Fodor's 1996

"When it comes to information on regional history, what to see and do, and shopping, these guides are exhaustive."
—*USAir Magazine*

"Usable, sophisticated restaurant coverage, with an emphasis on good value."
—*Andy Birsh, Gourmet Magazine columnist*

"Valuable because of their comprehensiveness."
—*Minneapolis Star-Tribune*

"Fodor's always delivers high quality...thoughtfully presented...thorough."
—*Houston Post*

"An excellent choice for those who want everything under one cover."
—*Washington Post*

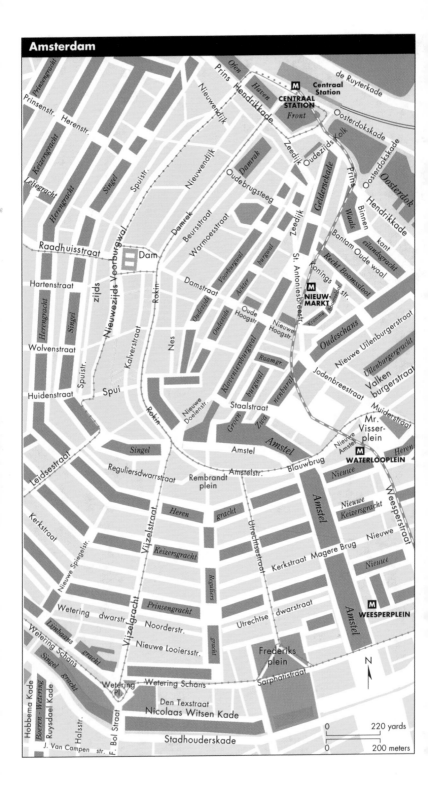

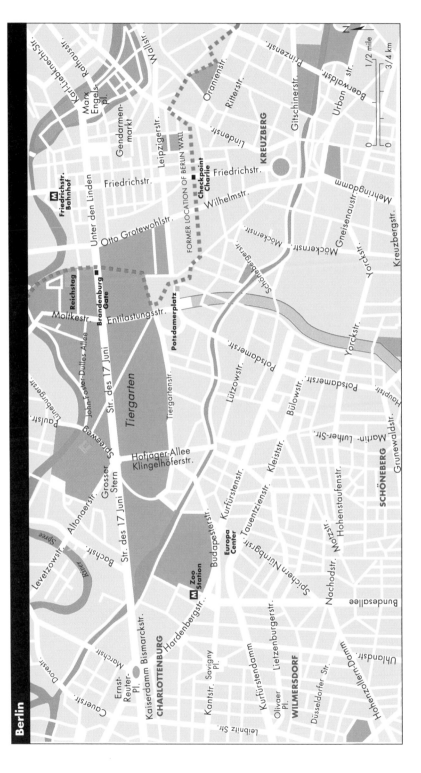

Berlin

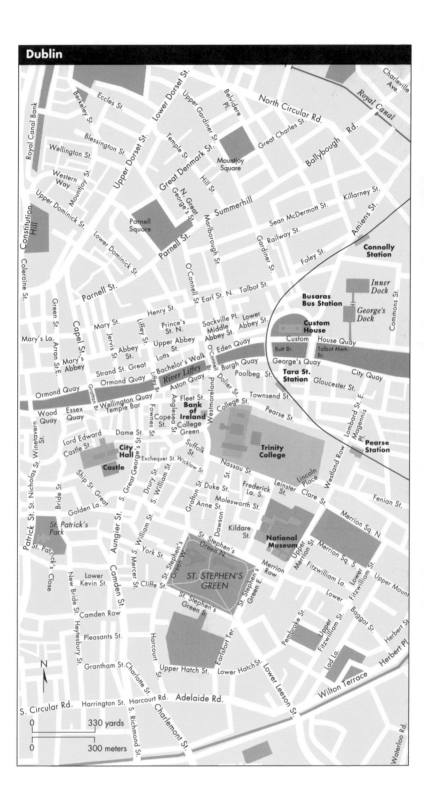

Dublin

Charleville Ave.

Royal Canal

Eccles St.

Berkeley St.

Lower Dorset St.

Upper Gardiner St.

Belvidere Pl.

North Circular Rd.

Royal Canal Bank

Blessington St.

Wellington St.

Upper Dorset St.

Temple St.

Great Charles St.

Ballybough Rd.

Western Way

Mountjoy St.

Great Denmark St.

Hill St.

Mountjoy Square

Killarney St.

Upper Dominick St.

Lower Dominick St.

N. Great George's St.

Summerhill

Sean McDermott St.

Amiens St.

Constitution Hill

Parnell Square

Parnell St.

Marlborough St.

Gardiner St.

Railway St.

Connolly Station

Coleraine St.

Green St.

Parnell St.

O'Connell St.

Foley St.

Inner Dock

Mary's La.

Arran St. E.

Capel St.

Henry St.

Mary St.

Prince's St. N.

Earl St. N.

Talbot St.

Sackville Pl.

Lower Middle Abbey St.

Abbey St.

Busaras Bus Station

Custom House

George's Dock

Commons St.

Mary's Abbey

Jervis St.

Liffey St.

Upper Abbey St.

Lotts

O'Connell St.

Eden Quay

Custom House Quay

Talbot Mem. Br.

Strand St. Great

Bachelor's Walk

Burgh Quay

Butt Br.

House Quay

City Quay

Ormond Quay

Ormond Quay

Liffey Br.

River Liffey

Aston Quay

Poolbeg St.

George's Quay

Tara St. Station

Gloucester St.

Wood Quay

Essex Quay

Grattan Br.

Wellington Quay

Temple Bar

Fownes St.

Anglesea St.

Fleet St.

D'Olier St.

Townsend St.

Lombard St. E.

Magennis

Winetavern St.

Nicholas St.

Lord Edward St.

Dame St.

Copeland St.

Bank of Ireland

College Green

Westmoreland St.

College St.

Pearse St.

Pearse Station

Castle St.

City Hall

Exchequer St.

Suffolk St.

Wicklow St.

Nassau St.

Trinity College

Patrick St.

Castle

Ship St. Great

S. Great George's St.

Drury St.

S. William St.

St. Andrew St.

Duke St.

Anne St.

Frederick La. S.

Lincoln Place

Leinster St.

Clare St.

Westland Row

Fenian St.

Bride St.

Golden La.

Molesworth St.

St. Patrick's Park

Aungier St.

William St.

S. York St.

Dawson St.

Grafton St.

Kildare St.

National Museum

Merrion Sq. N.

St. Patrick's Close

Lower Kevin St.

Camden St.

S. Mercer St.

Cliffe St.

St. Stephen's Green N.

St. Stephen's Green W.

ST. STEPHEN'S GREEN

St. Stephen's Green E.

Merrion Row

Upper Merrion St.

Merrion Sq. S.

Fitzwilliam La.

Lower Fitzwilliam St.

Upper Mount

New Bride St.

Camden Row

Harcourt St.

St. Stephen's Green S.

Earlsfort Ter.

Pembroke St.

Lower

Baggot St.

Herbert St.

Heytesbury St.

Pleasants St.

Upper Fitzwilliam St.

Lad La.

Herbert Pl.

N

Grantham St.

Charlotte St.

Upper Hatch St.

Lower Hatch St.

Lower Leeson St.

Wilton Terrace

S. Circular Rd.

Harrington St.

Harcourt Rd.

Adelaide Rd.

S. Richmond St.

Charlemont St.

Waterloo Rd.

0 — 330 yards

0 — 300 meters

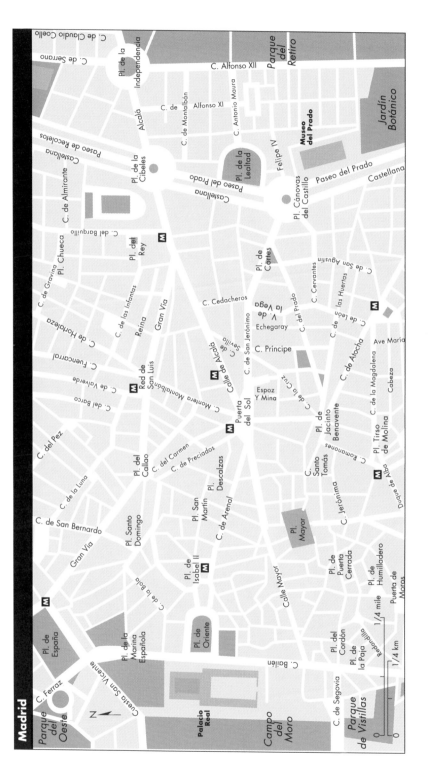

London

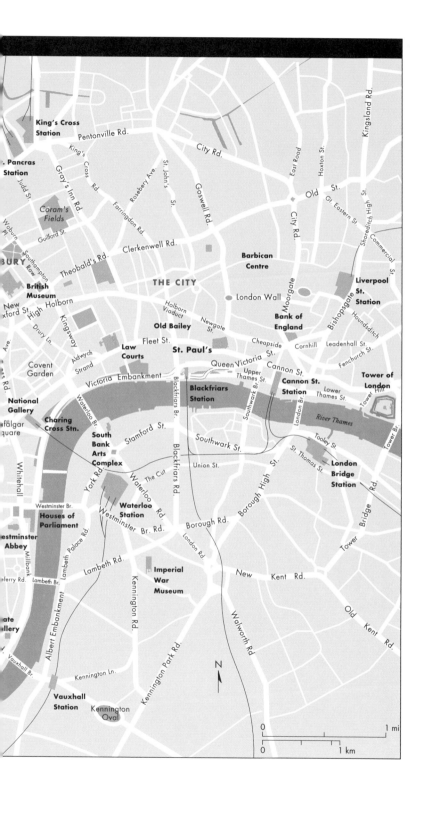

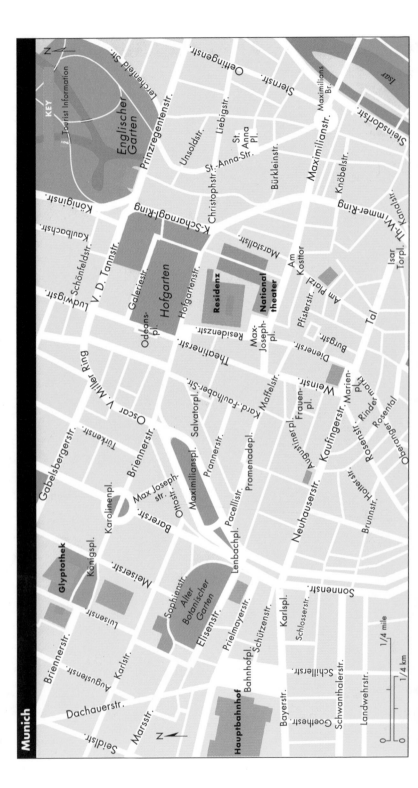

Munich

Prague

Pražský Hrad (Prague Castle)

STARÉ MĚSTO

MALA STRANA

Zlatnická
Na poříčí
Na Havlíčkova
Solnická
Truhlářská
Revoluční
Benediktská
Zlatnická
Dlouhá
Masná
Rybná
Jakubská
nám. Republiky
Hybernská
nám. M. Gorkého
Opletalova
Celetná
Nekázanka
Panská
Růžová
Politických vězňů
Ve Smečkách
Krakovská
Washingtonova
(Wenceslas Square)
Štěpánská
Jindřišská
Václavské náměstí
Na příkopě
Havířská
Železná
Pařížská
Maislova
Staroměstské nám.
Melantrichova
Malé nám.
Husova
Jilská
Na Perštýně
Marinská
Jungmannovo nám.
Vladislavova
Lazarská
Jungmannova
Vodičkova
Spálená
Kaprova
Platnéřská
Karlova
Liliová
Betlémské nám.
Bartolomějská
Národní tř.
Ostrovní
17. listopadu
nám. Jana Palacha
Veleslavínova
Křižovnická
Křižovnické nám.
Betlémská
Konviktská
Smetanovo nábř.
Masarykovo nábř.
Mánesův most
Pod Bruskou
Karlův most
Vltava
most Legii
Letenská
Jilská
Valdštejnská
Vojanovy Sady
Na Kampě
Velkopřevorské nám.
Malostranské nábř.
Janáčkovo nábř.
Zborovská
Thunovská
Nerudova
Malostranské nám.
Mostecká
Prokopská
Maltézské nám.
Hellichova
Všehrdova
Vítězná
Plaská
Petřínská
Tržiště
Karmelitská
Újezd
Jánský vršek
Petřín Gardens
N
0 250 yards
0 250 meters

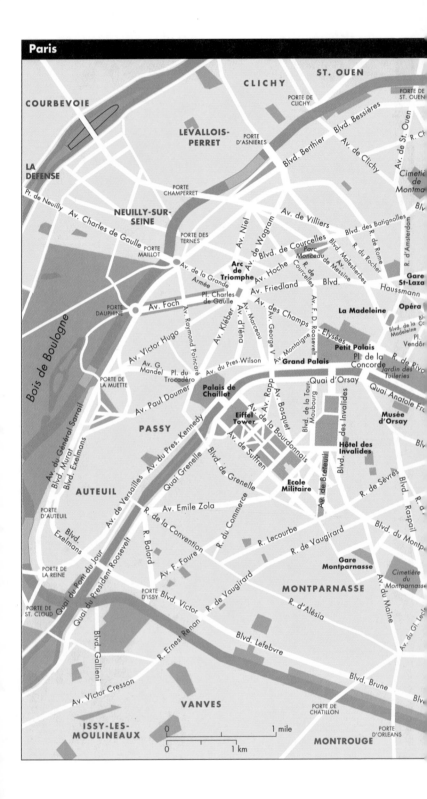

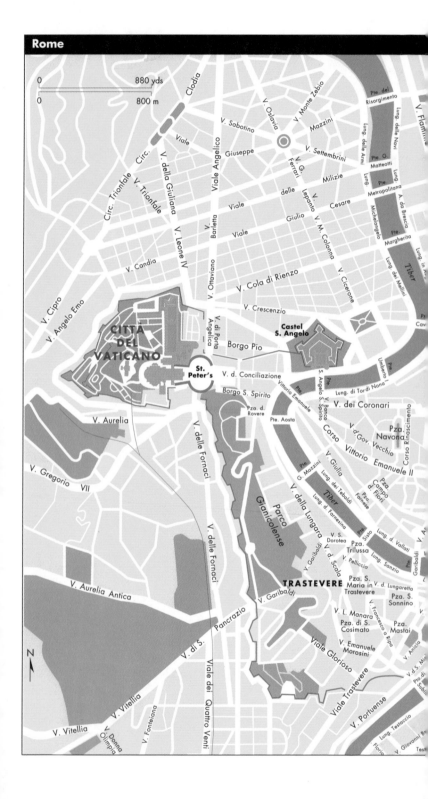

Rome

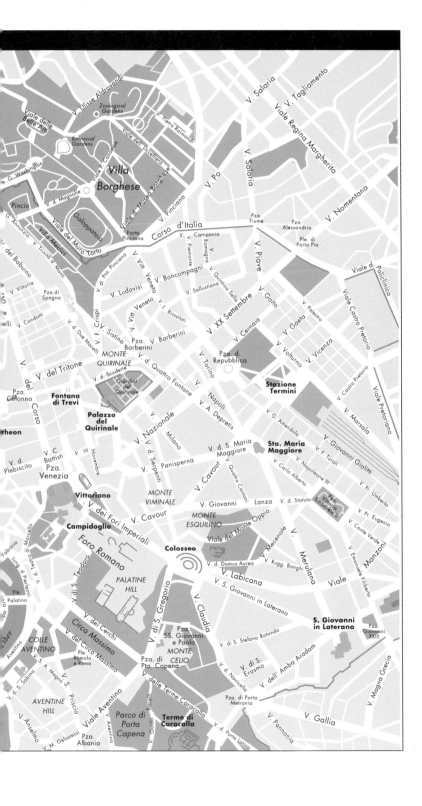

Vienna

N

Landesgerichtsstrasse
Grillparzerstr.

Rathaus

Josefstädter Str.
Stadiong.

Parlament

Auerspergstr.

Lerchen-felderstr.
Neustiftg.

Burggasse
Gutenbergg.
Siebensterng.
Spittelbergg.

Schotteng. Herrengasse
Freyung
Rosengasse
Schottenb.
Mölker-Steig
Oppolzerg.
Teinfaltstr.
Bankg.
Löwelstr.

Mölker
Bastei
Schrey-vogelg.

Burgtheater

Dr. Karl Lueger-Ring
Dr. K. Renner-Ring

Ballhaus-pl.
Schauflerg.
Landhausg.

Hofburg

Heldenpl.

Kunsthistorisches Museum

Maria-
Theresien-
Platz

Burgring
Messeplatz
Bellariastr.
Volkgartenstr.
Museumstrasse

Getreidemarkt
Babenbergerstr.
Eschenbachg.

Elisabethstr. Platz
Schillerpl.
Robert Stolz Platz

Operning
Burggarten
Goethegasse
Hanuschg.

Josefs-pl. Augustinerstr.

Am
Hof
Bognerg.
Naglerg.
Wallnerstr.

Renng.
Tiefer Graben
Seitzerg.
Tuchlauben
Judenpl.

Färberg. Schwertg.
Wipplingerstr.
Salvatorgasse
Sterng.
Salzgries
Morzin-pl.

Marc-Aurel-Str.
Judengasse
Rabensteig

Kohlmarkt
Habsburgerg.
Bräunerstr.
Graben
Dorotheerg.
Spiegelg.
Plankeng.
Dorotheerg.

Michaeler-pl.
Stallburgg.
Bräunerstr.

Stock-im-
Eisen-
Platz
Goldschm.g.
Jasomirg.
str.

Brandstätte
Bauernmkt.
Landskrong.
Hoher
Markt
Rotg.
Lugeck
Rotenturmstr.

Stephanspl.

Bäckerstr.
Wollzeile
Schulerstr.
Domg.
Blutg.
Lilieng.
Grünangerg.
Ball g.
Singerstr.
Rauhensteing.
Franziskaner-pl.

Köllnerhofg.
Sonnenfelsg.
Fleischmarkt
Köln
Raben Steig

Laurenzer berg
Postg.
Postg.
Lotreng.
Schönl.
Schwedenbr.
Schwedenpl.

Untere Donaustr.
Obere Donaustr.
Danube Canal
Franz Josefs Kai
Aspernbr.
Marienbr.
Palaistrasse

Radetzkystr.
Julius Raab Pl.
Georg-Coch-Pl.
Biberstr.
Rosenburserstr.
M. Wiesingerstr.
Dominikanerbastei

Bahnhof Wien-Mitte

Vord. Zollamtsstr.
Invalidenstr.
Hauptstrasse
Weiskchn.-str. Landstrasse
Wallnerstr.

Rechte Bahngasse
Beatrixgasse

Dr. Karl Luegerpl.
Stubenring
Parkring
Stubenbastei
Zedlitzg.
Riemerg.
Liebenbgg.
Wollzeile
Singerstr.

Stadtpark

Johannesg.

Weihburgg.
Seilerstätte
Himmelpfortg.
Johannesg.
Annag.
Wallfischg.
Krugerstr.
Mahlerstr.
Akademiestr.

Schellingg.
Fichteg.
Hegelg.
Weihburgg.

Schubertring
Schwarzenbergstr.

Neuer
Markt
M. d'Avianog.
Tegetthof-
str. richg.
Füh.
Seilergasse
Kärntner Strasse

Planteng.
Kärntner
Passage
Opern

Operng.

Albertina-pl.

Kunsthistorisches Museum

Kärntner Ring

1/4 mile
1/4 km

Fodor's 96
Europe

Fodor's Travel Publications, Inc.
New York • Toronto • London • Sydney • Auckland

Fodor's Europe '96

Editor: Linda Cabasin

Editorial Contributors: Steven Amsterdam, Rob Andrews, Barbara Walsh Angelillo, Corky Bastlund, Robert Blake, Toula Bogdanos, Rodney Bolt, Hannah Borgeson, Jules Brown, Roderick Conway-Morris, Samantha Cook, Fionn Davenport, Giuliano Davenport, Chris Drake, Mario Falzon, Nigel Fisher, Robert I. C. Fisher, George Hamilton, Emma Harris, Simon Hewitt, Catherine Hill-Herndon, Alannah Hopkin, Anto Howard, Holly Hughes, Laura M. Kidder, Ky Krauthamer, Corinne LaBalme, David Lakein, Lisa Leventer, David Low, Deborah Luhrman, Amy McConnell, Anne Midgette, Rebecca Miller, Anastasia Mills, Conrad Little Paulus, Kristen Perrault, Karina Porcelli, Mark Potok, Kathryn Sampson, Mary Ellen Schultz, M. T. Schwartzman, Kate Sekules, George Semler, Eric Sjogren, Fiona Smith, Timea Spitka, Dinah Spritzer, Katherine Tagge, Robert Tilley, Julie Tomasz, Ivanka Tomova, Meltem Türköz, Nancy van Itallie, Greg Ward, Daniel Williams, Stephen Wolf, Anna Yates.

Creative Director: Fabrizio La Rocca

Cartographer: David Lindroth

Cover Photograph: BKA/Network Aspen

Design: Between the Covers

Copyright

Copyright © 1995 by Fodor's Travel Publications, Inc.

Fodor's is a registered trademark of Fodor's Travel Publications, Inc.

All rights reserved under International and Pan-American Copyright Conventions. Published in the United States by Fodor's Travel Publications, Inc., a subsidiary of Random House, Inc., New York, and simultaneously in Canada by Random House of Canada Limited, Toronto. Distributed by Random House, Inc., New York.

No maps, illustrations, or other portions of this book may be reproduced in any form without written permission from the publisher.

ISBN 0–679–03002–6

Special Sales

Fodor's Travel Publications are available at special discounts for bulk purchases for sales promotions or premiums. Special editions, including personalized covers, excerpts of existing guides, and corporate imprints, can be created in large quantities for special needs. For more information, contact your local bookseller or write to Special Markets, Fodor's Travel Publications, 201 East 50th Street, New York, NY 10022. Inquiries from Canada should be directed to your local Canadian bookseller or sent to Random House of Canada, Ltd., Marketing Department, 1265 Aerowood Drive, Mississauga, Ontario L4W 1B9. Inquiries from the United Kingdom should be sent to Fodor's Travel Publications, 20 Vauxhall Bridge Road, London, England SW1V 2SA.

MANUFACTURED IN THE UNITED STATES OF AMERICA

10 9 8 7 6 5 4 3 2 1

CONTENTS

Italic entries are maps

On the Road with Fodor's '96 vii

What's New *vii*
How to Use This Guide *vii*
Please Write to Us *vii*

What's New in Europe '96 and Fodor's Choice ix

What's New in Europe '96 *x*
Fodor's Choice *xvi*
Map of Europe *xxii–xxiii*
Map of World Time Zones *xxiv–xxv*

1   The Gold Guide 1

Important Contacts A to Z 2
Smart Travel Tips A to Z 19

2   Andorra 32

Andorra 34

3   Austria 42

Austria 44
Vienna 54–55
Danube Valley 69
Salzburg 74
Innsbruck 79

4   Belgium 83

Belgium 85
Brussels 96–97
Antwerp 109
Brugge 114

5   Bulgaria 117

Bulgaria 119
Sofia 128
The Black Sea Golden Coast 135
Inland Bulgaria 141

6   Cyprus 145

Cyprus 147

7   The Czech Republic 159

The Czech Republic 162
Prague 170–171
Bohemia 178

8   Denmark   *181*

Denmark 183
Copenhagen 194–195
Fyn (Funen) and the Central Islands 206
Jylland (Jutland) 211

9   Finland   *217*

Finland 219
Helsinki 230–231
The Lakelands 240
Finnish Lapland 247

10   France   *251*

France 254–255
Paris Métro 266–267
Paris 272–273
Ile de France 290
Normandy 297
Rouen 299
Burgundy 306
The Loire Valley 312
The Riviera 319
Nice 322
Monaco 324

11   Germany   *328*

Germany 332–333
München (Munich) 348–349
Frankfurt 364–365
Hamburg 374–375
The Rhine 381
The Black Forest 394
West Berlin 408–409
East Berlin 412
Saxony and Thuringia 422

12   Great Britain   *432*

Great Britain 436–437
London Underground 448
London 454–455
Windsor to Bath 480
Oxford 483
Stratford-upon-Avon 485
Bath 488
Cambridge 494
York 500
York Environs 502
Edinburgh 507

13   Greece   *511*

Greece 514–515
Athens 526–527
The Peloponnese 539
Mainland Greece 547
The Greek Islands 553

14 Holland *559*

Holland 561
Amsterdam 572–573
Historic Holland 586
The Hague, Delft, and Rotterdam 594

15 Hungary *601*

Hungary 603
Budapest 614–615
The Danube Bend 626
Lake Balaton 630

16 Iceland *633*

Iceland 635
Reykjavík 641

17 Ireland *651*

Ireland 654–655
Dublin 666–667
Dublin to Cork 681
Cork to Galway 685
Northwest Ireland 691

18 Italy *695*

Italy 698–699
Roma (Rome) 712–713
Firenze (Florence) 734–735
Toscana (Tuscany) 745
Milano (Milan) 756
Venezia (Venice) 766–767
Campania 778

19 Luxembourg *786*

Luxembourg 788
Luxembourg City 794

20 Malta *801*

Malta 803

21 Norway *813*

Norway 815
Oslo 826–827
The Coast Road to Stavanger 835
Through Telemark to Bergen 840

22 Poland *847*

Poland 849
Warsaw 858–859
Kraków 865
Gdańsk and the North 869

23   Portugal   872

      Portugal 874
      Lisbon 885
      Belém 888
      The Portuguese Riviera 895
      The Algarve 900

24   Romania   908

      Romania 910
      Bucharest 920–921
      The Black Sea Coast 927

25   Slovakia   931

      Slovakia 933
      Bratislava 940
      The Tatras and Eastern Slovakia 944

26   Spain   947

      Spain 950–951
      Madrid 966–967
      Madrid Environs 977
      Barcelona 990–991
      Moorish Spain 1001
      Seville 1003
      Córdoba 1006
      Granada 1008
      Costa del Sol 1015
      Gibraltar 1020

27   Sweden   1031

      Sweden 1033
      Stockholm 1046–1047
      Stockholm Environs 1049
      Uppsala and the Folklore District 1059
      The West Coast and Glass Country 1063

28   Switzerland   1067

      Switzerland 1069
      Zürich 1080
      Geneva 1092–1093
      Luzern 1100
      Lugano 1107
      Bern 1112

29   Turkey   1122

      Turkey 1124
      Istanbul 1136–1137
      The Aegean Coast 1147
      The Mediterranean Coast 1154
      Central Anatolia and Cappadocia 1159

      Index   1162

ON THE ROAD WITH FODOR'S

A GOOD TRAVEL GUIDE is like a wonderful traveling companion. It's charming, it's brimming with sound recommendations and solid ideas, it pulls no punches in describing lodging and dining establishments, and it's consistently full of fascinating facts that make you view what you've traveled to see in a rich new light. In the creation of Europe '96, we at Fodor's have gone to great lengths to provide you with the very best of all possible traveling companions—and to make your trip the best of all possible vacations.

What's New

A New Design

If this is not the first Fodor's guide you've purchased, you'll immediately notice our new look. More readable and easier to use than ever? We think so—and we hope you do, too.

Travel Updates

Just before your trip, you may want to order a Fodor's Worldview Travel Update. From local publications all over Europe, the lively, cosmopolitan editors at Worldview gather information on concerts, plays, opera, dance performances, gallery and museum shows, sports competitions, and other special events that coincide with your visit. See the order blank at the back of this book, call 800/799–9609, or fax 800/799–9619.

How to Use this Guide

Organization

Chapter 1 is The Gold Guide, comprising two sections on gold paper that are chock-full of information about traveling within your destination and traveling in general. Both are in alphabetical order by topic. **Important Contacts A to Z** gives addresses and telephone numbers of organizations and companies that offer destination-related services and detailed information or publications. Here's where you'll find information about how to get to Europe from wherever you are. **Smart Travel Tips A to Z,** The Gold Guide's second section, gives specific tips on how to get the most

out of your travels, as well as information on how to accomplish what you need to in Europe.

Chapters in Europe '96 are in alphabetical order by country. Each chapter covers exploring, shopping, dining, lodging, and arts and nightlife, and begins with a section called Essential Information, which tells you how to get there and get around and gives you important local addresses and telephone numbers.

Hotel Facilities

Note that in general you incur charges when you use many hotel facilities. We wanted to let you know what facilities a hotel has to offer, but we don't always specify whether or not there's a charge, so when planning a vacation that entails a stay of several days, it's wise to ask what's included in the rate.

Dress Code in Restaurants

The **What to Wear** section in the Essential Information section of each chapter tells you what's most common in that area. In general, we note a dress code only when men are required to wear a jacket or a jacket and tie.

Credit Cards

The following abbreviations are used: **AE,** American Express; **DC,** Diners Club; **MC,** MasterCard; and **V,** Visa. Discover is not accepted outside the United States.

Please Write to Us

Everyone who has contributed to Europe '96 has worked hard to make the text accurate. All prices and opening times are based on information supplied to us at press time, and the publisher cannot accept responsibility for any errors that may have occurred. The passage of time will bring changes, so it's always a good idea to call ahead and confirm information when it matters—particularly if you're making a detour to visit specific sights or attractions. When making reservations at a hotel or inn, be sure to speak up if you have a disability or are traveling with children, if you prefer a private bath or a certain type of bed, or if you have specific dietary needs or any other concerns.

Were the restaurants we recommended as described? Did our hotel picks exceed your expectations? Did you find a museum we recommended a waste of time? We would love your feedback, positive and negative. If you have complaints, we'll look into them and revise our entries when the facts warrant it. If you've happened upon a special place that we haven't included, we'll pass the information along to the writers so they can check it out. So please send us a letter or postcard (we're at 201 East 50th Street, New York, New York 10022). We'll look forward to hearing from you. And in the meantime, have a wonderful trip!

Karen Cure
Editorial Director

What's New in Europe '96 and Fodor's Choice

WHAT'S NEW IN EUROPE '96

THE PERENNIAL ATTRACTIONS of Europe, from unspoiled historic villages to grand cosmopolitan capitals, continue to draw travelers eager to experience everything from a hike in the Alps to some of the world's most glittering nightlife. The challenge for visitors now is how to respond to fluctuating currencies—notably the dollar, which by mid-1995 had lost substantial ground against many European currencies, with the exception of the Italian lira. Fortunately, there are still ways to save on travel expenses large and small, whether by investigating special airfares, rail passes, or fly-drive packages, by booking ahead for discount hotel rates, or by visiting a favorite restaurant for a lunch that's less costly than dinner. The tips in Chapter 1, The Gold Guide, and the advice in individual chapters can help to make your travel dollars go farther in Europe.

By late 1994, super sleek Eurostar passenger trains—serving London, Paris, and Brussels—and car-carrying Le Shuttle trains were operating through the long-anticipated Channel Tunnel between Great Britain and France. The owners of these services hope to win over a good portion of the 60 million travelers who cross the Channel annually, although traditional ferry and air services are offering strong competition. The number of trains is increasing gradually, and time will reveal whether technological efficiency will deliver the passengers the tunnel needs for its financial well-being.

As a result of the Maastricht Treaty that went into effect in 1993, the European Community changed its name to the European Union (EU) and removed all trade barriers between the 12 member states, turning much of Europe into one huge tariff-free market, the largest economic grouping in the world. Austria, Finland, and Sweden joined the EU on January 1, 1995. Turkey, Cyprus, and Malta, all of which have applied (and were initially turned down for membership), should join the EU by the year 2000. Several Eastern European countries have or are negotiating association agreements.

In spring 1995, 7 of the 15 EU nations (Belgium, France, Germany, Luxembourg, the Netherlands, Portugal, and Spain), known as the Schengen group, officially agreed to lift border controls on land, so that people can travel among the countries and use special lines at airports without showing passports. Italy, Greece, and Austria are also considering joining the group. Travelers from the United States and countries outside the Schengen group will be required to produce passports only on initial entry into one of the countries. At that time, their names will be checked against a computer database. However, because airlines or various authorities can require proof of identity, it's still advisable to carry a passport. In some ways, the agreement merely confirms practices that have evolved over time in the EU. But the reluctance of some nations (notably Great Britain) to join the Schengen group highlights the separation of forces supporting the integration of Europe and those opposing it.

The collapse of communism in Eastern Europe has had the most tragic consequences in the former Yugoslavia. Heralded as the most open and "western" communist country under President Josip Broz Tito, this Balkan state has descended into a brutal war that has left tens of thousands of people dead and forced millions to flee their homes. At press time, U.S. State Department advisories were in effect for all republics except Slovenia. For the foreseeable future, travel is likely to be extremely hazardous in this once-beautiful region.

Austria

Austria will celebrate the thousandth year since its name first appeared in the written record; Vienna will lead an explosion of festivities throughout the country, hosting a series of special events including an exhibition on the Danube's history.

As usual, the old year will end and the new begin with the globally televised New Year's concert from Vienna's Musikverein concert hall, although other cities, including Salzburg and Innsbruck, field their own concerts featuring Strauss waltzes. In musical contrast, Vienna will also, together with St. Florian, mark the 100th anniversary of composer Anton Bruckner's death. The Bregenz festival, held on the shores of Lake Constance, will repeat its acclaimed production of Beethoven's only opera, *Fidelio,* on the great lakeside stage.

The sport of golf has caught on with immeasurable enthusiasm. This year, new courses are being added and existing ones expanded, with several set against magnificent Alpine panoramas. Cycling also continues to gain in popularity, so the number of tour packages that allow a leisurely biking day-trip while your baggage is forwarded is increasing; routes paralleling the Danube are particular favorites. Similar packages are available for Alpine hikers. Look for more combination attractions, such as those including rail and water travel, which give a bow to nostalgia in the form of steam-powered trains and sidewheelers.

Belgium

The **Golden Tree procession,** celebrating the wedding in 1468 of Charles the Bold, duke of Burgundy, and Margaret of York, will take place in **Brugge** on August 24 and 25. The first part of the pageant presents the legends of Flanders; the second, the ancestry of the couple; and the third, their joyful entry into the city. Dynastic marriages were of enormous importance in the Middle Ages, and the pageant recreates the pomp and circumstance of the occasion.

Brussels and Flanders will benefit from a **computerized tourist information system.** Sixty information centers are linked to the system, which supplies daily updates on accommodations and more than 2,000 events of specific interest to visitors. Eventually it will include a reservations service as well.

The Czech Republic

Like all of Eastern Europe, the Czech Republic is changing rapidly as the country pursues economic and cultural revitalization, aiming for membership in the EU by the year 2000. In increasing numbers, tourists are rediscovering **Prague** and its freshly restored Baroque churches and Art Nouveau hotels. The newest attraction in the city is the massive **Veletržní Palace**—one of Europe's most important 20th-century Constructivist monuments—which has recently been renovated and now houses a museum of modern art.

Denmark

The EU has designated Copenhagen **Cultural Capital of Europe for 1996.** Festivities begin New Year's Eve and continue throughout the year. The many restoration projects in anticipation of 1996 include an expansion of the Ny Carlsberg Glyptotek. The old naval military station, Holmen, will be a center of activity as its buildings and one ship, the *Kronborg,* are transformed into stages for dance and music.

In May, the Royal Danish Ballet kicks off a special festival with four of Europe's leading ballet companies, including the Kirov Ballet and the Royal Ballet London. The Royal Danish Ballet, the Royal Theater Orchestra, and the Danish rock band Sorte Sol (Black Sun) will present a world premiere of the ballet *Hamlet* in July, at Kronborg Castle (Hamlet's castle) in Helsingør. Finally, **Museet for Moderne Kunst, København** (the Museum of Modern Art, Copenhagen), specializing in Danish and Scandinavian art, will open north of the capital. It will mount an international painting and sculpture show in the summer and a major Picasso exhibit to end the year.

The $1 billion expansion of **Copenhagen Airport** will continue until the year 2005, but it has been organized to keep traffic flowing conveniently. A new expressway linking the center of the island of Amager to the airport should be open by the middle of the year. Completion of the high-speed rail link between the airport and Copenhagen center is expected by 1998.

Europe's other channel tunnel, linking the island of Fyn to Zealand, is due to be ready for train traffic by late in the year. Dredging of the sea bed has also begun, in anticipation of the long-awaited bridge that will link Denmark and Sweden by the year 2000.

Finland

Finland's decision to join the EU in 1995 and the signing of a cooperation agreement with NATO are two of the most important steps the country has taken since it declared independence from Russia in 1917. As a result of the revaluation of the Finnish mark in May 1993 and changes in the tax laws required by EU membership, Finland is now more affordable than in the past, although still not one of Europe's cheaper destinations. Helsinki has also become a popular base for those tourists wishing to visit the newly independent Baltic states, especially Estonia.

France

The opening of the **Channel Tunnel** and the start of high-speed passenger train service through it in November 1994 has put the French into closer touch with their neighbors across *La Manche* (the Channel).

The remodeling of the **Louvre** continues, with new sculpture halls in the Denon Wing and spectacular nighttime illumination the latest developments. The **Très Grand Bibliothèque** (Very Large Library), scheduled for completion in 1995, is intended to anchor previously undeveloped eastern Paris, which will be linked to central Paris by a new metro line in 1997.

Outside Paris, **Disneyland Paris** (as Eurodisney is now called) has been retrenching, offering lower rates for admissions, lodging, and dining. Elsewhere, too, the recession has kept prices down as the trend toward budget bistros continues.

Germany

The Germans who clamored for democracy in 1989 and 1990 are still waiting to enjoy its fruits. Inflation and unemployment are higher in the eastern part of the country than in the west, and wages are lower. The burden of unification weighed heavily on the Bonn government in 1995, testing the strength of the alliance between Chancellor Helmut Kohl's Christian Democrats and liberal Free Democrats, who challenged the Kohl cabinet's tax package and opened a split that could bring early elections, perhaps in 1996.

Berlin, which will take its historic place as capital from Rhineland Bonn, is adjusting slowly to its new role; in 1995 half the construction projects connected with the move still awaited official approval. Watch for the opening of the **Jewish Museum**, sure to be admired as much for its design (by

architect Daniel Libeskind) as its content. On Palm Sunday in 1996, **Festtage**, an annual music festival, will debut with Wagner's *Ring* cycle and related concerts.

Events commemorating the **450th anniversary of Martin Luther's death** are planned throughout the country, especially in eastern Germany.

In early 1995, the **Rhine** flooded severely for the second time in 13 months. At press time it was too early to know which establishments, if any, will have to close.

The number of attacks on immigrants in Germany is decreasing. Still, after triumphantly dismantling the barbed wire fences that separated East and West for nearly four decades, Germany is putting up new **border defenses** to keep out unwanted "refugees."

Great Britain

In April 1995, the **British telephone system** changed area codes for all numbers in the country, in most cases simply by inserting "1" after the initial "0"; for example, London's codes became 0171 and 0181. In the five cities of Bristol, Leicester, Leeds, Nottingham, and Sheffield, however, area codes changed according to a different system, and several rural areas were combined under new codes, with more digits in their local numbers. The numbers given in this book reflect these changes; British Telecom also planned to install phone messages telling callers what new codes were in effect.

The often-delayed **Channel Tunnel** now carries car, bus, and truck service on **Le Shuttle** trains; **Eurostar** passenger trains whisk passengers between London and Paris and London and Brussels.

At the popular **Tower of London,** a new $10 million-plus Jewel House was opened in March 1994, and a smoother flow of visitor traffic has cut down the time people spend waiting in line. To make space for the royal jewels, part of the Armouries Collection was moved from the Tower to the city of Leeds, where it will be displayed in the new $42.6-million **Royal Amouries Museum,** due to open in spring 1996.

Near Bankside Power Station, **Shakespeare's Globe,** ambitious dream scheme of the late American movie director and entrepreneur Sam Wanamaker, is set to open in summer 1996—a faithful reconstruction of Shakespeare's open-roof Globe Theater. Until then, visitors can tour the site under construction. Also in London, **Westminster Bridge** is currently undergoing an $8 million restoration, which will play havoc with one of London's favorite sights, not to mention its traffic flow.

Following its traditional four-year pattern, **York** will present its famous cycle of medieval Mystery Plays in summer 1996 at the Theatre Royal.

Greece

Sure to be a boost to Greek tourism are the 11 **casinos** the government has licensed for operation. It has already awarded three licenses for casinos in Thessaloniki, in the Halkidiki resort of Porto Carras, and in Palio Faliro, a coastal Athens suburb. Other permits have been allocated for casinos on Mt. Parnes in Athens, in Patras and Loutraki in the Peloponnese, and on the islands of Syros, Rhodes, Corfu, and Crete. Also helping tourism are the **faster ferries** now operating between Greece and Italy, making the trip in 18 rather than 28 hours.

In Athens the **metro extension** is still under construction, with a new projected completion date of 1998. This means downtown areas like Syntagma and Omonia squares are noisier and more congested. For the interim, the landmark glass statue decorating Omonia has been moved across from the Hilton. Thessaloniki will also start building its metro, as part of the government's campaign to reduce pollution and traffic in its cities. In spring 1995, a three-month ban on autos was put into effect in the downtown Athens triangle of Ermou, Athinas, and Stadiou streets. Only special minibuses and residents' autos will be allowed. If effective, the ban will become permanent.

Athens is hoping to become a model European capital, along with Stuttgart, Birmingham, and Torino, cities chosen by the EU to implement state-of-the-art traffic technology. The pilot program will rely on a more **modern traffic-light system** and a huge computer network to watch circulation through the city and provide continuous updates and alternate routes to motorists.

Holland

Two of the finest Dutch painters of the 17th century are the focus of major exhibitions in 1996. The **Rijksmuseum** in Amsterdam will be bursting with works by **Jan Steen,** best known for his anarchic tavern scenes and pictures of chaotic households. **The Hague** and **Delft** are host cities for a number of exhibitions and events centering on the life and work of **Jan Vermeer.** Culminating these is a spring exhibition at the **Mauritshuis Museum** in The Hague, where, for the first time ever, nearly all of the 35 known paintings by Vermeer will be on display under one roof.

Exhibitions begin early in 1996 in the lead-up to the 1997 celebration of the 300th anniversary of the visit of **Peter the Great** to The Netherlands. Most cities will have something to offer; precious works of art are coming to Holland from the Kremlin and Hermitage museums in Russia. Also in 1996, the **National Museum H. W. Mesdag** in The Hague reopens after an extensive renovation program.

Hungary

This year marks the country's **1,100th birthday**—the anniversary of the Magyar settlement of the Carpathian Basin. To celebrate, 1996 has been dubbed "The Year of Hungarian Tourism" by trade and cultural associations, which promise special museum exhibitions, heritage events, and other celebratory happenings centered in Budapest. The city's beloved yellow metro (continental Europe's oldest underground subway) and the proud monuments of Heroes' Square —both built one hundred years ago for the millennial celebration— will be spruced up and scrubbed down.

Major chain hotels are expanding and state-controlled hotels are going private and renovating. At press time, the Hungarian government was negotiating the sale of major state-run HungarHotels to an American group.

Travelers will still find Hungary a bargain compared to Western Europe, but strictly rock-bottom prices are a thing of the past. Restaurant and hotel rates are steadily creeping upward, and at press time, the annual inflation rate was at 25% and still rising.

Iceland

The real growth area in Icelandic tourism has been at the less expensive end of the market: farmhouses, guest houses, and camping holidays. Iceland has been going through a severe economic recession since the beginning of the 1990s, and this has led to efforts to keep prices down and attract more visitors from abroad. The cost of living is high, and the country remains an expensive destination, but visitors now have a larger range of options in terms of accommodations and services.

Icelanders are realizing that it's not enough to be on an island in the middle of the ocean—atmospheric and marine pollution can still occur. The increase in tourism and the fact that visitors tend to travel in the highlands, where the environment is very sensitive, have led to serious discussion about limiting access to the most vulnerable areas.

Ireland

Ireland used to rely on its unspoiled countryside and friendly, hospitable people to attract visitors. In the past six years, over IR £500 million has been invested in tourism, and the number of visitors is projected to double from 2 million to 4 million by 1996. Travelers can expect upgraded accommodations at all levels (most hotels and many bed-and-breakfasts now offer rooms with private bath, TV, and direct-dial phone), a wider choice of restaurants, better-organized cultural tourism, and greatly improved sporting facilities. Twenty-five new golf courses have been built, and as many again are in the making. Water sports, walking routes, fishing, cycling, and equestrian holidays have also been successfully developed.

Italy

After varying periods of quarantine, a number of Italy's major attractions will again be on view in 1996. Engineers have stabilized the tipsy foundations of the **Leaning Tower of Pisa,** and visitors may be allowed to make the dizzying climb to its top. After being evicted from the Baths of Caracalla, **Rome's Teatro dell'Opera** has found a new home for its summer season in a site near the famous ruins, and will resume mounting outdoor productions there. Major holdings from Rome's celebrated antique sculpture collections in the Museo Nazionale Romano have come to light in **Palazzo Altemps,** with the opening date of another section, in Palazzo Massimo, still indefinite at press time. The **Napoleonic Museum** in Rome has also reopened.

Naples is enjoying a renaissance. Avoided for years by many tour operators, the city is attracting streams of visitors again. The center has been spruced up, new hotels are welcoming guests, and special programs are opening the doors of churches and palaces formerly closed to the public. Restoration of the **Capodimonte Museum** should be completed during 1996; until then the museum's greatest masterpieces are on view in Villa Pignatelli.

Venice and the Veneto villas will be the focus of celebrations of the **300th anniversary of the birth of artist Giambattista Tiepolo,** whose paintings and fresco decorations embody the light and glory of his birthplace. In Genoa, the mammoth spring **Euroflora flower show,** held there every five years, attracts exhibitors and horticulture lovers from all over the world.

Luxembourg

The **Musée de la Ville de Luxembourg** (Luxembourg City Historical Museum) is the latest example of a farsighted municipal cultural policy that in previous years has given the capital a conservatory and two theaters. This exciting vertical museum plunges down from street level in the old town to the river valley below; a large, glass-wall elevator connects the eight levels. It is the outstanding legacy of Luxembourg's stint as European City of Culture in 1995.

Malta

The number of visitors to Malta now exceeds 1 million each year, and the country is establishing itself as one of the top cruise destinations in the Mediterranean. In response, the renovation of existing hotels and construction of new ones continues; facilities for water sports are being upgraded.

Norway

Norway is enjoying an unprecedented number of visitors in the wake of 1994's Winter Olympics. The government has made tourism one of its highest priorities, particularly in the depressed northern part of the country, and prices are still falling as a result of the heightened competition.

The heated debate about joining the EU ended in November 1994 when Norway narrowly rejected membership. Despite the decisions of its close neighbors, Sweden and Finland, in favor of the EU, the country has remained steadfast in its refusal to join, rendering it a Eurosceptics' mecca. Norway is a member of the European Economic Area, which has begun to exert a downward pressure on prices, including hotel and restaurant charges.

Poland

Upgrading of tourist facilities will continue in 1996, as more new hotels, including (if all goes according to schedule) the Sheraton in Warsaw, are opened and old ones are refurbished. The ongoing privatization of Orbis hotels should also bring more variety in prices and types of accommodations. Poles are getting used to their **new currency,** introduced in 1995; it is certainly easier for the tourist to handle than the old złoty, which had prices running into the millions.

Portugal

Although prices continue to rise, Portugal remains one of Europe's more affordable countries to visit. Some of the best values can be found at an increasing number of rural establishments—particularly in the Sintra area and in the north, where old manors, farmhouses, and even water mills have been converted into superior bed-and-breakfasts. Most of these are run within official programs, existing under a variety of names; local tourist offices can provide brochures and specific information.

In **Lisbon,** the new cultural center at Belém, the **Centro Cultural de Belém,** is successfully hosting a high-quality program of events and entertainment.

Be aware: Lisbon is continually improving its roads and transportation system; it always pays to request a room off main avenues and thoroughfares to avoid the sound of construction. Also, the national upgrading of the **telephone system** is still causing havoc for tourists and locals alike. Numbers throughout the country are changing in a rolling program, and official publications have been slow to catch up; always doublecheck.

Romania

Having established a democratic system, Romania is now trying to build a market economy. Peasants are being given back their land, and small private enterprises are being encouraged, leading to increasing variety in the shops and markets.

Spain

The 1993 recession in Spain led to a weakening of the peseta, which, in turn, led to a record year for tourism in 1994. Visitors in 1995 saw climbing hotel and restaurant prices brought on by that boom. Price hikes at the coastal resorts and in the Balearic and Canary Islands stabilized by mid-year; Madrid and Barcelona continue to offer good deals for tourists who schedule their city visits on weekends.

Rural Spain is an increasingly popular budget option. Farmhouses are being converted into charming **bed-and-breakfasts:** Besides providing a low-cost way to travel, they make it easier for visitors to absorb the local culture. Provincial tourism offices can supply brochures detailing rural tourism accommodations.

Nature lovers can now enjoy riverboat trips year-round into Europe's largest nature preserve: the **Coto de Doñana,** on the Guadalquivir delta in Andalucía.

The mayors of seven Spanish cities joined together in 1995 under the banner of **El Camino de Sefarad** (Journey through Sepharad) to communicate historical and cultural information about each of their *Juderías* (Jewish quarters). Look for new driving and walking tours and museum exhibits in Cáceres and Hervás (Extremadura), Córdoba (Andalucía), Girona (Catalunya), Ribadavia (Galicia), Toledo (Castilla-La Mancha), and Tudela (Navarra).

Sweden

Construction of the 18-kilometer bridge over the Öresund, the sound separating Sweden and Denmark, was to have begun in 1993. At press time (spring 1995), following lengthy environmental assessments, the Swedish Parliament had given final approval to the project, but environmental activists were still strongly opposed and were likely to create further delays. If constructed, this rail-and-road bridge will create the first physical link between Sweden and the Continent.

Visitors will find that Sweden, due to a weak krona and a unified effort by the travel industry to bring hotel, restaurant, and travel costs in line with Continental Europe, is a relative bargain. American travelers can expect to find the country less expensive than it was two years ago.

Switzerland

In voting against joining the **EU,** Switzerland has once more positioned itself apart from the countries that surround it. The vote has, for the time being, little impact on the traveler, aside from the increased presence of customs and immigration officials.

Thanks to the country's political stability, the **Swiss franc** has been steadily rising against the United States dollar and the British pound. With the exception of Scandinavia, Switzerland now ranks among Europe's most expensive countries to visit. Since hotels structure their prices by the time of year, visiting during the off-season— summer for ski resorts and winter for lake resorts—can be considerably cheaper.

Luzern's famous bridge, the **Kapellbrücke,** has been rebuilt after a disastrous fire that destroyed 80% of its structure. Of the 122 paintings in the gables of the bridge's roof, more than 20 were damaged beyond repair; polychrome substitutes have taken their place. The originals are being restored and will soon be displayed in a local museum.

The new sport of **snowshoe hiking** continues to enthrall the Swiss. With the newly refined lightweight plastic raquettes, walkers can leave the trail and take off over the surface of snowbound forests and fields.

Turkey

In Istanbul, the nation's first industrial museum has opened on the bank of the Golden Horn, in a Byzantine building that was once the foundry of the Ottoman Navy. The **Rahmi M. Koc Industrial Museum and Cultural Foundation** has assembled a collection of obsolete but treasured remnants of the mechanical age—displays of steam machinery, polished insides of old ships, and other obscure items. Ottoman splendor is the theme at another new museum in **Yildiz Place,** at the former residence of the late Sultan Abdulhamit. There are exhibits of priceless china, enormous, elaborately decorated vases, and more rarefied objects such as the sultan's coach and throne.

The **Darııca Kuş Cenneti** (Bird's Paradise), a small zoo and botanical park on the outskirts of Istanbul, should impress children and adults with its exotic population. The park is home to 300 species of birds and 375 types of tropical plants, as well as zebras, kangaroos, gazelles, and penguins.

Shoppers familiar with the **Grand Bazaar** in Istanbul will find a new kind of icon for sale: relics from churches of the former Soviet Union and its republics. The pieces vary greatly in size and sophistication, but, unlike many other Turkish antiques, are completely legal to take from the country.

FODOR'S CHOICE

No two people will agree on what makes a perfect vacation, but it's fun and can be helpful to know what others think. In compiling this list, we've included choices from each of the countries covered in the book, and we hope that you'll have a chance to experience some of them yourself. For more detailed information about each entry, refer to the appropriate chapters within this guidebook.

Sights to Remember

Belgium
The Burg and canals of Brugge at dusk

Bulgaria
The panorama from the ramparts of Veliko Târnovo

Denmark
Kronborg Castle overlooking the Baltic

Finland
Olavinlinna Castle, Savonlinna

France
Mont St-Michel at high tide

Germany
Tiny wine villages hugging the banks of the Rhine

Great Britain
Tower Bridge and the Tower of London in floodlights

Greece
Sunset over the Caldera on the island of Santorini

Holland
Amsterdam canals by night

Hungary
Parliament building at night, Budapest

Iceland
Ice floes drifting on the Jökulsárlon lagoon (Skaftafell)

Ireland
Dusk over the lakes of Killarney

Italy
The Grand Canal in Venice at dawn

Luxembourg
The castle of Vianden, seen from the memorial to the 6th U.S. Cavalry

Malta
The Grand Harbour in Valletta

Norway
The midnight sun at the North Cape

Romania
The view from the clock tower in Sighisoara

Spain
The villages of Andalucía, perched on hillsides

Sweden
Water Festival fireworks over the harbor in Stockholm

Switzerland
The Matterhorn from Gornergrat, Zermatt

Turkey
Istanbul's skyline at sunset from Camliça Hill

Hotels

Austria
Imperial, Vienna ($$$$)

Belgium
Radisson SAS, Brussels ($$$$)

Denmark
D'Angleterre, Copenhagen ($$$$)

Finland
Hotel Strand Inter-Continental, Helsinki ($$$$)

France
The Ritz, Paris ($$$$)

Any Logis et Auberges (Country Hotels and Inns) de France hotel ($)

Germany
Vier Jahreszeiten, Hamburg ($$$$)

Great Britain
Beaufort, London ($$$)

Greece
Any of the "paradosiakoi oikismoi" (traditional homes)

Holland
Amstel Inter-Continental, Amsterdam ($$$$)

Hungary
Gellért, Budapest ($$$)

Ireland
Park, Kenmare ($$$$)

Italy
Hassler-Villa Medici, Rome ($$$$)

Portugal
York House, Lisbon ($$$)

Spain
The Ritz, Madrid ($$$$)

Switzerland
Monte Rosa, Zermatt ($$$)

Turkey
Çirağan Palace, Istanbul ($$$$)

Restaurants

Austria
Landhaus Bacher, Mautern ($$$$)

Belgium
Comme Chez Soi, Brussels ($$$$)

Denmark
Kong Hans Kaelder, Copenhagen ($$$$)

Finland
Savoy, Helsinki ($$$$)

France
La Régalade, Paris ($$–$$$)

Great Britain
Bibendum, London ($$$$)

Greece
Bajazzo, Athens ($$$$)

Holland
Excelsior, Amsterdam ($$$$)

Hungary
Gundel, Budapest ($$$$)

Iceland
Perlan, Reykjavík ($$$)

Ireland
Arbutus Lodge, Cork ($$$)

Italy
El Toulà, Rome ($$$$)

Luxembourg
La Bergerie, Echternach ($$$$)

Malta
Pisces, Marsaxlokk ($$)

Norway
Theatercafeen, Oslo ($$$)

Portugal
Aviz, Lisbon ($$$$)

Spain
Set Portes, Barcelona ($$$$)

Sweden
Den Gyldene Freden, Stockholm ($$$)

Switzerland
Bierhalle Kropf, Zürich ($$$)

Monuments

The Czech Republic
Starý Źidovsky Hřbitov (Old Jewish Cemetery), Prague

Finland
The Sibelius Monument, Helsinki

Germany
Brandenburg Gate, Berlin

Great Britain
Scott Monument, Edinburgh

Ireland
The Rock of Cashel

Poland
The Solidarity Monument, Gdańsk

Portugal
Monumento dos Descobrimentos (Monument to the Discoveries), Lisbon

Spain
El Escorial monastery and Valle de los Caídos basilica, near Madrid

Museums and Galleries

Austria
Kunsthistorisches Museum, Vienna

Belgium
Groeninge Museum, Brugge

Bulgaria
National History Museum, Sofia

Denmark
Louisiana Museum of Modern Art, north of Copenhagen

Finland
The Finnish National Gallery, Helsinki

France
Fondation Maeght, St-Paul-de-Vence

Great Britain
The British Museum, London

Greece
The N. J. Goulandris Museum of Cycladic Art, Athens

Holland
Rijksmuseum, Amsterdam

Hungary
Műcsarnok (Art Gallery), Budapest

Luxembourg
Luxembourg City Historical Museum

Malta
National Museum of Fine Art, Valletta

Portugal
Fundação Calouste Gulbenkian, Lisbon

Romania
Museum of the Peasant, Bucharest

Spain
Museu de Picasso, Barcelona

Sweden
Vasa Museum, Stockholm

Switzerland
Musée International de la Croix-Rouge, Geneva

Turkey
Topkapi Palace and Harem, Istanbul

Festivals

Cyprus
Limassol Wine Festival

Denmark
The Copenhagen Jazz Festival

Finland
Savonlinna Opera Festival, Savonlinna

Germany
Oktoberfest, Munich

Great Britain
Edinburgh International Festival

Holland
Queen's Day, Amsterdam

Hungary
Spring Festival, Budapest

Ireland
St. Patrick's Day Parade, Dublin

Italy
Venice Carnivale

Norway
Bergen International Music Festival

Portugal
Santos Populares (Popular Saints) Festival, Lisbon

Sweden
Stockholm Water Festival

Churches, Temples, and Mosques

Andorra
Romanesque church of Sant Joan de Caselles, Canillo

Austria
Karlskirche, Vienna

The Czech Republic
St. Vitus Cathedral, Prague

Denmark
Rundetårn, Copenhagen

Finland
The Cathedral (Senate Square), Helsinki

France
Chartres Cathedral

Germany
Kölner Dom, Köln

Great Britain
St. Paul's Cathedral, London

Hungary
Mátyás Templom (Matthias Church), Budapest

Malta
St. John's Co-Cathedral, Valletta

Portugal
Jerónimos Monastery, Belém, Lisbon

Spain
The 10th-century Mezquita (Mosque), Córdoba

Classical Sights

Bulgaria
Roman amphitheater, Plovdiv

Cyprus
Ancient Curium and its amphitheater

Great Britain
The Roman baths, Bath

Greece
Delphi

Italy
Herculaneum and the temples of Paestum

Spain
Roman amphitheater, Mérida

Turkey
Ruins of Ephesus

Parks and Gardens

Austria
Hellbrunn, Salzburg

Denmark
Botanical Gardens, Copenhagen

Finland
Talvipuutarha, Helsinki

France
Monet's "Water Lily" garden, Giverny

Great Britain
Kensington Gardens, London

Holland
Palace Het Loo, Apeldoorn

Ireland
Japanese Gardens, Tully, County Kildare

Italy
Villa d'Este, Tivoli

Poland
Łazienki Park, Warsaw

Spain
Retiro Park, Madrid

Sweden
Linné Gardens, Uppsala

For Children

Denmark
Legoland, Billund

Finland
Santa Claus's Workshop, Arctic Circle, near Rovaniemi

France
Le Jardin d'Acclimatation, Paris
Ride to the top of the Eiffel Tower, Paris

Germany
Tierpark Hellabrun Zoo, Munich

Great Britain
Queen Mary's Dolls' House, Windsor

Holland
Musical Clock Museum, Utrecht

Italy
Exploring Castel Sant'Angelo, Rome

Norway
Cardamom Town, Kristiansand

Portugal
The beaches of the Algarve

Spain
Snowflake, the albino gorilla, Barcelona zoo

Sweden
Skansen in Stockholm

Shopping

Austria
Glass from the manufacturers at Neunagelberg

Belgium
Handmade Nihoul or Wittamer chocolates from Brussels

Denmark
Royal Copenhagen porcelain, Georg Jensen silver, Hans Wegner chairs

Finland
Iittala glass and Marimekko clothes

Great Britain
Cashmere sweaters from Edinburgh

Greece
Natural sponges from Kalymnos

Holland
Tulip bulbs, Schiphol Airport, Amsterdam

Iceland
Handmade woolen goods from Reykjavík

Ireland
Hand knits from Dublin, Cork, and Galway

Luxembourg
Villeroy & Boch porcelain

Portugal
Hand-embroidered carpets from Arraiolos

Romania
Art and craftwork from Transylvania

Spain
Pottery from Seville and Talavera de la Reina, outside Madrid

Sweden
Orrefors and Kosta Boda crystal

Turkey
Hand-woven carpets from Bodrum

Europe

Reykjavik
ICELAND

NORWAY
Bergen

SCOTLAND

NORTHERN
IRELAND

Edinburgh

North Sea

Skagerra

DENMARK

Belfast

IRELAND

Irish Sea

UNITED
KINGDOM

Dublin

WALES

Hamburg

Cardiff

ENGLAND

NETHERLANDS

London

The Hague

Amsterdam

Rotterdam

English Channel

Brussels

GERM

BELGIUM

Bonn

*ATLANTIC
OCEAN*

Paris

LUXEMBOURG

Frankfurt

FRANCE

Zürich

Munic

Bern
SWITZERLAND

LIECHTENSTE

Lyon

Milan

Ven

Monte
Carlo

Nice

PORTUGAL

ANDORRA

Marseille

MONACO

Florence

Madrid

Corsica

Lisbon

Barcelona

SPAIN

Seville

Granada

*Balearic
Islands*

Sardinia

Gibraltar

Mediterranean Sea

Tyrrheni

MOROCCO

ALGERIA

400 miles

TUNISIA

0

0

600 km

World Time Zones

Numbers below vertical bands relate each zone to Greenwich Mean Time (0 hrs.).
Local times frequently differ from these general indications,
as indicated by light-face numbers on map.

Algiers, **29**

Anchorage, **3**

Athens, **41**

Auckland, **1**

Baghdad, **46**

Bangkok, **50**

Beijing, **54**

Berlin, **34**

Bogotá, **19**

Budapest, **37**

Buenos Aires, **24**

Caracas, **22**

Chicago, **9**

Copenhagen, **33**

Dallas, **10**

Delhi, **48**

Denver, **8**

Djakarta, **53**

Dublin, **26**

Edmonton, **7**

Hong Kong, **56**

Honolulu, **2**

Istanbul, **40**

Jerusalem, **42**

Johannesburg, **44**

Lima, **20**

Lisbon, **28**

London
(Greenwich), **27**

Los Angeles, **6**

Madrid, **38**

Manila, **57**

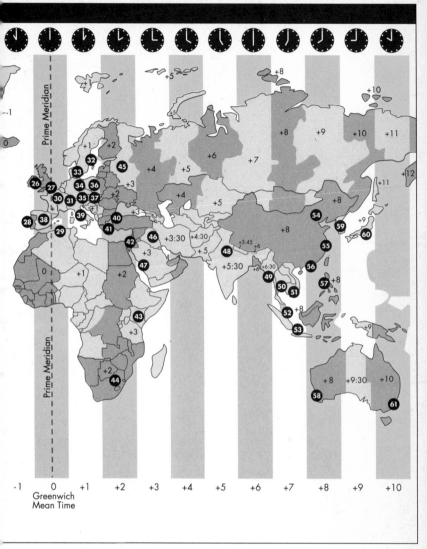

Mecca, **47**
Mexico City, **12**
Miami, **18**
Montréal, **15**
Moscow, **45**
Nairobi, **43**
New Orleans, **11**
New York City, **16**

Ottawa, **14**
Paris, **30**
Perth, **58**
Reykjavík, **25**
Rio de Janeiro, **23**
Rome, **39**
Saigon (Ho Chi Minh City), **51**

San Francisco, **5**
Santiago, **21**
Seoul, **59**
Shanghai, **55**
Singapore, **52**
Stockholm, **32**
Sydney, **61**
Tokyo, **60**

Toronto, **13**
Vancouver, **4**
Vienna, **35**
Warsaw, **36**
Washington, D.C., **17**
Yangon, **49**
Zürich, **31**

1 The Gold Guide

IMPORTANT CONTACTS / THE GOLD GUIDE

IMPORTANT CONTACTS A TO Z

An Alphabetical Listing of Publications, Organizations, and Companies That Will Help You Before, During, and After Your Trip

No single travel resource can give you every detail about every topic that might interest or concern you at the various stages of your journey—when you're planning your trip, while you're on the road, and after you get back home. The following organizations, books, and brochures will supplement the information in *Europe '96*. For related information, including both basic tips on visiting Europe and background information on many of the topics below, study Smart Travel Tips A to Z, the section that follows Important Contacts A to Z.

A
AIR TRAVEL

CARRIERS

U.S. airlines that serve major European cities include **American Airlines** (tel. 800/433–7300); **Continental** (tel. 800/231–0856); **Delta** (tel. 800/241–4141); **Northwest** (tel. 800/447–4747); **TWA** (tel. 800/892–4141); and **United** (tel. 800/538–2929).

European national airlines that fly directly from the United States: **Austria:** Austrian Airlines (tel. 800/843–0002); **Belgium:** Sabena Belgian World Airlines (tel. 800/955–2000); **Cyprus:** Cyprus Airways

(tel. 212/714–2190); **Czech Republic and Slovakia:** Czechoslovak Airlines (CSA, tel. 212/765–6022); **Denmark:** Scandinavian Airlines (SAS, tel. 800/221–2350); **Finland:** Finnair (tel. 800/950–5000); **France:** Air France (tel. 800/237–2747); **Germany:** Lufthansa (tel. 800/645–3880); **Great Britain:** British Airways (tel. 800/247–9297); Virgin Atlantic (tel. 800/862–8621); **Greece:** Olympic Airways (tel. 212/838–3600 or 800/223–1226 outside NY); **Holland:** KLM Royal Dutch Airlines (tel. 800/374–7747); **Hungary:** Malév Hungarian Airlines (tel. 212/757–6446); **Iceland:** Icelandair (tel. 800/223–5500); **Ireland:** Aer Lingus (800/223–6537); **Italy:** Alitalia (tel. 800/223–5730); **Malta:** Air Malta (tel. 415/362–2929); **Norway:** Scandinavian Airlines (SAS, tel. 800/221–2350); **Poland:** LOT Polish Airlines (tel. 212/869–1074); **Portugal:** TAP Air Portugal (tel. 800/221–7370); **Romania:** Tarom Romanian Airlines (tel. 212/687–6013); **Spain:** Iberia Airlines (tel. 800/772–4642); **Sweden:** Scandinavian Airlines (SAS, tel. 800/221–2350); **Switzerland:** Swissair (tel. 800/221–4750); and **Turkey:** THY Turkish Airlines (tel. 212/986–5050).

COMPLAINTS

To register complaints about charter and scheduled airlines, contact the U.S. Department of Transportation's **Office of Consumer Affairs** (400 7th St. NW, Washington, DC 20590, tel. 202/366–2220 or 800/322–7873).

CONSOLIDATORS

Established consolidators selling to the public include **Euram Tours** (1522 K St. NW, Suite 430, Washington, DC 20005, tel. 800/848–6789) and **TFI Tours International** (34 W. 32nd St., New York, NY 10001, tel. 212/736–1140 or 800/745–8000).

PUBLICATIONS

For general information about charter carriers, ask for the Office of Consumer Affairs brochure **"Plane Talk: Public Charter Flights."** The Department of Transportation also publishes a 58-page booklet, **"Fly Rights"** (Consumer Information Center, Dept. 133-B, Pueblo, CO 81009; $1.75).

For other tips and hints, consult the Consumers Union's monthly **"Consumer Reports Travel Letter"** (Box 53629, Boulder, CO 80322, tel. 800/234–1970; $39 annually) and the newsletter **"Travel Smart"**

(40 Beechdale Rd., Dobbs Ferry, NY 10522, tel. 800/327–3633; $37 annually); *The Official Frequent Flyer Guidebook,* by Randy Petersen (4715-C Town Center Dr., Colorado Springs, CO 80916, tel. 719/597–8899 or 800/487–8893; $14.99 plus $3 shipping); *Airfare Secrets Exposed,* by Sharon Tyler and Matthew Wonder (Universal Information Publishing; $16.95 plus $3.75 shipping from Sandcastle Publishing, Box 3070-A, South Pasadena, CA 91031, tel. 213/255–3616 or 800/655–0053); and *202 Tips Even the Best Business Travelers May Not Know,* by Christopher McGinnis (Irwin Professional Publishing, 1333 Burr Ridge Pkwy., Burr Ridge, IL 60521, tel. 708/789–4000 or 800/634–3966; $10 plus $3.00 shipping).

B
BETTER BUSINESS BUREAU

For local contacts in the home town of a tour operator you may be considering, consult the **Council of Better Business Bureaus** (4200 Wilson Blvd., Arlington, VA 22203, tel. 703/276–0100).

BUS TRAVEL

FROM THE U.K.
Eurolines links London with the English Channel ferry ports and Amsterdam, Paris, Antwerp, Brussels, and other points farther afield in Germany, France, and Italy. Night service to Paris takes

about 8 hours; the overnight journey time to Amsterdam is about 12 hours. **Citysprint** uses the Ramsgate–Oostende Jetfoil service en route to Amsterdam to reduce travel time to a little more than eight hours. **National Express** uses Sealink ferries (*see* Ferry Travel, *below*) to the Republic of Ireland. A connecting bus service in Ireland is operated by Bus Éireann. Sailings are from Fishguard to Rosslare—a 3½-hour crossing. Eurolines services can be booked in person at **National Express** offices at Victoria Coach Station or at 52 Grosvenor Gardens, London SW1W OAU, opposite Victoria Rail Station (tel. 0171/730–0202), at any National Express agent throughout Britain, and at **Eurolines** (23 Crawley Rd., Luton LU1 1HX, tel. 01582/404511). **Citysprint** services can be booked at Victoria Coach Station or by calling 01304/240241.

C
CAR RENTAL

Major car-rental companies represented in Europe include **Alamo** (tel. 800/327–9633, 0800/272-2000 in the United Kingdom), **Avis** (tel. 800/331–1084, 800/879–2847 in Canada), **Budget** (tel. 800/527–0700, 0800/181–181 in the United Kingdom), **Hertz** (tel. 800/654–3001, 800/263–0600 in Canada, 0181/679–1799 in the United Kingdom), and **National** (sometimes known as Europcar

InterRent outside North America; tel. 800/227–3876, 0181/950–5050 in the United Kingdom).

Car rental prices vary considerably throughout Europe, as does tax. Rates in London begin at $21 a day and $126 a week for an economy car with unlimited mileage (plus 17.5% tax). Rates in Paris begin at $180 a week for an economy car with unlimited mileage (plus 18.6% tax). In Madrid, rates start at $24 a day and $167 a week (plus 16% tax). In Rome, rates begin at $48 a day and $185 a week for an economy car with unlimited mileage (plus 19% tax). Many car rental agencies in Rome impose mandatory theft insurance on all rentals. Coverage costs $10–$15 a day.

RENTAL WHOLESALERS

Contact **Auto Europe** (Box 7006, Portland, ME 04112, tel. 207/828–2525 or 800/223–5555); **Europe by Car** in New York City (write 1 Rockefeller Plaza, 10020; visit 14 W. 49th St.; or call 212/581–3040, 212/245–1713, or 800/223–1516) or Los Angeles (9000 Sunset Blvd., 90069, tel. 800/252–9401 or 213/272–0424 in CA); **Foremost Euro-Car** (5658 Sepulveda Blvd., Suite 201, Van Nuys, CA 91411, tel. 818/786–1960 or 800/272–3299); or the **Kemwel Group** (106 Calvert St., Harrison, NY 10528, tel. 914/835–5555 or 800/678–0678).

THE CHANNEL
TUNNEL

For information, contact **Le Shuttle** (tel. 0990/353535 in the United Kingdom, 800/388–3876 in the United States), which transports cars, or **Eurostar** (tel. 01233/617575 in the United Kingdom, 800/942–4866 in the United States), the high-speed train service between London (Waterloo) and Paris (Gare du Nord). Eurostar tickets are available in the United Kingdom through **British Rail International** (BritRail Victoria Station, London, tel. 0171/834–2345 or 01233/617575 for credit-card bookings), and in the United States through **Rail Europe** (tel. 800/942–4866 or 800/438–7245) and **BritRail Travel** (1500 Broadway, New York, NY 10036, tel. 212/575–2667 or 800/677–8585).

CHILDREN
AND TRAVEL

FLYING

Look into **"Flying with Baby"** (Third Street Press, Box 261250, Littleton, CO 80126, tel. 303/595–5959; $5.95 plus $1 shipping), cowritten by a flight attendant. **"Kids and Teens in Flight,"** free from the U.S. Department of Transportation's Office of Consumer Affairs, offers tips for children flying alone. Every two years the February issue of *Family Travel Times* (*see* Know-How, *below*) details children's services on three dozen airlines.

KNOW-HOW

Family Travel Times, published 10 times annually by Travel with Your Children (TWYCH, 45 W. 18th St., New York, NY 10011, tel. 212/206–0688; annual subscription $55), covers destinations, types of vacations, and modes of travel.

The *Family Travel Guides* catalogue (tel. 510/527–5849; $1 postage) lists about 200 books and articles on family travel. Also check *Take Your Baby and Go! A Guide for Traveling with Babies, Toddlers and Young Children,* by Sheri Andrews, Judy Bordeaux, and Vivian Vasquez (Bear Creek Publications, 2507 Minor Ave., Seattle, WA 98102, tel. 206/322–7604 or 800/326–6566; $5.95 plus $1.50 shipping). *Innocents Abroad: Traveling with Kids in Europe,* by Valerie Wolf Deutsch and Laura Sutherland (Penguin USA, 120 Woodbine St., Bergenfield, NJ 07621, tel. 201/387–0600 or 800/253–6476; $15.95 or $4.95 paperback), covers child- and teen-friendly activities, food, and transportation.

LODGING

Novotel hotels (tel. 800/221–4542) permit up to two children to stay free in their parents' room. **Sofitel** hotels (tel. 800/221–4542) offer a free second room for children during July and August and over the Christmas holiday.

Holiday Fun with Kids, at more than 100 properties in Switzerland, offers programs for children at reduced prices; contact the Swiss National Tourist Office (608 5th Ave., New York, NY 10019, tel. 212/757–5944) for a brochure. The **Sol and Melia chains** (tel. 800/336–3542) in Spain permit children 12 and under to stay free with their parents. **Italy's CIGA hotels** (reservations, tel. 800/221–2340) welcome families as well.

RESORTS

Club Med (40 W. 57th St., New York, NY 10019, tel. 800/258–2633) has "Baby Clubs" (from age four months), "Mini Clubs" (for ages four to six or eight, depending on the resort), and "Kids Clubs" (for ages eight and up during school holidays) at many of its resort villages in France, Italy, Switzerland, and Spain.

TOUR OPERATORS

Contact **Grandtravel** (6900 Wisconsin Ave., Suite 706, Chevy Chase, MD 20815, tel. 301/986–0790 or 800/247–7651), which has tours for people traveling with grandchildren ages 7 to 17; **Families Welcome!** (21 W. Colony Pl., Suite 140, Durham, NC 27705, tel. 919/489–2555 or 800/326–0724); or **Rascals in Paradise** (650 5th St., Suite 505, San Francisco, CA 94107, tel. 415/978–9800 or 800/872–7225).

If you're outdoorsy, look into **American**

Wilderness Experience
(Box 1486, Boulder,
CO 80306, tel. 303/
444–2622 or 800/444–
0099), the **American
Museum of Natural
History** (79th St. and
Central Park W, New
York, NY 10024, tel.
212/769–5700 or 800/
462–8687), and **Wild-
land Adventures** (3516
N.E. 155th St., Seattle,
WA 98155, tel. 206/
365–0686 or 800/345–
4453).

CUSTOMS

U.S. CITIZENS

The **U.S. Customs
Service** (Box 7407,
Washington, DC
20044, tel. 202/927–
6724) can answer
questions on duty-free
limits and publishes a
helpful brochure,
"Know Before You
Go." For information
on registering foreign-
made articles, call
202/927–0540.

CANADIANS

Contact **Revenue
Canada** (2265 St.
Laurent Blvd. S, Ot-
tawa, Ontario, K1G
4K3, tel. 613/993–
0534) for a copy of
the free brochure **"I
Declare/Je Déclare"**
and for details on duties
on purchases exceeding
the standard duty-free
limit.

U.K. CITIZENS

**HM Customs and
Excise** (Dorset House,
Stamford St., London
SE1 9NG, tel. 0171/
202–4227) can answer
questions about U.K.
customs regulations and
publishes **"A Guide for
Travellers,"** detailing
standard procedures
and import rules.

D
FOR TRAVELERS
WITH DISABILITIES

COMPLAINTS

To register complaints
under the provisions of
the Americans with
Disabilities Act, contact
the U.S. Department of
Justice's **Public Access
Section** (Box 66738,
Washington, DC 20035,
tel. 202/514–0301, FAX
202/307–1198, TTY
202/514–0383).

ORGANIZATIONS

FOR TRAVELERS
WITH HEARING IMPAIR-
MENTS➤ Contact the
**American Academy
of Otolaryngology**
(1 Prince St., Alexan-
dria, VA 22314, tel.
703/836–4444, FAX
703/683–5100, TTY
703/519–1585).

FOR TRAVELERS
WITH MOBILITY PROB-
LEMS➤ Contact the
**Information Center for
Individuals with Dis-
abilities** (Fort Point Pl.,
27–43 Wormwood St.,
Boston, MA 02210, tel.
617/727–5540, 800/
462–5015 in MA, TTY
617/345–9743); **Mobil-
ity International USA**
(Box 10767, Eugene,
OR 97440, tel. and
TTY 503/343–1284,
fax 503/343–6812), the
U.S. branch of an
international organiza-
tion based in Belgium
(*see below*) that has
affiliates in 30 coun-
tries; **MossRehab
Hospital Travel Infor-
mation Service** (1200
W. Tabor Rd., Philadel-
phia, PA 19141, tel.
215/456–9603, TTY
215/456–9602); the
**Society for the Ad-
vancement of Travel
for the Handicapped**

(347 5th Ave., Suite
610, New York, NY
10016, tel. 212/447–
7284, fax 212/725–
8253); the **Travel
Industry and Disabled
Exchange** (TIDE, 5435
Donna Ave., Tarzana,
CA 91356, tel. 818/
344–3640, fax 818/
344–0078); and **Trav-
elin' Talk** (Box 3534,
Clarksville, TN 37043,
tel. 615/552–6670, fax
615/552–1182).

FOR TRAVELERS WITH
VISION IMPAIRMENTS➤
Contact the **American
Council of the Blind**
(1155 15th St. NW,
Suite 720, Washington,
DC 20005, tel. 202/
467–5081, fax 202/
467–5085) or the
**American Foundation
for the Blind** (15 W.
16th St., New York,
NY 10011, tel. 212/
620–2000, TTY 212/
620–2158).

IN THE U.K.

Contact the **Royal
Association for Disabil-
ity and Rehabilitation**
(RADAR, 12 City
Forum, 250 City Rd.,
London EC1V 8AF, tel.
0171/250–3222) or
Mobility International
(Rue de Manchester 25,
B–1070 Brussels, Bel-
gium, tel. 00–322/410–
62–97), an international
clearinghouse of travel
information for people
with disabilities.

PUBLICATIONS

Several free publications
are available from the
U.S. Information Center
(Box 100, Pueblo, CO
81009, tel. 719/948–
3334): **"New Horizons
for the Air Traveler
with a Disability"**
(address to Dept. 355A),
describing legally man-
dated changes; the

pocket-size **"Fly Smart"** (Dept. 575B), good on flight safety; and the Airport Operators Council's worldwide **"Access Travel: Airports"** (Dept. 575A).

The 500-page **Travelin' Talk Directory** ((Box 3534, Clarksville, TN 37043, tel. 615/552–6670; $35) lists people and organizations who help travelers with disabilities. For specialist travel agents worldwide, consult the **Directory of Travel Agencies for the Disabled** (Twin Peaks Press, Box 129, Vancouver, WA 98666, tel. 206/694–2462 or 800/637–2256; $19.95 plus $2 shipping).

TRAVEL AGENCIES AND TOUR OPERATORS

The Americans with Disabilities Act requires that travel firms serve the needs of all travelers. However, some agencies and operators specialize in making group and individual arrangements for travelers with disabilities, among them **Access Adventures** (206 Chestnut Ridge Rd., Rochester, NY 14624, tel. 716/889–9096), run by a former physical-rehab counselor. In addition, many general-interest operators and agencies (*see* Tours Operators, *below*) can arrange vacations for travelers with disabilities.

FOR TRAVELERS WITH MOBILITY PROBLEMS➤ A number of operators specialize in working with travelers with mobility impairments: **Accessible Journeys**

(35 W. Sellers Ave., Ridley Park, PA 19078, tel. 610/521–0339 or 800/846–4537, fax 610/521–6959), a registered nursing service that arranges vacations; **Flying Wheels Travel** (143 W. Bridge St., Box 382, Owatonna, MN 55060, tel. 507/451–5005 or 800/535–6790), a travel agency that specializes in European cruises and tours; **Hinsdale Travel Service** (201 E. Ogden Ave., Suite 100, Hinsdale, IL 60521, tel. 708/325–1335 or 800/303–5521), a travel agency that will give you access to the services of wheelchair traveler Janice Perkins; **Nautilus Tours** (5435 Donna Ave., Tarzana, CA 91356, tel. 818/344–3640 or 800/345–4654); and **Wheelchair Journeys** (16979 Redmond Way, Redmond, WA 98052, tel. 206/885–2210), which can handle arrangements worldwide.

FOR TRAVELERS WITH DEVELOPMENTAL DISABILITIES➤ Contact the nonprofit **New Directions** (5276 Hollister Ave., Suite 207, Santa Barbara, CA 93111, tel. 805/967–2841).

Options include **Entertainment Travel Editions** (Box 1068, Trumbull, CT 06611, tel. 800/445–4137; fee $28–$53, depending on destination), **Great American Traveler** (Box 27965, Salt Lake City, UT 84127, tel. 800/548–2812; $49.95 annually), **Moment's Notice Discount Travel Club** (163 Amsterdam

Ave., Suite 137, New York, NY 10023, tel. 212/486–0500; $25 annually, single or family), **Privilege Card** (3391 Peachtree Rd. NE, Suite 110, Atlanta GA 30326, tel. 404/262–0222 or 800/236–9732; $74.95 annually), **Travelers Advantage** (CUC Travel Service, 49 Music Sq. W, Nashville, TN 37203, tel. 800/548–1116 or 800/648–4037; $49 annually, single or family), and **Worldwide Discount Travel Club** (1674 Meridian Ave., Miami Beach, FL 33139, tel. 305/534–2082; $50 annually for family, $40 single).

AUTO CLUBS

In the United Kingdom, the **Automobile Association** (Box 128, Basingstoke, Hampshire RG21 1BR; tel. 0345/555577) and the **Royal Automobile Club** (RAC Travel Services, Box 499, Croydon CR2 6ZH, tel. 0800/550–550) operate on-the-spot breakdown and repair services across Europe. Replacement cars can be provided in case of accidents. U.S. citizens cannot use these services on the Continent.

E

Send a SASE to the **Franzus Company** (Customer Service, Dept. B50, Murtha Industrial Park, Box 142, Beacon Falls, CT 06403, tel. 203/723–6664) for a copy of the free brochure "Foreign Electricity Is No Deep Dark Secret."

F
FERRY TRAVEL

Ferry service from the United Kingdom to many European countries is provided by: **Brittany Ferries** (Millbay Docks, Plymouth PL1 3EW, tel. 01705/827701; to France, Spain); **Color Line** (International Ferry Terminal, Royal Quays, North Shields NE29 6EE, tel. 01912/961313; to Norway); **Eurolink Ferries** (Ferry Terminal, Sheerness, Kent ME12 1RX, tel. 01233/617575; to Germany, Holland); **Hoverspeed** (International Hoverport, Marine Parade, Dover, Kent CT17 9TG, tel. 01304/240241; to France); **Irish Ferries** (150 New Bond St., London W1Y 0AQ, tel. 0171/491–8682; to Ireland); **North Sea Ferries** (King George Dock, Hedon Rd., Hull HU9 5QA, tel. 01482/795141; to Holland); **P&O European Ferries** (Channel House, Channel View Rd., Dover, Kent CT17 9TJ, tel. 01304/203388 or 0181/575–8555 in London; to France, Spain, Northern Ireland); **Sally Line** (Argyle Centre, York St., Ramsgate CT11 9DS, tel. 01843/595522; to Belgium, France); **Scandinavian Seaways** (Scandinavia House, Parkeston Quay, Harwich, Essex CO12 4QG, tel. 01255/240240; to Denmark, Germany, Sweden); **Sealink** (Charter House, Park St., Ashford, Kent TN24 8EX, tel. 01233/647047; to France,

Germany, Holland, Ireland); and **Swansea Cork Ferries** (Kings Dock, Swansea SA1 8RU, tel. 01792/456116; to Ireland).

G
GAY AND
LESBIAN TRAVEL

ORGANIZATION

The **International Gay Travel Association** (Box 4974, Key West, FL 33041, tel. 800/448–8550), a consortium of 800 businesses, can supply names of travel agents and tour operators.

PUBLICATIONS

The premiere international travel magazine for gays and lesbians is *Our World* (1104 N. Nova Rd., Suite 251, Daytona Beach, FL 32117, tel. 904/441–5367; $35 for 10 issues). The 16-page monthly *"Out & About"* (tel. 212/645–6922 or 800/929–2268; $49 for 10 issues), covers gay-friendly resorts, hotels, cruise lines, and airlines.

TOUR OPERATORS

Cruises and resort vacations are handled by **RSVP Travel Productions** (2800 University Ave. SE, Minneapolis, MN 55414, tel. 800/328–7787) for gays, **Olivia** (4400 Market St., Oakland, CA 94608, tel. 800/631–6277) for lesbian travelers. For mixed gay and lesbian travel, contact **Hanns Ebensten Travel** (513 Fleming St., Key West, FL 33040, tel. 305/294–8174), one of the nation's oldest

operators in the gay market, and **Toto Tours** (1326 W. Albion Suite 3W, Chicago, IL 60626, tel. 312/274–8686 or 800/565–1241), which has group tours worldwide.

TRAVEL AGENCIES

The largest agencies serving gay travelers are **Advance Travel** (10700 Northwest Freeway, Suite 160, Houston, TX 77092, tel. 713/682–2002 or 800/695–0880), **Islanders/Kennedy Travel** (183 W. 10th St., New York, NY 10014, tel. 212/242–3222 or 800/988–1181), **Now Voyager** (4406 18th St., San Francisco, CA 94114, tel. 415/626–1169 or 800/255–6951), and **Yellowbrick Road** (1500 W. Balmoral Ave., Chicago, IL 60640, tel. 312/561–1800 or 800/642–2488). **Skylink Women's Travel** (746 Ashland Ave., Santa Monica, CA 90405, tel. 310/452–0506 or 800/225-5759) works with lesbians.

H
HEALTH ISSUES

FINDING A DOCTOR

For members, the **International Association for Medical Assistance to Travellers** (IAMAT, 417 Center St., Lewiston, NY 14092, tel. 716/754–4883; 40 Regal Rd., Guelph, Ontario, Canada N1K 1B5, tel. 519/836–0102; 1287 St. Clair Ave., Toronto, Ontario, Canada M6E 1B8, tel. 416/652–0137; 57 Voirets, 1212

THE GOLD GUIDE / IMPORTANT CONTACTS

Grand-Lancy, Geneva, Switzerland; membership free) publishes a worldwide directory of English-speaking physicians who meet IAMAT standards.

MEDICAL-ASSISTANCE COMPANIES

Contact **International SOS Assistance** (Box 11568, Philadelphia, PA 19116, tel. 215/244–1500 or 800/523–8930; Box 466, Pl. Bonaventure, Montréal, Québec, Canada H5A 1C1, tel. 514/874–7674 or 800/363–0263), **Medex Assistance Corporation** (Box 10623, Baltimore, MD 21285, tel. 410/296–2530 or 800/573–2029), **Near Services** (Box 1339, Calumet City, IL 60409, tel. 708/868–6700 or 800/654–6700), and **Travel Assistance International** (1133 15th St. NW, Suite 400, Washington, DC 20005, tel. 202/331–1609 or 800/821–2828). Because these companies also sell death-and-dismemberment, trip-cancellation, and other insurance coverage, there is some overlap with the travel-insurance policies sold by the companies listed under Insurance, *below.*

WARNINGS

The **National Centers for Disease Control** (Center for Preventive Services, Division of Quarantine, Traveler's Health Section, 1600 Clifton Rd., MSE03, Atlanta, GA 30333, automated hot line 404/332–4559) provides information on health risks abroad and vaccination require-

ments and recommendations.

I

INSURANCE

Travel insurance covering baggage, health, and trip cancellation or interruptions is available from **Access America** (Box 90315, Richmond, VA 23286, tel. 804/285–3300 or 800/284–8300), **Carefree Travel Insurance** (Box 9366, 100 Garden City Plaza, Garden City, NY 11530, tel. 516/294–0220 or 800/323–3149), **Near Services** (Box 1339, Calumet City, IL 60409, tel. 708/868–6700 or 800/654–6700), **Tele-Trip** (Mutual of Omaha Plaza, Box 31716, Omaha, NE 68131, tel. 800/228–9792), **Travel Insured International** (Box 280568, East Hartford, CT 06128, tel. 203/528–7663 or 800/243–3174), **Travel Guard International** (1145 Clark St., Stevens Point, WI 54481, tel. 715/345–0505 or 800/826–1300), and **Wallach & Company** (107 W. Federal St., Box 480, Middleburg, VA 22117, tel. 703/687–3166 or 800/237–6615).

IN THE U.K.

The **Association of British Insurers** (51 Gresham St., London EC2V 7HQ, tel. 0171/600–3333; 30 Gordon St., Glasgow G1 3PU, tel. 0141/226–3905; Scottish Provident Building, Donegall Sq. W, Belfast BT1 6JE, tel. 01232/249176; call for other locations) gives advice by phone and publishes the free **"Holiday Insurance,"** which

sets out typical policy provisions and costs.

L

LODGING

APARTMENT AND VILLA RENTAL

Among the companies to contact are **At Home Abroad** (405 E. 56th St., Suite 6H, New York, NY 10022, tel. 212/421–9165), **Europa-Let** (92 N. Main St., Ashland, OR 97520, tel. 503/482–5806 or 800/462–4486), **Hometours International** (Box 11503, Knoxville, TN 37939, tel. 615/588–8722 or 800/367–4668), **Interhome** (124 Little Falls Rd., Fairfield, NJ 07004, tel. 201/882–6864), **Property Rentals International** (1008 Mansfield Crossing Rd., Richmond, VA 23236, tel. 804/378–6054 or 800/220–3332), **Rental Directories International** (2044 Rittenhouse Sq., Philadelphia, PA 19103, tel. 215/985–4001), **Rent-a-Home International** (7200 34th Ave. NW, Seattle, WA 98117, tel. 206/789–9377 or 800/488–7368), **Vacation Home Rentals Worldwide** (235 Kensington Ave., Norwood, NJ 07648, tel. 201/767–9393 or 800/633–3284), **Villas and Apartments Abroad** (420 Madison Ave., Suite 1105, New York, NY 10017, tel. 212/759–1025 or 800/433–3020), and **Villas International** (605 Market St., Suite 510, San Francisco, CA 94105, tel. 415/281–0910 or 800/221–

2260). Members of the travel club **Hideaways International** (767 Islington St., Portsmouth, NH 03801, tel. 603/430–4433 or 800/843–4433; $99 annually) receive two annual guides plus quarterly newsletters, and arrange rentals among themselves.

HOME EXCHANGE

Principal clearinghouses include **HomeLink International/Vacation Exchange Club** (Box 650, Key West, FL 33041, tel. 305/294–1448 or 800/638–3841; $60 annually), which gives members four annual directories, with a listing in one, plus updates; **Intervac International** (Box 590504, San Francisco, CA 94159, tel. 415/435–3497; $65 annually), which has three annual directories; and **Loan-a-Home** (2 Park La., Apt. 6E, Mount Vernon, NY 10552, tel. 914/664–7640; $35–$45 annually), which specializes in long-term exchanges.

M
MONEY MATTERS

ATMS

For foreign **Cirrus** locations, call 800/424–7787; for foreign **Plus** locations, consult the Plus directory at your local bank.

CURRENCY EXCHANGE

If your bank doesn't exchange currency, contact **Thomas Cook Currency Services** (41 E. 42nd St., New York, NY 10017 or 511 Madison Ave., New York, NY 10022, tel.

212/757–6915 or 800/223–7373 for locations) or **Ruesch International** (tel. 800/424–2923 for locations).

WIRING FUNDS

Funds can be wired via **American Express MoneyGram℠** (tel. 800/926–9400 from the United States and Canada; when abroad, call collect 303/980–3340 for details and locations) or **Western Union** (tel. 800/325–6000 for agent locations or to send using Master-Card or Visa, 800/321–2923 in Canada).

P
PASSPORTS
AND VISAS

U.S. CITIZENS

For fees, documentation requirements, and other information, call the **Office of Passport Services** information line (tel. 202/647–0518).

CANADIANS

For fees, documentation requirements, and other information, call the Ministry of Foreign Affairs and International Trade's **Passport Office** (tel. 819/994–3500 or 800/567–6868).

U.K. CITIZENS

For information on fees and documentation requirements or to get an emergency passport call the **London Passport Office** (tel. 0171/271–3000).

PHOTO HELP

The **Kodak Information Center** (tel. 800/242–2424) answers consumer questions about film and photog-

raphy. The **Kodak Guide to Shooting Great Travel Pictures** explains techniques for getting the best shots (Fodor's Travel Publications, tel. 800/533–6478; $16.50).

R
RAIL TRAVEL

DISCOUNT PASSES

An excellent value if you plan to rack up the miles, **EurailPasses** provide unlimited first-class rail travel during their period of validity in Austria, Belgium, Denmark, Finland, France, Germany, Greece, Hungary, the Irish Republic, Italy, Luxembourg, the Netherlands, Norway, Portugal, Spain, Sweden, and Switzerland (but not England, Scotland, Northern Ireland, and Wales). Standard passes are available for 15 days ($498), 21 days ($648), one month ($728), two months ($1,098), and three months ($1,398). **Eurail Saverpasses, Eurail Youthpasses** (for those under 26), **Eurail Flexipasses,** and **Eurail Youth Flexipasses** offer additional choices. Another option is the **Europass,** featuring a minimum of 5 and a maximum of 15 days (within a two-month period) of unlimited rail travel in your choice of three to all five of the participating countries (France, Germany, Italy, Spain, and Switzerland). With Europass, if two people travel together first-class, the second receives a half-price pass. The second-class **Youth Europass,**

THE GOLD GUIDE / IMPORTANT CONTACTS

for travelers under 26, covers four countries for the price of three countries for 5–10 days' travel; a fifth country is free with 11–15 days' travel within a two-month period. Europass and Europass Youth purchasers can also receive discounts on Eurostar, the Channel Tunnel train. Apply through your travel agent or **Rail Europe** (226–230 Westchester Ave., White Plains, NY 10604, tel. 800/438–7245 or 800/848–7245 or 2087 Dundas E, Suite 105, Mississauga, Ontario, Canada L4X 1M2, tel. 416/602–4195), **DER Tours** (Box 1606, Des Plaines, IL 60017, tel. 800/782–2424, fax 800/282–7474), or **CIT Tours Corp.** (342 Madison Ave., Suite 207, New York, NY 10173, tel. 212/697–2100 or 800/248–8687; 310/670–4269 or 800/248–7245 in western United States).

Rail Europe also sells single-country passes for Austria, Bulgaria, the Czech Republic, Finland, France, Germany, Greece, Hungary, Norway, Poland, Portugal, Romania, Russia, Spain, and Switzerland, as well as multicountry passes.

Travelers under 26 who have resided in Europe for at least six months qualify for the **Inter Rail Card,** which offers discounted travel. Cards are available from rail stations.

If you plan to do a lot of rail traveling in Great Britain, look into the many **BritRail Passes**

offered by **BritRail Travel International** (1500 Broadway, New York, NY 10036, tel. 212/575–2667 or 800/677–8585 or 94 Cumberland St., Toronto, Ontario, Canada M5R 1A3, tel. 416/482–1777).

S
SENIOR CITIZENS

EDUCATIONAL TRAVEL

The nonprofit **Elderhostel** (75 Federal St., 3rd Floor, Boston, MA 02110, tel. 617/426–7788), for people 60 and older, has offered inexpensive study programs since 1975. The nearly 2,000 courses cover everything from marine science to Greek myths and cowboy poetry. Fees for two- to three-week international trips—including room, board, and transportation from the United States—range from $1,800 to $4,500.

For people 50 and over and their children and grandchildren, **Interhostel** (University of New Hampshire, 6 Garrison Ave., Durham, NH 03824, tel. 603/862–1147 or 800/733–9753) runs 10-day summer programs involving lectures, field trips, and sightseeing. Most last two weeks and cost $2,125–$3,100, including airfare.

ORGANIZATIONS

Contact the **American Association of Retired Persons** (AARP, 601 E St. NW, Washington, DC 20049, tel. 202/434–2277; $8 per person or couple annu-

ally). Its Purchase Privilege Program gets members discounts on lodging, car rentals, and sightseeing.

For more information on lodging, car rental, and other travel-product discounts, along with magazines and newsletters, contact the **National Council of Senior Citizens** (1331 F St. NW, Washington, DC 20004, tel. 202/347–8800; membership $12 annually) and **Mature Outlook** (6001 N. Clark St., Chicago, IL 60660, tel. 312/465–6466 or 800/336–6330; subscription $9.95 annually).

PUBLICATIONS

The 50+ Traveler's Guidebook: Where to Go, Where to Stay, What to Do, by Anita Williams and Merrimac Dillon (St. Martin's Press, 175 5th Ave., New York, NY 10010, tel. 212/674–5151 or 800/288–2131; $12.95), offers many useful tips. **"The Mature Traveler"** (Box 50400, Reno, NV 89513; $29.95, tel. 702/786–7419), a monthly newsletter, covers travel deals.

SHIP TRAVEL

Cunard Line (555 5th Ave., New York, NY 10017, tel. 800/221–4770) operates four ships that make transatlantic crossings. The *Queen Elizabeth 2* (*QE2*) makes regular crossings April–December, between Southampton, England, and Baltimore, Boston, and New York City. Arrangements for the *QE2* can include one-way airfare. Cunard Line also offers fly/cruise packages and pre- and post-land packages. For other ships that sail to Europe, **check the travel pages of your Sunday newspaper**.

STUDENTS

GROUPS

Major tour operators include **Contiki Holidays** (300 Plaza Alicante, Suite 900, Garden Grove, CA 92640, tel. 714/740–0808 or 800/466–0610) and **AESU Travel** (2 Hamill Rd., Suite 248, Baltimore, MD 21210, tel. 410/323–4416 or 800/638–7640).

HOSTELING

Contact **Hostelling International–American Youth Hostels** (733 15th St. NW, Suite 840, Washington, DC 20005, tel. 202/783–6161) in the United States, **Hostelling International–Canada** (205 Catherine St., Suite 400, Ottawa, Ontario K2P 1C3, tel. 613/237–7884) in Canada, and the **Youth Hostel Association of England and Wales** (Trevelyan House, 8 St. Stephen's Hill, St. Albans, Hertfordshire AL1 2DY, tel. 01727/855215 and 01727/845047) in the United Kingdom. Membership ($25 in the United States, C$26.75 in Canada, and £9 in the United Kingdom) gets you access to 5,000 hostels worldwide that charge $7–$20 nightly per person.

ID CARDS

For discounts on transportation and

admissions, get the **International Student Identity Card** (ISIC) if you're a bona fide student or the **International Youth Card** (IYC) if you're under 26. In the United States, the ISIC and IYC cards cost $16 each and include basic travel-accident and illness coverage, plus a toll-free travel hot line. Apply through the Council on International Educational Exchange (*see* Organizations, *below*). Cards are available for $15 each in Canada from **Travel Cuts** (187 College St., Toronto, Ontario M5T 1P7, tel. 416/979–2406 or 800/667–2887) and in the United Kingdom for £5 each at student unions and student travel companies.

ORGANIZATIONS

A major contact is the **Council on International Educational Exchange** (CIEE, 205 E. 42nd St., 16th Floor, New York, NY 10017, tel. 212/661–1450), with locations in Boston (729 Boylston St., 02116, tel. 617/266–1926), Miami (9100 S. Dadeland Blvd., 33156, tel. 305/670–9261), Los Angeles (1093 Broxton Ave., 90024, tel. 310/208–3551), 43 other college towns nationwide, and the United Kingdom (28A Poland St., London W1V 3DB, tel. 0171/437–7767). Twice a year, it publishes *Student Travels* magazine. The CIEE's Council Travel Service is the exclusive U.S. agent for several student-discount cards.

Campus Connections (325 Chestnut St., Suite 1101, Philadelphia, PA 19106, tel. 215/625–8585 or 800/428–3235) specializes in discounted accommodations and airfares for students. The **Educational Travel Centre** (438 N. Frances St., Madison, WI 53703, tel. 608/256–5551) offers rail passes and low-cost airline tickets, mostly for flights departing from Chicago. For air travel only, contact **TMI Student Travel** (100 W. 33rd St., Suite 813, New York, NY 10001, tel. 800/245–3672).

In Canada, also contact **Travel Cuts** (*see* ID cards, *above*).

PUBLICATIONS

See the *Berkeley Guide to Europe* (Fodor's Travel Publications, tel. 800/533–6478 or from bookstores; $18.95).

T

TAX

For information about value-added tax (VAT) refunds, see the individual country chapters. You can also obtain a refund before leaving Europe if you've shopped at the 90,000 stores affiliated with the refund service **Europe Tax-free Shopping** (ETS, 233 S. Wacker Dr., Chicago, IL, tel. 312/382–1101). You ask for a check at the store, have it validated at customs at the airport, and claim a cash refund (minus 20% handling) at an ETS booth.

THE GOLD GUIDE / IMPORTANT CONTACTS

For local access numbers abroad, contact **AT&T** USADirect (tel. 800/874–4000), **MCI** Call USA (tel. 800/444–4444 or 800/444–4141 for automated hot line), or **Sprint** Express (tel. 800/793–1153).

Among the companies selling tours and packages to Europe, the following have a proven reputation, are nationally known, and have plenty of options to choose from.

GROUP TOURS

Superdeluxe, escorted, motor-coach tours of Europe are available from **Abercrombie & Kent** (1520 Kensington Rd., Oak Brook, IL 60521, tel. 708/954–2944 or 800/323–7308) and **Travcoa** (Box 2630, Newport Beach, CA, 92658, tel. 714/476–2800 or 800/992–2003). For deluxe tours, try **Tauck Tours** (11 Wilton Rd., Westport CT 06881, tel. 203/226–6911 or 800/468–2825) or **Maupintour** (Box 807, Lawrence KS 66044, tel. 913/843–1211 or 800/255–4266). Another operator falling between deluxe and first-class is **Globus** (5301 S. Federal Circle, Littleton, CO 80123, tel. 303/797-2800 or 800/221–0090). For first-class and first-class superior programs, try **Caravan Tours** (401 N. Michigan Ave., Chicago, IL 60611, tel. 312/321–9800 or 800/227–2826), **Trafalgar Tours** (21 E. 26th St.,

New York, NY 10010, tel. 212/689–8977 or 800/854–0103), **Brendan Tours** (15137 Califa St., Van Nuys, CA 91411, tel. 818/785–9696 or 800/421–8446), and **Insight International** (745 Atlantic Ave., Boston, MA 0211, tel. 617/482-2000 or 800/582-8380). For budget and tourist-class programs, contact **Cosmos** (*see* Globus, *above*).

PACKAGES

Just about every airline that flies to Europe sells independent vacation packages that include round-trip airfare and hotel accommodations. Among U.S. carriers, contact **American Airlines Fly AAway Vacations** (tel. 800/321–2121), **Continental Airlines Grand Destinations** (tel. 800/634–5555), **Delta Dream Vacations** (tel. 800/872–7786), and **United Airlines Vacation Planning Center** (tel. 800/328–6877). Independent packages are also available from leading tour operators. Contact **CIE Tours** (108 Ridgedale Ave., Box 2355, Morristown, NJ 07962, tel. 201/292-3899 or 800/243–8687), **DER Tours** (11933 Wilshire Blvd., Los Angeles, CA 90025, tel. 310/479–4140 or 800/782–2424), and **Jet Vacations** (1775 Broadway, New York, NY 10019, tel. 212/474–8740 or 800/538–2762).

THEME TRIPS

Travel Contacts (45 Idmiston Rd., London SE27 9HL, tel. 011/44–81766–7868, fax 011/

44–81766–6123), which has 135 member operators, can satisfy just about any special interest in Europe.

ADVENTURE➤ From rafting on Turkey's Coruh River to climbing the Austrian Alps, adventure travel in Europe can mean hiking, walking, skiing, cycling—you name it. Contact **All Adventure Travel** (5589 Arapahoe, No. 208, Boulder, CO 80303, tel. 800/537–4025), **Mountain Travel-Sobek** (6420 Fairmount Ave., El Cerrito, CA 94530, tel. 510/527–8100 or 800/227–2384), **Wilderness Travel** (801 Allston Way, Berkeley, CA 94710, tel. 510/548–0420 or 800/368–2794), **Himalayan Travel** (112 Prospect St., Stamford, CT 06901, tel. 800/225–2380, fax 203/359–3669), and **Uniquely Europe** (2819 First Ave., No. 280, Seattle, WA 98121, tel. 206/441–8682 or 800/426–3610).

In the United Kingdom, **Top Deck Travel** (131–135 Earl's Court Rd., London SW5 9RH, tel. 0171/244–8641) offers tours to Europe, with activities including flotilla sailing and a variety of water sports, including rafting.

ART AND ARCHITECTURE➤ For a variety of programs, contact **4th Dimension Tours** (1150 N.W. 72nd Ave., Suite 250, Miami, FL 33126, tel. 305/477–1525 or 800/343–0020), **Five Star Touring** (60 E. 42nd St., Suite 612, New York,

NY 10165, tel. 212/818–9140 or 800/792–7827), **Esplanade Tours** (581 Boylston St., Boston, MA 02116, tel. 617/266–7465 or 800/628–4893), **Archeological Tours** (271 Madison Ave., New York, NY 10016, tel. 212/986–3054, fax 212/370–1561), and the **Smithsonian Institution's Study Tours and Seminars** (1100 Jefferson Dr. SW, Room 3045, Washington, DC 20560, tel. 202/357–4700).

In the United Kingdom, contact **Prospect Music & Art Tours Ltd.** (454–458 Chiswick High Rd., London W4 5TT, tel. 0181/995–2151) and **Swann Hellenic Treasures Tours** (77 New Oxford St., London WC1A 1PP, tel. 0171/800–2300).

BALLOONING➤ **European Bombard Balloon Adventures** (855 Donald Rd., Juno Beach, FL 33408, tel. 407/775–0039 or 800/862–8537) operates balloon holidays in France, Italy, Austria, Turkey, the Czech Republic, and Switzerland.

In the United Kingdom, **Air 2 Air** (Vauxhall House, Coronation Rd., Bristol BS3 1RN, tel. 0117/963–3333), a clearinghouse for balloon activities in Britain, has information about what's happening on the Continent.

BARGE TRAVEL➤ For barge vacations in Europe, contact **Avalon Tours** (1909 Alden Landing, Portsmouth, RI 02871, tel. 401/683–1782 or 800/662–

2628), **Abercrombie & Kent** (1520 Kensington Rd., Oak Brook, IL 60521, tel. 708/954–2944 or 800/323–7308), **Le Boat** (201/342–1838 or 800/922–0291), and **Barge & Voyage** (140 E. 56th St., Suite 4C, New York, NY 10022, tel. 800/438–4748).

BICYCLING➤ Bike tours are available from **Backroads** (1516 5th St., Suite A550, Berkeley, CA 94710, tel. 510/527–1555 or 800/462–2848), **Butterfield & Robinson** (70 Bond St., Toronto, Ontario, Canada M5B 1X3, tel. 416/864–1354 or 800/387–1147), **Euro-Bike** (Box 990-P, De Kalb, IL 60115, tel. 800/321–6060, fax 815/758–8851), and **Classic Adventures** (Box 153, Hamlin, NY 14464, tel. 800/777–8090, fax 716/964–7297).

CRUISING➤ **EuroCruises** (303 W. 13th St., New York, NY 10014, tel. 212/691–2099 or 800/688–3876) represents more than 20 European-based cruise lines and 60 ships, ranging from 32-passenger yachts to 2,500-passenger ocean liners.

FISHING➤ **Fishing International** (Box 2132, Santa Rosa, CA 95405, tel. 800/950–4242, fax 707/539–1320) has trout- and salmon-fishing packages in Ireland, France, and Norway.

FOLK ART➤ **The Texas Connection** (207 Arden Grove, San Antonio, TX, tel. 210/980–9538) visits tapestry and embroidery workshops;

leather and ceramic studios; and famous markets in Spain, Portugal, Morocco, Great Britain, Hungary, Romania, Greece, and Turkey.

HISTORY➤ History buffs should contact **Herodot Travel** (7 S. Knoll Rd., Mill Valley, CA 94941, tel. and fax 415/381–4031).

HORSEBACK RIDING➤ **FITS Equestrian** (685 Lateen Rd., Solvang, CA 93463, tel. 805/688–9494, fax 805/688–2943) has tours for every level of rider.

HORTICULTURE➤ Amateur and professional gardeners alike should contact **Expo Garden Tours** (145 4th Ave., Suite 4A, New York, NY 10003, tel. 212/677–6704 or 800/448–2685).

MOTORCYCLING➤ **Beach's Motorcycle Adventures** (2763 W. River Pkwy., Grand Island, NY 14072, tel. 716/773–4960, fax 716/773–5227) can take you on Alpine adventures through Germany, Austria, Italy, France, Switzerland, and Lichtenstein.

MUSIC➤ **Dailey-Thorp Travel** (330 W. 58th St., New York, NY 10019, tel. 212/307–1555; book through travel agents) specializes in classical music and opera programs throughout Europe; its packages include tickets that are otherwise very hard to get. Also try **Keith Prowse Tours** (234 W. 34th St., Suite 1000, New York, NY 10036, tel. 212/398–

1430 or 800/669–8687).

In the United Kingdom, **Travel for the Arts** (117 Regent's Park Rd., London NW1 8UR, tel. 0171/483–2290) takes groups to visit the musical highlights of regions throughout Europe. **Prospect Music & Art Tours** (see Art and Architecture, above) has tours to many of the famous annual festivals—Savonlinna, Prague, Bregenz, and Munich among them.

NATURAL HISTORY➤ **Questers Worldwide Nature Tours** (257 Park Ave. S, New York, NY 10010, tel. 800/468–8668) explores the wild side of Europe in the company of expert guides. **Earthwatch** (680 Mt. Auburn St., Watertown, MA 02272, tel. 617/926–8200) recruits volunteers to serve in its EarthCorps as short-term assistants to scientists or research expeditions.

In the United Kingdom, **Ramblers Holidays Ltd.** (Box 43, Welwyn Garden City, Hertfordshire AL8 6PQ, tel. 01707/331–133) arranges walking tours within Europe with guides who point out natural features of interest.

SINGLES AND YOUNG ADULTS➤ Travelers 18–35 looking to join a group should try **Club Europa** (802 W. Oregon St., Urbana, IL 61801, tel. 217/344–5863 or 800/331–1882) and **Contiki Holidays** (see Groups in Students, above). **Trafalgar Tours** (see Group Tours,

above) has a "Club 21" program of escorted bus tours through Europe and Great Britain for travelers ages 21 to 35.

SPAS➤ **DER Tours** (11933 Wilshire Blvd., Los Angeles, CA 90025, tel. 213/479–4411 or 800/937–1234) represents some of Europe's most acclaimed spa resorts. Some maintain sophisticated medical facilities; others are simply beautiful, healthy places to relax.

In the United Kingdom, **Moswin Tours Ltd.** (21 Church St., Oadby, Leicester LE2 5DB, tel. 0116/271–9922) has visits to health farms among its programs.

SPORTS➤ **Golf International** (275 Madison Ave., New York, NY 10016, tel. 212/986–9176 or 800/833–1389) has golf packages to the United Kingdom, Ireland, and France. **Championship Tennis Tours** (9 Antigua, Dana Point, CA 92629, tel. 714/661–7331 or 800/545–7717) has packages to the French Open, Wimbledon, the Volvo Monte Carlo Open and the Italian Open. For other participant and spectator sports, contact **Keith Prowse & Co.** (234 W. 44th St., Suite 100, New York, NY 10036, tel. 800/669–7469) or **Travel Concepts** (62 Commonwealth Ave., Suite 3, Boston, MA 02116, tel. 617/266–8450), which packages prestigious sporting events and can also enroll you in an English polo school or a Swedish tennis clinic.

In the United Kingdom, **Green Card Golf Holidays** (11a Queensdale Rd., London W11 4QF, tel. 0171/727–7287) arranges visits to greens and amateur tournaments suitable for every level of handicap throughout Western Europe. Companies offering Alpine skiing packages include **Top Deck Ski** (131 Earls Court Rd., London SW5 9RH, tel. 0171/244–8641) and **Crystal Holidays** (Arlington Rd., Surbiton KT6 6BW, tel. 0181/399–5144), both with a wide range of resorts at competitive prices.

TRAIN➤ **Abercrombie & Kent** (see Barge Travel, above) operates luxury tours aboard Europe's legendary trains, including the transcontinental *Venice-Simplon Orient Express* and the *Andalusian Express,* the luxury train of Spain. Less costly packages travel on regularly scheduled trains with stays in first-class and deluxe hotels; you are accompanied by a bellhop so you don't have to lug your bags from train to hotel.

WALKING➤ For walking tours of England, France, and Italy, contact **Backroads** and **Butterfield & Robinson** (see Bicycling, above).

WINE AND FOOD➤ For a culinary adventure, try **Annemarie Victory Organization** (136 E. 64th St., New York, NY 10021, tel. 212/486–0353, fax 212/751–3149) or **Travel Concepts** (see Sports, above). To attend a cooking school in

England, France, or Italy, contact **Cuisine International** (7707 Willow Vine Ct., Suite 219, Dallas, TX 75230, tel. 214/373–1161, fax 214/373–1162) or **Endless Beginnings** (9825 Dowdy Dr., Suite 105, San Diego, CA 92126, tel. 619/566–4166 or 800/822–7855).

In the United Kingdom, **Alternative Travel Group, Ltd.** (69–71 Banbury Rd., Oxford OX2 6PE, tel. 01865/310–334) has wine-tasting tours of France in the region of Alsace, as well as other countries. They also stage orchid, truffle, and mushroom hunts in Italy, France, and Portugal.

ORGANIZATIONS

The **National Tour Association** (546 E. Main St., Lexington, KY 40508, tel. 606/226–4444 or 800/682–8886) and **United States Tour Operators Association** (211 E. 51st St., Suite 12B, New York, NY 10022, tel. 212/750–7371) can provide lists of member operators and information on booking tours.

PUBLICATIONS

Consult the brochures **"Worldwide Tour & Vacation Package Finder"** from the National Tour Association (*see* Organizations, *above*) and the Better Business Bureau's **"Tips on Travel Packages"** (publication no. 24-195; 4200 Wilson Blvd., Arlington, VA 22203; $2).

TRAVEL AGENCIES

For names of reputable agencies in your area, contact the **American Society of Travel Agents** (1101 King St., Suite 200, Alexandria, VA 22314, tel. 703/739–2782).

U

U.S. GOVERNMENT TRAVEL BRIEFINGS

The U.S. Department of State's Overseas Citizens Emergency Center (Room 4811, Washington, DC 20520; enclose SASE) issues **Consular Information Sheets,** which cover crime, security, political climate, and health risks as well as embassy locations, entry requirements, currency regulations, and other routine matters. (Travel Warnings, which counsel travelers to avoid a country entirely, are issued in extreme cases.) For the latest information, stop in at any U.S. passport office, consulate, or embassy; call the interactive hot line (tel. 202/647–5225, fax 202/647–3000); or, with your PC's modem, tap into the Bureau of Consular Affairs' computer bulletin board (tel. 202/647–9225).

V

VISITOR INFORMATION

AUSTRIAN NATIONAL TOURIST OFFICE➤ In the United States: Telephone inquiries only, 500 5th Ave., Suite 2022, New York, NY 10110, tel. 212/944–6880, fax 212/730–

4568; 11601 Wilshire Blvd., Suite 2480, Los Angeles, CA 90025, tel. 310/477–3332, fax 310/477–5141. In Canada: 2 Bloor St. E, Suite 3330, Toronto, Ontario M4W 1A8, tel. 416/967–3381, fax 416/967–4101. In the United Kingdom: Telephone inquiries only, 30 St. George St., London W1R 0AL, tel. 0171/629–0461, fax 0171/499–6038.

BELGIAN NATIONAL TOURIST OFFICE➤ In the United States and Canada: 780 3rd Ave., New York, NY 10017, tel. 212/758–8130, fax 212/355–7675. In the United Kingdom: 29 Princes St., London W1R 7RE, tel. 01891/887799 (per minute charge), fax 0171/629–0454.

BRITISH TOURIST AUTHORITY➤ In the United States: 551 5th Ave., Suite 701, New York, NY 10179, tel. 212/986–2200, fax 212/986–1188; 625 N. Michigan Ave., Suite 1510, Chicago, IL 60611, tel. 312/787–0490, fax 312/787–7746; World Trade Center, 350 S. Figueroa St., Suite 450, Los Angeles, CA 90071, tel. 213/628–3525, fax 213/687–6621; 2850 Cumberland Pkwy., Suite 470, Atlanta, GA 30339, tel. 404/432–9635, fax 404/432–9641. In Canada: 111 Avenue Rd., Suite 450, Toronto, Ontario M5R 3J8, tel. 416/925–6326. In the United Kingdom: British Travel Centre, 12 Regent St., London SW1Y 4PQ (no information by phone, but you can call 0181/846–9000).

BULGARIAN NATIONAL TOURIST OFFICE➤ In the United States and Canada: Balkan Holidays (authorized agent), 41 E. 42nd St., Suite 508, New York, NY 10017, tel. 212/573–5530, fax 212/573–5538. In the United Kingdom: For information, contact Balkan Holidays, 19 Conduit St., London W1R 9TD, tel. 0171/491–4499.

CYPRUS TOURIST OFFICE➤ In the United States and Canada: 13 E. 40th St., New York, NY 10016, tel. 212/683–5280, fax 212/683–5282. In the United Kingdom: 213 Regent St., London W1R 8DA, tel. 0171/734–9822; **North Cyprus Tourist Office,** 28 Cockspur St., London SW1Y 5BN, tel. 0171/930–5069.

CZECH TRAVEL BUREAU AND TOURIST OFFICE (ČEDOK)➤ In the United States and Canada: 10 E. 40th St., New York, NY 10016, tel. 212/689–9720. In the United Kingdom: 49 Southwark St., London SE1 1RU, tel. 0171/378–6009, fax 0171/403–2321; the Czech Center, 30 Kensington Palace Gardens, London W8 4QY, tel. 0171/243–7981, fax 0171/727–9589.

DANISH TOURIST BOARD➤ In the United States: 655 3rd Ave., New York, NY 10017, tel. 212/949–2333, fax 212/983–5260. In Canada: c/o Helen Bergstrom, Box 636, Streetsville, Missis-

sauga, Ontario, L5M 2C2, tel. 519/576–6213, fax 519/576–7115. In the United Kingdom: 55 Sloane St., London SW1X 9SY, tel. 0171/259–5959, fax 0171/259–5955.

FINNISH TOURIST BOARD➤ In the United States and Canada: 655 3rd Ave., New York, NY 10017, tel. 212/949–2333, fax 212/983–5260; 1900 Ave. of the Stars, Suite 1070, Los Angeles, CA 90067, tel. 310/277–5226. In the United Kingdom: 30–35 Pall Mall, London SW1Y 5LP, tel. 0171/839–4048, fax 0171/321–0696.

FRENCH GOVERNMENT TOURIST OFFICE➤ In the United States: Nationwide, tel. 900/990–0040 (costs 50¢ per minute); 444 Madison Ave., 16th Floor, New York, NY 10022, tel. 212/838–7800, fax 212/247–6468; 645 N. Michigan Ave., Chicago, IL 60611, tel. 312/337–6301, fax 312/337–6339; 2305 Cedar Springs Rd., Dallas, TX 75201, tel. 214/720–4010, fax 214/720–0250; 9454 Wilshire Blvd., Beverly Hills, CA 90212, tel. 310/271–2358, fax 310/276–2835. In Canada: 1981 McGill College Ave., Suite 490, Montréal, Québec H3A 2W9, tel. 514/288–4264, fax 514/845–4868; 30 St. Patrick St., Suite 700, Toronto, Ontario M5T 3A3, tel. 416/593–4723, fax 416/979–7587. In the United Kingdom: 178 Piccadilly, London W1V 0AL, tel. 01891/244123 (per minute charge).

GERMAN NATIONAL TOURIST OFFICE➤ In the United States: 122 E. 42nd St., New York, NY 10168, tel. 212/661–7200, fax 212/661–7174; 11766 Wilshire Blvd., Suite 750, Los Angeles, CA 90025, tel. 310/575–9799, fax 310/575–1565. In Canada: 175 Bloor St. E, Suite 604, Toronto, Ontario M4W 3R8, tel. 416/968–1570. In the United Kingdom: Nightingale House, 65 Curzon St., London W1Y 7PE, tel. 01891/600100 (per minute charge).

GIBRALTAR GOVERNMENT TOURIST OFFICE➤ In the United States and Canada: 1155 15th St. NW, Room 710, Washington, DC 20005, tel. 202/452–1108, fax 202/872–8543. In the United Kingdom: Arundel Great Court, 179 The Strand, London WC2R 1EH, tel. 0171/836–0777.

GREEK NATIONAL TOURIST ORGANIZATION➤ In the United States: 645 5th Ave., New York, NY 10022, tel. 212/421–5777, fax 212/826–6940; 611 W. 6th St., Suite 2198, Los Angeles, CA 90017, tel. 213/626–6696, fax 213/489–9744; 168 N. Michigan Ave., Suite 600, Chicago, IL 60601, tel. 312/782–1084, fax 312/782–1091. In Canada: 1233 Rue de la Montagne, Suite 101, Montréal, Québec H3G 1Z2, tel. 514/871–1535, fax 514/871–1498; 1300 Bay St., Toronto, Ontario M5R 3K8, tel. 416/968–2220, fax 416/968–

6533. In the United Kingdom: 4 Conduit St., London W1R 0DJ, tel. 0171/734–5997.

HUNGARIAN NATIONAL TOURIST OFFICE (IBUSZ)➢ In the United States and Canada: 150 E. 58th St., New York, NY 10155, tel. 212/586–5230. In the United Kingdom: Box 4336, London SW18 4XE, tel. 01891/171200 (per minute charge), fax 01891/669970.

ICELAND TOURIST BOARD➢ In the United States and Canada: 655 3rd Ave., New York, NY 10017, tel. 212/949–2333, fax 212/983–5260. In the United Kingdom: 172 Tottenham Court Rd., 3rd Floor, London W1P 9LG, tel. 0171/388–7550.

IRISH TOURIST BOARD➢ In the United States: 345 Park Ave., New York, NY 10154, tel. 212/418–0800 or 800/223–6470, fax 212/371–9052. In Canada: 160 Bloor St. E, Suite 1150, Toronto, Ontario M4W 1B9, tel. 416/929–2777, fax 416/929–6783. In the United Kingdom: Ireland House, 150 New Bond St., London W1Y 0AQ, tel. 0171/493–3201, fax 0171/493–9065.

ITALIAN GOVERNMENT TRAVEL OFFICE (ENIT)➢ In the United States: 630 5th Ave., Suite 1565, New York, NY 10111, tel. 212/245–4822, fax 212/586–9249; 12400 Wilshire Blvd., Suite 550, Los Angeles, CA 90025, tel. 310/820–0098, fax 310/820–

6357. In Canada: 1 Pl. Ville Marie, Suite 1914, Montréal, Québec H3B 3M9, tel. 514/866–7667. In the United Kingdom: 1 Princes St., London W1R 8AY, tel. 0171/408–1254.

LUXEMBOURG TOURIST INFORMATION OFFICE➢ In the United States and Canada: 17 Beekman Pl., New York, NY 10022, tel. 212/935–8888, fax 212/935–5896. In the United Kingdom: 122 Regent St., London W1R 5FE, tel. 0171/434–2800.

MALTA NATIONAL TOURIST OFFICE➢ In the United States and Canada: 350 5th Ave., Suite 4412, New York, NY 10118, tel. 212/695–9520, fax 212/695–8229. In the United Kingdom: Mappin House, Suite 300, 4 Winsley St., London W1N 7AR, tel. 0171/323–0506.

MONACO GOVERNMENT TOURIST AND CONVENTION BUREAU➢ In the United States and Canada: 845 3rd Ave., New York, NY 10022, tel. 212/759–5227, fax 212/754–9320. In the United Kingdom: 3–18 Chelsea Garden Market, Chelsea Harbour, London SW10 0XE, tel. 0171/352–9962.

NETHERLANDS BOARD OF TOURISM➢ In the United States: 225 N. Michigan Ave., Suite 326, Chicago, IL 60601, tel. 312/819–0300, fax 312/819–1740. In Canada: 25 Adelaide St. E, Suite 710, Toronto, Ontario M5C 1Y2, tel. 416/363–1577, fax 416/363–1470. In the

United Kingdom: 25–28 Buckingham Gate, London SW1E 6LD, tel. 01891/200277 (per minute charge).

NORWEGIAN TOURIST BOARD➢ In the United States and Canada: 655 3rd Ave., New York, NY 10017, tel. 212/949–2333, fax 212/983–5260. In the United Kingdom: Charles House, 5–11 Lower Regent St., London SW1Y 4LR, tel. 0171/839–6255.

POLISH NATIONAL TOURIST OFFICE➢ In the United States and Canada: 275 Madison Ave., Suite 1711, New York, NY 10016, tel. 212/338–9412, fax 212/338–9283. In the United Kingdom: 82 Mortimer St., London W1N 8HN, tel. 0171/580–8028, fax 0171/436–6558.

PORTUGUESE NATIONAL TOURIST OFFICE➢ In the United States: 590 5th Ave., 4th Floor, New York, NY 10036, tel. 212/354–4403, fax 212/764–6137. In Canada: 60 Bloor St. W, Suite 1005, Toronto, Ontario M4W 3BS, tel. 416/921–7376, fax 416/921–1353. In the United Kingdom: 22–25A Sackville St., London W1X 1DE, tel. 0171/494–1441.

ROMANIAN NATIONAL TOURIST OFFICE➢ In the United States and Canada: 342 Madison Ave., Suite 210, New York, NY 10173, tel. 212/697–6971, fax 212/697–6972. In the United Kingdom: 83A Marylebone High St., London W1M 3DE, tel. 0171/224–3692.

SLOVAKIA➤ In the United States and Canada: Viktor Corporation, 10 E. 40th St., Suite 3601, New York, NY 10016, tel. 212/213–3862, fax 212/213–4461. In the United Kingdom: Embassy of the Slovak Republic, Information Dept., 25 Kensington Palace Gardens, London W8 4QY, tel. 0171/243–0803, fax 0171/727–5821.

SPANISH NATIONAL TOURIST OFFICE➤ In the United States: 665 5th Ave., New York, NY 10022, tel. 212/759–8822, fax 212/980–1053; 845 N. Michigan Ave., Chicago, IL 60611, tel. 312/642–1992, fax 312/642–9817; San Vicente Plaza Bldg., 8383 Wilshire Blvd., Suite 960, Beverly Hills, CA 90211, tel. 213/658–7188, fax 213/658–1061; 1221 Brickell Ave., Suite 1850, Miami, FL 33131, tel. 305/358–1992, fax 305/358–8223. In Canada: 102 Bloor St. W, Suite 1400, Toronto, Ontario M5S 1M8, tel. 416/961–

3131, fax 416/961–1992. In the United Kingdom: 57–58 St. James's St., London SW1A 1LD, tel. 0171/499–0901, fax 0171/629–4257.

SWEDISH TRAVEL AND TOURISM COUNCIL➤ In the United States and Canada: 655 3rd Ave., 18th Floor, New York, NY 10017, tel. 212/949–2333, fax 212/983–5260. In the United Kingdom: 73 Welbeck St., London W1M 8AN, tel. 0171/935–9784, fax 0171/935–5853.

SWISS NATIONAL TOURIST OFFICE➤ In the United States: 608 5th Ave., New York, NY 10020, tel. 212/757–5944, fax 212/262–6116; 222 N. Sepulveda Blvd., Suite 1570, El Segundo, CA 90245, tel. 310/335–5980, fax 310/335–5982; 150 N. Michigan Ave., Suite 2930, Chicago, IL 60601, tel. 312/630–5840, fax 312/630–5848. In Canada: 154 University Ave., Suite 610, Toronto, Ontario M5H 3Y9, tel. 416/

971–9734. In the United Kingdom: Swiss Centre, 1 New Coventry St., London W1V 8EE, tel. 0171/734–1921.

TURKISH TOURIST OFFICE➤ In the United States and Canada: 821 UN Plaza, New York, NY 10017, tel. 212/687–2194, fax 212/599–7568; 1717 Massachusetts Ave. NW, Suite 306, Washington, DC 20036, tel. 202/429–9844, fax 202/429–5649. In Canada: c/o Turkish Embassy, 197 Wurtemburg St., Ottawa, Ontario K1N 8L9, tel. 613/789–4044. In the United Kingdom: 170–173 Piccadilly, 1st Floor, London W1V 9DD, tel. 0171/734–8681.

W

WEATHER

For current conditions and forecasts, plus the local time and helpful travel tips, call the **Weather Channel Connection** (tel. 900/932–8437; 95¢ per minute) from a Touch-Tone phone.

SMART TRAVEL TIPS A TO Z

Basic Information on Traveling in Europe and Savvy Tips to Make Your Trip a Breeze

The more you travel, the more you know about how to make trips run like clockwork. To help make your travels hassle-free, Fodor's editors have rounded up dozens of tips from our contributors and travel experts all over the world, as well as basic information on visiting Europe. For names of organizations to contact and publications that can give you more information, *see* Important Contacts A to Z, *above.*

A

AIR TRAVEL

If time is an issue, **always look for non-stop flights,** which require no change of plane. If possible, **avoid connecting flights,** which stop at least once and can involve a change of plane, although the flight number remains the same; if the first leg is late, the second waits.

CUTTING COSTS

The Sunday travel section of most newspapers is a good source of deals. *See also* Travel Passes, *below.*

MAJOR AIRLINES➤ The least-expensive airfares from the major airlines are priced for round-trip travel and are subject to restrictions. You must usually **book in advance and buy the ticket within 24 hours** to get cheaper fares, and

you may have to **stay over a Saturday night.** The lowest fare is subject to availability, and only a small percentage of the plane's total seats are sold at that price. It's good to **call a number of airlines**—and **when you are quoted a good price, book it on the spot**—the same fare on the same flight may not be available the next day. Airlines generally allow you to change your return date for a $25 to $50 fee, but most low-fare tickets are nonrefundable. However, if you don't use your ticket, you can apply the cost toward the purchase price of a new one, again for a small charge.

CONSOLIDATORS➤ Consolidators, who buy tickets at reduced rates from scheduled airlines, sell them at prices below the lowest available from the airlines directly—usually without advance restrictions. Sometimes you can even get your money back if you need to return the ticket. Carefully read the fine print detailing penalties for changes and cancellations. If you doubt the reliability of a consolidator, **confirm your reservation with the airline.**

CHARTER FLIGHTS➤ Charters usually have the lowest fares and the most restrictions. De-

partures are limited and seldom on time, and you can lose all or most of your money if you cancel. (The closer to departure you cancel, the more you lose, although sometimes you will be charged only a small fee if you supply a substitute passenger.) The flight may be canceled for any reason up to 10 days before departure (after that, only if it is physically impossible to operate). The charterer may also revise the itinerary or increase the price after you have bought the ticket, but only if the new arrangement constitutes a "major change" do you have the right to a refund. Before buying a charter ticket, **read the fine print** about the company's refund policies. Money for charter flights is usually paid into a bank escrow account, the name of which should be on the contract, and if you don't pay by credit card, **make your check payable to the carrier's escrow account** (unless you're dealing with a travel agent, in which case, his or her check should be payable to the escrow account). The U.S. Department of Transportation's Office of Consumer Affairs has jurisdiction.

Charter operators may offer flights alone or with ground arrange-

SMART TRAVEL TIPS / THE GOLD GUIDE

ments that constitute a charter package. You typically must book charters through your travel agent.

TRAVEL PASSES> You can **save on air travel** within Europe if you plan on traveling to and from Europe aboard Air France (to Paris), Sabena (to Brussels), or Czechoslovak Airlines (to Prague). As part of their Euro Flier program, you can then buy between three and nine flight coupons, which are valid on those airlines' flights to more than 100 European cities. At $120 each, these coupons are a good deal, and the fine print still allows you plenty of freedom.

WITHIN EUROPE

Air travel within the EU countries was deregulated in 1993, spurring a slew of special deals from national carriers and from charter operators that now offer scheduled flights. The best require a round-trip purchase and Saturday-night stay-over. For one-way or midweek travel, the smaller airlines generally offer better prices. For air travel within one country, **check with your transatlantic carrier.** Many carriers offer an air travel pass at a reasonable price that is good for numerous domestic flights.

Airlines are developing hub-style services. The idea is that you take a transatlantic flight to an airline's hub, then continue on its service to other European cities. SAS is developing Copenhagen as a Scan-dinavian hub; KLM is doing the same at Amsterdam's Schiphol (and is working with Northwest to ease transatlantic connections); British Airways at London's Heathrow and Gatwick; and Lufthansa at Frankfurt. If you plan to fly to other European cities, **one of these hubs is your obvious choice.**

Before booking an internal flight, **compare different modes of transportation.** Flights from London to Edinburgh take about one hour—airport to airport—while the BritRail InterCity train takes just over four hours. But if you add in the hour needed to get from central London to the airport, the need to check in as much as one hour before departure, the inevitable flight delays, the time spent waiting for luggage, and the transfer time back into town from Edinburgh Airport—you'll find you may not have saved more than half an hour for a considerably higher fare.

For scheduled flights, you will be asked to check in at least one hour before departure; for charter flights, generally two hours. If you are traveling with just hand luggage, it is possible to check in as late as 30 minutes before takeoff.

The Green Channel/Red Channel customs system in operation at most western European airports and other borders is basically an honor system. If you have nothing to declare, walk through the Green Channel, where there are only spot luggage checks; if in doubt, go through the Red Channel. If you fly between two EU-member countries, you may go through the new Blue Channel, where there are no customs officers except the one who glances at baggage labels to make sure only people off EU flights get through.

ALOFT

AIRLINE FOOD> If you hate airline food, **ask for special meals when booking.** These can be vegetarian, low-cholesterol, or kosher, for example; commonly prepared to order in smaller quantities than standard catered fare, they can be tastier.

JET LAG> To avoid this syndrome, which occurs when travel disrupts your body's natural cycles, try to maintain a normal routine. At night, **get some sleep.** By day, move about the cabin to **stretch your legs, eat light meals, and drink water—not alcohol.**

SMOKING> Smoking is banned on all flights within the United States of less than six hours' duration and on all Canadian flights; the ban also applies to domestic segments of international flights aboard U.S. and foreign carriers. Delta has banned smoking system-wide. On U.S. carriers flying to Europe and other destinations abroad, a seat in a no-smoking section must be provided for every passenger who requests one, and the section must be enlarged to accommodate such passengers if necessary as long as they have complied with the airline's deadline for check-in and seat assignment. If smoking bothers you, request a seat far from the smoking section.

Foreign airlines are exempt from these rules but do provide no-smoking sections. British Airways has banned smoking, as has Virgin Atlantic, on most international flights; some nations have banned smoking on all domestic flights, and others may ban smoking on some international flights. Talks continue on the feasibility of broadening no-smoking policies.

B
BICYCLING

Some ferry lines transport bicycles free, others charge a nominal fee. Shop around. You can also transport your bicycle by air as checked baggage—you usually won't have to pay extra as long as you are within the 44-pound total baggage allowance.

Most European rail lines will transport bicycles free of charge or for a nominal fee, though you may have to book ahead. Check with the main booking office.

Local and regional tourist information offices will have information about renting bicycles. For bike tours of Europe, *see* Tour Operators *in* Important Contacts A to Z, *above*.

BUS TRAVEL

In Britain, France, Germany, and Holland, bus travel was, until recently, something of a poor man's option—slow, uncomfortable, but cheap. Today, though, fast modern buses travel on excellent highways and offer standards of service and comfort comparable to those on trains—but still at generally lower fares. Between major cities and over long distances, trains are almost always faster; but buses will take you to places that trains often do not reach.

In several southern European countries—including Portugal, Greece, much of Spain, and Turkey—the bus has supplanted the train as the main means of public transportation, and is often quicker and more comfortable, with more frequent service, than the antiquated national rolling stock. Unless there is a particular scenic rail route you want to see, **choose the bus over the train in southern Europe**—but be prepared to discover that the bus is more expensive. Competition among lines is keen, so **ask about air-conditioning and reclining seats** before you book.

National or regional tourist offices have information about bus services. For reservations on major lines before you go, contact your travel agent at home; do your legwork so you know the different services available.

C
CAMERAS, CAMCORDERS, AND COMPUTERS

LAPTOPS

Before you depart, **check your portable computer's battery,** because you may be asked at security to turn on the computer to prove that it is what it appears to be. At the airport, you may prefer to **request a manual inspection,** although security X-rays do not harm hard-disk or floppy-disk storage. Also, **register your foreign-made laptop with U.S. Customs.** If your laptop is U.S.-made, call the consulate of the country you'll be visiting to find out whether or not it should be registered with local customs upon arrival. You may want to **find out about repair facilities at your destination** in case you need them.

PHOTOGRAPHY

If your camera is new or if you haven't used it for a while, **shoot and develop a few rolls of film** before you leave. Always **store film in a cool, dry place**—never in the car's glove compartment or on the shelf under the rear window.

Every pass through an X-ray machine increases the chance that your film becomes cloudy. To protect it, carry it in a clear plastic bag and **ask for hand inspection at security.** Such requests are virtually always honored at U.S. airports, and are usually accommodated abroad. Don't depend on a lead-lined bag to protect film in checked luggage—the airline may increase the radiation to see what's inside.

VIDEO

Before your trip, **test your camcorder, invest in a skylight filter to protect the lens, and charge the batteries.** (Airport security personnel may ask you to turn on the camcorder to prove that it's what it appears to be.) The batteries of most newer camcorders can be recharged with a universal or worldwide AC adapter charger (or multivoltage converter), usable whether the voltage is 110 or 220. All that's needed is the appropriate plug.

Videotape is not damaged by X-rays, but it may be harmed by the magnetic field of a walk-through metal detector, so **ask that videotapes be hand-checked.** Videotape sold in Europe is based on the PAL standard, which is different from the one used in the United States (NTSC). You will not be able to view your tapes through the local TV set or view movies bought there in your home VCR. Blank tapes bought in Europe can be used for camcorder taping, but they are pricey. Some U.S. audiovisual shops convert foreign tapes to U.S. standards; contact an electronics dealer to find a store nearby.

THE CHANNEL TUNNEL

The Channel Tunnel provides the fastest route across the Channel—25 minutes from Folkestone to Calais, or 60 minutes from motorway to motorway. It consists of two large, 50-kilometer-long (31-mile-long) tunnels for trains, one in each direction, linked by a smaller service tunnel running between them.

Le Shuttle, a special car, bus, and truck train, operates continuously, with trains departing every 15 minutes at peak times and at least once an hour through the night. No reservations are necessary, although tickets may be purchased in advance from travel agents. Most passengers travel in their own car, staying with the vehicle throughout the "crossing," with progress updates via radio and display screens. Motorcyclists park their bikes in a separate section with its own passenger compartment, and foot passengers must book passage by coach. At press time, prices for a one-day roundtrip ticket began at £107–£154 for a car and its occupants. Prices for a five-day roundtrip ticket began at £115.

Eurostar operates high-speed passenger-only trains, which whisk riders between stations in Paris (Gare du Nord) and London (Waterloo) in 3 hours and between London and Brussels (Midi) in 3¼ hours. At press time, fares were $154 for a one-way, first-class ticket and $123 for an economy fare.

The Tunnel is reached from exit 11a of the M20. Tickets for either Tunnel service can be purchased in advance (*see* Important Contacts A to Z, *above*.)

CHILDREN AND TRAVEL

BABY-SITTING

For recommended local sitters, **check with your hotel desk.**

DRIVING

If you are renting a car, **arrange for a car seat when you reserve.** Sometimes they're free.

FLYING

Always **ask about discounted children's fares.** On international flights, the fare for infants under age 2 not occupying a seat is generally either free or 10% of the accompanying adult's fare; children ages 2 through 11 usually pay half to two-thirds of the adult fare. On domestic flights, children under 2 not occupying a seat travel free, and older children currently travel on the "lowest applicable" adult fare.

BAGGAGE➤ In general, the adult baggage allowance applies for children paying half or more of the adult fare. Before departure, **ask about carry-on allowances** if you are traveling with an infant. In general, those paying 10% of the adult fare are allowed one carry-on bag, not to exceed 70 pounds or 45 inches (length + width + height) and a collapsible stroller; you may be allowed less if the flight is full.

FACILITIES➤ When making your reservation, **ask for children's**

meals or a freestanding bassinet if you need them; the latter is available only to those with seats at the bulkhead, where there's enough legroom. If you don't need the bassinet, **think twice before requesting bulkhead seats**—the only storage for in-flight necessities is in the inconveniently distant overhead bins.

SAFETY SEATS➤ According to the Federal Aviation Administration (FAA), it's good to **use safety seats aloft.** Airline policy varies. U.S. carriers allow FAA-approved models, but airlines usually require that you buy a ticket, even if your child would otherwise ride free, because the seats must be strapped into regular passenger seats. Foreign carriers may not allow infant seats, may charge the child's rather than the infant's fare for their use, or may require you to hold your baby during takeoff and landing, thus defeating the seat's purpose.

LODGING

Most hotels allow children under a certain age to stay in their parents' room at no extra charge, while others charge them as extra adults; be sure to **ask about the cut-off age.**

CUSTOMS AND DUTIES

IN EUROPE

See individual country chapters for limits on imports.

BACK HOME

In the U.S. You may bring home $400 worth of foreign goods duty-free if you've been out of the country for at least 48 hours and haven't already used the $400 exemption, or any part of it, in the past 30 days.

Travelers 21 or older may bring back 1 liter of alcohol duty-free, provided the beverage laws of the state through which they reenter the United States allow it. In addition, 100 non-Cuban cigars and 200 cigarettes are allowed, regardless of your age. Antiques and works of art more than 100 years old are duty-free.

Duty-free, travelers may mail packages valued at up to $200 to themselves and up to $100 to others, with a limit of one parcel per addressee per day (and no alcohol or tobacco products or perfume valued at more than $5); outside, identify the package as being for personal use or an unsolicited gift, specifying the contents and their retail value. Mailed items do not count as part of your exemption.

IN CANADA➤ Once per calendar year, when you've been out of Canada for at least seven days, you may bring in C$300 worth of goods duty-free. If you've been away less than seven days but more than 48 hours, the duty-free exemption drops to C$100 but can be claimed any number of times (as can a C$20 duty-free exemption for absences of 24 hours or more). You cannot combine the yearly and 48-hour exemptions, use the C$300 exemption only partially (to save the balance for a later trip), or pool exemptions with family members. Goods claimed under the C$300 exemption may follow you by mail; those claimed under the lesser exemptions must accompany you.

Alcohol and tobacco products may be included in the yearly and 48-hour exemptions but not in the 24-hour exemption. If you meet the age requirements of the province through which you reenter Canada, you may bring in, duty-free, 1.14 liters (40 imperial ounces) of wine or liquor *or* 24 12-ounce cans or bottles of beer or ale. If you are 16 or older, you may bring in, duty-free, 200 cigarettes, 50 cigars or cigarillos, and 400 tobacco sticks or 400 grams of manufactured tobacco. Alcohol and tobacco must accompany you on your return.

An unlimited number of gifts valued up to C$60 each may be mailed to Canada duty-free. These do not count as part of your exemption. Label the package "Unsolicited Gift—Value under $60." Alcohol and tobacco are excluded.

IN THE U.K.➤ If your journey was wholly within EU countries, you no longer need to pass through customs when you return to the United Kingdom. If you plan to bring large quantities of alcohol or tobacco, check in advance on EU limits.

From countries outside the EU, you may import duty-free 200 cigarettes, 100 cigarillos, 50 cigars or 250 grams of tobacco; 1 liter of spirits or 2 liters of fortified or sparkling wine; 2 liters of still table wine; 60 milliliters of perfume; 250 milliliters of toilet water; plus £136 worth of other goods, including gifts and souvenirs.

D
FOR TRAVELERS WITH DISABILITIES

When discussing accessibility with an operator or reservationist, **ask hard questions.** Are there any stairs, inside *or* out? Are there grab bars next to the toilet *and* in the shower/tub? How wide is the doorway to the room? To the bathroom? For the most extensive facilities, meeting the latest legal specifications, **opt for newer accommodations,** which more often have been designed with access in mind. Older properties or ships must usually be retrofitted and may offer more limited facilities as a result. Be sure to **discuss your needs before booking.**

DISCOUNT CLUBS

Travel clubs offer members unsold space on airplanes, cruise ships, and package tours at as much as 50% below regular prices. Membership may include a regular bulletin or access to a toll-free hot line giving details of available trips departing from three or four days to several months in the future. Most also offer

50% discounts off hotel rack rates. Before booking with a club, **make sure the hotel or other supplier isn't offering a better deal.**

DRIVING

BORDERS

Many European countries have a relatively casual approach to border controls for drivers. At many frontiers, you may simply be waved through. There are, however, spot checks at all borders, and at some—particularly those checkpoints used by heavy commercial truck traffic—there can be long delays at peak times. Ask tourist offices or motoring associations for latest advice on ways to avoid these tie-ups.

DOCUMENTATION

If you are driving a rented car, the rental company will have provided you with all the necessary papers; if the vehicle is your own, you will need proof of ownership, a certificate of roadworthiness (known in the United Kingdom as a Ministry of Transport, or MOT, road vehicle certificate), up-to-date vehicle registration or tax (in the United Kingdom), and a Green Card proof of insurance, available from your insurance company (fees vary depending on destination and length of stay).

RULES OF THE ROAD

Speed limits in most countries are set much higher than those in the United States. Even on British motorways, where the upper limit is

a very conservative 112 kph (70 mph), it is not uncommon to be passed by vehicles traveling 24–32 kph (15–20 mph) faster than that. On German autobahns, French autoroutes, or Italian autostradas, cars in the fast lane are often moving at speeds of 167 kph (100 mph) and faster. Always **stay in the slower lane unless you want to pass,** and be sure to make way for faster cars wanting to pass you. Much of the time traffic is heavier than is common on U.S. freeways outside major city rush hours.

Most tourists will find it more rewarding to avoid the freeways and use the alternative main routes. Traffic moves more slowly, and this can also save money; many European freeways (such as those of France, Spain, Italy, and Greece) are toll roads, and a day's drive on them can be expensive. Wherever you're driving, be sure to carry a good map.

In the United Kingdom, the Republic of Ireland, Malta, Cyprus, and Gibraltar, cars drive on the left. In other European countries, traffic is on the right. Beware the transition when coming off ferries from Britain or Ireland to the Continent (and vice versa).

TRAFFIC

During peak vacation periods, main routes can be jammed with holiday traffic. In the United Kingdom, try to avoid driving during any of the long bank-holiday (public holiday) weekends, when motorways can be clogged. In

France, Spain, and Italy, huge numbers of people still take a fixed one-month vacation in August, so avoid driving during *le dé-part,* the first weekend in August, when vast numbers of drivers head south; or *le retour,* when they head back.

F

FERRY TRAVEL

Ferry routes for passengers and vehicles link the North Sea, English Channel, and Irish Sea ports with almost all of Britain's maritime neighbors. For ferry operators, *see* Important Contacts A to Z, *above.*

I

INSURANCE

Travel insurance can protect your investment, replace your luggage and its contents, or provide for medical coverage should you fall ill during your trip. Most tour operators, travel agents, and insurance agents sell specialized health-and-accident, flight, trip-cancellation, and luggage insurance as well as comprehensive policies with some or all of these features. Before you make any purchase, **review your existing health and homeowner's policies** to find out whether they cover expenses incurred while traveling.

BAGGAGE

Airline liability for your baggage is limited to $1,250 per person on domestic flights. On international flights, the airlines' liability is $9.07 per pound or $20 per kilogram for checked baggage (roughly $640 per 70-pound bag) and $400 per passenger for unchecked baggage. However, this excludes valuable items such as jewelry and cameras that are listed in your ticket's fine print. You can buy additional insurance from the airline at check-in, but first **see if your home-owner's policy covers lost luggage.**

FLIGHT

You should **think twice before buying flight insurance.** Often purchased as a last-minute impulse at the airport, it pays a lump sum when a plane crashes, either to a beneficiary if the insured dies or sometimes to a surviving passenger who loses eyesight or a limb. Supplementing the airlines' coverage described in the limits-of-liability paragraphs on your ticket, it's expensive and basically unnecessary. Charging an airline ticket to a major credit card often automatically entitles you to coverage and may also include travel by bus, train, and ship.

HEALTH

If your own health insurance policy does not cover you outside the United States, **consider buying supplemental medical coverage.** It can provide from $1,000 to $150,000 worth of medical and/or dental services incurred as a result of an accident or illness during a trip. These policies also may include a personal-accident or death-and-dismemberment provision (pays a lump sum ranging from $15,000 to $500,000 to your beneficiaries if you die or to you if you lose one or more limbs or your eyesight) and a medical-assistance provision, which may either reimburse you for the cost of referrals, evacuation, or repatriation and other services or may automatically enroll you as a member of a particular medical-assistance company. (*See* Health Issues *in* Important Contacts A to Z, *above.*)

FOR U.K. TRAVELERS➤ You can buy an annual travel-insurance policy valid for most vacations during the year in which it's purchased. If you go this route, make sure it covers you if you have a preexisting medical condition or are pregnant.

TRIP

Without insurance, you will lose all or most of your money if you must cancel your trip due to illness or any other reason. Especially if your airline ticket, cruise, or package tour is nonrefundable and cannot be changed, it's essential that you **buy trip-cancellation-and-interruption insurance.** When considering how much coverage you need, look for a policy that will cover the cost of your trip plus the nondiscounted price of a one-way airline ticket should you need to return home early. Read the fine print carefully, especially sections defining "family member" and "preexisting medical conditions."

Also **consider default or bankruptcy insurance,** which protects you against a supplier's failure to deliver. However, such policies often do not cover default by a travel agency, tour operator, airline, or cruise line if you bought your tour and the coverage directly from the firm in question.

L

LODGING

APARTMENT AND VILLA RENTALS

If you want a home base that's roomy enough for a family and comes with cooking facilities, **consider a furnished rental.** It's generally cost-wise, too, although not always—some rentals are luxury properties (economical only when your party is large). Home-exchange directories do list rentals—often second homes owned by prospective house swappers—and some services search for a house or apartment for you (even a castle if that's your fancy) and handle the paperwork. Some send an illustrated catalogue and others send photographs of specific properties, sometimes at a charge; up-front registration fees may apply.

HOME EXCHANGE

If you would like to find a house, an apartment, or other vacation property to exchange for your own while on vacation, **become a member of a home-exchange organization,** which will send you its annual directories listing available

exchanges and will include your own listing in at least one of them. Arrangements for the actual exchange are made by the two parties to it, not by the organization.

M

MEDICAL

ASSISTANCE

No one plans to get sick while traveling, but it happens, so **consider signing up with a medical assistance company.** These outfits provide referrals, emergency evacuation or repatriation, 24-hour hot lines for medical consultation, dispatch of medical personnel, relay of medical records, cash for emergencies, and other personal and legal assistance.

MONEY AND

EXPENSES

ATMS

Chances are that you can **use your bank card at ATMs** to withdraw money from an account and get cash advances on a credit-card account if your card has been programmed with a personal identification number, or PIN. Before leaving home, **check in on frequency limits** for withdrawals and cash advances. Also **ask whether your card's PIN must be reprogrammed** for use in Europe. Four digits are commonly used overseas. Note that Discover is accepted only in the United States.

On cash advances you are charged interest from the day you receive the money,

whether from an ATM or a teller. Although transaction fees for ATM withdrawals abroad may be higher than fees for withdrawals at home, Cirrus and Plus exchange rates are excellent because they are based on wholesale rates only offered by major banks.

EXCHANGING CURRENCY

For the most favorable rates, **change money at banks.** You won't do as well at exchange booths in airports, rail, and bus stations, or in hotels, restaurants, and stores, although you may find their hours more convenient. To avoid lines at airport exchange booths, **exchange a small amount of currency before you leave home.**

TRAVELER'S CHECKS

Whether or not to buy traveler's checks depends on where you are headed; **take cash to rural areas and small towns, traveler's checks to cities.** The most widely recognized are American Express, Citicorp, Thomas Cook, and Visa, which are sold by major commercial banks for 1% to 3% of the checks' face value—it pays to **shop around.** Both American Express and Thomas Cook issue checks that can be countersigned and used by you or your traveling companion, and they both provide checks, at no extra charge, denominated in various non-U.S. currencies. You can cash them in banks without paying a fee (which can be as much as 20%) and use them as readily as cash in many hotels, restaurants, and shops. So you won't be left with excess foreign currency, **buy a few checks in small denominations** to cash toward the end of your trip. Record the numbers of the checks, cross them off as you spend them, and keep this information separate from your checks.

WIRING MONEY

You don't need a bank account or a credit card to send or receive funds through the Money-Gram^{SM} money-wiring service. Go to one of more than 18,000 MoneyGram^{SM} service agents in retail outlets, bureaux de change, travel agencies, and selected Thomas Cook bureaux de change, plus many other locations, and a computerized money transfer will be complete in minutes. The sender pays a small, one-time transaction fee. You can send or receive up to $10,000. You can also send a free personal message to the recipient.

You can also send money using Western Union. Money sent from the United States or Canada will be available for pickup at agent locations in 100 countries within 15 minutes. Once the money is in the system, it can be picked up at any one of 25,000 locations. Fees range from 4% to 10%, depending on the amount you send.

P

PACKAGES

AND TOURS

A package or tour to Europe can make your vacation less expensive and more convenient. Firms that sell tours and packages purchase airline seats, hotel rooms, and rental cars in bulk and pass some of the savings on to you. In addition, the best operators have local representatives to help you out at your destination.

A GOOD DEAL?

The more your package or tour includes, the better you can predict the ultimate cost of your vacation. Make sure you know exactly what is included, and **beware of hidden costs.** Are taxes, tips, and service charges included? Transfers and baggage handling? Entertainment and excursions? These can add up.

Most packages and tours are rated deluxe, first-class superior, first class, tourist, or budget. The key difference is usually accommodations. If the package or tour you are considering is priced lower than in your wildest dreams, **be skeptical.** Also, **make sure your travel agent knows the hotels** and other services. Ask about location, room size, beds, and whether the hotel has a pool, room service, or programs for children, if you care about these. Has your agent been there or sent others you can contact?

BUYER BEWARE

Each year consumers are stranded or lose their money when operators go out of business—even very large ones with excellent reputations. If you can't afford a loss, take the time to **check out the operator**—find out how long the company has been in business, and ask several agents about its reputation. Next, **don't book unless the firm has a consumer-protection program.** Members of the United States Tour Operators Association and the National Tour Association are required to set aside funds exclusively to cover your payments and travel arrangements in case of default. Nonmember operators may instead carry insurance; look for the details in the operator's brochure—and the name of an underwriter with a solid reputation. Note: When it comes to tour operators, **don't trust escrow accounts.** Although there are laws governing those of charter-flight operators, no governmental body prevents tour operators from raiding the till.

Next, **contact your local Better Business Bureau and the attorney general's office** in both your own state and the operator's; have any complaints been filed? Last, **pay with a major credit card.** Then you can cancel payment, provided that you can document your complaint. Always **consider trip-cancellation insurance** (*see* Insurance, *above*).

BIG VS. SMALL➤ An operator that handles several hundred thousand travelers annually can use its purchasing power to give you a good price. Its high volume may also indicate financial stability. But some small companies provide more personalized service; because they tend to specialize, they may also be experts on an area.

USING AN AGENT

Travel agents are an excellent resource. In fact, large operators accept bookings only through travel agents. But it's good to **collect brochures from several agencies,** because some agents' suggestions may be skewed by promotional relationships with tour and package firms that reward them for volume sales. If you have a special interest, **find an agent with expertise in that area;** the American Society of Travel Agencies (*see* Travel Agents *in* Important Contacts A to Z, *above*) can give you leads in the United States. (Don't rely solely on your agent, though; agents may be unaware of small-niche operators, and some special-interest travel companies only sell direct).

SINGLE TRAVELERS

Prices are usually quoted per person, based on two sharing a room. If traveling solo, you may be required to pay the full double occupancy rate. Some operators eliminate this surcharge if you agree to be matched up with a roommate of the same sex, even if one is not found by departure time.

PACKING FOR EUROPE

What you pack depends more on the season than on any particular dress code. In general, northern and central Europe have cold, snowy winters, and the Mediterranean countries have mild winters, though parts of southern Europe can be bitterly cold, too. In the Mediterranean resorts you may need a warm jacket for mornings and evenings, even in summer. The mountains usually are warm on summer days, but the weather is unpredictable, and the nights are generally cool.

For European cities, **pack as you would for an American city;** formal outfits for first-class restaurants and nightclubs, casual clothes elsewhere. Jeans are perfectly acceptable for sightseeing and informal dining. Sturdy walking shoes are appropriate for the cobblestone streets and gravel paths that fill many of the parks and surround some of the historic buildings. For visits to churches, cathedrals, and mosques, avoid shorts and immodest outfits. In Italy, women cover their shoulders and arms (a shawl will do). Women, however, no longer need to cover their heads in Roman Catholic churches. In Turkey, though, women must have a head covering; a long-sleeved shirt and a long skirt are required.

To discourage purse snatchers and pickpockets, **take a handbag with long straps** that you can sling across your body, bandolier-style, and with a zippered compartment for money.

If you stay in budget hotels, **take your own soap.** Pack an extra pair of eyeglasses or contact lenses in your carry-on luggage, and if you have a health problem, **bring enough medication** to last the trip or have your doctor write a prescription using the drug's generic name, because brand names vary from country to country. In case your bags go astray, **don't put prescription drugs or valuables in luggage to be checked.** To avoid problems with customs officials, carry medications in original packaging. Also, don't forget the addresses of offices that handle refunds of lost traveler's checks.

ELECTRICITY

To use your U.S.-purchased electric-powered equipment, **bring a converter and an adapter.** The electrical current in Europe is 220 volts, 50 cycles alternating current (AC). Wall outlets in most of Europe take plugs with two round prongs; Great Britain uses plugs with two oversize round prongs.

If your appliances are dual voltage, you'll need only an adapter. Hotels sometimes have 110-volt outlets for low-wattage appliances marked "For Shavers Only" near the sink; don't use them for high-wattage appliances like blow-dryers. If your laptop computer is older, carry a converter; new laptops operate equally well on 110 and 220 volts, so you need only an adapter.

LUGGAGE

REGULATIONS➤ Free airline baggage allowances depend on the airline, the route, and the class of your ticket; ask in advance. In general, on domestic flights and on international flights between the United States and foreign destinations, you are entitled to check two bags—neither exceeding 62 inches, or 158 centimeters (length + width + height), or weighing more than 70 pounds (32 kilograms). A third piece may be brought aboard; its total dimensions are generally limited to less than 45 inches (114 centimeters), so it will fit easily under the seat in front of you or in the overhead compartment. In the United States, the FAA gives airlines broad latitude to limit carry-on allowances and tailor them to different aircraft and operational conditions. Charges for excess, oversize, or overweight pieces vary.

If you are flying between two foreign destinations, note that baggage allowances may be determined not by piece but by weight— generally 88 pounds (40 kilograms) in first class, 66 pounds (30 kilograms) in business class, and 44 pounds (20 kilograms) in economy. If your flight between two cities abroad *connects* with your transat-

lantic or transpacific flight, the piece method still applies.

SAFEGUARDING YOUR LUGGAGE➤Before leaving home, **itemize your bags' contents** and their worth, and label them with your name, address, and phone number. (If you use your home address, cover it so that potential thieves can't see it.) Inside your bag, **pack a copy of your itinerary.** At check-in, **make sure that your bag is correctly tagged** with the airport's three-letter destination code. If your bags arrive damaged or not at all, file a written report with the airline before leaving the airport.

PASSPORTS AND VISAS

If you don't already have one, **get a passport.** While traveling, **keep a photocopy of the data page** separate from your wallet and leave another copy with someone at home. If you lose your passport, promptly call the nearest embassy or consulate and the local police; having the data page can speed replacement.

U.S. CITIZENS

All U.S. citizens, even infants, need a valid passport to enter the countries covered in this guide. See the individual country chapters for any visa requirements or limits on the length of your stay. New and renewal application forms are available at any of the 13 U.S. Passport Agency offices and at some post offices and courthouses. Pass-

ports for adults are valid for 10 years and are usually mailed within four weeks; allow five weeks or more in spring and summer.

CANADIANS

You need a valid passport to enter the countries covered in this guide. See the individual country chapters for any visa requirements or limits on the length of your stay. Application forms are available at 28 regional passport offices as well as post offices and travel agencies. Whether for a first or a renewal passport, you must apply in person. Children under 16 may be included on a parent's passport but must have their own to travel alone. Passports are valid for five years and are usually mailed within two to three weeks of application.

U.K. CITIZENS

Citizens of the United Kingdom need a valid passport to enter the countries covered in this guide. See the individual country chapters for any visa requirements or limits on the length of your stay. Applications for new passports are available from main post offices as well as at the passport offices in Belfast, Glasgow, Liverpool, London, Newport, and Peterborough. You may apply in person at all passport offices, or by mail to all except the London office. Renewal passports must be applied for in person at passport offices. Children under 16 may travel on an accompanying parent's passport. All passports are valid for 10 years. Allow a month for processing.

R

RAIL TRAVEL

To save money, **look into rail passes** (*see* Rail Travel *in* Important Contacts A to Z, *above*). But be aware that if you don't plan to cover many miles, you may come out ahead by buying individual tickets.

Many travelers assume that rail passes guarantee them seats on the trains they wish to ride. Not so. You need to **book seats ahead even if you are using a rail pass;** seat reservations are required on some European trains, particularly high-speed trains, and are a good idea on trains that may be crowded—particularly in summer on popular routes. You will also need a reservation if you purchase overnight sleeping accommodations.

FROM THE U.K.

Boat trains timed to meet ferries at Channel ports leave London and connect with onward trains at the main French and Belgian ports. Calais and Boulogne have the best quick connections for Paris (total journey time about six to seven hours using the cross-Channel hovercraft); the Ramsgate–Oostende Jetfoil provides the fastest rail-sea connection to Brussels (about 5½ hours, station to station), with good rail connections to Germany and points east.

Boat trains connecting with ferries from Harwich to the Dutch and Danish North Sea ports leave from London/Liverpool Street; there are good rail connections from the Dutch ports to Amsterdam and onward to Germany and Belgium and south to France. For the Republic of Ireland, trains connecting with the ferry services across the Irish Sea leave from London/Euston and London/Paddington.

WITHIN EUROPE

International trains link most European capitals, including those of Eastern Europe; service is offered several times daily. Generally, customs and immigration formalities are completed on the train by officials who board when it crosses the frontier.

France, Germany, and the United Kingdom have all developed high-speed trains, although the latter has fallen behind the other two. The French National Railroad's (SNCF's) Train à Grande Vitesse (TGV), for example, takes just 4½ hours to cover the 871 kilometers (540 miles) from Paris to Marseille on the Mediterranean.

A number of European airlines and railways operate fast train connections to hub airports, and these can sometimes be booked through the airline's reservation service.

Most European systems operate a two-tier class system. First class costs substantially more; its only outstanding advantage is that it is likely to be less crowded on busier routes. Train journeys in Europe tend to be shorter than in the United States—trains are much faster and distances much shorter—so first-class rail travel is usually a luxury rather than a necessity. Some of the poorer European countries retain a third class, but avoid it unless you are on a rock-bottom budget.

For additional information on rail services and special fares, contact the national tourist office of the country (*see* Visitor Information *in* Important Contacts A to Z, *above*).

RENTING A CAR

CUTTING COSTS

To get the best deal, **book through a travel agent and shop around.** When pricing cars, **ask where the rental lot is located.** Some off-airport locations offer lower rates—even though their lots are only minutes away from the terminal via complimentary shuttle. You may also want to **price local car-rental companies,** whose rates may be lower still, although service and maintenance standards may not be up to those of a national firm. Also **ask your travel agent about a company's customer-service record.** How has it responded to late plane arrivals and vehicle mishaps? Are there often lines at the rental counter, and, if you're traveling during a holiday period, does a confirmed reservation guarantee you a car?

Always **find out what equipment is standard** at your destination before specifying what you want; **do without automatic transmission or air-conditioning** if they're optional. In Europe, manual transmissions are standard and air-conditioning is rare and often unnecessary.

Also in Europe, **look into wholesalers**—companies that do not own their own fleets but rent in bulk from those that do and often offer better rates than traditional car-rental operations. Prices are best during low-travel periods, and rentals booked through wholesalers must be paid for before you leave the United States. If you use a wholesaler, **know whether the prices are guaranteed** in U.S. dollars or foreign currency, and if unlimited mileage is available; find out about required deposits, cancellation penalties, and drop-off charges; and confirm the cost of any required insurance coverage.

INSURANCE

When you drive a rented car, you are generally responsible for any damage or personal injury that you cause as well as damage to the vehicle. Before you rent, **see what coverage you already have** by means of your personal auto-insurance policy and credit cards. For about $14 a day, rental companies sell insurance, known as a collision

damage waiver (CDW), that eliminates your liability for damage to the car; it's always optional and should never be automatically added to your bill.

REQUIREMENTS

Your driver's license is acceptable; an International Driver's Permit, available from the American or Canadian Automobile Association, is a good idea. Check the individual country chapters or call the country's tourist office for further information.

SURCHARGES

Before picking up the car in one city and leaving it in another, **ask about drop-off charges or one-way service fees,** which can be substantial. Note, too, that some rental agencies charge extra if you return the car before the time specified on your contract. To avoid a hefty refueling fee, **fill the tank just before you turn in the car.**

S

SENIOR-CITIZEN DISCOUNTS

To qualify for age-related discounts, **mention your senior-citizen status up front** when booking hotel reservations, not when checking out, and before you're seated in restaurants, not when paying your bill. Note that discounts may be limited to certain menus, days, or hours. When renting a car, **ask about promotional car-rental discounts**—they can net lower costs than your senior-citizen discount.

STUDENTS ON THE ROAD

To save money, **look into deals available through student-oriented travel agencies.** To qualify, you'll need to have a bona fide student ID card. *See* Students *in* Important Contacts A to Z, *above.*

T

TAX

If you shop in Europe, **get a value-added tax (VAT) refund.** For EU countries, have tax-refund forms from the store stamped at customs as you leave your final EU country; send the stamped form back to the store. See individual country chapters for information (*also see* Tax *in* Important Contacts A to Z, *above*).

TELEPHONES

LONG-DISTANCE

The long-distance services of AT&T, MCI, and Sprint make calling home relatively convenient and let you avoid hotel surcharges; typically, you dial an 800 number in the United States and a local number abroad. Before you go, **find out the local access codes** for your destinations.

W

WHEN TO GO

For information about travel seasons and for the average daily maximum and minimum temperatures of the major European cities, *see* Essential Information *in* each country chapter.

2 Andorra

THE 191-SQUARE-MILE MOUNTAIN PARADISE, tax haven, and commercial oasis known as the coprincipality of Andorra drafted a constitution—somewhat grandly titled the Carta Magna—and held elections in 1993, converting Europe's last bastion of feudalism into a full-fledged democratic state. The bishop of Urgell and the president of France assumed even more symbolic roles as the coprinces of this unique Pyrenean country. The area originally fell through the cracks between France and Spain when Charlemagne founded Andorra as an independent entity during his 8th-century battles with the Moors. In the 9th century, his heir, Carles el Calb (Charles the Bald), made the bishop of Urgell overlord of Andorra, a role contested by the French counts of Foix until a treaty providing joint suzerainty was agreed upon in 1278. The French monarchy inherited these rights and passed them on to the modern-day French presidents, while the bishop of Urgell's claim has remained rock-solid for the past thousand years. This dual protection has allowed Andorra to thrive as a low-tax, duty-free haven. Europe's new semiborderless unity, however, is eliminating this special status; the new Andorra aspires to an improved tourist industry and a more dignified economy than the smuggling and tax-evasion expertise for which it has acquired fame.

Winter sports, mountain climbing and hiking, and the cultural resources provided by a plethora of Romanesque chapels, bridges, and medieval farm and town houses are Andorra's once and future stock in trade, although numbered bank accounts will surely not be disappearing anytime soon.

ESSENTIAL INFORMATION

Before You Go

When to Go

Winter brings a huge influx of ski buffs, though any time of year has always attracted consumers with an eye on Andorra's now less advantageous tax- and duty-free shopping status. Andorra is a paradise for lovers of the outdoors. In winter there is reliable snowfall from December to early April, and efficient ski resorts at Soldeu, Arinsal, Pas de la Casa, and La Massana. In summer, hikers will find magnificent trails on the Grande Randonnée (GR) network and a score of shorter but still demanding routes. Botanists and bird-watchers should arrive by early April, in time for the bird migrations from Africa and the first flush of spring flowers on the slopes and in the valleys. Be warned that even in summer the nighttime temperatures can drop to freezing.

CLIMATE

The following are the average daily maximum and minimum temperatures for Andorra.

Jan.	43F	6C	May	62F	17C	Sept.	71F	22C
	30	− 1		43	6		49	10
Feb.	45F	7C	June	73F	23C	Oct.	60F	16C
	30	− 1		39	4		42	6
Mar.	54F	12C	July	79F	26C	Nov.	51F	10C
	35	2		54	12		35	2
Apr.	58F	14C	Aug.	76F	24C	Dec.	42F	6C
	39	4		53	12		31	− 1

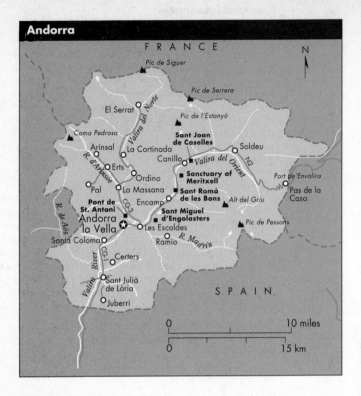

Andorra

(Map labels:) FRANCE, Pic de Siguer, Pic de Serrera, El Serrat, Pic de l'Estanyó, Coma Pedrosa, Arinsal, La Cortinada, Sant Joan de Caselles, Soldeu, Canillo, Valira del Orient, Erts, Ordino, Sanctuary of Meritxell, Port de l'Envalira, Pal, La Massana, Sant Romà de les Bons, Pas de la Casa, Encamp, Alt del Griu, Pont de St. Antoni, Sant Miguel d'Engolasters, Andorra la Vella, Pic de Pessons, Les Escaldes, Santa Coloma, Ramio, R. Madriu, Certers, Sant Julià de Lòria, Juberri, SPAIN, Valira del Norte, R. d'Arinsal, R. de Aós, Valira River, CG-3, CG-1

0 — 10 miles
0 — 15 km

Currency

The Spanish peseta is the major Andorran currency, but French francs are equally acceptable, and all prices are quoted in both currencies in Andorra. For exchange rates and coinage information, *see* Currency *in* Chapter 10, France, and Chapter 26, Spain.

What It Will Cost

Prices in Andorra are similar to those in neighboring France and Spain. The only bargains still available are products subject to state tax, such as tobacco, alcohol, perfume, and gasoline. Staples such as butter, cheese, and milk sold as surplus by member countries of the European Union (EU) are also cheaper in Andorra.

SAMPLE PRICES

Coca-Cola, 150 ptas.; cup of coffee, 100 ptas.; 1-mile taxi ride, 300 ptas.; ham sandwich, 350 ptas.

Customs

Andorra has traditionally been famous for its liberality in the matter of customs, duties, visas, and the like. Non-Europeans need a passport to cross the border; Europeans enter with only an identity card. But now that the French–Spanish border is virtually a wave-by (and usually not even that), Andorra's is less than a formality.

Language

Andorran nationalism is being invented, despite the fact that 82% of the country's population of 61,599, mainly Spanish and Portuguese nationals, are not native speakers of Catalan, the coprincipality's official language. Spanish, French, and English are also commonly spoken by merchants and service personnel. Catalonia's "linguistic normalization," the establishment of Catalan as the area's first language, has become a fact in the Andorran school system as well, and Andorra will join the more than 6 million Catalan-speakers on both sides of the Pyrenees from the Delta del Ebro south of Barcelona to Perpignan in the French Roussillon.

Getting Around

By Car

The maintenance of Andorran roads varies. The one main artery from France into Spain via Andorra la Vella is excellent and handles the heaviest traffic, as does the spur north toward the ski resorts at La Massana and Ordino. Elsewhere, roads are narrow, winding, and best suited to four-wheel-drive vehicles or, higher up, mules. In winter, snow tires or chains are essential. Although the Puymorens Tunnel that opened in fall 1994 does not surface in Andorra, it does eliminate the switchback Puymorens mountain pass. This pass is either dangerous or closed in bad weather and adds an extra 30 minutes to the Barcelona–Pas de la Casa trip. In good weather, though, don't miss the spectacularly scenic Puymorens pass.

By Bus

Minibuses connect the towns and villages, and fares are low; 100 ptas. will take you 5 kilometers (3 miles). Details on fares and services are available at hotels and from tourist offices.

On Foot

Mountainous Andorra is a mecca for hikers, hill-walkers, and backpackers. The mountains are high and the terrain is wild, so a degree of care and experience is advisable. There are two long-distance trails: the GR7, which runs from Portello Blanca on the French frontier to Escaldes on the road to Spain; and the GR75, also called the Ordino Route, a magnificent, high-mountain trail that stretches across the central range. Get details on local treks and walks from tourist offices.

Staying in Andorra

Telephones

LOCAL CALLS

For local directory assistance, dial 111. There are no regional area codes in Andorra. Most pay phones take phone cards issued by the telephone company; these may be purchased at *tabacs* (stores that sell tobacco and stamps).

INTERNATIONAL CALLS

For assistance, call the local operator at 111. To call Andorra from Spain, dial 07–376 and the six-digit local number; from France, dial 19–376.

COUNTRY CODE

The country code for Andorra is 376.

Mail

You can buy Andorran stamps with French francs or Spanish pesetas, though the postal service within the country is free. The Spanish post office in Andorra la Vella is at Carrer Joan Maragall 10; the French post office is at 1 rue Père d'Urg. There are no postal codes in Andorra but be sure to write "Principat d'Andorra" to distinguish the country from the Spanish town.

Opening and Closing Times

Banks are open weekdays 9–1 and 3–5, and Saturday 9–noon. They are closed Sunday.

Churches. Andorra is predominantly Catholic. Most chapels and churches are kept locked around the clock, with the key being left at the closest house. Check with the local tourist office for additional details.

Shops open daily 9–8, though many are closed between 2 and 4.

National Holidays
January 1; April 8 (Easter Monday); May 1 (Labor Day); May 27 (Pentecost Monday); June 23 (St. John); September 8 (La Verge de Meritxell); November 1 (All Saints' Day); December 25.

LOCAL HOLIDAYS
At Canillo: third Saturday in July and following Sunday and Monday; at Les Escaldes: July 25–27; at Sant Julià de Lòria: last Sunday in July and following Monday and Tuesday; at Andorra la Vella: first Saturday, Sunday, Monday in August; at Encamp and La Massana: August 15–17; at Ordino: September 16, 17.

Dining
Andorra is not known as a gastronomic paradise, but the quality of the food is improving. There are good restaurants serving French, Spanish, or Catalan cuisine and plenty of spots where the visitor will eat hearty Pyrenean fare at no great cost. Local dishes worth trying include *truite de carreroles* (a type of omelet with wild mushrooms); *trinchat,* a typical country specialty of potatoes and cabbage; and such local delicacies as *estofat d'isard* (stewed mountain goat); local cheeses, such as *formatge de tupi*; and *rostes amb mel* (ham baked with honey). Although most restaurants offer prix-fixe menus, a number of more expensive establishments are only à la carte.

MEALTIMES
True to the coprincipality's predominantly Spanish flavor, Andorrans eat late: Dinners don't usually get under way until 8:30 or 9, and lunch is a substantial meal served between 2 and 4.

WHAT TO WEAR
Casual dress is acceptable in all restaurants in Andorra, regardless of price category.

RATINGS
The following ratings are for a three-course meal for one person, excluding wine. Highly recommended restaurants are indicated by a star ★.

CATEGORY	COST
$$$$	over 5,000 ptas.
$$$	3,500–5,000 ptas.
$$	1,500–3,500 ptas.
$	under 1,500 ptas.

Lodging
The number of Andorran hotels continues to increase, and standards are rising. The decor is usually functional, but service is friendly and the facilities are excellent.

Most hotels are open year-round. Reservations are necessary during July and August. Hotel rates often include at least two meals.

RATINGS
The following price ratings apply for two people in a double room. Highly recommended lodgings are indicated by a star ★.

CATEGORY	COST
$$$$	over 9,000 ptas.
$$$	6,000–9,000 ptas.
$$	4,000–6,000 ptas.
$	2,500–4,000 ptas.

Tipping

Restaurants and cafés almost always tack on a 10%–15% service charge; it's customary to leave a similar amount in addition to the charge, but this is optional.

Arriving and Departing

By Plane

The nearest international airports are at Barcelona (200 km/125 mi), Perpignan (136 km/85 mi), and Toulouse-Blagnac (180 km/112 mi).

By Train

From Barcelona, take the train to Puigcerdà, then the bus to La Seu d'Urgell and Andorra la Vella; from Madrid, take the train to Lleida and then a bus to La Seu d'Urgell and Andorra la Vella; from Toulouse, take the train to Ax-les-Thermes and La Tour de Carol, then the bus to La Seu d'Urgell and Andorra la Vella. Alternatively, take the train from Toulouse to L'Hospitalet (the bus to Pas de la Casa and Andorra la Vella meets the morning train from Toulouse).

By Bus

A bus service runs twice daily from Barcelona (Ronda Universidad 4). In summer there are direct buses from Perpignan and Toulouse to Andorra. The ride from Barcelona, Perpignan, or Toulouse to Andorra la Vella takes about three hours.

By Car

The fastest, most direct course from Barcelona to Andorra la Vella—the route with the fewest curves and the most tolls (around 3,000 ptas. in all)—runs through the Tunel del Cadí and the Cerdanya Valley via Bellver and La Seu d'Urgell. The roads from Toulouse and Perpignan are beautiful but tortuous, approaching Andorra through its eastern Pas de la Casa entrance at the French border.

Important Addresses and Numbers

Tourist Information

Andorra La Vella. Sindicat d'Iniciativa (National Tourist Office, Carrer Dr. Vilanova, tel. 820214, fax 825823. Open Mon.–Sat. 10–1 and 3–7, Sun. and holidays 10–1).

Barcelona (Carrer Marià Cubí, 159, tel. 93/200–0655, 93/200–0787).

Canillo (Unió Pro-Turisme, Caseta Pro-Turisme, tel. and fax 851002).

Encamp (Unió Pro-Foment i Turisme, Plaça Consell General, tel. 831405, fax 831878).

Escaldes-Engordany (Unío Pro-Turisme, Plaça dels Co-Prínceps, tel. 820963).

La Massana (Unió Pro-Turisme, Plaça del Quart, tel. 835693).

Ordino (Oficina de Turisme, Cruïlla d'Ordino, tel. 836963).

Pas de la Casa (Unió Pro-Turisme, C. Bernat III, tel. 855292).

Sant Julià de Lòria (Unió Pro Turisme, tel. 844345, fax 844000).

Consulates

U.S. (Pg. Reina Elisenda 23, Barcelona, Spain, tel. 93/280–2227). **Canadian** (Nuñez de Balboa 35, Madrid, Spain, tel. 91/225–9119). **U.K.** (Apartado de Correos 12111, Barcelona, Spain, tel. 93/322–2151).

Emergencies
Doctor (tel. 118). **Police** (tel. 110). **Ambulance and Fire** (tel. 118).

Travel Agency
Relax Travel Agency/American Express (Roc dels Escolls 2, Andorra la Vella, tel. 822044, fax 827055).

Guided Tours
Tours of the Andorra la Vella and the surrounding countryside are offered by several firms; check with the tourist office for details or call **Excursion Nadal** (tel. 821138) or **Solineu Excursion** (tel. 823653).

EXPLORING ANDORRA

Exploring Andorra takes time. The roads are narrow and steep, the views compel frequent stops, and every village is worth examining. If possible, do as much sightseeing on foot as time permits.

Overlooking **Andorra la Vella's** main square is the stone bulk of the **Casa de la Vall** (House of the Valley), a medieval-looking building constructed in 1580 and the seat of the Andorran government in the capital city. A charmingly rustic spot, the Casa contains many religious frescoes of note, some of which were carefully transported here from village churches high in the Pyrenees. The kitchen is particularly interesting, with a splendid array of ancient copper pots and other culinary implements. *Carrer de la Vall s/n. Tours weekdays 10–1 and 3–7, Sat. 3–7.*

The spa town of **Les Escaldes** is about a 15-minute walk from Andorra la Vella. The Romanesque church of **Sant Miquel d'Engolasters** lies on a ridge northeast of the capital and can be reached on foot—allow half a day for the round-trip—or by taxi up a mountain road. The views are well worth the climb. Just beyond Encamp, 6 kilometers (4 miles) northeast, is the 12th-century church of **Sant Romà de les Bons,** situated in a particularly picturesque convergence of medieval buildings and mountain scenery.

Midway between Encamp and Canillo on CG-2 is the **Sanctuary of Meritxell,** the focal point of the country's religious fervor. The Blessed Virgin of Meritxell is the principality's patron saint, although, oddly enough for such a religious country, this patronage wasn't declared until the late-19th century. The original sanctuary was destroyed by fire in 1972; the new gray-stone building looks remarkably like a factory, but the mountain setting is superb. *Admission free. Open Wed.–Mon. 9–1 and 3–7.*

Another 3 kilometers (2 miles) farther, just before the town of Canillo, you will see a Gothic seven-arm stone cross (actually it has six arms, as one has broken off). A mile or so beyond is the Romanesque church of **Sant Joan de Caselles,** whose ancient walls have turned a lovely dappled brown hue over the centuries. The bell tower is stunning: three stories of weathered stone punctuated by rows of arched windows. Inside the main building is a good example of a reredos (a wall or screen positioned behind an altar). It dates from 1525 and depicts the life of St. John the Evangelist.

Retrace your way back to Andorra la Vella, and this time take CG-3 due north out of the capital. After just 3 kilometers (2 miles) you'll come to a Romanesque stone bridge, the **Pont de Sant Antoni,** which spans a narrow river. Three kilometers (2 miles) beyond is the picturesque mountain town of **La Massana;** take some time to stroll along its rustic streets. Another 5 kilometers (3 miles) farther is the tiny village of **Ordino.** Its medieval church is exceptionally appealing; to see it properly, go at night between 7 and 8, when mass is celebrated.

In **La Cortinada,** a mile or so to the northwest, is the **Can Pal,** another fine example of medieval Andorran architecture. This time the building is a privately owned manor house (strictly no admittance), with a dovecote attached. Note the turret perched high on the far side.

Backtrack once more to Andorra la Vella, then take CG-1 south. In 4 kilometers (2½ miles) you'll come to the pre-Romanesque church of **Santa Coloma,** in the village bearing the same name; parts of the church date from the 9th and 10th centuries, and there are Romanesque frescoes on the interior walls.

Shopping

Visitors to Andorra have traditionally listed shopping as one of the main attractions, but not all the goods displayed are actually at bargain prices. Moreover, Andorra's appeal to bargain-seekers may be ending. The French and Spanish come here to buy cigarettes, liquor, household items, and foodstuffs, but find electrical goods and cameras no cheaper than they are at home. Good buys are consumable items: perfume, cigarettes, whiskey, and gin. For cameras, tape recorders, and other imported items, compare prices and models carefully. The main shopping area is **Andorra la Vella,** but there are stores in all the new developments and in the towns close to the frontiers, at **Pas de la Casa** and **Sant Julià de Lòria.**

DINING AND LODGING

For details and price-category definitions, *see* Dining and Lodging *in* Staying in Andorra, *above.*

Andorra la Vella

DINING

Chez Jaques. The varied menu features both classical and nouvelle French dishes, though other international cuisines are handled with flair. With good food and a cozy ambience, it's very popular with the locals. *Av. Tarragona, Edificio Terra Vella, tel. 820325. Reservations accepted. AE, DC, MC, V. Closed July and Aug.* $$$

El Rusc. A smallish hideaway near La Massana is one of Andorra's best new options for fine dining. Chef Antoni Garrallá's Basque cuisine includes French and international specialties as well. Try the foie gras with onions or *besugo* (baked sea bream), a standard treat from the Basque country. Do make a reservation, as this flower-covered chalet can seat only 50 diners. *Carrer d'Arinsal, tel. 838200, fax 835180. Reservations advised. AE, DC, MC, V.* $$$

Molí dels Fanals. This quiet restaurant is built into an antique *borda* (typical Andorran mountain refuge) that's made of stone and has a fireplace and wooden paneling. The international cuisine here uses consistently high-quality ingredients. Try the chateaubriand with foie-gras sauce. *Carrer Dr. Vilanova (Borda Casadet), tel. 821381. Reservations advised. AE, DC, MC, V. Closed Sun. June–Aug.* $$$

Borda Estevet. Another borda with a very Pyrenean feel, this simple spot offers a selection of Spanish and Andorran dishes, beef cooked and served *a la llosa* (on hot slabs of slate), four private dining rooms, and a terrace for outside dining in summer. *Ctra. Comella 2, tel. 864026. AE, DC, MC, V.* $$

★ **Versailles.** A tiny and authentic French bistro with only a handful of tables, Versailles is always packed. Leave room for pastries after the *magret* (breast) of duck! *Cap del Carrer 1, tel. 821331. Reservations advised. AE, DC, MC, V. $$*

LODGING

★ **Andorra Palace.** The large, modern Palace is widely considered one of the capital's best hotels. The rooms are spacious and the furnishings smartly contemporary. The outdoor terrace is a pleasant spot in which to relax and watch the bustle below. *Carrer de la Roda, tel. 821072, fax 828195. 140 rooms with bath. Facilities: restaurant, parking, bar, sauna, fitness center, pool. AE, DC, MC, V. $$$$*

Andorra Park. The Park ranks with the Palace as one of Andorra la Vella's two top hotels. It's a grand building away from the city's congestion of traffic and pedestrians. The American Bar is a popular watering hole for local society. There's a pretty garden, as well as a terrace, and the deluxe guest rooms have private balconies. *Carrer Les Canals 24, tel. 820979, fax 820983. 40 rooms with bath. Facilities: restaurant, tennis courts, croquet, parking, bar, pool. AE, DC, MC, V. $$$$*

Hotel Eden Roc. Besides having all the amenities of larger hotels, the smaller Eden Roc offers an exceptional dining room and attentive personal service. *Av. Dr. Mitjavila 1, tel. 821000, fax 860319. 56 rooms with bath. Facilities: restaurant, bar, terrace. AE, V. $$$$*

Florida. For good value at relatively inexpensive rates, try this cheerful hotel. There's no on-site restaurant, but there are several nearby. *Carrer La Llacuna 15, tel. 820105, fax 861925. 52 rooms with bath. Facilities: bar, lounge. AE, DC, MC, V. $$*

Hotel La Mola. This friendly spot, midway between the ski slopes and the brightish lights of Andorra la Vella, is a comfortable choice with all the basic facilities at a fraction of the price of some of the better-known Andorra hotels. *Av. Co-Princep Episcopal 62, tel. 31181, fax 833046. 48 rooms with bath. Facilities: restaurant, pool, tennis courts. AE, DC, MC, V. $*

Les Escaldes

DINING

★ **1900.** This small, beautifully decorated restaurant serves some of the best food in the principality, with a mixture of French, Spanish, and Andorran cuisines. It's expensive for Andorra, but Chef Alain Despretz's inventive dishes are often worth it. *11 Carrer de la Unío, tel. 826716. Reservations advised. AE, DC, MC, V. Closed Mon. and July. $$$*

DINING AND LODGING

★ **Roc Blanc.** Sleek, modern, and luxurious trappings—and a wealth of facilities to pamper the body, from mud baths to acupuncture—are what the Roc Blanc is all about. The rooms are large, and the hotel's restaurant, El Pi, is consistently good. *Plaça Co-Princeps 5, tel. 821486, fax 860244. 250 rooms with bath. Facilities: restaurant, piano bar, 2 pools, sauna, tennis courts, health club, thermal baths, hairdresser, terrace. AE, DC, MC, V. $$$$*

Ordino

LODGING

Hotel Coma. Surrounded by woods and meadows, this Swiss chalet–style hideaway just outside the village offers scenery, silence, and simple Andorran fare at affordable prices. *Carretera General, tel. 835116, fax 837909. 48 rooms with bath. Facilities: bar, restaurant, terrace, pool. AE, DC, MC, V. $$*

Pas de la Casa

DINING

Le Grizzly. This is a popular French restaurant for lunch or dinner, especially during the ski season. The food is simple but well prepared, and it offers good value, with a choice of four prix-fixe menus from 800 ptas. to 1,300 ptas. Try the *entrecôte roquefort* (steak) and the thick Provençal soups. *Av. d'Encamp, tel. 855227. Reservations advised. AE, DC, MC, V. $*

Sant Julià de Lòria

LODGING

★ **Pol.** Gracefully modern surroundings and friendly staff are just two reasons this hotel is so popular. Its disco is a popular nightspot. *Av. Verge de Canólich 52, tel. 841122, fax 841852. 80 rooms with bath. Facilities: restaurant, bar, garden, terrace. AE, MC, V. $$$*

Santa Coloma

DINING

El Bon Racó. This is exactly what it says it is: a good corner, nook, or retreat. A traditional borda in design, it turns out good local cuisine at encouraging prices. Try to arrive early; the *racó* is popular and fills quickly, especially on weekends. *Av. Salou 86, tel. 822085. Reservations advised. AE, DC, MC, V. $$*

3 Austria

WHATEVER AUSTRIA may lack in size, it more than makes up for in diversity. Its Alps and mountain lakes in the central and southern provinces equal those of neighboring Switzerland; the vast Vienna Woods remind some of the Black Forest; the steppes of the province of Burgenland blend with those across the border in Hungary; and the vineyards along the Danube rival those of the Rhine and Mosel river valleys. And nowhere else is there a Vienna or a Salzburg—or such pastry shops!

Austria has become considerably more expensive in recent years. But there are still bargains to be found, and discovering them can be one of the diversions of a vacation in Austria.

The country is highly accessible. There are virtually no outposts that are not served by public transport of one form or another. The rail network is well maintained, and trains are fast, comfortable, and punctual. Highways are superb and well marked. Public transportation in cities, although not cheap, is safe, clean, and convenient. In short, the visitor to Austria spends more time having fun than coping with the logistics of getting from A to B.

Austrians are for the most part friendly and welcoming. Lovers of the outdoors, they are ever ready to pack off to the mountains, lakes, woods, or ski slopes at a moment's notice. At the same time, they can be as melancholy as their wine tavern songs suggest. For English-speaking travelers, communication is seldom a problem, since most Austrians speak another language beyond their native German, and English is the usual choice.

You'll discover in conversation with Austrians that they are more for evolution than revolution. As a result, change is gradual, and old values tend to be maintained. Graceful dancers do execute the tricky "left waltz" on balmy summer evenings in Vienna, and at any time you may find an entire town celebrating some event—brass band, lederhosen, and all.

ESSENTIAL INFORMATION

Before You Go

When to Go

Austria has two tourist seasons. Summer season technically starts around Easter, reaches its high in July, and winds down in September. May, June, September, and October are the most temperate months, and the most affordable. Aside from a few overly humid days when you may wish for wider use of air-conditioning, even Vienna is pleasant, and the city literally moves outdoors in summer. The winter cultural season starts in October and runs into June; winter sports get under way in December and last until the end of April, although you can ski in certain areas well into June and on some of the highest glaciers year-round. Some events—the Salzburg Festival is a prime example—cause a substantial increase in hotel and other costs.

CLIMATE

Summer can be warm; winter, bitterly cold. The southern region is usually several degrees warmer in summer, several degrees colder in win-

Austria

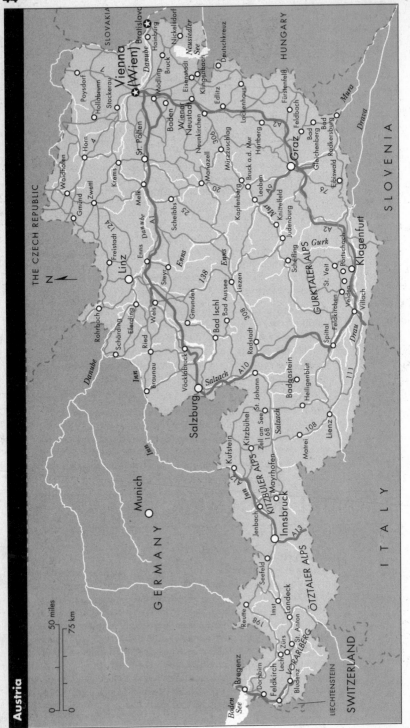

ter. Winters north of the Alps can be overcast and dreary, whereas the south basks in winter sunshine.

The following are the average daily maximum and minimum temperatures for Vienna.

Jan.	34F	1C	May	67F	19C	Sept.	68F	20C
	25	– 4		50	10		53	11
Feb.	38F	3C	June	73F	23C	Oct.	56F	14C
	28	– 3		56	14		44	7
Mar.	47F	8C	July	76F	25C	Nov.	45F	7C
	30	– 1		60	15		37	3
Apr.	58F	15C	Aug.	75F	24C	Dec.	37F	3C
	43	6		59	15		30	– 1

Currency

The unit of currency is the Austrian schilling (AS), divided into 100 groschen. There are AS20, 50, 100, 500, 1,000, and 5,000 bills; AS1, 5, 10, and 20 coins; and 1-, 2-, 10-, and 50-groschen coins. The 1-, 2-, and 5-groschen coins are rare, and the AS20 coins are unpopular—though useful for some cigarette machines. The 500- and 100-schilling notes look perilously similar; confusing the two can be an expensive mistake.

At press time (spring 1995), there were about AS9.41 to the dollar and about AS15.50 to the pound sterling.

Credit cards are widely used throughout Austria, although not all establishments take all cards, and some take cash only. American Express has money machines in Vienna at Parkring 10 (actually in Liebenberggasse, off Parkring) and at the airport. Many of the Bankomat money dispensers will also accept Visa cards if you have an international PIN encoded.

Exchange traveler's checks at a bank, post office, or American Express office to get the best rate. All charge a small commission; some smaller banks or "change" offices may give a poorer rate *and* charge a higher fee. All change offices at airports and at main train stations in major cities cash traveler's checks. Bank-operated change offices in Vienna with extended hours are located on Stephansplatz and in the Opernpassage. The Bank Austria machines on Stephansplatz and at Kärntnerstrasse 51 (to the right of the opera) and at the Raiffeisenbank on Kohlmarkt (at Michaelerplatz) change bills from other currencies into schillings, but rates are poor and a hefty commission is automatically deducted.

You may bring in any amount of foreign currency or schillings and take out any amount with you.

What It Will Cost

Austria is not inexpensive, but since inflation is relatively low, costs remain fairly stable. Vienna and Salzburg are the most expensive cities, along with fashionable resorts at Kitzbühel, Seefeld, Badgastein, Velden, Zell am See, Pörtschach, St. Anton, Zürs, and Lech. Many smaller towns offer virtually identical facilities at half the price.

Drinks in bars and clubs are considerably higher than in cafés or restaurants. Austrian prices include service and tax.

SAMPLE PRICES

Cup of coffee, AS25; half-liter of draft beer, AS27–AS40; glass of wine, AS35; Coca-Cola, AS25; open sandwich, AS25; theater ticket,

AS200–AS300; concert ticket, AS250–AS500; opera ticket, AS600 and up; 1-mile taxi ride, AS35.

Customs on Arrival

Austria's duty-free allowances are as follows: 200 cigarettes or 100 cigars or 250 grams of tobacco, 2 liters of wine and 1 liter of spirits, 1 bottle of toilet water (about 300-milliliter size), 50 milliliters of perfume for those aged 18 and over arriving from other European countries. Although Austria is a member of the European Union (EU), these limits may apply to EU citizens as well. Visitors arriving from the United States, Canada, or other non-European points may bring in twice the above amounts.

Language

German is the official national language. In larger cities and most resort areas, you will have no problem finding those who speak English; hotel and restaurant staff, in particular, speak English reasonably well. Most younger Austrians speak at least passable English, and fluency is increasing.

Getting Around

By Car

ROAD CONDITIONS

The highway system is excellent, and all roads are well maintained and well marked. Secondary mountain roads may be narrow and winding, but traffic is generally light. Check the condition of mountain roads in winter before starting out (tel. 0222/711–99–7). Many mountain passes are closed, though tunnels are kept open.

RULES OF THE ROAD

Drive on the right. Seat belts are compulsory in front. Children under 12 must sit in the back, and smaller children must have a restraining seat. Speed limits are as posted; otherwise, 130 kph (80 mph) on expressways, 100 kph (62 mph) on other main roads, 50 kph (31 mph) in built-up areas. Some city center areas have speed limits of 30 kph (19 mph). The right-of-way is for those coming from the right (especially in traffic circles) unless otherwise marked. A warning triangle—standard equipment in rental cars—must be set up in case of breakdown.

PARKING

Observe signs; tow-away in cities is expensive. Overnight parking in winter is forbidden on city streets with streetcar lines.

GASOLINE

Prices—AS10–AS11 per liter—are fairly consistent throughout the country. Only *bleifrei* (unleaded)—regular and premium—is sold, and smaller filling stations may not carry diesel fuel.

BREAKDOWNS

Emergency road service is available from **ARBÖ** (tel. 123 nationwide) or **ÖAMTC** (tel. 120) auto clubs. Special phones are located along autobahns and major highways.

By Train

Trains in Austria are fast and efficient, and most lines have now been electrified. Hourly express trains run on the key Vienna–Salzburg route. All principal trains have first- and second-class cars, as well as smoking and no-smoking areas. Overnight trains have sleeping compartments, and most trains have dining cars. Dining car service and quality are highly variable; alas, value for your money is rarer still, although the railroads have pledged improvement. If you're traveling at peak times, a reserved seat—available for a small additional fee—is always a good idea.

FARES

If you're visiting other European countries, a **Eurail Pass** (*see* Rail Travel *in* Chapter 1), valid throughout most of Europe, is the best deal. Austria has only two discount tickets, but half-price fares are available to families, with children up to 15 years traveling free. Adults need a passport photo to get the family pass at rail stations. A **Bundesnetzkarte** allows unlimited travel for a month and costs AS5,400 for first class and AS3,600 for second class. The alternative is an **Österreich Puzzle** ticket, which is valid for one or more of the four zones that cover the country. The ticket is good for unlimited travel on any four days within a 10-day period. For a single zone, a first-class Puzzle ticket costs AS1,485, second-class AS990. If you're 26 or under, the Puzzle Junior ticket costs AS900 first class, AS600 second class. Full details are available from travel agents or from the Austrian National Tourist Office. Prices are likely to be higher in 1996.

By Plane

Domestic service is expensive. **Austrian Airlines** flies between Vienna and Linz, Salzburg, Graz, and Klagenfurt. **Tyrolean Airlines** has service from Vienna to Innsbruck. **Rheintalflug** flies between Vienna and Altenhausen, just over the border in Switzerland, with bus connections to Feldkirch, Bregenz, and Bludenz in Vorarlberg.

By Bus

Service is available to virtually every community accessible by highway. Winter buses have ski racks. Vienna's central bus terminal (Wien-Mitte/Landstrasse Hauptstrasse, opposite the Hilton) is the arrival/departure point for international bus routes. In most other cities the bus station is adjacent to the train station. Bus services are run by both the post office and the railroads; tourist offices can help you resolve consequent confusions.

By Boat

Boats ply the Danube from Passau in Germany all the way to Vienna and from Vienna to Bratislava (Slovakia), Budapest (Hungary), and the Black Sea. Only East European boats run beyond Budapest. Overnight boats have cabins; all have dining. The most scenic stretches in Austria are from Passau to Linz and through the Danube—or Wachau—Valley (Melk, Krems). From Vienna, there are day trips you can take upstream to the Wachau and downstream to Bratislava and Budapest. There are also special moonlight dancing and jazz excursions. Make reservations from **DDSG** (the Danube Steamship Company, tel. 0222/727–50–0) in Vienna or travel agents.

By Bicycle

Bicycles can be rented at many train stations and returned to any of them. Most trains and some postal buses will take bikes as baggage. Bikes can be taken on the Vienna subway, with the exception of the U-6 (year-round Sun., holidays all day; May–Sept., weekdays 9–3 and after 6:30, Sat. after 9 AM). You'll need a half-fare ticket for the bike (*see* Getting Around *in* Vienna, *below*). Marked cycling routes parallel most of the Danube.

Staying in Austria

Telephones

LOCAL CALLS

Pay telephones take AS1, 5, 10, and 20 coins. A three-minute local call costs AS1. Emergency calls are free. Instructions are in English in most booths. Add AS1 when time is up to continue the connection. If you will be phoning frequently, get a phone card at a post office. This works in all *Wertkartentelefon* phones. The cost of the call will be deducted from the card automatically. Cards cost AS190 for AS200 worth of phoning, AS95 for AS100 in calls, AS48 for calls totaling AS50.

Phone numbers throughout Austria are being changed. A sharp tone indicates no connection or that the number has been changed. Calls to Vienna from *outside* Austria use the city prefix 01 or 1; from *inside* Austria, 0222.

INTERNATIONAL CALLS

It costs more to telephone *from* Austria than it does to telephone *to* Austria. Calls from post offices are least expensive. To avoid hotel charges, call overseas and ask to be called back; use an international credit card, available from AT&T, Sprint, MCI, and others; or use access codes to reach operators for **AT&T** (022/903–011) or **MCI** (022/903–012). To make a collect call—you can't do this from pay phones—dial the operator and ask for an R-Gespräch (pronounced air-ga-*shprayk*). For international information, dial 08, 1611, or 1614. Most operators speak English; if yours doesn't, you'll be passed to one who does.

COUNTRY CODE

The country code for Austria is 43.

Mail

POSTAL RATES

Airmail letters to the United States and Canada cost AS11.50 minimum; postcards cost AS8.50. Letters to the United Kingdom cost AS7, postcards cost AS6, and both automatically go by air. An aerogram costs AS12.

RECEIVING MAIL

American Express offices in Vienna, Linz, Salzburg, and Innsbruck will hold mail at no charge for those carrying an American Express credit card or American Express traveler's checks.

VAT Refunds

Value-added tax (VAT) at 20% is charged on all sales and is automatically included in prices. If you purchase goods worth AS1,000 or more and are not a citizen of an EU country, you can claim the tax back as you leave or once you've reached home. Ask store clerks to fill out and give you the necessary papers. Get them stamped at the airport or border by customs officials (who may ask to see the goods). You can get an immediate refund of the VAT at international airports or at main border points, less a service charge, or you can return the papers by mail to the shop(s), which will then deal with the details. The VAT refund can be credited to your credit-card account or paid by check.

Opening and Closing Times

Banks are open weekdays 8–noon or 12:30, and 1:30–3 or 4. Hours vary from one city to another. Principal offices in cities stay open during lunch.

Museums. Opening days and times vary considerably from one city to another and depend on the season, the size of the museum, budgetary constraints, and assorted other factors. Monday is often a closing day. Your hotel or the local tourist office will have current details.

Shops are open weekdays from 8 or 9 until 6 and Saturday until noon or 1 only, except the first Saturday of every month, when they stay open until 5. Some shops in larger cities are open on Thursday evening until 8. Many smaller shops close for one or two hours at midday.

National Holidays

January 1; January 6 (Epiphany); April 7–8 (Easter); May 1 (May Day); May 16 (Ascension); May 26–27 (Pentecost); June 6 (Corpus Christi); August 15 (Assumption); October 26 (National Day); November 1 (All Saints' Day); December 8 (Immaculate Conception); December 25–26.

Dining

Take your choice of sidewalk *Wurstl* (frankfurter) stands, *Imbissstube* (quick-lunch stops), cafés, *Heuriger* (wine restaurants), self-service restaurants, modest *Gasthäuser* (neighborhood establishments with local specialties), and full-fledged restaurants in every price category. Most places post their menus outside. Shops (such as Eduscho) that sell coffee beans also offer coffee by the cup at prices considerably lower than those in cafés. Many Anker bakery shops also offer tasty *Schmankerl* (snacks) and coffee. *Fleischer* or *Fleischhauer* (butchers) may also offer soup and a main course at noon. A growing number of shops and snack bars offer pizza by the slice. We recommend that you make dinner reservations.

MEALTIMES

Austrians often eat up to five meals a day: a very early Continental breakfast of rolls and coffee; *Gabelfrühstück,* a slightly more substantial breakfast with eggs or cold meat—possibly even a small goulash—at mid-morning (understood to be 9, sharp); a main meal at noon; afternoon *Jause* (coffee with cake) at teatime; and, unless dining out, a light supper to end the day.

WHAT TO WEAR

A jacket and tie are generally advised for restaurants in the top price categories. Otherwise casual dress is acceptable, although in Vienna formal dress (jacket and tie) is preferred in some **$$** restaurants at dinner. When in doubt, it's best to dress up.

RATINGS

Prices are per person and include soup and a main course, usually with salad, and a small beer or glass of wine. Meals in the top price categories will include a dessert or cheese and coffee. Prices include taxes and service (but leaving an additional 5%–7% is customary). Highly recommended restaurants are indicated by a star ★.

CATEGORY	MAJOR CITY	OTHER AREAS
$$$$	over AS800	over AS600
$$$	AS500–AS800	AS400–AS600
$$	AS200–AS500	AS170–AS400
$	under AS200	under AS170

Lodging

Austrian hotels and pensions are officially classified using from one to five stars. These grades broadly coincide with our own four-way rating system. No matter what the category, standards for service and cleanliness are high. All hotels in the upper three categories have either a bath or shower in the room; even the most inexpensive accommodations provide hot and cold water. Accommodations include castles and palaces, conventional hotels, *Gasthöfe* (country inns), motels (considerably less frequent), and the more modest pensions.

RATINGS

All prices quoted here are for two people in a double room. Though exact figures vary, a single room generally costs more than half the price of a comparable double. Breakfast—which can be anything from a simple roll and coffee to a full and sumptuous buffet—is usually included in the room rate. In top five-star hotels, however, it is extra (and expensive). Highly recommended lodgings are indicated by a star ★.

CATEGORY	MAJOR CITY	OTHER AREAS
$$$$	over AS2,500	over AS1,800
$$$	AS1,600–AS2,500	AS1,000–AS1,800
$$	AS900–AS1,600	AS700–AS1,000
$	under AS900	under AS700

Tipping

Railroad porters get AS10 per bag. Hotel porters or bellhops get AS10–AS20 per bag. Doormen get AS20 for hailing a cab and assisting. Room service gets AS10 for snacks and AS20 for full meals. Maids get no tip unless you stay a week or more, or special service is rendered. In restaurants, 10% service is included. Add anything from AS5 to AS50, depending on the restaurant and the size of the bill, or about 5%–7%.

VIENNA

Arriving and Departing

By Plane

All flights use Schwechat Airport (tel. 0222/71110–2231), about 16 kilometers (10 miles) southwest of Vienna.

BETWEEN THE AIRPORT AND DOWNTOWN

Buses leave from the airport for the city air terminal (tel. 0222/5800–35404, 9–5; otherwise 0222/5800–33369) by the Hilton on Wien-Mitte/Landstrasse Hauptstrasse every half hour from 5 to 6:30 AM and every 20 minutes from 6:50 AM to 11:30 PM; after that, buses depart every hour to 5 AM. Trains shuttle every half hour between the rail terminal in the airport and Wien-Mitte/Landstrasse Hauptstrasse; fare is AS34. Check schedules and fares, as a projected new rail service may mean a change in bus service. Buses also run every hour (every half hour on weekends and holidays Apr.–Sept.) from the airport to the Westbahnhof (west train station) and the Südbahnhof (south train station). Be sure you get on the right bus! The one-way fare for all buses is AS60. A taxi from the airport to downtown Vienna costs about AS330–AS350; agree on a price in advance. Cabs (legally) do not meter this drive, as airport fares are more or less fixed (legally again) at about double the meter fare. The cheapest cab service is C+K Airport Service (tel. 0222/60808), charging about AS270–AS300. A seat in a limousine costs less; book at the airport. **Mazur** (tel. 0222/711–10–6422 or 711–10–6491) offers cheaper pickup and delivery service by arrangement. If you are driving from the airport, follow signs to ZENTRUM.

By Train

Vienna has four train stations. The principal station, the Westbahnhof, is for trains to and from Linz, Salzburg, and Innsbruck, and arriving trains from Germany and France. The Südbahnhof is for trains to and from Graz, Klagenfurt, Villach, and Italy. Franz-Josefs-Bahnhof is for trains to and from Prague, Berlin, and Warsaw. Go to Wien-

Mitte (Landstrasse) for local trains to and from the north of the city. Budapest trains use the Westbahnhof and Südbahnhof, and Bratislava trains use Wien-Mitte and the Südbahnhof, so check.

By Bus

If you arrive by bus, it will probably be at the central bus terminal, Wien-Mitte, opposite the city air terminal (and the Hilton).

By Boat

All Danube riverboats dock at the DDSG terminal on Mexikoplatz. There's an awkward connection with the U-1 subway from here. Some boats also make a stop slightly upstream at Heiligenstadt, Nussdorf, from which there is an easier connection to the U-4 subway line.

By Car

Main access routes are the expressways to the west and south (West-autobahn, Südautobahn). Routes to the downtown area are marked ZENTRUM.

Getting Around

Vienna is fairly easy to explore on foot; as a matter of fact, much of the heart of the city—the area within the Ring—is largely a pedestrian zone. The Ring itself replaced the city ramparts, torn down just over a century ago to create today's broad, tree-lined boulevard.

Public transportation is comfortable, convenient, and frequent, though not cheap. Tickets for bus, subway, and streetcar are available in subway stations and from dispensers on buses and streetcars. Tickets in multiples of five are sold at cigarette shops, known as *Tabak-Trafik,* or at the window marked VORVERKAUF at central stations such as Karlsplatz or Stephansplatz. A block of five tickets costs AS85, a single ticket AS20. If you plan to use public transportation frequently, get a **24-hour ticket** (AS50), a **three-day tourist ticket** (AS130), or an **eight-day ticket** (AS265). Maps and information in English are available at Stephansplatz, Karlsplatz, and Praterstern U-Bahn stations.

By Bus or Streetcar

Inner-city buses are numbered 1A through 3A and operate weekdays until about 7:40 PM, Saturday until 2 PM. Reduced fares (buy a **Kurzstreckenkarte;** it gives four trips for AS34) are available for these routes as well as designated shorter stretches (roughly two to four stops) on all other bus or streetcar lines. Streetcars and buses are numbered or lettered according to route, and they run until about midnight. Night buses marked N follow special routes every hour on Saturdays and nights before holidays; service may be expanded to every night as more lines are added. The fare is AS25. The central terminal point is Schwedenplatz. Streetcars 1 and 2 run the circular route around the Ring, clockwise and counterclockwise, respectively.

By Subway

Subway (U-Bahn) lines—stations are marked with a huge blue U—are designated U-1, U-2, U-3, U-4, and U-6 and are clearly marked and color-coded. Additional services are provided by a fast suburban train, the S-Bahn, indicated by a stylized blue *S* symbol. Both are tied into the general city fare system.

By Taxi

Cabs can be flagged on the street if the FREI (free) sign is illuminated. You can also dial 1718, 60160, 31300, or 40100 to call for one. All rides around town are metered. The initial fare is AS24 days, AS25 nights, but expect to pay AS60 for an average city ride. There are additional charges for luggage and a night and Sunday surcharge of AS10. Tip the driver AS5–AS8 by rounding up the fare.

Important Addresses and Numbers

Tourist Information
City Tourist Office (Kärntnerstr. 38, behind the opera, tel. 0222/513–8892). Open daily 9–7.

Embassies
The **U.S. embassy** is at Boltzmanngasse 16; the **consulate** is at Gartenbaupromenade, Parkring 12A, in the Marriott building; the telephone number for both is 0222/313–39. The **Canadian embassy** is at Fleischmarkt 19, tel. 0222/533–3691. The **U.K. embassy and consulate** are at Jauresgasse 12; embassy tel. 0222/713–1575, consulate tel. 0222/714–6117.

Emergencies
Police (tel. 133), **Ambulance** (tel. 144), **Doctor:** ask your hotel, or in an emergency, phone your embassy or consulate (*see above*). **Pharmacies:** open weekdays 8–6, Saturday 8–noon.

English-Language Bookstores
Big Ben Bookshop (Porzellang. 24, tel. 0222/319–6412), **British Bookshop** (Weihburgg. 24–26, tel. 0222/512–1945), **Shakespeare & Co.** (Sterng. 2, tel. 0222/535–5053).

Travel Agencies
American Express (Kärntnerstr. 21–23, tel. 0222/515–4040); **Austrian Travel Agency** (Opernring 3–5, tel. 0222/588628); **Wagons-Lits** (Kärntner Ring 2, tel. 0222/501600).

Guided Tours

Orientation Tours
Vienna Sightseeing Tours (tel. 0222/712–468388–0) offers a short highlights tour or a lengthier one to the Vienna Woods, Mayerling, and other sights near Vienna. Tours start in front of or beside the opera house. **Cityrama** (tel. 0222/534130) provides city tours with hotel pickup; tours assemble opposite the Inter-Continental Hotel. **Citytouring Vienna** (tel. 0222/894–1417–0), with hotel pickup, starts from the city air terminal behind the Hilton hotel. Prices are similar, but find out which admissions are included or excluded, particularly to Schönbrunn and Belvedere palaces.

Special-Interest Tours
Tours are available to the Spanish Riding School, the Vienna Boys Choir, operettas and concerts, the wine suburb of Grinzing, nightclubs, and Vienna by night. Check with the city tourist office or your hotel for details.

Walking Tours
Vienna from A to Z (in English) is available for AS50 at most bookstores and tourist information offices; it explains the numbered plaques attached to all major buildings in Vienna. *In Search of Vienna: Walking Tours in the City* by Henriette Mandl outlines suggested routes and provides information on sights.

Excursions
Day bus trips are organized to the Danube Valley, the Hungarian border, the Alps south of Vienna, Salzburg, and Budapest; get information from the city tourist office.

Exploring Vienna

Vienna has been characterized as an "old dowager of a town"—an Austro-Hungarian empress, don't forget, widowed by the Great War. It's not just the aristocratic and courtly atmosphere, with monumental doorways and stately facades of former palaces at every turn. Nor is it just that Vienna (Wien in German) has a higher proportion of middle-aged and older citizens than any other city in Europe, with a concomitant sense of stability, quiet, and respectability. Rather, it's these factors, combined with a love of music; a discreet weakness for rich food (especially cakes); an adherence to old-fashioned and formal forms of address; a high, if unadventurous, regard for the arts; and a gentle mourning for lost glories, that preserve the stiff elegance of Old World dignity.

The Vienna Card, available for AS180 at tourist and transportation information offices and most hotels, will give you tips and discounts on various attractions and selected shopping throughout the city.

The Heart of Vienna

Most main sights are in the inner zone, the oldest part of the city, encircled by the **Ring,** once the city walls and today a broad boulevard. Carry a ready supply of AS10 coins; many places of interest have coin-operated tape machines that provide English commentaries. As you wander around, train yourself to look upward; some of the most memorable architectural treasures are on upper stories and roof lines.

Numbers in the margin correspond to points of interest on the Vienna map.

Vienna's role as imperial city is preserved in the complex of buildings that make up the former royal palace. Start your tour at Albertinaplatz, behind the opera house. Head down Augustinerstrasse. To the right is the "Memorial to Victims of Fascism," disputed in part because the sculptor was once an admitted Communist. On your left is the **Albertina,** home to the world's largest collection of drawings, sketches, engravings, and etchings. There are works here by Dürer—these are perhaps the highlight of the collection—Rembrandt, Michelangelo, Correggio, and many others. The holdings are so vast that only a limited number can be shown at one time. Some original works are so delicate that they can be shown only in facsimile. *Augustinerstr. 1, tel. 0222/534830. Closed for renovations, but check to see whether parts of collection are being shown elsewhere.*

Beethoven was a regular visitor at the Palais Lobkowitz across the street on Lobkowitzplatz. The renovated palace now houses the **Theater Museum.** Exhibits cover the history of theater in Vienna and the rest of Austria. A children's museum in the basement—alas, open only by appointment—is reached by a slide! *Lobkowitzpl. 2, tel. 0222/512–8800. Admission: AS40 adults, AS20 students and children. Open Tues.–Sun. 10–5.*

Go back to Augustinerstrasse to the 14th-century **Augustinerkirche,** a favorite on Sundays, when the 11 AM mass is sung in Latin. The Hapsburg rulers' hearts are preserved in a chamber here. Nearby is the **Nationalbibliothek** (National Library), with its stunning Baroque great hall. Don't overlook the fascinating collection of globes on the third floor. *Josefspl. 1, tel. 0222/534–10–397. Admission: AS20 adults, children free. Opening hours may vary, but generally May–Oct., Mon.–Sat. 10–4, Sun. and holidays 10–1; Nov.–Apr., Mon.–Sat. 11–noon. Globe museum: tel. 534–10–297. Admission: AS10. Open Mon.–Wed., Fri. 11–noon, Thurs. 2–3.*

Albertina, **1**
Augustinerkirche, **3**
Court Silver and
Tableware Museum, **10**
Donner Brunnen, **19**
Hofburg, **6**
Hofburgkapelle, **9**
Hoher Markt, **29**
Imperial
Apartments, **7**
Jewish Museum, **20**
Kapuzinerkirche, **18**
Karlskirche, **15**
Kirche am Hof, **26**
Kunsthistorisches
Museum, **13**
Maria am Gestade, **28**
Mozart
Erinnerungsräume, **24**
Nationalbibliothek, **4**
Naturhistorisches
Museum, **12**
Neue Hofburg, **11**
Pestsäule, **21**
Peterskirche, **22**
Ruprechtskirche, **30**
Sacher Hotel, **17**
Schatzkammer, **8**
Schloss Belvedere, **32**
Schönbrunn
Palace, **31**
Schottenkirche and
Museum, **25**
Spanische
Reitschule, **5**
Staatsoper, **16**
Stephansdom, **23**
Tabak Museum, **14**
Theater Museum, **2**
20th Century Museum, **33**
Uhrenmuseum, **27**

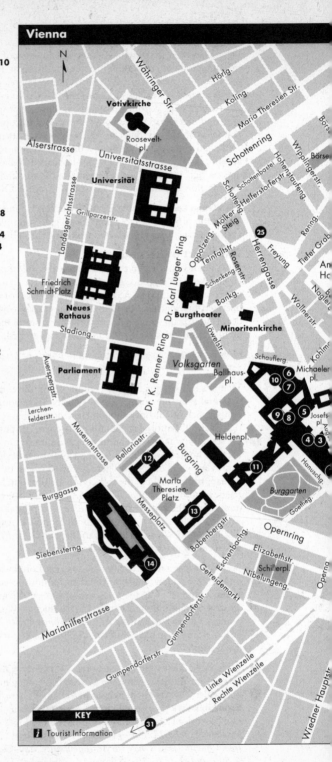

Vienna

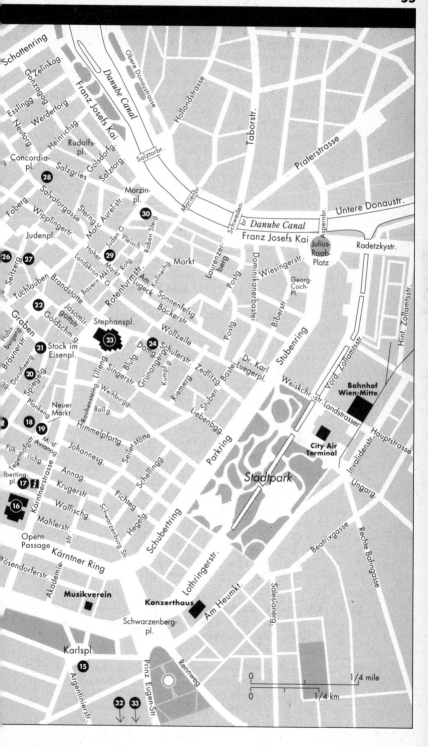

Josefsplatz is where much of *The Third Man* was filmed, specifically in and around the Palais Pallavicini across the street. The usual entrance

5 to the **Spanische Reitschule,** the Spanish Riding School, is here, too, though the famed white horses are actually stabled on the other side of the square. During renovations, the entrance to the school has been relocated in the main courtyard next to the Swiss Gate, beyond the Michaelertor rotunda dome. For tickets, write to the Spanische Reitschule (Hofburg, A-1010 Vienna) or Austrian Tourist Office (Friedrichstr. 7, A-1010 Vienna) *at least* three months in advance. There are generally performances on Sunday at 10:45 AM from March through June, and from September through October. Evening performances are occasionally given on Wednesdays at 7. Tickets for the few short training performances on Saturday mornings at 10 AM are available only from ticket offices and travel agencies. You can watch the 10 AM–noon training sessions Tuesday to Saturday during much of the performance season; tickets are available only at the door (Burghof, inner court; admission AS80 adults, AS20 children).

From here you're only a few steps from Michaelerplatz, the circular

6 square that marks the entrance to the **Hofburg,** the imperial palace. On one side of the square, opposite the entrance, on the corner of Herrengasse and Kohlmarkt, is the **Loos building** (1911), designed by Adolf Loos. Step inside—it's now a bank—to see the remarkable restoration of the foyer. Outside, it's no more than a simple stucco-and-glass structure, but architectural historians point to it as one of the earliest "modern" buildings in Europe—a building where function determines style. In striking contrast is the Baroque **Michaelertor,** opposite, the principal gateway to the Hofburg.

TIME OUT Some insist that no visit to Vienna is complete without a visit to **Demel,** on the left just down the Kohlmarkt. The pastries and lunch are expensive even by Viennese standards, but new management has sought to bring back quality and service to match the elegant tradition. *Tel: 0222/533-5516. Reservations advised. AE, D, MC, V. Closes 6 pm.*

7 Head through the domed gateway of the Michaelertor to visit the **imperial apartments** of Emperor Franz Josef and Empress Elisabeth. Among the exhibits is the exercise equipment used by the beautiful empress. Here, too, is the dress she was wearing when she was stabbed to death by a demented Italian anarchist on the shore of Lake Geneva in 1898; the dagger marks are visible. *Michaelerpl. 1, tel. 0222/587-5554-515. Admission: AS40 adults, AS20 children; combined admission with Court Silver and Tableware Museum: AS90 adult, AS45 children. Open Mon.–Sat. 8:30–noon, 12:30–4; Sun. and holidays 8:30–12:30.*

8 Be sure to see the **Schatzkammer,** the imperial treasury, home of the magnificent crown jewels. *Hofburg, Schweizerhof, tel. 0222/533-7931. Admission: AS60 adults, AS30 children. Open Wed., Fri.-Mon. 10-6, Thurs. 10-9.*

9 The **Hofburgkapelle,** the court chapel, is where the Vienna Boys Choir sings mass at 9:15 AM on Sunday mid-September through June. You'll need tickets to attend; they are available at the chapel from 5 PM Friday (queue up by 4:30 and expect long lines) or by writing two months ahead to Hofmusikkapelle, Hofburg, Schweizerhof, A-1010 Vienna. The city tourist office can sometimes help with ticket applications.

10 Diagonally across the main courtyard is the new **Court Silver and Tableware Museum,** a brilliant showcase of imperial table settings sparkling with light and mirrors reflecting period elegance. *Burghof (inner court), tel. 0222/523–4240. Admission: AS70 adults, AS35 children; combined admission with imperial apartments: AS90 adults, AS45 children. Open daily 9–5.*

Head south to Heldenplatz, the vast open square punctuated with oversized equestrian statues of Prince Eugene and Archduke Karl, which stand in front of the **Neue Hofburg.** The ponderously ornate 19th-century edifice—Hitler announced the annexation of Austria from the balcony in 1938—now houses a series of museums. Highlights are the Waffensammlung (the weapons collection), the collections of musical instruments (you can listen to the various instruments on wireless headphones as you move from room to room), the Ethnological Museum with Montezuma's feathered headdress, and the exciting Ephesus museum, with finds from the excavations at that ancient site. *Neue Hofburg, Heldenpl. 1, tel. 0222/521770. Admission: AS30 adults, AS15 children. Open Wed.–Mon. 10–6. Ethnological Museum open Wed.–Mon. 10–4.*

Walk west again under the unmonumental Hero's Monument archway and across the Ring. The **Naturhistorisches Museum** (Natural History Museum) is on your right, the **Kunsthistorisches Museum** (Art History Museum) is on your left. The latter is one of the great art museums of the world; this is not a place to miss. The collections focus on old master paintings, notably those by Brueghel, Cranach, Titian, Canaletto, Rubens, and Velázquez. But there are important Egyptian, Greek, Etruscan, and Roman exhibits, too. *Burgring 5, tel. 0222/521770. Admission: AS45 adults, AS30 children. Open Tues.–Sun. 10–6, limited galleries also Thurs. 10–9.*

TIME OUT Across the Messeplatz stretches Messepalast, the former court stables that now serve as a fair and exhibit space. Inside is one of Vienna's better-kept secrets, the **Glacis-Beisl** restaurant. Wine and the local specialties in the garden under the vine-clad arbors have to be experienced. *Tel. 0222/526–6795. Reservations advised. No credit cards. Closed Jan.–Feb., Sun., and holidays.*

At the Mariahilferstrasse end of the Messepalast complex is the small and fascinating **Tabak Museum,** the Tobacco Museum. *Mariahilferstr. 2, tel. 0222/526–1716. Admission: AS20 adults, AS10 children. Open Tues.–Fri. 10–5, weekends 10–2.*

Head east down the Getreidemarkt, with the Kunsthistorisches Museum on your left. Looming up ahead with the gilt cauliflower dome is the Sezession and beyond it a huge yellow and blue container. Both are art museums with changing exhibits. Beyond them, over Karlsplatz, is the heroic facade and dome, flanked by vast twin columns, of the **Karlskirche.** It was built around 1715 by Fischer von Erlach. The oval interior is surprisingly small, given the monumental facade: One expects something more on the scale of St. Peter's in Rome. The ceiling has airy frescoes, and stiff shafts of gilt radiate like sunbeams from the altar.

Take the pedestrian underpass back under the Ring to Opernplatz. This is the site of the **Staatsoper,** one of the best opera houses in the world and a focus of Viennese social life. Tickets are expensive and rare, so you may have to settle for a backstage tour. The tour schedule for the day is usually posted alongside the door under the right front arcade, on the Kärntnerstrasse side, and will depend on the activities going on inside.

17 Head up Kärntnerstrasse, Vienna's main thoroughfare, now a busy pedestrian mall. On your left is the creamy facade of the **Sacher Hotel.** Take a look inside at the plush red-and-gilt decor, a fin de siècle masterpiece. The hotel is also the home of the original Sachertorte—the ultimate chocolate cake. Back on Kärntnerstrasse, around the corner from the Sacher, is the city tourist office. Leading off Kärntnerstrasse, to the left,

18 is the little street of Marco d'Aviano-Gasse. Follow it to the **Kapuzinerkirche,** in whose crypt, called the **Kaisergruft,** or imperial vault, the serried ranks of long-dead Hapsburgs lie. The oldest tomb is that of Ferdinand II; it dates from 1633. The most recent tomb is that of Empress Zita, widow of Austria's last kaiser, dating from 1989. *Neuer Markt 1, tel. 0222/512–6853–12. Admission: AS30 adults, AS20 children. Open daily 9:30–4.*

19 In the center of the square is the ornate 18th-century **Donner Brunnen,** the Providence Fountain. Sculpted figures represent main rivers that flow into the Danube. Empress Maria Theresa thought the figures were obscene and wanted them removed or properly clothed.

TIME OUT Coffee or tea and what are said even by the French and Belgians to be the best pastries in the world are available at the **Konditorei Oberlaa.** *Neuer Markt 16. Open weekdays 9–7, Sat. 9–6, Sun. and holidays 10–6.*

20 Turn down Plankengasse to Dorotheergasse. On your right, in the former Eskeles palace, is the **Jewish Museum.** Permanent and changing exhibits try but regrettably fail to portray the richness of the Jewish culture and heritage that contributed to so much of Vienna and Austria. Don't consider it a priority if you're pressed for time. *Dorotheerg. 11, tel. 0222/535–0431. Admission: AS50 adults, AS25 children. Open Sun.–Wed., and Fri. 10–6, Thurs. 10–9.*

21 Continue north through Dorotheergasse to reach the pedestrians-only Graben. The **Pestsäule,** or Plague Column, shoots up from the middle of the street, looking like a geyser of whipped cream touched with gold. It commemorates the Black Death of 1697. A small turn to the right,

22 just past the column, leads to the Baroque **Peterskirche.** The little church, the work of Johann Lukas von Hildebrandt, finished in about 1730, has what is probably the most theatrical interior in the city. The pulpit is especially fine, with a highly ornate canopy, but florid and swirling decoration is everywhere. Many of the decorative elements are based on a tent form, a motif suggested by the Turkish forces that camped outside the city walls during the great siege of Vienna at the end of the 17th century.

23 Walk down Goldschmiedgasse to Stephansplatz, site of the **Stephansdom** (St. Stephen's Cathedral). Its towering Gothic spires and gaudy 19th-century tile roof are still the dominant feature of the Vienna skyline. The oldest part of the building is the 13th-century entrance, the soaring **Riesentor,** or Giant Doorway. Inside, the church is mysteriously dark, filled with an array of monuments, tombs, sculptures, paintings, and pulpits. Despite extensive wartime damage—and numerous Baroque additions—the building radiates an authentically medieval atmosphere. Climb up the 345 steps of **Alte Steffl,** Old Steven, the south tower, for a stupendous view over the city. An elevator goes up the north tower to the **Pummerin,** the Boomer, a 22-ton bell cast in 1711 from cannons captured from the Turks. Take a 30-minute tour of the crypt to see the copper jars in which the entrails of the Hapsburgs are carefully preserved.

㉔ On a narrow street east of the cathedral is the house where Mozart lived from 1784 to 1787. Today it contains the **Mozart Erinnerungsräume,** the Mozart Museum. It was here that the composer wrote *The Marriage of Figaro* (thus the nickname Figaro House) and here, some say, that he spent the happiest years of his life. *Domg. 5, tel. 0222/513–6294. Admission: AS15 adults, AS5 children. Open Tues.–Sun. 9–12:15 and 1–4:30.*

Other Corners of Vienna

Walk back down the Graben and the narrow Naglergasse and turn left into the Freyung. On your left is the **Palais Ferstl,** now a stylish shopping arcade. At the back is the skillfully restored **Café Central,** once headquarters for Vienna's leading literary figures. Next door to Palais Ferstl is **Palais Harrach,** part of which is now an outpost of the Museum of Fine Arts for special exhibits and overflow of tapestries and paintings from the main house.

㉕ Cross the Freyung to the imposing **Schottenkirche.** The monks who were brought to found it were actually Irish, not Scottish. The Benedictines have installed a small but worthwhile museum of mainly religious art including a late-Gothic winged altar removed from the church when it received a Baroque overlay in the mid-1600s. Entrance is in the courtyard to the left. *Freyung 6, tel. 0222/534–98–600. Admission AS40 adults, AS20 children. Open Thurs.–Sat. 10–5, Sun. 12–5.*

Turn back through the Freyung to **Am Hof,** a remarkable square with the city's Baroque central fire station, possibly the world's most ornate. You'll find occasional flea markets here on Thursdays and Fridays in summer and seasonal markets at other times. Cross the square
㉖ to the **Kirche am Hof.** The interior is curiously reminiscent of many Dutch churches.

TIME OUT For a tasty thick soup or snack, or just a glass of wine, beer, or coffee, go into Drahtgasse and turn into the tiny Ledererhof to discover **Bretzl G'wölb,** once a pretzel bakery, now a minicafé charmingly decorated with antique accents. *Ledererhof 9, tel. 0222/533-8811. Open daily 11:30 am–1 am.*

㉗ Continue to Judenplatz and turn right into Parisergasse to the **Uhrenmuseum** (Clock Museum), located in a lovely Renaissance house. Try to be there when the hundreds of clocks strike the noon hour. *Schulhof 2, tel. 0222/533-2265. Admission: AS30 adults, AS10 children. Open Tues.–Sun. 9–4:30.*

Turn down the Kurrentgasse and, via Fütterergasse, cross the Wipplingerstrasse into Stoss im Himmel (literally, a "thrust to heaven").
㉘ To your left down Salvatorgasse is **Maria am Gestade,** originally a church for fishermen on the nearby canal. Note the ornate "folded hands" spire.
㉙ Return along Wipplingerstrasse, across Marc Aurel-Strasse, to **Hoher Markt,** with a central monument celebrating the betrothal of Mary and Joseph. Underground are **Roman ruins,** remains of the 2nd-century Roman encampment. *Hoher Markt 3, tel. 0222/535–5606. Admission: AS15 adults, AS5 children; free on Fri. morning. Open Tues.–Sun. 9–12:15 and 1–4:30.*

On the north side of Hoher Markt is the amusing **Anker-Uhr,** a clock that tells time by figures moving across a scale. The figures are identified on a plaque at the lower left of the clock; it's well worth passing
㉚ by at noon to catch the show. Go through Judengasse to **Ruprechtskirche** (St. Rupert's). The oldest church in Vienna, dating from the 11th cen-

tury, is small, damp, dark, and, unfortunately, usually closed, though you can peek through a window.

Vienna Environs

 It's a 15-minute ride from the city center on subway line U-4 (stop either at Schönbrunn or Hietzing) to **Schönbrunn Palace,** the magnificent Baroque residence and formal gardens built between 1696 and 1713 for the Hapsburgs. Here Kaiser Franz Josef I was born and died. His "office" (kept as he left it in 1916) is a touching reminder of his spartan life. Other rooms, however, reflect the elegance of the monarchy. The ornate public rooms are still used for state receptions. A guided tour covers 45 of the palace's 1,441 rooms and is the best way to see the most of the Palace interior. Among the curiosities are the Chinese Room and the gym fitted out for Empress Elisabeth, where she exercised daily to keep her figure. Other rooms are occasionally open independent of tours. *Schönbrunner Schlosstr., tel. 0222/81113–238. Admission: AS95 adults, AS40 children with guided tour. AS80 adults, AS 30 children without tour. Open Nov.–Mar., daily 9–4:30; Apr.–Oct., daily 8:30–5.*

Once on the grounds, don't overlook the **Tiergarten** (zoo). It's Europe's oldest menagerie and, when established in 1752, was intended to amuse and educate the court. It contains an extensive assortment of animals, some of them in their original Baroque enclosures. *Tel. 0222/877–9294. Admission: AS80 adults, AS60 children. Open Nov.–Jan., daily 9–4:30; Feb. and Oct., daily 9–5; Mar., daily 9–5:30; Apr., daily 9–6; May–Sept., daily 9–6:30.*

Follow the pathways up to the **Gloriette,** that Baroque ornament on the rise behind Schönbrunn, and enjoy superb views of the city. Originally this was to have been the site of the palace, but projected construction costs were considered too high. The restored edifice again incorporates a café, as the original did. *Admission: AS20 adults, AS10 children. Open May–Sept., daily 9–6; Oct., daily 9–5.*

The **Wagenburg** (Carriage Museum), near the entrance to the palace grounds, holds some splendid examples of early transportation, from children's sleighs to funeral carriages of the emperors. *Tel. 0222/877–3244. Admission: AS30 adults, AS15 children. Open May–Sept., daily 9–6; Apr. and Oct., daily 9–5; Nov.–Mar., Tues.–Sun. 10–5.*

Take Streetcar D toward the Südbahnhof to reach **Schloss Belvedere** (Belvedere Palace), a Baroque complex often compared to Versailles. It was commissioned by Prince Eugene of Savoy and built by Johann Lukas von Hildebrandt in 1721–22. The palace is made up of two separate buildings, one at the foot and the other at the top of a hill. The lower tract was first built as residential quarters; the upper buildings were reserved for entertaining. The lavish gardens in between are considered among the finest showpieces of the Baroque period found anywhere. The buildings have contemporary significance: The State Treaty that gave Austria its independence in 1955 was signed in the great upper hall. The composer Anton Bruckner lived in an apartment to the north of the upper building until his death in 1896. Both sections now house outstanding art museums: the gallery of 19th-and 20th-century art in the Upper Belvedere (Klimt, Kokoschka, Schiele, Waldmüller, Markart) and the Baroque museum (including medieval Austrian art) in the Lower Belvedere. *Prinz-Eugen-Str. 27, tel. 0222/798–4158–0. Admission: AS60 adults, AS30 children. Open Tues.–Sun. 10–5.*

Continue across the Gürtel from the Upper Belvedere southward to the **20th Century Museum,** containing a small but extremely tasteful modern art collection. *Schweizer Garten, tel. 0222/799–6900–0. Admission: AS45 adults, AS25 children. Open Tues.–Sun. 10–6.*

You can reach a small corner of the **Vienna Woods** by streetcar and bus: Take a streetcar or the U-2 subway line to Schottentor/University and, from there, Streetcar 38 (Grinzing) to the end of the line. Grinzing itself is out of a picture book. Unfortunately, much of the wine offered in the taverns is less enchanting. (For better wine and ambience, try the area around Pfarrplatz and Probusgasse in Hohe Warte—Streetcar 37, Bus 39A—or the suburb of Nussdorf—Streetcar D.) To get into the woods, change in Grinzing to Bus 38A. This will take you to Kahlenberg, which provides a superb view over the Danube and the city. You can take the bus or hike to Leopoldsberg, the promontory over the Danube from which Turkish invading forces were repulsed during the 16th and 17th centuries.

Off the Beaten Track

Vienna's **Bermuda Triangle** (around Judengasse/Seitenstettengasse) is jammed with everything from good bistros to jazz clubs. Also check the tourist office's museum list carefully: There's something for everyone, ranging from Sigmund Freud's apartment to the Funeral and Burial Museum. The **Hundertwasserhaus** (Kegelgasse/Löwengasse; Streetcar N), an astonishing apartment complex designed by artist Friedenreich Hundertwasser, with turrets, towers, odd windows, and uneven floors, will be of interest to those who do not think that architectural form has to follow function. The nearby **KunstHaus Wien** art museum offers Hundertwasser plus changing exhibits of modern works. *Untere Weissbergerstr. 13, tel. 0222/712–0491. Admission: AS70 adults, AS40 children; half-price on Mon. Open daily 10–7.*

Children and adults alike will enjoy the charming **Doll and Toy Museum,** next door to the Clock Museum (*see* Exploring Vienna, *above*). It's filled with trains, dollhouses, and troops of teddy bears. *Schulhof 4, tel. 0222/535–6860. Admission: AS60 adults, AS30 children. Open Tues.–Sun. 10–6.*

Shopping

Antiques
The best (and most expensive) shops are in the inner city, many in and around **Dorotheergasse,** but there are good finds in some of the outer districts, particularly among the backstreets in the **Josefstadt** (eighth) district. A free brochure, "Wiener Kunst und Antiquitäten Führer," gives detailed information in English.

Boutiques
Name brands are found along the **Kohlmarkt** and **Graben** and their respective side streets, and the side streets off the **Kärntnerstrasse.**

Folk Costumes
A good selection at reasonable prices is offered by the **NÖ Heimatwerk** (Herrengasse 6); also try **Trachten Tostmann** (Schottengasse 3a) or **Loden-Plankl** (Michaelerplatz 6).

Shopping Districts
Tourists gravitate to the **Kärntnerstrasse,** but the Viennese do most of their shopping on the **Mariahilferstrasse.**

Food and Flea Markets
The **Naschmarkt** (between Rechte and Linke Wienzeile; weekdays 6 AM–mid-afternoon, Sat. 6–1) is a sensational open-air market, offer-

ing specialties from around the world. The **Flohmarkt** (flea market) operates year-round beyond the Naschmarkt (subway U-4 to Kettenbrückengasse) and is equally fascinating (Sat. 8–4). An **Arts and Antiques Market** with better offerings operates on Saturday (2–6) and Sunday (10–6) alongside the Danube Canal near the Salztorbrücke. Look for the seasonal markets in the Freyung square opposite Palais Ferstal.

Dining

In contrast to those of many cities, the leading Viennese hotels are in competition for the country's best cooks and therefore offer some of the city's best dining. Even the chain hotels have joined in the effort to see which can win over the leading chefs. The results are rewarding; you may not even have to leave your hotel to enjoy outstanding food and service. For details and price-category definitions, *see* Dining *in* Staying in Austria, *above.*

\$\$\$\$ **Korso.** You'll find outstanding food and atmosphere at this gourmet
★ temple of "New Vienna Cuisine." Chef Reinhard Gerer produces exquisite variations on Austrian standards such as pork and beef by borrowing accents from Asian cuisine. *Mahlerstr. 2, tel. 0222/51516–546. AE, DC, MC, V. Closed 3 wks in August. No lunch Sat.*

\$\$\$\$ **Palais Schwarzenberg.** The glassed-in restaurant with a view into the palace gardens is a perfect setting for the excellent fillet of beef, lamb in herb crust, or souffléd turbot. Wine prices are high, although special offers can be outstanding and reasonable. The house wines are good. *Schwarzenbergpl. 9, tel. 0222/798–4515. Reservations required. AE, DC, MC, V.*

\$\$\$\$ **Steirereck.** Acclaimed as Austria's best restaurant, the Steirereck successfully espouses the lighter New Vienna Cuisine in an elegant atmosphere, with service that cannot be faulted. Try Styrian venison, turbot crepes with asparagus, or even a schnitzel. The noontime prix-fixe lunch offers choices and is a good value. *Rasumofskyg. 2, tel. 0222/713–3168. Reservations required. AE, DC, V. Closed weekends and holidays.*

\$\$\$\$ **Zu den Drei Husaren.** This is one of Vienna's enduring monuments to tradition, complete with candlelight and live piano music (except on Sunday). Casual visitors (as opposed to regulars) may have to settle for more atmosphere than service, but the food—mainly Viennese standards such as variations on rump steak—is of top quality. Beware the enticing but uppriced hors d'oeurve trolley, which can easily double the lunch or dinner bill. *Weihburgg. 4, tel. 0222/512–1092. Reservations required. AE, DC, MC, V. Closed mid-July–mid-Aug.*

\$\$\$ **Plachutta.** The feature here is superb *Tafelspitz* (boiled beef), served in its own delicious soup, for which you can order the day's "supplement"—*Frittaten* (thin pancake strips), perhaps, or *Leberknödel* (liver dumpling). You choose the cut or type of beef you prefer (all are outstanding) or select a steak or grilled fish, and finish with a rhubarb strudel. The house wines are fine; service is less so. *Wollzeile 38, tel. 0222/512–1577. Dinner reservations required. AE, MC, V.*

\$\$\$ **Vier Jahreszeiten.** This restaurant effortlessly manages to achieve that
★ delicate balance between food and atmosphere. The service is attentive without being overbearing. The lunch buffet offers both excellent food and value. Evening dining includes grill specialties and live piano music. *Hotel Inter-Continental, Johannesg. 28, tel. 0222/71122–143. AE, DC, MC, V. Closed weekends and two wks in June.*

\$\$\$ **Zum Kuckuck.** Wood paneling and the patina of years mark this intimate restaurant, candlelit at night. Specials change daily but tend toward regional variations on pork, venison, or lamb. The fig cake with rum sauce is a house classic. *Himmelpfortg. 15, tel. 0222/512–8470,* *fax 0222/523–3818. Reservations required. AE, DC, MC, V. Closed weekends.*

\$\$ Bastei-Beisl. You'll find good, basic Viennese cuisine in this comfortable, wood-paneled restaurant. Outdoor tables are particularly pleasant on summer evenings. *Stubenbastei 10, tel. 0222/512–4319. AE, DC, MC. Closed Sun.*

\$\$ Bei Max. The decor is somewhat bland, but the tasty Carinthian specialties—*Käsnudeln* and *Fleischnudeln* (cheese and meat ravioli) in particular—keep this friendly restaurant packed. *Landhausg. 2/Herrengasse, tel. 0222/533–7359. No credit cards. Closed Sat., Sun., last wk in July, first 3 wks in Aug.*

\$\$ Gigerl. ★ It's hard to believe you're right in the middle of the city at this imaginative and charming wine restaurant that serves hot and cold buffets. The rooms are small and cozy but may get smoky and noisy when the place is full—which it usually is. The food is typical of wine gardens on the fringes of the city: roast meats, casserole dishes, cold cuts, salads. The wines are excellent. The surrounding narrow alleys and ancient buildings add to the charm of the outdoor tables in summer. *Rauhensteing. 3, tel. 0222/513–4431. AE, DC, MC, V. No lunch Sun.*

\$\$ Kaiserwalzer. The rooms in this once-private house radiate the elegance of the old empire. Austrian specialties are prominent; the beet soup, roast chicken, and paprika sauces are all splendid. *Esterházyg. 9, tel. 0222/587–0494. AE, DC, MC, V. Dinner only. Closed Sun.*

\$\$ Melker Stiftskeller. This is one of the city's half-dozen genuine *Weinkeller* (taverns). The food selection is limited but good, featuring pig's knuckle. House wine from the Wachau is excellent. *Schotteng. 3, tel. 0222/533–5530. MC. Dinner only; closed Sun.*

\$\$ Ofenloch. ★ This place is always packed, which speaks well not only of the excellent specialties from some Viennese grandmother's cookbook but also of the atmosphere. Waitresses are dressed in turn-of-the-century costume, and the furnishings add to the color. At times the rooms may be too smoky and noisy for some tastes. If you like garlic, try *Vanillerostbraten*, a rump steak with as much garlic as you request. *Kurrentg. 8, tel. 0222/533–8844. Reservations required. AE, DC, MC, V.*

\$\$ Stadtbeisl. Good standard Austrian fare is served at this popular eatery, which is comfortable without being pretentious. The service gets uneven as the place fills up, but if you are seated outside in summer, you probably won't mind. *Naglerg. 21, tel. 0222/533–3507. Reservations advised. V.*

\$\$ Zu den drei Hacken. This is one of the few genuine Viennese Gasthäuser in the city center; like the place itself, the fare is solid if not elegant. Legend has it that Schubert dined here; the ambience probably hasn't changed much since then. There are tables outside in summer, although the extra seating capacity strains both the kitchen and the service. *Singerstr. 28, tel. 0222/512–5895. AE, DC, V. Closed Sun.*

\$\$ Zu ebener Erde und erster Stock. ★ Ask for a table upstairs in this exquisite, tiny, utterly original Biedermeier house, which serves excellent Austrian fare; the downstairs space is really more for snacks. *Burgg. 13, tel. 0222/523–6254. AE. No lunch Sat. Closed Sun., Mon., and late July–late Aug.*

\$ Figlmüller. Known for its schnitzel, Figlmüller is always packed. Guests share the benches, the long tables, and the experience. Food choices are limited, but nobody seems to mind. Only wine is offered to drink, but it is good. The small "garden" is now enclosed and is just as popular as the tables inside. *Wollzeile 5 (passageway), tel. 0222/512–6177. No credit cards.*

$ **Königsbacher bei der Oper.** Its spaces are intimate and its tables close,
★ but portions are generous and the daily special (listed for the week) could be anything from roast pork to a ham-and-noodle casserole. Shaded outdoor tables are delightful in summer. *Walfischg. 5, tel. 0222/513–1210. No credit cards. No dinner Sat. Closed Sun.*

Lodging

Vienna's inner city is the best base for visitors because it's so close to most of the major sights, restaurants, and shops. This accessibility translates, of course, into higher prices. Try bargaining for discounts at the larger international chain hotels during the off season. For details and price-category definitions, *see* Lodging *in* Staying in Austria, *above.*

$$$$ **Bristol.** Opposite the opera house, the Bristol is classic Viennese, preferred by many for the service as well as the location. The bar is comfortable, though not overly private, and the restaurants associated with the hotel are outstanding, especially Korso. Back and upper guest rooms are quieter. *Kärntner Ring 1, tel. 0222/515160, fax 0222/515–16550. 146 rooms with bath. Facilities: 2 restaurants, bar. AE, DC, MC, V.*

$$$$ **Imperial.** This former palace represents elegant old and new Vienna at
★ its best, with such features as heated towel racks in some rooms. The location could hardly be better, although being on the Ring sometimes makes the front and lower rooms a bit noisy. The bar is intimate and pleasant. Lunch in the café is both reasonable and good; the hotel restaurant, Majestät, is still searching for its identity. *Kärntner Ring 16, tel. 0222/501100, fax 0222/501–10410. 145 rooms with bath or shower. Facilities: restaurant, café, bar, beauty parlor, conference rooms. AE, DC, MC, V.*

$$$$ **Inter-Continental.** Vienna's modern Inter-Continental has the reputation
★ of being one of the chain's very best. The rooms are a cut above standard; the main restaurant, exceptional. But whereas the hotel succeeds in acquiring some Viennese charm, the bar is impersonal, as is the less formal Brasserie. Rooms in front overlooking the park are quieter, particularly in winter when the ice-skating rink at the back is in operation. *Johannesg. 28, tel. 0222/711220, fax 0222/713–4489. 500 rooms with bath. Facilities: 2 restaurants, bar, sauna, health club, laundry, dry cleaning service, barber, hair stylist, garage. AE, DC, MC, V.*

$$$$ **Marriott.** The only Viennese aspect here is the service; all else is global modern. The atrium lobby, although pleasant, is anything but intimate. The restaurants are satisfactory if not quite up to the level of other top hotels, although Sunday brunch at the Marriott has become immensely popular (book at least a week in advance). *Parkring 12A, tel. 0222/515180, fax 0222/515–186722. 304 rooms with bath. Facilities: 2 restaurants, café, bar, sauna, health club, pool, shops, garage. AE, DC, MC, V.*

$$$$ **Palais Schwarzenberg.** The rooms are furnished with antiques and appropriately incorporated into a quiet wing of a Baroque palace, a 10-minute walk from the opera. The restaurant enjoys a good reputation; the view out over the formal gardens is glorious. *Schwarzenbergpl. 9, tel. 0222/798–4515, fax 0222/798–4714. 38 rooms with bath. Facilities: restaurant, bar, parking. AE, DC, MC, V.*

$$$$ **Sacher.** The hotel's reputation has varied considerably during recent years, but it remains one of the legendary addresses in Europe, with its opulent decor highlighted by original oil paintings, sculptures, and objets d'art. The Blue and Red bars are intimate and favored by nonguests as well, as is the café, particularly in summer when tables are set up outside. Guest rooms are spacious and elegantly appointed. *Philharmonikerstr. 4, tel. 0222/514560, fax 0222/514–57810. 117*

rooms with bath or shower. Facilities: restaurant, coffee shop, bars. AE, DC, MC, V.

$$$ Altstadt. You're one streetcar stop or a short walk from the main museums in this newly renovated old-Vienna residential building. Each of the spacious rooms is decorated individually, though the predominant scheme involves fine wood period furniture set against light blue-gray walls. The upper rooms have views out over the city roofline. *Kircheng. 41, tel. 0222/526–33990, fax 0222/423–4901. 25 rooms with bath or shower. Facilities: bar. AE, DC, MC, V.*

$$$ Astoria. Though the Astoria is one of Vienna's traditional old hotels, the rooms have been modernized considerably. The paneled lobby, however, has been preserved and retains an unmistakable Old World patina. The location is central, but because of the street musicians and the late-night crowds in the pedestrian zone, rooms overlooking the Kärntnerstrasse tend to be noisy in summer. *Fürichg. 1, tel. 0222/515770, fax 0222/515–7782. 108 rooms with bath or shower. Facilities: restaurant. AE, DC, MC, V.*

$$$ Capricorno. This establishment overlooks the Danube Canal in a fairly central location. Although its facade is modern and somewhat short on charm, the hotel nonetheless represents good value. *Schwedenpl. 3–4, tel. 0222/533–3104, fax 0222/533–76714. 46 rooms with bath or shower. Facilities: garage. AE, DC, MC, V.*

$$$ Europa. The location—midway between the opera house and the cathedral—is ideal, but the rooms on the Kärntnerstrasse side are noisy in summer; ask for a room overlooking Neuer Markt. The building is postwar modern and lacks the charm of older hotels, but the staff is friendly and helpful. The café is popular, particularly in summer when tables are put outdoors. *Neuer Markt 3, tel. 0222/515940, fax 0222/513–8138. 102 rooms with bath. Facilities: restaurant, coffee shop, bar. AE, DC, MC, V.*

$$$ König von Ungarn. This utterly charming, centrally located hotel is tucked away in the shadow of the cathedral. The historic facade belies the modern efficiency of the interior, from the atrium lobby to the guest rooms themselves. Insist on written confirmation of bookings. *Schulerstr. 10, tel. 0222/515840, fax 0222/515848. 32 rooms with bath or shower. Facilities: restaurant, bar. DC, MC, V.*

$$$ Mailberger Hof. This is a favorite of opera stars, conductors, and those who want a central but quiet location. Some rooms have limited kitchenette facilities. The arcaded courtyard is very pretty. *Annag. 7, tel. 0222/512–0641, fax 0222/512–064110. 40 rooms with bath or shower. Facilities: restaurant. AE, MC, V.*

$$ ★ Austria. This older hotel is on a quiet side street in a historic area. It is popular with tourists. *Wolfeng. 3/Fleischmarkt, tel. 0222/51523, fax 0222/515–23506. 46 rooms, 42 with bath or shower. Facilities: bar. AE, DC, MC, V.*

$$ ★ Kärntnerhof. Though tucked away in a tiny, quiet side street, Kärntnerhof is nevertheless centrally located. It's known for its particularly friendly staff. The rooms are functionally decorated but clean and serviceable. *Grashofg. 4, tel. 0222/512–1923, fax 0222/513–222833. 43 rooms, 41 with bath or shower. AE, DC, MC, V.*

$$ Pension Christina. This quiet pension, just steps from Schwedenplatz and the Danube Canal, offers mainly smallish modern rooms, warmly decorated with attractive dark-wood furniture set off against beige walls. Room 524 is particularly spacious and inviting. *Hafnersteig 7, tel. 0222/533–2961, fax 0222/533–296111. 32 rooms with bath or shower. DC, MC, V.*

$$ **Pension Zipser.** This 1904 house, with an ornate facade and gilt-
★ trimmed coat of arms, has become a favorite with regular visitors to
Vienna. It is slightly less central than some others, but very comfort-
able. *Lange Gasse 49, tel. 0222/404–5400, fax 0222/408–526613.
46 rooms with bath or shower. Facilities: bar. AE, DC, MC, V.*

$$ **Post.** Taking its name from the city's main post office, opposite, this
★ is an older but updated hotel that offers a fine location, a friendly staff,
and a good café. *Fleischmarkt 24, tel. 0222/515830, fax 0222/515–
83808. 107 rooms, 77 with bath or shower. AE, DC, MC, V.*

$$ **Wandl.** The house is old and some of the rooms are small, but Wandl's
location and reasonable prices compensate for most of its deficiencies.
*Peterspl. 9, tel. 0222/534550, fax 0222/534–5577. 134 rooms with
bath or shower. Facilities: bar. No credit cards.*

$ **Pension Kirschbichler.** This tidy family-run pension is simple but ade-
quate, and the location is excellent. There's no breakfast, but tea and
coffee are offered. *Landstrasser Haupstr. 33, tel. 0222/712–1068. 15
rooms with shower. No credit cards.*

The Arts

Theater and Opera

Check the monthly program published by the city; posters also show
opera and theater schedules. The **Staatsoper,** one of world's great
opera houses, features major stars in its almost-nightly performances
in the original languages. The **Volksoper** offers lighter opera, operetta,
and musicals, all in German. Performances at the **Burgtheater** and
Akadamietheater are in German. Tickets for the Staatsoper, Volk-
soper, and the Burg and Akademie theaters are available at the central
ticket office to the left rear of the Staatsoper (**Bundestheaterkassen,**
Hanuschg. 3, tel. 0222/514–442959, fax 0222/514–442969; open week-
days 8–6, Sat. 9–2, Sun. and holidays 9–noon). Tickets go on sale a
week before performances. Unsold tickets can be obtained at the
evening box office. Plan to be there at least one hour before the per-
formance; students can buy remaining tickets at lower prices, so they
are usually out in force. Tickets can be ordered three weeks or more
in advance in writing (or by fax) or six days in advance from anywhere
in the world by phone (tel. 0222/513–1513; AE, DC, MC, V). The-
ater is offered in English at **Vienna English Theater** (Josefsg. 12, tel.
0222/402–1260) and **International Theater** (Porzellang. 8, tel. 0222/319–
6272).

Music

Most classical concerts are in either the **Konzerthaus** (Lothringerstr.
20, tel. 0222/712–1211, fax 0222/712–2872) or **Musikverein** (Dum-
bastr. 3, tel. 0222/505–8190, fax 0222/505–9409). Tickets can be
bought at the box offices or ordered by phone (AE, DC, MC, V). Pop
concerts are scheduled from time to time at the **Austria Center** (Am Hu-
bertusdamm 6, tel. 0222/236–9150; U-1 subway to Vienna Interna-
tional Center stop). Tickets to various musical events are available via
Vienna Ticket Service (tel. 0222/587–9843, fax 0222/587–9844), or
at the Salettl gazebo ticket office on the Kärntnerstrasse next to the
opera (tel. 0222/588–85–81).

Film

Films are shown in English at **Burg Kino** (Opernring 19, tel. 0222/587–
8406), **de France** (Schottenring 5, tel. 0222/317–5236), **Top Kino**
(Rahlg. 1, tel. 0222/587–5557), **Votiv Kino** (Währinger Str. 12, tel.
0222/317–3571), and **Film Museum** (Augustinerstr. 1, tel. 0222/533–

7054). To find English-language movies, look for "OF" (original version) or "OmU" (original with subtitles) in the newspaper listings.

Nightlife

Cabarets
Most cabarets are expensive and unmemorable. Two of the best are **Casanova** (Dorotheerg. 6, tel. 0222/512–9845), which emphasizes striptease, and **Moulin Rouge** (Walfischg. 11, tel. 0222/512–2130).

Discos
Atrium (Schwarzenbergpl. 10, tel. 0222/505–3594) is open Thursday through Sunday and draws a lively younger crowd. **Queen Anne** (Johannesg. 12, tel. 0222/512–0203) is central, popular, and always packed. The **U-4** (Schönbrunnerstr. 222, tel. 0222/858307) ranks high among the young set. Live bands, dancing, and snacks are offered at **Chattanooga** (Graben 29, tel. 0222/533–5000).

Nightclubs
A casual '50s atmosphere pervades the popular **Café Volksgarten** (Burgring 1, tel. 0222/533–0518), situated in the city park of the same name; tables are set outdoors in summer. The more formal **Eden Bar** (Lilieng. 2, tel. 0222/512–7450) is considered one of Vienna's classiest night spots; don't expect to be let in unless you're dressed to kill.

Wine Taverns
For a traditional Viennese night out, head to one of the city's atmospheric wine taverns, some of which date from as far back as the 12th century. You can often have full meals at these taverns, but the emphasis is mainly on drinking. **Melker Stiftskeller** (*see* Dining, *above*) is one of the friendliest and most typical. Other well-known ones: **Antiquitäten-Keller** (Magdalenenstr. 32, tel. 0222/566–9533; closed Aug.), which has a backdrop of classical music; **Augustinerkeller** (Augustinerstr. 1, tel. 0222/533–1026), open at lunchtime as well as during the evenings, in the same building as the Albertina collection; **Esterházykeller** (Haarhof 1, tel. 0222/533–3482), a particularly mazelike network of rooms, with excellent wines; and **ZwölfApostelkeller** (Sonnenfelsg. 3, tel. 0222/512–6777), near St. Stephen's Cathedral, down, down, down underground.

THE DANUBE VALLEY

The Danube Valley stretches about 88 kilometers (55 miles) west of Vienna, and many visitors enjoy it as part of an excursion from the country's capital. What this region offers is magnificent countryside, some of Austria's best food and wine, and comfortable—in some cases elegant—accommodations. Above the river are the ruins of ancient castles. The abbeys at Melk and Göttweig, with their magnificent libraries, dominate their settings. Vineyards sweep down to the river, which is lined with fruit trees that burst into blossom every spring. People here live close to the land, and at certain times of year vintners open their homes to sell their own wines and produce. Roadside stands offer flowers, fruits, vegetables, and wines. And this is an area of legend: The Danube (Donau in German) shares with the Rhine the story of the mythical Nibelungen, defenders of Siegfried, hero of German myth.

Getting Around

By Car

If you're pressed for time, take the Autobahn to St. Pölten, turn north onto Route S-33, and follow the signs to Melk. For a more scenic route, leave Vienna along the south shore of the Danube via Klosterneuburg and Greifenstein, taking Routes 14, 19, 43, and 33. Cross the Danube at Melk, then return to Vienna along the north bank of the river (Route 3).

By Train

Depart from the Westbahnhof for Melk, then take the bus along the north bank of the Danube to Dürnstein and Krems. Side bus trips can be made from Krems to Göttweig.

By Boat

Travel upstream, with stops at Krems, Dürnstein, Melk, and points between. Return to Vienna by boat or by train from Melk (combination tickets available).

Guided Tours

Vienna travel agencies offer tours of the Wachau, as the Danube Valley is known. These range from one-day outings to longer excursions. For details, contact the **Lower Austria Tourist Office** (Heidenschuss 2, tel. 0222/533–3114–0, fax 0222/535–0319).

Tourist Information

Dürnstein (Parkpl. Ost, tel. 02711/219 or 02711/200, fax 02711/442).
Klosterneuburg (Niedermarkt 4, Postfach 6, tel. 02243/32038, fax 02243/86773).
Krems (Undstr. 6, tel. 02732/82676, fax 02732/70011—also covers **Stein an der Donau**).
Melk (Linzerstr. 3–5, tel. 02752/2307–32, fax 02752/2307–37).
Tulln (Albrechtsg. 32, tel. 02272/5836).

Exploring the Danube Valley

North of Vienna lies **Klosterneuburg**, whose huge **abbey** dominates the market town. The abbey's extensive vineyards produce excellent wines; the abbey itself is a major agricultural landowner in the region. *Guided tours every half hour (winter schedule may vary) Mon.–Sat. 9–11 and 1:30–5, Sun. 11 and 1:30–5.*

If you are driving, you have the choice of either following the riverbank or heading up over the village of St. Andrae and down to the river plain again. At **Tulln,** the **town hall** dominates the town square.

You will see **Stift Göttweig** long before you reach it. This impressive, 11th-century Benedictine abbey affords sensational views of the Danube Valley; walk around the grounds and view the impressive chapel. *Rte. 303, on south bank of Danube, opposite Krems.*

TIME OUT Have lunch at the **Stiftskeller.** If the weather is clear, sit out on the open terrace and enjoy the magnificent views of the Danube in the distance. The local wines are excellent. *Open daily Apr.–Oct.*

Farther along the valley is the abbey of **Melk,** holding a commanding position over the Danube. The library is rich in art as well as books; the ceiling frescoes are particularly memorable. *Tel. 02752/2312. Admission: AS45 adults, AS20 children. Admission (with guided tour):*

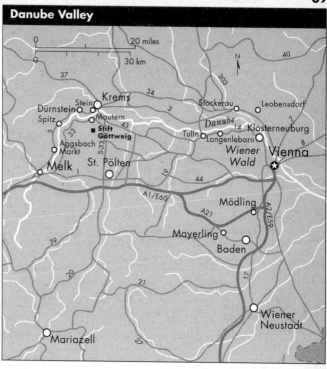

Danube Valley

AS55 adults, AS30 children. Open May–Sept., daily 9–5; Apr. and Oct., daily 9–4; Nov.–Mar., daily 11 and 2 (by tour only).

Cross to the north of the river and head back downstream. The beautiful medieval town of **Dürnstein** is known for having kept Richard the Lionhearted imprisoned in its now-ruined castle for 13 months. The town is also known for its fine hotels, restaurants, and wines. Virtually next door is **Stein,** with its former **Imperial Toll House** and the 14th-century **Minoritenkirche,** a church that now serves as an exhibition showcase. Stein and Krems sit at the center of Austria's foremost wine-growing region.

The road back to Vienna now wanders away from the Danube, crossing through some attractive woodlands. When you reach Leobensdorf, you'll spot **Burg Kreuzenstein,** perched to the left upon a nearby hilltop. The castle includes a small museum of armor. *Open mid-Mar.–mid-Nov. Tours daily 9–4, according to demand.*

Dining and Lodging

For details and price-category definitions, *see* Dining and Lodging *in* Staying in Austria, *above.*

Dürnstein

<u>DINING AND LODGING</u>
Richard Löwenherz. This former cloister sits perched above the Danube. Room furnishings include antiques and every comfort. The restaurant is excellent, as is the house wine. *Dürnstein 8, tel. 02711/222, fax 02711/22218. 40 rooms with bath or shower. Facilities: restaurant, bar, outdoor pool, parking. AE, DC, MC, V. Closed Nov.–mid-Mar.* $$$$

Krems

LODGING

Alte Post. A 16th-century house with an arcaded courtyard, the Alte Post is conveniently positioned right in the center of town. In good weather the courtyard is used for dining. *Obere Landstr. 32, tel. 02732/82276, fax 02732/84396. 20 rooms, most with bath. Facilities: restaurant (closed Wed.), bicycle rental, garage. No credit cards. Closed Jan. and Feb. $*

Langenlebarn

DINING

★ **Zum Roten Wolf.** This outstanding, elegant country restaurant serves traditional local foods and superb wines. *Bahnstr. 58, tel. 02272/2567. AE, DC, MC, V. Closed Mon. and Tues. $$$*

Mautern

DINING

★ **Landhaus Bacher.** The Landhaus Bacher is one of Austria's best restaurants, elegant but entirely lacking in pretension. Dining in the garden during the summer adds to the experience. *Südtirolerpl. 208, tel. 02732/829–370, fax 02732/74337. Reservations required. DC, V. Closed Mon., Tues., and mid-Jan.–mid-Feb. $$$$*

SALZBURG

Salzburg is best known as the birthplace of Wolfgang Amadeus Mozart and receives its greatest number of visitors during the annual Music Festival in July and August. Dominated by a fortress on one side and the Kapuzinerberg, a small mountain, on the other, this Baroque city is best explored on foot. Many areas are pedestrian precincts. Some of the most interesting boutiques and shops are found in the dozens of alleys and passageways that link streets and squares. Be sure to bring an umbrella: Salzburg is noted for sudden, brief downpours that start as abruptly as they stop.

Arriving and Departing

By Plane

For information, phone Salzburg airport, tel. 0662/852091.

BETWEEN THE AIRPORT AND DOWNTOWN

Buses leave for the Salzburg train station at Südtirolerplatz every 15 minutes during the day, every half hour at night to 10 PM. Journey time is 18 minutes. Taxi fare runs about AS150–AS170.

By Train

Salzburg's main train station is at Südtirolerplatz. For train information, call 0662/1717; for telephone ticket orders and seat reservations, call 0662/1700.

By Bus

The central bus terminal (post office bus information: tel. 0662/167; railroad bus information: tel. 0662/872150) is in front of the train station, although during construction of the underground garage in front of the rail station, bus stops may be moved to various points around the square.

By Car

Salzburg has several autobahn exits; study the map and decide which one is best for you. Parking is available in the cavernous garages under the Mönchsberg, and in other garages around the city; look for the large blue P signs.

Getting Around

By Bus and Trolleybus

Service is frequent and reliable; route maps are available from the tourist office or your hotel. Save money by buying an **Umwelttarif,** a 24-hour ticket that is good on all trolley and bus lines, on the funicular up to the fortress, on the Mönchsberg lift, and on the rail line north to Bergheim. Tickets for children 6–15 are half price. For local transportation information, call 0662/20551–533.

By Taxi

At festival time, taxis are too scarce to hail on the street, so order through your hotel porter or phone 0662/8111 or 0662/1716.

By Fiaker

Fiakers, or horse-drawn cabs, are available at the railroad station and at Residenzplatz (tel. 0662/872680).

By Car

Don't even think of it! The old part of the city is a pedestrian zone. Cars are totally forbidden in the entire Old City on weekends. Many other parts of the city have restricted parking (indicated by a blue pavement stripe), either reserved for residents with permits, or for a restricted period. Get parking tickets from coin-operated dispensers on street corners; instructions are also in English.

Guided Tours

Guided bus tours of the city and its environs are given by **Salzburg Sightseeing Tours** (Mirabellpl. 2, tel. 0662/881616), **Salzburg Panorama Tours** (Mirabellpl./St. Andrä Church, tel. 0662/874029), and **Bob's Special Tours** (Chiemseeg. 1/Kaig., tel. 0662/849511–0). All can organize chauffeur-driven tours for up to eight people. Your hotel will have details.

Tourist Information

Salzburg's official tourist office, **Stadtverkehrsbüro,** has an **information center** at Mozartplatz 5 (tel. 0662/847568) and at the main train station (tel. 0662/871712). The main office is at Auerspergstrasse 7 (tel. 0662/889870).

Exploring Salzburg

Numbers in the margin correspond to points of interest on the Salzburg map.

The Salzach River separates Salzburg's old and new towns; for the best perspective on the old, climb the **Kapuzinerberg** (follow pathways from Linzerstrasse or Steingasse). Once back down at river level, walk up through Markartplatz to the **Landestheater,** where operas and operettas are staged during winter months; the larger houses used in the festival are closed most of the year. Diagonally across from the theater is the reconstructed **Mozart's Wohnhaus** (residence), where the family lived for some years. The building now includes a small recital hall. Wander through the Baroque **Mirabell Gardens** in back of the theater and enjoy a dramatic view of the Old City, with the castle in the background. And at least look in on the **Baroque Museum.** *Admission: AS40 adults, AS20 children. Open Tues.–Sat. 9–noon and 2–5, Sun. 9–noon.*

❸ Be sure to look inside **Schloss Mirabell,** which houses public offices, including that of the city's registrar; many couples come here for the experience of being married in such a sumptuous setting. The foyer and staircase, decorated with cherubs, are good examples of Baroque excess. *Mirabellpl., tel. 0662/8072–2258. Open Mon.–Thurs. 8–4, Fri. 8–1.*

❹ Head left down Schwarzstrasse, back toward the center of the city. On your left is the famed **Mozarteum,** a music academy (Schwarzstr. 26, tel. 0662/889400) whose courtyard encloses the summerhouse in which Mozart wrote *The Magic Flute.* Cross the Markartsteg footbridge to the Old City side of the Salzach river. Turn right and walk a short dis-
❺ tance up the Kai to the **Carolino Augusteum Museum.** This is the city museum, whose collections include art, archaeology, and musical instruments. *Museumspl. 1, tel. 0662/843145. Admission: AS40 adults, AS15 children; combined ticket with toy museum in the Bürgerspital (see below), cathedral excavations, and Folklore Museum: AS60 adults, AS20 children. Open Tues. 9–8, Wed.–Sun. 9–5.*

TIME OUT   From the Carolinum, as the museum is called, turn the corner into Gstät-
tengasse. On your right is the Mönchsberg elevator, which will take you to the top of the promontory. Once here, follow the signs and path south to **Burgerwehr-Einkehr,** a café-restaurant with superb views of the city—the fortress is in the background. It's a delightful hike over the ridge to the fortress from here (making the trip in reverse, however, will save you an uphill climb). *Am Mönchsberg 19c, tel. 0662/841729. No credit cards. Closed mid-Oct.–Apr. $*

❻ Returning to city level, follow the Gstättengasse to the **Bürgerspital,** which houses a toy and musical instruments museum within its Renaissance arcades. *Bürgerspitalpl. 2, tel. 0662/847560. Admission: AS30 adults, AS10 children; combined ticket with the Carolino Augusteum, cathedral excavation, and Folklore Museum AS60 and AS20. Open Tues.–Sun. 9–5.*

Ahead is Herbert-von-Karajan-Platz, whose central **Pferdeschwemme** (Horse Fountain) is its most notable feature. Built into the side of the
❼ mountain itself is the **Festspielhaus,** a huge complex where many of the events of Salzburg's annual festival, the Festspiel, are held. *Hofstallg. 1, tel. 0662/80450.*

From the Festspielhaus, turn left into the Wiener-Philharmoniker-Strasse.
❽ The **Kollegienkirche** (Collegiate Church) on the left is the work of Fischer von Erlach and is one of the best examples of Baroque architecture anywhere; be sure to look inside. Cut under the covered passageway and turn right into Sigmund-Haffner Gasse. At the corner on the left
❾ stands the 13th-century **Franziskanerkirche** (Franciscan Church), an eclectic mix of architectural styles with Romanesque and Gothic accents. Nearby, at Domplatz, stands the magnificently proportioned Salzburg
❿ **Dom** (cathedral). Don't overlook the great bronze doors as you enter.

To reach the fortress on the hill above, walk under the arcade to the right side of the church and up the narrow Festungsgasse at the back end of Kapitalplatz. From here, you can either follow the footpath up the hill or take a five-minute ride on the Festungsbahn, an inclined railway cable car. On a sunny day, a far more pleasurable—and strenuous!—route is to hike up Festungsgasse, turning frequently to enjoy the changing panorama of the city below.

TIME OUT   **Stieglkeller** offers a wide choice of good Austrian fare, served outdoors in summer. The local beer is superb. Try *Salzburger Nockerln,* a heavenly meringue dessert. Stop here during the day; in the evenings they hold a *Sound of Music* dinner theater. *Festungsg. 10, tel. 0662/ 842681. Closed Oct.–Apr.*

⑪ Once you've reached the **Festung Hohensalzburg** itself, you can wander around on your own (admission: AS30 adults, AS15 children) or take a tour (AS30 adults, AS15 children in addition to admission). The views from the 12th-century fortress are magnificent in all directions. A main attraction is **St. George's Chapel,** built in 1501. A year later, in 1502, the chapel acquired the 200-pipe barrel organ, which plays daily in summer at 7 AM, 11 AM, and 6 PM. *Mönchsberg, tel. 0662/8042– 2133. Open July–Sept., daily 8–7; Apr.–June and Oct. daily 9–6; Nov.–Mar. 9–5. Guided tour schedule varies.*

⑫ Back down in the city, follow the wall to **Stiftskirche St. Peter** (St. Peter's Abbey). The cemetery lends an added air of mystery to the monks' caves cut into the cliff. The catacombs attached to the church can be visited by guided tour. *Just off Kapitalpl., tel. 0662/844–5780. Admission: AS12 adults, AS8 children. Tours hourly May–Sept., daily 10–5; Oct.–Apr., daily 11–noon and 1:30–3:30.*

⑬ Head around the cathedral to the spacious Residenzplatz, a vast and elegant square. The **Residenz** itself includes the prince-archbishop's living quarters and ceremonial rooms. *Residenzpl. 1, tel. 0662/8042–2690. Admission: AS45 adults, AS15 children. Tours Sept.–June, weekdays at 10–noon, 2, and 3; July–Aug., daily every 30 mins from 10 to 4:30.*

The **Residenzgalerie,** in the same building complex, has an outstanding collection of 16th- to 19th-century European art. *Residenzpl. 1, tel. 0662/840451. Admission: AS45 adults, AS15 children. Combined ticket with state rooms: AS70. Open daily 10–5. Closed on Wed. Oct.–Mar.*

⑭ From the lower end of Residenzplatz, cut across into the **Alter Markt,** which still serves as an open-air market. Salzburg's narrowest house is squeezed into the north side of the square. Turn left into Getreidegasse, a narrow street packed with boutiques and fascinating shops.
⑮ At the head of the tiny Rathausplatz is **Mozart's birthplace,** now a museum. *Getreideg. 9, tel. 0662/844313. Admission: AS62 adults, AS22 children. Open daily 9–6; during festival, daily 9–7.*

Wander along Getreidegasse, with its ornate wrought-iron shop signs and the Mönchsberg standing sentinel at the far end. Don't neglect the warren of interconnecting side alleys: These include a number of fine shops and often open onto impressive inner courtyards that, in summer, are guaranteed to be filled with flowers.

⑯ One popular excursion from Salzburg is to **Schloss Hellbrunn,** about 5 kilometers (3 miles) outside the city. Take Bus 55. The castle was built during the 17th century, and its rooms have some fine trompe l'oeil decorations. The castle's full name is Lustschloss Hellbrunn— Hellbrunn Pleasure Palace. It was designed for the relaxation of Salzburg's prince-archbishops and includes **Wasserspiele,** or fountains, conceived by someone with an impish sense of humor. Expect to get sprinkled as water shoots up from unlikely spots, such as the center of the table at which you're seated. The Baroque fountains are also fascinating. Both the palace and the fountain gardens can be included on a tour. *Tel. 0662/820372. Admission: AS48 adults, AS24 children. Tours Apr. and Oct., daily 9–4:30; May–Sept., daily 9–5. Evening tours July–Aug. on the hour 6–10.*

74

Alter Markt, **14**
Baroque Museum, **2**
Bürgerspital, **6**
Carolino Augusteum Museum, **5**
Dom, **10**
Festspielhaus, **7**
Festung Hohensalzburg, **11**
Franziskanerkirche, **9**
Kollegienkirche, **8**
Landestheater, **1**
Mozarteum, **4**
Mozart's Birthplace, **15**
Residenz, **13**
Schloss Hellbrunn, **16**
Schloss Mirabell, **3**
Stiftskirche St. Peter, **12**

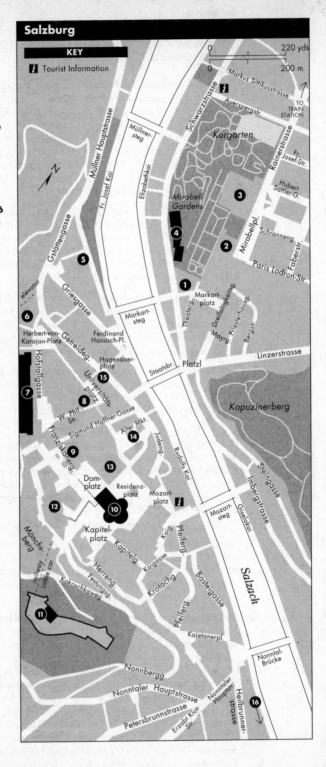

Salzburg

The Hellbrunn complex houses the **Tiergarten** (zoo), which is outstanding because of the way in which the animals have been housed in natural surroundings. You can also visit the small **folklore museum.** *Zoo: tel. 0662/820176. Admission: AS60 adults, AS25 children. Open Oct.–Mar., daily 8:30–4; Apr.–Sept., daily 8:30–6. Folklore museum: admission: AS20 adults, AS10 children. Open Easter–Oct., daily 9–5.*

Dining

Some of the city's best restaurants are in the leading hotels. This is a tourist town, and popular restaurants are always crowded, so make reservations well ahead, particularly during festival time. For details and price-category definitions, *see* Dining *in* Staying in Austria, *above.*

$$$ **Goldener Hirsch.** The return to more traditional Austrian and international cuisine suits the preferences of the musical and theater celebrities who regularly dine in these chic rooms. But don't overlook such specialties as fillet of catfish in anchovy sauce or game in season. The same kitchen serves the cheaper **s'Herzl** next door. *Getreideg. 37, tel. 0662/848511–861. Reservations required. AE, DC, MC, V.*

$$$ **Mirabell.** Although it's housed in a chain hotel (the Sheraton), the Mirabell is among the city's top restaurants. The menu mixes international dishes with adventurous versions of such local specialties as Wiener schnitzel and *Wildschwein* (wild boar). *Auerspergstr. 4, tel. 0662/889995. AE, DC, MC, V.*

$$$ **Zum Eulenspiegel.** The intimate rooms of an Old City house con-
★ tribute to the charm of this city restaurant. *Hagenauerpl. 2, tel. 0662/843180. MC, V. Closed Sun. except during festival, and early Jan.–mid-Mar.*

$$ **St. Peter Stiftskeller.** Allegedly Europe's oldest restaurant, offerings in this network of paneled rooms include the excellent St. Peter's fish, as well as traditional grilled and roast specialties. Finish with light-as-a-cloud meringue Salzburger Nockerln. *St. Peter District I/4, tel. 0662/841268. Reservations advised. AE, DC, MC, V.*

$$ **Zipfer Bierhaus.** Such standards as tasty roast pork with bread dumplings seem appropriate in this informal setting of arched ceilings and brick floors, one of the oldest Gasthäuser in town. *Sigmund-Haffner-Gasse 12/Universitätspl. 19, tel. 0662/840745. No credit cards. Closed Sun.*

$$ **Zum Mohren.** Arched ceilings in the lower rooms add atmosphere to
★ this historic house. Duck and venison are specialties. *Judeng. 9, tel. 0662/842387. No credit cards. Closed Sun. and holidays.*

$ **Sternbräu.** If you're not looking for anything too fancy, try the hearty sausages and roasted meats at this vast complex, which has a pleasant garden in summer. *Griesg. 23/Getreideg. 34, tel. 0662/842140. No credit cards.*

$ **Wilder Mann.** The atmosphere may be too smoky for some (choose the
★ outside courtyard in summer), but the beamed ceiling and antlers are genuine, as are the food and value. Try the *Tellerfleisch* (boiled beef) or game in season. *Getreideg. 20/Griesg. 17 (passageway), tel. 0662/841787. No credit cards. Closed Sun.*

Lodging

Reservations are always advisable and are essential at festival time (both Easter and summer). For details and price-category definitions, *see* Lodging *in* Staying in Austria, *above.*

$$$$ **Altstadt Radisson.** Rooms and suites are elegant and no two are alike in this handsomely converted Old City hostelry dating from 1377 with splendid views across the river or up to the fortress. Furnishings are individual and include antiques. The rooftop restaurant is excellent and offers stunning panoramas. *Judeng. 15/Rudolfskai 28, tel. 0662/848571–0, fax 0662/848571–6. 60 rooms with bath. Facilities: restaurant. AE, DC, MC, V.*

$$$$ ★ **Goldener Hirsch.** This old-timer—800 years old and an inn since 1564—is conveniently set right in the heart of the Old City. Arched corridors, vaulted stairs, rustic furniture, and antiques provide a medieval atmosphere; the essential modern appliances stay ingeniously hidden. The restaurant (*see* Dining, *above*) is excellent. *Getreideg. 35–37, tel. 0662/848511, fax 0662/843349. 75 rooms with bath. Facilities: restaurant, garage. AE, DC, MC, V.*

$$$$ **Österreichischer Hof.** Salzburg's grande dame occupies a lovely riverside location, and the favored rooms give views of the fortress and the Old City. The house restaurants are disappointing. *Schwarzstr. 5–7, tel. 0662/88977–0, fax 0662/88977–14. 120 rooms, 118 with bath or shower. Facilities: 4 restaurants, garage. AE, DC, MC, V.*

$$$$ **Schloss Mönchstein.** If you are a romantic with money to spend, look no further. With its sensational castle location overlooking the city, this is a top hotel. The restaurant is one of the best in the city. *Mönchsberg 26, tel. 0662/848555, fax 0662/848559. 17 rooms with bath. Facilities: restaurant, garage, tennis. AE, DC, MC, V.*

$$$$ **Sheraton.** A Sheraton is a Sheraton, but this one has one of Salzburg's best restaurants. Favored rooms at the back overlook the Mirabell Gardens. *Auerspergstr. 4, tel. 0662/889990, fax 0662/881776. 165 rooms with bath. Facilities: restaurant, garage, laundry, health spa, indoor pools. AE, DC, MC, V.*

$$$ ★ **Elefant.** This charming old inn in the heart of the Old City has been totally modernized without losing the carpets, country furniture, or resultant atmosphere. *Sigmund-Haffner-Gasse 4, tel. 0662/843397, fax 0662/840109–28. 36 rooms with bath or shower. Facilities: restaurant, garage. AE, DC, MC, V.*

$$$ **Stadtkrug.** This historic, family-run hotel is literally cut into the stone of the Capucine hill, creating a welcome garden terrace off the top floor. Dark wood accents and beamed ceilings in some rooms contrast with light walls and Oriental rugs. The pedestrian zone out front can be noisy in summer; choose a room on an upper floor. *Linzerg. 20, tel. 0662/873545, fax 0662/879588. 34 rooms with bath or shower. Facilities: restaurant. AE, DC, MC, V.*

$$ ★ **Markus Sittikus.** This hotel is reasonably priced and more than reasonably comfortable. The train station is within walking distance unless you're loaded with luggage. *Markus-Sittikus-Str. 20, tel. 0662/871121–0, fax 0662/871121–58. 41 rooms with bath or shower. AE, DC, MC, V.*

$$ ★ **Wolf.** The family touch reigns in this intimate, well-located hotel with spotless rooms in country decor. Book well ahead. *Kaig. 7, tel. 0662/843453–0, fax 0662/842423–4. 12 rooms with bath. AE.*

The Arts

Festivals

Tickets for the festival performances are almost impossible to get once you are in Salzburg. Write or fax ahead to **Salzburger Festspiele,** Postfach 140, A-5010 Salzburg, fax 0662/846682.

Opera, Music, and Art

Theater and opera are presented in the **Festspielhaus** (*see* Exploring, *above*), opera and operetta at the **Landestheater** (Schwarzstr. 22, tel. 0662/871–5120), and concerts at the **Mozarteum** (Schwarzstr. 26, tel. 0662/873154). Chamber music—in costume—is performed in **Schloss**

Mirabell. Special art exhibitions in the **Carolino Augusteum** (*see* Exploring, *above*) are often outstanding.

INNSBRUCK

Squeezed by the mountains and sharing the valley with the Inn River, Innsbruck is compact and very easy to explore on foot. The medieval city—it received its municipal charter in 1239—no doubt owes much of its fame and charm to its unique situation. To the north, the steep, sheer sides of the Alps rise like a shimmering blue-and-white wall from the edge of the city, an awe-inspiring backdrop to the mellow green domes and red roofs of the picturesque Baroque town.

Arriving and Departing

By Plane

The airport is 4 kilometers (2 miles) to the west of the city. For flight information, phone 0512/22525–304.

BETWEEN THE AIRPORT AND DOWNTOWN

Buses (Line F) to the city center (Maria-Theresien-Str.) run every 20 minutes and take about 20 minutes. Get your ticket from the bus driver; it costs AS18. Taxis should take no more than 10–15 minutes into town, and the fare is about AS120–AS150.

By Train

All trains stop at the city's main station at Südtiroler-Platz. Train connections are available to Munich, Vienna, Rome, and Zurich. For train information, phone 0512/1717. Ticket reservations, tel. 0512/1700.

By Bus

The terminal is to the right of the main train station.

By Car

Exit from the east–west autobahn or from the Brenner autobahn running south to Italy. Much of the downtown area is pedestrian zone or paid-parking only; get parking vouchers at tobacco shops, coin-operated dispensers, or the city tourist office at Burggraben 3.

Getting Around

By Bus and Streetcar

Most bus and streetcar routes begin or end at Südtiroler-Platz, site of the main train station. The bus is the most convenient way to reach the six major ski areas outside the city. Many hotels offer free transportation with direct hotel pickup; for those staying in the Old City, the buses leave from in front of the Landestheater.

By Taxi

Taxis are not much faster than walking, particularly along the one-way streets and in the Old City. To order a radio cab, phone 0512/1718, 0512/5311 or 0512/45500.

Guided Tours

Sightseeing Tours

Bus tours lasting two hours cover the city's highlights and leave from the hotel information office at the railroad station (Südtiroler-Pl.) daily at noon. In summer, additional buses are scheduled at 10 and 2, and there are shorter tours Monday through Saturday at 10:15, noon, 2, and 3:15. Your hotel or one of the tourist offices will have tickets and details.

Tourist Information

The two main tourist offices are at Burggraben 3 (tel. 0512/5356, fax 0512/535643, daily 8–7, Innsbruck) and Wilhelm-Greil-Strasse 17 (tel. 0512/5320–170, fax 0512/5320–174 weekdays 8:30–6, Sat. 9–noon, Tirol). Pick up a Club-Innsbruck card at your hotel for discounts. **American Express** (Brixnerstr. 3, tel. 0512/582491, fax 0512/573385). **Wagon-Lits Travel** (Brixnerstr. 2, tel. 0512/520790, fax 0512/520–7985).

Exploring Innsbruck

Numbers in the margin correspond to points of interest on the Innsbruck map.

Modern-day Innsbruck retains close associations with three historical figures: Emperor Maximilian I and Empress Maria Theresa, both of whom are responsible for much of the city's architecture, and Andreas Hofer, a Tirolean patriot. You will find repeated references to these names

❶ as you tour the city. A good starting point is the **Goldenes Dachl** (the Golden Roof), which made the ancient mansion and the balcony it covers famous. (It's actually made of copper tiles gilded with 31 pounds of gold.) The building now houses an **Olympic Museum,** which runs videotapes of the Innsbruck winter Olympics. *Herzog Friedrich-Str. 15, tel. 0512/536–0575. Admission: AS22 adults, AS11 children. Open daily 9:30–5:30. Closed on Mon. Nov.–Feb.*

❷ A walk up Hofgasse brings you to the **Hofburg,** the Rococo imperial palace with an ornate reception hall decorated with portraits of Maria Theresa's ancestors. *Rennweg 1, tel. 0512/587186. Admission: AS50 adults, AS10 children. Open May–Oct., daily 9–5; Nov.–Apr., Mon.–Sat. 10–5.*

❸ Close by, the **Hofkirche,** the Imperial Church, was built as a mausoleum for Maximilian. The emperor is surrounded by 24 marble reliefs portraying his accomplishments, as well as 28 oversize statues of his ancestors, including the legendary King Arthur. Andreas Hofer is also buried here. Don't miss the ornate altar of the 16th-century Silver Chapel. The **Tiroler Volkskunstmuseum** (Tirolean Folk Art Museum) is housed in the Hofkirche, too. It exhibits costumes, rustic furniture, and farmhouse rooms decorated in styles ranging from Gothic to Rococo. *Universitätsstr. 2, tel. 0512/584302. Admission: AS20 adults, children free (Hofkirche), AS40 adults, AS15 children (Volkskunstmuseum); combined ticket: AS50 adults. Hofkirche open Sept.–June, daily 9–5; July–Aug. daily 9–5:30. Volkskunstmuseum open Sept.–June, Mon.–Sat. 9–5, Sun. 9–noon; July–Aug., Mon.–Sat. 9–5:30, Sun. 9–noon.*

❹ Follow Museumstrasse to the **Ferdinandeum,** which houses Austria's largest collection of Gothic art and painting from the 19th and 20th centuries. *Museumstr. 15, tel. 0512/594–8971. Admission: AS50 adults, AS30 children. Open May–Sept., daily 10–5, Thurs. eve. 7–9; Oct.–Apr., Tues.–Sat. 10–noon and 2–5, Sun. and holidays 10–1.*

TIME OUT   Relax over coffee, excellent pastries, and a newspaper in just about any language you want under the crystal chandeliers at **Café Central,** in the Hotel Central, just off Wilhelm-Greil-Strasse. *Gilmstr. 5, tel. 0512/5920–0. AE, DC, MC, V. Closed Nov.*

❺
❻ Cut back down Wilhelm-Greil-Strasse to the **Triumphpforte** (Triumphal Arch), built in 1765, and walk up Maria-Theresien-Strasse past the **Annasäule** (Anna Column) for a classic view of Innsbruck with the Alps in the background.

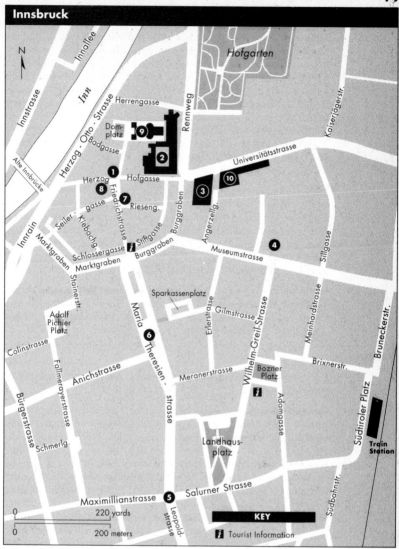

Innsbruck

Major Attractions
Annasäule, **6**
Ferdinandeum, **4**
Goldenes Dachl, **1**
Hofburg, **2**
Hofkirche, **3**
Triumphpforte, **5**
Other Attractions
Dom zu St. Jakob, **9**
Helblinghaus, **8**
Stadtturm, **7**
Tiroler Volkskunst-
museum, **10**

Off the Beaten Track

Schloss Ambras, one of Austria's finest and best-preserved castles, lies just 3 kilometers (2 miles) southeast of the city. It is easily reached by bus or streetcar. Dating from the 11th century, it was later rebuilt as a residence for the archduke Ferdinand of Tirol (from 1564 to 1582), so most of what you now see is in German Renaissance style. The collection includes numerous pictures (including the only known portrait of Count Dracula), weapons, armor, furniture, and other objects. *In village of Ambras (Streetcar 3 or the closer Bus K), tel. 0512/348446. Admission: AS60 adults, AS30 children. Open Apr.–Oct., Wed.–Mon. 10–5; Jan.–Mar. 2–3 only, by tour, for an additional AS20. Verify opening dates and times.*

In the mountains high above the city is the unique **Alpine Zoo,** with alpine animals and birds in their native environment and even an aquarium. And, of course, there's a restaurant at the top. You can either hike up or take the Hungerberg funicular, then the cable car. A combination funicular-cable entry card is available at the Hungerberg ticket office. *Weiherburgg. 37, tel. 0512/292323. Admission: AS60 adults, AS30 children. Open summer, daily 9–6; winter, daily 9–dusk.*

A visit to the 400-year-old, operating **Grassmayr Bell Foundry** shows how bells are cast and tuned. Take Bus J, K, or S south to Grassmayrstrasse. *Leopoldstr. 53, tel. 0512/59416. Admission: AS20 adults, AS10 children. Open weekdays 9–6, Sat. 9–noon.*

Dining

For details and price-category definitions, *see* Dining *in* Staying in Austria, *above.*

$$$ Europa-Stüberl. Regional specialties and the resplendent setting are two reasons why the Hotel Europa's (*see* Lodging, *below*) restaurant is highly regarded by locals and visitors. *Brixnerstr. 6, tel. 0512/593–1648. AE, DC, MC, V.*

$$$ Schwarzer Adler. This place drips with atmosphere, its massive-beamed rooms a perfect backdrop for typical Austrian dishes like *Knödeln* (dumplings) and Tafelspitz. *Kaiserjägerstr. 2, tel. 0512/587109. AE, DC, MC, V. Closed Sun. and mid-Jan.*

$$ Goethestube. The wine tavern of the city's oldest inn, the Goldener Adler (*see* Lodging, *below*), is one of Innsbruck's best. It was here that Goethe (who lent his name to the tavern) sipped quantities of red South Tirolean wine during his stays in 1786 and 1790. *Herzog Friedrich-Str. 6, tel. 0512/586334. Dinner only. AE, DC, MC, V.*

$$ Hirschenstuben. Old-fashioned hospitality and dark-wood trim are
★   found in force at this charming local favorite. Game is particularly good here. *Kiebachg. 5, tel. 0512/582979. Reservations advised. AE, DC, MC, V. Closed Sun.*

$$ Ottoburg. A warren of rooms in a 13th-century building, the Ottoburg
★   is exactly right for an intimate, cozy lunch or dinner. It's packed with Austriana and is 100% genuine. Go for the trout if it's available. *Herzog Friedrich-Str. 1, tel. 0512/574652. Reservations advised. AE, DC, MC, V.*

$$ Stieglbräu. Lovers of good beer will be delighted to find this popular rustic spot, which, in addition to its thirst-quenching brews, provides good, solid Austrian fare. Portions are substantial, the small garden exceptionally pleasant. *Wilhelm-Greil-Str. 25, 0512/584338. No credit cards.*

$ Gasthaus Steden. The substantial portions and unassuming (if occasionally smoky) atmosphere attract visiting businesspeople as well as many local regulars to this thoroughly genuine Gasthaus. Roast pork is particularly tasty and daily specials are a good value. *Anichstr. 15, tel. 0512/580890. No credit cards. Closed Sun.*

$ Schnitzel Paradies. Generous schnitzels are the feature in this spacious restaurant, although daily specials may include turkey or pasta. Cakes and desserts are homemade. *Innrain 25, tel. 0512/572972. Dinner reservations advised. No credit cards. Closed Sun.*

Lodging

Most hotels offer or can arrange transport to ski areas. For details and price-category definitions, *see* Lodging *in* Staying in Austria, *above.*

$$$$ Europa. The Europa is a postwar building blessed with a surprising amount of charm. Some rooms have period furnishings; others are 20th-century modern. *Südtiroler-Pl. 2, tel. 0512/5931, fax 0512/587800. 132 rooms with bath. Facilities: restaurant, bar, beauty salon, sauna, solarium, garage. AE, DC, MC, V.*

$$$$ Goldener Adler. The Golden Eagle has been an inn since 1390, and over
★ the centuries it has welcomed nearly every king, emperor, duke, or poet who passed through the city. The facade looks suitably medieval, and inside, passages and stairs twist romantically and rooms crop up when least expected. The several restaurants offer well-prepared seasonal and local dishes. *Herzog Friedrich-Str. 6, tel. 0512/586334, fax 0512/584409. 40 rooms with bath or shower. Facilities: 2 restaurants, Weinstube. AE, DC, MC, V.*

$$$$ Schwarzer Adler. Rooms are individual, warm, and inviting in this traditional Romantik Hotel. It's an easy stroll to the Old City. *Kaiserjägerstr. 2, tel. 0512/587109, fax 0512/561697. 27 rooms. Facilities: 2 restaurants, bar, garage. AE, DC, MC, V.*

$$$ Alpotel. Abundant space, comfort, and modern style are the keys in this new hotel on the edge of the Old City. The staff is particularly helpful. Many rooms have balconies with splendid views. The Tiroler Stuben restaurant (*see* Dining, *above*) is very good. *Innrain 13 (Ursulinenpassage), tel. 0512/577931, fax 0512/577931–15. 75 rooms with bath. Facilities: restaurant, bar, café, sauna, solarium, garage. AE, DC, MC, V.*

$$$ Scandic Crown. Innsbruck's newest major hotel belongs to the leading Scandinavian chain. The rooms are modern plush; the facilities, including sauna, are extensive. The buffet lunch is good value and abundant. The train station is nearby. *Salurnerstr. 15, tel. 0512/59350, fax 0512/593–5220. 176 rooms with bath. Facilities: 2 restaurants, bar, health club, pool, sauna, garage. AE, DC, MC, V.*

$$ Goldene Krone. The smallish rooms in this older hotel are clean and adequate, and the location on the main square is splendid, if not directly in the Old City. You can easily walk the two longish blocks from the railroad station. Rooms on the Maximilianstrasse side are noisier but look across to an attractive Art Deco building opposite. *Maria-Theresien-Str. 48, tel. 0512/586160, fax 0512/580189–6. 35 rooms with bath. Facilities: café. AE, DC, MC, V.*

$$ Weisses Kreuz. Occupying an honored position just steps away from
★ the famous Goldenes Dachl (*see* Exploring, *above*), the White Cross is a lovely inn that dates from 1465. Mozart stayed here in 1769. *Herzog Friedrich-Str. 31, tel. 0512/594790, fax 0512/59479–90. 39 rooms, 28 with bath or shower. Facilities: restaurant. AE, V.*

$ **Binder.** A short streetcar trip (Line 3) from the center of town should-n't be too high a price to pay for less-costly comfort at this small, friendly, family-run hotel. *Dr.-Glatz-Str. 20, tel. 0512/33436–0, fax 0512/33436–99. 32 rooms, most with bath or shower. Facilities: café-bar, parking. AE, DC, MC, V.*

$ **Riese Haymon.** You're outside the center in this one-time cloister (take Bus J, K, or S south to Grassmayrstr.). The furnishings are eclectic, but the rooms are neat. *Haymong. 4, tel. 0512/589837, fax 0512/586190, 22 rooms, 7 with shower. Facilities: restaurant, parking. No credit cards.*

The Arts

Most hotels have a monthly calendar of events (in English). Tickets to most events are available at the main tourist office (Burggraben 3, tel. 0512/5356, fax 0512/535643). Opera, operetta, musicals, and concerts take place at the **Tiroler Landestheater** (Rennweg 2, tel. 0512/520744) and **Kongresshaus** (Rennweg 3, tel. 0512/5936–0).

4 Belgium

BELGIUM COVERS A STRIP OF LAND just under 320 kilometers (200 miles) long and 160 kilometers (100 miles) wide bordering the North Sea between France and Holland. With more than 10 million people, it is the second most densely populated country in the world. Although influenced by the Dutch and the French, Belgium has a distinctive culture, or rather, two: Flemish and Walloon. The Flemings, who speak Dutch (Flemish), inhabit the northern half of the country; the French-speaking Walloons live in the south. Brussels, the capital, is officially designated a dual-language area.

Belgium is the world's most heavily industrialized country, with only 5% of the working population engaged in agriculture (though they still manage to produce 165 different cheeses and any number of fine sausages). Besides being natural entrepreneurs, the Belgians also work very hard—partly to make up for what has so long been denied them. In the course of history, the Belgians have been ruled by the Romans, French, Spanish, Austrians, Dutch, English, and Germans. Many of Europe's greatest battles have been fought on Belgian soil—from the Hundred Years' War to Waterloo to World War I. During World War II, this territory witnessed both the initial blitzkrieg of Nazi Panzer units and Hitler's final desperate counterattack against the advancing Allies in the Ardennes—an offensive that has gone down in history as the Battle of the Bulge.

The south of the country is a wild wooded area, with mountains rising to more than 2,000 feet. In the Dutch-speaking north, on the other hand, the land is flat and heavily cultivated, much as it is in neighboring Holland. Here stand the medieval Flemish cities of Ghent and Brugge, with their celebrated carillons and canals—not to mention the 68 kilometers (42 miles) of sandy beaches that make up the country's northern coastline. Due north of Brussels lies Antwerp, the country's dynamic seaport. This city, where the painter Rubens lived, is now the world's leading diamond-cutting center.

Brussels stands in the very center of the country. A booming, expanding, and often expensive city, it is the home of the European Commission, where most decisions affecting the European Union (EU) are made. The city hosts more ambassadors than any other in the world—approximately 160. Partly as a result of this concentration of power and partly because of the Belgians' celebrated love of good food, Brussels has won gastronomic renown around the world.

As befits a bourgeois culture, the Belgians are great believers in living well. In practice, this means that meals, parks, cars, and houses are large. Homes are highly individualistic and comfortable; trendy designer bars are cozy as well as chic. Except on the road, Belgians are generous and have time for old-fashioned courtesy.

But Belgians are not just creatures of the senses. A robust culture is celebrated in paintings by Brueghel and Rubens, Magritte, and Delvaux and by exciting Gothic, Renaissance, and Art Nouveau architecture. Belgium is no self-publicist, but quietly and confidently waits to be discovered.

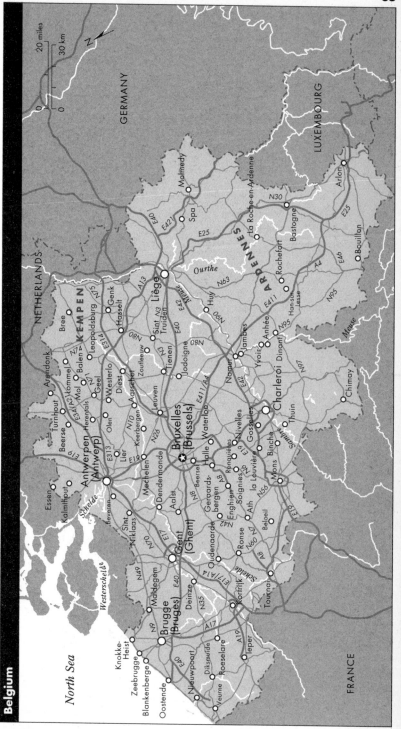

Belgium

ESSENTIAL INFORMATION

Before You Go

When to Go

The tourist season runs from early May to late September and peaks in July and August, when the weather is warmest. May and September offer the advantage of generally clear skies and smaller crowds. In the coastal resorts, some hotels and restaurants remain open all year.

CLIMATE

Temperatures range from around 65°F in May to an average 73°F in July and August. In winter, they drop to an average of about 40°F to 45°F. Snow is unusual except in the mountains of the Ardennes, where cross-country and alpine skiing are popular.

The following are the average daily maximum and minimum temperatures for Brussels.

Jan.	40F	4C	May	65F	18C	Sept.	69F	21C
	30	– 1		46	8		51	11
Feb.	44F	7C	June	72F	22C	Oct.	60F	15C
	32	0		52	11		45	7
Mar.	51F	11C	July	73F	23C	Nov.	48F	9C
	36	2		54	12		38	3
Apr.	58F	14C	Aug.	72F	22C	Dec.	42F	6C
	41	5		54	12		32	0

Currency

The unit of currency in Belgium is the franc (BF). There are bills of 100, 500, 1,000, 2,000, and 10,000 francs in addition to coins of 1, 5, 20, and 50 francs. At press time (spring 1995), the exchange rate was about BF28 to the dollar and BF45 to the pound sterling.

What It Will Cost

Brussels is a considerably less expensive city than Paris, Zürich, or Frankfurt and on par with London and New York. Deluxe hotels are very expensive but offer substantially discounted weekend and summer rates. There is also a wide selection of reasonably priced establishments, and hotels away from the capital are generally less pricey. Top restaurants are in the $100 range, but you can eat very well in this land of gourmets for a third of that sum. Note that all taxes and service charges are included in hotel and restaurant bills. Gasoline prices conform to the high European average, but the excellent highways are toll-free.

SAMPLE PRICES

A cup of coffee in a café will cost BF45–BF60; a glass of beer, BF35–BF85; and a glass of wine, about BF100. Train travel averages BF6 per mile, the average bus/metro/tram ride costs BF50, theater tickets cost about BF500, and movie tickets about BF250.

Customs on Arrival

Since the EU's 1992 agreement on a unified European market, the limits of what visitors from EU countries may bring in have become generous to the point of being meaningless. For example, travelers from EU nations may now bring in 120 bottles of wine, 10 liters of alcohol, and 800 cigarettes. Duty-free amounts, however, remain unchanged: 300 cigarettes, 5 liters of wine, and 1½ liters of spirits. Visitors from non-EU countries can bring in 200 cigarettes, or 50 cigars, or 250 grams of tobacco; 2 liters of still wine and 1 liter of spirits or 2 liters of aperitif wine; and 50 grams of perfume. Other goods from non-EU countries may not exceed a total value of BF2,000. There are no restrictions on the import or export of currency.

Language

Language is a sensitive subject that leads to frequent political crises. There are three national languages in Belgium: French, spoken primarily in the south of the country (Wallonia); Flemish, spoken in the north; and German, spoken in a small area in the east. Brussels is bilingual, with both French and Flemish officially recognized, though French predominates. Many people speak English in Brussels and in the north (Flanders). In addressing a Fleming, you're likely to get more cooperation if you speak English rather than French. In Wallonia you may have to muster whatever French you possess, but in tourist centers you will be able to find people with at least basic English.

Getting Around

By Car

ROAD CONDITIONS

Belgium has an excellent system of expressways, and the main roads are generally very good. Road numbers for main roads have the prefix *N;* expressways, the prefix *A* or *E.*

RULES OF THE ROAD

Drive on the right and pass on the left (passing on the right is forbidden). Seat belts are compulsory in both front and rear seats. Each car must have a warning triangle to be used in the event of a breakdown or accident. At intersections, particularly in cities, traffic on the right has priority. Adhere strictly to this rule because there are few stop or yield signs. In Brussels, the system of tunnels and ring roads is generally effective. Cars within a traffic circle have priority over cars entering it. Buses and streetcars have priority over cars. Maximum speed limits are 130 kph (80 mph) on highways, 90 kph (55 mph) on major roads, and 50 kph (30 mph) in cities.

ROAD SIGNS

Road signs are written in the language of the region, so you need to know that Antwerpen (Flemish) is Anvers (French) and Antwerp to us; likewise, Brugge and Brussel (Flemish) are Bruges and Bruxelles (French); Gent (Flemish) is Gand (French) and Ghent (English). Even more confusing, Liège and Luik are the same place, as are Louvain and Leuven and Namur and Namen. Even more difficult is Mons (French) and its Flemish equivalent, Bergen, or Tournai (French), which becomes Doornik in Flemish.

PARKING

Most cities have metered on-street parking (parking meters take 5- or 20-franc coins) and parking lots.

By Train

Fast and frequent trains connect all main towns and cities. If you intend to travel frequently, buy a **Benelux Tourrail Ticket,** which allows unlimited travel throughout Belgium, Luxembourg, and the Netherlands for any five days during a one-month period. The cost of the five-day pass is BF6,050 first class and BF4,040 second class. For those under 26, the pass costs BF3,030 second class (first class is not available). The **Belgian Tourrail Ticket** allows unlimited travel for five days in a one-month period at a cost of BF2,970 first class and BF1,980 second class. Young people from 12 to 26 can purchase a **Go Pass** for BF1,290, valid for 10 one-way trips in a six-month period on the Belgian rail network. All of the above are available at any Belgian train station.

Special weekend round-trip tickets are valid from Friday noon to Monday noon: A 40% reduction is available on the first traveler's ticket and a 60% reduction on companions' tickets. During the tourist season there are similar weekday fares to the seaside and the Ardennes.

By Bus
Intercity bus service is almost nonexistent. Details of services are available at train stations and tourist offices.

By Bicycle
You can rent a bicycle from Belgian railways at 48 stations throughout the country; train travelers get reduced rates. Bicycling is especially popular in the flat northern and coastal areas. Bicycle lanes are provided in many Flemish cities, but bicycling in Brussels is madness.

Staying in Belgium

Telephones

LOCAL CALLS
Pay phones work mostly with telecards, available in a number of denominations starting from BF200; some phones are coin-operated and take 5- and 20-franc coins. The telecards can be purchased at any post office and at many newsstands. Most phone booths that accept telecards have a list indicating where these cards are sold. An average local call costs BF20.

INTERNATIONAL CALLS
The least expensive method is to buy a high-denomination telecard and make a direct call from a phone booth. A five-minute phone call to the United States at a peak time will cost about BF750 by this method. To reach an **AT&T** long-distance operator, dial 078/11–0010; for **MCI**, 0800–10012; for **Sprint**, 0800–10014.

COUNTRY CODE
The country code for Belgium is 32.

Mail

POSTAL RATES
Airmail letters and postcards to the United States cost BF38 for the first 10 grams and BF4 more for each additional 10 grams. Airmail letters to the United Kingdom are BF16 for the first 20 grams.

RECEIVING MAIL
You can have mail forwarded directly to your hotel. If you're uncertain where you'll be staying, have mail sent in care of **American Express** (pl. Louise 1, B-1000 Brussels). Cardholders are spared the $2-per-letter charge.

Shopping

SALES-TAX REFUNDS
When you buy goods for export, you can ask most shops to fill out special forms covering VAT or sales tax. An itemized invoice showing the amount of VAT will also do. When you leave Belgium, you must declare the goods at customs and have the customs officers stamp the documents. Once you're back home, you simply send the stamped forms back to the shop and your sales tax will be refunded. This facility covers most purchases of more than BF2,000. There's a simpler option, but it requires trust. At the time of purchase by credit card, you pay only

the price without VAT, but you also sign, with your card, a guarantee in the amount of the sales tax. Have the invoice stamped by customs when you leave the last EU country on your itinerary. You have three months to return the stamped invoice to the store, where the guarantee is then disposed of. If you fail to do so, you forfeit the guarantee.

Opening and Closing Times

Banks are open weekdays from 9 to 4; some close for an hour at lunch. Exchange facilities are usually open on weekends, but you'll get a better rate during the week.

Museums are generally open from 10 to 5 six days a week. Closing day is Monday in Brussels and Antwerp, Tuesday in Brugge.

Shops are open weekdays and Saturdays from 10 to 6 and generally stay open later on Friday. Some shops close for lunch. Bakeries and some groceries are open Sunday and closed Monday.

National Holidays

January 1; April 8 (Easter Monday); May 1 (May Day); May 16 (Ascension); May 27 (Pentecost Monday); July 21 (National Holiday); August 15 (Assumption); November 1 (All Saints' Day); November 11 (Armistice); December 25.

Dining

Nearly all Belgians take eating seriously and are discerning about fresh produce and innovative recipes. They are prepared to spend a considerable amount on a celebratory meal. At the top end of the scale, the *menus de dégustation* offer a chance to sample a large selection of the chef's finest dishes. Prix-fixe menus are widely available and often represent considerable savings. Menus and prices are always posted outside.

Belgian specialties include *lapin à la bière* (rabbit in beer), *faisan à la brabançonne* (pheasant with chicory), *waterzooi* (a rich chicken or fish hot pot), and *carbonnades* (chunky stews). Belgians love their *frites* (french fries) so much that they think they invented them. *Steack et frites* can be found everywhere. For the best cut of beef, ask for *filet pur.*

Local specialties include marvelous asparagus from Mechelen, at their best in May; *salade Liègoise,* a hot salad with beans and bacon (Liège); wild strawberries and freshwater fish from the Meuse (Namur); different permutations of sprouts, chicory, and pheasant (Brussels); and shrimp, oysters, and mussels (Flanders).

Belgian snacks are equally appetizing. The *gaufre/wafel* (waffle) has achieved world fame, but *couques* (sweet buns), *speculoos* (spicy gingerbread biscuits), and *pain d'amandes* (nutty after-dinner biscuits) are less well known. For lunch, cold cuts, rich pâtés, and *jambon d'Ardennes* (Ardennes ham) are popular, often accompanied by goat cheese and rye or whole-wheat bread.

MEALTIMES

Most hotels serve breakfast until 10. Belgians usually eat lunch between 1 and 3, some making it quite a long, lavish meal. However, the main meal of the day is dinner, which most Belgians eat between 7 and 10; peak dining time used to be about 8, but is now creeping closer to 9.

WHAT TO WEAR

Belgians tend to be fairly formal and dress conservatively when dining out in the evenings. Generally speaking, though, a jacket and tie are required only in the most expensive establishments. Younger Belgians favor stylish, casual dress in most restaurants.

Prices are per person and include a first course, main course, dessert, tip, and sales tax, but no wine. Highly recommended restaurants are indicated by a star ★.

CATEGORY	COST
$$$$	over BF3,500
$$$	BF2,500–BF3,500
$$	BF1,500–BF2,500
$	under BF1,500

Lodging

You can trust Belgian hotels, almost without exception, to be clean and of a high standard. The more modern hotels in city centers can be very expensive, but there are smaller, well-appointed hotels offering lodging at excellent rates. The family-run establishments in out-of-the-way spots, such as the Ardennes, can be surprisingly inexpensive, especially if you are visiting them out of season.

PENSIONS

Pensions offer a double room with bath or shower and full board from BF2,500 to BF3,500 in Brussels and from BF2,000 to BF3,000 elsewhere. These terms are often available for a minimum stay of three days.

YOUTH HOSTELS

For information about youth hostels, contact **Fédération Belge des Auberges de la Jeunesse** (tel. 02/215–31–00).

CAMPING

Belgium is well supplied with camping and caravan (trailer) sites. For details, contact the **Royal Camping and Caravaning Club of Belgium** (av. de Villas 5, B–1060 Brussels, tel. 02/537–36–81).

RATINGS

Hotel prices are inclusive and are usually listed in each room. All prices are for two people in a double room. Highly recommended lodgings are indicated by a star ★.

CATEGORY	COST
$$$$	BF9,000–BF12,000
$$$	BF6,500–BF9,000
$$	BF3,500–BF6,500
$	under BF3,500

Tipping

Tipping has been losing its hold in Belgium because a service charge is almost always figured into the bill. For example, a tip of 16% is included in all restaurant and café bills. The tip is also included in taxi fares. If you want to give more, round the amount up to the nearest BF50 or BF100. Railway porters ask a fixed per-suitcase price, BF30 in the day and BF35 at night. For moderately priced hotels, BF50 should be an adequate tip for bellhops and doormen; in very expensive hotels, BF100 is more appropriate. At the movies, give the usher BF20, whether or not he or she shows you to your seat. In theaters, tip about BF50 for programs. Tip washroom attendants in public places BF10.

BRUSSELS

Arriving and Departing

By Plane

All international flights arrive at Brussels's Zaventem Airport, about a 30-minute drive or a 16-minute train trip from the city center. A new passenger terminal opened in December 1994. **Sabena, American, Delta, TWA,** and **United** all fly into Brussels from the United States. **Sabena, British Airways,** and **British Midland** dominate the short-haul London (Heathrow)–Brussels route. **Air UK** flies to Brussels from London (Stansted), and **British Airways** from London (Gatwick). Several regional centers in the United Kingdom also have direct flights to Brussels.

BETWEEN THE AIRPORT AND DOWNTOWN

Regular train service from the airport to the Gare du Nord (North Station) and the Gare Centrale (Central Station)leaves every 20 minutes. The trip takes 16 minutes and costs BF220 (first-class round-trip) and BF140 (second-class round-trip); you can buy a ticket on the train for a BF30 surcharge. The first train from the airport runs at 6:09 AM and the last one leaves at 11:46 PM. A taxi to the city center takes about half an hour and costs about BF1,000. You can save up to 25% on Autolux airport taxi fares by buying a voucher for the return trip at the same time. Beware freelance taxi drivers who offer their services in the arrival hall.

By the Channel Tunnel

Drivers can now piggyback on **Le Shuttle,** a special car, bus, and truck train, between Dover and Calais in 35 minutes. **Eurostar** passenger trains link London's Waterloo station with Brussels's Gare du Midi in 3¼ hours. Prices are still volatile in the new competitive situation. For Le Shuttle information in Brussels, call 02/512–79–79; for Eurostar, call 02/224–88–56.

By Train and Boat/Jetfoil

Conventional train services from London connect with the Ramsgate–Oostende ferry or Jetfoil, and from Oostende the train takes you to Brussels. The Channel crossing takes about two hours by Jetfoil, 4½ hours by ferry. Total train time on both sides of the Channel is close to three hours. For more information, call **British Rail International** in London (tel. 0171/834–2345) or **Sally Line** (tel. 01843/595522). In Belgium, tickets are available at railway stations and from travel agents; for information call 02/219–26–40.

By Bus and Hovercraft

From London, the Hoverspeed City Sprint bus connects with the Dover–Calais Hovercraft, and the bus then takes you on to rue Antoine Danseart 101 in Brussels. The journey takes 6½ hours; for reservations and times, contact **Hoverspeed** (tel. 01304/240241) in Great Britain; call 02/513–93–40 in Brussels.

Getting Around

By Metro, Tram, and Bus

The metro, trams (streetcars), and buses run as part of the same system. All three are clean and efficient, and a single ticket costs BF50. The best buy is a 10-trip ticket, which costs BF310, or a one-day card costing BF120. You need to stamp your ticket in the appropriate machine on the bus or tram; in the metro, your card is stamped as you pass through the automatic barrier. You can purchase these tickets in any metro station or at newsstands. Single tickets can be purchased on the bus.

Detailed maps of the Brussels public transportation network are available in most metro stations and at the Brussels tourist office in the Grand' Place (tel. 02/513–89–40). You get a map free with a **Tourist Passport** (also available at the tourist office), which for BF220 allows you a one-day transport card and BF1,000 worth of museum admissions.

By Taxi

Taxis are expensive, but tips are included in the fare. To call a cab, phone (or have the restaurant or hotel call) **Taxis Verts** (tel. 02/349–49–49) or **Taxis Oranges** (tel. 02/513–62–00) or catch one at a cabstand. The price per kilometer is BF38, but airport taxis charge higher rates.

Important Addresses and Numbers

Tourist Information

The **Tourist Information Brussels** (TIB) office (tel. 02/513–89–40) is in the Hôtel de Ville on the Grand' Place, open daily 9–6 during the main tourist season (off-season Sun. 10–2; Dec.–Feb. closed Sun.) The main tourist office for the rest of **Belgium** is near the Grand' Place (rue Marché-aux-Herbes 63, tel. 02/504–03–90) and is open weekdays 9–7, weekends 9–1 and 2–7 (in winter the office closes at 6 PM and is closed Sun. morning). There is a tourist office at **Waterloo** (chaussée de Bruxelles 149, tel. 02/354–99–10); it is open April–November 15, daily 9:30–6:30 and November 16–March, daily 10:30–5.

Embassies

U.S. (blvd. du Régent 27, B–1000 Brussels, tel. 02/513–38–30). **Canadian** (av. de Tervuren 2, B–1040 Brussels, tel. 02/741–06–11). **U.K.** (rue d'Arlon 85, B–1040 Brussels, tel. 02/287–62–11).

Emergencies

Police (tel. 101); **Accident** (tel. 100); **Ambulance** (tel. 02/649–11–22); **Doctor** (tel. 02/648–80–00 and 02/479–18–18); **Dentist** (tel. 02/426–10–26); **Pharmacy:** To find out which one is open on a particular night or on weekends, call 02/479–18–18.

English-Language Bookstores

House of Paperbacks (chaussée de Waterloo 813, Uccle, tel. 02/343–11–22) is open Tuesday–Saturday 10–6. **Librairie de Rome** (av. Louise 50b, tel. 02/511–79–37) is open Monday–Saturday 8 AM–10 PM, Sunday 9–6; the bookshop sells U.S. and U.K. newspapers, periodicals, and paperbacks. **W. H. Smith** (blvd. Adolphe Max 71–75, tel. 02/219–27–08) is open Monday–Saturday 9–6.

Travel Agencies

American Express (pl. Louise 2, B–1000 Brussels, tel. 02/512–17–40). **Wagons-Lits** (blvd. du Régent 27, tel. 02/513–38–30) and other locations).

Guided Tours

Orientation Tours

De Boeck Sightseeing (tel. 02/513–77–44) operates city tours (BF750) with multilingual cassette commentary. Passengers are picked up at major hotels and at the tourist office in the town hall. More original are the tours run by **Chatterbus,** rue des Thuyas 12. For reservations, call the Brussels tourist office at 02/513–89–40. Tours include visits on foot or by minibus to the main sights (BF600) and a walking tour that includes a visit to a bistro (BF250). Tours are operated early June–September.

Special-Interest Bus Tours

ARAU organizes thematic city bus tours (in English), including "Brussels 1900: Art Nouveau," "Alternative Brussels," and "Brussels 1930: Art Deco." Tours begin in front of rue du Midi 2 (next to the Bourse); call 02/513–47–61 for times and bookings. The cost is BF500 for a half-day tour.

Regional Tours

De Boeck Sightseeing Tours (rue de la Colline 8, Grand' Place, tel. 02/513–77–44) visits Antwerp, the Ardennes, Brugge, Ghent, Ieper, and Waterloo.

Exploring Brussels

Brussels is a city of individualists. Walk along almost any street, and you will be surprised at how different each house is from its neighbor. Stop in the Grand' Place during a sound-and-light show and your mood softens, or watch from a cozy bar, its tables stacked high with pancakes or covered with bottles of Duvel beer. Brussels is a provincial city at heart, even though it has assumed a new identity as capital of the EU. Underneath the bureaucratic surface, the city is a subtle meeting of the Walloon and Flemish cultures. As the heart of the ancient Duchy of Brabant, Brussels retains its old sense of identity and civic pride. A stone's throw from the steel-and-glass towers, there are cobbled streets and forgotten spots where the city's eventful and romantic past is plainly visible through its 20th-century veneer.

Numbers in the margin correspond to points of interest on the Brussels map.

The Grand' Place

❶ Begin in the **Grand' Place,** one of the most ornate market squares in Europe. There is a daily flower market and a colorful Sunday-morning bird market. On summer nights, the entire square is flooded with music and colored light. The Grand' Place also comes alive during local pageants, such as the *Ommegang,* a splendid historical pageant (early July); the biennial *Tapis de Fleurs,* when the square is covered by a carpet of flowers (mid-August 1996); and the traditional Christmas illumination, when there is also a life-size crib and real animals.

❷ The bombardment of the city by Louis XIV's troops left only the **Hôtel de Ville** (town hall) standing. Civic-minded citizens started rebuilding the Grand' Place immediately, but the highlight of the square remains the Gothic town hall. The central tower, combining boldness and light, is topped by a statue of St-Michel, the patron saint of Brussels. Among the magnificent rooms are the Salle Gothique, with its beautiful paneling; the Salle Maximilienne, with its superb tapestries; and the Council Chamber, with a ceiling fresco, *Assembly of the Gods,* painted by Victor Janssens in the early 15th century. *Tel. 02/512–75–54. Admission: BF80. English-speaking tours Tues. 11:30 and 3:15, Wed. 3:15, Sun. 12:15. No individual visits.*

❸ Opposite the town hall is the **Maison du Roi** (King's House)—though no king ever lived there—a 16th-century palace housing the **City Museum.** The collection includes important ceramics and silverware—Brussels is famous for both—church sculpture, and statues removed from the facade of the town hall, as well as an extravagant collection of costumes for Manneken Pis *(see below). Grand' Place, tel. 02/511–27–*

42. Admission: BF80. Open Mon.–Thurs. 10–12:30 and 1:30–5 (Oct.–Mar. until 4), weekends 10–1.

TIME OUT **La Rose Blanche** (Grand' Place 11, tel. 02/513–64–79) is in a renovated three-story town house beside the town hall. Try a *fondue au parmesan* (cheese in batter) with a strong Chimay or a light *bière blanche*. A sweeter combination is coffee and a *dame blanche* (vanilla ice cream coated with hot chocolate sauce).

Southwest of the town hall, on the corner of the rue de l'Etuve and rue du Chêne, stands the famous **Manneken Pis,** a fountain with a small bronze statue of a chubby little boy urinating. Made by Jerome Duquesnoy in 1619, the statue is known as "Brussels's Oldest Citizen" and is often dressed in costumes that are kept in the City Museum. The present Manneken is a copy; the original was kidnapped by 18th-century French and English invaders (soldiers, not tourists!).

Leaving the Manneken, cross the Grand' Place in the direction of the Marché-aux-Herbes. Opposite the tourist office, take the petite rue des Bouchers, the main restaurant street in the heart of the tourist maelstrom. Each establishment advertises its wares by means of large signs and carts packed with food. As a rule, remember that the more lavish the display, the poorer the cuisine. From here, explore the network of galleries called **Galeries St-Hubert,** which includes the Galerie de la Reine, Galerie du Roi, and Galerie des Princes, all built in 1847. The motto on the central galleries, "Omnibus Omnia" (Everything for Everyone), is not altogether appropriate, given the designer prices.

Head south along the rue Marché-aux-Herbes and the rue Madeleine until you come to the **equestrian statue of King Albert.** To the left of the statue is the Central Station and to the right, the **Bibliothèque Nationale** (National Library). Walk through the formal gardens next to the library and look back at the ornate clock, with moving figures, over the lower archway.

Place Royale

If you continue walking through the gardens, you will arrive at the **place Royale,** the site of the Coudenberg palace, where the sovereigns once lived. Here you have a superb view over the lower town. On the northwest corner of the square is the **Musée d'Art Moderne** (Museum of Modern Art), housed in an exciting feat of modern architecture. On entry, a vertiginous descent into the depths reveals a sudden well of natural light. Although there are a few paintings by Matisse, Gauguin, Degas, and Dali, the surprise lies in the quality of Belgian modern art. See Magritte's luminous fantasies, James Ensor's masks and still lifes, and Spilliaert's coastal scenes. Do not miss Permeke's deeply brooding *Fiancés* or Delvaux's Surrealist works. *Pl. Royale 1, tel. 02/508–32–11. Admission free. Open Tues.–Sun. 10–1 and 2–5.*

Next door is the **Musée Royale d'Art Ancien** (Royal Museum of Ancient Art). Here the collection is of Flemish and Dutch paintings, ranging from magnificent 15th- and 16th-century works—Cranach, Matsys, and Brueghel the Elder, among them—to Rubens (several fine canvases), Van Dyck, and David. Do not miss Brueghel's dramatic *La Chute d'Icare (The Fall of Icarus)* or Hieronymous Bosch's *Le Dernier Jugement (The Last Judgment)*, a malevolent portrayal of humanity. *Rue de la Régence 10, tel. 02/508–32–11. Admission free. Open Tues.–Sun. 10–12 and 1–5.*

If you decide to divide your exploration of Brussels into two walks, this is a good place to break. You can pick up again at the same spot on the neoclassical place Royale. The rue de la Régence runs from this square toward the Palais de Justice. The Sablon lies along this street,

10 on the right. The **Grand Sablon,** the city's most sophisticated square, is alive with cafés, restaurants, and antiques shops. Here, also, is the tempting Wittamer (Grand Sablon 12–16), the city's finest pastry shop. Toward the end of the square is the **church of Notre Dame du Sablon,** built in flamboyant Gothic style. Although much of the original workmanship was lost in restoration, it remains one of the city's best-loved churches. The stained-glass windows are illuminated from within at night, creating an extraordinary effect of kindly warmth.

11 A small garden square, the **Petit Sablon** is surrounded by 48 statues representing Brussels's medieval guilds. Each craftsman carries an object that reveals his trade: The furniture maker holds a chair, for instance; the wine merchant, a goblet.

On the Petit Sablon is the **Musée Instrumental** (Museum of Musical Instruments). A huge collection of more than 1,000 musical instruments is on display. Half of them are unique, and a few go back to the Bronze Age. The guide can often be persuaded to play one of the pianos. *Petit Sablon 17, tel. 02/511–35–95. Admission free. Open Tues.–Sun. 2:30–4:30.*

Immediately behind the Petit Sablon is the **Palais d'Egmont,** at different times the residence of Christina of Sweden, Louis XV, and Voltaire. It is now used by the Belgian Ministry of Foreign Affairs for official meetings. If security allows, you can enter the Jardin d'Egmont, another small park, on this side. Come out of the entrance on rue du Grand Cerf and turn left toward the boulevard de Waterloo, a wide street full of bars and designer shops.

TIME OUT Among the bars on your right, **Le Nemrod** (blvd. de Waterloo 61, near pl. Louise) is the most inviting. In summer, there is a sidewalk café. The interior is decorated like a Belgian hunting lodge.

Palais de Justice to the Black Tower

12 At the end of the rue de la Régence is the **Palais de Justice,** constructed during the reign of the empire-builder Leopold II. Often described as the ugliest building in Europe, the palais is designed to impress upon you the majesty of justice. It's on the site of the former Gallows Hill.

Down a rather steep hill from the Palais de Justice is the working-class **Marolles** district, where the artist Pieter Brueghel died in 1569. His im-

13 posing marble tomb is in **Notre Dame de la Chapelle,** his local church on rue Haute, which has just been splendidly restored. From the church, head back to the Sablon via the cobbled rue Rollebeek. If you would rather see more of the authentic Marolles district, ignore the cluster of chic restaurants and designer shops on rue Rollebeek. Instead,

14 from place de la Chapelle, take rue Blaes to the flea market in **place du Jeu de Balle** (*see* Shopping, *below*). On the way, you will pass a number of rough Belgian bars and North African food shops. Until this century, bourgeois Belgians considered this labyrinth of small alleys a haven for thieves and political refugees. Although the Marolles continues to welcome immigrants and outsiders, it has lost its danger but kept its slightly raffish character.

96

Bibliothèque Nationale, **7**

Bourse, **19**

Cathédrale St-Michel et Ste-Gudule, **17**

Cinquantenaire, **23**

Equestrian Statue of King Albert, **6**

European Commission Headquarters, **22**

Galeries St-Hubert, **5**

Grand' Place, **1**

Grand Sablon, **10**

Hôtel de Ville, **2**

Maison du Roi, **3**

Manneken Pis, **4**

Musée d'Art Moderne, **8**

Musée Royale d'Art Ancien, **9**

Notre Dame de la Chapelle, **13**

Palais de Justice, **12**

Palais de la Nation, **16**

Palais Royal, **15**

Petit Sablon, **11**

Place des Martyrs, **18**

Place du Jeu de Balle, **14**

Rue Antoine Dansaert, **21**

Toure Noir, **20**

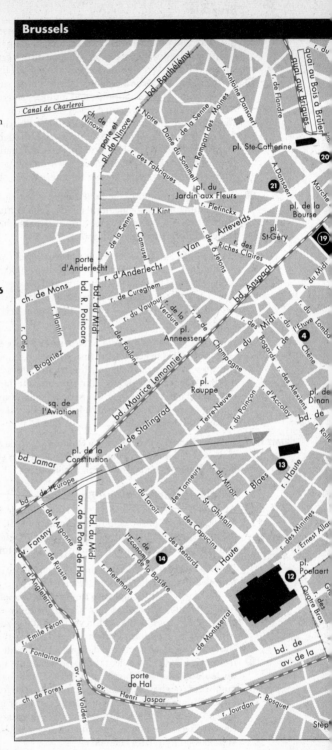

Brussels

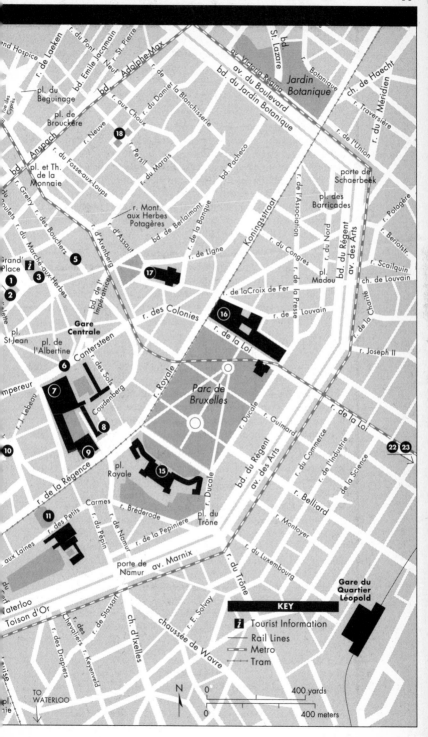

pl. du Beguinage

pl. de Brouckère

Anspach

bd.

pl. et Th. de la Monnaie

r. Grétry

r. du Fosse-aux-Loups

r. Neuve

r. Persil

r. du Marais

18

r. du Damier la Blanchisserie

av. Victoria Régina

av. du Boulevard

bd. du Jardin Botanique

St. Lazare

bd.

Botanique

Jardin Botanique

ch. de Haecht

r. Traversière

r. du Méridien

r. de l'Union

porte de Schaerbeek

pl. des Barricades

r. des Bouchers

Grand' Place

r. du Marché-aux-Herbes

5

3

2

1

pl. St-Jean

r. Mont. aux Herbes Potagères

bd. de l'Impératrice

bd. de Berlaimont

r. d'Arenberg

r. d'Assaut

17

r. de Ligne

r. de la Banque

Koningstraat

r. de l'Association

r. du Congres

r. de la Presse

r. du Nord

pl. Madou

r. de la Charité

r. Potagère

r. Berlafstr.

r. Scailquin

ch. de Louvain

r. des Colonies

16

r. de la Loi

r. de laCroix de Fer

Louvain

r. de

r. Joseph II

Gare Centrale

Cantersteen

pl. de l'Albertine

r. des Sols

6

7

8

9

Coudenberg

r. Royale

Parc de Bruxelles

r. Ducale

r. Guimard

r. de la Loi

10

r. de la Régence

pl. Royale

15

r. Ducale

bd. du Régent

av. des Arts

r. du Commerce

r. de l'Industrie

de la Science

22 23

Carmes

r. Bréderode

pl. du Trône

r. Belliard

11

r. des Petits

r. de Namur

r. du Pépin

r. de la Pepiniere

r. Montoyer

aux Laines

porte de Namur

av. Marnix

r. du Trône

r. du Luxembourg

Gare du Quartier Léopold

Waterloo

Toison d'Or

r. des Chevaliers

r. de Stassart

ch. d'Ixelles

r. E. Solvay

chaussée de Wavre

r. des Drapiers

r. Keyenveld

TO WATERLOO

N

0   400 yards

0   400 meters

KEY

ℹ Tourist Information

—— Rail Lines

═══ Metro

···· Tram

⑮ Return via the Sablon to the place Royale. Directly ahead of you is the **Parc de Bruxelles** (Brussels Park) with the **Palais Royal** (Royal Palace) at the end closer to you (open for visits from July 22 to early Septem-
⑯ ber). You can walk through the formal park to the **Palais de la Nation** (Palace of the Nation) at the opposite end, where the two houses of the Belgian Parliament meet. When Parliament is not sitting, you can visit the building. *Tel. 02/519–81–36. Admission free. Guided tours weekdays 9:30–noon.*

Surrounding the park are elegant turn-of-the-century houses. The prime minister's office is next to the Parliament building. A walk downhill (rue des Colonies) toward the downtown area and a short
⑰ right-hand detour bring you to the **Cathédrale St-Michel et Ste-Gud-ule.** The cathedral's chief treasures are the beautiful stained-glass windows designed by Bernard van Orley, an early 16th-century painter at the royal court. In summer the great west window is floodlighted from inside to reveal its glories. In the crypt, you can see the remnants of the original 12th-century church.

⑱ Continue downhill to the **place des Martyrs,** a dignified square over a mass grave for local patriots who died in the 1830 battle to expel the Dutch. Renovation of this nobly proportioned square is slowly progressing. Cross the rue Neuve and continue on to the boulevard
⑲ Adolphe-Max. Turn left and then right, in front of the imposing **Bourse** (stock exchange), to place Ste-Catherine.

⑳ The 12th-century **Tour Noire** (Black Tower) here is part of the city's first fortifications. Archaeological excavations have begun under this shamefully neglected monument. Under the square runs the river Senne, channeled underground in the last century. As a result of its watery past, place Ste-Catherine and the old fish market (quai aux Briques) that extends north from it still have the city's best seafood restaurants.
㉑ Return to the Bourse via the **rue Antoine Dansaert,** which has lately become a trendy shopping street with boutiques and galleries.

TIME OUT **Le Pain Quotidien** (rue Antoine Dansaert 16) is open all day and serves superior sandwiches on crusty bread, salads, and cakes at a communal table.

Parc du Cinquantenaire and Bois de la Cambre

㉒ To see the **European Commission** headquarters at the Rond Point Schuman, take the metro (Line 1) from the center. The vast 13-story cruciform building is now undergoing restoration to remove asbestos ceilings and partitions. The Council offices are nearby. The new European Parliament building is a couple of blocks away on Rue Wiertz. Near it is the **Musée des Sciences Naturelles** (Museum of Natural Sciences), recently spruced up, which features a great collection of iguanodon dinosaurs and many imaginative displays. *Rue Vautier 29, tel. 02/627–42–33. Admission: BF120. Open Tues.–Sat. 9:30–4:45, Sun. 9:30–6.*

㉓ The **Cinquantenaire** is a huge, decorative archway, built in 1905 in a pleasant park. The buildings on either side of the archway house the **Musées Royaux d'Art et d'Histoire** (Royal Museums of Art and History). Displays include Greek, Roman, and Egyptian artifacts and toys. Large-scale changing exhibitions are also mounted here. *Parc du Cinquantenaire 10, tel. 02/741–72–11. Admission free. Open weekdays 9:30–5, weekends 10–5.*

The new **Autoworld Museum,** also in the Cinquantenaire, has one of the world's handsomest collections of vintage cars. *Parc du Cinquan-*

tenaire 11, tel. 02/736–41–65. Admission: BF150. Open daily 10–6 (Nov.–Mar. until 5).

Waterloo

No history buff can visit Brussels without making the pilgrimage to the site of the **Battle of Waterloo,** where Napoléon was finally defeated on June 18, 1815. It is easily reached from the city and lies 19 kilometers (12 miles) to the south of the Forêt de Soignes; take a bus from place Rouppe or a train from Gare Centrale to Waterloo station.

Wellington's headquarters, now a museum, presents the complex battle through illuminated 3-D maps, scale models, and military memorabilia, including the general's personal belongings. Chaussée de Bruxelles 149, tel. 02/354–78–06. Admission: BF70. Open Apr.–Oct., daily 9:30–6:30; Nov.–Mar., daily 10:30–5.

Just south of town is the actual battlefield. Start at the **visitor center,** which has an audiovisual presentation that shows scenes of the battle. You can also book expert guides to take you around the battlefield. Route du Lion 252–254, tel. 02/385–19–12. Admission: BF300. Open Apr.–Oct., daily 9:30–6:30; Nov.–Mar., daily 10:30–4. Guides 1815: Route du Lion 250, tel. 02/385–06–25. 1 hr BF1,400; 3 hrs BF2,200.

Overlooking the battlefield is the **Butte de Lion,** a pyramid-shape monument erected by the Dutch. After climbing 226 steps, you will be rewarded with a great view of the site.

TIME OUT For a lunch of authentic Belgian cuisine, try the **Bivouac de l'Empereur,** an attractive 1720s farmhouse close to the Butte de Lion. Route de Lion 315, tel. 02/384-67-40. AE, DC, MC, V. $$

Off the Beaten Track

The **Atomium** is the trademark of Brussels, visible from all over the city. Erected in the hopeful 1950s as a symbol of science, it is an iron crystal molecule magnified 160 billion times, and from the highest sphere you have a panoramic view of Brussels. The structure also houses a futuristic medical exhibition, **"Biogenium."** Blvd. du Centenaire, tel. 02/477–09–77. Metro: Heysel. Admission: BF160. Open daily 9:30–6 (July and Aug. until 9:30).

In the same area are the **Brussels Trade Mart** and **Heysel Stadium,** the latter currently under renovation. Here, too, is Bruparck, including Kinepolis (a 26-cinema complex) and **Mini-Europe,** a great family attraction comprising 300 models (on a 1:25 scale) of famous European buildings and monuments. Blvd. du Centenaire 20, tel. 02/478–05–50. Admission: BF370. Open daily 10–6 (July–Aug. until 8).

The **Maison d'Erasme** is a beautifully restored 15th-century house where Erasmus, the great humanist, lived in 1521. Every detail of this atmospheric house is authentic, with period furniture, paintings by Holbein, Dürer, and Hieronymous Bosch, and early editions of Erasmus's works, including In Praise of Folly. Rue du Chapitre 31, tel. 02/521–13–83. Metro: Saint-Guidon. Admission: BF50. Open Wed.–Thurs. and Sat.–Mon., 10–noon and 2–5.

The **Centre Belge de la Bande Dessinée** (Belgian Comic-Strip Center) celebrates the comic strip, emphasizing such famous Belgian graphic artists as Hergé, Tintin's creator. Hergé pioneered the ligne claire, a simple, bold style of drawing. The display is housed in Victor Horta's splendid Art Nouveau building, once a department store. Rue des

Sables 20, tel. 02/219–19–80. Metro: Botanique; Trams 92, 93. Admission: BF150. Open Tues.–Sun. 10–6.

The **Musée Horta** (Horta Museum) was until 1919 the home of the Belgian master of Art Nouveau, Victor Horta. From attic to cellar, every detail of the house displays the exuberant curves of Art Nouveau style. Horta, who designed the house for himself, wanted to put nature back into daily life. Here his floral motifs give a sense of opulence and spaciousness where little space exists. *Rue Américain 25, tel. 02/537–16–92. Tram 92 or Bus 60. Admission: BF100. Open Tues.–Sat. 2–5:30.*

Shopping

Gift Ideas

CHOCOLATE

For "everyday" chocolate, try the Côte d'Or variety, available in any chocolate shop or larger store. For delicious pralines—rich chocolates filled with fruit, liqueur, or nuts—try the brands made by Godiva, Neuhaus, or Leonidas, available at shops scattered throughout the city. Godiva is the best known, Neuhaus the best-tasting, and Leonidas the best value for money. Exclusive handmade pralines can be bought at **Wittamer** (Grand Sablon 12–16) and **Nihoul** (av. Louise 300).

CRYSTAL

The Val-St-Lambert mark is the only guarantee of handblown, hand-carved lead crystal tableware. You can buy it in many stores, including **Art and Selection** (rue Marché-aux-Herbes 83) near the Grand' Place.

LACE

To avoid disappointment, ask the store assistant outright whether the lace is handmade Belgian or made in the Far East. As preparation, visit the **Lace Museum** (rue de la Violette 6, near the Grand' Place). **La Maison F. Rubbrecht,** on the Grand' Place, sells authentic, handmade Belgian lace. For a large choice of old and modern lace, try **Manufacture Belge de Dentelles** (Galerie de la Reine 6–8).

Shopping Districts

For boutiques and stores, the main districts are in the **ville basse** (low town), the **Galeries St-Hubert** (luxury goods or gift items), **rue Neuve** (inexpensive clothes), and **City 2** and the **Anspach Center** (large shopping malls). In City 2, **FNAC** is a cherished French institution: As well as being an outlet for books, records, cameras, and stereo equipment at the best prices in town, it is also a cultural and exhibition center.

You'll find designer names and department stores (such as **Sarmalux**) in the **ville haute** (high town). **Avenue Louise** is its center, complete with the arcades **Galerie Louise** and **Espace Louise,** while the **Galerie de la Toison d'Or** branches off from the appropriately named street of the Golden Fleece! To offset prices, many of these stores offer sales-tax refunds (*see* Shopping *in* Staying in Belgium, *above*). The **place du Grand Sablon** is an equally expensive but more charming shopping district. This is the center for antiques, small art galleries, and designer shops. Around the Sablon and its neighboring streets, **rue des Minimes** and **rue Lebeau,** it is possible to buy anything from Oriental rugs and African primitives to 18th-century paintings and Art Nouveau.

Markets

On Saturday (9–5) and Sunday (9–1), the Sablon square is transformed into an **antiques market.** The **flower market** (Tues.–Sun. 8–4) on the Grand' Place is a colorful diversion, as is the Sunday-morning **bird market** in the same square. **Midi Market** is far more exotic (by the Gare du

Midi train station). On Sunday (5 AM–1 PM) the whole area becomes a colorful souk as the city's large North African community gathers to buy and sell exotic foods and household goods. The **Vieux Marché** (Old Market) in place du Jeu de Balle is a flea market worth visiting for the authentic atmosphere of the working-class Marolles district. The market is open daily 7–2. To make real finds, get there as early in the morning as you can.

Dining

Brussels is proud of its foreign restaurants as well as those serving hearty Belgian dishes: Chefs from at least 50 countries work in the city, and many Asian restaurants provide a tasty and inexpensive alternative to European fare. The local cuisine is an imaginative variant of French cuisine. The ambience tends to be formal, dignified, and old-fashioned in the more exclusive restaurants and cozy or jovial in the simpler brasseries or bistros. Servings are plentiful everywhere.

For details and price-category definitions, *see* Dining *in* Staying in Belgium, *above.*

$$$$ **Comme Chez Soi.** Pierre Wynants, the perfectionist owner-chef, has dec-
★ orated the restaurant in art-nouveau style. Inventive French cuisine, an excellent wine list, and attentive service complement the warm decor. Specialties include fillets of sole with a white wine mousseline and shrimp; saddle of young rabbit with lemon and basil; venison; partridge; and pheasant. Many dishes are served for a minimum of two persons. Tables for two are very close together. You need to make reservations at least a couple of months ahead. *Pl. Rouppe, tel. 02/512–29–21, fax 02/511–80–52. Reservations required. Jacket and tie. AE, DC, MC, V. Closed Sun., Mon., July, and Christmas–New Year's.*

$$$$ **L'Ecailler du Palais Royal.** This fish restaurant just off the Grand Sablon seems more like a comfortable club, and many of the clients seem to have known each other and the staff for years. Risotto of prawns in champagne, baked lobster custard, and the best turbot you're likely to taste for a long time are among the delicacies on offer. There's no prix-fixe menu. *Rue Bodenbroek 18, tel. 02/512–87–51. Reservations required. Jacket and tie. AE, DC, MC, V. Closed Easter wk and Aug.*

$$$$ **Maison du Cygne.** With decor to match its classical cuisine, this restaurant is set in a 17th-century guildhall on the Grand' Place. The formal dining room upstairs features paneled walls hung with old masters, and a small room on the mezzanine floor contains two priceless Brueghels. Service is flawless in the grand manner of old. Typical French-Belgian dishes include *lotte aux blancs de poireaux,* a monkfish-and-leeks specialty. *Rue Charles Buyls 2, tel. 02/511–82–44. Reservations required. Jacket and tie. AE, DC, MC, V. Closed Sun. No lunch Sat.*

$$$ **Castello Banfi.** On the Grand Sablon, in beige-and-brown postmodern surroundings, you can enjoy classic dishes with small added refinements such as toasted pine nuts with the pesto. There's excellent carpaccio with Parmesan and celery, red mullet with ratatouille, and unbelievable mascarpone. The quality of the ingredients (sublime olive oil, milk-fed veal imported from France) is very high. *Rue Bodenbroek 12, tel. 02/512–87–94. Reservations advised. Jacket and tie. AE, DC, MC, V. Closed Mon. and second half of Aug. No dinner Sun.*

$$$ **Michel Meyers.** Only seafood is served in this tiny restaurant just off the fish market, which has been enlarged to serve all of 18 diners. The eponymous owner-chef is alone in the kitchen and goes to the nearby market twice daily for the freshest products of the sea. Don't hesitate to take the menu he proposes. It might consist of smoked salmon paté, lobster with five spices, medallion of monkfish with fresh garlic, and a dessert prepared by Madame la Patronne. *Pl. du Samedi 18, tel. 02/219–26–16. Reservations advised. AE, V. Closed Sun. and mid-July–mid-Aug.*

$$$ **Ogenblik.** With green-shaded lamps over marble-top tables, sawdust on the floor, ample servings, and a great ambience, Ogenblik is a true bistro. The long and imaginative menu changes frequently, but generally, includes such specialties as mille-feuille with lobster and salmon, and saddle or leg of lamb with fresh, young vegetables. *Galerie des Princes 1, tel. 02/511–61–51. No reservations after 8 PM. AE, DC, MC, V. Closed Sun.*

$$ **Aux Armes de Bruxelles.** This restaurant is one of the few to escape the "tourist trap" label in this hectic little street. Inside, a lively atmosphere fills three rooms: The most popular section overlooks the street theater outside, but locals prefer the cozy rotunda. Specialties include waterzooi *de volaille* (a rich chicken stew) and *moules au vin blanc* (mussels in white wine). *Rue des Bouchers 13, tel. 02/511–21–18. Reservations advised. AE, DC, MC, V. Closed Mon. and June.*

$$ **Brasserie Georges.** This hugely successful restaurant, open every day until past midnight, was the first of its kind in Brussels and is still the best. The brasserie formula calls for a splendid display of shellfish at the entrance, an art deco interior with tile floor and potted plants, fast and friendly service by waitresses in black and white, and traditional fare such as *choucroute* (sauerkraut), poached cod, and *confit de canard* (potted duck). *Av. Winston Churchill 259, tel. 02/347–21–00. Reservations advised. AE, DC, MC, V.*

$$ **La Quincaillerie.** The name means "the hardware store"—and the character has been retained, with tables perched on the balcony and a zinc oyster bar downstairs. The three-course *menu du patron* is a bargain. Excellent game dishes are nicely presented by staff members who, like the clientele, are young and pleasant. *Rue du Page 45, tel. 02/538–25–53. Reservations advised. AE, DC, MC, V.*

$ **Au Vieux Saint Martin.** When neighboring eateries on Grand Sablon are empty, this one remains busy, and you're equally welcome whether you order a full meal or a cup of coffee. The short menu features Belgian specialties, and portions are huge. Wines are sold by the glass or bottle. The walls are hung with bright contemporary paintings, and picture windows front on the pleasant square. *Grand Sablon 38, tel. 02/512–64–76. Open daily noon to midnight. No reservations. No credit cards.*

$ **Chez Leon.** Even though prices have been edging upward lately, this 100-year-old restaurant continues to do land-office business and has over the years expanded into a row of eight old houses. Heaping plates of mussels and other Belgian specialties, like eels in a green sauce, are served nonstop from noon to midnight. Chez Leon also offers a mean *filet américain* (steak tartare to you) and arguably the best french fries in town. *Rue des Bouchers 18, tel. 02/511–14–15. No reservations. AE, DC, MC, V.*

$ **Falstaff.** Some things never change, and Falstaff is one of them. This huge tavern, with an interior that is pure Art Nouveau, fills up for lunch and keeps going until 5 AM, with an ever-changing crowd from students to pensioners. Cheerful waitresses punch in your orders for onion soup, filet mignon, salads, and other straightforward dishes on electronic order pads. Falstaff II at No. 25 has the same food but not the ambience. *Rue Henri Maus 19, tel. 02/511–87–89. Reservations advised. AE, DC, MC, V.*

Lodging

The annual hotel guide published by Tourist Information Brussels provides reliable and up-to-date information on prices and services. You can obtain a copy by writing to TIB (Hôtel de Ville, B-1000 Brussels). In general, finding accommodations is not difficult; there has been a boom in hotel construction. Substantial weekend and summer rebates are available in many hotels; be sure to check when you book. The main hotel districts are in the Grand' Place area and around the avenue Louise shopping district. Avoid the cheap hotel districts near the Gare du Midi and Gare du Nord train stations. Hotels can be booked at the tourist office on the Grand' Place (tel. 02/513-89-40), and a deposit is required (deductible from the final hotel bill).

For details and price-category definitions, *see* Lodging *in* Staying in Belgium, *above*.

$$$$ **Conrad.** Opened in 1993, The Conrad seeks to combine the European grand hotel tradition with American taste and amenities and does a fine job. Rooms come in many different shapes but are uniformly spacious, with three telephones, bathrobes, and in-room checkout. The Maison de Maître restaurant is getting good notices in the gourmet press, and the large bar is pleasantly clublike. *Av. Louise 71, tel. 02/542-42-42, fax 02/542-43-42. 268 rooms with bath. Facilities: 2 restaurants, bar, conference facilities, parking. AE, DC, MC, V.*

$$$$ **Hilton International.** The 27-story Hilton was one of the first high- rises in Brussels back in the '60s and remains a distinctive landmark. Corner rooms are the most desirable. The top-floor restaurant, Plein Ciel (lunch only), has a terrific city view. The second-floor Maison du Boeuf is outstanding, and the ground-floor Café d'Egmont highly popular. Centrally located, the hotel is next to the main luxury shopping area and overlooks the Parc d'Egmont. *Blvd. de Waterloo 38, tel. 02/504-11-11, fax 02/504-21-11. 420 rooms with bath, 30 suites. Facilities: 2 restaurants, coffee shop, bar, health club, sauna, solarium. AE, DC, MC, V.*

$$$$ **Radisson SAS.** This 1990 hotel, a few minutes' walk through the Ga-
★ lerie de la Reine from Grand' Place, has guest rooms decorated in different styles: Scandinavian, Asian, Italian, and art deco. A portion of the city wall from 1134 forms part of the atrium. The Sea Grill has become one of the city's top seafood restaurants. Rooms for non-smokers and for guests with disabilities are available. Travelers age 65 or older qualify for discounts of at least 65%; children under 15 stay free. *Rue du Fossé-aux-Loups 47, tel. 02/219-28-28, fax 02/219-62-62. 281 rooms with bath. Facilities: 3 restaurants, 2 bars, valet parking, fitness center, in-room checkout, airline check-in, business center, meeting rooms. AE, DC, MC, V.*

$$$ **Amigo.** This world-famous, family-owned hotel, off the Grand' Place,
★ was built in the 1950s but has the charm of an older age. No one would guess that it stands on the former site of the city prison. Each room is individually decorated, often in silk, velvet, and brocades. A 1993 refurbishment has smartened up bedrooms and public rooms. The bar is very pleasant, though the restaurant is not memorable. Room rates vary considerably, with the less expensive options being on lower floors. *Rue d'Amigo 1, tel. 02/547-47-47, fax 02/513-52-77. 183 rooms with bath. Facilities: restaurant, bar, parking. AE, DC, MC, V.*

$$$ **Metropole.** A major restoration has returned the Metropole to the palace it was during the Belle Epoque. The lobby sets the tone, with its high coffered ceiling, chandeliers, and Oriental rugs. The theme extends seamlessly to the bar with its deep leather sofas, to the gourmet restaurant, and to the café, which opens onto a heated terrace on the place Brouckère. Most guest rooms have been discreetly done over in pastel shades and art-deco style, but the very high ceilings can be disconcerting. *Place de Brouckère 31, tel. 02/217–23–00, fax 02/218–02–20. 410 rooms with bath. Facilities: restaurant, bar, café, conference rooms, fitness room, airport shuttle. AE, DC, MC, V.*

\$\$\$ **Sofitel.** Opened in 1989, the six-floor Sofitel has a great location in the heart of a chic shopping district. There's even a boutique-lined arcade on the ground floor, and you reach the lobby on an escalator. Public rooms and bedrooms are decorated in warm brown and beige tones. Bathroom telephones and bathrobes are standard. The restaurant, at the back of the lobby, is good and getting better. *Av. de la Toison d'Or 40, tel. 02/514–22–00, fax 02/514–57–44. 171 rooms with bath. Facilities: restaurant, bar. AE, DC, MC, V.*

\$\$ **Alfa Louise.** Opened in 1994 on the prestigious avenue Louise, this hotel has large rooms with office-size desks and a sitting areas. Bathrobes and room safes are additional conveniences. There's a jazz piano bar off the lobby, but no restaurant. *Av. Louise 212, tel. 02/644–29–29, fax 02/644–18–78. 40 rooms with bath. Facilities: bar/breakfast room, small conference rooms, parking. AE, DC, MC, V.*

\$\$ **Cadettt.** This 1991 addition to the Swiss Mövenpick chain does spell its name with three *t*s. The large, bright rooms have blond wood furniture, modem jacks, and La-Z-Boy chairs. The atrium bar and restaurant serves ample Swiss breakfasts and a limited selection of specialties for lunch and dinner. The Caveau wine bar offers wine tasting and light snacks. *Rue Paul Spaak 15, tel. 02/645–61–11, fax 02/646–63–11. 128 rooms with bath. Facilities: restaurant, bars, café, sauna, fitness room, no-smoking rooms, parking. AE, DC, MC, V.*

\$\$ **Manos Stéphanie.** The Louis XV furniture, marble lobby, and plenti-
★   ful antiques set a standard of elegance rarely encountered in a hotel in this price category. Even the corridors are decorated with paintings and mirrors. This 1992 hotel occupies a converted town house, and most rooms have good-size sitting areas. Avenue Louise is just a few minutes' walk away. *Chaussée de Charleroi 28, tel. 02/539–02–50, fax 02/537–57–29. 55 rooms with bath. Facilities: restaurant, bar, parking. AE, DC, MC, V.*

\$ **Matignon.** Only the Belle Epoque facade of this family-owned-and-operated hotel, opposite the Bourse and a couple of blocks from the Grand' Place, was preserved when it was converted into a hotel in 1993. The lobby is tiny to make room for the large café/brasserie. Rooms are small but have large beds. The five duplex suites are a good value for families. *Rue de la Bourse 10, tel. 02/511–08–88, fax 02/513–69–27. 17 rooms with bath, 5 suites. Facilities: bar, restaurant (closed Mon.). AE, DC, MC, V.*

\$ **Mozart.** The entrance to the Mozart, which opened in 1993, is between two Greek pita joints; the reception is up a flight of stairs. The lack of an elevator is a drawback, but the spacious, oak-beam rooms, in shades of salmon, are attractive; each has a refrigerator and a shower. Complimentary breakfast is served in a cozy nook. The multilingual Moroccan owner, Ben, and his Swedish wife also own the remarkably inexpensive restaurant Boccaccio across the street. *Rue Marché aux Fromages 15a, tel. 02/502–66–61, fax 02/502–77–58. 23 rooms with bath. Facilities: breakfast room. AE, DC, MC, V.*

\$ **Welcome/Truite d'Argent.** Among the charms of the smallest hotel in
★   Brussels are the young owners, Michel and Sophie Smeesters. The six rooms, with king- or queen-size beds, are as comfortable as those in far more expensive establishments. This little hotel is much in demand, so book early. There's a downstairs breakfast-room-cum-dining room for

hotel guests, while the rather expensive Silver Trout around the corner on the fish market serves excellent seafood. *Rue du Peuplier 5, tel. 02/219–95–46, fax 02/217–18–87. 6 rooms with bath. Facilities: 2 restaurants, garage, seminar rooms. AE, DC, MC, V.*

The Arts

The best way to find out what's going on is to buy a copy of the English-language weekly magazine *The Bulletin*. It's published every Thursday and sold at newsstands for BF80.

Music

Major classical music concerts are generally held at the **Palais des Beaux-Arts** (rue Ravenstein 23, tel. 02/507–82–00). Alternatively, there are many free Sunday morning concerts at various churches, including the **Cathédrale St-Michel et Ste-Gudule** and the **Petite Église des Minimes** (rue des Minimes 62). Major rock and pop concerts are given at **Forest National** (av. du Globe 36, tel. 02/347–03–55).

Opera and Dance

The national opera company is based at the **Théâtre Royal de la Monnaie** (pl. de la Monnaie, tel. 02/218–12–02). The Monnaie is an attractive opera house, and its productions are of international quality. Tickets cost from BF500 to BF2,000 and are very hard to come by. Touring dance and opera companies often play at the **Cirque Royal** (rue de l'Enseignement 81, tel. 02/218–20–15).

Theater

At Brussels's 30 theaters, actors perform in French, Flemish, and occasionally in English. The loveliest theater is the **Théâtre Royal du Parc** (in Parc de Bruxelles at rue de la Loi 3, tel. 02/512–23–39), which has productions of Molière and other French classics. Avant-garde theater is performed at the enterprising **Théâtre Varia** (rue du Sceptre 78, tel. 02/640–82–58) and **Théâtre de Poche** (in Bois de la Cambre at Chemin du Gymnase, tel. 02/649–17–27). Puppet theater is a Belgian experience not to be missed. In Brussels, visit the intimate **Théâtre Toone VII** (impasse Schuddeveld, petite rue des Bouchers 21, tel. 02/511–71–37). In this atmospheric medieval house, satirical plays are performed in a Bruxellois dialect.

Film

Movies are mainly shown in their original language, so many are in English. **The Acropole** (Galeries de la Toison d'Or, tel. 077/34–97–30), the new **UCG** complex (pl. de Brouckère, tel. 077/34–97–30), and the multiscreen **Kinepolis** (av. du Centenaire 1, tel. 077/23–35–10) feature comfortable armchairs and first-run movies. For unusual movies or screen classics, visit the **Musée du Cinéma** (Cinema Museum; rue Baron Horta 9, tel. 02/507–83–70). Five movies are shown daily, for only BF80 each (BF50 if you buy tickets 24 hours in advance). Complete listings are published in *The Bulletin* and newspapers.

Nightlife

Disco

Griffin's (rue Duquesnoy 5, tel. 02/505–55–55) at the Royal Windsor Hotel appeals to young adults and business travelers. **Le Mirano** (chaussée de Louvain 38, tel. 02/218–57–72) attracts a self-styled jet set (Sat. only), while **Le Garage** (rue Duquesnoy 16, tel. 02/512–66–22) draws a younger crowd. The trendy favor **Jeux d'Hiver,** a members-only club in the Bois de la Cambre (Thurs. and Sat.); you'll be admitted if you look the part. In all of the above, the action starts at midnight.

Bars

The diversity is greater here than in many other European capitals. These are just a few of the best: **La Fleur en Papier Doré** (rue des Aléxiens 53, tel. 02/511–16–59) is a quiet bar that attracts an artistic audiences. **Cirio** (rue de la Bourse 18, tel. 02/512–13–95) is a pleasant bar with nice decor. **Rick's Café** (av. Louise 344, tel. 02/647–75–30) is as popular with homesick Americans as it is with the British expatriate community. It serves fairly expensive American and Tex-Mex food. **De Ultieme Hallucinatie** (rue Royale 316, tel. 02/217–06–14) is another popular Art Nouveau bar and restaurant that serves imaginative cocktails, a full range of beers, and a short but appealing menu. **Henry J. Bean's** (rue du Montagne-aux-Herbes-Potagères 40, tel. 02/219–28–28) is a 1950s-style bar and grill.

Jazz

Among the best venues are **Travers** (rue Traversière 11, tel. 02/218–40–86), **Preservation Hall** (Place de Londres 4, tel. 02/502–15–97), and **Sounds** (Rue de la Tulipe 28, tel. 02/512–92–50).

ANTWERP

Arriving and Departing

By Plane

Antwerp International Airport lies just 3 kilometers (2 miles) southeast of the city. For flight information, call 03/218–12–11. Antwerp is served by a small number of flights from neighboring countries. Most passengers arrive via Brussels National Airport (Zaventem), which is linked with Antwerp by hourly bus service (50 minutes one-way).

BETWEEN THE AIRPORT AND DOWNTOWN

Buses bound for Antwerp's Centraalstation (Central Station) leave about every 20 minutes; travel time is around 15 minutes. Taxis are readily available as well.

By Train

Express trains run between Antwerp and Brussels; the trip takes 35 minutes. There are four trains an hour in both directions. Central Station is at Koningin Astridplein 27 (tel. 03/233–39–15).

By Car

Several major highways converge on Antwerp's inner-city ring expressway. It's a 10-lane racetrack, so be sure you maneuver into the correct lane well before you exit. Antwerp is an easy 45-kilometer (28-mile) drive from Brussels on E19.

Getting Around

By Streetcar

In the downtown area, the streetcar (or tram) is the best, and most common, means of transportation. Some lines have been rebuilt underground (look for signs marked M); the most useful line runs between Central Station (metro stop Diamant) and the Groenplaats (for the cathedral). A single ride costs BF40, a 10-ride ticket BF250, and a day pass BF100. For detailed transportation maps, stop at the tourist office.

Guided Tours

Orientation tours by minibus (50 minutes) depart from the Grote Markt daily at 2, 3, and 4 (mid-Nov. to mid-Mar., weekends only). Tickets (BF330 adults, BF200 children) are sold on the bus. The tourist office operates a **Guide's Exchange** and, with a week's notice, is able to meet most requirements for city guides. Guides charge BF600 an hour, with a minimum of two hours.

Tourist Information

The **Toerisme Stad Antwerpen** (Antwerp City Tourist Office) is near the cathedral (Grote Markt 15, tel. 03/232–01–03, fax 03/231–19–37). It is open Monday–Saturday 9–6, Sunday 9–5. Ask for their booklet on self-guided tours, which includes the famous "Rubens Walk." Various other popular walks are signposted throughout the city.

Exploring Antwerp

Antwerp, lying on the Scheldt River 50 kilometers (31 miles) north of Brussels, is the world's fifth-largest port and the main city of Belgium's Flemish region. Its name, according to legend, is derived from *handwerpen,* or "hand throwing." It seems a Roman soldier once cut off the hand of a malevolent giant and flung it into the river; his feat is commemorated by a statue on the Grote Markt. In the 16th century, Emperor Charles V made Antwerp the world's most important trading center, and during the 17th century Rubens and other painters made their city an equally important center of the arts. Enterprising craftspeople began practicing diamond-cutting at about this time, and the city is still a world leader in the diamond trade. Antwerp's year as the Cultural Capital of Europe (1993) resulted in a much-improved cultural infrastructure.

Numbers in the margin correspond to points of interest on the Antwerp map.

1 Antwerp's **Centraalstation** (Central Station) is a good place to start exploring the city. This elegant neoclassical building, impeccably restored, was built early in this century as a virtual "railway cathedral."

2 To the east of the station is **Antwerp Zoo,** a huge, well-designed complex that includes a winter garden, a planetarium, a good restaurant, and a natural history museum. *Koningin Astridplein 26, tel. 03/231–16–40. Admission: BF390 adults, BF240 children. Open July–Aug., daily 8:30–6:30; Sept.–Feb., daily 9–5; Mar.–June, daily 8:30–6.*

Near Central Station, along the Pelikaanstraat and the streets running off it, lies the **Diamond Quarter.** You can visit the spectacular show**3** rooms of **Diamondland** to see both rough and polished diamonds, slide shows and films illustrating the history of the industry, and diamond cutters at work. Stones purchased here are accompanied by a Diamond High Council guarantee. *Appelmansstraat 33a, tel. 03/234–36–12. Admission free. Open Mon.–Sat. 9:30–5:30.*

The **Provinciaal Diamantmuseum** (Provincial Diamond Museum), farther along the same street, has three floors of maps, models, and videos about the diamond trade, besides a treasure room of jewelry. *Lange Herentalsestraat 31-33, tel. 03/202–48–90. Admission free. Open daily 10–5; cutting demonstrations Sat. afternoon.*

The broad De Keyserlei leads west from the train station to the main
4 shopping area, the **Meir.** South of the Meir, on Wapper, is **Rubenshuis**

(Rubens's House). The artist lived here from 1610 until his death in 1640. It is a patrician's home, enriched with paintings by Rubens and his contemporaries. *Wapper 9, tel. 03/232–47–51. Admission: BF75. Open Tues.–Sun. 10–4:45.*

On Meir, turn left at the **Torengebouw,** which Antwerpers claim to be Europe's first skyscraper, and you find yourself in a shopping district where the tone is set by the Antwerp Six, pioneers of "grunge" fash-
❺ ion. A few blocks south is the **Museum Mayer van den Bergh,** whose masterpiece is Brueghel's *Dulle Griet* (often referred to in English as "Mad Meg"), a powerful antiwar allegory that may be his greatest work. *Lange Gasthuisstraat 19, tel. 03/232–42–37. Admission: BF75. Open Tues.–Sun. 10–4:45.*

Turn back, and let yourself be guided by its white, 400-foot spire to
❻ the **Onze-Lieve-Vrouwekathedraal** (Cathedral of Our Lady), the largest church in the Low Countries. It is an inspiring Gothic monument, with four Rubens altarpieces among its art treasures. *Groenplaats 21, tel. 03/231–30–33. Admission: BF60. Open weekdays 10–5, Sat. 10–3, Sun. 1–4.*

The **Grote Markt,** flanked by the 16th-century city hall and surrounded by old guild houses, is just a few steps north of the cathedral. The area north of the square, with its narrow streets, churches, and old merchants' houses, is the heart of old Antwerp.

Returning to the cathedral, walk the short distance west along the Suik-
❼ errui to the river. To your right is the fortresslike **Steen,** the oldest building in Antwerp. From the terraces around the Steen, you can see the main port installations. For a close look, a 2½-hour **boat excursion** (from Easter to late September) around the port leaves from Quay 13 on weekdays and from the Steen Landing stage on Sunday. *Cost: BF375 adults, BF240 children. Information from N.V. Flandria, Steenplein 1, tel. 03/231–31–00.*

Walking along the river south of the Steen, you come to a foot tunnel,
❽ the **St. Annatunnel,** leading to the left bank of the river. Turn east and explore St. Jans Vliet, Hoogstraat, and Reyndersstraat, an area of old Antwerp full of shops, authentic bars, and excellent restaurants. Via
❾ Helig Geeststraat you reach Vrijdagmarkt and the **Plantin-Moretus Museum,** a famous printing works founded in the 16th century. The building is a fine example of Renaissance architecture and is magnificently furnished. Among its treasures are many first editions, engravings, and a copy of Gutenberg's Bible. Plantin was printer to Emperor Charles V, and his workshop produced thousands of liturgical books. The presses are still in working order, and you can purchase a copy of Plantin's "Ode to Happiness" printed on one of them. *Vrijdagmarkt 22, tel. 03/233–02–94. Admission: BF75. Open Tues.–Sun. 10–4:45.*

From the Plantin, walk through the Vrijdagmarkt and up the Oude
❿ Koornmarkt to the Groenplaats and catch Tram 8 to the **Koninklijk Museum voor Schone Kunsten** (Royal Museum of Fine Arts). It lies in the southern part of the old city and contains more than 1,500 paintings by old masters, including magnificent works by Rubens, Van Dyck, Hals, and Brueghel. The second floor houses one of the best collections of paintings by Flemish Primitives of the 15th and 16th centuries; the first floor has more modern paintings. *Leopold de Waelplaats 1–9, tel. 03/238–78–09. Admission free. Open Tues.–Sun. 10–4:45.*

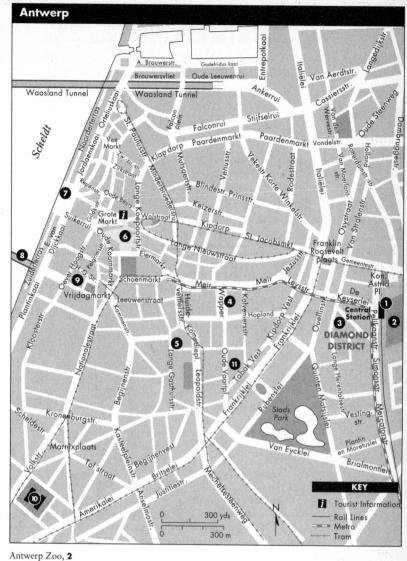

Antwerp Zoo, **2**

Centraalstation, **1**

Diamondland, **3**

Koninklijk Museum
voor Schone   Kun-
sten, **10**

Museum Mayer
van den Bergh, **5**

Onze-Lieve-
Vrouwekathedraal, **6**

Plantin-Moretus
Museum, **9**

Rubenshuis, **4**

St. Annatunnel, **8**

Steen, **7**

Vogelmarkt, **11**

⑪ On Sunday morning you can see the famous **vogelmarkt,** or bird market, a few blocks south of Rubenshuis on the Oude Vaartplaats. You'll find everything from domestic pets to plants, clothes, and food.

TIME OUT   More than 350 kinds of Belgian beer and 150 foreign brews are available in **Café Kulminator.** The beers are best accompanied by the excellent cheeses. *Vleminckveld 32, tel. 03/232–45–38. No credit cards. Closed Sun. $*

Dining

Local specialties include herring and eel dishes and *witloof* (endive) cooked in a variety of ways. As for drink, there are 20 local beers; a gin called *jenever*; and a strong liqueur, *Elixir d'Anvers*. For details and price-category definitions, *see* Dining *in* Staying in Belgium, *above*.

$$$$ **La Pérouse.** When the good ship *La Pérouse*, which carries tourists on pleasure trips in summer, ties up at the Steen for the winter season, it is converted into an outstanding restaurant. The emphasis is naturally on seafood, such as bass cooked in salt crust and served with saffron butter, but meat dishes are also excellent. *Steenplein, tel. 03/231–31–51. Reservations required. Jacket and tie. AE, DC, MC, V. Closed Sun., Mon., and May–mid-Sept.*

$$$ **De Matelote.** At a tiny restaurant in a small house down a narrow street,
★   the gifted chef concocts inventive dishes such as grilled asparagus with fresh morels and a poached egg, or langoustines in a light curry sauce. Local gourmets consider this the best fish restaurant in town. For dessert, try the outstanding crème brûlée. *Haarstraat 9, tel. 03/231–32–07. Reservations advised. Jacket and tie. AE, DC, MC, V. Closed Sun. and 3 wks in July. No lunch Mon. or Sat.*

$$$ **Petrus.** The prix-fixe theater menu at this small restaurant opposite the marvelous early 19th-century Bourla Theater is an especially good buy. One specialty is a terrine of duck's liver interleaved with *filet d'Anvers* (lightly smoked beef). The sliced, sautéed sea scallops on baked potato pancakes with olive oil and white truffles are a dream. *Kelderstraat 1, tel. 03/225–27–34. Reservations advised. Jacket and tie. AE, DC, MC, V. Closed Mon. and 2 wks in July. No lunch on weekends.*

$$ **Neuze Neuze.** Five tiny houses have been cobbled together to create
★   this handsome, split-level restaurant with whitewashed walls, dark brown beams, and a blazing fireplace. Warm smoked salmon with endive and a white beer sauce, scallops with rhubarb preserve, and monkfish rolls with caviar are some of the dishes executed with the flair of pricier establishments. *Wijngaardstraat 19, tel. 03/232–57–83. Reservations advised. AE, DC, MC, V. Closed Sun. and last 2 wks of July.*

$$ **Sir Anthony Van Dijck.** In 1992 the owner-chef cut prices in half, increased the number of tables, and introduced simpler, brasserie-type dishes based on less expensive products. Still, the food, including duck à a l'orange and tuna steak, is quite good, and the antiques-filled interior is appealing. *Vlaykensgang, Oude Koornmarkt 16, tel. 03/231–61–70. Reservations advised. Jacket and tie. AE, DC, MC, V. Closed Sun. and most of Aug.*

$ **Panaché.** At this Antwerp institution, you can savor the best sandwiches in town or, in the back room, simple but satisfying fare. *Statiestraat 17, tel. 03/232–69–05. No reservations. AE, DC, MC, V.*

$ **Zuiderterras.** A stark glass-and-black-metal construction, this riverside café and restaurant was designed by avant-garde architect bOb (his spelling) Van Reeth. Here you can have a light meal for about $15 and enjoy seeing the river traffic on one side and, on the other, a view of the cathedral and the old town. *Ernest Van Dijckkaai, tel. 03/234–12–75. No reservations. AE, DC, MC, V.*

Lodging

The city tourist office can reserve hotel rooms for you up to a week in advance for reduced prices. Write or fax for a reservation form. For details and price-category definitions, *see* Lodging *in* Staying in Belgium, *above.*

$$$$ De Rosier. A 17th-century mansion provides discreet luxury for the privileged few. Cloistered behind double doors on a narrow street, its presence announced only by a small brass plaque, De Rosier focuses instead on the aristocratic garden court and lavishly furnished interiors. Rooms vary from skylighted, modernized garrets to the beamed and leaded-glass Renaissance suite. *Rosier 21–23, tel. 03/225–01–40, fax 03/231–41–11. 12 rooms with bath. Facilities: breakfast room, garden terrace, indoor pool. AE, DC, MC, V.*

$$$$ Hilton. The newest contender among luxury hotels in Antwerp opened in 1993; its five stories are architecturally compatible with other buildings on Groenplaats. Afternoon tea is served in the marble-floor lobby; buffet breakfast, lunch, and dinner, in the Isabella and Helena restaurant, named for Rubens's two wives. Rooms are equipped with three telephones, safes, and desks. *Groenplaats, tel. 03/204–12–12, fax 03/204–12–13. 211 rooms with bath. Facilities: 2 restaurants, bar, sauna, fitness center, conference rooms, no-smoking floors, garage. AE, DC, MC, V.*

$$$ Alfa De Keyser. This well-maintained deluxe hotel is handily situated next to Central Station and near the diamond center. Ask for a room in the back, overlooking an AstroTurf "court." The restaurant prides itself on its adaptation of local ingredients to nouvelle cuisine. *De Keyserlei 66, tel. 03/234–01–35, fax 03/232–39–70. 117 rooms with bath. Facilities: restaurant, café, bar, nightclub, indoor pool, fitness center, sauna, parking. AE, DC, MC, V.*

$$ Firean. An Art Deco gem built in 1929 and restored in 1986, Firean offers the personal service of a family-owned and -operated hotel. Rooms are decorated in peaceful pastels, offset by rich fabrics. There's a tiny bar-cum-breakfast room, where eggs are brought to the table in floral-print cozies. The location is not central, but there's a tram to the old town outside the door. *Karel Oomsstraat 6, tel. 03/237–02–60, fax 03/238–11–68. 11 rooms plus 6 in annex next door, all with bath. Facilities: breakfast room-bar. AE, DC, MC, V. Closed first half of Aug. and Christmas Eve–weekend after Epiphany (Jan. 6).*

$$ Prinse. Opened in 1990, this hotel occupies a 400-year-old building surrounding an interior courtyard. Rooms are modern in decor; those on the top floor, with exposed beams, have more character. The Prinse offers peace and quiet, close to both sightseeing and shopping districts. *Keizerstraat 63, tel. 03/226–40–50, fax 03/225–11–48. 30 rooms with bath. Facilities: breakfast room, 3 conference rooms, parking. AE, DC, MC, V.*

$ Pension Cammerpoorte. In this simple but pleasant hotel, the rooms (some with a view of the cathedral) are full of bright pastels and sad-clown art. A buffet breakfast, included in the price, is served in the tidy brick-and-lace café downstairs. There's no elevator. *Steenhouwersvest 55, tel. 03/231–28–36, fax 03/226–29–68. 9 rooms with toilet and shower. Facilities: breakfast room. AE, DC, MC, V.*

$ Waldorf. This pleasant, modern hotel is near the diamond center. The smallish rooms are attractively decorated in gray and brown. *Belgielei*

36, tel. 03/230–99–50, fax 03/230–78–70. 100 rooms with bath. Facilities: restaurant, bar. AE, DC, MC, V.

BRUGGE

Arriving and Departing

By Train

Trains run hourly at 28 and 59 minutes past the hour from Brussels (Gare du Midi) to Brugge. The London–Brussels service stops here as well. The station is south of the canal that surrounds the downtown area; for train information, call 050/38–24–06. Travel time from Brussels is 53 minutes.

By Car

Brugge lies 97 kilometers (61 miles) northwest of Brussels. The most direct route between the two cities is the A10/E40.

Getting Around

The center of Brugge is best explored on foot, as car and bus access is restricted. **De Lijn** (tel. 078/11–36–63) has some minibuses in service. You can also rent bicycles; ask the tourist office for information.

By Horse-Drawn Cab

An expensive means of seeing the sights is provided by the horse-drawn cabs that congregate in the Burg square, March–November, daily 10–6. A 35-minute trip will cost BF800, and the cabs take as many as four people.

Guided Tours

Boat Trips

Boat trips along the city canals are run by several companies and depart from five separate landings. Boats ply the waters March–November, daily 10–6. They leave when enough people have gathered, but you'll never have to wait more than 15 minutes or so.

Orientation Tours

Fifty-minute minibus trips of the city center leave every hour on the hour from the Market Square in front of the post office. Tours are given in seven languages (individual headphones) and cost BF330, BF200 children.

Tourist Information

Toerism Brugge (Brugge Tourist Office) is on a central square (Burg 11, tel. 050/44–86–86).

Exploring Brugge

Brugge (also known by its French name, Bruges) is an exquisitely preserved medieval town. It had the good fortune to be linked with the sea by a navigable waterway, and the city became a leading member of the Hanseatic League in the 13th century. Brugge was ignored for centuries after the Zwin silted up in the 15th century, but this past misfortune is its present glory. Little has changed in this city of interlaced canals, overhung with humpback bridges. The Burg, an intimate medieval square, is the inspiring setting for summer classical concerts.

Numbers in the margin correspond to points of interest on the Brugge map.

❶ The best place to start a walking tour is the **Markt** (Market Square).

❷ From the top of the **Belfort** (Belfry) there's a panoramic view of the town. The belfry has a carillon notable even in Belgium, where they are a matter of civic pride. On summer evenings, the Markt is brightly lighted. *Belfort admission: BF100. Open Apr.–Sept., daily 9:30–5; Oct.–Mar., 9:30–12:30 and 1:30–5. Carillon concerts Oct.–mid-June, Wed. and weekends 2:15–3; mid-June–Sept., Mon., Wed., and Sat. 9–10 PM, Sun. 2:15–3.*

❸ On the eastern side of the Market Square stands the **Provinciaal Hof,** the neo-Gothic provincial government building. Walk east from the square along Breidelstraat, to the Burg, a square at the center of an-

❹ cient Brugge. On the left is the **Proostdijg** (Provost's House), built in

❺ 1665. Across the square is a row of magnificent buildings—the **Stadhuis** (town hall), dating from the 14th century, its wonderfully ornate

❻ facade covered with statues; **Oude Griffie,** the former Recorder's House dating from the 1530s, and also ornamented with impressive windows;

❼ and the **Heilig-Bloed Basiliek** (the Basilica of the Holy Blood), a double chapel consisting of a Romanesque 12th-century crypt and an upper chapel, rebuilt in Gothic style in the 15th century and decorated with 19th-century murals. In this chapel the relic of the Holy Blood is worshiped every Friday. Here, too, is a **Heilig-Bloed Museum** (Museum of the Holy Blood), with the reliquary and exhibits of vestments and paintings. The Procession of the Holy Blood on Ascension Day (May 16 in 1996) is a major pageant that combines religious and historical elements. *Stadhuis admission: BF60. Open Apr.–Sept., daily 9:30–5; Oct.–Mar., daily 9:30–12:30 and 2–5. Heilig-Bloed Museum admission: BF40. Open Apr.–Sept., daily 9:30–noon and 2–6; Oct.–Mar., daily 10–noon and 2–4. Closed Wed. afternoon.*

Walk through a passage between the town hall and the Oude Griffie

❽ and you'll come to the **Dijver,** the city canal. Canal boat trips leave from here. *Boats leave on demand. Average trip 30 minutes. Cost: BF150.*

Walking south along the Dijver, you'll soon reach a group of muse-

❾ ums. The **Groeninge Museum,** on the Dijver Canal, has a very rich, wide-ranging collection of Flemish masterpieces, with works by Van Eyck, Memling, Bosch, and Brueghel, among many others, plus some contemporary works. *Dijver 12, tel. 050/33–99–11. Admission: BF130; combination ticket for BF350 covers the Groeninge, Brangwyn, Gruuthuse, and Memling museums (see below). Open Apr.–Sept., daily 9:30–5; Oct.–Mar., Wed.–Mon. 9:30–12:30 and 2–5.*

The **Brangwyn Museum,** next door, is named for the artist Frank Brangwyn (1867–1956) and contains hundreds of his Brugge-inspired works, as well as a fine collection of old lace. *Dijver 16, tel. 050/33–99–11. Admission: BF130. Open Apr.–Sept., daily 9:30–5; Oct.–Mar., Wed.–Mon. 9:30–noon and 2–5.*

❿ The **Gruuthuse Museum,** in the 15th century a palace of the aristocratic Gruuthuse family, contains archaeological exhibitions and a large collection of Flemish sculpture, paintings, furniture, and tapestries. *Dijver 17, tel. 050/33–99–11. Admission: BF130. Open Apr.–Sept., daily 9:30–5; Oct.–Mar., Wed.–Mon. 9:30–12:30 and 2–5.*

⓫ Here, too, is the **Memling Museum,** dedicated to the work of one of Brugge's most famous sons, the painter Hans Memling (?1440–94), perhaps the most spiritual of all the Flemish Primitives, housed in the former Sint Jans Hospital (Hospital of St. John), where the artist was nursed back to health after being wounded in France. *Mariastraat 38,*

Brugge

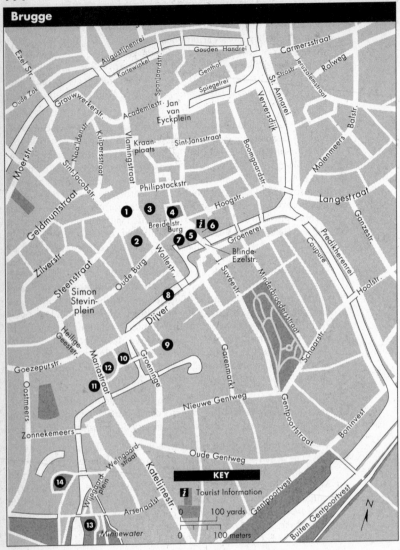

KEY

i Tourist Information

0 ———— 100 yards

0 ———— 100 meters

Begijnhof, **14**

Belfort, **2**

Dijver, **8**

Groeninge
Museum, **9**

Gruuthuse
Museum, **10**

Heilig–Bloed
Basiliek, **7**

Markt, **1**

Memling
Museum, **11**

Minnewater, **13**

Onze-Lieve-
Vrouwekerk, **12**

Oude Griffie, **6**

Proostdijg, **4**

Provinciaal Hof, **3**

Stadhuis, **5**

tel. 050/33–25–62. Admission: BF130. Open Apr.–Sept., daily 9:30–5; Oct.–Mar., Thurs.–Tues. 9:30–12:30 and 2–5.

⓬ Next to the Memling Museum is the **Onze-Lieve-Vrouwekerk** (Church of Our Lady), with, at 381 feet, the highest tower in Belgium, a notable collection of paintings and carvings—especially Michelangelo's small *Madonna*—and some splendidly colorful tombs. *Admission to mausoleum: BF30. Open Apr.–Sept., weekdays 10–11:30 and 2:30–5, Sun. 2:30–5; Oct.–Mar., weekdays 10–11:30 and 2:30–4:30, Sun. 2:30–4:30. Closed Sun. AM except to worshipers.*

TIME OUT Walk south on Katelijnestraat, turn right on the narrow Stoofstraat, and find yourself on Walplein, one of Brugge's many charming squares. Treat yourself to a **Straffe Hendrik** (Strong Henry) beer: crystal clear, natural, and indeed quite strong, at the eponymous brewery pub, or a snack at **Nieuw 't Walnutje** across the street.

⓭ Continue south to the enchanting **Minnewater** (Lake of Love Park). From the Minnewater visit the adjoining 16th-century lockkeeper's house, usually surrounded by contented white swans, the symbol of the city.

⓮ Beside Minnewater, a picturesque bridge leads to the **Begijnhof,** the former almshouses and the most serene spot in Brugge. Founded in 1245 by the countess of Constantinople, the Begijnhof was originally a home for widows of fallen Crusaders. These women took partial vows and lived a devout life while serving the community. Although the last Beguines left in 1930, a Benedictine community has replaced them. The Begijnhof has kept its cloistered charm.

Dining

For details and price-category definitions, *see* Dining *in* Staying in Belgium, *above.*

$$$$ **De Karmeliet.** One of Belgium's top culinary landmarks is in a lovely
★ 18th-century house. The talented chef serves up scallops of goose liver with truffled potatoes, turbot with bacon, crisp potato nests with Dublin Bay prawns, and fabulous desserts. *Langestraat 19, tel. 050/33–82–59. Reservations required. Jacket and tie. AE, DC, MC, V. Closed Mon. and 2 wks in Aug./Sept. No dinner Sun. No lunch Sun. in July and Aug.*

$$$ **'t Boergoensche Cruyce.** Claiming one of the most romantic canal-side
★ settings in Brugge, this restaurant has salmon-and-copper decor that is reflected in the water. The cuisine is equally romantic: lamb lightly flavored with fennel and cinnamon, delicate smoked halibut, saddle of hare. *Wollestraat 41, tel. 050/33–79–26. Reservations advised. Jacket and tie. AE, MC, V. Closed Tues., Feb., and mid-Nov.–mid-Dec. No lunch Wed.*

$$ **De Castillion.** The restaurant and hotel bears the name of Jean-Baptiste de Castillion, whose residence it was during the 18th century. Predinner drinks and postprandial coffee are served in a handsome Art Deco salon. Fillet of venison in a Pomerol stock, duck's liver, and a fricassée of turbot and wild salmon are among the offerings. The hotel side comprises 18 rooms and 2 suites. *Heilige Geeststraat 1, tel. 050/34–30–01, fax 050/33–94–75. Reservations advised. Jacket and tie. AE, DC, MC, V. Closed Tues. and first half of Jan.*

$ **Taverna Curiosa.** You have to descend a short but steep staircase to arrive at the cross-vaulted crypt. Snacks include very good omelets, sandwiches, and a smoked fish plate. *Vlamingstraat 22, tel. 050/34–23–34. No reservations. AE, MC, V. Closed Mon.*

Lodging

In proportion to its size, Brugge has a large number of hotels; in fact, many more than Antwerp. Prices are relatively high, but so are the standards. For details and price-category definitions, *see* Lodging *in* Staying in Belgium, *above.*

$$$ **De Tuileriëen.** A stately mansion with Venetian glass windows was con-
★   verted into this patrician hotel in 1988 and decorated with discreet antique reproductions. The bar is furnished with tartan wing chairs, and the breakfast room has a coffered ceiling. Canal-side rooms have great views; courtyard rooms are quieter. *Dijver 7, tel. 050/34–36–91, fax 050/34–04–00. 26 rooms with bath. Facilities: breakfast room, bar, indoor pool, whirlpool, sauna, solarium, parking. AE, DC, MC, V.*

$$$ **Holiday Inn Crowne Plaza.** This superbly located hotel has been successfully integrated into the heart of the city. The large, modern rooms are decorated in muted colors; the best ones have dark-wood ceiling beams. In the basement, next to the conference area, you can see remnants of the old ramparts, and a small museum contains objects found during construction. *Burg 10, tel. 050/34–58–34, fax 050/34–56–15. 96 rooms with bath. Facilities: restaurant, bar, fitness center, sauna, solarium, swimming pool. AE, DC, MC, V.*

$$ **Egmond.** There are garden views from every room—as well as parquet floors and the odd fireplace or dormer ceiling—in this manorlike inn on Minnewater. The hotel is a pleasant retreat from the tourist bustle of the center, 10 minutes away. *Minnewater 15, tel. 050/34–14–45, fax 050/34–29–40. 9 rooms with bath. Facilities: breakfast room. AE, DC, MC, V.*

$ **De Pauw.** At this spotless, family-run hotel, the warmly furnished rooms have names rather than numbers, and breakfast comes with six different kinds of bread, cold cuts, and cheese. The two rooms that share a shower down the hall are a super value. *St. Gilliskerkhof 8, tel. 050/33–71–18, fax 050/34–51–40. 8 rooms, 6 with bath. AE, DC, MC, V.*

$ **Fevery.** In this friendly, comfortable hotel you are made to feel like a personal guest. Rooms were upgraded in 1993 with new carpets and fresh chenille. *Collaert Mansionstraat 3, tel. 050/33–12–69, fax 050/33–17–91. 11 rooms with bath. Facilities: bar. AE, DC, MC, V.*

5 Bulgaria

BULGARIA, A LAND OF MOUNTAINS and seascapes, of austerity and rustic beauty, lies in the eastern half of the Balkan peninsula. From the end of World War II until recently, it was the closest ally of the former Soviet Union and presented a rather mysterious image to the Western world. This era ended in 1989 with the overthrow of Communist party head Todor Zhivkov. Since then, Bulgaria has gradually opened itself to the West as it struggles along the path toward democracy and a free-market economy.

Endowed with long Black Sea beaches, the rugged Balkan range in its interior, and fertile Danube plains, Bulgaria has much to offer the tourist year-round. Its tourist industry is quite well developed and is being restructured to better shield visitors from shortages of goods and services and the other legacies of rigid central planning.

The Black Sea coast along the country's eastern border is particularly attractive, with secluded coves and old fishing villages, as well as wide stretches of shallow beaches that have been developed into self-contained resorts. The interior landscape offers great scenic beauty, and the traveler who enters it will find a tranquil world of forested ridges, spectacular valleys, and rural communities where folklore is a colorful part of village life.

Founded in 681, Bulgaria was a crossroads of civilization even before that date. Archaeological finds in Varna, on the Black Sea coast, give proof of civilization from as early as 4600 BC. Bulgaria was part of the Byzantine Empire from AD 1018 to 1185 and was occupied by the Turks from 1396 until 1878. The combined influences are reflected in Bulgarian architecture, which has a truly Eastern feel. Five hundred years of Muslim occupation and nearly half a century of communist rule did not wipe out Christianity, and there are many lovely, icon-filled churches to see. The 120 monasteries, with their icons and many frescoes, provide a chronicle of the development of Bulgarian cultural and national identity, and several merit special stops on any tourist's itinerary.

The capital, Sofia, is picturesquely situated in a valley near Mt. Vitosha. There is much of cultural interest here, and the city has good hotels and restaurants serving traditional and international cuisine. Other main towns are Veliko Târnovo, the capital from the 12th to the 14th centuries and well worth a visit for its old, characteristic architecture; Plovdiv, southeast of Sofia, which has a particularly interesting old quarter; and Varna, the site of one of Europe's first cultural settlements and the most important port in Bulgaria.

ESSENTIAL INFORMATION

Before You Go

When to Go
The ski season lasts from mid-December through March; the Black Sea coast season runs from May to October, reaching its crowded peak in July and August. Fruit trees blossom in April and May; in May and early June the blossoms are gathered in the Valley of Roses (you have to be up early to watch the harvest); the fruit is picked in September, and in October the fall colors are at their best.

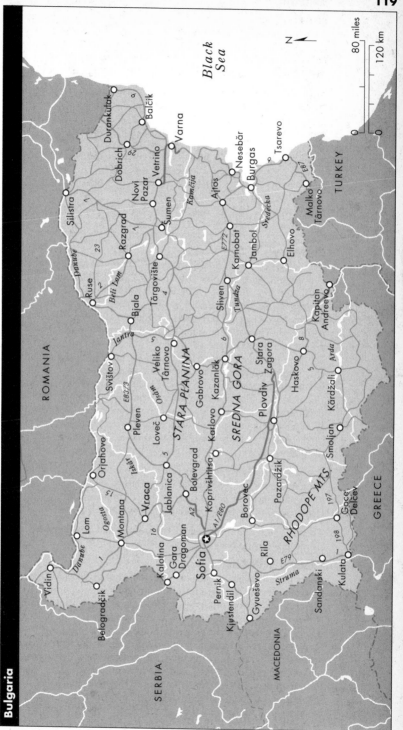

Black Sea

N

80 miles
120 km

TURKEY

Durankulak

Balčik

Varna

Nesebăr

Tsarevo

Dobrich

Vetrino

Burgas

Malko Tărnovo

Novi Pazar

Šumen

Kamčija

Ajtos

Razgrad

Silistra

Kamčija

E772

Karnobat

Jambol

Elhovo

Sredecka

Ruse

Târgovište

Bjala

Beli Lom

Sliven

Tundža

Kapitan Andreevo

Jantra

Svištov

Veliko Tărnovo

STARA PLANINA

Gabrovo

Kazanlăk

SREDNA GORA

Stara Zagora

Haskovo

Arda

Kărdžali

E83/3

Osăm

Pleven

Loveč

Karlovo

Plovdiv

Smoljan

Botevgrad

Koprivštitsa

Pazardžik

RHODOPE MTS.

Orjahovo

Iskăr

Vraca

Jablanica

A2

A1/E80

Borovec

Goce Delčev

Montana

Ogosta

Lom

Danube

Kalotina

Gara Dragoman

Sofia

Rila

Struma

Kulata

Sandanski

Vidin

Belogradčik

Pernik

Kjustendil

Gyueševo

E79

ROMANIA

SERBIA

MACEDONIA

GREECE

CLIMATE

Summers are warm, winters are crisp and cold. The coastal areas enjoy considerable sunshine, though March and April are the wettest months inland. Even when the temperature climbs, the Black Sea breezes and the cooler mountain air prevent the heat from being overpowering.

The following are the average daily maximum and minimum temperatures for Sofia.

Jan.	35F	2C	May	69F	21C	Sept.	70F	22C
	25	4		50	10		52	11
Feb.	39F	4C	June	76F	24C	Oct.	63F	17C
	27	3		56	14		46	8
Mar.	50F	10C	July	81F	27C	Nov.	48F	9C
	33	1		60	16		37	3
Apr.	60F	16C	Aug.	79F	26C	Dec.	38F	4C
	42	5		59	15		28	– 2

Currency

The unit of currency in Bulgaria is the lev (plural leva), divided into 100 stotinki. There are bills of 1, 2, 5, 10, 20, 50, 100, 200, 500, 1,000, and 2,000 leva; coins of 1, 2, and 5 leva; and coins of 5, 10, 20, and 50 stotinki. At press time (spring 1995), as part of efforts at economic reform, hard-currency payments for goods and services are no longer permitted. The only legal tender for commercial transactions and tourist services in Bulgaria is the lev. These services include air, train, and long-distance bus travel; accommodations, from camping to hotels; and car rentals and Balkantourist package tours. You may import any amount of foreign currency, including traveler's checks, and exchange it at branches of the Bulgarian State Bank, commercial banks, Balkantourist hotels, airports, border posts, and other exchange offices, all of which quote their daily selling and buying rates. The rate quoted by the Bulgarian State Bank is 66 leva to the U.S. dollar, 104 leva to the pound sterling.

It is forbidden either to import or to export Bulgarian currency. Unspent leva must be exchanged at frontier posts on departure before you go through passport control. You will need to present your official exchange slips to prove that the currency was legally purchased.

The major international credit cards are accepted in some of the larger stores, hotels, and restaurants.

What It Will Cost

Prices in Bulgaria have been low for years, but this is changing as the government tries to revive the economy and open it up to the West. If you choose the more moderate hotels, accommodations won't be very expensive. It is possible to cut costs even more by staying in a private hotel or private room in a Bulgarian house or apartment—also arranged by Balkantourist or other tourism companies—or by camping. The favorable cash exchange rate, linked to foreign-currency fluctuations, makes such expenses as taxi and public transport fares, museum and theater admission, and meals in most restaurants seem comparatively low by international standards. A little hard currency, exchanged at this rate, goes a long way. Shopping for imported and domestic wares in the duty-free shops also helps to keep travel expenses down. The following price list, correct as of spring 1995, can therefore be used only as a rough guide.

SAMPLE PRICES
Trip on a tram, trolley, or bus, 5 leva; theater ticket, 40 leva–60 leva; coffee in a moderate restaurant, 5 leva–20 leva; bottle of wine in a moderate restaurant, 120 leva–200 leva.

MUSEUMS
Museum admission is very inexpensive, ranging from 30 to 50 leva (less than $1).

Visas

All visitors need a valid passport. Those traveling in groups of six or more do not require visas, and many package tours are exempt from the visa requirement. Americans do not need visas when traveling as tourists. Other tourists, traveling independently, should inquire about visa requirements at a Bulgarian embassy or consulate before entering the country, since fees may be higher for visas obtained at the border.

Customs on Arrival

You may import duty-free into Bulgaria 250 grams of tobacco products, plus 1 liter of hard liquor and 2 liters of wine. Items intended for personal use during your stay are also duty-free. Travelers are advised to declare items of greater value—cameras, tape recorders, etc.—so there will be no problems with Bulgarian customs officials on departure.

Language

The official language, Bulgarian, is written in Cyrillic and is very close to Old Church Slavonic, the root of all Slavic languages. English is spoken in major hotels and restaurants, but is unlikely to be heard elsewhere. It is essential to remember that in Bulgaria, a nod of the head means "no" and a shake of the head means "yes."

Getting Around

By Car

ROAD CONDITIONS
Main roads are generally well engineered, although some routes are poor and narrow for the volume of traffic they have to carry. A large-scale expressway construction program has begun to link the main towns. Completed stretches run from Kalotina—on the Serbian border—to Sofia and from Sofia to Plovdiv. Highway tolls of some $20 total are paid at the border; be prepared for delays during the summer season at border points (open 24 hours) while documents are checked and stamped.

RULES OF THE ROAD
Drive on the right, as in the United States. The speed limits are 50 or 60 kph (31 or 36 mph) in built-up areas, 80 kph (50 mph) elsewhere, except on highways, where it is 120 kph (70 mph). The limits for a car towing a trailer are 50 kph (31 mph), 70 kph (44 mph), and 100 kph (62 mph), respectively. You must obtain a Green Card from your car insurance company, as recognized international proof that your car is covered by third-party insurance. You may be required to show one of these cards at the border. Balkantourist recommends that you also take out collision, or Casco, insurance. You are required to carry a first-aid kit, fire extinguisher, and breakdown triangle in the vehicle, and you must not sound the horn in towns. Front seat belts must be worn. The drunk-driving laws are strict—you are not expected to drive after you have had more than one drink.

PARKING

Park only in clearly marked parking places. If you are in doubt, check with the hotel or restaurant.

GASOLINE

Stations are regularly spaced on main roads but may be few and far between off the beaten track. All are marked on Balkantourist's free motoring map. As of press time (spring 1995) service stations sell unlimited quantities of fuel, supplies permitting, for leva (38¢ per liter, or $1.52 per gallon, for regular leaded). For motorist information contact the main office of the Bulgarian **Automobile Touring Association** at 3 Pozitano Street, Sofia (tel. 2/86–15–1) or **Shipka Tourist Agency** at 18 Lavele Street, Sofia (tel. 2/88–38–56).

BREAKDOWNS

In case of breakdown, telephone 146. The **SBA** (Bulgarian Automobile Touring Association) trucks carry essential spares, but it's wise to carry your own spare-parts kit. Fiat, Ford, Volkswagen, Peugeot, and Mercedes-Benz all have car-service operations in Bulgaria that offer prompt repairs by skilled technicians.

CAR RENTAL

The **Balkan Holidays/Hertz Rent-a-Car** organization has offices in most of the major hotels and at Sofia Airport (tel. 2/72–01–57). Its main headquarters in Sofia are at 8 Pozitano Street (tel. 2/83–50–49 or 2/31–80–45). Rental cars and fly/drive arrangements can be booked through Balkantourist agents abroad. These agents can also provide you with a driver for a small extra charge. **Avis** (tel. 2/87–34–12 or 2/73–80–23) and **Europe Car** (tel. 2/72–01–57) also have offices in Sofia.

By Train

Buy tickets in advance at a ticket office—there is one in each of the major centers—and avoid long lines at the station. Trains are very busy; seat reservations are obligatory on expresses. All medium- and long-distance trains have first- and second-class carriages and limited buffet services; overnight trains between Sofia and Black Sea resorts have first- and second-class sleeping cars and second-class couchettes. From Sofia there are six main routes—to Varna and Burgas on the Black Sea coast, to Plovdiv and on to the Turkish border, to Dragoman and the Serbian border, to Kulata and the Greek border, and to Ruse on the Romanian border. The main line is powered by electricity. Plans to electrify the rest are under way.

By Plane

Balkanair (Balkan Bulgarian Airlines) has regular services to Varna and Burgas, the biggest ports of the Black Sea. Book through Balkantourist offices; this can take time, however, and overbooking is not unusual. Group travel and air-taxi services are available through privately run Hemus Air and Air Via. Business flights to other destinations in the country are also arranged by Hemus Air.

By Bus

The routes of the crowded buses are mainly planned to link towns and districts not connected by rail. Within the cities, a regular system of trams and trolley buses operates for a single fare of 5 leva. Ticket booths, at most bus stops, sell single or season tickets; you can also pay the driver. Tourist information offices have full details of routes and times.

By Boat

Modern luxury vessels cruise the Danube from Passau in Austria to Ruse. Hydrofoils link main communities along the Bulgarian stretches of the Danube and the Black Sea, and there are coastal excursions from some Black Sea resorts. A ferry from Vidin to Calafat links Bulgaria with Romania.

Staying in Bulgaria

Country Code
For international calls to Bulgaria, the country code is 359. The access code for Sofia is 2.

Telephones
In Bulgaria, calls can be made from public telephones in the post office in each major town or resort or, at a surcharge, from hotels. To place a call to the United States via an AT&T USADirect international operator, dial 00–1800–0010; for Sprint Express, dial 00–800–0877. There is a new system of international telephones—modern, direct-dial phones with no coin slots—that operate only with special cards paid for in leva. Directions for buying the cards are given, often in English, on the phones.

Mail
Letters and postcards to the United States cost 17 leva, 15 leva to the United Kingdom.

Opening and Closing Times
Banks are open weekdays 9–3. **Museums** are usually open 9–6:30 but are often closed on Monday or Tuesday. **Shops** are open Monday–Saturday 9–7. Many shops are open on Sunday, and most grocery stores are open round-the-clock.

National Holidays
January 1; March 3 (Independence Day); April 14–15 (Orthodox Easter); May 1 (Labor Day); May 24 (Bulgarian Culture Day); December 24–26.

Dining
There is a choice of hotel restaurants with their international menus, Balkantourist restaurants, or the inexpensive restaurants and cafeterias run privately and by cooperatives. The best bets are the small folk-style restaurants that serve national dishes and local specialties. The word "picnic" in a restaurant name means that the tables are outdoors. Standards have improved, but food is still rarely served piping hot, and visitors should be prepared for loud background music.

SPECIALTIES
Bulgarian national dishes are closely related to their Greek and Slav counterparts: basic Balkan cooking relies mainly on lamb and potatoes. Other staples are pork, sheep cheese, peppers, eggplant, tomatoes, onions, carrots, and spices. Bulgarian melons, apples, and pears are in a class by themselves, as are the rich, amber-colored *bolgar* grapes and orange-red apricots. Bulgaria invented *kiselo mleko* (yogurt), with its promise of good health and longevity, and there are excellent *tarator* (cold yogurt soups) during the summer. *Banitsa*—rich cream cakes eaten with fruit or cheese—and syrupy baklava are served to round out a meal.

Bulgarian wines are good, usually full-bodied, dry, and inexpensive. The national drink is *rakia*—*slivova* (plum) or *grozdova* (grape) brandy—but vodka is popular, too. Coffee is strong and is often drunk along with a cold beverage, such as cola or a lemon drink. Tea is taken with lemon instead of milk and many Bulgarians love to drink a fragrant infusion of dried lime leaves.

In Sofia, formal dress (jacket and tie) is customary at **$$$** and **$$$$** restaurants. Casual dress is appropriate elsewhere.

Prices are per person and include a first course, main course, dessert, and tip, but no alcohol. Highly recommended restaurants are indicated by a star ★.

CATEGORY	ALL AREAS
$$$$	over 1000 leva
$$$	600 leva–1000 leva
$$	300 leva–600 leva
$	under 300 leva

Increasingly, even restaurants in the *$$* category are accepting credit cards, although the list of cards accepted may not always be correctly posted. Before you place an order, check to see whether you can pay with your card.

Lodging

There is a wide choice of accommodations, ranging from hotels—most of them dating from the '60s and '70s—to apartment rentals, rooms in private homes, hostels, and campsites. Although hotels are improving, they still tend to suffer from temperamental wiring and erratic plumbing, and it is a good idea to pack a universal drain plug, as plugs are often missing in hotel bathrooms. In *$$* and *$* hotels, bathrooms often look unusual. Don't be surprised if strangely placed plumbing turns the entire bathroom into a shower. Due to power cuts in the winter, flashlights and other battery-powered utilities are strongly recommended.

Until recently, most hotels used by Western visitors were owned by Balkantourist and Interhotels. At press time, many of the government-owned or -operated hotels listed below were on the verge of privatization. The conversion is expected to take up to five years. Hotels may be closed for renovation for extended periods or may be permanently shut down. Visitors are strongly urged to call ahead to hotels to get the latest information. Some hotels were always privately run or run by municipal authorities or organizations catering to specific groups (Shipka for motorists, Orbita for young people, Pirin for hikers). Most have restaurants and bars; the large, modern ones have swimming pools, shops, and other facilities.

Rented accommodations are a growth industry, with planned, modern complexes as well as picturesque cottages. Cooking facilities tend to be meager, and meal vouchers are included in the deal. An English-speaking manager is generally on hand.

A stay in a private home, an arrangement made by Balkantourist, is becoming a popular alternative to hotels as a means not only of cutting costs but also of offering increased contact with Bulgarians. There are one-, two-, and three-star private accommodations (ranked by Balkantourist). Some offer a bed or bed and breakfast only; some provide full board. Three-star rooms are equipped with kitchenettes. Booking offices are located in most main tourist areas. In Sofia, contact **Balkantourist** at 1 Vitosha Boulevard (tel. 2/43–331), or go to the private accommodations office at 27 Stambolijski Boulevard (tel. 2/88–52–56 or 2/88–44–30).

HOSTELS
Hostels are basic, but clean and cheap. Contact **Orbita** (48 Hristo Botev Blvd., Sofia, tel. 2/80–01–02).

CAMPSITES
There are more than 100 campsites, many near the Black Sea coast. They are graded one, two, or three stars (ranked by Balkantourist) and the best of them offer hot and cold water, grocery stores, and restaurants. Balkantourist provides a location map.

RATINGS
Prices are for two people in a double room with half-board (breakfast and a main meal). Highly recommended lodgings are indicated by a star ★. At the leading hotels, you can pay in either Western or local currency; many hotels, however, will only accept leva. Fortunately, at the exchange office—found at the receptionist desk of all hotels—foreign currency can be exchanged for local currency. Note that you must show your exchange slips to prove that the money was legally changed.

CATEGORY	SOFIA	OTHER AREAS
$$$$	over 9,000 leva	over 6,000 leva
$$$	6,000 leva–9,000 leva	4,000 leva–6,000 leva
$$	2,500 leva–6,000 leva	2,000 leva–4,000 leva
$	under 2,500 leva	under 2,000 leva

Tipping
Tipping is not frowned on. Tips are given to waiters, taxi drivers, hotel employees, but only tips on restaurant bills are more or less determined. You can round your bill up by 10%.

SOFIA

Arriving and Departing

By Plane
All international flights arrive at Sofia airport. For information on international flights, tel. 2/79–80–35 or 2/72–06–72; domestic flights, tel. 2/79–32–21–16 or 2/72–24–14.

BETWEEN THE AIRPORT AND DOWNTOWN
Bus 84 serves the airport. Fares for taxis taken from the airport taxi stand run about 150 leva for the 10-kilometer (6-mile) ride into Sofia. Avoid the taxi touts; they tend to overcharge or to insist on payment in hard currency.

By Train
The central station is at the northern edge of the city. For information, call 2/3–11–11 or 2/843–33–33. The ticket offices in Sofia are in the underpass of the National Palace of Culture (1 Bulgaria Sq., tel. 2/843–42–92) or at the Rila International Travel Agency (5 Gurko St., tel. 2/87–07–77 or 2/87–59–35). There is a taxi stand at the station.

By Car
Heading to or from Serbia, the main routes are E80, going through the border checkpoint at Kalotina on the Niš-Sofia road, or E871 going through the checkpoint at Gyueshevo. Traveling from Greece,

take E79, passing through the checkpoint at Kulata; from Turkey, take E80, passing through checkpoint Kapitan-Andreevo. Border crossings to Romania are at Vidin on E79 and at Ruse on E70 and E85.

Getting Around

By Bus

Buses, trolleys, and trams run fairly often. Buy a ticket from the ticket stand near the streetcar stop and punch it into the machine as you board. (Watch how the person in front of you does it.) For information, call 2/312–42–63 or 2/88–13–53.

By Taxi

Since private taxi drivers were given permission to operate in 1990, it has become easier to find cabs in Sofia. Hail them in the street or at a stand—or ask the hotel to call one. At press time, daytime taxi rates run about 10 leva per kilometer; it will cost about 12 leva per kilometer after 10 PM. There is a 10-leva surcharge for taxis ordered by phone. To order by phone, call 2122, 1280, 1282, or 1284. To tip, round out the fare by 5%–10%

By Rental Car

You can rent a car, with or without driver, through Balkantourist, at the airport, and at hotel reception desks.

On Foot

The main sights are centrally located, so the best way to see the city is on foot.

Important Addresses and Numbers

Since late 1990, a national commission has been working to rename cities, streets, and monuments throughout the country. Names given in the following sections were correct as of spring 1995 but are subject to change.

Tourist Information

Balkantourist Head Office (tel. 2/4–33–31) is at 1 Vitosha Boulevard; its tourist and accommodations office (tel. 2/88–52–56 or 2/88–44–30; 2/88–55–43; 2/88–06–55) is at 27 Stambolijski Boulevard. It also has offices or desks in all the main hotels. **Balkantourist** is also at 27 Stambolijski Boulevard (tel. 2/88–52–56). **Pirin** is at 30 Stambolijski Boulevard (tel. 2/88–41–22).

Embassies

U.S. (1 Suborna St., tel. 2/88–48–01); **Canadian,** c/o Canadian Embassy in Budapest, Budakeszi u. 32, 1121 Budapest, Hungary, tel. 36/1–1767–312; **U.K.** (38 Levski Blvd., tel. 2/88–53–61).

Emergencies

Police: Sofia City Constabulary (tel. 166); **Ambulance** (tel. 150); **Fire** (tel. 160); **Doctor:** Clinic for Foreign Citizens (Mladost 1, 1 Eugeni Pavlovski St., tel. 2/77–95–18) or Pirogov Emergency Hospital (tel. 2/5–15–31); **Pharmacies** (tel. 178 for information about all-night pharmacies).

Guided Tours

Orientation Tours

Guided tours of Sofia and environs are arranged by Balkantourist from either of the main Sofia offices or from Balkantourist desks at the major hotels. Among the possibilities are three- to four-hour tours of the principal city sights by car or minibus or a longer four- to five-hour tour that goes as far as Mt. Vitosha.

Excursions

Balkantourist offers 23 types of special-interest tours of various lengths, using Sofia as the point of departure. There are trips to the most beautiful monasteries, such as the Rila Monastery, 118 kilometers (74 miles) south of Sofia; to museum towns, such as Nesebâr and Koprivshtitsa; to sports areas and spas; to the Valley of Roses; and to other places of exceptional scenic or cultural interest.

Evening Tours

Balkantourist has a number of evening tours, from a night out eating local food and watching folk dances to an evening at the National Opera.

Exploring Sofia

Sofia is set on the high Sofia Plain, ringed by mountain ranges: the Balkan range to the north; the Lyulin Mountains to the west; part of the Sredna Gora Mountains to the southeast; and, to the southwest, Mt. Vitosha, the city's playground, which rises to more than 7,600 feet. The area has been inhabited for about 7,000 years, but the visitor's first impression is of a modern city with broad streets, light traffic, spacious parks, and open-air cafés. As recently as the 1870s it was part of the Turkish Empire, and one mosque still remains. Most of the city, however, was planned after 1880. There are enough intriguing museums and high-quality musical performances to merit a lengthy stay, but if time is short, you need only two days to see the main sights and another day, at least, for Mt. Vitosha.

Numbers in the margin correspond to points of interest on the Sofia map.

① **Ploshtad Sveta Nedelya** (St. Nedelya Square) is a good starting point for an exploration of the main sights. The south side of the square is **②** dominated by the 19th-century **Tzarkva Sveta Nedelya** (St. Nedelya Church). Go behind it to find Vitosha Boulevard, a lively pedestrian street with plenty of stores, cafés, and dairy bars.

The first building along this boulevard, on the west side of the street, **③** is the former Courts of Justice, now the **Natzionalen Istoricheski Musei** (National History Museum). Its vast collections, vividly illustrating the art history of Bulgaria, include priceless Thracian treasures, Roman mosaics, enameled jewelry from the First Bulgarian Kingdom, and glowing religious art that survived the years of Ottoman oppression. The courts are due to return to this location as soon as a new home is found for the National History Museum collection. *2 Vitosha Blvd., tel. 2/88–41–60. Admission: 50 leva. Open weekdays 9:30–4:30.*

Return to the northeast side of St. Nedelya Square, and in the court-**④** yard of the Sheraton Sofia Balkan Hotel you will see the **Rotonda Sveti Georgi** (Rotunda of St. George). Built in the 4th century as a Roman temple, it has served as a mosque and church, and recent restoration has revealed medieval frescoes. It is not open to the public. Head east to the vast Alexander Batenberg Square, which is dominated by the **⑤** **Partiyniyat Dom** (the former headquarters of the Bulgarian Communist party).

Facing the square, but entered via Alexander Stambolijski Boulevard, **⑥** is the former Great Mosque, which now houses the **Natzionalen Archeologicheski Musei** (National Archaeological Museum). The 15th-century building itself is as fascinating as its contents, which illustrate the

Sofia

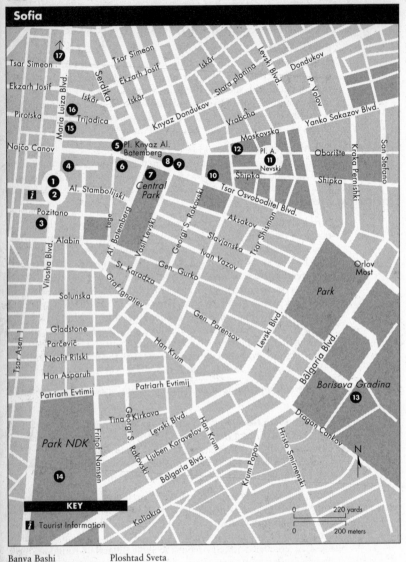

Tsar Simeon
Ekzarh Josif Blvd.
Pirotska
Najčo Canov
Al. Stamboliiski
Pozitano
Alabin
Vitoša Blvd.
Solunska
Gladstone
Parčevič
Neofit Rilski
Han Asparuh
Patriarh Evtimij
Tsar Asen
Park NDK

Tsar Simeon
Serdika
Iskâr
Maria Luiza Blvd.
Trijadica
Pl. Knyaz Al.
Batemberg
Central Park
Al. Batemberg
Iege
St. Karadza
Graf Ignatiev
Georgi S. Rakovski
Vasil Levski
Gen. Gurko
Tina
Georgi S. Rakovski
Fritiof Nansen

Tsar Simeon
Ekzarh Josif
Iskâr
Knyaz Dondukov
Stara planina
Vrabča
Moskovska
Shipka
Tsar Osvoboditel Blvd.
Aksakov
Slavjanska
Ivan Vazov
Gen. Parensov
Han Krum
Patriarh Evtimij
Kirkova
Levski Blvd.
Ljuben Karavelov
Bâlgaria Blvd.
Han Krum

Iskâr
Levski Blvd.
Dondukov
P. Volov
Yanko Sakazov Blvd.
Oborište
Shipka
Pl. A. Nevski
Tsar Shisman
Levski Blvd.
Bâlgaria Blvd.
Orlov Most
Park
Borisova Gradina
Dragan Cankov
Hristo Smirnenski
Krum Popov
Kaliakra
Kraka Pernishki
San Stefano

KEY

🛈 Tourist Information

0 ——— 220 yards
0 ——— 200 meters

N

Banya Bashi
Djamiya, **16**

Borisova Gradina, **13**

Hram-pametnik
Alexander Nevski, **11**

Mavsolei Georgi
Dimitrov, **7**

Natzionalen Dvoretz
na Kulturata, **14**

Natzionalen Archeo-
logicheski Musei, **6**

Natzionalen Etno-
grafski Musei, **8**

Natzionalen Istorich-
eski Musei, **3**

Natzionalna Hudozh-
estvena Galeria, **9**

Partiyniyat Dom, **5**

Ploshtad Sveta
Nedelya, **1**

Rotonda Sveti
Georgi, **4**

Tsentralen Univer-
salen Magazin, **15**

Tsentralni Hali, **17**

Tzarkva Sveta
Nedelya, **2**

Tzarkva Sveta
Sofia, **12**

Tzarkva Sveti Niko-
lai, **10**

cultures of the different peoples who inhabited Bulgaria up to the 19th century. *Tel. 2/88–24–06. Closed for renovations at press time.*

7 On the next block to the east is the former **Mavsolei Georgi Dimitrov** (Georgi Dimitrov Mausoleum), which until 1990 contained the embalmed body of the first general secretary of the Bulgarian Communist party, who died in Moscow in 1949 and was known as the "Father of the Nation." His remains have been moved to the Central Cemetery, and there is talk of converting the mausoleum into a museum, or destroying it.

8 Across from the mausoleum is the former palace of the Bulgarian tsar, which currently houses the **Natzionalen Etnografski Musei** (National Ethnographic Museum), with displays of costumes, handicrafts, and tools that illustrate the agricultural way of life of the country people until the 19th century. *1 Alexander Batenberg Sq., tel. 2/87–41–91. Admission: 50 leva. Open Wed.–Sun. 10–noon and 1:30–5:30.*

9 In the west wing of the same building is the **Natzionalna Hudozhestvena Galeria** (National Art Gallery). It houses a collection of the best works of Bulgarian artists, as well as a foreign art section that contains some prints and engravings of important artists. *1 Alexander Batenberg Sq., tel. 2/89–28–41. Admission: 50 leva. Open Tues.–Sun. 10:30–6.*

10 Nearby stands the ornate Russian **Tzarkva Sveti Nikolai** (Church of St. Nicholas), erected 1912–14.

11 From here you'll enter Tsar Osvoboditel Boulevard, with its monument to the Russians, topped by the equestrian statue of Russian Tsar Alexander II. It stands in front of the National Assembly. Behind the National Assembly, just beyond Shipka Street, you'll be confronted by the neo-Byzantine structure with glittering onion domes whose image you may recognize from almost every piece of tourist literature, and which really does dominate the city. This is the **Hram-pametnik Alexander Nevski** (Alexander Nevski Memorial Church), built by the Bulgarian people at the beginning of this century as a mark of gratitude to their Russian liberators. Inside are alabaster and onyx, Italian marble and Venetian mosaics, magnificent frescoes, and space for a congregation of 5,000. Attend a service to hear the superb choir, and, above all, don't miss the fine collection of icons in the **Crypt Museum**. *Alexander Nevski Sq., tel. 2/87–76–97. Admission: 50 leva. Open Wed.–Mon. 10:30–5.*

12 Cross the square to the west to pay your respects to the much older **Tzarkva Sveta Sofia** (Church of St. Sofia), which dates to the 6th century, though remains of even older churches have been found during excavations. Its age and simplicity contrast sharply with its more glamorous neighbor.

13 Return to Tsar Osvoboditel Boulevard and continue east to the **Borisova Gradina** (Boris's Garden), with its lake and fountains, woods and lawns, huge sports stadium, and open-air theater. From the park take Dragan Tsankov west (back toward St. Nedelya Square) briefly, before going left on Patriarh Evtimij, toward Južen Park. The formal gardens and extensive woodlands here are to be extended as far as Mt. Vitosha.

14 At the entrance to the park stands a large modern building, the **Natzionalen Dvoretz na Kulturata** (National Palace of Culture), with its complex of halls for conventions and cultural activities. Its multi-level underpass is equipped with a tourist information office, shops, restaurants, discos, and a bowling alley. *1 Bulgaria Sq., tel. 2/5–15–01. Admission: 50 leva. Open 10:30–6:30.*

Back at St. Nedelya Square, follow Knyaginya Maria-Luiza Boulevard to the train station. The large building on the right is the recently re-

⑮ furbished **Tsentralen Universalen Magazin** (Central Department Store, known as Tsum). *2 Knyaginya Maria-Luiza Blvd. Open Mon.–Sat. 8–8.*

Just beyond is a distinctive building, a legacy of Turkish domination, the

⑯ **Banya Bashi Djamiya** (Banja Basi Mosque); it is closed to visitors. Nearby you will see the public mineral baths. Across the boulevard is the busy

⑰ **Tsentralni Hali** (Central Market Hall), which is closed for renovations.

TIME OUT   Anyone doing the full tour is going to need at least one refreshment stop. There are several fast food restaurants and many cafés on the northern length of Vitosha Boulevard. A café huddles near the 14th-century church of **Sveta Petka Samardzijska** (St. Petka of the Saddles) in the underpass leading to the Central Department Store. Or take a break in a café in the underpass at the National Palace of Culture or on St. Nedelya Square itself at the Complex Rubin.

Off the Beaten Track

The little medieval church of **Boyana,** about 10 kilometers (6 miles) south of the city center, is well worth a visit as is the small, elegant restaurant of the same name, next door. The church itself is closed for restoration, but a replica, complete with copies of the exquisite 13th-century frescoes, is open to visitors.

The **Dragalevci Monastery** stands in beech woods above the nearby village of Dragalevci. The complex is currently a convent, but you can visit the 14th-century church with its outdoor frescoes. Shepherds can often be seen tending their flocks in the surrounding woods. From here take the chairlift to the delightful resort complex of **Aleko,** and another nearby chairlift to the top of Malak Rezen. There are well-marked walking and ski trails in the area. Both Boyana and Dragalevci can be reached by taking Bus 64.

Shopping

Gifts and Souvenirs

There are good selections of arts and crafts at the shop of the **Union of Bulgarian Artists** (6 Shipka St.) and at the **Bulgarian Folk Art Shop** (14 Vitosha Blvd.). You will find a range of souvenirs at **Sredec** (7 Lege St.), **Souvenir Store** (7 Stambolijski Blvd.), and **Prizma Store** (1 Vasil Levski St.). If you are interested in furs or leather, try the shops along Vitosha Boulevard, Levski Boulevard, and Tsar Osvoboditel Boulevard. For recordings of Bulgarian music, go to the **National Palace of Culture** (*see* Exploring Sofia, *above*).

Shopping Districts

The latest shopping center is in the underpass below the modern **National Palace of Culture,** where stores sell fashions, leather goods, and all forms of handicrafts. The pedestrian-only area along **Vitosha Boulevard** features many new, privately owned shops. The colorful small shops along **Graf Ignatiev Street** also merit a visit.

Department Stores

Sofia's biggest department store is the newly renovated **Central Department Store** (2 Knyaginya Maria-Luiza Boulevard).

Dining

Eating in Sofia can be enjoyable and even entertaining if the restaurant has a nightclub or folklore program. Be prepared to be patient and make an evening of it, as service can be slow at times. Or try a *mehana*, or tavern, where the atmosphere is informal and the service sometimes a bit quicker. For details and price-category definitions, *see* Dining *in* Staying in Bulgaria, *above.*

$$$$ **Deva Helios.** With an orchestra serenading diners most evenings, the Deva Helios—located across from Alexander Nevski Memorial Church—is one of the more elegant establishments in Sofia. Expect no epicurean revolutions, just fine service and traditional Bulgarian, Italian, and Spanish food. *95 Vasil Levski Blvd., tel. 2/88–03–85. No credit cards. Closed Sun.*

$$$$ **Dionyssos.** This club and restaurant above Tsum (the large Central Department Store), opposite the Sheraton Hotel, provides a rich selection of international and Bulgarian cuisine spiced with a three-hour floor show. House specialities include *kavarma* (highly seasoned fried pork). *2 Knyaginya Maria-Luiza Blvd., tel. 2/81–37–26. Reservations advised. DC, MC, V.*

$$$$ **Krim.** This Russian restaurant serves the best beef Stroganoff in town. *17 Slavjanska St., tel. 2/87–01–31. Reservations advised. AE.*

$$$$ **Valimpex.** There are wonderful days and nights of wine and roses here, and splendid food. Try the Italian specialties, which have been recently added to the customary menu of game, fish, and fowl. *31–33 Vitosha Blvd., tel. 2/87–94–65. Reservations essential. AE, DC, MC, V.*

$$$ **Mexicano (Casa del Arquitecto).** Mexican food and music make this place popular, but it also serves traditional Bulgarian dishes, including a spicy mussaka (baked minced meat and potatoes). *11 Krakra St., tel. 2/44–65–98 or 2/44–17–24. No credit cards.*

$$$ **Budapest.** This place enjoys a reputation as one of the best restaurants
★ in Sofia for good food, wine, and live music. As the name suggests, Hungarian food takes center stage—including a fine *kebap* (stewed meat with garlic and red peppers). *145 G. S. Rakovski St., tel. 2/87–27–50. No credit cards.*

$$$ **Havana.** Cuban food is featured in this popular restaurant near the center of town. *27 Vitosha Blvd., tel. 2/80–05–44. No credit cards.*

$$ **Boyansko Hanche.** Local and national specialties are the main features in this restaurant and folklore center, 8 kilometers (6 miles) from downtown (take Bus 64 or 107). *Near Bojanska Church, tel. 2/56–30–16. No credit cards.*

$$ **The Golden Dragon.** This new, centrally located restaurant is very popular for its wide selection of Chinese dishes. *86 Rakovski St., no phone. No credit cards.*

$$ **Phenyan.** This place is known for its Far Eastern ambience and Korean specialties. *24 Assen Zlatarov St., tel. 2/44–34–36. No credit cards.*

$$ **Rubin.** This eating complex in the center of Sofia has a snack bar and an elegant restaurant that serves Bulgarian and international food. A full meal can sometimes push the cost into the $$$ bracket. *4 St. Nedelya Sq., tel. 2/87–47–04. AE, DC, MC, V.*

$$ **Vodeničarski Mehani.** The English translation is "Miller's Tavern," which is appropriate, since it's made up of three old mills linked together. It is at the foot of Mt. Vitosha and features a folklore show and a menu of Bulgarian specialties. Try the *giuvech* (potatoes, tomatoes, peas, and onions baked in an earthenware pan). *Dragalevci district (Bus 64), tel. 2/67–10–21 or 2/67–10–01. No credit cards.*

$ Party Club. This restaurant features international and Chinese cuisines. *3 Vasil Levski Blvd., tel. 2/81–05–44 or 2/81–43–43. Reservations accepted. AE, DC, MC, V.*

$ Zheravna. This is a small, cozy place with a homey atmosphere. It serves tasty Bulgarian food. *67 Levski Blvd., tel. 2/87–21–86. No credit cards.*

$ Chepishev. At the foot of Mt. Vitosha, this spot offers Bulgarian specialities and live folk music in the evenings. *Boyana district, 23 Kumata St., tel. 2/550888. No credit cards.*

Lodging

The following hotels maintain a high standard of cleanliness and are open year-round unless otherwise stated. If you arrive in Sofia without reservations, go to the Interhotels Central Office (2 Sveta Sofia St.), Balkantourist (1 Vitosha Blvd.), the Bureau of Tourist Information and Reservations (22–24 Lavele St.), the National Palace of Culture (1 Bulgaria Sq.), or the central rail station. For details and price-category definitions, *see* Lodging *in* Staying in Bulgaria, *above.*

$$$$ Novotel Europa. This member of the prestigous French Novotel chain is on one of Sofia's main boulevards, near the train station, and not far from the center of the city. Among its many facilities are a conference center and casino. *131 Knyaginya Maria-Luiza Blvd., tel. 2/3–12–61, fax 2/32–00–11. 600 rooms with bath. Facilities: 2 restaurants, bar, coffee shop, shops. AE, DC, MC, V.*

$$$$ Sheraton Sofia Hotel Balkan. The former Grand Hotel Balkan has re-
★ cently been done up to Sheraton standards. It is now a first-class hotel with a central location that is hard to match. It also has excellent restaurants. *5 St. Nedelya Sq., tel. 2/87–65–41, fax 2/87–10–38. 188 rooms with bath. Facilities: 3 restaurants, 2 bars, nightclub, fitness center, whirlpool. AE, DC, MC, V.*

$$$$ Vitosha. There is a distinctly Asian flavor to this towering, trim Inter-
★ hotel—not surprising, as it was designed by a Japanese firm. It is hard to match the range of services and activities available here. With audio-visual and simultaneous translation facilities available, this is a prime option for business conferences. The Vitosha also has a shopping arcade and superb Japanese restaurant. *100 James Boucher Blvd., tel. 2/6–25–11, 2/68–12–25. 454 rooms with bath. Facilities: 5 restaurants, 6 bars, shopping and business center, tennis courts, sauna, fitness center, pool, nightclub, casino. AE, DC, MC, V.*

$$$ Grand Hotel Sofia. This five-story, centrally located Interhotel conveys an atmosphere of relative intimacy, compared with some of its larger rivals in the capital. Its Panorama Restaurant provides a fine view of Sofia. *4 Narodno Sobranie Sq., tel. 2/87–88–21, 2/88–13–08. 204 rooms with bath. Facilities: 3 restaurants, bar, coffee shop, folk tavern, nightclub, and shops. AE, DC, MC, V.*

$$$ Park Hotel Moskva. Twenty stories high, this hotel is equipped with the latest in technical services, including satellite television and a video channel for guest information. The pleasant park setting makes up for the fact that it's not as centrally located as some other comparable hotels. An excellent restaurant is hidden away on the rooftop. *25 Nezabravka St., tel. 2/7–12–61, 2/65–67–45. 390 rooms with bath. Facilities: 4 restaurants, bar, coffee shop, nightclub, sports center. AE, DC, MC, V.*

$$$ Rodina. Sofia's highest building is not far from the city center and near all of Sofia's government, cultural, and shopping centers. As one of the finest hotels in Sofia, the Rodina features the latest in modern facilities, including a sports center (pool, sauna, and solarium) and CNN news. Besides the main restaurant—complete with evening floorshow—

there is a Chinese eatery and Grill Room. *8 Tsar Boris III Blvd., tel. 2/5–16–31, fax 2/54–32–25. 536 rooms with bath. Facilities: 3 restaurants, bar, coffee shop, nightclub, pool, shops. AE, DC, MC, V.*

$$ Bulgaria. Despite its central location, this small hotel is quiet and a bit old-fashioned. *4 Tsar Osvoboditel Blvd., tel. 2/88–22–11 or 2/87–01–91, fax 2/88–05–85. 85 rooms with bath or shower. Facilities: restaurant, 2 bars, coffee shop. AE, DC, MC, V.*

$$ Deva-Spartak. A small hotel behind the National Palace of Culture, the Deva-Spartak offers guests convenient access to the adjoining Spartak sports complex, which includes indoor and outdoor pools. *4 Arsenalski Blvd., tel. 2/66–12–61, 2/66–25–37. 13 rooms with bath. Facilities: restaurant, access to Spartak sports complex, shop. No credit cards.*

$$ Hemus. Guests here can save money while availing themselves of the myriad facilities—including casino and nightclub—of the grander Vitosha Hotel, located within easy walking distance. *31 Cherni Vrah Blvd., tel. 2/6–39–51 or 2/66–13–19, fax 2/66–13–18. 240 rooms with bath or shower. Facilities: restaurant, folk tavern, nightclub, shops. AE, DC, MC, V.*

$$ Pliska-Cosmos. Part of the Balkan Airlines hotel chain, the Pliska-Cosmos, located at the entrance to Sofia, has been recently renovated. *87 Tsarigradsko Shose Blvd., tel. 2/71281, fax 2/72-39-52. 200 rooms with shower. Facilities: restaurant, bar, casino, shops. DC, MC, V.*

$$ Rila. A convenient, central downtown location makes the Rila a low-cost alternative to the Sheraton. *6 Kaloyan St., tel. 2/88–18–61, fax 2/65–01–06. 120 rooms with bath or shower. Facilities: restaurant, coffee shop, folk tavern, art gallery, fitness center. AE, DC, MC, V.*

$ Serdika. Just opposite the Vasil Levski Monument, the centrally located Serdika has a handy feature for travelers: a bureau for tourist services located on the premises. The restaurant serves some of the best German specialties in Sofia. *2 Yanko Sakazov Blvd., tel. 2/44–34–11, 2/46–52–96. 140 rooms, most with shower. Facilities: Restaurant, coffee lounge, banquet hall. DC, MC, V.*

The Arts

The standard of music in Bulgaria is high, whether it takes the form of opera, symphonic, or folk music, which has just broken into the international scene with its close harmonies and colorful stage displays. Contact Balkantourist or the **Concert Office** (2 Tsar Osvoboditel Blvd., tel. 2/87–15–88) for general information.

You don't need to understand Bulgarian to enjoy a performance at the **Central Puppet Theater** (14 Gen. Gurko St., tel. 2/88–54–16) or at the **National Folk Ensemble** (check with the tourist office for details).

There are a number of fine art galleries: The art gallery of the **Sts. Cyril and Methodius International Foundation** has a collection of Indian, African, Japanese, and Western European paintings and sculptures (Alexander Nevski Sq., tel. 2/88–49–22; open Wed.–Mon. 10:30–6). The art gallery of the **Union of Bulgarian Artists** has exhibitions of contemporary Bulgarian art (6 Shipka St., tel. 2/44–61–15; open daily 10:30–6). The **City Art Gallery** has both permanent exhibits of 19th-century and modern Bulgarian paintings as well as changing exhibits by contemporary artists (1 Gen. Gurko St., tel. 2/87–21–81).

The **Odeon, Serdika,** and **Vitosha cinemas** show recent foreign films in their original languages with Bulgarian subtitles.

Nightlife

Nightclubs

The following hotel bars have floor shows and a lively atmosphere:
Bar Sofia (Grand Hotel Sofia, 4 Narodno Sobranie Sq., tel. 2/87–88–
21); **Bar Variety Ambassador** (Vitosha Hotel, 100 James Boucher
Blvd., tel. 2/6–25–11); **Bar Variety** (Park Hotel Moskva, 25 Nez-
abravka St., tel. 2/7–12–61); **Bar Fantasy** (Sheraton Sofia Hotel
Balkan, 5 St. Nedelya Sq., tel. 2/87–65–41).

Discos

There is a disco, nightclub, and bowling alley at the **National Palace of
Culture** (1 Bulgaria Sq.). Other choices are **Orbylux** (76 James Boucher
Blvd., tel. 2/63–89–97), known as the classiest disco in town, **Excalibur,**
a new popular disco in the underpass of Sofia University, Kliment Ohrid-
sky St. (no phone), and **Yacht Club** (21 Aksakov St., tel. 2/88–12–97).

Casinos

Gamblers can try their luck at the casino in the **Vitosha Hotel,** (100
James Boucher Blvd., tel. 2/82–25–11) at the **Sheraton Sofia Hotel** (5
St. Nedelya Sq., tel. 2/87–65–41), or at **Pliska Cosmos** (87 Tsari-
gradsko Shose Blvd., tel. 2/71281). There is also a new casino at the
Grand Hotel Sofia (4 Narodno Sobranie Sq., tel. 2/87–88–21).

THE BLACK SEA GOLDEN COAST

Bulgaria's most popular resort area attracts visitors from all over Europe. Its sunny, sandy beaches are backed by the easternmost slopes
of the Balkan range and by the Strandja Mountains. Although the tourist
centers tend to be huge state-built complexes with a somewhat lean
feel, they have modern amenities. Slânčev Brjag (Sunny Beach), the largest
of the resorts, with more than 100 hotels, has plenty of children's amuse-
ments and play areas; baby-sitters are also available.

The historic port of Varna is a good center for exploration. It is a focal
point of land and sea transportation and has museums, a variety of
restaurants, and some nightlife. The fishing villages of Nesebâr and Sozopol are more attractive. Lodgings tend to be scarce in these villages,
so private accommodations, arranged on the spot or by Balkantourist,
are a good option. Whatever resort you choose, all offer facilities for
water sports and some have instructors. Tennis and horseback riding
are also available.

Getting Around

Buses make frequent runs up and down the coast and are inexpensive.
Buy your ticket in advance from the kiosks near the bus stops. **Cars**
and **bicycles** can be rented; bikes are particularly useful for getting around
such sprawling resorts as Sunny Beach. A **hydrofoil** service links Varna,
Nesebâr, Burgas, and Sozopol. A regular **boat** service travels the
Varna–Sveti Konstantin (St. Konstantin)–Zlatni Pjasâci (Golden
Sands)–Albena–Balčik route.

Guided Tours

A wide range of excursions can be arranged from all resorts. There are
bus excursions to Sofia from Golden Sands, Sveti Konstantin, Albena,
and Sunny Beach; a one-day bus and boat trip along the Danube from
Golden Sands, Sveti Konstantin, and Albena; and a three-day bus tour
of Bulgaria, including the Valley of Roses, departing from Golden Sands,

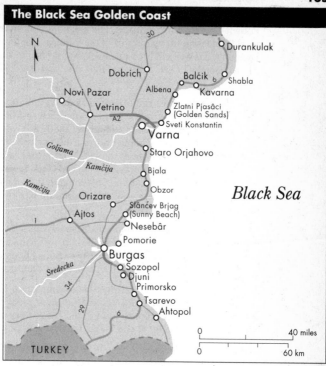

The Black Sea Golden Coast

N

Durankulak

Dobrich

Balčik 6 Shabla

Albena Kavarna

Novi Pazar

Vetrino

Zlatni Pjasâci
(Golden Sands)

Sveti Konstantin

Varna

Goljama

Staro Orjahovo

Kamčija

Bjala

Kamčija

Obzor

Black Sea

Orizare

Slânčev Brjag
(Sunny Beach)

Ajtos

Nesebâr

Pomorie

Burgas

Sredecka

Sozopol

Djuni

Primorsko

Tsarevo

Ahtopol

TURKEY

0   40 miles

0   60 km

Sveti Konstantin, and Albena. All tours are run by Balkantourist (*see* Tourist Information, *below,* or check with your hotel information desk).

Tourist Information

There is a Balkantourist office in most towns and resorts. Note that phone numbers are listed here; Many resort areas, however, do not have regular street names or numbers.

Albena (tel. 05722/2721).
Burgas (Hotel Primorets, 1 Knyaz Batenberg St., tel. 056/4–54–96).
Golden Sands (tel. 052/85–53–02 or 052/85–54–14).
Nesebâr (tel. 0554/58–30 or 0554/58–33).
Sunny Beach (tel. 0554/23–35 or 0554/25–10).
Sveti Konstantin (tel. 052/86–10–45).
Varna (main office, 3 Moussala Sq., tel. 052/22–34–84 or 052/22–22–72; private accommodations office, 3 Moussala Sq., tel. 052/22–55–24 or Slaveikov Sq., tel. 052/22–22–06).

Exploring the Black Sea Golden Coast

Varna

Varna, Bulgaria's third-largest city, is easily reached by rail (about 7½ hours by express) or road from Sofia. If you plan to drive, allow time to see the Stone Forest (Pobiti Kammani) just off the Sofia–Varna road between Devnya and Varna. The unexpected groups of monumental petrified tree trunks are thought to have been formed when the area was the bed of the Lutsian Sea. There is plenty to see in the port city of Varna. The ancient city, named Odessos by the Greeks, became a major Roman trading center and is now an important shipbuilding and industrial city. The main sights can be linked by a planned walk.

Begin with the **Archeologicheski Musei,** one of the great—if lesser known—museums of Europe. The splendid collection includes the world's oldest gold treasures from the Varna necropolis of the 4th millennium BC, as well as Thracian, Greek, and Roman treasures, and richly painted icons. *41 Osmi Primorski Polk Blvd., tel. 052/23–70–57. Open Tues.–Sat. 10–5.*

Near the northeastern end of Osmi Primorski Polk Boulevard are numerous shops and cafés; the western end leads to Mitropolit Simeon Square and the monumental **cathedral** (1880–86), whose lavish murals are worth a look. Running north from the cathedral is Vladislav Varnenchik Street, with shops, movie theaters, and eateries. Opposite the cathedral, in the city gardens, is the **Old Clock Tower,** built in 1880 by the Varna Guild Association. On the south side of the city gardens, on Nezavisimost Square, stands the magnificent Baroque **Stoyan Buch-varov National Theater.**

Leave the square to the east and walk past the Moussala Hotel. Nearby, on the corner of Knyaz Boris I Boulevard and Shipka Street, are the remains of the **Roman fortress wall.** Knyaz Boris I Boulevard is another of Varna's shopping streets where you can buy handcrafted souvenirs.

Walk south along Odessos Street to Han Krum Street. Here you'll find the Holy Virgin Church of 1602 and the substantial remains of the **Roman baths,** dating from the 2nd to the 3rd century AD. Buy the excellent English guidebook here to get the most out of your visit.

Not far from the baths as you walk west is old Drazki Street, recently restored and comfortingly lined with restaurants, taverns, and coffeehouses.

Head toward the sea and November 8 Street. Continue to Primorski Boulevard and follow it, with the sea on your right, to No. 2 for the **Naval Museum** (tel. 052/22–26–55; open weekdays 8–4), with its displays of the early days of navigation on the Black Sea and the Danube. The museum is at the edge of the extensive and luxuriant **Marine Gardens,** which command a wide view over the bay. In the gardens there are restaurants, an open-air theater, and the fascinating **Copernicus Astronomy Complex** (tel. 052/22–28–90; open weekdays 8–noon and 2–5) near the main entrance.

Sveti Konstantin

Eight kilometers (5 miles) north along the coast from Varna is **Sveti Konstantin,** Bulgaria's oldest Black Sea resort. Small and intimate, it spreads through a wooded park near a series of sandy coves. Warm mineral springs were discovered here in 1947, and the five-star **Grand Hotel Varna,** the most luxurious on the coast, offers all kinds of hydrotherapy under medical supervision (*see* Lodging, *below*).

In contrast to the sedate atmosphere of Sveti Konstantin is lively Zlatni Pjasâci, better known as **Golden Sands,** another 8 kilometers (5 miles) to the north, with its extensive leisure amenities, mineral-spring medical centers, and sports and entertainment facilities. Just over 4 kilometers (2 miles) inland from Golden Sands is **Aladja Rock Monastery,** one of Bulgaria's oldest, cut out of the cliff face and made accessible to visitors by sturdy iron stairways.

From Sveti Konstantin, if time permits, take a trip 16 kilometers (10 miles) north to **Balčik.** Part of Romania until just before World War II, it is now a relaxed haven for Bulgaria's writers, artists, and scientists. On its white cliffs are crescent-shaped tiers sprinkled with houses, and by the Balčik Palace, the beautiful **Botanical Gardens** contain some curious buildings, including a small Byzantine-style church.

Albena, the newest Black Sea resort, is located between Balčik and Golden Sands. It is well known for its long, wide beach and clean sea. The most luxurious among its 35 hotels is the **Dobrudja,** with extensive hydrotherapy facilities.

Sunny Beach

Another popular resort, this one 36 kilometers (22.5 miles) south of Varna, is Slânčev Brjag, more familiarly known as **Sunny Beach**. It is enormous and especially suited to families because of its safe beaches, gentle tides, and facilities for children. During the summer there are kindergartens for young vacationers, children's concerts, and even a children's discotheque. Sunny Beach has a variety of beachside restaurants, kiosks, and playgrounds.

Nesebâr is 5 kilometers (3 miles) south of Sunny Beach and accessible by regular excursion buses. It would be hard to find a town that exudes a greater sense of age than this ancient settlement, founded by the Greeks 25 centuries ago on a rocky peninsula reached by a narrow causeway. Among its vine-covered houses are richly decorated medieval churches. Don't miss the frescoes and the dozens of small, private, cozy pubs all over Nesebâr.

Continue traveling south along the coast. The next place of any size is **Burgas,** Bulgaria's second main port on the Black Sea. Burgas is rather industrial, with several oil refineries, though it does have a pleasant **Maritime Park** with an extensive beach below.

For a more appealing stopover, continue another 32 kilometers (20 miles) south to **Sozopol,** a fishing port with narrow cobbled streets leading down to the harbor. This was Apollonia, the oldest of the Greek colonies in Bulgaria. It is now a popular haunt for Bulgarian and, increasingly, foreign writers and artists who find private accommodations in the rustic Black Sea–style houses, so picturesque with their rough stone foundations and unpainted wood slats on the upper stories. It is also famous for the Apollonia Arts Festival, held each September.

Ten kilometers (6 miles) farther south is the vast, modern resort village of **Djuni,** where visitors can stay in up-to-date cottages, in the modern Monastery Compound, or in the Seaside Settlement. The wide range of amenities—cafés, folk restaurants, a sports center, a shopping center, a yacht club, and a marina—make it another attractive vacation spot for families.

Dining and Lodging

For details and price-category definitions, *see* Dining and Lodging *in* Staying in Bulgaria, *above*. Gradually, even restaurants in the $$ category are beginning to accept credit cards. To be safe, ask at the restaurant before you order.

Albena

DINING
Bambuka. This open-air restaurant serves international and Bulgarian cuisines and seafood. *Albena Resort, tel. 0572/24–04. No credit cards. $$*

LODGING
Dobrudja Hotel. The mineral-water health spa is a main attraction at this big, comfortable hotel. *Albena Resort, tel. 0572/20–20, fax*

0572/2216. 272 rooms with bath. Facilities: 2 restaurants, 2 bars, nightclub, coffee shops, indoor and outdoor swimming pools, fitness center, hydrotherapy, shops. DC, MC, V. $$

Burgas

DINING

Starata Gemia. The name of this restaurant translates to "old boat," appropriate for a beachfront restaurant that features fish specialties. *Next to the Primorets Hotel, tel. 056/45708. No credit cards. $$*

LODGING

Bulgaria. The Bulgaria is a high-rise Interhotel in the center of town. It features its own nightclub with floor show and a restaurant set in a winter garden. *21 Aleksandrovska St., tel. 056/4-28-20, fax 056/47291. 200 rooms, with bath or shower. DC, MC, V. $$*

Sunny Beach (Slânčev Brjag)

DINING

Hanska Šatra. In the coastal hills behind the sea, this combination restaurant and nightclub has been built to resemble the tents of the *Hans* (Bulgarian rulers) of old. It has entertainment well into the night. *4.8 km (3 mi) west of Slânčev Brjag, tel. 0554/2811. No credit cards. $$*

Ribarska Hiza. This lively beachside restaurant specializes in fish and has music until 1 AM. *Northern end of Slânčev Brjag Resort, tel. 0554/2186. No credit cards. $*

LODGING

Burgas. Large and comfortable, this hotel lies at the southern end of the resort. *Slânčev Brjag Resort, tel. 0554/2358, 0554/2524. 250 rooms with bath or shower. Facilities: restaurant, bar, coffee shop, 2 pools, gym. AE, DC, MC, V. $$*

Čajka. For its price category, this hotel offers the best location. *Slânčev Brjag Resort, tel. 0554/2308. 36 rooms with bath or shower. No credit cards. $$*

★ **Globus.** Considered by many to be the best in the resort, this hotel combines a central location with modern facilities. *Slânčev Brjag Resort, tel. 0554/22-45, fax 0554/2921. 100 rooms with bath or shower. Facilities: restaurant, bar, coffee shop, indoor pool, gym. AE, DC, MC, V. $$*

Kuban. Near the center of the resort, this large establishment is just a short stroll from the beach. *Slânčev Brjag Resort, tel. 0554/2309, fax 0554/2524. 216 rooms with bath or shower. Facilities: 2 restaurants, 2 coffee shops. AE, DC, MC, V. $$*

Sveti Konstantin

DINING

Bulgarska Svatba. This folk-style restaurant with dancing is on the outskirts of the resort; charcoal-grilled meats are especially recommended. *Sveti Konstantin Resort, tel. 052/86-12-83. No credit cards. $$*

Manastirska Izba. Centrally located, this eatery is a modest but pleasant restaurant with a sunny terrace. *Sveti Konstantin Resort, tel. 052/86-20-36. No credit cards. $$*

LODGING

★ **Grand Hotel Varna.** This Swedish-built hotel has a reputation for being the best hotel on the coast. It is set just 450 feet from the beach and offers a wide range of hydrotherapeutic treatments featuring the natural warm mineral springs. *Sveti Konstantin Resort, tel. 052/86-14-91, fax 052/86-19-20. 325 rooms with bath. Facilities: 3 restaurants, 2 bars, coffee shop, nightclub, 2 swimming pools, gym, tennis courts, bowling alley, shops. AE, DC, MC, V. $$$*

Čajka. Çajka means "seagull" in Bulgarian, and this hotel has a bird's-eye view of the entire resort from its perch above the northern end of the beach. *Sveti Konstantin Resort, tel. 052/86–13–32. 130 rooms with bath or shower. No credit cards. $$*

Varna

DINING

Orbita. Don't come here for the ambience (dark room, simple tables) but to experience the typical East European food in vast quantities. This cheap hole-in-the-wall is extremely popular with the locals, who come here for the lentil soup, grilled kebabs with potatoes, or Bulgarian sausage in a pot. *25 Tsar Osvoboditel, in Hotel Orbita, off Knyaz Boris I Blvd., tel. 052/22–52–75. No credit cards. $$*

Horizont. This restaurant near the Delphinerium has a good selection of seafood as well as a view of the Black Sea from its outside tables. It's not too busy during the day, but at night the live music draws a crowd. *Morskaya Gradina, tel. 052/88–45–30. No credit cards. $*

LODGING

★ **Černo More.** One of the more modern hotels in Varna, the Černo More offers panoramic vistas from the top floors of its 22-story-high tower. *33 Slivnitza Blvd., tel. 052/23–21–15. 230 rooms with bath or shower. Facilities: 3 restaurants, bar, ground-floor café with terraces, nightclub. AE, DC, MC, V. $$$*

INLAND BULGARIA

Inland Bulgaria is not as well known to tourists as the capital and the coast, but an adventurous traveler willing to put up with limited hotel facilities and unreliable transportation will find plenty to photograph, paint, or simply savor. Wooded and mountainous, the interior is dotted with attractive "museum" villages (entire settlements listed for preservation because of their historic cultural value) and ancient towns; the folk culture is a strong survivor from the past, not a tourist-inspired re-creation of it. The foothills of the Balkan Range, marked Stara Planina ("old mountains") on most maps, lie parallel with the lower Sredna Gora Mountains, with the verdant Rozova Dolina (Valley of Roses) between them. In the Balkan range is the ancient capital of Veliko Târnovo; south of the Sredna Gora stretches the fertile Thracian plain and Bulgaria's second-largest city, Plovdiv. Between Sofia and Plovdiv is the enchanting old town of Koprivshtitsa. To the south, in the Rila Mountains, is Borovec, first of the mountain resorts. A round-trip covering all these towns, with a side excursion to Rila Monastery, could be made in four or five days, although more time is recommended.

Getting Around

Rail and bus services cover all parts of inland Bulgaria, but the timetables are not easy to follow and there are frequent delays. The best bet is to rent a car. You may also prefer to hire a driver; Balkantourist can arrange this.

Guided Tours

Organized tours set out from Sofia, each covering different points of interest. Check with your Sofia hotel information desk or with Balkantourist for specific information.

Tourist Information

Plovdiv (106 Bulgaria Blvd., tel. 032/55–38–48).
Veliko Târnovo (2 Al. Penchev St., tel. 062/30571 or 2 Opâchenska St., tel. 062/30353).

Exploring Inland Bulgaria

Koprivshtitsa

Koprivshtitsa, one of Bulgaria's showpiece villages, is set in mountain pastures and pine forests, about 3,050 feet up in the Sredna Gora range. It is 105 kilometers (65 miles) from Sofia, reached by a minor road south from the Sofia–Kazanlak expressway. Founded during the 14th century, it became a prosperous trading center with close ties to Venice during the National Revival period 400 years later. The architecture of this period, also called the Bulgarian Renaissance, features carved woodwork on broad verandas and overhanging eaves, brilliant colors, and courtyards with studded wooden gates. Throughout the centuries, artists, poets, and wealthy merchants have made their homes here, and many of the historic houses can be visited. The town has been well preserved and revered by the Bulgarians as a symbol of freedom since April 1876, when the rebellion that led, two years later, to the end of Turkish occupation ignited.

Return to the main road and turn right. After 15 kilometers (9 miles) you'll reach **Klisura** and the beginning of the Valley of Roses. Here the famous Bulgarian rose water and attar, or essence, are produced. Each May and June, the whole valley is awash in fragrance and color. After another 17 kilometers (11 miles), turn at the village of Karnare; take the winding scenic road north over the Balkan range to the town of Trojan; and, a few miles away, you'll see the **Trojan Monastery,** built during the 1600s in the heart of the mountains. The Trojan Monastery Church was painstakingly remodeled during the 19th century, and its icons, wood carvings, and frescoes are classic examples of National Revival art. Back at Trojan, continue north on the mountain road until it meets highway E771, where you turn right for Veliko Târnovo, 82 kilometers (50 miles) away.

Veliko Târnovo

Veliko Târnovo, a town of panoramic vistas, rises up against steep mountain slopes through which the River Jantra runs its jagged course. From the 12th to the 14th century, this was the capital of the Second Bulgarian Kingdom. Damaged by repeated Ottoman attack, and again by an earthquake in 1913, it has been reconstructed and is now a museum city of marvelous relics. The town warrants two or three days of exploration, but even in a short visit some sights should not be missed. Ideally, you should begin at a vantage point above the town in order to get an overview of its design and character. Next, seek out **Tsarevec** to the west (Carevec on some maps), protected by a river loop. This is where medieval tsars and patriarchs had their palaces. The area is under restoration, and steep paths and stairways now provide opportunities to view the extensive ruins of the patriarchate and the royal palace. On summer evenings, there is a spectacular sound-and-light show that can be seen from nearby pubs.

The prominent feature to the south is **Baldwin's Tower,** the 13th-century prison of Baldwin of Flanders, onetime Latin emperor of Constantinople. Nearby are three important churches: the 13th-century **Church of the Forty Martyrs,** with its Târnovo school frescoes and two inscribed columns, one dating from the 9th century; the **Church of Sts.**

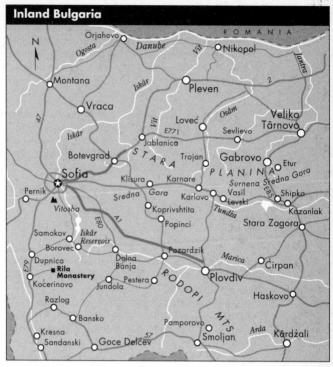

Peter and Paul, with vigorous murals both inside and out; and, across the river, reached by a bridge near the Forty Martyrs, the restored **Church of Saint Dimitrius,** built on the spot where the Second Bulgarian Kingdom was launched in 1185.

Back toward the center of town, near the Jantra Hotel, is Samovodene Street, lined with restored crafts workshops—a fascinating place to linger in and a good place to find souvenirs, Turkish candy, or a charming café. On nearby Rakovski Street are a group of buildings of the National Revival period. One of the finest is **Hadji Nikoli,** a museum that was once an inn. *17 Georgi Sava Rakovski, tel. 062/2–17–10. Closed for renovations at press time.*

Moving east from Veliko Târnovo toward Varna on E771, you can go back farther in time by visiting the ruins of the two capitals of the First Bulgarian Kingdom in the vicinity of **Šumen** (spelled Shoumen in some English translations). The first ruins are the fortifications at **Pliska,** 23 kilometers (14 miles) southeast of Šumen, and date from 681. At **Veliki Preslav,** 21 kilometers (13 miles) southwest of Šumen, there are ruins from the second capital that date from 893 to 927. The 8th- to 9th-century **Madara Horseman,** a bas-relief of a rider slaying a lion, appears 18 kilometers (11 miles) east of town on a sheer cliff face.

If you leave Veliko Târnovo by E85 and head south toward **Plovdiv,** you can make three interesting stops en route. The first, near the industrial center of Gabrovo—is the museum village of **Etur,** 8 kilometers (5 miles) to the southeast. Its mill is still powered by a stream, and local craftsmen continue to be trained in traditional skills. The second is **Shipka Pass,** with its mighty monument on the peak to the 200,000 Russian soldiers and Bulgarian volunteers who died here in 1877 during the Russian-Turkish Wars. The third is **Kazanlak,** at the eastern end of the Valley of Roses, where you can trace the history of rose production, Bulgaria's oldest industry. Here, in early June, young rose pickers dress in traditional costumes for rose parades and other carnival processions. There is also a highly decorated replica of a Thracian tomb of the 3rd or 4th century BC, set near the original, which remains closed for its preservation.

Plovdiv

From Kazanlak, take the road west through the **Valley of Roses** to either Vasil Levski or Karlovo, another rose festival town. Then turn south for **Plovdiv,** Bulgaria's second-largest city, one of the oldest cities in Europe and a major industrial center. The old town, on the hillier southern side of the Marica River, is worth a visit.

Begin at the **National Ethnographical Museum** in the House of Arghir Koyumdjioglu, an elegant example of the National Revival style that made its first impact in Plovdiv. The museum is filled with artifacts from that important period. *2 Čomakov St., tel. 032/22–56–56. Open Tues.–Sun. 9–noon and 1:30–5.*

Below the medieval gateway of Hissar Kapiya are the attractive **Georgiadi House,** on Starinna Street, and the steep, narrow **Strumna Street,** lined with workshops and boutiques, some reached through little courtyards. Follow Saborna Street westward to its junction with the pedestrians-only Knyaz Alexander I Street; here you'll find the remains of a **Roman stadium.** Nearby, the **Kapana District** has many restored and traditional shops and restaurants. Turn east off Knyaz Alexander I Street and walk to the fine hilltop **Roman amphitheater,** sensitively renovated and frequently used for dramatic and musical performances. On the other side of the old town, toward the river, is the **National Archaeological Museum,** which holds a replica of the 4th-century BC Panagjuriste Gold Treasure, the original of which is in Sofia. *1 Suedinenie Sq., Open Tues.–Sun. 9–12:30 and 2–5:30.*

Travel west along the E80 Sofia road. At Dolna Banja, turn off to **Borovec,** slightly more than 4,300 feet up the northern slopes of the Rila Mountains. This is an excellent walking center and winter sports resort, well equipped with hotels, folk taverns, and ski schools. The winding mountain road leads back to Sofia, 70 kilometers (44 miles) from here, past Lake Iskar, the largest in the country.

On the way back to Sofia, you should consider a visit to the **Rila Monastery,** founded by Ivan of Rila during the 10th century. Cut across to E79, travel south to Kočerinovo, and then turn east to follow the steep forested valley past the village of Rila. The monastery has suffered so frequently from fire that most of it is now a grand National Revival reconstruction, although a rugged 14th-century tower has survived. The atmosphere in this mountain retreat, populated by many storks, is still heavy with a sense of the past—although part of the complex has been turned into a museum and some of the monks' cells are now guest rooms. The visitor can see 14 small chapels with frescoes from the 15th and 17th centuries, a lavishly carved altarpiece in the new Assumption Church, the sarcophagus of Ivan of Rila, icons, and ancient manuscripts—a reminder that this was a stronghold of art and learning during the centuries of Ottoman rule. It is well worth the detour of 120 kilometers (75 miles)—or a special trip from Sofia.

Dining and Lodging

For details and price-category definitions, *see* Dining and Lodging *in* Staying in Bulgaria, *above*. In *$$* hotels and restaurants, check to see whether your credit card will be accepted.

Koprivshtitsa

DINING

Djedo Liben Inn. This attractive folk restaurant with a bar and night-club is built in the traditional style of the area—with half-timber, high stone walls. The menu reflects similar attention to traditional detail. *Tel. 997184/21–09. No credit cards. $$*

LODGING

Barikadite. This small hotel is located on a hill 15 kilometers (9 miles) from Koprivshtitsa. *Tel. 997184/20–91. 20 rooms with shower. Facilities: restaurant, bar, nightclub. No credit cards. $*

Koprivshtitsa. This good-value hotel is popular with vacationing Bulgarians and is just over the river from the center of town. *Tel. 997184/21–18. 30 rooms with bath or shower. No credit cards. $*

Plovdiv

DINING

Puldin. This is an attractive folk restaurant in the center of town. A video presentation in the lobby highlights the city's past. *3 Knyaz Tseretelev St., tel. 032/23–17–20. AE, DC, MC, V. $$$*

Alafrangite. This charming folk-style restaurant is in a restored 19th-century house with wood-carved ceilings and a vine-covered courtyard. One of the specialities is *kiopolu* (vegetable pureé of baked eggplant, peppers, and tomatoes). *17 Nektariev St., tel. 032/22–98–09 or 032/26–95–95. No credit cards. $$*

Filipopol. This is an elegant folk-style restaurant with a menu that combines traditional Bulgarian, Greek, and international cuisine (including seafood); the food is served by candlelight to the accompaniment of a jazz piano. Try the rich salads and *chushka byurek* (baked green peppers stuffed with cheese and eggs). *56 Stamat Matanov St., tel. 032/22–52–96. No credit cards. $*

Rhetora. This coffee bar is in a beautifully restored old house near the Roman amphitheater in the old part of the city. *8A G. Samodoumov St., tel. 032/22–20–93. No credit cards. $*

LODGING

Novotel Plovdiv. The large, modern, and well-equipped Novotel is across the river from the main town, near the fairgrounds. *2 Zlatju Boyadjiev St., tel. 032/55–51–71 or 032/5–58–92. 322 rooms with bath. Facilities: restaurant, bar, folk tavern, nightclub, gym, swimming pools, shop. AE, DC, MC, V. $$$*

Trimontium. This centrally located Interhotel built in the 1950s is comfortable and ideal for exploring the old town. *2 Kapitan Raico St., tel. 032/2–34–91. 163 rooms with bath or shower. Facilities: restaurant, bar, folk tavern, shop. AE, DC, MC, V. $$$*

Marica. This is a large, modern hotel that offers a less expensive alternative to its neighbor, the Novotel. *42 Vazrazhdane Blvd., tel. 032/55–27–35. 171 rooms with bath or shower. Facilities: restaurant, bar. AE, DC, MC, V. $*

Veliko Târnovo

DINING

Boljarska Izba. In the center of the busy district just north of the river, this is a popular place with the locals, many of whom order the house sarmi (vine leaves stuffed with pork). *Dimiter Blagoev St., no phone. No credit cards. $$*

<u>LODGING</u>

Veliko Târnovo. Located right in the middle of the most historic part of the town, this modern Interhotel boasts some of the best facilities for this class of hotel. *2 Emile Popov St., tel. 062/3–05–71. 195 rooms with bath or shower. Facilities: 2 restaurants, bar, coffee shop, disco, gym, indoor pool, shops. AE, DC, MC, V. $$$*

Etur. This moderate-size hotel's address near the more expensive Veliko Târnovo makes it a good base for sightseeing within town. *1 Ivailo St., tel. 062/2–68–51. 80 rooms with shower. Facilities: restaurant, bar, coffee shop. AE, DC, MC, V. $*

Jantra. The Jantra has some of the best views in town, looking across the river to Tsaravec. *1 Velchova Zavera Sq., tel. 062/2–03–91. 60 rooms, most with shower. Facilities: restaurant, bar, coffee shop. DC, MC, V. $*

6 Cyprus

THE MEDITERRANEAN ISLAND of Cyprus was once a center for the cult of Aphrodite, the Greek goddess who is said to have risen naked and perfect from the sea near what is now the beach resort of Paphos. Wooded and mountainous, with a 751-kilometer-long (466-mile-long) coastline, Cyprus lies just off the southern coast of Turkey. Oranges, olives, lemons, grapes, and cherries grow here, and fish are plentiful. The summers are hot and dry, the springs gentle. Snow covers the Troodos Mountains in winter, making it possible to ski in the morning and sunbathe on a beach in the afternoon.

Cyprus's strategic position in the eastern Mediterranean has made it subject to regular invasions by powerful countries. Greeks, Phoenicians, Assyrians, Egyptians, Persians, Romans, and Byzantines—all have ruled here. In the Middle Ages, King Richard I of England took Cyprus from the Byzantine Empire by force and gave it to Guy of Lusignan. Guy's descendants ruled the island until the late-15th century, when it was annexed by the Venetians. From the 16th century to the 19th century it was ruled by the Turks. It became a British colony in 1914.

The influence of diverse cultures adds to the island's appeal to tourists. Many fortifications built by the Crusaders and the Venetians still stand. The tomb of the Prophet Mohammed's aunt (Hala Sultan Tekke), on the shores of the great salt lake near Larnaca, is one of Islam's most important shrines. A piece of the true cross is said to exist in the Monastery of Stavrovouni, and Paphos has the remains of a pillar to which St. Paul was allegedly tied and beaten for preaching Christianity.

The upheavals are not over. Following independence in 1960, the island became the focus of Greek–Turkish contention. Currently nearly 80% of the population are Greek Cypriots and 18% are Turkish Cypriots. Since 1974 Cyprus has been divided by a thin buffer zone—occupied by United Nations (UN) forces—between the Turkish Cypriot north and the Greek Cypriot south. The zone cuts right through the capital city of Nicosia. Talks aimed at uniting the communities into one bizonal federal state have been going on for years, lately under the auspices of the UN's secretary general. Both communities offer comfortable tourist facilities.

ESSENTIAL INFORMATION

Before You Go

When to Go

The tourist season runs throughout the year, though prices tend to be lower from November through March. Spring and fall are best, usually warm enough for swimming but not uncomfortably hot.

CLIMATE

The rainy season is in January and February, and it often snows in the highest parts of the Troodos Mountains from January through March. January and February can be cold and wet; July and August are always very hot and dry.

The following are the average daily maximum and minimum temperatures for Nicosia.

Cyprus

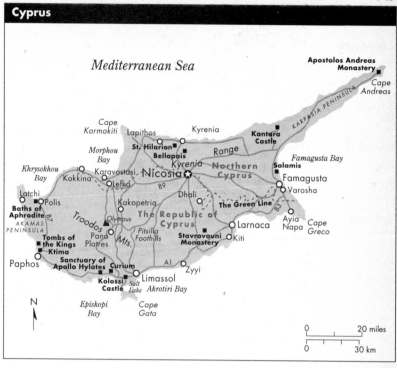

Jan.	59F	15C	May	85F	29C	Sept.	92F	33C
	42	5		58	14		65	18
Feb.	61F	16C	June	92F	33C	Oct.	83F	28C
	42	5		65	18		58	14
Mar.	66F	19C	July	98F	37C	Nov.	72F	22C
	44	7		70	21		51	10
Apr.	75F	24C	Aug.	98F	37C	Dec.	63F	17C
	50	10		69	21		45	7

Visas

No visas are necessary for holders of valid passports from the United States, Canada, the United Kingdom, and other European countries.

Customs on Arrival

Duty-free allowances are: 250 grams of tobacco, 1 liter of spirits, 750 milliliters of wine, 300 milliliters of perfume, and up to C£50 in other goods.

The export of antiques and historical artifacts is strictly forbidden unless a license is obtained from the Ministry of Tourism in Nicosia.

Language

Greek is the main language, but English is widely spoken in hotels, tavernas, and other tourist haunts. Off the beaten track, sign language may have to do.

THE REPUBLIC OF CYPRUS

Currency

The monetary unit in the Republic of Cyprus is the Cyprus pound (C£), which is divided into 100 cents. There are notes of C£20, C£10, C£5, and C£1 and coins of 50, 20, 10, 5, 2, and 1 Cyprus cents. At press time (spring 1995) there were C£0.39 to the U.S. dollar and C£0.70 to the pound sterling.

What It Will Cost

A cup of coffee or tea costs Cyprus 60¢–C£1; a glass of beer 75¢–C£1; a kebab around C£1–C£1.50; a bottle of local wine C£1–C£3. Admission to museums and galleries costs 50¢–C£1.

Arriving and Departing

By Plane

There are now direct flights between Larnaca and New York via **Gulf Air. Cyprus Airways** and **British Airways** fly direct from London, Birmingham, and Manchester to Larnaca and Paphos. Cyprus Airways also operates from Athens, Amsterdam, Brussels, Frankfurt, Munich, Paris, Vienna, and Zurich. **Alitalia** flies from Rome. **United Airlines** and **Swiss Air** have good connections.

By Boat

Passenger ships connect Cyprus with various Greek, Egyptian, Italian, and Middle Eastern ports.

Getting Around

By Car

An international or national license is acceptable for driving in Cyprus. Drive on the left. Main roads between large towns are good. Minor roads can be unsurfaced, narrow, and winding. Gas costs 37¢ per liter. Cars may be rented from C£20 per day; lower rates are available off season.

By Bus

This is the cheapest form of transportation in urban areas; the fare is 40¢. Buses operate every half hour and cover an extensive network. In Nicosia, buses run until 7:30 PM (winter 6:30 PM). In tourist areas during the summer, services are extended until midnight.

Intercity bus fares range between C£2 and C£3. For information on the Nicosia–Limassol–Paphos route, tel. 02/464636; or on the Limassol–Larnaca–Ayia Napa route, tel. 05/351031.

By Service Taxi

Shared taxis accommodate four to seven passengers and are a cheap, fast, and comfortable way of traveling between towns. Taxis operate between the main towns—Nicosia, Limassol, Larnaca, and Paphos. Tariffs are from C£1.65 to C£4.25. Seats must be booked by phone, and passengers may embark/disembark anywhere within the town boundaries. The taxis run every half hour (Mon.–Sat. 5:45 AM–6:30 PM). Sunday service is less frequent and rides must be booked one day ahead. Contact the **Kypros Taxi Office** (tel. 02/464811), **Karydas** (tel. 02/463126), or **Kyriakos** (tel. 02/444141).

By Private Taxi

Private taxis operate 24 hours throughout the island. They are generally very cheap within towns but far more expensive than service taxis between towns. Telephone from your hotel or hail one in the street. Urban taxis have an initial charge of 59¢ and charge 23¢ per kilometer (.6 mile) in the daytime, more at night. Drivers are bound by law to use and display a meter. Ask the driver what it will cost before you depart, and don't be afraid to barter. In-town journeys range from C£1.50 to about C£3.

Staying in the Republic of Cyprus

Telephones

LOCAL CALLS

Pay phones take 2¢, 10¢, and 20¢ coins. Some newer pay phones also take 5¢ coins, and others take telecards of C£2, C£5, and C£10, which can be purchased at post offices, souvenir shops, and kiosks. Cheaper rates apply from 10 PM to 8 AM and all day Sunday. For telephone inquiries service, dial 192 in all towns.

INTERNATIONAL CALLS

To reach an **AT&T** long-distance operator, dial 080–90010; for **MCI,** 080–90000; for **Sprint,** 080–90001. Public phones may require a deposit of a coin or phone card when you call these services.

COUNTRY CODE

The country code for Cyprus is 357.

Mail

A 20-gram letter to the United States costs 36¢, a postcard, 26¢. To Europe, a 20-gram letter costs 31¢, and a postcard 21¢. Post offices are open Mon.–Fri. 7:30 AM–2:30 PM. Stamps are also sold at hotels, newsstands, and kiosks.

Opening and Closing Times

Banks are open weekdays 8:15 AM–12:30 PM. Some have afternoon tourist services and will cash traveler's checks weekdays 3–6 in winter, 4–7 in summer, in addition to Saturday 8:30–noon year-round.

Museum hours vary greatly. It pays to check ahead. Generally, museums are closed for lunch and on Sunday. Most ancient monuments are open from dawn to dusk.

Shops are open Monday–Saturday 8–1 and 4–7 PM (summer); 2–5:30 PM (winter). Shops are closed Wednesday and Saturday afternoons and on Sundays year-round. In tourist areas shops generally maintain longer hours.

National Holidays

January 1; January 6 (Epiphany); April 12–15 (Greek Easter); May 1 (May Day); June 3 (Pentecost Monday); August 15 (Assumption); October 1 (Cyprus Independence Day); October 28 (Greek National Day); December 25, 26.

Tipping

A service charge of 10%, a 3% charge by the Cyprus tourist organization, and an 8% VAT are usually added to all bills. If service has been especially good, add 5%.

Important Addresses and Numbers

The main **tourist information office** is in Nicosia (19 Limassol Ave., tel. 02/337715, fax 02/331644). This is the head office; for personal and telephone inquiries, call the other Nicosia office at Laiki Yitonia (tel. 02/444264). There are local offices at all major resorts.

EMBASSIES OR HIGH COMMISSIONS
U.S. Embassy (Metochiou Ploutarchou, Box 4536, Engomi, Nicosia, tel. 02/476100, fax 02/465944). **British High Commission** (Alexander Pallis St., Nicosia, tel. 02/473131–7, fax 02/367198). **Consulate of Canada** (15 Them Dervis St., Box 2125, Nicosia, tel. 02/451630, fax 02/459096).

EMERGENCIES
Ambulance, Fire Brigade, and **Police** (tel. 199). **Doctor: Nicosia General Hospital** (tel. 02/451111); **Limassol Hospital** (tel. 05/330333); **Paphos Hospital** (tel. 06/240111). **Pharmacies** (tel. 192 for information about opening times in English). A list with additional opening details appears in the English-language *Cyprus Mail* and *Cyprus Weekly*.

Guided Tours

Guided tours are often the best way to see Cyprus and learn about its rich history. Try **National Sightseeing Tours** (c/o Louis Tourist Agency, 54–58 Evagoras Ave., Nicosia, tel. 02/442114) for half-day and full-day trips—expect to pay C£7–C£12. Night tours are quite popular, and typically include dinner at a local taverna, folk dancing, and bouzouki music. In Limassol, **Laikon Shipping** (124 Ayias Paraskevis St., tel. 05/326108) arranges coastal cruises on the *Lady Thetis* that usually include lunch on board; if passengers wish to go ashore to eat, they may do so independently.

Exploring the Republic of Cyprus

Nicosia

The capital, **Nicosia,** is twice divided. The picturesque Old City is contained within 16th-century Venetian fortifications that separate it from the wide, tree-lined streets, large hotels, and high-rises of the modern section. The second division is political and more noticeable. The so-called Green Line (set up by the UN) divides the island between the Republic of Cyprus and Turkish-occupied Northern Cyprus. It is possible, at press time (spring 1995), to arrange a day trip from the Greek to the Turkish sector through the official checkpoint in Nicosia (Ledra Palace), though it is essential to return by 5 PM. Visits in the other direction are not permitted.

In the Greek sector a good starting point is **Laiki Yitonia** at the southern edge of the Old City, an area of winding alleys and traditional architecture. Tavernas, cafés, and crafts workshops line the shaded, cobbled streets. Just to the west lies Ledra Street, where modern shops alternate with yet more crafts shops. Head north of the tourist information center (tel. 02/444264) in Laiki Yitonia to visit the tiny **Tripiotis Church.** This Greek Orthodox church, with its ornately carved golden iconostasis and silver-covered icons, dates from 1690.

The **Leventis Museum,** also in Laiki Yitonia, traces the history of Nicosia from 3000 BC to the present with exhibits on crafts and daily life. *17 Hippocratous St., tel. 02/451475. Admission free. Open Tues.–Sun. 10–4:30.*

Within the walls to the east of the Old City is a cluster of museums. Housed in a wing of the Archbishopric built in 1960 in neo-Byzantine style, the **Archbishop Makarios III Cultural Foundation** consists of the **Byzantine Art Museum,** with fine displays of icons spanning 1,000 years, and the **Greek War of Independence Gallery,** with a collection of maps, paintings, and mementos of 1821. *Archbishop Kyprianou Sq., tel. 02/ 456781. Admission: C£1. Open weekdays 9–1 and 2–5, Sat. 9–1.*

Next door, the **Museum of the National Struggle** has dramatic displays of the Cypriot campaigns against the British during the pre-independence years 1955–59. *Archbishop Kyprianou Sq., tel. 02/302465. Admission: 25¢. Open weekdays 8–2.*

Close by is the **Cyprus Folk Art Museum** (housed in the 14th-century part of the Archbishopric), which offers demonstrations of ancient weaving techniques and displays of ceramics, olive and wine presses. *Archbishop Kyprianou Sq., tel. 02/463205. Admission: 50¢. Open weekdays 8:30–4, Sat. 8:30–1.*

Don't miss **St. John's Cathedral** (Ayios Ioannis), built in 1662 within the courtyard of the Archbishopric. Look for the 18th-century wall paintings, which illustrate Cypriot moments of religious significance, including a depiction of the tomb of St. Barnabas. **Famagusta Gate** is just a short walk to the east. Now a cultural center, it houses exhibitions, a lecture hall, and a theater. *Athina St., tel. 02/430877. Open weekdays 8–1 and 4–7.*

To the west of the city stands the **Cyprus Museum.** Located outside the city walls near the Paphos Gate, it has extensive archaeological displays ranging from Neolithic to Roman times. This stop is essential to understanding the island's ancient sites. *Museum St., tel. 02/302189. Admission: C£1. Open Mon.–Sat. 9–5, Sun. 10–1.*

Across the street from the museum lie the neoclassical **Municipal Theatre** (1960) and the lush **Municipal Gardens.**

Larnaca

Many visitors choose to stay in the seaside resorts. Larnaca and Paphos, each of which has its own airport, make excellent centers. **Larnaca,** 51 kilometers (32 miles) southeast of Nicosia, is famous as the burial place of Lazarus and for its flamboyant Whitsuntide celebration, *Cataklysmos.* It has fine beaches, palm trees, and a modern harbor and marina, the starting point for boat trips. The tourist office at Democratias Square (tel. 04/654322; open weekdays, hours vary) is right at the marina district and just a short walk from **Larnaca Museum,** with its displays of treasures including outstanding sculptures and Bronze Age seals. *Kimon and Kilkis Sts., tel. 04/630169. Admission: 50¢. Open weekdays 7:30– 2:30, Thurs. 4–7 (winter 3–6).*

A short walk north from the museum, along Kyman Street, will bring you to the site of **Kition,** the old Larnaca of biblical times and one of the most important ancient city-kingdoms. Architectural remains of ancient temples date from the 13th century BC. *Admission: 50¢. Open weekdays 7:30–2:30 and 3–5.*

South of the marina is the 17th-century **Turkish fort,** open the same hours as the Larnaca Museum. The fort contains finds from Hala Sultan Tekke (*see below*) and Kition. On the way to the ancient fort is the **Pierides Collection,** a private collection of more than 3,000 pieces distinguished by Bronze Age terra-cotta figures. *Paul Zenon Kitieus St. near Lord Byron St., tel. 04/651345. Admission: C£1. Open Mon.–Sat. 9–1, Sun. 10–1 and 3–6.*

Walk inland from the fort to the town center and to one of the island's more important churches, **Ayios Lazarus,** resplendent with icons. It has a fascinating crypt containing Lazarus's sarcophagus.

South of Larnaca on the airport road is the 2½-square-mile **Salt Lake.** In winter it's a refuge for migrating birds. On the lake's edge, a mosque stands in an oasis of palm trees guarding the **Hala Sultan Tekke**—burial place of the prophet Mohammed's aunt. This is an important Muslim shrine.

Nearby, the **Panayia Angeloktistos Church,** in Kiti, is famous for its outstanding Byzantine wall mosaics, which date from the 6th and 7th centuries.

Ayia Napa

The formerly samll fishing village of **Ayia Napa,** 30 kilometers (19 miles) east of Larnaca, is anchored by a **16th-century monastery** and renowned for its white, sandy beaches and views of the brilliant sea. Today's emergence of tavernas, bars, restaurants, and fine hotels reflects the town's transformation into Cyprus's premier vacationland. Ayia Napa maintains the flavor of its historic past, however, and from the monastery's 14th-century sycamore tree, you can still enjoy the panoramic view of the Mediterranean.

Paphos

In the west of the island, **Paphos,** 142 kilometers (88 miles) southwest of Nicosia, combines superb sea-swimming with archaeological sites and a rich history. This town, the birthplace of Aphrodite—the Greek goddess of love and beauty—has a modern center with numerous ancient sights. Begin at the tourist office on Gladstone Street (tel. 06/232841; open weekdays, hours vary) in Upper Paphos.

The **Paphos District Museum** is famous for its pottery, jewelry, and statuettes from the Roman villas. *Grivas Dighenis Ave., Ktima, tel. 06/240215. Admission: 50¢. Open weekdays 7:30–2:30 and 4–6 (winter 7:30–2 and 3–5), weekends 10–1.*

Nearby are the notable icons in the **Byzantine Museum** (Andreas Ioannou St., tel. 06/232092) in the Archbishopric and the charming **Ethnographical Museum.** *1 Exo Vrysi, tel. 06/232010. Open 9–1 and 3–7 (winter 9–1 and 2–5).*

Don't miss the elaborate mosaics in the **Roman Villa of Theseus,** the **House of Dionysos,** and the **House of Aion,** all in New Paphos. The mosaics are considered by many to be among the finest in the eastern Mediterranean. The town bus stops nearby. Also worth seeing are the **Tombs of the Kings,** an early necropolis dating from 300 BC. Though the coffin niches are empty, a powerful sense of mystery remains. *Admission: C£1 (mosaics) and 50¢ (Tombs of the Kings). Open daily 7:30–sunset (winter 7:30–5:30).*

Limassol

A commercial port and wine-making center on the south coast, **Limassol,** 75 kilometers (47 miles) from Nicosia, is a bustling, cosmopolitan town popular with tourists. Luxury hotels, apartments, and guest houses stretch along 12 kilometers (7 miles) of seafront. The nightlife is the liveliest on the island. In central Limassol, the elegant modern shops of Makarios Avenue contrast with those of the old part of town, where you'll discover local handicrafts.

The tourist information office (Spyros Araouzos St., tel. 05/362756) is open Monday through Saturday; hours vary. A short walk takes you to **Limassol Fort,** near the old port. This 14th-century castle was built on the site of an earlier Byzantine fortification. According to tradition, Richard the Lionhearted married his future queen of England here in 1191. The **Cyprus Medieval Museum** is housed here and displays a variety of medieval armor and relics. *Tel. 05/330132. Admission: 50¢. Open weekdays 7:30–5, Sat. 9–5, Sun. 10–1.*

For a glimpse of Cypriot folklore, visit the **Folk Art Museum** on St. Andrew's Street. The collection includes national costumes and fine examples of the island's crafts and woven materials. *Tel. 05/362303. Admission: 30¢. Open Mon. and Wed.–Fri. 8:30–1:30 and 4–7 (winter 3–5:30); Tues. 8:30–1:30.*

At the annual **Limassol Wine Festival** in September, local wineries offer free samples and demonstrate traditional grape-pressing methods. There are open-air music and dance performances. If wine making interests you, try a nice side trip to the **KEO Winery,** just west of the town, which welcomes visitors daily. *Roosevelt Ave., toward new port, tel. 05/362053. Admission free. Tours given weekdays at 10.*

Troodos Mountains

The **Troodos Mountains,** north of Limassol, are popular in summer for the shade of their cedar and pine forests and the coolness of their springs. Small, painted churches in the Troodos and **Pitsilia foothills** are rich examples of a rare indigenous art form. **Asinou Church** and **St. Nicholas of the Roof,** south of Kakopetria, are especially noteworthy. Nearby is the **Tall Trees Trout Farm,** a shady oasis serving delicious fresh fish meals. In winter, skiers take over. **Platres,** in the foothills of Mt. Olympus, is the principal resort. Be sure to visit the **Kykko Monastery,** whose prized icon of the Virgin is reputed to have been painted by St. Luke.

Off the Beaten Track

Stavrovouni Monastery stands on a mountain west of Larnaca. It was founded by St. Helena (mother of Emperor Constantine) in AD 326, though the present buildings date from the 19th century. Ideally, it should be visited in a spirit of pilgrimage rather than sightseeing, out of respect for the monks, though the views of the island are splendid. Male visitors are allowed inside the monastery daily from sunrise to sunset, except between noon and 3 (noon and 1 in winter). The monks have decreed that female visitors will be admitted only on Sunday morning.

Curium (Kourion), west of Limassol, has numerous Greek and Roman ruins. There is an **amphitheater,** where actors occasionally present classical and Shakespearean drama. Next to the theater is the **Villa of Eustolios,** a summer house that belonged to a wealthy Christian. A nearby **Roman stadium** has been partially rebuilt. Three kilometers (2 miles) farther along the main Paphos road is the **Sanctuary of Apollo Hylates** (Apollo of the woodlands), an impressive archaeological site. *Admission: C£1. Open daily 7:30–sunset (winter 7:30–5:30).*

Other places to visit include **Kolossi Castle,** a Crusader castle of the Knights of St. John, a 15-minute drive outside Limassol; and the fishing harbor of **Latchi** on the west coast, 32 kilometers (20 miles) north of Paphos. Near Latchi are the **Baths of Aphrodite,** where the goddess of love is said to have seduced swains. The wild and undeveloped Akamas Peninsula is perfect for a hike.

Dining

Most hotels have restaurants, but these tend to serve bland international-style food garnished with french fries. Meals in local restaurants or tavernas start with a variety of mezes (appetizers). Kebabs are popular, as are dolmas, stews, fresh fish, and various lamb dishes. End with fruit or honey pastries and Greek coffee. Moderate establishments display a menu; in inexpensive ones it is customary to go into the kitchen and choose your meal. Food is cheap in Cyprus, and the quality is good.

WHAT TO WEAR
Casual dress is acceptable in all restaurants in Cyprus, regardless of price category.

RATINGS
Prices are for a three-course meal for one person, not including drinks or tip.

CATEGORY	ALL AREAS
$$$	over C£12
$$	C£6–C£12
$	under C£6

Larnaca
Miliges. This sea-view restaurant is popular with tourists and locals. It is near the old fort and has a typical village ambience. *Kleftico* (lamb and goat meat wrapped in bay leaves) cooked in traditional clay ovens is a specialty. *42 Bia-Pasha, tel. 04/655867. AE, DC, MC, V. $$*
Monte Carlo. The outdoor seating in this spot on the road to the airport is on a balcony extending over the sea. Service is efficient, and the dining area is clean. Particularly worthy Cypriot dishes are the fish and meat mezes and casseroles. *28 Piale Pashia, tel. 04/653815. AE, DC, MC, V. $$*

Limassol
Ladas. The old port is the site of this pleasant seafood restaurant. All the fish here is fresh; try the tender and sweet fried calamari and grilled *soupies* (ink fish). *1 Sadi St., tel. 05/365760. Closed Sunday. AE, DC, MC, V. $$*
Porta. A varied menu of international and Cypriot dishes, such as *foukoudha* barbecue (grilled strips of steak) and trout baked in prawn and mushroom sauce, is served in this restored warehouse. On many nights, you'll be entertained by soft live music. *17 Yenethliou Mitella, Old Castle, tel. 05/360339. MC, V. $$*

Nicosia
Archondiko. A lively meeting place for business or pleasure, Archondiko has tables on the walking path of the restored Laiki Yitonia area, indoors in cooler weather. Cypriot cuisine includes savory *lountza* (smoked fillet of pork) and grilled *haloumi* (a salty local cheese). *27 Aristokyprou St., Laiki Yitonia, tel. 02/450080. AE, DC, MC, V. $$*
Cellari. This romantic, candlelighted inn is lent a festive touch by a pair of guitarists strumming mellow Greek and Cypriot favorites. The highlight of this restaurant is the traditional Cypriot cooking, with dishes such as *souvla* (marinated lamb chunks cooked over charcoal). *22 Korai St., tel. 02/448338. No credit cards. $$*

Paphos
Chez Alex. A well-established tavern, Chez Alex serves only fresh fish (which varies with the catch of the day) and fish mezes. *7 Constantia St., Kato Paphos, tel. 06/234767. AE, DC, MC, V. $$*
Panicos Corallo Restaurant. Sheltered from the main road by grapevines, this traditional family-run restaurant is just outside Paphos on the northern coastal road toward Coral Bay. The veal is recommended, as is the swordfish, a house specialty. Meals are served with fresh vegetables, all of which are homegrown. *Peyia, tel. 06/621052. DC, MC, V. $$*

Lodging

All hotels listed below have private bath or shower, but check when making reservations. Most have at least partial air-conditioning. In resort areas, hotel/apartments are a convenient choice for groups or families—many have kitchens.

RATINGS

Prices are for two people sharing a double room and include breakfast.

CATEGORY	ALL AREAS
$$$	over C£60
$$	C£40–C£60
$	under C£40

Ayia Napa

Nissi Beach. This modern, fully air-conditioned, family-style hotel is set in magnificent gardens overlooking a sandy beach 3 kilometers (2 miles) outside town. Some of the accommodations are in bungalows, although these do not have kitchens. *Nissi Ave., Box 10, tel. 03/721021, fax 03/721623. 270 rooms. Facilities: pool, disco, restaurant. AE, MC, DC, V. $$$*

Pernera Beach Sun Hotel. Even on a budget, you can enjoy this hotel with a view of the beach. All rooms are air-conditioned. *Pernera Beach, Box 38, tel. 03/831011, fax 03/831020. 156 rooms. AE, DC, MC, V. $$*

Larnaca

Golden Bay. Comfort is high on the list at this beach hotel to the east of the town center. All rooms have balconies and views of the sea. The extensive range of sports facilities makes it ideal for summer or winter vacations. *Larnaca-Dhekelia Rd., Box 741, tel. 04/645444, fax 04/645451. 194 rooms. Facilities: 2 restaurants, pool, minigolf, tennis. AE, DC, MC, V. $$$*

Pasithea. This apartment/hotel near Salt Lake is a short stroll from the sandy beach. The management is friendly, the apartments spacious. *4 Michael Angelou, Box 309, Larnaca, tel. 04/658264, fax 04/625848. 14 1-bedroom apartments. AE, DC, MC, V. $$*

Cactus Hotel. The Cactus, near the airport in a popular tourist area, has a restaurant and bar. It's 20 minutes from the seafront and Larnaca's tavernas. *6–8 Shakespeare St., Box 188, tel. 046/27400, fax 046/26966. 58 rooms. Facilities: restaurant, bar, pool. AE, MC, V. $*

Limassol

Le Meridien. The striking lobby of this spacious, luxurious hotel is pink marble and glass. You'll find all the amenities expected in a first-class hotel—health and beauty club, gym, steam baths—as well as the island's largest swimming pool. *Old Limassol/Nicosia Rd., Box 6560, tel. 05/634000, fax 05/634222. 191 rooms and 60 villas. Facilities: 3 restaurants, pool, water sports including scuba diving. AE, DC, MC, V. $$$*

Azur Beach. This fine apartment/hotel has two restaurants, a sandy beach, and helpful management. *Potamios Yermasoyias, Box 1318, tel. 05/322667, fax 05/321897. 24 1-bedroom apartments, 12 studios, 60 rooms. DC, MC, V. $$*

Continental. A great sea view adds to the appeal of this family hotel close to the castle. *137 Spyros Araouzos Ave., Box 398, tel. 05/362530, fax 05/373030. 30 rooms. AE, V. $*

Nicosia

Cyprus Hilton. The Hilton is among the island's best hotels, with its own health spa, sports facilities, skylit indoor pool, dancing, and more. An executive wing with 84 rooms, opened in 1995, offers separate check-in, a business center, a club room, and exercise rooms. *Archbishop Makarios Ave., Box 2023, tel. 02/377777, fax 02/377788. 314 rooms. Facilities: 2 restaurants, disco, 2 pools, health spa, tennis and squash courts, gym. AE, DC, MC, V. $$$*

Holiday Inn. Centrally located in the Old City, near commercial and historic districts, this member of the chain opened in 1995, with amenities including Japanese, Greek, international, and health-food restaurants, a fitness center, and a sauna. *70 Regina St., Box 1212, tel. 02/475131, fax 02/473337. 140 rooms. Facilities: 3 restaurants, bar, rooftop pool and garden, indoor pool, fitness center, sauna. AE, DC, MC, V. $$$*

Cleopatra Hotel. Visitors to the Cleopatra enjoy its convenient location, cordial service, and well-prepared food served at poolside. *8 Florina St., Box 1397, tel. 02/445254, fax 02/452618. 90 rooms. Facilities: restaurant, pool. AE, DC, MC, V. $$*

Paphos

Paphos Beach. There are many facilities at this hotel surrounded by attractive gardens. Accommodations are either in the main hotel or in spacious bungalows on the grounds. *Posidonos St., Box 136, tel. 06/233091, fax 06/242818. 224 rooms. Facilities: pool, tennis. AE, DC, MC, V. $$$*

Amalthea Hotel. This hotel on the beach amid banana groves has a friendly, personal atmosphere fostered by the resident owner-managers. The impressive, open lobby, furnished with gray leather couches and large plants, overlooks the water, and the rooms have balconies with sea views. *Kissonerga Rd., Box 323, tel. 06/247777, fax 06/245963. 168 rooms. Facilities: restaurant, bar, indoor and outdoor pools, gym, sauna, tennis and squash courts. AE, DC, MC, V. $$*

Hilltop Gardens Hotel Apartments. All the apartments have a view of the sea, which is 500 yards away. The decor is a pleasant mixture of traditional Cypriot village style, including wooden furniture, and modern touches. *Off Tombs of the Kings Rd., Box 185, tel. 06/243111, fax 06/248229. 48 apartments. Facilities: bar, pool. AE, DC, MC, V. $$*

NORTHERN CYPRUS

Currency

The monetary unit in Northern Cyprus is the Turkish lira (TL). There are bills for 1,000,000, 500,000, 250,000, 100,000, 50,000, 20,000, and 10,000 TL and coins for 10,000, 5,000, 2,500, 1,000, and 500 TL. The Turkish lira is subject to considerable inflation, so most of the prices in this section are quoted in dollars.

What It Will Cost

Prices for food and accommodations tend to be lower than those in the Republic of Cyprus. Wine and spirits, on the other hand, are imported from Turkey, and drinks will be slightly more expensive.

SAMPLE PRICES

A cup of coffee should cost less than a dollar, a glass of beer about $1. Wine is good and cheap at around $3 per bottle. Taxis are also a bargain—an 80-kilometer (50-mile) ride costs about $12. Admission to museums costs less than $1.

Arriving and Departing

Turkish Airlines, Cyprus Turkish Airlines, and **Istanbul Airlines** run all flights via mainland Turkey, usually with a change of plane at Istanbul. There are also direct flights from Adana, Ankara, Antalya, and I(dt)zmir to Ercan Airport near Nicosia. Ferries run from Mersin and Tasucu in Turkey to Famagusta and Kyrenia, respectively. *It is not possible to enter Northern Cyprus from the Republic except for a day trip from Nicosia.*

Getting Around

By Car
See Getting Around by Car *in* the Republic of Cyprus, *above.*

By Bus
Buses and the shared *dolmuş* (taxis) are the cheapest forms of transportation. Service is frequent on main routes.

FARES
A bus from Nicosia to Kyrenia costs about U.S. 40¢, and to Famagusta about 70¢. A seat in a dolmuş for the same trips would cost about 90¢ and $3, respectively.

Exploring Northern Cyprus

The main **tourist information office** is at the Department of Tourism Marketing in Lefkoşa (Nicosia), Selçuklu Caddesi, tel. 90/392/228–3666, fax 90/392/228–5625. (The postal address is Selçuklu Cad., Lefkoşa-KKTC, Mersin–10, Turkey.) There are also regional tourism offices in Gazimagusa, Girne, and Lefkoşa.

There are two important things to bear in mind in Northern Cyprus. One is to obey the "no photographs" signs wherever they appear. The other is to note that as Turkish is the language used here, Turkish names designate the cities and towns: **Nicosia** is known as **Lefkoşa, Kyrenia** as **Girne,** and **Famagusta** as **Gazimagusa.** A useful map showing these and other Turkish names is available free from tourist offices.

Lefkoşa (Nicosia)
The Turkish half of **Nicosia** is the capital of Northern Cyprus. In addition to Venetian walls (*see* Exploring the Republic of Cyprus, *above*), it contains the **Selimiye Mosque** (Selimiye St.), originally the 13th-century Cathedral of St. Sophia and a fine example of Gothic architecture, to which a pair of minarets has been added. Near the Girne Gate is the **Mevlevi Tekke ve Etnografy Müzesi** (Mevlevi Sacred Place and Ethnographic Museum), the former home of the Mevlevi Dervishes, a Sufi order popularly known as Whirling Dervishes. The building now houses a museum of Turkish history and culture. *Girne St. Open Mon.–Fri. 8–1 and 2–5, Sat. 8–1, Sun. 10–1.*

A walk around the **Old City,** within the encircling walls, is rich with glimpses from the Byzantine, Lusignan, and Venetian past. There is a great deal of restoration and reconstruction work going on, especially in the parts of the city beyond the walls.

Girne (Kyrenia)
Of the coastal resorts, **Girne,** with its yacht-filled harbor, is the most appealing. There are excellent beaches to the east and west of the

town. **Girne Castle,** overlooking the harbor, is Venetian. It now houses the **Batık Gemi Müzesi** (Shipwreck Museum), whose prize possession is the remains of a ship that sank around 300 BC. *Open Mon.–Fri. 8–1 and 2–5, Sat. 8–1, Sun. 10–1.*

Gazimagusa (Famagusta)

The chief port of Northern Cyprus, **Gazimagusa,** has massive and well-preserved Venetian walls and the late-13th-century Gothic Cathedral of St. Nicholas, now **Lala Mustafa Pasha Mosque.** The **Old Town,** within the walls, is the most intriguing part to explore.

Off the Beaten Track

It is well worth making two short excursions from Girne—to **St. Hilarion** and to **Bellapais.** The fantastic ruins of the **Castle of St. Hilarion** stand on a hilltop 11 kilometers (7 miles) to the southwest. It's a strenuous walk, so take a taxi; the views are breathtaking. The ruins of the former **Abbey of Bellapais,** built in the 12th century by the Lusignans, are just as impressive. They lie on a mountainside 6 kilometers (4 miles) to the southeast.

Salamis, north of Gazimagusa, is an ancient ruined city and perhaps the most dramatic archaeological site on the island. St. Barnabas and St. Paul arrived in Salamis and set up a church near here. The present ruins date largely from the 12th-century Lusignan rulers of Cyprus, who came from France, but Salamis does contain relics of earlier civilizations, including Greek and Roman settlements. The setting is beautiful, and some of the ruins are sufficiently overgrown to give the visitor a satisfying sense of discovery.

7 The Czech Republic

JUST THREE YEARS after the dramatic but peaceful revolution that overthrew a Communist regime that had been in power for 40 years, Czechoslovakia again made world headlines in 1993 when its two constituent republics, Czech and Slovak, officially parted ways to form independent countries.

To observers from abroad, the rush to split the republics following federal elections in 1992 came as something of a surprise. Formed from the ruins of the Austro-Hungarian empire at the end of World War I, Czecho-Slovakia had portrayed itself to the world as a modern-day success story: a union of two peoples that had managed to overcome divisive nationalism in the higher interest of stabilizing a potentially volatile region.

Popular perceptions were reinforced by a long list of achievements. During the difficult 1930s, the Czechoslovak republic was the model democracy in central Europe. The 1968 Prague Spring, an intense period of cultural renewal, was centered largely on Czech territory, but was led by a courageous Slovak, Alexander Dubček. In 1989 the Communists were brought down by students and opponents of the regime in both Prague and Bratislava.

The forces for separation, however, proved too powerful. For all its successes, Czechoslovakia was ultimately an artificial creation, masking important and longstanding cultural differences between two outwardly similar peoples. The Czech Republic, linking the old Austrian crown lands of Bohemia and Moravia, can look to a rich cultural history going back some 600 to 700 years when the Bohemian kingdom was at the center of the Holy Roman Empire. Bohemia and Moravia played pivotal roles in the great religious and social conflicts of European history.

Slovakia, by contrast, languished for nearly a millennium as an agrarian outpost of the Hungarian empire. Although great strides were made in the years following World War II to bring Slovakia's schools and industries to the level of their cousins to the west, many Slovaks are still stung by the label of cultural inferiority. Given the state of the national ego, independence was probably inevitable.

Although officially separate as of January 1993, the two republics still present themselves to the visitor in many respects as one country. Combining a visit to Prague with an excursion to Slovakia's breathtaking High Tatras is as easy as it ever was.

Today, travelers have rediscovered Prague, and Prague has rediscovered the world. Not so long ago, the visitor was unhindered by crowds of tourists but had to struggle with a creeping sensation of melancholy and neglect that threatened to eclipse the city's beauty. At least on the surface, the atmosphere is changing rapidly. The revolution has brought enthusiasm, bustle, and such conveniences as English-language newspapers, attentive hotels, and restaurants that will try to find you a seat even if you don't have a reservation. Musicians and writers are finding new inspiration in the city that once harbored Mozart and Kafka. Countering the drab remnants of socialist reality—the lack of public services, the uncared-for buildings, the strange boxy cars with colors from the '60s—are the spectacular Gothic, Baroque, and Art Nouveau treasures to be found all over the city.

Outside the capital, travelers are now exploring regions rarely visited in recent years. The range of sights is startling, from imperial spas to modern industrial cities. Don't pass up the lovely towns and castles of southern Bohemia: many visitors rank the Renaissance river town of Český Krumlov as a must-see. News for the traveler is that more and more services are being privatized, possibly making them better, certainly making them more expensive. On the other hand, your bill is now more likely to come with a smile.

ESSENTIAL INFORMATION

Before You Go

When to Go

Organized sightseeing tours run from April or May through October (year-round in Prague). Some monuments, especially castles, either close entirely or open for shorter hours in winter. Hotel rates may drop during the off-season except during festivals. May, the month of fruit blossoms, is the time of the Prague Spring Music Festival. During the fall, when the forests are glorious, Brno—the cultural center of Moravia—holds its own music festival. For information about these events and tours, contact the state-owned (but soon to be privatized) tourist agency, Čedok; Their offices—located in cities throughout the country—offer a full range of tourist services from booking tickets to arranging guided tours.

CLIMATE

The following are the average daily maximum and minimum temperatures for Prague.

Jan.	3	2C	**May**	66F	19C	**Sept.**	68F	20C
	25	− 4		46	8		50	10
Feb.	37F	3C	**June**	72F	22C	**Oct.**	55F	13C
	27	− 3		52	11		41	5
Mar.	46F	8C	**July**	75F	24C	**Nov.**	46F	8C
	32	0		55	13		36	2
Apr.	58F	14C	**Aug.**	73F	23C	**Dec.**	37F	3C
	39	4		55	13		28	− 2

Currency

The unit of currency in the Czech Republic is the crown, or koruna, written as Kč, and divided into 100 haléřů (heller). There are bills of 20, 50, 100, 200, 500, 1,000, and 5,000 Kč and coins of 10, 20, and 50 hellers and 1, 2, 5, 10, 20, and 50 Kč. At press time (spring 1995), the koruna was trading at around 22 Kč to the dollar and 36 Kč to the pound sterling.

What It Will Cost

Costs are highest in Prague and only slightly lower in the main Bohemian resorts and spas, though even in these places you can now find very reasonable accommodations in private rooms. The least expensive area is southern Bohemia.

SAMPLE PRICES

Cup of coffee, 15 Kč; beer (1/2 liter), 10–25 Kč, Coca-Cola, 20 Kč; ham sandwich, 30 Kč; 1-mile taxi ride, 100 Kč.

MUSEUMS

Admission to museums, galleries, and castles ranges from 5 Kč to 50 Kč.

Czech Republic

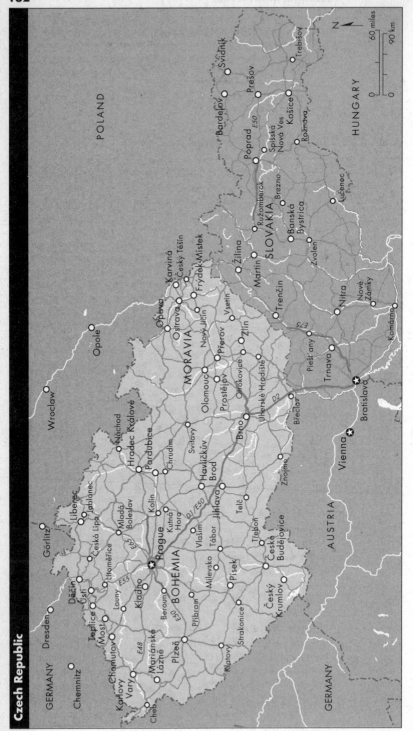

Visas

U.S. and British citizens do not need visas to enter the Czech Republic. Visa requirements have been temporarily reintroduced for Canadian citizens; check whether this is still the case with the consulate. Apply to the Embassy of the Czech Republic, 541 Sussex Drive, Ottawa, Ontario K1N 6Z6, tel. 613/562–3875, fax 613/562–3878.

Customs

ON ARRIVAL

Valuable items should be entered on your customs declaration. You can bring in 200 cigarettes, 100 cigars, 1 liter of alcohol, and gifts with a total value of 1,000 Kč.

ON DEPARTURE

Only antiques bought at specially appointed shops may be exported. To be on the safe side, hang on to all receipts.

Language

English is spoken fairly widely by the young and those associated with the tourist industry. You will come across English speakers elsewhere, though not frequently. German is generally understood throughout the country.

Getting Around

By Car

ROAD CONDITIONS

Main roads are usually good, if sometimes narrow, and traffic is light, especially away from main centers. An expressway links Prague, Brno, and Bratislava. Other highways are single-lane only.

RULES OF THE ROAD

Drive on the right. Speed limits are 60 kph (37 mph) in urban areas, 90 kph (55 mph) on open roads, and 110 kph (68 mph) on expressways. Seat belts are compulsory outside urban areas; drinking and driving is strictly prohibited.

PARKING

Except for those belonging to hotel guests, private cars are banned in much of the center of Prague. In some areas of the capital you can pay to park for a limited period. Whatever you do, don't park in a no-parking area; your car is likely to be towed away. Elsewhere in the country there's little problem.

GASOLINE

At about 81 Kč (or approximately $3) a gallon, gasoline is expensive. Look for service stations along main roads on the outskirts of towns and cities. Finding a station in Prague is notoriously difficult. Fill up on the freeway as you approach the city to avoid frustration. Lead-free gasoline, known as "natural," is still only available at select stations, so tank up when you see it.

BREAKDOWNS

The Yellow Angels (tel. 02/773455) operate a patrol service on main highways. The emergency telephone number for motorists is 154.

By Train

There is an extensive rail network throughout the country. As elsewhere in Eastern Europe, fares are relatively low and trains can be crowded. Also, you have to pay a supplement on all express trains. Most long-distance trains have dining cars; overnight trains between main centers have sleeping cars.

By Plane

Good internal air service links Prague with several other towns, including Ostrava in Moravia and Bratislava and Poprad (for the High Tatras) in Slovakia. Prices are reasonable.

Make reservations at Čedok offices or directly at **ČSA,** Czechoslovak Airlines (tel. 02/24815110).

By Bus

A wide-ranging bus network provides quicker service than trains at somewhat higher prices (though they are still very low by Western standards). Buses are always full, and, on long-distance routes especially, reservations are advisable.

Staying in the Czech Republic

Telephones

LOCAL CALLS

To use a public phone, buy a phone card at a newsstand or tobacconist. Cards cost 100 Kč for 50 units or 190 Kč for 100 units. Local calls cost one unit, and international rates vary according to destination. To place a call, lift the receiver, insert the card, and dial.

INTERNATIONAL CALLS

Automatic dialing is available to many parts of the world, including North America and the United Kingdom. Special international pay booths in central Prague will take 5 Kč coins, but your best bet is to go to the main post office at Jindřišská 14, near Václavské náměstí (Wenceslas Square). For international inquiries, dial 0132 for the United States, Canada, or the United Kingdom. To place a call via an **AT&T** USADirect international operator, dial 0042–000101; for **MCI,** dial 0042–000112; for **Sprint,** dial 0042–087187.

COUNTRY CODE

The country code for the Czech Republic is 42.

Mail

POSTAL RATES

Airmail letters to the United States and Canada cost 11 Kč up to 20 grams, postcards 6 Kč. Airmail letters to the United Kingdom cost 8 Kč up to 20 grams, postcards 5 Kč.

RECEIVING MAIL

Mail can be labeled "poste restante" and sent to the main post office in Prague (Jindřišská 14, window 28) or to any other main post office. There's no charge. The American Express office in Prague's Wenceslas Square will hold letters addressed to cardholders or holders of American Express traveler's checks for up to one month free of charge.

Opening and Closing Times

Banks are open weekdays 8–5. **Museums** are usually open Tues.–Sun. 10–5. **Shops** are generally open weekdays 9–6; some close for lunch between noon and 2. Many are also open till noon or later on Saturdays.

National Holidays

January 1; April 8 (Easter Monday); May 1 (Labor Day); May 8 (Liberation Day); July 5 (Saints Cyril and Methodius); July 6 (Jan Hus); October 28 (Independence Day); December 25, 26.

Dining

Dining options include restaurants, *vinárna* (wine cellars), the more down-to-earth *pivnice* (beer taverns), cafeterias, and a growing number of coffee shops and snack bars. Eating out is popular, and in summer you must make reservations. Part of privatization's legacy is more restaurants and more kinds of cuisine, especially in Prague.

Prague ham makes a favorite first course, as does soup, which is less expensive. The most typical main dish is roast pork (or duck or goose) with sauerkraut. Dumplings in various forms, generally with a rich gravy, accompany many dishes.

MEALTIMES
Lunch is usually from 11:30 to 2 or 3; dinner from 6 to 9:30 or 10. Some places are open all day, and you might find it easier to get a table during off-hours.

WHAT TO WEAR
A jacket and tie are recommended for **$$$$** and **$$$** restaurants. Informal dress is appropriate elsewhere.

RATINGS
Prices are reasonable by American standards, even in the more expensive restaurants. Czechs don't normally go for three-course meals, and the following prices apply only if you're having a first course, main course, and dessert (excluding wine and tip). Highly recommended restaurants are indicated by a star ★.

CATEGORY	PRAGUE	OTHER AREAS
$$$$	over 800 Kč	over 400 Kč
$$$	350 Kč–800 Kč	250 Kč–400 Kč
$$	200 Kč–350 Kč	100 Kč–250 Kč
$	under 200 Kč	under 100 Kč

Lodging

There's a choice of hotels, motels, private accommodations, and campsites. Many older properties are gradually being renovated, and the best have great character and style. There is still an acute shortage of hotel rooms during the peak season, so make reservations well in advance. Many private room agencies offer a variety of lodgings. The standards of facilities and services hardly match those in the West, so don't be surprised by faulty plumbing or indifferent reception clerks.

HOTELS
These are officially graded with from one to five stars, using the international classification system. Many hotels used by foreign visitors are affiliated with Čedok and are mainly in the three- to five-star categories. These will have all or some rooms with bath or shower. Čedok can also handle reservations for some non-Čedok hotels.

Bills can be paid in koruny (check to see if your hotel insists on hard currency; some hotels refuse to accept credit cards).

PRIVATE ACCOMMODATIONS
Prague is full of travel agencies that offer accommodation in private homes. Such rooms are invariably cheaper and often more comfortable than those in hotels, though you may have to sacrifice some privacy. The largest room-finding service is probably **AVE** in the main and Holešovice train stations, the airport (all open 7 AM–11 PM), and other locations. Insist on a room in the city center, however, or you may find yourself in a dreary, far-flung suburb. Another helpful agency is **Hello Ltd.** (Senovážné nám. 3, Prague 1, tel. 02/24214212). Elsewhere, look for signs declaring ROOM FREE or, more frequently, in German, ZIMMER FREI or PRIVATZIMMER along main roads. Čedok and the Prague Information Service (PIS) offices can also help in locating private accommodations.

CAMPING

Campsites are run by a number of organizations. A free map and list are available from Čedok.

RATINGS

Prices are for double rooms, generally including breakfast. Prices at the lower end of the scale apply to low season. At certain periods, such as Easter or during festivals, there may be an increase of 15%–25%. Highly recommended lodgings are indicated by a star ★.

CATEGORY	PRAGUE	OTHER AREAS
$$$$	over 5,400 Kč	over 2,700 Kč
$$$	2700–5,400 Kč	1350–2,700 Kč
$$	1350–2,700 Kč	675–1,350 Kč
$	under 1,350 Kč	under 675 Kč

Tipping

Reward good service in restaurants with a few koruny, given directly to the waiter on paying your bill. As a rule of thumb, round up to the nearest multiple of 10 (i.e., if the bill comes to 83 Kč, give the waiter 90 Kč). Give 10% on big or group tabs. For taxis, add 10 Kč. In the better hotels, doormen should get 5 Kč for each bag they carry to the check-in desk; bellhops get up to 10 Kč for taking them up to your rooms. In $$ or $ hotels, you'll have to lug baggage yourself.

PRAGUE

Arriving and Departing

By Plane

All international flights arrive at Prague's Ruzyně Airport, about 20 kilometers (12 miles) from downtown. For arrival and departure times, call 02/367814 or 02/367760.

BETWEEN THE AIRPORT AND DOWNTOWN

Czechoslovak Airlines provides shuttle bus service linking the airport with their Town Terminal Vltava (Revoluční 25). Buses depart every 20 minutes during the day, every half hour evenings and on weekends. The trip into Prague costs 30 Kč and takes about 30 minutes. The cheapest way to get into Prague is by regular Bus 119; the cost is 6 Kč, but you'll need to change to the subway at the Dejvická station to reach the center. By taxi, expect to pay 300 Kč.

By Train

The main station for international and domestic routes is Hlavní nádraží (tel. 02/24217654), Wilsonova, not far from Wenceslas Square. Some international trains arrive at and depart from Nádraží Holešovice (tel. 02/24615865), on the same metro line (C) as the main station.

By Bus

The main bus station is Florenc (at Na Florenci, tel. 02/24211060), not far from the main train station. Take Metro B or C to Florenc station.

Getting Around

Public transportation is a bargain. Jizdenky (tickets) cost 6 Kč and can be bought at hotels, newsstands, and from dispensing machines in the metro stations. For the metro, punch the ticket in the station before getting on the escalators; for buses and trams, punch the ticket inside the vehicle. You can also buy one-day passes allowing unlimited use of the system for 50 Kč, two-day for 85 Kč, three-day for 110 Kč, and five-day for 170 Kč. The passes can be purchased at the main metro stations and at some newsstands.

Understanding addresses is relatively simple once you know the basic street sign words: *ulice* (street, abbreviated to ul.; note that common usage often drops ulice in a printed address), *náměstí* (square, abbreviated to nám.), and *třída* (avenue).

By Subway

Prague's three modern metro lines are easy to use and relatively safe. They provide the simplest and fastest means of transportation, and most new maps of Prague mark the routes.

By Tram/Bus

You need to buy a new ticket every time you change vehicles. Trams 50–59 and Buses 500 and above run all night, after the metro shuts down at midnight.

By Taxi

Taxi scams are common. Avoid taxi stands in heavily touristed areas. Instead, hail cabs from the street or order them in advance by telephone. Reputable firms include **AAA** (tel. 02/3399) and **Profitaxi** (tel. 02/61045555). The basic charge is 10 Kč, increased by 12 Kč per kilometer. Be warned: Many drivers don't turn on the meter. Either agree on a price beforehand (no more than 100 Kč within the city) or ask the driver to start the meter. Some larger hotels have their own fleets, which are a little more expensive.

Important Addresses and Numbers

Tourist Information

The main **Čedok** office (Na přikopě 18, tel. 02/24197111) is close to Wenceslas Square. **PIS** (tel. 02/544444) has offices at Na přikopě 20 and Staroměstská náměstí 22 (Old Town Square).

Embassies

U.S. (Tržiště 15, Malá Strana, tel. 02/24510847). **Canadian** (Mickiewiczova 6, Hradčany, tel. 02/24311108). **U.K.** (Thunovská 14, Malá Strana, tel. 02/24510439).

Emergencies

Police (tel. 158). **Ambulance** (tel. 155). **Foreigners' Department of Na Homolce Hospital** (Roentgenova 2, Prague 5, weekdays tel. 02/52922146, evenings and weekends tel. 02/52922191); **First Medical Clinic of Prague** (Vyšehradská 35, Prague 2, tel. 02/292286, 298978; 24-hour emergency tel. 02/7921692, 02/0601225050, mobile phone). **24-Hour Pharmacies** (two close to the center are Štefánikova 6, Prague 5, tel. 02/24511112, and Koněvova 210, Prague 3, tel. 02/6441895). **Lost credit cards:** American Express (02/24219992); Diners Club, Visa (02/24125353); MasterCard (02/24423135).

English-Language Bookstores

The best selections are at the **Globe Bookstore and Coffeehouse** (Janovského 14, Prague 7) and **U Knihomola** (Mánesova 79, Prague 2). **Bohemian Ventures** (Nám. Jana Palacha 2) at the Philosophical Faculty of Charles University (near the Staroměstská metro station) stocks a large selection of paperbacks and modern fiction. For hiking maps and atlases, try **Orbis** (Václavské nám.).

Guided Tours

Čedok arranges a variety of tours in and around Prague; they can be arranged either before you leave home or during your stay in Prague.

Orientation Tours

Čedok offers a daily three-hour tour of the city, starting at 10 AM from the Čedok office at Bílkova 6 (tel. 02/2318255), opposite the Hotel Inter-Continental. Contact any Čedok office for the current schedule and itinerary. From April to October, the organization also operates an afternoon tour, starting at 2. Both tours cost about 500 Kč.

Martin-Tour (tel. 02/24212473) offers a similar but cheaper tour departing from Náměstí Republiky and three other Old Town points four times daily. **PIS** arranges guided tours at its Na přikopě and Old Town Square locations (tel. 02/24212844).

Special-Interest Tours

For cultural tours, call Čedok (*see above*). These include visits to the Jewish quarter, performances of folk troupes, Laterna Magika (*see* The Arts, *below*), opera, and concerts. You can save money by buying tickets—if available—at box offices.

Excursions

Čedok's one-day tours out of Prague cover principal historic and scenic sights and include lunch. The "Treasures of Bohemian Gothic" tour includes an excursion to the lovely medieval town of Kutná Hora; "Bohemian Paradise" features the bizarre sandstone and rock formations of northern Bohemia. Other tours include visits to famous spa towns and castles, wineries and the Terezín ghetto.

Personal Guides

Contact Čedok or PIS (*see above*) to arrange a personal walking tour of the city. Times, prices, and itinerary are negotiable. Prices start at around 400 Kč per hour.

Exploring Prague

Poets, philosophers, and the Czech-in-the-street have long sung the praises of *Praha* (Prague), also referred to as the "Golden City of a Hundred Spires." Like Rome, Prague is built on seven hills, which slope gently or tilt precipitously down to the Vltava River. The riverside location, enhanced by a series of graceful bridges, makes a great setting for two of the city's most notable features: its extravagant, fairy-tale architecture and its memorable music. Mozart claimed that no one understood him better than the citizens of Prague, and he was only one of several great masters who lived or lingered here.

It was under Charles IV (Karel IV) during the 14th century that Prague briefly became the seat of the Holy Roman Empire—virtually the capital of western Europe—and acquired its distinctive Gothic imprint. At times you'll need to look quite hard for this medieval inheritance; it's still here, though, under the overlays of graceful Renaissance and exuberant Baroque.

Prague escaped serious wartime damage, but it didn't escape neglect. Because of the long-term restoration program now under way, some part of the city is always under scaffolding. But what's completed—which is nearly all that's described in the following itineraries—is hard to find fault with as an example of sensitive and painstaking restoration.

Numbers in the margin correspond to points of interest on the Prague map.

The Nové Město and Staré Město (New Town and Old Town)

① **Václavské náměstí** (Wenceslas Square) is the Times Square of Prague. Confusingly, it's not actually a square at all but a broad boulevard that
② slopes down from the **Národní muzeum** (National Museum) and the
③ equestrian **statue of St. Wenceslas.** The lower end is where all the action is. Na příkopě, once part of the moat surrounding the Old Town, is now an elegant pedestrian mall. Čedok's main office is here, on your
④ way to the **Prašná brána** (Powder Tower), a 19th-century neo-Gothic restoration of the medieval original.

⑤ Turn into Celetná and you're on the old **Royal Route,** once followed by fabled coronation processions. This direction will lead you past the
⑥ foreboding Gothic spires of the Týn Church through **Staroměstské náměstí** (Old Town Square), down **Karlova,** across **Karlův most** (Charles Bridge), and up to the castle. As you explore this route, you can study every variety or combination of Romanesque, Gothic, Renaissance, and Baroque architecture. First, however, on Old Town Square, marvel at the the famous **Clock Tower,** where, on the hour, the complex five-century-old mechanism activates a procession that includes the Twelve Apostles. Note the skeleton figure of Death that tolls the bell.

⑦ **Franz Kafka's birthplace** is just north of Old Town Square on U radnice. Since the 1989 revolution, Kafka's popularity has soared, and the works of this German Jewish writer are now widely available in Czech. A fascinating little museum has been set up in the house. *U radnice 5. Closed Sunday and Monday.*

⑧ In the **Starý židovský hřbitov** (Old Jewish Cemetery) in **Josefov** (Joseph's Town, the former Jewish quarter), ancient tombstones lean and jostle one another; below them, in a dozen layers, are 12,000 graves. As you stand by the tomb of the scholar Rabbi Löw, who died in 1609, you may see, stuffed into the cracks, scraps of paper bearing prayers and requests. Be sure to visit the tiny Gothic **Staronová synagóga** (Old-New Synagogue), as well as the several other synagogues and exhibitions
⑨ comprising the **Židovské muzeum** (Jewish Museum). *Červená 101. Museum admission: 80 Kč. Open Sun.–Fri. 9–6 (9–4:30 in winter; last tour of cemetery at 3 in winter); closed Sat. and religious holidays.*

⑩ The **Betlémská kaple** (Bethlehem Chapel) has been completely reconstructed since Jan Hus thundered his humanitarian teachings from its pulpit in the early 15th century to congregations that could number 3,000. But the little door through which he came to the pulpit is original, as are some of the inscriptions on the wall. *Betlémské nám. Open daily 9–6.*

⑪ When you stand on **Karlův most** (Charles Bridge), you'll see views of Prague that would still be familiar to the 14th-century architect Peter Parler and to the sculptors who added the 30 statues in the early 18th century (most are copies—the Baroque-era originals have been brought indoors to prevent further deterioration from air pollution). They're worth a closer look, especially the 12th on the left (starting from the Old Town side of the bridge), which depicts St. Luitgarde, sculpted by Matthias Braun, circa 1710, and the 14th on the left, in which a Turk guards suffering saints, by F. M. Brokoff, circa 1714.

Malá Strana and Hradčany (Lesser Quarter and the Castle District)

Cross Charles Bridge and follow Mostecká up to Malostranské náměstí, the entry to **Malá Strana** (known as the Lesser Quarter or "Little Town,") one of Prague's most intriguing neighborhoods. Here, on this
⑫ square, you'll find the **Chrám svatého Mikuláše** (Church of St. Nicholas),

Prague

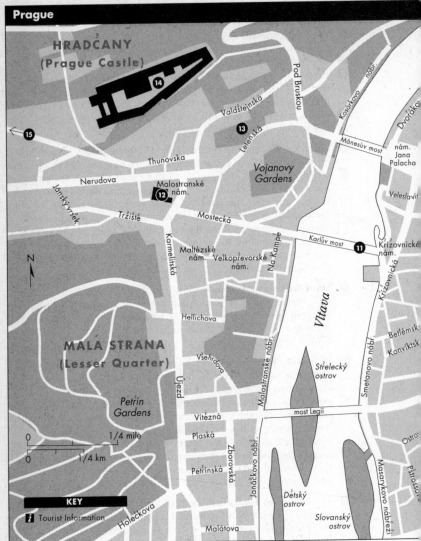

HRADČANY
(Prague Castle)

14

15

Pod Bruskou

Kazárkovo nábř.

Dvořák

Valdštejnská

13

Letenská

Mánesův most

nám.
Jana
Palacha

Thunovska

Vojanovy
Gardens

Veleslavír

Nerudova

Jánský vršek

Malostranské
nám.

12

Tržiště

Mostecká

Karlův most

11

Křižovnické
nám.

Maltézské
nám.

Velkopřevorské
nám.

Na Kampě

Karmelitská

Křižovnická

N

Hellichova

Betlémsk

Konviktsk

MALÁ STRANA
(Lesser Quarter)

Všehrdova

Malostranské nábř.

Vltava

Smetanovo nábř.

Střelecký
ostrov

Újezd

Petřín
Gardens

Vítězná

most Legií

0   1/4 mile

Plaská

Ostr

0   1/4 km

Zborovská

Janáčkovo nábř.

Masarykovo nábřeží

Přístavu

Petřínská

KEY

Dětský
ostrov

i Tourist Information

Holečkova

Malátova

Slovanský
ostrov

Betlémská kaple, **10**

Chrám svatého
Mikuláše, **12**

Kafka's Birthplace, **7**

Karlův most Charles
Bridge, **11**

Loreto, **15**

Národní muzeum, **2**

Starýžidovský-
hřbitov, **8**

Pražsky hrad (Prague
Castle), **14**

Prašná brána, **4**

Royal Route, **5**

Staroměstské
náměstí, **6**

Statue of
St.Wenceslas, **3**

Václavské náměstí, **1**

Wallenstein
Gardens, **13**

Židovské muzeum, **9**

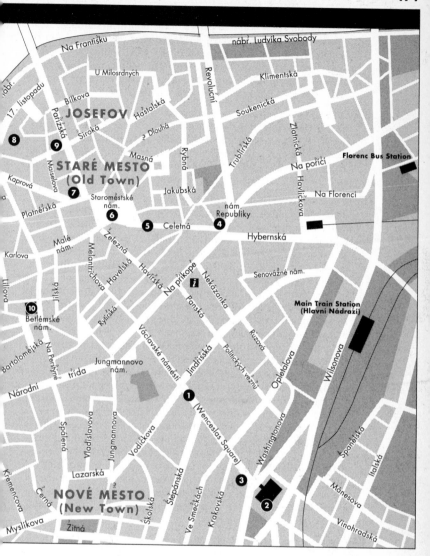

Na Františku

nábř. Ludvíka Svobody

U Milosrdných

Klimentská

Revoluční

Soukenická

17. listopadu

Bílkova

JOSEFOV

Hašťalská

Zlatnická

nábř.

Pařížská

Trubitřská

Na poříčí

Florenc Bus Station

Široká

Dlouhá

Rybná

8

9

Maiselova

Masná

STARÉ MESTO
(Old Town)

Na Florenci

Havličkova

Kaprová

Jakubská

7

Platnéřská

Staroměstské
nám.

nám.
Republiky

Karlova

Malé
nám.

6

5

Celetná

4

Hybernská

10

Jilská

Železná

Melantrichova

Havelská

Havířská

Na příkope

Nekázanka

Senovážné nám.

Betlémské
nám.

Rytířská

Panská

Main Train Station
(Hlavní Nádraži)

Bartolomějská

Na Perštýně

Václavské náměstí

Jindřišská

Ruzová

Opletalova

Wilsonova

Národní

Jungmannovo
nám.

třída

Policických veznů

Spálená

1

[Wenceslas Square]

Vladislavova

Jungmannova

Vodičkova

Washingtonova

Lazarská

Štěpánská

Krakovská

Španělská

Italská

Křemencova

Černá

NOVÉ MESTO
(New Town)

3

Školská

Ve Smečkách

Mánesova

2

Mysliková

Žitná

Vinohradská

designed by the architects Dientzenhofer, father and son. Many consider this the most beautiful edifice of the Bohemian Baroque, an architectural style that flowered in Prague after the turbulence of the Counter-Reformation at the start of the 17th century. If you're in Prague when a concert is being given in this church, fight for a ticket. The lavish sculptures and frescoes of the interior make for a memorable setting. *Malostranské nám. Open daily 10–4 (9–6 in summer).*

13 On busy Letenská a small door admits visitors to the large, formal **Wallenstein Gardens,** part of the huge palace built in the 1620s by the Hapsburgs' victorious commander, Albrecht of Wallenstein. A covered outdoor stage of late-Renaissance style dominates its western end. Music and theater pieces are occasionally performed here. *Entrance on Letenská ul. Admission free. Open May–September, daily 9–7.*

14 The monumental complex of **Pražský hrad** (Prague Castle) has witnessed the changing fortunes of the city for more than 1,000 years. The castle's physical and spiritual core, **Chrám svatého Víta** (St. Vitus Cathedral), took from 1344 to 1929 to build, so you can trace the whole gamut of styles from high Gothic to Art Nouveau. This is the final resting place for numerous Bohemian kings. Charles IV lies in the crypt. "Good King" Wenceslas (in reality a mere prince, later canonized) has his own chapel in the south transept, studded with semiprecious stones. Behind St. Vitus's, don't miss the miniature houses of the "Golden Lane." King Rudolph II used to lock up Europe's most renowned alchemists in these tiny laboratories, and command them to turn lead into gold. Knightly tournaments often accompanied coronation ceremonies in the **Královský palác** (Royal Palace), next to the cathedral, hence the broad Riders' Staircase leading up to the grandiose **Vladislavský sál** (Vladislav Hall) of the Third Courtyard. Oldest of all the buildings, though much restored, is the Romanesque complex of **Bazilika svatého Jiří** (St. George's Basilica and Convent). Behind a Baroque facade, it houses a superb collection of Bohemian art from medieval religious sculptures to Baroque paintings. Take a few minutes to appreciate the glorious vistas that the castle ramparts afford. Eastward, toward the Moldau, many of Prague's fabled spires rise above the rooftops, including the steeples of the Church of St. Nicholas. To the right are the gardens of the once-private palaces of the Lesser Quarter and the huge leafy **Kinského Zahrada** park. *Hradčanské nám. Admission: 80 Kč. Open Tues.–Sun. 9–5 (9–4 in winter).*

15 The Baroque church and shrine of **Loreto** is named for the Italian town to which the Virgin Mary's house in Nazareth was supposedly transported by angels to save it from the infidel. The crowning glory of its fabulous treasury is the glittering monstrance of the *Sun of Prague,* set with 6,222 diamonds. Arrive on the hour to hear the 27-bell carillon. *Loretánské nám. 7. Admission: 30 Kč. Open Tues.–Sun. 9–noon and 1–4:30.*

Off the Beaten Track

Cross the Vltava at the Hotel Inter-Continental (via the Čechův bridge) and climb the steps to the **Letenské sady** (Letná Park) for sweeping views of Prague.

Almost as old as the oldest parts of Prague Castle, the ruins of **Vyšehrad Castle** crown a rock bluff that rises from the Vltava, about 2 miles upstream from the Old Town. The quiet cemetery adjoining the **Church of Sts. Peter and Paul** is a place to pay homage to some of the nation's cultural giants, among them Bedřich Smetana and the writer Karel Čapek.

Across the river, in the Prague 5 district, Mozart stayed in the peaceful **Bertramka Villa** and completed his opera *Don Giovanni*. With luck, your trip will coincide with a concert here. If not, taped music will accompany your walk through the villa, restored to what it was in his day.

Franz Kafka's grave rests amid the overgrown **Židovské hřbitovy** (New Jewish Cemetery) in Vinohrady, a rather depressing part of Prague. Take Metro A to Želivského, turn right at the main cemetery gate, and follow the wall for about 100 yards. Kafka's thin, white tombstone lies at the front of section 21.

Shopping

Specialty Shops
Look for the name **Dílo** for objets d'art and prints; **Lidová Řemesla** for folk art. **Moser** (Na přikopě 12) is the most famous for glass and porcelain. Shops specializing in Bohemian crystal, porcelain, ceramics, and antiques abound.

Shopping Districts
Many of the main shops are in and around Wenceslas Square and Na přikopě, as well as along Celetná and Pařížská.

Department Stores
Four central stores are **Bílá Labuť** (Na poříčí 23), **Krone** (Václavské nám. 21), **Kotva** (Nám. Republiky 8), and **Kmart** (Narodní 26).

Dining

Eating out in Prague is a very popular pastime, so it's advisable to make reservations whenever possible, especially for dinner. For details and price-category definitions, *see* Dining *in* Staying in the Czech Republic, *above*.

$$$$ ★ **Opera Grill.** Though called a grill, this is one of the most stylish small restaurants in town, complete with antique Meissen candelabra and Czech specialties. *K. Světlé 35, Staré Město, tel. 02/265508. Reservations required. AE, DC, V. Dinner only.*

$$$$ **U Malířů.** This esteemed old restaurant now serves exclusively French food and wines at the highest prices you'll see in the entire country. The specialty of the house is lobster, but the chef prepares a couple of elaborate prix-fixe menus daily. *Maltézké nám. 11, Malá Strana, tel. 02/24510269. Reservations advised. AE, DC, MC, V. Closed Sun.*

$$$$ **U Zlaté Hrušky.** Careful restoration has returned this restaurant to its original 18th-century style. It specializes in Moravian wines, which go down well with fillet steaks and goose liver. *Nový Svět 3, Castle area, tel. 02/531133. Reservations required. AE, DC, MC, V.*

$$$$ **V Zátiší.** White walls and casual grace accentuate the subtle flavors of smoked salmon, roast beef, and other non-Czech specialties. It's a favorite spot with the expatriate crowd and visiting businesspeople on expense accounts. *Liliova 1, Staré Město, tel. 02/24228977. Reservations advised. AE, MC, V.*

$$$ ★ **U Mecenáše.** This wine restaurant manages to be both medieval and elegant despite the presence of an ancient gallows. Try to get a table in the back room. The chef specializes in thick, juicy steaks, served with a variety of sauces. *Malostranské nám. 10, Malá Strana, tel. 02/533881. Reservations advised. AE, DC, MC, V. Dinner only.*

$$$ **U Modré Kachničky.** The exuberant, eclectic decor is as attractive as the Czech and international dishes served, which include steaks, duck, and game in the autumn, and Bohemian trout and carp specialties.

Nebovidská 6, Malá Strana, tel. 02/539751. Dinner reservations required. No credit cards.

$$ **Myslivna.** They took the antlers off the walls of this rustic restaurant a year or so after the Velvet Revolution, but the cooks still know their way around pheasant, boar, and quail. Try leg of venison in wine sauce and walnuts or the seasonal variations on wild boar, all prepared to please both eye and palate. *Jagellonská 21, Vinohrady, tel. 02/6270209. Reservations advised. AE, V.*

$$ **Penguin's.** You'd expect to pay more for the setting and service at this popular spot. The muted mauve and matte-black walls make the atmosphere casual yet elegant. *Zborovská 5, Prague 5, tel. 02/545660. Reservations advised. AE, MC, V.*

$$ **Pezinok.** You'll get good, hearty fare served in a relaxed, no-frills atmosphere at this restaurant behind Národní třída in the New Town. The homemade sausage, accompanied by hearty Slovak wine, is excellent. The large *palačinky* (crepes) for dessert are some of the best in Prague. *Purkynova 4, tel. 02/291996. Reservations advised. AE, MC, V.*

$$ **U Lorety.** Sightseers will find this an agreeable spot—peaceful except for the welcoming carillon from neighboring Loreto Church. The service here is discreet but attentive, the tables are private, and the food is consistently good. Venison and steak are specialties. *Loretánské nám. 8, near the Castle, tel. 02/24510191. Reservations advised. No credit cards.*

$ **Na Zvonařce.** This bright beer hall serves very good traditional fare at unbeatable prices. In summer, sit on the terrace to escape the noisy crowd. Noteworthy dishes include fried chicken and English roast beef. Fruit dumplings for dessert are a rare treat. Service is slow. *Šafaříkova 1, Prague 2, tel. 02/254534. Reservations advised. No credit cards.*

$ **U Koleje.** The friendly staff at this popular, convivial restaurant—suitable for the whole family—serves good traditional pork and beef dishes and excellent beer. You may have to share a table. *Slavíkova 24, Prague 2 tel. 02/6274163. Reservations advised. No credit cards.*

$ **U Zlatého Tygra.** This impossibly crowded hangout is the last of a breed of authentic Czech pivnice. The smoke and stares preclude a long stay, but it's still worth dropping in for typical pub staples like ham and cheese plates or roast pork. The service is surly, but the beer is good. *Husova 17, Staré Město, no phone. No reservations. No credit cards.*

$ **V Krakovské.** This clean pub noted for its excellent traditional fare is the place to try Bohemian duck: It's cooked just right and offered at an excellent price. Wash it down with good light or dark Braník beer. *Krakovská 20, Nové Město, tel. 02/261537. No credit cards.*

Lodging

Many of Prague's older hotels—some of which have great style—have recently been or are due to be renovated. For details and price-category definitions, *see* Lodging *in* Staying in the Czech Republic, *above.*

$$$$ **Diplomat.** Completed in 1990 as part of a joint venture with an Aus-
★ trian company, the Diplomat succeeds in fusing elegance with "Western" efficiency. The effect is marred only by an unfortunate location, a 10-minute taxi or subway ride from the Old Town. *Evropská 15, Prague 6, tel. 02/24394111, fax 02/24394215. 387 rooms with bath. Facilities: nightclub, sauna. AE, DC, MC, V.*

$$$$ **Forum.** This modern 28-story high-rise is near ancient Vyšehrad Castle, two subway stops south of the city center. The Palace of Culture next door often hosts trade fairs and conferences. *Kongresová 1, Prague 4, tel. 02/61191111, fax 02/421669. 531 rooms with bath. Facilities: nightclub, pool, saunas, bowling alleys, gym. AE, DC, MC, V.*

$$$$ **Hoffmeister.** Situated on a picturesque (if a bit busy) corner near the Malostranská metro station, this is one of the most stylish small hotels in the city. The standard double rooms are not large but are decorated with a interior designer's eye. *Pod Bruskou 9, Malá Strana, tel. 02/538380, fax 02/530959. 38 rooms with bath. Facilities: restaurant, bar, parking. AE, DC, MC, V.*

$$$$ **Palace Praha.** Beautifully renovated, the Art Nouveau–style Palace is
★ Prague's most elegant and luxurious hotel. Its central location just off Wenceslas Square makes it an excellent choice. *Panská 12, tel. 02/24093111, fax 02/24221240. 125 rooms with bath. Facilities: restaurant, café, saunas. AE, DC, MC, V.*

$$$ **Atlantic.** Something of the 1970s hangs in the air of this well-run establishment, situated a stone's throw from the Powder Tower in central Prague. Dark, carpeted interiors and overstuffed leather chairs set the subdued mood. The slickly appointed rooms, all with television sets and clean, modern bathrooms, date from a 1989 renovation. *Na poříčí 9, tel. 02/24811084, fax 02/24812378. 60 rooms with bath. Facilities: restaurant, bar. AE, DC, MC, V.*

$$$ **U Páva.** Some rooms and suites in this svelte, neoclassical inn on a cobblestone street in the Lesser Quarter afford unforgettable views of Prague's Castle. The Old World staff is courteous, and the reception and public areas are elegant and discreet. *U lužického semináře 106, Prague 1, tel. 02/24510922, fax 02/533379. 11 rooms with bath. AE, DC, MC, V.*

$$ **Central.** Quite conveniently, this hotel lives up to its name, with a site near Celetná and Náměstí Republiky. Rooms are sparely furnished, but all have baths. The Baroque glories of the Old Town are steps away. *Rybná 8, tel. 02/24812041, fax 02/2328404. 62 rooms with bath. Facilities: restaurant, nightclub. MC, V.*

$$ **Kampa.** An early Baroque armory-turned-hotel, the Kampa is tucked away in a shady corner just south of the Lesser Quarter. The rooms are clean, if spare, but the bucolic setting compensates for any discomforts. *Všehrdova 16, tel. 02/24510409, fax 02/24510377. 85 rooms with bath. Facilities: restaurant, café. AE, DC, MC, V.*

$$ **Karl-Inn.** The neighborhood's nothing much but the rooms, though basic, are comfortable enough and all have televisions and telephones. Two tram lines and a metro station (Křižkova, line B) provide quick transport to the center and the Florenc bus terminal. *Šaldova 54, Prague 8, tel. 02/24811718, fax 02/24812681. 168 rooms with bath. Facilities: restaurant, conference rooms. AE, MC, V.*

The Arts

Prague's cultural life is one of its top attractions—and its citizens like to dress up for it—but performances are usually booked far ahead. You can get a monthly program of events from the PIS, Čedok, or many hotels. The English-language newspapers *The Prague Post* and *Prognosis* carry detailed entertainment listings. The main ticket agencies are **Bohemia Ticket International** (Salvátorská 6, tel. 02/24227832) and **Tiketpro** (main outlet at Štěpánská 61, Lucerna passage, tel. 02/24232110, fax 02/24232021; credit cards accepted). For major concerts, opera and theater, it's much cheaper, however, to buy tickets at the box office.

Concerts

Performances are held in many palaces and in nearly every church in town, notably the **churches of St. Nicholas** in both the Old Town Square and in the Lesser Quarter; **St. James's Church** on Malá Stupartská (Staré Město), where Bach cantatas are performed amid a flourish of Baroque statuary; the giant Wallenstein Palace in the Lesser

Quarter; and in the palace's **Garden on the Ramparts,** where music comes with a view.

The Czech Philharmonic, Prague Symphony, and Czech Radio Orchestra play in the intimate, lavish **Dvořák Hall** in the **Rudolfinum** (Nám. Jana Palacha, tel. 02/24893111). The other main concert venue, **Smetana Hall,** along with the rest of the Obecní dům building on Náměstí Republiky, will remain closed for repairs into 1997.

Opera and Ballet

Opera is of an especially high standard in the Czech Republic. The main venues in the grand style of the 19th century are the beautifully restored **National Theater** (Národní tř. 2, tel. 02/24912673) and the **State Opera of Prague** (Wilsonova 4, tel. 02/24227693; formerly the Smetana Theater). The even older **Theater of Estates** (Ovocný trh 1, tel. 02/24215001; formerly the Týl Theater) hosts opera, ballet, and theater performances.

Theater

Diverse kinds of multimedia theater, mime, and other nonverbal forms abound. Most famous is the "Black Theater" of **Laterna Magika** (Magic Lantern, Národní tř. 4, tel. 02/24914129), a popular extravaganza combining live actors, mime, and sophisticated film techniques.

Puppet Shows

This traditional form of Czech popular entertainment has been given new life thanks to the productions mounted at the **National Marionette Theater** (Žatecká 1) and the **Magic Theater of the Baroque World** (Celetná 13).

Nightlife

Cabaret

The Alhambra (Václavské nám. 5, tel. 02/24193692) has a three-part floor show. More moderately priced is **Variété Praha** (Vodičkova 30, tel. 02/24215945). You'll find plenty of fellow foreigners at both.

Discos and Clubs

Discos catering to a young crowd (mostly 14- to 18-year-olds) line Wenceslas Square. The best bet is to stroll down the square and listen for the liveliest music. Excellent jazz can be heard nightly in Prague at several venues. Try **Reduta** (Národní tř. 20, tel. 02/24912246) or **Agharta** (Krakovská 5, tel. 02/24212914). For live rock, check out the **Rock Cafe** (Národní tř. 20, tel. 02/24914416) or **Malostranská Beseda** (Malostranské nám. 21, tel. 02/539024).

BOHEMIAN SPAS AND CASTLES

The Bohemian countryside is a restful world of gentle hills and thick woods. It is especially beautiful during fall-foliage season or in May, when the fruit trees that line the roads are in blossom. In such settings lie the two most famous of the Czech Republic's scores of spas: Karlovy Vary and Mariánské Lázně. During the 19th and early 20th centuries, the royalty and aristocrats of Europe who came to ease their overindulged bodies (or indulge them even more!) knew these spas as Karlsbad and Marienbad.

To the south, the higher wooded hills of Šumava, bordering Germany, have their own folklore and give rise to the headwaters of the Vltava. You'll follow its tortuous course as you enter South Bohemia, which has probably spawned more castles than any other region of comparable size. The medieval towns of southern Bohemia are exquisite, though be prepared to find them in various stages of repair or decay. In such towns was the Hussite reformist movement born during the early 15th century, sparking off a series of religious conflicts that eventually embroiled all of Europe.

Getting Around

There are bus or train connections to every corner of this region. The service is cheap, and fairly frequent and reliable, though you may be frustrated by incomprehensible small print when trying to decipher timetables. The most convenient way to follow this itinerary is by car.

Guided Tours

Many of the attractions on this itinerary, and some additional ones in Moravia, are covered by one or more of Čedok's many escorted tours out of Prague. Most of the attractions can also be visited during a series of day trips from the capital.

Tourist Information

České Budějovice (Nám. Přem. Otakara II. 39, tel. 038/52127).
Česky´ Krumlov (Latrán 79, tel. 0337/3444).
Karlovy Vary (Moskevská 2, tel. 017/3222292).
Mariánské Lázně (Čedok, Tebízského 2/101, tel. 0165/2254; City Service, Hlavní 626/1, tel. 0165/3816).
Tábor (Tř. 9 května 1282, tel. 0361/22235).

Exploring Bohemian Spas and Castles

If you're traveling by car, the best—though not fastest—route is to head south from Prague on Highway 4, then west along minor roads up the Berounka Valley, taking in the magnificently picturesque castles of **Karlštejn** and **Křivoklát.** The first is an admirable restoration of the 14th-century castle built by Charles IV to protect the crown jewels of the Holy Roman Empire, which were housed in the castle's stunning Chapel of the Holy Rood. Currently being renovated, the chapel—covered with 128 Gothic paintings and encrusted with 2,000 gems—can only be glimpsed from its entrance portal. Křivoklát's main attractions are its glorious woodlands, a favorite royal hunting ground in times past. *Karlštejn, tel. 42–331–94617. Admission: 85 Kč. Open year-round, Tues.–Sun. 7–12, 1–4. In Apr. and Oct. open till 5 PM; in May, June, and Sept. open until 6 PM; in July and Aug. open until 7 PM. Křivoklát: open mid-March–December, Tues.–Sun. 9–4.*

Karlovy Vary, or Karlsbad, was named after Charles IV, who, while out hunting, was supposedly led to the main thermal spring of Vřídlo by a fleeing deer. In due course, the spa drew not only many of the crowned heads and much of the blue blood of Europe but also leading musicians and writers. For all its later buildings and proletarian patients, Karlovy Vary still has a great deal of elegance. The waters from the spa's 12 springs are uniformly foul-tasting. The thing to do is sip them while nibbling rich Karlovy Vary *oplatky* (wafers), then resort to the "13th spring," Karlovy Vary's tangy herbal liqueur called Becherovka.

Karlovy Vary and **Mariánské Lázně** have the Czech Republic's two best golf courses—the latter spa hosts the PGA European Tour event. As a spa, Mariánské Lázně is younger and smaller, yet its more open setting gives it an air of greater spaciousness. It was much favored by

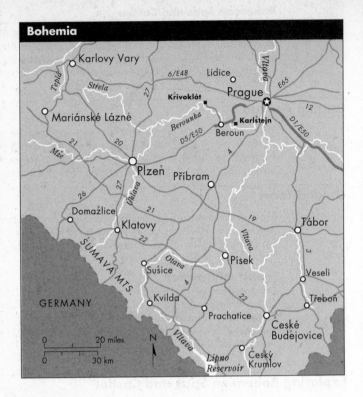

Bohemia

Britain's Edward VII, though from all accounts, he didn't waste too much time on strict diets and rigorous treatments.

The spas of west Bohemia have long catered to foreign travelers. As you head south to the higher Šumava Mountains bordering Germany, you'll be following much less frequented trails. **Domažlice** is the heart of the region of the Chods, for centuries guardians of Bohemia's frontiers, a function that earned them a number of privileges. Their special folk culture is still very much alive, not least in their pottery and their contagious dances accompanied by local bagpipes (main festival in mid-August). It is a bustling if neglected little town with a lovely arcaded square, old fortifications, and a castle that houses the **Chod Museum** of local folk culture, which is scheduled to reopen in the spring of 1996.

From Domažlice runs an intricate but extremely pretty route, mainly along minor roads, through Sušice along the upper Otava River and over the hills to Prachatice and back to **Kvilda,** where the road joins the young Vltava River. Downstream, the Vltava has been trapped to form the great reservoir and recreational area of **Lipno.** You skirt part of it before turning northeast to Český Krumlov.

This entire part of South Bohemia has strong associations with such feudal families as the Rožmberks, who peppered the countryside with their castles and created lake-size "ponds" in which to breed highly prized carp, still the main feature of a Czech Christmas dinner. Once the main seat of the Rožmberks, **Český Krumlov** is a magical town dominated by a forbidding Renaissance castle, complete with romantic elevated walkways and delicate towers. The Vltava River snakes through the town, which is steeply stacked on either bank, with flights of steps linking various levels and twisting narrow lanes that converge on

Svornosti náměstí, the main square of the Old Town. There are arcades, courtyards, and landscaped castle gardens with an 18th-century theater. The **Egon Schiele Center** has exhibitions of the work of Schiele, a frequent visitor to the town, and other 20th-century artists. *Široká 70–72. Open daily 10–6. Castle open Apr.–Oct. 9–4.*

České Budějovice is on a much larger scale, and here your main stop should be the massive but handsome **Přemysla Otakara II Square** (once called Žižka Square to honor the Hussite leader, its name was changed in 1991 to reflect historical reality—the town was firmly on the side of the Catholics). This is the home of the Czech version of Budweiser beer, known in Czech as Budvar and well worth trying.

Farther north along Highway 3 is **Tábor,** the very cradle of the Hussite movement. Its twisting streets were designed to confuse the enemy. A labyrinth of tunnels and cellars below the town were used both as living quarters and as links with the outer defenses. Their story is told in the **Hussite Museum** just off Přemysla Otakara II Square. *Křivkova 31. Admission: 40 Kč. Open daily 9–5 (Mon.–Fri. 9–3 in winter).*

Dining and Lodging

In many parts of Bohemia, the only real options for dining are the restaurants and cafés at the larger hotels and resorts; the following list is largely a selection of hotel/restaurants. For details and price-category definitions, *see* Dining and Lodging *in* Staying in the Czech Republic, *above.*

Český Krumlov

DINING AND LODGING

Krumlov. Centrally located on the main square, this is a pleasant, rambling old hotel occupying several renovated houses. Massive furniture and animal trophies give it a hunting-lodge feel, belied by the delicate pink tones of the Gothic-vaulted restaurant. *Svornosti nám. 14, tel. 0337/2255, fax 0337/3498. 36 rooms, 13 with bath. Facilities: restaurant. AE, MC, V. $–$$*

Růže. This former Renaissance monastery was lovingly restored in 1992, and now holds its own with other impressive sights in this enchanting town. Guest rooms are spacious and well-appointed; some are furnished in period style. *Horní ul. 153, tel. 0337/2245, fax 0337/3881. 50 rooms, most with bath. Facilities: restaurant, nightclub. AE, DC, MC, V. $$$*

Karlovy Vary

DINING AND LODGING

Dvořák. Opened in 1991, this Austrian-built hotel offers imaginative decor, friendly efficiency, and a superb array of facilities. *Nova louka 11, tel. 017/3224145, fax 017/3222814. 75 rooms with bath. Facilities: restaurant, pool, fitness room, spa center, casino. AE, DC, MC, V. $$$$*

★ **Grand Hotel Pupp.** Founded in 1701, the Pupp still has a fine 18th-century hall, Slavností sál. It's one of the oldest surviving hotels in Europe, with a glittering list of guests, both past and present. *Mírové nám. 2, tel. 017/209111, fax 017/3224032. 358 rooms with bath. Facilities: 2 restaurants, tavern, 2 nightclubs, saunas, tennis courts, golf, riding. AE, DC, MC, V. $$$$*

LODGING

Atlantic. This hotel in the middle of town is run by the nearby Hotel Central. The turn-of-the-century building still bears its landmark (and rather grotesque) porcelain statues on the roof. It may close in low season (November–March); if so, the Central has adequate rooms in just as excellent a location. *Atlantic, Tržiště 23; Central, Divadelní nám. 17.*

Tel. for both hotels 017/3225251, fax 017/3229086. Atlantic: 30 rooms, some with bath. Central: 110 rooms with bath. $$$

Mariánské Lázně
DINING AND LODGING
Palace. Built in 1875 during the spa's heyday, this elegant building is conveniently situated just within the resort center. Wheelchair-accessible and no-smoking rooms are available. *Hlavní tř. 67, tel. 0165/2222, fax 0165/4262. 45 rooms with bath. Facilities: restaurant. AE, DC, MC, V. $$$–$$$$*

Bohemia. Like its neighboring yellow-and-white hotels on Hlavní třída, this one concentrates on providing a full range of hotel services rather than functioning as a spa that also puts up hotel guests; it thus offers more amenities and comforts than some of the spa hotels do. *Hlavní tř. 100, tel. 0165/3251, fax 0165/2943. 100 rooms with bath. Facilities: restaurant, club, fitness center. AE, DC, MC, V. $$$*

8 Denmark

EBULLIENCE AND A SENSE OF HUMOR have earned the Danes a reputation as "the Italians of Scandinavia." While one might expect a country comprising more than 400 islands to develop an island mentality, the Danes are famous for their friendliness and have a word—*hyggelig*—for the feeling of well-being that comes from their own brand of cozy hospitality.

The stereotype of melancholic Scandinavia doesn't hold here: not in the café-studded streets of the larger cities, where musicians and fruit vendors hawk their wares to passersby; not in the tiny coastal towns, where the fishing boats are as brightly painted as fire trucks; not in the joyous "jam" sessions involved in the production of *smørrebrød* (the famous open-face Danish sandwich). Even the country's indoor/outdoor museums, where history is reconstructed through full-scale dwellings out in the open, indicate that Danes don't wish to keep life behind glass.

This is a land of well-groomed agriculture, where every acre is rich in orchard and field. Nowhere are you far from water, as you drive on and off the ferries and bridges linking the three regions of Jylland (Jutland), Fyn (Funen), and Sjælland (Zealand).

The sea surrounding the land has shaped Denmark's history. The Vikings, unparalleled seafarers, had seen much of the world by the 8th century. Today the Danes remain expert navigators, using the 4,480 kilometers (2,800 miles) of coastline for sport—regattas around Zealand and Funen—as well as for fishing and trading.

Long one of the world's most liberal countries, Denmark has a highly developed social welfare system. The hefty taxes are the subject of grumbles and jokes, but Danes remain proud of their state-funded medical and educational systems.

The country that gave the world Isak Dinesen, Hans Christian Andersen, and Søren Kierkegaard has a long-standing commitment to culture and the arts. In what other nation does the royal couple translate the writings of Simone de Beauvoir or the queen design costumes for the ballet? The Danish Ballet is world-renowned, and the provinces boast numerous theater groups and opera houses.

Perhaps Denmark's greatest charm is its manageable size—about half that of Maine. The ferry journey from Esbjerg, on the western coast of Jutland, to Copenhagen, on the eastern coast of Zealand, takes around five hours. From here you can make comfortable, unhurried expeditions by boat, car, bus, or train to cover what is one of the world's most civilized countries.

ESSENTIAL INFORMATION

Before You Go

When to Go

Most travelers visit Denmark during the warmest months, July and August, but there are advantages to going in May, June, or September, when sights are less crowded and many establishments offer off-season discounts. However, few places in Denmark are ever unpleasantly crowded, and when the Danes make their annual exodus to the beaches, the cities have even more breathing space. Visitors may want to avoid

Denmark

North Sea

Skagerrak

TO GREENLAND
TO FAROE ISLANDS

Skagen
Hirtshals
Hjørring
Frederikshavn
Sæby
Brønderslev
Hanstholm
Læsø
Thisted
Lim-fjord
Limfjord
Aalborg
Nykøbing
Hadsund
Aalborg Bugt
Kattegat
Lemvig
Skive
Struer
Viborg
Anholt
Holstebro
Jylland
Randers
Grenå
Ringkøbing
Herning
Silkeborg
Ebeltoft
Skanderborg
Århus
Grindsted
Horsens
Samsø
Tisvildeleje
Hornbæk
Skjern
Vejle
Nykøbing
Helsingør
Billund
Frederikssund
Hillerød
Esbjerg
Fredericia
Kalundborg
Holbæk
Copenhagen
Fanø
Holsted
Middelfart
Store-bælt
Jyderup
Roskilde
Kolding
Odense
Kerteminde
Slagelse
Sjælland
Amager
Ribe
Vojens
Assens
Fyn
Køge Bugt
Rømø
Haderslev
Nyborg
Ringsted
Køge
Skærbæk
Åbenrå
Fåborg
Næstved
St. Heddinge
Tønder
Svendborg
Langeland
Karrebæksminde
Sønderborg
Als
Troense
Vordingborg
Stege
Ærøskøbing
Rudkøbing
Tranekær
Nakskov
Møn
Ærø
Marstal
Nykøbing
Maribo
Falster
TO BORNHOLM
Rødby
Nysted
Lolland
Ostsee

GERMANY

N

0 ——— 50 miles
0 ——— 75 km

SWEDEN

Baltic Sea

Bornholm

Rønne

the winter months, when the days are short and dark and when important attractions, Tivoli included, close for the season.

CLIMATE

The following are the average daily maximum and minimum temperatures for Copenhagen.

Jan.	36F	2C	May	61F	16C	Sept.	64F	18C
	28	– 2		46	8		51	11
Feb.	36F	2C	June	67F	19C	Oct.	54F	12C
	28	– 2		52	11		44	7
Mar.	41F	5C	July	71F	22C	Nov.	45F	7C
	31	– 1		57	14		38	3
Apr.	51F	11C	Aug.	70F	21C	Dec.	40F	4C
	38	3		56	14		34	1

Currency

The monetary unit in Denmark is the krone (kr., DKr, or DKK), which is divided into 100 øre. At press time (spring 1995), the krone stood at about 5.2 kr. to the dollar, 3.9 kr. to the Canadian dollar, and 8.6 kr. to the pound sterling. Most well-known credit cards are accepted in Denmark, though the American Express card is accepted less frequently than others. Traveler's checks can be changed in banks and in many hotels, restaurants, and shops.

What It Will Cost

Denmark's economy is stable, and inflation remains reasonably low, without wild fluctuations in exchange rates. Although Denmark is slightly cheaper than Norway and Sweden, the standard and the cost of living are nonetheless high, especially for such luxuries as hard liquor and cigarettes. Prices are highest in Copenhagen; the least expensive areas are Funen and Jutland.

SAMPLE PRICES

Cup of coffee, 14 kr.–20 kr.; bottle of beer, 15 kr.–25 kr.; soda, 10 kr.–15 kr.; ham sandwich, 22 kr.–40 kr.; 1-mile taxi ride, 30 kr.

Customs on Arrival

If you purchase goods in a country that is a member of the European Union (EU) and pay that country's value-added tax (VAT) on those goods, you may import duty-free 1½ liters of liquor; 300 cigarettes or 150 cigarillos or 75 cigars or 400 grams of tobacco.

If you are entering Denmark from a non-EU country or if you have purchased your goods on a ferryboat or in an airport not taxed in the EU, you must pay Danish taxes on any amount of alcoholic beverages greater than 1 liter of liquor or 2 liters of strong wine, plus 2 liters of table wine. For tobacco, the limit is 200 cigarettes or 100 cigarillos or 50 cigars or 250 grams of tobacco. You are also allowed 50 grams of perfume. Other articles (including beer) are allowed up to a maximum of 1,350 kr.

Language

Danish is a difficult tongue for foreigners, except those from Norway and Sweden, to understand, let alone speak. Danes are good linguists, however, and almost everyone, except elderly people in rural areas, speaks English well.

Getting Around

By Car

Roads here are good and largely traffic-free (except around Copenhagen); you can reach many islands by toll-free bridges.

RULES OF THE ROAD

The driver needs a valid license, and, if you're using your own car, it must have a certificate of registration and national plates. A triangular hazard-warning sign is compulsory in every car and is provided with a rented car. The driver and all passengers traveling in cars must wear seat belts, and headlights must always be on—even in the daytime. Motorcyclists must always wear helmets and use headlights. All drivers must pay attention to cyclists, who drive on the outer right lane and have the right-of-way.

Drive on the right and give way to traffic from the left. A red-and-white triangular yield sign, or a line of white triangles across the road, means you must yield to traffic on the road you are entering. Do not turn right on a red light. Speed limits are 50 kph (30 mph) in built-up areas; on highways, 100 kph (60 mph); and on other roads, 80 kph (50 mph). If you are towing a trailer, you must not exceed 70 kph (40 mph). Speeding and, especially, drinking and driving, are punished severely.

PARKING

In areas with signs that say PARKERING/STANDSNING FORBUDT, (no parking and no stopping) you are allowed a three-minute grace period to load and unload. In towns, automatic parking-ticket machines are used. Drop in coins, push the silver button, and a ticket will drop down with the expiration time. Display the ticket clearly on the dash. Parking for an hour is 6 kr.–15 kr. in Copenhagen, 7 kr. elsewhere. In some areas, signs post parking regulations. All cars have a plastic dial inside, on the windshield. Set the dial to the time you leave your car.

GASOLINE

Gas costs around 5.90 kr. a liter.

BREAKDOWNS

Members of organizations affiliated with Alliance International de Tourisme (AIT), including American AAA and British AA, can get technical and legal assistance from the **Danish Motoring Organization** (**FDM**, Firskovej 32, DK 2800 Lyngby, tel. 45/93–08–00). All highways have emergency phones, and you can even phone the car-rental company for help. If you cannot drive your car to a garage for repairs, the rescue corps, **Falck** (tel. 44/92–22–22), can help anywhere, night or day.

By Train and Bus

Traveling by train or bus is easy because **Danish State Railways** (**DSB**, tel. 33/14–17–01) and a few private companies cover the country with a dense network of train services, supplemented in remote areas by buses. Hourly intercity trains connect the main towns in Jutland and Funen with Copenhagen and Zealand, using high-speed diesels, called IC–3s, on the most important stretches. All these trains make the one-hour ferry crossing of the Store Bælt (Great Belt), the waterway separating Funen and Zealand. You can reserve seats on intercity trains and Lyntog (the high-speed express), and you *must* have a reservation if you plan to cross the Great Belt. Buy tickets at stations for trains, buses, and connecting ferry crossings. You can usually buy tickets on the bus itself. For most cross-country trips, children between 4 and 11 accompanied by an adult travel free, though they must have a seat reservation (30 kr.). Ask about discounts for senior citizens and groups.

FARES

There are two types of **Scanrail passes.** The first can be purchased in the United States for either five days of travel within 15 days ($199 first class, $159 second class); 10 days within a month ($339 first class, $275 second class); or one month ($499 first class, $399 second class). Only the five-day pass can be purchased in Denmark. Call either RailEurope (800/849–7245) or DER (800/782–2424). The Scanrail pass available in Denmark is a good buy for 21 days of unlimited travel by rail and on most sea routes in Denmark, Norway, Sweden, and Finland. The price for adults traveling second class is 1,930 kr.; for young adults (12–25), 1,450 kr.; and for children (4–11), 965 kr. For details, call DER, RailEurope, or your travel agent. DSB also offers other discounts; ask, ask, ask!

By Boat

There is frequent service to Germany, Poland, Sweden, Norway, and the Faroe Islands (in the Atlantic Ocean, north of Scotland), as well as to Britain. Domestic ferries provide service between the three areas of Jutland, Funen, and Zealand and to the smaller islands, 100 of which are inhabited. Danish State Railways and several private shipping companies publish timetables in English, and you should reserve on domestic as well as overseas routes. Ask about off-season discounts.

By Bicycle

Some say the Danes have the greatest number of bikes per capita in the world. Indeed, with its flat landscape and uncrowded roads, Denmark is a cycler's paradise. You can rent bikes at some train stations and many tourist offices, as well as from private firms. Contact the **Danish Cyclists' Association** (Dansk Cyklist Forbund) (Rømersgade 7, DK 1362 Copenhagen, tel. 33/32–31–21) for additional information. Danish tourist offices publish the pamphlet "Cycling Holiday in Denmark."

Staying in Denmark

Telephones

LOCAL CALLS

Pay phones take 1-, 5-, and 10-kr. coins. You must use the area codes even when dialing a local number. Calling cards, which are sold at DSB stations, post offices, and some kiosks, cost 25, 50, or 100 kr., and are used at certain phones.

INTERNATIONAL CALLS

Dial 00, then the country code, the area code, and the number. To reach an **AT&T** long-distance operator, dial 8001–0010; for **MCI,** dial 8001–0022; and for **Sprint,** 8001–0877. Denmark's international telephone country code is 45.

OPERATORS AND INFORMATION

To speak to an operator, most of whom speak English, for local assistance, dial 118; for an international operator, dial 113.

Mail

POSTAL RATES

Surface and airmail letters, as well as aerograms, to the United States cost 5 kr. for 20 grams; postcards also cost 5 kr. Letters and postcards to the United Kingdom and other EU countries cost 3.75 kr. Stamps are sold at post offices and some shops.

RECEIVING MAIL

If you do not know where you will be staying, your mail can be addressed to "poste restante" and sent to any post office. If no post office is specified, letters will be sent to the main post office in Copenhagen (Tietgensgade 37, DK 1704). American Express holds mail free of charge, but only for card- and/or traveler's check–holders; otherwise there's a small fee.

Shopping

VAT REFUNDS

Visitors from a non-EU country can save about 20% by obtaining a refund of the value-added tax (VAT) at the more than 1,500 shops displaying TAX FREE signs. If the shop sends your purchase directly to your home address, you pay only the sales price, exclusive of VAT. If you want to take the goods home yourself, pay the full price in the shop and get a VAT refund at the Danish duty-free shopping center at the Copenhagen airport. Get a copy of the *Tax-Free Shopping Guide* from the tourist office.

Opening and Closing Times

Banks in Copenhagen are open weekdays 9:30–4 and Thursdays until 6. Several *bureaux de change,* including the ones at Copenhagen's central station and airport, stay open until 10 PM. Outside Copenhagen, banking hours vary.

Museums are generally open 10–3 or 11–4 and closed Mondays. In winter, opening hours are shorter, and some museums close for the season. Check the local papers or ask at tourist offices.

Small shops and boutiques are open weekdays 10–5:30; most stay open Thursday and Friday until 7 or 8 and close on Saturday at 1 or 2. The first Saturday of every month, most shops stay open until 4 or 5.

National Holidays

January 1; April 5–7 (Easter); May 3 (Common Prayer); May 16 (Ascension); June 26 (Pentecost); June 5 (Constitution Day; shops close at noon); and December 24–26.

Dining

Danes take their food seriously, and Danish food, however simple, is excellent, with an emphasis on fresh ingredients and careful presentation. Fish and meat are both of top quality in this farming and fishing country, and both are staple ingredients of the famous smørrebrød. Some smørrebrød are huge meals in themselves: Innocent snackers can find themselves faced with a dauntingly large (but nonetheless delicious) mound of fish or meat, slathered with pickle relish, all atop *rugbrød* (rye bread) and *franskbrød* (French bread). Another specialty is *wienerbrød* (a Danish pastry), an original far superior to anything billing itself "Danish pastry" elsewhere.

All Scandinavian countries have versions of the cold table, but Danes claim that theirs, *det store kolde bord,* is the original and the best. It's a celebration meal; the setting of the long table is a work of art—often with paper sculpture and silver platters—and the food itself is a minor miracle of design and decoration.

In hotels and restaurants the cold table is served at lunch only, though you will find a more limited version at hotel breakfasts—a good bet for budget travelers because you can eat as much as you like.

Denmark boasts more than 50 varieties of beer made by as many breweries; the best-known come from Carlsberg and Tuborg. Those who like harder stuff should try *snaps,* the aquavit traditionally drunk with cold food, especially herring. A note about smoking: Danes, like many Europeans, regard smoking as an inalienable right. Militant insistence that they abstain will be regarded as either hysteria or comedy. A polite tone requesting they blow their smoke away from you may prove more effective.

MEALTIMES
The Danes start work early, which means they generally eat lunch at noon. Evening meals are also eaten early, so visitors should make sure they have dinner reservations for 9 at the latest. Bars and cafés stay open later, and most offer at least light fare.

WHAT TO WEAR
The Danes are a fairly casual lot, and few restaurants require a jacket and tie. Even in the chicest establishments, the tone is elegantly casual.

RATINGS
Meal prices vary little between town and country. While approximate gradings are given below, remember that careful ordering can get you a moderate (**$$**) meal at a very expensive (**$$$$**) restaurant. Prices are per person and include a first course, main course, and dessert, plus taxes and tip, but not wine. Highly recommended restaurants are indicated by a star ★.

CATEGORY	COST
$$$$	over 400 kr.
$$$	200 kr.–400 kr.
$$	120 kr.–200 kr.
$	under 120 kr.

Lodging
Accommodations in Denmark range from the spare and comfortable to the resplendent. Even inexpensive hotels offer simple designs in good materials and good, firm beds. Many Danes prefer a shower to a bath, so if you particularly want a tub, ask for it, but be prepared to pay more. Except in the case of rentals, breakfast and taxes are usually included in prices, though this seems to be changing. Check when making a reservation.

HOTELS
Luxury hotels in the city or countryside offer rooms of a high standard, and in a manor-house hotel you may find yourself sleeping in a four-poster bed. Less expensive accommodations, however, are uniformly clean and comfortable.

INNS
A cheaper and charming alternative to hotels are the old stagecoach *kro* inns scattered throughout Denmark. You can save money by contacting **Kro Ferie** (Vejlevej 16, 8700 Horsens, tel. 75/64–87–00) to invest in a book of Inn Checks, valid at 86 inns. Each check costs 375 kr. per person or 550 kr. per couple and includes one overnight stay in a double room with bath, breakfast included. Family checks, for three (595 kr.) and four (685 kr.), are also available. Order a free catalogue from Kro Ferie and choose carefully; the organization includes some chain hotels bereft of even a smidgen of inn-related charm. Some establishments also tack a 100 kr. surcharge on to the price of a double.

FARM VACATIONS
These are perhaps the best way to see how the Danes live and work. You stay on a farm and share meals with the family; you can even get out and help with the chores. There's a minimum stay of three nights; bed and breakfast is 175 kr., and half board runs 245. (Full board can be arranged.) Children under 4 get 75% off; 4–11 get 50%. Contact

the **Horsens Tourist Office** (Søndergade 26, DK 8700 Horsens, Jutland, tel. 75/62–38–22, fax 75/62–61–51) for details.

YOUTH HOSTELS

The 100 youth hostels in Denmark are open to everyone regardless of age. If you have an International Youth Hostels Association card (obtainable before you leave home), the average rate is 60 kr. Without the card, there's a surcharge of 25 kr. For more information, contact **Danmarks Vandrehjem** (Vesterbrogade 39, 1620 KBH V, tel. 31/31–36–12).

RENTALS

Many Danes rent out their summer homes; it's a good way to see the countryside on your own terms. A simple house with room for four will cost from 1,000 kr. per week to twice as much during the summer high season. Contact the Danish Tourist Board for details.

CAMPING

Denmark has more than 500 approved campsites, with a rating system of one, two, or three stars. You need an International Camping Carnet or Danish Camping Pass (available at any campsite and valid for one year). For more details on camping and discounts for groups and families, contact **Campingrådet** (Hesseløgade 10, 2100 KBH 0 tel. 39/27–88–44).

RATINGS

Prices are for two people in a double room and include service and taxes and usually breakfast. Highly recommended lodgings are indicated by a star ★.

CATEGORY	COPENHAGEN	OTHER AREAS
$$$$	over 1,100 kr.	over 850 kr.
$$$	800 kr.–1,100 kr.	650 kr.–850 kr.
$$	670 kr.–800 kr.	450 kr.–650 kr.
$	under 670 kr.	under 450 kr.

Tipping

The egalitarian Danes do not expect to be tipped. The exception is hotel porters, who get around 5 kr. per bag; you should also leave 1 or 2 kr. for the use of a public toilet, if there is an attendant.

COPENHAGEN

Arriving and Departing

By Plane

The main airport for both international and domestic flights is Copenhagen Airport, 10 kilometers (6 miles) outside of town.

BETWEEN THE AIRPORT AND DOWNTOWN

There is frequent bus service to the city; the airport bus to the central station leaves every 15 minutes, and the trip takes about 25 minutes. You pay a 30-kr. fare on the bus. Public buses cost 15 kr. and run as often but take longer. Bus 250S takes you to Rådhus Pladsen, the city hall square. A taxi ride takes 15 minutes and costs about 120 kr.

By Train

Copenhagen's recently renovated central station is the hub of the train networks. Express trains leave hourly, on the hour, from 6 AM to 10 PM for principal towns in Funen and Jutland. Find out more from **DSB Information** (tel. 33/14–17–01) at the central station. You can make reservations at the central station (tel. 33/14–88–00) and most other stations and through travel agents. In Copenhagen, public shower facilities at the main train station are open 4:30 AM–2 AM and cost 15 kr.

Getting Around

By Bus and Suburban Train
The best bet for visitors is the **Copenhagen Card,** affording unlimited travel on buses and suburban trains (S-trains), admission to some 60 museums and sights around Zealand, and a reduction on the ferry crossing to Sweden. Buy the card, which costs about 140 kr. (one day), 230 kr. (two days), or 295 kr. (three days)—half price for children 5–11—at tourist offices, hotels, or from travel agents.

Buses and suburban trains operate on the same ticket system and divide Copenhagen and environs into three zones. Tickets are validated on the time system: On the basic ticket, which costs 10 kr. for an hour, you can travel anywhere in the zone in which you started. You can buy a clip-card, equivalent to 10 basic tickets, for 70 kr. Get zone information from the 24-hour information service: tel. 36/45–45–45 for buses, 33/14–17–01 for S-trains. (Disregard the Danish message, and just hang on until a human being answers.) Buses and S-trains run from 5 AM (6 AM on Sunday) to 12:30 AM.

By Car
Copenhagen is a city for walkers, not drivers. The charm of its pedestrian streets is paid for by a complicated one-way road system and difficult parking. Leave your car in the garage: Attractions are relatively close together, and public transportation is excellent.

By Taxi
Taxis are not cheap, but all are metered. The base charge is 12 kr., plus 8–10 kr. per kilometer. A cab is available when it displays the sign FRI (free); it can be hailed (though this can be difficult outside the center) or picked up at a taxi stand, or call 31/35–35–35. If you call, there is a surcharge of 20 kr.; additional fees apply at night.

By Bicycle
More than half the 5 million Danes are said to ride bikes, which are popular with visitors as well. Bike rental costs 30 kr.–50 kr. a day, with a deposit of 100 kr.–200 kr. Contact **Danwheel-Rent-a-Bike** (Colbjørnsensgade 3, tel. 31/21–22–27) or **Urania Cykler** (Gammel Kongevej 1, tel. 31/21–80–88).

Important Addresses and Numbers

Tourist Information
The main tourist information office is **Danmarks Turistråd** (Danish Tourist Board, Bernstoffsgade 1, DK–1577 V, Copenhagen, tel. 33/11–13–25). Located on the Tivoli grounds, it is open May, weekdays 9–6, Sat. 9–2, Sun. 9–1; June–Sept., daily 9–6; Oct.–Apr., weekdays 9–5, Sat. 9–noon, closed Sun. There are also offices at Helsingør, Hillerød, Køge, Roskilde, Gilleleje, Hundersted, and Tisvildeleje. Youth information in Copenhagen is available at **Huset** (Rådhusstraede 13, tel. 33/15–65–18).

Embassies
U.S. (Dag Hammarskjöldsallé 24, tel. 31/42–31–44). **Canadian** (Kristen Benikowsgade 1, tel. 33/12–22–99). **U.K.** (Kastelsvej 40, tel. 35/26–46–00).

Emergencies

Police, Fire, Ambulance (tel. 112). **Doctor** (after 4 PM, tel. 33/12–00–41. Fees payable in cash only; night fees around 400–500 kr.). **Dentist: Dental Emergency Service,** Tandlægevagten, 14, Oslo Plads, near Østerport station (no phone; emergencies only; cash only). **Pharmacies:** The following are open 24 hours in central Copenhagen: **Steno Apotek** (Vesterbrogade 6C, tel. 33/14–82–66); **Sønderbro Apotek** (Amagerbrogade 158, Amager area, tel. 31/58–01–40); **Glostrup Apotek** (Hovedvegen 101, Glostrup area, tel. 43/96–00–20). There is a nighttime surcharge of about 10–20 kr.

English-Language Bookstores

English-language publications are sold at the central-station newsstand and in most bookstores around town. **Boghallen** (Rådhus Pladsen 37) and **Arnold Busck** (Købmagergade 49) have particularly good selections.

Travel Agencies

American Express (Amagertorv 18, tel. 33/12–23–01). **Spies** (Nyropsgade 41, tel. 33/32–15–00) arranges charter flights and accommodations all over Europe.

Guided Tours

Orientation Tours

Tours are a good way to get acquainted with Copenhagen. The "Harbour and Canal Tour" (by boat; May–mid-Sept., daily every ½ hour 10–5) leaves from Gammel Strand and the east side of Kongens Nytorv. The following bus tours, conducted by **Copenhagen Excursions** (tel. 31/54–06–06), leave from the Lur Blowers' Column in Rådhus Pladsen: "City Tour" (mid-May–mid-Sept., daily at 10 and 4; June 15–Aug., daily at 10, 12, 4); "Grand Tour of Copenhagen" (Nov.–Mar., daily at 11, plus Sat. at 1:30; Apr.–Oct., daily at 11, 1:30, 3); "Royal Tour of Copenhagen" (June–mid-Sept., Tues., Thurs., Sat. at 10); "City and Harbour Tour" (combined bus and boat; May–mid-Sept., daily at 9:30, 1, 3). Tickets are available aboard the bus and boat or from travel agencies.

Special-Interest Tours

The "Carlsberg Brewery Tour," which includes a look into the draft-horse stalls, meets at the Elephant Gate (Ny Carlsbergvej 140) on weekdays at 11 and 2 or by arrangement for groups (tel. 33/27–13–14). Tuborg Breweries also provides tours (Strandvejen 54, Bus 6 or the Svanemøllen train station) weekdays at 10, 12:30, and 2:30 or by arrangement for groups (tel. 33/27–22–12). The "Royal Copenhagen Porcelain" tour (Smallegade 45, tel. 31/86–48–48) is given on weekdays at 9, 10, and 11.

Walking Tours

The tourist board supplies maps and brochures and can recommend a walking tour.

Regional Tours

The Danish Tourist Board has full details of excursions outside the city, including visits to castles (such as Hamlet's castle), the Viking Ship Museum, and Sweden.

Personal Guides

The tourist information center can recommend multilingual guides for individual needs, while travel agents have details on hiring a limousine and guide.

Exploring Copenhagen

When Denmark ruled Norway and Sweden in the 15th century, Copenhagen was the capital of all three countries. Today it is still a lively northern capital, with about 1 million inhabitants. It's a city meant for walking, the first in Europe to recognize the value of pedestrian streets in fostering community spirit. As you stroll through the cobbled streets and squares, you'll find that Copenhagen combines the excitement and variety of big-city life with a small-town atmosphere. If there's such a thing as a cozy metropolis, you'll find it here.

Nor are you ever far from water, be it sea or canal. The city itself is built upon two main islands, Slotsholmen and Christianshavn, connected by drawbridges. Walk down Nyhavn Canal, an area formerly haunted by a fairly salty crew of sailors. Now it's gentrified, and the 18th-century houses lining it are filled with chic restaurants. You should linger, too, in the five main pedestrian streets known collectively as "Strøget," with shops, restaurants, cafés, and street musicians and vendors. In summer Copenhagen moves outside, and the best views of city life are from the sidewalk cafés in the sunny squares.

Numbers in the margin correspond to points of interest on the Copenhagen map.

The best place to start a stroll is Rådhus Pladsen, the hub of Copenhagen's commercial district. The mock-Renaissance building dominating it is **Københavns Rådhus** (city hall), completed in 1905. A statue of Copenhagen's 12th-century founder, Bishop Absalon, sits atop the main entrance. Inside, you can see the first World Clock, an astrological timepiece invented and built by Jens Olsen and put in motion in 1955. If you're feeling energetic, take a guided tour partway up the 350-foot tower for a panoramic view. *Rådhus Pladsen, tel. 33/66–25–82. Open Mon.–Wed., Fri. 9:30–3, Thurs. 9:30–4, Sat. 9:30–1. Tours in English: weekdays at 3, Sat. at 10. Tower tours: Mon.–Sat. at noon; additional tours June–Sept. at 10 and 2. Admission: tour 20 kr., tower 10 kr.*

On the east side of Rådhus Pladsen is **Lurblæserne** (Lur Blowers' Column), topped by two Vikings blowing an ancient trumpet called a *lur*. The artist took a good deal of artistic license—the lur dates from the Bronze Age, 1500 BC, while the Vikings lived a mere 1,000 years ago. The monument is a starting point for sightseeing tours of the city.

If you continue to the square's northeast corner and turn right, you will be in Frederiksberggade, the first of the five pedestrian streets that make up **Strøget**, Copenhagen's shopping district. Walk past the cafés and trendy boutiques to the double square of **Gammeltorv** and **Nytorv**, where, farther along, the street is paved with mosaic tiles.

Turn down Rådhusstræde toward Frederiksholms Kanal, and continue to Ny Vestergade. Here you'll find the entrance to **Nationalmuseet** (the National Museum), with extensive collections that chronicle Danish cultural history to modern times and display Egyptian, Greek, and Roman antiquities. Viking enthusiasts may want to see the Runic stones in the Danish cultural history section. *Ny Vestergade 10, tel. 33/13–44–11. Admission: 30 kr. adults, 20 kr. students and senior citizens, children under 16 free. Open Tues.–Sun. 10–5.*

Cross Frederiksholms Kanal to Castle Island, dominated by the massive gray **Christiansborg Slot** (Christiansborg Castle). The complex, which contains the Folketinget (Parliament House) and the Royal Reception Chambers, is on the site of the city's first fortress, built by Bishop Absalon in 1167. While the castle was being built at the turn of the century, the National Museum excavated the ruins beneath the site. *Christiansborg ruins, tel. 33/92–64–92. Admission: 12 kr. adults, 5 kr. children. Open May–Sept., daily 9:30–3:30; closed Oct.–Apr., Mon. and Sat. Folketinget, tel. 33/37–55–00. Admission free. Tour times vary; call ahead. Reception Chambers: Admission: 27 kr. adults, 10 kr. children. Opening and tour times vary; call ahead. Closed Jan.*

6 Just north of the castle is **Thorvaldsens Museum.** The 19th-century Danish sculptor Bertel Thorvaldsen, buried at the center of the museum, was greatly influenced by the statues and reliefs of classical antiquity. In addition to his own works, there is a collection of paintings and drawings by other artists illustrating the influence of Italy on Denmark's Golden Age artists. *Porthusgade 2, tel. 33/32–15–32. Admission free. Open Tues.–Sun. 10–5.*

7 Nearby, **Det Kongelige Bibliotek** (the Royal Library) houses the country's largest collection of books, newspapers, and manuscripts. Look for early records of the Viking journeys to America and Greenland and the statue of the philosopher Søren Kierkegaard in the garden. *Christians Brygge 8, tel. 33/93–01–11. Admission free. Open weekdays 9–7, Sat. 10–7.*

8 Close to the library is **Teaterhistorisk Museet** (the Theater History Museum), in the Royal Court Theater of 1767. You can see extensive exhibits on theater and ballet history, then wander around the boxes, stage, and dressing rooms to see where it all happened. *Christianborg Ridebane 18, tel. 33/11–51–76. Admission: 20 kr. adults, 10 kr. senior citizens and students, 5 kr. children. Open Wed. 2–4, Sun. noon–4.*

9 Across the street that bears its name is **Tøjhusmuseet** (the Royal Armory), with impressive displays of uniforms, weapons, and armor in an arched hall 200 yards long. *Tøjhusgade 3, tel. 33/11–60–37. Admission: 20 kr. adults, 5 kr. children 6–17. Open Tues.–Sun. 10–4.*

10 A few steps from Tøjhusmuseet is the old stock exchange, **Børsen,** believed to be the oldest still in use—although it functions only on special occasions. It was built by the 16th-century monarch King Christian IV, a scholar and warrior, and architect of much of the city. The king is said to have had a hand in twisting the tails of the four dragons that form the structure's distinctive green copper spire. With its steep roofs, tiny windows, and gables, the building is one of Copenhagen's treasures.

From Børsen, look east across the drawbridge (Knippelsbro) that connects Slotsholmen with Christianshavn, one of the oldest parts of
11 Copenhagen, to the delicate green-and-gold spire of **Vor Frelsers Kirke** (Our Savior's Church). The Gothic structure was built in 1696. Local legend has it that the staircase encircling it was built curling the wrong way around, and that when its architect reached the top and saw what he had done, he jumped. *Skt. Annægade 9, tel. 31/57–27–98. Admission free. Open Mar. 15–May, Mon.–Sat. 9–3:30, Sun. noon–3:30; June–Sept., Mon.–Sat. 9–4:30, Sun. noon–4:30; Oct.–Mar. 14, Mon.–Sat. 10–1:30, Sun. noon–1:30.*

Head back to Strøget, turning left along the Amagertorv section. Toward the end and to the right (5 Niels Hemmingsens Gade) is the 18th-
12 century **Helligånds Kirken** (Church of the Holy Ghost). The choir contains a marble font by the sculptor Thorvaldsen.

In Østergade, the easternmost of the streets that make up Strøget, you
13 cannot miss the green spire of **Nikolaj Kirke** (Nikolaj Church). The build-

194

Amalienborg, **15**

Amalienhavn, **16**

Børsen, **10**

Botanisk Have, **28**

Christiansborg Slot, **5**

Den Hirschsprungske Samling, **30**

Den Lille Havfrue, **22**

Det Kongelige Bib-liotek, **7**

Frihedsmuseet, **20**

Helligånds Kirken, **12**

Kastellet, **21**

Københavns Rådhus, **1**

Københavns Synagoge, **25**

Københavns Universitet, **24**

Kongelig Teater, **14**

Kunstindustrimuseet, **19**

Lurblæserne, **2**

Marmorkirken, **17**

Nationalmuseet, **4**

Nikolaj Kirke, **13**

Ny Carlsberg Glyptotek, **33**

Rosenborg Slot, **27**

Rundetårn, **26**

Russiske Ortodoks Kirke, **18**

Statens Museum for Kunst, **29**

Strøget, **3**

Teaterhistorisk Museet, **8**

Thorvaldsens Museum, **6**

Tivoli, **32**

Tøjhusmuseet, **9**

Tycho Brahe Planetarium, **31**

Vor Frelsers Kirke, **11**

Vor Frue Kirke, **23**

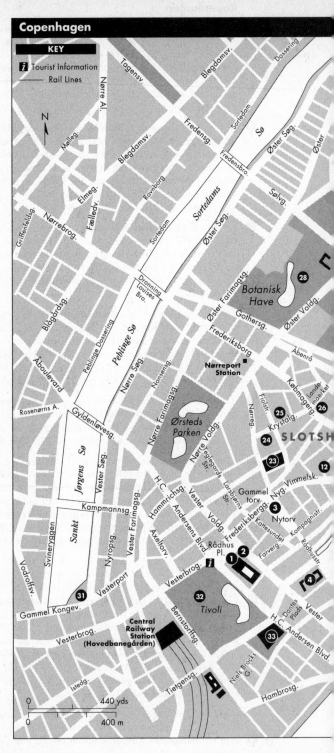

Copenhagen

KEY

i Tourist Information

Rail Lines

Farimagsg.
Dag Hammarskjölds Al.
Kristianiag.
Langeliniebrd.
Østbaneg.
Stockholmsg.
Øster Anlæg
Østerport Station
Oslo Plads
Oslo Folke Bernadottes Al.
22
Forbindelsev.
Langelinie
Yderhavn
21
Churchill-parken
30
Rigensg.
Fredericiag.
Grønningen
St. Kongensg.
29
Sølvg.
20
Esplanaden
27
Kongens Have
Kronprinsesseg.
Store Kongensg.
Dronningens Tværg.
Adelg.
Borgerg.
Bredg.
19
18
17
Bredg.
15
16
Amalieg.
Toldbodg.
Amalieg.
Sankt Annæ Plads
Vognmagerg.
Gammel mønt.
Pilestræde
Gothersg.
Ny Østerg.
Kr. Bernikg.
Bremerholm
OLMEN
Østerg.
Kongens Nytorv
Nyhavn
Nyhavn
Canal
Inderhavn
Amagertorv
13
Højbro
14
Heibergsg.
Læderstr.
Gammel Strand
Holmenskanal
Holbergsg.
Vindelbrog.
6
Christiansborg Slotsplads
Holmenskanal
Havnegade
5
10
Børsg.
Chr. IV's Bro
Knippelsbro
8
Tøjhusgade
7
9
Christians Brygge
Sankt Annæg.
CHRISTIANSHAVN
Frederiksholms Kanal
Voldg.
Torveg.
11
Langebro
Langerbrog.
Dronningensg.
Princessg.
Christianshavns Voldg.
Amagerbrog.
Amager Blvd.
Stadsgraven
Vermlandsg.

ing that currently stands was built in the 20th century; the previous structure, which dated from the 13th century, was destroyed by fire in 1728. Today the church's role is secular—it's an art gallery and an exhibition center.

TIME OUT **Café Nikolaj,** inside the old Nikolaj Kirke, is a good place to stop for a Danish pastry or a light meal. If you have toddlers, there's a small playground adjacent to the church with a slide shaped like a peacock.

Although Strøget is famous as a shopping area, and elegant stores abound, it's also where Copenhagen comes to stroll. Outside the posh displays of the fur and porcelain shops, the sidewalks have the festive aura of a street fair.

Kongens Nytorv (the King's New Market) is the square marking the ⑭ end of Strøget. The **Kongelig Teater** (Danish Royal Theater), home of Danish opera and ballet as well as theater, sits on the south side. The Danish Royal Ballet remains one of the world's great companies, with a repertoire ranging from classical to modern. On the western side of the square you'll see the stately facade of D'Angleterre, the grande dame of Copenhagen hotels.

The street leading southeast from Kongens Nytorv is **Nyhavn.** The recently gentrified canal was a longtime haunt of sailors. Now restaurants and boutiques outnumber the tattoo shops, but on hot summer nights the area still gets rowdy, with Scandinavians reveling amid a fleet of old-time sailing ships and well-preserved 18th-century buildings. Hans Christian Andersen lived at both numbers 18 and 20. Nearer the harbor are old shipping warehouses, including two—Nyhavn 71 and the Admiral—that have been converted into comfortable hotels.

Turn left at the end of Nyhavn to see the harbor front and then make an immediate left onto Sankt Annæ Plads. Take the third right onto ⑮ Amaliegade. Continue straight ahead for **Amalienborg,** the principal royal residence since 1784. When the royal family is in residence during the fall and winter, the Royal Guard and band march through the city at noon to change the palace guard. The second division of the Royal Collection (the first is at Rosenborg) is at Amalienborg. Among the museum's highlights are the study of King Christian IX (1818–1906) and the drawing room of his wife, Queen Louise. The collection also includes Rococo banquet silver, highlighted by a bombastic Viking ship centerpiece, and a small costume collection. *Amalienborg Museum, tel. 33/12–21–86. Admission 35 kr. adults, 5 kr. children. Open Mar.–late-Oct., daily 11–4; late-Oct.–Feb., Tues.–Sun. 11–4.*

Rest a moment on the palace's harbor side, amid the trees and foun- ⑯ tains of **Amaliehavn.** Across the square, it's just a step to Bredgade and ⑰ **Marmorkirken** (the Marble Church), a 19th-century baroque church with a dome that looks several sizes too large for the building.

⑱ Bredgade is also home to the exotic onion domes of the **Russiske** ⑲ **Ortodoks Kirke** (Russian Orthodox Church). Farther on is the **Kunstindustrimuseet** (Museum of Decorative Art), with a large selection of European and Asian handicrafts, as well as ceramics, silver, and tapestries. *Bredgade 68, tel. 33/14–94–52. Admission: 30 kr. adults, 20 kr. students and senior citizens, children under 16 free. Permanent exhibition open Tues.–Sun. 1–4; special exhibitions open Tues.–Sat. 10–4, Sun. 1–4.*

⑳ A little farther, turn right onto Esplanaden and you'll come to **Frihedsmuseet** (the Liberty Museum), in Churchillparken. It gives an evocative picture of the heroic Danish Resistance movement during World War II, which managed to save 7,000 Jews from the Nazis by hiding them in homes and hospitals, then smuggling them across to Sweden. *Churchillparken, tel. 33/13–77–14. Admission free. Open Sept. 16– April, Tues.–Sat. 11–3, Sun. 11–4; May–Sept. 15, Tues.–Sat. 10–4, Sun. 10–5.*

㉑ At the park's entrance stands the English church, St. Alban's, and, in the center, **Kastellet** (the Citadel), with two rings of moats. This was the city's main fortress in the 18th century, but, in a grim reversal during World War II, the Germans used it as headquarters during their occupation of Denmark. *Admission free. Open 6 AM to sunset.*

㉒ Continue on to the Langelinie, which on Sunday is thronged with promenading Danes, and at last to **Den Lille Havfrue** (The Little Mermaid), the 1913 statue commemorating Hans Christian Andersen's lovelorn creation, and the subject of hundreds of travel posters.

㉓ From Langelinie, take the train or bus from Østerport station to the center or wind back the 2.5 km (1.6 mi) through the pedestrian streets. Walk north from the Strøget on Nørregade until you reach **Vor Frue Kirke** (The Church of Our Lady), Copenhagen's cathedral since 1924. The site itself has been a place of worship since the 13th century, when Bishop Absalon built a chapel here. The spare neoclassical facade is a 19th-century revamp that repaired the damage incurred during Nelson's bombing of the city in 1801. If the church is open, you can see Thorvaldsen's marble sculptures of Christ and the Apostles. *Nørregade, Frue Plads, tel. 33/15–10–78. Opening times irregular.*

㉔ Head north up Fjolstræde until you come to the main part of **Københavns Universitet** (Copenhagen University), built in the 19th century on the site of the medieval bishops' palace. Past the university, turn
㉕ right onto Krystalgade. On the left is the **Københavns Synagoge** (Copenhagen Synagogue), designed by the contemporary architect Gustav Friedrich Hetsch. Hetsch drew on the Doric and Egyptian styles to create the arklike structure.

㉖ Just across Købmagergade is the **Rundetårn**, a round tower built as an observatory in 1642 by Christian IV. It is said that Peter the Great of Russia drove a horse and carriage up the 600 feet of the inner staircase. You'll have to walk, but the view is worth it. *Købmagergade, tel. 33/93–66–60. Admission: 15 kr. adults, 5 kr. children. Open Dec.–May and Sept.–Oct., Mon.–Sat. 10–5, Sun. noon–4; June–Aug., Mon.–Sat. 10–8, Sun. Observatory and telescope open, with astronomer on hand to answer questions, mid-Oct.–mid-Mar., Tues.–Wed. 7–10.*

㉗ Turn right at Rundetårn onto Landemærket, then left onto Åbenrå until you reach Nørre Voldgade, where you turn right and cross Gothersgade to Øster Voldgade, which will bring you to **Rosenborg Slot**. This Renaissance castle—built by Renaissance man Christian IV—houses the Crown Jewels, as well as a collection of costumes and royal memorabilia. Don't miss Christian IV's pearl-studded saddle. *Øster Voldgade 4A, tel. 33/15–32–86. Admission: 40 kr. adults, 5 kr. children. Castle open late-Oct.–Apr., Tues., Fri., and Sun. 11–2; treasury open daily 11–3. Both open May, Sept.–late-Oct., daily 11–3; June–Aug., daily 10–4.*

㉘ The palace is surrounded by gardens, and just across Øster Voldgade is the **Botanisk Have**, Copenhagen's 25 acres of botanical gardens, with a rather spectacular Palm House containing tropical and subtropical plants. There's also an observatory and a geological museum. *Admis-*

sion free. Open May–Aug., daily 8:30–6; Sept.–Apr., daily 8:30–4. Palm House open daily 10–3.

㉙ Leave the gardens through the north exit to get to the **Statens Museum for Kunst** (National Art Gallery), where the collection ranges from modern Danish art to works by Rubens, Dürer, and the Impressionists. Particularly fine are the museum's 20 Matisses. *Sølvgade 48–50, tel. 33/91–21–26. Admission: 20 kr. adults (30 kr. for special exhibitions), children under 16 free. Open Tues.–Sun. 10–4:30, Wed. until 9 PM.*

TIME OUT   The subterranean **cafeteria** in the museum makes an excellent place to stop for lunch or coffee. Art posters deck the walls, and a cheerful staff serves hearty lunches.

㉚ A nearby building houses **Den Hirschsprungske Samling** (the Hirschsprung Collection) of Danish 19th-century art. The cozy museum features works from the Golden Age, as well as a collection of paintings by the late-19th-century artists of the Skagen school. *Stockholmsgade 20, tel. 31/42–03–36. Admission: 20 kr. adults, 10 kr. students and senior citizens, children under 16 free. Admission prices are higher for special exhibitions. Open Thurs.–Mon. 10–5, Wed. 10–10; opening times may vary—call first.*

From Stockholmsgade, turn right onto Sølvgade and then left onto Øster Søgade, just before the bridge. Continue along the canal (the street name will change from Øster Søgade to Nørre Søgade to Vester Søgade) until you reach the head of the harbor.

㉛ Tucked between St. Jorgens Lake and the main arteries of Vester Søgade and Gammel Kongevej is the **Tycho Brahe Planetarium.** The modern cylindrical building is filled with astronomy exhibitions and an Omnimax Theater, which takes visitors on a visual journey up through space and down under the seas. *Gammel Kongevej 10, tel. 33/12–12–24. Admission: exhibition and theater, 65 kr.; exhibition only, 15 kr. Reservations advised for theater. (Because films can be disorienting, planetarium officials do not recommend them for children under 7.) Open daily 10:30–9; films shown 11–9.*

㉜ Walk straight ahead and turn left onto Vesterbrogade. On the right lies Copenhagen's best-known attraction, **Tivoli.** In the 1840s, the Danish architect Georg Carstensen persuaded King Christian VIII that an amusement park was the perfect opiate of the masses, preaching that "when people amuse themselves, they forget politics." In the season from May to September, about 4 million people come through the gates. Tivoli is more sophisticated than a mere funfair: It offers a pantomime theater and an open-air stage; elegant restaurants; and numerous classical, jazz, and rock concerts. On weekends there are elaborate fireworks displays. Try to see Tivoli at least once by night, when the trees are illuminated along with the Chinese Pagoda and the main fountain. *Tel. 33/15–10–01. Admission: 40 kr. adults, 20 kr. children. Open mid-Apr.–mid-Sept., daily 10 AM–midnight.*

㉝ At the southern end of the gardens, on Hans Christian Andersens Boulevard, is the **Ny Carlsberg Glyptotek** (New Carlsberg Picture Hall). This elaborate neoclassical building houses a collection of works by Gauguin and Degas and other Impressionists, as well as Egyptian, Greek, Roman, and French sculpture. *Dantes Plads 7, tel. 33/41–81–41. Admission: 15 kr. adults, children free; adults free on Wed. and Sun. Open Sept.–Apr., Tues.–Sat. noon–3, Sun. 10–4; May–Aug., Tues.–Sun. 10–4.*

Excursions from Copenhagen

Shakespeare immortalized town and castle when he chose **Helsingør's Kronborg Castle** as the setting for *Hamlet*. Completed in 1585, the gabled and turreted structure is about 600 years younger than the fortress we imagine from the setting of Shakespeare's tragedy. Inside are the 200-foot-long dining hall, the luxurious chapel, and the royal chambers. The ramparts and 12-foot walls are a reminder of the castle's role as coastal bulwark—Sweden is only a few miles away. The town—about 29 miles north of Copenhagen—has a number of picturesque streets with 16th-century houses. There is frequent train service to Helsingør station, and then it's a 20-minute walk around the harbor to the castle. *Helsingør, tel. 49/21–30–78. Admission: 30 kr. adults, 10 kr. children. Open Easter and May–Sept., daily 10:30–5; Oct. and Apr., Tues.–Sun. 11–4; Nov.–Mar., Tues.–Sun. 11–3.*

Louisiana is a world-class modern art collection housed in a spectacular building in Humlebæk on the "Danish Riviera," the North Zealand coast. Even if you can't tell a Rauschenberg from a Rembrandt, you should make the 35-kilometer (22-mile) trip to see the setting: It's an elegant, rambling structure set in a large park with views of the sound, and, on a clear day, Sweden. The new children's wing has pyramid-shape chalkboards, kid-proof computers, and weekend activities under the guidance of an artist or museum coordinator. It's a half-hour train ride from Copenhagen to Humlebæk. A 10-minute walk from the station, the museum is also accessible by the E4 highway and the more scenic coastal road, Strandvejen. *Gammel Strandvej 13, Humlebæk, tel. 42/19–07–19. Admission: 48 kr. adults, 15 kr. children. Open Mon., Tues., Thurs., and Friday 10–5, Wed. 10–10, weekends 10–6. Combined train and admission ticket, 77 kr. (from Copenhagen), available from DSB. Admission prices are higher for special exhibitions.*

For history, you can head 30 kilometers (19 miles) west of Copenhagen to the bustling market town of **Roskilde.** A key administrative center during Viking times, it remained one of the largest towns in northern Europe through the Middle Ages. Its population has dwindled, but the legacy of its 1,000-year history lives on in the spectacular cathedral. Built on the site of Denmark's first church, the **Domkirke** (cathedral) has been the burial place of Danish royalty since the 15th century. *Domkirkepladsen, Roskilde. Admission: 5 kr. adults, 2 kr. children. Open Apr.–Sept., weekdays 9–4:45, Oct.–Mar., weekdays 10–2:45; May–Aug., Sun. 12:30–4:45; Sept.–Apr., Sun. 12:30–3:45. For varying Sat. hrs and to confirm opening times, tel. 42/35–27–00.*

A 10-minute walk south and through the park takes you to the water and to the **Viking Ship Museum.** Inside are five Viking ships, discovered at the bottom of the Roskilde Fjord in 1962. Detailed placards in English chronicle Viking history. There are also English-language films on the excavation and reconstruction. *Strandengen, Roskilde, tel. 42/35–65–55. Admission: 30 kr. adults, 20 kr. children. Open Apr.–Oct., daily 9–5; Nov.–Mar., daily 10–4.*

About halfway between Copenhagen and Helsingør is **Rungstedlund,** the former manor of Karen Blixen. The author of *Out of Africa* and several accounts of aristocratic Danish life, Blixen wrote under the pen name Isak Dinesen. The manor, where she lived as a child and to which she returned in 1931, opened as a museum in 1991; it includes manuscripts as well as photographs and memorabilia documenting her years in Africa and Denmark. The estate is a half-hour train ride from Copenhagen and a 10-minute walk from Rungsted station. *Rungsted*

Strandvej 111, Rungsted Kyst, tel. 42/57–10–57. Admission: 30 kr. adults, children free. Open May–Sept., daily 10–5; Oct.–Apr., Wed.–Fri. 1–4, weekends 11–4.

Shopping

Specialty Shops

Synonymous with shopping are Strøget's pedestrian streets. For glass, try **Holmegaard** (Østergade 15, tel. 33/12–44–77), where hand-crafted bowls, glasses, and vases are available. Just off the street is Pistolstræde, a typical old courtyard that's been lovingly restored and filled with intriguing boutiques. **Magasin** (Kongens Nytorv 13, tel. 33/11–44–33), one of the largest department stores in Scandinavia, offers everything in terms of clothing and gifts, as well as an excellent grocery. **Illum** (Østergade 52, tel. 33/14–40–02) is similar to Magasin, with another fine basement grocery and eating arcade. Don't confuse Illum with **Illums Bolighus** (Amagertorv 10, tel. 33/14–19–41), where designer furnishings, porcelain, quality clothing, and gifts are displayed in near-gallery surroundings. **Royal Copenhagen Porcelain** (Amagertorv 6, tel. 33/13–71–81) carries both old and new china and porcelain patterns and figurines. **Georg Jensen** (Amagertorv 4 and Østergade 40, tel 33/11–40–80) is one of the world's finest silversmiths and gleams with a wide array of silver patterns and jewelry. Don't miss the **Georg Jensen Museum** (Amagertorv 6, tel. 33/14–02–29), which showcases glass and silver beauties, ranging from tiny, twisted-glass shot glasses to an $85,000 silver fish dish.

Off the eastern end of Strøget **Tin Centret** (Ny Østergade 2, tel. 33/14–82–00) has a large pewterware collection (*tin* means pewter in Danish), some pieces reminiscent of colonial designs, others fashioned in uniquely Scandinavian simplicity. Back along Strøget, at furrier **Birger Christensen** (Østergade 38, tel. 33/11–55–55), you can ogle chic furs. **A. C. Bang** (Østergade 27, tel. 33/15–17–26) upholds its Old World, old-money aura with impeccable quality. Mid-summer and after-Christmas fur sales offer real savings. **Otto Madsen** (Vesterbrogade 1, tel 33/13–41–10) has less astronomical prices, in a less ritzy, more tourist-oriented shop. **FONA** (Østergade 47, tel. 33/15–90–55) carries stereo equipment, including the superior design and sound of Bang & Olufsen. **Bang & Olufsen** (Østergade 3–5, tel. 33/15–04–22) offers excellent prices in its own upscale shop.

Dining

Food remains one of the great pleasures of a stay in Copenhagen, a city with more than 2,000 restaurants. Traditional Danish fare spans all the price categories: You can order a light lunch of the traditional smørrebrød, snack from a store kolde bord, or dine out on lobster and Limfjord oysters. If you are strapped for cash, you can enjoy fast food Danish style, in the form of *pølser* (hot dogs) sold from trucks on the street. Team any of this with some pastry from a bakery (look for them under the sign of the upside-down gold pretzel), and you've got yourself a meal on the go.

For details and price-category definitions, *see* Dining *in* Staying in Denmark, *above.*

$$$$ **Kong Hans Kaelder.** Five centuries ago, this was a Nordic vineyard, ★ but now it's one of Scandinavia's finest restaurants. Chef Daniel Letz's French-inspired cooking is superb, while the setting is subterranean and mysterious, with whitewashed arching ceilings, candles, and wood

carvings. *Vingårdstræde 6, tel. 33/11–68–68. Reservations advised. AE, DC, MC, V. Dinner only. Closed Sun., mid-July–mid-Aug., and Dec. 24–25.*

$$$$ **Krogs.** This elegant canal-front restaurant commands a loyal clientele—both foreign and local; it's decorated with pale green walls, mirrored ceilings, and paintings of old Copenhagen. The menu (printed in five languages) lists such specialties as Canadian lobster flambé and poached Norwegian salmon served with spinach, cranberries, and saffron. *Gammel Strand 38, tel. 33/15–89–15. Reservations required. AE, DC, MC, V. Closed Dec. 24–Jan. 1.*

$$$$ **Skt. Gertrude's Kloster.** The history of this monastery goes back 700
★ years. The dining room is bedecked with hundreds of icons, the only light provided by 2,000 candles. The French menu is extensive, with such specials as fresh fillet of halibut steamed in oyster sauce and duck breast in sherry vinaigrette. *Hauser Plads 32, tel. 33/14–66–30. Reservations required. AE, DC, MC, V. Dinner only.*

$$$ **Els.** When it opened in 1853, the intimate Els was the place to be seen
★ before the theater, and the painted muses on the walls still watch diners rush to make an 8 o'clock curtain. Antique wooden columns and Royal Copenhagen tile tables complement a nouvelle Danish/French menu. The menu changes daily and incorporates game, fish, and market-fresh produce. *Store Strandstæde 3, tel. 33/14–13–41. Reservations advised. AE, DC, MC, V. Closed Dec. 24–25 and 31, Jan. 1.*

$$$ **L'Alsace.** Set in the cobbled courtyard of Pistolstraede and hung with paintings by Danish surrealist Wilhelm Freddie, this restaurant is peaceful and quiet, attracting such diverse diners as Queen Margrethe and Pope Paul II. The hand-drawn menu includes a hearty *choucroute* (sauerkraut) with sausage, and pork, as well as superb fruit tarts and cakes. *Ny Østergade 9, tel. 33/14–57–43. Reservations advised. AE, DC, MC, V. Closed Sun. and holidays.*

$$$ **Pakhuskælderen.** Surrounded by thick white walls and raw timbers, Nyhavn 71 Hotel's intimate restaurant attracts a mix of business and holiday guests and is known for its fresh, classically prepared seafood. There's also an excellent Danish buffet at lunch. *Nyhavn 71, tel. 33/11–85–85. Reservations required. AE, DC, MC, V.*

$$ **Copenhagen Corner.** Diners get a great view of the Rådhus Pladsen here and terrific smørrebrød for a reasonable price, too—both of which compensate for often slack service provided by an overworked staff. Plants hang from the ceiling; waiters hustle platters of herring, steak, and other Danish/French dishes; and businesspeople clink glasses. In summer you can eat outside. *Rådhus Pladsen, tel. 33/91–45–45. Reservations advised. AE, DC, MC, V. Closed Dec. 24.*

$$ **El Meson.** Ceiling-hung pottery, knowledgeable waiters, and a top-notch menu make this Copenhagen's best Spanish restaurant. Choose carefully for a moderately priced meal, which might include beef spiced with spearmint, lamb with a honey sauce, or paella for two. *Hauser Plads 12, tel. 33/11–91–31. Reservations advised. AE, DC, MC, V. Dinner only. Closed Sun.*

$$ **Havfruen.** A life-size wooden mermaid swings decorously from the ceiling in this small, rustic fish restaurant in Nyhavn. Natives love the maritime-bistro ambience and the daily changing French-and-Danish menu. *Nyhavn 39, tel. 33/11–11–38. Reservations advised. DC, MC, V. Closed Sun.*

$$ **Ida Davidsen.** Five generations old, this world-renowned lunch place
★ has become synonymous with smørrebrød. Choose from creative open-face sandwiches, piled high with such ingredients as pâté, bacon, and steak tartare, as well as smoked duck, served with a beet salad and pota-

toes. *Skt. Kongensgade 70, tel. 33/91–36–55. Reservations required. DC, MC, V. Lunch only. Closed weekends and July.*

$$ **Peder Oxe.** On a historic square, this lively bistro is countrified, with rustic antiques and 15th-century Portuguese tiles. Grilled steaks and fish—and the best burgers in town—come with an excellent salad bar. *Gråbrødretorv 11, tel. 33/11–00–77. DC, MC, V.*

$$ **Victor.** This French-style corner café offers great people-watching and bistro fare. It's best during weekend lunches, when young and old gather for specialties like rib roast, homemade pâté, smoked salmon, and cheese platters. Careful ordering here can get you an inexpensive meal. *Ny Østergade 8, tel. 33/13–36–13. Reservations advised. AE, DC, MC, V.*

$ **Flyvefisken.** Silvery stenciled fish swim along blue-and-yellow stenciled walls in this funky Thai eatery. Among the city's more experimental (and spicy) restaurants, it offers chicken with cashews, spicy shrimp soup with lemongrass, and herring shark in basil sauce. There is also a less expensive café in the basement. *Larsbjørnsstræde 18, tel. 33/14–95–15. AE, DC, MC, V. Closed Sun., Dec. 24–26 and 31.*

$ **Quattro Fontane.** On a corner west of the lakes, one of Copenhagen's best Italian restaurants is a busy, noisy, two-story affair, packed tight with marble-top tables and a steady flow of young Danes. Served by chatty Italian waiters, the homemade food includes cheese or beef ravioli or cannelloni, linguine with clam sauce, and thick pizza. *Guldbersgade 3, tel. 31/39–39–31. Reservations advised, especially on weekends. No credit cards. Closed Dec. 24–25.*

$ **Riz Raz.** On a corner off Strøget, this Middle Eastern restaurant hops with young locals who pack it on weekends. The very inexpensive all-you-can-eat buffet is heaped with healthy dishes, including lentils, falafel, bean salads, and occasionally pizza. *Kompagnistræde 20, tel. 33/15–05–75. Reservations advised; weekend reservations required. DC, MC, V. Closed Dec. 24–25 and Jan. 1.*

Lodging

Copenhagen is well served by a wide range of hotels, and you can expect your accommodations to be clean, comfortable, and well run. Most Danish hotels include a substantial breakfast in the room rate, but this isn't always the case. In summer reservations are always recommended, but if you should arrive without one, try the hotel booking service in the tourist office. They can also give you a "same-day, last-minute price," which is about 200–250 kr. for a single hotel room. This service will also locate rooms in private homes, with rates starting at about 140 kr. for a single. Young travelers should head for Use It (Huset) at Rådhusstræde 13 (tel. 33/15–65–18). For details and price-category definitions, *see* Lodging *in* Staying in Denmark, *above.*

$$$$ **D'Angleterre.** The grande dame of Copenhagen hotels has undergone
★ major renovations and changes over the past couple of years, including the addition of a swimming pool and a nightclub. Luckily, the hotel still retains its Old World, old-money aura. The rooms are done in pinks and blues, with overstuffed chairs and antique escritoires and armoires. There's a liberal use of brass, mahogany, and marble in the bathrooms. *Kongens Nytorv 34, 1051 KBH K, tel. 33/12–00–95, fax 33/12–11–18. 130 rooms with bath. Facilities: 2 restaurants, bar, pool, barbershop, beauty salon, nightclub. AE, DC, MC, V.*

$$$$ **Nyhavn 71.** In a 200-year-old warehouse, this quiet hotel is a good choice for privacy-seekers. It overlooks the old ships of Nyhavn, and the maritime interiors have been preserved with the original plaster walls and exposed brick. The rooms are tiny but cozy, with warm woolen spreads, dark woods, soft leather furniture, and crisscrossing timbers.

Nyhavn 71, 1051 KBH K, tel. 33/11–85–85, fax 33/93–15–85. 82 rooms with bath. Facilities: restaurant, bar. AE, DC, MC, V.

$$$$ **SAS Scandinavia.** Near the airport, this is one of northern Europe's largest hotels and Copenhagen's token skyscraper. The immense lobby is streamlined and modern, as are the rooms—a good choice if you prefer convenience to character. *Amager Blvd. 70, 2300 KBH S, tel. 33/11–23–24, fax 31/57–01–93. 542 rooms with bath. Facilities: 4 restaurants, bar, coffee shop, pool, sauna, casino. AE, DC, MC, V.*

$$$ **Kong Frederik.** West of Rådhus Pladsen, near Strøget, this intimate hotel is a cozy version of its grand sister, D'Angleterre. The sunny Queen's Garden restaurant serves a breakfast buffet; the rooms are elegant with Oriental vases, mauve carpets, and plain blue spreads. *Vester Voldgade 25, 1552 KBH K, tel. 33/12–59–02, fax 33/93–59–01. 110 rooms with bath, 17 suites. Facilities: restaurant, bar, room service, meeting rooms, parking. Breakfast not included. AE, DC, MC, V.*

$$$ **Neptun.** The centrally situated Neptun has been in business for nearly 150 years and shows no signs of flagging. Guest rooms are decorated with blond wood and are usually reserved by American visitors. *Skt. Annæ Plads 18, 1250 KBH K, tel. 33/13–89–00, fax 33/14–12–50. 137 rooms with bath, 10 apartments. Facilities: restaurant, café, meeting rooms. AE, DC, MC, V. Closed Dec. 24–Jan. 2.*

$$$ **The Phoenix.** This luxury hotel welcomes guests with automatic glass doors, crystal chandeliers, and gilt touches everywhere. The staff switches languages as they register business and cruise guests. The suites and executive-class rooms have Biedermeier furniture and 18-karat-gold bathroom fixtures, but the standard rooms are very small, at barely 9'×15'. Light sleepers should ask for a room above the second floor to avoid street noise. *Bredgade 37, 1260 KBH K, tel. 33/95–95–00, fax 33/33–98–33. 212 rooms with bath, 7 suites. Facilities: restaurant, pub (closed Sun.), meeting room. AE, DC, MC, V.*

$$ **Ascot.** A charming old building downtown, this family-owned hotel has a classically columned entrance and an excellent breakfast buffet. The rooms have colorful geometric-pattern bedspreads and cozy bathrooms. A few have kitchenettes. All are so homey that repeat guests often ask for their regular rooms. *Studiestræde 61, 1554 KBH K, tel. 33/12–60–00, fax 33/14–60–40. 143 rooms with bath, 30 apartments. Facilities: restaurant (breakfast only), bar, exercise room, meeting rooms. AE, DC, MC, V.*

$$ **Copenhagen Admiral.** Overlooking old Copenhagen and Amalienborg, the monolithic Admiral was once a grain warehouse but now affords travelers no-nonsense accommodations. With massive stone walls broken by rows of tiny windows, it's one of the less expensive top hotels, cutting frills and prices. The guest rooms are spare, with jutting beams and modern prints. *Toldbodgade 24–28, 1253 KBH K, tel. 33/11–82–82, fax 33/32–55–42. 365 rooms with bath. Facilities: restaurant, bar, café, sauna, nightclub. AE, DC, MC, V.*

$$ **Triton.** Despite its seedy surroundings, this streamlined hotel attracts a cosmopolitan clientele thanks to a central location in Vesterbro. The large rooms, in blond wood and warm tones, have almost all been updated with new bathrooms and state-of-the-art fixtures. The buffet breakfast is exceptionally generous, the staff friendly. There are also family rooms, with a separate bedroom and foldout couch. *Helgolandsgade 7–11, 1653 KBH K, tel. 31/31–32–66, fax 31/31–69–70. 123 rooms with bath. Facilities: restaurant (breakfast only), bar. AE, DC, MC, V.*

$ **Cab-Inn Scandinavia.** Copenhagen's answer to Japanese-style hotel minirooms is more cozy than futuristic, with shiplike "berths" brightly decorated. All offer standard hotel furnishings, including a private shower and small wall-hung desks with chairs. The hotel is popular with business travelers in winter and kroner-pinching backpackers and families in summer. Around the corner, on Danasvej 32, is a sister hotel, the Cab-Inn Copenhagen, with 86 rooms. *Vodroffsvej 55, 1900 FR C, tel. 35/36–11–11, fax 35/36–11–14. 201 rooms with shower. Facilities: café, exercise room. AE, DC, MC, V.*

$ **Viking.** A comfortable, century-old former mansion near Amalienborg, Nyhavn, and Langelinie, this hotel is close to most sights and the Strøget—making it a favorite for inner-city guests. Though the halls are decorated with antiques, the rooms are filled with '60s and '70s furniture. Despite their dated decor, they are clean, comfortable and spacious. *Bredgade 65, 1260 KBH K, tel. 33/12–45–50, fax 33/12–46–18. 90 rooms, 22 with bath. Facilities: restaurant (breakfast only). AE, DC, MC, V.*

The Arts

Copenhagen This Week has good information on musical and theatrical events, as well as on special events and exhibitions. Concert and festival information is available from the **Dansk Musik Information Center** (**DMIC,** Gråbrødretorv 16, tel. 33/11–20–66). Copenhagen's main theater and concert season runs from September through May, and tickets can be obtained either directly from theaters and concert halls or from ticket agencies; ask your hotel concierge for advice. Billetnet (tel. 35/28-91-83), the post office box office, has tickets for most major events. Keep in mind that same-day purchases at the box office ARTE (near the Nørreport station) will be half price.

Tivoli Concert Hall (Vesterbrogade 3, tel. 33/15–10–12) offers more than 150 concerts each summer, featuring a host of Danish and foreign soloists, conductors, and orchestras.

The **Royal Theater** (Kongens Nytorv, tel. 33/14–10–02) regularly holds theater, ballet, and opera performances. For English-language theater, call either the professional **London Toast Theatre** (tel. 33/33–80–25) or the amateur **Copenhagen Theatre Circle** (tel. 31/62–86–20).

Copenhagen natives are avid **movie** buffs, and as the Danes rarely dub films or television imports, you can often see original American and British movies and TV shows.

Nightlife

Many of the city's restaurants, cafés, bars, and clubs stay open after midnight, some as late as 5 AM. Copenhagen is famous for jazz, but you'll find night spots catering to musical tastes ranging from bop to ballroom music. Younger tourists should make for the district around the **Nikolaj Kirke,** which has scores of trendy discos and dance spots, with admission ranging between 40 and 50 kr., and beer about half that. **Privé** (Ny Østergade 14, tel.33/13-75-20) is a trendy, Euro-techno-pop disco, favored by the young and painfully chic. **Rosie McGee's** (Vesterbrogade 2A, tel. 33/32-19-23) is hugely popular with a mixed crowd of young and old, who come for the international pop and rock, cavernous English-pub atmosphere, and good-natured rowdiness.

A few streets behind the railway station is Copenhagen's red-light district, where sex shops share space with grocers. Although the area is fairly well lighted and lively, women may feel uncomfortable here alone at night.

Nightclubs

Some of the most exclusive nightclubs are in the biggest hotels: **Fellini's** in the SAS Royal (Hammerichsgade 1, tel. 33/93–32–39) features modern, cabaret-style dancers that heaps of Scandinavian businessmen come to ogle while downing outrageously priced booze.

Jazz

Many of Copenhagen's sophisticated jazz clubs have closed in the past couple of years. **La Fontaine** (Kompagnistræde 11) is Copenhagen's quintessential jazz dive, with sagging curtains, impenetrable smoke, crusty lounge lizards and the random barmaid nymph; for jazz lovers, the bordello atmosphere and Scandinavian jazz talent make this a must. **Copenhagen Jazz House** (Niels Hemmingsensgade 10, tel. 33/15-26-00) is infinitely more upscale than La Fontaine, attracting European and some international names to its chic, modern barlike ambience. **Jazzhus Slukefter** (Vesterbrogade 3, tel. 33/11-11-13) is Tivoli's jazz club, and lures some of the biggest names in the world.

FUNEN AND THE CENTRAL ISLANDS

It was Hans Christian Andersen, the region's most famous native, who dubbed Fyn (Funen) "The Garden of Denmark." Part orchard, part farmland, Funen is sandwiched between Zealand and Jutland, and with its tidy, rolling landscape, seaside towns, manor houses, and castles, it is one of Denmark's loveliest islands. Its capital is 1,000-year-old Odense in the north, the birthplace of Hans Christian Andersen. It has two museums detailing his life and works. In a country crowded with castles, Funen has two of the best-preserved: the 12th-century Nyborg Slot, in the east, and the 16th-century Egeskov Slot, near Svendborg, in the south. From Svendborg it's easy to hop on a ferry and visit some of the smaller islands, such as Tåsinge, Langeland, and Ærø, whose main town, Ærøskøbing, with its twisting streets and half-timber houses, seems caught in a time warp.

Getting Around

The best starting point is Nyborg on Funen's east coast, just across the Great Belt from Korsør, on Zealand. (At press time, spring 1995, the "other chunnel," connecting Zealand to Funen, was scheduled to open for rail traffic some time at the end of 1995.) From Nyborg, the easiest way to travel is by car, though public transportation is good. Distances on Funen and its islands are short, but there is much to see and you can easily spend two or three days here. The choice is to circle the islands from Nyborg or to base yourself in Odense or Svendborg and make excursions.

Guided Tours

There are few organized tours of any area of Denmark outside Copenhagen. The Funen town of Odense has a two-hour tour that operates Monday through Saturday during July and August and focuses on native son Hans Christian Andersen.

A day trip to Odense leaves from Copenhagen's city-hall square at 9 AM every Sunday from mid-May to mid-September. Lasting about 11 hours, the trip includes stops at several picturesque villages and a lightning visit to Egeskov Slot.

Fyn (Funen) and the Central Islands

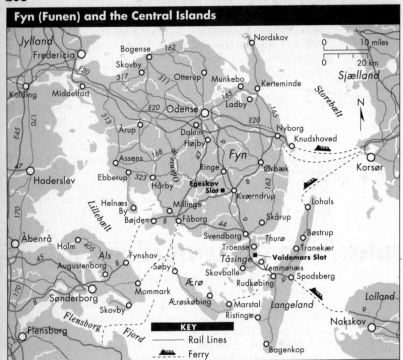

Tourist Information

Nyborg (Torvet 9, tel. 65/31–02–80); **Odense** (Rådhuset, tel. 66/12–75–20); **South Fyn Tourist Board** (Centrumpladsen, tel. 62/21–09–80).

Exploring Funen and the Central Islands

The 13th-century town of **Nyborg** was Denmark's capital during the Middle Ages, as well as an important stop on a major trading route between Zealand and Jutland. From 1200 to 1413, Nyborg housed the Danehof, the early Danish parliament. Nyborg's major landmark is its 12th-century castle, **Nyborg Slot.** It was here that Erik Glipping granted the first Danish constitution, the Great Charter, in 1282. *Slotspladsen, tel. 65/31–02–07. Admission: 20 kr. adults, 10 kr. children under 16. Open Mar.–June, Tues.–Sun. 10–3; July–Aug., daily 10–5; Sept.–Oct., Tues.–Sun. 10–3.*

Take Route 165 20 kilometers (12½ miles) along the coast to **Kerteminde,** Funen's most important fishing village and a picturesque summer resort. Stroll down Langegade to see its half-timber houses.

If you're a Viking enthusiast, head a few kilometers south to the village of **Ladby.** Stop here to see the **Ladbyskibet,** the 1,100-year-old underground remains of a Viking chieftain's burial, complete with his 72-foot-long ship. The warrior was equipped for his trip to Valhalla (the afterlife) with his weapons, 4 hunting dogs, and 11 horses. *Vikingsvej 123, tel. 65/32–16–67. Admission: 20 kr. adults, 10 kr. students and senior citizens, children under 16 free. Open Nov.–Mar., weekends 11–3; Apr.–mid-May and mid-Sept.–mid-Oct., daily 10–4; mid-May–mid-Sept., daily 10–6.*

Twenty kilometers (12½ miles) southwest on Route 165 lies **Odense,** Denmark's third-largest city. Plan on spending at least one night here; in addition to its museums and pleasant pedestrian streets, Odense gives a good feel for a provincial capital.

If you can't take quaintness, don't go to the **H. C. Andersens Hus** (Hans Christian Andersen Museum). The surrounding area has been carefully preserved, with cobbled pedestrian streets and low houses with lace curtains. Inside, exhibits use photos, diaries, drawings, and letters to convey a sense of the man and the time in which he lived. Attached to the museum is an extensive library with Andersen's works in more than 100 languages, where you can listen to fairy tales on tape. *Ramsherred, tel. 66/13–13–72. Admission: 20 kr. adults, 10 kr. children under 14. Open Sept.–May, daily 10–4; June–Aug., daily 9–6.*

Nearby is the **Carl Nielsen Museum,** a modern structure with multimedia exhibits on Denmark's most famous composer (1865–1931) and his wife, the sculptor Anne Marie Carl-Nielsen. *Claus Bergsgade 11, tel. 66/13–13–72, ext. 4671. Admission: 15 kr. adults, 5 kr. children. Open daily 10–4.*

Møntergården, Odense's museum of cultural and urban history, fills four houses built from the Renaissance to the 18th century, all grouped around a shady cobbled courtyard. Inside are dioramas, an extensive coin collection, clothed dummies, toys, and tableaus. *Overgade 48– 50. Admission: 15 kr. adults, 5 kr. children. Open daily 10–4.*

Brandt's Passage, off Vestergade, is a heavily boutiqued walking street. At the end of it, in what was once a textile factory, is a four-story art gallery, the Brandts Klædefabrik, incorporating the **Museum for Photographic Art,** the **Graphic Museum,** and other spaces, with temporary exhibits for video art. It's well worth the short walk to see Funen's version of a New York Soho loft. *37–43 Brandts Passage, tel. 66/13–78– 97. Admission: photography museum, 20 kr. adults, 10 kr. children; graphics museum, 20 kr. adults, children free. Open Tues.–Fri. 10–5, weekends 11–5.*

Don't neglect **Den Fynske Landsby** (Funen Village), 3 kilometers (2 miles) south; an enjoyable way of getting there is to travel down the Odense River by boat. The open-air museum-village is made up of 20 farm buildings, including workshops, a vicarage, a water mill, and a windmill. There's a theater, too, which in summer stages adaptations of Andersen's tales. *Sejerskovvej 20, tel. 66/13–13–72, ext. 4642. Admission: 20 kr. adults, 10 kr. children. Open Apr.–mid-May and mid-Sept.–Oct., daily 10–5; mid-May–mid-Sept., daily 10–7.*

Head 30 kilometers (18 miles) south on Route 43 to **Fåborg,** a lovely little town dating from the 12th century. Four times a day, it echoes with the dulcet chiming of Klokketårnet's (the belfry's) carillon, the largest in Funen. Dating from 1725, **Den Gamla Gård** (the Old Merchant's House) chronicles the cultural history of Funen. *Holkegade 1, tel. 62/61–33–38. Admission: 20 kr. adults, 10 kr. children under 14. Open May 15–Sept. 15, daily 10:30–4:30.*

Visit the **Fåborg Museum for Fynsk Malerkunst** (Gallery for Funen Artists), which has a good collection of paintings and sculpture—dating mainly from 1880 to 1920—by the Funen Painters, whose works are full of the dusky light that so often illuminates Scandinavian painting. *Grønnegade 75, tel. 62/61–06–45. Admission: 25 kr. adults, children under 15 free. Open Apr.–May and Sept.–Oct., daily 10–4; June–Aug., daily 10–5; Nov.–Mar., daily 11–3.*

From Fåborg, take the car ferry to Søby at the northern tip of **Ærø** Island, the "Jewel of the Archipelago," where roads wend through fertile fields and past thatched farmhouses. South from Søby 13 kilometers (8 miles) on Route 16 is the charming town of Ærøskøbing on the island's north coast. When you've spent an hour walking through its cobbled 17th- and 18th-century streets, you'll understand its great appeal.

From Ærøskøbing, the ferry takes just over an hour to reach Svendborg, Funen's southernmost town. It's also the gateway to the country's southern islands, so leave it for the moment and cross over the bridge onto the tiny island of **Tåsinge.**

Pretty **Troense** is one of Denmark's best-preserved villages. Once the home port for many sailing ships, both commercial and Viking, today the harbor is stuffed with pleasure yachts.

Dating from around 1640, **Valdemars Slot,** now a sumptuously furnished home, is one of Denmark's oldest privately owned castles. Upstairs, the rooms are furnished to the smallest detail. Downstairs is the castle church, illuminated only by candlelight. There's a restaurant (*see* Dining and Lodging, *below*) beneath the church. The café overlooks Lunkebugten, a bay with one of south Funen's best stretches of beach. *Slotsalleen 100, Troense, tel. 62/22–61–06. Admission: 45 kr. adults, 15 kr. children. Opening times vary greatly; call for details.*

Tåsinge is connected with the island of **Langeland** by a causeway-bridge. The largest island in the southern archipelago, Langeland is rich in relics of the past, and the beaches are worth scouting out.

Head back now, passing through Tåsinge, to Funen's **Svendborg.** Just north of town is **Egeskov Slot,** one of the best-preserved island castles in Europe. Egeskov means "Oak Forest," and an entire one was felled around 1540 to form the piles on which the rose-stone structure stands. The park contains noteworthy Renaissance, Baroque, English, and peasant gardens and an antique-car museum. Unfortunately, little of the castle is open to the public. *Egeskovgade 18, Kværndrup, tel. 62/27–10–16. Admission (to castle and museum): 95 kr. adults, 47.50 kr. children under 12. Castle open May 1–Sept. 30, daily 10–5. Museum open June 1–Aug. 31, daily 9–6.*

Dining and Lodging

Funen has a wide range of hotels and inns, many of which offer off-season (October through May) rates, as well as special weekend deals. The islands are also endowed with numerous campsites and youth hostels, all clean and attractively located. Some, like Odense's youth hostel, are set in old manor houses. For information, contact the local tourist office. For details and price-category definitions, *see* Dining and Lodging *in* Staying in Denmark, *above.*

Ærøskøbing
LODGING

Ærøhus. A half-timber building with a steep red roof, the Ærøhus looks like a rustic cottage on the outside, an old aunt's house on the inside. Hanging pots and slanted interiors fill the living areas, while pine furniture and cheerful curtains and duvets keep the guest rooms simple and bright. In an annex are apartments, all with kitchenettes. The garden's eight cottages have small terraces. *Vestergade 38, tel. 62/52–10–03, fax 62/52–21–23. 30 rooms, 18 with bath; 8 cottages; 37 apartments. Facilities: restaurant. Closed Dec. 24–Jan. 20. $$*

Fåborg

DINING AND LODGING

Falsled Kro. Once a smuggler's hideaway, the 500-year-old Falsled Kro is among Denmark's most elegant inns. A favorite among well-heeled Europeans, it has appointed its cottages sumptuously with European antiques and stone fireplaces. The restaurant combines French and Danish cuisines, using ingredients from its garden and markets in Lyon. *Assensvej 513, Falsled, 13 km (8 mi) northwest of Fåborg on the Millinge–Assens highway, tel. 62/68–11–11, fax 62/68–11–62. 14 rooms with bath, 3 apartments. Facilities: restaurant. AE, DC, MC. Closed Jan.–Feb. $$$$*

Steensgård Herregårdspension. A long avenue of beeches leads to this 700-year-old moated manor 7 kilometers (4½ miles) northwest of Fåborg. The rooms are elegant, with antiques, four-poster beds, and yards of silk damask. In the fine restaurant, wild game is served from the manor's own preserve. *Steensgård 4, Millinge (Funen), tel. 62/61–94–90, fax 62/61–78–61. 15 rooms, 13 with bath. Facilities: restaurant, tennis, horseback riding. AE, DC, MC, V. Closed Jan. $$$*

Nyborg

LODGING

Hesselet. This modern hotel looks like a brick slab outside, a refined English-cum-Oriental sanctuary inside. The guest rooms are furnished with cushy, modern furniture, and most have splendid views. *Christianslundsvej 119, 5800 Nyborg, tel. 65/31-30-29, fax 65/31-29-58. 46 rooms with bath and shower, 3 suites. Facilities: restaurant, room service, indoor pool, sauna, meeting rooms. AE, DC, MC, V. $$$*

Odense

DINING

Rudolf Mathis. You'll enjoy delectable fish and seafood specialties and a splendid view of Kerteminde Harbor at this traditional Danish restaurant. *Dosseringen 13, Kerteminde, 13 km (8 mi) northeast of Odense on Rte. 165, tel. 65/32–32–33. AE, DC, MC, V. Closed Mon.; Oct.–Dec., Sun.; Jan.-Mar. $$$*

Restaurant Provence. A few minutes from the pedestrian street, this cozy, blue-and-white dining room puts a Danish twist on Provençal cuisine, with such specialties as venison in blackberry sauce and duck breast cooked in sherry. *Pogstræde 31, tel. 66/12–12–96. Reservations advised. DC, MC, V. $$*

Målet. A lively crowd calls this sports club their neighborhood bar, and, next to steaming plates of schnitzel served in a dozen ways, soccer is the delight of the house. *Jernbanegade 17, tel. 66/17–82–41. No reservations. No credit cards. $*

LODGING

Grand Hotel. They don't make spacious, gracious places like this anymore. Dating from 1897, the Grand offers spruced-up fin-de-siècle elegance. The decor is cool and green, and there are lovely marble bathrooms in the rooms, as well as a sweeping staircase and a spectacular Pompeiian red dining room. *Jernbanegade 18, tel. 66/11–71–71, fax 66/14–11–71. 137 rooms with bath. Facilities: restaurant, bar, sauna, parking. AE, DC, MC, V. Closed Dec. 25–Jan. 1. $$$$*

Hotel Ydes. This bright, colorful hotel is a good bet for students and budget-conscious travelers tired of barracks-type accommodations. The plain, white, hospital-style rooms are clean and comfortable. *Hans Tausensgade 11, tel. 66/12–11–31. 30 rooms, 24 with shower. Facilities: bar. AE, DC, MC, V. $*

Svendborg

DINING

Sandig. This austere white eatery near the harbor is spartan, but food, not decor, is owner-chef-waiter-dishwasher Volkert Sandig's priority. His daily French-Danish menu includes inventive fish and beef specialties. Try the cod served with mussel and garlic sauce or the roast veal in a creamy mushroom ragout. *Kullinggade 1b, tel. 62/22–92–11. Reservations advised. DC, MC, V. Closed Sun. and Dec. 24–Jan. 4. $$*

Troense

DINING

Restaurant Valdemars Slot. Beneath the castle, this domed restaurant is ankle-deep in pink carpet and aglow with candlelight. Fresh ingredients from France and Germany and wild game from the castle's preserve are the essentials for an ever-changing menu. Wild venison with cream sauce and duck breast à l'orange are typical of the French-inspired cuisine. A less expensive annex, Den Gråa Dame, serves traditional Danish food. *Slotsalleen 100, tel. 62/22–59–00. Reservations advised. AE, MC, V. Closed Nov.–Mar. except to groups of 4 or more with several days' notice. $$$*

JUTLAND AND THE LAKES

The peninsula of Jylland (Jutland) is the only part of Denmark that is attached to the mainland of Europe; its southern boundary is the frontier with Germany. It's a region of carefully groomed pastures punctuated by stretches of rugged beauty. The windswept landscapes of Isak Dinesen's short stories are in northwest Jutland. One-tenth of the peninsula consists of moors and sand dunes; the remaining land is devoted to agriculture and forestry. To the east of the peninsula, facing Funen, lie well-wooded fjords, which run inland for miles. The region of rustic towns and stark countryside also boasts gracious castles, parklands, and the famed Legoland. Ribe, Denmark's oldest town, lies to the south, while to the east is Århus, Denmark's second-largest city, with its superb museums and new concert hall.

Getting Around

If you're following this itinerary directly after the tour around Funen, head northwest from Odense through Middlefart and then on to Vejle. By train, either from Odense or Copenhagen, the starting point is Kolding, to the south of Vejle. Although there are good train and bus services between all the main cities, this tour is best done by car. Delightful though they are, the offshore islands are suitable only for those with a lot of time, as many involve an overnight stay.

Guided Tours

Guided tours are scarce in these parts; stop by any tourist office for maps and suggestions for a walking tour. Århus also offers a "Round and About the City" tour, which leaves from the tourist office daily at 10 AM from mid-June to mid-Aug.

Tourist Information

Aalborg (Østerå 8, tel. 98/12–60–22); **Århus** (Rådhuset, tel. 86/12–16–00); **Billund** (c/o Legoland A/S, tel. 75/33–19–26); **Herning** (Bredgade 2, tel. 97/12–44–22); **Kolding** (Axeltorv 8, tel. 75/53–21–00); **Randers** (Erik Menveds Plads 1, tel. 86/42–44–77); **Ribe** (Torvet 3–5, tel. 75/42–15–00); **Silkeborg** (Godthåbsvej 4, tel. 86/82–19–

Jylland (Jutland)

11); **Vejle** (Søndergade 14, tel. 75/82–19–55); **Viborg** (Nytorv 9, tel. 86/61–16–66).

Exploring Jutland and the Lakes

If **Kolding** is your starting point, don't miss the well-preserved 13th-century **Koldinghus** castle, a royal residence during the Middle Ages. *Tel. 75/50–15–00. Admission: 30 kr. adults, children free. Open daily 10-5.*

Den Geografiske Have (the Geographical Garden) has a rose garden with more than 120 varieties, as well as some 2,000 plants from all parts of the world, arranged geographically. *Admission: 30 kr. adults, children free. Open June and Aug., daily 9–7; July, daily 9–8; Sept.–May, daily 10–6.*

Vejle, about 20 kilometers (12 miles) to the north of Kolding, is beautifully positioned on the fjord; amid forest-clad hills, the town looks toward the Kattegat, the strait that divides Jutland and Funen. You can hear the time of day chiming on an old Dominican monastery clock; the clock remains, but the monastery has long since given way to the town's imposing 19th-century city hall.

Leaving Vejle, take the road 10 kilometers (6 miles) north through the Grejs Valley to **Jelling.** Here you'll find two 10th-century burial mounds marking the seat of King Gorm the Old and his wife, Thyra. Between the mounds are the Jelling runic stones, one of which, "Denmark's Certificate of Baptism," shows the oldest known figure of Christ in Scandinavia. The stone was erected by Gorm's son, King Harald Bluetooth, who brought Christianity to the Danes in AD 960.

Head north toward **Silkeborg,** on the banks of the River Gudena in Jutland's lake district. The region stretches from Silkeborg in the west to Skanderborg in the east and contains some of Denmark's loveliest scenery, as well as one of the country's meager "mountains." The best way to explore the area is by water because the Gudena winds its way some 160 kilometers (100 miles) through lakes and wooded hillsides down to the sea. You can take one of the excursion boats or, better still, a rare, old coal-fired paddle steamer, *Hjejlen,* which runs in summer and is based at Silkeborg. Since 1861, it has paddled its way through narrow stretches of fjord, where the treetops meet overhead, to the foot of the Himmelbjerget at Lake Julso. From that point you can clamber up the narrow paths through the heather and trees to the top, where an 80-foot tower stands sentinel, placed there on Constitution Day in 1875 in memory of King Frederik VII.

Silkeborg's other attraction is housed in the **Silkeborg Kulturhistoriske Museum** (Museum of Culture and History): the 2,200-year-old Tollund Man, one of the so-called bog people, whose corpse was preserved by natural ingredients in the soil and water. *Hovedgaardsvej 7, tel. 86/82–14–99. Admission: 20 kr. adults, 5 kr. children. Open Apr. 15–Oct. 23, daily 10–5; Oct. 24–Apr. 14, Wed. and weekends noon–4.*

On the coast, lying directly east of Silkeborg, is **Århus,** Denmark's second-largest city. The town is at its liveliest during the 10-day Århus Festival in September, which brings together everything from classical concerts to jazz and folk music, clowning, theater, exhibitions, beer tents, and sports. The town's cathedral, the 15th-century **Domkirke,** is Denmark's longest church; it contains a beautifully executed three-panel altarpiece. Look up at the whimsical sketches on the ceiling.

Nearby is the **Vor Frue Kirke,** formerly a Dominican abbey. Underneath the 13th-century structure is the eerie but interesting crypt church, rediscovered in 1955 and, dating from 1060, one of the oldest preserved stone churches in Scandinavia. The vaulted room houses a replica of an old Roman crucifix.

Not to be missed is the town's open-air museum, **Den Gamle By** (The Old Town). A sophisticated version of Disneyland, it features 65 half-timber houses, a mill, and a millstream. The meticulously re-created period interiors range from the 15th to the early 20th century. *Viborgvej, tel. 86/12–31–88. Admission: 40 kr. adults, children under 16 free. Open Jan.–Mar. and Nov., daily 11–3; Apr. and Oct., daily 10–4; May and Sept., daily 10–5; June–Aug., daily 9–6; Dec., Mon.–Sat. 10–3, Sun. 10–4. Grounds always open.*

Set in a 250-acre forest in a park south of Århus is the indoor/outdoor **Moesgård Prehistoric Museum,** with exhibits on ethnography and archaeology, including the Grauballe Man, an eerie, well-preserved corpse from 2,000 years ago. Take the "Prehistoric Trail" through the forest, which leads past Stone and Bronze Age displays to some reconstructed houses from Viking times. *Ny Moesgård Allé 20, Højbjerg, tel. 86/27–24–33. Admission: 25 kr. adults, children under 15 free. Open mid-Sept.–Apr., Tues.–Sun. 10–4; May–mid-Sept., Tues.–Sun. 10–5.*

Heading north 21 kilometers (15 miles), you'll come to the medieval town of **Randers,** where, in 1340, the Danish patriot Niels Ebbesen killed the German oppressor, Count Gert the Bald of Holstein, whose army was then occupying most of Jutland. To the east of Randers is the Djursland Peninsula, a popular vacation area, with fine manor houses open to the public. If time is of the essence, choose **Gammel Estrup,** a grand 17th-century manor in the tiny village of **Auning;** it's full of rich period furnishings, including an alchemist's cellar. *Tel. 86/48–30–01. Admission: 20 kr. adults, 5 kr. children. Manor and farm open May–Oct., daily 10–5; Nov.–Apr., (manor) Tues.–Sun. 11–3, (farm) daily 10–5.*

Aalborg, 71 kilometers (44 miles) north of Randers, is set at the narrowest point of the Limfjord, the great waterway of northern Jutland and the gateway between north and south. You'll find charming combinations of new and old; twisting lanes filled with medieval houses and, nearby, broad modern boulevards. Jomfru Ane Gade, a tiny cobbled street in the center of Aalborg, is lined with restaurants, inns, and sidewalk cafés. Major sights include the magnificent five-story **Jens Bangs Stenhus** (Jens Bang's Stone House). Dating from 1642, it has an atmospheric restaurant and an excellent wine cellar. The Baroque cathedral, the **Budolfi Kirke,** is dedicated to the English saint Butolph. The 15th-century **Helligåndsklosteret** (Monastery of the Holy Ghost), one of Denmark's best-preserved, is now a home for the elderly.

If you have some time to spare, head north up to the tip of Jutland, to **Skagen,** where the picturesque streets and the luminous light have inspired painters and writers alike. The 19th-century Danish artist Holger Drachmann (1846–1908) and his friends founded the Skagen school of painting; you can see their efforts on display in the local **Skagens Museum.** *4 Brøndumsvej, tel. 98/44–64–44. Admission: 30 kr. adults, children free. Open Apr. and Oct., Tues.–Sun. 11–4; May and Sept., daily 10–5; June–Aug., daily 10–6; Nov.–Mar., Wed.–Fri. 1–4, Sat. 11–4, Sun. 11–3.*

Heading south once more, you next come to **Viborg,** a town whose history goes back to the 8th century, when it was a trading post and a place of pagan sacrifice. Later it became a center of Christianity, with monasteries and an episcopal residence. The 1,000-year-old **Haerve-jen,** the old military road that starts near here, was once Denmark's most important connection with the outside world. Legend has it that in the 11th century, King Canute set out from Viborg to conquer England; he succeeded and ruled from 1016 to 1035.

Built in 1130, Viborg's **Domkirke,** the cathedral, was once the largest granite church in the world. Today the crypt is all that remains of the original building, which was restored and reopened in 1876. The early 20th-century biblical frescoes are by Danish painter Joakim Skovgaard.

There's terrific walking country 8 kilometers (5 miles) south of Viborg, beside **Hald Sø** (Hald Lake) and on the heatherclad **Dollerup Bakker** (Dollerup Hills). Next head southwest 45 kilometers (28 miles) to **Herning,** an old moorland town. There you'll find a remarkable circular building, with an exterior frieze by Carl-Henning Pedersen; it houses the **Carl-Henning Pedersen and Else Afelt Museum.** Just next door is the **Herning Art Museum.** The inner exterior wall of the collar-shape building, a shirt factory until 1977, is lined with another enormous frieze 722 feet long. Both museums are set within a **sculpture park.** *Uldjydevej 3, tel. 97/12–10–33. Admission: 40 kr. adults, children free. Open Tues.–Sun. 12–5; May–Oct., extended weekend hours 10–5.*

About 100 kilometers (60 miles) to the south is Ribe, Denmark's oldest town, where the medieval center is preserved by the Danish National Trust. From May to mid-September, a night watchman goes around the town telling of its ancient history and singing traditional songs. Visitors can meet him nightly in the main square at 10.

Before heading back to Vejle, stop off at **Billund** to see the country's most famous tourist attraction. **Legoland** is a park filled with scaled-down versions of cities, towns, and villages, as well as working harbors and airports, a Statue of Liberty, a statue of Sitting Bull, Mt. Rushmore, a safari park, even a Pirate Land—all constructed of millions of Lego bricks. There are also exhibits of toys from pre-Lego days, including Legoland's high point, Titania's Palace, a sumptuous dollhouse built in 1907 by Sir Neville Wilkinson for his daughter. *Billund, tel. 75/33–13–33. Admission: 100 kr. adults, 90 kr. children under 14. Open April–Sept., daily 10–8.*

Dining and Lodging

For details and price-category definitions, *see* Dining and Lodging *in* Staying in Denmark, *above.*

Aalborg
DINING
★ **Duus Vinkælder.** This amazing cellar is part alchemist's dungeon, part neighborhood bar. Though most people come for a drink before or after dinner, you can also get a light bite. During the summer, the menu is mostly smørrebrød, but during the winter, grilled specialties include *pølser* (Danish sausages), *frikadeller* (Danish meatballs), *biksemad* (cubed potato, meat, and onion hash) and the restaurant's specialty, pâté. *9 Østerå, tel. 98/12–50–56. Reservations required. No credit cards. Closed Sun.* $$
Spisehuset Kniv og Gaffel. In a 400-year-old building parallel to Jomfru Ane Gade, this busy restaurant is crammed with oak tables, crazy slanting floors, and candlelight, and its year-round courtyard is a veritable greenhouse. Young waitresses negotiate the mayhem to deliver

inch-thick steaks, the house specialty. *Maren Turisgade 10, tel. 98/16–69–72. Reservations advised. DC, MC, V. Closed Sun. $$*

DINING AND LODGING

Helnan Phønix. At a central location in a sumptuous old mansion, this hotel is popular with international and business guests. The rooms are luxuriously furnished with plump chairs and polished dark-wood furniture; in some the original raw beams are still intact. The Halling restaurant serves excellent French and Danish cuisines. *Vesterbro 77, tel. 98/12–00–11, fax 98/16–31–66. 179 rooms with bath. Facilities: 2 restaurants, bar, café, sauna. AE, DC, MC, V. $$$$*

Århus

DINING

Medina. In this cozy, casual eatery, hearty Middle-Eastern fare includes hummus, shish kebab, couscous, falafel and other exotic specialties. *Vesterbrogade 36, tel. 86/13–16–37. Reservations advised. AE, DC, MC, V. Dinner only. $$*

LODGING

Royal Hotel. Open since 1838, Århus's grand hotel has welcomed such greats as Arthur Rubinstein and Marian Andersen. Guests are welcomed into a stately lobby appointed with Chesterfield sofas, modern paintings, and a winding staircase to the accommodations above. The plush rooms vary in style and decor, but all have rich drapery, velour- and brocade-covered furniture, and marble bathrooms. *Store Torv 4, tel. 86/12–00–11, fax 86/76–04–04. 105 rooms with bath. Facilities: restaurant, sauna, casino, nightclub. AE, DC, MC, V. $$$$*

Youth Hostel Pavilionen. As in all Danish youth and family hostels, the rooms here are clean, bright, and functional, and the secluded, wooded setting near the fjord is downright beautiful. Unfortunately, it can get a little noisy, with guests ranging from carousing business parties to budget-conscious backpackers. *Marienlundsvej 10, tel. 86/16–72–98, fax 86/10–55–60. 30 rooms, 11 with shower; 4 communal showers and toilets. Facilities: cafeteria (breakfast only), kitchen, parking. AE, MC, V. Closed mid-Dec.–mid-Jan. $*

Ribe

DINING AND LODGING

Hotel Dagmar. In the midst of Ribe's quaint center, this cozy, half-timber hotel encapsulates the charm of the 16th century, with stained-glass windows, frescoes, sloping floors, and carved chairs. The lavish rooms are all appointed with antique canopy beds, fat armchairs, and chaise longues. The fine French restaurant serves such specialties as fillet of salmon in sorrel cream sauce and marinated *foie gras de canard* (duck liver). *Torvet 1, tel. 75/42–00–33, fax 75/42–36–52. 50 rooms with bath. Facilities: restaurant (reservations advised). AE, DC, MC, V. $$$*

Skagen

DINING AND LODGING

Brøndums Hotel. A few minutes from the beach, this 150-year-old gabled inn is furnished with antiques and Skagen-school paintings. Although the hotel is full of charm, the rooms are beginning to show their age. The 21 guest rooms in the main building, without TVs or phones, are old-fashioned, with wicker chairs and Oriental rugs, pine and four-poster beds. The 25 annex rooms are more modern. The hotel has a fine Danish-French restaurant with a lavish cold table. *Anchersvej 3, tel. 98/44–15–55, fax 98/45–15–20. 46 rooms, 12 with bath. Facilities: restaurant (reservations advised). AE, DC, MC, V. $$$*

Vejle

DINING AND LODGING

Munkebjerg. Seven kilometers (4 miles) southeast of town, surrounded by a thick beech forest and majestic views of the Vejle Fjord, this elegant hotel attracts guests who prefer privacy. The rooms overlook the forest and are furnished in blond pine and soft green; the lobby is rustic. There are also two top-notch restaurants, one specializing in French cuisine, the other in very Danish fare. *Munkebjergvej 125, tel. 75/72–35–00, fax 75/72–08–86. 148 rooms with bath. Facilities: 2 restaurants, café, pool, sauna, golf course, tennis, exercise room, horseback riding, jogging, biking, casino, heliport. AE, DC, MC, V. $$$$*

9 Finland

IF YOU LIKE MAJESTIC OPEN SPACES, fine architecture, and civilized living—and can afford the prices—Finland is for you. It is a land of lakes, 187,888 at the last count, and forests. It is a land where nature is so prized that even the designs of urban centers reflect the soaring spaces of the countryside.

The music of Sibelius, Finland's most famous son, tells you what to expect from this Nordic landscape. Both can swing from the somber nocturne of midwinter darkness to the tremolo of sunlight slanting through pine and bone-white birch and from the crescendo of a sunset as it fades into the next day's dawn. Similarly, the Finnish people reflect the changing moods of their land and climate. They can get annoyed when described as "children of nature"—still, the description is apt. Their affinity with nature has produced some of the world's greatest designers and architects. Many American cities have buildings designed by Alvar Aalto and the Saarinens, Eliel and son Eero. In fact, Eliel and his family moved to the United States in 1923 and became American citizens—but it was to a lonely Finnish seashore that Saarinen had his ashes returned.

Until 1917, Finland (the Finns call it *Suomi*) was under the domination of its nearest neighbors, Sweden and Russia, who fought over it for centuries. After more than 600 years under Swedish rule and 100 under the czars, the country inevitably bears many traces of these two cultures, including a small (6%) but influential Swedish-speaking population and a scattering of Russian Orthodox churches.

But the Finns themselves are neither Scandinavian nor Slavic. All that is known of their origins is that they are descended from wandering groups of people who probably came from west of the Ural Mountains before the Christian era and settled on the swampy shores of the Gulf of Finland.

There is a tough, resilient quality in the Finns. No other people fought the Soviets to a standstill as the Finns did in the Winter War of 1939–40. This resilience, in part, stems from the turbulence of the country's past, but also comes from the people's strength and determination to work the land and survive the long winters. For the Finn is in a state of constant confrontation—with the weather, the land, and most recently a huge eastern neighbor that is engulfed in political and economic turmoil. The Finn is stubborn, patriotic, and self-sufficient, yet not aggressively nationalistic. Chiefly, the Finn is proud of finding ways to live independently and in peace.

The average Finn doesn't volunteer much information, but that's due to reserve, not indifference. Make the first approach and you may have a friend for life. Finns like their silent spaces, though, and won't appreciate back-slapping familiarity—least of all in the sauna, still regarded by many as a spiritual, as well as a cleansing, experience.

ESSENTIAL INFORMATION

Before You Go

When to Go

The tourist summer season runs from mid-June until mid-August, a magnificently sunny and generally dry time marked by unusually warm temperatures in recent years. Outside this period, many amenities and

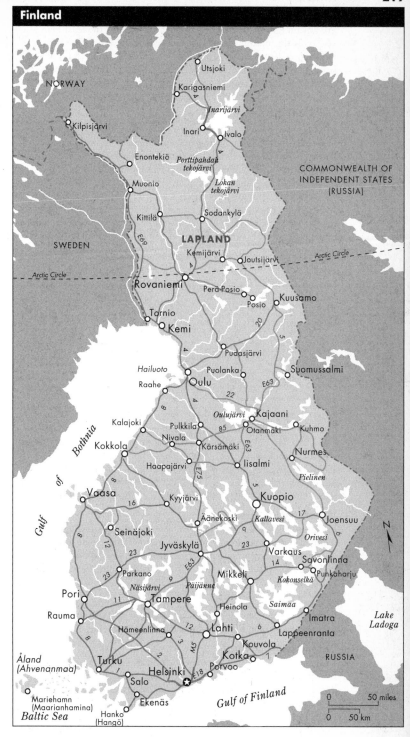

NORWAY

Utsjoki

Karigasniemi

Inarijärvi

Kilpisjärvi

Inari

Ivalo

Enontekiö

*Porttipahdak
tekojärvi*

COMMONWEALTH OF
INDEPENDENT STATES
(RUSSIA)

Muonio

*Lokan
tekojärvi*

Kittilä

Sodankylä

SWEDEN

LAPLAND

Kemijärvi

Joutsijärvi

Arctic Circle

Arctic Circle

Rovaniemi

Perä-Posio

Posio

Kuusamo

Tornio

Kemi

20

Pudasjärvi

Hailuoto

Puolanka

Suomussalmi

Raahe

Oulu

E63

22

Kalajoki

Oulujärvi

Kajaani

Kuhmo

Pulkkila

85

Otanmäki

Kokkola

Nivala

Kärsämäki

Nurmes

Haapajärvi

E75

Iisalmi

Pielinen

Vaasa

Kyyjärvi

Kuopio

16

Äänekoski

Kallavesi

17

Joensuu

Seinäjoki

Orivesi

N

12

23

Jyväskylä

23

Varkaus

Savonlinna

Parkano

E63

14

Punkaharju

Pori

9

Mikkeli

Kokonselkä

Näsijärvi

Päijänne

11

Tampere

Saimaa

Rauma

Heinola

Imatra

*Lake
Ladoga*

Hämeenlinna

12

Lahti

6

Lappeenranta

Åland
(Ahvenanmaa)

2

M5

Kouvola

1

RUSSIA

Turku

1

Helsinki

Kotka

Porvoo

Salo

E18

Mariehamn
(Maarianhamina)

Ekenäs

Gulf of Finland

0   50 miles

Baltic Sea

Hanko
(Hangö)

0   50 km

Gulf

of

Bothnia

8

8

8

attractions either close or operate on much-reduced schedules. But there are advantages to visiting Finland off-season, not the least being that you avoid the mosquitoes, which can be fearsome, especially in the north. Fall colors (from early September in the far north, October in the south) are spectacular. January through March (through April in the north) is the main cross-country skiing season. Spring is brief but magical, as the snows melt, the ice breaks up, and nature explodes into life almost overnight.

CLIMATE

Generally speaking, the spring and summer seasons begin a month earlier in the south of Finland than they do in the far north. You can expect warm (not hot) days in Helsinki from mid-May; in Lapland from mid-June. The midnight sun can be seen from May to July, depending on the region. In midwinter there is a corresponding period when the sun does not rise at all, but it is possible to see magnificent displays of the Northern Lights. Even in Helsinki, summer nights are brief and never really dark, whereas in midwinter daylight lasts only a few hours.

The following are average daily maximum and minimum temperatures for Helsinki.

Jan.	30F	– 1C	May	64F	18C	Sept.	53F	11C
	26	– 3		48	9		39	4
Feb.	34F	1C	June	60F	16C	Oct.	46F	8C
	24	– 4		48	9		36	2
Mar.	36F	2C	July	68F	20C	Nov.	32F	0C
	26	– 3		55	13		26	– 3
Apr.	46F	8C	Aug.	64F	18C	Dec.	32F	0C
	32	0		53	12		24	– 4

Currency

The unit of currency in Finland is the Finnmark, divided into 100 penniä. There are bills of FIM 20, 50, 100, 500, and 1,000. Coins are 10 and 50 penniä, and FIM 1, FIM 5, and FIM 10. At press time (spring 1995), the exchange rate was about FIM 3.97 to the dollar and FIM 6.73 to the pound sterling Credit cards are widely accepted, even in many taxicabs. Traveler's checks can be changed only in banks.

What It Will Cost

Prices are highest in Helsinki; otherwise they vary little throughout the country. Taxes are already included in hotel and restaurant charges, and there is no airport departure tax. However, the price of many goods includes an 18% sales tax, less on food (*see* Shopping *in* Staying in Finland, *below*).

SAMPLE PRICES

Cup of coffee, FIM 7; glass of beer, FIM 10–FIM 20; soft drink, FIM 10; ham sandwich, FIM 15–FIM 20; 1-mile taxi ride, FIM 25.

Customs on Arrival

Visitors to Finland may import goods for their own use from another European Union (EU) country duty-free, with the exception of tobacco and alcohol. Visitors over age 22 may bring in 1 liter of spirits or 3 liters of aperitifs (over 22% alcohol by volume) or 3 liters of sparkling wines, plus 5 liters of table wine and 15 liters of beer. Spirits containing over 60% alcohol by volume may not be brought in Finland. Visitors ages 18–22 may not bring in spirits, but may import other amounts listed above. If the items were purchased in a duty-free shop at an airport or harbor, or on board an airplane or ship, visitors may bring in 1 liter of spirits, 2 liters of aperitifs or sparkling wines, 2 liters of table wine and 15 liters of beer. Visitors over age 17 may bring in 300 cigarettes, 75 cigars or 400 grams (about 13 oz) of tobacco. If the items were purchased at a duty-free shop, 200 cigarettes, 50 cigars or 250 grams (about 8 oz) of tobacco are allowed.

Language

The official languages of Finland are Finnish and Swedish, though only a small minority (about 6%) speak Swedish. English is widely spoken among people in the travel industry and by many younger Finns, though they're often shy about using it. Nearly all tourist sites and attractions provide texts in English. In the north the Lapp people, called *Same* (pronounced Sah-me), have their own language.

Getting Around

By Car

ROAD CONDITIONS

Finland has no superhighways, but there is an expanding network of efficient major roads, some of which are multilane. In some areas, however, especially in the north, you can expect long stretches of dirt road. These roads are usually adequate to good, although during the spring thaw they become difficult to negotiate. Away from the larger towns, traffic is light, but take moose and reindeer warning signs seriously.

RULES OF THE ROAD

Drive on the right. At intersections, cars coming from the right have priority. Speed limits (usually marked) are 50 kph (30 mph) in built-up areas and between 80 kph and 100 kph (50 mph and 62 mph) in the country and on main roads. Low-beam headlights must be used at all times outside city areas, seat belts are compulsory (on rear as well as front seats), and you must carry a warning triangle in case of breakdown.

PARKING

Parking is a problem only in some city centers. Major cities offer multistory garages; most towns have on-street meters. In Helsinki, there is no free on-street parking. In areas with no meters, drivers must display *pysäkointlippu* (parking vouchers), purchased at **R-Kiosks** or gas stations, on their dashboard. Illegally parked cars may be towed away.

BREAKDOWNS AND ACCIDENTS

The **Automobile and Touring Club of Finland** (Autoliitto ry, Hämeentie 105 A, PL 35, 00550 Helsinki, tel. 90/774761) operates a 24-hour road patrol service (tel. 90/774–76400), and a weekend road patrol service (tel. 9700/8080) on the main roads from 6 PM Friday to 10 PM Sunday. If you're involved in an accident, report it without delay to the **Finnish Motor Insurers' Bureau** (Liikennevakutuskeskus, Bulevardi 28, Helsinki, tel. 90/680401) as well as to the police.

By Train

Finland's extensive rail system reaches all main centers of the country and offers high standards of comfort and cleanliness. A special **Finnrail Pass** entitles you to unlimited travel for three, five, or ten days within a four-week period; second-class prices are FIM 505 (three days), FIM 685 (five days), and FIM 945 (10 days); first-class tickets are FIM 760 (three days), FIM 1,030 (five days), and FIM 1,420 (10 days). Children pay half fare. These tickets can be purchased both inside and outside the country. In Finland, the Finnrail Pass is available from the Finnish State Railways (VR, tel. 90/010–0127). In the United States and Canada they can be purchased by calling **Rail Europe** (tel. 800/438–7245) in the United Kingdom, from **Finlandia Travel** (tel. 0171/409–7334).

By Plane

Finnair (tel. 90/818800) operates an elaborate network of flights linking 25 towns in Finland. A **Holiday Ticket** can be purchased outside of Finland for $425 (at press time) and includes 10 flight coupons valid for any domestic Finnair flights. Finnair grants visitors under age 25 a 60-percent **Youth Discount** on flights booked ahead. These tickets are available in most countries, and in Finland they can be purchased at major travel agencies.

By Bus

Bus travel plays a leading role in Finland, and the country's bus system provides the most extensive travel network of all; it can take you virtually anywhere. A **Coach Holiday Ticket,** available from bus stations and travel agencies, entitles you to 1,000 kilometers (625 miles) of bus travel for FIM 320 for two weeks.

By Boat

Helsinki and Turku have regular sea links with the Åland Islands in the Baltic Sea. From mid-June to mid-August you can cruise the labyrinthine lakes of the Finnish interior. Complete timetables are available from the Finnish Tourist Board.

By Bicycle

Planned bicycle routes are provided in many areas. The main advantages for the cyclist are the lack of steep hills and the absence of heavy traffic. Bikes can be rented in some youth hostels. The Finnish **Youth Hostel Association** (Yrjönkatu 38B, Helsinki, tel. 90/694–0377) offers accommodation packages of seven or 14 days to tie in with visitors' cycling tours.

Staying in Finland

Telephones
LOCAL CALLS

To avoid exorbitant hotel surcharges on calls, use the public pay phones. Have some FIM 1 and FIM 5 coins ready. Note that the Finnish letters å, ä, and ö come at the end of the alphabet; this may be useful when looking up names in the telephone book. For information about telephone charges, dial 92020; for number inquiries, dial 118.

INTERNATIONAL CALLS

You can dial directly to Britain and the United States from anywhere in Finland. Calls to other countries can be made from a telegraph office; these are marked LENNÄTIN or TELE and usually adjoin the post office. An operator will assign you a private booth and collect payment at the end of the call. To dial the numbers listed in this guide from outside of Finland, omit the "9" at the beginning of the city code. To make a direct international phone call from Finland, dial 990, then the appropriate country code and phone number. For an **AT&T** long-distance operator, dial 9800–10010; for **MCI**, 9800–10280; for **Sprint**, 9800–10284.

COUNTRY CODE

The country code for Finland is 358.

Mail
POSTAL RATES

At press time (spring 1995), airmail rates to North America were FIM 3.40 for a letter of up to 20 grams. Letters to the United Kingdom cost FIM 2.90.

If you're uncertain about where you'll be staying, be sure that mail sent to you is marked "poste restante" and addressed to the Main Post Office, Mannerheimintie 11, 00100 Helsinki, or to major post offices in other towns. American Express offers a free clients' mail service and will hold mail for up to one month (*see* Important Addresses and Numbers in Helsinki, *below*). The Finland Travel Bureau also provides a free mail service for foreigners: Mail should be addressed to Mail Department, Box 319, 00101 Helsinki, and collected from the office at Kaivokatu 10A.

Shopping
SALES TAX REFUNDS
Non-EU residents who purchase goods worth more than FIM 100 in any of the many shops marked "tax-free for tourists" can get a 12%–16% refund. Show your passport and the store will give you a check for the appropriate amount that you can cash at your final point of departure from the EU.

Opening and Closing Times
Banks are open weekdays 9:15–4:15. **Museums.** Opening hours vary considerably, so check individual listings. Many museums in the countryside are open only during the summer months. **Shops** are generally open weekdays 9–6, Saturday 9–2. Department stores and supermarkets stay open until 8 on weekdays. **Sightseeing.** Schedules for most attractions vary widely outside the main tourist season. Check local tourist offices for opening days and hours.

National Holidays
January 1; January 6 (Epiphany); April 5, 7–8 (Good Friday, Easter and Easter Monday); May 1 (May Day); May 16 (Ascension); May 22 (Pentecost); May 26 (Whit Sunday); June 21–22 (Midsummer's Eve and Day); November 2 (All Saints' Day); December 6 (Independence Day); December 25–26.

Dining
You can choose among restaurants, taverns, coffeehouses, and snack bars. As in other parts of Scandinavia, the *voileipäpöytä* (cold table) is often a work of art as well as a feast. Special Finnish dishes include *poronkäristys* (reindeer casserole; superb in Lapland); salmon, herring, and various freshwater fish; and *lihapullia* (meatballs) with a tasty sauce. Crayfish parties are popular between the end of July and early September. For a delicious dessert, try *lakka* (cloudberries) which are similar to blackberries and grow above the Arctic Circle in the midnight sun.

MEALTIMES
The Finns eat early; lunch runs from 11 or noon to 1 or 2, dinner from 4 to 7 (a bit later in Helsinki).

WHAT TO WEAR
Except for the most elegant restaurants, where a jacket and tie are preferred, casual attire is acceptable for restaurants in all price categories; however, jeans are not allowed in some of the more expensive establishments.

RATINGS
Prices are per person and include first course, main course, dessert, and service charge—but not wine. All restaurant checks include a *sisältää palvelupalkkion* (service charge). If you want to leave an additional tip—though it really isn't necessary—it's enough to round the figure

off to the nearest FIM 5 or FIM 10. Highly recommended restaurants are indicated by a star ★.

CATEGORY	HELSINKI	OTHER AREAS
$$$$	over FIM 200	over FIM 170
$$$	FIM 150–FIM 200	FIM 140–FIM 170
$$	FIM 80–FIM 150	FIM 80–FIM 140
$	under FIM 80	under FIM 80

If you select the prix-fixe menu, which usually covers two courses and coffee, and is served at certain hours in many establishments, the cost of the meal can be as little as half these prices.

Lodging

The range of accommodations available in Finland includes hotels, motels, boarding houses, private homes, rented chalets and cottages, farmhouses, youth hostels, and campsites. There is no official system of classification, but standards are generally high. If you haven't reserved a room in advance, you can make reservations at the **Hotel Booking Center** at the railway station (Rautatieasema, 00100 Helsinki, tel. 90/171133) or through a travel agency; the booking fee is FIM 10.

HOTELS

Nearly all hotels in Finland are modern or will have been recently renovated; a few occupy fine old manor houses. Most have rooms with bath or shower. Prices generally include breakfast and often a morning sauna and swim. The **Finncheque** voucher system, operating in many hotels from June through August, offers good discounts. Only the first night can be reserved from outside of Finland, but subsequent reservations can be made free from any Finncheque hotel. For additional information, inquire at the Hotel Booking Center or the Finnish Tourist Board (Eteläesplanadi 4, 00130 Helsinki, tel. 90/4030–1300 or 90/4030–1211).

SUMMER HOTELS

University students' accommodations are turned into "summer hotels" from June through August; they offer modern facilities at slightly lower-than-average prices.

BOARDINGHOUSES, PRIVATE HOMES, AND RENTALS

These provide the least expensive accommodations and are found only outside Helsinki. Local tourist offices have lists. The choice of rentals is huge, and the chalets and cottages are nearly always in delightful lakeside or seashore settings. For comfortable (not luxurious) accommodations, count on paying FIM 1,000–FIM 3,500 for a four-person weekly rental. A central reservations agency is **Lomarengas** (Malminkaari 23C, 00700 Helsinki, tel. 90/3516–1321, or Eteläesplanadi 4, 00130 Helsinki, tel. 90/170611).

FARMHOUSES

These are located in attractive settings, usually near water. A central reservations agency is **Suomen 4H-liitto** (Abrahaminkatu 7, 00180 Helsinki, tel. 90/642233).

YOUTH HOSTELS

These range from empty schools to small manor houses. There are no age restrictions, and prices range from FIM 50 to FIM 200 per bed. The Finnish Tourist Board can provide a list of hostels.

CAMPING

There are about 350 Finnish campsites, all classified into one of three grades. All offer showers and cooking facilities, and many include cottages for rent. A list is available from the Finnish Tourist Board.

RATINGS

Prices are for two people in a double room and include breakfast and service charge. Hotels in Helsinki, particularly in the middle range of prices, tend to be cheaper in the summer and on weekends. Highly recommended lodgings are indicated by a star ★.

CATEGORY	HELSINKI	OTHER AREAS
$$$$	over FIM 900	over FIM 700
$$$	FIM 600–FIM 900	FIM 550–FIM 700
$$	FIM 400–FIM 600	FIM 400–FIM 550
$	under FIM 400	under FIM 400

Tipping

The Finns are less tip-conscious than other Europeans. (For restaurant tips, *see* Dining, *above*.) You can give taxi drivers a few small coins, but it's not essential. Train and airport porters have a fixed charge. It's not necessary to tip hotel doormen for carrying bags to the check-in counter, but give bellhops FIM 5–FIM 10 for carrying bags to your room. The obligatory coat-check room fee of about FIM 5 is usually clearly indicated; if not, give FIM 5–FIM 10, depending on the number in your party. FIM 5 is a standard tip for all minor services.

HELSINKI

Arriving and Departing

By Plane

All international flights arrive at Helsinki's Vantaa Airport, 20 kilometers (12 miles) north of the city. For arrival and departure information, call 9700–8100.

BETWEEN THE AIRPORT AND DOWNTOWN

Finnair buses leave two to three times an hour for the city terminals, located at the Inter-Continental hotel (Töölönkatu 21, tel. 90/40551) and the main railway station. The trip takes about 30 minutes and costs FIM 22. A local bus service (No. 615), which takes about 40 minutes, goes to the train station and costs FIM 15. Expect to pay between FIM 100 and FIM 120 for a taxi into the city center. If you are driving, the way is well marked to Highway 137 (Tuusulantie) and Keskusta (downtown Helsinki).

By Train

Helsinki's railway station is in the heart of the city. For train information, call 90/010–0121.

By Bus

The terminal for many local buses is the railway station square, Rautatientori. The main long-distance bus station is located off Mannerheimintie between Salomonkatu and Simonkatu. For information, phone 9600–4000.

By Sea

The Silja Line terminal for ships arriving from Stockholm is at Olympialaituri, on the west side of the South Harbor. The Finnjet-Silja Line and Viking Lines terminal for ships arriving from Travemünde and Stockholm is at Katajanokka, on the east side of the South Harbor.

Getting Around

The center of Helsinki is compact and best explored on foot. If you want to use public transportation, your best buy is the **Helsinki Card,** which gives unlimited travel on city public transportation, as well as free entry to many museums, a free sightseeing tour, and a variety of other discounts. It's available for one, two, or three days (FIM 95, FIM 135, FIM 165; about half-price for children). You can buy it at some hotels, travel agencies, Stockmann's, and at the Helsinki City Tourist Office.

By Subway

Helsinki's only subway line runs from Ruoholahti, just west of the city center, to Mellunmäki, in the eastern suburbs. It runs from 5:15 AM (later on weekends) to 11:20 PM, and each ride costs FIM 9; you can transfer for free if you do so within an hour from the start of travel. Each trip costs FIM 7.50 if you buy a 10-trip ticket. Tickets are available from R-Kiosks and shops displaying the Helsinki city transport logo (2 curving black arrows on a yellow background) as well as subway stations.

By Streetcar

These run from 6 AM to 1:30 AM, depending on the line. They can be very handy and route maps and schedules are posted at most downtown stops. The fare is the same as for the subway; single tickets are sold on board. The Helsinki City Tourist Office distributes a pamphlet called "Helsinki Sightseeing: 3T" which describes points of interest along the 3T tram's downtown route.

By Taxi

Taxis are all marked "taksi." The meters start at FIM 18, with the fare rising on a kilometer basis. After 6 PM weekdays and after 4 PM on weekends, the meters start at FIM 29. Car services have a minimum charge and should be ordered well in advance. A listing of all taxi companies appears in the white pages under "Taksi"—try to choose one that is located nearby, because they charge from point of dispatch. Many accept credit cards.

By Boat

In summer there are regular boat services from the South Harbor market square to the islands of Suomenlinna and Korkeasaari.

Important Addresses and Numbers

Tourist Information

The **Helsinki City Tourist Office** is near the South Harbor (Pohjoisesplanadi 19, tel. 90/169–3757); open May 2–September, weekdays 8:30–6, weekends 10–3; October 1–April 28, 8:30–4, closed weekends. The **Finnish Tourist Board's Tourist Information Office** (covering all Finland) is nearby at Eteläesplanadi 4, tel. 90/4030–1211 or 90/4030–1300; open June–August, weekdays 8:30–5, Sunday 10–2; September–May, weekdays 8:30–4.

Embassies

U.S. (Itäinen Puistotie 14, tel. 90/171931). **Canadian** (Pohjoisesplanadi 25B, tel. 90/171141). **U.K.** (Itäinen Puistotie 17, tel. 90/661293).

Emergencies

General (tel. 112); **Police** (tel. 112); **Ambulance** (tel. 112); **Doctor** (tel. 10023); **Dentist** (tel. 90/736166); **Pharmacy: Yliopiston Apteekki,** Mannerheimintie 96, open 24 hours (tel. 90/415778).

English-Language Bookstores
You'll find a good selection of books and newspapers in English at **Aka-teeminen Kirjakauppa** (Keskuskatu 1) and **Suomalainen Kirjakauppa** (Aleksanterinkatu 23).

Travel Agencies
American Express (Area Travel Agency, Pohjoisesplanadi 2, 00170 Helsinki, tel. 90/628788). **Thomas Cook** (Finland Travel Bureau, Kaivokatu 10A, Box 319, tel. 90/18261).

Guided Tours

Orientation Tours
Suomen Turistiauto (tel. 90/588–5166) runs a "City Tour" that lasts 1½ hours. Tours start from Asemaaukio (opposite the main post office), Eteläsatama (South Harbor, near the Olympia Terminal), or the market square. October–April, Sunday 11 AM (from Asemaaukio); May–September, daily 9 AM from Eteläsatama and 11 AM from Ase-maaukio; and June–August, daily 10:30 AM, 12:30 PM, and 2:30 PM from the Market Square. You can buy tickets on the bus 15 minutes before departure. **Ageba Travel Agency** (tel. 90/669193) offers a similar tour (2 to 2½ hrs), starting from the Olympia Terminal (Apr.–Oct., daily 9:30 AM and 11 AM; Nov.–Mar., weekends 11 AM). **Royal Line Rautakorpi** (tel. 90/351–1885) operates "Helsinki by Sea" boat tours (1½ hrs; May 13–Aug., daily 11 AM, 1 PM, and 3 PM; with additional summer service June 10–Aug., daily 10 AM, noon, 2 PM, 4 PM, and 6 PM. Some tours are available in September; the 1996 schedule was not available at press time. The same agency runs "Porvoo Old Town Cruises" (seven hrs; June 10–Aug. 13, Tues., Thurs., and weekends 11 AM).

Excursions
Helsingin Matkailuyhdistys (Lönnrotinkatu 7B, Helsinki, tel. 90/645225) offers four-hour tours of historic homes of Finnish artists and the Old Town of Porvoo. No-visa trips by sea to St. Petersburg, Russia, and Tallinn, Estonia, are offered by **Finnsov Tours** (tel. 90/694–2011). **Atlas Cruising Center** offers visa-free cruises to Tallinn (one-day), and St. Petersburg (three-days) (tel. 90/651011).

Exploring Helsinki

Helsinki is a city of the sea, built on peninsulas and islands along the Baltic shoreline. Streets curve around bays, bridges arch over the nearby islands, and ferries carry traffic to destinations further offshore. The smell of the sea hovers over the city, while the huge ships that ply the Baltic constantly come and go from the city's harbors.

Helsinki has grown dramatically since World War II, and now accounts for about one-sixth of the Finnish population. The city covers a total of 433 square miles and includes 315 islands. Most of the city's sights, hotels, and restaurants, however, are located on one peninsula—forming a compact hub of special interest to the traveler.

Helsinki is a relatively young city compared with other European capitals. In the sixteenth century, the Swedish king, Gustavus Vasa, whose rule included present-day Finland, decided to woo trade from the Estonian city of Tallinn, and thus challenge the Hanseatic League's monopoly on Baltic trade. The city was founded on June 12, 1550, at the rapids of the Vantaa River, by people from four Finnish towns who were ordered to move there by the king.

Over the next three centuries, Helsinki had its ups and downs, suffering several fires and epidemics. Turku, on Finland's west coast, was the capital and the intellectual center. Helsinki did not take center stage until Finland was ceded by Sweden to Russia in 1809. The Russian czar, Alexander I, made Finland an autonomous grand duchy of Russia; he proclaimed Helsinki the capital in 1812. About the same time, much of Turku burned to the ground, forcing the university to move to Helsinki as well. From then on, Helsinki's position as Finland's first city was guaranteed.

Fire also played a role in Helsinki's fortunes. Just before the czar's proclamation, a fire destroyed many of Helsinki's traditional wooden buildings, necessitating the construction of a new city center. The German-born architect Carl Ludvig Engel was commissioned to rebuild the city, and, as a result, Helsinki has some of the purest neoclassical architecture in the world. Add to this foundation the stunning outlines of the Jugendstil period (early 20th century) and the modern buildings designed by talented Finnish architects, and you have a European capital city that is as architecturally eye-catching as it is different from its Scandinavian neighbors or the rest of Europe.

Numbers in the margin correspond to points of interest on the Helsinki map.

Across from the city tourist office and beside the South Harbor is the ❶ **Kauppatori** (Market Square) frequented by locals and tourists alike. All around are stalls selling everything from colorful, freshly cut flowers to ripe fruit, from vegetables trucked in from the hinterland to handicrafts made in small villages. Look at the fruit stalls—mountains of strawberries; raspberries; blueberries; and, if you're lucky, cloudberries. Closer to the dock are fresh fish, caught that morning in the Baltic Sea and still flopping. You can't miss the **statue of Havis Amanda** standing in the square.

The market ends at 2 PM, and, in the summer, the fruit and vegetable stalls are replaced with arts-and-crafts stalls. This happens at 3:30 PM and lasts until about 8 PM.

On the other side of the street, the **Pohjoisesplanadi** (North Esplanade), ❷ the political center of Finland, is the **Presidentinlinna** (President's Palace), built as a private home in 1818 and converted for use by the czars in 1843. It was the official residence of Finnish presidents from 1919–1993. It still houses President Martti Ahtisaari's offices and is the scene of official receptions. Just up the street is the city hall. Across from the palace is the waterfront, where ferries and sightseeing boats set out into the bay. On a summer's day it is a sailor's vision: sails hoisted and taut to the wind and island waters to explore. The redbrick edi- ❸ fice perched above the east side of the market is the Orthodox **Uspenskin Katedraali** (Uspenski Cathedral).

Just behind the cathedral is the district of **Katajanokka.** Here the 19th-century brick warehouses are slowly being renovated to form a complex of boutiques, arts-and-crafts studios, and restaurants. You'll find innovative designs at these shops, and the restaurants tend to offer lighter fare, which can make this a tempting area to stop for lunch. While in Katajanokka, you might enjoy a visit to **Wanha Satama,** a small complex of cafés and food stores attached to an art gallery.

❹ A one-minute stroll north of the city hall will take you into **Senaatin- tori** (Senate Square), the heart of neoclassical Helsinki, which is domi- ❺ nated by the domed **Tuomiokirkko** (Lutheran cathedral). The square is the work of Carl Ludvig Engel. The harmony created with the Tuomiokirkko, the university, and the state council building places you amid one of the purest styles of European architecture. Senaatintori has a dignified, stately air, enlivened in summer by sun-worshipers who gather on the wide steps leading up to Tuomiokirkko and throughout the year by the bustle around the **Kiseleff Bazaar** on the square's south side.

6 Back on the market, head southward along the western shore of the South Harbor on Eteläranta Street. You'll soon come to the old brick **Market Hall**—it's worth taking a look at the voluminous displays of meat, fish, and other gastronomic goodies (open weekdays 8–5, Saturday 8–2). A little farther on are the **Makasiini and Olympia terminals,** where the huge ferries from Sweden, Estonia, and Poland berth. Beyond this is **Kaivopuisto,** the elegant parkland district much favored by Russian high society during the 19th century. It is now popular as a residential area for diplomats and strolling ground for Helsinki's citizens.

TIME OUT Perched on the shore is the **Café Ursula.** However welcome the refreshments may be, the view of the harbor with its waterborne traffic is all the reason you need to stop here.

7 You can avoid the long walk back by cutting across Kaivopuisto to Tehtaankatu and catching Streetcar 3T to the Kauppatori: From here, there's a frequent ferry service to **Suomenlinna,** or "Finland's Castle." Finnish units of the Swedish army began construction of this fortress in 1748. The fortress's six islands, known as the "Gibraltar of the North," were Sweden's shield against Russia until the surrender to Russia, without a fight, by the Swedish commander during the War of Finland (1808–1819). The commander's motives for the surrender are not fully understood by historians. A heavy British naval attack in 1855, during the Crimean War, damaged the fortress.

8 Although still a military garrison, Suomenlinna is now also a collection of museums and parks. In early summer, it is engulfed in purple lilacs introduced from Versailles by the Finnish architect Augustin Ehrensvärd. One of the museums you may care to visit is the **Pohjoismainen Taidekeskus** (Nordic Arts Center), which exhibits work by Nordic artists. *Admission free. Open Tues.–Sun. 11–6.*

9 Back on the mainland, head west from the marketplace up Pohjoisesplanadi. To your left are the Esplanade gardens. On your right are the showrooms and boutiques of some of Finland's top fashion designers (*see* Shopping, *below*). The circular **Svenska Teatern** (Swedish Theater) marks the junction of the Esplanade and Helsinki's main artery, Mannerheimintie.

10 If you take a right up Keskuskatu, you'll come to **Stockmann's,** Helsinki's most famous department store, well worth a shopping stop.
11 Next you'll come to the **Railway Station** and its square, the bustling commuting hub of the city. The station's huge red-granite figures are by Emil Wikström, but the solid building they adorn was designed by Eliel Saarinen, one of the founders of the early-20th-century National **12** Romantic style. The **Valtion Taidemuseo Ateneum** (Finnish National Gallery) is on the south side of the square facing the **National Theater.** *Admission: FIM 10 adults, children free. Open Tues. and Fri. 9–6, Wed. and Thurs. 9–8, weekends 11–5.*

TIME OUT **Café Socis,** in the Seurahuone Hotel opposite the railway station, provides a restful turn-of-the-century atmosphere for a prix-fixe lunch or afternoon tea. **Café Ekberg,** at Bulevardi 9, is a favorite sipping ground

230

Finlandiatalo, **15**
Kauppatori, **1**
Market Hall, **6**
Parliament House, **14**
Pohjoismainen
Taidekeskus, **8**
Presidentinlinna, **2**
Railway Station, **11**
Senaatintori, **4**
Statue of Marshal
Mannerheim, **13**
Stockmann's, **10**
Suomen Kansallis-
museo, **17**
Suomen Kansalliso-
opera, **16**
Suomenlinna, **7**
Svenska Teatern, **9**
Temppeliaukion
Kirkko, **18**
Tuomiokirkko, **5**
Uspenskin
Katedraali, **3**
Valtion Taidemuseo
Ateneum, **12**

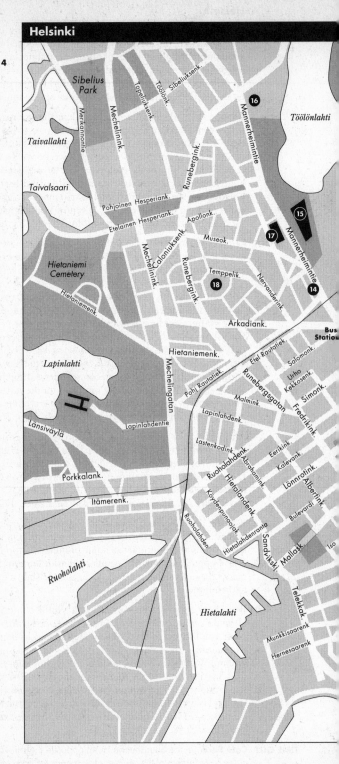

Helsinki

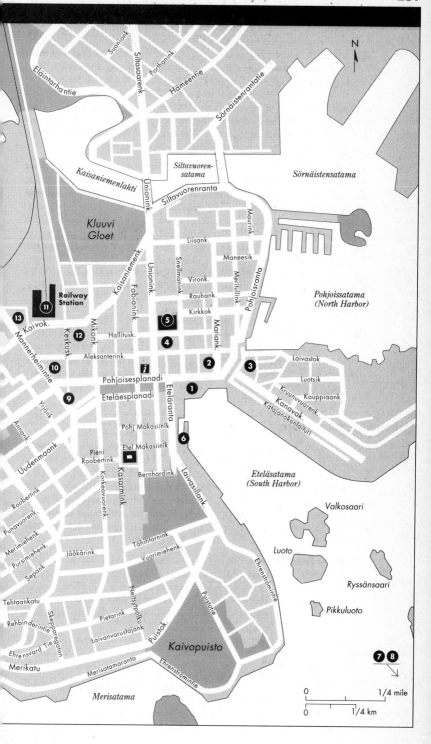

Suonionk.

Siltasaarenk.

Porthonink.

Eläintarhantie

Hämeentie

Siltavuoren-
satama

Sörnäistenrantatie

Kaisaniemenlahti

Unionink.

Siltavuorenranta

Sörnäistensatama

**Kluuvi
Gloet**

Liisank.

Maneesik.

Maurink.

Kaisaniemenk.

Unionink.

Snellmanink.

Vironk.

Meritullink.

Pohjoisranta

**Pohjoissatama
(North Harbor)**

Railway
Station

Fabianink.

Rauhank.

Kirkkok.

⑤

Mariank.

⑬ Kaivok.

Keskusk.

Mikonk.

Hallitusk.

④

Aleksanterink.

②

③

Laivastok.

Luotsik.

Kruunuvuorenk.

Kauppiaank.

Katajanokanlaituri

Kanavak.

⑪

⑫

⑩

ℹ

Pohjoisesplanadi

Eteläesplanadi

①

⑨

Yrjönk.

Mannerheimintie

Annank.

Pohj Makasiinik.

Etel Makasiinik.

⑥

Eteläranta

**Eteläsatama
(South Harbor)**

Pieni
Roobertink.

Bernhardink.

Laivasillank.

Kasarmink.

Korkeavuorenk.

Valkosaari

Uudenmaank.

Roobertink.

Punavuorenk.

Merimiehenk.

Pursimiehenk.

Jääkärink.

Tähtitornink.

Vuorimiehenk.

Luoto

Sepänk.

Ehrenströmintie

Ryssänsaari

Tehtaankatu

Rehbinderintie

Skepparegatan

Ehrensvard Tie

Merikatu

Pietarink.

Laivanvarustajank.

Neitsypolku

Puistok.

Puistotie

Pikkuluoto

Kaivopuisto

Merisatamaranta

Ehrenströmintie

⑦⑧

Merisatama

N

| 0 | | 1/4 mile |
| 0 | | 1/4 km |

of literati and the staffs from publishing houses in the neighborhood. The café's renowned line of traditional confections is also worth a visit.

⓭ In front of the main post office west of the station is the **statue of Marshal Mannerheim,** gazing down Mannerheimintie, the major thoroughfare named in his honor. Perhaps no man in Finnish history is so revered as Marshal Baron Carl Gustaf Mannerheim, the military and political leader who guided Finland through much of the turbulent 20th century. When he died in Switzerland on January 28, 1951, his body was flown back to lie in state in the cathedral. For three days, young war widows, children, and soldiers filed past his bier.

⓮ About half a mile along, past the colonnaded red-granite **Parliament**
⓯ **House,** stands **Finlandiatalo** (Finlandia Hall), one of the last creations
⓰ of Alvar Aalto, and, a bit farther up Mannerheimintie, the new **Suomen Kansallisoppera** (Finnish National Opera), a striking example of Scandinavian architecture. If you can't make it to a concert there, take a guided tour. Behind the hall and the opera house lies the inland bay of
⓱ Töölönlahti, and almost opposite the hall stands the **Suomen Kansallismuseo** (National Museum), another example of National Romantic exotica in which Eliel Saarinen played a part. *Admission: FIM 15 adults, children free. Open June–Aug., Wed.–Sun. 11–5, Tues. 11–8; Sept.–May, Wed.–Sun. 11–4, Tues. 11–8.*

Tucked away in a labyrinth of streets to the west is the strikingly modern **Temppeliaukion Kirkko** (Temple Square Church). Carved out of solid
⓲ rock and topped with a copper dome, this landmark is a center for church services and concerts. (From here it's only a short distance back to Mannerheimintie, where you can pick up any streetcar for the downtown area.) *Lutherinkatu 3. Open daily 11–8. Closed Tues. 1–2 PM and during concerts and services.*

Off the Beaten Track

In Espoo, Helsinki's next-door neighbor, is the garden city of **Tapiola,** one of Finland's architectural highlights. Designed by Alvar Aalto, the urban landscape of alternating high and low residential buildings, fountains, gardens, and swimming pools blends into the natural surroundings. What began as an experiment in communal, affordable housing has now lost its radical appeal, but Tapiola still holds interest for anyone interested in urban planning. Sightseeing tours are available from the Espoo City Tourist Office (tel. 90/460311).

Akseli Gallen Kallela (1865–1931) was one of Finland's greatest artists. His studio-home can be seen at Gallen-Kallelan tie 27, Tarvaspää. To get there, take Tram 4 to Munkkiniemi, then it's a 1½-mile walk through the woods. *Admission: FIM 35 adults, FIM 15 children. Open mid-May–Aug., Mon.–Thurs. 10–8, Fri.–Sun. 10–5; Sept.–mid-May, Tues.–Sat. 10–4, Sun. 10–5.*

Shopping

Shopping Districts and Specialty Shops

Helsinki's prime shopping districts run along **Pohjoisesplanadi** (North Esplanade) and **Aleksanterinkatu** in the city center. You can find a number of antique shops in the neighborhood behind Senate Square, called **Kruununhaka. The Forum** (Mannerheimintie 20) is a modern, multistory shopping center with a wide variety of stores, including clothing, gifts, books, toys. etc. You can also make purchases until 10 PM daily in the shops along the Tunneli underpass underneath the Railway Station. Some shops in the **Kiseleff Bazaar Hall** (Aleksanderinkatu 28), which once housed Stockmann's and now has shops selling handicrafts, toys and knitwear, are open on Sundays from noon to 4 in the summer. **Kaunis Koru,** which sells Finnish-designed jewelry, is next door to the Kiseleff Bazaar Hall. **Kalevala Koru** (Unioninkatu 25) has jewelry based on ancient Finnish designs.

Along Pohjoisesplanadi, and the other side of the street, Eteläesplanadi, you will find Finland's design houses. **Hackman Arabia** (Pohjoisesplanadi 25) sells Finland's well-known Arabia china, Iittala glass and other items. **Pentik** (Pohjoisesplanadi 27) features artful leather goods. **Aarikka** (Pohjoisesplanadi 25–27 and Eteläesplanadi 8) offers wooden jewelry, toys and gifts. **Artek** (Eteläesplanadi 18) is known for its Alvar Alto-designed furniture and ceramics. **Marimekko** (Pohjoisesplanadi 31 and Eteläesplanadi 18) sells women's clothing, household items and gifts made from its famous textiles. **Design Forum Finland** (Eteläesplanadi 8) which often hosts exhibits of the latest Finnish design innovations, can provide more information.

Department Stores
Stockmann's, a huge store that fills an entire block between Aleksanterinkatu, Mannerheimintie, and Keskuskatu, is your best bet for finding everything under one roof.

Markets
The **Kauppatori market** beside the South Harbor (*see* Exploring Helsinki, *above*) is an absolute must year-round. In favorable weather, there is a variety of goods at the **Hietalahti flea market,** located at the west end of Bulevardi on Hietalahti. (Open Mon.–Sat. 8 AM–2 PM; mid-May–Aug., also open weekdays 3:30 PM–8 PM and Sat. 10 AM–4 PM.)

Dining

For details and price-category definitions, *see* Dining *in* Staying in Finland, *above*. Highly recommended restaurants are indicated by a star ★.

$$$$ **Alexander Nevski.** In a city already famed for having the finest Rus-
★ sian cuisine in Scandinavia, it is hard to stand out as special. But the food, decor and service at Alexander Nevski, which is situated right across from the Havis Amanda statue, has come to be regarded as the best in Finland. The decor of the restaurant is dominated by hues of green and palm trees, in the Russian-French style of 19th-century St. Petersburg restaurants. Be sure to sample the blinis and the game specialties, often baked in clay pots. *Pohjoisesplanadi 17, tel. 90/639610. Reservations advised. AE, DC, MC, V. Closed Christmas and Midsummer.*

$$$$ **Amadeus.** In an old town house near the South Harbor, Amadeus specializes in game dishes such as snow grouse, wild duck and reindeer fillets. *Sofiankatu 4, tel. 90/626676. Reservations advised. AE, DC, MC, V. Closed Sun., Christmas, Easter, and Midsummer.*

$$$$ **Galateia.** Helsinki's best seafood restaurant is perched on top of the Inter-Continental hotel with a magnificent view of Töölönlahti. Try the lobster bisque with veal sweetbreads, or the poached sander, a fish found in Finnish waters. *Mannerheimintie 46, tel. 90/405–5900 or 90/40551. Reservations advised. AE, DC, MC, V. Dinner only. Closed weekends and holidays.*

$$$$ **Palace Gourmet.** One of Helsinki's top restaurants, Palace Gourmet
★ offers elegant surroundings with a splendid view of South Harbor. Chef Markus Maulavirta specializes in Finnish and French fare. Recommended

Finnish specialties include jellied roe of *muikku* (vendace, a kind of white-fish), with sour-cream dill sauce, and reindeer fillet and tongue with rowanberry sauce. *Eteläranta 10, tel. 90/134561. Reservations advised. AE, DC, MC, V. Closed weekends, holidays, and July.*

$$$$ **Savoy.** In keeping with its reputation as the favorite dining spot of Finnish
★ statesman Marshal Baron Carl Gustaf Mannerheim, the Savoy is Helsinki's first choice for business lunches or a festive splurge. The airy 1930s-style dining room with its grand view of Esplanade park was designed by architect Alvar Aalto. The Savoy still serves *Vorschmack* (minced lamb and anchovies) made according to the recipe said to have been introduced by Mannerheim himself. *Eteläesplanadi 14, tel. 90/176571. Reservations advised. AE, DC, MC, V. Closed weekends, Christmas, Easter, Midsummer, and other holidays.*

$$$ **Bellevue.** Established in 1917, Bellevue is one of Helsinki's oldest
★ restaurants. Despite its French name, the restaurant is Russian, both in decor and cuisine. Fillet à la Novgorod (a traditional ox fillet pre-pared with carrots, barley and sauerkraut), and chicken à la Kiev are the authentic articles here. *Rahapajankatu 3, tel. 90/179560. Reservations advised. AE, DC, MC, V. No lunch weekends. Closed Christmas, Easter, Midsummer.*

$$$ **Nylandskä Jaktklubben.** One of Finland's summer restaurants, the Ny-landska Jaktklubben (Swedish Yacht Club) is in a picturesque turn-of-the-century wooden building on an island in Helsinki's South Harbor. It is easily reached by motorboat, leaving from the small harbor just south of the Olympia Terminal. This restaurant specializes in fresh local fish, and is a beautiful spot for dinner during Finland's long summer days. *Valkosaari Island, tel. 90/636047. Reservations advised. AE, DC, MC, V. Dinner only. Closed Sept. 16–May 6.*

$$$ **Sipuli.** Sipuli, at the foot of the Russian Orthodox Uspenski Cathedral, gets its name from the golden onion-shape cupolas that adorn the cathe-dral. In a brick warehouse building dating from the late 19th century, French-style food is served with a Finnish flair. The skylight offers a spectacular view of the cathedral. *Kanavaranta 3, tel. 90/179900. Reservations advised. AE, DC, MC, V. Dinner only. Closed weekends, Christmas, Easter and Midsummer.*

$$$ **Troikka.** The Troikka takes you back to czarist times in decor, paint-ings, and music, and offers exceptionally good food and friendly ser-vice. Try the Siberian *pelmeny* (small meat pastries). *Caloniuksenkatu 3, tel. 90/445229. Reservations advised. AE, DC, MC, V. Closed Sun., weekends in summer, first wk in July, and holidays.*

$$$ **Villa Thai.** This Thai-run kitchen serves authentic Thai food in elegant and comfortable surroundings—patrons have a choice between west-ern and Thai-style seating. One exceptional dish is the prawn curry with coconut milk and pineapple. *Bulevardi 28, tel. 90/680–2778. Reservations advised. AE, DC, MC, V. Closed Christmas.*

$$ **Asia King.** The Asia King offers generous portions of authentic Indian food in a modest yet attractive setting. *Sepankatu 19, tel. 90/664521. Reservations advised. AE, DC, MC, V. Closed Christmas, Midsummer.*

$$ **Omenapuu.** A lunchtime favorite for shoppers and businesspeople, Om-enapuu has a varied menu and a central location for a quick stop. *Keskuskatu 6, 2nd floor, tel. 90/630205. Lunch reservations advised. AE, DC, MC, V. Closed Christmas.*

$ **Café Kobenhavn.** Generous open-face sandwiches are the specialty of Café Kobenhavn, Helsinki's only Danish restaurant; the menu in-cludes other traditional Scandanavian dishes as well. *Tehtaankatu 21, tel. 90/633997. DC, V. Closed Christmas, Easter.*

$ **Perho Mechelin.** This is the restaurant associated with Helsinki's catering school. During summer the emphasis is on Finnish food, offering myriad salmon options. *Mechelininkatu 7, tel. 90/493481. Reservations advised. AE, DC, MC, V. Closed Christmas, Easter, and Midsummer.*

$ **Pikku Satama.** The casual Pikku Satama, in the renovated warehouse complex Wanha Satama in Katajanokka, serves a variety of lunch and dinner specialties—pizza, baked potatoes with various toppings, and hot dishes. *Pikku Satamakatu 3, tel. 90/174093. AE, DC, MC, V. Closed holidays.*

Lodging

For details and price-category definitions, *see* Lodging *in* Staying in Finland, *above.*

$$$$ **Hesperia.** Enlarged and redecorated in 1986, the Hesperia is modern in the best Finnish tradition and just a short stroll from the center of the city. *Mannerheimintie 50, 00260, tel. 90/43101, fax 90/431–0995. 360 rooms, 287 with bath, 73 with shower. Facilities: sauna, pool, golf simulator, nightclub, helipad. AE, DC, MC, V. Closed Christmas.*

$$$$ **Inter-Continental.** This is the most popular hotel in the city—with
★ American visitors, at least. It's modern and centrally located—close to Finlandia Hall and the new opera house. Rooms are on the small side, though, and restaurant noise may disturb guests staying on the top floor. *Mannerheimintie 46–48, 00260, tel. 90/40551, fax 90/405–5255. 555 rooms with bath. Facilities: 2 restaurants, bar, coffee shop, sauna, pool, barber shop. AE, DC, MC, V.*

$$$$ **Palace.** The Palace has a splendid location overlooking the South Harbor—but make sure you ask for a room with a view; these rooms are on the ninth floor. *Eteläranta 10, 00130, tel. 90/134561, fax 90/654786. 50 rooms with bath or shower. Facilities: 2 restaurants, sauna. AE, DC, MC, V. Closed Christmas.*

$$$$ **Ramada Presidentti.** In addition to its spacious rooms, the hotel also offers a wide range of facilities that continues to draw repeat visitors. Finland's first international casino was inaugurated here in 1991 and has enjoyed tremendous success. The hotel's main restaurant, Four Seasons, serves a tasty buffet. *Eteläinen Rautatiekatu 4, 00100, tel. 90/6911, fax 90/694–7886. 495 rooms with bath. Facilities: 2 restaurants, 2 coffee shops, sauna, pool, nightclub, casino. AE, DC, MC, V.*

$$$$ **SAS Royal Hotel.** This luxury hotel is centrally located and a 10-minute walk from the Railway Station. The rooms are elegant and decorated in one of three styles: Scandinavian (light woods), Oriental (lots of bamboo), and Italian (strong colors). If you want more space and privacy, try the business-class rooms (art deco–style) located on the hotel's top floors. The Johan Ludvig restaurant specializes in dishes like prime rib of beef. The hotel's other restaurant, Ströget, is cheaper and serves pasta, salads, hamburgers, and Danish sandwiches. *Runeberginkatu 2, 00100, tel. 90/69580, fax 90/6958–7100. 260 rooms with bath. Facilities: 2 restaurants, sauna, bar, summer terrace. AE, DC, MC, V.*

$$$$ **Strand Inter-Continental.** Centrally located, the hotel is adjacent to the
★ Old City on the waterfront. The hotel's distinctive use of granite and marble in the central lobby is accentuated by a soaring atrium and softened by a cozy fireplace. There is a choice of restaurants—Pamir's elegant gourmet dishes of seafood, steak, and game or the Atrium Plaza's buffet restaurant for light meals. *John Stenbergin ranta 4, 00530, tel. 90/39351, fax 90/761362 or 90/393–5225. 200 rooms with bath. Facilities: 2 restaurants, sauna, indoor pool, lounge-bar. AE, DC, MC, V. Closed Christmas.*

$$$ **Lordhotel.** In a handsome stone castle built in 1903, each room offers contemporary furnishings in peaceful blue and gray tones. *Lönnrotinkatu 29, 00180, tel. 90/680–1680, fax 90/680–1315. 49 rooms with bath or shower (17 rooms with Jacuzzi). Facilities: restaurant, bar, saunas, banquet hall, conference rooms, free parking. AE, DC, MC, V. May be closed Christmas.*

$$$ **Rantasipi Airport Hotel.** The rooms here are rather small, but shuttle service is provided to the airport which is just 3.2 kilometers (2 miles) away. *Robert Huberintie 4, 01510 Vantaa, tel. 90/87051, fax 90/822846. 300 rooms with shower. Facilities: restaurant, sauna, pool, piano bar. AE, DC, MC, V.*

$$$ **Rivoli Jardin.** Rivoli Jardin is a central town house, with all rooms overlooking a quiet courtyard. The rooms are small but rich in design and detail. The only meal available here is the breakfast which is served each morning in the winter garden. *Kasarmikatu 40, 00130, tel. 90/177880, fax 90/656988. 53 rooms with shower. Facilities: sauna. AE, DC, MC, V. Closed Christmas.*

$$–$$$ **Hotel Grand Marina.** This renovated early 19th-century customs warehouse sits in the plush Katajanokka Island neighborhood. The hotel's choice location, friendly service, and ample modern facilities have made it a favorite among tourists. It's congress center across the street—considered the best-equipped in the country—has made it a favorite with conventioneers. *Katajanokkalaituri 7, 00160, tel. 90/16661, fax 90/664764. 462 rooms with bath or shower. Facilities: 5 restaurants, bar, pub, sauna. AE, DC, MC, V.*

$$ **Arthur.** A property of the Helsinki YMCA, the Arthur is located on a quiet, central street and is unpretentious and comfortable. *Vuorikatu 17B, 00100, tel. 90/173441, fax 90/626880. 143 rooms with bath or shower. Facilities: restaurant, sauna. AE, DC, MC, V. Closed Christmas.*

$$ **Aurora.** About a mile from the city center, the Aurora is just opposite the Linnanmäki amusement park. Reasonable prices, cozy rooms, and good facilities have made this hotel a favorite with families. *Helsinginkatu 50, 00530, tel. 90/717400, fax 90/714240. 76 rooms, 6 with bath, 70 with shower. Facilities: restaurant, sauna, squash courts, health spa. AE, DC, MC, V. Closed Dec. 23–Jan. 3.*

$$ **Marttahotelli.** The rooms here are small but pleasantly decorated. The hotel is only a 10-minute walk from the Railway Station. *Uudenmankatu 24, 00120, tel. 90/646211, fax 90/680–1266. 45 rooms with bath or shower. Facilities: sauna. AE, DC, MC, V. Closed Christmas, Easter, and Midsummer.*

$$ **Merihotelli.** Located on the seafront, the Merihotelli is a 10-minute walk from the center of town. The rooms are somewhat small and modern; those with a sea view get some traffic noise. *John Stenbergin ranta 6, 00530, tel. 90/69121, fax 90/760271. 87 rooms with shower. Facilities: 2 restaurants, coffee shop, sauna. AE, DC, MC, V. Closed Christmas.*

$$ **Seurahuone.** This is a traditional hotel built in 1914 and renovated in
★ 1992. The room decor ranges from sleek modern to crystal chandeliers and brass bedsteads. The street-side rooms that face the Railway Station are not always quiet. *Kaivokatu 12, 00100, tel. 90/170441, fax 90/664170. 118 rooms, 95 with bath, 23 with shower. Facilities: café, pub, sauna. AE, DC, MC, V. Usually closed Christmas.*

$ **Academica.** Fully renovated in 1992, this summer hotel is a standard student dormitory during the school year. However, its simple, adequate rooms, the 10-minute walk from the town center, and the impressive array of exercise facilities make staying here an excellent value. *Hietaniemenkatu 14, 00100, tel. 90/402–0206, fax 90/441201. 115 rooms with shower and kitchenette. Facilities: sauna, pool, indoor ten-*

nis, disco (weekends), self-service laundry, solarium. AE, DC, MC, V. Closed Sept.–May.

$ **Skatta.** In the elegant neighborhood of Katajanokka Island and just 3 kilometers (2 miles) from the Railway Station, the Skatta is modest and practical; each room has a kitchenette. *Linnankatu 3, 00160, tel. 90/659233 or 90/669984, fax 90/631352. 24 rooms with shower. Facilities: sauna, exercise room. AE, DC, MC, V. Sometimes closed at Christmas.*

The Arts

For a list of events, pick up the free publication *Helsinki This Week*, available in hotels and tourist offices. In summer, the guide lists a telephone number for recorded program information in English. A central reservations office for all events is **Lippupalvelu** (Mannerheimintie 5, tel. 9700–4700 or 90/664466 when calling from abroad). Call **Tiketti** (Yrjönkatu 29C, tel. 90/9700–4204) to book tickets for small concerts at clubs and restaurants.

Theater

Although all performances are in Finnish or Swedish, summertime productions in such bucolic settings as **Suomenlinna Island, Kekuspuisto Park, Mustikkamaa Island,** the **Rowing Stadium** (operettas), the **Indoor Ice Rink** (rock concerts), and the **Savoy Theater** (ballet and music performances) make enjoyable entertainment. The splendid **Kansallisooppera** (National Opera, tel. 90/4030–2211) opened in 1993 in a waterside park by Tööönlahti just a few hundred feet from Finlandia Hall.

Concerts

The main concert venues are **Finlandia Hall** (tel. 90/40241), **Temppeliaukion Church** (*see* Exploring, *above*), and the **Sibelius Academy** (tel. 90/405441).

Festivals

Finland holds many festivals throughout the country, especially during the summer months. The **Helsinki Festival** is said to be the biggest in Scandinavia. For more than two weeks during August and September, there are scores of musical happenings and art exhibitions. Contact Helsinki Festival (Rauhankatu 7E, tel. 90/135–4522); for more information on festivals, call Finland Festivals (Mannerheimintie 40, B49, tel. 90/445686, fax 90/445117).

Nightlife

Bars and Lounges

One of the most popular nightspots in Helsinki is **Happy Days** (Pohjoisesplanadi 2, tel. 90/657700), known also for its hamburgers and outdoor terrace. The historic **Kappeli Café-Brasserie** (Eteläesplanadi 1, tel. 90/179242) brews its own beer. **Kaarle XII** (Kasarmikatu 40, tel. 90/171312) is located in one of Helsinki's striking German Art Nouveau buildings. **Cantina West** (Kasarmikatu 23, tel. 90/6221500) is a Tex-Mex bar and restaurant with good food and live music nightly.

Jazz Clubs

Try **Storyville Happy Jazz Club** (Museokatu 8, tel. 90/408007), which features Finnish and foreign jazz musicians and New Orleans-style cuisine. Modern jazz brings a hip, young crowd to the **Hot Tomato Jazz Café** (Annankatu 6, tel. 90/680–1701).

Nightclubs

Helsinki's largest and most famous club is the **Hesperia Nightclub** (Hotel Hesperia, Kivelänkatu 2, tel. 90/43101). **Fennia** (Mikonkatu 17, tel. 90/666355) boasts dancing and live music on weekends. **Café Adlon** is another well-known disco. **Kaivohuone** (Kaivohuone Kaivopuisto, tel. 90/177881), in its attractive park setting, is a summertime favorite.

THE LAKELANDS

In southeastern and central Finland, the light has a softness that seems to brush the forests, lakes, and islands, changing the landscape throughout the day. For centuries, though, this beautiful region was actually a much-contested buffer between the warring empires of Sweden and Russia. The Finns of the Lakelands prevailed by sheer *sisu* (guts), and now their descendants thrive amid the rough beauty of the terrain.

Getting Around

Savonlinna is the best-placed town in the Lakelands and can make a convenient base from which to begin exploring. You can fly to the Savonlinna area from Helsinki in 40 minutes; a connecting bus takes you the remaining 16 kilometers (10 miles) into town. By train, the journey takes 5½ hours; by bus, six hours.

If you travel by car, you can do the lake trips as separate excursions. The alternative is to take advantage of the excellent network of air, rail, bus, and boat transportation. Take the boat from Savonlinna to Kuopio in 12 hours (**Roll Cruises,** tel. 971/262–6744). From Kuopio, take the 320-kilometer (200-mile) cross-country bus ride via Jyväskylä to Tampere. Continue by boat to Hämeenlinna for a little over eight hours (**Finnish Silverline,** tel. 931/124803). The final leg by bus or train back to Helsinki takes about 1¼ hours.

Guided Tours

A program of **Friendly Finland Tours,** available through a number of travel agencies, offers escorted lakeland packages from two to 11 days, starting from Helsinki. Brochures are available from the **Finnish Tourist Board** (Eteläesplanadi 4, tel. 90/4030–1300) and its overseas offices (*see* Important Addresses and Numbers *in* Helsinki, *above*).

Tourist Information

Hämeenlinna (Sibeliuksenkatu 5A, 13100, tel. 917/621–2388).
Kuopio (Haapaniemenkatu 17, 70110, tel. 971/182584).
Savonlinna (Puistokatu 1, 57100, tel. 957/273492).
Tampere (Verkatehtaankatu 2, 33211, tel. 931/212–6652).

Exploring the Lakelands

Savonlinna

The center of **Savonlinna** is a series of islands linked by bridges. First, stop at the tourist office for information; then cross the bridge east to the **open-air market** that flourishes alongside the main passenger quay. In days when waterborne traffic was the major form of transportation, Savonlinna was the central hub of the passenger fleet serving Saimaa, the largest lake system in Europe. Now the lake traffic is dominated by cruise and sightseeing boats.

A 10-minute stroll from the quay to the southeast brings you to Savonlinna's most famous sight, the castle of **Olavinlinna**. First built in 1475 to protect Finland's eastern border, the castle retains its medieval character and is one of Scandinavia's best-preserved historic monuments. Still surrounded by water that once formed part of its defensive strength, the fortress rises majestically out of the lake. The Savonlinna Opera Festival is held in the courtyard each July. You will need to make reservations well in advance (tel. 957/514700 or 957/21866), both for tickets and for hotel rooms. *Castle admission: FIM 20 adults, FIM 5 children; includes guided tours on the hr. Open June–Aug., daily 10–5; Sept.–May, daily 10–3.*

Close to the castle are the 19th-century steam schooners, **Mikko, Salama,** and **Savonlinna.** The *Salama* houses an excellent museum on the history of lake traffic, including the fascinating floating timber trains that are still a common sight on Saimaa today. *Admission: FIM 15 adults, FIM 5 children. Open June–Aug., daily 10–8 Closed Sept.–May.*

The most popular excursion from Savonlinna is to **Taidekeskus Retretti** (Retretti Art Center). You can take either a two-hour boat ride or a 30-minute, 29-kilometer (18-mile) bus trip. The journey by bus takes you along the 8-kilometer (5-mile) ridge of **Punkaharju.** This breathtaking ridge of pine-covered rocks, which rises out of the water and separates the lakes on either side, predates the Ice Age. At times it narrows to only 25 feet, yet it still manages to accommodate a road and train tracks. *Admission: FIM 60 adults, FIM 25 children 7–16, FIM 145 family (2 adults, 2 or more children). Open May 24–June 23 and Aug., daily 10–6. Open June 24–July, daily 10–7.*

Near Retretti is the **Punkaharju National Hotel.** The building started as a gamekeeper's lodge for Czar Nicholas I in 1845, but has been subsequently enlarged and restored; it is now a restful spot for a meal or an overnight visit.

Kuopio

The 12-hour boat trip from Savonlinna to **Kuopio** is probably the best opportunity you'll get to feel the soul of the Finnish lakeland. Meals are available on board. The boat arrives at Kuopio passenger harbor, where you'll find a small evening market in action daily from 3 to 10.

The Kuopio Tourist Office is located close to the **Tori** (marketplace). The Tori should be one of the places you visit first, for it is one of the most colorful outdoor markets in Finland. *Open May–Aug., weekdays 7–5, Sat. 7–2.; Sept.–April, Mon.–Sat. 7–2.*

Only a 15-minute walk from the heart of Kuopio is another picturesque market square by the Kuopio passenger harbor. *Open May 15–Aug. 31, daily noon–10.*

The **Orthodox Church Museum** has one of the most interesting and unusual collections of its kind in the world. When Karelia was ceded to the Soviet Union after World War II, religious art was taken out of the monasteries and brought to Kuopio. *Karjalankatu 1, tel. 971/261–8818. Admission: FIM 15 adults, FIM 5 children. Open May–Aug., daily 10–3; Sept.–Apr., weekdays noon–3, weekends noon–5.*

Visitors who are fascinated by the treasures in the museum will want to visit the Orthodox convent and **monastery of Valamo.** The monastery is a center for Russian Orthodox religious and cultural life in Finland. Precious 18th-century icons and sacred objects are housed in the main church and in the icon conservation center. The Orthodox library is the most extensive in Finland and is open to visitors. Church services

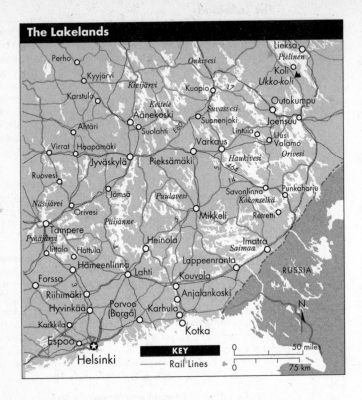

The Lakelands

[Map showing the Lakelands region of Finland with cities including: Perho, Kyyjärvi, Karstula, Ahtäri, Virrat, Haapamäki, Ruovesi, Jämsä, Orivesi, Tampere, Iittala, Hattula, Hämeenlinna, Forssa, Riihimäki, Hyvinkää, Karkkila, Espoo, Helsinki, Onkivesi, Kiivijärvi, Kuopio, Keitele, Äänekoski, Suolahti, Jyväskylä, Pieksämäki, Puulavesi, Heinola, Lahti, Porvoo (Borgå), Karhula, Kotka, Lieksa, Pielinen, Koli, Ukko-koli, Outokumpu, Suvasvesi, Suonenjoki, Varkaus, Lintula, Uusi Valamo, Orivesi, Haukivesi, Savonlinna, Kokonselkä, Punkaharju, Retretti, Mikkeli, Imatra, Saimaa, Lappeenranta, Kouvola, Anjalankoski, Russia. Näsijärvi, Pyhäjärvi, Päijänne lakes shown.]

KEY
— Rail Lines

0 — 50 miles
0 — 75 km

are held daily. There is a café-restaurant, and hotel and hostel accommodations are available at the monastery. It can be reached by car and bus routes from Kuopio, Joensuu, and Varkaus. *Uusi Valamo, tel. 972/570111 (972/561959 for hotel reservations). Admission free. Guided tours: FIM 20 adults, FIM 5 children. Open Mar.–Sept., daily 7:30 AM–9 PM; Oct.-Feb., Mon.-Sat. 7:30 AM–9 PM, Sun. 7:30–7.*

The **convent of Lintula** can be reached by boat from Valamo, or you can visit both the convent and the monastery by boat on scenic day excursions from Kuopio that run from June 13 through August 13. Tickets, available from the tourist office, cost FIM 275 (FIM 150 for children).

Puijo Tower is best visited at sunset, when the lakes shimmer with reflected light. The slender tower is located 3 kilometers (2 miles) northwest of Kuopio. It has two observation decks and a revolving restaurant on top where you can enjoy the marvelous views. *Open May–Sept., daily 11–11. Admission: FIM 15 adults, FIM 5 children. Open Oct.–Apr., daily 11–9. Admission free in winter.*

Tampere

The 320-kilometer (200-mile) journey from Kuopio to **Tampere** will take four to five hours, whether you travel by car or bus. Almost every guide will inform you that Tampere, the country's third-largest city, is Finland's Pittsburgh. However, the resemblance begins and ends with the concentrated presence here of industry—the settings themselves have little in common.

From about the year 1000, this part of Finland was a base from which traders and hunters set out on their expeditions to northern Finland and even to Lapland. But it was not until 1779 that a Swedish king, Gustav III, founded Tampere. One hundred and three years later, a Scotsman by the name of James Finlayson came to the infant city and established a factory for spinning cotton. The firm of Finlayson exists today and is still one of the country's large industrial enterprises.

An isthmus, little more than half a mile wide at its narrowest point, separates the lakes Näsijärvi and Pyhäjärvi, and at one spot the **Tammerkoski Rapids** provide an outlet for the waters of one to cascade through to the other. Called the "Mother of Tampere," these rapids provide a small part of the power on which the town's livelihood depends. Their natural beauty has been preserved in spite of the factories on either bank, and the distinctive public buildings of the city grouped around them enhance their general effect. Also in the heart of town is **Hämeensilta Bridge,** with its four statues by the well-known Finnish sculptor Wäinö Aaltonen.

Close to the Hämeensilta bridge, near the high-rise Hotel Ilves, are some old factory buildings that have been restored as shops and boutiques. Nearby, at Verkatehtaankatu 2, is the city tourist office, where you can buy a 24-hour **Tourist Ticket** (FIM 25 adults, FIM 20 children) that allows unlimited travel on city transportation.

Parts of the ridge of **Pyynikki,** which separates the two lakes, form a natural park that includes the Särkänniemi peninsula—all of this is just a 20-minute walk northwest from the city center. On the way there, visit one of Tampere's best small museums, **The Amuri Museum of Workers' Housing.** It consists of a block of old timber houses, with descriptions and illustrations of how the original tenants lived. *Makasiininkatu 12. Admission: FIM 15 adults, FIM 5 children. Open May 11–Sept. 19, Tues.–Sat. 9–5, Sun. 11–5.*

At Särkänniemi, not far from downtown Tampere, is Finland's tallest structure, the 550-foot **Näsinneula Observation Tower.** There is an observatory on top, as well as a revolving restaurant. The views are magnificent, commanding the lake, forest, and town. The contrast between the industrial maze of Tampere at your feet and the serenity of the lakes stretching out to meet the horizon is unforgettable. *Admission: FIM 12 adults, FIM 6 children. Open June–Aug., daily 10–10; Sept.–May, daily 10–5.*

The same building complex houses the first **planetarium** in Scandinavia and a well-planned **aquarium,** which includes a separate dolphinarium. Near this complex is another striking example of Finnish architecture, the **Sarah Hildén Art Museum,** where modern Finnish and international artists (including Miró, Leger, Picasso, and Chagall) are on display. There is also an amusement park in the area. *Joint admission: FIM 120 adults and children (admission for children not tall enough to go on amusement park rides is free); Hildén Museum only: FIM 15 adults, FIM 5 children. Open daily 11–6.*

On the east side of the town is the modern **Kaleva Church,** a soaring, spiritual monument to space and light. On the walls are some of the best-known masterpieces of Finnish art, including Magnus Encknell's frescoes, *The Resurrection,* and a few works by Hugo Simberg, such as *Wounded Angel* and *Garden of Death. Open May–Aug., daily 10–5; Sept.–Apr., daily 11–3.*

It was in Tampere that Lenin and Stalin first met, and this fateful occasion is commemorated with displays of photos and mementoes in the **Lenin Museum.** *Hämeenpuisto 28. Admission: FIM 10 adults, children free. Open weekdays 9–5, weekends 11–4.*

One of the most popular excursions from Tampere is the **Poet's Way** boat tour along Lake Näsijärvi. The boat passes through the agricultural parish of Ruovesi, where J. L. Runeberg, Finland's national poet, once lived. Shortly before the boat docks at Virrat, you'll pass through the straits of Visuvesi, where many artists and writers spend their summers. *Finnish Silverline and Poet's Way, PL 87, Verkatehtaankatu 2, tel. 931/212–4804. Round-trip fare: FIM 240.*

Hämeenlinna

The Finnish Silverline's white motor ships leave Tampere for **Hämeenlinna** from the Laukontori terminal. If you're traveling by car, take Highway 3 and stop en route at the famous **Iittala Glassworks,** which offers museum tours and has a shop. The magnificent glass is produced by top designers, and the seconds are bargains you won't find elsewhere. *Admission FIM 10 adults (FIM 7 in winter), FIM 7 children (FIM 5 in winter). Museum open May–Aug., daily 10–6; Sept.–Apr., weekdays 10–5, weekends 10–6. Shop opens June–Aug., daily 9–8; Sept.–May, daily 10–6.*

Hämeenlinna's secondary school has educated many famous Finns, among them composer Jean Sibelius (1865–1957). The only surviving timber house in the town center is the **birthplace of Sibelius,** a modest dwelling built in 1834. Here you can listen to tapes of his music and see the harmonium he played when he was a child. *Hallituskatu 11. Admission: FIM 10 adults, FIM 5 children; admission includes a guided tour. Open June–Aug., daily 10–4; Sept.–May, daily 12–4.*

The much-altered medieval **Häme Castle,** Finland's oldest castle, on the lakeshore half a mile north of the town center, doesn't compare with Savonlinna's, but it has seen a lot of action in its time and has been used as a granary as well as a prison. *Admission: FIM 15 adults, FIM 10 children. Open May–Aug. 15, daily 10–6; Aug. 16–Apr., daily 10–4.*

Hattula Church, 6 kilometers (3½ miles) to the north, is the most famous of Finland's medieval churches. The interior is a fresco gallery of biblical scenes whose vicious little devils and soulful saints are as vivid as when they were first painted around 1510. The admission fee includes entry to **Hämeenlinna Art Museum** (Viipurintie 2, tel. 917/621–2669) and to the **Hämeenlinna History Museum** (Lukionkatu 6, tel. 917/621–2560), which offers exhibitions on 19th-century life in the city. *Admission: FIM 15 adults, FIM 5 children. Open May 15–Aug. 15, daily 11–5.*

Rail and bus departures to Helsinki are frequent. If you're traveling by car, take the new Highway 12. As you pass by **Riihimäki,** you'll see signs to the **Finnish Glass Museum.** Follow them for an outstanding display of the history of glass from early Egyptian times to the present, artfully arranged in an old glass factory. *Admission: FIM 15 adults, FIM 10 children. Open Apr.–Sept., daily 10–6; Oct.–Dec., Feb., Mar., Tues.–Sun. 10–6.*

Dining and Lodging

For details and price-category definitions, *see* Dining and Lodging *in* Staying in Finland, *above.*

Hämeenlinna

DINING
Bistro Park. In a renovated old timber building, Bistro Park offers Finnish and international fare. *Kirkkorinne 2, tel. 917/612–1606. Reservations advised. AE, DC, MC, V. $$*

Huviretki. For lighter, more artful cuisine, try the salmon soup or the smoked reindeer salad in this friendly eatery. They also have a wide range of standard international cuisine, such as pepper steak and honey chicken—all with a focus on presentation. The restaurant is located inside the Cumulus Hotel. *Raatihuonentie 16–18, tel. 917/64881. Reservations advised. AE, DC, MC, V. $$*

LODGING

★ **Rantasipi Aulanko.** One of Finland's top hotels sits on the lakeshore in a beautifully landscaped park 6.4 kilometers (4 miles) from town. *13210 Hämeenlinna, tel. 917/658801, fax 917/21922. 245 rooms with bath. Facilities: saunas, pool, tennis, golf, riding, boating, nightclub, tax-free shop. AE, DC, MC, V. $$$*

Kuopio

DINING

Mustalammas. Located near the passenger harbor, Mustalammas has been attractively adapted from a beer cellar and features steaks and basic fish dishes. *Satamakatu 4, tel. 971/262–3494. Reservations advised. AE, DC, MC, V. $$$*

Sampo. The specialty here is muikku. Try the smoked variety. The atmosphere is unpretentious and lively and the location in the town center is convenient enough for a quick meal. *Kauppakatu 13, tel. 971/261–4677. AE, DC, MC, V. $$*

LODGING

Arctia. The most up-to-date and best equipped of local hotels, the Arctia has all the advantages of a lakefront location while being close to the center of town. *Satamakatu 1, 70100, tel. 971/195111, fax 971/195170. 141 rooms with bath or shower. Facilities: sauna, swimming pool, Jacuzzi, solarium, boat rental. AE, DC, MC, V. $$$*

Hotelli Iso-Valkeinen. The rooms are spacious and quiet at this lakeshore property, only 5 kilometers (3 miles) from the town center. *Päiväranta, 70420, tel. 971/364–1444, fax 971/364–1344. 100 rooms with shower. Facilities: 2 restaurants, nightclub, 2 saunas, pool, minigolf, tennis, swimming beach, fishing, boat rental. AE, DC, MC, V. $$*

Rauhalahti. Sports-oriented travelers and families flock to this high-energy setting. Close to the lakeshore and 4.8 kilometers (3 miles) from the town center, Rauhalahti offers lively activities and conveniences for all ages and interests. The hotel has three restaurants, including the tavern-style Vanha Apteekkari—a favorite with locals. *Katiskaniementie 8, 70700, tel. 971/361–1700, fax 971/361–1843. 106 rooms with bath or shower, 13 apartments, and 20 hostel rooms. Facilities: 3 restaurants, saunas, Jacuzzi, solarium, gymnasium, children's playroom, nightclub, tennis, horseback riding, badminton, spa, boat rental. AE, DC, MC, V. $–$$*

Savonlinna

DINING

Rauhalinna. This romantic turn-of-the-century timber villa was built by a general in the Imperial Russian Army. From town it's 16 kilometers (10 miles) by road, 40 minutes by boat. Both the food and atmosphere are old Russian, touched by Finnish accents. *Lehtiniemi, tel. 957/523119. Festival-season reservations required. AE, DC, MC, V. Closed Aug. 7– June 3. $$$*

Majakka. Centrally located, Majakka goes in for home cooking and a family atmosphere. *Satamakatu 11, tel. 957/21456. Festival-season reservations required. AE, DC, V. $$*

Paviljonki. An affiliate of the Savonlinna restaurant school, this convenient spot (just 1 kilometer west of the city) serves homemade Finnish dishes. *Rajalahdenkatu 4, tel. 957/520960. DC, V. $*

LODGING

Savonlinnan Seurahuone. This hotel is near the market and passenger harbor. A new extension opened in 1989. Some older rooms are small. An open-air summer restaurant has view of the harbor and the market. *Kauppatori 4–6, 57130, tel. 957/5731, fax 957/273918. 80 rooms with shower. Facilities: 6 restaurants, lobby bar, saunas, disco, nightclub. AE, DC, MC, V. $$$–$$$$*

Casino Spa. Built in the 1960s and renovated in 1986, the Casino Spa has a bucolic lakeside location on an island linked by a pedestrian bridge to the center of town. *Kylpylaitoksentie, Kasinosaari, 57130, tel. 957/57500, fax 957/272524. 80 rooms with shower. Facilities: restaurant, saunas, pool, marina, spa treatment. AE, DC, MC, V. $$$*

Vuorilinna Summer Hotel. Guests at this modern hotel enjoy the same island setting and facilities as guests at the more-expensive nearby Casino Spa Hotel. *Kasinonsaari, 57130, tel. 957/57500, fax 957/272524. 220 rooms, with shower for every 2 rooms. AE, DC, MC, V. Closed Sept.–May. $–$$*

Tampere

DINING

Tiiliholvi. Fish, meat, and game dishes are the specialties of this romantic converted cellar. *Kauppakatu 10, tel. 931/212–1220. Reservations advised. AE, DC, MC, V. $$$*

Astor. Dark wood and red tones provide romantic environs for trying the renowned reindeer and snow grouse dishes. In the evenings, candlelight and live piano music deepen the cozy ambience. *Aleksis Kivenkatu 26, tel. 931/213–3522. Reservations advised. AE, DC, MC, V. $$*

Bodega Salud. Bodega Salud has a well-earned reputation for Spanish specialties, though it also features such unconventional dishes as grilled alligator, rattlesnake soup, and stewed kangaroo. *Otavalankatu 10, tel. 931/223–5996. Reservations advised. AE, DC, MC, V. $$*

Silakka. Despite the casual and unpretentious atmosphere, Silakka (which means Baltic herring) is well-known for its Finnish fish specialties. *Hatanpään valtatie 1, Koskikeskus, tel. 931/214–9740. DC, MC, V. $$*

LODGING

Ilves. This hotel soars above a newly gentrified area of old warehouses near the city center. It is favored by Americans. *Hatanpään valtatie 1, 33100, tel. 931/212–1212, fax 931/213–2565. 336 rooms with bath or shower, no-smoking floor. Facilities: 3 restaurants, nightclub, gymnasium, saunas, pool, Jacuzzi whirlpool bath. AE, DC, MC, V. $$$$*

Cumulus Koskikatu. Overlooking the tamed rapids of Tammerkoski, Cumulus Koskikatu is central and modern. The Finnair terminal is in the same building. *Koskikatu 5, 33100, tel. 931/242–4111, fax 931/242–4399. 230 rooms with shower. Facilities: restaurant, wine bar, nightclub, saunas, pool. AE, DC, MC, V. $$$*

Domus Summer Hotel. About 3 kilometers (2 miles) from the center of town in the Kaleva district, the standard facilities here are a good value. *Pellervonkatu 9, 33540, tel. 931/550000, fax 931/222–5409. 197 rooms, 85 with shower. Facilities: saunas, pool. MC, V. Closed Sept.–May. $*

FINNISH LAPLAND

Lapland is often called Europe's last wilderness, a region of endless forests, fells, and great silences. So often the arrival of settlers has obliterated all that came before, but here people have walked gently and left the virgin solitude of this country almost unspoiled. Now easily accessible, this Arctic outpost offers the necessary comforts, yet you won't have to go very far to find an almost primordial solitude.

The oldest traces of human habitation in Finland have been found in Lapland, and hoards of Danish, English, and even Arabian coins indicate the existence of trade activities many centuries ago. There are only about 4,500 pure Same still living here; the remainder of the province's population of 220,000 is Finns. Until the 1930s, Lapland was still largely unexploited, still a region where any trip was an expedition. Then the Canadian-owned Petsamo Nickel Company completed the great road (now known as the Arctic Highway) that connects Rovaniemi with the Arctic Sea.

Summer has the blessing of daylight up to 24 hours long and often beautiful weather to go with it. In early fall the colors are so fabulous that the Finns have a special word for it: *ruskaa*. If you can take the intense but dry cold, winter is also fascinating, not only for the Northern Lights but also for such experiences as the reindeer roundups.

In December and January, reindeer owners bring together their herds from all over Lapland province and corral them by the thousands. Sometimes dressed in colorful costumes, the Same (and also many Finns) lasso the reindeer in true Wild West fashion, recognizing their own animals by brand marks on the ears. The roundups are attended by many buyers, for reindeer meat is considered a delicacy and is exported to the south and abroad.

To get to some of the more remote roundups, you may have to travel by taxi plane, though other corrals are near the road, especially around Ivalo, Inari, and Enontekiö. Most Same and northern Finns get there on the motorized sleds that have almost entirely replaced the much more attractive (and silent) reindeer-drawn *pulkka* (a kind of boat-shape sleigh on one runner). In southern Lapland especially, an increasing number of roundups occur in the fall. Finding out exactly when and where a roundup is taking place isn't easy, for much depends on the whims of the weather and the reindeer, so you must check locally.

A few words should be said about the Same, many of whom resent visitors who regard them as merely a tourist attraction. Modern influences (and intermarriage) have changed many aspects of their traditional way of life; for example, the attractive costumes are less frequently seen, except on festive occasions. The young, especially, have been affected by the changes, and many of them are far more interested in becoming teachers, lawyers, or engineers than in breeding reindeer or hunting from their remote homesteads. But most prefer to go about their daily lives, minding their own business. The Lady Day church festival in Enontekiö in March is a particularly colorful event, attended by many Same in their most brilliant costumes and usually featuring reindeer racing or lassoing competitions.

The experienced traveler who would like to roam through the wilds for days on end without meeting a fellow human being can still do so without any problem at all. Be warned, however, that weather here can change very fast. Always seek local advice and let your hotel and friends know where you're heading and how long you intend to be away.

An attractive alternative is provided by organized canoeing or hiking trips with nights in huts or tents in the wilderness.

Getting Around

Rovaniemi is the best base for traveling around the Arctic area. It connects with Helsinki and the south by road, rail, and air links; there is even a car-train from Helsinki. Within the area, driving is the easiest way to get around, although regular bus service connects most centers. There are also daily flights from Rovaniemi to Ivalo.

Guided Tours

Friendly Finland Tours (tel. 90/18261) features an escorted five-day "North Cape" tour in summer or a five-day "Winter's Tale" tour out of Helsinki. You can get details from the Finnish Tourist Board's overseas offices (*see* Important Addresses and Numbers *in* Helsinki, *above*) or at Eteläesplanadi 4, 00130 Helsinki (tel. 90/4030–1211).

Tourist Information

Ivalo (Ivalontie 12, 99800, tel. 9697/662521).
Rovaniemi (Koskikatu 1, 96200, tel. 960/356–2096). For further information on the region, contact **Lapland Travel** (Maakuntakatu 10, 96200, tel. 960/346052).
Saariselkä (Tunturihotelli, PL 22, 99831, tel. 9697/8111).
Sodankylä (Jäämerentie 9, 99600, tel. 9693/613474).

Exploring Lapland

Rovaniemi

Your best launching point is the town of **Rovaniemi,** where the Ounas and Kemi rivers meet almost on the Arctic Circle. Rovaniemi is the so-called Gateway to Lapland and the administrative hub and communications center of the province.

If you're expecting an Arctic shanty town, you're in for a surprise. Rovaniemi was nearly razed by the retreating German army in 1944, so what you'll see today is a modern city strongly influenced by Alvar Aalto's architecture. The old way of life is preserved in museums. During the process of rebuilding, the population rose from 8,000 to around 34,000, so be prepared for a contemporary city on the edge of the wilderness, with various amenities and some incredible architecture—notably **Lappia Hall,** the concert and congress center that also houses the world's northernmost professional theater, designed by Aalto.

After collecting information from the tourist office, find a window table in the restaurant of the nearby **Pohjanhovi Hotel,** and contemplate your next moves while gazing at the swiftly flowing Kemi River.

You can get a good instant introduction to the region and its natural history at the **Museum of the Province of Lapland** at the **Arktikum** (Arctic Research Center), located 1 kilometer (½ mile) north of Lappia House. The collection also includes exhibits of Same culture. *Pohjoisranta 4, Rovaniemi, tel. 960/317840. Admission: FIM 45 adults, FIM 10 children. Open Tues.–Sun., 10–6.*

You'll get more of a feel for the living past from the **Pöykkölä Museum,** located in 18th-century farm buildings just 3 kilometers (2 miles) from the town center. *Admission: FIM 5 adults, FIM 2 children. Open June–Aug., Tues.–Sun. 1–4. Bus service available.*

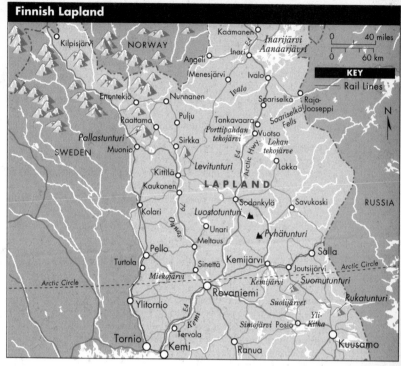

Finnish Lapland

Arctic Highway

The Arctic Highway (Highway 4) is the main artery of central and north-ern Lapland; you'll follow it north for most of this tour. Eight kilo-meters (5 miles) north of Rovaniemi, right on the Arctic Circle, is **Santa Claus's Village,** where gifts can be bought for shipping any time of year, with a special Santa Claus Land stamp. For most visitors, however, the main attractions are Santa Claus, the mountains of mail that pour in from all over, and the chance to mail postcards home from the special Arctic Circle post office. Yes, all of it gets answered. *Admission free. Open June–Aug., daily 8–8; Sept.–May, daily 10–5.*

Continue north, through the village of Vuotso, to **Tankavaara,** the most accessible and best developed of several gold-panning areas. The **Gold Museum** tells the century-old story of Lapland's hardy fortune seek-ers. For a small fee (FIM 20 per hr), authentic prospectors will show you how to sift gold dust and tiny nuggets from the dirt of an ice-cold stream. You can keep what you find, but don't expect to be able to re-tire early. *Summer admission: FIM 35 adults, FIM 10 children. Open June–Aug. 15, daily 9–6; Aug. 16–Oct., daily 9–5. Winter admission: FIM 20 adults, FIM 5 children. Open Nov.–May, daily 10–4.*

Thirty kilometers (19 miles) north of Tankavaara is the holiday cen-ter of **Saariselkä,** which has a variety of accommodations and makes a sensible base from which to set off on a trip (alone or in a group) into the true wilderness; during the snowy months, this is where to find the finest cross-country and downhill skiing in Finland. There are marked trails through forests and over fells where nothing much has changed since the last Ice Age and where you can experience the time-less silence of the Arctic landscape. More than 2,500 square kilometers (965 square miles) of this magnificent area has been named the **Urho Kekkonen National Park.**

Northern Lapland

Just south of the village of Ivalo, the highway passes the **Ivalo River** (Ivalojoki). Canoeing trips are organized on its fast waters down to Lake Inari, returning by bus. The village of **Ivalo** is the main center for northern Lapland. However, except for a first-class hotel, an airport, and the standard amenities of a modern community, it has little to offer the tourist in search of a wilderness experience.

The huge island-studded expanses of **Lake Inari** (Inarinjärvi), north of Ivalo, offer endless possibilities for wilderness exploration. It is a beautiful 40-kilometer (25-mile) drive northwest from Ivalo, along the lakeshore, to **Inari.** This is a good base for summer boat excursions. The **Sami Museum,** on the village outskirts, covers all facets of Same culture. *Admission: FIM 20 adults, FIM 5 children. Open June 1–Aug. 10, daily 8–10; Aug. 11–30, daily 8–8; Sept. 1–20, daily 9–3:30. Call ahead in winter (tel. 9697/51014).*

In recent years, a growing number of small holiday villages have blossomed near Inari and to the north of it, usually with a small restaurant and attached shop. Conveniences are simple, but the locations are often magnificent and bring you very close to the true pulse of Lapland. Usually there will be a boat at your disposal, fishing possibilities, and the experience of preparing your own sauna. From Kaamanen, north of Inari, a side road leads to **Sevettijärvi,** home of the Skolt Lapps, and eventually into Norway.

It is an attractive drive back south from Inari to **Menesjärvi** along a relatively new secondary road that passes through a wilderness of forest and swamp. Take every opportunity to leave your car and do some walking; it's the only way to experience the vastness of these Arctic spaces. The hills get gentler and the ride less dramatic as you continue south to Levitunturi, the last of the gently sloping fells before you reach the banks of the Ounas River and return to Rovaniemi via Highway 79.

Dining and Lodging

For details and price-category definitions, *see* Dining and Lodging *in* Staying in Finland, *above.*

Inari
LODGING
Kultahovi. This recently renovated old inn is located on the wooded banks of a swiftly flowing river. *99870 Inari, tel. 9697/51221, fax 9697/51250. 29 rooms with shower. Facilities: restaurant, saunas. DC, MC, V. $$*

Ivalo
LODGING
Hotel Ivalo. Fully modern and equipped, the Hotel Ivalo is right on the riverside about a kilometer (½ mile) from the village center. One of its two restaurants serves Lapland specialties, including *poronkäristys,* a reindeer casserole. *Ivalontie 34, 99800 Ivalo, tel. 9697/688111, fax 9697/661905. 94 rooms with bath or shower. Facilities: 2 restaurants, saunas, pool, boating. AE, DC, MC, V. $*

Kultahippu. Here is the home of the "northernmost nightclub in Finland." In addition to that facility (and its traffic), you will find cozy guest rooms in the heart of Ivalo, next to the Ivalo River. *Petsamontie 1, 99800 Ivalo, tel. 9697/661825, fax 9697/662510. 30 rooms with* *bath (7 with saunas). Facilities: restaurant, nightclub, sauna, Jacuzzi, swimming beach. AE, DC, MC, V. $*

Levitunturi

LODGING

Levitunturi. Built in traditional log style at the foot of the fells, Levitunturi is a particularly well-equipped and modern tourist complex. *99130 Sirkka, tel. 9694/641301, fax 9694/641434. 80 rooms with shower. Facilities: restaurant, café, no-smoking floor, saunas, pool, Jacuzzi, squash, gymnasium, tennis, boating, cross-country skiing, spa amenities. AE, DC, MC, V. $–$$*

Luostotunturi

LODGING

Arctia Hotel Luosto. Situated amid the fells southeast of Sodankylä, this small timber hotel has a traditional feel while still being modern and comfortable. *99600 Luostotunturi, tel. 9693/624400, fax 9693/624410. 54 cabins. Facilities: saunas, boating, cross-country skiing. AE, DC, MC, V. $$*

Rovaniemi

DINING

Fransmanni. Located at the Vakunna Hotel in the heart of Rovaniemi, the Fransmanni specializes in international, Finnish, and Same dishes. *Koskikatu 4, tel. 960/332211. Reservations advised. AE, DC, MC, V. $$*

Ounasvaaran Pirtit. The fare at this town favorite is traditional Finnish and Same food. Try the sautéed salmon with cream. *Antinmukka 4, tel. 960/369056. Reservations required; owner recommends that patrons order ahead if possible. AE, DC, MC, V. $$*

LODGING

Hotel Lapponia. Opened in 1992, Hotel Lapponia is one of the newest luxury hotels in Lapland. *Koskikatu 23, 96200 Rovaniemi, tel. 960/33661, fax 960/313770. 151 rooms with shower, 8 with sauna, and 8 with Jacuzzi. Facilities: 4 restaurants, pub, nightclub, lobby bar, saunas. AE, DC, MC, V. $$$*

Vaakuna. Opened in January 1992, the Vaakuna is a recent addition to the high-class hotel scene. The club here is reportedly the center of Rovaniemi nightlife. *Koskikatu 4, 96200 Rovaniemi, tel. 960/332211, fax 960/332–2199. 159 rooms (all doubles) with shower. Facilities: 4 restaurants, saunas, nightclub, pub, gymnasium. AE, DC, MC, V. $$$*

Hotelli Pohjanhovi. With its pleasant location overlooking the Kemi River, this hotel is an old favorite with travelers to the north. It has been expanded and modernized over the years. *Pohjanpuistikko 2, 96200 Rovaniemi, tel. 960/33711, fax 960/313997. 216 rooms with bath or shower. Some rooms in neighboring building. Facilities: no-smoking floor, saunas, pool, boating, disco. AE, DC, MC, V. $$*

Rudolf. Completely renovated, renamed, and under new management since spring 1995, the former Gasthof is still a comfortable small hotel with a traditional restaurant. *Koskikatu 41, 96100 Rovaniemi, tel. 960/342–3222, fax 960/342–3226. 41 rooms with shower. Facilities: restaurant, saunas, pool, no-smoking floor. AE, DC, MC, V. $$*

Sky Hotel Ounasvaara. The views of the town and the surrounding area are fantastic from this tranquil, full-service hotel. Since the Sky Hotel is perched on a hilltop 3 kilometers (2 miles) from the center of town, it's best if you have a car. *Hiihtokeskus, 96400 Rovaniemi, tel. 960/346001, fax 960/318789. 69 rooms with shower, 47 with sauna. Facilities: restaurant, saunas, cross-country skiing. AE, DC, MC, V. $$*

Oppipoika. As a member of the Hotel School of Rovaniemi, the focus here is on service. The rooms are spacious and comfortable, but the real reason to come here is for the food: chef Tapio Sointu has created the "Lappi à la Carte" program, featuring a variety of Lapland specialties. *Korkalonkatu 33, 96200 Rovaniemi, tel. 960/388–8111, fax 960/346969. 40 rooms with bath or shower. Facilities: restaurant, saunas, pool. AE, DC, MC, V. $*

Saariselkä
LODGING
Riekonlinna. This is the latest and best-equipped addition to this developing tourist complex on the fringes of the wilderness fells. *99830 Saariselkä, tel. 9697/668601, fax 9697/668602. 124 rooms with shower. Facilities: saunas, boating, squash, cross-country skiing. AE, DC, MC, V. $$$*

Tankavaara
DINING
Wanhan Waskoolimiehen Kahvila. Same specialties are featured in this attractive café and restaurant; try the gold prospector's reindeer beefsteak with mashed potatoes. *Tankavaara Gold Village, tel. 9693/626158. AE, DC, MC, V. $$*

10 France

THE FRENCH ARE a Mediterranean people—temperamental and spontaneous, closer to the Spanish and Italians than to the northern Europeans. At the same time, they are heirs to the Cartesian tradition of logic ("I think, therefore I am"), as well as being inveterate theorizers. Their reluctance to take a shortcut to an obvious solution often frustrates English-speaking pragmatists.

The essence of French *savoir-vivre* is simplicity. Everyday things count: eating, drinking, talking, dressing, shopping. Daily rituals are meant to be enjoyed. Dining is the best example. The French don't like rushing their meals. They plan them in advance, painstakingly prepare them, anticipate them over an aperitif, admire the loving presentation of each dish, and savor each mouthful. The pace is unhurried, and the wine flows steadily.

French towns and villages are quietly attractive and historic. Chances are that the ornate *mairie,* or *hôtel de ville* (town hall), has been there since the Revolution, and the church or cathedral since the Middle Ages. The main streets tend to be lined with sturdy trees planted before living memory. The 20th century is kept firmly at bay. Modern buildings—such as supermarkets—are banished to the outskirts or obliged to fit architecturally.

There is a bewildering variety of man-made marvels in France. Southern France is rich in Roman remains; western France is dotted with Romanesque churches from the 10th and 11th centuries. Gothic architecture was born in the Ile de France around Paris: Huge cathedrals like Notre Dame rank among the world's finest. The Renaissance yielded the sumptuous Loire châteaus and the palace of Fontainebleau, paving the way for the haughty Baroque of Versailles.

France boasts as much natural as man-made variety. You'll find ski slopes and towering peaks in the Alps and Pyrenees; beaches and cliffs in Brittany or along the Mediterranean; limitless horizons beyond the golden grain fields of the Beauce or the misty plains of the north; haunting evergreen forests stretching from the Ardennes down to the Midi (south); marsh and canals in "Green Venice," the Marais Poitevin; lush, softly lighted valleys along the Seine and the Loire; steep, climbing terraces above the Rhône; and wherever you go, the swirl and sway of ripening vines.

Whatever you've heard, France is a welcoming country. Don't be misled by superficial coldness: The French are a formal people who don't go out of their way to speak to strangers (except in anger). Above all, don't suppose that all Frenchmen are like Parisians—most are more approachable and friendly. Still, deep down, most of the French are chauvinists who are proud of *La douce France,* worship Napoléon, and feel that the "Liberty, Equality, Fraternity" motto of the French Revolution confers moral superiority upon their country.

ESSENTIAL INFORMATION

Before You Go

When to Go

June and September, free of the midsummer crowds, are the best months to be in France. June offers the advantage of long daylight hours, while slightly cheaper prices and frequent Indian summers (often lasting well into October) make September attractive. The second half of July and all of August are spoiled by inflated prices and huge crowds on the beaches, and the heat can be stifling in southern France. Paris, though pleasantly deserted, can be stuffy in August, too.

The ski season in the Alps and Pyrenees lasts from Christmas through Easter—steer clear of February (school vacation time) if you can. Anytime between March and November offers a good chance to soak up the sun on the Riviera. The weather in Paris and the Loire is unappealing before Easter. If you're dreaming of Paris in the springtime, May (not April) is your best bet.

CLIMATE

France's climate changes regionally. North of the Loire (including Paris), France has a northern European climate—cold winters, pleasant if unpredictable summers, and frequent rain. Southern France has a Mediterranean climate: mild winters, long, hot summers, and sunshine throughout the year. The more Continental climate of eastern and central France is a mixture of these two extremes: Winters can be very cold and summers mighty hot. France's Atlantic coast has a temperate climate even south of the Loire, with the exception of the much warmer Biarritz.

The following are the average daily maximum and minimum temperatures for Paris and Marseille.

Paris

Jan.	43F	6C	May	68F	20C	Sept.	70F	21C
	34	1		49	10		53	12
Feb.	45F	7C	June	73F	23C	Oct.	60F	16C
	34	1		55	13		46	8
Mar.	54F	12C	July	76F	25C	Nov.	50F	10C
	39	4		58	15		40	5
Apr.	60F	16C	Aug.	75F	24C	Dec.	44F	7C
	43	6		58	15		36	2

Marseille

Jan.	50F	10C	May	71F	22C	Sept.	77F	25C
	35	2		52	11		58	15
Feb.	53F	12C	June	79F	26C	Oct.	68F	20C
	36	2		58	14		51	10
Mar.	59F	15C	July	84F	29C	Nov.	58F	14C
	41	5		63	17		41	5
Apr.	64F	18C	Aug.	83F	28C	Dec.	52F	11C
	46	8		63	17		37	3

Currency

The unit of French currency is the franc, subdivided into 100 centimes. Bills are issued in denominations of 50, 100, 200, and 500 francs (frs); coins are 5, 10, 20, and 50 centimes and 1, 2, 5, 10, and 20 francs. The small, copper-color 5-, 10-, and 20-centime coins have considerable nuisance value, but they can be used for tips in bars and cafés.

International credit cards and traveler's checks are widely accepted throughout France, except in rural areas. At press time (spring 1995), the dollar bought 4.60 francs, and the pound sterling, 7.77 francs.

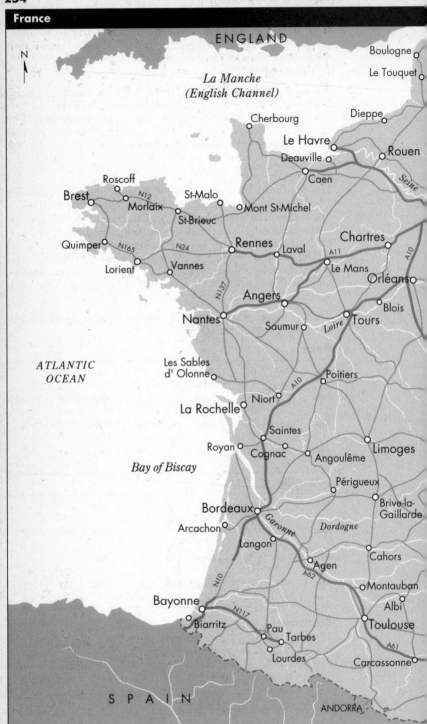

Calais

BELGIUM

Lille
A26

Arras
Amiens

Cambrai
St. Quentin

LUXEMBOURG

Beauvais

Laon

A16

A1

Reims

Metz

Corsica

Calvi

Bastia

Corte

Ajaccio

N198

Bonifacio

Paris

Châlons-sur-
Marne

Nancy
Strasbourg

GERMANY

Fontainebleau

Troyes

A5

Sens

A31

Colmar

Mulhouse

Auxerre

Belfort

A6

Dijon

A36

Besançon

Bourges

Nevers

Beaune

SWITZERLAND

Autun

A71

Saône

Montluçon

Mâcon

Bourg-en-
Bresse

Clermont-
Ferrand

Lyon

Rhône

ITALY

A72

A43

Chambéry

Aurillac

Le Puy

Grenoble

Rhône

Rodez

Montélimar

Gap

Millau

Avignon

Nîmes

Montpellier

Aix-en-Provence

A8

Monte Carlo
Nice
Cannes

A9

Narbonne

Marseille

Toulon

A19

Perpignan

0   50 mi

0   75 km

Mediterranean Sea

Corsica

What It Will Cost

Hotel and restaurant prices compensate for travel expenses. Prices are highest in Paris, on the Riviera, and in the Alps during the ski season. But even in these areas, you can find pleasant accommodations and excellent food for surprisingly reasonable prices.

All taxes must be included in posted prices in France. The initials TTC (*toutes taxes comprises,* which means taxes included) are sometimes included on price lists but, strictly speaking, they are superfluous. Restaurant and hotel prices must *by law* include taxes and service charges: If they are tacked onto your bill as additional items, you should complain.

SAMPLE PRICES

Prices vary greatly depending on the region, proximity to tourist sights, and—believe it or not—whether you're sitting down or standing up in a café! Here are a few samples: cup of coffee, 5–10 francs; glass of beer, 10–13 francs; soft drink, 10–15 francs; ham sandwich, 14–20 francs; 1-mile taxi ride, 35 francs.

Visas

Citizens of the United States, Canada, and Britain do not require a visa to visit France.

Customs on Arrival

There are two levels of duty-free allowance for travelers entering France: one for goods obtained (tax paid) within another EU country and the other for goods obtained anywhere outside the EU or for goods purchased in a duty-free shop within the EU.

In the first category, you may import duty-free: 300 cigarettes, or 150 cigarillos, or 75 cigars, or 400 grams of tobacco; 5 liters of table wine and (1) 1½ liters of alcohol over 22% volume (most spirits), (2) 3 liters of alcohol under 22% by volume (fortified or sparkling wine), or (3) 3 more liters of table wine; 90 milliliters of perfume; 375 milliliters of toilet water; and other goods to the value of 2,400 francs (620 frs for those under 15).

In the second category, you may import duty-free: 200 cigarettes, or 100 cigarillos, or 50 cigars, or 250 grams of tobacco (these allowances are doubled if you live outside Europe); 2 liters of wine and (1) 1 liter of alcohol over 22% volume, (2) 2 liters of alcohol under 22% volume, or (3) 2 more liters of table wine; 60 milliliters of perfume; 250 milliliters of toilet water; and other goods to the value of 300 francs (150 frs for those under 15).

Language

The French study English for a minimum of four years at school, and although few are fluent, their English is probably better than the French of most Americans. English is widely understood in major tourist areas, and in most hotels there is likely to be at least one person who can converse with you. Even if your own French is rusty, try to master a few words: The French will greatly appreciate that you are at least making an effort to speak their language.

Getting Around

By Car

ROAD CONDITIONS

France's roads are classified into five types, numbered and prefixed *A, N, D, C,* or *V.* Roads marked *A* (Autoroutes) are expressways. There are excellent links between Paris and most French cities, but poor ones between the provinces (the principal exceptions being A62 between Bordeaux and Toulouse and A9/A8 the length of the Mediterranean coast). It is often difficult to avoid Paris when crossing France—this need not cause too many problems if you steer clear of the rush hours (7–9:30 AM and 4:30–7:30 PM). A *péage* (toll) must be paid on most expressways: The rate varies but can be steep. The N (Route Nationale) roads—which are sometimes divided highways—and D (Route Départementale) roads are usually wide and fast, and driving along them can be a real pleasure. Don't be daunted by smaller (C and V) roads, either. The yellow regional Michelin maps—on sale throughout France—are invaluable.

RULES OF THE ROAD

You may use your own driver's license in France, but you must be able to prove you have third-party insurance. Drive on the right, and be aware of the French tradition of yielding to drivers coming from the right. Seat belts are obligatory for all passengers, and children under 12 may not travel in the front seat. Speed limits are 130 kph (80 mph) on expressways, 110 kph (70 mph) on divided highways, 90 kph (55 mph) on other roads, 50 kph (30 mph) in towns. French drivers break these limits and police dish out hefty on-the-spot fines with equal abandon.

PARKING

Parking is a nightmare in Paris and often difficult in other large towns. Meters and ticket machines (pay and display) are common: Make sure you have a supply of 1-franc coins. Parking is free during August in most of Paris, but be sure to check the signs. In smaller towns, parking may be permitted on one side of the street only—alternating every two weeks—so pay attention to signs.

GASOLINE

Fuel is more expensive on expressways and in rural areas. Don't let your tank get too low—you can go for many miles in the country without passing a gas station—and keep an eye on pump prices as you go. These vary enormously; anything from 5.50 to 6.25 francs per liter.

BREAKDOWNS

If your car breaks down on an expressway, go to the nearest roadside emergency telephone and call the breakdown service. If you have a breakdown anywhere else, find the nearest garage or contact the police (dial 17).

By Train

SNCF, the French national railroad, is generally recognized as Europe's best national train service: fast, punctual, comfortable, and comprehensive. The high-speed TGVs (trains à grande vitesse) with a top speed of 190 mph, are the best domestic trains, heading southeast from Paris to Lyon, the Riviera, and Switzerland; west to Nantes; southwest to Bordeaux; and north to Lille. Most TGV trains require passengers to pay a supplement—usually 20–40 francs, but a bit more during peak periods. Also, you need a seat reservation—easily obtained at the ticket window or from a machine. Seat reservations are reassuring but seldom necessary on other French trains, except at holiday times.

You must punch your train ticket in one of the orange machines you'll encounter alongside platforms. Slide your ticket in faceup and wait for a "clink" sound. (The small yellow tickets and automatic ticket barriers used for most suburban Paris trains are similar to those in the métro/RER.) The ticket collectors will present you with an on-the-spot fine of 100 francs if your ticket hasn't been validated before boarding.

If you take an overnight train, you have a choice between wagons-lits (private sleeping cars), which are expensive, and *couchettes* (bunks), which sleep six to a compartment in second class and four to a compartment in first class (sheet and pillow provided) and are more affordable (around 89 frs). Ordinary compartment seats do not pull together to enable you to lie down. In summer there are special night trains from Paris to Spain and the Riviera geared for a younger market, with discos and bars.

FARES

Various reduced-fare passes are available from major train stations in France and from SNCF travel agents. If you are planning a lot of train travel, buy a special **France Vacances** card (around 1,400 frs for nine days). Families and couples are also eligible for big discounts. So are senior citizens (over 60) and young people (under 26), who qualify for different discount schemes (**Carte Vermeil** and **Carrissimo**). You can get 50% discounts in blue periods (most of the time) and 20% most of the rest of the time (white periods: noon Friday to noon Saturday; 3 PM Sunday to noon Monday). On major holidays (red periods) there are no reductions. Calendars are available at stations. The **Carte Kiwi 4 x 4** (280 frs) enables children and up to four accompanying adults to make four trips at half price.

By Plane

Domestic flights from Paris, which are on **Air Inter,** leave from Orly. Contact your travel agent or Air Inter (tel. 45–46–90–00). Train service may be faster when you consider time spent getting to and from the airport.

By Bus

Because of the excellent train service, long-distance buses are rare; they're found mainly where train service is scarce. Bus tours are organized by the **SNCF** and other tourist organizations, such as **Horizons Européens:** Ask for their brochures at any major travel agent, or contact France-Tourisme at 3 rue d'Alger, 75001 Paris, tel. 42–61–85–50.

By Boat

France has Europe's most extensive inland waterway system. Canal and river vacations are popular: Visitors can either take an organized cruise or rent a boat and plan their own leisurely route. Contact a travel agent for details or ask for a "Tourisme Fluvial" brochure in any French tourist office. Some of the most picturesque stretches are in Brittany, Burgundy, and the Midi. The Canal du Midi between Toulouse and Sète, constructed in the 17th century, is a historic marvel. Contact the French national tourist offices or **Bourgogne Voies Navigables** (1 quai de la République, 89000 Auxerre, tel. 86–52–18–99).

By Bicycle

With plenty of wide, empty roads and rolling countryside, there is no shortage of suitable biking terrain. The French are great cycling enthusiasts—witness the Tour de France. For around 40 francs a day bikes can be rented from 260 train stations; you need to show your passport and leave a deposit of about 500 francs (unless you have a Visa or MasterCard). Bikes may be taken as accompanied luggage from any station in France; some trains in rural areas don't even charge for this. Tourist offices supply details on the more than 200 local shops that rent bikes, or you can get the SNCF brochure "Guide du Train et du Vélo" from any station.

Staying in France

Telephones

Because of a need for more telephone lines, in October 1996 France-Télécom will add two digits to all phone numbers; the digits will be determined by zone: Paris and the Ile de France, 01 (replacing the 16 + 1); the northwest, 02; the northeast, 03; the southeast, 04; and the southwest, 05.

LOCAL CALLS

The French telephone system is modern and efficient. Phone booths are plentiful; they are nearly always available at post offices and cafés. A local call in France costs 80 centimes per three minutes; half-price rates apply between 9:30 PM and 8 AM and between 1:30 PM Saturday and 8 AM Monday.

Some French pay phones take 1-, 2-, and 5-franc coins (1-fr minimum), but most phones are now operated by *télécartes* (phone cards), sold in post offices, métro stations, and cafés sporting a red TABAC (tobacco) sign outside (cost: 40 frs for 50 units; 96 frs for 120).

French phone numbers have eight digits; a code is required only when calling the Paris region from the provinces (dial 16–1, then the number) and for calling the provinces from Paris (dial 16, then the number).

INTERNATIONAL CALLS

Dial 19 and wait for the tone, then dial the country code, area code, and number. Calls from your hotel room are very expensive. To reach an **AT&T** long-distance operator, dial 19–0011; for **MCI,** dial 19–0019; and for **Sprint,** 19–0087. Dial 12 for local operators. France's country code is 33.

Mail

POSTAL RATES

Airmail letters to the United States and Canada cost 4.30 francs for 20 grams. Letters to the United Kingdom cost 2.80 francs for up to 20 grams, as do letters within France. Postcards cost 2.40 francs within France and if sent to EU countries (2.40 frs for surface or 3.80 frs for airmail to North America). Stamps can be bought in post offices and tabacs.

RECEIVING MAIL

If you're uncertain where you'll be staying, have mail sent to American Express (if you're a cardmember) or Thomas Cook; mail labeled "poste restante" is also accepted at most French post offices.

Precaution

Beware of thieves! Though no one likes to talk about it, burglaries, once confined to Paris and other major cities, have spread into the countryside.

Shopping

VAT REFUNDS

A number of shops, particularly large stores in cities and holiday resorts, offer value-added tax (VAT) refunds to foreign shoppers. You are entitled to an export discount of 13% or 23%, depending on the item purchased, though this often applies only if your purchases in the same store reach a minimum 2,800 francs (for residents of EU countries) or 1,200 francs (all others).

Shop prices are clearly marked and bargaining is not a way of life. Still, at outdoor markets, flea markets, and in antiques stores, you can try your luck. If you're thinking of buying several items in these places, you have nothing to lose in cheerfully suggesting to the proprietor, *"Vous me faites un prix?"* ("How about a discount?").

Hours

Banks are open weekdays 9:30–4:30, with variations. Most close for an hour to an hour and a half for lunch.

Museums are closed one day a week (usually Tuesday) and on national holidays. Usual times are from 9:30 to 5 or 6. Many museums close for lunch (noon–2); on Sunday many are open afternoons only.

Shops in big towns are open from 9 or 9:30 to 7 or 8 without a lunch break and have recently begun to open on Sunday. Smaller shops often open earlier and close later, but take a lengthy lunch break (1–4). This siesta-type schedule is more typical in the south of France. Corner grocery stores frequently stay open until around 10 PM.

National Holidays

January 1; April 8 (Easter Monday); May 1 (Labor Day); May 8 (VE Day); May 26 (Ascension); May 27 (Pentecost Monday); July 14 (Bastille Day); August 15 (Assumption); November 1 (All Saints' Day); November 11 (Armistice); December 25.

Dining

Eating in France is serious business, at least for two of the three meals each day. For a light meal, try an informal brasserie (steak and french fries remain the classic), a picnic (a baguette with ham, cheese, or pâté is a perfect combination), or one of the fast-food places that have sprung up in urban areas during recent years.

French breakfasts are relatively modest—strong coffee, fruit juice if you insist, and croissants. International chain hotels are likely to offer American or English breakfasts, but in cafés you will probably be out of luck if this is what you want.

MEALTIMES

Dinner is the main meal and usually begins at 8. Lunch begins at 12:30 or 1.

WHAT TO WEAR

Jacket and tie are recommended for **$$$$** and **$$$** restaurants, and at some of the more stylish **$$** restaurants as well. When in doubt, it's best to dress up. Otherwise casual dress is appropriate.

PRECAUTIONS

Tap water is perfectly safe, though not always very palatable (least of all in Paris). Mineral water is a good alternative; there is a vast choice of *eaux plates* (plain) as well as *eaux gazeuses* (fizzy).

RATINGS

Prices are per person and include a first course, main course, and dessert plus tax (18.6%) and service (which are always included in displayed prices), but not wine. Highly recommended restaurants are indicated by a star ★.

CATEGORY	COST: MAJOR CITY	COST: OTHER AREAS
$$$$	over 550 francs	over 500 francs
$$$	300–550 francs	250–500 francs
$$	175–300 francs	125–250 francs
$	under 175 francs	under 125 francs

Lodging

France has a wide range of accommodations, from rambling old village inns to stylishly converted châteaus. Prices must, by law, be posted at the hotel entrance and should include taxes and service. Prices are always by room, not per person. Breakfast is not always included, but you are usually expected to have it and often are charged for it whether you partake or not. In smaller rural hotels, you may be expected to have your evening meal at the hotel, too.

The quality of rooms, particularly in older properties, is uneven; if you don't like the room you're given, ask to see another. If you want a private bathroom, state your preference for *douche* (shower) or *baignoire* (tub)—the latter always costing more. Tourist offices in major train stations can reserve hotels for you, and so can tourist offices in most towns.

HOTELS

Hotels are officially classified from one-star to four-star-deluxe. France has—but is not dominated by—big hotel chains: Examples in the upper price bracket include Frantel, Holiday Inn, Novotel, and Sofitel. The Ibis and Climat de France chains are more moderately priced. Chain hotels, as a rule, lack atmosphere, with the following exceptions:

Logis de France. This is a group of small, inexpensive hotels that can be relied on for comfort, character, and regional cuisine. Look for its distinctive yellow and green sign. The Logis de France paperback guide is widely available in bookshops (around 75 frs) or from Logis de France (83 av. d'Italie, 75013 Paris, tel. 45–84–83–84, fax 44–24–08–74). **France-Accueil** is another chain of friendly low-cost hotels. You can get a free booklet from France-Accueil (163 av. d'Italie, 75013 Paris, tel. 45–83–04–22, fax 45–86–49–82).

Relais et Châteaux. You can stay in style at any of the 150 members of this prestigious chain of converted châteaus and manor houses. Each hotel is distinctively furnished, provides top cuisine, and often stands on spacious grounds. A booklet listing members is available in bookshops or from Relais et Châteaux (15 rue Galvani, 75017 Paris, tel. 45–72–90–00, fax 45–72–90–30).

RENTALS

Gîtes Ruraux offers families or small groups economical stays in a furnished cottage, chalet, or apartment. These can be rented by the week or month. Contact either the **Fédération Nationale des Gîtes de France** (35 rue Godot-de-Mauroy, 75009 Paris, tel. 49–70–75–75, fax 49–70–75–76; indicate the region that interests you), or the French Government Tourist Office in New York or London (*see* Visitor Info *in* Chapter 1).

BED-AND-BREAKFASTS

Known as *chambres d'hôte*, these are increasingly popular in rural areas and can be a great bargain. Check local tourist offices for details.

YOUTH HOSTELS

With inexpensive hotel accommodations in France so easy to find, you may want to think twice before staying in a youth hostel—especially as standards of French hostels don't quite approximate those in neighboring countries. Contact **Fédération Unie des Auberges de Jeunesse** (27 rue Pajol, 75018 Paris, tel. 44–89–87–27, fax 44–89–87–10).

The French Government Tourist Offices in London and New York publish extensive lists of agencies specializing in villa rentals. You can also write to **Rent-a-Villa Ltd.** (3 W. 51st St., New York, NY 10019) or, in France, **Interhome** (15 av. Jean-Aicard, 75011 Paris).

French campsites have a good reputation for organization and amenities but are crowded in July and August. Many campsites welcome reservations, and in summer, it makes sense to book in advance. A guide to France's campsites is published by the **Fédération Française de Camping et de Caravaning** (78 rue de Rivoli, 75004 Paris, tel. 42–72–84–08). They'll send it to you directly for 70 francs, plus shipping.

Prices are for standard double rooms and include tax (18.6%) and service charges. Highly recommended lodgings are indicated by a star ★.

CATEGORY	COST: MAJOR CITY	COST: OTHER AREAS
$$$$	over 1,200 francs	over 800 francs
$$$	750–1,200 francs	500–800 francs
$$	450–750 francs	250–500 francs
$	under 450 francs	under 250 francs

Tipping

The check in a bar or restaurant will include service, but it is customary to leave some small change unless you're dissatisfied. The amount varies, from 30 centimes for a beer to a few francs after a meal. Tip taxi drivers and hairdressers about 10%. Give ushers in theaters 1–2 francs. Cloakroom attendants will expect nothing if there is a sign saying POURBOIRE INTERDIT (tipping forbidden); otherwise give them 5 francs. Washroom attendants usually get 5 francs—a sum that is often posted. Bellhops should get 10 francs per item.

If you stay in a moderately priced hotel for more than two or three days, it is customary to leave something for the chambermaid—perhaps 10 francs per day. Expect to tip 10 francs for room service—but nothing is expected if breakfast is routinely served in your room.

Service station attendants get nothing for giving you gas or oil, and 5 or 10 francs for checking tires. Train and airport porters get a fixed sum (6–10 frs) per bag. Museum guides should get 5–10 francs after a guided tour. It is standard practice to tip guides (and bus drivers) after an excursion.

PARIS

Arriving and Departing

By Plane

International flights arrive at either Charles de Gaulle Airport (Roissy), 24 kilometers (15 miles) northeast of Paris, or at Orly Airport, 16 kilometers (10 miles) south of the city.

From Charles de Gaulle: Buses operated by **Air France** leave every 15 minutes from 5:40 AM to 11 PM. The fare is 48 francs and the trip takes 40 minutes (up to 1½ hours during rush hour). You arrive at the Arc de Triomphe or Porte Maillot, on the Right Bank by the Hôtel Concorde-Lafayette. Alternatively, the **Roissybus,** operated by Paris Transport Authority (RATP), runs directly to and from rue Scribe at the Paris Opera every 15 minutes and costs 35 francs.

From Orly: Buses operated by **Air France** leave every 12 minutes from 6 AM to 11 PM and arrive at the Air France terminal near Les Invalides on the Left Bank. The fare is 44 francs, and the trip takes between 30 and 60 minutes, depending on traffic. RATP also runs the **Orlybus** to and from Denfert-Rochereau and Orly every 15 minutes for 30 francs.

Both airports have their own train stations, from which you can take the RER service to Paris. The advantages of this are speed, price (44 frs to Paris from Charles de Gaulle in Roissy, 50 frs from Orly on the shuttle-train **Orlyval**), and the fact that the RER trains link up directly with the métro system. The disadvantage is having to lug your bags around. Taxi fares from airports to Paris range from 150 to 230 francs, with a 5-franc surcharge per bag. A new **Paris Airports Service** takes you by 8-passenger van to your destination in Paris from de Gaulle: 140 francs (one person) or 170 francs (two); Orly: 110 francs (one), 130 francs (two); less for groups. To book ahead (English-speaking clerks), call 33–1/49–62–78–78, fax 33–1/49–11–18–82; on arrival, 09–14–16–93.

By Train

Paris has five international stations: Gare du Nord (for northern France, northern Europe, and England via Calais or the Channel Tunnel); Gare de l'Est (for Strasbourg, Luxembourg, Basle, and central Europe); Gare de Lyon (for Lyon, Marseille, the Riviera, Geneva, and Italy); Gare d'Austerlitz (for the Loire Valley, southwest France, and Spain); and Gare St-Lazare (for Normandy and England via Dieppe). The Gare Montparnasse serves western France (mainly Nantes and Brittany) and is the terminal for the new TGV Atlantic service from Paris to Bordeaux. For train information, call 45–82–50–50. You can reserve tickets at any Paris station regardless of the destination. Go to the Grandes Lignes counter for travel within France or to the Billets Internationaux (international tickets) desk if you're heading out of France.

By Bus

Long-distance bus journeys within France are uncommon, which may be why Paris has no central bus depot. The leading Paris-based bus company is **Eurolines** (28 av. du Général-de-Gaulle, Bagnolet, tel. 49–72–51–51).

By Car

The highway system fans out from Paris. You arrive from the north (England/Belgium) via A1; from Normandy via A13; from the east via A4; from Spain and the southwest via A10; and from the Alps, the Riviera, and Italy via A7. Each of these expressways connects with the *périphérique* (beltway). Note that exits here are named by "Porte" and are not numbered. The "Périphe" can be extremely fast—but it gets very busy and is best avoided between 7:30 and 10 AM and between 4:30 and 7:30 PM.

Getting Around

Paris is relatively small as capital cities go, and most of its prize monuments and museums are within walking distance of one another. A river cruise is a pleasant way to get an overview. The most convenient form of public transportation is the métro; buses are a slower alternative, though they do allow you to see more of the city. Taxis are not expensive but are not always easy to hail, either. Car travel within Paris is best avoided because parking is chronically difficult.

By Métro

There are 13 métro lines crisscrossing Paris and the nearby suburbs, and you are seldom more than a five-minute walk from the nearest station. It is essential to know the name of the last station on the line you take, since this name appears on all signs within the system. A connection (you can make as many as you please on one ticket) is called a *correspondance*. At junction stations, illuminated orange signs bearing the names of each line terminus appear over the corridors that lead to the various correspondances.

The métro runs from 5:30 AM to 1:15 AM. Some lines and stations in the seedier parts of Paris are a bit risky at night—in particular, Line 2 (Porte-Dauphine–Nation) and the northern section of Line 13 from St-Lazare to St-Denis/Asnières. The long, bleak corridors at Jaurès and Stalingrad are a haven for pickpockets and purse snatchers. But the Paris métro is relatively safe, as long as you don't walk around with your wallet hanging out of your back pocket or travel alone (especially women) late at night.

The métro network connects at several points in Paris with RER trains that race across Paris from suburb to suburb: RER trains are a sort of supersonic métro and can be great time-savers. All métro tickets and passes are valid for RER and bus travel within Paris. Métro tickets cost 7 francs each, though a *carnet* (10 tickets for 41 frs) is a far better value. If you're staying for a week or more, the best deal is the *coupon jaune* (weekly) or *carte orange* (monthly) ticket, sold according to zone. Zones 1 and 2 cover the entire métro network (63 frs per week or 219 frs per month). If you plan to take a suburban train to visit monuments in the Ile de France, you should consider a four-zone ticket (Versailles, St-Germain-en-Laye; 113 frs per week) or a six-zone ticket (Rambouillet, Fontainebleau; 150 frs per week). For these weekly or monthly tickets, you need a pass (available from train and major métro stations), and you must provide a passport-size photograph.

Alternatively there are one-day (Formule 1) and three- and five-day (Paris Visite) unlimited travel tickets for the métro, bus, and RER. The advantage is that unlike the coupon jaune, which is good from Monday morning to Sunday evening, the latter are valid starting any day of the week and give you admission discounts to a limited number of museums and tourist attractions. The prices are 38, 95, and 150 francs for Paris only; 95, 210, and 285 francs for the suburbs including Versailles, St-Germain-en-Laye, and Disneyland Paris.

Access to métro and RER platforms is through an automatic ticket barrier. Slide your ticket in flat and pick it up as it pops up farther along. Keep your ticket; you'll need it again to leave the RER system.

By Bus

Most buses run from around 6 AM to 8:30 PM; some continue until midnight. Noctambus (night buses) operate from 1 AM to 6 AM between Châtelet and nearby suburbs. They can be stopped by hailing them at any point on their route. You can use your metro tickets on the buses, or you can buy a one-ride ticket on board. You need to show weekly/monthly/special tickets to the driver as you get on; if you have individual tickets, you should state your destination and be prepared to punch one or more tickets in the red and gray machines on board the bus.

By Taxi

There is no standard vehicle or color for Paris taxis, but all offer good value. Daytime rates (7 to 7) within Paris are about 2.80 francs per kilometer, and nighttime rates are around 4.50 francs, plus a basic charge of 12 francs. Rates outside the city limits are about 40% higher. It is best to ask your hotel or restaurant to call for a taxi, since cruising cabs can be hard to find. There are numerous taxi stands, but you have to know where to look. Note that taxis seldom take more than three people at a time.

Important Addresses and Numbers

Tourist Information

Paris Tourist Office (127 av. des Champs-Elysées, tel. 49–52–53–54). Open daily 9–8 (except Dec. 25, Jan 1.) Offices in major train stations are open daily 8–8.

Embassies

U.S. (2 av. Gabriel, 75008 Paris, tel. 42–96–12–02). **Canadian** (35 av. Montaigne, 75008 Paris, tel. 44–43–29–00). **U.K.** (35 rue du Faubourg St-Honoré, 75008 Paris, tel. 42–66–91–42).

Emergencies

Police: dial 17 for emergencies. Automatic phone booths can be found at various main crossroads for use in police emergencies (Police-Secours) or for medical help (Services Médicaux). **Ambulance:** tel. 15 or 43–78–26–26. **Doctor:** tel. 47–07–77–77. **Hospitals: American Hospital** (63 blvd. Victor-Hugo, Neuilly, tel. 47–45–71–00); **British Hospital** (3 rue Barbes, Levallois-Perret, tel. 47–58–13–12) **Dentist:** tel. 43–37–51–00; open 24 hours. **Pharmacies: Dhéry** (Galerie des Champs, 84 av. des Champs-Elysées, tel. 45–62–02–41; open 24 hours); **Drugstore** (corner of blvd. St-Germain and rue de Rennes, 6ᵉ; open until 2 AM); **Pharmacie des Arts** (106 blvd. Montparnasse, 6ᵉ; open until midnight).

English-Language Bookstores

W. H. Smith (248 rue de Rivoli); **Galignani** (224 rue de Rivoli); **Brentano's** (37 av. de l'Opéra); **Shakespeare & Co.** (rue de la Bûcherie).

Most newsstands in central Paris sell *Time, Newsweek,* and the *International Herald Tribune,* as well as the English dailies.

Travel Agencies

American Express (11 rue Scribe, 75009 Paris, tel. 47–77–77–07). **Wagons-Lits** (32 rue du Quatre-Septembre, 75002 Paris, tel. 42–66–15–80).

Guided Tours

Orientation Tours

Bus tours of Paris offer a good introduction to the city. The two largest operators are **Cityrama** (4 pl. des Pyramides, tel. 44–55–61–00) and **Paris Vision** (214 rue de Rivoli, tel. 42–60–31–25). Tours start from their respective offices. Both are in the first arrondissement (ward), opposite the Tuileries Gardens (toward the Louvre end). Tours are generally given in double-decker buses with either a live guide or tape-recorded commentary. They last two to three hours and cost about 150 francs. The same operators also offer a variety of other theme tours (historic Paris, modern Paris, Paris by night) that last from 2½ hours to all day and cost between 120 and 300 francs. For a more intimate tour of the city, Cityrama also runs minibus excursions that pick

Paris Metro

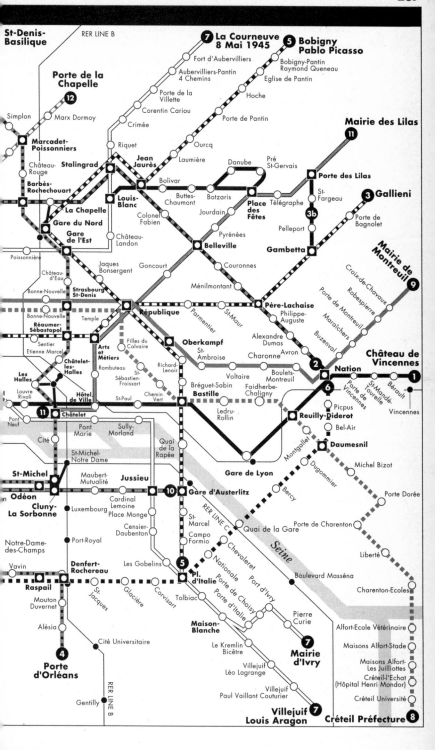

you up and drop you off at your hotel. Costs run between 210 and 350 francs per person; reservations are necessary.

Boat Trips

Boat trips along the Seine are a must for first-time Paris visitors. The two most famous services are the **Bâteaux Mouches,** which leaves from the Pont de l'Alma, at the end of the avenue George V, and the **Vedettes du Pont-Neuf,** which sets off from the square du Vert Galant, on the western edge of the Ile de la Cité. Price per trip is around 40 francs. Boats depart in season every half hour from 10:30 to 5 (slightly less frequently in winter). Evening cruises are available most of the year and, thanks to the boats' powerful floodlights, offer unexpected views of Paris's riverbanks.

Canauxrama (tel. 42–39–15–00) organizes canal tours in flat-bottom barges along the picturesque but relatively unknown St-Martin and Ourcq canals in East Paris. Departures from 5 bis quai de la Loire, 19e (métro Jaurès), or the Bassin de l'Arsenal, opposite 50 boulevard de la Bastille, 12e (métro Bastille). Times vary, so call to check hours. Tours cost from 75 francs, depending on the time of day and length of trip.

Walking Tours

There are numerous special-interest tours concentrating on historical or architectural topics. Most are in French, however. Charges vary between 40 and 60 francs, depending on fees that may be needed to visit certain buildings. Tours last about two hours and are generally held in the afternoon. Details are published in the weekly magazines *Pariscope* and *L'Officiel des Spectacles* under the heading "Conférences."

Bike Tours

Paris by Cycle organizes daily bike tours around Paris and the environs (Versailles, Chantilly, and Fontainebleau) for about 220 francs, 120 francs for bike rental (78 rue Ouest, 14e, tel. 43–35–28–63).

Excursions

The **RATP** organizes many guided excursions in and around Paris. Ask at its tourist service on the place de la Madeleine (north of place de la Concorde), or at the RATP office at St-Michel (53 quai des Grands-Augustins). **Cityrama** and **Paris Vision** (*see* Orientation Tours, *above*) organize half- and full-day trips to Chartres, Versailles, Fontainebleau, the Loire Valley, and Mont St-Michel at a cost of between 150 and 750 francs.

Personal Guides

International Limousines (182 blvd. Pereire, 17^e, tel. 45–74–77–12) and **Paris Bus** (16 av. du Château Vincennes, tel. 43–65–55–55) have limousines and minibuses that take up to seven passengers around Paris or to surrounding areas for a minimum of three hours. The cost starts at about 250 francs per hour. Call for details and reservations.

Exploring Paris

Paris is a compact city. With the possible exception of the Bois de Boulogne and Montmartre, you can easily walk from one sight to the next. Paris is divided in two by the River Seine, with two islands (Ile de la Cité and Ile St-Louis) in the middle. The south—or Left—Bank has a more intimate, bohemian flavor than the haughtier Right Bank. The east–west axis from Châtelet to the Arc de Triomphe, via the rue de Rivoli and the Champs-Elysées, is the principal thoroughfare for sightseeing and shopping on the Right Bank.

A special **Carte Musées et Monuments** pass, allowing access to most Paris museums and monuments, can be obtained from museums or métro stations (one-day pass, 60 frs; three days, 120 frs; five days, 170 frs).

Though attractions are grouped into four logical touring areas, there are several "musts." If time is a problem, explore Notre Dame and the Latin Quarter; head to place de la Concorde and enjoy the vista from the Champs-Elysées to the Louvre; then take a boat along the Seine for a waterside rendezvous with the Eiffel Tower. You could finish off with dinner in Montmartre and consider it a day well spent.

Numbers in the margin correspond to points of interest on the Paris map.

Notre Dame and the Left Bank

The most enduring symbol of Paris, and its historic and geographic heart, is **Notre Dame Cathedral,** around the corner from Cité métro station. This is the logical place from which to start any tour of the city—especially as the tour starts on the **Ile de la Cité,** one of the two islands in the middle of the Seine, where Paris's first inhabitants settled around 250 BC. Notre Dame has been a place of worship for more than 2,000 years; the present building is the fourth on this site. It was begun in 1163, making it one of the earliest Gothic cathedrals, although it was not finished until 1345. The facade seems perfectly proportioned until you notice that the north (left) tower is wider than the south. The interior is at its lightest and least cluttered in the early morning. Bay-by-bay cleaning is gradually revealing the original honey color of the stone. Window space is limited and filled with shimmering stained glass; the circular rose windows in the transept are particularly delicate. The 387-step climb up the towers is worth the effort for a perfect view of the famous gargoyles and the heart of Paris. *Cathedral admission free. Towers admission: 31 frs adults, 20 frs students, 7 frs children. Open daily 10–5. Treasury (religious and vestmental relics) admission: 15 frs adults, 10 frs students, 5 frs children. Open Mon.–Sat. 10–6, Sun. 2–6.*

The pretty garden to the right of the cathedral leads to a bridge that crosses to the city's second and smaller island, the **Ile St-Louis,** barely 600 meters long (1,968 feet) and an oasis of inner-city repose.

The rue des Deux-Ponts bisects the island. Head left over the Pont de la Tournelle. To your left is the **Tour d'Argent,** one of the city's most famous restaurants (*see* Dining, *below*).

Continue along quai de la Tournelle past Notre Dame, then turn left at rue St-Jacques. A hundred yards ahead, on the right, is the back end of the **Eglise St-Séverin,** an elegant and unusually wide 16th-century church. Note the spiraling column among the forest of pillars behind the altar.

Turn left out of the church, cross the bustling boulevard St-Germain, and take rue de Cluny to the left. This leads to the **Hôtel de Cluny,** which houses the **Musée National du Moyen-Age,** a museum devoted to the late Middle Ages and Renaissance. Look for the *Lady with the Unicorn* tapestries and the beautifully displayed medieval statues. *6 pl. Paul-Painlevé. Admission: 27 frs adults, 18 frs students and children; 18 frs for all on Sun. Open Wed.–Mon. 9:30–5:15.*

Head up rue de la Sorbonne to the **Sorbonne,** Paris's ancient university. Students here used to listen to lectures in Latin, which explains why the surrounding area is known as the Quartier Latin (Latin Quarter). The Sorbonne is the oldest university in Paris—indeed, one of the oldest in Europe—and has for centuries been one of France's principal institutions of higher learning.

6 Walking up rue Victor-Cousin and, turning left into rue Cujas, you come to the **Panthéon.** Its huge dome and elegant colonnade are reminiscent of St. Paul's in London but date from a century later (1758–89). The Panthéon was intended to be a church, but during the Revolution it was earmarked as a secular hall of fame. Its crypt contains the remains of such national heroes as Voltaire, Rousseau, and Zola. The interior is empty and austere, with principal interest centering on Puvis de Chavannes's late 19th-century frescoes, relating the life of Geneviève, patron saint of Paris. *Admission: 26 frs adults, 6 frs children, 17 frs senior citizens. Open daily 10–5:30.*

Behind the Panthéon is **St-Etienne du Mont,** a church with two claims to fame: its ornate facade and its curly Renaissance rood-screen (1521–35), the only one of its kind in Paris. Don't forget to check out the fine 17th-century glass in the cloister at the back of the church.

7 Take the adjoining rue Clovis, turn right into rue Descartes, then left at the lively place de la Contrescarpe down rue Rollin. Cross rue Monge to rue de Navarre. On the left is the **Arènes de Lutèce** (admission free, always open during daylight hours), a Gallo-Roman arena rediscovered only in 1869; it has since been landscaped and excavated to reveal parts of the original amphitheater, and counts as one of the least-known points of interest in Paris.

8 Rue de Navarre and rue Lacépède lead to the **Jardin des Plantes** (Botanical Gardens), which have been on this site since the 17th century. The gardens have what is reputedly the oldest tree in Paris, an *acacia Robinia* (allée Becquerel) planted in 1636, several natural history museums, plus a zoo, an alpine garden, hothouses, an aquarium, and a maze. Natural science enthusiasts will be in their element at the various museums, devoted to insects (Musée Entomologique), fossils and prehistoric animals (Musée Paléontologique), and minerals (Musée Minéralogique). The **Grande Galerie de l'Evolution,** with its mind-blowing collection of stuffed and mounted animals (some now extinct), reopened in 1994 to popular acclaim. *Admission: 12–40 frs. Museums open Wed.–Mon. 9–11:45, 1–4:45.*

Head back up Rue Lacépède from the Jardin des Plantes. Turn left into rue Gracieuse, then right into rue Ortolan, which soon crosses the rue Mouffetard—site of a colorful market and many restaurants. Continue along rue du Pot-de-Fer and rue Rataud. At rue Claude-Bernard, turn right; then make your first left up rue St-Jacques.

9 Set slightly back from the street is the **Val de Grâce,** a domed church designed by the great architect Jules Hardouin-Mansart and erected in 1645–67 (after the Sorbonne church but before the Invalides). Its two-tiered facade, with capitals and triangular pedestals, was directly inspired by the Counter-Reformation Jesuit architectural style found more often in Rome than in Paris. The Baroque style of the interior is epitomized by the huge twisted columns of the baldachin (ornamental canopy) over the altar.

10 From the crossroads by the Closerie des Lilas, there is an enticing view down the tree-lined avenue de l'Observatoire toward the **Palais du Luxembourg.** The palace was built by Queen Maria de' Medici at the beginning of the 17th century in answer to Florence's Pitti Palace. It now houses the French Senate and is not open to the public. In the surrounding gardens, mothers push their baby carriages along tree-lined paths among the majestic fountains and statues.

Head through the gardens to the left of the palace into rue de Vaugirard. Turn left, then right into rue Madame, which leads down to the (11) enormous 17th-century church of **St-Sulpice.** Stand back and admire the impressive, though unfinished, 18th-century façade, with its unequal towers. The interior is overwhelmingly impersonal, but the wall paintings by Delacroix, in the first chapel on the right, are worth a visit.

Rue Bonaparte descends to boulevard St-Germain. You can hardly miss (12) the sturdy pointed tower of **St-Germain-des-Prés,** the oldest church in Paris (begun around 1160, though the towers date from the 11th century). Note the colorful nave frescoes by the 19th-century artist Hippolyte Flandrin, a pupil of Ingres.

TIME OUT The spirit of writers Jean-Paul Sartre and Simone de Beauvoir still haunts the **Café de Flore** opposite the church, though this, and the neighboring **Les Deux Magots,** have more tourists than literary luminaries these days. Still, you can linger over a drink while watching what seems to be all of Paris walking by. *Blvd. St-Germain. No credit cards.*

Rue de l'Abbaye runs along behind St-Germain-des-Prés to place Fürstemberg, a charming little square where fiery Romantic artist Eugène Delacroix (1798–1863) had his studio. Turn left into rue Jacob and continue along rue de l'Université. You are now in the heart of the Carré Rive Gauche, the Left Bank's district of art dealers and galleries.

About a quarter of a mile along rue de l'Université, turn down rue (13) Poitiers. Ahead is the sandstone bulk of the **Musée d'Orsay.** Follow it around to the left to reach the main entrance. The new Musée d'Orsay—opened in late 1986—is already one of Paris's star tourist attractions, thanks to its imaginatively housed collections of the arts (mainly French) spanning the period 1848–1914. Exhibits take up three floors, but the visitor's immediate impression is one of a single, vast hall. This is not surprising: The museum was originally built in 1900 as a train station.

The chief artistic attraction, of course, is the Impressionist collection, transferred from the inadequate Jeu de Paume across the river. Other highlights include Art Nouveau furniture, a faithfully restored Belle Epoque restaurant (formerly part of the station hotel), and a model of the Opéra quarter beneath a glass floor. *1 rue Bellechasse, tel. 40–49–48–14. Admission: 35 frs adults, 24 frs students, senior citizens, and children. Open Tues., Wed., Fri., Sat. 10–5:30; Thurs. 10–9:30; Sun. 9–5:30.*

(14) Farther along on rue de l'Université is the 18th-century **Palais Bourbon,** home of the French National Legislature (Assemblée Nationale). The colonnaded façade commissioned by Napoléon is a sparkling sight after a recent cleaning program (jeopardized at one stage by political squabbles as to whether cleaning should begin from the left or the right). There is a fine view across to place de la Concorde and the Madeleine.

Follow the Seine down to the exuberant **Pont Alexandre III.** The Grand and Petit Palais are to your right, across the river. To the left, the sil- (15) houette of **L'Hôtel des Invalides** soars above expansive if hardly manicured lawns. The Invalides was founded by Louis XIV in 1674 to house wounded (or "invalid") war veterans. Although only a few old soldiers live here today, the military link remains in the form of the **Musée de l'Armée**—a vast, albeit musty, collection of arms, armor, uniforms, ban-

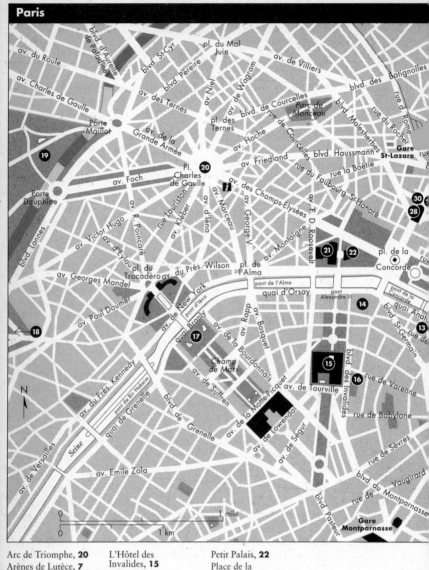

Arc de Triomphe, **20**

Arènes de Lutèce, **7**

Beaubourg, **39**

Bois de Boulogne, **19**

Eglise de la Madeleine, **28**

Eglise St-Séverin, **3**

Eiffel Tower, **17**

Fauchon's, **29**

Grand Palais, **21**

Hédiard's, **30**

Hôtel de Cluny, **4**

Hôtel de Ville, **44**

Jardin des Plantes, **8**

Jardin des Tuileries, **23**

Les Grands Magasins, **34**

Les Halles, **38**

L'Hôtel des Invalides, **15**

Louvre, **24**

Louvre des Antiquaires, **36**

Moulin Rouge, **27**

Musée d'Orsay, **13**

Musée Marmottan, **18**

Musée Picasso, **40**

Musée Rodin, **16**

Notre Dame Cathedral, **1**

Opéra, **33**

Palais Bourbon, **14**

Palais de Justice, **46**

Palais du Luxembourg, **10**

Palais-Royal, **35**

Panthéon, **6**

Petit Palais, **22**

Place de la Bastille, **42**

Place des Vosges, **41**

Place du Tertre, **26**

Place Vendôme, **31**

Ritz, **32**

Sacré-Coeur, **25**

St-Eustache, **37**

St-Germain-des-Prés, **12**

Saint-Paul-Saint-Louis, **43**

St-Sulpice, **11**

Sorbonne, **5**

Square du Vert Galant, **47**

Tour d'Argent, **2**

Tour St-Jacques, **45**

Val de Grâce, **9**

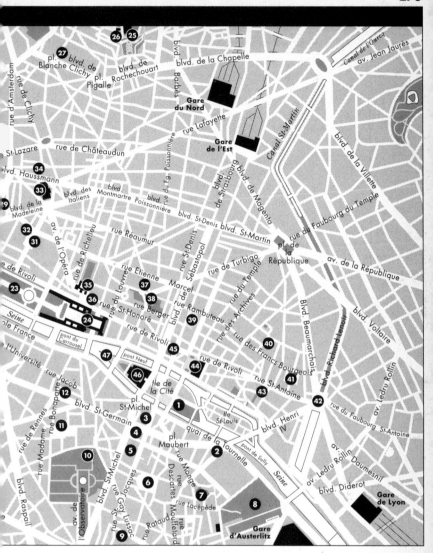

rue d'Amsterdam

rue de Clichy

pl. de
Blanche

blvd. de
Clichy

blvd. de
Rochechouart

pl.
Pigalle

blvd. Barbès

blvd. de la Chapelle

Canal de l'Ourcq

av. Jean Jaurès

27
26 **25**

St-Lazare

rue de Châteaudun

rue Lafayette

**Gare
du Nord**

**Gare
de l'Est**

Canal St-Martin

blvd. de la Villette

blvd. Haussmann

blvd. des
Italiens

blvd.
Montmartre

blvd.
Poissonnière

rue du Fg Poissonnière

blvd.
de Strasbourg

blvd. de Magenta

rue du Faubourg du Temple

34

blvd. de la
Madeleine

rue Réaumur

blvd. St-Denis

blvd. St-Martin

pl. de
la
République

av. de la République

33

32

31

av. de l'Opéra

rue de Richelieu

rue Etienne

rue St-Denis

blvd. Sébastopol

rue de Turbigo

rue du Temple

rue des Archives

Blvd Beaumarchais

blvd. Richard Lenoir

blvd. Voltaire

av. Ledru Rollin

de France

rue de Rivoli

23

rue du Louvre

Marcel

rue de Rambuteau

35

37

rue Berger

38

36

rue St-Honoré

39

rue des Francs-Bourgeois

40

24

rue de Rivoli

pont du
Carrousel

pont Neuf

45

rue de Rivoli

44

rue St-Antoine

41

l'Université

rue Jacob

47

12

46

Ile de
la Cité

43

blvd. Henri

rue du Faubourg St-Antoine

42

rue Bonaparte

rue de Rennes

blvd. St-Germain

pl.
St-Michel

1

Ile
St-Louis

V

11

3

4

pl.
Maubert

quai de la Tournelle

pont de Sully

av. Ledru Rollin

Daumesnil

blvd. Madame

5

2

Seine

av. de
l'Observatoire

10

blvd. St-Michel

rue St-Jacques

rue Gay Lussac

6

rue Monge

rue Descartes

rue Lacépède

7

blvd. Diderot

**Gare
de Lyon**

blvd. Raspail

rue Rataud

rue Mouffetard

8

9

**Gare
d'Austerlitz**

ners, and pictures. The **Musée des Plans-Reliefs** contains a fascinating collection of scale models of French towns made by the military architect Vauban in the 17th century.

The museums are far from being the only reason to visit the Invalides. It is an outstanding Baroque ensemble, designed by Bruand and Mansart, and its church possesses the city's most elegant dome as well as the tomb of Napoléon, whose remains are housed in a series of no less than six coffins within a tomb of red porphyry. *Admission to museums and church: 34 frs adults, 24 frs children and senior citizens. Open daily 10–6 (10–5 in winter).*

16 Alongside is the **Musée Rodin.** Together with the Picasso Museum in the Marais, this is the most charming of Paris's individual museums, consisting of an old house (built 1728) with a pretty garden, both filled with the vigorous sculptures of Auguste Rodin (1840–1917). The garden also has hundreds of rosebushes, with dozens of different varieties. *77 rue de Varenne. Admission: 27 frs, 18 frs Sun. Open Tues.–Sun. 10–5.*

Take avenue de Tourville to avenue de La Motte-Picquet. Turn left, and **17** in a few minutes you will come face-to-face with the **Eiffel Tower.** It was built by Gustave Eiffel for the World Exhibition of 1889. Recent restorations haven't made the elevators any faster—long lines are inevitable—but decent shops and two good restaurants have been added. Consider coming in the evening, when every girder is lighted in glorious detail. Such was Eiffel's engineering precision that even in the fiercest winds the tower never sways more than a few centimeters. Today, of course, it is the best-known Parisian landmark. Standing beneath it, you may have trouble believing that it nearly became 7,000 tons of scrap-iron when its concession expired in 1909. Only its potential use as a radio antenna saved the day; it now bristles with a forest of radio and television transmitters. The view from 1,000 feet up will enable you to appreciate the city's layout and proportions. *Admission: on foot, 12 frs; by elevator, 20–53 frs, depending on the level. Open July–Aug., daily 9 AM–midnight; Sept.–June, Sun.–Thurs. 9 AM–11 PM, Fri., Sat. 9 AM–midnight.*

West Paris and the Louvre

18 Our second itinerary starts at the **Musée Marmottan.** To get there, take the métro to La Muette, then head down chaussée de la Muette, through the small Ranelagh park to the corner of rue Boilly and avenue Raphaël. The museum is a sumptuous early 19th-century mansion, replete with many period furnishings, and probably is the most underestimated museum in Paris. It houses a magnificent collection of paintings by Claude Monet, along with other Impressionist works and some delicately illustrated medieval manuscripts. *2 rue Louis-Boilly. Admission: 35 frs adults, 15 frs children and senior citizens. Open Tues.–Sun. 10–5:30.*

Continue along rue Boilly and turn left on boulevard Suchet. The next **19** right takes you into the **Bois de Boulogne.** Class and style have been associated with "Le Bois" (The Wood) ever since it was landscaped into an upper-class playground by Haussmann in the 1850s. The attractions of this sprawling 2,200-acre wood include cafés, restaurants, gardens, waterfalls, and lakes. Pass Auteuil racetrack on the left and then walk to the right of the two lakes. An inexpensive ferry crosses frequently to an idyllic island. Rowboats can be rented at the far end of the lake. Just past the boathouse, turn right on the route de Suresnes and follow it to Porte Dauphine, a large traffic circle.

Cross over to avenue Foch, with the unmistakable silhouette of the Arc de Triomphe in the distance. Notice the original Art Nouveau iron-and-glass entrance to Porte Dauphine métro station, on the left. Continue along avenue Foch, the widest and grandest boulevard in Paris, **20** to the **Arc de Triomphe.** This 164-foot arch was planned by Napoléon to celebrate his military successes. Yet when Empress Marie-Louise entered Paris in 1810, it was barely off the ground and an arch of painted canvas had to be strung up to save appearances. Napoléon had been dead for 15 years when the Arc de Triomphe was finally finished in 1836.

Place Charles de Gaulle, referred to by Parisians as **L'Etoile** (The Star), is one of Europe's most chaotic traffic circles. Short of a death-defying dash, your only way to get over to the Arc de Triomphe is to take the pedestrian underpass from either the Champs-Elysées (to your right as you arrive from avenue Foch) or avenue de la Grande Armée (to the left). France's Unknown Soldier is buried beneath the archway; the flame is rekindled every evening at 6:30.

From the top of the Arc you can see the "star" effect of Etoile's 12 radiating avenues and admire two special vistas: one down the Champs-Elysées toward place de la Concorde and the Louvre, and the other down avenue de la Grande Armée toward La Tête Défense, a severe modern arch surrounded by imposing glass and concrete towers. Halfway up the Arc is a small museum devoted to its history. *Museum and platform. Admission: 31 frs adults, 6 frs children, 20 frs senior citizens. Open daily 10–5:30 (10–5 in winter).*

The **Champs-Elysées** is the site of colorful national ceremonies on July 14 and November 11; its trees are often decked with French tricolors and foreign flags to mark visits from heads of state. It is also where the cosmopolitan pulse of Paris beats strongest. The gracefully sloping 2-kilometer (1¼-mile) boulevard was originally laid out in the 1660s by André Le Nôtre as a garden sweeping away from the Tuileries. There is not much sign of that as you stroll past the cafés, restaurants, airline offices, car showrooms, movie theaters, and chic arcades that occupy its upper half, although the avenue was spruced up in the early 1990s, with wider sidewalks and an extra row of trees. **21** Farther down, on the right, is the **Grand Palais,** which hosts Paris's major art exhibitions. Its glass roof makes its interior remarkably bright. *Admission varies. Usually open daily 10:30–6:30.*

The Grand Palais also houses the **Palais de la Découverte,** with scientific and mechanical exhibits and a planetarium. Entrance is in the avenue Franklin-Roosevelt. *Admission: 25 frs adults, 15 frs students; additional 15 frs (10 frs students) for planetarium. Open Tues.–Sat. 9:30–6, Sun. 10–7.*

22 Directly opposite the main entrance to the Grand Palais is the **Petit Palais,** built at the same time (1900) and now home to an attractively presented collection of French paintings and furniture from the 18th and 19th centuries. *Admission: 26 frs adults, 14 frs students. Open Tues.–Sun. 10–5:40.*

Continue down to place de la Concorde, built around 1775 and the scene of more than 1,000 deaths at the guillotine, including those of Louis XVI and Marie Antoinette. The obelisk, a gift from the viceroy of Egypt, was erected in 1833.

23 To the east of the place de la Concorde is the **Jardin des Tuileries:** formal gardens with trees, ponds, and statues, currently undergoing renovations as part of the **Grand Louvre Project.** Standing guard on either side are the **Jeu de Paume** and the **Orangerie,** identical buildings erected in the mid-19th century. The Jeu de Paume, home of an Impressionist collection before its move to the Musee d' Orsay, has been completely transformed. Its spacious, austere, white-wall rooms now house temporary exhibits of contemporary art, usually at its most brazen. The Orangerie contains fine early 20th-century French works by Monet (including his *Water Lilies*), Renoir, Marie Laurencin, and others. *Admission to Jeu de Paume: 35 frs adults, 25 frs students. Open Tues. noon–9:30, Wed.–Fri. noon–7, weekends 10–7. Admission to Orangerie: 27 frs, 18 frs students, senior citizens, and Sun. Open Wed.–Mon. 9:45–5:45.*

Pass through the Tuileries to the Arc du Carrousel, a rather small triumphal arch erected more quickly (1806–08) than its big brother at the far end of the Champs-Elysées. Towering before you is the **Louvre,** with its glass pyramids. The Louvre, originally a royal palace, is today the world's largest and most famous museum. I. M Pei's pyramids are the highlight of a major modernization program begun in 1984 and scheduled for completion in 1996. The plans include the extension of the museum collections into the Richelieu wing and cleaning of the facades, restoration of the gardens between the Louvre and the Tuileries, and the construction of an underground garage and shopping arcade, the **Carrousel du Louvre.** In the course of construction, the medieval foundations of the palace were unearthed and are maintained and displayed as an integral part of the museum's collection.

The Louvre was begun as a fortress in 1200 (the earliest parts still standing date from the 1540s) and completed under Napoléon III in the 1860s. The Louvre used to be even larger; a wing facing the Tuileries Gardens was razed by rampaging revolutionaries during the bloody Paris Commune of 1871.

Whatever the aesthetic merits of Pei's new-look Louvre, the museum has emerged less cramped and more rationally organized. Yet its sheer variety can seem intimidating. The main tourist attraction is Leonardo da Vinci's *Mona Lisa* (known in French as *La Joconde*), painted in 1503. The latest research, based on Leonardo's supposed homosexuality, would have us believe that the subject was actually a man! The *Mona Lisa* may disappoint you: It's smaller than most imagine, it's kept behind glass, and it's invariably encircled by a mob of tourists.

Turn your attention instead to some of the less-crowded rooms and galleries nearby, where Leonardo's fellow Italians are strongly represented: Fra Angelico, Giotto, Mantegna, Raphael, Titian, and Veronese. El Greco, Murillo, and Velázquez lead the Spanish; Van Eyck, Rembrandt, Frans Hals, Brueghel, Holbein, and Rubens underline the achievements of northern European art. English paintings are highlighted by works of Lawrence, Reynolds, Gainsborough, and Turner. Highlights of French painting include works by Poussin, Fragonard, Chardin, Boucher, and Watteau—together with David's *Coronation of Napoléon,* Géricault's *Raft of the Medusa,* and Delacroix's *Liberty Guiding the People.*

Famous statues include the soaring *Victory of Samothrace,* the celebrated *Venus de Milo,* and the realistic Egyptian *Seated Scribe.* New rooms for sculpture were opened in the Denon Wing's former imperial stables in 1994. Be sure to inspect the Gobelins tapestries, the Crown Jewels (including the 186-carat Regent diamond), and the 9th-century bronze statuette of Emperor Charlemagne. *Admission 40 frs adults,*

*20 frs students and for all after 3 PM and Sun., children under 18 free.
Open Mon. and Wed. 9–9:45 PM, Thurs.–Sun. 9–6.*

Montmartre

If you start at the Anvers métro station and head up rue de Steinkerque,
with its budget clothing shops, you will be greeted by the most familiar and spectacular view of the Sacré Coeur basilica atop the Butte Mont-
(25) martre. The **Sacré-Coeur** was built in a bizarre, mock-Byzantine style
between 1876 and 1910. It is no favorite with aesthetes, yet it has become a major Paris landmark. It was built as an act of national peni-
tence after the disastrous Franco-Prussian War of 1870—a Catholic
show of strength at a time when conflict between church and state was
at its most bitter.

(26) Around the corner is the **place du Tertre,** full of would-be painters and
trendy, overpriced restaurants. The painters have been setting up their
easels on the square for years; avoid being talked into having your portrait done.

Despite its eternal tourist appeal and ever-growing commercialization,
Montmartre has not lost all its traditional bohemian color. Walk down
rue Norvins and descend the bustling rue Lepic to place Blanche and
one of the favorite haunts of Toulouse-Lautrec and other luminaries
(27) of the Belle Epoque—the legendary **Moulin Rouge** cabaret.

Montmartre is some distance from the rest of the city's major attractions, so go left up boulevard de Clichy as far as **place Pigalle,** then
take the métro to Madeleine.

Central Paris

(28) The **Eglise de la Madeleine,** with its array of uncompromising columns,
looks like a Greek temple. The only natural light inside comes from three
shallow domes; the walls are richly but harmoniously decorated, with
plenty of gold glinting through the dim interior. The church was designed
in 1814 but not consecrated until 1842, after efforts to turn the site into
a train station were defeated. The portico's majestic Corinthian colonnade supports a huge pediment with a sculptured frieze of the *Last Judgment.* From the top of the steps you can admire the vista down rue Royale
across the Seine. Another vista leads up boulevard Malesherbes to the
dome of **St-Augustin,** a mid-19th-century church noted for its innovative use of iron girders as structural support.

Place de la Madeleine is in the heart of Paris's prime shopping district:
(29) (30) Jewelers line rue Royale; **Fauchon's** and **Hédiard's,** behind the Madeleine,
are high-class delicatessens. Alongside the Madeleine is a **ticket kiosk**
(open Tues.–Sat. 12:30–8) that sells tickets for same-day theater performances at greatly reduced prices.

Continue down boulevard de la Madeleine and turn right into rue des
Capucines. This nondescript street leads to rue de la Paix. Immediately
(31) to the right is **place Vendôme.** This is one of the world's most opulent
squares, a rhythmically proportioned example of 17th-century urban
architecture that shines in all its golden-stone splendor since being sand-
blasted several years ago. Other things shine here, too, in the windows
of jewelry shops that are even more upscale (and understated) than those
(32) in rue Royale—fitting neighbors for the top-ranking **Ritz** hotel. The
square's central column, topped by a statue of Napoléon, is made from
the melted bronze of 1,200 cannons captured at the Battle of Austerlitz in 1805.

TIME OUT   Rue de la Paix leads, logically enough, to the **Café de la Paix** on the corner of the place de l'Opéra. There are few grander cafés in Paris, and fewer places where you can perch with as good a tableau before you.

㉝   Dominating the northern side of the square is the imposing **Opéra,** the first great work of the architect Charles Garnier, who in 1860 won the contract to build the opera house. He used elements of neoclassical architecture—bas-reliefs on facades and columns—in an exaggerated combination that borders on parody. The lavishly upholstered auditorium, with its delightful ceiling painted by Marc Chagall in 1964, seems small—but this is because the stage is the largest in the world, accommodating up to 450 players. It was the Opéra Garnier that inspired Gaston Leroux's penny dreadful, **The Phantom of the Opera,** as it was rumored that a diabolical genius who lived in the cellar lured the opera singers down to his murky chambers. *Tel. 47–42–57–50. Admission: 30 frs adults, 18 frs students and children. Open daily 10–4:30.*

㉞   Behind the Opéra are *les grands magasins,* Paris's most venerable department stores. The nearer of the two, the **Galeries Lafayette,** is the more outstanding because of its elegant turn-of-the-century glass dome. But **Printemps,** farther along boulevard Haussmann to the left, is better organized and has an excellent view from its rooftop cafeteria.

㉟   Take the métro at Chaussée d'Antin, near the Galeries Lafayette, and travel three stops (direction Villejuif) as far as **Palais-Royal.** This former royal palace, built in the 1630s, has a charming garden, bordered by arcades and boutiques, that many visitors overlook.

㊱   On the square in front of the Palais-Royal is the **Louvre des Antiquaires,** a chic shopping mall full of antiques dealers. It deserves a browse whether you intend to buy or not. Afterward, head east along rue St-Honoré and left into rue du Louvre. Skirt the circular **Bourse du Commerce** (Commercial Exchange) and head toward the imposing church

㊲   of **St-Eustache** (1532–1637), an invaluable testimony to the stylistic transition between Gothic and Classical architecture. It is also the

㊳   "cathedral" of **Les Halles**—the site of the central market of Paris until the much-loved glass-and-iron sheds were torn down in the late '60s. The area has since been transformed into a trendy—and already slightly seedy—shopping complex, Le Forum.

Head across the topiary garden and left down rue Berger. Pass the square des Innocents, with its Renaissance fountain, to boulevard de Sébastopol.

㊴   Straight ahead lies the futuristic, funnel-topped **Beaubourg** (also known as the Pompidou Center)—a must for lovers of modern art. The Beaubourg was built in the mid-1970s and named in honor of former French president Georges Pompidou (1911–74). This "cultural Disneyland" is always crowded, housing the **Musée National d'Art Moderne,** a huge library, experimental music and industrial design sections, a children's museum, and a variety of activities and exhibitions. Musicians, magicians, fire-eaters, and other street performers fill the large forecourt near the entrance. *Plateau Beaubourg, tel. 42–77–12–33. Admission free. Art museum admission: 30 frs; 20–50 frs for special exhibitions; 50 frs for daily pass covering all sectors of the center. Open Mon., Wed.–Fri. noon–10; weekends 10–10. Guided tours in English in summer and the Christmas season: weekdays 3:30 PM and weekends 11 AM.*

Note, on the right side of the Beaubourg as you face it, the large digital clock, dubbed the **Genitron,** which counts down the seconds to the year 2000 at what seems like an apocalyptic pace. Peek into the café-lined **square Stravinsky** just to the right; kids will delight in the lively fountain animated by the colorful and imaginative sculptures and aquatic mechanisms by French artists Niki de Saint-Phalle and Jean Tinguely. Continue east to the **Marais,** one of the most historic quarters of Paris. The spacious affluence of its 17th-century mansions, many of them beautifully restored, contrasts with narrow winding streets full of shops and restaurants. Rue de Rambuteau leads from the Beaubourg into rue des Francs-Bourgeois. Turn left on rue Elzévir—via the **Musée Cognacq-Jay** (devoted to the arts of the 18th century)—

40 to rue Thorigny, where you will find the Hôtel Salé and its **Musée Picasso.** This is a convincing experiment in modern museum layout, whether you like Picasso or not. Few of his major works are here, but many fine, little-known paintings, drawings, and engravings are on display. *5 rue Thorigny, tel. 42–71–25–21. Admission: 26 frs, 17 frs senior citizens and for all on Sun., under 18 free. Open Wed.–Mon. 9:30–6.*

Double back down rue Elzévir and turn left along rue des Francs-Bour-

41 geois until you reach the **place des Vosges.** Built in 1605, this is the oldest square in Paris. Its harmonious proportions, soft pink brick, and cloisterlike arcades give it an aura of calm. In the far corner is the **Maison de Victor Hugo,** containing souvenirs of the great poet's life and many of his surprisingly able paintings and ink drawings. *6 pl. des Vosges. Admission: 12 frs, 6.50 frs students and children. Open Tues.–Sun. 10–5:40.*

Rue Birague leads from the middle of the place des Vosges down to

42 rue St-Antoine. About 250 yards along to the left is the **place de la Bastille.** Unfortunately, there are no historic vestiges here; not even the soaring column, topped by the figure of Liberty, commemorates the famous storming of the Bastille in 1789 (the column stands in memory of Parisians killed in the uprisings of 1830 and 1848). Only the new **Opéra de la Bastille,** which opened in 1989, can be said to mark the bicentennial.

Retrace your steps down rue St-Antoine as far as the large Baroque church

43 of **Saint-Paul-Saint-Louis** (1627–41). Then continue down the rue de

44 Rivoli to the **Hôtel de Ville.** This magnificent city hall was rebuilt in its original Renaissance style after being burned down in 1871, during the violent days of the Paris Commune. The vast square in front of its many-statued facade has fountains and bronze lamps.

45 Avenue de Victoria leads to place du Châtelet. On the right is the **Tour St-Jacques.** This richly worked 170-foot stump is all that remains of a 16th-century church destroyed in 1802.

From Châtelet take the pont-au-Change over the Seine to the Ile de la

46 Cité and the **Palais de Justice** (law courts). Visit the turreted **Conciergerie,** a former prison with a superb vaulted 14th-century hall (Salles des Gens d'Armes) that often hosts temporary exhibitions. The **Tour de l'Horloge** (clock tower) near the entrance on the quai de l'Horloge has a clock that has been ticking off time since 1370. Around the corner in the boulevard du Palais, through the imposing law court gates, is the **Sainte-Chapelle,** built by St-Louis (Louis IX) in the 1240s to house the Crown of Thorns he had just bought from Emperor Baldwin of Constantinople. The building's lead-covered wood spire, rebuilt in 1854, rises 246 feet. The somewhat garish lower chapel is less impressive than the upper one, whose walls consist of little else but dazzling 13th-century stained glass. *Conciergerie and Sainte-Chapelle. Admission: joint ticket 40 frs; single ticket 26 frs, 17 frs students. Open daily 9:30–6:30 (winter 10–5).*

From boulevard du Palais turn right on quai des Orfèvres. This will
47 take you past the quaint place Dauphine to the **square du Vert Galant**
at the westernmost tip of the Ile de la Cité. Here, above a peaceful garden, you will find a statue of the Vert Galant: gallant adventurer Henry
IV, king from 1589 to 1610.

Off the Beaten Track

Few tourists venture into East Paris, but there are several points of interest tucked away here. The largest is the **Bois de Vincennes,** a less
touristy version of the Bois de Boulogne, with several cafés and lakes.
Rowboats can be taken to the two islands in Lac Daumesnil or to the
three in Lac des Minimes. There is also a zoo, cinder racetrack (the
hippodrome), and an extensive flower garden (Parc Floral, route de la
Pyramide). The **Château de Vincennes** (av. de Paris) is an imposing,
high-walled castle surrounded by a dry moat and dominated by a 170-
foot keep. It contains a replica of the Sainte-Chapelle on Ile de la Cité
and two elegant classical wings added in the mid-17th century. *Bois
de Vincennes, métro: Porte Dorée. Parc Floral and Château de Vincennes, métro: Château de Vincennes. Admission (garden and castle):
20 frs adults, 17 frs students and senior citizens, 7 frs children under
7. Open daily 10–6 in summer, 10–4 in winter.*

Cemeteries aren't every tourist's idea of the ultimate attraction, but **Père
Lachaise** is the largest, most interesting, and most prestigious in Paris.
It forms a veritable necropolis with cobbled avenues and tombs competing in pomposity and originality. Steep slopes and lush vegetation
contribute to a powerful atmosphere; some people even bring a picnic
lunch. Leading incumbents include Chopin, Molière, Proust, Oscar
Wilde, Sarah Bernhardt, Jim Morrison, Yves Montand, and Edith Piaf.
Get a map at the entrance and track them down. *Av. du Père-Lachaise,
20ᵉ. Métro: Gambetta. Open daily 8–6, winter 8–5.*

The **Canal St-Martin** starts life just south of the place de la Bastille but
really comes into its own during the 1.5-kilometer (1-mile) stretch north
across the 10ᵉ arrondissement. It has an unexpected flavor of Amsterdam, thanks to its quiet banks, locks, and footbridges. *Métro: Jaurès
to the north or Jacques-Bonsergent to the south.*

Hidden away in a grid of narrow streets, not far from the Opéra, is
Paris's central auction house, the **Hôtel Drouot.** It is open six days a
week (except at Christmas, Easter, and midsummer), and its 16
salesrooms make a fascinating place to browse, with absolutely no obligation to bid—though you may wish to do so! Everything from stamps
and toy soldiers to Renoirs and 18th-century commodes is available.
The mixture of fur-coated ladies with money to burn, penniless art lovers
desperate to unearth an unidentified masterpiece, and scruffy dealers
trying to look anonymous makes up Drouot's unusually rich social fabric. *Entrance at corner of rue Rossini and rue Drouot. Métro: Richelieu-Drouot. Viewing 11–noon and 2–6, auctions start at 2.*

Some of Paris's less-frequented arrondissements afford great walks. The
Bercy section of the 12ᵉ arrondissement (Métro: Bercy) is the focus of
a massive renovation project scheduled for completion in 1996. Once
filled with warehouses for the storing of wine from the provinces, the
neighborhood has seen a total transformation, which was kicked off
in the mid-'80s with the creation of the **Palais Omnisports,** the grassy-
walled, pyramid-shape sports complex and the installation in 1989 of
the **French Finance Ministry** in quayside, glass-and-steel offices. These
buildings serve as cornerstones for the **Parc de Bercy,** which is also bor-

dered by a large food and wine business complex and the new **American Center,** a venue for American art and cultural events designed by architect Frank Gehry.

Enjoy an afternoon stroll along the tree-lined streets of Paris's so-called **Beaux Quartiers,** which are in the 16ᵉ arrondissement (Métro: Eglise d'Auteil, Ranelagh, La Muette) and are punctuated with some superb examples of 20th-century architecture. Of greatest interest are the Art Nouveau buildings built by **Hector Guimard** (who designed the métro entrances)—particularly 34 rue Boileau; 8 av. de la Villa-de-la-Réunion; and 14, 17, and 19 rue de la Fontaine); and **Le Corbusier's** first private houses, featuring Villa La Roche (1923), on a small cul-de-sac off rue du Docteur-Blanche.

Finally, for those weary of monument gazing, Paris's **Chinatown**—concentrated between the high-rises of rue Tolbiac, avenue de Choisy, and boulevard Massena (Métro: Tolbiac) in the 13ᵉ—though not as ornamental as that of New York or San Francisco, boasts a delightful array of Chinese restaurants, supermarkets, and clothing stores.

Shopping

Gift Ideas
Paris is the home of fashion and perfume. Old prints are sold by *bouquinistes* (second-hand booksellers) in stalls along the Left Bank of the Seine. For state-of-the-art home decorations, the shop in the **Musée des Arts Décoratifs** in the Louvre (107 rue de Rivoli) is well worth visiting. Regional specialty foods, herbs, and pâtés can be found at **Fauchon** and **Hédiard,** two upscale grocers at 30 and 21 place de la Madeleine, 8ᵉ.

Antiques
Antiques dealers proliferate in the **Carré Rive Gauche** between St-Germain-des-Prés and the Musée d'Orsay. There are also several dealers around the Drouot auction house near the Opéra (corner of rue Rossini and rue Drouot; Métro: Richelieu-Drouot). The **Louvre des Antiquaires,** near the Palais-Royal (*see* Exploring, *above*), and the **Village Suisse,** near the Champ de Mars (78 av. de Suffren), are stylish shopping malls dominated by antiques.

Boutiques
Only Milan can compete with Paris for the title of Capital of European Chic. The top shops are along both sides of the Champs-Elysées, along the avenue Montaigne and the rue du Faubourg St-Honoré, and at place des Victoires. St-Germain-des-Prés, rue de Grenelle, and rue de Rennes on the Left Bank are centers for small specialty shops and boutiques. If you're on a tight budget, search for bargains along the shoddy streets around the foot of Montmartre (*see* Exploring, *above*), or in the designer discount shops (Cacharel, Rykiel, Dorotennis) along rue d'Alésia in Montparnasse. The streets to the north of the Marais, close to Arts-et-Métiers métro, are historically linked to the cloth trade, and some shops offer garments at wholesale prices.

Department Stores
The most famous department stores in Paris are **Galeries Lafayette** and **Printemps,** on boulevard Haussmann. Others include **Au Bon Marché** on the Left Bank (Métro: Sèvres-Babylone) and the **Samaritaine,** overlooking the Seine east of the Louvre (Métro: Pont-Neuf).

Food and Flea Markets

The sprawling **Marché aux Puces de St-Ouen,** just north of Paris, is one of Europe's largest flea markets. Best bargains are to be had early in the morning (open Sat.–Mon.; métro: Porte de Clignancourt). There are smaller flea markets at the Porte de Vanves and Porte de Montreuil (weekends only).

Dining

Eating out in Paris should be a pleasure, and there is no reason why choosing a less expensive restaurant should spoil the fun. After all, Parisians themselves eat out frequently and cannot afford haute cuisine every night, either. For details and prices-category definitions, *see* Dining *in* Staying in France, *above.*

Left Bank

$$$$ **L'Arpège.** This small, striking restaurant one block from the Rodin Mu-
★ seum is currently one of the most talked-about in Paris. Young chef-owner Alain Passard's cuisine is both original (lobster/turnip starter in a sweet-sour vinaigrette, stuffed sweet tomato) and classic (beef Burgundy, pressed duck). The problem here is inconsistency: one sublime meal can be followed by a mediocre experience. With its curving, hand-crafted wood panels and wrought-iron window frames, the decor is unusually minimalist. The staff, although young and energetic, sometimes falls behind. The prix-fixe lunch is a steal. *84 rue de Varenne, 7ᵉ, tel. 45–51–47–33. Métro: Varenne. Reservations advised. AE, DC, MC, V. Closed Sat. and Aug. No lunch Sun.*

$$–$$$ **La Timonerie.** Only a few steps along the quay from La Tour d'Argent,
★ this small, elegant restaurant avoids all theatrics and sticks to fine cooking. Philippe de Givenchy works with a small staff and his creations are consistently interesting and well executed. In his hands, a simple dish such as rosemary and lemon mackerel is turned into a high-class eating experience. *35 quai de la Tournelle, 5ᵉ, tel. 43–25–44–42. Métro: Maubert-Mutalité. Reservations advised. Jacket and tie. MC, V. Closed Sun. and Mon.*

$$ **Les Bookinistes.** Talented chef Guy Savoy's fifth bistro annex—his
★ first on the Left Bank—is a big success with the locals. The cheery post-modern room is painted peach, with red, blue, and yellow wall sconces, and it looks out on the Seine. The menu of French country cooking changes seasonally, and might include a mussel and pumpkin soup, ravioli stuffed with chicken and celery, or baby chicken roasted in a casserole with root vegetables. The reasonable prices are challenged by a somewhat pricey wine list. The service is friendly and efficient. *53 quai des Grands-Augustins, 6ᵉ, tel. 43–25–45–94. Métro: St-Michel. Reservations advised. AE, DC, MC, V. Closed Sun. No lunch Sat.*

$$ **Campagne et Provence.** This small establishment on the quay across
★ from Notre Dame specializes in country cooking. Fresh, colorful Provençal-inspired cuisine includes vegetables stuffed with *brandade* (creamed salt cod), ratatouille, and beer *daube* (stew) with olives. The list of reasonably priced regional wines helps keep the cost down. *25 quai de la Tournelle, 5ᵉ, tel. 43–54–05–17. Métro: Maubert-Mutualité. Reservations advised. MC, V. Closed Sun. No lunch Mon. or Sat.*

$$ **La Rotisserie d'En Face.** A long rotisserie is part of the attractive country-elegant decor at this bistro created by renowned chef Jacques Cagna. Overcrowding sometimes results in lowered standards, but this is one of the most popular of the "chef-bistros"—inexpensive bistros opened by well-known chefs—that continue to sprout throughout the city. The cuisine includes roast chicken with mashed potatoes and grilled salmon with spinach. The menu is prix-fixe only, and it's cheaper at lunch. There are only two seatings for dinner. *2 rue Christine, 6ᵉ, tel. 43–26–40–98. Métro: Odéon. MC, V. No dinner Sat.*

$ **Le Petit Plat.** Originally in a tiny space in the Latin Quarter, this bistro was so popular that the owners decided to seek out a bit more space in a quiet residential area; it's still small, but now the feel is intimate rather than crowded. Try the terrine of rabbit in tarragon aspic, sausage with potato salad in shallot vinaigrette or the roast chicken with sautéed mushrooms. The excellent wine list was selected by Henri Gault of Gault Millau, the famous French food guide (his daughter is one of the three owners). *45 av. Emile-Zola, 75015, tel. 45–78–24–20. Métro: Charles-Michel. Reservations advised. V. Closed Mon. No lunch Tues.*

$ **La Régalade.** This is one of the most talked-about new restaurants in
★ Paris. The location—in a remote, colorless residential neighborhood—is a nuisance, but Yves Camdeborde's cooking is stunning. Although a veteran of the Crillon, he has kept his prices remarkably low—$35 for a three-course feast. Tables are booked as much as a month in advance, but service does continue until midnight, and you can often sneak in late in the evening. *49 av. Jean-Moulin, 14ᵉ, tel. 45–45–68–58. Métro: Aléesia. Reservations 1 month in advance advised. MC, V. Closed Sun., Mon., Aug. No lunch Sat.*

West Paris

$$$$ **Guy Savoy.** Guy Savoy is one of a handful of top chefs in Paris today, and his four bistros have not managed to distract him too much from his handsome luxury restaurant near the Arc de Triomphe. Savoy's oysters in aspic, sea bass with spices, and poached and grilled pigeon reveal the magnitude of his talent. His mille-feuille is a contemporary classic. *18 rue Troyon, 16ᵉ, tel. 43–80–40–61. Métro: Charles de Gaulle-Etoile. Reservations advised. AE, MC, V. Closed Sun. No lunch Sat.*

$$$$ **Taillevent.** Many say this is the best restaurant in Paris. Within the wood-
★ paneled main dining rooms of this mid-19th-century mansion you will find exceptional service that is never overbearing, a stellar wine list, and the tempered classic cuisine of young chef Philippe Legendre. Among his signature dishes are lobster boudin and lamb with cabbage. Pastry chef Gilles Bajolle is one of the finest in Paris. Try his *nougatine glacée aux poires* (thin layers of nougat, pastry, and pear sherbet) or tarte Tatin with quince. Book three to four weeks ahead. *15 rue Lamennais, 8ᵉ, tel. 45–63–39–94. Métro: Charles de Gaulle/Etoile. Reservations essential. Jacket and tie. AE, MC, V. Closed weekends and Aug.*

$$$ **Le Cercle Ledoyen.** This luxury brasserie sits below the landmark restaurant Ledoyen. For about $50 a meal—wine included—you can sample chef Ghislaine Arabian's cooking, including the specials served at Ledoyen. The handsome, curved dining room with a view of the surrounding park is a pleasure year-round, and the terrace is a special treat in warm weather. *Carré des Champs-Elysées, 8ᵉ, tel. 47–42–23–23. Métro: Champs-Elysées–Clemenceau. Reservations advised. AE, DC, MC, V. Closed Sun.*

$ **Le Petit Yvan.** Personable Yvan, much loved by fashionable Paris, has opened a new annex to his eponymous restaurant nearby. The decor (unremarkable, but comfortable and casual) and menu are both simpler than at his star-studded main outpost, but this place has become very stylish for lunch. The prix-fixe menu offers very good value and might include such dishes as lemon-marinated salmon and steak tartare. *1 bis rue Jean-Mermoz, 8ᵉ, tel. 42–89–49–65. Métro: St-Philippe-du-Roule. Reservations advised. MC, V. Closed Sun. No lunch Sat.*

Right Bank

$$$$ **Le Grand Véfour.** Luminaries from Napoléon to Colette to Jean Cocteau have frequented this intimate address under the arcades of the Palais-Royal; you can request to be seated at their preferred table. This sumptuously decorated restaurant, with its mirrored ceiling and painted glass panels, is perhaps the prettiest in Paris, and its 18th-century origins make it one of the oldest. Chef Guy Martin impresses with his unique blend of sophisticated yet rustic dishes, including roast lamb in a juice of herbs. *17 rue Beaujolais, 1ᵉ, tel. 42–96–56–27. Métro: Palais-Royal. Reservations 1 wk in advance advised. Jacket and tie. AE, DC, MC, V. Closed Sat., Sun., and Aug.*

$$–$$$ **Pile ou Face.** This restaurant serves the most interesting and creative food around the stock exchange. Housed on two floors in a narrow building, it offers an intimate setting for discussing big business. The cooking is inventive, the service attentive. Try the rabbit pâté and the scrambled eggs with mushrooms, then move on to the sweetbreads and the exquisite roast chicken. *52 bis rue de Notre Dame des Victoires, 2ᵉ, tel. 42–33–64–33. Métro: Bourse. Reservations advised. MC, V. Closed Sat., Sun., and Aug.*

$$ **Chardenoux.** A bit off the beaten track but well worth the effort, this
★ cozy neighborhood bistro with amber walls, cut-glass windows, dark bentwood furniture, tile floors, and a long zinc bar attracts a cross section of savvy Parisians with its first-rate traditional cooking. Start with one of the delicious salads, such as the green beans and foie gras, and then try the veal chop with morels, or a game dish. Savory desserts and a nicely chosen wine list complete the experience. *1 rue Jules-Valles, 11ᵉ, tel. 43–71–49–52. Métro: Charonne. Reservations advised. AE, V. Closed Sat., Sun., and Aug.*

$ **L'Ebauchoir.** A trendy, laid-back, local crowd is complemented by a sprinkling of fashionable types who know a bargain when they see one, at this old-fashioned bistro with classic prewar decor. The salad with poached eggs and bacon bits and the confit *de canard* (duck) are delicious, as are the steaks and the homemade tarts for dessert. *43–45 rue des Citeaux, 20ᵉ, tel. 43–42–49–31. Métro: Faidherbe-Chaligny. Reservations advised. MC, V. Closed Sun.*

Lodging

For details and price-category definitions, *see* Lodging *in* Staying in France, *above.*

Left Bank and Ile St-Louis

$$$$ **L'Hôtel.** Rock idols and movie stars adore this expensive and eccentric
★ Left Bank hotel filled with flowers and antiques. Oscar Wilde died in Room 16 ("I am dying beyond my means," he wrote). One small double is covered entirely in leopard skin; another handsome suite features the mirrored Art Deco boudoir furniture that belonged to the music-hall star Mistinguett. Warning: Many rooms are extremely small. The hotel has a fine restaurant, Le Belier, whose decor includes a fountain with a live tree. The bar, open until 1 AM, is popular with a well-heeled international crowd. *13 rue des Beaux-Arts, 75006, tel. 43–25–27–22, fax 43–25–64–81. 24 rooms with bath or shower, 3 suites. Facilities: restaurant, bar, room service. AE, DC, MC, V.*

$$$ **Deux-Iles.** This cleverly converted 17th-century mansion on the resi-
★ dential Ile St-Louis has long won plaudits for charm and comfort. Flowers and plants are scattered around the stunning hall. The fabric-hung rooms, though small, have exposed beams and are fresh and airy. Ask for a room overlooking the little garden courtyard. The lounge, dominated by a fine chimneypiece, doubles as a bar. If the hotel is full, go

to the Lutèce down the road; it belongs to the same owners. *59 rue St-Louis-en-l'Ile, 75004, tel. 43–26–13–35, fax 43–29–60–25. 17 rooms with bath or shower. No credit cards.*

$$ **Grandes Ecoles.** This delightful hotel in three small old buildings is set far off the street in a beautiful garden. There are parquet floors and antiques, and a (non-working) piano in the breakfast area. Most rooms have beige carpets and flowery wallpaper. You won't find a quieter, more charming hotel for the price. There's a faithful American clientele, including some backpackers. The rooms with bathroom facilities on the well-lighted landings are inexpensive. *75 rue du Cardinal Lemoine, 75005, tel. 43–26–79–23, fax 43–25–28–15. 29 rooms with bath, 10 with shower, 9 with shared bath. AE, MC, V.*

$$ ★ **Jardin des Plantes.** Across the street from the lovely Jardin des Plantes botanical gardens on the edge of the Latin Quarter, this pleasant two-star hotel offers botanical-theme decor and very reasonable prices. There's a fifth-floor terrace where you can breakfast or sunbathe in summer, and a sauna and ironing room in the cellar. *5 rue Linné, 75005, tel. 47–07–06–20, fax 47–07–62–74. 33 rooms with bath or shower. Facilities: sauna, bar-tearoom, terrace. AE, DC, MC, V.*

West Paris

$$$$ ★ **Le Bristol.** The understated facade on rue du Faubourg St-Honoré might mislead the unknowing, but the Bristol ranks among Paris's top four hotels. Some of the air-conditioned and spaciously elegant rooms have authentic Louis XV and Louis XVI furniture, and the management has filled public areas with old master paintings, sculptures, sumptuous carpets, and tapestries. The marble bathrooms are simply magnificent. You can take tea in the vast garden or dine in the tented summer restaurant or the paneled winter restaurant even if you're not staying here; later, you can listen to the pianist in the bar, open till 1 AM. The service throughout is impeccable. *112 rue du Faubourg St-Honoré, 75008, tel. 42–66–91–45, fax 42–66–68–68. 155 rooms with bath, 45 suites. Facilities: restaurant, bar, pool, sauna, fitness machines, solarium, parking. AE, DC, MC, V.*

$$$$ **Crillon.** The Crillon is the crème de la crème of the Paris "palace hotels," set as it is in two 18th-century town houses on the place de la Concorde, site of the French Revolution's infamous guillotine. Marie Antoinette, who met her end there, took singing lessons at the Hôtel de Crillon, where one of the original *grands appartements,* now sumptuous salons protected by the French National Historic Landmark Commission, has been named for the queen. Guests must pay dearly for a balcony overlooking the great square, with seemingly all of Paris at their feet; only the suites have them. Lesser mortals still get magnificent digs, individually decorated with Rococo and Directoire antiques, crystal and gilt wall sconces, and gold fittings. Most double rooms have separate sitting rooms, and the bathrooms, stocked with wonderful Annick Goutal toiletries, are clad in marble. The staff anticipates your every need. *10 pl. de la Concorde, 75008, tel. 44–71–15–00, fax 44–71–15–02. 120 rooms with bath, 43 suites. Facilities: 2 restaurants, 2 bars, shop. AE, DC, MC, V.*

$$ ★ **Etoile-Pereire.** Pianist Ferrucio Pardi, owner and manager here, has created a unique small hotel, set behind a quiet, leafy courtyard in a chic residential district. All rooms and duplexes are decorated in soothing pastels—pinks, grays, and apricots—with Laura Ashley curtains and chair covers, and prints on the walls. There's no restaurant, but room service can be arranged. A copious breakfast is available, with 40 different jams and jellies. The bar is always busy in the evening. For a lively, personally run hotel, few places beat this likeable spot. *146 blvd.*

Pereire, 75017, tel. 42–67–60–00, fax 42–67–02–90. 21 rooms with bath or shower, 4 duplexes, 1 suite. Facilities: bar. AE, DC, MC, V.

$$ **Keppler.** Ideally located on the edge of the 8ᵉ and 16ᵉ arrondissements near the Champs-Elysées, this small two-star hotel in a 19th-century building bursts with amenities (room service, small bar) at extremely reasonable prices. The spacious, airy rooms are simply decorated with modern furnishings. Some rooms with shower are less expensive. *12 rue Keppler, 75116, tel. 47–20–65–05, fax 47–23–02–29. 49 rooms with bath or shower. Facilities: bar. AE, MC, V.*

$ **Argenson.** This friendly, family-run hotel provides what may well be the best value in the swanky 8ᵉ arrondissement. Some of the city's greatest sights are just a 10-minute walk away. Old furniture, molded ceilings, and skillful flower arrangements add to the charm. The best rooms have full baths, but they are pricier; reserve well in advance for one of these. The smallest rooms have shared baths. *15 rue d'Argenson, 75008, tel. 42–65–16–87, fax 47–42–02–06. 27 rooms, 24 with bath or shower. MC, V.*

Montmartre and Central Paris

$$$$ **Grand Hotel Inter-Continental.** Paris's biggest luxury hotel has endless hallways and a facade that seems as long as the Louvre. After a thorough restoration, completed mid-1991, this 1862 gem sparkles like new. The grand salon's Art Deco dome and the painted ceilings of the Opéra and Café de la Paix restaurants are registered landmarks; the latter, one of the city's great rendezvous and people-watching spots. Rooms are spacious and light, decorated in Art Nouveau style with pastel colors. *2 rue Scribe, 75009, tel. 40–07–32–32, fax 42–66–12–51. 470 rooms with bath, 23 suites. Facilities: 3 restaurants, 2 bars, health club, shops, parking. AE, DC, MC, V.*

$$$$ **Pavillon de la Reine.** The best hotel in the Marais, it's set around two
★   flower-filled courtyards behind the historic Queen's Pavilion on the 17th-century place des Vosges. Although this cozy mansion looks old, it was actually reconstructed from scratch in 1986 following original plans and using period timbers, rough-hewn paving stones, Louis XIII fireplaces, and antiques. Ask for a duplex with French windows over the first courtyard (there are no rooms overlooking the place des Vosges). Breakfast is served in a vaulted cellar. *28 pl. des Vosges, 75003, tel. 42–77–96–40, fax 42–77–63–06. 31 rooms with bath, 24 suites. Facilities: parking. AE, DC, MC, V.*

$$$$ **Ritz.** Surrounded by the city's finest jewelers, the Ritz is the crowning
★   gem on the newly sparkling place Vendôme. Festooned with gilt and ormolu, dripping with crystal chandeliers and tapestries, and swathed in heavy silk, this dazzling hotel— a sumptuous 18th-century town house—which opened in 1896, is the epitome of fin-de-siële Paris. It's suprisingly intimate, too. The hotel has no lobby, for the express purpose of discouraging paparazzi and sightseers who could annoy the privileged clientele. Legendary suites are named after former residents like Coco Chanel and Marcel Proust. The famous Hemingway Bar (which the writer claimed to have "liberated" in 1945) re-opened in 1994. The handsome Vendôme Bar and the Espadon restaurant remain chic meeting spots, and the lower-level health club has a magnificent indoor pool. There's warm-weather seating in the charming adjacent garden. *15 pl. Vendôme, 75001, tel. 42–60–38–30, fax 42–86–00–91. 142 rooms with bath, 45 suites. Facilities: 2 restaurants, 2 bars, health-sports complex, indoor pool. AE, DC, MC, V.*

$$ **Gaillon-Opéra.** The oak beams, stone walls, and marble tiles of the Gail-
★   lon-Opéra single it out as one of the most charming hotels in the Opéra neighborhood. The plants throughout and a flower-filled patio

also delight. *9 rue Gaillon, 75002, tel. 47–42–47–74, fax 47–42–01–23. 26 rooms with bath, 1 suite. AE, DC, MC, V.*

$ Castex. This family-run, two-star hotel in a 19th-century building is a real find. It was remodeled from top to bottom in 1989, and rooms are squeaky clean. The decor is strictly functional, but the extremely friendly owners and rock-bottom prices mean the Castex is often fully booked months ahead. There's a large American clientele. The eight least expensive rooms, two per floor, share toilets on the immaculate, well-lighted landings. There's no elevator, and the only TV is in the lobby. *5 rue Castex, 75004, tel. 42–72–31–52, fax 42–72–57–91. 4 rooms with bath, 23 with shower. MC, V.*

$ Place des Vosges. A loyal American clientele swears by this small hotel
★ on a charming street just off the exquisite square of the same name. Oak-beam ceilings and rough-hewn stone in public areas and some of the guest rooms add to the atmosphere. Ask for the top-floor room, the hotel's largest, with a view of Marais rooftops. There's a welcoming little breakfast room. *12 rue de Birague, 75004, tel. 42–72–60–46, fax 42–72–02–64. 16 rooms with bath or shower. AE, DC, MC, V.*

$ Regyn's Montmartre. Despite small rooms (all recently renovated), this owner-run hotel is rapidly gaining an enviable reputation for simple, comfortable accommodations. A predominantly young clientele and a correspondingly relaxed atmosphere have made this an attractive choice for some. Try for one of the rooms on the upper floors, with great views of either the Eiffel Tower or Sacré Coeur. All rooms have safes and hairdryers. *18 pl. des Abbesses, 75018, tel. 42–54–45–21, fax 42–23–76–69. 22 rooms with bath or shower. AE, MC, V.*

The Arts

The monthly English-language magazine *Paris Boulevard* and the weekly magazines *Pariscope, L'Officiel des Spectacles,* and *Figaroscope* give detailed entertainment listings. The Paris Tourist Office has set up a **24-hour English-language hot line** (tel. 49–52–53–56) with information about weekly events. Buy tickets at the place of performance; otherwise, try hotels, travel agencies (try **Paris-Vision** at 214 rue de Rivoli), and special ticket counters (in the **FNAC** stores at 26 av. des Ternes, near the Arc de Triomphe and the Forum des Halles). Half-price tickets for same-day theater performances are available at the ticket stand at the west side of the Madeleine church.

Theater

There is no Parisian equivalent to Broadway or the West End, although a number of theaters line the grand boulevards between the Opéra and République. Shows are mostly in French; classical drama is at the distinguished **Comédie Française** (by the Palais-Royal). A completely different charm is to be found in the tiny **Théâtre de la Huchette,** near St-Michel, where Ionesco's short modern plays make a deliberately ridiculous mess of the French language.

Concerts

The principal venues for classical music are the **Salle Pleyel** (252 rue du Faubourg St-Honoré), near the Arc de Triomphe, the new **Opéra Bastille,** and the **Châtelet** theater (pl. Châtelet). You can also attend one of the many inexpensive organ or chamber music concerts in churches throughout the city.

Opera

The "old" **Opéra,** or **Opéra Garnier** (pl. de l'Opéra, 9ᵉ), ceded its role as Paris's main opera house to the **Opéra Bastille** (pl. de la Bastille, tel. 47–42–53–71), which stages both traditional opera and symphony concerts. Getting a ticket for an opera or ballet performance is not easy, though, and requires either luck, much planning, or a well-connected hotel receptionist. The **Opéra Comique** (the French term for opera with spoken dialogue), close by in the rue Favart, is more accessible.

Dance

The highlights of the Paris dance year usually take place at the **Palais Garnier,** which, in addition to being the sumptuous home of the well-reputed Paris Ballet, also bills dozens of major foreign troupes ranging from classical to modern. Other major venues include the **Théâtre de la Ville** (tel. 42–74–22–77) at Châtelet and the **Palais des Congrès** (tel. 40–68–22–22) at Porte Maillot.

Film

There are hundreds of movie theaters in Paris, and some of them, especially in principal tourist areas such as the Champs-Elysées and the boulevard des Italiens near the Opéra, run English films marked *"version originale"* (VO, i.e., not dubbed). Admission is around 40–50 francs, with reduced rates on Monday. Movie fanatics should check out the **Beaubourg** and the **Musée du Cinéma** at Trocadéro, where old and rare films are often screened.

Nightlife

Cabaret

This is what Paris is supposed to be all about. Its nightclubs are household names—more so abroad than in France, it would seem, judging by the hefty percentage of foreigners present at most shows. Prices range from 200 francs (basic admission plus one drink) to 700 francs (dinner included). For 350–500 francs, you can get a good seat plus half a bottle of champagne.

The **Crazy Horse** (12 av. George-V, tel. 47–23–32–32) is one of the field leaders in pretty women and dance routines: It features lots of humor and a lot less clothes. The **Moulin Rouge** (pl. Blanche, tel. 46–06–00–19) is an old favorite at the foot of Montmartre. Nearby is the **Folies-Bergère,** (32 rue Richer, tel. 42–46–77–11), which reopened at the end of 1993 with an all-new show reminiscent of its music-hall origins. The **Lido** (116 bis av. des Champs-Elysées, tel. 40–76–56–10) underwent a $10-million face-lift in 1994 to put more razzle into its dazzle.

Bars and Nightclubs

Upscale nightclubs are usually private, so unless you have a friend who is a member, forget it. Give the wildly popular **Niel's** (27 av. Ternes, 17ᵉ) or **Sheherazade** (93 rue de Liège, 9ᵉ) a try on weeknights only, or you run the risk of spending the evening waiting in line on the sidewalk.

The Pigalle area in Montmartre is becoming the place to be, despite its reputation as a seedy red-light district. Among hot places here are: **Moloko** (26 rue Fontaine, 9ᵉ), a smoky late-night bar; **Le Dépanneur** (next door at 27 rue Fontaine), which caters to more of a gin-drinking yuppie crowd; **Lili la Tigresse** (98 rue Blanche, 9ᵉ), a sexy bar with a trendy crowd; and—not to be missed—the brasserie **Pigalle** (22 blvd. de Clichy, 18ᵉ), whose '50s frescoes and ceramics have been classified as a national treasure.

The nightlife is still hopping in and around the Bastille: the **China Club** (50 rue de Charenton, 12ᵉ) is a trendy bar with an Orient Express theme; **Le Casbah** (18 rue de la Forge Royale, 11ᵉ) is a bar and dance club with a touch of Casablanca; and **Le Piston Pelican** (15 rue de Bagnolet, 20ᵉ), a favorite among Beaux-Arts students, has a laid-back ambience and occasional live music.

For a more leisurely experience in an atmosphere that is part bar and part gentlemen's club, try an old haunt of Hemingway, the Fitzgeralds, and Gertrude Stein: **Harry's Bar** (5 rue Daunou, 2ᵉ), a cozy wood-paneled spot for Americans, journalists, and sportsmen.

Gay and Lesbian
Gay and lesbian bars and clubs are mostly concentrated in the Marais and include some of the most happening addresses in the city. The very trendy **Banana Café** (13 rue de la Ferronnerie, 1ᵉ) attracts an energetic and scantily clad mixed crowd; dancing on the tables is the norm. For men, **Le Quetzal** (10 rue de la Verrerie, 4ᵉ), which features a chrome-and-blue-light atmosphere, gets very crowded and smoky on weekends; **The Trap** (10 rue Jacob, 6ᵉ) contains a ground-floor video bar with a staircase leading to a darker, more social area. For a more relaxed atmosphere try **Subway** (35 rue Ste-Croix-de-la-Bretonnerie, 4ᵉ), a popular hangout that has pinball and pool.

For women, **La Champsmelé** (4 rue Chabanais, 2ᵉ) is the hub of lesbian nightlife with a back room reserved for women only; **Le Memorie's** (2 pl. de la Porte-Maillot, 17ᵉ), though in a staid neighborhood, is Paris's most renowned lesbian dance club.

Jazz Clubs
The Latin Quarter is a good place to track down Paris jazz, and the doyen of clubs is the **Caveau de la Huchette** (5 rue de la Huchette), where you can hear Dixieland in a hectic, smoke-filled atmosphere. **Le Slow Club** (130 rue de Rivoli), another favorite, tries to resurrect the style of early Bourbon Street, and it nearly succeeds.

Rock Clubs
Le Sunset (60 rue des Lombards) is a small, whitewashed cellar with first-rate live music and a clientele that's there to listen. **New Morning** (7 rue des Petites-Ecuries) is a top spot for visiting American musicians and good French bands.

Discos
Club Zed (2 rue des Anglais off blvd. St.-Germain) is the best place for rock and roll. The long-established **Balajo** (9 rue de Lappe, 11ᵉ) is crowded and lots of fun, with plenty of nostalgic '60s sounds on some nights. **Memphis** (3 impasse Bonne-Nouvelle) boasts some impressive lighting and video gadgetry.

ILE DE FRANCE

The area surrounding Paris is called the Ile (island) de France, reflecting the role it has played over the centuries as the economic, political, and religious center of the country. For many visitors to Paris, it is the first taste of French provincial life, with its slower pace and fierce devotion to the soil. Although parts of the area are fighting a losing battle to resist the encroaching capital, you can still see the countryside that was the inspiration for the Impressionists and other 19th-centur painters and is home to a wealth of architecture dating from the M dle Ages. The most famous buildings are Chartres—one of the beautiful of French cathedrals—and Versailles, the monumental of Louis XIV, the Sun King. Before the completion of Versa and court resided in the delightful château of St-Germain-e of Paris. This is within easy day-trip range of Paris, as a

Ile de France

of Vaux-le-Vicomte, Rambouillet, and Fontainebleau, and the newest Disney venture, Disneyland Paris.

Getting Around

The region is reached easily from Paris by car and by regular suburban train services. But you might find it convenient to group some sights together: Versailles, Rambouillet, and Chartres are all on the Paris–Chartres train line; Fontainebleau, Barbizon, and Vaux-le-Vicomte are all within a few miles of each other.

By Train

Three lines connect Paris with Versailles; on each, the trip takes about 30 minutes. Best for the château is RER-C5 to Versailles Rive Gauche station. Trains from Gare St-Lazare go to Versailles Rive Droite. Trains from Gare Montparnasse go to Versailles Chantiers and then on to Rambouillet and Chartres. Fontainebleau is served by 20 trains a day from Gare de Lyon; buses for Barbizon leave from the main post office in Fontainebleau. The RER-A4 line will take you to Disneyland Paris.

By Car

Expressway A13, from the Porte d'Auteuil, will take you from Paris to Versailles. Alternatively, you can get to Chartres on A10 or N10 south from Porte d'Orléans. For Fontainebleau, take A6 from Porte d'Orléans or, for a more attractive route through the forest of Sénart and the northern part of the forest of Fontainebleau, take N6 from Porte de Charenton via Melun. Vaux-le-Vicomte is 6 kilometers (4 miles) northeast of Melun via N36 and D215. The 32-kilometer (20-mile) drive along the A4 expressway from Paris to Disneyland Paris takes about 30 minutes, longer in heavy traffic. Disneyland is 4 kilometers (2½ miles) off the A4; follow the signs for the park.

Guided Tours

Two private companies, **Cityrama** and **Paris Vision,** organize regular half-day and full-day tours from Paris with English-speaking guides. Times and prices are identical. Tours are subject to cancellation, and reservations are suggested. Cityrama tours depart from 4 place des Pyramides, 1er (tel. 44–55–61–00). Paris Vision leaves from 214 rue de Rivoli, 1er (tel. 42–60–31–25).

Versailles and Les Trianons. Daily excursions starting at 9:30 include a complete tour of Paris in the morning followed by an afternoon at Versailles. Half-day excursions of Versailles leave mornings and afternoons daily (9:30 and 2:30, 300 frs) and include a guided tour of the château, Hall of Mirrors, and Queen's Suite. On Thursday only, you can extend the morning tour (450 frs) to include an afternoon visit (starting 1:30) to the Trianons, or take a separate afternoon visit there (1:30; 220 frs).

Chartres. Both companies organize half-day tours to Chartres on Tuesday, Thursday, and Saturday afternoons (1:30, 270 frs), but if you're short of time or cash, you'd be better off taking the **Versailles–Chartres** day trips on Tuesday and Saturday (9:30, 450 frs).

Fontainebleau and Barbizon. Half-day trips (1:30, 310 frs) on Wednesday, Friday, and Sunday run to Fontainebleau and nearby Barbizon (which is otherwise difficult to reach), but can be linked to a Versailles tour leaving at 9:30 on the same days.

Tourist Information

Barbizon (41 rue Grande, tel. 60–66–41–87).
Chartres (pl. de la Cathédrale, tel. 16/37–21–50–00).
Disneyland Paris (Central Reservations Office, Box 105, Marne-la-Vallée Cedex 4, 77777 France, tel. 60–30–60–30).
Fontainebleau (31 pl. Napoléon-Bonaparte, tel. 64–22–25–68).
Rambouillet (8 pl. de la Libération, tel. 34–83–21–21).
Versailles (7 rue des Réservoirs, tel. 39–50–36–22).

Exploring the Ile de France

Versailles

Versailles is the location of one of the world's grandest palaces and one of France's most popular attractions. Wide, tree-lined avenues, broader than the Champs-Elysées and bordered with massive 17th-century mansions, lead directly to the Sun King's château. From the imposing place d'Armes, you enter the Cour des Ministres, a sprawling cobbled forecourt. Right in the middle, the statue of Louis XIV stands triumphant, surveying the town that he built from scratch to house those of the 20,000 noblemen, servants, and hangers-on who weren't lucky enough to get one of the 3,000 beds in the château.

The building of the château in its entirety took 50 years. Hills were flattened, marshes drained, forests transplanted, and water for the magnificent fountains was channeled from the Seine several miles away. Visit the **Grands Appartements,** the six salons that made up the royal living quarters, and the famous **Galerie des Glaces** (Hall of Mirrors). Both can be visited without a guide, but you can get a cassette in English. There are also guided tours of the **Petits Appartements,** wh the royal family and friends lived in relative intimacy, and the m ture opera house—one of the first oval rooms in France, built *aile nord* (north wing) for Louis XV in 1770. *Grands Appa* *and Galerie des Glaces. Admission: 40 frs adults, 26 frs students and senior citizens. Open Tues.–Sun. 9–6:30 (9–5:30 in winter).*

The château's vast grounds are masterpieces of formal landscaping. At one end of the Petit Canal, which crosses the Grand Canal at right angles, is the **Grand Trianon,** a scaled-down pleasure palace built in the 1680s. The **Petit Trianon,** nearby, is a sumptuously furnished 18th-century mansion, commissioned by Louis XVI for Marie Antoinette, who would flee here to avoid the stuffy atmosphere of the court. Nearby, she built the village, complete with dairy and mill, where she and her companions would dress as shepherdesses and lead a make-believe bucolic life. *Château grounds: admission free. Open 8:30–dusk. Grand Trianon admission: 21 frs adults, 14 frs children and senior citizens. Open June–Sept., daily 10–6:30, Oct.–May, daily 10–12:30 and 2–5:30. Petit Trianon admission: 12 frs adults, 8 frs children and senior citizens. Open June–Sept., daily 10–6:30; Oct.–May, daily 2–5:30.*

Rambouillet

Just a little more than 20 kilometers (12 miles) southwest of Versailles is the small town of **Rambouillet,** home of a château, an adjoining park, and 34,000 acres of forest. Since 1897, the château has been a summer residence of the French president; today, it is also used as a site for international summits. You can visit the château only when the president is not in residence—fortunately, he's not there often.

French kings have lived in the château since it was built in 1375. Highlights include the **Appartements d'Assemblée,** decorated with finely detailed wood paneling, and Napoléon's bathroom, with its Pompeii-inspired frescoes. The park stretches way behind the château. Beyond the **Jardin d'Eau** (Water Garden) lies the English-style garden and the **Laiterie de la Reine** (Marie Antoinette's Dairy). This was another of her attempts to "get back to nature." *Château, tel. 34–83–00–25. Admission: 27 frs adults, 17 frs children and senior citizens. Open Wed.–Mon. 10–11:30 and 2–4:30 (till 5:30 Apr.–Sept.). Park admission free. Open sunrise–sunset. Marie Antoinette's Dairy admission 13 frs. Open same hrs as château; closes at 4 in winter.*

Chartres

From Rambouillet, N10 will take you straight to **Chartres.** Long before you arrive you will see its famous cathedral towering over the plain of the Beauce, France's granary. The attractive old town, steeped in religious history and dating from before the Roman conquest, is still laced with winding medieval streets.

Today's Gothic cathedral, **Notre Dame de Chartres,** is the sixth Christian church to have been built on the site; despite a series of fires, it has remained virtually the same since the 12th century. The **Royal Portal** on the main facade, presenting "the life and triumph of the Savior," is one of the finest examples of Romanesque sculpture in the country. Inside, the 12th- and 13th-century rose windows come alive even in dull weather, thanks to the deep Chartres blue of the stained glass: Its formula remains a mystery to this day. *Cathedral tours available. Ask at the Maison des Clercs, 18 rue du Cloître Notre Dame. Tours in English daily noon and 2:45.*

Since the rest of the tour is on another side of Paris, it is probably easier to return to the capital to continue (*see* Getting Around Ile de France, *above*).

Fontainebleau

In the early 16th century, the flamboyant François I transformed the medieval hunting lodge of **Fontainebleau** into a magnificent Renaissance palace. His successor, Henry II, covered the palace with his initials, woven into the *D* for his mistress, Diane de Poitiers. When he died, his queen, Catherine de' Medici, carried out further alterations, later extended under Louis XIV. Napoléon preferred the relative intimacy of Fontainebleau to the grandeur of Versailles. Before he was exiled to Elba, he bade farewell to his Old Guard in the courtyard now known as the **Cour des Adieux** (Farewell Court). The emperor also harangued his troops from the **Horseshoe Staircase.** Ask the curator to let you see the **Cour Ovale** (Oval Court), the oldest and perhaps most interesting courtyard. It stands on the site of the original 12th-century fortified building, but only the keep remains today.

The **Grands Appartements** (royal suites and ballroom) are the main attractions of any visit to the château. The **Galerie de François I** is really a covered bridge (built 1528–30) looking out over the Cour de la Fontaine. The overall effect inside the Galerie—and throughout Fontainebleau—is one of classical harmony and proportion, combining to create a sense of Renaissance lightness and order. François I appreciated the Italian Renaissance, and the ballroom is decorated with frescoes by Primaticcio (1504–70) and his pupil, Niccolò dell'Abbate. If you're here on a weekday, you will also be able to join a guided tour of the Petits Appartements, used by Napoléon and Josephine. *Pl. du Général-de-Gaulle, tel. 64–22–27–40. Admission: 31 frs adults, 20 frs 18–25, 20 frs on Sun. Open Wed.–Mon. 9:30–12:30 and 2–5.*

Barbizon

The **Rochers des Demoiselles,** a rocky outcrop just south of town, are good for an afternoon stroll. The **Gorges d'Apremont,** which offer the best views of the rocks, are near **Barbizon,** on the edge of the forest, 10 kilometers (6 miles) northwest of Fontainebleau. This delightful little village is scarcely more than a main street lined with restaurants and boutiques, but a group of landscape painters put it on the map in the mid-19th century. Théodore Rousseau and Jean-François Millet both had their studios here. Sculptor Henri Chapu's bronze medallion, sealed to one of the famous sandstone rocks in the forest nearby, pays homage to the two leaders of what became known as the Barbizon group.

Drop in at the **Ancienne Auberge du Père Ganne** (rue Grande), where most of the landscape artists ate and drank while in Barbizon. They painted on every available surface, and even now you can see some originals on the walls and in the buffet.

Next to the church, in a barn that Rousseau used as a studio, you'll find the **Musée de l'Ecole de Barbizon** (Barbizon School Museum), containing documents of the village as it was in the 19th century as well as a few original works. *55 rue Grande, tel. 60–66–22–38. Admission: 15 frs adults. Open Apr.–Sept., Wed.–Sun. 10:30–12:30 and 2–6; Oct.–Mar., Wed.–Sun. 10:30–12:30 and 2–5.*

From Barbizon, D64 offers a pleasant shortcut to Melun and then on to the château of **Vaux-le-Vicomte,** one of the greatest monuments of 17th-century French architecture. It was to have been Nicolas Fouquet's pride and joy, but turned out to be his downfall. This superintendent of France's finances under Louis XIV tended to use state resources for his own benefit—the château itself is damning evidence—and the Sun King eventually had him imprisoned for life. From the visitor's point of view, though, Fouquet's *folie de grandeur* is a treat. He had excellent taste (and a large budget) and chose the best-qualified team to build Vaux-le-Vicomte. Louis liked the results enough to reemploy them all when he built Versailles. Visit the kitchens, which have been preserved just as they were in the 17th century. The gardens (admission 22 frs) are open all day. *Guided tours of château. Admission: 43 frs. Open Apr.–Oct., daily 10–6; Nov.–Dec. and mid-Feb.–Mar., daily 11–5. Candlelight visits. Admission: 50 frs. Open May–Sept., Sat. 8:30–11:30.*

Disneyland Paris

The resort is on A4 (Exit 14—PARC DISNEYLAND PARIS). From Paris, the RER-A4 (40 min, 35 frs one way) runs directly to Marne-la-Vallée, a short walk from the theme park entrance; as of June 1994 a new TGV line connects Disneyland to Lille and Lyon.

Now you can get a dose of American pop culture in between visits to the Louvre and the Left Bank. In April 1992 the **Disneyland Paris** (formerly Euro Disney) complex opened in Marne-la-Vallée, just 32 kilometers (20 miles) east of Paris, much to the consternation of French cultural partisans. The complex is divided into several areas, including the pay-as-you-enter theme park that is the main reason for coming here. Occupying 136 acres, the park is less than half a mile across and ringed by a railroad with whistling steam engines. Although smaller than its U.S. counterparts, Disneyland Paris was built with great attention paid to the tiniest detail. Smack in the middle of the park is the soaring Sleeping Beauty Castle, which is surrounded by a plaza from which you can enter the four "lands" of Disney: **Frontierland, Adventureland, Fantasyland,** and **Discoveryland.** In addition, Main Street U.S.A. connects the castle to the entrance, under the pointed pink domes of the Disneyland Hotel. In June 1995 Disneyland Paris inaugurated its newest attraction, **Space Mountain,** aiming to catapult riders through the Milky Way. *Admission (prices vary according to season): 150–195 frs adults, 120–150 frs children under 12. Open mid-June–mid-Sept., daily 9 AM–10 PM; mid-Sept.–mid-June, daily 10–6; Dec. and spring school holidays, daily 10–9.*

There are six hotels in the 4,800-acre Disneyland Paris complex, just outside the theme park. The resort also comprises parking lots, a train station, and the Festival Disney entertainment center, with restaurants, a theater, dance clubs, shops, a post office, and a tourist office. Cheaper accommodations—log cabins and campsites—are available at Camp Davy Crockett, farther from the theme park.

Dining and Lodging

For details and price-category definitions, *see* Dining *and* Lodging *in* Staying in France, *above.*

Barbizon

DINING

Le Relais. The delicious specialties—particularly the beef and the game (in season)—are served in large portions, and there is a good choice of prix-fixe menus. The Relais is spacious, its walls covered with paintings and hunting trophies, and there is a big open fireplace. The owner is proud of the large terrace where you can eat in the shade of lime and chestnut trees. *2 av. Charles de Gaulle, tel. 60–66–40–28. Weekend reservations required. MC, V. Closed Wed. No dinner Tues.$–$$*

DINING AND LODGING

Auberge des Alouettes. This delightful 19th-century inn is set on 2 acres of grounds. The interior has been redecorated in '30s style, but many rooms still have their original oak beams. The restaurant, with a large open terrace, features nouvelle cuisine in sizable portions. *4 rue Antoine-Barye, tel. 60–66–41–98, fax 60–66–20–69. 22 rooms with bath or shower. Facilities: restaurant, tennis, parking, TV. Weekend dinner reservations required. AE, DC, MC, V. $$*

Chartres

DINING

Vieille Maison. Located in a recently refitted 14th-century building only a stone's throw from the cathedral, Vieille Maison offers excellent nouvelle cuisine as well as more traditional dishes. Try the regional *menu beauceron* for the homemade foie gras and duck dishes or the mouthwatering *menu gourmand,* if the wallet allows. *5 rue au Lait, tel. 16/37–34–10–67. Reservations advised. AE, MC, V. Closed Mon. No dinner Sun. $$$*

Buisson Ardent. Set in an attractive old oak-beam building within sight of the cathedral's south portal, Buisson Ardent is a popular restaurant providing inexpensive prix-fixe menus (especially good on weekdays) and a choice of imaginative à la carte dishes with delicious sauces. The wine list is comprehensive. *10 rue au Lait, tel. 16/37–34–04–66. Reservations advised. AE, DC, MC, V. No dinner Sun. $$*

LODGING

Grand Monarque. The most popular rooms in this 18th-century coaching inn are in a separate turn-of-the-century building overlooking a garden. Rooms have the level of comfort and consistency you would expect from a Best Western. The hotel also has an excellent reasonably priced restaurant. *22 pl. des Epars, tel. 16/ 37–21–00–72. 54 rooms with bath or shower. Facilities: restaurant. AE, DC, MC, V. $$$*

Disneyland Paris

DINING AND LODGING

Disneyland is peppered with places to eat, ranging from snack bars and fast-food joints to full-service restaurants—all with a distinguishing theme. In addition, all Disney hotels have restaurants that are open to the public. As these are outside the theme park, you may not want to waste time traveling to them for lunch. Disney now offers wine and beer in sit-down restaurants within the park. The resort has 5,000 rooms in six hotels, all a short distance from the park, ranging from the luxurious Disneyland Hotel to the not-so-rustic Camp Davy Crockett. *Disneyland Paris, Central Reservations Office, Box 105, Marne-la-Vallée Cedex 4, 77777 France, tel. 60–30–60–30, fax 49–41–49–49; for hotel/restaurant reservations, tel. 60–45–65–40. Hotels $$–$$$$; Sit-down restaurants (reservations advised; AE DC MC V) $$; Counter-service restaurants (no credit cards). $*

Fontainebleau

DINING

Le Table des Maréchaux. Two good-value prix-fixe menus (130 frs and 180 frs) mark this elegant restaurant on the town's main street, five minutes from the château. Traditional French dishes include gizzard salad and lamb with béarnaise sauce. *9 rue Grande, tel. 64–22–20–39. Reservations advised. AE, MC, V. $$*

LODGING

Londres. The balconies of this tranquil hotel look out over the palace and the Cour des Adieux; the 19th-century facade is preserved by government order. Inside, the decor is dominated by Louis XV furniture. *1 pl. du Général-de-Gaulle, tel. 64–22–20–21. Fax 60–72–39–16. 22 rooms with bath or shower. Facilities: restaurant, bar, tearoom, parking. AE, DC, MC, V. Closed Dec. 20–Jan. 5. $$*

Rambouillet

DINING

La Poste. Traditional, unpretentious cooking is the attraction of this former coaching inn, close to the château. The restaurant's two dining rooms are often packed with a lively group. The service is good, as is the selection of inexpensive prix-fixe menus, even on Sunday. *101 rue du Général-de-Gaulle, tel. 34–83–03–01. Reservations advised. AE, MC, V. Closed Mon. No dinner Sun.* $

Versailles

DINING

Trois Marches. This, the best-known restaurant in town, is also recognized as one of the best in France for its nouvelle cuisine. Don't miss Gerard Vié's bisque of lobster, salmon with fennel, or turbot galette. Vié's 1992 move here to the sumptuous Trianon Palace Hotel, overlooking the château park—and the restaurant's huge, spanking-new kitchens—seem to have inspired him. *1 blvd. de la Reine, tel. 39–50–13–21. Reservations required. AE, DC, MC, V. Closed Sun., Mon., and Aug.* $$$$

La Grande Sirène. An appealing lunch menu served every day but Sunday makes this pretty spot near the château a popular noontime choice. Zesty simmered snails and well-prepared fish are good choices here. *25 rue du Maréchal-Foch, tel. 39–53–08–08. Reservations advised. AE, MC, V. Closed Mon.* $$

Quai N° I. Fish enthusiasts don't have to spend a fortune in Versailles, as a visit to this atmospheric restaurant—awash in wood and brass and decked out in seafaring paraphernalia—will underline. Smoked salmon is the house specialty, and crème brûlée the pick of the desserts. *1 av. de St-Cloud, tel. 39–50–42–26. Reservations advised. MC, V. Closed Mon. No dinner Sun.* $$

NORMANDY

Jutting out into the Channel, Normandy has had more connections with the English-speaking world than any other part of France. The association continues today. Visitors flock here not only to see historic monuments but to relax in the rich countryside amid apple orchards, lush meadows, and sandy beaches.

The historic cities of Rouen and Caen, capitals of Upper and Lower Normandy, respectively, are full of churches, well-preserved buildings, and museums. The Seine Valley is lined with abbeys and castles from all periods: St-Wandrille, for example, dates from the 7th century. Richard the Lionhearted's 12th-century Château Gaillard, at Les Andelys, is still imposing, and memories of the D-Day landings are still fresh. Normandy also has one of France's most enduring tourist attractions: Mont St-Michel, a remarkable Gothic abbey perched on a rocky mount off the Cotentin peninsula.

Etretat and Fécamp on the Alabaster Coast and Deauville, Trouville, and Honfleur on the Côte Fleurie (Flowered Coast) are among Normandy's many seaside resorts. Hotels, restaurants, and beaches cater to the simpler pleasures of life, while casinos make the rich poor—and sometimes the other way around, too. Normandy is also recognized as one of France's finest gastronomic regions; try some of the excellent cheeses with local cider, calvados (apple brandy), or the wide range of seafood dishes.

Normandy

La Manche (English Channel)

Dieppe

D925

N27

Fécamp

Etretat

D39

N15

Baie de la Seine

Tancarville

St. Wandrille Abbey

D982

Cherbourg

Le Havre

Cotentin Peninsula

N13

Honfleur

Seine

Rouen

Trouville

N178

Jumièges Abbey

St-Martin de Boscherville

Arromanches

A13

Bayeux

N13

D513

Deauville

Les Andelys

D572

Caen

Giverny

St-Lô

N175

Lisieux

N13

To Mantes (20 miles)

Coutances

D971

N158

D840

Evreux

N174

Vire

Granville

N175

Villedieu-les-Poêles

Flers

N138

Argentan

Avranches

Mont St-Michel

Parc Naturel

0 — 20 miles

0 — 30 km

Getting Around

Normandy is best visited by car, although there are regular daily trains from Paris to Rouen, Caen, and Bayeux. Limited train connections make cross-country traveling difficult. Visiting many historic monuments and some towns—such as Honfleur, which has no train station—means using buses whose connections are not always convenient.

Guided Tours

Paris Vision (214 rue de Rivoli, 75001 Paris, 1er, tel. 42–60–31–25) and **Cityrama** (4 pl. des Pyramides, Paris, 1er, tel. 44–55–61–00) organize identical one-day excursions (990 frs) to Mont St-Michel from Paris, leaving at 7:15 Saturday morning and taking you by bus to Mont St-Michel in time for lunch at the Terrasse Poulard restaurant (*see* Dining and Lodging, *below*). There is a guided tour of the mount and the abbey, and you return by first-class train from Laval to Gare Montparnasse.

Tourist Information

Regional Centers

Caen (Lower Normandy, pl. du Canada, tel. 31–86–53–30).
Rouen (Upper Normandy, 2 bis rue du Petit-Salut, tel. 35–88–61–32).

Local Offices

Les Andelys (rue Philippe Auguste, tel. 32–54–41–93).
Bayeux (Pont St-Jean, tel. 31–92–16–26).
Caen (12 pl. St-Pierre, tel. 31–27–14–14).
Deauville (pl. de la Mairie, tel. 31–88–21–43).
Etretat (pl. de la Mairie, tel. 35–27–05–21).

Fécamp (pl. Bellet, tel. 35–28–20–51).
Honfleur (9 rue de la Ville, tel. 31–89–23–30).
Mont St-Michel (Corps de Garde des Bourgeois, tel. 33–60–14–30).
Rouen (25 pl. de la Cathédrale, tel. 35–71–41–77).

Exploring Normandy

Take Expressway A13 from Paris (Porte d'Auteuil) as far as Meulan or Mantes and cross the Seine to the right bank. Then follow D913 or make a short stop in the village of **Giverny,** where you can visit the house and gardens in which Claude Monet lived and worked. *Admission: 30 frs. Open Tues.–Sun. 10–6.*

D313 goes to **Les Andelys,** a small town on the banks of the Seine, dominated by the imposing **Château Gaillard,** the fortress built in 1196 by Richard the Lionhearted, King of England, and duke of Normandy. *Admission: 15 frs. Open mid-Mar.–mid-Nov., Thurs.–Mon. 10–12:30 and 2–5, Wed. 2–5.*

Numbers in the margin correspond to points of interest on the Rouen map.

Rouen

Rouen, the capital of Upper Normandy, has a remarkable number of
❶ historic churches, from the city's **Cathédrale Notre Dame,** dating from
❷ the 12th century, to the modern, fish-shape **Eglise Jeanne d'Arc** on the old market square, where Joan of Arc was burned at the stake in 1431. The tourist office organizes a guided tour leaving from place de
❸ la Cathédrale and visiting the city's main churches, the **Palais de Justice,** and the lively old quarter around the rue du Gros-Horloge, where you can see the giant Renaissance clock that was built in 1527. The most noteworthy churches are on the right bank, around the old quar-
❹ ter, and can be visited on foot. Try to visit **Eglise St-Maclou,** with its
❺ five-gable facade; **Abbaye St-Ouen,** a beautifully proportioned 14th-
❻ century abbey; and the **Eglise St-Godard,** with well-preserved stained-glass windows.

One ticket will get you into several of Rouen's best museums, notably
❼ the **Musée des Beaux Arts** (Fine Arts Museum), near Eglise St-Godard (on Square Vedral). This specializes in 17th- and 19th-century French paintings, with an emphasis on artists who lived and worked locally. There is an outstanding collection of macabre paintings by Romantic
❽ painter Géricault. Nearby museums include the **Musée Le Secq des Tour-nelles** (in the Eglise St-Laurent, rue Jacques Villon), which has an un-
❾ usual collection of wrought iron; the **Musée de la Céramique** (rue
❿ Faucon), which now houses Rouen's porcelain collections; and the **Musée du Gros-Horloge** (rue du Gros-Horloge), where you can study the mechanism of the Renaissance clock that gives its name to the museum. *Admission: 21 frs. Open Thurs.–Mon. 10–noon and 2–6, Wed. 2–6.*

Follow D982 across the Forest of Roumare and along the Seine via St-Martin de Boscherville, with its mighty 12th-century Romanesque abbey church of St-Georges, to **Jumièges Abbey,** once a powerful Benedictine center, founded in the 7th century. The abbey was dismantled during the Revolution, but you can still wander through the remains of the chapter house and several of the chapels. *Admission: 24 frs adults, 15 frs senior citizens, 10 frs children. Open Apr.–Sept., daily 10–noon and 2–6; Oct.–Mar., weekdays 10–noon and 2–4, weekends 2–5.*

The nearby **St-Wandrille Abbey,** off D982, founded in 649, still has a Benedictine community. Arrive early in the morning to hear the Gre-

Abbaye
St-Ouen, **5**

Cathédrale
Notre Dame, **1**

Eglise Jeanne
d'Arc, **2**

Eglise St-
Godard, **6**

Eglise St-
Maclou, **4**

Musée de la
Céramique, **9**

Musée des
Beaux Arts, **7**

Musée du
Gros-
Horloge, **10**

Musée Le
Secq des
Tournelles, **8**

Palais de
Justice, **3**

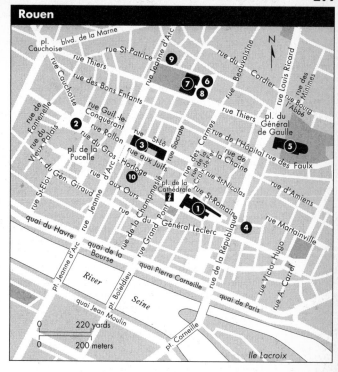

Rouen

gorian chants at Mass. *Mass Mon.–Sat. 9:30 AM; Sun. and holidays at 10. Guided tours (18 frs adults) weekdays 3 and 4 PM.*

Fécamp

Fécamp, at the foot of the highest cliffs in Normandy, was the region's first place of pilgrimage. Legend has it that in the first century, an abandoned boat washed ashore here with a bottle containing Christ's blood. The 11th-century **Eglise de la Trinité** was built to accommodate all the pilgrims. *Guided tours May–Oct., Sun. at 11, 3, and 5.*

Fécamp is also home of the famous Bénédictine liqueur. The museum devoted to its production—rebuilt in 1892 after a fire—is one of the most popular attractions in Normandy. *Musée de la Bénédictine. 110 rue Alexandre-le-Grand, tel. 35–28–00–06. Admission: 30 frs. Open Easter–Oct., daily 9:30–11:30 and 2–5:30; Nov.–Easter, daily 10–1:30 and 3:30–4:30.*

Follow the pretty coast road about 12 kilometers (7 miles) to **Etretat,** where the sea has cut into the cliff to create two immense archways that lead to the neighboring beaches at low tide. For a view over the bay and the **Aiguille,** which is an enormous rock towering in the middle, take the little path up the Falaise d'Aval cliff.

To avoid doubling back to Fécamp, take D39 to the Tancarville Bridge, which links Upper and Lower Normandy. Have some small change ready for the toll. Turn right on N178 and drive south for 14 kilometers (9 miles) to a major crossroads. Turn right and drive the same distance to Honfleur.

Honfleur

Once an important port for maritime expeditions, **Honfleur** became a favorite spot for painters, including the Impressionists. Today, Honfleur's lively cobbled streets, harbors full of colorful yachts, and the Eglise Ste-Catherine—a little 15th-century wooden church—make it the most picturesque town on the north coast. In summer or on weekends, be prepared for lines at restaurants and cafés, but even the crowds don't spoil Honfleur's perfection.

The popular resorts of **Trouville** and **Deauville** are 16 kilometers (10 miles) along the Côte de Grâce, on D513. Deauville is the swankier of the two, with its palaces, casino, horse racing, and film festival. Its more modest neighbor, Trouville, with its active fishing fleet, is easier to relax in and less damaging to the wallet.

Caen, slightly inland from these resorts, is the capital of Lower Normandy. It was badly bombed in 1944 but has been rebuilt with care and imagination. William the Conqueror was responsible for Caen's large **fortress** perched on a hill behind the town: Its ramparts now encircle the public garden. William and his queen, Mathilde, also built Caen's "his and hers" abbeys—**Abbaye aux Hommes** and **Abbaye aux Dames.** The city hall is alongside the Abbaye aux Hommes, which has hourly guided tours (admission 10 frs); Abbaye aux Femmes is now a hospital, and only the church is open to visitors. The **Mémorial,** a museum in the north of the city, has videos, photos, arms, paintings, and prints that detail the Normandy landings, the Battle of Normandy, and France's liberation, within a historical context from the 1930s to the 1960s. *Esplanade Général Eisenhower. Admission: 58 frs adults, 32 frs students. Open Wed.–Mon. 9–7.*

Bayeux

Bayeux, a few miles inland from the D-Day beach via N13, was the first French town freed by the Allies in June 1944. But it is known primarily as the home of **La Tapisserie de la Reine Mathilde** (the Bayeux Tapestry), which tells the epic story of William's conquest of England in 1066. It is on show at the **Centre Culturel Guillaume le Conquérant** (William the Conqueror Cultural Center). *Rue St-Exupère. Admission: 32 frs adults, 18 frs students. Open June–Sept., daily 9–7; Oct.–May, daily 9:30–12:30 and 2–7.*

Head up rue de Nesmond to rue Larchet, turning left into lovely place des Tribuneaux, where you'll find the **Musée Baron Gérard** with a fine collection of Bayeux porcelain and lace, ceramics from Rouen, a marvelous array of apothecary jars from the 17th and 18th centuries, and furniture and paintings from the 16th to 19th centuries. *1 rue la Chaine, tel. 31–92–14–21. Admission: 18 frs adults, 12 frs senior citizens. Open June–mid-Sept. daily 9–7; mid-Sept.–May, 10–12:30 and 2–6.*

Behind the museum, with an entrance on rue de Bienvenu, sits Bayeux's most important historic building, the **Cathédrale Notre Dame,** a harmonious mixture of Norman and Gothic architecture. Note the portal on the south side of the transept, which depicts the assassination of English Archbishop Thomas à Becket in Canterbury Cathedral in 1170.

The **Musée de la Bataille de Normandie** (Museum of the Battle of Normandy) traces the history of the Allied advance against the Germans in 1944. It overlooks the British Military Cemetery. *Blvd. Général-Fabian-Ware. Admission: 24 frs adults, 12 frs students. Open June–Aug., daily 9–7; Sept.–mid-Oct. and mid-Mar.–May, daily 9:30–12:30 and 2:30–6:30; mid-Oct.–mid-Mar., daily 10–12:30 and 2–6.*

Bayeux is a good base for excursions up the Cotentin coast, to Mont-St-Michel, and the D-Day beaches. In **Arromanches** harbor, you can see the remains of **Mulberry B,** an artificial port built for the British D-

Day landings. Mulberry A, where American troops landed farther up the coast on what is now known as **Omaha Beach,** was destroyed by a storm a few months after the landings. The **Musée du Débarquement** (Landings Museum) on Arromanches seafront shows the landing plan and a film (in English) on the operation. *Admission: 30 frs adults, 18 frs children. Open July–Aug., daily 9–7; Sept.–June, daily 9–11:30 and 2–6. Closed Jan. 1–22.*

Mont-St-Michel

Drive through the fertile heartland of Normandy, among the rolling hills and orchards that produce calvados and cider. Take D972 to **St-Lô** and then D999 to **Villedieu-les-Poêles,** a town famous for its kitchen copperware. Now join N175 and continue to **Avranches,** where you will have your first view of **Mont-St-Michel,** the Gothic abbey and village rising up from the sea. The mount's fame comes not just from its location—until the causeway was built, it was cut off from the mainland at high tide—but from the dramatic nature of its construction in the 8th century, when tons of granite were brought from the nearby Chausey Islands and Brittany and hauled up the 265-foot peak. It has been a pilgrimage center ever since.

For most of the year, Mont-St-Michel is surrounded by sandy beach. The best time to see it is during the high tides of spring and fall, when the sea comes pounding in—dangerously fast—and encircles the mount. **La Merveille** (the Wonder) is the name given to the collection of Gothic buildings on top. What looks like a fortress is in fact a series of architectural layers that trace the evolution of French architecture from Romanesque to late-Gothic. You can join a guided tour (in English). *Admission: 32 frs adults, 15 frs students and senior citizens, 7 frs children. Open mid-May–Sept., daily 9–11:30 and 1:30–6; Oct.–mid-May, Wed.–Mon. 9:30–11:45 and 1:45–4:15.*

Dining and Lodging

For details and price-category definitions, *see* Dining *and* Lodging *in* Staying in France, *above.*

Bayeux

DINING

L'Amaryllis. This small, simply decorated restaurant with fewer than 15 tables produces good Norman fare at very reasonable prices. For 98 francs you'll get a three-course dinner that might include a half dozen oysters, sole with a cider-based sauce, and pastries for dessert. *32 rue St-Patrice, tel. 31–22–47–94. AE, DC, MC, V. Closed Mon. and Dec. 20–Jan. 15. $*

DINING AND LODGING

Le Chenevière. This grand manor of the late 19th century, set in parkland between Bayeux and the coast, was converted into an elegant hotel in 1988. Its smooth operation sets out to challenge the nearby Château d'Audrieu. The rooms have modern furnishings, with plain draperies on the floor-to-ceiling windows and flowered bedspreads to give a splash of color. The marble bathrooms are spanking fresh. Chef Claude Esprabens strives for a Michelin star, and dinner is worth a detour. His Norman recipes are prepared with a lightness of style: The roasted scampi with sesame seed and fresh chanterelles is delicious; then you might try the justifiably famous rack of lamb with a truffle sauce. *Escures-Commes, 14520 Port-en-Bressin, tel. 31–21–41–96, fax 31–21–47–98. 19 rooms with bath. Facilities: restaurant, free parking. AE, MC, V. $$$*

Grand Hôtel du Luxembourg. Les Quatre Saisons, the restaurant at this fairly run-of-the-mill hotel, has the best kitchen in town. Chef Daniel Rivière's classical repertoire from Normandy includes a galette of salmon, chicken roasted with cider, and veal in a sauce strongly scented with calvados. The hotel's guest rooms are adequate. All but two face the courtyard garden, away from any street noise. *25 rue des Bouchers, 14403, tel. 31–92–54–26, fax 31–92–54–26. 19 rooms with bath, 3 suites. Facilities: restaurant, bar, free parking. AE, DC, MC, V. $$*

Churchill. This small family-run, friendly inn is within walking distance of all the attractions. Two old town houses were made into a hotel in 1986, so the rooms are of various shapes and sizes. Furnishings are modest and functional; bathrooms are compact. Hearty breakfasts are served in the veranda café. *14 rue St-Jean, 14400, tel. 31–21–32–80, fax 31–21–41–66. 32 rooms with bath or shower. AE, DC, MC, V. Closed mid-Nov.–mid-Mar. $–$$*

Caen

DINING

Bourride. Michel Bruneau, owner and chef of this famous restaurant set in one of the town's oldest streets, bases his inventive recipes almost exclusively on local and regional produce. Specialties include skate caramelized in honey and cider and meat pastry cooked in cider vinegar. *15 rue du Vaugueux, tel. 31–93–50–76. Reservations advised. AE, DC, MC, V. Closed Sun., Mon., Jan. 1–24, and Aug. 15–31. $$$*

DINING AND LODGING

Le Dauphin. Although small, the rooms in this old priory are clean and renovated. Many of them overlook the quiet hotel courtyard. Le Dauphin also has an excellent restaurant serving Norman dishes topped by unusually light sauces, with an emphasis on seafood. *29 rue Gémare, 14000, tel. 31–86–22–26, fax 31–86–35–14. 21 rooms with bath or shower. Facilities: restaurant (closed Sat.), parking. AE, DC, MC, V. Closed part of Feb. and mid-July–mid-Aug. $$*

Deauville

DINING

Spinnaker. Here is a handy—and affordable—restaurant in the center of this chic resort. The atmosphere is informal and the food is local, with special emphasis on seafood. Try the delicious fresh pasta and crab salad. *52 rue Mirabeau, tel. 31–88–24–40. Reservations advised. MC, V. Closed Wed. off-season, Thurs., and Jan. 15–Feb. 15. $$*

Etretat

DINING

Roches Blanches. Situated back from the sandy beach, this family-owned restaurant is a concrete post–World War II eyesore on the outside. Inside, it's another matter: There's a view of the sea and the cliffs, and the seafood is superbly fresh. Besides other dishes, such as veal escalope with mushrooms and flambéed in calvados, be sure to try the mussels. *Rue Abbé Cochet, tel. 35–27–07–34. Reservations required. MC, V. Closed Wed. in summer, Tues.–Thurs. in winter, and Oct. and Jan. $$*

DINING AND LODGING

Le Donjon. This charming little château, in a park overlooking the resort, offers lovely bay views. The individually furnished guest rooms are spacious, comfortable, and quiet. Reliable French cuisine is served with flair in a cozy, romantic restaurant. *Chemin de St-Clair, 76790, tel. 35–27–08–23, fax 35–29–92–24. 8 rooms, 6 with bath. Facilities: pool, parking. AE, DC, MC, V. $$*

Fécamp

DINING AND LODGING

Auberge de la Rouge. The quaint inn is in a little hamlet a mile or so south of Fécamp. Its menu features a good mix of classic and modern dishes and includes many local specialties—try the *coquilles St-Jacques* (scallops in the shell in a sherry cream sauce) or the pressed duck. *Commune de St-Léonard, 76400, tel. 35–28–07–59, fax 35–28–70–55. Reservations advised. 8 rooms with bath. Facilities: restaurant. AE, DC, MC, V. Closed Mon. No dinner Sun. $$*

Honfleur

DINING

Absinthe. The magnificent 17th-century dining room dominates the ground floor, where you will also find the pub-style bar, the Ivanhoe. But in warm weather, the place to be is on the sunny terrace on the quayside. The menu features both nouvelle and traditional cuisines, with the accent on seafood. *10 quai de la Quarantaine, tel. 31–89–39–00. Reservations advised. AE, DC, MC, V. Closed Mon. evening (except in midsummer), Tues., and mid-Nov.–Dec. 20. $$$*

L'Assiette Gourmande. Next door to the Cheval Blanc (*see below*) is Honfleur's unsung top restaurant. If Chef Gérard Bonnefoy should stir out of his kitchen into the dining room, you'll find he's a master at deciding what you would enjoy most after a few minutes of culinary conversation. The season influences the menu, but you may be lucky enough in the fall to have the superb coquilles St-Jacques grilled with sautéed asparagus in a raspberry vinaigrette and reduced orange sauce. Or you may enjoy lobster salad, tartare of smoked salmon in a caviar-based cream, roast turbot marinated in a basil mussel sauce, or roast lamb *pré-salé*, that is, lamb that has grazed on the salt marshes around Mont-St-Michel. *2 quai des Passagers, tel. 31–89–24–88. Reservations advised. Closed Mon. $$–$$$*

LODGING

Le Cheval Blanc. In a renovated, 15th-century building on the harbor front, owners Alain Petit and his wife run this friendly inn. All the guest rooms have recently been redecorated and offer fine views of the port across the main road. Room 34 (slightly more expensive than the others) has gabled ceilings supported by gable and cross beams pegged together, a small sitting area, and a whirlpool bath. *2 quai des Passagers, 14600, tel. 31–81–65–00, fax 31–89–52–80. 35 rooms, 14 with bath. Facilities: breakfast room, parking in nearby lot. MC, V. Closed Jan. $$*

Mont-St-Michel

LODGING

Terrasses Poulard. This collection of town houses, while still overpriced, is the less expensive sister hotel to the exorbitant Mère Poulard; each room takes the name of a famous Norman personality and is decorated accordingly. Several rooms have breathtaking views of the bay; others look out onto a little garden. The restaurant, crowded with American, British, and Canadian tourists, has its best views upstairs. *Grande Rue, 50116, tel. 33–60–14–09, fax 33–60–37–31. 29 rooms with bath. Facilities: restaurant. AE, DC, MC, V. $$$*

DINING AND LODGING

Le Manoir de la Roche Turin. An appealing alternative to the high-priced hotels in Mont-St-Michel is this small ivy-clad manor house 9 kilometers (6 miles) away. Rooms are pleasantly old-fashioned, but the bathrooms are modern, and the owners run a delightful dining room. The *agneau pré-salé* is superb, but lobster and fresh fish are also available on the 150-franc and 200-franc menus. *50220 Courtils, tel. 33–70–96–*

55, fax 33–48–35–20. 11 rooms with bath, 1 suite. Facilities: restaurant (closed Mon.), free parking. MC, V. Closed mid-Nov.–mid-Mar. $$

Rouen

DINING

La Couronne. Built in 1345, La Couronne claims to be the oldest inn in France. The oak beams, leather upholstery, and woodwork provide an attractive setting for a collection of sculptures. The traditional cuisine features homemade foie gras, duck à l'orange, and turbot in flaky pastry. Keep to the "menu Normand," for 180 francs, or expect a hefty bill if you order à la carte. 31 pl. du Vieux-Marché, tel. 35–71–40–90. Reservations required. AE, DC, MC, V. $$$

LODGING

Hôtel de la Cathédrale. On a narrow pedestrian street behind the cathedral stands a very appealing hotel in a medieval building. Rooms are petite, but neat and comfortable, and all have a private bath or shower. Guests can sleep soundly, too; the cathedral bells do not boom out the hour during the night. Breakfast is served in a wonderfully beamed dining room. The owner, who is on hand at the desk, is extremely cordial and will give you tips on exploring Rouen and advice on dining options. 12 rue St-Romain, 76000, tel. 35–71–57–95, fax 35–70–15–54. 25 rooms with bath or shower. Facilities: breakfast room, public parking nearby. MC, V. $–$$

BURGUNDY AND LYON

For a region whose powerful medieval dukes held sway over large tracts of Western Europe and whose current image is closely allied to its expensive wine, Burgundy is a place of surprisingly rustic, quiet charm. Its leading religious monument is the Romanesque basilica at Vézelay, once an important pilgrimage center, and today a tiny village hidden in rolling hills.

The heart of Burgundy is the dark, brooding Morvan Forest. Dijon, the region's only city, retains something of its medieval opulence, but its present reputation is essentially gastronomic. Top restaurants abound, and local industries produce mustard, cassis, snails, and—of course—wine. The vineyards leading down toward the ancient town of Beaune are among the world's most distinguished and picturesque.

The vines continue to flourish as you head south along the Saône Valley, through the Mâconnais and Beaujolais, toward Lyon, one of France's most appealing cities. The combination of frenzied modernity and unhurried joie de vivre gives Lyon a sense of balance. The only danger is a temptation to overindulge in its rich, robust cuisine.

Getting Around

Burgundy is a region best visited by car. Its meandering country roads invite leisurely exploration. There are few big towns, and traveling around by train is unrewarding, especially as the infrequent cross-country trains steam along at the speed of a legendary Burgundy snail.

Guided Tours

The Dijon branch of the regional tourism office organizes a series of tours using Dijon as a base. These include wine tastings and historic tours of the famous religious centers. Write to Comité Régional de Tourisme (21 blvd. Brosses, 21000 Dijon).

Tourist Information

Auxerre (1 quai de la République, tel. 86–52–06–19).
Beaune (rue de l'Hôtel-Dieu, tel. 80–26–31–30).
Dijon (29 pl. Darcy, tel. 80–30–35–39).
Lyon (pl. Bellecour, tel. 78–42–25–75).
Sens (pl. Jean-Jaurès, tel. 86–65–19–49).

Exploring Burgundy and Lyon

It makes sense for **Sens** to be your first stop on the way down to Burgundy, as it lies just 120 kilometers (75 miles) from Paris on N6—a fast, pretty road that hugs the Yonne Valley south of Fontainebleau. Sens is home to France's senior archbishop and is dominated by the 12th-century **Cathédrale St-Etienne.** This is one of the oldest cathedrals in France and has a foursquare facade topped by towers and an incongruous little Renaissance campanile. The vast, harmonious interior contains outstanding stained glass of various periods.

The 13th-century **Palais Synodal** alongside, with six grand windows and a vaulted hall, provides a first encounter with Burgundy's multicolored tiled roofs; from its courtyard, there is a fine view of the cathedral's south transept, constructed in the fluid Flamboyant Gothic style of the 16th century. It'a now a museum with statues, mosaics, and tapestries. *Rue des Déportés de la Résistance. Admission: 18 frs. Open Mar.–mid-Dec. daily 10–noon and 2–5; mid-Dec.–Feb., Thurs.–Tues. 2–4:30.*

Auxerre

N6 continues to **Auxerre,** a small, peaceful town with its own **Cathédrale St-Etienne,** perched on a steepish hill overlooking the Yonne. The muscular cathedral, built between the 13th and 16th centuries, has a powerful north tower similar to that at Clamecy. The former **abbey of St-Germain** nearby contains a crypt dating from the 9th century. *Rue Cochois. Admission: 20 fr covers St-Germain and crypt and the treasury at St-Etienne. Open Wed.–Mon. 10–noon and 2–5.*

Chablis, famous for its dry white wine, makes an attractive excursion 16 kilometers (10 miles) to the east of Auxerre, along N65 and D965. Beware of village tourist shops selling local wines at unpalatable prices. The surrounding vineyards are dramatic: Their towering, steeply banked hills stand in marked contrast to the region's characteristic gentle slopes.

Clamecy

From Auxerre, take N151 43 kilometers (27 miles) south along the Yonne to **Clamecy.** This sleepy town is not on many tourist itineraries, but its tumbling alleyways and untouched, ancient houses epitomize *la France profonde.* The many-shaped roofs of Clamecy, dominated by the majestic square tower of the **church of St-Martin,** are best viewed from the banks of the Yonne. The river played a crucial role in Clamecy's development: Trees from the nearby Morvan Forest were cut down and floated in huge convoys to Paris. The history of this curious form of transport (*flottage*), now extinct, is detailed in the town museum, in two mansions, the **Musée d'Art et d'Histoire Romain Rolland,** named for a native son, a Nobel laureate for literature in 1915. *Av. de la République, tel. 86–27–17–99. Admission: 10 frs. Open July–Sept., Wed.–Mon. 10–noon and 2–5; Oct.–June by appointment.*

Vézelay lies 24 kilometers (15 miles) east of Clamecy along D957. The **Basilica** is perched on a rocky crag, with commanding views of the surrounding countryside. It rose to fame in the 11th century as the rest-

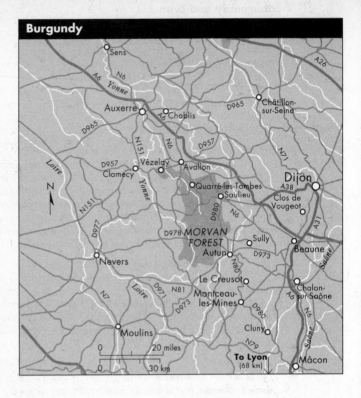

Burgundy

ing place of the relics of St. Mary Magdalene and became a departure point for the great pilgrimages to Santiago de Compostela in northwest Spain. The church was rescued from decay by the 19th-century Gothic Revival architect Eugène Emmanuel Viollet-le-Duc and counts as one of the foremost Romanesque buildings in existence. Its interior is long and airy, with superbly carved column capitals; the facade boasts an equally majestic tympanum.

Avallon is 13 kilometers (8 miles) farther along from Vézelay, via D957. Its site, on a promontory, is spectacular, and its old streets and ramparts make agreeable places to stroll. The imagination of medieval stone carvers ran riot at the portals of the venerable church of **St-Lazarus.**

The expressway passes close by Avallon and can whisk you along to Dijon, 96 kilometers (60 miles) away, in less than an hour. If you're in no rush, take the time to explore part of the huge **Morvan Regional Park;** the road twists and turns through lakes, hills, and forests. Take D944 out of Avallon and then turn left on D10 to reach **Quarré-les-Tombes**—so called because of the empty prehistoric stone tombs discovered locally and eerily arrayed in a ring around the church—before continuing southeast toward Saulieu. The **Rocher de la Pérouse,** 8 kilometers (5 miles) from Quarré-les-Tombes, is a mighty outcrop worth climbing for the view of the Cousin Valley. Continue to **Saulieu** via the N6, D264, and D977.

Saulieu's reputation belies its size (just 3,000 inhabitants). It is renowned for good food (Rabelais, that 16th-century authority, extolled its hospitality) and Christmas trees (a million are harvested each year). The **Basilica of St-Andoche** is almost as old as Vézelay's, though less imposing and much restored. The adjoining town **museum** (admission 20 frs.; open Wed.–Mon., 10–noon and 2–5) contains a room devoted to the sculptor of art deco animals, François Pompon.

Dijon

N6 and then D977 link Saulieu to the Dijon-bound A38 expressway to the east. **Dijon** is capital of both Burgundy and gastronomy. Visit its restaurants and the **Palais des Ducs** (Ducal Palace), testimony to bygone splendor and the setting for one of France's leading art museums (admission 12 frs; open Wed.–Mon. 10–6). The tombs of Philip the Bold and John the Fearless head a rich collection of medieval objects and Renaissance furniture. Outstanding features of the city's old churches include the stained glass of **Notre Dame,** the austere interior of the **cathedral of St-Bénigne,** and the chunky Renaissance facade of **St-Michel.** Don't miss the exuberant 15th-century gateway at the **Chartreuse de Champmol**—all that remains of a former charterhouse—or the adjoining **Puits de Moïse,** the so-called Well of Moses, with six large, realistic medieval statues on a hexagonal base.

Beaune

A31 connects Dijon to **Beaune,** 40 kilometers (25 miles) to the south, but you may prefer a leisurely trip through the vineyards. Take D122, then N74 at Chambolle-Musigny; just to the south is the Renaissance **Château du Clos de Vougeot,** famous as the seat of Burgundy's elite company of wine tasters, the Confrérie des Chevaliers du Tastevin, who gather here in November at the start of the three-day festival Les Trois Glorieuses—which includes a wine auction at the Hospices de Beaune. *Château du Clos de Vougeot. tel. 80–62–86–09. Admission: 22 frs. Open daily 9–11:30 and 2–5:30. Closed Dec. 24–Jan. 3. Guided tours daily.*

The **Hospices** (or Hôtel-Dieu) **de Beaune** owns some of the finest vineyards in the region yet was founded in 1443 as a hospital. Its medical history is retraced in a **museum** that also features Roger van der Weyden's medieval Flemish masterpiece *The Last Judgment,* plus a collection of tapestries, though a better series, relating the life of the Virgin, hangs in Beaune's main church, the **Collégiale Notre Dame**, which dates from 1120. *Hospices de Beaune tel. 80–24–45–00. Admission: 27 frs adults, 14 frs children. Open Apr.–Nov., daily 9–6:30; Dec.–Mar., daily 9–11:30 and 2–5:30.*

The history of local wines can be explored at the **Musée du Vin de Bourgogne** (admission 10 frs; open Apr.–Oct., daily 9–noon and 1:30–6; Nov.–Mar., daily 10–noon and 2–5:30), housed in a mansion built in the 15th and 16th centuries. The place to drink the stuff is in the candlelit cellars of the **Marché aux Vins** (wine market), on rue Nicolas Rolin, where you can taste as much as you please for 40 francs.

Autun

Autun is 48 kilometers (30 miles) west of Beaune along D973 but is worth a detour, if only for the Renaissance **château of Sully** (admission: 12 frs; visits to grounds only, daily in summer, 10–noon and 2–5) on the way. The town's importance dates back to Roman times, as you can detect at the **Porte St-André,** a well-preserved archway, and the **Théâtre Romain,** once the largest arena in Gaul. The leading monument in Autun is the church of **St-Lazarus,** a curious Gothic cathedral redone in the Classical style by 18th-century clerics trying to follow fashion. The building actually dates from the first half of the 12th century. Note the majestic picture by Ingres, the *Martyrdom of St-Symphorien,* in one of the side chapels. Across from the cathedral is the **Musée Rolin** (admission 14 frs; open Wed.–Mon. 10–noon and 2–5; Sun. 2–5), with several fine paintings from the Middle Ages.

Cluny

From Autun, head southeast along N80 and D980, via industrial Montceau-les-Mines, to **Cluny,** 80 kilometers (50 miles) away. The **Abbey** of Cluny, founded in the 10th century, was the largest church in Europe until St. Peter's was built in Rome in the 16th century. The ruins give an idea of its original grandeur. Note the **Clocher de l'Eau-Bénite,** a majestic bell tower, and the 13th-century **farinier** (flour mill) with its fine chestnut roof and collection of statues. *Guided tours of ruins. Admission: 29 frs adults, 9 frs children. Open Easter–Oct., daily 9– noon and 2–5; Nov.–Easter, daily, late morning–early afternoon.*

A model of the original abbey can be seen in the **Musée Ochier,** the 15th-century abbot's palace. *Rue Conant. Admission: 8 frs. Open Wed.–Mon. 10–noon and 2–5. Closed Jan. 1–15.*

Cluny is a mere 28 kilometers (16 miles) northwest of **Mâcon,** a bustling town best known for its wine fair in May and for its stone bridge across the Saône; the low arches are a headache for large river barges. At Mâcon take N6 or A6 due south to Lyon, where the River Rhône runs parallel to the Saône before the two converge south of the city center.

Lyon

In recent years, **Lyon** has solidified its role as a commercial center, thanks to France's policy of decentralization and the TGV train. Much of the city has an appropriate air of untroubled prosperity, and you will have plenty of choices when it comes to good eating. Enchanting Lyon is a human-size town; you can walk its pedestrian streets, explore Old Lyon and Presqu'Ile (almost island), lying between the two rivers, and in a few days visit all its seductive sights.

The clifftop silhouette of **Notre Dame de Fourvière** is the city's most striking symbol: The 19th-century basilica is an exotic mishmash of styles with an interior that's pure decorative overkill. Climb the Fourvière heights for the view, instead, and then go to the nearby Roman remains. *Théâtres Romains. Admission free. Open Mar.–Oct., weekdays 8–noon and 2–5, Sat. 9–noon and 3–6, Sun. 3–6; Nov.–Feb., weekdays 8–noon and 2–5.*

The pick of Lyon's museums is the **Musée des Beaux-Arts.** It houses sculpture, classical relics, and an extensive collection of old masters and Impressionists. Don't miss local artist Louis Janmot's 19th-century mystical cycle *The Poem of the Soul,* 18 canvases that took nearly 50 years to complete. *20 pl. des Terreaux, tel. 78–28–07–66. Admission: 20 frs adults, 10 frs students, children under 18 free. Open Wed.–Sun. 10:30–6.*

Dining and Lodging

For details and price-category definitions *see* Dining *and* Lodging *in* Staying in France, *above.*

Auxerre

DINING

Jardin Gourmand. As its name implies, the Jardin Gourmand has a pretty garden where you can eat *en terrasse* in warm weather. The interior, accented by light-colored oak, is equally congenial. The cuisine is innovative—try the ravioli and foie gras or the duck with black currants— and the service is unobtrusive. *56 blvd. Vauban, 89000, tel. 86–51–53–52. Reservations advised. MC, V. Closed Mon. No lunch Tues.* $$

LODGING

Normandie. This picturesque creeper-covered construction is right in the town center, with its own garden but no restaurant. The rooms are well equipped and unpretentious. *41 blvd. Vauban, 89000, tel. 86–52–57–80, fax 86–51–54–33. 47 rooms, some with bath or shower. AE, DC, MC, V. $*

Avallon

DINING AND LODGING

Moulin des Ruats. The hotel is housed in an old flour mill just southwest of Avallon along D427. The rooms, many with their own balcony, are rustic. Most look onto the sparkling River Cousin, and in the summer you can eat on the riverbank. The traditional dishes that make up the large menu are served in the wood-paneled restaurant at other times. Try the coq au vin. This hotel is popular, so make sure to have a reservation if you come in July or August. *Vallée du Cousin, 89200, tel. 86–34–07–14, fax 86–31–65–47. 27 rooms, some with bath or shower. Facilities: restaurant. AE, DC, MC, V. Closed winter. $$*

Beaune

DINING

L'Ecusson. Despite its unprepossessing exterior, L'Ecusson is a comfortable, friendly, thick-carpeted restaurant, with four prix-fixe menus offering outstanding value. For around 200 francs, you can have rabbit terrine with tarragon followed by leg of duck in oxtail sauce, then cheese, and dessert. *2 rue du Lieutenant-Dupuis, tel. 80–24–03–82. Reservations advised. AE, DC, MC, V. Closed Sun., mid-Feb.–mid-Mar. $$*

La Grilladine. At this small, warm restaurant, chef Pierre Lenko's fare, while not elaborate, is good and hearty Burgundy cooking with such items as beef bourguignonne and *oeufs en meurette* (eggs poached in a red wine and bacon sauce). One of the two cheerful dining rooms has rose-pink table cloths, exposed stone walls, and a mammoth ancient wood beam supporting the ceiling's center. The other is lighter, more open, and less rustic. *17 rue Maufoux, tel. 80–22–22–36. Reservations advised. MC, V. Closed Mon. $–$$*

LODGING

★ **Le Cep.** Within the ramparts and only a five-minute walk from the main square, Beaune's top hotel offers spacious, tastefully decorated rooms furnished with antiques and large tile bathrooms. Rooms facing the courtyard are quieter. The hotel is a combination of several ancient town houses—the oldest is circa 1547—and the courtyards have been made into a small garden. On the ground floor, the large beams are exposed. Service can become a little harried when tour groups, albeit of fairly small size, check in and out. *27 rue Maufoux, 21200, tel. 80–22–35–48, fax 80–22–76–80. 52 rooms with bath. Facilities: restaurant (closed Mon., no lunch Tues.), garage. AE, DC, MC, V. $$$*

Hôtel de la Cloche. It has become hard to find reasonably priced lodgings in the center of town. This hotel has only six rooms at 290 francs, each with a queen-size bed and a shower; the remainder are slightly larger, and in the 360-franc range. All are neat and clean, however. There is a reasonably good restaurant in the hotel and a couple of slightly less expensive eating places up the street. The staff is helpful and there is a parking lot across the road. *40–42 rue du Faubourg Madeleine, 21200, tel. 80–24–66–33, fax 80–24–04–24. 16 rooms with bath. Facilities: restaurant. MC, V. Closed Dec. 20–Jan. 20. $$*

Chablis

DINING AND LODGING

★ **Hostellerie des Clos.** Guest rooms at this inn are quite simple and ordinary, given color by the cheerful floral curtains and quilts on the beds. The attraction is Michel Vignaud's superb culinary art. His *sandre* (perch-like freshwater fish) is served with a chicken-based sauce that stands in tasty juxtaposition to the fish. The casserole of hare (available only in autumn) is wonderfully robust. Most exciting is the appetizer of *huîtres d'Isigny* (small oysters) in a dill-and-chablis sauce. Desserts are equally splendid; perhaps try the *feuilles de chocolat* with red fruit. *Rue Jules-Rathier, 89800, tel. 86–42–10–63, fax 86–42–17–11. 26 rooms with bath. Facilities: restaurant. AE, DC, MC, V. $$–$$$*

Cluny

DINING AND LODGING

Bourgogne. It is hard to find a better place to get into the medieval mood of Cluny than this old-fashioned hotel, right next door to the ruins of the famous abbey. There is a small garden and an atmospheric restaurant with sober pink decor and refined cuisine: foie gras, snails, and fish with ginger are specialties. *Pl. de l'Abbaye, 71250, tel. 85–59–00–58, fax 85–59–03–73. 14 rooms with bath or shower. Facilities: restaurant. AE, DC, MC, V. Closed Wed. lunch, Mon., and mid-Nov.–mid-Feb. $$–$$$*

Dijon

DINING

Jean-Pierre Billoux. M. Billoux's restaurant is reputedly the best of all in this most gastronomic of French cities. It is magnificently situated in a spacious, restored town house with garden, bar, and stone-vaulted rooms. Service is charming. Specialties include steamed frogs' legs served with cress pancakes, and guinea fowl with foie gras. *14 pl. Darcy, tel. 80–30–11–00. Reservations required. MC, V. Closed Mon., part of Feb., and first half Aug. No dinner Sun. $$$*

DINING AND LODGING

Chapeau Rouge. This is a good choice if you want to be sure of getting a quiet, tasteful room in the center of town—it's close to Dijon cathedral. The Chapeau is even a better choice for its restaurant, renowned as a haven of regional cuisine. Snails, pigeon, and veal in mustard top the list of specialties. *5 rue Michelet, 21000, tel. 80–30–28–10, fax 80–30–33–89. 29 rooms with bath or shower. Facilities: restaurant (reservations required). AE, DC, MC, V. $$–$$$*

Lyon

DINING

★ **Léon de Lyon.** A mixture of regional tradition (dumplings, hot sausages) and eye-opening innovation keep Léon de Lyon at the forefront of Lyon's restaurant scene. It consists of two floors in an old house full of alcoves and wood paneling. The blue-aproned waiters melt into the old-fashioned decor, and such dishes as fillet of veal with celery or leg of lamb with fava beans will linger in your memory. *1 rue Pléney, tel. 78–28–11–33. Reservations required. MC, V. Closed Aug. No dinner Sun., no lunch Mon. $$$*

A Ma Vigne. Here is a restaurant that's popular with tourists; it provides straightforward meals as a break from too much gourmet Lyonnais dining. French fries, *moules* (mussels), roast ham, and tripe lead the menu. Locals appreciate this place, too, so get there early, especially at lunchtime. *23 rue Jean-Larrivé, tel. 78–60–46–31. MC, V. Closed Sun., Aug. $$*

LODGING

Royal. The Royal is on the spacious and elegant place Bellecour in the very heart of Lyon. Beware of the huge range in room prices (590–890 frs); many rooms have been stylishly renovated and some of the most expensive (with their own Jacuzzi) are positively luxurious. *20 pl. Bellecour, 69002, tel. 78–37–57–31, fax 78–37–01–36. 80 rooms, most with bath or shower. Facilities: parking, restaurant. AE, DC, MC, V.* $$$

Sens

LODGING

Paris et Poste. This hotel makes a pleasant stop on the way to Burgundy from Paris. The helpful service and sumptuous breakfasts (rare in France) confirm a sense of well-being created by the robust evening meal (with prix-fixe menus including duck, snails, and steak) served in the large, solemn restaurant, whose decor can be described as rustic Burgundian. *97 rue de la République, 89100, tel. 86–65–17–43, fax 86–64–48–45. 25 rooms with bath or shower. Facilities: restaurant. AE, DC, MC, V.* $$

Vézelay

DINING AND LODGING

★ **L'Espérance.** In the small neighboring village of St-Père-sous-Vézelay, L'Espérance is one of France's premier restaurants. Chef Marc Meneau is renowned for the subtlety and originality of his cuisine. A second restaurant, **Le Pré des Marguerites,** offers more traditional fare, much simpler, and less expensive. L'Espérance also has 40 luxurious rooms. Thirteen are pretty, but rather small rooms in the main house; the others, slightly larger, are in nearby buildings. *St-Père-sous-Vézelay, 89450, tel. 86–33–20–45, fax 86–33–26–15. Reservations required. Jacket and tie. AE, DC, MC, V. Closed Tues., Wed. lunch, and Jan. 1–Feb. 15.* $$$$.

LOIRE VALLEY

The Loire is the longest river in France, rising near Le Puy in the east of the Massif Central and pursuing a broad northwest curve on its 1,000-kilometer (620-mile) course to the Atlantic Ocean near Nantes. The region traditionally referred to as the Loire Valley—château country—is the 225-kilometer (140-mile) stretch between Orléans, 113 kilometers (70 miles) south of Paris, and Angers, 96 kilometers (60 miles) from the Atlantic coast. Thanks to its mild climate, soft light, and lush meadowland, this area is known as the Garden of France. Its leading actor—the wide, meandering Loire—offers two distinct faces: fast-flowing and spectacular in spring, sluggish and sandy in summer.

To the north lies the vast grain plain of the Beauce; to the southeast the marshy, forest-covered Sologne, renowned for mushrooms, asparagus, and game. The star attractions along the rocky banks of the Loire and its tributaries—the Rivers Cher, Indre, Vienne, and Loir—are the famous châteaus: stately houses, castles, or fairy-tale palaces. Renaissance elegance is often combined with fortresslike medieval mass. The Loire Valley was fought over by France and England during the Middle Ages. It took the example of Joan of Arc, the "Maid of Orléans" (scene of her most rousing military successes), for the French finally to expel the English.

The Loire Valley's golden age came under François I (1515–47), France's flamboyant contemporary of England's Henry VIII. He hired Renaissance craftsmen from Italy and hobnobbed with the aging

The Loire Valley

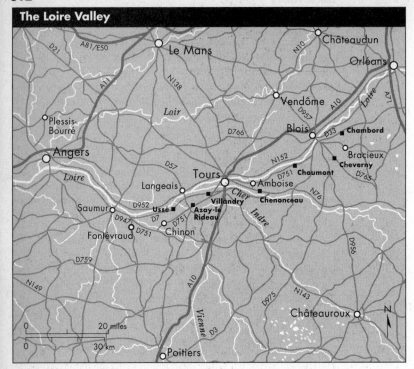

Leonardo da Vinci, his guest at Amboise. His salamander emblem is to be seen in many châteaus.

Getting Around

The easiest way to visit the Loire châteaus is by car; N152 hugs the riverbank and offers excellent sightseeing possibilities. Trains run along the Loire Valley every two hours, supplemented by local bus services. A peaceful way to explore the region is to rent a bicycle at one of the SNCF train stations (some trains even transport bikes for free).

Guided Tours

Bus tours for the main châteaus leave daily in summer from Tours, Blois, Angers, Orléans, and Saumur: Ask at the relevant tourist office for latest times and prices. Most châteaus insist that visitors follow one of their own tours anyway, but try to get a booklet in English before joining the tour, as most are in French only.

Tourist Information

Angers (pl. du Président Kennedy, tel. 41–91–96–56).
Blois (3 av. du Docteur Jean-Laigret, tel. 54–74–06–49).
Orléans (pl. Albert-Ier, tel. 38–53–05–95).
Tours (rue B. Palissy, tel. 47–05–58–08).

Exploring the Loire Valley

Châteaudun

Orléans, little more than an hour away by expressway (A10) or train, is the most obvious gateway to the Loire Valley if you're coming from

Paris. Apart from its art museum and majestic Ste-Croix cathedral, however, Orléans has little going for it. Instead take the expressway from Paris to Chartres, then N10 to **Châteaudun,** whose colossal château, standing resplendent on a steep promontory, contains graceful furniture and lavish tapestries. In its chapel are 15 statues produced locally in the 15th century. *Admission: 32 frs. Open daily, mid-Mar.–Sept. 9:30–11:45 and 2–6; Oct.–mid-Mar. 10–11:45 and 2–6.*

Continue along N10 to **Vendôme,** 40 kilometers (25 miles) southwest, where the Loir River (not to be confused with the larger and more famous Loire to the south) splits into many arms, lending the town a canal-like charm that harmonizes with its old streets and bridges. The large but little-known main church, **Eglise de la Trinité,** an encyclopedia of different styles, with brilliantly carved choir stalls and an exuberant west front, is the work of Jean de Beauce, best known for his spire at Chartres Cathedral. Vendôme also has a ruined **castle** with ramparts and pleasant, uncrowded gardens. *Admission to castle: 12 frs. Open Mar.–June, Wed.–Mon. 10–noon and 2–6; July and Aug., daily 10–noon and 2–6.*

Blois

Blois lies 32 kilometers (20 miles) southeast of Vendôme along D957. It is the most attractive of the major Loire towns, with its tumbling alleyways and its **château.** The château is a mixture of four different styles: Feudal (13th century); Gothic-Renaissance transition (circa 1500); Renaissance (circa 1520); and Classical (circa 1635). *Admission: 30 frs. Open May–Aug., daily 9–6:30; Sept.–Apr., daily 9–noon and 2–5.*

Blois makes an ideal launching pad for a visit to the châteaus of Chambord and Cheverny. **Chambord** (begun in 1519) is 20 kilometers (11 miles) east of Blois along D33, near Bracieux. It stands in splendid isolation in a vast forest and game park. There's another forest on the roof: 365 chimneys and turrets, representing architectural self-indulgence at its least squeamish. Grandeur or a mere 440-room folly? Judge for yourself, and don't miss the superb spiral staircase or the chance to saunter over the rooftop terrace. *Admission: 31 frs adults, 7 frs children. Open July–Aug., daily 9:30–6:30; Sept.–June, daily 9:30–11:45 and 2–sunset.*

About 20 kilometers (12 miles) south of Blois, along D751, stands the sturdy château of **Chaumont,** built between 1465 and 1510—well before Benjamin Franklin became a regular visitor. There is a magnificent Loire panorama from the terrace, and the stables—where purebreds dined like royalty—show the importance attached to fine horses, for hunting or just prestige. *Admission: 25 frs adults, 13 frs students and senior citizens. Open Apr.–Sept., daily 9–12:30 and 2–4:30; Oct.–Mar., daily 9:30–12:30 and 2–3:30.*

Amboise

Downstream (westward) another 16 kilometers (10 miles) lies the bustling town of **Amboise,** whose **château,** with charming grounds, a rich interior, and fine views over the river from the battlements, dates from 1500. It wasn't always so peaceful: In 1560, more than 1,000 Protestant "conspirators" were hanged from these battlements during the Wars of Religion. *Admission: 30 frs adults, 20 frs students, 10 frs children. Open July–Aug., daily 9–6:30; Sept.–June, daily 9–noon and 2–5.*

The nearby **Clos-Lucé,** a 15th-century brick manor house, was the last home of Leonardo da Vinci, who was invited to stay here by François I. Leonardo died here in 1519, and his engineering genius is illustrated by models based on his plans and sketches. *Admission: 34 frs adults,*

25 frs students and senior citizens. Same hrs as château, but open till 6:30 in winter.

The early 16th-century château of **Chenonceau,** 16 kilometers (10 miles) south of Amboise along D81 and then D40, straddles the tranquil River Cher like a bridge. It is surrounded by elegant gardens and a splendid avenue of plane trees. Inside, note the fine paintings, colossal fireplaces, and richly worked ceilings. A waxworks museum lurks in an outbuilding. *Admission: 45 frs adults, 25 frs children. Open mid-Feb.–mid-Nov., daily 9–sunset; mid-Nov.–mid-Feb., daily 9–4:30.*

Tours

Tours, 25 kilometers (15 miles) farther on, is the unofficial capital of the Loire. It retains a certain charm despite its sprawling size (250,000 inhabitants) and extensive postwar reconstruction. Its attractive old quarter, Vieux Tours, around place Plumereau, has been tastefully restored, while the **Cathedral of St-Gatien** (1239–1484) numbers among France's most impressive churches. The influence of local Renaissance sculptors and craftsmen is much in evidence on the ornate facade. The stained glass in the choir is particularly delicate; some of it dates from 1320.

The château of **Villandry,** 16 kilometers (10 miles) southwest of Tours along the River Cher, is known for its painstakingly relaid 16th-century gardens, with their long avenues of 1,500 manicured lime trees. The château interior, restored, like the gardens, in the mid-19th century, is equally beguiling. Note the painted and gilded ceiling from Toledo and the collection of Spanish pictures. *Admission: château and gardens, 37 frs; garden only, 24 frs. Open daily 9–6; gardens open 9–dusk.*

Langeais

Langeais is just 14 kilometers (9 miles) west of Villandry: Keep on D7 to Lignières before turning right onto D57 and crossing the Loire. A massive **castle** built in the 1460s and never altered dominates this small town. Its apartments contain a superb collection of tapestries, chests, and beds. *Admission: 35 frs adults, 25 frs senior citizens, 17 frs students and children. Open Easter–Oct., daily 9–6:30; Nov.–Easter, Tues.–Sun. 9–noon and 2–5. Closed Mon.*

Azay-le-Rideau (1518–29), one of the prettiest of the Loire châteaus, lies on the River Indre 10 kilometers (6 miles) south of Langeais along D57. It has harmonious proportions and exquisite grounds, with a domesticated moat that is really a lake. This graceful ensemble compensates for the château's spartan interior, as does the charm of the surrounding village. *Admission: 26 frs adults, 17 frs senior citizens, 6 frs children. Open Apr.–Sept., daily 9:30–noon and 2–6; Oct.–Mar., daily 9:30–noon and 2–4:15.*

A short ride down the Indre Valley (on D17 and then D7) from Azay will help you judge whether **Ussé** really is, as the brochures claim, the fairy-tale castle that inspired *Sleeping Beauty*. Its bristling roofs and turrets, flowered terraces, and forest backcloth have undeniable romance. Don't forget the **chapel** in the park, built 1520–38 in purest Renaissance proportions. *Admission: 54 frs adults, 25 frs students. Open mid-Mar.–Nov., daily 9–noon and 2–6.*

Chinon

Chinon, 13 kilometers (8 miles) from Ussé via D7 and D16, is an ancient town nestled by the River Vienne, with a rock-of-ages **castle** patrolling the horizon. This 12th-century fortress, with walls 370 meters (400 yards) long, is mainly in ruins, though small museums are installed in the Royal Chambers and sturdy Tour de l'Horloge (clock tower).

There are excellent views from the ramparts over Chinon and the Vienne Valley. *Admission: 23 frs adults, 18 frs senior citizens and children under 19. Open Nov.–mid-Mar., Thurs.–Tues. 9–noon and 2–5; mid-Mar.–June and Sept., daily 9–6; July and Aug., daily 9–7; Oct., daily 9–5.*

From just south of Chinon, D751 heads off up the Vienne Valley toward **Fontevraud,** 21 kilometers (13 miles) away. This quiet village is dominated by its medieval **abbey,** where English kings Henry II and Richard the Lionhearted are buried. The church, cloisters, Renaissance chapter house, long-vaulted refectory, and octagonal kitchen are all still standing. The guided tours are in French, but you can get a brochure in English to keep track of where you are. *Admission: 26 frs adults, 17 frs senior citizens, 7 frs children. Open May–mid-Sept., daily 9–noon and 2–6:30; mid-Sept.–Apr., daily 9:30–12:30 and 2–5:30.*

Saumur, 16 kilometers (10 miles) west along the Loire from Fontevraud via D947, is a prosperous town famous for its riding school, wines, and château—a white 14th-century castle that towers above the river. The château contains two outstanding museums: the **Musée des Arts Décoratifs** (Decorative Arts Museum), featuring porcelain and enamels, and the **Musée du Cheval** (Equine Museum), with saddles, stirrups, skeletons, and Stubbs engravings. *Admission: 33 frs adults, 24 frs students and senior citizens. Open July–Sept., daily 9–6:30; Oct. and Apr.–June, daily 9–11:30 and 2–6; Nov.–Mar., Wed.–Mon. 10–5.*

Angers

Angers is a large, historic town on the River Maine just to the north of the Loire. D952 runs along the Loire Valley from Saumur, 45 kilometers (28 miles) away. The feudal **château** was built by St-Louis (1228–38) and has a dry moat, drawbridge, and 17 round towers along its ½-mile-long walls. A modern, well-integrated gallery houses an exquisite tapestry collection, notable for the enormous *Tapestry of the Apocalypse,* woven in Paris around 1380. *Admission: 31 frs adults, 15 frs students and senior citizens, 6 frs children. Open July–Aug., daily 10–7; Sept.–June, daily 9:30–noon and 2–5:30.*

Dining and Lodging

For details and price-category definitions, *see* Dining *and* Lodging *in* Staying in France, above.

Amboise

DINING AND LODGING

Le Blazon. This delightful small hotel, enlivened by the enthusiasm of the owners, is behind the château, a four-minute walk from the center of town. The old building has been well converted into guest rooms of different shapes and sizes, whose compact prefabricated bathroom units have showers and toilets. Most rooms have twin beds, though a few have queens. Room 229, with exposed beams and a cathedral ceiling, has special charm; Room 109 is comfortably spacious and has a good view of the square. There's superior fare in the pretty little restaurant, with menus beginning at 95 francs. The menu changes with the seasons, and may include roast lamb with garlic and medallions of pork, and appetizers of salmon carpaccio with mustard dressing and air-dried duck breast scented with herbs and spices. *14 rue Joyeuse, 37400, tel. 47–23–22–41, fax 47–57–56–18. 29 rooms with bath. Facilities: restaurant. MC, V. $–$$*

Angers

DINING

La Treille. For traditional, simple fare, try this small two-story mom-and-pop restaurant just off the place Ste-Croix (next to the cathedral). The prix-fixe menu may start with a *salade au chèvre chaud* (warm goat cheese salad), followed by confit of duck and an apple tart. A bottle of local wine completes the meal. Madame runs the small bar while her husband serves the food with a warm welcoming smile. The upstairs dining room has a party atmosphere; downstairs is better for quiet conversation. *12 rue Montault, tel. 41–88–45–51. MC, V. Closed Sun.* $

DINING AND LODGING

Pavillon Paul Le Quéré. In 1992, Paul Le Quéré created a luxurious boutique hotel to complement his restaurant in a renovated mansion set back from the main avenue. The rooms, decorated by his wife, Martine, in classic modern style, have flashy marble bathrooms. The chef happily juggles tradition with modern innovations, be it roast lobster tails, fillet of sole sautéed in the juice of oysters, or diced beef with mussels. One opulent dining room is in a glass rotunda, splendid for lunch, while the formal dining room with a Charles X fireplace sets a classic tone for dinner. *3 blvd. du Maréchal-Foch, 49100, tel. 41–20–00–20, fax 41–20–06–20. 6 rooms with bath, 4 suites. Facilities: restaurant, parking. AE, DC, MC, V.* $$$

Blois

DINING

Au Rendez-vous des Pêcheurs. Located on the right bank of the Loire below the castle, this extremely modest restaurant has simple decor but offers excellent value in its creative cooking. Chef Eric Reithler has brought inventiveness to his fish-based specialties. *27 rue du Foix, tel. 54–74–67–48. MC, V. Closed Sun. No dinner Mon.* $$

DINING AND LODGING

Le Médicis. This is your best bet in Blois. The rooms at the smart and friendly hotel, 1,000 yards from the château, are comfortable, air-conditioned, and soundproofed from the main avenue. If you wish to splurge, the suite has a whirlpool; the regular rooms have simply modern bathrooms with such amenities as hair dryers. The rooms, newly decorated, are furnished individually, but all share a joyous color scheme. The restaurant itself makes staying here worthwhile. Chef-owner Christian Garanger makes each dish a presentation, and his cooking is innovative classical—coquille St-Jacques with a pear fondue, and thin slices of roast hare with black currant sauce, for example. *2 allée François 1ᵉʳ, 41000, tel. 54–43–94–04, fax 54–42–04–05. 12 rooms with bath, 1 suite. Facilities: restaurant (no dinner Sun. in low season). AE, DC, MC, V. Hotel closed Jan. 3–Jan. 24.* $$

Chambord

LODGING

Hôtel St-Michel. Considering its location right across from the château, the St-Michel offers good value. Some of its rooms afford splendid views of the château, its lawns, and the forest backdrop, as does the conveniently situated terrace, an ideal place for summer morning coffee before the tourist hordes arrive. *41250 Chambord, tel. 54–20–31–31. 38 rooms, some with bath or shower. Facilities: restaurant, tennis court, parking. MC, V. Closed Nov. 12–Dec. 19.* $$

Chenonceaux

DINING AND LODGING

★ **Bon Laboureur et du Château.** In 1882, it won Henry James's praise as a simple, rustic inn. Since then, through four generations of the Jeudi family, the Bon Laboureur has come up in the world. It's elegantly modern, with a few oak beams surviving, and a pretty kitchen garden. Rooms in the old house are comfortably traditional; rooms in the former stables are larger and have more contemporary appeal, and the largest rooms are in the converted manor house across the street. There is also a "honeymoon" room in the garden with the pool. The food is commendable. You can dine on excellent turbot with hollandaise or braised rabbit with dried fruit. The *poêle de St-Jacques* (sautéed scallops) with fresh ceps is a must in the autumn. Make your dinner reservations early for a table in the dining room rather than in the annex. *6 rue du Dr-Bretonneau, 37150, tel. 47–23–90–02, fax 47–23–82–01. 36 rooms with bath. Facilities: restaurant, garden, heated pool. AE, DC, MC, V. Closed Dec.–mid-Mar. $$*

Chinon

DINING AND LODGING

Château de Marçay. In a smartly renovated château whose early beginnings were a medieval fortress, a professional and efficient staff serve the fashion-conscious guests who come to stay and dine. Chef Pascal Bodin prepares an excellent carpaccio de canard for a starter and follows with, perhaps, tournedos of salmon bathed in a Chinon wine sauce and served with a confit of aubergine. Rooms in the château are furnished with valuable antiques; space is generous, beams and gables add warmth, and bathrooms are marbled and vast. Ground-floor rooms in the west wing have private patios. Rooms in the newly constructed Pavilion 50 yards from the château, though pleasantly furnished, have less charm. *Marçay (6 km/4 mi south of Chinon by D49 and D116), 37500 Chinon, tel. 47–93–03–47, fax 47–93–45–33. 35 rooms with bath (27 in château). Facilities: restaurant, gardens, pool, tennis, parking. AE, DC, MC, V. Closed 2nd wk of Jan.–mid-Mar. $$$*

Saumur

LODGING

Anne d'Anjou. Close to the center of town, this hotel facing the river offers views of the château (floodlit at night) perched above. Inside the 18th-century building the staircase has wrought-iron banisters that circle up to the top floor. Rooms are simple, with either old furniture or contemporary decor. Room 102 has wood panel paintings and Empire furnishings. The restaurant, Les Menestreles, offers traditional fare. *32–33 quai Mayaud, 49400, tel. 41–67–30–30, fax 41–67–51–00. 50 rooms. Facilities: restaurant, parking. AE, DC, MC, V. $$*

Tours

DINING AND LODGING

★ **Domaine de la Tortinière.** Ten kilometers (6 miles) due south of Tours and near Montbazon along N10, this turreted building dates from the mid-19th century. It stands proudly on a hill amid vast fields and woodland. The bedrooms are individually decorated in styles ranging from conventionally old-fashioned to brashly ultramodern. The airy restaurant looks out over the gardens. Salmon, pigeon, and rabbit with truffles are menu highlights. *10 route de Ballan, 37250 Veigné, tel. 47–26–00–19, fax 47–65–25–70. 14 rooms with bath. Facilities: restaurant (closed Tues. in Nov., Dec., and Mar. No lunch Wed.). MC, V. Closed mid-Dec.–Feb. $$$*

Hôtel de l'Univers. A complete renovation completed in 1993 has made the most of the building's old charm. The rooms vary slightly, but common to all is a clever use of space to form separate desk and sitting areas. The use of wood panels and soft colorings adds warmth. Bathrooms are spacious. Most rooms look onto a garden. The lobby is decorated with murals depicting some of the famous people who have stayed here, among them, Winston Churchill, Rudyard Kipling, and Maurice Chevalier. *5 blvd. Heurteloup, 37000, tel. 47–02–37–12, fax 47–61–51–80. 89 rooms with bath, 10 suites. Facilities: restaurant, bar, parking. AE, DC, MC, V. $$$*

THE RIVIERA

Few places in the world have the same pull on the imagination as France's fabled Riviera, the Mediterranean coastline stretching from St-Tropez in the west to Menton on the Italian border. Cooled by the Mediterranean in the summer and warmed by it in winter, the climate is almost always pleasant. Avoid the area in July and August, however—unless you love crowds.

While the Riviera's coastal resorts seem to live exclusively for the tourist trade and have often been ruined by high-rise blocks, the hinterlands remain relatively untarnished. The little villages perched high on the hills behind medieval ramparts seem to belong to another century. One of them, St-Paul-de-Vence, is the home of the Maeght Foundation, one of the world's leading museums of modern art.

Artists, attracted by the light, have played a considerable role in popular conceptions of the Riviera, and their presence is reflected in the number of modern art museums: the Musée Picasso at Antibes, the Musée Renoir and the Musée d'Art Moderne Mediterranée at Cagnes-sur-Mer, and the Musée Jean Cocteau near the harbor at Menton. Wining and dining are special treats on the Riviera, especially if you are fond of garlic and olive oil. Bouillabaisse, a spicy fish stew, is the most popular regional specialty.

The tiny principality of Monaco, which lies between Nice and Menton, is included in this section despite the fact that it is a sovereign state. Although Monaco has its own army and police force, its language, food, and way of life are French.

Getting Around

By Car
Expressway A8 is the only way to get around the Riviera quickly, but for the drama of mountains and sea, take one of the famous Corniche roads.

By Train
The train line follows the coast from Marseille to the Italian border, providing excellent access to the seaside resorts, but you will have to take local buses (marked GARE ROUTIÈRE) or guided tours to visit Grasse and the perched villages.

Guided Tours

SNCF runs many organized tours (contact the Nice Tourist Office, *below*) to areas otherwise hard to reach: St-Paul-de-Vence, Upper Provence, and the Verdon Gorges. Boats operate from Nice to Marseille; from St-Tropez to the charming Hyères Islands; and from Antibes, Cannes, and Juan-les-Pins to the Lérins Islands.

The Riviera

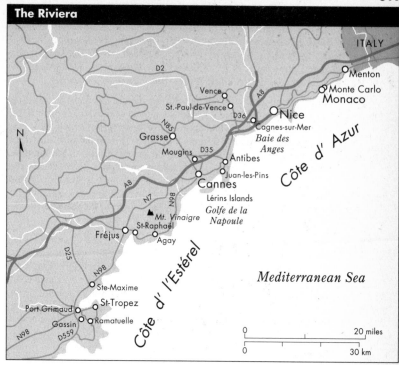

ITALY

Menton

Monte Carlo
Monaco

D2

Vence

St.-Paul-de-Vence

D36

Nice

Cagnes-sur-Mer

Baie des Anges

Grasse

N85

Mougins

D35

Antibes

Juan-les-Pins

Côte d' Azur

Cannes

Lérins Islands

Golfe de la Napoule

N7

N98

A8

Mt. Vinaigre

Fréjus

St-Raphaël

Agay

Côte de l'Estérel

D25

Mediterranean Sea

N98

Ste-Maxime

St-Tropez

Port Grimaud

Gassin

Ramatuelle

N98

D559

N

0   20 miles

0   30 km

Tourist Information

Cagnes-sur-Mer (6 blvd. du Mal-Juin, tel. 93–20–61–64).
Cannes (Palais des Congrès, La Croisette, tel. 93–39–24–53).
Fréjus (325 rue Jean-Jaurès, tel. 94–17–19–19).
Grasse (22 cours Honoré-Cresp, tel. 93–36–03–56).
Juan-les-Pins (51 blvd. Guillaumont, tel. 93–61–04–98).
Menton (Palais de l'Europe, Av. Boyer, tel. 93–57–57–00).
Monaco (2a blvd. des Moulins, tel. 92–16–61–16).
Nice (av. Thiers, tel. 93–87–07–07; 5 av. Gustave-V, tel. 93–87–60–60).
St-Paul-de-Vence (Maison Tour, rue Grande, tel. 93–32–86–95).
St-Tropez (quai Jean-Jaurès, tel. 94–97–45–21).
Vence (pl. du Grand-Jardin, tel. 93–58–06–38).

Exploring the Riviera

St-Tropez

St-Tropez was just another pretty fishing village until it was "discovered" in the 1950s by the "beautiful people," a fast set of film stars, starlets, and others who scorned bourgeois values while enjoying bourgeois bank balances. Today, its summer population swells from 6,000 to 60,000. In season, its top hotels, restaurants, nightclubs, and chic little shops are jammed. In the winter, it's hard to find a restaurant open. The best times to visit, therefore, are early summer or fall. May and June are perhaps the best months, when the town lets its hair down during two local festivals.

The **old port** is the liveliest part of town. You can kill time here at a café terrace, watching the rich and famous on their gleaming yachts.

Between the old and new ports is the **Musée de l'Annonciade,** set in a cleverly converted chapel, which houses paintings by artists drawn to St-Tropez between 1890 and 1940—including Paul Signac, Matisse, Derain, and Van Dongen. *Quai de l'Épi, tel. 94–97–04–01. Admission: 22 frs adults, 11 frs children. Open June–Sept., Wed.–Mon. 10–noon and 3–7; Oct.–May, Wed.–Mon. 10–noon and 2–6.*

Across the place de l'Hôtel de Ville lies the old town, where twisting, narrow streets, designed to break the impact of the terrible mistral (the cold, dry, northerly wind common to this region), open onto tiny squares and fountains. A long climb up to the **citadel** is rewarded by a splendid view over the old town and across the gulf to **Ste-Maxime,** a quieter, more working-class family resort with a decent beach and reasonably priced hotels. St-Tropez is also a good base for visiting **Port Grimaud,** a pastiche of an Italian fishing village (take D558), and the nearby hilltop villages: the old Provençal town of **Ramatuelle** and the fortified village of **Gassin.**

The **Corniche des Issambres** (N98) runs along the coast from Ste-Maxime to **Fréjus,** a Roman town built by Caesar in 49 BC, standing on a rocky plateau between the Maures and Estérel hills. Two main roads link Fréjus and Cannes. Tortuous N7, originally a Roman road, skirts the northern flank of the rugged Estérel hills. Look for an intersection called the "carrefour du Testannier" and follow the signs to **Forêt Domaniale de l'Estérel** and **Mont Vinaigre** for a magnificent view over the hills.

Cannes

In 1834, a chance event was to change the town of **Cannes** forever. Lord Brougham, Britain's lord chancellor, was en route to Nice when an outbreak of cholera forced the authorities to freeze all travel. Trapped in Cannes, he fell in love with the place and built himself a house there to use as an annual refuge from the British winter. The English aristocracy, czars, kings, and princes soon caught on, and Cannes became a community for the international elite. Grand palace hotels were built to cater to them, and Cannes came to symbolize dignified luxury. Today, Cannes is also synonymous with the **International Film Festival.**

Cannes is for relaxing—strolling along the seafront on the **Croisette** and getting tanned on the beaches. Almost all the beaches are private, but that doesn't mean you can't use them, only that you must pay for the privilege. The Croisette offers splendid views of the **Napoule Bay.** Only a few steps inland is the old town, known as the **Suquet,** with its steep, cobbled streets and its 12th-century watchtower.

Grasse is perched in the hills behind Cannes. Take N85 or just follow your nose to the town that claims to be the perfume capital of the world. A good proportion of its 40,000 inhabitants work at distilling and extracting scent from the tons of roses, lavender, and jasmine produced here every year. The various perfumers are only too happy to guide visitors around their fragrant establishments. Fragonard is the best known (20 blvd. Fragonard, tel. 93–36–44–65). The old town is attractive, with its narrow alleys and massive, somber **cathedral.** Three of the paintings inside the cathedral are by Rubens and one is by Fragonard, who lived here for many years.

Take N85 back down to the coast, but fork left at **Mougins,** an attractive fortified hilltop town, famous for one of France's best restaurants, Le Moulin de Mougins. D35 takes you to **Antibes** and **Juan-les-Pins,** originally two villages that now form one town on the west side of the **Baie des Anges** (Angels' Bay).

Antibes

Antibes, the older village, dates back to the 4th century BC, when it was a Greek trading port. Today, it is renowned throughout Europe for its commercial flower and plant production. Every morning except Monday, the market on the Cours Masséna comes alive with the colors of roses, carnations, anemones, and tulips. The Grimaldis, the family that rules Monaco, built **Château Grimaldi** here in the 12th century on the remains of a Roman camp. Today, the château's main attraction is the **Musée Picasso**—a bounty of paintings, ceramics, and lithographs inspired by the sea and Greek mythology. *Pl. du Château, tel. 92–90–54–20. Admission: 26 frs adults, 13 frs students and senior citizens. Open Dec.–Oct., Wed.–Mon. 10–noon and 2–6.*

Nice

With its population of 400,000, its own university, new congress hall, and nearby science park, Nice is the undisputed capital of the Riviera. Founded by the Greeks as Nikaia, it has lived through several civilizations and was attached to France only in 1860. It consequently boasts a profusion of Greek, Italian, British, and French styles. Tourism may not be the main business of Nice, but it is a deservedly popular center with much to offer. There is an eclectic mixture of old and new architecture, an opera house, museums, flourishing markets, and regular concerts and festivals, including the Mardi Gras festival and the Battle of Flowers.

Numbers in the margin correspond to points of interest on the Nice map.

❶ The **place Masséna** is the logical starting point for an exploration of Nice. This fine square was built in 1815 to celebrate a local hero: one of Napoléon's most successful generals. The **Promenade des Anglais,** **❷** built by the English community here in 1824, is only a short stroll past the fountains and the **Jardin Albert Iᵉʳ.** It now carries heavy traffic but **❸** still forms a splendid strand between town and sea.

❹ Just up rue de Rivoli is the **Palais Masséna,** a museum concerned with the Napoleonic era. *65 rue de France, tel. 93–88–11–34. Admission free. Open Dec.–Oct., Tues.–Sun. 10–noon and 2–5 (3–6 May–Sept.).*

Further west, along rue de France, and right up avenue des Baumettes **❺** is the **Musée des Beaux-Arts Jules-Chéret,** Nice's fine-arts museum, built in 1878 as a palatial mansion for a Russian princess. The rich collection of paintings includes works by Renoir, Degas, Monet; Oriental prints; sculptures by Rodin; and ceramics by Picasso. *33 av. des Baumettes, tel. 93–62–18–12. Admission free. Open May–Sept., Tues.–Sun. 10–noon and 3–6; Oct. and Dec.–Apr., Tues.–Sun. 10–noon and 2–5.*

The narrow streets in the old town are the prettiest part of Nice: Take **❻** the rue de l'Opéra to see **St-François-de-Paule** church (1750) and the **❼** **opera house.** At the northern extremity of the old town lies the vast **❽** **place Garibaldi**—all yellow-ocher buildings and formal fountains.

❾ The **Musée Chagall** is just off the boulevard de Cimiez, near the Roman ruins. The museum was built in 1972 to house the Chagall collection, including the 17 huge canvases of *The Message of the Bible,* which took 13 years to complete. *Av. du Dr-Ménard, tel. 93–81–75–75. Admission: 27 frs adults, 18 frs students and senior citizens. Open July–Sept., Wed.–Mon. 10–7; Oct.–June, Wed.–Mon. 10–12:30 and 2–5:30.*

A 17th-century Italian villa amid the Roman remains contains two museums: the **Musée Archéologique,** with a plethora of ancient objects, **❿**

322

Nice

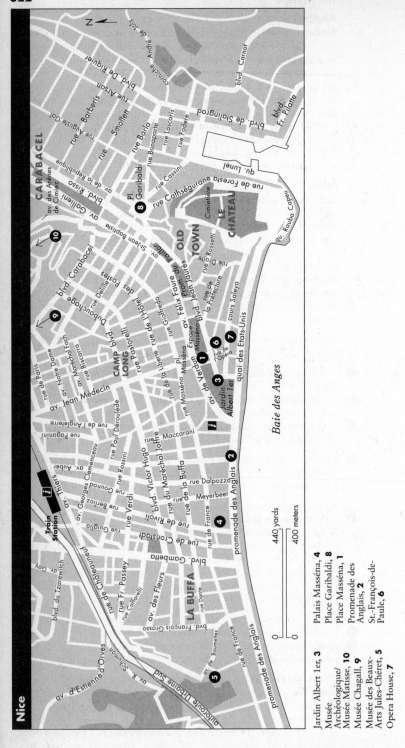

Baie des Anges

Jardin Albert 1er, **3**
Musée
Archéologique/
Musée Matisse, **10**
Musée Chagall, **9**
Musée des Beaux-
Arts Jules-Chéret, **5**
Opera House, **7**

Palais Masséna, **4**
Place Garibaldi, **8**
Place Masséna, **1**
Promenade des
Anglais, **2**
St-François-de-
Paule, **6**

and the renovated **Musée Matisse,** with paintings and bronzes by Henri Matisse (1869–1954). *164 av. des Arènes-de-Cimiez, tel. 93–81–08–08. Musée Matisse admission: 25 frs. Open Apr.–Sept., Wed.–Mon. 11–7; Oct.–Mar., Wed.–Mon. 10–5. Musée Archéologique, admission free. Open Dec.–Oct., Tues.–Sat. 10–noon and 2–5, Sun. 2–5.*

Monaco

Numbers in the margin correspond to points of interest on the Monaco map.

Sixteen kilometers (10 miles) along the coast from Nice is **Monaco.** For more than a century Monaco's livelihood was centered in its splendid copper-roof **casino.** The oldest section dates from 1878 and was conceived by Charles Garnier, architect of the Paris opera house. It's as elaborately ornate as anyone could wish, bristling with turrets and gold filigree, and masses of interior frescoes and bas-reliefs. There are lovely sea views from the terrace, and the gardens out front are meticulously tended. The main activity is in the American Room, where beneath the gilt-edged ceiling, busloads of tourists feed the one-armed bandits. *Pl. du Casino, tel. 92–16–21–21. Persons under 21 not admitted. Admission: 50 frs (American Room free). Open daily noon–4 AM. Closed May 1.*

The **Musée National des Automates et Poupées d' Autrefois** (Museum of Antique Dolls and Automatons) has a compelling collection of 18th- and 19th-century dolls and mechanical figures, the latter shamelessly showing off their complex inner workings. It's magically set in a 19th-century seaside villa (designed by Garnier). *17 av. Princesse-Grace, tel. 93–30–91–26. Admission: 26 frs adults, 15 frs children. Open daily 10–12:15 and 2:30–6:30.*

Monaco Town, the principality's old quarter, has many vaulted passageways and exudes an almost tangible medieval feel. The magnificent **Palais du Prince** (Prince's Palace), a grandiose Italianate structure with a Moorish tower, was largely rebuilt in the last century. Here, since 1297, the Grimaldi dynasty has lived and ruled. The spectacle of the **Changing of the Guard** occurs each morning at 11:55; inside, guided tours take visitors through the state apartments and a wing containing the **Palace Archives** and **Musée Napoléon** (Napoleonic Museum). *Pl. du Palais, tel. 93–25–18–31. Palace admission: 40 frs adults, 20 frs children. Open June–Oct., daily 9:30–12:30 and 2–6:30. Musée Napoléon and Palace Archives admission: 20 frs adults, 10 frs children. Open Tues.–Sun. 9:30–6:30.*

Monaco's **cathedral** (4 rue Colonel Bellando de Castro) is a late-19th-century neo-Romanesque confection in which Philadelphia-born Princess Grace lies entombed in splendor along with past members of the Grimaldi dynasty. Nearby is the **Musée Historial des Princes de Monaco** (Waxworks Museum), a Monégasque Madame Tussaud's, with none-too-realistic wax figures stiffly portraying various episodes in the Grimaldi history. The waxworks may not convince, but the rue Basse is wonderfully atmospheric. *27 rue Basse, tel. 93–30–39–05. Admission: 24 frs. Open May–Sept., daily 9–8; Oct.–Dec., daily 10:30–6; Jan.–Apr., daily 9–6:30.*

Next to the **St-Martin Gardens**—which contain an evocative bronze monument in memory of Prince Albert I (Prince Rainier's great-grandfather, the one in the sou'wester and flying oilskins, benignly guiding a ship's wheel)—is the **Musée Océanographique** (Oceanography Museum and Aquarium). This museum is also an internationally renowned research institute founded by the very Prince Albert who is remembered

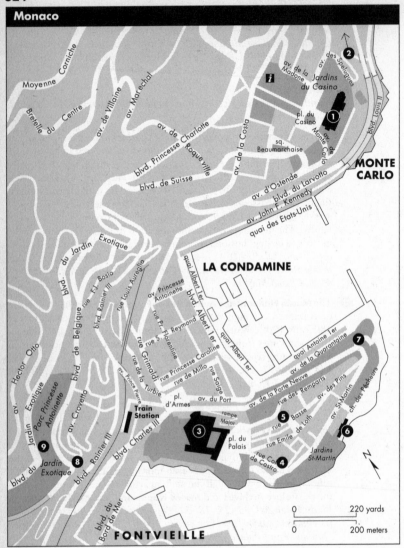

Casino, **1**

Cathedral, **4**

Fort Antoine The-
ater, **7**

Jardin Exotique, **8**

Musée Historial des
Princes de Monaco, **5**

Musée National des
Automates et Poupées
d'Autrefois, **2**

Musée
Océanographique, **6**

Museum of Prehis-
toric Anthropology, **9**

Palais du Prince, **3**

outside as an eminent marine biologist; the well-known underwater explorer Jacques Cousteau is the present director. The aquarium is the undisputed highlight, however, where a collection of the world's fish and crustacea—some colorful, some drab, some the stuff of nightmares—live out their lives in public. *Av. St-Martin, tel. 93–15–36–00. Admission: 60 frs adults, 30 frs children. Open Sept.–Oct. and May–June, daily 9:30–7; Nov.–Apr., daily 9:30–6; July and Aug., daily 9–8.*

7 Before heading back inland, take a stroll to the eastern tip of the rock, to the **Fort Antoine Theater** (av. de la Quarantaine, tel. 93–30–19–21), a converted 18th-century fortress that certainly looks a lot prettier now than it would have in more warlike times, covered as it is in ivy and flowering myrtle and thyme. In the summer, this is an open-air theater that seats 350.

8 The Moneghetti area is the setting for the **Jardin Exotique** (Garden of Exotic Plants), where 600 varieties of cacti and succulents cling to the rock face, their improbable shapes and sometimes violent coloring a further testimony to the fact that Mother Nature will try anything once. Your ticket also allows you to explore the **caves** next to the gardens, **9** and to visit the adjacent **Museum of Prehistoric Anthropology.** *Blvd. du Jardin Exotique, tel. 93–15–80–06. Admission: 39 frs adults, 26 frs senior citizens, 15 frs children. Open Oct.–May, daily 9–5:30; June–Sept., daily 9–7.*

Menton

Menton also once belonged to the Grimaldis and, like Nice, was attached to France only in 1860. Because of its popularity among British visitors, the western side of the town was developed at the turn of the century to cater to the influx of the rich and famous, with spacious avenues, first-class hotels, and the inevitable casino. The eastern side of town long remained the domain of the local fishermen but has been developed to cater to the needs of tourists. A large marina was built and the **Sablettes,** once a tiny beach, has been artificially extended.

Down by the harbor stands a small 17th-century fort, where Jean Cocteau, the artist, writer, and filmmaker, once worked. It now houses the **Musée Jean Cocteau,** with a collection of his work. *111 quai Napoléon, tel. 93–57–72–30. Admission free. Open Apr.–Oct., Wed.–Sun. 10–noon and 2–6; Nov.–Mar., Wed.–Sun. 10–noon and 3–6.*

Dining and Lodging

For details and price-category definitions, *see* Dining *and* Lodging *in* Staying in France, *above.*

Antibes

LODGING

Auberge Provençale. The rooms and service are sunny, partly a reflection of the manageable size of the hotel. Its popular restaurant serves lobster and shellfish as well as *boudin de rascasse,* a minced fish shaped into a sausage. *61 pl. Nationale, 06600. Tel. 93–34–13–24, fax 93–34–89–88. 6 rooms with bath. AE, DC, MC, V. Facilities: restaurant (reservations required, closed Mon., no lunch Tues.). Closed mid-Nov.–mid-Dec. $$*

Cagnes

DINING AND LODGING

Cagnard. This hotel is in an attractive 15th-century building in the old village. The restaurant—once the Grimaldi Château Guards Room—dates from the early 14th century. The hotel has several suites in two houses in the garden and a third up the road. The view from them all—over the Cap d'Antibes—is memorable. *54 rue Sous–Bari, 06800. Tel. 93–20–73–22, fax 93–22–06–39. 19 rooms and suites with bath. Facilities: restaurant (closed Nov.–mid-Dec., no lunch Thurs.). AE, DC, MC, V. $$$*

Cannes

DINING

Mirabelle. For many, this is a favorite restaurant in the Suquet. The cuisine is inventive, the sauces light, and the desserts special. *24 rue St-Antoine, tel. 93–38–72–75. Reservations advised. MC, V. Closed Tues., Jan. 15–Feb. 15, and Nov. 15–30. $$$*

LODGING

Majestic. Unlike most luxury hotels lining the Croisette on the seafront, the Majestic has a discreet atmosphere. The rooms are spacious and traditional but refreshingly decorated in pastels. The restaurant also offers a reasonably priced evening meal in winter. *14 La Croisette, 06400, tel. 92–98–77–00, fax 93–38–97–90. 283 rooms with bath. Facilities: private beach, swimming pool, air-conditioning, parking lot, tennis, golf, horseback riding. AE, DC, MC, V. Closed Nov. 11–Dec. 20. $$$*

Beverly. Despite extensive renovations and a 1993 name change, the Beverly (formerly the Bristol) continues to offer an intimate, wallet-friendly contrast to the big names nearby on La Croisette. Prices start at around 180 francs, but be prepared to go a bit higher if you fancy one of the 10 (quieter) rooms with a balcony at the back of the building. The beach, train station, and Palais des Festivals are all within a three-minute walk. *14 rue Hoche, 06400, tel. 93–39–10–66, fax 92–98–65–63. 19 rooms, 15 with bath or shower. AE, MC, V. Closed Dec.–mid-Jan. $–$$*

Grasse

LODGING

Panorama. The excellent views of the Massif de l'Estérel and right across to Cannes are the vindication of this hotel's name. It is modern and well run and has ample parking. Most rooms have good views, but there is no restaurant. *2 pl. du Cours, 06130, tel. 93–36–80–80, fax 93–36–92–04. 36 rooms with bath. MC, V. $$*

Menton

DINING AND LODGING

Princesse et Richmond. This classic hotel on the promenade is an excellent standby. Nothing fancy, but the rooms are bright and cheery, with lots of light coming through the windows. Most rooms have terraces looking out to sea. As a peaceful alternative to the often jam-packed beach, there is a roof terrace on the eighth floor, complete with a whirlpool bath. The hotel has no restaurant, but that releases you into the enormous range of Menton eateries. *617 prom. du Soleil, 06500, tel. 93–35–80–20, fax 93–57–40–20. 44 rooms with bath. Facilities: breakfast room. AE, DC, MC, V. Closed Nov.–early Dec. $$*

Monaco

DINING

★ **Louis XV.** A strong contender for the best-in-Monaco award, Louis XV's opulent decor and chef Alain Ducasse's beautifully conceived dishes, such as ravioli with foie gras and truffles, contribute to the formal atmosphere. The wine cellar is exceptional. *Hôtel de Paris, pl. du Casino, tel. 92–16–30–01. Reservations required. AE, DC, MC, V. $$$$*

Port. Harbor views from the terrace and top-notch Italian food make Port a good choice. A large, varied menu includes shrimp, pasta, lasagna, fettuccine, fish risotto, and veal with ham and cheese. *Quai Albert Ier, tel. 93–50–77–21. Reservations advised. AE, DC, MC, V. Closed Mon. and Nov. $$–$$$*

LODGING

★ **Hôtel de Paris.** An exceptional establishment, where elegance, luxury, dignity, and Old World charm are the watchwords. Built in 1864, it still exudes the gold-plated splendor of an era when kings and grand dukes stayed here. *Pl. du Casino, 98000, tel. 92–16–30–00, fax 93–15–90–03. 245 rooms with bath. Facilities: 2 restaurants, bar, pool, health club, shops, tennis court. AE, DC, MC, V. $$$$*

Balmoral. Despite the name, there's nothing even vaguely Scottish about this somewhat old-fashioned hotel overlooking the harbor. Rooms are a reasonable size, if bland; many have balconies. *12 av. de la Costa, 98000, tel. 93–50–62–37, fax 93–15–08–69. 75 rooms with bath or shower, half with air-conditioning. Facilities: restaurant (closed Nov.). AE, DC, MC, V. $$*

Mougins

DINING AND LODGING

Le Moulin de Mougins. Roger Vergé has created one of France's finest restaurants in a converted mill a short distance west of the village along D3. The cuisine ranges from apparently simple salads to rich, complicated sauces for lobster, salmon, or turbot. Considering that it is a gourmet favorite, the restaurant has a surprisingly informal atmosphere. There are five elegantly rustic guest rooms as well. *Quartier Notre-Dame-de-Vie, 424 Chemin du Moulin, 06250, tel. 93–75–78–24, fax 93–90–18–55. Reservations required. AE, DC, MC, V. Closed Thurs. lunch and Mon., hotel and restaurant closed Feb.–Mar. $$$$*

Nice

DINING

Ane-Rouge. Famous for generations as *the* place for Nice's best fish and seafood, this tiny, family-run restaurant is popular with locals, not least for the Vidalots, the pleasant couple who run it. *7 quai des Deux-Emmanuel, tel. 93–89–49–63. Reservations advised. MC, V. Closed weekends, mid-July–end of Aug. $$$*

DINING AND LODGING

★ **Négresco.** Opened in 1912, the Négresco is officially listed as a historic monument and is a byword for Old World elegance. The public rooms have antique coffered ceilings and magnificent fireplaces. No two bedrooms are alike, but they all have antique furniture and paintings. Its main restaurant, Le Chantecler, is without doubt the best in Nice. *37 promenade des Anglais, 06000, tel. 93–88–00–58, fax 93–88–35–68. 130 rooms with bath. Facilities: 2 restaurants (reservations required, closed mid-Nov.–mid-Dec.). AE, DC, MC, V. $$$$*

St-Tropez

DINING AND LODGING

Byblos. This hotel is unique. Its luxury rooms and suites are built around tiled courtyards, fragrant with magnolia and orange trees, like a miniature Provençal village. Each room is different, with amusing touches and subtle lighting. Les Caves du Roy, one of its two night-clubs, and Les Arcades, a restaurant run by Philipe Audibert, are considered among the best in town. *Av. Paul Signac, 83990, tel. 94–97–00–04, fax 94–97–40–52. 59 rooms with bath, 48 suites. Facilities: Restaurant, pool, gym, nightclub, sauna, hairdresser. AE, DC, MC, V. Closed mid-Oct.–Mar. $$$$*

11 Germany

AREUNITED GERMANY offers the traveler a unique experience. Today one country exists where there used to be two, and although the 40-year division was an artificial one, the differences that developed will take many years to even out. Technically, Germany is already one country: the same language, the same currency, the same federal political structure. But some of the differences can be quirky.

Rapid reunification—critics said it was too hasty—has had a damaging effect on the German economy, which had previously been unaffected by the recession in other parts of the Western world. The bid to quickly rejuvenate former East Germany and provide its 17 million inhabitants with better standards of living has so far proved difficult, while costing western German taxpayers billions of Deutschmarks. By the end of 1992, the effects of reunification had virtually stopped the great German economic locomotive, resulting in higher prices and the threat of higher taxes—and causing much grumbling in the west. And in January 1995, the government announced an additional 7.5% income tax (known as the solidarity tax) on top of regular income-tax levels to pay for the staggering cost of reunification. The determined effort of the powerful German federal bank, the Bundesbank, to curb inflation at all costs, has been blamed by neighboring western European governments for slowing their efforts to recover from the recession.

The problems of reunification, and the attendant social unrest in the east, also coincided with the massive influx of several hundred thousand "political" refugees as word spread far and wide that Germany had the most liberal asylum laws in the world, one of the central planks of a deliberately liberal post-Nazi constitution. The refugees—many of whom are believed to be economic rather than political—have added to the strains on the economy.

In the eastern part of the country, Germans still earn less than their fellow countrymen in the west. But many basic costs of living are lower. Overall, eastern German shops are less numerous and elegant, but they are filled with the sort of material goods that were unobtainable under the Communist regime. During the first six months after the fall of the Berlin Wall, the number of car owners in eastern Germany rose by 600,000.

Eastern Germany's emergence from communism has not so much inspired a new sense of nationhood there as it has revived regional traditions and identities. The villages south of Leipzig and Dresden have more in common with their neighbors in northern Bavaria, from whom they were cut off for four decades, than with Berlin bureaucrats. Six old states—with their capitals in Berlin, Dresden, Erfurt, Magdeburg, Potsdam, and Schwerin—have been re-created, making a total of 16 for all of reunited Germany.

Germans tend to rise very early; they may be found hammering away at a building site by 7 AM or seated at an office desk by 8 AM, but they take their leisure time just as seriously. Annual vacations of up to six weeks are the norm, and secular and religious festivals occupy at least another 12 days. Every town and village, and many city neighborhoods, manages at least one "Fest" a year, when the beer barrels are rolled out and sausages are thrown on the grill. The seasons have their own festivities: Fasching (carnival) heralds the end of winter, countless beer gardens open up with the first warm rays of sunshine; fall is celebrated with the Munich Oktoberfest; and Advent brings Christkindlmärket, colorful pre-Christmas markets held in town and city squares.

The great outdoors has always been an important escape hatch for the Germans, and *Lebensraum* (living space) is even more highly prized in the era of high technology and pressurized urban life. Germany does its best to meet the needs of its hardworking inhabitants. A Bavarian mountain inn, the glow of its lights reflected on the blanket of snow outside, may be only a short drive from Munich. The busy industrial city of Stuttgart lies at the gateway to the Schwarzwald (Black Forest), the popular region of spas, hiking trails, and tempting cake. Berlin is surrounded by its own lakes and green parklands.

The transportation system that links these various regions is a godsend to the visitor. German trains are fast, clean, and punctual; a drive on a speed limit–free autobahn will give you an idea of just how fast all those BMW and Mercedes sports cars are meant to go.

ESSENTIAL INFORMATION

Before You Go

When to Go

The main tourist season in Germany runs from May to late October, when the weather is best. In addition to many tourist events, there are hundreds of folk festivals during this period. Winter-sports season in the Bavarian Alps runs from Christmas to mid-March. Prices everywhere are generally higher in summer, so you may find considerable advantages in visiting out of season. Most resorts have *Zwischensaison* (between season) and *Nebensaison* ("edge-of-season") rates, and tourist offices can provide lists of hotels offering *Pauschalangebote* (special low-price inclusive weekly packages). Similarly, many winter resorts lower their rates for the periods immediately before and after the Christmas and New Year high season (*Weisse Wochen,* or "white weeks"). The other advantage of out-of-season travel is that there aren't as many crowds. The disadvantages of visiting out of season, especially in winter, are that the weather is often cold and gloomy, and many tourist attractions, especially in rural areas, are closed. Ski resorts are an exception. The major cities, especially Munich and Berlin, are active year-round.

CLIMATE

Germany's climate is generally temperate. Winters vary from mild and damp to very cold and bright. Particularly chilly regions include the Baltic coast, the Alps, the Harz Mountains, and the Black and Bavarian forests. Summers are usually sunny and warm, though you should be prepared for a few cloudy and wet days. In Alpine regions, spring often comes late, with snow flurries well into April. Fall is sometimes spectacular in the south: warm and soothing. The only real exception to the above is the strikingly variable weather in southern Bavaria (Bayern) caused by the *Föhn,* a warm Alpine wind that brings sudden barometric changes and gives rise to clear but oppressive conditions in summer and, in winter, can cause snow to disappear overnight.

The following are the average daily maximum and minimum temperatures for Munich.

Jan.	35F	1C	May	64F	18C	Sept.	67F	20C
	23	− 5		45	7		48	9
Feb.	38F	3C	June	70F	21C	Oct.	56F	13C
	23	− 5		51	11		40	4
Mar.	48F	9C	July	74F	23C	Nov.	44F	7C
	30	− 1		55	13		33	0
Apr.	56F	14C	Aug.	73F	23C	Dec.	36F	2C
	38	3		54	12		26	− 3

Currency

The unit of currency in Germany is the Deutschmark, written DM and generally referred to as the mark. It is divided into 100 pfennig. There are bills of 5 (rare), 10, 20, 50, 100, 200, 500, and 1,000 marks and coins of 1, 2, 5, 10, and 50 pf and 1, 2, and 5 marks. At press time (spring 1995), the mark stood strong at DM 1.29 to the U.S. dollar and DM 2.17 to the pound sterling.

The Deutschmark is legal tender throughout Germany. The cost of living is still somewhat lower in the former German Democratic Republic (GDR), where most people earn slightly less than their western colleagues doing the same jobs, and some of these lower costs benefit tourists. But a growing number of places that cater specifically to visitors are now charging Western rates.

Major credit cards are widely, though not universally, accepted in Germany. You can buy a seat on a Lufthansa flight with a credit card but not on a German train, for example. Most hotels, a significant number of restaurants, and all leading car-rental companies accept credit cards, however. A growing number of shops also honor them, but don't be surprised if you are offered a discount for cash.

What It Will Cost

Inflation has crept up in the 1990s (at press time, the annual rate of inflation was around 4%), primarily because of the cost of financing the rejuvenation and integration of the former East Germany. For example, a "reunification" tax has been levied on basic commodities such as gas, and telephone charges have risen. There were further modest increases in fares for most forms of public transportation.

The most expensive areas to visit are the major cities, notably Berlin, Frankfurt, Hamburg, and Munich. Out-of-the-way rural regions, such as northern and eastern Bavaria, the Saarland on the French border, and many parts of eastern Germany, offer the lowest prices.

SAMPLE PRICES
Cup of coffee in a café, DM 3.50, in a stand-up snack bar DM 1.80; mug of beer in a beer hall, DM 4.50, a bottle of beer from a supermarket, DM 1.50; soft drink, DM 2; ham sandwich, DM 4; 2-mile taxi ride, DM 12.

Visas

To enter Germany, only passports are required of visitors from the United States, Canada, and the United Kingdom, although U.S. citizens must obtain a visa if they plan to stay longer than three months. A passport is valid for travel throughout the country, and, of course, there are no limitations on movement between former East and West Germany.

Customs

The establishment in 1993 of a single, unrestricted market within the European Union (EU) means that there no longer are any restrictions

Germany

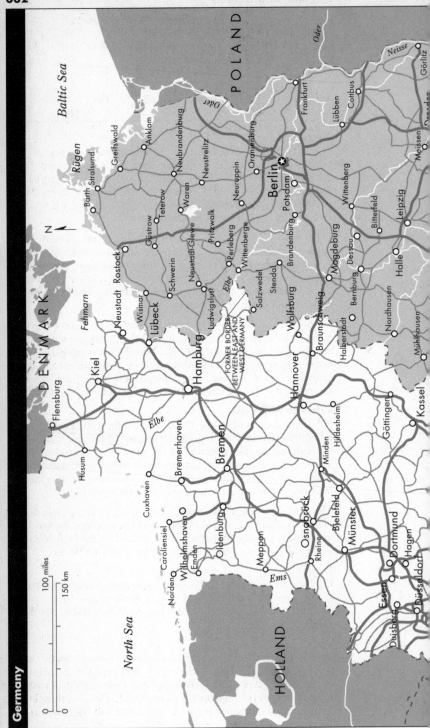

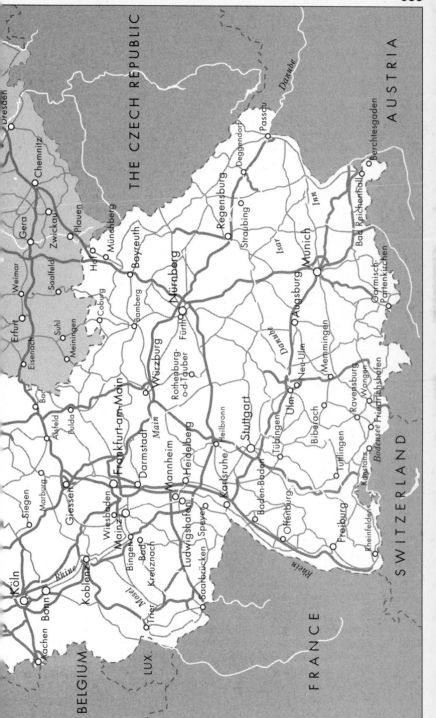

on importing items duty-free for citizens of the 12 member countries traveling among EU countries.

If you are entering Germany as a citizen of a country that does not belong to the EU, you may import duty-free: (1) 200 cigarettes, or 50 cigars, or 250 grams of tobacco; plus (2) 1 liter of spirits more than 22% proof or 2 liters of spirits less than 22% proof, and 2 liters of still wine; plus (3) 50 grams of perfume and ¼ liter of toilet water; plus (4) other goods with a total value of up to DM 115.

Tobacco and alcohol allowances are for visitors ages 17 and over. Other items intended for personal use may be imported and exported freely. There are no restrictions on the import and export of German currency.

Language

English has long been taught in high schools in the western part of Germany. Consequently, many people under age 40 speak some English, although the level of understanding varies considerably. Older people in rural areas are less familiar with the English language, but a substantial number have retained some basic words of communication from the immediate postwar years when American and British forces occupied the country. English is not as widely understood in eastern parts of the country where, before the collapse of communism, Russian was the first foreign language taught in many schools.

Germans who speak some English will take every opportunity to practice what they know, and they are delighted when someone makes an effort—no matter how elementary—to speak their language. For a visitor attempting to practice his or her German, the country's many dialects pose the biggest problem. Probably the most difficult to comprehend is Bavaria's, which is like another language—even books are written in *Bayerisch*. Nonetheless, except for older people in remote, rural districts, virtually everyone can also speak *Hochdeutsch,* the German equivalent of Oxford English. *Hochdeutsch* is always used on TV and radio.

Getting Around

By Car

ROAD CONDITIONS

The autobahn system in western Germany is of the highest standard. These roads are marked either A (on blue signs), meaning inter-German highways, or E (on green signs), meaning they form part of the Europe-wide *Europastrasse* network. All autobahns are toll-free. Local roads are called *Bundesstrassen* and are marked by their number on a yellow sign. All local roads are single lane and slower than autobahns.

The condition of the road system in eastern Germany has improved enormously. Many major roads have been repaired, and new autobahns are being added, most notably those linking Berlin with both western and eastern destinations.

RULES OF THE ROAD

Rules of the road are now the same in both parts of reunited Germany, with no difference in the speed limits. Officially, there's no speed limit on autobahns, although you'll find signs recommending that motorists stay below 130 kph (80 mph). You'll also find blue signs on autobahns stating the recommended minimum speed on that stretch. Germans are fast drivers, and autobahn speeds of more than 160 kph (100 mph) are common. Unless you're driving at that speed, stay in the right-hand lane on autobahns, using the faster-paced left-hand lanes only for passing. There are speed limits on other roads—100 kph (60 mph) on Bundesstrassen, 80 kph (50 mph) on country roads, between 30 kph (18 mph) and 60 kph (36 mph) in built-up urban areas. Fines for exceeding the speed limit can be heavy. Penalties for driving under the influence of alcohol are even more severe, so make sure to keep within the legal limit—equivalent to the consumption of two small beers or a glass of wine.

PARKING
Daytime parking in cities is very difficult. If you can find a parking lot, use it or you'll risk having your car towed. Parking restrictions are not always clearly marked and can be hard to understand when they are. At night, parking-meter spaces are free.

GASOLINE
Leaded and unleaded gas and diesel are generally available all over Germany. At press time (spring 1995), the price of a liter of gas ranged from DM 1.05 to DM 1.55, depending on the grade.

BREAKDOWNS
The **ADAC,** the major German automobile organization, gives free help and advice to tourists, though you have to pay for any spare parts and labor you need. All autobahns have regularly spaced telephones with which you can call for help. The contact address for the ADAC is Am Westpark 8, D-81373 Munich (tel. 089/76760).

By Train
The German railway system is being privatized, so routes and timetables may still change in some areas. The two separate rail networks of the former East and West Germany merged in 1994 into one entity known as **Deutsche Bahn** (**DB**), or German Rail, bringing Berlin and the cities of the old GDR much closer to the main railheads of the west. The electrification and renovation of the ancient tracks in eastern Germany also made big strides forward, allowing the extension there of the high-speed InterCity Express (ICE) service that previously linked only the cities of the west.

InterCity (IC) and EuroCity services were improved and expanded, and the regional InterRegio network was extended nationwide. Train travel times were reduced so dramatically that journeys between many cities—Munich–Frankfurt, for example—can be completed faster by rail than by plane. All overnight InterCity services and the slower D-class trains have sleepers, with a first-class service that includes breakfast in bed. All InterCity and InterCity Express trains have restaurant cars, and the Hamburg–Berchtesgaden service has introduced an onboard McDonald's as an experiment. A DM 6 (DM 12 round-trip) surcharge is added to the ticket price on all InterCity and EuroCity journeys irrespective of distance, while InterCity Express fares are about 20% more expensive than normal ones. Seat reservations are free of charge. Bikes cannot be transported on InterCity Express services, but InterCity, EuroCity, and most D-class trains have special storage facilities aboard, and InterRegio trains even have compartments where cyclists can travel next to their bikes.

FARES
The **German Rail Pass,** not available to Germans, allows travel over the entire German rail network for 5, 10, or 15 days within a single month; cost is $260, $410, and $530, respectively, in first class, and $178, $286, and $386 in second class (if purchased in Germany, the prices are DM 520, DM 720, and DM 900, and DM 350, DM 480,

and DM 600). A **Twin Pass** discounts these rates for two people traveling together; cost per person is $234, $369, and $477 for first class, and $160, $257, and $331 for second class (DM 400, DM 520, and DM 675, and DM 265, DM 360, and DM 450). A **Youth Pass,** sold to those age 12–25 for second-class travel, costs $138–$238 (DM 270–DM 450). These passes are also valid on all buses operated by the Deutsche Bahn, as well as on tour routes along the Romantic and Castle roads served by **Deutsche Touring Gesellschaft** (DTG, Am Römerhof 17, D-60486 Frankfurt/Main, tel. 069/ 79030) and Rhine, Main, and Mosel river cruises operated by the **Köln-Düsseldorfer (KD) Line** (*see* By Boat, *below*). Passes are sold by travel agents and DER Tours (Box 1606, Des Plaines, IL 60017, tel. 800/782–2424) in the U.S. and by Deutsche Bahn in Germany.

In 1995 a new and more comprehensive version of the popular **Inter-Rail** ticket became available. It's complicated, but there are big savings for young travelers (26 years old or younger) touring just one area of Europe. The system divides Europe into seven zones, with different InterRail tariffs within each one. Germany belongs to Zone C, along with Switzerland, Austria, and Denmark. A one-month InterRail ticket for travel within this zone and an additional zone of your choice costs DM 500, and a two-week ticket DM 420. Young travelers intending to tour only Germany can get an even better deal with a **Euro Domino** ticket, which allows rail travel on all German trains (including the high-speed InterCity Express) for 3, 5, or 10 days within one month (for DM 231, DM 257, and DM 378 respectively). No age limit is linked to other special deals, such as the **Sparpreis** and **ICE-Super Sparpreis** which offer big savings on return journeys made on off-peak days.

Travelers under 26 who do not have a rail pass should inquire about discount travel fares available under the **Billet International Jeune** (BIJ) scheme. The special one-trip tariff (also known as a **twen-tickets** fare) is offered by EuroTrain International, which has offices in 22 European cities. You can buy a EuroTrain ticket at one of these offices or at travel agencies, mainline rail stations, and youth-travel operators.

One tip: There is very little difference in comfort between first-and second-class compartments in the newer InterCity trains and all InterCity Express trains but there's a big difference in fares.

By Bus

Long-distance bus services in Germany are part of the Europe-wide Europabus network. Services are neither as frequent nor as comprehensive as those on the rail system, so make reservations. Be careful in selecting the service you travel on: All Europabus services have a bilingual hostess and offer small luxuries that you won't find on the more basic, though still comfortable, regular services. For details and reservations, contact DTG (*see* By Train, *above*). Reservations can also be made at any of the Deutsche Touring offices in Cologne, Hannover, Hamburg, Munich, Nürnberg, and Wuppertal and at travel agents.

Rural bus services are operated by local municipalities and some private firms, as well as by Deutsche Bahn and the post office. Services are variable, however, even when there is no other means to reach your destination by public transportation.

By Plane

Germany's national airline, **Lufthansa** (in the United States, tel. 800/645–3880; in Great Britain tel. 0171/495–2044; in Germany tel. 068/6907–1222), serves all major cities. **LTU International Airways** (in the United States, tel. 800/546–7334; in Germany, tel. 0211/941–8888) has connections between Düsseldorf and Munich and between Frankfurt and Munich. Regular fares are high, but you can save up to 40% with *Flieg und Spar* (fly-and-save) specials; several restrictions apply, such as a DM 100 penalty for changing flights. A British Airways subsidiary, **Deutsche BA** (Poststr. 4-5, D-10178 Berlin, tel. 030/4101–2647), competes with Lufthansa on many domestic routes, including those between Berlin and Munich and Köln/Bonn and Düsseldorf.

By Boat

For a country with such a small coastline, Germany is a surprisingly nautical nation: You can cruise rivers and lakes throughout the country. The biggest fleet, and most of the biggest boats, too, belongs to the Cologne-based KD line, the Köln-Düsseldorf Rheinschiffahrt. It operates services on the Rivers Rhine, Mosel, and Main, ranging from luxurious five-day trips from Amsterdam or Rotterdam in Holland all the way down the Rhine to Basel in Switzerland, to short "riverboat shuffles" with jazz bands and freely flowing wine. For details, contact **KD River Cruises of Europe** (Rhine Cruise Agency, 2500 Westchester Ave., Purchase, NY 10577, tel. 914/696–3600) or **KD German Rhine Line** (Frankenwerft 15, D-50667 Köln, tel. 0221/208–8288).

Services on the 160-kilometer (100-mile) stretch of the Danube (Donau) between the spectacular Kelheim Gorge and Passau on the Austrian border are operated by **Donauschiffahrt Wurm & Köck** (Höllgasse 26, D-94032 Passau, tel. 0851/929–292). The company has daily summer cruises on the Rivers Danube, Inn, and Ilz, which meet at Passau; some two-day cruises into Austria are also offered. The Bodensee (Lake Constance), the largest lake in Germany, located at the meeting point of Germany, Austria, and Switzerland, has up to 40 ships crisscrossing it in summer. **Deutsche Bahn** (Bodensee-Schiffsbetriebe, Hafenstr. 6, D-78462 Konstanz) also has information on cruises. Bavaria's five largest lakes—Ammersee, Chiemsee, Königsee, Tegernsee, and Starnbergersee—have regular summer cruises and excursions. Details are available from local tourist offices.

KD Line has two luxury cruise ships plying the Elbe. Several itineraries are offered, ranging from five to eight days. All cruises stop at Dresden, and some include free bus transfers to Hamburg, Berlin, and Prague.

By Bicycle

Bicycles can be rented at more than 370 train stations throughout Germany from April 1 to October 31. The cost is DM 11 or DM 13 (with gears) per day, DM 7 or DM 9 if you have a valid rail ticket. You can pick up a bike at one station and return it to another, provided both stations rent bikes. Mountain bikes can be rented for DM 20 a day at Garmisch-Partenkirchen Station and three other Alpine stations (Immenstadt, Oberstdorf, and Sonthoten). You will need to buy a *Fahrradkarte,* or bicycle ticket (DM 8.60 per journey), to take your bike on the train; InterCity Express trains do not carry bikes. Full details are given in German Rail's brochure "Radler-Bahn." Most cities also have companies that rent bikes for about DM 15 per day or DM 80– DM 90 a week.

Staying in Germany

Telephones

LOCAL CALLS

Since reunification, all phones in the east and west use the same coins: 10 pf, DM 1, and DM 5 for long-distance calls. A local call costs 30 pf and lasts six minutes. Card phones are rapidly replacing coin-operated phones: Cards cost DM 12 or DM 50 (for DM 60 worth of calls) and can be purchased at all post offices and many exchange places. If you need an operator, dial 010.

INTERNATIONAL CALLS

These can be made from public phones bearing the sign INLANDS UND AUSLANDSGESPRÄCHE. Using DM 5 coins is best for long-distance dialing; a four-minute call to the United States costs DM 15. To avoid weighing yourself down with coins, however, make international calls from post offices; even those in small country towns will have a special booth for international calls. You pay the clerk at the end of your call. To reach an **AT&T** long-distance operator, dial 0130–0010; for **MCI,** dial 0130–0012; for **Sprint,** 0130–0013. Dial 0010 for a local operator who handles international calls.

COUNTRY CODE

Germany's country code is 49.

Mail

Airmail letters to the United States and Canada cost DM 3; postcards cost DM 2. Airmail letters to the United Kingdom cost DM 1; postcards cost 80 pf.

You can arrange to have mail sent to you in care of any German post office; have the envelope marked "Postlagernd." This service is free. Alternatively, have mail sent to any American Express office in Germany. There's no charge to cardholders, holders of American Express traveler's checks, or anyone who has booked a vacation with American Express. Otherwise, you pay DM 2 per collection (not per item).

Shopping

VAT REFUNDS

German goods carry a 15% value-added tax (VAT). You can claim this back either as you leave the country or once you've returned home. When you make a purchase, ask the shopkeeper for a form known as an Ausfuhr-Abnehmerbescheinigung; he or she will help you fill it out. As you leave the country, give the form, plus the goods and receipts, to German customs, which will give you an official export certificate or stamp. In the unlikely event that there's a branch of the Deutsche Bank on the spot, you can take the stamped form to it, where you will receive the refund on the spot. Otherwise, send the form back to the shop, and it will send the refund.

Opening and Closing Times

Banks. Times vary from state to state and city to city, but banks are usually open weekdays from 8:30 or 9 to 2 or 3 (5 or 6 on Thursday). Some banks close from 12:30 to 1:30. Branches at airports and main train stations open as early as 6:30 AM and close as late as 10:30 PM.

Museums are generally open Tuesday to Sunday 9–5. Some close for an hour or more at lunch, and some are open on Monday. Many stay open until 9 on Thursday.

Most **shops** are open weekdays from 8:30 or 9 until 6:30 and Saturday until 1 or 2. On the first Saturday of each month, many larger shops and department stores stay open until 6. Some stores stay open until 8:30 on Thursday.

National Holidays

January 1; January 6 (Epiphany, Bavaria and Baden Württenberg only); April 5 (Good Friday); April 8 (Easter Monday); May 1 (Worker's

Day); May 16 (Ascension); May 27 (Pentecost Monday); June 6 (Corpus Christi, south Germany only); August 15 (Assumption Day, Bavaria and Saarland only); October 3 (German Unity Day); November 1 (All Saints' Day); November 20 (Day of Prayer and Repentance), December 24–26.

Dining

It's hard to generalize about German food beyond saying that standards are high and portions are large. In fact, the range of dining experiences is vast: everything from highly priced nouvelle cuisine to hamburgers. As a visitor, you should search out local restaurants if atmosphere and regional specialties are your priority. Beer restaurants in Bavaria, *Apfelwein* (alcoholic apple cider) taverns in Frankfurt, and *Kneipen*—the pubs-cum-local-cafés on the corner—in Berlin nearly always offer the best value and atmosphere. But throughout the country you'll find *Gaststätten, Gasthäuser,* and/or *Gasthöfe*—local inns—where atmosphere and regional specialties are always available. Likewise, just about every town will have a *Ratskeller*, a cellar restaurant in the town hall, where exposed beams, huge fireplaces, sturdy tables, and immense portions are the rule.

In larger towns and cities throughout the country, Germans like to nibble at roadside or market snack stalls, called *Imbisse*. Hot sausages, *Fleischpflanzerl* (spicy meatballs), *Leberkäs* (meatloaf topped with a fried egg), in the south, and sauerkraut are the traditional favorites. But foods eaten on the hoof are creeping in, too: french fries, pizzas, hamburgers, and the *Döner Kebab,* the Turkish gyro equivalent, which in many larger cities has become as much a part of the German diet as a bratwurst.

The most famous German specialty is sausage. Everyone has heard of frankfurters, but if you're in Munich, try *Weisswurst,* a delicate white sausage traditionally eaten only between midnight and noon. Nürnberg's sausage favorite is the Nürnberger bratwurst; its fame is such that restaurants all over Germany serve it. Look for the BRATWURST-STUBE sign. *Knödeln* (dumplings) can also be found throughout the country, though their natural home is probably Bavaria; farther north, potatoes often take their place.

The natural accompaniment to German food is either beer or wine. Munich is the beer capital of Germany, though there's no part of the country where you won't find the amber nectar. Say *"Helles"* or *"Export"* if you want light beer; *"Dunkles"* if you want dark beer. In Bavaria, try the sour but refreshing beer brewed from wheat, called *Weissbier.*

Germany is also a major wine-producing country, and much of it is of superlative quality. You will probably be happy with the house wine in most restaurants or with one of those earthenware pitchers of cold Mosel wine. If you want something more expensive, remember that all wines are graded in one of three basic categories: *Tafelwein* (table wine); *Qualitätswein* (fine wine); and *Qualitätswein mit Prädikat* (top-quality wine).

MEALTIMES

Breakfast, served anytime from 6:30 to 10 (in some cafés and Kneipen, until as late as 2 or 4 PM), is often a substantial meal, with cold meats, cheeses, rolls, and fruit. Many city hotels offer Sunday brunch, and the custom is rapidly catching on. Lunch is served from around 11:30 (especially in rural areas) to around 2; dinner is generally from 6 until 9:30, or earlier in some quiet country areas. Big-city hotels and popular restaurants serve later. Lunch tends to be the main meal, a fact reflected in the almost universal appearance of a lunchtime *Tageskarte,* or suggested menu; try it if you want maximum nourishment for minimum outlay. This doesn't mean that dinner is a rushed or skimpy affair, however; the Germans have too high a regard for food for any meal to be underrated.

WHAT TO WEAR
Jacket and tie are advised for restaurants in the **$$$$** and **$$$** categories. Casual dress is appropriate elsewhere.

RATINGS
Prices are per person and include a first course, main course, dessert, and tip and tax. Highly recommended restaurants are indicated by a star ★.

The following chart gives price ranges for restaurants in the western part of Germany. Food prices in the territory of former East Germany are still somewhat unstable, although in the bigger cities many of the better-quality restaurants already mimic "western" rates. Generally speaking, the prevailing price structure in the eastern part of the country, except for restaurants in the priciest hotels, falls into the **$** to **$$$** categories listed below. Bills in simple restaurants in country areas of the eastern region will, however, still come well below DM 35.

CATEGORY	MAJOR CITIES AND RESORTS	OTHER AREAS
$$$$	over DM 100	over DM 90
$$$	DM 75–DM 100	DM 55–DM 90
$$	DM 50–DM 75	DM 35–DM 55
$	under DM 50	under DM 35

Lodging
The standard of German hotels, from top-notch luxury spots (of which the country has more than its fair share) to the humblest pension, is excellent. Prices can be high, but not disproportionately so compared to other northern European countries. You can expect courteous service; clean and comfortable rooms; and, in rural areas especially, considerable old-German atmosphere.

In addition to hotels proper, the country has numerous *Gasthöfe* or *Gasthäuser* (country inns); pensions or *Fremdenheime* (guest houses); and, at the lowest end of the scale, *Zimmer,* meaning, quite simply, rooms, normally in private houses. Look for the sign ZIMMER FREI (rooms free) or ZU VERMIETEN (for rent). A red sign reading BESETZT means there are no vacancies.

Lists of hotels are available from the German National Tourist Office (Beethovenstr. 69, D-60325 Frankfurt/Main 1, tel. 069/75720), and from all regional and local tourist offices. Tourist offices will also make reservations for you—they usually charge a nominal fee—but may have difficulty doing so after 4 PM in peak season and on weekends. The German National Tourist Office also operates a reservations service (Allgemeine Deutsche Zimmer-reservierung, Cornelius-str. 34, D-60325 Frankfurt/Main, tel. 069/740–767), which is free of charge.

Most hotels have restaurants, but those describing themselves as *Garni* will provide breakfast only. Many larger hotels offer no-smoking rooms, and some even offer no-smoking floors, so it's always worth asking for one, if you're interested, when you check in.

Tourist accommodations in eastern Germany are beginning to blossom under free enterprise, although the choice and facilities are still far behind the western part of the country. The formerly state-owned Inter-hotel chain (34 hotels with several thousand rooms) has been dis-mantled, its components sold individually. Other hotel groups are keen to build new properties in the region or to convert old buildings with the potential for atmospheric lodgings. But for now, accommo-dations remain scarce at the top- and middle-quality levels. It cannot be too greatly stressed: If you want to stay in good hotels in eastern Germany, book well in advance (Berlin is the notable exception). Hotel rooms in the cities are in demand year-round because of the comings and goings of businesspeople involved in rebuilding the east's econ-omy. Traditional inn accommodations have become run down during the past 40 years—still, you may well come across the odd gem.

The real boom in lodgings has been at the inexpensive end of the mar-ket, where thousands of beds are now available for the adventurous traveler. For relatively few marks, every village can now provide some-where for the tourist to put his or her head and perhaps offer a sim-ple but wholesome evening meal. For a list of approved addresses, consult the local tourist office.

ROMANTIK HOTELS

Among the most delightful places to stay and eat in Germany are the aptly named Romantik Hotels and Restaurants. All are in historic buildings—this is a precondition of membership—and are personally run by the owners. The emphasis generally is on solid comfort, good food, and style. A detailed listing of all Romantik Hotels is available in the United States for $5 from **Harm Meyer Romantik Hotels** (Box 1278, Woodinville, WA 98072, tel. 206/486–9394 or 800/826–0015, reservations only).

CASTLE HOTELS

Gast im Schloss is a similar hotel association, though some of the sim-pler establishments lack a little in the way of comfort, and furnishings can be basic. But most can be delightful, with antiques, imposing in-teriors, and out-of-the-way locations setting the tone. Prices are mostly moderate. Ask the German National Tourist Office or your travel agent for the "Gast im Schloss" brochure that lists nearly 60 castle ho-tels in Germany; they can also advise on a number of good-value pack-ages, most for stays of four to six nights.

RINGHOTELS

This association groups 130 individually owned and managed hotels in the medium price range. Many are in the countryside or in pretty villages. Package deals of 2–3 days are available. Contact **Ringhotels** (Belfortstr. 8, D-81667 Munich, tel. 089/448–9206).

RENTALS

Apartments and hotel homes, most accommodating from two to eight guests, can be rented throughout Germany. Rates are low, with reductions for longer stays. Charges for gas and electricity, and sometimes water, are usually added to the bill. Local and regional tourist offices have lists of apartments in their areas; otherwise contact the German Na-tional Tourist Office (*see* Lodging *in* Staying in Germany, *above*).

FARM VACATIONS

Taking an *Urlaub auf dem Bauernhof,* as the Germans put it, has in-creased dramatically in popularity over the past four or five years. Al-most every regional tourist office has listings of farms, by area, offering bed and breakfast, apartments, or whole farmhouses to rent. Alter-natively, contact the **German Agricultural Association** (DLG, Eschborner Landstr. 122, D–60489 Frankfurt/Main, tel. 069/247–880). It produces an annual listing of more than 1,500 farms, all of them inspected and graded, that offer accommodations. The brochure costs DM 7.50.

CAMPING

There are 2,600 campsites in Germany, about 1,600 of which are listed by the **German Camping Club** (DCC, Mandlstr. 28, D-80802, Munich, tel. 089/380–1420). The German National Tourist Office also publishes a listing of sites. Most are open from May through October, with about 400 staying open year-round. They tend to become crowded during the summer, so it's always worthwhile to make reservations a day or two ahead. Prices range from DM 15 to DM 20 per night for two adults, a car, and trailer (less for tents).

YOUTH HOSTELS

Germany's *Jugendherberge* (youth hostels) are probably the most efficient and up-to-date in Europe. There are 600 in all, many located in castles, adding a touch of romance to otherwise utilitarian accommodations. There's an age limit of 27 in Bavaria; elsewhere, there are no restrictions, though those under 20 take preference if space is limited. You'll need a Hostelling International (HI) card to stay in a German youth hostel; write **American Youth Hostels Association** (Box 37613, Washington, DC 20013) or **Canadian Hostelling Association** (333 River Rd., Ottawa, Ontario K1L 8H9). In Great Britain, contact the **Youth Hostels Association** (22 Southampton St., London WC2). The HI card can also be obtained from the **Deutsches Jugendherbergswerk Hauptverband** (Bismarckstr. 8, D-32754 Detmold, tel. 05231/74010, or one of their regional offices), which provides a complete list of German hostels for DM 6.50.

Hostels must be reserved well in advance for midsummer, especially in eastern Germany. Bookings for hostels can only be made by calling the hostels directly; telephone numbers are listed in the Deutsches Jugendherbergswerk's listings (*see above*).

RATINGS

Service charges and taxes are included in all quoted room rates. Similarly, breakfast is usually, but not always, included, so check before you book. Rates are often surprisingly flexible in German hotels, varying considerably according to demand. Major hotels in cities often have lower rates on weekends or in other periods when business is quiet. If you're lucky, you can find reductions of up to 60%. Likewise, rooms reserved after 10 PM will often carry a discount. Although it's worthwhile to ask if your hotel will give you a reduction, don't count on finding rooms at lower rates late at night, especially in the summer. Prices are for two people in a double room. Highly recommended lodgings are indicated by a star ★.

The following chart is for hotels throughout Germany. In Berlin, hotel price categories are about DM 50 higher than those for major cities indicated below.

CATEGORY	MAJOR CITIES AND RESORTS	OTHER AREAS
$$$$	over DM 300	over DM 200
$$$	DM 200–DM 300	DM 160–DM 200
$$	DM 140–DM 200	DM 100–DM 160
$	under DM 140	under DM 100

Tipping

The Germans are as punctilious about tipping as they are about most facets of life in their well-regulated country. Overtipping is as frowned upon as not tipping at all, though the kind of abuse you risk in some countries for undertipping is virtually unknown here. Nonetheless, tips are expected, if not exactly demanded.

In restaurants, service is included (under the heading *Bedienung,* at the bottom of the check), and it is customary to round out the check to the next Mark or two, a practice also commonplace in cafés, beer halls, and bars. For taxi drivers, also round out to the next mark or two: for DM 11.20, make it DM 12; for DM 11.80, make it DM 13. Railway and airport porters (if you can find any) have their own scale of charges, but round out the requested amount to the next mark. Hotel porters get DM 1 per bag. Doormen are tipped the same amount for small services, such as calling a cab. Room service should be rewarded with at least DM 2 every time you use it. Maids should get about DM 1 per day. Double all these figures at luxury hotels. Service-station attendants get 50 pf or DM 1 for checking oil and tires or cleaning windshields.

MUNICH

Arriving and Departing

By Plane
Munich's Franz Josef Strauss (FJS) Airport, named after a former state premier, opened in 1992. It is 28 kilometers (17½ miles) northeast of the city center.

BETWEEN THE AIRPORT AND DOWNTOWN
The S-8 S-Bahn (suburban train line) links FJS Airport with the city's main train station (Hauptbahnhof). Trains depart in both directions every 20 minutes from 3:55 AM to 12:55 AM daily. Intermediate stops are made at the Ostbahnhof (good for hotels located east of the River Isar) and city-center stations such as Marienplatz. The 38-minute trip costs DM 10 if you purchase a multi-use strip ticket (*see* Getting Around, *below*) and use 8 strips; otherwise an ordinary one-way ticket is DM 12.80 per person. A tip for families: Up to five people (maximum of two adults) can travel to or from the airport for only DM 20 by buying a Tageskarte (*see* Getting Around, *below*). This is particularly advantageous if you are arriving in Munich, because you can continue to use the Tageskarte in the city for the rest of the day. The only restriction is that you cannot use this special day ticket before 9 AM weekdays.

A bus service was reintroduced in 1994, but it's slower and more expensive (DM 15) than the S-Bahn. A taxi will cost between DM 80 and DM 100. If you are driving from the airport into the city, follow the MÜNCHEN autobahn signs to A92 and A9.

By Train
All long-distance services arrive at and depart from the main train station, the Hauptbahnhof. Trains to and from destinations in the Bavarian Alps usually use the adjoining Starnbergerbahnhof. For information on train times, call 089/19419. For tickets and information, go to the station or to the ABR travel agency right by the station on Bahnhofplatz.

By Bus
Munich has no central bus station. Long-distance buses arrive at and depart from the north side of the train station on Arnulfstrasse.

By Car
From the north (Nürnberg, Frankfurt), leave the autobahn at the Schwabing exit and follow the STADTMITTE signs. The autobahn from

Stuttgart and the west ends at Obermenzing; again, follow the STADT-MITTE signs. The autobahns from Salzburg and the east, from Garmisch and the south, and from Lindau and the southwest all join up with the city beltway, the Mittlerer Ring. The city center is well posted.

Getting Around

Downtown Munich is only about 1 mile square, so it can easily be explored on foot. Other areas—Schwabing, Nymphenburg, the Olympic Park—are best reached on the efficient and comprehensive public transportation network, which incorporates buses, streetcars, U-Bahn (subways), and S-Bahn (suburban trains). Tickets are good for the entire network, and you can break your trip as many times as you like using just one ticket, provided you travel in one direction within a given period of time. If you plan to make only a few trips, buy strip tickets (Streifenkarten)—blue for adults, red for children. Fares were due to rise by up to 15% by 1996 but at press time (spring, 1995), an adult ticket of 12 strips cost DM 15; children got the same number for DM 8. For adults, short rides that span up to 4 stations cost 1 strip; trips spanning more than 4 stations cost 2 strips. Children pay 1 strip per ride. All tickets must be validated by time-punching them in the automatic machines at station entrances and on all buses and streetcars. The best buy is the Tageskarte: Up to two adults and three children can use this ticket for unlimited journeys between 9 AM and the end of the day's service (about 2 AM). It costs DM 10 for the inner zone, which covers central Munich. A Tageskarte for the entire system, extending to the Starnbergersee and Ammersee lakes, costs DM 20. Holders of a Eurail Pass, a Youth Pass, an InterRail Card, or a DB Tourist Card travel free on all S-Bahn trains.

By Taxi

Munich's cream-color taxis are numerous. Hail them in the street or call 089/21610 (there's an extra charge for the drive to the pickup point). Rates start at DM 3.90 and rise by DM 2.20 per kilometer (about DM 4 per mile). There are additional charges of DM 1 for each piece of luggage. Figure on paying around DM 12 for a short trip within the city.

Important Addresses and Numbers

Tourist Information

The address to write to for information in advance of your visit is **Fremdenverkehrsamt München**, 80310, München. This address also deals with lodging questions and bookings. Two other offices provide on-the-spot advice: at the Hauptbahnhof (tel. 089/233–0300, open Mon.–Sat. 8 AM–10 PM, Sun. and public holidays 11–7 PM) and at the corner of Rindermarkt and Pettenbeckstrasse, behind Marienplatz (tel. 089/233–0300, open Mon.–Thurs. 8:30–4, Fri. 8:30–2).

Consulates

U.S. Consulate General (Königinstr. 5, tel. 089/28880). **U.K. Consulate General** (Bürkleinstr. 10, tel. 089/211–090). **Canadian Consulate** (Tal 29, tel. 089/222–661).

Emergencies

Police (tel. 110). **Ambulance** and **emergency medical attention** (tel. 089/558–661). **Dentist** (tel. 089/723–3093). **Pharmacies: Internationale Ludwigs-Apotheke** (Neuhauserstr. 11, tel. 089/260–3021); **Europa-Apotheke,** (Schützenstr. 12, near the Hauptbahnhof, tel. 089/595–423). Open weekdays 8–6, Saturday 8–1. Outside these hours, call 089/594–475.

English-Language Bookstores

The **Anglia English Bookshop** (Schellingstr. 3, tel. 089/283–642) has the largest selection of English-language books in Munich. Also try the **Hugendubel** bookshops at Marienplatz and Karlsplatz. A library of English-language books is kept in **Amerika Haus** (Karolinenpl. 3, tel. 089/595–369).

Travel Agencies

American Express (Promenadepl. 6, tel. 089/21990). **ABR,** the official Bavarian travel agency, has outlets all over Munich; tel. 089/ 12040 for information.

Guided Tours

Orientation Tours

City bus tours are operated by **Panorama Tours** (Arnulfstr. 8, tel. 089/591–504). Tours run daily and take in the city center, the Olympic Park, and Nymphenburg. Departures are at 10 AM and 2:30 PM (and 11:30 AM in midsummer) from outside the Hertie department store across from the train station, and the cost is between DM 15 and DM 27 per person, depending on the duration of the tour.

Walking and Cycling Tours

Under the auspices of the city council, students conduct walking tours of the historic center on Monday, Tuesday, and Thursday at 10 AM. The walks start from the Fischbrunnen (Fish Fountain) at Marienplatz and cost DM 6. Bike tours of the city, including bike rentals, are offered through **City Hopper Touren** (tel. 089/272–1131). Charges run from DM 40 per person in a group of two to DM 20 for larger groups. Tours on foot, by bicycle, and by streetcar are organized by **Radius Touristik** (Arnulfstr. 3, north side of Hauptbahnhof, tel. 089/596–113).

Excursions

Panorama Tours (Arnulfstr. 8, tel. 089/591–504) organizes bus trips to most leading tourist attractions outside the city, including the "Royal Castles Tour" (Schlösserfahrt) of "Mad" King Ludwig's dream palaces. This tour, which takes in Neuschwanstein, costs DM 75 adults, DM 38 children. All tours leave from outside the Hertie department store in front of the Hauptbahnhof.

Exploring Munich

People who live in other parts of Germany sometimes refer to Munich (München in German) as the nation's "secret capital." This sly compliment may reflect the importance of Munich—it's the number-one tourist destination in Germany, as well as arguably the most attractive major German city—but there's nothing "secret" about the way Münchners make this brave claim. Flamboyant, easygoing Munich, city of beer and Baroque, is starkly different from the sometimes stiff Prussian influences to be found in Berlin, the gritty industrial drive of Hamburg, or the hard-headed commercial instincts of high-rise Frankfurt. This is a city to visit for its good-natured and relaxed charm—*Gemütlichkeit,* they call it here—and for its beer halls, its museums, its malls, its parks, and its palaces.

Munich is a crazy mix of high culture (witness its world-class opera house and art galleries) and wild abandon (witness the vulgar frivolity of the Oktoberfest). Its citizenry seems determined to perpetuate the lifestyle of the 19th-century king Ludwig I, the Bavarian ruler who brought so much international prestige to his home city after declaring: "I want to make out of Munich a town which does such credit to

Germany that nobody knows Germany unless he has seen Munich."
He kept his promise with an architectural and artistic renaissance—
before abdicating because of a wild romance with a half-caste Irish-
born dancing girl, Lola Montez (who died in exile in New York).

The Historic Heart
*Numbers in the margin correspond to points of interest on the München
(Munich) map.*

➊ Begin your tour of Munich at the **Hauptbahnhof,** the main train station and an important orientation point. The city tourist office is here,
too, ready with information and maps. Cross the street and you're at
the start of a kilometer (½ mile) of pedestrian shopping malls, the first
being Schützenstrasse. Facing you are **Hertie,** Munich's leading de-
➋ partment store, and **Karlsplatz** square, known locally as the "Stachus."
The huge, domed building on your left is the late-19th-century **Justizpalast** (Palace of Justice). It's one of Germany's finest examples of
Gründerzeit style, 19th-century versions of medieval and Renaissance
architecture.

Head down into the pedestrian underpass—it's another extensive shopping area—to reach the other side and one of the original city gates,
➌ the **Karlstor.** The city's two principal shopping streets—**Neuhauserstrasse**
and **Kaufingerstrasse**—stretch away from it on the other side. Two of
➍ ➎ the city's major churches are here, too: the **Bürgersaal** and the **Michaelskirche.** The latter is one of the most magnificent Renaissance churches
in Germany, a spacious and handsome structure decorated throughout in plain white stucco. It was built for the Jesuits in the late 16th
century and is closely modeled on their church (Il Gesù) in Rome. The
intention was to provide a large preaching space, hence the somewhat
barnlike atmosphere. Ludwig II is buried here; his tomb is in the crypt.
The large Neoclassical tomb in the north transept is the resting place
of Eugène de Beauharnais, Napoléon's stepson. The highly decorated
Rococo interior of the Bürgersaal makes a startling contrast with the
simplicity of the Michaelskirche. Guided tours of the Michaelskirche
are given every Wed. at 2 PM and cost DM 5.

A block past the Michaelskirche to your left is Munich's late-15th-cen-
➏ tury cathedral, the **Frauenkirche,** or Church of Our Lady. Towering
above it are two onion-shape domes, symbols of the city (perhaps because they resemble brimming beer mugs, cynics claim). They were added
in 1525 after the body of the church had been completed. Step inside
and you'll be amazed at the stark simplicity of the church. This is partly
the result of the construction that followed the severe bombing in
World War II. The crypt houses the tombs of numerous Wittelsbachs,
the family that ruled Bavaria for seven centuries until forced to abdicate in 1918. The cathedral—after a two-year, $17-million renovation—
reopened in 1994, just in time for the 500th anniversary of its
consecration.

➐ From the Frauenkirche, walk to the **Marienplatz** square, the heart of
the city, surrounded by shops, restaurants, and cafés. It takes its name
from the 300-year-old gilded statue of the Virgin in the center. When
it was taken down to be cleaned in 1960, workmen found a small casket containing a splinter of wood said to have come from the cross of
➑ Christ. The square is dominated by the 19th-century **Neues Rathaus,**
the new town hall, built in the fussy, turreted style so loved by Lud-
➒ wig II. The **Altes Rathaus,** or old town hall, a medieval building of great
charm, sits, as if forgotten, in a corner of the square. At 9 AM and 11
AM daily (also May–Oct. at 5 PM and 9 PM), the **Glockenspiel,** or chim-

ing clock, in the central tower of the new town hall, swings into action. Two tiers of dancing and jousting figures perform their ritual display. It can be worthwhile to schedule your day to catch the clock. Immediately after the war, an American soldier donated some paint to help restore the battered figures and was rewarded with a ride on one of the knight's horses, high above the cheering crowds. April through October, an elevator whisks visitors to an observation point near the top of one of the towers. On a clear day the view is spectacular. The elevator operates Monday–Saturday 10–5; the fare is DM 2, DM 1 children.

TIME OUT   If you're visiting Munich after mid-1996, ride one of the newly installed glass-enclosed elevators to the sixth-floor **Hoch-Cafe,** opposite the new town hall, where the view of the Glockenspiel is unbeatable. (The installation of the elevators and the renovation-enlargement of the café and Press Club began in 1995 and was scheduled for completion by mid-1996.) Claim a window-side table early, however—particularly on rainy days, when all Munich seems to have the same idea. The café is open daily until 10 PM and serves medium-priced light meals as well as morning coffee and afternoon tea.

⑩   Heading south down Rosenstrasse to Sendlingerstrasse, you come to the **Asamkirche** on your right. Some consider the Asamkirche a preposterously overdecorated jewel box; others consider it one of Europe's finest late-Baroque churches. One thing is certain: If you have any interest in church architecture, this is a place you shouldn't miss. It was built around 1730 by the Asam brothers—Cosmas Damian and Egid Quirin—next door to their home, the Asamhaus. They dedicated it to St. John Nepomuk, a 14th-century Bohemian monk who drowned in the Danube. Before you go in, pause to see the charming statue of angels carrying him to heaven from the rocky riverbank. Inside, there is a riot of decoration: frescoes, statuary, rich rosy marbles, billowing clouds of stucco, and gilding everywhere. The decorative elements and the architecture merge to create a sense of seamless movement and color.

⑪   Go back to Marienplatz and turn right for the **Viktualienmarkt,** the food market. Open-air stalls sell cheese, wine, sausages, fruit, and flowers. Fortified with Bavarian sausage and sauerkraut, plunge into **⑫** local history with a visit to the **Residenz,** home of the Wittelsbachs from the 16th century to their forced abdication at the end of World War I. From Max-Joseph-Platz you'll enter the great palace, with its glittering Schatzkammer, or treasury, and glorious Rococo theater, designed by court architect François Cuvilliès. Also facing the square is the **⑬** stern Neoclassical portico of the **Nationaltheater,** built at the beginning of the 19th century and twice destroyed. *Residenz and Schatzkammer, Max-Joseph-Pl. 3. Admission to each: DM 4 adults. Open Tues.–Sun. 10–4:30 PM. Cuvilliès Theater admission: DM 2.50 adults. Open Mon.–Sat. 2–5, Sun. 10–5.*

⑭   To the north of the Residenz is the **Hofgarten,** the palace gardens. Two sides of the gardens are bordered by sturdy arcades designed by Leo von Klenze, whose work for the Wittelsbachs in the 19th century helped transform the face of the city. Dominating the east side of the Hofgarten is the Bavarian state chancellery, an eclectic and controversial mixture of styles that incorporates the dome of Bavaria's former Army Museum, destroyed in World War II.

348

Alte Pinakothek, **20**
Altes Rathaus, **9**
Asamkirche, **10**
Bürgersaal, **4**
Englischer Garten, **18**
Feldherrnhalle, **16**
Frauenkirche, **6**
Hauptbahnhof, **1**
Haus der Kunst, **19**
Hofgarten, **14**
Karlsplatz, **2**
Karlstor, **3**
Marienplatz, **7**
Michaelskirche, **5**
Nationaltheater, **13**
Neue Pinakothek, **21**
Neues Rathaus, **8**
Residenz, **12**
Siegestor, **17**
Theatinerkirche, **15**
Viktualienmarkt, **11**

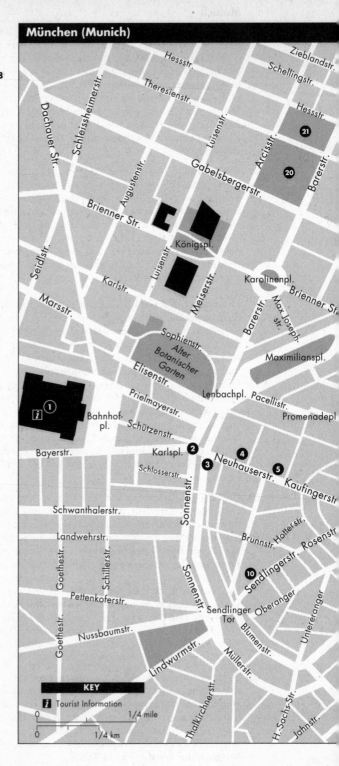

München (Munich)

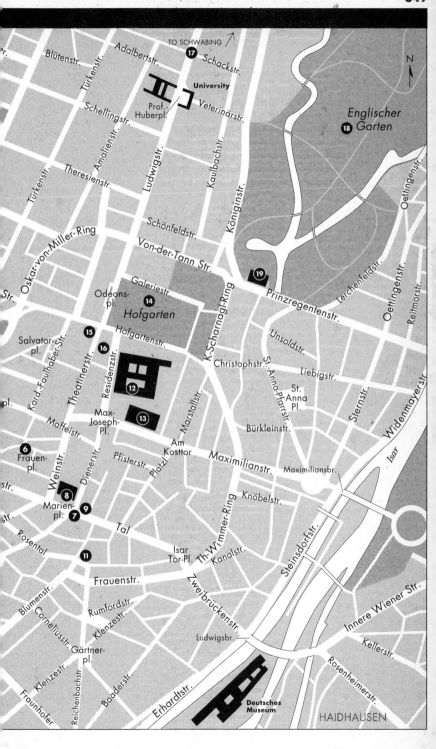

TO SCHWABING

Blütenstr.

Adalbertstr.

Türkenstr.

Schackstr.

⑰

Schellingstr.

Amalienstr.

University

Prof.-
Huberpl.

Veterinärstr.

Englischer
Garten

⑱

N

Türkenstr.

Theresienstr.

Ludwigstr.

Kaulbachstr.

Königinstr.

Oettingenstr.

Oskar-von-Miller-Ring

Schönfeldstr.

Von-der-Tann Str.

Str.

Prinzregentenstr.

⑲

Lerchenfeldstr.

Oettingenstr.

Reitmorstr.

Galeriestr.

Odeons-
pl.

⑭

Hofgarten

K.-Scharnagl-Ring

Unsoldstr.

Liebigstr.

Steinstr.

Salvator-
pl.

⑮

Hofgartenstr.

Christophstr.

St.-Anna-Pfarrstr.

St.
Anna
Pl.

Widenmayerstr.

Kard.-Faulhaber-Str.

Theatinerstr.

⑯

Residenzstr.

⑫

Marstallstr.

Bürkleinstr.

Isar

Maffeistr.

Max-
Joseph-
Pl.

⑬

Am
Kosttor

Maximilianstr.

Maximiliansbr.

⑥

Frauen-
pl.

Weinstr.

Dienerstr.

Pfisterstr.

Platzl

Str.

⑧

Marien-
pl.

⑦ ⑨

Tal

Knöbelstr.

Th.-Wimmer-Ring

Steinsdorfstr.

Rosental

⑪

Isar
Tor-Pl.

Kanalstr.

Innere Wiener Str.

Frauenstr.

Zweibrückenstr.

Blumenstr.

Rumfordstr.

Corneliusstr.

Klenzestr.

Gärtner-
pl.

Ludwigsbr.

Rosenheimerstr.

Kellerstr.

Klenzestr.

Reichenbachstr.

Baaderstr.

Fraunhofer

Erhardtstr.

Deutsches
Museum

HAIDHAUSEN

TIME OUT Munich's oldest café, the **Annast,** is on Odeonsplatz, right by the west entrance to the Hofgarten. Sit at one of the tables under the Hofgarten trees at the back of the café.

Odeonsplatz itself is dominated by two striking buildings. One is the ⑮ **Theatinerkirche,** built for the Theatine monks in the mid-17th century, though its handsome facade, with twin eye-catching domes, was added only in the following century. Despite its Italian influences, the interior, like that of the Michaelskirche, is austerely white. The other notable building here is the **Feldherrnhalle,** built by Ludwig I and modeled ⑯ on the Loggia dei Lanzi in Florence, and later used by the Nazis as a speakers' rostrum. For years it was a key Nazi shrine, for in the neighboring street, Residenz-Strasse, Hitler's unsuccessful 1923 putsch came to its bloody end.

The Feldherrnhalle looks north along one of the most imposing boulevards in Europe, the **Ludwigstrasse,** which in turn becomes the **Leopold-strasse.** Von Klenze was responsible for much of it, replacing the jumble of old buildings that originally stood here with the clean, high-windowed lines of his restrained Italianate buildings. The state library ⑰ and the university are located along it; halfway up it is the **Siegestor,** or Arch of Victory, modeled on the Arch of Constantine in Rome. Beyond this is **Schwabing,** once a student and artist quarter but now much glossier, with a mix of bars, discos (*see* Nightlife, *below*), trendy cafés, and boutiques. Nightlife centers around Wedekindplatz, near the Münchener Freiheit subway station.

Back on Leopoldstrasse, wander down to the university, turn on to Professor-Huber-Platz (he was a Munich academic executed by the Nazis for his support of an anti-Hitler movement), and take Veterinärstrasse. ⑱ It leads you to Munich's largest park, the magnificent **Englischer Garten.** You can rent a bike (tel. 089/282–500) at the entrance to the park on summer weekends (May–Oct.). The cost is DM 5 per hour and DM 25 for the day.

The Englischer Garten, 4½ kilometers (3 miles) long and more than ½ kilometer (¼ mile) wide, was laid out by Count Rumford, a refugee from the American War of Independence. He was born in England, but it wasn't his English ancestry that determined the park's name as much as its open, informal nature, a style favored by 18th-century English aristocrats. You can rent boats, visit beer gardens—the most famous is at the foot of a Chinese Pagoda—ride your bike (or ski in winter), or simply stroll around. Ludwig II loved to wander incognito along ⑲ the serpentine paths. A large section of the park right behind the **Haus der Kunst**—Munich's leading modern art gallery and a surviving example of Third Reich architecture—has been designated a nudist area. The building, which underwent major renovations in 1992, also houses one of the city's most exclusive discos, the P1. *Haus der Kunst, Prinzregentenstr. 1. Admission: DM 5 adults, DM 3 children; Sun. and holidays free. Open Tues.–Sun. 10–5, Thurs. until 8.*

Munich's two leading picture galleries, the Alte (old) and the Neue (new) Pinakothek, are on Barerstrasse, just to the west of the university. The ⑳ **Alte Pinakothek** is usually the repository of some of the world's most celebrated old master paintings; it is also an architectural treasure in its own right, though much scarred from wartime bomb damage. It was built by von Klenze at the beginning of the 19th century to house Ludwig I's collections. In 1994, the museum closed for renovations scheduled to take at least three years. Its most famous paintings (including most of the Dürers, Rembrandts, Rubenses, and two celebrated Murillos) are now on display at the Neue Pinakothek (*see below*) until the renovations are completed.

㉑ The **Neue Pinakothek** was another of Ludwig I's projects, built to house his "modern" collections, meaning, of course, 19th-century works. The building was destroyed during World War II, and today's museum opened in 1981. The low, brick structure—some have compared it with a Florentine palazzo—is an unparalleled environment in which to see one of the finest collections of 19th-century European paintings and sculpture in the world. *Barerstr. 29. Admission: DM 6 adults, DM 1 children; free Sun. and holidays. Open Tues.–Sun. 9–5, Tues. and Thurs. till 8 PM. Take Streetcar 18 or the U-2 subway to Königspl. from Karlspl.*

Suburban Attractions

There are a number of trips you can take to worthwhile sights not far from the city center. One is to the **Olympic Park,** a 10-minute U-Bahn ride (U-3); another is to **Nymphenburg,** 6 kilometers (4 miles) northwest and reached by the U-1 subway to Rotkreuzplatz, then Streetcar 12. The town of Dachau is a 20-minute ride from Marienplatz on the S-2 suburban railway line. To get to the **Dachau Concentration Camp Memorial** from the stop, take Bus 722 to Robert-Boschstrasse and walk along Alte Römerstrasse for 100 yards, or board Bus 720 and get off at Ratiborer Strasse.

Perhaps the most controversial buildings in Munich are the circus tent–shape roofs of the **Olympic Park.** Built for the 1972 Olympics, the park, with its undulating, transparent tile roofs and modern housing blocks, represented a revolutionary marriage of technology and visual daring when first unveiled. Sports fans might like to join the crowds in the Olympic Stadium when the local soccer team, Bayern Munich, has a home game. Call 089/699–310 for information and tickets. There's an amazing view of the stadium, the Olympic Park, and the city from the Olympic Tower. An elevator speeds you to the top in seconds. *Tower admission: DM 5 adults; DM 2.50 children; combined tower and park tour (until 5 PM) DM 7 adults, DM 4 children. Admission to stadium alone: DM 1 adults, 50 pf children. Tower open daily 9 AM–midnight. Stadium open daily 9–4:30.*

Schloss Nymphenburg was the summer palace of the Wittelsbachs. The oldest parts date from 1664, but construction continued for more than 100 years, the bulk of the work undertaken during the reign of Max Emmanuel between 1680 and 1730. The gardens, a mixture of formal French *parterres* (trim, ankle-high hedges and gravel walks) and English parkland, were landscaped during the same period. The interiors are exceptional, especially the Banqueting Hall, a Rococo masterpiece in green and gold. Make a point of seeing the Schönheits Galerie, the **Gallery of Beauties.** It contains more than 100 portraits of women who had caught the eye of Ludwig I; duchesses rub shoulders with butchers' daughters. Among them is Lola Montez. Seek out the **Amalienburg,** or Hunting Lodge, on the grounds. It was built by Cuvilliès, architect of the Residenz Theater in Munich. That the lodge was designed for hunting of the indoor variety can easily be guessed by the sumptuous silver and blue stucco and the atmosphere of courtly high life. The palace also contains the **Marstallmuseum** (Museum of Royal Carriages), containing a sleigh that belonged to Ludwig II, among the opulently decorated vehicles, and, on the floor above, the **Nymphenburger Porzellan,** with examples of the porcelain produced here between 1747 and the 1920s. *Schloss Nymphenburg. Admission: ticket to all Nymphenburg attractions DM 6 adults, DM 4 children;*

*ticket to Schloss, Gallery of Beauties, Amalienburg, and Marstallmu-
seum DM 2.50, DM 2 children; Botanic gardens: DM 1.50 adults. Open
Apr.–Sept., Tues.–Sun. 9–12:30 and 1:30–5; Oct.–Mar., Tues.–Sun.
10–12:30 and 1:30–4. Gardens open daily year-round.*

Although the 1,200-year-old town of **Dachau** attracted hordes of
painters and artists from the mid-19th century until World War I,
most people remember it as the site of Germany's first **concentration
camp.** From its opening in 1933 until its capture by American soldiers
in 1945, the camp greeted more than 206,000 political dissidents,
Jews, clergy, and other "enemies" of the Nazis; more than 32,000 prisoners died here. Photographs, contemporary documents, the few remaining cell blocks, and the grim crematorium create a somber and
moving picture of the vicious living and working conditions at the camp.
*Admission free. Open Tues.–Sun. 9–5; documentary (in English)
shown at 11:30 and 3:30.*

Off the Beaten Track

Even though the Olympic Tower is higher, romantics say the best view
of Munich and the Alps is from the top of the **Alte Peterskirche** tower
(DM 2.50 adults, DM 1.50 children); it's just off Marienplatz. Check
that a white disk is hanging on the wall outside the entrance: It means
that visibility is good. There are 302 steps to climb to the top. For the
most inexpensive sightseeing tour of the center, take Streetcar 19 from
outside the train station at Bahnhofplatz and ride it to **Wienerplatz,**
itself located in Haidhausen, one of Munich's most interesting areas.
On a fine day, join the chess players at their open-air boards in
Schwabing's **Münchener Freiheit** square. On a rainy day, pack your swim-
suit and splash around in the Art Nouveau setting of the **Müllersches
Volksbad** pool; it's on the corner of the Ludwigsbrücke, one of the bridges
over the Isar.

Shopping

Gift Ideas

Munich is a city of beer, and beer mugs and coasters make an obvious
gift to take home. Many shops specialize in beer-related souvenirs, but
Ludwig Mory (Marienplatz 8) is about the best. Munich is also the home
of the famous Nymphenburg porcelain factory; its major outlet is on
Odeonsplatz. You can also buy direct from the factory, which is on the
half-moon–shape road—Schlossrondell—in front of Nymphenburg
Palace. *Nördliche Schlossrondell 8, tel. 089/1791–9710. Salesroom open
Mon.–Fri. 8:30–noon and 12:30–5.*

Shopping Districts

From Odeonsplatz you are poised to plunge into the heart of the huge
pedestrian mall that runs through the center of town. The first street
you come to, **Theatinerstrasse,** is also one of the most expensive. In
fact, it has only one serious rival in the money-no-object stakes: **Maximilianstrasse,** the first street to your left as you head down Theatinerstrasse. Both are lined with elegant shops selling desirable German
fashions and other high-price goods from around the world. Leading
off to the right of Theatinerstrasse is **Maffeistrasse,** where **Loden-Frey**
has Bavaria's most complete collection of traditional wear, from green
"loden" coats to lederhosen. Maffeistrasse runs parallel to Munich's
principal shopping streets: **Kaufingerstrasse** and **Neuhauserstrasse,** the
one an extension of the other.

Department Stores

All the city's major department stores—other than **Hertie** (*see* Exploring, *above*)—are along Maffeistrasse, Kaufingerstrasse, and Neuhauserstrasse. **Kaufhof** and **Karstadt-Oberpollinger** are probably the best. Both have large departments stocking Bavarian arts and crafts, as well as clothing, household goods, jewelry, and other accessories.

Antiques

Antique hunters should visit **Blumenstrasse, Ottostrasse, Türkenstrasse,** and **Westenriederstrasse.** Also try the open-air Auer Dult fairs held on Mariahilplatz at the end of April, July, and October (Streetcar 25), or the Friday and Saturday markets at the old Riem airport (take the S-6 to Riem).

Dining

Münchners love to eat just as much as they love to drink their beer, and the range of food is as varied and rich as the local breweries' output. Some of Europe's best chefs are here, purveyors of French nouvelle cuisine in some of the most noted—and pricey—restaurants in Germany. But these restaurants are mainly for the gourmet. For those in search of local cuisine, the path leads to Munich's tried-and-true, wood-paneled, flagstone beer restaurants and halls where the food is as sturdy as the large measure of beer that comes to your table almost automatically. Provided your pockets are deep enough, the choice is limitless—from a mountainous roast pork knuckle with dumplings to delicate slivers of salmon and truffle salad. The highbrow restaurants offer a low-key, library-quiet atmosphere, while many of the lower-brow establishments provide ear-splitting conviviality. Try the Weisswurst, brought to your table in a tureen of boiling water to keep them fresh and hot. They are served with a sweet mustard and pretzels and are a breakfast or midmorning favorite. Equally good is Leberkäs, wedges of piping-hot meat loaf with a fried egg on top and panfried potatoes.

For details and price-category definitions, *see* Dining *in* Staying in Germany, *above.*

$$$$ **Aubergine.** German gourmets swear by the upscale nouvelle cuisine
★ of Eckart Witzigmann, chef and owner of this sophisticated restaurant. The decor is a bit loud, incorporating aubergine, white, and silver into the color scheme. If you want a gastronomic experience on the grand scale, try the turbot in champagne or the breast of pigeon with artichoke and truffle salad. The equally exotic wine list includes an 1832 Lafite-Rothschild. *Maximilianpl. 5, tel. 089/ 598–171. Reservations required. DC, MC, V. Closed Sun., Mon. lunch, public holidays, and first 3 wks of Aug.*

$$$$ **Königshof.** On the second floor of the postwar Königshof Hotel and overlooking the Karlstor at the northern entrance to the pedestrian-only center, the Königshof is without doubt Munich's most opulent restaurant. The neo-baroque style includes ceiling frescoes, subdued chandelier lighting, and heavy drapery. Nouvelle cuisine is served—breast of goose with truffles, or veal in basil cream and mushroom sauce, for example. *Karlspl. 25, tel. 089/551–360. Reservations advised. AE, DC, MC, V.*

$$$ **Hunsingers Bouillabaisse.** After establishing a nationwide reputation for excellent cuisine at a restaurant in Munich's southern suburbs, Werner Hunsinger is at work in the city center. The sleek and elegant decor of this place, just off fashionable Maximilianstrasse, is a change in style from the solid traditional look of his previous location, but the cuisine is the same. The predominantly French menu is full of light, imaginative dishes created from the simplest of ingredients—calves' tongue, for instance, with avocado vinaigrette, or black noodles with mussels. *Falkenturmstr. 10, tel. 089/297–909. Reservations advised. AE, DC, MC, V. Closed Sun. and last 3 wks of Aug.*

$$$ **Käferschanke.** Fresh seafood, including lobster, crab, salmon, trout, and halibut, imported daily, is the attraction here. Try the grilled prawns in a sweet-and-sour sauce. The rustic decor, complemented by some fine antique pieces, is also sure to delight. The restaurant is in the classy Bogenhausen suburb, a 10-minute taxi ride from downtown. *Prinzregentenstr. 73, tel. 089/416–8247. Reservations advised. AE, DC, MC. Closed Sun. and holidays.*

$$$ **Le Gourmet.** Imaginative combinations of French and Bavarian specialties
★ have made this small bistro a local favorite. Try chef Otto Koch's souf-flé of sole in lemongrass sauce, or filled marrowbones with *Rösti* (Swiss-style panfried potatoes). *Hartmannstr. 8, tel. 089/212–0958. Reservations advised. AE, DC, MC. Closed Sun., Mon., and first 10 days of Jan.*

$$$ **Preysing Keller.** Devotees of all that's best in modern German cook-
★ ing—food that's light and sophisticated but with recognizably Teutonic touches—will love the Preysing Keller, a hotel-restaurant. It's in a 16th-century cellar, though it has been so over-restored that there's prac-tically no sense of its age or original character. Never mind; it's the food, the extensive wine list, and the perfect service that make this place spe-cial. *Innere-Wiener-Str. 6, tel. 089/481–015. Reservations required. No credit cards. Closed Sun., Christmas, and New Year's Day.*

$$ **Augustiner Keller.** This 19th-century establishment is the flagship beer restaurant of one of Munich's oldest breweries, Augustiner. The decor emphasizes wood—from the refurbished parquet floors to the wooden barrels from which the beer is drawn. A full range of Bavarian spe-cialties comprises the daily changing menu, but try to order *Tellerfleisch*—cold roast beef with lashings of horseradish, served on a big wooden board. The communal atmosphere of the two baronial-hall–like rooms makes this a better place to meet locals than attempt a quiet meal for two. *Arnulfstr. 52, tel. 089/594–393. No credit cards.*

$$ **Grüne Gans.** This small, chummy restaurant near Viktualienmarkt is popular with local entertainers, whose photographs clutter the walls. International fare with regional German influences dominates the menu, although there are a few Chinese dishes. Try the chervil cream soup, followed by calves' kidneys in tarragon sauce. *Am Einlass 5, tel. 089/266–228. Reservations required. MC. Closed lunch and Sat.*

$$ **James Cafe.** Chef-owner James is an immigrant from Kenya, but you'll find no African specialties on his small but very fine menu. Instead, James cooks Italian, and so well that his cozy café is considered by aficiona-dos as one of *the* Italian eating places in town. One of Munich's lead-ing restaurant critics said the city's Italian cooks should turn "green, white, and red [the colors of Italy's flag] with shame." James changes his menu every day; if Italian-style pheasant is on it, then that's the dish to order. *Hochbrückenstr. 14, tel. 089/298–940. MC. No lunch Sun.*

$$ **Weinhaus Neuner.** Originally a seminary, this early 18th-century build-ing houses Munich's oldest surviving wine hostelry, in the Neuner family since 1852. There is a timeless atmosphere in the high-ceilinged dining rooms lined with dark oak paneling. Look for the herb-filled pork fillets with noodles, and veal with Morchela mushroom sauce. *Herzogspitalstr. 8, tel. 089/260–3954. Reservations required. AE, DC, MC, V. Closed Sun., and holidays.*

$ **Altes Hackerhaus.** This upscale beer restaurant on one of Munich's ritzi-
★ est shopping streets is full of bric-a-brac and mementos that harken back to its origins as a medieval brewery and one-time home of the

Hacker family. Since 1570, beer has been brewed or served here, the birthplace of one of the city's largest breweries—Hacker-Pschorr. On a cold day, duck into one of the cozy little rooms and choose from the selection of hearty soups, then try a plate of *Käsespätzle* (egg noodles with melted cheese). In the heat of summer, try for a table in the tiny, cool, inner courtyard, probably the smallest beer garden in Munich. *Sendlingerstr. 14, tel. 089/260–5026. No credit cards.*

$ **Baltzer.** Vegetarians say they eat better at this evenings-only restaurant than fellow epicurean omnivores do in their starred temples of haute cuisine. The dishes certainly have a flair not usually associated with vegetarian stringency (eggplant, for instance, stuffed with oyster mushrooms, mangold, and wild rice). The Baltzer team's credo, which you too will be convinced of after eating here, is that "Plants have a myriad different tastes." *Volkartstr. 70, tel. 089/1239–1919. Closed Mon and lunchtime, open Sun 9 AM–midnight. No reservations. No credit cards.*

$ **Brauhaus zur Brez'n.** This hostelry is bedecked in the blue-and-white of the Bavarian flag. The eating and drinking are spread over three floors and cater to a broad clientele—from local business lunchers to hungry night owls emerging from Schwabing's bars looking for a bite at 2 AM. Brez'n offers a big all-day menu of traditional roasts, to be washed down with a choice of three draft beers. *Leopoldstr. 72, tel. 089/390–092. MC.*

$ **Dürnbräu.** A fountain plays outside this picturesque old Bavarian inn. Inside, it's crowded and noisy. Expect to share a table; your fellow diners will range from businessmen to students. The food is resolutely traditional. Try the cream of spinach soup and the boiled beef. *Dürnbräug. 2, tel. 089/222–195. AE, DC, MC, V.*

$ **Franziskaner.** Vaulted archways, cavernous rooms interspersed with intimate dining areas, bold blue frescoes on the walls, and long wooden tables create a spic-and-span medieval atmosphere. Aside from the late-morning Weisswurst, look out for *Ochsenfleisch* (boiled ox meat) and dumplings. *Perusastr. 5, tel. 089/231–8120. No reservations. No credit cards.*

$ **Haxnbauer.** You can still order meat dishes here—Bratwurst (roast sausages), *Schweinshaxe* (roast pork knuckle)—that have been cooked over an open charcoal fire. And, surprisingly for a Munich beer restaurant, the beer is from a north German brewery. The decor in the series of interlocking rooms is plain, with chunky, dark wood furniture. *Sparkassenstr. 3, tel. 089/221–922. Reservations advised. MC, V.*

$ **Hofbräuhaus.** The heavy stone vaults of the Hofbräuhaus contain the most famous of the city's beer restaurants. Crowds of singing, shouting, swaying beer drinkers fill the cavernous, smoky hall. Picking their way past the tables are hefty waitresses in traditional garb bearing frothing steins. The menu is strictly Bavarian. If you're not here solely to drink, try the more subdued upstairs restaurant, where the service is not so brusque and less beer gets spilled. It's between Marienplatz and Maximilianstrasse. *Platzl 9, tel. 089/221–676. No reservations. No credit cards.*

$ **Hundskugel.** History practically oozes from the crooked walls at this tavern, Munich's oldest, which dates from 1440. If *Spanferkel*—roast suckling pig—is on the menu, make a point of ordering it. This is simple Bavarian fare at its best. *Hotterstr. 18, tel. 089/264–272. Reservations advised. No credit cards. Closed Sun.*

$ **Pfälzer Weinprobierstube.** A warren of stone-vaulted rooms of various sizes, wooden tables, glittering candles, dirndl-clad waitresses, ★ and a vast range of wines add up to an experience as close to your picture of timeless Germany as you're likely to get. The food is reliable rather than spectacular. Local specialties predominate. *Residenzstr. 1, tel. 089/225–628. No reservations. No credit cards.*

Lodging

Though Munich has a vast number of hotels in all price ranges, most are full year-round. If you plan to visit during the "fashion weeks" (Mode Wochen) in March and September or during the Oktoberfest at the end of September, make reservations at least several months in advance. Munich's tourist offices will handle only written or personal requests for reservations assistance. Write/fax: Fremdenverkehrsamt, Sendlinger-str. 1, D-80313 Munich, fax 089/ 239–1313. Your best bet for finding a room if you haven't reserved one is the tourist office at the Hauptbahnhof, by the Bayerstrasse entrance. The staff will charge a small fee.

Consider staying in a suburban hotel—where rates are often, but not always, lower—and taking the U-Bahn or S-Bahn into town. A 15-minute train ride is no obstacle to serious sightseeing. Check out the city tourist office "Key to Munich" packages. These include reduced-rate hotel reservations, sightseeing tours, theater visits, and low-cost travel on the U- and S-Bahn. Write to the tourist office (*see* Important Addresses and Numbers in Munich, *above*).

For details and price-category definitions, *see* Lodging *in* Staying in Germany, *above*.

$$$$ **Bayerischer Hof.** This is one of Munich's most traditional luxury hotels. Public rooms are decorated with antiques, fine paintings, marble, and painted wood. Old-fashioned comfort and class abound in the older rooms; some of the newer rooms are less ornate but functional. *Promenadepl. 2–6, tel. 089/21200, fax 089/212–0906. 383 rooms with bath and 45 apartments. Facilities: 3 restaurants, nightclub, rooftop pool, garage, sauna, masseur, hairdresser. AE, DC, MC, V.*

$$$$ **Kempinski Hotel Vier Jahreszeiten.** The Vier Jahreszeiten—it means the
★ Four Seasons—has been playing host to the world's wealthy and titled for more than a century. It has an unbeatable location on Munich's premier shopping street and is only a few minutes' walk from the heart of the city. Elegance and luxury set the tone throughout; many rooms have handsome antique pieces. *Maximilianstr. 17, tel. 089/ 230–390, fax 089/2303–9693. (Reservations in the U.S. from Kempinski International, tel. 800/426–3135.) 322 rooms with bath, 44 suites, presidential suite. Facilities: 2 restaurants, nightclub, rooftop pool, sauna, garage, car rental, Lufthansa check-in desk. AE, DC, MC, V.*

$$$$ **Rafael.** A character-laden lodging in the heart of the Old Town (close to the Hofbräuhaus), the Rafael, which opened in 1989, retains many of the architectural features of its building's late-19th-century origins, including a sweeping staircase and stuccoed ceilings. Rooms are individually furnished and extravagantly decorated. The hotel restaurant, Mark's, has made a name for itself with its new German cuisine. *Neuturmstr. 1, tel. 089/290–980, fax 089/222–539. 67 rooms and 7 suites with bath. Facilities: restaurant, bar, indoor pool, sauna. AE, DC, MC, V.*

$$$ **Eden Hotel Wolff.** Chandeliers and dark wooden paneling in the public rooms underline the old-fashioned elegance of this downtown favorite. It's directly across the street from the train station and the airport bus terminal. The rooms are comfortable, and most are spacious. Dine on excellent Bavarian specialties in the intimate Zirbelstube restaurant. *Arnulfstr. 4, tel. 089/551–150, fax 089/5511–5555. 210 rooms with bath. Facilities: restaurant, parking. AE, DC, MC, V.*

$$$ Hotel Erzgiesserei Europe. Its location on a dull little street in an uninteresting section of town is its only drawback, and one easily overcome: The nearby subway whisks you in five minutes to central Karlsplatz, convenient for the pedestrian shopping area and the main railway station. Rooms in this attractive hotel are particularly bright, decorated in soft pastel tones with good-quality art reproductions on the walls. The cobblestone garden café is a peaceful haven in summer. *Erzgiessereistr. 15, tel. 089/126–820, fax 089/123–6198. 106 rooms with bath. Facilities: restaurant, bar, garden café, parking. AE, DC, MC, V.*

$$$ Pannonia Hotel Königin Elisabeth. Housed in a 19th-century Neo-
★ classical building that was completely restored and opened for the first time as a hotel in 1989, the Elisabeth is modern and bright, with an emphasis on the color pink. The restaurant offers Hungarian specialties. The Elisabeth is a 15-minute streetcar ride northwest of the city center en route to Nymphenburg. *Leonrodstr. 79, tel. 089/ 126–860, fax 089/1268–6459. 80 rooms with bath. Facilities: bar, beer garden, sauna, solarium, and fitness equipment. AE, DC, MC, V.*

$$$ Platzl Ringhotel. This hotel manages to be both modern and Bavarian-rustic. It's in a building that dates from 1573 and is in the heart of Munich's historic quarter—next to the famous Hofbräuhaus beer hall. The rooms are smallish but comfortable. *Sparkassenstr. 10, tel. 089/237–030, fax 089/2370–3800 (toll-free booking in the U.S., tel. 800/448–8355). 167 rooms with bath. Facilities: sauna, solarium, fitness rooms, rooftop terrace, restaurant, bar, underground garage. AE, DC, MC, V.*

$$$ Torbräu. You'll sleep in the shadow of one of Munich's ancient city gates—the 14th-century Isartor—if you stay here. This snug hotel offers comfortable, Scandinavian-modern rooms and an excellent location between the Marienplatz and the Deutsches Museum (and around the corner from the Hofbräuhaus). There's an Italian restaurant and a coffee shop that bakes its own cakes. *Tal 41, tel. 089/225–016, fax 089/225–019. 82 rooms with bath, 4 suites. Facilities: restaurant, coffee shop, bowling alley. AE, MC, V.*

$$ Adria. This modern, comfortable hotel is ideally located in the upscale area of Lehel, in the middle of Munich's museum quarter. Rooms are large and tastefully decorated, with old prints on the pale-pink walls, Oriental rugs on the floors, and flowers beside the large double beds. A spectacular breakfast buffet (including a glass of sparking wine) is included in the room rate. There's no hotel restaurant, but the area is rich in good restaurants, bistros, and bars. *Liebigstr. 8a, tel. 089/293–081, fax 089/227–015. 47 rooms with bath. AE, DC, MC, V.*

$$ Amba. Families get an especially good deal at the Amba, a member of a hotel group that prides itself on being child-friendly. A modern, brightly furnished double room comes for as low as DM 110, and additional beds cost DM 35. The hotel is across the street from the main railway station and has its own porter service. A hotel bus collects guests from the airport. *Arnulfstr. 20, tel. 089/545–140, fax 089/5451–4555. 86 rooms, 73 with bath. Facilities: restaurant, coffee-bar, parking. AE, DC, MC, V.*

$$ Bauer. If the rustic Bavarian style of pinewood, blue-and-white check, and red geraniums appeals to you, you'll feel at home at the Bauer, a 20-minute ride east on the S-6 suburban train, or just a few miles by car along the A94 autobahn. The Bauer gives excellent value and facilities for the price. *Münchnerstr. 6, D-85622 Feldkirchen, tel. 089/90980, fax 089/909–8414. 103 rooms with bath. Facilities: restaurant, terrace café, solarium, sauna, indoor pool. AE, DC, MC, V.*

$$ Gästehaus am Englischer Garten. Though the rooms are slightly basic, you need to reserve well in advance to be sure of getting one in this converted, 200-year-old watermill. The hotel, complete with ivy-clad walls and shutter-frame windows, stands on the edge of the Englischer Garten, no more than a five-minute walk from the bars and shops of Schwabing. Be sure to ask for a room in the main building; the modern annex down the road is cheaper but charmless. There's no restaurant, but in summer, breakfast is served on the terrace. *Liebergesellstr. 8, tel. 089/392–034, fax 089/391–233. 30 rooms, 27 with bath. No credit cards.*

$$ Hotel Carlton. This is a diplomats' favorite—a small, elegant, discreet hotel on a quiet side street in the best area of downtown Munich. The American and British consulates are nearby, as are some of the liveliest Schwabing bars and restaurants. Art galleries, museums, and cinemas are also in the neighborhood. Rooms are on the small side, but there are also four apartments with cooking facilities. *Fürstenstr. 12, tel. 089/282–061, fax 089/284–391. 49 rooms with bath, 4 apartments. AE, DC, MC, V.*

$$ Tele-Hotel. This modern, well-appointed hotel on the outskirts of Munich is close to the television studios (hence the name) at Unterföhring, and is conveniently located along the airport S-8 line, only a 15-minute ride from downtown. TV types escape their studio cafeteria's drab fare by popping into the hotel's Bavarian Hackerbräu restaurant, where a lunchtime menu for less than DM 30 is a hot favorite. *Bahnhofstr. 15, Unterföhring, tel. 089/950–146, fax 089/950–6652. 60 rooms with bath, 1 apartment. Facilities: restaurant, bar, roof terrace, bowling alley, parking. AE, DC, MC, V.*

$ Fürst. On a quiet street just off Odeonsplatz on the edge of the university quarter, this very basic, clean guest house is constantly busy. Book early. *Kardinal-Döpfnerstr. 8, tel. 089/281–043. 19 rooms, 12 with bath. No credit cards.*

$ Hotel-Pension Beck. American and British guests receive a particularly warm welcome from the Anglophile owner of the rambling, friendly Beck. Rooms were recently refurnished in pinewood. The pension has a prime location in the heart of fashionable Lehel—handy for museums and the Englischer Garten. *Thierschstr. 36, tel. 089/220–708 or 089/225–768, fax 089/220–925. 44 rooms, 4 with shower. No credit cards.*

$ Mariandl. Large families are catered to at this rambling, friendly pension with huge rooms furnished in a variety of homey styles. The ground floor is taken up by a Viennese-style restaurant, with Biedermeier furnishings and a menu featuring every variety of Wiener-schnitzel. The large grand piano isn't in here just for decoration—evening soirees in the style of those once enjoyed by Franz Schubert and his friends in Vienna are held here Monday through Friday (portraits of the composer adorn the walls). If you like your schnitzel with Lieder, then you'll love this place. *Goethestr. 51, tel. 089/534–108 or 089/535–158. 30 rooms, 4 with shower. AE, V.*

The Arts

Details of concerts and theater performances are available from the "Vorschau" or "Monatsprogramm" booklets obtainable at most hotel reception desks. Some hotels will make ticket reservations; otherwise use one of the ticket agencies in the city center: **Hieber Konzertkasse** (Liebfrauenstr. 1, tel. 089/290–080) or the **Residenz Bücherstube** (Residenzstr. 1, concert tickets only, tel. 089/220–868). You can also book tickets at the two kiosks on the concourse below Marienplatz.

Concerts

Munich's Philharmonic Orchestra performs in Germany's biggest concert hall, the **Gasteig Cultural Center** (Rosenheimerstrasse, on a hill above Ludwigsbrücke Bridge, tel. 089/5481–8181). Tickets can be bought at the box office. The Bavarian Radio Orchestra performs Sunday concerts here. In summer, concerts are held at two Munich palaces, **Nymphenburg** and **Schleissheim,** and in the open-air interior courtyard of the **Residenz.**

Opera

Munich's **Bavarian State Opera** company is world-famous, and tickets for major productions in its permanent home, the State Opera House, are difficult to obtain. Book far in advance for the annual opera festival held in July and August; contact the tourist office for the schedule of performances and ticket prices. The opera house box office (Maximilianstr. 11, tel. 089/2185–1920) takes reservations one week in advance only. It's open weekdays 10–1 and 2–6, Saturday 10–1.

Dance

The ballet company of the Bavarian State Opera performs at the State Opera House. Ballet productions are also staged at the attractive late-19th-century **Gärtnerplatz Theater** (tel. 089/201–6767).

Film

Munich hosts a film festival each June. English-language films are shown regularly at several downtown cinemas: **Ricks and Hollywood** (Schwantalerstr. 2–6), **Cinema** (Nymphenburgerstr. 31), the **Film Museum** (St. Jakobs Pl.), and the **Museum Lichtspiele** (Ludwigsbrücke).

Theater

There are two state theater companies, one of which concentrates on the classics. More than 20 other theater companies (some of them performing in basements) are to be found throughout the city. Regular English-language productions, featuring an American cast and director, are staged at **America House** and the **Theater an der Leopoldstrasse** (Leopoldstr. 17, tel. 089/343–803).

Nightlife

Although it lacks the racy reputation of Hamburg, Munich has something for just about all tastes.

Bars, Cabaret, Nightclubs

Try **Schumann's** (Maximilianstr. 36) anytime after the curtain comes down at the nearby opera house (and watch the barmen shake those cocktails; closed Sat.), but wait till after midnight before venturing into the **Alter Simpl** (Turkenstr. 57) for a sparkling crowd despite the gloomy surroundings. Back on fashionable Maximilianstrasse, **O'Reilly's Irish Cellar Pub** offers escape from the German bar scene, and it serves genuine Irish Guinness. Great Caribbean cocktails and a powerful Irish-German Black and Tan (Guinness and strong German beer) are served at the English nautical-style **Pusser's** bar (Falkenturmstr. 9; it replaced Munich's own Harry's Bar). Stiff competition is nearby at **Havana** (Herrnstr. 3), which does its darnedest to look like a run-down Cuban dive, although the chic clientele spoils those pretensions.

Gone are the sixties-generation nightclubs combining a good restaurant, a dance combo, and high-class exotic dancers. In their place are tiny cabaret stages and even smaller strip bars. The cabarets, most of them in Schwabing, usually offer political satire, performed in dialects incomprehensible to non-Germans.

Jazz

The best jazz can be heard at the **Scala Music Bar** (Oscar-von-Miller Ring 3), the **Unterfahrt** (Kirchenstr. 96), and the **Podium** (Wagnerstr.

1). Or try **Jenny's Place in the Blue Note** (Moosacherstr. 24, tel. 089/351–0520), named for an English singer who settled in Munich.

Discos

Disco bars abound in the side streets off Freilitzschstrasse surrounding Münchener Freiheit in Schwabing. **Babalu** (Leopoldstr. 19) is among the best—a real old-timer on Munich's changing disco scene. More upscale are **Nachtcafe** (Maximilianspl. 5), open all night on weekends, and **P1** (in the Haus der Kunst, Prinzregentenstr. 1). **Nachtwerk** (Landsbergerstr. 185) has everything from punk to avant-garde, plus live bands.

For Singles

Every Munich bar is singles territory. Making contact at the **Wunder-bar** (Hochbrückenstr. 3) is made easier on Tuesday nights when telephones are installed on the tables and at the bar, and the place hums like a stygian switchboard. The lively (at any time) basement bar is run by an innovative young New Yorker. Munich's gay scene is found between Sendlingertorplatz and Isartorplatz. Its most popular bars are **Together** (Rumfordstr. 2), **Nil** (Hans-Sachs-Str. 2), **Ochsengarten** (Müllerstr. 47), and **Pimpernel** (Müllerstr. 56). For the student, beard, and pipe scene, try **Türkenstrasse,** behind the university (Cafe Puck, No. 33, and La Boheme, No. 79, are typical of the scene).

FRANKFURT

Arriving and Departing

By Plane

Frankfurt airport, the busiest in mainland Europe, is about 10 kilometers (6 miles) southwest of the city.

BETWEEN THE AIRPORT AND DOWNTOWN
Two suburban (S-Bahn) lines connect the airport and the center. The S-14 runs every 20 minutes, taking 15 minutes between the Hauptwache station and the airport. The S-15, from the main train station, the Hauptbahnhof, leaves every 10 minutes and takes 11 minutes. The trip costs DM 4.20 (DM 5.60 in rush hour, 6:30–8:30 AM and 4–6:30 PM. InterCity and InterCity Express trains also stop at the Frankfurt airport train station on hourly direct runs to Cologne, Dortmund, Hamburg, and Munich. Bus 61 runs from the airport to the Südbahnhof station in Sachsenhausen, where there is access to the U-Bahn (subway) lines U-1 and U-3; the fare is DM 4.20 (DM 5.60 during rush hours). Taxi fare from the airport to downtown is about DM 40. By rented car, follow the STADTMITTE signs to Frankfurt via the B43 main road.

By Train

Frankfurt's main train station, the Hauptbahnhof, and the airport station are directly linked with all parts of the country by fast Euro-City and InterCity services and by the high-speed ICE trains. For train information, call 069/19419. For tickets and general information, go directly to the station or to the DER travel office at the Hauptbahnhof.

By Bus

Long-distance buses connect Frankfurt with more than 200 European cities. Buses leave from the south side of the Hauptbahnhof. Tickets and information are available from **Deutsche Touring GmbH** (Am Römerhof 17, tel. 069/79030).

By Car

From the north, leave autobahn A5 at the Nordwestkreuz, join A66 and follow it to its end, in the Nordend district. From the east, A66 brings you into Enkheim, from where you follow the STADTMITTE signs to the downtown area. From the west, leave autobahn A3 at the Frankfurt-Süd (Frankfurt south) exit and enter the city on B43/44. From the south, leave the autobahn at the Anschluss-Stelle Offenbach (Offenbach exit) and enter the city on B459.

Getting Around

By Public Transportation

A combination of subway and suburban train, streetcar, and bus services provides speedy transportation. Tickets cover travel on the complete network, which is divided into tariff zones. A single ticket for travel within the city costs DM 2.20 (DM 2.80 during rush hour). A day ticket (for use during one calendar day) offers unlimited journeys in the inner zone for DM 6. Buy all tickets at newspaper kiosks or from blue dispensing machines. If you're caught without a ticket, you'll have to pay a fine of DM 60 to the plainclothes "controllers" who patrol the trains. For further information or assistance, call 069/269–462.

By Taxi

Taxi meters start at DM 3.80, and the fare is DM 2.15 per kilometer (about DM 3.50 per mile), or DM 2.35 on weekends. Count on paying DM 10 to DM 12 for a short city ride. Taxi drivers charge 50 pf for each piece of luggage carried. To order a taxi, call 069/250–001, 069/ 545–011, or 069/230–033.

Important Addresses and Numbers

Tourist Information

There are three **city information offices.** One is at the Hauptbahnhof, across from Platform 23 (tel. 069/2123–8849). It's open Monday–Friday 8 AM–9 PM; Saturday, Sunday, and holidays 9:30 AM–8 PM. Another is in the town hall in the Old Town at Römerberg 27 (tel. 069/2123–8708). It's open daily 9 AM–6 PM. Both offices will help you find accommodations. A third information office (tel. 069/690–6211), in the airport Arrival Hall B, is open daily 6:45 AM–10:15 PM. The **DER Deutsches Reisebüro**, Arrival Hall B6, can also help you find rooms. Open daily 8 AM–9 PM (tel. 069/693–071). For information in advance of your trip, contact the **Verkehrsamt Frankfurt/Main** (Kaiserstr. 52, 60329 Frankfurt, tel. 069/2123–8800).

Consulates

U.S. (Siesmayerstr. 21, tel. 069/75350). **U.K.** (Bockenheimer Landstr. 42, tel. 069/170–0020).

Emergencies

Police (tel. 110). Fire (tel. 112). **Dentist** (tel. 069/660–7271). **Pharmacy Information** (tel. 069/11500).

English-Language Bookstores

The **British Bookshop** (Börsenstr. 17, tel. 069/280–492) and the **American Book Center** (Jahnstr. 36, tel. 069/552–816) carry English-language titles.

Travel Agencies

American Express (Kaiserstr. 8, tel. 069/210–548). **DER Deutsches Reisebüro** (Emil-von-Behring Str. 6, tel. 069/9588–3560).

Guided Tours

Orientation Tours

English-speaking guides lead daily bus tours of the city, including visits to Goethe's House and the Europa Tower for a view over Frankfurt, throughout the year. In summer, tours leave at 1 PM weekdays from the tourist information office at the Römer, and 1:15 PM from the office at the train station; weekend tours leave twice daily, at 10 AM (Römer)/10:15 (train station) and 2 PM (Römer)/2:25 (train station). From November to March, tours are given on weekends and holidays only, at 1 PM (Römer)/1:15 (train station). The tour lasts about two and a half hours and costs DM 36 (under 16, half price). **Gray Line** (tel. 069/230–492) offers city tours four times a day; they cost DM 50 (DM 40 children). On weekend afternoons, a gaily painted old streetcar, *The Ebbelwei Express,* trundles around the city and Sachsenhausen, on the south side of the Main. The 40-minute ride—starting and ending at the Ostbahnhof train station, at Danzigerplatz in Frankfurt's Ostend district—includes a glass of *Ebbelwei* (apple cider) and a pretzel in the DM 4 fare. Further information and tickets can be obtained from the tourist offices (*see* Important Addresses and Numbers, *above*). For DM 12, visitors who like to go at their own pace can buy a cassette of a one-hour walking tour (in English) at the tourist office at the Römer and rent a Walkman for a DM 50 deposit.

Excursions

Bus tours of the surrounding countryside, as far as the Rhine, are offered by **Noblesse Limousine Service** (tel. 06101/12055) in Bad Vilbel, **Deutsche Touring GmbH** (Am Römerhof 17, tel. 069/790–3268), and **Gray Line** (*see above*). One-day excursions are also offered by German Railways, the Deutsche Bahn. These are described in a brochure, "Der Schöne Tag," obtainable from the main train station and the DER tourist office. A "Casino-Express" bus service runs daily from Frankfurt (departing from the south side of the train station) to the casino at Bad Homburg in the Taunus Mountains. The DM 9.50 fare includes the entrance charge to the casino. The bus departs hourly, from 2 to 11 PM. Pleasure boats of the **Primus Line** cruise the Main and Rhine rivers from Frankfurt, sailing as far as the Lorelei and back in a day; for schedules and reservations, contact **Frankfurter Personenschiffahrt** (Mainkai 36, tel. 069/281–884).

Exploring Frankfurt

Numbers in the margin correspond to points of interest on the Frankfurt map.

At first glance, Frankfurt-am-Main doesn't seem to have much to offer the tourist. Virtually flattened by bombs during the war, it now bristles with skyscrapers, the visible sign of the city's role as Germany's financial capital. Yet the inquisitive and discerning visitor will find many remnants of Frankfurt's illustrious past (besides being well placed for excursions to other historic cities, such as Heidelberg and Würzburg, and within easy reach of the Rhine).

Originally a Roman settlement, Frankfurt was later one of Charlemagne's two capitals (the other being Aachen). Still later, it was for centuries the site of the election and coronation of the emperors of that unwieldy entity the Holy Roman Empire, which was the forerunner of a united Germany. It was also the birthplace of the poet and dramatist Goethe (1749–1832). The house in which he was born is one of many restored and reconstructed old buildings that inject a flavor of bygone days into the center of this busy modern city.

Although the true center of Frankfurt is its ancient **Römerberg Square,** where the election of Holy Roman Emperors was traditionally proclaimed and celebrated, this tour of the city begins slightly to the north,

① at the **Hauptwache,** an 18th-century guardhouse that today serves a more peaceful purpose as a café. The ground floor houses Intertreff, an information office that assists young visitors with such tasks as finding moderately priced accommodations. *Open weekdays 10–6, Sat. 10–1.*

② Head south along Kornmarkt, passing on the left the **Katerinenkirche** (Church of St. Catherine), the historic center of Frankfurt Protestantism, in whose 17th-century font Goethe was confirmed. After

③ crossing Berlinerstrasse, still heading south, you'll pass the **Paulskirche** (Church of St. Paul). It was here that the first all-German parliament convened in 1848, and the church is therefore an important symbol of German unity and democracy. Continue down Buchgasse, and within a few minutes you're on the north bank of the River **Main.** Turn left toward the iron footbridge known as the **Eiserner Steg** and at the **Rententurm,** one of the city's medieval gates, bear left again and you'll

④ arrive at the spacious **Römerberg Square,** center of Frankfurt civic life over the centuries. In the center of the square stands the 16th-century **Fountain of Justitia** (Justice): At the coronation of Emperor Matthias in 1612, wine instead of water spouted from the stonework. Not long ago, city officials started restaging this momentous event for festive occasions, such as the annual Main Fest.

⑤ Compared with many city halls, Frankfurt's **Römer** is a modest affair, with a gabled Gothic facade. It occupies most of one side of the square and is actually three patrician houses (the Alt-Limpurg, the Römer—from which it takes its name—and the Löwenstein). The mercantile-minded Frankfurt burghers used the complex not only for political and ceremonial purposes, but also for trade fairs and commerce. The most important events to take place in the Römer, however, were the elections of the Holy Roman Emperors. The **Kaisersaal** (Imperial Hall) was last used in 1792 to celebrate the election of Emperor Francis II, who was later forced to abdicate by egomaniac Napoléon Bonaparte. (A 16-year-old Goethe smuggled himself into the banquet celebrating the coronation of Emperor Joseph II in 1765 by posing as a waiter.) Today, visitors can see the impressive full-length 19th-century portraits of the 52 emperors of the Holy Roman Empire that line the walls of the reconstructed banquet hall. *Admission: DM 3 adults, DM 1 children. Open Tues.–Sun. 11–3. Closed Mon. and during official functions.*

Charlemagne's son, Ludwig the Pious, established a church on the present site of the Römerberg in AD 850. His church was replaced by a much grander Gothic structure, one used for imperial coronations; it became

⑥ known as the **Kaiserdom,** the Imperial Cathedral. The cathedral suffered only superficial damage during World War II, and it still contains many of its original treasures, including a fine 15th-century altar.

⑦ On the south side of the square stands the 13th-century **Nikolaikirche** (St. Nicholas's Church). It's worth trying to time your visit to the square to coincide with the chimes of the Glockenspiel. *Carillon chimes daily at 9, noon, and 5. Nikolaikirche open Mon–Sat. 10–5.*

Frankfurt

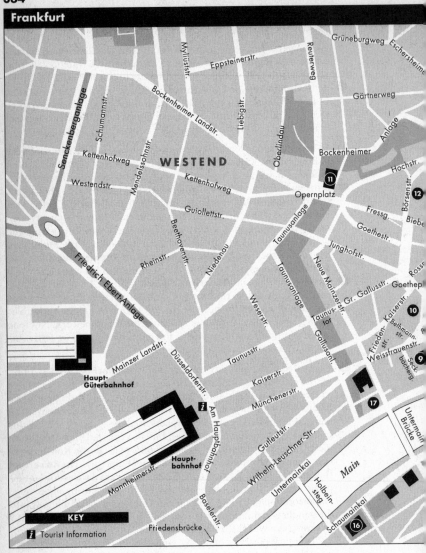

Alte Brücke, **14**

Alte Oper, **11**

Börse, **12**

Goethehaus und
Goethemuseum, **10**

Hauptwache, **1**

Jüdisches
Museum, **17**

Kaiserdom, **6**

Karmeliterkloster, **9**

Katerinenkirche, **2**

Kuhhirtenturm, **15**

Leonhardskirche, **8**

Museum für Moderne
Kunst, **13**

Nikolaikirche, **7**

Paulskirche, **3**

Römer, **5**

Römerberg, **4**

Städelsches Kunstin-
stitut und Städtische
Galerie, **16**

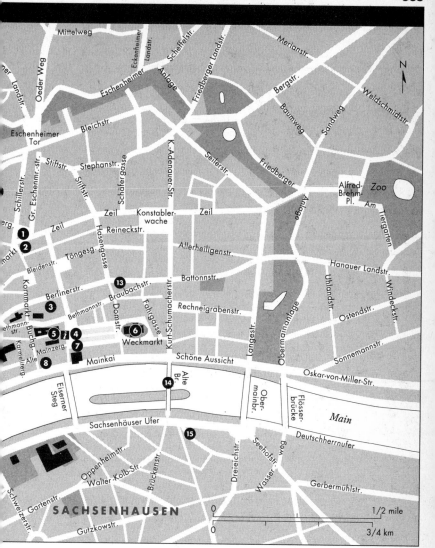

8 From the Römerberg, stroll south toward the river, but turn right this time. Walk past the riverside **Leonhardskirche** (St. Leonhard's Church), which is filled with wonderful things including a fine 13th-century porch and a beautifully carved circa 1500 Bavarian altar, and then into **9** the narrow Karmelitergasse to the **Karmeliterkloster** (Carmelite church and monastery). The secularized and renovated church houses the **Museum für Vor-und Frühgeschichte** (Museum of Prehistory and Early History); next door, the main cloister contains the largest religious fresco north of the Alps, a 16th-century representation of the birth and death of Christ. The cloister also hosts rotating exhibitions of modern art. *Admission to museum: DM 5 adults, DM 2.50 children. Open Tues.–Sun. 10–5, Wed. 10–8. Admission to art gallery in cloister: DM 3 adults, DM 1.50 children. Open Tues.–Sun. 11–6.*

10 From here, it's only a short way to the **Goethehaus und GoetheMuseum** (Goethe's House and Museum). It was here that the poet was born in 1749, and though the house was destroyed by Allied bombing, it has been carefully restored and is furnished with pieces from Goethe's time, some belonging to his family. The adjoining museum is closed for renovations. *Grosser Hirschgraben 23–25, tel. 069/282–824. Admission: DM 4 adults, DM 3 children. Open Apr.–Sept., Mon.–Sat. 9–6, Sun. 10–1; Oct.–Mar., Mon.–Sat. 9–4, Sun. 10–1.*

From the Goethehaus, retrace your steps to the Hauptwache via Rossmarkt. From there, take a window-shopping stroll past the elegant boutiques of Goethestrasse, which ends at Opernplatz and Frankfurt's **11** reconstructed opera house, the **Alte Oper.** Wealthy Frankfurt businessmen gave generously for the construction of the opera house during the 1870s (provided they were given priority for the best seats), and Kaiser Wilhelm I traveled from Berlin for the gala opening in 1880. Bombed in 1944, the opera house remained in ruins for many years while controversy raged over its reconstruction. The new building, in the classical proportions and style of the original, was finally opened in 1981.

Looking out from the Alte Oper, you'll see the skyscrapers that have earned Frankfurt its nickname of "Mainhattan"; some of these house the headquarters of Germany's biggest and richest banks. Cross Opernplatz and bear left down Grosse Bockenheimer Strasse (known locally as Fressgasse—literally "Eating Street"—because of its abundance of gourmet shops and restaurants), turn left into Börsenstrasse, and you'll hit the center of the financial district. Just around the corner from Fress- **12** gasse is the Frankfurt **Börse,** Germany's leading stock exchange and financial powerhouse. It was founded by Frankfurt merchants in 1558 to establish some order in their often chaotic dealings. Today's dealings can also be quite hectic; see for yourself by slipping into the visitors' gallery. *Admission free. Gallery open weekdays 11–1.*

From the Börse, turn right into Schillerstrasse, and within two minutes you're once again back at the Hauptwache. Here begins Frankfurt's main shopping street, the **Zeil,** which claims the highest turnover per square yard of stores in all Germany. Resist, if you can, the temptations in the shop windows on both sides of this crowded pedestrian zone and head eastward to the nearby point where it is crossed by Hasengasse. Turn right into Hasengasse and you'll see the striking wedge form **13** of Frankfurt's newest museum rising straight ahead of you. The **Museum für Moderne Kunst** (Museum of Modern Art), which was opened in 1991 and contains an important collection of works by such artists as Siah Armajani, Joseph Beuys, Walter de Maria, and Andy Warhol. *Domstr. 10, tel. 069/2123–8819. Admission: DM 7 adults, DM 3.50 children. Open Tues., Thurs.–Sat. 12–7, Sun. 10–5, Wed. 10–8.*

Across the Main lies the district of **Sachsenhausen.** It's said that Charlemagne arrived here with a group of Saxon families during the 8th century and formed a settlement on the banks of the Main. It was an important bridgehead for the crusading Knights of the Teutonic Order and, in 1318, officially became part of Frankfurt. Cross to Sachsenhausen over the **Alte Brücke.** Along the bank to your left you'll see the 15th-century **Kuhhirtenturm,** the only remaining part of Sachsenhausen's original fortifications. The composer Paul Hindemith lived and worked in the tower from 1923 to 1927.

The district still has a medieval air, with narrow back alleys and quiet squares that have escaped the destructive tread of city development. Here you'll find Frankfurt's famous Ebbelwei taverns. A green pine wreath over the entrance tells passersby that a freshly pressed—and alcoholic—apple wine or cider is on tap. You can eat well in these little inns, too.

TIME OUT The main street in Sachsenhausen, **Neuer Wall,** is lined with atmospheric old taverns offering home-brewed apple wine and solid local fare. A favorite is Dauth-Schneider (Neuer Wall 7, tel. 069/613–533).

No fewer than eight top-ranking museums line the Sachsenhausen side of the Main, on **Schaumainkai** (locally known as the **Museumsufer** or Museum Bank). These range from exhibitions of art and architecture to the German Film Museum. The **Städelsches Kunstinstitut und Städtische Galerie** (Städel Art Institute and Municipal Gallery) has one of the most significant art collections in Germany, with fine examples of Flemish, German, and Italian old masters, plus a sprinkling of French Impressionists. *Schaumainkai 63. Admission: DM 6 adults, DM 3 children; free on Sun. Open Tues.–Sun. 10–5, Wed. until 8.*

Across the river from this impressive lineup of museums (take the Untermain Bridge) is Frankfurt's **Jüdisches Museum** (Jewish Museum). The fine city mansion houses a permanent exhibit tracing the history of Frankfurt's Jewish community; its library is Germany's main registry for Jewish history. *Untermainkai 14–15, tel. 069/2123–5000. Admission DM 10 adults, DM 5 children. Open Tues–Sun. 10–5, Wed. until 8.*

Dining

Several Frankfurt restaurants close for the school summer vacation break, a six-week period that falls between mid-June and mid-September. Always check to avoid disappointment. For details and price-category definitions, *see* Dining *in* Staying in Germany, *above.*

$$$ Avocado. This classy restaurant is as ideal for a romantic dinner as for a business lunch. Excellent service and huge arrangements of fresh flowers help to create a fitting ambience for the fine French bistro food. *Hochstr. 27, tel. 069/292–867. Reservations advised. AE, MC, V. Closed Sun.*

$$$ Bistrot 77. Mainly Alsatian specialties are served at this bright, light, ★ cheerful French restaurant in Sachsenhausen. Chef-proprietor Dominique offers various special dinners during the week—bouillabaisse on Tuesdays, a three-course regional meal on Thursdays—and there's always one three-course lunch for DM 48. *Ziegelhüttenweg 1–3, tel. 069/614–040. Reservations advised. AE, MC, V. Closed Sun., mid-June–mid-July. No lunch Sat.*

$$$ Erno's Bistro. Small, chic, and popular with visiting power brokers, Erno's has become something of a Frankfurt institution. The menu features classy nouvelle specialties, with fish—flown in daily, often from

France—predominating. All the waiters speak English and are both able and happy to choose your meal for you. *Liebigstr. 15, tel. 069/721–997. Reservations required. AE, DC, MC, V. Closed weekends and mid-June–mid-July.*

$$$ **Weinhaus Brückenkeller.** This establishment offers magnificent German specialties in the sort of time-honored arched cellar that would have brought a lump to Bismarck's throat. What's more, though the food may be unmistakably Teutonic, it's light and delicate. In addition to the antique-strewn surroundings (the restaurant has been in business since 1652) and the classy food, there's a phenomenal range of wines from which to choose: The cellars—don't be shy about asking to see them—hold around 85,000 bottles. *Schützenstr. 6, tel. 069/284–238. Reservations advised. AE, DC, MC, V. Dinner only. Closed Sun.*

$$ **Altes Zollhaus.** In this beautiful, 200-year-old half-timber house, you can sample very good versions of traditional German specialties. Try a game dish. In summer, you can eat in the beautiful garden. *Friedberger Landstr. 531, tel. 069/472–707. Reservations advised. AE, DC, MC, V. Dinner only. Closed Mon.*

$$ **Börsenkeller.** Solid Germanic food, with just a hint of French style, is served here to fortify the business community from the nearby stock exchange. Soft lighting, heavy arches, and high-back booths establish the mood; steaks are a specialty. *Schillerstr. 11, tel. 069/281–115. AE, DC, MC, V. Closed Sun. No dinner Sat.*

$$ **Charlot.** The French cuisine of this very popular restaurant acquired an Italian touch with the arrival of chef Mario, but it survived the transition well. The Alte Oper is just across the street, so after the curtain falls you'll be fighting with the music buffs for a place in the French bistro–style dining rooms, spread over two floors. But you might also be sharing a table with Luciano Pavarotti. *Opernpl. 10, tel. 069/287–007. Reservations advised. AE, DC, MC, V. No lunch Sun.*

$$ **Zur Müllerin.** The *Müllerin* (miller's wife) is Lieselotte Müller, who has been running this restaurant since the 1950s. Her regulars are artists and actors from the nearby theaters; you'll find expressions of appreciation for the cooking skills of their beloved Müllerin decorating the restaurant walls. *Weissfrauenstr. 18, tel. 069/285–182. Reservations advised. AE, DC, MC, V. No lunch Sat. or Sun.*

$ **Café GegenwART.** "Gegenwart" means "the present," and the accent on ART means regularly changing exhibitions by local artists on the walls of this friendly, bustling café-restaurant. There's also art in the cooking; the menu changes as regularly as the paintings. In summer, the tables spill out onto the sidewalk. Try the freshly caught angler fish or tomato fondue if they are available. *Bergerstr. 6, tel. 069/497–0544. No credit cards.*

$ **Pelikan.** Inexpensive but imaginative dishes from a daily-changing menu are served up here on pink-linen-covered tables to students and professors from the nearby university. This is one place where vegetarians are not in the minority—the Pelikan offers an unusually good selection of meatless dishes. In summer a boulevard terrace opens for business. *Jordanstr. 19, tel. 069/701–287. No credit cards. Closed Sun., no lunch Sat., except during trade fairs.*

$ **Zum Gemalten Haus.** This is the real thing: a traditional wine tavern
★ in the heart of Sachsenhausen. Its name means "at the painted house," a reference to the frescoes that cover the place inside and out. In the summer and on fine spring and autumn days, the courtyard is the place to be (the inner rooms can get a bit crowded). But if you can't at first find a place at one of the bench-lined long tables, order an apple wine and hang around until someone leaves: It's worth the wait. *Schweizerstr. 67, tel. 069/614–559. No credit cards. Closed Mon. and Tues.*

Lodging

For details and price-category definitions, *see* Lodging *in* Staying in Germany, *above.*

$$$$ **An der Messe.** This place—the name means "at the fairgrounds"—is a small but stylish hotel with chicly appointed rooms. Comfort and attentive service push this venue into the quality class, despite the absence of a restaurant. *Westendstr. 104, tel. 069/747–979, fax 069/748–349. 46 rooms with bath. Facilities: garage. AE, DC, MC, V.*

$$$$ **Gravenbruch Kempinski.** The atmosphere of the 16th-century manor
★   house that this elegant, sophisticated hotel was built around still remains at this parkland sight in leafy Neu Isenburg (a 15-minute drive south of Frankfurt). Some of its luxuriously appointed rooms and suites are arranged as duplex penthouse apartments. Make sure you get a room overlooking the lake. *63243 Neu Isenburg, tel. 06102/5050, fax 06102/505–445. 287 rooms with bath. Facilities: 2 restaurants, indoor and outdoor pools, tennis courts, health spa, hairdresser, conference center, limo service to airport and city (both 15 mins away). AE, DC, MC, V.*

$$$$ **Hessischer Hof.** This former palace is still owned by a prince of Hesse, and fine antiques are deftly positioned in many guest rooms. A daily supply of fresh fruit delivered to all rooms is part of the outstanding service. One of the two bars, Jimmy's, numbers among Frankfurt's best, and the hotel restaurant, Sevres, is highly prized both for its gourmet cuisine and its refined ambience. *Friedrich-Ebert-Anlage 40, tel. 069/75400, fax 069/754–0924. 117 rooms with bath. Facilities: restaurant, 2 bars, garage. AE, DC, MC, V.*

$$$$ **Steigenberger Hotel Frankfurter Hof.** The Victorian Frankfurter Hof
★   is one of the city's oldest hotels. The atmosphere throughout is one of old-fashioned, formal elegance, with burnished woods, fresh flowers, and thick-carpeted hush. Kaiser Wilhelm once slept here. *Am Kaiserpl., tel. 069/21502, fax 069/215–860. 347 rooms with bath, 10 suites. Facilities: 4 restaurants, café, 2 bars. AE, DC, MC, V.*

$$$ **Dorint Hotel.** A palm-fringed, rooftop pool beckons after a day of touring downtown Frankfurt, which is a short walk across the river from this stylish member of the Dorint group. The hotel has all the comfort and facilities expected from this respected hotel chain. *Hahnstr. 9, tel. 069/663–060, fax 069/6630–6600. 183 rooms with bath, 8 suites, 29 no-smoking rooms. Facilities: restaurant, 2 bars, indoor pool, sauna, parking. AE, DC, MC, V.*

$$$ **Palmenhof.** Named for its proximity to the botanical garden, or Palmengarten, this luxuriously modernized hotel occupies a renovated *Jugendstil* (German Art Nouveau) building in Frankfurt's West End. In the basement is a cozy restaurant, the Bastei, which has an expensive nouvelle menu. *Bockenheimer Landstr. 89–91, tel. 069/753–0060, fax 069/7530–0666. 47 rooms with bath, 40 apartments. Facilities: restaurant, garage. AE, DC, MC, V.*

$$ **Attache.** This simple but comfortable downtown hotel has no restaurant, but a buffet breakfast provides a hearty start to the day. *Kölnerstr. 10, tel. 069/730–282, fax 069/739–2194. 46 rooms with shower or bath. Facilities: bar. AE, MC, V.*

$$ **Hotel Ibis Frankfurt Friedensbrücke.** This modern hotel on the north bank of the Main River is just a five-minute walk from the train station. It was recently acquired by the Ibis chain, known for providing modern comfort at affordable prices. *Speicherstr. 3–5, tel. 069/273–030, fax 069/237–024. 233 rooms with bath. Facilities: restaurant, bar, parking. AE, DC, MC, V.*

$$ **Maingau.** This excellent-value hotel is in the city's Sachsenhausen dis-
★   trict, within easy reach of the downtown area and just a stone's throw
from the lively Altstadt quarter. The rooms are spartanly furnished,
though clean and comfortable, and all have TV. Families with children
are welcome. *Schifferstr. 38–40, tel. 069/617–001, fax 069/620–790.
100 rooms with bath. Facilities: restaurant, garage. AE, MC.*

$ **Hotel-Schiff** *Peter Schlott.* Watch your step when returning to this un-
usual hotel after a night out in Frankfurt—it's a hotel ship, moored
on the Main River in the suburb of Höchst, a 15-minute train or tram
ride from the city center. Guest cabins are predictably on the small side,
but the marvelous river views more than compensate. *Mainberg, tel.
069/315–480, fax 069/307–671. 19 rooms, about half with shower.
Facilities: restaurant, parking. AE, MC.*

$ **Waldhotel "Hensel's Felsenkeller."** Helmut Braun's traditional old
hotel has the woods that ring Frankfurt as its backyard, yet the city
center is just a 15-minute tram ride away (the nearest stop is a three-
minute walk from the hotel). Rooms are quite basic. *Buchrainstr. 95,
tel. 069/652–086, fax 069/658–371. 15 rooms, 7 with bath. Facili-
ties: restaurant, parking. MC.*

HAMBURG

Arriving and Departing

By Plane
Hamburg's international airport, Fuhlsbüttel, is 11 kilometers (7 miles)
northwest of the city. Lufthansa flights connect Hamburg with all
other major German cities and European capitals.

BETWEEN THE AIRPORT AND DOWNTOWN
An Airport-City-Bus runs between Hamburg's main train station
(Hauptbahnhof) and the airport (stopping also at the hotels Atlantic,
Plaza, and Reichshof); it operates daily at 20-minute intervals between
5:40 AM and 10:30 PM. The first bus leaves the airport for the city at
6:30 AM. It takes about 25 minutes. One-way fare, including luggage,
is DM 8. There is also the Airport Express—Bus 110—which runs be-
tween the airport and the Ohlsdorf S-Bahn (suburban line) and U-Bahn
(subway) station. The fare is DM 3.60 for adults, DM 1.20 for chil-
dren. Taxi fare from the airport to the downtown area is about DM
30. By rented car, follow the STADTMITTE (downtown) signs, which ap-
pear immediately outside the airport area.

By Train
Hamburg is a terminus for main line services to northern Germany;
trains to Schleswig-Holstein and Scandinavia also stop here. There are
two principal stations: the Hauptbahnhof and Hamburg-Altona. Euro-
City, InterCity, and InterCity Express services connect Hamburg with
all German cities and the European rail network. For train informa-
tion, call 040/19419.

By Bus
Hamburg's bus station, the Zentral-Omnibus-Bahnhof, is in Aden-
auerallee, behind the Hauptbahnhof. For information, call 040/247–
575 or contact the **Deutsche Touring Gesellschaft** (Am Römerhof 17,
D–60486 Frankfurt/Main, tel. 069/79030).

By Car
Hamburg has proportionately fewer cars than most German cities and
an urban road system that is the envy of many of them. Incoming au-

tobahns end at one of Hamburg's three beltways, which then connect easily with the downtown area.

Getting Around

By Public Transportation

The comprehensive city and suburban transportation system includes a U-Bahn network, which connects efficiently with S-Bahn lines, and an exemplary bus service. Tickets cover travel by all three, as well as by harbor ferry. A ticket costs DM 2.30 (DM 3.60 for travel outside the inner city) and can be bought at the machines found in all stations and most bus stops. A day ticket, for unlimited travel in the entire Hamburg urban area from 9 AM to 1 AM, costs DM 6.90 for one adult and up to three children (DM 12.20 for a group of up to four adults and three children); a three-day ticket costs DM 19. The all-night buses (Nos. 600–640) tour the downtown area, leaving the Rathausmarkt and the Hauptbahnhof every hour. The one-and three-day **Hamburg CARD** allows free transport on all public transportation within the city, free admission to state museums, and discounts of approximately 30% on most bus, train, and boat tours. For information about this card, inquire at tourist offices (*see below*). Information about the public-transportation system can be obtained from the **Hamburg Passenger Transport Board** (HHV, Steinstr. 1, tel. 040/322–911; open daily 7 AM–8 PM).

By Taxi

Taxi meters start at DM 3.60, and the fare is DM 2.20 per kilometer (or about DM 3.50 per mile). To order a taxi, call 040/441–011, 040/686–868, or 040/611–061.

Important Addresses and Numbers

Tourist Information

The principal Hamburg tourist office is at Bieberhaus, Hachmann-platz, next to the Hauptbahnhof (tel. 040/3005–1244; open weekdays 7:30–6, Saturday 8–3). There's also a tourist information center inside the Hauptbahnhof itself (tel. 040/3005–1230, open daily 7 AM–11 PM) and in the arrivals hall of Hamburg Airport (tel. 040/3005–1240 open daily from 8 AM to 11 PM). Other tourist offices can be found in the Hanse-Viertel shopping arcade (tel. 040/3005–1220; open weekdays 10–6:30, Sat. 10–3) and at the Landungsbrücken (tel. 040/3005–1200; open daily 9:30–5:30). All centers will reserve hotel accommodations.

Consulates

U.S. (Alsterufer 28, tel. 040/411–710). **U.K.** (Harvestehuder Weg 8a, tel. 040/448–0320).

Emergencies

Police (tel. 110). **Ambulance** and **Fire Department** (tel. 112). **Medical Emergencies** (tel. 040/228–022). **Dentist** (tel. 040/11500).

English-Language Bookstores

Try **Frensche** (Spitalerstr. 26e, tel. 040/327–585) for a selection of English-language newspapers and books.

Travel Agencies

American Express (Rathausmarkt 5, tel. 040/33114). **Hapag-Lloyd** (Verkehrspavillon Jungfernstieg, tel. 040/3258–5640).

Guided Tours

Orientation Tours

Bus tours of the city, with an English-speaking guide, leave from Kirchenallee (in front of the Hauptbahnhof) at regular intervals (six times daily in summer). The 1¼-hour tour costs DM 24 for adults, DM 12 for children. A 2½-hour tour, taking in more of the city, starts at 10 and 2 daily from the same place. The fare is DM 30 for adults, DM 15 for children. For an additional DM 11 adults/5.50 children, either tour can be combined with a one-hour boat trip. A tour of the city's nightlife sets off from Kirchenallee at 8 and returns shortly after midnight (March–Oct., Tues.–Sat.; Fri. and Sat. only Nov.–Feb.). The fare of DM 99 includes all cover charges and three drinks. Tourist offices have additional tour information.

Boat Tours

Tours of the harbor leave every half hour in summer, less frequently during the winter, from Piers (Landungsbrücken) 1–7. The one-hour tour costs DM 15 (DM 7.50 children). A special harbor tour with an English-speaking guide leaves Pier 1 at 11:15 daily from March 1 to November 30 (same price). The Störtebeker line has a special party boat aboard which you can wine, dine (a six-course banquet), and dance. The boat casts off from Pier 6 every evening at 8. The all-inclusive cost of the four-hour cruise is DM 111, and reservations can be made by calling 040/2274–2375. Inquire at tourist offices about other special boat cruises.

Fifty-minute cruises of the Binnenalster and Aussenalster leave from the Jungfernstieg every half hour between 10 and 6 April–October, less frequently the rest of the year. The fare is DM 13 for adults, DM 7.50 for children. A three-hour cruise including canals leaves four times daily (DM 19 and DM 9.50, respectively). For information on these and other boat tours, call 040/341–141.

Excursions

Bus tours of the surrounding countryside are offered by **Jasper-Reisebüro** (Colonnaden 72, tel. 040/343–751).

Exploring Hamburg

The comparison that Germans like to draw between Hamburg and Venice is—like all such comparisons with the *Serenissima*—somewhat exaggerated. Nevertheless, Hamburg is, like Venice, a city on water: the great River Elbe, which flows into the North Sea; the small River Alster, which has been dammed to form two lakes, the Binnenalster and Aussenalster; and many canals. Once a leading member of the Hanseatic League of cities, which dominated trade on the North Sea and the Baltic during the Middle Ages, Hamburg is still a major port, with 33 individual docks and 500 berths for oceangoing vessels.

Within the remaining traces of its old city walls, Hamburg combines the seamiest, steamiest streets of dockland Europe with the sleekest avenues to be found anywhere between Biarritz and Stockholm. During World War II and afterward, Hamburg was wrecked from without and within—by fire, then by Allied bombing raids, and finally by philistine town planners, who tore down some of the remaining old buildings to make way for modernistic glass-and-steel boxes. The result is a city that is, in parts, ugly, but still a fascinating mixture of old and new.

It is also a city in which escaping the urban bustle is relatively easy, since it contains more than 800 kilometers (500 miles) of riverside and country paths within its boundaries. The following itinerary includes a few detours, some by boat, that will enhance your enjoyment of Hamburg.

Numbers in the margin correspond to points of interest on the Hamburg map.

❶ Hamburg's main train station, the **Hauptbahnhof,** is not only the start of the city tour but very much part of it. It's not often you are tempted to linger at a train station, but this is an exception. Originally built in 1906 and completely renovated earlier this decade, it has a remarkable spaciousness and sweep, accentuated by a 486-foot-wide glazed roof, the largest unsupported roof in Germany. Gather city travel guides and maps from the city tourist office here and ride one stop on the S-Bahn to the Dammtor station. Compare this Art Nouveau–style building (built in 1903) with the one you've just left. You'll find splendid examples of Germany's version of Art Nouveau, the *Jugendstil,* throughout your tour of Hamburg.

From the Dammtor station you emerge at the northern end of the **Wallringpark,** a stretch of parkland that runs for more than a kilometer alongside what was once the western defense wall of the city. The first
❷ two sections of the park—the **Alter Botanischer Garten** (Old Botani-
❸ cal Garden) and the **Planten un Blomen** (Plants and Flowers)—have lots to attract the attention of gardeners and flower lovers. In summer, the evening sky over the Planten un Blomen lake is lighted by the colored waters of its fountain, dancing what the locals romantically call a "water ballet."

The **Grosse Wallanlagen** section of the park—to the southwest—is interrupted abruptly by the northern edge of the **St. Pauli** district and its
❹ most famous—or infamous—thoroughfare, the **Reeperbahn** (*see* Nightlife, *below*). Unlike other business sections of Hamburg, this industrious quarter works around the clock; although it may seem quiet as you stroll down its tawdry length in broad daylight, any tourist who stops at one of its bars will discover that many of the girls who work this strip are on a day shift.

❺ If it's a Sunday morning, join the late revelers and the early joggers and dog-walkers for breakfast at the **Fischmarkt** (fish market), down at the Elbe riverside between the St. Pauli Landungsbrücken (the piers where the excursion boats tie up) and Grosse Elbstrasse. The citizens of Hamburg like to breakfast on pickled herring, but if that's not to your taste, there's much more than fish for sale, and the nearby bars have yet to close from the previous night. *Fish market held Sun. 5 AM–10 AM, 7 AM–10 AM in winter.*

❻ The nearby **Landungsbrücken** are the start of the many boat trips of the harbor that are offered throughout the year (*see* Guided Tours, *above*).

Along the north bank of the Elbe is one of the finest walks Hamburg has to offer. The walk is a long one, about 13 kilometers (8 miles) from the St. Pauli Landungsbrücken to the attractive waterside area of
❼ **Blankenese,** and that's only three-quarters of the route. But there are S-Bahn stations and bus stops along the way, to give you a speedy return to the downtown area. Do, however, try to reach Blankenese, even if you have to catch an S-Bahn train from downtown to Blankenese station and walk down to the riverbank from there.

Blankenese is another of Hamburg's surprises—a city suburb that has the character of a quaint fishing village. If you've walked all the way

Hamburg

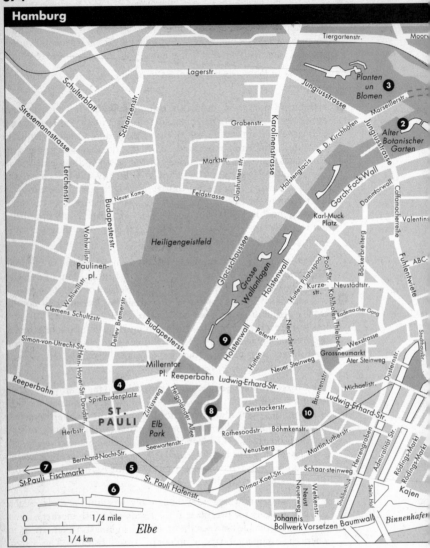

Alter Botanischer
Garten, **2**

Bismarckdenkmal, **8**

Blankenese, **7**

Fischmarkt, **5**

Hauptbahnhof, **1**

Jungfernstieg, **13**

Kunsthalle, **14**

Landungsbrücken, **6**

Michaeliskirche, **10**

Museum für Hamburgische Geschichte, **9**

Planten un Blomen, **3**

Rathaus, **12**

Rathausmarkt, **11**

Reeperbahn, **4**

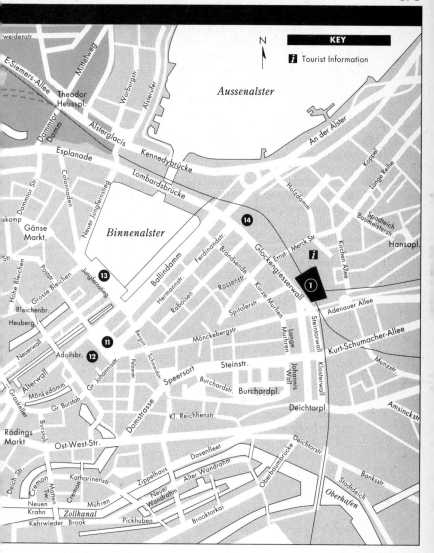

N

weidenstr.

E.Siemers-Allee

Theodor
Heusspl.

Dammtor Damm

Alsterglacis

Esplanade

Colonnaden

Dammtor Str.

skamp

Gänse
Markt.

Str.

Hohe Bleichen

Poststr.

Grosse Bleichen

Bleichenbr.

Heuberg

Neuerwall

Adolfsbr.

Alterwall

Mönkedamm

Grasskeller

Gr. Burstah

Burstah

Rödings
Markt

Ost-West-Str.

Mittelweg

Warburgstr.

Alsterufer

Aussenalster

Kennedybrücke

Lombardsbrücke

Binnenalster

Neuer Jungfernstieg

Jungfernstieg

Ballindamm

Ferdinandstr.

Brandsende

Hermannstr.

Rabaisen

Rossenstr.

Spitalerstr.

Mönckebergstr.

Bergstr.

Schmiedstr.

Pelzerstr.

Gr. Johannisstr.

Speersort

Steinstr.

Burchardstr.

Domstrasse

Kl. Reichhenstr.

Burchardpl.

An der Alster

Holzdamm

Glockengiesserwall

Ernst Merck Str.

Kurze Mühren

Lange Mühren

Steintorwall

Johannis Wall

Klosterwall

Deichtorpl.

Koppel

Lange Reihe

Kirchen Allee

Spaldeich
Baumeisterstr.

Hansapl.

Adenauer Allee

Kurt-Schumacher-Allee

Munzstr.

Amsinckstr.

Bankstr.

14

13

11

12

1

Deichtorstr.

Dovenfleet

Zippelhaus

Katharinenstr.

Cremon Tw.

Matten Twt.

Cremon

Mühren

Neuer
Wandrahm

Alter Wandrahm

Brooktorkai

Oberbaumbrücke

Oberhafen

Stadtdeich

Deich Str.

Neuen
Krahn

Zollkanal

Kehrwieder

Brook

Pickhuben

from St. Pauli, you may not be able to face the 58 flights of stairs (nearly 5,000 individual steps) that crisscross through Blankenese between its heights and the river. But by all means attempt an exploratory prowl through some of the tiny lanes, lined with the retirement retreats of Hamburg's sea captains and the cottages of the fishermen who once toiled here.

A ferry connects Blankenese with Hamburg's St. Pauli, although the S-Bahn ride back to the city is much quicker. Back at St. Pauli, resume your tour at the riverside and head back toward the downtown area

⑧ through Elb Park, crossing Helgolander Allee to the **Bismarckdenkmal** (Bismarck Memorial)—an imposing statue of the Prussian "Iron Chancellor," the guiding spirit of the 19th-century unification of Germany.

⑨ Cross the square ahead of you and make for the **Museum für Hamburgische Geschichte** at Holstenwall 24. A visit to this museum is highly recommended—it gives an excellent overall perspective of the forces that have guided Hamburg from its origins in the 9th century to the present. The museum's Historic Emigration Office, at the St. Pauli Landungsbrücken, tel. 040/3005–1250) is of great interest to American descendants of German immigrants, who can arrange to have called up from the microfilm files information about any ancestors who set out for the New World from Hamburg. *Holstenwall 24, tel. 040/3504–2360. Admission: DM 6 adults, DM 1 children. Open Tues.–Sun. 10–6.*

Cross Holstenwall to Peterstrasse, where you'll find a group of finely restored, 18th-century, half-timber houses. Turn right down Neanderstrasse and cross Ludwig-Erhard-Strasse to Hamburg's principal

⑩ Protestant church, the **Michaeliskirche** (St. Michael's Church), the finest Baroque church in northern Germany. Twice in its history, this well-loved 17th-century church has given the people of Hamburg protection—during the Thirty Years' War and again in World War II. From its 440-foot tower, there is a magnificent view of the city and the Elbe, and twice a day the watchman blows a trumpet solo from up there. *Michaeliskirche: open Apr.–Sept. daily 9–6, Thurs. until 10; Oct.–March daily 10–5, Thurs. until 10. St. Michael's Tower: open Apr.–Sept. daily 9–6, Sun 11:30–6; Oct.–March daily 10–5. Elevator or staircase (449 steps) admission: DM 4 adults, DM 2.50 children.*

From the Michaeliskirche, return to Ludwig-Erhard-Strasse, turn right, then left down Brunnenstrasse to Wexstrasse. Follow Wexstrasse to Grosse Bleichen, turn right down Heugberg, and cross the Bleichenbrücke and Adolphsbrücke over two of Hamburg's canals (known as

⑪ the Fleete). Make a left into Alter Wall, and you'll come to the **Rathausmarkt**, town hall square. The designers of the square deliberately set out to create a northern version of the Piazza San Marco in Venice and, to a certain extent, succeeded. The rounded glass arcade bordered by

⑫ trees was added in 1982. The 100-year-old **Rathaus** is built on 4,000 wooden piles sunk into the marshy ground beneath. It is the home not only of the city council but also of the Hamburg state government, for Hamburg is one of Germany's federal, semiautonomous states. The sheer opulence of its interior is hard to beat. It has 647 rooms, 6 more than Buckingham Palace. Only the state rooms are open to visitors; on a tour you'll see tapestries, huge staircases, glittering chandeliers, coffered ceilings, and gilt-frame portraits that convey forcefully the wealth of the city in the last century and give rich insight into the bombastic municipal taste. *English-language tours: DM 1 adults, 50 pf children. Mon.–Thurs. hourly 10:15–3:15, Fri.–Sun. hourly 10:15–1:15.*

If you've had enough sightseeing by this time, you've ended up at the right place, for an arcade at the western edge of the Rathausmarkt signals the start of Europe's largest covered shopping area, nearly a kilometer of airy arcades, cool in summer and warm in winter, bursting with color and life. Three hundred shops, from cheap souvenir stores to expensive fashion boutiques, are crammed into this consumer-age labyrinth. There are expensive restaurants and cozy cafés, among them an opportunity rare in Germany (or anywhere)—eating lobster and sipping good wine at a fast-food outlet. It's easy to get lost here, but all the arcades lead, at some point, to the wide, seasidelike promenade, ⓭ the **Jungfernstieg,** which borders Hamburg's smaller artificial lake, the **Binnenalster** (to its north is the larger, Aussenalster). Although called lakes, they are really dammed-up sections of the Alster River. The original dam, built at the beginning of the 13th century to form a millrace before the river spilled into the Elbe, is today the elegant Jungfernstieg promenade. From the Jungfernstieg, you can take a boat tour of the two Alster lakes and the canals beyond (*see* Guided Tours, *above*), passing some of Hamburg's most ostentatious homes, with their extensive grounds rolling down to the water's edge (the locals call it "Millionaires' Coast").

Hamburg has its share of millionaires, enriched by the city's thriving commerce and industry. But they, in turn, can claim to have enriched the artistic life of Hamburg. For example, it was a group of wealthy merchants who, in 1817, founded the Kunstverein, from which grew Hamburg's ⓮ famous Kunsthalle collection. The **Kunsthalle** is well placed at the end of our Hamburg tour, next to the Hauptbahnhof, and its collection of paintings is one of Germany's finest. You'll find works by practically all the great northern European masters from the 14th to the 20th century, as well as by such painters as Goya, Tiepolo, and Canaletto. Masterpieces in the gallery's possession include the oldest known representation of the murder of Thomas à Becket, the head of the English church in the 12th century. This painting, called the *Thomas Altar,* was done by Meister Francke in 1424 and depicts Becket's death in Canterbury Cathedral. *Glockengiesserwall 1, tel. 040/2486–2612. Admission: DM 6 adults, DM 1 children. Open Tues.–Sun. 10–6, Thurs. until 9.*

Dining

For details and price-category definitions, *see* Dining *in* Staying in Germany, *above*.

$$$ La Mer. The elegant restaurant of Hotel Prem, on the southeast bank of the Aussenalster, La Mer offers a fine and varied menu. Try the marinated enoki mushrooms with imperial oysters and salmon roe or the spring venison with elderberry sauce. *An der Alster 9, tel. 040/245–454. Reservations advised. AE, DC, MC, V. Closed Sat. No lunch Sun.*

$$$ Landhaus Dill. A fine fin-de-siècle building with views of the Elbe is home for this restaurant. It has an air of cool elegance, with crisp linen and glistening tiled floors, and a high standard of cuisine. The lobster salad is prepared at your table; the rack of lamb comes hot from the kitchen with an aromatic thyme sauce. For dessert try the rhubarb compote with vanilla cream, a dream of a dish. *Elbchaussee 94, tel. 040/390–5077. Reservations advised. AE, DC, MC, V. Closed Mon.*

$$$ Landhaus Scherrer. A popular, country house–style restaurant in the city's Altona district, Landhaus Scherrer fuses sophisticated specialties with more down-to-earth local dishes and prides itself on its extensive wine list. It has a separate bistro for lunches. *Elbchaussee 130, tel. 040/880–1325. Reservations advised. AE, DC, MC, V. Closed Sun.*

$$$ **L'Auberge Française.** Generally regarded as Hamburg's most authentic French restaurant, L'Auberge Française specializes in traditional seafood dishes and fine wines. *Rutschbahn 34, tel. 040/410–2532. Reservations advised. AE, DC, MC, V. Closed Sun.*

$$$ **Peter Lembcke.** There's no better place to eat eel soup or the traditional
★ Hamburg dish *Labskaus*—a stew made from pickled meat, potatoes, and (sometimes) herring, garnished with a fried egg, sour pickles, and lots of beets. The best of German cuisine is served in this small, traditional restaurant just north of the train station. *Holzdamm 49, tel. 040/243–290. Reservations advised. AE, DC, MC, V. Closed Sun. No lunch Sat.*

$$ **Ahrberg.** Located on the river in Blankenese, the Ahrberg has a pleas-
★ ant terrace for summer dining, and a cozy, wood-paneled dining room for colder days. The menu features a range of traditional German dishes and seafood specialties—often served together. Try the shrimp and potato soup and fresh carp in season. *Strandweg 33, tel. 040/860–438. Reservations advised. AE, DC, MC, V. Closed Sun.*

$$ **Fischerhaus.** Hamburg's famous fish market is right outside the door of this traditional old restaurant, which accounts for the variety and quality of fish dishes on its menu. Meat-eaters are also catered to, and the soups are legendary; fish soup is understandably the pride of the house. It's always busy, so be sure to reserve a table and get there on time—you have a 10-minute grace period before your table is given away. *St. Pauli Fischmarkt 14, tel. 040/314–053. Reservations advised. AE, DC, MC, V.*

$$ **Noblesse.** The Ramada Renaissance Hotel's stylish restaurant is among the choicest in the city center. The extensive menu combines German traditional and nouvelle cuisine; the wine list embraces the best labels from Germany, France, and Italy. The buffet is a particularly good value. *Grosse Bleichen, tel. 040/349–180. Reservations advised. AE, DC, MC, V.*

$ **At Nali.** This is one of Hamburg's oldest and most popular Turkish restaurants; it has the advantage of staying open till 1 AM, handy for those hankering after a late-night kebab. Prices are low, service is reliable and friendly, and the menu is extensive. *Rutschbahn 11, tel. 040/410–3810. Weekend reservations advised. AE, DC, MC, V.*

$ **Avocado.** This popular, modern restaurant offers excellent value and an imaginative vegetarian menu, and it's Hamburg's only no-smoking restaurant. Try the salmon in Chablis. *Kanalstr. 9, tel. 040/220–4599. Reservations required. No credit cards. Dinner only. Closed Mon.*

$ **Sagres.** Portuguese and Spanish restaurants are part of the city's seafaring tradition, and this is one of the best. The mood is busy and cheerful, the decor simple. Try swordfish for an adventurous meal. Fight your way through the Portuguese dockworkers to find a place at the bar, where you'll probably have to wait for a table. *Vorsetzen 46, tel. 040/371–201. Weekend reservations advised. No credit cards.*

Lodging

For details and price-category definitions, *see* Lodging *in* Staying in Germany, *above.*

$$$$ **Atlantic Hotel Kempinski Hamburg.** Since it first opened in 1909, the luxuriously appointed Atlantic has been a focal point of the Hamburg social scene. The rooms, whether traditionally or more modernly furnished, exude an understated luxury, the suites are just short of palatial, and the service is swift and hushed. The Atlantic Restaurant, stunning with its bird's-eye maple Empire-style decor and inlaid marble floor, serves haute cuisine with a complimentary view of the Aussenalster. *An der Alster 72, tel. 040/28880, fax 040/247–129. 243 rooms with bath, 13 suites. Facilities: 2 restaurants, bar, lobby snack bar, indoor pool, sauna, solarium, masseur, beauty salon, boutique, 24-hr room service, garage. AE, DC, MC, V.*

$$$$ **Hamburg Marriott.** The U.S. Marriott group chose downtown Hamburg, amid the city's shopping arcades and smart restaurants, as the site of its first hotel in Germany, and it remains the showpiece: a luxury establishment from the extraordinary barrel-roof ceiling of the reception area to the expansive comfort of its guest rooms. Among its many refinements are the attractive American Place restaurant and two floors reserved for nonsmokers. *ABC-Str. 52, tel. 040/35050, fax 040/3505–1777. 277 rooms with bath, 10 suites, no-smoking rooms. Facilities: restaurant, piano bar, indoor pool, whirlpool, sauna, solarium, masseur, fitness center, beauty salon, 24-hr room service, boutiques, garage. AE, DC, MC, V.*

$$$$ **Vier Jahreszeiten.** This handsome 19th-century town-house hotel, ★ with its antique-style rooms, impeccable service, and excellent food, is rated among the world's best. It is continually being refurbished to maintain an exemplary standard, but you won't notice a blip in the hotel's smooth routine. Centrally located on Hamburg's "Millionaires' Coast," it has scenic views of the Binnenalster. *Neuer Jungfernstieg 9–14, tel. 040/34940, fax 040/349–4602. 148 rooms and 23 apartments, all with bath. Facilities: 3 restaurants, bar, solarium, beauty salon, patisserie, wine shop, 24-hr room service, boutique, garage. AE, DC, MC, V.*

$$$ **Aussen Alster.** Crisp and contemporary in design, this boutique hotel prides itself on giving personal attention to its guests. Rooms are compact; most have a full bathroom, and a few have a shower only. The cool, modern decor is given warmth by a fireplace and friendly bar. *Schmilinskystr. 11, tel. 040/241–557, fax 040/280–3231. 27 rooms with bath or shower. Facilities: restaurant, bar, sauna, solarium, garden, free bike use. AE, DC, MC, V.*

$$ **Baseler Hof.** Centrally located near the Binnenalster and the State Opera House, this hotel offers friendly and efficient service and neatly furnished rooms. There is no charge for children under 10 sharing a room with parents. *Esplanade 11, tel. 040/359–060, fax 040/3590–6918. 140 rooms with bath. Facilities: 2 restaurants, bar, room service. AE, DC, MC, V.*

$$ **Hotel Graf Moltke.** The sturdy old Graf Moltke rules majestically over central Steindamm Street (a short walk from the main railway station). All rooms are equipped with soundproofing. Special weekend deals are offered for families. *Steindamm 1, tel. 040/280–1154, fax 040/280–2562. 97 rooms with bath or shower. Facilities: bar, boutiques. AE, DC, MC, V.*

$$ **Kronprinz.** For its down-market position (on a busy street opposite the railway station) and its moderate price, the Kronprinz is a surprisingly attractive hotel, with a whiff of five-star flair. Rooms are individually styled, modern but homey; ask for Number 45, with its mahogany and red-plush decor. *Kirchenallee 46, tel. 040/243–258, fax 040/280–1097. 69 rooms with bath or shower. Facilities: restaurant, bar, terrace. AE, DC, MC, V.*

$ **Alameda.** The Alameda offers guests good, basic accommodations. The upstairs rooms are more spacious, but all rooms have TV, radio, and minibar. *Colonnaden 45, tel. 040/344–000, fax 040/343–439. 18 rooms with shower. AE, DC, MC, V.*

$ **Hotel-Garni Emde.** If you're touring northern Germany by car, this small, friendly hotel is an ideal base for exploring Hamburg; it's just 5 minutes from the autobahn A7 Bahrenfeld exit. It can also be reached by rail, from the S-1 S-Bahn line's Hamburg-Othmarschen stop. If you're willing to forgo a central location, you can have suburban peace and quiet here, in a charming mansion set on its own grounds. *Lüdemannstr. 1, tel. 040/893–626, fax 040/810–0689. 10 rooms with bath or shower, 2 suites. Facilities: parking. AE, DC, MC, V.*

Nightlife

Few visitors can resist taking a look at the **Reeperbahn,** if only by day. From about 10 PM onward, however, the place really shakes itself into life, and *everything* is for sale. Among the Reeperbahn's even rougher side streets, the most notorious is the Grosse Freiheit, which means "Great Freedom." A stroll through this small alley, where the attractions are on display behind plate glass, will either tempt you to stay or send you straight back to your hotel. The Reeperbahn area is not just a red-light district, however. Side streets are rapidly filling up with a mixture of yuppie bars, restaurants, and theaters that are somewhat more refined than the seamen's bars and sex shops. The **Hans-Albers-Platz** is a center of this revival; here the stylish bar La Paloma provides contrast to the Hans-Albers-Ecke, an old sailors' bar. The **Theater Schmidt** (Spielbudenpl. 23, tel. 040/311–231) offers variety shows most evenings to a packed house.

A few tips for visiting the Reeperbahn: Avoid going alone; ask for a price list wherever you drink (legally, it has to be on display), and pay as soon as you're served; if you have trouble, threaten to call the cops. If that doesn't work, call the cops.

THE RHINE

None of Europe's many rivers is so redolent of history and legend as the Rhine. For the Romans, who established forts and colonies along its western banks, the Rhine was the frontier between civilization and the barbaric German tribes. Roman artifacts can be seen in museums throughout the region. Throughout the Middle Ages, the river's importance as a trade artery made it the focus of sharp, often violent, conflict between princes, noblemen, and archbishops. Many of the picturesque castles that crown its banks were the homes of robber barons who held up passing ships and barges and exacted heavy tolls to finance even grander fortifications.

For poets and composers, the Rhine—or *Vater Rhein,* (Father Rhine) as the Germans call it—has been an endless source of inspiration. As legend has it, the Lorelei, a treacherous, craggy rock, was home to a beautiful and bewitching maiden who lured sailors to a watery grave. Wagner based four of his epic operas on the lives of the medieval Nibelungen, said to have inhabited the rocky banks.

The Rhine does not belong to Germany alone, but it is in Germany—especially the stretch between Mainz and Köln (Cologne) known as the Middle Rhine—that the riverside scenery is most spectacular. This is the "typical" Rhine: a land of steep and thickly wooded hills, terraced vineyards, tiny villages hugging the banks, and a succession of brooding castles.

In early 1995, the Rhine flooded severely for the second time in 13 months. Many establishments did all they could to pull through the first floods, leaving little or no resources for the second go-round. At press time it was too early to know which, if any, places will have to close. To avoid disappointment and inconvenience, be sure to call ahead.

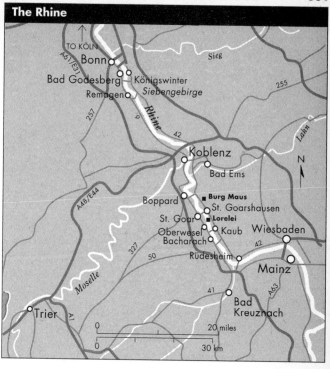

The Rhine

Getting Around

By Train

One of the best ways to visit the Rhineland in very limited time is to take the scenic train journey from Mainz to Köln along the western banks of the river. The views are spectacular, and the entire trip takes less than two hours. Choose an InterCity train for its wide viewing windows. If you're traveling north toward Köln, make sure you get a window seat on the right-hand side. Contact Deutsche Bahn *Reisedienst,* Friedrich-Ebert-Anlage 43, tel. 069/19419, or get details at any big train-station travel office.

By Boat

Passenger ships traveling up and down the Rhine and its tributaries offer a pleasant and relaxing way to see the region. **Köln-Düsseldorfer Rheinschiffahrt** (Frankenwerft 15, 50667 Köln, tel. 0221/258–3011; in the U.S., **KD River Cruises of Europe** 2500 Westchester Ave., Purchase, NY 10577, tel. 914/696–3600; 323 Geary St., Suite 603, San Francisco, CA 94102, tel. 415/392–8817) has ships that travel daily between Düsseldorf and Frankfurt, from Easter to late October. They also offer cruises along the entire length of the Rhine. Passengers have a choice of buying an excursion ticket or a ticket to a single destination. This company also offers trips up the Mosel as far as Trier. From March through November, the **Hebel-Line** (tel. 06742/2420) in Boppard cruises the Lorelei Valley; night cruises have music and dancing. For information about Neckar River excursions, contact **Neckar Personen Schiffahrt** in Stuttgart, tel. 0711/541–073 or 0711/541–074.

By Car

If you choose to drive, you'll take in some of the region's most spectacular scenery on the Rhineland's comprehensive highway network. Roads crisscross the entire province, from the historic vineyards of the Mosel Valley to the beautiful castle and wine-growing country of the Rhine's west bank. For information about routes, contact the **German Automobile Club** (AVD, Lyonerstr. 16, 60528 Frankfurt-am-Main, tel. 069/66060).

By Bicycle

Tourist offices in all the larger towns will provide information and route maps. Deutsche Bahn rents bikes at numerous stations. For information, call 069/19419 or ask for the *"Fahrrad am Bahnhof"* ("Bikes for Rent") brochure at any station.

Tourist Information

For general information on the region, contact the Fremdenverkehrsverband Rheinland-Pfalz, Löhrstr. 103, Koblenz, tel. 0261/31079.

Bacharach (Fremdenverkehrsamt, Oberstr. 1, tel. 06743/2968).
Boppard (Verkehrsamt, Karmeliterstr. 2, tel. 06742/10319).
Koblenz (Fremdenverkehrsamt Pavillon am Hauptbahnhof, tel. 0261/31304).
Köln (Verkehrsamt, Unter Fettenhennen 19, tel. 0221/221–3340).
Mainz (Verkehrsverein, Bahnhofstr. 15, tel. 06131/286–210).
Rüdesheim (Verkehrsamt, Rheinstr. 16, tel. 06722/2962).
St. Goarshausen (Verkehrsamt, Bahnhofstr. 8, tel. 06771/427).

Guided Tours

In addition to a number of special-interest cruises, **KD River Cruises of Europe** (*see* Getting Around, *above*) operates a series of guided excursions covering the towns along its routes. A host of local shipping lines do the same, including **Personenschiffahrt Merkelbach** (Emserstr. 87, Koblenz-Pfaffendorf, tel. 0261/76810) or **Rhein und Moselschiffahrt Gerhard Collee-Holzbein** (Rheinzollstr. 4, Koblenz, tel. 0261/37744). The tourist offices in Mainz, Köln, and Koblenz also offer tours (in English) of their respective cities; Köln even has one in a horse-drawn carriage April–October.

Exploring the Rhine

Köln

Köln (Cologne) is the largest city on the Rhine, marking the northernmost point of the river's scenic stretch before it becomes a truly industrial waterway through the Ruhr Valley. It's a very old city—first settled by the Romans in 38 BC. It derives its name from the Latin Colonia Claudia Ara Agrippinensium, the title given to it by the Roman emperor Claudius in honor of his wife, Julia Agrippina, who was born there. The Franks and Merovingians followed the Romans before Charlemagne restored the city's fortunes in the 9th century, appointing its first archbishop and ensuring its ecclesiastical prominence for centuries.

By the Middle Ages, Köln was the largest city north of the Alps, and, as a member of the powerful Hanseatic League, it was more important commercially than either London or Paris. Ninety percent of the city was destroyed in World War II, and the rush to rebuild it after the war shows in some of the blocky, uninspired architecture. Still, attempts were made to restore many of the old buildings. Whatever the city's aesthetic drawbacks, the Altstadt (Old Town), within the line of the medieval city walls, has great charm, and at night it throbs with life.

Towering over the Old Town is the extraordinary Gothic cathedral, the **Kölner Dom,** dedicated to Sts. Peter and Mary. It's comparable to the best French cathedrals; a visit to it may prove a highlight of your trip to Germany. What you'll see is one of the purest expressions of the Gothic spirit in Europe. Spend some time admiring the outside of the building (you can walk almost all the way around it). Notice that there are practically no major horizontal lines—all the accents of the building are vertical. It may come as a disappointment to learn that the cathedral, begun in 1248, was not completed until 1880. Console yourself with the knowledge that it was still built to original plans. At 515 feet high, the two western towers of the cathedral were by far the tallest structures in the world when they were finished. The length of the building is 469 feet; the width of the nave is 148 feet; and the highest part of the interior is 139 feet.

The cathedral was built to house what were believed to be the relics of the Magi, the three kings or wise men who paid homage to the infant Jesus. Today the relics are kept just behind the altar, in the same enormous gold-and-silver **reliquary** in which they were originally displayed. The other great treasure of the cathedral is the **Gero Cross,** a monumental oak crucifix dating from 971. Impressive for its simple grace, it's in the last chapel on the left as you face the altar.

Other highlights to admire are the stained-glass windows, some of which date from the 13th century; the 15th-century altar painting; and the early 14th-century high altar with its surrounding arcades of glistening white figures and its intricate choir screens. The choir stalls, carved from oak around 1310, are the largest in Germany, seating 104 people. There are more treasures to be seen in the **Dom Schatzkammer,** the cathedral treasury, including the silver shrine of Archbishop Engelbert, who was stabbed to death in 1225. *Admission: DM 3 adults, DM 1.50 children. Open Mon.–Sat. 9–5, Sun. 1–5.*

Outside again, you have the choice of either more culture or commerce. Köln's **shopping district** begins at nearby **Wallrafplatz.** Grouped around the cathedral is a collection of superb museums. If your priority is painting, try the ultramodern **Wallraf-Richartz-Museum** and **Museum Ludwig** complex. Together, they form the largest art collection in the Rhineland. The Wallraf-Richartz-Museum's pictures span the years 1300 to 1900, with Dutch and Flemish schools particularly well represented (Rubens, who spent his youth in Köln, has a place of honor). The Museum Ludwig is devoted exclusively to 20th-century art. Its Picasso collection is so outstanding that construction on a new, all-Picasso museum will begin in the near future. *Bischofsgartenstr. 1, tel. 0221/221–2372 or 3491. Admission to both museums: DM 8 adults, DM 4 children. Open Tues.–Fri. 10–6, weekends 11–6.*

Opposite the cathedral is the **Römisch-Germanisches Museum,** built from 1970 to 1974 around the famous Dionysus mosaic that was uncovered at the site during the construction of an air-raid shelter in 1941. The huge mosaic, more than 300 feet square, once covered the dining-room floor of a wealthy Roman trader's villa. Its millions of tiny earthenware and glass tiles depict some of the adventures of Dionysus, the Greek god of wine and, to the Romans, the object of a widespread and sinister religious cult. The pillared first-century tomb of Lucius Publicius, a prominent Roman officer, some stone Roman coffins, and a series of memorial tablets are among the museum's other exhibits.

Roncallipl. 4, tel. 0221/221–4438. Admission: DM 5 adults, DM 2.50 children. Open Tues.–Fri. 10–4, weekends 11–4.

Now head south to the nearby **Alter Markt** and its **Altes Rathaus,** the oldest town hall in Germany (if you don't count the fact that the building was entirely rebuilt after the war). The square has a handsome assembly of buildings—the oldest dating from 1135—in a range of styles. There was a seat of local government here in Roman times, and directly below the current Rathaus are the remains of the Roman city governor's headquarters, the Praetorium. Go inside to see the 14th-century **Hansa Saal,** whose tall Gothic windows and barrel-vaulted wooden ceiling are potent expressions of medieval civic pride. The figures of the prophets, standing on pedestals at one end, are all from the early 15th century. Ranging along the south wall are nine additional statues, the so-called *Nine Good Heroes,* carved in 1360. Charlemagne and King Arthur are among them.

Cross Unter Käster to get to the river and one of the most outstanding of Köln's 12 Romanesque churches, the **Gross St. Martin.** Its massive 13th-century tower, with distinctive corner turrets and an imposing central spire, is another landmark of Köln. Gross St. Martin is the parish church of Köln's colorful old city, the **Martinsviertel,** an attractive combination of reconstructed, high-gabled medieval buildings, winding alleys, and tastefully designed modern apartments and business quarters. Head here at night—the place comes alive at sunset.

To complete your daytime Köln tour, however, leave the Martinsviertel along Martinstrasse and turn right into Gürzenichstrasse, passing the crenellated Gothic-style Gürzenich civic reception/concert hall. Take a left turn into Hohestrasse and another right turn into Cäcilienstrasse. At Number 29, you'll find the 12th-century St. Cecilia Church, and within its cool, well-lighted interior one of the world's finest museums of medieval Christian art, the **Schnütgen Museum.** The museum is named after the cathedral capitular Alexander Schnütgen, who bequeathed his collection of religious art to the city in 1906. Enlarged considerably over the years, the collection was moved to St. Cecilia's in 1956. Although the main emphasis of the museum falls on early and medieval sacred art, the collection also covers the Renaissance and Baroque periods. *Cäcilienstr. 29, tel. 0221/221–2310. Admission: DM 5 adults, DM 2.50 children. Open Tues.–Fri. 10–6, weekends 11–6. Guided tours (in German) on Sun. at 11.*

Around the corner, on Leonhard-Tietz-Strasse, is **St. Peter's Church,** where the painter Peter Paul Rubens was christened. There's a fine Rubens painting in the altar recess, joined recently by a modern triptych by the British painter Francis Bacon.

A few steps away is the expansive **Neumarkt** square, at whose western end is one of Köln's finest Romanesque basilicas, **St. Aposteln.** The Neumarkt was an early trading center; the church was built in the 11th century amid the hustle and bustle of a daily market. Today, its weighty eastern front, surmounted by two graceful hexagonal towers and the more traditional four-sided western steeple, dominates a very different scene—a green city park lined with elegant shops and offices.

Not far south of Köln is the staid city of **Bonn,** the former capital of West Germany, now preparing to hand most of its legislative and administrative functions over to Berlin. The **Beethovenhaus** (Beethoven Museum, Bonngasse 20, tel. 0228/635–188) displays scores, a grand piano, and an ear trumpet or two in the house where the composer was born. The city also has a respectable **Münster** (cathedral) and a trio of new museums, including the **Federal Kunsthalle,** which brings Bonn more into the swing of things, culturally speaking.

The diplomats' ghetto of **Bad Godesberg,** just south of Bonn, is across the river from **Königswinter,** site of one of the most visited castles on the Rhine, the **Drachenfels.** Its ruins crown the highest hill in the **Siebengebirge** (Seven Hills), commanding a spectacular view of the river. The castle was built during the 12th century by the archbishop of Köln. Its name commemorates a dragon said to have lived in a nearby cave. As legend has it, the dragon was slain by Siegfried, hero of the epic poem *The Nibelungenlied.*

Koblenz

In the heart of the Middle Rhine region, at the confluence of the Rhine and Mosel rivers, lies the city of **Koblenz,** the area's cultural and administrative center and the meeting place of the two great wine-producing districts. Here you are ideally placed to sample and compare the light, fruity Mosel wines and the headier Rhine varieties. At **Weindorf,** or "wine village," just south of the **Pfaffendorfer Bridge,** you can try the wines in traditional Römer glasses, with their symbolic amber and green bowls.

The city of Koblenz began as a Roman camp—Confluentes—more than 2,000 years ago. The vaults beneath **St. Florin's Church** contain an interesting assortment of Roman remains. A good place to begin your tour of Koblenz is the **Deutches Eck,** or "Corner of Germany," the tip of the sharp peninsula separating the Rhine and Mosel rivers. In the 12th century, the Knights of the Teutonic Order established their center here. The towering equestrian statue of Kaiser Wilhelm here was destroyed by Allied bombs during World War II; the decision to replace it in 1993 aroused controversy, as some thought this a misplaced celebration of Prussian military might. On summer evenings, concerts are held in the nearby **Blumenhof Garden.** Most of the city's historic churches are also within walking distance of the Deutsches Eck. The **Liebfrauenkirche** (Church of Our Lady), completed in the 13th century but later much modified, incorporates Romanesque, late Gothic, and Baroque elements. **St. Florin,** a Romanesque church built around 1100, was remodeled in the Gothic style in the 14th century. Gothic windows and a vaulted ceiling were added in the 17th century. The city's most important church, **St. Kastor,** also combines Romanesque and Gothic elements and features some unusual altar tombs and rare Gothic wall paintings.

Although the city lost 85% of its buildings during wartime air raids, some of the old buildings survived, and others have been built in complementary styles. Much of the **Old Town** of Koblenz is now a pedestrian district, an attractive area for a leisurely stroll. Many of the ancient cellars beneath the houses have been rediscovered and now serve as wine bars and jazz clubs.

Koblenz is also the site of an assortment of castles and palaces. The former residence of the archbishop of Trier now houses the city administrative offices. The original 18th-century building was demolished during the war; today only the interior staircase remains. Across the river, on the Rhine's east bank, towers the city's most spectacular castle, **Ehrenbreitstein.** The fortifications of this vast structure date from the 1100s, although the bulk of it was built much later, in the 16th and 17th centuries. To reach the fortress, take the *Sesselbahn* (cable car) or, if you're in shape, try walking up. The view alone is worth the trip. The fortress contains an interesting museum, the **Landesmuseum,** with exhibits tracing the industrial development of the Rhine Valley, including a reconstructed 19th-century tobacco factory and a pewter works. *Admission free. Open Mar.–Nov., daily 9–12:30 and 1–5.*

One of Koblenz's two noteworthy art galleries, the **Ludwig Museum**—opened in 1992—presents rotating exhibitions of contemporary art, much of it from the enormous collection of Koblenz-born tycoon Peter Ludwig, Germany's top collector (also responsible for the Museum Ludwig in Köln). The setting is spectacular—converted rooms of the historic Deutschherrenhaus on Danziger Freiheit square. *Admission: DM 5 adults, DM 3 students. Open Tues.–Sun. 11–5, Thurs. until 8, Sun. until 6.*

The other gallery, the **Mittelrhein Museum,** features Rhenish art and artifacts from the Middle Ages to the present day. *15 Florinsmarkt. Admission: DM 5 adults. Open Tues.–Sun. 11–5, Wed. until 8, Sun. until 6.*

Rhine Gorge

Between the cities of Koblenz and Mainz, the Rhine flows through the 64-kilometer (40-mile) stretch known as the **Rhine Gorge.** It is here that the Rhine lives up to its legends and lore and where the river, in places, narrows to a width of 200 yards. Once it was full of treacherous whirlpools, sudden shallows, and stark rock outcroppings that menaced passing ships. Today, vineyards occupy every inch of available soil on the steep, terraced slopes. High above, ancient castles crown the rocky shelves.

South of Koblenz, at a wide, western bend in the river, lies the quiet old town of **Boppard,** once a bustling city of the Holy Roman Empire. Now the remains of its Roman fort and castle are used to house a museum of Roman artifacts and geological specimens. There are also several notable churches, including the **Carmelite Church,** with its fine Baroque altar, and the Romanesque church of **St. Severus.** From Boppard is a wonderful view across the Rhine to the ruined castles of **Liebenstein** and **Sterrenberg,** known as the "hostile brothers." As legend has it, the castles were built by two feuding brothers to protect their respective interests.

Continuing south from Boppard, you come to the little town of **St. Goar,** crowded against the steep gorge cliff and shadowed by the imposing ruin of **Rheinfels Castle.** Rheinfels was built in the mid-13th century by Count Dieter von Katzenelnbogen (whose name means "cat's elbow"). The count's enormous success in collecting river tolls provoked the other river barons to join and lay siege to his castle. What transpired is unclear, but through the years Rheinfels survived numerous sieges. It was finally destroyed by the French in 1797. During the 19th century, the ruins served as a source of inspiration for a host of Romantic poets and artists. It is now being restored, and a luxury hotel has been built on the site (*see* Dining and Lodging, *below*). *Admission: DM 5, children DM 4. Open Apr.–Oct., daily 9–5.*

On the east bank of the river, just across from the town of St. Goar, lies its sister village, **St. Goarshausen.** An hourly ferry service links the two. St. Goarshausen is dominated by **Burg Katz** (Cat Castle), a massive fortress built by a later count von Katzenelnbogen. Tourists are not permitted inside, but the top of the cliff offers a lovely view of the famous Lorelei rock. About 3.2 kilometers (2 miles) north of St. Goarshausen is the **Burg Maus,** or Mouse Castle. Legend has it that an archbishop of Trier built the fortress to protect a strip of land he owned at the base of the cliff. The count von Katzenelnbogen, annoyed at what he considered an intrusion into his territory, sent the archbishop a message explaining that his "cat" (Burg Katz) was sufficient to protect the electoral "mouse." Hence the nickname, Burg Maus.

Many tourists visit St. Goarshausen for its location—only a few kilometers from the legendary **Lorelei rock.** To get to the Lorelei, follow the road marked with LORELEI-FELSEN signs. Here the Rhine takes a sharp turn around a rocky, shrub-covered headland. This is the narrowest and shallowest part of the Middle Rhine, full of treacherous currents. According to legend, the beautiful maiden, Lore, sat on the rock here, combing her golden hair and singing a song so irresistible that passing sailors forgot the navigational hazards and were swept to their deaths.

Oberwesel, on the west bank, is a medieval wine town encircled by ancient walls and towers. Sixteen of the original 21 towers remain. Two churches deserve a visit: **St. Martin,** built in the 14th and 15th centuries, features a distinctive, brightly painted nave; the **Liebfrauenkirche** (known as the "red church" because of its fiery facade) contains a magnificent choir screen, some fine sculpture, and an altarpiece depicting the magnanimous deeds of St. Nicholas.

One of the most photographed sites of the Middle Rhine region is the medieval village of **Kaub,** just south of Oberwesel on the east side of the river. Its unusual castles are well worth a visit. The **Pfalzgrafenstein,** on a tiny island in the middle of the Rhine, bristles with sharp-pointed towers and has the appearance of a small sailing ship. In the 14th century, the resident *Graf,* or count, was said to have strung chains across the Rhine to stop riverboats and collect his tolls. A special boat takes visitors to the island. *Ferry runs every ½-hour 9–1 and 2–5 (in season). Fare: DM 2.50 adults, DM 2 children; castle admission: DM 4 adults, DM 1.50 children.*

On a hillside above Kaub hovers another small castle: **Burg Gutenfels.** Built in the 13th century, Gutenfels was renovated completely at the end of the 18th century and is now an exquisite hotel (*see* Dining and Lodging, *below*).

The picturesque little village of **Bacharach,** encircled by 15th-century walls, is the best-preserved town of the Middle Rhine. It takes its name from the Roman Baccaracum (altar of Bacchus)—a great stone that stood here until it was dynamited by river engineers during the last century. As its name implies, Bacharach is also a wine-trade center.

Farther south, on the Rhine's east bank and at the center of the Rhine Gorge region, lies another famous wine town. According to legend, **Rüdesheim's** first vines were planted by Charlemagne. More recent vintages can be enjoyed in the many taverns lining **Drosselgasse,** a narrow, colorful street in the heart of town. Rüdesheim is a tourist magnet—about the most popular destination on the Rhine—so if you plan to stay overnight, be sure to reserve well in advance. Besides its half-timber houses, hidden courtyards, and medieval castles, Rüdesheim offers an interesting museum, the **Rheingau und Weinmuseum,** devoted to the history of wine making and local lore. *Rheinstr. 2. Admission: DM 3 adults, DM 2 children. Open mid-Mar.–Oct., daily 9–6.*

Mainz

On the west side of the Rhine, at the mouth of the Main River, stands the city of **Mainz,** an old university town that's the capital of the Rhineland-Palatinate state. During Roman times, Mainz was a camp called Moguntiacum. Later it was the seat of the powerful archbishops of Mainz. It's also the city in which, around 1450, printing pioneer Johannes Gutenberg established his first movable-type press. (He's such an important figure in Mainz that he has his own festival, Johannisnacht, celebrated in mid-June.) He is commemorated by a monument and square bearing his name and a museum containing his press and one of his Bibles. *Liebfrauenpl. 5. Admission free. Open Tues.–Sat. 10–6, Sun. and holidays 10–1. Closed Jan.*

Today, Mainz is a bustling, modern city of nearly 200,000 inhabitants. Although it was heavily bombed during World War II, many of the buildings have been faithfully reconstructed, and the pedestrian zones of the Old Town, lined with medieval-style buildings that house taverns and shops, are charming. A focal point is the city's **Dom** (cathedral), one of the finest Romanesque churches in Germany. On **Gutenbergplatz** in the **Old Town** stand two fine Baroque churches, **Seminary Church** and **St. Ignatius.** The Old Town also claims the country's oldest Renaissance fountain—**the Marktbrunnen**—and the **Dativius-Victor-Bogen**, an arch dating from Roman times. The **Römisch-Germanisches Museum,** in the **Kurfürstliches Schloss** (Elector's Palace), contains a notable collection of archaeological finds. *Rheinstr. Admission free. Open Tues.–Sun. 10–6.*

A newer touch is provided in the Gothic church of **St. Stephan,** standing on a hilltop to the south of the Old Town; in the choir are six stained-glass windows by French artist Marc Chagall.

Dining and Lodging

When it comes to cuisine, the Rhineland offers a number of regional specialties. Be sure to sample the wide variety of sausages available, the goose and duck dishes from the Ahr Valley, and Rhineland sauerbraten—accepted by many as the most succulent of pot roasts. Hotels in the Rhineland range from simple little inns to magnificent castle hotels. Many smaller towns have only small hotels and guest houses, some of which close during the winter months. During the peak summer season and in early autumn—wine festival time—accommodations are scarce, so it is advisable to reserve well in advance.

For details and price-category definitions, *see* Dining and Lodging *in* Staying in Germany, *above.*

Bacharach
DINING
Hotel-Restaurant Steeger Weinstube. Less than 20 marks buys you three hearty courses at this friendly, family-run tavern/restaurant just off the Rhine tourist route. The menu changes daily, but Rhineland-style sauerbraten, homemade potato dumplings, and venison (in season) are often featured. *Blucherstr. 149, Bacharach-Steeg, tel. 06743/1240. AE, MC. Closed Wed. $*

DINING AND LODGING
Altkölnischer Hof. This small but cozy half-timber hotel was built at the turn of the century. Its rustic restaurant serves typical local dishes and some excellent wines. *Blücherstr. 2, tel. 06743/1339, fax 06743/2793. 18 rooms with bath. Facilities: restaurant, parking. AE, V. Closed Nov.–Easter. $$*

Bonn
DINING
Haus Daufenbach. The stark white exterior of the Daufenbach, near the church of St. Remigius, conceals one of the most distinctive restaurants in Bonn. The mood is rustic, with simple wooden furniture and antlers on the walls. Specialties include Spanferkel and a range of

imaginative salads. Wash them down with wines from the restaurant's own vineyards. *Brüderg. 6, tel. 0228/637–944. Reservations advised. No credit cards. Closed Mon. In summer, no Sun. dinner. $$*

Em Hottche. Travelers have been dining at this tavern since the late 14th century; today, it offers one of the best-value lunches in town. The tone is decidedly rustic, the food hearty, and the portions are large. *Markt 4, tel. 0228/690–009. No reservations. No credit cards. $*

LODGING

Domicil. A group of buildings around a quiet central courtyard has been stylishly converted into a hotel of great charm and comfort. The rooms are decorated in styles from fin-de-siècle romantic to Italian modern. *Thomas-Mann-Str. 24-26, tel. 0228/729–090, fax 0228/691–207. 42 rooms with bath. Facilities: restaurant, coffee bar, sauna, game room, hairdresser. AE, DC, MC, V. Closed Christmas–New Year's Day. $$$$*

Rheinland. This modest lodging has the advantage of being a short walk from the center of the Old Town. Rooms are comfortable, and although there is no restaurant, a good buffet breakfast greets the day. *Berliner Freiheit 11, 53111, tel. 0228/658–096, fax 0228/472–844. 31 rooms with bath. AE, MC. $$*

Sternhotel. For good value, solid comfort, and a central location in the Old Town, the family-run Stern is tops. Rooms can be small, but all are pleasantly furnished. There's no restaurant, but snacks are available at the bar. *Markt 8, tel. 0228/72670, fax 0228/726–715. 81 rooms with bath. Facilities: bar. AE, DC, MC, V. $$*

Boppard
LODGING

Bellevue Rheinhotel. This is one of the most majestic hotels of the Rhineland, an imposing turn-of-the-century building whose elegant white-and-yellow facade, under steep slate eaves, faces directly onto the river. *Rheinallee 41–42, tel. 06742/1020, fax 06742/102–602. 94 rooms with bath. Facilities: restaurant, beer cellar, bar, indoor pool, sauna, Turkish bath, fitness center, tennis courts. AE, DC, MC, V. $$$*

Kaub
LODGING

★ **Burg Gutenfels.** The terrace of this luxurious castle hotel offers one of the finest views in the Rhine Valley (*see* Exploring, *above*). Guests can also enjoy wine from the hotel's own vineyard. Be sure to reserve well in advance. *Tel. 06774/220, fax 06774/1760. 10 rooms with bath. Facilities: restaurant, private chapel. AE, DC, MC, V. $$$–$$$$*

Koblenz
DINING

Wacht am Rhein. The name of this attractive riverside restaurant, Watch on the Rhine, sums it up. In summer, take a table on the terrace and watch the river traffic roll by; in winter, choose a window table and dine with the Rhine outside and the atmospheric warmth of the fin-de-siècle fittings and furnishings inside. Fish is the basis of the extensive menu. *Adenauer-Ufer 6, tel. 0261/15313. AE. $$*

Weinhaus Hubertus. This restaurant, named for the patron saint of hunting, lives up to its sporting image. Its decor is 17th-century rustic; its specialty, fresh game in season. Guests enjoy generous portions and a congenial atmosphere. *Florinsmarkt 6, tel. 0261/31177. Reservations advised. No credit cards. Closed Tues. No lunch. $$*

LODGING

Scandic Crown. This modern, somewhat charmless hotel stands directly on the banks of the Rhine; most rooms have fine views of the river and the Ehrenbreitstein fortress. A lovely garden and terrace also overlook the river. *Julius-Wegeler-Str. 6, tel. 0261/1360, fax 0261/136–1199. 159 rooms with bath. Facilities: 2 restaurants, bar, sauna, whirlpool. AE, DC, MC, V. $$$$*

Kleiner Reisen. This is a well-run, straightforward hotel that gives value for the money. Another plus is the quiet riverside location that's still within walking distance of the train station and Old Town. There's no restaurant. *Kaiserin-Augusta-Anlagen 18, tel. 0261/32077, fax 0261/160–725. 27 rooms with bath. Facilities: parking. AE, DC, MC, V. $$–$$$*

Köln

DINING

★ **Bado-La Poêle d'Or.** At first glance, the heavy furnishings and hushed atmosphere of the Poêle d'Or make it seem like the last place you'd find light and sophisticated nouvelle cuisine in Germany. But for some years, those in the know have been savoring mouthwatering dishes as simple as onion soup here. Order salmon with lemon-ginger sauce to taste the place's capabilities. *Komödienstr. 50–52, tel. 0221/134–100. Reservations required. AE, DC, MC, V. Closed Sun. No lunch Mon. $$$*

★ **Weinhaus im Walfisch.** The black-and-white gabled facade of this 400-year-old restaurant lets you know what to expect inside—though here the local offerings are spruced up for an up-market clientele. The menu presents quasitraditional dishes with a French accent: fine fare at corresponding prices, and a wide range of wines. The restaurant is tucked away between the Heumarkt (Haymarket) and the river. *Salzg. 13, tel. 0221/258–0397. Reservations advised. AE, DC, MC, V. Closed weekends and holidays. $$$*

Gaststätte Früh am Dom. For real down-home German food, there are few places to compare with this time-honored former brewery. Bold frescoes on the vaulted ceilings establish the mood, and such dishes as *Hämmchen* (pork shank) provide an authentically Teutonic experience. The beer garden is delightful for summer dining. *Am Hof 12–14, tel. 0221/258–0394. Reservations advised. No credit cards. $$*

DINING AND LODGING

★ **Dom-Hotel.** The Dom is in a class of its own. Old-fashioned, formal, and gracious, with a stunning location right by the cathedral, it offers the sort of elegance and discreetly efficient service few hotels even aspire to these days. The antique-filled bedrooms are subdued in color, high-ceilinged, and spacious. The view of the cathedral is something to treasure; enjoy it from the glassed-in Atelier am Dom, where you can dine on anything from wild boar served with chanterelle ragout to tofu piccata with ratatouille and curried rice. *Domkloster 2A, tel. 0221/20240, fax 0221/202–4444. 126 rooms with bath. Facilities: 2 restaurants, terrace café, bar, parking. AE, DC, MC, V. $$$$*

★ **Excelsior Hotel Ernst.** The Empire-style lobby in sumptuous royal blue, bright yellow, and gold is striking, and a similar boldly conceived grandeur extends to all the public rooms in this 1863 hotel. Old master paintings (including a Van Dyck) are everywhere; you'll be served breakfast in a room hung with Gobelin tapestries. Guest rooms are appropriately more intimate in scale, with spectacular marble bathrooms and ultramodern fixtures. The lacquered-wood-paneled restaurant serves classic French cuisine imaginatively prepared. All this comes with convenience as well—the hotel is just down the street from the main train station and across from the cathedral. *Trankg. 1-5, tel. 0221/2701, fax 0221/135–150. 160 rooms with bath. Facilities: restaurant, piano bar, hair salon, masseuse, fitness room. AE, DC, MC, V. $$$$*

Stapelhäuschen. One of the few houses along the riverbank to have survived World War II bombings, this is one of the very oldest buildings in Köln. You can't beat the location, overlooking the river and right by Gross St. Martin; yet rooms are reasonably priced, making up in quaintness for what they lack in luxury. The restaurant is in a slightly higher price bracket, but does a respectable enough job with spruced-up versions of German specialties. *Fischmarkt 1-3, tel. 0221/257–7862, fax 0221/257–4232. AE, DC, MC, V.* $$

LODGING

★ **Altstadt.** Close to the river and in the Old Town, this is the place for charm and low rates. Each room is furnished differently, and the service is impeccable—both welcoming and efficient. There's no restaurant. *Salzg. 7, tel. 0221/257–7851, fax 0221/257–7853. 28 rooms with bath. Facilities: sauna. AE, DC, MC, V. Closed Christmas–New Year's Day.* $$

Königswinter

DINING

Zum Alten Bräuhaus. In a pleasant, shady garden in the center of town, Zum Alten Bräuhaus serves German fare with a selection of local wines and beers. *Hauptstr. 454, tel. 02223/22528. No credit cards.* $$

Mainz

DINING

★ **Drei Lilien.** This beautifully appointed restaurant has antique furnishings and excellent nouvelle cuisine. *Ballpl. 2, tel. 06131/225–068. Reservations advised. AE, DC, MC, V. Closed Sun. and Mon.* $$$

Rats- und Zunftstuben Heilig Geist. Although the decor is predominantly modern, this popular restaurant also incorporates some Roman remains and offers a traditional atmosphere. The cuisine is hearty German fare. *Renteng. 2, tel. 06131/225–757. Reservations required. AE, DC, MC, V. Closed Sun.* $$

LODGING

Hotel-Restaurant Am Lerchenberg. The location isn't ideal—some 4 miles from the city center—but there's a bus stop right outside the door and open countryside only short steps away. Family-run, the hotel is friendly, comfortable, and peaceful. *Hindemithstr. 5, tel. 06131/934–300, fax 06131/934–3099. 53 rooms with bath. Facilities: restaurant, sauna, solarium, fitness room. AE, DC, MC, V. Closed Christmas–New Year's.* $$–$$$

Hotel Stadt Coblenz. In the heart of the town, this attractive hotel offers budget rooms (bath in the hall) at budget prices—ask for a room facing the back. The rustic restaurant serves local and German specialties. *Rheinstr. 49, tel. 0631/227–602. Facilities: restaurant. No credit cards.* $

Rüdesheim

DINING

Krone. The extensive restoration work carried out on the 450-year-old Krone included a complete renovation of its restaurant, which now ranks among the most outstanding in the region. Chef Herbert Pucher's terrines and pâtés draw regular customers from as far away as Frankfurt. His fish dishes are supreme, and the Rhine wines are the best. *Rheinuferstr. 10, Assmannshausen, tel. 06722/4030. Reservations advised. AE, DC, MC, V. Closed Jan.–Feb.* $$–$$$

LODGING

Hotel Jagdschloss Niederwald. This is not so much a place to overnight as a luxury resort hotel where you might want to spend your entire vacation. It's set in the hills 5 kilometers (3 miles) out of Rüdesheim, with predictably good views over the Rhine and the Rhine Gorge. The former hunting lodge of the dukes of Hesse, it has a lavish, baronial atmosphere. *Auf dem Niederwald 1, 65383, tel. 06722/1004, fax 06722/47970. 52 rooms with bath. Facilities: restaurant, bar, indoor pool, sauna, gym, tennis courts, horseback riding. AE, DC, MC, V. Closed Jan. 1–Feb. 14. $$$–$$$$*

Hotel und Weinhaus Felsenkeller. Just around the corner from Drossel-gasse, Hotel und Weinhaus Felsenkeller is a traditional 18th-century es-tablishment offering modern comforts. *Oberstr. 39–41, tel. 06722/2094, fax 06722/47202. 60 rooms with shower. AE, MC, V. $$*

Rüdesheimer Hof. For a taste of Rheingau hospitality, try this typical inn. There's a terrace for summer dining on excellent local specialties, which you can enjoy along with any of the many wines offered. *Geisen-heimerstr. 1, tel. 06722/2011, fax 06722/48191. 42 rooms with bath. Facilities: restaurant, terrace, parking. AE, DC, MC, V. Closed mid-Nov.–mid-Feb. $$*

St. Goar, St. Goarshausen

DINING

Roter Kopf. This is a historic wine restaurant brimming with rustic Rhineland atmosphere. *Burgstr. 5, St. Goarshausen, tel. 06771/2698. Reservations advised. No credit cards. $$*

LODGING

Schlosshotel-Burg Rheinfels. High above St. Goar, on a hill com-manding spectacular river views, the Schlosshotel-Burg Rheinfels rises from the ruins of the adjacent castle (*see* Exploring, *above*). *Schloss-berg 47, tel. 06741/8020, fax 06741/7652. 58 rooms with shower. Fa-cilities: restaurant, pool, sauna. AE, DC, MC, V. $$$*

Hermannsmühle. This rustic, chalet-style hotel just outside of town has heavy furniture decorated with painted, floral patterns. Herr Her-mann, the host, extends a warm welcome to all, and his place offers good value at low prices. *Forstbachstr. 46, 56346 St. Goarshausen, tel. 06771/7317. 10 rooms with bath. Facilities: restaurant. MC, V. Closed mid-Nov.–Feb. $*

THE BLACK FOREST

Only a century ago, the Black Forest (Schwarzwald) was one of the wildest stretches of countryside in Europe. But then, the deep hot springs first discovered by the Romans were rediscovered, and small forgotten villages became wealthy spas. Hikers treasured the lonely trails that cut through the forests and rolling uplands, skiers opened the world's first lift on the slopes of the region's highest mountain, and horseback riders cut bridle paths through the tangle of narrow river valleys. Today, the region is friendly and hospitable, still ex-tensively forested but with large, open valleys and stretches of ver-dant farmland.

The Black Forest is the southernmost German wine region and the cus-todian of some of the country's best traditional foods. Black Forest smoked ham and Black Forest cake are world-famous. The region re-tains its vibrant clock-making tradition, and local wood-carvers haven't yet died out. Best of all, though, it's still possible to stay overnight in a Black Forest farmhouse and eat a breakfast hearty enough to last the day, all for the price of an indifferent meal at a restaurant in, say, Mu-nich or Frankfurt.

Getting Around

The Rhine Valley autobahn, the A5, runs the entire length of the Black Forest and connects at Karlsruhe with the rest of the German expressway network. Well-paved, single-lane highways traverse the region. A main north–south train line follows the Rhine Valley, carrying Euro-City and InterCity trains that call at hourly intervals at Freiburg and Baden-Baden, connecting those two centers directly with Frankfurt and many other German cities. Local lines connect most Black Forest towns, and two local east–west services, the Black Forest Railway and the Höllental Railway, are spectacular scenic runs. The nearest airports are at Stuttgart; Strasbourg, in the neighboring French Alsace; and the Swiss border city of Basel, just 64 kilometers (40 miles) from Freiburg.

Tourist Information

Baden-Baden (Augustapl. 8, tel. 07221/275–200).
Freiburg (Rotteckring 14, tel. 0761/368–9090).
Freudenstadt (Promenadenpl. 1, tel. 07741/86420).
Pforzheim (Marktpl. 1, tel. 07231/302–314).

Guided Tours

Guided bus tours of the Black Forest begin in both Freiburg and Baden-Baden. A choice of 25 day tours from Freiburg includes the French Alsace region, the Swiss Alps, and various attractions in the Black Forest. Prices start at DM 32 and include English-speaking guides. In Baden-Baden, a range of day tours to the Black Forest, France, and Switzerland are offered by **Armbruster Reisen** (Jahnstr. 1, 77830 Bühlertal, tel. 07223/72227).

Exploring the Black Forest

The regional tourist authority has worked out a series of scenic routes covering virtually every attraction the visitor is likely to want to see (obtainable from the **Fremdenverkehrsverband,** Bertoldstr. 45, D-79098 Freiburg, tel. 0761/31317). The following itinerary is accessible by all means of transportation and takes in parts of the Black Forest High Road, Low Road, Spa Road, Wine Road, and Clock Road.

The ancient Roman city of **Pforzheim** is the starting point here, accessible either from the Munich–Karlsruhe autobahn or by train from Karlsruhe, Frankfurt, or Stuttgart. Known even beyond Germany's borders as the Gold City because of its association with the jewelry trade, Pforzheim has the world's finest museum collection of jewelry in the **Schmuckmuseum** (Jewelry Museum in the **Reuchlinhaus,** Jahnstr. 42, tel. 07231/392–126; admission DM 5 adults, DM 3 children; Tues.–Sun. 10–5). Pforzheim was almost completely destroyed by wartime bombing and is a fine example of reconstruction work: Visit the centrally located parish church of **St. Michael** to see how faithfully the experts stuck to the original mixture of sturdy Romanesque and later, finer Gothic styles.

On the way out of Pforzheim, toward B463, the Nagold Valley road, gardening enthusiasts should make a detour to the **Alpine Garden** on the Tiefenbronn road. More than 100,000 varieties of plants, including the rarest Alpine flowers, are found here, and many are for sale. *Open mid-Apr.–Oct., daily 8–7.*

Bad Liebenzell, our first stop on B463, is one of the Black Forest's oldest spas, with the remains of 15th-century installations. Visitors are welcome to take the waters at the **Paracelsus Baths** on the Nagold riverbank.

The Black Forest

Karlsruhe

A8

Pforzheim

Bad Liebenzell

FRANCE

294

Calw

Stuttgart

29

Baden-Baden

Zavelstein

Talmühle

B463

0 20 miles

0 30 km

A5/E35

Kehl

Mummelsee

3

Baiersbronn

Nagold

Offenburg

Freudenstadt

Neckar

N

Alpirsbach

27

415

Zell

B294

Lahr

Wolfach

Gutachtal Valley

Schiltach

B294

Rottweil

Kaiserstuhl

Triberg

Danube

Freiburg

Furtwangen

A81/E41

Tuttlingen

Himmelreich

Titisee

Staufen

Schluchsee

Radolfzell

Zell

Friedrichshafen

Rheinfelden

34

Bodensee

S W I T Z E R L A N D

Rhine

Tel. 07052/408–250. Admission (for 3 hrs): DM 11.50 adults, DM 5 children. Open Mon. 8:30–5; Tues., Wed., Sat. 8:30–8; Sun. 8:30–7.

Take some time to explore **Calw** (pronounced calve), the next town on the road south. Its famous native son, the novelist and poet Hermann Hesse, called it the "most beautiful [town] of all I know." And Hesse, who died in Switzerland in 1962, had seen more than a few in his extensive travels. Pause on the town's 15th-century bridge over the rushing Nagold River—you might see a local tanner spreading hides over the river wall to dry, as his ancestors did in centuries past.

Back on the main road south, turn off at Talmühle for the **Neubulach silver mine.** Once the most productive workings of the Black Forest, the mine closed in 1924 but is now open to visitors. *Admission: DM 4 adults, DM 3 children (includes entry to mineral museum). Open Apr.–Oct., daily 10–4:15.*

TIME OUT In the town of **Nagold**, visit the 1697-built half-timber **Alte Post** inn at Bahnhofstrasse 2. Kings and queens have taken refreshment here on journeys through the Black Forest. Enjoy the local beer and a plate of Black Forest smoked ham or a pot of strong coffee and a slice of delectable Black Forest cake.

From Nagold, the road travels on through lush farmland to **Freudenstadt,** another war-flattened German city that has been painstakingly restored. It was originally built during the early 17th century as a model city to house not only workers in nearby silver mines but also refugees from religious persecution in what is now Austrian Carinthia. The streets are still laid out in the grid pattern decreed by the original planners, while the vast central square continues to wait for the palace that was intended to stand here. It was to have been built for the city's founder,

Prince Frederick I of Württemberg, but he died before work could begin. Don't miss Freudenstadt's **Protestant parish church,** just off the square. It's L-shape is a rare architectural liberty during the early 17th century, when this imposing church was built.

Quench your thirst at nearby **Alpirsbach,** where the unusually soft water gives the local beer an especially smooth quality. The brewery was once part of a monastic settlement; its pretty **Romanesque church** next to the brew house is well worth a visit. The brewery still produces *Klosterbock* (a strong monastery beer) and maintains the tradition of brewing a special Christmas beer.

From here, take B294 to **Wolfach** and visit one of the last Black Forest factories where glass is blown by centuries-old techniques once common throughout the region. *Die Dorotheen-Glashütte, Glashüttenweg 4, tel. 07834/751. Admission (tour of works): DM 4 adults, DM 3 children. Open weekdays 9–4:30, Sat. 9–2.*

The valley of **Gutachtal,** south of Wolfach, is famous for its traditional costumes, and if you're here at the right time (holidays and some Sundays), you'll see the married women sporting black pom-poms on their hats to denote their matronly status (red pompoms are for the unmarried). At the head of the valley, at **Triberg,** are Germany's highest waterfalls, which reach a height of nearly 509 feet. This is also cuckoo-clock country. The **Clock Museum** (Uhrenmuseum) at Furtwangen is the largest in Germany. Its collection includes an astronomical timepiece weighing more than one ton. *Gerwigstr. 11, tel. 07723/920–117. Admission: DM 4 adults, DM 2 children. Open Apr.–Oct., daily 9–5; Nov.–Mar., daily 10–5.*

From Furtwangen, the road leads to the lakeland of the Black Forest. The two largest lakes, **Titisee** and **Schluchsee,** are beautifully set amid fir-clad mountains, but try to avoid them at the height of the summer holidays, when they are quite crowded. From here, it's a short run to Freiburg, capital of the Black Forest. The most direct route goes via the aptly named Höllental (Hell Valley). The first stop outside the narrow, gorgelike valley, **Himmelreich,** is said to have been named by railway engineers who were grateful finally to have run a line through Hell Valley (the town's name means "Kingdom of Heaven"). The Black Forest railway, more than 100 years old, still tackles the mountainous route, connecting Freiburg and the resort of Hinterzarten; details and tickets are available from the **Deutsche Bahn** in Freiburg (tel. 0761/19419).

Perched on the western slopes of the Black Forest, **Freiburg,** now one of the Black Forest's largest and loveliest cities, was founded as a free market town in the 12th century. It was badly bombed in World War II. Towering over the rebuilt medieval streets of the city is its most famous landmark, the cathedral, or **Münster.** The cathedral took three centuries to build and has one of the finest spires in the world. April through October the English-language walking tours of the Old Town include an explanation of the Münster's numerous architectural styles (Contact the tourist office). *Tours: Mon. and Fri. 2:30, Wed., Thurs., Sat., Sun. 10:30. Admission: DM 8 adults, DM 2 children.*

On weekdays, the square in front of the cathedral becomes a mass of color and movement; it's the town market, where you can buy everything from herbs to hot sausage. A fitting backdrop is provided by the **Kaufhaus,** a 16th-century market house.

TIME OUT Stroll up to Oberlinden Square and stop in at **Zum Roten Bären** (The Red Bear), reputedly Germany's oldest inn; it has a documented history dating from 1091. Order a *Viertel* of the local wine and perhaps a plate of locally smoked ham—and if you like the atmosphere, why not stay the night?

Once you've braved Hell Valley to get to Freiburg, a visit to the nearby town where Dr. Faustus is reputed to have made his deal with the devil should hold no horrors. **Staufen,** which claims the inquisitive doctor as one of its early burghers, is some 19 kilometers (12 miles) south of Freiburg. Local records show there really was an alchemist named Faustus who blew himself up in his laboratory. According to legend, the devil dragged him off to hell from the **Gasthof zum Löwen** (Hauptstr. 47, tel. 07633/7078), an old inn in the village center. The inn has a tap room named for Faust, and there are comfortable guest rooms if you fancy staying the night.

From Staufen, turn northward to Baden-Baden along the **Wine Road,** skirting the French border to your left, through the southernmost vineyards of Germany, source of the prized Baden wine. Some of the best vineyards are situated on a volcanic outcrop known as the **Kaiserstuhl** (Emperor's Chair). Sample a glass of wine in the village of **Achkarren,** which has a fascinating **wine museum.** *Admission: DM 2 adults, DM 1 children. Open Apr.–Oct., weekdays 2–5, weekends 10:30–4 (and by arrangement).*

All the vineyards along the Wine Road offer tastings, so don't hesitate to drop in and try one or two. To continue on our tour, leave the Wine Road at the town of Lahr and head inland, on B415, through the narrow Schuttertal valley to Zell, and from there to the Black Forest **High Road.** This is the land of fable and superstition, and if you're here during the misty days of autumn, stop off at the mystery-shrouded lake of **Mummelsee,** immortalized by the poet Mörike in his ballad *The Spirits of the Mummelsee.* Legend has it that sprites and other spirits of the deep live in the cold waters of the small, round lake in its forest setting. It's true that no fish are found in the lake, but scientific sorts say this is a result of the high mineral content of the water.

From the Mummelsee, it's downhill all the way to fashionable **Baden-Baden,** idyllically set in a wooded valley of the northern Black Forest and sitting atop the extensive underground hot springs that gave the city its name (*Bad,* German for "baths"). The Romans first exploited the springs, which were then rediscovered by wealthy 19th-century travelers. By the end of the 19th century, there was scarcely a crowned head of Europe who had not dipped into the healing waters of Baden-Baden. The town became the unofficial summer residence of numerous royal and titled families, and they left their imprint in the form of palatial houses that grace its tree-lined avenues.

One of the grand buildings of Baden-Baden's belle epoque is the pillared **Kurhaus,** home of Germany's first casino, which opened its doors to the world's gamblers in 1853. Entrance costs a modest DM 5, though visitors are required to sign a declaration that they enter with sufficient funds to settle subsequent debts! *Open Sun.–Fri. 2 PM–2 AM, Sat. 2 PM–3 AM. Daily tours (DM 3) from Apr.–Sept., daily 9:30–noon; Oct.–Mar., 10–noon. Jacket and tie required. Passport necessary as proof of identity.*

If jackets and ties are customary attire at the casino, no clothes at all are de rigueur at Baden-Baden's famous Roman baths, the **Friedrichsbad.** You take the waters here just as the Romans did nearly 2,000 years ago—nude. The remains of the Roman baths that lie beneath the

Friedrichsbad can be visited (Admission: DM 2) from April through October. *Römerpl. 1, tel. 07221/275–920. Admission: DM 28 for 3 hours (DM 38 with massage). Children under 18 not admitted. Open Mon.–Sat. 9 AM–10 PM, Sun. 2–10 PM.*

TIME OUT Step into the warm elegance of the **Café König** in the nearby Lichten-talerstrasse pedestrian zone. Order a pot of coffee and a wedge of Black Forest cake and listen to the hum of contentment from the monied spa crowd who have made this quiet corner their haunt.

The attractions of the Friedrichsbad are rivaled by the neighboring **Cara-calla Baths,** renovated and enlarged in 1985. The huge, modern complex has five indoor pools, two outdoor ones, numerous whirlpools, a solarium, and what is described as a "sauna landscape"—you look out through windows at the countryside while steaming. *Römerpl. 11, tel. 07221/275–940. Admission: DM 18 for 2 hours, DM 24 for 3 hours. Open daily 8 AM–10 PM.*

Dining and Lodging

For details and price-category definitions, *see* Dining and Lodging *in* Staying in Germany, *above.*

Baden-Baden

DINING

Stahlbad. The Gallo-Germanic menu here is echoed by the restaurant's furnishings—19th-century French oils adorn the walls, and French and German china are reflected in the mahogany gleam of antique tables and sideboards. An abundance of green velvet catches the tone of the parklike grounds of the stately house that accommodates this elegant restaurant. *Augustapl. 2, tel. 07221/ 24569. Reservations advised. AE, DC, MC, V. Closed Sun. and Mon. $$$*

DINING AND LODGING

★ **Der Kleine Prinz.** Each room of this beautifully modernized 19th-century mansion is decorated in a different style, from romantic Art Nouveau to Manhattan modern (owner Norbert Rademacher was director of New York's Waldorf-Astoria for several years). Chef Berthold Krieger is in charge of the kitchen, and by combining nouvelle cuisine flair with unmistakable German thoroughness, he has elevated the restaurant to a leading position in demanding Baden-Baden. *Lichtentalerstr. 36, tel. 07221/3464, fax 07221/38264. 39 rooms with bath. Facilities: restaurant (closed first 2 wks of Jan.). AE, DC, MC, V. $$$*

Pospisil's Merkurius. A log fire on cool days adds to the already warm atmosphere of this country-style restaurant and small hotel in the district of Varnhalt on the southern fringe of Baden-Baden. The menu offers classic and regional dishes with a light touch—goose-liver soufflé and imaginative preparations of wild hare and pheasant, for example. The wine list has an extensive selection of very fine vintages. *Klosterbergstr. 2, tel. 07223/5474, fax 07223/60996. Reservations required. No credit cards. Closed Mon. No lunch Tues. $$$*

Gasthaus zur Traube. Regional specialties such as smoked bacon and homemade noodles take pride of place in this cozy inn, south of the city center in the Neuweier district. If you like the food, you can also spend the night in one of the 18 neatly furnished and moderately priced rooms. *Mauerbergstr. 107, tel. 07223/57216. MC, V. Closed Wed. $$*

LODGING

Brenner's Park Hotel. This exceptional stately mansion is set in spacious private grounds. All rooms are luxuriously furnished and appointed—as they should be for the price. *Schillerstr. 6, tel. 07221/9000, fax 07221/38772. 68 rooms with bath and balcony, 32 suites. Facilities: 2 restaurants, beauty salon, indoor pool, sauna, bridge room, bicycles. AE, DC, MC. $$$$*

Deutscher Kaiser-Etol. This centrally located, old, established hotel, a few minutes' stroll from the Kurhaus, offers homey and individually styled rooms at comfortable prices in an otherwise expensive town. All the double rooms have balconies on a quiet street off one of the main thoroughfares. *Merkurstr. 9, tel. 07221/2700, fax 07221/ 270–270. 44 rooms with bath. Facilities: restaurant (No Sun. dinner in winter), bar, wine and beer tavern, bicycles. AE, DC, MC, V. $$*

Hotel am Markt. The Bogner family has run the place for more than three decades—a relatively short amount of time for this 250-plus-year-old building. It's friendly, popular, and right in the center of town. *Marktpl. 17–18, tel. 07221/22747, fax 07221/391–887. 28 rooms, 14 with bath or shower. Facilities: restaurant, terrace. AE, DC, MC, V. $*

Bad Liebenzell

LODGING

Thermen-Hotel. This luxurious spa hotel, on the edge of Bad Liebenzell's spa park, is an old half-timber mansion spruced up with a modern face. The Black Forest creeps to the very edge of the garden. Rooms are spacious and comfortable and most have pergolalike balconies. *Am Kurpark, tel. 07052/408–300, fax 07052/408–305. 23 rooms with bath or shower. Facilities: restaurant, garden café, terrace, fitness center, sauna, parking. MC. $$$*

Baiersbronn

DINING AND LODGING

Bareiss. The beautiful mountain resort of Baiersbronn is blessed with two of Germany's leading restaurants. The most notable is the Bareiss, in the luxury hotel of the same name. Its dark wood furniture and tapestry-papered walls are warmly lighted by candles and traditional lamps. Guests, some from across the border in Alsace, are lured by the light, classic cuisine and carefully selected wines (30 brands of champagne alone). The hotel itself is among the most luxurious and best-equipped in the Black Forest. *Gärtenbühlweg 14, Mitteltal, tel. 07442/470, fax 07442/47320. 51 rooms with bath, 42 apartments, 7 suites. Facilities: 2 restaurants, bar, 3 swimming pools, fitness room, sauna, solarium, billiards room, bowling, bikes, tennis. AE, DC, MC, V. $$$$*

Traube Tonbach. Baiersbronn's second world-class restaurant, the Schwarzwaldstube, is also part of a luxurious hotel, the Traube Tonbach. The hotel has two outstanding restaurants, and if the fabulous Schwarzwaldstube is full or too pricey, then the Köhlerstube is an acceptable alternative. In both, you dine beneath beamed ceilings at tables bright with fine silver and glassware. The hotel is a harmonious blend of old and new furnishings and decor, each room enjoying sweeping views of the Black Forest. *Tonbachstr. 237, Tonbach, tel. 07442/4920, fax 07442/492–692. 134 rooms with bath, 38 apartments, 8 suites. Facilities: 2 restaurants, bars, cafeteria, terraces, gardens, 3 swimming pools, sauna, solarium, fitness room, bowling, bikes, tennis. AE, DC, MC, V. $$$$*

Hotel Lamm. The half-timber exterior of this 200-year-old building presents a clear picture of the traditional Black Forest hotel within. Rooms are furnished with heavy oak fittings and some fine antiques. In winter, logs flicker in the open fireplace of the lounge, a welcome sight for guests coming in from the slopes (the ski lift is nearby). In its beamed restaurant, you can order fish taken from the hotel's trout pools. *Ellbacherstr. 4, tel. 07442/4980, fax 07442/49878. Facilities: restaurant, indoor pool, sauna, solarium, billiards room, table tennis. AE, DC, MC, V. $$*

Calw

DINING AND LODGING

Hotel Kloster Hirsau. This country-house hotel on the wooded outskirts of Calw stands on the site of a 900-year-old monastery, whose Gothic cloisters are still largely intact. The hotel prides itself on its award-winning restaurant, where owner-chef Joachim Ulrich's menu changes daily. The emphasis is on regional dishes enhanced with a light French touch: featured are Swabian farmhouse noodles along with truffle vinaigrette. *Wildbaderstr. 2, tel. 07051/56213, fax 07051/51795. 43 rooms with bath. Facilities: restaurant, bar, indoor pool, garden terrace, parking. DC, MC, V. $$$*

Ratsstube. Most of the original features, including 16th-century beams and brickwork, are still intact at this historic house in the center of Calw. Rooms aren't spacious but they are brightly decorated, with pastel colors and floral patterns. The restaurant offers sturdy, traditional German fare, such as marinated beef and noodles, thick soups, and Black Forest sausage. *Marktpl. 12, tel. 07051/1864, fax 07051/70826. 13 rooms with bath. Facilities: restaurant, parking. No credit cards. $$*

Freiburg

DINING

Enoteca. Three dining possibilities are now offered by the Enoteca: Lunch is served in the crowded, friendly bistro; dinner is a more leisurely affair in the adjacent restaurant, where subdued lighting glistens on honey-color paneling; and late-night diners can get light meals at the Enoteca bar, which is open until 1:30 AM. Proprietor Manfred Schmitz can be relied on to recommend just the right vintage to accompany such imaginative Italian specialties as veal roulade with Gorgonzola. *Gerberau 21–23, tel. 0761/30751. Reservations advised. AE, MC, V. Closed Sun. $$–$$$*

Oberkirchs Weinstuben. The landlord of this tavern in a small hotel facing the cathedral personally bags some of the game that ends up in the kitchen. Fresh trout is another specialty. In summer, the dark oak dining tables spill onto an outdoor terrace. *Münsterpl. 22, tel. 0761/31011. MC, V. Closed Sun., holidays, and mid-Jan.–Feb. $$*

DINING AND LODGING

Colombi. Freiburg's most luxurious hotel also has the city's finest and most original restaurant and two reconstructed 18th-century Austrian farmhouse guest cottages, now luxuriously furnished and decorated with antiques. In the rustic section of the restaurant, you can order hearty local dishes, such as lentil soup and venison, while its more elegant section's menu goes decidedly upscale combining traditional meat and fish dishes with innovative sauces. The hotel is centrally located and quiet. *Am Colombi Park/Rotteckring 16, tel. 0761/21060, fax 0761/31410. 80 rooms with bath, 12 suites. Facilities: restaurant (reservations required; closed Sun). AE, DC, MC, V. $$$–$$$$*

Zum Roten Bären. Now a showpiece of the Ring group, this inn, which dates from 1311, has retained its character with very comfortable lodging and excellent dining in a cozy warren of four restaurants and taverns. If it's a chilly evening, order a table next to the large tiled oven, which dominates the main, beamed restaurant. A tour of the two basement floors of cellars, dating from the original 12th-century foundation of the town of Freiburg and now well stocked with fine wines, is also recommended. *Oberlinden 12, tel. 0761/36913, fax 0761/36916.*

19 rooms with bath, 3 apartments. Facilities: restaurant, wine tavern, sauna, parking. AE, DC, MC, V. $$$

Markgräfler Hof. Even the French make the pilgrimage to dine in Hans Leo Kempchen's restaurant in this traditional old hotel in Freiburg's quaint pedestrian zone. Kempchen rewards travelers with special gourmet menus and unbeatable two-day deals that include accommodations, a wine tasting, and a guided tour of the city. Call well in advance to reserve rooms. *Gerberau 22, tel. 0761/32540, fax 0761/37947. 18 rooms with bath or shower. Facilities: restaurant, parking. AE, DC, MC, V. $$*

LODGING

Park Hotel Post. Good old-fashioned service gives away the age of this century-old hotel. It's on the main street between the train station and the Old Town. The Jugendstil facade, with stone balconies and copper-dome tower, has earned the building landmark status. *Eisenbahnstr. 35, tel. 0761/385–480, fax 0761/31680. 41 rooms with bath. AE, DC, MC, V. $$$*

Gasthaus und Pension Hirschen. This charming converted farmhouse has been in the possession of the Winterhalter family for four centuries, and today's Winterhalters take as much care in making their guests feel at home as did their ancestors. The pension is in the village of Wittnau, a 10-minute drive or 15-minute bus trip from Freiburg, but the disadvantages of its distance from the city are more than offset by its peaceful location amid open countryside—a walker's paradise. *Schönberg 11, 7801 Wittnau, tel. 0761/402–137. 20 rooms, most with bath. Facilities: restaurant, bowling alley, parking. No credit cards. $$*

Rappen Hotel. The Rappen is in the center of the traffic-free Old Town overlooking the marketplace and the cathedral (and overhearing the bustle of the former and the bells of the latter). A farmhouse theme dominates here, with rustic furnishings in every room. In the countrified but comfortable restaurant, patrons have the choice of more than 200 regional wines. *Am Münsterpl. 13, tel. 0761/31353, fax 0751/382–252. 25 rooms, 13 with bath. Facilities: bar-restaurant, terrace. AE, DC, MC, V. $$*

Freudenstadt

DINING

Ratskeller. If it's cold outside, ask for a place near the Ratskeller's *Kachelofen,* a large, traditional, tiled heating stove. Swabian dishes and venison are prominent on the menu, but if the homemade trout roulade with crab sauce is available, go for it. *Marktpl. 8, tel. 07441/2693. Reservations advised. MC, V. Closed Mon. $$*

DINING AND LODGING

Bären. The sturdy old Gasthof Bären has been owned by the same family since 1878, and it strives to maintain tradition and service with a personal touch. Rooms are modern but with homey touches such as farmhouse-style bedsteads and cupboards. The beam-ceiling restaurant is a favorite with the locals; its menu combines heavy German dishes (roasts and hearty sauces) and lighter international fare. *Langestr. 33, tel. 07441/2779, fax 07441/2887. 23 rooms with bath. Facilities: restaurant, parking. MC. $$–$$$*

Lutz Posthotel. This old coaching inn in the heart of town has been managed by the same family since 1809. But there's nothing old-fashioned about the rooms, which are both modern and cozy. The restaurant offers Swabian delicacies. In summer there's a coffee terrace. *Stuttgarterstr. 5, tel. 07441/2421, fax 07441/ 84533. 45 rooms with bath, some with balcony. Facilities: wine bar, library. AE, DC, MC, V. $$*

Warteck. The centrally located Warteck's Biedermeier-style restaurant is first a feast for the eye—freshly picked posies adorn the linen-covered tables and the nooks and crannies between the handsome, lead-pane windows. The imaginative menu offers succulent lamb in meadow herbs, venison with Swabian noodles, or veal in mushroom sauce. The Biedermeier style extends to the comfortable furnishings of the hotel's guest rooms as well. *Stuttgarterstr. 14, tel. 07441/7418, fax 07441/2957. 13 rooms with bath. Restaurant closed Tues.; restaurant and hotel closed November and 3 wks after Easter. DC, V. $$*

Gutach
LODGING
★ **Romantik Hotel Stollen.** The flower-bedecked balconies and low roofs of this hotel disguise a distinctive and luxurious interior, where understated comfort—some rooms have four-poster beds—is combined with attentive service. You are treated as if you were staying in a family's home rather than a hotel. The restaurant—complete with a roaring log fire—serves regional food with nouvelle touches. The hotel is 21 kilometers (15 miles) northeast of Freiburg. *79261 Gutach im Elztal, tel. 07685/207, fax 07685/1550. 11 rooms with bath and balcony, 1 suite. AE, MC, V. $$–$$$*

Hinterzarten
LODGING
★ **Park Hotel Adler.** Since 1446, when an early ancestor of the hotel's present owners gave 17 schillings for the original property, it has been developing into one of Germany's finest hotels. The hotel complex stands on nearly 10 acres of grounds ringed by the Black Forest. Among the seven rooms devoted to eating and drinking are a French restaurant and a paneled 17th-century dining room. An orchestra accompanies dinner and later moves to the bar for dancing. *Adlerpl. 3, tel. 07652/1270, fax 07652/127–717. 84 rooms with bath. Facilities: 2 restaurants, bar, pool, sauna, solarium, tennis (indoor/outdoor), horseback riding, bicycles, beauty salon, library, game rooms, child-care facilities. AE, DC, MC, V. $$$$*

Nagold
DINING
Romantik Restaurant Alte Post. This centuries-old half-timber inn has the kind of atmosphere lesser establishments believe can be built in with false beams. The menu ranges from Swabian traditional to pricey French, so stay with the local dishes (veal in a rich mushroom sauce or, in season, venison in the Baden-Baden style) and you won't be shocked by the bill. *Bahnhofstr. 2, tel. 07452/4221. Reservations required. AE, DC, MC, V. Closed two wks in Jan. and two wks in July–Aug. No lunch Fri. $$–$$$*

LODGING
Hotel Post Gästehaus. Run by the former proprietors of the adjacent Alte Post restaurant, this hotel is made up of an old coaching inn and modern additions. It offers a high degree of comfort—and homemade preserves for breakfast. *Bahnhofstr. 3, tel. 07452/4048, fax 07452/4040. 24 rooms with bath. Facilities: English-language cable TV. AE, DC, MC, V. $$–$$$*

Pforzheim
DINING
Silberburg. This is a rustic restaurant offering classic and regional cooking at bargain prices. For best value, ask to see the *Tagesempfehlungen*—the chef's daily recommendations. *Dietlingerstr. 27, tel.*

07231/41159. Reservations required. AE, DC, MC, V. Closed Mon. and 3 wks in Aug. No lunch Tues. $

Titisee

DINING AND LODGING

Romantik Hotel Adler Post. This hotel is in the Neustadt district of Titisee, about 4½ kilometers (3 miles) from the lake. The solid old building has been in the possession of the Ketterer family for more than 140 years. The guest rooms are comfortably and traditionally furnished. The hotel's restaurant, the Rôtisserie zum Postillon, is noted for its regional cuisine. *Hauptstr. 16, tel. 07651/5066, fax 07651/3729. 24 rooms, 4 apartments, all with bath. Facilities: restaurant, pool, sauna, solarium, game room, library. AE, DC, MC, V. Closed mid-Mar.–early Apr. $$*

Triberg

DINING AND LODGING

Park Hotel Wehrle. The Wehrle family has owned this enchanting building in the center of town since 1707; its vine-covered facade dominates the marketplace. The comfortable rooms are individually furnished, the service is impeccable, the restaurant is outstanding, and the prices are surprisingly low for this kind of luxury. *Am Marktpl. 1, tel. 07722/86020, fax 07722/860–290. 52 rooms, 2 apartments, 2 suites, all with bath. Facilities: cable TV, indoor/outdoor pools, sauna, fitness room, parking. AE, DC, MC, V. $$–$$$*

Römischer Kaiser. The "Roman Emperor" exudes Black Forest tradition. Rooms are comfortably furnished in solid Black Forest style, with heavy wooden bedsteads and painted furniture. The restaurant serves German and international dishes, all with a perceptible French flair. Fresh mountain trout is almost always on the menu. *Sommerauerstr. 35, Nussbach, tel. 07722/4418, fax 07722/4401. 26 rooms with bath. Facilities: restaurant (closed Mon.; no dinner Sun.), terrace, parking. AE, DC, MC, V. $$*

BERLIN

Berlin is now a united metropolis—again the largest in continental Europe—and only four small sections of the Wall have been left in place to remind visitors and residents of the hideous barrier that divided the city for nearly 30 years. Old habits die hard, however, and it will be a long time before Germans and even Berliners themselves become accustomed to regarding Berlin as one entity with one identity. You'll still hear Berliners in the western, more prosperous half talking about "those Ossies over there" when referring to people in the still down-at-the-heels eastern part. All restrictions on travel within and beyond the city have, of course, disappeared. But there's still a strong feeling of passing from one world into another when crossing the scar that marks the line where the Wall once stood. It's not just the very visible differences between the glitter of west Berlin and the relative shabbiness of the east. Somehow the historical heritage of a long-divided city permeates the place and penetrates the consciousness of every visitor.

Arriving and Departing

By Plane

Tegel (tel. 030/410–2306) airport is only 7 kilometers (4 miles) from downtown. Airlines flying to Tegel include Delta, United, Air France, British Airways, Deutsche BA, Lufthansa, and some charter specialists. Because of increased air traffic at Tegel following unification, the former military airfield at **Tempelhof** (tel. 030/691–510), even closer to downtown, is being used more and more. **Schönefeld** (tel. 030/60910) airport is about 24 kilometers (15 miles) outside the downtown area.

Bus 109 runs every 10 minutes between Tegel airport and downtown. The journey takes 30 minutes and the fare is DM 3.70 for adults, DM 2.50 for children and covers all public transportation throughout Berlin. A taxi will cost about DM 25. If you're driving from the airport, follow signs for the STADTAUTOBAHN highway. Tempelhof is right on the U-6 subway line, in the center of the city. A shuttle bus leaves Schönefeld airport every 10–15 minutes for the nearby S-Bahn station. S-Bahn trains leave every 20 minutes for the Friedrichstrasse and Zoologischer Garten stations. The trip takes about 30 minutes, and you can get off at whatever stop is nearest your hotel. The fare for this trip is DM 3.70. Taxi fare to your hotel will be about DM 40–DM 55, and the trip will take about 40 minutes. By car, follow the signs for STADTZENTRUM BERLIN.

By Train

There are six major rail routes to Berlin from the western part of the country (from Hamburg, Hannover, Köln, Frankfurt, Munich, and Nürnberg), and the network has expanded considerably, making the rest of eastern Germany more accessible. For the latest information on routes call **Deutsche Bahn** (tel. 030/19419) or inquire at the local main train station. Three people or more can often travel at discounted group rates.

Some trains now arrive at and depart from all of Berlin's four main train stations, but generally trains originating from the north and the west arrive at Friedrichstrasse and Zoologischer Garten, and those from the south and the east arrive at the Hauptbahnhof and Lichtenberg.

By Bus

Long-distance bus services link Berlin with numerous German and European cities. For travel details, if you're in Berlin, call the main bus station (Messedam, tel. 030/301–8028); if you're in other parts of Germany, inquire at the local tourist office.

By Car

The eight former "transit corridor" roads linking the western part of Germany with Berlin have been incorporated into the country-wide autobahn network, but some are ill prepared for the vast increase of motor traffic between east and west that has followed unification. Be prepared for large traffic jams, particularly on weekends. At the time of writing, speed restrictions of 100 kph (60 mph) still applied on some autobahn sections, but on others they had been raised to 120 kph (74 mph) or 130 kph (81 mph).

Getting Around

By Public Transportation

Berlin is surprisingly large, and only the center can comfortably be explored on foot. Fortunately, the city has an excellent public transportation system: A combination of U-Bahn and S-Bahn lines, buses, streetcars (in east Berlin only), and even a ferry across the Wannsee lake allows easy access to the whole city. Extensive all-night bus and streetcar services (they are marked by the letter N next to their number) operate all week, and the subway lines U-9 and U-12 run all night on weekends. For DM 3.70 (DM 2.50 children) you can buy a ticket that covers travel on the entire system for 2 hours. If you are just making a short trip, buy a **Kurzstreckentarif.** It allows you to ride six bus stops or three U-Bahn or S-Bahn stops for DM 2.50 (DM 2.00 children). A multiple ticket, valid for four trips on the entire system, costs DM 12.50 (DM 8.50 children). Or, you can pay DM 15 for a **Day Card** (no children's discount), good for 30 hours of unlimited public-transportation travel (except on the Wannsee lake ferries). The **Group Day Card,** for DM 20, offers the same benefits for two adults and as many as three children. If you're staying for more than a few days, the **Tourist Pass,** valid for a week and costing DM 40 is the best bargain. The **Berlin-WelcomeCard,** for DM 27, entitles one adult and up to three children to three days of unlimited travel and free or reduced admission for sightseeing trips, museum, theater, and other events and attractions.

All regular tickets are available from vending machines at U-Bahn and S-Bahn stations. Punch your ticket in the red machine on the platform. The Day Card, Tourist Pass, and BerlinWelcomeCard can only be bought from the main **BVG** ticket offices at the Zoologischer Garten station (Berliner Verkehrsbetriebe, tel. 030/752–7020) and at the Kleistpark U-Bahn station. For information, call the BVG or go to the information office on Hardenbergplatz, directly in front of the Bahnhof Zoo train station. If you're caught without a ticket, the fine is DM 60.

By Taxi
The base rate is DM 4, after which prices vary according to a complex tariff system. A drive along the Kurfürstendamm will cost about DM 15. Hail cabs in the street or at taxi stands, or order one by calling 030/9644, 030/210–202, 030/691–001, or 030/261–026. U-Bahn employees will call a taxi for passengers after 8 PM.

Important Addresses and Numbers

Tourist Information
The main tourist office, **Verkehrsamt Berlin,** is at the Europa Center (Budapesterstr., tel. 030/262–6031). It's open Monday–Saturday 8 AM–10:30 PM, Sunday 9–9. There are other offices at the main hall of **Tegel** airport (tel. 030/4101–3145, open daily 8 AM–11 PM); at the **Zoologischer Garten,** (tel. 030/313–9063, open Mon.–Sat. 8 AM–11 PM); and at the **Hauptbahnhof** (tel. 030/279–5209; open daily 8–8) in east Berlin.

Accommodations can be reserved at all offices, which also issue a free English-language information brochure, "Berlin Turns On." Pretravel information on Berlin can be obtained by writing to the Verkehrsamt Berlin (Martin-Luther-Str. 105, 10825 Berlin). Berlin has an information center especially for women that helps with finding accommodations and provides information on upcoming events. Contact **Fraueninfothek Berlin** (Dirchsenstr. 47, tel. 030/282–3980; open Tues.–Sat. 9–9, Sun. and public holidays 9–3.)

TIPS FOR TRAVELERS WITH DISABILITIES
Many S- and U-Bahn stations have elevators and a few buses have hydraulic lifts. Check the public transportation maps or call the **BVG** (*see above*). **Service-Ring-Berlin e.V.** (tel. 030/859–4010 or 030/9389–2410) and **Verband Geburts- und anderer Behinderter e.V.** (tel. 030/341–1797) provide information and van and wheelchair rentals.

Consulates
U.S. (Clayallee 170, tel. 030/819–7454). **Canadian** (International Trade Center, Friedrichstr. 95, tel. 030/261–1161). **U.K.** (Unter den Linden 32–34, tel. 030/201–8401). **Irish** (Ernst-Reuter-Pl. 10, tel. 030/3480-0822).

Emergencies
Police (tel. 030/110). **Ambulance and emergency medical attention** (tel. 030/310–031). **Dentist** and **emergency pharmaceutical assistance** (tel. 030/01141).

English-Language Bookstores
Marga Schoeller (Knesebeckstr. 33, tel. 030/881–1112) and **Buch-handlung Kiepert** (Hardenbergstr. 4–5, tel. 030/311–0090) sell English-language publications.

Guided Tours

By Bus
Severin & Kühn (Kurfürstendamm 216, tel. 030/883–1015); **Berliner Bären Stadtrundfahrt** (**BBS,** Rankestr. 35, corner of Kurfürstendamm, tel. 030/214–8790); **Berolina Stadtrundfahrten** (Kurfürstendamm 22, corner Meinekestr., tel. 030/882–2091); and **Bus Verkehr Berlin (BVB,** Kurfürstendamm 225, tel. 030/885–9880) offer more or less identical tours in English, covering all the major sights in Berlin, as well as day tours to Potsdam and Dresden. The Berlin tours cost DM 25–DM 45, those to Potsdam and Sanssouci Palace, the favorite residence of Frederick the Great, DM 50–DM 70. Inquire about tour operators that offer specialty (cultural, historical, walking) tours at the main city tourist office at the Europa-Center (Budapesterstr., tel. 030/262–6031).

By Boat
Berlin is a city of waterways, and boat trips can be made on the Spree River, on the canals that connect the city's network of big lakes, and on the lakes themselves. For details, contact the main city tourist office.

Exploring Berlin

Visiting Berlin is still a bittersweet experience, as so many of the triumphs and tragedies of the past are tied up with the bustling present. The result can be either dispiriting or exhilarating. By European standards, Berlin isn't that old: Köln was more than 1,000 years old when Berlin was born from the fusion of two tiny settlements on islands in the Spree River. Although already a royal residence in the 15th century, Berlin really came into its own three centuries later, under the rule of King Friedrich II—Frederick the Great—whose liberal reforms and artistic patronage led the way as the city developed into a major cultural capital.

What Berlin was forced to endure in the 20th century would have crushed the spirit of most other cities. Hitler and his supporters destroyed the city's reputation for tolerance and plunged Berlin headlong into the war that led to the wholesale destruction of monuments and houses. And after World War II, Berlin was still to face the bitter division of the city and the construction of the infamous Wall in 1961. But a storm of political events, beginning in 1989, brought the downfall of the East German communist regime; the establishment of democracy in the east; and finally, in October 1990, the unification of Berlin and of all Germany.

Numbers in the margin correspond to points of interest on the West Berlin map.

West Berlin

The **Kurfürstendamm,** or Ku'damm as the Berliners call it, is one of Europe's busiest thoroughfares, throbbing with activity day and night. At its eastern end is the **Kaiser Wilhelm Gedächtniskirche** (Kaiser Wilhelm Memorial Church). This landmark had come to symbolize West Berlin, and it still is a dramatic reminder of the futile destructiveness of war. The shell of the tower is all that remains of the church that was built at the end of the 19th century and dedicated to Kaiser Wilhelm. Surrounding the tower are the new church and bell tower, referred to as the "powder box" and the "lipstick" by Berliners. Inside is a historical exhibition of the devastation of World War II. *At Breitscheidpl., tel. 030/218–5023. Admission free. Open Tues.–Sat. 10–5, closed holidays.*

Cross Budapesterstrasse to enter the **Zoologischer Garten,** Berlin's zoo. It has the world's largest variety of individual types of fauna along with a fascinating aquarium. *Budapesterstr. 34, tel. 030/254–010. Admission to zoo only: DM 10 adults, DM 5 children; admission to aquarium only: DM 9 adults, DM 4.50 children; admission to zoo and aquarium: DM 15 adults, DM 7.50 children. Open daily 9–6:30, or to dusk in winter.*

Double back across Breitscheidplatz and take Tauentzienstrasse to Wittenbergplatz to catch Bus 142 to Kemperplatz. Among the buildings that comprise the **Kulturforum** (Cultural Forum) on the large square is the **Philharmonie** (Philharmonic Hall), home of the famous Berlin Philharmonic orchestra. You'll recognize it by its roof, which resembles a great wave. *Matthäikirchstr. 1, tel. 030/261–4383. Box office open weekdays 3:30–6, weekends 11–2.*

Opposite is the **Kunstgewerbemuseum** (Museum of Decorative Arts), which displays arts and crafts of Europe from the Middle Ages to the present day. Among its treasures is the Welfenschatz (Guelph Treasure), a collection of 16th-century gold and silver plate from Nürnberg. *Matthäikirchpl. 6, tel. 030/266–2902. Admission: DM 4 adults, DM 2 children. Free Sun. Open Tues.–Fri. 9–5, weekends 10–5.*

Leave the museum and walk south past the mid-19th-century church of St. Matthew to the **Neue Nationalgalerie** (New National Gallery), a modern glass-and-steel building designed by Mies van der Rohe and built in the mid-1960s. The gallery's collection consists of paintings, sculptures, and drawings from the 19th and 20th centuries, with an accent on works by the Impressionists. *Potsdamerstr. 50, tel. 030/266–2651. Admission: DM 4 adults, DM 2 children. Free Sun. Open Tues.–Fri. 9–5, weekends 10–5.*

A Tageskarte (Day Card), covers 1-day admission to all museums at Kulturforum. Cost: DM 8 adults, DM 4 children. Card is available at each museum.

The Kulturforum is adjacent to the 630-acre **Tiergarten** (Animal Park), once the Elector's hunting grounds, which has at last recovered from the war, when it was not only ripped apart by bombs and artillery, but was also stripped of its woods by desperate, freezing Berliners in the bitterly cold winter of 1945–46. The column in the center of a large traffic circle in the park is the **Siegessäule** (Victory Column), erected in 1873 to commemorate four Prussian military campaigns against the French. The granite and sandstone monument originally stood in front of the Reichstag (parliament building), but was moved to its present site in 1938 as part of the Nazis' grand architectural designs for Berlin. Climb the 285 steps to its 213-foot summit, and you'll be rewarded with a fine view of Berlin. *Am Grossen Stern, Admission: DM 1.50 adults, DM 1 children. Open Mon. 3–6, Tues.–Sun. 9–6.*

The wide Strasse des 17. Juni (June 17th Street) runs past the base of the Siegessäule. This street's name memorializes the day in 1953 when 50,000 East Germans staged an uprising that was put down by Soviet tanks. On the left as you come from the column, at the eastern end of **❺** the park, you'll pass the **Sowjetisches Ehrenmal** (Soviet War Memorial), a semicircular colonnade topped with a statue of a Russian soldier and flanked by what are said to be the first Soviet tanks to have fought their way into Berlin in 1945.

❻ Ahead of you is the **Brandenburger Tor** (Brandenburg Gate), built in 1788 as a victory arch for triumphant Prussian armies. The horse-drawn chariot atop the arch was reerected after the war. The monumental gate was cut off from West Berlin by the Wall, and it became a focal point of celebrations marking the reunification of Berlin and of all Germany.

❼ Just north of the Brandenburg Gate is the **Reichstag,** which served as Germany's parliament building from its completion in 1894 until 1933, when it was gutted by fire under suspicious circumstances. When the federal government relocates to Berlin (scheduled for 2000), the Bundestag, the lower house of parliament, will convene here. At the Reichstag's northeastern corner, white wooden crosses hang on a low metal fence—grim reminders of the 80 East Germans who lost their lives trying to escape to the west after the Wall was built.

❽ Walk south along where the Wall used to stand to **Potsdamer Platz** (Potsdam Square). It was one of prewar Berlin's busiest squares, but then had the distinction of being the widest expanse of no-man's-land separating East and West Berlin. Follow farther along the Wall's former course to see the real thing, one of four still-standing segments of the **❾** **❿** famous **Berliner Mauer** (Berlin Wall), just north of the **Prince-Albert-Gelände** (Prince Albert Grounds) along Niederkircherstrasse. Buildings that once stood here housed the headquarters of the Gestapo and other Nazi security organizations from 1933 until 1945. After the war, they were leveled and remained so until 1987, when what was left of the buildings was excavated and an exhibit documenting their history and Nazi atrocities was opened. *Exhibit: "Topography of Terrors," Stresemannstr. 110, tel. 030/2548–6703. Admission free. Open Tues.–Sun. 10–6. Tours by appointment only.*

The history of the hideous frontier fortification can be followed in the museum that arose at its most famous crossing point, at Friedrichstrasse, the second cross street heading east. Checkpoint Charlie, as it was known, **⓫** disappeared along with the Wall, but the **Haus am Checkpoint Charlie** (House at Checkpoint Charlie–The Wall Museum) is still there. Be sure to give yourself at least a few hours to see the many excellent exhibits and films. *Friedrichstr. 44, tel. 030/251–1031. Admission: DM 7.50 adults, DM 4.50 children. Open daily 9 AM–10 PM.*

TIME OUT Try to visualize the former Checkpoint Charlie crossing and the Wall from a window seat at **Café Adler** (Friedrichstr. 206), which bumped right up against the Wall here. The soups and salads are all tasty and cheap.

Find the nearby Hallesches Tor U-Bahn station and go four stops west on the U-3 line to Nollendorfplatz. Switch to the southbound U-4 to **⓬** get to **Rathaus Schöneberg,** the former West Berlin city hall. (In 1991 the city administration moved back to the Rotes Rathaus in the Mitte

West Berlin

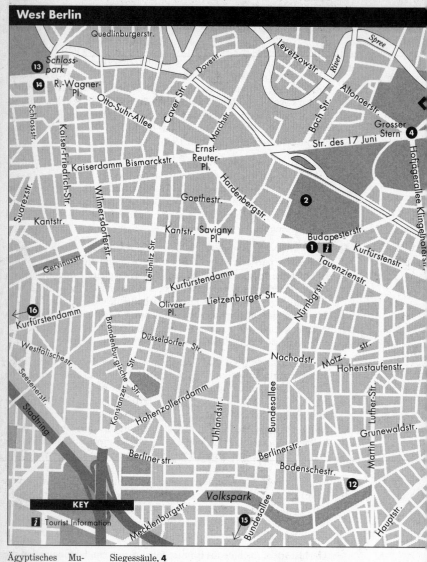

Ägyptisches Museum, **14**

Berliner Mauer, **9**

Brandenburger Tor, **6**

Gemäldegalerie, **15**

Grunewald, **16**

Haus am Checkpoint Charlie, **11**

Kaiser Wilhelm Gedächtniskirche, **1**

Kulturforum, **3**

Potsdamer Platz, **8**

Prinz-Albert-Gelände, **10**

Rathaus Schöneberg, **12**

Reichstag, **7**

Schloss Charlottenburg, **13**

Siegessäule, **4**

Sowjetisches Ehrenmal, **5**

Zoologischer Garten, **2**

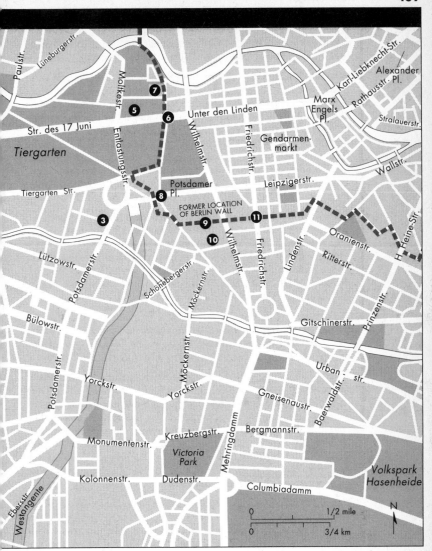

district.) In the belfry of the Rathaus is a replica of the Liberty Bell, donated to Berliners in 1950 by the United States and rung every day at noon. It was in front of the Rathaus that President Kennedy made his famous *"Ich bin ein Berliner"* speech, in the spring of 1963.

Take the U-Bahn north one stop from Rathaus Schöneberg station and change to the U-7 line for eight stops, to Richard-Wagner-Platz station.
⑬ From the station, walk east along Otto-Suhr-Allee to the handsome **Schloss Charlottenburg** (Charlottenburg Palace) and its beautiful, calming grounds, which have French and English gardens and a swan-filled pond. Built at the end of the 17th century by King Frederick I for his wife, Queen Sophie Charlotte, the palace was progressively enlarged for later royal residents. Frederick the Great's suite of rooms can be visited. *Luisenpl., tel. 030/320–911. Admission: DM 4 adults, DM 2 children. Free Sun. Open Tues.–Fri. 9–5, weekends 10–5.*

⑭ Opposite the palace is the **Ägyptisches Museum** (Egyptian Museum), home of perhaps the world's best-known portrait sculpture, the beautiful Nefertiti. The 3,300-year-old queen is the centerpiece of a fascinating collection of Egyptian antiquities that includes one of the finest preserved mummies outside Cairo. *Schlosstr. 70, tel. 030/320–911. Admission: DM 4 adults, DM 2 children. Free Sun. Open Mon.–Thurs. 9–5, weekends 10–5. Closed Fri.*

A Tageskarte (Day Card), available at the Ägyptisches Museum and the nearby Antikensammlung and Museum für Vor- and Frühgeschichte covers 1-day admission to all three museums and includes a guided tour of Schloss Charlottenburg. Cost: DM 8 adults, DM 4 children.

Take U-Bahn line U-7 back toward Schöneberg to Fehrbelliner Platz, where you change to line U-1 southwest for five stops to Dahlem-Dorf station. This is the stop for the magnificent **Dahlem museums,** chief of
⑮ which is west Berlin's leading picture gallery, the **Gemäldegalerie.** The collection includes many works by the great European masters, with 26 pieces by Rembrandt and 14 by Rubens. *Arnimallee 23/27, tel. 030/83011. Admission: DM 4 adults, DM 2 children. Combined day pass to 8 Dahlem museums: DM 8 adults, DM 4 children. Free Sun. Open Tues.–Fri. 9–5, weekends 10–5.*

No visit to west Berlin is complete without an outing to the city's out-
⑯ door playground, the **Grunewald** (Green Forest). Bordering the Dahlem district to the west, the park is a vast green space, with meadows, woodlands, and lakes. There is a string of 60 lakes within Berlin's boundaries; some are kilometers long, others are no more than ponds. The total length of their shorelines—if stretched out in one long line—is 209½ kilometers (130 miles), longer than Germany's Baltic Coast. There are nudist beaches on the banks of the Wannsee lake, and in winter a downhill ski run and even a ski jump operate on the modest slopes of the Teufelsberg hill.

East Berlin

The infamous Wall is now gone, but the specter of division remains in a city that was physically split for 28 years. The stately buildings in the former East Berlin were not as overwhelmed by new high-rise construction as their counterparts on the other side of the wall, but the east's postwar architectural blunders are just as monumental in their own way. These will be obvious—along with the sad shabbiness of years of neglect—as you explore the side streets and the main thoroughfares.

Numbers in the margin correspond to points of interest on the East Berlin map.

⑰ For a sense of times past, enter the eastern part of Berlin at **Checkpoint Charlie,** the most famous crossing point between the two Berlins during the Cold War; American and Soviet tanks faced each other here during the tense months of the Berlin Blockade in 1948. At this point both ends of Friedrichstrasse—north and south—are lined with attractive new shops and trendy restaurants.

Walk along Friedrichstrasse and turn right onto Mohrenstrasse and you'll

⑱ arrive at the **Gendarmenmarkt,** with its beautifully reconstructed **Schauspielhaus**—built in 1818, and now one of the city's main concert halls—and the twin **Deutsche und Französische Dome** (German—south side, undergoing restoration—and French cathedrals). In the

⑲ latter, you'll find the **Hugenottenmuseum** (Huguenot Museum), which has some interesting collections of the history and art of the French Protestant Huguenots who took refuge in Germany after being expelled from Catholic France in 1685. *Gendarmenmarkt, tel. 030/229–1760. Admission: DM 2 adults, DM 1 children. Open Wed., Thurs., Sat. noon–5, Sun. 1–5.*

TIME OUT The **Arkade Café** (Französischer Str. 25) on the northwest corner of the plaza is perfect for a light snack; some excellent pastry; and a beer, coffee, or tea.

Continue east along the Französischer Strasse and turn left into Hed-

⑳ wigskirchgasse to reach Bebelplatz. The peculiar round shape of **St. Hedwigs Kathedrale** (St. Hedwig's Cathedral) calls to mind Rome's Pantheon. The tiny street named Hinter der Katholischen Kirche (Behind the Catholic Church) is a reminder that though Berlin was very much a Protestant city, St. Hedwig's was built (about 1747) for Catholics.

Walk north across Bebelplatz to Unter den Linden, the elegant central

㉑ thoroughfare of Old Berlin. On your right is the **Deutsche Staatsoper** (German State Opera), the great opera house of Berlin, now with an entirely new interior. Just after Oberwallstrasse is the former crown prince's palace, the **Kronprinzenpalais,** now restored and used to house official government visitors.

Look back down the street to the western sector and you'll see the

㉒ monumental **Brandenburger Tor** (Brandenburg Gate), its chariot-and-horses sculpture now turned to face the east. Cross Unter den Linden

㉓ and look into the courtyard of **Humboldt Universität** (Humboldt University): It was built as a palace for the brother of Friedrich II of Prussia but became a university in 1810, and today is one of Germany's largest institutions of higher learning. Marx and Engels were its two most famous students. Beyond the war memorial, housed in a one-

㉔ time arsenal (built 1695–1730), is the **Deutsches Historisches Museum** (German Historical Museum), which has an exhibit tracing German history from the Middle Ages to the present. *Unter den Linden 2, tel. 030/215–020. Admission: DM 4 adults, DM 2 children. Open Thurs.–Tues. 10–6.*

Turning left along the Spree Canal (along Am Zeughaus and Am Kupfergraben) will bring you to east Berlin's museum complex, at the northern end of what is known as **Museumsinsel** (Museum Island). The

㉕ first of the Big Four that you'll encounter is the **Altes Museum** (entrance on Lustgarten), an austere neoclassical building just to the north of Schlossplatz (formerly Marx-Engels-Platz). The collections here include postwar art from some of Germany's most prominent artists and numerous etchings and drawings from the old masters. Next comes

East Berlin

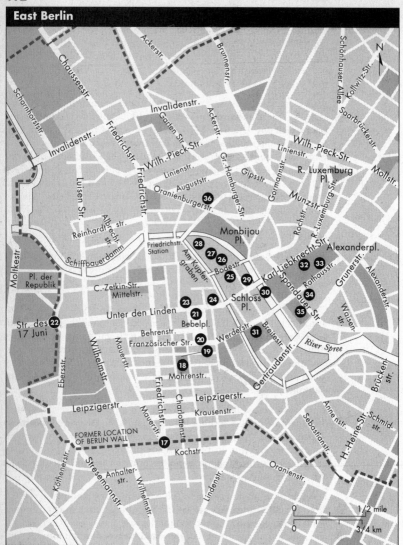

Altes Museum, **25**

Berliner Dom, **29**

Bodemuseum, **28**

Brandenburger
Tor, **22**

Checkpoint
Charlie, **17**

Deutsche
Staatsoper, **21**

Deutsches
Historisches
Museum, **24**

Fernsehturm, **33**

Gendarmenmarkt, **18**

Hugenotten
museum, **19**

Humboldt
Universität, **23**

Marienkirche, **32**

Nationalgalerie, **26**

Neue Synagoge, **36**

Nikolaikirche, **35**

Palast der
Republik, **30**

Pergamon
Museum, **27**

Rotes Rathaus, **34**

St. Hedwigs
Kathedrale, **20**

Staatsrat, **31**

㉖ the **Nationalgalerie,** on Bodestrasse, which displays 19th- and 20th-
㉗ century paintings and sculptures. The **Pergamon Museum,** on Am
Kupfergraben, is one of Europe's greatest museums. Its name is derived
from the museum's principal exhibit, the Pergamon Altar, a monumental
Greek altar dating from 180 BC that occupies an entire city block. Almost as impressive is the Babylonian Processional Way. The Pergamon
Museum also has vast Egyptian, early Christian, and Byzantine collections, plus a fine array of sculpture from the 12th to 18th centuries.
㉘ To the north is the **Bodemuseum** (also on Am Kupfergraben, but with
its entrance on Monbijoubrücke), with an outstanding collection of early
Christian, Byzantine, and Egyptian art, as well as exhibits of Italian
old masters' paintings. *For all of Museumsinsel: tel. 030/ 203–550.*
Admission to each museum: DM 4 adults, DM 2 children. Combined
day pass to 4 Museumsinsel museums: DM 8 adults, DM 4 children.
Free Sun. Museum complex open Tues.–Sun. 9–5.

From the museum complex, follow the Spree River south to Unter den
㉙ Linden and the vast **Berliner Dom** (Berlin Cathedral). The cathedral's
impressive nave was reopened in June 1993 after a 20-year renovation.
The hideous modern building in bronze mirrored glass opposite is the
㉚ **Palast der Republik** (Palace of the Republic), a postwar monument to
socialist progress that also housed restaurants, a theater, and a dance
hall. Since 1991 the Palast has been closed while the politicians argue
about whether it should be torn down or used for other purposes. It
formerly housed the Volkskammer, East Germany's People's Chamber
(parliament). The building at the south end of Schlossplatz used to house
㉛ East Germany's **Staatsrat** (federal senate). From the balcony of the preserved older entrance, on November 9, 1919, Karl Liebknecht declared the birth of the doomed German Communist Republic.

Head east on Karl-Liebknecht-Strasse for a closer look at the 13th-cen-
㉜ tury **Marienkirche** (Church of St. Mary), especially noting its late-
Gothic *Dance of Death* fresco. You are now at the lower end of
㉝ Alexanderplatz. Just ahead is the massive **Fernsehturm** (TV Tower), which
stands 1,198 feet high (not accidentally 710 feet *higher* than west
Berlin's broadcasting tower). Its observation deck affords the best
view of Berlin; the city's highest café, which rotates, is also up there.
Alexanderpl., tel. 030/242–3333. Admission: 6 DM adults, 3 DM chil-
dren. Open daily 9 AM–midnight.

TIME OUT If it's a cold day, escape the keen wind that almost always seems to
sweep across Alexanderplatz in the winter months and dodge into **Café
Mosaik** (Rathausstr. 5) for one of their tasty coffee specialties. In summer
enjoy a glass of one of their superb French wines. This cozy café has a
thoroughly French feel, and serves breakfast until 8 PM for later risers.

㉞ The red building southwest of the tower is the **Rotes Rathaus** (Red
City Hall). The redbrick building's design and the frieze depicting scenes
from the city's history are impressive. In the fall of 1991 the city administration and seat of the governing mayor were transferred from
Rathaus Schöneberg back to the Rotes Rathaus, renewing its prewar
function. The area adjacent to the Rathaus, known as the **Nikolai Viertel** (Nikolai Quarter), has been handsomely rebuilt and is now filled
with delightful shops, cafés, and restaurants. On the quarter's Probst
㉟ Strasse is Berlin's oldest building, the **Nikolaikirche** (St. Nicholas
Church). Dating from 1230, it was heavily damaged in the war, but
has been beautifully restored and is now a museum. Wander back
down Muhlendamm into the area around the Breitestrasse—there are
some lovely old buildings here—and on over to the **Fischerinsel** area.

The throbbing heart of Old Berlin of 750 years ago, Fischerinsel retains a tangible medieval flavor.

Take the U-2 subway from Märkisches Museum station three stops to Stadtmitte, then change to the U-6, traveling three stops to Oranienburger Tor. Walk a few blocks down Oranienburger Strasse to reach the **Neue Synagoge.** Completed in 1866, in Middle Eastern style, the synagogue was one of Germany's most beautiful until it was seriously damaged on November 9, 1938, the infamous *Kristallnacht* (crystal night) when synagogues and Jewish stores across Germany were vandalized, looted, and burned. Nearly destroyed by Allied bombing in 1943, it remained a ruin until renovation began under the East German regime in the mid-'80s. Today only the facade remains and it is connected to the Centrum Judaicum (Jewish Center)—a center for Jewish culture and learning.

The area to the northeast of the synagogue is known as the **Scheunenviertel** (Stable Quarters) or **Jüdisches Viertel** (Jewish Quarter). Jews, brought into the country by the Great Elector to improve his trade and finance situation, first moved here during the second half of the 17th century. In the 1880s many Eastern European Jews escaping pogroms settled here, and by the 20th century, the quarter had a number of bars, stores, and small businesses. Jewish religious and business life flourished here until 1933, when the Nazis conducted their first raid and made arrests. After the conference on "The Final Solution of the Jewish Question" in 1942, deportation of the city's Jews began in earnest.

Shopping

Fine porcelain is still produced at the former Royal Prussian Porcelain Factory, now called **Staatliche Porzellan Manufactur,** or KPM. This delicate, handmade, hand-painted china is sold at KPM's store at Kurfürstendamm 26A (tel. 030/881–1802), but it may be more fun to visit the factory salesroom at Wegelystrasse 1. It sells seconds at reduced prices. If you long to have the Egyptian queen Nefertiti on your mantlepiece at home, try the **Gipsformerei der Staatlichen Museen Preussicher Kulturbesitz** (Sophie-Charlotte-Str. 17, tel. 030/321–7011, open weekdays 9–4). It sells plaster casts of this and other treasures from the city's museums.

Shopping Districts

The liveliest and most famous shopping area in west Berlin is the **Kurfürstendamm** and its side streets, especially between **Breitscheidplatz** and **Oliver Platz.** The **Europa Center** at Breitscheidplatz encompasses more than 100 stores, cafés, and restaurants—this is not a place to bargain-hunt, though! Running east from Breitscheidplatz is **Tauenzientstrasse,** another shopping street. Elegant malls include the **Gloria Galerie** (opposite the Wertheim department store on the Ku'damm) and the **Uhland-Passage** (connecting Uhlandstrasse and Fasanenstrasse). In both, you'll find leading name stores as well as cafés and restaurants.

For trendier clothes, try the boutiques along **Bleibtreustrasse.** One of the more avant-garde fashion boutiques is **Durchbruch** (Schlutterstr. 54), around the corner. Less trendy and much less expensive is the shopping strip along **Wilmersdorferstrasse** (U-7 station of same name), where price-conscious Berliners do their shopping. It's packed on weekends.

East Berlin's chief shopping areas are along the **Friedrichstrasse, Unter den Linden,** and in the area around **Alexanderplatz.** The **Berliner Markthalle** (corner Karl-Liebknecht-Str. and Rosa-Luxemburg-Str.) is one of the east's newest and largest malls.

Department Stores

The classiest department store in Berlin is **KaDeWe,** the Kaufhaus des Westens (Department Store of the West, as it's modestly known in English), at Wittenbergplatz. Be sure to check out the food department, which occupies the whole sixth floor. The other main department store downtown is **Wertheim** on the Ku'damm. Neither as big nor as attractive as KaDeWe, Wertheim nonetheless has a large selection of fine wares. The main department store in east Berlin is **Kaufhof** (formerly Centrum), at the north end of Alexanderplatz. Under the old regime, you could find ridiculously cheap subsidized prices here. Now it is filled with mainly Western-made products—superior, but more expensive.

Antiques

On Saturdays and Sundays from 10 to 5, the colorful and lively antiques and handicrafts fair on Strasse des 17. Juni swings into action. Don't expect to pick up any bargains—or to have the place to yourself. Not far from Wittenbergplatz is **Keithstrasse,** a street given over to antiques stores. Eisenacherstrasse, Fuggerstrasse, Kalckreuthstrasse, Motzstrasse, and Nollendorfstrasse—all close to Nollendorfplatz—have many antiques stores of varying quality. Another good street for antiques is **Suarezstrasse,** between Kantstrasse and Bismarckstrasse. Antiques are also sold in the Nikolai Quarter, at the **Berliner Antikenmarkt** under the tracks at Friedrichstrasse, and in the restored Husemannstrasse. Some private stores along the stretch of Friedrichstrasse north of the Spree Bridge sell old books and prints.

Dining

Dining in Berlin can mean sophisticated nouvelle creations in upscale restaurants with linen tablecloths and hand-painted porcelain plates or hearty local specialties in atmospheric and inexpensive inns. The range is as vast as the city. Specialties include *Eisbein mit* (with knuckle of pork) sauerkraut, *Rouladen* (rolled stuffed beef), Spanferkel, *Berliner Schüsselsülze* (potted meat in aspic), *Schlachtplatte* (mixed grill), *Hackepeter* (ground beef), and *Kartoffelpuffer* (fried potato cakes). *Bockwurst* is a chubby frankfurter that's served in a variety of ways and sold in restaurants and at Bockwurst stands all over the city. *Schlesisches Himmlreich* is roast goose or pork served with potato dumplings in rich gravy. *Königsberger Klopse* consists of meatballs, herring, and capers—it tastes much better than it sounds.

East Berlin now has some of the city's most fashionable and expensive restaurants, ranging from French and new German cuisine to even more exotic fare, such as Japanese, Thai, and Indonesian; most of the restaurants featuring the national cuisine of other onetime socialist states are now gone. Wines and spirits imported from other former East Bloc countries can still be found in many restaurants, however, and are quite good; try Hungarian, Balkan, and Bulgarian wines (the whites are lighter), and Polish and Russian vodkas.

For details and price-category definitions, *see* Dining *in* Staying in Germany, *above.*

$$$$ **Bamberger Reiter.** Considered by Berliners to be one of the city's best
★ restaurants, Bamberger Reiter is the pride of its chef, Tyrolean Franz Raneburger. He relies heavily on fresh market produce for his *neue deutsche Küche* (new German cuisine), so the menu changes from day to day. Fresh flowers, too, abound in his attractive, oak-beamed restaurant. *Regensburgerstr. 7, tel. 030/218–4282. Reservations required. AE, DC, V. Dinner only. Closed Sun., Mon., Jan. 1–15.*

$$$$ Ermeler-Haus. The rococo grandeur of this wine restaurant reflects the elegance of the restored patrician home whose upper floors it occupies. The restaurant's atmosphere is subdued and formal, the wines are imported, and the service and German cuisine are excellent. There's dancing every Saturday evening. *Märkisches Ufer 12, tel. 030/279–4028. Reservations advised. AE, DC, MC, V. Closed Mon.*

$$$$ Frühsammer's Restaurant an der Rehwiese. From your table you can watch chef Peter Frühsammer at work in his open kitchen. He's ready with advice on the daily menu; salmon is always a treat here. The restaurant is in the annex of a turn-of-the-century villa in the southern district of Zehlendorf (U-Bahn to Krumme Lanke and then Bus 53 to Rehwiese). *Matterhornstr. 101, tel. 030/803–8032. Reservations advised. AE, MC. Dinner only.*

$$$ Borchardt. This fashionable meeting place has columns, red plush benches, and an art nouveau mosaic, all of which help create the impression of a 1920s salon. The restaurant serves entrées that are prepared with a French accent, and it's also well known for its luscious seafood platter (DM 58). Try the whiskey parfait with honey sauce for dessert. *Französischer Str. 47, tel. 030/229–3144. Reservations advised. AE, MC, V.*

$$$ Paris Bar. This top-class restaurant in Charlottenburg attracts a polyglot clientele of film stars, artists, entrepreneurs, and executives. The cuisine is high-powered, high-quality French. *Kantstr. 152, tel. 030/313–8052. Reservations advised. AE.*

$$ Alt-Nürnberg. Step into the tavernlike interior and you could be in Bavaria: The waitresses even wear dirndls. The Bavarian colors of blue and white are everywhere, and such Bavarian culinary delights as *Schweinshaxe* (knuckle of pork) are well represented on the menu. If you prefer to eat in the Prussian style, the calves' liver *Berliner Art* (Berlin style) is recommended. *Europa Center, tel. 030/261–4397. Reservations advised. AE, DC, MC, V.*

$$ Blockhaus Nikolskoe. Prussian King Frederick Wilhelm III built this
★ Russian-style wooden lodge for his daughter Charlotte, wife of Russia's Czar Nicholas I. In character with its history and appearance, the Blockhaus features game dishes. It's in the southwest of the city, on the eastern edge of Glienicke Park, with an open terrace (in summer) overlooking the Havel River. *Nikolskoer Weg, tel. 030/805–2914. Reservations advised. DC, MC, V. Closed Thurs.*

$$ Reinhard's. This restaurant in the Nikolai Quarter is one the city's newer popular eating establishments. Berliners of all stripes meet here to enjoy the carefully prepared entrées and to sample spirits from the amply stocked bar. It's all served to you by friendly waiters wearing bright ties. The honey-glazed breast of duck is one of the house specialties. *Poststr. 28, tel. 030/242–5295. Dinner reservations advised. AE, DC, MC, V.*

$$ Samâdhi. This quaint restaurant just north of Savigny Platz serves a wide variety of vegetarian Southeast Asian food. The soft lighting and sparse interior don't exactly transport you to Asia, but you'll feel its presence once you sample some of the delicately prepared food. One of eight soups the restaurant offers, the Thai coconut soup with tofu is smoothness embodied, and at DM 5 their fried banana dessert is a bargain. *Goethestr. 6, tel. 030/313–1067. Dinner reservations advised. No credit cards.*

$$ Turmstuben. Tucked away below the cupola of the French Cathedral,
★ which sits on the north side of the beautiful Gendarmenmarkt, this restaurant is approached by a long, winding staircase. The reward at the top of the stairs is a table in one of Berlin's most original and attractive restaurants. The menu is as short as the stairway is long, but there's

an impressive wine list. *Gendarmenmarkt, tel. 030/229–9313. Weekend reservations advised (the frustration of being turned away after that climb could spoil anyone's day). MC, V.*

$$ **Zur Rippe.** This famous eating place in the Nikolai Quarter serves wholesome food in an intimate oak-paneled, ceramic-tile setting. Specialties include Eisbein and herring casserole. *Poststr. 17, tel. 030/242–4248. AE, DC, MC, V.*

$ **Alt-Cöllner Schankstuben.** A tiny restaurant and Kneipe are contained within this charming, historic Berlin house. The menu is relatively limited, but the quality, like the service, is good. *Friedrichsgracht 50, tel. 030/242–5972. AE, DC, MC, V.*

$ **Eierschale (II).** This is one of the better breakfast cafés, just off the Ku'-damm. In the evenings, it serves mostly Berlin fare and features jazz bands in an adjoining room. Sunday mornings are Frühschoppen time, when live jazz accompanies the buffet brunch. *Rankestr. 1, tel. 030/882–5305. AE, DC, MC, V.*

$ **Thürnagel.** The great food served in this vegetarian restaurant in the Kreuzberg district makes healthful eating fun. The *seitan* (vegetable protein) in sherry sauce and the tempeh curry are good enough to convert a seasoned carnivore. *Gneisenaustr. 57, tel. 030/691–4800. Reservations advised. No credit cards. Dinner only.*

$ **Zur Letzten Instanz.** Established in 1621, Berlin's oldest restaurant
★ combines the charming atmosphere of Old-World Berlin with a limited (but tasty) choice of dishes. The emphasis here is on beer, both in the recipes and in the mug. Service can be erratic, though engagingly friendly. *Waisenstr. 14–16, tel. 030/242–5528. Reservations advised. AE, DC, MC, V.*

Lodging

Berlin lost all its grand old luxury hotels in the bombing during World War II; though some were rebuilt, many of the best hotels today are modern. For first-class or luxury accommodations, east Berlin is easily as good as the western part of the city, because the East German government, eager for hard currency, built several elegant hotels—the Grand, Radisson, and Hilton—which are up to the very best international standards and place in the very top price category. For something more moderate, the better choice may be west Berlin, where there are large numbers of good-value pensions and small hotels, many of them in older buildings with some character. The hostels run by the Evangelical Lutheran church in east Berlin also offer outstanding value for your money.

Business conventions year-round and the influx of summer tourists mean that you should make reservations well in advance. If you arrive without reservations, consult the board at Tegel Airport that shows hotels with vacancies, or go to the tourist office.

Add DM 50 to the price chart categories given in Lodging *in* Staying in Germany, *above.*

$$$$ **Berlin Hilton.** One of Berlin's newer hotels, the Hilton is on the beautiful Gendarmenmarkt in the center of east Berlin. The rooms have heated tubs; house facilities are equally plush. *Gendarmenmarkt, tel. 030/23820, fax 030/2382–4269. 355 rooms with bath, 24 suites. Facilities: 3 restaurants, cafeteria, winter garden, pub, 2 bars, discotheque, pool, sauna, solarium, masseur, health club, bowling, squash, beauty salon, shop, 24-hr room service, garage, car rental. AE, DC, MC, V.*

$$$$ Bristol Hotel Kempinski. This grand hotel in the heart of the city has the best of Berlin's shopping on its doorstep. All the rooms and suites are luxuriously decorated and equipped, with marble bathrooms, air-conditioning, and cable TV. English-style furnishings give the "Kempi" an added touch of class. Children under 12 stay for free if they share their parents' room. *Kurfürstendamm 27, tel. 030/884–340, fax 030/883–6075. 315 rooms with bath, 52 suites. Facilities: 3 restaurants, bar, garden room, winter garden, indoor pool, sauna, fitness room, solarium, masseur, hairdresser, boutiques, 24-hr room service, limousine service. AE, DC, MC, V.*

$$$$ Grand Hotel Esplanade. The Grand Hotel Esplanade exudes luxury. Uncompromisingly modern architecture, chicly styled rooms, and works of art by some of Berlin's most acclaimed artists are some of its outstanding visual aspects. Then there are the superb facilities and impeccable service. *Lützowufer 15, tel. 030/254–780, fax 030/265–1171. 369 rooms with bath, 33 suites. Facilities: 2 restaurants, pub, bar, poolside bar, pool, sauna, whirlpool, steam bath, solarium, fitness center, masseur, hairdresser, boutique, 24-hr room service, bicycles, library. AE, DC, MC, V.*

$$$$ Inter-Continental Berlin. In conjunction with the recent addition of a
★ major conference center, the whole hotel was substantially improved. Rooms and suites are all of the highest standard and their decor shows exquisite taste. The lobby is a quarter the size of a football field, opulently furnished, and just the place for afternoon tea and pastries. The newly opened L.A. Cafe serves California cuisine. *Budapesterstr. 2, tel. 030/26020, fax 030/2602–80760. 511 rooms with bath, 70 suites. Facilities: 3 restaurants (including rooftop garden), 2 bars, indoor pool, whirlpool, sauna, no-smoking floor, 24-hr room service, boutiques. AE, DC, MC, V.*

$$$$ Maritim Grand Hotel. East Berlin's most expensive hotel lives up to its
★ name—it's grand in every sense of the word. From the moment you step into the atrium lobby, you're surrounded by luxury. You'll wonder how this grandiose bit of capitalist decadence ever fit into a socialist society. *Friedrichstr. 158–164, corner Behrenstr., tel. 030/23270, fax 030/2327–3362. 358 rooms with bath, 36 suites. Facilities: 4 restaurants, concert café, 2 bars, pool, sauna, solarium, fitness room, shopping arcade, hairdresser, 24-hr room service, no-smoking floor, garage. AE, DC, MC, V.*

$$$$ Maritim proArte Hotel Berlin. French designer Philippe Starck (responsible for Manhattan's Paramount and Royalton hotels) took the old Metropol Hotel and transformed it into this modern, futuristic hotel. It's still a choice facility for business travelers, with a large desk, two telephones, and fax and PC connections in every room, but you don't have to be one to enjoy the luxury. *Friedrichstr. 150–153, tel. 030/23875, fax 030/2387–4209. 403 rooms with bath, 29 suites. Facilities: 3 restaurants, bar, pool, sauna, solarium, masseur, fitness room, hairdresser, boutiques, no-smoking floors, garage. AE, DC, MC, V.*

$$$$ Steigenberger Berlin. The Steigenberger group's exemplary Berlin hotel is only a few steps from the Ku'damm, but inside it's remarkably quiet. Small touches that lift the hotel above the usual run of chain establishments include a safe in every room and complimentary shoe-shine service. *Los-Angeles-Pl. 1, tel. 030/21270, fax 030/212–7117. 397 rooms with bath, 11 suites. Facilities: 2 restaurants, 2 cafés, 2 bars, tavern, indoor pool, poolside bar, sauna, solarium, masseur, hairdresser, boutique, 24-hr room service, no-smoking floor. AE, DC, MC, V.*

$$$ Berlin Excelsior Hotel. The Ku'damm is just a five-minute walk from this modern establishment. It's well-run—office staff will arrange sightseeing tours and will try to obtain hard-to-get theater and concert tickets—and rooms are comfortable, with dark teak furnishings. *Hardenbergerstr. 14, tel. 030/31550, fax 030/3155–1002. 320 rooms with bath. Facilities: 2 restaurants, bar, garden terrace, winter garden, garage. AE, DC, MC, V.*

$$$ **Berlin Hilton Krone.** The Krone is part of the Hilton Hotel complex, sharing the Hilton's excellent location on east Berlin's beautiful Gendarmenmarkt but not its high prices. The rooms are not as lavish, but they are all comfortable and adequately furnished, and Krone guests can use all the Hilton facilities free of charge. *Mohrenstr. 30, tel. 030/23820, fax 030/2382–4269. 148 rooms with bath. Facilities:* see *Berlin Hilton,* above. *AE, DC, MC, V.*

$$$ **Forum Hotel.** With its 40 stories, the Forum Hotel competes with the nearby TV tower for the title of premier downtown landmark. As the city's largest hotel, it is understandably somewhat impersonal, although a recent renovation of all public areas has made the atmosphere more welcoming. The high-level dining room, Panorama 37, has good food, good service, and stunning views; reservations are essential. *Alexanderpl., tel. 030/23890, fax 030/2389–4305. 943 rooms with bath, 14 suites. Facilities: 3 restaurants, bar, casino, solarium, fitness room, no-smoking floors, garage. AE, DC, MC, V.*

$$$ **Hotel Berlin.** The hotel that bears Berlin's name has a bright and light look, furnished in enduring, understated good taste. The location is handy for both the Ku'damm and Unter den Linden. *Lützowpl. 17, tel. 030/260–50, fax 030/260–52716. 490 rooms with bath, 21 suites. Facilities: restaurant, beer tavern, piano bar, summer terrace, sauna, solarium, masseur, fitness room, beauty center, boutiques. AE, DC, MC, V.*

$$ **Hotel Casino.** Large, comfortable, well-equipped rooms here belie the hotel's former role—as a Prussian military barracks. The soldiers never had it so good. The hotel is in the Charlottenburg district. *Königin-Elisabeth-Str. 47a, tel. 030/303–090, fax 030/303–0945. 23 rooms with bath. Facilities: all-night snack bar. AE, DC, MC, V.*

$$ **Märkischer Hof.** All of downtown Berlin is within walking distance of this small hotel conveniently located just off Friedrichstrasse. The rooms are fairly large and cheerfully furnished. *Linienstr. 133, tel. 030/282–7155, fax 030/282–4331. 20 rooms, most with bath. AE, MC, V.*

$$ **Ravenna.** This small, friendly hotel is in the Steglitz district, close to
★ the Botanical Garden and the Dahlem museums. All the rooms are well equipped, but Suite 111B is the best bargain: It includes a large living room and kitchen for the rate of only DM 305. *Grunewaldstr. 8–9, tel. 030/790–910, fax 030/794–412. 55 rooms with bath or shower, 4 suites. Facilities: restaurant, bar. AE, DC, MC, V.*

$$ **Riehmers Hofgarten.** A few minutes' walk from the Kreuzberg hill and surrounded by the colorful district's bars and restaurants, this hotel also has fast connections to the center of town. The 19th-century building's high-ceiling rooms are elegantly furnished. *Yorckstr. 83, tel. 030/781–011, fax 030/786–6059. 21 rooms with bath or shower. Facilities: restaurant, bar. AE, DC, MC, V.*

$ **Econtel.** Families are well cared for here, but lone travelers will also appreciate the touches in the rooms, which come with free closet safes and cable. The breakfast buffet offers a dazzling array of choices and will fill you up for a day of sightseeing—perhaps at nearby Charlottenburg Palace. *Sommeringstr. 24, tel. 030/346–810, fax 030/344–7034. 205 rooms with bath or shower. Facilities: bar. AE, MC, V.*

$ **Gendarm Garni Hotel.** This well-run hotel is also near the Gendarmenmarkt. All the rooms are neat and pleasantly furnished. Ask for the corner suite facing the square; the view and the large living room make it one of the better deals in town (DM 225). *Charlottenstr. 60, tel. 030/200–4180, fax 030/208–2482. 25 rooms with bath, 4 suites. Facilities: lobby bar. AE, MC, V.*

$ Hotel Merkur. Service at this small hotel is friendly, and the rooms are comfortable, equipped with such extras as minibars, safes, radio, and TVs. The Merkur is in central east Berlin's Prenzlauerberg district, within walking distance of downtown east Berlin and Museum Island. *Torstr. 156, tel. 030/282–8297. 16 rooms, some with bath. AE, DC, MC, V.*

The Arts

The quality of opera and classical concerts in Berlin is high. Tickets are available at the theaters' own box offices, either in advance or an hour before the performance, at many hotels, and at numerous ticket agencies, including **Ticket Counter** (in Europa Center, tel. 030/264–1138); **Hekticket** (Alexanderpl.); **Theaterkasse Centrum** (Meinekestr. 25, tel. 030/882–7611); and the **Top Ticket** branches (in all major stores, such as Hertie, Wertheim, and KaDeWe). Check the monthly publication *Berlin Programm* for a detailed guide to what's going on in the arts while you're here.

Concerts
The Berlin Philharmonic, one of the world's leading orchestras, performs in the **Philharmonie** (Matthäikirchstr. 1, tel. 030/261–4383). It plays a major role in the annual festival months of August, September, and October. The east's venue is **Konzerthaus Berlin** (in the Schauspielhaus at Gendarmenmarkt, tel. 030/2030–92100).

Opera and Ballet
The **Deutsche Oper** (Bismarckstr. 35, tel. 030/341–0249), by the U-Bahn stop of the same name, is the home of opera and ballet companies. Other performances are given at **Deutsche Staatsoper** (Unter den Linden 7, tel. 030/200–4762) and **Komische Oper** (Behrenstr. 55–57, tel. 030/229–2555).

Musicals
Metropol Theater (Friedrichstr. 101, tel. 030/2036–4117).

Nightlife

Nightlife in west Berlin is no halfhearted affair. It starts late (from 9 PM) and runs until breakfast. Almost 50 Kneipen have live music of one kind or another, and there are numerous small cabaret clubs and discos. The heart of this nocturnal scene is the Kurfürstendamm, but some of the best bars and discos are around Nollendorfplatz (try the **Metropol** for late-night dancing on weekends, Nollendorfpl. 5) in Schöneberg, and along Oranienstrasse and Wienerstrasse in Kreuzberg (head straight for the secret back room at **Bierhimmel,** Oranienstr. 183).

West Berlin is still Germany's drag-show capital, as you'll see if you go to **Chez Nous** (Marburgerstr. 14). It's essential to book ahead (tel. 030/213–1810). The women are for real next door (No. 15) at the **Scotch Club 13.**

Berlin is a major center for jazz in Europe. If you're visiting in the fall, call the tourist office for details of the annual international Jazz Fest. Throughout the year a variety of jazz groups appear at the **Eierschale** (Podbielskiallee 50) and **Quasimodo** (Kantstr. 12a).

Nightlife in east Berlin offers just as much excitement and variety as that in the west, and new bars and clubs open almost weekly. Most of

the action is in Mitte along Oranienburgerstrasse and points north—
Zosch (Tucholskystr. 30) has a great basement bar—and in Prenz-
lauerberg along Knaackstrasse and around Kollwitzpl. **Café Westfall**
(Kollwitzstr. 64) is one of few places left over from communist days.
For clubs with music and atmosphere, try one of the following: **Check-
point** (Leipzigerstr. 55); **Franz** (Schönhauser Allee 36–39); **Knaack**
(Greifswalderstr. 224); **Sophienklubb** (Sophienstr. 6); **Tacheles** (Oranien-
burgerstr. 53–56).

SAXONY AND THURINGIA

Saxony and Thuringia—just those names conjure up images of kingdoms and forest legends, of cultural riches and booming industrial enterprises. Today's reality is markedly less glamorous. Isolated from the
West for decades, these two regions in eastern Germany are now strug-
gling to make the transition from state-planned economies to a free-
market system.

Since German reunification, Saxony has thrown open its doors to visitors. Tourists are proudly conducted around the world-famous
porcelain factory in Meissen. In Colditz, a small town southeast of
Leipzig, foreigners are courteously shown the town's forbidding castle, which during World War II housed captured Allied officers.
Leipzig may be renowned for its East–West trade fairs, but its true
fame lies in its music and literary tradition, proudly upheld by the
internationally famous Gewandhaus Orchestra and by its annual
book fair.

Thuringia's fame, it is sometimes said, begins and ends with its vast
green forests, an unfair assessment given its many other historical
facets and the fact that for centuries it was the home of dozens of kingdoms. Back in the 14th century, Thuringia was known as the Rynestig
or Rennsteig (literally, "fast trail"), when it attracted traders from the
dark forested depths of the Thüringer Wald (Woods) to the prosper-
ing towns of Erfurt (today the state capital), Eisenach, and Weimar,
then already 600 years old. It was in Weimar in 1777 that the privy
councillor and poet Johann Wolfgang von Goethe was inspired by the
pristine beauties of the 168 kilometers (104 miles) of the Rennsteig to
write that "tranquility crowns all its peaks."

Getting Around

By Car
Some 1,600 kilometers (1,000 miles) of autobahn and 11,300 kilometers
(7,000 miles) of secondary roads crisscross the five new federal states
in the east. Resurfacing of some of the communist-built highways has
now resulted in the lifting of the previous strictly enforced 100 kph
(62 mph) speed limits on autobahns. Gas stations can be scarce on back
roads, so be careful not to let fuel reserves get too low.

By Train
The railway systems of the former East and West Germany have now
been completely fused, although many stretches of line in Saxony and
Thuringia are still being modernized and electrified. InterCity and EuroCity trains connect Dresden and Leipzig with Berlin and other major
German cities, with InterRegio services completing the express network;
older and slower D- and E-class trains connect smaller towns.

Saxony and Thuringia

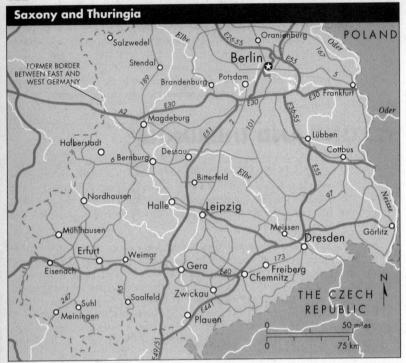

Leipzig has an S-Bahn system. Tickets must be obtained in advance, at various prices according to the number of rides in a block. Get S-Bahn tickets at the main railway station.

By Bus and Streetcar

Within Saxony and Thuringia, most areas are accessible by bus, but service is infrequent and serves chiefly to connect with rail lines. Check schedules carefully. In Dresden, Leipzig, and Weimar, public buses and streetcars are cheap and efficient.

By Taxi

Taxis in Dresden are inexpensive, but the city is small and walking is the best way to discover its hidden surprises. Leipzig has more cabs than any other eastern German city because of the number needed to cope with peak traffic at fair time. Weimar's chief attractions are within walking distance, but you may want to take a taxi from the main train station, which is somewhat removed from the city center.

By Boat

The **Weisse Flotte** (White Fleet) of inland boats, including paddle side-wheelers, ply the river Elbe, starting in Dresden or at the beautiful forested border town of Bad Schandau, and on into the Czech Republic. **KD River Cruises of Europe** (2500 Westchester Ave., Purchase, NY 10577, tel. 914/696–3600; 323 Geary St., Suite 603, San Francisco, tel. 415/392–8817) operates luxury cruises in both directions on the Elbe from May to October.

Tourist Information

Dresden (Pragerstr. 10–11, tel. 0351/495–5025). A museum card good for one day and covering admission to all museums in the

Staatlichen Kunstsammlungen, including the museums at the Albertinum and the Zwinger, is available at the participating institutions. The card costs DM 10 for adults, DM 5 for children.

Leipzig (Sachsenpl. 1, tel. 0341/71040).

Weimar (Marktstr. 4, tel. 03643/24000).

Guided Tours

The tourist information office in **Leipzig** leads regularly scheduled bus and tram tours of the city. Daily two-hour bus tours leave from near the tourist office at Am Brühl at 1:30 PM (additional tours in summer at 10 AM); reservations are advised (tel. 0341/79590). The cost is DM 20 adults, DM 10 children. Walking tours start from the Thomaskirche at 4 and 7, and cost DM 10.

Nine tours daily of **Dresden** and the surrounding countryside (as far as Pillnitz Palace) are organized by the tourist office. Buses depart from the central Postplatz (near the main post office) and stop en route at the Augustusbrücke. Two-hour city tours (10:30, 12:30, and 2:30) cost DM 29 (DM 15 children). Day tours to Prague (DM 89) and Meissen (DM 58) are also offered.

Walking tours of **Weimar** start from outside the tourist office, Weimar-Information, daily at 11 and 4. Cost is DM 5 adults and DM 2.50 children. The tourist office can also arrange individual tours of the city.

Exploring Dresden

Dresden, superbly located on the banks of the River Elbe, suffered appalling damage during World War II but has been lovingly rebuilt. Italianate influences are everywhere, most pronounced in the glorious Rococo and Baroque buildings in pastel shades of yellow and green. Although many of Dresden's architectural and cultural treasures were destroyed during a fateful night of British bombing in 1945, some gems still remain.

The **Semper Opera House,** at Theaterplatz in the center of Dresden, is a mecca for music lovers. Named after its architect, Gottfried Semper, the hall has premiered Wagner's *The Flying Dutchman* and *Tannhäuser* (conducted by the composer) and nine operas of Richard Strauss. Dating from 1871–78 (the first building by Semper burned down in 1869), the opera house fell victim to the 1945 bombings, but fortunately Semper's architectural drawings had been preserved, so it was rebuilt on the same lines and reopened with much pomp in 1985. Tickets are in great demand at the Semper (tel. 0351/484–2323 or 0351/484–2328); try booking through your travel agent before you go or ask at your hotel. As a last resort, line up at the Abendkasse (evening box office) half an hour before the performance begins. Tours of the opera house are also included in one of the daily guided tours of the city.

From Theaterplatz, stroll down the Sophienstrasse to the largely 18th-century **Zwinger** palace complex, which remains one of the city's cultural wonders in the heart of the Altstadt. Completely enclosing a central courtyard of lawns and pools, the complex consists of six linked pavilions decorated with a riot of garlands, nymphs, and other Baroque ornamentation and sculpture, all created under the direction of Matthäus Daniel Pöppelmann.

The Zwinger complex is the home of the world-renowned **Sempergalerie** (Gemäldegalerie Alte Meister) collection of old master paintings, among them works by Dürer, Holbein the Younger, Rembrandt, Vermeer, Raphael, Correggio, and Canaletto. The Zwinger's other treasures include the Porzellansammlung (Porcelain Collection)—famous for its Meissen pieces—the Zoological Museum, and the salon that displays marvelous old scientific instruments (Mathematisch-Physikalischer Salon). *Tel. 0351/484–0620. Gemäldegalerie Alte Meister admission: DM 7 adults, DM 3.50 children. Open Tues.–Sun. 10–6. Porzellansammlung admission: DM 3 adults, DM 1.50 children. Open Fri.–Wed. 10–6. Mathematisch-Physikalischer Salon admission: DM 3 adults, DM 1.50 children. Open Fri.–Wed. 9:30–5. Zoological Museum admission: DM 3 adults, DM 1.50 children. Open Mon.–Wed., Fri. 9:30–5, weekends 9:30–12:30, 1–5.*

After leaving the Zwinger, head eastward along Ernst-Thälmann-Strasse and turn into the **Neumarkt** (New Market), which is, despite its name, the historic heart of old Dresden. The ruined shell on the right is all that remains of the mighty Baroque **Frauenkirche,** once Germany's greatest Protestant church, after the bombing raids of February 1945. The ruined church is being rebuilt. Work is scheduled to be completed in time for the 800th anniversary of the foundation of Dresden in 2006.

Behind the Frauenkirche looms Dresden's leading art museum, the **Albertinum.** This large, imperial-style building gets its name from Saxony's King Albert, who between 1884 and 1887 converted a royal arsenal into a convenient setting for the treasures he and his forebears had collected.

Permanent exhibits at the Albertinum include the **Gemäldegalerie Neue Meister** (New Masters Gallery), which displays outstanding 19th- and 20th-century European pictures that include French Impressionist and Postimpressionist works and Caspar David Friedrich's haunting *Das Kreuz im Gebirge.*

Despite the rich array of paintings, it is the **Grünes Gewölbe** (Green Vault) that invariably attracts most attention. Named after a green room in the palace of August the Strong, this part of the Albertinum (entered from Georg-Treu-Platz) contains an exquisite collection of unique objets d'art fashioned from gold, silver, ivory, amber, and other precious and semi-precious materials. Next door is the **Skulpturensammlung** (Sculpture Collection), which includes ancient Egyptian and classical objects and Italian Mannerist works. *Tel. 0351/495–3056. Admission to all three galleries: DM 7 adults, DM 3.50 children. Open Fri.–Wed. 10–6.*

The southern exit of the Albertinum, at Augustus-Strasse, brings you back to the Neumarkt and leads you to another former royal building now serving as a museum, the 16th-century **Johanneum,** once the royal stables. Instead of horses, the Johanneum now houses the **Verkehrsmuseum** (Transport Museum), a collection of historical vehicles, including vintage automobiles and engines. *Am Neumarkt, tel. 0351/495–3002. Admission: DM 4 adults, DM 2 children. Admission half-price on Fri. Open Tues.–Sun. 10–5.*

On the outside wall of the Johanneum is a prime example of Meissen porcelain art: a 335-foot-long painting on Meissen tiles of a royal procession. More than 100 members of the royal Saxon house of Wettin, half of them on horseback, are depicted on the giant jigsaw made up of 25,000 porcelain tiles, painted from 1904 to 1907.

Follow this unusual procession to the end and you arrive at the former royal palace, the **Herzogschloss,** where major restoration work will continue until the late-1990s behind the fine Renaissance facade. Rooms now in use host historical exhibitions. *Sophienstr., tel. 0351/495–3110. Admission: DM 3 adults, DM 1.50 children. Open Fri.–Wed. 10–6.*

Standing next to the Herzogschloss is the **Katholische Hofkirche,** also known as the Cathedral of St. Trinitas, Saxony's largest church. The son of August the Strong, Frederick Augustus II (ruled 1733–63) brought architects and builders from Italy to construct this Catholic church, consecrated in 1754, in a city that had been the first large center of Lutheranism. In the cathedral's crypt are the tombs of 49 Saxon rulers and a precious vessel containing the heart of August the Strong.

Moving away from the treasures near the river, along the St. Petersburger Strasse, make a left into Lingnerplatz. The **Deutsches Hygiene-Museum** (German Health Museum) reflects Dresden's important role in the history of medicine. The most famous object is a glass model of a human, which caused a sensation when it was first displayed in 1930. *Lingnerpl. 1, tel. 0351/48460. Admission: DM 4 adults, DM 2 children. Open Tues.–Sun. 9–5.*

Two fine examples of Baroque architecture, both designed by Pöppelmann, general designer of the Zwinger palace, are within easy reach from Dresden. Take Bus 85 from Schillerplatz to the chinoiserie-bedecked **Schloss Pillnitz** (tel. 0351/39325), once the summer residence of the Saxon court and situated in a huge park on the Elbe that embodies both Baroque and English landscape styles. The complex consists of two major palaces—the Wasserpalais (admission: DM 3 adults, DM 1.50 children; open Easter–Oct., Wed.–Mon. 9:30–5:30) and the Bergpalais (DM 3 adults, DM 1.50 children; open Easter–Oct., Tues.–Sun. 9:30–5:30)—both housing arts and crafts collections. The palace park is open throughout the year. Schloss Moritzburg, an imposing 17th-century hunting lodge once used by the Saxon royal family, was renovated and enlarged by Pöppelmann in the baroque style and is now called the Jägerhof (Hunter's Court). Today it is home to the **Folk Art Museum,** where a decorative arts collection, much of the building's original furniture, and a collection of hunting trophies is displayed. You can get there by taking the Grossenhein bus from the main train station in Dresden. *Köpckestr. 1, tel. 0352/07439. Admission: DM 5 adults, DM 3 children. Open Apr.–Oct., Tues.–Sun. 10–5; Nov., Tues.–Sun., 10–4; Dec., Tues.–Sun. 10–3.*

Exploring Leipzig

With a population of about 560,000, Leipzig is the second-largest city (after Berlin) in eastern Germany. Since the Middle Ages, it has been an important market town and a center for printing, book publishing, and the fur industry. Nowadays, its twice-yearly fairs, staged in March and September, maintain Leipzig's position as a commercial center. Yet it is music and literature that most people associate with Leipzig. Johann Sebastian Bach (1685–1750) was the organist and choir director at St. Thomas's church. The composer Richard Wagner was born in Leipzig in 1813. The writers Johann Wolfgang von Goethe (1749–1832) and Friedrich von Schiller (1759–1805) are also closely associated with the city and its immediate area. Trade and the arts are just two aspects of the city's fame. One of the greatest battles of the Napoléonic Wars—the Battle of the Nations—was fought here in 1813 and was instrumental in leading to the French general's defeat. Little remained of old Leipzig following the devastation of World War II, but reminders of its medieval and Renaissance character are still to be found in the city center.

Railroad buffs may want to start their tour of Leipzig at the **Hauptbahnhof,** the main train station. With its 26 platforms, majestic staircase, and great arched ceiling, it is Europe's biggest and is unique among German railway stations.

Cross the Platz der Republik to the pedestrian area, leading to Sachsenplatz and the **Markt,** the old market square. Here, in the rebuilt 12th-century marketplace, you will find the **Altes Rathaus,** the Renaissance town hall, now housing the municipal museum, where Leipzig's illustrious past is well documented. *Markt 1, tel. 0341/ 70921. Admission: DM 3 adults, DM 1.50 children. Open Tues–Fri. 10–6, weekends 10–4.*

On all sides of the Markt, small streets leading from the square attest to Leipzig's rich trading past. Tucked in among them are glass-roofed arcades of surprising beauty and elegance. At the **Apotheke** at Hainstrasse 9, you enter surroundings that haven't changed for 100 years or more, redolent of powders and perfumes, home cures and foreign spices. It's spectacularly Jugendstil, all stained glass and rich mahogany. Nearby, on Grimmaischestrasse, is Leipzig's finest arcade, the **Mädlerpassage.** Here, at Number 2, you'll find the **Auerbachs Keller** restaurant (*see* Dining and Lodging, *below*), built in 1530 and made famous in Goethe's tale of Faust.

Continuing west, Grimmaischestrasse becomes Thomasgasse, site of the **Thomaskirche,** where Johann Sebastian Bach worked for 27 years; he composed most of his cantatas for the church's boys' choir. Once the heart of a 13th-century monastery, rebuilt in the 15th century, the tall Gothic church now stands by itself, with only the names of adjacent streets recalling the cloisters that once surrounded it. The great composer's burial place, it is to this day the home of the Thomasknabenchor (St. Thomas boys choir) and a center of Bach tradition.

Another church of more than historic interest is the **Nikolaikirche,** behind Grimmaischestrasse on Nikolaistrasse, where tens of thousands of East Germans demanding reform gathered in the months before the collapse of the Communist regime. *"Wir sind das Volk"* (We are the people) was their chant as they defied the government's efforts to silence them. The church, more impressive inside than outside, has an ornate 16th-century pulpit and an unusual diamond-pattern ceiling supported by classical pillars that are crowned with palm-tree-like flourishes.

Looming above the Nikolaikirche in the city center is the 470-foot-high **Leipzig University Tower,** dubbed the "Jagged Tooth" by students. Using the university skyscraper as a landmark, you come to **Augustus-Platz,** on which stands the modernistic **Opera House** and **Neues Gewandhaus** concert hall, both centers of Leipzig's musical life. By heading across the Ring and up the Grimmaisch Steinweg, you reach the **Grassimuseum** (Johannespl. 5–11) complex, built in the late-1920s in striking Art Deco style. It includes the **Museum of Arts and Crafts** (tel. 0341/214–2114; admission: DM 4 adults, DM 2 children; open Tues.–Fri. 10–6, Wed. until 8, weekends 10–5), the **Geographical Museum** (admission DM 5 adults, DM 2 children; open Tues.–Fri. 10–5:30, weekends 10–4), and the **Musical Instruments Museum** (enter from Taubchenweg 2; admission DM 3 adults, DM 1.50 children; open Tues.–Fri. 9–5, Sat. 10–5, Sun. 10–1).

Back on the Ring and heading clockwise (west), turn left into Harkorstrasse. You'll come to the city's most outstanding museum, the **Museum der Bildenden Künste,** an art gallery of international stature that is especially strong in German and Dutch painting. *Georgi-Dimitroff-Pl. 1, tel. 0341/216–9914. Admission: DM 5 adults, DM 2.50 children; free Sun. Open Tues. and Thurs.–Sun. 9–5, Wed. 1–9:30.*

Still further out, reached by Streetcars 15, 20, 21, and 25, is the **Exhibition Pavilion** at Pragerstrasse 210 (admission: DM 2 adults, DM 1 children; open May–Sept., Wed.–Sun. 10–6; Oct.–Apr., Wed.–Sun.

9–4). Its main feature is a vast diorama portraying the Battle of the Nations of 1813. Nearby on Pragerstrasse is the massive **Völkerschlachtdenkmal** (open May–Oct., daily 10–5; Nov.–Apr., daily 9–4) a 300-foot-high granite-and-concrete memorial in a formal park; it, too, commemorates the battle. You must climb 500 steps to take in the view from the platform near the top. The Prussians did make one concession to Napoléon in designing the monument: A stone marks the spot where he stood during the battle.

Exploring Weimar

Weimar sits prettily on the Ilm River between the Ettersberg and Vogtland hills, and has a place in German political and cultural history out of all proportion to its size (population 63,000). Its civic history, not long by German standards, began as late as 1410, but by the early 19th century Weimar had become one of Europe's most important cultural centers, where Goethe and Schiller were neighbors, Carl Maria von Weber wrote some of his best music, and Liszt was director of music, presenting the first performance of Wagner's *Lohengrin*. Walter Gropius founded his Staatliches Bauhaus design school in Weimar in 1919, and it was there in 1919–20 that the German National Assembly drew up the constitution of the Weimar Republic. After the collapse of the ill-fated Weimar government, Hitler chose the city as the site for the first national congress of his new Nazi Party, and later built—or forced prisoners to build for him—the notorious Buchenwald concentration camp on the city's outskirts.

Weimar's greatness is bound up with the activity of the widowed Countess Anna Amalia, who in the late-18th century set about attracting cultural figures to enrich the glittering court her Saxon forebears had set up in the town. Goethe, who served the countess as a councillor, advising on financial matters and town design, was one of them; Schiller was another. In front of the National Theater on **Theaterplatz,** a statue of the famous pair, showing Goethe with a patronizing hand on the shoulder of the younger Schiller, commemorates them.

Adjacent to the National Theater is the Baroque **Wittumspalais,** once the home of Countess Anna Amalia. In the exquisite drawing room where her soirees were held, you find the original cherry-wood table at which company sat. In the east wing is a small museum that is a fascinating memorial to her cultural gatherings. *Theaterpl. 9. Admission: DM 6 adults. Open Mar.–Oct., Tues.–Sun. 9–noon and 1–5; Nov.–Feb., Tues.–Sun. 9–noon and 1–4.*

Goethe spent 57 years in Weimar, 47 of them in the house that has since become a shrine for millions of visitors. The **Goethehaus** is two blocks south of Theaterplatz on a street called the Frauenplan. The museum it contains is testimony not only to the great man's literary might but also his interest in the sciences, particularly medicine, and his administrative skills (and frustrations) as Weimar's exchequer. Here you find the desk at which Goethe stood to write (he liked to work standing up), his own paintings (he was an accomplished watercolorist), and the modest bed on which he died. *Frauenplan 1, tel. 03643/ 62041. Admission: DM 8 adults. Open Mar.–Oct., Tues.–Sun. 9–5; Nov.–Feb., Tues.–Sun. 9–4.*

On a tree-shaded square around the corner from Goethe's house is Schiller's green-shuttered home, the **Schillerhaus,** in which he and his family spent a happy, all-too-brief three years (Schiller died there in 1805). The poet and playwright's study, dominated by the desk where he probably completed *William Tell,* is tucked up underneath the mansard roof. *Schillerstr. 17, tel. 03643/62041. Admission: DM 6 adults. Open Mar.–Oct., Wed.–Mon. 9–5; Nov.–Feb., Wed.–Mon. 9–4.*

Another historic house worth visiting is found on the **Marktplatz,** the central town square. It was the home of the painter Lucas Cranach the Elder, who lived there during his last years, 1552–53. Its imposing facade, richly decorated, bears the coat of arms of the Cranach family. In its ground floor is a private modern art gallery.

Around the corner and to the left is Weimar's 16th-century castle, the **Stadtschloss,** with its restored classical staircase, festival hall, and falcon gallery. The castle's impressive art collection includes several fine paintings by Cranach the Elder and many early 20th-century works by such artists as Böcklin, Liebermann, and Beckmann. *Burgpl. Admission: DM 3 adults, DM 2 children. Open May–Sept., Tues.–Sun. 9–6; Oct.–Apr., Tues.–Sun. 9–5.*

In Weimar's old, reconstructed town center stands the late-Gothic **Herderkirche,** with its large winged altarpiece started by Lucas Cranach the Elder and finished by his son in 1555. Nearby in Jakobstrasse you'll spot the Baroque facade of the **Kirms-Krackow** house.

A short walk south, past the Goethehaus and across Wieland Platz, brings you to the **Historischer Friedhof** (Historic Cemetery), where Goethe and Schiller are buried. Their tombs are in the classical-style chapel. The Goethe-Schiller vault can be visited daily 9–1 and 2–5.

On the other side of the Ilm, amid meadowlike parkland, is Goethe's beloved **Gartenhaus** (Garden House, admission: DM 4 adults, DM 1.50 children; open daily 9–noon and 1–5; Nov.–Feb., 9–noon and 1–4), where he wrote much poetry and began his masterpiece *Iphigenie auf Tauris.* Goethe is said to have felt very close to nature here, and you can soak up the same rural atmosphere today on footpaths along the peaceful little river, where time seems to have stood still.

Just south of the city (take Bus 1 from Goetheplatz) is the lovely 18th-century hunting and pleasure palace, **Schloss Belvedere,** which now houses a museum of Baroque art and an exhibition of coaches and other old vehicles. The formal gardens were in part laid out according to Goethe's concepts. *Tel. 0621/661–831. Admission: DM 4 adults, DM 2 children. Open Apr.–Oct., Tues.–Sun. 10–6. Closed Nov.–Mar.*

North of Weimar, in the Ettersberg Hills, is a blighted patch of land that contrasts cruelly with the verdant countryside that so inspired Goethe: **Buchenwald,** where, from 1937 to 1945, 65,000 men, women, and children from 35 countries met their deaths through disease, starvation, and gruesome medical experiments. Each is commemorated today by a small stone placed on the outlines of the former barracks (no longer existing), and by a massive memorial tower. Buses to the camp depart at least hourly between 9 and 3:30 from the main railway station, or you can take the more frequent Bus 6 to Ettersburg. *Contact Weimar Tourist Information, tel. 03643/24000. Admission free. Open Tues.–Sun. 8:45–4:30.*

Dining and Lodging

Many of the best restaurants in Saxony and Thuringia are in the larger hotels. You can expect hearty food in both regions. Roast beef, venison, and wild boar are often on Saxon menus, and in the Vogtland you'll find *Kaninchentopf* (rabbit stew). In Thuringia, regional specialties include *Thüringer Rehbraten* (roast venison); roast mutton served in a delicate cream sauce; tasty grilled Thuringian sausages; *Thüringer Sauerbraten mit Klössen* (marinated beef with dumplings); *Bören-schinken* (cured ham); and roast mutton shepherd-style, with beans and vegetables. The light Meissner Wein, wine from the Meissen region, is splendid.

Dining out in Saxony and Thuringia can still be relatively inexpensive, but hotel prices are high because of the constant shortage of accommodations. Although hotels are being built at a brisk pace, building costs are so high that they are directly reflected in room rates. Cheaper hotels tend to be the unimproved and sometimes substandard holdovers from the old German Democratic Republic; it's often better to seek cheap but clean accommodation from the lists of private bed-and-breakfasts available at most tourist offices.

For details and price-category definitions, *see* Dining and Lodging *in* Staying in Germany, *above.*

Dresden

DINING

Kügelhaus. A combination grill/coffee shop/restaurant/beer cellar, the Kügelhaus is extremely popular, so either get there early or reserve your table in advance. You'll find the usual hefty local dishes, but prepared with a deft touch. *Str. der Befreiung 13, tel. 0351/ 52791. Reservations advised. No credit cards. $$*

Haus Altmarkt. The choice of cuisine in this busy corner of the colonnaded Altmark is enormous—from the McDonald's which has wormed itself into the landscape to the upscale Amadeus restaurant on the first floor. In between are a jolly bistrolike café and, downstairs, a vaulted restaurant, Zum Humpen, with a secluded bar. The restaurant offers good value, with midday menus under DM 20. In warm weather you can eat outside on a terrace and watch the marketplace's bustle. *Am Altmarkt 1, tel. 0351/495–1212. No credit cards. $–$$*

LODGING

Maritim Hotel Bellevue. Across the river from the Zwinger palace, opera, and main museums, this modern hotel cleverly incorporates an old restored mansion. The hotel views of the historic center are terrific, the rooms luxurious, and the service good. Its Cafe Pöppelmann is especially recommended for its atmosphere and hearty dishes. *Grosse-Meissner-Str. 15, tel. 0351/56620, fax 0351/55997. 328 rooms with bath. Facilities: 5 restaurants, wine cellar, café, beer pub, bar, nightclub, shops, sauna, solarium, jogging course. AE, DC, MC, V. $$$$*

Leipzig

DINING

★ **Auerbachs Keller.** A visit to this 1530 restaurant, which is immortalized in Goethe's *Faust,* is a must. The menu features regional dishes from Saxony, often with Faustian names. There is also a good wine list. *Mädler-Passage 2–4, tel. 0341/216–1040. Reservations required. Jacket and tie required. AE, DC, MC, V. $$$*

★ **Paulaner.** This intimate restaurant is recommended for its quiet atmosphere and good regional cooking. *Klosterg. 3, tel. 0341/211–3115. Reservations advised. AE, MC, V. $$*

Zill's Tunnel. The tunnel refers to the barrel-ceiling ground-floor restaurant, where foaming glasses of excellent local beer are cheerily served by the friendly staff who can also help you decipher the Old Saxon descriptions of the menu's traditional dishes. Upstairs there's a larger wine restaurant, with a welcoming open fireplace. Goose in a variety of forms is a staple here and among the soups is a potent mixture of vegetables, beer, and gin. *Barfussgässchen 9, tel. 0341/200–446. Reservations advised. No credit cards. $$*

Thüringer Hof. This fine old tavern-restaurant has been in business for centuries and its dark-paneled walls have history carved deep within the wood. The roast wild boar is served just as Leipzigers would have ordered it in ages past, and the traditional Thüringer dishes couldn't be more authentic—marinated beef, Thüringer dumplings, and red cabbage sweetened with apple, to name just one. *Burgstr. 19–23, tel. 0341/209–884. No credit cards. Closed Fri. No dinner, Sat. $*

LODGING

Hotel Inter-Continental Leipzig. The city's most luxurious accommodation is imposing for its high-rise profile as well as its Japanese restaurant and garden. Rooms have every comfort, including marble-walled and -floored bathrooms and air-conditioning. The hotel is close to the main rail station. *Gerberstr. 15, tel. 0341/9880, fax 0341/988–1229. 429 rooms with bath, 18 suites. Facilities: 4 restaurants, 2 bars, coffee bar, nightclub, indoor pool, sauna, solarium, bowling, billiards, jogging course, fitness club, casino, shops, garage. AE, DC, MC, V. $$$$*

Maritim Hotel Astoria. This older, well-worn hotel is still preferred by many for its genteel ambience and central location next to the main rail station. Traffic in the area is considerable; ask for a room at the rear. *Pl. der Republik 2, tel. 0341/72220, fax 0341/722–4747. 323 rooms with bath. Facilities: 2 restaurants, bar, café, nightclub, sauna, fitness room, parking. AE, DC, MC, V. $$$$*

Corum. In 1993, the former, and slightly seedy, Hotel Zum Löwen was dazzlingly transformed into a smart and very comfortable hotel. Unchanged is the excellent location, across the street from Leipzig's main railway station. Rooms still tend to be small but lack nothing in terms of comfort and facilities. *Rudolf-Breitscheid-Str. 3, tel. 0341/125–100, fax 0341/1251–0100. 108 rooms, 14 suites. Facilities: restaurant, bar, sauna, fitness room, parking. AE, DC, MC, V. $$$*

Hotel Garni Silencium. This newly opened hotel is part of the Silencium group, which guarantees its guests a peaceful night's sleep. So although it's on a busy thoroughfare, a hush permeates Leipzig's Silencium, a beautifully restored old city mansion. The hotel is about 3 kilometers (2 miles) from the city center, but tram stops are nearby. The modern, comfortable rooms have satellite TV and fax/modem outlets. *Georg-Schumann-Str. 268, Leipzig-Möckern, tel. 0341/901–2990, fax 0341/901–2991. 34 rooms with bath. AE, DC, MC, V. $$$*

Zum Goldenen Adler. Up-to-date comfort and facilities are contained within the handsome framework of this old Leipzig inn. Rooms are bright and modern, with dark woods and red upholstery dominating the decor. The bistro-bar, Day & Night, is a popular nightspot in town, and though conveniently part of the hotel, it's well soundproofed. *Portitzerstr. 10, tel. 0341/61031, fax 0341/66326. 20 rooms with bath. Facilities: restaurant, bistro-bar, parking. AE, MC, V. $$$*

Weimar

DINING

Weisser Schwan. This historic restaurant in the center of town, right by the Goethehaus, dates from 1500. It offers high-quality international cuisine and Thuringian specialties, particularly fish and grilled meats. *Frauenstorstr. 23, tel. 03643/61715. Reservations required. AE, DC, MC, V. Closed Mon. $$$*

Hotel Thüringen. The plush elegance of the Thüringen's restaurant, complete with velvet drapes and chandeliers, makes it seem expensive, but there's a pleasant surprise in store: The menu of international and regional dishes is remarkably moderately priced. An excellent Thüringer roast beef, for instance, costs less than DM 20. *Brennerstr. 42, tel. 03643/3675 or 03643/62900. AE, DC, MC, V. $$*

Scharfe Ecke. Thuringia's traditional Knödeln (dumplings) are best here. But be patient; they are made to order and take at least 20 minutes to make the journey from kitchen to table. The Knödel come with just about every dish, from roast pork to venison stew. And the ideal accompaniment to any of the choices here is the locally brewed beer. *Eisfeld 2, tel. 03643/202–430. No reservations. Closed Mon. No dinner Sun. No credit cards. $*

LODGING

Flamberg Hotel Elephant. The historic Elephant, dating from 1696, is now a member of the Flamberg group, which has, thankfully, kept the original charm that made the hotel one of Germany's most famous, even in the communist years. Goethe, Schiller, and Liszt (after whom the friendly hotel bar is named) are some of the illustrious names in the hotel register. If you want to share the "Elephant" experience, book well in advance. *Am Markt 19, tel. 03643/8020, fax 03643/65310. 87 rooms with bath, 5 suites. Facilities: 2 restaurants, bar, nightclub, sauna, solarium, parking. AE, DC, MC, V. $$$$*

Weimar Hilton. Weimar's most modern hotel combines luxury with smooth-running service. The riverside Belvedere park—which Goethe helped to lay out—is just across the road, and the rococo Belvedere Palace, with its museum of ancient vehicles, is a short walk away. Weimar town center *is* quite a hike from here, but bus service is frequent. *Belvederer Allee 25, tel. 03643/7220, fax 03643/722–741. 300 rooms with bath. Facilities: 2 restaurants, café, beer tavern, 3 bars, indoor pool, sauna, solarium, fitness room, spa, parking. AE, DC, MC, V. $$$$*

Hotel Russischer Hof. Franz Liszt, Hector Berlioz, Richard Wagner, and a group of other well-known friends founded a Weimar cultural society here in 1848. The rooms are furnished and decorated in pastel shades, light woods, and floral prints. The restaurant has a reputation far beyond Weimar; an airy, enclosed garden-terrace and a beer tavern in the vaulted cellar are two other favorite meeting places. *Goethepl. 2, tel. 03643/7740, fax 03643/62337. 87 rooms with bath. Facilities: 2 restaurants, bar, beer cellar, garden/terrace, parking. AE, DC, MC, V. $$$*

12 Great Britain

GREAT BRITAIN is a small country with a long history spread out for all to see. Two factors have helped to ensure the preservation of so much of the nation's past. The first is the absence of fighting on British soil. Although for centuries Britain's armies crossed the Channel to take part in European wars and during the 18th and 19th centuries the nation won for itself an extensive worldwide empire, the physical fact of the English Channel has kept Britain's shores free from invasion for more than 900 years, blocking the process of destruction and reconstruction seen in much of the rest of Europe. In addition, the nation's internal conflicts, though bloody, have generally been brief. The second factor is the innate sense of history (some would call it conservatism) of the British, who generally prefer the old to the new and are often reluctant to contemplate any kind of change, especially in their physical surroundings.

All this means that Great Britain is an ideal holiday destination for anyone with a feel for the past. Here you'll find soaring medieval cathedrals, tributes to the faith of the churchmen and masons who built them; grand country mansions of the aristocracy filled with treasures—paintings, furniture, tapestries—and set in elegantly landscaped grounds; and grim fortified castles, their gray stone walls set fast against all challengers.

But Britain is not merely a historical theme park, and the visitor who concentrates solely on such traditional sights misses the essence of the land and the people. Many of the pleasures of exploration away from the main tourist routes derive from the constantly changing variety of the countryside. A day's drive from York, for example, will take you through long stretches of wild, heather-covered moorland, ablaze with color in the fall, or past the steep, sheep-dotted mountainsides of the Dales, cut by deep valleys and scattered with isolated stone-built hamlets.

Wandering off the beaten track will also allow you to discover Britain's many distinctive small country towns and villages, which move at a notably slower pace than the metropolitan centers. A medieval parish church, a high street of 18th-century buildings interrupted by occasional survivors from earlier centuries, and a grandiose Victorian town hall, all still in use today, help to convey a sense of a living past.

This direct continuity of past into present can be experienced in such a celebrated and tourist-filled place as Stratford-upon-Avon, but even more in such communities as the little town of Chipping Campden, set in the rolling Cotswold Hills, and Bury St. Edmunds, in the gentle Suffolk countryside east of Cambridge. In such places, the visitor's understanding is often helped by small museums devoted to explaining local history, full of intriguing artifacts and information on trade, traditions, and social life. Such towns, too, are the places to look for specialty goods, such as knitwear, pottery, glass, and pictures, the product of a 1980s renaissance in craftsmanship.

In contrast is the hectic, at times aggressive, pace of life in London. This is a city with a vibrant artistic, cultural, and commercial life. Yet here, too, the links with the past are plain for all to see. For instance, despite all the recent rebuilding, the basic street pattern of the City (the financial quarter between St. Paul's Cathedral and the Tower of London) is the one that evolved in the Middle Ages, more than 600 years ago, and still standing is much of the work of Christopher Wren, the master architect chiefly responsible for reconstruction after the disastrous Great Fire of 1666. Most notable of these works is St. Paul's itself. Here again, exploration off the beaten track will reward you with the discovery of a London relatively untouched by tourists.

Finally, it is important to remember that Great Britain consists of three nations—England, Scotland, and Wales—and that 640 kilometers (400 miles) north of London lies another capital city, Edinburgh, whose streets and monuments bear witness to the often turbulent and momentous history of the Scottish people. Cardiff, 272 kilometers (170 miles) west of London, is a busy port and the focal point of two of the famous Welsh passions—singing and rugby.

ESSENTIAL INFORMATION

Before You Go

When to Go

The main tourist season runs from mid-April to mid-October. In recent years, however, parts of the winter—especially December—have been almost as busy. Winter is also the height of London's theater, ballet, and opera season. Springtime reveals the countryside at its most verdant and beautiful, while fall offers soft vistas of muted, golden color. May, September, and October are the months to visit the northern moorlands and Scottish highlands, while June is best for Wales and the Lake District. Most British people take their vacations during July and August, when costs are high and accommodations at a premium.

CLIMATE

On the whole, Britain's winters are rarely bitter, except in northern Scotland. Recent summers have been scorchers all over the country. Wherever you are, and whatever the season, be prepared for sudden changes. What begins as a brilliant, sunny day often turns into a damp and dismal one by lunchtime. Take an umbrella and raincoat wherever you go, particularly in Scotland, where the temperatures are somewhat cooler.

The following are the average daily maximum and minimum temperatures for London.

Jan.	43F	6C	May	62F	17C	Sept.	65F	19C
	36	2		47	8		52	11
Feb.	44F	7C	June	69F	20C	Oct.	58F	14C
	36	2		53	12		46	8
Mar.	50F	10C	July	71F	22C	Nov.	50F	10C
	38	3		56	13		42	6
Apr.	56F	13C	Aug.	71F	22C	Dec.	45F	7C
	42	6		56	13		38	3

Currency

The British unit of currency is the pound sterling, divided into 100 pence (p). Bills are issued in denominations of 5, 10, 20, and 50 pounds (£). Coins are £1, 50p, 20p, 10p, 5p, 2p, and 1p; the 10p and 5p are the size of a quarter and a dime, respectively. Scottish banks issue Scottish currency, of which all coins and notes—with the exception of the £1 notes—are accepted in England. At press time (spring 1995), exchange rates were approximately US$ 1.71 to the pound.

Traveler's checks are widely accepted in Britain, and many banks, hotels, and shops offer currency-exchange facilities. You will probably lose from 1¢ to 4¢ on the dollar, however, depending on where you change them; banks offer the best rates. In London and other big cities, *bureaux de change* abound, but it definitely pays to shop around:

They usually have a minimum charge of £1 and often a great deal more. Credit cards are universally accepted, too. The most commonly used are MasterCard and Visa.

What It Will Cost

In general, transportation in Britain is expensive in comparison with other countries. You would be well advised to take advantage of the many reductions and special fares available on trains, buses, and subways. Always ask about these when buying your ticket. Gasoline prices are about the same as those on the Continent.

London now ranks with Tokyo as one of the world's most expensive hotel capitals. Finding budget accommodations—especially during July and August—can be difficult; you should try to book well ahead if you are visiting during these months. Many London hotels offer special off-season (October–March) rates, however. Dining out, even in moderate restaurants, can be prohibitively expensive, but a large number of pubs and ethnic restaurants offer excellent food at reasonable prices, and fast-food facilities are widespread.

Remember that the gulf between prices in the capital and outside is wide. Be prepared to pay a value-added tax (VAT) of 17½% on almost everything you buy; in nearly all cases it is included in the advertised price.

SAMPLE PRICES
For London: cup of coffee, £1–£2; pint of beer, £1.70–£2.20; glass of wine, £2–£5; soda, 60p; 1-mile taxi ride, £2.50; ham sandwich, £1.75.

Customs on Arrival

There are two levels of duty-free allowance for people entering the United Kingdom: one, for goods bought outside the European Union (EU) or for goods bought in a duty-free shop within the EU; two, for goods bought in an EU country.

In the first category, you may import duty-free 200 cigarettes or 100 cigarillos or 50 cigars or 250 grams of tobacco (*note:* If you live outside Europe, these allowances are doubled), plus 1 liter of alcoholic drinks over 22% volume or 2 liters of alcoholic drinks not over 22% volume or fortified or sparkling wine, plus 2 liters of still table wine, plus 60 cc/ml of perfume, plus 250 cc/ml of toilet water, plus other goods to the value of £36.

In the second category, you may import duty-free a considerable amount of liquor and tobacco—800 cigarettes, 400 cigarillos, 200 cigars, 1 kilogram of pipe tobacco, 10 liters of spirits, 90 liters of wine, and 110 liters of beer.

In addition, no animals or pets of any kind may be brought into the United Kingdom without a six-month quarantine. Penalties for evading this regulation are severe and strictly enforced.

Getting Around

By Car

ROAD CONDITIONS
Britain has superhighways (called motorways) running almost the length of the country, with links connecting them in the South, Midlands, and North. Motorways, given the prefix M on maps and road signs, have two or three lanes in each direction and are designed for high-speed rather than scenic travel.

The main north–south road between London and Leeds is M1. Other principal routes are M5, running from the Midlands to the Southwest,

Great Britain

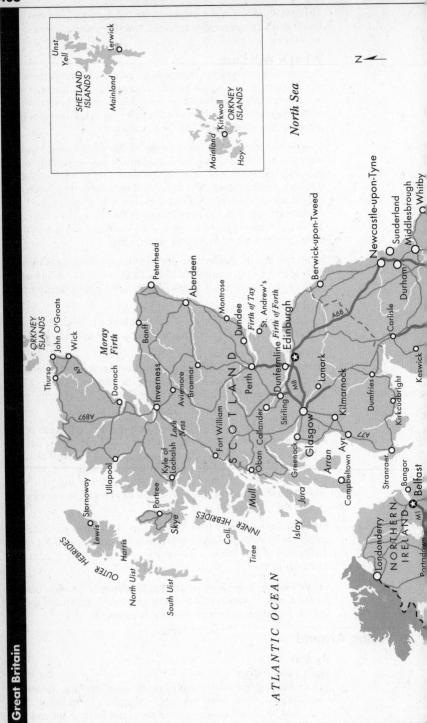

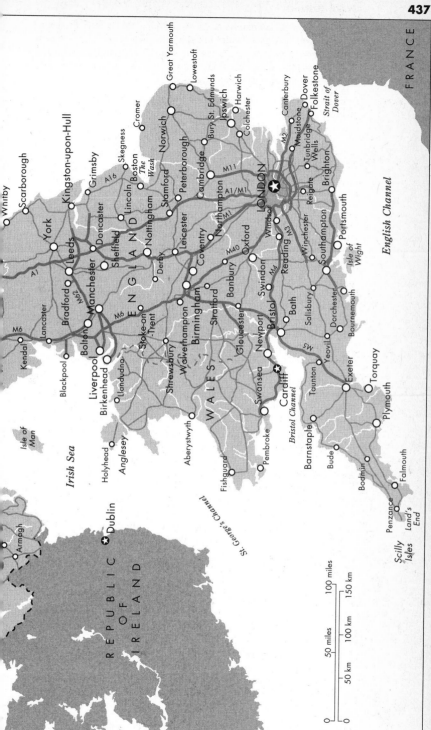

and M6, from the Midlands north to Scotland. M4 covers the route from London to Wales via Bristol. Encircling London is M25, which provides access to the countryside and southeast coast. It is, however, heavily traveled and not capable of supporting the volume of traffic it sees. Be ready for lengthy traffic jams.

Divided A roads are usually shown on maps as thick, red lines and, except for occasional traffic lights, are similar to motorways. Most other major routes are the 19th-century coach and turnpike roads designed for horses and carriages. Although they—and the even narrower, winding village roads—will allow you to see much more of the real Britain, your journey could end up taking twice the time. In remote country areas, road travel can be slow, especially in an icy winter. Good planning maps are available from the **AA** (Automobile Association) and the **RAC** (Royal Automobile Club); for in-depth exploring, try the Ordnance Survey 1:50,000-series maps. These show every road, track, and footpath in the country. You might also consult the very useful Ordnance Survey *Motoring Atlas*.

RULES OF THE ROAD

You can use either your driver's license or an International Driving Permit in Britain. Drive on the left-hand side of the road and pay close attention to the varying—and abruptly changing—speed limits. Seat belts are obligatory for front-seat passengers (and back-seat ones when the cars are fitted with them). In general, speed limits are 30 mph in the center of cities and built-up areas, 40 mph in suburban areas, 70 mph on motorways and divided highways, and 60 mph on all other roads.

PARKING

Parking in London and other large cities can be a nightmare. On-street meters are hard to find and can be very expensive. Cheaper pay-and-display lots (the driver inserts money into a machine to receive a sticker for the car with the amount of time allowed for parking) are common in smaller towns and suburban areas. But wherever you are, in town or city, beware of yellow or red lines. A single yellow line denotes no parking during the daytime. Double yellow lines or red lines indicate a more extensive prohibition on stopping. The exact times can always be ascertained from nearby signs, usually attached to lamp posts. Illegal parking can result in having your vehicle removed or wheelclamped, which can lead to a great deal of inconvenience as well as a hefty fine. Be sure to check street signs carefully before parking. In central London, where there is good bus and underground service and taxis are plentiful, the use of a car is not recommended.

GASOLINE

In Britain gas (called petrol) comes in three grades; the price difference among them is negligible. Though most gas stations advertise prices by the gallon, pumps actually measure in liters. A British Imperial gallon is larger than its American equivalent—four of the former equal five of the latter. At press time (spring 1995), the price of gasoline was about £2.60 per gallon, less for lead-free. A recent campaign to promote lead-free gas has been fairly successful, helped by the fact that it's slightly cheaper (£2.05 per gallon) than the leaded variety.

By Train

Britain's rail system is somewhat overpriced, but it no longer deserves its reputation for being unreliable. All in all, it is one of the fastest, safest, and most comfortable rail services in the world. At press time (spring 1995), trains were still run by the state-owned **British Rail (BR)**, although this is due to change, as various routes are sold off to private operators. BR expects half its lines to be franchised by mid-1996.

The country's principal—and most efficient—service is the InterCity network, linking London with every major city in the country. The most modern high-speed trains travel up to 200 kph (125 mph) and offer comfortable, fully air-conditioned cars, both first- and second-class, with restaurant or buffet facilities. Local train services are not quite as reliable, particularly around congested city centers such as London. In general, seat reservations are not necessary except during peak vacation periods and on popular medium- and long-distance routes. Reserving a standard-class seat costs £1.

FARES

British Rail fares are high when compared with those in other countries. However, the network does offer a wide, and often bewildering, range of ticket reductions, and these can make a tremendous difference. The information office in each station is generally the most reliable source of information. Information and tickets can also be obtained from British Rail Travel Centers within the larger train stations and from selected travel agents displaying the double-arrow British Rail logo.

One of the best bargains available to overseas visitors is the **BritRail Pass** or the **BritRail Youth Pass,** the U.K. equivalent of the Eurail ticket. It provides unlimited standard and first-class travel over the entire British Rail network (and associated ferry and bus routes) for periods of 8, 15, or 22 days, or one month. The cost of a **BritRail adult pass** for 8 days is $230 standard and $315 first-class; for 15 days, $355 standard and $515 first-class; for 22 days, $445 and $645; and for a month, $520 and $750. The **Youth Pass,** for those aged 16 to 25, provides unlimited second-class travel and costs $189 for 8 days, $280 for 15 days, $355 for 22 days, and $415 for one month. The **Senior Citizen Pass,** for passengers over 60, costs $209 for 8 days (first-class $295), $320 for 15 days (first-class $479), $399 for 22 days (first-class $585), and $465 for one month (first-class $675). There is also a **Flexi Pass,** which allows 4, 8, or 15 days' travel in one month. These passes can be purchased only outside Britain, either in the United States, before you leave, or in one of 46 other countries. British Rail has its own information offices in New York, Los Angeles, Chicago, Dallas, Vancouver, and Toronto. The quoted prices are in U.S. dollars. Canadian tickets are slightly higher-priced.

If you are planning to travel only short distances, be sure to buy inexpensive same-day return tickets ("cheap day returns"). These cost only slightly more than ordinary one-way, standard-class tickets but can be used *only* after 9:30 AM and on weekends. Other special offers are regional **Rover** tickets, giving unlimited travel within local areas, and **Saver** returns, allowing greatly reduced round-trip travel during off-peak periods. For information about routes and fares, contact the **British Travel Centre** (12 Regent St., London SW1Y 4PQ, no information given by phone). Also inquire at main rail stations for details about reduced-price tickets to specific destinations.

By Plane

For a comparatively small country, Britain offers an extensive network of internal air routes. These are run by about six different airlines. Hourly shuttle services operate every day between London and Glasgow, Edinburgh, Belfast, and Manchester. Seats are available on a no-reservations basis, and you can generally check in about half an hour before flight departure time. Keep in mind, however, that Britain's internal air services are not as competitive as those in the United States. And with modern, fast trains and relatively short distances, it is often much cheaper—and not much more time-consuming—to travel by train.

By Bus

Buses provide the most economical form of public transportation in Britain. Prices are invariably half those of train tickets, and the network is just as extensive. In recent years, both short- and long-distance buses have improved immeasurably in speed, comfort, and frequency. There is one important semantic difference to keep in mind when discussing bus travel in Britain. **Buses** (either double- or single-decker) are generally part of the local transportation system in towns and cities and make frequent stops. **Coaches,** on the other hand, are comparable to American Greyhound buses and are used only for long-distance travel.

National Express offers the largest number of routes of any coach operator in Britain. It also offers a variety of discount tickets, including the **BritExpress Card** and the **Tourist Trail Pass** for overseas visitors. The BritExpress Card (£7) is a discount card that provides a reduction on every journey made in any 30-day period. The Tourist Trail Pass costs £49 for 3 consecutive days' travel, £79 for 5 days' travel out of 10 consecutive days, £119 for 8 days out of 16, and £179 for 15 days out of 30. Passes can be bought from travel agents in the United States; in London, at the Victoria Coach Station (Buckingham Palace Rd., SW1 9TP) or at main train stations in Edinburgh and Glasgow. Information about all services can be obtained from the National Express Information Office at Victoria Coach Station (tel. 0171/730–0202) or from **SMT** (St. Andrew Sq., tel. 0131/556–8464) in Edinburgh.

By Boat

Britain offers more than 2,400 kilometers (1,500 miles) of navigable inland waterways—rivers, lakes, canals, locks, and loughs—for leisure travel. Particular regions, such as the Norfolk Broads in East Anglia, the Severn Valley in the West Country, and the sea lochs and canals of Scotland, are especially popular among the nautically minded. Although there are no regularly scheduled waterborne services, hundreds of yachts, canal boats, and motor cruises are available throughout the year. The **British Tourist Authority's** booklet "U.K. Waterway Holidays" is a good source of information. You can also contact the **Inland Waterways Association** (114 Regents Park Rd., London NW1 8UQ, tel. 0171/586–2510) or the **British Waterways Board** (Willow Grange, Church Rd., Watford WD1 3QA, tel. 01923/226422).

By Bicycle

Cycling provides an excellent way to see the countryside, and most towns—including London—offer bike-rental facilities. Any bike shop or tourist information center should be able to direct you to the nearest rental firm. Rental fees generally start at £15 per day, plus a fairly large deposit, though this can often be put on your credit card. If you're planning a tour and would like information on rental shops and special holidays for cyclists, contact a British Tourist Authority office in the United States before you leave home. In Britain, contact the **Cyclists' Touring Club** (Cotterell House, 69 Meadrow, Godalming, Surrey GU7 3HS, tel. 01483/417217).

On Foot

Many organizations conduct group walking holidays during the summer months. These are especially popular in the Welsh mountains, the Lake District, Dartmoor, and Exmoor. Details are available from the British Tourist Authority.

Staying in Great Britain

Telephones

In spring 1995, an extra digit was added to area codes nationwide. This may not yet be reflected on every business card or listing, so if a phone number doesn't work, try adding a "1" after the initial "0."

LOCAL CALLS

Public telephones are plentiful in British cities, especially London, and you will find fewer out of order these days than in years past. Other than on the street, the best place to find a bank of pay phones is in a hotel or large post office; pubs usually have a pay phone, too. As part of British Telecom's modernization efforts, the distinctive red phone booths are gradually being replaced by generic glass and steel cubicles, but the red boxes still remain in more remote areas of the country. The workings of coin-operated telephones vary, but there are usually instructions in each unit. Most take 10p, 20p, 50p, and £1 coins. A Phonecard is also available; it comes in denominations of 10, 20, 40, and 100 units and can be bought in a number of retail outlets. Cardphones, which are clearly marked with a special green insignia, will not accept coins.

A local call before 6 PM costs 15p for three minutes. A daytime call to the United States will cost 47p a minute. Each large city or region in Britain has its own numerical prefix, which is used only when you are dialing from outside the city. In provincial areas, the dialing codes for nearby towns are often posted in the booth.

INTERNATIONAL CALLS

The cheapest way to make an overseas call is to dial it yourself. But be sure to have plenty of coins or Phonecards close at hand. After you have inserted the coins or card, dial 010 (the international code), then the country code—for the United States, it is 1—followed by the area code and local number. To reach an **AT&T** long-distance operator, dial 0500890011 ; for **MCI**, dial 0800890202 , and for **Sprint,** dial 0800890877 (from a British Telecom phone) or 0500890877 (from a Mercury Communications phone). To make a collect or other operator-assisted call, dial 155.

COUNTRY CODE

When you're dialing overseas, the United Kingdom's country code is 44.

OPERATORS AND INFORMATION

For information anywhere in Britain, dial either 142 or 192. For the operator, dial 100. For assistance with international calls, dial 155.

Mail

POSTAL RATES

Airmail letters to the United States and Canada cost 41p for 10 grams; postcards, 35p; aerograms, 36p. Letters and postcards to Europe weighing up to 20 grams cost 30p (25p to EU-member countries). Letters within the United Kingdom: first-class, 25p; second-class and postcards, 19p. These rates are likely to have risen by early 1996.

RECEIVING MAIL

If you're uncertain where you'll be staying, you can arrange to have your mail sent to American Express (6 Haymarket, London SW1Y 4BS). The service is free to cardholders; all others pay a small fee. You can also collect letters at London's main post office. Ask to have them addressed to "poste restante" and mailed to the Main Post Office, London. The point of collection is King Edward Building (King Edward St., London EU1A 1AA). Hours are Monday, Tuesday, Thursday, and

Friday 8:30–6:30; Wednesday 9–6:30; closed weekends. You'll need your passport or other official form of identification.

Shopping

VAT REFUNDS

Foreign visitors can avoid Britain's crippling 17½% value-added tax (VAT) by taking advantage of a variety of special refund and export schemes. The easiest and most common way of getting a refund is the Over-the-Counter method. To qualify for this, you must buy goods worth £75 or more (stores vary; if you are from the EU, it can be as much as £420). The shopkeeper will attach a special paper—Form VAT 407— to the invoice, and upon leaving the United Kingdom, you present the goods, form, and invoice to the customs officer. Allow plenty of time to do this at the airport; there are often long lines. The form is then returned to the store, and the refund forwarded to you, minus a small service charge. The Direct Export method is another option. With this method, you are also issued Form VAT 407, but your purchases are sent home separately, and upon returning home, you must have the form certified by customs or a notary public. You then return the form to the store, and your money is refunded.

Opening and Closing Times

Banks. Most banks are open weekdays 9:30–4:30. Some have extended hours on Thursday evenings, and a few are open on Saturday mornings.

Museums. Museum hours vary considerably from one part of the country to another. In large cities, most are open Tuesday–Saturday 10–5; many are also open on Sunday afternoons. The majority close one day a week. Be sure to double-check the opening times of historic houses, especially if the visit involves a difficult trip.

Shops. Usual business hours are Monday–Saturday 9–5:30, but many shops are now open Sundays. Outside the main centers, most shops observe an early closing day once a week, often Wednesday or Thursday; they close at 1 PM and do not reopen until the following morning. In small villages, many also close for lunch. In large cities—especially London—department stores stay open for late-night shopping (usually until 7:30 or 8) one day midweek.

National Holidays

England and Wales: January 1; April 5 (Good Friday); April 8 (Easter Monday); May 1 (May Day); May 6 (Spring Bank Holiday); August 26 (Summer Bank Holiday); December 25–26. Scotland: January 1–2; April 5, 8; May 1 (May Day); May 27 (Spring Bank Holiday); August 26; December 25–26.

Dining

British food was once condemned the world over for its plainness and mediocrity. But nowadays the problem is not so much bad food as expensive food; you might want to check prices on the menu, which by law must be displayed outside the restaurant, before committing yourself. The best of traditional British cooking relies on top-quality, fresh local ingredients: wild salmon, spring lamb, orchard apples, and countless varieties of seasonal vegetables. Nearly all restaurant menus also include some vegetarian dishes, and interesting ethnic cuisines, especially Asian, provide variety even in quite small towns. In the capital, restaurants have taken such giant steps during the past decade that London is now one of the world's greatest cities for dining out.

MEALTIMES

These vary somewhat, depending on the region of the country you are visiting. But in general, breakfast is served between 7:30 and 9 and lunch between noon and 2. Tea—a famous British tradition and often a meal in itself—is generally served between 4 and 5:30. Dinner or supper is served between 7:30 and 9:30, sometimes earlier, but rarely later outside the metropolitan areas. High tea, at about 6, replaces dinner in some areas, and in large cities, after-theater suppers are often available.

WHAT TO WEAR

Jacket and tie are suggested for the more formal restaurants in the top price categories, but, in general, casual chic or informal dress is acceptable in most establishments.

RATINGS

Prices quoted here are per person and include a first course, a main course, and dessert, but not wine or service. Highly recommended restaurants are indicated by a star ★.

CATEGORY	LONDON AND SOUTHERN ENGLAND	OTHER AREAS
$$$$	over £50	over £40
$$$	£30–£50	£25–40
$$	£20–£30	£15–25
$	under £20	under £15

Lodging

Britain offers a wide variety of accommodations, ranging from enormous, top-quality, top-price hotels to simple, intimate farmhouses and guest houses.

HOTELS

British hotels vary greatly, and there is no reliable official system of classification. Most have rooms with private bathrooms, although there are still many—usually older hotels—that offer some rooms with only wash basins; in this case, showers and bathtubs (and toilets) are usually just down the hall. Many also have "good" and "bad" wings. Be sure to check the room before you take it. Generally, British hotel prices include breakfast, but beware: Many offer only a Continental breakfast—often little more than tea and toast. A hotel that includes a traditional British breakfast in its rates is usually a good bet. Hotel prices in London can be significantly higher than in the rest of the country, and sometimes the quality does not reflect the extra cost. Tourist information centers all over the country will reserve rooms for you, usually for a small fee. A great many hotels offer special weekend and off-season bargain packages.

BED-AND-BREAKFASTS

In Britain these are small, simple establishments, not the upscale option Americans know by this name. They offer modest, inexpensive accommodations, usually in a family home. Few have private bathrooms, and most offer no meals other than breakfast. Guest houses are a slightly larger, somewhat more luxurious, version. Both provide the visitor with an excellent glimpse of everyday British life.

FARMHOUSES

Farmhouses rarely offer professional hotel standards, but they have a special appeal: the rustic, rural experience. Prices are generally very reasonable. Ask for the British Tourist Authority booklets "Farmhouse Vacations" and "Stay on a Farm." A car is vital for a successful farmhouse stay. The **Farm Holiday Bureau** (National Agricultural Centre, Stoneleigh, Kenilworth, Warwickshire CV8 2LZ, tel. 01203/696909), a network of farming and country people who offer B&B accommodation, is a good source for regional tourist board inspected and approved properties.

HOLIDAY COTTAGES

Furnished apartments, houses, cottages, and trailers are available for weekly rental in all areas of the country. These vary from quaint, cleverly converted farmhouses to brand-new buildings set in scenic surroundings. For families and large groups, they offer the best value for the money. Lists of rental properties are available free of charge from the British Tourist Authority. Discounts of up to 50% apply during the off-season (October to March). A useful publication on the subject is the *Good Holiday Cottage Guide* (Swallow Press).

HISTORIC BUILDINGS

Do you dream of spending your vacation in a gothic banqueting house, an old lighthouse, or maybe in a gate house that sheltered Mary, Queen of Scots, in 1586? There are some half-dozen organizations in Great Britain that have specially adapted historic buildings to rent. Most of them have cooking facilities, so for a short while you can pretend to have lived there all your life. Two of the leading charities that have such buildings for rent are **The Landmark Trust** (Shottesbrooke, Maidenhead, Berkshire SL6 3SW, tel. 01628/825925) and the **National Trust** (Box 101, Western Way, Melksham, Wiltshire SN12 8EA, tel. 01225/705676). All the buildings have been adapted and modernized, with due respect to their historic status, so you don't have to worry about medieval plumbing or Tudor kitchens. There are, however, no TVs in the Landmark Trust properties. Other organizations are **Portmeirion Cottages** (Portmeirion, Gwynedd, Wales LL48 6ER, tel. 01766/770228) and the rather upscale **Rural Retreats** (Retreat House, Station Rd., Blockley, Moreton-in-Marsh, Gloucestershire GL56 9DZ, tel. 01386/701177).

UNIVERSITY HOUSING

In larger cities and in some towns, certain universities offer their residence halls to paying vacationers. The facilities available are usually compact sleeping units, and they can be rented on a nightly basis. For information, contact the **British Universities Accommodation Consortium** (Box 880, University Park, Nottingham NG7 2RD, tel. 01602/504571).

YOUTH HOSTELS

There are more than 350 youth hostels throughout England, Wales, and Scotland. They range from very basic to very good. Many are located in remote and beautiful areas; others can be found on the outskirts of large cities. Despite the name, there is no age restriction. The accommodations are inexpensive and generally reliable and usually include cooking facilities. For additional information, contact the **YHA Headquarters** (Trevelyan House, 8 St. Stephen's Hill, St. Albans, Hertfordshire AL1 2DY, tel. 01727/855215).

CAMPING

Britain offers an abundance of campsites. Some are large and well equipped; others are merely small farmers' fields, offering primitive facilities. For information, contact the British Travel Authority in the United States or the **Camping and Caravan Club, Ltd.** (Greenfields House, Westwood Way, Coventry CV4 8JH, tel. 01203/694995).

RATINGS

Prices are for two people in a double room and include all taxes. Highly recommended lodgings are indicated by a star ★.

CATEGORY	LONDON AND SOUTHERN ENGLAND	OTHER AREAS
$$$$	over £150	over £110
$$$	£80–£150	£60–£110
$$	£60–£80	£50–£60
$	under £60	under £50

Tipping

Some restaurants and most hotels add a service charge of 10%–15% to the bill. If this has been done, you're under no obligation to tip further. If no service charge is indicated, add 10%–15% to your total bill. Taxi drivers should also get 10%–15%. You are not expected to tip theater or cinema ushers, elevator operators, or bartenders in pubs. Hairdressers and barbers should receive 10%–15%.

LONDON

Arriving and Departing

By Plane

International flights to London arrive at either Heathrow Airport, 19.4 kilometers (12 miles) west of London, or at Gatwick Airport, 40.3 kilometers (25 miles) south of the capital. Most flights from the United States go to Heathrow. Gatwick generally serves European destinations. American Airlines flights from Chicago and AirTransit flights from Toronto and Vancouver land at a third airport, Stansted.

BETWEEN THE AIRPORT AND DOWNTOWN

The Piccadilly Line serves Heathrow (all terminals) with a direct Underground (subway) link. The 40-minute ride cost £3.10 at press time (spring 1995). Three special buses also serve Heathrow: A1 leaves every 30 minutes for Victoria Station and takes about an hour; A2 goes to Euston Station every 30 minutes and takes 80 minutes. The one-way cost for either bus is £6. Bus 390 runs to Victoria eight times daily and costs £5 one-way.

From Gatwick, the quickest way to London is the nonstop rail Gatwick Express, costing (at press time) £8.90 one-way and taking 30 minutes to reach Victoria Station. Regular bus services are provided by Greenline Coaches, including the Flightline 777 to Victoria Station. This takes about 70 minutes and costs £6 one-way.

Cars and taxis drive into London on M4; the trip can take more than an hour, depending on traffic. The taxi fare is about £25, plus tip. From Gatwick, the taxi fare is at least £35, plus tip; traffic can be very heavy.

By Train

London is served by no fewer than 15 train stations, so be absolutely certain of the station for your departure or arrival. All have Underground stops either in the train station or within a few minutes' walk from it, and most are served by several bus routes. The principal routes that connect London to other major towns and cities are on an Inter-City network. Seats can be reserved by phone only with a credit card. You can, of course, apply in person to any British Rail Travel Centre or directly to the station from which you depart. Below is a list of the major London rail stations and the areas they serve.

Charing Cross (tel. 0171/928–5100) serves southeast England, including Canterbury, Margate, Dover/Folkestone.

Euston/St. Pancras (tel. 0171/387–7070) serves East Anglia, Essex, the Northeast, the Northwest, and North Wales, including Coventry, Stratford-upon-Avon, Birmingham, Manchester, Liverpool, Windermere, Glasgow, and Inverness.

King's Cross (tel. 0171/278–2477) serves the east Midlands; the Northeast, including York, Leeds, and Newcastle; and north and east Scotland, including Edinburgh and Aberdeen.

Liverpool Street (tel. 0171/928–5100) serves Essex and East Anglia.

Paddington (tel. 0171/262–6767) serves the south Midlands, west and south Wales, and the west country, including Reading, Bath, Bristol, Oxford, Cardiff, Swansea, Exeter, Plymouth, and Penzance.

Victoria (tel. 0171/928–5100) serves southern England, including Gatwick Airport, Brighton, Dover/Folkestone (from May), and the south coast.

Waterloo (tel. 0171/928-5100) serves the southwestern United Kingdom, including Salisbury, Bournemouth, Portsmouth, Southampton, Isle of Wight, Jersey, and Guernsey.

FARES

The fare structures are slowly changing as the formerly nationalized British Rail is sold off to various independent operators. Generally speaking, though, it is less expensive to buy a return (round-trip) ticket, especially for day trips not far from London, and you should always inquire at the information office to find out what discount fares are available for your route. You can hear a recorded summary of timetable and fare information to many destinations by calling the appropriate "dial and listen" numbers listed under British Rail in the telephone book.

Via the Channel Tunnel

If you're combining a trip to Great Britain with stops on the Continent, you can either drive your car onto a Le Shuttle train through the Channel Tunnel (35 minutes from Folkestone to Calais), or book a seat on the Eurostar high-speed train service that zips through the tunnel (3 hours from London's Waterloo Station to Paris, 3¼ hours from London to Brussels). For details, *see* the Channel Tunnel *in* Chapter 1.

By Bus

The **National Express** coach service has routes to more than 1,000 major towns and cities in the United Kingdom. It's considerably cheaper than the train, although the trips usually take longer. National Express offers two types of service: an ordinary service, which makes frequent stops for refreshment breaks, and a Rapide service, which has hostess and refreshment facilities on board. Day returns are available on both, but booking is advised on the Rapide service. National Express coaches leave Victoria Coach Station (Buckingham Palace Rd.) at regular intervals, depending on the destination. For travel information and credit card reservations, dial 0171/730–0202.

Getting Around

By Underground

Known as "the tube," London's extensive Underground system is by far the most widely used form of city transportation. Trains run both beneath and above ground out into the suburbs, and all stations are clearly marked with the London Underground circular symbol. (A

SUBWAY sign refers to an under-the-street crossing.) Trains are all one class; smoking is *not* allowed on board or in the stations.

There are 10 basic lines—all named—plus the East London line, which runs from Shoreditch and Whitechapel across the Thames south to New Cross, and the Docklands Light Railway, which runs from Stratford in London's East End to Greenwich, with an extension to the Royal Docks to be completed. The Central, District, Northern, Metropolitan, and Piccadilly lines all have branches, so be sure to note which branch is needed for your particular destination. Electronic platform signs tell you the final stop and route of the next train, and most signs also indicate how many minutes you'll have to wait for the train to arrive.

From Monday to Saturday, trains begin running around 5:30 AM; the last services leave central London between midnight and 12:30 AM. On Sundays, trains start two hours later and finish about an hour earlier. The frequency of trains depends on the route and the time of day, but normally you should not have to wait more than 10 minutes in central areas.

A pocket map of the entire tube network is available free from most Underground ticket counters. There should also be a large map on the wall of each platform, and the new computerized database, "Routes," is available at 14 London Transport (LT) Travel Information Centres (*see below*).

FARES

For both buses and tube fares, London is divided into six concentric zones; the fare goes up the farther afield you travel. Ask at Underground ticket counters for the LT booklet "Tickets," which gives details of all the various ticket options and bargains for the tube; after some experimenting, you'll soon know which ticket best serves your particular needs. Till then, here is a brief summary of the major ticket categories, but note that these prices are subject to increases.

Singles and Returns. For one trip between any two stations, you can buy an ordinary single (one-way ticket) for travel anytime on the day of issue; if you're coming back on the same route the same day, then an ordinary return (round-trip ticket) costs twice the single fare. Singles vary in price from £1 in the central zone to £3.10 for a six-zone journey—not a good option for the sightseer who wants to make several journeys.

One-Day Travelcards. These allow unrestricted travel on the tube, most buses, and British Rail trains in the Greater London zones and are valid weekdays after 9:30 AM, weekends, and all public holidays. They cannot be used on airbuses, night buses, or for certain special services. The price is £2.80–£3.80.

Visitor's Travelcard. These are the best bet for visitors, but they must be bought before leaving home (they're available in both the United States and Canada). They are valid for periods of three, four, or seven days ($25, $32, $49 adults; $11, $13, $21 children) and can be used on the tube and virtually all buses and British Rail services in London. One-day Visitor's Travelcards can be bought at hotels in London for £3.90. All these cards also include a set of money-saving discounts to many of London's top attractions. Apply to travel agents or to BritRail Travel International (1500 Broadway, New York, NY 10036, tel. 212/382–3737).

For more information, there are **LT Travel Information Centres** at the following tube stations: Euston (open Sat.–Thurs. 7:15–6, Fri. to

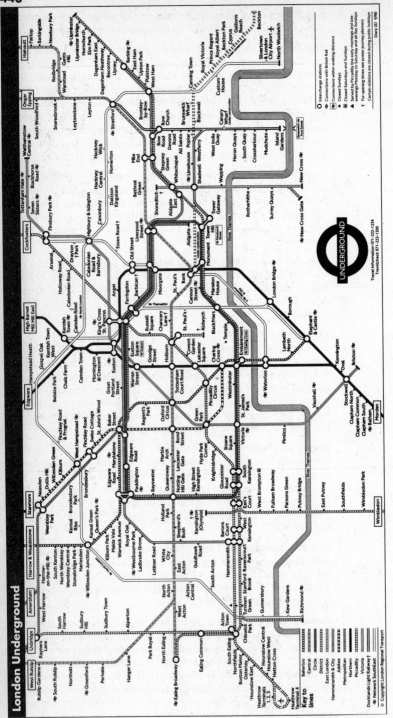

London Underground

7:30); King's Cross (open Sat.–Thurs. 8:15–6, Fri. to 7:30); Oxford Circus (open Mon.–Sat. 8:15–6); Piccadilly Circus (open Mon.–Sun. 8:15–6); Victoria (open Mon.–Sun. 8:15–9:30); and Heathrow (open Mon.–Sun. to 9 or 10 PM in Terminals 1 and 2). For information on all London bus and tube times, fares, and so on, dial 0171/222–1234.

By Bus

London's bus system consists of bright red double- and single-deckers, plus other buses of various colors. Destinations are displayed on the front and back, with the bus number on the front, back, and side, though not all buses run the full length of their route at all times. Some buses are still operated with a conductor whom you pay after finding a seat, but these days you will more often find one-man buses, in which you pay the driver upon boarding.

Buses stop only at clearly indicated stops. Main stops—at which the bus should stop automatically—have a plain white background with a red LT symbol on it. There are also request stops with red signs, a white symbol, and the word REQUEST added; at these you must hail the bus to make it stop. Smoking is not allowed on any bus. Although you can see much of the town from a bus, *don't* take one if you want to get anywhere in a hurry; traffic often slows travel to a crawl, and during peak times you may find yourself waiting at least 20 minutes for a bus and not being able to get on it once it arrives. If you intend to go by bus, ask at a Travel Information Centre for a free "Londonwide Bus Map."

FARES

Single fares start at 50p for short distances (90p in the central zone). Travelcards are good for tube, bus, and British Rail trains in the Greater London Zones. There are also a number of bus passes available for daily, weekly, and monthly use, and prices vary according to zones. A photograph is required for weekly or monthly bus passes; this also applies to children and older children who may need a child-rate photocard to avoid paying the adult rate.

By Taxi

London's black taxis are famous for their comfort and for the ability of their drivers to remember the mazelike pattern of the capital's streets. Hotels and main tourist areas have ranks (stands) where you wait your turn to take one of the taxis that drive up. You can also hail a taxi if the flag is up or the yellow FOR HIRE sign is lighted. Fares start at £1 and increase by units of 20p per 291 yards or 1 minute. A surcharge of 60p is added in the evenings until midnight, on Sundays, and on holidays.

By Car

The best advice is to avoid driving in London because of the illogical street patterns and the chronic parking shortage. A constantly changing system of one-way streets adds to the confusion.

Important Addresses and Numbers

Tourist Information

The main **London Tourist Information Centre** at Victoria Station Forecourt provides details about London and the rest of Britain, including general information; tickets for tube and bus; theater, concert, and tour bookings; and accommodations (open Apr.–Oct., daily 9–8:30; Nov.–Mar., Mon.–Sat. 9–7, Sun. 9–5). Other information centers are located in **Harrods** (Brompton Rd., SW1 7XL) and **Selfridges** (Oxford St., W1A 2LR) and are open store hours only; at **Tower of London** (West Gate, EC3W 4AB), open summer months only; and **Heathrow Airport**

(Terminals 1, 2, and 3). **Visitorcall** is the London Tourist Board's phone service—a premium-rate (49p per minute; 39p off-peak) recorded information line, with different numbers for theater, events, museums, sports, getting around, and so on. To access the list of options, call 01839/123456, or see the display advertisement in the phone book. An events calendar is also available via fax, tel. 01839/401278.

Embassies and Consulates
American Embassy (24 Grosvenor Sq., W1A 1AE, tel. 0171/499–9000). Inside the embassy is the **American Aid Society,** a charity set up to help Americans in distress. Dial the embassy number and ask for extension 570 or 571.

Canadian High Commission (McDonald House, 1 Grosvenor Sq., W1, tel. 0171/258–6600).

Emergencies
For **police, fire brigade,** or **ambulance,** dial 999.

The following **hospitals** have 24-hour emergency rooms: **Charing Cross** (Fulham Palace Rd., W6, tel. 0181/846–1234); **Guys** (St. Thomas St., SE1, tel. 0171/955–5000); **Royal Free** (Pond St., Hampstead, NW3, tel. 0171/794–0500); and **St. Thomas's** (Lambeth Palace Rd., SE1, tel. 0171/928–9292).

Pharmacies
Chemists (drugstores) with late opening hours include **Bliss Chemist** (5 Marble Arch, W1, tel. 0171/723–6116, open daily 9 AM–midnight) and **Boots** (44 Piccadilly Circus, W1, tel. 0171/734–6126, open Mon.–Sat. 8:30–8, also the branch at 439 Oxford St., W1, tel. 0171/409–2857, open Thurs. 8:30–7).

Travel Agencies
American Express (6 Haymarket, SW1, tel. 0171/930–4411; 89 Mount St., W1, tel. 0171/499–0288; and other branches). **Thomas Cook** (4 Henrietta St., WC2, tel. 0171/240–4872; 1 Marble Arch, W1, tel. 0171/706–4188; and branches).

Credit Cards
Should your credit cards be lost or stolen, here are some numbers to dial for assistance: **Access (MasterCard,** tel. 0181/450–3122); **American Express** (tel. 0171/222–9633, 24 hours, or 01800/521313 for traveler's checks); **Barclaycard (Visa,** tel. 01604/230230); **Diners Club** (tel. 01252/516261).

Guided Tours

Orientation Tours
BY BUS
LT's London Plus sightseeing tours (tel. 0171/828–7395) offer passengers a good introduction to the city from double-decker buses (seating capacity 64–72). Tours run daily every half hour 9:30–5:30 April–October (on the hour 10–4, November–March), departing from Marble Arch, Haymarket, Baker Street, or Embankment. There are about 21 stops, where you may board and alight to view the sights and then get back on the next bus. Tickets cost £10 (£5 for those under 16 years old) and can be bought from the driver, any LT Travel Information Centre, or Tourist Information Centres. Other reputable agencies offering half- and full-day bus tours include **Evan Evans** (tel. 0171/930–2377), **Frames Rickards** (tel. 0171/837–3111), and **The Big Bus Company** (tel. 0181/944–7810). These tours have a smaller seating capacity of approximately 50 passengers and include stops at places such as St. Paul's Cathedral and

Westminster Abbey. Prices and pick-up points vary according to the sights visited, but many pick-up points are at major hotels.

BY RIVER

From April to October, boats cruise up and down the Thames, offering a different view of the London skyline. Most leave from Westminster Pier (tel. 0171/930–4097), Charing Cross Pier (Victoria Embankment, tel. 0171/839–3312), or Tower Pier (tel. 0171/488–0344). Downstream routes go to the Tower of London, Greenwich, and Thames Barrier; upstream destinations include Kew, Richmond, and Hampton Court. Most of the launches seat between 100 and 250 passengers, have a public-address system, and provide a running commentary on passing points of interest. Depending upon the destination, river trips may last from one to four hours. For more information, call **Catamaran Cruisers** (tel. 0171/839–3572), or **Tidal Cruises** (tel. 0171/928–9009).

BY CANAL

During summer, narrow boats and barges cruise London's two canals, the Grand Union and Regent's Canal; most vessels (seating about 60) operate on the latter, which runs between Little Venice in the west (the nearest tube is Warwick Ave. on the Bakerloo Line) and Camden Lock (about 200 yards north of Camden Town tube station). **Jason's Trip** (tel. 0171/286–3428) operates one-way and round-trip narrow boat cruises on this route. During April, May, and September, there are two cruises per day; from June to August there are four. Trips last 1½ hours. **Canal Cruises** (tel. 0171/485–4433) also offers cruises from March to October on the *Jenny Wren* and all year on the cruising restaurant *My Fair Lady*.

Walking Tours

One of the best ways to get to know London is on foot, and there are many guided walking tours from which to choose. **The Original London Walks** (tel. 0171/624–3978), **City Walks** (tel. 0171/700–6931), and **Citisights** (tel. 0181/806–4325) are just a few of the better-known firms, but your best bet is to peruse a variety of leaflets at the London Tourist Information Centre at Victoria Station. The duration of the walks varies (usually 1–3 hours), and you can generally find one to suit even the most specific of interests—Shakespeare's London, say, or a Jack the Ripper tour. Prices are around £4 for adults.

If you'd rather explore on your own, then the City of London Corporation has laid out a **Heritage Walk** that leads through Bank, Leadenhall, and Monument; follow the trail by the directional stars set into the sidewalks. A map of this walk can be found in *A Visitor's Guide to the City of London,* available from the City Information Centre across from St. Paul's Cathedral. Another option is to follow the **Silver Jubilee Walkway,** created in 1977 in honor of the 25th anniversary of the reign of the present queen. The entire route covers 16 kilometers (10 miles) and is marked by a series of silver crowns set into the sidewalks; Parliament Square makes a good starting point. Several guides offering further London walks to follow are available in bookshops.

Excursions

LT, Evan Evans, and Frames Rickards (*see* Orientation Tours, *above*) all offer day excursions (some combine bus and boat) to places of interest within easy reach of London, such as Windsor, Hampton Court, Oxford, Stratford, and Bath. Prices vary and may include lunch and admission prices or admission only.

Personal Guides

British Tours (tel. 0171/629–5267) will pick you up from your hotel and take you anywhere in the United Kingdom. Tour prices include car and driver-guide expenses and range from £100 for two people in a medium-size car going on a three-hour tour of London to £295 for four people in a large car taking in Bath and Stonehenge (10 hours). A good choice of tours, for one to six people, is available all year. Details of similar private operators can be found at the London Tourist Information Centre in Victoria Station or at Heathrow.

Exploring London

Traditionally London has been divided between the City, to the east, where its banking and commercial interests lie, and Westminster to the west, the seat of the royal court and of government. Today the distinction between the two holds good, and even the briefest exploration will reveal each area's distinct atmosphere. It is also in these two areas that you will find most of the grand buildings that have played a central role in British history: the Tower of London and St. Paul's Cathedral, Westminster Abbey and the Houses of Parliament, Buckingham Palace, and the older royal palace of St. James's.

These sights are natural magnets for visitors to London, as the crowds of people and the ubiquitous tourist coaches demonstrate. But visitors who restrict their sightseeing to these well-known tourist areas miss much of the best the city has to offer. Within a few minutes' walk of Buckingham Palace, for instance, lie St. James's and Mayfair, two neighboring quarters of elegant town houses built for the nobility in the 17th and early 18th centuries and now notable for the shopping opportunities they house. The same lesson applies to the City, where, tucked away in quiet corners, stand many of the churches Christopher Wren built to replace those destroyed during the Great Fire of 1666.

Other parts of London worth exploring include Covent Garden, a former fruit and flower market converted into a lively shopping and entertainment center where you can wander for hours enjoying the friendly bustle of the streets. Hyde Park and Kensington Gardens, by contrast, offer a great swathe of green parkland across the city center, preserved by past kings and queens for their own hunting and relaxation. A walk across Hyde Park will bring you to the museum district of South Kensington, with three major national collections: the Natural History Museum, the Science Museum, and the Victoria and Albert Museum, which specializes in costume and the fine and applied arts.

The south side of the River Thames has its treats as well. A short stroll across Waterloo Bridge brings you to the South Bank Arts Complex, which includes the National Theatre, the Royal Festival Hall, the Hayward Gallery (with changing exhibitions of international art), the National Film Theatre, and the Museum of the Moving Image (MOMI)—a must for movie buffs. The views from here are stunning—to the west are the Houses of Parliament and Big Ben; to the east the dome of St. Paul's is just visible on London's changing skyline.

London, although not simple of layout, is a rewarding walking city, and this remains the best way to get to know its nooks and crannies. The infamous weather may not be on your side, but there's plenty of indoor entertainment to keep you amused if you forgot the umbrella. More than in most cities, though, London's centuries of history are revealed as much in the quotidian street life and residential districts as in the grand national monuments, so keep your eyes peeled, and discover it for yourself.

Numbers in the margin correspond to points of interest on the London map.

Westminster

Westminster is the royal backyard—the traditional center of the royal court and of government. Here, within a kilometer or so of each other, are virtually all London's most celebrated buildings (St. Paul's Cathedral and the Tower of London excepted), and there is a strong feeling of history all around you. Generations of kings and queens and their offspring have lived here since the end of the 11th century, in no less than four palaces, three of which (Buckingham, St. James's, and Westminster) still stand.

① Start at **Trafalgar Square,** which is on the site of the former Royal Mews. Both the square's name and its present appearance date from about 1830. A statue of Lord Nelson, victor over the French in 1805 at the Battle of Trafalgar, at which he lost his life, stands atop a column. Huge stone lions guard the base of the column, which is decorated with four bronze panels depicting naval battles against France and cast from French cannons captured by Nelson. The bronze equestrian statue on the south side of the square is of the unhappy Charles I; he is looking down Whitehall toward the spot where he was executed in 1649.

② In the **National Gallery,** which occupies the long neoclassical building on the north side of the square, is a comprehensive collection of paintings, with works from virtually every famous artist and school from the 14th to the 19th century. The gallery is especially strong on Flemish and Dutch masters, Rubens and Rembrandt among them, and on Italian Renaissance works. The Sainsbury Wing houses the early Renaissance collection. *Trafalgar Sq., tel. 0171/839–3321; 0171/839–3526 (recorded information). Admission free; charge for Sainsbury Wing exhibitions. Open Mon.–Sat. 10–6, Sun. 2–6; June–Aug., Wed. until 8.*

③ Around the corner, at the foot of Charing Cross Road, is a second major art collection, the **National Portrait Gallery,** which contains portraits of well-known (and not so well-known) Britons, including monarchs, statesmen, and writers. *2 St. Martin's Pl., tel. 0171/930–1552. Admission free. Open weekdays 10–5, Sat. 10–6, Sun. 2–6.*

④ The Gallery's entrance is opposite the distinctive neoclassical church of **St. Martin-in-the-Fields,** built in about 1730. Regular lunchtime music recitals are held here.

TIME OUT Both **The Brasserie** in the Sainsbury Wing of the National Gallery and **Café in the Crypt** in St. Martin's serve ambitious hot meals at lunchtime, as well as sandwiches, salads, snacks, cakes, and coffee.

⑤ **Admiralty Arch** guards the entrance to **The Mall,** the great ceremonial way that leads alongside **St. James's Park** to Buckingham Palace. The Mall takes its name from a game called "pell mell," a version of croquet that society people, including Charles II and his courtiers, used to play here in the late 1600s. The park—with its duck-filled lake, deck chairs, bandstand, and perfectly maintained flower beds—was developed by successive monarchs, most recently by George IV in the 1820s, having originally been used for hunting by Henry VIII. Join office workers relaxing with a lunchtime sandwich, or stroll here on a summer's evening when the illuminated fountains play and Westminster Abbey and the Houses of Parliament beyond the trees are floodlit.

London

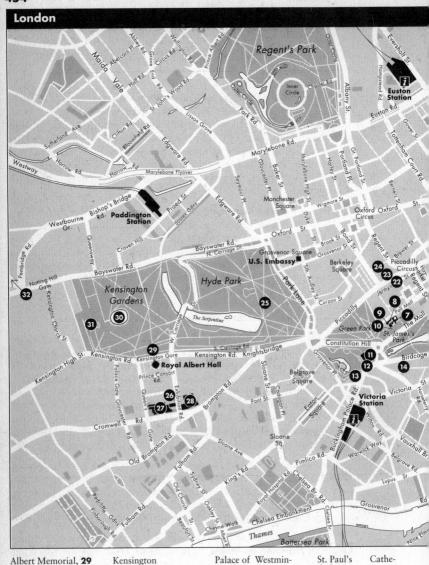

Albert Memorial, **29**

Bank of England, **45**

Banqueting House, **20**

Barbican, **42**

British Museum, **38**

Buckingham Palace, **11**

Cabinet War Rooms, **15**

Carlton House Terrace, **6**

Cenotaph, **19**

Clarence House, **10**

Covent Garden, **33**

Guildhall, **43**

Horse Guards Parade, **21**

Hyde Park, **25**

Kensington Palace, **31**

Lancaster House, **9**

Leadenhall Market, **48**

Lloyd's of London, **49**

London Transport Museum, **35**

The Mall, **5**

Mansion House, **47**

Museum of London, **41**

Museum of Mankind, **24**

National Gallery, **2**

National Portrait Gallery, **3**

Natural History Museum, **27**

Palace of Westminster, **17**

Parliament Square, **16**

Portobello Road, **32**

Queen's Gallery, **12**

Round Pond, **30**

Royal Academy, **23**

Royal Exchange, **46**

Royal Mews, **13**

Royal Opera House, **37**

St. James's Church, **22**

St. James's Palace, **7**

St. Martin-in-the-Fields, **4**

St. Mary-le-Bow, **44**

St. Paul's Cathedral, **40**

St. Paul's Church, **34**

Science Museum, **26**

Sir John Soane's Museum, **39**

Theatre Museum, **36**

Tower of London, **50**

Trafalgar Square, **1**

Victoria and Albert Museum, **28**

Wellington Barracks, **14**

Westminster Abbey, **18**

York House, **8**

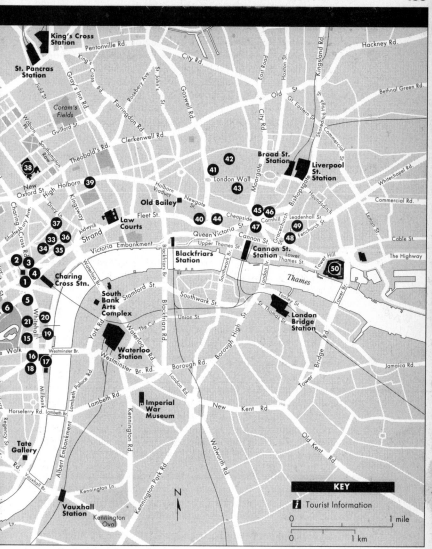

King's Cross
Station

St. Pancras
Station

Pentonville Rd.

City Rd.

Hackney Rd.

King's Cross Rd.

Rosebery Ave.

St. John's St.

Goswell Rd.

City Rd.

Old St.

East Road

Hoxton St.

Kingsland Rd.

Shoreditch High St.

Gt. Eastern St.

Commercial St.

Bethnal Green Rd.

Coram's
Fields

Guilford St.

Gray's Inn Rd.

Judd St.

Woburn

Southampton Row

Theobald's Rd.

Clerkenwell Rd.

Farringdon Rd.

38

New
Oxford St.

High Holborn

39

Holborn
Viaduct

41

London Wall

42

43

Moorgate

Broad St.
Station

Liverpool
St.
Station

Whitechapel Rd.

Bishopsgate

Houndsditch

Commercial Rd.

Charing
Cross Rd.

Shaftesbury Ave.

Gt. Russell St.

Drury Lane

Kingsway

37

33 **36**

34 **35**

Ashwych

Strand

**Law
Courts**

Fleet St.

Old Bailey

Newgate
St.

40 **44**

Cheapside

45 **46**

47

Cornhill

Leadenhall St.

Fenchurch St.

48

49

Lemon St.

Cable St.

The Highway

Queen Victoria St.

Cannon St.

**Cannon St.
Station**

Upper Thames St.

Lower
Thames St.

Tower Hill

50

Victoria Embankment

Blackfriars Br.

Southwark Br.

London Br.

Tower Br.

**Blackfriars
Station**

Thames

2 **3**

4

1

**Charing
Cross Stn.**

Waterloo Br.

**South
Bank
Arts
Complex**

Stamford St.

Southwark St.

Tooley St.

St. Thomas St.

**London
Bridge
Station**

Jamaica Rd.

5

6

21 **20**

15 **19**

York Rd.

Blackfriars Rd.

The Cut

Union St.

Borough High St.

Borough Rd.

Tower
Bridge Rd.

Walk

Whitehall

16 **17**

18

Westminster Br.

**Waterloo
Station**

Westminster Br. Rd.

London Rd.

New

Kent

Rd.

Old Kent Rd.

Horseferry Rd.

Lambeth Br.

Millbank

Lambeth Palace Rd.

Lambeth Rd.

Kennington Rd.

**Imperial
War
Museum**

Walworth Rd.

**Tate
Gallery**

Regency St.

Albert Embankment

Vauxhall Br.

Kennington Ln.

Kennington Park Rd.

**Vauxhall
Station**

Kennington
Oval

N

| **KEY** |

i Tourist Information

0 _____ 1 mile

0 _____ 1 km

On the other side of the Mall, you'll pass along the foot of the imposing
⑥ **Carlton House Terrace,** built in 1827–32 by John Nash. A right turn
up Marlborough Road brings you to the complex of royal and gov-
⑦ ernment buildings known collectively as **St. James's Palace.** Although
the earliest parts of this lovely brick building date from the 1530s, it
had a relatively short career as the center of royal affairs, from the destruction of Whitehall Palace in 1698 until 1837, when Victoria became queen and moved the royal household down the road to
Buckingham Palace. A number of royal functionaries have offices here,
however, and various court functions are held in the state rooms.

At the end of Marlborough Road, beyond the open-sided **Friary Court,**
⑧ turn left along **Cleveland Row,** and walk past **York House,** the London
home of the duke and duchess of Kent. Another left turn into **Stable**
⑨ **Yard Road** takes you to **Lancaster House,** built for the duke of York
by Nash in the 1820s and used today for government receptions and
⑩ conferences. On the other side of Stable Yard is **Clarence House,** designed and built by Nash in 1825 for the duke of Clarence, who later
became King William IV. It was restored in 1949 and is now the home
of the Queen Mother. Inside the palace is the **Chapel Royal,** said to have
been designed for Henry VIII by the painter Holbein; it was heavily
redecorated in the mid-19th century. The ceiling still has the initials *H*
and *A*, intertwined, standing for Henry VIII and his second wife, Anne
Boleyn, the mother of Elizabeth I and the first of his wives to lose her
head. The public can attend Sunday morning services here between the
first week of October and Good Friday.

⑪ **Buckingham Palace,** at the end of the Mall, is the London home of the
queen and the administrative hub of the entire royal family. When the
queen is in residence (normally on weekdays except in January, August,
September, and part of June), the royal standard flies over the east front.
Inside there are dozens of splendid state rooms used on such formal occasions as banquets for visiting heads of state. The private apartments
of Queen Elizabeth and Prince Philip are in the north wing. Behind the
palace lie some 40 acres of private gardens, a wildlife haven.

The ceremony of the **Changing of the Guard** takes place in front of the
palace at 11:30 daily, May through July, and on alternate days during
the rest of the year. It's advisable to arrive early, since people are invariably stacked several-deep along the railings, whatever the weather.

Parts of **Buckingham Palace** are open to the public during August and
September; the former chapel, bombed during World War II, rebuilt
⑫ in 1961, and now the **Queen's Gallery,** shows paintings from the vast
royal art collections from March through December. *Buckingham
Palace Rd., tel. 0171/493–3175. Admission: £8 adults, £4 children,
£5.50 senior citizens. Queen's Gallery, tel. 0171/799–2331. Admission: £3 adults, £1.50 children, £2 senior citizens. Open Tues.–Sat. and
bank holidays 10–5, Sun. 2–5; closed between exhibitions.*

Just along Buckingham Palace Road from the Queen's Gallery is the
⑬ **Royal Mews,** where some of the queen's horses are stabled and the elaborately gilded state coaches are on view. *Tel. 0171/799–2331. Admission:
£3 adults, £1.50 children, £2 senior citizens. Combined ticket with
Queen's Gallery: £5 adults, £2.20 children, £3.50 senior citizens.
Open Oct.–Mar., Wed. noon–4; April–Sept., Tues.–Thurs. noon–4; closed
March 25–30, Oct. 1–6, Dec. 23–Jan. 5.*

Birdcage Walk, so called because it was once the site of the royal
⑭ aviaries, runs along the south side of St. James's Park, past the **Wellington Barracks.** These are the regimental headquarters of the Guards Di-

vision, the elite troops that traditionally guard the sovereign and mount the guard at Buckingham Palace. The **Guards Museum** relates the history of the Guards from the 1660s to the present; paintings of battle scenes, uniforms, and a cat-o'-nine-tails are among the items on display. *Tel. 0171/414–3428. Admission: £2 adults, £1 children under 16 and senior citizens. Open Sat.–Thurs. 10–4.*

⑮ The **Cabinet War Rooms,** between the Foreign Office and the Home Office, are the underground offices used by the British High Command during World War II. Among the rooms on display are the Prime Minister's Room, from which Winston Churchill made many of his inspiring wartime broadcasts, and the Transatlantic Telephone Room, from which he spoke directly to President Roosevelt in the White House. *Clive Steps, King Charles St., tel. 0171/930–6961. Admission: £3.90 adults, £1.90 children under 16, £3 senior citizens. Open daily 10–5:15.*

⑯ **Parliament Square** is flanked, on the river side, by the Palace of Westminster. Among the statues of statesmen long since dead are those of Churchill, Abraham Lincoln, and Oliver Cromwell, the Lord Protector of England during the country's brief attempt at being a republic (1648–60).

⑰ The **Palace of Westminster** was the monarch's main residence from the 11th century until 1512, when the court moved to the newly built Whitehall Palace. The only part of the original building to have survived, however, is **Westminster Hall,** which has a fine hammer-beam roof. Westminster Hall is used only on rare ceremonial occasions. The rest was destroyed in a disastrous fire in 1834 and was rebuilt in the newly popular mock-medieval Gothic style with ornate interior decorations. The architect, Augustus Pugin, provided many delightful touches, such as Gothic umbrella stands. This newer part of the palace contains the debating chambers and committee rooms of the two Houses of Parliament—the Commons (whose members are elected) and the Lords (whose members are appointed or inherit their seats). There are no tours of the palace, but the public is admitted to the Public Gallery of each House; expect to wait in line for several hours (the line for the Lords is generally much shorter than that for the Commons).

The most famous features of the palace are its towers. At the south end is the 341-foot **Victoria Tower.** At the other end is **St. Stephen's Tower,** better known, but inaccurately so, as Big Ben. That name properly belongs to the 13-ton bell in the tower on which the hours are struck; Big Ben himself was probably Sir Benjamin Hall, commissioner of works when the bell was installed in the 1850s. A light shines from the top of the tower during a night sitting of Parliament.

⑱ **Westminster Abbey** is the most ancient of London's great churches and the most important, for it is here that Britain's monarchs are crowned. It is unusual for a church of this size and national importance not to be a cathedral. The abbey dates largely from the 13th and 14th centuries, although **Henry VII's Chapel,** an exquisite example of the heavily decorated late-Gothic style, was not built until the early 1600s, and the twin towers over the west entrance are an 18th-century addition. There is much to see inside, including the touching tomb of the Unknown Warrior, a nameless World War I soldier buried, in memory of the war's victims, in earth brought with his corpse from France; and the famous Poets' Corner, where England's great writers—Milton, Chaucer, Shakespeare, et al—are memorialized, and some are actually buried. Behind the high altar are the royal tombs, including those of Queen Elizabeth I; Mary, Queen of Scots; and Henry V. In the Chapel of Edward the Confessor stands the Coronation Chair. Among the royal weddings that have taken place here are those of the present queen and most recently, in 1986, the duke and duchess of York.

It is all too easy to forget, swamped by the crowds trying to see the abbey's sights, that this is a place of worship. Early morning is a good moment to catch something of the building's atmosphere. Better still, take time to attend a service. *Broad Sanctuary, tel. 0171/222–5152. Admission to the nave is free; to Poets' Corner and Royal Chapels: £4 adults, £1 children, £2 students and senior citizens (Royal Chapels, free Wed. 6–7:45 PM). Open weekdays 9–4, Sat. 9–2 and 3:45–5; Sun. all day for services only; museum and cloisters open Sun.; closed weekdays to visitors during services; Royal Chapels closed Sun. No photography except Mon. eve.*

The Norman **Undercroft,** off the original monastic cloisters, houses a small museum with exhibits on the abbey's history. In the **Pyx Chamber** next door, the original strongroom, the Abbey's treasure is housed. The nearby **Chapter House** was where the English Parliament first met. *Tel. 0171/222–5152. Joint admission: £2.10 adults, £1.65 students and senior citizens, £1.05 children. Open daily 10:30–1:45.*

From Parliament Square, walk up **Parliament Street** and **Whitehall** (this is a single street—its name changes), past government offices, toward
🄳 Trafalgar Square. The **Cenotaph,** in the middle of the road, is the national memorial to the dead of both world wars. On the left is the entrance to **Downing Street,** an unassuming row of 18th-century houses. The prime minister's office is at No. 10 (he has a private apartment on the top floor). The chancellor of the exchequer, the finance minister, occupies No. 11.

🄴 On the right side of Whitehall is the **Banqueting House,** built by the architect Inigo Jones in 1625 for court entertainments. This is the only part of Whitehall Palace, the monarch's principal residence in the 16th and 17th centuries, that was not burned down in 1698. It has a magnificent ceiling by Rubens, and outside there is an inscription that marks the window through which King Charles I stepped to his execution. *Tel. 0171/930–4179. Admission: £2.90 adults, £2.20 students and senior citizens, £1.90 children. Open Tues.–Sat. 10–5, Sun. 2–5.*

🄵 Opposite is the entrance to **Horse Guards Parade,** the former tiltyard of Whitehall Palace. This is the site of the annual ceremony of Trooping the Colour, when the queen takes the salute in the great military parade that marks her official birthday on the second Saturday in June (her real one is on April 21). There is also a daily guard-changing ceremony outside the guard house, at 11 AM (10 on Sunday).

St. James's and Mayfair

After such a concentrated dose of grand, historical buildings, it's time to explore two of London's elegant shopping areas. Start by walking west from Piccadilly Circus along **Piccadilly,** a busy street lined with some grand and very English shops (including **Hatchards,** the booksellers; **Swaine, Adeney Brigg,** the equestrian outfitters; and **Fortnum and Mason,** the department store that supplies the queen's groceries).

🄶 **St. James's Church** was designed by the 17th-century architect Christopher Wren and contains beautiful wood carvings by Grinling Gibbons.

TIME OUT   **The Wren** at St. James's is a friendly café in the church precincts. Coffee, pastries, and light lunches are served.

Jermyn Street, south of Piccadilly, is famous for upscale shops that sell accessories for the gentleman's wardrobe, from handmade shoes to bespoke hats (his suits come from nearby Savile Row). Shops along **Duke Street** and **Bury Street** specialize in paintings, the former in old masters, the latter in early English watercolors. Don't be put off by the exclusive appearance of these establishments—anyone is free to enter, and there is no obligation to buy. **King Street** is home to **Christie's,** the fine art auctioneer, and to **Spink and Son,** renowned for Oriental art.

㉓ On the north side of Piccadilly, **Burlington House** contains the offices of many learned societies and the headquarters of the **Royal Academy.** The RA, as it is generally known, stages major visiting art exhibitions. The best known is the Summer Exhibition (May–Aug.), featuring a chaotic hodge-podge of works by living British artists.

Burlington Arcade, beside the RA, is a covered walkway that dates from 1819, where quaint shops sell luxury: cashmere sweaters, silk scarves, handmade chocolates, leather-bound books. A uniformed beadle is on duty to ensure that no one runs, whistles, or sings here.

㉔ The **Museum of Mankind,** behind the RA, contains the British Museum's ethnographic collection, though this will shortly be transferred to the British Museum when the British Library moves to its new premises in St. Pancras. There are displays on the South Seas, the Arctic, and other regions of the world. *6 Burlington Gardens, tel. 0171/323–8043. Admission free. Open Mon.–Sat. 10–5, Sun. 2:30–6.*

There are three special shopping streets in this section of Mayfair, each with its own specialties. **Savile Row** is the home of gentlemen's tailors. Nearby **Cork Street** has many dealers in modern and classical art. **Bond Street** (divided into two parts, Old and New, though both are some 300 years old) is the classiest shopping street in London, the home of haute couture, with such famous names as **Gucci, Hermès,** and **Chanel,** and costly jewelry from such shops as **Asprey, Tiffany,** and **Cartier.**

Some of the original 18th-century houses survive on the west side of **Berkeley Square** (currently being renovated). Farther along is **Curzon Street,** which runs along the northern edge of **Shepherd Market,** a maze of narrow streets full of antiques shops, restaurants, and pubs.

TIME OUT **L'Artiste Musclé** is a popular bistro serving French food with a few picturesque tables outside in summer. *1 Shepherd Market.*

Hyde Park and Beyond

㉕ A great expanse of green parkland begins at **Hyde Park Corner** and cuts right across the center of London. **Hyde Park,** which covers about 340 acres, was originally a royal hunting ground, while **Kensington Gardens,** which adjoins it to the west, started life as part of the royal Kensington Palace. These two parks contain many fine trees and are a haven for wildlife. The sandy track that runs along the south edge of the parks has been a fashionable riding trail for centuries. Though it's called **Rotten Row,** there's nothing rotten about it. The name derives from *route du roi* (the King's Way)—the route William III and Queen Mary took from their home at Kensington Palace to the court at St. James's. There is boating and swimming in the **Serpentine,** the S-shaped lake formed by damming a stream that used to flow here. Refreshments can be had at the lakeside tearooms, and the **Serpentine Gallery** holds noteworthy exhibitions of modern art (tel. 0171/402–6075).

㉖ Leave the park at **Exhibition Road** and visit three of London's major museums. The **Science Museum** is the leading national collection of science and technology, with extensive hands-on exhibits on outer space, astronomy, computers, transportation, and medicine. *Tel. 0171/938–8000; 0171/938–8123 (recorded information). Admission: £4.50 adults, £2.40 children under 15 and senior citizens. Open Mon.–Sat. 10–6, Sun. 11–6.*

㉗ The **Natural History Museum** is housed in an ornate late-Victorian building with striking modern additions. As in the Science Museum, its displays on topics such as human biology and evolution are designed to challenge visitors to think for themselves. *Cromwell Rd., tel. 0171/938–9123; 0142/692–7654 (recorded information). Admission: £5 adults, £2.50 children under 15 and senior citizens; free weekdays 4:30–5:50. Open Mon.–Sat. 10–6, Sun. 2:30–6.*

㉘ The **Victoria and Albert Museum** (or V&A) originated in the 19th century as a museum of decorative art and has extensive collections of costumes, paintings, jewelry, and crafts from every part of the globe. The collections from India, China, and the Islamic world are especially strong. *Cromwell Rd., tel. 0171/938–8500; 0171/938–8441 (recorded information). Suggested voluntary contribution: £4.50 adults, £1 children and senior citizens. Open Mon.–Sat. 10–5:50, Sun. 2:30–5:50.*

TIME OUT   The **V&A restaurant** has morning coffee, hot lunchtime dishes, Sunday brunch, or afternoon tea.

㉙ Back in Kensington Gardens, the **Albert Memorial** commemorates Queen Victoria's much-loved husband, Prince Albert, who died in 1861 at the age of 42. The monument, itself the epitome of high Victorian taste, commemorates the many socially uplifting projects of the prince, among them the Great Exhibition of 1851, whose catalog he is holding. The Memorial, which has been badly eroded by pollution, is currently being restored.

From the **Flower Walk,** behind the Albert Memorial, carefully planted so that flowers are in bloom virtually throughout the year, strike out
㉚ across Kensington Gardens to the **Round Pond,** a favorite place for children to sail toy boats.

㉛ **Kensington Palace,** across from the Round Pond, has been a royal home since the late 17th century—and is one still, for Princess Margaret. From the outside it looks less like a palace than a country house, which it was until William III bought it in 1689. Inside, however, are state rooms on a grand scale, mostly created in the early 18th century. Such distinguished architects as Wren, Hawksmoor, Vanbrugh, and William Kent were all employed here. Queen Victoria spent a less-than-happy childhood at Kensington Palace, moving to Buckingham Palace as soon as she was crowned. Kensington Palace is currently closed for refurbishment. *Tel. 0171/937–9561.*

North of Kensington Gardens is the lively **Notting Hill** district, full of restaurants and cafés where young people gather. The best-known at-
㉜ traction in this area is **Portobello Road,** where the lively antiques and bric-a-brac market is held each Saturday (arrive early in the morning for the best bargains). The street is also full of regular antiques shops that are open most weekdays.

TIME OUT   **Geales** (2 Farmer St.) is a superior Notting Hill fish-and-chips restaurant, popular with locals and visitors alike.

Covent Garden

33 You could easily spend a half day exploring the block of streets north of the Strand known as **Covent Garden.** The heart of the area is a former wholesale fruit and vegetable market, established in 1656. The market moved to more modern and accessible premises only in 1974. **The Piazza,** the Victorian Market Building, is now a vibrant shopping center, with numerous boutiques, crafts shops, and cafés. On the south side of the market building is the lively and much less formal **Jubilee market,** with crafts and clothing stalls.

34 Look for the open-air entertainers performing under the portico of **St. Paul's Church**—you can enjoy an excellent show for the price of a few coins thrown in the hat that's passed among the onlookers. The church, entered from Bedford Street, is known as the Actors' Church, and inside are numerous memorials to theater people. The **Royal Opera House** and the **Theatre Royal Drury Lane,** two of London's oldest theaters, are close by.

TIME OUT Around here, you can scarcely move for restaurants jostling to feed you. Try **Maxwell's,** on James Street near the tube station, for one of London's best burgers, or **Crank's** in the Piazza for vegetarian alternatives.

For interesting specialty shops, head north of the Market Building. Shops on **Long Acre** sell maps, art books, clothing, and glass; shops on **Neal Street** sell clothes, pottery, jewelry, tea, housewares, and goods from the Far East.

35 The collection of vehicles at the **London Transport Museum** includes a steam locomotive, a tram, a subway car, and an Underground train simulator. Visitors are encouraged to operate many of the vehicles, and the exhibits and the space were recently upgraded. The shop sells T-shirts, books, and souvenirs. *The Piazza (southeast corner), tel. 0171/379–6344. Admission: £3.95 adults, £2.50 children 5–16 and senior citizens, children under 5 free. Open daily 10–5:15.*

36 The **Theatre Museum** contains a comprehensive collection of material on the history of the English theater—not merely the classic drama but also opera, music hall, pantomime, and musical comedy. Scripts, playbills, costumes, and props are displayed; there is even a re-creation of a dressing room filled with memorabilia of former stars. *Russell St., tel. 0171/836–7891. Admission: £3 adults, £1.50 children under 14, students, and senior citizens. Open Tues.–Sun. 11–7.*

37 On **Bow Street** is the **Royal Opera House,** home of the Royal Ballet and the Royal Opera Company. The plush interior captures the richness of Victorian England.

Bloomsbury

Bloomsbury is a semiresidential district to the north of Covent Garden that contains some spacious and elegant 17th- and 18th-century squares. It could claim to be the intellectual center of London, since both the British Museum and the University of London are found here. The area also gave its name to the Bloomsbury Group, a clique of writers and painters who thrived here in the early 20th century. The antiquarian and specialist bookshops, publishing houses, restaurants, and pubs frequented by the local literati add to the academic-cum-bohemian ambience of the area.

38 The **British Museum** houses a vast and priceless collection of treasures, including Egyptian, Greek, and Roman antiquities; Renaissance jewelry; pottery; coins; glass; and drawings from virtually every European school since the 15th century. It's best to pick out one section that particularly interests you—to try to see everything would be an overwhelming and exhausting task. Some of the highlights are the **Elgin Marbles,** sculptures that formerly decorated the Parthenon in Athens; the **Rosetta Stone,** which helped archaeologists to interpret Egyptian script; a copy of the **Magna Carta,** the charter signed by King John in 1215 to which is ascribed the origins of English liberty; and the **Mildenhall treasure,** a cache of Roman silver found in East Anglia in 1842. *Great Russell St., tel. 0171/636–1555; 0171/580–1788 (recorded information). Admission free. Open Mon.–Sat. 10–5, Sun. 2:30–6.*

39 On the border of London's legal district, **Sir John Soane's Museum** is an eccentric and delightful collection of art and artifacts in the former home of the architect of the Bank of England. Soane's great sense of humor and keen eye for visual perspective are equally apparent. *13 Lincoln's Inn Fields, tel. 0171/405–2107. Admission free. Open Tues.–Sat. 10–5.*

The City

The **City,** the traditional commercial center of London, is the most ancient part of the capital, having been the site of the great Roman city of Londinium. Since those days, the City has been built and rebuilt several times. The wooden buildings of the medieval City were destroyed in the Great Fire of 1666. There were further waves of reconstruction in the 19th century, and then again after World War II to repair the devastation wrought by air attacks. The 1980s saw the construction of many mammoth office developments, some undistinguished, others incorporating adventurous and exciting ideas.

Throughout all these changes, the City has retained its unique identity and character. The lord mayor and Corporation of London are still responsible for the government of the City, as they have been for many centuries. Commerce remains the lifeblood of the City, which is a world financial center rivaled only by New York, Tokyo, and Zurich. The biggest change has been in the City's population. Until the first half of the 19th century, many of the merchants and traders who worked in the City lived there, too. Today, despite its huge daytime population, scarcely 8,000 people live in the 677 acres of the City. Try, therefore, to explore the City on a weekday morning or afternoon. On weekends its streets are deserted, and many of the shops and restaurants, even some of the churches, are closed.

40 Following the Great Fire, **St. Paul's Cathedral** was rebuilt by Sir Christopher Wren, the architect who was also responsible for designing 50 City parish churches to replace those lost in the Great Fire. St. Paul's is Wren's greatest work. Fittingly, he is buried in the crypt under a simple Latin epitaph, composed by his son, which translates as: "Reader, if you seek his monument, look around you." The cathedral has been the site of many famous state occasions, including the funeral of Winston Churchill in 1965 and the ill-fated marriage of the prince and princess of Wales in 1981. Note the fine choir stalls by the great 17th-century wood-carver Grinling Gibbons, a rare decorative flourish in an otherwise surprisingly restrained interior, with relatively few monuments and tombs. Among those commemorated are George Washington; the essayist and lexicographer Samuel Johnson; and two military heroes—Nelson, victor over the French at Trafalgar in 1805, and Wellington, who defeated the French on land at Waterloo 10 years later. In the ambulatory (the area behind the high altar) is the American Chapel, a memorial to the 28,000 U.S. citizens stationed in Britain during World War II who lost their lives while on active service.

The greatest architectural glory of the cathedral is the dome. This consists of three distinct elements: an outer, timber-frame dome covered with lead; an interior dome built of brick and decorated with frescoes of the life of St. Paul by the 18th-century artist Sir James Thornhill; and, in between, a brick cone that supports and strengthens both. There is a good view of the church from the **Whispering Gallery,** high up in the inner dome. The gallery is so called because of its remarkable acoustics, whereby words whispered on one side can be clearly heard on the other, almost 115 feet away. Above this gallery are two others, both external, from which there are fine views over the City and beyond. *Tel. 0171/248–2705. Admission to cathedral free; Ambulatory (American Chapel), Crypt, and Treasury: £3 adults, £2.50 senior citizens and students, £2 children; to galleries: £2.50 adults, £2 senior citizens and students, £1.50 children, combined ticket: £5 adults, £4 senior citizens and students, £3 children. Cathedral open Mon.–Sat. 7:30–6, Sun. 8–6; the Ambulatory, Crypt, and Galleries weekdays 10–4:15, Sat. 11–4:15. Tours weekdays 11, 11:30, 2, 2:30.*

A short walk north of the cathedral, to **London Wall,** so called because it follows the line of the wall that surrounded the Roman settlement, brings you to the **Museum of London.** Its displays enable you to get a real sense of what it was like to live in London at different periods of history, from Roman times to the present day. Among the highlights are the Lord Mayor's Ceremonial Coach, an imaginative reconstruction of the Great Fire, and the Cheapside Hoard, jewelry hidden during an outbreak of plague in the 17th century and never recovered by its owner. The 20th-century exhibits include a Woolworth's counter and elevators from Selfridges; both stores were founded by Americans. A new introductory gallery uses computer graphics to illustrate London's growth from prehistoric times to the present day. *London Wall, tel. 0171/600–3699. Admission £3 adults, £1.50 under 18 and senior citizens. Open Tues.–Sat. 10–6, Sun. 2–6.*

The **Barbican** is a vast residential complex and arts center built by the City of London. It takes its name from the watchtower that stood here during the Middle Ages, just outside the City walls. The arts center contains a concert hall, where the London Symphony Orchestra is based, two theaters, an art gallery, a cinema, and several cafés and restaurants. The theaters are the London home of the Royal Shakespeare Company.

On the south side of London Wall stands **Guildhall,** the much reconstructed home of the Corporation of London; the lord mayor of London is elected here each year with ancient ceremony. *King St., tel. 0171/606–3030. Admission free. Open weekdays 10–5.*

Now walk south to **Cheapside.** This was the chief marketplace of medieval London (the word *ceap* is Old English for "to barter"), as the street names hereabouts indicate: Milk Street, Ironmonger Lane, etc. Despite rebuilding, many of the streets still run on the medieval pattern. The church of **St. Mary-le-Bow** in Cheapside was rebuilt by Christopher Wren after the Great Fire; it was built again after being bombed during World War II. It is said that to be a true Cockney, you must be born within the sound of Bow bells.

TIME OUT **The Place Below** (St Mary-le-Bow, Cheapside) serves a very high standard of meatless soup-quiche-salad lunches, then metamorphoses into a fancy restaurant two nights a week. *Closed weekends.*

A short walk east along Cheapside brings you to a seven-way intersection. The **Bank of England,** which regulates much of Britain's financial
life, is the large windowless building on the left. At the northern side
of the intersection, perpendicular to the bank, is the **Royal Exchange,**
originally built in the 1560s as a trading hall for merchants. The
present building, opened in 1844 and the third on the site, is now occupied by the **London International Financial Futures Exchange.** *Tel.
0171/623–0444. Admission free. Visitors' Gallery open by appointment to groups from relevant organizations.*

The third major building at this intersection, on its south side, is the
Mansion House, the official residence of the lord mayor of London.

Continue east along **Cornhill,** site of a Roman basilica and of a medieval
grain market. Turn right into Gracechurch Street and then left into **Leadenhall Market.** There has been a market here since the 14th century;
the present building dates from 1881.

Just behind the market is one of the most striking pieces of contemporary City architecture: the headquarters of **Lloyd's of London,** built by
the modernist architect Richard Rogers, whose other famous work is
Paris's Pompidou Center; Rogers' firm has also won the competition
to redesign the South Bank arts complex (*see* Concerts, *below*). The un-
derwriters of Lloyd's provide insurance for everything imaginable, from
oil rigs to a pianist's fingers, though they suffered a crash in 1993, with
most of the so-called Names, whose millions formed the Lloyd's backbone, losing major money. *1 Lime St., tel. 0171/623–7100. Admission
free. Open by appointment to groups from recognized organizations.*

From here it's a short walk east to the **Tower of London,** one of London's most famous sights and one of its most crowded, too. Come as
early in the day as possible and head for the Crown Jewels so you can
see them before the crowds arrive.

The tower served the monarchs of medieval England as both fortress
and palace. Every British sovereign from William the Conqueror in the
11th century to Henry VIII in the 16th lived here, and it remains a royal
palace, in name at least. The **History Gallery,** south of the White Tower,
is a walk-through display designed to answer questions about the inhabitants of the tower and its evolution over the centuries.

The **White Tower** is the oldest and also the most conspicuous building
in the entire complex. Inside, the **Chapel of St. John** is one of the few
unaltered parts. A structure of great simplicity, it is almost entirely lack-
ing in ornamentation. The **Royal Armories,** England's national collection of arms and armor, occupies the rest of the White Tower. Armor
of the 16th and 17th centuries forms the centerpiece of the displays,
including pieces belonging to Henry VIII and Charles I.

Among other buildings worth seeing is the **Bloody Tower.** This name
has been traced back only to 1571; it was originally known as the Garden Tower. Sir Walter Raleigh was held prisoner here, in relatively comfortable circumstances, between 1603 and 1616, during which time
he wrote his *History of the World;* his rooms are furnished much as
they were during his imprisonment. The little princes in the tower—
the boy king Edward V and his brother Richard, duke of York, supposedly murdered on the orders of the duke of Gloucester, later crowned
Richard III—certainly lived in the Bloody Tower, and may well have
died here, too. Another bloody death is alleged to have occurred in the
Wakefield Tower, when Henry VI was murdered in 1471 during England's medieval civil war, the Wars of the Roses. It was a rare honor

to be beheaded in private inside the tower; most people were executed outside, on **Tower Hill,** where the crowds could get a much better view. Important prisoners were held in the **Beauchamp Tower;** the walls are covered with graffiti and inscriptions carved by prisoners.

The **Crown Jewels** are a breathtakingly beautiful collection of regalia, precious stones, gold, and silver. The Royal Scepter contains the largest cut diamond in the world. The Imperial State Crown, made for the 1838 coronation of Queen Victoria, contains some 3,000 precious stones, largely diamonds and pearls. The Jewels moved to their new home in the Duke of Wellington's Barracks in spring 1993. Look for the ravens whose presence at the tower is traditional. It is said that if they leave, the tower will fall and England will lose her greatness. *Tower Hill, tel. 0171/709–0765. Admission: £7.95 adults, £5.95 students and senior citizens, £5.25 children under 16, family ticket £19. Reduced admission charges apply during Feb. when Jewel House is closed. Small additional admission charge to Fusiliers Museum only. Open Mar.–Oct., Mon.–Sat. 9:30–6, Sun. 10–6; Nov.–Feb., Mon.–Sat. 9:30–4. Yeoman Warder guides conduct tours daily from Middle Tower, no charge, but a tip is always appreciated. Subject to weather and availability of guides, tours are conducted about every 30 minutes until 3:30 in summer, 2:30 in winter.*

Off the Beaten Track

Camden Lock

Walk along the bank of the **Grand Union Canal** (Regent's Canal) from the northwest corner of Regent's Park eastward to **Camden Lock,** where scores of shops sell gifts, secondhand clothes, crafts, and antiques in a frenetic atmosphere that's half shanty town, half souk. On weekends there's an outdoor market. You can extend the excursion in two different directions from Camden Lock. Either walk east along the canal towpath through the elegant streets of Islington, then through increasingly less prosperous areas until you reach the Thames at Limehouse, or turn north to **Hampstead** and **Hampstead Heath.**

Hampstead

Hampstead is a village within the city, where many famous poets and writers have lived. Today it is a fashionable residential area, with a main shopping street and some rows of elegant 18th-century houses. The heath is one of London's largest and most attractive open spaces. In **Keats Grove,** on the southern edge of the heath, is the house where the Romantic poet John Keats (1795–1821) lived. *Wentworth Pl., tel. 0171/435–2062. Admission free. Call in advance for exact opening times.*

Standing alone in its own landscaped grounds on the north side of the heath is **Kenwood House,** built in the 17th century and remodeled by Robert Adam, the talented exponent of classical decoration, at the end of the 18th. The house contains a collection of superb paintings by such masters as Rembrandt, Vermeer, Turner, Reynolds, Van Dyck, and Gainsborough, which gain enormously from being displayed in the grand country-house setting for which they were originally intended. The lovely landscaped grounds, with lake, provide the setting for symphony concerts in summer. *Hampstead La., tel. 0181/348–1286. Admission free. Open Apr.–Oct., weekdays 2–6, Sat. 10–1 and 2–5, Sun. 2–5; Nov.–Mar., weekdays 1–5, Sat. 10–1 and 2–5 , Sun. 2–5.*

Greenwich

The historical and maritime attractions at **Greenwich,** on the Thames, some 8 kilometers (5 miles) east of central London, make it an ideal place for a day out. You can get to Greenwich by riverboat from Westminster and Tower Bridge piers, by ThamesLine's high-speed river buses, or by train from Charing Cross station. You can also take the Docklands Light Railway from Tower Gateway to Island Gardens and walk a short distance along a pedestrian tunnel under the river.

Visit the **National Maritime Museum,** a treasure house of paintings; maps; models; sextants; and, best of all, ships from all ages, including the ornate royal barges. *Romney Rd., tel. 0181/858–4422. Joint admission with the Royal Observatory: £4.95 adults, £2.95 children, £3.95 senior citizens. Open late-Mar.–late-Oct., Mon.–Sat. 10–6, Sun. 2–6; late-Oct.–late-Mar., Mon.–Sat. 10–5, Sun. 2–5.*

Two ships now in dry dock are the glorious 19th-century clipper ship **Cutty Sark** and the tiny **Gipsy Moth IV,** which Sir Francis Chichester sailed single-handed around the world in 1966. *Cutty Sark, King William Walk, tel. 0181/858–3445. Admission: £3.25 adults, £2.25 children under 16 and senior citizens. Open late-Mar.–Sept., Mon.–Sat. 10–5:30, Sun. noon–5:30; Oct.–late-Mar., Mon.–Sat. 10–4:30, Sun. noon–4:30. Gipsy Moth IV, King William Walk, tel. 0181/853–3589. Admission: 50p adults, 30p children and senior citizens. Open Apr.–Oct., Mon.–Sat. 10–5:30, Sun. noon–5:30.*

The **Royal Naval College** was built in 1694 as a home, or hospital, for old sailors. You can see the magnificent **Painted Hall,** where Nelson's body lay in state following the Battle of Trafalgar, and the College Chapel. *Tel. 0181/858–2154. Admission free. Open Fri.–Wed. 2:30–4:30.*

Behind the museum and the college is **Greenwich Park,** originally a royal hunting ground and today an attractive place in which to wander and relax. On top of the hill is the **Old Royal Observatory,** founded in 1675, where original telescopes and other astronomical instruments are on display. The prime meridian—zero degrees longitude—runs through the courtyard of the observatory. *Greenwich Park, tel. 0181/858–4422. Joint admission with National Maritime Museum: £4.95 adults, £2.95 children, £3.95 senior citizens. Open Apr.–Oct., Mon.–Sat. 10–6, Sun. 2–6; Nov.–Mar., Mon.–Sat. 10–5, Sun. 2–5.*

Shopping

Shopping is one of London's great pleasures. Different areas retain their traditional specialties, as described below, but there are also numerous pockets of local shops to explore, and it's fun to seek out the small crafts, antiques, and gift stores, designer clothing resale outlets, and national department-store chains.

Shopping Districts

Chelsea centers on the King's Road, once synonymous with ultrafashion; it still harbors some designer boutiques, plus antiques and home furnishings stores.

Covent Garden is a something-for-everyone neighborhood, with clothing chain stores and top designers, stalls selling crafts, and shops selling gifts of every type—bikes, kites, herbs, beads, hats, you name it.

Crowded **Oxford Street** is past its prime and lined with tawdry discount shops. Selfridges, John Lewis, and Marks and Spencer are good department stores, though, and there are interesting boutiques secreted off Oxford Street, just north of the Bond Street tube stop, in little St. Christopher's Place and Gees Court.

Perpendicular to Oxford Street lies **Regent Street,** with possibly London's most pleasant department store, Liberty's, as well as Hamley's, the capital's toy mecca. Shops around once-famous **Carnaby Street** stock designer youth paraphernalia and 57 varieties of T-shirt.

In **Mayfair** is Bond Street, Old and New, with desirable dress designers and jewelers, plus fine art. South Molton Street offers high-price high-style fashion—especially at Browns—and the tailors of Savile Row are of worldwide repute.

In **St. James's,** the English gentleman buys the rest of his gear: handmade hats, shirts, and shoes, silver shaving kits and hip flasks. Here is also the world's best cheese shop, Paxton & Whitfield. Nothing in this neighborhood is cheap, in any sense.

Kensington's main drag, Kensington High Street, is a smaller, classier version of Oxford Street, with some larger stores at the eastern end. Try Kensington Church Street for expensive antiques, plus a little fashion.

Neighboring **Knightsbridge** has Harrods, of course, but also Harvey Nichols, the top clothes stop, and many expensive designers' boutiques along Sloane Street, Walton Street, and Beauchamp Place.:

Markets

Street markets are one aspect of London life not to be missed. Here are some of the more interesting markets:

Bermondsey. Arrive as early as possible for the best treasure—that's what the dealers do. *Tower Bridge Rd., SE1. Open Fri. 4:30 AM–noon. Take the tube to London Bridge and walk, or take Bus 15 or 25 to Aldgate and then Bus 42 over Tower Bridge to Bermondsey Square.*
Camden Lock. The youth center of the world, apparently, and good for cheap leather boots. The canal-side antiques, crafts, and junk markets are also picturesque in their fashion, and very crowded. *Chalk Farm Rd., NW1. Open Sat.–Sun. 9:30–5:30. Take the tube or Bus 24 or 29 to Camden Town.*
Camden Passage. The rows of little antiques shops are a good hunting ground for silverware and jewelry. Stalls open Wednesday and Saturday, a books and prints market opens Thursdays, and shops open the rest of the week. *Islington, N1. Open Wed.–Sat. 8:30–3. Take the tube or Bus 19 or 38 to the Angel, Islington.*
Petticoat Lane. Look for budget-priced leather goods, gaudy knitwear, and fashions, plus cameras, videos, stereos, antiques, books, and bric-a-brac. *Middlesex St., E1. Open Sun. 9–2. Take the tube to Liverpool Street, Aldgate, or Aldgate East.*
Portobello Market. Saturday is the best day for antiques, though this neighborhood is London's melting pot, becoming more vibrant every year. Find fabulous small shops, the city's trendiest restaurants, and a Friday and Saturday flea market at the far end. *Portobello Rd., W11. Open Fri. 5–3, Sat. 8–5. Take the tube or Bus 52 to Notting Hill Gate or Ladbroke Grove, or Bus 15 to Kensington Park Rd.*

Dining

For details and price-category definitions, *see* Dining *in* Staying in Great Britain, *above.*

Bloomsbury

$$ **Chez Gerard.** This purveyor of *steak-frites* and similarly simple gallic offerings is reliable, relaxed, and usefully located near Oxford Street. Some say these shoestring fries are London's best French fries. *8 Charlotte St., tel. 0171/636–4975. Reservations advised. AE, DC, MC, V. Closed Dec. 25. Tube: Goodge St.*

$ **The North Sea Fish Restaurant.** Good old British fish 'n' chips—battered and deep-fried fish with thick fries—cooked to a turn and always fresh—is served in this popular haunt. It's a bit tricky to find—three blocks south of St. Pancras station, down Judd Street. You can eat in or take out. *7–8 Leigh St., tel. 0171/387–5892. Reservations advised. AE, DC, MC, V. Closed Sun., holidays, 10 days at Christmas. Tube: Russell Sq.*

$ **Wagamama.** Japanese noodles here are fast and delicious, served in
★   soup, topped with meat or fish, or supplemented by rice and vegetable dishes. The staff takes your order on hand-held computers for fast, high-tech service. You will have to share a table, such is its popularity. *4 Streatham St., tel. 0171/323–9223. No reservations. No credit cards. Closed Dec 25. Tube: Tottenham Court Rd.*

Chelsea

$$$$ **La Tante Claire.** This spot is justly famous for Pierre Koffmann's superb haute cuisine: hot foie gras on shredded potatoes with a sweet wine and shallot sauce or his famous signature dish of pig's trotter stuffed with sweetbreads and wild mushrooms. The set-price lunch is a relative bargain. *68 Royal Hospital Rd., tel. 0171/352–6045. Reservations 3–4 wks in advance. AE, DC, MC, V. Closed weekends, 10 days at Easter and Christmas, 3 wks in Aug.–Sept. Tube: Sloane Sq.*

$$$ **Chutney Mary.** London's only Anglo-Indian restaurant provides a fantasy version of the British Raj, with colonial cocktails and authentic re-creations of comforting, rich dishes like Country Captain (chicken with almonds, raisins, chilis, and spices) and Masala roast lamb. *535 King's Rd., tel. 0171/351–3113. Reservations advised. AE, DC, MC, V. Closed Dec. 26. No dinner Dec. 25. Tube: Fulham Broadway.*

$ **Henry J. Bean's.** Hamburgers and Tex-Mex food are served to American oldies music. Order food at the bar, then wait—in the big patio garden if you're lucky. *195–197 King's Rd., tel. 0171/352–9255. No reservations. No credit cards. Closed Dec. 25–26, 31. Tube: Sloane Sq.*

The City

$$$ **Bill Bentley's.** Once a wine merchant's vault with bare walls and arched ceiling, this atmospheric institution has a menu dominated by seafood of many varieties and tables filled with lunching City workers. *Swedeland Ct., 202 Bishopsgate, tel. 0171/283–1763. Reservations required. AE, DC, MC, V. Lunch only. Closed weekends. Tube: Liverpool St.*

$$ **Sri Siam City.** This easterly cousin of a well-liked Soho Thai place turns down the chili fire a little. The Thai staples—green or red chicken curry, pad Thai (noodles stir-fried with vegetables and shrimp)—are good, or try squid salad with lemongrass, lime, and chili. *85 London Wall, tel. 0171/628–5772. Lunch reservations advised. AE, DC. MC. V. Closed weekends and Dec. 25. Tube: Moorgate.*

$$ **Sweetings.** City gents stand in line to lunch at this tiny, basic Victorian restaurant where nothing has changed for years, let alone the menu, which is fish cooked however you want (it's best grilled), served with potatoes and peas. The service is Old World courteous, the food comforting and well prepared. *39 Queen Victoria St., tel. 0171/248–3062. No reservations. No credit cards. Lunch only. Closed weekends, Dec. 25, and holidays. Tube: Cannon St.*

Covent Garden

$$$$ **The Savoy Grill.** Continuing to attract more than its fair share of
★   mostly male power-brokers, from newspaper editors to tycoons, this paneled French-English salon exudes comfort, from the avuncular, yet deferential, service to the traditional British food, which most choose over the more modern, more French side of the menu. The daily dish

is the way to go—or something British, like jugged hare (a stew of hare, with blood), or the omelet Arnold Bennett (with cheese and smoked fish), invented here for that novelist. *Strand, tel. 0171/836–4343. Lunch and Thurs.–Sat. dinner reservations essential. AE, DC, MC, V. No lunch Sat. Closed Sun. and Aug. Tube: Aldwych.*

$$$ **The Ivy.** The epitome of style without pretentiousness, this restaurant
★ beguiles everybody, including media, literary, and theatrical movers and shakers. The menu's got it all—fish-and-chips, sausage-and-mash, squid-ink risotto, bang-bang chicken, sticky toffee pudding—and all are good. *1 West St., tel. 0171/836–4751. Reservations required. AE, DC, MC, V. Closed Dec. 25–26. Tube: Covent Garden.*

$$$ **Rules.** This city's oldest restaurant (it's been here since 1798) is tradi-tional from soup to nuts, or rather, from venison (disconcertingly listed on the menu as "deer") and Dover sole to trifle and Stilton. Nowa-days there's the odd nod to newer cuisines, but the clientele of expense-accounters and tourists in search of olde London Towne remains. *35 Maiden La., tel. 0171/836–5314. Reservations at least 1 day in ad-vance. AE, DC, MC, V. Closed Sun., Dec. 25. Tube: Covent Garden.*

$$ **Bertorelli's.** Opposite the stage door of the Royal Opera House,
★ Bertorelli's is a favorite with operagoers. Chic decor complements Maddalena Bonino's modern Italian food—try the poached *cotechino* sausage on lentils, followed by the monkfish, fennel, and tomato ragout. *44a Floral St., tel. 0171/836–3969. Reservations advised. AE, DC, MC, V. Closed Sun., Dec. 25. Tube: Covent Garden.*

$–$$ **Joe Allen.** This basement restaurant behind the Strand Palace Hotel fol-
★ lows the style of its New York counterpart, is descended on by packs of theatrical types after curtain, and is forever noisy. The menu, too, is straight from the Manhattan parent—there's a great Caesar, barbecue ribs with black-eye peas and wilted greens, brownies with ice cream—and it's open late. *13 Exeter St., tel. 0171/836–0651. Reservations re-quired. No credit cards. Closed Dec. 25. Tube: Covent Garden.*

$–$$ **Le Palais du Jardin.** This is a fair imitation of a Parisian brasserie, com-plete with a seafood bar offering lobsters for £10 or so, though there's plenty else—duck confit with apples and prunes; coq au vin; tuna with a black olive potato cake. Neither as chic nor as expensive as it looks, but always busy. *136 Long Acre, tel. 0171/379–5353. Reservations advised. AE, DC, MC, V. Closed Dec. 25. Tube: Covent Garden.*

$ **Food for Thought.** This is a simple downstairs vegetarian restaurant,
★ with seats for only 50. The menu—stir-fries, casseroles, salads, and dessert—changes daily, and each dish is freshly made. No alcohol is served here. *31 Neal St., tel. 0171/836–0239. No reservations. No credit cards. Closed Sun., Sat. after 4:30 PM, weekdays after 8 PM, 2 wks at Christmas, holidays. Tube: Covent Garden.*

Kensington

$$$$ **Bibendum.** Upstairs in the renovated 1911 Michelin building, this ex-
★ cellent restaurant has been the flavor of the month for some time now with chef Simon Hopkinson continually showered with well-deserved accolades. From the scallops in a citrus sauce to the passion-fruit *bavarois* (Bavarian cream), all the dishes are unpretentious but perfectly done every time. *81 Fulham Rd., tel. 0171/581–5817. Reservations 2–3 wks in advance. MC, V. Closed Dec. 25 and holidays. Tube: South Kensington.*

$$ **Bistrot 190.** Chef-restaurateur Antony Worral-Thompson seems to
★ know exactly what the people want, which, in this case, is big plates of happy, hearty food from southern Europe (liver and wild mushroom terrine; grilled squid with red and green salsa; lemon tart). The decor incorporates hardwood floors and art-laden walls. Next door is **Down-**

stairs at 190—similar, but offering fish and seafood. *190 Queensgate, tel. 0171/581–5666. No reservations. AE, DC, MC, V. No lunch Sat. Closed Sun., Dec. 25–26, Jan. 1. Tube: Gloucester Rd.*

$$ **Wodka.** This modern Polish restaurant in a quiet back street serves stylish
★ food to a fashionable group and often has the relaxed atmosphere of a dinner party. Try herring blinis, roast duck with figs and port, and the several flavored vodkas. *12 St. Albans Grove, tel. 0171/937–6513. Reservations advised. AE, DC, MC, V. No lunch weekends. Closed Dec. 25–26. Tube: Kensington High St.*

Knightsbridge

$$ **St. Quentin.** This is a popular French spot just a few blocks west of Harrods. Every inch of the Gallic menu is explored—Gruyère quiche, escargots, cassoulet, lemon tart—in the bourgeois provincial comfort so many London chains (the Dômes, the Cafés Rouges) try hard, yet fail, to achieve. *243 Brompton Rd., tel. 0171/589–8005. Reservations advised. AE, DC, MC, V. Closed Dec. 25. Tube: South Kensington.*

$ **Stockpot.** Speedy service is the mark of this large, jolly restaurant full of students and shoppers. The food is filling and wholesome; try the homemade soups, the Lancashire hot pot, and the apple crumble. Breakfast is also served Monday–Saturday. *6 Basil St., tel. 0171/589–8627. No credit cards. Closed Dec. 25, Jan. 1. Tube: Knightsbridge.*

Mayfair

$$$$ **Chez Nico at Ninety Park Lane.** Those with refined palates and very
★ deep pockets should not miss Nico Ladenis's exquisite gastronomy. He is one of the world's great chefs, and is famous for knowing it. Nowhere is food taken more seriously; the menu is in French (untranslated); vegetarians and children are not welcome. *90 Park La., tel. 0171/409–1290. Reservations required. AE, DC, MC, V. Closed weekends, public holidays, 3 wks in Aug. Tube: Marble Arch.*

$$$$ **Le Gavroche.** Long regarded as a top temple of haute cuisine, this dark
★ and rich dining room dropped its third *Michelin* star when Albert Roux's son, Michel, took over the kitchen in '93, but no drop in quality seemed to ensue. Dining here is an unashamedly sybaritic and costly experience, punctuated with foie gras, oysters, and lobster, but one that becomes accessible with the three-course lunch for £36, inclusive of coffee, wine, and service. *43 Upper Brook St., tel. 0171/408–0881. Reserve at least 1 wk in advance. AE, DC, MC, V. Closed weekends, 10 days at Christmas, holidays. Tube: Marble Arch.*

$$$ **Mulligans.** At this friendly and relaxing slice of Dublin, the cooking is
★ unpretentious and satisfying—London's finest black pudding served with calvados and spiced apples; steak, Guinness, and kidney pie; and, of course, a sublime Irish stew. *13–14 Cork St., tel. 0171/409–1370. Reservations advised. AE, DC, MC, V. No lunch Sat., no dinner Sun. Closed Dec. 25–26, Jan. 1. Tube: Green Park.*

$–$$ **Criterion.** This welcome oasis in the Piccadilly desert offers an uninspired but unobjectionable Mediterranean menu (garlic roast chicken, poached salmon with leeks and lemon, chocolate marquise) afternoon tea, and sanctuary. The setting is a palatial neo-Byzantine mirrored, marbled hall with a splendid gold mosaic ceiling. An admirable innovation offers any two of the marked dishes on the menu for £10. *Piccadilly Circus, tel. 0171/925–0909. Reservations advised. AE, DC, MC, V. Closed Dec. 25. Tube: Piccadilly Circus.*

$ **The Chicago Pizza Pie Factory.** Huge pizzas with salad and garlic bread are served at reasonable prices in this loud basement. These pies are American-style with a thick chewy base and a somewhat limited choice of toppings. *17 Hanover Sq., tel. 0171/629–2669. Reservations advised for lunch. No credit cards. Closed Dec. 25, 26. Tube: Oxford Circus.*

Notting Hill Gate

$$$ **Clarke's.** There's no choice of dishes at dinner (and only a limited choice at lunch); chef Sally Clarke plans the meal according to what is freshest and best in the market each day. Her style is natural and unfussy West Coast cuisine. *124 Kensington Church St., tel. 0171/221–9225. Reservations advised. MC, V. Closed weekends, 10 days at Christmas, Easter, 3 wks in Aug. Tube: Notting Hill Gate.*

$$$ **Kensington Place.** Trendy and loud, this ever-popular place features enormous plate-glass windows through which to be seen, and plenty of fashionable food. Try the foie gras with sweet-corn pancake, rack of lamb, and baked tamarillo with vanilla ice cream. *201 Kensington Church St., tel. 0171/727–3184. Reservations advised. MC, V. Closed Aug. bank holiday, Dec. 25–26. Tube: Notting Hill Gate.*

$$ **192.** A noisy, buzzy wine bar-restaurant just off the Portobello Road,
★ this is a social hangout for the local media mafia, and the food's always ahead of fashion. The best part of the menu is the appetizer list; also try the risottos, the seasonal salad, or whatever sounds unusual. *192 Kensington Park Rd., tel. 0171/229–0482. Reservations required. AE, MC, V. Closed holidays. Tube: Notting Hill Gate.*

$ **Tootsies.** A useful burger joint characterized by loudish rock and vintage advertisements on the walls, Tootsies serves some of London's better burgers, as well as chili, chicken, BLTs, taco salad, apple pie, fudge cake, and ice cream. There are five other branches. *115 Notting Hill Gate, tel. 0171/727–6562. MC, V. Tube: Holland Park.*

St. James's

$$$$ **The Ritz.** The British menu here hasn't always lived up to its setting, but since this Louis XVI marble, gilt, and trompe l'oeil treasure, with its view over Green Park, is known as London's most magnificent dining room, that's not such a crime. The latest chef retains the French accent and ingredients as rich as the decor (foie gras terrine with fig preserve; lobster thermidor), and also offers British specialties—Irish stew, braised oxtail, steak-and-kidney pie, and a daily roast. Prix-fixe menus make the check more bearable, but the wine list is pricey. *Picadilly, tel. 0171/493–8181. Jacket and tie. Reservations required. AE, DC, MC, V. Tube: Green Park.*

$$$ **Le Caprice.** The cool and elegant decor here matches the often well-known clientele exactly. The international menu should appeal to all tastes, with dishes from North Africa, France, and the Far East. Finish with a mousse of dark and white chocolate. *Arlington House, Arlington St., tel. 0171/629–2239. Reservations required. AE, DC, MC, V. Closed 10 days at Christmas. Tube: Green Park.*

Soho

$$$ **Alastair Little.** A favorite among table-hopping media types, here the eponymous Little—one of Britain's most innovative and exciting chefs—serves his much-imitated eclectic (with influences from Japan, via Sicily to Scandinavia), seafood-dominated fare. The set lunch is, at £25 for three courses, a more affordable way to enjoy the constantly changing menu. The decor is functional and space at a premium. *49 Frith St., tel. 0171/734–5183. Reservations required. AE, MC, V. No lunch Sat. Closed Sun., Dec. 25, Easter. Tube: Leicester Sq.*

$$ **Bistrot Bruno.** Although his long-awaited L'Odeon must by now be open, there's little doubt that this spot, ex-Four Seasons star chef Bruno Loubet's first restaurant, will still be charming the crowds. Here are big, fat flavors in large portions: smoked fish cannelloni, salt cod on minestrone vegetables, and sautéed rabbit with Swiss chard, olives, and rosemary. Next door is the bargain Café Bruno. *63 Frith St., tel.*

0171/734–4545. Reservations required. AE, D, MC, V. No lunch Sat. Closed Sun., Dec. 25, Jan. 1. Tube: Leicester Sq.

\$\$ Chiang Mai. The interior is modeled on a traditional Thai stilt house. The food is delicious and spicy, all easy to order from an English menu. Try a *tom yum* (hot-and-sour soup) or a *pad kra prow* (beef, pork, or chicken with fresh Thai basil and chili). *48 Frith St., tel. 0171/437–7444. Reservations advised. AE, MC, V. Closed Sun. and holidays. Tube: Leicester Sq.*

\$–\$\$ dell'Ugo. At this three-story Mediterranean café-restaurant from the Antony Worral-Thompson stable (*see* Bistrot 190, *above*), heart-warming country food is the style—spaghetti with roasted peppers, anchovy, and chili; tuna tartare with spicy gazpacho; and bruschetta with pears, watercress, and Gorgonzola. *56 Frith St., tel. 0171/734–8300. Reservations required for restaurant, not accepted for café. AE, MC, V. Closed Sun., Dec. 25. Tube: Leicester Sq.*

\$ Crank's. This restaurant belongs to a popular vegetarian chain that has weathered the storms of food fashion since the '60s, despite (or because of) a certain worthiness of menu—mixed salads and thick soups; dense, grainy breads; and sugarless cakes. It is self-service, and many branches, though not this one, close at 8 PM. *8 Marshall St., tel. 0171/437–9431. Dinner reservations advised. AE, DC, MC, V. Closed Sun., Dec. 25. Tube: Leicester Sq.*

\$ Poon's. A popular Chinese restaurant (there are long lines in the evening), Poon's specializes in wind-dried meats. *4 Leicester St., tel. 0171/437–1528. Reservations required. Closed Sun., Dec. 25–26. Tube: Leicester Sq.*

Lodging

Although British hotels traditionally included breakfast in their nightly tariff, these days many of London's most expensive establishments charge extra for breakfast. For details and price-category definitions, *see* Lodging *in* Staying in Great Britain, *above*.

Bayswater

\$\$\$\$ Whites. This cream-faced Victorian "country mansion" has a wrought-
★ iron portico that looks especially grand when floodlit at night. Thick carpets, gilt and mirrors, marble balustrades, swagged silk draperies, and Louis XV-style furniture all help to give a sense of deep luxury. Some of the bedrooms have balconies with a wonderful view of Kensington Gardens, across the road; all have seating areas and personal safes. Colors are muted: powder blue, old rose, and pale green. *90–92 Lancaster Gate, W2 3NR, tel. 0171/262–2711, fax 0171/262–2147. 54 rooms with bath. Facilities: restaurant, lounge, valet service, free in-house movies. AE, DC, MC, V. Tube: Lancaster Gate.*

\$\$\$ Abbey Court. A short walk from Kensington Gardens brings you to this luxury bed-and-breakfast establishment in a historic 1850 building. Each bedroom is individually designed with 19th-century French furniture, Venetian mirrors, and oil portraits; some have four-poster beds. *20 Pembridge Gardens, W2 4DU, tel. 0171/221–7518, fax 0171/792–0858. 22 rooms with bath. Facilities: Jacuzzis, conservatory, drawing room, garden. AE, DC, MC, V. Tube: Notting Hill Gate.*

\$\$\$ Portobello. A faithful core of visitors returns again and again to this eccentric hotel in a Victorian terrace near the Portobello Road antiques market. Some rooms are tiny, but the suites have sitting rooms attached, and the atmosphere is relaxed and informal. *22 Stanley Gardens, W11 2NG, tel. 0171/727–2777, fax 0171/792–9641. 25 rooms with bath or shower. Facilities: restaurant, 24-hr bar. AE, DC, MC, V. Closed 10 days at Christmas. Tube: Ladbroke Grove.*

$$ **Camelot.** This affordable hotel, recently refurbished and extended, has
★ beautifully decorated rooms and a friendly staff. The few bathless single rooms are bargains. *45–47 Norfolk Sq., W2 1RX, tel. 0171/723–9118, fax 0171/402–3412. 43 rooms, 33 with bath or shower. Facilities: lounge, free in-house videos. MC, V. Tube: Paddington.*

Bloomsbury–Regent's Park

$$$$ **The Regent.** The onetime Great Central Hotel and former BritRail headquarters was resuscitated by a three-year injection of £75 million, and transformed into London's latest most elegant and understated luxury hotel. The palm-filled, six-story "Winter Garden" atrium is overlooked by guest rooms; even standard rooms here are among the largest in London. This Hong Kong-based hotel group is famous for glamorous bathrooms—these are marble and chrome, complete with robes and hair dryers. Not surprisingly, the Regent is very near Regent's Park; it's also near Madame Tussaud's. The West End is a 15-minute walk away. *222 Marylebone Rd., NW1 6JO, tel. 0171/631–8000, fax 0171/631–8080. 309 rooms with bath. Facilities: restaurant, 2 bars, health club with pool, cable TV, VCR and personal fax on request, business center. AE, DC, MC, V. Tube: Marylebone.*

$$–$$$ **Academy.** Convenient to the British Museum and area shops, the Academy is in a Georgian building and has a bar, library/lounge, and patio garden. *17–21 Gower St., WC1E 6HG, tel. 0171/631–4115, fax 0171/636–3442. 32 rooms, 24 with bath. Facilities: restaurant, lounge, bar. AE, DC, MC, V. Tube: Russell Sq.*

$$–$$$ **Morgan.** This charming family-run hotel in an 18th-century terrace house has rooms that are small and comfortably furnished, but friendly and cheerful. The tiny paneled breakfast room is straight out of a doll's house. The back rooms overlook the British Museum. *24 Bloomsbury St., WC1B 3QJ, tel. 0171/636–3735. 14 rooms with bath or shower. No credit cards. Tube: Russell Sq.*

$ **Ridgemount.** The kindly owners, Mr. and Mrs. Rees, make you feel at home in this tiny hotel by the British Museum. There's a homey, cluttered feel in the public areas and some bedrooms overlook a leafy garden. *65 Gower St., WC1E 6HJ, tel. 0171/636–1141. 15 rooms, none with bath. Facilities: lounge. No credit cards. Tube: Russell Sq.*

Chelsea and Kensington

$$$$ **Blakes.** Patronized by musicians and film stars, this hotel is one of the
★ most exotic in town. Its Victorian exterior contrasts with the rather 1980s ultrachic interior, with its arty mix of Biedermeier and bamboo, four-poster beds, and chinoiserie, all lit as dramatically as film noir. The bedrooms have individual designs ranging from swaths of black moiré silk to an entirely pink suite. *33 Roland Gardens, SW7 3PF, tel. 0171/370–6701. 52 rooms with bath. Facilities: restaurant, bar, satellite TV. AE, DC, MC, V. Tube: Gloucester Rd.*

$$$ **The Gore.** Every wall of every room in this very friendly and quiet hotel
★ near the Albert Hall is smothered in prints and etchings, and antiques pepper the rooms. Some of these are spectacular follies—like Tudor-style Room 101, with its minstrel gallery and four-poster, or Room 211, with its ceramic Greek goddess mural. Despite all that, it manages to remain most elegant, and certainly unique. *189 Queen's Gate, SW7 5EX, tel. 0171/584–6601, fax 0171/589–8127. 54 rooms with bath. Facilities: lounge. AE, DC, MC, V. Tube: Gloucester Rd.*

$ **Abbey House.** Standards are high and the rooms unusually spacious in this hotel in a fine residential block near Kensington Palace and Gardens. *11 Vicarage Gate, W8 4AG, tel. 0171/727–2594. 15 rooms without bath. Facilities: orthopedic beds. No credit cards. Tube: Kensington High St.*

$ **Vicarage Hotel.** This genteel establishment, run by the same husband/wife team for the past 40 years, has high standards of cleanliness throughout. Bedrooms are traditional and comfortable with solid English furniture. It attracts many repeat visitors from the United States and welcomes single travelers. *10 Vicarage Gate, W8 4AG, tel. 0171/229–4030. 20 rooms without bath. Facilities: small TV lounge. No credit cards. Tube: Kensington High St.*

Knightsbridge, Belgravia, and Victoria

$$$$ **Berkeley.** This is a luxurious, spacious, air-conditioned modern building into which a period country mansion has been decanted. One very special feature is the penthouse health club, with a pool whose roof opens in good weather. Bedrooms are elegant and sophisticated and there are some spectacular suites, including one with a sauna. *Wilton Pl., SW1X 7RL, tel. 0171/235–6000. 160 rooms with bath. Facilities: 2 restaurants, bar, lounges, health club, hairdresser, florist, movie theater. AE, DC, MC, V. Tube: Knightsbridge.*

$$$$ **Goring.** Around the corner from Buckingham Palace and often used by visiting VIPs, this hotel was built in 1910 and is now run by the third generation of Gorings. The atmosphere remains opulently Edwardian: marble fixtures in the bathrooms, with brass trim and the original fitted closets in some of the bedrooms. *17 Beeston Pl., Grosvenor Gardens, SW1W 0JW, tel. 0171/834–8211. 90 rooms with bath. Facilities: restaurant, bar, lounge. AE, DC, MC, V. Tube: Victoria.*

$$$$ **Halkin.** This peaceful, ultramodern haven for the design-conscious has
★ many high-tech features in the bedrooms, like personal fax, video player, two phone lines, and a keypad for operating lights and TV. Everything is cool and beautiful, from the charcoal gray curved corridors to the Armani staff uniform. But it's surprisingly friendly. *Halkin St., SW1X 7DJ, tel. 0171/333–1000. 41 rooms with bath. Facilities: restaurant, cable TV, video library, fax (on request), Reuters news service. AE, DC, MC, V. Tube: Hyde Park Corner.*

$$$$ **The Lanesborough.** Brocades and Regency stripes, moiré silks and fleurs-de-lys, antiques, oils, and reproductions in gilded splendor—everything undulates with richness in this multimillion-pound conversion of the old St. George's Hospital at Hyde Park Corner. To register you just sign the book, then retire to your room to find a personal butler, business cards with your in-room fax and phone numbers, VCR and CD player, umbrella, robe, huge flacons of unguents for bath time, and a drinks tray. Such a palace should be nearer the shops. *1 Lanesborough Pl., SW1X 7TA, tel. 0171/259–5599, fax 0171/259–5606. 95 rooms with bath. Facilities: 2 restaurants, bar, satellite TV, video and CD library. AE, DC, MC, V. Tube: Hyde Park Corner.*

$$$ **Basil Street.** Family-run for some 75 years, this is a gracious Edwardian hotel on a quiet street. The rooms are filled with antiques, as are the various lounges, hushed like libraries with polished wooden floors and Oriental rugs. It sounds swanky, but Basil Street is more like home. *Basil St., SW3 1AH. tel. 0171/581–3311. 96 rooms, 72 with bath. Facilities: 2 restaurants, wine bar, lounge, ladies' club. AE, DC, MC, V. Tube: Knightsbridge.*

$$$ **Beaufort.** "Hotel" would be a misnomer for this elegant pair of coun-
★ try house-style Victorian houses; there's a sitting room instead of a reception area, and guests have a front door key. The rates include drinks, breakfast, and anything from the 24-hour service menu, plus membership at a local health club. *33 Beaufort Gardens, SW3 1PP, tel. 0171/584–5252, fax 0171/589–2834. 29 rooms with bath. Facilities: sitting room with complimentary bar, video library, access to health club. AE, DC, MC, V. Tube: Knightsbridge.*

$$$ **Claverley.** Located on a quiet, tree-lined street, the Claverley offers friendly, attractive surroundings, some four-poster beds, and the wealthy world of Knightsbridge shopping just around the corner. *13–14 Beaufort Gardens, SW3 1PS, tel. 0171/589–8541, fax 0171/584–3410. 31 rooms with bath. AE, V. Tube: Knightsbridge.*

$$$ **The Pelham.** Eighteenth-century pine paneling in the drawing room, glazed chintz and antique lace, four-posters in some rooms, fireplaces in others—this is another hotel that feels more like an elegant home. It's opposite South Kensington tube, near the big museums, and there's a garden nearby with a heated pool for guests' use. *15 Cromwell Pl., SW7 2LA, tel. 0171/589–8288, fax 0171/584–8444. 37 rooms with bath. Facilities: restaurant, air-conditioning, access to garden with pool, valet. AE, MC, V. Tube: South Kensington.*

West End

$$$$ **Brown's.** Close to Bond Street, Brown's is like a country house in the middle of town, with wood paneling, grandfather clocks, and large fireplaces. Both Roosevelts used to stay here and it has remained popular with Anglophile Americans ever since. *34 Albemarle St., W1A 4SW, tel. 0171/493–6020, fax 0171/493–9381. 133 rooms with bath. Facilities: restaurant, bar, lounge, writing room. AE, DC, MC, V. Tube: Green Park.*

$$$$ **Claridges.** This legendary hotel has one of the world's classiest guest
★ lists. The liveried staff are friendly, not at all condescending, and the rooms are luxurious. The hotel was founded in 1812, but present decor is either 1930s Art Deco or country-house style. Have a drink or afternoon tea in the Foyer and hear the Hungarian mini-orchestra. The rooms are spacious, the sweeping staircase grand. *Brook St., W1A 2JQ, tel. 0171/629–8860, fax 0171/499–2210. 200 rooms with bath. Facilities: 2 restaurants, lounge (with orchestra), hairdresser, valet, AE, DC, MC, V. Tube: Bond St.*

$$$$ **Duke's.** This small Edwardian hotel in a cul-de-sac in St. James's enjoys a distinct Old World character, helped by the portraits of dukes adorning the walls. The top-floor bedrooms are the most spacious. *35 St. James's Pl., SW1A 1NY, tel. 0171/491–4840, fax 0171/493–1264. 62 rooms with bath. Facilities: restaurant, bar. AE, DC, MC, V. Tube: Green Park.*

$$$$ **Four Seasons.** Once one of Howard Hughes's hideaways, this opulent hotel with its polished marble entrance hall has strikingly decorated rooms with gigantic beds and plenty of extras, such as guest bathrobes and phone extensions in the bathrooms. *Hamilton Pl., Park La., W1A 1AZ, tel. 0171/499–0888, fax 0171/493–1895. 228 rooms with bath. Facilities: 2 restaurants, coffee shop, bar, lounge, fitness center, shopping arcade, free in-house movies, garden. AE, DC, MC, V. Tube: Hyde Park Corner.*

$$$$ **Savoy.** This grand, historic late-Victorian hotel has been the byword
★ for luxury for just over a century. Spacious bedrooms have antiques and cream plasterwork, and the best ones overlook the Thames. More than a hint of 1920s style remains, not least in the bathrooms with their original splendid fittings. The Fitness Gallery is a more recent addition, situated on top of the freshly restored historic Savoy Theatre. *Strand, WC2R 0EU, tel. 0171/836–4343, fax 0171/240–6040. 202 rooms with bath. Facilities: 3 restaurants, 2 bars, grill room, health club, coffee shop, florist, theater-ticket desk, free in-house movies. AE, DC, MC, V. Tube: Aldwych.*

$$$ **Chesterfield.** This former town house of the earls of Chesterfield is very popular with U.S. visitors, who are often return guests. It is deep in the heart of Mayfair, with welcoming, paneled public rooms; a good restaurant; spacious bedrooms; and an outstandingly helpful staff. *35 Charles St., W1X 8LX, tel. 0171/491-2622, fax 0171/491-4793. 113 rooms with bath. Facilities: restaurant, in-house movies. AE, DC, MC, V. Tube: Green Park.*

$$$ **Dorset Square.** The same husband (architect) and wife (interior designer)
★ team who own the Pelham (*see above*), created this stunning, comfortable small hotel in a fine pair of Regency town houses north of Oxford Street almost a decade ago, but it remains fresh. Service is personal and charming; there's an "honesty bar" in the parlor, where you help yourself and own up later, and you can be chauffered in the owner's vintage Bentley on request. *39-40 Dorset Sq., NW1 6QN, tel. 0171/723-7874, fax 0171/724-3328. 37 rooms with bath. Facilities: bar/restaurant, garden, 24-hr room service, air-conditioning. AE, MC, V. Tube: Baker St.*

$$$ **Hazlitt's.** Still Soho's sole hotel, this, the last home of Hazlitt the essayist (1778-1830), is crammed with prints on every wall, Victorian claw-foot baths, assorted antiques, plants, and bits of art. There's no elevator, the sitting room is minuscule, floors can be creaky and bedrooms tiny, but Hazlitt's legion of devotees don't mind. And who needs room service when you live on Restaurant Row? *6 Frith St., W1V 5TZ, tel. 0171/434-1771, fax 0171/439-1524. 23 rooms with bath. AE, DC, MC, V. Tube: Tottenham Court Rd.*

$$–$$$ **Bryanston Court.** Three 18th-century houses have been converted into a traditional English family-run hotel with open fires and comfortable armchairs; the bedrooms are more contemporary. *56-60 Great Cumberland Pl., W1H 7FD, tel. 0171/262-3141, fax 0171/262-7248. 56 rooms with bath or shower. Facilities: restaurant, bar, lounge, satellite TV. AE, DC, MC, V. Tube: Marble Arch.*

$$–$$$ **The Fielding.** Tucked away in a quiet alley, steps from the Royal Opera House, this funny little place is so adored by its regulars, you'd better book ahead. It's shabby-homey in decor and attitude—there's no elevator, only one room with a bathtub (most have showers), and no room service or restaurant, but it's cute and so handy for the theater. *4 Broad Ct., Bow St., WC2B 5OZ, tel. 0171/836-8305, fax 0171/497-0064. 26 rooms, 1 with bath, 23 with showers. Facilities: bar, breakfast room. AE, DC, MC, V. Tube: Covent Garden.*

$$ **Edward Lear.** The former home of Edward Lear, the artist and writer of nonsense verse, this hotel has barely anything in the way of amenities, but it's a good value for the area, which is very central. The peacefulness of the rooms varies—ask for a quieter room to the rear—as does their size (Room 14 is the smallest). *28-30 Seymour St., W1H 5WD, tel. 0171/402-5401, fax 0171/706-3766. 32 rooms, 12 with bath or shower. V. Tube: Marble Arch.*

The Arts

For a list of events in the London arts scene, visit a newsstand or bookstore to pick up the weekly magazine *Time Out.* The city's evening paper, the *Evening Standard,* carries listings, as do the major Sunday papers; the daily *Independent* and *Guardian*; and, on Friday, *The Times.*

Theater

London's theater life can more or less be divided into three categories: the government-subsidized national companies; the commercial, or "West End," theaters; and the fringe.

The main national companies are the **Royal National Theatre Company** (NT) and the **Royal Shakespeare Company** (RSC). Each has its own custom-designed facilities, in the South Bank arts complex and in the

Barbican Arts Centre, respectively. Each presents a variety of plays by writers of all nationalities, ranging from the classics of Shakespeare and his contemporaries to specially commissioned modern works. Box office: NT, tel. 0171/928–2252; RSC, tel. 0171/638–8891.

The West End theaters largely stage musicals, comedies, whodunits, and revivals of lighter plays of the 19th and 20th centuries, often starring television celebrities. Occasionally there are more serious productions, including successful productions transferred from the subsidized theaters, such as RSC's *Les Liaisons Dangereuses* and *Les Misérables*.

The two dozen or so established fringe theaters, scattered around central London and the immediate outskirts, frequently present some of London's most intriguing productions, if you're prepared to overlook occasional rough staging and uncomfortable seating.

Most theaters have an evening performance at 7:30 or 8 daily, except Sunday, and a matinee twice a week (Wednesday or Thursday and Saturday). Expect to pay from £7 to £10 for a seat in the upper balcony and at least £20 for a good seat in the stalls (orchestra) or dress circle (mezzanine)—more for musicals. Tickets may be booked in person at the theater box office; over the phone by credit card; or through ticket agents, such as **First Call** (tel. 0171/497–9977). In addition, the ticket booth in Leicester Square sells half-price tickets on the day of performance for about 45 theaters; there is a small service charge. Beware of unscrupulous ticket agents who sell tickets at four or five times their box-office price (a small service charge is legitimate) and scalpers, who stand outside theaters offering tickets for the next performance; they've been known to charge £200 for a sought-after show.

Concerts

Ticket prices for symphony orchestra concerts are still relatively moderate—between £5 and £15, although you can expect to pay more to hear big-name artists on tour. If you can't book in advance, arrive half an hour before the performance for a chance at returns.

The London Symphony Orchestra is in residence at the **Barbican Arts Centre** (tel. 0171/638–8891), although other top symphony and chamber orchestras also perform here. The **South Bank arts complex** (tel. 0171/928–8800), which includes the **Royal Festival Hall** and the **Queen Elizabeth Hall,** is another major venue for choral, symphonic, and chamber concerts. For less expensive concert going, try the **Royal Albert Hall** (tel. 0171/589–8212) during the summer Promenade season; special tickets for standing room are available at the hall on the night of performance. **The Wigmore Hall** (tel. 0171/935–2141) is a small auditorium, ideal for recitals. Inexpensive lunchtime concerts take place all over the city in smaller halls and churches, often featuring string quartets, singers, jazz ensembles, and gospel choirs. **St. John's, Smith Square** (tel. 0171/222–1061), a converted Queen Anne church, is one of the more popular venues. It has a handy crypt cafeteria.

Opera

The **Royal Opera House** ranks alongside the New York Met. Prices range from £8.50 (in the upper balconies, from which only a tiny portion of the stage is visible) to £392 for a box in the Grand Tier. Bookings are best made at the box office (tel. 0171/240–1066). The **Coliseum** (tel. 0171/836–3161) is the home of the English National Opera Company; productions are staged in English and are often innovative and exciting. Tickets range from £8 to £48.

Ballet

The Royal Opera House also hosts the **Royal Ballet.** The prices are slightly more reasonable than for the opera, but be sure to book well ahead. The **English National Ballet** and visiting companies perform at the Coliseum from time to time, especially during the summer. **Sadler's Wells Theatre** (tel. 0171/278–8916) hosts regional ballet and international modern dance troupes. Prices here are reasonable.

Film

Most West End cinemas are in the area around Leicester Square and Piccadilly Circus. Tickets run from £5 to £8. Matinees and Monday evenings are cheaper. Cinema clubs screen a wide range of films: classics, Continental, underground, rare, or underestimated masterpieces. A temporary membership fee is usually about £1. One of the best-value clubs is the **National Film Theatre** (tel. 0171/928–3232), part of the South Bank arts complex.

Nightlife

London's night spots are legion, and there is only space here to list a few of the best known. For up-to-the-minute listings, buy *Time Out* magazine.

Jazz

Bass Clef (85 Coronet St., tel. 0171/729–2476), situated in an out-of-the-way warehouse on the northern edge of the City (the nearest tube is Old Street), offers some of the best live jazz in town and a mainly vegetarian menu. **Ronnie Scott's** (47 Frith St., tel. 0171/439–0747) is the legendary Soho jazz club where international performers regularly take the stage.

Nightclubs

The Wag (33–35 Wardour St., tel. 0171/437–5534) is a tenacious entry in Soho's notoriously fickle club circuit—it's still hip, though it changes according to who's hosting and which DJ is spinning. Be under 30. Glitzy **Stringfellows** (16 Upper St. Martin's Lane, tel. 0171/240–5534) has an art deco upstairs restaurant, mirrored walls, and a dazzling light show in the downstairs dance floor. **The Limelight** (136 Shaftesbury Ave., tel. 0171/434–0572), in a converted church, is one of London's enduringly popular nightspots, with lots of one-nighter shows.

Casinos

By law, you must apply in person for membership in a gaming house; in many cases, clubs prefer an applicant's membership to be proposed by an existing member. Approval usually takes about two days.

Crockford's (30 Curzon St., tel. 0171/493–7771) is a civilized and unflashy 150-year-old club with a large international clientele; American roulette, punto banco, and blackjack are played. **Sportsman Club** (3 Tottenham Court Rd., tel. 0171/637–5464) has a dice table as well as punto banco, American roulette, and blackjack.

Discos

Camden Palace (1A Camden High St., tel. 0171/387–0428) is perennially popular with both Londoners and visiting youth. This multitier place, following a recent overhaul, has two major dance floors, plus at least three bars, and a colorful light show. American-style food is served. The **Hippodrome** (Cranbourn St., tel. 0171/437–4311) is a hugely popular and lavish disco with an exciting sound-and-laser light system, live bands and dancing acts, a video screen, bars, and a restaurant.

Rock

The Forum (9–17 Highgate Rd., Kentish Town, tel. 0171/284–0303), a little out of the way, is a premier venue for medium-to-big acts. **The Rock Garden** (67 The Piazza, Covent Garden, tel. 0171/240–3961) is famous for encouraging younger talent: Talking Heads, U2, and The Smiths are among those who played here while still virtually unknown. Music is in the standing-room-only basement. **The Marquee** (105 Charing Cross Rd., tel. 0171/437–6603), Soho's original rock club, has moved house since its heyday; at least two bands perform every night.

Cabaret

The best comedy in town can be found in the bigger, brighter, new-look **Comedy Store** (Haymarket House, Oxendon St., near Piccadilly Circus, tel. 01426/914433). There are two shows, at 8 and midnight on Friday and Saturday, at 8 only Tuesday to Thursday. **Madame Jo Jo's** (8 Brewer St., tel. 0171/734–2473) is possibly the most fun of any London cabaret, with its outrageous, glittering drag shows. The place is luxurious and civilized. There are two shows, at 12:15 and 1:15 AM.

WINDSOR TO BATH

The Thames, England's second-longest river, winds its way toward London through an accessible and gracious stretch of countryside. An excursion west from the capital, roughly following the river toward its source in the Cotswold Hills, allows you to explore historic townships such as Windsor, where the castle is still regularly used by the royal family; Oxford, home of the nation's oldest university; and Stratford-upon-Avon, Shakespeare's birthplace. Traveling south, you come to Bath, whose 18th-century streets recall an age more elegant than our own.

Getting Around

By Train

Suburban services run from London (Waterloo and Paddington stations) to Windsor. Regular fast trains run from Paddington to Oxford and Bath, and less frequent and slower services requiring at least one change, to Stratford. For information, call 0171/262–6767. An alternative route to Stratford is from London's Euston Station to Coventry, from which there are hourly bus connections on the Stratford Blue line; call 01788/535555 for details.

By Bus

Regular long-distance services leave from Victoria Coach Station. For information, call 0171/730–0202.

By Car

M4 and M40 are the main highways out of London serving Oxford, the Cotswolds, and Bath. Once you're clear of London, take to the country roads and explore tiny villages and the best of the English countryside.

Tourist Information

Bath (The Colonnades, 11–13 Bath St., tel. 01225/462831).
Chipping Campden (open Apr.–Sept., Woolstaplers Hall Museum, High St., tel. 01386/840101).
Oxford (The Old School, Gloucester Green, tel. 01865/726871).
Stratford (Bridgefoot, next to the canal bridge, tel. 01789/293127).
Warwick (The Court House, Jury St., tel. 01926/492212).
Windsor (Central Station, Thames St., tel. 01753/852010).

Windsor to Bath

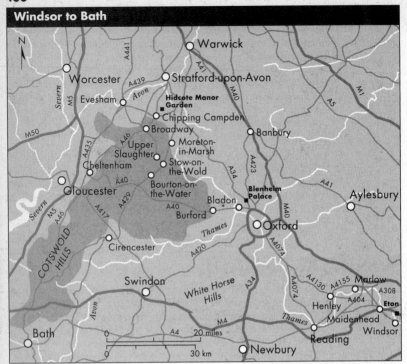

Guided Tours

National Holidays operates five-day trips in the Cotswolds, some in Bath. There are agents throughout the country. **Frames Rickards** (tel. 0171/837–3111) runs full-day sightseeing tours to Windsor, Stratford-upon-Avon, Oxford, and Bath. **Guide Friday** (Windsor: tel. 01753/855755; Oxford: tel. 01865/790522; and Stratford: tel. 01789/294466) offers excellent tours of Windsor, Oxford, and Shakespeare country.

Exploring Windsor to Bath

Windsor

Windsor, some 40 kilometers (25 miles) west of London, has been a royal citadel since the days of William the Conqueror in the 11th century. In the 14th century, Edward III revamped the old castle, building the Norman gateway, the great round tower, and new apartments. Almost every monarch since then has added new buildings or improved existing ones; over the centuries, the medieval fortification has been transformed into the lavish royal palace the visitor sees today.

The following are some of the highlights of the castle: **St. George's Chapel,** more than 230 feet long with two tiers of great windows and hundreds of gargoyles, buttresses, and pinnacles, is one of the noblest buildings in England. Inside, above the choir stalls, hang the banners, swords, and helmets of the Knights of the Order of the Garter, the most senior Order of Chivalry. The many monarchs buried in the chapel include Henry VIII and George VI, father of the present queen. The magnificent art collection at Windsor contains paintings by such masters as Rubens, Van Dyck, and Holbein; drawings by Leonardo da Vinci;

and Gobelin tapestries. There are splendid views across to Windsor Great Park, the remains of a former royal hunting forest. Make time to view **Queen Mary's Dolls' House,** a charming toy country house with every detail complete, including electricity, running water, and miniature books on the library shelves. It was designed in 1921 by the architect Sir Edwin Lutyens for the present queen's grandmother.

The terrible fire of November 1992, which started in the Queen's private chapel, completely destroyed some of the **State Apartments.** Miraculously, a swift rescue effort meant that hardly any works of art were lost. Repairs are likely to last until 1999, though all but two of the state rooms previously visitable were open at press time (spring 1995), along with all the other public areas. *Windsor Castle, tel. 01753/868286. Admission: £8 adults, £4 children, £5.50 senior citizens, £18 family ticket; Dolls' House £1 extra; Carriages £1.60 adults, 80p children, £1.40 senior citizens. Open daily Mar.–Oct. 10–4 (last admissions at 3); Nov.–Feb. 10–5:30 (last admissions at 4).*

After seeing the castle, stroll around the town and enjoy the shops; antiques are sold in cobbled Church Lane and Queen Charlotte Street.

TIME OUT The **Adam and Eve** pub (Thames St.) opposite the walls of Windsor Castle serves hot snacks and ploughman's lunches, while **The Courtyard** (8 King George V Pl.) is an inviting spot for lunch or a cream tea.

A short walk over the river brings you to **Eton,** Windsor Castle's equally historic neighbor and home of the famous public school. (In Britain, so-called public schools are private and charge fees.) Classes still take place in the distinctive redbrick Tudor-style buildings; the oldest are grouped around a quadrangle called School Yard. The **Museum of Eton Life** has displays on the school's history, and a guided tour is also available. *Brewhouse Yard, tel. 01753/671177. Admission: £2.30 adults, £1.60 children; with tour: £3.40 adults, £2.80 children. Open daily 2–4:30 during term, 10:30–4:30 on school holidays. Guided tours Mar.–Oct., daily at 2:15 and 3:15.*

A relatively uncrowded route from Windsor to Oxford is along the river through Marlow and Henley on A308, then A4155, A4130, and A4074. In **Marlow,** there are some stylish 18th-century houses on Peter and West streets, and several princes of Wales have lived in Marlow Place on Station Road, which dates from 1721. Mary Shelley wrote her celebrated horror story *Frankenstein* in the town.

Henley has been famous since 1839 for the rowing regatta it holds each year around the first Sunday in July. The social side of the regatta is as entertaining as the races themselves; elderly oarsmen wear brightly colored blazers and tiny caps, businessmen entertain wealthy clients, and everyone admires the ladies' fashions. The town is worth exploring for its small but good selection of specialty shops, such as Saffron on Bell Street (crafts items) and Thames Gallery on Thameside (Georgian and Victorian silver). The Red Lion Hotel near the 200-year-old bridge has been visited by kings, dukes, and writers; the duke of Marlborough stayed there while Blenheim Palace was being built. St. Mary's Church has a 16th-century "checkerboard" tower made of alternate squares of flint and stone, and the **Chantry House,** built in 1420 as a school for poor boys, is an unspoiled example of the rare overhanging timber-frame design. *Hart St., tel. 01491/577340. Admission free. Open Thurs. and Sat. 10–noon (other times by appointment).*

Oxford

Numbers in the margin correspond to points of interest on the Oxford map.

Continue along A4130 and A4070 northwest to **Oxford.** The surest way to absorb Oxford's unique blend of history and scholarliness is to wander around the tiny alleys that link the honey-colored stone buildings topped by elegant "dreaming" spires, exploring the colleges where the undergraduates live and work. Oxford University, like Cambridge University, is not a single building but a collection of 35 independent colleges; many of their magnificent chapels and dining halls are open to

❶ visitors—times are displayed at the entrance lodges. **Magdalen College** (pronounced maudlin) is one of the most impressive, with cloisters more than 500 years old and lawns leading down to a deer park and

❷ the River Cherwell. **St. Edmund Hall,** the next college up the High Street, has one of the smallest and most picturesque quadrangles, with

❸ an old well in the center. **Christ Church,** on St. Aldate's, has the largest quadrangle, known as Tom Quad; hanging in the medieval dining hall are portraits of former pupils, including John Wesley, William Penn, and no fewer than 14 prime ministers. The doors between the inner and outer

❹ quadrangles of **Balliol College,** on Broad Street, still bear the scorch marks from the flames that burned Archbishop Cranmer and Bishops Latimer and Ridley at the stake in 1555 for their Protestant beliefs.

❺ The **Oxford Story** on Broad Street is a dramatic multimedia presentation of the university's 800-year history, in which visitors travel through depictions of college life. *Broad St., tel. 01865/790055. Admission: £4.50 adults, £3.25 children, £3.95 senior citizens, £14 family ticket. Open Apr.–June and Sept.–Oct., daily 9:30–5; Jul.–Aug., daily 9:30–7; Nov.–Mar., daily 10–4.*

❻ Also on Broad Street is the **Sheldonian Theatre,** which St. Paul's architect Christopher Wren designed to look like a semicircular Roman amphitheater. Graduation ceremonies are held here. *Broad St., tel. 01865/277299. Admission: 50p adults, 25p children. Open Mon.–Sat. 10–12:45 and 2–4:45; closes at 3:45 mid-Nov.–Feb.*

❼ The **Ashmolean Museum,** which you encounter by turning right out of Broad Street into Magdalen Street, then taking the first left, is Britain's oldest public museum, holding priceless collections of Egyptian, Greek, and Roman artifacts; Michelangelo drawings; and European silverware. *Beaumont St., tel. 01865/278000. Admission free. Open Tues.–Sat. 10–4, Sun. 2–4.*

For a relaxing walk, make for the banks of the River Cherwell, either through the University Parks area or through Magdalen College to Addison's Walk, and watch the undergraduates idly punting a summer's afternoon away, or rent one of these narrow flat-bottom boats yourself. But be warned: Navigating is more difficult than it looks!

TIME OUT   The **St. Aldate's Coffee House** (94 St. Aldate's) is run by the church next door and is a great place for lunch or coffee. The **Eagle and Child** is a historic pub on St. Giles. On the outskirts of the city are two excellent pubs, the **Perch** at Binsey and the **Trout** at Godstow.

Blenheim Palace, about 13 kilometers (8 miles) north of Oxford on A44 (Woodstock Road), is a vast mansion in neoclassical style built in the early 18th century by the architect Sir John Vanbrugh; it stands in 2,500 acres of beautiful gardens landscaped later in the 18th century by "Capability" Brown, the famous English landscape gardener. Soldier and statesman John Churchill, first duke of Marlborough,

Oxford

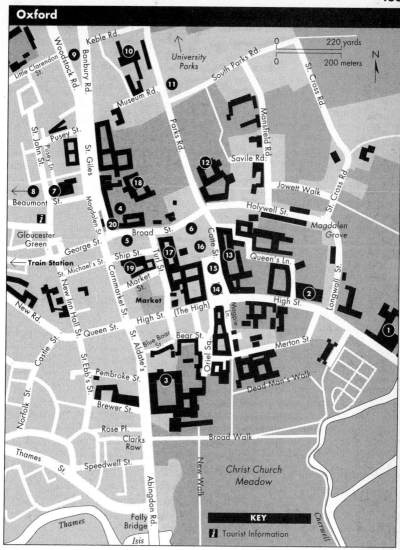

Major Attractions
Ashmolean Museum, **7**
Balliol College, **4**
Christ Church, **3**
Magdalen College, **1**
Oxford Story, **5**
St. Edmund Hall, **2**
Sheldonian Theatre, **6**

Other Attractions
All Souls College, **13**
Bodleian Library, **16**
Exeter College, **17**
Jesus College, **19**
Keble College, **10**
Radcliffe Camera, **15**
St. Giles' Church, **9**

St. Mary Magdalen Church, **20**
Trinity College, **18**
University Church (St. Mary's), **14**
University Museum, **11**
Wadham College, **12**
Worcester College, **8**

built the house on land given to him by Queen Anne and with money voted him by Parliament on behalf of a "grateful nation" as a reward for his crushing defeat of the French at the Battle of Blenheim in 1704. The house is filled with fine paintings, tapestries, and furniture. Winston Churchill, a descendant of Marlborough, was born in the palace; some of his paintings are on display, and there is an exhibition devoted to his life. *Woodstock, tel. 01993/811091. Admission to grounds free; admission to house £7 adults, £3.50 children 5–15, £4.90 senior citizens, £19 family ticket. Open mid-Mar.–Oct., 10:30–5:30. Grounds open year-round 9–4:45. Restaurant and cafeteria.*

Sir Winston Churchill (1874–1965) is buried in the nearby village of **Bladon.** His grave in the small tree-lined churchyard is all the more touching for its simplicity.

Stratford-upon-Avon

A34 runs northwest from Oxford and Blenheim across the Cotswold Hills to **Stratford-upon-Avon,** the home town of William Shakespeare. Even without its most famous son, Stratford would be worth visiting. The town's timbered buildings bear witness to its prosperity in the 16th century, when it was a thriving craft and trading center, and attractive 18th-century buildings are also of note.

Numbers in the margin correspond to points of interest on the Stratford-upon-Avon map.

The main places of Shakespearean interest are run by the **Shakespeare Birthplace Trust.** They all have similar opening times (mid-Mar.–mid-Oct., Mon.–Sat. 9–6, Sun. 9:30–6; mid-Oct.–mid-Mar., Mon.–Sat. 9:30–4:30, Sun. 10–4:30; last entry always 30 mins before closing) and you can get a combination ticket for them all—£8 adults, £3.60 children, £7 senior citizens, £21 family ticket—or pay separate entry fees

❶ ❷ if you want to visit only one or two. The **Shakespeare Centre** and **Shakespeare's Birthplace** contain the costumes used in the BBC's versions of the plays and an exhibition of the playwright's life and work. *Henley St., tel. 01789/204016. A Shakespeare Birthplace Trust property.*

TIME OUT **Mistress Quickly** (59–60 Henley Street) serves light refreshments and meals throughout the day; an unusual feature is the jigsaw tree sculpture on the stairs. The **Black Swan**—better known locally as the Dirty Duck—is a riverside pub beside the theater, serving good ales and bar meals.

Two very different attractions reveal something of the times in which Shakespeare lived. Originally a farmhouse, the girlhood home of Shake-

❸ speare's mother, **Mary Arden's House,** is now an extensive museum of farming and country life. It was built in the 16th century and many of the original outbuildings are intact, together with a 600-nesting-hole dovecote. There is a garden planted with trees mentioned in Shakespeare's plays. *Wilmcote (5.5 km/3½ mi northwest of Stratford, off A3400 and A46), tel. 01789/204016. Also reachable by train in a few minutes from Stratford. A Shakespeare Birthplace Trust property.*

❹ A complete contrast is **Hall's Croft,** a fine Tudor town house that was the home of Shakespeare's daughter Susanna and her doctor husband; it is furnished in the decor of the day, and the doctor's dispensary and consulting room can also be seen. *Old Town, tel. 01789/292107. A Shakespeare Birthplace Trust property.*

❺ The **Royal Shakespeare Theatre** occupies a perfect position on the banks of the Avon—try to see a performance if you can. The company (always referred to as the RSC) performs several Shakespeare plays each

Major Attractions

Anne Hathaway's Cottage, **9**

Hall's Croft, **4**

Holy Trinity Church, **8**

Mary Arden's House, **3**

The Other Place, **7**

Royal Shakespeare Theatre, **5**

Shakespeare Centre, **1**

Shakespeare's Birthplace, **2**

Swan, **6**

Other Attractions

American Fountain, **15**

Grammar School and Guildhall, **11**

Guild Chapel, **12**

Harvard House, **14**

Shakespeare Institute, **10**

Town Hall, **13**

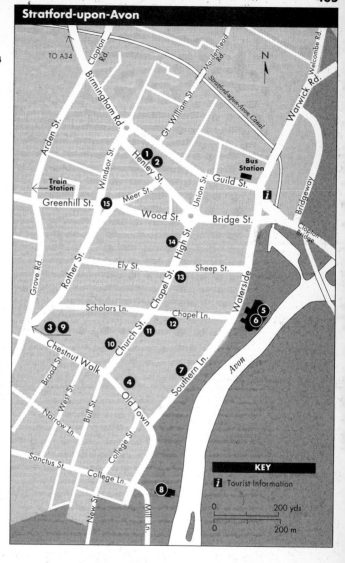

Stratford-upon-Avon

season, as well as plays by a wide variety of other playwrights, between March and January. For a fascinating insight into how the theater operates, join one of the backstage tours, led twice daily (four times on

❻ Sundays). Beside the main theater there is the smaller **Swan**, the gift of an Anglophile American, Frederick Koch. Modeled on an Elizabethan theater, the Swan provides a very exciting auditorium for in-the-round staging. The Swan also provides entry to the RSC Collection, comprising paintings, props, and memorabilia; visit it either on one of the backstage tours or on your own. A new auditorium for experimental pro-

❼ ductions, **The Other Place,** is located just down the street. It's best to book well in advance for RSC productions, but a very few tickets for the day of performance are always available, and it is also worth asking if there are any returns. *Programs are available starting in February from the Royal Shakespeare Theatre, Stratford-upon-Avon, Warwickshire CV37 6BB, tel. 01789/295623; call 01789/296655 for details on backstage tours and RSC Collection.*

8 It is in **Holy Trinity Church**, close to the Royal Shakespeare Theatre, that Shakespeare and his wife are buried.

9 **Anne Hathaway's Cottage,** in Shottery on the edge of the town, is the early home of the playwright's wife. *Tel. 01789/292100. A Shakespeare Birthplace Trust property.*

Warwick

Warwick, some 13 kilometers (8 miles) north of Stratford along A46, is an unusual mixture of Georgian redbrick and Elizabethan half-timber buildings, although some unattractive postwar developments have spoiled the town center. **Warwick Castle** is one of the finest medieval structures of its kind in England, towering on a precipice above the River Avon. Most of the present buildings date from the 14th century; look for the remarkable gate house, which consists of a pair of towers above the doorway passage, and two massive towers, Guy's and Caesar's, both about 130 feet tall, the latter with a system of double battlements. The interior contains magnificent collections of armor, paintings, and furniture and a waxworks display by Madame Tussaud's, while, outside, peacocks strut in the 60 acres of landscaped riverside gardens. A restored Victorian boathouse has a flora-and-fauna exhibition and a nature walk. *Castle Hill, tel. 01926/495421. Admission: £8.25 adults, £4.95 children 4–16, £5.95 senior citizens, £22 family ticket. Open Apr.–mid-Oct., daily 10–6; mid-Oct.–Mar., daily 10–5 (last entry 30 mins before closing); open until 7 PM Aug. weekends.*

TIME OUT The paneled bar in the **Zetland Arms** (11 Church St.) serves good local beer and simple meals. There is also a quiet, attractive little garden.

The Cotswolds

From Stratford take an easy detour via A3400 and B4632 into the **Cotswolds**—high, bare hills patterned by patches of ancient forest and stone walls that protect the sheep that have grazed here from the earliest times. In the Middle Ages, English wool commanded high prices, and the little towns and villages nestling in valleys and on hillsides grew in prosperity. Although the wool trade has now dwindled in importance, the legacy of those days remains in the solid, substantial churches, cottages, and manor houses built of the mellow, golden-gray local stone. Burford, Stow-on-the-Wold, Upper Slaughter, Bourton-on-the-Water, Broadway, and Moreton-in-Marsh are just a few of the picturesque towns connected by pleasant country roads. If you have time to visit only one Cotswold town, make it **Chipping Camden.** Its broad High Street is lined with houses in an attractive disarray of styles, many dating from the 17th century. Look for the group of almshouses built in 1624 and raised above street level and for the gabled **Market Hall** built three years later for the sale of local produce.

One of the town's earliest buildings, dating from the 14th century, is the **Woolstaplers Hall,** which contains a museum of local history; besides material on the wool trade, there is a 1920s cinema and collections of medical equipment. *High St., tel. 01386/840101. Admission: £2.50 adults, £1.50 children. Open Apr.–Oct., daily 10–5.*

Five kilometers (3 miles) outside Chipping Campden is **Hidcote Manor Garden,** a 20th-century garden created around a Cotswold manor house (not open to the public). The garden consists of a series of open-air rooms divided by walls and hedges, each in a different style. *Hidcote Bartrim, tel. 01386/438333. Admission: £5 adults, £2.50 children, £13.75 family ticket. Open Apr.–Oct., Sat.–Mon., Wed., Thurs. 11–7. Last admission 6 PM or 1 hr before sunset.*

B4632 runs along the western edge of the gently rolling Cotswold Hills, as far as **Cheltenham,** once the rival of Bath in its Georgian elegance. Although it's now marred by modern developments, there are still some fine examples of the Regency style in its graceful secluded villas, lush gardens, and leafy crescents and squares.

Bath

Bath lies at the southern end of the Cotswolds (at the end of A46), some 112 kilometers (70 miles) from Stratford. A perfect 18th-century city, perhaps the best preserved in all Britain, it is a compact place, easy to explore on foot; the museums, elegant shops, and terraces of magnificent town houses are all close to one another.

Numbers in the margin correspond to points of interest on the Bath map.

It was the Romans who first took the waters at Bath, building a temple in honor of their goddess Minerva and a sophisticated series of baths to make full use of the curative hot springs. To this day, these springs gush from the earth at a constant temperature of 115.7°F (46.5°C). In

❶ the **Roman Baths Museum,** underneath the 18th-century Pump Room, you can see the excavated remains of almost the entire baths complex. *Abbey Churchyard, tel. 01225/477000, ext. 2785. Admission: £5 adults, £3 children, £13 family ticket. Combined ticket for Roman Baths and Museum of Costume: £6.60 adults, £3.50 children, £16 family ticket. Open Apr.–July and Sept., daily 9–6; Aug. 8 PM–10 PM; Oct.–Mar., Mon.–Sat. 9:30–5, Sun. 10:30–5.*

❷ Next to the Pump Room is the **Abbey,** built in the 15th century. There are superb fan-vaulted ceilings in the nave.

In the 18th century, Bath became the fashionable center for taking the waters. The architect John Wood created a harmonious city from the mellow local stone, building beautifully executed terraces, crescents, and
❸ villas. The heart of Georgian Bath is the perfectly proportioned **Circus**
❹ and the Royal Crescent. On the corner, **No. 1 Royal Crescent** is furnished as it might have been when Beau Nash, the master of ceremonies and arbiter of 18th-century Bath society, lived in the city. *Tel. 01225/428126. Admission: £3 adults, £2.50 children and senior citizens. Open Mar.–Oct., Tues.–Sun. 10:30–5; Nov.–mid-Dec., Tues.–Sun. 11–4.*

❺ Also near the Circus are the **Assembly Rooms,** frequently mentioned by Jane Austen in her novels of early 19th-century life. This neoclassical villa now houses a Museum of Costume that displays dress styles from Beau Nash's day to the present. *Bennett St., tel. 01225/477000, ext. 2785. Admission: £3.20 adults, £2 children, £9 family ticket. Open Mon.–Sat. 10–5, Sun. 11–5.*

❻ Across the Avon, in an elegant 18th-century building, is the **Holburne Museum and Crafts Study Centre,** which houses a superb collection of 17th- and 18th-century fine art and decorative arts. *Great Pulteney St., tel. 01225/466669. Admission: £3.50 adults, £1.50 children, £3 senior citizens, £7 family ticket. Open mid-Feb.–Easter, Tues.–Sat. 11–5, Sun. 2:30–6; Easter–mid-Dec., Mon.–Sat. 11–5, Sun. 2:30–5:30.*

TIME OUT Try the **Pump Room** (Abbey Churchyard) for morning coffee or afternoon tea in grand surroundings, perhaps listening to the music of a string quartet, or, in nearby North Parade Passage, **Sally Lunn's,** where the famous Sally Lunn bun is still baked.

Major Attractions

Abbey, **2**

Assembly Rooms, **5**

Circus, **3**

Holburne Museum and Crafts Study Center, **6**

No. 1 Royal Crescent, **4**

Roman Baths Museum, **1**

Other Attractions

Camden Works Museum, **7**

Carriage Museum, **8**

Octagon and National Center of Photography, **10**

Pulteney Bridge, **11**

Sally Lunn's, **12**

Theatre Royal, **9**

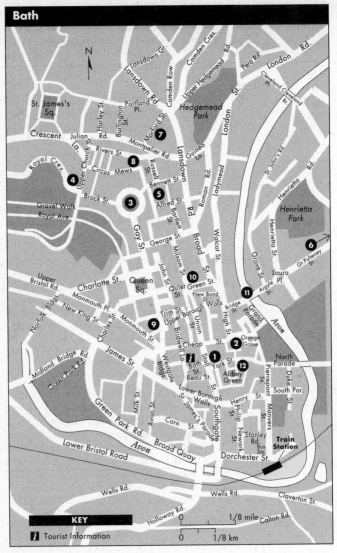

Dining and Lodging

For details and price-category definitions, *see* Dining and Lodging *in* Staying in Great Britain, *above*.

Bath

DINING

Popjoys Restaurant. Beau Nash entertained the best of 18th-century society here, and Popjoys retains its air of elegance, though its recently-opened downstairs Brasserie has a more contemporary, relaxed tone. *Sawclose, tel. 01225/460494. Reservations advised. AE, MC, V. Closed Sun. and Mon. $$*

Number Five. This candlelit bistro off Pulteney Bridge has a relaxed ambience and offers simple pasta with olive oil and grilled eggplant or more elaborate dishes such as confit of duck or roast breast of chicken with sun-dried tomatoes. *5 Argyle St., tel. 01225/444499. Reservations advised. DC, MC, V. Closed Sun. No lunch Mon. $–$$*

Rascals. Located in a mazelike cellar of interconnecting rooms just south of the abbey, Rascals is a cheerful bistro-style restaurant offering excellent food, fine wines at low prices, and a noisy, relaxed atmosphere. Chef and proprietor Nick Anderson provides an international range of dishes, such as breast of Barbary duck and goujons of brill, though the menu changes regularly. Vegetarian dishes are also available, and homemade ice cream features among the desserts. *8 Pierrepoint Pl., tel. 01225/330201. Reservations advised. MC, V. No lunch Sun. $*

Theatre Vaults. These busy stone cellars house a very handy restaurant that serves light meals at lunchtime and early evening or full-scale dinner menus later. *Sawclose, tel. 01225/442265. AE, DC, MC, V. Closed Sun. $*

LODGING

Royal Crescent. The Royal Crescent is the ultimate in luxury living, in a gracious, lavishly converted building, situated on one of England's most famous terraces. Each bedroom has been individually designed to recapture the elegance of Bath's heyday. The hotel's formal Dower House restaurant wins consistent praise. *16 Royal Crescent, BA1 2LS, tel. 01225/319090, fax 01225/339401. 29 rooms with bath, 17 suites. Facilities: restaurant, whirlpool bath, garden, croquet, parking garage. AE, DC, MC, V. $$$–$$$$*

Francis Hotel. Overlooking one of Bath's attractive Georgian squares, the Francis consists of six Georgian houses and a new wing. Bedrooms in the old building are decorated in period style. *Queen Sq., BA1 2HH, tel. 01225/424257, fax 01225/319715. 93 rooms with bath. AE, DC, MC, V. $$$*

Pratt's. Just a few minutes' walk from the center of town and the main sights, Pratt's is a fine Georgian house. Once the home of novelist Sir Walter Scott, it is now a comfortable hotel with an innovative restaurant. *South Parade, BA2 4AB, tel. 01225/460441, fax 01225/448807. 46 rooms with bath. Facilities: restaurant, bar, conference rooms. AE, DC, MC, V. $$*

The Tasburgh Hotel. This refurbished Victorian house, surrounded by gardens with beautiful views over the Avon Valley, has tastefully furnished rooms complete with every modern comfort. It's a mile from city center. *Warminster Rd., Bathampton, BA2 6SH, tel. 01225/425096, fax 01225/463842. 14 rooms, 10 with bath. Facilities: extensive gardens, fishing and mooring rights. AE, DC, MC, V. $$*

Oxford

DINING

Elizabeth's. These small, elegant dining rooms in a 16th-century bishop's palace overlook Christ Church and have the best views of any restaurant in Oxford. Salmon quenelles and roast lamb are among the Spanish chef's specialties, and there are outstanding wines. *82 St. Aldates, tel. 01865/242230. Reservations advised. AE, DC, MC, V. Closed Mon. $$*

Fifteen North Parade. Just outside the city center, this is an intimate, stylish restaurant with cane furniture and a bright, open feeling. The menu changes regularly and may feature lobster ravioli, potted partridge, or pumpkin pie with nutmeg. *15 North Parade, tel. 01865/513773. Reservations advised. MC, V. Closed Sun. eve and Mon. $$*

Gee's. This brasserie is in a conservatory just north of the town center. The large menu features Italian food and is very popular with both town and gown. *61 Banbury Rd., tel. 01865/53540. Reservations required. MC, V. $$*

Munchy Munchy. A constantly changing menu of spicy Malaysian dishes and a good selection of fresh fruit and vegetables make this a refreshing and popular spot. The surroundings are unpretentious and the prices are reasonable. *6 Park End St., tel. 01865/245710. MC, V. Closed Sun., Mon., 2 wks in Aug.–Sept and 2 wks in Dec.–Jan. $*

LODGING

The Randolph. Oxford's only large central hotel has undergone extensive restoration of its elaborate Victorian Gothic interior. It's across from the Ashmolean Museum. *Beaumont St., OX1 2LN, tel. 01865/247481, fax 01865/791678. 105 rooms with bath, 4 suites. Facilities: restaurant, bar, parking garage. AE, DC, MC, V. $$$–$$$$*

Eastgate Hotel. This welcoming hotel has the traditional style of an inn. Its bar is a favorite with undergraduates and is a good place for getting an insight into university life. *The High, OX1 4BE, tel. 01865/248244, fax 01865/791681. 43 rooms with bath. Facilities: restaurant, bar. AE, DC, MC, V. $$$*

Old Parsonage. It's rare to find an attractive country house-hotel, with stone gables and mullioned windows, in the middle of a city, but that is just what awaits at the Old Parsonage. Just a few yards behind St. Giles church, close to Somerville and Keble colleges, the Old Parsonage was established in 1660 and was completely restored and refurbished in 1991. Open fires, fascinating pictures, comfortable rooms, and immaculate service make this a hotel to remember. *1 Banbury Rd., OX2 6NN, tel. 01865/310210, fax 01865/311262. 30 rooms with bath. Facilities: restaurant, bar, garden. AE, DC, MC, V. $$$*

Stratford

DINING

Box Tree Restaurant. In the Royal Shakespeare Theatre, this elegant restaurant overlooks the river and is a favored spot for pre- and post-theater dining. Specialties include noisettes of lamb and poached Scotch beef fillet. *Waterside, tel. 01789/293226. Reservations required. AE, DC, MC, V. Closed when theater is closed. $$$*

The Opposition. Located near the Royal Shakespeare Theatre, the Opposition caters to the pre- and post-theater dining crowd (as do all sensible restaurants in Stratford). It is extremely popular with the locals, so book in advance. The American and Continental dishes change constantly—if you're lucky there'll be Cajun chicken or a lasagna made with courgettes (zucchini) and aubergine (eggplant). *13 Sheep St., tel. 01789/269980. Reservations advised. MC, V. $$*

River Terrace. For less expensive fare at the theater, this spot provides informal meals and light refreshments. Hot dishes include lasagna and shepherd's pie, and there are also salads, cakes, and sandwiches. *Waterside, tel. 01789/293226. No reservations. No credit cards. $*

The Slug and Lettuce. Don't let the name put you off—this pine-paneled pub serves excellent meals. Long-standing favorites are chicken breast baked in avocado and garlic, and salmon escalope. *38 Guild St., tel. 01789/299700. Reservations advised. MC, V. $*

LODGING

Falcon Hotel. Licensed as an alehouse since 1640, it still has a friendly inn atmosphere. The heavily beamed rooms in the older part are small and quaint; those in the modern extension are in standard international style. *Chapel St., CV37 6HA, tel. 01789/205777, fax 01789/414260. 73 rooms with bath. Facilities: restaurant, 2 bars, parking, garden. AE, DC, MC, V. $$$*

Shakespeare Hotel. For a touch of typical Stratford, stay at this timbered Elizabethan town house in the heart of the town, close to the theater and to most of the attractions. It has been luxuriously modernized while still retaining its Elizabethan character. *Chapel St., CV37 6ER, tel. 01789/294771, fax 01789/415411. 63 rooms with bath. AE, DC, MC, V. $$$*

Caterham House. Built in 1830, this elegantly furnished building is in the center of town, within an easy walk of the theater. You may spot an actor or two among the guests. Its French restaurant, Bonaparte, is recommended. *58 Rother St., CV37 6LT, tel. 01789/267309, fax 01789/414836. 10 rooms with bath or shower. Facilities: restaurant, parking. MC, V. $–$$*

Windsor and Eton

DINING

The Cockpit. Cockfighting once took place in the courtyard of this smart 500-year-old inn with oak beams, located on Eton's quiet main street. Specialties include guinea fowl and fish cooked with fresh asparagus. *47–49 High St., Eton, tel. 01753/860944. Reservations advised. AE, DC, MC, V. Closed Sun. eve and Mon. lunch. $$–$$$*

The Courtyard. An idyllic setting near the river and castle makes this a pleasant spot for light lunches and teas. *8 King George V Pl., tel. 01753/858338. No credit cards. $*

LODGING

Oakley Court. This Victorian mansion is set in leafy grounds beside the river, just outside Windsor. Most of the bedrooms are in a bright wing of converted stables. It has the excellent Oak Leaf Room restaurant. *Windsor Rd., Water Oakley, SO21 2LT, tel. 01628/74141, fax 01628/37011. 92 rooms with bath. Facilities: 2 restaurants, tennis, putting green, croquet, helipad, gardens. AE, DC, MC, V. $$$$*

Sir Christopher Wren's House. As the name suggests, this house was built by the famous architect, though modern additions have been made to convert it into a hotel. The restaurant overlooks the river, and the cream teas served on the terrace are renowned. *Thames St., Windsor, SL4 1PX, tel. 01753/861354, fax 01753/860172. 39 rooms with bath. Facilities: restaurant. AE, DC, MC, V. $$$*

Christopher Hotel. The owners have done a good job of converting this former coaching inn on Eton High Street; some of the rooms in the courtyard annexes have been redecorated as well. It is also a good spot for solid, home-cooked meals. *110 High St., Eton, SL4 6AN., tel. 01753/852359, fax 01753/830914. 34 rooms with bath. Facilities: restaurant, bar. AE, DC, MC, V. $$*

CAMBRIDGE

Cambridge, home of England's second-oldest university, is an ideal place to explore. Students began studying here in the late 13th century, and virtually every generation since then has produced fine buildings, often by the most distinguished architects of its day. The result is a compact gallery of the best of English architecture. There is also good shopping in the city, and you can enjoy relaxing riverside walks.

A short excursion outside Cambridge will introduce you to some characteristic East Anglian landscapes. To the north, on the edge of the Fens, is **Ely,** which boasts an impressive medieval cathedral. To the east is **Bury St. Edmunds,** a bustling market town rich with 17th- and 18th-century buildings and surrounded by cornfields, gentle hills, and tiny villages, each with its medieval church.

Getting Around

By Train

Hourly trains from London's Liverpool Street Station (tel. 0171/928–5100) and King's Cross Station (tel. 0171/278–2477) run to Cambridge. Average journey time varies from 1 to 1½ hours, depending on the day of week or time of day. Regular local services connect Cambridge with both Ely and Bury St. Edmunds.

By Bus

There are 14 buses daily from Victoria Coach Station that take just under two hours. Call 0171/730–0202.

By Car

M11 is the main highway from London to Cambridge. This connects with the fast A45 road east to Bury St. Edmunds. Ely is reached along A10 from Cambridge. The main car rental companies have offices in Cambridge.

Tourist Information

Bury St. Edmunds (6 Angel Hill, tel. 01284/764667).
Cambridge (Wheeler St., off King's Parade, tel. 01223/322640).
Ely (Oliver Cromwell's House, 29 St. Mary's St., tel. 01353/662062).

Guided Tours

The **Cambridge Tourist Information Center** offers two-hour guided walking tours of the city and the colleges daily; tickets (£3.10) are available up to 24 hours in advance (tel. 01223/463290). Various theme tours are also offered, including combined walking/punting tours and 1½-hour evening pub tours. Booking is essential—the tours are very popular. **Guide Friday** (tel. 01223/62444), in Cambridge, operates a city open-top bus tour every 15 minutes throughout the day (Oct.–May, half-hourly); tickets (£6.50 adults, £4.50 students and senior citizens, £2 children) can be bought from the driver or the office at Cambridge train station. You can join the tours at the station or at any of the specially-marked bus stops throughout the city.

Exploring Cambridge

The university is in the very heart of **Cambridge.** It consists of a number of colleges, each of which is a separate institution with its own distinct character and traditions. Undergraduates join an individual college and are taught by dons attached to the college, who are known as "fellows." Each college is built around a series of courts, or quadrangles; because students and fellows live in these quadrangles, access is sometimes restricted, especially during examination weeks (April to mid-June). Visitors are not normally allowed into college buildings other than chapels and halls. It is best to check first with the city tourist office to find out which colleges may be visited.

Numbers in the margin correspond to points of interest on the Cambridge map.

❶ King's College, off King's Parade, is possibly the best known of all the colleges. Its chapel, started by Henry VI in 1446, is a masterpiece of late-Gothic architecture, with a great fan-vaulted roof supported only by a tracery of soaring side columns. Behind the altar hangs Rubens's painting *Adoration of the Magi*. Every Christmas Eve the college choir sings the Festival of Nine Lessons and Carols, which is broadcast all over the world. King's runs down to the "Backs," the tree-shaded grounds on the banks of the River Cam, which is the background of many of the colleges. From King's make your way along the river and through **②** **③** **④** the narrow lanes past **Clare College** and **Trinity Hall** to **Trinity.** This is the largest college, established by Henry VIII in 1546. It has a handsome 17th-century Great Court, around which are the chapel, hall, gates, and a library by Christopher Wren. In the massive gate house is Great Tom, a large clock that strikes each hour with high and low notes. Prince Charles was an undergraduate here during the late 1960s.

⑤ Beyond Trinity lies **St. John's,** the second-largest college. The white crenellations of the enormous mock-Gothic **New Building** of 1825 have earned it the nickname "the wedding cake." To reach it, cross a bridge that's a facsimile of Venice's Bridge of Sighs. Among St. John's build- **⑥** ings is one of the oldest houses in Cambridge, **Merton Hall,** with its origins in the 12th century (although the building itself largely dates from the 16th century).

Up Northampton and across **Magdalene** (pronounced maudlin) **Street** **⑦** you come to **Magdalene College,** with its pretty redbrick courts. The **Pepys Library** contains the 17th-century diarist's own books and desk. *Admission free. Open Oct.–Mar., daily 2:30–3:30; Apr.–Sept., daily 11:30–12:30 and 2:30–3:30.*

⑧ Beyond Magdalene is **Kettle's Yard.** This was originally the home of Jim Ede, a connoisseur of 20th-century art. Here he displayed his collections to the public; a gallery extension now houses temporary exhibits. *Castle St., tel. 01223/352124. Admission free. House open Tues.–Sun. 2–4; gallery open Tues.–Sat. 12:30–5:30, Sun. 2–5:30.*

Returning the way you've just come, along the Backs from King's, you'll **⑨** see **Queen's College,** where Isaac Newton's **Mathematical Bridge** crosses the river. This arched wooden structure was originally held together by gravitational force; when it was taken apart to see how Newton did it, no one could reconstruct it without using nails. Back from the **⑩** river, on Trumpington Street, sits **Pembroke College,** which contains **⑪** some 14th-century buildings and a chapel by Wren, and **Peterhouse,** **⑫** the oldest college, dating from 1281. Next to Peterhouse is the **Fitzwilliam Museum,** which contains outstanding art collections (including paintings by Constable, Gainsborough, and the French Impressionists) and antiquities (especially from ancient Egypt). *Trumpington St., tel. 01223/332900. Admission free. Open Tues.–Sat. 10–5; Sun. 2:15–5.*

⑬ Other colleges worth visiting include **Downing College,** which has a unique collection of neoclassical buildings dating from about 1800, and **⑭** **Emmanuel College,** whose chapel and colonnade are by Christopher Wren. Emmanuel's spacious gardens have a pretty duck pond with several unusual breeds.

⑮ If you have time, hire a punt at **Silver Street Bridge** or at **Magdalene Bridge** and navigate down past St. John's or upstream to **Grantchester,** the pretty village made famous by the Edwardian poet Rupert Brooke. On a sunny day, there's no better way to absorb Cambridge's unique atmosphere.

TIME OUT The coffee shop in the **Fitzwilliam Museum** is an excellent choice for a pastry or a light lunch. So is **The Copper Kettle** (King's Parade), a traditional students' hangout. The **Fort St. George,** on Jesus Green, is a riverside pub with plenty of outdoor space for summer drinking.

Cambridge

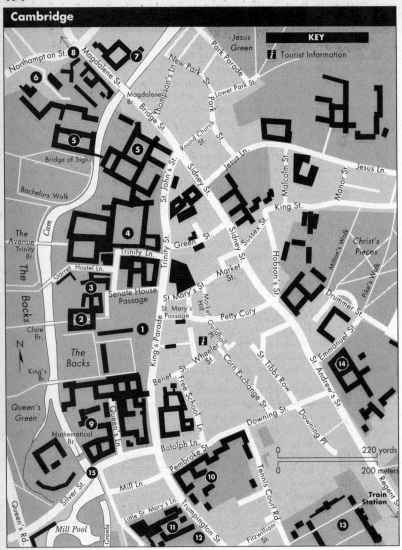

KEY

i Tourist Information

Clare College, **2**
Downing College, **13**
Emmanuel College, **14**
Fitzwilliam Museum, **12**
Kettle's Yard, **8**
King's College, **1**
Magdalene College, **7**
Merton Hall, **6**
Pembroke College, **10**
Peterhouse, **11**
Queen's College, **9**
St. John's, **5**
Silver Street Bridge, **15**
Trinity, **4**
Trinity Hall, **3**

From Ely to Bury St. Edmunds

Some 24 kilometers (15 miles) north of Cambridge, on A10, is the compact town of **Ely.** Dominating the town is the **Cathedral,** whose commanding position atop one of the few Fenland ridges makes it visible from kilometers away; not for nothing is it nicknamed "the ship of the Fens." Within the cathedral, which was begun by the Normans in 1083, is a marvel of medieval construction—the octagonal lantern, a sort of stained-glass skylight of colossal proportions, which was built to replace the central tower after it collapsed in 1322. The **Lady Chapel,** restored during the 1970s with financial help from the United States, contains delicate decorative carving and a superb fan-vaulted ceiling. There is also a **Stained-Glass Museum.** *Chapter Office, The College, tel. 01353/667735. Cathedral admission: £2.80 adults, £2 senior citizens; up to 2 children free; free Sun. Open Mon.–Sat. 7:30–6, Sun. 7:30–5. Stained-Glass Museum admission: £1.80 adults, £1 children and senior citizens. Open weekdays 10:30–4, Sat. 10:30–4:30, Sun. noon–3:30; closed weekdays Nov.–Feb.*

Around the cathedral are the well-preserved buildings of the cathedral courtyard, where many of the clergy live, and of the **King's School,** which provides the cathedral with its choristers. To the north is the little market square and shopping streets that lead down to the attractive riverside.

TIME OUT The **Steeplegate Café and Gallery** (Steeplegate St.), on a street that connects the cathedral grounds with High Street, is a convenient spot for lunch.

The route from Cambridge to Bury St. Edmunds, 47 kilometers (29 miles) along A45, passes **Newmarket,** headquarters of British horse racing. The town is known both for its first-class racecourse and as a breeding and training center. The **National Horseracing Museum** traces the history of the sport in entertaining detail and has a fine collection of paintings. The museum also operates daylong tours of all of Newmarket's equestrian attractions (Apr.–Nov., Tues.–Sat. starting at 9:30; £20 adults, £16 senior citizens, £12 children, £8 for additional children in family). *High St., tel. 01638/667333. Admission: £3.30 adults, £2 senior citizens, £1 children. Open Apr.–Nov., Tues.–Sat. 10–5, Sun. noon–4.*

Newmarket is the home of Britain's **National Stud,** one of the country's premier institutions for breeding champion racehorses. You can tour its 500 acres of pastureland; in spring and early summer you're likely to see young foals taking their first faltering steps across the meadows. *Tel. 01638/663464. Tours Apr.–Sept., Mon.–Fri. 11:15 and 2:30, Sat. 11:15, Sun. 2:30. Admission: £3.50 adults, £2.50 children, students, and senior citizens. Reservations essential.*

Bury St. Edmunds is a quintessential English country town with a picturesque gate tower and the ruins of a great 11th-century Norman abbey, which are located on **Angel Hill.** Medieval buildings along one side of the street face elegant 18th-century houses on the other; there are also some striking public buildings along **Abbeygate Street.**

Farther along Angel Hill from the abbey and then to the left, down Honey Hill, is the **Manor House Museum.** Housed in a Georgian mansion facing the abbey grounds are excellent art and horological collections: clocks, watches, paintings, furniture, and ceramics from the 17th to the 20th centuries. *Honey Hill, tel. 01284/757072. Admission:*

£2.50 adults, £1.50 senior citizens, students, and children. Open Mon.–Sat. 10–5, Sun. 2–5.

TIME OUT The lounge of the **Angel Hotel** (Angel Hill) makes a restful spot for an old-fashioned English tea.

The **Theatre Royal,** built in 1819 and now owned by the National Trust, is a perfect example of a working Georgian theater. The auditorium is usually "dark" for a month in mid-summer, but for the rest of the year its 350 seats make it a delightfully intimate place to watch a performance. If rehearsals are not taking place, you can look around during the day. *Westgate St., tel. 01284/755127. Admission free. Open Mon.–Sat. 10–8. Reservations advised for tours.*

As if to remind visitors that Bury St. Edmunds remains a working town, not a museum piece, a livestock market is held every Wednesday and Saturday off **Risbygate.**

Dining and Lodging

For details and price-category definitions, *see* Dining and Lodging *in* Staying in Great Britain, *above.*

Dining

$$ **Midsummer House.** A classy restaurant set beside the River Cam, Mid-
★ summer House is lovely in summer. There's a comfortable conservatory. Set-price menus for lunch and dinner parade a selection of gourmet haute cuisine—one current favorite is a delicious mille-feuille of scallops and langoustines, served with orange and saffron butter sauce and squid-ink noodles. There's always a soufflé on the menu, and desserts are a specialty—try the pear tart with honey ice cream. *Midsummer Common, Cambridge, tel. 01223/69299. Reservations required. AE, DC, MC, V. No lunch Sat., no dinner Sun. Closed Mon.*

$$ **Three Horseshoes.** This is an early 19th-century thatched cottage with a recently added conservatory. A pub restaurant serves beautifully prepared grilled fish, and the conservatory menu offers traditional English fare and seafood, also beautifully presented. *Madingley, tel. 01954/210221 (3 mi southwest of Cambridge). AE, DC, MC, V.*

$$ **Twenty-Two.** This intimate restaurant occupies a modest house ½ mile west of the city center. There's an extremely good-value prix-fixe dinner, featuring eclectic and innovative dishes from all quarters, together with modern British specialties such as baked salmon with herb crust. *22 Chesterton Rd., Cambridge, tel. 01223/351880. Reservations advised. AE, MC, V. Dinner only. Closed Sun., Mon., and Dec. 25–26.*

$–$$ **Brown's.** This huge, airy French-American style brasserie-diner was converted from the outpatient department of the old Addenbrooke's Hospital opposite the Fitzwilliam Museum. Large fans still keep things cool in the pale yellow dining room. The wide-ranging menu runs from toasted tuna sandwiches, steak-mushroom-and-Guinness pie, hamburgers, and salads up to venison or lamb steaks; check the daily specials, too—there's usually fresh fish. *23 Trumpington St., tel. 01223/461655. No reservations. AE, MC, V. Closed Dec. 25–26.*

$ **Hobbs Pavilion.** Housed in an old cricket pavilion on the western edge of Parker's Piece, this cheery place has wooden walls decorated with cricketing memorabilia and a small terrace ideal for watching players in summer. The specialty is pancakes, both sweet and savory. The ice cream is also recommended, homemade from free-range eggs, double cream, and honey. Three-course prix-fixe menus are a special bargain. *Park Terrace, Cambridge, tel. 01223/67480. No credit cards. Closed Sun. and Mon.*

Lodging

$$$ De Vere University Arms Hotel. There has been continuing refurbishment of the public areas and bedrooms in this city-center hotel; most rooms have now been attractively upgraded without impairing the hotel's original 19th-century elegance. Guest rooms are comfortable and well-appointed without being large, though views of Parker's Piece from many rooms compensate. The central lounge provides a cozy and comfortable place for afternoon tea, where you can sit by the fire enjoying a pot of Darjeeling and smoked salmon sandwiches. *Regent St., Cambridge CB2 1AD, tel. 01223/351241, fax 01223/315256. 115 rooms with bath. Facilities: restaurant, 3 bars, 24-hr room service. AE, DC, MC, V.*

$$$ **Garden House Hotel.** Set among the colleges, this fairly luxurious, mod-
★ ern hotel makes the most of its riverside location. Its gardens, lounge, cocktail bar, and conservatories all have river views, as do most of the guest rooms—if you want one, make it clear when you make your reservation, as some of the rooms at the rear of the L-shaped hotel have less desirable views. The brightly furnished guest rooms are comfortable, with minibars, TVs, and fine bathrooms. *Granta Pl., Mill La., Cambridge CB2 1RT, tel. 01223/63421, fax 01223/316605. 118 rooms with bath. Facilities: restaurant, bar, punt rentals, garden. AE, DC, MC, V.*

$$ Arundel House. This hotel occupies a converted terrace of Victorian houses overlooking the river. The bedrooms are comfortably furnished with locally made mahogany furniture. A videotape tour of the city can be viewed on the hotel's TV information channel. *53 Chesterton Rd., Cambridge CB4 3AN, tel. 01223/67701, fax 01223/67721. 105 rooms with bath or shower. Facilities: restaurant, bar, videos, garden. AE, DC, MC, V.*

YORK AND ENVIRONS

Once England's second city, the ancient town of York has survived the ravages of time, war, and industrialization to remain one of northern Europe's few preserved walled cities. It was King George VI, father of the present queen, who remarked that the history of York is the history of England. Even in a brief visit to the city, you can see evidence of life from every era since the Romans, not only in museums but also in the very streets and houses. On a more contemporary note, the city also boasts some upscale shops.

York is surrounded by some of the grandest countryside England has to offer. A fertile plain dotted with ancient abbeys and grand aristocratic mansions leads westward to the hidden valleys and jagged, windswept tops of the Yorkshire Dales and northward to the brooding mass of the North York Moors. This is a land quite different from the south of England—it's friendlier, emptier, and less aggressively materialistic. No visitor to Britain should overlook it.

Getting Around

By Train
Regular fast trains run from London's King's Cross Station to York. The trip takes two hours. For information, call 0171/278–2477.

By Bus
Regular Rapide buses leave from Victoria Coach Station daily. The trip takes 4½ hours. For information, call 0171/730–0202.

By Car

Take A1, the historic main route from London to the north, which branches east onto A64 near Tadcaster for the final 19½ kilometers (12 miles) to York. Alternatively, take M1, then M18, and finally A1. The drive from London takes a minimum of four hours. The main car rental companies have offices in York.

The best way to explore the area around York is by car—although it's inadvisable, and sometimes impossible, to take a car into the crowded city center. Bus tours (*see* Guided Tours, *below*) visit most of the nearby attractions.

Tourist Information

There is a tourist information office at **De Grey Rooms** (Lendel Bridge, Exhibition Square, North Yorkshire Y01 2HB, tel. 01904/621756) and smaller ones at the **York railway station** (tel. 01904/643700) and 6 Rougier Street (tel. 01904/620557).

Guided Tours

Guide Friday (8 Tower St., tel. 01904/640896) runs frequent city tours that allow you to get on and off the bus as you please (£6 adults, £1.50 children, £4.50 senior citizens, £12 family ticket). They also conduct tours of the surrounding countryside, including Fountains Abbey and Castle Howard. The **York Association of Voluntary Guides** (in De Grey Rooms, Exhibition Square, tel. 01904/640780) arranges short walking tours around the city (free, but a gratuity is appreciated) each morning at 10:15, with additional tours at 2:15 PM from April through October, and one at 7 PM from July through August.

Exploring York

Numbers in the margin correspond to points of interest on the York map.

❶ York's greatest glory is the **Minster,** the largest Gothic church in England and one of the finest in Europe. Take time to gaze at the soaring columns and intricate tracery of the 14th-century nave, the choir screen portraying whimsical images of the kings of England, and the imposing tracery of the mighty rose window—just one of 128 stained-glass windows in the Minister—which commemorates the marriage of Henry VII and Elizabeth of York. Visit the exquisite 13th-century **Chapter House** and the Roman and Saxon remains in the **Undercroft Museum and Treasury.** Climb the 275 steps of the **Central Tower** for an unrivaled view of the city and the countryside beyond. The **Crypt** features some of the cathedral's oldest and most valuable treasures, among them the Romanesque 12th-century statue of a heavy-footed Virgin Mary. *York Minster Undercroft Museum and Treasury, Chapter House, Central Tower, and Crypt, tel. 01904/624426. Admission: Minster free (£1.50 donation appreciated); Foundations £1.80 adults, 70p children, £1.50 senior citizens, £4 family ticket; Chapter House 70p adults, 30p children; Central Tower £2 adults, £1 children; Crypt 60p adults, 30p children and senior citizens. Minster open summer daily 7–8:30; winter 7–5; Undercroft, Chapter House, Central Tower, and Crypt open Mon.–Sat. 10–6:30, Sun. 1–6:30.*

❷ At the **Jorvik Viking Centre,** south of the Minster through tiny medieval streets, you can take another journey into history—whisked back in little "time cars" to the sights, sounds, and even the smells of a Viking street, which archaeologists have re-created in astonishing detail. *Cop-*

pergate, tel. 01904/643211. Admission: £3.95 adults, £2 children, and (Nov.–Mar. only) £3 senior citizens. Open Apr.–Oct., daily 9–7; Nov.–Mar., daily 9–5:30.

3 Walk south down Castlegate and onto Tower Street, where you'll find the **Castle Museum,** housed in an 18th-century prison. It has a series of realistic period displays that bring the past to life. Highlights include a Victorian street scene, an 18th-century dining room, and a moorland farmer's cottage. Don't miss the Coppergate Helmet, one of only three Anglo-Saxon helmets ever found. The welcoming tearoom serves drinks and simple snacks. *Clifford St., tel. 01904/653612. Admission: £4 adults, £2.90 children and senior citizens, family ticket £11. Open Apr.–Oct., Mon.–Sat. 9:30–5:30, Sun. 10–5:30; Nov.–Mar., Mon.–Sat. 9:30–4, Sun. 10–4.*

Even more than the wealth of museums, it is the streets and city walls that bring York's past to life. A walk along the **walls,** most of which date from the 13th century, though with extensive restoration, provides delightful views across rooftops and gardens and the Minster itself. The narrow paved path winds between various fortified gates where the old roads ran out of the city.

4 Within the walls, the narrow streets still follow the complex medieval pattern. The **Shambles,** in the heart of this walled city, is a well-preserved example; the half-timbered shops and houses have such large overhangs that you can practically reach from one second-floor win- **5** dow to another. **Stonegate** is a narrow pedestrian street of 18th-century (and earlier) shops and courts. Along a narrow passage off Stonegate, at 52A, you will find the remains of a 12th-century Norman stone house—one of the very few surviving in England.

6 The **Merchant Adventurers' Hall** is a superb medieval building (1357– 68) built and owned by one of the richest medieval guilds; it contains the largest timber-framed hall in York. *Fossgate, tel. 01904/654818. Admission: £1.80 adults, 50p children under 15, £1.50 senior citizens. Open mid-Mar.–mid-Nov., daily 8:30–5; mid-Nov.–mid-Mar., Mon.–Sat. 8:30–3.*

7 One very different attraction is the **National Railway Museum,** the largest railway museum in the world, just outside the city walls, by the train station. This houses Britain's national collection of railway loco- motives, including such giants of the steam era as *Mallard,* holder of the world speed record for a steam engine (126 mph), early rolling stock, and pioneer diesel and electric locomotives. *Leeman Rd., tel. 01904/621261. Admission: £4.20 adults, £2.10 children under 16, £2.80 senior citizens, £11.50 family ticket. Open Mon.–Sat. 10–6, Sun. 11–6.*

TIME OUT In St. Helens Square, **Betty's** has been a York institution since 1912, serving teas with mouth-watering cakes and desserts as well as light meals and a splendid selection of exotic coffees. On Peaseholme Green, the 15th-century **Black Swan** pub—reputedly York's oldest inn—makes genuine Yorkshire pudding.

Outside York

Traveling west on A59, once a Roman road, you soon reach the **York- shire Dales,** made world-famous by the writings of a local veterinar- ian, the late James Herriot, and inspiration for, among others, the poet William Wordsworth and the quintessentially English painter J. M. Turner. The fertile river valleys of the Dales are separated from one another by areas of wild, high moorland that offers many opportuni-

York

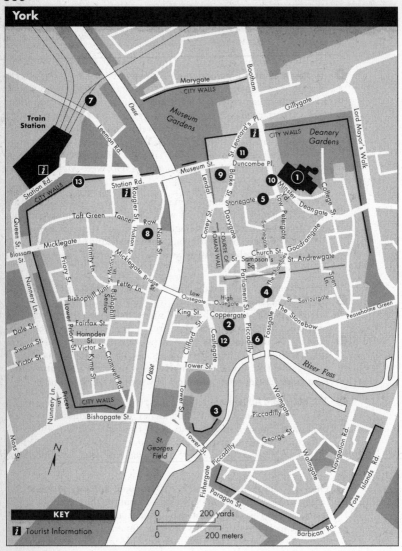

KEY

i Tourist Information

0 — 200 yards
0 — 200 meters

Major Attractions
Castle Museum, **3**
Jorvik Viking Centre, **2**
Merchant Adventurers' Hall, **6**
Minster, **1**
National Railway Museum, **7**
Shambles, **4**
Stonegate, **5**

Other Attractions
All Saints, **8**
Assembly Rooms, **9**
Cholera Burial Ground, **13**
St-Michael-le-Belfry, **10**
Theater Royal, **11**
York Story (Heritage Center), **12**

ties for exhilarating walks and drives. At **Bolton Abbey,** about 57 kilometers (36 miles) west of York, the ruins of a 13th-century priory lie on a grassy embankment contained within a great curve of the River Wharfe. (There's unrestricted access during daylight.) Explore the ruins and walk through some of the most romantic woodland scenery in England, past the legendary **Strid,** where the river plunges through a rocky chasm only a few yards wide.

Northwest from Bolton Abbey, off B6160, is **Grassington,** a village of stone houses with an ancient, cobbled marketplace—a convenient center from which to explore the wild landscapes of Upper Wharfedale. The **National Park Centre** has a wide choice of guidebooks, maps, and bus schedules to help you enjoy a day in the Dales. Organized tours depart from the center with qualified guides who explain the botanical and geological features of the area. *Colvend, Hebdon Rd., tel. 01756/752748. Open Apr.–Oct., daily 9:30–5:30; Nov.–Mar., Fri. 1–4, weekends 10–5, Mon. 10–1.*

About 24 kilometers (15 miles) east from Grassington, along B6265, across the moors, is **Fountains Abbey and Studley Royal,** on the very edge of the hills. Here, the extensive ruins of a 12th-century monastery are set beside an 18th-century landscaped water garden and deer park, complete with lakes, half-moon ponds, statuary, and pseudo-Greek temples. *Tel. 01756/608888. Admission: £4 adults, £2 children, family ticket £10. Open Feb.–Mar. daily 10–5 or dusk; Apr.–Sept., daily 10–7; Oct. daily 10–5 or dusk. Guided tours daily Apr.–Oct. at 2:30.*

Nearby **Newby Hall**—5 kilometers (3 miles) due east of Fountains Abbey along pleasant country roads—has some restored interiors by the 18th-century master architect Robert Adam and some equally celebrated gardens with a collection of old breeds of roses and rare shrubs. There is a handy restaurant. *Skelton-on-Ure, tel. 01423/322583. Admission: £5.20 adults, £3 children, £4 senior citizens, family tickets £14.90 and £17.50; gardens only, £3.30 adults, £2.20 children, £2.60 senior citizens, family tickets £8.50 and £10.50. Open Apr.–Sept., Tues.–Sun., grounds 11–5:30, house noon–5.*

To the northeast, across the Vale of York, lie the **North York Moors,** dominated by a vast expanse of dense woodland and heather moorland that in late summer turns a rich blaze of crimson and purple. Nestled in deep valleys are charming villages built of brownstone—a contrast with the gray stone of the Dales.

Helmsley is a pleasant market town on the southern edge of the Moors. It is not far, by road (B1257 north) or footpath, from the ruins of **Rievaulx Abbey,** a medieval seat of monastic learning whose graceful arches occupy a dramatic riverside setting. The ruins are best seen from the **Rievaulx Terraces,** a long grassy walkway on the hillside above, terminating in the remains of several classical temples. *Rievaulx Abbey, tel. 01439/798228. Admission: £2.20 adults, £1.10 children, £1.65 senior citizens. Open Apr.–Sept., daily 10–6; Oct.–Mar., daily 10–4. Rievaulx Terrace, tel. 01439/798340. Admission: £2.10 adults, 90p children. Open Apr.–Oct., daily 10:30–6.*

Returning south to York, stop off at **Nunnington Hall** (off B1257), a largely late-17th-century manor house set on the River Rye containing a paneled hall with a carved chimneypiece, fine tapestries and china, and a superb collection of miniature rooms with intricate dollhouse furniture of different periods. *Nunnington, tel. 01439/748243. Admission: £3.50 adults, £1.50 children, £7 family ticket; gardens only,*

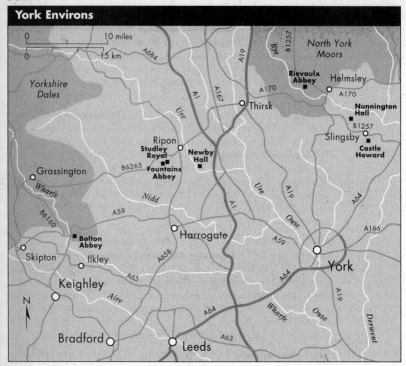

York Environs

£1, children free. Open Apr.–June and Sept.–Oct., Tues.–Thurs. and weekends 2–6; July–Aug., Tues.–Fri. 2–6, weekends noon–6.

TIME OUT Teas (and light lunches on summer weekends) can be enjoyed at Nunnington Hall's excellent **tearoom.**

In marked contrast to Nunnington is the palatial majesty of **Castle Howard** (south off B1257 at Slingsby), the setting for the TV series "Brideshead Revisited." The great central domed tower, flanked by two huge and richly decorated wings, took 60 years—from 1699 to 1759—to build. The central hall, with its painted ceiling, leads to a series of grand state rooms and galleries, filled with paintings, sculpture, furniture, and porcelain. *Coneysthorpe, tel. 01653/648333. Admission to castle: £5.50 adults, £3 children, £5 senior citizens. Grounds only: £3 adults, £1.50 children and senior citizens. House open mid-Mar.–Oct. daily 11–4:30. Grounds open mid-Mar.–Oct., daily 10–4:30; Nov.–mid-Mar. Sun. 10–4.*

Dining and Lodging

For details and price-category definitions, *see* Dining and Lodging *in* Staying in Great Britain, *above.*

Dining

\$\$–\$\$\$ **Melton's.** Just 10 minutes from the Minster, this unfussy restaurant has local art on the walls and an open kitchen. The excellent seasonal menu, cooked up by chef Michael Hjort, an alumnus of the Roux empire, offers modern English, Continental, and fish dishes. *7 Scarcroft Rd., York, tel. 01904/634341. Reservations advised. MC, V. No dinner Sun., no lunch Mon. Closed 3 wks at Christmas and 1 wk in Sept.*

$$–$$$ **19 Grape Lane.** The narrow, slightly cramped restaurant is housed in a typically leaning timbered York building in the heart of town. Hugely popular, it serves modern English food from a blackboard of specials such as medallions of hare with field mushrooms in a red wine sauce. *19 Grape La., York, tel. 01904/636366. Reservations advised. MC, V. Closed Sun. and Mon., 2 wks in Feb., 2 wks in Sept.*

$$–$$$ **Partners.** The restaurateur is Polish, so you'll find the occasional Eastern European dish among the modern English cuisine in this simple, elegant restaurant, tucked well off the road and arranged around a pretty paved courtyard. Try the Kulibiaka Russian fish pie of smoked salmon, prawns, rice, and egg, served with a creamy white wine sauce. *13a High Ousegate, York, tel. 01904/627929. Reservations advised. AE, DC, MC, V. Closed Sun.*

$$ **Kites.** Climb a steep, narrow staircase to find an innovative restaurant serving offbeat, health-conscious food. Try the chicken *garda*, filled with raisins, parmesan, and oregano and served in a tamarind sauce. *13 Grape La., York, tel. 01904/640750. Reservations advised. AE, DC, MC, V. Closed Sun.*

$–$$ **Four Seasons.** This cheery restaurant in the heart of York's medieval center serves homemade pies and traditional English meat dishes in a 16th-century beamed hall with a wood-block floor. The cheese-and-lentil loaf is highly recommended for vegetarians. *45 Goodramgate, York, tel. 01904/633787. Reservations advised. AE, DC, MC, V.*

$–$$ **Hudson's Below Stairs.** Eat traditional roast beef and Yorkshire pudding in this atmospheric Victorian hotel restaurant five minutes' walk from the Minster. Fresh fish is also served, and there's a choice of prix-fixe menu or a la carte. *60 Bootham, York, tel. 01904/621267. Reservations advised. AE, DC, MC, V.*

Dining and Lodging

$$$–$$$$ **Middlethorpe Hall.** This handsome, superbly restored 18th-century mansion is located on the edge of the city, about 1½ miles from the center, beside the racetrack. The individually decorated rooms, some in cottage-style accommodations around an 18th-century courtyard, are filled with antiques, paintings, and fresh flowers, and the extensive grounds boast a lake, a 17th-century dovecote, and "ha-ha's"— drops in the garden level that create cunning views. The large garden grows fresh vegetables for the hotel's award-winning wood-paneled Anglo-French restaurant. *Bishopthorpe Rd., York YO2 1QB, tel. 01904/641241, from the U.S. toll-free 800/260–8338, fax 01904/620176. 30 rooms with bath. Facilities: restaurant (reservations required; jacket and tie), garden, croquet. AE, DC, MC, V.*

$$–$$$ **Mount Royale Hotel.** Two elegant town houses dating from the 1830s have been furnished in a traditional English country-cottage style to make a very attractive hotel about 15 minutes from the town center. The open-plan "garden suites" open out onto the hotel's lovely grounds; semitropical plants, including oranges and figs, decorate the approach to these suites. The fine Anglo-French restaurant, in a lovely sunny room, serves dishes based on local produce. *119 The Mount, York Y02 2DA, tel. 01904/628856, fax 01904/611171. 23 rooms with bath. Facilities: restaurant, lounges, garden, health center, open-air pool, satellite TV. AE, DC, MC, V. Closed Dec. 24–31.*

Lodging

$$$ **Dean Court.** This establishment in a Victorian house has comfortably furnished rooms with plump sofas, TVs, and great views overlooking the Minster. Parking is a few minutes from the hotel, but there is a valet parking service. The restaurant serves good English cuisine, including a hearty Yorkshire breakfast. *Duncombe Place, York YO1 2EF, tel.*

01904/625082, fax 01904/620305. 40 rooms with bath. Facilities: coffee shop, bar, lounge, in-house movies. AE, DC, MC, V.

$$–$$$ **Curzon Lodge and Stable Cottages.** This attractive white 17th-century house was once owned by York's famous Terry chocolate family. It sits on the edge of town, near the racetrack, a mile or so from the train station. The house itself is beautifully furnished with antiques, four-poster beds, and Victorian brass bedsteads; delightful oak-beamed "cottages," in the old coach house and stables, offer two-room family suites. Breakfast is served in the cozy, rustic dining room. *23 Tadcaster Rd., Dringhouses, YO2 2QG, tel. 01904/703157. 10 rooms with bath or shower. Facilities: garden, lounge, parking. MC, V.*

$$ **Savages.** Despite its name, this small hotel on a leafy road near the town center is eminently refined, with a reputation for attentive service. Once a Victorian home, it has a stylish and comfortable interior, and there's a bar in which to relax. *15 St. Peter's Grove, YO3 6AQ, tel. 01904/610818, fax 01904/627729. 18 rooms with bath or shower. Facilities: restaurant, bar, garden, baby-listening service. AE, DC, MC, V.*

$ **Abbey Guest House.** This quaint, pretty guest house is a 10-minute walk from the train station and town center. Although small, it's very clean and friendly, with a peaceful garden right on the river. *14 Earlsborough Terr., Marygate, YO3 7BQ, tel. 01904/627782. 7 rooms with shared baths. Facilities: baby-sitting service, parking, picnic lunches and evening meal on request. AE, MC, V.*

EDINBURGH

Scotland and England *are* different—and let no Englishman tell you otherwise. Although the two nations have been united in a single state since 1707, Scotland retains its own marked political and social character, with, for instance, legal and educational systems quite distinct from those of England. And by virtue of its commanding geographic position, on top of a long-dead volcano, and the survival of a large number of outstanding buildings carrying echoes of the nation's history, Edinburgh ranks among the world's greatest capital cities.

Getting Around

By Train

Regular fast trains run from London's King's Cross Station to Edinburgh Waverley; the fastest journey time is just over four hours. For information in London, call 0171/278–2477; in Edinburgh, 0131/556–2451 (recorded information lines: weekday service 0131/557–3000; Saturday service 0131/557–2737; Sunday service 0131/557–1616).

By Plane

British Airways operates a shuttle service from London's Heathrow Airport to Edinburgh; reservations are not necessary, and you are guaranteed a seat. Flying time from London is one hour, 15 minutes. For information, call 0181/759–2525 or 01345/222111. **British Midland** also flies from Heathrow (tel. 0181/745–7321 or 01345/554554). **Air UK** flies from Gatwick (tel. 01293/567977) and Stansted (tel. 01279/662816)—both airports are far less crowded than Heathrow, and are as easy to reach by rail. From Edinburgh, call 01345/666777 for Air UK flights to both Gatwick and Stansted. Transatlantic flights direct to Scotland use Glasgow Airport, from which there are regular rail connections to Glasgow city center and on to Edinburgh.

By Bus

Regular services are operated by **National Express** between Victoria Coach Station, London, and St. Andrew Square bus station, Edinburgh, three times a day. The 405-mile journey takes approximately eight hours.

By Car

London and Edinburgh are 640 kilometers (400 miles) apart; allow a comfortable nine hours for the drive. The two principal routes to the Scottish border are A1 (mostly a small but divided road) or the eight-lane M1, then M6. From there, the choice is between the four-lane highway A74, which can be unpleasantly busy, followed by A701 or A702, or the slower but much more scenic A7 through Hawick. All the main car-rental agencies have offices in Edinburgh.

Tourist Information

The **Edinburgh and Scotland Information Centre** (3 Princes St., tel. 0131/557–1700) gives expert advice on what to see and do in Edinburgh and throughout Scotland. Services include information and literature, accommodation reservations, route planning, coach tour tickets, entertainment reservations, a Scottish bookshop, and currency exchange. Visitors can also buy National Trust, Historic Scotland, and Great Britain Heritage passes.

Guided Tours

Both **Lothian Region Transport** (dark-red-and-white buses) and **SMT** (green buses) operate tours in and around the city. For information, call 0131/220–4111 (Lothian) or 0131/313–1515 (SMT; for SMT bus times, call 0131/556–8464). Tickets allowing unlimited travel on city buses for various periods are also available.

The Cadies and **Witchery Tours** (352 Castlehill, 3rd Floor, tel. 0131/225–6745) offer a highly popular murder and mystery tour, and historical and other special-interest tours.

Exploring Edinburgh

The key to understanding Edinburgh is to make the distinction between the Old and New Towns. Until the 18th century, the city was confined to the rocky crag on which its castle stands, straggling between the fortress at one end and the royal residence, the Palace of Holyroodhouse, at the other. In the 18th century, during a civilizing time of expansion known as the "Scottish Enlightenment," the city fathers fostered the construction of another Edinburgh, one a little to the north. This is the New Town, whose elegant squares, classical facades, wide streets, and harmonious proportions remain largely intact and lived-in today.

Numbers in the margin correspond to points of interest on the Edinburgh map.

The Royal Mile

❶ **Edinburgh Castle,** the brooding symbol of Scotland's capital and the nation's martial past, dominates the city center. The castle's attractions include the city's oldest building—the 11th-century **St. Margaret's Chapel;** the **Crown Room,** where the Regalia of Scotland are displayed; **Old Parliament Hall;** and **Queen Mary's Apartments,** where Mary, Queen of Scots, gave birth to the future King James VI of Scotland (who later became James I of England). In addition, military features of interest include the **Scottish National War Memorial** and the **Scottish United**

Services Museum. Tel. 0131/244–3101. Admission: £5 adults, £3 senior citizens, £1 children under 16. Open Apr.–Sept., daily 9:30–5; Oct.–Mar., daily 9:30–4:15.

② The **Royal Mile,** the backbone of the Old Town, starts immediately below the **Castle Esplanade,** the wide parade ground that hosts the annual Edinburgh Military Tattoo—a grand military display staged during a citywide festival every summer (*see below*). The Royal Mile consists of a number of streets, running into each other—**Castlehill, Lawnmarket, High Street,** and **Canongate**—leading downhill to the Palace of Holyroodhouse, home to the Royal Family when they visit Edinburgh. Tackle this walk in leisurely style; the many original Old Town "closes," narrow alleyways enclosed by high tenement buildings, are rewarding to explore and give a real sense of the former life of the city.

③ In Lawnmarket, the six-story tenement known as **Gladstone's Land** dates from 1620. It has a typical arcaded front and first-floor entrance and is furnished in the style of a merchant's house of the time; there are magnificent painted ceilings. *747B Lawnmarket, tel. 0131/226–5856. Admission: £2.50 adults, £1.30 children and senior citizens. Open Apr.–Oct., Mon.–Sat. 10–5, Sun. 2–5 (last admission 4:30).*

④ Close by is **The Writers' Museum,** housed in Lady Stair's House, a town dwelling of 1622 that recalls Scotland's literary heritage with exhibits on Sir Walter Scott, Robert Louis Stevenson, and Robert Burns. *Lady Stair's Close, Lawnmarket, tel. 0131/225–2424, ext. 4901. Admission free. Open June–Sept., Mon.–Sat. 10–6; Oct.–May, Mon.–Sat. 10–5, Sun. 2–5 during the festival.*

⑤ A heart shape set in the cobbles of the High Street marks the site of the **Tolbooth,** the center of city life until it was demolished in 1817.
⑥ Nearby stands the **High Kirk of St. Giles,** Edinburgh's cathedral; parts of the church date from the 12th century, the choir from the 15th. *High St. Admission free. Open Mon.–Sat. 9–5 (7 in summer), Sun. 2–5 and for services.*

⑦ Farther down High Street you'll see **John Knox House.** Its traditional connections with Scotland's celebrated religious reformer are tenuous, but it gives a flavor of life in the Old Town during Knox's time. *45 High St., tel. 0131/556–2647. Admission: £1.25 adults, 75p children, £1 senior citizens. Open Mon.–Sat. 10–4:30.*

Next door is the **Netherbow Arts Centre** (tel. and opening hours as for John Knox House), with a theater, an art gallery, and a café .

⑧ **Canongate** was formerly an independent burgh, or trading community, outside the city walls of Edinburgh. **Huntly House,** built in 1570, is a museum featuring Edinburgh history and social life. *142 Canongate, tel. 0131/225–2424, ext. 4143. Admission free. Open June–Sept., Mon.–Sat. 10–6; Oct.–May, Mon.–Sat. 10–5, Sun. 2–5 during the festival.*

⑨ Some notable Scots are buried in the graveyard of the **Canongate Kirk** nearby, including the economist Adam Smith and the poet Robert Fergusson.

TIME OUT Two places that serve a good cup of tea and a sticky cake (a notable Scottish indulgence) are **Clarinda's** in Canongate and the **Abbey Strand Tearoom,** near the palace gates.

⑩ The **Palace of Holyroodhouse,** still the Royal Family's official residence in Scotland, was founded by King James IV at the end of the 15th century and was extensively remodeled by Charles II in 1671. The state

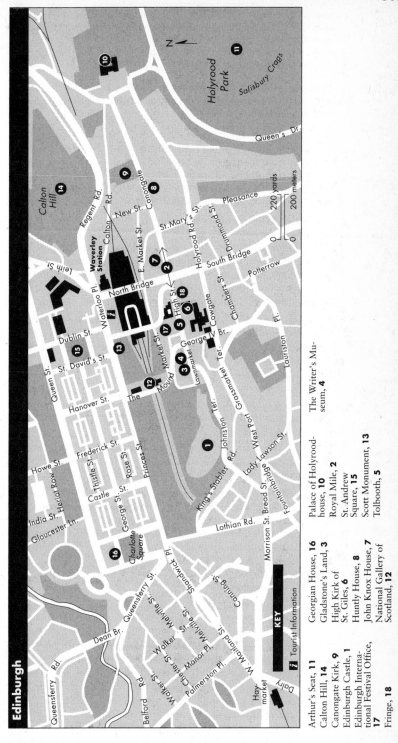

Edinburgh

Arthur's Seat, **11**
Calton Hill, **14**
Canongate Kirk, **9**
Edinburgh Castle, **1**
Edinburgh International Festival Office, **17**
Fringe, **18**

Georgian House, **16**
Gladstone's Land, **3**
High Kirk of St. Giles, **6**
Huntly House, **8**
John Knox House, **7**
National Gallery of Scotland, **12**

Palace of Holyroodhouse, **10**
Royal Mile, **2**
St. Andrew Square, **15**
Scott Monument, **13**
Tolbooth, **5**

The Writer's Museum, **4**

KEY

i Tourist Information

apartments, with their collections of tapestries and paintings, can be visited. *Tel. 0131/556–7371. Admission: £3.50 adults, £1.75 children, £3 senior citizens, £8.50 family ticket. Open Apr.–Oct., Mon.–Sat. 9:30–5:15, Sun. 10:30–4:30; Nov.–Mar., Mon.–Sat. 9:30–3:45, Sun. 10–3:45; closed during royal and state visits.*

⑪ The open grounds of **Holyrood Park** enclose Edinburgh's distinctive, originally volcanic minimountain, **Arthur's Seat,** with steep slopes and miniature crags.

In 1767, the competition to design the New Town was won by a young and unknown architect, James Craig. His plan was for a grid of three east–west streets, balanced at each end by a grand square. The plan survives today, despite all commercial pressures. Princes, George, and Queen streets are the main thoroughfares, with St. Andrew Square at one end and Charlotte Square at the other.

⑫ The **National Gallery of Scotland,** on the Mound, the street that joins the Old and New Towns, contains works by the old masters and the French Impressionists and has a good selection of Scottish paintings. This is one of Britain's best national galleries, and is small enough to be taken in easily on one visit. *Tel. 0131/556–8921. Admission free; charge for special exhibitions. Open Mon.–Sat. 10–5, Sun. 2–5. Print Room, weekdays 10–noon and 2–4 by arrangement.*

⑬ To the east along Princes Street is the unmistakable soaring Gothic spire of the 200-foot-high **Scott Monument,** built in the 1840s to commemorate the celebrated novelist of Scots history. There is a statue of Sir Walter and his dog within. The views from the top are well worth the 287-step climb. *Tel. 0131/225–2424. Admission: £1. Open Apr.–Sept., Mon.–Sat. 9–6; Oct.–Mar., Mon.–Sat. 9–3.*

⑭ There are more splendid views from **Calton Hill:** north across the Firth (or estuary) of Forth to the Lomond Hills of Fife and to the Pentland Hills that enfold the city from the south. Among the various monuments on Calton Hill are a partial reproduction of the **Parthenon,** in Athens, begun in 1824 but left incomplete because the money ran out; the **Nelson Monument;** and the **Royal Observatory.**

⑮ Make your way to **St. Andrew Square,** then along George Street, where there is a wide choice of shops, and on to **Charlotte Square,** whose north side was designed by the great Scottish classical architect Robert Adam.

⑯ The rooms of the elegant **Georgian House** are furnished to show the domestic arrangements of a prosperous late-18th-century Edinburgh family. *7 Charlotte Sq., tel. 0131/225–2160. Admission: £3 adults, £1.50 children and senior citizens. Open Apr.–Oct., Mon.–Sat. 10–5, Sun. 2–5 (last admission 4:30).*

TIME OUT   Bianco's, in Hope Street, close to the Georgian House, is good for coffee and croissants.

Finally, a word about the **Edinburgh International Festival,** the celebration of music, dance, and drama that the city stages each summer (the 1996 dates are Aug. 11–31), featuring international artists of the highest caliber. The **Festival Fringe,** the unruly child of the official festival, spills out of halls and theaters all over town, offering visitors a cornucopia of theatrical and musical events of all kinds—some so weird that they defy description. Although the official festival is the place to see top-flight performances by established artists, at a Fringe event you might catch a new star, or a new art form, or a controver-

sial new play. Advance information, programs, and ticket sales for the
⑰ festival are available from the **Edinburgh International Festival Office**
⑱ (21 Market St., tel. 0131/226–4001), and for the **Fringe** from its office (180 High St., tel. 0131/226–5257 or 5259).

Dining and Lodging

For details and price-category definitions, *see* Dining and Lodging *in*
Staying in Great Britain, *above*.

Dining

$$$$ **The Pompadour.** The decor in this Caledonian Hotel restaurant is inspired by the France of Louis XV, with ornate gilts and reds prevail-
ing. A sophisticated French menu in the evening is balanced by a Scots
flavor at lunchtime. The Caledonian has a second, less pricey restau-
rant, **Carriages ($$$)** that also offers a Scottish menu. *Caledonian
Hotel, Princes St., Edinburgh, tel. 0131/225–2433. Reservations ad-
vised. Jacket and tie. AE, DC, MC, V.*

$$$ **Jackson's Restaurant.** Intimate and candlelit in a historic Old Town
close halfway down the Royal Mile, Jackson's offers good Scots fare.
Aberdeen Angus steaks and Border lamb are excellent; there are vegetarian and seafood specialties, too. *2 Jackson Close, 209–213 High
St., Edinburgh, tel. 0131/225–1793. Reservations advised. AE, MC,
V. No lunch weekends.*

$$$ **L'Auberge.** An established restaurant, L'Auberge is comfortably old-
fashioned. The French-style cuisine uses the best Scottish ingredients.
Try the brill with oysters or the tender venison. There are excellent three-
course, prix-fixe menus available. *56–58 St. Mary's St., Edinburgh,
tel. 0131/556–5888. Reservations advised. AE, DC, MC, V.*

$$$ **Martin's.** This very small spot is good for imaginative vegetarian dishes,
game, and fresh seafood. Try the succulent halibut with leeks and car-
rot-and-basil coulis, or the breasts of mallard and pigeon with red cabbage and raisins. There's a good-value set-price lunch. *70 Rose St., North
La. (between Castle and Frederick Sts.), Edinburgh, tel. 0131/225–3106.
Reservations essential. Jacket and tie advised. AE, DC, MC, V. No lunch
Sat. Closed Sun., Mon.*

$$ **Howie's.** Howie's is a simple, neighborhood bistro, unlicensed, so you
have to bring your own bottle. The steaks are tender Aberdeen beef,
the Loch Fyne herring are sweet-cured to Howie's own recipe, and the
clientele's lively. *75 St. Leonard's St., Edinburgh, tel. 0131/668–2917,
and 63 Dalry Rd., Edinburgh, tel. 0131/313–3334. Reservations ad-
vised. MC, V. No lunch Mon.*

$ **Henderson's.** This friendly place claims to be the city's original vege-
tarian restaurant, long before such places became fashionable. Try the
vegetarian haggis! *94 Hanover St., Edinburgh, tel. 0131/225–2131.
AE, MC, V.*

$ **Pierre Victoire.** There are four branches of this very popular bistro chain
in Edinburgh. They are fairly chaotic, friendly, enjoyable eateries, serv-
ing healthy portions at low prices. The fish is fresh and especially
good. *38 Grassmarket, Edinburgh, tel. 0131/226–2442; 10 Victoria
St., Edinburgh, tel. 0131/225–1721 (closed Sun.); 8 Union St., Edin-
burgh, tel. 0131/557–8451 (closed Mon.); 5 Dock Pl., Leith, tel.
0131/556–6178 (closed Sun.) MC, V.*

Lodging

$$$$ **The Caledonian Hotel.** Popularly known as "the Caley," this hotel
echoes the days of the traditional great railway hotel, though its neigh-
bor station has long since closed. The imposing Victorian decor has
been preserved in a total refurbishment. There are also two excellent

restaurants (*see* Pompadour, *above*). *Princes St., EH1 2AB, tel. 0131/225–2433, fax 0131/225–6632. 239 rooms with bath. Facilities: 2 restaurants, in-house movies. AE, DC, MC, V.*

$$$$ **George Hotel.** This extensively refurbished city-center hotel has elegant 18th-century features in the public rooms and up-to-date bedrooms. Though busy, the staff takes time to be helpful. *19 George St., Edinburgh, EH2 2PB, tel. 0131/225–1251, fax 0131/226–5644. 195 rooms with bath. Facilities: 2 restaurants, bar. AE, DC, MC, V.*

$$$$ **Scandic Crown.** One of the latest hotels to open in Edinburgh, the Scandic Crown has been designed to blend in with the surrounding ancient buildings. The bedrooms are roomy and follow the color scheme of each floor. If what you want is modern ambience but proximity to the sights, this is the place. *80 High St., The Royal Mile, Edinburgh EH1 1TH, tel. 0131/557–9797, fax 0131/557–9789. 238 rooms with bath. AE, DC, MC, V.*

$$$ **The Albany Hotel.** Three fine 18th-century houses with many original features have been carefully converted into a comfortable city-center hotel. There's a good restaurant in the basement. *39 Albany St., Edinburgh EH1 3QY, tel. 0131/556–0397, fax 0131/557–6633. 20 rooms with bath. Facilities: restaurant. MC, V.*

$$$ **Mount Royal Hotel.** This modern hotel is ideally located for sightseeing and shopping. The front rooms have views of the castle. It has a friendly staff. *53 Princes St., Edinburgh EH2 2DG, tel. 0131/225–7161, fax 0131/220–4671. 160 rooms with bath. AE, DC, MC, V.*

$$ **Brunswick Hotel.** This bed-and-breakfast, close to the city center and near the Playhouse Theatre, is in a fine Georgian building that offers easy parking. All rooms have tea/coffee making facilities and TVs; two of them have four posters. *7 Brunswick St., Edinburgh EH7 5JB, tel. and fax 0131/556–1238. 10 rooms with shower. AE, MC, V.*

$$ **Dorstan Private Hotel.** A Victorian villa in a quiet area, the Dorstan has fully modernized rooms decorated in bright, country-cottage colors. *7 Priestfield Rd., Edinburgh EH16 5HJ, tel. 0131/667–6721, fax 0131/668–4644. 14 rooms, 9 with bath or shower. MC, V.*

13 Greece

YOU CANNOT TRAVEL FAR across the land in Greece without meeting the sea or far across the sea without meeting one of its roughly 2,000 islands. About the size of New York State, Greece has 15,019 kilometers (9,312 miles) of coastline, more than any other country of its size in the world. The sea is everywhere, not on three sides only but at every turn, reaching through the shoreline like a probing hand. The land itself is stunning, dotted with cypress groves, vineyards, and olive trees, carved into gentle bays or dramatic coves with startling white sand, rolling hills, and rugged mountain ranges that plunge straight into the sea. This natural beauty and the sharp, clear light of sun and sea, combined with plentiful archaeological treasures, make Greece one of the world's most inviting countries.

Poetry, music, architecture, politics, medicine, law—all had their Western birth here in Greece centuries ago, alongside the great heroes of mythology who still seem to haunt this sun-drenched land. Among the great mountains of mainland Greece are the cloud-capped peak of Mt. Olympus, fabled home of the Greek gods, and Mt. Parnassus, favorite haunt of the sun-god Apollo and the nine Muses, goddesses of poetry and science. The remains of the ancient past—the Acropolis and the Parthenon, the temples of Delphi, the Tombs of the Kings in Mycenae—and a later procession of Byzantine churches, Crusader castles and fortresses, and Turkish mosques are spread throughout the country.

Of the hundreds of islands and islets scattered across the Aegean Sea in the east and the Ionian Sea in the west, fewer than 250 are still inhabited. This world of the farmer and seafarer has largely been replaced by the world of the tourist. More than 10 million vacationers visit Greece each year, almost as many as the entire native population; in fact, tourism has overtaken shipping as the most important element in the nation's economy. Once-idyllic beaches have become overcrowded and noisy, and fishing harbors have become flotilla sailing centers. On some of the islands, the impact of the annual influx of visitors has meant the building of a new Greece, more or less in their image. But traditionalism survives: Pubs and bars stand next door to *ouzeri,* discos are as popular as *kafeneia,* and pizza and hamburger joints compete with tavernas. Prices rose steeply after Greece joined the European Community (today's European Union) in 1981, and the simplicity and hardships of a peasant economy have largely disappeared from the islands' way of life.

Although mass tourism has taken over the main centers, it is still possible to strike out and find your own place among the smaller islands and the miles of beautiful mainland coastline. Except for some difficulty in finding accommodations (Greek families on vacation tend to fill the hotels in out-of-the-way places during high summer), this is the ideal way to see traditional Greece. Those who come only to worship the classical Greeks and gaze at their temples, seeing nothing but the glory that was, miss today's Greece. If you explore this fascinating country with open eyes, you'll enjoy it in all its forms: its slumbering cafés and buzzing tavernas; its elaborate religious rituals; its stark, bright beauty; and the generosity, curiosity, and kindness of its people.

ESSENTIAL INFORMATION

Before You Go

When to Go

Although the tourist season runs from May through October, the heat can be unpleasant in July and August, particularly in Athens. On the islands, a brisk northwesterly wind, the *meltemi,* can make life more comfortable. If you want to move about the country and avoid all the other tourists, the ideal months are May, June, and September. The winter months tend to be damp and cold virtually everywhere.

The following are the average daily maximum and minimum temperatures for Athens.

Jan.	55F	13C	May	77F	25C	Sept.	84F	29C
	44	6		61	16		67	19
Feb.	57F	14C	June	86F	30C	Oct.	75F	24C
	44	6		68	20		60	16
Mar.	60F	16C	July	92F	33C	Nov.	66F	19C
	46	8		73	23		53	12
Apr.	68F	20C	Aug.	92F	33C	Dec.	58F	15C
	52	11		73	23		47	8

Currency

The Greek monetary unit is the drachma (dr.). Banknotes are in denominations of 50, 100, 500, 1,000, and 5,000 dr.; coins, 5, 10, 20, 50, and 100. At press time (spring 1995), there were approximately 208 dr. to the U.S. dollar and 352 dr. to the pound sterling. Daily exchange rates are prominently displayed in banks.

What It Will Cost

Inflation in Greece is rather high—just under 11% a year—and fluctuations in currency make it impossible to do accurate budgeting long in advance, so keep an eye on exchange rates. On the whole, Greece offers good value compared with many other European countries.

There are few regional price differences for hotels and restaurants. A modest hotel in a small town will charge only slightly lower rates than a modest hotel in Athens, with the same range of amenities. The same is true of restaurants. The spread of tourism has made Rhodes, Corfu, and Crete as affordable as many other islands. Car rentals are expensive in Greece, but taxis are inexpensive even for long-distance runs.

SAMPLE PRICES

At a central-city café, you can expect to pay about 500 dr. for a cup of coffee or a bottle of beer, 300 dr. for a soft drink, and around 400 dr. for a grilled cheese sandwich. A 1½-kilometer (1-mile) taxi ride costs about 300 dr.

Customs on Arrival

You may take in one carton of cigarettes or cigars or ¼ pound of smoking tobacco; 1 liter of alcohol, or 2 liters of wine; and gifts up to a total value of 51,000 dr. There's no duty on articles for personal use. The only restrictions applicable to tourists from European Union (EU) countries are those for cigarettes, cigars and tobacco. Foreign bank notes amounting to more than $2,500 must be declared for re-export. There are no restrictions on traveler's checks. Foreign visitors may take in 100,000 dr. in Greek currency and export up to 40,000 dr.

Greece

FORMER YUGOSLAV
REPUBLIC OF
MACEDONIA

BULGARIA

Stavroupoli

ALBANIA

Sidirókastro
Séres

Philippi

Eleftheroúpoli

Kilkís

Amfípoli

Kaval

E86

Edessa

Florina

Gianitsa

Thessaloniki

Kastoria

Alexandria

Thérmi

E90

Nea
Apolonia

Vatopedi

Ptolemaïda

Veria

Polygyros

Ormylia

Ivirio

Kozáni

Katerini

Dafni

Siatista

*Gulf of
Thermaikos*

 Athos

Konitsa

Grevena

Mount
Olympus

E75

Gulf of Kassandra

Delvinákio

Elassona

Kalithéa

Metsovo

Palioúri

Kerkira
Corfu

Igoumenítsa

Ioanina

Kalambaka

Tirnavos

Agia

Paramythia

Trikala

Larissa

Parga

Arta

Karditsa

Aliki

Stavros

Farsala

Volos

SPORADES

Skiathos

Preveza

Almiros

Skopelos

Lefkas
Vassiliki

Karpenissi

Lamia

Skyros

N

Kephalonia

Ithaki

Agrinio

Orhomenos

EVIA

Kymi

Itea

Delphi

Lixouri

Sami

Messolongi

Nafpaktos

Livadia

Halkida

E55

Patras

Galaxidi

Thebes

Gulf of Corinth

Diakofto

Megara

Rafina

Kary

Killini

Corinth

Piraeus

Athens

Loutra

Nemea

Glyfada

Zakynthos

Amalias

Argos

Aegina

Voula

Lavrio

Kea

Zakynthos

Pyrgos

Olympia

Tripoli

Nauplion

Poros

Sounio

Kaiafas

Andritsena

Toló

Kyparissia

PELOPONNESE

Ermioni

Ydra

Kythnos

Spetses

Serifos

Ionian Sea

Messini

Sparta

Leonidio

Gargaliani

Kalamata

Mystras

Geraki

Kyparíssi

*Mirtoan
Sea*

Pilos

Methoni

Koroni

Skala

Milos

Areopoli

Gythio

Monemvassia

Agía Pelagia

Kythira

Kythira

Mediterranean Sea

Hania

0 ——— 100 miles

0 ——— 150 km

CRETE

Black Sea

T U R K E Y

Istanbul

Sea of
Marmara

Kastanies

Didymótiho
E90

Xanthi

T H R A C E

Avdira   Makri   Alexandroupoli

Thassos

Samothrace

Troy

Límnos

Aegean Sea

Lesvos   Mytilini

Plomari

T U R K E Y

Hios   Hios
Mésta
Pirgi

stos

Andros
Andros

Izmir (Smyrna)

Samos

Ephesus

Tinos

Ikaria

Samos

Ermoupoli Tinos

Agios
Kirykos

Pythagorio

Syros
Mykonos

Delos

Patmos

Paros

Naxos

Leros

Bodrum
(Halicarnassus)

Kos

C Y C L A D E S   Amorgos

Kos

Ios   Astypalea

Nissyros   Symi

Oia Fira

Santorini   Anafi

D O D E C A N E S E

Tilos

Kameiros

Rhodes

Halki

Lindos

Rhodes

Sea of Crete

Karpathos

Heraklion

Mallia

Siteia

Knossos

Ayios Nikolaos

Phaestos   Ierapetra

Kassos

Language

English is widely spoken in hotels and elsewhere, especially by young people, and even in out-of-the-way places someone is always happy to lend a helping hand.

In this guide, names are given in the Roman alphabet according to the Greek pronunciation except when there is a familiar English form, such as "Athens."

Getting Around

By Car

ROAD CONDITIONS

Driving in Greek cities is not recommended unless you have iron nerves. Red traffic lights are frequently ignored, and it is not unusual to see motorists passing on hills and while rounding corners. For the ratio of collisions to the number of cars on the road, Greece has one of the worst accident rates in Europe. This is due, in part, to extremely varied road conditions. Motorways tend to be good; tolls are between 200 dr. and 700 dr. and are charged according to distance. Many country roads are narrow but free of traffic.

RULES OF THE ROAD

Unless you are a citizen of an EU country, you must have an international driver's license. The **Automobile and Touring Club of Greece** (*see below*) issues them for 17,700 dr.; they're good for three years. Bring a photo and your driver's license. Driving is on the right, and although the vehicle on the right has the right-of-way, don't expect this or any other driving rule to be obeyed. The speed limit is 120 kph (74 mph) on the National Road, 80 kph (49 mph) outside built-up areas, and 50 kph (31 mph) in town. Seat belts are compulsory, as are helmets for motorcyclists, though many natives ignore the laws. In downtown Athens do not drive in the bus lanes marked by a yellow divider.

PARKING

In Greece's half-dozen large cities, parking spaces are hard to find. In Athens or Thessaloniki, you can pay to use one of the few temporary parking areas set up in vacant lots, but you're better off leaving your car in the hotel garage and walking or taking a cab. Elsewhere, however, parking is easy.

GASOLINE

At press time gas cost about 178 dr.–184 dr. a liter. Gas pumps and service stations are everywhere, and lead-free gas is widely available. Be aware that many stations close at 7 PM.

BREAKDOWNS

The **Automobile and Touring Club of Greece** (ELPA, Athens Tower, Messoghion 2–4, Athens, tel. 01/779–1615 or fax 01/778–6642; in an emergency, tel. 104) assists tourists with breakdowns free of charge for those who are ELPA members; otherwise, there is a charge, depending on the agreement made between ELPA and the driver's own automobile association.

By Motorcycle and Bicycle

Dune buggies, bicycles, mopeds, and motorcycles can be rented on the islands. Use extreme caution. Helmets, although technically compulsory for motorcyclists, are not usually available, and injuries are common.

By Train

Few tourists use the trains because they are slow and railway networks are limited. The main line runs north from Athens to the former Yugoslavia. It divides into three lines at Thessaloniki. The main line continues on to Belgrade, a second line goes east to the Turkish border and Istanbul, and a third line heads northeast to Bulgaria. The Peloponnese in the south is served by a narrow-gauge line dividing at Corinth into the Mycenae–Argos section and the Patras–Olympia–Kalamata section. For information, call 01/524–0601.

By Plane

Olympic Airways (Syngrou 96, Athens, tel. 01/966–6666) has service between Athens and several cities and islands. Thessaloniki is also linked to the main islands, and there are several interisland connections. Reservations can be made by telephone daily from 7 AM to 10 PM. For information on arrivals and departures for Olympic Airways flights (West Terminal), call 01/936–3363; for other carriers (East Terminal), call 01/969–9466 or 01/969–9467.

By Bus

Travel by bus is inexpensive, usually comfortable, and relatively fast. The journey from Athens to Thessaloniki takes roughly the same time as the slow train, though the express covers the distance 1¼ hours faster. In the Peloponnese, however, buses are much faster than trains. Bus information and timetables are available at tourist information offices. Make reservations at least one day before your planned trip, earlier for holiday weekends. Railway-operated buses leave from the Peloponnisos railway station in Athens. All other buses leave from one of two bus stations: Liossion 260—for central and eastern Greece and Evia; Kifissou 100—for the Peloponnese and northwestern Greece.

By Boat

There are frequent car ferries and hydrofoils from Piraeus, the port of Athens, to the central and southern Aegean islands and Crete. Nearby islands are also served by hydrofoils and ferries from Rafina, east of Athens. Ships to the Ionian islands sail from ports nearer to them, such as Patras. Connections from Athens/Piraeus to the main island groups are good, connections from main islands to smaller ones within a group less so, and services between islands of different groups or areas—such as Rhodes and Crete—are less frequent. Travel agents and shipping offices in Athens and Piraeus and in the main towns on the islands have details. Buy your tickets two or three days in advance, especially if you are traveling in summer or taking a car. Reserve your return journey or continuation soon after you arrive.

Timetables change very frequently, and boats may be delayed by weather conditions, so your plans should be flexible.

Staying in Greece

Telephones

LOCAL CALLS

Many curbside kiosks have pay telephones for local calls only. You pay the kiosk owner 20 dr. per call after you've finished. It's easier, though, to buy a phone card from the Telecommunications Office (OTE), kiosks, or convenience shops and use it at the now ubiquitous card phones. If you're calling within Greece, the price is reduced by 30% daily 3 PM–5 PM and on weekends from 3 PM Saturday to 9 AM Monday.

INTERNATIONAL CALLS

Although you can buy phone cards with up to 5,000 dr. credit, if you plan to make and pay for several international phone calls, go to an OTE office, usually in the center of towns and villages. There are several branches in Athens. Calls to the United States and Canada cost

348 dr. a minute during the day and 295 dr. nightly from 11 PM to 8
AM. Calls to Great Britain cost 159 dr. a minute during the day and
120 dr. between 10 PM and 6 AM. There is a three-minute minimum
charge for operator-assisted station-to-station calls, a four-minute minimum for person-to-person connections. For an **AT&T** long-distance operator, dial 00/800–1311; **MCI**, 00/800–1211; **Sprint**, 00/800–1411.

OPERATORS AND INFORMATION

There are English-speaking operators on the International Exchange.
Ask your hotel reception desk or an employee at the OTE for help in
reaching one. It takes up to an hour for the operator to connect you.

COUNTRY CODE

The country code for Greece is 30.

Mail

POSTAL RATES

Airmail letters or postcards for delivery within Europe cost 90 dr. for
20 grams and 180 dr. for 50 grams; outside Europe the cost is 120 dr.
for 20 grams and 220 dr. for 50 grams. If you are mailing a package,
you must bring it open with your wrapping materials to the post office so it can be inspected. In Athens, parcels over a kilogram must be
brought to the station at Mitropoleos 60.

RECEIVING MAIL

Except for the main offices at **Aeolou 100** and on **Syntagma Square**
(both open weekdays 7:30 AM–8 PM, Sat. 7:30–2, Sun. 9–1:30), most
post offices are open weekdays 8–2. You can have your mail addressed to "poste restante" and sent to Aeolou 100, Athens 10200 (take
your passport to pick up your mail), or to American Express, Ermou
2, Athens, 10225. For holders of American Express cards or traveler's
checks, there is no charge for the service. Others pay 400 dr. for each
pickup.

Shopping

Prices quoted in shops include the value-added tax (VAT). There are
no VAT refunds. Prices in large stores are fixed. Bargaining may take
place in small, owner-managed souvenir and handicrafts shops and in
antiques shops. In flea markets, bargaining is expected.

EXPORT PERMITS

Antiques and Byzantine icons require an export permit (not normally
given if the piece is of any value), but beautiful replicas can be bought
fairly cheaply, although even these require a certificate stating they are
copies.

Opening and Closing Times

Office and shopping hours vary considerably and may also change according to the season. Check with your hotel for up-to-the-minute information on opening and closing times.

Banks are open weekdays 8–2, except Fridays, when they close at 1:30;
closed weekends and public holidays. ATM machines are becoming more
numerous in most cities.

Museums and archaeological sites are open 8:30–3, with longer hours
in summer. Generally, museums are closed on Monday. Admission is
free on Sunday and holidays. EU students enjoy free admission, students from other countries pay half the fee, and senior citizens often
get a discount as well. Hours vary; always check with tourist offices
or travel agencies before visiting.

Shops are usually open Tuesday, Thursday, and Friday 9–2 and 5:30–8; Monday, Wednesday, and Saturday 9–2. Supermarkets are open 8–8 on weekdays and 8–2 on Saturdays.

National Holidays

January 1; January 6 (Epiphany); February 26 (Clean Monday); March 25 (Independence); April 12 (Good Friday); April 14 (Greek Easter Sunday); April 15 (Greek Easter Monday); May 1 (Labor Day); June 2 (Pentecost); August 15 (Assumption); October 28 (Ochi Day); December 25–26.

Dining

The principal elements of Greek cuisine are such fresh vegetables as eggplants, tomatoes, and olives, inventively combined with lots of olive oil and seasoned with lemon juice, garlic, and oregano. Meat dishes are limited (pork, lamb, and chicken being the most common); fish is often the better, though more expensive choice, particularly on the coast. Your best bet is to look for tavernas and *estiatoria* (restaurants) and choose the one frequented by the most Greeks. The estiatorio serves oven-baked dishes called *magirefta*, precooked and left to stand, while tavernas offer similar fare plus grilled meats and fish. Another alternative is an *ouzeri* or *mezedopolion*, where you can order several plates of appetizers instead of an entrée. The decor of these establishments may range from simple to sophisticated, with prices to match.

Traditional fast-food in Greece consists of the gyro (slices of grilled lamb with tomato and onions in pita bread), souvlakia (shish kebab), and pastries filled with a variety of stuffings (spinach, cheese, or meat)—but hamburgers and pizzas can now be found everywhere.

MEALTIMES

Lunch in Greek restaurants is served from 12:30 until 3. Dinner begins at about 9 and is served until 1 in Athens and until midnight outside Athens.

PRECAUTIONS

Tap water is safe to drink everywhere, but it is often heavily chlorinated. Excellent bottled mineral water, such as Loutraki, is available.

WHAT TO WEAR

Throughout the Greek islands you can dress informally for dinner, even at expensive restaurants; in Athens, you may want to wear a jacket at some of the top-price restaurants.

RATINGS

Prices are per person and include a first course, main course, dessert (generally fruit and cheese or a sweet pastry, such as baklava), and the 12%–15% service charge. They do not include drinks. Highly recommended restaurants are indicated by a star ★.

CATEGORY	ATHENS/ THESSALONIKI	OTHER AREAS
$$$$	over 10,000 dr.	over 7,000 dr.
$$$	6,000 dr.–10,000 dr.	5,000 dr.–7,000 dr.
$$	3,500 dr.–6,000 dr.	2,500 dr.–5,000 dr.
$	under 3,500 dr.	under 2,500 dr.

Lodging

Most accommodations are in standard hotels, sometimes called motels. There are a number of "village" complexes, especially at the beaches and as part of some hotels. On islands and at beach resorts, large hotels are complemented by family-run pensions and guest houses—usually clean, bright, and recently built—and self-catering apartment and bungalow complexes. In a very few places, there are state-organized "traditional settlements"—houses with guest accommodations in buildings that are representative of the local architecture.

Greek hotels are classified as Luxury (L) and A–E. Within each category, which is set by the government, quality varies greatly, but prices usually don't. Still, you may come across an A-class hotel that charges less than a B-class, depending on facilities. In this guide, hotels are classified according to price. All very expensive (**$$$$**) and expensive (**$$$**) hotels are assumed to have air-conditioning, so listings in these categories mention it only when it is absent. If a moderate (**$$**) or an inexpensive (**$**) hotel is air-conditioned, this is indicated. All have been built or completely renovated during the past 20 years, and, unless indicated, all have private baths.

Prices quoted by hotels usually include service, local taxes, and VAT; many hotels include breakfast. At certain times, though, you can negotiate the price, sometimes by eliminating breakfast. The official price should be posted on the back of the door or inside a closet. Booking a room through a travel agency may reduce the price substantially. Seaside hotels, especially those in the **$$$$** and **$$$** categories, frequently insist that guests take half board (lunch or dinner included in the price).

RATINGS

Prices quoted are for a double room in high season, including taxes and service, but not breakfast unless noted. Rates are the same throughout the country for each category. Highly recommended lodgings are indicated by a star ★.

CATEGORY	ALL AREAS
$$$$	over 40,000 dr.
$$$	23,000 dr.–40,000 dr.
$$	15,000 dr.–23,000 dr.
$	under 15,000 dr.

Tipping

In restaurants, cafés, and tavernas, leave a tip of around 10%. This should be left on the table for your waiter and not on the plate, where it will be taken by the head waiter. In hotels, tip porters 100 dr. per bag for carrying your luggage—more in a top hotel. For taxi drivers, Greeks usually round off the fare. Hairdressers usually get 10% or slightly more. In legitimate theaters, tip ushers 100 dr. if you are shown to your seat. In movie theaters, tip about 50 dr. if you receive a program from the usher. On cruises, cabin and dining-room stewards get about 500 dr. per day; guides receive about the same.

ATHENS

Arriving and Departing

By Plane

Most visitors arrive by air at **Ellinikon Airport,** about 10 kilometers (6 miles) from the city center. All Olympic Airways flights, both international and domestic, use the West Terminal next to the ocean. All other flights arrive and depart from the East Terminal on the opposite side of the airport.

BETWEEN THE AIRPORT AND DOWNTOWN

A bus service connects the two air terminals, Syntagma Square, Omonia Square, and Piraeus. Between the East Terminal and Athens, the express bus (No. 91) runs every 20 minutes 6 AM–12:30 AM; from the West Terminal, Bus 90 runs every 30 minutes 6:30 AM–9:30 PM. The fare is 160 dr. The night express buses (200 dr.) run at irregular intervals; ask for a schedule from a Greek National Tourist Organization office (*see* Important Addresses and Numbers, *below*). You can catch either bus to the airport on Syntagma Square in front of the Bank of Macedonia Thrace or off Omonia Square on Stadiou. From the terminals to Karaiskaki Square in Piraeus and between the terminals, the express bus (No. 19) runs about every 50 minutes (5 AM–11:20 PM)and costs 160 dr. The night bus (200 dr.) runs hourly. In most cases it's easier to take taxis: about 1,500 dr. to Piraeus; 900 dr. between terminals; 1,300–1,600 dr. to the center, depending on which terminal. The price goes up by about two-thirds between midnight and 5 AM.

By Train

Athens has two railway stations, side by side, not far from Omonia Square. International trains from the north arrive at, and depart from, **Stathmos Larissis** (tel. 01/823–7741). Take Trolley 1 from the terminal to Omonia Square. Trains from the Peloponnese use the marvelously ornate and old-fashioned **Stathmos Peloponnisos** (tel. 01/513–1601) next door. To Omonia and Syntagma squares, take Bus 57. Since the phones are almost always busy and agents often don't speak English, it's easier to get information and buy tickets at a railway office downtown (Sina 6, tel. 01/362–4402 through 01/362–4406; Filellinon 17, tel. 01/323–6747; or Karolou 1, tel. 01/524–0646 through 01/524–0648).

By Bus

Greek buses arrive either at **Terminal A** (100 Kifissou, tel. 01/512–4910) or **Terminal B** (Liossion 260, tel. 01/831–7153). From Terminal A, take Bus 51 to Omonia Square; from Terminal B, take Bus 24 downtown. To take public transportation to the stations, catch Bus 51 at Zinonos and Menandrou off Omonia Square and Bus 24 on Amalias Avenue in front of the National Gardens. International buses drop their passengers off on the street, usually in the Omonia or Syntagma Square areas or at Stathmos Peleponnisos.

By Car

Whether you approach Athens from the Peloponnese or from the north, you enter by the National Road (as the main highways going north and south are known) and then follow signs for the center. Leaving Athens, routes to the National Road are well marked; signs usually name Lamia for the north and Corinth or Patras for the southwest.

By Ship

Except for cruise ships, few passenger ships from other countries call at Piraeus, the port of Athens, 10 kilometers (6 miles) from Athens's center. If you do dock at the main port in Piraeus, you can take the nearby metro right into Omonia Square. The trip takes 20 minutes and costs 100 dr. Alternatively, you can take a taxi, which may well take longer due to traffic and will cost around 1,100 dr. If you arrive by hydrofoil in the smaller port of Zea Marina, take Bus 905 or Trolley 20 to the metro.

Getting Around

Many of the sights you'll want to see, and most of the hotels, cafés, and restaurants, are within a fairly small central area. It's easy to walk everywhere.

By Metro

An electric (partially underground) railway runs from Piraeus to Omonia Square and then on to Kifissia. It is not useful for getting around the central area. The standard fare is 75 dr. or 100 dr., depending on the distance. There are no special fares or day tickets for visitors, and there is, as yet, no public transport map.

By Bus

The fare on blue buses and the roomier yellow trolley buses is 75 dr. Tickets should be purchased beforehand at one of the curbside kiosks, or from booths at the main terminals. Validate your ticket on the bus by stamping it in the orange machine, or you may be fined 1,500 dr. Buses run from the center to all suburbs and suburban beaches until about midnight. For suburbs beyond central Kifissia, you have to change at Kifissia. Attica has an efficient bus network. Most buses to the east Attica coast, including those for Sounion (tel. 01/823–0179; 1,000 dr.) and Marathon (tel. 01/821–0872; 600 dr.), leave from the KTEL terminal, Platia Aigyptiou on Mavromateon, at the corner of Patission and Alexandras avenues.

By Taxi

Taxis are plentiful except during rush hours, public transportation strikes, and rainstorms. Although you will eventually find an empty taxi, it's often more successful to shout your general destination to one carrying passengers; if the taxi is going in that direction, the driver will pick you up. Note the fare on the meter, so you can subtract your charge from the original amount. Most drivers speak basic English and are familiar with the city center, though not necessarily with the suburbs. The meter starts at 200 dr., and even if you join other passengers, you must add this amount to your final charge. There is a 300 dr. minimum and a basic charge of 54 dr. per kilometer; this increases to 105 dr. between midnight and 5 AM. There is an additional 260 dr. charge for trips from the airport, and 140 dr. for trips from the port, the train stations, and the bus terminals. There is also a 50 dr. charge per item for baggage over 10 kilograms. Waiting time is 1,400 dr. per hour. Some drivers overcharge foreigners, especially on trips from the airport or from Piraeus; insist that they turn on the meter as soon as you get in, and make sure they use the high tariff ("Tarifa 2") only between midnight and 5 AM. You can also call a radio taxi, which charges you an additional 200 dr.–300 dr. for the pickup if you call a few hours ahead and 300 dr.–400 dr. if you want a taxi immediately. Some reliable companies are **Kosmos** (tel. 01/420–7244, 01/420–7261, or 01/420–7247) and **Lycabettus** (tel. 01/502–3583, 01/502–3783, or 01/502–0357).

Important Addresses and Numbers

Tourist Information

There are **Greek National Tourist Organization (EOT)** offices at Karageorgi Servias 2, in the bank, tel. 01/322–2545; at the East Terminal of Ellinikon Airport, tel. 01/961–2722; and at Piraeus, EOT Building, 1st floor, Zea Marina, tel. 01/413–5716.

Embassies

U.S. (Vasilissis Sofias 91, tel. 01/721–2951); **Canadian** (Gennadiou 4, tel. 01/725–4011); **U.K.** (Ploutarchou 1, tel. 01/723–6211).

Emergencies

Police: Tourist Police (tel. 171); Traffic Police (tel. 01/523–0111); and City Police (tel. 100). **Fire** (tel. 199). **Ambulance:** Tel. 166, but a taxi is often faster. Not all hospitals are open nightly; dial 106 (in Greek) or check the English-language *Athens News,* which lists emergency hospitals daily. **Doctors:** Any hotel will call one for you. You can also call your embassy. **Dentist:** Ask your hotel or embassy. **Pharmacies:** Many pharmacies in the central area have someone who speaks English. Try **Marinopoulos** (Kanari 23, tel. 01/361–3051). For information on late-night pharmacies, dial 107 (Greek), or check the *Athens News.*

English-Language Bookstores

Pantelides (Amerikis 9–11, tel. 01/362–3673); **Eleftheroudakis** (Nikis 4, tel. 01/323–1051); **Compendium** (Nikis 28, upstairs, tel. 01/322–1248); **Reymondos** (Voukourestiou 18, tel. 01/354–8188).

Travel Agencies

American Express (Ermou 2, tel. 01/324–4975); **CHAT Tours** (Stadiou 4, tel. 01/322–2886); **Condor Travel** (Stadiou 47, off Omonia Sq., tel. 01/321–2453); **Travel Plan** (Christou Lada 9, tel. 01/323–8801 through 01/323–8804).

Guided Tours

Orientation Tours

All tour operators offer a four-hour morning bus tour of Athens, including a guided tour of the Acropolis, for around 7,700 dr. Make reservations at your hotel or at a travel agency; besides those agents already mentioned, there are hundreds of others, many situated around Filellinon and Nikis streets off Syntagma Square.

Special-Interest Tours

For those interested in folk dancing, there is a four-hour evening tour (April–October) for around 7,000 dr. that begins with a sound-and-light show of the Acropolis from Filopappou Hill and then goes on to a performance of Greek folk dances in the open-air theater nearby. Another evening tour offers a dinner show at a taverna in the Plaka area, after the sound and light, for around 10,500 dr. Any travel agency can arrange these tours—and the excursions below—for you, but go first to **CHAT Tours** (*see* Important Addresses and Numbers, *above*) for reliable and efficient service.

Excursions

The choice is almost unlimited. A one-day tour to Delphi will cost up to 16,500 dr., with lunch included; a two-day tour to Corinth, Mycenae, Nauplion, and Epidaurus, around 27,500 dr., including half board in first-class hotels. A full-day cruise from Piraeus, visiting three islands—Aegina, Poros, and Ydra—costs around 15,000 dr. (including buffet lunch on the ship), and a three-day classical tour to Delphi and the breathtaking Meteora monasteries costs from 69,500 dr. (including half board in first-class hotels).

Personal Guides

All the major tourist agencies can provide English-speaking guides for personally organized tours. Only hire one licensed by the EOT.

Exploring Athens

Athens is essentially a village that outgrew itself, spreading out from the original settlement at the foot of the Acropolis. Back in 1834, when it became the capital of modern Greece, the city had a population of fewer than 10,000. Now it houses more than a third of the Greek population—around 4 million. A modern concrete city has engulfed the old village and now sprawls for 388 square kilometers (244 square miles), covering almost all the surrounding plain from the sea to the encircling mountains.

The city is crowded, dusty, and overwhelmingly hot during the summer. It also has an appalling air-pollution problem, caused mainly by traffic fumes; in an attempt to lessen the congestion, it is forbidden to drive private cars in central Athens on alternate workdays. Still, Athens is an experience not to be missed. Its tangible vibrancy makes it one of the most exciting cities in Europe, and the sprawling cement has failed to overwhelm the few astonishing reminders of ancient Athens.

The central area of modern Athens is small, stretching from the Acropolis to Mt. Lycabettus, with its small white church on top. The layout is simple: Three parallel streets—Stadiou, Venizelou (a.k.a. Panepistimiou), and Akademias—link two main squares—Syntagma and Omonia. Try to wander off this beaten tourist track: Seeing the Athenian butchers in the central market near Monastiraki sleeping on their cold marble slabs during the heat of the afternoon siesta may give you more of a feel for the city than seeing hundreds of fallen pillars.

Keep in mind that most museums and archaeological sites are free on Sundays and holidays. There may be a 500 dr. charge if you want to use your camera's flash.

Numbers in the margin correspond to points of interest on the Athens map.

The Historic Heart

1 At the center of modern Athens is **Syntagma (Constitution) Square.** It has several leading hotels, airline and travel offices, and numerous cafés.

2 Along one side of the square stands the **Parliament Building,** completed in 1838 as the royal palace for the new monarchy. In front of the palace, you can watch the changing of the vividly costumed **Evzone guard** at the **Tomb of the Unknown Soldier.** On Sundays there is a more elaborate ceremony at 11:15 AM. Amalias Avenue, leading out of Syntagma, will take you to the **National Gardens.**

3 Across Vasilissis Olgas, at the far end of the National Gardens, you will see the columns of the once-huge **Temple of Olympian Zeus.** This famous temple was begun in the 6th century BC, and, when it was finally completed 700 years later, it exceeded in magnitude all other temples in Greece. It was destroyed during the invasion of the Goths in the 4th century, and today only a few towering sun-browned columns remain. *Vas. Olgas 1, tel. 01/922–6330. Admission: 500 dr. Open Tues.– Sun. 8:30–2:45.*

4 Nearby stands **Hadrian's Arch,** built at the same time as the temple by the Roman emperor. It consists of a Roman archway, with a Greek superstructure of Corinthian pilasters. Visiting heads of state are officially welcomed here.

5 About three-quarters of a kilometer (a half mile) east, down Vasilissis Olgas, you'll come to the marble **Panathenaic Stadium** built for the first modern Olympic Games in 1896; it is a blindingly white, marble reconstruction of the ancient Roman stadium of Athens and can seat 80,000 spectators.

6 From Hadrian's Arch, take Dionysiou Areopagitou a few blocks west to the **Theater of Dionysos,** built during the 6th century BC. Here the famous ancient dramas and comedies were originally performed in conjunction with bacchanalian feasts. *Tel. 01/322–4625. Admission: 500 dr. Open daily 8:30–2:45.*

7 A little farther along, on the right, you'll see the massive back wall of the much better preserved **Odeon of Herod Atticus,** built by the Romans during the 2nd century AD. Here, on pine-scented summer evenings, the **Athens Festival** takes place. It includes opera, ballet, drama, and concerts (*see* The Arts, *below*). *It is not otherwise open to the public.*

8 Beyond the theater, a steep, zigzag path leads to the **Acropolis.** After a 30-year building moratorium at the time of the Persian wars, the Athenians built this complex during the 5th century BC to honor the goddess Athena, patron of the city. It is now undergoing conservation as part of an ambitious 20-year rescue plan launched with international support in 1983 by Greek architects. The first ruins you'll see are the **Propylaea,** the monumental gateway that led worshipers from the temporal world into the spiritual world of the sanctuary; now only the columns of Pentelic marble and a fragment of stone ceiling remain. Above, to the right, stands the graceful **Temple of Wingless Victory** (or Athena Nike), so called because the sculptor depicted the goddess of victory without her wings in order to prevent her from flying away. The elegant and architecturally complex **Erechtheion temple,** most sacred of the shrines of the Acropolis and later turned into a harem by the Turks, has now emerged from extensive repair work. Dull, heavy copies of the Caryatids (draped maidens) now support the roof. The Acropolis Museum houses five of the six originals, their faces much damaged by acid rain; only four are on display, since one is being restored. The sixth is in the British Museum in London.

9 The **Parthenon** dominates the Acropolis and indeed the Athens skyline. Designed by Ictinus, with Phidias as master sculptor, it was completed in 438 BC and is the most architecturally sophisticated temple of that period. Even with hordes of tourists wandering around the ruins, you can still feel a sense of wonder. The architectural decorations were originally picked out in vivid red and blue paint, and the roof was of marble tiles, but time and neglect have given the marble pillars their golden-white shine, and the beauty of the building is all the more stark and striking. The British Museum houses the largest remaining part of the original 532-foot frieze (the Elgin Marbles). The building has 17 fluted columns along each side and 8 at the ends, and these lean slightly inward and bulge to cleverly counterbalance the natural optical distortion. The Parthenon has had a checkered history: It was made into a brothel by the Romans, a church by the Christians, and a mosque by the Turks. The Turks also stored gunpowder in the Propylaea, and when this was hit by a Venetian bombardment in 1687, a fire raged for two days and 28 columns of the Parthenon were blown out, leaving the temple in its present condition. *Tel. 01/321–0219. Admission: 2,000 dr., joint ticket to Acropolis and museum. Open weekdays 8–6:30 (8–4:30 in winter), weekends and holidays 8:30–2:30.*

10 The **Acropolis Museum,** just below the Parthenon, contains some superb sculptures from the Acropolis, including the Caryatids and a large collection of colored korai (statues of women dedicated by wor-

526

Academy, **16**
Acropolis, **8**
Acropolis Museum, **10**
Agora, **11**
Byzantine Museum, **23**
Evzone Guards'
barracks, **20**
Hadrian's Arch, **4**
Hephaisteion, **12**
Little Cathedral, **15**
Mt. Lycabettus, **24**
Museum of Agora
Excavations, **13**
Museum of Cycladic
Art, **22**
National
Archaeological
Museum, **19**
National Library, **18**
Odeon of Herod
Atticus, **7**
Panathenaic Sta-
dium, **5**
Parliament Building, **2**
Parthenon, **9**
Plaka, **14**
Presidential Palace, **21**
Senate House of the
University, **17**
Syntagma
(Constitution)
Square, **1**
Temple of Olympian
Zeus, **3**
Theater of Dionysos, **6**

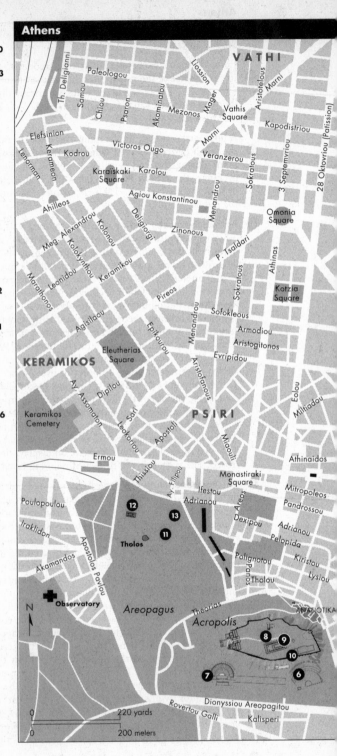

Athens

Strefi

NEAPOLIS

Tossitsa

Stournara

Solomou

Kapodistriou

Kaningos
Kaningos
Square

Themistokleous

Em. Benaki

Zoodohou Pigis

Harilaou Trikoupi

Navarinou

Panepistimiou (Venizelou)

Akademas

Asklepiou

Skoufa

Didotou

Methonis

Eressou

Dervenion

Arachovis

Mavromichali

Ippokratous

Kallidromiou

Isavron

Smolenski

Tsimiski

Youlgarokotonou

Vatatzi

Lastareos

N. Ouranou

Dafnomili

Chesanos

Sarantapichou

LIKAVITOS

**Ayios ■
Giorgios**

Marasli

24

Municipal
Cultural
Center

18

17

Stadiou

Korai

16

Massalias

Sina

Solonos

Omirou

Lykavitou

Anagnostopoulou

Aristidou

Dragatsaniou

Klafthmonos
Sq.

Papariopoulou

Amerikis

Dimokritou

Voukourestiou

Pindarou

Aristipou

Kleomenous

Loukianou

Spefsipou

Patriarhou Ioakim

Alopekis

Karneadou

Ploutarchou

Ypsilantou

KOLONAKI

Praxitelous

**Schliemann's
Mansion**

Kolokotroni

Kanari

Merlin

Kolonaki
Square

Irodotou

Karageorgi
Servias

Perikleos

Ermou

Georgiou I

i

Vasilissis Sofias

Koumbari

Vasilissis

Sofias

22

23

15

Apollonos

14

PLAKA

Nikis

Filellinon

Amalias

Syntagma
Square

1

2

20

Herod Atticus

Rigillis

Mitropoleos

Nikodimou

Adrianou

Scholiou

Tripodon

Thespidos

Kidathineon

Sourt

National

Gardens

Vasileos Georgiou B'

21

Vasileos Konstantinou

Eratosthenous

Arianou

Patsaniou

Amalias Ave.

Epimenidou

Vironos

Goura

Lysikratous

Pitakou

Vasilissis Olgas

Zappion

4

3

5

Agros

**Ardittos
Hill**

Plastira
Square

shipers to the goddess Athena, patron of the ancient city). *Tel. 01/323–6665. Admission: 2,000 dr., joint ticket to the Acropolis. Open weekdays 8–6:30 (8–4:30 in winter), weekends and holidays 8–2:30.*

On **Areopagus,** the rocky outcrop facing the Acropolis, St. Paul preached to the Athenians; the road leading down between it and the hill of Pnyx is called Agiou Pavlou (St. Paul). To the right stands the **⑪ Agora,** which means "marketplace," the civic center and focal point of community life in ancient Athens. The sprawling confusion of stones, slabs, and foundations is dominated by the best-preserved temple in Greece, the **Hephaisteion** (often wrongly referred to as the Theseion), built during the 5th century BC. Nearby, the impressive Stoa of Attalos II, reconstructed by the American School of Classical Studies **⑬** in Athens with the help of the Rockefeller Foundation, houses the **Museum of the Agora Excavations.** *Tel. 01/321–0185. Admission: 1,200 dr. Open Tues.–Sun. 8:30–2:45.*

⑭ Stretching east from the Agora is **Plaka,** almost all that's left of 19th-century Athens. During the 1950s and '60s, the area became garish with neon as nightclubs moved in and residents moved out. Renovation in recent years has restored Plaka, with its winding lanes, neoclassical houses, and sights like the **Greek Folk Art Museum** (Kidathineon 17), the **Tower of the Winds** (a first-century BC water clock near the Roman agora), and the **Monument of Lysikrates** (in a park off Lysikratous). Above Plaka, at the base of the Acropolis, is **Anafiotika,** the closest thing you'll find to a village in Athens. To escape the city bustle, take some time to wander among its whitewashed, bougainvillea-framed houses and its tiny churches.

Below Plaka, in Cathedral Square, stands a 12th-century Byzantine **⑮** church known as the Old or **Little Cathedral,** whose outer walls are covered with reliefs. It nestles below the vast structure of the 19th-century **Cathedral of Athens.** From here, a short walk up Mitropoleos will take you back to Syntagma.

TIME OUT   Visit the **De Profundis Tea Room** in an old mansion at Hatzimichali 1 for pastries and a large variety of teas. **Kostis,** on the main square in Plaka at Kidathineon 18, is good for a Greek lunch—wild greens, roast chicken, *imam* (a spicy eggplant dish). Go around the corner to **Glikis** at Aggelou Geronta 2 for an inexpensive Greek coffee or ouzo and a *mikri pikilia* (a small plate of appetizers, including cheese, sausage, olives, and dips).

Downtown Athens

If you walk along Venizelou Avenue (Panepistimiou) from Syntagma, you will pass, on the right, three imposing buildings in classical style: **⑯ ⑰ ⑱** the **Academy,** the **Senate House of the University,** and the **National Library.** When you reach **Omonia Square,** a bedlam of touts and tourists, you are in the heart of downtown Athens.

⑲ Make time to see the **National Archaeological Museum.** Despite being somewhat off the tourist route, a good 10-minute walk north of Omonia Square, it is well worth the detour. It houses one of the most exciting collections of antiquities in the world, including sensational archaeological finds made by Heinrich Schliemann at Mycenae; 16th-century BC frescoes from the Akrotiri ruins on Santorini; and the 6½-foot-tall bronze sculpture *Poseidon,* an original work of circa 470 BC, possibly by the sculptor Kalamis, which was found in the sea off Cape Artemision in 1928. *28 Oktovriou (Patission) 44, tel. 01/821–7717.*

Admission: 2,000 dr. Open Mon. 11–5, Tues.–Fri. 8–7 (8–5 in winter), weekends and holidays 8:30–3.

Alternatively, from Syntagma you can take Vasilissis Sofias along the
20 edge of the National Gardens to reach the **Evzone Guards' barracks.**
From here you can turn right onto Herod Atticus, which leads to the
21 **Presidential Palace,** used by Greece's kings after the restoration of 1935
and now by the head of state.

22 Or you can cross the street and turn up Neofytou Douka to the **Museum of Cycladic Art.** The collection spans 5,000 years, with nearly 100
exhibits of the Cycladic civilization (3000–2000 BC), including many
of the slim marble figurines that so fascinated artists like Picasso and
Modigliani. *Neofytou Douka 4, tel. 01/722–8321. Admission: 400 dr.
Open Mon. and Wed.–Fri. 10–4, Sat. 10–3.*

23 A little farther along Vasilissis Sofias is the **Byzantine Museum,** housed
in an 1848 mansion built by an eccentric French aristocrat. Since the
museum is undergoing renovation, not all its pieces are on display, but
it has a unique collection of icons and the very beautiful 14th-century
Byzantine embroidery of the body of Christ, in gold, silver, yellow, and
green. Sculptural fragments provide an excellent introduction to Byzantine architecture. *Vasilissis Sofias 22, tel. 01/721–1027. Admission: 500
dr. Open Tues.–Sun. 8:30–3.*

Kolonaki, the chic shopping district and one of the most fashionable
24 residential areas, occupies the lower slopes of **Mt. Lycabettus** and is
only a 10-minute walk northeast of Syntagma; it's worth a stroll
around if you enjoy window-shopping and people-watching. Three
times the height of the Acropolis, Lycabettus can be reached by funicular railway from the top of Ploutarchou; Minibus 60 from Kolonaki Square drops you at the station (fare: 400 dr. round-trip; open daily
8:45 AM–12:45 AM, until 12:15 AM from October through March).
The view from the top—pollution permitting—is the finest in Athens.
You can see all Athens, Attica, the harbor, and the islands of Aegina
and Poros laid out before you.

TIME OUT Take a cappuccino break at one of the many trendy but friendly cafés,
such as **Peros** or **Da Capo** at the start of the pedestrian zone off Kolonaki Square. Sip an ouzo with your *mezedes* (appetizers) on Mt. Lycabettus at **I Prasini Tenta** (the Green Awning), with its resplendent view of
the city and the Acropolis. To get there, take the funicular to the top and
walk back down the road about 10 minutes.

Off the Beaten Track

Outside central Athens, on the slopes of Mt. Ymittos (ancient Mt. Hymettus), is one of the city's most evocative Byzantine remains, the **Kaisariani monastery.** Take a taxi or Bus 224 from the terminal on Akademias
(across from the Municipal Cultural Center) for 6 kilometers (4 miles)
east of central Athens until you pass through the working-class suburb of Kaisariani. The monastery is an additional 30-minute walk
along the paved road that climbs Mt. Ymittos. The well-restored 11th-century church, built on the site of a sanctuary of Aphrodite, has some
beautiful frescoes dating from the 17th century. If you feel particularly
energetic, you can continue walking up Mt. Ymittos—the roads wind
through the forested slopes for 19 kilometers (12 miles)—and take your
pick of the many picnic spots. *Tel. 01/723–6619. Admission 800 dr.
Open Tues.–Sun. 8:30–3.*

Beyond the port of Piraeus, **Mikrolimano** is famed for its many seafood restaurants—22 at last count—but has lost favor with some Athenians because its pretty, crescent-shaped harbor suffers from pollution. The delightful atmosphere remains intact, however, and the harbor is crowded with elegant yachts. While it's not a particularly cheap place to eat, the freshness and quality of the fish and seafood here matches any elsewhere in Greece. If you don't like seafood, you'll still be enchanted by the terraces of lovely houses tucked up against the sloping hillsides. To get there from Athens, take the metro from Omonia Square to Neo Faliron or a bus from Filellinon to the Neo Faliron train station; it's only five minutes' walk from there. Alternatively, a relatively expensive (1,800 dr.) taxi ride will take you 20 kilometers (13 miles) from downtown along the coastal road toward **Glyfada,** where the fish restaurants give you wonderful views of the Saronic Gulf.

Shopping

Gift Ideas

Better tourist shops sell copies of traditional Greek jewelry, silver filigree, enamel, Skyrian pottery, onyx ashtrays and dishes, woven bags, attractive rugs (including flokatis—shaggy wool rugs, often brightly colored), worry beads in amber or silver called *koboloi,* good leather items, and furs. Furs made from scraps are inexpensive. Some museums sell replicas of small items that are in their collections. The best handicrafts are sold in the **National Welfare Organization shop** (Ypatias 6) near the Cathedral of Athens and the **Center of Hellenic Tradition** (Pandrossou 36, in Monastiraki), which also has a café on the upper floor. Other shops sell dried fruit, packaged pistachios, and canned olives. Natural sponges also make good gifts.

Antiques

Many shops, especially on **Pandrossou,** sell small antiques and icons. Keep in mind that there are many fakes, and that you must have permission from the government to export genuine objects from the Greek, Roman, or Byzantine periods.

Shopping Areas

The central shopping area lies between Syntagma and Omonia. The **Syntagma** area has good jewelers, shoe shops, and handicrafts and souvenir shops, especially along **Voukourestiou. Stadiou** is the best bet for men's clothing. Try **Ermou** for shoes and the fascinating small streets that lead off it for fabrics and housewares. Go to **Mitropoleos** for rugs and souvenirs. Most of the moderately priced fur shops are here also, including **Hydra** (Mitropoleos 3–5) and **Voula Mitsakou** (Mitropoleos 7). Nearby is **Karamichos Flokati** (Voulis 31–33) where you'll find a large selection of flokatis. Ermou runs west to **Monastiraki,** a crowded market area popular with Athenians. Below the cathedral, **Pandrossou** has antiques, sandals (an especially good buy), and inexpensive souvenirs. **Kolonaki** has the most expensive shops. Here you'll find unique jewelry from the famous **LALAoUNIS** (Panepistimiou 6), with **La Chrysoteque Zolotas** just down the street (Panepistimiou 10), and **PentheRoudakis** (Voukourestiou 19) in a pedestrian zone lined with jewelry shops. Kolonaki also has designer boutiques, such as **Gianni Versace** (Anagnostopoulou 3) and **Gianfranco Ferre** (Anagnastopoulou 4), as well as Greek designers like **Sotris** (Leventi 3), **Aslanis** (Anagnostopoulou 16), and **Makis Tselios** (Solonos 2). For a broader selection, try **Bettina** (Voukourestiou 4) for women's clothing and **Artisti Italiani** (Kanari 5) for men's.

Flea Market

The flea market, based on **Pandrossou** and **Ifestou streets,** operates on Sunday mornings and sells almost anything: secondhand clothes, cooking pots and pans, old books, guitars, and backgammon sets. Pontians—Greeks who lived in the former Soviet Union—sell Russian caviar, vodka, and table linens. However little it costs, you should haggle. Ifestou, where coppersmiths have their shops, is more interesting on a weekday—and you can pick up copper wine jugs, candlesticks, cooking ware, and more for next to nothing.

Dining

Search for places with at least half a dozen tables occupied by Athenians—they're discerning customers. If you'd like a change of cuisine and don't object to higher prices, pick up the weekly English-language magazine *Athenscope*, available at most bookshops and central kiosks. It lists all kinds of ethnic restaurants. For details and price-category definitions, *see* Dining *in* Staying in Greece, *above.*

$$$$ **Bajazzo.** If you can splurge only once in Greece, this is the place. The
★ restaurant recently moved, but chef Klaus Feuerbach is still in charge. The beef fillets layered with foie gras and served with cognac-cream sauce; the fillet of sole with smoked salmon mousse, mascarpone, and chive sauce; and the langoustine with ricotta, tomatoes, and garlic-butter-lemon sauce are mouth-watering. *Anapafseos 14, Mets, tel. 01/921–3013. Reservations required. AE, DC, MC, V. Closed Sun. No lunch.*

$$$ **Aglamair.** The most expensive fish restaurant on Mikrolimano harbor is also one of the best in Athens, and you can dine watching the lights shimmer across the bay. The menu includes lobster, shrimp, prawns, octopus, and squid, as well as house specialties like the *saganaki garides* (fried cheese with shrimp) appetizer and *ekmek,* a dessert made with shredded wheat and ice cream. *Akti Koumoundourou 54–56, Mikrolimano, tel. 01/411–5511 through 01/411–5515. Reservations advised. AE, DC, MC, V.*

$$$ **La Fenice.** For those staying near the coast, this is the place to spend a romantic evening dining on beautifully presented, imaginative Italian food. Try the spaghetti with lobster, gnocchi with spinach and Gorgonzola, crawfish wrapped in pastry, salmon fillet in champagne sauce, or fillet of beef with balsamic vinegar. *Zisimopoulou 10, Glyfada, tel. 01/894–9454. Reservations required. AE, DC, V. Closed Sun. No lunch.*

$$$ **Melrose.** An anomaly in the student neighborhood of Exarchia, Melrose serves up the only Pacific Rim cuisine in Athens, in a understated setting punctuated with striking modern art. Choices range from seviche to Molokai venison with raspberry sauce and litchis. Other excellent dishes are the honey-glazed duck, with black currants, pineapple, and red peppers, and the Japanese salad—fresh spinach drizzled with rice wine vinegar and toasted sesame oil and topped with shrimp and scallops. *Zosimadou 16, at top of stairs off Kallidromiou 68, Exarchia, tel. 01/825–1627. Reservations advised. AE, V. Closed Sun. and June–Sept. No lunch.*

$$$ **Symposio.** After a show at the nearby Odeon of Herod Atticus, sit in the glass-enclosed dining room and enjoy crepes with spinach and Cretan *mizithra* cheese, fillets of St. Peter's fish with saffron, or venison with wild cherries. The menu changes weekly. *Erecthiou 46, Makriyanni, tel. 01/922–5321, 01/996–0501 for reservations. Reservations advised. AE, DC, MC, V. Closed Sun and Aug. 15. No lunch.*

$$ **Apotsos.** A famous ouzerie, close to Syntagma Square but hidden away down an arcade, this is an echoing barn of a place—truly Athenian in atmosphere. Politicians, journalists, and artists gather here at lunchtime.

As well as ouzo, wine and beer are served, along with dishes of mezedes—three or four of these will add up to a substantial meal. *Panepistimiou 10 in the arcade, Syntagma, tel. 01/363–7046. No credit cards. Closed Sun. Lunch only (11–5).*

$$ Kaldera. Island specialties here include Chios *tsiro* salad (made with small, marinated fish resembling anchovies), *fava* dip (mashed chickpeas with pepper and tomato) from Santorini, and hot mussels in mustard sauce from Skopelos. That's just for starters: If you can manage an entrée, try the *makaronada thalassina* (pasta with a jumble of crab, shrimp, and mussels) or the day's catch. *Poseidonos 54, Palio Faliro, tel. 01/982–9647. Weekend reservations advised. AE, DC, MC, V.*

$$ Kostoyiannis. One of the oldest and most popular tavernas in the area, located behind the Archaeological Museum, this authentic establishment has an impressively wide range of Greek dishes—including excellent shrimp salads, stuffed mussels, rabbit *stifado* (a stew), and sautéed brains. *Zaimi 37, Exarchia, tel. 01/821–2496. Summer reservations advised. No credit cards. Closed Sun. and Aug. No lunch.*

$$ Socrates' Prison. Amiable owner Socrates declares, "This is my prison; I'm here every day." He eschews run-of-the-mill taverna fare in lieu of his own creations: pork rolls stuffed with carrots and celery in lemon sauce, lamb with garlic and mushrooms, zucchini with ham and bacon topped with béchamel, and the house salad—dill, carrots, olives, and eggs. It's ideal for a late dinner after a show at the nearby Herod Atticus theater. *Mitseon 20, Makriyanni, tel. 01/922–3434. Weekend reservations advised. V. Closed Sun. and latter half of Aug. No lunch.*

$$ ★ Vlassis. Relying on recipes from Thrace, Roumeli, Thessaly, and the islands, the cooks here whip up Greek home cooking in generous portions. Order several appetizers for a meal: Musts are the fava dip and the octopus stifado, tender and sweet with lots of onions. Also good are the kebabs, oven-baked pork, and *katsiki ladorigani* (goat with oil and oregano). For dessert, the *galaktobouriko* (custard in phyllo) is delicious. In summer, the restaurant moves to the resort area of Porto Karras. *Armatolon and Klefton 20, Ambelokipi, tel. 01/642–5337. Reservations advised. No credit cards. Closed Sun. and July–Sept. No lunch.*

$$ Xynos. Enter a time warp in this Plaka taverna: Athens in the '50s. Nothing's changed much since then, including the excellent food. Start with the classic stuffed grape leaves, then move on to cooked dishes like lamb *yiouvetsi,* made with tiny noodles called *kritharakia,* and *tsoutsoukakia,* spicy meat patties laced with cinnamon. Roving musicians charm the crowd of regulars as they croon ballads of yesteryear. *Aggelou Geronta 4, Plaka (entrance down walkway next to kafenion Glikis), tel. 01/322–1065. Reservations advised. No credit cards. Closed weekends and part of July. No lunch.*

$ Karavitis. A neighborhood favorite, this taverna near the Olympic Stadium has outdoor garden seating and a winter dining room decorated with huge wine casks. The classic Greek cuisine is well prepared, including pungent *tzatziki* (yogurt-garlic dip), *bekri meze* (lamb chunks in a spicy red sauce), and *stamnaki* (beef baked in a clay pot). *Arktinou 35 and Pausaniou 4, Pangrati, tel. 01/721–5155. No credit cards. Closed a few days around Greek Easter. No lunch.*

$ Leuka. Start an evening of barhopping in Exarchia at this humble taverna that serves all the Greek classics. The grill offers souvlakia, tender lamb ribs, and pork chops sprinkled with oregano. Appetizers are numerous—fava, garlicky lamb livers, marinated black-eyed peas, delicious beans caled *gigantes,* and grilled green peppers. *Mavromichalis 121, Exarchia, tel. 01/361–4038. No credit cards. Closed Sun. and 3 wks in Aug. No lunch.*

$ **O Platanos.** This is one of the oldest tavernas in the area, with a shady
★ courtyard for outdoor dining. Don't miss the oven-baked potatoes, the
roast lamb, and the exceptionally cheap but delicious barrel retsina.
Although the place is extremely friendly, not much English is spoken.
Diogenous 4, Plaka, tel. 01/322–0666. No credit cards. Closed Sun.

$ **Sigalas.** Run by the Bairaktaris family for more than a century, this is
★ the best place to eat in Monastiraki Square. Go to the window case to
view the day's magirefta—beef *kokkinisto* in red sauce, tsoutsoukakia
spiked with clove and cinnamon—or sample the gyro platter. Appetizers include small cheese pies with sesame seeds, tender mountain
greens, and fried zucchini with garlicky dip. *Platia Monastiraki 2,
Monastiraki, tel. 01/321–3036. No credit cards.*

$ **Vasilenas.** Come here ravenously hungry with friends, so you can do
★ justice to the set menu of 16 dishes. Zesty shrimp yiouvetsi and prawn
croquettes are two standouts, as is the dessert called *tiganites,* a sort
of fried bread filled with walnuts. *Etolikou 72, Agia Sofia, Piraeus, tel.
01/461–2457. Weekend and group reservations required. No credit
cards. Closed Sun. and 3 wks in Aug. No lunch.*

Lodging

It's always advisable to reserve a room ahead. Both traditional and modern hotels can be found in the center of town and out along the sea-
coast toward the airport. Modern hotels are more likely to be
air-conditioned in summer, but in winter, look for double-glazed windows; the center of Athens can be so noisy that it's hard to sleep. Except where noted, breakfast is not included in the rate, though it is often
provided—sometimes in the form of a lavish buffet. For details and
price-category definitions, *see* Lodging *in* Staying in Greece, *above.*

$$$$ **Andromeda Athens Hotel.** Athens's newest luxury hotel caters to business travelers. The spacious rooms have a salmon color scheme, with
quilted headboards, wall-to-wall carpeting, minibars, and TVs (computers and fax machines are available on request). The hotel is on a
quiet street near the U.S. Embassy, and the bedrooms have double-glazed
windows. The White Elephant Polynesian restaurant is excellent. *Tim-
oleondos Vassou 22, Mavili Sq., 11521, tel. 01/643–7302 through
01/643–7304, fax 01/646–6361. 23 rooms with bath, 4 suites, 3
penthouses. Facilities: 2 restaurants, meeting rooms, secretarial services,
convention space. AE, DC, MC, V.*

$$$$ **Athenaeum Inter-Continental.** The plush Inter-Continental has a marble atrium lobby that displays a private art collection. Its spacious rooms
have sitting areas and marble bathrooms; ask for one with an Acropolis view. Except for the eighth and ninth floors, which will have been
renovated by November 1995, all floors were recently redone. In the
morning a shuttle takes guests to the airport, and the rest of the day
until 9:30 PM it travels hourly between the hotel and Syntagma Square,
15 minutes away. *89–93 Syngrou Ave., Neos Kosmos, 11745, tel.
01/902–3666, fax 01/924–3011. 520 rooms with bath, 38 suites. Facilities: 3 restaurants, 2 bars, health club, outdoor pool, secretarial services, meeting rooms. AE, DC, MC, V.*

$$$$ **Athens Hilton.** A 200-year-old olive tree with a Turkish cannonball in
its branches stands near what is still one of the city's top hotels after
nearly 30 years. It is about a 20-minute walk to Syntagma, but a shuttle takes guests downtown and to the airport. The spacious rooms all
have balconies and double-glazed windows, as well as fine views of either the Acropolis or Mt. Ymittos. The executive floor has private check-
in and checkout, business facilities, and a private lounge. *Vasilissis Sofias
46, 11528, tel. 01/725–0201, fax 01/725–3110. 434 rooms with*

bath, 19 suites. Facilities: 3 restaurants, 2 bars, outdoor pool, sauna, health club, massage, bank, meeting rooms. AE, DC, MC, V.

$$$$ **Grande Bretagne.** The G. B., as it is known, is centrally located on Syntagma Square. An internationally famous landmark and the hub of Athenian social life, this distinguished hotel had a face-lift in 1992. Ask for an inside room overlooking the courtyard to escape the noise of the traffic, or try one of the coveted Syntagma rooms with large balconies and Acropolis views. *Syntagma Square, 10563, tel. 01/331–4444, fax 01/322–8034. 341 rooms with bath, 23 suites. Facilities: restaurant, 2 bars, lounge, meeting rooms. AE, DC, MC, V.*

$$$$ **St. George Lycabettus.** High on Mt. Lycabettus in upscale Kolonaki, this hotel has a splendid view. Getting there, however, involves a steep short walk or a ride up (remember, taxis are inexpensive). In 1992 plush new rooms and suites were added, and older rooms were freshened up in late 1994. Le Grand Balcon, a two-tier rooftop restaurant, has good food, a terrace, and a wonderful view. There's also an attractive ground-floor bistro. Continental breakfast is included in the price. *Kleomenous 2, Kolonaki, 10675, tel. 01/729–0711, fax 01/724–7610 or 01/729–0439. 152 rooms with bath, 10 suites. Facilities: 2 restaurants, bar, outdoor pool, roof garden. AE, DC, MC, V.*

$$$ **Electra Palace.** At the edge of Plaka, this hotel offers cozy rooms in warm hues—with TVs, hair dryers, balconies, and minibars—for comparatively low prices. Rooms from the fifth floor up are smaller but have bigger balconies; all were recently renovated. The best feature, however, is the rooftop pool, where you can spend hours sunning, sipping a cool drink, and gazing at the nearby Acropolis. *Nikodimou 18, Plaka, 10557, tel. 01/324–1401 through 01/324–1407, fax 01/324–1875. 101 rooms with bath, 5 suites. Facilities: restaurant, bar, pool, meeting rooms. AE, DC, MC, V.*

$$$ **Novotel Athenes.** Although not central, this hotel is just a 10-minute walk to the rail station or the national museum. One of the city's better values, it has an elegant lobby and quiet rooms with sofas, minibars and TVs. The rooftop pool is beside a Greek restaurant from which, in summer, you can watch the sun set behind the Acropolis. *M. Voda 4–8, Vathis Sq., 10439, tel. 01/825–0422, fax 01/883–7816. 190 rooms with bath, 5 suites. Facilities: 2 restaurants, bar, pool, meeting rooms. AE, DC, MC, V.*

$$ **Acropolis View Hotel.** This hotel in a quiet neighborhood below the
★ Acropolis has agreeable rooms, some with Parthenon views; the first, second, and fourth floors were recently renovated. Staff members in the homey lobby are efficient and friendly, and major sights lie a stone's throw away. American breakfast (cornflakes, egg, ham, cheese) is included in the price. *Webster 10, Acropolis, 11742, tel. 01/921–7303 through 01/921–7305, fax 01/923–0705. 32 rooms with bath. Facilities: bar (summer), roof garden, air-conditioning. AE, MC.*

$$ **Astor.** The no-frills Astor is a good choice if you want to stay very close to Syntagma Square and enjoy the standard amenities—TV, air-conditioning, room service—without paying a fortune. In 1995 new air-conditioning and elevators were installed, and rooms were outfitted with more modern furniture. If possible, request a room on the sixth floor and up for a memorable view of the Acropolis. Continental breakfast is included in the price. *Karageorgi Servias 16, Syntagma, 10562, tel. 01/325–5111, fax 01/325–5115. 131 rooms with bath. Facilities: restaurant, bar, air-conditioning. AE, DC, V.*

$$ **Austria.** This small, unpretentious hotel on Filopappou Hill, opposite the Acropolis, is ideal as a base for exploring the heart of ancient Athens. Austria has no restaurant, but it is at the bottom of the price range and is well worth considering. Continental breakfast is included in the quoted rate but is not required (700 dr. per person). *Mouson 7, Filopappou, 11742, tel. 01/923–5151, fax 01/924–7350. 38 rooms with bath. Facilities: air-conditioning, breakfast room. AE, DC, MC, V.*

$$ Plaka Hotel. Convenient for sightseeing and the Monastiraki Square metro, this hotel has a roof garden with a view to the Parthenon. Double-glazed windows cut down the noise; the fifth and sixth floors are the quietest. All rooms have TV and are simply furnished; those in back have Acropolis views. *Kapnikareas 7, Plaka, 10556, tel. 01/322–2096 through 01/322–2098, fax 01/322–2412. 67 rooms with bath. Facilities: air-conditioning. AE, DC, MC, V.*

$$ President. Perhaps the most inexpensive A-class hotel in Athens, the President is a favorite with athletic teams and tourist groups. The staff is helpful, and the rooms, though unexceptional, are quiet, air-conditioned, and have city views (the Acropolis is visible from the sixth floor and up). Taxis stop often at the hotel, and there are trolley and bus stops nearby for the 20-minute journey to the center. Continental breakfast is included in the price. *Kifissias 43, Ambelokipi, 11523, tel. 01/692–4600, fax 01/692–4968. 513 rooms with bath. Facilities: restaurant, grill, bar, outdoor roof pool. AE, DC, MC, V.*

$ Acropolis House. This landmark family-run villa in Plaka is popular with visiting students and faculty. Note Belle Epoque accents such as the painting behind the reception desk. Although the decor may be somewhat cluttered and the wallpaper elderly, clients feel the hotel's nurturing service and friendly atmosphere more than compensate. *Kodrou 6–8, Plaka, 10558, tel. 01/322–2344 or 01/322–6241, fax 01/324–4143. 23 rooms, 20 with bath. Facilities: TV room. V.*

$ Aphrodite Hotel. Near Syntagma and perfectly comfortable, the Aphrodite has quiet and tidy, if rather spare, rooms. With all the facilities of more costly hotels, it offers excellent value, with rates at the low end of the category. The gleaming white marble lobby ends in a bar, where guests often relax in the evenings. *Apollonos 21, Syntagma, 10557, tel. 01/323–4357 through 01/323–4359, fax 01/322–5244. 84 rooms with bath. Facilities: bar, air-conditioning. AE, DC, MC, V.*

$ Art Gallery Pension. On a quiet side street near the Acropolis, this
★ friendly place, much prized by visiting students and single travelers, draws a congenial crowd. The handsome house has an old-fashioned look with family paintings on the muted white walls, comfortable beds, hardwood floors, and overhead fans to make up for the lack of air-conditioning. Most rooms have balconies with views of Filopappou or the Acropolis. *Erecthiou 5, Koukaki, 11742, tel. 01/923–8376, fax 01/923–3025. 21 rooms with bath. Facilities: bar. No credit cards. Closed Nov.–Feb.*

$ Attalos Hotel. The market area, where the Attalos is located, is full of life and color by day, but deserted at night. The hotel has an exceptionally fine view of the Acropolis and Mt. Lycabettus. Try to get a room on the fifth or sixth floor or in the rear, where the street noise is less. Half of the rooms have air-conditioning. *Athinas 29, Psiri, 10554, tel. 01/321–2801 through 01/231–2803, fax 01/324–3124. 80 rooms with bath. Facilities: bar, roof garden (summer only) V.*

$ Erechtheon. This quiet budget hotel is close to the ancient sites, the metro, and the many bars and restaurants of the Thission district. Rooms have carpeting, double-glazed windows, and, except for the singles, an Acropolis view; the best are the corner rooms with balconies. Half are air-conditioned. *Flamarion 8, Thission, 11851, tel. 01/345–9606 or 01/345–9626, fax 01/346–2756. 22 rooms with bath. Facilities: TV room. AE, MC, V.*

$ Marble House. This popular pension, in a cul-de-sac about 15 minutes' walk from the Acropolis, has a steady, satisfied clientele—even in winter, when it offers low monthly room rates. Rooms are quiet, with ceiling fans and basic furniture. The international staff is always willing to help out, and the courtyard is a lovely place to relax. Take Trolleys 1, 5, or 9 from Syntagma and get off at the Zinni stop. *A. Zinni 35, Koukaki, 11741, tel. 01/923–4058 or 01/922–6461. 16 rooms, 12 with bath. Facilities: breakfast room. No credit cards.*

The Arts

The **Athens Festival** runs from late June through September and includes concerts, recitals, opera, ballet, folk dancing, and drama. Performances are in various locations, including the open-air theater of Herod Atticus at the foot of the Acropolis, nearby Filopappou Hill, and Mt. Lycabettus. Tickets are available a few days before the performance from the festival box office in the arcade at Stadiou 4 (tel. 01/322–1459). Admission ranges from 1,500 dr. to 10,000 dr.

Though rather corny, the **sound-and-light** shows showcase the Acropolis with dramatic lighting and a brief narrated history. Performances are given nightly from April through October, in English, at 9 PM (the time is subject to change), and admission is 1,000 dr. The entrance is on Dionysiou Areopagitou, opposite the Acropolis.

The lively Dora Stratou Troupe performs Greek and Cypriot **folk dances** at its theater atop Filopappou Hill from mid-May through mid-September. Daily performances begin at 10:15 PM; there are also 8:15 PM shows on Wednesday and Sunday. Tickets, which range from 1,900 to 2,200 dr. (1,200 dr. for students; free for children under 7), can be purchased at the box office before the show. For information, call the theater at 01/921–4650 or the troupe's offices at 01/324–4395.

Cultural activity has improved enormously with the opening in 1991 of the **Megaron Athens Concert Hall** (tel. 01/728–2333), with two auditoriums equipped with state-of-the-art acoustics. Daily listings are published year-round in *The Athens News,* available in hotels and at newsstands. Both it and the weeklies *Athenscope* and *Greek News* list concerts, exhibitions, and showings of films in English.

Concerts
Concerts are given September through June at the Megaron by Greek and world-class international orchestras. Information and tickets are available from the Megaron (Vasilissis Sofias and Kokkali, tel. 01/728–2333, weekdays 10–4), next to the U.S. embassy. Prices range from 2,000 dr. to 20,000 dr, with lower rates for students and children. Tickets go on sale a few weeks in advance but popular events sell out within hours. On the first day of sales, they can be purchased by credit card in person at the Megaron; sales begin at 8 AM, but try to arrive an hour before. Tickets remaining the next day may be purchased by phone with a credit card. From the second day on, tickets are also sold at the Megaron's downtown box office in the arcade at Stadiou 4.

Opera
The **Lyriki Skini Opera Company** has a winter season (Oct.–May) and a small—not very good—ballet season at the Olympia Theater (Akademias 59, tel. 01/361–2461). In summer they perform at the Herod Atticus theater. The best seats cost about 7,000 dr.

Films
Almost all cinemas now show foreign films; *The Athens News, Athenscope,* and *Greek News* list them in English. Downtown cinemas are the most comfortable and best equipped. Near Syntagma try the **Astor** (Stadiou 28, tel. 01/323–1297) or the **Apollon** (Stadiou 19, tel. 01/323–

6811); near Omonia, the **Ideal** (Panepistimiou 46, tel. 01/362–6720) has the best seats in Athens. Unless they have air-conditioning, most cinemas close June–September, giving way to wonderful outdoor movie theaters, such as the **Thission** (Pavlou 7, tel. 01/342–0864 or 01/347–0980), where you have a view of the Acropolis as a backdrop, and **Cine Paris** (Kidathineon 22, tel. 01/322–2071) in Plaka. At both, the films change every few days, and you can order drinks from the bar during the screening.

Nightlife

Athens has an active nightlife; one way to get a taste is to take an "Athens by Night" guided tour, which can be arranged for you by any good travel agent (*see* Important Addresses and Numbers, *above*). If you want to go on your own, try a *bouzoukia* (a club with live bouzouki music) or a taverna with a floor show. Tavernas with floor shows are concentrated in Plaka.

Be forewarned that you will have to pay for an overpriced, second-rate meal at most places. At the bouzoukia, there is usually a per-person minimum or a prix-fixe menu; a bottle of whiskey costs about 24,000 dr.–29.000 dr. Ask your hotel for recommendations, and check ahead for summer closings.

Bars
Balthazar (Tsoha 27, Ambelokipi, tel. 01/644–1215), in a neoclassical house, has a lush garden courtyard where Athenians come to escape the summer heat.

Café Parastasi (Valtetsiou 15 at Ippokratous, Exarchia, tel. 01/645–0166) offers poetry readings, concerts, and philosophy lectures. There is a 2,500 dr. minimum per person during performances.

In the gallery-bar **Ileana Tounda** (Armatolon and Klefton 48, tel. 01/643–9466, Ambelokipi, closed Aug.), diners and drinkers will enjoy the modern paintings, live music, and beautiful people.

Stavlos (Hraklidou 10, Thission, tel. 01/345–2502), in the former royal stables, often features live music, art shows, and Sunday afternoon jazz in its restaurant-bar-gallery complex.

Strofilia (Karitsi 7, Kolokotronis Square, tel. 01/323–4803, closed May–Aug.) is one of the city's few wine bars; it offers vintages from about 50 small Greek producers, about 20 of them by the glass.

Bouzoukias
Diogenes Palace (Syngrou 259, Nea Smyrni, tel. 01/942–4267) is currently the "in" place with Athenians who want to hear Greece's most popular singers, such as Leftheris Pantazis, Iannis Parios, and Konstantina; it's also the most expensive.

Decadence reigns at **Posidonio** (Posidonios 18, Elliniko, tel. 01/894–1033) as diners dance the seductive *tsifteteli* with enthusiasm and order flower vendors to shower gardenias on their favorite singers.

Rembetika Clubs
Rembetika, the blues sung by Asia Minor refugees who came to Greece in the 1920s, still enthralls Greeks. At **Anifori** (Vas. Georgiou 47, Pasalimani, Piraeus, tel. 01/411–5819) a small upstairs club, the band usually starts off slowly, but by 1 AM, they're wailing to a packed dance floor. You don't need to order a complete dinner; a bottle of wine or drinks will do.

Amid the bars of Exarchia, **Frangosyriani** (Arachovis 57, Exarchia, tel. 01/380–0693) has a band specializing in the songs of rembetika great

Markos Vamvakaris. On weekends there is a 4,000 dr. minimum per person; 2,000 dr. on weekdays.

Tavernas

At **Stamatopoulou Palia Plakiotiki Taverna** (Lysiou 26, tel. 01/322–8722), in a 1822 Plaka house, you'll find good food along with an acoustic band of three guitars, bouzouki, and accordion playing old Athenian songs. In summer the show moves to a cool garden.

THE PELOPONNESE

Suspended from the mainland of Greece like a large leaf, with the Isthmus of Corinth as its stem, the ancient land of Pelops offers beautiful scenery—rocky coasts, sandy beaches, and mountains—and a fascinating variety of ruins: temples, theaters, mosques, churches, palaces, and medieval castles built by crusaders.

Legend and history meet in Mycenae, where Agamemnon, Elektra, and Orestes played out their grim family tragedy. This city dominated the entire area from the 18th to the 12th century BC, and may even have conquered Minoan Crete. According to Greek mythology, Paris, son of the king of Troy, abducted the beautiful Helen, wife of Menelaus, the king of Sparta. Agamemnon, the king of Mycenae, was Menelaus's brother. This led to the Trojan War and the defeat of Troy. The story of the war is told in Homer's *Iliad*. Following Heinrich Schliemann's discoveries of gold-filled graves and a royal palace during excavations in 1874, Mycenae has become a world-class archaeological site and, of all the sites in the Peloponnese, is most worthy of a visit.

Sparta, once a powerful city-state, is today, unfortunately, devoid of charm or character. Like Corinth, once the largest, richest, and most pleasure-loving city of ancient Greece, Sparta now appears sadly lifeless and unattractive. Neither of these modern townships seems to bear any relation to their original vibrancy; Corinth, in fact, was destroyed by earthquakes in 1858 and 1928, and each time experienced a more practical and banal reconstruction, the last of which left it 5 kilometers (3 miles) from its original site.

During the Middle Ages, the Peloponnese was conquered by leaders of the Fourth Crusade and ruled as a feudal state by French and Italian nobles. It formed the cornerstone of Latin (Christian) power in the eastern Mediterranean during the 13th and 14th centuries. In 1821, the Peloponnese played a key role in the Greek War of Independence. Nauplion was, for a short time during the 1800s, the capital of Greece. Among the region's many contributions to humanity are the Olympic Games, begun in 776 BC in Olympia.

Getting Around

The best way to see all the important sights of the Peloponnese at your own pace is by car. If you take the car ferry from Italy to Patras, capital of the Peloponnese, or if you rent a car in Patras, you can visit the area on the way to Athens. Otherwise, your tour will begin in Athens (*see* Exploring the Peloponnese, *below*).

Guided Tours

CHAT Tours (4 Stadiou, Athens, tel. 01/322–2886) and **Key Tours** (Kallirois 4, Athens, tel. 01/923–3166) both organize tours in the Peloponnese. A four-day tour of the Peloponnese and Delphi, including the sites, a qualified guide, and half-board accommodations at first-

Peloponnese

class hotels, costs around 92,000 dr. A two-day tour, again including accommodations, to Corinth, Mycenae, and Epidauros, will cost around 27,500 dr. A six-day grand tour of the Peloponnese costs around 167,000 dr.

Tourist Information

In **Patras,** visit the Greek National Tourist Organization (Iroon Polytechniou 110, Glyfada, tel. 061/653–358) or the American Express representative at Albatros Travel (Othonos 48, tel. 061/220–993); Albatros can assist with all travel arrangements. The Tourist Police are in the welcome station on the harbor (Norman-Iroon Politechniou, tel. 061/651–833, 061/651–893, or 061/652–502). The Olympic Airlines office is at Ayios Andreou 16 (tel. 061/222–901). The Automobile and Touring Club of Greece (ELPA) has an office at Patroon Athinon 18 in Patras (tel. 061/425–411 and 061/426–416). In **Olympia** you'll find the Municipal Tourist Office at Kondili 75 (tel. 0624/23–100). The Tourist Police are at Spiliopoulou 5 (tel. 0624/22–550). **Nauplion** also has a Municipal Tourist Office (25th Martiou across from OTE, tel. 0752/24–444); its Tourist Police are at Fotamara 16 (tel. 0752/28–131).

Exploring the Peloponnese

Daphni

Eleven kilometers (7 miles) northwest of Athens, after you have passed the last houses of the Athenian urban sprawl, you'll come to the 6th-century monastery of **Daphni.** It was sacked in 1205 by Frankish crusaders, who later installed Cistercian monks from Burgundy to rebuild it. The monastery has superb mosaics. *End of Iera Odos, tel. 01/581–1558. Admission: 800 dr. Open daily 8:30–2:45.*

Eleusis

Descending from Daphni to the sea, you face the narrow straits of Salamis, where the Persian fleet of Xerxes was defeated in 480 BC by Athens and its allies. Shortly beyond are the ruins of **Eleusis,** site of antiquity's most important harvest celebrations, the Eleusinian Mysteries, where participants underwent rites commemorating the gift of corn cultivation given by Demeter, goddess of grain. Now the area is unattractive, surrounded by factories and their pollution, and there is almost nothing left of the ancient Eleusis but a few fallen pillars and overgrown pathways. Admission to the site includes entrance to a small museum. *Iera Odos 2, tel. 01/554–6019. Admission: 500 dr. Open Tues.–Sun. 8:30–3.*

Corinth

When you cross the **Corinth Canal,** about 84 kilometers (52 miles) from Athens, you will have entered the **Peloponnese.** Modern **Corinth** lies by the sea; the ancient Greek city stood higher up. An important ruin is the **Doric Temple of Apollo,** built during the 6th century BC and one of the few buildings that still stood when Julius Caesar decided to restore Corinth. In AD 51, St. Paul fulminated against the sacred prostitutes who served Aphrodite on the **Acrocorinth,** the peak behind the ancient city. A museum beside the ruins contains finds from the excavations. *Tel. 0741/31–207. Admission: 1,200 dr. Open daily 8–7 (8:45–3 in winter).*

Drive from the square of ancient Corinth or hire a taxi to take you to the **Fort of Acrocorinth,** then continue on to explore the imposing Franco-Turkish fortifications. *Tel. 0741/31–207. Admission: 500 dr. Open daily 8:30–5.*

Mycenae

Mycenae, 44 kilometers (28 miles) from Corinth, was the fabulous stronghold of the Achaean kings of the 13th century BC. Destroyed in 468 BC, it was forgotten until 1874 when German archaeologist Heinrich Schliemann, who discovered the ruins of ancient Troy, uncovered the remains of this ancient fortress city. Mycenae was the seat of the doomed House of Atreus—of King Agamemnon and his wife, Clytemnestra (sister of Helen of Troy), and of their tragic children, Orestes and Elektra. When Schliemann uncovered six shaft graves (so named because the kings were buried standing up) of the royal circle, he was certain that one was the tomb of Agamemnon. The gold masks and diadems, daggers, jewelry, and other treasures found in the graves are now in the National Archaeological Museum in Athens; the new local museum is dedicated to archaeological studies. Along with the graves, you'll find the astounding beehive tombs built into the hillsides outside the reconstructed wall, the **Lion Gate,** dating to 1250 BC, and the castle ruins crowning the bleak hill, all remnants of the first great civilization in continental Europe. The tombs, the acropolis, the palace, and the museum can all be explored for the cost of admission. *Tel. 0751/76–585. Admission: 1,500 dr. Open weekdays 8–7 (8–5 in winter), weekends and holidays 8–3.*

Argos

Moving south, 11 kilometers (7 miles) from Mycenae, you'll pass **Argos,** prominent during the 8th century BC, and the Cyclopean ramparts (huge, irregular stones) of **Tiryns.** One version of the legend has Tiryns as the birthplace of Hercules, but the present remains, including the walls, date mostly from the 13th century BC when Tiryns was one of the most important Mycenaean cities.

Nauplion

Farther on is **Nauplion**, a picturesque town below the Venetian fortifications. Modern Greece's first king lived for a year or two within the
walls of the higher fortress when Nauplion was capital of Greece. His
courtiers had to climb 999 steps to reach him; you can still climb the
long staircase or drive up to the **fortress.** *Tel. 0752/28–036. Admission: 800 dr. Open weekdays 8–7 (8–4:45 in winter), weekends and
holidays 8:30–2:45.*

The **Venetian naval arsenal** on the town square houses a museum with
Mycenaean finds, including a 7th-century BC gorgon mask from Tiryns.
Tel. 0752/27–502. Admission: 500 dr. Open Tues.–Sun. 8:30–3.

Epidauros

Epidauros, 24 kilometers (15 miles) east of Nauplion, was the sanctuary of Asklepios, the Greek god of healing. You can visit the foundations of the temples and ancient hospital. The most important site is
the ancient open-air theater, which seats 14,000. In summer, during
the **Epidauros Festival,** ancient Greek plays are staged here (*see* The
Arts, *below*). The theater merits a visit at any time of year. The acoustics are so good that you can sit in the top row and hear a whisper on
stage. *Tel. 0753/22–009. Admission: 1,500 dr. Theater open weekdays
7:30–7 (7:30–5 in winter), weekends and holidays 8:30–7 (8:30–3
in winter). Museum open same hours except Mon. 12:30–7 (10:30–
7 in winter).*

Olympia

From here you can return to Athens along the coast, a lovely drive, or
continue on to **Olympia** by way of the rugged mountains of Arcadia.
The site of ancient Olympia lies a few kilometers from the sea, northwest of **Megalopolis,** where a huge assembly hall was built to hold the
Ten Thousand representatives of the Arcadian League. The first Olympic
Games were held in Olympia in 776 BC and continued to be celebrated
every four years until AD 393, when the Roman emperor Theodosius
I, with his Christian sensibility, banned these "pagan rites." Women
were excluded from watching the games under penalty of death, although no one was ever executed. They always held their own games
a few weeks prior. Archaeologists still uncover statues and votive offerings among the pine trees surrounding **Olympic Stadium** and the imposing **ruins of the temples of Zeus and Hera** within the sacred precinct.
*Stadium tel. 0624/22–517, museum tel. 0624/22–742. Admission: 1,200
dr. museum; 1,200 dr. stadium. Stadium open weekdays 7:30–7 (7:30–
5 in winter), weekends and holidays 8:30–3. Museum open same
hours except Mon. 11–7 (11–5 in winter).*

The **International Olympic Academy,** 6.4 kilometers (4 miles) east,
houses the **Museum of the Olympic Games,** with its collection of commemorative postage stamps and mementos. *Tel. 0624/22–544. Admission: 500 dr. Open weekdays 8–3:30, weekends 9–4:30.*

Patras

North of Olympia, 122 kilometers (76 miles) away, is **Patras,** the
third-largest city in Greece, its main western port, and the hub of the
business world in the Peloponnese. Walk up to the **Byzantine kastro,**
built on the site of the ancient acropolis, to take a look at the fine view
along the coast. The **Cathedral of St. Andrew's,** reputedly the largest
in Greece and built on the site of the crucifixion of St. Andrew, is also
worth exploring. Its treasure is the saint's silver-mounted skull, returned
to Patras in 1964 after 500 years in St. Peter's, Rome. The cathedral
is on the far west side of the harbor at the end of Ayios Andreou. Apart

from the kastro and the cathedral, there is little of particular interest here. The city's prettiest features are its arcaded streets and its squares, surrounded by neoclassical buildings.

The shortest route back to Athens follows the National Road along the southern shore of the Gulf of Corinth, an exceptionally beautiful drive. You could instead cross the entrance to the gulf and visit Delphi (*see* Exploring Mainland Greece, *below*) on your way back to Athens.

Dining and Lodging

Many of the hotels in the Peloponnese have good dining rooms, so try these as well as the local tavernas. For details and price-category definitions, *see* Dining and Lodging *in* Staying in Greece, *above*.

Nauplion
DINING

O Arapakos. Settle in on the waterfront and start with grilled octopus; then move on to *giouvetsi ton arapi* (lamb with potatoes, tomatoes, carrots, and eggplant) or *arnaki exohiko* (lamb stuffed with feta and potatoes). Fresh fish is also available, including charcoal-grilled sea bream. *Bouboulinas 81, tel. 0752/27–675. V. $$*

Savouras. Fresh seafood is served in this unpretentious taverna overlooking the bay; it is generally regarded as one of the area's best fish restaurants. Specialties are red mullet and dorado. *Bouboulinas 79, tel. 0752/27–704. No credit cards. $$*

Karamanlis. This simple taverna near the courthouse is crowded at lunch with civil servants who come for its tasty though limited number of magirefta. The light fish soup makes a good appetizer, followed by *yiouvelakia* (meat-rice balls) with egg-lemon sauce, baked potatoes, wild greens, and barrel wine. Fresh fish is also available at very good prices. *Bouboulinas 1, tel. 0752/27–668. No credit cards. $*

★ **Ta Fanaria.** Sit at one of the tables in the narrow alley beside the restaurant and ask what's best that night. The restaurant is known for its *ladera*, vegetables cooked in olive oil, but equally delicious are the charcoal-grilled lamb ribs, lamb baked with vegetables like okra or green beans, and the imam. *Staikopoulos 13, tel. 0752/27–141. V. $*

LODGING

★ **Candia House.** This beautifully decorated hotel 17 kilometers (10½ miles) south of Nauplion on Candia Beach weds good taste with comfort. Fresh flowers, antiques, paintings by Greek artists, and handcrafted mirrors are just some of the special touches. All suites have balconies, sitting rooms, television, and a refrigerator. Buffet breakfast is included in the price. *Candia-Irion, 21100, tel. 0752/94–060 through 0752/94–063, fax 0752/94–480. 10 suites. Facilities: restaurant, gym, pool, hydromassage, game room. AE, DC, MC, V. $$$$*

Xenia Palace. Compulsory half board boosts the price and some of the furniture could use reupholstering, but this hotel has an unbeatable location on the ruins of the Frankish fortification atop Acronauplia. Modern art adorns the lobby, the relatively spacious rooms have exposed stonework and marble bathrooms, and the bougainvillea-framed pool overlooks the harbor. An elevator tunneled through the rock takes you to the town below. *Acronauplia, 21100, tel. 0752/28–981 through 0752/28–985, fax 0752/28–783. 48 rooms with bath, 3 suites, 50 bungalows (the latter only available weekends during Nov.–Feb.) Facilities: restaurant, bar, pool. AE, MC, V. $$$$*

Amalia. The attractive Amalia occupies a fine neoclassical building in large gardens 3 kilometers (2 miles) outside town, on the sea, near ancient Tiryns. The public rooms are spacious and comfortable, the service attentive, and the swimming pool very inviting. With a beach nearby, this makes the ideal base for a relaxing stay, and a buffet breakfast is included in the price. *National Road to Argos outside Nauplion, 21100, tel. 0752/24–401, fax 0752/24–400. 171 rooms with bath. Facilities: 3 restaurants, cafeteria, bar, outdoor pool, meeting rooms. AE, DC, MC, V. $$$*

Dioscouri. This family-run hotel above the old town, with a fine view across the gulf of Nauplion, is cool and quiet, and Continental breakfast is included in the price. *Zigomala 6, 21100, tel. 0752/28–550, fax 0752/21–202. 51 rooms with bath. Facilities: restaurant, bar. V. $*

Olympia

DINING

★ **Pete's Den.** Run by a Greek-German couple, this well-known restaurant serves some of the region's finest cooking. You can feast on the appetizers alone, including *saganaki* (baked cheese) flambé with brandy, crisp zucchini pies, *bourekakia* (cheese pastries), and local sausage made with wine and orange peel. Don't pass up the yogurt dessert topped with homemade strawberry syrup. *Stephanopoulou near National Bank of Greece, tel. 0624/22–066. AE, MC, V. Closed Nov.–Feb. No lunch. $$*

Taverna Praxitelous. This taverna offers tasty appetizers: Order the *pikilia* (variety) plate, which includes zucchini fritters, *bourekakia tirolates* (ham and cheese fingers), marinated red peppers, stuffed grape leaves, tzatziki, eggplant dip, and moussaka. The prix-fixe Greek menu includes a variety plate, stifado or a grilled meat, and a pan dessert like baklava. *Spiliopoulou 7, tel. 0624/23–570. V. $*

Thraka. This family-run taverna has a large variety of home-cooked food including *lahanokeftedes* (fried vegetable balls), *arnaki giouvetsi* (lamb with bite-size noodles), and beef stifado made the old-fashioned way, with vinegar and garlic. Desserts are from the family's pastry shop. Off-season, the cook (and family matriarch) will still prepare meals for you; just call. *Main St., tel. 0624/22–575; off-season, 0624/22–475, fax 0624/23–150. AE, DC, MC, V. Closed Dec.–Mar. $*

LODGING

Hotel Europa. Run by the friendly Spiliopoulos family, this Best Western hilltop hotel overlooks ancient Olympia, the mountains of Arcadia, Alfios Valley, and the sea in the distance. Rooms have large beds, flokati rugs, hair dryers, and marble bathrooms. Most face the pool, but try to book one of the six that look onto the archaeological site. Buffet breakfast is included in the price. *Off road to ancient Olympia, at Oikismou Drouba, 27065, tel. 0624/22–650 or 0624/22–700, fax 0624/23–166. 42 rooms with bath. Facilities: restaurant, bar, taverna (summer), tennis court, horseback riding, pool. AE, DC, MC, V. $$$*

Altis. The Altis is conveniently located opposite the old museum and near the archaeological site. The rooms have balconies and plenty of light, and the garden is ideal for enjoying the restaurant's hearty *spesiota* (perch baked with onion). Continental breakfast is included in the price. *Platia Dimarchiou (town hall sq.), 27065, tel. 0624/23–101 and 0624/23–102, fax 0624/22–525. 61 rooms with bath. Facilities: cafeteria-style restaurant, air-conditioning. AE, DC, MC, V. Closed Nov.–Mar. $$*

Apollon. Although the rooms are not exceptional, the wood furnishings and white walls create a cheerful beach bungalow atmosphere. The owner keeps things in good shape, renovating bit by bit every year. The hotel is in the center of the modern town, near the bus and train stations. Buffet breakfast is included in the price. *Douma 13, 27065, tel.*

0624/22–513 or 0624/22–522, fax 0624/23–068. 96 rooms with bath. Facilities: restaurant, rooftop pool. AE, DC, MC, V. $

Pelops. Australian owner Susan Spiliopoulou has taken a standard '60s Greek hotel and decked the rooms in chintz and lace curtains for an old-fashioned feel. Across from the main church, this fairly quiet hotel offers rooms with orthopedic mattresses and telephones; most have a balcony. Guests without a balcony can use those at the end of each floor, complete with café tables, or the vine-shaded terrace. *Varela 2, 27065, tel. 0624/22–543, fax 0624/22–213. 25 rooms with bath. Facilities: restaurant, bar. MC, V. Closed Feb.–Oct. $*

Patras

DINING

Kalypso. In the beach area of Porto Rio about 2 kilometers (1½ miles) from Patras, Kalypso offers fresh grilled red mullet and dorado, its specialty, *mides saganaki* (mussels with fried cheese), and a lemon-fish soup, in addition to grilled meats and the usual Greek magirefta. Top it off with a baked apple with whipped cream. *Posidonios 21, Porto Rio, tel. 061/994–739. Reservations advised. AE, DC, MC, V. $$*

Trikoyia. The Trikoyia family cooks delicious food in its traditional taverna, where a typical menu showcases *kalofaga* (beef baked with ham) and fresh grilled fish. Enjoy the ocean view as you complete your meal with a piece of baklava. *Amalias 46, tel. 061/279–421. AE, DC, MC, V. $$*

Faros. During the day, the owner is out hauling in his catch, which he serves up to locals that night. If it's atmosphere you want, forget it: This is a bare-bones, often noisy place, without a menu or even tablecloths, but it serves the freshest fish at the lowest prices. Nobody speaks English, but all you have to do is point (you pay by weight), round out your meal with a Greek salad, sit back, and enjoy. *Othonos-Amalias 101, tel. 061/336–500. No credit cards. No lunch. $*

LODGING

★ **Porto Rio.** There's a varied selection of rooms and cottages with a wide range of prices at this hotel complex on the sea at Rion, about 8 kilometers (5 miles) from Patras. Some rooms have outstanding views across the narrow entrance to the Gulf of Corinth. American breakfast is included. *National Road, 26500, tel. 061/992—212, fax 061/992–115. 218 rooms with bath, 7 suites, 42 cottages. Facilities: 2 restaurants, 2 outdoor pools, 4 tennis courts, playground, gym, sauna. AE, DC, MC, V. $$$*

Astir. Recently renovated, this large hotel enjoys an excellent location on the waterfront near the center of town. Spacious and pleasant, it looks out on the busy harbor and to the mountains across the gulf. *Ag. Andreou 16, 26223, tel. 061/277–502, fax 061/271–644. 120 rooms with bath (about 80 with TV). Facilities: restaurant, roof garden, bar, outdoor pool, conference rooms, sauna, air-conditioning. AE, DC, V. $$*

Adonis. For its price and convenient location, Adonis has very good rooms, with TV and air-conditioning; all bathrooms were renovated in 1994. Rooms have balconies, many with gulf and Adriatic views. Because the hotel is across from the bus terminal, some rooms may be noisy during the day. The price includes buffet breakfast. *Zaimi and Kapsali 9, tel. 061/226–715 or 061/224–235, fax 061/226–971. 56 rooms with bath. Facilities: bar, air-conditioning. AE, MC, V. $*

The Arts

The **Festival of Ancient Drama** in the theater at Epidauros takes place from mid-July to mid-September, weekends only, at 9 PM. Tickets can be bought either at the theater itself before performances or in advance from the festival box office in Athens (Stadiou 4, tel. 01/322–1459). Patras also stages a lively summer arts festival. Check with the Greek National Tourist Organization (tel. 061/653–358 and 061/653–359) for details. In the several weeks before Lent there are masquerade balls, fireworks, and on the last Sunday the Grand Parade, with entrants competing for the best costume. Buy tickets for seats at the Grand Parade (3,200 dr.) at the Carnival office in the Municipal Cultural Center (Koryllon 1, tel. 061/226–063).

MAINLAND GREECE

The dramatic rocky heights of mainland Greece provide an appropriate setting for man's attempt to approach divinity. The ancient Greeks placed their gods on snowcapped Mt. Olympus and chose the precipitous slopes of Parnassus, "the navel of the universe," as the site for Delphi, their most important religious center. Many centuries later, pious Christians built a great monastery (Hosios Loukas) in a remote mountain valley. Others settled on the rocky mountain peninsula of Athos, the Holy Mountain. Later, devout men established themselves precariously on top of strange, towerlike rocks and, to be closer to God, built monasteries like those at Meteora. In fact, many of mainland Greece's most memorable and interesting sites are closely connected with religion—including the remarkable Byzantine churches of Thessaloniki.

In this land of lonely mountain villages, narrow defiles, and dark woods, bands of *klephts* (a cross between brigands and guerrillas) earned their place in folk history and song during the long centuries of Turkish rule. The women of Souli, one of the mountain strongholds of the klephts, threw themselves dancing and singing over a cliff rather than be captured by the Turks. During the German occupation of World War II, guerrilla bands descended from these same mountains to the valleys and plains to harry and attack the occupying army.

Since Greece joined the EU farmers have flourished, and few villages, even those tucked away in the hills, are still poor and isolated. But despite the arrival of video clubs and discos, the traditional way of life still survives. The mainland Greeks see fewer tourists and have more time for those they do see, hotels are unlikely to be full, and the sights—steep, wooded mountains, cypress trees like candles, narrow gorges, the soaring monasteries of Meteora—are beautiful.

Getting Around

This proposed itinerary begins in Athens. It can be done by public transportation, car, or guided tour. A one-day trip to Delphi is rushed; two days will give you more leisure time. Your best bet is a three-day trip that includes Delphi and Meteora. The five-day tour takes in more remote parts of western Greece, Epirus, and other main sights. A longer trip through the mainland should include Hosios Loukas. Thessaloniki is usually included only in lengthy guided tours of northern Greece. If you don't have a car, you can leave the Delphi–Meteora tour at Trikala, take the train to Thessaloniki, and return to Athens by plane or train. In September, during the Thessaloniki International Trade Fair, make hotel reservations well in advance.

Guided Tours

Travel agencies in Athens with tours of mainland Greece include **American Express** (Ermou 2, tel. 01/324–4975), **CHAT Tours** (Stadiou 4, tel.

01/322–2886), and **Key Tours** (Kallirois 4, tel. 01/923–3166). American Express also has a representative in Thessaloniki at **Memphis Travel** (Nikis 23, tel. 031/222–795, fax 031/281–508). A one-day tour to Delphi, with lunch, costs around 16,500 dr.; without lunch 14,500 dr. A three-day trip to Delphi and Meteora with half board (hotel, breakfast, and lunch or dinner) costs 69,500 dr. A nine-day tour of northern and central Greece, including Delphi, Meteora, Thessaloniki, Philippi, Kavala, Pella, and Vergina costs around 209,000 dr. with half-board accommodations. Athens travel agencies can also arrange a four-day Macedonia tour via plane (about 97,000 dr. and airfare).

Tourist Information

In **Delphi,** visit the Delphi Tourist Office on Vas. Pavlou and Friderikis 12 for helpful service (tel. 0265/82–900); the Tourist Police is at Apollonos 46 (tel. 0265/82–220). At **Kalambaka,** the Tourist Police can be found at Hatzipetrou 10–11 (tel. 0432/22–813). In **Thessaloniki,** visit the Greek National Tourist Organization (Mitropoleos 34 on Platia Aristotelous, tel. 031/222–935, or at the airport, tel. 031/471–170); here, the Tourist Police is at Dodekanissou 4 (tel. 031/254–871) and Taxiarchou 1, Kalamaria (tel. 031/453–223).

Exploring Mainland Greece

Thebes and Livadia

To get from Athens to Delphi, take the National Road toward Thessaloniki and turn off to **Thebes** (Thiva), the birthplace of the legendary Oedipus, who unwittingly fulfilled the prophesy of the Delphic Oracle by slaying his father and marrying his mother. Little now remains of the ancient city. At **Livadia,** 45 kilometers (28 miles) farther along the road, the ruins of a medieval fortress tower above the springs of Lethe (Oblivion) and Mnemosyne (Remembrance). Halfway between Livadia and Delphi is the crossroads where, according to mythology, Oedipus killed his father.

The road to the left leads to a serene upland valley and the **Monastery of Hosios Loukas,** a fine example of Byzantine architecture and decoration. Built during the 11th century to replace the earlier shrine of a local saint, it has some of the world's finest Byzantine mosaics. *Tel. 0267/22–797. Admission: 800 dr. Open daily 8–2 and 4–7 (8–6 in winter).*

Arahova

Back on the road to Delphi, you'll climb a spur of Mt. Parnassus to reach the village of **Arahova,** 32 kilometers (20 miles) from Livadia, known for handmade items in brightly colored wools, especially rugs. From Arahova, a short, spectacular drive down to Delphi will take you across the gorge of the Pleistos. You'll see the twin cliffs called the Phaedriades split by the **Castalian spring,** which gushes with cool, pure water. It was here that pilgrims to the Delphic Oracle came for purification.

Delphi

The ancient Greeks believed that **Delphi** was the center of the universe because two eagles released by the gods at opposite ends of Earth met here. For hundreds of years, the worship of Apollo and the pronouncements of the Oracle here made Delphi the most important religious center of ancient Greece. As you walk up the Sacred Way to the **Temple of Apollo,** the **theater,** and the **stadium,** you'll see Mt. Parnassus above; silver-green olive trees below; and, in the distance, the blue Gulf of Itea. This is one of the most rugged and lonely sites in

Mainland Greece

Greece, and one of the most striking; if you can get to the site in the early morning or evening, avoiding the busloads of tourists, you will feel the power and beauty of the place. You may even see an eagle or two. First excavated in 1892, most of the ruins date from the 5th to the 3rd century BC. *Tel. 0265/82–313. Admission: 1,200 dr. Open Tues.–Fri. 8–7 (7:30–5:30 in winter), Mon. 11–7 (11–5:30 in winter), weekends and holidays 8–3.*

Don't miss the famous bronze charioteer (early 5th century BC) in the **Delphi Museum.** Other interesting and beautiful works of art here include a statue of Antinoüs, Emperor Hadrian's lover; fragments of a 6th-century BC silver-plated bull, the largest example of an ancient statue in precious metal; the stone *omphalos,* representing the navel of the earth; fragments from the site's Sifnian Treasury, depicting scenes from the Trojan War; and the statues of Kleobis and Viton. According to legend, they pulled their mother 50 miles by chariot to the Temple of Hera so she could worship, then died when Hera rewarded them with eternal sleep. It was said of them, "Those whom the gods love die young." *Tel. 0265/82–313. Admission: 1,200 dr. Open Tues.–Fri. 8–7 (7:30–5:30 in winter), Mon. 11–7 (11–5:30 in winter), weekends and holidays 8–3.*

Kalambaka

From Delphi, the road descends in sharp bends past groves of gnarled, ancient olive trees. Continue 17 kilometers (11 miles) to Amfissa and over the Pournaraki (Bralos) Pass to the town of **Lamia.** Follow the road to Karditsa and around the Thessalian plain to Trikala. You will then arrive at **Kalambaka** (139 kilometers, or 86 miles, from Lamia), the base for visits to the monasteries of **Meteora,** which sit atop gigantic rocks that tower almost 1,000 feet above the plain. Monks and supplies once reached the top of the slopes by ladders or baskets. Today steps are cut into the boulders, and some of the monasteries can easily be reached by car. Of the original 24 monasteries, only six can now be visited. Female visitors should wear skirts to the knee, not shorts, and men should wear long pants.

The fortresslike **Varlaam** monastery is easy to reach and has beautiful Byzantine frescoes. To get a better idea of what living in these monasteries was like 300 years ago, climb the steep rock steps to the **Megalo Meteoron,** the largest of the monasteries. Make sure that you allow time for the trek up if it's nearing closing time. The monasteries are all closed during midday. The hours vary from place to place, but they are generally open 9–1 and 3–6, although to complicate matters Varlaam is closed on Friday and Megalo Meteoron on Tuesday. *Tel. 0432/22–277 (Varlaam), tel. 0432/22–278 (Megalo Meteoron). Admission: 400 dr. each.*

Thessaloniki

En route to Thessaloniki, the road east from Trikala crosses the plain of Thessaly (one of Europe's hottest places during the summer) and joins the National Road at Larissa. Eventually you will see Mt. Olympus, Greece's highest mountain. The road runs for 154 kilometers (96 miles) through the valley of Tempe and then goes up the coast to **Thessaloniki**—Greece's second-largest city, its second port after Piraeus, and the capital of northern Greece. It is the cocapital of the country as a whole; as a shopping center it is possibly superior to Athens.

Although Thessaloniki still has some remains from the Roman period, it is best known for its fine Byzantine churches. The city is compact enough for you to see the main sights on foot. Start at the 15th-century grayish **White Tower,** landmark and symbol of Thessaloniki, previously named "Tower of Blood," referring to its use as a prison. Now it houses a museum, with an exhibition on the history and art of Byzantine Thessaloniki, including pottery, mosaics, and ecclesiastical objects. *Pavlou Mela and Nikis, tel. 031/267–832. Admission: 800 dr. Open Mon. 10:30–5, Tues.–Fri. 8–7 (8–5 in winter), weekends 8:30–3.*

Then walk up Pavlou Mela toward Tsimiski, the elegant tree-lined shopping street, and cut across to the green-domed basilica-style church of **Aghia Sophia,** which dates from the 8th century and has beautifully preserved mosaics.

Walk to Egnatia, which partially traces the original Roman road leading from the Adriatic to the Bosphorous. Continue north along the **Roman Agora** (town center) to **Agios Dimitrios,** the principal church. Though it is only a replica of the original 7th-century church that burned down in 1917, it is adorned with many 8th-century mosaics that were in the original building. Follow Aghiou Dimitriou east to **Agios Georgios,** a rotunda built by Roman emperor Galerius as his tomb during the 4th century AD. His successor, Constantine the Great, the first Christian emperor, turned it into a church. If the current restoration has been completed and it's open, have a look at the superb 4th-century mosaics of flowers, birds, and fish.

Return to Egnatia and the **Arch of the Emperor Galerius,** built shortly prior to the rotunda to commemorate the Roman victories of Galerius over forces in Persia, Armenia, and Mesopotamia. A short walk downhill to Tsimiski, where you turn left, will eventually bring you to the **Archaeological Museum.** Among its many beautiful objects are a huge bronze vase and a delicate, gold myrtle wreath from Derveni, as well as gold artifacts from recent excavations of the royal tombs of Vergina, including a gold casket that contains bones thought to be those of Philip

II, father of Alexander the Great. *Platia Hanth, tel. 031/830–538. Admission: 1,500 dr. Open Mon. 10:30–7 (10:30–5 in winter), Tues.–Fri. 8–7 (8–5 in winter), weekends and holidays 8:30–3.*

Dining and Lodging

For details and price-category definitions, *see* Dining and Lodging *in* Staying in Greece, *above.*

Delphi

DINING

Topiki Gefsi. Traditional Greek cuisine, with many local specialties, is what this excellent *mezedopolion* (a place serving appetizers) offers. In winter, warm yourself at the fireplace; in summer, dine on the veranda overlooking Delphi. Especially good are the regional *kokkora krasato* (rooster stewed in wine), pork with celery, *hortopites* (vegetable pies), lamb on the spit, and *mides saganaki* (mussels in fried cheese). *Vas. Pavlou and Friderikis 19, tel. 0265/82–710, fax 0265/82–480. Reservations advised. AE, DC, MC, V. $$–$$$*

Vakhos. From the large veranda, decorated with murals of Bacchus (for whom the restaurant is named), you have a view of the Gulf of Itea; enjoy it with the local retsina, kokkora krasato, vegetable croquettes, souvlakia, and for the adventurous, boiled goat. There are also seven fixed-price menus. *Apollonos 32, tel. 0265/82–448. Closed weekdays Nov.–mid-Mar., except holidays. V. $*

DINING AND LODGING

Kastalia. Fedriades' *(see below)* sister hotel has simple rooms with paintings of the area and views either over Mt. Parnassus or to the Gulf of Itea. The restaurant serves Greek food with a twist; lamb fricassee, for example, has lettuce rather than the typical cabbage. Be sure to sample the local sweet cheese, *formaella*. The price includes Continental breakfast. *Vas. Pavlou and Friderikis 13, 33054, tel. 0265/82–205 through 0265/82–207, fax 0265/82–208. 26 rooms with bath. Facilities: restaurant. AE, DC, MC, V. Closed weekdays Nov.–Mar. $$*

LODGING

★ **Hotel Vouzas.** The hotel sits on the edge of a gorge and has wonderful views from every room. It was renovated in 1991, and rooms now all have air-conditioning and TVs. There's a cozy living room with a fireplace, which fills up on winter weekends with Athenians who come to ski Mt. Parnassus. *Vas. Pavlou and Friderikis 1, 33054, tel. 0265/82–232, fax 0265/82–033. 51 rooms with bath, 8 suites. Facilities: restaurant. MC, V. $$$*

Apollo. The *saloni* (living room) here has traditional wall hangings and old prints among its carefully selected furnishings. The light wood furniture in the cheerful bedrooms is set off by blue quilts and striped curtains. Many rooms have balconies with iron railings; all have hair dryers and TVs. A full breakfast is included. *Vas. Pavlou and Friderikis 59B, 33054, tel. 0265/82–580 or 0265/82–244, fax 0265/82–455. 21 rooms with bath. Facilities: bar, breakfast room, minibars. MC, V. Closed weekdays Nov.–Mar. except Christmas and Carnival. $$*

Fedriades. Named after Delphi's famous rocks, this 1992 hotel has a neoclassical exterior, which gives way to a light, airy lobby and rooms done in marble and wood with views of the Gulf of Itea. Buffet breakfast is included in the price. *Vas. Pavlou and Friderikis 38, 33054, tel. 0265/82–919 or 0265/82–370, fax 0265/82–208. 24 rooms with bath. Facilities: cafeteria, bar. AE, DC, MC, V. Closed weekdays Nov.–Mar. $$*

★ **Acropole.** This friendly, family-run hotel has a garden and a spectacular view—bare mountainside and a sea of olive groves—so that guests feel as though they're completely secluded. All but a few rooms have balconies; about 10 have air-conditioning, minibars, and TVs. *Filellinon 13, tel. 0265/82–675, fax 0265/83–171. 42 rooms with bath. Facilities: bar, breakfast room, TV lounge. AE, MC, V. $*

Kalambaka

DINING

★ **Gertzos.** A local favorite since 1925, this family restaurant relies on the cooking of matriarch Ketty Gertzos, who prepares such succulent dishes as tsoutsoukakia, rabbit stew, and chicken in wine with green peppers and garlic. The wine list is heavily regional. *Ekonomou 4, on town hall sq., tel. 0432/22–316. No credit cards. Closed Nov.–Mar. $*

Vachos. This traditional taverna is decorated with ceramics and ironwork; its flower-filled garden has a view of Meteora. Try the mincemeat-stuffed squash with egg-lemon sauce, baked perch, or *pilino Vachos* (beef and vegetables or noodles topped with cheese and baked in ornamental crockery). *Platia Riga Fereou, tel. 0432/24–678. Closed Nov.–Feb. except for Christmas. No credit cards. $*

LODGING

★ **Amalia.** The area's best hotel is about 4 kilometers (2½ miles) outside of Kalambaka. Built in 1991, the low-lying complex has spacious, handsomely decorated public rooms that vary in style from the sitting room with its floral murals to the poolside bar with glistening blue tiles and rustic ceiling rafters. Rooms are done in soothing colors and have large beds and art prints. Buffet breakfast is included. *Trikalon 14, Theopetra, 42200, tel. 0432/81–216 and 0432/81–217, fax 0432/81–457. 171 rooms with bath, 2 suites. Facilities: 2 restaurants, bar, cafeteria, TV/game room, pool, meeting rooms. AE, DC, MC, V. $$$*

Motel Divani. In spite of its name, this is actually an A-class hotel. Rooms are quiet and rather plain, but the hotel's advantage over the Amalia is that half the rooms have views of the rocks. The professional reception staff can arrange for a taxi driver to take you to the various monasteries. Buffet breakfast is included in the price (half board is available for another 1,300 dr. per person). *Trikalon 1, 42200, tel. 0432/22–583, fax 0432/23–638. 165 rooms with bath. Facilities: restaurant, snack bar, outdoor pool, tea shop, air-conditioning. AE, DC, MC, V. $$*

Hotel Edelweiss. Bright and clean, this hotel shines like a new pin. About half of its comfortable rooms (with TVs and minibars) look out over the swimming pool to the daunting Meteora rocks towering beyond. The hotel bar is a lively and crowded local meeting spot. *E. Venizelou 3, 42200, tel. 0432/23–966, fax 0432/24–733. 58 rooms with bath. Facilities: restaurant, outdoor pool, snack bar, dance club, air-conditioning. MC, V. $*

Thessaloniki

DINING

Vita-Vita. For a romantic evening made memorable by a flawless meal, try this trendy favorite with a decidedly French influence. Don't miss the fresh mushrooms in parsley-and-fennel sauce before moving on to lamb with artichokes in an egg-lemon sauce, or the fresh salmon diablo. There's an international wine list, and nightly piano music sets the mood. *Tsimiski 46, tel. 031/287–443. Reservations advised. AE, DC, MC. Closed Sun. and July–Aug. No lunch. $$$*

Krikelas. A Thessaloniki landmark, this family-run taverna has been serving classic Greek dishes for more than half a century. Its homemade eggplant dip has a faint smoky taste, and its gyros are heaped high with succulent lamb. In winter, Krikelas specializes in game like wild pig and venison; fresh fish is served year-round. *Ethnikis Antistasis 32, Kala-maria, tel. 031/451–690 or 031/451–289. Reservations advised. AE, DC, MC, V. $$*

O Ragias. Known for Macedonian cooking, this restaurant with a sea view offers unusual dishes like *yiaourtlou ragias* (veal in yogurt-garlic sauce), *hungar begiendi* (veal casserole with eggplant purée), and grilled mussels. For dessert, try the Macedonian crepe with honey, walnuts, and ice cream. Except for Monday, there is piano music nightly. *Nikis 13, tel. 031/279–993 or 031/227–468. AE, DE, MC. Closed Sun. No lunch. $$*

★ **O Kipos ton Pringipon.** The Milos enclave, a former mill complex in the city's slaughterhouse area, is now a nightlife center, with a café, bars playing everything from light jazz to Greek music, and exhibition spaces for art shows and live performances. The ouzeri has traditional appetizers—saganaki and croquettes made with *kasseri* cheese—as well as such specialties as diced beef in a mushroom and red-wine sauce topped with cheese. *Andrea Georgiou 56, Sfagia, tel. 031/251–838, 031/516–945, or 031/251–836. Reservations advised. No credit cards. $*

LODGING

Capsis. Two blocks from the rail station, this hotel is popular with Greek business travelers for its convenient downtown location. There's a roof garden, and the renovated rooms all have TVs. During the two weeks of the International Trade Fair, the room price increases by about 30%, as it does for most of the hotels listed here. *Monastiriou 18, 54629, tel. 031/521–321 or 031/521–421, fax 031/510–555. 421 rooms with bath, 7 suites. Facilities: restaurant, pool, minibars, air-conditioning, meeting rooms. AE, DC, MC, V. $$$*

★ **Electra Palace.** This hotel is built in a neo-Byzantine style to match the other buildings on the square. It's conveniently located in the center of town, and it has a no-smoking floor, rare in Greece. Rooms have refrigerators and TV; buffet breakfast is included in the price. *Platia Aristotelous 9, 54624, tel. 031/232–221 through 031/232–230, fax 031/235–947. 125 rooms with bath, 6 suites. Facilities: restaurant, bar, meeting rooms. AE, DC, MC, V. $$$*

Panorama. If you don't mind taking a taxi, this is a delightful hotel tucked into the wealthy, foothill suburb of Panorama, about 10 kilometers (6 miles) from downtown. In 1995, the rooms underwent a major renovation and now have Italian lighting and furniture, TVs, and three telephones, including one in the bathroom. On the terrace you can enjoy the city view unhurriedly with an iced coffee or frozen sherbet. *Analipseos 26, Panorama, 55236, tel. 031/341–871, fax 031/341–229. 47 rooms with bath, 3 suites. Facilities: restaurant, bar, minibar. AE, DC, MC, V. $$$*

Queen Olga Hotel. Though it's starting to show its age, this hotel is slowly being renovated. The location near the International Fairgrounds and the helpful staff make it appealing to the budget-minded traveler. Rooms in front have a sea view. *Vas. Olgas 44, 54641, tel. 031/824–621 through 031/824–629, fax 031/868–581. 148 rooms with bath. Facilities: restaurant, bar, air-conditioning, minibars. AE, MC, V. $$*

Pella. This quiet hotel between city hall and the Ministry of Northern Greece was renovated in 1992. It offers small but spotless rooms at very low prices, so book early. *Ionos Dragoumi 63, 54630, tel. 031/524–221, 031/524–222, or 031/524-224, fax 031/524–223. 79 rooms with bath. MC, V. $*

THE GREEK ISLANDS

The islands of the Aegean have colorful legends of their own—the Minotaur in Crete; the lost continent of Atlantis, which some believe was Santorini; and the Colossus of Rhodes, to name a few. Each island has its own personality. Mykonos has windmills, dazzling whitewashed buildings, hundreds of tiny churches and chapels on golden hillsides, and small fishing harbors. Visitors to volcanic Santorini sail into what was once a vast volcanic crater and anchor near the island's forbidding cliffs. Crete, with its jagged mountain peaks, olive orchards, and vineyards, contains the remains of the Minoan civilization. In Rhodes, a bustling modern town surrounds a walled town with a medieval castle.

Getting Around

The simplest way to visit the Aegean Islands is by cruise ship. Visitors might consider a three-day cruise to the four most popular islands—Mykonos, Rhodes, Crete, and Santorini. Car and passenger ferries sail to these main destinations from Piraeus, the port of Athens; other ferries sail from Rafina, 20 miles north of Athens. (*See* Getting Around, By Boat, *in* Essential Information, *above.*) There is also frequent air service from Athens, and most flights are full, especially in summer. It's vital to book well in advance and to reconfirm.

Guided Tours

Aegean Cruises

From April through October there are many cruises to the Greek Islands from Piraeus. Try any of the following: **Chandris Cruises** (Akti Miaouli 95, Piraeus, 18538, tel. 01/429–0300); **Epirotiki** (Akti Miaouli 85, Piraeus, 18538, tel. 01/429–1000); **Hydrodynamic Cruises** (Xenofontos 14, Athens, 10557, tel. 01/323–4292); **Royal Cruise Lines** (Akti Miaouli 1, Piraeus, 18538, tel. 01/428–2440 or 800/227–0925 in the U.S.); or **Sun Line** (Iasonas 3, Piraeus, 18537, tel. 01/452–3417 or 800/872–6400 in the U.S.). They offer cruises ranging from one to seven days. In the United Kingdom, contact **Epirotiki** (Westmoreland House, 127/131 Regent St., London WIR 7HA, tel. 0171/734–0805).

Tourist Information

There are **Greek National Tourist Organization** offices on **Crete,** at Kriari 40, Hania (tel. 0821/92–624 or 031/92–943), and at Xanthoudidou 1, Heraklion (tel. 081/244–462); and on **Rhodes,** at Archibishop Makarios and Papagou, Rhodes town (tel. 0241/23–655, 0241/23–255, or 0241/27–466. Much more helpful as well as closer to the Old Town is the **Rhodes Municipal Tourism Office** off Platia Rimini (tel. 0241/35–945; closed Nov.–Apr.)

Exploring the Greek Islands

The Cyclades

Cruise ships and car ferries to Mykonos leave from Piraeus or Rafina. If you sail from Piraeus, you will be able to see one of the great sights of Greece: the Temple of Poseidon looming on a hilltop at the edge of Cape Sounion, at the tip of mainland Greece.

MYKONOS

Mykonos is the name of the island and also of its chief village—a colorful maze of narrow, paved streets lined with whitewashed houses, many with bright blue doors and shutters. Every morning, women scrub

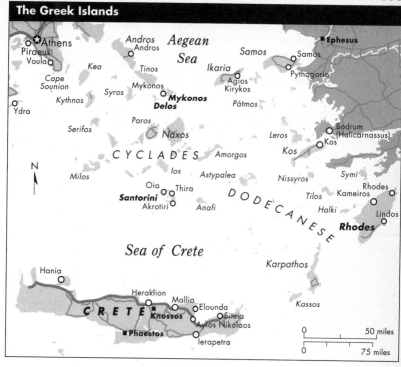

the sidewalks and streets in front of their homes, undaunted by the many donkeys that pass by each day. During the 1960s, the bohemian jet set discovered Mykonos, and most of the old houses along the waterfront are now restaurants, nightclubs, bars, and discos—both gay and straight, all blaring loud music until the early morning; a quiet café or taverna is hard to find. Mykonos is still a favorite anchorage with the international yacht set, as well as being *the* holiday destination for the young, lively, and liberated—finding yourself alone on any of its beaches is unlikely.

DELOS

About 40 minutes by boat from Mykonos and its 20th-century holiday pleasures is the ancient isle of Delos, the legendary sanctuary of Apollo. Its **Terrace of the Lions,** a remarkable group of nine Naxian marble sculptures from the 7th century BC, is a must. Worth seeing, too, are some of the houses of the Roman period, with their fine floor mosaics. The best of these mosaics are in the **Archaeological Museum.** *Tel. 0289/22–259. Admission to archaeological site (including entrance to the museum): 1,200 dr. Open Tues.–Sun. 8:30–3.*

SANTORINI

The best way to approach Santorini is to sail into its harbor, once the vast crater of its volcano, and dock beneath its black and red cliffs. In some parts, the cliffs rise more than 1,000 feet above the sea. The play of light across them can produce strange color effects. The white houses and churches of the main town, **Thira** (Fira), cling inside the rim in dazzling white contrast to the somber cliffs.

Most passenger ferries now use the new port, Athinios, where visitors are met by buses, taxis, and a gaggle of small-hotel owners hawking rooms. The bus ride into Thira takes about a half hour, and from there you can make connections to **Oia,** the serene town at the northern tip, and to other towns on the island. Despite being packed with visitors in the summer, the tiny town is charming and has spectacular views. It has the usual souvenir and handicrafts shops and several reasonably priced jewelry shops. Be sure to try the local wines. The volcanic soil produces a unique range of flavors from light and dry to rich and aromatic.

The island's volcano erupted during the 15th century BC, destroying its Minoan civilization. At **Akrotiri,** on the south end of Santorini, the remains of a Minoan city buried by volcanic ash are being excavated. The site, believed by some to be part of the legendary Atlantis, is well worth visiting. *Tel. 0286/81–366. Admission: 1,200 dr. Open Tues.–Sun. 8:30–3.*

At **Ancient Thira,** a clifftop site on the east coast of the island, a well-preserved ancient town includes a theater and agora, houses, fortifications, and ancient tombs. *No phone. Admission free. Open Tues.–Sun. 8:30–3.*

For an enjoyable but slightly unnerving excursion, take the short boat trip to the island's still-active small offshore volcanoes called the **Kamenes** (Burnt Islands). You can descend into a small crater, hot and smelling of sulfur, and swim in the nearby water that has been warmed by the volcano.

The Dodecanese

RHODES

The large island of Rhodes, 170 kilometers (106 miles) southeast of Mykonos and 11 kilometers (7 miles) off the coast of Turkey, is the chief island of the group of 12 called the Dodecanese. The northern end of the island is one of Greece's major vacation centers, and the Old Town of Rhodes is full of crooked cobbled streets, charming cityscapes, and echoes of antiquity. It's also full of the trappings of tourism, mainly evident in the pubs and bars that cater to the large Western European market. The island as a whole is not particularly beautiful, but it has fine beaches and an excellent climate. It makes a good base for visiting other islands of the Dodecanese, with their mixture of Aegean and Turkish architecture.

The town of Rhodes has an attractive harbor with fortifications; the gigantic bronze statue of the Colossus of Rhodes, once supposed to have straddled the entrance, was one of the wonders of the ancient world. The fascinating **old walled city,** near the harbor, was built by crusaders—the Knights of St. John—on the site of an ancient city. The knights ruled the island from 1309 until they were defeated by the Turks in 1522. Within the fine medieval walls, on the Street of the Knights, stands the **Knights' Hospital,** now the Archaeological Museum, housing ancient pottery and sculpture, including two famous statues of Aphrodite. *Tel. 0241/27–657. Admission: 800 dr. Open Tues.–Fri. 8:30–7 (8:30–3 in winter), weekends and holidays 8:30–3.*

Another museum that deserves your attention is the restored and moated medieval **Palace of the Grand Master.** Destroyed in 1856 by a gunpowder explosion, the palace was renovated by the Italians as a summer retreat for Mussolini. Note its splendid Hellenstic and Roman floor mosaics. *Tel. 0241/23–359. Admission: 1,200 dr. Open Tues.–Fri. 8:30–7 (8:30–3 in winter), weekends and holidays 8:30–3.*

The walls of Rhodes's Old Town are among the greatest medieval monuments in the Mediterranean. For 200 years the knights strengthened them, making them up to 40 feet thick in places and curving the walls to deflect cannon balls. You can take a guided walk on part of the 4-kilometer (2½-mile) road along the top of the walls every Tuesday and Saturday (call 0241/21–954 for information).

Many attractive souvenir and handicrafts shops in the Old Town and just outside the walls sell decorative Rhodian pottery, local embroidery, sea sponges, and relatively inexpensive jewelry.

From the town of Rhodes, drive about 60 kilometers (37 miles) down the east coast to the enchanting village of **Lindos.** Take a donkey from the village center and ride, or put on your comfortable shoes and walk up the steep hill to the ruins of the ancient **Acropolis of Lindos,** which is slowly being restored. The sight of its beautiful colonnade with the sea far below is unforgettable. Look for little St. Paul's Harbor, beneath the cliffs of the acropolis; seen from above, it appears to be a lake, as the tiny entrance from the sea is obscured by the rocks. *Tel. 0244/31–258. Admission: 1,200 dr. Open Tues.–Sun. 8:30–2:40.*

Crete

Greece's largest island, situated in the south Aegean, was the center of Europe's earliest civilization, the Minoan, which flourished from about 2000 BC to 1200 BC. It was struck a mortal blow in about 1450 BC by some unknown cataclysm, now thought to be political.

The most important Minoan remains are to be seen in the **Archaeological Museum in Heraklion,** Crete's largest (and least attractive) city. The museum houses many Minoan treasures, including some highly sophisticated frescoes and elegant ceramics depicting Minoan life. *Plateia Eleftherias, tel. 081/226–092. Admission: 1,500 dr. Open Mon. 12–3, Tues.–Fri. 8–7 (8–5 in winter), weekends and holidays 8:30–3.*

Not far from Heraklion is the partly reconstructed **Palace of Knossos,** which will also give you a feeling for the Minoan world. Note the simple throne room, which contains the oldest throne in Europe, and the bathrooms with their efficient plumbing. The palace was the setting for the legend of the Minotaur, a monstrous offspring of Queen Pasiphae and a bull, which King Minos confined to the Labyrinth under the palace. *Tel. 081/231–940. Admission: 1,500 dr. Open Tues.–Sun. 8:30–3.*

Crete belonged to Venice from 1210 until 1669, when it was conquered by the Turks. The island became part of Greece early in this century. The **Venetian ramparts** that withstood a 24-year Turkish siege still surround Heraklion. In addition to archaeological treasures, Crete can boast beautiful mountain scenery and a large number of beach resorts along the north coast. One is **Mallia,** which contains the remains of another Minoan palace and has good sandy beaches. Two other beach resorts, **Ayios Nikolaos** and the nearby **Elounda,** are farther east. The south coast offers good, quieter beaches.

Dining and Lodging

For details and price-category definitions, *see* Dining and Lodging *in* Staying in Greece, *above.*

Crete

DINING

Old Mill. This outdoor restaurant disproves the rule of mediocre hotel food. The Elounda Mare is part of the Relais et Châteaux chain, with its emphasis on gastronomic excellence. The specialty is flambéed Continental cuisine—prawns flambé with raki (a Turkish liqueur), chicken fillets with whiskey, beef in cognac. *Elounda Mare Hotel, Ayios Nikolaos, tel. 0841/41–102 and 0841/41–103. Reservations required. Jacket required. AE, MC, V. Closed Nov.–Mar./Apr., depending on weather. No lunch.* $$$$

Kyriakos. This popular taverna, with pink tablecloths and green chairs, offers a wide range of salads, fish dishes, and such Cretan specialties as snail stew with *pligouri* (cracked wheat), artichokes baked with tomatoes and broad beans, and *tiropitakia* (pies with honey and creamy, mild Cretan cheese). *Leoforos Dimokratias 53, Heraklion, tel. 081/224–649. AE, DC, V. Closed Wed. and June 15–July 15.* $$

Minos Taverna. Specialties at this outdoor restaurant include lamb in yogurt, stifado, fresh seafood, stuffed squash blossoms, and homemade *rizogalo* (rice pudding made from sheep's milk). Service is prompt and attentive. *Daedelou 10, Heraklion, tel. 081/244–827 or 081/246–466. Closed 2 months in winter, usually Nov.–Jan. AE, MC, V.* $$

★ **Vassilis.** Watch the boats bobbing along the jetty at this classic taverna. Don't miss Cretan dishes like *koukouvayia* (a local roll soaked in wine, tomato, oil and herbs) and lamb fricassee stewed with lettuce. They owners also make their own wine. *Nearchou 10, old harbor, Rethymnon, tel. 0831/22–967 or 0831/52–135. AE, DC, MC, V.* $$

LODGING

Elounda Beach. Located 9 kilometers (7 miles) north of Ayios Nikolaos, this seaside resort is spacious, attractive, and spotlessly maintained. The complex is set in beautiful grounds—the pool is cleverly landscaped among carob trees—and has a private beach. Half board, including buffet breakfast, is required. *Elounda Beach, 72053, tel. 0841/41–812 or 0841/41–412, fax 0841/41–373. 120 rooms with bath, 143 bungalows, 15 suites. Facilities: 3 restaurants, 3 bars, outdoor pool, miniature golf, 2 tennis courts, dance club. AE, DC, MC, V. Closed Nov.–Mar.* $$$$

Casa Delfino. In the heart of Hania's old town, this small, tranquil hotel was once part of a Venetian Renaissance palace. Rooms decorated in cool pastel colors with modern furniture surround a courtyard paved in pebble mosaic. *Theofanous 9, Palio Limani, 73131, tel. 0821/93–098 or 0821/87–400, fax 0821/96–500. 12 rooms with bath. Facilities: kitchenettes, air-conditioning. DC, MC, V.* $$

★ **Mediterranean.** This is another comfortable hotel in the center of Heraklion and 4.8 kilometers (3 miles) from the beach. More than half of the rooms have air-conditioning, and Continental breakfast is included in the price. *Smyrnis 1, 71201, tel. 081/289–331, fax 081/289–335. 55 rooms with bath. Facilities: restaurant, roof garden. AE, DC, MC, V.* $$

Mykonos

DINING

Chez Cat'rine. A favorite with Greeks as well as foreigners, this is where you can enjoy simple but superbly cooked French dishes and Greek fare, in an informal, brightly furnished dining room. *Delos and Drakopoulou, opposite St. Gerasimos's church, tel. 0289/22–169. Reservations required. AE, MC, V. Closed Nov.–Apr. No lunch.* $$$

Pilafas. This friendly taverna just behind the waterfront (follow the signs) is patronized by locals for its good grilled dishes, salads, and reasonably priced seafood. *Chora, tel. 0289/24–120. No credit cards. No lunch.* $–$$

LODGING

★ **Cavo Tagoo.** Within walking distance of the center of town, this small, charming hotel sits above a beach. All rooms have balconies with sea views. American breakfast is included in the price, and half board is available. *Tagoo Beach, 84600, tel. 0289/23–692 through 0289/23–694, fax 0289/24–923; in Athens tel. 01/643–0233, fax 01/644–5237. 67 rooms with bath. Facilities: restaurant, outdoor pool, 2 bars, baby-sitting, airport and harbor shuttle. AE, DC, MC, V. Closed Nov.–mid-Apr. $$$*

Kamari. This family-run hotel looks like new and is 4 kilometers (2½ miles) from Mykonos town, between two sheltered sandy beaches that are each a five-minute walk away. The hotel has added 11 more up-scale rooms, with TV, refrigerator, and air-conditioning. Buffet breakfast is included in the price. *Platy Gialos, 84600, tel. 0289/23–424, 0289/23–982, or 0289/25–054, fax 0289/24–414. 55 rooms with bath. Facilities: breakfast room, bar, airport shuttle. AE, MC, V. Closed Nov.–Mar. $$*

Kouneni Hotel. The Kouneni is a comfortable family-run hotel in the town center, and it's quieter than most. It is set in a cool green garden, a rarity on Mykonos, the ideal place to linger over the Continental breakfast included in the price. Rooms are fairly large and the lobby is cozy. *Tria Pigadia, across from public school, 84600, tel. 0289/22–301, fax 0289/26–559. 20 rooms with bath. Facilities: bar. No credit cards. $$*

Rhodes

DINING

★ **Alexis.** The owner spares no expense or effort to bring his clientele the very best seafood. A side dish might be sautéed squash with local greens such as *vlita* (notchweed) and *glistrida* (purslane). Finish your meal on the quiet, shady terrace with *hilli*, a kind of baklava with ice cream. *Sokratous 18, Old Town, tel. 0241/29–347 or 0241/26–717. Dinner reservations advised. AE, V. Closed Nov. $$$*

★ **Ta Kioupia.** Antique farm implements hang on the walls here, and tables are elegantly set with linens, fine china, and crystal. Food arrives on large platters and you select what pleases your eye: pine-nut salad, cheese dip with garlic, *tiropites* (four-cheese pie), wafer-thin pastry with clotted cream and nuts, rooster kebab. *Tris, about 7 km (4¼ mi) from Rhodes town, tel. 0241/91–824. Reservations advised. AE, V. Closed Sun Oct.–May. No lunch. $$$*

Dinoris. Set in a great hall built in 1530 as a stable for the knights, this establishment has long specialized in fish. For mezedes, try the variety platter, which includes *psarokeftedakia* (fish balls made from a secret recipe) as well as mussels, shrimp, and lobster. *Platia Mouseou 14A, Rhodes Old Town, tel. 0241/25–824 or 0241/35–530. Garden reservations required. Summer weekend reservations advised. AE, MC, V. $$*

★ **Palia Istoria.** Ensconced in an old house with genteel murals, this mezedopolion is a visual treat. Begin your meal with a few appetizers such as feta saganaki, very lightly fried with the potent red pepper *bukova*, or the plump mussels served with piquant *tsouska* peppers. Entrées include pork in garlic and wine sauce, and shrimp ouzo with orange juice. *Mitropoleos 108 and Dendrinou, Ammos Marasia area south of Old Town (about 850 dr. by taxi), tel. 0241/32–421. Reservations advised. MC, V. No lunch. $$*

LODGING

Grand Hotel Summer Palace. This resort hotel in Rhodes town offers easy access to the beach across the street, the Old Town (20 minutes on foot), and the New Town's vibrant nightlife. The best rooms are in the new wing, with its pink marble floors and paintings of nymphs and goddesses. Rooms have either a sea or a garden view; the higher you are, the better. Buffet breakfast is included. *Akti Miaouli 1, Rhodes, 85100, tel. 0241/26–284, fax 0241/35–589; in Athens tel. and fax 01/291–7027. 350 rooms with bath, 18 suites. Facilities: restaurant,* bar, nightclub, 4 pools (1 indoor, 1 children's), tennis court, sauna, exercise room, meeting rooms. AE, DC, MC, V. $$$

★ **Rhodos Imperial.** Stacked red, blue, and yellow boxes zigzag down the hillside at this Grecotel establishment opened in 1993. Linked by pedestrian tunnel to the beach, it offers excellent value for a resort setting just 4 kilometers (2½ miles) from Rhodes town. The crisp, modern rooms are in shades of peach and gray or blue and sea green; all have balconies, about half with sea views. Buffet breakfast is included. *Ialyssou Ave, Ixia, 85100, tel. 0241/37–489, fax 0241/25–390; in Athens tel. 01/725–3219, fax 01/721–7739. 356 rooms with bath, 48 suites. Facilities: 2 restaurants, 4 tennis courts, 3 pools (1 indoor), water sports, exercise room, sauna, squash, children's programs, meeting rooms. AE, DC, MC, V. Closed mid-Nov.–mid-Mar. $$$*

St. Nikolis Hotel. This hotel within the Old Town is away from the most crowded tourist area. The rooms are small, outfitted with dark, rustic furniture, and look out toward the spacious courtyard or old city walls. A roof terrace lets you breakfast with a view over the entire town. Buffet breakfast is included. *Ippodamou 61, Rhodes, 85100, tel. 0241/34–561, 0241/36–238, 0241/34–747, fax 0241/32–034. 10 rooms with bath, 8 apartments. Facilities: breakfast room, bar. AE, DC, MC, V. $$*

Spartalis Hotel. Many rooms in this simple but lively hotel near the city's port have balconies overlooking the bay. Note that the rooms on the street are noisy. *Plastira 2, Rhodes, 85100, tel. 0241/24–371 and 0241/24–372, fax 0241/20–406. 79 rooms with bath. Facilities: breakfast room, bar. AE, DC, MC, V. $*

Santorini

DINING

Camille Stefani. This is one of the island's best restaurants, where you can enjoy seafood, Greek and Continental cuisine, and the local wines. A taste of the mellow Santorini Lava red wine, a product of the volcanic ash, is a must! *Main St., Thira, tel. 0286/22–265. Reservations advised. AE, MC, V. Closed Nov.–Mar. $$*

★ **Nikolas.** You can't go wrong at this simple taverna, one of the few places in town that stays open in winter. The menu, which changes daily, offers a limited but delicious choice of classic Greek dishes, including stifado, stuffed cabbage rolls, and mountain greens. *Erithrou Stavrou, Thira, no phone. No credit cards. $*

LODGING

Perivolas. This group of traditional houses in the beautiful village of Oia has been carefully restored by the Greek National Tourist Organization. They overlook the sea and the volcano and offer comfortable accommodations in an authentic island setting. *Oia, 84700, tel. 0286/71–308, fax 0286/71–309. 12 houses, each with 2 rooms and bath. Facilities: kitchenettes. AE, MC, V. Closed Nov.–Mar. $$$*

Matina. Near the beach at Kamari, this pleasant family-run hotel is set among vineyards. Prices are at the bottom of the category; half the rooms have air-conditioning. *Kamari, 84700, tel. 0286/31–491 or 0286/32–275, fax 0286/31–860. 27 rooms with bath. Facilities: bar. AE, DC, MC, V. Closed mid-Nov.–mid-Mar. $$*

14 Holland

IF YOU COME TO HOLLAND expecting to find its residents shod in wooden shoes, you're years too late; if you're looking for windmills at every turn, you're looking in the wrong place. The bucolic images that brought tourism here in the decades after World War II have little to do with the Netherlands (the country's proper name, though Holland remains in popular use) of the '90s. Sure, tulips grow in abundance in the bulb district of Noord and Zuid Holland provinces, but today's Netherlands is no backwater operation: This tiny nation has an economic strength and cultural wealth that far surpass its size and population. Sophisticated, modern Netherlands has more art treasures per square mile than any other country on earth, as well as a large number of ingenious, energetic people with a remarkable commitment to quality, style, and innovation.

The 41,526 square kilometers (15,972 square miles) of the Netherlands are just about half the number in the state of Maine, and its population of 15 million is slightly less than that of the state of Texas. Size is no measure of international clout, however. The Netherlands is second only to Great Britain and Japan as an investor in the American economy. The Netherlands encourages internal accomplishments as well, particularly of a cultural nature. Within a 120-kilometer (75-mile) radius are 10 major museums of art and several smaller ones that together contain the world's richest and most comprehensive collection of art masterpieces from the 15th to the 20th centuries, including the majority of paintings by Rembrandt and Vincent van Gogh. In the same small area are a half dozen performance halls offering music, dance, and internationally known performing arts festivals.

The marriage of economic power and cultural wealth is nothing new to the Dutch; in the 17th century, for example, money raised through their colonial outposts overseas was used to buy or commission portraits and paintings by young artists such as Rembrandt, Hals, Vermeer, and van Ruisdael. But it was not only the arts that were encouraged: The Netherlands was home to the philosophers Descartes, Spinoza, and Comenius; the jurist Grotius; the naturalist van Leeuwenhoek, inventor of the microscope; and others like them who flourished in the country's enlightened tolerance. The Netherlands continues to subsidize its artists and performers, and it supports an educational system in which creativity in every field is respected, revered, and given room to express itself.

The Netherlands is the delta of Europe, located where the great Rhine and Maas rivers and their tributaries empty into the North Sea. Near the coast, it is a land of flat fields and interconnecting canals; in the center it is surprisingly wooded, and in the far south are rolling hills. The country is too small for there to be vast natural areas, and it's too precariously close to sea level, even at its highest points, for there to be dramatic landscapes. (In fact, about half of the Netherlands is below sea level.) Instead, the country is what the Dutch jokingly call a big green city. Amsterdam is the focal point of the nation; it also is the beginning and end point of a 60-kilometer (37½-mile) circle of cities that includes The Hague (the Dutch seat of government and the world center of international justice), Rotterdam (the industrial center of the Netherlands and the world's largest port), and the historic cites of Haarlem, Leiden, Delft, and Utrecht. The northern and eastern provinces are rural and quiet; the southern provinces that hug the Belgian border are lightly industrialized and sophisticated. The great rivers that cut through the heart of the country provide both geographical and

Holland

North Sea

W a d d e n   I s l a n d s

Schiermonnikoog

Ameland

Terschelling

Delfzijl

Dokkum

Groningen

Winschoten

Leeuwarden

N7/E22

Vlieland

Harlingen

Drachten

Assen

N34

Bolsward

Sneek

Emmen

Texel

A32

N371

N28/E32

Hoogeveen

Den Helder

IJsselmeer

Meppel

N48

N34

N36

Enkhuizen

Zwolle

Almelo

Hoorn

Lelystad

Hengelo

Alkmaar

N35

Deventer

Enschede

Purmerend

A6

A28/E232

Zaanstad

A1/E30

Amsterdam

Apeldoorn

Haarlem

Bussum

Winterswijk

A9

Hilversum

Amersfoort

Arnhem

Doetinchem

A4/E14

A2

Leiden

Rijn

Utrecht

Rijn

A12/E35

Den Haag
(The Hague)

E30

A12

Lek

Tiel

Nijmegen

Rhine

GERMANY

Delft

E25

A50

Rotterdam

A15/E31

Oss

'Hertogenbosch

Dordrecht

Waal

Maas

Veghel

A59

Haringvliet

Overflakkee

A16/E19

A67/E34

Grevelingen

Breda

Tilburg

Eindhoven

Schouwen/
Duiveland

Tholen

Steenbergen

A2/E25

Oosterschelde

Weert

Roermond

Goes

A58

Bergen op Zoom

Walcheren *Beveland*

Middelburg

Westerschelde

Schelde

Sittard

Breskens

Terneuzen

Antwerp

Maastricht

Aachen

Vaals

KEY

--- Ferry

BELGIUM

Liège

0 —— 40 miles

0 —— 60 km

Brussels

sociological borders. The area "above the great rivers," as the Dutch phrase it, is peopled by tough-minded and practical Calvinists; to the south are more ebullient Catholics. A tradition of tolerance pervades this densely populated land; aware that they cannot survive alone, the Dutch are bound by common traits of ingenuity, personal honesty, and a bold sense of humor.

ESSENTIAL INFORMATION

Before You Go

When to Go
The prime tourist season in Holland runs from April through October and peaks during school vacation periods (Easter, July, and August), when hotels may impose a 20% surcharge. Dutch bulb fields bloom from late March to the end of May—not surprisingly, the hotels tend to fill up then, too. June is the ideal time to catch the warm weather and miss the crowds, but every region of the Netherlands has its season. Delft is luminous after a winter storm, and fall in the Utrecht countryside can be as dramatic as in New England.

CLIMATE
Summers are generally warm, but beware of sudden showers and blustery coastal winds. Winters are chilly and wet but are not without clear days. After a cloudburst, notice the watery quality of light that inspired Vermeer and other great Dutch painters.

The following are the average daily maximum and minimum temperatures for Amsterdam.

Jan.	40F	4C	**May**	61F	16C	**Sept.**	65F	18C
	34	1		50	10		56	13
Feb.	41F	5C	**June**	65F	18C	**Oct.**	56	13C
	34	1		56	13		49	9
Mar.	47F	8C	**July**	70F	21C	**Nov.**	47F	8C
	38	3		59	15		41	5
Apr.	52F	11C	**Aug.**	68F	20C	**Dec.**	41F	5C
	43	6		59	15		36	2

Currency
The unit of currency in Holland is the guilder, written as NLG (for Netherlands guilder), Fl., or simply F. (from the centuries-old term for the coinage, florin). Each guilder is divided into 100 cents. Bills are in denominations of 10, 25, 50, 100, 250, and 1,000 guilders. Denominations over Fl. 100 are rarely seen, and many shops refuse to change them. Coins are 1, 2.5, and 5 guilders and 5, 10, and 25 cents. Be careful not to confuse the 1- and 2.5-guilder coins and the 5-guilder and 5-cent coins. Bills have a code of raised dots that can be identified by touch; this is for people who are blind.

At press time (spring 1995), the exchange rate for the guilder was Fl. 1.48 to the U.S. dollar and Fl. 2.45.

What It Will Cost
Holland is a prosperous country with a high standard of living, so overall costs are similar to those in other northern European countries. Prices for hotels and other services in major cities are 10%–20% above those in rural areas. Amsterdam and The Hague are the most expensive. Hotel and restaurant service charges and the 6% value-added tax (VAT) are usually included in the prices quoted.

The cost of eating varies widely in Holland, from a snack in a bar or a modest restaurant offering a *dagschotel* (day special), or "tourist menu" at around Fl. 25 to the considerable expense of gourmet cuisine. A traditional Dutch breakfast is usually included in the overnight hotel price.

One cost advantage Holland has over other European countries is that because it is so small, traveling around is inexpensive—especially if you use the many money-saving transportation deals available.

SAMPLE PRICES

Half bottle of wine, Fl. 25; glass of beer, Fl. 3.50; cup of coffee, Fl. 2.75; ham and cheese sandwich, Fl. 5; 1-mile taxi ride, Fl. 10.

MUSEUMS

The **Museumkaart,** which can be purchased from some museums and all tourist offices, provides a year's free admission to about 350 museums. It costs Fl. 45, Fl. 32.50 if you're over 65, and Fl. 15 if you're under 18. A photo and passport are required for purchase. If your time is limited, you might want to check the list; not all museums participate.

Customs on Arrival

For travelers arriving from a country that is not a member of the European Union (EU) or those coming from an EU country who have bought goods in a duty-free shop, the allowances are (1) 200 cigarettes, or 50 cigars, or 100 cigarillos, or 250 grams of tobacco, (2) 1 liter of alcohol more than 22% by volume or 2 liters of liqueur wine or 2 liters of sparkling wine, (3) 50 grams of perfume or 25 centiliters of toilet water, and (4) other goods with a total value of Fl. 380.

Since January 1, 1993, allowances for travelers within the EU member states have been effectively removed, provided that goods have been bought duty-paid (i.e., not in a duty-free shop) and are for personal use.

All personal items are considered duty-free, provided you take them with you when you leave Holland. Tobacco and alcohol allowances are for those 17 and older. There are no restrictions on the import and export of Dutch currency.

Language

Dutch is a difficult language for foreigners, but luckily the Dutch are fine linguists, so almost everyone speaks at least some English, especially in larger cities and tourist centers.

Getting Around

By Car

ROAD CONDITIONS

Holland has one of the best road systems in Europe, and even the longest trips between cities take only a few hours. Multilane expressways (toll-free) link major cities, but the smaller roads and country lanes provide more varied views of Holland. In towns many of the streets are narrow, and you'll have to contend with complex one-way systems and cycle lanes. Information about weather and road conditions can be obtained by calling 06/9622.

RULES OF THE ROAD

The speed limit on expressways is 120 kph (75 mph); on city streets and in residential areas it is 50 kph (30 mph) or less, according to the signs. Driving is on the right.

PARKING

Parking in the larger towns is difficult and expensive, with illegally parked cars quickly towed away or subject to a wheel clamp. Fines for recovery can reach Fl. 300. So consider parking on the outskirts of a town and using public transportation to get to the center.

Gas, *benzine* in Dutch, costs around Fl. 1.86 per liter for regular, Fl. 1.92 for super, and Fl. 2.03 for leaded.

Experienced, uniformed mechanics of the **Wegenwacht** patrol the highways in yellow cars 24 hours a day. Operated by the Royal Dutch Touring Club (ANWB), they will help if you have car trouble. On major roads, ANWB also maintains phone boxes from which you can call for assistance. To use these services, you may be asked to take temporary membership in ANWB.

By Train

Fast, frequent, comfortable trains operate throughout the country. All trains have first- and second-class cars, and many intercity trains have buffet or dining-car services. Intercity trains run every 30 minutes and regular trains run to the smaller towns at least once an hour. Sometimes one train contains two separate sections that divide during the trip, so be sure you are in the correct section for your destination. Trains have specially designed entryways for people using wheelchairs.

To get the best value out of rail travel it is advisable to purchase one of the three available rail passes before you leave. The **Benelux Tourrail** gives you unlimited travel throughout Holland, Belgium, and Luxembourg on any five days within one month ($230 first class, $153 second class). A **Holland Rail Pass** (known in the Netherlands as a EuroDomino Holland) ticket allows unlimited travel throughout Holland for 3, 5, or 10 days within any 30-day period (first class: 3-day $84, 5-day $135, 10-day $250; second class: 3-day $64, 5-day $100, 10-day $178). A **Rail Rover** entitles you to unlimited travel within Holland for seven consecutive days (first class $144, second class $96). A **Transport Link** ticket, which offers free travel on buses and trams as well, may be bought in conjunction with the Holland Rail Pass and the Rail Rover (with Holland Rail Pass: 3-day $12, 5-day $19, 10-day $31; with Rail Rover: $17). Your rail pass is also valid on **Interliner,** a fast bus network that operates 16 intercity lines between towns that have no direct rail link. The Netherlands Board of Tourism's (NBT) offices abroad have information on train services, as do overseas offices of Netherlands Railways. Your passport may be needed when you purchase these tickets. The Benelux Tourrail and the Rail Rover must be bought abroad, but the others are available in the Netherlands. **Dagtochtkaartjes** are special combined tickets covering train, boat, and bus trips. Ask about these fares at railway information bureaus or local tourist offices.

By Plane

KLM Royal Dutch Airlines, under the banner of CityHopper, operates several domestic services connecting major cities. In this small country, however, you'd probably travel just as fast by car or train.

By Bus

Holland has an excellent bus network between towns that are not connected by rail and also within towns. Bus excursions can be booked on the spot and at local tourist offices. In major cities, the best buy is a **strippenkaart** ticket (Fl. 11), which can be used for all bus, tram, and metro services. Each card has 15 strips, which are canceled either by the driver as you enter the buses or by the stamping machine at each door of the trams. More than one person can travel on a strippenkaart—it just gets used up more quickly. A strippenkaart with 45 strips is available for Fl. 32.25. You can buy it at train stations, post offices, and some tourist offices, or in Amsterdam at the national bus system (GVB) ticket office in the plaza in front of the central railway station and at many newsagents. A **Dagkaart,** a travel-anywhere ticket, covers all urban bus/streetcar routes and costs Fl. 12 for one day, Fl. 16 for two days, and Fl. 19.75 for three days.

By Bicycle

Holland is a cyclist-friendly country with specially designated cycle paths, signs, and picnic areas. Bikes can usually be rented at train stations in most cities and towns, and Dutch trains are cycle-friendly, too, with extra-spacious entryways designed to accommodate bicycles. You will need an extra ticket for the bike, however. There are some restrictions on carrying bicycles on trains, so it is worthwhile to check first. The flat-rate single fare for a bike to anywhere in the country is Fl. 10, but this can rise to Fl. 25 depending on the day of the week, the season, and what kind of ticket you hold. (It's most expensive to transport a bike on Monday and Friday in July or August.) Rental costs for bicycles are around Fl. 10 per day or from Fl. 40 per week, plus a deposit of Fl. 50–Fl. 200. Many larger railway stations rent bicycles to holders of valid train tickets at Fl. 6 per day and Fl. 24 per week. Advice on rentals and routes is available from offices of the Netherlands Board of Tourism in North America or in Holland, or from local tourist offices; cycling packages can be booked at the larger offices.

Staying in Holland

Telephones

LOCAL CALLS

The telephone system in Holland is excellent and reliable. All towns and cities have area codes that are used only when you are calling from outside the area. Most pay phones take 25¢ or Fl. 1 coins, though newer ones also accept other denominations. Increasingly, public phone booths are being converted to a phone-card system. Phone cards may be purchased from post offices, railway stations, and some newsagents for Fl. 5, Fl. 10, or Fl. 25. Lines at coin-operated boxes tend to be longer, so a phone card is worth the investment, especially if you intend to make international calls. Dial 06/0410 for an English-speaking operator.

INTERNATIONAL CALLS

Direct-dial international calls can be made from any phone booth. Lower rates to the United States are charged from 7 PM to 10 AM weekdays, and from 7 PM Friday to 10 AM Monday. The average cost per minute to the U.S. is Fl. 1.70 (Fl. 1.50 nights and weekends). To reach an **AT&T** long-distance operator, dial 06/022–9111; for **MCI,** dial 06/022–9122; for **Sprint,** dial 000–999.

COUNTRY CODE

The country code for Holland is 3l.

Mail

POSTAL RATES

The Dutch post office is as efficient as the telephone network. Airmail letters to the United States cost Fl. 1.60 for the first 20 grams; postcards cost Fl. 1; aerograms cost Fl. 1.30. Airmail letters to the United Kingdom cost Fl. 1 for the first 20 grams; postcards cost 80¢; aerograms cost Fl. 1.30.

If you're uncertain where you'll be staying, have mail sent to "poste restante, GPO," in major cities along your route, or to American Express offices, where a small charge is made on collection to non-American Express customers.

Shopping
VAT REFUNDS
Purchases of goods in one store on one day amounting to Fl. 300 or more qualify for a value-added tax (VAT) refund of 17.5%, which can be claimed at the airport or main border crossing when you leave Holland, or by mail. Ask the salesperson for a VAT refund form when you buy anything that may qualify.

BARGAINING
The prices in most shops are fixed, but you can try to bargain for items in any of the open-air markets.

Opening and Closing Times
Banks are open weekdays from 9 to 4. You can also change money at GWK Border Exchange Offices at major railway stations and Schiphol Airport, which are open Monday–Saturday 8–8 and Sunday 10–4. GWK offices in major cities or at border checkpoints are open 24 hours. Many tourist offices exchange funds, too.

Museums now close on Monday, but not all, so check with local tourist offices. In rural areas, some museums close or operate shorter hours during winter. Usual hours are 10–5.

Shops are open weekdays and Saturdays from 8:30 or 9 to 5:30 or 6, but outside the cities, some close for lunch. Department stores and most shops, especially in shopping plazas (in The Hague and Amsterdam) do not open on Monday until 1 PM, and a few close one afternoon a week on whichever day they choose. Late-night shopping usually can be done until 9 PM on Thursday or Friday. Few shops are open Sunday.

National Holidays
January 1; April 5–8 (Easter); April 30 (Queen's Day; shops are open unless it falls on Sunday); May 5 (Liberation); May 16 (Ascension); May 26–27 (Pentecost); December 25–26.

Dining
Of the many earthly pleasures in which the Dutch indulge, eating probably heads the list. There is a wide variety of cuisines from traditional Dutch to Indonesian—the influence of the former Dutch colony.

Breakfast is hearty and substantial—including several varieties of bread, butter, jam, ham, cheese, chocolate, boiled eggs, juice, and steaming coffee or tea. Dutch specialties for later meals include *erwtensoep* (a rich, thick pea soup with pieces of tangy sausage or pigs' knuckles) and *hutspot* (a meat, carrot, and potato stew); both are usually served only in winter. *Haring* (herring) is particularly popular, especially the "new herring" caught between May and September and served raw in brine, garnished with onions. If Dutch food begins to pall, try an Indonesian restaurant, where the chief item is rijsttafel, a meal made up of rice and 20 or more small meat, seafood, or vegetable dishes, many of which are hot and spicy.

The indigenous Dutch liquor is potent and warming *jenever* (gin), both "old" and "new." Dutch liqueurs and beers are also popular.

Eating places range from snack bars, fast-food outlets, and modest local cafés to gourmet restaurants of international repute. Of special note are the "brown cafés," traditional pubs of great character that normally offer snack-type meals.

MEALTIMES

The Dutch tend to eat dinner around 6 or 7 PM, especially in the country and smaller cities, so many restaurants close at about 10 PM and accept final orders at 9. In larger cities dining hours vary, and some restaurants stay open until midnight.

WHAT TO WEAR

Jacket and tie are advised for restaurants in the **$$$$** and **$$$** categories. The Dutch are tolerant, and casual outfits are acceptable in most eateries.

RATINGS

Prices are per person including three courses (appetizer, main course, and dessert), service, and sales tax but not drinks. For budget travelers, many restaurants offer a tourist menu at an officially controlled price, currently Fl. 25. Highly recommended restaurants are indicated by a star ★.

CATEGORY	AMSTERDAM	OTHER AREAS
$$$$	over Fl. 100	over Fl. 85
$$$	Fl. 70–Fl. 100	Fl. 55–Fl. 85
$$	Fl. 40–Fl. 70	Fl. 35–Fl. 55
$	under Fl. 40	under Fl. 35

Lodging

Holland offers a wide range of accommodations, from the luxurious Dutch-owned international Golden Tulip hotel chain to traditional, small-town hotels and family-run guest houses. For young or adventurous travelers, the provinces abound with modest hostels, camping grounds, and rural bungalows. Travelers with modest budgets may prefer to stay in friendly bed-and-breakfast establishments; these are in short supply and must be booked well ahead at local tourist offices.

HOTELS

Dutch hotels are generally clean, if not spotless, no matter how modest their facilities, and service is normally courteous and efficient. There are many moderate and inexpensive hotels, most of which are relatively small. In the provinces, the range of accommodations is more limited, but there are pleasant, inexpensive family-run hotels that are usually centrally located and offer a friendly atmosphere. Some have good—if modest—dining facilities. English is spoken or understood almost everywhere. Hotels usually quote room prices for double occupancy, and rates usually include breakfast, service charges, and VAT.

To book hotels in advance, you can use the free **National Reservation Center** (Box 404, 2260 AK Leidschendam, tel. 070/3202500, fax 070/3202611). Alternatively, for a small fee, tourist offices can usually make reservations at short notice. Bookings must be made in person, however.

RATINGS

Prices are for two people sharing a double room. Highly recommended lodgings are indicated by a star ★.

CATEGORY	AMSTERDAM	OTHER AREAS
$$$$	over Fl. 500	over Fl. 350
$$$	Fl. 300–Fl. 500	Fl. 200–Fl. 350
$$	Fl. 200–Fl. 300	Fl. 150–Fl. 200
$	under Fl. 200	under Fl. 150

Tipping

Hotels and restaurants almost always include 10%–15% service and 6% VAT in their charges. Give a doorman Fl. 3 for calling a cab. Bell-hops in first-class hotels should be tipped Fl. 2 for each bag they carry. Hat-check attendants expect at least 25¢, and washroom attendants get 50¢. Taxis in almost every town have a tip included in the meter charge, but you round the fare to the nearest guilder nevertheless.

AMSTERDAM

Arriving and Departing

By Plane

Most international flights arrive at Amsterdam's Schiphol Airport, one of Europe's finest. Immigration and customs formalities on arrival are relaxed, with no forms to be completed.

BETWEEN THE AIRPORT AND DOWNTOWN

The best transportation between the airport and the city center is the direct rail link to the central train station, where you can get a taxi or tram to your hotel. The train runs every 10 to 15 minutes throughout the day and takes about half an hour. Second-class fare is Fl. 5.75.

Taxis from the airport to central hotels cost about Fl. 60.

By Train

The city has excellent rail connections with the rest of Europe. Fast services link it to Paris, Brussels, Luxembourg, and Cologne. Centraal Station (Central Station) is conveniently located in the center of town.

Getting Around

By Bus, Tram, and Metro

A zonal fare system is used. Tickets (starting at Fl. 3) are bought from automatic dispensers on the metro or from the drivers on trams and buses; or buy a money-saving **strippenkaart** (*see* Getting Around, By Bus, *in* Essential Information, *above*). Even simpler is the **dagkaart,** which covers all city routes for Fl. 12. These discount tickets can be obtained from the main GVB ticket office in front of Centraal Station and from many newsstands, along with route maps of the public transportation system. The **Canalbus,** which travels between the central train station and the Rijksmuseum, is Fl. 22 for a hop-on, hop-off day card.

By Taxi

Taxis are expensive: A short 3-mile ride costs around Fl. 20. Taxis are not usually hailed on the street but are picked up at stands near stations and other key points. Alternatively, you can dial 020/6777777. Water taxis (tel. 020/6222181) are even more expensive (standard-size water taxis—for up to eight people—cost Fl. 60 for the first half hour plus Fl. 30 pickup charge and Fl. 2 per minute).

By Car

Parking in Amsterdam has always been difficult. Frequent attempts to ban cars from the city center are scuppered by the opposition of local big business. The city's concentric ring of canals, one-way systems, and lack of parking facilities will continue to plague drivers. It's best to put your car in one of the parking lots on the edge of the old center and abandon it for the rest of your stay.

By Bicycle

Rental bikes are readily available for around Fl. 10 per day with a Fl. 50–Fl. 200 deposit. Bikes are an excellent and inexpensive way to explore the city. Several rental companies are close to the central station, or ask at tourist offices for details. Lock your bike up at all times, preferably to something immovable; thieves have been known to abscond with them in fewer than 30 seconds. Also, check with the rental company what your liability is under their insurance terms.

By Boat

The **Museum Boat** (*see* Guided Tours, *below*), which makes seven stops near major museums, is Fl. 19 for adults, Fl. 15 for children.

On Foot

Amsterdam is a small, congested city of narrow streets, which makes it ideal for exploring on foot. The tourist office issues seven excellent guides that detail walking tours around the center. The best are "The Jordaan," a stroll through the lively canal-side district, and "Jewish Amsterdam," a walk past the symbolic remains of Jewish housing and old synagogues.

Important Addresses and Numbers

Tourist Information

There are two locations for the **VVV Amsterdam Tourist Office:** one in front of Central Station (Stationsplein 10, in the Old Dutch Coffee House; open daily 9–5) and another at Leidseplein 1 (open fall–spring, daily 9–7; summer, daily 9–9). VVV is the acronym for information offices; you'll see it on signposts throughout the country. The general number for telephone inquiries in Amsterdam is 06/34034066, but you are charged 75¢ per minute and kept waiting in an electronic line.

Consulates

U.S. (Museumplein 19, tel. 020/6645661). **Canadian** (7 Sophialaan, The Hague, tel. 070/3614111). **U.K.** (Koningslaan 44, tel. 020/6764343).

Emergencies

The general number for emergencies is 06/11, but note direct numbers. **Police** (tel. 020/6222222); **Ambulance** (tel. 020/5555555). For emergency medical service, call **Doctor Academisch Medisch Centrum** (Meibergdreef 9, tel. 020/5669111). **Central Medical Service** (tel. 020/6123766 or 06/35032042) will give you names of pharmacists and dentists as well as doctors.

English-Language Bookstores

American Discount Book Center (Kalverstraat 185, 020/6255537). **Athenaeum Boekhandel** (Spui 14, tel. 020/6233933). **English Bookshop** (Lauriergracht 71, tel. 020/6264230).

Travel Agencies

American Express (Damrak 66, tel. 020/5207777; Van Baerlestraat 38, tel. 020/6738550); **De Vries & Co.** (Dam 6, tel. 020/5550900); **Holland International** (Leidseplein 43, tel. 020/6262660); **Key Tours** (Dam 19, tel. 020/6247310); **Thomas Cook** (Bureau de Change, Leidseplein 31a, tel. 020/6267000; Van Baerlestraat 40, tel. 020/6766101).

Guided Tours

Boat Tours

The most enjoyable way to get to know Amsterdam is by taking a boat trip along the canals. There are frequent departures from points opposite Central Station, along the Damrak, and along the Rokin and Stadhouderskade (near the Rijksmuseum). For a tour lasting about one hour, the cost is around Fl. 12.50, but the student guides expect a small tip for their multilingual commentary. On summer evenings, longer cruises include wine and cheese or a full buffet dinner. A few tours feature increasingly drunken stops for wine tastings in canal-side bars. A candlelight dinner cruise costs upward of Fl. 39.50. Trips can be booked through the tourist office.

Alternatively, you may want to rent a pedal boat and make your own canal tour. At **Canal-Bike** (tel. 020/6239886), a pedal boat for four costs FL. 29.50 per hour.

The **Museum Boat** (Stationsplein 8, tel. 020/6222181) combines a scenic view of the city with seven stops near 20 museums. Tickets, good for the entire day, are Fl. 19; a combination ticket for Fl. 35 includes entrance to three museums.

Bus Tours

Guided bus tours around the city are also available and provide an excellent introduction to Amsterdam. A combined bus-and-boat tour includes the inevitable trip to a diamond factory. Costing Fl. 25–Fl. 35, the comprehensive three-hour tour can be booked through **Lindbergh** (Damrak 26–27, tel. 020/6222766) or **Key Tours** (Dam 19, tel. 020/6247310).

Exploring Amsterdam

Amsterdam is a gem of a city for the visitor. Small and densely packed with fine buildings, many dating from the 17th century or earlier, it is easily explored on foot or by bike. The old heart of the city consists of canals, with narrow streets radiating out like the spokes of a wheel. The hub of this wheel and the most convenient point to begin sightseeing is Central Station. Across the street, in the same building as the Old Dutch Coffee House, is a tourist information office that offers helpful advice.

Amsterdam's key points of interest can be covered within two or three days, with each walking itinerary taking in one or two of the important museums and galleries. The following exploration of the city center can be broken up into several sessions.

Around the Dam

Numbers in the margin correspond to points of interest on the Amsterdam map.

① Start at **Centraal Station** (Central Station). Designed by P. J. H. Cuijpers and built in 1884–89, it is a good example of Dutch architecture at its most flamboyant. The street directly in front of the station square is Prins Hendrikkade. To the left, a good vantage point for
② viewing the station, is **St. Nicolaaskerk** (Church of St. Nicholas), consecrated in 1888.

Around the corner from St. Nicolaaskerk, facing the harbor, is the
③ **Schreierstoren** (Weepers' Tower), a lookout tower for women whose men were out at sea. The tower was erected in 1480, and a tablet marks the point from which Henrik (a.k.a. Henry) Hudson set sail on the *Half*

Moon on April 4, 1609, on a voyage that eventually took him to what is now New York and the river that still bears his name. Today the Weepers' Tower is used as a combined reception and exhibition center, which includes a maritime bookshop.

④ Three blocks to the southwest along the Oudezijds Voorburgwal is the **Museum Amstelkring,** whose facade carries the inscription *"Ons Lieve Heer Op Solder"* ("Our Dear Lord in the Attic"). In 1578, Amsterdam embraced Protestantism and outlawed the church of Rome. So great was the tolerance of the municipal authorities, however, that secret Catholic chapels were allowed to exist; at one time there were 62 in Amsterdam alone. One such chapel was established in the attics of these three neighboring canal-side houses, built around 1661. The lower floors were used as ordinary dwellings, while services were held in the attics regularly until 1888, the year St. Nicolaaskerk was consecrated for Catholic worship. Of interest are the Baroque altar with its revolving tabernacle, the swinging pulpit that can be stowed out of sight, and the upstairs gallery. *Oudezijds Voorburgwal 40, tel. 020/6246604. Admission: Fl. 5. Open Mon.–Sat. 10–5, Sun. 1–5.*

⑤ Just beyond, you can see the **Oude Kerk** (Old Church), the city's oldest church. Built during the 14th century but badly damaged by iconoclasts after the Reformation, the church still retains its original bell tower and a few remarkable stained-glass windows. From the tower, there is a typical view of Old Amsterdam stretching from St. Nicolaaskerk to medieval gables. Rembrandt's wife, Saskia, is buried here. *Oudekerksplein 23, tel. 020/6249183. Admission: Fl. 5. Open Apr.–Oct., Mon.–Sat. 11–5, Sun. 1:30–5; Nov.–Mar., Fri.–Sun. 1–5.*

This area, bordered by Amsterdam's two oldest canals (Oudezijds Voorburgwal and Oudezijds Achterburgwal), is the heart of the *rosse buurt,* the red-light district. In the windows at canal level, women in sheer lingerie slouch, stare, or do their nails. Although the area can be shocking, with its sex shops and porn shows, it is generally safe, but midnight walks down dark side streets are not advised. If you do decide to explore the area, take care; purse snatchers and pickpockets are a problem.

⑥ Return to the Damrak and continue to the **Dam** (Dam Square), the broadest square in the old section of the town. It was here that fishermen used to come to sell their catch. Today it is circled with shops and people, and bisected with traffic; it is also a popular center for outdoor performers. At one side of the square you will notice a simple monument to Dutch victims of World War II. Eleven urns contain soil from the 11 provinces of Holland, while a 12th contains soil from the former Dutch East Indies, now Indonesia.

⑦ In a corner of the square is the **Nieuwe Kerk** (New Church). A huge Gothic church, it was gradually expanded until 1540, when it reached its present size. Gutted by fire in 1645, it was reconstructed in an imposing Renaissance style, as interpreted by strict Calvinists. The superb oak pulpit, the 14th-century nave, the stained-glass windows, and the great organ (1645) are all shown to great effect on national holidays, when the church is bedecked with flowers. As befits Holland's national church, the Nieuwe Kerk is the site of all inaugurations (as the Dutch call their coronations), including that of Queen Beatrix in 1980. But in democratic Dutch spirit, the church is also used as a meeting place and is the home of a lively café, temporary exhibitions, and concerts. *Dam, tel. 020/6268168. Admission free, except for special exhibitions (Fl. 12.50). Open daily 11–5; exhibitions daily 10–6.*

Amsterdam Historisch Museum, **12**

Anne Frankhuis, **10**

Begijnhof, **13**

Centraal Station, **1**

Concertgebouw, **27**

Dam, **6**

Dokwerker, **22**

Flower Market, **16**

Gouden Bocht, **17**

Het Koninklijk Paleis te Amsterdam, **8**

Joods Historisch Museum, **23**

Jordaan, **28**

Leidseplein, **14**

Muntplein, **15**

Museum Amstelkring, **4**

Museum Het Rembrandthuis, **19**

Muziektheater/ Stadhuis, **20**

Nederlands Theater Instituut, **18**

Nieuwe Kerk, **7**

Noorderkerk, **11**

Oude Kerk, **5**

Portugees Israelitische Synagogue, **21**

Rijksmuseum, **24**

Rijksmuseum Vincent van Gogh, **25**

St. Nicholaaskerk, **2**

Schrierstoren, **3**

Stedelijk Museum, **26**

Westerkerk, **9**

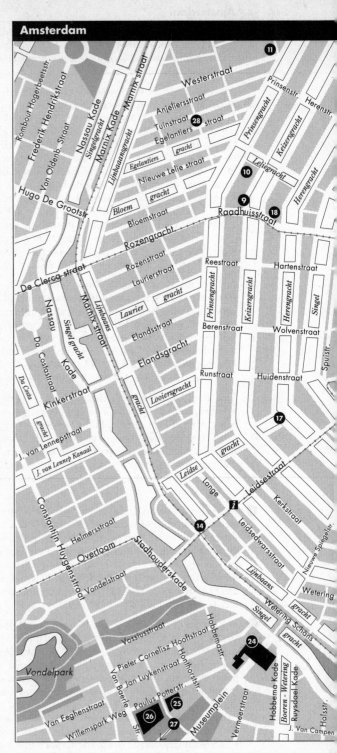

Amsterdam

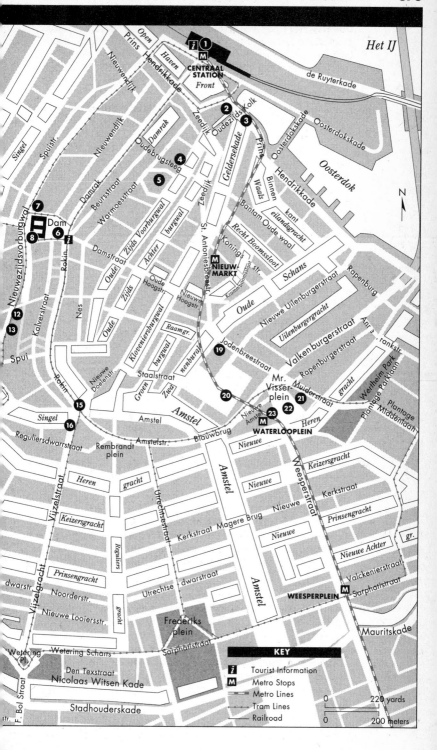

Het IJ

de Ruyterkade

CENTRAAL
STATION
Front

Oosterdokskade

Oosterdok

Open Haven

Prins Hendrikkade

Zeedijk

Oudezijds Kolk

Geldersekade

Prins Hendrikkade

Binnen kant

Binnen Waals

eilandsgracht

Bantammerstraat

Oude waal

Recht Boomssloot

Oosterdokskade

Singel

Spuistr.

Nieuwendijk

Damrak

Oudebrugsteeg

Beurstraat

Warmoesstraat

Oude

Damrak

Zeedijk

Zijds Voorburgwal

Achter

St. Antoniesbreestr.

burgwal

Oude Hoogstr.

Konings str.

Kromboomsloot

Schans

Rapenburg

Dam

Nieuwezijdsvoorburgwal

Damstraat

Oude

Zijds Voorburgwal

Achter

burgwal

Oude Hoogstr.

NIEUW
MARKT

Oude

Nieuwe Uilenburgerstraat

Uilenburgergracht

Rokin

Nes

Oude

Zijds

Nieuwe Hoogstr.

Raamgr.

venburgwal

Jodenbreestraat

Valkenburgerstraat

Rapenburgerstraat

Anna. ranksir.

gracht

Wertheim Park

Plantage Parklaan

Spui

Kalverstraat

Nieuwe Doelenstr.

Klovemiersburgwal

Groen burgwal

Zwad

Staalstraat

Amstel

Mr.
Visser-
plein

Muiderstraat

Plantage Middenlaan

Singel

Reguliersdwarrstraat

Rokin

Amstel

Blauwbrug

Amstelstr.

Nieuwe Amstel

WATERLOOPLEIN

Heren

Weesperstraat

Rembrandt
plein

Nieuwe

Keizersgracht

Kerkstraat

Vizelstraat

Heren

gracht

Amstel

Nieuwe

Nieuwe

Prinsengracht

Keizersgracht

Utrechtestraat

Kerkstraat Magere Brug

Nieuwe

Nieuwe Achter

gr.

Regulers

Nieuwe

Valckenierstraat

Vijzelgracht

Prinsengracht

gracht

Utrechtse

dwarstraat

Amstel

Sarphatistraat

WEESPERPLEIN

dwarstr.

Noorderstr.

Frederiks
plein

Mauritskade

Nieuwe Looiersstr.

Wetering
Pl

Wetering Schans

Sarphatistraat

Den Texstraat

Nicolaas Witsen Kade

F. Bol Straat

Stadhouderskade

KEY	
🛈	Tourist Information
Ⓜ	Metro Stops
	Metro Lines
	Tram Lines
	Railroad

0 ——— 220 yards
0 ——— 200 meters

In a house on a crooked, medieval street behind the Nieuwe Kerk, **De Drie Fleschjes** (The Three Bottles) is one of the most typical 17th-century *proeflokalen* (wine- and spirit-tasting houses). The tone is set by the burnished wood interior, the candlelighted bar, and the profusion of kegs and taps. Although the main emphasis is on drink, light snacks are also available. *Gravenstraat 18. Open Mon.–Sat. noon–8.*

⑧ Dominating Dam Square is the **Het Koninklijk Paleis te Amsterdam** (Royal Palace at Amsterdam), a vast, well-proportioned structure on Dam Square that was completed in 1655. It is built on 13,659 pilings sunk into the marshy soil. The great pedimental sculptures are an allegorical representation of Amsterdam surrounded by Neptune and mythological sea creatures. *Dam, tel. 020/6248698. Admission: Fl. 5. Open Tues.–Thurs. 1–4; daily noon–4 during Easter, summer, and fall holidays. Sometimes closed for state events.*

⑨ From behind the palace, Raadhuisstraat leads west across three canals to the Westermarkt and the **Westerkerk** (West Church), built in 1631. The church's 279-foot tower is the highest in the city. It also features an outstanding carillon. Rembrandt and his son Titus are buried in the church. On summer afternoons, you can climb to the top of the tower for a fine view over the city. *Prinsengracht (corner of Westermarkt), tel. 020/6247766. Tower open June–Sept., Tues., Wed. and Fri.–Sat. 2–5.*

⑩ Opposite, at Westermarkt 6, is the house where René Descartes, the great 17th-century French philosopher (*"Cogito, ergo sum"*—"I think, therefore I am") lived in 1634. Another more famous house lies farther down Prinsengracht. This is the **Anne Frankhuis** (Anne Frank House), immortalized by the poignant diary kept by the young Jewish girl from 1942 to 1944, when she and her family hid here from the German occupying forces. A small exhibition on the Holocaust can also be seen in the house. *Prinsengracht 263, tel. 020/5567100. Admission: Fl. 8. Open June–Aug., Mon.–Sat. 9–7, Sun. 10–7; Sept.–May, Mon.–Sat. 9–5, Sun. 10–5.*

⑪ Continuing across the Prinsengracht, you'll reach the **Noorderkerk** (North Church), built in 1623. In the square in front of the church, the Noorderplein, a bird market is held every Saturday.

South of the Dam

Turn down Kalverstraat, a shopping street leading from the Royal Palace. You will notice a striking Renaissance gate (1581) that guards a series of tranquil inner courtyards. In medieval times, this area was an island devoted to piety. Today the bordering canals are filled in.

⑫ The medieval doorway just around the corner in St. Luciensteeg leads to the former Burgerweeshuis (City Orphanage), once a nunnery but now the **Amsterdam Historisch Museum** (Amsterdam Historical Museum). The museum traces the city's history from its origins as a fishing village through the 17th-century Golden Age of material and artistic wealth to the decline of the trading empire during the 18th century. The engrossing story unfolds through a display of old maps, documents, and paintings, often aided by a commentary in English. *Kalverstraat 92, tel. 020/5231822. Admission: Fl. 7.50. Open weekdays 10–5, weekends 11–5.*

⑬ A small passageway and courtyard link the museum with the **Begijnhof** (Beguine Court), an enchanting, enclosed square of almshouses founded in 1346 that is an oasis of silence beside the hectic Kalverstraat. The Beguines were women who chose to lead a form of convent life, often taking the vow of chastity. The last Beguine died in 1974 and her house, Number 26, has been preserved as she left it. Number 34, dating from the 15th century, is the oldest and the only one to keep its wooden Gothic facade. *Begijnhof 29, tel. 020/6233565. Admission free. Open weekdays 11–4.*

In the center of the square is a church given to Amsterdam's English and Scottish Presbyterians more than 300 years ago. On the church wall and also in the chancel are tributes to the Pilgrim Fathers who sailed from Delfshaven to the New World in 1620. Opposite the church is another of the city's secret Catholic chapels, built in 1671.

Continuing along Kalverstraat, you soon come to Spui, a lively square in the heart of the university area. It was a center for student rallies in revolutionary 1968. Now it is a center for bookstores and bars, including the cozy brown cafés.

Beyond is the Singel Canal and, following the tram tracks, Leidsestraat, an important shopping street that terminates in the **Leidseplein,** a lively square that is one of the nightlife centers of the city.

If you continue straight along Kalverstraat instead of turning at Spui, you'll soon reach the **Muntplein,** with its **Munttoren** (Mint Tower, built in 1620), a graceful structure whose clock and bells still seem to mirror the Golden Age. Beginning at the Muntplein is the floating **Flower Market** on the Singel Canal, which is open Monday–Saturday 9:30–5.

From the Singel, take Leidsestraat to the Herengracht, the city's most prestigious "Gentlemen's Canal." The stretch of canal from here to Huidenstraat is named the **Gouden Bocht** (Golden Bend) for its sumptuous patrician houses with double staircases and grand entrances. Seventeenth-century merchants moved here from the Amstel River to escape the disadvantageous byproducts of their wealth: the noisy warehouses, the unpleasant smells from the breweries, and the risk of fire in the sugar refineries. These houses display the full range of Amsterdam facades: from houses with gables in a variety of shapes to grander Louis XIV–style houses with elaborate cornices and frescoed ceilings. These houses are best seen from the east side of the canal. For more gables, turn down Wolvenstraat into the Keizersgracht, the Emperor's Canal. Walk northward toward Westerkerk and the Anne Frankhuis (*see above*).

TIME OUT On the corner of Keizersgracht and Reestraat is the **Pulitzer Hotel** and restaurant complex. Inside, you can wander around quiet inner courtyards and a modern art gallery before sitting down in the **Café Pulitzer,** which overlooks the canal, for a well-deserved apple tart or pastry. *Keizersgracht 236. Open daily 11–4.*

Along Herengracht, parallel to the Westerkerk, is the **Nederlands Theater Instituut.** This theater museum is a dynamic find on such a genteel canal. Two frescoed Louis XIV–style merchants' houses form the backdrop for a history of the circus, opera, musicals, and drama. Miniature theaters and videos of stage productions are just two entertaining features. In summer, the large garden is open for buffet lunches. *Herengracht 168, tel. 020/6235104. Admission: Fl. 5. Open weekdays 11–5, weekends 1–5.*

Jewish Amsterdam

Take the Museum Boat or the metro from Central Station to Waterlooplein and walk east to Jodenbreestraat. This is the heart of **Jodenbuurt,** the old Jewish district and an important area to all Amsterdammers. The original settlers here were wealthy Sephardic Jews from Spain and Portugal, later followed by poorer Ashkenazic refugees from Germany and Poland. At the turn of the century, this was a thriving community of Jewish diamond polishers, dyers, and merchants. During World War II, the corner of Jodenbreestraat marked the end of the *Joodse wijk* (Jewish neighborhood), by then an imposed ghetto. Although the character of the area was largely destroyed by highway construction in 1965, and more recently by construction of both the metro and the Muziektheater/Stadhuis complex (*see below*), neighboring Muiderstraat has retained much of the original atmosphere. Notice the gateways decorated with pelicans, symbolizing great love; according to legend, the pelican will feed her starving young with her own blood.

From 1639 to 1658, Rembrandt lived at Jodenbreestraat 4, now the **19 Museum Het Rembrandthuis** (Rembrandt's House). For more than 20 years, the ground floor was used by the artist as living quarters; the sunny upper floor was his studio. It contains a superb collection of his etchings. From St. Antonies Sluis bridge, just by the house, there is a canal view that has barely changed since Rembrandt's time. *Jodenbreestraat 4–6, tel. 020/6249486. Admission: Fl. 7.50. Open Mon.–Sat. 10–5, Sun. 1–5.*

After visiting Rembrandt's House, walk back to the canal and go left to pass the Waterlooplein flea market. Ahead of you is the Amsterdam **20 Muziektheater/Stadhuis** (Music Theater/Town Hall) complex, which presents an intriguing combination of bureaucracy and art. Amsterdammers come to the town hall section of the building by day to obtain driving licenses, to pick up welfare payments, and to be married. They return by night to the rounded part of the building facing the river to see opera and ballet by Holland's well-known performing companies. Feel free to wander into town hall (there are some interesting sculptures and other displays to see). Opera and ballet fans can go on a tour of the Muziektheater, which takes you around the dressing rooms, dance studios, and even the wig departmeant. *Amstel 3, tel. 020/5518054. Cost: Fl. 8.50. Guided tours every Wed. and Sat. at 3.*

Walk through the flea market behind the Muziektheater, and across a **21** busy traffic junction you come to the 17th-century **Portugees Israelitische Synagogue** (Portuguese Israelite Synagogue). As one of Amsterdam's four neighboring synagogues, it was part of the largest Jewish religious complex in Europe. The austere interior is still intact, even if the building itself is marooned on a traffic island. *Mr. Visserplein 3, tel. 020/6245351. Admission: Fl. 5. Open Apr.–Oct., Sun.–Fri. 10–4; Nov.–Mar., Mon.–Thurs. 10–4, Fri. 10–3, Sun. 10–noon. Closed daily 12:30–1.*

Jonas Daniël Meijerplein is a square behind the synagogue. In the cen- **22** ter is a statue of the **Dokwerker** (Dockworker), a profession that has played a significant part in the city's history. The statue commemorates the 1942 strike by which Amsterdam dockworkers expressed their solidarity with persecuted Jews. A memorial march is held every year on February 25.

23 On the other side of the square is the intriguing **Joods Historisch Museum** (Jewish History Museum), set in a complex of three ancient synagogues. These synagogues once served a population of 100,000 Jews, which shrank to fewer than 10,000 after 1945. The new museum, founded by American and Dutch Jews, displays religious treasures in a clear cultural and historical context. Since the synagogues lost most of their treasures in the war, their architecture and history are more compelling than the individual exhibits. *Jonas Daniël Meijerplein 2–4, tel. 020/6269945. Admission: Fl. 7. Open daily 11–5.*

TIME OUT In the oldest part of the Jewish History Museum, **Cafeteria Kosher** (open daily 11–5) is built above the former kosher meat halls that later became ritual baths. It still looks like part of a clandestine Catholic church, the original model for the synagogue. Jewish delicacies include fish cakes, cheese tarts, bagels, and spicy cakes with gingerbread and almond cream filling.

Instead of returning on foot, you can catch the Museum Boat from the Muziektheater to the central station or to a destination near your hotel. If you feel like a breath of fresh air, stroll along Nieuwe Herengracht, once known as the "Jewish Gentlemen's Canal." In Rembrandt's day, there were views of distant windjammers sailing into port, but today the canal is oddly deserted.

The Museum Quarter

By crossing the bridge beyond the Leidseplein and walking a short distance to the left on Stadhouderskade, you'll find three of the most distinguished museums in Holland—the Rijksmuseum, the Stedelijk Museum, and the Rijksmuseum Vincent van Gogh. Of the three, the

㉔ **Rijksmuseum** (State Museum), easily recognized by its towers, is the most important, so be sure to allow adequate time to explore it. It was founded in 1808, but the current, rather lavish, building dates from 1885. The museum contains significant collections of furniture, textiles, ceramics, sculpture, and prints, as well as Italian, Flemish, and Spanish paintings, many of which are of the highest quality. But the museum's fame rests on its unrivaled collection of 16th- and 17th-century Dutch masters. Of Rembrandt's masterpieces, make a point of seeing *The Nightwatch,* concealed during World War II in caves in Maastricht. The painting was misnamed because of its dull layers of varnish; in reality it depicts the Civil Guard in daylight. Also worth searching out are Frans Hals's family portraits, Jan Steen's drunken scenes, Van Ruysdael's romantic but menacing landscapes, and Vermeer's glimpses of everyday life bathed in his usual pale light. *Stadhouderskade 42, tel. 020/6732121. Admission: Fl. 12.50. Open Tues.–Sun. 10–5.*

㉕ A few blocks beyond is the **Rijksmuseum Vincent van Gogh** (Vincent van Gogh Museum). This museum contains the world's largest collection of the artist's works—200 paintings and nearly 500 drawings—as well as works by some 50 of his contemporaries. *Paulus Potterstraat 7, tel. 020/5705200. Admission: Fl. 10 adults, Fl. 5 children. Open daily 10–5.*

㉖ Next door is the **Stedelijk Museum** (Municipal Museum), with its neo-Renaissance facade. The museum has a stimulating collection of modern art and ever-changing displays of contemporary art. Before viewing the works of Cézanne, Chagall, Kandinsky, and Mondrian, check the list of temporary exhibitions in Room 1. Museum policy is to trace the development of the artist rather than merely to show a few masterpieces. Don't forget the museum's restaurant overlooking a garden filled with modern sculptures. *Paulus Potterstraat 13, tel. 020/5732911. Admission: Fl. 7.50. Open daily 11–5.*

Diagonally opposite the Stedelijk Museum, at the end of the broad Museumplein, is the **Concertgebouw,** home of the country's foremost orchestra, ㉗ the world-renowned Concertgebouworkest. Many visiting orchestras also perform here. The building has two auditoriums, the smaller of which is used for chamber music and recitals. A block or two in the opposite direction is **Vondelpark,** an elongated rectangle of paths, lakes, and pleasant shade trees. A monument honors the 17th-century epic poet Joost van den Vondel, for whom the park is named. From Wednesday to Sunday in summer, free concerts and plays are performed in the park.

The Jordaan

28 One old part of Amsterdam that is certainly worth exploring is the **Jordaan,** the area bordered by Prinsengracht, Lijnbaansgracht, Brouwersgracht, and Raadhuisstraat. The canals and side streets here are all named for flowers and plants. Indeed, at one time, when this was the French quarter of the city, the area was known as *le jardin* (the garden), a name that over the years has become Jordaan. The best time to explore this area is on a Sunday morning, when there are few cars and people about, or in the evening. This part of the town has attracted many artists and is something of a bohemian quarter, where run-down buildings are being renovated and converted into restaurants, antiques shops, boutiques, and galleries.

TIME OUT   The Jordaan is the best part of Amsterdam for relaxing in a brown café, so named because of the rich wooden furnishings and—some say—the centuries-old pipe-tobacco stains on the ceilings. You can while away a rainy afternoon chatting with friendly strangers over homemade meatballs or apple tarts. Spend an hour or three over a beer or coffee at either **'t Doktorje** (Rozenboomsteeg 4) or **De Gijs** (Lindegracht 249).

Off the Beaten Track

Another "see-worthy" district is the burgeoning **Maritime Quarter.** To reach it, walk from Central Station along the Prins Hendrikkade and the Eastern Harbor, the hub of shipping activity during Holland's Golden Age. A growing permanent collection of restored vessels is moored at the **Rijksmuseum Nederlands Scheepvaart** (State Museum of Netherlands Shipping), a former naval complex at Kattenburgerplein 1. A short stroll farther down the Kattenburgergracht-Wittenburgergracht to the footbridge over the canal leads to the **Kromhout Museum** (Hoogte Kadijk 147). Many early steamships were built at this wharf, where models and motors are on display.

About three blocks from Central Station, at **Haarlemmerstraat 75,** a plaque commemorates the occasion, in 1623, when the directors of the Dutch West India Company planned the founding of Nieuw Amsterdam on the southernmost tip of the island of Manhattan. In 1664, this colony was seized by the English and renamed New York.

An otherwise unremarkable building at **Singel 460** (near Herengracht) has special significance for Americans. In this building John Adams raised the first foreign loan ($2 million) for the United States from the banking house of Van Staphorst in 1782. Additional loans from this and other banks soon followed, for a total of $30 million—a gesture of Dutch confidence in the future of America.

Beer lovers—or anyone with an interest in the production of a world-class product—will want to take time to visit the **Heinekenontvangstgebouw,** formerly the Heineken Brewery. The guided weekday tours (year-round 9:30 and 11, additional summer tours at 1 and 2:30) take in a slide presentation, the old brewery stables, and, of course, include free beer at the end of the tour. *Van der Helstraat, tel. 020/5239436. Admission: Fl. 2. Children under 18 not admitted.*

Shopping

Amsterdam is a cornucopia of interesting markets, quirky specialist shops, antiques, art, and diamonds.

Gift Ideas

Diamonds. Since the 17th century, "Amsterdam cut" has been synonymous with perfection in the quality of diamonds. You can see this craftsmanship at any of the diamond-cutting houses. The cutters explain how the diamond's value depends on the four cs—carat, cut, clarity, and color—before encouraging you to buy. There is a cluster of diamond houses on the Rokin.

Porcelain. The Dutch have been producing Delft, Makkum, and other fine porcelain for centuries. **Focke and Meltzer** stores have been selling it since 1823. The objects vary from affordable, newly painted tiles to expensive Delft blue-and-white pitchers. One store is near the Rijksmuseum (P. C. Hooftstraat 65–67, tel. 020/6642311).

Shopping Districts

Amsterdam's chief shopping districts, which have largely been turned into pedestrian-only areas, are the **Leidsestraat, Kalverstraat,** and **Nieuwendijk.** The **Rokin,** hectic with traffic, houses a cluster of boutiques and renowned antiques shops selling 18th- and 19th-century furniture, antique jewelry, Art Deco lamps, and statuettes. By contrast, some of the **Nieuwe Spiegelstraat's** old curiosity shops sell a less expensive range. Haute couture and other fine goods are at home on P. C. Hooftstraat, Van Baerlestraat, and Beethovenstraat. For trendy small boutiques and unusual crafts shops, locals browse through the Jordaan. For A-to-Z shopping in a huge variety of stores, visit the new **Magna Plaza** shopping center, built inside the glorious old post office behind the Royal Palace. When leaving Holland, remember that Schiphol Airport is Europe's best tax-free shopping center.

Department Stores

De Bijenkorf (Dam Square), the city's number-one department store, is excellent for contemporary fashions and furnishings. Running a close second is **Vroom and Dreesman** (Kalverstraat 201), with well-stocked departments carrying all manner of goods. More sedate is **Maison de Bonneterie en Pander** (Rokin 140–142 and Beethovenstraat 32). The restaurants and cafés in these department stores are also worth trying.

Markets

There is a lively open-air **flea market** on Waterlooplein around the Musiektheater (Mon.–Sat. 9:30–4). The **floating flower market** on the Singel is popular with locals and visitors alike (Mon.–Sat. 9:30–5). An unusual Saturday **bird market** is held in the Noordermarkt. Philatelists will not want to miss the **stamp market** at Nieuwezijds Voorburgwal (Wed. and Sat. 1–4). For antiques, especially silver and toys, visit the **Antiekmarkt de Looier** (Elandsgracht 109; Sun.–Wed. 11–5, Thurs. 11–9). During the summer, art lovers can buy etchings, drawings, and watercolors at the Sunday **art markets** on Thorbeckeplein and the Spui.

Dining

Amsterdammers are less creatures of habit than are the Dutch in general. Even so, set menus and early dinners are preferred by these health-conscious citizens. For travelers on a diet or a budget, the blue-and-white TOURIST MENU sign guarantees an economical (Fl. 25) yet imaginative set menu created by the head chef. For traditionalists, the NEDERLANDS

DIS soup tureen sign is a promise of regional recipes and seasonal ingredients. "You can eat in any language" is the city's proud boast, so when Dutch restaurants are closed, Indonesian, Chinese, and Turkish restaurants are often open. For details and price-category definitions, *see* Dining *in* Staying in Holland, *above*.

$$$$ **Amstel Inter-Continental.** This world-class restaurant in a 125-year-old
★ grand hotel is fit for royalty. The French cuisine, with an awe-inspiring "truffle menu" of dishes prepared with exotic (and expensive) ingredients, is nonpareil and can be tailored to meet your every whim. Epicureans seeking the ultimate should inquire about the "chef's table": With a group of six you can sit in the heart of the kitchen and watch chefs describe each of your courses as it is prepared. *Professor Tulpplein 1, tel. 020/6226060. Reservations advised. Jacket and tie. AE, DC, MC, V.*

$$$$ **Excelsior.** The Hôtel de l'Europe's renowned restaurant offers a var-
★ ied menu of French cuisine that is based on local ingredients. There is a splendid array of seafood dishes and an elaborate vegetarian menu. The service is discreet and impeccable. *Nieuwe Doelenstraat 2–4, tel. 020/6234836. Reservations required. Jacket and tie. AE, DC, MC, V. No lunch Sat.*

$$$$ **'t Swarte Schaep.** The Black Sheep is named after a proverbial 17th-
★ century sheep that once roamed the area. With its creaking boards and array of copper pots, the interior is reminiscent of a ship's cabin. The Dutch chef uses seasonal ingredients to create classical French dishes with regional flourishes. Dinner orders are accepted until 11 PM—unusually late even for Amsterdam. *Korte Leidsedwarsstraat 24, tel. 020/6223021. Reservations required. Jacket and tie. AE, DC, MC, V.*

$$$ **De Silveren Spiegel.** In an alarmingly crooked 17th-century house, you
★ can have an outstanding meal while you enjoy the personal attention of the owner at one of just a small cluster of tables. Local ingredients such as Texel lamb and wild rabbit are cooked with subtlety and flair. *Kattengat 4–6, tel. 020/6246589. Reservations advised. Jacket and tie. AE, MC, V.*

$$$ **Le Tout Court.** This small, meticulously appointed restaurant features seasonal specialties (spring lamb, summer fruits, game during autumn and winter) personally prepared by owner-chef John Fagel, who hails from a well-known Dutch family of chefs. *Runstraat 13, tel. 020/6258637. Reservations advised. AE, DC, MC, V.*

$$$ **Yamazoto.** Japanese expatriates laud this as the top Japanese restaurant in town. An award-winning chef blends the freshest local ingredients with exotica flown in daily from the Land of the Rising Sun. The full seasonal set menu will cost you more than Fl. 100, but there are scores of less pricey options. At a separate bar fresh sushi is prepared before your eyes. The adjoining Sazanaka Restaurant specializes in *teppanyaki* (food grilled at the table). *Hotel Okura, Ferdinand Bolstraat 333, tel. 020/6787111. Reservations advised. Jacket and tie. AE, DC, MC, V.*

$$–$$$ **Eerst Klas.** Amsterdam's best-kept secret is in the most obvious of places: the former first-class waiting lounge of the central train station. The classic, dark-wood paneling and soft interior lighting create the perfect hideaway from the city's hustle and bustle. Diners munch their way through tasty salads, steaks, and fish dishes. *Stationsplein 15, Spoer 2b, tel. 020/6250131. Reservations advised. Jacket and tie. AE, DC, MC, V.*

$$–$$$ **Lucius.** Outstanding fish and seafood are simply served in a plain setting. Choices range from fish burgers with Gorgonzola to grilled lobster. Not for the queasy, though—as you tuck into your fish, its live cousins eye you from a tank along the wall. *Spuistraat 247, tel. 020/6241831. Reservations advised. AE, DC, MC, V. Closed Sun.*

$$–$$$ **Oesterbar.** The Oyster Bar specializes in seafood, grilled, baked, or fried. The upstairs dining room is more formal than the downstairs bistro, but prices don't vary. Salmon, wollfish, and halibut are favorite seafood entrées; oysters are a good, if pricey, appetizer. *Leidseplein 10, tel. 020/6232988. Reservations advised. AE, DC, MC.*

$$–$$$ **Pier 10.** Perched on the end of a pier behind Central Station, this in-
★ timate restaurant was built in the '30s as a shipping office. Water laps gently just beneath the windows, and the harbor lights twinkle in the distance. Culinary adventures might include Victoria bass in phyllo with caviar or a handsome platter of dove, duck, and partridge with cran-berry sauce. *De Ruyterkade Steiger 10, tel. 020/6248276. Reservations required. AE, MC, V.*

$$ **Haesje Claes.** Traditional Dutch food is served here in a traditional Dutch environment, with prices that are easy on the wallet; it sounds like a tourist's dream and, in ways, it is. There's a cozy feeling here and a re-laxed simplicity. Menu choices can be as basic as traditional *stamppot* (mixed potatoes and sauerkraut) or as elaborate as filet of salmon with lobster sauce. There is a tourist menu. *Spuistraat 273–275, tel. 020/6249998. Reservations advised. AE, DC, MC, V. No lunch Sun.*

$$ **Rose's Cantina.** This perennial favorite of the sparkling set offers spicy Tex-Mex food, lethal cocktails, and a high noise level. Pop in for a full meal or a late afternoon drink. *Reguliersdwarsstraat 38, tel. 020/6259797. Weekend reservations required. AE, DC, MC, V.*

$$ **Speciaal.** Although set in the Jordaan area, this Indonesian restaurant is slightly off the beaten track. Along with the usual rijsttafel, chicken, fish, and egg dishes provide tasty variants on a sweet-and-sour theme. *Nieuwe Leliestraat 142, tel. 020/6249706. Reservations accepted. AE, MC, V.*

$$ **Toscanini.** This cavernous, noisy Italian restaurant has superb cuisine.
★ Try the pasta with game sauce, the scrumptious selection of antipasti, the rabbit, or the fresh fish dishes. *Lindengracht 75, tel. 020/6232813. Reservations required. No credit cards. No lunch.*

$ **De Keuken van 1870.** "The Kitchen of 1870" was a soup kitchen through the Great Depression and two world wars and now serves up hearty Dutch food at unbeatably low prices. Plates are borne from the steamy kitchen piled high with good, nutritious meat and vegetables doused in gravy. *Spuistraat 4, tel. 020/6248965. No reservations. AE, DC, MC, V.*

$ **Eettuin.** This "eating garden" in the heart of the arty Jordaan area has something for everyone—from vegetarian dishes to spare ribs and the house special, pork. Unusual for Europe is the salad bar. *Tweede Tuindwarsstraat 10, tel. 020/6237706. Reservations advised. No credit cards. No lunch.*

$ **Pancake Bakery.** Here is a chance to try a traditionally Dutch way of keeping eating costs down. The name of the game is pancakes—for every course including dessert, for which the topping can be ice cream, fruit, or liqueur. The Pancake Bakery is not far from Anne Frankhuis. *Prin-sengracht 191, tel. 020/6251333. No reservations. No credit cards.*

Lodging

Accommodations are tight from Easter to summer, so early booking is advised. Since few hotels have parking lots, cars are best abandoned in a multistory parking ramp for the duration of your stay. Many vis-itors like to stay inside the concentric ring of canals, an atmospheric area of historic gable-roof merchants' houses. Others prefer the quieter museum quarter, convenient for the Rijksmuseum and near enough to the Vondelpark for light jogging. For details and price-category definitions, *see* Lodging *in* Staying in Holland, *above*.

$$$$ **Amstel Inter-Continental.** Amsterdam's grand dame opened in 1867 and ★ was spectacularly renovated in late 1992. The spacious rooms have Oriental rugs, brocade upholstery, Delft lamps, and a color scheme that borrows from the warm tones of Makkum pottery. The Amstel is frequented by many of the nation's top businesspeople and visited at times by the royal family. *Professor Tulpplein 1, tel. 020/6226060, fax 020/6225808. 79 rooms with bath. Facilities: 2 restaurants, fitness center, pool. AE, DC, MC, V.*

$$$$ **Golden Tulip Barbizon Palace.** The newest Golden Tulip hotel in Amsterdam combines past and present with fantasy and flair. The exterior blends in with neighboring old houses; inside, a towering atrium stretches across the length of the hotel. Rooms are small but are decorated nicely. *Prins Hendrikkade 59–72, tel. 020/5564564, fax 020/6243353. 263 rooms with bath, 5 suites. Facilities: 2 restaurants, fitness center. AE, DC, MC, V.*

$$$$ **Grand Amsterdam.** In 1991, Amsterdam's former city hall was converted into a luxury hotel. Parts of the building date from the 16th century, but most of it belongs to the early part of the 20th, when the country's best artists and architects were commissioned to create a building the city could be proud of. The rooms are pamperingly luxurious and the kitchens are under the supervision of the incomparable Albert Roux. *Oudezijds Voorburgwal 197, tel. 020/5553111, fax 020/5553222. 182 rooms with bath. Facilities: restaurant, spa, garden. AE, DC, MC, V.*

$$$$ **Hôtel de l'Europe.** This 100-year-old hotel hides a full complement of ★ modern facilities behind its stately facade. The rooms are larger than is usual for Amsterdam, and each is decorated according to its shape and location. Bright rooms overlooking the Amstel are done in pastel colors; others have warm, rich colors and antiques. Apart from its world-renowned Excelsior restaurant (*see* Dining, *above*), de l'Europe houses a sophisticated leisure complex. *Nieuwe Doelenstraat 2–4, tel. 020/6234836, fax 020/6242962. 100 rooms with bath. Facilities: restaurant, sauna, solarium, fitness room, pool. AE, DC, MC, V.*

$$$ **Grand Hotel Krasnapolsky.** This fine, Old World hotel is enhanced by the Winter Gardens restaurant, which dates from 1818. During 1995, the hotel expanded into the building next door, increasing its size by half. The cosmopolitan atmosphere carries through all the rooms, with decor ranging from Victorian to art deco. *Dam 9, tel. 020/5549111, fax 020/6228607. 429 rooms with bath. Facilities: restaurant, parking. AE, DC, MC, V.*

$$$ **Pulitzer.** The Pulitzer succeeds in making living in the past a positive ★ pleasure. This is one of Europe's most ambitious hotel restorations, using the shells of a row of 17th-century merchants' houses. Inside, the refined atmosphere is sustained by the modern art gallery, the lovingly restored brickwork, oak beams, and split-level rooms—no two are alike. *Prinsengracht 315–331, tel. 020/5235235, fax 020/6276753. 230 rooms with bath. Facilities: restaurant, bar. AE, DC, MC, V.*

$$ **Ambassade.** With its beautiful canal-side location, its Louis XV–style ★ decoration, and its Oriental rugs, the Ambassade seems more like a stately home than a hotel. Service is attentive and room prices include breakfast. For other meals, the neighborhood has a good choice of restaurants. *Herengracht 341, tel. 020/6262333, fax 020/6245321. 49 rooms with bath. Facilities: lounge. AE, DC, MC, V.*

$$ **Atlas Hotel.** Renowned for its friendly atmosphere, this small hotel has moderate-size rooms decorated in art nouveau style. It's also very handy for Museumplein, whose major museums are within easy walking distance. *Van Eeghenstraat 64, tel. 020/6766336, fax 020/6717633. 22 rooms with bath. Facilities: bar, restaurant. AE, DC, MC, V.*

$$ **Het Canal House.** The American owners of this canal-side hotel opt for antiques rather than televisions as furnishings. Spacious rooms overlook the canal or the illuminated garden. A hearty Dutch breakfast is included in the price. *Keizergracht 148, tel. 020/6225182, fax 020/6241317. 26 rooms with bath or shower. Facilities: breakfast room. AE, DC, MC, V.*

$$ **Hotel de Filosoof.** In a quiet street near Vondelpark, this hotel attracts artists, thinkers, and people looking for something a little unusual. Each room is decorated in a different cultural motif—there's an Aristotle room, and a Goethe room adorned with texts from *Faust*. *Anna van den Vondelstraat 6, tel. 020/6833013, fax 020/6853750. 29 rooms, 25 with bath. Facilities: bar. AE, MC, V.*

$-$$ **Agora.** Near the Singel flower market, this small hotel reflects the cheer-
★ ful bustle. The rooms are light and spacious, some decorated with vintage furniture; the best overlook the canal or the university. Refurbished in 1993, this 18th-century house has a considerate staff, and a relaxed neighborhood ensures the hotel's popularity. Book well in advance. *Singel 462, tel. 020/6272200, fax 020/6272202. 15 rooms, 11 with bath or shower. AE, DC, MC, V.*

$ **Amstel Botel.** This floating hotel moored near Central Station is an appropriate place to stay in watery Amsterdam. The rooms are small, but the windows are large, offering fine views across the water to the city. Make sure you don't get a room on the land side of the vessel, or you'll end up staring at an ugly postal sorting office. *Oosterdokskade 224, tel. 020/6264247, fax 020/6391952. 176 rooms with shower. Facilities: bar. AE, DC, MC, V.*

$ **Hotel Seven Bridges.** Named for the scene beyond its front steps, this small canal-house hotel offers rooms decorated with individual flair. Oriental rugs are laid out on wooden floors, and there are comfy antique armchairs and custom-built marble washstands. The Rembrandtsplein is nearby. For a stunning view of the city, request one of the two large double rooms. *Reguliersgracht 31, tel. 020/6231329. 6 rooms with bath. No credit cards.*

$ **Quentin Hotel.** A stone's throw from the hectic Leidseplein is this small, family-run hotel. It is simply decorated with plain colors and modern prints, and flooded with light through large windows. The best rooms are the spacious corner ones that overlook a canal. *Leidsekade 89, tel. 020/6262187, fax 020/6220121. 23 rooms, 15 with shower and toilet. AE, MC, V.*

The Arts

The arts flourish in tolerant and cosmopolitan Amsterdam. The best sources of information about performances are the monthly publications *Time Out Amsterdam* (in English) and *Uit Krant* (in Dutch) and the biweekly *What's On in Amsterdam,* which you can get at the tourist office, where you can also secure tickets for the more popular events. Tickets must be booked in person from Monday to Saturday, 10 to 4. You also can book at the **Amsterdam Uit Buro** (Stadsschouwburg, Leidseplein 26, tel. 020/6211211).

Classical Music

Classical music is featured at the **Concertgebouw** (Concertgebouwplein 2–6), home of one of Europe's finest orchestras. A smaller auditorium in the same building is used for chamber music, recitals, and even jam sessions. While ticket prices for international orchestras are fairly high, most concerts are good values and the Wednesday lunchtime concerts are free. The box office is open from 9:30 to 7; you can make telephone bookings (020/6718345) from 10 to 5.

Opera and Ballet

The Dutch national ballet and opera companies are housed in the new **Muziektheater** (tel. 020/6255455) on Waterlooplein. Guest companies from foreign countries perform here during the three-week Holland Festival in June.

Theater

At the **Stalhouderij Theater** (1e Bloemdwarsstraat 4, tel. 020/6262282), an international cast performs a wide range of English-language plays in a former stable in the Jordaan. For experimental theater and colorful cabaret in Dutch, catch the shows at **Felix Meritis House** (Keizersgracht 324, tel. 020/6231311).

Film

The largest concentration of movie theaters is around Leidseplein and near Muntplein. Most foreign films are subtitled rather than dubbed, which makes Amsterdam a great place to catch up on movies you missed at home. The **City 1–7** theater near Leidseplein is the biggest (seven screens), but the Art Deco–era **Tuschinski** on Reguliersbreestraat is the most beautiful cinema house.

Nightlife

Amsterdam has a wide variety of discos, bars, and exotic shows. The more respectable—and expensive—after-dark activities are in and around Leidseplein and Rembrandtsplein; fleshier productions are on Oudezijds Achterburgwal and Thorbeckeplein. Names and locations change from year to year, but most bars and clubs are open every night from 5 PM to 2 AM or 5 AM. On weeknights, very few clubs charge admission, though the more lively ones sometimes ask for a "club membership" fee of Fl. 20 or more.

Bars

De Jaren (Nieuwe Doelenstraat 20, tel. 020/6255771) is a spacious café with a canal-side terrace. The smart young business set comes in for a drink after work; arts and media people use it as a communal sitting room; and the trendy pass through on their way out nightclubbing.

Jazz Clubs

Set in a converted warehouse, the **Bimhuis** (Oude Schans 73–77, tel. 020/6233373; open Thurs.–Sat. from 9 PM) is currently the most fashionable jazz club. Ticket holders can sit in the adjoining BIM café and enjoy a magical view across Oude Schans to the port. If you long for good Dixieland jazz, go to **Joseph Lam Jazz Club** (Van Diemenstraat 242, tel. 020/6228086); it's only open on Saturday.

Rock Clubs

Paradiso (Weteringschans 6–8, tel. 020/6264521) is an Amsterdam institution; converted from a church, it has become a vibrant venue for rock, New Age, and even contemporary classical music.

Discos

Mostly only hidden in cellars around the Leidseplein, the discos fill up after midnight. **Roxy** (Singel 465, tel. 020/6200354) is the current hot spot; also popular are **Escape** (Rembrandtsplein 11–15, tel. 020/6223542) and **It** (Amstelstraat 24, tel. 020/6250111, generally straight Thurs., Sun.; gay Fri.–Sat.). **Mazzo** (Rozengracht 114, tel.

020/6267500) uses dramatic lighting and slick videos to attract gay and straight student poseurs, would-be musicians, and artists.

Casinos

Blackjack, roulette, and slot machines have come lately—but not lightly—to the thrifty Dutch. Now everyone wants to play. The newest and most elegant venue, **Holland Casino** (Max Euweplein 62, tel. 020/6201006), just off Leidseplein, opened in 1991. You'll need your passport to get in; the minimum age is 18.

Gay and Lesbian Bars

Amsterdam has a vibrant gay and lesbian community, concentrated principally on Warmoestraat, Reguliersdwarsstraat, Amstelstraat, and Kerkstraat near Leidseplein. The **Gay & Lesbian Switchboard** (tel. 020/6236565) can provide information on the city's nightlife.

HISTORIC HOLLAND

This circular itinerary can be followed clockwise or counterclockwise. There are the historic towns of Leiden and Utrecht and the major museums in Haarlem; in between these towns, you'll see some of Holland's windmill-dotted landscape and pass through centers of tulip growing and cheese production.

Getting Around

The most convenient way to cover the following itinerary is by rented car out of Amsterdam. If you want someone else to do the navigating, then all the towns listed below can be reached by bus or train. From Amsterdam there are, for example, three direct trains per hour to Haarlem, Leiden, and Utrecht. Check with the tourist office in Amsterdam for help in planning your trip, or inquire at Central Station.

Guided Tours

Alternatively, these towns are covered, in various combinations, by organized bus tours out of Amsterdam. Brochures for tour operators are available from the **VVV Amsterdam Tourist Offices** at Stationsplein 10 or Leidseplein 1; the central telephone number is 06/34034066.

The VVV office in Utrecht organizes several excursions, including a boat trip along the canals and a sightseeing flight over the city. There are also day trips to country estates, castles, and gardens.

Tourist Information

Amersfoort (Stationsplein 9–11, tel. 033/635151).
Apeldoorn (Stationstraat 72, tel. 06/91681636).
Gouda (Markt 27, tel. 01820/13666).
Haarlem (Stationsplein 1, tel. 06/32024043).
Leiden (Stationsplein 210, tel. 071/146846).
Lisse (Grachtweg 53a, tel. 02521/14262).
Utrecht (Vredenburg 90, tel. 06/34034085).

Exploring Historic Holland

Amersfoort

Traveling southeast from Amsterdam, 90 kilometers (56 miles) along highway A1, you will reach Apeldoorn; but if you have time, stop off at **Amersfoort** en route. Although today it is a major industrial town, Amersfoort still manages to retain much of its medieval character and

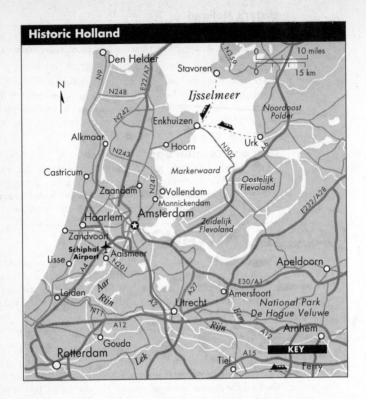

charm. Starting at the **Koopelport,** the imposing water gate across the Eem that dates from 1400, walk down Kleine Spui. On the right is **St. Pieters-en-Bloklands Gasthuis,** a hospice founded in 1390. Close by is the **Museum Flehite,** with its unusual medieval collections that give a fascinating insight into the history of the town. There's a large model of the Old Town. *Westsingel 50, tel. 033/619987. Admission: Fl. 7.50 summer, Fl. 5 winter. Open Tues.–Fri. 10–5, weekends 2–5.*

Continuing along Breestraat, you'll come to the graceful, 335-foot-high **Onze Lieve Vrouwetoren** (Tower of Our Lady). The musical chimes of this Gothic church can be heard every Friday between 10 and 11 AM. Turning left down Langstraat, past the Gothic **St. Joriskerk,** you will come to the **Kamperbinnenpoort,** the turreted land gate dating from the 15th century. Making your way left down Muurhuizen, you'll come to a short canal, the **Hovik,** which was once the old harbor.

Apeldoorn

The main attraction at **Apeldoorn** is the **Rijksmuseum Paleis Het Loo.** This former royal palace was built during the late-17th century for Willem III and has been beautifully restored to illustrate the domestic surroundings enjoyed by the House of Orange for more than three centuries. The museum, which is housed in the stables, has a fascinating collection of royal memorabilia, including cars and carriages, furniture and photographs, silver and ceramics. The formal gardens and the surrounding parkland offer attractive walks. *Koninklijk Park 1, tel. 055/212244. Admission: Fl. 12.50. Open Tues.–Sun. 10–5.*

From Apeldoorn, it is well worth the 5-kilometer (3-mile) drive on N304 to the **Kröller-Muller Museum.** In the woods in the middle of a national park, it displays one of the finest collections of modern art in the world. It possesses 278 works by Vincent van Gogh, as well as paintings, drawings, and sculptures by such masters as Seurat, Redon, Braque, Picasso, and Mondrian. The building, too, is part of the experience; it seems to bring the museum's wooded setting right into the galleries with you. The major sculptures are shown in the garden; don't miss them. *National Park De Hoge Veluwe, tel. 08382/1041. Admission: Fl. 7.50. Open Tues.–Sun. 10–5. Sculpture garden closes ½ hr earlier.*

Arnhem

If you have children in tow, consider a visit to the **Nederlands Openlucht Museum** (Open-Air Museum) in **Arnhem,** 15 kilometers (9 miles) from Apeldoorn on A90. In a 44-acre park, the curators have brought together original buildings and furnishings from all over the Netherlands to establish a comprehensive display of Dutch rural architectural styles and depict traditional ways of living. There are farmhouses and barns, workshops, and windmills—animals, too. *Schelmseweg 89, tel. 085/576111. Admission: Fl. 15 adults, Fl. 10 children under 13. Open Apr.–Oct., weekdays 9:30–5, weekends 10–5.*

Utrecht

The city of **Utrecht** is 72 kilometers (44 miles) west of Apeldoorn. The gabled houses of the Nieuwegracht, the canals with their water gates, the 13th-century wharves and storage cellars of the Oudegracht, and the superb churches and museums are just some of the key attractions, most of which are on the main cathedral square. The **Domkerk** is a late-Gothic cathedral containing a series of fine stained-glass windows. The **Domtoren** (cathedral tower) opposite the building was connected to the cathedral until a hurricane hit in 1674. The bell tower is the tallest in the country, and it has 465 steep steps that lead to a magnificent view. A guide is essential in the labyrinth of steps and passageways. *Domplein, tel. 030/310403. Admission to Domkerk free; tours on the hr Fl. 2.25. Open May–Sept., weekdays 10–5, Sat. 10-3:30, Sun. 2–4; Oct.–Apr., weekdays 11–4, Sat. 11-3:30, Sun. 2–4. Admission to Domtoren: Fl. 4. Open Apr.–Oct., weekdays 10–5, weekends noon–5; Nov.–Mar., weekends noon–5.*

Not far from the cathedral is the merry **Rijksmuseum van Speelklok tot Pierement** (National Museum of Mechanical Musical Instruments) devoted solely to music machines—from music boxes to street organs and even musical chairs. During the guided tour, music students play some of the instruments. The museum is housed in Utrecht's oldest parish church. *Buurkerkhof 10, tel. 030/312789. Admission: Fl. 7.50. Open Tues.–Sat. 10–5, Sun. 1–5.*

Behind the museum is **Pieterskerk,** the country's oldest Romanesque church, built in 1048. The grandeur of the city's churches reflects the fact that Utrecht was Holland's religious center during the Middle Ages. Most churches are open in summer and a church concert is held almost every day.

Walk south out of Domplein, down Lange Nieuwstraat. Halfway down is the **Rijksmuseum Het Catharijneconvent.** In addition to its collection of holy relics and vestments, this museum contains the country's largest display of medieval art. *Nieuwegracht 63, tel. 030/317296. Admission: Fl. 6. Open Tues.–Fri. 10–5, weekends 11–5.*

There are more museums to be explored on Agnietenstraat, which crosses Lange Nieuwstraat. The **Centraal Museum** houses a rich collection of contemporary art and other city exhibits. Amid the clutter is an original Viking ship (discovered in 1930) and a 17th-century dollhouse complete with period furniture, porcelain, and miniature old master paintings. *Agnietenstraat 1, tel. 030/362362. Admission: Fl. 6. Open Tues.–Sat. 11–5, Sun. noon–5.*

An important part of the museum's collection is a house that is a 15-minute walk away in Utrecht's eastern suburbs; it is known as the **Rietveld-Schröder House.** In 1924 the architect Gerrit Rietveld, working with Truus Schröeder, designed what is considered to be the architectural pinnacle of de Stijl (The Style). The use of primary colors (red, yellow, blue) and black and white, and the definition of the interior space are unique and innovative even today. The experience of the house is, as one art historian phrased it, "like wandering into a Mondrian painting." *Prins Hendriklaan 50a, tel. 030/362310. Admission: Fl. 9. Open Wed.–Sat. 11–5, Sun. noon–5. Call for appointment.*

Gouda

West of Utrecht, 36 kilometers (22 miles) along the A12, you'll come to **Gouda,** famous for its cheese. Try to be there on a Thursday morning in July or August, when the cheese market is held in front of the **Waag,** or Weigh House. Brightly colored farm wagons are loaded high with cheeses. The Weigh House is due to open as a cheese museum in late 1995. Take a good look at the **Stadhuis** (Town Hall), parts of which date from 1449 (admission: Fl. 1; open weekdays 9–4, weekends 11–3). After trying all five types of Gouda cheese, leave some space for syrup waffles, the city's other specialty.

By the side of the market square is **Sint Janskerk** (Church of St. John); what you see today was built during the 16th century. It has the longest nave in the country and 70 glorious stained-glass windows, the oldest of which is from 1555. Around the corner from the cathedral is the Catharina Gasthuis, now the **Stedelijk Museum Het Catharina Gasthuis,** the municipal museum that houses many unusual exhibits, including a fearsome medieval torture chamber and an equally horrific operating room. *Oosthaven 9, Achter de Kerk 14, tel. 01820/88440. Admission: Fl. 4. Open Mon.–Sat. 10–5, Sun. noon–5.*

Leiden

Heading north on N11, you'll come to the ancient city of **Leiden,** renowned for its spirit of religious and intellectual tolerance and known for its university and royal connections. Start at the **De Lakenhal,** built in 1639 for the city's cloth merchants and now an art gallery, cloth, and antiques museum. Pride of place in the collection goes to the 16th- and 17th-century Dutch paintings, with works by Steen; Dou; Rembrandt; and, above all, Lucas van Leyden's *Last Judgment*—the first great Renaissance painting in what is now the Netherlands. Other rooms are devoted to furniture and to the history of Leiden's medieval guilds: the drapers, tailors, and brewers. *Oude Singel 32, tel. 071/165361. Admission: Fl. 5. Open Tues.–Fri. 10–5, weekends noon–5.*

Near the De Lakenhal is the **Molenmuseum de Valk** (Windmill Museum), housed in an original windmill built in 1747, which was worked by 10 generations of millers until 1964. The seven floors still contain the original workings, an old forge, washrooms, and living quarters. *2e Binnenvesstgracht 1, tel. 071/165353. Admission: Fl. 5. Open Tues.–Sat. 10–5, Sun. 1–5.*

Crossing the canal and walking into bustling Breestraat and then down the narrow Pieterskerk-Choorsteeg, you'll come to the imposing **St. Pieterskerk,** with its memories of the Pilgrim Fathers who worshiped here and of their spiritual leader, John Robinson, who is buried here. A narrow street by the **Persijnhofje** almshouse, dating from 1683, takes you downhill to the gracious, tree-lined Rapenburg canal, crossed by triple-arch bridges and bordered by stately 18th-century houses. To the right is the **Rijksmuseum van Oudheden** (National Museum of Antiquities), the country's leading archaeological museum. The prize exhibit is the entire 1st-century AD Temple of Taffeh, donated by the Egyptian government. There is also a floor devoted to finds in the Netherlands. *Rapenburg 28, tel. 071/163163. Admission: Fl. 5; Fl. 3 surcharge for special exhibitions. Open Tues.–Sat. 10–5, Sun. noon–5.*

On the other side of the canal, a little farther down, you find the **Academie** (university) and the **Hortus Botanicus** gardens. The university was founded by William the Silent as a reward to Leiden for its victory against the Spanish in the 1573–74 siege. During the war, the dikes were opened and the countryside flooded so that the rescuing navy could sail right up to the city walls. Founded in 1587, the botanical gardens are among the oldest in the world. The highlights are a faithful reconstruction of a 16th-century garden, the herb garden, the colorful orangery, and the ancient trees. *Rapenburg 73. Admission: Fl. 3.50. Open Apr.–Oct., Mon.–Sat. 9–5, Sun. 11–5; Nov.–Mar., weekdays 9–4:30.*

Follow Keizerstraat out of Rapenburg and turn left into Boisotkade. On your left is the **Pilgrim Fathers Documentatie Centrum.** This tiny museum contains photocopies of documents and maps related to the Pilgrims during their stay in Leiden, before they went to Delfshaven on the first stage of their arduous voyage to the New World. The documentation center will be closed in late 1995/early 1996 for renovations, but there may be temporary exhibitions from the collection at the De Lakenhal (*see above*). *Vliet 45, tel. 071/120191. Admission free. Open weekdays 9:30–4:30.*

Lisse/Aalsmeer

North from Leiden toward Haarlem, you can stop to visit (in spring only) the 70-acre **Keukenhof.** Set in a park intersected by canals and lakes, the world's largest flower show draws huge spring crowds to its regimental lines of tulips, hyacinths, and daffodils. (A lazier way to see the flowers is from the windows of the Leiden–Haarlem train.) *Lisse, tel. 02521/19034. Admission: Fl. 15. Open late Mar.–late May, daily 8–7:30.*

During the rest of the year, or certainly as a complement to a spring visit to Keukenhof, you will want to see how flowers are marketed. Flowers are very big business to the Dutch, and the Netherlands is home to the world's largest complex of flower auction houses. The biggest of these auction facilities (it also is the single largest in the world) is the **Bloemenveiling** (Flower Auction) in the town of Aalsmeer near the national airport and not far from Amsterdam. In a building the size of three football fields, there are three separate auction rooms all functioning at the same time. Get there early; it's all over by 10 AM. *Legmeerdijk 313, tel. 02977/34567. Open weekdays 7:30 AM–11 AM. Closed weekends and holidays.*

Haarlem

With its secret inner courtyards and pointed gables, **Haarlem** can resemble a 17th-century canvas, even one painted by Frans Hals, the city's greatest painter. The area around the **Grote Markt,** the market square, provides an architectural stroll through the 17th and 18th centuries. Some of the facades are adorned with such homilies as "The body's sickness is a cure for the soul." Haarlem's religious faith can also be sensed in any of its 20 almshouses. The **Stadhuis** was once a hunting lodge. Nearby is the **Vleeshal,** or meat market, which has an especially fine gabled front. This dates from the early 1600s and is now used as an art gallery and a museum of local history. *Lepelstraat. Admission: Fl. 4. Open Mon.–Sat. 11–5, Sun. 1–5.*

Across from the Vleeshal is the **Grote Kerk,** dedicated to St. Bavo. The church, built between 1400 and 1550, houses one of Europe's most famous organs. This massive instrument has 5,000 pipes, and both Mozart and Handel played on it. It is still used for concerts, and an annual organ festival is held here in July. Make your way down Damstraat, behind the Grote Kerk, and turn left at the **Waag** (Weigh House). On the left is the **Teylers Museum,** which claims to be the oldest museum in the country. It was founded by a wealthy merchant in 1778 as a museum of science and the arts; it now houses a fine collection of The Hague school of painting as well as a collection of drawings and sketches by Michelangelo, Raphael, and other non-Dutch masters. Since the canvases in this building are shown in natural light, try to see the museum on a sunny day. *Spaarne 16, tel. 023/319010. Admission: Fl. 6.50. Open Tues.–Sat. 10–5, Sun. 1–5.*

Follow the Binnen Spaarn and turn right onto Kampervest and then onto Gasthuisvest. On your right, on Groot Heiligland, you'll find the **Frans Hals Museum.** This museum, in what used to be a 17th-century hospice, contains a marvelous collection of the artist's work; his paintings of the guilds of Haarlem are particularly noteworthy. The museum also has works by Hals's contemporaries. *Groot Heiligland 62, tel. 023/319180. Admission: Fl. 7.50. Open Mon.–Sat. 11–5, Sun. 1–5.*

Dining and Lodging

In towns such as Apeldoorn and Gouda, which have few good hotels, B&B accommodations, booked through the VVV tourist office, make a more interesting choice. Rooms in Utrecht are often in short supply, so book in advance or immediately upon arrival. For details and price-category definitions, *see* Dining and Lodging *in* Staying in Holland, *above.*

Apeldoorn

DINING

De Echoput. Near Het Loo, this delightful restaurant is a member of the Alliance Gastronomique Nederlandaise, a guarantee of an excellent meal. Game from the surrounding forest is a specialty. There is an attractive terrace, overlooking fountains and greenery, for summer dining. *Amersfoortseweg 86, tel. 05769/1248. Reservations required. Jacket and tie. AE, DC, MC, V. Closed Mon. No lunch Sat. $$$$*

LODGING

Hotel de Keizerskroon. A perfect complement to the nearby royal palace is a stay at the Keizerskroon (the name means Emperor's Crown). In style and amenities it is a business hotel; in comfort and cordiality it is a traveler's hotel; in setting—at the edge of the city on a quiet street leading toward the woods—it is a weekend getaway inn. *Koningstraat 7, tel. 055/217744, fax 055/214737. 100 rooms with bath. Facilities: sauna, solarium, pool. AE, DC, MC, V. $$$*

Gouda

DINING

Goudsche Salon. Wooden floors, a big table of newspapers and magazines, and a friendly atmosphere combine with tasty cuisine to make this an ideal place for a lunch or dinner break. There are healthy salads and a good-value, seasonally changing set menu that might include such delights as lamb cooked with rosemary and garlic and served on a tomato and herb risotto. *Wijdstraat 13, tel. 01820/12330. AE, MC, V. $$*

Haarlem

DINING

Café Restaurant Brinkman. This elegant, classic grand café overlooks the magnificent Grote Kerk. You can while away the afternoon over a single coffee or choose from a wide menu of casseroles and grills with salad. *Grote Markt 9–13, tel. 023/323111. AE, DC, MC, V. $$*

LODGING

Golden Tulip Lion d'Or. Just five minutes from the old city center and conveniently near the railway station, this comfortable but unprepossessing hotel offers all the luxuries associated with a Golden Tulip hotel. Special weekend deals include reduced room prices, gourmet evening meals, and free cocktails. *Kruisweg 34–36, tel. 023/321750, fax 023/329543. 36 rooms with bath. Facilities: restaurant, conference rooms. AE, DC, MC, V. $$$*

Leiden

DINING

Jill's. A delightful, bright restaurant just a few minutes' walk from the De Valk windmill, this spot is ideal for a relaxing meal. A variety of set menus with Italian, Asian, and Dutch influences allows you to find something to satisfy almost every palate. There is fresh fish daily. *Morsstraat 6, tel. 071/143722. Reservations advised. AE, DC, MC, V. $$*

Annie's Verjaardag. A low, arched cellar full of cheery students and a water-level canal-side terrace make Annie's popular in all weather. There is a modest but well-prepared selection of salads and baguettes and usually at least one daily special of something more substantial (such as mussels or pork medallions in a creamy casserole). *Oude Rijn 1a, tel. 071/125737. No reservations. No credit cards. $–$$*

DINING AND LODGING

★ **Nieuw Minerva.** This family-run hotel is a conversion of eight 15th-century buildings. The original part of the hotel is decorated in Old Dutch style; the newer part is better equipped but has slightly less character. Many of the rooms overlook a quiet tributary of the Rhine. The restaurant caters to most tastes and pockets. The excellent three-course tourist menu offers vegetarian as well as meat and fish selections. *Boommarkt 23, tel. 071/126358, fax 071/142674. 40 rooms, 30 with bath or shower. Facilities: restaurant. AE, DC, MC, V. $$*

LODGING

Hotel De Doelen. The spartan decor of this small hotel is in keeping with its origins as a 15th-century house, but the rooms are comfortable and much sought after. *Rapenburg 2, tel. 071/120527, fax 071/128453. 16 rooms with bath or shower. AE, DC, MC, V. $$*

Utrecht

DINING

Town Castle Oudaen/"Between Heaven and Earth." In medieval times Utrecht's Oudegracht (Old Canal) was lined with many "town castles" such as this fine one. You may be confused by the clublike atmosphere as you enter, but you'll find the dining room on the second floor (which may be why it is called "Between Heaven and Earth") and an excellent café at ground level. Another unique feature is that the owners brew their own beer in the basement. *Oudegracht 99, tel. 030/311864. AE, DC, MC, V. No lunch (except café). $$*

De Soepterrine. This snug restaurant offers steaming bowls of home-made soups. Ten varieties are made daily, usually including Dutch specialties such as thick erwtensoep. Each bowl comes with crusty bread and herb butter. Quiches and generous salads fill up those extra corners. *Zakkendragerssteeg 40, tel. 030/317005. No reservations. AE, MC, V. $*

LODGING

Malie. The Malie is in a 19th-century row house on a quiet leafy street a 15-minute walk from the old center. Rooms are brightly decorated though simply furnished. This small, friendly hotel has an attractive breakfast room overlooking the garden and terrace. *Maliestraat 2–4, tel. 030/316424, fax 030/340661. 29 rooms with bath or shower. Facilities: bar, breakfast room. AE, DC, MC, V. $$*

THE HAGUE, DELFT, AND ROTTERDAM

Within this itinerary you can visit the Netherlands' most dignified and spacious city—the royal, diplomatic, and governmental seat of Den Haag (better known as The Hague)—and its close neighbor, the leading North Sea beach resort of Scheveningen. Also nearby are Delft, a historic city with many canals and ancient buildings, and the energetic and thoroughly modern international port city of Rotterdam. The latter is known to the Dutch as "Manhattan on the Maas," for its office towers as well as its cultural attractions.

Getting Around

The Hague and Delft are each about 60 kilometers (37½ miles) southwest of Amsterdam and can be reached within less than an hour by fast, frequent trains. The heart of both towns is compact enough to be explored on foot. Scheveningen is reached from The Hague's center by bus or tram. Travelers will find public transportation more convenient than driving because of severe parking problems at the resort. The RET Metro is an easy-to-use option for getting around Rotterdam. There are two main branches (north–south and east–west), and they cross in the heart of the business district at a major transfer center.

Guided Tours

Boat Trips

From The Hague, various boat companies run short day trips and longer candlelight dinner cruises. These can be booked at The Hague tourist office or through **Rondvaartbedrijf RVH** (Spui 256, tel. 070/3462473). Scheveningen offers fishing-boat tours around the Dutch coast. Contact **Sportsviscentrum Trip 30** (Scheveningen, tel. 070/3541122). In Delft, the tourist office organizes boat tours along the unspoiled canal system.

You can cruise the port of Rotterdam on a basic tour of 1¼ hours (year-round) or choose one that lasts as long as nine hours (midsummer only). **Spido Havenrondvaarten** (Willemsplein, tel. 010/4135400), the main boat company, also operates summer evening music-and-dinner cruises of the inner harbor. The 1¼-hour tour costs Fl. 12.50. The pier can be reached by taking the RET Metro blue line toward Spijkenisse to the Leuvehaven station and walking to the end of the boulevard.

Orientation Tours

City sightseeing tours of The Hague can be arranged by or through the main VVV tourist office next to the train station. The size and diversity of the city make a bus tour a logical choice. The "Royal Bus Tour" leaves from outside the office at 1 PM every day between April and September. The 2½- to 3-hour trip includes background on the royal family and takes passengers past Queen Beatrix's residences. Book in advance at the tourist office (cost: Fl. 22).

Scheveningen and Delft are best seen on foot. The VVV Delft Tourist Office organizes tours, while the Scheveningen office will advise on coastal strolls.

In the long summer season (April through September), there are daily two-hour bus tours of Rotterdam conducted by the VVV Rotterdam Tourist Office. The tours, which leave from the office at 1:30 PM, cost Fl. 25.

Tourist Information

Delft (Markt 85, tel. 015/126100).
The Hague (Babylon Center, Koningin Julianaplein 30, next to the train station, tel. 06/34035051).
Rotterdam (Coolsingel 67, tel. 06/34034065).
Scheveningen (Gevers Deynootweg 1134, tel. 06/34035051).

If you're planning to spend a few days in The Hague or Rotterdam, ask for the VVV brochure on city events and entertainment. Tickets for concerts and other activities can be reserved in person at the VVV tourist office.

Exploring The Hague, Delft, and Rotterdam

The Hague

During the 17th century, when Dutch maritime power was at its zenith, **The Hague** was known as "The Whispering Gallery of Europe" because it was thought to be the secret manipulator of European politics. Although the Golden Age is over, The Hague remains a powerful world diplomatic capital, quietly boastful of its royal connections. It also is the seat of government for the Netherlands.

The city's heart is the **Hofvijver** reflecting pool and the complex of gracious **Parliament Buildings** reflected in it. At the center of it all is the **Ridderzaal** (Knights' Hall). Inside are vast beams spanning a width of 59 feet, flags, and stained-glass windows. A sense of history pervades the 13th-century great hall. It is now used mainly for ceremonies: Every year the queen's gilded coach brings her here to open Parliament. The two government chambers sit separately in buildings on either side of the Ridderzaal and can be visited by guided tour only when Parliament is not in session. Tours in English are conducted by Stichting Bezoekerscentrum Binnenhof, located just to the right of the Ridderzaal. *Binnenhof 8a, tel. 070/3646144 (for tours; reservations required). Admission: tour Fl. 5.50, Parliament exhibition free. Open Mon.–Sat. 10–4.*

On the far side of the **Binnenhof,** the inner court of the complex, is a small, well-proportioned Dutch Renaissance building called the **Mauritshuis,** one of the finest small art museums in the world. This diminutive 17th-century palace contains a feast of art from the same period, including six Rembrandts; of these the most powerful is *The Anatomy Lesson of Dr. Tulp,* a theatrical work graphically depicting a dissection of the lower arm. Also featured are Vermeer's celebrated *Girl Wearing a Turban* and the glistening *View of Delft. Korte Vijverberg 8, tel. 070/3469244. Admission: Fl. 7.50. Open Tues.–Sat. 10–5, Sun. 11–5.*

Outside the Mauritshuis, follow the Korte Vijverberg past the reflecting pool, which is bordered by patrician houses with revamped 18th- and 19th-century facades, a sign of the area's continuing popularity with the local aristocracy.

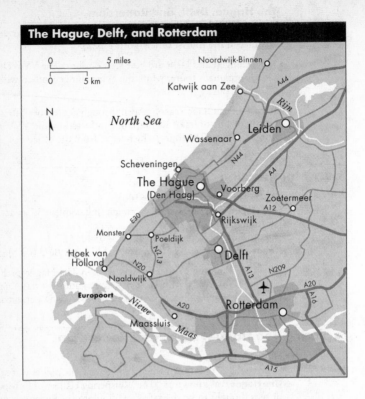

The Hague, Delft, and Rotterdam

0 ___ 5 miles
0 ___ 5 km

N

North Sea

Noordwijk-Binnen

Katwijk aan Zee

A44

Rijn

Leiden

Wassenaar

N44

A4

Scheveningen

The Hague
(Den Haag)

Voorberg

Zoetermeer

A12

Rijkswijk

E30

Monster

Poeldijk

N213

Delft

A13

N209

Hoek van
Holland

N20

A20

A16

Naaldwijk

Europoort

Niewe

A20

Rotterdam

Maassluis

Maas

A15

Turn right at Lange Vijverberg and walk a short way until you come to Lange Voorhout, a large L-shape boulevard. During the last century, horse-drawn trams clattered along its cobbles and deposited dignitaries outside the various palaces. Apart from the trams, not much has changed. Diplomats still eat in the historic Hotel des Indes at Numbers 54–56. For more than 100 years, it has hosted ambassadors and kings, dancers and spies. Memories of famous guests remain in the form of Emperor Haile Selassie's gold chair and the ballerina Anna Pavlova's silver candlesticks. Lange Voorhout 34 once belonged to William I, the first king of the Netherlands, but later it became the royal library; it is now the **Supreme Court.** With its clumsy skewed gable, the headquarters of the Dutch Red Cross at Number 6 seems out of place on this stately avenue. A few doors down, at the corner of Parkstraat, is The Hague's oldest church, the **Kloosterkerk,** built in 1400. During spring, the adjoining square is covered with yellow and purple crocuses; on Thursday during the summer, it is the scene of a colorful antiques market.

North of Lange Voorhout is the **Panorama Mesdag,** a 400-foot painting-in-the-round that shows the nearby seaside town of Scheveningen as it looked in 1880. Hendrik Mesdag was a late-19th-century marine painter, and he used the typically melancholic colors of The Hague school in his calming seascape. Mesdag was assisted by his wife, who painted much of the fishing village, and by a friend, who painted the sky and dunes. *Zeestraat 65b, tel. 070/3642563. Admission: Fl. 5. Open Mon.–Sat. 10–5, Sun. noon–5.*

Just around the corner in Laan van Meerdervoort is the painter's home, now transformed into the **Rijksmuseum H. W. Mesdag.** Paintings by Mesdag and members of The Hague school are hung beside those of Corot, Courbet, and Rousseau. These delicate landscapes represent one of the finest collections of Barbizon School painting outside France. At press time (spring 1995) the museum was closed for renovation and was scheduled to reopen sometime in 1996. *Laan van Meerdervoort 7f. For information, contact the Vincent van Gogh Museum in Amsterdam, tel. 020/5705200.*

The **Vredespaleis** (Peace Palace), near Laan van Meerdervoort, is a monument to world peace through negotiation. Following the first peace conference at The Hague in 1899, the Scottish-American millionaire Andrew Carnegie donated $1.5 million for the construction of a building to house a proposed international court. The Dutch government donated the grounds, and other nations offered furnishings and decorations. Although it still looks like a dull multinational bank, the building has been improved by such gifts as Japanese wall hangings, a Danish fountain, and a grand staircase presented by The Hague. Today the **International Court of Justice,** consisting of 15 jurists, has its seat here. There are guided tours when the court is not in session. *Carnegieplein 2, tel. 070/3469680. Admission: Fl. 5. Open June–Sept., weekdays 10–4; Oct.–May, weekdays 10–3. Guided tours at 10, 11, 2, 3, and 4.*

The nearby **Haags Gemeentemuseum** (Hague Municipal Museum) is the home of the largest collection of Mondrians in the world plus two vast collections of musical instruments—European and non-European. The 1935 building itself is fascinating as an example of the International Movement in modern architecture. *Stadhouderslaan 41, tel. 070/3512873. Admission: Fl. 8. Open Tues.–Sun. 11–5.*

Behind the Gemeentemuseum, overlooking Zorgvliet (the westernmost park of the Scheveningse Bosjes, a vast stretch of green that separates The Hague from Scheveningen), is the IMAX theater **Omniversum.** It is housed in a cylindrical building with a 75-foot dome that acts as a screen for the projection of 6–10 daily video presentations about outer space and nature. *President Kennedylaan 5, tel. 070/3545454 for reservations and show times. Admission: Fl. 16. Shows Tues.–Thurs. hourly 11–4, Fri.–Sun. hourly 11–9 (except 6).*

Between The Hague and Scheveningen is **Madurodam,** a miniature Holland where the country's important buildings and facilities are duplicated at a scale of 1:52. None of the details has been forgotten, from the lighthouse and quay-side cranes in a harbor to the hand-carved furniture in the gabled houses. In July and August, there is also an after-dark sound-and-light presentation. *Haringkade 175, tel. 070/3520930. Admission: Fl. 15 adults, Fl. 12 children. Open late-March–June and Sept., daily 9–7; July–Aug., daily 9 AM–10 PM.*

Scheveningen is adjacent to The Hague along the North Sea coast. A fishing village since the 14th century, it became popular as a beach resort during the last century, when the grand Kurhaus Hotel, still a focal point of this beach community, was built. The beach itself, protected from tidal erosion by stone jetties, slopes gently into the North Sea in front of a high promenade whose function is to protect the boulevard and everything behind it from winter storms. The surface of the beach is fine sand, and you can bicycle or walk for miles to the north.

At the turn of the century, the **Kurhaus Hotel** stood alone at the center of the beach as a fashionable, aristocratic resort. Now it is modern and bustling, with a casino among its new attractions. There is a fancifully painted ceiling over the large central court and buffet restaurant.

Part of the new design around the Kurhaus area includes the Golfbad, a surf pool complete with artificial waves. **The Pier,** completed in 1962, stretches 1,220 feet into the sea. Its four circular end buildings provide a sun terrace and restaurant, an observation tower, an amusement center with a children's play area, and an underwater panorama. At 11 on summer evenings, the Pier is the scene of dramatic fireworks displays.

A newcomer to the beachfront is the **Sea Life Center,** an ingeniously designed aquarium complex that includes a transparent underwater tunnel. You walk through it as if you were on the sea floor, with sharks, rays, eels, and octopuses swimming inches above your head. *Strandweg 13, tel. 070/3542100. Admission: Fl. 13.50 adults, Fl. 8.50 children. Open Sept.–June, daily 10–6; July–Aug., daily 10–9.*

Delft

Thirteen kilometers (8 miles) along the A13 from The Hague, you'll enter **Delft.** There is probably no town in the Netherlands that is more intimate, more attractive, or more traditional than this minimetropolis, whose famous blue-and-white earthenware is popular throughout the world. Compact and easy to explore despite its web of canals, Delft is best discovered on foot—although canal boat excursions are available April through October, as are horse-drawn trams that leave from the marketplace. Every street is lined with attractive Gothic and Renaissance houses.

In the marketplace, the only lively spot in this tranquil town, is the **Nieuwe Kerk** (New Church), built during the 14th century, with its tall Gothic spire and a magnificent carillon of 48 bells. The mausoleum of Prince William the Silent, a massive, ornate structure of black marble and alabaster, dominates the chancel. Nearby in the floor is a stone that covers the entry to a crypt containing the remains of members of the Orange-Nassau line, including all members of the royal family since King William I ascended the throne during the mid-16th century. *Markt, tel. 015/123025. Admission: Fl. 2.50. Tower: Fl. 2.50. Open Apr.–Oct., Mon.–Sat. 9–6; Nov.–Mar., Mon.–Sat. 11–4.*

Walk around the right side of the Nieuwe Kerk, then left at the back and along the Vrouwenregt canal for a few steps before taking another left turn into Voldersgracht. To the left, the backs of the houses rise straight from the water as you stroll to the end of the street, which is marked by the sculptured animal heads and outdoor stairs of the old **Meat Market** on the right. Cross the Wijnhaven and turn left along its far side to the Koornmarkt, a stately canal spanned by a high, arching bridge that is one of the hallmarks of Delft.

Turn right at the Peperstraat to reach the **Oude Delft,** the city's oldest waterway. A few blocks farther along the canal is the **Prinsenhof,** formerly the Convent of St. Agatha, founded in 1400. The chapel inside dates from 1471; its interior is remarkable for the wooden statues under the vaulting ribs. Today the Prinsenhof is a museum that tells the story of the liberation of the Netherlands after 80 years of Spanish occupation (1568–1648). For Dutch royalists, the spot is significant for the assassination of Prince William of Orange in 1584; the bullet holes can still be seen in the wall. *St. Agathaplein 1, tel. 015/602358. Admission: Fl. 5. Open Tues.–Sat. 10–5, Sun. 1–5.*

Across the Oude Delft canal is the **Oude Kerk** (Old Church), a vast Gothic monument of the 13th century. Its beautiful tower, surmounted by a brick spire, leans somewhat alarmingly. *Heilige Geest Kerkhof, tel. 015/123015. Admission: Fl. 2.50. Open Apr.–Oct., Mon.–Sat. 10–5.*

Beyond the Prinsenhof on the same side of the Oude Delft canal is the **Lambert van Meerten Museum,** a mansion whose timbered rooms are filled with the country's most complete collection of old Dutch tiles as well as Delft pottery. *Oude Delft 199, tel. 015/602358. Admission: Fl. 3.50. Open Tues.–Sat. 10–5, Sun. 1–5.*

While in Delft, you will want to see the famous local specialty—Delftware. Decorated porcelain was brought to Holland from China on East India Company ships and was so much in demand that Dutch potters felt their livelihood was being threatened. They therefore set about creating pottery to rival Chinese porcelain. There are only two manufacturers that still make hand-painted Delftware: **De Delftse Pauw** and the more famous "Royal" **De Porceleyne Fles.** *De Delftse Pauw: Delftweg 133, tel. 015/124920. Admission free. Open Apr.–mid-Oct., daily 9–4; mid-Oct.–Mar., weekdays 9–4, weekends 11–1. De Porceleyne Fles: Rotterdamsweg 196, tel. 015/560234. Admission: Fl. 2.50. Open Apr.–Oct., Mon.–Sat. 9–5, Sun. 10–4; Nov.–Mar., weekdays 9–5, Sat. 10–4.*

Rotterdam

One of the few thoroughly modern cities in the Netherlands and the site of the world's largest and busiest port, **Rotterdam** is 13 kilometers (8 miles) south of Delft on the A13. Art lovers know Rotterdam for its extensive and outstanding collection of art; philosophers recall it as the city of Erasmus. It is a major stop on the rock-and-roll concert circuit, and its soccer team is well known, but the city's main claim to fame is its extraordinary concentration of adventurous modern architecture. Among the most intriguing buildings are a series of cube-shape apartments, turned to balance on one corner at the top of a tall stem. One of these precarious-looking houses, the **Kijk-Kubus,** just east of the center, is open to the public. *Overblaak 70, tel. 010/4142285. Admission: Fl. 2.50. Open Apr.–Dec., Tues.–Fri. 10–5, weekends 11–5; Jan.–Mar., Fri.–Sun. 11–5.*

The biggest surprise in Rotterdam is the remarkable 48-kilometer-long (30-mile-long) **Europoort,** which handles more than 250 million tons of cargo every year and more ships than any other port in the world. It is the delta for three of Europe's most important rivers (the Rhine, the Waal, and the Meuse/Maas) and a seemingly endless corridor of piers, warehouses, tank facilities, and efficiency. You can get to the piers at Willemsplein by tram or metro (blue line to the Leuvehaven station) from the train station. The 1¼-hour harbor tour (*see* Boat Trips *in* Guided Tours, *above*) illuminates Rotterdam's vital role in world trade.

As an alternative to the boat tour, you also can survey the harbor from the vantage point of the **Euromast** observation tower. Get there via the RET Metro red line to Dijkszicht. *Parkhaven 20, tel. 010/4364811. Admission: Fl. 14.50. Open Apr.–June and Sept., daily 10–7; July and Aug., Sun. and Mon. 10–7, Tues.–Sat. 10 AM–10:30 PM; Oct.–Mar., daily 10–5.*

After the harbor tour, walk down the boulevard past the metro station into Leuvehaven. On your right as you stroll along the inner harbor is **IMAX Rotterdam,** a gigantic theater in which films are projected onto a six-story screen. There are earphones for English translation. *Leuvehaven 77, tel. 010/4048844. Admission: Fl. 15. Shows Tues.–Sun. 2, 3, 4, 5:45; Mon. also during holiday periods. Non-IMAX films (from the regular commercial circuit) shown daily at 7:45 PM and 9:30 PM.*

Past the theater is a hodgepodge of cranes, barges, steamships, and old shipbuilding machines, even a steam-operated grain elevator. What looks at quick glance to be a sort of maritime junkyard is in fact a work in progress: Volunteers are working daily to restore these vessels and machines. The whole operation is an open-air museum of shipbuilding, shipping, and communications that is part of the **Prins Hendrik Maritime Museum,** housed in a large gray building at the head of the quay. Also moored in this inner harbor adjacent to the museum is the historic 19th-century Royal Dutch Navy warship *De Buffel.* Within the museum are exhibits devoted to the history and activity of the great port outside. *Leuvehaven 1, tel. 010/4132680. Admission: Fl. 6. Open Tues.–Sat. 10–5, Sun. 11–5.*

From the nearby Churchillplein metro station, take the red line toward Marconiplein to the first stop at Eendrachtsplein, where you will walk along the canal toward the Museumpark. As a welcome contrast to the industrial might of the Europoort and Holland's maritime history, the **Boymans–van Beuningen Museum** is an impressive refresher course in Western European art history. There is an Old Arts section that includes the work of Brueghel, Bosch, and Rembrandt and a renowned print gallery with works by artists such as Dürer and Cézanne. Dali and Magritte mix with the Impressionists in the Modern Arts collection. *Mathenesserlaan 18–20, tel. 010/4419400. Admission: Fl. 7.50. Open Tues.–Sat. 10–5, Sun. 11–5.*

Beside this long-established museum is the spanking-new **Nederlands Architectuurinstituut,** which houses changing exhibitions in the field of architecture and interior design. Across the park is the recently built **Kunsthal,** which hosts all manner of major temporary exhibitions—from Andy Warhol retrospectives to rows of compact cars. *Nederlands Architectuurinstituut, Museumpark 25, tel. 010/4401200. Admission: Fl. 7.50. Open Tues.–Sat. 10–5, Sun. 11–5. Kunsthal, Westzeedijk 341, tel. 010/4400300. Admission: Fl. 10. Open Tues.–Sat. 10–5, Sun. 11–5.*

Three stops farther west along the metro line is Delfshaven, the last remaining nook of old Rotterdam. (From the station double back along Schiedamseweg, then turn right down Aelbrechtskolk.) Rows of gabled buildings line the waterfront, and there is even a windmill. Nowadays Delfshaven is an up-and-coming area of trendy galleries, cafés, and restaurants.

Dining and Lodging

For details and price-category definitions, *see* Dining and Lodging *in* Staying in Holland, *above.*

Delft

DINING

Spijshuis De Dis. Seafood is a house specialty at this favorite neighborhood spot, where a friendly staff serves typically Dutch cuisine. The mussels with garlic sauce are delicious, and you can also get such delicacies as roast quail. *Beestenmarket 36, tel. 015/131782. Reservations advised. AE, MC, V. $–$$*

DINING AND LODGING

★ **Hotel de Plataan.** Converted in 1994 from a rather grand old post office building, Hotel de Plataan was decorated by a local artist in 1950s-style cream and green. Most rooms have a kitchen nook where you can prepare you own breakfast. You can also have meals in Het Establissement, an excellent restaurant with meaty casseroles as well as imaginative vegetarian dishes. *Verwersdijk 48a, tel. 015/126046, fax*

015/157327. 26 rooms with bath or shower. Facilities: restaurant (tel. 015/121687) AE, DC, MC, V. $

LODGING

Hotel De Ark. This bright, airy hotel in the center of old Delft comprises three canal houses joined so that nearly every room has a view of the canal or the large garden in back. Rooms are clean and modern. *Koornmarkt 59–65, tel. 015/157999, fax 015/144997. 16 rooms with bath, 9 apartments. Facilities: covered parking. AE, DC, MC, V. $$–$$$*

Hotel Leeuwenbrug. On one of the prettiest canals in Delft, you'll find this traditional Dutch family-style hotel. There are two buildings, one of which is simpler, with smaller, cheaper rooms; the annex is more contemporary and businesslike. Everyone enjoys breakfast overlooking the canal, however, and rooms on the top floor of the annex overlook the city. *Koornmarkt 16, tel. 015/147741, fax 015/159759. 38 rooms with bath or shower. Facilities: lounge, bar. AE, MC, V. $$*

The Hague

DINING

Djawa. Whether or not it is a result of the city's diplomatic heritage is unknown, but The Hague is said to have Holland's highest concentration of Indonesian restaurants. Among them is this cozy, family-run, neighborhood restaurant located not far from the center. *Mallemolen 12a, tel. 070/3635763. AE, DC, MC, V. No lunch. $$–$$$*

Le Haricot Vert. What was built in 1638 as a staff house for the nearby palace is nowadays an intimate, candlelighted restaurant in the city center. Dishes combine Dutch simplicity with French flair. Succulent meats swimming in sauce appear on large white plates with a colorful tangle of vegetables. Owner Herman van Overdam can be seen chatting at diners' tables, or flitting back into the kitchen to create one of his sinfully laden dessert platters. Menus change frequently according to what is in season. *Molenstraat 9a–11, tel. 070/3652278. Reservations advised. Jacket and tie. AE, MC, V. $$–$$$*

DINING AND LODGING

Corona. Overlooking a charming square in the center of the city is this pride and joy of The Hague. Rooms are restfully decorated in a muted scheme of white, cream, and dove gray. The restaurant is one of the best in town; for less expensive meals, try the brasserie. *Buitenhof 39–42, tel. 070/3637930, fax 070/3615785. 26 rooms with bath. Facilities: 2 restaurants. AE, DC, MC, V. $$$*

Rotterdam

DINING

Zocher's. Resplendent beside a lake in the city's Maas Park, this airy 19th-century building has one of the most attractive positions—and the sunniest terrace–in town. In one wing is a restaurant serving such tantalizing dishes as guinea fowl stuffed with salmon. In the café on the other side of the building, the same kitchen creates inexpensive, lighter meals. On Sunday the restaurant has live classical music over breakfast. *Baden-Powelllaan 12, tel. 010/4364249. Reservations advised for restaurant; no reservations for café. AE, MC, DC, V. Restaurant $$$; café $*

Inn the Picture. This trendy café offers a wide selection of typical Dutch fare. The salads are especially inviting. In summer, tables offer a view of passing crowds in the shopping district. *Karel Doormanstraat 294, tel. 010/4133204. AE, DC, MC, V. $$*

DINING AND LODGING

Hotel New York. For more than 90 years, the twin towers of the Hotel New York have been a feature of Rotterdam's skyline. Before a 1993 renovation, though, the building was the headquarters of the Holland-America Line. Today some rooms retain the original walnut paneling and restored Art Nouveau carpets, while others are modern in design. Downstairs, the huge café-restaurant (it seats 400) offers everything from English afternoon tea to a selection of five different types of oyster. The hotel is 15 minutes' walk from the Rijnhaven metro station, or you can take one of the hotel's water taxis direct from Veerhaven or Leuvehaven. *Koninginnenhoofd 1, tel. 010/4390500, fax 010/4842701. 73 rooms with bath. Facilities: restaurant, gym, meeting rooms. AE, DC, MC, V. Hotel $$; Restaurant $$–$$$*

15 Hungary

HUNGARY SITS, proudly but precariously, at the crossroads of Central Europe—long a meeting place and battleground of many peoples—having somehow retained its own identity despite countless invasions and foreign occupations by great powers of the East and West. Its industrious, resilient people have a history of brave but doomed uprisings: against the Turks in the 17th century, the Hapsburgs in 1848, and the Soviet Union in 1956. Each has resulted in a period of readjustment, a return to politics as the art of the possible.

The '60s and '70s saw matters improve politically and materially for the majority of Hungarians. Communist party leader János Kádár remained relatively popular at home and abroad, allowing Hungary to expand and improve trade and relations with the West. The bubble began to burst in the 1980s, however, when the economy stagnated and inflation escalated. The peaceful transition to democracy began when young reformers in the party shunted aside the aging Mr. Kádár in 1988 and began speaking openly about multiparty democracy, a market economy, and cutting ties with Moscow. Events quickly gathered pace, and by spring 1990, as the Iron Curtain fell, Hungarians went to the polls in the first free elections in 40 years. A center-right government took office, sweeping away the communists and their renamed successor party, the Socialists, who finished fourth. Ironically, four years later, in the nation's next elections, Hungarians voted out the ailing center-right party in favor of none other than the Hungarian Socialist party, which now rules in coalition with the Free Democrats. *Plus ça change* . . .

In dull mathematical terms, the total landmass of Magyarország (Hungary) is less than twice that of New York state; but every square foot seems packed with natural beauty and charm. Two rivers cross the country. The famous Duna (Danube) flows from the west through Budapest on its way to the southern frontier, while the smaller Tisza flows from the northeast across the Nagyalföld (Great Plain). Western Hungary is dominated by the largest lake in Central Europe, Lake Balaton. Although some overdevelopment has blighted its splendor, its shores are still lined with Baroque villages, relaxing spas, and a hillside tapestry of magnificent vineyards. In eastern Hungary, the Nagyalföld is steeped in the romance of the Magyars (the Hungarians' name for themselves and their language) with its spicy food, strong wine, and proud *csikós* (horsemen).

However, it is Budapest, a city of more than 2 million people, that draws travelers from all over the world. The hills of Buda rise from the brackish waters of the Danube, which bisects the city; on the flatlands of Pest are an imposing array of hotels, restaurants, and shopping areas. Throughout Hungary, comfortable accommodations can be found for comparatively modest prices, and there's an impressive network of inexpensive guest houses.

Hungarians are known for their hospitality and love talking to foreigners, although their strange language, which has almost no links to Indo-European tongues, can be a problem. Today, however, everyone seems to be learning English, especially young people. Trying out a few words of German will delight the older generation. But what all Hungarians share is a deep love of music, and the calendar is star-studded with it, from Budapest's famous opera to its annual spring music festival and the serenades of gypsy violinists during evening meals.

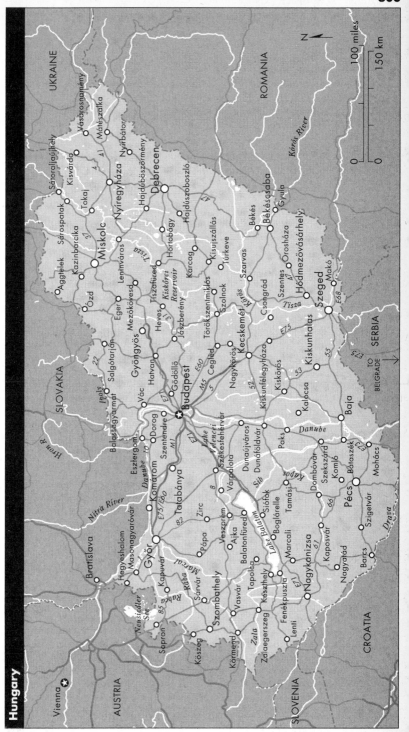

ESSENTIAL INFORMATION

Before You Go

When to Go

Many of Hungary's major fairs and festivals take place in the spring and fall. During July and August, Budapest can be hot and the resorts at Lake Balaton crowded, so spring (May) and the end of summer (September) are the ideal times to visit.

CLIMATE

The following are average daily maximum and minimum temperatures for Budapest.

Jan.	34F	1C	May	72F	22C	Sept.	73F	23C
	25	– 4		52	11		54	12
Feb.	39F	4C	June	79F	26C	Oct.	61F	16C
	28	– 2		59	15		45	7
Mar.	50F	10C	July	82F	28C	Nov.	46F	8C
	36	2		61	16		37	3
Apr.	63F	17C	Aug.	81F	27C	Dec.	39F	4C
	45	7		61	16		30	– 1

Currency

The unit of currency is the forint (Ft.), divided into 100 fillérs (f.). There are bills of 50, 100, 500, 1,000, and 5,000 forints; coins of 1, 2, 5, 10, and 20 forints; and coins of 10, 20, and 50 fillérs. A newly designed series of the forint coins—including new but rare 100- and 200-forint pieces—was introduced into the system in late 1993, precipitating mild confusion and general frustration with pay phones and other coin-operated machines that still accept only the old coins. Until the old coins are phased out entirely, it helps to know that *új* means "new" and *régi* means "old." The exchange rate was approximately 92 Ft. to the dollar and 151 Ft. to the pound sterling at press time (spring 1995). Note that official exchange rates are adjusted at frequent intervals.

Most credit cards are accepted, though don't rely on them in smaller towns or less expensive accommodations and restaurants. Eurocheque holders can cash personal checks in all banks and in most hotels. American Express has a full-service office in Budapest (V, Deák Ferenc u. 10, tel. 1/267–2024, 1/267–2022, or 1/266–8680; fax 1/267–2029), which also dispenses cash to its cardholders.

There is still a black market in hard currency, but changing money on the street is illegal and the bank rate almost always comes close. Stick with official exchange offices.

What It Will Cost

Although first-class hotel chains in Budapest charge standard international prices, quality hotels are still modest by Western standards. Even though the introduction of a value-added tax (VAT) in 1988 has increased many of the prices in the service industry by up to 25%, and the annual inflation rate is more than 25%, enjoyable vacations with all the trimmings remain less expensive than in nearby Western cities like Vienna.

SAMPLE PRICES

Cup of coffee, 60 Ft.; bottle of beer, 100 Ft.–120 Ft.; soft drinks, 20 Ft.–50 Ft.; ham sandwich, 100 Ft.; 1-mile taxi ride, 90 Ft.; museum admission, 50 Ft.–100 Ft.

Visas

Only a valid passport is required of U.S., British, and Canadian citizens. For additional information, contact the Hungarian Embassy in the United States (3910 Shoemaker St. NW, Washington, DC 20008, tel. 202/362–6730) or Canada (7 Delaware Ave., Ottawa K2P OZ2, Ontario, tel. 613/234–8316), or the Hungarian Embassy in London (35b Eaton Pl., London SW1X 8BY, tel. 0171/235–2664).

Customs

ON ARRIVAL

Objects for personal use may be imported freely. If you are over 16, you may also bring in 250 cigarettes or 50 cigars or 250 grams of tobacco, plus 2 liters of wine, 1 liter of spirits, and .25 liters of perfume. A customs charge is made on gifts valued in Hungary at more than 8,000 Ft.

ON DEPARTURE

Take care when you leave Hungary that you have the right documentation for exporting goods. Keep receipts of any items bought from Konsumtourist, Intertourist, or Képcsarnok Vállalat. A special permit is needed for works of art, antiques, or objects of museum value. You are entitled to a VAT refund on new goods (i.e., not works of art, antiques, or objects of museum value) valued at more than 25,000 Ft. (VAT inclusive). But applying for the refund may rack up more frustration than money: cash refunds are given only in forints and you may find yourself in the airport minutes before boarding with a handful of soft currency, of which no more than 1,000 forints may be taken out of the country. If you made your purchases by credit card you can file for a credit to your card or to your bank account (again in forints), but just don't expect it to come through in a hurry. If you intend to apply for the credit, make sure you get customs to stamp the original purchase invoice before you leave the country. For more information, pick up a tax refund brochure from any tourist office or hotel or contact Intel Trade Rt. (I, Csalogány u. 6-10, tel. 1/156–9800).

For further information, inquire at the **National Customs and Revenue Office** (VIII, Keleti train station arrivals area, tel. 1/114–0203 or 1/114–0280). If you have trouble communicating, ask **Tourinform** (tel. 1/117–9800) for help.

Language

Hungarian (Magyar) tends to look and sound intimidating to every one at first because it is a non-Indo-European language. However, there is a major trend, especially among young people, to learn English, and most people in the tourist trade, from bus drivers to waiters, speak some English or German.

Getting Around

By Car

DOCUMENTATION

To drive in Hungary, U.S. and Canadian visitors need an International Driver's License—although their domestic licenses are usually accepted anyway—and U.K. visitors may use their own domestic licenses.

ROAD CONDITIONS

There are three classes of roads: highways (designated by the letter M and a single digit), secondary roads (designated by a two-digit number), and minor roads (designated by a three-digit number). Highways and secondary roads are generally excellent. The conditions of minor roads vary considerably; keep in mind that tractors and horse-drawn carts may slow your route down in rural areas. There are no toll charges on highways.

RULES OF THE ROAD
Hungarians drive on the right and observe the usual Continental rules of the road. Unless otherwise noted, the speed limit in developed areas is 50 kph (30 mph), on main roads 90 kph (55 mph), and on highways 120 kph (75 mph). Seat belts are compulsory and drinking alcohol is totally prohibited—the penalties are very severe.

GASOLINE
Gas stations are plentiful in and around major cities, and major chains have opened modern all-service stations on highways in the provinces. A gallon of *benzin* (gasoline) costs about $3.50. Unleaded gasoline, only slightly more expensive, is usually available at all stations, as is diesel. Interag Shell and Áfor stations at busy traffic centers stay open all night; elsewhere, they're open from 6 AM to 8 PM.

BREAKDOWNS
The **Hungarian Automobile Club** runs a 24-hour "Yellow Angels" breakdown service from Budapest (XI, Francia út 38/A, tel. 1/252–8000; when outside Budapest, tel. 088). There are repair stations in all the major towns and emergency telephones on the main highways.

By Train
Travel by train from Budapest to other large cities or to Lake Balaton is cheap and efficient. Remember to take a *gyorsvonat* (express train) and not a *személyvonat* (local), which is extremely slow. A *helyjegy* (seat reservation), which costs about 45 Ft. (160 Ft. for Inter-City trains) and is sold up to 60 days in advance, is advisable for all express trains, especially for weekend travel in summer. It is also worth paying a little extra for first-class tickets.

FARES
Only Hungarian citizens are entitled to student and senior citizen discounts. InterRail cards are available for those under 26, and the Rail Europe Senior Travel Pass entitles senior citizens to a 30% reduction on all train fares. Snacks and drinks can be purchased on all express trains, but the supply often runs out quickly, especially in summer, so pack a lunch just in case. For more information about rail travel, contact the **MÁV Passenger Service** (VI, Andrássy út 35, tel. 1/322–8049 or 1/322–8275).

By Bus
Long-distance buses link Budapest with many main cities in Eastern and Western Europe. Services to the eastern part of the country leave from Népstadion station (tel. 1/252–0696). Buses to the west and south leave from the main Volán bus station at Erzsébet tér in the Inner City (tel. 1/118–2122). Although inexpensive, they tend to be crowded, so reserve your seat.

By Boat
Hungary is well equipped with nautical transport, and Budapest is situated on a major international waterway—the Danube. Vienna is five hours away by hydrofoil, and many Hungarian resorts are accessible by hydrofoil or boat. For information about excursions or pleasure cruises, contact **MAHART Tours** (V, Belgrád rakpart, tel. 1/118–1704, 1/118–1586, or 1/118–1743) or **IBUSZ** (Hungarian Travel Bureau; VII, Károly körút 3/C, tel. 1/321–1000 or 1/321–2932).

By Bicycle

A land of rolling hills and flat plains, Hungary lends itself to bicycling. A few of the larger train stations around Lake Balaton rent bicycles (in various states of repair) for about 200 Ft. a day; but the sad truth is that insurance difficulties have led to a serious, nationwide dearth of bicycle rental outlets. For information about renting in Budapest, contact **Tourinform** (V, Sütő u. 2, tel. 1/117–9800). For brochures and general information on bicycling conditions and suggested routes, contact the Bicycle Touring Association of Hungary (IX, Kávin tér 9, tel. 1/217–7208). The **IBUSZ Riding and Hobbies** department provides a variety of guided bicycle tours (V, Ferenciek tere 10, tel. 1/118–2967).

Staying in Hungary

Telephones

LOCAL CALLS

Pay phones use 10 Ft. coins—the cost of a three-minute local call—and also accept 5 Ft. and 20 Ft. coins. At press time (spring 1995), pay phones had still not been converted to accept Hungary's new coins. Most towns in Hungary can be dialed directly—dial 06 and wait for the buzzing tone, then dial the local number. It is unnecessary to use the city code, 1, when dialing within Budapest.

Gray card-operated telephones outnumber coin-operated phones in Budapest and the Balaton region. The cards—available at post offices and most newsstands and kiosks—come in units of 50 (500 Ft.) and 120 (1,200 Ft.) calls. Don't be surprised if a flock of kids gathers around your pay phone while you talk—collecting and trading used phone cards is a raging fad.

INTERNATIONAL CALLS

Direct calls to foreign countries can be made from Budapest and all major provincial towns by dialing 00 and waiting for the international dialing tone; on pay phones the initial charge is 40 Ft. To reach an **AT&T** long-distance operator, dial 00–800–01111; for **MCI,** dial 00–800–01411; for **Sprint,** dial 00–800–01877.

OPERATORS

International calls can be made through the operator by dialing 09; for operator-assisted calls within Hungary, dial 01. Be patient: The telephone system is antiquated, especially in the countryside.

Dial 1/117–0170 for directory assistance. Some operators speak English and, depending on their mood, may assist you in English.

COUNTRY CODE

The country code for Hungary is 36.

Mail

The post offices near Budapest's Keleti (East) (VII, Baross tér 11c) and Nyugati (West) (VI, Teréz körút 51) train stations are open 24 hours.

POSTAL RATES

An airmail postcard to the United States, the United Kingdom, and the rest of Western Europe costs 47 Ft., and an airmail letter costs from 67 Ft. Postcards to the United Kingdom and the rest of Western Europe cost 40 Ft., letters from 60 Ft.

RECEIVING MAIL

A poste restante service, for general delivery, is available in Budapest. The address is Magyar Posta, H-1052 Budapest, Petőfi Sándor utca

17–19. The roman numeral prefix listed in a Budapest address refers to one of the city's 22 districts.

Opening and Closing Times

Banks are generally open weekdays 8–4, often with a one-hour lunch break at around noon; many close at noon on Fridays.

Museums are generally open daily from 10 to 6 and are closed on Mondays.

Department stores are open weekdays 10 to 5 or 6, Saturday until 1.

Grocery stores are generally open weekdays from 7 or 8 to 7, Saturday until 1 PM; **"non-stops"** or *éjjeli-nappali* are open 24 hours.

National Holidays

January 1; March 15 (Anniversary of 1848 Revolution); April 7–8 (Easter and Easter Monday); May 1 (Labor Day); June 26–27 (Pentecost); August 20 (St. Stephen's and Constitution Day); October 23 (1956 Revolution Day); December 24–26.

Dining

There are plenty of good, affordable restaurants offering a variety of Hungarian dishes. Meats, rich sauces, and creamy desserts predominate, but the health-conscious will also find salads, even out of season. Visitors can eat at a *önkiszolgáló étterem* (self-service restaurant), *bistró étel bár* (sit-down snack bar), *büfé* (snack counter), *eszpresszó* (café), or a *drink-bár* (bar). Be sure to visit a *cukrászda* (pastry shop).

In almost all restaurants, an inexpensive prix-fixe lunch, called a *menü*, is available, usually for as little as 350 Ft. It includes soup or salad, an entrée, and a dessert.

MEALTIMES

Hungarians eat early—you risk offhand service and cold food after 9 PM. Lunch, the main meal for many, is served from noon to 2.

WHAT TO WEAR

At most moderately priced and inexpensive restaurants, casual but neat dress is acceptable.

RATINGS

Prices are per person and include a first course, main course, and dessert, but no wine or tip. Prices in Budapest tend to be a good 30% higher than elsewhere in Hungary. Highly recommended restaurants are indicated by a star ★.

CATEGORY	ALL AREAS
$$$$	over 2,500 Ft.
$$$	1,750 Ft.–2,500 Ft.
$$	1,000 Ft.–1,750 Ft.
$	under 1,000 Ft.

Lodging

HOTELS

There are few expensive hotels outside Budapest, but the moderately priced hotels are generally comfortable and well-run. Inexpensive establishments—more numerous every year as Hungarians convert unused rooms or second apartments into rental units for tourists—seldom have private baths, but plumbing is adequate almost everywhere.

RENTALS

Apartments in Budapest and cottages at Lake Balaton are available for short- and long-term rental, and can make the most economic lodging for families—particularly for those who prefer to cook their own meals. Rates and reservations can be obtained from tourist offices in Hungary and abroad. A Budapest apartment might cost 5,000 Ft. a day; a luxury cottage for two on Lake Balaton costs around the same. Bookings can be made in Budapest at the **IBUSZ** at Petőfi tér 3 (tel. 1/118–5707 or 1/118–4842), which is open 24 hours a day, or through IBUSZ offices in the United States and Great Britain (*see* Visitor Info *in* Chapter 1). Some enterprising locals stand outside the IBUSZ office and offer tourists their apartments for lower than official rates, and are usually willing to bargain. If you choose this route, insist on seeing the place before you hand over any cash. Ask for a written agreement and be sure to get the owner's contact telephone number and address should anything go wrong. Other rental agencies in Budapest include **Cooptourist** (I, Atilla u. 107, tel. 1/175–2846 or 1/175–2937) and **Charles Apartments** (I, Hegyalja út 23, tel. 1/201–1796 or 1/212–3830).

GUEST HOUSES
Also called pensions, these offer simple accommodations—well suited to people on a budget. Many offer simple breakfast facilities. Arrangements can be made through local tourist offices or travel agents abroad.

In the provinces it is safe to accept rooms that you are offered directly: They will almost always be clean and in a relatively good neighborhood, and the prospective landlord will probably not cheat you. SZOBA KIADÓ (or the German ZIMMER FREI) means "Room to Rent." The rate per night for a double room in Budapest or at Lake Balaton is around 1,500 Ft.–2,000 Ft., which usually includes the use of a bathroom but not breakfast. Reservations and referrals can also be made by any tourist office, and if you go that route, you have someone to complain to if things don't work out.

CAMPING
Most of the 140 campsites in Hungary are open from May through September. As rates are no longer state-regulated, prices vary. An average rate is about 650 Ft. a day. There's usually a small charge for hot water and electricity plus an accommodations fee—around 100 Ft. per person per night. Children often get a 50% reduction. Camping is forbidden except in appointed areas. Information can be obtained through travel agencies or through the **Hungarian Camping and Caravanning Club** (VIII, Üllői út 6, tel. 1/133–6536), which publishes an informative brochure listing campsites and their facilities in English.

RATINGS
The following price categories are for a double room with bath and breakfast during the peak season; rates are even lower off-season and in the countryside, sometimes under 1,500 forints for two. For single rooms with bath, count on about 80% of the double-room rate. Most large hotels require payment in hard currency. Highly recommended lodgings are indicated by a star ★.

CATEGORY	BUDAPEST	BALATON AND DANUBE BEND
$$$$	over 24,000 Ft.	over 11,000 Ft.
$$$	16,000 Ft.–24,000 Ft.	9,000 Ft.–11,000 Ft.
$$	9,000 Ft.–16,000 Ft.	5,000 Ft.–9,000 Ft.
$	under 9,000 Ft.	under 5,000 Ft.

During the peak season (June through August), full board may be compulsory at some of the Lake Balaton hotels. During the off-season (in Budapest, September through March; at Lake Balaton and the Danube Bend, in May and September), rates can be considerably lower than those given above.

Tipping

Four decades of socialism didn't alter the Hungarian habit of tipping generously. Cloakroom and gas-pump attendants, hairdressers, waiters, and taxi drivers all expect tips. At least 10% should be added to a restaurant bill or taxi fare. If a gypsy band plays exclusively for your table, you can leave 100 Ft. in the plate discreetly provided for that purpose.

BUDAPEST

Arriving and Departing

By Plane

Hungary's international airport, **Ferihegy** (tel. 1/157–9123), is about 22 kilometers (14 miles) southeast of the city. All **Malév** and **Lufthansa** flights operate from the new Terminal 2; other airlines use Terminal 1. For same-day flight information, call the airport authority (tel. 1/157–7155); you can also call for general information on arrivals (tel. 1/157–8460) and departures (tel. 1/157–8768). The staff takes its time to answer calls, and may not be cordial; be prepared.

BETWEEN THE AIRPORT AND DOWNTOWN

Minibuses to and from Erzsébet tér station (Platform 1) in downtown Budapest leave every half hour from 5:30 AM to 9 PM. The trip takes 30–40 minutes (longer in rush hours) and costs around 200 Ft. The modern minivans of the fast, friendly, and reliable LRI Airport Shuttle service (tel. 1/157–8555 or 1/157–6283) transport you to any destination in Budapest, door to door, for around 600 Ft., even less than the least expensive taxi—and most employees speak English. At the airport, buy tickets at the LRI counter in the arrivals hall near baggage claim; for your return trip, just call ahead for a pick-up. There are also approved taxi stands outside both terminals.

By Train

There are three main train stations in Budapest: Keleti, Nyugati, and Déli (South). Trains from Vienna usually operate from the Keleti station, while those to the Balaton depart from the Déli.

By Bus

Most buses to Budapest from the western region of Hungary, including those from Vienna, arrive at **Erzsébet tér** station.

By Car

The main routes into Budapest are the M1 from Vienna (via Győr) and the M7 from the Balaton.

Getting Around

Budapest is best explored on foot. The maps provided by tourist offices are not very detailed, so arm yourself with one from any of the bookshops in Váci utca or from downtown stationery shops and newsstands.

By Public Transportation

The Budapest Transportation Authority runs the public transportation system—a metro (subway) with three lines, buses, streetcars, and trolleybuses—and it's cheap, efficient, and simple to use but closes down around 11:30 PM. However, certain trams and buses run on a limited schedule all night. A *napijegy* (day ticket) costs 200 Ft. (three-day, 400 Ft.) and allows unlimited travel on all services within the city limits. You can also buy tickets for single rides for 25 Ft. from metro stations or newsstands. You can travel on all trams, buses, and on the subway with this ticket, but you can't change lines.

Bus, streetcar, trolleybus, and M1 metro tickets must be canceled on board—watch how other passengers do it; M2 and M3 metro tickets are canceled at station entrances. Don't get caught without a ticket: Spot checks are frequent, often targeting tourists, and you can be fined several hundred forints.

By Taxi

Taxis are plentiful and are a good value, but make sure that they have a meter that is working. The average initial charge is 30 Ft.–50 Ft., plus 70 Ft. per kilometer plus 14 Ft. per minute of waiting time. There are too many taxis in Budapest, but some drivers try to charge outrageous prices. Avoid unmarked, "freelance" taxis; stick with those affiliated with an established company. Your safest and most reliable bet is to do what the locals do: Order a taxi by phone; it will arrive in about five to 10 minutes. The best rates are with **Fötaxi** (tel. 1/222–2222), **6 X 6** (tel. 1/266–6666), **Citytaxi** (tel. 1/153–3633 or 1/211–1111), **Volántaxi** (tel. 1/166–6666), and **Teletaxi** (tel. 1/155–5555).

By Boat

In summer the Budapest Transportation Authority runs a not-so-regular boat service that links the north and south of the city, stopping at points on both banks, including Margit-sziget (Margaret Island); contact Tourinform for current schedules. From May through October boats leave from the quay at Vigadó tér on 1½-hour cruises between the Árpád and Petőfi bridges. The trip, organized by **MAHART**, runs twice a day and costs around 400 Ft. (tel. 1/118–1586, 1/118–1743, or 1/118–1704).

Important Addresses and Numbers

Tourist Information

Tourinform (V, Sütő u. 2, tel. 1/117–9800) is open April–October daily 8–8 and November–March weekdays 8–8, weekends 8–3. **IBUSZ Accommodation Office** (V, Petőfi tér 3, tel. 1/118–5707 or 1/118–4842) is open 24 hours. **Budapest Tourist** (V, Roosevelt tér 5, tel. 1/117–3555) is also helpful. *The Budapest Sun*, an English-language weekly newspaper that covers news, business, and culture, carries general orientation tips for tourists and listings of concerts and foreign-language films. It's sold at newsstands, bookstores, and hotels.

Embassies

U.S.: V, Szabadság tér 12 (tel. 1/112–6450). **Canadian:** XII, Budakeszi út 32 (tel. 1/275–1200). **U.K.:** V, Harmincad utca 6 (tel. 1/266–2888).

Emergencies

Police (tel. 07). **Ambulance** (tel. 04) or call **SOS** (VII, Kerepesi út 15, tel. 1/118–8212 or 1/118–8288), a 24-hour private ambulance service with English-speaking personnel. **Doctor:** Ask your hotel or embassy for recommendations or visit the **International Medical Services** (IMS, XIII, Váci út 202, tel. 1/129–8423), a private clinic staffed by

English-speaking doctors offering 24-hour medical service. U.S. and Canadian visitors are advised to take out full medical insurance. U.K. visitors are covered for emergencies and essential treatment.

English-Language Bookstores

Libri International Bookstore (V, Váci u. 32), **Central Secondhand Bookshop** (V, Múzeum körút 15), **Idegennyelvű Könyvesbolt** (V, Petöfi Sándor u. 2), **Longman ELT** (VIII, Kölcsey u. 2), **Litea Bookshop and Tea Salon** (I, Hess András tér 4), **Bestsellers** (V, Október 6 u. 11), and **Atlantisz Book Island** (V, Váci u. 31–33). Foreign publications—including those in English—can be bought at the reception desks of major hotels and at newsstands at major traffic centers.

Travel Agencies

American Express (V, Déak Ferenc u. 10, tel. 1/267–2024, 1/267–2022, or 1/266–8680, fax 1/267–2029). **Getz International** (V, Falk Miksa u. 5, tel. 1/112–0645 or 1/112–0649, fax 1/112–1014). **Vista** (VII, Károly körút 21, tel. 1/269–6032, 1/342–9316, or 1/342–1534, fax 1/269–6031).

Guided Tours

Orientation Tours

IBUSZ (*see* Important Addresses and Numbers, *above*) sponsors three-hour bus tours of the city that operate all year and cost about 2,000 Ft. Starting from Erzsébet tér, they take in parts of both Buda and Pest. **Gray Line Cityrama** (V, Báthori u. 22, tel. 1/132–5344) also offers a three-hour city bus tour (2,000 Ft. per person), as well as the three-hour "Budapest Potpourri" boat tour from April to September (2,500 Ft. per person), which includes a stop to look inside Parliament.

Special-Interest Tours and Excursions

IBUSZ, Cityrama, and **Budapest Tourist** organize a number of unusual tours, including trips to the Buda Hills and goulash parties as well as visits to the National Gallery and Parliament and other traditional sights. These tour companies will provide personal guides on request. Several enterprising tour operators now offer oddities such as day trips to former Soviet army bases and historical excursions focusing on Budapest's remaining communist monuments. Also check at your hotel's reception desk.

Excursions farther afield include day-long trips to the *Puszta* (another term for the Great Plain), the Danube Bend, and Lake Balaton. IBUSZ's **Riding and Hobbies** department (*see* Getting Around *in* Essential Information, *above*) offers a variety of special-interest tours, including horseback riding, bicycling, and angling, as well as special stays in many of Hungary's historic castles and mansions.

Exploring Budapest

Budapest, situated on both banks of the Danube, unites the colorful hills of Buda and the wide boulevards of Pest. Though it was the site of a Roman outpost in the 1st century, the city was not actually created until 1873, when the towns of Óbuda, Pest, and Buda were joined. The cultural, political, intellectual, and commercial heart of the nation beats in Budapest; for the 20% of the nation's population who live in the capital, anywhere else is simply "the country."

Much of the charm of a visit to Budapest lies in unexpected glimpses into shadowy courtyards and in long vistas down sunlit cobbled streets. Although some 30,000 buildings were destroyed during World War II and in 1956, the past lingers on in the often crumbling architectural details of the antique structures that remain and in the memories and lifestyles of Budapest's citizens.

The principal sights of the city fall roughly into three areas, each of which can be comfortably covered on foot. The Budapest hills are best explored by public transportation. Note that many street names have been changed to purge all reminders of the communist regime. If the street you're looking for seems to have disappeared, ask any local— though he or she may well be as bewildered as you are.

Numbers in the margin correspond to points of interest on the Budapest map.

①
② Take a taxi or bus (No. 16 from **Erzsébet tér** or the *Várbusz*—castle minibus—from **Moszkva tér**) to **Dísz tér,** at the top of **Várhegy** (Castle Hill), where the painstaking work of reconstruction has been in progress since World War II. Having made their final stand in the Royal Palace itself, the Nazis left behind them a blackened wasteland. Under the rubble, archaeologists discovered the medieval foundations of the palace of King Matthias Corvinus, who, in the 15th century, presided over one of the most splendid courts in Europe.

③ The **Királyi Palota** (Palace), now a vast museum complex and cultural center, can be reached on foot from Dísz tér—it is one block to the south—or by *Sikló* (funicular railway) from Clark Ádám tér. Until recently, the northern wing of the building was devoted to the **Legújabbkori Történeti Múzeum** (Museum of Contemporary History), but at press time (spring 1995) plans were underway to close it by 1996 and transfer the entire collection to the "most recent" end of the National Museum's epic Hungarian history exhibit. The **Ludwig Múzeum** (Ludwig Museum), with a collection of more than 200 pieces of Hungarian and contemporary world art, including works by Picasso and Lichtenstein, has shared the northern wing with the Museum of Contemporary History since 1991 and was bidding to spread eventually into the building's vacated areas. The central block houses the **Magyar Nemzeti Galeria** (Hungarian National Gallery), exhibiting a wide range of Hungarian fine art, from medieval paintings to modern sculpture. Names to look for are Munkácsy, a 19th-century Romantic painter, and Csontváry, an early Surrealist whom Picasso much admired. *Ludwig Museum: Buda Castle (Wing A), Dísz tér 17, tel. 1/175– 7533. Admission: 80 Ft. Open Tues.–Sun. 10–6. Hungarian National Gallery: Buda Castle (Wing C), Dísz tér 17, tel. 1/175–7533. Admission: 100 Ft. adults, 50 Ft. children; free on Sat; tour with Englishspeaking guide, 800 Ft. Open Mar.–Nov., Tues.–Sun. 10–6; Dec.–Feb., Tues.–Sun. 10–4; closed Mon.*

The southern block contains the **Budapesti Történeti Múzeum** (Budapest History Museum). Down in the cellars are the original medieval vaults of the palace, portraits of King Matthias and his second wife, Beatrice of Aragon, and many late-14th-century statues that probably adorned the Renaissance palace. *Buda Castle (Wing E), Szt. György tér 2, tel. 1/175–7533. Admission: 100 Ft. adults, 50 Ft. children. Open Mar.–Oct., Wed.–Mon. 10–6; Nov.–Dec., Wed.–Mon. 10–5; Jan.–Feb., Wed.–Mon. 10–4.*

④ The **Mátyás templom** (Matthias Church), northeast of Dísz tér, with its distinctive patterned roof, dates from the 13th century. Built as a mosque by the occupying Turks, it was destroyed and reconstructed in the 19th century, only to be bombed during World War II. Only the south porch is from the original structure. The Hapsburg emperors were

Állami Operaház, **18**

Belvárosi plébánia
templom, **12**

Dísz tér, **2**

Erzsébet tér, **1**

Hadtörténeti
Múzeum, **8**

Halászbástya, **5**

Királyi Palota, **3**

Magyar Nemzeti
Múzeum, **14**

Március 15 tér, **11**

Mátyás templom, **4**

Medieval synagogue, **7**

Mezőgazdasági
Múzeum, **22**

Millenniumi
Emlékmű, **19**

Műcsarnok, **21**

Néprajzi Múzeum, **16**

Parliament, **15**

Roosevelt tér, **9**

Szépművészeti
Múzeum, **20**

Szt. István Bazilika, **17**

Váci utca, **13**

Vigadó tér, **10**

Zenetörténeti
Múzeum, **6**

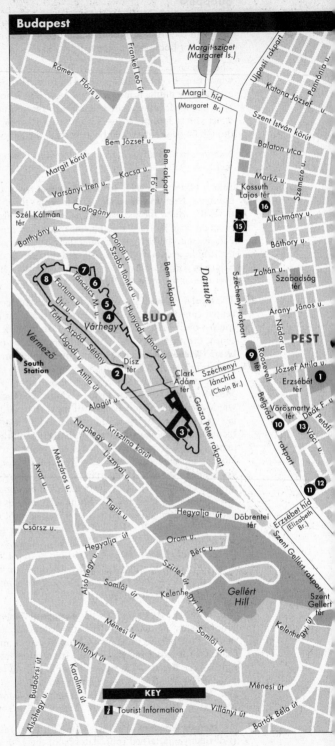

Budapest

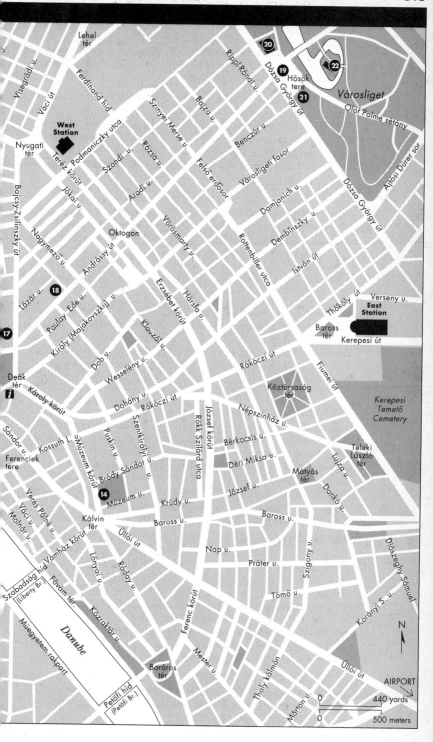

Lehel tér

Visegrádi u.

Váci út

Ferdinánd híd

Rippl-Rónai u.

Dózsa György út

⑳

⑲ Hősök tere

㉒

Városliget

⑳

Olof Palme sétány

Szinyei Merse u.

Bajza u.

Benczúr u.

West Station

Nyugati tér

Teréz körút

Podmaniczky utca

Szondi u.

Rózsa u.

Felső erdősor

Városligeti fasor

Damjanich u.

Attősi Dürer sor

Dózsa György út

Bajcsy-Zsilinszky út

Jókai u.

Aradi u.

Nagymező u.

Oktogon

Andrássy út

Vörösmarty u.

Rottenbiller utca

Dembinszky u.

István út

⑱

Lázár u.

Paulay Ede u.

Erzsébet körút

Hársfa u.

Király (Majakovszkij) u.

Thököly út

Verseny u.

East Station

⑰

Klauzál u.

Rákóczi út

Fiumei út

Baross tér

Kerepesi út

Deák tér

ℹ

Károly körút

Dob u.

Wesselényi u.

Dohány u.

Rákóczi út

Köztársaság tér

Népszínház u.

Kerepesi Temető Cemetery

Sándor u.

Kossuth L.

Múzeum körút

Puskin u.

Szentkirályi u.

József körút

Rökk Szilárd utca

Bérkocsis u.

Déri Miksa u.

Teleki László tér

Luzsa u.

Ferenciek tere

Veres Pálné u.

Bródy Sándor u.

Mátyás tér

Dankó u.

⑭

Múzeum u.

Krúdy u.

József u.

Kálvin tér

Baross u.

Baross u.

Molnár u.

Váci u.

Üllői út

Nap u.

Szigony u.

Diószeghy Sámuel

Lónyai u.

Ráday u.

Práter u.

Korányi S. u.

Szabadság híd (Liberty Br.)

Fővám tér

Közraktár u.

Tömő u.

N

Müegyetem rakpart

Danube

Ferenc körút

Mester u.

Thaly Kálmán u.

Üllői út

AIRPORT

Boráros tér

Petőfi híd (Petőfi Br.)

Márton u.

0   440 yards

0   500 meters

crowned kings of Hungary here, including Charles IV in 1916. High mass is celebrated every Sunday at 10 AM with an orchestra and choir, and organ concerts are often held in the summer on Friday at 8 PM. Tourists are asked to remain at the back of the church during services. *I, Szentháromság tér 2, tel. 1/155–5657. Open daily 7–8. Admission free, except during concerts.*

❺ The turn-of-the-century **Halászbástya** (Fishermen's Bastion) is on your left as you leave the church. It was built as a lookout tower to protect what was once a thriving fishing settlement. Its neo-Romanesque columns and arches frame views over the city and river. Near the church, in Hess András tér, are remains of the oldest church on Castle Hill, built by Dominican friars in the 13th century. These have now been tastefully integrated into the modern Hilton hotel.

The town houses lining the streets of the Castle district are largely occupied by offices, restaurants, and diplomatic residences, but the house
❻ where Beethoven stayed in 1800 is now the **Zenetörténeti Múzeum** (Museum of Music History), which hosts intimate classical music recitals and displays rare manuscripts and antique instruments. *I, Táncsics Mihály u. 7, tel. 1/175–9011. Admission: 40 Ft. Open mid-Mar.–mid-Nov., Mon. 4–8, Wed.–Sun. 10–6; mid-Nov.–mid-Mar., Mon. 3–6, Wed.–Sun. 10–5.*

❼ The remains of a **medieval synagogue** are also in the neighborhood and open to the public. On display are a number of objects relating to the Jewish community, including religious inscriptions, frescoes, and tombstones dating from the 15th century. *Táncsics Mihály u. 26, tel. 1/155–8764. Admission: 40 Ft. adults, 20 Ft. children. Open May–Oct., Tues.–Fri. 10–2, weekends 10–6. Group tours (arrange 2 days in advance) Oct.–May.*

❽ The **Hadtörténeti Múzeum** (Museum of Military History) is at the far end of Castle Hill. The collection includes uniforms and regalia, many belonging to the Hungarian generals who took part in the abortive uprising against Austrian rule in 1848. Other exhibits trace the military history of Hungary from the original Magyar conquest in the 9th century through the period of Ottoman rule and right to the middle of this century. *I, Tóth Árpád sétány 40, tel. 1/156–9522 or 1/156–9770. Admission: 50 Ft.; free Sat. Open Mar.–Nov., Tues.–Sat. 9–5, Sun. 10–6; Dec.–Feb., Tues.–Sat. 10–4, Sun. 10–6.*

The Heart of the City

Cross the **Széchenyi lánchíd** (Chain Bridge) from Clark Ádám tér to
❾ reach **Roosevelt tér** in Pest, with the 19th-century neoclassical Academy of Sciences on your left, and directly in front, the 1907 Gresham Palace, a crumbling temple to the age of Art Nouveau. Pest fans out from the **Belváros** (Inner City), which is bounded by the **Kiskörút** (Little Ring Road). The **Nagykörút** (Grand Ring Road) describes a wider semicircle from the Margaret Bridge to Petőfi Bridge. To your right, an elegant promenade, the **Korzó,** runs south parallel to the river, providing postcard views of Castle Hill, the Chain Bridge, and Gellért Hill on the other side of the Danube.

TIME OUT The **Bécsi Kávéház** (Viennese Café) in the Fórum Hotel serves the best coffee and cream pastries in town. *V, Apáczai Csere János u. 12–14, tel. 1/117–8088. Open daily 9–9.*

⑩ A square called **Vigadó tér** is dominated by the Danube view and Vigadó concert hall, built in a Romantic mix of Byzantine, Moorish, and Romanesque styles, with Hungarian motifs thrown in for good measure. Liszt, Brahms, and Bartók all performed here. Completely destroyed during World War II, it has been rebuilt in its original style. Another

⑪ square, **Március 15 tér,** commemorates the 1848 struggle for independence from the Hapsburgs with a statue of the poet Petőfi Sándor, who died in a later uprising. Every March 15, the national holiday commemorating the revolution, the square is packed with patriotic Hun-

⑫ garians. Behind the square is the 12th-century **Belvárosi plébánia templom** (Inner-City Parish Church), the oldest in Pest. The church has been redone in a variety of western architectural styles; even Turkish influences, such as the Muslim prayer niche, remain. Liszt, who lived only a few yards away, often played the organ here.

⑬ Parallel to the Korzó, lies Budapest's most upscale shopping street, **Váci utca. Vörösmarty tér,** a handsome square in the heart of the Inner City, is a good spot to sit and relax. Street musicians and sidewalk cafés make it one of the liveliest places in Budapest.

TIME OUT **Gerbeaud,** an elegant pastry shop founded in 1857, retains the old imperial style and has a terrace overlooking the square. A fashionable meeting place, it always seems crowded with tourists and locals devouring the rich chocolate cake known as *dobos torta,* their pleasure undiminished by the surliness of the waitresses. *V, Vörösmarty tér 7, tel. 1/118-1311. Open daily 9-9.*

⑭ A slight detour back down the river and deeper into Pest brings you to the steps of the stern, Classical edifice of the **Magyar Nemzeti Múzeum** (Hungarian National Museum), built between 1837 and 1847. On these steps, on March 15, 1848, Petőfi Sándor recited his revolutionary poem, the *"Nemzeti Dal"* ("National Song"), and the "12 Points," a list of political demands by young Hungarians calling upon the people to rise up against the Hapsburgs. Celebrations of the national holiday—long banned by the communist regime—are now held here (and throughout the city) every year on March 15. You'll find the museum's most sacred treasure, the Szent Korona (Holy Crown)—it's the one that looks like a great golden soufflé resting on a Byzantine band of enamel, pearls, and other gems—with a host of other royal relics in the domed Hall of Honor off the main lobby. The museum's epic Hungarian history exhibit has been closed for renovations but is scheduled to reopen by August 1996, when the addition of the post-1989 exhibits will be complete. *IX, Múzeum körút 14–16, tel. 1/138–2122. Admission: 80 Ft. adults, 40 Ft. children. Open mid-Mar.–mid-Oct., Tues.–Sun. 10– 6; mid-Oct.–mid-Mar., Tues.–Sun. 10–5.*

⑮ North of Roosevelt tér is the riverfront's most striking landmark, the imposing neo-Gothic **Parliament,** now minus the red star on top (open for tours only; call IBUSZ, tel. 1/118–5776 or 1/118–4842, or Budapest Tourist, tel. 1/117–3555 or 1/118–1453). To its left sits an expressive statue of József Attila (1905–37), who, in spite of his early death, became known as one of Hungary's greatest poets.

⑯ Across from the Parliament is the majestic **Néprajzi Múzeum** (Museum of Ethnography), with impressive exhibits—captioned in English—depicting folk costumes and traditions. These are the authentic pieces you can't see at touristy folk shops. *V, Kossuth Lajos tér 12, tel. 1/132– 6340. Admission: 80 Ft. Open Tues.–Sun. 10–6.*

17 Dark and massive, the 19th-century **Szent István Bazilika** (St. Stephen's Basilica) is one of the chief landmarks of Pest. It was planned early in the 19th century as a neoclassical building, but was in the neo-Renaissance style by the time it was completed more than 50 years later. During World War II, the most precious documents from the Municipal archives were placed in the cellar of the basilica—one of the few available bombproof sites. The mummified right hand of St. Stephen, Hungary's first king and patron saint, is preserved in the Szent Jobb chapel as a relic. Extensive restorations have been underway at the aging basilica for years, with a target completion date of 2010, and some part of the structure is likely to be under scaffolding when you visit. *V, Szt. István tér, tel. 1/117–2859. Open Mon.–Sat. 7–7, Sun 1–5.*

Andrássy út runs 3.2 kilometers (2 miles) from the basilica to **Hősök tere** (Heroes' Square). About one quarter of the way up on the left, at **18** Hajós utca, is the **Állami Operaház** (State Opera House), with its statues of the Muses in the second-floor corner niches. Completed in 1884, it was the crowning achievement of architect Miklós Ybl. It has been restored to its original ornate glory—particularly inside—and has been spared attempts at modernization. Foreign-language tours, held daily at 3 PM and 4 PM, meet in front of the opera house, but call ahead to confirm that there is a tour on the day you want to visit (tel. 1/131–2550 ext. 156). The cost is about 300 Ft. There are no performances in summer, except for the week-long BudaFest international opera and ballet festival in mid-August.

Heroes' Square and Városliget

19 In the center of Heroes' Square stands the 120-foot **Millenniumi Emlékmű** (Millennium Monument), begun in 1896 to commemorate the 1,000th anniversary of the Magyar Conquest. Statues of Prince Árpád and six other founders of the Magyar nation occupy the base of the monument, while Hungary's greatest rulers and princes are between the columns on either side.

20 The **Szépművészeti Múzeum** (Fine Arts Museum) stands on one side of the square. Egyptian, Greek, and Roman artifacts dominate an entire section of the museum, and the collection of ceramics includes many rare pieces. The institution's largely unknown Spanish collection, which includes many works by El Greco and a magnificent painting by Velásquez, is considered the best of its kind outside Spain. *XIV, Dózsa György út 41, tel. 1/142–9759. Admission: 60 Ft. Open Tues.–Sun. 10–5:30; closed Jan.–Mar.*

After four years of being boarded up for exhaustive renovations, the **21** striking 1895 **Műcsarnok** (Art Gallery), on the other side of the square, reopened its doors to the public during the 1995 Budapest Spring Festival. It's program of events includes exhibitions of contemporary Hungarian and international art and rich series of films, plays, and concerts. *XIV, Dózsa György út 37, tel. 1/267–8776 or 1/267–8777. Admission: 60 Ft. Open Tues.–Sun. 10–6.*

The **Városliget** (City Park) extends beyond the square; on the left as you enter it are the zoo, state circus, amusement park, and outdoor swimming pool of the Széchenyi mineral baths. On the right is the **Vajdahunyad Castle,** an art historian's Disneyland, created for the Millennial celebration in 1896 that blends elements from all of Hungary's historic architectural past. Housed in one building is the surprisingly **22** interesting **Mezőgazdasági Múzeum** (Agricultural Museum), with displays on subjects including animal husbandry, forestry, and horticulture. *XIV, Városliget, Széchenyi Island, tel. 1/142–3198. Admission:*

60 Ft.; Tues. free. Open Mar.–Nov., Tues.–Sat. 10–5, Sun. 10–6; Dec.–Feb., Tues.–Fri. 10–4, weekends 10–5.

Off the Beaten Track

A *libegő* (chairlift) will take you to the highest point in Budapest, **Jánoshegy** (János Hill), where you can climb a lookout tower for the best view of the city. *Take Bus 158 from Moszkva tér to last stop, Zugligeti út, tel. 1/156–7975 or 1/176–3764. Admission: 80 Ft. one way, 140 Ft. round-trip. Open mid-May–mid-Sept., daily 9–5; mid-Sept.–mid-May (depending on weather), daily 9:30–4. Closed alternate Mons.*

Farther up the Danube, after a somewhat strenuous climb up the steep, dilapidated sidewalks of a hill in Óbuda, you'll find the **Kiscelli Múzeum,** an elegant, mustard-yellow Baroque mansion, built between 1744 and 1760 as a Trinitarian monastery with funds donated by the wealthy Zichy family. Today it is a museum housing an eclectic mix of paintings, sculptures, engravings, and sundry items related to the history of Budapest, including the printing press on which poet and revolutionary Petőfi Sándor printed his famous *"Nemzeti Dal"* ("National Song"), in 1848, inciting the Hungarian people to rise up against the Hapsburgs. *III, Kiscelli u. 108, tel. 1/188–8560. Admission: 100 Ft. adults, 30 Ft. children. Open Nov.–Mar., Tues.–Sun. 10–4; Apr.–Oct., Tues.–Sun. 10–6.*

Shopping

You'll find plenty of folk art and souvenir shops, foreign-language bookshops, and classical record shops in or around **Váci utca,** but a visit to some of the smaller, more typically Hungarian shops on **Erzsébet tér,** Kossuth Lajos utca, and **Teréz boulevard** and to the modern **Skála-Metro** department store near the Nyugati train station may prove more interesting.

The magnificent **Vásárcsarnok** (Central Market Hall) (IX, Vámhaz körút 1–3) was reopened in late 1994 after years of renovation (and disputes over who would foot the bill). The cavernous, three-story hall once again teems with shoppers browsing among stalls packed with salamis and red paprika chains, crusty bread, fresh fish, and other tastes of Hungary. Upstairs you can buy folk embroideries and souvenirs.

You'll also encounter Transylvanian women dressed in colorful folk costume standing on busy sidewalks selling their own hand-made embroideries and ceramics at rock-bottom prices. Another good way to find bargains (and adventure) is to make an early-morning trip out to **Ecseri Piac,** a vast, colorful, chaotic flea market on the outskirts of Budapest. The place is an arsenal of secondhand goods of every conceivable form and function including frayed Russian military fatigues, authentic (and counterfeit) Herend and Zsolnay porcelain, and individual— that is, half a pair of—cowboy boots. The best selection is on Saturday mornings, but foreigners are a favorite target for over-charging, so prepare to bargain tough. *IX, Nagykőrösi út (take Bus 54 from Boráros tér). Open weekdays 8–4, Sat. 8–3.*

Dining

Private restaurateurs are breathing excitement into the Budapest dining scene. You can choose among Chinese, Mexican, Italian, French, and Indian cuisines—there is even a vegetarian restaurant. Or you can stick to solid, traditional Hungarian fare. Be sure to check out the less expensive spots favored by locals. For price-category definitions, *see* Dining *in* Staying in Hungary, *above.*

$$$$ **Gundel.** Kings, prime ministers, and Communist party bosses have dined
★ in this turn-of-the-century palazzo in City Park since it was founded in 1894, but its elegance and grandeur dissipated under state control. Now relaunched by New York-based restaurateur George Lang, it showcases all that's best in Hungarian cuisine—here prepared with less fat and salt than is usual elsewhere. The interior was redesigned by world-famous designers Adam Tihany, Milton Glaser, and Emery Roth, and is one of the most handsome in Budapest, with dark-wood paneling, navy-blue upholstered chairs and love seats, and tables set with Zsolnay porcelain and sterling silver. Waiters in black tie serve traditional favorites such as tender veal in a paprika-and-sour-cream sauce and carp *Dorozsma* (panfried with mushrooms) to the accompaniment of gypsy music led by one of Hungary's legendary gypsy violinists. Don't forget to try a glass of Tokaj Aszu, Hungary's famous sweet, amber desert wine. *XIV, Allatkerti út 2, tel. 1/321–3550, fax 1/342–2917. Reservations advised. Jacket and tie. AE, DC, MC, V.*

$$$$ **Kisbuda Gyöngye.** This venerable Budapest favorite, hidden away on a small street in Óbuda, is decorated with mixed antique furniture, and its walls are creatively adorned with a patchwork of antique carved wooden cupboard doors. A violin-piano duo with a repertoire favoring Mozart set a romantic mood, but on a typically crowded evening, try to avoid being seated immediately next to the piano; it can get a little overpowering. Try the chicken Cumberland (grilled boneless breasts marinated in basil and spices) or the fresh trout smothered in a cream sauce with mushrooms and capers. In warm weather, guests can dine outdoors in the cozy back garden. *III, Kenyeres u. 34, tel. 1/168–6402 or 1/168–9246. Reservations advised 2 days ahead. AE. No dinner Sun.*

$$$$ **Vadrózsa.** The name means "wild rose," and there are always fresh ones on the table at this restaurant in an old villa in Buda's exclusive Rózsadomb district. It's elegant to the last detail—even the service is white-glove—and the garden is delightful in summer. *II, Pentelei Molnár u. 15, tel. 1/135–1118. Reservations advised. Jacket and tie. AE, DC, MC, V.*

$$$ **Kacsa.** Hungarian and international dishes with a focus on duck are done with a light touch and served by candlelight, with quiet traditional Hungarian music in the background, in this small, celebrated restaurant just a few steps from the river. Try the crisp wild duck stuffed with plums. *II, Fő u. 75, tel. 1/201–9992. Reservations advised. Dinner only. AE, DC, MC, V.*

$$$ **Múzeum.** Fans swear that this elegant, candlelit salon with mirrors, mosaics, and swift-moving waiters has the best dining in Budapest. The salads are generous, the Hungarian wines excellent, and the chef dares to be creative. *VIII, Múzeum körút 12, tel. 1/267–0375. Reservations advised. AE.*

$$ **Fészek.** Hidden away inside the nearly 100-year-old Fészek Artists' Club in downtown Pest, you'll find this large, neoclassical dining room with eye-catching details including high ceilings hung with brass and glass chandeliers, and mustard-color walls trimmed with ornate molding and dark wood panels. In summer, guests dine outdoors at candlelit tables set in a Venetian-style courtyard. The extensive, almost daunting menu is shared with the sister restaurant Kispipa (*see below*), and features all the Hungarian classics with specialties such as turkey stuffed with goose liver and a variety of game dishes. *VII, Dob u. 55 (corner of Kertész* *u.), tel. 1/322–6043. Reservations accepted. 50 Ft. Artists' Club cover charge. AE.*

$$ Kispipa. The street outside, a lane full of crumbling old buildings, makes this restaurant's gleaming brass fixtures, stylish art deco chairs, and convivial crowd seem that much more polished. On the extensive menu, the game dishes stand out, and the venison stew with tarragon is outstanding. *VII, Akácfa u. 38, tel. 1/342–2587. Reservations required. AE. Closed Sun. and holidays.*

$$ Tabáni Kakas. Situated just below Castle Hill, this popular restaurant has a distinctly warm and friendly atmosphere. It specializes in large helpings of poultry dishes, particularly goose. Try the catfish *paprikás* (fresh catfish fried in the powder of crushed, sun-dried red peppers) or the roast duck with steamed cabbage. A pianist entertains every evening except Monday. *I, Attila út 27, tel. 1/175–7165. AE, MC.*

$ Bohémtanya. There's always a wait for a table at this rustic, lively hangout, but it pays to be patient. The reward: heaping plates of stuffed cabbage, fried pork chops filled with goose liver, and other Hungarian specialties. The trilingual menu is extra budget-conscious. *VI, Paulay Ede u. 6, tel. 1/122–1453. No credit cards.*

$ Szerb. Down a sawdust-covered stairway, this lively cellar serves grilled meats on a skewer and other Serbian dishes for a song, along with giant pitchers of beer. *V, Nagy Ignác u. 16, tel. 1/269–3139. AE, MC. No dinner Sun.*

Lodging

Some 30 million tourists come to Hungary every year, and the boom has encouraged hotel building; yet there is sometimes a shortage of rooms, especially in summer. If you arrive in Budapest without a reservation, go to the IBUSZ travel office at Petőfi tér (tel. 1/118–5707 or 1/118–4842) or to one of the tourist offices at any of the train stations or at the airport. For details and price-category definitions, *see* Lodging *in* Staying in Hungary, *above.*

$$$$ Budapest Hilton. Built in 1977 around a 13th-century monastery adjacent to the Matthias Church, this perfectly integrated architectural wonder overlooks the Danube from the choicest site on Castle Hill. Every ample, contemporary room has a remarkable view; Danube vistas cost more. Service and facilities are of the highest caliber. Note: breakfast is not included in room rates. *I, Hess András tér 1–3, tel. 1/175–1000, fax 1/156–0285; in U.S. and Canada, tel. 800/445–8667. 323 rooms with bath, 28 suites. Facilities: 3 restaurants, café, 2 bars, wine cellar, casino, hairdresser, cosmetic salon, business center, ballroom, parking, gift shops, flower shop, boutiques, antiques shop, IBUSZ travel agency. AE, DC, MC, V.*

$$$$ Budapest Marriott. Bought by the Marriott chain in 1993, this sophisticated yet friendly hotel near downtown Pest on the Danube has just under gone a $13 million overhaul and it's evident in every detail of the place, including the marble floors, brass lamps, and dark wood paneling in the lobby, and the expansive beds, floral bedspreads, and etched glass in the rooms. Stunning vistas of Gellért Hill, the Chain and Elizabeth bridges, and Castle Hill are available from every guest room, the ballroom, and even the swimming pool. Most rooms have a balcony. *V, Apáczai Csere János u. 4, tel. 1/266–7000, fax 1/266–5000. 362 rooms with bath, 20 suites. Facilities: 3 restaurants, bar, pool, fitness center, squash court, sauna, solarium, business center, ballroom, parking, laundry, gift shop, baby-sitting. AE, DC, MC, V.*

$$$$ **Fórum.** This boxy, modern riverside hotel consistently wins applause for its gracious appointments, friendly service, and gorgeous views across the Danube to Castle Hill. The Fórum's is among the most modern hotel fitness facilities in the country, and considering how addictive the Viennese Café's pastries are, you might need to use it. The central location makes it popular with businesspeople. Note: breakfast is not included in the room rates. *V, Apáczai Csere János u. 12–14, tel. 1/117–8088, fax 1/117–9808. 392 rooms with bath, 16 suites. Facilities: 2 restaurants, café, bar, fitness center, business center, airport transfer, drugstore, car rental, doctor. AE, DC, MC, V.*

$$$ **Alba Hotel.** Tucked behind an alleyway at the foot of Castle Hill, this spotless, modern gem of a hotel is a short walk via the Chain Bridge from lively business and shopping districts. Swiss management ensures efficient service. *I, Apor Péter u. 3, tel. 1/175–9244, fax 1/175–9899. 95 rooms with bath. Facilities: bar, no-smoking rooms, conference room, underground parking. AE, DC, MC, V.*

$$$ **Gellért.** Nowadays, this plump, grand old lady of city hotels is shin-
★ ing. The turn-of-the-century architecture is regal, and the famous thermal baths are wonderfully ornate. (They're like regular swimming pools but more elegant; jets of water come shooting up through the floor at odd moments, and fountains dribble hot water onto the heads of bathers.) Rooms have early-20th-century furnishings, including some Jugendstil pieces, along with views across the Danube or up Gellért Hill. *XI, Gellért tér 1, tel. 1/185–2200, fax 1/166–6631. 233 rooms with bath, 13 suites. Facilities: restaurant, brasserie, café, spa, thermal pools, business center, baby-sitting, parking. AE, DC, MC, V.*

$$$ **Grand Hotel Corvinus Kempinski.** Opened in August 1992, this sleek, luxury hotel has already become a focal point of elite goings-on—such as hosting Sotheby's debut art auction in Hungary—and the favored lodging of visiting VIPs—from rock superstars to foreign dignitaries. The location offers no Danube views but is about as city-central as you can get. The building's dramatic modern design alternates surfaces of glass and polished stone arrayed in stylish geometries. Room decor is understated, with an emphasis on functional touches such as three phones in every room. Note: breakfast is not included in the room rates. *V, Erzsébet tér 7–8, tel. 1/266–1000; in the U.S. and Canada, tel. 800/426–3135; fax 1/266–2000. 340 rooms with bath, 28 suites. Facilities: 3 restaurants, 3 bars, business center, conference room, indoor swimming pool, sauna, fitness center, private parking, airport transfer, gift shop, boutiques. AE, DC, MC, V.*

$$$ **Korona.** Modern and functional, this Austrian-built hotel is on busy Kálvin tér, near the river and close to the National Museum and other sights. *V, Kecskeméti u. 14, tel. 1/117–4111, fax 1/118–3867. 433 rooms with bath. Facilities: restaurant, bar, pool, sauna, solarium, fitness club, massage, business center, parking garage. AE, DC, MC, V.*

$$$ **Ramada Grand Hotel.** This venerable 100-year-old hotel is completely modern, yet retains its period look, with high ceilings and Old World furnishings. It's in a tranquil park, surrounded by gardens on a car-free island in the Danube; the city is closer than it seems. *XIII, Margit-sziget, tel. 1/111–1000, fax 1/153–3029; for reservations, tel. 1/131–7769; in the U.S. and Canada, tel. 800/228–9898. 162 rooms with bath, 10 suites. Facilities: restaurant, ice cream parlor, bar, thermal baths, fitness center, beauty shop. AE, DC, MC, V.*

$$$ **Thermal Hotel Helia.** A sleek Scandinavian design and quiet location away from downtown pollution make this spa hotel on the Danube a relaxing retreat. Special health packages—including anything from Turkish baths to electrotherapy and fitness tests—are available. *XIII, Kárpát u. 62–64, tel. 1/270–3277, fax 1/270–2262; in the U.S. and Canada, tel.*

800/223–5652. 254 rooms with bath; 8 suites, 4 with sauna. Facilities: 2 restaurants (1 with summer terrace), café, bar, pool, spa, fitness center, tennis courts, beauty salon, business center. AE, DC, MC, V.

$$ Astoria. Revolutionaries and intellectuals once gathered in the marble-and-gilt Art Deco lobby here. Recent renovations have remained faithful to the Empire-style decor and furnishings and have not obscured the 82-year-old hotel's distinct charm; rather, they have meant the addition of other comforts—most notably soundproofing, essential since the Astoria is located at the city's busiest intersection. *V, Kossuth Lajos u. 19–21, tel. 1/117–3411, fax 1/118–6798. 123 rooms with bath or shower, 5 suites. Facilities: restaurant, bar, café, nightclub, business center, parking. AE, DC, MC, V.*

$$ Hotel Centrál. Relive history—stay in this hotel, well situated in a leafy diplomatic quarter just one block from Heroes' Square, as visiting communist dignitaries once did. The architecture and furnishings are straight out of the 1950s, but rooms are comfortable and have unusually large bathrooms. Suites are classically elegant, with turn-of-the-century Hungarian eclectic furnishings; ask for Rudolf Nureyev's favorite. *VI, Munkácsy Mihály u. 5–7, tel. 1/321–2000, fax 1/321–2008. 36 rooms with bath, 6 suites. Facilities: restaurant. AE, DC, MC, V.*

$$ Nemzeti. The baby-blue Baroque facade stands out in this dingy neighborhood, which turns seedy after dark. The high-ceilinged lobby and public areas with pillars, arches, and wrought-iron railings are elegant, but rooms are small and unexceptional. For a quieter night, ask for a room facing the inner courtyard. The homey atmosphere is the real draw. *VIII, József Körút 4, tel. 1/269–9310, fax 1/114–0019. 76 rooms with bath. Facilities: restaurant, brasserie, piano bar, meeting room. AE, DC, MC, V.*

$$ Victoria. The dark, stately Parliament building and city lights twinkling
★ over the river can be seen from every room at this three-year-old establishment right on the Danube that mixes the charm of a country inn with ultramodern comforts. The absence of conventions is a plus. *II, Bem rakpart 11, tel. 1/201–8644, fax 1/2015–816. 24 rooms with bath, 2 with balcony; 1 suite. Facilities: 24-hr. room service, bar, sauna, conference room, garage. AE, DC, MC, V.*

$ Ifjúság. The concrete "Youth" hotel is a boxy remnant of socialist architecture, but the location—a quiet, residential street at the top of a hill—is lovely and the rooms are modern and clean. Ask for a room with a view and a balcony, and you won't be sorry. *II, Zivatar u. 3, tel. 1/135–3331, fax 1/135–3989. 100 rooms with bath. Facilities: restaurant. AE, DC, MC, V.*

$ Kulturinnov. One wing of what looks like a Gothic castle now houses basic budget accommodations. Rooms come with two or three beds and are clean, and the neighborhood—one of Budapest's most famous squares in the luxurious Castle district—is unbeatable. *I, Szentháromság tér 6, tel. 1/155–0122 or 1/175–1651, fax 1/175–1886. 17 rooms with shower. Facilities: snack bar, reading room. AE.*

$ Medosz. One of Budapest's better small hotels, the Medosz provides a central location near Oktogon, a major transport hub, and lovely Andrássy út; the opera house is a block away. Rooms are neat but very basic, with small, low beds, worn upholstery, and a leftover 1950s institutional feel. Request a room facing the rear if you prefer quiet. *VI, Jókai tér 9, tel. 1/153–1700 or 1/153–1434, fax 1/132–4316. 63 rooms with bath, 7 suites. Facilities: restaurant (for groups only). No credit cards.*

The Arts

Budapest's English-language newspapers are the most up-to-date sources for arts information. The "Style" section of *The Budapest Sun* maps out the week's entertainment happenings, gallery exhibits, and all else going on culturally. *The Sun* is sold for about $1 at many newsstands in well-trafficked areas. Hotels and tourist offices will provide you with a copy of the monthly publication *Programme,* which contains details of all cultural events in the city. Tickets can be bought at venue box offices, your hotel desk, many tourist offices, or any of several ticket agencies, the biggest of which are the **National Philharmonic Ticket Office** (V, Vörösmarty tér 1, tel. 1/117–6222) and the **Central Theater Booking Office** (VI, Andrássy út 18, tel. 1/112–0000).

There are two opera houses, the **Magyar Állami Operaház** or Hungarian State Opera House (VI, Andrássy út 22) and the **Erkel Színház** or Erkel Theater (VIII, Köztársaság tér), for which dress can be informal. Concerts are given all year at the **Academy of Music** on Liszt Ferenc tér, the **Pesti Vigadó** on Vigadó tér, and at the **Old Academy of Music** on Vörösmarty utca. Displays of Hungarian folk dancing are held at the **Cultural Center** on Corvin tér, and regular participatory folk dance evenings—with instructions for beginners—are held at district cultural centers. Ask your hotel clerk for the latest programs at the center nearest you.

Arts festivals fill the calendar beginning in early spring. The season's first and biggest, the **Budapest Spring Festival** (beginning in early to mid-March), showcases Hungary's best opera, music, theater, fine arts, and dance, as well as visiting foreign artists. It's followed by the smaller annual **Jazz Festival** (April), and, after the opera season ends, by the week-long **BudaFest** opera and ballet festival (mid-August) at the opera house. Information and tickets are available from the ticket sources, above.

Nightlife

Budapest is a lively city by night. Establishments stay open late and Western European–style drink-bárs have sprung up all over the city. For quiet conversation, there are such bars in most hotels, but beware of the inflated prices. Hotel nightclubs are convenient but pricey and not usually among the "in" places to be. The life span of a Budapest nightspot can be very brief, and although the bars and clubs listed here are popular and seem to be here to stay, you should check *The Budapest Sun* and other local publications for the more transient "in" spots.

Bars and Clubs

The Jazz Café hosts local jazz bands every night in a small basement space of blue neon lights and funky papier-mâché statues. *V, Ballasi Bálint u. 25, tel. 1/269–5506. Open Mon.–Sat. 5 PM–3 AM.*

Mad Block is a popular disco in the ornate Baroque theater that once housed the Moulin Rouge nightclub. Live bands play weekdays, but the disco on weekends is what draws the crowds. *VI, Nagymező u. 17, tel. 1/112–4492. Open daily 9 PM–6 AM.*

Made Inn Mine, is a prime example of the nearly schizophrenic atmosphere of many new Budapest clubs. Housed in a old stone mansion near Heroes' Square, it has an elaborate decor modeled on an underground mine shaft, a kitchen specializing in Mediterranean foods, a large bar, and a disco dance floor packed with local and international Beautiful People. *VI, Andrássy út 112, tel. 1/111–3437. Open Sun.–Thurs. 8 PM–4 AM, Fri.–Sat. 8 PM–5 AM.*

Piaf is popular with arts sophisticates; it's classy and just a touch pretentious, with red velvet chairs and low, candlelit tables in cozy brick rooms. The downstairs room tends to get noisier. Open only from 10 PM, it often is still serving enthusiasts at 6 and 7 in the morning. You have to ring the bell to get in. *VI, Nagymező u. 20, tel. 1/112–3823. Open daily 10 PM–5 AM (or when last person leaves).*

Picasso Point, a very popular, spacious bar with a hip, coffeehouse feel and Pablo-themed decor, hosts local art exhibits and live jazz ensembles. *V, Hajós u. 31, tel. 1/269–5544. Open daily noon–4 AM.*

Café Pierrot, an elegant café and piano bar on a small street on Castle Hill, is well suited to a secret rendezvous. *I, Fortuna u. 14, tel. 1/175–6971. Open 11 AM–1 AM.*

Casinos

Gresham Casino. *In Gresham Palace, V, Roosevelt tér 5, tel. 1/117–2407. Open daily 2 PM–4 AM.*

Las Vegas Casino. *V, Roosevelt tér 2, tel. 1/117–6022. Open 24 hours.*

Várkert Casino. *I, Miklós Ybl tér 9, tel. 1/202–4244. Open daily 2 PM–5 AM.*

THE DANUBE BEND

About 40 kilometers (25 miles) north of Budapest, the Danube abandons its eastward course and turns abruptly south toward the capital, cutting through the Börzsöny and Visegrád hills. This area is called the Danube Bend and includes the Baroque town of Szentendre, the hilltop castle ruins and town of Visegrád, and the cathedral town of Esztergom. The attractive combination of hillside and river should dispel any notion that Hungary is one vast, boring plain.

Here, in the heartland, are traces of the country's history—the remains of the Roman Empire's frontiers, the battlefields of the Middle Ages, and the relics of the Hungarian Renaissance. Although the area can be covered by car in a day—the round-trip from Budapest is only 124 kilometers (78 miles)—two days, with a night in Visegrád or Esztergom, would be a better way to savor its charms.

Getting Around

The most pleasant way to get around is by boat or hydrofoil on the Danube. The three main centers—Szentendre, Esztergom, and Visegrád—all have connections with one another and with Budapest. Contact MAHART (tel. 1/118–1586, 1/118–1743, or 1/118–1704) for schedules. There is also regular bus service connecting all three with one another and with Budapest. Szentendre can also be reached by HÉV commuter rail, departing from the Batthyány tér metro; the trip takes about 40 minutes and costs around 65 Ft.

Guided Tours

IBUSZ (tel. 1/118–1139 or 1/118–1043) organizes daylong bus trips from Budapest along the Danube stopping in Esztergom, Visegrád, and Szentendre on Tuesdays and Fridays from May through October, and Saturdays only from November through April: the cost, including lunch, is about 5,500 Ft. Full-day boat tours of Szentendre and Visegrád run May through October on Wednesdays and Saturdays and cost about 6,600 Ft., including lunch and a cocktail.

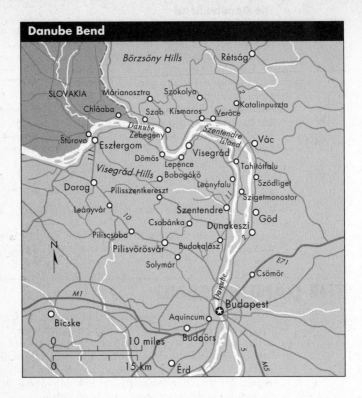

Danube Bend

Tourist Information

Budapest (Dunatours, VI, Bajcsy-Zsilinszky út 17, tel. 1/131–4533 or 1/111–5630, fax 1/111–6827).

Esztergom (Grantours, Széchenyi tér 25, tel. and fax 33/313–756; Komtourist Lőrinc u. 6, tel. 33/312–082).

Szentendre (Tourinform, Dumsta J. u. 22, tel. and fax 26/317–965; Dunatours, Bogdányi út 1, on the quay, tel. 26/311–311).

Exploring the Danube Bend

Heading north from Budapest toward Szentendre, 19 kilometers (12 miles) by car on Road 11, or by train, on your right look for the reconstructed remains of **Aquincum,** capital of the Roman province of Pannonia. Careful excavations have unearthed a varied selection of artifacts and mosaics, giving a tantalizing inkling of what life was like on the northern fringes of the Roman Empire.

Szentendre, nowadays a flourishing artists' colony with a lively Mediterranean atmosphere, was first settled by Serbs and Greeks fleeing the advancing Turks in the 14th and 17th centuries. There is a Greek Orthodox church in the main square and a dark crimson Serbian Orthodox cathedral on the hill. The narrow cobbled streets are lined with cheerfully painted houses. Part of the town's artistic reputation can be traced to the life and work of the ceramic artist Margit Kovács, whose work blended Hungarian folk art traditions with motifs from modern art. The **Margit Kovács Pottery Museum,** devoted to her work, is housed in a small 18th-century merchant's house with an attractive courtyard. *Vastag György u. 1, tel. 26/310–244. Admission: 100 Ft. adults,*

25 Ft. children. Open mid-Mar.–Oct., daily 10–6; Nov.–mid-Mar., Tues.–Sun. 10–4.

A short drive up Szabadság Forrás út, or a bus ride from the train station, will take you to the **Szabadtéri Néprajzi Múzeum** (Open-Air Ethnography Museum), where a collection of buildings has been designed to show Hungarian peasant life and folk architecture in the 19th century. Regular crafts demonstrations are held in summer. *Szabadság Forrás út, tel. 26/312–304. Admission: 100 Ft. Open Apr.–Oct., Tues.–Sun. 10–5.*

Visegrád, 23 kilometers (14 miles) from Szentendre, was the seat of the kings of Hungary in the 14th century. The ruins of the palace of King Matthias on the main street have been excavated and reconstructed, and there are jousting tournaments here in June. A winding road leads up to a haunting late-medieval fortress, from which you have a fine view of the Danube Bend.

Esztergom, 21 kilometers (13 miles) farther upriver, stands on the site of a Roman fortress. St. Stephen, the first Christian king of Hungary, was crowned here in the year 1000. The kings are long gone, but Esztergom is still the home of the archbishop of Esztergom, the cardinal primate, head of the Catholic church in Hungary.

Thousands of pilgrims visit the imposing **bazilika** (basilica), the largest in Hungary, which stands on a hill overlooking the town. It was here, in the center of Hungarian Catholicism, that the famous anti-communist cleric, Cardinal József Mindszenty, was finally reburied in 1991, ending an era of religious intolerance and prosecution and a sorrowful chapter in Hungarian history. The cathedral also houses a valuable collection of ecclesiastical art. Below it are the streets of Viziváros (Watertown), lined with Baroque buildings. The **Keresztény Múzeum** (Museum of Christian Art) is in the Primate's Palace. It is the finest art gallery in Hungary, with a large collection of early Hungarian and Italian paintings. The Italian collection of 14th- and 15th-century works is unusually large for a museum outside Italy. This collection, coupled with the extensive number of early Renaissance paintings from Flanders and the Lower Rhine, provides insights into the transition of European sensibilities from medieval Gothic to the humanistic Renaissance. *Berényi u. 2, tel. 33/313–880. Admission: 70 Ft. Open mid-Mar.–Sept., Tues.–Sun. 10–6; Oct.–early Jan., Tues.–Sun. 10–5.*

Dining and Lodging

For details and price-category definitions, *see* Dining *and* Lodging *in* Staying in Hungary, *above.*

Esztergom
DINING

Primáspince. Arched ceilings and exposed brick walls make a charming setting for refined Hungarian fare at this restaurant just below the cathedral. Try the tournedos Budapest style, tender beef with sautéed vegetables and paprika, or the thick stuffed turkey breast Fiaker style (stuffed with ham and melted cheese). *Szent István tér 4, tel. 33/313–495. Reservations advised. AE, DC, MC, V. Closed Jan.–Feb. $$$*
Fili Falatozó. The hearty German fare is heavy on meat and potatoes. The location is on Esztergom's most pleasant old cobblestone street, just a short stroll from the Danube. *Bajcsy-Zsilinszky u. 51 (no phone). No reservations. No credit cards. Closed Tues. and Jan.–Feb. $*

LODGING

Alabárdos Panzió. Conveniently located downhill from the basilica, this cozy, remodeled home provides an excellent view of Castle Hill, topped by the oldest royal castle in Hungary. A 1995 expansion has increased the capacity and all rooms (doubles and quads) are large. *Bajcsy-Zsilinsky u. 49, tel. and fax 33/312–640. 21 rooms with bath. Facilities: parking. No credit cards. $$*

Ria Panzió. In this small, friendly guest house near the cathedral, all rooms face a garden courtyard. The very reasonable room rates include a filling breakfast and plans are underway to expand the pension into the house next door. *Batthyány u. 11, tel. 33/313–115. 9 rooms with bath. No credit cards. $*

Szentendre

DINING

Angyal Borozó. This wine bar, also a restaurant, serves hefty portions of Hungarian food. *Alkotmány u. 1, tel. 26/310–160. No credit cards. $$*

Rab Ráby. Fish soup and fresh grilled trout are the specialties in this popular restaurant with wood beams and equestrian decorations. *Péter Pál u. 1, tel. 26/310–819. Summer reservations advised. No credit cards. $$*

LODGING

Bükkös Panzió. Impeccably clean, this stylishly modernized old house is on a small canal just a few minutes' walk from the town center. The narrow staircase and small rooms give it a homey feel. *Bükkös part 16, tel. 26/312–021 or tel. and fax 26/310–782. 16 rooms with bath. Facilities: restaurant. No credit cards. $$*

Visegrád

LODGING

Silvanus. Set high up on Fekete hill, this hotel is renowned for its spectacular views. Located at the end of a long, steep road, it's recommended for motorists (though the bus from town does stop here) and offers trails through the forest for the more active. Rooms are bright and clean and you'll pay extra for a Danube view. *Fekete-hegy, tel. and fax 26/398–311 or 26/398–170. 74 rooms, 60 with bath; 4 suites. Facilities: restaurant, brasserie, terrace café, tennis court, bowling alley, gift shop, parking. AE, DC, MC, V. $$*

Haus Honti. This intimate, alpine-style pension, named after its owner, József Honti, is situated in a quiet residential area far from the main highway but close to the Danube ferry. A stream running close to the house creates a rustic ambience. *Fő u. 66, tel. 26/398–120. 5 rooms with bath. No credit cards. $*

LAKE BALATON

Lake Balaton, the largest lake in Central Europe, stretches 80 kilometers (50 miles) across western Hungary. It is within easy reach of Budapest by any means of transportation. Sometimes known as the nation's playground, it goes some way toward making up for Hungary's much-lamented lack of coastline. On its hilly northern shore, ideal for growing grapes, is **Balatonfüred,** the country's oldest and most famous spa town.

The national park on the Tihany Peninsula is just to the south, and regular boat service links Tihany and Balatonfüred with Siófok on the southern shore. This shore is not as attractive as the northern one—being flatter and more crowded with resorts, cottages, and high-rise hotels once used as communist trade-union retreats. Still, it is worth visiting for its shallower—you can walk out for nearly 2 kilometers (1¼ miles) before it deepens—warmer waters, which make it a better choice for swimming than other locations.

A circular tour taking in Veszprém, Balatonfüred, and Tihany could be managed in a day, but two days, with a night in Tihany or Balatonfüred, would be more relaxed and allow for detours to Herend and its porcelain factory, or to the castle at Nagyvázsony.

The region gets more crowded every year (July and August are the busiest times) but a few steps along any side road will still lead you to a serene, picturesque, hilly landscape of vineyards punctuated by old stone houses and wine cellars.

Getting Around

Trains from Budapest serve all the resorts on the northern shore; a separate line links the resorts of the southern shore. Road 71 runs along the northern shore; M7 covers the southern. Buses connect most resorts. Regular ferries link the major ones. On summer weekends, traffic can be heavy and driving slow around the lake, and bus and train tickets should be booked in advance. In winter, note that schedules are curtailed, so check before making plans.

Guided Tours

IBUSZ has several tours to Balaton from Budapest; inquire at the main office in Budapest (*see* Important Addresses and Numbers *in* Budapest, *above*). Other tours more easily organized from hotels in the Balaton area include boat trips to vineyards, folk music evenings, and overnight trips to local inns.

Tourist Information

Budapest (Balatontourist, VIII, Üllői út 52/A, tel. 1/133–6982, fax 1/210–0363).
Balatonfüred (Balatontourist, Blaha L. u. 5, tel. 87/343–471 or 87/342–822, fax 87/343–435).
Tihany (Balatontourist, Kossuth u. 20, tel. 86/348–519).
Veszprém (Balatontourist, Kossuth Lajos u. 21, tel. 88/429–630).

Exploring Lake Balaton

Hilly **Veszprém** is the center of cultural life in the Balaton region. **Várhegy** (Castle Hill) is the most attractive part of town, north of Szabadság tér. **Hősök Kapuja** (Heroes' Gate), at the entrance to the Castle, houses a small exhibit on Hungary's history. Just past the gate and down a little alley to the left, is the **Tűztorony** (Fire Tower); note that the lower level is medieval while the upper stories are Baroque. There is a good view of the town and surrounding area from the balcony. *Exhibit admission: 10 Ft. Open May–Oct., Tues.–Sun. 10–6.*

Vár utca, the only street in the castle area, leads to a small square in front of the **Bishop's Palace** and the **cathedral;** outdoor concerts are held here in the summer. Vár utca continues past the square up to a terrace erected on the north staircase of the castle. Stand beside the modern statues of St. Stephen and his queen, Gizella, for a far-reaching view of the old quarter of town.

If you are traveling by car, go 5 kilometers (3 miles) west to the village of **Nemesvámos,** where you can slake your thirst or conquer your hunger at the **Vámosi Betyár Csárda** (Highwayman's Inn). This 18th-century

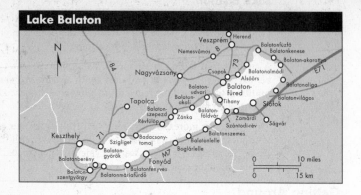

Baroque building takes its name from Savanyu Jóska ("Sour Joe"), an infamous 19th-century highwayman who claimed it as one of his bases. Go down to the cellar to see the tables and seats made from tree trunks—a local architectural feature.

Herend, 16 kilometers (10 miles) northwest of Veszprém on Road 8, is the home of Hungary's renowned hand-painted porcelain. The factory, founded in 1839, displays many valuable pieces in its **museum.** *Tel. 88/361–144. Admission: 80 Ft. Open Apr.–Sept., daily 9–4; Oct.–Mar., weekdays 10–3.*

From Veszprém, take Road 73 about 20 kilometers (12 miles) south to **Balatonfüred,** a spa and resort with good beaches. It is also one of the finest wine-growing areas of Hungary. Above the main square, where medicinal waters bubble up under a colonnaded pavilion, the hillsides are thick with vines. Down at the shore, the Tagore sétány (Tagore Promenade) is a wonderful place to stroll and watch the local swans glide by.

A seven-minute boat trip takes you from Balatonfüred to the **Tihany Peninsula,** a national park rich in rare flora and fauna and an ideal place for strolling. From the ferry port, follow green markers to the springs (Oroszkút) or red ones to the top of **Csúcs-hegy,** a hill from which there is a good view of the lake.

The village of **Tihany,** with its famous **abbey,** is on the eastern shore. The abbey building houses a **museum** with exhibits related to the Balaton area. Also worth a look are the pink angels floating on the ceiling of the abbey church, and the abbey organ, on which recitals are given in summer. Consider a special detour to the Rege pastry shop at Batthyány út 38, not far from the abbey. *Első András tér 1, tel. 87/348–405. Admission: 60 Ft.; Open free Sun. May–Sept., daily 10–3; Nov.–Mar., daily 10–4:30; Apr. and Oct., daily 10–4:30.*

The castle of **Nagyvázsony,** about 20 kilometers (12 miles) northwest of Balatonfüred, dates to the early 15th century. The 92-foot-high keep is the oldest part, and its upper rooms now house the **Castle Museum.** Try to get to the highest balcony in late afternoon for the best view. The surrounding buildings, preserved in their original style, date from the period when post horses were changed here. *Tel. 88/331–015. Museum admission: 30 Ft. Open Tues.–Sun. 10–6.*

Dining and Lodging

For details and price-category definitions, *see* Dining *and* Lodging *in* Staying in Hungary, *above*. Note that off-season lodging is significantly cheaper at Lake Balaton.

Balatonfüred

DINING

Tölgyfa Csárda. A prime hilltop location gives this eatery, named for the large oak tree nearby, breathtaking views over the steeples and rooftops of Balatonfüred and the Tihany peninsula. The menu and decor are worthy of a first-class Budapest restaurant, and there's live gypsy music in the evenings. *Meleghegy (walk north on Jókai Mór út and turn right on Mérleg út), tel. 87/343–036. Reservations advised. AE. $$$*

Baricska Csárda. From its perch atop a hill at the southwestern end of town, this rambling, reed-thatched, rustic inn overlooks a smooth carpet of vineyards scarred only by the winding river. The hearty yet ambitious fare includes roasted trout and *fogas* (a freshwater fish particular to the Balaton region), creamy fish paprikás with gnocchi, and desserts crammed with sweet poppy seed filling. *Baricska dülő, off Rd. 71 (Széchenyi út) behind Shell station, tel. 87/343–105. Reservations advised. AE, V. Closed mid-Nov.–mid-Mar. $$*

LODGING

Annabella. The cool, spacious guest quarters in this large, Miami-style high rise are especially pleasant during summer heat. Overlooking the Tagore Promenade and Lake Balaton, it has excellent swimming and water-sports facilities and is just around the corner from the main square in town. *Deák Ferenc u. 25, tel. 87/342–222, fax 87/343–084. 390 rooms; all 360 double rooms have bath. Facilities: restaurant, brasserie, bar, café, nightclub, banquet hall, indoor pool, sauna, solarium, windsurfing, hairdresser, laundry, gift shop, baby-sitting, parking. AE, DC, MC, V. Closed mid-Oct.–mid-Apr. $$*

Blaha Lujza. This sober summer house in the historic section of town, built in classic Roman villa style, was formerly owned by legendary Hungarian actress Blaha Lujza. Today it's a friendly, unassuming bed-and-breakfast inn with clean, functional rooms. *Blaha Lujza u. 4, tel. and fax 87/342–603. 19 rooms, 17 with shower. Facilities: restaurant, coffee shop, parking. No credit cards. $$*

★ **Margaréta.** This attractive apartment-hotel stands across the street from the lakefront Hotel Marina and, unfortunately, behind a large gas station. It is smaller and more intimate than most of its neighbors, and its restaurant is popular locally. Each room has a kitchen, a balcony, a phone, a TV, and a radio. *Széchenyi út 29, tel. and fax 87/343–824. 52 rooms with bath. Facilities: restaurant, bar, snack bar, laundry, parking. AE, DC, MC, V. Closed mid-Nov.–mid-Mar. (but open over New Year's holiday). $$*

Tihany

DINING

Halásztánya. A quaint setting on a twisting, narrow street plus the relaxed atmosphere and evening gypsy music help contribute to the popularity of the Halásztánya, which specializes in fish. *Visszhang u. 11 (no phone). No reservations. Closed Nov.–Mar. $$*

Pál Csárda. Two thatched cottages tucked away off a narrow street make up this simple restaurant, where cold fruit soup and fish stew are the specialties. Or you can eat in the garden, which is decorated with gourds and strands of the peppers from which paprika is made. *Vis-*

szhang u. 19 (no phone). No reservations. No credit cards. Closed Dec.–Mar. $$

<u>LODGING</u>

★ **Park.** Lush landscaped gardens surround this stately mansion on the water's edge. Inside, it's all understated elegance; rooms have balconies, views, and crisp sheets. *Fürdötelepi út 1, tel. 87/348–611, fax 87/348–409. 76 rooms with bath. Facilities: restaurant, café, bar, tennis court, miniature golf, fitness center, sauna, hairdresser, laundry, gift shop, private beach, water sports, parking. AE, DC, MC, V. $$$*

Kolostor. The cozy, wood-paneled rooms are built into an attic above a popular restaurant and brewery in the heart of Tihany village. *Kossuth u. 14, tel. 87/348–408. 7 rooms with bath. Facilities: breakfast room. No credit cards. $$*

Veszprém

<u>DINING</u>

★ **Diana.** The Diana is just a little southwest of the town center, but worth the trip if you want to experience the old-fashioned charm of a small provincial Hungarian restaurant. The decor could be called "cozy traditional," and the fish and game specialties are perennial favorites. There is also a 10-room pension on the premises. *József Attila u. 22, tel. 88/421–061. Reservations advised. No credit cards. $$*

Club Skorpio. This city-center eatery might look like an Alpine hut, but the menu is top class and features grilled meats and specialties such as pheasant soup and steamed wild duck. *Virág Benedek u. 1/b, tel. 88/420–319. Reservations advised. No credit cards. $*

<u>LODGING</u>

Veszprém. This modern, comfortable hotel in the center of town is in one of the less attractive buildings in Veszprém, but is convenient to all the major sights and to the bus station. *Budapesti u. 6, tel. 88/424–677, fax 88/424–076. 72 rooms with bath, 4 suites. Facilities: restaurant, café, bar, hairdresser, gift shop. No credit cards. $*

16 Iceland

CELAND IS ANYTHING BUT ICY. Though glaciers cover about 10% of the country, summers in Iceland are relatively warm, and the winter climate is milder than New York's. Coastal farms lie in green, pastoral lowlands, where cows, sheep, and horses graze alongside raging streams. Distant waterfalls plunge from heather-covered mountains with great spiked ridges and snowcapped peaks.

Iceland's name can be blamed on Hrafna-Flóki, a 9th-century Norse settler who failed to plant enough crops to see his livestock through their first winter. Leaving in a huff, he passed a northern fjord filled with pack ice and cursed the country with a name that's kept tourism in cold storage for 1,100 years.

The second-largest island in Europe, Iceland is in the middle of the North Atlantic, where the warm Gulf Stream from the south meets cold currents from the north, providing a choice environment for the fish on which the nation depends for 80% of its export revenue. Beneath some of the country's glaciers are burning fires that become visible during volcanic eruptions—fires that heat the country's hot springs and geysers. The springs, in turn, provide heat to the country's homes, hospitals, and public swimming pools, keeping the nation's air smokeless and smogless. Except for fish and agricultural products, almost all consumer goods are imported, making the cost of living high.

The first permanent settlers arrived from Norway in 874, though some Irish monks had arrived a century earlier. The country came under foreign rule in 1262 and did not win complete independence until 1944. Today nearly three-fifths of the country's 260,000 people live in Reykjavík and its suburbs.

ESSENTIAL INFORMATION

Before You Go

When to Go
The best time to visit is from May through November; from June through July, the sun never sets. Weather is unpredictable: In June, July, and August, sunny days alternate with spells of rain showers and driving winds. Winter weather fluctuates bewilderingly, with temperatures as high as 50°F (10°C) or as low as –14°F (–10°C.). In December the sun shines for only three hours a day, but on a clear and cold evening you can see the Northern Lights dancing among the stars.

CLIMATE
Iceland enjoys a temperate ocean climate with cool summers and mild winters. In the northern part of the country, the weather is more stable than in the windy, rainy south. The following are the average daily maximum and minimum temperatures for Reykjavík.

Jan.	35F	2C	May	50F	10C	Sept.	52F	11C
	28	– 2		39	4		43	6
Feb.	37F	3C	June	54F	12C	Oct.	45F	7C
	28	– 2		34	7		38	3
Mar.	39F	4C	July	57F	14C	Nov.	39F	4C
	30	– 1		48	9		32	0
Apr.	43F	6C	Aug.	56F	14C	Dec.	36F	2C
	33	1		47	8		29	– 2

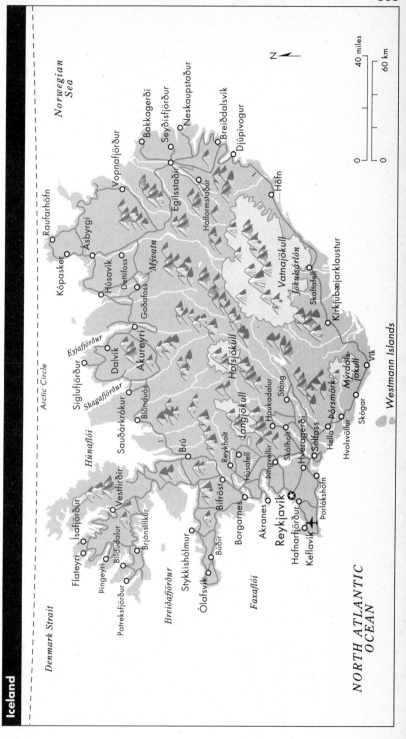

Currency

The Icelandic monetary unit is the króna (plural krónur), which is equal to 100 aurar, and is abbreviated ISK. Coins are the ISK 1, 5, 10, and 50. There are krónur bills in denominations of 100, 500, 1,000, and 5,000. At press time (spring 1995), the rate of exchange was ISK 65 to the dollar and ISK 102 to the pound sterling, but in the generally unstable economic climate, considerable fluctuation occurs. No limitations apply to import and export of currency, and you may bring any amount of foreign currency, which is easily exchanged for krónur at the Icelandic banks. Major credit cards are widely accepted in the capital and by most businesses in the countryside.

What It Will Cost

Iceland is expensive. Hotels and restaurants cost about 20% more in Reykjavík than elsewhere in the country. The airport departure tax is about ISK 1,300.

SAMPLE PRICES

A cup of coffee or soft drink costs about ISK 150; a bottle of beer costs ISK 300; a sandwich or snack about ISK 400; and a 2-mile taxi ride, about ISK 500.

Customs on Arrival

Tourists can bring in 6 liters of beer or 1 liter of wine containing up to 21% alcohol, 1 liter of liquor with up to 47% alcohol content, and 200 cigarettes.

Language

The official language is Icelandic, brought to the country by early Norse settlers. It's a highly inflected North Germanic tongue that has changed little over the centuries. English is widely understood and spoken, particularly by the younger generation.

Getting Around

By Car

Most of the Ring Road, which encircles the island, is asphalt. Elsewhere, driving can be very bumpy, often along lava track or dirt and gravel surfaces—but the scenery is superb. Although service stations and garages are rare, the main roads are patrolled, and fellow motorists are helpful. You'll need a four-wheel-drive vehicle for remote roads. An international driver's license is required.

By Plane

Icelandair, Íslandsflug, Norlandair, and a few other airlines have domestic flights to some 50 towns and villages. Special discounts are available on certain combinations of domestic air routes.

By Bus

A comprehensive network of buses compensates for the lack of any train network. A good buy, if you want to explore extensively, is the **Omnibus Passport,** which permits you to travel on all scheduled bus routes for one to four weeks for ISK 14,000–ISK 30,000. The **Full Circle Passport,** which costs ISK 13,500 and is valid for a trip around Iceland on the Ring Road, will take you to some of the most popular attractions; but if you want to see more, you'll have to pay extra for the scheduled bus tours. An **Air/Bus Rover Ticket** entitles the bearer to additional discounts on certain Central Highland tours, camping grounds, youth hostels, and ferries. For further information, contact **Reykjavik Central Bus Terminal,** BSÍ (Vatnsmýrarvegur 10, tel. 552–2300, fax 552–9973).

Staying in Iceland

Telephones

LOCAL CALLS

All phone numbers in Iceland contain seven digits; there are no city codes. Pay phones take ISK 10 and ISK 50 coins and are found in hotels, shops, bus stations, and post offices. There are few outdoor telephone booths in the towns and villages. Phone cards cost ISK 500 and are sold at post offices, hotels, etc.

INTERNATIONAL CALLS

To call Iceland from abroad, dial the country code, 354, followed by the Icelandic telephone number. You can dial direct to almost anywhere in Europe and the United States. Use the following international access codes for a long-distance operator: **AT&T** (800–9001), **MCI** (999–002), **Sprint** (800–9003).

OPERATORS AND INFORMATION

For collect calls and assistance with overseas calls, dial 09; for local calls dial 02; for information dial 03; for direct international calls dial 00.

COUNTRY CODE

The country code for Iceland is 354.

Mail

POSTAL RATES

Airmail letters to the United States cost ISK 65; letters to Europe, ISK 35.

RECEIVING MAIL

You can have your mail sent to the post office in any town or village in Iceland. In Reykjavík, have mail sent to the downtown post office (R/O Pósthússtræti, 101 Reykjavík).

Opening and Closing Times

Banks are open weekdays 9:15–4. Some branches are also open Thursday 5–6. The bank at Hotel Loftleiðir in Reykjavík is open weekends for foreign exchange only.

Museums are usually open 1–4:30, but some open as early as 10 and others stay open until 7.

Shops are open weekdays 9–6 and Saturdays 9–noon (shopping malls 9–4). Many grocery stores are open longer hours, including Sunday afternoons.

National Holidays

January 1; April 4–8 (Easter); April 25 (first day of summer); May 1 (Labor Day); May 16 (Ascension); May 26–27 (Pentecost); June 17 (National Day); August 5 (public holiday); December 24–26.

Dining

Seafood and lamb are local specialties. Restaurants are small and varied—Asian, Lebanese, Indian, French, and Italian. Many are located in interesting old buildings. Although pizzas and hamburgers are widely available, the favorite local food is a tasty version of a hot dog, served with fried onions.

MEALTIMES

Dinner, served between 6 and 9, is the main meal; a light lunch is usually served between noon and 2. Most restaurants are open from mid-morning until midnight.

Casual dress is acceptable in all but the most expensive restaurants, where a jacket and tie are recommended.

RATINGS
The following ratings are for a three-course meal for one person. Prices include taxes and service charges but not wine or cocktails. Highly recommended restaurants are indicated by a star ★.

CATEGORY	REYKJAVÍK	OTHER AREAS
$$$	over ISK 4,000	over ISK 3,500
$$	ISK 3,000–ISK 4,000	ISK 2,500–ISK 3,500
$	under ISK 3,000	under ISK 2,500

Lodging

Hotels are clean, quiet, and friendly. Reykjavík and most villages have guest houses and private accommodations. Hostels are few and only functional. Lodging in farmhouses is highly recommended: More than 100 participating farms are listed with **Icelandic Farm Holidays** (tel. 551–9200 or 562–3640, fax 562–3644), and many offer fishing, guided tours, and horseback riding. Outside Reykjavík, the **Icelandic Touring Club** (Mörkin 6, tel. 568–2533, fax 568–2535) operates a number of huts for mountaineers and hikers in remote areas, available during the summer months only; club members have priority. If you tour Iceland on your own, get a list of hotels and guest houses in the regions from the **Tourist Information Center** (Bankastræti 2, tel. 562–3045, fax 562–4749). The **Iceland Tourist Board** (tel. 552–7488, fax 562–4749) offers additional information on where to stay.

RATINGS
Prices are for two people sharing a double room. Highly recommended lodgings are indicated by a star ★.

CATEGORY	REYKJAVÍK	OTHER AREAS
$$$	over ISK 11,000	over ISK 9,000
$$	ISK 8,000–ISK 11,000	ISK 6,000–ISK 9,000
$	under ISK 8,000	under ISK 6,000

Tipping

Tipping is not customary in Iceland.

REYKJAVÍK

Arriving and Departing

By Plane

Flights from the United States and Europe arrive at Keflavík Airport, 50 kilometers (30 miles) from Reykjavík. For information on arrivals and departures at Keflavík Airport, call 569–0100.

BETWEEN THE AIRPORT AND DOWNTOWN
Buses connect with all flights to and from Keflavík. The drive takes 45 minutes and costs ISK 500. Taxis are also available, but they cost at least ISK 4,500.

By Boat

During the summer, the North Atlantic ferry **Norröna** sails from the Faroe Islands, Denmark, and Norway to Seyðisfjörður, one of the magnificent fjords on the east side of Iceland, 720 kilometers (450 miles) from Reykjavík. From Seyðisfjörður, Reykjavík is a one-hour flight or a 10-hour drive. For information, contact **Smyril Line Passenger Department** (Box 370, 3800 Torshavn, Faroes, or Norræna ferðaskrifstofan, Laugavegur 3, Reykjavík, tel. 562–6362, fax 552–9450).

Getting Around

Most interesting sights are in the city center, within easy walking distance of one another. Sightseeing tours are also reccommended.

By Bus

Buses run from 7 AM to midnight. The flat fare for Reykjavík and suburbs is ISK 100 for adults and ISK 25 for children under 13. Exact change is required. Strips of tickets are available from bus drivers and at bus stations.

By Taxi

Rates start at about ISK 300; few taxi rides exceed ISK 700. The best taxis to call are: **Hreyfill** (tel. 568–5522), **BSR** (tel. 561–1720), and **Bæjarleiðir** (tel. 553–3500).

Important Addresses and Numbers

Tourist Information

The tourist information center, Bankastræti 2 (tel. 562–3045, fax 562–4749), is adjacent to the main shopping district. It's open summer, weekdays 8:30–6, Sat. 8:30–2, Sun. 10–2; fall–spring, weekdays 10–4, Sat. 10–2.

Embassies

U.S. (Laufásvegur 21, tel. 552–1900). **Canadian Consulate** (Suðurlandsbraut 10, tel. 568–0820). **U.K.** (Laufásvegur 49, tel. 551–5883).

Emergencies

Police (tel. 551–1166). **Ambulance** (tel. 551–1100). **Doctors and dentists** (weekdays 8 AM–5 PM, tel. 569–6600; weekdays 5 PM–8 AM and weekends, tel. 552–1230). **Pharmacies** operate in shifts at night and on weekends; for information, call 551–8888.

English-Language Bookstores

Eymundsson-Penninn (Austurstræti, tel. 552–7077). **Mál og menning** (Laugavegur 18, tel. 552–4240).

Travel Agencies

Iceland Tourist Bureau (Skógarhlíð 18, tel. 562–3300, fax 562–5895). **Samvinn Travel** (Austurstræti 12, tel. 552–7077, fax 569–1095). **Úrval–Útsýn Travel** (Lágmúli 4, tel. 569–9300, fax 567–0202).

Guided Tours

For information on tour operators, call the tourist information center (tel. 562–3045).

Orientation Tours

Reykjavík Excursions (tel. 562–4422, fax 562-4450) offers "Reykjavík City Sightseeing," a daily tour that takes about 2½ hours and includes commercial centers, folk museums, and art centers.

Excursions

Reykjavík Excursions (*see above*) offers many different types of tours. Perhaps the most interesting are the daily "Gullfoss/Geysir" tours, an eight-hour visit to volcanic craters, geysers, and waterfalls; a half-day trip that includes a visit to the unique **Blue Lagoon,** where you can bathe in hot mineral-rich springs from the depths of the earth; and three-hour pony-trekking trips. For trout-fishing excursions, contact **Úrval–Útsýn Travel** (*see above*). For inexpensive, guided hikes that can last from an afternoon to several weeks, try the **Touring Club of Iceland** (Mörkin 6, tel. 568–2533) or **Outdoor Life Tours** (Grófin 1, tel. 551–4606).

Exploring Reykjavik

Numbers in the margin correspond to points of interest on the Reykjavík map.

❶ The heart of Reykjavík is **Austurvöllur,** a small square in the center of the city. The 19th-century **AlÐingi** (Parliament building), one of the oldest stone buildings in Iceland, faces the square. In the center of the square is a statue of Jón Sigurðsson (1811–79), the national hero who led Iceland's fight for independence, which it achieved fully in 1944.

❷ Next to AlÐingi is the **Dómkirkjan** (Lutheran cathedral), a small,
❸ charming stone church. Behind it is **Tjörnin,** a natural pond next to **Reykjavík City Hall.** One corner of the pond does not freeze; here thermal springs feed warm water, making it an attraction for birds year-round.
❹ Overlooking Tjörnin stands the **National Gallery,** which houses a collection of Icelandic art.

❺ Head back along Lækjargata, beyond Austurvöllur to **Lækjartorg** square. On the right is the **Bernhöftstorfa** district, a small hill with colorful two-story wooden houses from the mid-19th century, where no modernizing efforts have been made. For a century and a half, the largest building has housed the oldest educational institution in the country,
❻ **Menntaskólinn í Reykjavík,** a college whose graduates have from the early days dominated political and social life in Iceland.

TIME OUT Café Paris, on the corner of Austurvöllur square and Pósthússtræti, is a Parisian-style bistro with sidewalk dining in the summer. *Austurstræti 14. tel. 551-1020. $$*

Leading west out of the square is Austurstræti, a semipedestrian shopping street with the main post office on the right. From here you can take Buses 10 or 110 from the bus station for a 20-minute ride to the
❼ **Arbæjarsafn** (Open-Air Museum), a "village" of 18th- and 19th-century houses. *Tel. 558–4094. Admission: ISK 300 adults, ISK 150 children 12–18. Open June–Aug., Tues.–Sat. 10–6; Sept., weekends 10–6; Oct.–May, by appointment.*

❽ You can also take Bus 4 from the square to the **Ásmundur Sveinsson Gallery.** A few originals of this social realist sculptor are in the surrounding garden, which is accessible at all times free of charge. *v/Sigtún, tel. 553-2155. Admission: ISK 200. Open June–Sept., daily 10–4; Oct.–May, Tues., Thurs., and weekends 1–4.*

❾ Most downtown buses pass the **Náttúrufræðistofnun** (Museum of Natural History), located on Hlemmtorg square along with the city's main bus station. The exhibits here vary from stuffed peacocks to giant sea turtles. *Tel. 552–9822. Admission free. Open Tues. and Thurs.–Sun. 1:30–4:30.*

Leading east out of Lækjartorg square is Bankastræti. On the left-hand
❿ side is an 18th-century white building, **Government House,** which houses the offices of Iceland's president and prime minister.

⓫ Walk left toward Arnarhóll hill: At the top is a statue of Viking **Ingólfur Arnarson,** Iceland's first settler, who arrived in 874. Nearby is the mod-
⓬ ern Central Bank. Across the hill is the new **High Court** building, now

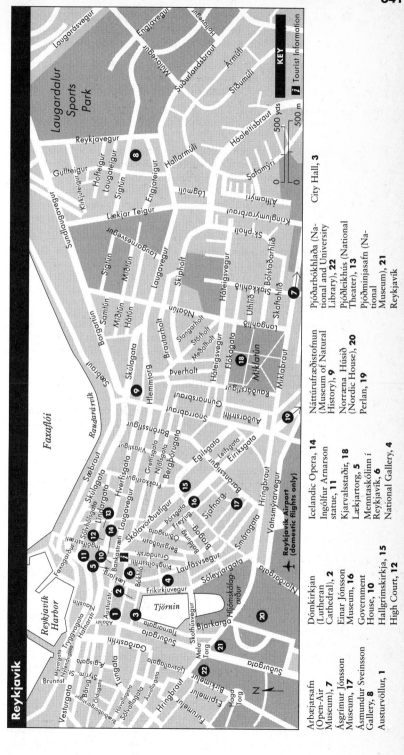

Reykjavik

Arbæjarsafn (Open-Air Museum), **7**

Ásgrímur Jónsson Museum, **16**

Ásmundur Sveinsson Gallery, **8**

Austurvöllur, **1**

Dómkirkjan (Lutheran Cathedral), **2**

Einar Jónsson Museum, **17**

Government House, **10**

Hallgrímskirkja, **15**

High Court, **12**

Icelandic Opera, **14**

Ingólfur Arnarson statue, **11**

Kjarvalsstaðir, **18**

Lækjartorg, **5**

Menntaskólinn í Reykjavik, **6**

National Gallery, **4**

Náttúrufræðistofnun (Museum of Natural History), **9**

Norræna Húsið (Nordic House), **20**

Perlan, **19**

Þjóðarbókhlaða (National and University Library), **22**

Þjóðleikhús (National Theater), **13**

Þjóðminjasafn (National Museum), **21** Reykjavik

City Hall, **3**

⑬ under construction. Adjacent to it are the **Þjóðleikhús** (National Theater), built during the 1940s, and the old **National Library** building, which dates from the beginning of the 20th century.

⑭ Walk along Ingólfsstræti. To the right is the **Icelandic Opera** building, which was Iceland's first cinema and later its first opera house. A bit farther up, across Bankastræti, is the tourist information center.

TIME OUT **Café Solon Islandus.** A bar, light snacks, art shows, live music, and intimate theater are the draws here. *Bankastræti 7A, tel. 551–2666. $$*

To continue the tour from Bankastræti, turn right onto Skólavörðustígur.
⑮ At the end of that street towers the **Hallgrímskirkja,** a church with a 210-foot gray stone tower that dominates the city's skyline. The church, which took more than 40 years to build and was completed in the '80s, is open to the public. The **church tower** offers a panoramic view of the city and its spacious suburbs. *Tel. 551–0745. Admission to tower: ISK 200 adults, ISK 100 children under 12. Open daily 10–6.*

⑯ The neighboring **Einar Jónsson Museum** is devoted to the works of Iceland's leading early-20th-century sculptor. His monumental sculptures have a strong symbolic and mystical content. *v/Skólavörðuholt. Admission: ISK 100. Open weekends, 1:30–4. Sculpture garden open daily, 11–4.*

⑰ Nearby is the **Ásgrímur Jónsson Museum,** which features the works of the popular post-Impressionist painter Ásgrímur Jónsson (1870–1968). *Bergstaðastræti 74. Admission free. Open weekdays 4–10, weekends 2–10.*

⑱ **Kjarvalsstaðir,** a municipal art gallery named in honor of Jóhannes Kjarval (1889–1972), the nation's best-loved painter, is a 10-minute walk away from the Hallgrímskirkja. It is pleasantly situated in the **Miklatún,** one of two spacious parks in Reykjavík. Temporary exhibits show the work of Icelandic and visiting artists. *v/Flókagata, tel. 552–6131. Admission free, except for private exhibitions. Open daily 2–8.*

From Kjarvalsstaðir, cross Miklabraut and head south along any one of
⑲ the short side streets to the reflective glass dome of the atrium, **Perlan,** perched high on a hill atop five huge hot-water reservoirs that heat the capital area. There's a fine restaurant here, as well as a coffee shop, an ice cream bar, and a balcony with splendid views. *Öskjuhlíð, tel. 562–0200. Admission free. Open daily 11:30 AM–10 PM.*

Return to Miklabraut and walk west until you reach the city's other major
⑳ park, Hljómskálagarður. On your left is **Norræna Húsið** (Nordic House), a cultural center with exhibitions, lectures, concerts, and a coffee shop. *Call for information, tel. 551–7030. Open daily 2–7.*

Northwest of the Nordic House are the campus of the **University of**
㉑ **Iceland** (founded 1911) and the outstanding **Þjóðminjasafn** (National Museum). On display are Viking artifacts, national costumes, weaving, wood carving, and silver works. *Suðurgata 41, tel. 552–8888. Small admission fee. Open June–Sept., daily 1:30–4; Oct.–May, Tues., Thurs., and weekends 1:30–4.*

Across Suðurgata from the National Museum, you can't miss the new
㉒ red aluminum-clad **Þjóðarbókhlaða** (National and University Library). *(Hringbraut, tel. 563–5600. Open weekdays 9–7, Sat. 9–5).* From the National Museum, it is a 10-minute walk back to the pond and the city center.

Shopping

Many of the shops that sell the most attractive Icelandic woolen goods and arts and crafts are on Aðalstræti, Hafnarstræti, and Vesturgata streets. The **Icelandic Handcrafts Center** (Falcon House, Hafnarstræti 3, tel. 551–1784) stocks Icelandic woolens, knitting and tapestry materials, handmade pottery, glassware, and jewelry. At the **Handknitting Association of Iceland,** (Skólavörðustígur 9, tel. 552–1890 or 552–1912) you can buy high-quality hand-knits through a knitters' cooperative. **Rammagerðin** (Hafnarstræti 19, tel. 551–7910) stocks a wide range of Icelandic-made clothes, souvenirs, and books. For original Icelandic arts and crafts direct from the artists, try **Hjá Peim** (Skólavörðustigur 6b, tel. 551–2350). On weekends, try the harborside **Kolaport** flea market (tel. 562–5030).

Dining

Most Reykjavík restaurants feature excellent seafood dishes. Many serve European cuisine as well as local fish and lamb specialties. Reservations are vital on weekends in the better restaurants. Jacket and tie are rarely required. Most are open from noon to midnight, and most take major credit cards. Some offer discount lunch or tourist menus. For details and price-category definitions, *see* Dining *in* Staying in Iceland, *above.*

$$$ Holt. In this hotel setting of Icelandic art chosen from the owner's private collection, diners indulge in mouthwatering seafood such as gravlax and grilled halibut, and a wine list to match. *Bergstaðastræti 37, tel. 552–5700. Reservations advised. AE, DC, MC, V.*

$$$ Perlan. In this slightly formal rotating restaurant under the Perlan
★ dome, you may pay a bit more for the food, but the splendid view, especially at sunset, more than compensates for the price. Jacket and tie are reccommended. *Öskjuhlíð, tel. 562–0200. Reservations advised. No lunch. AE, DC, MC, V.*

$$$ Vid Tjörnina. The classic Icelandic seafood cuisine here includes mar-
★ inated cod cheeks and *tindabikkja* (starry ray) with grapes, capers, and Pernod. It's on the second floor of a typical corrugated-iron-clad early 20th-century house. *Templarasund 3, tel. 551–8555. Reservations advised. AE, MC, V.*

$$ Hornið. Pizzas and pasta are the draw, but good meat and fish dishes also are served at this cosmopolitan bistro. *Hafnarstræti 15, tel. 551–3340. Reservations advised. AE, DC, MC, V.*

$$ Oðinsvé. On the first floor of a hotel, this cozy restaurant specializes in Scandinavian-French fare, mostly seafood. Don't miss the fish chowder or the hot apple strudel. *Oðinstorg, tel. 552–5090. Reservations advised. AE, DC, MC, V.*

$$ Potturinn og Pannan. The service at this small restaurant on the edge of the downtown area is efficient but friendly. Lamb and fish dishes and American-style salads are the specialties. *Brautarholt 22, tel. 551–1690. Reservations advised. AE, MC, V.*

$$ Þrír Frakkar Hjá Úlfari. An interesting selection of seafood includes whale meat. Beef dishes are also recommended. *Baldursgata 14, tel. 552–3939. Reservations advised. AE, DC, MC, V.*

$ Café Hressó. This is the place for a quick snack and some local color. Tasty cakes are served, and the back garden is open in good weather. *Austurstræti 20, tel. 551–4353. MC, V.*

$ Coffee Wagon. Here on the waterfront in West Reykjavík, local fishermen enjoy hearty lunches. Try the filling "fish of the day." *Grandagarði 10, tel. 551–5932. No credit cards.*

Lodging

For details and price-category definitions, *see* Lodging *in* Staying in Iceland, *above.*

$$$ **Holt.** One of Reykjavík's finest hotels, the Holt is in a central residen-
★   tial district. Many of the rooms are furnished with Icelandic works of
art. The restaurant (*see* Dining, *above*) is especially good; jacket and
tie are reccommended. *Bergstaðastræti 37, tel. 552–5700, fax 562–
3025. 40 rooms with bath or shower, 9 suites. Facilities: restaurant,
lobby lounge. AE, DC, MC, V.*

$$$ **Ísland.** This modern luxury hotel in the eastern part of the city has su-
perb sea and mountain views. *Ármúli 9, tel. 568–8999, fax 568–9957.
119 rooms with bath, 3 suites. Facilities: restaurant, bar, nightclub. AE,
DC, MC, V.*

$$$ **Saga.** All the rooms of this business-oriented hotel are above the fourth
★   level and have spectacular views. It's within walking distance of most
museums, shops, and restaurants. The restaurant has live music and
dancing. *Hagatorg, tel. 552–9900, fax 562–3980. 162 rooms with bath.
Facilities: restaurant, 6 bars, grill, in-room VCRs, sauna, meeting
rooms. AE, DC, MC, V.*

$$$ **Scandic Loftleiðir.** The Scandic Loftleiðir accommodates both tourists
and conventioneers. Located near the domestic airport, it's 15 minutes
from the center of town. *Reykjavík Airport, tel. 552–2322, fax 552–
5320. 218 rooms with bath. Facilities: 2 restaurants, indoor pool,
sauna. AE, DC, MC, V.*

$$ **City Hotel.** On a quiet street, this comfortable hotel is convenient to
the center of town. *Ránargata 4A, tel. 551–8650, fax 552–9040. 31
rooms with bath or shower. Facilities: restaurant, meeting rooms. AE,
DC, MC, V.*

$$ **Hotel Leifur Eiríksson.** Adjacent to the hilltop church, Hallgrímskirkja,
this hotel is an easy walk from all the city's main attractions.
*Skólavörðustígur 45, tel. 562–0800, fax 562–0804. 29 rooms with
shower. Facilities: restaurant. AE, DC, MC, V.*

$$ **Lind.** Near the Hlemmur city bus station and a 10-minute walk from
downtown, the Lind offers few frills but plenty of clean rooms and easy
access to the city center. *Rauðarárstígur 18, tel. 562–3350, fax 562–
3150. 44 rooms with bath. Facilities: restaurant, lobby lounge, meet-
ing rooms. AE, DC, MC, V.*

$ **Garður.** This is a student residence, open as a hotel only during the sum-
mer, when students are on vacation. Its basic but comfortable rooms
are adequate for travelers on a tight budget. It's within easy reach of
the National Museum and other attractions. *Hringbraut, tel. 551–5656.
44 rooms without bath. No credit cards. Closed in winter.*

$ **Snorra Guest House.** The rooms are basic but clean, and all have wash-
basins. The main bus station is close by. *Snorrabraut 52, tel. 551–6522.
18 rooms without bath. No credit cards.*

THE ICELANDIC COUNTRYSIDE

The real beauty of Iceland is in the countryside: the fjords of the east,
the stark mountains of the north, the sands of the south, the rough coast-
line of the west, and the lava fields of the interior.

Getting Around

There are daily flights to most of the large towns. Although flights are
expensive, special family fares and vacation tickets are available. There
are car-rental agencies in Reykjavík and in many towns. The few sched-

uled ferries travel mainly to the Westmann Islands, from Þorlákshöfn on the south coast, and to Akranes, from Reykjavík. If you do not have your own car, consider buying one of the special bus tickets that cover scheduled routes throughout the country (*see* Getting Around *in* Staying in Iceland, *above*).

Guided Tours

Many people prefer guided bus tours to driving on the rough roads; both day excursions and longer journeys are available. Such tours are an excellent way to relax and enjoy Iceland's spectacular scenery. Most longer tours operate between June and September and cost from ISK 25,000 to ISK 150,000 per person, including overnight accommodations and three meals a day. On some tours you'll stay in hotels; on others you'll camp out or sleep in tents. Tours typically last from 3 to 19 days and can be booked from abroad through **Icelandair** or travel agencies. For information on tour operators, contact the **Iceland Tourist Board** (Gimli, Lækjargata 3, Reykjavík, tel. 552–9488, fax 562–4749).

Local Tours

One-day tours can be arranged through agencies in Reykjavík (*see* Important Addresses and Numbers, *above*).

From Akureyri, tours to **Lake Mývatn** take about 10 hours and cost about ISK 3,500 per person. The four-hour "Midnight Sun Tour" along Eyjafjörður costs about ISK 3,000 per person.

From Egilsstaðir, a strenuous eight-hour journey to Mjóifjörður costs about ISK 2,500 per person. From Höfn in Hornafjörður you can go by bus on a "Glacier Tour," which lasts 10 hours and costs about ISK 5,000 per person. Reasonably priced sightseeing trips by boat are available in the Westmann Islands. Boat tours also depart from Stykkishólmur in West Iceland and from Isafjörður in the nearby fjords.

Tourist Information

Akureyri (Tourist Center, Hafnarstræti 82, tel. 462–7733, fax 461–1817).
Egilsstaðir (campsite, tel. 471–2320).
Höfn (campsite, Hafnarbraut, tel. 478–1701).
Ísafjörður (Tourist Bureau, Hafnarstræti 6, tel. 456–5121, fax 456–5122).
Lake Mývatn (Eldá Travel, Mývatnssveit, tel. 464–4220).
Ólafsvík (Gamlapakkhúsið, tel. 436–1543).
Seyðisfjörður (Austfar, Fjarðargata 8, tel. 472–1111).

Exploring the Icelandic Countryside

The South

Iceland is not a crowded place. There can be up to 80 kilometers (50 miles) between tourist accommodations, so you must be prepared for some considerable traveling every day. Start your tour around Iceland from Reykjavík, heading east on the main Ring Road around the country (Road 1), which you will follow for most of your tour.

In **Hveragerði,** some 40 kilometers (25 miles) away, there are some interesting hot springs and botanic greenhouses where fruits and vegetables are grown. When you have passed **Selfoss,** 8 kilometers (5 miles) farther, you'll be in the heartland of Icelandic farming, and soon you'll cross the longest river in the country, the Þjórsá. For an overnight stop in this area, the Edda hotels in **Skógar,** 120 kilometers (75 miles) east of Selfoss, and **Kirkjubæjarklaustur,** 80 kilometers (50 miles) farther east on Road 205, offer pleasant lodging in school dormitories. (*see* Dining and Lodging, *below*).

The landscape around Kirkjubæjarklaustur is shaped by 200-year-old lava deposits. When the volcano Laki erupted in 1783, it produced the greatest amount of lava from a single eruption in recorded history.

The landscape of the south coast is a major tourist attraction. Don't miss the **Skaftafell National Park,** where you can put down your tent for ISK 400 a night. The park is at the foot of the glacier Svínafells-jökull; farther up is the highest peak in Iceland, Hvannadalshnjúkur, rising to 6,950 feet. About 32 kilometers (20 miles) east of the park is the adventure world of the **Jökulsárlón** glacial lagoon, with its eerie ice floes. Boat tours can be arranged on arrival for about ISK 1,000. Information is available from Fjönir Torfason (tel. 478–1065) and at Skaftafell National Park.

One-day downhill skiing and snowmobiling tours of great nature spots in **Vatnajökull** are scheduled from June through September from **Höfn** in Hornafjörður, Road 99. Details and general tourist information are available from Glacier Tours (tel. 478–1701, fax 478–1901) in Höfn.

The East

From Höfn the journey continues to Djúpivogur, Road 98, and along the east coast, where one fjord lies beside another. From **Breiðdalsvík** there are two alternative routes. The coastal one runs through the fishing villages of **Stöðvarfjörður, Fáskrúðsfjörður,** and **Reyðarfjörður,** which can be reached via Roads 97, 96, and 92, respectively.

From Reyðarfjörður the Ring Road continues for 32 kilometers (20 miles) to **Egilsstaðir.** If you decide not to follow the coastline from Breiðdalsvík, you'll reach Egilsstaðir across Breiðdalsheiði, which, at approximately 2,500 feet, is the highest mountain road in Iceland. The road is steep and badly engineered. In Egilsstaðir you are about 768 kilometers (480 miles) from Reykjavík, or halfway around the island, so you can either turn back or continue north. The Egilsstaðir campsite has a tourist information center (tel. 471–2320).

Some 24 kilometers (15 miles) south of Egilsstaðir on Road 931 is **Hallormsstaðarskógur,** the largest forest in Iceland. There you can stop for the night at an Edda hotel, or pitch a tent by the Lögur lagoon, where Iceland's Loch Ness monster is said to live.

From there you can travel around the **Hérað district** and to **Seyðisfjörður,** 48 kilometers (30 miles) from Egilsstaðir on Road 93. Check with the tourist office for information on such activities as boat trips and pony trekking. Here the Faroese ferry *Norröna* docks weekly on its North Atlantic summer sailing route.

From Egilsstaðir the Ring Road continues for more than 160 kilometers (100 miles) across remote highlands to **Lake Mývatn.** On this daylong journey through a remote area, you will pass the highest inhabited farm in the country, Möðrudalur, approximately 1,350 feet above sea level. Lake Mývatn, with its incredibly rich variety of waterfowl, is a mecca for bird lovers and also offers fantastic geological formations. Information about bike rentals, fishing, and other activities is available at Hótel Reynihlíð (tel. 464–4170) and Eldá Travel (tel. 464–4220).

From Lake Mývatn there are two possible routes. One is to go directly along Road 1 to **Akureyri,** the capital of the north, a journey of 96 kilometers (60 miles). A key attraction on this route is the graceful waterfall **Goðafoss.**

The other alternative is to go to **Húsavík** (Road 87) and **Tjörnes** (Road 85) for a day or so, a detour of more than 160 kilometers (100 miles). The major attractions in this area are the thundering waterfall **Dettifoss** (Road 864) and the great rocky haven of **Ásbyrgi,** which legend says is a giant hoofprint left by Sleipnir, the eight-legged horse of the ancient Norse god Odin.

The North and the West

The natural surroundings in **Akureyri** are unequaled by any other Icelandic town. Late-19th-century wooden houses give the city center a sense of history, as well as architectural variety. The **Botanic Gardens** (admission free, open daily 8 AM–11 PM) have a fine collection of arctic flora. Akureyri also has the northernmost 18-hole golf course in the world, host of the **Midnight Sun Open Golf Tournament** each year around midsummer. For information, call the Iceland Tourist Board (tel. 562–3300, fax 562–5895).

From Akureyri you can go for an evening tour north along the coast of **Eyjafjörður** (Road 82) to see the midnight sun; June and July are the brightest months. Information for traveling in the north is available at the Akureyri tourist center and Nonni Travel (tel. 461–1841).

Driving from Akureyri to Reykjavík, a journey of 400 kilometers (250 miles) takes an entire day, so if there is time to spare, a stay in **Sauðárkrókur** (Roads 75 and 76), **Blönduós,** or **Borgarnes** can be both pleasant and peaceful. Holders of the Omnibus Passport (*see* Getting Around in Iceland, *above*) should not miss the 320-kilometer (200-mile) detour to the peninsula of **Snæfellsnes,** via Roads 54 and 57. A night in the presence of the glacier Snæfellsjökull, where Jules Verne's *Journey to the Center of the Earth* begins, is recommended.

Trips to the top of the glacier by snowmobile can be arranged from **Ólafsvík,** north of the glacier, or **Arnarstapi,** to the south. The trip costs around ISK 3,000 per person. Information is available from Pálmar Einarsson in Ólafsvík (tel. 438–6678) and Snjófell, at Arnarstapi (tel. 435–6783, fax 435–6795).

Another interesting detour, which can take up to a week, is to **Vestfirðir** (the West Fjords) (Roads 68, 69, and 61). From Ísafjörður, trips to the inhabitable parts of Strandasýsla may be of interest to hikers and mountaineers. Information is available at the Vestfirðir Tourist Bureau (Aðalstræti 11, tel. 456–3457).

Dining and Lodging

Since most restaurants outside Reykjavík are in hotels, the following list is a selection of hotel-restaurants. For details and price-category definitions, *see* Lodging in Staying in Iceland, *above*.

Akureyri

$$$ **Hótel KEA.** Here you'll receive first-class hotel service at surprisingly rea-
★ sonable prices. In addition to the rooftop restaurant that serves Danish haute cuisine, there's an inexpensive cafeteria on the ground floor. *Hafnarstræti 97, 600 Akureyri, tel. 462–2200, fax 461–2285. 72 rooms with shower. Facilities: restaurant, cafeteria, minibars. AE, MC, V.*

$$$ **Hótel Norðurland.** Rooms here are pleasantly decorated with floral prints and Danish furniture. On the ground floor is the separately run Bing-Dao restaurant, serving Asian food. *Geislagata 7, 600 Akureyri, tel.*

462–2600, fax 462–7962. 28 rooms with bath. Facilities: restaurant, minibars. AE, DC, MC, V.

$$ Hótel Edda. This summer hotel in a school dormitory is known for its quality service. *Menntaskólinn, 600 Akureyri, tel. 461–1434. 77 rooms without bath. Facilities: restaurant. AE, MC, V. Closed Sept.–May.*

Blönduós

$ Hótel Blönduós. This small hotel, in the center of town a stone's throw from the seashore, has a large restaurant where the specialty is locally caught fresh trout. *Aðalgata 6, 540 Blönduós, tel. 452–4126, fax 452–4989. 18 rooms, 11 with shower. Facilities: restaurant. AE, MC, V.*

Borgarnes

$$$ Hótel Borgarnes. One of the biggest and most popular hotels on the west coast, this offers both a cafeteria, an elegant restaurant, and a bar. *Egilsgata 14–16, 310 Bogarnes, tel. 437–1119, fax 437–1443. 36 rooms with shower. Facilities: restaurant, bar, cafeteria, minibars. AE, DC, MC, V.*

Breiðdalsvík

$ Hótel Bláfell. Though it's only a few years old, this small hotel in a fishing village on Route 96 has a cozy, rustic interior and an award-winning seafood restaurant. *Sólvellir 14, 760 Breiðdalsvík, tel. 475–6770, fax 475–6668. 15 rooms without bath. Facilities: restaurant. AE, MC, V.*

Búðir

$$ Hótel Búðir. Under the magical glacier Snæfellsjökull and close to a beach of black lava and golden sand, this rustic hotel has an excellent restaurant. *Staðarsveit, Snæfellsnes 355, tel. 435–6700, fax 435–6701. 22 rooms without bath. Facilities: restaurant. AE, DC, MC, V. Closed Aug.–June.*

Djúpivogur

$$ Hótel Framtíð. In an old fishing village where 19th-century Danish merchant homes still stand, this small hotel by the harbor has a friendly dining room where home-style food is served. *Vogaland 4, 765 Djúpivogur, tel. 478–8887, fax 478–8187. 10 rooms without bath. Facilities: restaurant. AE, MC, V.*

Egilsstaðir

$$ Hótel Valaskjálf. Large and practical, this hotel has a restaurant and a cafeteria. Breakfast is included in the room rate, and there is dancing on the weekends. *Skógarlönd, 700 Egilsstaðir, tel. 471–1500, fax 471–1501. 66 rooms with shower. Facilities: restaurant, cafeteria, minibars. AE, MC, V.*

Hallormsstaður

$$ Hótel Edda. The hotel is merely adequate, but the harmony of forest, lake, and quiet bays is the real attraction. A good restaurant is on the premises. *707 Hallormsstaður, tel. 471–1705. 20 rooms without bath. Facilities: restaurant. AE, DC, V. Closed Oct.–Apr.*

Höfn

$$ Hótel Höfn. This clean and comfortable hotel has a restaurant with good service and tasty food; try the excellent almond trout. Fast food is also available at the grill, and there is dancing on the weekends. *780 Hornafjörður, tel. 478–1240, fax 478–1996. 40 rooms, half with shower. Facilities: restaurant, grill. AE, MC, V.*

Húsavík

$$$ Hótel Húsavík. Popular as a ski hotel during winter, this comfortable hotel has both a restaurant and a cafeteria. *Ketilsbraut 22, 640 Húsavík, tel. 464–1220, fax 464–2161. 33 rooms with shower. Facilities: restaurant, cafeteria. AE, DC, MC, V.*

Hveragerði

$$$ Hótel Örk. Newly built with a health spa, the Örk has expensive rooms, but meals in the ground-floor restaurant are reasonable. Three- to seven-day "spa cure" retreat packages are available. *Breiðamörk 1, 810 Hveragerði, tel. 483–4700, fax 483–4775. 81 rooms with shower. Facilities: restaurant, pool, sauna, 9-hole golf course, tennis court, exercise room. AE, MC, V.*

Ísafjörður

$$ Hótel Ísafjörður. This is a good family hotel. The restaurant offers a great variety of tasty seafood. *Silfurtorg 2, 400 Ísafjörður, tel. 456–4111, fax 456–4767. 20 rooms with shower. Facilities: restaurant, minibars. AE, MC, V.*

Kirkjubæjarklaustur

$$ Hótel Edda. This standard Edda facility, in a modern building with a restaurant and a swimming pool, is open all year round. *880 Kirkjubæjarklaustur, tel. 487–4799, fax 487–4614. 55 rooms with shower. Facilities: restaurant, pool. AE, MC, V.*

Mývatn

$$$ Hótel Reykjahlíð. This small hotel and restaurant sits next to a lake. *Reykjahlíð, 660 Mývatnssveit, tel. 464–4142. 7 rooms without bath. Facilities: restaurant. AE, MC, V. Closed Oct.–Apr.*

$$$ Hótel Reynihlíð. This popular hotel offers a helpful tourist information service and a restaurant. *Reykjahlíð, 660 Mývatnssveit, tel. 464–4170, fax 464–4371. 41 rooms with shower. Facilites: restaurant. AE, DC, MC, V.*

Ólafsvík

$$ Höfði Guesthouse. This family-style, harborside hotel has a small restaurant that offers fresh local delicacies such as trout and halibut. *Ólafsbraut 20, Ólafsvík, tel. 436–1650. 14 rooms without bath. Facilities: restaurant. No credit cards.*

Sauðárkrókur

$$ Hótel Mælifell. This attractive hotel has a restaurant, plus dancing on weekends. *Aðalgata 7, 550 Sauðárkrókur, tel. 453–5265, fax 453–5640. 16 rooms without bath. Facilities: restaurant. AE, MC, V.*

Seyðisfjörður

$$ Hótel Snæfell. In an old wooden house, this new hotel has a glassed-★ in restaurant and a picturesque pond. *Austurvegur 3, 710 Seyðisfjörður, tel. 472–1460, fax 472–1570. 9 rooms with shower. Facilities: restaurant. AE, MC, V.*

Skógar

$$ Hótel Edda. Close to the waterfall Skógafoss, this summer hotel has views of the sea, mountains, and glaciers. *Skógar, 861 Hvolsvöllur, tel. 487–8870. 36 rooms without bath. Facilities: restaurant. AE, MC, V. Closed Oct.–Apr.*

Lodging

The cost of lodging in the countryside is less than in Reykjavík. For details and price-category definitions, *see* Lodging *in* Staying in Iceland, *above.*

Akureyri

$ Lónsá Youth Hostel. It's the bare basics, but kitchen facilities are available. *Glæsibæjarhreppur, 601 Akureyri, tel. 462–5037. 16 rooms without bath. Facilities: kitchen. AE, MC, V. Closed Sept.–June.*

Djúpivogur

$ Berunes Youth Hostel. This small summer hostel offers lodging for 15 people. *Beruneshreppur, 765 Djúpivogur, tel. 478–8988. No credit cards. Closed Sept.–May.*

Egilsstaðir

$ Hótel Egilsstaðir. This charming farmhouse hotel is on the outskirts of town. *Egilsstaðir, tel. 471–1114. 10 rooms without bath. No credit cards.*

$ Húsey Youth Hostel. A distance from town, this hostel offers lodging only. *Hróarstunga, Tunguhreppur, 701 Egilsstaðir, tel. 471–3010, fax 471–3009. Facilities: fishing, horseback riding. No credit cards.*

Hveragerði

$ Ból Youth Hostel. This is a basic youth hostel with two, three, or five beds to a room, as well as kitchen facilities. *Hveramörk 14, 810 Hveragerði, tel. 483–4198. 24 beds. No credit cards. Closed Aug.–June.*

Skaftafell

$$ Hótel Skaftafell. This newly built guest house is adjacent to Skaftafell National Park. *Skaftafell, 785 Fagurhólsmýri, tel. 478–1945, fax 478–1946. 21 rooms with bath. MC, V.*

17 Ireland

IRELAND, ONE OF THE WESTERNMOST COUNTRIES in Europe, is a small island on which you are never more than an hour's drive from the sea. It's actually two countries in one. The northeast corner of the island, Northern Ireland, remains a part of the United Kingdom, while the Republic, with a population of only 3½ million, has been independent since 1921.

The Republic of Ireland is virtually free from the "troubles" that have dominated the news from Northern Ireland. Over the past few years, millions of pounds have been spent on upgrading tourist facilities, but the attractions of Ireland as a vacation destination remain the same as ever: those of a small, friendly country with a mild climate and a relaxed pace of life, where simple pleasures are to be found in its scenery, its historical heritage, its sporting opportunities, and the informal hospitality of its loquacious inhabitants.

Dublin, the capital, is a thriving modern city. It's a strikingly elegant city, too, a fact of which Dubliners are well aware. Trinity College, Dublin Castle, and the magnificent public buildings and distinctive Georgian squares of the city have all been restored, allowing the elegance of 18th-century Dublin to emerge again after 200 years of neglect.

The Irish way of life is unpretentious and informal. In a country where pubs play a key role in social gatherings, the Irish will be found at their most convivial when seated in front of a pint of their famous black ale, Guinness, consumed here in vast quantities. Even if you do not usually frequent bars, a visit to an Irish pub or two will add greatly to the enjoyment of your visit.

The pace of life outside Dublin is even more relaxed. When a local was asked for the Irish-language equivalent of *mañana,* the reply came that there is no word in Irish to convey quite the same sense of urgency. An exaggeration, of course, but the farther you travel from the metropolis, the more you will be inclined to linger. Apart from such sporting attractions as championship golf, horse racing, deep-sea fishing, and angling, the thing to do in Ireland is to take it easy, and look around you.

The lakes of Killarney—a chain of deep-blue lakes surrounded by romantic, boulder-strewn mountains—are justifiably among the country's most famous attractions. The Ring of Kerry provides the motorist with a day-long tour through lush coastal vegetation. By contrast, you will have to explore County Clare's eerie limestone desert, the Burren, on foot to find its rare alpine and Mediterranean flowers. Likewise, if you want to stand on the summit of the Cliffs of Moher to watch the Atlantic breakers pounding on the rocks 712 feet below you, you'll have to walk a bit first. The blue hills of Connemara remain the inspiration for many paintings. The history buff will delight in the Shannon region, peppered with numerous castles, some of which have been meticulously restored. Throughout the country, there are prehistoric and early Christian remains to be discovered. You can also seek out the places made famous by James Joyce, William Butler Yeats, John Millington Synge, and other well-known writers, and gain a new insight into the land and the people who inspired them.

ESSENTIAL INFORMATION

Before You Go

When to Go

The main tourist season runs from June to mid-September. The attractions of Ireland are not as dependent on the weather as those in most other northern European countries, and the scenery is just as attractive in the off-peak times of fall and spring. Accommodations are more economical in winter, although some of the smaller attractions are closed from October through March. In all seasons the visitor can expect to encounter rain.

CLIMATE

Winters are mild though wet; summers can be warm and sunny, but there's always the risk of a sudden shower. No one ever went to Ireland for a suntan.

The following are the average daily maximum and minimum temperatures for Dublin.

Jan.	46F	8C	May	60F	15C	Sept.	63F	17C
	34	1		43	6		48	9
Feb.	47F	8C	June	65F	18C	Oct.	57F	14C
	35	2		48	9		43	6
Mar.	51F	11C	July	67F	19C	Nov.	51F	11C
	37	3		52	11		39	4
Apr.	55F	13C	Aug.	67F	19C	Dec.	47F	8C
	39	4		51	11		37	3

Currency

The unit of currency in Ireland is the pound, or punt (pronounced poont), written as IR£ to avoid confusion with the pound sterling. The currency is divided into the same denominations as in Britain, with IR£1 divided into 100 pence (written *p*). There is likely to be some variance in the rates of exchange between Ireland and the United Kingdom (which includes Northern Ireland). Change U.K. pounds at a bank when you get to Ireland (pound coins not accepted); change Irish pounds before you leave.

Although the Irish pound is the only legal tender currency in the Republic, U.S. dollars and British currency are often accepted in large hotels and shops licensed as bureaux de change. Banks give the best rate of exchange. The rate of exchange at press time (spring 1995) was 65 pence to the U.S. dollar and 95 pence to the British pound sterling.

What It Will Cost

Dublin is one of Europe's most expensive cities—an unfortunate state of affairs that manifests itself most obviously in hotel and restaurant rates. You can generally keep costs lower if you visit Ireland on a package tour. Alternatively, consider staying in a guest house or one of the multitude of bed-and-breakfasts; they provide an economical and atmospheric option (*see* Lodging *in* Staying in Ireland, *below*). The rest of the country—with the exception of the better-known hotels and restaurants—is less expensive than Dublin. That the Irish themselves complain bitterly about the high cost of living is partly attributable to the high rate of value-added tax (VAT)—a stinging 21% on "luxury" goods and 10% on hotel accommodations. Some sample costs make the point. For instance, while a double room in a moderately priced Dublin hotel will cost about IR£90, with breakfast sometimes another IR£9

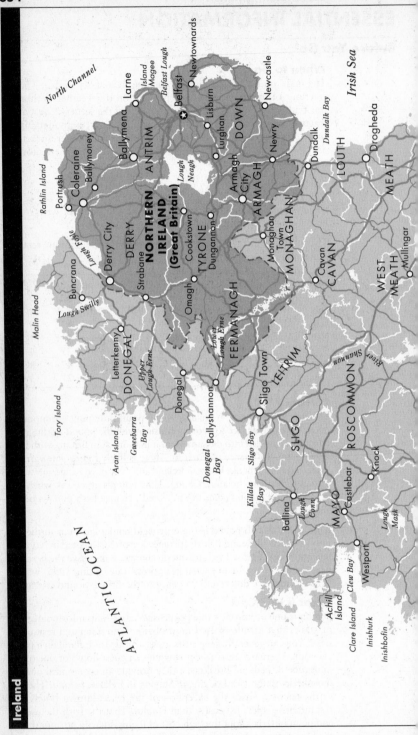

ATLANTIC OCEAN

North Channel

Irish Sea

Rathlin Island

Tory Island

Malin Head

Buncrana

Letterkenny

DONEGAL

Upper Lough Erne

Donegal

Ballyshannon

Lough Swilly

Lough Foyle

Derry City

Strabane

DERRY

NORTHERN IRELAND (Great Britain)

TYRONE

Omagh

Cookstown

Dungannon

FERMANAGH

Lower Lough Erne

Portrush

Coleraine

Ballymoney

Ballymena

ANTRIM

Lough Neagh

Larne

Island Magee

Belfast Lough

Belfast

Lisburn

Lurgan

Lurgan

Newtownards

Newcastle

DOWN

Armagh City

ARMAGH

Newry

Monaghan Town

MONAGHAN

Dundalk

Dundalk Bay

LOUTH

Drogheda

MEATH

River Shannon

Cavan

CAVAN

WEST MEATH

Mullingar

LEITRIM

Sligo Town

SLIGO

Sligo Bay

Killala Bay

ROSCOMMON

Knock

Ballina

Lough Conn

MAYO

Castlebar

Lough Mask

Westport

Clew Bay

Achill Island

Clare Island

Inishturk

Inishbofin

Gweebarra Bay

Aran Island

Donegal Bay

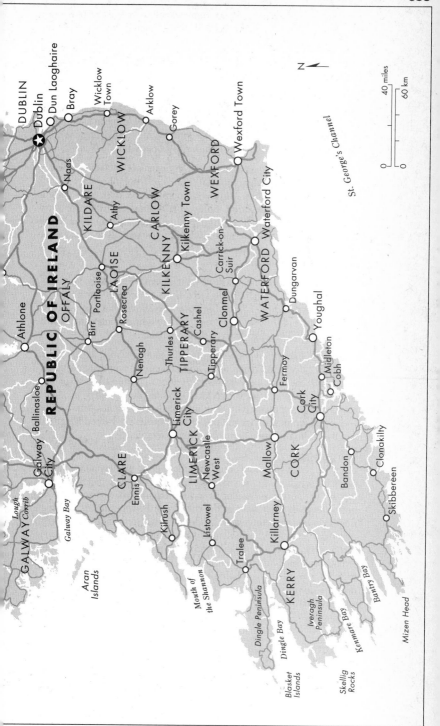

REPUBLIC OF IRELAND

DUBLIN
Dublin
Dun Laoghaire
Bray
Wicklow Town
Arklow
Gorey
Wexford Town

Naas
KILDARE
Athy
CARLOW
Kilkenny Town
WEXFORD
Waterford City

LAOISE
OFFALY
Portlaoise
Birr
Rosecrea
KILKENNY
Carrick-on-Suir
Clonmel
WATERFORD
Dungarvan

Athlone
Nenagh
Thurles
TIPPERARY
Cashel
Tipperary
Fermoy
Youghal
Midleton
Cobh

Ballinasloe
Galway City
REPUBLIC OF IRELAND

Limerick City
LIMERICK
Newcastle West
Mallow
Cork City
CORK
Clonakilty

CLARE
Ennis
Kilrush
Listowel
Killarney
Bandon
Skibbereen

Lough Corrib
Galway Bay
GALWAY
Aran Islands

Tralee
KERRY

Mouth of the Shannon
Dingle Peninsula
Dingle Bay
Blasket Islands
Iveragh Peninsula
Skellig Rocks
Kenmare Bay
Bantry Bay
Mizen Head

St. George's Channel

N

40 miles
60 km

per person, the current rate for a country B&B is around IR£16 per person. A modest small-town hotel will charge around IR£25 per person.

SAMPLE PRICES
Cup of coffee, 70p; pint of beer, IR£2; Coca-Cola, 95p; ham sandwich, IR£1.80; 1-mile taxi ride, IR£3.50.

Customs on Arrival
Two categories of duty-free allowance exist for travelers entering the Irish Republic: one for goods obtained outside the European Union (EU), on a ship or aircraft, or in a duty-free store within the EU; and the other for goods bought in the EU, with duty and tax paid.

In the first category, you may import duty-free: (1) 200 cigarettes, or 100 cigarillos, or 50 cigars, or 250 grams of smoking tobacco; (2) 2 liters of wine, and either 1 liter of alcoholic drink over 22% volume or 2 liters of alcoholic drink under 22% volume (sparkling or fortified wine included); (3) 50 grams of perfume and ¼ liter of toilet water; and (4) other goods to a value of IR£34 per person (IR£17 per person for travelers under 15 years of age); you may import 12 liters of beer as part of this allowance.

Duty paid allowances increased substantially in 1993. Travelers are now entitled to purchase (1) 800 cigarettes, (2) 10 liters of spirits, (3) 45 liters of wine, and (4) 55 liters of beer. The allowances apply only to goods bought in shops in EU countries, including Britain and Northern Ireland, which already have the duty paid.

Goods that cannot be freely imported include firearms, ammunition, explosives, drugs (e.g., narcotics, amphetamines) and drug paraphernalia, indecent or obscene books and pictures, oral smokeless tobacco products, meat and meat products, poultry and poultry products, plants and plant products (including shrubs, vegetables, fruit, bulbs, and seeds), domestic cats and dogs from outside the United Kingdom, and live animals from outside Northern Ireland.

Language
Officially, Irish (Gaelic) is the first language of the Republic, but the everyday language of the vast majority of Irish people is English. Except for the northwest and parts of Connemara, where many signs are not translated, most signs in the country are written in Irish with an English translation underneath. There is one important exception to this rule, with which all visitors should familiarize themselves: FIR (pronounced *fear*) and MNÁ (pronounced muh-*naw*) translate, respectively, into "men" and "women." The *Gaelteacht* (pronounced *gale-tocked*)—areas in which Irish *is* the everyday language of most people—comprises only 6% of the land, and all its inhabitants are, in any case, bilingual.

Getting Around

By Car
ROAD CONDITIONS
Ireland is one country in which a car is more or less essential for successful travel. Despite improvements in public transportation, both the train and bus networks are limited, and many of the most intriguing areas are accessible only by car. Roads are reasonable, though the absence of turnpikes means that trip times can be long; on the other hand, you'll soon find that driving past an ever-changing and often dramatic series of unspoiled landscapes can be very much part of the fun. There's a bonus in the fact that traffic is normally light, though you can eas-

ily find yourself crawling down country lanes behind an ancient tractor or a flock of sheep. This is not a country for those with a taste for life in the fast lane.

All principal roads are designated by the letter *N*, meaning National Primary Road. Thus, the main highway north from Dublin is N1, the main highway northwest is N2, and so on. Road signs are usually in both Irish and English; in the northwest and Connemara, most are in Irish only, so make sure you have a good road map. Distances on the new green signposts are in kilometers; the old white signposts give distances in miles.

RULES OF THE ROAD
Driving is on the left. There is a general speed limit of 96 kph (60 mph) on most roads; in towns, the limit is 48 kph (30 mph). In some areas, the limit is 64 kph (40 mph); this is always clearly posted. At traffic circles, traffic from the right takes priority.

Seat belts must be worn by the driver and front-seat passengers. Children under 12 must ride in the back. The new (and controversial) drunk-driving laws are strict, restricting the driver to less than one pint of beer.

PARKING
Despite the relative lack of traffic, parking in towns is a real problem. Signs with the letter P indicate parking lots, but if there's a stroke through the P, keep away or you'll collect a stiff fine, normally around IR£25. After 6 PM, restrictions are lifted. Give lot attendants about 50p when you leave.

By Train
Iarnód Eireann (Irish Rail) and **Bus Eireann** (Irish Bus) are independent components of the state-owned public transportation company **Coras Iompair Eireann** (CIE). The rail network, although much cut back in the past 25 years, is still extensive, with main routes radiating from Dublin to Cork, Galway, Limerick, Tralee, Killarney, Westport, and Sligo; there is also a line for the north and Belfast. All trains are diesel; cars on principal expresses have air-conditioning. There are two classes on many trains—Super Standard (first class) and Standard (second class). Dining cars are carried on main expresses. There are no sleeping cars.

Speeds are slow in comparison with those of other European trains. Dublin, however, has a modern commuter train—the DART (Dublin Area Rapid Transit)—that runs south from the suburb of Howth through the city to Bray on the Wicklow coast and makes many stops along the way.

FARES
There is a **Rambler** ticket (rail and bus) for IR£78, valid for any eight days in a 15-day period. One- and four-day round-trip train tickets are also available at discounted rates. The **Irish Rover** ticket includes travel in Northern Ireland via rail, bus, and Ulsterbus; it costs IR£70 for five days' travel out of 15 consecutive days.

By Plane
Distances are not great in Ireland, so airplanes play only a small role in internal travel. There are daily flights from Dublin to Shannon, Cork, Waterford, Kerry, Knock, and Galway; all flights take around 30 minutes. There is frequent service to the Aran Islands, off Galway Bay, from Connemara Airport, Galway. The flight takes five minutes.

By Bus

For the strictly independent traveler, the 15-day **Rambler** ticket gives unlimited travel by bus and is an excellent value at IR£95. It can be purchased from any city bus terminal and is valid for travel on any 15 days in a 30-day period. The provincial bus system operated by Bus Eireann is widespread—more so than the train system—although service can be infrequent in remote areas. But the routes cover the entire country and are often linked to the train services. *See* By Train, *above,* for details of combined train and bus discount tickets.

By Boat

Exploring Ireland's lakes, rivers, and canals is a delightful, offbeat way to get to know the country. Motor cruisers can be chartered on the Shannon, the longest river in the British Isles. Bord Fáilte (the Irish Tourist Board, pronounced Board *Fall*-cha) has details of the wide choice of trips and operators available.

For drifting through the historic Midlands on the Grand Canal and River Barrow, contact **Celtic Canal Cruisers,** 24th Lock, Tullamore, County Offaly, tel. 0506/21861.

By Bicycle

Biking can be a great way to get around Ireland. Details of bicycle rentals are available from the Bord Fáilte. Rates average IR£7.50 per day or IR£35 per week. You must pay a IR£30 deposit. Be sure to make reservations, especially in July and August. If you rent a bike in the Republic, you may *not* take it into Northern Ireland; nor may you take a bike rented in Northern Ireland into the Republic.

Staying in Ireland

Telephones
LOCAL CALLS

There are pay phones in all post offices and most hotels and bars, as well as in street booths. Local calls cost 20p for three minutes, calls within Ireland cost about 50p for three minutes, and calls to Britain cost about IR£1.75 for three minutes. Telephone cards are available at all post offices and most newsagents. Prices range from IR£2 for 10 units to IR£8 for 50 units. Card booths are as common as coin booths. Rates go down by about a third after 6 PM and all day Saturday and Sunday.

INTERNATIONAL CALLS

For calls to the United States and Canada, dial 001 followed by the area code. For calls to the United Kingdom, dial 0044 followed by the number, dropping the beginning zero. To reach an **AT&T** long distance operator, dial 1–800/550–000; for **MCI,** dial 1–800/551–001; and for **Sprint,** dial 1–800/552–001.

COUNTRY CODE

The country code for the Republic of Ireland is 353.

Mail
POSTAL RATES

Airmail rates to the United States, Canada, and the Commonwealth are 52p for the first 10 grams, air letters 45p, and postcards 38p. Letters to Britain and continental Europe cost 32p, postcards 28p.

RECEIVING MAIL

A general delivery service is operated free of charge from Dublin's General Post Office (O'Connell St., Dublin 1, tel. 01/872–8888).

Shopping
VAT REFUNDS

Visitors from outside Europe can take advantage of the "cash-back" system on value-added tax (VAT) if their purchases total more than IR£50. A cash-back voucher must be filled out by the retailer at the point of sale. The visitor pays the total gross price, including VAT, and receives green and yellow copies of the invoice; both must be retained. These copies are presented to and stamped by customs, as you leave the country. Take the stamped form along to the cashier, and the VAT will be refunded.

Opening and Closing Times

Banks are open weekdays 10–4, and until 5 on selected days. In small towns they may close for lunch from 12:30–1:30.

Museums are usually open weekdays 10–5, Saturday 10–1, Sunday 2–5. Always make a point of checking, however, as hours can change unexpectedly.

Shops are open Monday–Saturday 9–5:30, closing earlier on Wednesday, Thursday, or Saturday, depending on the locality.

National Holidays

January 1 (New Year's); March 18 (St. Patrick's Day); April 5 (Good Friday); April 8 (Easter Monday); May 1 (May Day); June 3 (Whit Monday); August 5 (August Holiday); October 28 (October Holiday); and December 25–26 (Christmas). If you're planning a visit at Easter, remember that theaters and cinemas are closed for the last three days of the preceding week.

Dining

When it comes to food, Ireland has some of the best raw materials in the world: prime beef, locally raised lamb and pork, free-range poultry, game in season, abundant fresh seafood, and locally grown seasonal vegetables. Despite the near-legendary awfulness of much Irish cooking in the recent past, times are definitely changing, and a new generation of chefs is beginning to take greater advantage of this abundance of magnificent produce. In almost all corners of the country, you'll find a substantial choice of restaurants, many in hotels, serving fresh local food that is imaginatively prepared and served.

If your tastes run toward traditional Irish dishes, there are still a few old-fashioned restaurants serving substantial portions of excellent, if plain, home cooking. Look for boiled bacon and cabbage, Irish stew, and colcannon (cooked potatoes diced and fried in butter with onions and either cabbage or leeks and covered in thick cream just before serving). The best bet for daytime meals is "pub grub"—a choice of soup and soda bread, two or three hot dishes of the day, salad platters, or sandwiches. Most bars serve food, and a growing number offer coffee and tea as an alternative to alcohol. Guinness, a dark ale (also known as "stout") brewed with malt, is the Irish national drink. Even if you never go out for a drink at home, you should visit at least one or two pubs in Ireland. The pub is one of the pillars of Irish society, worth visiting as much for entertainment and conversation as for drinking.

MEALTIMES

Breakfast is served between 8 and 10—earlier by special request only—and is a substantial meal of cereal, bacon, eggs, sausage, and toast. Lunch is eaten between 12:30 and 2. The old tradition of "high tea" taken around 5, followed by a light snack before bed, is still encountered in many Irish homes, including many B&Bs. Elsewhere, however, it is generally assumed that you'll be eating between 7 and 9:30 and that this will be your main meal of the day.

WHAT TO WEAR
A jacket and tie or upscale casual dress are suggested for expensive restaurants. Otherwise casual dress is acceptable.

RATINGS
Prices are per person and include a first course, a main course, and dessert, but no wine or tip. Sales tax at 10% is included in all Irish restaurant bills. Some places, usually the more expensive establishments, add a 12% or 15% service charge, in which case no tip is necessary; elsewhere a tip of 10% is adequate. Highly recommended restaurants are indicated by a star ★.

CATEGORY	COST
$$$	over IR£28
$$	IR£16–IR£28
$	under IR£16

Lodging
Accommodations in Ireland range all the way from deluxe castles and renovated stately homes to thatched cottages and farmhouses to humble B&Bs. Standards everywhere are high, and they continue to rise. Pressure on hotel space reaches a peak between June and September, but it's a good idea to make reservations in advance at any time of the year, particularly at the more expensive spots. Rooms can be reserved directly from the United States; ask your travel agent for details. Bord Fáilte has a Central Reservations Service (14 Upper O'Connell St., Dublin 1, tel. 01/874–7733, fax 01/874–3660) that can make reservations, as can local tourist board offices.

Bord Fáilte has an official grading system and publishes a detailed price list of all approved accommodations, including hotels, guest houses, farmhouses, B&Bs, and hostels. No hotel may exceed this price without special authorization from Bord Fáilte; prices must also be displayed in every room. Don't hesitate to complain either to the manager or to Bord Fáilte, or both, if prices exceed this maximum.

In general, hotels charge per person. In most cases (but not all, especially in more expensive places), the price includes a full breakfast. VAT is included, but some hotels—again, usually the more expensive ones—add a 10–15% service charge. This should be mentioned in their price list. If it's not, a tip of between 10% and 15% is customary—if you think the service is worth it. In $$ and $ hotels, be sure to specify whether you want a private bath or shower; the latter is cheaper. Off-season (October–May) prices are reduced by as much as 25%.

GUEST HOUSES
Some smaller hotels are graded as guest houses. To qualify, they must have at least five bedrooms. A few may have restaurants; those that do not will often provide evening meals by arrangement. Few will have a bar. Otherwise these rooms can be as comfortable as those of a regular hotel, and in major cities they offer very good value for the money, compared with the $ hotels.

BED-AND-BREAKFASTS
Bed-and-breakfast means just that. The bed can vary from a four-poster in the wing of a castle to a feather bed in a whitewashed farmhouse or the spare bedroom of a modern cottage. Rates are generally around IR£16 per person, though these can vary significantly. Although many

larger B&Bs offer rooms with bath or shower, in some you'll have to use the bathroom in the hall and, in many cases, pay 50p–IR£1 extra for the privilege.

CAMPING

There are a variety of beautifully sited campgrounds and trailer parks, but be prepared for wet weather! All are listed in *Guest Accommodation* (IR£4), available from Bord Fáilte.

RATINGS

Prices are for two people in a double room, based on high season (June–September) rates. Highly recommended lodgings are indicated by a star ★.

CATEGORY	COST
$$$$	over IR£160
$$$	IR£120–IR£160
$$	IR£80–IR£120
$	under IR£80

Tipping

Other than in upscale hotels and restaurants, the Irish are not really used to being tipped. Some hotels and restaurants will add a service charge of about 12% to your bill, so tipping isn't necessary unless you've received particularly good service.

Tip taxi drivers about 10% of the fare if the taxi has been using its meter. For longer journeys, where the fare is agreed in advance, a tip will not be expected unless some kind of commentary (solicited or not) has been provided. In luxury hotels, porters and bellhops will expect IR£1; elsewhere, 50p is adequate. Hairdressers normally expect a tip of about IR£1. You don't tip in pubs, but if there is waiter service in a bar or hotel lounge, leave about 20p.

DUBLIN

Arriving and Departing

By Plane

All flights arrive at Dublin's Collinstown Airport, 10 kilometers (6 miles) north of town. For information on arrival and departure times, call individual airlines.

BETWEEN THE AIRPORT AND DOWNTOWN

Buses leave every 20 minutes from outside the Arrivals door for the central bus station in downtown Dublin. The ride takes about 30 minutes, depending on the traffic, and the fare is IR£2.50. A taxi ride into town will cost from IR£9 to IR£14, depending on the location of your hotel.

By Train

There are three main stations. Heuston Station (at Kingsbridge) is the departure point for the south and southwest; Connolly Station (at Amiens Street), for Belfast, the east coast, and the west; Pearse Station (on Westland Row), for Bray and connections via Dun Laoghaire to the Liverpool/Holyhead ferries. Call 01/836–6222 for information.

By Bus

The central bus station, Busaras, is at Store Street near the Custom House. Some buses terminate near O'Connell Bridge. Call 01/873–4222 for information on city services (Dublin Bus); dial 01/836–6111 for express buses and provincial services (Bus Eireann).

By Car
The main access route from the north is N1; from the west, N4; from the south and southwest, N7; from the east coast, N11. On all routes there are clearly marked signs indicating the center of the city:AN LÁR.

Getting Around

Dublin is small as capital cities go—the downtown area is positively compact—and the best way to see the city and soak in the full flavor is on foot.

By Train
An electric train commuter service, DART, serves the suburbs out to Howth, on the north side of the city, and to Bray, County Wicklow, on the south side. Fares are about the same as for buses. Street-direction signs to DART stations read STAISIUM/STATION. The **Irish Rail** office is at 35 Lower Abbey Street; for rail inquiries, call 01/836–6222.

By Bus
Most city buses originate in or pass through the area of O'Connell Street and O'Connell Bridge. If the destination board indicates AN LÁR, that means that the bus is going to the city center. Timetables (IR£2) are available from the **Dublin Bus** office (59 Upper O'Connell St., tel. 01/873–4222) and give details of all routes, times of operation, and price codes. The minimum fare is 55p.

By Taxi
Taxis do not cruise, but are located beside the central bus station, at train stations, at O'Connell Bridge, at St. Stephen's Green, at College Green, and near major hotels. They are not of a uniform type or color. Make sure the meter is on. The initial charge is IR£2; the fare is displayed in the cab. A one-mile trip in city traffic costs about IR£3.50.

Important Addresses and Numbers

Tourist Information
There is a tourist information office in the entrance hall of the **Bord Fáilte** headquarters (Baggot St. Bridge, tel. 01/676–5871; open weekdays 9–5). More conveniently located is the office at 14 Upper O'Connell Street (tel. 01/874–7733); open weekdays 9–5:30, Saturday 9–1. There is also an office at the airport (tel. 01/844–5387). From mid-June to September, there is an office at the Ferryport, Dun Laoghaire (tel. 01/280–6984).

Embassies
U.S. (42 Elgin Rd., Ballsbridge, tel. 01/688–8777), **Canadian** (65 St. Stephen's Green, tel. 01/478–1988), **U.K.** (33 Merrion Rd., tel. 01/269–5211).

Emergencies
Police (tel. 999), **Ambulance** (tel. 999), **Doctor** (tel. 01/679–0700), **Dentist** (tel. 01/679–4311), **Pharmacy** (Hamilton Long, 5 Upper O'-Connell St., tel. 01/874–8456).

Travel Agencies
American Express (116 Grafton St., tel. 01/677–2874), **Thomas Cook** (118 Grafton St., tel. 01/677–1721).

Guided Tours

Orientation Tours

Both **Bus Eireann** (tel. 01/836–6111) and **Gray Line Sightseeing** (tel. 01/661–9666) offer bus tours of Dublin and its surrounding areas. Both also offer three- and four-hour tours of the main sights in the city center. In summer **Dublin Bus** (tel. 01/873–4222) has a daily three-hour city-center tour using open-top buses in fine weather (IR£7). From mid-April through September Dublin Bus runs a continuous guided open-top bus tour (IR£5) that allows you to hop on and off the bus as often as you wish and visit some 15 sights along its route.

Special-Interest Tours

Bus Eireann has a "Traditional Irish Music Night" tour. **Elegant Ireland** (tel. 01/475–1665) organizes tours for groups interested in architecture and the fine arts; these include visits with the owners of some of Ireland's stately homes and castles.

Walking Tours

Most tourist offices have leaflets giving information on a selection of walking tours, including "Literary Dublin," "Georgian Dublin," and "Pub Tours." **Bord Fáilte** has a "Tourist Trail" walk, which takes in the main sites of central Dublin and can be completed in about three hours.

Excursions

Bus Eireann (tel. 01/836–6111) and **Gray Line Sightseeing** (tel. 01/661–9666) offer day-long tours into the surrounding countryside and longer tours elsewhere; price includes accommodations, breakfast, and admission costs. **CIE Tours International** offers vacations lasting from one to 10 days that include touring by train or bus, accommodations, and main meals. Costs range from around IR£240 (IR£345, including round-trip airfare from London) to IR£370 (IR£410 from London) for an eight-day tour in July and August.

Exploring Dublin

Numbers in the margin correspond to points of interest on the Dublin map.

Dublin is a small city with a population of just over 1 million. For all that, it has a distinctly cosmopolitan air, one that complements happily the individuality of the city and the courtesy and friendliness of its inhabitants. Originally a Viking settlement, Dublin is situated on the banks of the River Liffey. The Liffey divides the city north and south, with the more lively and fashionable spots, such as the Grafton Street shopping area, to be found on the south side. Most of the city's historically interesting buildings date from the 18th century, and, although many of its finer Georgian buildings disappeared in the overenthusiastic redevelopment of the '70s, enough remain, mainly south of the river, to recall the elegant Dublin of the past. The slums romanticized by writers Sean O'Casey and Brendan Behan have virtually been eradicated, but literary Dublin can still be recaptured by those who want to follow the footsteps of Leopold Bloom's progress, as described in James Joyce's *Ulysses*. And Trinity College, alma mater of Oliver Goldsmith, Jonathan Swift, and Samuel Beckett, among others, still provides a haven of tranquillity.

O'Connell Street

❶ Begin your tour of Dublin at **O'Connell Bridge,** the city's most central landmark. Look closely and you will notice a strange feature: The bridge is wider than it is long. The north side of O'Connell Bridge is dominated by an elaborate memorial to Daniel O'Connell, "The Liberator," erected as a tribute to the great 19th-century orator's achievement in securing Catholic Emancipation in 1829. Today **O'Connell Street** is the city's main shopping area. Turn left just beyond the General Post Office and take a look at Henry Street. This pedestrian-only shopping area leads to the colorful **Moore Street Market,** where street vendors recall their most famous ancestor, Molly Malone, by singing their wares—mainly flowers and fruit—in the traditional Dublin style.

2 The **General Post Office,** known as the GPO, occupies a special place in Irish history. It was from the portico of its handsome classical facade that Padraig Pearse read the Proclamation of the Republic on Easter Monday, 1916. You can still see the scars of bullets on its pillars from the fighting that ensued. The GPO remains the focal point for political rallies and demonstrations and is used as a viewing stand for VIPs during the annual St. Patrick's Day parade.

3 **The Gresham Hotel** has played a part in Dublin's history since 1817, although, along with the entire O'Connell Street area, it is less fashionable now than it was during the last century. Just south of the Gresham is the Bord Fáilte information office; drop in for a free street map, shopping guides, and information on all aspects of Dublin tourism. Opposite is the main office of Bus Eireann, which can supply bus timetables and information on excursions.

4 At the top of O'Connell Street is the **Rotunda,** the first maternity hospital in Europe, opened in 1755. Not much remains of the once-elegant Rotunda Assembly Rooms, a famous haunt of fashionable Dubliners until the mid-1800s. The **Gate Theater,** housed in an extension of the Rotunda Assembly Rooms, however, continues to attract crowds to its fine repertoire of classic Irish and European drama.

5 Beyond the Rotunda, you will have a fine vista of **Parnell Square,** one of Dublin's earliest Georgian squares. You will notice immediately that the first-floor windows of these elegant brick-face buildings are much larger than the others and that it is easy to look in from street level. This is more than simply the result of the architect's desire to achieve perfect proportions on the facades: These rooms were designed as reception rooms, and fashionable hostesses liked passersby to be able to peer in and admire the distinguished guests at their luxurious, candlelighted receptions.

6 **Charlemont House,** whose impressive Palladian facade dominates the top of Parnell Square, now houses the **Hugh Lane Municipal Gallery of Modern Art.** Sir Hugh Lane, a nephew of Lady Gregory, who was Yeats's curious, high-minded aristocratic patron, was a keen collector of Impressionist paintings. The gallery also contains some interesting works by Irish artists, including Yeats's brother Jack. *Parnell Sq., tel. 01/674–1903. Admission free. Open Tues.–Fri. 9:30–6, Sat. 9:30–5, Sun. 11–5.*

7 The Parnell Square area is rich in literary associations. They are explained and illustrated in the **Dublin Writers Museum,** which opened in 1991 in two carefully restored 18th-century buildings. Paintings, letters, manuscripts, and photographs relating to Joyce, O'Casey, Shaw, Yeats, Behan, Synge, and others are on permanent display. There are also temporary exhibitions, lectures, and readings, as well as a bookshop. *18–19 Parnell Sq. N, tel. 01/872–2077. Admission: IR£2.25. Open Mon.–Sat. 10–5, Sun. 1–5.*

⑧ Return to O'Connell Street, where a sign on the left will direct you to **St. Mary's Pro Cathedral,** the main Catholic church of Dublin. Try to catch the famous Palestrina Choir on Sunday at 11 AM. John McCormack is one of many famous voices to have sung with this exquisite

⑨ ensemble. Turn right, down Marlborough Street, to get to the **Abbey,** Ireland's national theater. Founded by W. B. Yeats and Lady Gregory in 1904, the original building was destroyed in a fire in 1951; the present theater was built in 1966. It has some noteworthy portraits and mementos in the foyer. Seats are usually available at about IR£12, and with luck you may just have a wonderful evening.

TIME OUT On Westmoreland Street is **Bewley's Coffee House** (there's another one nearby on Grafton Street), an institution that has been supplying Dubliners with coffee and buns since 1842. The aroma of coffee is irresistible, and the dark interior—with marble-top tables, original wood fittings, and stained-glass windows—evokes a more leisurely Dublin of the past. *12 Westmoreland St. and 78 Grafton St. Open Mon.–Sat. 9–5:30.*

Trinity and Stephen's Green

⑩ It is only a short walk across O'Connell Bridge to **Parliament House.** Today this stately, early 18th-century building is no more than a branch of the Bank of Ireland; originally, however, it housed the Irish Parliament. The original House of Lords, with its fine coffered ceiling and 1,233-piece Waterford glass chandelier, is open to the public during banking hours (weekdays 10–12:30 and 1:30–3). It's also worth taking a look at the main banking hall, whose judicial character—it was previously the Court of Requests—has been sensitively maintained.

⑪ Across the road is the facade of **Trinity College,** whose memorably atmospheric campus is a must for every visitor. Trinity College, Dublin (familiarly known as TCD) was founded by Elizabeth I in 1592 and offered a free education to Catholics—provided that they accepted the Protestant faith. As a legacy of this condition, right up until 1966, Catholics who wished to study at Trinity had to obtain a dispensation from their bishop or face excommunication. Today more than 70% of Trinity's students are Catholics, a clear indication of how far away those days seem to today's generation.

The facade, built between 1755 and 1759, consists of a magnificent portico with Corinthian columns. The design is repeated on the interior, so the view from outside the gates and from the quadrangle inside is the same. On the sweeping lawn in front of the facade are statues of two of the university's illustrious alumni—statesman Edmund Burke and poet Oliver Goldsmith. Other famous students include the philosopher George Berkeley, (who gave his name to the San Francisco-area campus of the University of California), Jonathan Swift, Thomas Moore, Oscar Wilde, John Millington Synge, Henry Grattan, Wolfe Tone, Robert Emmet, Bram Stoker, Edward Carson, Douglas Hyde, and Samuel Beckett.

The 18th-century building on the left, just inside the entrance, is the chapel. There's an identical building opposite, the Examination Hall. The oldest buildings are the library in the far right-hand corner and a row of redbrick buildings known as the Rubrics, which contain student apartments; both date from 1712.

Ireland's largest collection of books and manuscripts is housed in the **Trinity College Library.** There are 3 million volumes gathering dust here; about half a mile of new shelving has to be added every year to keep pace with acquisitions. The library is entered through the library shop.

666

Abbey Theatre, **9**

Archbishop Marsh's Library, **23**

Brown Thomas, **20**

Christ Church Cathedral, **25**

City Hall, **27**

Civic Museum, **22**

Custom House, **34**

Dublin Castle, **26**

Dublin Writers Museum, **7**

Four Courts, **33**

Genealogical Office, **18**

General Post Office, **2**

Gresham Hotel, **3**

Guinness Brewery, **29**

Ha'penny Bridge, **35**

Hugh Lane Municipal Gallery of Modern Art, **6**

Irish Whiskey Corner, **32**

Kilkenny Design Workshops, **12**

Leinster House, **15**

Merrion Square, **13**

National Gallery, **14**

National Library, **17**

National Museum, **16**

O'Connell Bridge, **1**

Parliament House, **10**

Parnell Square, **5**

Phoenix Park, **30**

Powerscourt Town House, **21**

Rotunda, **4**

Royal Hospital Kilmainham, **36**

Royal Irish Academy, **19**

St. Mary's Pro Cathedral, **8**

St. Michan's, **31**

St. Patrick's Cathedral, **24**

Temple Bar, **28**

Trinity College, **11**

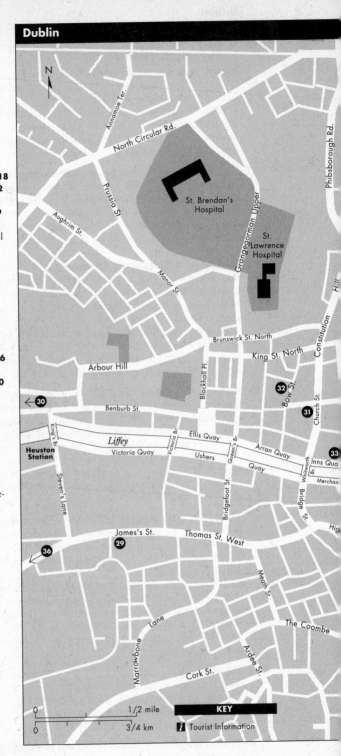

Dublin

N

North Circular Rd.

Annamoe Ter.

Prussia St.

Aughrim St.

St. Brendan's Hospital

Grangegorman Upper

St. Lawrence Hospital

Phibsborough Rd.

Manor St.

Constitution Hill

Brunswick St. North

King St. North

Arbour Hill

Blackhall Pl.

Bow St.

Church St.

32

31

Benburb St.

30 ←

King's Br.

Liffey

Ellis Quay

Victoria Br.

Arran Quay

Inns Qua

33

Heuston Station

Victoria Quay

Queen's Br.

Ushers

Quay

Merchan

Whitworth

Steven's Lane

Bridgefoot St.

Bridge St.

Hig

James's St.

Thomas St. West

Meath St.

36

29

Marrowbone Lane

The Coombe

Cork St.

Ardee St.

0 ___ 1/2 mile

0 ___ 3/4 km

KEY

i Tourist Information

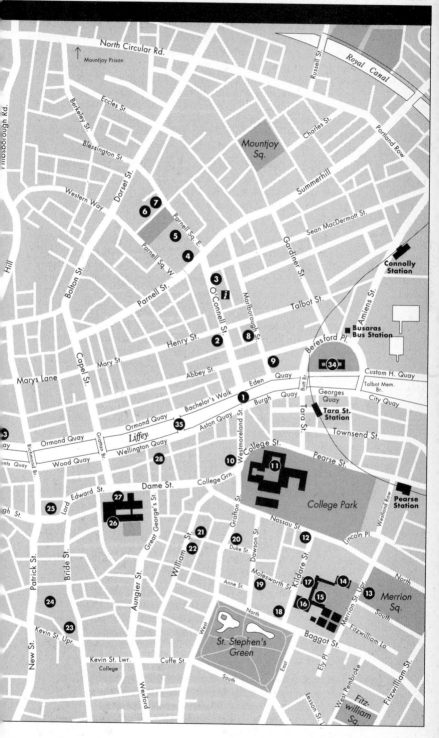

Its principal treasure is the **Book of Kells,** a beautifully illuminated manuscript of the Gospels dating from the 8th century. Because of the beauty and the fame of the Book of Kells, at peak hours you may have to wait in line to enter the library; it's less busy early in the day. Apart from the many treasures it contains, the aptly named **Long Room** is impressive in itself, stretching for 213 feet and housing 200,000 of the library's volumes, mostly manuscripts and old books. Originally it had a flat plaster ceiling, but the perennial need for more shelving resulted in a decision to raise the level of the roof and add the barrel-vaulted ceiling and the gallery bookcases. *Tel. 01/677–2941. Admission: IR£2.50. Open Mon.–Sat. 9:30–4:45, Sun. noon–5.*

In the Thomas Davis Theatre in the Arts Building, The **"Dublin Experience"** is an audiovisual presentation devoted to the history of the city over the last 1,000 years. *Tel. 01/677–2941. Admission: IR£2.75 (IR£5 with library). Open May–Oct., daily 10–5. Shows every hr on the hr.*

Leave Trinity by the Nassau Street exit, a covered way beside the Arts Block. Shoppers will find a detour along Nassau Street in order here. As well as being well endowed with bookstores, it contains the **Kilkenny Design Workshops,** which, besides selling the best in contemporary Irish design for the home, also holds regular exhibits of exciting new work by Irish craftsmen. *Nassau St. Open Mon.–Sat. 9–5.*

TIME OUT The **Kilkenny Kitchen,** a self-service restaurant on the first floor of the Kilkenny Design Workshops, overlooking the playing fields of Trinity, is an excellent spot for a quick, inexpensive lunch in modern, design-conscious surroundings. The emphasis is on natural fresh foods and home baking. *Nassau St. Open Mon.–Sat. 9–5.*

Nassau Street will lead you into **Merrion Square,** past a distinctive corner house that was the home of Oscar Wilde's parents. Merrion Square is one of the most pleasant in Dublin. Its flower gardens are well worth a visit in summer. Note the brightly colored front doors and the intricate fanlights above them—a distinctive feature of Dublin's domestic architecture.

The **National Gallery** is the first in a series of important buildings on the west side of the square. It is one of Europe's most agreeable and compact galleries, with more than 2,000 works on view, including a major collection of Irish landscape painting, 17th-century French works, paintings from the Italian and Spanish schools, and a collection of Dutch masters. *Merrion Sq., tel. 01/661–5133. Admission free. Open Mon.–Sat 10–5:30, Thurs. until 8:30, Sun. 2–5.*

Next door is **Leinster House,** seat of the Irish Parliament. This imposing 18th-century building has two facades: Its Merrion Square facade is designed in the style of a country house, while the other facade, in Kildare Street, is in the style of a town house. Visitors may be shown the house when Dáil Eireann (pronounced dawl Erin), the Irish Parliament, is not in session.

TIME OUT A half-block detour to your left, between Merrion Square and Stephen's Green, will bring you to the door of **Doheny & Nesbitt's,** an old Victorian-style bar whose traditional "snugs"—individual wood-paneled booths—are popular any time. Usually noisy and smoky, but always friendly, it is one of the few authentic pubs left in the city.

Stephen's Green, as it is always called by Dubliners, suffered more from the planning blight of the philistine '60s than did its neighbor, Merrion Square. An exception is the magnificent **Shelbourne Hotel,** which dominates the north side of the green. It is still as fashionable—and as expensive—as ever.

TIME OUT Budget-conscious visitors should put on their finery and try afternoon tea in the elegant splendor of the Shelbourne's **Lord Mayor's Room.** You can experience its old-fashioned luxury for around IR£9 (including sandwiches and cakes) per head.

Around the corner on Kildare Street, the town-house facade of Leinster House is flanked by the **National Museum** (admission free; open Tues.–Sat. 10–5, Sun. 2–5) and the **National Library,** each featuring a massive colonnaded rotunda entrance built in 1890. The museum houses a remarkable collection of Irish treasures from 6000 BC to the present, including the Tara Brooch, the Ardagh Chalice, and the Cross of Cong. Every major figure in modern Irish literature, from James Joyce onward, studied in the National Library at some point. In addition to a comprehensive collection of Irish authors, it contains extensive newspaper archives. *Kildare St., tel. 01/661–8811. Admission free. Open Mon. 10–9, Tues.–Wed. 2–9, Thurs.–Fri. 10–5, Sat. 10–1.*

The **Genealogical Office**—the starting point for ancestor-tracing—also incorporates the **Heraldic Museum,** which features displays of flags, coins, stamps, silver, and family crests that highlight the uses and development of heraldry in Ireland. *2 Kildare St., tel. 01/661–8811. Genealogical Office: Open weekdays 10–5. Heraldic Museum: Admission free. Open weekdays 10–12:30 and 2:30–4. Guided tours Mar.–Oct., cost IR£1.*

The **Royal Irish Academy,** on Dawson Street, is the country's leading learned society; it has many important manuscripts in its unmodernized 18th-century library (open weekdays 9:30–5:15). Just below the academy is **Mansion House,** the official residence of the Lord Mayor of Dublin. Its Round Room was the location of the first assembly of Dáil Eireann in January 1919. It is now used mainly for exhibitions.

Grafton Street, which runs between Stephen's Green and Trinity College, has inherited O'Connell Street's reputation as the city's premier shopping street. Check out **Brown Thomas,** Ireland's most elegant and old-fashioned department store; it has an extremely good selection of sporting goods and Waterford crystal—an odd combination. Many of the more stylish boutiques are just off the main pedestrian-only areas, so be sure to poke around likely—and unlikely— corners. Don't miss the **Powerscourt Town House,** an imaginative shopping arcade installed in and around the covered courtyard of an impressive 18th-century building. Nearby is the **Civic Museum,** which contains drawings, models, maps of Dublin, and other civic memorabilia. *58 S. William St., tel. 01/679–4260. Admission free. Open Tues.–Sat. 10–6, Sun. 11–2.*

A short walk from Stephen's Green will bring you to one of the smaller and more unusual gems of old Dublin, **Archbishop Marsh's Library.** It was built in 1701, and access is through a tiny but charming cottage garden. Its interior has been unchanged for more than 300 years and still contains "cages" into which scholars who wanted to peruse rare books were locked. (The cages were to discourage students who, often impecunious, may have been tempted to make the books their own.) *St. Patrick's Close, tel. 01/454–8511. Open Mon., Wed., and Fri. 10–12:45 and 2–4, Sat. 10:30–12:45.*

Opposite, on Patrick Street, is **St. Patrick's Cathedral.** Legend has it that St. Patrick baptized many converts at a well on the site of the cathedral in the 5th century. The building dates from 1190 and is mainly early English Gothic in style. At 305 feet, it is the longest church in the country. Its history has not always been happy. In the 17th century, Oliver Cromwell, dour ruler of England and no friend of the Irish, had his troops stable their horses in the cathedral. It wasn't until the 19th century that restoration work to repair the damage was begun. St. Patrick's is the national cathedral of the Protestant Church of Ireland and has had many illustrious deans. The most famous was Jonathan Swift, author of *Gulliver's Travels,* who held office from 1713 to 1745. Swift's tomb is in the south aisle, and Dean Swift's corner at the top of the north transept contains his pulpit, his writing table and chair, his portrait, and his death mask. Memorials to many other celebrated figures from Ireland's past line the walls of St. Patrick's. *Patrick St., tel. 01/475–4817. Admission: IR£1.*

㉕ St. Patrick's originally stood outside the walls of Dublin. Its close neighbor, **Christ Church Cathedral** (Christ Church Rd.), on the other hand, stood just within the walls and belonged to the See of Dublin. It is for this reason that the city has two cathedrals so close to one another. Christ Church was founded in 1172 by Strongbow, a Norman baron and conqueror of Dublin for the English crown, and it took 50 years to build. Strongbow himself is buried in the cathedral beneath an impressive effigy. The vast, sturdy **crypt** is Dublin's oldest surviving structure and should not be missed.

㉖ Signs in the Christ Church area will lead you to **Dublin Castle.** Guided tours of the lavishly furnished state apartments are offered every half hour and provide one of the most enjoyable sightseeing experiences in town. Only fragments of the original 13th-century building survive; the elegant castle you see today is essentially an 18th-century building. The state apartments were formerly the residence of the English viceroys and are now used by the president of Ireland to entertain visiting heads of state. The state apartments are closed when in official use, so phone first to check. *Off Dame St., tel. 01/677–7129. Admission: IR£2.50. Open weekdays 10–12:15 and 2–5, weekends 2–5.*

㉗ Step into the **City Hall** on Dame Street to admire the combination of grand classical ornament and understated Georgian simplicity in its circular main hall. It also contains a good example of the kind of gently curving Georgian staircase that is a typical feature of most large town houses in Dublin.

㉘ Between Dame Street and the River Liffey is a new semipedestrianized area known as **Temple Bar,** the city's version of the Latin Quarter, which should interest anyone who wants to discover "young Dublin." The area is chock-full of small, imaginative shops; innovative art galleries; and inexpensive restaurants.

㉙ The **Guinness Brewery,** founded by Arthur Guinness in 1759 and covering 60 acres, dominates the area to the west of Christ Church. Guinness is proud of its brewery and invites visitors to attend a 30-minute film shown in a converted hops store next door to the brewery itself. After the film, you can sample the famous black beverage. *Guinness Hop Store, Crane St., tel. 01/453–6700. Admission: IR£2.50. Open weekdays 10–3.*

Phoenix Park and the Liffey

㉚ Across the Liffey is the **Phoenix Park,** 1,760 acres of green open space. Though the park is open to all, it has only two residents: the president of Ireland and the American ambassador. The park is dominated by a 210-foot-tall obelisk, a tribute to the first duke of Wellington. Sunday is the best time to visit: Games of cricket, soccer, polo, baseball, hurling—a combination of lacrosse, baseball, and field hockey—or Irish football will be in progress.

Returning to the city's central area along the north bank of the Liffey, you pass through a fairly run-down section that's scheduled for major **③** redevelopment. A diversion up Church Street to **St. Michan's** will be relished by those with a macabre turn of mind. Open coffins in the vaults beneath the church reveal mummified bodies, some more than 900 years old. The sexton, who can be found at the church gate on weekdays, will guide you around the church and crypt.

③ **Irish Whiskey Corner** is just behind St. Michan's. A 90-year-old warehouse has been converted into a museum to introduce visitors to the pleasures of Irish whiskey. There's an audiovisual show and free tasting. *Bow St., tel. 01/872–5566. Admission: IR£3. Tours weekdays at 3:30 or by appointment.*

The Liffey has two of Dublin's most famous landmarks, both of them the work of 18th-century architect James Gandon and both among the **③** city's finest buildings. The first is the **Four Courts,** surmounted by a massive copper-covered dome, giving it a distinctive profile. It is the seat of the High Court of Justice of Ireland. The building was completed between 1786 and 1802, then gutted in the Civil War of the '20s; it has since been painstakingly restored. You will recognize the same ar-**③** chitect's hand in the **Custom House,** farther down the Liffey. Its graceful dome rises above a central portico, itself linked by arcades to the pavilions at either end. Behind this useful and elegant landmark is an altogether more workaday structure, the central bus station, Busaras.

Midway between Gandon's two masterpieces is the Metal Bridge, oth-**③** erwise known as the **Ha'penny Bridge,** so called because, until early in this century, a toll of a half-penny was charged to cross it. The poet W. B. Yeats was one among many Dubliners who found this too high a price to pay—more a matter of principle than of finance—and so made the detour via O'Connell Bridge. Today no such high-minded concern need prevent you from marching out to the middle of the bridge to admire the view up and down the Liffey as it winds its way through the city.

③ The **Royal Hospital Kilmainham** is a short ride by taxi or bus from the center; it's well worth the trip. The hospital is considered the most important 17th-century building in Ireland and has recently been renovated. It was completed in 1684 as a hospice—the original meaning of the term "hospital"—for veteran soldiers. Note especially the chapel with its magnificent Baroque ceiling. It also houses the **Irish Museum of Modern Art,** which opened in 1991. Parts of the old building, used as a national cultural center, are occasionally closed to the public. *District of Kilmainham, tel. 01/671–8666. Exhibitions: open Tues.–Sat. 10–5:30, Sun. noon–5:30. Tours: Sun. noon–5 and holidays 2–5; cost IR£2.*

Off the Beaten Track

It is all too easy for the visitor to forget how close Dublin is to the sea: Take advantage of fine weather and visit the fishing village of **Howth**— it's easily reached on the DART train—and watch the fishermen mending their nets on the pier. Or take the DART in the opposite direction to **Sandycove,** where intrepid all-weather swimmers brave the waves at the men-only **Forty Foot** bathing beach.

Devotees of James Joyce may find Sandycove a worthwhile detour, for it was here, in a Martello tower (a circular fortification built by the British as a defense against possible invasion by Napoléon at the beginning of the 19th century), that the maverick Irish genius lived for some months in 1904. It now houses the **Joyce Museum.** *Sandycove Coast. Admission: IR£1.50 adults, 60p children. Open Apr.–Oct., Mon.–Sat. 10–1 and 2–5, Sun. 2:30–6. Also by appointment, tel. 01/280–8571.*

The **Irish Jewish Museum** was opened in 1985 by Chaim Herzog, former president of Israel and an ex-Dubliner himself, and displays memorabilia of the Irish-Jewish community covering approximately 120 years of history. *3–4 Walworth Rd., tel. 01/453–1797. Open Sun. 10:30–2:30. Also by appointment, tel. 01/676–0737 or 01/455–5452.*

Shopping

Although the rest of the country is well supplied with crafts shops, Dublin is the place to seek out more specialized items—antiques, traditional sportswear, haute couture, designer ceramics, books and prints, silverware and jewelry, and designer hand-knit items.

Shopping Districts
The most sophisticated shopping area is around **Grafton Street:** The new **St. Stephen's Green Center** contains 70 stores, large and small, in a vast Moorish-style glass-roof building on the Grafton Street corner. **Molesworth** and **Dawson streets** are the places to browse for antiques; **Nassau** and **Dawson streets,** for books; the smaller cross side streets for jewelry, art galleries, and old prints. The pedestrianized **Temple Bar** area, with its young, offbeat ambience, has a number of small art galleries, specialty shops (including music and books), and inexpensive and adventurous clothes shops. The area is further enlivened by buskers (street musicians) and street artists.

Department Stores
The shops north of the river tend to be less expensive and less design-conscious; chain stores and lackluster department stores make up the bulk of them. The **ILAC Shopping Center,** on Henry Street, is worth a look, however. **Clery's,** on O'Connell Street (directly opposite the GPO), was once the city's most fashionable department store and is still worth a visit, despite its rapidly aging decor. **Switzers** and **Brown Thomas** are Grafton Street's main department stores; the latter is Dublin's most elegantly decorated department store, with many international fashion labels on sale. **Arnotts,** on Henry Street, is Dublin's largest department store and has a good range of cut crystal. Visit **Kilkenny Design Workshops** on Nassau Street for the best selection of Irish designs for the home.

Tweeds and Woolens
Ready-made tweeds for men can be found at **Kevin and Howlin,** on Nassau Street, and at **Cleo Ltd.,** on Kildare Street. The **Blarney Woollen Mills,** on Nassau Street, has a good selection of tweed, linen, and woolen sweaters in all price ranges. The **Woolen Mills,** at Ha'penny Bridge, has a good selection of handknits and other woolen sweaters at competitive prices.

Dining

The restaurant scene in Dublin has improved beyond recognition in recent years. Though no one is ever likely to confuse the place with, say, Paris, the days of chewy boiled meats and soggy, tasteless vegetables are long gone. Food still tends to be substantial rather than subtle, but more and more restaurants are at last taking advantage of the magnificent livestock and fish that Ireland has in such abundance. For details and price-category definitions, *see* Dining *in* Staying in Ireland, *above.*

$$$ Celtic Mews. This long-established oasis of calm is in a Georgian mews off Baggot Street. A deep wine-color interior is the backdrop for a collection of fine antiques, and tuxedo-clad waiters provide full silver service at polished or white-clothed tables. Despite the elegance of the setting, the atmosphere is cozy and informal. The chefs have successfully blended classical French and Irish cooking styles, with cuisine ranging from the very rich—Celtic filet mignon, cooked at the table and served in a whiskey-and-cream sauce—to upscale versions of traditional dishes such as Irish stew made with center loin chops. *109A Lower Baggot St., tel. 01/676–0796. Reservations advised. AE, DC, MC, V. Closed Sun. and holidays. No lunch Sat.*

$$$ The Commons Restaurant. In the basement of the Georgian showplace Newman House, you will find this elegantly modern restaurant, where the cream-and-dark-blue walls are hung with specially commissioned Irish art, and French windows open onto a patio used for al fresco lunches. The menu is international with French and Middle-Eastern influences; main courses lean toward fish, but other favorites include lamb cutlets roasted in garlic and thyme. *85–86 St. Stephen's Green, tel. 01/478–0530. Reservations required. AE, DC, MC, V. Closed Sun. and holidays. No lunch Sat.*

$$$ Ernie's. This luxurious place is built around a small floodlighted courtyard shaded by an imposing mulberry tree. The rustic interior's granite walls and wood beams are adorned by 135 paintings of Kerry, where, for generations, the late Ernie Evans's family ran the famous Glenbeigh Hotel. The Evans family serves generous portions of the very best seafood—try scallops Mornay or prawns in garlic butter—and steaks. *Mulberry Gardens, Donnybrook, tel. 01/269–3300. Reservations advised. AE, DC, MC, V. Closed Sun., Mon. No lunch Sat.*

$$$ King Sitric. Owner-chef Aidan MacManus's quay-side restaurant in the
★ fishing village-cum-suburb of Howth is a 20-minute ride north of Dublin by DART or cab. It's worth the journey to taste the succulent selection of locally caught seafood; try the turbot with saffron or the wild Irish salmon steaks with Hollandaise sauce. You eat in the quietly elegant Georgian dining room of the former harbormaster's house. *East Pier, Howth, tel. 01/832–5235. Reservations advised. AE, DC, MC, V. Dinner only. Closed Sun., holidays, Dec. 24–Jan. 1, and wk preceding Easter.*

$$$ Le Coq Hardi. Award-winning owner-chef John Howard is noted for
★ his wine cellar and for such specialties as Coq Hardi smokies—smoked haddock marbled with tomato, cream, and cheese—and (in season) roast loin of venison with fresh cranberries and port wine. The seriousness of the cooking is complemented by the polished wood and brass and the gleaming mirrors of the sumptuous interior. *35 Pembroke Rd., Ballsbridge, tel. 01/268–9070. Reservations required. AE, DC, MC, V. Closed Sun.*

$$$ Patrick Guilbaud. This is an authentic, rather formal French restaurant with a consistently good reputation, decked out in a refreshing combination of pink, white, and green with hanging plants. The emphasis is firmly on traditional bourgeois cuisine; the Gallic connection is reinforced by the all-French staff. *46 James Pl., tel. 01/676–4192. Reservations advised. AE, DC, MC, V. Closed Sun., Mon., and holidays.*

$$ Elephant & Castle. American visitors may be familiar with the New York cousin of this "Left Bank" restaurant. Traditional American food on an eclectic and flavorful menu incorporates everything from spicy nachos to ginger-laced stir fry and a wide assortment of tasty omelets. The diner-style decor is sparse, the noise level high, and the portions large—but this suits the typically voracious clientele. The central location attracts a young crowd. *18 Temple Bar, tel. 01/679–3121. No reservations. AE, DC, MC, V.*

$$ La Pigalle. This is a charming, unpretentious French restaurant in an old and crooked building that forms part of the archway leading to the Ha'penny Bridge. It is in the heart of, and very much part of, the Temple Bar area scene. The decor is old-fashioned and well-worn, the atmosphere relaxed and the food authentically French, with a menu that changes daily. Typical dishes include fresh asparagus tart, sea trout fillet with sorrel and muscadet, and duck breast with apples and calvados. *14 Temple Bar, tel. 01/671–9262. Reservations advised. MC, V. No lunch Sat. Closed Sun.*

$$ Le Caprice. This Italian restaurant with busy decor and white linen tablecloths is right in the city center. The menu includes traditional Continental dishes such as prawn cocktail, deep-fried scampi, and roast duckling a l'orange, as well as an interesting selection of authentic Italian dishes including pasta and veal. This place can develop a real party atmosphere later in the evening if the pianist is in the right mood. *12 St. Andrew's St., tel. 01/679–4050. Reservations accepted. AE, DC, MC, V. Dinner only.*

$ Bad Ass Café. Definitely one of Dublin's loudest restaurants, this barnlike place in the trendy Temple Bar area, between the Central Bank and the Ha'penny Bridge, is always a fun place to eat. American-style fast food—burgers, chili, and pizzas—and the pounding rock music attract a lively crowd, both the young and the young at heart. Look out for the old-fashioned cash shuttles whizzing around the ceiling! *9–11 Crown Alley, tel. 01/671–2596. Reservations for large parties advised. AE, MC, V. Closed Good Fri., and Dec. 25–26.*

$ Cornucopia Wholefoods. This recently refurbished vegetarian restaurant above a health-food shop provides good value for the money in simple rustic surroundings. It's popular with students from nearby Trinity College. The menu includes red lentil soup, avocado quiche, vegetarian spring rolls, and vegetarian curry—all of them regular favorites. *19 Wicklow St., tel. 01/677–7583. No reservations. No credit cards. Closed Sun.*

$ Gallagher's Boxty House. Located behind the Central Bank in the lively Temple Bar area, this highly original Irish eatery has a country cottage ambience, with antique pine furniture complementing the dark green decor. Boxty is a traditional Irish potato bread or cake that is served here as a pancake thin enough to wrap around savory fillings such as bacon and cabbage, chicken with leeks, and smoked fish. Follow these with "Bailey's and brown bread" ice cream or the superb bread-and-butter pudding. *20 Temple Bar, tel. 01/677–2762. No reservations. V.*

$ Pizzeria Italia. This tiny, one-room pizza-bar and restaurant is decorated in the red, white, and green of the Italian flag and adorned by a nostalgia-provoking collection of Italian travel posters. It is all delightfully cheap and cheerful: Either take a place at the one large central table or perch on a bar stool at a wall-side counter. The delicious herbal aromas signal a good selection of freshly prepared pizzas and classic pasta dishes, but there is also a choice of light snacks, steaks, ribs, and chicken at very reasonable prices. *22 Temple Bar, tel. 01/677–8528. No reservations. No credit cards. Closed Sun.and Mon.*

Pub Food

All the pubs listed here serve food at lunchtime; some also have food in the early evening. They form an important part of the dining scene in Dublin and make a pleasant and informal alternative to a restaurant meal. In general, a one-course meal should not cost much more than IR£4–IR£5, but a full meal will put you in the lower range of the **$$** category. In general, credit cards are not accepted.

Barry Fitzgerald's. Salads and a freshly cooked house special are available in the upstairs bar at lunch on weekdays. Pretheater dinners are served in the early evening. *90 Marlborough St., tel. 01/677–4082.*

Davy Byrne's. James Joyce immortalized Davy Byrne's in his sprawling novel *Ulysses*. Nowadays it's more akin to a cocktail bar than a Dublin pub, but it's good for fresh and smoked salmon, salads, and a hot daily special. Food is available at lunchtime and in the early evening. *21 Duke St., tel. 01/671–1298.*

Kitty O'Shea's. Kitty O'Shea's cleverly, if a little artificially, recreates the atmosphere of old Dublin. *23–25 Grand Canal St., tel. 01/660–9965.*

Thomas Read's. This new Continental-style bar serves a wide variety of atypical pub grub, including hot bagels, danishes, and Parma ham. The coffees, especially the megaccino (a jumbo-size cappuccino), are particularly good. *Corner of Dame and Parliament Sts., tel. 677–2504.*

Old Stand. Located conveniently close to Grafton Street, the Old Stand offers grilled food, including steaks. *37 Exchequer St., tel. 01/677–0821.*

Lodging

Although only a few major hotels have opened in Dublin in the past few years, considerable investment in redevelopment, updating of facilities, and refurbishing of some of the older establishments is taking place. As in most major cities, there is a shortage of mid-range accommodations. For value-for-the-money, try one of the registered guest houses; in most respects they are indistinguishable from small hotels. Most economical of all is the B&B. Both guest houses and B&Bs tend to be in suburban areas—generally a 10-minute bus ride from the center of the city. This is not in itself a great drawback, and savings can be significant.

Bord Fáilte (14 Upper O'Connell St.) can usually help if you find yourself without reservations.

For details and price-category definitions, *see* Lodging *in* Staying in Ireland, *above.*

$$$$ **Berkeley Court.** The most quietly elegant of Dublin's large modern hotels, Berkeley Court is located in Ballsbridge—a leafy suburb about a 10-minute cab ride from the center of town. Its new conservatory gives freshness and spaciousness to the atmosphere of the public rooms; among the other new features are five luxury suites, each with its own Jacuzzi. *Lansdowne Rd., Ballsbridge, Dublin 4, tel. 01/660–1711, fax 01/661–7238. 157 rooms with bath, 29 suites. Facilities: 2 restaurants, bar, minigym, conference center, parking. AE, DC, MC, V.*

$$$$ **Conrad.** A subsidiary of Hilton Hotels, the Conrad is firmly aimed at the international business executive. The seven-story redbrick and smoked-glass building is well located just off Stephen's Green. The spacious rooms are decorated in light brown and pastel shades of green, and the bathrooms are fitted in Spanish marble. Alfie Byrne's, the main bar, attempts to re-create the traditional Irish pub atmosphere in spite of its high-powered clientele. *Earlsfort Terrace, tel. 01/676–5555, fax 01/676–5076. 190 rooms with bath. Facilities: restaurant, 2 bars, cof-*

fee shop, sauna, gym, sporting facilities available by arrangement, parking. AE, DC, MC, V.

$$$$ **Shelbourne.** The Shelbourne is one of Europe's grand old hotels whose
★ guest book contains names ranging from the Dalai Lama and Princess Grace to Laurel and Hardy, Richard Burton, and Peter O'Toole. In the bustling open lobby, the blazing open fire—flanked by two huge rose brocade sofas—is proof that the Shelbourne has not lost the sense of grandeur of its past. Between 1986 and 1988, IR£7 million was lavished on major refurbishment, which included restoring many original Georgian features and emphasizing them with luxurious drapes and a prominently displayed collection of fine antiques and heirlooms. A supplement is charged for rooms overlooking the leafy but busy green; the back bedrooms without views are far quieter, however. 27 Stephen's Green, tel. 01/676–6471, fax 01/661–6006. 165 rooms with bath. Facilities: 2 bars, restaurant, sporting facilities available by arrangement. AE, DC, MC, V.

$$$ **Burlington.** Dublin's largest hotel is popular with American tour groups and Irish and European business travelers. It is about five minutes by car from the city's central area. At night the Burlington's disco and Irish cabaret turn it into a lively spot for overseas visitors. Bedrooms are the usual modern plush in neutral tones. Upper Leeson St., tel. 01/660–5222, fax 01/660–8496. 477 rooms with bath. Facilities: restaurant, 2 bars, disco, and cabaret. AE, DC, MC, V.

$$$ **Hibernian.** An early 20th-century Edwardian nurses' home was converted into this hotel in 1993. The distinctive red-and-amber brick facade has been retained, and every room is a different shape, decorated in light pastel shades with deep-pile carpets. The public rooms are slightly small, but are attractively done in cheerful chintz and stripes. There is a library off the lobby and a small restaurant that provides intimate dinners and lunches. Eastmoreland Pl., off Upper Baggot St., Dublin 4, tel. 01/668–7666, fax 01/660–2655. 30 rooms. Facilities: restaurant, bar. AE, DC, MC, V.

$$$ **Jury's.** This lively, fashionable spot has more atmosphere than most comparable modern hotels. It's a short cab ride from the center of town. Bedrooms are relatively spacious, and each comes with a picture-window view of town. Exclusive facilities for businesspeople are provided in the 100-room Towers annex. Ballsbridge, Dublin 4, tel. 01/660–5000, fax 01/660–5540. 390 rooms with bath. Facilities: 3 restaurants, 2 bars, cabaret May–Oct., indoor/outdoor pool, Jacuzzi. AE, DC, MC, V.

$$$ **Westbury.** This comfortable, modern hotel has an excellent location right off the fashionable shopping mecca of Grafton Street. The spacious main lobby on the mezzanine level is furnished with attractive antiques and large sofas, on which guests sit to take afternoon tea. Bedrooms are rather utilitarian with pastel color schemes; the suites, which combine European decor with Japanese prints and screens, are more inviting. The flowery Russell Room serves formal lunches and dinners; the Sandbank, a ground floor seafood bar is less enticing. Grafton St., Dublin 2, tel. 01/679–1122, fax 01/679–7078. 195 rooms with bath, 8 suites. Facilities: 2 restaurants. AE, DC, MC, V.

$$ **Ariel Guest House.** This is Dublin's leading guest house, just a block
★ from the elegant Berkeley Court and a 10-minute walk from Stephen's Green. The lobby lounge and restaurant of this Victorian villa are furnished with leather and mahogany heirlooms, as are most of the spacious bedrooms, 13 of which were added to the house in 1991. This is a good bet if you're in town for a leisurely, relaxing holiday. 52 Lansdowne Rd., tel. 01/668–5512, fax 01/668–5845. 27 rooms with bath. Facilities: refreshments, parking. MC, V. Closed Dec. 21–Jan. 31.

$$ Lansdowne. In the leafy suburb of Ballsbridge, convenient to the city center, this small establishment offers a very friendly ambience. The cozy, modest rooms are painted in pastel shades, and have all the basics. The basement bar is a popular hangout for local businesspeople and fans of the international rugby matches held at nearby Lansdowne Road; photos of sporting personalities hang on the walls. Parker's Restaurant is better than the average hotel spot and specializes in steaks and seafood. *27 Pembroke Rd., Dublin 4, tel. 01/688–4079, fax 01/688–5585. 28 rooms. Facilities: restaurant, bar. AE, DC, MC, V.*

$$ Temple Bar. Previously a city center bank, these premises were converted into this well-appointed hotel in 1993. Although the decor is unexceptional, the triangular shape of the building on the corner of two streets makes the layout rather interesting. It is just around the corner from Trinity College and on the edge of the lively Temple Bar district. Busker's Pub is a popular street-level bar, and there is also a quieter lounge bar and a conservatory-style restaurant and coffee shop. *Fleet St., Temple Bar, Dublin 2, tel. 01/677–3333, fax 01/677–3088. 108 rooms with bath. Facilities: restaurant, 2 bars. AE, DC, MC, V.*

$ Dublin International Youth Hostel. Housed in a converted convent, it offers dormitory accommodations (up to 25 people per room) and also family-size rooms that can take up to four people. This is a spartan, low-cost alternative to hotels. Nonmembers of the youth hostelling organization can stay for a small extra charge. The hostel is north of Parnell Square, near the Mater Hospital. *51 Mountjoy St., Dublin 1, tel. 01/830–1766, fax 01/830–1600. 500 beds. Facilities: restaurant. No credit cards.*

$ Isaac Tourist Hotel. This cheap cheerful alternative for budget travelers provides either bunk beds in small dormitories or private rooms from about IR£6 per person. At the top of the range here—about IR£17 per night—there are eight rooms en suite available for singles and doubles. *2 Frenchman's La., Dublin 1, tel. 01/836–3877, fax 01/874–1574. 21 private rooms, 16 dormitory rooms. Facilities: restaurant. No credit cards.*

$ Jury's Christchurch Inn. Jury's has now introduced functional budget hotels into its hitherto upscale hotel chain. There are very few frills, but this hotel does offer good value for sharers, with a fixed room rate for up to three adults or two adults and two children. The main advantage is the pleasant location, facing Christ Church Cathedral and within walking distance of most city center attractions. The rooms are decorated in pastel colors with utilitarian furniture. A bar offers a pub lunch, and the restaurant serves breakfast and dinner. *Christchurch Pl., Dublin 8, tel. 01/475–0111, fax 01/475–0488. 183 rooms. Facilities: restaurant, bar, parking (fee). AE, DC, MC, V.*

$ Kilronan House. This guest house, a five-minute walk from St. Stephen's Green, is a favorite with vacationers. The large, late-19th-century terraced house is well converted, and the decor and furnishings are updated each year by the Murray family, who have run the place for the past 30 years. The bedrooms are pleasantly furnished with plush carpeting and pastel colored walls. *70 Adelaide Rd., Dublin 2, tel. 01/475–5266, fax 01/478–2841. 12 rooms with bath. Facilities: restaurant (wine license only). MC, V. Closed Dec. 21–Jan. 1.*

$ Mount Herbert Guest House. Located close to the swank luxury hotels in the tree-lined inner suburb of Ballsbridge, a 10-minute bus ride from Dublin's center, the Mount Herbert is popular with budget-minded American visitors in the high season. Bedrooms are small, but all have 10-channel TVs and hair dryers. There is no bar on the premises, but there are plenty to choose from nearby. *7 Herbert Rd., Ballsbridge, tel.*

01/668–4321, fax 01/660–7077. 135 rooms with bath. Facilities: restaurant (wine license only). AE, DC, MC, V.

The Arts

The fortnightly magazine *In Dublin* contains comprehensive details of upcoming events, including ticket availability. In peak season, consult the free Bord Fáilte leaflet "Events of the Week."

Theaters

Ireland has a rich theatrical tradition. The **Abbey Theatre,** Marlborough Street, is the home of Ireland's national theater company, its name forever associated with J. M. Synge, W. B. Yeats, and Sean O'Casey. The **Peacock Theatre** is the Abbey's more experimental small stage. The **Gate Theatre,** Parnell Square, is an intimate spot for modern drama and plays by Irish writers. The **Gaiety Theatre,** South King Street, features musical comedy, opera, drama, and revues. The **Olympia Theatre,** Dame Street, has seasons of comedy, vaudeville, and ballet. The **Project Arts Centre,** East Essex Street, is an established fringe theater. The **National Concert Hall,** in Earlsfort Terrace, just off Stephen's Green, is the place to go for classical concerts.

Nightlife

Dublin does not have sophisticated nightclubs in the international sense. Instead, there is a choice of discos (often billed as nightclubs) and cabarets, catering mainly to visitors. There is also a very animated bar-pub scene—some places with live music and folksinging. No visit to this genial city will be complete without spending at least one evening exploring them.

Discos

Annabels (Mespil Rd., tel. 01/660–5222) is a popular late-evening spot; so is **The Pink Elephant** (S. Frederick St., tel. 01/677–5876).

Cabarets

The following all offer Irish cabaret, designed to give visitors a taste of Irish entertainment: **Burlington Hotel** (Upper Leeson St., tel. 01/660–5222, open May–Oct.); **Jury's Hotel** (Ballsbridge, tel. 01/660–5000, open May–mid-Oct.); **Abbey Tavern** (Howth, Co. Dublin, tel. 01/839–0307).

Pubs

Check advertisements in evening papers for "sessions" of folk, ballad, Irish traditional, or jazz music. The **Brazen Head** (20 Lower Bridge St., tel. 01/677–9549)—Dublin's oldest pub, dating from 1688—and **O'Donoghue's** (15 Merrion Row, tel. 01/661–4303) feature some form of musical entertainment on most nights. Several of Dublin's centrally located pubs are noted for their character and ambience; they're usually at their liveliest from 5 to 7 PM and again from 10 to 11:30. The **Bailey** (2 Duke St.) is mentioned in *Ulysses* (under its original name, Burton's) and retains something of its Edwardian character, while **William Ryan's** (28 Parkgate St.) is a beautifully preserved Victorian gem. **Henry Grattan** (47–48 Lower Baggot St.) is popular with the business and sporting crowd; **O'Neill's Lounge Bar** (37 Pearse St.) is always busy with students and faculty from nearby Trinity College; and the **Palace Bar** (21 Fleet St.) is a journalists' haunt. You can eavesdrop on Dublin's social elite and their hangers-on at the expensive **Horseshoe Bar** in the Shelbourne Hotel or bask in the theatrical atmosphere of **Neary's** (Chatham St.)

For details on pubs serving food, *see* Dining *in* Staying in Ireland, *above.*

DUBLIN TO CORK

Ireland can be covered in three itineraries that, taken together, form a clockwise tour of the country, starting and ending in Dublin. Distances in Ireland seem short—the total mileage of the three itineraries combined is less than 960 kilometers (600 miles)—but roads are small and often twisty and hilly, and side attractions are numerous, so you should aim for a daily mileage of no more than 240 kilometers (150 miles). The consistently dazzling scenery, intriguing ruins, and beguiling villages will lead to many impromptu stops and explorations along the way. (We have tried to provide full addresses for hotels, restaurants, and sights, though many of Ireland's villages and towns are so tiny they barely have street names, much less numbers. If in doubt, just ask for directions.)

The first tour takes you southwest from Dublin to hilly Cork, the Republic's second-largest city. On the way, you'll see the lush green fields of Ireland's famous stud farms and imposing Cashel, where Ireland built its reputation as the "Land of Saints and Scholars" while most of Europe was slipping into the Dark Ages.

Getting Around

By Train

The terminal at Cork is Kent Station. There are direct services from Dublin and Tralee and a suburban line to Cobh; call 021/506–766 for information.

By Bus

The main bus terminal in Cork is at Parnell Place (tel. 021/508–188).

By Car

All the main car-rental firms have desks at Cork Airport. Be sure to get a map of Cork's complicated one-way street system.

By Bicycle

Bicycles can be rented from **Isaac's** (48 MacCurtain St., Cork, tel. 021/505–399).

Guided Tours

CIE operates a number of trips from Parnell Place in Cork (tel. 021/506–066).

Tourist Information

Tourist House (Grand Parade, Cork, tel. 021/273–251, fax 021/273–504).

Exploring Dublin to Cork

Leaving Dublin by N7 for **Naas** (pronounced nace), you will pass through the area known as The Pale—that part of Ireland in which English law was formally acknowledged up to Elizabethan times. Beyond Naas, the road takes you to the center of the Irish racing world. **Goff's Kildare Paddocks** at Kill sells more than 50% of all Irish-bred horses. Naas has its own racecourse and lies just 4.8 kilometers (3 miles) from Punchestown, famous for its steeplechases. The **Curragh** begins just after Newbridge and is the biggest area of common land in Ireland, containing about 31 square kilometers (12 square miles). You will see the **Curragh Racecourse,** home of the Irish Derby, on your right-hand side; to your left is the training depot of the Irish army.

If you are interested in horses, **Kildare,** the traditional home of St. Brigid, is not to be missed. The main attraction is the **National Stud and Horse Museum** and its **Japanese Gardens.** *Tel. 045/21617. Admission: IR£2. Open Easter–Oct., Mon.–Sat. 10–5, Sun. 2–6. Tours on request.*

At Portlaoise (pronounced portleash)—the location of Ireland's top-security prison—follow N8 to **Cashel.** Your first glimpse of the famous **Rock of Cashel** should be an unforgettably majestic sight: It rises imposingly to a height of 200 feet above the plains and is crowned with a magnificent group of gray-stone ruins. The kings of Munster held it as their seat for about seven centuries, and it was here that St. Patrick reputedly plucked a shamrock from the ground, using it as a symbol to explain the mystery of the Trinity, giving Ireland, in the process, its universally recognized symbol. The central building among the ruins is a 13th-century Gothic cathedral; next to it is the Romanesque Cormac's chapel. *Tel. 062/61437. Admission: IR£1.50 adults, 60p children and senior citizens. Open June–Sept., daily 9–7:30; mid-Mar.–May, daily 9:30–5:30; Oct.–mid-Mar., daily 9:30–4.*

Cashel and the next town, **Cahir** (pronounced care), are both popular stopping places to break the Dublin–Cork journey. In the center of Cahir, you will discover a formidable **medieval fortress** with a working portcullis, the gruesome barred gate that was lowered to keep out attackers. An audiovisual display can be seen in the castle complex. *Tel. 052/41011. Admission: IR£1 adults, 40p children and senior citizens. Open Apr.–June and late Sept., daily 10–6; June–mid-Sept., daily 9–7:30; Nov.–Mar., daily 10–1 and 2–4; closed Oct.*

The road continues through Mitchelstown and Fermoy, both of them busy market towns serving Cork's dairy farmers. A short detour at Mitchelstown will allow you to visit former President Reagan's ancestral home, **Ballyporeen,** a pretty little village with wide streets built to accommodate the open-air cattle markets held there until the '60s.

The road to **Cork City** passes through the beautiful wooded glen of Glanmire and along the banks of the River Lee. In the center of Cork, the Lee divides in two, giving the city a profusion of picturesque quays and bridges. The name Cork derives from the Irish *corcaigh* (pronounced corky),meaning a marshy place.The city received its first charter in 1185 and grew rapidly in the 17th and 18th centuries with the expansion of its butter trade. It is the major metropolis of the south, and, with a population of about 138,000, the second-largest city in Ireland.

The main business and shopping center of Cork lies on the island created by the two diverging channels of the Lee, and most places of interest are within walking distance of the center. **Patrick Street** is the focal point of Cork. Here, you will find the city's most famous statue, that of **Father Theobald Mathew** (1790–1856), who led a nationwide temperance crusade, no small feat in a country as fond of a drink (or two) as this one. In the hilly area to the north of Patrick Street is the famous 120-foot **Shandon Steeple,** the bell tower of **St. Anne's Church.** It is shaped like a pepper pot and houses the bells immortalized in the song "The Bells of Shandon." Visitors can climb the tower; read the inscriptions on the bells; and, on request, have them rung over Cork. *Admission: IR£1, with bell tower IR£1.50. Open May–Oct., Mon.–Sat. 9:30–5; Nov.–Apr., Mon.–Sat. 10–3:30.*

Patrick Street is the main shopping area of Cork, and here you will find the city's two major department stores, **Roches** and **Cash's.** Cash's has a good selection of Waterford crystal. The liveliest place in town to shop is just off Patrick Street, to the west, near the city center parking lot, in

the pedestrian-only **Paul Street** area. **Mendows & Byrne** of Academy Street stocks the best in modern Irish design, including tableware, ceramics, knitwear, hand-woven tweeds, and high fashion. The **Donegal Shop** in Paul Street Piazza specializes in made-to-order tweed suits and rainwear. At the top of Paul Street is the **Crawford Art Gallery,** which has an excellent collection of 18th- and 19th-century views of Cork and mounts adventurous exhibitions by modern artists. *Emmet Pl., tel. 021/273–377. Admission free. Open weekdays 10–5, Sat. 9–1.*

One of Cork's most famous sons was William Penn (1644–1718), founder of the Pennsylvania colony. He is only one of thousands who sailed from Cork's port, the Cove of Cork, on Great Island, 24 kilometers (15 miles) down the harbor. **Cobh** (pronounced cove), as it is known nowadays, can be reached by train from Kent Station, and the trip provides excellent views of the magnificent harbor. Cobh is an attractive hilly town dominated by its 19th-century **cathedral.** It was the first and last European port of call for transatlantic liners, one of which was the ill-fated *Titanic.* Cobh has other associations with shipwrecks: It was from here that destroyers were sent out in May 1915 to search for survivors of the *Lusitania,* torpedoed by a German submarine with the loss of 1,198 lives. Cobh's maritime past and its links with emigration are documented in a new IR£2 million heritage center known as **The Queenstown Project,** which opened in the town's old railway station in 1993. *Tel. 021/813–591. Admission: IR£3.50 adults, IR£2 children and senior citizens. Open Feb.–Nov., daily 10–6.*

Fota Island, midway between Cork and Cobh, is a recent and very welcome addition to Cork's tourist attractions. The Royal Zoological Society has created a 238-square-kilometer (70-acre) wildlife park here.

Tel. 021/812–678. Admission: IR£3.50 adults, IR£2 children and senior citizens. Open Feb.–Nov., daily 10–6. Parking: IR£1 per car.

Most visitors to Cork want to kiss the famous **Blarney Stone** in the hope of acquiring the "gift of the gab." Blarney itself, 8 kilometers (5 miles) from Cork City, should not, however, be taken too seriously as an excursion. All that is left of **Blarney Castle** is its ruined central keep containing the celebrated stone. This is set in the battlements, and to kiss it, you must lie on the walk within the walls, lean your head back, and touch the stone with your lips. Nobody knows how the tradition originated, but Elizabeth I is credited with giving the word *blarney* to the language when, commenting on the unfulfilled promises of Cormac MacCarthy, Lord Blarney of the time, she remarked, "This is all Blarney; what he says, he never means." In Blarney village there are several good crafts shops, and the outing provides a good opportunity to shop around for traditional Irish goods at competitive prices. *Tel. 021/385–252. Admission: IR£3 adults, IR£1 children, IR£1.50 senior citizens. Open Mon.–Sat. 9 to sundown, Sun. 9–5:30.*

Dining and Lodging

For details and price-category definitions, *see* Dining and Lodging *in* Staying in Ireland, *above.*

Cahir

DINING AND LODGING

Kilcoran Lodge Hotel. Set on its own grounds on the main road, Kilcoran Lodge Hotel is an ideal place to break the journey with coffee or a plainly cooked lunch. It occupies a bucolic country setting on the southern slope of the Galtees. *Co. Tipperary, on N8, tel. 052/41288, fax 052/41994. 23 rooms with bath. Facilities: indoor pool, sauna. AE, DC, MC, V. $$*

Cashel

DINING

Chez Hans. Fresh local produce cooked with a French accent is served in this converted chapel at the foot of the famous rock. *Tel. 062/61177. MC, V. Dinner only. Closed Sun., Mon., first 3 wks in Jan. $$$*

LODGING

Cashel Palace. This elegant Palladian mansion was once a bishop's palace. It has luxurious rooms and a beautiful garden. *Main St., Co. Tipperary, tel. 062/61411, fax 062/61521. 20 rooms with bath. AE, DC, MC, V. Closed Dec. 25–26. $$$$*

Cork

DINING

Clifford's. Cork's most fashionable restaurant, just a short walk from Jury's hotel, serves seriously good food in a fun atmosphere. The ground floor of a Georgian house has been strikingly modernized and decorated in black and white. Choose from the owner-chef's small set menu (four or five choices for each course), which includes items such as black sole and prawns in a pepper and lime sauce or medallions of veal garnished with apples and walnuts. *18 Dyke Parade, tel. 021/275–333. Reservations advised. AE, DC, MC, V. Closed Sun. and Mon. No lunch Sat. $$$*

Isaac's. In an old warehouse with cast-iron pillars, this popular brasserie-style spot has a Continental atmosphere echoed by the food, which combines Mediterranean influences with excellent local produce. Worth a try, whatever your budget. *48 MacCurtain St., tel. 021/503–805. Weekend reservations advised. MC, V. $*

DINING AND LODGING

★ **Arbutus Lodge.** This exceptionally comfortable hotel has an outstanding restaurant and panoramic views of the city and the river. The restaurant Ireland's most highly acclaimed restaurants, not least for its excellent wine list.*Middle Glanmire Rd., Montenotte, tel. 021/501–237, fax 021/502–893. 20 rooms with bath. Facilities: restaurant, bar, 1 tennis court. AE, DC, MC, V. Closed 1 wk at Christmas. $$$*

★ **Ballymaloe House.** This rambling house on 400 acres has been developed into an informal, easygoing hotel over the past few years. Each guest room is decorated elegantly in variations on the country-house style. The restaurant—run by Myrtle Allen, a world expert on Irish cookery—is outstanding. *Shanagarry, Midleton, tel. 021/652–531. 30 rooms with bath. Facilities: restaurant (jacket and tie), bar, outdoor heated pool, tennis court, deep-sea fishing by arrangement. No TV in rooms. AE, DC, MC, V. $$$*

LODGING

Fitzpatrick's Silver Springs. Situated on its own grounds overlooking the River Lee, five minutes' drive from the town center, this modern low rise reopened in 1989 after major refurbishment. A popular choice for tour groups, it also has the most up-to-date leisure facilities in town. *Tivoli, tel. 021/507–533, fax 021/507–641. 110 rooms with bath. Facilities: 2 restaurants, 2 bars, indoor pool, sauna, gym, squash, tennis (1 outdoor, 2 indoor), bowling, 9-hole golf course. AE, DC, MC, V. $$$*

Jury's. This modern two-story hotel has a lively bar and occupies a riverside location a five-minute walk from the downtown area. *Western Rd., tel. 021/276–622, fax 021/274–477. 185 rooms with bath. Facilities: 2 restaurants, indoor and outdoor pools, health club, sauna, squash, 2 tennis courts. AE, DC, MC, V. Closed Dec. 25–26. $$$*

Jury's Inn. Opened in 1994, the newest member of Jury's budget chain provides modern, well-equipped rooms in the city center that can accommodate three adults or two adults and two children. *Anderson's Quay, tel. 021/276–444, fax 021/276–144. 133 rooms with bath. AE, DC, MC, V. $*

★ **Victoria Lodge.** Originally built in the early 20th century as a Capuchin monastery, this exceptionally well-appointed B&B is a five-minute drive from the town center; it is also on several bus routes. The rooms are simple but comfortable, with views over the lodge's own grounds. Breakfast is served in the spacious old refectory. *Victoria Cross, tel. 021/542–233, fax 021/542–572. 20 rooms with bath. Facilities: restaurant (wine license only), TV lounge. MC. V. $*

CORK TO GALWAY

The trip from Cork to Galway is about 300 kilometers (188 miles) and includes stops in Killarney and Limerick. Killarney and the mysterious regions of the Burren are two very different areas of outstanding natural beauty. The Shannon region around Limerick is littered with castles, both ruined and restored.

Getting Around

By Train

Trains run from Cork to Tralee, via Killarney, and from Cork to Limerick, changing at Limerick Junction.

By Bus

Buses offer more flexible service than do trains; details are available from local tourist information offices.

By Car

All major rental companies have facilities at Shannon Airport. **Killarney Autos Ltd.** (Park Rd., tel. 064/31355) is the major firm in Killarney. Taxis do not operate on meters; agree on the fare beforehand.

By Bicycle

You can rent bicycles from **O'Callaghan Bros.** (College St., Killarney, tel. 064/31175), **D. O'Neill** (Plunkett St., Killarney, tel. 064/31970), and **Emerald Appliances** (1 Patrick St., Limerick, tel. 061/416–983).

Guided Tours

Bus Eireann offers day tours by bus from Killarney and Tralee train stations; check with the tourist office or rail station for details. **Shannon Castle Tours** (tel. 061/61788) and **Destination Killarney** (tel. 064/32638) also operate tours.

Tourist Information

All tourist information offices are open weekdays 9–6, Sat. 9–1.

Killarney (Town Hall, tel. 064/31633, fax 064/34506).
Limerick (Arthur's Quay, tel. 061/317–522, fax 061/315–634).
Shannon Airport (tel. 061/471–664).
Tralee (Ashe Memorial Hall, tel. 066/21288).

Exploring Cork to Galway

Beyond Macroom, the main Cork–Killarney road passes through the west-Cork **Gaeltacht**—a predominantly Irish-speaking region—and begins its climb into the Derrynasaggart Mountains. A detour to the left at Macroom will take you to the lake of **Gougane Barra,** source of the River Lee and now a national park. The 6th-century monk St. Finbarr, founder of Cork, had his cell on an island in the lake; this island can now be reached by causeway.

Killarney itself is an undistinguished market town, well developed to handle the tourist trade that flourishes here in the peak season. To find the famous scenery, you must head out of town toward the lakes that lie in a valley running south between the mountains. Part of Killarney's lake district is within **Killarney National Park.** At the heart of the park is the 10,000-acre **Muckross Estate** (open daily, daylight hours). Cars are not allowed in the estate, so if you don't want to walk, rent a bicycle in town or take a trip in a jaunting car—a small two-wheeled horse-drawn cart whose operators can be found at the gates to the estate and in Killarney. At the center of the estate is **Muckross House,** a 19th-century manor that contains the **Kerry Folklife Center.** On the adjoining grounds is an Old World farm. *Tel. 064/31440. Admission: IR£2.50 adults, IR£1 children. Combined farm and house: IR£3.50 adult, IR£1.50 children. Open Sept.–June, daily 9–5:30; July and Aug., daily 9–7. Closed 1 wk. At Christmas.*

To get an idea of the splendor of the lakes and streams—and of the massive glacial sandstone and limestone rocks and lush vegetation that characterize the Killarney district—take one of the day-long tours of the **Gap of Dunloe, the Upper Lake, Long Range, Middle** and **Lower lakes,** and **Ross Castle.** The central section, the Gap of Dunloe, is not suitable for cars, but horses and jaunting cars are available at **Kate Kearney's Cottage,** which marks the entrance to the gap.

The **Ring of Kerry** will add about 176 kilometers (110 miles) to your trip, but in good weather it provides a pleasant experience. Leave Kil-

Cork to Galway

larney by the Kenmare Road. **Kenmare** is a small market town 34 kilometers (21 miles) from Killarney at the head of Kenmare Bay. Across the water, as you drive out along the Iveragh Peninsula, will be views of the gray-blue mountain ranges of the Beara Peninsula. **Sneem,** on the estuary of the River Ardsheelaun, is one of the prettiest villages in Ireland. Beyond the next village, Caherdaniel, is **Derrynane House,** home of the 19th-century politician and patriot Daniel O'Connell, "The Liberator," and completed by him in 1825. It still contains much of its original furniture. *Tel. 066/75113. Admission: IR£1 adults, 40p children and senior citizens. Open mid-June–Sept., daily 10–1 and 2–7; Oct.–mid-June, Tues.–Sat. 10–1, Sun. 2–5. Park: admission free. Open year-round.*

The village of **Waterville** is famous as an angling center; it also has a fine sandy beach and a championship golf course. Charles de Gaulle, the French statesman, used to come to Waterville for the fishing; he intended to retire here, but died before ever taking up residence. Offshore, protruding in conical shapes from the Atlantic, are the **Skellig Rocks,** which contain the cells of early Christian monks. To learn more about the history and bird life of these islands, visit **The Skellig Experience,** an interpretative center situated where the bridge joins Valentia Island. Landing is prohibited on the Skelligs without a special permit, but the 1½-hour boat cruise (weather permitting) offered at the center is a good substitute. *Tel. 064/31633. Admission: IR£3 adults, IR£1.50 children; with cruise, IR£15 adults, IR£8 children. Open Apr.–June and Sept., daily 9:30–5; July–Aug., daily 9:30–7. Call to confirm cruise times.*

Beyond Cahirciveen, you are on the other side of the Ring, with views across Dingle Bay to the rugged peaks of the Dingle Peninsula. At the head of the bay is **Killorglin**, which has a three-day stint of unbridled merrymaking the first weekend in August—including the crowning of a goat as monarch of the town—known as Puck Fair.

If time and the weather are on your side, turn off the main Killorglin–Tralee road and make a tour of the **Dingle Peninsula**—one of the wildest and least spoiled regions of Ireland—taking in the **Connor Pass, Mount Brandon, the Gallarus Oratory,** and stopping at **Dunquin** to hear some of Ireland's best traditional musicians. For an adventure off the beaten path, arrange for a boat ride to the **Blasket Islands** and spend a few blissful hours wandering along the cliffs. Dingle town is a handy touring base, with a surprisingly wide choice of good restaurants, open Easter–October.

Tralee is the commercial center of Kerry, but has little to recommend it unless you happen to be visiting in September, when the "Rose of Tralee" is selected from an international lineup of young women of Irish descent. Listowel is similarly transformed during its race week in October. From **Tarbert** (where a ferry provides a handy shortcut directly to County Clare and the Burren), the road skirts the estuary of the River Shannon. **Limerick** is the fourth-largest city in the Republic, with a population of 60,000; it's also arguably the least attractive city in Ireland. Its Newtown area, however, is dominated by handsome Georgian buildings.

Bunratty Castle is a famous landmark midway between Limerick and Shannon Airport. It is one of four castles in the area that offer nightly medieval banquets, which, though as fake as they come, at least offer some fairly uninhibited fun. The castle was the stronghold of the princes of Thomond and is the most complete and—despite its ye-Olde-World banquets—authentic medieval castle in Ireland, restored in such a way as to give an idea of the 15th- and 16th-century way of life. The **Folk Park** on its grounds has farm buildings and crafts shops typical of the 19th century. *Tel. 061/361–511. Admission: IR£4.10 adults, IR£3.75 students and senior citizens, IR£2 children. Open daily 9:30–dusk (last entry 1 hr before closing).*

TIME OUT Drop in to **Durty Nelly's,** beside Bunratty Castle—it's one of Ireland's most popular old-time bars.

There is an incredible number of castles—almost 900—in the Shannon area, ranging from such fully restored examples as **Knappogue** at Quin, 14 kilometers (9 miles) from Bunratty, to the multitude of crumbling ruins that loom up all over the area.

Beyond Shannon Airport is County Clare and its principal town, **Ennis,** the campaigning base of Eamon de Valera, the New York–born politician whose character and views dominated the Republic from independence until the mid-'50s. Just beyond Ennis, a detour to **Corofin** will take you to the **Clare Heritage Center,** which explains the traumatic story of Ireland in the 19th century, a story of famines and untold misery that resulted in the mass emigrations of the Irish to England and the United States. *Tel. 065/37955. Admission: IR£1.75 adults, 75p children. Open Apr.–Oct., daily 10–6; Nov.–Mar. by appointment.*

Ennistymon and Lisdoonvarna, both quiet villages with an old-fashioned charm, make excellent bases for touring the Burren. **Lisdoonvarna** has developed something of a reputation over the years as a matchmaking center, with bachelor farmers and single women converging here each year around harvesttime for a **Bachelors' Festival.** This strange, rocky, limestone district is a superb nature reserve, with a profusion of unique wildflowers that are at their best in late May. Huge colonies of puffins, kittiwakes, shags, guillemots, and razorbills nest along its coast. The **Burren Display Center** at **Kilfenora** explains the extraordinary geology and wildlife of the area in a simple audiovisual display. *Tel. 065/88030. Admission: IR£2 adults, IR£1 children. Open mid-Mar.–Apr.and Sept.–Oct., daily 10–5; May–Aug., daily 10–6.*

The dramatic **Cliffs of Moher** are a must: They rise vertically out of the sea in a wall that stretches 8 kilometers (5 miles) and varies in height from 710 to 1440 feet, with **O'Brien's Tower** at their highest point. There is a visitor center beside the parking lot (open Mar.–Oct., daily 10–6). On a clear day, the **Aran Islands** are visible from the cliffs, and in summer there are regular day trips to them from **Doolin,** a small village popular with young travelers and noted for its spontaneous traditional music sessions.

At **Ailwee Cave** near Ballyvaughan, you can take a guided tour into the underworld of the Burren, where 3,415 feet of cave, formed millions of years ago, can be explored. *Tel. 065/77036. Admission: IR£3.50 adults, IR£2 children. Open early Mar.–June and Sept.–early Nov., daily 10–6 (last tour 5:30); July and Aug., daily 10–7 (last tour 6:30).*

The coast road continues into County Galway, through the pretty fishing village of Kinvara. Galway City itself is approached through **Clarinbridge,** the village that hosts Galway's annual Oyster Festival, which is held in September and features the superlative products of the village's oyster beds.

Dining and Lodging

For details and price-category definitions, *see* Dining and Lodging *in* Staying in Ireland, *above.*

Clarinbridge
DINING
Moran's of the Weir. This waterside, traditional, thatched cottage is one of Ireland's simplest yet most famous seafood eateries. The specialty here is oysters, but they also serve crab, prawns, mussels, and smoked salmon. *The Weir, Kilcolgan, Co. Galway, tel. 091/96113. AE, MC, V. $*

Dingle
DINING
Beginish. The best of several small but sophisticated restaurants in town, this relaxing place serves local meat and seafood in a generous version of nouvelle cuisine. *Green St., tel. 066/51588. AE, DC, MC, V. Closed Mon. and Nov. 1–Mar. $$*
Doyle's Seafood Bar. This is Dingle's best-known seafood restaurant, specializing in simply prepared local fish and shellfish. *John St., tel. 066/51174. Reservations advised. DC, MC, V. Closed Sun. and mid-Nov.–early Mar. $$*

LODGING
Benner's. This busy town-center hotel has been beautifully restored with country-pine antique furniture in all bedrooms. *Main St., tel. 066/51638, fax 066/51412. 25 rooms with bath. Facilities: 2 bars, restaurant. AE, DC, MC, V. $$*

Ennis
LODGING
★ **Old Ground.** This rambling creeper-clad building in the town center, dating from the early 18th century and much added to over the years,

is a comfortable, well-established hotel that has retained its past elegance. The lodging serves as a popular base for Americans, especially golfers. *O'Connell St., tel. 065/28127, fax 065/28112. 60 rooms with bath. Facilities: restaurant, bar. AE, DC, MC, V. $$$*

West County. This is a lively modern hotel with adequate rooms and Irish cabaret nightly in summer. *On N18 Limerick road, tel. 065/28421, fax 065/28801. 110 rooms with bath. Facilities: 2 restaurants, 2 bars, nightclub with live entertainment. AE, DC, MC, V. $$*

Kenmare

DINING AND LODGING

★ **Park.** A guest feels truly pampered at this antique-laden hotel, widely considered to be one of Ireland's best. Be sure to sample the seafood on the nouvelle-cuisine menu of the renowned French restaurant (jacket and tie). *Tel. 064/41200, fax 064/41402. 50 rooms with bath. Facilities: restaurant, 1 tennis court, fishing, 18-hole golf course, horseback riding, bicycles. TV in rooms on request. AE, DC, MC, V. $$$$*

Killarney

DINING

★ **Foley's.** This popular eatery specializes in seafood, steaks, and Kerry mountain lamb. *23 High St., tel. 064/31217. AE, DC, MC, V. $$*

★ **Gaby's.** For simple and fresh seafood, Gaby's can't be beat. *17 High St., tel. 064/32519. AE, DC, MC, V. Closed Sun. and Dec.–mid-Mar. No lunch Mon. $$*

LODGING

Aghadoe Heights. This luxury hotel overlooks the lakes and has the most romantic view of all the hotels in Killarney. The restaurant is outstanding. *Aghadoe Heights, tel. 064/31766, fax 064/31345. 57 rooms with bath. Facilities: restaurant, bar, indoor heated pool, sauna, Jacuzzi, 1 tennis court, fishing. AE, DC, MC, V. $$$$*

Europe. This large, luxurious, modern hotel has a secluded lakeside location and excellent sporting facilities. *Killorglin Rd., Fossa, tel. 064/31900, fax 064/32118. 205 rooms with bath. Facilities: restaurant, bar, gymnasium, indoor pool, sauna, 1 tennis court, fishing, horseback riding, bicycles. AE, DC, MC, V. Closed Nov.–Feb. $$$*

Arbutus. Newly refurbished and centrally located, Arbutus benefits from a lively bar and an Old World atmosphere. *College St., tel. 064/31037, fax 064/34033. 35 rooms with bath. AE, DC, MC, V. $$*

Lahinch

LODGING

Aberdeen Arms. Golfers abound among the clientele of this comfortably refurbished Victorian seaside hotel. *Lahinch, Co. Clare, tel. 065/81100, fax 065/81228. 55 rooms with bath. Facilities: 2 restaurants, 2 bars, snooker, sauna, Jacuzzi, 10 tennis courts, bicycles. AE, DC, MC, V. $$*

Limerick

DINING

De La Fontaine. The French owner-chef uses only the best local produce to present imaginative "cuisine moderne" creations in this intimate hideaway. *12 Gerald Griffin St., tel. 061/414–461. Reservations advised. AE, DC, MC, V. Closed Sun. Lunch served only on Fri. $$*

LODGING

Castletroy Park. High standards of comfort are the rule at this well-designed modern hotel on the outskirts of town. *Dublin Rd., tel.*

061/335–566, fax 061/331–117. 107 rooms with bath. Facilities: 2 restaurants, bar, indoor pool, gymnasium, sauna, steam room, Jacuzzi. AE, DC, MC, V. $$$$

Greenhills. This suburban, modern low rise is convenient for Shannon Airport and also makes a good touring base. The friendly owner-manager welcomes families. *Ennis Rd., tel. 061/453–033, fax 061/453–307. 55 rooms with bath. Facilities: restaurant, bar, coffee shop, indoor heated pool, sauna, Jacuzzi, steam room, gym, tennis court. AE, DC, MC, V. $$*

Lisdoonvarna

<u>LODGING</u>

Ballinalacken Castle. It's not a castle, but a converted Victorian shooting lodge on the very edge of the Burren that commands a breathtaking view of the Atlantic. Rooms are modest but full of character. *Co. Clare, tel. 065/74025. 12 rooms with bath. Facilities: restaurant, bar. MC, V. Closed early Nov.–Easter. $*

Sheedy's Spa View. This is a friendly, family-run establishment with open turf fires and an excellent restaurant. *Lisdoonvarna, tel. 065/74026, fax 065/74555. 11 rooms with bath. Facilities: restaurant, tennis. AE, DC, MC, V. $*

THE NORTHWEST

This route from Galway to Sligo and then back to Dublin, via Kells, takes you through the rugged landscape of Connemara to the fabled Yeats country in the northwest and then skirts the borders of Northern Ireland before returning to Dublin. The entire trip is about 400 kilometers (250 miles) and passes through some of the wildest and loneliest parts of Ireland.

Getting Around

By Train

Trains to Galway, Westport, and Sligo operate from Dublin's Heuston or Connolly (Sligo) stations. There is no train service north of Sligo.

By Bus

Travel within the area is more flexible by bus; details are available from local tourist information offices.

By Car

In Galway, cars can be rented from **Avis** (tel. 091/68886), **Budget** (tel. 091/66376), or **Murray's** (tel. 091/62222). Taxis do not operate on meters; agree on the fare beforehand.

By Bicycle

You can rent bikes from **Celtic Cycles** (Victoria Place, Galway City, tel. 091/66606), **John Mannion** (Railway View, Clifden, tel. 095/21160), or **Gary's Cycles** (Quay St., Sligo, tel. 071/45418).

Guided Tours

CIE Tours International operates day tours of Connemara out of Galway City and bus tours into the Donegal highlands from Sligo train station; details are available from local tourist offices. **CIE/Bus Eireann** (tel. 01/830–2222) and **Gray Line** (tel. 01/661–9666) offer tours of the Boyne Valley and County Meath out of Dublin.

Tourist Information

All are open weekdays 9–6, Sat. 9–1.

Galway (off Eyre Sq., tel. 091/63081, fax 091/65201).
Sligo (Temple St., tel. 071/61201, fax 071/60360).
Westport (The Mall, tel. 098/25711, fax 098/26709).

Exploring the Northwest

Galway City is the gateway to the ancient province of Connacht, the most westerly seaboard in Europe. Galway City was well established even before the Normans arrived in the 13th century, rebuilding the city walls and turning the little town into a flourishing port. Later its waterfront was frequented by Spanish grandees and traders. The salmon fishing in the River Corrib, which flows through the lower part of the town, is unsurpassed. In early summer, you can stand on the **Weir Bridge** beside the town's cathedral and watch thousands of salmon as they leap and twist through the narrow access to the inner lakes. **Lynch's Castle** on Shop Street, now a bank, is a good example of a 16th-century fortified house—fortified because the neighboring Irish tribes persistently raided Galway City, whose commercial life excluded them. Nowadays the liveliest part of town is around the area between **Eyre Square** (the town's center) and the **Spanish Arch.**

TIME OUT Drop in at **Noctan's** pub on the corner of Abbeygate Street for food at lunchtime and the latest news of what's on in town.

On the west bank of the Corrib estuary, just outside of the Galway town walls, is **Claddagh,** said to be the oldest fishing village in Ireland. **Salthill Promenade,** with its lively seaside amenities, is the traditional place "to sit and watch the moon rise over Claddagh, and see the sun go down on Galway Bay"—in the words of the city's most famous song.

Connemara is a land of romantic, underpopulated landscapes, and rugged craggy coastlines, where the Irish language is still used by many people. **Rossaveale,** a port on the coast road beyond Spiddal, is the handiest port for a trip to the Aran Islands, 48 kilometers (30 miles) off the coast, where J. M. Synge drew the inspiration for his play *Riders to the Sea.* The islands are still 100% Irish speaking and retain an atmosphere distinct from that of the mainland, which will be appreciated by those in search of the peace and quiet of a past century. **Inishmaan,** the middle island, is considered the most unspoiled of the three and will delight botanists, ornithologists, and walkers. *Sailings daily from Rossaveale and less frequently from Galway; round-trip fare about IR£12. Details from Galway Tourist Information Office. Also accessible by air from Connemara Airport (tel. 091/93034): daily flights, round-trip fare about IR£32.*

Oughterard is an important angling center on Lough Corrib. Boats can be rented for excursions to the lake's many wooded islands. The road to Clifden runs between the Maamturk and the Cloosh Mountains beside a string of small lakes. **Clifden,** the principal town of Connemara, has an almost alpine setting, nestling on the edge of the Atlantic with a spectacular mountain backdrop. Just beyond Clifden is the **Connemara National Park,** with its many nature trails offering views of sea, mountain, and lake. Its visitor center features an audiovisual presentation and a collection of farm furniture. *Tel. 095/41054. Admission free. Open Apr.–Oct., daily 10–6.*

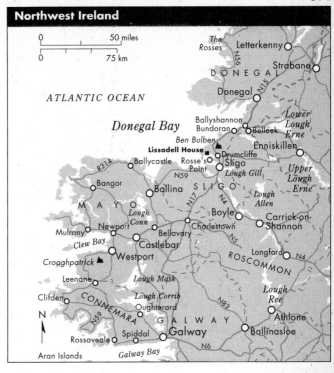

Westport is a quiet, mainly 18th-century town overlooking Clew Bay—a wide expanse of water studded with nearly 400 islands. The distinctive silhouette of **Croaghpatrick,** a 2,540-foot mountain, dominates the town. Today some 25,000 pilgrims climb it on the last Sunday in July in honor of St. Patrick, who is believed to have spent 40 days fasting on its summit in AD 441. Whether he did or not, the climb is an exhilarating experience and can be completed in about three hours; it should be attempted only in good weather, however.

County Sligo is noted for its seaside resorts, the famous golf course at Rosse's Point (just outside Sligo Town), and its links with Ireland's most famous 20th-century poet, W. B. Yeats who is buried just north of **Sligo Town** at Drumcliffe. An important collection of paintings by the poet's brother, Jack B. Yeats, can be seen in the **Sligo Museum** (Stephen St., tel. 071/42212), which also has memorabilia of Yeats, the poet. Take a boat from Sligo up to **Lough Gill** and see the **Lake Isle of Innisfree** and other places immortalized in Yeats's poetry. His grave is beneath the slopes of Ben Bulben, just north of the town. Nearby is **Lissadell House,** a substantial mansion dating from 1830 that features prominently in his writings. It was the home of Constance Gore-Booth, later Countess Markeviecz, who took part in the 1916 uprising. *Tel. 071/63150. Admission: IR£2 adults, 50p children. Open June–Sept., Mon.–Sat. 10:30–noon, 2–4:30.*

Bundoran, the southernmost town of Donegal, is one of Ireland's major seaside resorts, with excellent sandy beaches. From **Donegal Town,** you can set off to tour the ever-changing landscape of Donegal's rugged coastline and highlands, visiting the "tweed villages" on the coast at the Rosses, where the famous Donegal tweed is woven.

This route heads back to Dublin through **Belleek,** on the borders of Counties Donegal and Fermanagh, known for its fragile, lustrous china; a factory visit can be arranged (tel. 08036/565–501). For the remaining towns on this tour, *see* the Ireland country map. Belleek is a frontier post on an approved road that skirts the shores of Lower Lough Erne in Northern Ireland, passing through Enniskillen and reemerging in Belturbet, County Cavan, on the main N3 Dublin road. The N3 continues across a beautiful patchwork of lakes, the heart of the low-lying lakelands. In **Cavan** you may want to visit the **Crystal Factory,** which runs daily tours of the premises, showing visitors the techniques for blowing and cutting glass. *Dublin Rd., tel. 049/31800. Admission free. Guided tours: weekdays 9:30, 10:30, 11:30, 12:30, 2:30.*

The N3 returns you to Dublin by way of **Kells,** in whose 8th-century abbey the Book of Kells was completed; a facsimile can be seen in **St. Columba's Church.** Among the remains of the abbey is a well-preserved round tower and a rare example of a stone-roof church dating from the 9th century. There are five richly sculptured stone crosses in Kells. Just south of **Navan** is the **Hill of Tara,** the religious and cultural capital of Ireland in ancient times. Its importance waned with the arrival of Christianity in the 5th century, and today its crest is, appropriately enough, crowned with a statue of the man who brought Christianity to Ireland—St. Patrick.

Dining and Lodging

For details and price-category definitions, *see* Dining and Lodging *in* Staying in Ireland, *above.*

Cashel Bay

<u>LODGING</u>

Cashel House. One of Ireland's outstanding country-house hotels, luxurious and secluded, Cashel House attracts an affluent outdoor-loving international clientele as well as Ireland's elite. *Cashel Bay, Connemara, Co. Galway, tel. 095/31001, fax 095/31077. 32 rooms with bath. Facilities: restaurant, bar, horseback riding, tennis, private beach, bicycles, fishing. AE, MC, V. $$$*

Clifden

<u>LODGING</u>

Abbeyglen Castle. This comfortable hotel is quietly set about 1 kilometer (½ mile) west of town, featuring panoramic views over the rolling green hillsides. The secluded garden is a haven for travel-weary souls. *Sky Rd., tel. 095/21201, fax 095/21797. 46 rooms with bath. Facilities: heated pool, tennis, horseback riding, 9-hole golf course, bicycles. AE, DC, MC, V. Closed Jan. $$*

Rock Glen Manor House. Dating from 1815, this converted hunting lodge is 1½ kilometers (1 mile) south of town in exceptionally peaceful surroundings. *Tel. 095/21035, fax 095/21737. 29 rooms with bath. AE, DC, MC, V. Closed Oct.–mid-Mar. $$*

Collooney

<u>DINING AND LODGING</u>

Markree Castle. This magnificent 17th-century castle, which also houses the renowned Knockmuldowney Restaurant, is situated on a 1,000-acre estate. The host family offers bed and breakfast, delectable home-cooked French food at dinner, and a traditional Sunday lunch. *11 km (7 mi) south of Sligo Town on N4, Co. Sligo, tel. 071/67800, fax 071/67840. 11 rooms with bath. AE, DC, MC, V. $$$*

Cong

DINING AND LODGING

★ **Ashford Castle.** This imposing castle is set in its own park on the edge of Lough Corrib and has a superb restaurant, the Connaught Room. President Reagan stayed here in 1984. *Tel. 092/46003, fax 092/46260. 83 rooms with bath. Facilities: 2 restaurants, 2 bars, 9-hole golf course, 2 tennis courts, fishing, horseback riding, jaunting car, bicycles, clay-target shooting. AE, DC, MC, V. $$$$*

Galway City

DINING

de Burgos. This Old World basement restaurant serves an extensive French-influenced menu focused around local seafood and char-grilled steaks. *15 Augustine St., tel. 091/62188. AE, DC, MC, V. Closed Sun. $$*

Noctan's. This excellent, small French restaurant is above a popular pub. *17 Cross St., tel. 091/66172. MC, V. Dinner only. Closed Sun.–Mon. $$*

LODGING

Great Southern. Recently refurbished, this old-style town hotel enjoys a convenient central location. *Eyre Sq., tel. 091/64041, fax 091/66704. 115 rooms with bath. Facilities: rooftop heated pool, sauna, health complex. AE, DC, MC, V. $$$*

Ardilaun House. This hotel is set in pleasant grounds midway between Galway City and the seaside suburb of Salthill. *Taylors Hill, tel. 091/21433, fax 091/21546. 89 rooms with bath. AE, DC, MC, V. $$*

Moycullen

DINING

Drimcong House. The chef-owner prepares his award-winning meals in a 300-year-old lakeside house, 13 kilometers (8 miles) from Galway City. *Northwest on N59, tel. 091/85115. AE, DC, MC, V. Open Tues.– Sat., dinner only. Closed Christmas–mid-Mar. $$$*

Oughterard

LODGING

Connemara Gateway. This modern low rise makes a convenient touring base and has relatively spacious rooms with views of the Connemara hills. *Oughterard, Co. Galway, tel. 091/82328, fax 091/82332. 62 rooms with bath. Facilities: restaurant, indoor pool, sauna,1 tennis court. DC, MC, V. Closed Dec. and Jan. $$$*

Sligo Town

DINING AND LODGING

Ballincar House Hotel. Just outside of town, this converted country house with gardens has a highly recommended restaurant that specializes in fresh seafood. *Rosses Point Rd., tel. 071/45361, fax 071/44198. 25 rooms with bath. Facilities: restaurant, squash, tennis, sauna, solarium. AE, DC, MC, V. $$$*

LODGING

Silver Swan Hotel. In the town center overlooking the Garavogue River, this '60s-style hotel has recently been refurbished, with quite effective results. *Hyde Bridge, tel. 071/43231, fax 071/42232. 29 rooms with bath. Facilities: restaurant, bar. AE, DC, MC, V. $$*

Sligo Park. This is a modern two-story building, set on spacious grounds. *Pearse Rd., tel. 071/60291, fax 071/69556. 89 rooms with bath. Facilities: restaurant, indoor pool, 1 tennis court. AE, DC, MC, V. $$*

Westport

Asgard. The Asgard is a pub with award-winning food in both its bar and second-floor restaurant. *The Quay, tel. 098/25319. AE, DC, MC, V. $$*

Hotel Westport. A modern low rise, this quiet hotel is five minutes' walk from the town center and overlooks the grounds of Westport House. *Newport Rd., tel. 098/25122, fax 098/26739. 49 rooms with bath. $$*

18 Italy

WHERE ELSE IN EUROPE can you find the blend of great art, delicious food and wine, and sheer verve that awaits you in Italy? This Mediterranean country has made a profound contribution to Western civilization, producing some of the world's greatest thinkers, writers, politicians, saints, and artists. Impressive traces of their lives and works can still be seen in the great buildings and lovely countryside.

The whole of Italy is one vast attraction, but the triangle of its most-visited cities—Rome (Roma), Florence (Firenze), and Venice (Venezia)—gives a good idea of the great variety to be found here. In Rome and Florence, especially, you can feel the uninterrupted flow of the ages, from the Classical era of the ancient Romans to the bustle and throb of contemporary life carried on in centuries-old settings. Venice, by contrast, seems suspended in time, the same today as it was when it held sway over the eastern Mediterranean and the Orient. Each of these cities presents a different aspect of the Italian character: the Baroque exuberance of Rome, Florence's serene stylishness, and the dreamy sensuality of Venice.

The uninhibited Italian lifestyle can be entertaining or irritating, depending on how you look at it. Rarely do things run like clockwork here; you are more likely to encounter unexplained delays and incomprehensible complications. Relax: There's usually something you can smile about even in the most trying circumstances.

Trying to soak in Italy's rich artistic heritage is a great challenge. The country's many museums and churches draw hordes of visitors, all wanting to see the same thing at the same time. From May through September, the Sistine Chapel, Michelangelo's *David,* St. Mark's Square, and other key sights are more often than not swamped by mobs of tourists. Try to see the highlights at off-peak times in the day. If they are open during lunch—and many are not—that is often a good time. Again, relax: Seeing some attractions—such as the scrubbed facades of Rome's glorious Baroque churches—entails no opening hours and no lines at all.

Along with hordes of tourists, large Italian cities are plagued by automobiles. Recent regulations barring some traffic from the centers of Rome and Florence have made them less noisy in spots, but air pollution remains a serious problem. Plans are now afoot to curtail the auto traffic that swirls around the Colosseum, sparing it some of the pollution and vibration it has suffered as perhaps the world's most extravagant *spartitraffico* (traffic circle).

Even in the major tourist cities, Italians generally take a friendly interest in their visitors. Only the most blasé waiters and salespeople will be less than courteous and helpful. However, the persistent attention some Italian Casanovas pay to foreign females can be oppressive and annoying. If you're not interested, the best tactic is to ignore them. It's important to be attentive to matters of personal security in certain parts of the country; always be on guard against pickpockets and purse snatchers in the main tourist cities and in Naples. Especially in Rome and Florence, watch out for bands of gypsy children, expert at lifting wallets. Small cities and towns are usually safe.

Making the most of your time in Italy doesn't mean rushing through it. To gain a rich appreciation for Italy, don't try to see everything all at once. Do what you really want to do, and if that means skipping a museum to sit at a pretty café, enjoying the sunshine and a cappuccino, you're getting into the Italian spirit. Art—and life—are to be enjoyed, and the Italians can show you how.

ESSENTIAL INFORMATION

Before You Go

Tourist Information

Contact the **Italian Government Travel Office (ENIT)** at 630 5th Ave., Suite 1566, New York, NY 10111, tel. 212/245–4822, fax 212/586–9249; 500 N. Michigan Ave., Chicago, IL 60611, tel. 312/644–0990, fax 312/644–3019; 12400 Wilshire Blvd., Suite 550, Los Angeles, CA 90025, tel. 310/820–0098, fax 310/820–6357. In Italy, this helpful agency is known as **Azienda di Promozione Turismo (APT)** and **Ente Provinciale per il Turismo (EPT)**, with offices found in most cities and towns.

When to Go

The main tourist season in Italy runs from mid-April to the end of September. The best months for sightseeing are April, May, June, September, and October, when the weather is generally pleasant and not too hot. Foreign tourists crowd the major cities at Easter, when Italians flock to resorts and the countryside. Avoid traveling in August, when the heat can be oppressive and when vacationing Italians cram roads, trains, and planes, as well as beach and mountain resorts. Especially around the August 15 holiday, such cities as Rome and Milan are deserted, and many restaurants and shops close. Except for such year-round resorts as Taormina and a few on the Italian Riviera, coastal resorts close up tight from October or November to April. The best time for resorts is June and September, when the weather is usually fine and everything is open but not crowded.

The hottest months are July and August, when brief afternoon thunderstorms are common in inland areas. Winters are relatively mild in most places on the tourist circuit, but there are always some rainy spells.

Although low-season rates do not officially apply in Rome, Florence, and Milan you can usually bargain for discounted rates in Rome and Milan in summer (when business travelers are few) and in Florence in winter. Ask for *"la tariffa scontata."* You can save on hotel accommodations in Venice and in such resorts as Sorrento and Capri during their low seasons—the winter, early spring, and late-autumn months.

CLIMATE

The following are average daily maximum and minimum temperatures for Rome.

Jan.	52F	11C	May	74F	23C	Sept.	79F	26C
	40	5		56	13		62	17
Feb.	55F	13C	June	82F	28C	Oct.	71F	22C
	42	6		63	17		55	13
Mar.	59F	15C	July	87F	30C	Nov.	61F	16C
	45	7		67	20		49	9
Apr.	66F	19C	Aug.	86F	30C	Dec.	55F	13C
	50	10		67	20		44	6

The following are average daily maximum and minimum temperatures for Milan.

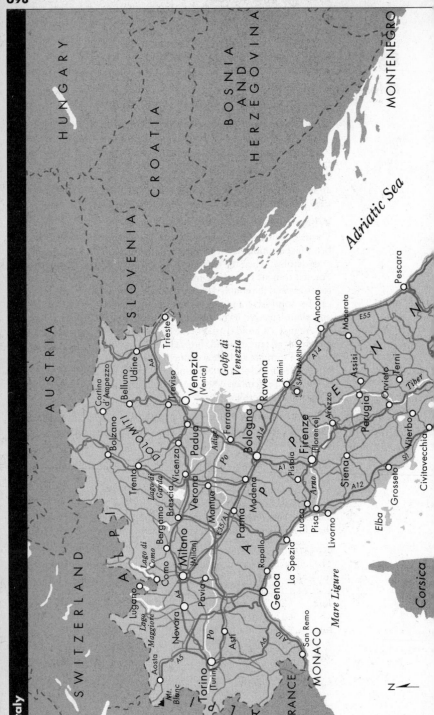

Italy

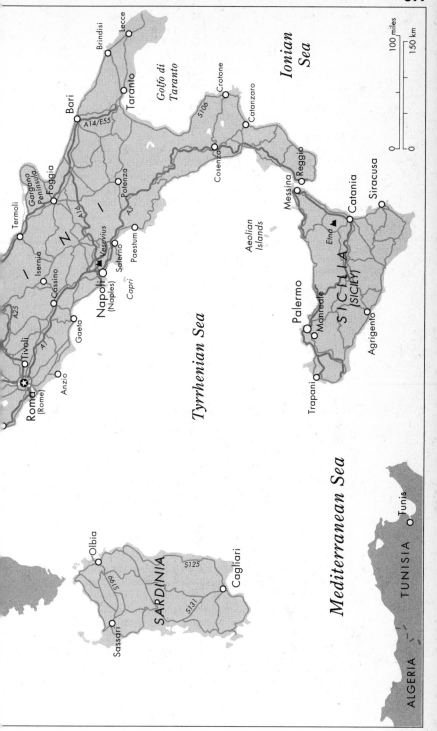

100 miles
150 km

Ionian Sea

Lecce

Brindisi

Taranto

Bari

A14/E55

Golfo di Taranto

Crotone

S106

Catanzaro

Cosenza

Reggio

Messina

Catania

Siracusa

Etna

S I C I L I A
(SICILY)

Palermo

Monreale

Agrigento

Trapani

Gargano Peninsula

Foggia

Termoli

Polenza

A16

Vesuvius

Salerno

Paestum

Isernia

Cassino

A25

Napoli
(Naples)

Capri

Gaeta

A3

Aeolian Islands

A7

Tivoli

Roma
(Rome)

Anzio

Tyrrhenian Sea

Mediterranean Sea

Olbia

S199

S A R D I N I A

S125

Cagliari

S131

Sassari

Mediterranean Sea

Tunis

TUNISIA

ALGERIA

Jan.	40F	5C	May	74F	23C	Sept.	75F	24C
	32	0		57	14		61	16
Feb.	46F	8C	June	80F	27C	Oct.	63F	17C
	35	2		63	17		52	11
Mar.	56F	13C	July	84F	29C	Nov.	51F	10C
	43	6		67	20		43	6
Apr.	65F	18C	Aug.	82F	28C	Dec.	43F	6C
	49	9		66	16		35	2

Currency

The unit of currency in Italy is the lira (plural, lire). There are bills of 1,000, 2,000, 5,000, 10,000, 50,000, and 100,000 lire; coins are worth 10, 20, 50, 100, 200, and 500 lire. At press time (spring 1995), the exchange rate was about 1,621 lire to the dollar and 2,575 lire to the pound sterling. Sooner or later the zeros will be lopped off the lire in order to simplify money dealings and life in general. The long-heralded move has not yet been made, but it seems imminent. If it does come to pass, 5,000 lire would become 5 lire, 50 lire would become 50 centesimi. When it does happen, both old and new values will be in effect until people become accustomed to the new system.

While the present system continues, especially when your purchases run into hundreds of thousands of lire, beware of being shortchanged, a dodge that is practiced at ticket windows and cashiers' desks, as well as in shops and even banks. *Always count your change before you leave the counter.*

Always carry some smaller-denomination bills for sundry purchases; you're less likely to be shortchanged, and you won't have to face the eye-rolling dismay of cashiers chronically short of change.

Credit cards are generally accepted in shops and hotels, but may not always be welcome in restaurants, so always look for those little signs in the window or ask when you enter to avoid embarrassing situations. When you wish to leave a tip beyond the 15% service charge (*see* Tipping *in* Staying in Italy, *below*) that is usually included with your bill, leave it in cash rather than adding it to the credit card slip.

What It Will Cost

Rome, Milan, and Venice are the more expensive Italian cities to visit. Taxes are usually included in hotel bills; a cover charge may appear as a separate item in restaurant checks, as does the service charge, usually about 15%, if added. There is a 19% tax on car rentals.

SAMPLE PRICES

A cup of espresso consumed while standing at a bar costs from 1,200 lire to 1,400 lire, triple that for table service. A bottle of beer costs from 2,200 lire to 3,800 lire, a soft drink about 2,200 lire. A *tramezzino* (small sandwich) costs about 2,200 lire, a more substantial one about 3,500. You will pay about 10,000 lire for a short taxi ride in Rome and Florence, more in Milan. Admission to a major museum is about 12,000 lire; a three-hour sightseeing tour, about 40,000 lire.

Customs on Arrival

Two still cameras and one movie camera can be brought in duty-free. Travelers arriving in Italy from a European Union (EU) country are allowed, duty-free, a total of 800 cigarettes (or 400 cigarillos or 400 cigars), 10 liters of spirits plus 90 liters of still wine, if duty and taxes have been paid on them at the time of purchase. Visitors traveling directly from non-EU countries are allowed 200 cigarettes and cigars or tobacco not exceeding 250 grams, 1 liter of spirits, and 2 liters of still wine.

Not more than 20 million lire in Italian bank notes may be taken into or out of the country.

Language

Italy is accustomed to English-speaking tourists, and in major cities you will find that many people speak at least a little English. In smaller hotels and restaurants, a smattering of Italian comes in handy.

Getting Around

By Car

ROAD CONDITIONS

The extensive network of *autostrade* (toll superhighways) connecting all major towns is complemented by equally well-maintained but toll-free *superstrade* (express highways), *strade statali* (main roads), and *strade provinciali* (secondary roads).

All are clearly signposted and numbered. The ticket issued on entering an autostrada must be returned on leaving, along with the toll. On some shorter autostrade, mainly connections, the toll is payable on entering. Have small bills and change handy for tolls; shortchanging is a risk, so always count your change before leaving the toll booth. If you will be using autostrade extensively, buy a Viacard, an automatic toll card, for 50,000 or 100,000 lire at autostrada locations.

The Autostrada del Sole (A1, A2, and A3) crosses the country from north to south, connecting Milan to Reggio Calabria. The A4 from west to east connects Turin to Trieste.

RULES OF THE ROAD

Driving is on the right. The speed limit on an autostrada for a medium-size car is 130 kph (81 mph). On other roads it is 90 kph (56 mph). Other regulations are largely as in the United States except that the police have the power to levy on-the-spot fines—even as high as $500!

PARKING

Check with your hotel to determine the best place to park. Parking is greatly restricted in the center of most cities. Parking in a "Zona Disco" is for limited periods. City garages cost up to 30,000 lire per day.

GASOLINE

Gas costs the equivalent of more than $4 per U.S. gallon, or about 1,700 lire per liter. Except on the autostrade, most gas stations are closed Sunday; they also close from 12:30 PM to 3:30 PM and at 7 PM for the night. Self-service pumps can be found in most cities and towns.

BREAKDOWNS

Dial 116 for towing and repairs; breakdown service (emergency repairs and towing on autostrada) is free for tourists with foreign license plates or with cars rented in Italy that have breakdown insurance. Dial 113 for ambulance and highway police.

By Train

The fastest service on the FS (Ferrovie dello Stato), the state-owned railroad, are the Pendolino, or ETR 450, trains for which you pay a special supplement and for which seat reservations are required in both first and second class; service includes optional airline-type meals. Also fast are Intercity (IC) and Eurocity (EC) trains, for which you pay a supplement in both classes and for which reservations may be required. Trains designated Interregionale are slower, making more stops. Regionale trains are locals, serving a single region. You can buy tickets and make seat reservations at travel agencies displaying the FS symbol up to two months in advance, thereby avoiding long lines at station ticket windows. You pay a 20% penalty if you purchase your ticket on board the train. Tickets within a 100-kilometer (62-mile) range can be purchased at any *tabacchi* (tobacconist's shop). They also must be stamped in the yellow machines before boarding. There is a refreshment service on all long-distance trains. Tap water on trains is not drinkable. Carry compact bags for easy overhead storage. Trains are very crowded at holiday times; always reserve.

By Plane

Alitalia and domestic affiliate **ATI,** plus some privately owned companies such as **Meridiana,** provide service throughout Italy. Alitalia offers several types of discount fares; inquire at travel agencies or at Alitalia agencies in major cities.

By Bus

Regional bus companies provide service over an extensive network of routes throughout Italy. Route information and timetables are usually available at tourist information offices and travel agencies, or at bus company ticket offices. Among the interregional companies providing long-distance service is **SITA** (Viale Cadorna 105, Florence, tel. 055/47821).

By Boat

Ferries connect the mainland with all the major islands. Car ferries operate to Sicily, Sardinia, Elba, Ponza, Capri (though cars are not advised), and Ischia, among others. Lake ferries connect the towns on the shores of the Italian lakes: Como, Maggiore, and Garda.

Staying in Italy

Telephones

LOCAL CALLS

Most local calls cost 200 lire. Pay phones take either 100-, 200-or 500-lire coins, a *gettone* (token), or *schede* (magnetic card). Tokens can be purchased from the token machine or from the cashier of the store, bar, or other facility where the phone is located. Local calls cost 200 lire for a minimum of 4 minutes. For *teleselezione* (long-distance direct dialing), place several coins in the slot; unused coins are returned when you push the large yellow knob. Buy magnetic cards (costing either 5000 or 10,000 lire) that are increasingly being used to replace coin-operated phones throughout Italy—at tobacconists and post offices. For information and operators in Europe and the Mediterranean area, dial 15; for intercontinental service, dial 170.

INTERNATIONAL CALLS

To place international calls, many travelers go to the Telefoni telephone exchange, where the operator assigns you a booth, can help place your call, and will collect payment when you have finished. Telefoni exchanges (usually marked TELECOM) are found in all cities. To dial an international call, insert a phone card, dial 00, then the country code, area code, and phone number. The cheaper and easier option, however, will be to use your AT&T, MCI, or Sprint calling card. For **AT&T,** dial access number 172–1011; for **MCI,** dial access number 172–1022; for **Sprint,** dial access number 172–1877. You will be connected directly with an operator in the United States.

COUNTRY CODE

The country code for Italy is 39.

Mail

The Italian mail system is notoriously erratic and often excruciatingly slow. Allow up to 15 days for mail to and from the United States and Canada, almost as much to and from the United Kingdom, and much longer for postcards.

POSTAL RATES

Airmail letters to the United States cost 1,250 lire for up to 20 grams; postcards with a short greeting and signature cost 1,000 lire, but cost letter rate if the message is lengthy. Airmail letters to the United Kingdom cost 750 lire, postcards 650 lire.

RECEIVING MAIL

You can have mail sent to American Express offices or to Italian post offices, marked "fermo posta" and addressed to you c/o Palazzo delle Poste, with the name of the city in which you will pick it up. In either case you must show your passport and pay a small fee.

Shopping

SALES-TAX REFUNDS

Italy's value-added tax, known as the IVA-refund system, is complicated. Foreign tourists who have spent more than 300,000 lire (before tax) in one store can take advantage of it, however. At the time of purchase, with passport or ID in hand, ask the store for an invoice describing the article or articles and price. If your destination when you leave Italy is a non-EU country, you must have the invoice stamped at customs upon departure from Italy; if your destination is another EU country, you must obtain the customs stamp upon departure from that country. Once back home—and within 90 days of the date of purchase—you must send the stamped invoice back to the store, which should forward the IVA rebate directly to you. If the store participates in the Europe Tax-Free Shopping System (those that do display a sign to the effect), things are simpler. The invoice provided is a Tax-Free Cheque in the amount of the tax refund, which can be cashed at the Tax-Free Cash Refund window in the transit area of major airports and border crossings.

BARGAINING

Most shops now have *prezzi fissi* (fixed prices), but you may be able to get a discount on a large purchase. Always bargain with a street vendor or at a market (except for food).

Opening and Closing Times

Banks. Banks are open weekdays 8:30–1:30 and 2:45–3:45.

Churches. Churches are usually open from early morning to noon or 12:30, when they close for about two hours or more, opening again in the afternoon until about 7 PM.

Museums. National museums are usually open from 9 AM until 2 and are often closed on Monday, but there are many exceptions. Nonnational museums have entirely different hours, which may vary according to season. Archaeological sites are usually closed on Monday. At all museums and sites, ticket offices close an hour or so before official closing time. Always check with the local tourist office for current hours and holiday closings.

Shops. Shops are open, with individual variations, from 9 to 1 and from 3:30 or 4 to 7 or 7:30. They are open from Monday through Saturday, but close for a half day during the week; for example, in Rome most shops (except food shops) are closed on Monday morning (Saturday afternoon in July and August), though a 1995 ordinance allows greater freedom. Some tourist-oriented shops are open all day, every day, as in downtown Rome, Florence, and Venice.

National Holidays

Offices, shops, and museums are closed on the following dates: January 1; January 6 (Epiphany); April 7 (Easter Sunday); April 25 (Liberation Day); May 1 (May Day); August 15 (the religious feast of the Assumption, known as Ferragosto); November 1 (All Saints Day); December 8 (Immaculate Conception); December 25-26. Services are also closed during local feast days in major cities, such as Venice (April 25, St. Mark), Florence (June 24, St. John the Baptist), and Rome (June 29, Sts. Peter and Paul).

Dining

Generally speaking, a *ristorante* pays more attention to decor, service, and menu than does a trattoria, which is simpler and often family-run. An *osteria* used to be a lowly tavern, though now the term may be used to designate a chic and expensive eatery. A *tavola calda* offers hot dishes and snacks, with seating. A *rosticceria* offers the same, to take out.

The menu is always posted in the window or just inside the door of an eating establishment. Check to see what is offered, and note the charges for *coperto* (cover) and *servizio* (service), which will increase your check. Many restaurants offer a *menu turistico*, usually a complete dinner, limited to a few entrées, at a reasonable price (including taxes and service, with beverages extra).

MEALTIMES

Lunch hour in Rome lasts from 1 to 3, dinner from 8 to 10. Service begins and ends a half hour earlier in Florence and Venice, later in the south. Practically all restaurants close one day a week; some close for winter or summer vacation.

PRECAUTIONS

Tap water is safe in large cities and almost everywhere else unless noted *non potabile*. Bottled mineral water is available everywhere, *gassata* (with bubbles) or *non gassata* (without). If you prefer tap water, ask for *acqua semplice*.

WHAT TO WEAR

Except for restaurants in the **$$$$** and occasionally in the **$$$** categories, where jacket and tie are advisable, casual attire is acceptable.

RATINGS

Prices are per person and include first course, main course, dessert or fruit, and house wine, where available. Highly recommended restaurants are indicated by a star ★.

CATEGORY	ROME, MILAN*	OTHER AREAS
$$$$	over 120,000 lire	over 80,000 lire
$$$	65,000 lire–120,000 lire	45,000 lire–80,000 lire
$$	40,000 lire–65,000 lire	25,000 lire–45,000 lire
$	under 40,000 lire	under 25,000 lire

Note that restaurant prices in Venice are slightly higher than those in Rome and Milan; in small cities prices are usually lower.

Lodging

Italy, and especially the main tourist capitals of Rome, Florence, and Venice, offers a good choice of accommodations. Room rates are on a par with most European capitals, although porters, room service, and in-house laundering are disappearing in all but the most elegant hotels. Taxes and service are included in the room rate. Although breakfast is usually quoted in the room rate, it's actually an extra charge that you can decline. The desk might not be happy about it, but make your preference clear when booking or checking in. Air-conditioning also may be an extra charge. In older hotels, room quality may be uneven; if you don't like the room you're given, ask for another. This applies to noise, too; some front rooms are bigger and have views but get street noise. Specify if you care about having either a bathtub or shower, as not all rooms have both. In **$$** and **$** places, showers may be the drain-in-the-floor type guaranteed to flood the bathroom. Major cities have hotel reservation service booths in the rail stations.

HOTELS

Italian hotels are classified by regional tourist boards from five-star (deluxe) to one-star (modest hotels and small inns). The established price of the room appears on a rate card on the back of the door of your room or inside the closet door, though you may be able to get a lower rate by asking. Any variations above the posted rate should be cause for complaint and should be reported to the local tourist office. CIGA, Jolly, Space, Atahotels, Best Western, and Italhotels are among the reliable chains or groups operating in Italy, with CIGA among the most luxurious. Sheraton hotels are making an impact in Italy in a big way, though most, located in Rome, Florence, Bari, Padua, and Catania, tend to be geared toward convention and business travel. There are a few Relais et Châteaux member hotels that are noted for individual atmosphere, personal service, and luxury; they are also expensive. The AGIP chain is found mostly on main highways. The Family Hotels group, composed mostly of small **$$** and **$** family-run hotels, offers good value, reliability, and special attention to families.

Standards in one-star hotels are very uneven. At best, rooms are usually spotlessly clean but basic, with shower and toilets down the hall.

RENTALS

More and more people are discovering the attractions of renting a house, cottage, or apartment in the Italian countryside. These are ideal for families or for groups of up to eight people looking for a bargain—or just independence. Availability is subject to change, so it is best to ask your travel agent or the nearest branch of ENIT, the Italian tourist board, about rentals.

CAMPING

Italy has a wide selection of campgrounds, and the Italians themselves have taken to camping by the thousands, which means that beach or mountain sites will be crammed in July and August. It's best to avoid these peak months. An international camping *carnet* (permit) is required; get one from your local association before leaving home. You can buy a campsite directory such as the detailed guide published by the Touring Club Italiano (available in bookstores) or obtain the free directory of campsites published by the Federazione Italiana del Campeggio (Casella Postale 23, 50041 Calenzano, Florence, fax 055/882–5918) in tourist information offices or by mail from the organization if you send three international reply coupons.

RATINGS

The following price categories are determined by the cost of two people in a double room. Highly recommended lodgings are indicated by a ★.

CATEGORY	ROME, MILAN*	OTHER AREAS
$$$$	over 450,000 lire	over 350,000 lire
$$$	280,000 lire– 450,000 lire	200,000 lire– 350,000 lire
$$	160,000 lire– 280,000 lire	120,000 lire– 200,000 lire
$	under 160,000 lire	under 120,000 lire

As with restaurant prices, the cost of hotels in Venice may be slightly more than those shown here.

Tipping

Tipping practices vary depending on where you are. Italians tip smaller amounts in small cities and towns, often not at all in cafés and taxis north of Rome. The following guidelines apply in major cities.

In restaurants, a 15% service charge is usually added to the total, but it doesn't all go to the waiter. In large cities and resorts it is customary to give the waiter a 5% tip in addition to the service charge made on the check.

Charges for service are included in all hotel bills, but smaller tips to staff members are appreciated. In general, in a **$$** hotel, chambermaids should be given about 1,000 lire per room per day, 4,000 lire–5,000 lire per week; bellhops 1,000 lire–2,000 lire. Tip a minimum of 1,000 lire for room service and valet service. Tip breakfast waiters 500 lire–1,000 lire per day per table (at end of stay). These amounts should be increased by 40% in **$$$** hotels, doubled in **$$$$** hotels. Give the concierge about 15% of his bill for services. Tip doormen about 500 lire for calling a cab.

Taxi drivers are happy with 5%–10%. Porters at railroad stations and airports charge a fixed rate per suitcase; tip an additional 500 lire per person, more if the porter is very helpful. Service-station attendants are tipped 500 lire–1,000 lire if they are especially helpful. Tip guides about 2,000 lire per person for a half-day tour, more if they are very good.

ROME

Arriving and Departing

By Plane

Rome's principal airport is at Fiumicino, 29 kilometers (18 miles) from the city. Though its official name is Leonardo da Vinci Airport, everybody calls it Fiumicino. For flight information, call 06/659-53640. The smaller airport of Ciampino is on the edge of Rome and is used as an alternative by international and domestic lines, especially for charter flights. For flight information, call 06/794941.

BETWEEN THE AIRPORT AND DOWNTOWN

To get to downtown Rome from Fiumicino Airport you have a choice of two trains. Inquire at the airport (at EPT or train information counters) as to which takes you closest to your hotel. The nonstop Airport-Termini express takes you directly to Track 22 at Termini Station, Rome's main train terminal, well served by taxis and the hub of Metro (subway) and bus lines. The ride to Termini takes 30 minutes; departures are hourly, beginning at 7:50 AM, with the final departure at 10:25 PM. Tickets cost 12,000 lire. The other airport train (FM1) runs to Rome and beyond to Monterotondo, a suburban town to the east. The main stops in Rome are at Trastevere, Ostiense, and Tiburtina Stations. At each of these you can find taxis and bus and/or Metro connections to various parts of Rome. This train runs from 6:55 AM to 8:15 PM, with departures every 20 minutes. The ride to Tiburtina takes 40 minutes. Tickets cost 7,000 lire. For either train you buy your ticket at automatic vending machines (you need Italian currency). There are ticket counters at some stations (Termini Track 22, Trastevere, Tiburtina).

A taxi to or from Fiumicino costs about 65,000 lire, including supplements. At a booth inside the terminal you can hire a four-or five-passenger car with driver for a little more. If you decide to take a taxi, use only the yellow or the newer white cabs, which must wait outside the terminal; make sure the meter is running. Gypsy cab drivers solicit your business as you come out of customs; they're not reliable, and their rates may be rip-offs.

Ciampino is connected with the Anagnina Station of the Metro A by bus (every half hour). A taxi between Ciampino and downtown Rome costs about 35,000 lire.

By Train
Termini Station is Rome's main train terminal, while Tiburtina and Ostiense Stations serve some long-distance trains, many commuter trains and the FM1 line to Fiumicino Airport. For train information, try the English-speaking personnel at the Information Office in Termini, or at any travel agency. Tickets and seats can be reserved and purchased at travel agencies bearing the "FS" (Ferrovie dello Stato) emblem. Short-distance tickets are also sold by tobacconists and from ticket machines (instructions in English) in the stations.

By Bus
There is no central bus station in Rome; long-distance and suburban buses terminate either near Tiburtina Station or near strategically located Metro stops.

By Car
The main access routes from the north are the Autostrada del Sole (A1) from Milan and Florence, and the Aurelia highway (SS 1) from Genoa. The principal route to or from points south, such as Naples, is the southern leg of the Autostrada del Sole (A2). All highways connect with the GRA (Grande Raccordo Anulare), a beltway that encircles Rome and funnels traffic into the city. Markings on the GRA are confusing; take time in advance to study which route into the center best suits you.

Getting Around

The best way to see Rome is to choose an area or a sight that you particularly want to see, reach it by bus or Metro, then explore the area on foot, following one of our itineraries or improvising one to suit your mood and interests. Wear comfortable, sturdy shoes, preferably with thick rubber soles to cushion you against the cobblestones. Heed our advice on security, and try to avoid the noise and polluted air of heavily trafficked streets, taking parallel byways wherever possible.

You can buy transportation route maps at newsstands and at ATAC (bus company) information and ticket booths.

Metrebus
Rome's integrated Metrebus transportation system includes buses and trams (ATAC), Metro and suburban trains and buses (COTRAL), and some other suburban trains (FS) run by the state railways. A ticket valid for 75 minutes on any combination of buses and trams and one admission to the Metro costs 1,500 lire (date-stamp your ticket when boarding the first vehicle and stamp it again when boarding for the last time).

Tickets are sold at tobacconists, newsstands, some coffee bars, automatic ticket machines in Metro stations, some bus stops, and at ATAC and COTRAL ticket booths. A BIG tourist ticket, valid for one day on all public transport, costs 6,000 lire. A weekly ticket (Settimanale, also known as CIS) costs 24,000 lire and can be purchased only at ATAC and Metro booths.

By Metro

The Metro provides the easiest and fastest way to get around. It opens at 5:30 AM, and the last train leaves each terminal at 11:30 PM. Metro A runs from the eastern part of the city to Termini Station and past Piazza di Spagna and Piazzale Flaminio to Ottaviano, near St. Peter's and the Vatican Museums. Metro B serves Termini, the Colosseum, and the Tiburtina Station (also the terminal of the Fiumicino Airport train).

By Bus

Orange ATAC (tel. 06/4695–4444) city buses (and a few streetcar lines) run from about 6 AM to midnight, with night buses (indicated N) on some lines (night service may be eliminated entirely; check locally). When entering a bus, remember to board at the rear and exit at the middle.

By Taxi

Taxis wait at stands and, for a small extra charge, can also be called by telephone. The meter starts at 6,400 lire; there are supplements for service after 10 PM, on Sundays and holidays, and for each piece of baggage. Use the yellow or the newer white cabs only, and be very sure to check the meter. To call a cab, phone 06/3570, 06/3875, 06/4994, or 06/88177.

By Bicycle

Bikes provide a pleasant means of getting around when traffic isn't heavy. There are bike-rental shops at Via di Porta Castello 43, near St. Peter's, and at Piazza Navona 69, next to Bar Navona. Rental concessions are at the Piazza di Spagna and Piazza del Popolo Metro stops, and at Largo San Silvestro and Largo Argentina. There are also some in Villa Borghese, at Sector III of the underground parking lot and at Viale della Pineta and Viale del Bambino on the Pincio.

By Moped

You can rent a moped or scooter and mandatory helmet at **Scoot-a-Long** (Via Cavour 302, tel. 06/678–0206) or **St. Peter Moto** (Via di Porta Castello 43, tel. 06/687–5714).

Important Addresses and Numbers

Tourist Information

The main **EPT** (Rome Provincial Tourist) office is at Via Parigi 5, 00185 (tel. 06/488–3748, open weekdays 8:15–7:15, Sat. 8:15–1:15). There are also EPT booths at Termini Station and Fiumicino Airport. A booth on the main floor of the **ENIT** (National Tourist Board) building at Via Marghera 2 (tel. 06/497–1293, open Mon., Wed., Fri. 9–1 and 4–6; Tues., Thurs. 9–1) can provide information on destinations in Italy outside Rome.

White municipal tourist information booths are located at Largo Goldoni (corner of Via Condotti and Via del Corso in the Spanish Steps area), Via dei Fori Imperiali (opposite the entrance to the Roman Forum) and Via Nazionale (at Palazzo delle Esposizioni). They're open Tuesday–Saturday 10–6, Sunday 10–1.

Consulates

U.S. (Via Veneto 121, tel. 06/46741). **Canadian** (Via Zara 30, tel. 06/445981). **U.K.** (Via Venti Settembre 80a, tel. 06/482–5441).

Emergencies

Police (tel. 06/4686; also known as Polizia Urbana and Polizia Statale, responsible for traffic violations, theft, etc.); **Carabinieri** (tel. 06/112; responsible for general crime); **Ambulance** (tel. 06/118). **Doctor:** for a recommendation call your consulate, the private **Salvator Mundi Hospital** (tel. 06/588961), or the **Rome American Hospital** (tel. 06/22551), which has English-speaking staff members. **Pharmacies:** You will find American and British medicines (or their equivalents) and English-speaking personnel at **Farmacia Internazionale Capranica** (Piazza Capranica 96, tel. 06/679–4680), **Farmacia Internazionale Barberini** (Piazza Barberini 49, tel. 06/482–5456), and **Farmacia Cola di Rienzo** (Via Cola di Rienzo 213, tel. 06/324–3130), among others. They are open 8:30–1 and 4–8; some stay open all night.

English-Language Bookstores

You'll find English-language books and magazines at newsstands in the center of Rome, especially on Via Veneto. Also try the **Economy Book and Video Center** (Via Torino 136, tel. 06/474–6877), the **Anglo-American Bookstore** (Via della Vite 102, tel. 06/679–5222), or the **Lion Bookshop** (Via del Babuino 181, tel. 06/322–5837).

Travel Agencies

American Express (Piazza di Spagna 38, tel. 06/67641). **CIT** (Piazza della Repubblica 64, tel. 06/482–7052). **CTS** (youth and budget travel, discount fares; Via Genova 16, tel. 06/46791; for information tel. 06/467–9271).

Guided Tours

Orientation Tours

American Express (tel. 06/67641), **CIT** (tel. 06/47941), and **Appian Line** (tel. 06/488–4151) offer three-hour tours in air-conditioned buses with English-speaking guides, covering Rome with four separate itineraries: "Ancient Rome" (including the Roman Forum and Colosseum), "Classic Rome" (including St. Peter's Basilica, Trevi Fountain, and the Janiculum Hill, with its panorama of the city), "Christian Rome" (some major churches and the Catacombs), and the "Vatican Museums and Sistine Chapel." Most tours cost about 39,000 lire, though the Vatican Museums tour is about 52,000 lire. American Express tours depart from Piazza di Spagna, CIT from Piazza della Repubblica, and Appian Line picks sightseers up at their hotels. The least expensive organized bus tour is run by **ATAC,** the municipal bus company, and lasts three hours. Book tours for about 10,000 lire at the ATAC information booth in front of Termini Station. There is at least one tour daily, departing at 2:30 (3:30 in summer).

American Express can provide a car for up to three persons, limousine for up to seven, and minibus for up to nine, all with English-speaking driver. Guide service is extra. A minibus costs about 500,000 lire for three hours. Almost all operators offer "Rome by Night" tours, with or without dinner and entertainment. Reservations can be made through travel agents.

Special-Interest Tours

You can make your own arrangements (at no cost) to attend a public papal audience in the Vatican or to be at the Sunday blessing at the Pope's summer residence at Castel Gandolfo, or do it through **CIT** (tel.

06/47941), **Appian Line** (tel. 06/488–4151), or **Carrani** (tel. 06/488–0510). **Secret Walks** (tel. 06/397–28728) conducts small groups on theme walks led by English-speaking connoisseurs of the city.

Excursions

Most operators offer half-day excursions to Tivoli to see the Villa d'Este's spectacular fountains and gardens; Appian Line's and CIT's half-day tours to Tivoli also include Hadrian's Villa and its impressive ancient ruins. Most operators have all-day excursions to Assisi, to Pompeii and/or Capri, and to Florence.

Personal Guides

Visitors can arrange for a personal guide through **American Express** (tel. 06/67641), **CIT** (tel. 06/47941), or the main **EPT** tourist office (tel. 06/488–3748).

Exploring Rome

Antiquity is taken for granted in Rome, where successive ages have piled the present on top of the past—building, layering, and overlapping their own particular segments of Rome's 2,500 years of history to form a remarkably varied urban complex. Most of the city's major sights are located in a fairly small area known as the *centro*. At its heart lies ancient Rome, where the Forum and Colosseum stand. It was around this core that the other sections of the city grew up through the ages: medieval Rome, which covered the horn of land that pushes the Tiber toward the Vatican and extended across the river into Trastevere; and Renaissance Rome, which was erected upon medieval foundations and extended as far as the Vatican, creating beautiful villas on what was then the outskirts of the city.

The layout of the centro is highly irregular, but several landmarks serve as orientation points to identify the areas that most visitors come to see: the Colosseum, the Pantheon and Piazza Navona, St. Peter's, the Spanish Steps, and Villa Borghese. You'll need a good map to find your way around; newsstands offer a wide choice. Energetic sightseers will walk a lot, a much more pleasant way to see the city now that some traffic has been barred from the centro during the day; others might choose to take taxis, buses, or the Metro. The important thing is to relax and enjoy Rome. Don't try to see everything, but do take time to savor its pleasures. If you are in Rome during a hot spell, do as the Romans do: Start out early in the morning, have a light lunch and a long siesta during the hottest hours, then resume sightseeing in the late afternoon and end your evening with a leisurely meal outdoors, refreshed by cold Frascati wine and the *ponentino*, the cool evening breeze.

Ancient Rome

Numbers in the margin correspond to points of interest on the Roma (Rome) map.

❶ Start your first tour at the city's center, in **Piazza Venezia.** Behind the enormous marble monument honoring the first king of unified Italy, ❷ Victor Emmanuel II, stands the **Campidoglio** (Capitol Square) on the Capitoline Hill. The majestic ramp and beautifully proportioned piazza are Michelangelo's handiwork, as are the three palaces. **Palazzo Senatorio** at the center is still the ceremonial seat of Rome's city hall; it was built over the Tabularium, where ancient Rome's state archives were kept.

③ The palaces flanking the Palazzo Senatorio contain the **Capitoline Museums.** On the left, the **Museo Capitolino** holds some fine classical sculptures, including the gilded bronze equestrian statue of Marcus Aurelius that once stood on the pedestal in the piazza, as well as the *Dying Gaul,* the *Capitoline Venus,* and a fascinating series of portrait busts of an**④** cient philosophers and emperors. In the courtyard of the **Palazzo dei Conservatori,** on the right of the piazza, you can use the mammoth fragments of a colossal statue of the emperor Constantine as amusing props for snapshots. Inside you will find splendidly frescoed salons, as well as sculptures and paintings. *Piazza del Campidoglio, tel. 06/671–002475. Admission: 10,000 lire, free last Sun. of month. Open May–Sept., Tues. 9–1:30, 5–8; Wed.–Fri. 9–1:30; Sat. 9–1:30, 8–11; Sun. 9–1. Oct.–Apr., Tues. and Sat. 9–1:30, 5–8; Wed.–Fri. 9–1:30; Sun. 9–1.*

⑤ The Campidoglio is also the site of the very old church of the **Aracoeli,** which you can reach by way of the stairs on the far side of the Museo Capitolino. Stop in to see the medieval pavement; the Renaissance gilded ceiling that commemorates the victory of Lepanto; some Pinturicchio frescoes; and a much-revered wooden statue of the Holy Child. The Campidoglio gardens offer some good views of the heart of ancient Rome, the Imperial Fora, built when the original Roman Forum became too small for the city's burgeoning needs.

⑥ In the valley below the Campidoglio, the **Foro Romano** (Roman Forum), once only a marshy hollow, became the political, commercial, and social center of Rome, studded with public meeting halls, shops, and temples. As Rome declined, these monuments lost their importance and eventually were destroyed by fire or the invasions of barbarians. Rubble accumulated (though much of it was carted off later by medieval home-builders as construction material), and the site reverted to marshy pastureland; sporadic excavations began at the end of the 19th century.

You don't really have to try to make sense of the mass of marble fragments scattered over the area of the Roman Forum. Just consider that 2,000 years ago this was the center of the Mediterranean world. Wander down the Via Sacra and climb the Palatine Hill, where the emperors had their palaces and where 16th-century cardinals strolled in elaborate Italian gardens. From the belvedere you have a good view of the Circus Maximus. *Entrances on Via dei Fori Imperiali, Piazza Santa Maria Nova and Via di San Gregorio, tel. 06/699–0110. Admission: 12,000 lire. Open Apr.–Sept., Mon.–Sat. 9–6, Sun. 9–1; Oct.–Mar., Mon.–Sat. 9–3, Sun. 9–1.*

Leave the Forum from the exit at Piazza Santa Maria Nova, near the **⑦** Arch of Titus, and head for the **Colosseum,** inaugurated in AD 80 with a program of games and shows that lasted 100 days. On opening day alone 5,000 wild animals perished in the arena. The Colosseum could hold more than 50,000 spectators; it was faced with marble, decorated with stuccos, and had an ingenious system of awnings to provide shade. Try to see it both in daytime and at night, when yellow floodlights make it a magical sight. The Colosseum, by the way, takes its name from a colossal, 118-foot statue of Nero that stood nearby. You must pay a fee to explore the upper levels. *Piazza del Colosseo, tel. 06/700–4261. Admission: 8,000 lire to upper levels. Open Apr.–Sept. Mon., Tues., and Thurs.–Sat. 9–7; Sun. and Wed. 9–1. Oct.–Mar. Mon., Tues., Thurs.–Sat. 9–3.*

TIME OUT For delicious *gelati* (ice cream) try **Ristoro della Salute,** one of Rome's best *gelaterie. Piazza del Colosseo 2a.*

712

Aracoeli, **5**

Arch of Constantine, **8**

Baths of Caracalla, **9**

Campidoglio, **2**

Campo dei Fiori, **32**

Castel Sant' Angelo, **21**

Church of Santa Maria della Concezione, **19**

Church of the Gesù, **27**

Colosseum, **7**

Fabricio Bridge, **36**

Fontana di Trevi, **16**

Foro Romano (Roman Forum), **6**

Galleria Borghese, **20**

Museo Capitolino, **3**

Palazzo Barberini, **18**

Palazzo dei Conservatori, **4**

Palazzo Farnese, **34**

Pantheon, **29**

Piazza Barberini, **17**

Piazza del Popolo, **10**

Piazza Farnese, **33**

Piazza Navona, **31**

Piazza San Pietro, **22**

Piazza Venezia, **1**

San Luigi dei Francesi, **30**

Santa Maria del Popolo, **11**

Santa Maria Sopra Minerva, **28**

Spanish Steps, **15**

St. Peter's Basilica, **24**

Tiberina Island, **35**

Trinità dei Monti, **14**

Vatican Gardens, **25**

Vatican Museums, **26**

Vatican Palace, **23**

Via Condotti, **13**

Via del Babuino, **12**

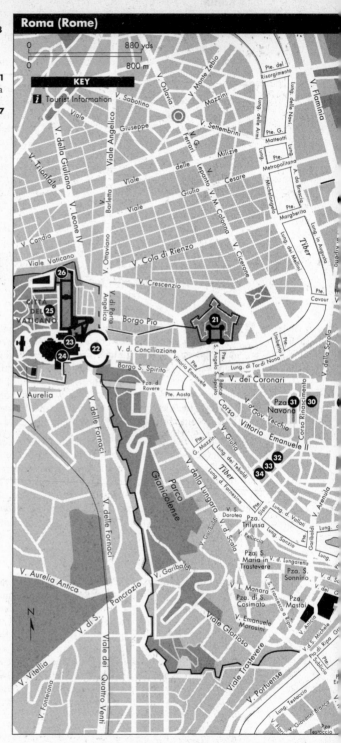

Roma (Rome)

KEY

ℹ️ Tourist Information

8 Stroll past the **Arch of Constantine.** The reliefs depict Constantine's victory over Maxentius at the Milvian Bridge. Just before this battle in AD 312, Constantine had a vision of a cross in the heavens and heard the words, "In this sign thou shalt conquer." The victory led not only to the construction of this majestic marble arch but also to a turning point in the history of Christianity: Soon afterward a grateful Constantine decreed that it was a lawful religion and should be tolerated throughout the empire.

9 A fairly long but pleasant walk takes you to the **Baths of Caracalla,** which numbered among ancient Rome's most beautiful and luxurious, inaugurated by Caracalla in 217 and used until the 6th century. An ancient version of a swanky athletic club, the baths were open to the public; citizens could bathe, socialize, and exercise in huge pools and richly decorated halls and libraries, now towering ruins. *Via delle Terme di Caracalla. Admission: 8,000 lire. Open Apr.–Sept., Tues.–Sat. 9–6, Sun. and Mon. 9–1; Oct.–Mar., Tues.–Sat. 9–3, Sun.–Mon. 9–1.*

Piazzas and Fountains

10 **Piazza del Popolo** is one of Rome's most vast and airy squares, but for many years it was just an exceptionally beautiful parking lot with a 3,000-year-old obelisk in the middle. Now most traffic has been barred, **11** and the piazza is open to strollers. The church of **Santa Maria del Popolo** over in the corner of the piazza near the arch stands out more, now that it has been cleaned, and is rich in art, including two stunning Caravaggios in the chapel to the left of the main altar.

12 If you're interested in antiques, stroll along **Via del Babuino.** If trendy fashions and accessories suit your fancy, take Via del Corso and turn into **13** **Via Condotti,** Rome's most elegant and expensive shopping street. Here you can ogle fabulous jewelry, designer fashions, and accessories in the windows of Buccellati, Ferragamo, Valentino, Gucci, and Bulgari.

TIME OUT The more-than-200-year-old **Antico Caffè Greco** is the haunt of writers, artists, and well-groomed ladies toting Gucci shopping bags. With its small marble-topped tables and velour settees, it's a nostalgic sort of place—Goethe, Byron, and Liszt were regulars here, and even Buffalo Bill stopped in when his road show came to town. Table service is expensive. *Via Condotti 86. Closed Sun.*

14 Via Condotti gives you a head-on view of the Spanish Steps in **Piazza di Spagna,** and of the church of **Trinità dei Monti.** In the center of the piazza is Bernini's **Fountain of the Barcaccia** (Old Boat), around which Romans and tourists cool themselves on hot summer nights. The 200-**15** year-old **Spanish Steps,** named for the Spanish Embassy to the Holy See, opposite the American Express office, are a popular rendezvous, especially for the young people who throng this area. On weekend afternoons, Via del Corso is packed with wall-to-wall teenagers, and McDonald's, tucked away in a corner of Piazza di Spagna beyond the American Express office, is a mob scene. In contrast, **Babington's Tea Room,** to the left of the Spanish Steps, is a stylish institution that caters to an upscale clientele.

To the right of the Spanish Steps is the **Keats and Shelley Memorial House.** Once the home of these romantic poets, it's now a museum. *Piazza di Spagna 26, tel. 06/678–4235. Admission: 5,000 lire. Open June–Sept., weekdays 9–1 and 3–6; Oct.–May, weekdays 9–1 and 2:30–5:30.*

Head for Via del Tritone and cross this heavily trafficked shopping street **16** into narrow Via della Stamperia, which leads to the **Fontana di Trevi** (Trevi Fountain), a spectacular fantasy of mythical sea creatures and cascades of splashing water. Legend has it that visitors must toss a coin into the fountain to ensure their return to Rome, but you'll have to force your way past crowds of tourists and aggressive souvenir vendors to do so. The fountain as you see it was completed in the mid-1700s, but there had been a drinking fountain on the site for centuries. Pope Urban VIII almost sparked a revolt when he slapped a tax on wine to cover the expenses of having the fountain repaired.

⑰ At the top of Via del Tritone, **Piazza Barberini** boasts two fountains by Bernini: the jaunty **Triton** in the middle of the square and the **Fountain of the Bees** at the corner of Via Veneto. Decorated with the heraldic Barberini bees, this shell-shaped fountain bears an inscription that was immediately regarded as an unlucky omen by the superstitious Romans, for it erroneously stated that the fountain had been erected in the 22nd year of the reign of Pope Urban VIII, who had commissioned it, while in fact the 21st anniversary of his election was still some weeks away. The wrong numeral was hurriedly erased, but to no avail: Urban died eight days before the beginning of his 22nd year as pontiff.

⑱ A few steps up Via delle Quattro Fontane is **Palazzo Barberini,** Rome's most splendid 17th-century palace, now surrounded by rather unkempt gardens and occupied in part by the **Galleria Nazionale di Arte Antica.** Visit the latter to see Raphael's *Fornarina,* many other good paintings, some lavishly frescoed ceilings, and a charming suite of rooms decorated in 1782 on the occasion of the marriage of a Barberini heiress. *Via delle Quattro Fontane 13, tel. 06/481–4591. Admission: 8,000 lire. Open Tues.–Sat. 9–2, Sun. 9–1.*

⑲ One of Rome's oddest sights is the **crypt** of the **Church of Santa Maria della Concezione** on Via Veneto, just above the Fountain of the Bees. In four chapels under the main church, the skeletons and scattered bones of some 4,000 dead Capuchin monks are arranged in decorative motifs, a macabre practice peculiar to the Baroque age. *Via Veneto 27, tel. 06/462850. Admission free, but donations encouraged. Open daily 9–noon and 3–6.*

The lower reaches of Via Veneto are quiet and sedate, but at the intersection with Via Bissolati, otherwise known as "Airline Row," the avenue comes to life. The big white palace on the right is the U.S. Embassy, and the even bigger white palace beyond it is the luxurious **Hotel Excelsior.** Together with Doney's next door and the Café de Paris across the street, the Excelsior was a landmark of La Dolce Vita, that effervescent period during the 1950s when movie stars, playboys, and exiled royalty played hide-and-seek with press agents and paparazzi, ducking in and out of nightclubs and hotel rooms along the Via Veneto. The atmosphere of Via Veneto is considerably more sober now, and its cafés cater more to tourists than to the rich and famous.

Via Veneto ends at **Porta Pinciana,** a gate in the 12-mile stretch of defensive walls built by Emperor Aurelian in the 3rd century; 400 years later, when the Goths got too close for comfort, Belisarius reinforced the gate with two massive towers. Beyond is **Villa Borghese,** most famous of Rome's parks, studded with tall pines that are gradually dying off as pollution and age take their toll. Inside the park, strike off to

⑳ the right toward the **Galleria Borghese,** a pleasure palace created by Cardinal Scipione Borghese in 1613 as a showcase for his fabulous sculpture collection. In the throes of structural repairs for several years, the now-public gallery is, at press time, only partially open to visitors. It's still worth a visit to see the seductive reclining statue of Pauline Borghese by Canova, and some extraordinary works by Bernini, among them the unforgettable *Apollo and Daphne,* in which marble is transformed into flesh and foliage. With restorations dragging on, perhaps into 1996, a few of the best works, including Caravaggio's, have been moved from the upstairs picture gallery, which is closed, to the San Michele complex in Trastevere, where they are on view (Via di San Michele, tel. 06/581–6732; admission: 4,000 lire; open Tues.–Sat. 9–7, Sun.–Mon. 9–1). *During reconstruction, entrance to Galleria Borghese is on Via Raimondi, reached from Via Pinciana. Via Pinciana (Piazzale Museo Borghese–Villa Borghese), tel. 06/854–8577. Admission: 4,000 lire. Open May–Sept., Tues.–Sat. 9–7, Sun. 9–1; Oct.–Apr., Tues.–Sat. 9–1:30, Sun. 9–1.*

Castel Sant'Angelo–St. Peter's

Ponte Sant'Angelo, an ancient bridge spanning the Tiber, is decorated with lovely Baroque angels designed by Bernini. From the bridge there are fine views of St. Peter's, in the distance, and of the nearby **Castel Sant'Angelo,** a formidable fortress that was originally built as the tomb of Emperor Hadrian in the 2nd century AD. In its early days, it looked much like the **Augusteo,** or Tomb of Augustus, which still stands more or less in its original form across the river. Hadrian's Tomb was incorporated into the town walls and served as a military stronghold during the barbarian invasions. According to legend it got its present name in the 6th century, when Pope Gregory the Great, passing by in a religious procession, saw an angel with a sword appear above the ramparts to signal the end of the plague that was raging. Enlarged and fortified, the castle became a refuge for the popes, who fled to it along the **Passetto,** an arcaded passageway that links it with the Vatican. Inside the castle you see ancient corridors, medieval cells and Renaissance salons, a museum of antique weapons, courtyards piled with stone cannonballs, and terraces with great views of the city. There's a pleasant bar with outdoor tables on one level. The highest terrace of all, under the newly restored bronze statue of the legendary angel, is the one from which Puccini's heroine, Tosca, threw herself. *Lungotevere Castello 50, tel. 06/687–5036. Admission: 8,000 lire. Open Mon.–Sat. 9–2, Sun. 9–noon. Closed 2nd Tues. and Fri. of month.*

Via della Conciliazione, the broad avenue leading to St. Peter's Basilica, was created by Mussolini's architects by razing blocks of old houses. This opened up a vista of the basilica, giving the eye time to adjust to its mammoth dimensions, and thereby spoiling the effect Bernini sought when he enclosed his vast square (which is really oval) in the embrace of huge quadruple colonnades. In **Piazza San Pietro** (St. Peter's Square), which has held up to 400,000 people at one time, look for the stone disks in the pavement halfway between the fountains and the obelisk. From these points the colonnades seem to be formed of a single row of columns all the way around.

When you enter St. Peter's Square (completed in 1667), you are entering Vatican territory. Since the Lateran Treaty of 1929, **Vatican City** has been an independent and sovereign state, which covers about 108 acres and is surrounded by thick, high walls. Its gates are watched over by the Swiss Guards, who still wear the colorful dress uniforms designed by Michelangelo. Sovereign of this little state is John Paul II, 264th Pope of the Roman Catholic Church. At noon on Sunday, the Pope appears at his third-floor study window in the **Vatican Palace,** to the right of the basilica, to bless the crowd in the square. (Note: Entry to St. Peter's, the Vatican Museums, and all other sites within Vatican City, e.g., the Gardens, is barred to those wearing shorts, miniskirts, sleeveless T-shirts, and otherwise revealing clothing. Women should carry scarves to cover bare shoulders and upper arms or wear blouses that come to the elbow. Men should dress modestly, in slacks and shirts.) Free 90-minute tours of St. Peter's Basilica are offered in English daily (usually starting about 10 AM and 3 PM) by volunteer guides. They start at the information desk under the basilica portico.

㉔ **St. Peter's Basilica** is one of Rome's most impressive sights. It takes a while to absorb the sheer magnificence of it, however, and its rich decoration may not be to everyone's taste. Its size alone is overwhelming, and the basilica is best appreciated when providing the lustrous background for ecclesiastical ceremonies thronged with the faithful. The original basilica was built in the early 4th century AD by the emperor Constantine, over an earlier shrine that supposedly marked the burial place of St. Peter. After more than a thousand years, the old basilica was so decrepit it had to be torn down. The task of building a new, much larger one took almost 200 years and employed the architectural genius of Alberti, Bramante, Raphael, Peruzzi, Antonio Sangallo the Younger, and Michelangelo, who died before the dome he had planned could be completed. Finally, in 1626, St. Peter's Basilica was finished.

The basilica is full of extraordinary works of art. Among the most famous is Michelangelo's *Pietà* (1498), seen in the first chapel on the right just as you enter the basilica. Michelangelo has four *Pietà*s to his credit. The earliest and best known can be seen here. Two others are in Florence, and the fourth, the *Rondanini Pietà,* is in Milan.

At the end of the central aisle is the bronze statue of **St. Peter,** its foot worn by centuries of reverent kisses. The bronze throne above the altar in the apse was created by Bernini to contain a simple wood and ivory chair once believed to have belonged to St. Peter. Bernini's bronze *baldacchino* (canopy) over the papal altar was made with metal stripped from the portico of the Pantheon at the order of Pope Urban VIII, one of the powerful Roman Barberini family. His practice of plundering ancient monuments for material to implement his grandiose schemes inspired the famous quip, *"Quod non fecerunt barbari, fecerunt Barberini"* ("What the barbarians didn't do, the Barberini did").

As you stroll up and down the aisles and transepts, observe the fine mosaic copies of famous paintings above the altars, the monumental tombs and statues, and the fine stucco work. Stop at the **Treasury** (Historical Museum), which contains some priceless liturgical objects.

Vatican Grottoes

The entrance to the so-called **Vatican Grottoes,** or crypt, is in one of the huge piers at the crossing. It's best to leave this visit for last, as the crypt's only exit takes you outside the church. The crypt contains chapels and the tombs of many popes. It occupies the area of the original basilica, over the necropolis, the ancient burial ground where evidence of what may be St. Peter's burial place has been found. You can book special tours of the necropolis. To see the roof and dome of the basilica take the elevator or climb the stairs in the courtyard near the exit of the Vatican Grottoes. From the roof you can climb a short interior staircase to the base of the dome for an overhead view of the interior of the basilica. Only if you are in good shape should you attempt the very long, strenuous, and claustrophobic climb up the narrow stairs to the balcony of the lantern atop the dome, where the view embraces the Vatican Gardens as well as all of Rome. *St. Peter's Basilica, tel. 06/6988–4466. Open daily Apr.–Sept., 7–7, Oct.–Mar. 7–6. Treasury (Museo Storico-Artistico): entrance in Sacristy. Admission: 3,000 lire. Open Apr.–Sept., daily 9–6:30; Oct.–Mar., daily 9–5:30. Roof* *and Dome: entrance in courtyard to the left as you leave basilica. Admission: 6,000 lire, including use of elevator to roof, 5,000 lire if you climb spiral ramp on foot. Open Apr.–Sept., daily 8–6; Oct.–Mar., daily 8–5. Vatican Grottoes (Tombs of the Popes): entrance alternates among piers at crossing. Admission: free. Open Apr.–Sept., daily 7–6; Oct.–Mar., daily 7–5. Necropolis: Apply a few days in advance to Ufficio Scavi, left beyond Arco delle Campane entrance to Vatican, or try in the morning for the same day, tel. 06/6988–5318. Admission: 10,000 lire for 2-hr guided visit, 6,000 lire with tape cassette. Ufficio Scavi office hrs: Mon.–Sat. 9–5; closed Sun. and religious holidays.*

For many visitors, a **papal audience** is the highlight of a trip to Rome. Mass audiences take place on Wednesday morning in a modern audience hall (capacity 7,000) off the left-hand colonnade. Tickets are necessary, but you can also see the Pope when he appears at the window of the **Vatican Palace** to bless the crowd in the square below at noon on Sunday. He also blesses the public on summer Sundays when he's at the papal residence at **Castel Gandolfo.** *For audience tickets, write well in advance to Prefettura della Casa Pontificia (00120 Vatican City), indicating the date you prefer, language you speak, and hotel in which you will stay. Pick up free tickets from 4–6 PM at North American College, Via dell 'Umiltà 30 (tel. 06/678–9184), or apply to Papal Prefecture (Prefettura), which you reach through Bronze Door in right-hand colonnade, tel. 06/6988–4466. Open Mon. and Tues. 9–1. Or arrange for tickets through a travel agent: Carrani Tours, Via V. E. Orlando 95, tel. 06/488–0510; Appian Line, Via Barberini 109, tel. 06/488–4151. Admission: about 40,000 lire (including transportation) if booked through an agent or hotel concierge.*

㉕ Guided tours through the **Vatican Gardens**—an hour by bus and an hour on foot—show you some attractive landscaping, a few historical monuments, fountains, and the lovely 16th-century house of Pius IV by Pirro Ligorio. These tours give you a different perspective on the basilica itself. *Tickets at information office, on left side of St. Peter's Square, tel. 06/6988–4466. Open Mon.–Sat. 8:30–7. Garden tour cost: 16,000 lire. Available Mon., Tues., and Thurs.–Sat.*

From the St. Peter's Square information office you can take a shuttle bus (cost: 2,000 lire) directly to the Vatican Museums. This operates every morning, except Wednesday and Sunday, gives you a glimpse of the Vatican Gardens, and saves you the 15-minute walk that goes left from the square and continues along the Vatican walls.

㉖ The collections in the **Vatican Museums** cover nearly 8 kilometers (5 miles) of displays. If you have time, allow at least half a day for Castel Sant'Angelo and St. Peter's, and another half day for the museums. Posters at the museum entrance plot out a choice of four color-coded itineraries; the shortest takes about 90 minutes, the longest more than four hours, depending on your rate of progress.

Sistine Chapel

No matter which tour you take, it will include the famed **Sistine Chapel.** In 1508, Pope Julius II commissioned Michelangelo to fresco the more than 10,000 square feet of the chapel's ceiling. For four years Michelangelo dedicated himself to painting over fresh plaster, and the result was his masterpiece. Recent cleaning operations, now completed, have removed centuries of soot and revealed its original and surprisingly brilliant colors.

You can try to avoid the tour groups by going early or late, allowing yourself enough time before the closing hour. In peak season, the crowds definitely detract from your appreciation of this outstanding artistic achievement. To make sense of the figures on the ceiling, buy an illustrated guide or rent a taped commentary. A pair of binoculars also helps.

The Vatican collections are so rich that unless you are an expert in art history, you will probably want only to skim the surface, concentrating on pieces that strike your fancy. If you really want to see the museums thoroughly, you will have to come back again and again. Some of the highlights that might be of interest on your first tour include the newly reorganized Egyptian collection and the *Laocoön*, the *Belvedere Torso*, and the *Apollo Belvedere*, which inspired Michelangelo. The Raphael Rooms are decorated with masterful frescoes, and there are more Raphaels in the *Pinacoteca* (Picture Gallery). At the Quattro Cancelli, near the entrance to the Picture Gallery, a rather spartan cafeteria provides basic nonalcoholic refreshments. *Viale Vaticano, tel. 06/6988–3332. Admission: 13,000 lire, free on last Sun. of the month. Open Easter period and July–Sept., weekdays 8:45–5, Sat. 8:45–2; Oct.–June, Mon.–Sat. 8:45–2. Ticket office closes 1 hr before museums close. Closed Sun., except last Sun. of the month, and religious holidays: Jan. 1, Jan. 6, Feb. 11, Mar. 19, Easter Sun. and Mon., May 1, Ascension Thurs., Corpus Christi, June 29, Aug. 15–16, Nov. 1, Dec. 8, Dec. 25–26.*

TIME OUT Near the Vatican are many good neighborhood trattorias that are preferable to the touristy eateries opposite the Vatican Museums entrance. At moderately priced **La Caravella** (Via degli Scipioni 32, corner of Via Vespasiano, off Piazza Risorgimento, closed Thurs.) you can lunch on pizza or try the homemade pasta and other specialties of Roman and Abruzzo cooking. **Dino e Toni** (Via Leone IV 60, near Largo Trionfale; closed Sun.) is a typical Roman trattoria, hospitable and moderately priced. There are also several trattorias on and around Borgo Pio.

Old Rome

27 Take Via del Plebiscito from Piazza Venezia to the huge **Church of the Gesù.** This paragon of Baroque style is the tangible symbol of the power of the Jesuits, who were a major force in the Counter-Reformation in Europe. Encrusted with gold and precious marbles, the Gesù has a fantastically painted ceiling that flows down over the pillars, merging with painted stucco figures to complete the three-dimensional illusion.

28 On your way to the Pantheon you will pass **Santa Maria Sopra Minerva,** a Gothic church built over a Roman temple. Inside there are some beautiful frescoes by Filippo Lippi; outside there is a charming elephant by Bernini with an obelisk on its back.

29 Originally built in 27 BC by Augustus's general Agrippa and rebuilt by Hadrian in the 2nd century AD, the **Pantheon** is one of Rome's finest, best-preserved, and perhaps least appreciated ancient monuments. Romans and tourists alike pay little attention to it, and on summer evenings it serves mainly as a backdrop for all the action in the square in front. It represents a fantastic feat of construction, however. The huge columns of the portico and the original bronze doors form the entrance to a majestic hall covered by the largest dome of its kind ever built, wider even than that of St. Peter's. In ancient times the entire interior was encrusted with rich decorations of gilt bronze and marble, plundered by later emperors and popes. *Piazza della Rotonda. Open Mon.–Sat. 9–2, Sun. 9–1.*

TIME OUT There are several sidewalk cafés on the square in front of the Pantheon, all of which are good places to nurse a cappuccino while you observe the scene. Serious coffee drinkers also like **Tazza d'Oro** (Via degli Orfani 84), just off Piazza della Rotonda. And for a huge variety of ice cream in natural flavors, **Giolitti** (Via Uffici del Vicario 40; closed Mon.) is generally considered by gelato addicts to be the best in Rome. It also has good snacks and a quick-lunch counter.

30 On Via della Dogana Vecchia, stop in at the church of **San Luigi dei Francesi** to see the three paintings by Caravaggio in the last chapel on the left; have a few hundred-lire coins handy for the light machine. The clergy of San Luigi considered the artist's roistering and unruly lifestyle scandalous enough, but his realistic treatment of sacred subjects was just too much for them. They rejected his first version of the altarpiece and weren't particularly happy with the other two works either. Thanks to the intercession of Caravaggio's patron, an influential cardinal, they were persuaded to keep them—a lucky thing, since they are now recognized to be among the artist's finest paintings. *Open Fri.–Wed. 7:30–12:30 and 3:30–7, Thurs. 7:30–12:30.*

31 Just beyond San Luigi is **Piazza Navona,** an elongated 17th-century piazza that traces the oval form of the underlying Circus of Diocletian. At the center, Bernini's lively **Fountain of the Four Rivers** is a showpiece. The four statues represent rivers in the four corners of the world: the Nile, with its face covered in allusion to its then unknown source; the Ganges; the Danube; and the River Plate, with its hand raised. And here we have to give the lie to the legend that this was Bernini's mischievous dig at Borromini's design of the facade of the church of **Sant'Agnese in Agone,** from which the statue seems to be shrinking in horror. The fountain was created in 1651; work on the church's facade began some time later. The piazza dozes in the morning, when little groups of pensioners sun themselves on the stone benches and children pedal tricycles around the big fountain. In the late afternoon the sidewalk cafés fill up for the aperitif hour, and in the evening, especially in good weather, the piazza comes to life with a throng of street artists, vendors, tourists, and Romans out for their evening *passeggiata* (promenade).

TIME OUT The sidewalk tables of the **Tre Scalini** café (Piazza Navona 30; closed Wed.) offer a grandstand view of this gorgeous piazza. Treat yourself to a *tartufo,* the chocolate ice-cream specialty that was invented here. The restaurant is a pleasant place for a moderately priced lunch. For a salad or light lunch, go to **Cul de Sac** (Piazza Pasquino 73, just off Piazza Navona) or to **Insalata Ricca** (Via del Paradiso, next to the church of Sant'Andrea della Valle). Both are informal and inexpensive.

32 Across Corso Vittorio is **Campo dei Fiori** (Field of Flowers), the site of a crowded and colorful daily morning market. The hooded bronze figure brooding over the piazza is philosopher Giordano Bruno, who was **33** burned at the stake here for heresy. The adjacent **Piazza Farnese,** with fountains made of Egyptian granite basins from the Baths of Caracalla, **34** is an airy setting for **Palazzo Farnese,** now the French Embassy, one of the most beautiful of Rome's many Renaissance palaces. There are several others in the immediate area: **Palazzo Spada,** a Wedgwood kind of palace encrusted with stuccos and statues; **Palazzo della Cancelleria,** a massive building that is now the Papal Chancellery, one of the many Vatican-owned buildings in Rome that enjoy extraterritorial privileges; and the fine old palaces along Via Giulia.

This is a section to wander through, getting the feel of daily life carried on in a centuries-old setting, and looking into the dozens of antiques shops. Stroll along Via Arenula into a rather gloomy part of Rome bounded by Piazza Campitelli and Lungotevere Cenci, the ancient Jewish ghetto. Among the most interesting sights here are the pretty **Fountain of the Tartarughe** (Turtles) on Piazza Mattei, the **Via Portico d'Ottavia,** with medieval inscriptions and friezes on the old buildings, and the **Teatro di Marcello,** a theater built by Julius Caesar to hold 20,000 spectators.

35
36 A pleasant place to end your walk is on **Tiberina Island.** To get there, walk across the ancient **Fabricio Bridge,** built in 62 BC, the oldest bridge in the city.

Off the Beaten Track

If the sky promises a gorgeous sunset, head for the **Terrazza del Pincio** above Piazza del Popolo, a vantage point prized by Romans.

For a look at a real patrician palace, see the **Galleria Doria Pamphili,** still the residence of a princely family. You can visit the gallery housing the family's art collection and part of the magnificently furnished private apartments, as well. *Piazza del Collegio Romano 1/a, near Piazza Venezia, tel. 06/679–7323. Admission: 10,000 lire; additional 5,000 lire for guided visit of private rooms. Open Mon., Tues., Fri., weekends 10–1; closed Wed., and Thurs.*

Make an excursion to **Ostia Antica,** the well-preserved Roman port city near the sea, as rewarding as an excursion to Pompeii and much easier to get to from Rome. There's a regular train service from the Ostiense Station (Piramide Metro stop). *Via dei Romagnoli, Ostia Antica, tel. 06/565–1405. Admission: 8,000 lire. Open daily 9–1 hr before sunset.*

Delve into the world of the Etruscans, who inhabited Italy even in pre-Roman times and have left fascinating evidence of their relaxed, sensual lifestyle. Visit the **Museo Nazionale di Villa Giulia,** in a gorgeous Renaissance mansion with a full-scale Etruscan temple (and a small coffee bar) in the garden. You'll see a smile as enigmatic as that of the Mona Lisa on deities and other figures in terra cotta, bronze, and gold. Ask especially to see the **Castellani collection of ancient jewelry** (and copies) hidden away on the upper floor. *Piazza di Villa Giulia 9, tel. 06/320–1951. Admission: 8,000 lire. Open Wed. 9–7:30, Tues. and Thurs.–Sat. 9–2, Sun. 9–1.*

Shopping

Shopping is part of the fun of being in Rome, no matter what your budget. The best buys are leather goods of all kinds, from gloves to handbags and wallets to jackets; silk goods; and high-quality knitwear. Shops are closed on Sunday and on Monday morning; in July and August, they close on Saturday afternoon as well.

Antiques

A well-trained eye will spot some worthy old prints and minor antiques in the city's fascinating little shops. For prints, browse among the stalls at **Piazza Fontanelle Borghese** or stop in at **Casali** (Piazza della Rotonda 81a), at the Pantheon, or at **Tanca** (Salita dei Crescenzi 10), also near the Pantheon. For minor antiques, **Via dei Coronari** and other streets in the **Piazza Navona** area are good. The most prestigious antiques dealers are situated in **Via del Babuino** and its environs.

Boutiques

Via Condotti, directly across from the Spanish Steps, and the streets running parallel to Via Condotti, as well as its cross streets, form the most elegant and expensive shopping area in Rome. Lower-price fashions may be found on display at shops on **Via Frattina** and **Via del Corso.**

Shopping Districts

In addition to those mentioned, Romans themselves do much of their shopping along **Via Cola di Rienzo** and **Via Nazionale.** Among the huge new shopping malls dotting Rome's outskirts, CinecittàDue is easiest to reach; just take Metro A to the Subaugusta stop. It has 100 shops, as well as snack bars and cafés.

Religious Articles

These abound in the shops around St. Peter's, on **Via di Porta Angelica** and **Via della Conciliazione,** and in the souvenir shops tucked away on the roof and at the crypt exit in St. Peter's itself.

Food and Flea Markets

The open-air markets at **Campo dei Fiori** and in many neighborhoods throughout the city are colorful sights. The flea market held at **Porta Portese** on Sunday morning is stocked mainly with new or secondhand clothing. If you go, beware of pickpockets and purse snatchers.

Dining

There are plenty of fine restaurants in Rome serving various Italian regional cuisines and international specialties with a flourish of linen and silver, as well as a whopping *conto* (check) at the end. If you want family-style cooking and prices, try a trattoria, a usually smallish and unassuming, often family-run place. Fast-food places and Chinese restaurants are proliferating in Rome. Prix-fixe tourist menus can be scanty and unimaginative. During August many restaurants close for vacation. A few hotels (such as the Hassler, Hilton, and De la Ville) serve Sunday brunch. For details and price-category definitions, *see* Dining *in* Staying in Italy, *above.*

$$$$ **El Toulà.** On a little byway off Piazza Nicosia in Old Rome, El Toulà
★ has the warm, welcoming atmosphere of a 19th-century country house, with white walls, antique furniture in dark wood, heavy silver serving dishes, and spectacular arrangements of fruits and flowers. There's a cozy little bar off the entrance where you can sip a *prosecco,* the aperitif best suited to the chef's Venetian specialties, among them the classic pasta *e fagioli* (pasta-and-bean soup), risotto with radicchio, and *fegato alla veneziana* (calves' liver with onions). *Via della Lupa 29/b, tel. 06/687–3750. Reservations required. AE, DC, MC, V. No lunch Sat. Closed Sun., Aug., and Dec. 24–26.*

$$$$ **La Pergola.** A fabulous view of Rome whets your appetite for imaginatively prepared cuisine in this rooftop restaurant, located atop the Hilton on Monte Mario, one of the highest hills surrounding the city. If you take your eyes off the splendid vista, you will find what might be called a Tuscan garden ambience—potted lemon trees and discreet floral motifs, fresh herbs and candles on every table. The menu is fresh and changes with the seasons. It might include pasta with shrimp and *rucola* (arugula) or breast of guinea hen on a red wine onion confit. A special three-course menu is priced at about 65,000 lire, a four-course menu at 90,000. *Cavalieri Hilton. Via Cadlolo 101, tel. 06/35091. Reservations advised. Jacket and tie. AE, DC, MC, V. Dinner only. Closed Sun., Mon.*

$$$ **Andrea.** Ernest Hemingway and King Farouk used to eat here; FIAT
★ supremo Gianni Agnelli and other Italian power brokers still do. A half
block off Via Veneto, Andrea offers classic Italian cooking in an inti-
mate, clubby ambience in which snowy table linens gleam against a
discreet background of dark green paneling. The menu features deli-
cacies such as homemade *tagliolini* (thin noodles) with shrimp and
spinach sauce, spaghetti with seafood, and mouthwatering *carciofi al-
l'Andrea* (artichokes simmered in olive oil). *Via Sardegna 26, tel.
06/482–1891. Reservations advised. AE, DC, MC, V. No lunch Sat.
Closed Sun. and most of Aug.*

$$$ **Coriolano.** The only tourists who find their way to this classic restau-
rant near Porta Pia are likely to be gourmets looking for quintessen-
tial Italian food—that means light homemade pastas, choice olive oil,
and market-fresh ingredients, especially seafood. Although seafood dishes
vary, tagliolini *all'aragosta* (with lobster sauce) is usually on the menu,
as are porcini mushrooms (in season) cooked to a secret recipe. The
wine list is predominantly Italian but includes some French and Cali-
fornian wines. *Via Ancona 14, tel. 06/855–1122. Reservations advised.
AE, DC, MC, V. Closed Sun. and Aug. 1–25.*

$$$ **Ranieri.** On a quiet street off fashionable Via Condotti near the Span-
★ ish Steps, this historic restaurant was founded by a former chef of Queen
Victoria's. It remains a favorite with tourists for its traditional atmo-
sphere and decor, with damask-covered walls, velvet banquettes, crys-
tal chandeliers, and old paintings. Among the many specialties on the
vast menu are gnocchi *alla parigina* (souffléed gnocchi with cheese sauce)
and *mignonettes alla Regina Vittoria* (veal with pâté and an eight-cheese
sauce). *Via Mario dei Fiori 26, tel. 06/678–6505. Reservations advised.
AE, DC, MC, V. Closed Sun.*

$$ **Colline Emiliane.** Located near Piazza Barberini, the Colline Emiliane
is an unassuming trattoria offering exceptionally good food. Behind
an opaque glass facade, there are a couple of plain little dining rooms
where you are served light homemade pastas, a very special chicken
broth, and meats ranging from pot roast to *giambonetto di vitello* (roast
veal) and *cotoletta alla bolognese* (veal cutlet with cheese and tomato
sauce). *Via degli Avignonesi 22, tel. 06/481–7538. Reservations advised. No credit cards. Closed Fri. and Aug.*

$$ **La Campana.** An inconspicuous trattoria off Via della Scrofa, this is a
place with a long tradition of hospitality; there has been an inn on this
spot since the 15th century. The atmosphere is now that of a classic
Roman eating place, with friendly but businesslike waiters and a menu
that offers Roman specialties such as *vignarola* (sautéed fava beans,
peas, and artichokes), rigatoni with prosciutto and tomato sauce, and
olivette di vitello (tiny veal rolls, served with mashed potatoes). *Vicolo
della Campana 18, tel. 06/686–7820. Dinner reservations advised. AE,
DC, MC, V. Closed Mon. and Aug.*

$$ **Orso 80.** A bustling trattoria in Old Rome, near Piazza Navona, it is
known for a fabulous antipasto table. The egg pasta is freshly made,
and the *bucatini all'amatriciana* (thick spaghetti with a tangy tomato
and bacon sauce) is a classic Roman pasta. There's seafood on the menu,
but it can be pricey. For dessert, try the ricotta cake, a Roman specialty.
*Via dell'Orso 33, tel. 06/686–4904. Reservations advised. AE, DC,
MC, V. Closed Mon. and Aug. 10–20.*

$$ **Paris.** Off Piazza Santa Maria in Trastevere, Paris is reassuring and un-
derstated, with none of the flamboyant folklore of so many eateries in
Trastevere, a characteristically colorful but clearly gentrified neigh-
borhood. "Paris" is a traditional man's name in Rome, and this restau-
rant remains true to classic Roman cuisine, serving, among other
things, homemade fettuccine and delicate fritto misto. Before or after

your meal, take a stroll through the neighborhood. *Piazza San Callisto 7/a, tel. 06/581–5378. Dinner reservations advised. AE, DC, MC, V. Closed Sun. eve, Mon. and Aug.*

$$ Pierluigi. Pierluigi, in the heart of Old Rome, is a longtime favorite. On busy evenings it's almost impossible to find a table, so make sure you reserve well in advance. Seafood predominates, but traditional Roman dishes are offered, too, such as *orecchiette con broccoli* (disk-shaped pasta with greens) and *abbacchio* (roast lamb). In warm weather ask for a table in the piazza. *Piazza dei Ricci 144, tel. 06/687–8717. Reservations advised. AE. Closed Mon. and 2 wks in Aug.*

$$ Romolo. Generations of Romans have enjoyed the romantic garden court-
★ yard and historic dining room of this charming Trastevere haunt, re-
putedly once home of Raphael's ladylove, *La Fornarina*. In the evening, a guitarist serenades diners. The cuisine is appropriately Roman; specialties include mozzarella *alla fornarina* (deep-fried with ham and an-
chovies) and *braciolette d'abbacchio scottadito* (grilled baby lamb chops). Alternatively, try one of the vegetarian pastas featuring carciofi or radicchio. *Via di Porta Settimiana 8, tel. 06/581–8284. Reservations advised. AE, DC, V. Closed Mon. and Aug. 2–23.*

$ Baffetto. Rome's best-known inexpensive pizza restaurant is plainly dec-
orated and *very* popular; you'll probably have to wait in line outside on the *sampietrini*—the cobblestones. The interior is mostly given over to the ovens, the tiny cash desk, and the simple paper-covered tables. *Bruschetta* (toast) and *crostini* (canapés) are the only variations on the pizza theme. Expect to share a table. *Via del Governo Vecchio 114, tel. 06/686–1617. No reservations. No credit cards. Dinner only. Closed Sun. and Aug.*

$ Fratelli Menghi. A neighborhood trattoria that has been in the same family as long as anyone can remember, Fratelli Menghi consists of sev-
eral modest dining rooms off the busy kitchen, which produces typi-
cal Roman fare for faithful customers, many of whom work nearby. There's usually a thick, hearty soup such as minestrone, pasta *e ceci* (with chick peas), and other Roman standbys including *involtini* (meat roulades). *Via Flaminia 57, tel. 06/320–0803. No reservations. No credit cards. Closed Sun.*

$ Grappolo d'Oro. Located off Campo dei Fiori and close to Piazza Navona, this trattoria has been a favorite for decades with locals and foreign residents, one of whom immortalized it in a *New Yorker* pro-
file not so many years ago. This measure of notoriety has not spoiled the place at all. The graying owners are still friendly and patient, and the menu still leans heavily on Roman classics such as pasta all'amatriciana and scaloppini any way you want them. *Piazza della Cancel-
leria 80, tel. 06/686–4118. Dinner reservations advised. AE, MC, V. Closed Sun.*

$ Hostaria Farnese. This is a tiny trattoria between Campo dei Fiori and Piazza Farnese, in the heart of Old Rome. Papa serves, Mamma cooks, and depending on what they've picked up at the Campo dei Fiori mar-
ket, you may find rigatoni with tuna and basil, spaghetti with vegetable sauce, *spezzatino* (stew), and other homey specialties. *Via dei Baullari 109, tel. 06/654–1595. Reservations advised. AE, V. Closed Thurs.*

$ Pollarola. Located near Piazza Navona and Campo dei Fiori, this typ-
ical Roman trattoria has flowers (artificial) on the tables and an an-
tique Roman column embedded in the rear wall, evidence of its historic site. You can eat outdoors in fair weather. Try a pasta specialty such as fettuccine *al gorgonzola* (with creamy Gorgonzola sauce) and a mixed plate from the temptingly fresh array of antipasti. The house wine, white or red, is good. *Piazza della Pollarola 24 (Campo dei Fiori), tel. 06/6880–1654. Reservations advised for groups. AE, V. Closed Sun.*

Lodging

The list below covers mostly those hotels that are within walking distance of at least some sights and that are handy to public transportation. Those in the **$$** and **$** categories do not have restaurants but serve Continental breakfast. Rooms facing the street get traffic noise throughout the night, and few hotels in the lower price categories have double glazing. Ask for a quiet room, or bring earplugs.

We strongly recommend that you always make reservations, even if only a few days in advance, by phone or fax. Always inquire about special low rates, often available in both winter and summer and when occupancy is low. Should you find yourself in the city without reservations, however, contact **HR,** a hotel reservation service (tel. 06/699–1000; English-speaking operator available daily 7 AM–10 PM), with desks at Termini Station and Fiumicino Airport or one of the following **EPT** offices: at Fiumicino Airport (tel. 06/650–10255); Termini Station (tel. 06/487–1270); or the main information office at Via Parigi 5 (tel. 06/488–3748), which is near Piazza della Repubblica. The Rome municipal tourist information booths also will help you find a room. For details and price-category definitions, *see* Lodging *in* Staying in Italy, *above.*

$$$$ **Cavalieri Hilton.** Though it is outside the main part of Rome and a taxi or courtesy shuttle-bus ride to wherever you are going, this is a large, comfortable, elegant hotel, fresh from a stylish renovation and set in its own park, with two excellent restaurants. *Via Cadlolo 101, 00136, tel. 06/35091, fax, 06/315–12241. 378 rooms with bath. Facilities: 2 restaurants, pool, terrace. AE, DC, MC, V.*

$$$$ **Eden.** Totally renovated and reopened in 1994 under the aegis of the Forte hotel group, the historic Eden, a haunt of Hemingway, Ingrid Bergman, and Fellini, merits superlatives for dashing elegance and stunning vistas of Rome from the rooftop restaurant and bar (also seen from some of the most expensive rooms). Precious but discreet antique furnishings, sensuous Italian fabrics, fine linen sheets, and marble baths contribute to an atmosphere of understated opulence. *Via Ludovisi 49, 00187, tel. 06/474–3551, fax 06/482–1584. 112 rooms and suites with bath. Facilities: restaurant, bar, fitness center. AE, DC, MC, V.*

$$$$ **Hassler-Villa Medici.** Guests can expect a cordial atmosphere and mag-
★ nificent service at this hotel, just at the top of the Spanish Steps. The public rooms have an extravagant, somewhat dated decor, especially the first-floor bar (a chic city rendezvous), and the glass-roof lounge, with gold marble walls and hand-painted tile floors. The elegant bedrooms are decorated in a variety of classic styles (the best feature frescoed walls). The restaurant (with a panoramic view of Rome) is world famous. *Piazza Trinità dei Monti 6, 00187, tel. 06/678–2651, fax 06/678–9991. 100 rooms with bath. Facilities: 2 restaurants, bar, garage. AE, MC, V.*

$$$ **Forum.** A centuries-old palace converted into a fine hotel, the Forum is on a quiet street within hailing distance of the Roman Forum and Piazza Venezia. The wood-paneled lobby and street-level bar are warm and welcoming, as are the smallish, pink-and-beige bedrooms. The view of the Colosseum from the rooftop restaurant is superb: Breakfast here—or a nightcap at the roof bar—can be memorable. *Via Tor dei Conti 25, 00184, tel. 06/679–2446, fax 06/678–6479. 76 rooms with bath. Facilities: restaurant, bar. AE, DC, MC, V.*

$$$ **Victoria.** Oriental rugs, oil paintings, welcoming armchairs, and fresh
★ flowers add charm to the slightly dated public rooms of this hotel, a favorite of American businesspeople who prize the personalized service and restful atmosphere. Some upper rooms and the roof terrace

overlook the Villa Borghese. *Via Campania 41, 00187, tel. 06/473931, fax 06/487–1890. 110 rooms with bath. Facilities: restaurant, bar. AE, DC, MC, V.*

$$ ★ **Britannia.** A quiet location off Via Nazionale is only one of the attractions of this small and special hotel, where guests are coddled with luxury touches such as English-language dailies and local weather reports delivered to their room each morning. The sybaritic bathrooms and well-furnished rooms, especially the clubby tartan-and-wood decor on the second floor, indicate that the management really cares about giving guests superior service and value. *Via Napoli 64, 00184, tel. 06/488–3153, fax 06/488–2343. 32 rooms with bath. Facilities: bar. AE, DC, MC, V.*

$$ **D'Este.** Within hailing distance of Santa Maria Maggiore and close to Termini Station, the hotel occupies a solidly renovated and roomy 19th-century building. The fresh, pleasing decor evokes turn-of-the-century comfort with brass bedsteads and lamps and walnut furniture. Rooms are quiet, light, and spacious; many can be adapted to suit families. The attentive owner-manager makes sure everything works, and he encourages inquiries about special rates, particularly during the slack summer months. *Via Carlo Alberto 4/b, 00185, tel. 06/446–5607, fax 06/446–5601. 37 rooms with bath. Facilities: bar, garden. AE, DC, MC, V.*

$$ **La Residenza.** A converted town house near Via Veneto, this hotel offers good value and first-class comfort at reasonable rates. Public areas are spacious and furnished nicely and have a private-home atmosphere. Guest rooms are comfortable and have large closets, TV, minifridges, and air-conditioning. The color scheme throughout the property is aquamarine and beige. The hotel's clientele is mainly American, and rates include a generous buffet breakfast. *Via Emilia 22, 00187, tel. 06/488–0797, fax 06/485721. 27 rooms with bath. Facilities: bar, roof terrace, parking. No credit cards.*

$ **Amalia.** Handy to the Vatican and the Cola di Rienzo shopping district, this small, former *pensione* is owned and operated by the Consoli family—Amalia and her brothers. On several floors of a 19th-century building, it has 21 newly renovated rooms with TV sets, direct-dial telephones, and gleaming marble bathrooms (hair dryers included). The Ottaviano stop of Metro A is a block away. *Via Germanico 66, 00192, tel. 06/397–23354, fax 06/397–23365. 25 rooms, 21 with bath or shower. Facilities: bar. AE, MC, V.*

$ ★ **Margutta.** Near the Spanish Steps and Piazza del Popolo, this small hotel has an unassuming lobby but bright, attractive bedrooms with wrought-iron bedsteads and modern baths. *Via Laurina 34, 00187, tel. 06/322–3674. 21 rooms with bath. AE, DC, MC, V.*

$ **Romae.** Located near Termini Station, this mid-size hotel has clean, spacious rooms with light-wood furniture and small but bright bathrooms. The cordial, helpful management offers special winter rates and welcomes families. TVs and hair dryers in the rooms plus low rates that include breakfast make this a good value. *Via Palestro 49, 00185, tel. 06/446–3554, fax 06/446–3914. 20 rooms with bath. AE, MC, V.*

The Arts

You will find information on scheduled events and shows at EPT and municipal tourist offices or booths. The biweekly booklet "Un Ospite a Roma," free from concierges at some hotels, is another source of information, as is "Wanted in Rome," available at newsstands. There are listings in English in the back of the weekly "Roma c'è" booklet, with handy bus information for each listing; it is sold at newsstands.

If you want to go to the opera, the ballet, or a concert, it's best to ask your concierge to get tickets for you. They are sold at box offices only, just a few days before performances.

Opera

The **Teatro dell'Opera** is on Via del Viminale (tel. 06/481–7003); its summer season from May through August is famous for spectacular open-air performances. After having been evicted from the ancient ruins of the Baths of Caracalla, performances are now scheduled to be held in Villa Pepoli, a parklike area adjacent to the ruins of the Baths. Tickets are sold at the opera box office.

Concerts

The main concert hall is the **Accademia di Santa Cecilia** (Via della Conciliazione 4, tel. 06/688–1044). The Santa Cecilia Symphony Orchestra has a summer season of concerts.

Film

The only English-language movie theater in Rome is the **Pasquino** (Vicolo del Piede, just off Piazza Santa Maria in Trastevere, tel. 06/580–3622). The program is listed in Rome's daily newspapers. Several other movie theaters show films in English on certain days of the week; the listings in "Roma c'è" are reliable.

Nightlife

Rome's "in" nightspots change like the flavor of the month, and many fade into oblivion after a brief moment of glory. The best sources for an up-to-date list are the weekly entertainment guide, "Trovaroma," published each Thursday in the Italian daily *La Repubblica,* and "Roma c'è."

Bars

Jacket and tie are in order in the elegant **Blue Bar** of the Hostaria dell'Orso (Via dei Soldati 25, tel. 06/686–4250), and in **Le Bar** of Le Grand Hotel (Via Vittorio Emanuele Orlando 3, tel. 06/482931). **Jazz Club** (Via Zanardelli 12, tel. 06/686–1990), near Piazza Navona, is an upscale watering hole open from 7 PM to 2 AM, with a happy hour from 7 to 10. **Flann O'Brien** (Via Napoli 29, tel. 06/488–0418) has the look and atmosphere of a good Irish pub but also serves cappuccino.

Informal wine bars are popular with young Romans. Near the Pantheon is **Spiriti** (Via Sant'Eustachio 5, tel. 06/689–2499); both **Enoteca Roffi** (Via della Croce 76/a, tel. 06/679–0896) and **Trimani Wine Bar** (Via Cernaia 37/b, tel. 06/446–9630) offer light meals. **Birreria Marconi** (Via di Santa Prassede 9c, tel. 06/486636), near Santa Maria Maggiore, is a beer-hall pizzeria. Near the Pantheon, a hub of fashionable after-dark activity is **Antico Caffè della Pace** (Via della Pace 3, tel. 06/686–1216). Brazilian music is big in Rome; Trastevere especially draws Carioca clubs. **Clarabella** (Piazza San Cosimato 39, tel. 0337/801772) has live music and is open from 10 PM to 4 AM. **Mambo** (Via dei Fienaroli 30/a, tel. 06/589–7196) lives up to its name with lively Latin music and dancing.

Discos and Nightclubs

There's deafening disco music for an under-30 crowd at the **Tatum** (entrance at Via Luciani 52, tel. 06/322–1251). Special events such as beauty pageants and theme parties are a feature, and there's a restaurant on the premises. **Gilda** (Via Mario dei Fiori 97, tel. 06/678–4838) is a combination supper club-disco-piano bar, often featuring theme parties and special events. **Spago** (Via di Monte Testaccio, tel. 06/574–4999) has a trendier atmosphere, with late-night dining, piano bar and dancing to disco music, funk, and soul; it's not easy to find, so take a taxi.

Singles Scene

Locals and foreigners of all ages gather at Rome's cafés in **Piazza della Rotonda** in front of the Pantheon, in **Piazza Navona,** and **Piazza Santa Maria in Trastevere.** The cafés on **Via Veneto** and the bars of the big hotels draw tourists mainly and are good places to meet other travelers in the over-thirty age group. In fair weather, under-thirties will find crowds of contemporaries on the **Spanish Steps,** where it's easy to strike up a conversation.

FLORENCE

Arriving and Departing

By Plane

The airport that handles most arrivals is Galileo Galilei Airport—more commonly known as Pisa-Galilei Airport—at Pisa (tel. 050/500707), connected with Florence by train direct from the airport to the Santa Maria Novella Station. Service is hourly throughout the day and takes about 60 minutes. When departing, you can buy train tickets for the airport and check in for all flights leaving from Pisa-Galilei Airport at the Florence Air Terminal at Track 5 of Santa Maria Novella Station (flight information tel. 055/216073). Some domestic and European flights use Florence's Vespucci Airport at Peretola (tel. 055/333498), connected by SITA bus to the downtown area.

By Train

The main train station is Santa Maria Novella Station, abbreviated SMN on signs. There is an Azienda Transporti Autolinee Fiorentine (ATAF) city bus information booth across the street from the exit on the left side of the station (and also at Piazza del Duomo 57/r). Inside the station is an Informazioni Turistiche Alberghiere (ITA) hotel association booth, where you can get hotel information and bookings. The booking fee is from 3,000 to 10,000 lire, depending on the category.

By Bus

The SITA bus terminal is on Via Santa Caterina da Siena, near Santa Maria Novella train station. The CAP bus terminal is at Via Nazionale 13, also near the station.

By Car

The north–south access route to Florence is the Autostrada del Sole (A1) from Milan or Rome. The Florence–Mare autostrada (A11) links Florence with the Tyrrhenian coast, Pisa, and the A12 coastal autostrada.

Getting Around

On Foot

You can see most of Florence's major sights on foot, as they are packed into a relatively small area in the city center. It's best not to plan to use a car in Florence; most of the center is off-limits and ATAF buses will take you where you want to go. Wear comfortable shoes and wander to your heart's content. It is easy to find your way around in Florence. There are so many landmarks that you cannot get lost for long. The system of street addresses is unusual, with commercial addresses (those with an r in them, meaning *rosso*, or red) and residential addresses numbered separately (32/r might be next to or a block away from plain 32).

By Bus
ATAF city buses run from about 5:15 AM to 1 AM. Buy tickets before you board the bus; they are on sale singly or in books of eight at many tobacco shops and newsstands. The cost is 1,400 lire for a ticket good for 60 minutes on all lines, 1,900 lire for 120 minutes, and 5,400 lire for a book of four 60-minute tickets, called a *multiplo.* An all-day ticket (*turistico*) costs 5,000 lire.

By Taxi
Taxis wait at stands. Use only authorized cabs, which are white with a yellow stripe or rectangle on the door. The meter starts at 3,200 lire. To call a taxi, phone 055/4798 or 055/4390.

By Bicycle
You can rent a bicycle at **Alinari** (Via Guelfa 85/r, tel. 055/280500), which has several locations in Florence; **Motorent** (Via San Zanobi 9/r, tel. 055/490113); and at city concessions in several locations, including Piazza della Stazione, Piazza Pitti, and Fortezza da Basso.

By Moped
For a moped, go to **Alinari** or **Motorent** (*see* By Bicycle, *above*), or to **Ciao e Basta** (Lungarno Pecori Girardi 1, tel. 055/234–2726).

Important Addresses and Numbers

Tourist Information
The municipal tourist office is at Via Cavour 1/r (tel. 055/276–0382; open 8:30–7), with a branch next to the train station and another information office near Piazza della Signoria, at Chiasso dei Baroncelli 17/r (tel. 055/230–2124). The **Azienda Promozione Turistica (APT)** tourist board has its headquarters and an information office at Via Manzoni 16, 50121 (tel. 055/234–6284; open Mon.–Sat. 8:30–1:30).

Consulates
U.S. (Lungarno Vespucci 38, tel. 055/239–8276). **U.K.** (Lungarno Corsini 2, tel. 055/284133). **Canada** (citizens should refer to their consulate in Rome).

Emergencies
Police (tel. 113). **Ambulance** (tel. 118 or 055/212222). **Doctor:** Call your consulate for recommendations, or call the **Tourist Medical Service** (tel. 055/475411), associated with IAMAT, for English-speaking medical assistance 24 hours a day. **Pharmacies:** There are 24-hour pharmacies at Via Calzaiuoli 7/r (tel. 055/289490); Piazza San Giovanni 20/r (tel. 055/284013); and at the train station (tel. 055/289435).

English-Language Bookstores
You'll find English-language magazines and paperbacks on the newsstands in Piazza della Repubblica. **The Paperback Exchange** (Via Fiesolana 31/r, tel. 055/247–8154), in the Santa Croce area, has new and used paperbacks for sale. **The BM Bookshop** (Borgo Ognissanti 4/r, tel. 055/294575) has a good selection of books.

Travel Agencies
American Express (Via Guicciardini 49/r, tel. 055/288751; branch at Via Dante Alighieri 20/r, tel. 055/50981.) **CIT** (Via Cavour 54/r, tel. 055/294306). **Wagons-Lits** (Via del Giglio 27/r, tel. 055/218851).

Guided Tours

Orientation Tours

A bus consortium (through hotels and travel agents) offers three-hour tours in air-conditioned buses. Two tours cover most of the important sights: The morning itinerary gives you a look at the outside of the cathedral, baptistry, and bell tower, takes you to the Accademia to see Michelangelo's *David,* to Piazzale Michelangelo for the view, and perhaps then to the Palazzo Pitti to visit the Palatine Gallery; the afternoon tour includes Piazza della Signoria, a visit to the Uffizi Gallery and to Santa Croce, and an excursion to Fiesole. The cost is about 47,000 lire for a three-hour tour, including entrance fees, and bookings can be made through travel agents.

Personal Guides

American Express (tel. 055/288751) can arrange for limousine or mini-tours and personal guide services. **Europedrive** (Via Bisenzio 35, tel. 055/422–2839) will provide cars with English-speaking drivers.

Special-Interest Tours

Inquire at travel agents or at **Agriturist Regionale** (Piazza San Firenze 3, tel. 055/287838) for visits to villa gardens around Florence from April through June, or for visits to farm estates during September and October.

Excursions

Operators offer a half-day excursion to Pisa, usually in the afternoon, costing about 45,000 lire, and a full-day excursion to Siena and San Gimignano, costing about 63,000 lire. Pick up a timetable at ATAF information offices near the train station, at SITA (Via Santo Caterina da Siena 17, tel. 055/214721), or at the APT Tourist Office (*see* Tourist Information *in* Important Addresses and Numbers, *above*).

Both ATAF and tourist information offices may offer a free booklet containing information on interesting excursions in the vicinity of Florence, complete with timetables of local bus and train services.

Exploring Florence

Founded by Julius Caesar, Florence has the familiar grid pattern common to all Roman colonies. Except for the major monuments, which are appropriately imposing, the buildings are low and unpretentious. It is a small, compact city of ocher and gray stone and pale plaster; its narrow streets open unexpectedly into spacious squares populated by strollers and pigeons. At its best, it has a gracious and elegant air, though it can at times be a nightmare of mass tourism. Plan, if you can, to visit Florence in late fall, early spring, or even in winter, to avoid the crowds.

A visit to Florence is a visit to the living museum of the Italian Renaissance. The Renaissance began right here in Florence, and the city bears witness to the proud spirit and unparalleled genius of its artists and artisans. In fact, there is so much to see that it is best to savor a small part rather than attempt to absorb it all in a muddled vision.

For 10,000 lire you can purchase a special museum ticket valid for six months at seven city museums, including Palazzo Vecchio, the Museum of Firenze Com'Era (museum of Florentine history), and the Museum of Santa Maria Novella. Inquire at any city museum.

Numbers in the margin correspond to points of interest on the Firenze (Florence) map.

Piazza del Duomo and Piazza della Signoria

The best place to begin a tour of Florence is **Piazza del Duomo,** where the cathedral, bell tower, and baptistry stand in the rather cramped square. The lofty **cathedral of Santa Maria del Fiore** is one of the longest in the world. Begun by master sculptor and architect Arnolfo di Cambio in 1296, its construction took 140 years to complete. Gothic architecture predominates; the facade was added in the 1870s but is based on Tuscan Gothic models. Inside, the church is cool and austere, a fine example of the architecture of the period. Among the sparse decorations, take a good look at the frescoes of equestrian monuments on the left wall; the one on the right is by Paolo Uccello, the one on the left by Andrea del Castagno. The dome frescoes by Vasari take second place to the dome itself, Brunelleschi's greatest architectural and technical achievement. It was also the inspiration of such later domes as Michelangelo's dome for St. Peter's in Rome and even the Capitol in Washington. You can climb to the cupola gallery, 463 fatiguing steps up between the two skins of the double dome for a fine view of Florence and the surrounding hills. *Dome entrance is in left aisle of cathedral. Admission: 5,000 lire. Open Mon.–Sat. 10–5. Cathedral (small admission fee may be charged) open Mon.–Sat. 10–5:30, Sun. 1–5.*

Next to the cathedral is Giotto's 14th-century **bell tower,** richly decorated with colored marble and sculpture reproductions (the originals are in the Museo dell'Opera del Duomo). The 414-step climb to the top is less strenuous than that to the cupola. *Piazza del Duomo. Admission: 5,000 lire. Open Mar.–Oct., daily 8:30–7; Nov.–Feb., daily 9–4:30.*

In front of the cathedral is the **baptistry** (open Mon.–Sat. 1:30–6:30, Sun. 9–1), one of the city's oldest and most beloved edifices, where, since the 11th century, Florentines have baptized their children. The most famous of the bapistry's three portals are Ghiberti's east doors (facing the Duomo), dubbed the "gates of Paradise" by Michelangelo; gleaming copies now replace the originals, which have been removed to the **Museo dell'Opera del Duomo** (Cathedral Museum). The museum contains some superb sculptures by Donatello and Luca della Robbia—especially their *cantorie,* or choir decorations—as well as an unfinished *Pietà* by Michelangelo, which was intended for his own tomb. *Piazza del Duomo 9, tel. 055/230–2885. Admission: 5,000 lire. Open Mar.–Oct., Mon.–Sat. 9–6; Nov.–Feb., Mon.–Sat. 9–5:30.*

Stroll down fashionable Via Calzaiuoli to the church of **Orsanmichele,** for centuries an odd combination of first-floor church and second-floor wheat granary. The statues in the niches on the exterior (many of which are now copies) constitute an anthology of the work of eminent Renaissance sculptors, including Donatello, Ghiberti, and Verrocchio, while the tabernacle inside is an extraordinary piece by Andrea Orcagna. Some of the original statues can be seen in the Bargello or Palazzo della Signoria.

Continuing another two blocks along Via Calzaiuoli you'll come upon **Piazza della Signoria,** the heart of Florence, and the city's largest square. During the long and controversial process of replacing the paving stones over the past few years, well-preserved remnants of Roman and medieval Florence came to light and were thoroughly examined and photographed before being buried again and covered with the new paving. In the center of the square a slab marks the spot where in 1497 Savonarola—the Ayatollah Khomeini of the Middle Ages—induced the Florentines to burn their pictures, books, musical instruments, and other worldly objects—and where a year later he was hanged and then burned at the stake as a heretic. The square, the **Neptune Fountain** by Ammanati, and the surrounding cafés are popular gathering places for Florentines and for tourists who come to admire the massive **Palazzo della Signoria** (better known as the **Palazzo Vecchio**), the copy of Michelangelo's *David* on its steps, and the frescoes and art in its impressive salons. *Piazza della Signoria, tel. 055/276–8465. Admission: 8,000 lire; Sun. free. Open Mon.–Wed., Fri.–Sat. 9–7, Sun. 8–1.*

TIME OUT Stop in at *Rivoire*, a Florentine institution, for some of its delectable ice cream and/or chocolate goodies. *Piazza della Signoria 5/r.*

If you'd like to do a little shopping, make a brief detour off Piazza della **7** Signoria to the **Loggia del Mercato Nuovo** on Via Calimala. It's crammed with souvenirs and straw and leather goods at reasonable prices; bargaining is acceptable here. *Open Mon.–Sat. 8–7 (closed Mon. AM).*

8 If time is limited, this is your chance to visit the **Uffizi Gallery,** which houses Italy's most important collection of paintings. (Try to see it at a leisurely pace, though—it's too good to rush through!) The Uffizi Palace was built to house the administrative offices of the Medicis, onetime rulers of the city. Later their fabulous art collection was arranged in the Uffizi Gallery on the top floor, which was opened to the public in the 17th century—making this the world's first public gallery of modern times. The emphasis is on Italian art of the Gothic and Renaissance periods. Make sure you see the works by Giotto, and look for the Botticellis in Rooms X–XIV, Michelangelo's *Holy Family* in Room XXV, and the works by Raphael next door. In addition to its art treasures, the gallery offers a magnificent close-up view of Palazzo Vecchio's tower from the little coffee bar at the end of the corridor. Authorities have done wonders in repairing the damage caused by a bomb in 1993. *Loggiato Uffizi 6, tel. 055/23885. Admission: 12,000 lire. Open Tues.–Sat. 9–7, Sun. 9–2.*

Accademia, San Marco, San Lorenzo, Santa Maria Novella

9 Start at the **Accademia Gallery,** and try to be first in line at opening time so you can get the full impact of Michelangelo's *David* without having to fight your way through the crowds. Skip the works in the exhibition halls leading to the *David;* they are of minor importance and you'll gain a length on the tour groups. Michelangelo's statue is a tour de force of artistic conception and technical ability, for he was using a piece of stone that had already been worked on by a lesser sculptor. Take time to see the forceful *Slaves,* also by Michelangelo; the rough-hewn, unfinished surfaces contrast dramatically with the highly polished, meticulously carved *David.* Michelangelo left the *Slaves* "unfinished" as a symbolic gesture, to accentuate the figures' struggle to escape the bondage of stone. *Via Ricasoli 60, tel. 055/214375. Admission: 12,000 lire. Open Tues.–Sat. 9–7, Sun. 9–2.*

You can make a detour down Via Cesare Battisti to Piazza Santissima Annunziata to see the arcade of the **Ospedale degli Innocenti** (Hospital of the Innocents) by Brunelleschi, with charming roundels by An-**10** drea della Robbia, and the **Museo Archeologico** (Archaeological Museum) on Via della Colonna, under the arch. The latter has some fine Etruscan and Roman antiquities, and a pretty garden. *Via della Colonna 36, tel. 055/247–8641. Admission: 8,000 lire. Open Tues.–Sat. 9–2, Sun. 9–1.*

11 Retrace your steps to Piazza San Marco and the **Museo di San Marco,** housed in a 15th-century Dominican monastery. The unfortunate

Savonarola meditated on the sins of the Florentines here, and Fra Angelico decorated many of the austere cells and corridors with his brilliantly colored frescoes of religious subjects. (Look for his masterpiece, *The Annunciation*.) Together with many of his paintings arranged on the ground floor, just off the little cloister, they form an interesting collection. *Piazza San Marco 1, tel. 055/238–8608. Admission: 8,000 lire. Open Tues.–Sat. 9–2, Sun. 9–1.*

⑫ Lined with shops, Via Cavour leads to **Palazzo Medici Riccardi,** a massive Renaissance mansion (*see* Off the Beaten Track, *below*). Turn right **⑬** here to the elegant **Church of San Lorenzo,** with its Old Sacristy designed by Brunelleschi, and two pulpits by Donatello. Rounding the church, you'll find yourself in the midst of the sprawling **San Lorenzo Market,** dealing in everything and anything, including some interesting leather items. *Piazza San Lorenzo, Via dell'Ariento. Open Tues.–Sat. 8–7.*

TIME OUT In the big covered food market near San Lorenzo, **Nerbone** is a favorite with market workers for a quick sandwich or plate of pasta, which they usually eat standing at the counter. You can sit at the tables across the way, too. It's impossibly crowded between 1 and 1:30. *Mercato Centrale. Closed Sun.*

⑭ Enter the **Medici Chapels** from Piazza Madonna degli Aldobrandini, behind San Lorenzo. These remarkable chapels contain the tombs of practically every member of the Medici family, and there were a lot of them, for they guided Florence's destiny from the 15th century to 1737. Cosimo I, a Medici whose acumen made him the richest man in Europe, is buried in the crypt of the Chapel of the Princes, and Donatello's tomb is next to that of his patron. The chapel upstairs is decorated in a dazzling array of colored marble. In Michelangelo's New Sacristy, his tombs of Giuliano and Lorenzo de' Medici bear the justly famed statues of *Dawn* and *Dusk*, and *Night* and *Day*. *Piazza Madonna degli Aldobrandini, tel. 055/213206. Admission: 9,000 lire. Open Tues.–Sat. 9–2, Sun. 9–1.*

You can take either Via Panzani or Via del Melarancio to the large square **⑮** next to the massive church of **Santa Maria Novella,** a handsome building in the Tuscan version of Gothic style. See it from the other end of Piazza Santa Maria Novella for the best view of its facade. Inside are some famous paintings, especially Masaccio's *Trinity*, a Giotto crucifix in the sacristy, and Ghirlandaio's frescoes in the apse. *Piazza Santa Maria Novella, tel. 055/210113. Open daily 7–11:30 and 3:30–6.*

Next door to the church is the entrance to the **Museum of Santa Maria Novella,** worth a visit for its serene atmosphere and the restored Paolo Uccello frescoes in the Green Cloister. *Piazza Santa Maria Novella 19, tel. 055/282187. Admission: 4,000 lire. Open Mon.–Thurs., Sat. 9–2, Sun. 8–1.*

Only a few blocks behind Piazza della Signoria is the **Bargello,** a fortresslike palace that served as residence of Florence's chief magistrate in medieval times, and later as a prison. Don't be put off by its **⑯** grim look, for it now houses Florence's **Museo Nazionale** (National Museum), a treasure house of Italian Renaissance sculpture. In a historically and visually interesting setting, it displays masterpieces by Donatello, Verrocchio, Michelangelo, and many other major sculptors. This museum is on a par with the Uffizi, so don't shortchange yourself on time. *Via del Proconsolo 4, tel. 055/238–8606. Admission: 8,000 lire. Open Tues.–Sat. 9–2, Sun. 9–1.*

734

Accademia Gallery, **9**

Baptistry, **3**

Bell Tower, **2**

Boboli Gardens, **20**

Casa Guidi, **21**

Cathedral of Santa Maria del Fiore (Duomo), **1**

Church of San Lorenzo, **13**

Loggia del Mercato Nuovo, **7**

Medici Chapels, **14**

Museo Archeologico, **10**

Museo dell'Opera del Duomo, **4**

Museo di San Marco, **11**

Museo Nazionale, **16**

Orsanmichele, **5**

Palazzo Medici Riccardi, **12**

Palazzo Pitti, **19**

Palazzo Vecchio, **6**

Ponte Vecchio, **18**

Santa Croce, **17**

Santa Maria del Carmine, **23**

Santa Maria Novella, **15**

Santo Spirito, **22**

Uffizi Gallery, **8**

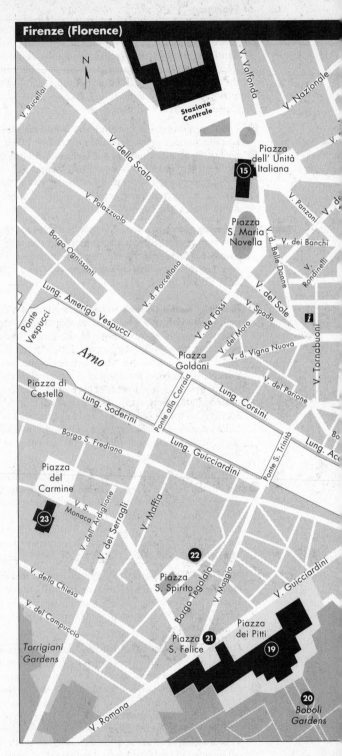

Firenze (Florence)

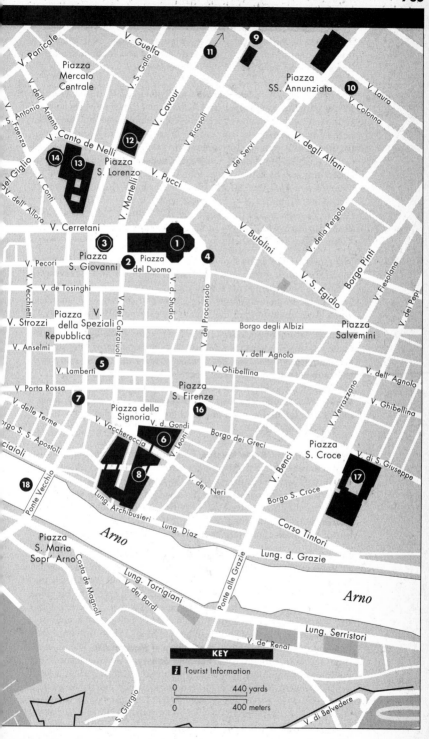

V. Panicale

V. Guelfa

Piazza
Mercato
Centrale

V. S. Gallo

V. dell' Ariento

V. S. Antonio

V. Faenza

V. Canto de Nelli

del Giglio

V. Conti

V. dell' Allora

Piazza
S. Lorenzo

V. Cerretani

V. Pecori

Piazza
S. Giovanni

V. de Tosinghi

V. Vecchietti

V. Strozzi

Piazza
della
Repubblica

V.
Speziali

V. Anselmi

V. Lamberti

V. Porta Rossa

V. delle Terme

Borgo S. S. Apostoli

ciaioli

V. Cavour

V. Ricasoli

V. dei Servi

Piazza
SS. Annunziata

V. Laura

V. Colonna

V. degli Alfani

V. Martelli

V. Pucci

V. della Pergola

Borgo Pinti

V. Fiesolana

V. dei Pepi

V. Bufalini

V. d. Studio

V. del Proconsolo

Piazza
del Duomo

V. dei Calzaiuoli

Borgo degli Albizi

V. dell' Agnolo

V. Ghibellina

Piazza
Salvemini

V. S. Egidio

V. dell' Agnolo

V. Ghibellina

V. Verrozzano

Piazza
S. Firenze

Piazza della
Signoria

V. Vacchereccia

V. d. Gondi

V. Leoni

Borgo dei Greci

V. dei Neri

Piazza
S. Croce

V. di S. Giuseppe

V. Benci

Borgo S. Croce

Corso Tintori

Ponte Vecchio

Piazza
S. Maria
Sopr' Arno

Costa de Magnoli

V. dei Bardi

Lung. Archibusieri

Lung. Diaz

Arno

Lung. Torrigiani

Ponte alle Grazie

Lung. d. Grazie

Arno

V. de' Renai

Lung. Serristori

S. Giorgio

V. di Belvedere

KEY

ℹ️ Tourist Information

0 ————— 440 yards

0 ————— 400 meters

TIME OUT From Piazza San Firenze follow Via degli Anguillara or Borgo dei Greci toward Piazza Santa Croce. Don't miss the chance to taste what's held by many to be the best ice cream in Florence, at **Vivoli,** on a little side street, the second left off Via degli Anguillara as you head toward Santa Croce. *Via Isole delle Stinche 7/r. Closed Mon.*

⑰ The mighty church of **Santa Croce** was begun in 1294; inside, Giotto's frescoes brighten two chapels and monumental tombs of Michelangelo, Galileo, Machiavelli, and other Renaissance luminaries line the walls. In the adjacent museum, you can see what remains of a Giotto crucifix, irreparably damaged by a flood in 1966, when water rose to 16 feet in parts of the church. The **Pazzi Chapel** in the cloister is an architectural gem by Brunelleschi. *Piazza Santa Croce, tel. 055/244619. Church open Apr.–Sept., Mon.–Sat. 8–6:30, Sun. 8–12:30 and 3–6:30; Oct.–Mar., Mon.–Sat. 8–12:30 and 3–6:30, Sun. 3–6. Opera di Santa Croce (Museum and Pazzi Chapel), tel. 055/244619. Admission: 3,000 lire. Open Mar.–Sept., Thurs.–Tues. 10–12:30 and 2:30–6:30; Oct.–Feb., Thurs.–Tues. 10–12:30 and 3–5.*

The monastery of Santa Croce harbors a leather-working school and showroom, with entrances at Via San Giuseppe 5/r and Piazza Santa Croce 16. The entire Santa Croce area is known for its leather factories and inconspicuous shops selling gold and silver jewelry at prices much lower than those of the elegant jewelers near Ponte Vecchio.

TIME OUT You have several eating options here. For ice cream, the **bar** on Piazza Santa Croce has a tempting selection. If it's a snack you're after, the **Fiaschetteria** (Via dei Neri 17/r) makes sandwiches to order and has a choice of antipasti and a hot dish or two. And if you're homesick for brownies and chocolate chip cookies, head for **Carlie's American Bakery** (Via delle Brache, aka Via dei Legnaioli, 12/r, a narrow street off Via dei Neri between Via dei Benci and Via dei Rustici; open 10–1:30 and 3:30–7:30).

⑱ Now head for the **Ponte Vecchio,** Florence's oldest bridge. It seems to be just another street lined with goldsmiths' shops until you get to the middle and catch a glimpse of the Arno flowing below. Spared during World War II by the retreating Germans (who blew up every other bridge in the city), it also survived the 1966 flood. It leads into the **Oltrarno district,** which has its own charm and still preserves much of the atmosphere of old-time Florence, full of fascinating craft workshops.

But for the moment you should head straight down Via Guicciardini ⑲ to **Palazzo Pitti,** a 15th-century extravaganza that the Medicis acquired from the Pitti family shortly after the latter had gone deeply into debt to build the central portion. The Medicis enlarged the building, extending its facade on the immense piazza. Solid and severe, it looks like a Roman aqueduct turned into a palace. The palace houses several museums: One displays the fabulous Medici collection of objects in silver and gold; another is the **Gallery of Modern Art.** The most famous museum, though, is the **Palatine Gallery,** with an extraordinary collection of paintings, many hung frame-to-frame in a clear case of artistic overkill. Some are high up in dark corners, so try to go on a bright day. *Piazza dei Pitti, tel. 055/210323. Gallery of Modern Art. Admission: 4,000 lire. Palatine Gallery. Admission: 12,000 lire. Monumental Royal Apartments. Admission 8,000 lire. Silver Museum. Admission: 8,000 lire (includes admission to Historical Costume Gallery and Porcelain Museum at top of the Boboli Gardens, if open). All open Tues.–Sat. 9–2, Sun. 9–1.*

② Take time for a refreshing stroll in the **Boboli Gardens** behind Palazzo Pitti, a typical Italian garden laid out in 1550 for Cosimo de' Medici's wife, Eleanor of Toledo. *Piazza dei Pitti, tel. 055/213440. Admission: 4,000 lire. Open daily, except first and last Mon. of the month. Apr., May, and Sept., 9–6:30; June–Aug., 9–7:30; Oct. and Mar.–Apr., 9–5:30; Nov.–Feb., 9–4:30.*

② In the far corner of Piazza dei Pitti, poets Elizabeth Barrett and Robert Browning lived in the **Casa Guidi,** facing the smaller Piazza San Felice. *Piazza San Felice 8, tel. 055/284393. Admission free. Open by appointment.*

TIME OUT From Piazza San Felice it's not far to the **Caffè Notte,** a wine and sandwich shop featuring a different salad every day (corner of Via delle Caldaie and Via della Chiesa, closed Mon.). For more substantial sustenance, go to the **Cantinone del Gallo Nero,** an atmospheric wine cellar where Chianti is king and locals lunch on soups, pastas, and salads (Via Santo Spirito 6/r. Closed Mon.). A block from the church of Santo Spirito, **Casalinga** (Via dei Michelozzi 9, closed weekends) is a large, popular trattoria, fine for a hearty, inexpensive lunch.

② The church of **Santo Spirito** is important as one of Brunelleschi's finest architectural creations, and it contains some superb paintings, including a Filippino Lippi *Madonna.* Santo Spirito is the hub of a colorful neighborhood of artisans and intellectuals. An **outdoor market** enlivens the square every morning except Sunday; in the afternoon, pigeons, pet owners, and pensioners take over. An arts and crafts fair is held in the square on the second Sunday of the month. The area is definitely on an upward trend, with new cafés, restaurants, and upscale shops opening every day.

② Walk down Via Sant'Agostino and Via Santa Monaca to the church of **Santa Maria del Carmine,** of no architectural interest but of immense significance in the history of Renaissance art. It contains the celebrated frescoes painted by Masaccio in the **Brancacci Chapel,** unveiled not long ago after a lengthy and meticulous restoration. The chapel was a classroom for such artistic giants as Botticelli, Leonardo da Vinci, Michelangelo, and Raphael, since they all came to study Masaccio's realistic use of light and perspective and his creation of space and depth. *Piazza del Carmine, tel. 055/212331. Admission: 5,000 lire. Open Mon. and Wed.–Sat. 10–5, Sun. 1–5.*

Off the Beaten Track

Few tourists get to see one of Florence's most precious works of art, Benozzo Gozzoli's glorious frescoes in the tiny chapel on the second floor of **Palazzo Medici Riccardi,** representing the Journey of the Magi as a spectacular cavalcade with Lorenzo the Magnificent on a charger. *Via Cavour 1, tel. 055/276–0340. Admission: 6,000 lire. Open Mon.–Tues., Thurs.–Sat. 9–1 and 3–6, Sun. 9–1.*

The **English Cemetery** is on a cypress-studded knoll in the middle of heavily trafficked Piazza Donatello, not far from the botanical garden. Here you can walk with the shades of Elizabeth Barrett Browning, Algernon Swinburne, and other poets. You will need to ask the custodian to let you into the cemetery. It is kept locked. *Piazza Donatello. Ring bell at entrance for admission.*

See some of Florence's smaller museums. The **Davanzati Museum** is a dusky and imposing medieval palazzo furnished with antiques from the 14th century on. *Via Porta Rossa 13, tel. 055/238–8610. Admission: 4,000 lire. Open Tues.–Sun. 9–2.*

Casa Buonarroti, which was Michelangelo's home from 1508 until his death in 1564 and subsequently belonged to his heirs, highlights the artist's early works and drawings in evocative surroundings. *Via Ghibellina 70, tel. 055/241752. Admission: 8,000 lire. Open Wed.–Mon. 9:30–1:30.*

The **Stibbert Museum,** a Victorian mansion full of objets d'art and armor, was donated to Florence by 19th-century collector Frederick Stibbert. This is the city's most eclectic and bizarre museum. *Via Stibbert 26, tel. 055/486049. Admission: 5,000 lire. Open Mon.–Wed., Fri., and Sat. 9–2, Sun. 9–12:30.*

Take Bus 12 or 13 from the train station or cathedral up to Piazzale Michelangelo, then walk along Viale dei Colli and climb to **San Miniato al Monte,** a charming green-and-white marble Romanesque church full of artistic riches.

Visit the **synagogue** on Via Farini and the **Jewish Museum** next door, which contains antique scrolls and ritual objects. *Via Farini 4; tel. 055/245252. Call in morning for opening hrs.*

Shopping

Florence offers top quality for your money in leather goods, linens and upholstery fabrics, gold and silver jewelry, and cameos. Straw goods, gilded wooden trays and frames, hand-printed paper desk accessories, and ceramic objects make good inexpensive gifts. Many shops offer fine old prints.

Shopping Districts

The most fashionable streets in Florence are **Via Tornabuoni** and **Via della Vigna Nuova.** Goldsmiths and jewelry shops can be found on and around the **Ponte Vecchio** and in the **Santa Croce area,** where there is also a high concentration of leather shops.

Antiques

Most of Florence's many antiques dealers are located in **Borgo San Jacopo** and **Borgo Ognissanti,** but you'll find plenty of small shops throughout the center of town.

Department Stores

Principe, in Piazza Strozzi, is a high-quality apparel store that incorporates several designer boutiques. At the other end of the price range, **UPIM,** in Piazza della Repubblica and various other locations, has inexpensive goods of all types.

Markets

The big food market at **Piazza del Mercato Centrale** is open in the morning (Mon.–Sat.) and is worth a visit. The **San Lorenzo market** on Piazza San Lorenzo and Via dell'Ariento is a fine place to browse for buys in leather goods and souvenirs (open Tues. and Sat. 8–7; also Sun. in summer). The **Mercato Nuovo,** Via Calimala, which is sometimes called the **Mercato del Porcellino** because of the famous bronze statue of a boar at one side, is packed with stalls selling souvenirs and straw goods (open Tues.–Sat. 8–7; closed Sun. and Mon. mornings in winter). There's a colorful neighborhood market at **Sant'Ambrogio,** Piazza Ghiberti (open Mon.–Sat. mornings), and a permanent flea market at **Piazza Ciompi** (open Mon.–Sat. 9–1 and 4–7, Sun. 9–1 in summer).

A huge weekly market takes over Viale Lincoln in the Cascine park every Tuesday morning.

Dining

Mealtimes in Florence are 12:30 to 2 and 7:30 to 9 or later. Many **$$** and **$** places are small, and you may have to share a table. Reservations are always advisable; to find a table at inexpensive places, get there early. For details and price-category definitions, *see* Dining *in* Staying in Italy, *above.*

$$$$ **Enoteca Pinchiorri.** In the beautiful Renaissance palace and its charm-
★ ing garden courtyard that was home to Giovanni da Verrazano (a 15th-century Florentine navigator), husband-and-wife team Giorgio Pinchiorri and Annie Feolde have created an exceptional restaurant that ranks as one of Italy's best. Guests can enjoy Annie's rediscoveries of traditional Tuscan dishes, or her own brand of imaginatively creative nouvelle cuisine, while Giorgio oversees the extraordinary wine cellar. At upward of 150,000 lire per person, meals here are for real connoisseurs; a prix-fixe menu costs about 95,000 lire. *Via Ghibellina 87, tel. 055/242777. Reservations required. AE, MC, V. Closed Sun., Aug., and Dec. 24–28. No lunch Mon.*

$$$ **Terrazza Brunelleschi.** The rooftop restaurant of the hotel Baglioni has
★ the best view in town. The dining room, decorated in pale blue and creamy tones, has big picture windows; the summer-dining terrace is charming, with tables under arbors and turrets for guests to climb to get an even better view. The menu offers such traditional Tuscan dishes as *minestra di fagioli* (bean soup) and other more innovative choices, such as a pâté of peppers and tomato. *Hotel Baglioni, Piazza Unità Italiana 6, tel. 055/215642. Reservations advised, especially in summer. AE, DC, MC, V.*

$$ **Alle Murate.** Between the Duomo and Santa Croce, this sophisticated but informal restaurant features creative versions of classic Tuscan food, along with specialties of other regions, such as the Calabrian *cavatelli con broccoli* (pasta with broccoli and cheese). In a smaller room called the *vineria*, the menu and service are simpler and prices lower. *Via Ghibellina 52/r, tel. 055/240618. Reservations advised. No credit cards. Dinner only. Closed Mon.*

$$ **Angiolino.** This bustling little trattoria has a real charcoal grill and an
★ old wood-burning stove to keep its customers warm on nippy days. Glowing with authentic atmosphere, Angiolino offers such specialties as *ribollita* (a Tuscan version of minestrone) and juicy *bistecca alla fiorentina* (T-bone steak basted in olive oil and black pepper). The bistecca will push the bill up, as you pay by weight (order one for two). *Via Santo Spirito 36/r, tel. 055/239–8976. Dinner reservations advised. No credit cards. No dinner Sun. Closed Mon. and last 3 wks in July.*

$$ **Cavallini.** It makes sense that this restaurant, with its outdoor café, is touristy, particularly since it's situated right on Piazza della Signoria. But it is also consistently good, it's open on Sundays, and it's so handy for collapsing in after a hard day at the Uffizi. The cooking is pure Tuscan, with broad pappardelle, bean soup, and grilled meat on the menu. *Via delle Farina 6/r, tel. 055/215818. Reservations advised, especially for outdoor tables. AE, DC, MC, V. No dinner Tues. Closed Wed. and Aug. 1–22.*

$$ **Il Cibreo.** The young chefs of this upscale trattoria near the Sant'Am-
★ brogio market prepare updated versions of traditional Florentine dishes and present them with flair, as in *passato di peperoni gialli* (yellow-pepper soup) and *anatra farcita* (boned duck with a meat, raisin, and pine-nut stuffing). Tables are set outdoors in June and July. It has a

café annex across the street and an inexpensive tavern annex around the corner. *Via dei Macci 118/r, tel. 055/234–1100. Dinner reservations advised. AE, DC, MC, V. Closed Sun., Mon., July 25–Sept. 5, and Dec. 31–Jan. 7.*

$$ **La Giostra.** A five-minute walk from the back of the cathedral or from Santa Croce, the Giostra has the typically unpretentious and rustic look of a Florentine trattoria, but with a difference: the gourmet touch of the courteous owner-chef. Try his ravioli or veal *agli agrumi* (with an unusual and delicate citrus sauce) or *spianata di carne* (a generous portion of thinly sliced beef redolent of herbs). Like the menu, the wine list offers good value. Service is informal. *Borgo Pinti 10/r, tel. 055/241341. Dinner reservations advised. AE, MC, V.*

$$ **Le Fonticine.** This roomy restaurant near Santa Maria Novella has a warm, rustic atmosphere, with paintings and ceramics covering the walls. Owner Silvano Bruci and his staff are cordial, the homemade pasta is exquisite (try the tortellini or *tortelli,* with meat or cheese stuffing), and the menu offers a good choice of main courses. *Via Nazionale 79/r, tel. 055/282106. Dinner reservations advised. AE, DC, MC, V. Closed Sun., Mon., and July 25–Aug. 25.*

$$ **Mario da Ganino.** Highly informal, rustic, and cheerful, this trattoria greets you with a taste of mortadella. An array of pastas follows, plus a heavenly cheesecake for dessert. There are plenty of other taste-tempters on the menu. It's tiny, seating only 35, double that in summer at outdoor tables. *Piazza dei Cimatori 4/r, tel. 055/214125. Reservations advised. AE, DC. Closed Sun. and Aug. 15–25.*

$ **La Maremmana.** A lavish display of produce at the entrance holds promise of what's in store at this typical Florentine trattoria near Santa Croce. The fixed-price menu includes generous servings of local favorites such as ribollita and stracotto. There is an à la carte menu, too, and there are tables in the garden. *Via dei Macci 77/r, tel. 055/241226. Reservations advised. MC, V. Closed Sun.*

$ **Za-Za.** Near the San Lorenzo market, this is an informal but trendy trattoria with posters of movie stars on the walls and a lively Italian clientele. The food is classic Florentine: ribollita, fagioli served several ways, and good steaks, with everything fresh from the market. *Piazza Mercato Centrale 16/r, tel. 055/215411. Reservations advised. AE, DC, MC, V. Closed Sun. and Aug.*

Lodging

What with mass tourism and trade fairs, rooms are at a premium in Florence for most of the year. Make reservations well in advance. If you arrive without a reservation, the ITA office in the railway station (open 8:20 AM–9 PM) can help you, but there may be a long line. Now that much traffic is banned in the downtown area, many central hotel rooms are quieter. Local traffic and motorcycles can still be bothersome, however, so check the decibel level before you settle in. From November through March ask for special low winter rates. For details and price-category definitions, *see* Lodging *in* Staying in Italy, *above.*

$$$$ **Grand.** A Florentine classic with Old World elegance and truly luxu-
★ rious amenities. Smaller and more intimate than the Excelsior, its sister hotel across the square, the Grand has public areas and most rooms decorated in rich Renaissance style. Some rooms have balconies overlooking the Arno. *Piazza Ognissanti 1, 50123, tel. 055/288781, fax 055/217400. 107 rooms with bath. Facilities: restaurant, bar, winter garden, parking. AE, DC, MC, V.*

$$$$ Regency. One of the Ottaviani family's small, select hotels, the Regency has the intimate and highly refined atmosphere of a private villa, luxuriously furnished with antiques and decorated with great style. Just outside the historic center of the city, it has a charming garden and the pleasant Le Jardin restaurant. *Piazza Massimo d'Azeglio 3, 50121, tel. 055/245247, fax 055/234–2938. 33 rooms with bath. Facilities: garage. AE, DC, MC, V.*

$$$$ Villa Cora. In a residential area on a hill overlooking the Oltrarno section of Florence and across the Arno to the Duomo and bell tower, the Villa Cora is a converted private villa. Furnishings are exquisite and the atmosphere is quietly elegant. There are gardens in which to stroll, a pool in which to wallow, and a formal but charming restaurant in which to dine. There is a Mercedes shuttle service between the hotel and the center of Florence. *Viale Machiavelli 18, 50125, tel. 055/229–8451, fax 055/229086. 48 rooms with bath. Facilities: restaurant, bar, pool, garden. AE, DC, MC, V.*

$$$ Baglioni. Spacious, elegant, and a favorite of businesspeople, the Baglioni has well-proportioned rooms tastefully decorated in antique Florentine style. The hotel also has a charming roof terrace, and the splendid Terrazza Brunelleschi restaurant (*see* Dining, *above*), which has the best view in all Florence. *Piazza Unità Italiana 6, 50123, tel. 055/23580, fax 055/235–8895. 197 rooms with bath. Facilities: restaurant, garage. AE, DC, MC, V.*

$$$ Brunelleschi. This unique hotel in the heart of Florence encompasses
★ a Byzantine tower, a medieval church, and an 18th-century palazzo. Sections of ancient stone walls and brick arches set off the tasteful contemporary decor in the public rooms. Bedrooms are decorated with textured, coordinated fabrics in soft colors, and the beige marble bathrooms are luxurious. *Piazza Sant'Elisabetta (Via dei Calzaiuoli), 50122, tel. 055/562068, fax 055/219653. 94 rooms with bath. Facilities: restaurant, bar. AE, DC, MC, V.*

$$$ Monna Lisa. Staying here is like living in an aristocratic palace in the
★ heart of Florence. American visitors in particular are fond of its smallish but homey bedrooms and sumptuously comfortable sitting rooms. Ask for a room on the quiet 17th-century courtyard, especially the one with the delightful balcony. A lavish buffet breakfast is included in the price. Reserve well in advance. *Borgo Pinti 27, 50121, tel. 055/247–9751, fax 055/247–9755. 30 rooms with bath. Facilities: bar, garden, parking. AE, DC, MC, V.*

$$ Hermitage. Comfort and charm are the attributes of this hotel occupying the top two floors of a palazzo next to the Ponte Vecchio and the Uffizi. In the inviting living room overlooking the Arno, the bright breakfast room, the flowered roof terrace, and the well-lighted bedrooms, decor and atmosphere are those of a well-kept Florentine home. Double glazing, air conditioning, and attentive maintenance sustain the relaxing ambience. (The hotel is served by an elevator located at the top of a short flight of stairs). *Vicolo Marzio 1 (Piazza del Pesce–Ponte Vecchio), 50122, tel. 055/287216, fax 055/212208. 30 rooms with bath. Facilities: breakfast room, roof terrace. AE, MC, V.*

$$ Loggiato dei Serviti. You'll find the Loggiato dei Serviti tucked under
★ an arcade in one of the city's quietest and most attractive squares. Vaulted ceilings and tasteful furnishings (some of them antiques) go far to make this hotel a real find for those who want to get the genuine Florentine feel and who will appreciate the 19th-century town house surroundings while enjoying modern creature comforts. There is no restaurant. *Piazza Santissima Annunziata 3, 50122, tel. 055/239–8280, fax 055/289595. 29 rooms with bath. Facilities: bar. AE, DC, MC, V.*

$$ **Morandi alla Crocetta.** This charming and distinguished residence near
★ Piazza Santissima Annunziata was once a monastery, and access is up
a flight of stairs. It is furnished in the classic style of a gracious Flo-
rentine home, and guests feel like privileged friends of the family. Small
and exceptional, it is also a good value and must be booked well in
advance. *Via Laura 50, 50121, tel. 055/234–4747, fax 055/248–
0954. 9 rooms with bath. Facilities: bar. AE, DC, MC, V.*

$$ **Villa Azalee.** In a residential area about five minutes from the train station, this century-old mansion is set in a large garden. It has a private-
home atmosphere and comfortable living rooms. Bedrooms are decorated
individually and are air-conditioned. *Viale Fratelli Rosselli 44, 50123,
tel. 055/214242, fax 055/268264. Facilities: air-conditioning, garden.
24 rooms with bath. AE, DC, MC, V.*

$ **Apollo.** A hospitable Italian-Canadian couple owns and manages this
conveniently located hotel near the station, offering good value in spacious rooms decorated in Florentine style, with gleaming new bathrooms
that, though compact, have such amenities as hair dryers. The staff is
helpful and attentive to guests' needs. *Via Faenza 77, 50123, tel.
055/284119, fax 055/210101. 15 rooms with bath. Facilities: bar. AE,
DC, MC, V.*

$ **Bellettini.** Very centrally located, this small hotel occupies two floors
★ of an old but well-kept building near the Church of San Lorenzo, in
an area with plenty of inexpensive eating places. Rooms are ample, with
Venetian or Tuscan decor, and bathrooms are modern. The management is friendly and helpful. *Via dei Conti 7, 50123, tel. 055/213561,
fax 055/283551. 27 rooms, 23 with bath. Facilities: bar, lounge. AE,
DC, MC, V.*

The Arts

For a list of events, pick up a "Florence Concierge Information" booklet from your hotel desk, or the monthly information bulletin published
by the **Comune Aperto** city information office (Via Cavour 1/r). This
information is also available at information offices at the station, at
Via Cavour 1/r, and at Chiasso dei Baroncelli.

Music and Ballet

Most major musical events are staged at the **Teatro Comunale** (Corso
Italia 16, tel. 055/277–9236). The box office (closed Sun. and Mon.)
is open from 9 to 1, and a half hour before performances. It's best to
order your tickets by mail, however, as they're difficult to come by at
the last minute. You can also order concert and ballet tickets through
Universalturismo (Via degli Speziali 7/r, tel. 055/217241). **Amici della
Musica** (Friends of Music) puts on a series of concerts at the **Teatro della
Pergola** (box office, Via della Pergola 10a/r, tel. 055/247–9651). For
program information, contact the Amici della Musica directly at Via
Sirtori 49 (tel. 055/608420).

Film

English-language films are shown at the **Cinema Astro,** on Piazza San
Simone near Santa Croce. There are two shows every evening, Tuesday through Sunday. It closes in July.

Nightlife

Bars

Many of the top hotels have piano bars; that of the **Plaza Lucchesi** (Lungarno della Zecca Vecchia 38, tel. 055/264141) is particularly spacious
and pleasant. The terrace of the hotel **Baglioni** (*see* Lodging, *above*)
has no music but has one of the best views in Florence, candlelit ta-

bles, and a wonderful atmosphere. Music is on tape at the **Champag-neria** (Via Lambruschini 15/r, tel. 055/490804, closed Sun.), a bistro-type meeting place for a fairly sophisticated mélange of young Florentines and an international crowd. **Caffè Voltaire** (Via della Scala 9/r, tel. 055/218255; closed Mon.) serves Brazilian food and drink and plays Latin music to a lively crowd.

Nightclubs
The River Club (Lungarno Corsini 8, tel. 055/282465) has winter-garden decor and a large dance floor (closed Mon.). **Meccanò** (in the Cascine park at Viale degli Olmi 1, tel. 055/331371, closed Mon.) offers a multimedia experience, with videos, art, and music, in a high-tech disco with a late-night restaurant, the Pomodoro d'Acciaio.

Discos
Jackie O (Via dell'Erta Canina 24a, tel. 055/234–2442) is a glittering art deco disco with lots of mirrors and marble and a trendy clientele (closed Wed.). **Space Electronic** (Via Palazzuolo 37, tel. 055/239–3082) is exactly what its name implies: ultramodern and psychedelic (closed Mon., except from Mar. to Sept., when it's open every night). **Yab** (Via Sassetti 5/r, tel. 055/282018) is another futuristic-style disco popular with the young international set. It's closed Sunday and Monday.

TUSCANY

Tuscany is a blend of rugged hills, fertile valleys, and long stretches of sandy beach that curve along the west coast of central Italy and fringe the pine-forested coastal plain of the Maremma. The gentle, cypress-studded green hills may seem familiar: Leonardo and Raphael often painted them in the backgrounds of their masterpieces. The cities and towns of Tuscany were the cradle of the Renaissance, which during the 15th century saw its greatest flowering in nearby Florence. Come to Tuscany to enjoy its unchanged and gracious atmosphere of good living, and, above all, its unparalleled artistic treasures, many still in their original settings in tiny old churches and patrician palaces.

Getting Around

By Train
The main train network connects Florence with Arezzo and Prato. Another main line runs to Pisa, while a secondary line goes from Prato to the coast via Lucca. Trains also connect Siena with Pisa (via Empoli), a two-hour ride.

By Bus
The region is crisscrossed by bus lines, good alternatives to trains, especially from Florence to Prato, a half-hour trip, and from Florence to Siena, which can take from 1¼ (by express bus) to 2 hours. Use local buses to tour the many pretty hill towns around Siena, such as San Gimignano, and then take a Tra-In or Lazzi bus from Siena to Arezzo, where you can get back onto the main Rome–Florence train line.

By Car
The main autostrade run parallel to the train routes. Roads throughout Tuscany are in good condition, though often narrow.

Guided Tours

A local bus consortium (book through travel agencies and hotels) operates one-day excursions to Siena and San Gimignano out of Florence. **American Express** (Via Guicciardini 49/r, Florence, tel. 055/288751) also can arrange for cars, drivers, and guides for special-interest tours in Tuscany. **CIT** (Via Cavour 54/r, tel. 055/294306) has a three-day Carosello bus tour from Rome to Florence, Siena, and San Gimignano, as well as a five-day tour that also takes in Venice.

Tourist Information

Arezzo (Piazza della Repubblica 28, tel. 0575/377678).
Cortona (Via Nazionale 72, tel. 0575/630557).
Lucca (Piazza Guidiccione 2, tel.. 0583/491205).
Pisa (Piazza della Stazione 11, tel. 050/42291; Piazza del Duomo 8, tel. 050/560464).
Pistoia (Piazza del Duomo 4, tel. 0573/21622).
Prato (Via Cairoli 48, tel. 0574/24112).
San Gimignano (Piazza del Duomo, tel. 0577/940008).
Siena (Via di Città 43, tel. 0577/42209; Piazza del Campo 56, tel. 0577/280551).

Exploring Tuscany

Starting from Florence, you can go west to Prato and Pistoia, workaday cities with a core of fine medieval buildings, then to the historic cities of Lucca and Pisa. Lucca makes a good base for an excursion to Pisa, which is only about a half hour away by car, bus, or train. Heading south from Florence you can explore the Chianti district by car. You can make Siena your base for excursions by car or local bus to some picturesque hill towns: San Gimignano, Montepulciano, and Pienza.

Prato

Since the Middle Ages, **Prato,** 21 kilometers (13 miles) northwest of Florence, has been Italy's major wool-producing center, and it remains one of the world's largest manufacturers of cloth. Ignore the drab industrial outskirts and devote some time to the fine old buildings in the downtown area, crammed with artwork commissioned by Prato's wealthy merchants during the Renaissance. The **Duomo** (cathedral), erected during the Middle Ages, was decorated with paintings and sculptures by some of the most illustrious figures of Tuscan art, among them Fra Filippo Lippi, who took 12 years to complete the frescoes in the apse (perhaps because in the meantime he was being tried for fraud and was also wooing a nun with whom he then eloped). Look in particular for his passionate portrayals of *Herod's Feast* and *Salome's Dance*. *Piazza del Duomo. Open daily May–Oct. 6:30–noon and 4–7; Nov.–Apr. 7:30–noon and 4–6.*

In the former bishop's palace, now the **Museo dell'Opera del Duomo,** you can see the original reliefs by Donatello for the Pulpit of the Holy Girdle (Mary's belt, supposedly given to Doubting Thomas as evidence of her assumption; the relic is kept in a chapel of the cathedral). *Piazza del Duomo 49, tel. 0574/29339. Admission: 5,000 lire (ticket valid for other Prato museums). Open Mon. and Wed.–Sat. 9:30–12:30 and 3–6:30, Sun. 9:30–12:30.*

Architects and architecture buffs rhapsodize over the church of **Santa Maria delle Carceri,** off Via Cairoli. Built by Giuliano Sangallo in the 1490s, it was a landmark of Renaissance architecture. Next to it, the formidable **castle** built for Frederick II of Hohenstaufen is another impressive sight, the only castle of its type to be seen outside southern Italy. *Piazza Santa Maria delle Carceri. Admission free. Open May–Sept., Mon.*

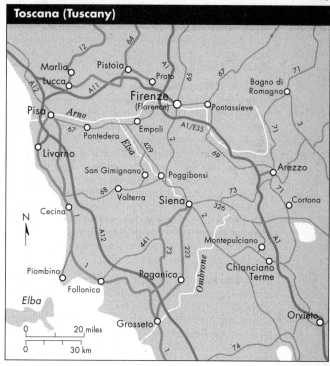

Toscana (Tuscany)

and Wed.–Sat. 9:30–12:30 and 3–6:30, Sun. 9:30–12:30; Oct.–Apr., Mon. and Wed.–Sat. 9:30–11:30 and 3–5:30, Sun. 9:30–11:30.

Pistoia

Pistoia lies about 15 kilometers (9 miles) northwest of Prato. A floricultural capital of Europe, it's surrounded by greenhouses and plant nurseries. Flowers aside, Pistoia's main sights are all in the downtown area, so you can easily see them on the way to Lucca. The Romanesque **Duomo** (cathedral) is flanked by a 13th-century bell tower, while in a side chapel dedicated to San Jacopo (St. James) there's a massive **silver altar** that alone makes the stop in Pistoia worthwhile. Two hundred years in the making, it's an incredible piece of workmanship, begun in 1287. *Piazza del Duomo. Illumination of altarpiece: 2,000 lire.*

Take a look at the unusual Gothic baptistry opposite the Duomo, then follow Via delle Pappe (to the left behind the Duomo) to admire the superb frieze by Giovanni della Robbia on the Ospedale del Ceppo. Continue on to the church of **Sant'Andrea** (Via Sant'Andrea) to see Pistoia's greatest art treasure, Giovanni Pisano's powerfully sculpted 13th-century **pulpit.** Heading back toward the train station and bus terminal, stop on the way to take in the green-and-white marble church of **San Giovanni Fuorcivitas** (Via Francesco Crispi, off Via Cavour). Highlights here include a *Visitation* by Luca della Robbia, a painting by Taddeo Gaddi, and a holy water font by Giovanni Pisano.

Lucca

Your next destination is **Lucca,** Puccini's hometown and a city well-loved by sightseers who appreciate the careful upkeep of its medieval look. Though it hasn't the number of hotels and other tourist trappings that, say, Pisa does, for that very reason it's a pleasant alternative. You can easily make an excursion to Pisa from here—it's only 22 kilometers (14 miles) away. First enjoy the views of the city and countryside from the tree-planted 16th-century ramparts that encircle Lucca. Then explore the city's marvelously elaborate Romanesque churches, fronted with tiers and rows of columns, and looking suspiciously like oversize marble wedding cakes.

From vast **Piazza Napoleone,** a swing around the Old Town will take you past the 11th-century **Duomo** on Piazza San Martino, with its 15th-century tomb of Ilaria del Carretto by Jacopo della Quercia. Don't neglect a ramble through the **Piazza del Mercato,** which preserves the oval form of the Roman amphitheater over which it was built, or the three surrounding streets that are filled with atmosphere: **Via Battisti, Via Fillungo,** and **Via Guinigi.** In addition to the Duomo, Lucca has two other fine churches. **San Frediano** (Piazza San Frediano) is graced with an austere facade ornamented by 13th-century mosaic decoration. Inside, check out the exquisite reliefs by Jacopo della Quercia in the last chapel on the left. **San Michele in Foro** (Piazza San Michele) is an exceptional example of the Pisan Romanesque style and decorative flair peculiar to Lucca: Note its facade, a marriage of arches and columns crowned by a statue of St. Michael.

The **Villa Reale** is 8 kilometers (5 miles) outside town, at Marlia. Once the home of Napoléon's sister, and recently restored by the Counts Pecci-Blunt, this villa is celebrated for its spectacular gardens, laid out in the 18th and 19th centuries. Gardening buffs adore the legendary *teatro di verdura,* a theater carved out of hedges and topiaries; concerts are occasionally offered there. *Marlia, tel. 0583/30108. Admission: 7,000 lire. Guided visits on the hr, July–Sept., Tues.–Thurs. and Sun. 10, 11, 4, 5, and 6; Oct. and Mar.–June, Tues.–Sun. 10, 11, 3, 4, and 5. Closed Nov.–Feb.*

Pisa

As you drive southwest, the next Tuscan town of note you'll come to is **Pisa,** a dull, overcommercialized place, though even skeptics have to admit that the **Torre Pendente** (Leaning Tower) really is one of the world's more amazing sights. Designed by Bonanno Pisano (the first of three architects to work on the structure), the tower began to tilt even before it was finished, as its foundations shifted under its weight. A 294-step staircase spirals its way up the tower, and now that the tower has been firmly anchored to the earth to keep it from tilting too far, it may be reopened to visitors in 1996 on a limited basis. If you want a two-foot marble imitation of the Leaning Tower, perhaps even illuminated from within, this is your chance to grab one at a souvenir stand. *Campo dei Miracoli.*

Pisa's **Duomo** is elegantly simple, its facade decorated with geometric and animal shapes. The cavernous interior is supported by a series of 68 columns, while the pulpit is a prime example of Giovanni Pisano's work and one of the major monuments of the Italian Gothic style. Be sure to note the suspended lamp that hangs across from the pulpit; known as Galileo's Lamp, it's said to have inspired his theories on pendular motion. *Piazza del Duomo. Admission: 2,000 lire. Open Mon.–Sat. 10–5, Sun. 1–5.*

Also in Campo dei Miracoli are the **baptistry** and the **Camposanto** (cemetery), with important frescoes. Adjacent are the Museo dell'Opera del Duomo, full of medieval sculpture, and the Museo delle Sinopie, the latter—comprising examples of wall sketches used to make frescoes—of limited interest to most visitors. The baptistry was begun in 1153 but not completed until 1400; the celebrated Pisano family did most of its decoration. Test out the excellent acoustics (occasionally the guard will slam the great doors shut and then sing a few notes—the resulting echo is very impressive, and costly, too, since he'll expect a tip). *Admission to any two: 10,000 lire; admission to any four: 15,000 lire. Baptistry and Camposanto open Apr.–Sept., daily 8–7:40; Oct.–Mar., daily 9–5:40. Museo delle Sinopie, Piazza del Duomo, tel. 050/560547. Open daily 9–5:40.*

Visitors may find it more convenient to take a train back to Florence and get a bus or train there for the nearly 1½-hour trip to Siena. For a more leisurely look at the Tuscan countryside, investigate the possibility of taking local trains from Pisa to Siena, changing trains at Empoli and then passing through **Certaldo,** a pretty hill town that's the birthplace of Giovanni Boccaccio, 14th-century author of the *Decameron.*

Siena

Siena is one of Italy's best-preserved medieval towns, rich both in works of art and in expensive antique shops. The famous **Palio** is held here, a breakneck, 90-second horse race that takes place twice each year in the Piazza del Campo, on July 2 and August 16. Built on three hills, Siena is not an easy town to explore, for everything you'll want to see is either up or down a steep hill or stairway. But it is worth every ounce of effort. Siena really gives you the chance of seeing and feeling what the Middle Ages must have been like: dark stone palaces that look like fortresses, Gothic church portals, and narrow streets opening out into airy squares.

Siena was a center of learning and art during the Middle Ages, and almost all the public buildings and churches in the town have enough artistic or historical merit to be worth visiting. Unlike most churches, Siena's **Duomo** has a mixture of religious and civic symbols ornamenting both its interior and exterior. The cathedral museum in the unfinished transept contains some fine works of art, notably a celebrated *Maestà* by Duccio di Buoninsegna. The animated frescoes of papal history in the Piccolomini Library (with an entrance off the left aisle of the cathedral) are credited to Pinturicchio and are worth seeking out. *Piazza del Duomo. Cathedral Museum. Admission: 5,000 lire. Open Mar. 14–Sept., daily 9–7:30; Oct.–Nov. 3, daily 9–6; Nov. 4–Dec., daily 9–1:30; Jan. 2–Mar. 13, daily 9–1. Library. Admission: 2,000 lire. Open mid-Mar.–Sept., daily 9–7:30; Oct.–Nov. 3, 9–6:30; Nov. 4–mid-Mar., daily 10–1 and 2–5.*

Nearby, the fan-shaped **Piazza del Campo** is Siena's main center of activity, with 11 streets leading into it. Farsighted planning has preserved it as a medieval showpiece, containing the 13th-century **Palazzo Pubblico** (City Hall) and the **Torre del Mangia** (Bell Tower). Try to visit both these buildings, the former for Lorenzetti's frescoes on the effects of good and bad government, the latter for the wonderful view (you'll have to climb 503 steps to reach it, however). *Piazza del Campo, tel. 0577/292111. Bell Tower. Admission: 5,000 lire. Open Mar. 15–Nov. 15, daily 10–1 hr before sunset; Nov. 16–Mar. 14, daily 10–1. Palazzo Pubblico (including the Civic Museum). Admission: 6,000 lire. Open Mar. 15–Nov. 15, Mon.–Sat. 9–7, Sun. 9–1:30; Nov.–Mar., daily 9–1:30.*

TIME OUT　There are several **gelaterie** on Piazza del Campo, but if you need something more substantial, walk east from Piazza del Campo to **Verrocchio** (Logge del Papa 2; closed Wed.), a restaurant serving local fare.

San Gimignano

From Siena, **San Gimignano** is only about a half hour away by car and an hour by Tra-In bus (change buses in Poggibonsi). "San Gimignano-of-the-Beautiful-Towers—to use its original name—is perhaps the most delightful of the Tuscan medieval hill towns. There were once 79 tall towers here, symbols of power for the wealthy families of the Middle Ages. Thirteen are still standing, giving the town its unique skyline. The bus stops just outside the town gates, from which you can stroll down the main street to the picturesque Piazza della Cisterna.

Just around the corner is the church of the **Collegiata.** Its walls, and those of its chapel dedicated to Santa Fina, are decorated with radiant frescoes (have plenty of 100-lire coins at hand for the light machines; to get a closer look at the chapel frescoes, buy a ticket for the Municipal Museum in Palazzo del Popolo, admission 5,000 lire). From the steps of the church you can observe the town's countless crows as they circle the tall towers. In the pretty courtyard on the right as you descend the church stairs, there's a shop selling Tuscan and Deruta ceramics, which you'll also find in other shops along the Via San Giovanni. The excellent San Gimignano wine could be another souvenir of your visit; it's sold in gift cartons from just about every shop in town.

If you have a car, you can drive northeast of Siena on Route 222, through hilly Chianti country, or southeast of Siena to the Abbey of Monte Oliveto Maggiore and the hill towns of Montepulciano and Pienza, each worth seeing and much less crowded than San Gimignano. You can also reach Montepulciano and Pienza by bus from Siena, though service is often haphazard.

Arezzo

A local bus takes you from Siena to **Arezzo,** about 48 kilometers (30 miles) east. The route meanders past thickly wooded hills, past vineyards and wheat fields, and past the broad ribbon of the Autostrada del Sole in the fertile Chiana Valley, known for its pale beef cattle that provide the classic bistecca alla fiorentina. Arezzo is not a particularly beautiful town, though the old, upper town still has a good assortment of medieval and Renaissance buildings. What makes Arezzo worth a visit, however, is its fine array of Tuscan art treasures, including frescoes, stained glass, and ancient Etruscan pottery.

The **Museo Archeologico** (Archaeological Museum) is near the train station, next to what's left of an ancient **Roman amphitheater.** The museum has a rich collection of Etruscan art, artifacts, and pottery, which has been copied by Arezzo's contemporary artisans and is sold in the local ceramic shops. *Via Margaritone 10, tel. 0575/20882. Admission: 8,000 lire. Open Tues.–Sat. 9–2, Sun. 9–1.*

Via Guido Monaco, named after the 11th-century originator of the musical scale, leads to the church of **San Francesco,** in which sit some of the town's main attractions, among them the famous frescoes by Piero della Francesca, which depict the Legend of the True Cross. Due for restoration after intensive studies of suitable methods, these frescoes may be at least partially hidden for a few years. Though faded, they still rank among the outstanding examples of Renaissance painting, and art lovers are looking forward to seeing them in renewed splendor. *Push button on black box for light. Via Cavour.*

Now you enter the old part of Arezzo, where the poet Petrarch (1304–74), the artist Vasari (1511–74), and the satirical author Pietro Aretino (1492–1556) all lived. Climb Via Cesalpino uphill to the fine Gothic **cathedral** (Piazza del Duomo), then stroll past **Petrarch's House** to Pi-

azza Grande, an attractive, sloping square where an extensive open-air fair of antiques and old bric-a-brac is held the first weekend of every month. The shops around the piazza also specialize in antiques, with prices lower than those you will encounter in Florence. The colonnaded apse and bell tower of the Romanesque church of **Santa Maria della Pieve** grace one end of this pleasant piazza.

Cortona

A full day may be enough for you to get the feel of Arezzo, but you may wish to stay overnight, especially during the antiques fair, or if you want to use the town as a base for an excursion to **Cortona,** about 30 kilometers (18 miles) south. This well-preserved, unspoiled medieval hill town is known for its excellent small art gallery and a number of fine antiques shops, as well as for its colony of foreign residents. Cortona has the advantage of being on the main train line, though you will have to take a local bus from the station up into the town, passing the Renaissance church of **Santa Maria del Calcinaio** on the way.

The heart of Cortona is formed by **Piazza della Repubblica** and the adjacent **Piazza Signorelli.** Wander into the courtyard of the picturesque **Palazzo Pretorio,** and, if you want to see a representative collection of Etruscan bronzes, climb its centuries-old stone staircase to the **Museo dell'Accademia Etrusca** (Gallery of Etruscan Art). *Piazza Signorelli 9, tel. 0575/630415. Admission: 5,000 lire. Open Apr.–Sept., Tues.–Sun. 10–1 and 4–7; Oct.–Mar., Tues.–Sun. 9–1 and 3–5.*

The nearby **Museo Diocesano** (Diocesan Museum) houses an impressive number of large and splendid paintings by native son Luca Signorelli, as well as a beautiful *Annunciation* by Fra Angelico, a delightful surprise to find in this small, eclectic town. *Piazza del Duomo 1, tel. 0575/62830. Admission: 5,000 lire. Open Apr.–Sept., Tues.–Sun. 9–1 and 3–6:30; Oct.–Mar., Tues.–Sun. 9–1 and 3–5.*

Dining and Lodging

For details and price-category definitions, *see* Dining *and* Lodging *in* Staying in Italy, *above.*

Arezzo
DINING

★ **Buca di San Francesco.** Travelers and passing celebrities come to this rustic and historic cellar restaurant for the 13th-century cantina atmosphere, but locals love it for the food, especially ribollita and *sformato di verdure* (vegetable pie). *Piazza San Francesco 1, tel. 0575/23271. Dinner reservations advised. AE, DC, MC, V. No dinner Mon. Closed Tues. and July. $$*

Tastevin. Arezzo's purveyor of creative *nuova cucina* serves traditional Tuscan dishes as well, in two attractive rooms in warm Tuscan provincial style and one in more sophisticated art deco. At the cozy bar the talented owner plays and sings Sinatra songs in the evening. Specialties are risotto Tastevin, with cream of truffles, and *tagliata* Tastevin (sliced beef with olive oil and rosemary). *Via dei Cenci 9, tel. 0575/28304. Dinner reservations advised. AE, DC, MC, V. Closed Mon., (Sun. in summer), and Aug. $$*

Spiedo d'Oro. Cheery red-and-white tablecloths add a colorful touch to this large, reliable trattoria near the Archaeological Museum. The menu offers such Tuscan home-style specialties as *zuppa di pane* (bread soup), pappardelle *oll'ocio* (with duck sauce), and osso buco *aretina* (sautéed veal shank). *Via Crispi 12, tel. 0575/22873. No credit cards. Closed Thurs. and first 2 wks in July. $*

LODGING

Continental. The circa-1950 Continental has fairly spacious rooms decorated in white and bright yellow, gleaming bathrooms, and the advantage of a central location within walking distance of all major sights. *Piazza Guido Monaco 7, 51200, tel. 0575/20251, fax 0575/340485. 74 rooms with bath. Facilities: restaurant. AE, DC, MC, V. $$*

Cortona

DINING

★ **Tonino.** The place to eat in Cortona, it's known for its delicious antipasto and for succulent steaks of Chiana Valley beef. It's best on weekdays, when it's quieter. Both service and food have a touch of class. The dining rooms, on two floors, have large picture windows overlooking the valley. *Piazza Garibaldi, tel. 0575/630500. Weekends reservations advised. AE, DC, MC, V. No dinner Mon. Closed Tues. $$*

Lucca

DINING

★ **La Mora.** You'll need a car or a taxi to take you to this charming old way station 10 kilometers (6 miles) outside Lucca, but its authentic local cooking is worth every effort. It is widely considered to be one of the best regional restaurants in Italy. *Via Sesto di Moriano 1748, Ponte a Moriano, tel. 0583/406402. Reservations advised. AE, DC, MC, V. Closed Wed., June 25–July 8, Oct. 10–30. $$–$$$*

★ **Buca di Sant'Antonio.** A Lucca favorite, located near the church of San Michele, Buca di Sant'Antonio was around more than a century ago, and it still retains something of its rustic look. It specializes in traditional local dishes, some unfamiliar but well worth trying, among them ravioli *di ricotta alle zucchine* (with cheese and zucchini) and kid or lamb roasted with herbs. *Via della Cervia 3, tel. 0583/55881. Dinner reservations advised. AE, DC, MC, V. No dinner Sun. Closed Mon. and July 9–29. $$*

Il Giglio. Off vast Piazza Napoleone, Il Giglio has a quiet, turn-of-the-century charm and a dignified atmosphere. In the summer the tables outdoors have a less formal air. The menu is classic: *crostini di fegatini* (savory Tuscan chicken liver, anchovy and caper paste on small pieces of toast), steaks, and seafood, as well. *Piazza del Giglio 3, tel. 0583/494058. Dinner reservations advised. AE, DC, MC, V. No dinner Tues. Closed Wed. $$*

LODGING

★ **Villa La Principessa.** This pretty 19th-century country mansion, 3½ kilometers (2 miles) outside Lucca, is an exclusive hotel with a deluxe annex, Principessa Elisa (**$$$$**). All rooms are individually and tastefully decorated. Antique floors, furniture, and portraits set the tone, and the restaurant is known for its fine Tuscan dishes. *Massa Pisana, 55100, tel. 0583/370037, fax 0583/379019. 44 rooms with bath. Facilities: restaurant, pool, park. AE, DC, MC, V. Closed Nov. 1–Mar. 31. $$$*

La Luna. There's an aura of Old World charm in this family-run hotel on one of Lucca's most central and historic streets. Recent, extensive renovations have endowed the establishment with gleaming modern bathrooms, leaving the atmosphere intact. A plus for anyone touring by car is the hotel's own garage and parking area. *Corte Compagni 12 (corner of Via Fillungo), 55100, tel. 0583/493634, fax 0583/490021. 30 rooms with bath. Facilities: parking. AE, DC, MC, V. Closed Dec. 24–Jan. 6. $$*

Ilaria. This small, family-run hotel sits in a pretty location on a minuscule canal within easy walking distance of the main sights. The rooms are smallish but fresh and functional. *Via del Fosso 20, 55100, tel. 0583/47558. 17 rooms, 12 with bath or shower. AE, DC, MC, V. $*

Montepulciano
DINING
Cittino. A few plants outside the door mark this plain, family-run trattoria off one of the town's main streets. *Pici* (homemade spaghetti) with meat sauce and local pecorino cheese are good choices. The house wine is local, too. *Vicolo Via Nuovo 2 (Via Voltaia), tel. 0578/757335. No reservations. No credit cards. Closed Wed. $*

Pievescola (Casolad'Elsa)
DINING AND LODGING
La Suvera. In this luxurious hotel in the Tuscan countryside, 27 kilometers (17 miles) from Siena and 56 kilometers (35 miles) from Florence, you can savor living on an aristocratic estate that was once owned by Pope Julius II. Rooms and suites are magnificently furnished with antiques and endowed with up-to-the-minute comforts. With salons, a library, Italian garden, swimming pool, and L'Oliviera restaurant (serving estate wines) to enjoy, guests find it hard to tear themselves away. *Pievescola (Casola d'Elsa), off Rte. 541, 53030, tel. 0577/960300, fax 0577/960220. 19 rooms with bath, 13 suites. Facilities: restaurant, bar, park, heated pool, garden, sauna, tennis court, horseback riding, helipad, meeting rooms. AE, DC, MC, V. Closed Nov. 1–Mar. 31. $$$*

Pisa
DINING
Bruno. A country-inn look, with beamed ceilings and soft lights, makes Bruno a pleasant place to lunch on classic Tuscan dishes, from *zuppa alla pisana* (vegetable soup) to *baccalà con porri* (cod with leeks). It's just outside the old city walls and only a short walk from the bell tower and cathedral. *Via Luigi Bianchi 12, tel. 050/560818. Reservations advised. AE, DC, MC, V. No dinner Mon. Closed Tues. $$*

Osteria dei Cavalieri. Just off Piazza dei Cavalieri, in Pisa's medieval center, this popular tavern occupies the ground floor of a centuries-old tower. It offers a one-course lunch menu and a wide range of vegetarian, meat, and fish dishes, including tagliata *di manzo* (sliced steak, usually served with mushrooms). *Via San Frediano 16, tel. 050/580858. Reservations advised. AE, DC, MC, V. No lunch Sat. Closed Sun. and Aug. $$*

Pistoia
DINING
La Casa degli Amici. The name means "the house of friends," and that's the atmosphere that the two industrious ladies who own it succeed in creating in this restaurant, located outside Pistoia's old walls, on the road toward the A11 autostrada exit. They offer homey specialties, such as ribollita, pasta e fagioli, and *coniglio alla Vernaccia* (rabbit in white wine). There's a terrace for outdoor dining in the summer. *Via Bonellina 111, tel. 0573/380305. Reservations advised. AE, DC, MC, V. No dinner Sun. Closed Tues. and Aug. $$*

Leon Rosso. To find this little restaurant, take Via Roma off Piazza del Duomo, and walk straight ahead to Via Panciatichi. Usually crowded with locals, it serves typical Tuscan specialties, among them appetizing crostini served with liver pâté. For dessert, try *panna cotta* (bread pudding). *Via Panciatichi 4, tel. 0573/29230. Reservations advised. AE, DC, MC, V. Closed Sun., Aug. $$*

Prato
DINING
Stefano. At the lower end of the moderate price range, this trattoria is popular with the locals. A simple place, it serves regional dishes such as ribollita, fagioli laced with local olive oil, and grilled meat. *Via Pomeria 23, tel. 0574/34665. No reservations. No credit cards. Closed Sun. $$*

San Gimignano
DINING
Bel Soggiorno. Bel Soggiorno is attached to a small hotel. It has fine views, refectory tables set with linen and candles, and leather-covered chairs. Specialties are pappardelle *alla lepre* (with hare sauce) and herbed grilled meat. *Via San Giovanni 89, tel. 0577/940375. Reservations advised. AE, DC, MC, V. Closed Mon. and Jan. 7–Feb. 7. $$*

DINING AND LODGING
Pescille. This rambling stone farmhouse, about 3 kilometers (2 miles) outside San Gimignano, with a good view of the town, has been restored as a hotel and furnished in attractive rustic-chic style. The upscale Cinque Gigli restaurant serves Tuscan *zuppe* (soups), *arrosti* (roasted meats), and other local specialties. *Località Pescille, 53037, tel. 0577/940186, fax 0577/940186. 40 rooms with bath. Facilities: restaurant (closed Wed.), bar, garden, pool, tennis court. AE, DC, MC, V. Closed Nov. 15–Feb. 28. $$*

Siena
DINING
★ **Ai Marsili.** In a medieval palace near the Duomo, Ai Marsili is a spacious, brick-vaulted wine cellar with refectory tables and excellent Tuscan cuisine; it's a place for a leisurely meal accompanied by classic Chianti wines. Specialties include pici with mushroom sauce, and *piccione* (squab). *Via del Castoro 3, tel. 0577/47154. Reservations advised. AE, DC, MC, V. Closed Mon. $$*

Osteria Le Logge. Just off Piazza del Campo, this is a fine choice for an informal but memorable meal. Get there early to claim a table. Among the specialties are *pennette all'Osteria* (creamy pasta) and *tagliata alla rucola* (sliced steak with arugula). *Via del Porrione 33, tel. 0577/48013. Reservations advised. DC, MC, V. Closed Sun., June 10–23 and Nov. 6–24. $$*

Tullio Tre Cristi. To find this historic trattoria, take Via dei Rossi from Via Banchi di Sopra. Even though it was discovered by tourists long ago, it remains true to typical Sienese cooking and atmosphere. Try spaghetti *alle briciole,* a poor-man's pasta with bread crumbs, tomato, and garlic. *Vicolo di Provenzano 1, tel. 0577/280608. Reservations advised. MC, V. No dinner Sun. Closed Mon., and Jan. $$*

Le Tre Campane. Boasting a convenient location between Piazza del Campo and the Duomo, this small trattoria displays the colorful banners of Siena's 17 districts. Popular with the locals, it specializes in Tuscan fare and a *trittico* (trio) of pastas. *Piazzetta Bonelli 5, tel. 0577/286091. Reservations advised. No credit cards. Closed Tues. and Jan.–Feb. $*

LODGING
Certosa di Maggiano. An easy and attractive walk (less than a mile) southeast of Siena takes you to this old Carthusian monastery, which has been converted into a sophisticated oasis furnished in impeccable style. The bedrooms have every comfort, and the atmosphere is that of an aristocratic family villa. *Strada di Certosa 82, 53100, tel.*

0577/288180, fax 0577/288189. 18 rooms with bath. Facilities: pool, tennis court. AE, DC, MC, V. Closed Dec.–Feb. $$$$

★ **Park Hotel.** Just outside the walls of the old city, this is a handsome 15th-century villa on its own grounds. Furnished in classic Tuscan style, with antiques and luxuriant plants in gleaming copper planters on highly polished terra-cotta floors, it has a simple but sophisticated ambience, in which you can pretend you're a house guest of the Medicis. There's a fine restaurant and garden terrace. *Via di Marciano 18, 53100, tel. 0577/44803, fax 0577/49020. 69 rooms with bath. Facilities: restaurant, pool, tennis court, garden. AE, DC, MC, V. $$$$*

Antica Torre. A cordial young couple runs this hotel in a restored centuries-old tower, a 10-minute walk from Piazza del Campo. Rooms are smallish and are furnished sparingly but in good taste. Beamed ceilings throughout and original brick vaults here and there are reminders of the tower's venerable history. *Via Fieravecchia 7, tel. 0577/222255, fax 0577/222255. 8 rooms with bath. AE, MC, V. $$*

★ **Duomo.** Occupying the top floor of a 17th-century building in the center of Siena, near Piazza del Campo, the hotel is quiet and is furnished in a neat contemporary style, with traces of the past showing in the artfully exposed brickwork in the breakfast room. Many rooms have superb views of the city's towers and the hills beyond. Two rooms are endowed with balconies. *Via Stalloreggi 38, 53100, tel. 0577/289088, fax 0577/43043. 23 rooms with bath. AE, MC, V. $–$$*

MILAN

Arriving and Departing

As Lombardy's capital and the most important financial and commercial center in northern Italy, Milan is well connected with Rome and Florence by fast and frequent rail and air service, though the latter is often delayed in winter by heavy fog.

By Plane

Linate Airport, 11 kilometers (7 miles) outside Milan, handles mainly domestic and European flights (tel. 02/7485–2200). Malpensa, 50 kilometers (30 miles) from the city, handles intercontinental flights (tel. 02/7485–2200).

BETWEEN THE AIRPORT AND DOWNTOWN

Buses connect both airports with Milan, stopping at the central station and at the Porta Garibaldi Station. Fare from Linate is 4,000 lire on the special airport bus or 1,400 lire on municipal Bus 73 (to Piazza San Babila); from Malpensa, 12,000 lire. A taxi from Linate to the center of Milan costs about 30,000 lire, from Malpensa, about 120,000 lire.

By Train

The main train terminal is the central station in Piazzale Duca d'Aosta (tel. 02/67500). Several smaller stations handle commuter trains. There are several fast Intercity trains daily between Rome and Milan, stopping in Florence. A nonstop Intercity leaves from Rome or Milan morning and evening, taking about four hours to go between the two cities.

By Car

From Rome and Florence, take the A1 Autostrada. From Venice, take the A4. With bans on parking throughout the center of Milan, it's easier to park on the outskirts and use public transportation.

Getting Around

By Subway

Milan's subway network, the Metropolitana, is modern, fast, and easy to use. MM signs mark Metropolitana stations. There are, at present, three lines. The ATM (city transport authority) has an information office on the mezzanine of the Duomo Metro Station (tel. 02/875495). Tickets are sold at newsstands at every stop, and in ticket machines *for exact change only*. The fare is 1,400 lire, and the subway runs from 6:20 AM to midnight.

By Bus and Streetcar

Buy tickets at newsstands, tobacco shops, and bars. The fare is 1,400 lire. One ticket is valid for 75 minutes on all surface lines, and one subway trip. Daily tickets valid for 24 hours on all public transportation lines are sold at the Duomo Metro Station ATM information office, and at Stazione Centrale Metro Station. Twenty-four-hour tickets cost 4,800 lire; 48-hour tickets cost 8,000 lire.

By Taxi

Use yellow cabs only. They wait at stands or can be telephoned in advance (tel. 6767, 8585, or 8388).

Important Addresses and Information

Tourist Information

The main **APT Tourist Offices** are at Stazione Centrale (tel 02/669–0532), open Monday–Saturday 8–7, Sun. 9–12:30 and 1:30–6, and in Palazzo del Turismo at Via Marconi 1, Piazza del Duomo (tel 02/809662), open Monday–Saturday 8–8, Sunday 9–12:30 and 1:30–5.

Consulates

U.S. (Via Prinicpe Amedeo 2, tel. 02/290351); **Canadian** (Via Pisani 19, tel. 02/6697451); **U.K.** (Via San Paolo 7, tel. 02/723001).

Emergencies

Police, tel 02/113; **Carabinieri,** tel. 02/112; **Ambulance,** tel. 02/7733; **Medical Emergency,** Fatebenefratelli Hospital, Corso di Porta Nuova 23, 02/63631.

Travel Agencies

Compagnia Italiana Turismo (CIT) (Galleria Vittorio Emanuele, tel. 02/866661); **American Express Travel Agency** (Via Brera 3, tel. 02/809645).

Guided Tours

City Tours

Three-hour morning or afternoon sightseeing tours depart Tues.–Sun. from Piazzetta Reale, next to the Duomo; the cost is about 50,000 lire and tickets can be purchased from APT offices (*see* Tourist Information, *above*) or aboard the bus.

Excursions

From April through September the **Autostradale** bus company (Via Pompeo Marchesi 55, tel. 02/4820–3177) and **AutostradaleViaggi** (Piazza Castello 1, tel. 02/801161) offer an all-day tour of Lake Maggiore, including a boat trip to the Borromean Islands and lunch. The cost is about 105,000 lire.

Exploring Milan

Milan, capital of all that is new in Italy, has a history that goes back at least 2,500 years. Its fortunes ever since, both as a great commercial trading center and as the object of regular conquest and occupation, are readily explained by its strategic position at the center of the Lombard Plain. Virtually every invader in European history—Gaul, Roman, Goth, Longobard, and Frank—as well as every ruler of France, Spain, and Austria, has taken a turn at ruling the city and the region. So if you are wondering why so little seems to have survived from Milan's antiquity, the answer is simple—war. Thanks to the great family dynasties of the Visconti and the Sforza, however, there are still great Gothic and Renaissance treasures to be seen, including Leonardo's unforgettable *Last Supper*. And thanks to new names—Valentino, Versace, and Armani, among them—the city now dazzles as the design and fashion center of the world. Old and new come together at Milan's La Scala—Europe's most important opera house—where audiences continue to set sail for passion on the high C's.

Numbers in the margin correspond to points of interest on the Milano (Milan) map.

1 The center of Milan is the Piazza del Duomo. The massive **Duomo** is one of the largest churches in the world, a mountain of marble fretted with statues, spires, and flying buttresses. The interior is a more solemn Italian Gothic. Take the elevator or walk up 158 steps to the roof, from which—if it's a clear day—you can see over the city to the Lombard Plain and the Alps beyond, all through an amazing array of spires and statues. The **Madonnina,** a gleaming gilt statue on the highest spire, is a Milan landmark. *Entrance to elevator and stairway outside cathedral, to the right. Admission: stairs, 5,000 lire; elevator, 7,000 lire. Open Mar.–Oct., daily 9–5:45; Nov.–Feb., daily 9–4:30.*

2 Outside the cathedral to the right is the elegant, glass-roofed **Galleria,** where the Milanese and visitors stroll, window-shop, and sip pricey
3 cappuccinos at trendy cafés. At the other end of the Galleria is **Piazza**
4 **della Scala,** with Milan's city hall on one side and **Teatro alla Scala,** the world-famous opera house, opposite.

5 Via Verdi, flanking the opera house, leads to Via Brera, where the **Pinacoteca di Brera** houses one of Italy's great collections of paintings. Most are of a religious nature, confiscated in the 19th century when many religious orders were suppressed and their churches closed. *Via Brera 28, tel. 02/862634. Admission: 8,000 lire. Open Tues.–Sat. 9–5:30, Sun. 9–12:45.*

After an eyeful of artwork by Mantegna, Raphael, and many other Italian masters, explore the Brera neighborhood, dotted with art galleries,
6 chic little restaurants, and such offbeat cafés as the **Jamaica** (Via Brera 26), once a bohemian hangout. Take Via dei Fiori Chiari in front of
7 the Brera and keep going in the same direction to the moated **Castello Sforzesco,** a somewhat sinister 19th-century reconstruction of the imposing 15th-century fortress built by the Sforzas, who succeeded the Viscontis as lords of Milan in the 15th century. It now houses wide-ranging collections of sculptures, antiques, and ceramics, including Michelangelo's *Rondanini Pietà,* his last work, left unfinished at his death. *Piazza Castello, tel. 02/6208391. Admission free. Open Tues.–Sun. 9:30–5:30.*

8 From the vast residence of the Sforzas it's not far to the church of **Santa Maria delle Grazie.** Although portions of the church were designed by

Milano (Milan)

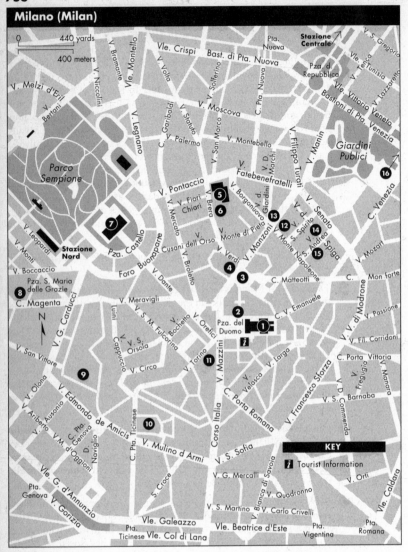

Castello Sforzesco, **7**

Corso Buenos
Aires, **16**

Duomo, **1**

Galleria, **2**

Jamaica, **6**

Piazza della Scala, **3**

Pinacoteca di Brera, **5**

San Lorenzo Maggiore, **10**

San Satiro, **11**

Santa Maria delle
Grazie, **8**

Sant'Ambrogio, **9**

Teatro alla Scala, **4**

Via della Spiga, **14**

Via Manzoni, **13**

Via Monte
Napoleone, **12**

Via Sant'Andrea, **15**

Bramante, it plays second fiddle to the **Refectory** next door, where, over a three-year period, Leonardo da Vinci painted his megafamous fresco, *The Last Supper*. The fresco has suffered more than its share of disaster, beginning with the experiments of the artist, who used untested pigments that soon began to deteriorate. *The Last Supper* is now a mere shadow of its former self, despite meticulous restoration that proceeds at a snail's pace. To save what is left, visitors are limited in time and number, and you may have to wait in line to get a glimpse of this world-famous work. *Piazza Santa Maria delle Grazie 2, tel. 02/498–7588. Admission: 6,000 lire. Open Tues.–Sun. 8–2. (Hrs may vary; call to confirm hrs.)*

If you are interested in medieval architecture, go to see the medieval church of **Sant'Ambrogio** (Piazza Sant'Ambrogio). Consecrated by St. Ambrose in AD 387, it's the model for all Lombard Romanesque churches, and contains some ancient works of art, including a remarkable 9th-century altar in precious metals and enamels, and some 5th-century mosaics. On December 8, the day after the feast day of St. Ambrose, the streets around the church are the scene of a lively flea market. Another noteworthy church is **San Lorenzo Maggiore** (Corso di Porta Ticinese), with 16 ancient Roman columns in front and some 4th-century mosaics in the Chapel of St. Aquilinus. Closer to Piazza del Duomo on Via Torino, the church of **San Satiro** is another architectural gem in which Bramante's perfect command of proportion and perspective, a characteristic of the Renaissance, made a small interior seem extraordinarily spacious and airy.

TIME OUT Stop in at the **Peck** shops a few steps from San Satiro. One is a gourmet delicatessen; another has a tempting array of snacks to eat on the premises. *Via Spadari 9; Via Cantù 3.*

Now head for Milan's most elegant shopping streets: **Via Monte Napoleone, Via Manzoni, Via della Spiga,** and **Via Sant'Andrea.** The **Café Cova** (Via Monte Napoleone 8) is famous for its pastries; Hemingway loved them. And the **Sant'Ambroeus,** not far away, is the epitome of a genteel tearoom (Corso Matteotti 7). If the chic goods of this area are a shock to your purse, make your way to **Corso Buenos Aires,** near the central station, which has hundreds more shops and accessible prices, too.

Dining

For details and price-category definitions, *see* Dining *in* Staying in Italy, *above*.

$$$ **Biffi Scala.** The elegant Biffi Scala caters mainly to the after-opera crowd that pours in around midnight. Built in 1861, it features a high ceiling and polished wood walls. Specialties include *crespelle alle erbette* (pancakes stuffed with wild mushrooms and other vegetables) and *carpaccio alla* Biffi Scala (thin slices of cured raw beef with a tangy sauce). *Piazza della Scala, tel. 02/866651. Dinner reservations required, especially after the opera. AE, DC, MC, V. Closed Sun., Aug. 10–20, and Dec. 24–Jan. 6. No lunch Sat.; no dinner Sat. mid-June–mid-July.*

$$$ **Boeucc.** Milan's oldest restaurant is situated not far from La Scala and
★ is subtly lighted, with fluted columns, chandeliers, thick carpet, and a garden for warm-weather dining. In addition to the typical Milanese foods, it also serves such exotica as penne *al branzino e zucchine* (with sea bass and zucchini sauce) and gelato *di castagne con zabaglione caldo* (chestnut ice cream with hot zabaglione). *Piazza Belgioioso 2, tel.*

02/760–20224. *Reservations required. AE. Closed Sat., Dec. 24–Jan. 2, Easter, and Aug. No lunch Sun.*

\$\$\$ **Don Lisander.** This 17th-century chapel has been drastically redecorated, and now features designer lighting, abstract prints, and a modern terra-cotta tile floor, creating an uncompromisingly contemporary effect. Try the *scaloppe di fegato con menta* (calves' liver scaloppini with fresh mint leaves) or else go for the *branzino al timo* (sea bass with thyme). *Via Manzoni 12A, tel. 02/760–20130. Reservations required. AE, DC, MC, V. Closed Sun., 2 wks in mid-Aug., and 2 wks at Christmas. No dinner Sat.*

\$\$\$ **Savini.** Red carpets and cut-glass chandeliers characterize the classy
★ Savini, a typical, Old World Milanese restaurant whose dining rooms spread over three floors. There's also a "winter garden" from which patrons can people-watch shoppers in the Galleria. The risotto *al salto* (rice cooked as a pancake, tossed in the pan, a Milanese specialty) is excellent here, as is the *cotoletta di vitello* (breaded veal cutlets). *Galleria Vittorio Emanuele, tel. 02/720–03433. Dinner reservations advised. AE, DC, MC, V. Closed Sun., 10 days in Aug., and 1 wk at Christmas.*

\$\$ **Antica Trattoria della Pesa.** Though the management has changed, the turn-of-the-century decor and atmosphere, dark wood paneling, and old-fashioned lamps still look much as they must have when it opened one hundred years ago. This is authentic Old Milan, and the menu is right in line, with risotto, minestrone, and osso buco. *Viale Pasubio 10, tel. 02/655–5741. Dinner reservations advised. AE, DC, MC, V. Closed Sun. and 2 wks in Aug.*

\$\$ **Nabucco.** This is a smart restaurant in the Brera district, tastefully furnished. Highlights on the menu include risotto con porcini, an excellent range of salads, and homemade pastries and desserts. The prix-fixe lunches are particularly good values. *Via Fiori Cjoaoro 10, tel. 02/860663. Reservations advised. AE, DC, MC, V. Closed Sun. No lunch Mon.*

\$\$ **Trattoria Milanese.** Situated between the Duomo and the Basilica of Sant' Ambrogio, this small, popular trattoria has been run by the same family for more than 80 years. It's invariably crowded, especially at dinner, when the regulars love to linger. Food is classic regional in approach, with risotto and cotoletta *alla milanese* (veal milanese-style) good choices. *Via Santa Marta 11, tel. 02/864-51991. Reservations advised. AE, D, MC, V. Closed Tues., Aug., and Dec. 25.*

\$ **Al Cantinone.** Operagoers still come to the Cantinone bar for a drink after the final curtain, just as they did a century ago. The decor is basic, the atmosphere lively, the service fast, and the food reliable. The proprietor stocks 240 different wines. Try the cotoletta *al Cantinone* (veal cutlets with mushrooms, olives, and a cream and tomato sauce). *Via Agnello 19, tel. 02/864–61338. Reservations advised. AE, MC, V. No lunch Sat. Closed Sun., Aug., and Dec. 25.*

\$ **Birreria-Bistro San Tomaso.** A popular lunch spot for trendy Milanese, this place has the informal atmosphere of an old beer hall. At the self-service counter you can have a salad made to order, a cheese platter, or other light fare. It's usually quieter at night, and the kitchen stays open until 1 AM. *Via San Tomaso 5, tel. 02/874510. Dinner reservations advised. No credit cards. Closed Sun.*

\$ **La Bruschetta.** A winning partnership of Tuscans and Neapolitans runs this tiny, busy, and first-class pizzeria near the Duomo. It features the obligatory wood-burning stove, so you can watch your pizza being cooked, though there are plenty of other dishes to choose from as well— try the spaghetti *alle cozze e vongole* (with clams and mussels). *Piazza*

Beccaria 12, tel. 02/869–2494. Reservations advised. No credit cards. Closed Mon., 3 wks in Aug, a few days at Christmas and Easter.

$ La Giara. At this tavern with bare wooden tables and benches, the menu offers a limited selection of southern Italian specialties, notably a varied vegetable antipasto. Meat is grilled on a range at the front of the restaurant and served with crusty bread and dense olive oil from the Puglia region. It is located in the vicinity of Piazzale Loreto. You may be asked to share a table. *Viale Monza 10, tel. 02/261–43835. No credit cards. Closed Wed.*

$ Taverna Moriggi. When there's a bad day on the nearby stock exchange, this dusky, wood-paneled wine bar is particularly crowded: it serves a prix-fixe lunch for a reasonable 30,000 lire. *Via Moriggi 8, tel. 02/864–50880. Reservations advised. DC, MC, V.*

Lodging

Make reservations well in advance, particularly when trade fairs are on, which can be most of the year except for August (when many hotels close) and mid-December to mid-January. March and October are months with the highest concentration of fairs, and it's virtually impossible to find a room at this time. For details and price-category definitions, *see* Lodging *in* Staying in Italy, *above*.

$$$$ ★ Duomo. Just 20 yards from the cathedral, this hotel's first-, second-, and third-floor rooms all look out onto the church's Gothic gargoyles and pinnacles. The rooms are spacious and snappily furnished in contemporary style. *Via San Raffaele 1, 20121, tel. 02/8833, fax 02/864–62027. 160 rooms with bath. Facilities: restaurant, bar. AE, DC, MC, V. Closed Aug.*

$$$$ Four Seasons. The elegant restoration of a 14th-century monastery on an exclusive shopping street in the center of Milan has produced a gem, and a precious one, at the highest rates in the city. The hotel blends European class with American comfort. Individually furnished rooms have opulent marble bathrooms; most rooms face the quiet courtyard. Downstairs is the hotel's Il Teatro restaurant. *Via Gesù 8, 20121, tel. 02/77088, fax 02/770–85000. 98 rooms with bath. Facilities: restaurant, bar, convention facilities. AE, DC, MC, V.*

$$$$ Pierre. Luxury keynotes rooms individually furnished with elegant fabrics and an assortment of modern and antique furniture. Electronic gadgetry controls curtains and lights. The Pierre is located near the medieval church of Sant'Ambrogio. *Via De Amicis 32, 20123, tel. 02/720–00581, fax 02/805–2157. 47 rooms with bath. Facilities: restaurant, bar. AE, DC, MC, V.*

$$$$ Principe di Savoia. The most fashionable and glitzy hotel in Milan, this is where fashion buyers and expense-account businesspeople stay. Dark wood paneling and period furniture, brass lamps, and a stucco lobby are all reminiscent of early 1900s Europe. *Piazza della Repubblica 17, 20124, tel. 02/6230, fax 02/659–5838. 287 rooms with bath. Facilities: restaurant, bar. AE, DC, MC, V.*

$$$ Carlton-Senato. This hotel is in the heart of Milan's chic shopping district. The atmosphere is light and airy, and there are lots of little touches (such as complimentary chocolates and liqueurs in the rooms) to make up for the rather functional furnishings. *Via Senato 5, 20121, tel. 02/760–15535, fax 02/783–300. 79 rooms with bath. Facilities: restaurant, bar, parking. AE, MC, V. Closed Aug.*

$$ Canada. This friendly, small hotel is close to Piazza del Duomo on the edge of a district full of shops and restaurants. Recently renovated, it offers good value; all rooms have TV, air-conditioning, and minifridge.

Via Santa Sofia 16, 20122, tel. 02/583–04844, fax 02/583–00282. 35 rooms with bath. Facilities: bar. AE, DC, MC, V.

$$ Casa Svizzera. A faithful clientele considers this one of Milan's best moderately priced small hotels, so it's advisable to make early reservations. The location, adjacent to the Duomo and a few yards from the Galleria, is central and handy to Metro and bus lines. The hotel has been totally renovated and soundproofed. Rooms have air conditioning, TV, and minifridge, and they are decorated in cheery floral-printed fabric. *Via San Raffaele 3, 20123, tel. 02/869–2246, fax 02/7200–4690. 45 rooms with bath. Facilities: bar. AE, DC, MC, V. Closed Aug.*

$$ Gritti. This bright, clean hotel has a cheerful atmosphere. Rooms are adequate, with picturesque views from the upper floors over the tiled roofs to the gilt Madonnina on top of the Duomo, only a few hundred yards away. *Piazza Santa Maria Beltrade 4 (north end of Via Torino), 20123, tel. 02/801056, fax 02/890–10999. 48 rooms with bath. Facilities: bar. AE, DC, MC, V.*

$ Città Studi. Near the University and Piazzale Susa, this hotel is modern and functionally furnished, undistinguished but with a reputation as a reliable, reasonably comfortable place to stay. Most rooms have private showers. *Via Saldini 24, 20133, tel. 02/744666, fax 02/713122. 45 rooms, 38 with shower. AE, MC, V.*

$ London. Close to the Duomo, the London has clean, good-size, simply furnished rooms and an English-speaking staff. It also has an arrangement with the Opera Prima restaurant in the same building, where guests may take their meals if they wish. *Via Rovello 3, 20121, tel. 02/720–20166, fax 02/805–7037. 29 rooms with shower. Facilities: bar. MC, V. Closed Dec. 25–Jan. 3, Aug.*

$ San Francisco. In a residential area between the central station and the university, this medium-size pension is handy to subway and bus lines. It also has the advantages of a friendly management, rooms that are bright and clean, and a charming garden. *Viale Lombardia 55, 20131, tel. 02/236–1009, fax 02/266–80377. 31 rooms with bath or shower. Facilities: bar, garden. AE, DC, MC, V.*

The Arts

The most famous spectacle in Milan is **La Scala,** which presents some of the world's most impressive operatic productions. The opera season begins December 7 (St. Ambrose Day) and ends in May. The concert season runs from May to the end of June and from September through November. There is a brief ballet season in September. Programs are available at principal travel agencies and tourist information offices in Italy and abroad. Tickets are usually hard to come by, but your hotel may be able to help obtain them. For information on schedules, ticket availability, and how to buy tickets, there is an Infotel Scala Service in operation (with English-speaking staff) at the ticket office (Teatro alla Scala, Ufficio Biglietteria, Via Filodrammatici 2, tel. 02/720–03744, open daily, 10–7).

Telephone bookings are not accepted, but travelers from abroad can book in advance—within a short specified period before each presentation (these dates are published at the beginning of the season)—through postal bookings, for which a certain percentage of tickets are set aside, allocated on a first-come, first-served basis. Apply for a reservation by mail or fax (transmitted 9–6 local time, with time and date of transmission, and sender's fax number to 02/877–996, or 8051625). You may also be able to book at CIT or other travel agencies (no more than 10 days before performance). There is a 15% advance booking charge.

VENICE

Arriving and Departing

By Plane

Marco Polo International Airport is situated about 10 kilometers (6 miles) northeast of the city on the mainland. For flight information, call 041/260–9260.

BETWEEN THE AIRPORT AND DOWNTOWN

Blue ATVO buses make the 25-minute trip in to Piazzale Roma, where the road to Venice terminates; the cost is around 5,000 lire. From Piazzale Roma visitors will most likely have to take a vaporetto (water bus) to their hotel (*see* Getting Around, *below*). The Cooperative San Marco motor launch (fare 20,000 lire) can be a more convenient way to reach the city, depending on where your hotel is located. It runs from the airport, via the Lido, dropping passengers across the lagoon at Piazza San Marco. (It works on a limited schedule in winter.) Land taxis are available, running the same route as the buses; the cost is about 50,000 lire. Water taxis (slick high-power motorboats) are very expensive: Negotiate the fare in advance, usually upward of 100,000 lire (the official scale of tariffs is published in the "Guest in Venice" booklet; *see* The Arts, *below*).

By Train

Make sure your train goes all the way to Santa Lucia Station in Venice's northwest corner; some trains leave passengers at the Mestre Station on the mainland. All trains traveling to and from Santa Lucia stop at Mestre, so to get from Mestre to Santa Lucia, or vice versa (a journey of about 10 minutes), take the first available train, remembering there is a *supplemento* (extra charge) for traveling on Intercity and Eurocity trains, and that if you board one of these trains without having paid in advance for this part of the journey, you are liable for a hefty fine. For train information, call 041/715555, 7:15 AM–9:30 PM. Since most tourists arrive in Venice by train, tourist services are conveniently located at Santa Lucia, including an APT information booth (tel. 041/719078, open daily 8–8) and baggage depot. If you need a hotel room, the station has a Venetian Hoteliers Association (AVA) desk (open Apr.–Oct., daily 8 AM–10 PM; Nov.–Mar., daily 8 AM–9:30 PM), with others at the airport and at the city garage at Piazzale Roma. Directly outside the train station are the main vaporetto landing stages; from here, vaporetti can transport you to your hotel's general neighborhood. It's easy to lose your way in Venice, so it's best to get advance telephone instructions from the hotel. A good map of Venice will also prove useful. When all else fails, however, the staff at the railroad station and central vaporetti stops can help.

By Car

If you bring a car to Venice, you will have to pay for a garage or parking space during your stay. Do not on any account allow yourself to be waylaid by illegal touts, often wearing fake uniforms, who will try to flag you down and offer to arrange parking and hotels; keep driving until you reach the automatic ticket machines. Parking at Piazzale Roma (in the Autorimessa Comunale run by the city) costs between 15,000 and 25,000 lire, depending on the size of the car; at the private Garage San Marco (next door), rates are between 30,000 and 45,000 lire per 24 hours, also depending on the size of the car. Parking at the Tronchetto parking area (privately run) costs around 35,000 lire per day under cover, and 18,000 outside. (Do not leave valuables in your car. There is a left-luggage office next door to the Pullman Bar on the ground floor of the Municipal Garage in Piazzale Roma.) The AVA has arranged a discount of around 40% for hotel guests who use the official Tronchetto parking facility. Ask for a voucher on checking into your hotel. Present the voucher at Tronchetto when you pay the parking fee.

There is a vaporetto (currently No. 82) from Tronchetto to Piazzale Roma and Piazza San Marco (including the Lido in summer). (In thick fog or when tides are extreme, a bus runs instead to Piazzale Roma, where you can pick up a vaporetto.)

Getting Around

First-time visitors find that getting around Venice presents some unusual problems: the complexity of its layout (the city is made up of more than 100 islands, all linked by bridges); the bewildering unfamiliarity of waterborne transportation; the apparently illogical house numbering system and duplication of street names in its six districts; and the necessity of walking whether you enjoy it or not. It's essential to have a good map showing all street names and water bus routes; buy one at any newsstand.

By Vaporetto

ACTV water buses run the length of the Grand Canal and circle the city. There are several lines, some of which connect Venice with the major and minor islands in the lagoon. **Line 1** is the Grand Canal local, calling at every stop, and continuing via San Marco to the Lido. (It takes about 45 minutes from the station to San Marco.) As the result of recent (extremely confusing and unpopular) rerouting, there are now two **Line 52** routes: one, running from the railway station to San Zaccaria, skirting the north of the city, via Fondamente Nove (where boats leave for the islands of the northern lagoon) and Murano, and continuing via the Arsenal; the other acting as a fast service via Zattere on the Giudecca Canal, south of the city, to San Marco and the Lido. There are also two **Line 82** routes from the Tronchetto: one going via Piazzale Roma, the railway station, and Rialto, and continuing, during the day, down the Grand Canal, with fewer stops than the Line 1, to San Marco and, in the summer, on to the Lido; the other taking the southern route through the Giudecca Canal, via Zattere and also stopping on Giudecca, to San Marco, and again, in the summer, continuing to the Lido. The fare is 3,500 on most lines. A 24-hour tourist ticket costs 14,000 lire, while a 3-day tourist ticket costs 20,000; these are especially worthwhile if you are planning to visit the islands. Timetables are posted at every landing stage, but there is not always a ticket booth operating. You may get on a boat without a ticket, but you will have to pay a higher fare on the boat. For this reason, it may be useful to buy a *blochetto* (book of tickets) in advance. Landing stages are clearly marked with name and line number, but check before boarding, particularly with the 52 and 82, to make sure the boat is going in your direction.

By Water Taxi

Known as *motoscafi,* or "taxi," these are excessively expensive, and the fare system is as complex as Venice's layout. A minimum fare of about 50,000 lire gets you nowhere, and you'll pay three times as much to get from one end of the Grand Canal to the other. *Always agree on the fare before starting out.* It's probably worth considering taking a water taxi only if you are traveling in a small group.

By Traghetto

Few tourists know about the two-man gondolas that ferry people across the Grand Canal at various fixed points. It's the cheapest and shortest gondola ride in Venice, and it can save a lot of walking. The fare is 600 lire, which you hand to one of the gondoliers when you get on. Look for TRAGHETTO signs.

By Gondola

Don't leave Venice without treating yourself to a gondola ride, preferably in the quiet of the evening when the churning traffic on the canals has died down, the palace windows are illuminated, and the only sounds are the muted splashes of the gondolier's oar. Make sure he understands that you want to see the *rii,* or smaller canals, as well as the Grand Canal. There's supposed to be a fixed minimum rate of about 50,000 lire for 50 minutes. (Official tariffs are quoted in the "Guest in Venice" booklet; *see* The Arts, *below.*) Come to terms with your gondolier *before* stepping into his boat.

On Foot

This is the only way to reach many parts of Venice, so wear comfortable shoes. Invest in a good map that names all the streets, and count on getting lost more than once.

Important Addresses and Numbers

Tourist Information

The main Venice **APT Tourist Office** (tel. 041/522–6356, fax 041/5298730) is at Palazzetto Selva, on the waterfront near the San Marco vaporetto stop. Open in summer and during Carnival every day (except public holidays), 9:30–1 and 2–5; in winter, Mon.–Sat. 9–1 and 2–4. There are APT information booths at the Santa Lucia Station (tel. 041/719078) and on the Lido (Gran Viale S. M. Elisabetta 6A, tel. 041/526–5721, fax 041/529–8720).

Consulates

There is no U.S., Canadian, or U.K. consular service in Venice. The nearest consulates for all three countries are in Milan (*see* Important Addresses and Numbers *in* Milan, *above.*)

Emergencies

Police (tel. 113). **Carabinieri** (tel. 112). English-speaking officers are available 24 hours a day to deal with any kind of emergency. **Ambulance** (tel. 041/523–0000). **Doctor:** Try the emergency room at Venice's hospital (tel. 041/529–4517). **Red Cross First Aid Station** (Piazza San Marco 55, near Caffè Florian, tel. 041/5228–6346, open Mon.–Sat. 8:30–1). **Pharmacies: Farmacia Italo-Inglese** (Calle della Mandola, tel. 041/522–4837); **Farmacia Internazionale** (Calle Larga XXII Marzo, tel. 041/522–2311). Pharmacies are open weekdays 9–12:30 and 4–7:45; Saturday 9–12:45; A roster of where to get late-night and Sunday service is posted outside every pharmacy.

Travel Agencies

American Express (San Moisè 1471, tel. 041/520–0844, fax 041/522-9937). **Wagons-Lits Travel** (Piazzetta dei Leoncini 289, tel. 041/522–3405, fax 041/522–8508).

Guided Tours

Orientation Tours

American Express and other operators offer two-hour walking tours of the San Marco area, taking in the basilica and the Doge's Palace.

The cost is about 35,000 lire. American Express also has an afternoon walking tour from April through October that ends with a gondola ride. The cost is about 35,000 lire.

Special-Interest Tours

Some tour operators offer group gondola rides with serenade. The cost is about 40,000 lire. During the summer free guided tours of the Basilica di San Marco are offered by the Patriarchate of Venice; information is available at a desk in the atrium of the church (tel. 041/520–0333). There are several tours daily, except Sunday, and some tours are in English, including one at 11 AM.

Excursions

The Cooperativa San Marco organizes tours of the islands of Murano, Burano, and Torcello with daily departures at 9:30 and 2:30 from the landing stage in front of Giardini Reali near Piazza San Marco; tours last about three hours and cost about 25,000 lire. However, tours tend to be annoyingly commercial and emphasize glass factory showrooms, pressuring you to buy, often at higher prices than normal. You can visit these islands on your own if you have a little more time and are feeling a bit more adventurous. To get to Burano and Torcello, take Vaporetto 52 to Fondamente Nuove and change to Vaporetto 12. For Murano, take Vaporetto 52 all the way to Murano. (You can also pick up the Vaporetto 12 at Murano to continue to Burano and Torcello.) In summer there is a Line 23 from San Zaccaria (near Piazza San Marco) to Murano, circling back to Venice via Sant'Elena around the eastern end of the city. **American Express** offers a day trip by car to the Venetian Villas, Padua and Asolo, available all year round. The cost is about 140,000 lire per person, and bookings need to be made the day before.

Personal Guides

American Express can provide guides for walking or gondola tours of Venice, or cars with driver and guide for excursions on the mainland. Pick up a list of licensed guides and their rates from the main **APT** Information Office at Calle dell'Ascensione 71C (tel. 041/522–6356, fax 041/529–8730).

Exploring Venice

Venice—La Serenissima, the Most Serene—is disorienting in its complexity, an extraordinary labyrinth of narrow streets and waterways, opening now and again onto some airy square or broad canal. The majority of its magnificent palazzi are slowly crumbling; though this sounds like a recipe for a down-at-the-heels slum, somehow in Venice the shabby, derelict effect is magically transformed into one of supreme beauty and charm, rather than horrible urban decay. The place is romantic, especially at night when the lights from the vaporetti and the stars overhead pick out the gargoyles and arches of the centuries-old facades. For hundreds of years Venice was the unrivaled mistress of trade between Europe and the Orient, and the staunch bulwark of Christendom against the tide of Turkish expansion. Though the power and glory of its days as a wealthy city-republic are gone, the art and exotic aura remain.

To enjoy the city, you will have to come to terms with the crowds of day trippers, who take over the center around San Marco, from May through September. Hot and sultry in the summer, Venice is much more welcoming in early spring and late fall. Romantics like it in the winter when prices are much lower, the streets are often deserted, and the sea mists impart a haunting melancholy to the *campi* (squares) and canals. Piazza San Marco (St. Mark's Square) is the pulse of Venice, but after joining with the crowds to visit the Basilica di San Marco and the Doge's Palace, strike out on your own and just follow where your feet take you—you won't be disappointed.

A new program, called "Dal Museo alla Città" (From Museum to City) was begun in 1995 to encourage visitors to seek out artwork not only in museums but also within the city itself—primarily in the churches and *scuole* (charitable confraternity halls) for which they were originally commissioned. More than a dozen places selected for their artistic importance now have fixed visiting hours when tourists can be sure of admission and of not intruding on church services. At these times, given below as "Special visiting hours," information, a free leaflet, and an opportunity to purchase souvenirs and booklets will be available (English texts will be ready in 1996). New lighting systems have been installed, taking 500-lire coins. Churches in this program—and many other churches—are also usually open 10–12 AM and 4–6 PM in winter, or 5–7 PM in summer.

Numbers in the margin correspond to points of interest on the Venezia (Venice) map.

Piazza San Marco and the Accademia

➊ Even the pigeons have to fight for space on **Piazza San Marco,** the most famous piazza in Venice, and pedestrian traffic jams clog the surrounding byways. Despite the crowds, San Marco is the logical starting place of each of our various itineraries. The short side of the square, facing the Basilica of San Marco, is known as the Ala Napoleonica, a wing built by order of Napoléon to complete the much earlier palaces on either side of the square, enclosing it to form what he called "the most beautiful drawing room in all of Europe." Upstairs is the

➋ **Museo Correr,** with eclectic collections of historical objects and a picture gallery of fine 13th–17th-century paintings. *Piazza San Marco, Ala Napoleonica, tel. 041/522–5625. Admission: 8,000 lire. Open Apr.–Oct., Wed.–Mon. 10–5; Nov.–Mar., Wed.–Mon. 9–4.*

➌ The **Basilica di San Marco** (St. Mark's Basilica) was begun in the 11th century to hold the relics of St. Mark the Evangelist, the city's patron saint, and its richly decorated facade is surmounted by copies of the four famous gilded bronze horses (the originals are in the basilica's upstairs museum). Inside, golden mosaics sheathe walls and domes, lending an extraordinarily exotic aura, half Christian church, half Middle Eastern mosque. Be sure to see the **Pala d'Oro,** an eye-filling 10th-century altarpiece in gold and silver, studded with precious gems and enamels. From the atrium, climb the steep stairway to the museum: The bronze horses alone are worth the effort. *Basilica is open from early morning, but tourist visits are allowed Mon.–Sat. 9:30–5, Sun. 2–5. No admission to those wearing shorts or other revealing clothing. Pala d'Oro and Treasury tel. 041/522–5205. Admission: 3,000 lire. Open Apr.–Sept., Mon.–Sat. 9:30–5, Sun. 2–5; Oct.–Mar., Mon.–Sat. 10–4, Sun. 2–4, although these times may vary slightly. Gallery and Museum admission: 3,000 lire. Open Apr.–Sept., daily 9:30–5; Oct.–Mar., daily 10–4.*

➍ Next to St. Mark's is the **Palazzo Ducale** (Doge's Palace), which, during Venice's prime, was the epicenter of the Serene Republic's great empire. More than just a palace, it was a combination White House, Senate, Supreme Court, torture chamber, and prison. The building's exterior is striking; the lower stories consist of two rows of fragile-seeming arches, while above rests a massive pink-and-white marble wall whose solid-

Venezia (Venice)

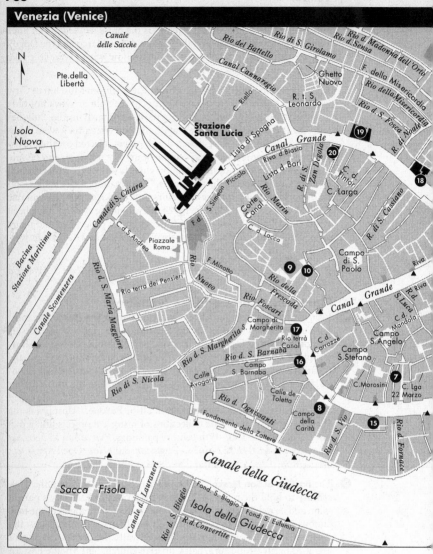

Basilica di San
Marco, **3**

Ca' d'Oro, **18**

Ca' Foscari, **17**

Ca' Rezzonico, **16**

Campanile di San
Marco, **5**

Fondaco dei
Turchi, **20**

Frari, **10**

Galleria dell'Ac-
cademia, **8**

Museo Correr, **2**

Palazzo Ducale, **4**

Palazzo Vendramin
Calergi, **19**

Peggy Guggenheim
Museum, **15**

Piazza San Marco, **1**

Rialto Bridge, **14**

San Moisè, **6**

San Zanipolo, **13**

Santa Maria
Formosa, **11**

Santa Maria dei
Miracoli, **12**

Santa Maria del
Giglio, **7**

Scuola di
San Rocco, **9**

Sacca
della
Misericordia

Canale delle Navi

San
Michele

| 0 | 440 yards |
| 0 | 400 meters |

C. Racchetta
Fondamente R.d.
Rio S. Caterina
Gesuiti Nuove

Strada
Nuova
Rio d' Santi Apostoli
Rio della Panada
C.d Testa
C.d Squero
R: dei Mendicanti

Campo d.
Pescheria
Erberia
del Vin

12

Campo Santi
Giovanni e Paolo

13

R.i Barbaria delle Tole

14
del Carbon

Rio di S.Marina
R.d Fava
Sal. di S.Lio
Riga
C.d.Bande
Giuffa
R.d S.Severo
R.d.S.Lorenzo

R.d S.
Giustina

R.d S.
Francesco

Canale d. Galeazze

11

Campo
Manin

Fabbri

Frezzaria

R.d. Palazzo

Fond.
Osmarin

R.d Greci

R.d. Pietà

C.Lion
C.d.
Furlani
R.d Scudi
R.d.Corna

Darsena
Grande

Rio d. Vergini

Rio d. S. Daniele

di S. Pietro

2 **1** **3**
5 **4**
Molo
Riva degli
Schiavoni

6

R.d.
S. Moisè

Piazza
San Marco

R.d.Arsenale

Rio della Tana

V. Garibaldi

Riva dei Sette Martiri

Rio d.S.Anna

R.d.S.Giuseppe

Viale Trieste

Rio dei Giardini

Can.

Canale di S. Marco

Fond.
delle Zitelle

Isola di
S. Giorgio
Maggiore

i

Calle
Michelangelo

KEY

⎯⎯ Rail Lines
▲ Boat stop
i Tourist Information

ity is barely interrupted by its six great Gothic windows. The interior is a maze of vast halls, monumental staircases, secret corridors, and the sinister prison cells and torture chamber. The palace is filled with frescoes, paintings, and a few examples of statuary by some of the Renaissance's greatest artists. Don't miss the famous view from the balcony, overlooking the piazza and St. Mark's Basin and the church of San Giorgio Maggiore across the lagoon. *Piazzetta San Marco, tel. 041/522–4951. Admission: 10,000 lire. Open Apr.–Oct., daily 9–7; Nov.–Mar., daily 9–4. Last entry 1 hr before closing time.*

For a pigeon's-eye view of Venice take the elevator up to the top of the
⑤ Campanile di San Marco (St. Mark's bell tower) in Piazza San Marco, a reconstruction of the 1,000-year-old tower that collapsed one morning in 1912, practically without warning. Fifteenth-century clerics found guilty of immoral acts were suspended in wooden cages from the tower, sometimes to live on bread and water for as long as a year, sometimes to die of starvation and exposure. (Look for them in Carpaccio's paintings of the square that hang in the Accademia). *Piazza San Marco, tel. 041/522–4064. Admission: 5,000 lire. Open Easter–Sept., daily 9:30–7; Oct., daily 10–6; Nov.–Easter, daily 10–4:30. Closed most of Jan.*

TIME OUT Caffè Florian is a Venetian landmark located on the square. It's a great place to nurse a Campari or a cappuccino. The pleasure of relaxing amid so much history does not come cheap. A pot of hot chocolate indoors runs about $6—and there's an extra charge if you're served when the orchestra is playing. If you drink sitting at the bar, there is no service charge. Florian's is closed Wednesday.

Armed with a street map, head west out of San Marco (with the facade of the basilica to your back), making your way past the American Express office, across the bridge in front of **San Moisè's** elaborate
⑥ Baroque facade, and on to Calle Larga 22 Marzo. Continue on to the
⑦ church of **Santa Maria del Giglio**, behind the **Gritti Palace** hotel. Across the bridge behind the church, **Piazzesi** on Campiello Feltrina is famous for its hand-printed paper and desk accessories.

Join the stream of pedestrians crossing the Grand Canal on the wooden
⑧ Accademia Bridge, and head straight on for the **Galleria dell'Accademia** (Accademia Gallery), Venice's most important picture gallery and a must for art lovers. Try to spend at least an hour viewing this remarkable collection of Venetian art, which is attractively displayed and well lighted. Works range from 14th-century Gothic to the Golden Age of the 15th and 16th centuries, including oils by Giovanni Bellini, Giorgione, Titian, and Tintoretto, and superb later works by Veronese and Tiepolo. *Campo della Carità, tel. 041/522–2247. Admission: 12,000 lire. Open Fri.–Mon. 9–2, Tues.–Thurs. 9–7. Admission to recently opened top floor (displaying works previously held in storage) by guided visit only. For details, telephone or ask at desk.*

Once again consulting your map, make your way through Calle Contarini, Calle Toletta, and Campo San Barnaba to Rio Terra Canal, where **Mondonovo** ranks as one of the city's most interesting mask shops (Venetians, who originated Italy's most splendid carnival, love masks of all kinds, from gilded lions to sinister death's heads). Just around the corner is Campo Santa Margherita, which has a homey feel.

Continue past Campo San Pantalon to Campo San Rocco, just beside the immense church of the Frari. In the 1500s, Tintoretto embellished
⑨ the **Scuola di San Rocco** with more than 50 canvases; they are an im-

pressive sight, dark paintings aglow with figures hurtling dramatically through space amid flashes of light and color. *The Crucifixion* in the Albergo (the room just off the great hall) is held to be his masterpiece. *Campo di San Rocco, tel. 041/523–4864. Admission: 8,000 lire. Open weekdays 9–5:30, weekends 10–4 in winter, 9–5:30 in summer.*

The church of Santa Maria Gloriosa dei Frari—known simply as the **Frari**—is one of Venice's most important churches, a vast soaring Gothic building of brick. Since it is the principal church of the Franciscans, its design is suitably austere to reflect that order's vows of poverty, though paradoxically it contains a number of the most sumptuous pictures in any Venetian church. Chief among them are the magnificent Titian altarpiece, the immense *Assumption of the Virgin* over the main altar. Titian was buried here at the ripe old age of 88, the only one of 70,000 plague victims to be given a personal church burial. *Campo dei Frari. Admission: 1,000 lire. Special visiting hrs: Mon.–Sat. 2:30– 6. Open Apr.–Oct., Mon.–Sat. 9–noon, Sun. 3–6; Nov.–Mar., Mon.–Sat. 9:30–noon, Sun. 3–5:30.*

San Zanipolo and the Rialto

Backtracking once again to Piazza San Marco, go to the arch under the Torre dell'Orologio (Clock Tower) and head northeast into the **Merceria,** one of Venice's busiest streets and, with the **Frezzeria** and **Calle dei Fabbri,** part of the shopping area that extends across the Grand Canal into the **Rialto district.** At Campo San Zulian, turn right into Calle della Guerra and Calle delle Bande to the graceful white marble church of **Santa Maria Formosa;** it's situated right on a lively square (of the same name) with a few sidewalk cafés and a small vegetable market on weekday mornings.

Use your map to follow Calle Borgoloco into Campo San Marina, where you turn right, cross the little canal, and take Calle Castelli to **Santa Maria dei Miracoli** (Campo dei Miracoli). Perfectly proportioned and sheathed in marble, this late-15th century building embodies all the classical serenity of the early Renaissance. The interior is decorated with marble reliefs by the church's architect, Pietro Lombardo, and his son Tullio.

Retrace your steps along Calle Castelli and cross the bridge into Calle delle Erbe, following signs for SS. GIOVANNI E PAOLO. The massive Dominican church of Santi Giovanni e Paolo—**San Zanipolo,** as it's known in the slurred Venetian dialect—is the twin (and rival) of the Franciscan Frari. The church is a kind of pantheon of the doges (25 are buried here), and contains a wealth of artwork. (Special visiting hrs: Mon.–Sat. 9–12, 3–6.) Outside in the campo stands Verrocchio's magnificent equestrian statue of Colleoni, who fought for the Venetian cause in the mid-1400s.

Cross the canal in front of the church, and continue along Calle Larga Giacinto Gallina, crossing a pair of bridges to Campiello Santa Maria Nova. Take Salizzada San Canciano to Salizzada San Giovanni Crisostomo to find yourself once again in the mainstream of pedestrians winding their way to the **Rialto Bridge.** Street stalls hung with scarves and gondolier's hats signal that you are entering the heart of Venice's shopping district. Cross over the bridge, and you'll find yourself on the edge of the famous market. Try to visit the Rialto market when it's in full swing (Tues.–Sat. mornings; Mondays are quiet because the fish market is closed), with fruit and vegetable vendors hawking their wares in a colorful and noisy jumble of sights and sounds. Not far beyond is the fish market, where you'll probably find sea creatures you've never seen before (and possibly won't want to see again). A left turn into Ruga San Giovanni and Ruga del Ravano will bring you face to face with scores of shops: At **La Scialuppa** (Calle Saoneri 2695) you'll find hand-carved wooden models of gondolas and their graceful oar locks known as *forcole*.

The Grand Canal

Just off Piazzetta di San Marco (the square in front of the Doge's Palace) you can catch Vaporetto 1 at either the San Marco or San Zaccaria landing stages (on Riva degli Schiavoni), to set off on a boat tour along the **Grand Canal.** Serving as Venice's main thoroughfare, the canal winds in the shape of an S for more than 3½ kilometers (2 miles) through the heart of the city, past some 200 Gothic-Renaissance palaces. Although restrictions have been introduced to diminish the erosive effect of wash on buildings, this is still the route taken by vaporetti, gondolas, water taxis, mail boats, police boats, fire boats, ambulance boats, barges carrying provisions and building materials, bridal boats, and funeral boats. Your vaporetto tour will give you an idea of the opulent beauty of the palaces and a peek into the side streets and tiny canals where the Venetians go about their daily business. *Vaporetto 1. Cost: 3,500 lire.*

Here are some of the key buildings that this vaporetto tour passes, as it departs from the San Marco landing: the **Accademia Gallery,** with its fine collection of 14th- to 18th-century Venetian paintings (which were visited earlier). The **Peggy Guggenheim Museum,** housed in the incomplete Palazzo Venier dei Leoni, has an exceptional modern art collection (*see* Off the Beaten Track, *below*). The **Ca' Rezzonico**—the most spectacular palace in all of Venice—was built between the mid-17th and 18th centuries and is now a museum of sumptuous 18th-century Venetian paintings and furniture. The Ca' Rezzonico is the best chance to glimpse Venetian splendor and is a must-see. *Ca' Rezzonico, tel. 041/522–4543. Admission: 8,000 lire. Open Apr.–Oct., Sat.–Thurs. 10–5; Nov.–Mar., Sat.–Thurs. 10–4.*

Ca' Foscari is a 15th-century Gothic building that was once the home of Doge Foscari, who was unwillingly deposed and died the following day! Today it's the headquarters of Venice's university. **Ca' d'Oro** is the most flowery palace on the canal; it now houses the Galleria Franchetti. *Ca' d'Oro, tel. 041/523–8790. Admission: 4,000 lire. Open daily 9–2.*

The **Palazzo Vendramin Calergi** is a opulent Renaissance building where Wagner died in 1883. It's also the winter home of the municipal casino. The **Fondaco dei Turchi** was an original Byzantine "house-warehouse" of a rich Venetian merchant, but the building suffered some fanciful remodeling during the 19th century. It is now the Natural History Museum. *Fondaco dei Turchi, tel. 041/524–0885. Admission: 5,000 lire. Open Tues.–Sat. 9–1.*

Off the Beaten Track

Explore the **Ghetto,** where Venice's Jewish community lived in cramped quarters for many centuries, and visit the **Museo Ebraico** (*Jewish Museum, Campo del Ghetto Nuovo, tel. 041/715359; admission 4,000 lire; with tour, every half hr from 10:30–3:30, 10,000 lire; open June–Sept., Sun.–Fri. 10–7, Oct.–May, Sun.–Fri. 10–4:30*) and the Ghetto's several synagogues.

Visit late heiress Peggy Guggenheim's house and collection of modern art at the **Palazzo Venier dei Leoni** on the Grand Canal. *Entrance: Calle San Cristoforo, Dorsoduro, tel. 041/520–6288. Admission: 10,000 lire. Open Sun.–Mon., Wed.–Sat. 11–6.*

At **Palazzo Labia,** you'll find the prettiest ballroom in Venice, magnificently adorned with Giambattista Tiepolo's 18th-century frescoes of Anthony and Cleopatra. This palace, once the home of Venice's most ostentatiously rich family, is now the Venetian headquarters of RAI, Italy's National Broadcasting Corporation, which occasionally host concerts in the Tiepolo ballroom. *Campo San Geremia, Cannaregio, tel. 041/524–2821. Admission to ballroom free Mon., Thurs., and Fri. 3– 4; tour of ballroom and other rooms (available in English): 10,000 lire, by prior arrangement, Mon.–Fri. 10–4.*

To discover the Venetian equivalent of World's End, explore the magical island of **Torcello** in the Venetian lagoon. Settled 1,500 years ago and a thriving city during the Byzantine era, the island is now deserted but remains a pilgrimage spot for art lovers due to two great 11th-century churches (the cathedral of Santa Maria Assunta has a world-famous mosaic of the Virgin). Locanda Cipriani, a favored restaurant of Hemingway and the Duke of Windsor, still lures gourmands. Katherine Hepburn and Rossanzo Brazzi fell in love during a picnic on Torcello in the film classic, *Summertime.* To get to Torcello, take Vaporetto 12 from Venice.

Shopping

Glass
Venetian glass is as famous as the city's gondolas, and almost every shop window displays it. There's a lot of cheap glass for sale; if you want something better, among the top showrooms are **Venini** (Piazzetta dei Leoncini 314), **Pauly** (Piazza San Marco 73–77), and **Salviati** (Piazza San Marco 79B). Carlo Moretti's chic, contemporary designs are on show at **L'Isola** (Campo San Moisè 1468, near Piazza San Marco). On the island of Murano, where prices are generally no lower than in Venice, **Domus** (Fondamenta dei Vetrai) has a good selection.

Fabrics
Norelene (Calle della Chiesa 727, in Dorsoduro, near the Guggenheim) has stunning hand-painted fabrics that make wonderful wall-hangings or elegantly styled jackets and chic scarves, while **Venetia Studuim** (Calle Larga XXII Marzo 2430), is famous for Fortuny-inspired lamps, furnishings, clothes, and accessories.

Shopping District
The main shopping area extends from Piazza San Marco through the Mercerie and Calle dei Fabbri toward the Rialto.

Dining

Venetians love seafood, which figures prominently on most restaurant menus, sometimes to the exclusion of any meat dishes. However, fish is generally expensive, and you should bear this in mind when ordering: The price given on menus for fish as a main course is often per 100 grams, not the total cost of what you are served, which could be two or three times that amount. This is not sharp practice, but a conventional way of pricing fish in Italy. Venice is not a particularly cheap place to eat, but there are good restaurants huddled along Venice's squares and seemingly endless canals. City specialties include pasta e fagioli; risotto and all kinds of seafood; and the delicious fegato alla veneziana served with grilled polenta. For details and price-category definitions, *see* Dining *in* Staying in Italy, *above.*

$$$$ Da Fiore. Long a favorite with Venetians, Da Fiore has been discov-
★ ered by tourists, so reservations are imperative. It's known for its excellent seafood dinners, which might include such specialties as *pasticcio
di pesce* (fish pie) and *seppioline* (little cuttlefish). Not easy to find, it's
just off Campo San Polo. *Calle dello Scaleter 2202, San Polo, tel.
041/721308. Reservations required. AE, DC, MC, V. Closed Sun., Mon.,
Aug. 10–early Sept., and Dec. 25–Jan. 15.*

$$$$ Grand Canal. The Hotel Monaco's restaurant is a favorite with Vene-
★ tians, who enjoy eating on the lovely canal-side terrace on sunny days,
looking across the mouth of the Grand Canal to the island of San Giorgio Maggiore, and in the cozy dining room in winter. All the pasta is made
fresh daily on the premises, and the smoked and marinated salmon are
also produced in the restaurant's kitchen. The traditional Venetian dishes
are very well prepared; the chef, Fulvio De Santa, also offers delicious
meat and fish dishes, such as scampi *alla Ca' d'Oro* (in cognac sauce,
served with rice). *Calle Vallaresso 1325, San Marco, tel. 041/520–0211.
Reservations advised. Jacket required. AE, DC, MC, V.*

$$$$ La Caravella. La Caravella is decorated like the dining saloon of an
old Venetian sailing ship, with lots of authentic touches and has a pretty
garden courtyard used during summer. The menu is long and slightly
intimidating, though the highly competent maître d' will advise you
well. The *granseola* (crab) is marvelous in any of several versions. *Calle
Larga XXII Marzo 2397, San Marco, tel. 041/520–8901. Reservations
required. AE, DC, MC, V. Closed Wed. Nov.–Apr.*

$$$ Da Arturo. The tiny Da Arturo is a refreshing change from the numerous
seafood restaurants of which Venetians are so fond. The cordial pro-
prietor prefers, instead, to offer varied and delicious seasonal veg-
etable and salad dishes, tasty, tender and generous meat courses like
braciola alla veneziana (pork chop schnitzel with vinegar), and an au-
thentic, creamy homemade *tiramisù* (espresso-soaked biscuits layered
with zabiglione, mascarpone cheese, whipped cream, and dusted with
cocoa). *Calle degli Assassini 3656, San Marco, tel. 041/528–6974. Reser-
vations required. No credit cards. Closed Sun., 3 wks in Aug.*

$$$ Fiaschetteria Toscana. Once a storehouse for a 19th-century wine mer-
chant from Tuscany, this popular restaurant has long favorite of Vene-
tians and visitors from terra firma, especially so in the summer when
they can sit under the arbor out front. Courteous, cheerful waiters serve
such specialties as *rombo* (turbot) with capers and an exceptionally good
pasta *alla buranella* (with shrimp, au gratin). *Campo San Giovanni
Crisostomo 5719, Cannaregio, tel. 041/528–5281. Reservations advised. AE, DC, MC, V. Closed Tues. and first 2 wks in July.*

$$ Al Mondo Novo. This fish restaurant is owned by a fish wholesaler in
the Rialto market, so you can be sure that everything is absolutely fresh.
Specialties prepared by Signora Trevisan, the owner's wife, include *cape
sante* (pilgrim scallops) and *cape longhe* (razor clams), risotto and pasta
dishes, and charcoal-grilled fish. Meat dishes are also available. *Saliz-
zada San Lio 5409, Castello, tel. 041/520–0698. Reservations advised.
AE, MC, V. Closed Wed. Feb.–Mar.*

$$ Da Gigio. Just off the Strada Nuova, this is an attractive, friendly, family-run trattoria on the quayside of a canal. Da Gigio is popular with
those who appreciate the affable service and excellently cooked, homemade pasta, fish and meat dishes, and high-quality draft wine. Its bar-
room makes a pleasant, informal setting for simple lunches. *Fondamenta
de la Chiesa 3628A, Cannaregio, tel. 041/528–5140. Dinner reservations advised. AE, DC, MC, V. No dinner Sun. Closed Mon., 2 wks
in mid-Jan., and 2 wks in Aug.*

$ L'Incontro. This trattoria has a faithful clientele who are attracted by good food (excellent meat–no fish) at reasonable prices. Menu choices include freshly made Sardinian pastas, juicy steaks, wild duck, boar, and (with advance notice) roast suckling pig. L'Incontro is between San Barnaba and Campo Santa Margherita. *Rio Terra Canal 3062A, Dorsoduro, tel. 041/522–2404. Reservations advised. MC, V. Closed Mon.*

$ Metropole Buffet. Here at the Hotel Metropole's buffet, in a charming, comfortable room overlooking the waterfront by the Pietà Church, you can eat a substantial and tasty lunch or dinner, helping yourself from a varied selection of starters, soup, pastas, hot and cold fish and meat dishes, and desserts, all for around 50,000 lire. The price even includes a highly drinkable Bianco di Custoza (a light white wine from the Veneto region) on draft. *Riva degli Schiavoni 4149, Castello, tel. 041/520–5044. Reservations advised. AE, DC, MC, V.*

$ Montin. Peggy Guggenheim used to wine and dine the greatest artists of the 20th century here after showing them the collection at her nearby Palazzo Venier dei Leoni. Since those days, Montin has become more of an institution, less a bohemian hang-out. Service can sometimes be erratic, but crowds still pack the place—especially at Biennale times—to enjoy the rigatoni *ai quattro formaggi* (with four cheeses, mushrooms, and tomato) and antipasto Montin (seafood antipasto). *Fondamenta di Borgo 1147, Dorsoduro, tel. 041/522–7151. Reservations advised. AE, DC, MC, V. No dinner Tues. Closed Wed., 15 days in Jan., and 15 days in Aug.*

Lodging

Venice is made up almost entirely of time-worn buildings, so it stands to reason that the majority of hotels are in renovated palaces. However, space is at a premium in this city, and even in the best hotels, rooms can be small and with little natural light. Preservation restrictions on buildings often preclude the installation of such amenities as elevators, air-conditioning systems, and satellite dishes (if any of these facilities is of paramount importance to you, check on their availability before booking). So don't come to Venice expecting to find the standard modern hotel room—you will almost certainly be disappointed. On the other hand, Venice's luxury hotels can offer rooms of fabulous opulence and elegance, and even in the more modest hotels you can find comfortable rooms of great charm and character, sometimes with stunning views.

Venice attracts visitors all year round, although the winter months are generally much quieter, and most hotels offer lower rates during this period. It is always worth booking in advance, but if you haven't, the AVA desk at the railway station (tel. 041/715016 and 041/715288; open Apr.–Oct., daily 8 AM–10 PM; Nov.–Mar., daily 8 AM–9:30 PM), at the airport (open Apr.–Oct., daily 10–9; Nov.–Mar., daily 10:30–6:30), or at the municipal parking garage at Piazzale Roma (open Apr.–Oct., daily 9 AM–10 PM; Nov.–Mar., daily 9–9) will help you find a room after your arrival in the city. For details and price-category definitions, *see* Lodging *in* Staying in Italy, *above.*

$$$$ Cipriani. A sybaritic oasis of stunningly decorated rooms and suites with marble baths and Jacuzzis, the Cipriani is located across St. Mark's Basin on the island of Giudecca (pronounced joo-*dek*-ka), offering a panorama of romantic views of the entire lagoon. The hotel launch whisks guests back and forth to Piazza San Marco at any hour of the day or night. Cooking courses and fitness programs are offered as special programs to occupy the guests. Some rooms have pretty garden patios. The newly restored Palazzo Vendramin annex of the Cipriani (with 7 suites and 3 double rooms) is open all year. *Giudecca 10, tel. 041/520–7744, fax 041/520–3930. 104 rooms with bath. Facilities: restaurant, bar, air-conditioning, pool, tennis court, health club. AE, DC, MC, V. Closed Dec.–mid-Mar.*

$$$$ **Danieli.** Parts of this rather large hotel are built around a 15th-century palazzo bathed in sumptuous Venetian colors, though the Danieli also has several modern annexes that some find bland and impersonal, and the lower-price rooms can be exceedingly drab. Still, it's a favorite with celebrities and English-speaking visitors, and the dining terrace does have a fantastic view of St. Mark's Basin. *Riva degli Schiavoni 4196, Castello, tel. 041/522–6480, fax 041/520–0208. 231 rooms with bath. Facilities: restaurant, bar, roof terrace, air-conditioning, access to tennis court and pool at the Hotel Exclesior and/or Hotel des Bains on the Lido. AE, DC, MC, V.*

$$$$ **Gritti Palace.** The atmosphere of an aristocratic private home is what
★   the management is after here, and they succeed beautifully. Fresh flowers, fine antiques, sumptuous appointments, and Old World service make this a terrific choice for anyone who wants to be totally pampered. The dining terrace overlooking the Grand Canal is best in the evening when boat traffic dies down. *Campo Santa Maria del Giglio 2467, San Marco, tel. 041/794611, fax 041/520–0942. 88 rooms with bath. Facilities: restaurant, bar, air-conditioning, canal-side terrace, access to tennis court and pool at Hotel Excelsior and/or Hotel des Bains on Lido. AE, DC, MC, V.*

$$$ **Londra Palace.** You get the obligatory view of San Giorgio and St. Mark's Basin at this distinguished hotel whose rooms are decorated in dark paisley prints, with such sumptuous touches as canopied beds. French chefs preside over Les Deux Lions restaurant, now a haven of *cuisine française,* and the piano bar is open late. The hotel offers a complimentary Mercedes for one-day excursions and free entrance to the casino. *Riva degli Schiavoni 4171, Castello, tel. 041/520–0533, fax 041/522–5032. 69 rooms with bath. Facilities: restaurant, piano bar, air-conditioning, solarium. AE, DC, MC, V.*

$$$ **Metropole.** Guests can step from their water taxi or gondola into the
★   lobby of this small, very well-run hotel, rich in precious antiques, just five minutes from Piazza San Marco. Many rooms have a view of the lagoon, others overlook the garden at the back, but all are furnished with style. *Riva degli Schiavoni 4149, Castello, tel. 041/520–5044, fax 041/522–3679. 73 rooms with bath. Facilities: buffet restaurant (see Dining, above), bar, air-conditioning. AE, DC, MC, V.*

$$ **Accademia.** Hidden within the heart of Venice, this miniature Palla-
★   dian villa—complete with canal-side garden—is the city's most enchanting hotel. There's plenty of atmosphere here, with just a touch of romance, though there are indications that it may be becoming a little too well-worn: Readers have reported chairs with broken springs. Many rooms overlook the gardens, where you can sit in warm weather. *Fondamenta Bollani 1058, Dorsoduro, tel. 041/523–7846, fax 041/523–9152. 27 rooms, most with bath. Facilities: bar, air-conditioning, gardens. AE, DC, MC, V.*

$ **Alboretti.** This small hotel is simply but attractively furnished. Despite its size and central location, it has a little garden courtyard off the breakfast room and a lounge upstairs from the tiny lobby and bar area. There is no elevator. Together with its moderately priced restaurant, the Alboretti is a good value. *Rio Terra Sant'Agnese 882, Dorsoduro, tel. 041/523–0058, fax 041/521–0158. 19 rooms with bath. Facilities: restaurant, bar, air-conditioning. AE, MC, V.*

$ Bucintoro. Whistler once stayed here and, today, the Bucintoro is still favored by artists, drawn by the lagoon views outside each room. Slightly off the tourist track, this friendly, family-run hotel has clean and simple rooms. The price is unbeatable for such spectacular vistas. *Riva San Biagio 2135, Castello, tel. 041/522–3240, fax 041/523–5224. 28 rooms, 18 with bath. Facilities: restaurant, bar. No credit cards. Closed Jan.–mid-Feb.*

$ La Residenza. A Gothic palace makes a delightful setting for this charming hotel, set on a an attractive square off the waterfront and just a 10-minute walk from San Marco. Breakfast is served in a real antique-furnished Venetian salon. With a decidedly subdued atmosphere, this is not the place for children, or for the high-spirited. Make reservations well in advance. *Campo Bandiera e Moro 3608, Castello, tel. 041/528–5315, fax 041/523–8859. 17 rooms, 14 with bath. AE, DC, MC, V. Closed mid-Jan.–mid-Feb., mid-Nov.–early Dec.*

$ Locanda Fiorita. Just off Campo Sant Stefano, near the Accademia Bridge, you'll find this welcoming, newly refurbished hotel, tucked away in a sunny little square (where breakfast is served in summer). The location is a big plus: it's very central for sightseeing. The rooms have beamed ceilings and are simply furnished. *Campiello Novo 3457, San Marco, tel. 041/523–4754, fax 041/522–8043. 10 rooms, 7 with shower. AE, MC, V. Closed 2 wks Nov.–Dec.*

$ Paganelli. The lagoon views here so impressed Henry James that he wrote the Paganelli up in the preface to his *Portrait of a Lady*. This charming, small hotel on the waterfront near Piazza San Marco has an annex on the quiet square of Campo San Zaccaria and is tastefully decorated in the Venetian style. Three rooms overlook the lagoon, and six have good views over the square. *Riva degli Schiavoni 4182, Castello, tel. 041/522–4324, fax 041/523–9267. 22 rooms, 19 with bath or shower. Facilities: bar. AE, DC, MC, V.*

The Arts

For a program of events, pick up the free "Un Ospite di Venezia" ("Guest in Venice") booklet, available from the Assessorato al Turismo (Ca' Giustinian, 2nd Floor, Calle del Ridotto), near Piazza San Marco, or at most hotel desks. Your hotel may also be able to get you tickets for some events.

Concerts

There are regular concerts at the Pietà Church, with an emphasis on Vivaldi, and at San Stae and San Barnaba. Concerts, sometimes free, are also held by visiting choirs and musicians in other churches. For information on these often short-notice events, ask at the APT office, and look for posters on walls and in restaurants and shops. The **Kele e Teo Agency** (Piazza San Marco 4930, tel. 041/520–8722) and **Box Office** (Calle Loredan 4127, off Salizzada San Luca, tel. 041/988369) handle tickets for many of the city's musical events.

Opera

The season at **Teatro La Fenice** (Campo San Fantin, tel. 041/521–0161, fax 041/522–1768) runs all year, except for August, with opera or concert performances most months. The box office is open September to July, Monday–Saturday 9:30–12:30 and 4–6, except when there's a performance on Sunday, in which case the box office is open Sunday and remains closed the following Monday. A 20% charge is levied on all reservations made more than one week before the performance.

Nightlife

The **Martini Scala Club** (Calle delle Veste, near Teatro La Fenice, tel. 041/522–4121) is an elegant piano bar with late-night restaurant. The bars of the top hotels stay open as long as their customers keep on drinking. Dedicated nighthawks should get a copy of "Fuori Orario: di Notte a Venezia e Mestre" ("Out of Hours: By Night in Venice and Mestre"), a guide to live music venues, discos, and late bars in and around Venice, published by the Assessorato alla Gioventù, the municipality's Youth Department (Corte Contarini 1529, 4th Floor, near Piazza San Marco). It's available free at APT information offices, at present only in Italian, but with useful maps and easy-to-follow notes. Night spots popular with young people are **Ai Canottieri** (Fondamenta San Giobbe 690, Cannaregio, tel. 041/71548, live music Thurs. and Sat., closed Sun. and in summer) and **Paradiso Perduto** (Fondamenta Misericordia 2540, Cannaregio, tel. 041/720581, live music usually on weekends, closed Wed. and first half of Aug.).

CAMPANIA

Campania (the region of Naples, the Amalfi coast, and other sights) is where most people's preconceived ideas of Italy become a reality. You'll find lots of sun, good food that relies heavily on tomatoes and mozzarella, acres of classical ruins, and gorgeous scenery. The exuberance of the locals doesn't leave much room for efficient organization, however, and you may have to revise your concept of real time; here minutes dilate into hours at the drop of a hat.

Once a city that rivaled Paris as a brilliant and refined cultural capital, Napoli (Naples) is afflicted by acute urban decay and chronic delinquency. You need patience, stamina, and a healthy dose of caution to visit Naples on your own, but it's worth it for those who have a sense of adventure and the capacity to discern the enormous riches the city has accumulated in its 2,000-year existence.

On the other hand, if you want the fun without the hassle, head for Sorrento, Capri, and the Amalfi coast, legendary haunts of the sirens who tried to lure Odysseus off course. Sorrento is touristy but has some fine old hotels and beautiful views; it's a good base for a leisurely excursion to Pompeii. Capri is a pint-size paradise, though sometimes too crowded for comfort, while the Amalfi coast has some enchanting towns and spectacular scenery.

Getting Around

By Plane

There are several daily flights between Rome and Naples's Capodichino Airport (tel. 081/709–2815), 8 kilometers (5 miles) north of the downtown area. During the summer months there's a direct helicopter service between Capodichino, Capri, and Ischia; for information, tel. 081/789–6273 or 081/584–1481.

By Train

A great number of trains run between Rome and Naples every day; Intercity trains make the journey in less than two hours. There are several stations in Naples, and a network of suburban trains connects the city with diverse points of interest in Campania—most usefully the **Circumvesuviana** line, which runs to Ercolano (Herculaneum), Pompeii, and Sorrento. The central station is at Piazza Garibaldi. For train information, tel. 081/553–3188. Naples has a Metropolitana (subway);

though it's old and trains are infrequent, it beats the traffic. The fare is 1,500 lire.

By Bus

For bus information, call **SITA** (tel. 081/552–2176) or the Naples Transport Board (tel. 081/553–3188).

By Car

The Naples–Pompeii–Salerno toll road has exits at Ercolano (Herculaneum) and Pompeii, and connects with the tortuous coastal road to Sorrento and the Amalfi coast at the Castellamare exit. Parking within Naples is not recommended: Window smashing and robbery are not uncommon.

By Boat

Most boats and hydrofoils for the islands, the Sorrento peninsula, and the Amalfi coast leave from the Molo Beverello, near Naples's Piazza Municipio. **Caremar** (tel. 081/551–3882), **Navigazione Libera del Golfo** (tel. 081/552–7209), and **Lauro** (tel. 081/551–3236) operate frequent passenger and car ferry services, while hydrofoils of the Caremar, Navigazione Libera del Golfo, and **Alilauro** (tel. 081/552–2838) lines leave from both Molo Beverello and the hydrofoil station at Mergellina pier, from which **SNAV** (tel. 081/761–2348) also operates.

Guided Tours

Aside from the one-, two-, or three-day guided tours of the area departing from Rome, offered by **American Express** (tel. 06/67641), **Carrani** (tel. 06/488–0510 and 06/474–2501), **Appian Line** (tel. 06/488–4151) and other operators, **CIT** in Naples (Piazza Municipio 72, tel. 081/552–5426) has a wide range of half-day and all-day tours on the mainland and to the islands. Similar tours are offered by **Tourcar** (Piazza Matteotti 1, tel. 081/552–0429).

Tourist Information

Capri (Marina Grande pier, tel. 081/837–0634; Piazza Umberto I, Capri town, tel. 081/837–0686).

Naples. EPT Information Offices (Piazza dei Martiri 58, tel. 081/405311; central station, tel. 081/268779; hydrofoil station, Mergellina, summer only, tel. 081/761–4585; Capodichino Airport, tel. 081/780–5761). Azienda Autonoma di Cura Soggionale Turismo Information Office (AACST, Piazza del Gesù, tel. 081/552–3328).

Sorrento (Via De Maio 35, tel. 081/807–4033).

Exploring Campania

Naples

Founded by the Greeks, **Naples** became a playground of the Romans and was ruled thereafter by a succession of foreign dynasties, all of which left traces of their cultures in the city and its environs. The most splendid of these rulers were the Bourbons, who were responsible for much of what you will want to see in Naples, starting with the 17th-century **Palazzo Reale** (Royal Palace), still furnished in the lavish Baroque style that suited them so well. *Piazza del Plebiscito, tel. 081/413888. Admission: 8,000 lire. Open Apr.–Oct., Tues.–Sun. 9–7:30; Nov.–Mar., Tues.–Sun. 9–1:30.*

Across the way is the massive stone **Castel Nuovo**, which was built by the city's Aragon rulers in the 13th century; some rooms recently opened to the public contain sculptures and frescoes that date from

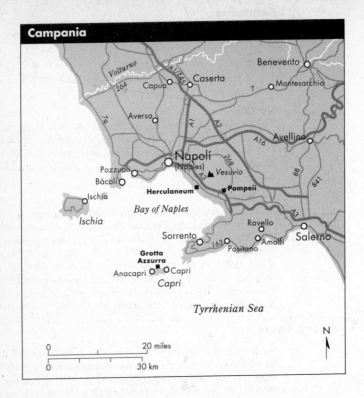

Campania

the 14th and 15th centuries. *Admission: 5,000 lire. Open weekdays 9–2, Sat. 9–1, closed Sun.*

Walk up Via Toledo, keeping an eye on the antics of the Neapolitans, whose daily lives are fraught with theatrical gestures and fiery speeches. They all seem to be actors in their own human comedy.

Continue along Via Toledo, also known as Via Roma, and make a detour to the right to see the oddly faceted stone facade and elaborate Baroque interior of the church of the **Gesù** (Via Benedetto Croce) and, directly opposite, the church of **Santa Chiara,** built in the early 1300s in Provençal Gothic style. A favorite Neapolitan song celebrates the quiet beauty of its cloister, decorated in delicate floral tiles.

TIME OUT For an authentic Neapolitan pizza in a genuine pizzeria, stop in at **Lombardi,** where you can have a classic pizza made in a wood-fired brick oven or a full meal in a tiny, crowded setting with no frills and lots of atmosphere. *Via Benedetto Croce 59.*

Another detour off Via Toledo, to the left this time, takes you from **Piazza Dante** to the Montesanto funicular, which ascends the Vomero hill, where you can see the bastions of **Castel Sant'Elmo** and visit the museum in the **Certosa di San Martino,** a Carthusian monastery restored in the 17th century. It contains an eclectic collection of Neapolitan landscape paintings, royal carriages, and *presepi* (Christmas crèches). Check out the view from the balcony off Room 25. *Certosa di San Martino, tel. 081/578–1769. Admission: 8,000 lire. Open Tues.–Sun. 9–2.*

Return to Piazza Dante and follow Via Pessina (an extension of Via Toledo) to the **Museo Archeologico Nazionale.** Dusty and unkempt, the museum undergoes perpetual renovations, but it holds one of the world's great collections of antiquities. Greek and Roman sculptures, vividly colored mosaics, countless objects from Pompeii and Herculaneum, and an equestrian statue of the Roman emperor Nerva are all worth seeing. *Piazza Museo, tel. 081/440166. Admission: 12,000 lire. Open May–Sept., Mon.–Sat. 9–7, Sun. 9–1; Oct.–Apr., Mon.–Sat. 9–2, Sun. 9–1.*

About a mile north on the same road (take a bus or a taxi), you'll come to the **Museo di Capodimonte,** housed in an 18th-century palace built by Bourbon king Charles III, and surrounded by a vast park that must have been lovely when it was better cared for. In the picture gallery are some fine Renaissance paintings; climb the stairs to the terrace for a magnificent view of Naples and the bay. Downstairs you can visit the State Apartments and see the extensive collection of porcelain, much of it produced in the Bourbons' own factory right here on the grounds. *Parco di Capodimonte, tel. 081/744–1307. Admission: 12,000 lire. Open Apr.–Oct., Tues.–Sun. 9–7:30; Nov.–Mar., Tues.–Sun. 9–2.*

Herculaneum

Herculaneum (Ercolano) lies 10 kilometers (6 miles) southeast of Naples. Reputed to have been founded by the legendary Hercules, the elite Roman resort was devastated by the same volcanic eruption that buried Pompeii in AD 79. Recent excavations have revealed that many died on the shore in an attempt to escape, as a slow-moving mud slide embalmed the entire town by covering it with an 36-foot-deep blanket of volcanic ash and ooze. While that may have been unfortunate for Herculaneum's residents, it has helped to preserve the site in pristine detail for nearly two millennia. *Corso Ercolano, tel. 081/739–0963. Admission: 8,000 lire. Open daily 9–1 hr before sunset (ticket office closes 2 hrs before sunset).*

Pompeii

Pompeii, a larger community 12 kilometers (8 miles) farther to the east, lost even more residents. An estimated 2,000 of them perished on that fateful August day. The ancient city of Pompeii was much larger than Herculaneum, and excavations have progressed to a much greater extent (though the remains are not as well preserved, due to some 18th-century scavenging for museum-quality artwork, most of which you are able to see at Naples's Museo Archeologico Nazionale; *see above*). This prosperous Roman city had an extensive forum, lavish baths and temples, and patrician villas richly decorated with frescoes. It's worth buying a detailed guide of the site to give meaning and understanding to the ruins and their importance. Be sure to see the **Villa dei Misteri,** whose frescoes are in mint condition. Perhaps that is a slight exaggeration, but the paintings are so rich with detail and depth of color that one finds it difficult to believe that they are 1,900 years old. Have lots of small change handy to tip the guards at the more important houses so they will unlock the gates for you. *Pompeii Scavi, tel. 081/861–0744. Admission: 10,000 lire. Open daily 9–1 hr before sunset (ticket office closes 2 hrs before sunset).*

Sorrento

Another 28 kilometers (18 miles) southwest is **Sorrento,** in the not-too-distant past a small, genteel resort for a fashionable elite. Now the town has spread out along the crest of its fabled cliffs. Once this was an area full of secret haunts for the few tourists who came for the beauty of this coastline. Now, it has been "discovered" and the secret haunts are the playground for package tours. In Sorrento's case, however, the change is not as grim as it sounds, since nothing can dim the delights of the marvelous climate and view of the Bay of Naples. For the best views go to the **Villa Comunale,** near the old church of **San Francesco** (in itself worth a visit), or to the terrace behind the **Museo Correale.** The museum, an attractive 18th-century villa, houses an interesting collection of decorative arts (furniture, china, and so on) and paintings of the Neapolitan school. *Via Correale. Admission: 5,000 lire; gardens only, 3,000 lire. Open Apr.–Sept., Mon. and Wed.–Sat. 9–12:30 and 4–6, Sun. 9–12:30; Oct.–Mar., Mon. and Wed.–Sat. 9–12 and 3–5, Sun. 9–8.*

Capri

Sorrento makes a convenient jumping-off spot for a boat trip to **Capri.** No matter how many day-trippers crowd onto the island, no matter how touristy certain sections have become, Capri remains one of Italy's loveliest places. Incoming visitors disembark at Marina Grande, from where you can take some time out for an excursion to the **Grotta Azzurra** (Blue Grotto). Be warned that this must rank as one of the country's all-time great rip-offs: Motorboat, rowboat, and grotto admissions are charged separately, and if there's a line of boats waiting, you'll have little time to enjoy the grotto's marvelous colors. At Marina Grande you can also embark on a boat excursion around the island.

A cog railway or bus service takes you up to the town of Capri, where you can stroll through the **Piazzetta,** a choice place from which to watch the action, and window-shop expensive boutiques or browse in souvenir shops along Via Vittorio Emanuele on your way to the **Gardens of Augustus,** which have gorgeous views. The town of Capri is deliberately commercial and self-consciously picturesque. To get away from the crowds, hike to **Villa Jovis,** one of the many villas that Roman emperor Tiberius built on the island, at the end of a lane that climbs steeply uphill. The walk takes about 45 minutes, with pretty views all the way and a final spectacular vista of the entire Bay of Naples and part of the Gulf of Salerno. *Villa Jovis, Via Tiberio. Admission: 4,000 lire. Open daily 9–1 hr before sunset.*

Or take the bus or a jaunty open taxi to **Anacapri** and look for the little church of **San Michele,** off Via Orlandi, where a magnificent hand-painted majolica tile floor shows you an 18th-century vision of the Garden of Eden. *Open Easter–Oct., daily 7–7; Nov.–Easter., 10–3.*

From Piazza della Vittoria, picturesque Via Capodimonte leads to **Villa San Michele,** charming former home of Swedish scientist-author Axel Munthe. *Via Axel Munthe. Admission: 5,000 lire. Open May–Sept., daily 9–6; Nov.–Feb., daily 10:30–3:30; Mar., daily 9:30–4:30; Apr. And Oct., daily 9:30–5.*

Amalfi and Positano

From Sorrento, the coastal drive down to the resort town of Amalfi provides some of the most dramatic and beautiful scenery you'll find in all of Italy. **Positano's** jumble of pastel houses, topped by whitewashed cupolas, clings to the mountainside above the sea. The town—the prettiest along this stretch of coast—attracts a sophisticated group of visitors and summer residents who find that its relaxed and friendly atmosphere more than compensates for the sheer effort of moving about this exhaustingly vertical town, most of whose streets are stairways. This former fishing village has now opted for the more regular and lucrative rewards of tourism and commercialized fashion. Practically every other shop is a boutique displaying locally made casual wear. The beach is the town's main focal point, with a little promenade and a multitude of café-restaurants.

Amalfi itself is a charming maze of covered alleys and narrow byways straggling up the steep mountainside. The piazza just below the cathedral forms the town's heart—a colorful assortment of pottery stalls, cafés, and postcard shops grouped around a venerable old fountain. The cathedral's exterior is its most impressive feature, so there's no need to climb all those stairs unless you really want to.

Ravello

Do not miss **Ravello,** 8 kilometers (5 miles) north of Amalfi. Ravello is not actually on the coast, but on a high mountain bluff overlooking the sea. The road up to it is a series of switchbacks, and the village itself clings precariously on the mountain spur. The village flourished during the 13th century and then fell into a tranquillity that has remained unchanged for the past six centuries. The center of the town is **Piazza Duomo,** with its cathedral, founded in 1087 and recently restored. Note the fine bronze 12th-century doors and, inside, two pulpits richly decorated with mosaics: one depicting the story of Jonah and the whale; the other—more splendid—carved with fantastic beasts and resting on a pride of lions.

To the right of the cathedral is the entrance to the 11th-century **Villa Rufolo.** The composer Richard Wagner once stayed in Ravello, and there is a Wagner festival every summer on the villa's garden terrace. There is a Moorish cloister with interlacing pointed arches, beautiful gardens, an 11th-century tower, and a belvedere with a fine view of the coast. *Admission: 3,000 lire. Open summer, daily 9:30–1 and 3–7:30; winter, daily 9:30–1, 2–4:30.*

Across the square from the cathedral is a lovely walk leading to the **Villa Cimbrone.** At the entrance to the villa complex is a small cloister that looks medieval but was actually built in 1917, with two bas-reliefs: one representing nine Norman warriors, the other illustrating the seven deadly sins. Then, the long avenue leads through peaceful gardens scattered with grottoes, small temples, and statues to a belvedere and terrace where, on a clear day, the view stretches out over the Mediterranean Sea. *Admission: 5,000 lire. Open daily 8:30–1 hr before sunset.*

Dining and Lodging

For details and price-category definitions, *see* Dining *and* Lodging *in* Staying in Italy, *above.*

Amalfi

DINING

La Caravella. Tucked away under some arches lining the coast road, the Caravella has a nondescript entrance but a pleasant interior decorated in a medley of colors and paintings of old Amalfi. It's small and intimate, and proprietor Franco describes the cuisine as *"sfiziosa"* (taste-tempting). Specialties include *scialatielli* (homemade pasta with shellfish sauce) and *pesce al limone* (fresh fish with lemon sauce). *Via M. Camera 12, tel. 089/871029. Reservations advised. AE, MC, V. Closed Tues. and Nov. 10–30. $*

LODGING

★ **Santa Caterina.** A large mansion perched above terraced and flowered hillsides on the coast road just outside Amalfi proper, the Santa Caterina is one of the best hotels on the entire coast. The rooms are tastefully decorated, and most have small terraces or balconies with great views. There are lounges and terraces for relaxing, and an elevator whisks guests down to the seaside saltwater pool, bar, and swimming area. Amid lemon and orange groves, there are two romantic villa annexes. Some rooms and suites are in the **$$$$** category. *Strada Amalfitana 9,* tel. 089/871012, fax 089/871351. 54 rooms with bath. Facilities: restaurant, bar, pool, beach bar, parking. AE, DC, MC, V. $$$–$$$$

Capri

DINING

La Capannina. Only a few steps away from Capri's social center, the Piazzetta, La Capannina has a delightful vine-hung courtyard for summer dining and a reputation as one of the island's best eating places. Antipasto features fried ravioli and eggplant stuffed with ricotta, and house specialties include chicken, scaloppini and a refreshing, homemade lemon liqueur. Via Botteghe 14, tel. 081/837–0732. Reservations advised. AE, MC, V. Closed Wed. (except during Aug.) and Nov.–mid-Mar. $$–$$$

Da Gemma. One of Capri's favorite places for a homey atmosphere and a good meal, Da Gemma features pappardelle all'aragosta and fritto misto. If you're on a budget, forgo the fish that you pay for by weight—it's always expensive. Pizza makes a great starter in the evening. Via Madre Serafina 6, tel. 081/837–0461. Reservations advised. AE, DC, MC, V. Closed Mon. and Nov. $

★ **Al Grottino.** This small family-run restaurant, with a handy location near the Piazzetta, sports autographed photographs of celebrity customers. House specialties are gnocchi with mozzarella and linguine con gamberini (with shrimp sauce). Via Longano 27, tel. 081/837–0584. Dinner reservations advised. AE, MC, V. Closed Tues. and Nov. 3–Mar. 20. $

LODGING

Quisisana. One of Italy's poshest hotels is right in the center of the town of Capri. The rooms are spacious, and many have arcaded balconies with views of the sea; the decor is traditional or contemporary, with some antique accents. From the small terrace at the entrance you can watch all Capri go by, but the enclosed garden and pool in the back are perfect for getting away from it all. The bar and restaurant are casual in a terribly elegant way. Via Camerelle 2, tel. 081/837–0788, fax 081/837–6080. 143 rooms with bath. Facilities: restaurant, pool, tennis court. AE, DC, MC, V. Closed Nov.–mid-Mar. $$$$

★ **Villa Brunella.** The glassed-in bar of this family-run hotel is on the lane leading to Punta Tragara and the Faraglioni. From that level you descend to the restaurant, with the rooms and the swimming pool all on lower levels. Furnishings are tastefully casual and comfortable, and the views from all levels are wonderful. Be prepared to climb stairs; there's no elevator. Via Tragara 24, tel. 081/837–0122, fax 081/837–0430. 18 rooms with bath. Facilities: restaurant, bar, pool. AE, DC, MC, V. Closed Nov.–Mar. $$$

Villa Sarah. Just a 10-minute walk from the Piazzetta, the Sarah is a whitewashed Mediterranean villa with bright, simply furnished rooms. There's a garden and small bar, but no restaurant. Via Tiberio 3/A, tel. 081/837–7817, fax 081/837–7215. 20 rooms with bath. Facilities: bar, garden. AE, MC, V. Closed Nov.–Mar. $$

Naples

DINING

La Sacrestia. This lovely restaurant is in an elevated position, above Mergellina, with a fine view and a delightful summer terrace. The menu offers traditional Neapolitan cuisine; among the specialties are sea bass, either steamed or baked, and linguine in salsa di scorfano (scorpion-fish sauce). Via Orazio 116, tel. 081/761–1051. Reservations advised. AE, DC, MC, V. Closed Mon. Sept.–June, Sun. in July, and Aug. $$$

★ **Ciro a Santa Brigida.** Centrally located off Via Toledo near the Castel Nuovo, this no-frills restaurant is a favorite with businesspeople, artists, and journalists. Tables are arranged on two levels, and the decor is classic trattoria. This is the place to try traditional Neapolitan *sartù di riso* (a rich rice dish with meat and peas) and *melanzane alla parmigiana* or scaloppe *alla Ciro* (eggplant or veal with prosciutto and mozzarella). There's pizza, too. *Via Santa Brigida 71, tel. 081/552–4072. Reservations advised. AE, DC, MC, V. Closed Sun. and 2 wks in Aug. $$*

La Bersagliera. This restaurant has been making tourists happy for years, with a great location on the Santa Lucia waterfront, cheerful waiters, mandolin music, and good spaghetti *alla disgraziata* (with tomatoes, capers, and black olives) and fried mozzarella in *carrozza* (batter). *Borgo Marinaro 10, tel. 081/764–6016. Reservations advised. AE, DC, MC, V. Closed Tues. $$*

<u>LODGING</u>

Excelsior. Splendidly located on the shore drive, the Excelsior has views of the bay from its front rooms. The spacious bedrooms are well furnished in informal floral prints or more formal Empire style; all have a comfortable, traditional air. The salons are formal, with chandeliers and wall paintings, and the excellent Casanova restaurant is elegant. *Via Partenope 48, tel. 081/764–0111, fax 081/764–9743. 102 rooms with bath. Facilities: restaurant, bar, sauna, parking. AE, DC, MC, V. $$$$*

★ **Jolly Ambassador.** This hotel occupies the top 14 floors of a downtown skyscraper, and its rooms and roof restaurant have wonderful views of Naples and the bay. It's furnished in the functional, modern style typical of this reliable chain, which promises comfort and efficiency in a city where these are scarce commodities. *Via Medina 70, tel. 081/416000, fax 081/551–8010. 251 rooms with bath. Facilities: restaurant, bar, parking. AE, DC, MC, V. $$–$$$*

Rex. This hotel occupies a fairly quiet location near the Santa Lucia waterfront. It is situated on the first two floors of an Art Nouveau building and lacks an elevator. The decor ranges from 1950s modern to fake period pieces and even some folk art, haphazardly combined. Although it has no restaurant, there are many in the area. *Via Palepoli 12, tel. 081/764–9389, fax 081/764–9227. 40 rooms, 37 with bath or shower. Facilities: bar, parking. AE, DC, MC, V. $$*

Positano

<u>DINING</u>

Capurale. Among all the popular restaurants on the beach promenade, Capurale (just around the corner) has the best food and lowest prices. Tables are set under vines on a breezy sidewalk in the summer, upstairs and indoors in winter. Spaghetti con melanzane and crepes *al formaggio* (cheese-filled crepes) are good choices here. *Via Regina Giovanna 12, tel. 089/875374. Reservations advised for outdoor tables. AE, DC, MC, V. Closed Tues. Nov.–Mar. $$*

<u>LODGING</u>

Le Sirenuse. The most fashionable hotel in Positano, this renovated 18th-century villa has been in the same family for eight generations. The hotel is set into the hillside about 200 feet above Positano's harbor. Most of the bedrooms face the sea—these are the best. Because of the hotel's location, the dining room is like a long, closed-in terrace overlooking the village of Positano—a magnificent view. The cuisine varies from acceptable to excellent. *Via Cristoforo Colombo 30, tel. 089/875066, fax 081/811798. 60 rooms with bath or shower. Facilities: restaurant, bar, pool, sauna, parking. AE, DC, MC, V. $$$$*

San Pietro. Situated on the side of a cliff, this is quite possibly one of the world's most attractive hotels because of its magnificent views of the sea and the Amalfi coast. The decor of the hotel is eclectic, with unusual antiques and, everywhere, hanging bougainvillea. The furnishings are perfectly arranged to give a sense of openness and create a feeling of opulence. The guest rooms are decorated with an eye to detail but the window views steal the show. Verdant with plants, the light, open dining room offers fine Italian cuisine. An elevator takes guests to the hotel's small beach area. *Via Laurito 2, tel. 089/875455, fax 089/811449. 60 rooms with bath. Facilities: restaurant, pool, beach, tennis. AE, DC, MC, V. Closed Nov.–Mar. $$$$*

Palazzo Murat. The location is perfect, in the heart of town, near the beachside promenade and set within a walled garden. The old wing is a historic palazzo, with tall windows and wrought-iron balconies; the newer wing is a whitewashed Mediterranean building with arches and terraces. Guests can relax in antiques-strewn lounges or on the charming vine-draped patio. *Via dei Mulini 23, tel. 089/875177, fax 089/811419. 28 rooms with bath. Facilities: bar, garden. AE, DC, MC, V. Closed Nov. 5–Mar. $$$*

Santa Caterina. There is more to this newly refurbished hotel than meets the eye, with rooms descending on three levels down the steep slope. The exquisite view over the town and seashore can be relished from each of the somewhat cramped rooms as well as the generous balconies and terraces. On street level (the top floor), there is also a good fish restaurant, well patronized by the locals. It's quite a hike down to the beach—a good 15 minutes down the steps—but that's nothing new in Positano. *Via Pasitea 113. tel. 089/857019. 10 rooms with bath or shower. Facilities: restaurant, bar. AE, DC, MC, V. Closed Nov.–Mar. $*

Ravello

LODGING

Hotel Palumbo. Of all the hotels on the Amalfi coast, the Hotel Palumbo is the most genteel—and one of its most costly. Occupying a 12th-century patrician palace furnished with antiques and endowed with modern comforts, this hotel has an elegant, warm atmosphere. With lovely garden terraces, breathtaking views, and a sumptuous upstairs dining room, the hotel is a memorable one. Some of the bedrooms are small, but they are full of character. The rooms facing the sea are the choice ones—and the more expensive. With the greatest of ease, guests quickly come to view the Hotel Palumbo as their private palazzo. *Via Toro 28, tel. 089/857244, fax 089/857347. 12 rooms with bath. Facilities: restaurant, bar, garden. AE, DC, MC, V. $$$$*

Sorrento

DINING

Antica Trattoria. This is a homey, hospitable place with a garden for summer dining. The specialties of the house are a classic pennette *al profumo di bosco* (with a creamy mushroom and ham sauce), fish (which can be expensive), and *gamberetti freschi* Antica Trattoria (shrimp in a tomato sauce). *Via Giuliani 33, tel. 081/807–1082. Dinner reservations advised. No credit cards. Closed Mon., Jan. 10–Feb. 10. $$*

La Belle Epoque. Occupying a 19th-century villa perched on the edge of the vine-covered gorge of the Mulini, this is an elegant veranda restaurant. Try the scialatielli *alla siciliana* (with mozzarella and eggplant). *Via Fuorimura 7, tel. 081/878–1216. Reservations advised. AE, DC, MC, V. Closed Mon. $$*

★ **Parrucchiano.** One of the town's best and oldest, Parrucchiano features greenhouse-type dining rooms dripping with vines and dotted with plants. Among the antipasti, try the *panzarotti* (pastry crust filled with mozzarella and tomato), and for a main course, the scaloppe *alla sorrentina*, again with mozzarella and tomato. *Corso Italia 71, tel. 081/878–1321. Weekend and Aug. reservations advised. MC, V. Closed Wed. Nov.–May. $$*

LODGING

Cocumella. In a lovely cliff-side garden in a quiet residential area just outside Sorrento, this historic old villa (it features a 17th-century chapel) has been totally renovated for comfort. Furnishings are a tasteful blend of antique and modern; there are vaulted ceilings and archways, a dining veranda, and stunning tiled floors. Cocumella has an exclusive, elegant atmosphere without being stuffy. *Via Cocumella 7, tel. 081/878–2933, fax 081/878–3712. 60 rooms with bath. Facilities: restaurant, pool, garden, tennis court, parking. AE, DC, MC, V. Closed Jan.–Feb. $$$$*

Excelsior Vittoria. In the heart of Sorrento, but removed from the main square by an arbored walk, the Excelsior Vittoria is right on the cliff and has old-fashioned, Art Nouveau furnishings, some very grand, though faded. Tenor Enrico Caruso's bedroom is preserved as a relic; guest bedrooms are spacious and elegant in a turn-of-the-century way. It overlooks the bay and is recommended for those who like a lot of atmosphere with their views. *Piazza Tasso 34, tel. 081/807–1044, fax 081/877–1206. 106 rooms with bath. Facilities: restaurant, pool, garden, parking. AE, DC, MC, V. $$$$*

Imperial Hotel Tramontano. Incorporating the birthplace of the poet Torquato Tasso—the first of an impressive list of literary credentials—this palatial villa lies within a semitropical garden in the center of Sorrento. The sumptuous furnishings and Belle Epoque tone are set off by the spectacular views out to sea. *Via Veneto 1, tel. 081/878–2588, fax 081/807–2344. 120 rooms with bath or shower. Facilities: restaurant, bar, garden, private beach, meeting rooms, parking. Closed Dec.–Mar. AE, DC, MC, V. $$$*

Eden. Eden occupies a fairly quiet but central location, with a garden. The bedrooms are bright but undistinguished; the lounge and lobby have more character. It's an unpretentious but friendly hotel, although it can get crowded in high season. *Via Correale 25, tel. 081/878–1909, fax 081/807–2016. 60 rooms with bath. Facilities: restaurant, bar, pool, parking. AE, MC, V. Closed Nov.–Feb. $$*

City. The central location and excellent value-for-money are the best reasons to stay in this modest establishment, close to the bus and train stations. Bedrooms are small and functional, but the atmosphere is relaxed and the management always ready with information and advice. *Corso Italia 221, tel. 081/877–2210, fax 081/877–2210. 13 rooms with shower. AE, MC, V. $*

19 Luxembourg

ENTERING THE EPONYMOUS CAPITAL of tiny Luxembourg across the Grand Duchess Charlotte Bridge, first-time visitors are greeted by an awe-inspiring panorama of medieval stonework fortifications and massive gates. Then the visitors turn left—and enter the 20th century. The boulevard Royal, crowded with luxury automobiles, glitters with glass-and-concrete office buildings. Luxembourg, until recently little more than a cluster of meager farms and failing mines, flaunts new wealth, new political muscle, and the fourth-highest standard of living in the world.

One of the smallest countries in the United Nations, Luxembourg measures only 2,587 square kilometers (999 square miles), less than the size of Rhode Island. It is dwarfed by its neighbors—Germany, Belgium, and France—yet from its history of invasion, occupation, and siege, you might think those square miles were built over solid gold. In fact, it was Luxembourg's very defenses against centuries of attack that rendered it all the more desirable: From AD 963, when Siegfried built a castle on the high promontory of the Bock, the once-grander duchy encased itself in layer upon layer of fortifications until by the mid-19th century its very invulnerability was considered a threat to those not commanding its thick stone walls. After successive invasions—by the Burgundians, the Spanish, the French, the Austrians, the French again, the Dutch, and the Prussians—Luxembourg was ultimately dismantled in the name of peace, its neutrality guaranteed by the 1867 Treaty of London, and its function reduced to that of a buffer zone. What remains of its walls, while impressive, is only a reminder of what was one of the strongholds of Europe—the "Gibraltar of the North."

Luxembourg is besieged again, this time by bankers and Eurocrats. Its boulevard Royal bristles with international banks—enough to rival Switzerland—and just outside the old city, a new colony has been populated by *fonctionnaires* for the European Union (EU), the heir to the Common Market. Fiercely protecting its share of the expanding bureaucracy from competitive co-capitals Strasbourg and Brussels, Luxembourg digs its heels in once again, vying not only for political autonomy but also for its newfound prosperity and clout. In this it will be helped by the new president of the union's powerful European Commission, Jacques Santer, who was the prime minister of Luxembourg for a decade. Thus the national motto takes on new meaning: *Mir wëlle bleiwe wat mir sin,* or "We want to stay what we are"—nowadays, a viable Grand Duchy in the heart of modern Europe.

Visitors will find evidence of Luxembourg's military past scattered around the Grand Duchy's luxurious countryside: There are castles by the dozen, set in the densely wooded hills of La Petite Suisse (Little Switzerland) to the east, in the crests and valleys of the Ardennes to the north, and along the riverbanks of the Our and the Moselle.

ESSENTIAL INFORMATION

Before You Go

When to Go

The main tourist season in Luxembourg is the same as in Belgium—early May to late September, with spring and fall the nicest times. But temperatures in Luxembourg tend to be cooler than those in Belgium, particularly in the hilly north, where there is frequently snow in winter.

Luxembourg

CLIMATE

In general, temperatures in Luxembourg are moderate. It does drizzle frequently, however, so be sure to bring a raincoat. The following are the average daily maximum and minimum temperatures for Luxembourg.

Jan.	37F	3C	May	65F	18C	Sept.	66F	19C
	29	– 1		46	8		50	10
Feb.	40F	4C	June	70F	21C	Oct.	56F	13C
	31	– 1		52	11		43	6
Mar.	49F	10C	July	73F	23C	Nov.	44F	7C
	35	1		55	13		37	3
Apr.	57F	14C	Aug.	71F	22C	Dec.	39F	4C
	40	4		54	12		32	0

Currency

In Luxembourg, as in Belgium, the unit of currency is the franc (abbreviated *Flux*). Luxembourg issues its own currency in bills of 100, 500, 1,000 and 5,000 francs and coins of 1, 5, 20, and 50 francs. Belgian currency can be used freely in Luxembourg, and the two currencies have exactly the same value. However, Luxembourg currency is not valid in Belgium. At press time (spring 1995), the exchange rate was Flux 28 to the U.S. dollar and Flux 45 to the pound sterling.

What It Will Cost

Luxembourg is a developed and sophisticated country with a high standard and cost of living. Luxembourg City is an international banking center, and a number of European institutions are based there, a fact that tends to push prices slightly higher in the capital.

SAMPLE PRICES

Cup of coffee, Flux 50; glass of beer, Flux 40–Flux 60; movie ticket, Flux 170–Flux 200; 3-mile taxi ride, Flux 600.

Customs on Arrival

For information on customs regulations, *see* Essential Information *in* Chapter 4, Belgium.

Language

Native Luxembourgers speak three languages fluently: Luxembourgish, German, and French. Many also speak English.

Staying in Luxembourg

Telephones

LOCAL CALLS

You can find public phones both on the street and in city post offices. A local call costs Flux 5 per three-minute period from a public phone (slightly more from restaurants and gas stations). No area codes are needed when you call within the Grand Duchy. Post offices also sell a Telekaart, in units of Flux 50 and Flux 150, that can be used in nearly half the booths in the Grand Duchy. For operator-assisted calls, dial 0010.

INTERNATIONAL CALLS

The cheapest way to make an international call is to dial direct from a public phone; in a post office, you may be required to make a deposit before the call. To reach an **AT&T** long-distance operator, dial 0800–0111; for **MCI**, dial 0800–0112; for **Sprint,** dial 0800–0115.

COUNTRY CODE

The country code for Luxembourg is 352.

Mail

POSTAL RATES

Airmail postcards and letters weighing less than 20 grams cost Flux 22 to the United States. Letters and postcards to the United Kingdom cost Flux 14.

RECEIVING MAIL

Holders of American Express cards or traveler's checks can have mail sent in care of American Express (34 av. de la Porte-Neuve, 2227 Luxembourg).

Shopping

SALES TAX REFUNDS

Purchases of goods for export may qualify for a sales tax (TVA) refund of 12%. Ask the shop to fill out a refund form. You must then have the form stamped by customs officers on leaving either Luxembourg, Belgium, or Holland.

Opening and Closing Times

Banks. These are generally are open weekdays 8:30–noon and 1:30–4:30, though more and more remain open through the lunch hour.

Museums. Opening hours vary, so check individual listings. Many close on Monday, and most also close for lunch between noon and 2.

Shops. Large city department stores and shops are generally open weekdays, except Monday morning, and Saturday 9–noon and 2–6. A few small family businesses are open Sunday morning from 8 to noon.

National Holidays

January 1; February 19, 20 (Carnival); April 8 (Easter Monday); May 1 (May Day); May 16 (Ascension); May 27 (Pentecost Monday); June

23 (National Day); August 15 (Assumption); November 1 (All Saints' Day); November 2 (All Souls' Day); December 25, 26.

Dining

Restaurants in Luxembourg offer their best deals at lunch, when you can find a *plat du jour* (one-course special) or *menu* (two or three courses included in price) at bargain rates. Pizzerias offer an excellent and popular source of cheap food, with pasta, risottos, and wood-oven pizzas making a full meal. Light lunches—easy on the stomach if not always the wallet—can be found in chic pastry shops, where you point to the dishes on display, then take your number to the *salon de consommation*, where your drink order will be taken and your meal served.

MEALTIMES

Most hotels serve breakfast until 10. Lunch hours are noon–2, sometimes extending until 3. Long accustomed to the Continental style of dining heavily at midday, business-conscious Luxembourgers now eat their main meal in the evening between 7 and 10.

Lodging

HOTELS

Most hotels in Luxembourg City are relatively modern and vary from the international style, mainly near the airport, to family-run establishments in town. Outside the capital, many hotels are housed in more picturesque buildings. Prices vary considerably between town and country, but as Luxembourg City is an important business center, many of its hotels offer reduced rates on weekends.

YOUTH HOSTELS

Inexpensive youth hostels are plentiful; many are set in ancient fortresses and castles. For information, contact **Centrale des Auberges de Jeunesse** (18 pl. d'Armes, L-1136 Luxembourg, tel. 225588).

CAMPING

The Grand Duchy is probably the best-organized country in Europe for camping. It offers some 120 sites, all with full amenities. Listings are published annually by the national tourist office (*see* Important Addresses and Numbers *in* Staying in Luxembourg City, *below.*)

Tipping

In Luxembourg hotels and restaurants, taxes and service charges are included in the overall bill. If you wish to tip, round off the sum to the nearest Flux 50 or Flux 100. Bellhops and doormen should receive between Flux 50 and Flux 100, depending on the grade of the hotel. At the movies, tip the usher Flux 20 if you are seated personally. In theaters, tip about Flux 20 for checking your coat, and the same to the program seller. Public washroom attendants receive between Flux 5 and 10. Taxi drivers expect a tip; add about 15% to the amount on the meter.

LUXEMBOURG CITY

Arriving and Departing

By Plane

All international flights arrive at Luxembourg's Findel Airport, 6 kilometers (4 miles) from the city.

BETWEEN THE AIRPORT AND DOWNTOWN

Bus 9 leaves the airport at regular intervals for the city center; it then continues to the main bus depot, next to the train station. Individual tickets cost Flux 35. A taxi will cost you Flux 700–Flux 800. If you are driving, follow the signs for the Centre Ville (city center).

By Train

Luxembourg is served by frequent direct trains from Paris and Brussels. From Paris, travel time is about four hours; from Brussels, just under three hours. From Amsterdam, the journey is via Brussels and takes about six hours. There are connections from most German cities via Koblenz. Outside Luxembourg City, three major train routes extend north, south, and east into the Moselle Valley. For all train information, phone 492424. All service is from Gare Centrale in place de la Gare.

Getting Around

One of the best transportation options is the **Oeko-Carnet,** a block of five one-day tickets good for unlimited transportation on trains and buses throughout the country. Cards are on sale for Flux 540 at Gare Centrale (the main train station) in Luxembourg City, or at Aldringen Center, located underground in front of the central post office.

By Bus

Luxembourg City has a highly efficient bus service. The blue-and-yellow buses outside the city train station will take you all around the city and also to some of the outlying areas. Get details about services at the information counter in the station arrivals hall. Fares are low, but the best bet is to buy a 10-ride ticket (Flux 270), available from banks or from the bus station in the Aldringen Center. Other buses, connecting Luxembourg City with towns throughout the country, leave from Gare Centrale.

By Car

A car is a liability in this small, walkable city. You can easily see the rest of the country in a day or two, and you might want to rent a car for this purpose. Major highways and smaller roads are excellent and fairly uncrowded. Speed limits are 120 kph (70 mph) on highways, 90 kph (55 mph) on major roads, and 50 kph (30 mph) in built-up areas.

Street parking in Luxembourg City is difficult. Make use of one of the underground parking lots, or park at the sizable Parking Glacis next to the Municipal Theater, five minutes' walk from the city center.

By Bicycle

Bicycling is an excellent way to see the city and outlying regions. A brochure, "Cycling Tracks," is available from the Luxembourg National Tourist Office (Box 1001, L-1010 Luxembourg, tel. 481199). Bikes can be rented in Luxembourg City at **Luxembourg DELTA** (8 Bisserwee, tel. 4796–2383), from March 30 through October 31; in Reisdorf, Diekirch, and Echternach, rent bikes at the tourist office (**Syndicat d'Initiative**). Maps are available from the local tourist offices.

By Taxi

There are taxi stands near Gare Centrale and the main post office; it is almost impossible to stop one in the streets. To call a taxi, phone 480058 or 482233.

Important Addresses and Numbers

Tourist Information

The main **Luxembourg National Tourist Office (ONT)** in Luxembourg City (Aerogare bus depot, pl. de la Gare, tel. 481199) is open daily (except Sun. Nov.–Mar.) 9–noon and 2–6:30 (July–mid-Sept., 9–7).

The **Luxembourg City Tourist Office** (pl. d'Armes, tel. 222809) is open mid-September–mid-June, Monday–Saturday 9–1 and 2–6; mid-June–mid-September, weekdays 9–7, Saturday 9–1 and 2–7, Sunday 10–noon and 2–6.

Embassies

U.S. (22 blvd. Emmanuel Servais, tel. 460123). **Canada:** The Belgian embassy (av. de Tervuren 2, B-1040 Brussels, Belgium, tel. 00322/741–06–11) covers Luxembourg. **U.K.** (14 blvd. F. D. Roosevelt, tel. 229864).

Emergencies

Police (tel. 113). **Ambulance, Doctor, Dentist** (tel. 112). **Pharmacies** in Luxembourg stay open nights on a rotation system. Signs listing late-night facilities are posted outside each pharmacy.

Books in English

For books and magazines in English, try **Magasin Anglais** (13 allée Scheffer, tel. 224925).

Travel Agencies

American Express (34 av. de la Porte-Neuve, tel. 228555). **CIT** (pl. de la Gare, tel. 485102). **Emile Weitzel** (15 rue Notree-Dame, tel. 22931). **Keiser Tours** (34 rue Philippe II, tel. 472717). **Sotour** (including youth travel; 15 pl. du Theatre, tel. 461514). **Wagons-Lits (Thomas Cook)** (99 Grand'rue, 460315).

Guided Tours

Orientation Tours

Sales-Lentz (26 rue du Curé, L-1368, tel. 46181) offers tours every morning from April through October. The tours leave from Platform 5 of the bus station (next to the railway station) or from the war memorial in place de la Constitution. They visit the historic sights of the center, the area housing various branches of the EU, and some of the villas on the city outskirts. Tours cost Flux 290. Another tour takes in the monuments of Luxembourg City, the cemeteries, and the castle of Bourglinster (Apr., May, and Oct., weekends 2:30–5:45; June–Sept., Tues., Thurs., Sat., and Sun. 2:30–5:45; Flux 320). Other more complete tours of the Grand Duchy are available to groups of 10 or more.

Special-Interest Tours

From April through October, guided minitrain tours of the Old Town and the Pétrusse Valley start from the place de la Constitution (tel. 461617; Flux 230 adults, Flux 160 children under 17).

Walking Tours

The guided walking tour "1,000 Years in 100 Minutes" was introduced in 1995; check with the Luxembourg City Tourist Office in the place d'Armes. You can rent a self-guided city tour with headphones and cassette at the bus booth on the place de la Constitution for Flux 180 (a refundable deposit of Flux 1,000 is required). For information on weekend walking tours, contact the tourist office or the **Fédération Luxembourgeoise des Marches Populaires** (Boite Postale 794, L-2018 Luxembourg). Also consult the **Agenda Touristique,** published by the ONT.

Excursions

Pick up the booklet "Circuits Auto-Pedestres," available at newsstands, bookstores, and the ONT (Flux 895), for information on combination driving-walking tours outside the city.

Exploring Luxembourg City

This walk takes in the ancient military fortifications and Old Town, with its cobbled streets and inviting public squares. In 1994 the United Nations Educational, Scientific, and Cultural Organization (UNESCO) declared these areas part of the world's architectural heritage.

Numbers in the margin correspond to points of interest on the Luxembourg City map.

① Start on the **Passerelle,** a 19th-century road bridge that links the station with the valley of the Pétrusse. The Pétrusse is more of a brook than a river and is now contained by concrete, but the valley has become a singularly beautiful park. From here you'll see the rocky ledges—partly natural, partly man-made—on which the city was founded.

② At the cathedral end of the Passerelle, on the right, take the steps and curving sidewalk up to **Monument de la Solidarité Nationale** (National Monument to Luxembourg Unity) and admire its perpetual flame. It was erected in 1971 to commemorate Luxembourg's sacrifices and intact survival following World War II.

③ To the right of the monument, follow the road along the remains of the old city fortifications, known as the **Citadelle du St-Esprit** (Citadel of the Holy Spirit). This 17th-century citadel was built by Vauban, the French military engineer, in the typical style of thrusting wedges. From the end you can see the three spires of the cathedral, the curve of the Alzette, and the incongruous white tower of the European Parliament secretariat.

④ Retrace your steps along the old city fortifications, cross boulevard F. D. Roosevelt, and continue on to the **place de la Constitution,** marked by a war memorial, the striking gilt *Gëlle Fra,* or Golden Woman. Here you'll find the entrance to the ancient **Pétrusse casemates,** military tunnels carved into the bedrock. During the many phases of the fortress's construction, the rock itself was hollowed out to form a honeycomb of passages running for nearly 24 kilometers (15 miles) below the town. These were used both for storage and as a place of refuge when the city was under attack. Two sections of the passages are open to the public. These sections contain former barracks, cavernous abattoirs, bakeries, and a deep well. *Pl. de la Constitution. Admission: Flux 50 adults, Flux 30 children. Open July–Sept.*

⑤ Take rue de l'ancien Athénée alongside the former Jesuit college, now the National Library. In rue Notre-Dame to your right is the main entrance to the 17th-century **Cathédrale Notree-Dame,** with its Baroque organ gallery and crypt containing the tomb of John the Blind, the 14th-century king of Bohemia and count of Luxembourg, as well as those of the grand-ducal family. The valley side of the church was rebuilt in 1935; the main tower was reroofed after a fire in 1985. *Open Easter–Oct., weekdays 10–5, Sat. 8–6, Sun. 10–6; Nov.–Easter, weekdays 10–11:30 and 2–5, Sat. 8–11:30 and 2–5, Sun. 10–5.*

⑥ Just east of the cathedral and past place Clairefontaine with its graceful statue of Grand Duchess Charlotte is the new **Musée d'Histoire de la Ville de Luxembourg** (Luxembourg City Historical Museum), which opened in 1995. This interactive multimedia museum traces the development of the city over 1,000 years and is partially underground, with the lowest five levels showing the town's preserved ancient stonework. A glass-wall elevator gives a wonderful view of the ravine

Luxembourg City

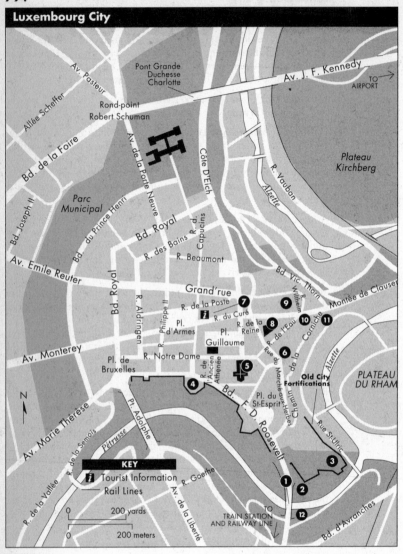

KEY

🛈 Tourist Information

— Rail Lines

0 ⊢———⊣ 200 yards

0 ⊢———⊣ 200 meters

Bock, **11**

Cathédrale
Notre-Dame, **5**

Chapelle de
St-Quirin, **12**

Citadelle du
St-Esprit, **3**

Grand Ducal
Palace, **8**

Maquette, **7**

Monument de la
Solidarité
Nationale, **2**

Musée d'Histoire de
la Ville de Luxem-
bourg, **6**

Musée National, **9**

Passerelle, **1**

Place de la
Constitution, **4**

St-Michel, **10**

from the upper floors. *38 rue du Marché-aux-Herbes. Open Tues.–Sun. 10–6, Thurs. until 8. Admission and tel. not available at press time.*

A couple of blocks northwest via the rue du Fossé is place Guillaume, known as the Knuedler, a name derived from the girdle worn by Franciscan monks who had a monastery on the site. On market days (Wednesday and Saturday mornings) the square is noisy and colorful.

The lively place d'Armes, with its cafés and restaurants, lies just beyond the place Guillaume. Open-air concerts are held every evening in summer. The city tourist office is on the square, and on rue du Curé **❼** there is a small museum that houses the **Maquette,** a model of the fortress at various stages of its construction: It provides a fascinating glimpse of the historical city. *Tel. 4796–2496. Admission: Flux 40 adults, Flux 20 children. Open July–Aug. only, daily 10–12:30 and 2–6.*

❽ From place Guillaume, rue de la Reine leads to the glorious **Grand Ducal Palace,** which dates from the 16th century. There is a distinct Spanish-Moorish influence in its elaborate ornamentation. Behind the palace is the oldest part of town, the Marché-aux-Poissons, site of the old fish market and originally the crossing point of two Roman roads.

❾ On the left is the **Musée National** (National Museum), set in an attractive row of 16th-century houses. The museum contains many objects that shed light on daily life during Gallo-Roman and Frankish times. The art gallery includes a fine Cranach and two Turner watercolors of the Luxembourg fortress. In the modern art collection, the major discovery for a visitor is the work of the expressionist Joseph Kutter, probably Luxembourg's greatest artist. The museum also hosts the spectacular Bentinck-Thyssen collection of 15th- to 19th-century art, including works by Brueghel, Rembrandt, Canaletto, and other masters. *Marché-aux-Poissons, tel. 479330. Admission free. Open Tues.–Fri. 10–4:45, Sat. 2–5:45, Sun. 10–11:45 and 2–5:45.*

TIME OUT In the rue Wiltheim, which runs alongside the National Museum, is the **Welle Man** (12 rue Wiltheim, tel. 471783), the quintessentially Luxembourgish museum bar. Sit on the tiny terrace and enjoy the magnificent view. Sip a glass of Elbling or Rivaner, local white wines, or try a *kir*, made from black-currant liqueur and white wine.

❿ At the bottom of rue Wiltheim is the gate of **St-Michel** and its Trois Tours (Three Towers), the oldest of which was built around 1050. During the French Revolution, the guillotine was set up in these towers. From here you can clearly see the source of Luxembourg's strength as a fortress.

⓫ To your right is the **Bock** promontory, the site of the earliest castle (AD 963) and always the Grand Duchy's most fortified point. From the Bock, steep cliffs plunge to the Alzette Valley. The Bock also has a series of passages similar to the Pétrusse casemates. *Casemates admission: Flux 50 adults, Flux 30 children. Open Mar.–Oct., daily 10–5.*

The scenic ramparts of the Bock's **corniche** provide a view over the lower town, known as the Grund. Many of the houses on the right were refuges, used in times of danger by nobles and churchmen from the surrounding area. The massive towers on the far side of the valley date to the Wenceslas fortifications, which, in 1390, extended the protected area, and the blocklike *casernes* (barracks) were built in the 17th century by the French.

At the ruined fortifications of the Citadelle du St-Ésprit, take the elevator down to the Grund, and turn right on leaving the tunnel. As you follow the valley below the cliffs, you'll see two signs marking the high-water points of two devastating floods; that's why the rivers have been tamed with locks and concrete today. Turn right into the green Pétrusse **⑫** Valley park. On the left, the little **Chapelle de St-Quirin** (Chapel of St. Quirin) is built into the rock near the Passerelle. The cave it surrounds is said to have been carved by the Celts; it is known to have housed a chapel since at least the 4th century. The relics of St. Quirin, transferred in 1050 from Avignon to Deutz-on-Rhine, spent a night in the chapel. At Pont Adolphe, walk back up to city level and you are suddenly face-to-face with the 20th century. The boulevard Royal, once the main moat of the fortress, is now Luxembourg's Wall Street, packed with the famous names of the international banking scene. Take the **Grand'rue** to the right. It widens to become a prosperous pedestrian shopping street, with boutiques bearing the same names as those on Fifth Avenue or Bond Street, sidewalk cafés, and tempting pastry shops.

Off the Beaten Track

Walk up boulevard Royal to rond-point Robert Schuman, named for one of the founders of the European Common Market, and cross the Pont Grande Duchesse Charlotte (with stunning views of the valley) to **Plateau Kirchberg,** a moonscape of modern architecture housing the European Court of Justice and various branches of the EU. The most prominent structure—at 23 stories, Luxembourg's only skyscraper— is home to the secretariat of the European Parliament. The area is increasingly adorned with modern sculpture and architecture. Recent additions include a work by Henry Moore near the Court of Justice, a replica of Carl Fredrik Reutersward's *Nonviolence* in front of the Jean Monnet Building, and a sculpture by Frank Stella in front of Frank Meier's Hypo Bank on rue Alphonse Weicker. Note also German architect Gottfried Boehm's Deutsche Bank Building on boulevard Konrad Adenauer. There are usually art exhibitions in its vast atrium.

Shopping

Luxembourg City has two main shopping areas: the **Grand'rue** and the **avenue de la Gare.** Jewelry and designer fashions are particularly well represented in the Grand'rue. There are a few small department stores near the train station, but most of the stores in this area are specialty shops. Luxembourg chocolates, called *knippercher,* are popular purchases, available from the best pastry shops. A leading patisserie is Oberweis (19 Grand'rue). Luxembourg's most famous product is Villeroy and Boch porcelain, available in most gift shops here. Feast your eyes at the glossy main shop at 2 rue du Fossé, then buy—at a 20% discount—at the excellent second-quality factory outlet (330 rue Rollingergrund).

Excursions from Luxembourg City

Diekirch

It would be a shame to leave Luxembourg without having explored some of the areas around the capital. To see the Ardennes, take Route N7 to **Diekirch,** where there is a church dating from the 7th century with Frankish tombs in the crypt. There are traces here of even older civilizations: the **Devil's Altar,** a Celtic dolmen, and some 4th-century Roman mosaics from nearby villas.

Echternach

Another rewarding drive is northeast on Route E29 to **Echternach,** where St. Willibrord, a 7th-century English missionary, founded a Benedictine abbey. Many of the abbey buildings are now schools, but each year on the Tuesday after Pentecost, 15,000 pilgrims flock to the basilica, on the site of the original chapel. In the crypt are frescoes dating from the 11th century and St. Willibrord's original sarcophagus. There's a charming, small hotel in Echternach, La Bergerie (47 route de Luxembourg, tel. 728504, fax 728508). A shuttle service links the hotel with the very expensive restaurant of the same name, a true gem set in the woods 7 kilometers (4 miles) away (1 Geyershof, tel. 79464). Between Echternach and Luxembourg City, a detour via Gorge de Loup (direction Diekirch) and Mullerthal takes you through the **Petite Suisse** and Luxembourg's prettiest scenery.

Northeast to Vianden

To take in some of Luxembourg's best castles, allow a full day to take E27 northeast toward Junglinster, then cut north to **Bourglinster,** complete with café; **Larochette,** its castle still inhabited, although the owners allow visitors to wander the older ruins out back; and **Beaufort,** a dramatic mix of ruins and restored chambers. Then follow the German border north to **Vianden,** perhaps the most spectacular of all; until recently it was in the possession of the grand duke's family.

Dining

"French quality, German quantity"—that's an apt and common description of Luxembourg cuisine. Yet this tiny country has its own earthy specialties, fresh off the farm: *judd mat gardebounen* (salted pork with fava beans); *Eslecker ham* or *jambon d'Ardennes* (pearly pink smoked ham served cold with pickled onions); *choucroute* (sauerkraut); *treipen* (blood pudding); and batter-fried *merlan* (whiting). A few restaurants still feature them, though nowadays you're as likely to find Chinese, Thai, Japanese, Indian, and—leading the ethnic selection by several laps— Italian. And there are more star-studded restaurants in Luxembourg per capita than in any other European country. Many restaurants— including some of these world-class venues—offer an accessibly priced menu at lunch. Crisp, fruity white wines range from the humble Elbling and Rivaner to fine Pinot Gris and Riesling.

WHAT TO WEAR

Stylish, casual dress is generally acceptable in most restaurants, but when in doubt, err on the formal side. In expensive French restaurants, formal dress (jacket and tie) is taken for granted.

RATINGS

Prices quoted here are per person and include a first course, main course, and dessert, but not wine. Highly recommended restaurants are indicated by a star ★.

CATEGORY	ALL AREAS
$$$$	over Flux 3,000
$$$	Flux 1,500–3,000
$$	Flux 750–1,500
$	under Flux 750

$$$$ **Clairefontaine.** This lavish but dignified dining spot attracts luminar-
★ ies who are pampered by chef Tony Tintinger. His inspirations include a showcase of foie gras specialties, innovative fish dishes (soufflé of langoustines perfumed with star anise), and game novelties (tourne-

dos of doe with wild mushrooms). There's a business lunch, a three-course prix-fixe, and a thorough tasting menu. *9 pl. de Clairefontaine, tel. 462211. Reservations required. Jacket and tie. AE, DC, MC, V. Closed Sun., 3 wks in Aug., and 1st wk in Nov. No dinner Sat.*

\$\$\$ ★ **Am Pays.** Seriously good fish, such as grilled sea bass infused with basil, and saffron-flavored monkfish, is served in this bandbox bistro, which has booths downstairs and a more formal dining room up a winding staircase. In August, Am Pays is the only ambitious restaurant to stay open. *20 rue du Curé, tel. 222618. Reservations advised. AE, DC, MC, V. Closed Sun. and Feb. No lunch Sat.*

\$\$\$ **La Lorraine.** Strategically placed on the place d'Armes, this restaurant specializes in outstanding seafood. A retail shop around the corner shows off the coast-fresh quality of their wares: heaps of briny oysters, glistening turbot and sole, wriggling crabs. Baked skate (in hazelnut butter with capers) and puff pastry with sole and morels are good bets. *7 pl. d'Armes, tel. 474620. Reservations advised. Jacket required. AE, DC, MC, V. Closed Sun. and 3 wks in Aug./Sept. No lunch Sat.*

\$\$\$ **Speltz.** In a chic, restored 17th-century home in the middle of the pedestrian shopping area, this stylish restaurant caters to a young business crowd, serving a reasonable prix-fixe lunch that may include Vosges quail in Armagnac gelée, or venison stew with herbed *spätzle* (small dumplings). *8 rue Chimay, tel. 474950. Reservations advised. Jacket and tie. AE, DC, MC, V. Closed Sat., Sun., Easter wk, and 2 wks in July/Aug.*

\$\$ **Ancre d'Or.** This tidy, friendly brasserie, just off the place Guillaume, serves a wide variety of old-time Luxembourgish specialties. Try their judd mat gardebounen, *kuddelfleck* (breaded tripe), or treipen. The apple tart (Luxembourgish style, with custard base) is homemade. Portions are generous, service is friendly, and the clientele is local. *23 rue du Fossé, tel. 472973. Reservations advised at lunch. MC, V. Closed Sun.*

\$\$ **Kamakura.** If heavy Western cuisine palls, take the elevator from the Citadelle du St-Esprit to the up-and-coming Grund and try this chic Japanese restaurant. A number of prix-fixe menus offer delicate, nouvelle-accented dishes, artfully presented and graciously served. À la carte specialties, considerably more expensive, include impeccably fresh sashimi (raw fish) and light tempura vegetables. *2–4 rue Munster, tel. 470604. Reservations advised. AE, DC, MC, V. Closed Sun.*

\$\$ **Mousel's Cantine.** Directly adjoining the great Mousel brewery, this fresh, comfortable café serves up heaping platters of local specialties—braised and grilled ham, sausage, fava beans, and fried potatoes—to be washed down with crockery steins of creamy *Gezwickelte Béier* (unfiltered beer). The front café is brighter, but the tiny fluorescent-lighted dining room has windows into the brewery. *46 montée de Clausen, tel. 470198. Reservations advised. MV, V. Closed Sun.*

\$\$ ★ **Times.** On a pedestrian-only street of art galleries and boutiques, you'll also find food that's an excellent value. The narrow dining room is lined with glass and Canadian cherrywood and often filled with artists and journalists. The cuisine is French with a Luxembourg accent, featuring ambitious creations like fillet of suckling pig cooked with tea, and five variations on the carpaccio theme. *8 rue Louvigny, tel 222722. Reservations advised. AE, DC, MC, V.*

\$ **Ems.** Across the street from the train station, this lively establishment with vinyl booths and posted specials draws a loyal clientele for its vast portions of *moules* (mussels) in a rich wine-and-garlic broth, accompanied by *frites* (french fries) and a bottle of sharp, cold Auxerrois or Rivaner. For dessert, try one of the huge ice-cream specialties. Food is served until 1 AM. *30 pl. de la Gare, tel. 487799. AE, DC, MC, V.*

$ Taverne Bit. With wooden tabletops and dark-wood banquettes, this is a cozy and very local pub, where you can drink a *clensch* (stein) of draft Bitburger beer (from just across the German border) and have a plate of sausage with good potato salad, a plate of cold ham, or *kachkeis,* the pungent local cheese spread, served with baked potatoes. It's just off the Parking Glacis. *43 allée Scheffer, tel. 460751. No credit cards. Closed Sun. No dinner Sat.*

Lodging

Hotels in Luxembourg City are in three main areas: the town center, near the train station, and close to the airport. By far the largest number are around the station. Most hotels are modern, but a warm welcome and high standards compensate for the relative lack of character.

RATINGS

Price categories are determined by the cost of a double room (Continental breakfast is sometimes included in the room price). Highly recommended lodgings are indicated by a star ★.

CATEGORY	COST
$$$$	over Flux 8,000
$$$	Flux 5,000–8,000
$$	Flux 2,500–5,000
$	under Flux 2,500

$$$$ Le Royal. In the city center, on the Wall Street of Luxembourg and within
★ steps of parks, shopping, and the Old Town, Le Royal is the best choice for luxury. It's solid, modern (opened 1984), and sleek, with a great deal of lacquer, marble, and glass, and pleasant lobbies on each floor. Opt for a quiet back room toward the park. The piano bar is popular, as is the brasserie Le Jardin, especially when the fountain terrace is open. The main restaurant, Le Relais Royal, is *the* place for power dining. *12 blvd. Royal, tel. 41616, fax 225948. 180 rooms with bath. Facilities: 2 restaurants, piano bar, exercise equipment, pool, hairdresser, sauna, and tennis. AE, DC, MC, V.*

$$$ Alviss-Parc. This modern hotel complex, with extensive conference facilities and an outdoor swimming pool, is just outside the city limits and traffic-clogged streets. It is especially useful as a base for excursions to the Ardennes. Rooms are restful, and the restaurant quite acceptable. *120 route d'Echternach, Dommeldange, tel. 435643, fax 436903. 271 rooms with bath. Facilities: restaurant, bar, conference rooms, parking. AE, DC, MC, V.*

$$$ Cravat. This charming Luxembourg relic—moderately grand, modestly
★ glamorous—straddles the valley and the Old Town in the best location in the city. Though corridors have a dated, institutional air, the rooms are fresh and welcoming in a variety of tastefully retro styles. The art deco coffee shop has been freshened up but despite its younger look still draws fur-hatted ladies of a certain age to tea. The prime minister and his cabinet can be found in the hotel tavern every Friday afternoon. *29 blvd. F. D. Roosevelt, tel. 221975, fax 226711. 60 rooms with bath. Facilities: restaurant, coffee shop, bar. AE, DC, MC, V.*

$$ Arcotel. Opened in 1985 on the busy shopping street between the Old Town and the train station, this airtight, modernized hotel provides a quiet refuge. Decorated in warm beige and rose, with polished wood and brass, it offers solid baths and extra comforts—hair dryers in the bathroom, drinks in the Bokhara-lined lounge—to make up for typically small rooms. *43 av. de la Gare, tel. 494001, fax 405624. 30 rooms with bath. Facilities: breakfast room. AE, DC, MC, V.*

$$ Auberge du Coin. At the edge of a quiet residential area but within easy reach of the station and the Old Town, this pleasant hotel has stone and terra-cotta floors, wood-frame double windows, polished oak, Oriental rugs, and tropical plants. Rooms are freshly furnished in bright knotty pine with new tile baths. There's a lovely French restaurant and a comfortable oak-and-stone bar. The nine rooms in the annex down the street cost slightly less, but the ground-floor rooms are in the basement, and there's no elevator. *2 blvd. de la Pétrusse, tel. 402101, fax 403666. 32 rooms with bath. Facilities: restaurant, bar. AE, DC, MC, V.*

$$ Hostellerie du Grunewald. A member of the Romantik group, the
★ Grunewald is just outside the city and at the high end of this category. The old-fashioned lounge is crammed with wing chairs, knickknacks, and old prints; rooms have Oriental rugs, rich fabrics, and Louis XV–style furniture. Garden-side rooms are worth booking ahead, although street-side windows are triple-glazed. The expensive restaurant serves rich, classic French cuisine. *10–14 route d'Echternach, Dommeldange, tel. 431882, fax 420646. 26 rooms with bath. Facilities: restaurant (closed Sun., no lunch Sat.), garden terrace. AE, DC, MC, V.*

$$ Italia. This is a valuable and remarkably inexpensive find: a former private apartment converted into hotel rooms, some with plaster details and cabinetry left behind. Rooms are solid and freshly furnished, all with private, tile bathrooms. The somewhat pricey restaurant downstairs is one of the city's better Italian eateries. *15–17 rue d'Anvers, tel. 486626, fax 480807. 20 rooms with bath. Facilities: restaurant, bar, garden. AE, DC, MC, V.*

$$ Sieweburen. At the northwestern end of the city is this attractively rus-
★ tic hotel, opened in 1991; the clean, large rooms have wooden beds and armoires. There are woods in the back and a playground in front. The brasserie-style tavern, older than the rest of the property, is hugely popular, especially when the terrace is open. *36 rue des Septfontaines, tel. 442356, fax 442353. 13 rooms with bath. Facilities: restaurant, garden, parking. AE, DC, MC, V.*

$ Bristol. Though on a street near the train station that is lined with strip joints and flophouses (as well as legitimate shops and restaurants), this modest hotel offers comfortable, secure lodging and fresh decor. The lobby-bar is warm and familial, and baths have been refurbished. A few bathless rooms on the first and fourth floors go for bargain rates. *11 rue de Strasbourg, tel. 485830, fax 486480. 30 rooms, 22 with shower/toilet. Facilities: bar for guests only. AE, DC, MC, V.*

$ Carlton. In this vast 1918 hotel, buffered from the rue de Strasbourg scene by a rank of stores and opening onto a quiet inner court, budget travelers will find roomy, quiet quarters. The beveled glass, oak parquet, and terrazzo floors are original—but so are the toilets, all down the hall. Each room has antique beds, floral-print comforters, and a sink; wooden floors, despite creaks, are white-glove clean. *9 rue de Strasbourg, tel. 484802, fax 486480. 50 rooms without toilet, 8 with shower. Facilities: breakfast room, bar. No credit cards.*

20 Malta

THE MEDITERRANEAN ISLAND OF MALTA and its two sister islands, Gozo and Comino, enjoy a mild, sunny climate and attractive bays and beaches—a fitting setting for such a festive and hospitable people.

For those interested in history and archaeology, tiny Malta—with only 28 kilometers (17 miles) between its two farthest points—displays the remains of a long and eventful past. Among the most fascinating ruins are Neolithic temples and stone megaliths left by prehistoric inhabitants. In AD 60, St. Paul, shipwrecked here, converted the people to Christianity. Other, less welcome visitors, attracted by Malta's strategic position, conquered and ruled. These included the Phoenicians, Carthaginians, Romans, Arabs, Normans, and Aragonese.

The Knights of the Order of St. John of Jerusalem arrived here in 1530 after they had been driven from their stronghold on the island of Rhodes by the Ottoman emperor Suleyman the Magnificent. In 1565, with only a handful of men, the knights held Malta against the Ottoman Turks in a dramatic and bloody siege. They left massive fortifications and rich architecture—including Valletta, Malta's capital—and ruled the islands until Napoléon arrived in 1798.

The British drove the French out in 1800 and gave the island a distinctive British feel, which it retains today. In 1942, during World War II, King George VI awarded the Maltese people the George Cross for their courage in withstanding repeated German and Italian attacks, especially from the air. Malta gained independence from Britain in 1964 and was declared a republic within the Commonwealth in 1974. On December 2–3, 1989, the island hosted the first Bush–Gorbachev summit, marking the beginning of improved relations between the two superpowers.

ESSENTIAL INFORMATION

Before You Go

When to Go

The archipelago is a year-round delight, but May through October is the main tourist season. April and May are the months for spring freshness; the summer months can be very hot, though sometimes tempered by sea breezes. August is just too hot for touring. If you visit in the winter, you'll find the climate pleasant and mild, but you may encounter sudden rainstorms.

CLIMATE

The following are the average daily maximum and minimum temperatures for Valletta.

Jan.	58F	14C	May	71F	22C	Sept.	81F	27C
	50	10		61	16		71	22
Feb.	59F	15C	June	79F	26C	Oct.	75F	24C
	51	10		67	19		66	19
Mar.	61F	16C	July	84F	29C	Nov.	67F	20C
	52	11		72	22		60	16
Apr.	65F	18C	Aug.	85F	29C	Dec.	61F	16C
	56	13		73	23		54	12

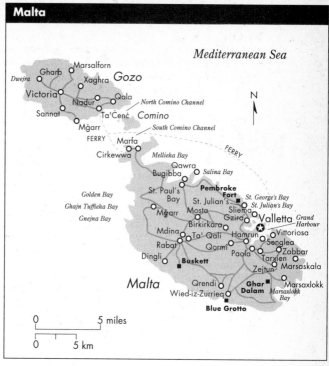

Malta

Mediterranean Sea

N

Marsalforn
Gharb *Xaghra* Gozo
Dwejra *Victoria* *Nadur* *Qala* *North Comino Channel*
Sannat *Ta'Ċenċ* Comino
Mġarr *South Comino Channel*
FERRY *Marfa*
Cirkewwa *Mellieha Bay* FERRY
Qawra
Bugibba *Salina Bay*
Golden Bay St. Paul's **Pembroke**
Bay **Fort** *St. George's Bay*
Ghajn Tuffieha Bay St. Julian's *St. Julian's Bay*
Gnejna Bay *Mġarr* *Mosta* *Gzira* Sliema Valletta *Grand*
Birkirkara *Harbour*
Mdina *Ta' Qali* *Hamrun* Vittoriosa
Rabat *Qormi* Senglea
Dingli *Paola* Zabbar
Buskett *Tarxien* Marsaskala
Zejtun
Malta *Qrendi* **Ghar** Marsaxlokk
Wied-iz-Zurrieq **Dalam** *Marsaxlokk*
Blue Grotto *Bay*

0 ———— 5 miles
0 ———— 5 km

Currency

The unit of currency is the Maltese lira (Lm), also sometimes referred to as the pound. It's divided into 100 cents, and the cents are divided into 10 mils; but in recent years the mils have dropped out of circulation. There are Lm 2, Lm 5, Lm 10, and Lm 20 bills; coins—1¢, 2¢, 5¢, 10¢, 25¢, 50¢, and Lm 1—are bronze and silver. At press time (spring 1995), the exchange rate was Lm .32 to the dollar and Lm .54 to the pound sterling.

What It Will Cost

Malta is one of the cheapest holiday destinations in Europe, though with the rapid development of tourism, prices are inevitably rising. Prices tend to be uniform across the island, except in Sliema and Valletta, the capital, where they are slightly higher. There is a value-added tax (VAT) of 15% on most services and goods purchased; restaurant meals have a 10% VAT.

SAMPLE PRICES
Cup of coffee, 25¢ (Maltese); bottle of beer, 25¢; Coca-Cola, 20¢.

Customs on Arrival

You may bring into Malta, duty-free, 200 cigarettes, one bottle of liquor, one bottle of wine, and one bottle of perfume. Up to Lm 50 in currency may be brought in.

Language

The spelling of many Maltese words can be bewildering. Fortunately, both Maltese and English are the official languages on the island, so you shouldn't experience any problems. Italian is widely spoken, too.

Getting Around

By Car
The roads around Valletta are busy most mornings, but a new road network has made it easier to reach Sliema and St. Julian's from the airport. Road conditions are fairly good, but driving around the island can be a trial. Driving is on the left-hand side of the road. Speed limits are 40 kph (25 mph) in towns, 65 kph (40 mph) elsewhere. International and British driving licenses are acceptable. Be careful on roundabouts, or traffic circles.

By Bus
Most routes throughout the island are via Valletta, which facilitates travel out of the capital but makes cross-country trips a bit longer. Public transportation is very inexpensive. Though some of the old green buses show their age, they are usually on time. Plans are in the works to renew the fleet and the shabby terminal at Valletta.

By Boat
Daily car-passenger ferries operate year-round from Cirkewwa to Mğarr on Gozo. Telephone 243964 in Malta; 571884 in Cirkewwa; and 556114 or 556743 in Gozo for details. The crossing from Marfa to Mğarr in Gozo lasts 25 minutes, with shuttle service in summer and departures every hour in winter. The round-trip fare is Lm 1.50 adults, 50¢ children. There is also one service weekdays from Pietà (near Valletta) to Gozo, leaving in the morning and taking an hour and 15 minutes each way. The round-trip fare from Mğarr (passenger plus car) is Lm 4.50. A daily ferry service links the tourist resort town of Sliema to Valletta.

By Helicopter
Malta Air Charter (tel. 882916 or 882920) flies to and from Gozo several times daily and offers helicopter sightseeing tours. Flight time to Gozo from Luqa Airport is 10 minutes and costs Lm 17 round-trip (open return date) and Lm 15 (same-day return). Twenty- and 40-minute tours cost Lm 12 and Lm 20, respectively.

By Taxi
There are plenty of metered taxis available, and fares are reasonable compared with those in other European countries. Be sure the meter is switched on when your trip starts, or bargain first. Tip the driver 10%.

Staying in Malta

Telephones
LOCAL CALLS
There are no regional area codes in Malta. For a time check, dial 195; for flight inquiries, dial 249600.

INTERNATIONAL CALLS
There is direct dialing to most parts of the world from Malta. The overseas operator is 194; the international dialing access code is 00. You may place calls from the Overseas Telephone Division of Telemalta at St. Julian's, Qawra, St. Paul's Bay, Sliema, Valletta, and Luqa International Airport. For an **AT&T** long-distance operator, dial 0800–890110; public phones may require a deposit.

COUNTRY CODE
The country code for Malta is 356.

Mail
Airmail letters to the United States cost 20¢; postcards cost 20¢. Airmail letters to the United Kingdom cost 14¢; postcards 14¢.

Opening and Closing Times
Banks are open weekdays 8:30–12:45, Tuesday and Friday 2:30–4, Saturday 8:30–noon (11:30 in summer). Banks in tourist areas are also open in the afternoon. The currency-exchange booth at the airport is open 24 hours.

Museums run by the Museums Department are generally open mid-June through September, daily 8–2; October through mid-June, daily 8:30–5; closed holidays. Valletta's museums are closed on Sunday in August and September but are open in the afternoon on Tuesday and Friday. Other museums' hours may vary slightly, so check locally.

Shops are open Monday–Saturday 9–1 and 4–7.

National Holidays
January 1; February 10 (St. Paul's shipwreck); March 19 (St. Joseph's Day); March 31 (Freedom Day); April 5 (Good Friday); May 1 (Workers' Day); June 7 (Sette Giugno); June 29 (Sts. Peter and Paul); August 15 (Assumption, or Santa Marija); September 8 (Our Lady of Victories); September 21 (Independence Day); December 8 (Immaculate Conception); December 13 (Republic Day); December 25.

Dining
There is a good choice of restaurants, ranging from expensive hotel restaurants to fast-food hamburger joints. Local specialties include *torta tal-lampuki* (dorado fish pie), *dentici* (sea bream), and tuna. *Minestra* is the local variant of minestrone soup, and the *timpana* (baked macaroni and meat) is filling. Rabbit, stewed or fried, is a national dish. Accompany your meal with the locally produced red, white, or rosé wine—*marsovin* or *lachryma vitis*—and sample the house wines, too. Maltese beers are excellent; highly popular are Cisk Lager and Hop Leaf. Lowenbrau recently began brewing in Malta, as well. Another choice is Kinnie, a refreshing, local, nonalcoholic citrus and herb drink.

PRECAUTIONS
The water in Malta is safe to drink, with the only drawback being its salty taste: Many prefer bottled mineral water.

WHAT TO WEAR
A jacket and tie are suggested for higher-priced restaurants. Otherwise, casual dress is acceptable.

RATINGS
Prices are person for a three-course meal, not including wine, VAT, and tip. Highly recommended restaurants are indicated by a star ★.

CATEGORY	COST*
$$$	over Lm 9
$$	Lm 6–Lm 9
$	under Lm 6

10% VAT is charged on meals; 15% VAT on beverages

Lodging
Malta has a variety of lodgings, from modern hotels to modest guest houses. Some self-contained complexes are geared to package tours.

RATINGS
Prices are for two people sharing a double room and exclude the 15% VAT.

CATEGORY	COST
$$$$	over Lm 35
$$$	Lm 22–Lm 35
$$	Lm 12–Lm 22
$	under Lm 12

Tipping
A tip of 10% is expected when a service charge is not included.

VALLETTA

Arriving and Departing

By Plane
There are no direct flights from the United States, but several airlines, including **Air Malta,** fly from London, Paris, Frankfurt, Athens, and Rome to Luqa Airport, 6 kilometers (4 miles) south of Valletta.

BETWEEN THE AIRPORT AND DOWNTOWN
There is local bus service (Bus 8) that passes through the town of Luqa on its way to Valletta, with a stop in front of the airport. It operates every 10 or 15 minutes from 6 AM to 11 PM; the trip takes about 30 minutes, and the fare is about 10¢. Taxis are also available and prices are posted on a board at the taxi stand.

By Boat
The **Gozo Channel Co.** (tel. 243964) operates weekly car and passenger ferries from Catania, Sicily, during the summer. **Euro Malta Express** (Flagstone Wharf, Marsa, tel. 25994213) operates ferries year-round via Otranto, Catania, and Syracusa in Italy.

Virtu (tel. 318854) runs an express passenger ferry service from Catania (Tuesday, Thursday, Saturday, Sunday); Pozzallo (Monday, Thursday, Sunday); and Licata (Wednesday, Sunday).

Important Addresses and Numbers

Tourist Information
Gozo (Mġarr Harbor, tel. 553343; Victoria, tel. 558106).
St. Julian's (Balluta Bay, tel. 342671 or 342672).
Sliema (Bisazza St., tel. 313409).
Valletta (1 City Gate Arcade, tel. 237747; Luqa Airport, tel. 249600; or 280 Republic St., tel. 224444 or 228282).

Embassies and High Commissions
U.S. Development House (St. Anne St., Floriana, tel. 243653). **British High Commission** (7 St. Anne St., Floriana, tel. 233134). **Canadian Embassy** (in Rome; Via G. B. de Rossi 27, tel. 06/445981).

Emergencies
Hospital: St. Luke's (Gwardamangia, tel. 241251) or Craig Hospital (Gozo, tel. 556851). **Police** (tel. 191). **Ambulance** (tel. 196). **Fire Brigade** (tel. 199).

Travel Agencies
American Express (representative) (Brockdorff, 14 Zachary St., Valletta, tel. 232141). **Thomas Cook** (Il-Pjazzetta, Tower Rd., Sliema, tel. 344225).

Guided Tours

Orientation

Sightseeing tours are arranged by local travel agents and the large hotels. There are half-day, full-day, and "Malta by Night" coach tours; rates vary. Contact the tourist offices (*see* Important Addresses and Numbers, *above*) for details. Beware of cheap tours: These usually turn out to be rip-offs, the guide being the driver himself, who is far from qualified. Officially licensed guides should wear an identification tag.

One-hour boat tours of the harbor of Valletta leave regularly from Sliema jetty. Prices vary; buy tickets at most travel agencies.

Personal Guides

Licensed guides can be hired through local travel agencies represented at most hotels.

Exploring Valletta

The minicity of Valletta, with ornate palaces and museums, protected by massive fortifications of honey-color stone, was built by the Knights of the Order of St. John, who occupied the island from 1530 to 1798. The main entrance is through the **City Gate** (where all bus routes end), which leads onto Republic Street, the spine of the city and the main shopping street. From Republic Street, other roads are laid out on a grid pattern; some are stepped. Houses along the narrow streets have overhanging wooden balconies, which visiting artists love to paint.

Valletta's small size makes it ideal to explore on foot. Before setting out along Republic Street, stop at the tourist information office for maps, brochures, and a copy of *What's On*. Two blocks farther, on your left, is the Auberge de Provence (the hostel of the knights from Provence), which now houses the **National Museum of Archaeology.** Its collection includes finds from Malta's many prehistoric sites—Tarxien, Hagar Qim, and the Hypogeum at Paola. You'll see pottery, statuettes, temple carvings, and, on the upper floor, finds from Punic and Roman tombs. *Republic St., tel. 225577. Admission: Lm 1. Open mid-June–July, daily 8–2; Aug.–Sept., Mon. Wed., Thurs., and Sat. 8–2, Tues. and Fri. 8–5; Oct.–mid-June, daily 8:30–5; closed holidays.*

From Republic Street, turn right at the Inter-Flora kiosk and head to St. John's Square. Dominating the square is **St. John's Co-Cathedral.** This was the Order of St. John's own church, completed in 1578. It is by far Malta's most important treasure. A side chapel was given to each national group of knights, who decorated it in their own distinctive way. The cathedral **museum** includes the oratory in which hangs *The Beheading of St. John*, the masterpiece painted by Caravaggio when he was staying on Malta in 1608. In the museum, you'll find a rich collection of Flemish tapestries based on drawings by Poussin and Rubens, antique embroidered vestments, and illuminated manuscripts. *Cathedral museum admission: 60¢. Open weekdays 9:30–12:30 and 1:30–4:30, Sat. 9:30–12:30.*

While in St. John's Square, visit the **Government Craft Center** for traditional, handmade goods. *Open weekdays 8:30–12:30 and 2–5.*

Continue along Republic Street to the **Grand Master's Palace,** where Malta's parliament sits. You can walk through the shady courtyards. Inside, friezes in the sumptuously decorated state apartments depict scenes from the history of the knights. There is also a gallery with Gobelin tapestries. At the back of the building is the **Armoury of the Knights,** with displays of arms and armor down through the ages. *Admission to state apartments and Armoury: Lm 1 each. Open mid-June–July, daily 8–2; Aug.–Sept., Mon., Wed., Thurs., and Sat. 8–2, Tues. and Fri. 8–5; Oct.–mid-June, 8:30–5; closed holidays.*

Also on Republic Street, spend some time at **Casa Rocca Piccola,** a traditional 16th-century Maltese house. Continue to **Ft. St. Elmo,** built by the knights to defend the harbor. Though completely destroyed during the siege of 1565, it was rebuilt by succeeding military leaders. Today part of the fort houses the **War Museum,** with its collection of military objects largely related to World War II. Here you can see an Italian E-boat and *Faith,* one of three Gloster Gladiator biplanes that defended the island. The other two, *Hope* and *Charity,* were shot down in the air battles of 1940–1941. *Ft. St. Elmo. Admission: Lm 1. Open mid-June–July, daily 8–2; Aug.–Sept., Mon., Wed., Thurs., and Sat. 8–2, Tues. and Fri. 8–5; Oct.–mid-June, daily 8:30–5; closed holidays.*

Continue along the seawall to the **Hospital of the Order** at the end of Merchants Street. This gracious building has been converted into the Mediterranean Conference Center. For an excellent introduction to the island, see the "Malta Experience," a multimedia presentation (admission: Lm 2) on the history of Malta that is given here daily. *Admission to center: 50¢. Open weekdays 9–4.*

Walk along the seawall past the siege bell memorial and climb up to the **Upper Barrakka Gardens.** Once part of the city's defenses, they're now a pleasant area from which to watch the comings and goings in the Grand Harbour. The War Rooms below, from which World War II operations were planned, are open to the public.

Next, stroll down to this end of Merchants Street, which is dominated by an open-air market. Here, with some haggling, you may snap up a good bargain. Then cut along South Street, across Republic Street, to the **National Museum of Fine Art.** The former 18th-century palace has paintings that date from the 15th century to the present, including works by Tintoretto, Preti, and de Favray, as well as local artists. *South St., tel. 225769. Admission: Lm 1. Open mid-June–July, daily 8–2; Aug.–Sept., Mon., Wed., Thurs., and Sat. 8–2, Tues. and Fri. 8–5; Oct.–mid-June, daily 8:30–5; closed holidays.*

Valletta's neighboring towns of **Sliema** and **St. Julian's** offer seaside resort facilities. **Ta' Xbiex** is equipped for yachts.

Dining

For details and price-category definitions, *see* Dining *in* Staying in Malta, *above.*

\$\$ **Bologna.** This restaurant situated in the heart of the city specializes in Italian cuisine. *59 Republic St., tel. 246149. AE, DC, MC, V.*

\$\$ **Giannini.** Atop Valletta's mighty bastions, this is one of the city's most
★ elegant restaurants. Leading local politicians and the fashionable set dine here on Maltese-Italian cuisine, especially seafood, while enjoying the marvelous view. *23 Windmill St., tel. 237121 or 236575. Reservations required. AE, DC, MC, V.*

\$\$ **Pappagall.** This restaurant is popular with locals and visitors alike. Tra-
★ ditional Maltese food is featured, and the bustling atmosphere is warm and friendly. *Melita St., tel. 236195. Reservations advised. AE, DC, MC, V. Closed Sun.*

\$\$ **Scalini.** An attractive cellar restaurant with walls of Malta's golden lime-stone, it features seafood and Italian-style pastas. The prix-fixe menu is a good value. *32B South St., tel. 246221. Reservations advised. AE, DC, MC, V.*

$$ **Ta' Kolina.** This waterfront restaurant overlooking Malta's casino specializes in Maltese food and fish, including *bragioli* (rolled slices of beef stuffed with mincemeat and stewed in tomato sauce) and baked and grilled swordfish. *151 Tower Rd., Sliema, tel. 335106. AE, DC, MC, V.*

$ **The Lantern.** Two brothers run this friendly spot. The 18th-century townhouse location may not win any design awards, but the food is delicious and served in a traditional Maltese atmosphere. *20 Sappers St., tel. 237521. Reservations advised. Closed Sun.*

$ **Pizzeria Bologna.** A street-level pizza house beside the Grand Master's Palace serves delicious pizzas with an interesting choice of ingredients. *59B Republic St., tel. 238014. Open until 9 PM.*

Lodging

For details and price-category definitions, *see* Lodging *in* Staying in Malta, *above.*

$$$$ **Holiday Inn Crowne Plaza.** This large resort hotel is in Sliema, close to the sea and the major shopping area. It offers a full range of activities from swimming and windsurfing to dining and dancing. *Tigne St., Sliema, tel. 341173, fax 311292. 182 rooms with bath. Facilities: restaurant, bar, pool, tennis, gym, sauna. AE, DC, MC, V.*

$$$ **Grand Hotel des Lapins.** A modern building on the banks of the Ta' Xbiex seafront, this hotel has contemporary decor and overlooks a yacht marina. It's popular with businesspeople but has resort facilities, too. *Ta' Xbiex Seafront, tel. 342551, fax 343902. 191 rooms with bath. Facilities: restaurant, bar, pool, tennis. AE, DC, MC, V.*

$$ **Castille.** For a touch of old Malta, stay at the Castille in what used to be a 16th-century palazzo. This is a gracious, comfortable, Old World hotel with a friendly, relaxed ambience. It has an ideal central location, close to the museums and the bus terminal. There's a good rooftop restaurant with an excellent prix-fixe menu. A pianist plays most evenings during dinner, and the views across the harbor are stunning. *St. Paul St., tel. 243677 or 243678, fax 243679. 38 rooms with bath. Facilities: coffee shop-bar, sun terrace. AE.*

$$ **Osborne.** The centrally located Osborne has spacious rooms but undistinguished decor. Spend a few minutes in the rooftop lounge and enjoy the view. *South St., tel. 243656, fax 232120. 60 rooms with bath. Facilities: restaurant. AE, DC, MC, V.*

BEYOND VALLETTA

It is impractical to attempt a tour of Malta and Gozo in one day. Allow at least two days for the main island—three to include Valletta—and one full day for Gozo. The rest of Malta has much to offer, ranging from unique prehistoric sites to richly decorated churches.

The Southeast

Leaving Valletta, head first for the **Hypogeum** at **Paola,** 6 kilometers (3½ miles) south of the capital. This massive area of underground chambers was used for burials more than 4,000 years ago. Built on three levels, the chambers descend to 40 feet beneath the ground, and there are examples of fine carving to be seen. *Admission: Lm 1. Closed for restoration at press time; check with tourist office in Valletta.*

Nearby is **Tarxien,** an ordinary suburban town with extraordinary megalithic monuments. The **Tarxien Temples** are three interconnecting temples with curious carvings, oracular chambers, and altars, all dating from about 2800 BC. There are also remains of an earlier temple from about 4000 BC. *Admission: Lm 1. Open mid-June–Sept., daily 8–2; Oct.–mid-June, daily 8:30–5; closed holidays.*

Northeast of Paola, across the Grand Harbour from Valletta, lie evidences of the reign of the Knights of St. John: the **Cottonera Lines**—massive coastal defensive walls—and the city of **Vittoriosa,** dominated by the looming Ft. St. Angelo and site of a 17th-century church as well as the Inquisitor's Palace built by the knights.

Turning southward, you can visit the fishing and resort towns of **Marsaskala** and **Marsaxlokk** on the southeast coast and then head west to **Ghar Dalam.** A cave here was found to contain the semifossilized remains of long-extinct species of dwarf elephants and hippopotamuses that roamed the island when it was still joined to Europe, about 125,000 years ago. You can visit the cave and see the fossils on display in the small museum. *Admission: Lm 1. Open mid-June–Sept., daily 8–2; Oct.–mid-June, daily 8:30–5; closed holidays.*

Follow the coast first south through **Birzebbugia,** a beach town, and **Kalafrana,** where the U.S. and Russian leaders met in 1989, and then west to the **Blue Grotto,** near Wied-iz-Zurrieq. This is part of a group of water-filled caves made vivid by the phosphorescent marine life that colors the water a distinctive, magical blue. You can reach the grotto only by sea. Boatmen will take you there for Lm 2.

Nearby, within walking distance of each other, are the imposing prehistoric temples of **Hagar Qim** and **Mnajdpa.** Some of the stones weigh 20 tons. *Admission: Lm 1. Open mid-June–Sept., daily 8–2; Oct.–mid-June, daily 8:30–5; closed holidays.*

Central Malta
Take the northwest route to Rabat and Mdina, visiting **Buskett,** a very old and colorful garden, along the way. This trip is best in the spring when the orange and lemon trees are in blossom. In **Rabat,** visit the beautiful **St. Paul's Church,** built above a grotto where St. Paul is said to have taken refuge when he was shipwrecked on Malta in AD 60. Also of interest are the 4th-century **catacombs** of St. Paul and St. Agatha, unusual for their rock tables where mourners held celebratory meals for the dead. *Admission: Lm 1. Open mid-June–Sept., daily 8–2; Oct.–mid-June, daily 8:30–5; closed holidays.*

The Crafts Village at Ta' Qali is geared mainly toward tourists. Browse through the shops, but be cautious when buying. Here, in this converted World War II aerodrome, you can see filigree silver, gold jewelry, and handblown Mdina glass being made using age-old methods. There are also leather workshops and pottery shops selling gaily colored items. Some of the seconds in the glass workshops are good buys.

Adjoining Rabat is **Mdina,** Malta's ancient walled capital. The Maltese have a special love for what is often called the Silent City. It certainly lives up to its sobriquet: Traffic here is limited to residents' cars, and the noise of the busy world outside somehow doesn't penetrate the thick, golden walls. Visit the serene Baroque cathedral of **St. Peter and St. Paul** for a look at Preti's 17th-century wall painting, *The Shipwreck of St. Paul,* and the **Cathedral Museum** nearby to see the Dürer woodcuts and illuminated manuscripts. *Museum admission: 60¢. Open Mon.–Sat. 9–1 and 2–5.*

On your way out of the city you can visit the **National Museum of Natural History** (Vilhena Palace, tel. 455951) and the **Mdina Dungeons** (St. Publius Sq., tel. 450267) for a feel of the old Malta.

Continue to **Mosta** to see the **Church of St. Mary.** The Rotunda, as it is also known, has the third-largest unsupported dome in Europe, after St. Peter's in Rome and Hagia Sophia in Istanbul. You can also see a replica of the bomb that crashed through the dome during a service in 1942 and fell to the ground without exploding.

Gozo

Head for the northwest tip of the island through the beach and watersports centers near **St. Paul's Bay** and along Mellieha Bay, and take a ferry from Cirkewwa to **Gozo,** Malta's lusher, quieter sister island. The capital, Victoria, is a charming old town with attractive cafés and bars around the main square. In it lies the hilltop citadel of **Gran Castello,** with an impressive Baroque cathedral famous for a trompe l'oeil ceiling that makes the flat roof appear to be a dome. The museum here offers displays of ceremonial silver and manuscripts. *Admission: Lm 1. Open mid-June–Sept., daily 8–2; Oct.–mid-June, daily 8:30–5; closed holidays.*

The town also has a **Folklore Museum** (Milite Bernardo St.) and a collection of objects from various periods in the **Archaeological Museum** (Cathedral Square). *Admission to each: Lm 1. Open mid-June–Sept., daily 8–2; Oct.–mid-June, daily 8:30–5; closed holidays.*

On Xaghra plateau stands the extraordinary pair of megalithic **Ggantija Prehistoric Temples,** dating from 3500 BC. *Admission: Lm 1. Open mid-June–Sept., daily 8–2; Oct.–mid-June, daily 8:30–5; closed holidays.*

In the town of **Xaghra** itself, there are two underground alabaster caves with delicately colored stalagmites and stalactites. Visit the parish church of St. Mary, famous for its alabaster interiors. In the cliffs nearby is the cave where the sea nymph Calypso, mentioned in Homer's *Odyssey,* is said to have lived; with such stunning views and the sandy beach, it's easy to imagine that the myth might be true.

Dining and Lodging

For details and price-category definitions, *see* Dining and Lodging *in* Staying in Malta, *above.*

Gozo

LODGING

Ta' Cenc. Surprisingly, the little island of Gozo harbors one of the best hotels in this part of the Mediterranean. The Ta' Cenc is a luxurious paradise, and its location on the coast about 6 kilometers (4 miles) out of Victoria ensures guests' privacy and accommodates a full range of water sports. *Ta' Cenc, near Sannat, tel. 561522 or 561525, fax 558199. 82 rooms with bath. Facilities: restaurant, bar, 2 pools, tennis, disco. AE, DC, MC, V. $$$$*

Calypso. This modern hotel has so many services and facilities that it's almost like a small town in itself. The choice of dining spots includes a Chinese restaurant. The rooms are comfortably furnished and have balconies, most with sea views. *Marsalforn, tel. 562000, fax 562012. 92 rooms with bath. Facilities: restaurants, nightclub, rooftop splash pool, boutique, bank. AE, DC, MC, V. $$*

Cornucopia. For pleasant, personal service and a restful vacation, try this lovingly restored farmhouse near the village of Xaghra—it's an ideal base for exploring the island, and the sea is just a short drive away. There's a good restaurant, with barbecues in the summer. *10 Gnien Imrik St., Xaghra, tel. 556486 or 553866, fax 552910. 52 rooms with bath. Facilities: restaurant, pool. AE, DC, MC, V. $$*

Marsaxlokk

DINING

Pisces. Diners can enjoy a superb view across Malta's largest fishing village. Seafood specialties include *aljotta* (a soup with chunks of fish), *pagell* (red bream, baked or grilled), and risotto with mussels. *49/50 Xatt is-Sajjieda, tel. 684956. MC, V. $$*

Qawra

LODGING

Suncrest Hotel. At this modern, seven-story turquoise-and-white complex overlooking Salina Bay in the northern part of the island, the atmosphere is relaxed and informal. Rooms have fresh white walls and marble-tile floors that are covered with rugs in winter. *Qawra Coast Rd., tel. 577101, fax 575478. 427 rooms with bath. Facilities: café, 3 restaurants, bar, pool, tennis, gym, sauna, beach, conference hall. AE, DC, MC, V. $$$$*

Rabat

LODGING

Medina. This is a good value near Mdina. It is not luxurious but is quite comfortable. *Labour Ave., tel. 453230, fax 455738. 40 rooms with bath. Facilities: fitness center, indoor pool. MC, V. $$*

St. Julian's

DINING

★ **San Giuliano.** St. Julian's and Sliema are Malta's smartest seaside resorts and main entertainment districts. The San Giuliano offers terrace dining in a harborside setting. On the menu are Maltese-Italian dishes, as well as pasta, steak, lobster, prawns, and squid. *Spinola Bay, tel. 332000. Reservations required. AE, DC, MC, V. $$$*

★ **Barracuda.** This old house perched precariously on columns—thus commanding a superb view of St. Julian's Bay—is now one of Malta's most delightful and efficiently run restaurants. Seafood, not surprisingly, is the drawing card here, with dentici and baked barracuda as options. *194/5 Main St., tel. and fax 337370. AE, DC, MC, V. $$*

21 Norway

NORWAY HAS some of the most remote and dramatic scenery in Europe. Along the west coast, deep fjords knife into steep mountain ranges. Inland, cross-country ski trails follow frozen trout streams and downhill trails career through forests whose floors teem with wildflowers and berries during the summer. In older villages, wooden houses spill down toward docks where Viking ships—and later, whaling vessels—once were moored. Today the maritime horizon is dominated by tankers and derricks, for oil is now Norway's economic lifeblood. Fishing and timber, however, still provide many Norwegians with a stable income.

Inhabited since 1700 BC, Norway is today considered a peaceful nation. This was hardly so during the Viking period (the 8th–10th centuries AD), when, apart from vicious infighting at home, the Vikings were marauding as far afield as Seville and the Isle of Man. This fierce fighting spirit remained, despite Norway's subsequent centuries of subjugation by the Danes and Swedes. Independence came early this century but was put to the test during World War II, when the Germans occupied the country. Norwegian Resistance fighters rose to the challenge, eventually quashing Nazi efforts to develop atomic weapons.

The foundations for modern Norwegian culture were laid in the 19th century, during the period of union with Sweden, which lasted until 1905. Oslo blossomed at this time, and Norway produced its three greatest men of arts and letters: composer Edvard Grieg (1843–1907), dramatist Henrik Ibsen (1828–1906), and painter Edvard Munch (1863–1944). The polar explorers Roald Amundsen and Fridtjof Nansen also lived during this period.

All other facts aside, Norway is most famous for its fjords, which were formed during an ice age a million years ago. The ice cap burrowed deep into existing mountain-bound riverbeds, creating enormous pressure. There was less pressure along the coast, so the entrances to most fjords are shallow, about 500 feet, while inland depths reach 4,000 feet. Although Norway's entire coastline is notched with fjords, the most breathtaking sights are on the west coast between Stavanger and Trondheim.

Oil-prosperous or fisherman-poor, friendly or taciturn, Norwegians remain outdoors fanatics, firmly in the grip of their country's natural beauty. Norway's high prices and its vastness (it is more than 3,200 difficult road-kilometers long) are the only reasons the country isn't overrun with tourists. Norway is not quite as expensive as it was a few years ago because low inflation and increased competition in the tourist industry have kept prices stable. There are discount schemes and travel strategies that can lower the cost of traveling here even more (*see* What It Will Cost *in* Before You Go, *below*).

ESSENTIAL INFORMATION

Before You Go

When to Go

Cross-country skiing was born in Norway, and the country remains an important winter sports center. Although much of the terrain is dark and impassable through the winter, you can cross-country or downhill ski within Oslo's city limits. January, February, and early March are good skiing months, and hotel rooms are plentiful then. Avoid April,

Norway

0   200 miles
0   300 km

ATLANTIC OCEAN

North Cape

Vardø
Vadsø
Hammerfest
Kirkenes
Alta
Masi
Tromsø
Kantokeino

FINLAND

Norwegian Sea

Bardu
Narvik
Svolvoer

Vestfjorden

Bodø   Fauske
Saltdal

Arctic Circle

Mo i Rana   Umbukta
Sandnessjøen
Mosjøen
Brønnøysund

E6

S W E D E N

Vikna
Namsos
Steinkjer

Trondheim
Meråker
Støren
Kristiansund N.
70   Oppdal
Ålesund   Røros
E69   Tynset
Dombås
Nordfjord   Otta
Florø   Koppang
Jostedalsbreen
Lillehammer   Rena
Sognefjorden
Voss   *Lake Mjøsa*   Hamar
E58   Eidsvoll
Bergen   7
Hønefoss
Hardangerfjorden   40

Gulf of Bothnia

★ Oslo

Kongsberg
Drammen   Sarpsborg
Larvik   Fredrikstad
Haugesund   Skien
Sandefjord
Oslofjord
Stavanger

Baltic Sea

Egersund   Evje
Arendal
Grimstad
Mandal   Kristiansand S.
Skagerrak   *Kattegat*

when sleet, rain, and countless thaws and refreezings may ruin the good skiing snow and leave roads—and spirits—in bad shape. Bear in mind that the country virtually closes down for the five-day Easter holiday, when Norwegians make their annual migration to the mountains. If you plan to visit at this time, reserve well in advance. May is one of the best times to visit—the days are long and sunny, the cultural life is still going strong, and *Syttende mai* (Constitution Day, May 17), with all its festivities, is worth a trip in itself.

Summers are generally mild. Then there's the famous midnight sun: Even in the "southern" city of Oslo, night seems more like twilight around midnight, and dawn comes by 2 AM. The weather can be fickle, however, and rain gear and sturdy waterproof shoes are recommended even during the summer. Norwegians themselves are on vacation in July and the first part of August.

CLIMATE

The following are the average daily maximum and minimum temperatures for Oslo.

Jan.	28F	– 2C	May	61F	16C	Sept.	60F	16C
	19	– 7		43	6		46	8
Feb.	30F	– 1C	June	68F	20C	Oct.	48F	9C
	19	– 7		50	10		38	3
Mar.	39F	4C	July	72F	22C	Nov.	38F	3C
	25	– 4		55	13		31	– 1
Apr.	50F	10C	Aug.	70F	21C	Dec.	32F	0C
	34	1		54	12		25	– 4

Currency

The unit of currency in Norway is the krone, written as Kr. on price tags but officially written as NOK (bank designation), NKr, or kr. It is divided into 100 øre. Bills of NKr 50, 100, 200, 500, and 1,000 are in general use. Coins are 50 øre and 1, 5, 10, and 20 kroner. Credit cards are accepted in most hotels, stores, restaurants, and many gas stations and garages, but generally not in smaller shops and inns in rural areas. The exchange rate at press time (spring 1995) was NKr 5.9 to the dollar, NKr 4.4 to the Canadian dollar, and NKr 9.79 to the pound sterling.

What It Will Cost

Norway has a high standard—and cost—of living, but there are ways to save money by taking advantage of special offers for accommodations and travel during the tourist season and on weekends throughout the year.

Hotels in larger towns have special summer rates from late June to early August, and some chains have their own discount schemes—see Norway's annual accommodation guide at the tourist office. Discounts in rural hotels are offered to guests staying several days; meals are then included in the rate. Meals are generally expensive, so take hotel breakfast when it's offered. Alcohol is very expensive and is sold only during strictly regulated hours at state-owned *vinmonopol* stores.

SAMPLE PRICES

Cup of coffee, NKr 12–NKr 25; a half-liter of beer, NKr 30–NKr 50; soft drink, NKr 15–NKr 25; ham sandwich, NKr 20–NKr 40; 1-mile taxi ride, NKr 40 (for night rates, add 15%).

Customs on Arrival

Residents of non-European countries who are over 16 may import duty-free into Norway 200 cigarettes or 500 grams of other tobacco goods, souvenirs, and gifts to the value of NKr 1,200. Residents of European countries who are over 16 may import 200 cigarettes or 250 grams of tobacco or cigars, a small amount of perfume or eau de cologne, and goods to the value of NKr 1,200. Anyone over 20 may bring in 1 liter of wine and 1 liter of liquor or 2 liters of wine and beer.

Language

In larger cities and in most commercial establishments, people speak English. Younger Norwegians generally speak it well—English is the main foreign language taught in schools, and movies and cable TV reinforce its popularity.

There are two official forms of the Norwegian language—bokmål and nynorsk—plus many dialects, so don't be disappointed if you've studied it but find that you can't understand everyone. Typical of Scandinavian languages, Norwegian's additional vowels—æ, ø, and å—come at the end of the alphabet.

Getting Around

By Car

ROAD CONDITIONS

Away from the major routes, roads are narrow and winding, so don't expect to cover more than 240 kilometers (150 miles) a day, especially in fjord country. The climate plays havoc with the roads: Even the best roads suffer from frost, and the mountain passes may be closed in winter. Snow tires (preferably studded) are compulsory in winter; if you're planning to rent a car, choose a smaller model with front-wheel drive.

RULES OF THE ROAD

Driving is on the right. The speed limit is 90 kph (55 mph) on highways, 80 kph (50 mph) on main roads, 50 kph (30 mph) in towns, and 30–40 kph (18–25 mph) in residential areas. The use of headlights at all times is mandatory. For assistance contact **Norges Automobil Forbund (NAF)**—the Norwegian Automobile Association (Storgt. 2, 0155 Oslo, tel. 22341400). It is important to remember to yield to the vehicle approaching from the right. Passing areas on narrow roads are marked with a white *M* (for *møteplass*) on a blue background.

PARKING

Street parking in cities and towns is clearly marked. There are also municipal parking lots. You cannot park on main roads or on bends. Details can be found in the leaflet "Parking in Oslo," available free from tourist offices and gas stations.

GASOLINE

Gas costs 8–9 NKr per liter. Gas stations are plentiful and not hard to find in remote areas.

BREAKDOWNS

The NAF patrols main roads and has emergency telephones on mountain roads. For NAF 24-hour service, dial 22341600.

By Train

Trains are punctual and comfortable, and most routes are scenic. They fan out from Oslo and leave the coasts (except in the south) to buses and ferries. Reservations are required on all *ekspresstog* (express trains) and night trains. The Oslo–Bergen route is superbly scenic, while the Oslo–Trondheim–Bodø route takes you within the Arctic Circle. Do not miss the side trips from Myrdal to Flåm from the Oslo–Bergen line, and Dombås to Åndalsnes from the Oslo–Trondheim line. The trains leave Oslo from Sentralstasjonen (Oslo S or Central Station) on Jern-banetorget (at the beginning of Karl Johans gate).

FARES

In addition to the Europe-wide passes (**Eurail** and **Inter-Rail**), **ScanRail** passes, good in Norway, Sweden, Denmark, and Finland, are also available. ScanRail passes offer set numbers of travel days within a spec-ified period or one month of unlimited travel. They are available in the United States through **Rail Europe** (tel. 914/682–2999) and **DER Travel Service** (tel. 310/479–4411), and in Great Britain through **NSB Travel,** the Norwegian State Railway (21–24 Cockspur St., London SW1Y 5DA, tel. 0171/930–6666). A **Norway Rail Pass** is available for one or two weeks' unlimited rail travel within Norway. In the United States the ticket is available through **ScanAm** (tel. 800/545–2204), and in London, at **NSB Travel.** Reduced fares during off-peak times ("green" routes) are also available if booked in advance.

By Plane

As so much of Norway is remote, air travel is a necessity for many in-habitants. The main Scandinavian airline, **SAS,** operates a network, along with **Braathens SAFE** and **Widerøe.** Fares are high, so be sure and ask about the special rates available year-round within Norway. For longer distances, flying can be cheaper than driving a rented car, especially once you've paid for gas and incidentals. Inquire about "Visit Norway" passes, which give you relatively cheap domestic-flight coupons. Nor-wegian airlines can be contacted at the following addresses: **SAS** (Oslo City, Stenersgt. 1A, 0184 Oslo, tel. 81003300); **Braathens SAFE AS** (Haakon VII's gt. 2, 0161 Oslo, tel. 67597000 or 22834470); **Norsk Air** (Torp Airport, Sandefjord, tel. 33469000); and **Widerøe** (Mustads vei 1, 0283 Oslo, tel. 22736600).

By Bus

The Norwegian bus network makes up for some of the limitations of the country's train system, and several of the routes are particularly scenic. For example, the north Norway bus service, starting at Fauske (on the train line to Bodø), goes right up to Kirkenes on the Russian-Norwe-gian border, covering the 1,000 kilometers (625 miles) within four days. Long-distance bus routes also connect Norway with all its Scandinavian neighbors. Most buses leave from Bussterminalen (Galleri Oslo, Schweigaardsgt. 10, tel. 22170166), close to Oslo's Central Station.

By Ferry

Norway's long, fjord-indented coastline is served by an intricate and essential network of ferries and passenger ships. A wide choice of ser-vices is available, from simple hops across fjords (saving many miles of traveling) and excursions among the thousands of islands to luxury cruises and long journeys up the coast. Most ferries carry cars. Reser-vations are required on journeys of more than one day but are not needed for simple fjord crossings. Many ferries have limited space, so book ahead if possible; this will allow you to drive onto the ferry ahead of the cars that are waiting in line. Fares and exact times of departures depend on the season and availability of ships. Contact the main Nor-wegian travel office, Nortra, or the Norway Information Center (*see* Important Addresses and Numbers *in* Oslo, *below*) for details.

One of the world's great sea voyages is aboard the mail-and-passen-ger *Hurtigruten* ships, that run up the Norwegian coast from Bergen to Kirkenes, a town well above the Arctic Circle. Contact the **Bergen**

Line (405 Park Ave., New York, NY 10022, tel. 800/323–7436), or the **Tromsø Main Office** (tel. 77686088).

Nortra (Norwegian Travel Association; Postboks 499, Sentrum, 0150 Oslo, tel. 22925200, fax 22560505) will answer your queries about long-distance travel.

Staying in Norway

Telephones

Norway's phone system is not as expensive as one might fear. Domestic rates are reduced 5 PM–8 AM weekdays and all day on weekends. Also, avoid using room phones in hotels. Cheap rates for international calls apply only after 10 PM. In public booths, place coins in the phone before dialing. The largest coins generally accepted are NKr 10, although some new phones take NKr 20 coins. Most older phones take only NKr 1 or NKr 5 coins, so make sure you have enough small change. The minimum deposit is NKr 2 or NKr 3, depending on the phone.

LOCAL CALLS

The cost of calls within Norway varies according to distance: Within Oslo, the cost goes up according to the amount of time used after the three-minute flat fee. Check the Oslo phone book for dialing information. In 1993, telephone numbers throughout Norway changed from six digits to eight digits; area codes were eliminated.

INTERNATIONAL CALLS

These can be made from any pay phone. For calls to North America, dial 095–1, then the area code and number. When dialing the United Kingdom, omit the initial zero on area codes (for Central London you would dial 095 followed by 44, then dial 171 and the local number). Beginning in November 1995, you will need to dial 00 for an international connection. To reach an **AT&T** long-distance operator, dial 80019011; for **MCI**, dial 180019912; and for **Sprint**, 180019877.

OPERATORS AND INFORMATION

For local information, dial 180. For international information, dial 181.

Mail

Post offices throughout the country are open weekdays 8:30–5, and Sat. 8:30–noon. They cash traveler's checks and exchange foreign currency as well as offering postal services.

POSTAL RATES

Letters and postcards to the United States cost NKr 5.50 for the first 20 grams. For the United Kingdom, the rate is NKr 4.50 for the first 20 grams.

RECEIVING MAIL

If you're uncertain about where you'll be staying, have your mail marked "poste restante" and sent to the town where you plan to pick it up. Your last name should be underlined. The service is free; letters are directed to the nearest main post office, where you'll need your passport to pick up your mail. American Express offices will also hold mail (nonmembers pay a small charge on collection).

Shopping

VAT REFUNDS

Much of the 23% Norwegian value-added tax (VAT) will be refunded to visitors who spend more than NKr 300 in any single store. Ask for a special tax-free check and show your passport to confirm that you are not a resident. All purchases must be sealed and presented together with the tax-free check at the tax-free counter at ports, on ferries destined for abroad, and at airports and border posts. The VAT will be refunded, minus a service charge. General information about the tax-free system is available by calling 67149901.

Opening and Closing Times

Banks are open weekdays 8–3:30; summer hours are 8:15–3. (All post offices change money.)

Museums are usually open Tuesday to Sunday 10–3 or 4. Many, but not all, are closed on Monday.

Shops are usually open weekdays 9 or 10–5 (Thursday until 7) and Saturday 9–1 or 2, though times vary. Shopping malls are often open until 8 on weeknights.

National Holidays

January 1; April 4–8 (Easter); May 1 (Labor Day); May 16 (Ascension); May 17 (Constitution Day); May 26 and 27 (Pentecost); December 25–26.

Dining

The Norwegian diet emphasizes protein and carbohydrates. Breakfast is usually a large buffet of smoked fish, cheeses, sausage, cold meats, and whole-grain breads accompanied by tea, coffee, or milk. Lunch is simple, usually *smørbrød* (open-face sandwiches). Restaurant and hotel dinners are usually three-course meals, often starting with soup and ending with fresh fruit and berries. The main course may be salmon, trout, or other fish; alternatives can include lamb or pork, reindeer, or even ptarmigan. Remember that the most expensive part of eating is drinking (*see* What It Will Cost *in* Before You Go, *above*) and that spirits are not served on Sundays, although beer and wine are available in most establishments.

MEALTIMES

Lunch is from noon to 3 at restaurants featuring a *koldtbord*. This is a Scandinavian buffet, primarily for special occasions and visitors. Dinner has traditionally been early, but in hotels and major restaurants it is now more often from 6 to 11. Some rural places still serve dinner from 4 to 7, however.

WHAT TO WEAR

Unless otherwise indicated, jacket and tie or high-fashion casual wear are recommended for restaurants in the **$$$$** and **$$$** price categories, although during the summer, neat casual dress is acceptable in most places.

Ratings

Prices are per person and include a first course, main course, and dessert, without wine or tip. Outside the major cities, prices are considerably less. Service is always included (*see* Tipping, *below*). Highly recommended restaurants are indicated by a star ★.

CATEGORY	OSLO
$$$$	over NKr 450
$$$	NKr 300–NKr 450
$$	NKr 150–NKr 300
$	under NKr 150

Lodging

HOTELS

Accommodations in Norway are usually spotless, and smaller establishments are often family-run. Service is thoughtful and considerate, right down to blackout curtains to block out the midnight sun. Passes are available for discounts in hotels. The **Scandinavian Bonus Pass,** costing approximately $25 and also valid in Denmark, Sweden, and Finland, gives up to 50% discounts in 120 Norwegian hotels during summer (May 15–Oct. 1). In addition, children under 15 may stay in their parents' room at no extra charge. Contact **Inter Nor Hotels** (Dronningensgt. 40, 0154 Oslo, tel. 22334200), or consult Norway's accommodations guide, free from any tourist office. **Fjord Pass** (Fjord Tours, Box 1752, 5024 Bergen, tel. 55326550), which costs about $11, is valid at 250 establishments.

CAMPING

Camping is a popular way to keep costs down. There are more than 900 authorized campsites in the country, many in spectacular surroundings. Prices vary according to the facilities provided: A family with a car and tent can expect to pay about NKr 100 per night. Some campsites have log cabins available from NKr 250 per night. *Camping Norway* is available from tourist offices and the **NAF** (Storgt. 2, 0155 Oslo, tel. 22341400).

YOUTH HOSTELS

There are about 90 youth hostels in Norway; some are schools or farms doing extra summer duty. Members of the Youth Hostel Association (YHA) get a discount. Contact **Norske Vandrerhjem (NoVa,** Dronningensgt. 26, 0154 Oslo, tel. 22421410).

International YHA guides are available to members in the United Kingdom and North America. (There are no age restrictions for membership.) In the United States, contact **American Youth Hostels Inc.** (733 15th St. NW, Suite 840, Washington, DC 20005, tel. 202/783–6161, fax 202/783–6171). In Canada, contact **Canadian Hostelling Association** (1600 James Naismith Dr., Suite 608, Gloucester, Ontario K1B 5N4, tel. 613/748–5638).

RENTALS

Norwegians escape to mountain cabins whenever they have a chance. Stay in one for a week or two and you'll see why—magnificent scenery; pure air; edible wild berries; and the chance to hike, fish, or cross-country ski. For information on renting cabins, farms, or private homes, write to Den Norske Hytteformidling A.S (Box 3404, Bjølsen, 0406 Oslo, tel. 22356710), or get the brochure "Norsk Hytteferie" from tourist offices. An unusual alternative is to rent a *rorbu* (fisherman's dwelling) in the northerly Lofoten Islands. Contact Destination Lofoten (Box 210, N–8301 Svolvær, tel. 76073000).

RATINGS

Prices are summer rates and are for two people in a double room with bath and include breakfast, service, and all taxes. Best bets are indicated by a star ★.

CATEGORY	MAJOR CITIES	OTHER AREAS
$$$$	over NKr 1,300	over NKr 1,000
$$$	NKr 1,000–NKr 1,300	NKr 850–NKr 1,000
$$	NKr 800–NKr 1,000	NKr 650–NKr 850
$	under NKr 800	under NKr 650

Tipping

A 10%–12% service charge is added to most bills at hotels and restaurants. If you have had exceptional service, then give an additional 5% tip. Round off a taxi fare to the next higher unit, or a little more if the driver has been particularly helpful with luggage. If a doorman hails a taxi for you, you can give NKr 5. On sightseeing tours, tip the guide NKr 10–NKr 15 if you are satisfied. Tip with local currency only.

OSLO

Arriving and Departing

By Plane

Oslo's Fornebu Airport, about 20 minutes west of Oslo, has international and domestic services. Charter flights go to Gardermoen Airport, about 50 minutes north of the city.

BETWEEN THE AIRPORT AND DOWNTOWN

Flybussen departs from its terminal under Galleri Oslo shopping center every 10 minutes during scheduled hours and from several other places in the city. Flybussene make round-trips to Fornebu and the fare is NKr 35; call 67596220 for more information. Alternatively, take Bus 31 from Jernbanetorget, marked SNARØYA. The fare is NKr 20; the bus makes a round-trip once hourly. Buses meet flights to Gardermoen and take passengers to the central station; the fare is NKr 60. Taxis between Fornebu and downtown cost NKr 130.

By Train

Trains on international or domestic long-distance and express routes arrive at Oslo Central Station. Suburban trains depart from Oslo Central Station, Stortinget, and National Theater Station.

Getting Around

By Public Transportation

The **Oslo Card**—valid for one, two, or three days—entitles you to free admission to museums and galleries; unlimited travel on the Oslo transport system and Norwegian Railways commuter trains within the city limits; free parking; free admission to the Tusenfryd amusement park, public swimming pools, and racetracks; and discounts at various stores, cinemas, and sports centers. You can get the card at Oslo's tourist information offices and hotels (*see* Important Addresses and Numbers in Oslo, *below*). A one-day card costs NKr 110 adults, NKr 55 children; two days NKr 190 adults, NKr 80 children; three days NKr 240 adults, NKr 110 children.

If using public transportation only occasionally, you can get tickets (adults NKr 15, children NKr 7.50) at bus and subway (T-bane) stops. For NKr 35, the **Tourist Ticket** gives 24 hours' unlimited travel on any means of public transportation, including the summer ferries to Bygdøy. The **Flexikort** gives you 10 subway, bus, or *trikk* (streetcar) rides for NKr 130, including transfers.

By Taxi

A taxi is available if the roof light is on. There are taxi stands at Oslo Central Station and usually alongside Narvesen newsstands, or call 22388090; during peak hours, though, you may have to wait.

Important Addresses and Numbers

Tourist Information

The **Oslo Tourist Information Office** (tel. 22830050) is at the **Norway Information Center,** Vestbaneplassen 1. Open Oct.–Apr., Mon.–Sat. 9–4; May and Sept., Mon.–Sat. 9–6; June, Mon.–Sat. 9–6, Sun. 9–4; July and Aug., daily 9–8. **Oslo Central Station,** tel. 22171124. Open

8 AM–11 PM. **Trafikanten,** Oslo Central Station, tel. 22177030. Open weekdays 7 AM–11 PM, weekends 8 AM–11 PM.

Embassies
U.S. (Drammensvn. 18, tel. 22448550). **Canadian** (Oscarsgt. 20, tel. 22466955). **U.K.** (Thos. Heftyesgt. 8, tel. 22552400).

Emergencies
Police (Grønlandsleiret 44, tel. 112 or 22669050; 24-hour service). **Ambulance** (tel. 113 or 22117070; 24-hour service). **Dentist** (Oslo Kommunale Tannlegevakt, Tøyen Center, Kolstadsgt. 18, tel. 22673000; for emergencies, 8 PM–11 PM, weekends and holidays 11 AM–2 PM). **Pharmacy: Jernbanetorgets Apotek** (Jernbanetorget 4B, tel. 22412482; open 24 hours).

Post Office
The main post office, located at Dronningensgate 15, is open weekdays 8–8, Saturday 9–3. The **Telegraph Office** is at Kongensgate 21.

English Language Bookstores
Tanum Libris (Karl Johans gt. 37–41, tel. 22411100), **Erik Qvist** (Drammensvn. 16, tel. 22445269, beside the U.S. Embassy).

Travel Agencies
Winge (agent for American Express): Karl Johans gate 33/35, tel. 22412030. **Bennett:** Pilestredet 35, tel. 22943600. **Berg-Hansen** (agent for Thomas Cook): 3 Arbiensgate, tel. 22551901. **NSB Travel Agency:** Stortingsgate 28, tel. 22838850.

Guided Tours

Orientation Tours
HMK provides three three-hour tours and one full-day tour departing from Rådhuset (the city hall; harbor side). Tickets are available on the bus or from Oslo Tourist Information Office (*see* Important Addresses and Numbers, *above*). The "Oslo Highlights" morning tour goes to the Vigeland Sculpture Park, Holmenkollen ski jump, the Viking Ship Museum, and the *Kon-Tiki*. The "Art and History tour" includes Akershus Castle and Church, Gamle Aker Church, the National Gallery, the Stave Church at the Norwegian Folk Museum, and Holmenkollen ski jump. *Each tour costs NKr 175 adults, NKr 85 children. Tours start daily at 10.*

The "Afternoon Tour" goes to Holmenkollen ski jump, Vigeland Sculpture Park, the Viking ships, and the polar ship *Fram* at Bygdøy. *Each tour costs NKr 175 adults, NKr 85 children. Tours start at 1:15 daily Feb. 1–Oct. 14; Tue., Thur., weekends Oct. 15–Dec. 31.*

The "Full Day Sightseeing Tour" lasts from 10 to 4:30 and includes most of what Oslo has to offer. *Tel. 22208206. Tour: NKr 320 adults, NKr 160 children under 12.*

Båtservice Sightseeing (Rådhusbrygge 3, tel. 22200715) has seven boat and/or bus tours—from a 40-minute minicruise (NKr 55 adults, NKr 25 children; May to mid-Sept.) to an all-day grand tour of Oslo by boat and bus (NKr 285 adults, NKr 145 children).

Walking Tours

The "Oslo Guide" brochure (free from the tourist office) has several walking tours on its map. Some go farther afield and link up with public transportation.

Personal Guides

Taxi drivers give sightseeing tours in English for NKr 250 per hour. Call 22388070 for reservations.

Exploring Oslo

Although it's one of the world's largest capital cities in area, Oslo has only about 475,000 inhabitants. In recent years, the city has taken off: shops are open late, and pubs, cafés, and restaurants are crowded at all hours. The downtown area is compact, but the geographic limits of Oslo spread out to include forests, fjords, and mountains, which give the city a pristine airiness that complements its urban dignity. Explore downtown on foot, then venture beyond via bus, streetcar, or train.

Numbers in the margin correspond to points of interest on the Oslo map.

Oslo's main street, **Karl Johans gate,** runs right through the center of town, from Oslo Central Station uphill to the Royal Palace. Half its length is closed to traffic, and it is in this section that you will find many of the city's shops and outdoor cafés.

❶ Start at **Slottet** (the Royal Palace), the king's residence. The neoclassical palace, completed in 1848, is as sober, sturdy, and unpretentious as the Norwegian character. The surrounding park is open to the public, though the palace is not. The changing of the guard happens daily at 1:30. When the king is in residence—signaled by a red flag—the Royal Guard strikes up the band.

❷ Walk down Karl Johans gate to the **Universitet** (University), which is made up of the three big buildings on your left. The main hall of the university is decorated with murals by Edvard Munch (1863–1944), Norway's most famous artist. The *aula* (hall) is open only during July. The Nobel Peace Prize is presented there each year on December 10. *Admission to hall free. Open July, weekdays noon–2.*

❸ Behind the University is **Nasjonalgalleriet** (the National Gallery), Norway's largest public gallery. It has a small but high-quality selection of paintings by European artists, but of particular interest is the collection of works by Scandinavian Impressionists. Edvard Munch is represented here, although most of his work is in the Munch Museum (*see below*), east of the center. *Universitetsgt. 13. Admission free. Open Mon., Wed., Fri., and Sat. 10–4, Thurs. 10–8, Sun. 11–3.*

❹ The **Historisk Museum** (Historical Museum) is in back of the National Gallery. In addition to displays of daily life and art from the Viking period, the museum has an ethnographic section with a collection related to the great polar explorer Roald Amundsen, the first man to reach the South Pole. *Frederiksgt. 2. Admission free. Open summer, Tues.–Sun. 11–3; winter, Tues.–Sun. noon–3.*

❺ Return to Karl Johans gate and cross over for a closer look at **Nationaltheatret** (the National Theater), watched over by the statues of Bjørnstjerne Bjørnson and Henrik Ibsen. Bjørnson was the nationalist poet who wrote Norway's anthem. Internationally lauded playwright Ibsen wrote *Peer Gynt* (he personally requested Edvard Grieg's musical accompaniment), *A Doll's House,* and *Hedda Gabler,* among others. He worried that his plays, packed with allegory, myth, and sociological and emotional angst, might not have appeal outside Norway. Instead, they were universally recognized and changed the face of modern theater.

TIME OUT Inside the Grand Hotel, in the informal **Palmen,** salads and light meals are served along with pastries and cakes.

❻ At the far end of the pond is **Stortinget** (the Parliament), a bow-fronted yellow-brick building stretched across the block. It is open to visitors by request when Parliament is not in session: A guide will take you around the frescoed interior and into the debating chamber. *Karl Johans gt. 22, tel. 22313050. Admission free. Guided tours July–Aug. Public gallery open weekdays 11–1.*

❼ Karl Johans gate is closed to traffic near the staid **Oslo Domkirke** (cathedral). The much-renovated cathedral, consecrated in 1697, is modest by the standards of those in some other European capital cities, but the interior is rich with treasures, such as the Baroque carved wooden altarpiece and pulpit. The ceiling frescoes by Hugo Lous Mohr were done after World War II. Behind the cathedral is an area of arcades, small restaurants, and street musicians. *Stortorvet 1. Admission free. Open weekdays 10–3.*

❽ Facing the cathedral, turn right at Kirkegata. Three blocks down, turn right onto Rådhusgate and then almost immediately left onto Kongens gate. This takes you to **Akershus Slott,** a castle on the harbor. It was built during the Middle Ages but restored in 1527 by Christian IV of Denmark—Denmark then ruled Norway—after it was damaged by fire. He then laid out the present city of Oslo (naming it Christiania, after himself) around his new residence; Oslo's street plan still follows his design. Some rooms are open for guided tours, and the grounds form a park around the castle. The grounds also house **Forsvarsmuseet** and **Hjemmefrontmuseum** (the Norwegian Defense and Resistance museums). Both give you a feel for the Norwegian fighting spirit throughout history and especially during the German occupation, when the Nazis set up headquarters on this site and had a number of patriots executed here. *Akershus Castle and museums. Entrance from Festningspl., tel. 22412521. Admission: NKr 15 adults, NKr 5 children. Guided tours of the castle, May–Sept., Mon.–Sat. 11, 1, and 3, Sun. 1 and 3. Forsvarsmuseet and Hjemmefrontmuseum open June–Aug., weekdays 10–6; Sept.–May, weekdays 10–4.*

❾ Just behind Akershus Castle, in the direction of Oslo Central Station, is **Museet for Samtidskunst** (the Museum of Contemporary Art), housed in the former Bank of Norway building. *Bankpl. 4, tel. 22335820. Admission free. Open Tues.–Fri. 11–7, weekends 11–4.*

❿ Continue along the waterfront toward the central **harbor**—the heart of Oslo and head of the fjord. **Aker Brygge,** the new quayside shopping and cultural center, with a theater, cinemas, and galleries among the shops, restaurants, and cafés, is a great place to hang out late into summer nights. You don't have to buy anything—just sit amid the fountains and statues and watch the activities.

⓫ The large redbrick **Rådhuset** (city hall) is on the waterfront, too: Note the friezes in the courtyard, depicting scenes from Norwegian folklore, then go inside and see murals depicting daily life in Norway, historical events, and Resistance activities. You can set your watch by the astronomical clock in the inner courtyard. *Admission free. Open May–Aug. Mon.–Sat. 9–5, Sun. noon–4; Sept.–Apr. Mon.–Sat. 9–3:30. Tours Mon.–Fri. 10, 12, 2.*

The **Norway Information Center** is on the right side across the street when facing the harbor. From nearby Pipervika Bay, you can board a ferry in the summertime for the seven-minute crossing of the fjord to

KEY

i Tourist Information

—— Rail Lines

Vigelandsparken

Kirkeveien
Glydenløves gt.
Tidemands gt.
Prof. Dahls gt.
Bogstadveien
Nordraaks gt.
Eilert Sundts gt.
Holte
Gt.
Gabenborgveien
Industrigt.
Frognerveien
Eckerbergs gt.
Arno Bergs Plass
Gyldenløves gt.
Camilla Colletts vei
Oscars gt.
Halvdan Svartes gt.
Nobels gt.
Thomas Heftyes
Gimleveien
Løvenskiolds gt.
Lille Frogner Allé
Skovveien
Riddervolds gt.
Bygdøy allé
veien
Baders Gate
Kruse gate
Elisenberg
Bygdøy allé
Parkveien
Drammensveien
Thomas
Gabels gt.
Lapsetorget
Heftyes gt.
Fred. Stangs gt.
Drammensveien
U.S. Embas
Niels Juels gate
Parkveien
Cort Adelers
Munkedamsveien

Sjølystveien

Dronning Blancas vei

Drammensstranda

Frognerstranda

Frognerkilen

E18

Filipstadveien

Filipstadkaia

BYGDØY

Oscarshallveien
Museumsveien
Dronninghavn veien

(12)

(13) Huk aveny

Langvikbukta

Bygdøynes- Løkenveien

(14) (15)

0   1 mile

0   1 km

N

Aker Brygge and harbor, **10**

Akershus Slott, **8**

Fram-Museet, **15**

Historisk Museum, **4**

Kon-Tiki Museum, **14**

Munch-Museet, **16**

Museet for Samtidskunst, **9**

Nasjonalgalleriet, **3**

Nationaltheatret, **5**

Norsk Folkemuseum, **12**

Oslo Domkirke, **7**

Rådhuset, **11**

Slottet, **1**

Stortinget, **6**

Universitet, **2**

Vikingskipshuset, **13**

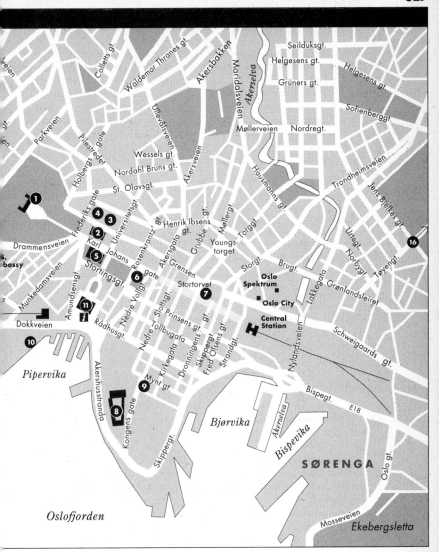

the **Bygdøy** peninsula, where there is a complex of seafaring museums. *Ferries run May–Sept., daily every half hour 8:15–5:45.*

⑫ The first ferry stop is Dronningen. From here, walk up a well-marked road to the **Norsk Folkemuseum** (Norwegian Folk Museum), a large park where centuries-old historic farmhouses have been collected from all over the country and reassembled. A whole section of 19th-century Oslo was moved here, as was a 12th-century wooden stave church. Look for the guides in period costume throughout the park, and on Sundays, there are displays of weaving and sheepshearing. *Museumsvn. 10, tel. 22437020. Admission: NKr 50 adults, NKr 10 children. Open summer, daily 10–6; winter, daily noon–4.*

⑬ Signs lead you around the corner to a second museum. **Vikingskipshuset** (the Viking Ship Museum) contains 9th-century ships used by Vikings as royal burial chambers, which have been excavated from the shores of the Oslofjord. Also on display are the treasures and jewelry that accompanied the royal bodies on their last voyage. The ornate craftsmanship evident in the ships and jewelry dispels any notion that the Vikings were skilled only in looting and pillaging. *Huk aveny 35. Admission: NKr 20 adults, NKr 10 children. Open Nov.–Mar., daily 11–3; Apr. and Oct., daily 11–4; May–Aug., daily 9–6; Sept., daily 11–5.*

⑭ Reboard the ferry or follow signs for the 20-minute walk to the **Kon-Tiki Museum,** where the *Kon-Tiki* raft and the reed boat *RA II* are on view. Thor Heyerdahl made no concessions to the modern world when he crossed the Pacific (*Kon-Tiki*) and the Atlantic (*RA II*) in these boats. *Admission: NKr 25 adults, NKr 10 children. Open Oct.–Mar., daily 10:30–4; Apr.–May 17 and Sept., daily 10:30–5; May 18–Aug. 31, daily 9–6.*

⑮ Directly across from the Kon-Tiki Museum is a large triangular building, **Fram-Museet.** This museum is devoted to the polar ship *Fram,* the sturdy wooden vessel that belonged to polar explorer Fridtjof Nansen. In 1893 Nansen led an expedition that reached latitude 86°14′N, the most northerly latitude to have been reached at that time. The book *Farthest North* tells his story. Active in Russian famine-relief work, Nansen received a Nobel Peace Prize in 1922. You can board the ship and imagine yourself in one of the tiny berths, and that outside a force-9 gale is blowing and the temperature is dozens of degrees below freezing. *Admission: NKr 20 adults, NKr 10 children. Open Apr., daily 11–2:45; May 1–15, daily 10–4:45; May 16–Sept., daily 9–5:45; Oct., daily 10–2:45; Nov., weekends 11–2:45; Dec.–Mar., weekends 11–4.*

TIME OUT Before catching the ferry back to the center of Oslo, consider a meal or snack at **Lanternen Kro.** In summer you can sit on the terrace, which commands a view of the entire harbor. Or you can stop at **Rodeløkken Kafé** for homemade heart-shape Norwegian waffles with preserves and whipped cream and coffee.

⑯ Back at City Hall, board Bus 29 to **Tøyen,** the area northeast of Oslo where you'll find **Munch-museet** (the Munch Museum). In 1940, four years before his death, Munch bequeathed much of his work to the city of Oslo; the museum opened in 1963, the centennial of his birth. Although only a fraction of its 22,000 items—books, paintings, drawings, prints, sculptures, and letters—are on display, you can still get a sense of the tortured expressionism that was to have such an effect on European painting. *Tøyengt. 53. Admission: NKr 40 adults, NKr 15 children. Open June–Sept. 15, Tues.–Sat. 10–6, Sun. noon–6; Sept. 16–May, Tues., Wed., Fri, Sat. 10–4, Thurs. 10–6, Sun. noon–6.*

Off the Beaten Track

Vigelandsparken

Gustav Vigeland's sculptures *Wheel of Life,* a circle in stone depicting the stages of human life, and *Monolith,* nearly 50 feet (15 meters) high and covered with more than 100 linked human forms, are the focal point of **Vigelandsparken,** in northwest Oslo, which is filled with his works. Open-air restaurants, tennis courts, and swimming pools provide additional diversions. To get there, take Trikk 2 or T-bane trains 13, 14, 15, or 16 and get off at Majorstuen. *Free. Park open 24 hours.*

Walk down Frognerveien to Krusesgate and turn left for a view of what Oslo looked like 100 years ago. The decorative gingerbread houses are on the historic preservation list.

Holmenkollen

The **Holmenkollen ski jump,** at 203 feet above ground level, is one of the world's highest and the site of an international contest each March. At the base is a ski museum carved into the rock. To get there, board any Frognerseter/Holmenkollen trikk from Nationaltheatret; get off at Holmenkollen and walk uphill to the jump. The half-hour trikk ride sweeps from underground up to 1,322 feet above sea level.

The forests within Oslo's vast city limits include 11 sports chalets geared to exercise and the outdoor life. The areas around **Skullerudstua** and **Skistua** are recommended for their walking and skiing trails. Contact Oslo Kommune (Forestry Services, Skogvesenet, tel. 22381870). Or, for winter or summer "safaris" through the forest by Land-Rover, contact the main tourist office (*see* Important Addresses and Numbers, *above*).

Ekebergsletta Park

Head east on Trikk 9 (from Nationaltheatret or Jernbanetorget) to the Sjømannsskolen stop to see 5,000-year-old runic carvings on the stones near **Ekebergsletta park.** They are across the road from the park on Karlsborgveien and marked by a sign reading FORTIDSMINNE. Walk through the park and take Oslogate and then Bispegata to the **Oslo Ladegård,** which has scale models of old Oslo on the site of the 13th-century Bispegård (Bishop's Palace). *St. Hallvards Plass, Oslo gt. 13, tel. 22194468. Admission: NKr 20 adults, NKr 10 children. Open May–Sept.; guided tours Wed. at 6 and Sun. at 1. Tours must be booked in advance.*

Lillehammer

Beyond Oslo lies **Lillehammer,** at the top of the long finger of **Lake Mjøsa.** It is reached by train from Oslo Central Station in about two hours. A paddle steamer, **D/S Skibladner,** travels the length of the lake (six hours each way) in summer, making several stops. Site of the 1994 Winter Olympics, Lillehammer is also home of **Maihaugen,** one of the largest open-air museums in northern Europe (tel. 61288900). Why not try out the Olympic bobsled track while you're there? It's in Hunderfossen about 3 miles from town. You can book at the Lillehammer Tourist Office (tel. 61259299). There's even a specially adapted sleigh ride for summer fun.

At the southern tip of the lake is **Eidsvoll,** where the Norwegians announced their new constitution in 1814, marking the end of centuries of domination by Denmark. There are limitless possibilities for outdoor activities in the region, all within reach of Oslo.

Shopping

Gift Ideas

Oslo is the best place to do your shopping since prices on handmade articles are government-controlled and selection is widest here: Pewter, silver, glass, sheepskin, leather, and knitwear are all appealing.

Shopping Districts

Many of the larger stores are in the area between Stortinget and the cathedral; much of this area is for pedestrians only. The **Basarhallene,** at the back of the cathedral, is an art and handicrafts boutique center. Oslo's newest shopping area, **Aker Brygge,** was once a shipbuilding wharf. Located right on the waterfront, it is a complex of booths, offices, and sidewalk cafés. Check out **Bogstadveien/Hegdehaugsveien,** which runs from Majorstua to Parkveien. This street offers a good selection of stores and has plenty of places to rest your tired feet and quench your thirst. Shops stay open until 5 (Thursday until 7).

Department Stores and Malls

Oslo's department stores, **Steen & Strøm** and **Christiania Glasmagasin,** are both in the shopping district near the cathedral. **Paléet** on Karl Johans gate has 40 shops and 10 restaurants. Across the street from Oslo Central Station you will find Oslo's largest shopping mall—**Oslo City**—with more than 100 stores and businesses including a bank, a travel agency, and a grocery store on the lower level; hours are 9–8 weekdays and 9–6 weekends. Also check out **Grønlands Torg** behind the Oslo Plaza Hotel, a market with produce, jewelry, and other goods.

Food and Flea Markets

Every Saturday during spring, summer, and fall, there is a flea market at Vestkanttorget, two blocks from Frogner Park at the junction of Professor Dahls gate and Eckerbergs gate. Check the papers for local flea markets.

Dining

For details and price-category definitions, *see* Dining *in* Staying in Norway, *above.*

$$$$ **Bagatelle.** Bagatelle was the first restaurant with a Norwegian chef serv-
★ ing Norwegian food to receive international recognition. Choose the seven-course menu for the full range of chef Hellstrøm's talents. The chairs are comfortable, service is impeccable, and Norwegian contemporary art adorns the walls. *Bygdøy allé 3, tel. 22446397. Reservations advised. AE, DC, MC, V. Dinner only. Closed Sun.*

$$$$ **D'Artagnan.** Among gourmands, D'Artagnan is a favorite. Stellar food
★ and excellent service make this a place to remember. Try chef Freddie Nielsen's Grand Menu with an appropriate wine from the well-stocked cellar. *Øvre Slottsgt. 16, tel. 22415062. Reservations required. AE, DC, MC, V. Closed weekends.*

$$$$ **De Fem Stuer.** Chef Frank Halvorsen prepares food that is even better
★ than the view. Enjoy modern versions of Norwegian specialties, with the accent on fish and game. *Holmenkollen Park Hotel, Kongevn. 26, tel. 22146090. Reservations advised. AE, DC, MC, V.*

$$$$ **Feinschmecker.** Located in a fashionable residential area only minutes from the center of town, this restaurant specializes in modern Scandinavian cuisine. The desserts are especially good. Lars Erik Underthun, the silver medal winner at the 1991 Bocuse d'Or World Championships for Chefs, is in charge here. *Balchensgt. 5, tel. 22441777. Dinner reservations required. AE, DC, MC, V. Closed Sun.*

$$$ **Babette's Gjestehus.** This warm and intimate restaurant has an international menu with a French accent. *Rådhuspassasjen, tel. 22416464. Reservations required. AE, DC, MC, V. Closed Sun. No lunch weekdays.*

$$$ **Theatercafeen.** This Oslo institution is one of the last Viennese-style
★ cafés in northern Europe and is a favorite with the literary and entertainment crowd. Save room for dessert, which the pastry chef also makes for Norway's royal family. *Hotel Continental, Stortingsgt. 24/26, tel. 22333200. AE, DC, MC, V.*

$$ **Det Gamle Raadhus.** The "old city hall," Oslo's oldest restaurant, is in a building that dates from 1641. Specialties include stockfish and shellfish casserole. *Nedre Slottsgt. 1, tel. 22420107. Reservations advised. AE, DC, MC, V. Closed Sun.*

$$ **Dinner.** Though its name is not the best for a restaurant specializing in
★ Szechuan-style cuisine, this is the best place for Chinese food, both hot and not so pungent. The mango pudding for dessert is wonderful. Don't bother with the other Chinese restaurants. *Arbeidergt. 2, tel. 22426890. Reservations advised. AE, DC, MC, V. Dinner only.*

$$ **Frognerseteren.** Located just above the Holmenkollen ski jump, this restaurant looks down on the entire city. Take the Holmenkollbanen to the end station and then walk downhill to the restaurant. Follow the signs. The newly renovated upstairs room has the same view as the more expensive panorama veranda. There is also an outdoor café. *Holmenkollenvn., tel. 22143736. AE, DC, MC, V.*

$$ **Kastanjen.** The short menu at this neighborhood restaurant changes often and features all seasonal ingredients. The three-course prix-fixe dinner is an excellent value. *Bygdøy allé 18, tel. 22434467. Reservations advised. AE, DC, MC, V. Closed Sun.*

$$ **A Touch of France.** The bouillabaisse at this intimate, French brasserie is out of this world. *Øvre Slottsgt. 16, tel. 22425697. Weekend reservations advised. AE, DC, MC, V.*

$ **Kaffistova.** This cafeteria serves Norwegian "country-style" cooking at
★ reasonable prices. *Rosenkrantz' gt. 8, tel. 22429530. No reservations. AE, DC, MC, V.*

$ **Lofotstua.** This rustic fish restaurant has a cozy atmosphere and good food. Typical specialties include fresh cod and seafood from the Lofoten Islands in northern Norway. *Kirkevn. 40, tel. 22469396. Reservations advised. AE, DC, MC, V. Closed Sat.*

$ **Vegeta.** Next to the Nationaltheatret bus and trikk station, this is a popular spot for hot and cold vegetarian meals and salads. It is a no-smoking restaurant. The all-you-can-eat specials offer top value. *Munkedamsvn. 3B, tel. 22834020. No reservations. AE, DC, V.*

Lodging

The tourist office's accommodations bureaus (open daily 8 AM–11 PM) in Oslo Central Station can help you find rooms in hotels, pensions, and private homes. You must apply in person and pay a fee of NKr 20 (NKr 10 children) plus 10% of the room rate, which will be refunded when you check in. For details and price-category definitions, *see* Lodging *in* Staying in Norway, *above.*

$$$$ **Grand Hotel.** It's hard to beat the Grand's location on Oslo's main street,
★ opposite the Parliament. The hotel has comforts and history to match its name: Ibsen had a permanent table in Grand Caféen, a famous Oslo rendezvous. Palmen, just off the lobby, is where Oslo matrons drink their afternoon tea. *Karl Johans gt. 31, tel. 22429390, fax 22421225. 215 rooms with bath and shower, 60 suites. Facilities: 3 restaurants, 2 bars, indoor pool, health club, parking (fee). AE, DC, MC, V.*

$$$$ **Holmenkollen Park Rica.** Near the ski jump, this hotel is an imposing
★ building in the old romantic folkloric style with a luxurious annex. The
rooms are bright, and most have balconies with excellent views of the
city and the fjord. The hotel runs a shuttle bus for its guests since it's
a 20-minute drive from downtown. It's probably the best place for anyone hoping to do some skiing. *Kongevn. 26, tel. 22922000, fax
22141692. 191 rooms with bath. Facilities: 2 restaurants, bar, hot tub,
sauna, indoor pool, cross-country skiing, nightclub. AE, DC, MC, V.*

$$$$ **SAS Scandinavia Hotel.** The SAS is a comfortable business hotel with
impeccable service. The airport bus stops right outside. Summit 21 is
the rooftop lunch bar, with views of the entire city. *Holbergs gt. 30,
tel. 22113000, fax 22113017. 491 rooms with bath, 12 suites. Facilities: restaurant, 2 bars, indoor pool, health club, shopping arcade, dance
club, nightclub. AE, DC, MC, V.*

$$$ **Ambassadeur.** Located just behind the Royal Palace, this hotel has in-
dividually designed rooms and personalized service. The Ambassadeur
restaurant serves modern Scandinavian food. *Camilla Colletts vei 15,
tel. 22441835, fax 22444791. 41 rooms with bath or shower, 8 suites.
Facilities: restaurant, bar, indoor pool, sauna, AE, DC, MC, V.*

$$$ **SAS Park Royal Hotel.** Ten minutes from Oslo, this hotel is clean, effi-
cient, and convenient to Fornebu Airport. The rooms are American hotel-
style, and the top-class facilities, including direct airport check-in, are
well suited to business stays. *Fornebuparken, Lysaker, tel. 67120220,
fax 67120011. 254 rooms with bath, 14 suites. Facilities: restaurant,
health club, tennis courts, meeting rooms. AE, DC, MC, V.*

$$$ **Stefan.** The service is cheerful and accommodating in this hotel in the
center of Oslo. One of its main attractions is the popular restaurant on
the top floor, with Oslo's best buffet lunch, featuring traditional Nor-
wegian dishes. *Rosenkrantz' gt. 1, tel. 22429250, fax 22337022. 130
rooms with bath or shower. Facilities: restaurant. AE, DC, MC, V.*

$$ **Bondeheimen.** Oslo's most Norwegian hotel has modern, comfortable
rooms and a staff that wears national costumes. *Rosenkrantz' gt. 8,
tel. 22429530, fax 22419437. 76 rooms with shower. Facilities: café,
meeting rooms. AE, DC, MC, V.*

$$ **Cecil Hotel.** Built in 1989, just off Stortingsgata right in the heart of
★ town, this hotel is a good value for the money. *Stortingsgt. 8, tel.
22427000, fax 22422670. 110 rooms with bath. Facilities: breakfast
room. AE, DC, MC, V.*

$$ **Europa.** This centrally located modern hotel is a moderately priced alternative to its next-door neighbor, the SAS Scandinavia. The rooms
are comfortable (all have color TV), and there are special reductions
for children. *St. Olavsgt. 31, tel. 22209990, fax 22112727. 158 rooms
with bath. Facilities: breakfast room. AE, DC, MC, V.*

$$ **Gabelshus Hotel.** Only five minutes from the center of town, the
Gabelshus is a moderate-size hotel on an attractive side street. The rooms
are spacious and airy, and the hotel has the feel of a large country house.
*Gabels gt. 16, tel. 22552260, fax 22442730. 45 rooms with bath. Fa-
cilities: restaurant. AE, DC, MC, V.*

$ **Gyldenløve.** This hotel on Bogstadveien—renovated in 1992—offers
quality at a reasonable price and well-equipped rooms with all con-
veniences. *Bogstadvn. 20, tel. 22601090, fax 22603390. 169 rooms
with bath or shower. Facilities: breakfast room. AE, DC, MC, V.*

$ **Haraldsheim.** Oslo's youth hostel is one of Europe's largest. Most of
the rooms have four beds, and those in the new wing all have show-
ers. It is 4 kilometers (2½ miles) from the city center on Trikk 1 or 7
to Sinsen. Breakfast is included. *Haraldsheimvn. 4, tel. 22155043, fax
22347197. 264 beds. No credit cards.*

$ Munch. This B&B hotel, renovated in 1994, has large but rather basic rooms. It's a 10-minute walk from downtown. *Munchsgt. 5, tel. 22424275, fax 22206469. 180 rooms with shower. AE, DC, MC, V.*

The Arts

Considering the size of the city, Oslo has a surprisingly good arts scene. Consult the "Oslo Guide" or "Oslo This Week" for details. Winter is *the* cultural season, with the **Nationaltheatret** featuring modern plays (all in Norwegian), classics, and a good sampling of Ibsen. **Det Norske Teatret** (Kristian IV's gate 8), one of Europe's most modern theater complexes, has musicals and plays.

Oslo's modern **Konserthuset** (Concert Hall), at Munkedamsveien 14, is the home of the Oslo Philharmonic, famous for its recordings of Tchaikovsky's symphonies. A smaller hall in the same building has folk dancing, held Monday and Thursday at 9 in July and August. In addition to the **Museum of Contemporary Art** (*see* Exploring Oslo, *above*), there's a good modern collection at the **Henie-Onstad Kunstsenter** (Høvikodden, tel. 67543050; open Mon. 11–5, Tue.–Fri. 9–9, weekends, 11–7), a gift from the Norwegian Olympic skater Sonja Henie and her husband, shipowner Niels Onstad. If you want to go to the movies, note that all films are screened in the original language with Norwegian subtitles. Tickets cost NKr 45.

Nightlife

Karl Johans gate is a lively place into the wee hours. There are loads of music cafés and clubs, as well as more conventional nightspots. A few good ones are **Barock** (Universitetsgt. 26, tel. 22424420), **Smuget** (Rosenkrantz' gt. 22, tel. 22425262), **Lipp** (Roald Amundsensgt. 2, tel. 22414400), **Barbeint** (Drammensvn. 20, tel 22445974), and **Kristiania** (Kristian IV's gt. 12, tel. 22425660) the hottest new place in town.

THE COAST ROAD TO STAVANGER

This tour follows the Sørlandet coast south of Oslo toward the busy port Kristiansand and then west to Stavanger. It is an area where whaling has given way to canneries, lumber, paper production, and petrochemicals. Yet the beauty of this 608-kilometer (380-mile) route has not been greatly marred, and you'll find seaside towns, rocky headlands, and stretches of forest (fjord country does not begin until north of Stavanger). The route outlined here follows the coast, but it is also possible to reach Stavanger on an inland route through Telemark.

Getting Around

By Car

Driving is recommended because it gives visitors the chance to stop at coastal villages that are either not served by trains or have only sporadic service. The route is simple: E18 as far as Flekkefjord, then Route 44 to Stavanger.

By Train

The best train service is the Sørland line, which leaves Oslo Central Station and goes all the way to Stavanger. The Oslo–Drammen stretch is an engineering feat and features Norway's longest tunnel, an 11-kilometer (7-mile) construction through sheer rock.

By Bus

Local buses cover the entire route, but they take much longer than the train. For details on fares and schedules, check with the tourist offices listed below or the main one in Oslo (*see* Important Addresses and Numbers in Oslo, *above*).

Guided Tours

In summer there is a daily boat excursion from Oslo to the coastal resorts of Kragerø, Jomfruland, and Risør southwest of the capital. Sightseers return the same day, and refreshments are served on board. The excursion is organized by the Norway Information Center (*see* Important Addresses and Numbers *in* Oslo, *above*).

Tourist Information

Arendal (Friholmsgt. 1, tel. 37022193); **Drammen** (Rådhuset, tel. 32806210); **Flekkefjord** (tel. 38324254); **Kristiansand** (Dronningensgt. 2, tel. 38026065); **Larvik** (Storgt. 48, tel. 33130100); **Mandal** (Bryggetgate, tel. 38260820); **Risør** (tel. 37158560); **Stavanger** (Stavanger Kulturhus, Sølvberget, tel. 51896200); **Tønsberg** (Nedre Langgt. 36B, tel. 33310220).

Exploring the Coast Road to Stavanger

From Oslo, take E18 west for about 40 kilometers (25 miles) to the bustling port of **Drammen.** Located at the mouth of a large timber-floating river, Drammen operates as a processing and shipping center for lumber and paper products. Take a short detour west of town on Route 11, turn right on Kongsgate, and climb the mile-long series of spiraling tunnels leading to **Spiraltoppen** at **Bragernes Hill.** During the '50s, locals decided against any further quarrying of building stone and turned instead to tunneling for it. The result is this scenic and dramatic road with panoramic views of **Drammensfjord** and **Oslofjord**.

Return to E18 and continue to the coastal town of **Åsgårdstrand,** an unspoiled summer resort where Edvard Munch painted many of his best works. His small yellow frame house is open to visitors during the summer (admission: NKr 15). Farther along is **Tønsberg,** which inhabitants claim is Norway's oldest town, founded in AD 870. The steep hill, Slottsfjellet, beside the train station leads to the ruins of **Tønsberghus,** an extensive fortress and abbey. The outlook tower, built in 1870 to commemorate the town's millennium, has a good view of the coast. The rise of Oslo as Norway's capital led to the decline of Tønsberg, although it thrived as a whaling port in the 1700s.

Attractive **Sandefjord,** 15 kilometers (9 miles) down E18, is a port that served as the base for the Norwegian whaling fleet until after World War II, when large-scale competition from the Soviet Union and Japan made the operation uneconomical. The port remains busy as a depot for timber shipping.

Just beyond Sandefjord, E18 crosses the important lumbering River Lågen and then follows it to the port of **Larvik,** which is the terminus for ferries to Frederikshavn in Denmark. Like Tønsberg and Sandefjord, Larvik once looked to whaling for its livelihood, but it, too, has turned to lumber and ferrying for employment.

The **Maritime Museum** is in the former customs house and chronicles Larvik's seafaring history. It emphasizes Thor Heyerdahl's voyages, with models of the *Kon-Tiki* and *RA II. Admission charges and opening times vary; check with the tourist office.*

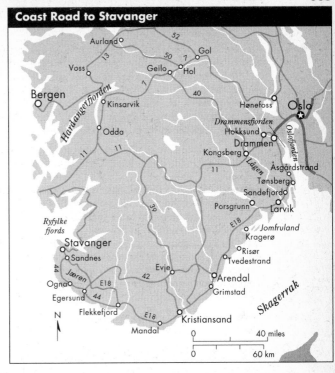

Coast Road to Stavanger

After Larvik, progress is faster, as E18 cuts across some of the narrower peninsulas on its way south. Side roads offer the chance to explore the smaller coastal village of **Kragerø,** where Edvard Munch spent many summers painting. Next is **Risør,** a sailing center with picturesque, white-painted, patrician 19th-century harbor-front houses. If you happen to be here in late summer, don't miss the wooden sailboat festival this town hosts every August. After **Risør** comes **Tvedestrand,** which has charming historic sections.

Arendal, 120 kilometers (75 miles) beyond Larvik, was once called the Venice of Scandinavia, but the canals have now been turned into wide streets. The atmosphere of bygone whaling prosperity in this and other Sørland ports is like that of Nantucket, with tidy cottages and grandiose captains' houses all within shouting distance of the docks. Explore Arendal's **Tyholmen quarter** for a glimpse into this 19th-century world.

Kristiansand is another 50 kilometers (31 miles) along the coast from Arendal. It is the largest town in Sørlandet and has important air, sea, road, and rail links. It was laid out during the 17th century in a grid pattern, with the imposing **Christiansholm Festning** guarding the eastern harbor approach. (Exhibitions are sometimes held inside the fort during the summer.) Just to the northeast of Kristiansand is the open-air **Vest-Agder Fylkesmuseum** (county museum), with 30 old buildings and farms rebuilt in the local style of the 18th and 19th centuries. There are also displays of folklore and costumes. *Admission: NKr 20 adults, NKr 10 children. Open June 20–Aug. 20, Mon.–Sat. 10–6, Sun. noon–6; winter open Sun. noon–5 or by appointment (tel. 38090228).*

A must for children is a visit to the nearby **Kardemomme By** (Cardamom Town) and the zoo and leisure park. *Tel. 38049700. Admission: NKr*

150 adults, NKr 130 children. Open summer, daily 9–6; off-season, daily 10–3.

Continue along E18 for another 30 kilometers (19 miles) to **Mandal**, Norway's most southerly town, famous for its beach, salmon, and 18th- and 19th-century houses. Every year, seafood lovers flock here for the shellfish festival the second weekend in August. For the next 30 kilometers (19 miles), the road climbs and weaves its way through steep, wooded hills and then descends to the fishing port of **Flekkefjord,** with its charming **Hollenderbyen,** or Dutch Quarter.

E18 heads inland here to Stavanger, but it is more rewarding to follow the coast road (Route 44) past the fishing port of **Egersund,** 40 kilometers (25 miles) ahead, and a little farther to **Ogna,** known for the stretch of sandy beach that has inspired so many Norwegian artists, among them Kitty Kjelland. Here you will find some of the most beautiful and unspoiled beaches in the south of Norway. Camping is an option to consider, available at Brusand and Ogna. For the last hour or so before Stavanger, you will be in the region known as the **Jæren.** Flat and stony, it is the largest expanse of level terrain in this mountainous country. The mild climate and the absence of good harbors mean that the population here turned to agriculture, and the miles of stone walls are a testament to their labor.

Stavanger, at the end of the tour, is a former trading town that became a focus (some environmentalists say victim) of the oil boom. It is now the fourth-largest city in Norway. Drilling platforms and oil tankers take the place of fishing boats in the harbor. In sharp contrast to the new high-rise complexes, there is an old quarter with narrow, cobbled lanes and clapboard houses at odd angles. The town is believed to date from the 8th century; its Anglo-Norman **Stavanger Domkirke** (cathedral), next to the central market, was established in 1125 by the bishop of Winchester in England. (Trading and ecclesiastical links between Norway and England were strong throughout the Middle Ages.)

Ledaal (Eiganesvn. 45, tel. 51520618) is a fine patrician mansion where the king resides when he's visiting Stavanger. It houses relics from the area and a special maritime display. Across the street is **Breidablikk** manor house (Eiganesvn. 40A, tel. 51526035), built by a Norwegian shipping magnate. An outstanding example of what Norwegians call "Swiss style" architecture, it has been perfectly preserved since the 1960s. Nearby **Ullandhaug** (Grannesvn., Ullandhaug, tel. 51534140) is a reconstructed Iron Age farm. The **Norsk Hermetikkmuseum** (Canning Museum; Øvre Strandgt. 88A, tel. 51534989), in the heart of Old Stavanger, is a reconstructed sardine factory in use between 1890 and 1920; here you'll get a lesson in the production of sardines and fish conserves.

The **Norwegian Emigration Center** specializes in genealogy and family research, helping to bridge the gap between Norway and the families of Norwegians who emigrated to America. *Bergjelandsgt. 30, tel. 51501267. Open weekdays 9–3.*

The **Ryfylke fjords** north and east of Stavanger form the southern end of the fjord country. The city is a good base for exploring this region, with the "white fleet" of low-slung sea buses making daily excursions into even the most distant fjords of Ryfylke. The Lysefjord excursion is superb. Great for a heart-stopping view is **Prekestolen** (Pulpit Rock), a huge cube of rock with a vertical drop of 2,000 feet. You can join a tour to get there or you can do it on your own from mid-June to late August by taking the ferry from Fiskepiren across Hildefjorden to Tau, riding a bus to the Pulpit Rock Lodge, and walking 1½ to 2 hours to the rock. If you're here between January and April, try skiing in Sirdal, 2½ hours from Stavanger. Special ski buses leave the Stavanger bus station weekends at 8:30 AM; contact SOT Reiser (tel. 51556066) for information.

Dining and Lodging

For details and price-category definitions, *see* Dining and Lodging *in* Staying in Norway, *above.*

Arendal

DINING

Madam Reiersen. This authentic restaurant on the waterfront serves good food in an informal atmosphere. *Nedre Tyholmsvn. 3, tel. 37021900. No reservations. AE, DC, MC, V. $$*

LODGING

Inter Nor Tyholmen. This new maritime hotel is located at Tyholmen, with the sea at close quarters and a splendid view of the fjord. Try the open-air restaurant, Bryggekanten. *Teaterpl. 2, tel. 37026800, fax 37026801. 60 rooms with bath. Facilities: 2 restaurants, bar. AE, DC, MC, V. $$*

Drammen

DINING

Spiraltoppen Café. Located at the top of Bragernes Hill, this café offers excellent views as well as good food. *Bragernesåsen, tel. 32837815. No reservations. AE, DC, MC, V. Closed weekdays in winter. $$*

LODGING

Rica Park. This comfortable and centrally located hotel has well-equipped rooms and a traditional Norwegian atmosphere. *Gamle Kirkepl. 3, tel. 32838280, fax 32895207. 103 rooms with bath or shower. Facilities: 2 restaurants, bar, nightclub. AE, DC, MC, V. $$*

Kristiansand

DINING

Sjøhuset. Seafood and fish are best bets in this rustic waterfront restaurant. *Østre Strandgt. 12a, tel. 38026260. No reservations. AE, DC, MC, V. Open May–Sept. $$–$$$*

LODGING

Rica Fregatten. You're right in the center of town in this medium-size hotel, a stone's throw from the town hall and cathedral. The rooms are quite comfortable, and there is a good restaurant, the Captain's Table. *Dronningens gt. 66, tel. 38021500, fax 38020119. 47 rooms with shower. Facilities: restaurant, bar. AE, DC, MC, V. $$*

Larvik

DINING AND LODGING

Grand. The rooms are spotless and service is attentive in this large hotel overlooking the fjord. Sample the local fish soup and smoked meat platters in the hotel's restaurant, Alexander, particularly good for lunch. *Storgt. 38–40, tel. 33187800, fax 33187045. 94 rooms with bath. Facilities: restaurant. AE, DC, MC, V. $$*

Sandefjord

DINING

★ **Edgar Ludl's Gourmet.** Enjoy fish specialties prepared by master chef Ludl in the best restaurant outside Oslo. The eight- and five-course menus are an excellent choice. *Rådhusgt. 7, tel. 33462741, fax 33462017. Reservations advised. AE, DC, MC, V. Closed Sun. $$–$$$*

★ **Rica Park.** Overlooking Sandefjord's attractive harbor, the imposing Rica Park is one of the best hotels in Norway. The rooms are large and comfortable, with excellent views over the water. The service is flawless. *Strandpromenaden 9, tel. 33465550, fax 33467900. 185 rooms with bath or shower. Facilities: 2 restaurants, 4 bars, pool, sauna. AE, DC, MC, V. $$$*

Stavanger

DINING

Sjøhuset Skagen. A restored 17th-century wharf house, this spot specializes in seafood plus lots of atmosphere. *Skagen 16, tel. 51895180, fax 51895181. Reservations advised. AE, DC, MC, V. $$*

Harry Pepper. This restaurant has two levels—the first has a trendy, popular bar that adjoins a Mexican restaurant. The color schemes are gaudy as are the displays of tacky South American souvenirs. In contrast, the decor upstairs is subtle and modern, and the emphasis is on meat dishes with an Italian touch. *Øvre Holmegate 15, tel. 51893993. AE, DC, V. $$*

Straen. In the oldest part of town, this famous fish restaurant offers a wide selection of delicious fresh seafood. There is a night club, a rock café, and a pub on the premises. *Nedre Strandgt. 15, tel. 51526230, fax 51567798. AE, DC, MC, V. Closed Sun. $$*

LODGING

Skagen Brygge. This hotel incorporates three rehabilitated old sea houses. Almost all rooms are different, from modern to old-fashioned maritime with exposed beams and brick-and-wood walls; many have harbor views. The hotel has an arrangement with 15 restaurants in the area—it makes the reservations and the tab ends up on your bill. *Skagenkaien 30, tel. 51894100, fax 51895883. 106 rooms with bath, 2 suites. Facilities: bar, pool, exercise room, meeting rooms. AE, DC, MC, V. $$–$$$*

Grand Hotel. This hotel on the edge of the town center doesn't aim to be fancy: Rooms are comfortable and bright, done in pastels and white. In summer the rates drop significantly. *Klubbgt. 3, tel. 51895800, fax 51895710. 92 rooms with bath. Facilities: breakfast room, bar. AE, DC, MC, V. $–$$*

THROUGH TELEMARK TO BERGEN

Bergen is Norway's second-largest city. To get there from Oslo, you can detour south through the Telemark area. This region is marked by steep valleys, pine forests, lakes, and fast-flowing rivers full of trout. Morgedal, the cradle of skiing, is here. You'll go on to Hardangervidda, a wild mountain area and national park that was the stronghold of Norway's Resistance fighters during World War II, and then down to the beautiful Hardangerfjord. Few places on earth match western Norway for spectacular scenic beauty—this is the fabled land of the fjords.

Fjord transportation is good, as crossing fjords is a necessary as well as scenic way to travel in Norway. Hardangerfjorden, Sognefjord, and Nordfjord are three of the deepest and most popular fjords. Local tourist offices will be able to recommend excursions and travel routes.

Guided Tours

Bergen is the gateway to the fjords, and excursions cover most of the last half of the tour below as well as the fjords farther north. Contact the tourist information offices (*see below*) for details of these constantly changing tours.

Tourist Information

Bergen (Bryggen 7, tel. 55321480); **Drammen** (Rådhuset, tel. 32806210); **Kinsarvik** (Public library bldg., mid-June–mid–Aug., tel. 53663112); **Kongsberg** (Storgt. 35, tel. 32735000); **Røldal** (tel. 53647259).

Exploring Through Telemark to Bergen

Take E18 west from Oslo to nearby Drammen (*see* Exploring the Coast Road to Stavanger, *above*). Follow Route 11 through Drammen and continue west for about 40 kilometers (25 miles) to **Kongsberg,** by the fast-flowing Lågen River. Kongsberg was founded in 1624 as a silver-mining town. Although there is no more mining, the old mines at Saggrenda are open for guided tours. The **Norsk Bergverksmuseum** includes the Silver Mines Collection, the Ski Museum, and the Royal Mint Museum. In the center of town is an 18th-century Rococo church, which reflects the town's former source of wealth—silver.

Kongsberg is one of the gateways to Telemark, which is just beyond Meheia on the county border. Forests give way to rocky peaks and desolate spaces farther into the plateau. **Heddal** is the first stop in Telemark. Norway's largest stave church, the Heddal church, is here. Stave churches are built with wooden planks staked vertically into the ground or base and usually have some carved ornamentation on the doors and around the aisle. These churches date from the medieval period and are found almost exclusively in southern Norway.

Route 11 climbs from Heddal and skirts the large Telemark plateau. You'll see the **Lifjell** area's highest peak, Røydalsnuten, 4,235 feet, on the left before descending toward **Seljord,** on the lake of the same name. The countryside by the lake is richer than that on the plateau; meadows and pastureland run down to the lakefront. The attractive village of Seljord has ornamented wooden houses and a medieval church.

Continue south from Seljord, making sure to stay right (on Route 11) at the Brunkeberg crossroads, while the other road continues south to Kristiansand. You are now entering the steep valley of **Morgedal.** It was here in the last century that Sondre Nordheim developed the Telemark method of skiing. You can get the full story on the development of skiing at the **Olav Bjåland's Museum,** named for the south polar explorer and ski hero. *Admission NKr 15. Open mid-June–mid-Aug., daily 10–5.*

Turn left at Høydalsmo for a scenic diversion to mountain-bound **Dalen.** At Dalen is **Tokke I,** one of Europe's largest hydroelectric power stations. From here it's an 8-kilometer (5-mile) drive to **Eidsborg,** where there is a stave church and a dramatic view of the Dalen valley.

Take Route 38 from Dalen along the Tokke valley to **Åmot.** The 305-foot Hyllandfoss Falls were destroyed by the hydroelectric project, but the drive is still spectacular.

Rejoin Route 11 at Åmot. At the next crossroads (**Haukeligrend**), Route 11 really begins to climb, and you'll see why the Norwegians are so proud of keeping this route open all year. Before you leave Telemark, you'll pass through the 6-kilometer (4-mile) Haukeli Tunnel and then begin a long descent to **Røldal,** another lakefront village with a hydroelectric plant.

Through Telemark to Bergen

Turn north on Route 13 a few miles after Røldal, and drive to the **Sørfjord** at Odda. Continue along the fjord to the attractive village of **Kinsarvik.** For the best view of the junction of the Sørfjord and the mighty Hardangerfjord, take the ferry across the Sørfjord to Utne. On the dramatic 30-minute ferry crossing from Utne to Kvanndal, you will know why this area was such a rich source of inspiration for Romantic composer Edvard Grieg.

At Kvanndal, turn left on Route 7. The road follows the fjord west, then veers right to **Norheimsund.** After climbing another coastal mountain spur, it winds through the wild **Tokagjel Gorge** and across the mountains of **Kvamskogen,** then descends tortuously into Bergen, capital of the fjords.

Bergen, founded in 1070, is now Norway's second-largest city, with a population of 219,000. Before oil brought an influx of foreigners to Stavanger, it was the most international of the country's cities, having been an important trading and military center when Oslo was an obscure village. Bergen was a member of the medieval Hanseatic League and offered an ice-free harbor and convenient trading location on the west coast. Natives of Bergen still think of Oslo as a dour provincial town.

Despite numerous fires in its past, much of medieval Bergen has remained. Seven surrounding mountains set off the weathered wooden houses, cobbled streets, and Hanseatic-era warehouses of **Bryggen** (the harbor area).

The best way to get a feel for Bergen's medieval trading heyday is to visit the **Hanseatisk Museum** on the Bryggen. One of the oldest and best-preserved of Bergen's wooden buildings, it is furnished in 16th-century style. The guided tour is excellent. *Admission: NKr 30 adults, NKr 15 children. Open June–Aug., daily 9–5; May and Sept., daily 11–2; Oct.–Apr., Mon., Wed., Fri., Sun. 11–2.*

On the western end of the Vågen is the **Rosenkrantz tårnet** (tower), part of the **Bergenhus,** the 13th-century fortress guarding the harbor entrance. The tower and fortress were destroyed during World War II, but were meticulously restored during the '60s and are now rich with furnishings and household items from the 16th century. *Admission: NKr 15 adults, NKr 5 children. Open mid-May–mid-Sept., daily 10–4; mid-Sept.–mid-May, Sun. noon–3, or upon request.*

From Øvregaten, the back boundary of Bryggen, you can walk through the meandering back streets to the popular **Fløybanen,** the funicular (a cable railway in which ascending cars counterbalance descending cars). It climbs a steep 1,070 feet to the top of Fløyen, one of the seven mountains guarding the city.

Troldhaugen manor on Nordås Lake, once home to Edvard Grieg, is now a museum and includes a new chamber music hall. Recitals are held each Wednesday and Sunday at 7:30 PM from late June through early August. *Troldhaugsvn, Hop, Bergen, tel. 55911791. Admission: NKr 30 adults, NKr 15 children. Open May–Sept., daily 9:30–5:30.*

Dining and Lodging

For details and price-category definitions, *see* Dining and Lodging *in* Staying in Norway, *above.*

Bergen
DINING

★ **Lucullus.** This French-inspired seafood restaurant is, appropriately enough, in the Hotel Neptun. It has an excellent wine cellar, with special emphasis on white wines to go with the fish. *Walckendorffsgt. 8, tel. 55901000, fax 55233202. Reservations advised. AE, DC, MC, V. Closed weekends. $$$$*

★ **Finnegaardstue.** This classic Norwegian restaurant near Bryggen has four small rooms that make for a snug, intimate atmosphere. Some of the timber interior dates from the 18th century. The emphasis here is on seafood, but the venison and reindeer are outstanding. Traditional Norwegian desserts such as cloudberries and cream are irresistible. *Rosenkrantzgt. 6, tel. 55313620, fax 55315811. Reservations advised. AE, DC, MC, V. Closed Sun. $$$*

Munkestuen Café. The locals regard this tiny mom-and-pop place as a hometown legend. Try the monkfish with hollandaise sauce or the fillet of roe deer with morels. Reserve a table early; sometimes they're booked up to four weeks in advance. *Klostergt. 12, tel. 55902149. Reservations required. AE, DC, MC, V. Dinner only. Closed Sat. and 3 wks in July. $$–$$$*

LODGING

SAS Royal. Located right at the harbor, the SAS Royal was opened in 1982 on the site of old warehouses. Ravaged by nine fires since 1170, the warehouses have been rebuilt each time in the same style, which SAS has incorporated into this well-equipped hotel. *Bryggen, tel. 55543000, fax 55324808. 273 rooms with bath. Facilities: 2 restaurants, bar, pub, pool, sauna, dance club, convention center. AE, DC, MC, V. $$–$$$$*

Augustin. This small but excellent hotel in the center of town has been recently restored to its original late–Art Nouveau character, complete with period furniture in the lobby. *C. Sundtsgt. 24, tel. 55230025, fax 55233130. 38 rooms with bath. AE, DC, MC, V. $–$$*

Bryggen Orion. Facing the harbor in the center of town, the hotel is surrounded by Bergen's most famous sights. *Bradbenken 3, tel. 55318080, fax 55329414. 229 rooms with bath. Facilities: restaurant, bar, nightclub. AE, DC, MC, V. $–$$*

Kinsarvik
LODGING

Kinsarvik Fjord Hotel. This handsome hotel near the busy ferry port offers good views of Hardangerfjord and the glacier. The rooms are bright and spacious. *Kinsarvik, tel. 53663100, fax 53663374. 62 rooms with bath or shower. Facilities: restaurant, bar. AE, MC, V. $$*

Kongsberg

<u>DINING</u>

Gamle Kongsberg Kro. Located by the waterfall at Nybrofossen, with a mini-golf course nearby, this newly restored café offers hearty Norwegian dishes at moderate prices. *Thornesvn. 4, tel. 32731633, fax 32732603. No reservations. AE, DC, MC, V. $$*

Utne

<u>DINING AND LODGING</u>

Utne Hotel. The white frame house dates from 1722, and the hotel, the oldest in Norway, has been run by the same family since 1787. The Utne has all the cared-for atmosphere of an old home. The dining room is wood paneled and hand painted, decorated with copper pans, old china, and paintings. The rooms are filled with period furniture. The Utne makes a good base for hiking or cycling. *Utne, tel. 5366983, fax 5366950. 24 rooms with bath or shower. AE, DC, MC, V. $$*

ABOVE BERGEN: THE FAR NORTH

The fjords continue northward from Bergen all the way to Kirkenes, at Norway's border with the Republic of Russia. Norway's north is for anyone eager to hike, climb, fish, bird-watch (seabirds), see Sami-land—the land of the Sami ("Lapps")—or experience the unending days of the midnight sun in June and July. The Lofoten Islands present the grand face of the "Lofoten Wall"—a rocky, 96-kilometer-long (60-mile-long) massif surrounded by the sea and broken into six pieces. Svolvær, the most populated island, has a thriving summer artists' colony. It's also known for Lofotfisket, the winter cod fishing.

The major towns north of Bergen are Ålesund, Trondheim, Bodø, Narvik, Tromsø, Hammerfest, and Kirkenes. Cheaper accommodations are the rule in the north, whether you stay in a cabin, campsite, or guest house, or in rorbuer—fishermen's huts in the islands that are available for rent outside the January to April fishing season. These days, many rorbuer are built to be motels.

Getting Around

By Ship

One of the best ways to travel in northern Norway is the **Hurtigrute,** or coastal steamer, which begins in Bergen and turns around 2,000 nautical kilometers (1,250 miles) later at Kirkenes. Many steamers run this route, so you can stay at any of the ports for any length of time and pick up the next one coming through. Major tourist offices have schedules, and reservations are essential as far in advance as a year (*see* Important Addresses and Numbers in Oslo, and Getting Around by Ferry, *above*).

By Car

E6 and its feeder roads are the only route available north of Trondheim, where the country narrows dramatically.

By Train

Major train routes are Oslo–Bergen and Oslo–Trondheim–Bodø (the Trondheim–Bodø leg takes one day). From Bodø there are tours to the Lofoten and Vesterålen islands and to the Væren Islands, two tiny, remote islands at the tail of the Lofoten chain. You can get to Svolvær, the Lofotens' main port, via ferry from Skutvik.

To get all the way to Nordkapp (the North Cape, the northernmost mainland point in Norway and Europe) and the Land of the Midnight Sun, you must continue your trip by bus from Fauske.

Tourist Information

Ålesund (Rådhuset , tel. 70121202); **Bodø** (Sjøgt. 21, tel. 75526000); **Hammerfest** (tel. 78412185); **Harstad** (Torvet 8, tel. 77063235); **Kirkenes** (off E6 in a wooden hut behind Rica Hotel, on Pasvikvn., tel. 78992544); **Narvik** (Kongensgt. 66, tel. 76943309); **Svolvær** (Torget 6, tel. 76073000); **Tromsø** (Storgt. 61, tel. 77610000); **Trondheim** (Munkegata 19, tel. 73929394).

Exploring the Far North

See the Norway country map (above) for towns in the Far North.

The steamer is probably the best route from Ålesund to Trondheim because no main road connects them directly. **Ålesund,** a much-overlooked coastal city flanked by fjords, is perhaps the only example you'll find of true architectural eccentricity in Norway. After a fire here during the early 1900s, anyone who had any aspirations to architecture designed his or her own new home, and the result is a rich, playful mixture of styles ranging from austere to Art Nouveau. There are excellent tours of the Romsdal, Geiranger, and Hjørund fjords. Pick up the free "Ålesund Guide" and "On Foot in Ålesund" from the tourist office (*see* Tourist Information, *above*).

Trondheim sits at the southern end of Norway's widest fjord, Trondheimsfjord. This water-bound city is the third-largest in the country and is where Norwegian rulers are traditionally crowned. Construction of what is Scandinavia's largest medieval building, **Nidaros Domkirke** (cathedral), started here in 1320 but was not completed until the early 1920s. For centuries it served as a goal for religious pilgrims. There is a historic fish market worth seeing. Scandinavia's two largest wooden buildings are in Trondheim. One is the rococo **Stiftsgården,** a royal palace built in 1774, and the other is a student dormitory.

After Trondheim, the country thins into a vertebral cord of land hugging the border with Sweden and hunching over the top of Finland. **Bodø,** the northern terminus of the Nordland railway, is the first major town above the Polar Circle. It is bathed in midnight sun from early June to mid-July. For those who want boat excursions to **coastal bird colonies** (the Væren Islands), Bodø is the best base. The city was bombed by the Germans in 1940. The stunning, contemporary **Bodø Cathedral,** its spire separated from the main building, was built after the war. Inside are rich, modern tapestries; outside is a war memorial. The **Nordland County Museum** depicts the life of the Sami, as well as regional history. *Prinsengt. 116, tel. 75526128. Admission free. Open weekdays 9–3, weekends noon–3.*

If you want to see a real maelstrom—a furious natural whirlpool—inquire at the tourist office (*see* Tourist Information, *above*) about **Saltstraumen.**

TIME OUT Alongside the maelstrom is **Saltstraumen Hotel.** Try the poached halibut—delicious!

Bodø is considered a gateway to the Lofoten and Vesterålen islands; the tourist office will make the necessary arrangements.

The **Lofoten** islands are a 190-kilometer (118-mile) chain of mountaintops rising from the bottom of the sea like open jaws. During the summer, the farms, fjords, and fishing villages make it a major tourist attraction. Between January and March, thousands of fishermen from all over the country head for Lofoten to the annual Lofotfisket, the world's largest annual cod fishing event.

Narvik is a rebuilt city, an "ice-free" seaport, and a major shipping center for iron ore. An excellent railway connects it to the mines across the Swedish border. The **Krigsminnemuseet** (War Memorial Museum) has gripping displays on wartime intrigue and suffering. *Kongensgt., near the main square. Admission: NKr 25. Open Mar.–Oct., Mon.–Sat. 10–10, Sun. 11–5.*

Northeast of Lofoten on Hinnøya, Norway's largest island, is **Harstad,** where the population of 22,000 swells to 42,000 during the annual June cultural festival and its July deep-sea fishing festival.

Farther north on the mainland is **Tromsø,** self-dubbed "Paris of the North" for the nightlife inspired by the midnight sun. Looming over this remote arctic university town are 6,100-foot peaks with permanent snowcaps. Tromsø trails off into the islands: Half the town lives offshore. Its population is about 50,000. Be sure to see the spectacular **Ishavskatedral** (cathedral), with its eastern wall made entirely of stained glass, across the long stretch of **Tromsø bridge.** Coated in aluminum, the bridge's triangular peaks make a bizarre mirror for the midnight sun.

Be sure to walk around old Tromsø (along the waterfront) and to visit the **Tromsø Museum,** which concentrates on science, the Sami, and northern churches. *Lars Thøringsvei 10, Folkeparken; take Bus 27 or 22. Admission: NKr 10 adults, NKr 5 children. Open June–Aug., daily 9–9; Sept.–May, weekdays 8:30–3:30, Sat. noon–3, Sun. 11–4.*

Hammerfest is the world's northernmost town. It is surrounded by Sami settlements and is home to the **Royal and Ancient Polar Bear Society.** Don't visit the society if you don't like real stuffed bears. *Town Hall basement. Admission free. Open June-Aug., weekdays 8–8, weekends 10–5.*

Hammerfest is an elegant, festive-looking port town despite having been razed twice in its history. During the late-19th century the town was leveled by fire. Years later, defeated German troops destroyed the town as they retreated to avoid leaving anything to the Russians.

Dining and Lodging

For details and price-category definitions, *see* Dining and Lodging *in* Staying in Norway, *above.*

Ålesund

DINING

Fjellstua. This mountaintop restaurant has tremendous views over the surrounding peaks, islands, and fjords. There are several different eating facilities here, but the main restaurant serves a variety of dishes and homemade desserts. *Fjellstua, tel. 70126582. AE, DC, V. Closed Dec.–Easter. $$*

Sjøbua. Located at Brunholmen on an old wharf, Sjøbua offers an excellent seafood selection. You can even pick your own dinner from a saltwater aquarium. *Brunholmgt. 1, tel. 70127100. Reservations advised. AE, DC, MC, V. $$*

LODGING

Bryggen. This dockside warehouse was converted into a hotel in 1990. There are splendid views over the water. *Apotekergt. 1–3, tel. 70126400, fax 70121180. 83 rooms with bath or shower. Facilities: sauna. AE, DC, MC, V. $$*

Hotel Scandinavie. The impressive building with towers and arches dates from 1905, but the rooms are newly refurbished. *Løevenvoldgt. 8, tel. 70123131, fax 70132370. 63 rooms with bath. Facilities: restaurant, pizzeria, bar. AE, DC, MC, V. $$*

Rica Parken. Renovated in 1990, this is the largest and best-equipped hotel in Ålesund. *Storgt. 16, tel. 70125050, fax 70122164. 138 rooms with bath. Facilities: restaurant, bar, disco, exercise room. AE, DC, MC, V. $$*

Bodø

DINING

Marlene Restaurant. Set within the SAS Royal hotel, the Marlene offers a superb seafood buffet throughout the summer. Be sure to try one of the salmon dishes. *Storgt. 2, tel. 75524100. Reservations advised. AE, DC, MC, V. $$–$$$*

Turisthytta. This mountaintop lodge (accessible by taxi) is a fine place to eat if you want to bask in the midnight sun. There is a good range of dishes, from snacks and open-faced sandwiches to fresh fish. *Turisthytta, tel. 75583300. Reservations advised. No credit cards. Closed in winter. $$*

LODGING

SAS Royal. This grandiose hotel is throbbing with life and has enough amenities to keep you entertained virtually around the clock. *Storgt. 2, tel. 75524100, fax 75527493. 190 rooms with bath. Facilities: restaurant, wine bar, nightclub, health club, sauna. AE, DC, MC, V. $$$*

Norrøna. This hotel is comfortable, with a location just as grand as that of the SAS Royal next door. *Storgt. 4B, tel. 75525550, fax 75527493. 190 rooms with bath or shower. Facilities: breakfast room. AE, DC, V. $$*

Hammerfest

DINING AND LODGING

Hammerfest Hotel. On the pleasant Rådhusplassen, this guest house has handsome, harbor-view rooms for tolerable prices in a town where hotels are expensive. *Strandgt. 2–4, tel. 78411622, fax 78412127. 53 rooms with bath or shower. Facilities: restaurant, cafeteria. AE, DC, MC, V. $$$*

Narvik

DINING AND LODGING

Inter-Nor Grand Royal Hotel. This is a classy, handsome hotel, enhanced by a staff that is eager to please. The location, right by the train station, is a plus, and there are many chances to try the skiing and fishing nearby. *Kongensgt. 64, tel. 76941500, fax 76945531. 108 rooms with bath. Facilities: 2 restaurants, 3 bars, sauna, nightclub. AE, DC, MC, V. $$$*

Svolvær

DINING AND LODGING

Nyvågar Rorbu. Built in 1990, this hotel and recreation complex is a 15-minute drive from the Svolvær airport. Activities include fishing trips, eagle safaris, and deep-sea rafting. *Kabelvåg, tel. 76078900, fax 76078950. 60 rooms with showers. Facilities: 2 restaurants, conference rooms. AE, DC, MC, V. $$–$$$*

Tromsø

DINING AND LODGING

SAS Royal. Each room in this beautifully set hotel gives splendid views over Tromsø's shoreline, although the location is in the heart of town. *Sjøgt. 7, tel. 77600000, fax 77656221. 195 rooms with bath. Facilities: 3 restaurants, bar, nightclub. AE, DC, MC, V. $$$–$$$$*

Saga. On a pretty town square, the Saga combines its central location with the staff's expertise. Its restaurant has affordable, hearty meals, and the rooms—although somewhat basic—are quiet and comfortable. *Richard Withs pl. 2, tel. 77681180, fax 77682380. 54 rooms with bath. Facilities: restaurant, cafeteria. AE, DC, MC, V. $$*

Trondheim

DINING

★ **Bryggen.** This popular restaurant, set near the Gamle Bybro (Old Town Bridge), serves a feast of Norwegian gourmet specialties with a Gallic flourish. They also have a creperie and a wine and cheese room. *Ø Bakklandet 66, tel. 73520230. Reservations advised. AE, DC, MC, V. $$$*

Hos Magnus. The price:value ratio is excellent at this old-fashioned, cozy restaurant in the new part of Bryggen. The menu includes such modern dishes as rosette of salmon cured and marinated with aquavit and brandy sauce, and lamb roulade stuffed with cheese and mushrooms. *Kjøpmannsgt. 63, tel. 73524110. Reservations advised. AE, DC, MC, V. $$*

★ **Tavern på Sverresborg.** Outside the city, at the open-air Folk Museum, this restaurant serves Norwegian specialties. *Sverresborg, tel. 73520932. V. $$*

LODGING

Royal Garden. Trondheim's finest hotel has excellent facilities for sports and fitness, as well as many features to help guests with disabilities. *Kjøpmannsgt. 73, tel. 73521100, fax 73531766. 297 rooms with bath. Facilities: 3 restaurants, bar, sauna, indoor pool, exercise room. AE, DC, MC, V. $$$*

Ambassadeur. Take in the panoramic view from the roof terrace of this first-rate modern hotel, about 300 feet from the market square. The deep blue waters of the Trondheimsfjord reflect the dramatic and irregular coastline. Most rooms in the Ambassadeur have fireplaces, and some have balconies. *Elvegt. 18, tel. 73527050, fax 73527052. 34 rooms with bath. Facilities: restaurant, bar. AE, DC, MC, V. $–$$*

★ **Bakeriet.** Built as a bakery in 1863, Trondheim's newest hotel opened in March 1991. Few rooms look alike, but all are large and stylish in their simplicity, with natural wood furniture and beige-and-red textiles. Although there's no restaurant, a hot evening meal is included in the room rate. *Brattørgt. 2, tel. 73525200, fax 73502330. 98 rooms with bath or shower. Facilities: sauna. AE, DC, MC, V. $$*

22 Poland

POLES ARE FOND OF QUOTING, with a wry grimace, the old Chinese saying, "May you live in interesting times." The times are certainly interesting in 1990s Poland, the home of the Solidarity trade union movement that sent shock waves through the Soviet bloc in 1980, and the first of the Eastern European states to shake off communist rule. But as the grimace implies, being on the firing line of history—something that the Poles are well used to—can be an uncomfortable experience. You will be constantly reminded that the current return to free-market capitalism after more than 45 years of state socialism is an experiment on an unprecedented scale that brings inconveniences and surprises as well as benefits.

With 38 million inhabitants living in a territory of 121,000 square miles, Poland entered the 1990s suspended between the old world and the new, and the images can be confusing. You will see bright, new, privately owned shops with smiling assistants next to shabby state-sector outlets with the old "take it or leave it" attitudes. Glowing new billboards advertise goods that most Poles cannot afford. Public services, such as transportation, can be cut off suddenly without warning, as local authorities discover that they have insufficient funds to keep the show on the road.

The official trappings of the communist state were quickly dismantled after the Solidarity victory in the 1989 elections. But communism never sat easily with the Poles. It represented yet another stage in their age-old struggle to retain their identity in the face of pressure from the lifestyles of neighbors to the west and east. Founded as a unified state during the 10th century on the great north European plain, Poland lay for a thousand years at the heart of Europe, precisely at the halfway point on a line drawn from the Atlantic coast of Spain to the Ural Mountains. This has never been an enviable position. During the Middle Ages, Poland fought against German advance; in the Golden Age of Polish history during the 16th and 17th centuries—of which you will be reminded by splendid Renaissance buildings in many parts of the country—Poland pushed eastward against her Slavic neighbors, taking Kiev and dreaming of a kingdom that stretched to the Black Sea. By the end of the 18th century, Poland's territories were divided among the Austrian, Prussian, and Russian empires.

During the 20th century, Poland fell victim to peculiarly vicious forms of the old struggle between east and west: the Nazi occupation and Stalin's postwar settlement. Despite this history of hardships, Poland remains a fascinating place for the visitor with an inquiring mind. Its historic cities—Kraków, Warsaw, Gdańsk—tell much of the tale of European history and culture. Its countryside offers unrivaled possibilities of escape from the 20th century. Paradoxically, communism—which after 1956 dropped attempts to collectivize agriculture and left the Polish farmer on his small, uneconomic plot—has preserved rural Poland in a romantic, preindustrial state. Despite pollution, cornflowers still bloom, storks perch atop untidy nests by cottage chimneys, and horsepower still frequently comes in the four-legged variety. While the Poles have a certain wary reserve, they will win you over with their strong individualism—expressed through their well-developed sense of humor and their capacity for conviviality.

Poland

ESSENTIAL INFORMATION

Before You Go

When to Go

The official tourist season runs from May through September. The best times for sightseeing are late spring and early fall. Major cultural events usually take place in the cities during the fall. The early spring is often wet and windy.

Below are the average daily maximum and minimum temperatures for Warsaw.

Jan.	32F	0C	May	67F	20C	Sept.	66F	19C
	22	6		48	9		49	10
Feb.	32F	0C	June	73F	23C	Oct.	55F	13C
	21	− 6		54	12		41	5
Mar.	42F	6C	July	75F	24C	Nov.	42F	6C
	28	− 2		58	16		33	1
Apr.	53F	12C	Aug.	73F	23C	Dec.	35F	2C
	37	3		56	14		28	− 3

Currency

The monetary unit in Poland is the złoty (zł), which is subdivided into 100 groszy (gr). By 1994, inflation had driven groszy, and coins in general, out of circulation; amazingly, there were notes of 50, 100, 200, 500, 1,000, 2,000, 5,000, 10,000, 20,000, 50,000, 100,000, 200,000, 500,000, 1,000,000, and 2,000,000 złotys. However, owing to a more recent currency reform, which has knocked four noughts (or zeroes) off the numeration of the złoty, there are now notes of 10, 20, 50, 100, and 200 złotys, and coins have been reintroduced in values of 1, 2, 5, 10 złotys and 1, 5, 10, and 50 groszys. Today, there is a new official system—listing currency in the simplified form of zł 2.4 (to use the current exchange rate to the U.S. dollar)—and the old traditional system, which continues to refer to zł 2.4 as zł 24,000. These older denominations will remain in circulation until 1997, causing confusion among Poles and visitors alike. At press time (spring 1995), the bank exchange rate was about zł 2.17 (24,000) to the dollar and zł 3.7 (37,000) to the pound sterling.

Since spring 1989, the złoty has been legally exchangeable at a free-market rate in banks (Bank Narodowy and Pekao are the largest) and *kantory* (private exchange bureaus) which sometimes offer slightly better rates than do banks. If you run out of złotys, you will find that Polish taxi drivers, waiters, and porters usually accept dollars or any other Western currency.

CREDIT CARDS
American Express, Diners Club, MasterCard, and Visa are accepted in all major hotels, in the better restaurants and nightclubs, and for other tourist services. In small cafés and shops, credit cards may not be accepted.

What It Will Cost

At press time, it was still illegal to import or export złotys. This may change if the Polish government goes through with plans to make the złoty fully exchangeable on the international market. Still, don't buy more złotys than you need, or you will have to go to the trouble of changing them back at the end of your trip.

Poland is now one of the more expensive countries of Eastern Europe, and, despite the reforms of 1990, inflation is still high by Western standards. Prices are highest in the big cities, especially in Warsaw. The farther you stray from the tourist track, the cheaper your vacation will be.

SAMPLE PRICES
A cup of coffee, zł 1.5–zł 4.5 (15,000–45,000); a bottle of beer, zł 2–zł 4.5 (20,000–45,000); a soft drink, zł 1–zł 4.5 (10,000–45,000); a ham sandwich, zł 2–zł 5 (20,000–50,000); a 1-mile taxi ride, zł 3 (30,000).

MUSEUMS

Admission to museums and other attractions is also rising. At press time, fees ranged from zł 1 (10,000) to zł 10 (100,000).

Visas

Citizens of the U.S. and the United Kingdom are no longer required to obtain visas for entry to Poland; Canadian citizens and citizens of other countries that have not yet abolished visas for Poles must pay the equivalent of $35 (more for multiple-entry visas). Apply at any Orbis office (the official Polish tourist agency), at an affiliated travel agent, or at the Polish Consulate General in any country. Each visitor from Canada and other countries that require visas must complete three visa application forms and provide two photographs. They should allow about two weeks for processing. Such visas are issued for 90 days but can be extended in Poland, if necessary, either through the local county police headquarters or through Orbis.

You can contact the **Polish Consulate General** at the following addresses: **United States:** 233 Madison Ave., New York, NY 10016, tel. 212/391–0844; 1530 N. Lake Shore Dr., Chicago, IL 60610, tel. 312/337–8166; 2224 Wyoming Ave., Washington DC 20008, tel. 202/234–2501. **Canada:** 1500 Pine Ave West., Montréal, Québec H3G 1B4, tel. 514/937–9481; 2603 Lakeshore Blvd. W, Toronto, Ontario M8V 1G5, tel. 416/252–5471. **United Kingdom:** 73 New Cavendish St., London W1, tel. 0171/636–4533.

Customs on Arrival

Persons over 17 may bring in duty-free: personal belongings, including musical instruments, typewriter, radio, 2 cameras with 24 rolls of film; up to 250 cigarettes or 50 cigars and ½ liter each of wine and spirits; and goods with a total value of $200. Any amount of foreign currency may be brought in but must be declared on arrival.

Language

Polish is a Slavic language that uses the Roman alphabet but has several additional characters and diacritics. Because it has a much higher incidence of consonant clusters than English, most English speakers find it a difficult language to decipher, much less pronounce. Most older Poles know German; the younger generation usually knows some English. In the big cities you will find people who speak English, especially in hotels, but you may have difficulty in the provinces and countryside.

Getting Around

By Car

ROAD CONDITIONS

Despite the extensive road network, driving conditions, even on main roads, have deteriorated in the past few years. Minor roads tend to be narrow and cluttered with horse-drawn carts and farm animals. Drivers in a hurry should stick to roads marked E or T.

RULES OF THE ROAD

Driving is on the right, as in the United States. The speed limit on highways is 110 kph (68 mph) and on roads in built-up areas, 60 kph (37 mph). A built-up area is marked by a white rectangular sign with the name of the town on it.

GASOLINE

The price of gas is between zł 13.20 (132,000) and zł 15.60 (156,000)—or approximately between $5.50 and $6.50—for 10 liters of high octane. Filling stations are located every 30 kilometers (20 miles) or so and are usually open 6 AM–10 PM; there are some 24-hour stations.

BREAKDOWNS

Poland's **Motoring Association** (PZMot) offers breakdown, repair, and towing services to members of various international insurance organizations. For names of affiliated organizations, check with Orbis before you leave home. Carry a spare-parts kit. For emergency road help, call 981.

CAR RENTALS

You can rent cars from Avis or Hertz at international airports or through Orbis offices. Rates vary according to season, car model, and mileage. Fly-drive vacations are also available through Orbis.

By Train

Poland's PKP railway network is extensive and inexpensive. Most trains have first- and second-class accommodations, but Western visitors usually prefer to travel first-class. You should arrive at the station well before departure time. The fastest trains are intercity and express trains, which require reservations. Some Orbis offices furnish information, reservations, and tickets. Overnight trains have first- and second-class sleeping cars and second-class couchettes. Most long-distance trains carry buffets, but the quality of the food is unpredictable; you may want to bring your own.

FARES

Polish trains run at three speeds—*ekspresowy* (express), *pośpieszny* (fast), and *osobowy* (slow)—and fares vary according to the speed of the train. You pay more for intercity and express and, unlike lower return-trip fares in other European countries, return-trip tickets cost exactly twice the single fare.

By Plane

LOT, Poland's national airline, operates daily flights linking five main cities: **Warsaw, Kraków, Gdańsk, Wrocław,** and **Rzeszów.** Fares begin at about $60 round-trip. Tickets and information are available from LOT or Orbis offices. All flights booked through Orbis in the United Kingdom carry a discount, but it is cheaper to pay in local currency in Poland. Be sure to book well in advance, especially for the summer season.

By Bus

PKS, the national bus company, offers long-distance service to most cities. Express buses, on which you can reserve seats, are somewhat more expensive than trains but often—except in the case of a few major intercity routes—get to their destination more quickly. For really out-of-the-way destinations, the bus is often the only means of transportation. PKS bus stations are usually near railway stations. Tickets and information are best obtained from Orbis. Warsaw's central bus terminal is located at aleje Jerozolimskie 144.

Staying in Poland

Telephones

LOCAL CALLS

Public phone booths take *żetony* (tokens) or coins for gr 20 (zł 2,000) for local calls and gr 50 (zł 5,000), zł (10,000) or zł (20,000) for long-distance calls, which must be made from special booths, usually in post offices. Place a token in the groove on the side or top of the phone, lift the receiver, and dial the number. Many phones automatically accept the token; in others you must push it into the machine when the call is answered. Phone cards are gradually being introduced and can be used for both local and long-distance calls. Cards, which cost zł 5 (50,000) or 10 (100,000), are available at post offices and some newspaper kiosks. When making a call, first dial 0, wait for the dial tone, then dial your number. To place a domestic long-distance call, dial 900.

INTERNATIONAL CALLS
Post offices and first-class hotels have assigned booths, at which you pay after the completion of your call. To place a call via an **AT&T** US-ADirect international operator, dial 0, wait for dial tone, then 010–480–0111; from major hotels in Warsaw, dial 010–480–0111. To place a call via **MCI,** dial 01–04–800–222; via **Sprint,** dial 0010–480–0115.

COUNTRY CODE
To place phone calls to Poland from abroad, the international country code for Poland is 48.

INFORMATION
For general information (including international codes), dial 913.

Mail
POSTAL RATES
Airmail letters to the United States cost gr 85 (zł 8,500); postcards, gr 65 (zł 6,500). Letters to the United Kingdom or Europe cost gr 65 (zł 6,500); postcards, gr 55 (zł 5,500). Post offices are open weekdays 8 AM–8 PM. At least one post office is open 24 hours in every major city. In Warsaw the post office is located at ulica Świętokrzyska 31.

Opening and Closing Times
Banks are open weekdays 8 or 9 AM–3 or 6 PM.

Museum hours vary greatly but are generally Tuesday–Sunday 9–5.

Shops. Food shops are open weekdays 7–7, Saturday 7 AM–1 PM; many are now open on Sunday, and there are a few all-night stores in most districts. Other stores are open weekdays 11 AM–7 PM and Saturday 9 AM–1 PM.

National Holidays
January 1; April 7, 8 (Easter Sunday and Monday); May 1 (Labor Day); May 3 (Constitution Day); June 20 (Corpus Christi); August 15 (Assumption); November 1 (All Saints Day); November 11 (rebirth of Polish state, 1918); December 25, 26.

Dining
Polish food and drink are basically Slavic with Baltic overtones. There is a heavy emphasis on soups and meat (especially pork) as well as freshwater fish. Much use is made of cream, and pastries are rich and often delectable.

The most popular soup is *barszcz* (known to many Americans as borscht), a clear beet soup often served with such Polish favorites as sausage, cabbage, potatoes, sour cream, coarse rye bread, and beer. Other dishes include pierogi, which may be stuffed with savory or sweet fillings; *gołąbki,* cabbage leaves stuffed with minced meat; *bigos,* sauerkraut with meat and mushrooms; and *flaki,* a select dish of tripe, served boiled or fried. Polish beer is good; vodka is a specialty and is often downed before, during, and after meals.

Zajazdy (roadside inns), which are less expensive than regular restaurants, serve more traditional food. As elsewhere in central Europe, cafés are a way of life in Poland and are often stocked with delicious pastries and ice creams.

MEALTIMES

At home, Poles eat late lunches (their main meal, usually around 4 PM) and late suppers (a light dinner around 10 PM). Restaurants—especially in major cities—are increasingly operating on a earlier timetable, more in line with American custom. Many establishments only begin service at 2 PM, but more sophisticated restaurants have been opening their doors around noon to offer a luncheon distinct from the late afternoon meal; they then serve a regular dinner between 7–10 PM. Athough many restaurants continue to close at 9 PM—especially in the provinces—more cosmopolitan establishments are staying open to 10 or 11 PM; Most hotel restaurants serve the evening meal until 10:30.

PRECAUTIONS

Tap water is unsafe, so ask for mineral water. Beware of meat dishes served in cheap snack bars. Avoid the food on trains.

WHAT TO WEAR

In Warsaw and Kraków, formal dress is customary at **$$$** restaurants. Casual dress is appropriate elsewhere.

RATINGS

Prices are for one person and include three courses and service but not drinks. Highly recommended restaurants are indicated by a star ★.

CATEGORY	WARSAW	OTHER AREAS
$$$$	over zł 70 (700,000)	over zł 60 (600,000)
$$$	zł 50–70 (500,000–700,000)	zł 40–60 (400,000–600,000)
$$	zł 25–50 (250,000–500,000)	zł 20–40 (200,000–400,000)
$	under zł 25 (250,000)	under zł 20 (200,000)

Lodging

HOTELS

The government rates hotel accommodations on the basis of one to five stars. Orbis hotels, owned by the state tourist office and currently undergoing privatization, have almost all been accorded four or five stars and guarantee a reasonable standard of cleanliness and service (although some travelers will find them characterless). They range in price from **$$** to **$$$$** and include a number of foreign-built luxury hotels, such as the InterContinental. In recent years Orbis hotels have faced competition from a growing number of privately owned lodgings, often part of international chains and mostly at the top end of the price range.

Municipal hotels and Dom Turysty hotels are run by local authorities or the Polish Tourist Association. They are often rather old and have limited bath and shower facilities. Prices are in the **$** category.

ROADSIDE INNS

A number of roadside inns, many of which are very attractive, offer inexpensive food and a few guest rooms at moderate rates.

PRIVATE ACCOMMODATIONS

Rooms can be arranged either in advance through Orbis or on the spot at the local tourist information office. Villas, lodges, rooms, or houses are available, and the prices are often negotiable. Rates vary from about $6 for a room to more than $150 for a villa.

RATINGS

The following chart is based on a rate for two people in a double room, with bath or shower and breakfast. These prices are in U.S. dollars; Most hotels in Poland quote prices in American dollars or German marks because of the fluctuations in Polish currency and the complicated twin systems of Polish denominations. Highly recommended lodgings are indicated by a star ★.

CATEGORY	COST
$$$$	over $200
$$$	$100–$200
$$	$50–$100
$	under $50

Tipping

Waiters get a standard 10% of the bill. Hotel porters and doormen should get about zł 2 (20,000). In Warsaw and other big towns frequented by foreign tourists, waiters also often expect a tip to help find you a table. If you choose to tip in foreign currency (readily accepted), remember that $1 is about an hour's wage.

WARSAW

Arriving and Departing

By Plane

All international flights arrive at Warsaw's Okęcie Airport (Port Lotniczy) just southwest of the city. Terminal 1 serves international flights; Terminal 2 serves domestic flights. For flight information, contact the airlines, or call the airport at tel. 02/650–42–20.

BETWEEN THE AIRPORT AND DOWNTOWN

LOT operates a regular bus service into Warsaw. Orbis cars and minivans also transport visitors to their hotels. Warsaw city transport Bus 175, which runs past almost all major downtown hotels, leaves Okęcie every 10 minutes during peak hours, and every 14 minutes at other times. The trip takes about 15 minutes and the fare is gr 60 (zł 6,000). There is also a direct airport–city bus to the main hotels at a fare of zł 2.5 (25,000).

By Train

Trains to and from Western Europe arrive at Dworzec Centralny (Central Station) on aleje Jerozolimskie in the center of town. For tickets and information, contact Orbis.

By Car

There are seven main access routes to Warsaw, all leading to the center of the city. Drivers heading to or from the West will use the E8 or E12 highways.

Getting Around

By Tram and Bus

These are often crowded, but they are the cheapest way of getting around. Trams and buses (including express buses) cost gr 60 (zł 6,000). The bus fare goes up to zł 2 (20,000) between 11 PM and 5:30 AM. Tickets must be bought in advance from **Ruch** newsstands or certain shops. You must cancel your own ticket in a machine on the tram or bus when you get on; watch others do it.

By Taxi

Taxis are a relatively cheap ride—about zł 3 (30,000) per mile (1.6 kilometers)—and are readily available at stands downtown; the Marriott and Victoria hotels have their own monogrammed fleets. There is an efficient radio taxi service (tel. 919) that is much cheaper than taxis at stands.

By Buggy

Horse-drawn carriages can be rented at a negotiated price from the Old Town Market Square.

Important Addresses and Numbers

Tourist Information

The **Center for Tourist Information** is open 9 to 6 weekdays, and 11 to 6 weekends; it is at plac Zamkowy 1, tel. 02/635–18–81. **Orbis** offices in Warsaw include: ulica Bracka 16, tel. 022/26–02–71; and ulica Marszałkowska 142, tel. 022/27–80–31 or 022/27–36–73.

Embassies

U.S. (al. Ujazdowskie 29–31, tel. 02/628–30–41). **Canadian** (ul. Matejki 1/5, tel. 022/29–80–51). **U.K.** (al. Róż 1, tel. 02/628–10–01). **U.K. Consulate** (ul. Emilii Plater 28, tel. 02/625–30–30).

Emergencies

Police (tel. 997). **Ambulance** (tel. 998). **Doctor** (tel. 998 or call your embassy).

Travel Agencies

American Express (ul. Bagińskiego 1, tel. 02/635–20–02). **Thomas Cook** (ul. Nowy Świat 64, tel. 022/26–47–29). **Polish Motoring Association** (PZMot, al. Jerozolimskie 63, tel. 022/29–45–50).

Guided Tours

Bus tours of the city depart in the morning and afternoon from the major hotels. **Orbis** also has half-day excursions into the surrounding countryside. These usually include a meal and some form of traditional entertainment. Check for details with your hotel, the Orbis office, or the tourist information office.

Exploring Warsaw

At the end of World War II, Warsaw lay in ruins, a victim of systematic Nazi destruction. Only one-third of its prewar population survived the horrors of German occupation. The experience left its mark on the city and is visible everywhere in the memorial plaques describing mass executions of civilians and in the bullet holes on the facades of buildings. Against all the odds, Warsaw's survivors have rebuilt their historic city. The old districts have been painstakingly reconstructed according to old prints and paintings, including those of Bernardo Bellotto and Canaletto from the 18th century. The result, a city of warm pastel colors, is remarkable.

Surrounding the old districts, however, is the modern Warsaw, built since the war in utilitarian Socialist-Realist and later styles. Whether you like it or not is your business, but it is worth noting as a testimony to one approach to urban life. The sights of Warsaw are all relatively close to one another, making most attractions accessible by foot.

Numbers in the margin correspond to points of interest on the Warsaw map.

The Stare Miasto (Old Town)

A walking tour of the old historic district takes about two hours. **①** Begin in the heart of the city at **plac Zamkowy** (Castle Square), where you will see a slender column supporting the **statue of Zygmunt (Sigismund) III Wasa,** the king who made Warsaw his capital in the early 17th century. It is the city's oldest monument and, symbolically, the first to be rebuilt after the wartime devastation. Dominating the square **②** is the **Zamek Królewski** (Royal Castle). Restoring the interior was a herculean task, requiring workers to relearn traditional skills, match ancient woods and fabrics, and even reopen abandoned quarries to find just the right kind of stone. *Plac Zamkowy 4, tel. 02/635–39–95. Admission: zł 8 (80,000) adults, zł 4 (40,000) children. Tours leave hourly from side entrance. Open Tues.–Sat. 10–2:30, Sun. 9–2:30.*

Enter the narrow streets of the **Stare Miasto** (Old Town), with its colorful medieval houses, cobblestone alleys, uneven roofs, and wrought-iron grillwork. On your right as you proceed along ulica Świętojańska **③** is the **Bazylika świętego Jana** (Cathedral of St. John), the oldest church in Warsaw, dating from the 14th century. Several Polish kings were **④** crowned here. Soon you will reach the **Rynek Starego Miasta** (Old Market Square), the charming and intimate center of the Old Town. The town hall, which once stood in the middle, was pulled down in the 19th century. It was not replaced, and today the square is full of open-air cafés, tubs of flowering plants, and the inevitable artists displaying their talents for tourists. At night the brightly lighted Rynek is the place to go for good food and atmosphere.

Continue along ulica Nowomiejska until you reach the pinnacled red- **⑤** brick **Barbakan,** a fine example of a 16th-century defensive fortification. From here you can see the partially restored wall that was built to enclose the Old Town, and enjoy a splendid view of the Vistula River, with the district of Praga on its east bank.

Follow the street called ulica Freta to Warsaw's **Nowe Miasto** (New Town), which was founded at the turn of the 15th century. Rebuilt after the war in 18th-century style, this district has a more elegant and spacious **⑥** feeling to it. Of interest here is the **Muzeum Marii Skłodowskiej-Curie,** where the woman who discovered radium and polonium was born. *Ul. Freta 16, tel. 022/31–80–92. Admission: zł 1 (10,000) adults, gr 50 (zł 5,000) children. Open Tues.–Sat. 10–4:30, Sun. 10–2:30.*

The Royal Route

All towns with kings had their Royal Routes; the one in Warsaw—the Trakt Królewski— stretched south from Castle Square down Krakowskie Prze dmieście, curving through Nowy Świat and on along aleje Ujaz- **⑦** dowskie to the **Pałac Belweder** (Belvedere Palace) and Łazienki Park. Some of Warsaw's finest churches and palaces are found along this route, as well as the names of famous Poles. A few blocks south of plac **⑧** Zamkowy on Krakowskie Przedmieście, you'll come to the **University ⑨** of Warsaw** on your left. Farther down, on your right, the **Kościoł świętego Krzyża** (Holy Cross Church) contains a pillar in which the heart of the great Polish composer Frédéric Chopin is entombed. As you pass the statue of Polish-born Nicolaus Copernicus, the great astronomer, you enter the busy Nowy Świat thoroughfare. Crossing aleje Jerozolimskie, on your left is the **former headquarters of the Polish Communist Party.** This large, solid, gray building, done in the Socialist-Realist architectural style, now houses banks and Poland's new stock exchange.

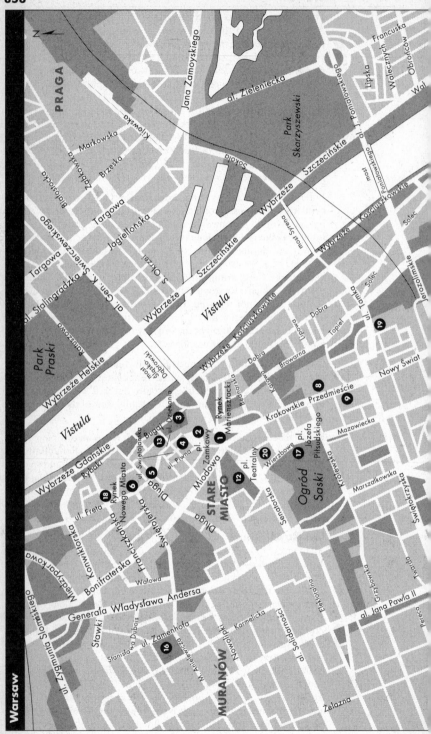

859

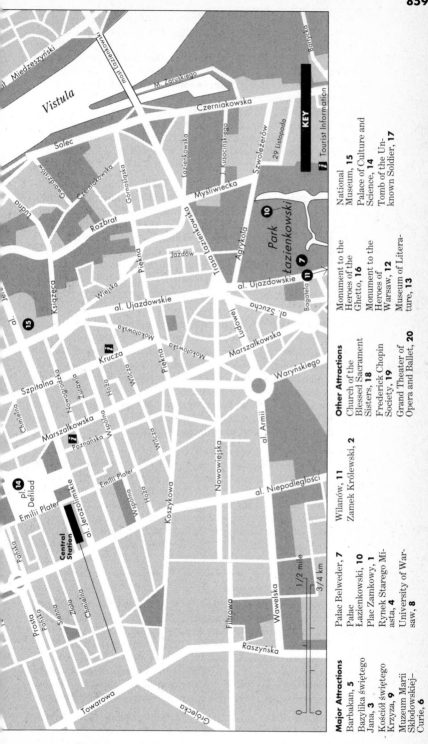

Major Attractions
Barbakan, **5**
Bazylika świętego
Jana, **3**
Kościół świętego
Krzyza, **9**
Muzeum Marii
Skłodowskiej-
Curie, **6**

Pałac Belweder, **7**
Pałac
Łazienkowski, **10**
Plac Zamkowy, **1**
Rynek Starego Mi-
asta, **4**
University of War-
saw, **8**

Wilanów, **11**
Zamek Królewski, **2**

Other Attractions
Church of the
Blessed Sacrament
Sisters, **18**
Frederick Chopin
Society, **19**
Grand Theater of
Opera and Ballet, **20**

Monument to the
Heroes of the
Ghetto, **16**
Monument to the
Heroes of
Warsaw, **12**
Museum of Litera-
ture, **13**

National
Museum, **15**
Palace of Culture and
Science, **14**
Tomb of the Un-
known Soldier, **17**

Aleje Ujazdowskie is considered by many locals to be Warsaw's finest street. It is lined with magnificent buildings and has something of a French flavor to it. At its southern end, before the name inexplicably changes to Belwederska, the French-style landscaped **Park Łazienkowski** (Łazienki Park), with pavilions and a royal palace, stands in refreshing contrast to the bustling streets. The **Pałac Łazienkowski** (Łazienki Palace), a gem of Polish neoclassical style, was the private residence of Stanisław August Poniatowski, the last king of Poland. It overlooks a lake stocked with huge carp. At the impressionistic Chopin monument nearby, you can stop for a well-deserved rest and, on summer Sundays, listen to an open-air concert. *Tel. 02/621–62–41. Admission: zł 3 (30,000) adults, zł 1.5 (15,000) children. Open Tues.–Sat. 9:30–3.*

The Royal Route extends along ulica Belwederska, ulica Jana Sobieskiego, and aleja Wilanowska to the **Wilanów,** 10 kilometers (6 miles) from the town center. This charming Baroque palace was the summer residence of King Jan III Sobieski, who, in 1683, stopped the Ottoman advance on Europe at the Battle of Vienna. The palace interior is open and houses antique furniture and a fine poster museum. *Ul. Wiertnicza 1l, tel. 022/42–07–95. Admission: zł 3 (30,000) adults, zł 1.5 (15,000) children. Open Wed.–Mon. 10–2:30.*

Off the Beaten Track

Some 3 million Polish Jews were put to death by the Nazis during World War II, ending the enormous Jewish contribution to Polish culture, tradition, and achievement. A simple monument to the **Heroes of the Warsaw Ghetto,** a slab of dark granite with a bronze bas-relief, stands on ulica Zamenhofa in the Muranów district, the historic heart of the old prewar Warsaw Jewish district and ghetto under the Nazi regime. The Warsaw Ghetto uprising that broke out in April 1943 was put down with unbelievable ferocity, and the Muranów district was flattened. Today there are only bleak gray apartment blocks here.

With ironic humor, Warsaw locals tell you that the best vantage point from which to admire their city is atop the 37-story **Palace of Culture and Science.** Why? Because it is the only point from which you can't see the Palace of Culture and Science. This wedding-cake-style skyscraper was a personal gift from Stalin. Although it is disliked by Poles as a symbol of Soviet domination, it does afford a panoramic view and is the best example in Warsaw of 1950s "Socialist Gothic" architecture. *Plac Defilad, tel. 02/656–67–77. Admission: zł 7.5 (75,000) adults, zł 2.5 (25,000) children. Open daily 9–5.*

Shopping

Nowy Świat, Krakowskie Przedmieście, and ulica Chmielna are lined with boutiques selling good-quality leather goods, clothing, and trinkets. Try the **Cepelia** stores (plac Konstytucji 5 and Rynek Starego Miasta 8–10) for a wide range of handicrafts, such as glass, enamelware, amber, and handwoven woolen rugs. **Orno** shops (Marszałkowska 83 and Nowy Świat 52) offer handmade jewelry and silverware. **Desa** (Marszałkowska 34) specializes in ornaments and objets d'art. Polish and imported wines and spirits can be found at most large delicatessens.

For the more adventurous there is a flea market, **Bazar Różyckiego,** at ulica Targowa 55, where you can find almost anything. An even bigger market, where visitors from all over Eastern Europe sell their wares, is open daily at the **Stadion Tysiąclecia** sports stadium, near Rondo Waszyngtona.

Dining

More and more interesting restaurants have been opening throughout the city, but some of the best and most atmospheric dining rooms are still to be found on and around the Rynek Starego Miasta in the Old Town. The brightly lighted area is a pleasant place to walk before or after dinner. Reservations for dinner can be made by telephone (by your hotel receptionist if you don't speak Polish); in the case of expensive and fashionable restaurants, this is usually necessary. For details and price-category definitions, *see* Dining *in* Staying in Poland, *above.*

$$$ Bazyliszek. Dimly lighted and elegant, the Bazyliszek excels in such game as boar, venison, and duck. A good café and snack bar are downstairs. *Rynek Starego Miasta 7/9, tel. 022/31–18–41. Reservations advised. AE, DC, MC, V.*

$$$ Canaletto. Located in the Victoria Inter-Continental hotel, this restau-
★ rant serves Polish specialties with a good selection of European wines. The two paintings of old Warsaw on the walls are reputed to be by Canaletto himself. *Pl. Piłsudskiego, tel. 022/27–92–91. Reservations advised. AE, DC, MC, V.*

$$$ Flik. A new restaurant in Mokotów, Flik is light and spacious and boasts
★ a lantern-lighted terrace overlooking the Morskie Oko park. The proprietors are devoted to serving good food and tend toward nouvelle cuisine. Try the fresh salmon to start. *Ul. Puławska 43, tel. 022/49–43–34. Reservations advised. AE, DC, MC, V.*

$$$ Forum. Another good hotel restaurant, the Forum offers traditional Polish mixed with conventional Central European meat dishes. Like Canaletto, it is frequented by Western businesspeople and tourists. *Ul. Nowogrodzka 24, tel. 02/621–01–19. Reservations advised. AE, DC, MC, V.*

$$ Kamienne Schodki. This intimate, candlelighted restaurant is in one of the Old Market Square's medieval houses. Its specialty is duck; also try the pastries. *Rynek Starego Miasta 26, tel. 022/31–08–22. Reservations advised. AE, DC, MC, V.*

$$ Pod Samsonem. This small restaurant, decorated in wood, has a smoke-filled Warsaw atmosphere and friendly waitresses. The fish and pierogi are good when available. *Ul. Freta 3/5, tel. 022/31–17–88. Reservations accepted. No credit cards.*

Lodging

Orbis hotels are recommended for convenience and high standards. The rooms are comfortable though standardized, with functional, nondescript carpeting and furniture. Some rooms are beginning to show signs of wear. Private accommodations are cheap and hospitable, and are available through Orbis, through the Center for Tourist Information, or Warszawska i Krajowa Informacja Noclegowa (tel. 02/643–95–92). There is no off-season for tourism. For details and price-category definitions, *see* Lodging *in* Staying in Poland, *above.*

$$$$ Bristol. Warsaw's most famous hotel was reopened in December 1992 after more than a decade of renovation and modernization. Once owned by Ignacy Paderewski, the concert pianist who served as Poland's prime minister in 1919–1920, the Bristol was always at the center of Warsaw's social life. Distinguished guests have included Charles de Gaulle and Marlene Dietrich. *Krakowskie Przedmieście 42–44, tel. 02/625–25–25, fax 02/625–25–77. 163 rooms with bath, 43 suites. Facilities: 2 restaurants, 2 bars, café, satellite TV in suites, sauna, solarium, pool. AE, DC, MC, V.*

$$$$ **Marriott.** The Warsaw Marriott was completed in late 1989, and at 40
★ stories (20 make up the hotel; the rest are set aside for office and retail shopping space), it is also the city's tallest building. Luxuries include 11 restaurants, 24-hour room service, and a color TV in every
room. *Al. Jerozolimskie 65, tel. 02/630–63–06, fax 022/30–52–39.
525 rooms with bath. Facilities: restaurants, bars, casino, health club,
swimming pool, sauna, shopping arcade. AE, DC, MC, V.*

$$$ **Holiday Inn.** This five-story hotel in the center of the city opened in
1989. All its rooms are equipped with color TV offering four satellite
programs. One floor is reserved for nonsmokers. *Ul. Złota 2, tel.
022/20–03–41, fax 022/30–05–69. 338 rooms with bath. Facilities:
restaurants, bars, business center, health club, sauna. AE, DC, MC, V.*

$$$ **Victoria Inter-Continental.** Frequented by Western travelers, this is a large
1970s hotel in an ideal location in the center of town. It has a variety
of facilities, including a fine restaurant and nightclub. Try to get a room
facing Victory Square. *Ul. Królewska 11, tel. 022/27–92–71, fax
022/27–98–56. 370 rooms, most with bath or shower. Facilities:
restaurant, nightclub, casino, sauna, indoor pool. AE, DC, MC, V.*

$$ **Hotel Europejski.** This fine old Warsaw hotel is in the heart of the city.
★ It was built in the 19th century in neo-Renaissance style, and its decor
is elegant and refined. The rooms are spacious and attractive; some have
hosted kings, presidents, and diplomats. The hotel takes pride in its
restaurant. *Krakowskie Przedmieście 13, tel. 022/26–50–51, fax
022/26–11–11. 279 rooms, most with bath or shower. Facilities:
restaurant. AE, DC, MC, V.*

$$ **Orbis Grand.** Conveniently located in the center of the city, this large
hotel was built in the 1950s and is a prime example of the Socialist-
Realist architecture of the period. It has a rooftop restaurant-café and
offers live jazz, dancing, or cabaret in the evening. *Ul. Krucza 28, tel.
022/29–40–51, fax 02/621–97–24. 415 rooms, some with shower.
Facilities: restaurant, café, nightclub, indoor pool, hairdresser. AE,
DC, MC, V.*

$$ **Zajazd Napoleoński.** This small, privately owned inn has an excellent
★ restaurant and deluxe facilities. Napoléon reputedly stayed here when
his Grand Army passed through Warsaw on its way to Russia. It is about
12.8 kilometers (8 miles) outside of town. Book well in advance. *Ul.
Płowiecka 83, tel. 022/15–30–68, fax 022/15–22–16. 22 rooms with
bath, 3 suites. Facilities: restaurant. AE, DC, MC, V.*

The Arts

For information, buy the newspaper *Życie Warszawy* or *Gazeta Wybor-
cza* at Ruch newsstands. Tickets can be ordered by your Orbis hotel
receptionist, through the tourist information center (pl. Zamkowy 1,
tel. 02/635–18–81), or at the ticket office at ulica Marszałkowska 104.

Theaters

There are 17 theaters in Warsaw, attesting to the popularity of this art
form, but none offers English performances. **Teatr Narodowy,** opened
in 1764 and the oldest in Poland, is on plac Teatralny; after a major
fire, it was scheduled to be closed for repairs and may reopen during
1996. **Teatr Polski Kameralny** (Foksal 16) has a small stage. **Współczesny**
(Mokotowska 13) shows contemporary works.

Concerts

The **National Philharmonic** is regarded as the country's best orchestra.
The hall is at ulica Sienkiewicza 12. An excellent new concert hall, opened
in 1992, is the **Studio Concertowe Polskiego Radia** (Woronicza 17). In
summer, free Chopin concerts take place both at the Chopin monu-

ment in **Łazienki Park** and each Sunday at **Żelazowa Wola,** the composer's birthplace, 58 kilometers (36 miles) outside Warsaw.

Opera
Teatr Wielki (plac Teatralny) hosts the Grand Theater of Opera and Ballet. Its stage is superb—one of the largest in Europe.

Nightlife

Cabaret
The Victoria, Forum, Grand, Europejski, and Marriott hotels all have nightclubs that are popular with Westerners. The acts vary, so check listings in the press. These clubs also present striptease and jazz.

Bars
Gwiazdeczka (Piwna 42) is a noisy, hip, upscale joint, popular with chic young Warsovians. The **Irish Pub** (Koszykowa 1) is a fashionable recent addition to Warsaw's nightspots. **Harenda** (Krakowskie Przedmieście 4–6), with an outdoor terrace in summer, is open until 4 AM.

Jazz Clubs
Akwarium (ul. Emilii Platter 49) and **Wanda Warska's Modern Music Club** (ul. Watowa 7) are popular jazz clubs. A new jazz club that is winning a major following is **Jazz Club 77** (Marszałkowska 77–79).

Discos
Apart from those in the hotels, the most popular discos are **Hybrydy** (Złota 7) and **Stodoła** (Batorego 10); note that the press has reported that violent incidents have occurred outside these establishments.

Cafés
Warsaw is filled with *kawiarnie* (cafés), which move outdoors in summer. They are popular meeting places and usually serve delicious coffee and pastries in the best Central European style.

Ambassador is an elegant, brightly lighted café with a tree-lined terrace that's open in the summer. *Ul. Matejki 4.*

Nowe Miasto, the former **Bonbonierka,** is a vegetarian café-cum-restaurant, with cane furniture and a resident harpist. *Rynek Nowego Miasta 13–15.*

Le Petit Trianon is an intimate 18th-century French-style restaurant and café. It is difficult to find a seat here, but worth it once you do. *Ul. Piwna 40.*

Telimena is a small corner café with an art gallery on the ground floor. *Krakowskie Przedmieście 27.*

Wilanowska has definitely seen better days, but its crumbling elegance has a certain appeal. *Pl. Trzech Krzyży 3.*

KRAKÓW AND ENVIRONS

Kraków (Cracow), seat of Poland's oldest university and once the capital of the country (before losing the honor to Warsaw in 1611), is one of the few Polish cities that escaped devastation during World War II. Today Kraków's fine ramparts, towers, facades, and churches, illustrating seven centuries of Polish architecture, make it a major attraction for visitors. Its location—about 270 kilometers (160 miles) south of Warsaw—also makes it a good base for hiking and skiing trips in a mountains of southern Poland.

Also within exploring range from Kraków are the famous Polish shrine to the Virgin Mary at Częstochowa, and, at Auschwitz (Oświęcim), a grim reminder of man's capacity for inhumanity.

Getting Around

Kraków is reached by major highways—E7 direct from Warsaw and E82 from Częstochowa. Trains link Kraków with most major destinations in Poland; the station is in the city center near the Old Town, on ulica Pawia. The bus station is nearby.

Guided Tours

Bus or walking tours of Kraków and its environs are provided by **Orbis.** Horse-drawn carriages can be rented at the main market square for a negotiated price.

Tourist Information

Częstochowa (al. najświętszej Marii Panny 37/39, tel. 034/24–71–34). **Kraków** (ul. Pawia 8, tel. 012/22–95–10).

Exploring Kraków

Numbers in the margin correspond to points of interest on the Kraków map.

Kraków's old city is ringed by a park called the **Planty.** The park replaced the old walls of the town, which were torn down in the mid-19th century. Begin your tour at **Brama Floriańska** (St. Florian's Gate), which leads to the Old Town. The gate is guarded by an imposing 15th-century fortress called the **Barbakan.** Enter the city, passing along ulica Floriańska, the beginning of the Royal Route through town.

TIME OUT Don't pass up the chance to stop for refreshments at Kraków's most famous café, **Jama Michalikowa** (ul. Floriańska 45), which now has a no-smoking area. It serves good coffee and excellent ice cream.

❷ Ulica Floriańska leads to the **Rynek Główny** (main market square), one of the largest and finest Renaissance squares in Europe. The calm of this spacious square, with its pigeons and flower stalls, is interrupted every hour by four short bugle calls drifting down from the spire of ❸ the **Kościół Mariacki** (Church of the Virgin Mary). The plaintive notes recall a centuries-old tradition in memory of a trumpeter whose throat was pierced by a well-aimed enemy arrow as he was warning his fellow citizens of an impending Tartar attack. The square Church of the Virgin Mary contains a 15th-century wooden altarpiece—the largest in the world—carved by Veit Stoss. The faces of the saints are reputedly those of Cracovian burghers. In the center of the square stands a ❹ covered market called **Sukiennice** (Cloth Hall), built in the 14th century but remodeled during the Renaissance. The ground floor is still in business, selling trinkets and folk art souvenirs. *Open Mon.–Sat. 10–6, Sun. 10–5.*

From the main market square, turn down ulica świętej Anny to No. ❺ 8, the **Collegium Maius,** the oldest building of the famous **Jagiellonian University** (founded 1364). Its pride is the Italian-style arcaded courtyard. Inside is a museum where you can see the Copernicus globe, the first on which the American continents were shown, as well as astronomy instruments belonging to Kraków's most famous graduate. *Admission*

Kraków

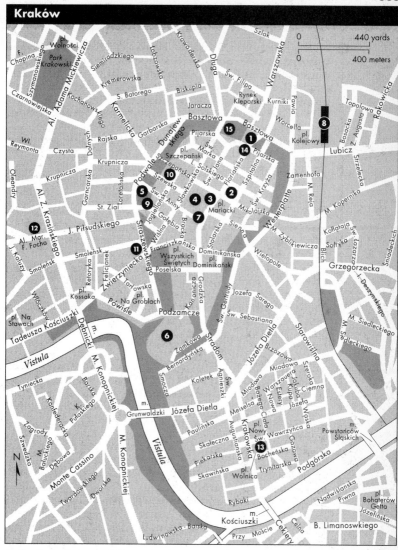

Major Attractions
Brama Floriańska, **1**
Jagiellonian University, **5**
Kościół Mariacki, **3**
Rynek Główny, **2**
Sukiennice, **4**
Wawel Castle and Cathedral, **6**

Other Attractions
Barbakan, **14**
Central Station, **8**
Czartoryski Museum, **15**
Ethnographic Museum, **13**
Helena Modrzejewska Stary Theater, **10**

Jagiellonian University Museum, **9**
K. Szymanowski State Philharmonic Hall, **11**
National Museum, **12**
St. Adalbert Romanesque Church, **7**

free. Courtyard open Mon.–Sat. 8–6. Museum shown by appointment only, 10–noon.

❻ Backtracking on ulica Grodzka will lead you to the **Wawel Castle and Cathedral.** This impressive complex of Gothic and Renaissance buildings stands on fortifications dating from as far back as the 8th century. Inside the castle is a museum with an exotic collection of Oriental tents that were captured from the Turks at the Battle of Vienna in 1683 and rare 16th-century Flemish tapestries. Wawel Cathedral is where, until the 18th century, Polish kings were crowned and buried. Until 1978, the cathedral was the principal church of the see of Archbishop Karol Wojtyła, now Pope John Paul II. *Ul. Grodzka, tel. 012/22–51–55. Castle. Admission: zł 5 (50,000) adults, zł 2.5 (25,000) children. Open Tues., Thurs., Sat., Sun. 9:30–3, Wed. and Fri. noon–6. Cathedral Museum. Admission: zł 2 (20,000). Open Tues.–Sun. 10–3.*

Schindler's List, Steven Spielberg's award-winning 1993 film, has inspired visitors to Kraków to retrace the steps of German industrialist Oskar Schindler, who saved the lives of more than 1,200 Jews during the Holocaust by hiring them to work in his enamel factory at ulica Lipowa 4. For those eager to learn the true history of the Jewish community that once made up one-third of the population of Kraków, "Schindler's List" tours are offered by Orbis and the Judaica bookstore, Jordan. The two-hour minibus tours include such landmarks as the Kazimierz district, the Liban quarry, the Plaszow concentration camp (now a city park), and the Vitula River bridge. *"Schindler's List" tours: Jordan Book Shop, ul. Szeroka 2, Miodowa 41, tel. 012/21–71–66, and Orbis, ul. Bracka 16, tel. 022/26–02–71.*

About 50 kilometers (30 miles) west of Kraków is Oświęcim, better known by its German name, **Auschwitz.** Here 4 million victims, mostly Jews, were executed by the Nazis in the Auschwitz and Birkenau concentration camps. Auschwitz is now a museum, with restored crematoria and barracks housing dramatic displays of Nazi atrocities. The buildings at Birkenau, a 15-minute walk away, have been left just as they were found in 1945 by the Soviet Army. Oświęcim itself is an industrial town with good connections from Kraków; buses and trains leave Kraków approximately every hour, and signs in Oświęcim direct visitors to the camp. *Auschwitz: ul. Więźniów Oświęcimia 20, tel. 0381/321–33. Admission free. Open Mar. and Nov., Tues.–Sun. 8–4; Apr. and Oct., Tues.–Sun. 8–5; May and Sept., daily 8–6; June–Aug., daily 8–7; Dec.–Feb., Tues.–Sun. 8–3. Birkenau: admission free, open all times.*

Wieliczka, about 8 kilometers (5 miles) southeast of Kraków, is the oldest salt mine in Europe, in operation since the end of the 13th century. It is famous for its magnificent underground chapel hewn from crystal rock, the **Chapel of the Blessed Kinga** (Queen Kinga was a 14th-century Polish queen, later beatified). *Ul. Daniłowicza 10, tel. 012/22–08–52, admission: zł. 10 (100,000) adults, zł 5 (50,000) children. Open daily 9–4.*

Częstochowa, 120 kilometers (70 miles) from Kraków and reached by regular trains and buses, is the home of the holiest shrine in a country that is more than 90% Catholic. Inside the 14th-century **Pauline monastery** on Jasna Góra (Light Hill) is the famous *Black Madonna,* a painting of Our Lady of Częstochowa attributed by legend to St. Luke. It was here that an invading Swedish army met herioc resistance from the Poles in 1655. About 25 miles southwest of Kraków is the little town of **Wadowice,** birthplace of Pope John Paul II. *Wadowice Mu-*

seum. Admission: zł 2 (20,000) adults, zł 1 (10,000) children. Open Tues.–Sat. 10–3, Sun. 10–5.

Dining and Lodging

For details and price-category definitions, *see* Dining and Lodging *in* Staying in Poland, *above.*

Częstochowa

LODGING

Polonia. The Polonia makes a good base for exploring the Pauline monastery, and since most of the other guests are pilgrims, the atmosphere is an interesting mixture of piety and good fun. *Ul. Piłsudskiego 9, tel. 034/24–40–67, fax 034/65–11–05. 62 rooms, most with bath or shower. Facilities: restaurant, café. AE, DC, MC, V. $*

Kraków

DINING

Staropolska. Traditional Polish cuisine is served in a medieval setting. Try the pork, duck, or veal. *Ul. Sienna 4, tel. 012/22–58–21. Reservations advised. AE, DC, MC, V. $$$*

★ **Wierzynek.** One of the best restaurants in the country, Wierzynek serves traditional Polish specialties and excels in soups and game. It was here, after a historic meeting in 1364, that the king of Poland wined and dined the Holy Roman Emperor Charles IV, five kings, and a score of princes. *Rynek Główny 15, tel. 012/22–14–04. Reservations advised. AE, DC, MC, V. $$$*

DINING AND LODGING

Francuski. This small hotel is just inside the Old Town's ramparts, within walking distance of all the main sights. Built at the turn of the century, it offers an intimate atmosphere and friendly service. The rooms are elegant in a homey, Eastern European way. The excellent restaurant is tranquil and plush and has a café with dancing. The hotel reopened in late 1991 after extensive renovations. *Ul. Pijarska 13, tel. 012/22–51–22, fax 012/22–52–70. 42 rooms, most with bath or shower. Facilities: restaurant, café. AE, DC, MC, V. $$$*

★ **Cracovia.** This large, Orbis-run, five-story 1960s hotel boasts one of the best restaurants in town—the chef specializes in an internationalized Polish cusine; try the *krem z pieczarek* (thick and creamy mushroom soup), followed by chateaubriand. There is also a lively nightclub where Western tourists like to meet. *Al. Marszałka F. Focha 1, tel. 012/22–86–66, fax 012/21–95–86. 427 rooms with bath. Facilities: restaurant, nightclub. AE, DC, MC, V. $$*

Holiday Inn. This was the first Holiday Inn in Eastern Europe. Rather bland but comfortable, this high-rise establishment is pleasantly located on the far side of Kraków Common, making it a good choice for those who want to combine sightseeing with a little exercise. *Ul. Koniewa 7, tel. 012/37–50–44, fax 012/37–59–38. 310 rooms with bath. Facilities: restaurant, solarium, sauna, indoor pool. AE, DC, MC, V. $$*

LODGING

Forum. Opened in 1988, this Orbis hotel stands on the south bank of the Vistula, commanding a fine view of Wawel Castle. *Ul. Marii Konopnickiej 28, tel. 012/66–95–00, fax 012/66–58–27. 280 rooms with bath. Facilities: restaurant, sauna, indoor pool, tennis courts, beauty salon. AE, DC, MC, V. $$$*

★ **Grand.** Reopened in 1990 after a 12-year renovation, this late-19th-century hotel in the heart of the Old Town is elegant and comfortable. It has reproduction period furniture but modern bathrooms and facilities. *Ul. Sławkowska 5–7, tel. 012/21–72–55, fax 012/21–83–60.*

50 rooms with bath. Facilities: restaurant, café, exercise room. AE, DC, MC, V. $$$

Europejski. This small, older hotel overlooking the Planty park has now been renovated, and most of the rooms have shower or bath. *Ul. Lubicz 5, tel. 012/22–09–11, fax 012/22–89–25. 55 rooms, most with bath. No credit cards. $*

GDAŃSK AND THE NORTH

In contrast to Kraków and the south, Poland north of Warsaw is a land of medieval castles and châteaus, dense forests and lakes, and fishing villages and beaches. If you don't have a car, consider going straight to Gdańsk and making excursions from there.

Getting Around

Gdańsk is a major transportation hub, with an airport just outside town (and good bus connections to downtown) and major road and rail connections with the rest of the country.

Guided Tours

Orbis arranges an eight-day tour of Warsaw, Toruń, Gdańsk, and Poznań. It also handles group and individual tours of Toruń, Gdańsk, and the surrounding areas.

Tourist Information

Elbląg (ul. 3 Maja 1, tel. 050/247–76; Orbis, ul. Hetmańska 23, tel. 050/223–64).
Gdańsk (ul. Heweliusza 8, tel. 058/31–03–38; Orbis, pl. Górskiego 1, tel. 058/31–49–44).
Ostróda (Orbis, ul. Czarnieckiego 10, tel. 088/35–57).
Płock (ul. Tuńska 4, tel. 024/226–00; Orbis, al. Jachowa 47, tel. 024/229–89).
Toruń (ul. Kopernika 27, tel. 056/272–99; Orbis, ul. Żeglarska 31, tel. 056/261–30).

Exploring Gdańsk and the North

From Warsaw, follow routes E81 and 107 through **Płock.** Once you get through Płock's industrial area, you'll find a lovely medieval city that was, for a short time, the capital of Poland. Worth seeing are the 12th-century cathedral, where two Polish kings are buried, and the dramatic 14th-century Teutonic castle. Continue through Włocławek to Toruń, where an overnight stay is recommended.

Toruń

Toruń, birthplace of Nicolaus Copernicus, is an interesting medieval city that grew wealthy due to its location on the north–south trading route along the Vistula. Its Old Town district is a remarkably successful blend of Gothic buildings—churches, the town hall, and burghers' homes—with Renaissance and Baroque patricians' houses. The Town Hall's tower (1274) is the oldest town hall tower in Poland. Don't leave without trying some of Toruń's famous gingerbread and honey cakes.

The route leading north from Toruń to Gdańsk passes through some of the oldest towns in Poland. Along the way are many medieval castles, manor houses, and churches that testify to the wealth and strategic importance of the area. Two short detours are a must: one is to

Gdańsk and the North

Kwidzyń to see the original 14th-century castle and cathedral complex, which is free and open to the public. The other is to **Malbork.** This huge castle, 58 kilometers (36 miles) from Gdańsk, was one of the most powerful strongholds in medieval Europe. From 1308 to 1457, it was the residence of the Grand Masters of the Teutonic Order. The Teutonic Knights were a thorn in Poland's side until their defeat at the Battle of Grunwald in 1410. Inside Malbork Castle is a museum with beautiful examples of amber—including lumps as large as melons and pieces containing perfect specimens of prehistoric insects. *Tel. 055/3364. Admission to Malbork, zł 4.5 (45,000) adults, zł 3.5 (35,000) children. Open Tues.–Sat. 10–3, Sun. 10–5.*

Gdańsk

Gdańsk, once the free city of Danzig, is another of Poland's beautifully restored towns, displaying a rich heritage of Gothic, Renaissance, and Mannerist architecture. This is where the first shots of World War II were fired and where the free trade union Solidarity was born after strikes in 1980. The city's Old Town has a wonderful collection of historic town houses and narrow streets. The city's axis is formed by splendid Długa Street (best for shopping) and Długi Targ Square—great starting points for walks into other districts. The evocative **Solidarity Monument**—erected in honor of workers killed by the regime during strikes in 1970—stands outside the Lenin shipyards. The nearby town of **Sopot** is Poland's most popular seaside resort.

For a different route back to Warsaw, follow highway E81 southeast through Poland's scenic forest and lake district. The area is rich in nature and wildlife attractions, as well as places of historical interest. Recommended is a side trip 42 kilometers (26 miles) east of Ostróda to the medieval town of **Olsztyn.** The Old Town was once administered and fortified by Copernicus.

About 30 kilometers (19 miles) farther south on E81 is **Olsztynek,** where the **Museum of Folk Buildings** has a collection of timber buildings from different parts of the country. They include a small Mazurian thatch-roofed church, an inn, a mill, a forge, old windmills, and thatched cottages, some of which have period-style furnishings. *Tel. 089/19–24–64. Admission: zł 4 (40,000) adults, zł 2 (20,000) children. Open May–Sept., Tues.–Sun. 9–4; closed Mon.*

Another diversion, 17 kilometers (10½ miles) west of Olsztynek, is the **site of the Battle of Grunwald,** possibly the greatest battle of the Middle Ages. Here on July 15, 1410, Władysław Jagiełło and his Polish Lithuanian army annihilated the Grand Master of the Teutonic Order, Ulrich von Jungingen, and thousands of his knights. A small museum on the site (open summer only, 10–10) graphically explains the course of the battle.

Dining and Lodging

For details and price-category definitions, *see* Dining and Lodging *in* Staying in Poland, *above.*

Elbląg
DINING

Karczma Słupska. This is the best restaurant in town. It's usually crowded and specializes in fresh fish. *Ul. Krótka 1. No reservations. No credit cards. $$*

Gdańsk
DINING

Pod Łososiem. The name of this restaurant refers to salmon, which, if available on the day you visit, is highly recommended. *Ul. Szeroka 51, tel. 058/31–76–52. Reservations advised. AE, DC, MC, V. $$$*

★ **Kaszubska.** The specialties here come from Kashubia. Smoked fish dishes are highly recommended. *Ul. Kartuska 76, tel. 058/32–06–02. Reservations advised. AE, DC, MC, V. $$*

★ **Tawerna.** This well-established restaurant overlooking the river serves traditional Polish and Germanic dishes such as pork cutlets and seafood. Yes, it's touristy, but the food is delicious. *Ul. Powroźnicza 19–20, off Długi Targ, tel. 058/31–92–48. Reservations advised. AE, DC, MC, V. $$*

LODGING

Hewelius. This large, modern, high-rise hotel is within walking distance of the Old Town. The spacious, blandly furnished rooms have all the modern conveniences. *Ul. Heweliusza 22, tel. 058/31–56–31, fax 31 058/31–19–22. 250 rooms, most with bath. Facilities: restaurant, nightclub. AE, DC, MC, V. $$*

★ **Marina.** Built in 1982, this large high-rise, popular with Western businesspeople, is one of the newer hotels in Poland and probably the best in town. Upper floors have splendid views. *Ul. Jelitkowska 20, tel. 058/53–20–79, fax 058/53–04–60. 193 rooms with bath or shower. Facilities: restaurant, nightclub, indoor pool, sauna, tennis courts, bowling alley. AE, DC, MC, V. $$*

Olsztyn
LODGING

Orbis Novotel. This standard 1970s hotel is typical of the kind found in Poland. It is, however, the most comfortable lodging in the area and

PARIS?
ROME?
WARSAW.

Don't just read about the changes in Eastern Europe. See them for yourself.
Stroll along the cobbled streets and vistas of Old Town. Enjoy coffee in the Old
Market square. And everywhere, experience a new birth of freedom
and enterprise in Warsaw, your best gateway to the splendors of Krakow,
Budapest, and Prague. Let us show you our passion for Poland.
With LOT Polish Airlines' Boeing 767s, the only non-stops to Warsaw, from New York,
Newark and Chicago, Business and Economy Class. Call your travel agent
today for new lower fares for the spring season, or call us direct at 1-800-223-0593.

LOT

THE   POLISH   AIRLINE

Reality check. Call home.

—— *AT&T USADirect® and World Connect®. The fast, easy way to call most anywhere.* ——

Take out AT&T Calling Card or your local calling card.** Lift phone. Dial AT&T Access Number for country you're calling from. Connect to English-speaking operator or voice prompt. Reach the States or over 200 countries. Talk. Say goodbye. Hang up. Resume vacation.

Austria*†††.....................022-903-011	Luxembourg 0-800-0111	Turkey* 00-800-12277
Belgium* 0-800-100-10	Netherlands* 06-022-9111	United Kingdom.............0500-89-0011
Czech Republic* 00-420-00101	Norway 800-190-11	
Denmark 8001-0010	Poland†◆‡.............0◊010-480-0111	
Finland 9800-100-10	Portugal† 05017-1-288	
France.................................19-0011	Romania* 01-800-4288	
Germany.........................0130-0010	Russia*†(Moscow) 155-5042	
Greece*...........................00-800-1311	Slovak Rep.* 00-420-00101	
Hungary*..............00◊-800-01111	Spain● 900-99-00-11	
Ireland 1-800-550-000	Sweden 020-795-611	
Italy*....................................172-1011	Switzerland* 155-00-11	

AT&T
Your True Choice

**You can also call collect or use most U.S. local calling cards. Countries in bold face permit country-to-country calling in addition to calls to the U.S. World Connect® prices consist of USADirect® rates plus an additional charge based on the country you are calling. Collect calling available to the U.S. only. *Public phones require deposit of coin or phone card. †May not be available from every phone. †††Public phones require local coin payment during call. ◆Not available from public phones. ◊Await second dial tone. ‡Dial 010-480-0111 from major Warsaw hotels. ●Calling available to most European countries. ©1995 AT&T.

For a free wallet sized card of all AT&T Access Numbers, call: 1-800-241-5555.

is situated in beautiful surroundings on the shores of lake Ukiel. *Ul. Sielska 4A, tel. 089/27–40–81, fax 089/27–54–03. 98 rooms with bath. Facilities: restaurant, pool. AE, DC, MC, V. $$*

Ostróda

LODGING

This town is not visited by many foreign tourists and is lacking in good-quality facilities. The undistinguished but inexpensive **Panorama Hotel** (Ul. Krasickiego 23, tel. 088/82–22–27) is the best, unless Orbis can locate private lodging for you.

Toruń

DINING

★ **Pod Kurantem.** Regional cuisine is featured in this attractive old wine cellar. Slow service is the penalty for popularity. *Rynek Staromiejski 28. No phone. No reservations. No credit cards. $$$*

Wodnik. This large café along the banks of the Vistula is very popular with locals. *Blwd. Filadelfijski, tel. 056/287–55. AE, DC, MC, V. $$*

Zajazd Staropolski. This restaurant serves excellent meat dishes and soups in a restored 17th-century interior. *Ul. Żeglarska 10/14, tel. 056/260–60. Reservations advised. AE, DC, MC, V. $$*

DINING AND LODGING

Helios. This friendly, medium-size hotel is in the city center and offers a good restaurant (albeit with slow service). *Ul. Kraszewskiego 1, tel. 056/250–33, fax 056/235–65. 140 rooms, most with bath or shower. Facilities: restaurant, sauna, nightclub, beauty parlor. AE, DC, MC, V. $$*

LODGING

Kosmos. A functional 1960s hotel, Kosmos is beginning to show signs of wear and tear. It is near the river, in the city center. *Ul. Portowa 2, tel. 056/270–85. 180 rooms, most with bath or shower. AE, DC, MC, V. $$*

23 Portugal

GIVEN ITS LONG ATLANTIC COASTLINE, it isn't surprising that Portugal has been a maritime nation
for most of its history. The valor of its seamen is
well known; from the charting of the Azores archipelago in 1427 to
the discovery of Japan in 1542, Portuguese explorers unlocked the major
sea routes to southern Africa, India, the Far East, and the Americas.
To commemorate the *descobrimentos,* this great era of exploration, a
period that reached its height in the 15th century under the influence
of Prince Henry the Navigator, the years 1988 to 2000 have been set
aside for various celebrations throughout the country.

Despite its sailors' worldwide adventures, Portugal itself has remained
relatively undiscovered. Although it shares the Iberian Peninsula with
Spain, it attracts far fewer visitors—a strange fact, because Portugal
has much to recommend it to tourists: fine beaches, beautiful castles,
charming fishing villages, well-maintained hotels and *pousadas* (government-owned inns), excellent restaurants, and colorful folk traditions.

About the size of Indiana, Portugal is so small that its main attractions
can be seen during a short visit; the country's widest point (the distance between the Atlantic and Spain) is a mere 240 kilometers (150
miles). Short distances don't mean monotony, however, for this narrow coastal strip of land has more geographic and climatic variations
than virtually any other nation in western Europe.

Although Portugal has seen numerous divisions in modern times, the
country has traditionally been divided into 11 historic provinces. Most
visitors head for the low-lying plains of the southern Algarve or the
region around the Lisbon/Estoril coast, but as traditional tourist destinations become more crowded, adventurous travelers are exploring
in other directions. The northern and central provinces—Minho, Beiras,
and Trás-os-Montes—are largely unspoiled, full of tiny villages and splendid scenery. The major drawbacks here are the comparative lack of first-
class accommodations and poor secondary roads. With the recent
infusion of substantial European Union (EU) funds, however, this condition has been improving rapidly. The main highways from Lisbon
to the north and the frontier are now in good shape. In the south the
once fearsome N125, which spans the Algarve from east to west, has
been widened and largely tamed, and a high-speed trans-Algarve expressway is under construction.

Observant visitors are likely to notice differences between Portugal's northern and southern regions and people. The northern character is decidedly more Celtic, while in the south, Moorish ancestry is apparent. But
throughout the country, the Portuguese are a welcoming people.

We have concentrated our Exploring sections on the southern part of
the country—the section most frequented by foreign visitors—including Portugal's sophisticated capital of Lisbon, its coastal and wooded
environs, and the Algarve.

ESSENTIAL INFORMATION

Before You Go

When to Go

The tourist season runs from spring through autumn, but some parts
of the country—especially the Algarve, which boasts 3,000 hours of

Portugal

50 miles
50 km

N

Minho
Valença
Viana do Castelo
Lima
Barcelos
Serra do Gerês N103
Chaves
Bragança
N101
Braga
Guimarães
Tâmega
N15
Mirandela
Póvoa de Varzim
Amarante
Vila Real
Mogadouro
Vila do Conde
Penafiel
Douro
Sabor
Oporto
Douro
Lamego
Moimenta da Beira
Duoro
Espinho
Oliveira dos Azeméis
S. Pedro do Sul
Albergaria-a-Velha
Vouga
Viseu
Pinhel
Aveiro
Mealhada
Sta. Comba Dão
Guarda
Mira
Cantanhede
Mondego
Coimbra
Serra da Estrêla
Covilhã
Figueira da Foz
Arganil
Fundão
Zêzere
Penamacor
E1/A1
Pombal
Serra da Gardunha
N233
N110
Proença-a-Nova
Castelo Branco
Leiria
Batalha
Ourém
Nazaré
Tomar
Abrantes
Nisa
Alcobaça
Fátima
Tagus N118
Caldas da Rainha
Sra. do Aire
Torres Novas
Obidos
Aveiras de Cima
Portalegre
Torres Vedras
Tejo
Santarém
Mafra
Ponte de Sor
Sintra
Vila Franca de Xira
Sorraia
Avis
Cascais
N8
Lisbon
N10
Estoril
Montemor-o-Novo
Arraiolos
Estremoz
Elvas
Seixal
A2
Sra. de Ossa
Vila Viçosa
Guadiana
Setúbal
Sado
Alcácer do Sal
Évora
Reguengos
Cabo Espichel
N2

TO THE AZORES

Ferreira do Alentejo
Moura
E1
Sines
Santiago do Cacém
Beja
Vilaverde de Ficalho
Cabo de Sines
Serpa
N122
TO MADEIRA ISLAND
Odemira
Ourique
Castro Verde
Mira
Mértola
Guadiana
N120
Almodôvar
Monchique
Chança
ALGARVE
Portimão EN125
Albufeira
S. Brás de Aportel
Vila do Bispo
Lagos
Tavira
Vila Real de S. António
Cabo de S. Vicente
Sagres
Faro
Olhão

ATLANTIC OCEAN

S P A I N

sunshine annually—are balmy even in winter. Hotel prices are greatly reduced between November and February, except in Lisbon where business visitors keep prices uniformly high throughout the year.

CLIMATE

Since Portugal's entire coast is on the Atlantic Ocean, the country's climate is temperate year-round. Portugal rarely suffers the extremes of heat that Mediterranean countries do. Even in August, the hottest month, the Algarve and the Alentejo are the only regions where the midday heat may be uncomfortable, but most travelers go to the beaches there to swim and soak up the sun. What rain there is falls from November to March; December and January can be chilly outside the Algarve, and very wet to the north, but there is no snow except in the mountains of the Serra da Estrela in the northeast. The almond blossoms and vivid wildflowers that cover the countryside start to bloom early in February. The dry months, June–September, can turn much of the landscape the tawny color of a lion's hide, but there is always a breeze in the evening in Lisbon, as well as along the Estoril coast west of the capital.

The following are the average daily maximum and minimum temperatures for Lisbon.

Jan.	57F	14C	May	71F	21C	Sept.	79F	26C
	46	8		55	13		62	17
Feb.	59F	15C	June	77F	25C	Oct.	72F	22C
	47	8		60	15		58	14
Mar.	63F	17C	July	81F	27C	Nov.	63F	17C
	50	10		63	17		52	11
Apr.	67F	20C	Aug.	82F	28C	Dec.	58F	15C
	53	12		63	17		47	9

Currency

The unit of currency in Portugal is the *escudo,* which can be divided into 100 *centavos.* Escudos come in bills of 500$00, 1,000$00, 2,000$00, 5,000$00, and 10,000$00. (In Portugal the dollar sign stands between the escudo and the centavo.) Coins come in 1$00, 2$50, 5$00, 10$00, 20$00, 50$00, 100$00, and 200$00.

At press time (spring 1995), the exchange rate was about 136$00 to the U.S. dollar and 228$00 to the pound sterling. Owing to the complications of dealing in millions of escudos, 1,000$00 is always called a *conto,* so 10,000$00 is referred to as 10 contos. You can change money in hotels and in larger shops and restaurants, but banks and *cambios* (exchange offices) usually give better rates.

What It Will Cost

Although the cost of hotels and restaurants in Portugal is still reasonable, inflation is pushing prices up. Some of Portugal's best food bargains are to be enjoyed in its many simple seaside restaurants. The most expensive areas are Lisbon, the Algarve, and the tourist resort areas along the Tagus estuary. The least expensive areas are country towns, which all have reasonably priced hotels and *pensões,* or pensions, as well as numerous café-type restaurants. A sales, or value-added, tax (called IVA) of 16% is imposed on hotel and restaurant bills, car rentals, and services such as car repairs.

SAMPLE PRICES

Cup of coffee, 150$00; bottle of beer, 150$00; soft drink, 175$00; bottle of house wine, 500$00–750$00; ham sandwich, 225$00; 1-mile taxi ride, 425$00; city bus ride, 150$00; museum entrance, 250$00–400$00.

Customs on Arrival

Non-EU visitors over age 17 are allowed to bring the following items into Portugal duty-free: 200 cigarettes or 250 grams of tobacco, 1 liter of liquor (over 22% volume) or 2 liters (under 22% volume), 2 liters of wine, 100 milliliter of perfume, and a reasonable amount of personal effects (camera, binoculars, etc). There is no limit on money brought into the country. However, no more than 100,000$00 in Portuguese currency or the equivalent of 500,000$00 in foreign currency may be taken out without proof that an equal amount or more was brought into Portugal. Computerized customs services make random and often thorough checks on arrival.

Language

Portuguese is easy to read by anyone with even slight knowledge of a Latin language, but it is difficult to pronounce and understand (most people speak quickly and elliptically). But in large cities and major resorts many people, especially the young, speak English and, occasionally, French.

Getting Around

By Car

ROAD CONDITIONS

The few turnpikes (moderate tolls) and the major highways between Lisbon and the coast, the Algarve, and Oporto are in good shape. For the most part, road conditions in Portugal have greatly improved, but minor roads are often poor and winding with unpredictable surfaces.

New highways have made the once grueling drive between the Algarve and Lisbon a pleasure. EN 125, the principal east–west Algarve highway, has been widened and resurfaced, while construction of the new Algarve highway continues. New bridges have eliminated the formerly horrendous bottlenecks at Portimão and replaced the ferry across the Guadiana River from Vila Real de Santo António to Spain.

In the north, the IP5 makes the drive from Aveiro to the border with Spain, near Guarda, a pleasant one, and the IP4 connects Oporto through Vila Real to once-remote Bragança.

There's no superhighway from Lisbon leading east to the nearest frontier post at Badajoz, Spain, but the route over the Tagus bridge through Setúbal (turnpike from Lisbon), via Montemor-o-Novo and Estremoz, is good and fast.

RULES OF THE ROAD

Driving is on the right. At the junction of two roads of equal size, traffic coming from the right has priority. Vehicles already in a traffic circle have priority over those entering it from any point. Traffic in the country is light, but local people are apt to walk in the road, and in very out-of-the-way places occasional horse- or donkey-drawn carts may hold things up. The use of seat belts is obligatory. Horns should not be used in built-up areas, and a reflective red warning triangle, for use in a breakdown, must be carried. The speed limit on turnpikes is 120 kph (72 mph); on other roads it is 90 kph (54 mph), and in built-up areas, 50–60 kph (30–36 mph).

PARKING

Lisbon, Coimbra, and Oporto are experimenting with parking meters, although these are still rare. Parking lots and underground garages abound in major cities, but those in Lisbon and Oporto are no longer cheap. Parking on side streets is usually chaotic, and in Lisbon and Oporto it's often very difficult to find a parking space near city-center hotels.

GASOLINE

Gas prices are among the highest in Europe: 175$00 per liter for super and 160$00 for regular. Unleaded gas is now available for 160$00. Many gas stations around the country are self-service. Credit cards are widely accepted.

BREAKDOWNS

All large garages in and around towns have breakdown services. Special orange emergency (SOS) telephones are located at intervals on turnpikes and highways. Motorists in Portugal are very helpful; if your car breaks down, aid from a passing driver is usually forthcoming. The national automobile organization, **Automóvel Clube de Portugal** (Rua Rosa Araújo 24/26, 1200 Lisbon, tel. 01/356–3931) provides reciprocal membership with AAA and other European automobile associations, provided the membership is current.

By Train

The Portuguese railway system is surprisingly extensive for such a small country. Trains are clean and leave on time, but there are few express runs except between Lisbon and Oporto, which takes just over three hours for the 210-mile (338-kilometer) journey. Most trains have first-and second-class compartments; some of the Lisbon–Oporto expresses are first-class only; suburban lines around Lisbon have a single class. Overall, tickets are reasonably priced (though expresses can cost up to twice as much as local trains) and should be bought, and seats reserved, at the stations or through travel agents, two or three days in advance. Advance reservations are essential on Lisbon–Oporto express trains. Timetables are generally the same on Saturday and Sunday as on weekdays, except on suburban lines. **Wasteels–Expresso** (Av. António Augusto Aguiar 88, 1000 Lisbon, tel. 01/579655 or 01/579180) is reliable for all local and international train tickets and reservations.

Special **tourist passes** can be obtained through travel agents or at main train stations. These are valid for periods of 7, 14, or 21 days for first- and second-class travel on any domestic train service; mileage is unlimited. At press time (spring, 1995), the cost was 17,000$00 for 7 days; 27,000$00 for 14 days; and 38,000$00 for 21 days. Child passes cost exactly half those amounts.

International trains to Madrid, Paris, and other parts of Europe depart from the Santa Apolonia Station in Lisbon and Campanhã in Oporto.

By Plane

The internal air services of **TAP Air Portugal** are good. Lisbon is linked at least four times daily with Oporto and Faro; daily with Funchal (Madeira), more at peak periods; weekly with Porto Santo, an island some way off Madeira; and several times a week with the archipelago of the Azores. TAP (Praça Marquês de Pombal 3, 1200 Lisbon, tel. 01/386–1020) also has flights to Viseu, Vila Real and Bragança. Other internal services are provided by LAR, Portugália, and SATA-Air Açores (which flies to the Azores), all of whose schedules change according to season. Any travel agent can provide up-to-date prices and timetables.

By Bus

The main bus company, **Rodoviaria Nacional,** has passenger terminals in Lisbon (Av. Casal Ribeiro 18, tel. 01/545439), with regular bus services throughout Portugal. Several private companies also offer luxury service between major cities. It is three hours to Oporto and five hours to the Algarve. For information and reservations in Lisbon, contact the main tourist office (*see* Important Addresses and Numbers *in* Lisbon, *below*) or **Marcus & Harting** (Rossío 45–50, tel. 01/346–9271). Most long-distance buses have toilet facilities, and the fares are often lower than those for trains.

By Boat

Ferries across the River Tagus (Lisbon) leave from Praça do Comércio, Cais do Sodré, and Belém. From April to October, a two-hour boat excursion leaves the ferry station at Praça do Comércio in Lisbon daily at 2:30 PM. The price is 3,500$00. In the United States, contact **Sea Air Holidays Ltd.** (733 Summer St., Stamford, CT 06901, tel. 800/732–6247) about cruises on the Douro River in an 80-cabin vessel, with weekly departures.

One-hour boat trips on the River Douro (Oporto) are organized from May through October by **Porto Ferreira** (Rua da Cavalhosa 19, Vila Nova de Gaia, Oporto, tel. 02/300866). They leave every day on the hour, 10–6 except Saturday afternoon and Sunday. Overnight cruises up the River Douro are also available. Contact **Endouro** (Rua da Reboleira 49, 4000 Oporto, tel. 02/208–4161, fax 02/317260).

By Bicycle

You can rent bicycles at certain Algarve resorts, though heavy traffic on the main roads can make cycling an exhausting experience. There aren't any cycle rental outfits in downtown Lisbon, which is just as well—if the hills don't defeat you, the careering taxis, trams, and buses will. **Tip Tours** (Av. Costa Pinto 91-A, 2750 Cascais, tel. 01/483–5150 and 01/483–5159) rents bicycles by the day or half day. **Cycling through the Centuries** (Box 877, San Antonio, FL 33576, tel. 800/425–4226, fax 904/588–4158 or, in Portugal, tel. 01/486–2044, fax 01/486–1409) offers bicycle tours in the Alentejo, Minho, and the Algarve with accommodations in first-class hotels and romantic country inns. Each tour is accompanied by a guide, a mechanic, and a van for luggage.

Staying in Portugal

Telephones

LOCAL CALLS

Pay phones take 10$00, 20$00, and 50$00 coins; 10$00 is the minimum payment for short local calls. Pay phones marked CREDIFONE will accept plastic phone cards, which can be purchased at post offices and most tobacconist shops.

INTERNATIONAL CALLS

Long-distance calls cost less from 8 PM to 7 AM. Collect calls can also be made from post offices. Some telephone booths accept international calls. Access numbers to reach American long-distance operators are: for **AT&T**, 050–171288; for **MCI**, 0010–480–0112; for **Sprint**, 050–171877.

COUNTRY CODE

The country code for Portugal is 351.

Mail

Postal rates, both domestic and foreign, increase twice a year. Country post offices close for lunch and at 6 PM on weekdays; they are not open on weekends. Main post offices in towns are open weekdays 8:30 to 6. In Lisbon, the post office in the Praça dos Restauradores is open daily from 8 AM until 10 PM.

RECEIVING MAIL

Mail can be sent in care of American Express Star (**Top Tours,** Av. Duque de Loulé 108, 1000 Lisbon, tel. 01/315–5877, fax 01/352–3227); there is no service charge. Main post offices also accept poste restante letters.

Shopping

Bargaining is not common in city stores or shops, but it is sometimes possible in flea markets, antiques shops, and outdoor markets that sell fruit, vegetables, and household goods. The **Centro de Turismo Artesanato** (Rua Castilho 61, 1200 Lisbon, tel. 01/353–4879) will ship goods abroad even if they were not bought in Portugal. By air to the United States, parcels take about three weeks; by sea, two months.

IVA REFUNDS

IVA tax on items over a certain value can be reclaimed, although the methods are time-consuming. For Americans and other non-EU residents, the tax paid on individual items costing more than 10,000$00 can be reclaimed in cash on presentation of receipts and a special *Tax-Free Shopping Cheque* to special departments in airports (in Lisbon, near Gate 23). You can also have the check stamped at any border crossing and receive the refund by mail or credit card. Shops specializing in IVA-refund purchases are clearly marked throughout the country, and shop assistants can help with the forms. For details consult the main tourist information center in Lisbon (see Important Addresses and Numbers, *below*).

Opening and Closing Times

Banks are open weekdays 8:30 to 3; they do not close for lunch. There are automatic currency-exchange machines in Lisbon in the Praça dos Restauradores and in other cities.

Museums are usually open 10–12:30 and 2–5. Most close on Sunday afternoon, and they are all closed on Monday. Most palaces close on Tuesday.

Shops are open weekdays 9–1 and 3–7, Saturdays 9–1. Shopping malls and supermarkets in Lisbon and other cities remain open until 10 PM or midnight and are often open on Sunday.

National Holidays

January 1; April 5 (Good Friday); April 25 (Anniversary of the Revolution); May 1 (Labor Day); June 6 (Corpus Christi); June 10 (National Day); August 15 (Feast of the Assumption); October 5 (Day of the Republic); November 1 (All Saints' Day); December 1 (Independence Day); December 8 (Immaculate Conception); December 25.

Dining

Eating is taken quite seriously in Portugal, and, not surprisingly, seafood is a staple including *sardinhas assadas* (fresh-grilled sardines), a local favorite. Freshly caught lobster, crab, shrimp, tuna, sole, and squid are prepared in innumerable ways, and *caldeirada* is a piquant seafood stew made with a little bit of everything. In the Algarve, *cataplana* is a must: It's a mouthwatering mixture of clams, ham, tomatoes, onions, garlic, and herbs, named for the dish in which it is cooked.

Meat lovers wax rhapsodic over northern-style *leitão da Bairrada* (roast suckling pig), *coelho á caçadora* (rabbit with potatoes, onions, garlic, and a splash of wine), and the tasty spiced sausages and smoked ham. There are some excellent local wines, and in modest restaurants even the *vinho da casa* (house wine) is usually very good. Desserts feature *doces de ovos* (egg and sugar confections), *pudim flan* (egg custard), egg and almond tarts, and always fruit. Water is generally safe, but visitors may want to drink bottled water—*sem gas* for still, *com gas* for fizzy—from one of the many excellent Portuguese spas. Unless noted, reservations are not necessary.

MEALTIMES
Lunch usually begins around 1 PM; dinner is served at about 8 PM.

WHAT TO WEAR
Jacket and tie are advised for most restaurants in the **$$$** and **$$$$** categories, but otherwise casual dress is acceptable.

RATINGS
Prices are per person, without alcohol. Taxes and service are usually included, but a tip of 5%–10% is always appreciated. Highly recommended restaurants are indicated by a star ★.

CATEGORY	ALL AREAS
$$$$	over 6,000$00
$$$	3,500$00–6,000$00
$$	2,000$00–3,500$00
$	under 2,000$00

Lodging
Visitors have a wide choice of lodging in Portugal, which offers some of the lowest rates in Europe for accommodations. The government grades hotels with one-to-five stars. Smaller inns called *estalagems* or *albergarias*, which usually provide breakfast only are also rated. Pensões go up to four stars and often include meals (though they don't usually insist that you take them). The state-subsidized pousadas, most of which are in castles, old monasteries, or have been built where there is a particularly fine view, are five-star luxury properties. *Residenciais* (between a pensão and a hotel) are in most towns and larger villages; most rooms have private baths or showers, and breakfast is usually included. They are an extremely good value (around 5,000$00–7,000$00), but since they usually have only a few rooms, we don't review many residenciais.

For more information about pousadas, contact **Enatur Pousadas de Portugal** (Av. Santa Joana Princesa 10, 1700 Lisbon, tel. 01/848–1221, fax 01/805846), or the national tourist organization in your home country. **Abreu Tours** (317 E. 34th St., New York, NY 10016, tel. 800/223–1580) can make pousada bookings and arrange tailor-made vacations.

A recent innovation is *Turismo no Espaço Rural* (Tourism in the Country), in which private homeowners all over the country offer visitors a room and breakfast (and sometimes provide dinner on request). This is an excellent way to experience life on a country estate or in a small village. Details are available from several agencies, including **Associação Portuguesa de Turismo de Habitação** (Rua João Penha 10, 1200 Lisbon, tel. 01/690549, fax 01/388–8115).

Tourist offices can help with reservations and will provide lists of the local hostelries without charge. In Lisbon, there's a hotel reservations desk at the airport and at the downtown tourist information center. Few international chains have hotels in Portugal.

Aparthotels, with double rooms, bath, and kitchenette, can be found in the main resorts and are good value. Villas can be rented by the week or longer in the Algarve from various agents. Among the better-run complexes are the Luz Bay Club and Luz Ocean Club, at Luz near Lagos, whose well-designed villas have daily maid service.

CAMPING

Camping has become increasingly popular in Portugal in recent years, and there are now more than 150 campsites throughout the country offering a wide range of facilities. The best equipped have markets, swimming pools, and tennis courts. For additional information, contact **Federação Portuguesa do Campismo** (Av. 5 Outubro 15-3, 1000 Lisbon, tel. 01/315–2715).

RATINGS

Prices quoted are for two people in a double room based on high-season rates, including tax and service. Highly recommended lodgings are indicated by a star ★.

CATEGORY	COST
$$$$	over 40,000$00
$$$	20,000$00–40,000$00
$$	14,000$00–20,000$00
$	under 14,000$00

Tipping

In Portugal, modest tips are usually the rule. Service is included in bills at hotels and most restaurants. In luxury hotels, give the porter who carries your luggage 200$00; in less expensive establishments, 100$00. If the maid brings your breakfast, give her 100$00 a day or 500$00 for a stay of a week. If you dine regularly in the hotel, give your waiter between 500$00 and 1,000$00 at the end of your stay; give the wine waiter somewhat less if you order wine with every meal. Otherwise tip 5%–10% on restaurant bills, except at inexpensive establishments, where you may just leave any coins given in change. Taxi drivers get 10%; cinema and theater ushers who seat you, 50$00; train and airport porters, 100$00 per bag; service-station attendants, 20$00 for gas, 50$00 for checking tires and cleaning windshields; hairdressers, around 10%.

LISBON

Arriving and Departing

By Plane

Lisbon's Portela Airport (tel. 01/802262) is only about 20 minutes from the city by car or taxi.

BETWEEN THE AIRPORT AND DOWNTOWN

A special bus, called Aerobus (400$00), runs every 20 minutes, 7:30 AM–10 PM, from outside the airport into the city center. Taxis here are so cheap, however, that visitors would be wise to take one straight to their destination. The cost into Lisbon is about 1,500$00–2,000$00, and to Estoril or Sintra, 6,000$00. There are no trains or subways between the airport and the city, but there are car-rental desks.

By Train

International trains from Paris and Madrid arrive at Santa Apolonia Station (tel. 01/888–4025), just east of the city center. There is a tourist office at the station and plenty of taxis and porters, but no car-rental firms. To get to the central Praça dos Restauradores by public transport, take Bus 9, 39, or 46.

Getting Around

Lisbon is a hilly city, and the sidewalks are paved with cobblestones, so walking can be tiring, even when you're wearing comfortable shoes. Fortunately, Lisbon's tram service is one of the best in Europe and buses go all over the city. A **Tourist Pass** for unlimited rides on the tram or bus costs 400$00 for one day's travel; four-day passes (1,350$00) and seven-day passes (2,050$00) are also valid on the metro. Tourist passes can be purchased at the Cais do Sodré Station and other terminals. Otherwise, there's a flat fee of 150$00 every time you ride a bus, tram, or the *elevador* (funicular railway system).

By Tram and Bus
Buses and trams operate from 6 AM to midnight. Try tram routes 12 or 28 for an inexpensive tour of the city; Buses 52 and 53 cross the Tagus bridge. In summer, old-fashioned trams run on tours (350$00 per person) through the city, departing from Pracça do Comércio; tel. 01/363–9343 for details.

By Subway
The subway, called the Metropolitano, operates from 6:30 AM to 1 AM; it is modern and efficient but covers a limited route. Tickets cost 65$00. If you use it, watch out for pickpockets during rush hour.

By Taxi
Taxis can be easily recognized by a lighted sign on green roofs. There are ranks in the main squares, and you can usually catch one cruising by, though this can be difficult late at night. Taxis are metered and take up to four passengers at no extra charge. Rates start at 300$00, with an extra charge for luggage.

By Ferry
Ferries cross the Tagus River from the Fluvial terminal, adjacent to Praça do Comércio, to the suburb of Cacilhas, famous for its fish restaurants; it's a 10-minute crossing and costs 95$00 (daily 7 AM–9:30 PM). Alternately, ferries from the quay at Cais do Sodré to Cacilhas run all night.

Important Addresses and Numbers

Tourist Information
The main Lisbon tourist office (tel. 01/346–3314) is in the Palácio Foz, Praça dos Restauradores, at the Baixa (Lower Town) end of the Avenida da Liberdade, the main artery of the city; open daily 9–8. The tourist office at Lisbon airport (tel. 01/849–4323 or 01/849–3689) is open daily 6 AM–2 AM.

Embassies
U.S. **(Av. Forças Armadas, tel. 01/726–6600); Canadian** (Av. da Liber-dade 144-3, tel. 01/347–4892); **U.K.** (Rua S. Domingos â Lapa 37, tel. 01/396–1191).

Emergencies
SOS Emergencies **(tel. 115). Police** (tel. 01/346–6141). **Ambulance** (tel. 01/301–7777). **Fire Brigade** (tel. 01/606060). **Doctor:** British Hos-pital (Rua Saraiva de Carvalho 49, tel. 01/395–5067). **Pharmacies:** open weekdays 9–1, 3–7, Saturday 9–1; consult the notice on the door for the nearest one open on weekends or after hours, or call tel. 118 for additional listings.

Travel Agencies

American Express **(c/o Top Tours, Av. Duque de Loulé 108, tel. and fax 01/315–5877). Marcus & Harting** (Rossío 45–50, tel. 01/346–9271). **Wagons-Lits** (Av. da Liberdade 103, tel. 01/342–6434 or 01/346–3872). **Viagens Rawes** (Travessa do Corpo Santo 15, tel. 01/347–4089).

Guided Tours

Orientation Tours and Excursions

Various companies organize half-day tours of Lisbon and environs and also full-day trips to more distant places of interest. Those listed below are reliable and offer similar trips and prices. Reservations can be made through any travel agent or hotel. A half-day tour of Lisbon will cost about 5,500$00. A full-day trip north to Obidos, Nazaré, and Fatima will run about 12,000$00, as will a full day east on the "Roman Route" to Évora and Monsaraz. Companies are **RN Gray Line Tours** (Av. Fontes Pereira de Melo 14, tel. 01/352–2594)Citirama (Av. Praia da Vitória 12–b, tel. 01/355–8567); and **Top Tours** (Rua Luciano Cordeiro 116, tel. 01/352–0028).

Personal Guides

Contact the main Lisbon tourist office (*see* Important Addresses and Numbers, *above*). Another source is the **Syndicate of Guide Interpreters** (Rua do Telhal 4, tel. 01/346–7170), or you can ask at your hotel; the front desk may have a list of bilingual guides. Beware of unauthorized guides who will approach you at popular attractions and try to "guide" you to a particular shop or restaurant.

Exploring Lisbon

North of the River Tagus estuary, spread out over a string of hills, Portugal's capital presents unending treats for the eye. Its wide boulevards are bordered by black-and-white mosaic sidewalks made of tiny cobblestones called *calçada*. Modern, pastel-colored apartment blocks vie for attention with Art Nouveau houses faced with decorative tiles. Winding, hilly streets provide scores of *miradouros,* natural vantage points that offer spectacular views of the river and the city.

Lisbon is not easy to explore on foot. The steep inclines of many streets present a tough challenge to the casual tourist, and places that appear to be close to one another on a map are sometimes on different levels. Yet the effort is worthwhile—judicious use of trams, the funicular railway, and the majestic city-center vertical lift (also called the elevador)make walking tours enjoyable even on the hottest summer day.

With a population of around a million, Lisbon is a small capital by European standards. Its center stretches north from the spacious Praça do Comércio, one of the largest riverside squares in Europe, to the Rossío, a smaller square lined with shops and sidewalk cafés. This district is known as the Baixa (Lower Town), and it is one of the earliest examples of town planning on a large scale. The grid of parallel streets between the two squares was built after an earthquake and tidal wave destroyed much of the city in 1755. The Alfama, the old Moorish quarter that survived the earthquake, lies just east of the Baixa, while Belém, where many royal palaces and museums are, is about 5 kilometers (3 miles) west.

Numbers in the margin correspond to points of interest on the Lisbon map.

Castelo de São Jorge and the Alfama

The Moors, who imposed their rule on most of the southern Iberian Peninsula during the 8th century, left their mark on Lisbon in many ways. The most visible examples are undoubtedly the imposing castle, set on one of the city's highest hills, and the Alfama, a district of narrow, twisting streets that wind their way up toward the castle. The best way to tour this area of Lisbon is to take a taxi to the castle and walk down.

❶ Although the **Castelo de São Jorge** (St. George's Castle) is Moorish in construction, it stands on the site of a fortification used by the Visigoths in the 5th century. Today its idyllic atmosphere is disturbed only by the shrieks of the many peacocks that strut through the well-tended grounds, which are also home to swans, turkeys, ducks, ravens, and other birds. The castle walls enclose the ruins of a Muslim palace that was the residence of the kings of Portugal until the 16th century; there is also a small village with a surviving church, a few simple houses, and souvenir shops. Panoramic views of Lisbon can be seen from the walls, but visitors should take care, because the footing is uneven and slippery. *Admission free. Open Apr.–Sept., daily 9–9; Oct.– Mar., daily 9–7.*

After leaving the castle by its impressive gate, wander down through
❷ the warren of streets that make up the **Alfama.** This jumble of whitewashed houses, with their flower-laden balconies and red-tile roofs, rests on a foundation of dense bedrock. It's a notorious place for getting lost, but it's relatively compact, and you'll keep coming upon the same main squares and streets. Find your way to the Largo Rodrigues
❸ de Freitas, a street to the east of the castle, then take a look at the **Museu da Marioneta** (Puppet Museum) at No. 19A (Admission: 300$00. Open Tues.–Sun. 10–1 and 2–6). From there head south along the Rua
❹ de São Tomé to the Largo das Portas do Sol, where you'll find the **Museu de Artes Decorativas** (Museum of Decorative Arts) in the 17th-century mansion housing the FundaçãoRicardo Espirito Santo. More than 20 workshops teach rare handicrafts—bookbinding, ormolu, carving, and cabinetmaking. *Largo das Portas do Sol 2. Admission: 500$00. Open Tues.-Sun. 10-5:30.*

Head southwest past the Largo de Santa Luzia along the Rua do Limoeiro, which eventually becomes the Rua Augusto Rosa. This route takes you
❺ past the **Sé** (cathedral), founded in 1150, to commemorate the defeat of the Moors three years earlier. The Sé has an austere Romanesque interior enlivened by a splendid 13th-century cloister. *Largo da Sé. Admission to cathedral free, cloister 300$00. Open daily 9–noon and 2–6.*

Continue northwest from the cathedral along the Rua de Santo António da Sé, turn left along the Rua da Conceiçao, then right and north up the Rua Augusta. A 10-minute stroll along this street takes you through the **Baixa,** one of Lisbon's main shopping and banking districts, a small crafts market, some of the best shoe shops in Europe, glittering jewelry stores, and a host of delicatessens selling anything from game birds to *queijo da serra*—a delicious mountain cheese from the Serra da Estrela range north of Lisbon.

Avenida da Liberdade

❻ Rua Augusta leads into the **Rossío** (officially, Praça Dom Pedro IV), Lisbon's principal square, which in turn opens on its northwestern end into the Praça dos Restauradores. This can be considered the beginning of modern Lisbon, for here the broad, tree-lined **Avenida da Liberdade** begins its northwesterly ascent, and ends just over 1.6 kilometers (1 mile)
❼ away at the green expanses of the **Parque Eduardo VII.**

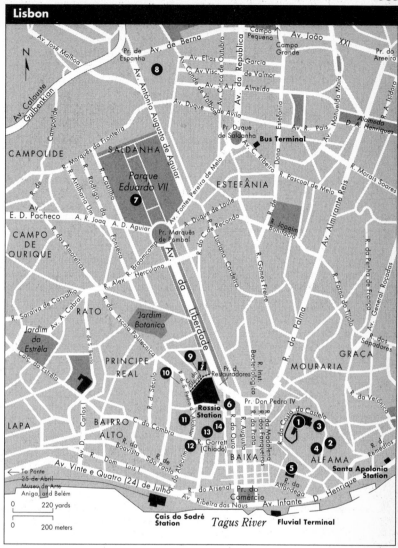

Lisbon

Tagus River

Alfama, **2**

Castelo de São Jorge, **1**

Elevador da Glória, **9**

Elevador de Santa Justa, **14**

Fundação Calouste Gulbenkian , **8**

Igreja do Carmo, **13**

Igreja de São Roque, **11**

Instituto do Vinho do Porto, **10**

Largo do Chiado, **12**

Museu de Artes Decorativas, **4**

Museu da Marioneta, **3**

Parque Eduardo VII, **7**

Rossío, **6**

Sé, **5**

A leisurely stroll from the Praça dos Restauradores to the park takes about 45 minutes. As you make your way up the Avenida da Liberdade, you'll find several cafés at its southern end. Most notable is the open-air café situated in the central esplanada, which splits the avenue. You'll also pass through a pleasant mixture of ornate 19th-century architecture and Art Deco buildings from the '30s. In the park, rare flowers, trees, and shrubs thrive in the *estufa fria* (cold greenhouse) and the *estufa quente* (hot greenhouse). *Parque Eduardo VII. Admission to greenhouses: 75$00. Open winter, daily 9–5; summer, daily 9–6.*

Walk through the park to the northeast corner and then head north along the Avenida António Augusto de Aguiar. A 15-minute walk will bring you to the busy Praça de Espanha, to the right of which, in the Parque de Palhavã, is the renowned **Fundação Calouste Gulbenkian,** a cultural trust whose museum houses treasures collected by Armenian oil magnate Calouste Gulbenkian (1869–1955) and donated to the people of Portugal. There are superb examples of Greek and Roman coins, Persian carpets, Chinese porcelain, and paintings by such old masters as Rembrandt and Rubens, as well as impressionist and pre-Raphaelite works. *Av. de Berna 45, tel. 01/795–0236. Admission: 200$00, free Sun. Open June–Sept., Tues., Thurs., Fri., and Sun. 10–5, Wed. and Sat. 2–7:30; Oct.–May, Tues.–Sun. 10–5; closed Mon. year-round.*

The complex also houses a good modern art museum (same times and price as the main museum) and two concert halls where music and ballet festivals are held during the winter and spring. Modestly priced tickets are available at the box office in the main building. Pick up an events brochure at the reception desk.

Bairro Alto

Lisbon's **Bairro Alto** (Upper Town) is largely made up of 18th-and 19th-century buildings that house an intriguing mixture of restaurants, theaters, nightclubs, churches, bars, and antiques shops. The best way to start a tour of this area is via the **Elevador da Glória** (funicular railway), on the western side of Avenida da Liberdade by the Praça dos Restauradores. The trip takes about a minute and drops passengers at the São Pedro de Alcântara miradouro, a viewpoint that looks toward the castle and the Alfama (cost: 150$00; open 7 AM–midnight).

Across the street from the miradouro is the **Instituto do Vinho do Porto** (Port Wine Institute), where, in its cozy, clublike lounge, visitors can sample from more than 300 types and vintages of Portugal's most famous beverage—from the extra-dry white varieties to the older ruby-red vintages. *Rua S. Pedro de Alcântara 45, tel. 01/342–3307. Admission free. Prices of tastings vary, starting at 160$00. Open Mon.–Sat. 10–10.*

From the institute, turn right and walk down Rua de São Pedro de Alcântara. On your left is the Largo Trindade Coelho, site of the highly decorative **Igreja de São Roque** (Church of St. Roque). The church is best known for the flamboyant 18th-century **Capela de São João Baptista** (Chapel of St. John the Baptist), but it is nonetheless a showpiece in its own right. Adjoining the church is the **Museu de Arte Sacra** (Museum of Sacred Art). *Church open daily 8:30–6. Museum admission: 250$00. Open Tues.–Sun. 10–5.*

Continue south down Rua de São Pedro de Alcântara until you reach the **Largo do Chiado** on your left. The Chiado, once Lisbon's chic shopping district, was badly damaged by a fire in August 1988, but it still houses some of the city's most fashionable department stores.

TIME OUT The Chiado's wood-paneled coffee shops attract tourists and locals alike; the most popular of these is the **Brasileira,** which features a life-size statue of Fernando Pessoa, Portugal's national poet, at one of the sidewalk tables. *Rua Garrett 120, tel. 01/346-9541. Closed Sun. $*

⑬ North of the Chiado, on the Largo do Carmo, lies the partially ruined **Igreja do Carmo** (Carmo Church), one of the few structures in the area to have survived the 1755 earthquake. Today its sacristy houses an **archaeological museum.** *Museu ArqueológicoLargo do Carmo. Admission: 300$00. Open Oct.–Mar., Tues.–Sat. 10–1 and 2–5; Apr.–Sept., Tues.–Sat. 10–6.*

⑭ Return directly to the Praça dos Restauradores via the nearby **Elevador de Santa Justa** (Santa Justa elevator), which is enclosed in a Gothic tower created by Raul Mesnier, the Portuguese protégé of Gustave Eiffel. *Cost: 150$00. Open 7 AM–midnight.*

Belém

Numbers in the margin correspond to points of interest on the Belém map.

To see the best examples of that uniquely Portuguese, late-Gothic architecture known as Manueline, head for Belém, at the far southwestern edge of Lisbon. If you are traveling in a group of three or four, taxis are the cheapest means of transportation; otherwise take Tram 15, 16, or 17 from the Praça do Comércio for a more scenic, if bumpier, journey.

⑮ Trams 15 and 16 stop directly outside the **Mosteiro dos Jerónimos,** (Jerónimos Monastery), in the Praça do Império. This impressive structure was conceived and planned by King Manuel I at the beginning of the 16th century to honor the discoveries of Vasco da Gama. Construction began in 1502, and was largely financed by treasures brought back from the so-called descobrimentos—the "discoveries" made by the Portuguese in Africa, Asia, and South America. Don't miss the stunning double cloister with its arches and pillars heavily sculpted with marine motifs. *Admission to church free, cloisters: 400$00. Open June–Sept., Tues.–Sun. 10–6:30; Oct.–May, Tues.–Sun. 10–1 and 2:30–5.*

⑯ The **Museu de Marinha** (Maritime Museum) is at the west end of the monastery. Its huge collection reflects Portugal's long seafaring tradition, and exhibits range from early maps, model ships, and navigational instruments to entire fishing boats and royal barges. *Admission: 300$00, free Sun. Open Tues.–Sun. 10–5.*

TIME OUT There are a number of small restaurants and inexpensive cafés close to the monastery on Rua de Belém. Stop for coffee at the **Fabrica dos Pasteis de Belém** (Belém Pastry Factory) to sample the delicious custard pastries served hot with cinnamon and powdered sugar. *Rua de Belém 86–88.*

⑰ Across from the monastery at the water's edge stands the **Monumento dos Descobrimentos,** a tall, white angular slab. Built in 1960, this modern tribute to the seafaring explorers stands on what was the departure point of many of their voyages. An interesting mosaic, surrounded by an intricate wave pattern of black and white stones, lies at the foot. Take the elevator to the top for river views. *Admission: 275$00. Open Tues.–Sun. 9:30–7.*

Monumento
dos Desco-
brimentos, **17**

Mosteiro dos
Jerónimos, **15**

Museu de
Marinha, **16**

Museu Na-
cional dos
Coches, **19**

Palácio
da Ajuda, **20**

Torre de
Belém, **18**

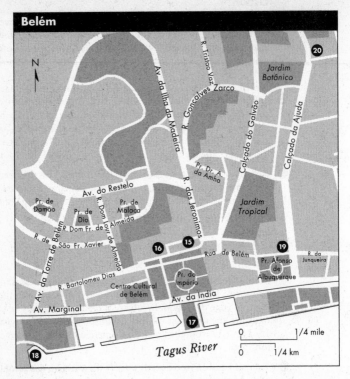

Belém

A 15-minute walk west of the monument brings you to the **Torre de Belém** (Belém Tower), another fine example of Manueline architecture with openwork balconies, loggia, and domed turrets. Although it was built in the early 16th century on an island in the middle of the River Tagus, today the tower stands near the north bank—the river's course has changed over the centuries. *Av. de India. Admission: 400$00 June–Sept.; 250$00 Oct.–May. Open June–Sept., Tues.–Sun. 10–6:30; Oct.–May, Tues.–Sun. 10–1 and 2:30–5.*

Away from the Tagus and east of the monastery, on the Praça Afonso de Albuquerque, is the **Museu Nacional dos Coches** (National Coach Museum), which houses one of the largest collections of coaches in the world. The oldest vehicle on display was made for Philip II of Spain in the late 16th century, but the most stunning exhibits are three golden Baroque coaches made in Rome for King John V in 1716. *Admission: June–Sept. 400$00, Oct.–May 250$00; free Sun. Open June–Sept., Tues.–Sun. 10–1 and 2:30–6:30; Oct.–May, Tues.–Sun. 10–1 and 2:30–5:30.*

Head north of the coach museum on Calçada da Ajuda to the **Palácio da Ajuda** (Ajuda Palace). Once a royal residence, this impressive building now contains a collection of 18th- and 19th-century paintings, furniture, and tapestries. *Largo da Ajuda. Admission: 250$00; free Sun. 10–2. Guided tours arranged on request. Open Thurs.–Tues. 10–5. Closed Wed.*

Off the Beaten Track

North of the city in the suburb of São Domingos de Benfica is one of the most beautiful private houses in the capital. The **Palácio da Fronteira,** built in the late 17th century, contains splendid reception rooms with 18th-century figurative tiles, contemporary furniture, and paintings, but it is the gardens that are unique. A long rectangular water tank is backed by 17th-century tiled panels of heroic-size knights on prancing horses. Stone steps at either side lead to a terraced walk above, between pyramid pavilions roofed with copper-colored tiles. This beautiful conceit is surrounded by a topiary garden, statuary, fountains, and terraces. *Largo de S. Domingos de Benfica 1. Admission to gardens: 300$00; to palace and gardens: 1,000$00. Open Mon.–Fri. for 1-hr. tour, but visitors must arrive between 10:45 and 11 AM. On Sat. a full guided tour costs 1,000$00 (gardens) or 1,500$00 (palace and gardens); arrive at 10:45 AM.*

In the wealthy district of Lapa, halfway between the Bairro Alto and Belém, stands the **Museu de Arte Antiga** (Ancient Art Museum) in a 17th-century palace, the only museum in Lisbon to rival the Gulbenkian. It has a beautifully displayed collection of Portuguese art, mainly 15th–19th century. The highlight is undoubtedly the St. Vincent altarpiece (1467–1470), masterpiece of Nuno Gonçalves. Its six panels show Vincent, the patron saint of Lisbon, receiving the homage of king, court, and citizens, and 60 different figures can be identified, including Henry the Navigator himself. *Rua das Janelas Verdes 95, Lapa. Tram 19 from Praça do Comércio. Admission 250$00, free Sun. 10–1. Open Tues.–Sun. 10–1 and 2–5.*

Shopping

Shopping Districts

Since the fire that destroyed much of the Chiado in 1988, an extensive reconstruction project has made some progress. Another important shopping area is in the **Baixa** quarter (between the Rossío and the River Tagus). On Avenida Engeneiro Duarte Pacheco, west of Parque Eduardo VII, the blue-and-pink towers of the **Amoreiras,** a huge modern shopping center (open daily 9 AM–11 PM), dominate the Lisbon skyline.

Flea Markets

The **feira da ladra** (flea market) is held on Tuesday morning and all day Saturday in the Largo de Santa Clara behind the Church of São Vicente, near the Alfama district.

Gift Ideas

LEATHER GOODS

Fine leather handbags and luggage are sold at **Galeão** (Rua Augusta 190) and at **Casa Canada** (Rua Augusta 232). Shoe stores abound in Lisbon, but they may have a limited selection of large sizes (the Portuguese have relatively small feet); the better shops can make shoes to order, on short notice, however. Leather gloves can be purchased at a variety of specialty shops on Rua do Carmo and Rua Aurea.

HANDICRAFTS

Viúva Lamego (Largo do Intendente 25) has the largest selection of tiles and pottery, while **Fabrica Sant'Ana** (Rua do Alecrim 95), in the Bairro Alto, sells wonderful hand-painted ceramics and tiles. For embroidered goods and baskets, try **Casa Regional da Ilha Verde** (Rua Paiva de Andrade 4) or **Tito Cunha** (Rua Aurea 286). **Casa Quintão** (Rua Ivens 30) probably has the largest selection of *arraiolos,* the traditional, hand-embroidered Portuguese carpets, in town. For fine porcelain, visit **Vista Alegre** (Largo do Chiado 18), and for handcrafted pottery, try **Casa Ribeiro da Silva** (Trav. Fiéis de Deus 69, Bairro Alto).

JEWELRY AND ANTIQUES

Antonio da Silva (Praça Luis de Camões 40), at the top of the Chiado, specializes in antique silver and jewelry, as does **Barreto e Gonçalves** (Rua das Portas de Santo Antão 17). Most of the antiques shops are along the Rua Escola Politecnica, Rua Dom Pedro IV, Rua da Misericódia and Rua do Alecrim. Look for characteristic Portuguese gold- and silver-filigree work at **Sarmento** (Rua Aurea 251) in the Baixa.

Dining

For details and price-category definitions, *see* Dining *in* Staying in Portugal, *above.*

$$$$ **António Clara.** Housed in an attractive Art Nouveau building in north Lisbon, this restaurant serves French and international dishes with a flourish. The elegant dining room has a decorated ceiling, heavy draperies, and huge chandelier. The menu is seasonal and there's a fine wine list. *Av. República 38, tel. 01/796–6380. Reservations required. AE, DC, MC, V. Closed Sun.*

$$$$ **Aviz.** One of the best and classiest restaurants in Lisbon, Aviz has a Belle
★   Epoque decor—even the rest rooms are impressive—and an excellent French and international menu. The restaurant is hidden on a side street off the Baixa's Rua Garrett. *Rua Serpa Pinto 12, tel. 01/342–8391. Reservations required. AE, DC, MC, V. Closed Sat. lunch and Sun.*

$$$$ **Casa da Comida.** A flower-filled patio is the centerpiece of this converted private home, where one can find imaginative French and Portuguese fare. *Travessa das Amoreiras 1, tel. 01/685376. Reservations advised. AE, DC, MC, V. Closed Sat. lunch and Sun.*

$$$$ **Gambrinus.** One of Lisbon's older restaurants, Gambrinus is noted for its fish and shellfish. Enter through an inconspicuous door on a busy street to one of the restaurant's numerous small dining rooms. *Rua das Portas de S. Antão 23–25, tel. 01/346–8974. Reservations advised. AE, DC, MC, V.*

$$$$ **Tagide.** Delicious Portuguese food and wine are served in this fine old tile house that looks out over the Baixa and the river. Try to secure a window table. *Largo Academia das Belas Artes 18–20, tel. 01/342–0720. Reservations advised. AE, DC, MC, V. Closed weekends.*

$$$$ **Tavares Rico.** A seasonal, French-inspired menu, an excellent wine list,
★   and handsome Edwardian furnishings have made this dining room (originally founded as a café in the 18th century) one of Lisbon's most famous restaurants. *Rua Misericórdia 37, tel. 01/342–1112. Reservations required. AE, DC, MC, V. Closed Sat. and Sun. lunch.*

$$$ **Michel.** Innovative French cooking and an intimate atmosphere can be found in this attractive restaurant in the village within the walls of St. George's Castle. *Largo S. Cruz do Castelo 5, tel. 01/886–4338. Reservations advised. AE, DC, MC, V. Closed Sat. lunch and Sun.*

$$$ **O Madeirense.** Lisbon's only Madeiran restaurant, this rustic-style room is inside the Amoreiras shopping center. The *espedata* is famously traditional—a skewer of fillet steak is hung above the table from a stand so that you can serve yourself at will. *Loja 3027, Amoreiras Shopping Center, Av. Eng. Duarte Pacheco, tel. 01/690827. Reservations advised. AE, DC, MC, V.*

$$$ **Solmar.** This large restaurant near the Rossío, Lisbon's main square, is best known for its seafood and shellfish, but try the wild boar or venison in season. *Rua das Portas de S. Antão 108, tel. 01/342–3371. AE, DC, MC, V.*

$$$ **Sua Excêlencia.** There's no written menu in this cozy little restaurant
★   in the Lapa district. The English-speaking owner will personally talk you through the outstanding Portuguese dishes that are offered. *Rua*

do Conde 42, tel. 01/603614. Reservations advised. MC, V. Closed Wed., Sept., and weekend lunch.

$$ Brasuca. A comfortable Brazilian restaurant set in an old mansion on the edge of the Bairro Alto, the Brasuca serves a splendid *caipirinha* (rum cocktail), grilled meats, and spicy meat stews. *Rua João Pereira da Rosa 7, tel. 01/342–3506. Reservations advised. AE, DC, MC, V. Closed Mon.*

$$ Cervejaria Trindade. Prepare for hearty Portuguese cuisine served in a
★ 19th-century Lisbon beer hall-restaurant adorned with colorful tiles. It specializes in seafood and is open until 2 AM. *Rua Nova da Trindade 20, tel. 01/346–3506. AE, DC, MC, V.*

$$ Farah's Tandoori. A small simple place, Farah's is known as one of the best and friendliest Indian restaurants in Lisbon. All the curries, which are served with Indian bread, are sure bets for a good meal. *Rua de Sant'Ana a Lapa 73, tel. 01/609219. MC, V. Closed Tues.*

$$ O Alexandre. This tiny restaurant in Belém has outdoor tables from which diners, mostly local, soak up the superb views of the monastery. Try one of the grilled fish dishes, or even the more unusual squid and octopus dishes if they're available. (Note that the restaurant closes at 10 PM.) *Rua Vieria Portuense 84, Belém, tel. 01/363–4544. No reservations. MC, V. Closed Sat.*

$$ Ribadouro. This bustling basement restaurant serves notable seafood to a discerning local clientele. The crabs, crayfish, and other shellfish are all excellent. *Av. de Liberdade 155, tel. 01/549411. AE, DC, MC, V.*

$ Bonjardim. Known as "Rei dos Frangos" (King of Chickens), the Bon-
★ jardim specializes in the spit-roasted variety. Just off the Restauradores, it gets very crowded at peak hours; you may have to wait in line for a table, but it's worth it. *Travessa S. Antão 11, tel. 01/342–7424. AE, DC, MC, V.*

$ Vá e Volta. This is a splendid place for one-plate, budget, Bairro Alto fare—fried or grilled meat or fish dishes served with gusto and good humor. *Rua do Diario de Noticias 100, tel. 01/342–7888. MC, V.*

Lodging

Lisbon has a good array of accommodations in all price categories, ranging from some of the major international chain hotels to charming little family-run establishments. During peak season reservations should be made well in advance. For details and price-category definitions, *see* Lodging *in* Staying in Portugal, *above.*

$$$$ Lisboa Sheraton and Towers. This is a typical Sheraton hotel with a huge reception area and medium-size rooms. The 79 deluxe units in the Towers section, which has a separate reception desk in the lobby and a private lounge, are about the same size but are more luxuriously appointed. The hotel is centrally located and is just across the street from a large shopping center. *Rua Latino Coelho 1, tel. 01/575757, fax 01/547164. 384 rooms with bath. Facilities: restaurant, grill, bar, garage, pool, health club, sauna. AE, DC, MC, V.*

$$$$ Meridien Lisboa. The rooms in this luxury hotel are on the small side, but they are soundproofed and attractively decorated; the front ones overlook the Parque Eduardo VII, which means the hotel is ideally situated for downtown exploration. *Rua Castilho 149, tel. 01/690400, fax 01/693231. 331 rooms with bath. Facilities: health club with sauna, shops, garage. AE, DC, MC, V.*

$$$$ Ritz Lisboa. One of the finest hotels in Europe, this Inter-Continental is
★ renowned for its excellent service. The large, handsomely decorated guest rooms all have terraces, and the elegantly appointed public rooms feature tapestries, antique reproductions, and fine paintings. The best

rooms are in the front overlooking Parque Eduardo VII. There's convenient dining at the Veranda restaurant, which has a summer terrace. *Rua Rodrigo da Fonseca 88, tel. 01/692020, fax 01/691783. 304 rooms with bath. Facilities: 2 restaurants, bar, shops, garage. AE, DC, MC, V.*

$$$ **As Janelas Verdes.** This late-18th-century mansion has marvelously re-
★ stored, individually furnished guest rooms. There's a lovely ivy-covered patio garden where you can eat breakfast—and you're not far from the Sua Excêlencia restaurant (*see* Dining, *above*). Reservations are vital at this hotel, since it's as popular as it is small. *Rua das Janelas Verdes 47, tel. 01/396–8143, fax 01/396–8144. 17 rooms with bath. Facilities; patio garden, lounge, parking. AE, DC, MC, V.*

$$$ **Sofitel Lisboa.** Tasteful modern architecture and a convenient location make this hotel a favorite with the international business community. Moderately sized guest rooms are comfortably furnished in pleasing colors. The small elegant lobby is bordered by an intimate piano bar. *Av. da Liberdade 123–125, tel. 01/342–9202, fax 01/342–9222. 170 rooms with bath. Facilities: restaurant, bar, garage. AE, DC, MC, V.*

$$$ **Tivoli Lisboa.** Located on Lisbon's main avenue, this comfortable, well-
★ run establishment has a large public area furnished with inviting armchairs and sofas. The guest rooms are all pleasant, but the ones in the rear are quieter. There's also a good restaurant, and the grill on the top floor has wonderful views of the city and the Tagus. *Av. da Liberdade 185, tel. 01/353–0182, fax 01/579461. 326 rooms with bath. Facilities: restaurant, grill, bar, outdoor pool, tennis courts, shops, garage. AE, DC, MC, V.*

$$$ **York House.** A former 17th-century convent, this residência is set in a
★ shady garden, up a long flight of steps, near the Museu de Arte Antiga. It has a good restaurant, and full or half board is available. Book well in advance: This atmospheric place is small and has a loyal following. *Rua das Janelas Verdes 32, tel. 01/396–2435, fax 01/397–2793. 36 rooms with bath. Facilities: restaurant, bar, garden. AE, DC, MC, V.*

$$ **Albergaria Senhora do Monte.** The rooms in this unpretentious little
★ hotel, located in the oldest part of town near St. George's Castle, have terraces that offer some of the loveliest views of Lisbon, especially at night when the castle and Carmo ruins in the middle distance are softly illuminated. The top-floor grill has a picture window. *Calçada do Monte 39, tel. 01/886–6002, fax 01/877783. 28 rooms with bath. Facilities: restaurant, bar, grill. AE, DC, MC, V.*

$$ **Flamingo.** Another good-value choice near the top of the Avenida da Liberdade, this hotel has a friendly staff and pleasant guest rooms, though those in the front tend to be noisy. There's a pay parking lot right next door, which is a bonus in this busy area. *Rua Castilho 41, tel. 01/386–2191, fax 01/386–1216. 39 rooms with bath. Facilities: restaurant, bar, shops. AE, DC, MC, V.*

$$ **Fenix.** Located at the top of Avenida da Liberdade, this hotel with elegant interiors has largish guest rooms—many with fine views—and a pleasant first-floor lounge. Its restaurant serves good Portuguese food. *Praça Marquês de Pombal 8, tel. 01/386–2121, fax 01/386–0131. 119 rooms with bath. Facilities: restaurant, bar, parking. AE, DC, MC, V.*

$$ **Florida.** This centrally located hotel is close to the downtown restaurants and has a restful atmosphere and guest rooms with marble-clad bathrooms. *Rua Duque de Palmela 32, tel. 01/576145, fax 01/543584. 112 rooms with bath. Facilities: bar. AE, DC, MC, V.*

$$ **Novotel Lisboa.** There's an attentive staff and a quiet, welcoming atmosphere at this pleasant, modern hotel near the U.S. Embassy. The public rooms are spacious and all benefit from recent renovation; guest rooms are spruce and comfortably equipped. *Av. Jose Malhoa*

Lote 1642, tel. 01/726–6022, fax 01/726–6496. 246 rooms with bath. Facilities: restaurant, bar, pool, garage. AE, MC, V.

$ **Duas Nações.** This basic, noisy pensão has a superb location in the heart of the Baixa grid. Guest rooms are plain and functional (ask for one at the rear to minimize street noise) although an impressive dining room retains its original large dimensions and fine decor. *Rua da Vitória 41, tel. 01/346–0710. 66 rooms, 42 with bath. Facilities: bar, dining room. No credit cards.*

$ **Hotel Borges.** In the heart of the Chiado district, convenient for shopping, this dependable, old-fashioned hotel has good service and a charm that transcends its limited facilities. You're also only a step away from the famous Brasileira café, an excellent breakfast spot. *Rua Garrett 108–110, tel. 01/346–1951, fax 01/342–6617. Facilities: breakfast room, bar. MC, V.*

The Arts

Two local newspaper supplements provide listings of music, theater, ballet, film, and other entertainment in Lisbon: *Sete,* published on Wednesday, and *Sabado,* published on Friday.

Plays are performed in Portuguese at the **Teatro Nacional de D. Maria II** (Praça Dom Pedro IV, tel. 01/342–2210) year-round except in July. Classical music, opera, and ballet are presented in the beautiful **Teatro Nacional de Opera de São Carlos** (Rua Serpa Pinto 9, tel. 01/346–5914). Classical music and ballet are also staged from autumn to summer by the **Fundação Calouste Gulbenkian** (Av. Berna 45, tel. 01/793–5131). Of particular interest is the annual Early Music and Baroque Festival held in churches and museums around Lisbon every spring. The new cultural center, the **Centro Cultural de Belém** (Av. da India, tel. 01/301–9606) at Belém, also hosts a full range of concerts and exhibitions—pick up a monthly program of events from the reception desk. Otherwise, there are free recitals held regularly at the Bairro Alto churches of Carmo and São Roque, and at the Sé. The **Nova Filarmonica,** one of Portugal's national orchestras, performs concerts around the country throughout the year; consult local papers for details.

Nightlife

The most popular nightspots in Lisbon are the *adegas tipicas* (wine cellars), where customers dine on Portuguese specialties, drink wine, and listen to the haunting melodies of *fado* (traditional Portuguese folk music). Most of these establishments are scattered throughout the Alfama and Bairro Alto districts. Try the **Senhor Vinho** (Rua do Meio a Lapa 18, tel. 01/397–7456; closed Sun.), **Lisboa à Noite** (Rua das Gaveas 69, tel. 01/346–8557; closed Sun.), or the **Machado** (Rua do Norte 91, tel. 01/346–0095; closed Mon.). The singing starts at 10 PM, and reservations are advised. Lisbon's top spot for live jazz is **The Hot Clube** (Praça da Alegria 39, tel. 01/346–7369; closed Sun.–Mon.), where sessions don't usually begin until 11 PM.

Bars and Discos

The main areas for bars and discos are the Bairro Alto or along Avenida 24 de Julho, northwest of Cais do Sodre station. In the former, the best place to start is the refined **Instituto do Vinho do Porto** (Rua de São Pedro de Alcântara 45, tel. 01/347–5707), where you choose drinks from a menu of port wines. Also, **Cena de Copas** (Rua da Barroca 103–105, tel. 01/347–3372) is still loud and fashionable, while **Pavilhão Chines** (Rua Dom Pedro V 89, tel. 01/342–4729) is decorated with extraordinary bric-a-brac from around the world. Along Avenida 24 de

Julho, current favorites include **Café 24 de Julho** (No. 114) and **Café Central** (No. 110), and the nearby **Kremlin** disco (Rua Escadinhas da Praia 5, tel. 01/608768) continues to attract the trendiest Lisboetas. **Trumps** (Rua Imprensa Nacional 104b, tel. 01/397–1059) is the city's biggest gay disco; **Memorial** (Rua Gustavo Sequeira 42, tel. 01/396–8891) is popular with both gay and lesbian visitors.

THE PORTUGUESE RIVIERA, SINTRA, AND QUELUZ

Extending 32 kilometers (20 miles) west of Lisbon is a stretch of coastline known as the Portuguese Riviera. Over the years, the casino at Estoril and the beaches, both there and in Cascais, have provided playgrounds for the wealthy, as well as homes for expatriates and exiled European royalty.

Beaches here differ both in quality and cleanliness. Some display the blue Council of Europe flag, which signals a high standard of unpolluted water and sands, but others leave much to be desired. The waters off Cascais and Estoril are calm, though sullied as a result of their proximity to the meeting of the sea and Lisbon's Tagus estuary. To the north, around Guincho's rocky promontory and the Praia de Maças coast, the Atlantic Ocean is often windswept and rough but provides good surfing and windsurfing.

To the north of Cascais and Estoril lie the lush, green mountains of Sintra and to the northeast, the historic town of Queluz, dominated by its 18th-century rococo palace and formal gardens. The villas, châteaus, and luxury *quintas* (country properties) of Sintra contrast notably with Cascais and Estoril, where life revolves around the sea. The entire region offers comprehensive sporting possibilities: golf courses, horseback riding, fishing, tennis, squash, swimming, water sports, grand prix racing, mountain climbing, and country walks.

Getting Around

The area is served by three main roads—the often congested four-lane coastal road (the N6 Avenida Marginal), the N117/N249 to Sintra, and the A5 expressway, which links Lisbon with Cascais. A commuter train leaves every 15 to 30 minutes (5:30 AM–2:30 AM) from Cais do Sodré Station in Lisbon for the trip to Estoril and then to Cascais, four stops farther. The 30-minute journey affords splendid sea views as it traces the shore. A one-way ticket costs 160$00. Trains from Lisbon's Rossío station run every quarter of an hour to Queluz (145$00), taking 20 minutes, and on to Sintra (155$00), which takes 40 minutes. For current information about train services, call 01/888–4025.

Guided Tours

Catur (Largo da Academia Nacional de Belas Artes 12, tel. 01/346–7974) offers a nine-hour excursion that takes in principal sights; it costs 12,000$00 and includes lunch. **Citirama Viagens e Turismo SA** (Av. Praia de Vitória 12-B, tel. 01/355–8567) offers a similar tour at a lower price. Both tours have daily departures.

Tourist Information

Cascais (Viscount Luz 14–r/c, tel. 01/486–8204).
Estoril (Arcadas do Parque, tel. 01/468–0113).
Sintra (Praça da Republica 3, tel. 01/923–3919).

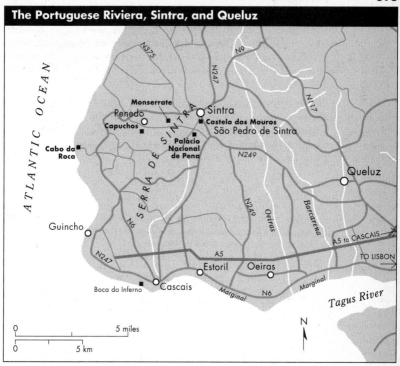

The Portuguese Riviera, Sintra, and Queluz

Exploring the Portuguese Riviera, Sintra, and Queluz

Leave Lisbon by car via the Estrada Marginal highway (following signs for Cascais/Estoril) and take the curving coastal route (the N6) to Estoril. Both Estoril and Cascais are favored residential areas; thanks to their special microclimate, they boast milder winters than does nearby Lisbon.

Estoril

Estoril is filled with grand homes and gardens, and many of its large mansions date from the last century when it was a favorite with the European aristocracy. People-watching is the favored pastime, and one of the best places for it is on the **Tamariz esplanade,** especially from an alfresco restaurant. A palm-studded coastline, plush accommodations, sports facilities, and restaurants are among Estoril's other attractions, but it is perhaps best known for its **casino,** (3 PM–3 AM) an excellent gambling hall and nightspot that has a restaurant, a bar, a theater, and an art gallery. A major open-air handicrafts and ceramics fair is held each summer (July–September), and many music concerts and ballets are staged here during the Estoril Festival each summer.

TIME OUT The luxurious **Hotel Palácio** (*see* Dining and Lodging, *below*), in Parque do Estoril, is worth a visit simply to take tea in one of its ample salons. During World War II, it was an espionage center where the Germans and Allies kept watch on each other in neutral Portugal, and where exiled European courts waited out the war.

Cascais

Cascais lies less than 3.2 kilometers (2 miles) west of Estoril. A pretty but heavily developed tourist resort, it is packed with shopping centers, cinemas, and hotels. The three beaches are small and crowded, and in summer, parking is a headache. Even so, there are sights worth seeing, including the **Igreja de Nossa Senhora da Assunção** (Church of Our Lady of the Assumption), which contains paintings by Portuguese artist Josefa de Óbidos. *Largo da Assunção. Admission free. Open daily 9–1 and 5–8.*

Opposite the church is one of the entrances to the **Parque do Marachal Carmona** (open daily 9–6), in which there's a shallow lake, a café, and a small zoo. Walk through the park to its southern edge and you'll find the **Museu Conde de Castro Guimarães** (Museum of the Count of Castro Guimarães), a large stately home set on spacious grounds. It houses some good paintings, ceramics, furniture, and archaeological artifacts excavated locally. *Estrada da Boca do Inferno. Admission: 150$00, free Sun. Open Tues.–Sun. 11–12:30 and 2–5.*

Continue west from the museum along the coastal road (N247), and it's less than 2 kilometers (about 1¼ miles), in the direction of Guincho beach, to the notorious **Boca do Inferno,** or Hell's Mouth. This rugged section of coastline is made up of many stunning tide-swept grottoes.

A scenic 9-kilometer (5½-mile) drive along the coastal road from Boca do Inferno brings you to the superb rocky surfing beach at **Guincho.** From here, the road cuts inland north to the turnoff for **Cabo da Roca,** whose lighthouse marks continental Europe's westernmost landfall.

Back on the main road, turn into the hills at the end of Praia do Guincho (Guincho Beach). This is the beginning of the **Serra de Sintra** (Sintra Mountains), and here, at **Capuchos,** you can visit the tiny friary, built in 1560 by Franciscan monks. The 12 diminutive cells, hacked out of solid rock, are lined with cork for warmth and insulation—hence the nickname the "Cork Convent." *Admission 200$00. Open June–Sept., daily 10–6; Oct.–May, daily 10–5.*

Return to the main road and follow its winding course through the village of **Penedo,** which offers terrific views of the sea and the surrounding mountains, until you reach the world-renowned gardens of **Monserrate,** 5½ kilometers (3 miles) from the superb Palácio de Seteais hotel (*see below*). This botanical wonderland was laid out by Scottish gardeners in the mid-1800s and is the site of an exotic and architecturally extravagant domed Moorish-style palace (closed to visitors). In addition to a dazzling array of tree and plant species, the gardens have one of the largest collections of fern varieties in the world. *Admission: 200$00. Open June–Sept., daily 10–6; Oct.–May, daily 10–5.*

TIME OUT   Follow signs to Seteais and stop for a meal at the **Palácio de Seteais** (Seteais Palace), built by the Dutch consul in Portugal in the 18th century. Now a luxury hotel (*see* Dining and Lodging, *below*), the Seteais has an excellent but expensive restaurant, and its stately rooms are decorated with delicate wall and ceiling frescoes.

Sintra

From here, the main road gently winds down toward **Sintra.** One of Portugal's oldest towns, Sintra is full of history. At the center of the **Old Town** near the Hotel Tivoli Sintra stands the 14th-century **Palácio Nacional de Sintra** (Sintra Palace). This twin-chimneyed building, a combination of Moorish and Gothic architectural styles, was once the summer residence of the House of Avis, Portugal's royal line. Today it's a museum that houses some fine examples of Moorish-Arabic *azulejos* (hand-painted tiles). *Admission: June–Sept. 400$00, Oct.–May 200$00, free Sun. morning. Open Thurs.–Tue. 10–1 and 2–5.*

If you stand on the steps of the palace and look up toward the Sintra Mountains, you can spot the 8th-century ruins of the **Castelo dos Mouros** (Moors' Castle), which defied hundreds of invaders until it was finally conquered by Dom Afonso Henriques in 1147. Follow the steep, partially cobbled road that leads up to the ruins; or rent one of the horse-drawn carriages outside the palace. From the castle's serrated walls, you can see why its Moorish architects chose the site: The panoramic views falling away on all sides are breathtaking. *Estrada da Pena. Admission free. Open June–Sept., daily 10–6; Oct.–May, daily 10–5.*

Farther up the same road you'll reach the **Palácio Nacional de Pena** (Pena Palace), a Wagnerian-style extravaganza built by the King Con-sort Ferdinand of Saxe-Coburg in 1840. It is a cauldron of clashing styles, from Arabian to Victorian, and was home to the final kings of Portugal. The nucleus of the palace is a convent commissioned by Dom Fernando, consort to Dona Maria II. The palace is surrounded by a park filled with a variety of trees and flowers brought from every cor-ner of the Portuguese empire by Dom Fernando in the 1840s. *Admis-sion for guided tour: June–Sept. 400$00, Oct.–May 200$00, free Sun. 10–2. Open Tues.–Sun. 10–5.*

Back in downtown Sintra, the **Museu do Brinquedo** (Toy Museum) houses an enjoyable collection of dolls and traditional toys from this region of Portugal. *Largo Latino Coelho 9. Admission: 200$00. Open Tues.–Sun. 10–12:30 and 2:30–5.*

If you're in the area on the second or fourth Sunday of the month, visit the **Feira de Sintra** (Sintra Fair) in the nearby village of **São Pedro de Sintra,** 2 kilometers (about 1¼ miles) to the southeast. This is one of the best-known fairs in the country.

Queluz

From the fairgrounds, drive past a gas station to the traffic circle and take N249 back toward Lisbon, keeping an eye out for the left turnoff to **Queluz.** As soon as you swing off the main road, you'll be confronted by the magnificent **Palácio Nacional de Queluz** (Queluz Palace). Par-tially inspired by Versailles, this salmon-pink rococo palace was begun by Dom Pedro III in 1747 and took 40 years to complete. The formal landscaping and waterways that surround it are the work of the French designer Jean-Baptiste Robillon. Restored after a disastrous fire in 1934, the palace is used today for formal banquets, music festivals, and as accommodations for visiting heads of state. Visitors may walk through the elegant state rooms, including the Music Salon, the Hall of the Ambassadors, and the mirrored Throne Room with its crystal chandeliers and gilt trimmings. *Admission: June–Sept. 400$00, Oct.–May 200$00. Open Wed.–Mon. 10–1 and 2–5.*

Dining and Lodging

For details and price-category definitions, *see* Dining and Lodging *in* Staying in Portugal, *above.*

Cascais

DINING

João Padeiro. This restaurant in the town center serves the best sole in the region—and other seafood as well—amid cheerful surroundings. *Rua Visconde da Luz 12, tel. 01/483–0232. AE, DC, MC, V. Closed Tues. $$$*

Beira Mar. This well-established restaurant behind the fish market has a wide variety of fish and meat dishes. The atmosphere is comfortable and unpretentious. *Rua das Flores 6, tel. 01/483–0152. AE, DC, MC, V. Closed Tues. $$*

★ **Hotel Albatroz.** Situated on a rocky outcrop, this attractive old house, converted from an aristocrat's summer residence, is the most luxurious of Cascais's hotels. Though it's been extended and modernized, it has retained its character, with charming bedrooms and a pleasant terrace bar. The restaurant boasts superior views of the sea and over the coast toward Lisbon; it specializes in fish dishes. *Rua Frederico Arouca 100, tel. 01/483–2821, fax 01/484–4827. 40 rooms with bath. Facilities: bar, restaurant (reservations required), pool, garage. AE, DC, MC, V. Hotel $$$$; Restaurant $$$*

★ **Restaurante/Estalagem Muchaxo.** The sound of the sea accompanies your meal at this restaurant nestled on the rocks overlooking Guincho beach, 10 kilometers (6 miles) from Cascais. It is one of the region's oldest and best-known eating places, and the Portuguese and fish specialties here are beautifully cooked and presented. There are also 24 rooms available for guests; prices are discounted heavily in winter. *Praia do Guincho, tel. 01/487–0221, fax 01/487–0444. Restaurant reservations advised. AE, DC, MC, V. Inn $$; Restaurant $$$*

Estoril
DINING

★ **Restaurant Grill Four Seasons.** This famous, elegant establishment in the Hotel Palácio (*see below*) serves buffets around the garden pool in summer and seeks perfection with the freshest food. *Parque do Estoril, tel. 01/468–0400. Reservations advised. AE, DC, MC, V. $$$–$$$$*

A Choupana. Just outside town toward Lisbon, this restaurant overlooks the beach. You can sample high-quality fresh fish, seafood, and other local dishes and dance to a live band until 2 AM. *Estrada Marginal, São João de Estoril, tel. 01/468–3099. Reservations advised. AE, DC, MC, V. $$$*

The English Bar. This mock-Tudor-style establishment serves good international cuisine in friendly, comfortable surroundings. There are beautiful views over the beach to Cascais and an excellent wine list. *Av. Saboia, off Av. Marginal, Monte Estoril, tel. 01/468–0413. Reservations advised. AE, DC, MC, V. Closed Sun. $$$*

Restaurante Frolic. Situated next to the Hotel Palácio, the Frolic is a friendly restaurant-bar with a covered, outdoor terrace. Try the delectable cakes, or stop longer for a Portuguese meal or pizza. *Av. Clotilde, tel. 01/468–1219. AE, DC, MC, V. $$*

DINING AND LODGING

★ **Hotel Palácio.** During World War II, exiled European courts came here to wait out the war in grand style. The pastel rooms are decorated in Regency style and the hotel contains one of Portugal's most famous restaurants (*see above*). It's a two-minute walk to the beach, and golfers can tee off at the Estoril golf course. *Parque do Estoril, tel. 01/468–0400, fax 01/468–4867. 162 rooms with bath. Facilities: outdoor pool, restaurant, bar, gardens, sports facilities. AE, DC, MC, V. $$$–$$$$*

Queluz
DINING

★ **Restaurante de Cozinha Velha.** This restaurant, housed in what were once the great kitchens of the adjoining Queluz Palace, is dominated by an open fireplace. There are some fine wines in the cellar to go with the traditional Portuguese cooking—a spicy dish with salmon, monkfish, clams, and shrimp is just one superb main course. *Palácio Na-*

cional de Queluz, tel. 01/435–0232. Reservations advised. AE, DC, MC, V. $$$

Sintra

DINING

Solar de São Pedro. Highly recommended by its habitués, this restaurant specializes in Portuguese and French country cooking. Its English-speaking host adds to the warm, friendly atmosphere. *Largo da Feira 12, São Pedro de Sintra, tel. 01/923–1860. Reservations advised. AE, DC, MC, V. Closed Wed. $$–$$$*

Alcobaça. Excellent value for classic Portuguese home cooking is offered at this central restaurant—try the grilled chicken or the *arroz de marisco* (seafood rice). *Rua das Padarias 7–11, tel. 01/923–1651. MC, V. $$*

LODGING

Palácio de Seteais. This luxurious former palace set on its own grounds a kilometer from Sintra (*see* Exploring the Portuguese Riviera, *above*) houses a splendid restaurant. *Rua Barbosa do Bocage 8, tel. 01/923–3200, fax 01/923–4277. 30 rooms with bath. Facilities: restaurant, bar, pool, tennis courts, gardens, horseback riding, parking. AE, DC, MC, V. $$$$*

Tivoli Sintra. From its perch in the center of Sintra, the Tivoli has excellent views over the local valleys. *Praça da República, tel. 01/923–3505, fax 01/923–1572. 75 rooms with bath. Facilities: restaurant, bar, garage. AE, DC, MC, V. $$$*

Quinta das Sequóias. This lovely old antique-filled manor house (formerly known as the Casa da Tapada) is down a side road just beyond the Palácio de Seteais and makes an excellent touring base. Reservations are essential. *Apartado 4, tel. and fax 01/923–0342. 6 rooms with bath. Facilities: bar, dinner on request, breakfast served, gardens, pool, sauna, parking. AE, DC, MC, V. $$–$$$*

THE ALGARVE

The Algarve, Portugal's southernmost holiday resort, encompasses some 240 kilometers (150 miles) of sun-drenched coast below the Serra de Monchique and the Serra do Caldeirão. It is the top destination for foreign visitors to Portugal. During the past three decades, this area, indelibly marked by centuries of Arab occupation, has been heavily developed in an effort to create a playground for international sun worshipers. Well known by Europeans as a holiday center of clean, sandy beaches, championship golf courses, and local color, this section of Portugal is only now being discovered by Americans. Although some parts of the coastline have been seriously overbuilt, there are still fishing villages and secluded beaches that remain untouched.

Getting Around

Faro, the capital of the Algarve, is only 45 minutes from Lisbon by air. **TAP Air Portugal** has daily service from Lisbon, and there are frequent international flights to Faro from London, Frankfurt, and Brussels. There is also daily bus and rail service between Lisbon and the major towns in the Algarve; trips take four to six hours, depending on your destination. The trip by car from Lisbon to Faro or Portimão takes about four hours.

The main east–west highway in the Algarve is the two-lane N125, which extends 165 kilometers (100 miles) from Vila Real de Santo António, on the Spanish border, to Vila do Bispo, north of Cabo de São Vicente.

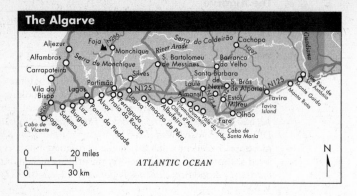

The Algarve

ATLANTIC OCEAN

0 — 20 miles
0 — 30 km

N

This road does not run right along the coast, but turnoffs to beach-side destinations mentioned here are posted along the route. Local rail and bus services link most of the villages and towns in the Algarve, and organized guided bus tours of some of the more noteworthy villages and towns depart from Faro, Quarteira, Vilamoura, Albufeira, Portimão, and Lagos.

Tourist Information

Local tourist offices can be found in the following towns:

Albufeira (Rua 5 de Outubro, tel. 089/512144).
Armação de Pêrá (Av. Marginal, tel. 082/312145).
Faro (Airport, tel. 089/818582; Rua da Misericódia 8/12, tel. 089/803604; Rua Ataide de Oliveira 100, tel. 089/803667).
Lagos (Largo Marquês de Pombal, tel. 082/763031).
Loulé (Edifico do Castelo, tel. 089/63900).
Monte Gordo (Av. Marginal, tel. 081/44495).
Olhão (Largo da Lagoa, tel. 089/713936).
Portimão (Largo 1° de Dezembro, tel. 082/23695).
Praia da Rocha (Av. Tomás Cabreira, tel. 082/22290).
Quarteira (Av. Infante de Sagres, tel. 082/312217).
Sagres (Promontório de Sagres, tel. 082/64125).
Silves (Rua 25 de Abril, tel. 082/442255).
Tavira (Praça da República, tel. 081/22511).
Vila Real de Santo António (Praça Marquês de Pombal, tel. 081/44495; Frontier Tourist Post, tel. 081/43272).

Exploring the Algarve

To reach the Algarve from Lisbon, cross the Tagus bridge and take the A2 toll road to Setúbal. Beyond here, the main IP1 (E1) highway runs via Alcácer-do-Sal, Grandola, and Ourique, eventually joining with the east–west N125. Albufeira is straight ahead; head east for Faro and the Spanish border, or west for Lagos. The trip to Albufeira from Lisbon takes about four hours; allow another hour to reach either Faro or Lagos.

Visitors coming to the Algarve from Spain by car can drive from Ayamonte, the Spanish frontier town, across a new suspension bridge over the River Guadiana to **Vila Real de Santo António.** This showcase of 18th-century Portuguese town planning is set out on a grid pattern, similar to the Baixa section of Lisbon, though there isn't really much to see here. A few miles west of this border town, pine woods and orchards break up the flat landscape around **Monte Gordo**, a town of brightly colored houses and extensive tourist facilities. The long, flat stretch of beach here is steeply sloped, and swimmers quickly find themselves in deep water.

Tavira

Continuing west past the excellent **Praia Verde** and **Manta Rota** beaches, you come to **Tavira,** which many people think the prettiest town in the Algarve. Situated at the mouth of the River Gilão, it is famous for its figs, cobbled old town streets, a seven-arched Roman bridge, old Moorish defense walls, and interesting churches. There are good sand beaches on nearby **Tavira Island,** which is reached by ferry (May–mid-Oct., every 30–60 min; 150$00 round-trip) from the jetty at Quatro Águas, 2 kilometers (1¼ mile) east of the town center. Another 22 kilometers (14 miles) west lies the fishing port and market town of **Olhão.** Founded in the 18th century, Olhão is notable for its North African–style architecture—cube-shaped whitewashed buildings—and the best food markets in the Algarve, found down on the harborside. There are also ferries (July–Aug., 9 a day; Sept.–June, 3–4 a day; 200$00 round-trip) from Olhão to the nearby sandy islands of **Armona** and **Culatra,** which both have excellent beaches.

Faro

From Olhão it's just 9 kilometers (6 miles) to **Faro,** the provincial capital of the Algarve. This city was finally taken by Afonso III in 1249, ending the Arab domination of Portugal; remnants of the medieval walls and gates that surrounded the city then can still be seen in the older district, the **Cidade Velha.** One of the gates, the **Arco da Vila,** with a white marble statue of St. Thomas Aquinas in a niche at the top, leads to the grand Largo da Sé. The Gothic **Sé** (admission free; open weekdays 10–noon, Sat. at 5 for service, Sun. 8–1) here has a stunning interior decorated with 17th-century tiles. There are also several fascinating museums in Faro, notably the **Museu do Etnografia Regional** (Algarve Ethnographic Museum) on Rua do Pé da Cruz (admission: 150$00; open weekdays 9–noon and 2–6), with good historical and folkloric displays; and the **Museu Maritimo** (Maritime Museum) on Rua Comunidade Lusiada near the yacht basin, next to the Hotel Eva (admission: 150$00; open Mon.–Sat. 10–11 and 2:30–4:30). The **Museu Municipal** (Municipal Museum) on Largo Afonso III (admission: 150$00; open Mon.–Sat. 9:30–noon and 2–5) has a section dedicated to the Roman remains found at Milreu. But best of the sights is really the **Capela dos Ossos** (Chapel of the Bones) in the Igreja do Carmo on Largo do Carmo (admission: 50$00; open Mon.–Sat. 10–1 and 3–5), decorated with human bones taken from the monks' cemetery. There's a large sand beach on Faro Island, the **Praia de Faro,** which is connected to land by road (Bus 16 from the harbor gardens); or take the ferry from the jetty below the old town to the beach at Farol on Culatra island (*see* Olhão, *above*).

About 9 kilometers (6 miles) north of Faro, a road branches east from N2 to the village of **Estói,** where you'll find the 18th-century **Palácio do Visconde de Estói.** The palace itself is closed to the public, but visitors can stroll around the gardens (admission free; open Tues.–Sat. 9–12:30 and 2–5:30). Close by, a 10-minute walk down the main road, are the extensive 1st-century **Roman ruins** at **Milreu** (admission free; open Tues.–Sun. 10–12:30 and 2–5). Another worthwhile excursion from Faro is to **Loulé,** about 17 kilometers (10 miles) away; take N125–4 northwest from N125. This little market town in the hills was once a Moorish stronghold and is now best known for its crafts and decorative white smokestacks on its houses. You can usually see coppersmiths and leather craftsmen toiling in their workshops along the narrow streets.

You can also visit the restored ruins of a medieval Saracen **castle** (within which is the town's museum) and the recently restored 13th-century parish church nearby, which is decorated with handsome tiles and wood carvings and features an unusual wrought-iron pulpit. *Castle and museum at Largo D. Pedro I: admission free; open daily 9–12:30 and 2:30–5. Church at Largo Pr. C. da Silva: admission free; open Mon.–Sat. 9–12 and 2–5:30.*

Back on N125, in the town of **Almansil,** stop at the 18th-century baroque chapel of **São Lourenço,** (admission: 200$00; open Mon.–Sat. 10–1 and 2–5) with its blue-and-white tile panels and intricate gilt work. The cottages next to the church have been transformed into a lovely art gallery. As you continue west, look for turnoffs to the south for local beach resorts. The tennis center at **Vale do Lobo,** one of the Algarve's earliest resort developments, is among the best in Europe. **Quarteira,** once a quiet fishing village, is now a bustling high-rise resort, with golf courses and tennis courts, as well as an excellent beach. **Vilamoura** is one of the most highly developed resort centers in the Algarve: There's a large yacht marina, several golf courses, a major tennis center, one of Europe's largest shooting centers, and other sports facilities, as well as modern luxury hotels and a casino.

Albufeira

If you continue on N125, you'll soon arrive at the **Albufeira** turnoff. At one time an attractive fishing village, the town has long since mushroomed into the Algarve's largest and brashest resort. Even the dried-up riverbed has been turned into a parking lot. But with its steep, narrow streets and hundreds of whitewashed houses snuggled on the slopes of nearby hills, Albufeira retains a distinctly Moorish flavor. Its attractions include the lively fish market (held daily); striking cave and grottoes; and plenty of nightlife. Just about 14 kilometers (8 miles) west of the town is the erstwhile fishing village of **Armação de Pêra,** now a bustling resort that claims the largest beach in the Algarve.

At **Lagoa,** a market town known for its wine, turn north to **Silves,** 8 kilometers (5 miles) up the N124-1. Once the Moorish capital of the Algarve, Silves lost its importance after it was almost completely destroyed by the 1755 earthquake. The 12th-century sandstone **fortress** (admission free, always open) together with its impressive parapets, was restored in 1835 and still dominates the town. Below the fortress stands the 12th–13th-century **Santa Maria da Sé** (Cathedral of Saint Mary; admission free; open daily 8:30–1 and 2:30–6), which was built upon the site of a Moorish mosque. The excellent **Museu Arqueologia,** below the cathedral in Rua das Portas de Loulé (admission: 300$00; open Mon.–Sat. 10–12:30 and 2–6), features artifacts from prehistoric times through the 17th century. The **Cruz de Portugal,** a 16th-century limestone cross, stands on the road to Messines.

Portimão

Return to N125 and continue to **Portimão,** the most important fishing port in the Algarve. There was a settlement here at the mouth of the River Arade even before the Romans arrived. This is a cheerful, busy town and a good center for shopping. Although the colorful fishing boats now unload their catch at a modern terminal across the river, the open-air restaurants along the quay are pleasant places to sample the local specialty: charcoal-grilled sardines with chewy fresh bread and red wine. Across the bridge, in **Ferragudo,** are the ruins of a 16th-century castle, and 3 kilometers (about 2 miles) south of Portimão is **Praia da Rocha.** Now dominated by high-rise apartments and hotels, this was the first resort in the Algarve to be developed; it can still boast of an excellent beach, made all the more interesting by a series of huge, colored rocks that have been worn by sea and wind into strange shapes.

For a different view, drive north from Portimão on routes N124 and 266 about 24 kilometers (15 miles) into the hills of the Serra de Monchique to the spa town of **Caldas de Monchique.** Besides its charming 19th-century buildings, in a shady wood there's a therapeutic spa that dates from Roman times (though the current spa building is resolutely modern).

Lagos

Return to N125 to continue your route west through **Lagos,** a busy fishing port with an attractive harbor and some startling cove beaches in the vicinity that attract a bustling holiday crowd. Lagos has a venerable history—Henry the Navigator maintained a base here—most evident in its grand surviving **city walls** and the 17th-century harborside fort at **Ponta da Bandeira** (admission: 200$00; open Tues.–Sat. 10–1 and 2–6, Sun. 10–1). The 18th-century Baroque **Igreja de Santo António** (Church of Santo António), off Rua General Alberto Silveira, is renowned for its gilt, carved wood, and exuberant decoration. An amusing regional museum is alongside (admission 200$00; open Tues–Sun. 9:30–12:30 and 2–5). Lagos is the western terminus of the coastal railway that runs from Vila Real de Santo António.

Sagres

After Lagos, the terrain becomes more rugged as you approach the windy headland at **Sagres,** where some think Prince Henry established his famous school of navigation—the first of its kind—in the 15th century. Take N268 south from N125 at Vila do Bispo to the promontory hundreds of feet above the sea. From here, a small road leads through the tunnel-like entrance to the **Fortaleza de Sagres** (Sagres Fortress), which was rebuilt in the 17th century. The **Rosa dos Ventos** (compass rose), made of stone and earth, was uncovered in this century in the courtyard, but is believed by some to have been used by Prince Henry in his calculations. The **Graça Chapel** is also inside the fortress (which is always open), as is a building believed to have been Henry's house.

There are spectacular views from **Cabo de São Vicente** (Cape St. Vincent) 6 kilometers (4 miles) to the west, where most historians think Henry the Navigator founded his school. This point, the most southwesterly tip of the European continent, is sometimes called, *"o fim do mundo"* (the end of the world). The lighthouse at Cabo de São Vicente is said to have the strongest reflectors in Europe, casting a beam 96 kilometers (60 miles) out to sea; it is open to the public. From this breathtaking spot, Pedro Álvares Cabral, Vasco da Gama, Ferdinand Magellan, and other great explorers learned their craft 500 years ago.

Dining and Lodging

For details and price-category definitions, *see* Dining and Lodging *in* Staying in Portugal, *above.* In winter, particularly January–March, hotel rates are discounted by as much as 40%.

Albufeira

DINING

Cabaz da Praia. This long-established restaurant has a spectacular view of the main beach from its cliffside terrace. There's fine French-Portuguese cooking here—fish soup, imaginatively served fish, and chicken with seafood. *Praça Miguel Bombarda 7, tel. 089/512137. Reservations advised. AE, MC, V. Closed Sat. lunch and Thur. $$$*

A Ruína. A rustic restaurant on the beach, built on several levels, this is the place for good views and charcoal-grilled seafood. *Cais Herculano, Praia dos Pescadores, tel. 089/512094. No credit cards. $$–$$$*

DINING AND LODGING

★ **Estalagem Vila Joya.** One of the most luxurious restaurants and elegant inns in the Algarve has 14 Moorish-style rooms and three suites if you'd like to stay the night. The French-inspired food in the restaurant continues to impress. The inn is 4 kilometers (2½ miles) west of town. *Praia da Galé, tel. 089/591839, fax 089/591201. 14 rooms with bath. Facilities: restaurant (reservations and jacket and tie required), bar, pool. AE, DC. $$$$*

LODGING

★ **Sheraton Algarve.** This new luxury hotel has a spectacular cliff-top location 8 kilometers (5 miles) east of town: It overlooks the sea and has access to some of the Algarve's finest beaches. The architecture and decor blend traditional Moorish features with modern elements. *Praia da Falésia, tel. 089/501999, fax 089/501950. 215 rooms with bath. Facilities: restaurant, bar, 9-hole golf course, indoor and outdoor pools, gym, sauna, tennis. AE, DC, MC, V. $$$$*

Hotel Cerro Alagoa. The smartly decorated guest rooms have private balconies; be sure to request a sea view. It's a 10-minute walk to the town center, but there's courtesy bus service to both Albufeira and the local beaches. *Via Rápida, tel. 089/588261, fax 089/588262. 310 rooms with bath. Facilities: restaurant, bar, outdoor pool, fitness center, shop, garage. AE, DC, MC, V. $$$*

Alvor

LODGING

★ **Golfe da Penina.** This impressive golf hotel, on 360 well-maintained, secluded acres off the main road between Portimão and Lagos, has spacious, elegant public rooms, pleasant guest rooms, and offers attentive service. Most of the guest rooms have balconies; those in the back of the hotel face the Serra de Monchique and have the best views. The excellent golf courses were designed by Henry Cotton, and golf greens fees are waived for hotel guests. There's a special bus to the beach. *Montes de Alvor, tel. 082/415415, fax 082/415000. 192 rooms with bath. Facilities: restaurant, grill, bar, 18-hole championship golf course plus two 9-hole courses, tennis, Olympic-size pool, private beach, small private airport, sauna, billiards room, shops, water sports, horseback riding. AE, DC, MC, V. $$$$*

Aparthotel Torralta. This large complex, offering good-size rooms, fully equipped kitchens, and daily maid service, is a very good value and has exceptionally low winter rates. *Praia de Alvor, tel. 082/459211, fax 082/459171. 655 units. Facilities: pools, horseback riding, restaurants, discos, tennis, shop. AE, DC, MC, V. $$*

Armação de Pêra

DINING

A Santola. This well-established restaurant overlooking the beach is probably the best in town. All dishes are good, especially the seafood ones. Try the excellent cataplana. *Largo da Fortaleza, tel. 082/312332. Reservations advised. MC, V. Closed Sun. $$*

LODGING

Hotel Garbe. The bar, lounge, and restaurant—all with terraces that provide unhindered views of the sea—maximize the superb location of this squat, white, central hotel. Rooms are modern and smartly furnished, and steps lead from the hotel to the beach below. *Av. Marginal, tel. 082/312194, fax 082/312087. 140 rooms with bath. Facilities: restaurant, bar, coffee shop, pool, garage. AE, DC, MC, V. $$$*

Caldas de Monchique

DINING AND LODGING

Albergaria do Lageado. This hotel right in the center of the spa town has rather small guest rooms, though they're attractively furnished and some overlook the lush gardens. The traditionally tiled dining room serves good home cooking, and there's a terrace for summer dining. *Caldas de Monchique, tel. 082/92616. 19 rooms with bath. Facilities: dining room, lounge, pool, gardens. No credit cards. Closed Nov.–Apr. $*

Faro

DINING

Cidade Velha. Located in an 18th-century house within the walls of the Old City, this intimate restaurant serves excellent international cuisine. *Rua Domingos Guieiro 19, tel. 089/27145. Reservations advised. June–Sept. dinner only; closed Sun. MC, V. $$$*

Dos Irmãos. A friendly staff in this central, cheery setting serves up an array of cataplana dishes. Save room for the homemade *pudim caseiro* (creme caramel). *Largo do Terreiro do Bospo 14–15, tel. 089/823337. MC, V. $$*

LODGING

Hotel Eva. This well-appointed, modern hotel block is on the main square overlooking the yacht basin. The best rooms face the sea, and there's a courtesy bus to the beach. *Av. da República 1, tel. 089/803354, fax 089/802304. 150 rooms with bath. Facilities: pool, restaurant, disco. AE, DC, MC, V. $$*

Casa de Lumena. This 150-year-old Faro mansion has been tastefully converted into a small hotel. Each room has a unique ambience, and the courtyard Grapevine Bar is a pleasant place for a drink. *Praça Alexandre Herculano 27, tel. 089/801990, fax 089/804019. 12 rooms with bath. Facilities: restaurant, courtyard bar. AE, DC, MC, V. $*

Lagos

DINING

Alpendre. This is one of the oldest and best restaurants in the Algarve. French-influenced dishes complement the local fish and shellfish. *Rua António Barbosa Viana 17, tel. 082/762705. Reservations advised. AE, MC, V. $$$*

★ **Dom Sebastião.** Portuguese cooking and charcoal-grilled specials and fish are the main attractions at this cheerful restaurant. It has a wide range of aged Portuguese wines. *Rua 25 de Abril 20, tel. 082/762795. Reservations advised. AE, DC, MC, V. Closed Sun. in winter. $$–$$$*

LODGING

★ **Hotel de Lagos.** This modern hotel stretches out at the eastern edge of the old town and is within easy walking distance of all the sights and restaurants. The terraced rooms overlook the pool or across the river to the coast, and tiling is used effectively throughout, even on lamps and tabletops. There is a regular courtesy bus to the beach, where the hotel has outstanding club facilities. *Rua Nova da Aldeia, tel. 082/769967, fax 082/769920. 317 rooms with bath. Facilities: restaurant, bar, health club, pool, windsurfing, tennis, billiards, garage. AE, DC, MC, V. $$$*

Monchique

DINING

★ **Restaurant Teresinha.** Simply decorated, this modest restaurant serves good country cooking: Try the local ham or one of the chicken recipes. Desserts are outstanding. The terrace overlooks a lovely valley and the coastline. *Estrada da Foia, tel. 082/92392. MC, V. Closed Mon. $*

DINING AND LODGING

Estalagem Abrigo da Montanha. This bucolic inn, noted for its garden of magnolias and camellias, serves excellent regional dishes. It also has six rooms, for which you'll need a reservation. *Estrada da Foia, tel. 082/92131, fax 082/93660. 6 rooms with bath. AE, DC, MC, V. $$.*

Monte Gordo

DINING

Mota. The Mota is a lively, unpretentious restaurant with a covered terrace, right on the sand. Noted for its seafood and regional cuisine, it has live music in the evenings. *On the beach at Monte Gordo, tel. 081/42650. No credit cards. $*

LODGING

Alcazar. This is one of the most attractive hotels in town, with unusual architecture and interior design—the sinuous arches and low molded ceilings recall a cave interior or that of an Arab tent. *Rua de Ceuta 9, tel. 081/512184, fax 081/512242. 95 rooms with bath. Facilities: restaurant, bar, shops, pool. AE, DC, MC, V. $$*

Vasco da Gama. This long, relatively low-lying hotel occupies a choice position on the extensive, sandy beach—rooms with sea views cost more but are worth the extra expense. The staff is friendly and helpful. *Av. Infante Dom Henrique, tel. 081/511321, fax 081/511622. 200 rooms with bath. Facilities: restaurant, pool, tennis, bowling, disco, water sports. AE, DC, MC, V. $$*

Olhos d'Agua

DINING

La Cigale. Nine kilometers (5½ miles) east of Albufeira, this restaurant—one of the best—combines French and native Portuguese cuisine. *On the beach, tel. 089/501637. Reservations advised. DC, MC, V. Closed Dec.–Feb. $$$*

Portimão

DINING

A Lanterna. This well-run restaurant is just over the bridge at Parchal, on the Ferragudo side. Its specialty is duck, but try the exceptional fish soup or smoked fish. *Parchal, tel. 082/23948. Reservations advised. MC, V. Closed Sun. $$*

A Vela. A pleasant restaurant decorated in Moorish fashion, A Vela has a spacious open kitchen that produces a varied selection of tasty Portuguese and international specialties. *Rua Dr. Manuel de Almeida 97, tel. 082/414016. Reservations advised in summer. AE, DC, MC, V. Closed Sun. $$*

Praia da Rocha

DINING

Safari. This lively Portuguese seafront restaurant has a distinctly African flavor. Seafood and delicious Angolan recipes are the specialties. *Rua António Feu, tel. 082/415540. Reservations advised. AE, DC, MC, V. $$*

LODGING

Algarve. This modern, luxurious hotel is perched on a cliff top. Decorated in Moorish style, it has good-size rooms and a large, attentive staff. Leisure facilities are particularly good here, and there is easy access to the fine beach below. *Av. Tomás Cabreira, tel. 082/415001, fax 082/415999. 220 rooms with bath. Facilities: restaurant, grill, 2 pools, disco, tennis courts, health center, bar. AE, DC, MC, V. $$$$*

Hotel Bela Vista. A small, tastefully decorated beachfront hotel with magnificent traditional tiles, Hotel Bela Vista is one of the most delightful accommodations on the Algarve. *Av. Tomás Cabreira, tel. 082/24055, fax 082/415369. 14 rooms with bath. Facilities: bar, terrace, live music in summer. Early reservations essential. AE, DC, MC, V. $$$*

Sagres

DINING AND LODGING

★ **Pousada do Infante.** Housed in a sprawling, traditional-style, red-tile-roof building, this pousada affords spectacular views of the sea and craggy rock cliffs. The moderate-size rooms are well appointed and have small balconies. The restaurant has excellent fresh fish, good desserts, and more marvelous sea views. *8650 Sagres, tel. 082/64222, fax 082/64225. 39 rooms with bath. Facilities: restaurant, bar, tennis, pool. AE, DC, MC, V. $$$*

Santa Barbara de Nexe

DINING AND LODGING

★ **Hotel Apartamento La Reserve.** This intimate luxury hotel in the hills, 10 kilometers (6 miles) inland from Faro and set within a 6-acre park, offers high-class accommodations, including small apartments with verandas and sea views. Don't pass up the restaurant, which serves elegant cuisine with a French accent; local game is a specialty, and the wine list is very good. *Santa Barbara de Nexe, 8000 Faro, tel. 089/90234 or 089/90474, fax 089/90402. 12 rooms with bath, 8 apartments. Facilities: restaurant (dinner only; reservations required; closed Tues.), bar, pool, tennis. No credit cards. $$$$*

Vale do Lobo

DINING AND LODGING

Dona Filipa. The Dona Filipa has a lavish and striking interior, pleasant rooms, and first-rate service. Set in extensive, beautifully landscaped grounds near the beach, the hotel houses a chic restaurant that offers an excellent international menu. Greens fees for the nearby 18-hole golf course are included in room rates. *Vale do Lobo/Almansil, tel. 089/394141, fax 089/394288. 147 rooms with bath. Facilities: golf, pool, restaurant, tennis center. AE, DC, MC, V. $$$$*

Vilamoura

LODGING

Hotel Dom Pedro Golf. Situated in the heart of this successful vacation complex, the Dom Pedro is close to the casino and not far from the beach. Each room is attractively furnished and has its own balcony. *Vilamoura, 8125 Quarteira, tel. 089/389650, fax 089/315482. 263 rooms with bath. AE, DC, MC, V. $$$*

Vila Real de Santo António

DINING

Caves do Guadiana. Located in a large, old-fashioned building facing the fishing docks, this restaurant is well known for its seafood and Portuguese specialties. *Av. República 90, tel. 081/44498. No reservations. DC, MC. Closed Thurs. $*

24 Romania

ROMANIA CAN BE A CHALLENGING DESTINATION for the tourist, but it is perhaps the most beautiful country in Eastern Europe. Its natural tourist attractions are varied, from the summer resorts on the Black Sea coast to the winter ski resorts in the rugged Carpathian Mountains; but perhaps even more surprising are the numerous medieval towns and traditional rural villages that are among the most unspoiled and unchanged in Europe.

Comparable in size to the state of Oregon, Romania is made up of the provinces of Walachia, Moldavia, and Transylvania and borders the Ukraine, Moldova, Bulgaria, Serbia, and Hungary. With a population of 23 million, Romania is a "Latin Island" in a sea of Slavs and Magyars—its people are the descendants of the Dacian tribe and of the Roman soldiers who garrisoned this easternmost province of the Roman Empire. Barbarian invasions, struggles against the Turks, the Austro-Hungarian domination of Transylvania, and a strong French cultural influence have endowed them with a rich heritage to add to a folk culture that survives to this day.

Romania's leading attractions are its largest metropolis, Bucharest—with its wide, tree-lined avenues, Arcul de Triumf, and lively café life, the city was once known as the Paris of the East—and the Romanian Riviera of the Black Sea Coast, with the spectacular wildlife sanctuaries of the Danube Delta nearby. Transylvania, a region wrapped in myth, is home to a sizable minority of Hungarians and a small minority of Germans with their own folk traditions and distinctive building styles. This area has long drawn travelers interested in the real and fictional sites associated with Dracula.

After Albania, Romania is the poorest country in Europe, so travelers should keep certain precautions in mind. Petty theft remains a widespread problem. If you are traveling independently, you may wish to take some food supplies with you. Vegetarians are warned that there is a limited range of produce available (especially in winter) and dairy products remain in short supply. Visitors should use water purification tablets or boil their tap water, since hepatitis is a danger in Romania. Alternatively, drinking-water fountains in most towns provide natural spring water, and bottled mineral water is available in many restaurants. All visitors should bring an emergency supply of toilet paper, a full first-aid kit, a flashlight for poorly lighted streets and corridors, and, in summer, insect repellent. Since medical facilities do not meet Western standards, it is best to take along your own vitamins and medication (including needles and syringes for injections).

Romania is likely to remain underexplored until the serious economic problems caused by the overthrown Ceaușescu regime are resolved, but, in the meantime, the package tourist is still assured a good price, while the intrepid independent traveler (who should remember to be low-key in both behavior and dress) will experience a part of Europe rich in tradition, one that has largely avoided the pressures and complexities of modern times.

Romania

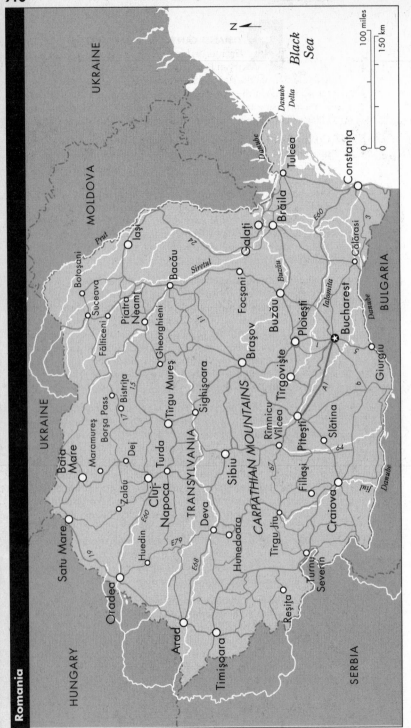

ESSENTIAL INFORMATION

Before You Go

When to Go

Bucharest, like Paris, is at its best during the spring and fall. The Black Sea resorts open in mid- to late May and close at the end of September. Winter ski resorts in the Carpathians such as Poiana Braşov, Predeal, and Buşeni, are now well developed and increasingly popular, while the best time for touring the interior is late spring to fall.

CLIMATE

The Romanian climate is temperate and generally free of extremes, but snow as late as April is not unknown, and the lowlands can be very hot in midsummer.

The following are the average daily maximum and minimum temperatures for Bucharest.

Jan.	34F	1C	May	74F	23C	Sept.	78F	25C
	19	− 7		51	10		52	11
Feb.	38F	4C	June	81F	27C	Oct.	65F	18C
	23	− 5		57	14		43	6
Mar.	50F	10C	July	86F	30C	Nov.	49F	10C
	30	− 1		60	16		35	2
Apr.	64F	18C	Aug.	85F	30C	Dec.	39F	4C
	41	5		59	15		26	− 3

Currency

The unit of currency is the *leu* (plural *lei*). There are coins of 1, 3, 5, 10, 20, 50, and 100 lei. Banknotes come in denominations of 200, 500, 1,000, 5,000, and 10,000 lei. The Romanian currency is expected to continue to drop in value, causing inflation and frequent price increases; costs are therefore best calculated in hard currency—for instance, international convertible currencies such as U.S. dollars, German marks, and Swiss francs. Cash dollar bills are the most readily negotiated currency and it is a good idea to always have some with you, especially in smaller denominations. At press time (spring 1995), the official exchange rate was approximately 1,900 lei to the dollar and 3,790 to the pound sterling. Prices of basic items, artificially low from Communism, are gradually increasing.

Coins of smaller denominations than 20 and 50 lei are seldom used and not always accepted. There is no longer an obligatory currency exchange, and an increasing number of licensed *casă de schimb* (exchange offices) have been competing to offer rates far higher than official rates, almost equal to those available on the illegal and risky black market. Retain your exchange receipts, as you may need to prove your money was changed legally. Except for air tickets, foreigners must pay in lei by law, though hard currency is widely accepted. The local police—rather than the *garda financiară* (financial police)—are useful if you experience difficulty. You may not import or export lei.

CREDIT CARDS

Major credit cards are welcome in a number of major hotels and their restaurants, but are not accepted in most shops and independent restaurants.

What It Will Cost

Prices of hotels and restaurants can be as high as those in Western Europe as far as the independent traveler is concerned. Those with prepaid arrangements, however, may enjoy substantial reductions.

SAMPLE PRICES

Museum admission usually costs less than 50¢, a bottle of imported beer in a restaurant around $2.50 or about 75¢ in a kiosk; a bottle of good local wine in a top restaurant around $6. A one-mile taxi ride will cost around 60¢.

Visas

Visas are not required for U.S. citizens for stays of less than 30 days. The only requirement is a valid American passport, with an expiration date more than three months beyond the date of departure from Romania. All other visitors entering Romania must have a visa, but no formal application or photograph is needed for British and Canadian citizens. The visa is stamped onto the passport and is valid for a minimum of three months from the date of entry into Romania. This visa can be issued from any Romanian diplomatic or consular office abroad, or at any Romanian customs station at the border when entering the country. Visa fees vary widely. For persons with prepaid hotel vouchers or for those on organized or escorted tours: $1 or its equivalent—bring a copy of your voucher to the Romanian diplomatic or consular office, or send a copy of the hotel voucher when ordering the visa by mail; free if issued at the border (show your hotel/reservation voucher). For individual tourists: without hotel voucher, $22 at diplomatic offices and Otopeni, the Bucharest airport; $15 if issued at any other border point. For persons on business or study trips: $32 at diplomatic offices and Otopeni; $25 if issued at any other border point. Send the visa fee, a stamped, self-addressed envelope, and your passport to the relevant office: in **Canada,** Romanian Consulate (111 Peter St., Suite 530, Toronto, Ontario M5V 2H1, tel. 416/585–5802, fax 416/585–9117), Romanian Consulate (1111 Street Urbain, Suite M-01, Montreal, Quebec H2Z 1Y6, tel. 514/876–1793, fax 514/876–1797), or Embassy of Romania (655 Rideau St., Ottawa, Ontario K1N 6A3, tel. 613/789–3709, fax 613/789–4365); in the **United Kingdom,** Consular Section of the Romanian Embassy (4 Palace Green, London W84QD, tel. 0171/937–9667, fax 0171/937–8069). In the **United States,** questions on visas and passports can be addressed to the Embassy of Romania (1607 23rd St. NW, Washington DC 20008, tel. 202/387–6902, fax 202/232–4748) or the Romanian Consulate (200 E. 38th St., New York, NY 10016, tel. 212/682–9122, fax 212/972–8463).

Customs

You may bring in a personal computer and printer, 2 cameras, 10 rolls of film, 1 small camcorder/video camera and VCR, 10 rolls of video film, a typewriter, binoculars, a radio/tape recorder, a small television set, a bicycle, a stroller for a child, 200 cigarettes, 2 liters of liquor, and 4 liters of wine or beer. Gifts are permitted, though you may be charged duty for some electronic goods. Camping and sports equipment may be imported freely. Declare video cameras, personal computers, and expensive jewelry on arrival.

Souvenirs and gifts may be taken out of Romania, provided their value does not exceed 50% of the currency you have changed legally—so keep your receipts.

Language

Romanian sounds pleasantly familiar to anyone who speaks a smattering of French, Italian, or Spanish. French is widely spoken and understood in Romanian cities, with German and Russian less so. Romanians involved with the tourist industry and the staff in most hotels and major resorts usually speak English.

Getting Around

By Car

ROAD CONDITIONS

An adequate network of main roads covers the country, though the great majority are still a single one-lane wide in each direction. Some roads have many potholes and a few roads have not been paved. Progress may be impeded by convoys of farm machinery or slow-moving trucks, by horses and carts, or by herds of animals. Night driving can be dangerous: Roads and vehicles are lighted either poorly or not at all.

RULES OF THE ROAD

Driving is on the right, as in the United States. Speed limits are 60 kph (37 mph) in built-up areas and 80 kph–90 kph (50 mph–55 mph) on all other roads. Driving after drinking any alcohol whatsoever is prohibited. Seat belts are now mandated by law and should always be worn. Police are empowered to levy on-the-spot fines, which are now huge. Vehicle spot checks are frequent. Road signs are the same as in Western Europe.

GASOLINE

State gas stations, usually found at the edge of towns on main roads, remain scarce, but there are many new private gas stations that charge a bit more money than the state stations. Most gas stations sell regular (90-octane), premium (98-octane), and *motorina* (diesel), but rarely unleaded gas. Prices remain well below those in Western Europe, but shortages sometimes cause waits of several hours. The Automobil Clubul Roman (*see below*) and tourist offices can provide visitors with a useful Tourist and Motor Car Map that pinpoints the location of each gas station.

BREAKDOWNS

Automobil Clubul Roman (ACR, Str. Tache Ionescu 27, Bucharest, tel. 01/6502595, fax 01/3120434) offers mechanical assistance in case of breakdowns, and medical and legal assistance at fixed rates in case of accidents. (It also arranges bus and driving tours and hotel bookings.) For breakdowns, dial 927 in Bucharest and 12345 elsewhere. Spare parts are scarce, so carry extras. Thefts of parts from vehicles under repair are frequent.

CAR RENTALS

A number of international car rental companies have opened offices in Bucharest and other major towns. **Hertz** is in the former ACR building (Str. Cihoski 2, Bucharest, tel. 01/2120040, and also at Bucharest's Otopeni Airport, tel. 01/2120122). **Europcar** is in the ONT Carpaţi building (B-dul Magheru 7, tel. 01/6131540, fax 01/3120915).

By Train

Romanian Railways (CFR) operates an extensive network of trains. *Rapid* and *accelerat* trains are the fastest, with limited stops; *Personal* trains are slow and have immumerable stops. *Expres* designates special international express trains, such as the Dacia Expres to Vienna. Note that when the conductor checks tickets, your ticket can occasionally be mixed up with another ticket and destination, so double check. Trains are inexpensive and often crowded, with carriages in poor repair. First class is worth the extra cost. A *vagon de dormit* (sleeper) or cheap *cuşeta,* with bunk beds, is available on longer journeys. It is always advisable to reserve a seat, but you cannot buy the ticket itself at a train station more than one hour before departure. If your reserved seat is already occupied, it may have been sold twice. If you're in Bucharest and want to buy your ticket ahead of time, contact either a travel agency or the Advance Booking Office (Strada Domniţa Anastasia 10–14, tel. 01/6132642/3/4) or, for international reservations, contact CFR International (B-dul I. C., Brătianu 44, tel. 01/6134008). You will be charged a small commission, but the process is less time-consuming than buying your ticket at the railway station.

By Plane

Tarom operates daily flights to major Romanian cities from Bucharest's Baneasa Airport. In summer, additional flights link Constanţa with major cities, including Cluj and Iaşi. Be prepared for delays and cancellations. Prices average $90 round-trip. External flights can be booked at the central reservations office, Strada Brezoianu 10, and at some major hotels. For domestic flights go to Piaţa Victoriei 1, tel. 01/6594125.

By Bus

Bus stations, or *autogara,* are usually near train stations. Buses are generally crowded and far from luxurious. Tickets are sold at the stations up to two hours before departure.

By Boat

Regular passenger services operate on various sections of the Danube; tickets are available at the ports (e.g., Giurgiu, Turnu Severin).

Staying in Romania

Telephones

LOCAL CALLS

The Romanian telephone system is antiquated and overextended: Local calls can be dialed directly, but you may have to order and wait a long time for long-distance calls. Coin-operated telephones at roadsides, airports, and train stations usually work only for local calls: Older phones use a 20 lei coin, newer ones 50 and 100. It is less expensive to telephone from the post office than from hotels. Post offices have a waiting system whereby you order your call and pay at the counter. When your call is ready, the name of the town you are phoning is announced, together with the number of the cabin you should proceed to for your call. In some large towns, private business services have opened; they offer phone, fax and telex services.

The area code for Bucharest is 01, and telephone numbers in the city have 2, 3, 6, or 7 as a prefix, followed by a six-digit number. Long-distance calls within Romania should be prefixed with a 0 followed by the area code for the county or region. For information, dial the relevant area code, then 11515: in Bucharest, dial 931 (A–L) and 932 (M–Z); for international calls, dial 971; for internal long distance, dial 991; for local information, dial 951. Your hotel's front desk or a phone book can be much more helpful.

INTERNATIONAL CALLS

International direct dialing is slowly being introduced in Bucharest, where international calls can be made from hotels, the train station, the phone company building on Calea Victoriei, and local post offices (*see* Local Calls, *above*). To place long distance calls out of Romania, dial 00, then country code and number. To place a call from Romania via an **AT&T** USADirect international operator, dial 01–800–4288; for **MCI,** dial 01–800–1800; for **Sprint,** dial 01–800–01–877.

COUNTRY CODE
The country code for Romania is 40. The locality prefix for Bucharest is 1.

Mail

The central post office in Bucharest is at Matei Millo 10 (open Mon.–Thurs. 7:30–7:30, Fri.–Sat. 8 AM–2 PM). The telephone section is open 24 hours a day.

POSTAL RATES
Rates are increasing regularly in line with inflation, so check before you post.

Opening and Closing Times

Banks are open weekdays 9 to 12:30 or 1. Exchange offices are usually open weekdays and Saturday mornings, though private bureaus could have other hours.

Museums are usually open from 10 to 6, but it's best to check with local tourist offices. Most museums are closed on Monday, and some are also closed on Tuesday.

Shops are generally open Monday–Friday from 9 or 10 AM to 6 or 8 PM and close between 1 and 3, though some food shops open earlier. Many shops are closed on Saturday afternoons.

National Holidays

January 1–2; April 8 (Easter Monday); May 1 (Labor Day); December 1 (National Day); December 25–26; December 31 (New Year's Eve).

Dining

Shortages have eased and poor standards have now improved sufficiently for the better hotels and restaurants to offer reasonable cuisine and menu choices. Traditional Romanian foods are *mamaliga* (corn porridge), *ciorbă* (a soup stock, slightly spicy and sour), and sheep cheeses. Featured meats are usually pork or beef. There are ready-to-eat treats to be sampled from street vendors, for instance, roasted chestnuts. Overcharging is a hazard outside the bigger restaurants with printed menus. You can insist on seeing the prices, but small establishments may genuinely not have a menu prepared for just one or two dishes.

MEALTIMES
Outside Bucharest and the Black Sea and Carpathian resorts, many restaurants will have stopped serving by 9 PM, although an increasing number have begun staying open until 11 PM or later. Restaurants usually open at midday.

PRECAUTIONS
The far less expensive *bufet expres* (beer and snack bar), *lacto vegetarian* snack bars (often serving meat, however), and *autoservire* (cafeteria) cannot always be recommended; the food may be inexpensive but sanitary conditions may be poor. The best bet is often found at the better *cofetarie* (coffee shops). Romanian coffee is served with grounds; instant coffee is called *nes*. Some travelers bring their own coffee creamer, as milk is sometimes in short supply.

WHAT TO WEAR
There are no dress rules as such, but jacket and tie are advised for the best restaurants and business lunches and dinners. Casual, but conservative, dress is appropriate at other times.

RATINGS

Prices are per person and include first course, main course, and dessert, plus wine and tip. Because high inflation means local prices frequently change, ratings are given in dollars, which remain reasonably constant. Your bill will be in lei. Highly recommended restaurants are indicated by a star ★.

CATEGORY	COST
$$$$	over $30
$$$	$20–$30
$$	$10–$20
$	under $10

Lodging

Prices are highly variable depending on booking arrangements. Prepaid arrangements through travel agencies abroad often benefit from discounted prices. Some schemes, such as fly-drive holidays, give bed-and-breakfast accommodation vouchers (these cannot be bought in Romania). Most places take vouchers; in deluxe hotels, you have to pay a little extra. Otherwise, book accommodations directly with hotels or through tourist agencies. Some agencies deal only with their local areas; those spawned from the formerly monolithic *agenţis de turism* (national tourism office) now known as ONT and from the former youth tourism bureau, now known as the **Biroul de Turism Şi Tranzacţii** (BTT), offer nationwide services. Travelers staying at less expensive hotels have sometimes encountered unacceptable basic conditions and even perilous circumstances.

HOTELS

The international star system of hotel classification has recently been introduced in Romania, and now ranks hotels with one to five stars, ranging from inexpensive to deluxe categories. Standards of facilities, including plumbing and hot water, decline rapidly through the categories and may not be ideal even in expensive accommodations. Ask at the front desk when hot water will be available. In principle, at least, all hotels leave a certain quota of rooms unoccupied until 8 PM for unexpected foreign visitors.

RENTALS

Rustic cottages may be rented at such ski resorts as Sinaia and Predeal. Details are available from Romanian tourist offices abroad (*see* Important Addresses and Numbers *in* Bucharest, *below*).

RATINGS

The following hotel price categories are for two people in a double room. Guests staying in single rooms are charged a supplement. Prices are estimated for high season. Because of inflation, ratings are given according to hard-currency equivalents—but you must usually pay in lei. (Note that hotels may insist on your buying lei from them to pay your bill, unless you can produce an exchange receipt to prove you changed your money legally.) Rates in Bucharest are usually much higher than in the rest of the country. Highly recommended lodgings are indicated by a star ★.

CATEGORY	BUCHAREST	BLACK SEA COAST
$$$$	over $200	over $80
$$$	$125–$200	$50–$80
$$	$70–$125	$30–$50
$	under $70	under $30

Tipping

A 12% service charge is added to meals at most restaurants. Elsewhere, a 10% tip is welcomed, and is expected by taxi drivers.

BUCHAREST

Arriving and Departing

By Plane

All international flights to Romania land at Bucharest's Otopeni Airport (tel. 01/6333137), 16 kilometers (9 miles) north of the city.

BETWEEN THE AIRPORT AND DOWNTOWN

Express Bus 783 leaves the airport every 30 minutes between 7 AM and 10 PM, stopping in the main squares before terminating in Piata Unirii. The journey takes an hour and costs 25¢. Your hotel can arrange transport by car from the airport. Taxi drivers at the airport seek business aggressively and usually demand payment in dollars. Note that the "official" fare is in lei, the equivalent of about $12 with tip, so bargain.

By Train

There are five main stations in Bucharest, though international lines operate from Gara de Nord (tel. 01/952). For tickets and information, go to the Advance Booking Office (Str. Domniţa Anastasia 10–14, tel. 01/6132642). For international trains, go to CFR International (B-dul I. C. Brătianu 44, tel. 01/6134008).

By Car

There are three main access routes into the city—E70 west from the Hungarian border, E60 north via Braşov, and E70/E85 south to Bulgaria. Bucharest has few street signs and many one-way systems. A handy question is *Unde este centrul* ("Where is the town center," pronounced *oon*-day *yes*-tay *tchen*-trul).

Getting Around

Bucharest is spacious and sprawling. Though the old heart of the city and the two main arteries running the length of it are best explored on foot, long, wide avenues and vast squares make some form of transportation necessary. New tourist maps are being printed and can be found in bookstores; they may also be available at tourism agencies and hotels. It is generally safe on the streets at night, but watch out for unlighted vehicles and hidden potholes.

By Subway

Four lines of the subway system are now in operation. Change is available from kiosks inside stations, and you may travel any distance. The present price is 100 lei (usually paid with two 50 lei coins). The system closes at 11:45 PM.

By Tram, Bus, and Trolley Bus

These are uncomfortable, crowded, and infrequent, but service is extensive. A ticket valid for two trips of any length can be purchased from kiosks near bus stops or from tobacconists; validate your ticket when you board. There are also *abonaments* (day and week passes) but more expensive *maxi taxis* (minibuses that stop on request) and express buses take fares on board. The system shuts down at midnight.

By Taxi

Hail in the street, or phone 01/953—they speak English. Taxis charge from 35¢ to over $1.00 per kilometer depending on pick-up point.

Important Addresses and Numbers

Tourist Information

There are many new travel agencies in Bucharest and throughout the country. The main branch of **ONT** (formerly the Romanian National Tourist Office, and now privatized) is at 7 Boulevard General Magheru, Bucharest (tel. 01/3122598, fax 01/3122594) and deals with all inquiries related to tourism (open weekdays 8–8 and weekends 8–2). There are also ONT offices at Otopeni Airport (open 24 hours) and at the Gara de Nord (open 8–8 Monday–Saturday). ONT is currently being broken up and privatized, so its office signs in most Romanian towns now read AGENŢIA DE TURISM.

For information before your trip, write or call the Romanian National Tourist Office; in the **United States** (342 Madison Ave., Suite 210, New York, NY 10016, tel. 212/697–6971, fax 212/697–6972); in the **United Kingdom** (17 Nottingham St., London W1M 3RD, tel. and fax 0171/224–3692).

Emergencies

Police (tel. 955). **Ambulance** (tel. 961). **Fire** (tel. 981).

Travel Agencies

Ambassador Tours, Str. Pitar Moş 27, Bucharest, tel. 01/6147589; **Arcadia Tour srl,** Str. Scitu Măgureanu 8, Bucharest, tel. 016505959, fax 01/3126860; **Bravo Tour,** Piaţa Unirii 1, Bucharest, tel. 01/6145803; **Magic Tours,** Str. Traian Vasile 28, Bucharest, tel. 01/6652544, fax 01/3128518; **Marshal Travel,** B-dul Nicolae Bălcescu 36, Bucharest, tel. 01/6147951, fax 01/3124657; **Olympic International Tourism,** Str. Visana 5, Bucharest, tel. 01/6768356, fax 01/3306152; **Romextur,** Str. Luterană 4, Bucharest, tel. 01/6136983; **Touring ACR,** Str. Tache Ionescu 27, Bucharest, tel. 01/6502595, fax 01/3120434.

Guided Tours

Tours are available from the growing number of tourist agencies, many of which maintain desks in the larger hotels. Tours range from sightseeing in the city—by car with your own driver, if you prefer—to weekend excursions to the Danube Delta or the monasteries of Bukovina.

Travel Agencies

Carpati International (Gypsy Trail Rd., Carmel, NY 10512, tel. 914/225–2215 or 800/766–2642, fax 914/225–2215) works with tour operators in Romania, America, and Canada to offer comprehensive services, including customized itineraries, general and special interest/events packages (Dracula/spas), and transportation to and within the country.

Exploring Bucharest

The old story goes that a simple peasant named Bucur settled on the site upon which the city now stands. True or not, the name Bucureşti was first officially used only in 1459 by none other than Vlad Ţepeş, the real-life Dracula (sometimes known as Vlad the Impaler for his blood-thirsty habit of impaling unfortunate victims on wooden stakes). Two centuries later, this citadel on the Dîmboviţa (the river that flows through Bucharest) became the capital of Walachia, and after another 200 years, it was named the capital of Romania. The city gradually developed into a place of bustling trade and gracious living, with ornate and varied architecture, landscaped parks, busy, winding streets, and wide boulevards. It became known before World War II as the Paris of the Balkans, but its past glory is now only hinted at.

The high-rise Hotel Inter-Continental now dominates the main cross-roads at Piaţa Universităţii; northwards, up the main shopping streets of Bulevardul Nicolae Bălcescu, Bulevardul General Magheru, and Bulevardul Ana Ipătescu, only the occasional older building survives. However, along Calea Victoriei, a flavor of Bucharest's grander past can be savored, especially at the former royal palace opposite the Romanian senate (formerly Communist Party headquarters) in Piaţa Revoluţiei. Here, one also sees remains of the domed National Library, gutted by fire, and bullet holes on walls nearby. Modest, touching monuments to the more than 1,000 people killed in the 1989 revolution can be found here, and Piaţa Universităţii has a wall still festooned with protest posters.

South along Calea Victoriei is the busy Lipscani trading district, a remnant of the old city that used to sprawl farther southward before it was bulldozed in Nicolae Ceauşescu's megalomaniacal drive to redevelop the capital. Piaţa Unirii was the hub of his enormously expensive and impractical vision, which involved the forced displacement of thousands of people and the demolition of many priceless early houses, churches, and synagogues and other irreplaceable buildings. Construction cranes now stand eerily idle above unfinished tower blocks with colonnaded, white marble frontages. They flank a lengthy boulevard leading to the enormous, empty, and unfinished Palace of the People (the second largest building in the world, after Washington DC's Pentagon). With such a massive diversion of resources, it is not surprising that Bucharest is pot-holed and faded, and suffers shortages and erratic services, although the city is redirecting its energy and money to remedying the situation. Happily, Bucharest continues to offer many places of historic interest, as well as cinemas, theaters, concert halls, and an opera house.

Numbers in the margin correspond to points of interest on the Bucharest map.

Historic Bucharest

A tour of this city should start at one of its most fascinating sites, the **❶ Curtea Veche** (old Princely Court) and the Lipscani District. The Princely Court now houses **Muzeul Curtea Veche-Palatul Voievodal,** a museum exhibiting the remains of the palace built by Vlad Ţepeş during the 15th century. One section of the cellar wall presents the palace's history from the 15th century onward. Prisoners were once kept in these cellars, which extend far into the surrounding city; a pair of ancient skulls of two young *boyars* (aristocrats), decapitated at the end of the 17th century, will interest some. *Str. Iuliu Maniu 31, tel. 01/6140375. Admission: 900 lei. Open Tues.–Sun. 10–6.*

❷ The **Biserica din Curtea Veche** (Curtea Veche Church), beside the Princely Court, was founded during the 16th century and remains an **❸** important center of worship in the city. Nearby, **Hanul lui Manuc** (Manuc's Inn), a renovated 19th-century inn arranged in the traditional Romanian fashion around a courtyard, now houses a small hotel and restaurant. Manuc was a wealthy Armenian merchant who died in Russia by poisoning—at the hand of a famous French fortune-teller who, having forecast Manuc's death on a certain day, could not risk ruining her reputation. The 1812 Russian-Turkish Peace Treaty was signed here. From here, some visitors may wish to journey across the river to view **Queen Marie of Romania's Cotroceni Palace** on the Dîmboviţa River corniche near the Botanical Gardens.

Bucharest

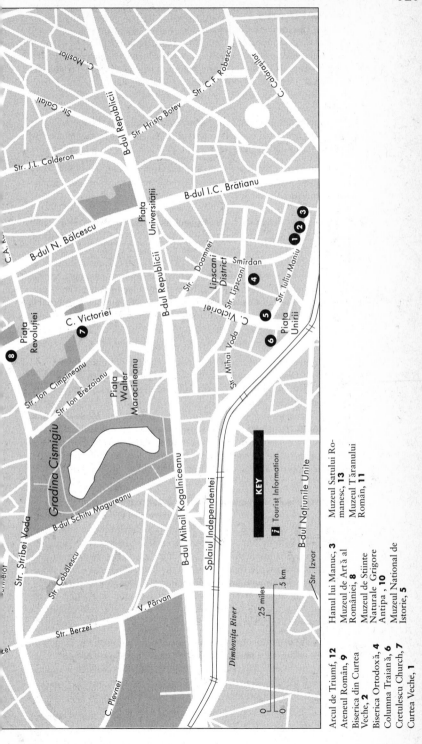

Str. Mosilor

C. Mosilor

Str. Galații

Str. C.F. Robescu

B-dul Republicii

Str. Hristo Botev

C. Călărașilor

Str. J.L. Calderon

B-dul I.C. Brătianu

Piața Universității

1 **2** **3**

B-dul N. Bălcescu

Str. Doamnei

Smîrdan

Lipscani District

Str. Lipscani

4

Str. Iuliu Maniu

B-dul Republicii

Str.

C. Victoriei

5

C. Victoriei

Piața Unirii

Piața Revoluției

7

Str. Mihai Vodă

6

8

Str. Ion Cîmpineanu

Str. Ion Brezoianu

Piața Walter Maracineanu

Gradina Cismigiu

B-dul Schitu Magureanu

B-dul Mihail Kogalniceanu

Str. Stirbei Voda

Splaiul Independenței

B-dul Națiunile Unite

Str. Izvor

KEY

7 Tourist Information

Str. Cobălcescu

V. Pârvan

Dimbovita River

Str. Berzei

.5 km

.25 miles

0

0

C. Plevnei

C. Plevnei

Arcul de Triumf, **12**
Ateneul Român, **9**
Biserica din Curtea Veche, **2**
Biserica Ortodoxă, **4**
Columna Traianǎ, **6**
Cretulescu Church, **7**
Curtea Veche, **1**

Hanul lui Manuc, **3**
Muzeul de Artă al României, **8**
Muzeul de Stiinte Naturale Grigore Antipa , **10**
Muzeul National de Istorie, **5**

Muzeul Satului Romanesc, **13**
Muzeul Tǎranului Român, **11**

Lipscani District

Nearby, **Lipscani** is a bustling area of narrow streets, open stalls, and small artisans' shops that combine to create the atmosphere of a bazaar. In Hanul cu Tei, off Strada Lipscani, you'll find many galleries and crafts
❹ and gift shops. On Strada Stavropoleos, a small but exquisite **Biserica Ortodoxă** (Orthodox church) combines late-Renaissance and Byzantine styles with elements of the Romanian folk-art style. Go inside to look at the superb wood and stone carvings and a richly ornate iconostasis, the painted screen that partitions off the altar. Boxes on either side of the entrance contain votive candles—for the living on the left, for the "sleeping" on the right.

TIME OUT   Down the road, at Strada Stavropoleos 3, is the historic—and now shiningly restored—**Carul cu Bere,** serving half-liter tankards of beer, appetizers, and Turkish coffee.

❺ At the end of the street is the **Muzeul Național de Istorie** (Romanian History Museum), which contains a vast collection of exhibits from Neolithic to modern times. The Treasury, which can be visited and paid for separately, has a startling collection of objects in gold and precious stones—royal crowns, weapons, plates, and jewelry—dating from the 4th millennium BC through the 20th century. Opposite the Treasury is
❻ a full-size replica of **Columna Traiană** (Trajan's Column; the original is in Rome), commemorating a Roman victory over Dacia in AD 2. *Calea Victoriei 12, tel. 01/6157056. Admission: 900 lei. Treasury open Tues.–Sun. 10–5, last ticket at 4 PM. Museum open Wed.–Sun. 10–4.*

Turning north along the Calea Victoriei, you'll pass a military club and
❼ academy before reaching the pretty little **Crețulescu Church** on your left. Built in 1722, the church and some of its original frescoes were restored during the 1930s. Immediately north is a massive building, once the
❽ royal palace and now the Palace of the Republic. The **Muzeul de Artă al României** (National Art Museum) is housed here, with its fine collection of Romanian art, including works by the world-famous sculptor Brâncuși. The foreign section has a wonderful collection of the Brueghel school and is well worth a visit. *Str. Știrbei Vodă 1, tel. 01/6155193. Admission: 1,000 lei. Open Wed.–Sun. 10–6.*

Around Piața Revoluției (Revolutionary Square)

Opposite the palace, the former headquarters of the Romanian Communist party was based in Piața Revoluției. Before the revolution in December 1989, no one was allowed to walk in front of this building. During the uprising the square was a major site of the fighting that destroyed the National Library, parts of the Palace, and the Cina restau-
❾ rant next to the **Ateneul Român** (Romanian Athenaeum Concert Hall). The Ateneul, dating from 1888, with its Baroque dome and Greek columns, survived the upheavals and still houses the George Enescu Philharmonic Orchestra.

Follow Calea Victoriei for some distance until you reach the Piața Vic-
❿ toriei. Opposite is the **Muzeul de Științe Naturale "Grigore Antipa"** (Natural History Museum), with its exceptional butterfly collection and the skeleton of the dinosaur *Dinotherium gigantissimum. Șoseaua Kiseleff 1, tel. 01/6504710. Admission: 800 lei. Open Tues.–Sun. 10–5.*

⓫ Next door, in an imposing redbrick building, is the impressive **Muzeul Țăranului Român** (Museum of the Romanian Peasant). This museum, which reopened in 1990, has an excellent collection of costumes, icons, carpets, and other artifacts from rural life, including reconstructed interiors from two 19th-century wooden churches. Şoseaua Kiseleff 3, tel. 01/6595655. Admission: 1,000 lei. Open Tues.–Sun. 10–6.

⑫ Şoseaua Kiseleff, a pleasant tree-lined avenue, brings you to the **Arcul de Triumf,** built in 1922 to commemorate the Allied victory in World War I. Originally constructed of wood and stucco, it was rebuilt during the 1930s and carved by some of Romania's most talented sculptors.

Still farther north lies Herăstrău Park, accommodating the fascinating
⑬ **Muzeul Satului Romanesc** (Village Museum), as well as Herăstrău Lake. The museum is outstanding, with more than 300 authentic exhibits of objects and fully furnished rooms from peasants' houses, with folk styles taken from all over Romania. Şoseaua Kiseleff 28, tel. 01/6171732. Admission: 1,000 lei. Open winter, daily 8–4; summer, daily 10–7.

Shopping

Gifts and Souvenirs
New private shops are bringing extra style and choice to Bucharest, but note the customs restrictions (see Customs in Before You Go, above). Keep receipts of all purchases, regardless of their legal export status. The **Apollo** gallery, in the National Theater building next to the Hotel Inter-Continental and the galleries in the fascinating **Hanul cu Tei** off Strada Lipscani sell art that you may legally take home with you. You can make delightful purchases such as stuffed toy dolphins and Christmas icons.

Market
A main food market is in Piaţa Amzei, open seven days a week and best visited during the morning. If you decide to visit outlying flea markets such as Piaţa Obor, be careful of inflated prices.

Dining

The restaurants of the better hotels (including the Continental, Bucureşti, and Inter-Continental) are recommended for a reasonable meal in pleasant surroundings. Some, like the **Balada,** at the top of the Inter-Continental, offer a folklore show or live music. Although prices are not unreasonable, it is possible to rack up quite a total. Many restaurants have no menu, and waiters' recommendations can be expensive. Also note that most places will serve wine only by the bottle and not by the glass. For details and price-category definitions, see Dining in Staying in Romania, above.

$$$$ **Casa Doina.** Recently refurbished, this historic restaurant—popular with the Bucharest elite between the wars—is once again one of the best in town. It serves Romanian and international cuisine in a relaxing atmosphere. In summer you can enjoy the terrace, which backs onto Kiseleff Park. Şos. Kiseleff 4, tel. 01/6176715. Reservations advised. AE, DC, MC, V.

$$$$ **La Premiera.** One of Bucharest's most popular restaurants is conveniently located at the back of the National Theatre. The good selection of Romanian and French cuisine includes excellent salads, even in winter. In summer, you can enjoy La Premiera's terrace. Str. Arghezi 9, tel. 01/3124397. Reservations advised. AE, DC, V.

$$$$ **Madrigal.** Located on the ground floor of the modern Hotel Inter-Continental, this is a quiet, elegant restaurant with a pianist in the evenings. There is a wide choice of authentic Romanian and international dishes. B-dul Nicolae Bălcescu 4–6, tel. 01/6140400. AE, DC, MC, V.

$$$ **Bar Grecesc.** A new German-run restaurant is in the basement of a turn-of-the-century building off Calea Victoriei. It serves mainly international

cuisine, including a good-value Sunday brunch in intimate surroundings. *Str. Occidentului 44, tel. 01/6596155. Reservations advised. AE, DC, MC, V.*

$$$ **Hanul lui Manuc.** Authentic Romanian cuisine is served within a beau-
★   tifully restored 19th-century inn, which was built in the traditional Romanian fashion around a courtyard. *B-dul Iuliu Maniu 30, tel. 01/6131415. Reservations advised. AE, DC, MC, V.*

$$$ **Select Restaurant.** Located in the Cartierul Primaverii (Primavera District)—one of the more well-to-do residential areas of Bucharest—this restaurant offers good Romanian food at reasonable prices in a friendly atmosphere. *Aleea Alexandru 18, tel. 01/6794120. Reservations advised. No credit cards.*

$$ **Dong Hai.** Of the many recently opened Chinese restaurants in Bucharest,
★   this one is one of the most authentic. *Str. Blánari 14, tel. 01/6156494. No credit cards.*

$$ **Maramureş.** You'll find this popular spot tucked in a corner behind the Hotel Bucareşti. Seated in booths in the garden, you can dine outside in summer and fall on typical Romanian dishes. The restaurant also has a small disco/bar. *Str. G-ral Berthelot at corner of Str. T. Aman, tel. 01/6644983. No credit cards.*

$ **Pani Pat.** If your weakness is delicious pastries, you won't want to miss the desserts offered by these take-out eateries. A selection of pizzas comprises the main menu. *Str. C.A. Rosetti 1, tel. 01/2107128; Ştefan Ştefan Cel Mare 4, tel. 01/2103469; Şoş. Dorobanti, tel. 01/2103874. No credit cards.*

Lodging

Hotels in Bucharest are often heavily booked during the tourist season. If you don't have reservations, the ONT office will be of help in suggesting available alternatives. For details and price-category definitions, *see* Lodging *in* Staying in Romania, *above.*

$$$$ **Helveţia.** The Helveţia has established itself as one of the capital's best hotels since opening in mid-1993. This is a small, quiet hotel with an emphasis on individual service and comfort. It is located a little north of the city center but is easily accessible by metro or taxi. *Str. Uruguay 29, tel. 01/3110566, fax 01/3110567. 30 rooms with bath. Facilities: restaurant, bar, café. AE, DC, MC, V.*

$$$$ **Hotel Inter-Continental.** Designed principally for business clients, the four-star Inter-Continental offers American-style accommodation in the city's tallest building. Every room is air-conditioned and has a balcony. *B-dul N. Bălcescu 4–6, tel. 01/6140400, fax 01/3120486. 423 rooms with bath. Facilities: 4 restaurants, 3 bars, nightclub, minicasino, fitness center, pool, sun terrace. AE, DC, MC, V.*

$$$$ **Sofitel.** With all the amenities and modern conveniences this chain is
★   known for, this five-star hotel—constructed in 1994—is out of the city center but located near the airport in a surprisingly tranquil area of parks and lakes. *Free Press Square, B-dul Expoziţiei 2, tel. 01/6182828, fax 01/2120646. 190 rooms with bath, 13 suites, some wheelchair-accessible rooms. Facilities: 2 restaurants, bar, café, nightclub, shops, meeting rooms, nearby fitness center (pool, gym, tennis courts), airport shuttle. AE, DC, MC, V.*

$$$ **Continental.** This small, turn-of-the-century four-star hotel recalls
★   Bucharest's more gracious past. Furnishings are traditional, but the rooms have air-conditioning. It is excellently located in the city center, just north of the lively Lipscani district. *Calea Victoriei 56, tel. 01/6385022, fax 01/3120134. 53 rooms with bath. Facilities: restaurant, coffee shop, bar. AE, DC, MC, V.*

$$$ Flora. The four-star Flora, on the outskirts of the city near Herăstrău Park, offers its cosmopolitan clientele modern facilities for antiaging treatments. The sun terraces are havens of relaxation. Many find this a quiet, restful refuge. *B-dul Poligrafiei 1, tel. 01/6184640, fax 01/3128344. 155 rooms with bath. Facilities: restaurant, pool, spa-care unit, health club, sauna. AE, DC, MC, V.*

$$ Ambassador. The three-star, 13-story Ambassador was built in 1937 and enjoys a fine central location. Most rooms are comfortably furnished and there is a good café. *B-dul General Magheru 6–8, tel. 01/6159080, fax 01/3121239. 233 rooms with bath. Facilities: restaurant, café. AE, DC, MC, V.*

$$ Lido. Conveniently located in the center of the city, this prewar three-star hotel has been recently privatized and renovated to offer comfortable rooms and good facilities, including an outdoor swimming pool and terrace. *B-dul Magheru 5, tel. 01/6144930, fax 01/3126544. 92 rooms with bath. Facilities: restaurant, bar, nightclub, outdoor pool, terrace. AE, DC, MC, V.*

$$ Parc. Located near Herău Park and the Flora Hotel, the Parc is modern and within easy reach of the airport; many guests stay here before moving on to the Black Sea resorts. There's a good restaurant that provides music every evening. *B-dul Poligrafiei 3, tel. 01/6180950, fax 01/3128419. 314 rooms with bath. Facilities: restaurant, pool, sauna. AE, DC, MC, V.*

$ Capitol. The circa-1900, two-star Capitol is in a lively part of town near the Cişmigiu Gardens. In days gone by, it was the stomping ground of Bucharest's mainstream artists and writers. Today the Capitol is modernized and offers comfortable rooms. *Calea Victoriei 29, tel. 01/6158030, fax 01/3124169. 70 rooms with bath. Facilities: restaurant. No credit cards.*

$ Central. This small, two-star hotel on a quiet side street in the middle of town near Cişmigiu gardens has recently been refurbished. *Strada Brezoianu 13, tel. 01/6155637, fax 01/6155635. 65 rooms. DC, MC, V.*

$ Triumf. This comfortable hotel is set on its own grounds slightly out-
★ side the city center near the Arcul de Triumf. Formerly the President, it used to serve only the Communist elite. This hotel is a good value. The more expensive rooms are miniapartments. *Şoseaua Kiseleff 12, tel. 01/6184110, fax 01/3128411. 98 rooms, 49 with bath. Facilities: restaurant, bar, tennis court. AE, DC, V.*

The Arts

You can enjoy Bucharest's lively theater and music life at prices well below those in the West. Tickets can be obtained directly from the theater or hall or from your hotel (for a fee). Performances usually begin at 7 PM (6 in winter). **Opera Română** (The Opera House, B-dul Mihail Kogălniceanu 70) has some good productions, but don't expect the same quality you would find in Prague or Budapest. The George Enescu Philharmonic Orchestra holds concerts at the **Ateneul Român** (Romanian Athenaeum in Piaţa Revoluţiei) or at the more modern **Studioul de Concerte al Radioteleviziunii** (Radio Concert Hall, Str. General Berthelot 62–64). The **Teatrul de Operetă** (Operetta House) is now at the **Teatrul National** (National Theater, B-dul N. Bălcescu 2), which also offers serious drama. For lighter entertainment, try the **Teatrul de Comedie** (Comedy Theater, Str. Mandinesti); despite the language barrier, there is often enough spectacle to ensure a very good evening's entertainment. **Teatrul Tăndărică** (Tandarica Puppet Theater, Calea Victoriei 50) has an international reputation, and the **Teatrul Evreesc de Stat** (State Jewish Theater, Str. Barasch 15) stages Yiddish-language performances. Don't miss the fine folkloric show at the **Rapsodia Română Artistic Ensemble** (Str. Lipscani 53). The **Cinematica Romana** (Str. Eforie 5) runs a daily program of old, undubbed American and English films.

Nightlife

Increasing numbers of bars and restaurants stay open late. Coffee shops, however, are usually closed after 8 PM.

Nightclubs

The **Lido, Ambassador,** and **Inter-Continental** hotels have nightclubs with floor shows, and many others are popping up as well. **Vox Maris** (Piaţa Victoriei); **Salonul Spaniol** (116 Calea Victoriei); and **Club A** (Str. Blănari) are among several late-night discos. **Şarpele Roşu** (Str. Icoanei Piaţa Galaţi), or "Red Snake," has a bohemian atmosphere.

Cafés

Cafés with outdoor terraces remain a feature of the city. Try the **Lido** or, in winter, the excellent indoor **Ana Café** (Str. Aviator Radu Beller 6), just north of Piaţa Dorobanţi.

THE BLACK SEA COAST AND DANUBE DELTA

The southeastern Dobrogea region, only 45 minutes by air from Bucharest, 210 kilometers (130 miles) by road, is one of the major focal points of Romania's rich history. Within a clearly defined area are the historic port of Constanţa; the Romanian Riviera pleasure coast; the Murfatlar vineyards; Roman, Greek, and earlier ruins; and the Danube Delta, one of Europe's leading wildlife sanctuaries. The rapid development of the Black Sea resorts and increasing interest in the delta region mean that tourist amenities (such as hotels and restaurants) and train, bus, and plane connections are good.

Getting Around

By Bus

Bus trips from the Black Sea resorts and Constanta to the Danube Delta, the Murfatlar vineyards, Istria, and the sunken city of Adamclisi are arranged by tourism agencies.

By Car

Rental cars, with or without drivers, are available through ONT offices, hotels, and specialized agencies.

By Boat

Regular passenger and sightseeing boats operate along the middle and southern arms of the Danube Delta. Motorboats are available for hire, or rent one of the more restful fishermen's boats.

Guided Tours

Tours always involve some hours on the road, so it is better to go for more than one day. The **Societatea Comercială Litoral** has the most tour experience. Try trips to the Bukovina monasteries, the Prahova Mountains, or, especially, the Danube Delta.

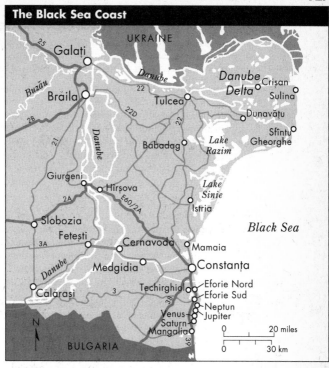

The Black Sea Coast

Tourist Information

Constanţa. Societatea Comercială Litoral (B-dul Tomis 69, tel. and fax 041/611429). **BTT** (Hotel Tineretului, B-dul Tomis 20–26, tel. 041/613590, fax 041/616624).

Mamaia. Societatea Comercială Mamaia (Hotel Bucureşti, B-dul Mamaia, tel. 041/831780).

Tulcea. Societatea Comercială Deltarom (Hotel Delta, Str. Isaccei 2, tel. 040/614720, fax 040/515776). **BTT** (Str. Babadag Bloc B1, tel. 040/512496, fax 040/616842).

Exploring the Black Sea Coast and Danube Delta

Tulcea, the main town of the Danube Delta, is the gateway to the region. Built on seven hills and influenced by Turkish styles, this former market town is now an important sea and river port, as well as the center of the Romanian fish industry, which centers on caviar-bearing sturgeon. The **Muzeul Deltei Dunării** (Danube Delta Museum) provides a good introduction to the flora, fauna, and way of life of the communities in the area. *Str. Progresului 32, tel. 040/158666. Admission: 700 lei. Open daily 10–6.*

The Danube Delta

The **Delta Dunării** (Danube Delta) is Europe's largest wetlands reserve, covering 1,676 square miles, with a sprawling, watery wilderness that stretches from the Ukrainian border to a series of lakes north of the Black Sea resorts. It is Europe's youngest land—more than 47 square yards are added each year by silting action. Today, it is prized as an ecosystem offering visitors the opportunity to see habitats endangered throughout the rest of Europe. Romanians have committed themselves to the restoration of this ecological treasure, now suffering from environmental stresses. Among other things, the Danube Delta is a refuge for hundreds of species of seasonal and migratory birds, and home to natives like the pelican. Within the reserve can still be found a small population of largely "Old Believer" inhabitants.

As it approaches the Delta Dunării, the great Danube divides into three. The northernmost branch forms the border with the Ukraine, the middle arm leads to the busy port of Sulina, and the southernmost arm meanders gently toward the little port of Sfintu Gheorghe, a simple holiday spot. From these channels, countless canals widen into tree-fringed lakes, reed islands, and pools covered with water lilies; there are sand dunes and pockets of lush forest. More than 300 bird species visit the area; 70 of these species come from as far away as China and India.

There are good roads to the Black Sea resorts from Tulcea that take you to **Babadag** via the strange, eroded Măcin hills. It was here, according to local legend, that Jason and the Argonauts cast anchor in their search for the mythical Golden Fleece. Farther south is **Istria,** founded in 6 BC by Greek merchants from Miletus. There are traces of early Christian churches and baths and even of residential, commercial, and industrial districts.

Istria lies only 60 kilometers (37 miles) from **Mamaia,** the largest of the Black Sea resorts. Mamaia is on a strip of land bordered by the Black Sea and fine beaches on one side and the fresh waters of the Mamaia Lake on the other. All the resorts along this stretch of the coast have high-rise modern apartments, villas, restaurants, nightclubs, and discos. There are cruises down the coast to Mangalia and along the new channel linking the Danube with the Black Sea near Constanţa. Sea-fishing expeditions can also be arranged for early risers, with all equipment provided. These resorts offer everything necessary for a complete vacation by the sea.

Constanţa

Constanţa is Romania's second-largest city and only a short ride by trolley bus from Mamaia, with a polyglot flavor characteristic of so many seaports. The famous Roman poet Ovid was exiled here from Rome in AD 8; a statue of the poet presides over a city square. The **Muzeul Naţional de Istorie şi Arheologie** (National History and Archaeological Museum) features statues from the Neolithic Hamangian culture (4000 to 3000 BC) and collections from the Greek, Roman, and Daco-Roman cultures. *Piaţa Ovidiu 12, tel. 041/614562. Admission: 500 lei. Open Tues.–Sun. 10–6.*

Near the museum is **Edificiu Roman cu Mozaic,** a Roman complex of warehouses and shops from the 4th century AD, including a large mosaic floor (Piaţa Ovidiu 1). Not far away are the remains of the Roman baths from the same period. The **Parcul Arheologic** (Archaeology Park) on Bulevardul Republicii contains items dating from the 3rd and 4th centuries AD and from a 6th-century tower. Modern-day attractions include an **Acvariul,** or aquarium (Str. Februarie 16), and **Delfinariul,** the dolphinarium (B-dul Mamaia 265), which offers aquatic displays by trained dolphins.

A string of seaside resorts lies just south of Constanţa. **Eforie Nord** is an up-to-date thermal treatment center. A series of resorts built during the 1960s are named for the coast's Greco-Roman past—**Neptun, Jupiter, Venus,** and **Saturn.** Not in any way typically Romanian, these resorts offer good amenities for relaxed, seaside vacations. The old port of **Mangalia** is the southernmost resort.

Most of the old Greek city of **Callatis** lies underwater now, but a section of the walls and the remains of a Roman villa are still visible.

There are regular excursions from the seaside resorts to the **Podgorile Murfatlar** (Murfatlar vineyards) for wine tastings and visiting the ruins of the Roman town at **Tropaeum Trajani.**

Dining and Lodging

For details and price-category definitions, *see* Dining and Lodging *in* Staying in Romania, *above.* Travelers are advised not to rely on credit cards in this region since many resorts are not yet equipped to accept them.

Constanţa

DINING

Cazinou. A turn-of-the-century former casino close to the aquarium, the Cazinou is decorated in an ornate 20th-century style; there's an adjoining bar by the sea. Seafood dishes are the house specialties. *Str. Februarie 16, tel. 041/617416. Reservations advised. No credit cards. $$$$*

LODGING

Continental. Older and slightly less luxurious than the Palace, the two-star Continental is conveniently situated near the open-air archaeological museum in the downtown area. *B-dul Republicii 20, tel. 041/616064. 140 rooms with bath. AE. $$$*

Palace. Located near the city's historic center, the large and gracious two-star Palace has recently been renovated. It has a good restaurant and a terrace overlooking the sea and the tourist port of Tomis. *Str. Remus Opreanu 5–7, tel. 041/614696. 132 rooms with bath. Facilities: restaurant. No credit cards. $$$*

Crişan

LODGING

Lebăda. This comfortable two-star hotel is convenient for those who plan to make fishing trips into the more remote parts of the delta. *Sulina Canal, mile 14.5, tel. 040/514720. 74 rooms with bath. Facilities: restaurant, currency exchange. No credit cards. $$*

Mamaia

DINING

Insula lui Ovidiu. This is a reed-thatched complex of rustic-style buildings with lively music every evening. A relaxed, informal atmosphere provides a good setting for delicious seafood dishes. *Lake Siutghiol. No phone. No credit cards. $$*

LODGING

Rex. One of King Carol's former residences, this four-star hotel is the largest and grandest of all hostelries in Mamaia. *Tel. 041/831595, fax 041/862292. 102 rooms with bath. Facilities: restaurant, cafeteria, bar, outdoor pool. AE, DC, MC, V. $$$$*

Ambasador, Lido, and Savoy. Among the many modern hotels, these three are all newly built and moderately priced. They are grouped in a horseshoe around open-air pools near the beach at the north end of the resort. Contact them through the Societatea Comercială Mamaia (Hotel Bucrureşti, tel. 041/531025). $$

Tulcea

LODGING

Delta. Located on the banks of the Danube, this spacious, modern hotel has good two-star facilities. *Str. Isaacei 2, tel. 040/514720, fax 040/516260. 117 rooms with bath. Facilities: restaurant, cafeteria, bar. No credit cards. $$*

Venus

LODGING

Dana. This is a new, privately run three-star hotel at the popular Venus resort. All rooms have balconies and showers. *Venus Resort, tel. 041/731503, fax 041/731465. 110 rooms with shower. Facilities: restaurant, terrace, shop, currency office. $$$*

25 Slovakia

EVEN IF IT HAD NOT DEVELOPED separately for nearly a millennium under Hungarian and Hapsburg rule, the newly independent Slovak Republic would be different from its Czech neighbor (*see* Chapter 7) in a great many respects. The mountains are higher here; the veneer less sophisticated. The people seem more outgoing, and the folk culture is particularly rich.

Although they speak a language closely related to Czech, the Slovaks have a strong sense of national identity, and indeed the two Slavic groups developed quite separately. Although united in the 9th century as part of the Great Moravian Empire, the Slovaks were conquered a century later by the Magyars and remained under Hungarian domination until 1918. After the Tartar invasions of the 13th century, many Saxons were invited to resettle the land, exploit its rich mineral resources, and thereby develop the economy. In the 15th and 16th centuries, Romanian shepherds migrated from Wallachia through the Carpathians into Slovakia, and the merging of these varied groups with the resident Slavs bequeathed to the region a rich folk culture and some unique forms of architecture, especially in the east.

Bratislava, the capital of Hungary for nearly 250 years until 1784, and now the capital of the new republic, was once a city filled with picturesque streets and Gothic churches. The 40 years of communist rule left a clear mark on the city, hiding its ancient beauty with hulking, and now dilapidated, futurist structures. Take time, however, to walk the streets of the Old Town, now undergoing frenzied revitalization. The city has many good concert halls, restaurants, and wine bars.

Most visitors head for the great peaks of the High Tatras. The smallest Alpine range in the world—and the reason Slovakia can claim to be the Switzerland of Central Europe—the Tatras rise magnificently from the foothills of northern Slovakia. The tourist infrastructure here is very good, catering especially to hikers and skiers. Visitors who come to admire the peaks, however, often overlook the exquisite medieval towns of the Spiš region in the plains and valleys below the Tatras and the beautiful 18th-century wood churches farther east.

ESSENTIAL INFORMATION

Before You Go

When to Go

Organized sightseeing tours run from April or May through October. Many tours are run by Satur Tours and Travel; Once a division of Čedok (the government-owned travel agency of former Czechoslovakia), Satur will probably be privatized in the future. Today, Satur is still often referred to as Čedok within Slovakia. Some monuments, especially castles, either close entirely or have shorter hours in winter. Hotel rates drop during the off-season except during festivals. The High Tatra mountains come into their own in winter (Dec.–Feb.), when skiers from all over Eastern Europe crowd the slopes and resorts. If you're not into skiing, visit the mountains in late spring (May or June) or fall, when the hills bloom with flowers, and you'll have the hotels and restaurants pretty much to yourself.

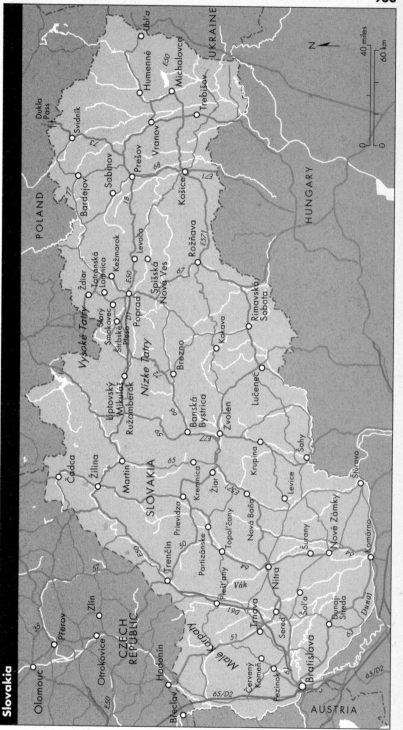

Slovakia

N

40 miles

60 km

UKRAINE

POLAND

HUNGARY

CZECH
REPUBLIC

AUSTRIA

SLOVAKIA

Vysoké Tatry

Nízke Tatry

Malé Karpaty

Dukla
Pass

Ubľa

Humenné

Michalovce

Trebišov

Svidník

Vranov

Sabinov

Prešov

Bardejov

Košice

Rožňava

Levoča

Spišská
Nová Ves

Ždiar

Tatranská
Lomnica

Kežmarok

Rimavská
Sobota

Starý
Smokovec

Štrbské
Pleso

Poprad

Kokava

Brezno

Liptovský
Mikuláš

Banská
Bystrica

Lučenec

Ružomberok

Zvolen

Čadca

Šahy

Žilina

Martin

Kremnica

Krupina

Žiar

Levice

Šurany

Prievidza

Nová Baňa

Štúrovo

Trenčín

Partizánske

Topoľčany

Nové Zámky

Komárno

Nitra

Piešťany

Šaľa

Dunajská
Streda

Přerov

Zlín

Trnava

Sereď

Otrokovice

Pezinok

Červený
Kameň

Bratislava

Olomouc

Hodonín

Břeclav

Dunaj

Váh

E50

E50

E71

E571

E77

D1

D61

65/D2

65/D2

CLIMATE

The following are the average daily maximum and minimum temperatures for Bratislava.

Jan.	36F	2C	May	70F	21C	Sept.	72F	22C
	27	− 3		52	11		54	12
Feb.	39F	4C	June	75F	24C	Oct.	59F	15C
	28	− 2		57	14		45	7
Mar.	48F	9C	July	79F	26C	Nov.	46F	8C
	34	1		61	16		37	3
Apr.	61F	16C	Aug.	79F	26C	Dec.	39F	4C
	43	6		61	16		32	0

Currency

The unit of currency in Slovakia is the crown, or koruna, written as Sk., and divided into 100 halér. There are bills of 20, 50, 100, 500, and 1,000 Sk. and coins of 10, 20, and 50 halér and 1, 2, 5, and 10 Sk.

At press time (spring 1995), the koruna was trading at around 29 Sk. to the American dollar and 47 Sk. to the pound sterling.

What It Will Cost

Costs are highest in Bratislava and only slightly less in the High Tatra resorts and main spas, although even in those places you can now find bargain private accommodations. The prices at tourist resorts in the outlying areas and off the beaten track are incredibly low. The least expensive areas are central and eastern Slovakia.

SAMPLE PRICES

Cup of coffee, 10 Sk.; beer (½ liter), 15 Sk.; Coca-Cola, 10 Sk.–15 Sk.; ham sandwich, 30 Sk.; 1-mile taxi ride, 100 Sk.

MUSEUMS

Admission to museums, galleries, and castles ranges from 5 Sk. to 50 Sk.

Visas

U.S. and British citizens do not need visas to enter Slovakia. Visa requirements have been temporarily reintroduced for Canadian citizens; check with the consulate to determine whether this is still the case. Apply to the Consulate of the Slovak Republic (50 Rideau Terrace, Ottawa, Ontario K1M 2A1, tel. 613/749–4442).

Customs

ON ARRIVAL

Valuable items should be entered on your customs declaration. You can bring in 250 cigarettes (or their equivalent in tobacco), 2 liters of wine, 1 liter of spirits, ½ liter of eau de cologne, and gifts with a total value of 1,000 Sk.

ON DEPARTURE

Crystal not purchased with hard currency may be subject to a tax of 100% of its retail price. To be on the safe side, hang on to all receipts. Only antiques bought at specially designated shops may be exported.

Language

Slovak, a western-Slavic tongue closely related to both Czech and Polish, is the official language of Slovakia. Czech and Slovak are mutually comprehensible; if you speak Czech, you'll have little problem in Slovakia. Learning English is popular among young people, but German is still the most useful language for tourists.

Getting Around

By Car

ROAD CONDITIONS

Main roads are usually good, if sometimes narrow, and traffic is light, especially away from main centers. **Bratislava** is not a good city for drivers, and finding a parking space can be a problem. Hence, for touring the capital, walking is the best option. It's very useful to have a car when exploring central and eastern Slovakia, however, where many of the interesting sights are outside the larger towns and difficult to reach with mass transit.

RULES OF THE ROAD

Drive on the right. Speed limits are 60 kph (37 mph) in built-up areas, 90 kph (55 mph) on open roads, and 110 kph (68 mph) on expressways. Seat belts are compulsory outside built-up areas; drinking and driving is strictly prohibited.

GASOLINE

Gasoline is expensive, averaging $2.50 a gallon. Service stations are usually located along main roads on the outskirts of towns and cities. Finding a station in Bratislava is difficult. Fill up on the freeway as you approach the city to avoid frustration. Lead-free gasoline, known as "natural," is still available only at select stations, so tank up when you see it.

BREAKDOWNS

For accidents, call the emergency number (tel. 155). In case of an auto breakdown, in Bratislava contact the 24-hour service (tel. 07/249404). The *Auto Atlas SR* (available at any bookstore) has a list of emergency road-repair numbers in various towns.

By Train

Train service is erratic to all but the largest cities—**Poprad, Prešov, Košice,** and **Banská Bystrica.** Good, if slow, electric rail service, however, connects Poprad with the resorts of the **High Tatras.** If you're going just to the Tatras, you won't need any other kind of transportation.

By Bus

Bus service in Bratislava is very cheap and reasonably frequent, and you can use it with confidence to reach any of the places in the tours below. You may have trouble reading the detailed information on the timetable, so ask if you're not sure where a particular bus is headed.

The bus network in Slovakia is dense, linking all the towns on the tours given here. Leave a couple of extra days, however, to compensate for the infrequent service to the smaller towns.

Staying in Slovakia

Telephones

LOCAL CALLS

These cost 2 Sk. from a pay phone. Lift the receiver, place the coin in the holder, dial, and insert the coin when your party picks up. Public phones are on street corners; unfortunately, they're often out of order. Try asking in a hotel if you're stuck. If you plan to make several local or out-of-town calls, it would be advisable to consider buying a phone card. They can be bought at most newsstands or at any post office and cost 150 Sk. for 75 local calls.

INTERNATIONAL CALLS

There's automatic dialing to many countries, including North America and the United Kingdom. For international inquiries, dial 0132 for the United States, Canada, or the United Kingdom. To place a call via an **AT&T** USADirect international operator, dial 00–420–00101; for **MCI,** dial 00–42–000112; for **Sprint,** dial 0042–087–187.

COUNTRY CODE
The country code for Slovakia is 42.

Mail

POSTAL RATES
Airmail letters to the United States and Canada cost 11 Sk. up to 10 grams, postcards 6 Sk. Airmail letters to the United Kingdom cost 8 Sk. up to 20 grams, postcards 5 Sk.

RECEIVING MAIL
Mail can be sent to "poste restante" at any main post office; there's no charge to claim it.

Opening and Closing Times
Banks are open weekdays 8–3. **Museums** are usually open Tues.–Sun. 10–5. **Shops** are generally open weekdays 9–6 (Thurs. 9–8); some close between noon and 2. Many are also open Sat. 9–noon (department stores, 9–4).

National Holidays
January 1; April 8 (Easter Monday); May 1 (Labor Day); July 5 (Sts. Cyril and Methodius); August 29 (anniversary of the Slovak National Uprising); September 1 (Constitution Day); December 25, 26.

Dining
The options in Slovakia include restaurants, wine cellars, the more down-to-earth beer taverns, cafeterias, and a growing number of coffee shops and snack bars. Most restaurants are remarkably reasonable, but privatization is beginning to push up prices in a few places.

The most typical main dish is roast pork (or duck or goose) with sauerkraut. Dumplings in various forms or potatoes, generally with a rich gravy, accompany many dishes. Peppers are frequently used as well to spice up bland entrées. Look for *halušky,* a tasty Slovak noodle dish, usually served with sheep cheese. Fresh green vegetables and salads are still rare, but there are plenty of the pickled variety. Be sure to try *palačinky,* a delicious treat of crepes stuffed with fruit and ice cream or jam.

WHAT TO WEAR
A jacket is suggested for higher-priced restaurants. Otherwise, casual dress is acceptable.

MEALTIMES
Lunch is usually from 11:30 to 2 or 3; dinner from 6 to 9:30 or 10. Some places are open all day, and in Bratislava you might find it easier to find a table during off hours.

RATINGS
Prices are reasonable by American standards, even in the more expensive restaurants. The following prices are for meals made up of a first course, main course, and dessert (excluding wine and tip). Highly recommended restaurants are indicated by a star ★.

CATEGORY	COST
$$$$	over 600 Sk.
$$$	400 Sk.–600 Sk.
$$	200 Sk.–400 Sk.
$	under 200 Sk.

Lodging

Slovakia's hotel industry has been slow to react to the political and economic changes that have taken place since 1989. Few new hotels have been built, and many of the older hotels are still majority-owned by the state. The good news is that many older properties are gradually being renovated, and the best have great character and style. There is still an acute shortage of hotel rooms during the peak season, so make reservations well in advance. Many private room agencies are now in operation, and as long as you arrive before 9 PM, you should be able to get a room. The standards of facilities and services hardly match those in the West, so don't be surprised by faulty plumbing or indifferent reception clerks.

HOTELS

These are officially graded with from one to five stars by Satur, the country's largest travel agency. Many foreign visitors stay at Interhotels—often owned by Satur—which are mainly in the three- to five-star categories. Most of the rooms in these hotels have baths or showers.

PRIVATE ACCOMMODATIONS

Satur and other tourist information services can help you find a private room in Bratislava and other large cities. These accommodations are invariably cheaper (around $20) and often more comfortable than hotels, though you may have to sacrifice some privacy. You can also wander the main roads looking for signs declaring ROOM FREE, or more frequently, in German, ZIMMER FREI or PRIVATZIMMER.

RATES

Prices are for double rooms, generally not including breakfast. Prices at the lower end of the scale apply to low season. At certain periods, such as Easter or during festivals, there may be an increase of 15%–25%. Highly recommended lodgings are indicated by a star ★.

CATEGORY	COST
$$$$	over 3,200 Sk.
$$$	1,600 Sk.–3,200 Sk.
$$	480 Sk.–1,600 Sk.
$	under 480 Sk.

Tipping

Small sums of hard currency will certainly be most welcome. To reward good service in a restaurant, round up the bill to the nearest multiple of 10; 10% is considered appropriate on very large tabs. Tip porters 20 Sk. For room service, a 20 Sk. tip is enough. In taxis, round up the bill to the nearest multiple of 10. Give tour guides and helpful concierges between 20 Sk. and 30 Sk. for services rendered.

BRATISLAVA

Arriving and Departing

By Plane

As few international airlines land in Bratislava, the most convenient international airport for Slovakia is Vienna's Schwechat Airport, approximately 50 kilometers (30 miles) away from Bratislava. Four buses a day stop at Schwechat en route to Bratislava, or you could even take a taxi; the journey takes just over an hour, depending on the border crossing. From Prague's Ruzyně Airport you can take a ČSA flight to Bratislava; the flight takes about an hour.

If time is a factor during your stay in Slovakia, consider flying to the relatively far-flung Tatras and eastern Slovakia. ČSA has reasonably priced daily flights from Prague and Bratislava to Poprad (the regional airport for the Tatras). For further information, contact the ČSA offices in Prague (tel. 02/2146) or Bratislava (tel. 07/311205).

By Train

Reasonably efficient train service connects Prague and Bratislava. Trains leave from Prague's main station (Hlavní nádraží), and the journey takes from five to six hours depending on the train. There are four trains a day to and from Vienna's Wien-Mitte and Südbahnhof Stations, with the journey lasting just over an hour.

By Bus

There are numerous buses from Prague to Bratislava; the journey costs less than 200 Sk. and takes about five hours. From Vienna, there are four buses a day from Autobusbahnhof Wien-Mitte. The journey takes between 1½ and two hours. The **Autobus Stanica** (station) in Bratislava is just outside the center; you can take Trolleybus 217 to Miérové námestie or Bus 107 to the castle (Hrad).

By Car

There are good freeways from Prague to Bratislava via Brno (D1 and D2); the 315-kilometer (203-mile) journey takes about 3½ hours. From Vienna, take the A4 and then Route 8 to Bratislava. The 60-kilometer (37-mile) trip will take about 1½ hours.

Getting Around

By Car

Driving can be difficult in Bratislava and parking spaces at a premium in the city center; hence, for touring the republic's capital, foot power will be the most effective way of seeing the sights. If you do need to rent a car, you can do so either at Satur or at the Hotel Forum.

By Bus

Bus service in Bratislava is very cheap and reasonably frequent, and you can use it with confidence to reach any of the main sights. Buy tickets ahead of time at any newspaper stand or at automatic ticket dispensers for 5 Sk. each and stamp them when you enter the bus.

Important Addresses and Numbers

Tourist Information

Bratislava has its own tourist information service, **Bratislava Tourist Information** (BIS, Panská 18, tel. 07/333715 or 07/334370). The office is in the Old Town, a few steps down from Hlavné námestie, and can supply visitors with information about accommodations. It's open weekdays 8–4:30 (8–6 in summer) and Saturday 8–1. With 54 offices throughout the country, **Satur Tours and Travel** is the largest travel agency in Slovakia. The main office is in Bratislava (Jesenské 5, tel. 07/367613 or 07/367624, fax 07/368624; open weekdays 9–6, Sat. 9–noon). Although more a travel agent than a tourist information office, it can supply you with hotel and tour information, and book air, rail, and bus tickets. Satur's U.S. representative is **Slovakia Travel Service**, 10 E. 40th St., Suite 3601, New York, NY 10016, tel. 212/213–3865, fax 212/213–4461.

Emergencies

Police: tel. 158. **Ambulance:** tel. 155.

Lekárna (pharmacies) take turns staying open late or on Sunday. Look for the list posted on the front door of each pharmacy. For after-hours service, ring the bell; you will be served through a little hatch-door.

Guided Tours

The best tours of Bratislava are offered by **BIS** (*see* Tourist Information, *above*), although out of the summer season they are given only in German and only on weekends. These tours start at 2 PM at the National Theater; they last two hours and cost 270 Sk. per person. **Satur** offers tours from May through September on Wednesday and Saturday, starting at 1:45 from the Devin Hotel (Riečna ul. 4, tel. 07/330851). You can combine these with an afternoon tour of the Small Carpathians (departing at 4:45 PM, also from the Devin), which includes dinner at Zochová Chata one of Slovakia's best restaurants. Satur can also arrange an individual guide at a cost of around 150 Sk.

Exploring Bratislava

Expecting a Slovak version of Prague or Vienna, many visitors to Bratislava are disappointed to discover instead a city with more than its fair share of high-rise housing projects, faded supermodern structures, and less-than-inspiring monuments to carefully chosen acts of heroism. But Europe's newest capital city is on the move. Everywhere you look new shops are opening and older buildings are being renovated—as if the city's residents were trying to forget as quickly as possible the past 40 years, during which Bratislava played second fiddle to Prague. Avoid the newer, and shabbier, parts of the city and head toward the Danube River to discover the peace and beauty of the Staré Mesto (Old Town) and its Gothic and Renaissance architectural treasures.

Numbers in the margin correspond to points of interest on the Bratislava map.

① Begin your tour of the city at the modern square **Námestie SNP.** An abbreviation for Slovenské Národné Povstanie (Slovak National Uprising), these three letters appear on streets, squares, bridges, and posters throughout Slovakia. This anti-Nazi resistance movement involved partisan fighting, organized partly but not exclusively by the communists, in Slovakia's mountainous areas during the final years of the war. In 1992 this was the center for demonstrations in support of Slovak independence, and you can often see the Slovak flag (red, blue, and white with a double cross) flying from a partisan's gun.

② From here walk up toward a bustling town square, **Hurbanovo námestie.** Across the road, unobtrusively located between a large shoe store and a bookshop, is the enchanting entrance to the Old Town. A small bridge, decorated with wrought-iron railings and statues of St. John Nepomuk and St. Michael, takes you over the old moat, now blossoming with trees and fountains, into the intricate barbican, a set of gates and houses that were part of the Old Town's medieval fortifications. After

③ going through the first archway, you come to the narrow **Michalská ulica;** in front of you is the **Michalská brána** (Michael's Gate), the last remaining of the city's three original gates.

④ A little farther down Michalská ulica on the right is the **Palác Uhorskej král'ovskej komory** (Hungarian Royal Chamber), a Baroque palace that housed the Hungarian nobles' parliament from 1802 until 1848; it is now used as the university library. Go through the arched passageway

Dóm Sv. Martina, **5**

Hrad, **7**

Hurbanovo Námestie, **2**

Jezuitský Kostol, **9**

Michalská Brána, **3**

Most SNP, **6**

Námestie SNP, **1**

Palác Uhorskej Kráľovskej Komory, **4**

Primaciálny Palác, **11**

Stará Radnica, **10**

Židovská Ulica, **8**

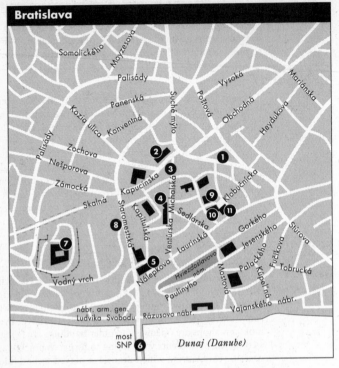

Bratislava

at the back of this building, and you'll emerge in a tiny square dominated by the **Church and Convent of the Poor Clares.**

⑤ Follow Farská ulica up to the corner, and turn left on **Kapitulská ulica,** noticing the ground stone depicting two kissing lizards. At the bottom of the street is the side wall of the **Dóm svätého Martina** (St. Martin's Cathedral). Construction of this massive plain Gothic church, with its 280-foot steeple twinkling with gold trim, began in the 14th century. Between the 16th and 19th centuries, the cathedral saw the coronation of 17 Hungarian royals.

⑥ As you leave the church and walk around to the front, the freeway leading to the futuristic spaceship bridge, **Most SNP,** is the first thing you see. Follow the steps under the passageway and up the other side in the direction of the historic castle, Bratislavský Hrad.

TIME OUT At the top of the wooden stairs, you come to the **Arkadia** restaurant and café, one of Bratislava's better private establishments, situated in a beautiful old house. Here you can get good coffee and desserts or a full meal before your ascent to the Castle.

⑦ Continue up the steps, through a Gothic arched gateway built in 1480, until you reach the **Bratislavský Hrad** (castle) area. The original fortifications date from the 9th century. The Hungarian kings expanded the castle into a large royal residence, and the Hapsburgs turned it into a very successful defense against the Turks. Its current design, square with four corner towers, stems from the 17th century, although the existing castle had to be completely rebuilt after a disastrous fire in 1811. In the castle, you'll find the **Slovenské národné múzeum** (Slovak National Museum). The exhibits cover glassmaking, medieval warfare, and coin making. *Zámocká ul., tel. 07/332985. Admission: 40 Sk. adults, 10 Sk. children and students. Open Tues.–Sun., 10–5.*

⑧ Leave the castle by the same route, but instead of climbing the last stairs by the Arkadia restaurant, continue down the Old-World Beblaveho thoroughfare. Continue along **Židovská ulica.** The name, Jews' Street, marks this area as the former Jewish ghetto. Walk up Židovská until you come to a thin concrete bridge that connects with the reconstructed city walls across the freeway.

Across the road you'll find steps leading down into the Old Town. Go through Františkánske námestie into the adjoining square, **Hlavné námestie,** which is lined with old houses and palaces representing the spectrum of architectural styles from Gothic (No. 2), through Baroque (No. 4) and Rococo (No. 7), to a wonderfully decorative example of Art Nouveau at No. 10. To your immediate left as you come into the square is
⑨ the richly decorated **Jezuitský kostol** (Jesuit Church). Next door is the colorful agglomeration of Gothic and Renaissance arcades, archways,
⑩ and audience halls that makes up the **Stará radnica** (Old Town Hall). Walk through the arched passageway, still with early Gothic ribbing, into a wonderfully cheery Renaissance courtyard with romantic gables. Toward the back of the courtyard, you'll find the entrance to the **Mestské múzeum** (City Museum), which documents Bratislava's varied past. *Primaciálne nám., tel. 07/334742. Admission: 10 Sk. adults, 5 Sk. children and students. Open Tues.–Sun. 10–5.*

⑪ Leaving the back entrance of the Old Town Hall, you come to the **Primaciálne námestie** (Primates' Square), with the glorious pale pink, classical elegance of the **Primaciálny palác** (Primates' Palace) taking pride of place. If the building is open, go up to the dazzling Hall of Mirrors. In this room, Napoléon and Hapsburg Emperor Francis I signed the Peace of Bratislava of 1805, following Napoléon's victory at the Battle of Austerlitz.

Dining

Prague may have its Slovak rival beat when it comes to architecture, but when it's time to eat, you can thank those lucky red stars you still see around town that you're in Bratislava. The long-shared history with Hungary gives Slovak cuisine an extra fire that Czech cooking—many gourmands will admit—generally lacks. Bratislava's proximity to Vienna, moreover, has lent something of grace and charm to the city's eateries. The happy result is that you'll seldom see pork and dumplings on the menu. Instead, prepare for a variety of shish kebabs, grilled meats, steaks, and pork dishes, all spiced to enliven the palate and served (if you're lucky) with those special noodles Slovaks call halušky. Keep in mind that the city's many street stands provide a price-conscious alternative to restaurant dining. In addition to the ubiquitous hot dogs and hamburgers (no relation to their American namesakes), try some *langoš*—flat, deep-fried, and delicious pieces of dough, usually seasoned with garlic.

For details and price-category definitions, *see* Dining *in* Staying in Slovakia, *above.*

$$$$ **Arkadia.** The elegant setting, at the threshold of Bratislava Castle, sets the tone for a luxurious evening. There are several dining rooms to choose from, ranging from the intimate to the more boisterous, all decorated with period 19th-century furnishings. A standard repertoire of Slovak and international dishes, including shish kebabs and steaks, is prepared to satisfaction. It is a 15-minute walk from the town center; take a taxi here and enjoy the mostly downhill walk back into town. *Zámocké schody, tel. 07/335650. Reservations advised. Jacket and tie. AE, DC, MC, V.*

$$$ **Klaštorná Vináreň.** Old Town dining can be a delight in the vaulted
★ cellars of this old monastery. The spiciness of Slovak cooking comes alive in dishes like *čikós tokáň*, a fiery mixture of pork, onions, and peppers. Wash it down with a glass of mellow red wine and a fire hose. *Bravcové ražníci* is milder, a tender pork shish kebab and fried potatoes. *Františkánská ul. 1, tel. 07/330430. Reservations advised. No credit cards. Closed Sun.*

$$ **Modrá Hviezda.** The first of a new breed of small, privately owned wine cellars, the "Blue Star" eschews the international standards in favor of regional Slovak fare. Be sure to try the *bryndza* (baked sheep-cheese) pie and the tasty goulash. *Beblavého 14, tel. 07/332747. Reservations advised. No credit cards.*

$ **Pekná Brána.** With more than 75 main-course meals from which to choose, this is not the place to go if you have trouble making up your mind. The menus at this old-fashioned, cozy restaurant include Chinese and vegetarian cuisines, as well as traditional Slovak specialities. It's open daily from 9:30 to midnight. *Obchodná ul. 39, tel 07/323008. Reservations advised. MC, V.*

$ **Stará Sladovňa.** This mammoth beer hall is known lovingly, and fittingly, as "Mamut" to Bratislavans. Locals come here for the Bohemian beer on tap and for inexpensive, filling meals. The place seats almost 2,000, so don't worry about reservations. *Cintorínska ul. 32, tel. 07/324050. No credit cards.*

Lodging

For details and price-category definitions, *see* Lodging *in* Staying in Slovakia, *above.*

$$$$ **Danube.** Opened in 1992, this French-run hotel on the bank of the
★ Danube has quickly developed a reputation for superior facilities and service. The modern rooms are done in tasteful pastels; the gleaming public areas are everything you expect from an international hotel chain. Of all the hotels in Bratislava, this one wins hands down on location— alongside the river, with a stunning view of the castle out the front door. *Rybné nám. 1, tel. 07/340833, fax 07/314311. 280 rooms with bath. Facilities: restaurants, nightclub, health club, pool, sauna, solarium. AE, DC, MC, V.*

$$$$ **Forum Bratislava.** The Forum opened in 1989 in downtown Bratislava, offering top facilities. It houses a French as well as a Slovak restaurant and several cafés and bars. *Hodžovo nám. 2, tel. 07/348111, fax 07/314645. 219 rooms with bath. Facilities: 3 restaurants, 2 bars, nightclub, café, saunas, pool, solarium, health club. AE, DC, MC, V.*

$$ **Hotel Echo.** This small, bright, affordable hotel is near the center of Bratislava. It has a friendly staff, great breakfasts, and rooms that are wheelchair-accessible. *Presovská ul. 39, tel. 07/329174, fax 07/329174. 66 rooms with bath. Facilities: restaurant. MC, V.*

HIGHLIGHTS OF SLOVAKIA

Outside of Bratislava, the great peaks of the High Tatras remain the prime destination for most travelers. In this resort region, the hotels are excellent and many tours are custom-tailored to introduce visitors to one of the most beautiful mountain ranges in Europe. The mountains *are* spectacular, but also worth seeing are the brooding medieval towns of the **Spiš region** in the plains and valleys below the High Tatras and the lovely 18th-century country churches farther east. Away from main centers, these areas are short on tourist amenities, so if creature comforts are important to you, stick to the Tatras.

Getting Around

If you want to travel by plane, **ČSA's** 40-minute flights from Bratislava to Poprad connect with services from Prague once or twice daily and are priced reasonably. For information on other transportation in Slovakia, *see* Getting Around *in* Essential Information, *above*.

Guided Tours

Satur's seven-day **Grand Tour of Slovakia,** which leaves from Bratislava every other Saturday from June through September, stops in the High Tatras, Kežmarok, Košice, and Banská Bystrica. The tour includes all meals and accommodations. For more information, contact the Satur office in Bratislava (tel. 07/367613).

Slovair offers a novel biplane flight over the Tatras from Poprad airport. Contact the Satur office in Poprad (tel. 092/23651). The Satur office in Starý Smokovec (tel. 0969/2417) is also helpful in arranging tours of the Tatras and the surrounding area.

Tourist Information

Bardejov (Radnicné nam. 21, tel. 0935/3271).
Bratislava (Panská 18, tel. 07/333715).
Prešov (Hlavná ul. 8, tel. 091/731113).
Smokovec (Starý Smokovec V/22, tel. 0969/3127).
Žilina (Burianová medzierka 4, tel. 089/23171).
Košice (Hlavná 8, tel. 095/186).

Exploring Slovakia

Despite its charms, there's no denying that Bratislava is intensely industrial. If you're not going on to the mountains and fresh air of the High Tatras, a good one- or two-day natural respite can be had less than an hour north of the city, in the **Malé Karpaty** (Small Carpathian) mountains. Drive or take the bus to the dusty wine-making town of **Modra,** and from there, follow the signs to **Zochová Chata,** some 8 kilometers (5 miles) away in the hills. The *chata* is really a cozy mountain chalet, with big rooms, plenty of period furniture, and a romantic *koliba* (tavern) that serves the best roast chicken in Slovakia. Trails fan out in all directions from the chata. For a full day's walk, follow the yellow-marked path about three hours to the Renaissance castle **Červený Kameň** ("red rock"). The blue-marked path will take you back to Zochová Chata.

The Spiš Region

Whether you travel by car, bus, or train, your route will follow the Vah Valley for most of the way to **Poprad,** a transit point for Slovakia's most magnificent natural treasure, the High Tatras. Although Poprad itself is a dreary place, its suburb of **Spišská Sobota,** reached by Buses 2, 3, or 4, is a little gem. It was one of 24 small Gothic towns in the medieval region known as **Spiš.** Steep shingled roofs, high timber-framed gables, and arched brick doorways are the main features of the Spišská Sobata's historic dwellings. The lovely old square—itself nearly a perfect ensemble of Renaissance houses—features a Romanesque church, **Sv. Juraj** (St. George's), rebuilt in the early 16th century. The church's ornate altar is the work of Pavel of Levoča, one of the great

The Tatras and Eastern Slovakia

woodcarvers of the 16th century. The **museum** is worth a visit. *Admission: 4 Sk. Open Mon.–Sat. 9–4.*

The High Tatras

Both an electric train network and a winding highway link Poprad with the resorts spread about on the lower slopes of the High Tatras. **Štrbské Pleso** is the highest of the towns and the best launching point for mountain excursions. A rewarding two-hour trek of moderate difficulty leads from here to **Popradské Pleso,** one of dozens of tiny, isolated Alpine lakes that dot the Tatras. **Smokovec** is really three resorts in one (Starý, Nový, and Horný) and has the most varied amenities. For the most effortless high-level trip, though, go to **Tatranská Lomnica,** from which a two-stage cable car will take you via Skalnaté Pleso to Lomnický štít, which at 8,635 feet is the second-highest peak in the range. From Skalnaté Pleso, you can take the red-marked Magistrale trail down to **Hrebienok,** where you can board a funicular and ride down to Starý Smokovec. The **Museum of the Tatra National Park** at Tatranská Lomnica offers an excellent introduction to the area's natural and human history. *Admission: 6 Sk., 2 Sk. for children. Open weekdays 8:30–noon and 1–5, weekends 8–noon.*

Levoča

Leave Poprad on Highway 18 east. Restoration work on **Levoča,** the most famous of the Spiš towns, is well under way, and the overlays of Renaissance on Gothic are extremely satisfying to the eye (note especially Nos. 43, 45, 47, and 49 on the main square). Pavel of Levoča's work on the main altar of **Sv. Jakub** (St. James's) on the main square is both monumental in size and exquisite in its detail. The surrounding countryside is dotted with more medieval towns. About 16 kilometers (10 miles) to the east, the massive, partly restored ruins of **Spiš**

Castle, above Spišské Podhradie, dominate the surrounding pastures and orchards. Some of **Prešov's** fortifications survive, and its spindle-shape main square is lined with buildings in the Gothic, Renaissance, and Baroque styles.

The Šariš Region

You have now left Spiš and entered **Šariš,** a region whose proximity to the Orthodox east has left a unique legacy of both Orthodox and Greek Catholic (Uniate) churches. **Bardejov** is a splendid walled town and makes the best center from which to set out on a journey of exploration, as long as you're prepared to get lost along some rough minor roads while seeking out the 17th- and 18th-century wooden churches of **Bodružal, Ladomirová, Mirola,** and **Šemetkovce**—and the right person to open them up for you. You'll find these churches east and northeast of **Svidník,** near the border with Poland (follow the road to Dukla Pass). These churches jostle for attention with the dramatic collection of Nazi and Soviet tanks and planes dotted around this area to commemorate the fighting that took place in 1944. Easier to find is the 15th-century church of **Hvervartov** (Roman Catholic), 10 kilometers (6 miles) southwest of Bardejov—a fascinating example of timber Gothic with some famous 17th-century frescoes.

Dining and Lodging

Despite the steady influx of visitors, finding a satisfying meal in the Tatras is about as tough as making the 1,000-foot climb from Starý Smokovec to Hrebienok. The best option is eating in one of the hotels; both the Grand in Smokovec and the Grandhotel Praha in Tatranská Lomnica have decent restaurants that make up in style what they might lack in culinary excellence. For lunch, local grocery stores, which stock basic sandwich fixings, are an alternative to restaurants.

If you are looking to splurge on accommodations, you will find no better place than the Tatras. That noted, ask to see several rooms in your hotel before selecting one, as reader reports indicate rooms can be quite quirky.

For details and price-category definitions, *see* Dining and Lodging *in* Staying in Slovakia, *above.*

Bardejov

LODGING

Minerál. This rather sterile modern hotel lies in a quiet location in the spa town of Bardejovské kúpele, 2¼ kilometers (1½ miles) from Bardejov proper. *Bardejovské kúpele, tel. 0935/4122, fax 0935/4124. 60 rooms with shower. Facilities: tennis courts. No credit cards. $$*

Levoča

LODGING

Hotel Satel. Levoča, the hub of the historic Spiš region, is busily preserving its heritage while building a future based on tourism, and this beautifully renovated hotel is a fine case in point. Housed in an 18th-century mansion, it's centered around a picturesque courtyard that conjures up all the charm of fairy-tale Levoča. The guest rooms are bright and modern. *Tel. 0966/2943, fax 0966/4486. 21 rooms with bath, 2 suites. Facilities: restaurant. No credit cards. $$*

Smokovec

DINING

Tatranská Kúria. The Tatranská's rustic decor and Slovak specialties will provide some insight into local life. Dishes include *rezeň kúria* (pork cutlets with a cheese and ham filling in a cheese pastry) and *bryndzové pirohy* (cheese-filled pastry served with cream and bacon). *Starý Smokovec, tel. 0969/2806. Reservations not necessary. No credit cards. Closes early.* $$

LODGING

Bellevue. This modern high-rise with well-appointed rooms lies about 200 yards from the resort center, although a good 15-minute walk away from the city's grocers and bars. Rates include breakfast and dinner. *Horný Smokovec, tel. 0969/2941, fax 0969/2719. 103 rooms, 63 with bath. Facilities: restaurant, bar, saunas, pool. AE, DC, MC, V.* $$$

Grand Hotel. The town's oldest hotel has a wonderful air of faded fin-de-siècle elegance. The location, at the commercial and sports center of the region, is a mixed blessing, however, due to crowds. The hotel has a reasonably priced restaurant. Rooms without bath have lower room rates. *Starý Smokovec, tel. 0969/2154, fax 0969/2157. 83 rooms, some with bath. Facilities: restaurant, nightclub, pool, sauna. AE, DC, MC, V.* $$$

Tatranská Lomnica

DINING

Zbojnícka Koliba. This tavern offers a small range of Slovak specialties prepared over an open fire, amid rustic decor and accompanied by folk music. *Near Grandhotel Praha, tel. 0969/967630. Reservations not necessary. No credit cards. Dinner only. Closed Sun.* $$

LODGING

Grandhotel Praha. Housed in a multiturreted turn-of-the-century building often acclaimed as one of the wonders of the Tatras, the Grandhotel Praha offers visitors spacious but slightly shabby guest rooms decorated with a traditional touch. The restaurant has an air of elegance that is unusual in Slovakia. *Tel. 0969/967941, fax 0969/967891. 92 rooms with bath. Facilities: restaurant, nightclub. AE, DC, MC, V.* $$$

26 Spain

SPAIN HAS LONG had a rather schizophrenic reputation as a vacation destination among English-speaking tourists. On the one hand, as Europe's premier package-vacation destination, the country is almost instinctively associated in many minds with the worst excesses of the cheap-holiday-in-the-sun, an image conjured up by the vast numbers of faceless hotels along the Mediterranean coasts. The other half of the equation is infinitely more appealing. For Spain is also the land of the fountain-singing courtyards of Moorish Granada and Córdoba, of dusty plains where Don Quixote fought imaginary enemies, and of timeless hilltop towns. Spain also acquired a new gloss on the international scene in 1992, when it played host to two major events of world stature: the Olympic Games in Barcelona, and the International Exposition in Seville. Both events brought with them major face-lifts to the cities and regions hosting them, as well as quite dramatic improvements to their infrastructures.

Still, if it's beaches you're after, there is the jet-set Costa del Sol in the south, or San Sebastián in the Basque country, formerly the summer capital of Spain. Farther west is the resort city of Santander and La Coruña, a long-standing favorite of British visitors. In the east is the Costa Brava, while to the south, around Alicante, is the Costa Blanca, with its most popular tourist center at Benidorm. When you tire of roasting in the sun, rent a car and head for one of the thousands of castles, ruins, or museums. Perhaps the number-one tourist attraction is the Alhambra, in Granada. Following close behind it come the Mosque of Córdoba, and the Alcázar (Moorish fortified palace) and cathedral of Seville. Àvila is a historic walled town and Segovia boasts a Roman aqueduct and proud Alcázar. Madrid, the capital, contains some of the greatest art collections in the world, while Toledo, home of El Greco and boasting a cathedral, synagogues, and startling views, is one of Spain's greatest treasures. Finally, Barcelona, capital of Catalonia, has a sophistication built on its obsession with design, from Gaudí at the turn of the century right up to the present day.

ESSENTIAL INFORMATION

Before You Go

When to Go

The tourist season runs from Easter to mid-October. The best months for sightseeing are May, June, September, and early October, when the weather is usually pleasant and sunny without being unbearably hot. During July and August try to avoid Madrid or the inland cities of Andalucía, where the heat can be stifling and many places close down at 1 PM. If you visit Spain in high summer, the best bet is to head for the coastal resorts or to mountain regions such as the Pyrenees or Picos de Europa. The one exception to Spain's high summer temperatures is the north coast, where the climate is similar to that of northern Europe.

Visitors should be aware of the seasonal events that can clog parts of the country, reserving in advance if traveling during peak periods. Easter is always a busy time, especially in Madrid, Barcelona, and the main Andalucían cities of Seville, Córdoba, Granada, Málaga, and the Costa del Sol resorts. July and August, when most Spaniards and other Europeans take their annual vacations, see the heaviest crowds, particularly in coastal resorts. Holiday weekends are naturally busy, and major fiestas, such as Pamplona's running of the bulls cause prices to soar. Off-season travel offers fewer crowds and lower rates in many hotels.

CLIMATE

The following are the average daily maximum and minimum temperatures for Madrid.

Jan.	47F	9C	**May**	70F	21C	**Sept.**	77F	25C
	35	2		50	10		57	14
Feb.	52F	11C	**June**	80F	27C	**Oct.**	65F	18C
	36	2		58	15		49	10
Mar.	59F	15C	**July**	87F	31C	**Nov.**	55F	13C
	41	5		63	17		42	5
Apr.	65F	18C	**Aug.**	85F	30C	**Dec.**	48F	9C
	45	7		63	17		36	2

Currency

The unit of currency in Spain is the peseta (pta.). There are bills of 1,000, 2,000, 5,000, and 10,000 ptas. Coins are 1, 5, 25, 50, 100, 200, and 500 ptas. The 2- and 10-pta. coins and the old 100-pta. bills are rare but still legal tender. Note that pay phones in Spain won't accept the new, smaller 5- and 25-pta. coins first minted in 1991. Following the recent European currency shakeup, which resulted in several devaluations of the peseta, most foreigners find that their currency now goes farther in Spain than it had in recent years. At press time (spring 1995), the exchange rate was about 131 ptas. to the U.S. dollar and 186 ptas. to the pound sterling.

CREDIT CARDS

Most hotels, restaurants, and stores accept payment by credit card. Visa is the most widely accepted piece of plastic, followed by MasterCard (called EuroCard in Spain). More expensive establishments may also take American Express and Diners Club.

CHANGING MONEY

The word to look for is CAMBIO (exchange). Most Spanish banks take a 1½% commission, though some less scrupulous places charge more; always check, as rates can vary greatly. To change money in a bank, you need your passport and a lot of patience, because filling out the forms takes time. Hotels offer rates lower than banks, but they rarely make a commission, so you may well break even. Restaurants and stores, with the exception of those catering to the tour bus trade, do not usually accept payment by dollars or traveler's checks. If you have a credit card with a Personal Identification Number (PIN), you'll be able to make withdrawals or get cash advances at most cash machines at Spanish banks.

CURRENCY REGULATIONS

Visitors may take any amount of foreign currency in bills or traveler's checks into Spain as well as any amount of pesetas. When leaving Spain, you may take out only 100,000 ptas. per person in Spanish bank notes and foreign currency up to the equivalent of 500,000 ptas., unless you can prove you declared the excess at customs on entering the country.

What It Will Cost

Prices rose fast during the first decade of Spain's democracy, and Spain's inflation rate was one of the highest in Europe. By the 1990s, however, inflation had been curbed; in 1994, it was just a little over 5%. Generally speaking, the cost of living in Spain is now on a par with that of most other European countries, and the days when Spain was the bargain basement of Europe are truly over, although the weakness of the peseta has somewhat improved the buying power of visi-

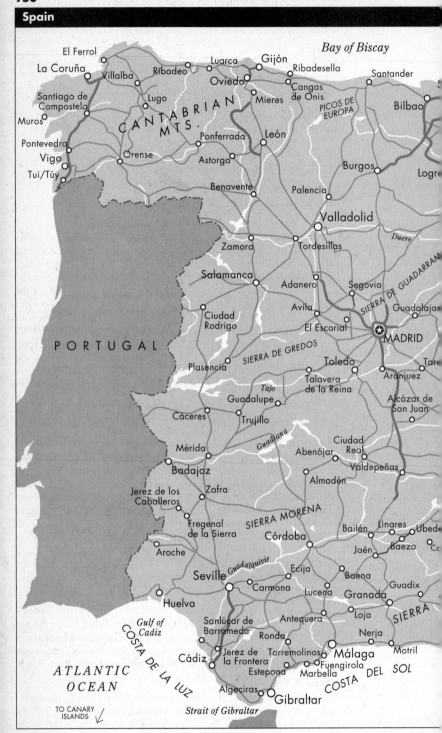

El Ferrol
La Coruña
Villalba
Ribadeo
Luarca
Gijón
Ribadesella
Santander
Bay of Biscay
Oviedo
Cangas de Onis
Santiago de Compostela
Lugo
Mieres
PICOS DE EUROPA
Bilbao
Muros
CANTABRIAN MTS.
León
Pontevedra
Ponferrada
Burgos
Logr
Vigo
Orense
Astorga
Tui/Túy
Benavente
Palencia
Valladolid
Zamora
Tordesillas
Duero
Salamanca
Adanero
Segovia
SIERRA DE GUADARRAM
Ciudad Rodrigo
Avila
Guadalajara
El Escorial
MADRID
PORTUGAL
SIERRA DE GREDOS
Toledo
Tare
Plasencia
Talavera de la Reina
Aranjuez
Tajo
Guadalupe
Alcázar de San Juan
Cáceres
Trujillo
Guadiana
Mérida
Ciudad Real
Abenójar
Badajaz
Zafra
Valdepeñas
Jerez de los Caballeros
Almadén
Fregenal de la Sierra
SIERRA MORENA
Córdoba
Bailén
Linares
Ubed
Aroche
Jaén
Baeza
Seville
Guadalquivir
Ecija
Baena
Guadix
Huelva
Carmona
Lucena
Granada
SIERRA
Gulf of Cadiz
Sanlúcar de Barrameda
Antequera
Loja
COSTA DE LA LUZ
Jerez de la Frontera
Ronda
Nerja
Cádiz
Torremolinos
Málaga
Motril
ATLANTIC OCEAN
Estepona
Fuengirola
Marbella
COSTA DEL SOL
Algeciras
Gibraltar
TO CANARY ISLANDS
Strait of Gibraltar

tors from North America and the United Kingdom. The 1992 completion of the country's integration into the European Union (EU) and the euphoria that accompanied the Olympic games and Seville's Expo '92 were, unfortunately, accompanied by sometimes shocking price increases. These have been reversed to a certain extent, though Seville and Barcelona are still quite expensive. In general, the cost of lodging is roughly comparable to that in France and Great Britain. You can still eat fairly cheaply in Spain, but if you go to high-quality restaurants, it will cost you dearly; in general, the cost of lodging has risen to make up for the peseta devaluation, while restaurant prices have remained stable. Snacks in cafés and bars are expensive by American or British standards, and alcohol is generally reasonable, except for cocktails in hotel bars. Trains and long-distance buses are relatively inexpensive, and car-rental rates are lower than in some European countries. City buses and subways are a good value, and cab fares are bargains compared with rates in the United States.

TAXES

A value-added tax known as IVA was introduced in 1986 when Spain joined the EU. IVA is levied at 6% on most goods and services, but it's 7% on hotels and 15% on car rentals. IVA is always included in the purchase price of goods in stores, but for hotels and car rentals, the tax will be added to your bill. Many restaurants include IVA in their menu prices, but plenty—usually the more expensive ones—do not. Large stores, such as the Corte Inglés and Galerías Preciados, operate a tax refund plan for foreign visitors who are not EU nationals; but to qualify for this refund, you need to spend at least 48,000 ptas. in any one store and, in theory, on any one item. There is no airport tax in Spain.

SAMPLE PRICES

A cup of coffee will cost around 125 ptas., a Coca-Cola 150 ptas., bottled beer 150 ptas., a small draught beer 100 ptas., a glass of wine in a bar 100 ptas., an American-style cocktail 400 ptas., a ham sandwich 300 ptas., an ice-cream cone about 150 ptas., a local bus or subway ride 125 ptas., and a 1-mile taxi ride about 350 ptas.

Language

In major cities and coastal resorts you should have no trouble finding people who speak English. In such places, reception staff in hotels of three or more stars are required to speak English. Don't expect the man in the street or the bus driver to speak English, although you may be pleasantly surprised.

Getting Around

By Car

ROAD CONDITIONS

Roads marked A (*autopista*) are toll roads. N stands for national or main roads, and C for country roads. A huge road improvement scheme has been largely completed, but many N roads are still single-lane and the going can be slow. Tolls vary but are high; for example, Bilbao–Zaragoza 2,930 ptas., Salou–Valencia 2,065 ptas., Seville–Jerez 585 ptas.

RULES OF THE ROAD

Driving is on the right, and horns and high-beam headlights may not be used in cities. Front seat belts are compulsory. Children under age 10 may not ride in front seats. At traffic circles, give way to traffic coming from the right unless your road has priority. Your home driving license is essential and must be carried with you at all times, along with your car insurance and vehicle registration document. You will also need an International Driving License and a proof-of-insurance Green Card if you are bringing your own car into Spain. Speed limits are 120 kph (74 mph) on autopistas, 100 kph (62 mph) on N roads, 90 kph (56 mph) on C roads, and 60 kph (37 mph) in cities unless otherwise signed.

PARKING
Parking restrictions should be checked locally. In many cities, a blue line on the street indicates residents-only parking; other cars are towed promptly. In other places, curbside signs inform you of legal parking times. Never leave *anything* on view inside a parked car. Thefts are common, and it is safer to leave your car in one of the many staffed parking lots; charges are reasonable.

GASOLINE
At press time (spring 1995), gas cost 106 ptas. a liter for super and 99 ptas. a liter for regular. *Sin plomo* (unleaded) gas is now available at a steadily increasing number of pumps. There is attendant service at most pumps, but there's no need to tip for just a fill-up. Most gas stations accept payment by credit card.

By Train
The Spanish railroad system, known usually by its initials RENFE, has greatly improved in recent years. Air-conditioned trains are now widespread but by no means universal. Most overnight trains have first- and second-class sleeping cars and second-class *literas* (couchettes). Dining, buffet, and refreshment services are available on most long-distance trains. There are various types of trains—*Talgo* (ultramodern), electric unit expresses (ELT), diesel rail cars (TER), and ordinary *expresos* and *rápidos*. Fares are determined by the kind of train you travel on and not just by the distance traveled. Talgos are by far the quickest, most comfortable, and the most expensive trains; expresos and rápidos are the slowest and cheapest of the long-distance services. In spring 1992, a high-speed train known as the Alto Velocidad Español (AVE) began service between Madrid and Seville, reducing travel time between these cities from 6 to 2½ hours (fares vary, but the AVE can cost almost as much as flying). A few lines, such as the narrow-gauge FEVE routes along the north coast from San Sebastián to El Ferrol and on the Costa Blanca around Alicante, do not belong to the national RENFE network, and international rail passes are not valid on these lines.

TICKET PURCHASE AND SEAT RESERVATION
Tickets can be bought from any station (regardless of your point of departure), and from downtown RENFE offices and travel agents displaying the blue and yellow RENFE sign. The latter are often best in the busy holiday season. At stations, buy your advance tickets from the window marked LARGO RECORRIDO, VENTA ANTICIPADA (Long Distance, Advance Sales). Seat reservation can be made up to 60 days in advance and is obligatory on all the better long-distance services.

FARE SAVERS
The **RENFE Tourist Card** is an unlimited-kilometers pass, valid for 3, 5, or 15 days' travel, and can be bought by anyone who lives outside Spain. It is available for first- or second-class travel and can be purchased from selected travel agencies and main railroad stations abroad; and in Spain at RENFE travel offices and major long-distance stations such as those in Madrid, Barcelona, Port Bou, and Irún. At press time (spring 1995) the second-class pass cost 15,650 ptas. for 3 days, 24,955 ptas. for 5 days, and 44,020 ptas. for 10 days. RENFE has no representative in the United States.

Prices are determined according to when the train leaves. There are three price categories: *valle* (low), *llano* (regular), and *punto* (high). On the most heavily used runs, Madrid–Barcelona or Madrid–Seville, for example, there is one valle and one punto train each day. The rest are in the llano price category. The cheapest train generally departs early in the morning, while the most expensive leaves at midday.

By Plane

Iberia and its subsidiary **Aviaco** operate a wide network of domestic flights, linking all the main cities and the Balearic Islands. Distances are great and internal airfares are high by U.S. standards, although deregulation is pushing prices lower. Flights from the mainland to the Balearics are heavily booked in summer, and the Madrid–Málaga route is frequently overbooked at Easter and in high season. A frequent shuttle service operates between Madrid and Barcelona. Iberia has its own offices in most major Spanish cities and acts as agent for Aviaco. In Madrid, Iberia headquarters are at Velázquez 130 (tel. 91/411–1011 for domestic reservations, and 91/329–4353 for international, or call Inforiberia for flight information, tel. 91/329–5767). Flights can also be booked at most travel agencies. Air Europa (91/305–5130) offers slightly cheaper service between Madrid and Barcelona as well as flights to the Canary Islands. For information on other airlines' flights to and within Spain, call the airline itself, or call the airport (tel. 91/305–8343, -44, -45, or -46) and ask for your airline.

By Bus

Spain has an excellent bus network, but there is no national or nationwide bus company. The network simply consists of numerous *empresas* (private regional bus companies) and there are therefore no comprehensive bus passes. Some of the buses on major routes are now quite luxurious, although this is not always the case in some of the more rural areas. Buses tend to be more frequent than trains, are sometimes cheaper, and often allow you to see more of the countryside. On major routes and at holiday times it is advisable to buy your ticket a day or two in advance. Some cities have central bus stations but in many, including Madrid and Barcelona, buses leave from various boarding points. Always check with the local tourist office. Bus stations, unlike train stations, usually provide luggage storage facilities.

Staying in Spain

Telephones

LOCAL CALLS

Pay phones are supposed to work with coins of 25 and either 50 or 100 ptas. (smaller 5- and 25-ptas. coins do not work in the machines). The minimum charge for short local calls is 25 ptas. In the older blue phones, place several coins in the slot, or in the groove on top of the phone, lift the receiver, and dial the number. Coins then fall into the machine as needed. In the newer green phones, place several coins in the slot, watch the display unit and feed as needed. These phones take 100-pta. coins. Area codes always begin with a 9 and are different for each province. In Madrid province, the code is 91; in Cantabria, it's 942. If you're dialing from outside the country, drop the 9.

INTERNATIONAL CALLS

Calling abroad can be done from any pay phone marked TELÉFONO INTERNACIONAL. Use 50-pta. (or 100-pta. if the phone takes them) coins initially, then coins of any denomination to prolong your call. Dial 07 for international, wait for the tone to change, then 1 for the United States, 0101 for Canada, or 44 for England, followed by the area code and number. For calls to England, omit the initial 0 from the area code. For lengthy international calls, go to the *telefónica*, a telephone office found in all sizable towns, where an operator assigns you a private booth and collects payment at the end of the call; this is the least expensive and by far the easiest way of phoning abroad.

OPERATORS AND INFORMATION

For the operator and information for any part of Spain, dial 003. If you're in Madrid, dial 008 to make collect calls to countries in Europe; 005 for the rest of the world. Private long-distance companies now have special access numbers: **AT&T** (tel. 900/99–00–11), **MCI** (tel. 900/99–00–14), **Sprint** (tel. 900/99–00–13).

Mail

POSTAL RATES

To the United States, airmail letters up to 15 grams and postcards each cost 90 ptas. (These were the rates at press time, spring 1995). To the United Kingdom and other EU countries, letters up to 20 grams and postcards each cost 45 ptas. To non–EU European countries, letters and postcards up to 20 grams cost 60 ptas. If you wish to expedite your overseas mail, send it *urgente* for 160 ptas. more than the regular airmail cost. Within Spain, letters and postcards each cost 27 ptas.; within a city in Spain, letters and postcards cost 17 ptas. Mailboxes are yellow with red stripes, and the slot marked EXTRANJERO is the one for mail going abroad. Buy your *sellos* (stamps) at a *correos* (post office) or in a *estanco* (tobacco shop).

RECEIVING MAIL

If you're uncertain where you'll be staying, have mail sent to American Express or addressed to "poste restante" or *lista de correos* and mailed to the local post office. To claim your mail, you'll need to show your passport. American Express has a $2 service charge per letter for non-cardholders. The Spanish mail is notoriously slow and not always very efficient.

Shopping

SALES TAX REFUNDS

If you purchase goods up to a value of 48,000 ptas. or more in any one store (and in theory this should be on only one item), you are entitled to a refund of the IVA tax paid (usually 6% but more in the case of certain luxury goods), provided that you leave Spain within three months. You will be given two copies of the sales invoice, which you must present at customs together with the goods as you leave Spain. Once the invoice has been stamped by customs, mail the blue copy back to the store, which will then mail your tax refund to you. If you are leaving via the airports of Madrid, Barcelona, Málaga or Palma de Mallorca, you can get your tax refund immediately from the Banco Exterior de España in the airport. The above does not apply to residents of EU countries, who must claim their IVA refund through customs in their own countries. The Corte Inglés and Galerías Preciados department stores operate the above system, but don't be surprised if other stores are unfamiliar with the tax-refund procedure and do not have the necessary forms.

BARGAINING

Prices in city stores and produce markets are fixed; bargaining is possible only in flea markets, some antiques stores, and with gypsy vendors, with whom it is *essential*, though you'd do best to turn them down flat as their goods are almost always fake and grossly overpriced.

Opening and Closing Times

Banks are open Monday to Saturday 9–2 from October to June; during the summer months they are closed on Saturdays.

Museums and churches. Opening times vary. Most are open in the morning, and most museums close one day a week, often Monday.

Post offices are usually open weekdays 9–2, but this can vary; check locally.

Stores are open weekdays from 9 or 10 until 1:30 or 2, then again in the afternoon from around 5 to 8. In some cities, especially in summer, stores close on Saturday afternoon. The Corte Inglés and Galerías Preciados department stores in major cities are open continuously from 10 to 8, and some stores in tourist resorts also stay open through the siesta.

National Holidays

January 1; January 6 (Epiphany); April 5 (Good Friday); May 1 (May Day); July 25 (St. James); August 15 (Assumption); October 12 (National Day); November 1 (All Saints' Day); December 6 (Constitution); December 8 (Immaculate Conception); December 25. Other holidays include May 2 (in the province of Madrid) and March 19 (St. Joseph). These holidays are not celebrated in every region; always check locally.

Dining

Visitors have a choice of restaurants, tapas bars, and cafés. Restaurants are strictly for lunch and dinner; they do not serve breakfast. Tapas bars are ideal for a glass of wine or beer accompanied by an array of tapas. Cafés, called *cafeterías,* are basically coffee shops that serve snacks, light meals, tapas, pastries, and coffee, tea, and alcoholic drinks. They also serve breakfast and are perfect for afternoon tea.

MEALTIMES

Mealtimes in Spain are much later than in any other European country. Lunch begins between 1 and 2:30, with 2 being the usual time, and 3 more normal on Sunday. Dinner is usually available from 8:30 onward, but 10 PM is the usual time in the larger cities and resorts. Lunch is the main meal, not dinner. Tapas bars are busiest between noon and 2 and from 8 PM on. Cafés are usually open from around 8 AM to midnight.

PRECAUTIONS

Tap water is safe to drink in all but the remotest villages (in Madrid, tap water, from the surrounding Guadarrama Mountains, is excellent; in Barcelona, it's safe but tastes terrible). However, most Spaniards drink bottled mineral water; ask for either *agua sin gas* (without bubbles) or *agua con gas* (with bubbles). A good paella should be served only at lunchtime and should be prepared to order (usually 30 minutes); beware the all-too-cheap version.

TYPICAL DISHES

Paella—a mixture of saffron-flavored rice with seafood, chicken, and vegetables—is Spain's national dish. Gazpacho, a cold soup usually made of crushed garlic, tomatoes, and olive oil and garnished with diced vegetables, is a traditional Andalucían dish and is served mainly in summer. The Basque Country and Galicia are the gourmet regions of Spain, and both serve outstanding fish and seafood. Asturias is famous for its *fabadas* (bean stews), cider, and dairy products; Extremadura for its hams and sausages; and Castile for its roasts, especially *cochinillo* (suckling pig), *cordero asado* (roast lamb), and *perdiz* (partridge). The best wines are those from the Rioja and Penedés regions. Valdepeñas is a pleasant table wine, and most places serve a perfectly acceptable house wine; ask for *vino de la casa*. Sherries from Jerez de la Frontera make fine aperitifs; ask for a *fino* or a *manzanilla;* both are dry. In summer you can try *horchata,* a sweet white drink made from ground nuts, or *granizados de limón* or *de café,* lemon juice or coffee served over crushed ice. *Un café solo* is a small, black, espresso coffee, and *café con leche* is coffee with cream, cappuccino-style; weak black American-style coffee is hard to come by.

WHAT TO WEAR
In **$$$$** and **$$$** restaurants, jacket and tie are the norm. Elsewhere, casual dress is appropriate.

RATINGS
Spanish restaurants are officially classified from five forks down to one fork, with most places falling into the two- or three-fork category. In our rating system, prices are per person and include a first course, main course, and dessert, but not wine or tip. Sales tax (IVA) is usually included in the menu price; check the menu for *IVA incluído* or *IVA no incluído.* When it's not included, an additional 6% (15% in the fancier restaurants) will be added to your bill. Most restaurants offer a prix-fixe menu called a *menú del día;* however, this is often offered only at lunch, and at dinner tends to be merely a reheated midday offering. This is usually the cheapest way to eat; à la carte dining is more expensive. Service charges are never added to your bill; leave around 10%, less in **$** restaurants and bars. Major centers such as Madrid, Barcelona, Marbella, and Seville tend to be a bit more expensive. Highly recommended restaurants are indicated by a star ★.

CATEGORY	COST
$$$$	over 9,000 ptas.
$$$	6,000 ptas.–9,000 ptas.
$$	3,000 ptas.–6,000 ptas.
$	under 3,000 ptas.

Lodging
Spain has a wide range of accommodations, including luxury palaces, medieval monasteries, converted 19th-century houses, modern hotels, high rises on the coasts, and inexpensive hostels in family homes. All hotels and hostels are listed with their rates in the annual *Guía de Hoteles* available from bookstores and kiosks for around 1,000 ptas., or you can see a copy in local tourist offices. Rates are always quoted per room, and not per person. Single occupancy of a double room costs 80% of the normal price. Breakfast is rarely included in the quoted room rate; always check. The quality of rooms, particularly in older properties, can be uneven; always ask to see your room *before* you sign the acceptance slip. If you want a private bathroom in a less expensive hotel, state your preference for shower or bathtub; the latter usually costs more though many hotels have both.

HOTELS AND HOSTELS
Hotels are officially classified from five stars (the highest) to one star, hostels from three stars to one star. Hostels—not the youth hostels associated with the word in most countries—are usually family homes converted to provide accommodations that often occupy only part of a building. If an R appears on the blue hotel or hostel plaque, the hotel is classified as a *residencia,* and full dining services are not provided, though breakfast and cafeteria facilities may be available. A three-star hostel is usually comparable to a two-star hotel; two- and one-star hostels offer simple, basic accommodations.

The main hotel chains are Husa, Iberotel Melia, Sol, and Tryp, and the state-run *paradores* (tourist hotels; paradors). Holiday Inn, Inter-Continental, and Forte also own some of the best hotels in Madrid, Barcelona, and Seville; only these and the paradors have any special character. The others mostly provide clean, comfortable accommodation in the two- to four-star range.

In many hotels, rates vary fairly dramatically according to the time of year. The hotel year is divided into *temporada alta, media,* and *baja* (high, mid, and low season); high season usually covers the summer and Easter and Christmas periods, plus the major fiestas. IVA is rarely included in the quoted room rates, so be prepared for an additional 6% to be added to your bill. Service charges are never included.

PARADORS

There about 100 state-owned-and-run paradors, many of which are in magnificent medieval castles or convents or in places of great natural beauty. Most of these fall into the four-star category and are priced accordingly. Most have restaurants that specialize in local regional cuisine and serve a full breakfast. The most popular paradors are booked far in advance. For more information or to make reservations, contact **Paradores** (Requena 3, 28013 Madrid, tel. 91/559–0069, fax 91/559–3233), **Keytel International** (402 Edgware Rd., London, W2 1ED, tel. 0171/402–8182) or **Marketing Ahead Inc.** (433 5th Ave., New York, NY 10016, tel. 212/686–9213).

VILLAS

Villas are plentiful all along the Mediterranean coast, and cottages in Cantabria and Asturias on the north coast are available from a few agencies. Several agencies in both the United States and United Kingdom specialize in renting property; check with the Spanish National Tourist Office.

CAMPING

There are approximately 530 campsites in Spain, with the highest concentration along the Mediterranean coast. The season runs from April through October, though some sites are open year-round. Sites are listed in the annual publication *Guía de Campings* available from bookstores or local tourist offices, and further details are available from the Spanish National Tourist Office. Reservations for the most popular seaside sites can be made either directly with the site or through camping reservations at: Federación Española de Campings, Príncipe de Vergara 85, 2°-dcha, 28006 Madrid, tel. 91/562–9994.

RATINGS

Prices are for two people in a double room and do not include breakfast. Highly recommended lodgings are indicated by a star ★.

CATEGORY	MAJOR CITY	OTHER AREAS
$$$$	over 20,000 ptas.	over 18,000 ptas.
$$$	14,000 ptas.–20,000 ptas.	12,000 ptas.–18,000 ptas.
$$	9,000 ptas.–14,000 ptas.	7,000 ptas.–12,000 ptas.
$	under 9,000 ptas.	under 7,000 ptas.

In Gibraltar, **$$$**: *£65–£75 ($104–$120);* **$$**: *£40–£46 ($64–$74) (not including tax).*

Tipping

Spaniards appreciate being tipped, though the practice is becoming less widespread. Restaurants and hotels are by law not allowed to add a service charge to your bill, though confusingly, your bill for both will most likely say *servicios e impuestos incluídos* (service and tax included). Ignore this unhelpful piece of advice, and leave 10% in most restaurants where you have had a full meal; in humbler eating places, bars, and cafés, 5%–10% is enough, or you can round out the bill to the nearest 100 ptas. A cocktail waiter in a hotel will expect at least 30 ptas. a drink, maybe 50 ptas. in a luxury establishment. Tip taxi drivers about 5% to 10% when they use the meter, otherwise *nothing*—they'll have seen to it themselves. Gas station attendants get no tip for pumping gas, but they get about 50 ptas. for checking tires and oil and cleaning windshields. Train and airport porters usually operate on a fixed rate of 60 ptas.–100 ptas. a bag. Coat-check attendants get 25 ptas.–50 ptas., and rest-room attendants get 10 ptas.–25 ptas. In top hotels, doormen get 100 ptas.–150 ptas. for carrying bags to the check-in counter or for hailing taxis, and bellhops get 100 ptas. for room service or for each bag they carry to your room. In moderate hotels about 50 ptas. is adequate for the same services. Leave your chambermaid about 300 ptas. for a week's stay. There's no need to tip for just a couple of nights.

MADRID

Arriving and Departing

By Plane

All international and domestic flights arrive at Madrid's Barajas Airport (tel. 91/305–8343), 16 kilometers (10 miles) northeast of town just off the N-II Barcelona highway. For information on arrival and departure times, call **Inforiberia** (tel. 91/329–5767) or the airline concerned.

BETWEEN THE AIRPORT AND DOWNTOWN

Buses leave the national and international terminals every 15 minutes from 5:40 AM to 2 AM for the downtown terminal at Plaza de Colón just off the Paseo de la Castellana. The ride takes about 20 minutes and the fare at press time (spring 1995) was 325 ptas. Most city hotels are then only a short taxi ride away. The fastest and most expensive route into town (usually about 1,500 ptas., but up to 2,000 ptas. plus tip in traffic) is by taxi. Pay what is on the meter plus 350 ptas. surcharge and 150 ptas. for each suitcase. By car, take the N-II, which becomes Avenida de América, into town, then head straight into Calle María de Molina and left on either Calle Serrano or the Castellana.

By Train

Madrid has three railroad stations. Chamartín, in the northern suburbs beyond the Plaza de Castilla, is the main station, with trains to France and the north (including Barcelona, Segovia, El Escorial, Santiago, and La Coruña). Most trains to Valencia, Alicante, and Andalucía now leave from here, too, but stop at Atocha station, at the southern end of Paseo del Prado on the Glorieta del Emperador Carlos V. Also departing from Atocha, where a new station was built in 1989, are trains to Toledo, Granada, Extremadura, and Lisbon. In 1992, a convenient new metro stop (Atocha RENFE) was opened in Atocha station, connecting it to the city subway system. The old Atocha station, designed by Eiffel, was refurbished and reopened in 1992 as the Madrid terminus for a new high-speed rail service to Seville. Norte (or Príncipe Pío), on Paseo de la Florida, in the west of town below the Plaza de España, is the departure point for local trains to the Madrid suburbs.

For all train information, call RENFE (tel. 91/563–0202, in Spanish and English), or go to its offices at Alcalá 4, or on the second floor of Torre de Madrid in the Plaza de España, right above the main tourist office (open weekdays 9–7, Sat. 9:30–1:30). There's another RENFE office at Barajas Airport in the International Arrivals Hall, or you can purchase tickets at any of the three main stations, or from travel agents displaying the blue and yellow RENFE sign.

By Bus

Madrid has no central bus station. The two main bus stations are the Estación del Sur (Canarias 17, tel. 91/468–4200), near the metro Palos de la Frontera, for buses to Toledo, La Mancha, Alicante, and Andalucía; and Auto-Rés (Plaza Conde de Casal 6, tel. 91/551–7200), near the metro Conde de Casal, for buses to Extremadura, Cuenca, Salamanca, Valladolid, Valencia, and Zamora. Auto-Rés has a central ticket and information office at Salud 19 near the Hotel Arosa, just off Gran Vía. Buses to other destinations leave from various points, so check with the tourist office. The Basque country and most of north central Spain is served by Auto Continental (Alenza 20, near the metro Ríos Rosas, tel. 91/533–0400). For Àvila, Segovia, and La Granja, Empresa La Sepulvedana (tel. 91/527–9537) leaves from Paseo de la Florida 11, next to the Norte station, a few steps from the Norte metro stop. Empresa Herranz (tel. 91/543–3645 or 91/543–8167), serving San Lorenzo de El Escorial and the Valley of the Fallen, departs from the base of Calle Fernandez de los Ríos, a few yards from the Moncloa metro stop. La Veloz (Avda. Mediterraneo 49, tel. 91/409–7602) serves Chinchón.

By Car

The main roads are north–south, the Paseo de la Castellana and Paseo del Prado; and east–west, Calle de Alcalá, Gran Vía, and Calle de la Princesa. The M30 ring road circles Madrid and the M40 is an outer ring road scheduled to have been completed in 1995. For Burgos and France, drive north up the Castellana and follow the signs for the N-I. For Barcelona, head up the Castellana to Plaza Dr. Marañón, then right onto María de Molina and the N-II; for Andalucía and Toledo, head south down Paseo del Prado, then follow the signs to the N-IV and N401, respectively. For Segovia, Ávila, and El Escorial, head west along Princesa to Avenida Puerta de Hierro and onto the N-VI La Coruña road.

Getting Around

Madrid is a fairly compact city and most of the main sights can be visited on foot. But if you're staying in one of the modern hotels in the north of town off the Castellana, you may well need to use the bus or subway. As a rough guide, the walk from the Prado to the Royal Palace at a comfortable sightseeing pace but without stopping takes around 30 minutes; from Plaza del Callao on Gran Vía to the Plaza Mayor, it takes about 15 minutes.

By Metro

The metro offers the simplest and quickest means of transport and is open from 6 AM to 1:30 AM. Metro maps are available from ticket offices, hotels, and tourist offices. Fares at press time (spring 1995) were 125 ptas. a ride. Savings can be made by buying a 10-ride ticket for 625 ptas. Keep some change (5, 25, 50, and 100 ptas.) handy for the ticket machines, especially after 10 PM; the machines give change and are handy for beating often long lines for tickets.

By Bus

City buses are red and run from 6 AM to midnight (though check, as some stop earlier). Again there is a flat-fare system, with each ride costing 125 ptas. Route plans are displayed at *paradas* (bus stops), and a map of the entire system is available from Empresa Municipal de Transportes (EMT) booths on Plaza de la Cibeles, Callao, or Puerta del Sol. Savings can be made by buying a **Bonobus** (625 ptas.), good for 10 rides, from EMT booths or any tobacco shop.

By Taxi

Madrid has more than 18,000 taxis, and fares are low by New York or London standards. The meter starts at 170 ptas. and each additional kilometer costs 70 ptas. The average city ride costs about 500 ptas., and there is a surcharge of 150 ptas. between 11 PM and 6 AM and on holidays from 6 AM to 11 PM. A supplemental fare of 150 ptas. applies to trips to the bullring or soccer matches, and there is a charge of 150 ptas. per suitcase. The airport surcharge is 350 ptas. Cabs available for hire display a LIBRE sign during the day and a green light at night. They hold four passengers. Make sure the driver puts his meter on when you start your ride, and tip from 5% to 10% of the fare.

Important Addresses and Numbers

Tourist Information

The main Madrid tourist office (tel. 91/541–2325) is on the ground floor of the Torre de Madrid in Plaza de España, near the beginning of Calle de la Princesa, and is open weekdays 9–7, Saturdays 9:30–1:30. Another Madrid Provincial Tourist Office (Duque de Medinacelli 2, tel. 91/429–4951) is on a small street across from the Palace Hotel. The much less useful municipal tourist office is at Plaza Mayor 3 (tel. 91/366–4874) and is open weekdays 10–8, Saturdays 10–2. A third office is in the International Arrivals Hall of Barajas Airport (tel. 91/305–8656) and is open weekdays 8–8, Saturdays 9–1.

Embassies

U.S. (Serrano 75, tel. 91/577–4000), **Canadian** (Núñez de Balboa 35, tel. 91/431–4300), **U.K.** (Fernando el Santo 16, tel. 91/319–0200).

Emergencies

Police: (emergencies, tel. 091; Municipal Police, tel. 092 for towed cars or traffic accidents). To report lost passports, go to Los Madrazos 9 just off the top of Paseo del Prado (tel. 91/521–9350). **Ambulance:** tel. 91/522–2222 or 91/588–4400. **Doctor:** Your hotel reception will contact the nearest doctor for you. Emergency clinics: **Hospital 12 de Octubre** (Avda. Córdoba, tel. 91/390–8000) and **La Paz Ciudad Sanitaria** (Paseo de la Castellana 261, tel. 91/358–2600). English-speaking doctors are available at British-American Medical Unit (Conde de Aranda 7, tel. 91/435–1823). **Pharmacies:** A list of pharmacies open 24 hours (*farmacias de guardia*) is published daily in *El País*. Hotel receptions usually have a copy. **Company** (Puerta del Sol 14, tel. 91/521–3625) has English-speaking pharmacists. It does not stock American medicines but will recognize many American brand names.

English-Language Bookstores

Booksellers (José Abascal 48, tel. 91/442–8104) and **Turner's English Bookshop** (Génova 3, tel. 91/319–0926) both have large selections of English-language books.

Travel Agencies

American Express (Plaza de las Cortes 2, tel. 91/322–5500), **Marsans** (Gran Vía 59, tel. 91/547–7300), **Wagons-Lits** (Alcalá 23, tel. 91/522–4334).

Airlines

Iberia (Velázquez 130, tel. 91/411–1011 for domestic reservations or tel. 91/329–4353 for international flights; for flight information, call Inforiberia, tel. 91/329–5767), **British Airways** (Serrano 60, 5th Floor, tel. 91/431–7575), **TWA** (Plaza de Colón 2, tel. 91/310–1905 or 91/305–4290), and **United** (Goya 6, tel. 91/578–0177).

Guided Tours

Orientation Tours

City sightseeing tours are run by **Julià Tours** (Gran Vía 68, tel. 91/559–9605), **Pullmantur** (Plaza de Oriente 8, tel. 91/541–1807), and **Trapsatur** (San Bernardo 23, tel. 91/302–6039). All three run the same tours, mostly in 48-seat buses and conducted in Spanish and English. Book tours directly with the offices above, through any travel agent, or through your hotel. Departure points are from the addresses above, though in many cases you can be picked up at your hotel. "Madrid Artístico" is a morning tour of the city with visits to the Royal Palace and Prado Museum, entrance fees included. The "Madrid Panorámico" tour includes the University City, Casa del Campo park, and the northern reaches of the Castellana. This is a half-day tour, usually in the afternoon, and makes an ideal orientation for the first-time visitor. Also offered are "Madrid de Noche," a night tour combining a drive around the illuminations, dinner in a restaurant, a flamenco show, and cabaret at La Scala nightclub; and "Panorámico y Toros," on bullfight days only (usually Sunday), a panoramic drive and visit to a bullfight. Trapsatur also runs the *Madridvision* tourist bus, which makes a one-hour sightseeing tour of the city with recorded commentary in English. No reservation is necessary. Catch the bus in front of the Prado Museum every 1½ hours beginning at 12:30 Monday through Saturday or 10:30 Sunday. A round-trip ticket costs 1,500 ptas. and a day pass, which allows you to get on or off at various attractions, is 2,000 ptas.

Walking and Special-Interest Tours

Those who understand Spanish can take advantage of a hugely popular selection of tours recently launched by the **Ayuntamiento** (city hall) under the title "Discubre Madrid." Walking tours are held most mornings year-round and visit many of the capital's hidden corners, as well as the major sights. Special-interest tours include "Madrid's Railroads," "Medicine in Madrid," "Goya's Madrid," and "Commerce and Finance in Madrid." Some tours are by bus, others on foot. Schedules are listed in the "Discubre Madrid" leaflet available from the municipal tourist office and tickets can be purchased at the Patronato de Turismo (Calle Mayor 69, 91/588–2900).

Excursions

Julià Tours, Pullmantur, and **Trapsatur** run full- or half-day trips to El Escorial, Ávila, Segovia, Toledo, and Aranjuez, and in summer to Cuenca and Salamanca; for additional details, *see* Madrid Environs, *below.* The "Tren de la Fresa" (Strawberry Train) is a popular excursion on summer weekends; a 19th-century train carries passengers from the old Delicias Station to Aranjuez and back. Tickets can be obtained from RENFE offices, travel agents, and the Delicias Station (Paseo de las Delicias 61). Other one- or two-day excursions by train to such

places as Àvila, Cuenca, or Salamanca are available on summer weekends. Contact RENFE for details.

Exploring Madrid

*Numbers in the margin correspond to points of interest on the Madrid
map.*

You can walk the following route in a day, or even half a day if you
stop only to visit the Prado and Royal Palace. Two days should give
you time for browsing. Begin in the Plaza Atocha, more properly
known as the Glorieta del Emperador Carlos V, at the bottom of the

❶ Paseo del Prado, and check out what's showing in the **Centro de Arte
Reina Sofía** (Queen Sofía Arts Center) opened by Queen Sofía in 1986.
This converted hospital, home of art and sculpture exhibitions and symbol of Madrid's new cultural pride, is fast becoming one of Europe's
most dynamic venues—a Madrileño rival to Paris's Pompidou Center.
It is also home to Picasso's *Guernica,* the horrific painting depicting
the April 1937 carpet bombing of the Basque Country's traditional capital by Nazi warplanes aiding Franco during the Spanish Civil War
(1936–39). The main entrance is on Calle de Santa Isabel 52. *Tel.
91/467–5062. Admission: 400 ptas. Open Mon., Wed.–Sat. 10–9; Sun.
10–2:30. Admission free Sat. 2:30–9 and Sun.*

Walk up Paseo del Prado to Madrid's number-one sight, the famous

❷ **Museo del Prado** (Prado Museum), one of the world's most important
art galleries. Plan to spend half a day here, though it will take at least
two full days to view its treasures properly. Brace yourself for the crowds.
The greatest treasures—the Velázquez, Murillo, Zurbarán, El Greco,
and Goya galleries—are all on the upper floor. Two of the best works
are Velázquez's *Surrender of Breda* and his most famous work, *Las
Meninas,* which occupies a privileged position in a room of its own.
The Goya galleries contain the artist's none-too-flattering royal portraits—Goya believed in painting the truth—his exquisitely beautiful
Marquesa de Santa Cruz, and his famous *Naked Maja* and *Clothed
Maja,* for which the 13th duchess of Alba was said to have posed. Goya's
most moving works, the *Second of May* and the *Fusillade of Moncloa*
or *Third of May,* vividly depict the sufferings of Madrid patriots at the
hands of Napoléon's invading troops in 1808. Before you leave, feast
your eyes on the fantastic flights of fancy of Hieronymus Bosch's *Garden of Earthly Delights* and his triptych *The Hay Wagon,* both on the
ground floor. *Paseo del Prado s/n, tel. 91/420–2836. Admission: 400
ptas. Open Tues.–Sat. 9–7, Sun. 9–2.*

❸ Across the street is the **Ritz,** the grand old lady of Madrid's hotels, built
in 1910 by Alfonso XIII when he realized that his capital had had no
hotels elegant enough to accommodate the guests at his wedding in 1906.
The Ritz garden is a delightfully aristocratic place to lunch in summer.

❹ The **Museo Thyssen-Bornemisza** across the plaza Neptuno was opened
in 1992 in the Villahermosa Palace—elegantly renovated to include plenty
of airy spaces and natural light. This ambitious collection of 800 paintings attempts to trace the history of Western art with examples from
all the important movements beginning with 13th-century Italy. Among
the museum's gems are the *Portrait of Henry VIII* by Hans Holbein,
purchased from Princess Diana's grandfather, who used the money to
buy a new Bugatti sports car. Two halls are devoted to the Impressionists and Post-Impressionists and contain many works by Pissarro and
canvases by Renoir, Monet, Degas, Van Gogh, and Cézanne. Among
the more recent movements represented are terror-filled examples of Ger-

man Expressionism, but there are also soothing paintings by Georgia O'Keeffe and Andrew Wyeth. *Paseo del Prado 8, tel. 91/420–3944. Admission: 600 ptas., under 12 free. Open Tues.–Sun. 10–7.*

⑤ The **Parque del Retiro** (Retiro Park) once a royal retreat, is today Madrid's prettiest park. Visit the beautiful rose garden, **La Rosaleda,** and enjoy the many statues and fountains. You can hire a carriage, row a boat on **El Estanque,** gaze up at the monumental **statue to Alfonso XII,** one of Spain's least notable kings though you wouldn't think so to judge by its size, or wonder at the **Monument to the Fallen Angel—** Madrid claims the dubious privilege of being the only capital to have a statue dedicated to the Devil. The **Palacio de Velázquez** and the beautiful steel-and-glass **Palacio de Cristal,** built as a tropical plant house in the 19th century, now host art exhibits.

⑥ Leaving the Retiro via its northwest corner, you come to the Plaza de la Independencia, dominated by the **Puerta de Alcalá,** a grandiose gateway built in 1779 for Charles III. A customs post once stood beside the gate, as did the old bullring until it was moved to its present site at Las Ventas in the 1920s. At the turn of the century, the Puerta de Alcalá more or less marked the eastern limits of Madrid.

⑦ Continue to the **Plaza de la Cibeles,** one of the great landmarks of the city, at the intersection of its two main arteries, the Castellana and Calle de Alcalá. If you can see it through the roar and fumes of the thundering traffic, the square's center is the **Cibeles Fountain,** the unofficial emblem of Madrid. Cybele, the Greek goddess of fertility, languidly rides her lion-drawn chariot, overlooked by the mighty **Palacio de Comunicaciónes,** a splendidly pompous cathedral-like post office.

TIME OUT To rest your feet and sip a cup of coffee or a beer, head about one block up the center boulevard of the Paseo Recoletos and pull up a chair on the shady terrace or inside the air-conditioned, stained-glass-windowed bar of **El Espejo** (Paseo Recoletos 31).

⑧ Now head down the long and busy Calle de Alcalá toward the Puerta del Sol, resisting the temptation to turn right up the Gran Vía, which beckons temptingly with its mile of stores and cafés. Before reaching the Puerta del Sol, art lovers may want to step inside the **Real Academia de San Fernando** at Alcalá 13. This recently refurbished fine arts gallery boasts an art collection second only to the Prado's and features all the great Spanish masters: Velázquez, El Greco, Murillo, Zurbarán, Ribera, and Goya. *Alcalá 13, tel. 91/532–1546. Admission: 200 ptas., free Sat and Sun. Open Tues.–Fri. 9-7; Sat.–Mon. 9–2:30.*

⑨ The **Puerta del Sol** is at the very heart of Madrid. Its name means Gate of the Sun, though the old gate disappeared long ago. It's easy to feel you're at the heart of things here—indeed, of all of Spain—for the kilometer distances for the whole nation are measured from the zero marker in front of the Police Headquarters. The square was expertly revamped in 1986 and now accommodates both a copy of **La Mariblanca** (a statue that 250 years ago adorned a fountain here) and, at the bottom of Calle Carmen, the much-loved statue of the **bear and madroño** (strawberry tree). The Puerta del Sol is inextricably linked with the history of Madrid and of the nation. Here, half a century ago, a generation of literati gathered in the long-gone cafés to thrash out the burning issues of the day; and if you can cast your thoughts back almost 200 years, you can conjure up the heroic deeds of the patriots' uprising immortalized by Goya in the *Second of May.*

This is a good place to break the tour if you've had enough sightseeing for one day. Head north up Preciados or Montera for some of the busiest shopping streets in the city or southeast toward Plaza Santa Ana for tavern-hopping in Old Madrid.

TIME OUT If it's teatime (6–7 PM), don't miss **La Mallorquina** (Calle Mayor 2, tel. 91/521-1201), an old pastry shop between Calle Mayor and Arenal. Delicious pastries are sold at the downstairs counter; the old-fashioned upstairs tea salon offers an age-old tea ritual and unbeatable views over the Puerta del Sol.

❿ Art lovers will want to make a detour to the **Convento de las Descalzas Reales** on Plaza Descalzas Reales just above Arenal. It was founded by Juana de Austria, daughter of Charles V, and is still inhabited by nuns. Over the centuries the nuns, daughters of the royal and noble, endowed the convent with an enormous wealth of jewels, religious ornaments, superb Flemish tapestries, and the works of such great masters as Titian and Rubens. A bit off the main tourist track, it's one of Madrid's better-kept secrets. Your ticket includes admission to the nearby, but less interesting, **Convento de la Encarnación.** *Plaza de las Descalzas Reales, tel. 91/559–7404. Admission: 600 ptas. Open Tues.–Thurs., Sat. 10:30–12:30 and 4–5:30; Fri. 10:30–12:30, and Sun. 11–1:30. Guided tours in Spanish only.*

⓫ Walk up **Calle Mayor,** the Main Street of Old Madrid, past the shops full of religious statues and satins for bishops' robes, to the **Plaza Mayor,** the capital's greatest architectural showpiece. It was built in 1617–19 for Philip III—that's Philip on the horse in the middle. The plaza has witnessed the canonization of saints, burning of heretics, fireworks and bullfights, and is still one of the great gathering places of Madrid.

⓬ If you're here in the morning, take a look inside the 19th-century steel-and-glass San Miguel market, a colorful provisions market, before continuing down Calle Mayor to the **Plaza de la Villa.** The square's notable cluster of buildings includes some of the oldest houses in Madrid. The **Casa de la Villa,** the Madrid city hall, was built in 1644 and has also served as the city prison and the mayor's home. Its sumptuous salons are occasionally open to the public; ask about guided tours, which are sometimes offered in English. An archway joins the Casa de la Villa to the **Casa Cisneros,** a palace built in 1537 for the nephew of Cardinal Cisneros, primate of Spain and infamous inquisitor general. Across the square, the **Torre de Lujanes** is one of the oldest buildings in Madrid. It once imprisoned Francis I of France, archenemy of the Emperor Charles V.

TIME OUT If it's lunchtime, close by is a moderately priced restaurant with turn-of-the-century decor: **Fuente Real** (Calle de las Fuentes 1, tel. 91/559-6613).

⓭ The last stop on the tour, but Madrid's second most important sight, is the **Palacio Real** (Royal Palace). This magnificent granite and limestone residence was begun by Philip V, the first Bourbon king of Spain, who was always homesick for his beloved Versailles, the opulence and splendor of which he did his best to emulate. His efforts were successful, to judge by the 2,800 rooms with their lavish Rococo decorations, precious carpets, porcelain, time pieces, mirrors, and chandeliers. From 1764, when Charles III first moved in, till the coming of the Second Republic and the abdication of Alfonso XIII in 1931, the Royal Palace proved a very stylish abode for Spanish monarchs. Today King Juan Carlos, who lives in the far less ostentatious Zarzuela Palace outside Madrid, uses it only for official state functions. Allow 1½–2 hours for

966

Major Attractions

Centro de Arte
Reina Sofía, **1**
Cibeles Fountain, **7**
Convento de las
Descalzas Reales, **10**
Museo del Prado, **2**
Museo Thyssen-
Bornemisza, **4**
Palacio Real, **13**
Parque del Retiro, **5**
Plaza de la Villa, **12**
Plaza Mayor, **11**
Puerta de Alcalá, **6**
Puerta del Sol, **9**
Real Academia de San
Fernando, **8**
Ritz, **3**
Royal Carriage Mu-
seum, **14**

Other Attractions

Biblioteca Nacional, **19**
Municipal Museum, **16**
Museo   Arque-
ológico, **20**
Museo de Artes Deco-
rativas, **21**
Museo de Cera
(Wax Museum), **18**
Museo Romántico, **17**
Torre de Madrid, **15**

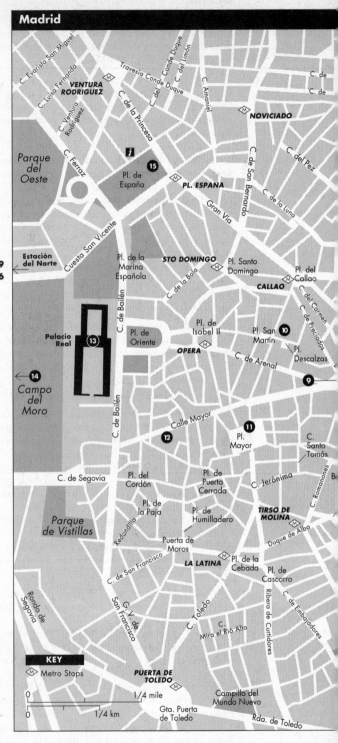

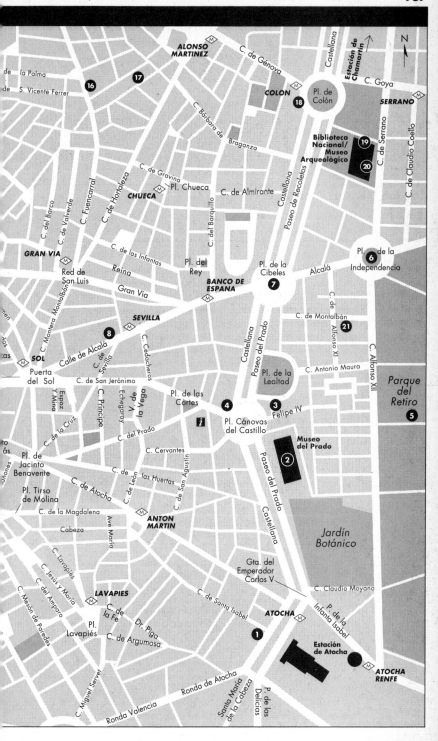

a visit that includes the Royal Pharmacy and other outbuildings. *Bailén s/n, tel. 91/559–7404. Admission: 800 ptas. Open Mon.–Sat. 9:30–5, Sun. 9–2. Closed during official functions.*

⑭ The **Royal Carriage Museum,** which belongs to the palace, has a separate entrance on Paseo Vírgen del Puerto. One of its highlights is the wedding carriage of Alfonso XIII and his English bride, Victoria Eugenia, granddaughter of Queen Victoria, which was damaged by a bomb thrown at it in the Calle Mayor during their wedding procession in 1906; another is the chair that carried the gout-stricken old Emperor Charles V to his retirement at the remote monastery of Yuste. The museum has been closed for several years for restoration, so make sure to check at the Royal Palace to find out if it is open.

Off the Beaten Track

Stroll around the narrow streets of the **Chueca** between Hortaleza and Paseo de Recoletos. Look for the architectural features of the old houses; the dark, atmospheric bars and restaurants well known to discerning Madrileños; and the small stores with their wooden counters and brass fittings, many of which have been run by the same families for generations. Calle de las Infantas has some real gems: the **Bolsa de los Licores** at No. 13, selling wines and liqueurs from every corner of Europe; the splendid silver shop at No. 25; the old world grocery store **Casa Jerez** at No. 32. And don't miss the **Tienda de Vinos** restaurant in Augusto Figueroa, affectionately nicknamed "El Comunista" and long famed for its rock-bottom prices. The whole quarter seems to come straight from the pages of a 19th-century novel.

For a dramatic view of the northwest quadrant of the city and the adjoining Casa de Campo park, take the metro to the Moncloa stop and climb the Faro de Moncloa, a recently opened 285-foot observatory. *Tel. 91/644–8104. Admission: 200 ptas. Open Tues.–Sun. 10:30–1:45.*

The old **Lavapiés** quarter, between Calle Atocha and Embajadores, is another area with plenty of atmosphere. Traditionally one of the poorest parts of Old Madrid, it is now the home of artists and actors, writers and musicians. Health-food restaurants—a novelty in Spain generally—have flourished. You can get a good cheap lunch at **La Biotika,** Amor de Diós 3 (tel. 91/429–0780). Don't miss a restored old tenement building, **La Corrala,** Mesón de Paredes 32, where in summer you can watch a *zarzuela* (light or comic opera) performance in the ancient courtyard.

Shopping

Gift Ideas
There are no special regional crafts associated with Madrid itself, but traditional Spanish goods are on sale in many stores. The **Corte Inglés** and **Galerías Preciados** department stores both stock good displays of Lladró porcelain, as do several specialist shops on the Gran Vía and behind the Plaza hotel on Plaza de España. Department stores stock good displays of fans, but for really superb examples, try the long-established **Casa Diego** in Puerta del Sol. Two stores opposite the Prado on Plaza Cánovas del Castillo, **Artesanía Toledana** and **El Escudo de Toledo,** have a wide selection of souvenirs, especially Toledo swords, inlaid marquetry ware, and pottery. Carefully selected handicrafts from all over Spain—ceramics, furniture, glassware, rugs, embroidery, and more—are sold at **Aretespanä** (Hermosilla 14), a government-run crafts store.

Antiques
The main areas to see are the Plaza de las Cortes, the Carrera San Jerónimo, and the Rastro flea market, along the Ribera de Curtidores and the courtyards just off it.

Boutiques
Calle Serrano has the largest collection of smart boutiques and designer fashions. Another up-and-coming area is around Calle Argensola, just south of Calle Génova. **Loewe,** Spain's most prestigious leather store, has boutiques on Serrano 26 and Gran Vía 8. **Adolfo Dóminguez,** one of Spain's top designers, has several boutiques in Salamanca, and another on Calle Orense in the north of town.

Shopping Districts
The main shopping area in the heart of Madrid is around the pedestrian streets of **Preciados** and **Montera,** between Puerta del Sol and Plaza Callao on Gran Vía. The smartest and most expensive district is the **Barrio de Salamanca** northeast of Cibeles, centered around Serrano, Velázquez, and Goya. **Calle Mayor** and the streets to the east of **Plaza Mayor** are lined with fascinating old-fashioned stores straight out of the 19th century.

Department Stores
El Corte Inglés is the biggest, brightest, and most successful Spanish chain store. Its main branch is on Preciados, just off the Puerta del Sol. **Galerías Preciados** is its main rival, with branches on Plaza Callao right off Gran Vía, Calle Arapiles, Goya corner of Conde de Peñalver, Serrano and Ortega y Gasset, and its newest branch at La Vaguada. Both stores are open Monday–Saturday 10–8, and neither closes for the siesta.

Food and Flea Markets
The Rastro, Madrid's most famous flea market, operates on Sundays from 9 to 2 around the Plaza del Cascorro and the Ribera de Curtidores. A **stamp and coin** market is held on Sunday mornings in the Plaza Mayor, and there's a **secondhand book** market most days on the Cuesta Claudio Moyano near Atocha Station.

Bullfighting

The Madrid bullfighting season runs from March to October. Fights are held on Sunday, and sometimes also on Thursday; starting times vary between 4:30 and 7 PM. The pinnacle of the spectacle may be seen during the three weeks of daily bullfights held during the San Isidro festivals in May. The bullring is at Las Ventas (formally known as the Plaza de Toros Monumental), Alcalá 237 (metro Ventas). You can buy your ticket there shortly before the fight, or, with a 20% surcharge, at the agencies that line Calle Victoria, just off Carrera San Jerónimo and Puerta del Sol.

Dining

For details and price-category definitions, *see* Dining *in* Staying in Spain, *above.*

$$$$ **Horcher.** Housed in a luxurious mansion at the edge of Retiro Park, ★   this classic restaurant is renowned for its hearty but elegant fare, served with impeccable style. Specialties include the types of game dishes favored by Spanish aristocracy. Try the wild boar, venison, or roast wild duck with almond croquettes. The star appetizer is lobster salad with truffles. Other dishes such as stroganoff with mustard, pork chops with sauerkraut, and a chocolate-covered fruit and cake dessert called *baumkuchen* betray the Germanic roots of this restaurant, which originally opened in Berlin at the turn of the century. The dining room is intimate, with rust brocade fabric on the walls and antique Austrian porcelains. A wide selection of French and German wines rounds out the menu. *Alfonso XII 6, tel. 91/532–3596. Reservations required. AE, DC, MC, V. Closed Sun.*

$$$$ Viridiana. The trendiest of Madrid's gourmet restaurants, Viridiana has the relaxed atmosphere of a bistro and a black and white decor highlighted by photograms from Luis Buñuel's classic anti-clerical film of the same name. Iconoclast chef Abraham Garcia says "market-based" is too narrow a description of his creative menu, which changes every two weeks and includes such varied fare as red onions stuffed with *morcilla* (black pudding); soft flour tortillas wrapped around marinated fresh tuna; and filet mignon in white truffle sauce. If it's available, be sure to try the superb duck pâté drizzled with sherry and served with tokay wine. The tangy grapefruit sherbet for dessert is a marvel. *Juan de Mena 14, tel. 91/531–5222. Reservations required. No credit cards. Closed Sun., Easter wk, and Aug.*

$$$$ Zalacaín. A deep apricot color scheme, set off by dark wood and gleaming silver, gives this restaurant the atmosphere of an exclusive villa. Zalacaín introduced nouvelle cuisine to Spain and continues to set the pace after 20 years at the top. Splurge on dishes such as prawn salad in avocado vinaigrette; scallops and leeks in Albariño wine; and roast pheasant with truffles. Service is somewhat stuffy. A prix-fixe tasting menu allows you to sample the best of Zalacaín for about 6,500 ptas. *Alvarez de Baena 4, tel. 91/561–5935. Reservations required. AE, DC, V. No lunch Sat. Closed Sun., Easter wk, and Aug.*

$$$ El Cenador del Prado. The Cenador's innovative menu features French
★ and Oriental touches, as well as exotic Spanish dishes not often found in restaurants. Dine in a baroque salmon-and-gold salon or a less formal plant-filled conservatory. The house specialty is *patatas a la importancia* (sliced potatoes fried in a sauce of garlic, parsley, and clams). Other possibilities include shellfish consommé with ginger ravioli, veal and eggplant in béchamel, or wild boar with prunes. For dessert try the cream-filled pastry called *cañas fritas*—a treat once served only at Spanish weddings. *Calle del Prado 4, tel. 91/429–1561. Reservations advised. AE, DC, MC, V. No lunch Sat. Closed Sun., Easter wk, and 1st half of Aug.*

$$$ Gure-Etxea. In the heart of Old Madrid on the Plaza de Paja, this is one of the capital's most authentic Basque restaurants. The ground floor dining room is airy, high-ceilinged, and elegant; brick walls line the cellar eating area, giving it a rustic, farmhouse feel. As in the Basque country, you are waited on by women. Classic dishes here include *bacalao pil-pil* (spicy cod fried in garlic and oil, making the "pil-pil" sound), *rape en salsa verde* (monkfish in garlic and parsley sauce), and for dessert *leche frita* (fried custard). On weekdays a hearty and inexpensive plate of the day is added to the lunchtime menu. *Plaza de Paja 12, tel. 91/365–6149. Reservations advised. AE, DC, V. Closed Sun., Easter wk, and Aug.*

$$$ La Trainera. Fresh seafood—the best money can buy—is what La Trainera is all about. For decades this informal restaurant, with its nautical decor and maze of little dining rooms, has reigned as the queen of Madrid's seafood houses. Crab, lobster, shrimp, mussels, and a dozen other types of shellfish are served by weight in *raciones* (large portions). While many Spanish diners share several plates of these delicacies as their entire meal, the grilled hake, sole, or turbot make an unbeatable second course, and it's a treat to watch the waiter expertly debone the fish at the table. Skip the listless house wine and go for a bottle of Albariño from the cellar. *Lagasca 60, tel. 91/576–8035. Reservations advised. AE, MC, V. Closed Sun. and Aug.*

$$ Café Balear. A sophisticated yet informal eatery that attracts a crowd of creative types from the fashion and advertising worlds, the Café Balear serves some of the best paella in Madrid. Art prints and potted palms are the only nods to decoration in the stark white dining room. Specialties include paella *centolla* (with crab) and a perfectly prepared paella *mixta* (with seafood, pork, and vegetables). *Sagunto 18, tel. 91/447–9115. Reservations advised. AE, V. Closed Sun. No dinner Mon.*

$$ Casa Botín. Madrid's oldest and most famous restaurant, just off the
★ Plaza Mayor, has been catering to diners since 1725. Its decor and food are traditionally Castilian, as are the wood-fired ovens used for cooking. Cochinillo asado and cordero asado are the specialties. It was a favorite with Hemingway and is somewhat touristy, but fun. Try to be seated in the basement or the upstairs dining room. *Cuchilleros 17, tel. 91/366–4217. Reservations strongly advised. AE, DC, MC. V.*

$$ Casa Vallejo. With its homey dining room, friendly staff, creative menu, and reasonable prices, this restaurant is the well-kept secret of Madrid's budget gourmets. Try the tomato, zucchini, and cheese tart or artichokes and clams for starters, then follow up with duck breast in prune sauce or meatballs made with lamb, almonds, and pine nuts. Their fudge-and-raspberry pie is worth a trip in itself. *San Lorenzo 9, tel. 91/308–6158. Reservations required. AE, MC, V. Closed Sun. No lunch Mon.*

$$ La Cacharrería. The name of this restaurant in Old Madrid means junkyard, and it's reflected in the decor, which is a funky mix of dusty calico, old lace, and gilt mirrors. The cooking, however, is surprisingly upscale with a market-based menu that changes daily and an excellent selection of wines. Venison stew and fresh tuna steaks with *cava* (Spanish sparkling wine) and leeks are among the specialties. Save room for the homemade lemon tart. *Moreria 9, tel. 91/365–3930. Reservations advised. AE, DC, MC, V. Closed Sun.*

$$ La Gamella. American-born chef Dick Stephens has created a new rea-
★ sonably priced menu at this hugely popular dining spot. The sophisticated rust-red dining room, batik tablecloths, oversized plates, and attentive service remain the same. But much of the nouvelle cuisine has been replaced by more traditional fare, such as chicken in garlic, beef bourguignonne, or steak tartar à la Jack Daniels. A few signature dishes such as sausage and red pepper quiche and the bittersweet chocolate pâté for dessert remain, and the lunchtime menú del día, at 1,700 ptas., is a great value. *Alfonso XII 4, tel. 91/532–4509. Reservations advised. AE, DC, MC, V. Closed Sun., Mon., and Aug. 15–31.*

$ Café La Plaza. Strategically positioned between the Prado and Thyssen-Bornemisza art museums and open continuously from 10 AM to midnight, the Café La Plaza is an indispensable rest stop for tourists exploring Madrid. It's an upscale, self-service restaurant with a green-and-white garden-party decor, set among the exclusive boutiques of the Galería del Prado shopping center. Food is arranged on several circular tables. There's a salad bar, a pasta bar, and an economical menú del día, which, depending on the day, might be Spanish-style chicken, breaded fish, or beef stew served with vegetables, bread, and wine. Breakfast, including bacon and eggs, is available until 12:30 and the café is also a good place to remember for afternoon coffee and pastries. *Plaza de las Cortes 7, tel. 91/429–6537. No reservations. AE, V. Closed Sun.*

$ Casa Mingo. Resembling an Asturian cider tavern, Casa Mingo is built
★ into a stone wall beneath the Norte train station. It's a bustling place and the only dishes offered are succulent roast chicken, salad, and sausages, all washed down with numerous bottles of *sidra* (hard cider).

Inside, you'll share long plank tables with other diners; in summer small tables are set up on the sidewalk. *Paseo de la Florida 2, tel. 91/547–7918. No reservations. No credit cards.*

Lodging

Madrid hotel prices have come down greatly since the glory days of 1992, especially in the upper price brackets. The Ritz and Villamagna hotels, which once charged more than $600 a night, can now be enjoyed for $250 to $300. If that's still too steep, try bargaining. Surveys show that only 15% of hotel guests pay the posted room rate in Madrid; more savvy customers take advantage of a dizzying array of special offers. Be sure to ask for a business or professional discount, often up to 40% off. You can generally save 50% on a Friday, Saturday, or Sunday night, and many hotels throw in extras, like meals or museum admissions. There are hotel reservation desks in the national and international terminals of the airport, and at Chamartín station (tel. 91/315–7894). Or you can contact **La Brújula** (tel. 91/559–9705) on the sixth floor of the Torre de Madrid in Plaza de España, which is open 9–9. Its staff speaks English and can book hotels anywhere in Spain for a fee of 250 ptas.

For details and price-category definitions, *see* Lodging *in* Staying in Spain, *above.*

$$$$ **Palace.** This dignified turn-of-the-century hotel opposite parliament and the Prado is a slightly less dazzling stepsister of the nearby Ritz but is full of charm and style. It has long been a favorite of politicians and journalists. Its Belle Epoque decor—especially the glass dome over the lounge—is superb. *Plaza de las Cortes 7, 28014, tel. 91/429–7551, fax 91/420–2547. 480 rooms with bath, 20 suites. Facilities: restaurant, bar, hair salon, shops, parking. AE, DC, MC, V.*

$$$$ **Ritz.** Spain's most exclusive hotel is elegant and aristocratic with beau-
★ tiful rooms, spacious suites, and sumptuous public salons furnished with antiques and handwoven carpets. Its palatial restaurant is justly famous, and its garden terrace is the perfect setting for summer dining. There are brunches with harp music on weekends, and tea or supper chamber-music concerts from February through May. Close to the Retiro Park and overlooking the famous Prado Museum, it offers pure unadulterated luxury. *Plaza Lealtad 5, 28014, tel. 91/521–2857, fax 91/532–8776. 158 rooms with bath. Facilities: restaurant, bar, hair salon, parking. AE, DC, MC, V.*

$$$$ **Villamagna.** Second in luxury only to the Ritz, the Villamagna's modern facade belies a palatial interior exquisitely furnished with 18th-century antiques. Set in a delightful garden, it offers all the facilities one would expect in a hotel of international repute. *Paseo de la Castellana 22, 28046, tel. 91/576–7500, fax 91/575–9504. 164 rooms with bath, 18 suites. Facilities: restaurant, bar, hair salon, sauna, shops, parking. AE, DC, MC, V.*

$$$$ **Villa Real.** Aubusson tapestries from the 19th century and English antiques set the tone in the lobby of this very personal hotel. The emphasis is on service and luxurious details, such as three telephones in every room and teletext service on TV. All rooms have both an upstairs and a downstairs and slightly clubby masculine decor with leather sofas and dark red floral fabrics. The hotel looks over the Plaza de las Cortes and is convenient to almost everything. *Plaza de las Cortes 10, 28014, tel. 91/420–3767, fax 91/420–2547. 94 rooms with bath, 20 suites. Facilities: bar, shops, parking. AE, DC, MC, V.*

$$$ El Prado. Wedged in among the classic buildings of Old Madrid, this skinny hotel is within stumbling distance of the city's best bars and nightclubs. Rooms are soundproofed with double-pane glass and are surprisingly spacious. Decor includes pastel floral prints and gleaming marble baths. *Calle Prado 11, 28014, tel. 91/369–0234, fax 91/429–2829. 50 rooms with bath. Facilities: cafeteria, parking. AE, DC, MC, V.*

$$$ Lagasca. Opened in 1993 in the heart of the elegant Salamanca neighborhood, this hotel combines large, brightly furnished rooms with an unbeatable location two blocks from Madrid's main shopping street, Calle Serrano. The marble lobbies border on the functional, but are fine to use as a meeting place. *Lagasca 64, 28001, tel. 91/575–4606, fax 91/575–1694. 100 rooms with bath. Facilities: restaurant, bar, parking. AE, DC, MC, V.*

$$$ Reina Victoria. One of Madrid's most historic and best loved hotels,
★ the Reina Victoria faces two of the city's liveliest squares. Once a haven for bullfighters, the hotel now attracts a more upscale clientele who are treated to large renovated rooms with a comfortable feel and magnificent views. *Plaza del Angel 7, 28014, tel. 91/531–4500, fax 91/522–0307. 110 rooms with bath. Facilities: bar. AE, DC, MC, V.*

$$$ Tryp Ambassador. In the refurbished palace of the Dukes of Granada, this hotel sits on a quiet old street near the Royal Palace. A magnificent front door and three-story spiral staircase in the entryway greet visitors. Rooms are large and luxurious with separate sleeping and sitting areas. *Cuesta de Santo Domingo 5, 28013, tel. 91/541–6700, fax 91/559–1040. 182 rooms with bath. Facilities: restaurant, bar, parking. AE, DC, MC, V.*

$$ Atlántico. Hidden away on the third floor of a rather shabby building on Gran Via, this hotel will surprise you with its clean and modern rooms, each one decorated in a different color scheme and all with tile baths. Windows are soundproofed, and the hotel is always filled with an interesting assortment of international visitors. *Gran Via 38, 28013, tel. 91/522–6480, fax 91/531–0210. 60 rooms with bath. Facilities: snack bar. AE, MC, V.*

$$ Carlos V. If you like to be right in the center of things, this classic Madrid hotel on a quiet, pedestrians-only street is just a few steps away from the Puerta del Sol and Plaza Mayor. A suit of armor decorates the tiny lobby, and crystal chandeliers add elegance to a second-floor guest lounge. All rooms are bright and carpeted. *Maestro Victoria 5, 28013, tel. 91/531–4100, fax 91/531–3761. 67 rooms with bath. AE, MC, V.*

$$ Inglés. The exterior may seem shabby, but don't be deterred. The In-
★ glés is a long-standing budget favorite. Its rooms are comfortable, with good facilities, and the location is a real bonus: You're a short walk from the Puerta del Sol one way, and from the Prado the other; inexpensive restaurants and atmospheric bars are right at hand. *Echegaray 10, 28014, tel. 91/429–6551, fax 91/420–2423. 58 rooms with bath. Facilities: cafeteria, bar, exercise room, parking. AE, DC, MC, V.*

$$ Paris. Overlooking the Puerta del Sol, the Paris is a stylish hotel full
★ of old-fashioned appeal. It has an impressive turn-of-the-century lobby and a restaurant where you can dine for around 1,500 ptas. Recently refurbished, the hotel has managed to retain its character while adding modern amenities. *Alcalá 2, 28014, tel. 91/521–6496, fax 91/531–0188. 114 rooms with bath. Facilities: restaurant. MC, V.*

$ Lisboa. Clean, small, and central, the Lisboa is a well-kept secret in the lively bar-and-restaurant neighborhood of Plaza Santa Ana. Rooms have tile floors and are sparsely furnished. They vary greatly in size and quality, so be sure to ask to see your room before taking it. *Ven-*

tura de la Vega 17, 28014, tel. 91/429–9894. 22 rooms with bath. AE, DC, MC, V.

$ Monaco. An eccentric and opulent delight, this hotel was once a haunt of the court of Alfonso XIII. All of the rooms are different, and many retain crumbling signs of grandeur such as murals on the ceiling, bas-relief figures, and gilt mirrors. Monaco is located in the lively but drug-infested neighborhood off Plaza Chueca. *Barbieri 5, 28004, tel. 91/522–4630, fax 91/521–1601. 33 rooms with bath. Facilities: cafeteria, bar. AE, MC, V.*

Bars and Cafés

Bars

Mesónes. The most traditional and colorful taverns are on Cuchilleros and Cava San Miguel just west of Plaza Mayor, where you'll find a whole array of mesónes with such names as **Tortilla, Champiñón,** and **Boqueron.**

Old Madrid. Wander the narrow streets between Puerta del Sol and Plaza Santa Ana, which are packed with traditional tapas bars. Favorites here are the **Cervecería Alemana** (Plaza Santa Ana 6), a beer hall founded more than 100 years ago by Germans and patronized, inevitably, by Hemingway; **Los Gabrieles** (Echegaray 17), with magnificent ceramic decor; **La Trucha** (Manuel Fernández y González 3), with loads of atmosphere; and **Viva Madrid** (Fernández y González 7), a lovely old bar.

Calle Huertas. Fashionable bars with turn-of-the-century decor and chamber or guitar music, often live, line this street. **La Fídula** at No. 57 and **El Hecho** at No. 56 are two of the best.

Plaza Santa Barbara. This area just off Alonso Martínez is packed with fashionable bars and beer halls. Stroll along Santa Teresa, Orellana, Campoamor, or Fernando VI and take your pick. The **Cervecería Santa Barbara** in the plaza itself is one of the most colorful, a popular beer hall with a good range of tapas.

Cafés

If you like cafés with an old-fashioned atmosphere, dark wooden counters, brass pumps, and marble-topped tables, try any of the following: **Café Comercial** (Glorieta de Bilbao 7); **Café Gijón** (Paseo de Recoletos 21), a former literary hangout and the most famous of the cafés of old, now one of the many café-terraces that line the Castellana; **Café León** (Alcalá 57), just up from Cibeles; and **El Espejo** (Paseo de Recoletos 31), with art-nouveau decor and an outdoor terrace in summer. And don't forget **La Mallorquina**'s tearooms on Puerta del Sol (*see* Exploring, *above*).

The Arts

Details of all cultural events are listed in the daily newspaper *El País* or in the weekly *Guía del Ocio.*

Concerts and Opera

The main concert hall is the new **Auditorio Nacional de Madrid** (Príncipe de Vergara 146, tel. 91/337–0100; metro Cruz del Royo), which opened at the end of 1988. The old **Teatro Real** on the Plaza de Oriente opposite the Royal Palace is being converted into Madrid's long-needed opera house and may have reopened in 1995; inquire at the tourist office.

Zarzuela

Zarzuela, a combination of light opera and dance ideal for non-Spanish speakers, is held at the **Teatro Nacional Lírico de la Zarzuela** (Jovellanos 4, tel. 91/429–8225). The season runs from October through July.

Theater

If language is no problem, check out the fringe theaters in Lavapiés (*see* Off the Beaten Track, *above*) and the **Centro Cultural de la Villa** (tel. 91/575–6080) beneath the Plaza Colón, and the open-air events in the Retiro Park. Other leading theaters—you'll also need reasonable Spanish—include the **Círculo de Bellas Artes** (Marqués de Casa Riera 2, just off Alcalá 42, tel. 91/531–7700); the **Teatro Español** (Príncipe 25 on Plaza Santa Ana, tel. 91/429–0318 or 429–9193) for Spanish classics; and the **Teatro María Guerrero** (Tamayo y Baus 4, tel. 91/310–2949), home of the Centro Dramático Nacional, for plays by García Lorca. Most theaters have two curtains, at 7 and 10:30 PM, and close on Mondays. Tickets are inexpensive and often easy to come by on the night of performance.

Films

Foreign films are mostly dubbed into Spanish, but movies in English are listed in *El País* or *Guía del Ocio* under "VO," meaning *versión original.* A dozen or so theaters now show films in English; some of the best bets are **Alphaville** and **Cines Renoir,** both in Martín de los Heros, just off Plaza España, and the **Filmoteca Español** (Santa Isabel 3), a city-run institution where classic VO films change daily.

Nightlife

Cabaret

Florida Park (tel. 91/573–7805), in the Retiro Park, offers dinner and a show that often features ballet, Spanish dance, or flamenco and is open Monday through Saturday from 9:30 PM, with shows at 10:45 PM. **Berlin** (Costanilla de San Pedro 11, tel. 91/366–2034) opens at 9:30 PM for a dinner that is good by most cabaret standards, followed by a show and dancing until 4 AM. **La Scala** (Rosario Pino 7, tel. 91/571–4411), in the Meliá Castilla hotel, is Madrid's top nightclub, with dinner, dancing, cabaret at 8:30, and a second, less expensive show around midnight. This is the one visited by most night tours.

Flamenco

Madrid offers the widest choice of flamenco shows in Spain; some are good, but many are aimed at the tourist trade. Dinner tends to be mediocre and overpriced, but it ensures the best seats; otherwise, opt for the show and a *consumición* (drink) only, usually starting around 11 PM and costing 3,000 ptas.–3,500 ptas. **Arco de Cuchilleros** (Cuchilleros 7, tel. 91/266–5867), behind the Plaza Mayor, is one of the better, cheaper ones. **Café de Chinitas** (Torija 7, tel. 91/547–1502) and **Corral de la Morería** (Morería 17, tel. 91/365–8446 and 91/265–1137) are two of the more authentic places where well-known troupes perform. Another choice is **Corral de la Pacheca** (Juan Ramón Jiménez 26, tel. 91/359–2660). **Zambra** (Velázquez 8, tel. 91/435–4928), in the Hotel Wellington, is one of the smartest (jacket and tie essential), with a good show and dinner served into the small hours.

Jazz

The city's best-known jazz venue is **Café Central** (Plaza de Angel 10), followed by **Clamores** (Albuquerque 14). Others include **Café Jazz Populart** (Huertas 22) and **Café del Foro** (San Andrés 38). Excellent jazz frequently comes to Madrid as part of city-hosted seasonal festivals; check the local press for listings and venues.

Casino
Madrid's Casino (tel. 91/856–1100) is 28 kilometers (17 miles) out at Torrelodones on the N-VI road to La Coruña. *Open 5 PM–4 AM. Free transportation service from Plaza de España 6.*

MADRID ENVIRONS

The beauty of the historic cities surrounding Madrid and the role they have played in their country's history rank them among Spain's most worthwhile sights. Ancient Toledo, the former capital; the great palace-monastery of El Escorial; the sturdy medieval walls of Ávila; Segovia's Roman aqueduct and fairy-tale Alcázar; and the magnificent Plaza Mayor of the old university town of Salamanca all lie within an hour or so from the capital.

All the towns below, with the possible exception of Salamanca, can easily be visited on day trips from Madrid. But if you've had your fill of the hustle and bustle of Spain's booming capital, you'll find it far more rewarding to tour from one place to another, spending a day or two in one or more of these fascinating locales. Then, long after the day-trippers have gone home, you can enjoy the real charm of these small provincial towns and wander at leisure through their medieval streets.

Getting There from Madrid

Trains to Toledo leave from Madrid's Atocha Station; to Salamanca, Avila, Segovia and El Escorial from Chamartín station.

Getting Around

There's a direct train line between El Escorial, Ávila, and Salamanca; otherwise, train connections are poor and you'll do better to go by bus. All places are linked by bus services and the local tourist offices will advise on schedules. Toledo's bus station is on the Ronda de Castilla la Mancha (tel. 925/215850) just off the road from Madrid. Ávila's bus station is on Avenida de Madrid (tel. 920/220154); Segovia's is on Paseo Ezequiel González (tel. 911/427725); and Salamanca's is on Filiberto Villalobos 73 (tel. 923/236717). The N403 from Toledo to Ávila passes through spectacular scenery in the Sierra de Gredos mountains, as does the C505 Ávila–El Escorial route. From El Escorial to Segovia, both the Puerto de León and Puerto de Navacerrada mountain passes offer magnificent views. The N501 from Ávila to Salamanca will take you across the tawny plain of Castile.

Tourist Information

Ávila (Plaza de la Catedral 4, tel. 920/211387); open weekdays 8–3 and 4–6 (5–7 in summer), Saturday 9–1:30.
El Escorial (Floridablanca 10, tel. 91/8901554); open weekdays 10–2 and 3–4:45, Saturday 10–1:45.
Salamanca (Casa de las Conchas, Rua Mayor 70, tel. 923/270340); open weekdays 9:30–2 and 4:30–8, Saturday 10–2. There's also an information booth on the Plaza Mayor (market side).
Segovia (Plaza Mayor 10, tel. 921/430328); open Monday–Saturday 9–2; also weekdays 4–6 in summer only.
Toledo (Puerta Nueva de Bisagra, tel. 925/220843); open Monday–Saturday 9–3 and 4–7, Sunday 9–3.

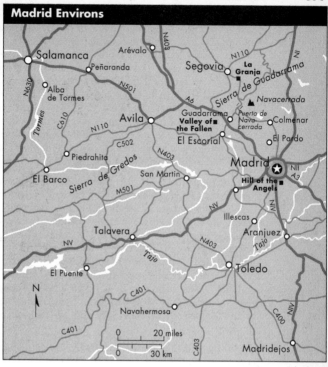

Madrid Environs

Exploring the Madrid Environs

Toledo

Head south from Madrid on the road to Toledo. About 20 minutes from the capital look left for a prominent rounded hill topped by a statue of Christ. This is the **Hill of the Angels,** which marks the geographical center of the Iberian Peninsula. After 90 minutes of drab, industrial scenery, the unforgettable silhouette of **Toledo** suddenly rises before you, the imposing bulk of the Alcázar and the slender spire of the cathedral dominating the skyline. This former capital, where Moors, Jews, and Christians once lived in harmony, is now a living national monument, depicting all the elements of Spanish civilization in hand-carved, sun-mellowed stone. For a stunning view and to capture the beauty of Toledo as El Greco knew it, begin with a panoramic drive around the Carretera de Circunvalación, crossing over the Alcántara bridge and returning by way of the bridge of San Martín. As you gaze at the city rising like an island in its own bend of the Tagus, reflect how little the city skyline has changed in the four centuries since El Greco painted *Storm Over Toledo*.

Toledo is a small city steeped in history and full of magnificent buildings. It was the capital of Spain under both Moors and Christians until some whim caused Philip II to move his capital to Madrid in 1561. Begin your visit with a drink in one of the many terrace cafés on the central **Plaza Zocodover,** study a map, and try to get your bearings, for a veritable labyrinth confronts you as you try to find your way to Toledo's great treasures. While here, search the square's pastry shops for the typical *mazapanes* (marzipan candies) of Toledo.

Begin your tour with a visit to the 13th-century **Cathedral,** seat of the Cardinal Primate of Spain, and one of the great cathedrals of Spain. Somber but elaborate, it blazes with jeweled chalices, gorgeous ecclesiastical vestments, historic tapestries, some 750 stained-glass windows, and paintings by Tintoretto, Titian, Murillo, El Greco, Velázquez, and Goya. The cathedral has two surprises: a **Mozarabic chapel,** where Mass is still celebrated on Sundays according to an ancient Mozarabic rite handed down from the days of the Visigoths (AD 419–711); and its unique **Transparente,** an extravagant Baroque roof that gives a theatrical glimpse into heaven as the sunlight pours down through a mass of figures and clouds. *Admission: 400 ptas. Open Tues.–Sat. 10:30–1 and 3:30–6 (7 in summer), Sun. 10:30–1 and 4–6.*

En route to the real jewel of Toledo, the **Chapel of Santo Tomé,** you'll pass a host of souvenir shops on Calle Santo Tomé, bursting with damascene knives and swords, blue-and-yellow pottery from nearby Talavera, and El Greco reproductions. In the tiny chapel that houses El Greco's masterpiece, *The Burial of the Count of Orgaz,* you can capture the true spirit of the Greek painter who adopted Spain, and in particular Toledo, as his home. Do you recognize the sixth man from the left among the painting's earthly contingent? Or the young boy in the left-hand corner? The first is El Greco himself, the second his son Jorge Manuel—see 1578, the year of his birth, embroidered on his handkerchief. *Admission: 100 ptas. Open daily 10–1:45 and 3:30–5:45 (6:45 in summer).*

Not far away is **El Greco's House,** a replica containing copies of his works. *Tel. 925/224046. Closed for restoration until 1996.*

The splendid **Sinagoga del Tránsito** stands on the corner of Samuel Levi and Reyes Católicos. Commissioned in 1366 by Samuel Levi, chancellor to Pedro the Cruel, the synagogue shows Christian and Moorish as well as Jewish influences in its architecture and decoration—look at the stars of David interspersed with the arms of Castile and León. There's also a small **Sephardic Museum** chronicling the life of Toledo's former Jewish community. *Admission: 400 ptas. Open Tues.–Sat. 10–2 and 4–6, Sun. 10–2.*

Another synagogue, the incongruously named **Santa María la Blanca** (it was given as a church to the Knights of Calatrava in 1405), is just along the street. Its history may have been Jewish and Christian, but its architecture is definitely Moorish, for it resembles a mosque with five naves, horseshoe arches, and capitals decorated with texts from the Koran. *Admission: 100 ptas. Open daily 10–2 and 3:30–6 (until 7 in summer).*

Across the road is **San Juan de los Reyes,** a beautiful Gothic church begun by Ferdinand and Isabella in 1476. Wander around its fine cloisters and don't miss the iron manacles on the outer walls; they were placed there by Christians freed by the Moors. The Catholic Kings originally intended to be buried here, but then their great triumph at Granada in 1492 changed their plans. *Admission: 100 ptas. Open daily 10–1:30 and 3:30–5:45 (6:45 in summer).*

Walk down the hill through the ancient **Cambrón Gate** and your visit to Toledo is over. Should you have more time, however, head for the **Museum of Santa Cruz,** just off the Zocodover, with its splendid El Grecos. *Tel. 925/221036. Admission: 200 ptas. Open Mon. 10–2 and 4–6:30, Tues.–Sat. 10–6:30, Sun. 10–2.*

Also consider a visit to the **Hospital de Tavera,** outside the walls, where you can see Ribera's amazing *Bearded Woman. Tel. 925/220451. Admission: 500 ptas. Open daily 10:30–1:30 and 3:30–6.*

El Escorial

In the foothills of the Guadarrama Mountains, 50 kilometers (31 miles) to the northwest of Madrid, and 120 kilometers (74 miles) from Toledo, lies **San Lorenzo del Escorial,** burial place of Spanish kings and queens. The **Monastery,** built by the religious fanatic Philip II as a memorial to his father, Charles V, is a vast rectangular edifice, conceived and executed with a monotonous magnificence worthy of the Spanish royal necropolis. It was designed by Juan de Herrera, Spain's greatest Renaissance architect. The **Royal Pantheon** contains the tombs of monarchs since Carlos I save three. Only those queens who bore sons later crowned lie in the same crypt; the others, along with royal sons and daughters who never ruled, lie in the nearby **Pantheon of the Infantes.** The monastery's other highlights are the magnificent **Library of Philip II,** with 40,000 rare volumes and 2,700 illuminated manuscripts, including the diary of Santa Teresa, and the **Royal Apartments.** Contrast the spartan private apartment of Philip II and the simple bedroom in which he died in 1598 with the beautiful carpets, porcelain, and tapestries with which his less austere successors embellished the rest of his somber monastery-palace. *San Lorenzo de El Escorial, tel. 91/890–5905. Admission: 800 ptas. Open Tues.–Sun. 10–6 (7 in summer). Last entry is 45 mins before closing time.*

Valley of the Fallen

Eight kilometers (5 miles) along the road to Segovia, the mighty cross of the **Valley of the Fallen** looms up on your left. This vast basilica hewn out of sheer granite was built by General Franco between 1940 and 1959 as a monument to the dead of Spain's Civil War of 1936–39. Buried here are 43,000 war dead and Franco himself, who died in 1975. A funicular to the top of the monument costs 300 ptas. *Tel. 91/890–5611. Admission: 600 ptas. Open Tues.–Sun. 10–7 (6 in winter).*

A spectacular drive lies ahead for those who use the local road rather than the autoroute, from the resort of Navacerrada up through the Guadarrama Mountains by way of the **Navacerrada pass** at 6,000 feet. The steep descent through fragrant pine forests via the hairpin bends of the Siete Revueltas (Seven Curves) brings you straight into La Granja.

La Granja

The **Palace of La Granja,** with its splendid formal gardens and fountains, was built between 1719 and 1739 by the homesick Philip V, first Bourbon king of Spain and grandson of France's Louis XIV, to remind him of his beloved Versailles. The whole place is like an exquisite piece of France in a Spanish wood, and it's small wonder that Philip chose to be buried here in the splendor of his own creation rather than in the austerity of El Escorial. The splendid gardens are open until dusk and you can stroll around them for free except when the fountains are running. *Tel. 921/470020. Palace admission: 600 ptas. Open Tues.–Sun. 10–6; winter, Tues.–Sat. 10–1:30 and 3–5, Sun. 10–2.*

Segovia

From La Granja, a 10-minute drive will bring you to the golden-stone market town of **Segovia.** In front of you rises the majestic Roman **aqueduct,** its huge granite blocks held together without mortar. At its foot is a small bronze statue of Romulus and the wolf, presented by Rome in 1974 to commemorate the 2,000-year history of Spain's most complete Roman monument.

Drive around the base of the rock on which Segovia stands. The Ronda de Santa Lucía leads to the most romantic view of the Alcázar, perched high on its rock like the prow of a mighty ship. Return via the Carretera de los Hoyos for yet another magical view, this time of the venerable cathedral rising from the ramparts. Next, fend off the pestering gypsies around the aqueduct and make for the **Calle Real,** the main shopping street. As you climb, you'll pass the Romanesque church of **San Martín,** with its porticoed outer gallery. Continue to the picturesque **Plaza Mayor** with its colorful ceramic stalls (good bargains) and pleasant cafés set against the backdrop of ancient arcaded houses and one of the loveliest, externally, at least, Gothic cathedrals in Spain.

Segovia **cathedral** was the last Gothic cathedral to be built in Spain (the one in Ávila was the first). Begun in 1525 by order of Charles V, its interior is sadly disappointing, as many of its treasures were carried off by Napoléon's troops in the Peninsular War of the early 1800s. Its museum has the first book printed in Spain (1472). You should also seek out the tomb of Don Pedro, two-year-old son of Henry IV who slipped from his nurse's arms and tumbled to his death over the battlements of the Alcázar (his distraught nurse cast herself over after him). *Admission: 200 ptas. Open daily in summer, 10–7; in winter, Mon.–Sat. 10–1 and 3–6, Sun. 9:30–6.*

The turreted **Alcázar** is largely a fanciful re-creation from the 1880s, the original 13th-century castle having been destroyed by fire in 1862. The view from its ramparts—and, even better, from its tower if you can manage the 156 steps—is breathtaking. The Alcázar served as a major residence of the Catholic Kings. Here Isabella met Ferdinand, and from here she set out to be crowned Queen of Castile. The interior successfully re-creates the era of this dual monarchy that established Spain's Golden Age. *Tel. 911/430176. Admission: 350 ptas. Open daily 10–6 in winter, 10–7 in summer.*

Ávila

Ávila, almost 4,100 feet above sea level, is the highest provincial capital in Spain. Alfonso VI and his son-in-law, Count Raimundo de Borgoña, rebuilt the town and walls in 1090, bringing it permanently under Christian control. It is these walls, the most complete military installations of their kind in Spain, that give Ávila its special medieval quality. Thick and solid, with 88 towers tufted with numerous untidy storks' nests, they stretch for 2½ kilometers (1½ miles) around the entire city and make an ideal focus for the start of your visit. For a superb overall view and photo spot, drive out to the **Cuatro Postes,** ¾ kilometer (½ mile) out on the road to Salamanca.

The personality of Santa Teresa the Mystic, to whom the city is dedicated, lives today as vividly as it did in the 16th century. Several religious institutions associated with the life of the saint are open to visitors, the most popular of which is the **Convent of Santa Teresa,** which stands on the site of her birthplace. There's an ornate Baroque chapel, a small gift shop, and a museum with some of her relics: her rosary, books, walking stick, a sole of her sandal, and her finger wearing her wedding ring. *Plaza de la Santa, just inside the southern gate, tel. 918/211030. Admission free. Open daily 9:30–1:30 and 3:30–8.*

Ávila's other ecclesiastical monuments are far older and more rewarding than those that commemorate the saint. The impregnable hulk of the **cathedral** is in many ways more akin to a fortress than a house of God. Though of Romanesque origin—the Romanesque sections are recognizable by their red and white brickwork—it is usually claimed as Spain's first Gothic cathedral. Inside is the ornate alabaster tomb of Cardinal Alonso de Madrigal, a 15th-century bishop whose swarthy complexion earned him the nickname of "El Tostado" (the toasted one). *Tel. 918/211641. Admission free. Open daily in summer 9–1:30 and 3:30–6:30, in winter 9–1:30 and 3:30–5. Museum admission: 200 ptas.*

The **Basilica of San Vicente,** just outside the walls, is one of Ávila's finest Romanesque churches, standing on the spot where St. Vincent and his sisters Sabina and Cristeta were martyred in AD 306. Here, too, Santa Teresa is said to have experienced the vision that told her to reform the Carmelite order. *Admission: 50 ptas. Open Tues.–Sun. 10–2 and 4–8.*

Before continuing to the **Monastery of Santo Tomás,** you can relax in the pleasant **Plaza de Santa Teresa** with its outdoor cafés and statue of the saint erected for Pope John Paul's visit in 1982. Built between 1482 and 1493 by Ferdinand and Isabella, who used it as a summer palace, the monastery houses the tomb of their only son, Prince Juan—who died at the age of 19 while a student at Salamanca—as well as the tomb of that far less lovable character, the notorious Inquisitor General Tomás de Torquemada. *Admission: monastery free, cloisters 50 ptas., Museum of Eastern Art 100 ptas. Open daily 11–1 and 4:30–7.*

Alba de Tormes

From Ávila it's straight sailing all the way to Salamanca unless you're a devotee of Santa Teresa and choose to take a small detour to the old ducal town of **Alba de Tormes** to visit the **Carmelite Convent** (open daily 9–2 and 4–8), where the saint is buried.

Salamanca

Salamanca is an ancient city, and your first glimpse of it is bound to be unforgettable. Beside the road flows the Tormes River and beyond it rise the old houses of the city and the golden walls, turrets, and domes of the Plateresque cathedrals. "Plateresque" comes from *plata* (silver) and implies that the stone is chiseled and engraved as intricately as that delicate metal. A superb example of this style is the facade of the Dominican **Monastery of San Esteban** (150 ptas.; open daily 9–1 and 4–7, 5–8 in summer), which you'll pass on your way to the cathedrals. The **old cathedral** far outshines its younger sister, the **new cathedral.** Inside the sturdy Romanesque walls of the old cathedral is a stunning altarpiece with 53 brightly painted panels. Don't miss the splendid **cloisters,** which now house a worthwhile collection of religious art, and the **Degree Chapel,** where anxious students sought inspiration on the night before their final exams. *New cathedral free; old cathedral and cloisters 200 ptas. Open daily 10–2 and 4–7.*

Founded by Alfonso IX in 1218, **Salamanca University** is to Spain what Oxford University is to England. On its famous **doorway** in the Patio de las Escuelas, a profusion of Plateresque carving surrounds the medallions of Ferdinand and Isabella. See if you can find the famous frog and skull, said to bring good luck to students in their examinations. Inside, the **lecture room** of Fray Luis de León has remained untouched since the days of the great scholar, and the prestigious **library** boasts some 50,000 parchment and leather-bound volumes. *Tel. 923/294400, ext. 1150. Admission: 200 ptas. Open Mon.–Sat. 9:30–1:30 and 4–6, Sun. 10–1.*

Now make for Salamanca's greatest jewel, the elegant 18th-century **Plaza Mayor.** Here you can browse in stores offering typical *charro* jewelry (silver and black flowerheads), head down the steps to the market in search of colorful tapas bars, or simply relax in an outdoor café. In this, the city's crowning glory, and the most exquisite square in Spain, you've found the perfect place to end your tour of Salamanca and Castile.

Dining and Lodging

For details and price-category definitions, *see* Dining and Lodging *in* Staying in Spain, *above.*

Ávila
DINING
El Fogón de Santa Teresa. Traditional Castilian roasts, lamb chops, and trout feature on the menu of this attractive restaurant in the vaults of the Palacio de Valderrábanos. *Alemania 3, tel. 920/211023. AE, DC, MC, V. $$*

★ **El Molino de la Losa.** Situated on a spit of land jutting into the Adaja River, this restaurant occupies a restored 15th-century mill and has splendid views of Avila's walls. Specialties include lamb roasted in a medieval-style wood oven and fresh river trout. *Bajada de la Losa 12, tel. 920/211101. AE, MC, V. Closed Mon. in winter. $$*

★ **Mesón del Rastro.** This ancient inn tucked into the city walls is Ávila's most atmospheric place to dine. Local specialties include Ávila's famous *ternera* (veal) and *yemas de Santa Teresa*, a dessert made from candied egg yolks. *Plaza del Rastro 1, tel. 920/211218. AE, DC, MC, V. $$*

LODGING
★ **Palacio de Valderrábanos.** Ávila's best hotel is located in a 15th-century mansion opposite the cathedral. It was once the residence of the first bishop of Ávila. *Plaza Catedral 9, 05001, tel. 920/211023, fax 920/256191. 73 rooms with bath. Facilities: restaurant, bar, meeting room. AE, DC, MC, V. $$$*

Parador Raimundo de Borgoña. The location of this parador in a 15th-century palace just inside the northern walls of the city is superb. The rooms are decorated in traditional Castilian style and have spacious, well-equipped bathrooms. Some rooms also have four-poster beds and a view of the city walls. Its dining room is atmospheric and serves local Ávilan dishes, including the inevitable yemas, and its garden offers the only access to the walls. Closed for renovation until spring 1996. *Marqués de Canales y Chozas 16, 05001, tel. 920/211340, fax 920/226166. 62 rooms with bath. Facilities: restaurant, meeting room. AE, DC, MC, V. $$$*

El Escorial
DINING
★ **Charolés.** This elegant restaurant has a terrace above the street for summer dining. Its meat dishes are famous throughout the region. Try the *charolés a la pimienta* (pepper steak). Fresh fish is brought in daily from Spain's north coast. *Floridablanca 24, tel. 91/890–5975. Weekend reservations usually required. AE, DC, MC, V. $$$*

Mesón de la Cueva. Founded in 1768, this atmospheric mesón has several small, rustic dining rooms. This inn is a must for ambience, and the food is good, too. *San Antón 4, tel. 91/890–1516. Weekend reservations advised. AE, DC, MC, V. $$–$$$*

El Candil. One of the best of the many middle-range restaurants in El Escorial, El Candil is situated above a bar on the corner of Plaza San Lorenzo on the village's main street. In summer you can dine outdoors in the square, a delightful spot. *Reina Victoria 12, tel. 91/890–4103. AE, DC, MC, V. $$*

LODGING

Victoria Palace. The rooms at the back of this grand old-world hotel close to the monastery have balconies and a splendid view toward Madrid; there's a garden and pool, too. *Juan de Toledo 4, tel. 91/890–1511, fax 91/890–1248. 89 rooms with bath. AE, DC, MC, V. $$$*

Miranda Suizo. Rooms are comfortable in this charming old hotel on the main street, and the hotel café, with its dark wood fittings and marble tables, is right out of the 19th century. *Floridablanca 20, tel. 91/890–4711, fax 91/890–4358. 47 rooms with bath. AE, DC, MC, V. $$*

Salamanca

DINING

★ **Chapeau.** This chic spot offers both meat and fish carefully roasted in its wood-fired ovens. Try their *pimientos relleños* (stuffed peppers) and orange mousse for dessert. *Gran Vía 20, tel. 923/271833. Reservations advised. AE, DC, MC, V. Closed Sun. in summer. $$$*

El Mesón. There's plenty of colorful atmosphere and good traditional Castilian food in this typical mesón just off the Plaza Mayor, beside the Gran Hotel. *Plaza Poeta Iglesias 10, tel. 923/217222. AE, MC, V. Closed Jan. $$*

Río de la Plata. This small, atmospheric restaurant close to El Mesón and the Gran Hotel serves superb *farinato* sausage; it's a great find. *Plaza del Peso 1, tel. 923/219005. AE, MC, V. Closed Mon., July. $$*

LODGING

Gran Hotel. The grande dame of Salamanca's hotels got a face-lift in 1994 and now offers stylishly baroque lounges and refurbished yet old-fashioned, oversized rooms just steps from the Plaza Mayor. *Poeta Iglesias 3, 37001, tel. 923/213500, fax 923/213501. 109 rooms with bath. Facilities: restaurant, bar. AE, DC, MC, V. $$$*

Palacio del Castellanos. Opened in 1992 in an immaculately restored 15th-century palace, this hotel offers a much-needed alternative to Salamanca's national parador (probably the ugliest of them all). There is an exquisite interior patio and an equally beautiful restaurant. *San Pablo 58, tel. 923/261818, fax 923/261819. 69 rooms with bath. Facilities: restaurant. AE, DC, MC, V. $$$*

Las Torres. Overlooking the Plaza Mayor, the down-at-the-heels look of this hotel is more than made up for by fabulous views of Spain's most beautiful square. The rooms are spartan but adequate; be sure to ask for one with balconies on the plaza. *Plaza Mayor 26, 37001, tel. 923/212100, fax 923/212101. 26 rooms. No credit cards. $$*

Segovia

DINING

Casa Duque. At the end of the main shopping street, this restaurant has several floors of beautifully decorated traditional dining rooms and is the main rival to the famous Cándido. There's plenty of local atmosphere, and the food is pure Castilian—roasts are the house specialty. *Cervantes 12, tel. 921/430537. Weekend reservations advised. AE, DC, MC, V. $$–$$$*

★ **Mesón de Cándido.** Segovia's most prestigious restaurant has seven dining rooms pulsating with atmosphere and decorated with bullfighting memorabilia and photos of the dignitaries who have dined here over the years. Specialties are cochinillo and cordero asado. *Plaza Azoguejo 5, tel. 921/425911. Sun. lunch reservations required. AE, DC, MC, V. $$–$$$*

La Oficina. Traditional Castilian dishes are served in two delightful dining rooms that date back to 1893. It's just off Plaza Mayor. *Cronista Lecea 10, tel. 921/431643. AE, DC, MC, V. $$*

LODGING

Los Linajes. The advantages of this pleasant, modern hotel, built in Castilian style, are its central location and its superb views from some rooms. *Dr. Velasco 9, 40003, tel. 921/431201, fax 921/431501. 53 rooms with bath. Facilities: restaurant, bar, meeting room, disco. AE, DC, MC, V. $$$*

★ **Parador.** To the north of town is this modern parador offering comfortable, spacious rooms and pools. The views of the city, especially when illuminated, are magnificent. The restaurant offers superior parador cooking. *Carretara de Valladoid s/n, 40003 (off the N601 toward Valladolid), tel. 921/443737, fax 921/437362. 103 rooms with bath. Facilities: restaurant, indoor and outdoor pools, meeting room, business services. AE, DC, MC, V. $$$*

Infanta Isabel. A recently restored building with a Victorian feel houses this small, centrally located hotel—it's two steps off the Plaza Mayor and offers great views of Segovia's cathedral. Guest rooms are feminine and light, with white painted furnishings. *Plaza Mayor s/n, 40001, tel. 921/443105, fax 921/433240. 29 rooms. Facilities: coffee shop. AE, MC, V. $$*

Toledo

DINING

Asador Adolfo. This restaurant is near the cathedral and is well known for its good food (try the superb roast meat and the pimentos rellenos) and service. *Calle de la Granada 6, tel. 925/227321. AE, DC, MC, V. No dinner Sun. $$$*

★ **Hostal del Cardenal.** Toledo's best restaurant is set in the 17th-century palace of Cardinal Lorenzana, up against the city ramparts, and boasts five dining rooms and a delightful garden for summer dining. The first choice of every tourist, both food and service are excellent (try the cochinillo asado). *Paseo Recaredo 24, tel. 925/220862. Reservations required in high season. AE, MC, V. $$$*

La Abadia. Perfect for a light lunch, a sandwich, or a round of tapas, this stylish bar-restaurant has vaulted stone ceilings and a huge old wooden door. The dining room downstairs specializes in shish-kebabs, grilled meats, and salads. *Plaza San Nicolás 3. No phone. No reservations. No credit cards. $$*

Venta de Aires. A century-old inn on the edge of town and not far from the Tajo River, this is where Toledanos go to eat partridge. Steaks and lamb are also expertly prepared. *Circo Romano 35, tel. 925/220545. Weekend reservations advised. MC, V. $$*

LODGING

Hostal del Cardenal. Built in the 18th century as a summer palace for a cardinal, this quiet and beautiful hotel has some rooms that overlook a wooded garden. It's difficult to believe that the main Madrid road is a short distance away. *Paseo de Recaredo 24 45004, tel. 925/224900, fax 925/222991. 27 rooms. Facilities: restaurant. AE. $$$*

★ **Parador Conde de Orgaz.** This is one of Spain's most popular paradores, and the best and most expensive hotel in Toledo (a 15-minute drive from city center). It's a modern parador built in traditional Toledo style and stands on a hill across the river, commanding magnificent views of the city. Book far ahead. *Paseo Emperador s/n, 45001, tel. 925/221850, fax 925/225166. 77 rooms with bath. Facilities: pool. AE, DC, MC, V. $$$*

Pintor El Greco. Next door to the famous painter's house-museum, this friendly hotel occupies a building that was once a 17th-century bakery. Extensive renovation has resulted in a light and modern interior, with some antique touches such as exposed brick vaulting. *Alamillos* *del Transito 13, 45002, tel. 925/214250, fax 925/215819. 35 rooms. AE, DC, MC, V. $$*

BARCELONA

Arriving and Departing

By Plane

All international and domestic flights arrive at El Prat de Llobregat airport, 14 kilometers (8½ miles) south of Barcelona just off the main highway to Castelldefels and Sitges. For information on arrival and departure times, call the airport (tel. 93/478–5000 or 478–5032) or Inforiberia (tel. 93/412–5667).

BETWEEN THE AIRPORT AND DOWNTOWN
The airport–city train leaves every 30 minutes between 6:30 AM and 11 PM and reaches the Barcelona Central (Sants) Station in 15 minutes; an extension carries you to the Plaça de Catalunya, at the head of the Rambla, in the heart of the old city. Taxis will then take you to your hotel. The Aerobus service connects the airport with Plaza Catalunya every 15 minutes between 6:25 AM and 11 PM; pay the driver the fare of 375 ptas. RENFE provides a bus service to the Central Station during the night hours. A cab from the airport to your hotel, including airport and luggage surcharges, will cost about 2,500 ptas.

By Train

The old Terminal (or França) Station on Avenida Marquès de l'Argentera reopened in 1992 after major renovations and now serves as the main terminal for trains to France and some express trains to points in Spain. The Central Station, which had been the main station, serves suburban destinations as well as most cities in Spain. Inquire at the tourist office to find out which station you need. Many trains also stop at the Passeig de Gràcia underground station at the junction of Aragó. This station is closer to the Plaça de Catalunya and Rambla area than Central, but though tickets and information are available here, luggage carts and taxi ranks are not. Check with tourist offices for current travel information and phone numbers. For RENFE information, call 93/490–0202 (24 hours).

By Bus

Barcelona has no central bus station, but many buses operate from the old Estació Vilanova (or Norte) at the end of Avenida Vilanova. **Julià,** Ronda Universitat 5, runs buses to Zaragoza and Montserrat; and **Alsina Graëlls,** Ronda Universitat 4, to Lérída and Andorra.

Getting Around

Modern Barcelona above the Plaça de Catalunya is mostly built on a grid system, though there's no helpful numbering system as in the United States. The Gothic Quarter from the Plaça de Catalunya to the port is a warren of narrow streets, however, and you'll need a good street map to get around. Most sightseeing can be done on foot—you won't have any other choice in the Gothic Quarter—but you'll need to use the metro or buses to link sightseeing areas.

By Metro

The subway is the fastest way of getting around, as well as the easiest to use. You pay a flat fare of 135 ptas. no matter how far you travel, or purchase a **tarjeta multiviatge,** good for 10 rides (700 ptas.). Plans of the system are available from main metro stations or from branches of the Caixa savings bank.

By Bus

City buses run from about 5:30 or 6 AM to 10:30 PM, though some stop earlier. Again, there's a flat-fare system (135 ptas.). Plans of the routes followed are displayed at bus stops. A reduced-rate tarjeta multiviatge, good for 10 rides, can be purchased at the transport kiosk on Plaça de Catalunya (700 ptas.).

By Taxi

Taxis are black and yellow, and when available for hire show a LIBRE sign in the daytime and a green light at night. The meter starts at 350 ptas., and there are small supplements for luggage (100 ptas. per case), Sundays and fiestas, rides from the airport, a station, or the port (varies according to zone), and for going to or from the bullring or a soccer match. There are cab stands all over town; cabs may also be flagged down on the street. Make sure the driver puts on his meter.

By Cable Car and Funicular

Montjuïc Funicular is a cog railroad that runs from the junction of Avenida Parallel and Nou de la Rambla to the Miramar Amusement Park on Montjuïc. It runs only when the amusement park is open (11– 8:15 in winter, noon–2:45 and 4:30–9:25 in summer). A *teleferic* (cable car) then runs from the amusement park up to Montjuïc Castle (noon–8 daily in summer; winter, weekends only, 11–7:30).

A **Transbordador Aeri Harbor Cable Car** runs from Miramar on Montjuïc across the harbor to the Torre de Jaume I on Barcelona *moll* (quay), and on to the Torre de Sant Sebastià at the end of Passeig Joan de Borbó in Barceloneta. You can board at either stage; the fare is 850 ptas. (1000 ptas. round-trip). Operates Oct.–June, weekdays noon to 5:45, weekends noon to 6:15; June to Oct., daily 11 to 9.

To reach Tibidabo summit, take either Bus 58 or the Ferrocarrils de la Generalitat train from Plaça de Catalunya to Avenida Tibidabo, then the *tramvía blau* (blue tram) to Peu del Funicular, and the Tibidabo Funicular from there to the Tibidabo Fairground. The funicular runs every half hour from 7:15 AM to 9:45 PM.

By Boat

Golondrinas harbor boats operate short harbor trips from the Portal de la Pau near the Columbus Monument between 10 AM and 1:30 PM weekends only in winter, daily in summer between 10 and 8. A one way ticket lets you off at the end of the breakwater for a 2½-mi stroll, surrounded by the Mediterranean, back into Barceloneta.

Important Addresses and Numbers

Tourist Information

The city's three main tourist offices are at the **Central** (Sants) train station (tel. 93/491–4431; open daily 8–8), the **França** train station (tel. 93/319–5758; open daily 8–8), and at the **airport** (tel. 93/478–4704; open Mon.–Sat. 9:30–8).

Information on the province and city can be found at the office at Gran Vía 658 (tel. 93/301–7443; open weekdays 9–7, Sat. 9–2, closed holidays).

During special events and conferences, a tourist office is open at the **Palau de Congressos** (Avda. Maria Cristina, tel. 93/423–3101, ext. 8356); a small office with some pamphlets and maps is at the **Ajunta-**

ment (Plaça Sant Jaume, tel. 93/402–7000, ext. 433; open summer, daily 9–8; and cultural information is available at the **Palau de la Virreina** (Rambla 99, tel. 93/301–7775; open Mon.–Sat. 9–9, Sun. 10–2).

American Visitors' Bureau (Gran Vía 591 between Rambla de Catalunya and Balmes, 3rd floor, tel. 93/301–0150 or 301–0032).

Consulates
U.S. (Pg. Reina Elisenda 23, tel. 93/280–2227), **Canadian** (Vía Augusta 125, tel. 93/209–0634), **U.K.** (Diagonal 477, tel. 93/419–9044).

Emergencies
Police: (National Police, tel. 091; Municipal Police, tel. 092; Main Police/Policía Nacional Station, Vía Laietana 43, tel. 93/301–6666). **Medical emergencies:** (tel. 061). **Pharmacies:** (tel. 010). **Tourist Attention:** (La Rambla 43, tel. 93/301–9060) is a 24-hr service offered by the police department to provide assistance to crime victims.

English-Language Bookstores
Several bookstalls on the Rambla sell English guidebooks and novels, but the bookstore at the **Palau de la Virreina** (Rambla 99) has the best selection. Also try **Librería Laie** (Pau Claris 85), **Librería Francesa** (Passeig de Gràcia 91), or **Come In** (Provença 203).

Travel Agencies
American Express (Rosello 257, on the corner of Passeig de Gràcia, tel. 93/217–0070), **Wagons-Lits Cook** (Passeig de Gràcia 8, tel. 93/317–5500), **Viajes Iberia** (Rambla 130, tel. 93/317–9320), and **Bestours** (Diputación 241, tel. 93/487–8580).

Guided Tours

Orientation Tours
City sightseeing tours are run by **Julià Tours** (Ronda Universitat 5, tel. 93/317–6454) and **Pullmantur** (Gran Viá de les Corts Catalanes 635, tel. 93/318–5195). Tours leave from the above terminals, though it may be possible to be picked up at your hotel. The content and price of tours are the same with both agencies. A morning sightseeing tour visits the Gothic Quarter and Montjuïc; an afternoon tour concentrates on Gaudí and the Picasso Museum. Visits to Barcelona's Olympic sites are scheduled from May through October.

Excursions
These are run by **Julià Tours** and **Pullmantur** and are booked as above. Principal trips are a half-day tour to **Montserrat** to visit the monastery and shrine of the famous Black Virgin; a full-day trip to the **Costa Brava** resorts, including a boat cruise to the Medes Isles; and, from June to September, a full-day trip to **Andorra** for tax-free shopping.

Exploring Barcelona

Numbers in the margin correspond to points of interest on the Barcelona map.

Barcelona, capital of Catalonia, thrives on its business acumen and industrial muscle. Its hardworking citizens are proud to have and use their own language—with street names, museum exhibits, newspapers, radio programs, and movies all in Catalan. A recent milestone was the realization of their long-cherished goal to host the Olympic Games, held in Barcelona in summer 1992 after a massive building program. The Games' legacy to the city includes a vastly improved ring road and several other highways; four new beaches and an entire new neighborhood in what used to be the run-down industrial district of Poble Nou; an adjoining marina; and a new sports stadium and pools on the hill of Montjuïc. This thriving metropolis also has a rich history and an abundance of sights. Few places can rival the narrow alleys of its Gothic Quarter for medieval atmosphere, the elegance and distinction of its Moderniste Eixample area, or the fantasies of Gaudí's whimsical imagination.

It should take you two full days of sightseeing to complete the following tour. The first part covers the Gothic Quarter, the Picasso Museum, and the Rambla. The second part takes you to Passeig de Gràcia, the Sagrada Família, and Montjuïc.

Start on Plaça de la Seu, where on Sunday morning the citizens of Barcelona gather to dance the *Sardana*, a symbol of Catalan identity.

1 Step inside the magnificent Gothic **cathedral** built between 1298 and 1450, though the spire and Gothic facade were not added until 1892. Highlights are the beautifully carved **choir stalls,** Santa Eulàlia's tomb in the crypt, the battle-scarred crucifix from Don Juan's galley in the **Lepanto Chapel,** and the cloisters. *Tel. 93/315–1554. Admission free. Open daily 7:45–1:30 and 4–7:45.*

2 Around the corner is the **Museu Frederic Marès,** where you can browse for hours among the miscellany of sculptor-collector Frederic Marès. Displayed here is everything from polychrome crucifixes to hat pins, pipes, and walking sticks. *Plaça Sant Iu 5, tel. 93/310–5800. Admission: 350 ptas., Wed. 175 ptas., 1st Sun. of every month free. Open Tues.–Sat. 10–5, Sun. 10–2.*

3 The neighboring **Plaça del Rei** embodies the very essence of the Gothic Quarter. Following Columbus's first voyage to America, the Catholic Kings received him in the **Saló de Tinell,** a magnificent banqueting hall built in 1362. Other ancient buildings around the square are the **Lieutenant's Palace;** the 14th-century **Chapel of St. Agatha,** built right into the Roman city wall; and the **Padellás Palace,** which houses the City History Museum.

Cross Vía Laietana, walk down Princesa, and turn right into Montcada, where you come to one of Barcelona's most popular attractions,

4 the **Museu Picasso.** Two 15th-century palaces provide a striking setting for the collections donated in 1963 and 1970, first by Picasso's secretary, then by the artist himself. The collection ranges from early childhood sketches to exhibition posters done in Paris shortly before his death. Of particular interest are his Blue Period pictures and his variations on Velázquez's *Las Meninas. Carrer Montcada 15–19, tel. 93/319–6310. Admission: 650 ptas; Wed. half price, free 1st Sun. of every month. Open Tues.–Sat. 10–8, Sun. 10–3.*

TIME OUT   At the bottom of Montcada, on the left, is **La Pizza Nostra** (Arc de Sant Vicens 2, tel. 93/319-9058), an ideal spot for a cup of coffee, a slice of cheesecake, or a pizza and a glass of wine. Or you may prefer the colorful **Xampanyet** across the street.

5 **Santa Maria del Mar** is the best example of a Mediterranean Gothic church, and is widely considered Barcelona's loveliest. It was built between 1329 and 1383 in fulfillment of a vow made a century earlier by Jaume I to build a church for the Virgin of the Sailors. Its simple beauty is enhanced by a stunning rose window and magnificent soaring columns. *Open Mon.–Fri. 9–12:30 and 5–8; closed weekends.*

6 Continue up Carrer Argentería, cross Vía Laietana, and walk along Jaume I till you come to **Plaça Sant Jaume,** an impressive square built in the 1840s in the heart of the Gothic Quarter. The two imposing buildings facing each other across the square are very much older. The 15th-century **Ajuntament,** or City Hall, has an impressive black and gold mural (1928) by Josep María Sert (who also painted the murals for New York's Waldorf Astoria) and the famous **Saló de Cent,** from which the Council of One Hundred ruled the city from 1372 to 1714. You can wander into the courtyard, but to visit the interior, you will need to ask permission in the office beforehand. The **Palau de la Generalitat,** seat of the Catalan Regional Government, is a 15th-century palace open to the public on Sunday mornings only.

7 Continue along the Carrer Ferrán, with its attractive 19th-century shops and numerous Moderniste touches, to the **Plaça Reial.** Here in this splendid 19th-century square, arcaded houses overlook the wrought-iron **Fountain of the Three Graces** and lampposts designed by a young Gaudí in 1879. Watch out for drug pushers here; the most colorful time to come is on a Sunday morning when crowds gather at the stamp and coin stalls and listen to soap-box orators.

TIME OUT Nearby are two atmospheric restaurants, **Los Caracoles** (Esudellers 14) and **Can Culleretes** (Quintana 15).

8 Head to the bottom of Rambla and take an elevator to the top of the **Monument a Colon** (Columbus Monument) for a breathtaking view over the city. Columbus faces out to sea, pointing, ironically, east. (Nearby you can board the cable car that crosses the harbor to Barceloneta or goes up to Montjuïc.) *Admission: 300 ptas. adults, 150 ptas. children. Open Tues.–Sat. 10–2 and 3:30–6:30, Sun. 10–7.*

9 Our next stop is the **Museu Marítim** (Maritime Museum) housed in the 13th-century Drassanes Reiales, the old Royal Shipyards. The museum is packed with ships, figureheads, nautical paraphernalia, and several early navigation charts, including a map by Amerigo Vespucci, and the 1439 chart of Gabriel de Valseca from Mallorca, the oldest chart in Europe. *Plaça Portal de la Pau 1, tel. 93/318–3245. Admission: 350 ptas., Wed. 175 ptas., 1st Sun. of every month free. Open Tues.–Sat. 10–2 and 4–7, Sun. 10–2.*

10 Turn back up the Rambla to Nou de la Rambla. At No. 3 is Gaudí's **Palau Güell.** Gaudí built this mansion between 1885 and 1890 for his patron, Count Eusebi de Güell, and it's the only one of his houses that is open to the public. *Admission: 350 ptas. Open Tues.–Sat. 10–1:30 and 4–7:30.*

11 Our next landmark, the **Gran Teatre del Liceu,** Barcelona's famous opera house, was tragically gutted by fire in early 1994. Built between 1845 and 1847, the Liceu claims to be the world's oldest opera house; it was also one of the world's most beautiful, with ornamental gilt and plush red velvet fittings. Anna Pavlova danced here in 1930, and Maria Callas sang here in 1959. The Liceu is being restored and is expected to open again in 1997. *Visits to certain rooms that were not damaged can be arranged (tel. 93/318–9122).*

12 This next stretch of the **Rambla** is one of the most fascinating. The colorful paving stones on the Plaça de la Boquería were designed by Joan Miró. Glance up at the swirling Moderniste dragon and the Art Nouveau street lamps. Then take a look inside the bustling **Boqueria Market** and the **Antiga Casa Figueras,** a vintage pastry shop on the corner of Petxina, with a splendid mosaic facade.

990

Casa Milà, **16**

Catedral, **1**

Fundació Miró, **19**

Gran Teatre del Liceu, **11**

Mançana de la Discòrdia, **15**

Monument a Colon, **8**

Museu Nacional d'Art de Catalunya, **18**

Museu Frederic Marès, **2**

Museu Marítim, **9**

Museu Picasso, **4**

Palau de la Virreina, **13**

Palau Güell, **10**

Plaça de Catalunya, **14**

Plaça del Rei, **3**

Plaça Reial, **7**

Plaça Sant Jaume, **6**

Rambla, **12**

Santa Maria del Mar, **5**

Temple Expiatori de la Sagrada Família, **17**

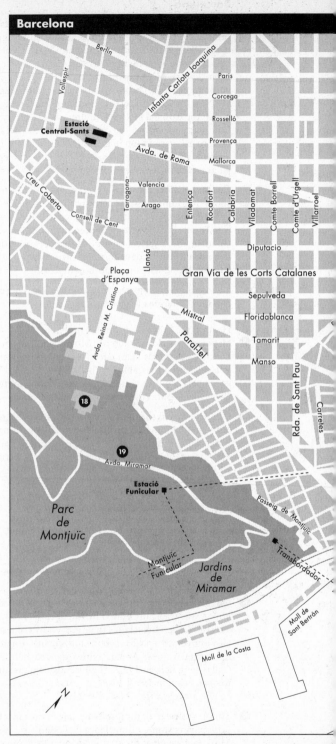

Barcelona

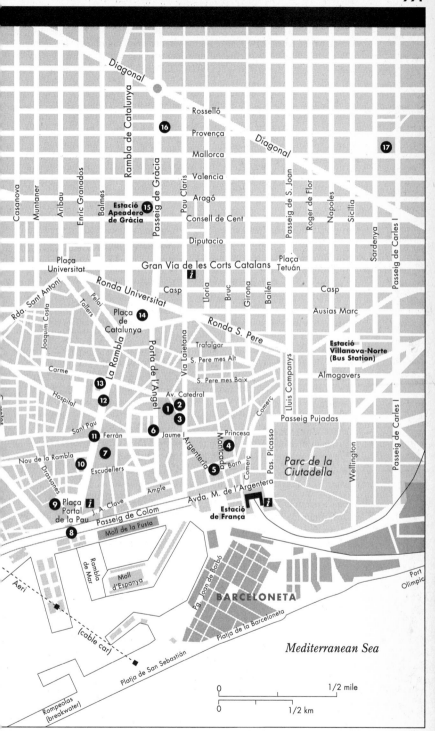

Diagonal

Rosselló
Provença
Mallorca
Valencia
Aragó
Consell de Cent
Diputacio

16

Rambla de Catalunya

Passeig de Gràcia

Pau Claris

Diagonal

Passeig de S. Joan

Roger de Flor

Napoles

Sicilia

Sardenya

Passeig de Carles I

17

Estació Apeadero de Gràcia **15**

Plaça Universitat

Gran Vía de les Corts Catalans

Plaça Tetuán

i

Ronda Universitat

Casp

Lloria

Bruc

Girona

Bailén

Casp

Ausias Marc

Rda. Sant Antoni

Joaquim Costa

Tallers

Pelai

Plaça de Catalunya **14**

Porta de l'Angel

Via Laietana

Ronda S. Pere

Trafalgar

S. Pere mes Alt

S. Pere mes Baix

Estació Villanova-Norte (Bus Station)

Almogavers

Casanova

Muntaner

Aribau

Enric Granados

Balmes

Carme

La Rambla

Hospital

13

12

Av. Catedral

1 **2**

3

Lluis Companys

Passeig Pujadas

Passeig de Carles I

Sant Pau

11 Ferràn

6 Jaume I

Princesa

4

Montcada

Comerç

7

Nou de la Rambla

10

Escudellers

Argenteria

Born

5

Comerç

Pas. Picasso

Parc de la Ciutadella

Wellington

Drassanes

Ample

Avda. M. de l'Argentera

9 Plaça Portal de la Pau *i*

J. A. Clave

Estació de França

i

8

Passeig de Colom

Moll de la Fusta

Aeri

Rambla de Mar

Moll d'Espanya

Pg. Joan de Borbó

BARCELONETA

Platja de la Barceloneta

Port Olímpic

(cable car)

Platja de San Sebastián

Mediterranean Sea

Rompeolas (breakwater)

0   1/2 mile

0   1/2 km

⑬ The **Palau de la Virreina** was built by a viceroy from Peru in 1778. It's recently been converted into a major exhibition center, and you should check to see what's showing while you're in town. *Rambla de les Flors 99, tel. 93/301–7775. Admission: 500 ptas., Wed. 250 ptas. Open Tues.–Sat. 10–2 and 4:30–9, Sun. 10–2, Mon. 4:30–9. Last entrance 30 mins before closing.*

⑭ The final stretch of the Rambla brings us past the lively bird market and out onto the busy **Plaça de Catalunya,** the frantic business center and transport hub of the modern city. The first stage of the tour ends here. You may want to head for the Corte Inglés department store across the square or for any of the stores on the nearby **Porta de l'Angel.** Alternatively, you can relax on the terrace of the ancient **Café Zurich** on the corner of Pelai, or stop at the colorful beer hall, the **Cervecería,** opposite the Hotel Continental.

Above the Plaça de Catalunya you come into modern Barcelona and an elegant area known as the **Eixample,** which was laid out in the late 19th century as part of the city's expansion scheme. Much of the building here was done at the height of the **Moderniste** movement, a Spanish and mainly Catalan offshoot of Art Nouveau, whose leading exponents were the architects Gaudí, Domènech i Montaner, and Puig i Cadafalch. The principal thoroughfares of the Eixample are the Rambla de Catalunya and the Passeig de Gràcia, where some of the city's most elegant shops and cafés are found. Moderniste houses are one of Barcelona's special drawing cards, so walk up **Passeig de Gràcia** until
⑮ you come to the **Mançana de la Discòrdia,** or Block of Discord, between Consell de Cent and Aragó. Its name is a pun on the word *mançana,* which means both "block" and "apple." The houses here are quite fantastic: The floral **Casa Lleó Morera** at No. 35 is by Domènech i Montaner. The pseudo-Gothic **Casa Amatller** at No. 41 is by Puig i Cadafalch. At No. 43 is Gaudí's **Casa Batlló.** Farther along
⑯ the street on the right, on the corner of Provença, is Gaudí's **Casa Milà** (Passeig de Gràcia 92), more often known as **La Pedrera.** Its remarkable curving stone facade with ornamental balconies actually ripples its way around the corner of the block. To arrange a guided tour of Gaudí's phantasmagorical roof, call 93/488–3592.

TIME OUT   You can ponder the vagaries of Gaudí's work over a drink in **Amarcord,** a terrace café on the sidewalk in front of the Pedrera building at Provença 261. For a more sedate, old-world tearoom, head for the **Salón de Té Mauri** on the corner of Rambla de Catalunya and Provença.

⑰ Now take the metro at Diagonal or walk 20 minutes to Barcelona's most eccentric landmark, Gaudí's **Temple Expiatori de la Sagrada Família** (Expiatory Church of the Holy Family). Far from finished at his death in 1926—Gaudí was run over by a tram and died in a pauper's hospital—this striking creation will cause consternation or wonder, shrieks of protest or cries of rapture. In 1936 during the Spanish Civil War the citizens of Barcelona loved their crazy temple enough to spare it from the flames that engulfed all their other churches except the cathedral. An elevator takes visitors to the top of one of the towers for a magnificent view of the city. Gaudí is buried in the crypt. *Tel. 93/455–0247. Admission: 700 ptas. Open Sept.–May, daily 9–7; June–Aug., daily 9–9.*

Back across town to the south, the hill of **Montjuïc** was named for the Jewish cemetery once located on its slopes. Montjuïc is home to a castle, an amusement park, several delightful gardens, a model Spanish village, an illuminated fountain, the recently rebuilt Mies van der Rohe Pavilion, and a cluster of museums—all of which could keep you busy for a day or more. This was the principal venue for the 1992 Olympics.

⑱ One of the leading attractions here is the **Museu Nacional d'Art de Catalunya** (National Museum of Catalan Art) in the Palau Nacional atop a long flight of steps. The collection of Romanesque and Gothic art treasures—medieval frescoes and altarpieces, mostly from small churches and chapels in the Pyrenees—is simply staggering. Just three rooms were open at press time (spring 1995), but the entire museum was expected to open by late 1995 after extensive renovations; ask at the tourist office for current information.

⑲ Nearby, on Avigunda de Miramar, is the **Fundació Miró** (Miró Foundation), a gift from the artist Joan Miró to his native city. One of Barcelona's most exciting contemporary galleries, it has several exhibition areas, many of them devoted to Miró's works. *Tel. 93/329–1908. Admission: 650 ptas. Open Tues.–Sat. 11–7 (9:30 on Thurs.), Sun. 10:30–2:30.*

Off the Beaten Track

If you're hooked on **Moderniste** architecture, you can follow a walking trail around the **Dreta de l'Eixample,** the area to the right of Rambla de Catalunya. Ask at a tourist office for a Gaudí or Modernisme trail brochure for the Eixample. Attend a concert at Domènech i Montaner's fantastic **Palau de la Música.** Make a trip to the **Parc Güell,** Gaudí's magical attempt at creating a garden city. *Open May–Aug., daily 10–9; Sept.–Apr., daily 10–7.*

Explore the **Gràcia** area, above the Diagonal. It's a small, once independent village within a large city, a warren of narrow streets, changing name at every corner, and filled with tiny shops where you'll find everything from old-fashioned tin lanterns to feather dusters.

Take a stroll around **Barceloneta,** the old fishermen's quarter built in 1755 below the Estació de França and the Ciutadella Park. There are no-frills fish restaurants on the Passeig Joan de Borbó and beach restaurants along the Passeig Marítim. Hike out to the end of the *rompeolas* (breakwater), extending 2½ miles southeast into the Mediterranean, for a panoramic view of the city and a few breaths of fresh air.

Hunt out the tiny **Shoe Museum** in Plaça Sant Felip Neri, in a hidden corner of the Gothic Quarter, between the cathedral and Bishop's Palace. The collection includes clowns' shoes and a pair worn by Pablo Casals. *Plaça de Sant Felip Neri. Admission: 300 ptas. Open Tues.–Sun. 11–2.*

Shopping

Gift Ideas

There are no special handicrafts associated with Barcelona, but you'll have no trouble finding typical Spanish goods anywhere in town. If you're into fashion and jewelry, then you've come to the right place, as Barcelona makes all the headlines on Spain's booming fashion front. **Xavier Roca i Coll,** Sant Pere mes Baix 24, just off Laietana, specializes in silver models of Barcelona's buildings.

Barcelona and Catalonia have passed along a playful sense of design ever since Antoni Gaudí began creating shockwaves over a century ago. Stores and boutiques specializing in design items (jewelry, furnishings, knickknacks) include **Gimeno** (Passeig de Gracia 102), **Vinçon** (Passeig de Gràcia 96), **Bd** (Barcelona Design, at Mallorca 291–293), and **Dos i Una** (Rosselló 275).

Antiques

Carrer de la Palla and Banys Nous in the Gothic Quarter are lined with antiques shops where you'll find old maps, books, paintings, and furniture. An **antiques market** is held every Thursday, 10–8, in Plaça del Pi. The **Centre d'Antiquaris,** Passeig de Gràcia 57, has some 75 antiques stores. **Gothsland,** Consell de Cent 331, specializes in Moderniste designs.

Boutiques

The most fashionable boutiques are in the **Galerías** on Passeig de Gràcia and Rambla de Catalunya. Others are on Gran Vía between Balmes and Pau Claris; and on the Diagonal between Ganduxer and Passeig de Gràcia. **Adolfo Domínguez,** Spain's top designer, is at Passeig de Gràcia 89 and Valencia 245; **Loewe,** Spain's top leather store, is at Passeig de Gràcia 35 and Diagonal 570; **Joaquín Berao,** a top jewelry designer, is at Rosselló 277.

Shopping Districts

Elegant shopping districts are the Passeig de Gràcia, Rambla de Catalunya, and the Diagonal. For more affordable, more old-fashioned, and typically Spanish-style shops, explore the area between Ramblas and Vía Laietana, especially around C. Ferran. The area around Plaça del Pi from Boquería to Portaferrisa and Canuda is recommended for young fashion stores and imaginative gift shops.

Department Stores

El Corte Inglés is on the Plaça de Catalunya 14 (tel. 93/302–1212) and at Diagonal 617 (tel. 93/419–2828) near the María Cristina metro stop. **Galerías Preciados** is at Porta de l'Angel 19 just off the Plaça de Catalunya; Diagonal 471 on the Plaça Francesc Macià; and Avenida Meridiana 352. All are open Monday through Saturday 10–8.

Food and Flea Markets

The **Boquería** or **Sant Josep Market** on the Ramblas between Carme and Hospital is a superb, colorful food market, held every day except Sunday. **Els Encants,** Barcelona's wild-and-woolly flea market, is held every Monday, Wednesday, Friday, and Saturday, 8–7, at the end of Dos de Maig on the Plaça Glòries Catalanes. **Sant Antoni Market,** at the end of Ronda Sant Antoni, is an old-fashioned food and clothes market, best on Sundays when there's a secondhand **book market** with old postcards, press cuttings, lithographs, and prints. There's a **stamp and coin market** in the Plaça Reial on Sunday mornings, and an **artists' market** in the Placeta del Pi just off the Rambla and Boquería on Saturday morning.

Bullfighting

Barcelona has two bullrings, the **Monumental** on Gran Vía and Carles I, and the smaller **Les Arenes** on the Plaça d'Espanya, now mainly used for rock concerts. Bullfights are held on Sundays between March and October; check the newspaper for details. The official ticket office, where there is no markup on tickets, is at Muntaner 24 (tel. 93/453–3821) near Gran Vía. There's a **Bullfighting Museum** at the Monumental ring, open March–October, daily 10–1 and 5:30–7.

Dining

For details and price-category definitions, *see* Dining *in* Staying in Spain, *above.*

$$$$ Beltxenea. There is an air of intimacy in this redecorated Eixample apartment, now converted to a series of elegant dining rooms. In summer you can dine outside in the formal garden. Chef Miguel Ezcurra's excellent cuisine is one of Barcelona's top Basque dining opportunities; a specialty is his *merluza con kokotxas y almejas* (hake and clams fried in garlic then simmered in stock). *Mallorca 275, tel. 93/215–3024. Reservations advised. AE, DC, MC, V. No lunch Sat. Closed Sun., Aug. 15– 30, Dec. 20–Jan. 7.*

$$$ Agut d'Avignon. This venerable Barcelona institution takes a bit of finding; it's near the junction of Ferran and Avinyó in the Gothic Quarter. The ambience is rustic and it's a favorite with businesspeople and politicians from the nearby Generalitat. The cuisine is traditional Catalan and game specialties are recommended in season. *Trinidat 3, tel. 93/317–3693. Reservations required. AE, DC, MC, V. Closed Holy Wk.*

$$$ La Cuineta. This small intimate restaurant in a 17th-century house just off Plaça Sant Jaume and its sister location behind the cathedral specialize in Catalan nouvelle cuisine. The decor is elegant and traditional; the service, professional; and the cuisine, impeccable. *Paradis 4, tel. 93/315– 0812; Pietat 12, tel. 93/315–4156. AE, DC, MC, V. Closed Mon.*

$$$ Quo Vadis. Located just off the Ramblas, near the Boquería Market and Betlem Church, is an unimpressive facade camouflaging one of Barcelona's most respected restaurants. Its much-praised cuisine includes delicacies like pot pourri *de setas* (wild mushrooms), *lubina al hinojo* (sea bass in fennel), and *hígado de ganso con ciruelas* (goose liver with plums). *Carmen 7, tel. 93/317–7447. Reservations advised. AE, DC, MC, V. Closed Sun.*

$$$ Tram-Tram. With prominent chef Isidro Soler at the helm in the kitchen
★ and Reyes Lizán as hostess and pastry chef, Tram-Tram is one of Barcelona's culinary stars. The excursion to the northwestern suburb of Sarrià, a village swallowed up by the city, is a delight. Order the taster's menu and let Isidro have his way with your palate. You won't regret it. *Major de Sarrià 121, tel. 93/204–8518. Reservations advised. AE, MC, V. Closed Sun. and Dec. 24–Jan. 6.*

$$ Can Culleretes. This picturesque old restaurant began life as a pastry shop in 1786, and it is one of the most atmospheric and reasonable finds in Barcelona. Located on an alleyway between Ferran and Boquería, its three dining rooms are decorated with photos of visiting celebrities. It serves real Catalan cooking and is very much a family concern; don't be put off by the street life that might be raging outside. *Quintana 5, tel. 93/317–3022. AE, MC, V. No lunch Sun. Closed Mon.*

$$ Los Caracoles. Just below the Plaça Reial is Barcelona's best known tourist haunt, crawling with Americans having a terrific time. Its walls are hung thick with photos of bullfighters and visiting celebrities; its specialties are mussels, paella and, of course, *caracoles* (snails). *Escudellers 14, tel. 93/309–3185. AE, DC, MC, V.*

$$ Set Portes. With plenty of old-world charm, this delightful restaurant
★ near the waterfront has been going strong since 1836. The cooking is Catalan, the portions enormous, and specialties are paella *de pescado* (with seafood) and *zarzuela Set Portes* (a mixed grill of seafood). *Passeig Isabel II 14, tel. 93/319–3033. Weekend reservations advised. AE, DC, MC, V.*

$$ Sopeta Una. Dining in this delightful small restaurant with old-fash-
★ ioned decor and intimate atmosphere is more like eating in a private home. All the dishes are Catalan, and the atmosphere is very genteel and middle class. For dessert, try the traditional Catalan *música*—a plate of raisins, almonds, and dried fruit served with a glass of muscatel. It's near the Palau de la Música; don't be put off by the narrow street. *Verdaguer i Callis 6, tel. 93/319–6131. V. Closed Sun.*

$ **Agut.** Simple, hearty Catalan fare awaits you in this unpretentious restau-
★ rant in the lower reaches of the Gothic Quarter. Founded in 1924, its
popularity has never waned. There's plenty of wine to wash down the
traditional home cooking, but you won't find frills like coffee or
liqueurs. *Gignàs 16, tel. 93/319–3315. No credit cards. Closed Mon.
and July. No dinner Sun.*

$ **Egipte.** This small, friendly restaurant hidden away in a very conve-
★ nient location behind the Boquería Market—though it's far better
known to locals than to visitors—is a real find. Its traditional Catalan
home cooking, huge desserts, and swift personable service all contribute
to its popularity and good value. *Jerusalem 12, tel. 93/301–6208. No
reservations. No credit cards.*

Lodging

Hotels around the Rambla and in the Gothic Quarter have plenty of
old-world charm, but are less strong on creature comforts; those in the
Eixample are mostly '50s or '60s buildings, often recently renovated;
and the newest hotels are found out along the Diagonal or beyond, in
the residential districts of Sarriá and Pedralbes. There are hotel reservation desks at the airport and Central Station.

For details and price-category definitions, *see* Lodging *in* Staying in Spain,
above.

$$$$ **Condes de Barcelona.** As this is one of Barcelona's most popular ho-
★ tels, rooms must be booked well in advance. The decor is stunning,
with marble floors and columns, an impressive staircase, and an outstanding bar area, but no restaurant. Guest rooms are on the small side.
*Passeig de Gràcia 75, 08008, tel. 93/487–3737; for reservations,
93/215–7931, fax 93/216–0835. 183 rooms with bath. Facilities:
restaurant, bar, parking. AE, DC, MC, V.*

$$$$ **Hotel Arts.** This luxurious Ritz-Carlton monolith overlooks Barcelona
from the new Olympic Port, providing unique views of the Mediterranean, the city, and the mountains behind. A short taxi ride from the
center of the city, the hotel is virtually a world of its own. The hotel
has three restaurants that respectively serve Mediterranean cuisine, Cal-
ifornian cooking, and tapas, like *gambas al ajillo* (baby shrimp fried
in garlic). *Calle de la Marina 19–21, tel. 93/221–1070. 455 rooms
and suites. Facilities: 3 restaurants, bar, pool, hair salon, beach, shops,
parking. AE, DC, MC, V.*

$$$$ **Hotel Claris.** Widely considered Barcelona's best hotel, the Claris is a
fascinating melange of design and tradition. The rooms come in 60 different layouts, all furnished in classical 18th-century English style.
Wood and marble furnishings and decorative details are everywhere,
along with a Japanese water garden, a first-rate restaurant, and a
rooftop pool—all close to the center of Barcelona. *Carrer Pau Claris
150, tel. 93/487–6262, fax 93/215–7970. 124 rooms and suites. Facilities: restaurant, bar, pool, garden. AE, DC, MC, V.*

$$$$ **Princesa Sofia.** The Barcelona hotel most convenient to the airport, the
Princesa Sofia is somewhat far from the hue and cry of downtown. For
business, comfort, and convenience, though, it's one of the city's best
guarantees. *Plaça Pius XII 4, tel. 93/330–7111, fax 93/411–2106. 505
rooms. Facilities: 3 restaurants, shops, fitness center, sauna, 2 pools.
AE, DC, MC, V.*

$$$$ **Ritz.** Founded in 1919 by Caesar Ritz, this is still the grand old lady
★ of Barcelona hotels. Extensive refurbishment has now restored it to its
former splendor. The entrance lobby is awe-inspiring, the rooms spacious, and the service impeccable. *Gran Vía 668, 08010, tel. 93/318–*

5200, fax 93/318–0148. 158 rooms with bath. Facilities: restaurant, bar. AE, DC, MC, V.

$$$ **Colón.** This cozy, older hotel has a unique charm and intimacy remi-
★ niscent of an English country hotel that recent refurbishing has left in-
tact. It's in an ideal location right in the heart of the Gothic Quarter,
and the rooms on the front overlook the cathedral and square. It was
a great favorite of Joan Miró. *Avda. Catedral 7, 08002, tel. 93/301–
1404, fax 93/317–2915. 148 rooms with bath. Facilities: restaurant,
bar. AE, DC, MC, V.*

$$$ **Regente.** This smallish hotel on the corner of Valencia has a rooftop
pool, plenty of style and charm, and a wonderful Modernista lobby. *Ram-
bla de Catalunya 76, 08008, tel. 93/215–2570, fax 93/487–3227. 78
rooms with bath. Facilities: 2 restaurants, bar, pool. AE, DC, MC, V.*

$$ **España.** This hotel with modern, large bedrooms—the best and qui-
etest overlook the bright interior patio—has stunning Art Nouveau pub-
lic rooms. The high-ceilinged downstairs has a breakfast room decorated
with mermaids, elaborate woodwork, and an Art Nouveau sculpted
chimney in the cafeteria. The rooms have been recently refurbished,
and the neighborhood is seedy but safe. *Sant Pau 9–1, 08001, tel.
93/318–1758, fax 93/317–1134. 76 rooms with bath. Facilities:
restaurant, breakfast room, cafeteria. AE, DC, MC, V.*

$$ **Gran Vía.** Architectural features are the special charm of this 19th-cen-
tury mansion, close to the main tourist office. The original chapel has
been preserved, and you can have breakfast in a hall of mirrors, climb
its Moderniste staircase, and make calls from elaborate Belle Epoque phone
booths. *Gran Vía 642, 08007, tel. 93/318–1900, fax 93/318–9997. 53
rooms with bath. Facilities: breakfast room, parking. AE, DC, MC, V.*

$$ **Oriente.** Barcelona's oldest hotel opened in 1843. Its public rooms are
★ a delight—the ballroom and dining rooms have lost none of their
19th-century magnificence—though the bedrooms have undergone
rather featureless renovation. It's located just below the Liceu, and its
terrace café is the perfect place for a drink. *Rambla 45, 08002, tel.
93/302–2558, fax 93/412–3819. 142 rooms with bath. Facilities:
restaurant, bar. AE, DC, MC, V.*

$ **Continental.** Something of a legend among cost-conscious travelers, this
comfortable hostel with canopied balconies stands at the top of Ram-
blas, just below Plaça Catalunya. The rooms are homey and comfort-
able, the staff is friendly, and the location's ideal. Buffet breakfasts are
a plus. *Rambla 136, 08002, tel. 93/301–2570, fax 93/302–7360. 35
rooms with bath. Facilities: breakfast room. AE, DC, MC, V.*

$ **Jardí.** With views over the adjoining traffic-free and charming squares,
★ Plaçdel Pi and Plaça Sant Josep Oriol, this hotel's renovated bedrooms
have white-tile floors, pine furniture, and powerful showers. Exterior
rooms are the quietest. *Plaça Sant Josep Oriol 1, 08002, tel. 93/301–
5900, fax 93/318–3664. 40 rooms with bath. Facilities: breakfast
room, bar. AE, DC, MC, V.*

Bars and Cafés

Cafés and Tearooms

Zurich (Plaça de Catalunya 1), at the head of La Rambla, on the cor-
ner of Pelai, is one of the oldest and most traditional cafés, perfect for
watching the world go by. Near the Picasso Museum, don't miss the
Textil Café in the Museu Textil's lovely medieval courtyard (Montcada
12–14). The **Croissant Show** (Santa Anna 10 just off the Rambla), is
a small coffee and pastry shop, ideal for a quick mid-morning or af-
ternoon break. **Salón de Té Mauri,** on the corner of Rambla de Catalunya
and Provença, and **Salón de Té Libre i Serra** (Ronda Sant Pere 3), are

both traditional tearooms with a good selection of pastries. **Carrer Petritxol** (from Portaferrissa to Plaça del Pi) is famous for its *chocolaterías*, hot chocolate, and tearooms.

Tapas Bars

Alt Heidelberg (Ronda Universitat 5) has German beer on tap and German sausages; **Cal Pep** on Plaça de les Olles (near Santa Maria del Mar) is another popular spot, as is **Casa Tejada** at Tenor Viñas (near Plaça Francesc Macià).

Cocktail Bars

The two best areas are the **Passeig del Born,** which is near the Picasso Museum and very fashionable with the affluent young, and the **Eixample,** near Passeig de Gràcia. A bar called **Dry Martini** (Aribau 162) has more than 80 different gins; **Ideal Cocktail Bar,** at Aribau 89, has some good malt whiskeys. **El Paraigua,** on Plaça Sant Miquel, in the Gothic Quarter behind the city hall, serves cocktails in a stylish setting with classical music.

Champagne Bars

Xampanyerías, serving sparkling Catalan cava, are something of a Barcelona specialty. Try **Brut** (Trompetas 3), in the Picasso Museum area; **La Cava del Palau** (Verdaguer i Callis 10), near the Palau de la Música; or **La Folie** (Bailén 169), one of the best.

Special Cafés

Els Quatre Gats (Montsiò 5, off Porta de l'Angel) is a reconstruction of the original café that opened in 1897, and a real Barcelona institution. Literary discussions, jazz, and classical music recitals take place in this café where Picasso held his first show. **Café de l'Opera** (Ramblas 74), opposite the Liceu, is a long-standing Barcelona tradition, ideal for a coffee or drink at any time of day.

The Arts

To find out what's on in town, look in the daily papers or in the weekly *Guía del Ocio,* available from newsstands all over town. *Actes a la Ciutat* is a weekly list of cultural events published by the Ajuntament and available from its information office on Plaça Sant Jaume or at the Virreina at La Rambla 99.

Concerts

Catalans are great music lovers, and their main concert hall is the **Palau de la Música** (Sant Francesc de Paula 2, tel. 93/268–1000). The ticket office is open weekdays 11–1 and 5–8 and Saturday 5–8 only. Its Sunday morning concerts are a popular tradition. Tickets are reasonably priced and can usually be purchased just before the concert.

Dance

L'Espai de Dansa i Mùsica de la Generalitat de Catalunya (Travessera de Gràcia 63, tel. 93/201–2906), usually listed simply as "L'Espai" (the Space), is now Barcelona's prime venue for ballet and contemporary dance. **El Mercat de les Flors** (Lleida 59, tel. 93/426–1875), not far from Plaça d'Espanya, continues to offer its traditionally rich program of modern dance and theater, as does the **Teatre Victoria** (Av. Paral.lel 67, tel. 93/443–2929).

Theater

Most theater performances are in Catalan, but Barcelona is also known for its experimental theater and for its mime troupes such as **Els Joglars** and **La Claca** (language is not always an impediment). The best-known modern theaters are the **Teatre Lliure** (Montseny 47, in Gràcia, tel.

93/218–9251), **Mercat de les Flors** (*see* Dance, *above*), **Teatre Romea** (Hospital 51, tel. 93/317–7189), **Teatre Tívoli** (Casp 10, tel. 93/412–2063), and **Teatre Poliorama** (Rambla Estudios 115, tel. 93/317–7599).

Film

Many theaters show foreign movies in their original languages. The **Filmoteca** (av. Sarrià 33, tel. 93/430–5007) often includes English films in its schedule.

Nightlife

Cabaret

Belle Epoque (Muntaner 246, tel. 93/209–7385) is a beautifully decorated music hall with sophisticated shows. **El Mediévolo** (Gran Vía 459, tel. 93/243–1566) has medieval feasts and entertainment; it's all geared to tourists but fun.

Casino

The **Gran Casino de Barcelona** (tel. 93/893–3866), 42 kilometers (26 miles) south in Sant Pere de Ribes, near Sitges, also has a dance hall and some excellent international shows in a 19th-century atmosphere. Jacket and tie essential.

Discos

The two top discos are **Otto Zutz** (Lincoln 15, tel. 93/238–0722), just below Via Augusta, and **Up and Down** (Numancia 179, tel. 93/280–2922)—ask for " 'pen-dow." **Oliver and Hardy** (Diagonal 593, next to the Barcelona Hilton, tel. 93/419–3181) is kind to persons over 35; **La Tierra** (Aribau 230, tel. 93/200–7346) and **El Otro** (Valencia 166, tel. 93/323–6759) also accept post-graduates.

Flamenco

The best place is **El Patio Andaluz** (Aribau 242, tel. 93/209–3378). **El Cordobés** (Ramblas 35, tel. 93/317–6853) is aimed at tour groups but can be fun. **Los Tarantos** (Plaça Reial 17, tel. 93/318–3067) is presently the hippest flamenco venue.

Jazz Clubs

Try **L'Auditori** (Balmes 245); **La Cova del Drac** (Vallmajor 33, tel. 93/200–7032); or the Gothic Quarter's **Harlem Jazz Club** (Comtessa Sobradiel 8, tel. 93/310–0755).

Music Bars

The *bar musical* is Spanish for any bar that plays modern music loud enough to drown out conversation. Current top choices are the **Universal** (Marià Cubí 182–184, tel. 93/200–7470), the **Mas i Mas** (Marià Cubí 199, tel. 93/209–4502), and **Nick Havanna** (Rosselló 208, tel. 93/215–6591).

Rock

Check out **Zeleste** (Almogávares 122, tel. 93/309–1204) for performances of all kinds. Major concerts are usually held in sports stadiums; keep an eye out for posters.

Ports and Beaches

The Barcelona waterfront has undergone a major overhaul since 1992. The **Port Vell** (Old Port) now includes an extension of the Rambla, the **Rambla de Mar,** crossing the inner harbor from just below the Columbus Monument. This boardwalk connects the Rambla with the **Moll d'Espanya,** where a shopping mall, a dozen restaurants, aquarium, cinema complex, and Barcelona's two yacht clubs are located. A walk around the Port Vell leads past the marina to Passeig Joan de Borbon, both lined with restaurants that have outdoor tables. From here, you can go south out to sea along the rompeolas, a two-mile excursion, or north (left) down the San Sebastian beach to the Passeig Maritim that leads to the **Port Olympic.** Except for the colorful inner streets of Barceloneta, the traditional fisherman's quarter, all of this new construction is devoid of character. Take the Golondrina boat (*see* Getting Around By Boat, *above*) to the end of the breakwater and walk in to Barceloneta for a paella; the rest is generic entertainment aimed not so much as visitors as at local weekenders.

The beaches that stretch down to and past the Port Olympic are much improved although generally dusty and crowded; water quality is erratic.

MOORISH SPAIN

Stretching from the dark mountains of the Sierra Morena in the north, west to the plains of the Guadalquivir valley, and south to the mighty snowcapped Sierra Nevada, Andalucía rings with echoes of the Moors. In the kingdom they called Al-Andalus, these Muslim invaders from North Africa dwelt for almost 800 years, from their first conquest of Spanish soil (Gibraltar) in 711 to their expulsion from Granada in 1492. And to this day the cities and landscapes of Andalucía are rich in their legacy. The great Mosque of Córdoba, the magical Alhambra Palace in Granada, and the Giralda tower, landmark of Seville, were the inspired creations of Moorish architects and craftsmen working at the behest of Al-Andalus's Arab emirs. The brilliant white villages with narrow streets and sturdy-walled houses clustered round cool inner patios, the whitewashed facades with heavily grilled windows, and the deep wailing song of Andalucía's flamenco, so reminiscent of the muezzin's call to prayer, all stem from centuries of Moorish occupation.

Getting There from Madrid

Seville, Córdoba, and Granada all lie on direct train routes from Madrid. Service is frequent from both Chamartín and Atocha stations in Madrid, and includes overnight trains (to Seville and Granada), slower day trains, and express talgos. In addition, the high-speed AVE train connecting Seville and Atocha Station began service in 1992 on entirely new track; it's more expensive but has cut traveling time on that route from 5½–6 hours to about 2½ hours. Most bus service from Madrid to Moorish Spain operates out of the Estación del Sur (*see* Arriving and Departing *in* Madrid, *above*). If you drive, follow the N-IV, which takes you through the scorched orange plains of La Mancha to Córdoba, then along the Guadalquivir River to Seville. The N323 road, which splits from the N-IV at Bailén, takes you past lovely olive groves and rolling hills to Granada.

Getting Around

Seville and Córdoba are linked by direct train service. Buses are a better choice between Seville and Granada, and between Córdoba and Granada, as trains are relatively slow and infrequent and often involve a time-consuming change. **Seville's** older bus station (tel. 95/441–7111) is between José María Osborne and Manuel Vazquez Sagastizabal; a new bus station is closer to downtown (Arjona, next to the Cachorro Bridge, tel. 95/490–8040). Check with the tourist office to determine which one you'll need. The city also has a spanking new train station, Santa Justa (at José Laquillo and Avda. Kansas City, tel.

Moorish Spain

95/454–0202), built in conjunction with the 1992 International Exposition. In **Granada,** the main bus station is Alsina Gräells (Camino de Ronda 97, tel. 958/251358). The train station is at the end of Avenida Andaluces; the RENFE office is located at Reyes Católicos 63, tel. 958/271272. **Córdoba** has no central bus depot, so check at the tourist office for the appropriate company. The train station is on the Glorieta Conde de Guadalorce (RENFE office: Ronda de los Tejares 10, tel. 957/475884).

Driving in Moorish Spain, long anathema to travelers, has been largely transformed by improvements made for the 1992 festivities. If you like winding roads and gorgeous landscapes, consider driving.

Guided Tours

Guided tours of Seville, Córdoba, Granada, and Ronda are run by **Juliá Tours, Pullmantur,** and **Trapsatur,** both from Madrid and resorts of the Costa del Sol; check with travel agents. Local excursions may be available from Seville to the sherry bodegas and equestrian museum of Jerez de la Frontera. From Granada, there's a weekly day trip to the villages of the Alpujarras; check details with tourist offices.

Tourist Information

Córdoba (Plaza de Judá Leví, tel. 957/200522, and Palacio de Congresos y Exposiciones, Torrijos 10, tel. 957/471235).
Granada (Plaza Mariana Pineda 10, tel. 958/226688, and the less useful office at Corral del Carbón, Calle Mariana Pineda, tel. 958/225990).
Seville (Av. Constitución 21B, tel. 95/422–1404, not far from the cathedral and Archives of the Indies, and the smaller office at Costurero de la Reina, Paseo de las Delícias 9, tel. 95/423–4465).

Exploring Moorish Spain

The downside to a visit here, especially to Seville, is that petty crime, much of it directed against tourists, is rife. Purse snatching and thefts from cars, frequently when drivers are in them, are depressingly familiar. *Always* keep your car doors *and* trunk locked. *Never* leave any valuables in your car. Leave your passport, traveler's checks, and credit cards in your hotel's safe, *never* in your room. Don't carry expensive cameras or wear jewelry. Take only the minimum amount of cash with you. There comes a point, however—if your windshield is smashed or your bag is snatched, for example—when all the precautions in the world will prove inadequate. If you're unlucky, it's an equally depressing fact that the police, again especially in Seville, have adopted a distinctly casual attitude to such thefts, and often combine indifference to beleaguered tourists with rudeness in about equal measure.

Numbers in the margin correspond to points of interest on the Seville map.

Seville

Lying on the banks of the Guadalquivir, **Seville**—Spain's fourth-largest city and capital of Andalucía—is one of the most beautiful and romantic cities in Europe. Here in this city of the sensuous Carmen and the amorous Don Juan, famed for the spectacle of its Holy Week processions and April Fair, you'll come close to the spiritual heart of Moorish Andalucía. Begin your visit in the **cathedral,** begun in 1402, a century and a half after St. Ferdinand delivered Seville from the Moors. This great Gothic edifice, which took just over a century to build, is traditionally described in superlatives. It's the biggest and highest cathedral in Spain, the largest Gothic building in the world, and the world's third-largest church after St. Peter's in Rome and St. Paul's in London. And it boasts the world's largest carved wooden altarpiece. Despite such impressive statistics, the inside can be dark and gloomy with too many overly ornate Baroque trappings. But seek out the beautiful Virgins by Murillo and Zurbarán, and reflect on the history enshrined in these walls. In a silver urn before the high altar rest the precious relics of Seville's liberator, St. Ferdinand. You'll want to pay your respects to Christopher Columbus, whose mortal vestiges are enshrined in a flamboyant mausoleum in the south aisle. Borne aloft by statues representing the four medieval kingdoms of Spain, it's to be hoped the great voyager has found peace at last, after the transatlantic quarrels that carried his body from Valladolid to Santo Domingo and from Havana to Seville. *Admission to cathedral and Giralda (see below): 550 ptas. Open Mon.–Sat. 10–5, Sun. 10–4. Cathedral also open for Mass.*

Every day the bell that summons the faithful to prayer rings out from a Moorish minaret, relic of the Arab mosque whose admirable tower of Abu Yakoub the Sevillians could not bring themselves to destroy. Topped in 1565–68 by a bell tower and weather vane and called the **Giralda,** this splendid example of Moorish art is one of the marvels of Seville. In place of steps, a gently sloping ramp climbs to the viewing platform 230 feet high. St. Ferdinand is said to have ridden his horse to the top to admire the view of the city he had conquered. Seven centuries later your view of the Golden Tower and shimmering Guadalquivir will be equally breathtaking. Try, too, to see the Giralda at night when the floodlights cast a new magic on this gem of Islamic art. *Open same hours as cathedral and visited on same ticket.*

The high fortified walls of the **Alcázar** belie the exquisite delicacy of the palace's interior. It was built by Pedro the Cruel—so known be-

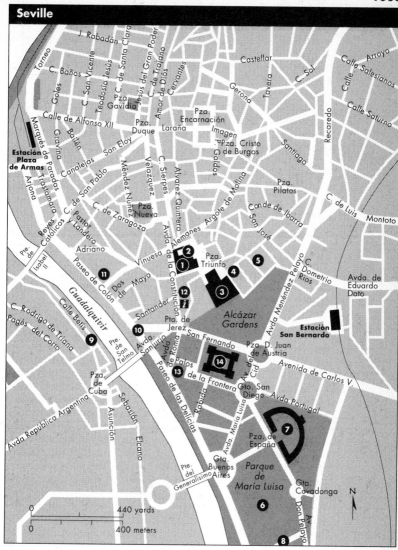

Seville

Major Attractions

Alcázar, **3**

Barrio de
Santa Cruz, **5**

Calle Betis, **9**

Catedral, **1**

Giralda, **2**

Maestranza
Bullring, **11**

Parque de
María Luisa, **6**

Patio de las
Banderas, **4**

Plaza de America, **8**

Plaza de España, **7**

Torre de Oro, **10**

Other Attractions

Museo Arte
Comtemporaneo, **12**

San Telmo Palace, **13**

Tobacco Factory
(University), **14**

cause he murdered his stepmother and four of his half-brothers—who lived here with his mistress María de Padilla from 1350 to 1369. Don't mistake this for a genuine Moorish palace as it was built more than 100 years after the reconquest of Seville; rather, its style is Mudéjar— built by Moorish craftsmen working under orders of a Christian king. The Catholic Kings (Ferdinand and Isabella), whose only son, Prince Juan, was born in the Alcázar in 1478, added a wing to serve as administration center for their New World empire, and Charles V enlarged it further for his marriage celebrations in 1526. Pedro's Mudéjar palace centers around the beautiful **Patio de las Doncellas** (Court of the Damsels), whose name pays tribute to the annual gift of 100 virgins to the Moorish sultans whose palace once stood on the site. Resplendent with the most delicate of lacelike stucco and gleaming azulejo decorations, it is immediately reminiscent of Granada's Alhambra, and is in fact the work of Granadan artisans. Opening off this are the apartments of María de Padilla.

The **Alcázar Gardens** are fragrant with jasmine and myrtle, an orange tree said to have been planted by Pedro the Cruel, and a lily pond well stocked with fat, contented goldfish. The end of your visit brings you ❹ to the **Patio de las Banderas** for an unrivaled view of the Giralda. *Plaza del Triunfo, tel. 95/422–7163. Palace and gardens admission: 600 ptas. Open Tues.–Sat. 10:30–5, Sun. 10–1.*

❺ The **Barrio de Santa Cruz,** with its twisting alleyways, cobbled squares, and whitewashed houses, is a perfect setting for an operetta. Once the home of Seville's Jews, it was much favored by 17th-century noblemen and today boasts some of the most expensive properties in Seville. All the romantic images you've ever had of Spain will come to life here: Every house gleams white or deep ocher yellow; wrought-iron grilles adorn the windows, and every balcony and patio is bedecked with geraniums and petunias. Ancient bars nestle side by side with antiques shops. Don't miss the famous **Casa Román** bar in Plaza de los Venerables Sacerdotes with its ceilings hung thick with some of the best hams in Seville, or the **Hostería del Laurel** next door, where in summer you can dine in one of the loveliest squares in the city. Souvenir and excellent ceramic shops surround the **Plaza Doña Elvira,** where the young of Seville gather to play guitars around the fountain and azulejo benches. And in the **Plaza Alianza,** with its well-stocked antiques shops and **John Fulton Gallery** (Fulton is the only American ever to qualify as a fullfledged bullfighter), stop a moment and admire the simplicity of the crucifix on the wall, framed in a profusion of bougainvillea.

Take a cab, or better still, hire a horse carriage from the Plaza Virgen de ❻ los Reyes, below the Giralda, and visit **Parque de María Luisa** (María Luisa Park), whose gardens are a delightful blend of formal design and wild vegetation, shady walkways and sequestered nooks. In the 1920s the park was redesigned to form the site of the 1929 Hispanic-American exhibition, and the impressive villas you see here today are the fair's ❼ remaining pavilions. Visit the monumental **Plaza de España,** whose grandiose pavilion of Spain was the centerpiece of the exhibition. At the opposite end of the park you can feed the hundreds of white doves that ❽ gather round the fountains of the lovely **Plaza de America;** it's a magical spot to while away the sleepy hours of the siesta.

❾ An early evening stroll along the **Calle Betis** on the far side of the Guadalquivir is a delight few foreigners know about. Between the San Telmo and Isabel II bridges, the vista of the sparkling water, the palmlined banks, and the silhouette of the **Torre de Oro** (Tower of Gold, ❿ built 1220; admission: 100 ptas., open Tues.–Fri. 10–2, weekends

11 11–2) and the **Maestranza Bullring** (built 1760–63), one of Spain's oldest, is simply stunning. *Admission for plaza tours and bullfighting museum: 250 ptas. Open Mon.–Sat. 10–1:30.*

Thirty kilometers (19 miles) from Seville, the N-IV brings you to **Carmona.** This unspoiled Andalucían town of Roman and Moorish origin is worth a visit, either to stay at the parador or to enjoy its wealth of Mudéjar and Renaissance churches, and its streets of whitewashed houses of clear Moorish influence. Most worthwhile is the **Church of San Pedro,** begun in 1466, whose extraordinary interior is an unbroken mass of sculptures and gilded surfaces, and whose tower, erected in 1704, is an unabashed imitation of Seville's famous Giralda. Carmona's most moving monument is its splendid **Roman Necropolis,** where in huge underground chambers some 900 family tombs dating from the 2nd to the 4th century AD have been chiseled out of the rock. *Calle Enmedio, tel. 95/414–0811. Admission: 250 ptas. Open Tues.–Fri. 9–2 and 4–6, weekends 10–2.*

A little farther along the N-IV brings you to **Ecija,** a dazzling white cluster reputed to be the hottest town in Spain—its nickname is *sarten de Andalucía,* "Andalucía's frying pan." With its history going back to Greek and Roman times, you'll find plenty of Renaissance and Baroque palaces here and a bewildering array of churches whose towers and turrets rise before you as you approach along the main road.

Numbers in the margin correspond to points of interest on the Córdoba map.

Córdoba

Ancient **Córdoba,** city of the caliphs, is one of Spain's oldest cities and the greatest embodiment of Moorish heritage in all Andalucía. From the 8th to the 11th centuries, the Moorish emirs and Caliphs of the West held court here, and the city became one of the Western world's greatest centers of art, culture, and learning. Moors, Christians, and Jews lived together in harmony within its walls. It is for its famous **1 Mezquita** (mosque), one of the finest built by the Moors, that Córdoba is known. Its founder was Abd ar-Rahman I (756–788), and it was completed by Al Mansur (976–1002) around the year 987. As you step inside you'll face a forest of gleaming pillars of precious marble, jasper, and onyx, rising to red-and-white horseshoe arches, one of the most characteristic traits of Moorish architecture. Not even the heavy Baroque cathedral that Charles V so mistakenly built in its midst—and later regretted—can detract from the overpowering impact and mystery wrought by the art of these Moorish craftsmen. The Mezquita was indeed a fitting setting for the original copy of the Koran and a bone from the arm of the Prophet Mohammed, holy relics once housed in the Mezquita that were responsible for bringing thousands of pilgrims to its doors in the great years before St. Ferdinand reconquered Córdoba for the Christians in 1236. The mosque opens onto the **Patio de los Naranjos** (Orange Tree Courtyard) and the bell tower, which served as the mosque's minaret. It's well worth climbing the uneven steps to the top for the view of the Guadalquivir river and the tiled rooftops of the old city. *Torrijos and Cardinal Herrero, tel. 957/470512. Admission: 700 ptas. Open daily May–Sept., 10–7; Oct.–Apr., 10–5.*

Near the mosque, the streets of Torrijos, Cardenal Herrero, and Deanes are lined with tempting souvenir shops specializing in local handicrafts, especially the filigree silver and embossed leather for which Córdoba **2** is famous. In her niche on Cardenal Herrero, the **Virgen de los Faroles** (Virgin of the Lanterns) stands demurely behind a lantern-hung grille.

Córdoba

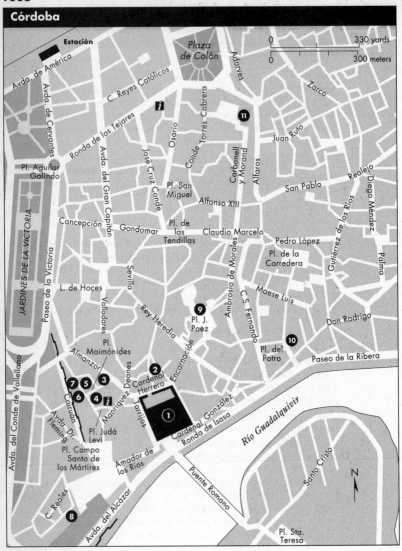

Major Attractions

Judería, **3**

Maimónides Statue, **6**

Mezquita, **1**

Museo Taurino, **5**

Plaza Judá Levi, **4**

Synagogue, **7**

Virgen de los
Faroles, **2**

Other Attractions

Alcázar, **8**

Cristo de los
Faroles, **11**

Museo
Arqueológico, **9**

Museo de
Bellas Artes, **10**

❸ Now make your way westward to the old **Judería,** or Jewish quarter.
❹ On the **Plaza Judá Leví** you'll find the municipal tourist office.

❺ Overlooking the Plaza Maimónides (or Bulas) is the **Museo Taurino** (Museum of Bullfighting), housed in two delightful old mansions. You'll see a well-displayed collection of memorabilia, paintings, and posters by early 20th-century Córdoban artists, and rooms dedicated to great Córdoban *toreros*—even the hide of the bull that killed the legendary Manolete in 1947. *Tel. 957/472000, ext. 211. Admission: 400 ptas. Open Tues.–Sat. 9:30–1:30 and 5–8 (4–7 in winter), Sun. 9:30–1:30.*

❻
❼ A statue of the great Jewish philosopher **Maimónides** stands in the Plaza Tiberiades. A few paces along Judíos, you come to the only **synagogue** in Andalucía to have survived the expulsion of the Jews in 1492. It's one of only three remaining synagogues in Spain—the other two you saw in Toledo—built before 1492, and it boasts some fine Hebrew and Mudéjar stucco tracery and a women's gallery. *Calle Judíos, tel. 957/298133. Admission: 75 ptas. Open Tues.–Sat. 10–2 and 3:30–5:30, Sun. 10–1:30.*

Across the way is the courtyard of El Zoco, a former Arab souk, with some pleasant shops and stalls, and sometimes a bar open in summer.

As you leave Córdoba and head for Granada, the N432 climbs from the Guadalquivir valley up into the mountains of central Andalucía. It is 63 kilometers (39 miles) to **Baena,** a picturesque Andalucían town of white houses clustered on the hillside, where you may want to stop for a drink and wander the narrow streets and squares as yet largely untouched by tourism. Mountain views line the route as the road twists toward its highest point, 3,000-foot Puerto del Castillo, before dropping down onto the *vega* (fertile plain) of Granada. At Pinos Puente, you can take a short detour to the village of **Fuente Vaqueros** where Federico García Lorca was born on June 5, 1898. In 1986, to commemorate the 50th anniversary of his assassination in Granada at the outbreak of the Civil War, his birthplace was restored as a museum. The nearby village of Valderrubio inspired his *Libro de Poemas* and *La Casa de Bernarda Alba. Museo de Lorca, open Jan., Feb., and July–Sept., Tues.–Sun. 10–1 and 6–8; Apr.–June, Tues.–Sun. 10–1 and 5–7; Oct.–Dec. and Mar., Tues.–Sun. 10–1 and 4–6. Tours every hr on the hr.*

Numbers in the margin correspond to points of interest on the Granada map.

Granada

The city of **Granada** rises majestically on three hills dwarfed by the mighty snowcapped peaks of the Sierra Nevada, which boasts the highest roads in Europe. Atop one of these hills, the pink-gold palace of the Alhambra, at once splendidly imposing yet infinitely delicate, gazes out across the rooftops and gypsy caves of the Sacromonte to the fertile vega rich in orchards, tobacco fields, and poplar groves. Granada, the last stronghold of the Moors and the most treasured of all their cities, fell finally to the Catholic Kings in January 1492. For Ferdinand and Isabella, their conquest of Granada was the fulfillment of a long-cherished dream to rid Spain of the Infidel, and here they built the flamboyant
❶ **Capilla Real** (Royal Chapel) where they have lain side by side since 1521, later joined by their daughter Juana la Loca. Begin your tour in the nearby Plaza de Bib-Rambla, a pleasant square with flower stalls and outdoor
❷ cafés in summer, then pay a quick visit to the huge Renaissance **cathedral** commissioned in 1521 by Charles V who thought the Royal Chapel "too small for so much glory." A grandiose and gloomy monument, not completed until 1714, it is far surpassed in beauty and historic value

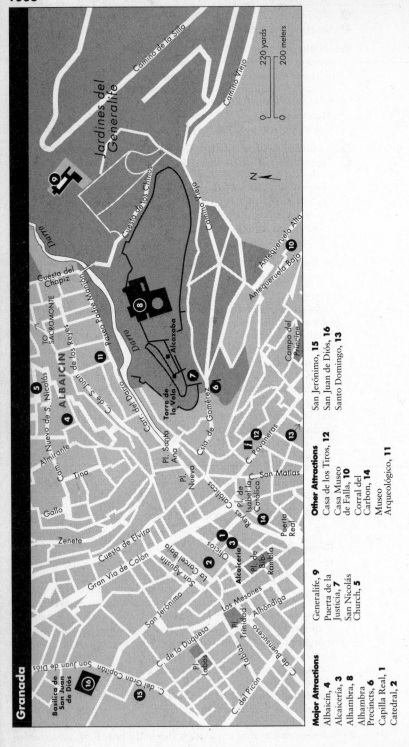

Granada

1008

Major Attractions

Albaicín, **4**
Alcaicería, **3**
Alhambra, **8**
Alhambra
Precincts, **6**
Capilla Real, **1**
Catedral, **2**

Generalife, **9**
Puerta de la
Justicia, **7**
San Nicolás
Church, **5**

Other Attractions

Casa de los Tiros, **12**
Casa Museo
de Falla, **10**
Corral del
Carbon, **14**
Museo
Arqueológico, **11**

San Jerónimo, **15**
San Juan de Diós, **16**
Santo Domingo, **13**

by the neighboring Royal Chapel, which, despite the great emperor's plans, still houses the tombs of his grandparents and less fortunate mother. *Tel. 958/229239. Admission to Royal Chapel and cathedral: 200 ptas. each. Open Mar.–Sept., Mon.–Sat. 10:30–1 and 4–7; Oct.–Feb., Mon.–Sat. 11–1 and 3:30–6, Sun. 3:30–6.*

3 The adjacent streets of the **Alcaicería,** the old Arab silk exchange, will prove a haven for souvenir hunters. Across the Gran Vía de Colón, Granada's main shopping street, the narrow streets begin to wind up **4** the slopes of the **Albaicín,** the old Moorish quarter, which is now a fascinating mixture of dilapidated white houses and beautiful *cármenes,* luxurious villas with fragrant gardens. Few visitors find their way to **5** the balcony of **San Nicolás Church,** which affords an unforgettable view of the Alhambra, particularly when it is floodlit at night.

6 The Cuesta de Gomérez climbs steeply to the **Alhambra precincts,** where the Duke of Wellington planted shady elms and Washington Irving tarried among the gypsies from whom he learned the Moorish legends so evocatively recounted in his *Tales of the Alhambra.* Above the **7** **Puerta de la Justicia,** the hand of Fatima, her fingers evoking the five laws of the Koran, beckons you inside the mystical Alhambra, the most imposing and infinitely beautiful of all Andalucía's Moorish monuments.

8 The history of the **Alhambra** is woven through the centuries. Once inside its famous courts the legends of the Patio of the Lions, the Hall of the Two Sisters, and the murder of the Abencerrajes spring to life in a profusion of lacy walls, frothy stucco, gleaming tiles, and ornate domed ceilings. Here in this realm of myrtles and fountains, festooned arches and mysterious inscriptions, every corner holds its secret. Here the emirs installed their harems, accorded their favorites the most lavish of courts, and bathed in marble baths. In the midst of so much that is delicate the Baroque palace of Charles V seems an intrusion, heavy and incongruous, were it not for the splendid acoustics that make it a perfect setting for Granada's summer music festival.

9 Wisteria, jasmine, and roses line your route to the **Generalife,** the nearby summer palace of the caliphs, where crystal drops shower from slender fountains against a background of stately cypresses. The view of the white, clustered houses of the Albaicín, the Sacromonte riddled with gypsy caves, and the imposing bulk of the Alhambra towering above the tiled roofs of the city will etch on your memory an indelible image of this most beautiful setting and greatest Moorish legacy. *Admission to Alhambra and Generalife: 625 ptas., free Sun. after 3. Open Nov.–Feb., daily 9–6, Mar.–Oct., daily 9–8. Floodlit visits Tues., Thurs., and Sat. 10 PM–midnight (Sat. 8–10 PM in winter). Ticket office closes 45 mins before closing times.*

If you have a day to spare, you can drive to the mountains of the nearby **Sierra Nevada.** The ski resort itself, where you can ski from December through May, is truly unmemorable, but the surrounding scenery viewed from the highest mountain route in Europe makes for a memorable day out. A bus leaves Granada daily at 9 AM and returns at around 5 PM; ask at the tourist office for details. Above the resort the road climbs to the Pico de Veleta, Spain's second-highest mountain at 3,100 meters (10,000 feet), and the view across the Alpujarra range to the sea at Motril is simply stunning. Away to the left rises the mighty Mulhacén; at 11,673 feet, it is Spain's highest peak.

If you opt instead for a trip to the villages of the high **Alpujarras,** leave Granada on the N323 toward Motril, then branch east to **Lanjarón,** a delightful old spa town with an air of faded gentility. From **Orgiva,** the main town of the Alpujarras, the highest road in Europe ascends to picturesque villages like **Bubión, Capileira** beneath the summit of the Veleta, and **Trevélez,** Europe's highest village, on the slopes of Mulhacén. These ancient villages, only recently brushed by modern tourism, became the final refuge of the Moors as they fled the Conquest of Granada, and here they remained until their expulsion from Spain in 1609. With their squat, square houses and flat roofs so reminiscent of the land across the Straits of Gibraltar, they are the last vestige of Andalucía's great Moorish past.

Dining and Lodging

For details and price-category definitions, *see* Dining and Lodging *in* Staying in Spain, *above.*

Carmona

LODGING

★ **Parador Alcázar del Rey Don Pedro.** The beauty of this modern parador is its splendid, peaceful setting in the ruins of the old Moorish Alcázar on top of the hill above Carmona, and its magnificent views across the vast fertile plain below. *41410, tel. 95/414–1010, fax 95/414–1712. 59 rooms with bath. Facilities: restaurant, bar, pool. AE, DC, MC, V. $$$*

Córdoba

DINING

★ **El Caballo Rojo.** The Red Horse, located close to the mosque, is Córdoba's most outstanding restaurant, famous throughout Andalucía and all of Spain. The decor resembles a cool Andalucían patio, and the menu features traditional specialties such as *rabo de toro* (bull's tail); *salmorejo,* a local version of gazpacho with chunks of ham and egg; and other exotic creations inspired by Córdoba's Moorish heritage. *Cardenal Herrero 28, tel. 957/475375. Reservations advised. AE, DC, MC, V. $$$*

El Blasón. Under the same management as El Caballo Rojo, this charming restaurant is fast gaining a name for fine food and unbeatable ambience. In an old inn with a pleasant tapas patio and a whole array of restaurants upstairs, its specialties include *salmón con naranjas* (salmon in oranges) and ternera *con salsa de alcaparrones* (in caper sauce). *José Zorrilla 11, tel. 957/480625. AE, DC, MC, V. $$*

El Cardenal. Close to the mosque, beside the Marisa hotel, this restaurant in the heart of Córdoba's tourist center offers a stylish setting for lunch or dinner. A marble staircase with Oriental rugs leads up to the second-floor dining room. *Cardenal Herrero 14, tel. 957/480346. AE, DC, MC, V. Closed Mon. in winter, no dinner Sun. $$*

★ **El Churrasco.** Ranking second only to El Caballo Rojo, this atmospheric restaurant with a patio is famous for its grilled meat dishes. Specialties are, of course, *churrasco,* a pork dish in pepper sauce, and an excellent salmorejo. *Romero 16, tel. 957/290817. AE, DC, MC, V. Closed Aug. $$*

La Almudaina. This attractive restaurant is located in a 15th-century house and former school that overlooks the Alcázar at the entrance to the Judería. It has an Andalucían patio, and the decor and cooking are both typical of Córdoba. *Campo Santo de los Mártires 1, tel. 957/474342. AE, DC, MC, V. No dinner Sun. $$*

LODGING

★ **Conquistador.** This delightful contemporary hotel on the east side of the mosque is built in Andalucían Moorish style with a charming patio and ceramic decor. The hotel itself has no restaurant, but guests can dine in the attractive Mesón del Bandolero in Calle Torrijos on the opposite side of the mosque. *Magistral González Francés 15, 14003, tel. 957/481102, fax 957/475079. 100 rooms with bath, 3 suites. Facilities: bar, sauna. AE, DC, MC, V. $$$–$$$$*

El Califa. This is a small, modern hotel in a reasonably quiet, central location in the heart of the old city. It accepts no tour groups, only individual guests, and is a comfortable place to stay, with the sights and shops close at hand. *Lope de Hoces 14, 14003, tel. 957/299400. 66 rooms with bath. Facilities: cafeteria, bar. MC, V. $$–$$$*

Marisa. This hotel is in a charming old Andalucían house whose location in the heart of the old town overlooking the mosque's Patio de los Naranjos is its prime virtue. You'll find the decor quaint and charming, and the rates reasonable. *Cardenal Herrero 6, 14003, tel. 957/473142. 28 rooms with bath. MC, V. $$*

Granada

DINING

★ **Baroca.** Located one block above the Camino de Ronda, the locals consider this Granada's best restaurant. The menu favors international cuisine; desserts are especially good. Service is professional and the ambience agreeable. *Pedro Antonio de Alarcón 34, tel. 958/265061. Reservations advised. AE, DC, MC, V. Closed Sun. and Aug. $$$*

Carmen de San Miguel. This is a restaurant to visit for its superb setting in a villa with an outdoor terrace and magnificent views over Granada. Located on the Alhambra hill beside the Alhambra Palace hotel, the setting is unbeatable; the food is average Continental-style cuisine. *Paseo Torres Bermejas 3, tel. 958/226723. AE, DC, MC, V. No dinner Sun. $$$*

Cunini. Located in the center of town, close to the cathedral, Cunini has long been famous for the quality of its seafood. *Pescadería 9, tel. 958/250777. Reservations advised. AE, DC, MC, V. Closed Mon. $$$*

Sevilla. This is a very atmospheric, colorful restaurant located in the Alcaicería beside the cathedral. There's a superb tapas bar at the entrance, and the dining room is picturesque but rather small and crowded. The menu can be rather tourist-oriented, but try their *sopa Sevillana* (fish soup). *Oficios 12, tel. 958/221223. AE, DC, MC, V. Closed Sun. $$*

Los Manueles. This old inn is one of Granada's long-standing traditions. The walls have ceramic tiles, and the ceiling is hung with hams. There's lots of atmosphere, good old-fashioned service, and plenty of traditional Granadan cooking. *Zaragoza 2, tel. 958/223413. AE, DC, MC, V. $*

LODGING

Parador de San Francisco. Magnificently located in an old convent right within the Alhambra precincts, the parador was where Queen Isabella was entombed before the completion of the Royal Chapel. It's one of Spain's most popular hotels, and you need to book at least four months in advance. *Alhambra, 18009, tel. 958/221440, fax 958/222264. 38 rooms with bath. Facilities: restaurant, bar. AE, DC, MC, V. $$$$*

★ **Alhambra Palace.** This flamboyant ocher-red Moorish-style palace was built about 1910 and sits halfway up the hill to the Alhambra. The mood is more harried than at the more isolated parador. Though recently renovated, it remains a conversation piece with rich carpets, tapestries, and Moorish tiles. Rooms overlooking the town are preferable. The terrace is the perfect place for an early evening drink as the sun sets over the Sierra Nevada. *Peña Partida 2, 18009, tel. 958/221468, fax 958/226404. 123 rooms with bath, 9 suites. Facilities: restaurant, 2 bars. AE, DC, MC, V. $$$–$$$$*

América. A simple but charming hotel within the Alhambra precincts. It's very popular so you'll need to reserve a room months ahead. The location is magnificent, and guests can linger over breakfast on a delightful patio. *Real de la Alhambra 53, 18009, tel. 958/227471. 14 rooms with bath. Facilities: restaurant. No credit cards. Closed Nov.–Feb. $$*

★ **Victoria.** An absolute gem of an Old World hotel, it overlooks the Puerta Real—from which noise might be a disadvantage. Carpeted bedrooms have dark polished furniture. *Puerta Real 3, 18005, tel. 958/25–77–00. 66 rooms with bath, 3 suites. Facilities: 2 restaurants, 2 bars. AE, DC, MC, V. $$*

Inglaterra. Set in a period house just two blocks above the Gran Vía de Colón in the heart of town, this is a hotel that will appeal to those who prefer Old World charm to creature comforts, though accommodations are perfectly adequate for the reasonable rates. *Cetti Meriem 6, tel. 958/221559, fax 958/221586. 36 rooms with bath. AE, DC, MC, V. $*

Seville

DINING

★ **Egaña-Oriza.** This is currently one of Seville's most fashionable restaurants. Basque specialties include *merluza con almejas en salsa verde* (white fish and clams in green sauce) and *solomillo con foie en salsa de trufas* (steak with goose liver pâté in truffle sauce). It's opposite the old tobacco factory, now Seville University. *San Fernando 41, tel. 95/422–7271. Reservations required. AE, DC, MC, V. No lunch Sat. Closed Sun. and Aug. $$$*

La Albahaca. Set in an attractive old house in the heart of the Barrio Santa Cruz, the Albahaca offers plenty of style and atmosphere and original, imaginative cuisine. Specialties of the chef, who was formerly in the Hotel Alfonso XIII, are *suprema de lubina al hinojo fresco* (sea bass with fresh fennel) and *filetitos de ciervo con ciruelas* (venison and cherries). *Plaza Santa Cruz 12, tel. 95/422–0714. Reservations advised. AE, DC, MC, V. Closed Sun. $$$*

La Isla. Located in the center of town between the cathedral and the Convent of La Caridad, La Isla has long been famous for its superb seafood and paella. *Arfe 25, tel. 95/421–5376. AE, DC, MC, V. Closed Mon. and Aug. $$$*

San Marco. The brothers Ramacciotti serve Italian-influenced cuisine in an 18th-century mansion with a classic Andalucían patio—a wonderful spot for a summer meal. Try the ravioli *rellenos de lubina en salsa de almejas* (with stuffed with sea bass in a clam sauce), *cordero relleno de espinacas y setas* (lamb stuffed with spinach and forest mushrooms), or any of a delectable array of desserts. *Cuna 6, tel. 95/421–2440. Reservations advised. AE, DC, MC, V. Closed Mon. and Aug. $$$*

El Bacalao. This popular fish restaurant, opposite the church of Santa Catalina, is in an Andalucían house decorated with ceramic tiles. As its name suggests, the house specialty is *bacalao* (cod); try it *con arroz* (with rice) or al pil-pil. *Plaza Ponce de León 15, tel. 95/421–6670. Reservations advised. V. Closed Sun. $$*

★ **La Judería.** This bright, modern restaurant near the Hotel Fernando III is fast gaining recognition for the quality of its Andalucían and international cuisine and reasonable prices. Fish dishes from the north of Spain and meat from Ávila are specialties. Try *cordero lechal asado* (roast baby lamb) or *urta a la Roteña* (a fish dish unique to Rota). *Cano y Cueto 13, tel. 95/441–2052. Reservations required. AE, DC, MC, V. Closed Sun. in Aug. $$*

★ **Mesón Don Raimundo.** In an old convent close to the cathedral, the Mesón has an atmosphere and decor that are deliberately Sevillian. Its bar is the perfect place to sample some splendid tapas, and the restaurant, when not catering to tour groups, is one of Seville's most delightful. *Argote de Molina 26, tel. 95/422–3355. Reservations advised. AE, DC, MC, V. No dinner Sun. $$*

Mesón Castellano. This recently refurbished old house opposite the church of San José is an ideal place for lunch after a morning's shopping on Calle Sierpes. Specialties are Castilian meat dishes. *Jovellanos 6, tel. 95/421–4028. AE, DC, MC, V. Lunch only. Closed Sun. $*

LODGING

Alfonso XIII. This ornate Mudéjar-style palace was built for Alfonso XIII's visit to the 1929 exhibition. It is worth a visit for its splendid Moorish decor, despite the fact that parts of the hotel are faded and fall short of five-star expectations. The restaurant is elegant but falls short of expectations also. *San Fernando 2, 41004, tel. 95/422–2850, fax 95/421–6033. 128 rooms with bath and 21 suites. Facilities: 2 restaurants, bar, pool, shops, meeting rooms. AE, DC, MC, V. $$$$*

Colón. The rooms and suites have been modernized to a high degree of comfort while retaining much of their style. It's right in the heart of town, close to the main shopping center. You can dine in the elegant El Burladero restaurant or in the more casual La Tasca. *Canalejas 1, 41001, tel. 95/422–2900, fax 95/422–0938. 204 rooms with bath and 14 suites. Facilities: 2 restaurants, 2 bars, hair salon, meeting rooms. AE, DC, MC, V. $$$$*

★ **Doña María.** Close to the cathedral, this is one of Seville's most charming hotels. Some rooms are small and plain; others are tastefully furnished with antiques. Room 310 has a four-poster double bed, 305 has two single four-posters, and both have spacious bathrooms. There's no restaurant, but there's a rooftop pool with a good view of the Giralda. *Don Remondo 19, tel. 95/422–4990, fax 95/421–9546. 60 rooms with bath. AE, DC, MC, V. $$$*

Bécquer. This functional, modern hotel with attentive service is convenient for the shopping center and offers comfortable if unexciting accommodations. It's one of the best mid-range bets, with a parking garage but no restaurant. *Reyes Católicos 4, 41001, tel. 95/422–8900, fax 95/421–4400. 120 rooms with bath. Facilities: bar, breakfast room. AE, DC, MC, V. $$*

Giralda. Recently modernized and extensively renovated, this is a comfortable, functional hotel with spacious, light rooms decorated in typical Castilian style. Located in a cul-de-sac off Avenida Menéndez Pelayo, it lies on the edge of the old city; rooms on the fifth floor are best. *Sierra Nevada 3, 41003, tel. 95/441–6661, fax 95/441–9352. 65 rooms with bath, 5 suites. Facilities: restaurant, bars, meeting rooms. AE, DC, MC, V. $$*

Internacional. Well maintained and charming, this Old World hotel lies in the narrow streets of the old town near Casa Pilatos. *Aguilas 17, tel. 95/421–3207. 26 rooms. No credit cards. $*

Murillo. This picturesque hotel in the heart of the Barrio Santa Cruz was redecorated in 1987. The rooms are simple and small, but the setting is a virtue. You can't reach the hotel by car, but porters with trolleys will fetch your luggage from your taxi. *Lope de Rueda 7, 41004, tel. 95/421–6095, fax 95/421–9616. 61 rooms with bath or shower. Facilities: bar, breakfast room. AE, DC, MC, V. $*

The Arts and Nightlife

Granada

FLAMENCO

There are several "impromptu" flamenco shows in the caves of the Sacromonte, but these can be dismally bad and little more than tourist rip-offs. Go only if accompanied by a Spanish friend who knows his way around or with a tour organized by a local agency. **Jardines Neptuno** (Calle Neptuno, tel. 958/522533) is a regular but colorful flamenco club that caters largely to tourists. **Reina Mora** (Mirador de San Cristo-bal, tel. 958/272228), though somewhat smaller than Jardines Nep-tuno, offers regular flamenco shows known as *tablaos*.

Seville
FLAMENCO
Regular flamenco clubs cater largely to tourists and cost a little more than 3,000 ptas. per person, but their shows are colorful and offer a good introduction for the uninitiated. **El Arenal** (Rodo 7, tel. 95/421–6492) is a flamenco club in the back of the picturesque Mesón Dos de Mayo. **Los Gallos** (Plaza Santa Cruz 11, tel. 95/421–6981) is a small intimate club in the heart of the Barrio Santa Cruz offering fairly pure flamenco. There are shows of flamenco and other regional dances nightly at **El Patio Sevillano** (Paseo de Colón, tel. 95/421–4120), which caters largely to tour groups.

BULLFIGHTS
Corridas take place at the Maestranza bullring on Paseo de Colón, usu-ally on Sunday from Easter through October. The best are during the April Fair. Tickets can be bought in advance from the windows at the ring (one of the oldest and most picturesque in Spain) or from the kiosks in Calle Sierpes (these charge a commission). The ring and a bullfighting museum may be visited year-round. *Tel. 95/422–4577. Admission: 250 ptas. Open Mon.–Sat. 10–1:30.*

COSTA DEL SOL

What were impoverished fishing villages in the 1950s are now retire-ment villages and package-tour meccas for northern Europeans and Americans. Behind the hideous concrete monsters you'll come across old cottages and villas set in gardens that blossom with jasmine and bougainvillea. The sun still sets over miles of beaches and the lights of small fishing craft still twinkle in the distance. Most of your time should be devoted to indolence—sunbathing and swimming. When you need something to do, you can head inland to the historic town of Ronda and the perched white villages of Andalucía. You can also make a day trip to Gibraltar or Tangier.

Getting There

Daily flights on Iberia and Aviaco connect Málaga with Madrid and Barcelona. Iberia (tel. 95/213–6166 or 213–6167), British Airways, and charter airlines such as Dan Air offer frequent service from Lon-don; most other major European cities also have direct air links. You'll have to make connections in Madrid for all flights from the United States. Málaga Airport (tel. 95/224–0000) is 12 kilometers (7 miles) west of the city. City buses run from the airport to the city every 20 minutes (fare: 115 ptas., 6:30 AM–midnight); the Portillo bus company (tel. 95/236–0191) has frequent service from the airport to Torremolinos. A suburban train serving Málaga, Torremolinos, and Fuegirola also stops at the airport every half hour. From Madrid, Málaga is easily reached by a half-dozen rapid trains a day.

Getting Around

Buses are the best means of transportation on the Costa del Sol (as well as from Seville or Granada). Málaga's long-distance station is on the Paseo de los Tilos (tel. 95/235–0061); nearby, on Muelle de Heredía, a smaller station serves suburban destinations. The main bus company

Costa del Sol

serving the Costa del Sol is **Portillo** (offices at the bus station, tel. 95/236–0191). **Alsina Gräells** (at the station, tel. 95/231–8295) has service to Granada, Córdoba, Seville, and Nerja. The train station in Málaga (Explanada de la Estación, tel. 95/236–0202) is a 15-minute walk from the city center, across the river. The **RENFE** office (Strachan 2, tel. 95/221–4127) is more convenient for tickets and information.

Guided Tours

Organized one- and two-day excursions to places such as Seville, Granada, Córdoba, Ronda, Gibraltar, and Tangier are run by **Julià Tours, Pullmantur,** and numerous smaller companies from all the Costa del Sol resorts and can be booked through your hotel desk or any travel agent.

Tourist Information

The most helpful tourist offices, by far, are in Málaga and Marbella. The Málaga office covers the entire province.

Estepona (Paseo Marítimo Pedro Manrique, tel. 95/280–0913).
Fuengirola (Av. Jesús Santos Rein 6, tel. 95/246–7457).
Gibraltar (On Cathedral Square, tel. 9567/74950).
Málaga (Pasaje de Chinitas 4, tel. 95/221–3445, and at the airport in both national and international terminals).
Marbella (Glorieta de la Fontanilla, tel. 95/277–1442).
Nerja (Puerta del Mar 2, tel. 95/252–1531).
Ronda (Plaza de España 1, tel. 95/287–1272).
Torremolinos (Guetaria 517, tel. 95/238–1578).

Exploring the Costa del Sol

Nerja

Nerja is a small but expanding resort that so far has escaped the worst excesses of the property developers. Its growth to date has been largely confined to villages such as El Capistrano, one of the showpieces of the Costa del Sol. There's pleasant bathing here, though the sand is gray and gritty. The **Balcón de Europa** is a fantastic lookout, high above the sea. The famous **Cuevas de Nerja** (a series of stalactite caves) are off the road to Almuñecar and Almería. A kind of vast underground cathedral, they contain the world's largest known stalactite (203 feet long). *Tel. 95/252–9520. Admission: 400 ptas. Open daily summer 10:30–6, winter 10:30–2 and 3:30–6.*

Málaga

Málaga is a busy port city with ancient streets and lovely villas set among exotic foliage, but it has little to recommend it to the overnight visitor. The central Plaza de la Marina, overlooking the port, is a pleasant place for a drink. The main shops are along the Calle Marqués de Larios.

The **Alcazaba** is a fortress begun in the 8th century when Málaga was the most important port of the Moorish kingdom. The ruins of the Roman amphitheater at its entrance were uncovered when the fort was restored. The inner palace dates from the 11th century when, for a short period after the breakup of the Caliphate of the West in Córdoba, it became the residence of the Moorish emirs. Today you'll find the **Archaeological Museum** here and a good collection of Moorish art. *Entrance on Alcazabilla, tel. 95/222–0043. Admission: 30 ptas. Open Mon.–Sat. 11–2 and 5–8 (4–7 in winter), Sun. 10–2.*

Energetic souls can climb through the Alcazaba gardens to the summit of **Gibralfaro.** Others can drive by way of Calle Victoria or take the parador minibus that leaves roughly every 1½ hours from near the cathedral on Molina Lario. The Gibralfaro fortifications were built for Yusuf I in the 14th century. The Moors called it Jebelfaro, which means "rock of the lighthouse," after the beacon that stood here to guide ships into the harbor and warn of invasions by pirates. Today the beacon is gone, but there's a small parador that makes a delightful place for a drink or a meal and has some stunning views.

Torremolinos

As you approach **Torremolinos** through an ocean of concrete blocks, it's hard to grasp that as recently as the early 1960s this was an inconsequential fishing village. Today, this grossly overdeveloped resort is a prime example of 20th-century tourism run riot. The town center, with its brash Nogalera Plaza, is full of overpriced bars and restaurants. Much more attractive is the district of La Carihuela, farther west, below the Avenida Carlota Alexandra. You'll find some old fishermen's cottages here, a few excellent seafood restaurants, and a traffic-free esplanade for an enjoyable stroll on a summer evening.

Benalmádena, Fuengirola, and Mijas

Head west from Torremolinos, toward the similar but more staid resorts of **Benalmádena** and **Fuengirola,** both retirement havens for British and American senior citizens. A short drive from Fuengirola up into the mountains takes you to the picturesque—and over-photographed—village of **Mijas.** Though the vast tourist-oriented main square may seem like an extension of the Costa's tawdry bazaar, there are hillside streets of whitewashed houses where you'll discover an authentic village atmosphere that has changed little since the days before the tourist boom of the 1960s. Visit the bullring, the nearby church, and the chapel of Mijas's patroness, the Virgen de la Peña (to the side of the main square), and enjoy shopping for quality gifts and souvenirs.

Marbella

Marbella is the most fashionable and sedate resort area along the coast. It does have a certain Florida land boom feel to it, but development has been controlled, and Marbella will, let's hope, never turn into another Torremolinos. The town's charming old Moorish quarter may be crowded with upmarket boutiques and a modern, T-shirt-and-fudge section along the main drag; but when people speak of Marbella they refer both to the town and to the resorts—some more exclusive than others—stretching 16 kilometers (10 miles) or so on either side of town, between the highway and the beach. If you're vacationing in southern Spain, this is the place to stay. There are championship golf courses and tennis courts, fashionable waterfront cafés, and trendy shopping arcades.

Ojén

A short drive up into the hills behind Marbella brings you to the village of **Ojén.** Its typical streets are a far cry from the promenades of the coastal resorts. Look out for the traditional pottery sold here and for the picturesque cemetery, with its rows of burial-urn chambers.

Back on the coastal highway, Marbella's Golden Mile, with its mosque, Arab banks, and residence of King Fahd of Saudi Arabia, proclaims the ever-growing influence of wealthy Arabs in this playground of the rich. In **Puerto Banús,** Marbella's plush marina, with its flashy yachts, fashionable people, and expensive restaurants, the glittering parade outshines even St. Tropez in ritzy glamour.

Ronda

Ronda is reached via a spectacular mountain road from San Pedro de Alcántara. One of the oldest towns in Spain and the last stronghold of the legendary Andalucían bandits, Ronda's most dramatic feature is its ravine, known as **El Tajo,** which is 915 feet across and divides the old Moorish town from the "new town" of El Mercadillo. Spanning the gorge is the **Puente Nuevo,** an amazing architectural feat built between 1755 and 1793, whose parapet offers dizzying views of the River Guadalevín way below. Ronda is visited more for its setting, breathtaking views, and ancient houses than for any particular monument. Stroll the old streets of **La Ciudad;** drop in at the historic **Reina Victoria** hotel, built by the English from Gibraltar as a fashionable resting place on their Algeciras–Bobadilla railroad line; and visit the **bullring,** one of the oldest and most beautiful rings in Spain. Here Ronda's most famous native son, Pedro Romero (1754–1839), father of modern bullfighting, is said to have killed 5,600 bulls during his 30-year career; and in the **Bullfighting Museum** you can see posters dating back to the very first fights held in the ring in May 1785. The ring is privately owned now, but three or four fights are still held in the summer months. Tickets are exceedingly difficult to come by (tel. 95/287–4132; admission to ring and museum: 200 ptas.; open daily 10–6:30, until 7 in summer). Above all, don't miss the cliff-top walk and the gardens of the **Alameda del Tajo,** where you can contemplate one of the most dramatic views in all of Andalucía.

Estepona

Returning to the coast road, the next town is **Estepona,** which until recently marked the end of the urban sprawl of the Costa del Sol. Estepona lacks the hideous high-rises of Torremolinos and Fuengirola, and, set back from the main highway, it's not hard to make out the old fishing village it's once was. Wander the streets of the Moorish village, around the central food market and the **Church of San Francisco**, and you'll find a pleasant contrast to the excesses higher up the coast.

Casares

Nineteen kilometers (11¾ miles) northwest of Estepona, the mountain village of **Casares** lies high in the Sierra Bermeja. Streets lined with ancient white houses perch on the slopes beneath a ruined Moorish castle. Admire the view of the Mediterranean and check out the village's thriving ceramics industry.

Between Estepona and Gibraltar, the highway is flanked by prosperous vacation developments known as *urbanizaciones*. The architecture here is much more in keeping with traditional Andalucían style than the concrete blocks of earlier developments. The new **Puerto de Sotogrande** near Manilva is one of the showpieces of the area.

Gibraltar

To enter **Gibraltar,** simply walk or drive across the border at La Línea and show your passport. In theory car drivers need an International Driver's License, insurance certificate, and registration book; in practice, these regulations are usually waived. It is also possible to fly into Gibraltar on daily flights from London but, as yet, there are no flights from Spanish airports. There are, however, plenty of bus tours from Spain. **Julià Tours, Pullmantur,** and many smaller agencies run daily tours (not Sunday) to Gibraltar from most Costa del Sol resorts. Alternatively, you can take the regular Portillo bus to La Línea and walk across the border. In summer, Portillo runs an inexpensive daily tour to Gibraltar from the Torremolinos bus station. Once you reach Gibraltar the official language is English and the currency is the British pound sterling, though pesetas are also accepted.

The Rock of Gibraltar acquired its name in AD 711 when it was captured by the Moorish chieftain Tarik at the start of the Arab invasion of Spain. It became known as Jebel Tariq (Rock of Tariq), later corrupted to Gibraltar. After successive periods of Moorish and Spanish domination, Gibraltar was captured by an Anglo-Dutch fleet in 1704 and ceded to the British by the Treaty of Utrecht in 1713. This tiny British colony, whose impressive silhouette dominates the straits between Spain and Morocco, is a rock just 5⅘ kilometers (3⅗ miles) long, ¾ kilometers (½ mile) wide, and 1,394 feet high.

On entering Gibraltar by road you have to cross the airport runway on the narrow strip of land that links the Rock with La Línea in Spain. Here you have a choice. You can either plunge straight into exploring Gibraltar town, or opt for a tour around the Rock. Several minibus tours are readily available at this point of entry.

Numbers in the margin correspond to points of interest on the Gibraltar map.

The tour around the Rock is best begun on the eastern side. As you enter

❶ Gibraltar, turn left down Devil's Tower Road, and drive as far as **Catalan Bay,** a small fishing village founded by Genoese settlers in the 18th century, and now one of the Rock's most picturesque resorts. The road continues on beneath water catchments that supply the colony's drink-

❷ ing water, to another resort, **Sandy Bay,** and then plunges through the Dudley Ward Tunnel to bring you out at the Rock's most southerly tip,

③ **Punta Grande de Europa** (Europa Point). Stop here to admire the view across the Straits to the coast of Morocco, 22½ kilometers (14 miles) away. You are standing on what in ancient times was called one of the two Pillars of Hercules. Across the water in Morocco, a mountain between the cities of Ceuta and Tangier formed the second pillar. Plaques explain the history of the gun installations here, and, nearby on Europa **④** Flats, you can see the **Nun's Well,** an ancient Moorish cistern, and the **⑤** **Shrine of Our Lady of Europe,** venerated by sailors since 1462.

⑥ Europa Road winds its way high on the western slopes above **Rosia Bay,** to which Nelson's flagship, HMS *Victory,* was towed after the Battle of Trafalgar in 1805. Aboard were the dead of the battle, who are now buried in Trafalgar Cemetery on the southern edge of town, and the body of Admiral Nelson himself, preserved in a barrel of rum. He was then taken to London for burial.

⑦ Continue on Europa Road as far as the **casino** (Europa Rd., tel. 9567/76666, open daily 9 PM–4 AM) above the Alameda Gardens. Make **⑧** a sharp right here up Engineer Road to **Jews Gate,** an unbeatable lookout point over the docks and Bay of Gibraltar to Algeciras in Spain. Here you can gain access to the **Upper Nature Preserve,** which includes St. Michael's Cave, the Ape's Den, the Great Siege Tunnel, and the Moor- **⑨** ish Castle (*see below*). Queens Road leads to **St. Michael's Cave,** a series of underground chambers adorned with stalactites and stalagmites, which provides an admirable setting for concerts, ballet, and drama. *Admission to preserve, including all sites: £4.50 adults, £2.25 children 5 or under, plus £1.50 per vehicle. Open daily 10–6.*

⑩ Drive down Old Queen's Road to the **Apes' Den** near the **Wall of Charles V.** The famous Barbary apes are a breed of cinnamon-colored, tailless monkeys, natives of the Atlas Mountains in Morocco. Legend holds that as long as the apes remain, the British will continue to hold the Rock. Winston Churchill himself issued orders for the maintenance of the ape colony when its numbers began to dwindle during World War II.

Passing beneath the cable car that runs to the Rock's summit, drive **⑪** up to the **Great Siege Tunnel** at the northern end of the Rock. These huge galleries were carved out during the Great Siege of 1779–1783. Here, in 1878, the Governor, Lord Napier of Magdala, entertained ex-President Ulysses S. Grant at a banquet in **St. George's Hall.** From here, the **Holyland Tunnel** leads out to the east side of the Rock above Catalan Bay.

The last stop before the town is at the **Moorish Castle** on Willis Road. **⑫** Built by the successors of the Moorish invader Tarik, the present **Tower of Homage** was rebuilt by the Moors in 1333. Admiral Rooke hoisted the British flag from its top when he captured the Rock in 1704, and here it has flown ever since. The castle has been closed to the public and can be seen only from the outside.

Willis Road leads steeply down to the colorful, congested town of Gibraltar where the dignified Regency architecture of Britain blends with the shutters, balconies, and patios of southern Spain. Apart from the attraction of shops, restaurants, and pubs on Main Street, you'll want **⑬ ⑭** to visit some of the following: the **Governor's Residence;** the **Law Courts,** where the famous case of the *Mary Celeste* sailing ship was heard in **⑮ ⑯** 1872; the Anglican **Cathedral of the Holy Trinity;** the Catholic **Cathe- ⑰** dral of St. Mary the Crowned;** and the recently refurbished **Gibraltar Museum,** whose exhibits recall the history of the Rock throughout the ages. *Gibraltar Museum, Bomb House La., tel. 9567–74289. Admission: £1.50 adults, £1 children. Open weekdays 10–6, Sat. 10–2.*

Apes' Den, **10**

Casino, **7**

Catalan Bay, **1**

Cathedral of the Holy Trinity, **15**

Cathedral of St. Mary the Crowned, **16**

Gibraltar Museum, **17**

Governor's Residence, **13**

Great Siege Tunnel, **11**

Jews Gate, **8**

Koehler Gun, **19**

Law Courts, **14**

Nefusot Yehudada Synagogue, **18**

Nun's Well, **4**

Punta Grande de Europa, **3**

Rosia Bay, **6**

St. Michael's Cave, **9**

Sandy Bay, **2**

Shrine of Our Lady of Europe, **5**

Tower of Homage, **12**

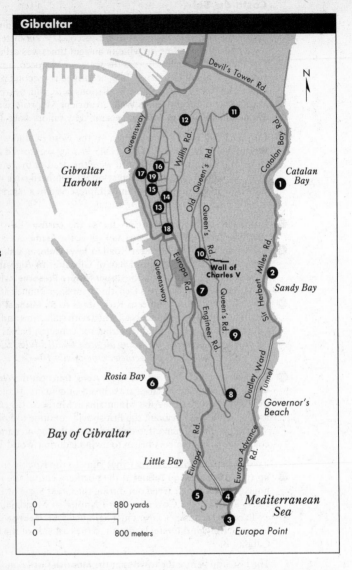

Gibraltar

---

18 Finally, the **Nefusot Yehudada Synagogue** on Line Wall Road is worth a look for its inspired architecture, and, if you're interested in guns, the

19 **Koehler Gun** in **Casemates Square** at the northern end of Main Street is an impressive example of the type of gun developed during the Great Siege.

Dining and Lodging

For details and price-category definitions, *see* Dining and Lodging *in* Staying in Spain, *above.*

Estepona

DINING

El Molino. In an old windmill, this restaurant has offered classic French cuisine for some three decades. Try the lubina al hinojo or the delicious Chateaubriand steak. *Carretera N340 at km 166, tel. 95/288–*

2135. *Reservations advised. AE, DC, MC, V. No lunch. Closed Sun., Tues., and Jan.* $$$

Alcaría de Ramos. José Ramos, winner of the National Gastronomy Prize, opened this restaurant outside town in 1990, and it has quickly garnered a large and loyal following. Try the *ensalada de lentejas con salmón ahumado* (lentil salad with smoked salmon), followed by cordero asado and the chef's justly famous fried ice cream. *Rte. N340, km. 167, tel. 95/288–6178. Reservations advised. MC, V. No lunch. Closed Sun., and June 15–July 15.* $$–$$$

LODGING

Santa Marta. This is a small, quiet hotel with just 37 rooms in chalet bungalows set in a large, peaceful garden. Some rooms are a little faded after 30 years, but the tranquil setting is a plus. Good lunches are served by the pool. *Rte. N340, km. 173, 29680, tel. 95/288–8180. 37 rooms with bath. AE, MC, V. Closed Oct.–Mar.* $$

Gibraltar

DINING

La Bayuca. One of the Rock's best-established restaurants, La Bayuca is renowned for its onion soup and Mediterranean dishes. Prince Charles and Prince Andrew have dined here while on naval service. *21 Turnbull's La., tel. 9567/75119. Reservations advised. AE, DC, MC, V. No lunch Sun. Closed Tues.* $$$

Country Cottage. Opposite the Catholic cathedral, this is the place to go for a taste of Old England. Enjoy steak and kidney pie, Angus steak, and roast beef, by candlelight. *13 Giro's Passage, tel. 9567/70084. Reservations advised. AE, MC, V. Closed Sun.* $$–$$$

LODGING

★ **The Rock.** The Rock has undergone a massive refurbishment program with the aim of bolstering its reputation as Gibraltar's supreme luxury hotel. You'll find a comfortable, old-fashioned English atmosphere, along with a pool, sun terrace, and gardens. Located on Gibraltar's western slopes, the hotel overlooks the town and harbor. *3 Europa Rd., tel. 9567/73000. 143 rooms with bath, 10 suites. Facilities: restaurant, bar, pool, hair salon. AE, DC.* $$$

Bristol. This colonial-style hotel is just off Gibraltar's main street, right in the heart of town. Rooms are large and comfortable, and the tropical garden is a real haven for those guests who want to relax in peaceful isolation. *10 Cathedral Sq., tel. 9567/76800. 60 rooms with bath. Facilities: breakfast room, bar, pool. AE, DC, MC, V.* $$

Málaga

DINING

Café de Paris. The owner of this stylish restaurant in the Paseo Marítimo area was a chef at Maxim's in Paris, and La Hacienda in Marbella. The *menú degustación* (tasting menu) lets you try a little of everything. Specialties include *rodaballo con espinacas* (turbot and spinach). *Vélez Málaga 8, tel. 95/222–5043. Reservations advised. AE, DC, MC, V. Closed Sun.* $$$

Casa Pedro. It's crowded and noisy, but Malgueños have been flocking to this no-frills fish restaurant for more than 50 years. In the seaside suburb of El Palo, the restaurant has a huge, bare dining room that overlooks the ocean. Try joining the hordes of local families who come here for lunch on Sundays. It's quieter at other times. *Quitapenas 121, El Paso beach (Bus 11), tel. 95/229–0003. Sun. reservations advised. AE, DC, MC, V. Closed Nov. No dinner Mon.* $$

Rincon de Mata. This is one of the best of many restaurants in the pedestrian shopping streets between Calle Larios and Calle Nueva. Its menu is more original than most, and in summer there are tables outside on the sidewalk. *Esparteros 8, tel. 95/222–3135. V. $$*

La Cancela. This is a colorful restaurant in the center of town, just off Calle Granada. Dine indoors or alfresco. *Denís Belgrano 5, tel. 95/222–3125. AE, DC, MC, V. $*

LODGING

Los Naranjos. This small hotel owned by the Luz chain is on a pleasant avenue in a residential district a little to the east of the city center. There's a small garden in front, but rooms overlooking the street can be noisy. *Paseo de Sancha 35, 29016, tel. 95/222–4317. 41 rooms with bath. Facilities: breakfast room, bar. AE, DC, V. $$$*

★ **Parador de Gibralfaro.** In a small wood on top of Gibralfaro mountain 3½ kilometers (2 miles) above the city, this tiny parador offers spectacular views over the city and bay. The Parador has been closed for major renovations but was expected to reopen in spring 1995; check first with the tourist office. *Gibralfaro, 29016, tel. 95/222–1902, fax 95/222–1904. 12 rooms. Facilities: restaurant, bar. AE, DC, MC, V. $$$*

Las Vegas. In a pleasant, though noisy, part of town, just east of the center, this recently renovated hotel has a dining room overlooking the Paseo Marítimo, a pool, and a large leafy garden. Rooms at the back enjoy a good view of the ocean. *Paseo de Sancha 22, 29016, tel. 95/221–7712. 107 rooms with bath. Facilities: restaurant, bar, pool. AE, DC, MC, V. $$*

Victoria. This small, renovated hostel in an old house just off Calle Larios offers excellent budget accommodations in a convenient central location. *Sancha de Lara 3, 29015, tel. 95/222–4223. 13 rooms. AE, V. $*

Marbella

DINING

★ **La Hacienda.** This restaurant, owned by chef Paul Schiff, belongs to the Relais Gourmand group and is one of the highest rated in Spain. The menu reflects the influence of both Schiff's native Belgium and his adopted home, Andalucía. The menú degustación at around 6,500 ptas. will enable you to sample the very best creations of this famous European chef. *Las Chapas, Rte. N340, km. 193, 12 km (7 mi) east of Marbella on the road to Málaga; tel. 95/283–1116. Reservations required. AE, DC, MC, V. Closed Mon., Tues., and mid-Nov.–mid-Dec. $$$$*

La Meridiana. Another of Marbella's most outstanding restaurants and a favorite with the local jet set, La Meridiana is located just west of town, toward Puerto Banús, and is famous for its original Bauhaus-type architecture and the superb quality and freshness of the ingredients. *Camino de la Cruz, tel. 95/277–6190. Reservations required. AE, DC, MC, V. Closed Mon. No lunch Tues., no lunch in summer. $$$$*

★ **La Fonda.** In a beautiful 18th-century house with antique furniture, and located in one of the loveliest old squares in Marbella, La Fonda is owned by one of Madrid's leading restaurateurs. Its cuisine combines the best of Spanish, French, and Austrian influences. A delightful patio filled with potted plants makes a perfect setting for summer dining. *Plaza del Santo Cristo 9, tel. 95/277–2512. Reservations advised. AE, DC, MC, V. No lunch. Closed Sun. $$$*

La Tricycleta. In an old house on a narrow alley in the center of town, English-owned La Tricicleta has become an institution. You can have a predinner drink in the downstairs bar, which is heated by a log fire in winter, and then dine upstairs or outside on the covered rooftop patio. A long-standing favorite is the duck in beer sauce. *Buitrago 14, tel. 95/277–7800. Reservations advised in summer. AE, MC, V. Closed Sun. $$–$$$*

Mesón del Pollo. This small, charming "house of chicken" illustrates how Marbella, despite tourism, remains truly Spanish. Porcelain lamp shades, azulejo tiles, a dozen tables, and the scent of roasting chicken fill this popular lunch spot. Try the *pollo a la sevillana* (roast chicken with squid, fried potatoes, salad, and cider) dinner or *fritura malagueña* (Málaga's famous fried fish), or sample tapas of octopus or meatballs. *Antonio Martín, across from the El Fuerte Hotel, no phone. No reservations. No credit cards.* $

LODGING

★ **Los Monteros.** Situated 2½ kilometers (1½ miles) east of Marbella, on the road to Málaga, this deluxe hotel offers all the facilities of a top hotel, including golf, tennis, pools, horseback riding, and gourmet dining in its famous El Corzo Grill restaurant. This is the third most expensive hotel in Spain, after the Ritz and Villa Magna in Madrid. Eighty percent of the guests are British, which may explain the somewhat starched formality of the rooms. *Urb. Los Monteros, 29600, tel. 95/277–1700, fax 95/282–5846. 161 rooms with bath. Facilities: 2 restaurants, 1 indoor and 2 outdoor pools, exercise room, sauna, 10 tennis courts, 5 squash courts, horseback riding, hair salon, shops, nightclub. AE, DC, MC, V.* $$$$

Marbella Club. The grande dame of Marbella tends to attract an older clientele. The bungalow-style rooms run from cramped to spacious, and the decor varies considerably; specify the type you prefer, but ask for a room that's been recently renovated. The grounds are exquisite. Breakfast is served on a patio where songbirds flit through the vegetation. *Rte. N340, km. 178, 29600, tel. 95/277–1300. 76 rooms with bath. Facilities: restaurant, bar, nightclub, 2 pools, exercise room, sauna, tennis, hair salon. AE, DC, MC, V.* $$$$

★ **Puente Romano.** A spectacular, modern hotel and apartment complex of low, white-stucco buildings located 3¼ kilometers (2 miles) west of Marbella on the road to Puerto Banús. The "village" has a Roman bridge in its beautifully landscaped grounds as well as two pools, a tennis club, and a disco run by Régine. *Rte. N340, km. 184, 29600, tel. 95/277–0100. 220 rooms with bath. Facilities: 2 restaurants, indoor and outdoor pool, tennis, shops, nightclub. AE, DC, V.* $$$$

El Fuerte. This is the best of the few hotels in the center of Marbella, with simple, adequate rooms. It's in a 1950s-type building in the midst of a large garden with an outdoor pool. *Avda. El Fuerte, 29600, tel. 95/286–1500. 263 rooms with bath. Facilities: indoor and outdoor pools, tennis. AE, DC, V.* $$

Mijas
DINING

Valparaíso. *Pato a la naranja* (duck in an orange sauce) is one of the specialties served in a pleasant villa with garden and terrace on the road from Fuengirola to Mijas. *Tel. 95/248–5996. AE, MC, V. No lunch. Closed Sun. Nov.–May.* $$$

Mirlo Blanco. Here you can sample Basque specialties such as *txangurro* (crab) and *merluza a la vasca* (hake with asparagus, eggs, and clam sauce). *Plaza Constitución 13, tel. 95/248–5700. AE, DC, MC, V.* $$

LODGING

★ **Byblos Andaluz.** In this new luxury hotel set in a huge garden of palms, cypresses, and fountains, you'll find every comfort. Facilities include pools, saunas, tennis, and an 18-hole golf course. Its Le Nailhac restaurant is famous for its French cuisine; special low-calorie meals are also available. *Urbano Mijas-Golf, 29640, tel. 95/247–3050, fax 95/247–6783. 144 rooms with bath. Facilities: indoor and outdoor pools, 18-*

hole golf course, exercise room, sauna, spa, hair salon, tennis, shops. *AE, DC, MC, V. $$$$*

Nerja
DINING
Casa Luque. This is one of the most authentically Spanish of Nerja's restaurants, in a charming old Andalucían house behind the Balcón de Europa church. *Plaza Cavana 2, tel. 95/252–1004. AE, V. Closed Mon. and Feb. $$*

Udo Heimer. A genial German is your host at this Art Deco villa. His menu is a combination of traditional German dishes and local produce. Try ham-stuffed pumpkin or prawns wrapped in bacon and served in a curried banana sauce. *Pueblo Andaluz 27, tel. 95/252–0032. AE, DC, MC, V. Reservations advised. No lunch. Closed Wed. and Jan.–Feb. $$*

LODGING
Mónica. Opened in 1986, the Mónica is spacious and luxurious, with cool, Moorish-style architecture and lots of marble. Popular with package tours, it's within walking distance of the center of town. *Playa Torrecilla, 29780, tel. 95/252–1100. 234 rooms with bath. Facilities: restaurant, bar, pool, tennis, nightclub, disco. AE, DC, MC, V. $$$*

★ **Parador.** All the rooms in this small parador a little to the east of the center of Nerja have balconies that overlook the sea. There's a pleasant leafy garden and outdoor pool, and an elevator takes you down to the beach. *El Tablazo, 29780, tel. 95/252–0050, fax 95/252–1997. 73 rooms with bath. Facilities: restaurant, outdoor pool. AE, DC, MC, V. $$$*

Ronda
DINING
Don Miguel. Located by the bridge over the Tajo gorge, the restaurant's terrace offers spectacular views of the ravine. Baby lamb, reared on the owner's farm, is a specialty; it's called *pierna de cordero lechal Don Miguel. Villanueva 4, tel. 95/287–7410. Reservations advised. AE, DC, MC, V. Closed Sun. and Wed. in summer and mid-Jan.–mid-Feb. $$$*

Pedro Romero. Located opposite the bullring, this restaurant is, not surprisingly, packed with colorful taurine decor. The restaurant serves traditional regional recipes; the *tocino del cielo al coco* (sweet caramel custard flavored with coconut) is a treat. *Virgen de la Paz 18, tel. 95/287–1110. AE, DC, MC, V. $$*

LODGING
Reina Victoria. A spectacularly situated Old-World hotel with a distinctly British air, the Reina Victoria sits atop the very rim of the gorge. Its views and style are tops, but its facilities are often overwhelmed by tour groups. *Jerez 25, 29400, tel. 95/287–1240, fax 95/287–1075. 89 rooms with bath. Facilities: restaurant, pool. AE, DC, MC, V. $$–$$$*

Polo. A cozy, old-fashioned hotel in the center of town, Polo sports a reasonably priced restaurant. The staff is friendly and the rooms simple but comfortable. *Mariano Soubiron 8, 29400, tel. 95/287–2447. 33 rooms. Facilities: restaurant. AE, DC, V. $$*

Torremolinos
DINING
Casa Guaquin. Casa Guaquin is widely known as the best seafood restaurant in the region. Changing daily catches and menu stalwarts such as *coquillas al ajillo* (sea cockles in garlic sauce) are served on a seaside patio. *Paseo Maritimo 63, tel. 95/238–4530. AE, MC, V. Closed Thurs. and mid.-Dec.–mid-Jan. $$*

El Atrio. This small, stylish restaurant is located in the Pueblo Blanco. Its cuisine is predominantly French. In summer, you can dine on the terrace. *Casablanca 9, tel. 95/238–8850. AE, MC, V. No lunch. Closed Sun. and Dec. $$*

Europa. A short walk from the Carihuela, this villa in a large garden has leafy dining in pleasant surroundings. It's best on Sundays, when local families flock here for a leisurely lunch. *Via Imperial, tel. 95/238–8022. Sunday reservations advised. AE, MC, V. $$*

Juan. This is a good place to enjoy seafood in summer, with a sunny outdoor patio facing the sea. The specialties include the great Costa del Sol standbys: *sopa de mariscos* (shellfish soup), *dorada al horno* (oven-roasted giltheads), and *fritura malagueña. Paseo Marítimo 29, La Carihuela, tel. 95/238–5656. AE, DC, MC, V. $$*

LODGING

Cervantes. This busy cosmopolitan hotel in the heart of town has comfortable rooms, good service, and a well-known dining room on its top floor. *Las Mercedes, 29620, tel. 95/238–4033, fax 95/238–4857. 393 rooms with bath. Facilities: restaurant, pool, sauna, nightclub. AE, DC, MC, V. $$$*

Tropicana. Located on the beach at the far end of the Carihuela is a comfortable, relaxing resort hotel with several good restaurants nearby. *Trópico 6, 29620, tel. 95/238–6600, fax 95/238–0568. 86 rooms with bath. Facilities: pool. AE, DC, MC, V. $$*

★ **Miami.** Set in an old Andalucían villa in a shady garden to the west of the Carihuela, this is something of a find amid the ocean of concrete blocks. *Aladino 14, 29620, tel. 95/238–5255. 29 rooms with bath. Facilities: pool. No credit cards. $*

CANARY ISLANDS

Traditionally a popular spot for winter holidays, Spain's Canary Islands are becoming a year-round destination favored by sun-seekers and nature lovers alike. The Canaries lie 70 miles off the coast of southern Morocco in the Atlantic Ocean and enjoy mild, sunny weather throughout the year, except for the north coast of Tenerife, which has above-average rainfall for the Canaries and below-average temperatures, year-round. Each of the seven volcanic islands in the archipelago is distinct. Some have lush tropical vegetation, poinsettias as tall as trees, and banana plantations, while others are arid and resemble an exotic moonscape of lava rock and sand dunes. Mt. Teide (12,198 feet), Spain's highest peak and snowcapped for much of the year, is here. The islands are also home to six national parks and dozens of other protected ecological zones in which visitors can hike through mist-shrouded forests of virgin laurel trees, climb mountains, eat food cooked by nature over volcanic craters, or scuba dive off long stretches of unspoiled coastline.

Important Addresses and Numbers

Tourist Offices

Each of the Canary Islands has its own tourist offices that are generally open 9 to 2:

Tenerife (Plaza de España 1, Santa Cruz, tel. 922/60–55–92).

Gran Canaria (Parque Santa Catalina, Las Palmas, tel. 928/26–46–23).

Lanzarote (Parque Municipal, Arrecife, tel. 928/85–10–24).

La Palma (Palacio Salazar, Calle O'Daly 22, Santa Cruz de la Palma, tel. 922/41–21–06).

La Gomera (Calle del Medio 20, San Sebastian, tel. 922/87–01–03).

El Hierro (Dr. Quintero 11, Valverde, tel. 922/55–00–78).

Arriving and Departing

By Plane

Iberia and its sister carrier **Aviaco** have several direct flights a day to Tenerife, Gran Canaria, and Lanzarote from most cities in mainland Spain. **Air Europa** and **Spanair** have fewer flights but slightly lower prices.

From the United States, **Air Europa** (tel. 212/888–7010) flies once a week directly to Tenerife.

By Boat

Transmediterranea (tel. 91/431–0700) operates a slow, comfortable ferry service between Cádiz and the Canary Islands.

Getting Around

By Plane

All the Canary Islands are served by air except La Gomera. Tenerife has two airports: Reina Sofia is in the south, and Los Rodeos is in the north. As a general rule, long-distance flights arrive at the southern terminal and interisland flights use the northern one. Driving time from one airport to the other is 1½ hours.

Airport information: Tenerife (Reina Sofia, tel. 922/77–00-50; Los Rodeos, tel. 922/25–23–50), Gran Canaria (tel. 928/25–41–40), Lanzarote (tel. 928/81–14–50), Fuerteventura (tel. 928/85–08–52), La Palma (tel. 922/44–04–27), and El Hierro (tel. 922/55–02–78).

Interisland flights are handled by **Iberia** and its regional subsidiary, **Binter Airlines.**

By Boat

Transmediterranea operates interisland car ferries. Trips often take all night; ferries have sleeping cabins. The company also runs passenger-only hydrofoil service three times a day between Las Palmas and Tenerife. One hydrofoil a day links southern Fuerteventura with Las Palmas and Tenerife. La Gomera can be reached by hydrofoil from southern Tenerife.

By Bus

In Tenerife, buses meet all arriving Iberia flights at Reina Sofia airport and transfer passengers to the bus terminal in the outskirts of Santa Cruz de Tenerife. Buses also meet the Gomera hydrofoil and ferry.

By Car

Most visitors rent a car or jeep for at least part of their stay—it is by far the best way to explore the countryside. Reservations for car rentals are necessary only during the Christmas and Easter holidays. **Hertz** and **Avis** have representatives in all the islands, though better rates can be obtained from the Spanish company **Cicar** (tel. 928/27–73–08)), located at all the airports except El Hierro. The only airport rental agency in El Hierro is **Cruz Alta** (tel. 922/55–00–04).

Guided Tours

One-day tours of Tenerife and sightseeing excursions to other islands can be arranged through **Viajes Insular** (tel. 922/38–02–62), which has branches on every island except La Gomera and El Hierro.

Exploring the Canary Islands

Tenerife

Of all the Canary Islands **Tenerife** is the most popular and has the greatest variety of scenery to offer visitors. Its beaches are small, though, with volcanic black sand or sand imported from the Sahara Desert.

The south coast resort of **Playa de las Americas,** built chock-a-block with hotels, is where the majority of tourists stay. Located in the most arid and barren zone of the island, it offers little apart from sprawling hotel swimming pools and sizzling nightlife.

An hour northeast by super-highway is the pleasant provincial capital, **Santa Cruz,** known as the site of Spain's wildest fiesta, the pre-lenten Carnival, which takes place the weekends before and after Ash Wednesday. The **Museo Arqueológico Provincial** (Provincial Archeology Museum, Bravo Murillo 5, tel. 922/24–20–90) contains ceramics and mummies from the stone-age culture of the Guanches, the native people who inhabited the islands before they were conquered and colonized by the Spanish in the 15th century. The best thing to visit in Santa Cruz is the colorful weekday morning market, **Mercado de Nuestra Señora de Africa,** which sells everything from tropical fruits and flowers to canaries and parrots. (Avenida de San Sebastín; open 5 AM–noon, Monday–Saturday).

North of Santa Cruz are the university town of La Laguna and the island's first resort village, **Puerto de la Cruz.** High-rise hotels and hawkers of plastic bananas are encroaching on the small-town feel of the village and the beauty of the flower-filled central square.

Inland the road rises through banana plantations, almond groves, and pine forests to the entrance to **Mt. Teide National Park** (visitors center open daily 9–4). Before arriving at the foot of the mountain, you pass through a stark landscape called Las Cañadas del Teide, a violent jumble of rocks and minerals created by millions of years of volcanic activity. A cable car (admission 1,000 ptas.; open daily 9–5, last trip up at 4) will take you within 534 feet of the top of Mt. Teide, where there are good views of the southern part of the island and neighboring Gran Canaria.

Also worth a visit are the north coast towns of **Icod de los Vinos,** which boasts a 3,000-year-old, 57-foot-tall dragon tree once worshipped by the ancient Guanches and a plaza surrounded by typical wood-balconied Canarian houses; and farther west, **Garachico,** the most peaceful and best-preserved village on this touristy isle.

Gran Canaria

The "in" spot of the '60s and '70s, **Gran Canaria** has better beaches than Tenerife. Most visitors base themselves in the south coast resorts of **Playa del Inglés** and **Maspalomas,** where the white sand beach extends for 4 kilometers (2½ miles).

The central highlands of Gran Canaria provide a glimpse of rural island life. The road passes through numerous villages, and it is common to see farmers walking along the road laden with burlap sacks of potatoes. The **Parador Cruz de Tejada** specializes in traditional Canarian cuisine. Twenty-one kilometers (13 mi) beyond the parador is the **Mirador Los Pechos,** the highest viewpoint on the island.

Gran Canaria's capital, **Las Palmas,** is a vibrant Spanish city with an interesting old quarter called La Vegueta. Here you can wander cobblestone streets and visit the **Casa Museo Colón** (Columbus House and

Museum, Colón 1; admission free), where the great navigator is said to have stayed when he stopped to repair the mast on the Pinta before leaving and discovering America. Lots of nautical paraphernalia is on display, as are ceramics and jewelry brought back by the Spanish from Mexico and Colombia. The real jewel of the capital, however, is **Las Canteras beach,** a sparkling-clean strand of white sand perfect for swimming or strolling.

Lanzarote

Stark and dry, with landscapes of volcanic rock, **Lanzarote** enjoys good beaches and tasteful architecture—low-rise with a green-and-white color scheme—the latter due to the efforts of the late artist, César Manrique, a Lanzarote native who is all but worshipped for single-handedly saving the island from mass development. The **Jameos del Agua** (Water Cavern, Rte. GC710, 21 km/13 mi north of Arrecife) is a natural wonder created when molten lava streamed through an underground tunnel and hissed into the sea. Ponds in the caverns are home to a unique species of albino crab. The site also features an auditorium with fantastic acoustics for concerts and a restaurant-bar.

The **Parque National Timanfaya,** popularly known as the fire mountains, takes up much of the southern part of the island. Here you can have a camel ride, take a guided coach tour of the volcanic zone, and eat lunch at one of the world's most unusual restaurants, **El Diablo,** where meat is cooked over the crater of a volcano using the earth's natural heat.

Fuerteventura

The island of **Fuerteventura** was only recently discovered by tourists—mostly Germans—who come to windsurf and to enjoy the dunes of **Corralejo** and the endless white sand beaches of the **Sotovento** coast. Diving is good along the lengthy and lonely **Jandía Peninsula,** while the arid interior is largely the domain of goatherds.

La Palma

Called the garden isle, **La Palma** has luxuriant foliage, tropical storms, rainbows, and black crescents of beach, the best known of which is **Los Cancajos.** Its capital, **Santa Cruz de la Palma,** was burned to the ground by pirates in 1533. It was rebuilt with assistance from the king of Spain and today remains one of the most beautiful and harmonious examples of Spanish colonial architecture.

La Gomera

Tiny **La Gomera** is a paradise for the backpacking crowd. Ruggedly mountainous, it offers good hiking, and UNESCO protects its misty primeval laurel forests. La Gomera has a laid-back tropical feel with black sand beaches fringed by banana plantations. It is also the only island in the chain that has no airport and must be reached by ferry from Tenerife.

El Hierro

The smallest and least-visited island in the Canaries, **El Hierro** is only for those who thrive on solitude. It is cool and windswept with a few black sand beaches, a highland pine forest for hiking, and good scuba diving around the volcanic southern tip of the island.

Dining and Lodging

For price-category definitions *see* Dining and Lodging *in* Staying in Spain, *above.*

Gran Canaria

DINING

Tenderete II. Canarian cuisine is cherished at this unassuming little restaurant in a shopping center. Typical soups and stews are always available for the first course, and it is one of the only restaurants in the islands that serves *gofio*, a traditional corn and barley pudding. The main course is always fish, grilled or baked in rock salt. *Av. de Tirajan, Edificio Aloe, Maspalomas, tel. 928/76–14–60. Reservations advised. AE, DC, MC, V. $$*

LODGING

Hotel Palm Beach. The Palm Beach, one of the most sophisticated and luxurious hotels in the Canary Islands, is in the middle of a 1,000-year-old palm oasis at the edge of Maspalomas Beach. Spacious rooms have dark bamboo furniture, large marble baths, and terraces that overlook the sea or pool area. *Av. del Oasis s/n, 35106, Maspalomas, tel. 928/14–08–06, fax 928/14–51–08. 358 rooms with bath. Facilities: restaurant, bar, pool, tennis, shops, discotheque. AE, MC, V. $$$*

Lanzarote

DINING

La Era. One of only three buildings that survived the eruption of the volcano that wiped out the town of Yaiza in 1730, this farmhouse restaurant offers simple dining rooms with blue-and-white checked tablecloths arranged around a center patio. This is a great place to try regional dishes such as goat stew, or Canarian cheeses. *Barranco 3, behind city hall (Ayuntamiento), Yaiza, tel. 928/83–00–16. AE, DC, MC, V. $–$$*

DINING AND LODGING

Melia Salinas. A stunning hotel built around an interior tropical garden, the Melia Salinas offers a chance to rub elbows with vacationing business and political leaders from all over Europe. Rooms have a tropical feel thanks to louvered closets and doors, and all include large, flower-filled terraces that face the sea. The hotel's restaurant, **La Graciosa,** Lanzarote's swankiest dining spot, overlooks the garden. A German chef prepares international cuisine with fresh island ingredients such as giant prawns, duck breast in plum sauce, and halibut wrapped in chard. *35509 Costa Teguise, 35509, tel. 928/59–00–40, fax 928/59–03–90. 310 rooms with bath. Facilities: 2 restaurants, 2 bars, pool, beach, tennis, squash, sauna, exercise room, hair salon, 5-hole golf course, basketball, football, archery, shops. AE, DC, MC, V. $$$$*

Tenerife

DINING

Mesón El Drago. In the village of El Socorro halfway between Santa Cruz and Puerto de la Cruz, this green-and-white 18th-century farmhouse with its brick floors and flower-filled patio has been converted into a showcase of typical Canarian cookery. Among the best dishes are *puchero canario*, a tangy stew of vegetables and meats, and fish casserole. *Urbanizacion San Gonzalo, El Socorro, tel. 922/54–30–01. Weekend reservations advised. AE, MC, V. Open Tues.–Sun. for lunch, Fri. and Sat. for dinner. $$$*

Piscis. There's no menu here; you simply point and choose from a vast array of fresh fish and shellfish in a big refrigerated case. Add a salad and a bottle of white wine to the order, and then find a seat on a wide terrace that overlooks Las Caletas cove (about 5 kilometers [3 miles] west of Playa de las Americas), and enjoy a simple feast of the best food the Canary Islands has to offer. *Caleta de Adeje, tel. 922/71–08–95. MC, V. $$*

LODGING

Gran Hotel Bahia del Duque. This sprawling hotel is a jumble of pastel colored houses and palaces, with Renaissance windows, loggias, and quiet courtyards. Rooms have oversize beds, summery wicker and pine furnishings, and rich architectural details such as scalloped plaster work and hand-painted ceramics. *38660 Adeje, tel. 922/71–30–00, fax 922/71–26–16. 362 rooms with bath. Facilities: 5 restaurants, bars, 4 pools, exercise room, squash, sauna, tennis, sailing, diving, hair salon. AE, MC, V. $$$*

Hotel Monopol. One of the town's first inns, this hotel has been lodging tourists for more than a century. Before that it was a private home built in 1742 in the Canarian patio style. Tropical plants fill the center courtyard. Rooms are simple but have good views of the sea or main plaza. *Quintana 15, 38400, Puerto de la Cruz, tel. 922/38–46–11, fax 922/37–03–10. 110 rooms with bath. Facilities: restaurant, 2 bars, pool. AE, MC, V. $$*

27 Sweden

SWEDEN'S 450,707 SQUARE KILOMETERS (173,349 square miles) contain only 8.5 million people, so its population density ranks among Europe's lowest. Its vast open spaces and well-paved, uncrowded roads allow you to escape the frantic pace of modern life. But the long, narrow shape of the country means that on a typical visit it is possible to explore only a relatively small area; it is unwise to be overly ambitious when planning your trip. The distances are considerable, especially by European standards—almost 1,600 kilometers (1,000 miles) as the crow flies, from north to south. The 2,128-kilometer (1,330-mile) train line from Trelleborg, in the far south, through endless birch forests to Riksgränsen, in the Arctic north, is the world's longest stretch of continuously electrified railroad.

Visitors to Sweden usually return home raving about its high standards of lodging and dining. Even the most modest establishment is spotless, and your hosts will welcome you warmly (almost certainly in excellent English, too).

Sweden's scenic attractions may not be as spectacular as the Norwegian fjords across the border, but the country offers a varied landscape, with forests, mountains, rushing rivers, more than 96,000 lakes, and a jagged coastline with countless archipelagoes. Although Sweden is very much a modern country, it zealously guards its rural heritage. Most city dwellers retreat to houses in the country as often as possible. Traditional arts and crafts are also highly prized.

The cities make the most of their natural settings and are carefully planned, with an emphasis on light and open spaces. Stockholm, one of the most beautiful of European capitals, is the major metropolitan attraction; Göteborg (Gothenburg), on the west coast, and Malmö, across the sound from Denmark, are worthy of visits as well.

ESSENTIAL INFORMATION

Before You Go

When to Go

In an attempt to encourage visitors from abroad, Sweden has extended the main tourist season to run from mid-May through mid-September. Bear in mind, however, that many attractions close in late August when the Swedes' own vacation season ends and children return to school. The weather can be magnificent in the spring and fall, and many visitors prefer sightseeing when fewer people are around.

The concentrated nature of the Swedes' own vacation period—Sweden virtually shuts up shop for the entire month of July—can sometimes make it difficult to get hotel reservations during July and early August. On the other hand, the big city hotels, which cater mainly to business travelers, reduce their rates drastically in summer, when their ordinary clients are on vacation. (If you're traveling fall through spring, the high season for business travel, be forewarned that prices are high.) Ask your travel agent about special discounts offered by the major hotel groups, or contact the tourist information center, **Next Stop Sweden** (Box 3030, 103 61 Stockholm, tel. 08/725–5500, fax 08/725–5531). Once you're in Sweden, you might also pay a visit to **Upptäck Sverige Resor** (Discover Sweden Travel Agency, Sveavägen 16, Stockholm, tel. 08/791–8085, fax. 08/791–8889) for well-priced seasonal package tours.

Sweden

Riksgränsen
Kiruna
Gällivare
Jokkmokk
Luleälven
400
Arctic Circle
Norwegian
Sea
Arjeplog
Töre
Törneå
Tärnaby
Arvidsjaur
Kalix
E79
Sorsele
95
Piteå
Luleå
Storuman
Lycksele
Skellefteå
342
Åsele
Umeälven
Strömsund
80
91
Umeå
Åre
Östersund
E75
Tännäs
Ljungan
Sundsvall
NORWAY
84
Gulf
of
Idre
Hudiksvall
Bothnia
FINLAND
70
Bollnäs
Mora
Söderhamn
62
Klarälven
Falun
Gävle
80
Borlänge
Avesta
Åland
Fagersta
Uppsala
Karlstad
Mellerud
Västerås
Gotska
Sandön
E18
Mälaren
Stockholm
Strömstad
Örebro
Gulf of Finland
Vänern
Uddevalla
Trollhättan
Norrköping
Göteborg
Vättern
Linköping
Baltic
ESTONIA
(Gothenburg)
40
Jönköping
Sea
Borås
Visby
Gulf of
Riga
Falkenberg
E6
Nässjö
E93
Värnamo
Oskarshamn
Gotland
Halmstad
Växjö
Öland
LATVIA
23
Helsingborg
Kalmar
Karlskrona
Malmö
Kristianstad
LITHUANIA
DENMARK
Trelleborg
Ystad

CLIMATE

Like the rest of northern Europe, Sweden has unpredictable summer weather, but, as a general rule, it is more likely to be rainy on the west coast than on the east. When the sun shines, the climate is usually agreeable; it is rarely hot. In Stockholm it never really gets dark in midsummer, while in the far north, above the Arctic Circle, the sun doesn't set between the end of May and the middle of July.

The following are the average daily maximum and minimum temperatures for Stockholm.

Jan.	30F	– 1C	May	58F	14C	Sept.	60F	15C
	23	– 5		43	6		49	9
Feb.	30F	– 1C	June	67F	19C	Oct.	49F	9C
	22	– 5		51	11		41	5
Mar.	37F	3C	July	71F	22C	Nov.	40F	5C
	26	– 4		57	14		34	1
Apr.	47F	8C	Aug.	68F	20C	Dec.	35F	3C
	34	1		55	13		28	– 2

Currency

The unit of currency in Sweden is the krona (plural kronor), which is divided into 100 öre and is written as SKr, SEK, or kr. Coins come in values of 50 öre and 1, 5, or 10 kronor, while bills come in denominations of 20, 100, 500, and 1,000 kronor. Traveler's checks and foreign currency can be exchanged at banks all over Sweden and at post offices bearing the NB Exchange sign. At press time (spring 1995), the exchange rate was 6.9 kronor to the dollar, 5.1 kronor to the Canadian dollar, and 11.39 kronor to the pound sterling.

What It Will Cost

Sweden is seen as an expensive country but, in recent years, hotel prices have fallen in line with the European average. As in most countries, the most expensive hotels are found in major cities. Restaurant prices are generally high, but there are bargains to be had: Look for the *dagens rätt* (dish of the day) in many city restaurants. This costs about SKr 40–SKr 65 and can include a main dish, salad, soft drink, bread and butter, and coffee.

Many hotels have special low summer rates and cut prices on weekends in winter. Because of heavy taxes and excise duties, liquor prices remain among the highest in Europe. It pays to take in your maximum duty-free allowance (although prices on wine in Systembolaget, the state liquor stores, are not unreasonable). Value-added tax (known as *Moms* in Swedish) is imposed on most goods and services at a rate of 25%, with the exception of a 21% Moms on food, hotels, restaurants, and transportation. You can get a refund for most of the tax on goods if you take advantage of the tax-free shopping service offered at more than 13,000 stores throughout the country (*see* Shopping *in* Staying in Sweden, *below*).

SAMPLE PRICES

Cup of coffee, SKr 10–SKr 15; bottle of beer, SKr 30–SKr 40; Coca-Cola, SKr 12–SKr 15; ham sandwich, SKr 25–SKr 35; 1-mile taxi ride, SKr 70 (depending on the taxi company).

Customs on Arrival

Travelers from the United States may import duty-free: 1 liter of liquor or 2 liters of fortified wine; 2 liters of wine; 15 liters of beer; 200 cigarettes or 100 cigarillos or 50 cigars or 250 grams of tobacco; 50 grams of perfume; 0.25 liter of aftershave; and other goods up to the value of SKr 1,700. Travelers from the United Kingdom or other European Union countries may import duty-free: 1 liter of liquor or 3 liters of fortified wine; 5 liters of wine; 15 liters of beer; 300 cigarettes or 150 cigarillos or 75 cigars or 400 grams of tobacco; and other goods, including perfume and aftershave, of any value. Duties are applied according to the traveler's point of origin, not citizenship—for example, if a U.S. citizen traveling from New York to Sweden were to break the trip for a few days in London, then the more generous U.K. limitations would be applied. There are no limits on the amount of foreign currency that can be imported or exported.

Language
Virtually all Swedes you are likely to meet will speak English, for it is a mandatory subject in all schools. Some of the older people you encounter in the rural areas may not be so familiar with English, but you'll soon find someone who can help out.

Getting Around

By Car
ROAD CONDITIONS
Sweden has an excellent highway network of more than 80,000 kilometers (50,000 miles). The fastest routes are those with numbers prefixed with an *E* (for "European"), some of which are the equivalent of American superhighways or British motorways—for part of the way, at least. Road E4, for instance, covers the entire distance from Malmö, in the south, to Stockholm, and on to Sundsvall and Umeå, in the north, finishing at Haparanda, on the border with Finland. All main and secondary roads are well surfaced, but some minor roads, particularly in the north, are gravel.

RULES OF THE ROAD
You drive on the right and, no matter where you sit in a car, you must wear a seat belt. You must also have at least low-beam headlights on at all times. Signs indicate five basic speed limits, ranging from 30 kph (19 mph) in school or playground areas to 110 kph (69 mph) on long stretches of *E* roads.

PARKING
Park on the right-hand side of the road, but if you want to park overnight, particularly in suburban areas, be sure not to do so on the night the street is being cleaned; signs should indicate when this occurs. Parking meters and, increasingly, timed ticket machines, are available for use in larger towns, usually between 8 AM and 6 PM. The fee varies from about SKr 4 to SKr 20 per hour. Parking garages in urban areas are mostly automated, often with machines that accept credit cards; LEDIGT on a garage sign means space is available. On the street, a circular sign with a red cross on a blue background with a red border means parking is prohibited. A yellow plate with a red border means restricted parking. The fees for parking tickets are extraordinarily high in Sweden. City "Trafikkarta" maps, available at gas stations, include English explanations of parking signs and systems.

GASOLINE
Sweden has some of the highest gasoline rates in Europe, about SKr 7.85 per liter, depending on the grade. Lead-free gasoline is readily available. Gas stations are self-service: pumps marked SEDEL are automatic and accept SKr 20 and SKr 100 bills; pumps marked KASSA are paid

for at the cashier; the KONTO pumps are for customers with Swedish gas credit cards.

The **Larmtjänst** organization, run by a confederation of Swedish insurance companies, provides a 24-hour breakdown service. Its phone numbers are listed in all telephone books. A toll-free emergency number, tel. 020/910040, is also available.

By Train

Sweden's rail network, mostly electrified, is highly efficient, and trains operate frequently, particularly on the main routes linking Stockholm with Gothenburg and Malmö. First- and second-class cars are provided on all main routes, and sleeping cars are available in both classes on overnight trains. On long-distance trains, there is usually a buffet or dining car. Seat reservations are advisable, and on some trains—indicated with *R, IN,* or *IC* on the timetable—they are compulsory. Reservations can be made right up to departure time at a cost of SKr 30 per seat (tel. 020/757575). In addition, the Swedish rail network operates several daily high-speed trains called the X2000 from Stockholm to Gothenburg, Jönköping, Karlstad, Falun, and Malmö.

FARES

On "Low price" or "Red" departures, fares are reduced by 50%, but careful planning and the Reslust discount card, which costs SKr 150, are necessary. Passengers paying low fares cannot make stopovers, and the tickets are valid for only 36 hours.

By Plane

Sweden's domestic air network is highly developed. Most major cities are served by **SAS** (tel. 020/727000). From Stockholm, there are flights to about 30 points around the country. SAS offers cut-rate round-trip "Jackpot" fares every day of the week on selected flights, and these fares are available on most services during the peak tourist season, from late June to mid-August. Some even more favorable offers on domestic flights are frequently available from the end of June through early August and during the Christmas and Easter seasons.

By Bus

Sweden has an excellent network of express bus services that provides an inexpensive and relatively speedy way of getting around the country. **Swebus** (tel. 08/237190) offers daily bus service from most major Swedish cities to various parts of Sweden. Other private companies operate weekend-only service on additional routes. In the far north, post buses delivering mail to remote areas also carry passengers, providing an offbeat and inexpensive way to see the countryside.

By Boat

The classic boat trip in Sweden is the four-day journey along the Göta Canal between Gothenburg and Stockholm, operated by **Göta Kanal,** Gothenburg, tel. 031/806315, fax 031/158311.

By Bicycle

Cycling is popular in Sweden, and the country's uncongested roads make it ideal for extended bike tours. Bicycles can be rented throughout the country; inquire at the local tourist information office. Rental costs average around SKr 80 per day or SKr 400 per week. The **Swedish Touring Club** (STF) in Stockholm (Drottninggatan 31–33, tel. 08/790–3100) can give you information about cycling packages that include bike rental, overnight accommodations, and meals. **Cykelfrämjandet** (tel. 08/321680, fax 08/310305) has an English-language guide to cycling trips.

Staying in Sweden

Telephones

LOCAL CALLS

Sweden has plenty of pay phones, and there are special offices marked TELE or TELEBUTIK from which you can make calls. To make calls from a pay phone, you should have SKr 1 or SKr 5 coins available. You can also purchase a *telefonkort* (telephone card) from a Telebutik, hospital, or *Pressbyrån* store for SKr 30, SKr 55 or SKr 95; this can be cheaper if you plan to make numerous domestic calls. For a local call, you need two SKr 1 coins. Telephone numbers beginning with 020 are toll-free within Sweden.

INTERNATIONAL CALLS

These can be made from any pay phone. For calls to the United States and Canada, dial 009, then 1 (the country code), then wait for a second dial tone before dialing the area code and number. When dialing the United Kingdom, omit the initial zero on area codes (for Central London you would dial 009 followed by 44, wait for the second tone, then dial 171 and the local number). You can make calls from Telebutik offices. To reach an **AT&T** long-distance operator, dial 020/795611; for **MCI**, dial 020/795922; and for **Sprint**, 020/799011.

OPERATORS AND INFORMATION

For international calls, the operator assistance number is 0018; directory assistance is 07977. Within Sweden, dial 90130 for operator assistance and 07975 for directory assistance.

COUNTRY CODE

If you're calling Sweden from another country, the country code is 46.

Mail

POSTAL RATES

Airmail letters and postcards to the United States and Canada weighing less than 20 grams cost SKr 7.50. Postcards and letters within Europe cost SKr 6.

RECEIVING MAIL

If you're uncertain where you will be staying, have your mail addressed to "poste restante" and sent to S-101 10 Stockholm. Collection is at the Central Post Office, Vasagatan 28–32, tel. 08/781–2040. A poste-restante service is also offered free to its clients by American Express (*see* Important Addresses and Numbers in Stockholm, *below*) or for a small fee to others.

Shopping

Swedish goods have earned an international reputation for elegance and quality, and any visitor to the country should spend some time exploring the many impressive shops and department stores. The midsummer tourist season is as good a time as any to go shopping, for that is when many stores have their annual sales. The best buys are glassware, stainless steel, pottery and ceramics, leather goods, and textiles. You will find a wide selection of goods available in such major stores as **NK, Åhléns,** and **PUB,** which have branches all over the country.

High-quality furniture is a Swedish specialty, and it is worthwhile to visit one of the many branches of **IKEA,** a shop usually located on the outskirts of major towns. For glassware at bargain prices, head for the "Kingdom of Glass" (*see* The West Coast and the Glass Country, *below*). All the major glassworks, including **Orrefors** and **Kosta Boda,** have large factory outlets where you can pick up seconds at only a fraction of the normal retail price. For clothing, the best center is Borås, not far from Gothenburg. Here you can find bargains from the leading mail-order companies. In country areas, look for the local **Hemslöjd** craft centers, featuring high-quality clothing and needlework items.

VAT REFUNDS

About 13,000 Swedish shops—1,000 in Stockholm alone—participate in the tax-free shopping program for visitors, enabling you to claim a refund on most of the value-added tax (Moms) that you have paid. Shops taking part in this service display a distinctive black, blue, and yellow sticker in the window. (Some stores offer the service only on purchases worth more than SKr 200.) Whenever you make a purchase in a participating store, the store wraps and seals your purchase and you are given a "Tax-Free Shopping Check" equivalent to the tax paid, less a handling charge. This check can be cashed when you leave Sweden and show your unopened packages, either at the airport or aboard ferries. You should have your passport with you when you make your purchase and when you claim your refund.

Opening and Closing Times

Banks are open weekdays 9:30–3; some stay open until 5:30 in larger cities. Banks at Stockholm's Arlanda Airport and Gothenburg's Landvetter Airport are open every day, with extended hours. **Forex** and **Valuta Specialisten** currency-exchange offices operate in downtown Stockholm, Gothenburg, and Malmö, also with extended hours.

Hours vary widely, but **museums** are typically open weekdays 10–4 or 10–5. Many are also open on weekends but may close on Monday.

Shops are generally open weekdays 9 or 9:30–6 and Saturday 9–1 or 9–4. Some department stores remain open until 8 or 10 on certain evenings, and some are also open Sunday noon–4 in major cities. Many supermarkets open on Sunday.

National Holidays

January 1; January 6 (Epiphany); April 5 (Good Friday); April 8 (Easter Monday); May 1 (Labor Day); May 16 (Ascension); May 27 (Whit Monday); June 22 (Midsummer Day); November 2 (All Saints' Day); December 25–26. Hotels and restaurants may close for some of these holidays and for the week between Christmas and New Year's.

Dining

Swedish cuisine has lately become much more cosmopolitan. The inevitable fast-food outlets, such as McDonald's and Burger King, have come on the scene, as well as Clock, the homegrown version. But there is also a good range of more conventional restaurants, from topclass establishments to less expensive places where you can pick up a cheaper lunch or snack. Snacks can also be enjoyed in a *konditori,* which offers inexpensive sandwiches, pastries, and pies with coffee, tea, or soft drinks. A cross between a café and a coffee shop, the konditori can be found in every city and town.

Many restaurants all over the country specialize in *husmanskost*—literally "home cooking"—which is based on traditional Swedish recipes.

Sweden is best known for its *smörgåsbord,* a word whose correct pronunciation defeats non-Swedes. It consists of a tempting buffet of hot and cold dishes, usually with a strong emphasis on seafood, notably herring, prepared in a wide variety of ways. Authentic smörgåsbord can be enjoyed all over the country, but the best is found in the many inns in Skåne, where you can eat as much as you want for about SKr 300. Many Swedish hotels serve a lavish smörgåsbord-style breakfast, often included in the room price. Do justice to your breakfast and you'll probably want to skip lunch!

MEALTIMES
Swedes eat early. Restaurants start serving lunch at about 11 AM, and outside the main cities you may find that they close quite early in the evening (often by 9) or may not open at all for dinner. Don't wait too long to look for someplace to have a meal. In major cities, especially on weekends, it's advisable to make reservations for dinner.

WHAT TO WEAR
Except for the most formal restaurants, where a jacket and tie are preferable, casual—or casual chic—attire is perfectly acceptable for restaurants in all price categories. Swedish dress, however, like other Europeans', tends to be a bit more formal and a bit less flamboyant than that of Americans.

RATINGS
Prices are per person and include a first course and main course, but no drinks. Service charges and Moms are included in the meal, so there is no need to tip. Highly recommended restaurants are indicated by a star ★.

CATEGORY	COST
$$$$	over SKr 350
$$$	SKr 250–SKr 350
$$	SKr 120–SKr 250
$	under SKr 120

Lodging
Sweden offers a wide range of accommodations, from simple village rooms and campsites to hotels of the highest international standard. Except at the major hotels in the larger cities that cater mainly to a business clientele, rates are fairly reasonable. Prices are normally on a per-room basis and include all taxes and service and usually breakfast. Apart from the more modest inns and the cheapest budget establishments, private baths and showers are standard features, although it is just as well to double-check when making your reservation. Whatever their size, virtually all Swedish hotels provide scrupulously clean accommodations and courteous service. In Stockholm, there is a hotel reservation office—**Hotellcentralen**—at the central train station (tel. 08/240880, fax 08/791–8666) and at the Stockholm Tourist Center in Sweden House. In other areas, local tourist offices will help you with hotel reservations.

HOTELS
You can get a good idea of the facilities and prices at a particular hotel by consulting the official annual guide, "Hotels in Sweden," obtainable free from the Swedish Travel and Tourism Council (Box 101 34, S–121 28 Stockholm–Globen, tel. 08/725–5500, fax 08/649–8882). There is a good selection of hotels in all price categories in every town and city, though major international chains such as Sheraton have made only small inroads in Sweden thus far. The main national chains are Scandic and RESO. The Sweden Hotels group has about 100 independently owned hotels and offers a central reservation office (tel. 08/789–8900). The group also has its own classification scheme—*A, B,* or *C*—based on the facilities available at each establishment. **Countryside Hotels** (Box 69, 830 13 Åre, tel. 0647/51860, fax 0647/51920) is a group of 33 handpicked resort hotels, some of them restored manor houses or centuries-old inns.

HOUSE-RENTAL VACATIONS

In Sweden, these are popular among other Europeans, particularly the British and Germans. There are about 250 chalet villages with amenities, such as grocery stores, restaurants, saunas, and tennis courts. You can often arrange such accommodations on the spot at local tourist information offices. An alternative is a package, such as the one offered by **Scandinavian Seaways,** that combines a ferry trip from Britain across the North Sea with a stay in a chalet village. Scandinavian Seaways is based in the United Kingdom at Parkeston Quay, Harwich, Essex (tel. 01255/240240), with a second office in London (tel. 0171/409–6060). Their number in Gothenburg is 031/650600.

CAMPING

Camping is also popular in Sweden. About 750 officially approved sites dot the country, most next to the sea or a lake and offering such activities as windsurfing, riding, and tennis. They are generally open between June 1 and September 1, though some are available year round. The Swedish Campsite Owners'Association (Box 255, S–451 17 Uddevalla, tel. 0522/39345) publishes, in English, a free abbreviated list of sites.

RATINGS

Prices are for two people in a double room, based on standard rates; tax and breakfast are included. Highly recommended lodgings are indicated by a star ★.

CATEGORY	COST
$$$$	over SKr 1,200
$$$	SKr 970–SKr 1,200
$$	SKr 725–SKr 970
$	under SKr 725

Tipping

Swedes seldom expect tips. In hotels, tip the porter about SKr 5 per item. Taxi drivers do not expect a tip. A consistent feature of the Swedish restaurant scene is that you must often dispose of your coat or sports jacket, whether you want to or not; the fee for leaving a coat in the checkroom is between SKr 6 and SKr 15.

STOCKHOLM

Arriving and Departing

By Plane

All international flights arrive at Arlanda Airport, 40 kilometers (25 miles) north of the city. The airport is linked to Stockholm by a major highway. For information on arrival and departure times, call the individual airlines.

BETWEEN THE AIRPORT AND DOWNTOWN

Buses leave both the international and domestic terminals every 10–15 minutes, from 6:30 AM to 11 PM, and run to the city terminal at Klarabergsviadukten next to the central train station. The bus costs SKr 50 per person. A bus-taxi package is available (tel. 08/670–1010) for SKr 120 per person inside city limits and SKr 180 anywhere in the Stockholm area; additional passengers in a group pay only the bus portion of the fare. A taxi directly from the airport will cost at least SKr 200 (be sure to ask the driver if he offers the standard SKr 200 airport-to-city rate before you get into the taxi), but a possible alternative if you are not traveling alone is the SAS limousine service to any point in greater

Stockholm. It operates as a shared taxi at SKr 274 per person. If two or three people travel together in a limousine to the same address, only one pays the full rate; all others pay SKr 130. The Moms will be deducted if the limousine is booked ahead of time through a travel agent in connection with an international arrival.

By Train

Major domestic and international trains arrive at Stockholm Central Station on Vasagatan, in the heart of the city. This is also the terminus for local commuter services. For train information and ticket reservations 6 AM–11 PM, tel. 020/757575. At the station there is a ticket and information office where you can make seat or sleeping-car reservations. An automatic ticket-issuing machine is also available. Seat reservations on the regular train cost SKr 30, couchettes SKr 85, and beds from SKr 165. Seat reservations on the X2000, the high-speed trains, cost from SKr 130 to SKr 295 depending on your destination.

By Bus

Long-distance buses, from such places as Härnösand and Sundsvall, arrive at Norra Bantorget, a few blocks north of the central train station, and all others at Klarabergsviadukten, just beside the train station. Bus tickets can also be bought at the railroad reservations office.

By Car

The two main access routes from the west and south are the E20 main highway from Gothenburg and E4 from Malmö, which continues as the main route to Sundsvall, the far north, and Finland. All routes to the city center are well marked.

Getting Around

The most cost-effective way of getting around Stockholm is to use **Stockholmskortet** (the Key to Stockholm card). Besides unlimited transportation on city subway, bus, and rail services, it offers free admission to 60 museums and several sightseeing trips. The card costs SKr 175 for 24 hours, SKr 350 for two days, and SKr 525 for three days. It is available from the tourist information centers at Sweden House and the Kaknäs TV tower, and at the Hotellcentralen accommodations bureau at the central train station.

Maps and timetables for all city transportation networks are available from the Stockholm Transit Authority (SL) information desks at Sergels Torg, the central train station, and Slussen in Gamla Stan. You can also obtain information by phone (tel. 08/600–1000).

By Bus and Subway

The SL operates both the bus and subway systems. Tickets for the two networks are interchangeable.

The subway system, known as T-banan (the *T* stands for tunnel), is the easiest and fastest way of getting around the city. Station entrances are marked with a blue T on a white background. The T-banan has about 100 stations and covers more than 60 route-miles. Trains run frequently between 5 AM and 2 AM.

The subway and bus fare system is based on zones. The basic fare is SKr 13, good for travel within one zone, such as downtown, for one hour. You pay more if you travel in more than one zone.

Tickets are available at ticket counters, but it is cheaper to buy the SL Tourist Card, a significant savings compared with buying separate tickets each time you travel. The cards, valid on both bus and subway and in some cases including free entry to an array of museums and sights, are available at Pressbyrån newsstands and SL information desks. A card for the entire Greater Stockholm area costs SKr 54 for 24 hours or SKr 107 for 72 hours. People under 18 or over 65 pay SKr 33 for one day and SKr 70 for three days. Also available from the Pressbyrån newsstands are SKr 85 coupons, good for at least 10 bus and subway rides in the central zone.

The Stockholm bus network provides service not only within the central area but also to out-of-town points of interest, such as Waxholm, with its historic fortress, and Gustavsberg, with its porcelain factory. In greater Stockholm, buses run throughout the night.

By Train
SL operates conventional train service from Stockholm Central Station to a number of nearby points, including Nynäshamn, a departure point for ferries to the island of Gotland. Trains also run from the Slussen station to the fashionable seaside resort of Saltsjöbaden.

By Taxi
Typically, a trip of 10 kilometers (6 miles) will cost SKr 93 between 6 AM and 7 PM on weekdays and SKr 103 on weekday nights; weekend prices are SKr 110, including Moms. Major taxi companies are Taxi Stockholm (tel. 08/150000), Taxikurir (tel. 08/300000), and Taxi 020 (tel. 020/850400).

Important Addresses and Numbers

Tourist Information
The main tourist center for Stockholm is at **Sweden House** (Kungsträdgården, Hamngatan 27, tel. 08/789–2490). During the peak tourist season (June through August), it is open weekdays 8–6; weekends 9–5. The current off-season hours are 9–6 and 10–3, respectively. Besides providing information, it is the main ticket center for sightseeing excursions. There are also information centers at the central train station, in the city hall (summer only), and in the Kaknäs TV Tower. When planning to visit any of the tourist attractions in Stockholm, be sure to call ahead, as opening times and prices are subject to change.

Embassies
U.S. (Strandvägen 101, tel. 08/783–5300). **Canadian** (Tegelbacken 4, tel. 08/613–9900). **U.K.** (Skarpögatan 6–8, tel. 08/671–9000).

Emergencies
Police (tel. 08/769–3000; emergencies only: 90000); **Ambulance** (tel. 90000); **Doctor** (Medical Care Information, tel. 08/644–9200)—travelers can get hospital attention in the district where they are staying or can contact the private clinic, **City Akuten** (tel. 08/411–7102); **Dentist** (8 AM–9 PM tel. 08/654–1117, 9 PM–8 AM tel. 08/644–9200); **24–hour Pharmacy:** C. W. Scheele (tel. 08/218934; all pharmacies are indicated by the sign APOTEKET).

English-Language Bookstores
Most bookstores have a good selection of English books. **Akademibokhandeln** (Mäster Samuelsgatan 32, tel. 08/613–6100), part of a chain of bookstores, has the widest selection of paperbacks, dictionaries, and maps in many languages.

Travel Agencies
American Express (Birger Jarlsgatan 1, tel. 08/679–5200, fax 08/611–6214). **Thomas Cook** (Kottbygatan 5, Kista, tel. 08/632–2200).

Guided Tours

Orientation Tours

Some 30 different tours—by foot, boat, bus, or a combination of these—are available during the summer. Some last only 30 minutes, others an entire day. A popular three-hour bus tour, costing SKr 230, runs daily at 9:45 AM. The tour includes City Hall, Storkyrkan in Gamla Stan, the Vasa Ship, and the Royal Palace, among other stops. Tickets can be purchased from the Excursion Shop at Sweden House. A convenient budget-price bus tour, at SKr 40 per adult, is SL's "Tourist Route" (Turistlinjen) on Line 87. The tour departs every 15 minutes during peak vacation periods and every 30 minutes at other times; you can get on and off at any one of the 14 stops. This tour is free for holders of the Key to Stockholm card but is conducted in Swedish only, with a printed text in English.

Boat Tours

You'll find a bewildering variety of tours available at Stockholm's quay. The **Waxholm Steamship Company** (tel. 08/679–5830) operates scheduled service to many islands in the archipelago on its white steamers. Trips range from one to three hours each way. Popular one-day excursions include Waxholm, Utö, Sandhamn, and Möja. Conventional sightseeing tours include a one-hour circular city tour run by the **Strömma Canal Company** (tel. 08/233375). It leaves from the Nybroplan quay every hour on the half-hour between 10:30 and 5:30 in summer.

Special-Interest Tours

Among the special-interest tours in the Stockholm area, especially in summer, are a weekend at a chalet in the archipelago, rental of a small fishing boat, or the chance to buy porcelain at the Gustavsberg porcelain factory, just outside Stockholm. Several outstanding 17th-century villas and estates within an hour or two of Stockholm have been converted into quaint, high-quality hotels, such as the stately Ulvhälls Herrgård in Strängnäs on Lake Mälaren. Contact the tourist center at Sweden House for details.

Excursions

Don't miss the boat trip to the 17th-century palace of **Drottningholm,** the private residence of the Swedish royal family and a smaller version of Versailles. Departures are every hour on the hour from 10 to 4 and at 6 PM during the summer from City Hall Bridge (Stadshusbron). Another popular trip goes from Stadshusbron to the ancient towns of Sigtuna and Skokloster. By changing boats you can continue to Uppsala to catch the train back to Stockholm. Information is available from the **Strömma Canal Company** (tel. 08/233375) or the Tourist Center at Sweden House.

Personal Guides

Contact the **Guide Center** at **Stockholm Information Service** (tel. 08/789–2496).

Exploring Stockholm

Numbers in the margin correspond to points of interest on the Stockholm map.

Because Stockholm's main attractions are concentrated in a relatively small area, the city itself can be explored in a few days. If you want to take advantage of some of the full-day excursions offered, it is worthwhile to devote a full week to your visit.

The city of Stockholm, built on 14 small islands among open bays and narrow channels, is a handsome, civilized place, full of parks, squares, and airy boulevards, yet it is also a bustling, modern metropolis. Glass-and-steel skyscrapers abound, but in the center you are never more than five minutes' walk from twisting, medieval streets and waterside walks.

The first written mention of Stockholm dates from 1252, when a powerful regent named Birger Jarl is said to have built a fortified castle here. This strategic position, where the calm, fresh waters of Lake Mälaren meet the salty Baltic Sea, must have prompted King Gustav Vasa to take over the city in 1523, and King Gustavus Adolphus to make it the heart of an empire a century later.

During the Thirty Years' War (1618–48), Sweden gained importance as a Baltic trading state, and Stockholm grew commensurately. But by the beginning of the 18th century, Swedish influence had begun to wane, and Stockholm's development slowed. It did not pick up until the Industrial Revolution, when the hub of the city moved north from the Old Town area.

City Hall and the Old Town

Anyone in Stockholm with limited time should give priority to a tour of **Gamla Stan** (the Old Town), a labyrinth of narrow, medieval streets, alleys, and quiet squares on the island just south of the city center. From the central station, take Vasagatan down to the waterfront. Ideally, you should devote an entire day to this district, but it's worthwhile starting with a detour along the quay and across Stadshusbron to the modern-day **Stadshuset** (city hall), constructed in 1923 and now one of the symbols of Stockholm. Lavish mosaics adorn the walls of the **Golden Hall,** and the **Prince's Gallery** features a collection of large murals by Prince Eugen, brother of King Gustav V. Take the elevator halfway up, then climb the rest of the way to the top of the 348-foot tower for a magnificent view of the city. *Tel. 08/785–9074. Admission: SKr 30. Tours daily at 10 and noon; also at 11 and 2 in summer. Tower admission: SKr 15. Tower open May–Sept., daily 10–4:30.*

Retrace your steps over Stadshusbron and head for the stairway leading up from the quay onto the Gångbro (footbridge). Crossing into the Old Town, the first thing you'll see is the magnificent **Riddarholms Kyrka** (Riddarholm Church), where a host of Swedish kings are buried. *Tel. 08/789–8500. Admission: SKr 10. Open May–Aug, daily 10–3; Sept., Wed. and weekends noon–3.*

Proceed across Riddarhusbron to the **Kungliga Slott** (Royal Palace), preferably by noon, when you can see the colorful changing-of-the-guard ceremony. The smartly dressed guards seem superfluous, as tourists wander at will into the palace courtyard and around the grounds. Several separate attractions are open to the public. Be sure to visit the **Royal Armory,** with its outstanding collection of weaponry and royal regalia. The **Treasury** houses the Swedish crown jewels, including the regalia used for the coronation of King Erik XIV in 1561. You can also visit the **State Apartments,** where the king swears in each successive government. *Tel. 08/789–8500. Admission: SKr 50 for Armory; SKr 30 for Treasury; SKr 30 for State Apartments. Call ahead for opening hours, as they are subject to change.*

From the palace, stroll down **Västerlånggatan,** one of the main streets in the Old Town. This popular shopping area brims with boutiques and antiques shops. Walk down to the Skeppsbron waterfront, then head back toward the center over the Ström bridge, where anglers cast for salmon. If you feel like a rest, stop off at **Kungsträdgården** and watch the world go by. Originally built as a royal kitchen garden, the property was turned into a public park in 1562. In summer, you can watch people playing open-air chess with giant chess pieces. In winter, the park has a skating rink.

Djurgården

Be sure to spend at least a day visiting the large island of **Djurgården.** Although it's only a short walk from the city center, the most pleasant way to approach it is by ferry from Skeppsbron, in the Old Town. The ferries drop you off near two of Stockholm's best-known attractions, Vasamuseet and Gröna Lund Tivoli. Or you might want to take the streetcar that runs from Norrmalmstorg, near the city center, to **Waldemarsudde,** (tel. 08/662–2800), an art museum in the former summer residence of Swedish prince Eugen, on a peninsula in Djurgården. The *Vasa,* a restored 17th-century warship, is one of the oldest preserved war vessels in the world and has become Sweden's most popular tourist sight. It sank ignominiously in Stockholm Harbor on its maiden voyage in 1628, reportedly because it was not carrying sufficient ballast. Recovered in 1961, the ship has been restored to its original appearance and is housed in a spectacular museum, **Vasamuseet,** which opened in 1990. It has guided tours, films, and displays. *Gälarvarvet, tel. 08/666–4800. Admission: SKr 45 adults, SKr 30 students. Open Thurs.–Tues. 10–5, Wed. 10–8.*

6 **Gröna Lund Tivoli,** Stockholm's version of the famous Copenhagen amusement park, is a family favorite, with roller coasters as well as tamer delights. *Tel. 08/670–7600. Open late Apr.–early Sept. Call ahead for prices and hours, as they are subject to change.*

7 Just across the road is **Skansen,** a large, open-air folk museum showcasing 150 reconstructed traditional buildings from Sweden's different regions. Here you can see a variety of handicraft displays and demonstrations. There is also an attractive zoo—with many native Scandinavian species, such as lynxes, wolves, reindeer, and brown bears—as well as an excellent aquarium and a carnival area for children. *Tel. 08/442–8000. Call ahead for prices and times, as they are subject to change.*

TIME OUT For a mediocre snack and a great view, try the **Solliden Restaurant** at Skansen. Skansen also offers a selection of open-air snack bars and cafés; Gröna Lund has four different restaurants and many snack bars.

8 From Skansen, head back toward the city center. Just before Djurgårdsbron, you come to **Nordiska Museet** (the Nordic Museum), which, like Skansen, provides insight into the way Swedish people have lived over the past 500 years. The collection includes displays of peasant costumes, folk art, and Sami culture. Families with children should visit the delightful "village life" play area on the ground floor. *Tel. 08/666–4600. Admission: SKr 40 adults, SKr 10 children. Open Tues.–Sun. 11–5.*

9 Once you're back on the "mainland," drop into **Historiska Museet** (the Museum of National Antiquities). Though its name is uninspiring, it houses some remarkable Viking gold and silver treasures. **The Royal Cabinet of Coin,** in the same building, boasts the world's largest coin. *Narvavägen 13–17, tel. 08/783–9400. Admission: SKr 55. Open Tues.–Sun. 11–5.*

Stockholm

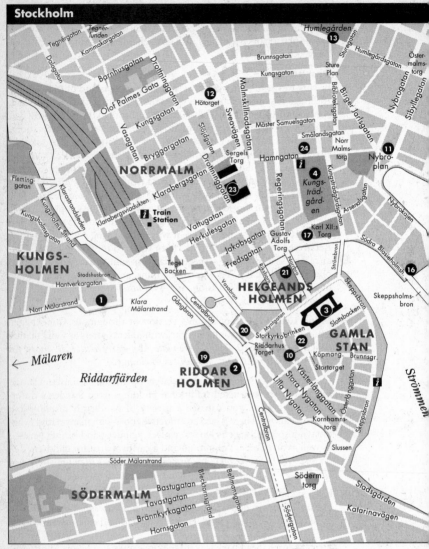

Major Attractions
Gröna Lund Tivoli, **6**
Historiska Museet, **9**
Kungliga Slott, **3**
Kungsträdgården, **4**
Nordiska Museet, **8**
Riddarholms
Kyrka, **2**
Skansen, **7**
Stadshuset, **1**
Vasamuseet, **5**

Other Attractions
Cathedral, **22**
House of Nobles, **20**
Kaknäs TV Tower, **15**
Konserthuset, **12**
Kulturhuset, **23**
Museum of Far
Eastern
Antiquities, **18**
Museum of Modern
Art, **14**

National Museum, **16**
NK, **24**
Operan, **17**
Parliament, **21**
Royal Dramatic
Theater, **11**
Royal Library, **13**
Stock Exchange, **10**
Supreme Court, **19**
Waldemarsudde, **25**

ÖSTERMALM

Sibyllegatan

Kommendörsgatan

Karlaplan

Narvavägen

Banérgatan

Karlavägen

LADUGÅRDSGÄRDET

Linnégatan

Oxenstiernsgatan

Artillerigatan

Skeppargatan

Grevgatan

Styrmangatan

Storgatan

Linnégatan

Riddargatan

9

Cladegatan

Starggatan

15

Strandvägen

Strandvägen

Djurgårdsbron

Djurgårdsbrunnsviken

8

Rosendalsvägen

5

18

14

DJURGÅRDEN

SKEPPSHOLMEN

Svensksundsvägen

Alkärret

Djurgårdsvägen

7

Sirishovsvägen

Falkenbergsg.

Djurgårds
Slätten

Soltidsbacken

Singelbacken

Allmänna Gränd

KASTELL-
HOLMEN

6

25

Saltsjön

BECKHOLMEN

Baltic →

N

KEY

i Tourist Information

—— Rail Lines

0   500 yards

0   500 meters

Around Stockholm

The region surrounding Stockholm offers many attractions that can easily be seen on day trips from the capital.

Gripsholm and the *Mariefred*

One "must" is the trip to the majestic 16th-century **Gripsholm Slott** (castle), at Mariefred, on the southern side of Lake Mälaren about 64 kilometers (40 miles) from Stockholm. Gripsholm, with its drawbridge and four massive round towers, is one of Sweden's most romantic castles. There had been a castle on the site as early as the 1380s, but it was destroyed, and King Gustav Vasa had the present building erected in 1577. Today the castle is best known for housing the Swedish state collection of portraits and is one of the largest portrait galleries in the world, with some 3,400 paintings.

The most pleasant way of traveling to Gripsholm from Stockholm is on the vintage steamer *Mariefred,* the last coal-fired ship on Lake Mälaren. Departures, between mid-June and late August, are from the city hall daily, except Monday, at 10 AM, leaving from Mariefred at 4:30. The journey takes 3½ hours each way, and there is a restaurant on board. *Mariefred tel. 08/669–8850. Round-trip fare: SKr 140. Castle tel. 0159/10194. Admission: SKr 30. Open Apr.–Sept., Tue.–Sun. 10–3.*

Skokloster

Another popular boat trip goes to **Skokloster Slott** (Skokloster Palace), about 70 kilometers (44 miles) from Stockholm. Departures are from the city hall bridge (Stadshusbron) daily, except Monday and Friday, between early June and mid-August. The route follows the narrow inlets of Lake Mälaren along the "Royal Waterway" and stops at **Sigtuna,** an ancient trading center. You can get off the boat here; visit the town, which has medieval ruins and an 18th-century town hall; and catch the boat again on the return journey. Or stay on board and continue to Skokloster, an impressive palace dating from the 1650s. Built by the Swedish field marshal Carl Gustav Wrangel, it contains many of his trophies from the Thirty Years' War. Other attractions include what is reckoned to be the largest private collection of arms in the world, as well as some magnificent Gobelin tapestries. Next door to the palace is a motor museum that houses Sweden's largest collection of vintage cars and motorcycles. The round-trip boat fare is SKr 165, and there are a restaurant and a cafeteria on board. *Strömma Canal Company, tel. 08/233375. Palace tel. 018/386077. Admission to palace: SKr 40. Admission to motor museum: SKr 35. Open daily noon–6.*

Archipelago

Lovers of the sea could easily spend an entire week cruising among the 24,000 islands in **Stockholms Skärgården** (archipelago). The **Båtlufffarkortet** (Inter-Skerries Card), available from early June to mid-August, gives you 16 days' unlimited travel on Waxholmsbolaget (the Waxholm Steamship Company) boats, which operate scheduled services throughout the archipelago. The card is on sale in the Excursion Shop at Sweden House and at the Waxholm Steamship Company terminal at Strömkajen, in front of the Grand Hotel. It costs SKr 230.

Off the Beaten Track

Just over 508 feet tall, the **Kaknäs TV Tower** at Gärdet is the highest structure in Scandinavia. From the top you can catch a magnificent view of the city and the surrounding archipelago. Facilities include a cafeteria, a restaurant, and a gift shop. *Ladugårdsgärdet, tel. 08/667–8030.*

Stockholm Environs

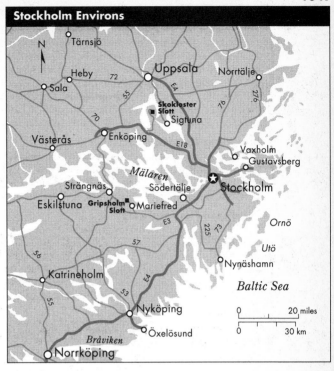

Admission: SKr 20. Open Apr., daily 9–6; May–Aug., daily 9–8; Sept.–May, daily 10–5.

You can see the world's largest variety of water lilies at the **Bergianska Botaniska Trädgården** (Bergianska Botanical Garden), just north of the city center. The largest lily's leaves are more than 7 feet in diameter. Frescati, tel. 08/162853. Admission: SKr 10 to the garden, free to the park. Greenhouse open daily 11–5; herbal garden open daily 8–5; Victoria House open May–Sept., daily 11-5; park never closed.

Fjäderholmarna (the Feather Islets), the collective name for a group of four secluded islands in the Stockholm archipelago only 20 minutes by boat from downtown, have been open to the public since the early '80s, after 50 years as a military zone. There is a museum depicting life in the archipelago, as well as the largest aquarium in Scandinavia, housing many species of Baltic marine life. Other facilities include a cafeteria, handicraft studios and shops, a restaurant (Fjäderholmarnas Krog, tel. 08/718–3355), and an unusual pirate-ship playground. Boats leave from Slussen, Strömkajen, and Nybroplan (Apr. 29–Sept. 17). Strömma Canal Co., tel. 08/233375. Fjäderholmarna information, tel. 08/7180100.

Shopping

Gift Ideas
Stockholm is an ideal place to find items that reflect the best in Swedish design and elegance, particularly glass, porcelain, furs, handicrafts, home furnishings, and leather goods. The quality is uniformly high, and you can take advantage of tax-free shopping in most stores (see Shopping in Staying in Sweden, above).

Department Stores

The largest is **NK** (Hamngatan 18–20, tel. 08/762–8000), where you can find just about anything at the impressive collection of independently operated boutiques; a large selection of Swedish crafts is available here, as well. Other major stores are **PUB** (Hötorget, tel. 08/791–6000) and **Åhléns City** (Klarabergsgatan 50, tel. 08/246000). All three are open Sundays. **Sturegallerian** is an elegant covered shopping gallery built on the site of the former public baths at Stureplan. There are about 50 shops, plus a number of restaurants.

Shopping Districts

The center of Stockholm's shopping activity is **Hamngatan,** a wide boulevard along which a huge, covered shopping complex called **Gallerian** (Hamngatan 37, tel. 08/796–9340) has been built. The **Old Town** area is best for handicrafts, antiquarian bookshops, and art shops.

Food and Flea Markets

One of the largest flea markets in northern Europe, **Loppmarknaden** is in **Skärholmen** shopping center's parking garage, a 20-minute subway ride from downtown. Market hours are weekdays 11–6, Saturday 9–3, Sunday 10–3, with an entry fee of SKr 10 on weekends. Superior food markets selling such Swedish specialties as marinated salmon and reindeer can be found at **Östermalmstorg** and **Hötorget.**

Glassware

For the best buys, try **Nordiska Kristall** (Kungsgatan 9, tel. 08/104372). **Arioso** (Västerlånggatan 59, tel. 08/213810) in the Old Town, is good for modern crystal and ceramics. **Duka** (corner of Kungsgatan and Sveavägen, tel. 08/104530), specializes in crystal as well as porcelain.

Handicrafts

A good center for all kinds of Swedish handicrafts in wood and metal is **Svensk Hemslöjd** (Sveavägen 44, tel. 08/232115), which also sells embroidery kits and many types of weaving and knitting yarn. For elegant home furnishings and timeless fabrics, Stockholmers tend to favor **Svensk Tenn** (Strandvägen 5A, tel. 08/670–1600), best known for its selection of designer Josef Franck's furniture and fabrics. **Stockholms Läns Hemslöjdsförening** (Drottninggatan 14, tel. 08/761–1717), has a wide selection of Swedish folk costumes and handicraft souvenirs from different parts of Sweden.

Dining

For details and price-category descriptions, *see* Dining *in* Staying in Sweden, *above.*

$$$$ **Operakällaren.** Located in part of the elegant Opera House, this is one of Stockholm's best-known traditional restaurants, featuring both Scandinavian and Continental cuisine. It is famed for its smörgåsbord, available from June 1st onward, with seasonal variations, through Christmas. In summertime, the veranda is opened for service as the Operabryggan, facing Kungsträdgården, the waterfront, and the Royal Palace. *Operahuset, tel. 08/676–5801. Reservations advised. AE, DC, MC, V. Main dining room closed July.*

$$$$ **Paul and Norbert.** A very cozy, 32-seat restaurant on Stockholm's most elegant avenue, Paul and Norbert is noted for its French-style cuisine, using indigenous wild game such as reindeer, elk, partridge, and grouse, as well as fish. The decor is rustic but refined. *Strandvägen 9, tel. 08/663–8183. Reservations required. AE, DC, MC, V. Closed weekends. Call for yearly closing dates.*

$$$$ Ulriksdals Värdshus. This beautifully situated country inn, built in 1868, is set in a castle park on the outskirts of town. It offers both Swedish and international cuisines but is particularly noted for its lunchtime smörgåsbord. *Ulriksdals Slottspark, tel. 08/850815. Reservations advised. AE, DC, MC, V. No dinner Sun.*

$$$ Clas på Hörnet. Just outside the city center, Clas på Hörnet is a small, ★ intimate establishment occupying the ground floor of a restored 200-year-old townhouse, now a hotel (*see* Lodging, *below*). It offers a choice of international or Swedish cuisine. *Surbrunnsgatan 20, tel. 08/165136. Reservations advised. AE, DC, MC, V. Closed July.*

$$$ Den Gyldene Freden. Once a favorite haunt of Stockholm's artists and ★ composers, the 1722 Den Gyldene Freden has Old Town ambience. The cuisine is a tasteful combination of French and Swedish. Every Thursday, the Swedish Academy meets for lunch on the second floor. *Österlånggatan 51, tel. 08/249760. Reservations advised. AE, DC, MC, V. Closed Sun.*

$$$ Stallmästaregården. A historic old inn with an attractive courtyard and ★ garden, Stallmästaregården is in the Haga Park, some distance from the city center. But the fine French and Swedish cuisine is well worth the journey. In summer, meals are served in the courtyard overlooking Brunnsviken Lake. A prix-fixe business lunch is available. *Norrtull, near Haga, tel. 08/610–1301. Reservations advised. AE, DC, MC, V. Closed Sun.*

$$$ Wedholms Fisk. Serving only fresh fish and shellfish, this open and high-ceilinged restaurant is in Berzelii Park, across from the Royal Dramatic Theater. The tartare of salmon and grilled sole are noteworthy. Portions are generous. The artwork featuring Scandinavian artists is part of the owner's personal collection. *Nybrokajen 17, tel. 08/611–7874. Reservations advised. AE, DC, MC, V. Closed Sun. and July.*

$$ Bakfickan. The name means "hip pocket" and is appropriate because ★ this restaurant is tucked around at the back of the Opera House complex. It's a budget-price alternative to the nearby Operakällaren and is particularly popular at lunchtime, offering Swedish home cooking and a range of daily dishes. Counter and table service are available. *Operahuset, tel. 08/207745. No reservations. AE, DC, MC, V. Closed Sun.*

$$ Cassi. This downtown restaurant, with an espresso bar dominating the front room, specializes in French cuisine at reasonable prices. *Narvavägen 30, tel. 08/661–7461. DC, MC, V. Closed Sat.*

$$ Eriks Bakficka. An extremely popular dining spot among locals, this eatery serves a wide variety of Swedish dishes. It's a block from the elegant waterside street Strandvägen, a few steps down from street level. A lower-priced menu is available in the pub section. The same owner operates Eriks Gamla Stan, one of Stockholm's most exclusive restaurants. *Frederikshovsgatan 4, tel. 08/660–1599. Reservations advised. AE, DC, MC, V. Closed weekends in July.*

$$ Gondolen. Suspended under the gangway of the Katarina elevator at Slussen, Gondolen offers a magnificent view over the harbor, Lake Mälaren, and the Baltic Sea. The cuisine is international, and a range of prix-fixe menus is available. *Stadsgården 6, tel. 08/641–7090. Reservations advised. AE, DC, MC, V. Closed Sun.*

$$ Martini. This popular, centrally located Italian restaurant is a great people-watching hangout. Patrons line up to get a seat during the summer, when the terrace is open. The main restaurant is below street level, but the decor is light and the atmosphere bustling. *Norrmalmstorg 4, tel. 08/679–8220. Reservations advised. AE, DC, MC, V.*

$$ Nils Emil. Frequented by members of the Swedish royal family, this unpretentious yet elegant restaurant is noted for its delicious Swedish cuisine and generous helpings. Walls are decorated with paintings of the Stockholm archipelago, birthplace of chef-owner Nils Emil. He likes to visit his patrons' tables to keep tabs on the quality of the meals and service. *Södermalm, Folkungagatan 122, tel. 08/640–7209. Reservations required. AE, DC, MC, V. Closed July. No lunch Sat.*

$$ Sturehof. After 97 years in business, Sturehof is Sweden's oldest fish restaurant. The seafood is served in an unpretentious, nautical ambience. There's also an English-style pub. *Stureplan 2, tel. 08/679–8750. Reservations advised. AE, DC, MC, V.*

$ Open Gate. This popular, trendy, art deco Italian-style trattoria is near ★ the Slussen locks, on the south side of Stockholm Harbor. Pasta dishes are the house specialty. *Högbergsgatan 40, tel. 08/643–9776. No reservations. AE, DC, MC, V. Closed Sun.*

$ Örtagården. This vegetarian, no-smoking restaurant is one floor up from the Östermalmshallen market hall. It offers an attractive buffet of soups, salads, hot dishes, and homemade bread—not to mention the five-kronor bottomless cup of coffee—in a turn-of-the-century atmosphere. *Nybrogatan 31, tel. 08/662–1728. AE, MC, V.*

Lodging

Stockholm has plenty of hotels in higher price brackets, but summer rates—some as much as 50% off—can make even very expensive hotels affordable. The major chains also have a number of bargain plans available on weekends throughout the year and daily in summer.

More than 50 hotels offer the "Stockholm Package," providing accommodations for one night, costing between SKr 360 and SKr 760 per person, including breakfast and a Key to Stockholm card (*see* Getting Around, *above*). The package is available June through mid-August, at Christmas and Easter, and Thursday–Monday year-round; get details from the **Stockholm Information Service** (Excursion Shop, Box 7542, S-103 93 Stockholm, tel. 08/789–2415). The package can also be reserved through travel agents or through **Hotellcentralen** (Central Station, S-111 20, tel. 08/240880, fax 08/791–8666).

If you arrive in Stockholm without a hotel reservation, **Hotellcentralen** will also arrange accommodations for you. The office is open November–March, weekdays 8–5 and weekends 8–2; April and October, daily 8–5; May and September, daily 8–7; and June–August, daily 7 AM–9 PM; telephone reservations can be made after 9 AM. There is a reservations office in Sweden House (*see* Important Addresses and Numbers, *above*) as well. A small fee is charged for each reservation, but advance telephone reservations are free. **Hotel Booking** (tel. 08/116–0380) is an independent agency that can reserve free for you in any Swedish hotel. Or phone one of the central reservations offices run by the major hotel groups: RESO (tel. 08/720–8100), Scandic (tel. 08/610–5050), Sweden Hotels (tel. 08/789–8900), or Best Western (tel. 08/330600 or 020/792752).

For details and price-category definitions, *see* Lodging *in* Staying in Sweden, *above*.

$$$$ Amaranten. Only five minutes' walk from the central train station, Amaranten is a large, modern hotel that was built in 1969. Rooms with air-conditioning and soundproofing are available at a higher rate. Guests can enjoy a brasserie and a piano bar. *Kungsholmsgatan 31, S-104 20, tel. 08/654–1060, fax 08/652–6248. 360 rooms with bath, 50 rooms with bath, air-conditioning, soundproofing. Facilities: restaurant, piano bar, no-smoking rooms, pool, sauna, meeting rooms. AE, DC, MC, V.*

$$$$ Continental. In the city center across from the central train station, the ★ Continental is popular with American visitors. It was opened in 1966 and was renovated in 1992. *Klara Vattugränd 4, S-101 22, tel. 08/244020, fax 08/411–3695. 268 rooms with bath. Facilities: restaurant, no-smoking rooms, sauna, meeting rooms. AE, DC, MC, V.*

$$$$ Diplomat. This elegant hotel within easy walking distance of Djurgår-
★ den Park and Skansen offers magnificent views over Stockholm Harbor. The building itself is a turn-of-the-century town house that accommodated foreign embassies in the 1930s and was converted into a hotel in 1966. The Teahouse Restaurant is a popular spot for light meals. *Strandvägen 7C, S-104 40, tel. 08/663–5800, fax 08/783–6634. 133 rooms with bath. Facilities: restaurant, no-smoking rooms, sauna. AE, DC, MC, V.*

$$$$ Grand. Opposite the Royal Palace on the waterfront in the center of town, the Grand is a large, gracious, Old World–style hotel dating from 1874. Most rooms have waterfront views, and guests are entitled to relax at the nearby Sturebadet Health Spa. The two restaurants—French and Swedish—offer harbor views. The bar serves light snacks. *Blasieholmshamnen 8, S-103 27, tel. 08/679–3500, fax 08/611–8686. 320 rooms with bath. Facilities: 2 restaurants, bar, no-smoking rooms, sauna, meeting room. AE, DC, MC, V.*

$$$$ Lady Hamilton. As charming, desirable, and airily elegant as its name-
★ sake, the Lady Hamilton opened in 1980 as a modern hotel inside a 15th-century building, so close to the Royal Palace in Gamla Stan that some rooms afford a view of the changing of the guard. Swedish antiques accent the light, natural-toned decor in all the guest rooms and common areas. Romney's "Bacchae" portrait of Lady Hamilton hangs in the foyer, where a large, smiling figurehead from an old ship supports the ceiling. The breakfast room, furnished of course with captain's chairs, looks out onto the lively cobblestone street, while the subterranean sauna rooms, in whitewashed stone, provide a secluded fireplace and a chance to take a dip in the building's original, medieval well. *Storkyrkobrinken 5, S-111 28, tel. 08/234680, fax 08/411–1148. 34 rooms with shower. Facilities: bar, no-smoking rooms, sauna, meeting rooms. AE, DC, MC, V.*

$$$$ Radisson SAS Strand. Acquired in 1986 by the SAS group, this is a gracious, Old World hotel. It was built in 1912 but was modernized in 1983. No two rooms are the same, but all are furnished with antiques. The Piazza is an indoor restaurant with an outdoor feel to it; its specialty is Italian cuisine, and it has a superb wine list. An SAS check-in counter for business-class travelers adjoins the main reception area. *Nybrokajen 9, S-103 27, tel. 08/678–7800, fax 08/611–2436. 138 rooms with bath. Facilities: restaurant, no-smoking rooms, sauna, meeting rooms. AE, DC, MC, V.*

$$$$ Reisen. This 17th-century building, on the waterfront in the Old Town, has been a hotel since 1819; it has a fine restaurant, a grill, tea and coffee service in the library, and possibly the best piano bar in town. The swimming pool is built under the medieval arches of the foundation. *Skeppsbron 12–14, S-111 30, tel. 08/223260, fax 08/201559. 114 rooms with bath. Facilities: 2 restaurants, piano bar, no-smoking floor, pool, sauna, library, meeting rooms. AE, DC, MC, V.*

$$$$ Scandic Crown. A modern hotel with a panoramic view of the Old Town and City Hall, the Scandic Crown is on Stockholm's increasingly trendy south side. Noteworthy is the Couronne d'Or, a French eatery, and a cellar with wines for tasting, some dating from 1650. *Guldgränd 8, S-104 65 tel. 08/702–2500, fax 08/642–8358. 264 rooms with bath. Facilities: 2 restaurants, piano bar, no-smoking rooms, pool, hair salon, sauna, meeting rooms. AE, DC, MC, V.*

$$$ **Birger Jarl.** A short bus ride from the city center, and half a block from the new Museum of Modern Art, the Birger Jarl is a contemporary, conservative, thickly carpeted refuge for business travelers, catered conferences, and tourists requiring unfussy comforts. Breakfast is an extensive buffet just off the lobby, but room service is also available. Rooms are not large, but they are well furnished; there are heated towel racks in the bathrooms and bathtubs for all double rooms. Four family-style rooms have extra floor space and sofabeds. *Tulegatan 8, S-104 32, tel. 08/151020, fax 08/673–7366. 225 rooms with bath. Facilities: coffee shop (closed summer), no-smoking rooms, sauna, meeting rooms. AE, DC, MC, V.*

$$$ **City.** A large, modern-style hotel built in the 1940s but completely rebuilt in 1984, City is near the city center and Hötorget market. It is owned by the Salvation Army, so alcohol is not served. Breakfast is served in the Winter Garden atrium. *Slöjdgatan 7, S-111 81, tel. 08/222240, fax 08/208224. 290 rooms with bath. Facilities: restaurant, no-smoking rooms, sauna, meeting rooms. AE, DC, MC, V.*

$$$ **Clas på Hörnet.** An 18th-century inn converted into a small hotel in
★ 1982, Clas på Hörnet is just outside the city center. Its rooms, furnished with antiques of the period, go quickly. If you can't manage to reserve a night, at least have a meal in the excellent restaurant (*see* Dining, *above*). *Surbrunnsgatan 20, S-113 48, tel. 08/165130, fax 08/612–5315. 10 rooms with bath. Facilities: restaurant. AE, DC, MC, V. Closed July.*

$$$ **Gamla Stan.** A quiet, cozy hotel in one of Old Town's 17th-century houses, the Gamla Stan was renovated in 1986, and each room is uniquely decorated. *Lilla Nygatan 25, S-111 28, tel. 08/244450, fax 08/216483. 51 rooms with shower. Facilities: no-smoking floor, meeting rooms. AE, DC, MC, V.*

$$$ **Karelia.** In a turn-of-the-century building on one of the main shopping streets, Karelia has Finnish owners, a Finnish atmosphere, and a Finnish restaurant for dining and dancing. *Birger Jarlsgatan 35, S-111 83, tel. 08/247660, fax 08/241511. 86 rooms with bath or shower. Facilities: restaurant, 2 no-smoking floors, pool, sauna, meeting room. AE, DC, MC, V.*

$$$ **Stockholm.** You can't get much closer to the center of Stockholm than this modern yet traditionally furnished hotel, which occupies the sixth and seventh floors of an office building on one of the city's main squares. It's a clean, efficient lodging intended for those who want to spend their waking hours shopping, sightseeing, or on business. *Norrmalmstorg 1, S-111 46, tel. 08/678–1320, fax 08/611–2103. 93 rooms with shower or bath. Facilities: no-smoking rooms, meeting room. AE, DC, MC, V.*

$$ **Aldoria.** Clean, modern, and simply furnished, the Aldoria has a loyal clientele of business travelers and academics who appreciate the convenient location at Fridhemsplan. The hotel occupies two floors of an office building in a busy commercial neighborhood on Kungsholmen; rooms overlooking the courtyard are spared the street noise. *St. Eriksgatan 38, S-112 34, tel. 08/654–1885, fax 08/652–2963. 22 rooms with shower. Facilities: no-smoking rooms. AE, DC, MC, V.*

$$ **Alexandra.** In the Södermalm area, to the south of the Old Town, the Alexandra is only five minutes by subway from the city center. It is a small, modern hotel that opened in the early 1970s. Only breakfast is served. *Magnus Ladulåsgatan 42, S-118 27, tel. 08/840320, fax 08/720–5353. 85 rooms with bath. Facilities: no-smoking rooms, sauna. AE, DC, MC, V.*

$$ **Arcadia.** On a hilltop near a large waterfront nature preserve, this converted dormitory is still within 15 minutes of downtown by bus or subway, or 30 minutes on foot along pleasant shopping streets. The rooms

are furnished in a spare, light style. The adjoining restaurant serves meals on the terrace in summer. *Körsbärsvägen 1, S-114 89, tel. 08/160195, fax 08/166224. 82 rooms with shower. Facilities: restaurant, no-smoking rooms, sauna, meeting rooms. AE, DC, MC, V.*

$$ August Strindberg. A narrow, frescoed corridor leads from the street to the flagstone courtyard, where the Strindberg's restaurant serves in summertime. New parquet flooring and high ceilings distinguish the rooms, which are otherwise plainly furnished. Kitchenettes are available to all guests; some rooms can be combined into family apartments. With four floors and no elevator, this may be appropriate mostly for younger travelers, but there is one large room on the ground floor. *Tegnérgatan 38, S-113 59, tel. 08/325006, fax 08/209085. 19 rooms with shower. Facilities: restaurant, bar. AE, DC, MC, V.*

$$ Långholmen. This former prison, built in 1724, was converted into a combined hotel and hostel in 1989. It sits on the island of Långholmen, which has popular beaches and a prison museum. The Inn, next door, serves Swedish home cooking, the Jail Pub offers light snacks, and a garden restaurant operates in the summertime. *Långholmen, Box 9116, 102 72, tel. 08/668–0500, fax 08/841096. 101 rooms with shower. Facilities: 3 restaurants, meeting room. AE, DC, MC, V.*

$$ Örnsköld. Just behind the Royal Dramatic Theater in the heart of the
★ city, this hidden gem has the atmosphere of an old private club, with a brass-and-leather lobby and Victorian-style furniture in the moderately spacious, high-ceilinged rooms. Breakfast is served in the rooms; those over the courtyard are quieter, but those facing the street—not a busy one, in any case—are sunnier. The hotel is often frequented by actors appearing at the Royal Theater. *Nybrogatan 6, S-114 34, tel. 08/667–0285, fax 08/667–6991. 30 rooms with shower. AE, MC, V.*

$$ Prize. This sleek hotel appeals to train lovers; the ultramodern rooms are as compactly efficient as train compartments. Some have no windows but are fitted with backlit shoji screens to simulate daylight. The building is part of the World Trade Center, above one end of the central train station, but a shock-absorbent base eliminates noise and vibrations from the trains below. Breakfast is available for SKr 55. *Kungsbron 1, S-111 22, tel. 08/149450, fax 08/149848. 158 rooms with shower. Facilities: no-smoking rooms. AE, DC, MC, V.*

$$ Tegnérlunden. A quiet city park fronts this modern hotel a 10-minute walk from the downtown hub of Sergelstorg, with the shops of Sveavägen along the way. Although the rooms are small and sparely furnished, they are clean and well maintained. The lobby is bright with marble, brass, and greenery, as is the sunny rooftop breakfast room. *Tegnérlunden 8, S-113 59, tel. 08/349780, fax 08/327828. 104 rooms with shower. Facilities: no-smoking rooms, sauna, meeting room. AE, DC, MC.*

$ Gustav af Klint. A "hotel ship" moored at Stadsgården quay, near Slussen subway station, the Gustav af Klint is divided into two sections—a hotel and a hostel. You can dine on deck in summer. Breakfast, at SKr 40, is not included. *Stadsgårdskajen 153, S-116 45, tel. 08/640–4077, fax 08/640–6416. 14 cabins with showers; 80 hostel beds. Facilities: restaurant, cafeteria. AE, MC, V.*

The Arts

Stockholm's main theater and concert season runs from September through May or June, so there are not many major performances during the height of the tourist season. For a list of events, pick up the free monthly booklet "Stockholm This Week," available from hotels and tourist information offices. For tickets to theaters and shows try **Biljettdirekt** at Sweden House or any post office.

Concerts

The city's main concert hall is the **Konserthuset** (Hötorget 8, tel. 08/786–0200), home of the Stockholm Philharmonic Orchestra. The season runs from mid-September to mid-May. In addition to full-scale evening concerts, there are lunchtime concerts some days. In summer, many city parks have free concerts; listings appear in the "Events" section of "Stockholm This Week."

Opera

The season at **Operan** (the Royal Opera House; tel. 08/248240), just across the bridge from the Royal Palace, runs from mid-August to early June and offers world-class performances. From May to early September, there are performances of opera, ballet, and orchestral music at the exquisite **Drottningholm Court Theater** (tel. 08/660–8225), which was the setting for Ingmar Bergman's film *The Magic Flute*. The original 18th-century stage machinery is still used in these productions. You can get to Drottningholm by subway and bus or by special theater-bus (leaving from the Grand Hotel or opposite the central train station).

Theater

Stockholm has about 20 top-rank theaters, but productions are in Swedish. A better option is to go to a musical; several city theaters hold regular performances. Productions by the English Theatre Company are occasionally staged at the **Vasan** (Vasagatan 19, tel. 08/102363).

Film

English and American films predominate, and they are screened with the original soundtrack and Swedish subtitles. Programs are listed in the local evening newspapers, though titles are usually in Swedish. Movie buffs should visit **Filmstaden** (Film City; Mäster Samuelsgatan 25, tel. 08/840500), where 15 cinemas under one roof show a variety of films from noon until midnight. Bear in mind that most, if not all, cinemas take reservations over the phone; it's best to make one or you may find a show sold out well ahead of time.

Nightlife

Cabaret

Stockholm's biggest nightclub, **Börsen** (Jakobsgatan 6, tel. 08/787–8500), offers high-quality Swedish and international cabaret shows. Another popular spot is the **Cabaret Club** (Barnhusgatan 12, tel. 08/411–0608); although it can accommodate 450 guests, reservations are advised.

Bars and Nightclubs

Café Opera (Operahuset, tel. 08/411–0026) is a popular meeting place for young and old alike; at the waterfront end of Kungsträgården, it has the longest bar in town, plus dining and roulette, and dancing after midnight. **Riche** (Birger Jarlsgatan 4, tel. 08/611–8450) is another popular watering hole in the city center. Piano bars are also an important part of the Stockholm scene. Try the **Anglais Bar** at the Hotel Anglais (Humlegårdsgatan 23, tel. 08/614–1600). The **Clipper Club** at the Hotel Reisen, (Skeppsbron 12–14, tel. 08/223260) is another good spot. Not to be forgotten is the renovated restaurant/bar **Berns' Salonger** (Berzelii Park 9, tel. 08/614–0550); the Red Room, on the second floor, is where playwright August Strindberg once held court. **Sture Compagniet** (Sturegatan 4, tel. 08/611–7800) is a popular club. **Café Victoria** (Kungsträdgården, tel. 08/101085) draws club lovers as well.

Irish pubs are trendy among happy-hour crowds. **Limerick** (Tegnérgatan 10, tel. 08/673–4398) has the right atmosphere. **Dubliner** (Birger

Jarlspassagen, tel. 08/679–7707) attracts Irish beer lovers. **Bagpiper's Inn** (Rörstrandsgatan 21, tel. 08/311855) is also a current hit.

Jazz Clubs
Fasching (Kungsgatan 63, tel. 08/216267) is Stockholm's largest, with a jazz lunch weekdays and soul music Saturday nights. Get to **Stampen** (Stora Nygatan 5, tel. 08/205793) in good time if you want a seat, but call first to be sure it hasn't been reserved for a private party.

Discos
Galaxy (Strömsborg, tel. 08/215400) is one of the most popular nightspots; there is an outdoor bar and dining area in summer. **Downtown** (Norrlandsgatan 5A, tel. 08/411–9488) is popular. **Karlsson** (Kungsgatan 65, tel. 08/411–9298) attracts a lively crowd.

UPPSALA AND THE FOLKLORE DISTRICT

The part of Sweden known as the "Folklore District"—essentially the provinces of Dalarna (sometimes called Darlecarlia in English) and Värmland—is easily accessible from Stockholm and the best region in which to see some of the country's enduring folk traditions. This itinerary takes you to Dalarna through the ancient city of Uppsala and returns to Stockholm through the Bergslagen region, the heart of the centuries-old Swedish iron industry.

Getting Around

The route can be covered entirely by train. The ride from Stockholm to Uppsala takes only 50 minutes, and the service is fairly frequent. A car, however, will give you the flexibility to explore some of the attractions that are not easily accessible by public transportation.

Guided Tours

Uppsala is compact enough to explore on foot, and guided sightseeing tours are available; you can book a tour in advance by calling the Guide Service (Uppsala Tourist Information office, tel. 018/274818).

Tourist Information

Falun (Stora Torget, tel. 023/83637); **Ludvika** (Fredsgatan 10, tel. 0240/86050); **Mora** (Ångbåtskajen, tel. 0250/26550); **Örebro** (Slottet, tel. 019/212121); **Rättvik** (Torget, tel. 0248/70200); **Uppsala** (Fyris Torg 8, tel. 018/117500 and 018/274800, and at Uppsala Castle in summer).

Exploring Uppsala and the Folklore District

Uppsala is really the cradle of Swedish civilization, so it is well worth spending a day or two exploring it. If you opt for a guided tour of the city, you should first stop by **Gamla Uppsala** (Old Uppsala), which is dominated by three huge burial mounds. During the 5th century AD, Aun, Egil, and Adils, the first Swedish kings, were buried here. Adjoining the burial mounds are a church, the seat of Sweden's first archbishop, built on the site of a former pagan temple, and the Odinsborg restaurant, where you can sample local mead, brewed from a 14th-century recipe. Check all prices and times listed below with the local tourist office, as they are subject to change.

Back in **Uppsala** itself, your first stop should be the enormous **cathedral,** whose twin towers dominate the city skyline. The cathedral has been the seat of the archbishop of the Swedish church for 700 years. Its present appearance owes much to major restoration work completed during the late 19th century. Make a point of visiting the **Cathedral Museum** in the north tower, where you can see one of Europe's finest collections of ecclesiastical textiles. *Cathedral open daily 8–6. Museum admission: SKr 10. Open May–Aug., daily 9–5; Sept.–Apr., Sun. 12:30–3.*

Nearby, in a strategic position atop a hill, is **Uppsala Castle.** This impressive structure was built during the 1540s by King Gustav Vasa. Having broken his ties with the Vatican, the king was eager to show who was actually running the country. He arranged to have the cannons aimed directly at the archbishop's palace. *Admission: SKr 35. Open mid-Apr.–mid-June, daily 11–3; mid-June–mid Aug., daily 10–5.*

Uppsala is also the site of Scandinavia's oldest university, founded in 1477. Be sure to visit one of its most venerable buildings, the **Gustavianum,** near the cathedral. Just below the cupola is the anatomical theater, where public dissections of executed convicts were a popular 17th-century tourist attraction.

One of Uppsala's most famous sons was Carl von Linné, known as **Linnaeus.** A professor of botany at the university during the 1740s, he developed a system of plant and animal classification that is still used today. You can visit the **gardens** he designed, as well as his former residence, now a **museum.** *Garden admission: SKr 10. Open May–Aug., daily 9–9; Sept., daily 9–7. Museum admission: SKr 10. Open June–Aug., Tue.–Sun. noon–4; May and Sept., weekends noon–4.*

From Uppsala, the route heads northwest through a pleasant agricultural landscape into the province of Dalarna, passing through **Säter,** one of the best-preserved wooden villages in Sweden. This is a pleasant spot in which to just wander around. For an overnight stop it is best to head for Falun, Dalarna's capital.

Falun is best known for a huge hole in the ground, referred to as the **"Great Pit."** The hole has been there since 1687, when an abandoned copper mine collapsed. Other mines on the site are still working today. You can take a guided tour (wear your boots) down into some of the old shafts and hear the gruesome story of 17th-century miner Fat Mats, whose body was perfectly preserved in brine for 40 years following a cave-in. There is also a museum that tells the story of the local mining industry. *Mine admission: SKr 55. Open May–Aug., daily 10–4:30; Sept.–mid-Nov. and Mar.–Apr., weekends 12:30–4:30. Museum admission: free with mine tour, or SKr 5. Open May–Aug., daily 10–4:30, Sept.–Apr., daily 12:30–4:30.*

Just outside Falun, at **Sundborn,** is the former home of Swedish artist Carl Larsson. Here, in an idyllic lakeside setting, you can see a selection of his paintings, which owe much to local folk-art traditions. His great-grandchildren still use the house on occasion. *Admission: SKr 55; guided tours only, in groups of 15 every 10 minutes (may be a wait in summer). Open May–Sept., daily 10–5; Oct.–Apr. Tues. at 11.*

The real center of Dalarna folklore is the area around **Lake Siljan,** by far the largest of the 6,000 lakes in the province. Begin your tour at the attractive lakeside village of **Tällberg,** or at **Mora,** toward the north end of the lake. In the neighboring village of **Rättvik,** hundreds of people wearing traditional costumes arrive in longboats to attend Midsummer church services. Mora itself is best known as the home of the artist **Anders Zorn.** His **house** and a **museum** exhibiting his paintings are open to the public. *Museum admission SKr 25. Open May 15–Sept.15, Mon.–Sat. 9–5, Sun. 11–5; Sept. 16–May 14, Mon.–Sat. 10–5, Sun.*

Uppsala and the Folklore District

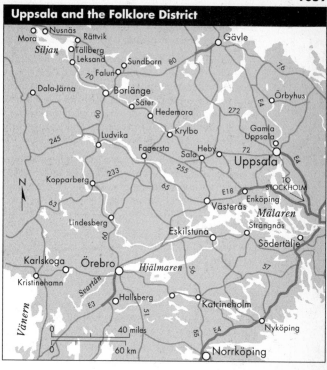

1–5. House admission: SKr 30, guided tours only. Open May 15–Sept. 15, Mon.–Sat. 10–4, Sun. 11–4; Sept. 16–May 14, Mon.–Sat. 12:30–4, Sun. 1–4.

Near Mora is the village of **Nusnäs,** where the famous, brightly colored **Dalarna wooden horses** are produced. You can visit either of the two workshops where they are made.

Heading south again you'll come to **Ludvika,** an important center of the old Bergslagen mining region. This region stretches from the forests of Värmland in the west to the coastal gorges in the east. Ludvika has a notable open-air mining museum, **Gammelgården.** Check times and prices with the Ludvika tourist office. There is also a **Railway Engine Museum** that features three steam turbine–driven iron-ore engines, the only ones of their kind in the world. *Admission: SKr 20. Open June 1–Sept. 3, daily 10–6.*

Another local attraction is **Luosa Cottage.** The poet Dan Andersson lived here in the early part of the century so he could experience for himself the rigorous life of the local charcoal burners. Music and poetry festivals are held in nearby towns in Andersson's memory; check with the Ludvika tourist office. *Admission to cottage: SKr 20. Open mid-May–Aug., daily 11–5.*

Continuing south from Ludvika, you'll come to **Örebro,** a sizable town at the western edge of **Lake Hjälmaren,** which is connected to Lake Mälaren and the sea by the Hjälmare Canal. Örebro received its charter in the 13th century and developed as a trading center for the farmers and miners of the Bergslagen region. Rising from a small island in the Svartån River, right in the center of town, is an imposing **castle,** parts of which date from the 13th century. The castle is now the residence of the regional governor. Guided tours run from mid-June to the end of August. Check with the Örebro tourist office for further information. An added attraction is the excellent restaurant in the castle.

To get a feel for the Örebro of bygone days, wander around the **Wadköping** district, where a number of old houses and crafts workshops have been painstakingly preserved. At the north end of town is **Svampen** (The Mushroom), a water tower that rises 193 feet into the air. If you take the elevator to the top, you'll get a magnificent view of the surrounding countryside. There is also a cafeteria and a tourist office. *Tower open Apr. 30–May 31 daily 10–10, June 1–Sept. 4 daily 10–8.*

Direct train service from Örebro back to Stockholm operates at two-hour intervals, and the journey takes just under three hours. You can also take the hourly train to Hallsberg and change there to the frequent Gothenburg–Stockholm service.

Dining and Lodging

For details and price-category definitions, *see* Dining and Lodging *in* Staying in Sweden, *above.*

Falun
LODGING
Bergmästaren. In the town center, Bergmästaren is a small, cozy hotel built in traditional Dalarna style and filled with antique furnishings. *Bergskolegränd 7, S-791 26, tel. 023/63600, fax 023/22524. 88 rooms, most with bath. Facilities: restaurant, no-smoking rooms, hot tub, sauna, meeting room. AE, DC, MC, V. $$$*
Hotel Falun. In the center of the city, Hotel Falun is a medium-size hotel built in the 1950s. The front desk closes at 9 PM. *Centrumhuset, Trotzgatan 16, S-791 71, tel. 023/29180, fax 023/13006. 17 rooms with shower, 10 with WC only (2 hallway showers). Facilities: no-smoking rooms, meeting rooms. AE, DC, MC, V. $$*

Ludvika
LODGING
Grand. A medium-size, modern-style hotel, the Grand is located in the town center. *Eriksgatan 6, S-771 31, tel. 0240/18220, fax 0240/611018. 102 rooms with bath. Facilities: restaurant, no-smoking rooms, sauna, disco, meeting rooms. AE, DC, MC, V. $$$*
Rex. The Rex is a fairly basic but modern hotel near the city center. It was built in 1960. Its restaurant serves breakfast only. *Engelbrektsgatan 9, S-771 30, tel. 0240/13690. 28 rooms, 15 with shower. Facilities: breakfast room. AE, DC, MC, V. Closed 1 wk in summer. $*

Mora
LODGING
★ **Siljan.** Taking its name from the nearby lake, the Siljan is a popular, small but modern-style hotel. *Moragatan 6, S-792 01, tel. 0250/13000, fax 0250/13098. 43 rooms with shower, 2 with WC only. Facilities: restaurant, bar, no-smoking floor, sauna, exercise room, disco, meeting room. AE, DC, MC, V. $$*

Örebro
DINING AND LODGING
RESO Grand. In the heart of town, the Grand is the city's largest hotel. It was built in 1985 and offers all the modern comforts. *Fabriksgatan 23, S-700 08, tel. 019/150200, fax 019/185814. 219 rooms with shower. Facilities: 2 restaurants, no-smoking rooms, sauna, meeting rooms. AE, DC, MC, V. $$$*

Stora Hotellet. Across the street from the castle on the Svartån River, this Best Western hotel is one of the oldest in Sweden, dating from 1858. There is a cozy 13th-century cellar restaurant, Slottskällaren, and an English pub, the Bishop's Arms. *Drottninggatan 1, S-701 45, tel. 019/124360, fax 019/611–7890. 103 rooms with bath or shower. Facilities: restaurant, pub, no-smoking rooms, sauna, meeting rooms. AE, DC, MC, V. $$$*

Tällberg
LODGING
★ **Åkerblads.** Near the shores of Lake Siljan, Åkerblads is a real rural Swedish experience. The hotel occupies a typical Dalarna farmstead, parts of which date from the 16th century. It is run by the 19th generation of the Åkerblad family. A hotel since 1910, it was modernized in 1987. *Sjögatu, S-793 70, tel. 0247/50800, fax 0247/50652. 58 rooms with bath, 6 rooms with shared WC/shower. Facilities: restaurant, pub, no-smoking rooms, sauna, meeting rooms. AE, DC, MC, V. $$*

Uppsala
DINING
★ **Domtrappkällaren.** One of the city's most popular restaurants, Domtrappkällaren is in a 14th-century cellar near the cathedral. The cuisine is a mixture of French and Swedish. *St. Eriksgränd 15, tel. 018/130955, fax 018/101740. Reservations required. AE, DC, MC, V. $$$*

LODGING
Sara Gillet. A centrally located, medium-size hotel, the Sara Gillet was opened in 1971 and renovated most recently in 1994. *Dragarbrunnsgatan 23, S-753 20, tel. 018/155360, fax 018/153380. 170 rooms with bath. Facilities: restaurant, bistro, no-smoking rooms, pool, sauna, meeting rooms. AE, DC, MC, V. $$$$*

Grand Hotel Hörnan. An Old World, medium-size hotel opened in 1906, the Grand Hotel Hörnan is in the city center near the train station, with a view of the castle and the cathedral. Only breakfast is served. *Bangårdsgatan 1, S-753 20, tel. 018/139380, fax 018/120311. 37 rooms with shower. Facilities: no-smoking rooms, meeting room. AE, DC, MC, V. Closed July. $$*

THE WEST COAST AND THE GLASS COUNTRY

For many visitors traveling to Sweden by ferry, Gothenburg is the port of arrival. If you arrive in Stockholm, don't miss making a side trip to this great shipping city and Sweden's scenic western coast. This itinerary combines a western trip with a route through the Glass Country to the medieval fortress town of Kalmar, on the east coast.

Getting Around

The route can be followed by both train and car. Regular trains for Gothenburg depart from Stockholm's central train station about every hour, and normal travel time is about 4½ hours. There are also daily high-speed trains (the X2000), which take about three hours between the two cities, but these require a supplementary fare. X2000 first-class seats include breakfast, lunch or dinner depending on departure time. Seat reservations are compulsory on all trains to Gothenburg. There are also hourly flights to Gothenburg from Stockholm's Arlanda Airport between 7 AM and 10 PM on weekdays, slightly less frequently on weekends. The trip by air takes 55 minutes.

For getting around the city of Gothenburg itself, the best transportation option for the visitor is **Göteborgskortet** (the Key to Gothenburg card), similar to the Key to Stockholm card. This entitles the user to free travel on all public transportation, free parking, and free admission to the Liseberg amusement park and all city museums. Prices for the card are SKr 120 for one day, SKr 200 for two days, and SKr 250 for three days. Cards for children under 18 are SKr 60 for one day, SKr 100 for two days, and SKr 140 for three days.

Guided Tours

In summer, sightseeing tours of Gothenburg leave regularly from Kungsportsplatsen, just beside the city tourist office. They must be reserved at the office in advance. Tour boats run frequently in summer (*see* Exploring, *below*).

Tourist Information

Gothenburg (Kungsportsplatsen 2, tel. 031/100740); **Jönköping** (Djurläkartorget, tel. 036/105050); **Kalmar** (Larmgatan 6, tel. 0480/15350); **Malmö** (Central Station, Skeppsbron, tel. 040/300150); **Växjö** (Kronobergsgatan 8, tel. 0470/41410).

Exploring the West Coast and the Glass Country

Visitors arriving in **Göteborg** (Gothenburg) by car often drive straight through the city in their haste to reach their coastal vacation spots, but this attractive harbor city is a destination in its own right. A quayside jungle of cranes and warehouses attests to the city's industrial might, yet within 10 minutes' walk of the waterfront is an elegant, modern city of broad avenues, green parks, and gardens. Most of the major attractions are within walking distance of one another, and there is an excellent streetcar network. In summer, you can take a sightseeing trip on a vintage open-air streetcar.

Gothenburg's development was pioneered mainly by British merchants in the 19th century, when it acquired the nickname "Little London." But a more accurate name would have been "Little Amsterdam," for the city was designed during the 17th century by Dutch architects, who gave it its extensive network of straight streets divided by canals. There is only one major canal today, but you can explore it on one of the popular "Paddan" sightseeing boats. The boats got their name, Swedish for toad, because of their short, squat shape, necessary for negotiating the city's 20 low bridges. You embark for the one-hour tour at the **Paddan terminal** at Kungsportsplatsen. *Fare: SKr 60. Departures: late Apr.–late June and mid-Aug.–early Sept., daily 10–5; late June–mid-Aug., daily 10–9; early Sept.–Oct. 1, daily 12–3; closed Oct.–Apr.*

The hub of Gothenburg is **Kungsportsavenyn,** better known as "Avenyn" (The Avenue). It is a broad, tree-lined boulevard flanked with elegant shops, restaurants, and sidewalk cafés. In summer it has a distinctly Parisian air. The avenue ends at **Götaplatsen,** home of the municipal theater, concert hall, art museum, and library (where there's an excellent selection of English-language newspapers). Just off the avenue is **Trädgårds-föreningen** (The Garden Association), an attractive park with a magnificent Palm House that was built in 1878 and recently restored, and a Butterfly House (tel. 031/611911) that contains 40 different species. *Admission to park: SKr 10. Admission to Palm House and Butterfly House : SKr 25 each. Open Apr., Tue.–Sun. 10–4; May and Sept., daily 10–4; June–Aug., daily 10–5; Oct.–Mar., Tue.–Sun. 10–3.*

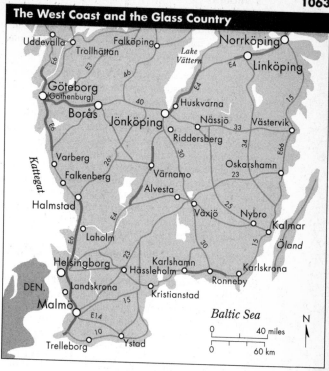

If you're interested in shopping, the best place to go is **Nordstan,** a covered complex of shops near the central train station. Many of its businesses participate in the tax-free shopping service.

On the harbor near the Nordstan shopping complex you will find the new **Maritime Center** (Packhuskajen 8, tel. 031/101035). The center houses a historic collection of ships, including a destroyer, a lightship, a trawler, and tugboats. *Admission: SKr 35. Open Mar.–Apr. and Sept.–Nov., daily 10–4; May–June, daily 10–6; July–Aug., daily 10–9.*

To reach Jönköping, the next stop on the journey, take the train from Gothenburg's central train station and change at Falköping.

Jönköping is an attractive town on the southern shores of **Lake Vättern,** Sweden's second-largest lake. The town, celebrated its 700th anniversary in 1984. It was here, during the 19th century, that the match-manufacturing industry got its start. **Tändsticksmuseet** (the Matchstick Museum), built on the site of the first factory, has an exhibition on the development and manufacture of matches. *Tel. 036/105543. Admission: SKr 25. Open June–Aug., Mon.–Fri. 10–5, weekends 10–3; Sept–May, Tues.–Thurs. 12–4, weekends 11–3.*

To the southeast of Jönköping lies **Växjö,** Kronoberg County's main town and the best center for exploring Sweden's Glass Country. It is also an important destination for some 10,000 American visitors each year, for it was from this area that their Swedish ancestors set sail during the 19th century. The **Emigrants' House** (tel.0470/20120), in the town center, tells the story of the migration period, during which close to 1 million Swedes—one-quarter of the entire population—departed for the promised land. The museum exhibits provide a vivid sense of the rigorous journey, and an archive room and research center allow

American visitors to trace their ancestry. On the second Sunday in August, Växjö celebrates "Minnesota Day." Swedes and Swedish-Americans come together to commemorate their common heritage with American-style square dancing and other festivities.

Many of Sweden's most famous glassworks are within easy reach of Växjö, and it is usually possible to take an organized tour of the facilities. Inquire at the tourist office for information. The manufacture of Swedish glass dates from 1556, when Venetian glassblowers were first invited to the Swedish court. But it was another 200 years before glass manufacturing became a real Swedish industry. The area between Växjö and Kalmar was chosen for its dense forest, which offered limitless wood supplies for heating the furnaces. All the major Swedish glass companies, including **Orrefors** and **Kosta Boda,** still have their works in this area, and all of them are open to the public. They also have shops where you can pick up near-perfect seconds at bargain prices. *Open weekdays 9–6, Sat. 9–3, Sun. noon–4 (no glass manufacturing on weekends in winter).*

An attractive coastal town, **Kalmar** is dominated by its imposing seaside castle. The town was once known as the "lock and key" of Sweden, for it is situated on the southern frontier of the kingdom, and thus open to constant enemy invasion. The castle's history goes back 800 years, although the present building dates only from the 16th century, when it was rebuilt by King Gustav Vasa. *Admission: SKr 40. Open June 15–Aug. 15, Mon.–Sat. 10–6, Sun. 12–6; Apr.–June 14 and Aug. 16–Oct., weekdays 10–4, weekends 12–4; Nov.–Mar., Sun. 1–3.*

To return to Stockholm from Kalmar, catch the train to Alvesta (the service runs every two hours) and change there for the Stockholm service. Two trains—one day service and one night service—run direct to Stockholm each day. The journey takes about 6½ hours. **SAS** (tel. 020/727000) operates several flights a day to Stockholm from the Kalmar airport, 5 kilometers (3 miles) from the town center. The trip takes about 45 minutes.

Dining and Lodging

For details and price-category definitions, *see* Dining and Lodging *in* Staying in Sweden, *above.*

Gothenburg
DINING
★ **Sjömagasinet.** In a 200-year-old renovated shipping warehouse, this waterfront restaurant, with its view of the harbor and the suspension bridge, specializes in seafood. During the summer, an outdoor terrace is open. A less expensive prix-fixe menu is available. *Klippanskulturreservat, tel. 031/246510. Reservations required. AE, DC, MC, V. $$$$*
Åtta Glas. A casual, lively restaurant in what was formerly a barge, Åtta Glas offers excellent views of the river and of Kungsportsbron, a bridge spanning the canal in the center of town. The two standard specials—ox fillet or grilled salmon—are the best deals at SKr 69, and a children's menu, which includes ice cream, is popular with families. The second floor houses a bar, especially popular with the younger crowd on weekends. *Kungsportsbron, tel. 031/136015. Reservations advised. AE, DC, MC, V. $$$*
★ **Räkan.** An informal and popular restaurant, Räkan makes the most of an unusual gimmick. The tables are arranged around a long tank, and if you order shrimp, the house specialty, they arrive at your table in radio-controlled boats you navigate yourself. Less expensive prix-

fixe menus are available. *Lorensbergsgatan 16, tel. 031/169839. Reservations required. AE, DC, MC, V. No lunch weekends. $$$*

Weise. A centrally located restaurant with a German beer-cellar atmosphere, Weise was once a haunt of local painters and intellectuals and still retains something of that ambience. The tables and chairs date from 1892. It specializes in traditional Swedish home cooking, serving such dishes as pork and brown beans. *Linnégatan 54, tel. 031/131402. Reservations advised. AE, DC, MC, V. $$*

LODGING

★ **Sheraton Hotel and Towers.** Opened in 1986, the Sheraton Hotel and Towers is Gothenburg's most modern and spectacular international-style hotel. It centers on an atrium lobby and a restaurant renovated in 1995. Guests receive a 20% discount at the well-appointed health club on the premises. *Södra Hamngatan 59–65, S-401 24, tel. 031/806000, fax 031/159888. 344 rooms with bath. Facilities: restaurant, bar, no-smoking rooms, hair salon, convention center, travel services. AE, DC, MC, V. $$$$*

★ **Eggers.** Dating from 1859, the Best Western Eggers has more Old World character than other hotels in the city. It is near the train station and was probably the last port of call in Sweden for many emigrants to the United States. Most rooms contain antique furnishings. Only breakfast is served. *Drottningtorget, S-411 03, tel. 031/806070, fax 031/154243. 65 rooms with bath. Facilities: no-smoking rooms, meeting rooms. AE, DC, MC, V. $$$*

Liseberg Heden. Not far from the famous Liseberg amusement park, Liseberg Heden is a popular modern, family hotel. *Sten Sturegatan, S-411 38, tel. 031/200280, fax 031/165283. 160 rooms with bath. Facilities: restaurant, no-smoking rooms, sauna, meeting rooms. AE, DC, MC, V. $$$*

Jönköping

DINING

★ **Mäster Gudmunds Källare.** Nestled in cozy, 16th-century cellar vaults and only two minutes from the train station is this particularly inviting restaurant. The cuisine is international. *Kapellgatan 2, tel. 036/100640. Reservations advised. AE, DC, MC, V. $$*

LODGING

John Bauer Hotel. This modern, family-run Best Western in the center of town overlooks Munksjön. It was named for a local artist famous for his fairy-tale illustrations of trolls and mystical landscapes. *Södra Strandgatan 15, S-553 20, tel. 036/700500, fax 038/712788. 100 rooms with shower or bath. Facilities: restaurant, bar, no-smoking rooms, sauna, billiards, meeting room. AE, DC, MC, V. $$$*

Stora Hotellet. Stora Hotellet is an old-fashioned establishment opened in 1861 and most recently renovated in 1995. *Hotellplan, S-553 20, tel. 036/719300, fax 036/719320. 112 rooms with shower or bath. Facilities: 3 restaurants, bar, no-smoking rooms, sauna, meeting rooms. AE, DC, MC, V. $$$*

Kalmar

LODGING

Slottshotellet. Occupying a gracious old house on a quiet street, Slottshotellet faces a waterfront park and is a few minutes' walk from both the train station and Kalmar Castle. Inside, you'll find a host of modern facilities wrapped in a 19th-century atmosphere. Only breakfast is served year-round, but in summer, full restaurant service is offered on the terrace. *Slottsvägen 7, S-392 33, tel. 0480/88260, fax*

0480/88266. *36 rooms with shower. Facilities: restaurant, bar, no-smoking rooms, sauna, meeting room. AE, DC, MC, V. $$$*

Stadshotellet. This Best Western in the city center is a large, Old World hotel. The main building dates from 1907. *Stortorget 14, S-392 32, tel. 0480/15180, fax 0480/15847. 139 rooms with bath or shower. Facilities: restaurant, bar, no-smoking rooms, sauna, meeting rooms. AE, DC, MC, V. $$$*

Växjö

Sara Statt. A conveniently located, traditional hotel, this Best Western is popular with tour groups. The building dates from 1853, but the rooms themselves are modern, and the hotel has a cozy Irish pub and two restaurants. *Kungsgatan 6, S-352 33, tel. 0470/13400, fax 0470/44837. 130 rooms with bath or shower. Facilities: 2 restaurants, pub, sauna, meeting rooms. AE, DC, MC, V. $$$*

Esplanad. Centrally located, the Esplanad is a small, family hotel offering basic amenities. Only breakfast is served. *Norra Esplanaden 21A, S-352 31, tel. 0470/22580, fax 0470/26226. 27 rooms, most with shower. Facilities: no-smoking rooms. MC, V. $*

28 Switzerland

THE SWISS keep their coziness under strict control: An electric eye beams open a sliding glass door into a room lined with carved wood, copper, and old-fashioned rafters. That is the paradox of the Swiss, whose two primary aesthetics pitch high-tech urban efficiency against rustic Alpine comfort. Fiercely devout, rigorously clean, prompt as their world-renowned watches, the Swiss are a people who drink their eau-de-vie in firelit *Stübli* (cozy little pubs)—but rarely on Sunday. Liquors here are measured with scientific precision into glasses marked for one or two centiliters, and the local wines come in sized carafes that are reminiscent of laboratory beakers. And as for passion—well, the "double" beds have separate mattresses and sheets that tuck firmly down the middle. (Foreigners with more lusty Latin tastes may request a French—that is, a standard—double bed.) Politically isolated, culturally self-contained, Switzerland remains economically aloof . . . even Europhobic. As their neighbors pull their wagons in a circle, breaking down internal borders to present a unified front to the world, the Swiss continue to choose their apples from bins marked *Inländ* (domestic), while the *Ausländ* varieties, from abroad, rot humbly beside them. Yet Switzerland itself is a country of contrasts: While cowbells tinkle on the slopes of Klewenalp, the hum of commerce in Zürich isn't far away. As befurred and bejeweled socialites shop in Geneva, across the country, in Appenzell, women stand beside their husbands on the Landsgemeinde-Platz to raise their hands in the local vote—a right they didn't win until 1990.

Switzerland combines most of the attractions of its larger European neighbors—Alpine grandeur, urban sophistication, ancient villages, scintillating ski slopes, and all-around artistic excellence. It's the heartland of the Reformation, the homeland of William Tell; its cities are full of historic landmarks, its countryside strewn with castles. Its varied cuisine reflects the best of French, Italian, and German influences.

All these assets have combined to create a major center of tourism, and the Swiss are happy to pave the way. A welcoming if reserved people, many of them well versed in English, they have earned their age-old reputation as fine hosts. Their hotels and inns are famous for cleanliness and efficiency, and the notorious prices—rivaling the highest in the world—are somewhat offset by the knowledge that what you pay accurately reflects the relative value of your purchase.

ESSENTIAL INFORMATION

Before You Go

When to Go

Switzerland functions as a year-round tourist attraction. Winter sports begin around Christmas and usually last until mid-April, depending on snow conditions. The countryside is a delight in spring when the wildflowers are in bloom, and the fall colors rival those in New England. In the Ticino (the Italian-speaking area) and around Lake Geneva (Lac Léman), summer stays late: There is often sparkling weather in September and October, and the popular resorts are less crowded then. After that, though, beware: Throughout Switzerland, resorts may close up altogether in November and May. Always check with the local tourist office.

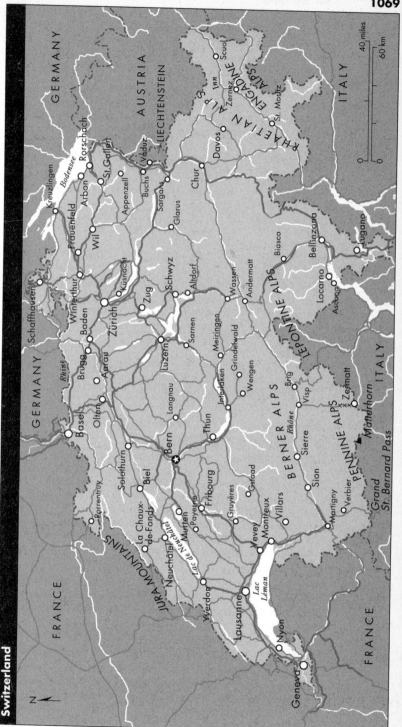

Switzerland

CLIMATE

Summer in Switzerland is generally warm and sunny, though the higher you go, the cooler it gets, especially at night. Winter is cold everywhere: In low-lying areas the weather is frequently damp and overcast; in the Alps, days are brilliantly clear, but invariably cold and snowy—especially above 4,600 feet.

Summer or winter, some areas of Switzerland are prone to an Alpine wind that blows from the south and is known as the *Föhn*. This gives rise to clear but rather oppressive weather, which the Swiss claim causes headaches. The only exception to the general weather patterns is the Ticino which, because it's protected by the Alps, has a positively Mediterranean climate—even in winter.

The following are the average daily maximum and minimum temperatures for Zürich.

Jan.	36F	2C	May	67F	19C	Sept.	69F	20C
	26	– 3		47	8		51	11
Feb.	41F	5C	June	73F	23C	Oct.	57F	14C
	28	– 2		53	12		43	6
Mar.	51F	11C	July	76F	25C	Nov.	45F	7C
	34	1		56	14		35	2
Apr.	59F	15C	Aug.	75F	24C	Dec.	37F	3C
	40	– 4		56	14		29	– 2

Currency

The unit of currency is the Swiss franc (SF), divided into 100 rappen (known as centimes in French-speaking areas). There are coins of 5, 10, 20, and 50 rappen and of 1, 2, and 5 francs. The bills are of 10, 20, 50, 100, 500, and 1,000 francs.

At press time (spring 1995), the Swiss franc stood at 1.12 to the dollar and 1.68 to the pound sterling.

All banks will change your money, though many impose a minimum and a slight fee. Traveler's checks get a better exchange rate, as do cash advances on major credit cards. Main airports and train stations have exchange offices (bureaux de change) that are open longer hours than banks and often offer equally good rates of exchange. Most hotels and some restaurants will change money but usually at a far less favorable rate. Most major credit cards are generally, though not universally, accepted at hotels, restaurants, and shops.

What It Will Cost

High standards of living mean that Switzerland is generally expensive: If it's luxury you're after, you'll pay more for it here than in almost any other European country. Though inflation has been less than 2% for years, the Swiss currency has gained appreciably against the U.S. dollar, resulting in price increases of up to 20% You'll find plenty of reasonably priced hotels and restaurants, however, if you look for them.

As in any other European country, the cities are more expensive than the smaller towns. Zürich and Geneva are the priciest; Basel, Bern, and Lugano are also quite expensive. Holiday resorts—especially the better-known Alpine ski centers—rival cities for high prices. Elsewhere, prices drop appreciably, particularly off the beaten track and in the northeast.

SAMPLE PRICES

Cup of coffee, 3 SF; bottle of beer, 3 SF; soft drink, 3 SF; ham sandwich, 7 SF; a 1-mile taxi ride, 10 SF (more in Geneva, Lugano, or Zürich).

Customs on Arrival

There are two levels of duty-free allowance for visitors to Switzerland. Residents of non-European countries may import 400 cigarettes or 100 cigars or 500 grams of tobacco, plus 2 liters of alcoholic beverage below 15% and 1 liter of alcoholic beverage in excess of 15%. Residents of European countries may import 200 cigarettes or 50 cigars or 250 grams of tobacco, plus 2 liters of alcoholic beverage below 15% and 1 liter of alcoholic beverage in excess of 15%. These allowances apply only to those age 17 and above.

There are no restrictions on the import or export of any currency.

Language

French is spoken in the southwest, around Lake Geneva, and in the cantons of Fribourg, Neuchâtel, Jura, Vaud, and the western portion of Valais; Italian is spoken in the Ticino, and lilting dialects of German are spoken everywhere else—in more than 70% of the country, in fact. The Romance language called Romansh has regained a firm foothold throughout the Upper and Lower Engadine regions of the canton Graubünden, where it takes the form of five different dialects. English, however, is spoken widely. Many public signs are in English, as well as in the regional language, and all hotels, restaurants, tourist offices, train stations, banks, and shops have at least a few English-speaking employees.

Getting Around

By Plane

Swissair connects the cities of Zürich, Basel, and Geneva. The airline's in-house tour operator, **Swisspack,** arranges flexible packages (106 Calvert St., Hamson, NY 10528, tel. 800/688–7947) for the independent traveler who flies at least one way between North America and Europe on Swissair or Delta. "The Swiss Travel Invention" allows visitors to tailor-fit their Swiss holiday to include hotels, car rentals, rail vacations, and guided tours at great savings. **Crossair** is Switzerland's domestic airline, flying between local airports and bringing in visitors from various Continental cities as well, incuding Rome, Barcelona, Berlin, and Amsterdam, as well as London.

By Car

ROAD CONDITIONS

Swiss roads are usually well surfaced but wind about considerably—especially in the mountains. Don't plan to achieve high average speeds. When estimating likely travel times, look carefully at the map: There may be only 32.3 kilometers (20 miles) between one point and another, but there could also be a mountain pass along the way. There is a well-developed highway network, though some notable gaps still exist in the south along an east–west line, roughly between Lugano and Sion. Under some mountain passes, there are tunnels through which cars can be transported by train while passengers remain in the cars—an experience not unlike riding through the world's longest car wash.

A combination of steep or winding routes and hazardous weather conditions may close some roads during the winter. Dial 120 or 163 for bulletins and advance information on road conditions.

RULES OF THE ROAD

Driving is on the right. In built-up areas, the speed limit is 50 kph (30 mph), and on main highways, it's 120 kph (75 mph). On other roads outside built-up areas, the limit is 80 kph (50 mph). Fines for speeding are exorbitant and foreigners must pay on the spot—in cash.

Children under 12 are not permitted to sit in the front seat. Driving with parking lights is prohibited, and the use of headlights is mandatory in heavy rain and under other conditions of poor visibility; you *must* use headlights in road tunnels.

To use the main highways, you must display a disk or *vignette,* which you can buy for 40 SF from the Swiss National Tourist Office (SNTO) before you leave home or at the border stations when you enter the country. Cars rented within Switzerland already have these disks.

Traffic going up a mountain has priority, except for postal buses coming down. A sign with a yellow post horn on a blue background means that postal buses have priority.

During the winter, snow chains are advisable—sometimes mandatory. They can be rented in all areas, and snow-chain service stations have signs marked SERVICE DE CHAÎNES À NEIGE or SCHNEEKETTENDIENST.

PARKING
Parking areas are clearly marked. Parking in public lots normally costs about 1 SF per hour.

GASOLINE
Sans plomb or *bleifrei* (lead-free) gas costs 1.14 SF per liter, and super costs 1.30 per liter. Leaded regular is no longer available.

BREAKDOWNS
Assistance is available through the telephone exchange: Ask for "Autohilfe." The Touring Club Suisse has a 24-hour breakdown service. Useful organizations are the **Automobile Club de Suisse** (ACS, Wasserwerkegasse 39, Bern) and the **Touring Club Suisse** (TCS, 9 rue Pierre Fatio, Geneva), both of which have branches throughout Switzerland.

By Train
Switzerland's trains are among Europe's finest. Generally, they are swift (except through the mountains), immaculate, and unnervingly punctual. Don't linger between international connections: The Swiss don't wait for languorous travelers. If you plan to use the trains extensively, get a timetable ("Offizieles Kursbuch" or "Horaire"), which costs 20 SF, or a portable, pocket version called "Fribo" for 10.80 SF. A useful booklet called "Switzerland by Train," available from the SNTO, describes passes, itineraries, and discounts available to rail travelers. Apply for tickets through your travel agent or **Rail Europe** (tel. 800/438-7245).

Trains described as Inter-City or Express are the fastest, stopping only at principal towns. *Regionalzug* means a local train, often affording the most spectacular views. Meals, snacks, and drinks are provided on most main services; there are even McDonald's dining cars on some routes. Seat reservations are useful during rush hours and high season, especially on international trains.

FARES
There are numerous concessions for visitors. The **Swiss Pass** is the best value, offering unlimited travel on Swiss Federal Railways, postal buses, lake steamers, and the local bus and tram services of 30 cities. It also gives reductions on many privately owned railways, cable cars, and mountain railways. It's available from the SNTO and from travel agents outside Switzerland. The card is valid for eight days (196 SF second class, 280 SF first class), 15 days (226 SF second class, 328 SF first class), or one month (312 SF second class, 452 SF first class). There is also a new three-day **Flexi Pass** (156 SF second class, 224 SF first

class), which offers the same unlimited travel options of a regular Swiss Pass for any three days within a 15-day period.

Within some popular tourist areas, **Regional Holiday Season Tickets,** issued for 15 days, give five days of free travel by train, postal buses, steamers, and mountain railways, with half fare for the rest of the validity of the card. Central Switzerland offers a similar pass for seven days, with two days of free travel. Prices vary widely, depending upon the region and period of validity, but if you like to cover a lot of ground, they do assure you of savings over full fare. Increasingly popular with tourists is a **Swiss Half-Fare Travel Card,** which allows half-fare travel for 30 days (85 SF) or one year (150 SF).

The new **Swiss Card,** which can be purchased in the United States through Rail Europe (226–230 Westchester Ave., White Plains, NY 10604, tel. 800/438–7245) and at train stations at the Zürich and Geneva airports and in Basel, is valid for 30 days and grants full round-trip travel from your arrival point to any destination in the country, plus a half-price reduction on any further excursions during your stay (104 SF second class, 126 SF first class). For more information about train travel in Switzerland, get the free "Swiss Travel System" or "Discover Switzerland" brochures from the SNTO.

For 20 SF per bag round-trip, travelers holding tickets or passes on Swiss Federal Railways can forward their luggage to their final destination and can then make stops on the way unencumbered.

By Bus
Switzerland's famous yellow postal buses link main cities with villages off the beaten track. Both postal and city buses follow posted schedules to the minute: You can set your watch by them. Free timetables can be picked up at any post office.

The Swiss Pass (*see above*) gives unlimited travel on the postal buses, which venture well beyond rail routes. "The Best River and Lakeside Walks," a free booklet available from the SNTO, describes 28 walks you can enjoy by hopping on and off postal buses. Most walks take around three hours.

By Boat
Drifting across a Swiss lake and stopping off here and there at picturesque villages nestling by the water makes a relaxing day's excursion, especially if you are lucky enough to catch one of the elegant old paddle steamers. Trips are scheduled on most of the lakes, with increased service in summer. Unlimited travel is free to holders of the Swiss Pass (*see above*). For those not traveling by train, there is also a **Swiss Boat Pass,** which allows half-fare travel on all lake steamers for the entire calendar year.

By Bicycle
Bikes can be rented at all train stations and returned to any station. Rates are 19 SF per day or 76 SF per week for a conventional bike, 31 SF per day and 124 SF per week for a mountain bike. Families can rent two adult bikes and bikes for the children for 48 SF per day, 208 SF per week. Groups get reductions according to the number of bikes involved. Reservations are necessary by 6 PM the day before use by individuals and a week ahead for groups. **Touring Club Suisse** (9 rue Pierre Fatio, CH-1211 Geneva 3, tel. 022/7851222) also rents bikes from its local offices at prices ranging from 14 SF to 24 SF per day.

Staying in Switzerland

Telephones
LOCAL CALLS
There is direct dialing to every location in Switzerland. For local and international codes, consult the pink pages at the front of the telephone book.

INTERNATIONAL CALLS
You can dial most international numbers direct from Switzerland, adding a 00 before the country's code. If you want a number that cannot be reached directly, dial 114 for a connection. Dial 191 for international numbers and information. It's cheapest to use the booths in train stations and post offices; calls made from your hotel cost a great deal more. The PTT phone card, available in 10 SF and 20 SF units, allows you to call from any adapted public phone. You can buy cards at the post office or train station. A convenient alternative is to use the international access codes for the major telephone companies: for **AT&T,** dial 155/0011; for **MCI,** dial 155/0222; for **Sprint,** dial 155/9777. These will put you directly in touch with an operator, who will place your call. Telephone rates are lower between 5 PM and 7 PM, after 9 PM, and on weekends. Calls to the United States cost 1.80 SF per minute, to the United Kingdom 1 SF per minute.

OPERATORS AND INFORMATION
All telephone operators speak English, and instructions are printed in English in all telephone booths.

COUNTRY CODE
The country code for Switzerland is 41.

Mail
POSTAL RATES
Mail rates are divided into first class (air mail) and second class (surface). Letters and postcards to the United States up to 20 grams cost 1.80 SF first class, .90 SF second class; to the United Kingdom, 1 SF first class, .80 SF second class.

RECEIVING MAIL
If you're uncertain where you'll be staying, you can have your mail, marked "poste restante" or "Postlagernd," sent to any post office in Switzerland. The sender's name and address must be on the back, and you'll need proof of identity to collect it. You can also have your mail sent to American Express for a small fee, payable when you collect it, or free for holders of American Express cards or traveler's checks.

Shopping
VAT REFUNDS
A 6.5% value-added tax (VAT) is included in the price of all goods. Nonresidents who have spent at least 500 SF at one time at a particular store may claim a VAT refund at the time of purchase, or the shop will send the refund to your home. To qualify for a refund, you *must* sign a form at the time of purchase and present it to Swiss customs on departure.

BARGAINING
Don't try bargaining: Except at the humblest flea market, it just doesn't work. As with everything in Switzerland, prices are efficiently controlled.

Opening and Closing Times
Banks are open weekdays 8:30–4:30 or 5.

Museum times vary considerably, though many close on Monday. Check locally.

Shops are generally open 8–noon and 1:30–6:30. Some close at 4 on Saturday, and some are closed Monday morning. In cities, many large stores do not close for lunch. In train stations, some shops remain open until 9 PM, and in Geneva and Zürich airports, shops remain open on Sunday.

National Holidays

January 1–2; April 14 (Good Friday); April 7–8 (Easter Sunday and Easter Monday); May 16 (Ascension); May 26 (Whitsunday/Pentecost Sunday); August 1 (National Day); December 25–26. May 1 (Labor Day) is also celebrated, though not throughout the country.

Dining

Options range from luxury establishments to modest cafés, Stübli, and restaurants specializing in local cuisine.

Because the Swiss are so good at preparing everyone else's cuisine, it is sometimes said that they have none of their own, but there definitely is a distinct and characteristic Swiss cuisine. Switzerland is the home of great cheeses—Gruyère, Emmentaler, Appenzeller, and Vacherin—which form the basis of many dishes. *Raclette* is cheese melted over a fire and served with potatoes and pickles, *Rösti* are hash brown potatoes, and fondue is either a bubbling pot of melted cheeses flavored with garlic and kirsch, into which you dip chunks of bread, or a pot of boiling broth into which you dip various meats. Other Swiss specialties are *geschnetzeltes Kalbfleisch* (veal bits in cream sauce), polenta in the Italian region, and fine game in autumn. A wide variety of Swiss sausages make both filling and inexpensive meals, and in every region the breads are varied and superb.

MEALTIMES

At home, the main Swiss meal of the day is lunch, followed by a light snack in the evening. Restaurants are open at midday and during the evening; often limited menus are offered all day. Watch for *Tagesteller* or *menus* (prix-fixe lunch platters or menus), which enable you to experience the best restaurants without paying high à la carte rates.

WHAT TO WEAR

Jacket and tie are suggested for restaurants in the **$$$$** and **$$$** categories; casual dress is acceptable elsewhere.

RATINGS

Prices are per person, without wine or coffee, but including tip and taxes. Highly recommended restaurants are indicated by a star ★.

CATEGORY	ZÜRICH/GENEVA	OTHER AREAS
$$$$	over 90 SF	over 70 SF
$$$	50 SF–90 SF	40 SF–70 SF
$$	30 SF–50 SF	20 SF–40 SF
$	under 30 SF	under 20 SF

Lodging

Switzerland's accommodations cover a broad range, from the most luxurious hotels to the more economical rooms in private homes. Pick up the "Schweizer Hotelführer" (Swiss Hotel Guide) from the SNTO before you leave home. The guide is free and lists all the members of the Swiss Hotel Association (SHA), which comprises nearly 90% of the nation's accommodations. Some hotels choose not to pay dues to the SHA guide or to the local tourist office; standards may be lower, but so may the prices.

Most hotel rooms today have private bath and shower; those that don't are usually considerably cheaper. Single rooms are generally about two-thirds the price of doubles, but this can vary considerably. Remember that the no-nonsense Swiss sleep in separate beds or, at best, a double with separate bedding. If you prefer more sociable arrangements, ask for the rare "matrimonial" or "French" bed. Service charges and taxes are included in the price quoted and the bill you pay. Breakfast is included unless there is a clear notice to the contrary. In resorts especially, half pension (choice of a noon or evening meal) may be included in the room price. If you choose to eat à la carte or elsewhere, the management will generally reduce your price. Give them plenty of notice, however.

All major towns and train stations have hotel-finding services, which sometimes charge a small fee. Local tourist offices will also help.

HOTELS
The Swiss Hotel Association grades hotels from one star (the lowest) to five stars. Always confirm what you are paying before you register, and check the posted price when you get to your room. Major credit cards are generally accepted, but make sure beforehand.

Two important hotel chains are the Romantik Hotels and Restaurants and Relais et Châteaux, with premises that are generally either in historic houses or houses that have some special character. Another chain with a good reputation is Best Western, affiliated with the familiar American chain. Relais du Silence hotels are usually isolated in a peaceful, natural setting with first-class comforts. The Check-In E and G ("Einfach und Gemütlich" or "Cheap and Cozy") Hotels are dependable small hotels, boardinghouses, and mountain lodges that offer accommodations at reasonable prices. Details are available from the SNTO, which also offers pamphlets recommending family hotels and a list of hotels and restaurants that cater specifically to Jewish travelers.

RENTALS
Switzerland has thousands of furnished chalets. Off-season, per-day prices are around 50 SF per person for four sharing a chalet; in peak season, prices double. Deluxe chalets cost much more. For more information, pick up an illustrated brochure from the **Swiss Touring Club** (9 rue Pierre Fatio, CH-1211 Geneva 3) or from **Uto-Ring AG** (Beethovenstr. 24, CH-8002 Zürich). In the United States, write to **Interhome** (36 Carlos Dr., Fairfield, NJ 07006). In Britain, contact **Interhome** (383 Richmond Rd., Twickenham, Middlesex TW1 2EF). You may save considerably if you write directly to the village or resort you wish to rent in, specifying your projected dates and number of beds needed: Prices start at around 20 SF per person without an agency's commission.

RATINGS
Prices are for two people in a double room with bath or shower, including taxes, service charges, and breakfast. Highly recommended lodgings are indicated by a star ★.

CATEGORY	ZÜRICH/GENEVA	OTHER AREAS
$$$$	over 450 SF	over 300 SF
$$$	250 SF–450 SF	200 SF–300 SF
$$	120 SF–250 SF	120 SF–200 SF
$	under 120 SF	under 120 SF

Tipping

Although restaurants include service charges of 15% with the taxes in your hotel and restaurant bill, you will be expected to leave a small additional tip: 1 SF or 2 SF per person for a modest meal, 5 SF for a first-class meal, and 10 SF at one of the exclusive gastronomic restaurants in the **$$$$** range. When possible, tip in cash. Elsewhere, give bathroom attendants 1 SF and hotel maids 2 SF. Theater and opera-house ushers get 2 SF. Hotel porters and doormen should get about 2 SF per bag in an upmarket hotel; 1 SF elsewhere.

ZÜRICH

Arriving and Departing

By Plane

Kloten (tel. 01/8127111) is Switzerland's most important airport and is among the most sophisticated in the world. Several airlines fly directly to Zürich from major cities in the United States, Canada, and the United Kingdom.

Swissair flies nonstop from New York, Chicago, Toronto, Montreal, Atlanta, Los Angeles, and Boston. "Fly Rail Baggage" allows Swissair passengers departing Switzerland to check their bags at any of 120 rail or postal bus stations throughout the country; luggage is automatically transferred to the airplane. At eight Swiss railway stations, passengers may complete all check-in procedures for Swissair flights, including boarding-pass issuance and baggage forwarding.

BETWEEN THE AIRPORT AND DOWNTOWN
Beneath the air terminals, there's a train station with an efficient, direct service into the Hauptbahnhof (main station) in the center of Zürich. Fast trains run every 10–15 minutes, and the trip takes about 10 minutes. The fare is 4.80 SF, and the ticket office is in the airport. There are express trains to most Swiss cities at least every hour. Trains run from 6 AM to midnight.

Taxis are very expensive: about 40 SF into town. Some hotels provide their own bus service. Cars can be rented at the airport.

By Bus

All bus services to Zürich will drop you at the Hauptbahnhof. There are also hotel bus services that charge 17 SF per person.

By Train

Zürich is the northern crossroads of Switzerland, with swift and timely trains arriving from Basel, Geneva, Bern, and Lugano. All routes lead to the Hauptbahnhof in the city center.

By Car

Highways link Zürich directly to France, Germany, and Italy. The quickest approach is from Germany.

Getting Around

Although Zürich is Switzerland's largest city, it has an estimated population of only 362,000 and is small by European standards. That's one of its nicest features: You can explore it comfortably on foot.

By Bus and Streetcar

The city's transportation network is excellent. **VBZ Züri-Line** (Zürich Public Transport) buses run from 5:30 AM to midnight, every six minutes on all routes at peak hours, and about every 12 minutes at other times. Before you board the bus, you must buy your ticket from the automatic vending machines found at every stop. A ticket for all travel for 24 hours is a good buy at 6.40 SF. Free route plans are available from VBZ offices.

By Taxi

Taxis are very expensive, with an 8 SF minimum, and should be avoided unless you have no other means of getting around.

Important Addresses and Numbers

Tourist Information

The tourist office is at Bahnhofplatz 15 (tel. 01/2114000. Open Apr.–Oct., weekdays 8:30–9:30, weekends 8:30–8:30; Nov.–Mar., weekdays 8:30–7:30, weekends 8:30–6:30).

Consulates

U.S. (Zollikerstr. 141, tel. 01/4222566). **Canadian** (Kirchenfeldstr. 88, tel. 031/3526321) **U.K.** (Dufourstr. 56, tel. 01/2611520).

Emergencies

Police (tel. 117). **Ambulance** (tel. 144). **Doctor/Dentist Referral** (tel. 01/2616100). **Pharmacy: Bellevue** (Theaterstr. 14, tel. 01/2525600) offers an all-night service.

English-Language Bookstores

For books and magazines, try **Payot** (Bahnhofstr. 9) or **Travel Book Shop** (Rindermarkt 20).

Travel Agencies

American Express (Bahnhofstr. 20, tel. 01/2118370). **Kuoni Travel** (Bahnhofpl. 7, tel. 01/2213411).

Guided Tours

Orientation Tours

Three bus tours are available. The daily "Sights of Zürich" tour (27 SF adults, 13 SF children) gives a good general idea of the city in two hours. "In and Around Zürich" covers more ground and includes an aerial cableway trip to Felsenegg; it takes 2½ hours and costs 35 SF adults, 20 SF children. The May-to-October tour, "Zürich by Night," takes in everything from folklore to striptease in 3½ hours (69 SF). All tours start from the main station. Contact the tourist office for reservations.

Walking Tours

From May through October, daily guided walking tours (16 SF adults, 8 SF children 6–12) start from the tourist office and take roughly two hours.

Excursions

There are many bus excursions to other areas, such as the Bernese Oberland, St. Gotthard, the Ticino, Luzern, and Geneva. Since these depend on the season and weather, it's best to book them after you arrive.

Exploring Zürich

Zürich is not what you'd expect. Stroll around on a fine spring day and you'll ask yourself if this can really be one of the great business centers of the world: the lake glistening and blue in the sun, the sidewalk cafés, the swans gliding in to land on the river, the hushed and haunted old squares of medieval guild houses. There's not a gnome (a mocking nickname for a Swiss banker) in sight. For all its economic importance, Zürich is a place where people enjoy life. Hardworking when need be, the Swiss love the good things in life and have the money to enjoy them.

Zürich started in 15 BC as a Roman customs post on the Lindenhof overlooking the River Limmat, but its growth really began around the 10th century AD. It became a free imperial city in 1336, a center of the Reformation in 1519, and gradually assumed commercial importance during the 1800s. Today there is peace as well as prosperity here, and since Zürich is so compact, you can take it in a morning's stroll.

Numbers in the margin correspond to points of interest on the Zürich map.

❶ Collect your map (it's essential) from the tourist office (Bahnhofpl. 15), then start your walk from the nearby **Bahnhofstrasse,** famous for its shops and cafés and as the center of the banking network—though you'd be unlikely to guess it. Take Rennweg on your left, and then turn left **❷** again into the Fortunagasse, a quaint medieval street leading to the **Lindenhof,** a square where there are remains of Zürich's Roman origins.

❸ An alley on the right leads to a picturesque square dating from the Middle Ages, with the **Peterskirche,** Zürich's oldest parish church (13th century), which also happens to have the largest clock face in Europe. Walk **❹** down to the river and follow it to the 13th-century church **Fraumünster,** which has modern stained-glass windows by Chagall. There are two handsome guildhalls nearby: the **Zunfthaus zur Waag,** hall of the linen weavers (Münsterhof 8), built in 1637, and the **Zunfthaus zur Meise** (Münsterhof 20), built during the 18th century for the wine merchants.

TIME OUT Head away from the river to the Bahnhofstrasse, then to Paradelplatz to visit **Sprüngli,** the famous café-sweets shop where glossy Zürichers gather to see and be seen. The chocolate truffles are sinfully rich.

Continue along Bahnhofstrasse to Bürkliplatz and cross the **Quai Bridge** to take in the impressive views of the lake and town. Art lovers **❺** might want to first continue up Rämistrasse to the **Kunsthaus** (Art Gallery), with its varied high-quality collection of medieval paintings, Dutch and Italian Baroque, and Impressionist works, as well as its excellent representation of Swiss artists, including nearly 100 works by Hodler. *Heimpl. 1, tel. 01/2516755. Admission varies with exhibitions. Open Tues.–Thurs. 10–9, Fri.–Sun. 10–5.*

❻ Now head left to the **Wasserkirche** (Water Church), which dates from the 15th century and is a lovely example of late-Gothic architecture. It is attached to the **Helmhaus,** originally an 18th-century cloth market.

❼ Now turn right toward the **Grossmünster** church, which dates from the 11th century. During the 3rd century AD, St. Felix and his sister Regula were martyred by the Romans. Legend maintains that having been beheaded, they then walked up the hill carrying their heads and collapsed on the spot where the Grossmünster now stands. On the south tower you can see a statue of Charlemagne (768–814), emperor of the West, who founded the church when his horse stumbled on the same site. During the 16th century, the Zürich reformer Huldreich Zwingli preached sermons here that were so threatening in their promise of fire and brimstone that Martin Luther himself was frightened.

❽ Back at the river on the **Limmatquai** are some of Zürich's most enchanting old buildings. Today most of them are restaurants. In the **Haus zum Ruden,** a 13th-century nobleman's hall, you can eat under a 300-year-

Main Attractions

Altstadt (Old Town), **9**
Bahnhofstrasse, **1**
Fraumünster, **4**
Grossmünster, **7**
Kunsthaus, **5**
Limmatquai, **8**
Lindenhof, **2**
Niederdorf, **10**
Peterskirche, **3**
Schweizerisches Landesmuseum, **11**
Wasserkirche, **6**

Other Attractions

Centre Le Corbusier, **19**
Federal Institute of Technology, **12**
Opernhaus, **15**
Rathaus, **17**
Stadthaus, **18**
University of Zürich, **13**
Wohnmuseum, **16**
Zoo, **14**

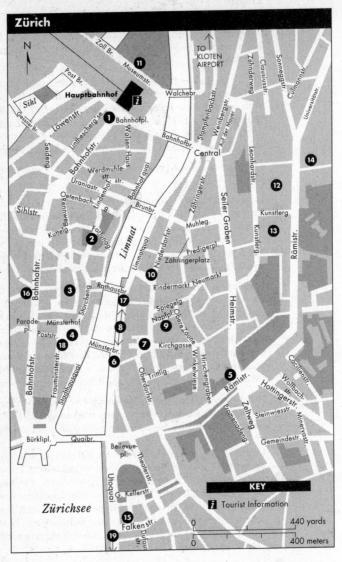

old wooden ceiling. Other notable buildings here are the **Zunfthaus zur Saffran**, built in 1723 for haberdashers; and the **Zunfthaus zur Zimmerleuten,** built in 1708 for carpenters. The 17th-century Baroque **Rathaus** (town hall) is nearby.

9 Turn right into the **Altstadt** (Old Town), and you will enter a maze of fascinating medieval streets where time seems to have stood still. The Rindermarkt, Napfplatz, and Kirchgasse all have their charming old houses.

10 Head back to the river through **Niederdorf** (Zürich's nightlife district) and cross the bridge to the Hauptbahnhof. On the northern edge of **11** the Hauptbahnhof, go to the **Schweizerisches Landesmuseum,** housed in a curious 19th-century building, for a look at Swiss history. There are fascinating pre-Romanesque and Romanesque church art, glass paintings from the 15th to the 17th century, splendid ceramic stoves, gold and silver from Celtic times, and weapons from many ages. *Museumstr. 2, tel. 01/2186565. Admission free. Open Tues.–Sun. 10–5.*

Off the Beaten Track

One of Zürich's most outstanding museums is the **Stiftung Sammlung E. G. Bührle** (Collection of the E. G. Bührle Foundation), a once-private collection of European art housed in a suburban mansion. Especially noteworthy are its French Impressionist and early modern paintings. *Zollikerstr. 172 (Tram 2 or 4 from Wildbachstr.), tel. 01/4220086. Admission: 9 SF adults, 7 SF children. Open Tues. and Fri. 2–5, Wed. 5–8.*

The **Museum Rietberg** is a wonderful gathering of art from India, China, Africa, Japan, and Southeast Asia, contained in the neoclassical Villa Wesendonck, where Richard Wagner (as in *Wesendonck Songs*) once lived. *Gablerstr. 15 (Tram 7), tel. 01/2024528. Admission: 10 SF adults, children 5 SF. Open Tues., Thurs.–Sun. 10–5, Wed. 10–9.*

The **Graphiksammlung** (Graphics Collection) of the Eidgenössische Technische Hochschule (Federal Institute of Technology) displays portions of its vast library of woodcuts, etchings, and engravings by European masters such as Dürer, Rembrandt, Goya, and Picasso. From time to time there are good thematic exhibitions drawn from the collection. *Rämistr. 101, tel. 01/6324046. Admission free. Open Mon., Tues., Thurs., Fri. 10–5; Wed. 10–8.*

Shopping

Gift Ideas
Typical Swiss products, all of the highest quality, include watches in all price categories, clocks, jewelry, music boxes, embroidered goods, wood carvings, and the famous multiblade Swiss army pocket knife. You'll also find fine household linens, delicate cotton or woolen underclothes, and Zürich-made Fogal hosiery.

Shopping Districts
The **Bahnhofstrasse** is one of the most bountiful shopping streets in Switzerland. Here you'll find **Jelmoli** (Seideng. 1), Switzerland's largest department store, carrying a wide range of tasteful Swiss goods. **Heimatwerk** (Bahnhofstr. 2) specializes in handmade Swiss crafts, all of excellent quality. For high fashion, go to **Trois Pommes** (Storcheng. 6/7) and **Grieder** (Bahnhofstr. 30), and for the finest porcelain, glass, and silverware, visit **Sequin-Dormann** (Bahnhofstr. 69a). If you have a sweet tooth, stock up on truffles at **Sprüngli** (Paradepl.), or **Teuscher** (Old Town 9).

In the **Old Town** and off the **Limmatquai**, you'll find boutiques, antiques shops, bookstores, and galleries in picturesque byways. The **Löwenstrasse** has a diversity of upscale shops; the **Langstrasse** is another good shopping area and often has slightly lower prices. Under the central train station, **Shopville** offers a variety of less expensive stores and snack bars.

Food and Flea Markets
In many parts of town, there are lively markets where fruit, vegetables, and flowers are competitively priced. The best are at **Bürkliplatz, Helvetiaplatz,** and **Milkbuckstrasse** (open Tues. and Fri. 6 AM–11 AM).

At Bürkliplatz, at the lake end of the Bahnhofstrasse, there's a flea market that's open Saturdays from 6 AM to 3:30 PM May through October, and a curio market is held at **Rosenhof** every Thursday and Saturday between April and Christmas.

Dining

You're likely to be served seconds in Zürich's generous restaurants, where the rest of your Rösti and *Geschnetzeltes Kalbfleisch* simmer in copper pans by your table while you relish the hefty first portion. This is a Germanic city, though its status as a minor world capital means that most international cuisines are represented as well. But brace yourself: The cash register rings portentously when the waiter places your order. Watch for posted Tagesteller lunch specials, a good source of savings. For details and price-category definitions, *see* Dining *in* Staying in Switzerland, *above*.

$$$$ Königstuhl. This trendy, tongue-in-cheek take on Zürich's *Zunfthäuser*
★ (guildhalls) has caught on with a vengeance. Itself the Zunfthaus zur Schneidern (Tailors' Guildhall), with a relatively traditional meeting hall on the top floor, this complex consisting of bar, bistro, and first-class restaurant functions more as an anti-Zunfthaus: It's been entirely redone in cool gray graphite and glass, with halogen lighting and broad, droll allusions to Zürich's heavy Teutonic taste. The cuisine is equally irreverent, with light, moderately priced suppers (appetizers, pastas) downstairs in the bistro and superb international experiments in the soigné restaurant upstairs (dress accordingly). There's a lovely courtyard terrace for summer dining. *Stüssihofstatt 3, tel. 01/2617618. Bistro reservations advised. Restaurant reservations required. AE, DC, MC, V.*

$$$$ La Rotonde. Even when it's not illuminated by candlelight, the Dolder Grand Hotel's haute cuisine restaurant is one of the most romantic spots in Zürich. Housed in a great arc of a room, La Rotonde provides sweeping park views that attract the lunchtime business crowd. The 70 SF prix-fixe dinner is a particularly good value. For those who love hors d'oeuvres, there's a Sunday afternoon buffet of nothing but starters. *Dolder Grand Hotel, Kurhausstr. 65, tel. 01/2516231. Reservations advised. Jacket and tie. AE, DC, MC, V.*

$$$$ Petermann's Kunststuben. This is one of Switzerland's gastronomic mec-
★ cas, and although it's south of the city center—in Küssnacht on the lake's eastern shore—it's more than worth the 8-kilometer (5-mile) pilgrimage. The ever-evolving, fish-based menu may include lobster with artichoke and almond oil, grilled turbot with lemon sauce and capers, or Tuscan dove with pine nuts and herbs. The high-rolling, jacket-clad clientele rarely blinks an eye at the prix-fixe menus, which start at 98 SF and climb to 185 SF. *Seestr. 160, Küssnacht, tel. 01/9100715. Reservations required. AE, DC, MC, V. Closed Sun. and Mon., 2 wks in Feb., and 3 wks in late July–early Aug.*

$$$$ Tübli. Tucked into a back alley in the more adventurous Niederdorf neighborhood, this intimate, fairly formal little Züricher secret continues to draw insiders for some of the best and most innovative cuisine in the city center. Eschewing à la carte standbys for ever-changing weekly seven-course menus, chef Martin Surbeck experiments with almost indiscriminate pleasure with literally far-fetched ingredients: Portuguese *chocolat* for his fish carpaccio, Norwegian reindeer with mulberry-flower mousseline, or passion-fruit soufflé. *Schneggeng. 8, tel. 01/2512471. Reservations advised. AE, DC, MC, V. Closed weekends.*

$$$–$$$$ Kronenhalle. From Stravinsky, Brecht, and Joyce to Nureyev, Deneuve,
★ and St-Laurent, this beloved landmark has always drawn a stellar crowd for its genial, formal but relaxed atmosphere, hearty cooking, and astonishing collection of 20th-century art. Try the herring in double cream, tournedos with truffle sauce, or duck à l'orange with red cabbage and *Spätzli* (tiny dumplings). And be sure to have a cocktail

in the adjoining bar: *Le tout* Zürich drinks here. *Rämistr. 4, tel. 01/2516669. Reservations advised. AE, DC, MC, V.*

$$$ **Blaue Ente.** Part of a shopping gallery in a converted mill south of the
★ city center, this modern, upmarket restaurant and bar draw well-dressed crowds from advertising and the arts. In a setting of whitewashed brick and glass, with jazz filtering through from the adjoining bar, guests sample a pot-au-feu of clams, prawns, and saffron, or lamb with potato pancakes and eggplant. Take Tram 2 toward Tiefenbrunnen. *Mühle Tiefenbrunnen, tel. 01/4227706. Reservations required. AE, DC, MC, V.*

$$$ **Veltliner Keller.** Though its rich, carved-wood decor borrows from Graubünden Alpine culture, this ancient and atmospheric dining spot is no tourist trap: The house, built in 1325 and functioning as a restaurant since 1551, has always stored Italian-Swiss Valtellina wines, which were carried over the Alps and imported to Zürich. The traditional kitchen favors heavy meat standards, but is reasonably deft with seafood as well. *Schlüsselg. 8, tel. 01/2213228. Reservations advised. AE, DC, MC, V. Closed weekends.*

$$ **Bierhalle Kropf.** Under the giant boar's head and century-old murals,
★ businesspeople, workers, and shoppers crowd shared tables to feast on generous hot dishes and a great selection of sausages. The *Leberknödli* (liver dumplings) are tasty, *Apfelköchli* (fried apple slices) tender and sweet, and the bread chewy and delicious—though you pay for every chunk you eat. *In Gassen 16, tel. 01/2211805. Reservations advised. AE, DC, MC, V. Closed Sun. and holidays.*

$$ **Oepfelchammer.** This was once the haunt of Zürich's beloved writer
★ Gottfried Keller, and, now restored, it still draws unpretentious literati. The bar is dark and graffiti-marked, with sagging timbers and slanting floors; the welcoming little dining room has carved oak paneling, a coffered ceiling, and pink damask linens. The traditional meats—calf's liver, veal, tripe in white wine sauce—come in generous portions; salads are fresh and seasonal. It's always packed, and service can be slow, so stake out a table and spend the evening. *Rindermarkt 12, tel. 01/2512336. Reservations advised. MC, V. Closed Sun.*

$$ **Rheinfelder Bierhaus.** Dark and smoky, with every wooden table squeezing in mixed parties of workers, bikers, shoppers, and tourists, this is a solid old institution in the Niederdorf area. There's rich *Rindpfeffer* (preserved beef stew) with homemade Spätzli, tender liver with Rösti, sausage dishes, and once a month, the chef's pride: an incongruous but homemade paella. *Marktgasse 19, tel. 01/2512991. No credit cards.*

$$ **Zeughauskeller.** Built as an arsenal in 1487, this enormous stone and
★ beam hall offers hearty meat platters and a variety of beers and wines amid comfortable and friendly chaos. Waitresses are harried and brisk, especially at lunchtime, when crowds are thick. They're not unaccustomed to tourists, but locals consider this their home away from home. *Bahnhofstr. 28 (at Paradepl.), tel. 01/2112690. Lunch reservations advised. No credit cards.*

$$ **Zunfthaus zur Schmiden.** The sense of history and the magnificent mix of Gothic wood, leaded glass, and tile stoves justify a visit to this popular landmark, the guild house of blacksmiths and barbers since 1412. All the classics are served in enormous portions, and there's a considerable selection of alternatives, fish among them. The guild's own house wine is fine. *Marktgasse 20, tel. 01/2515287. Reservations advised. AE, DC, MC, V.*

Lodging

Zürich has an enormous range of hotels, from some of the most chic and prestigious in the country to modest guest houses. Prices tend to be higher than anywhere else in Europe, but you can be sure that you will get what you pay for: Quality and good service are guaranteed. For details and price-category definitions, *see* Lodging *in* Staying in Switzerland.

$$$$ **Baur au Lac.** This is the hoary, highbrow patrician of Swiss hotels, with
★ luxury facilities but none of the glitz associated with the flashier upstarts among prestige resorts—aside from the Rolls Royce limousine service. Its broad back is turned to the commercial center, and its front rooms overlook the lake, canal, and manicured lawns of the hotel's private park. Decor is posh, discreet, and firmly fixed in the Age of Reason. In summer, meals are served in the glassed park Pavilion along the canal; in winter, in the glowing Restaurant Français; and the Grill Room is a business tradition. *Talstr. 1, CH-8022, tel. 01/2211650, fax 01/2118139. 156 rooms with bath. Facilities: 3 restaurants, bar, disco, AE, DC, MC, V.*

$$$$ **Dolder Grand.** A cross between Camp David and Maria Theresa's
★ summer palace, this sprawling Victorian fantasy-palace sits high on a wooded hill over Zürich, quickly reached from Römerhof by funicular railway (free for guests). It was opened in 1899 as a summer resort, a picturesque hodgepodge of turrets, cupolas, half-timbers, and mansards; the uncompromisingly modern wing was added in 1964, but from inside the connection is seamless. The garden and forest views behind nearly match those of the golf course, park, and city itself. Restaurant La Rotonde excels in traditional French cuisine (*see* Dining, *above*). *Kurhausstr. 65, CH-8032, tel. 01/2516231, fax 01/2518829. 207 rooms with bath. Facilities: restaurant, bar, café, hair salon, outdoor swimming pool, 9-hole golf course, ice-skating, 5 tennis courts, free parking. AE, DC, MC, V.*

$$$$ **Savoy Baur en Ville.** The oldest hotel in Zürich, built in 1838, this luxurious downtown landmark was gutted in 1975 and reconstructed as an airtight urban gem. It's directly on the Paradeplatz and at the hub of the banking, shopping, and sightseeing districts. The rooms have a warm, postmodern decor, with pear-wood cabinetry, brass, and chintz, and there are two fine restaurants—one French, the other Italian—as well as a city-slick café. *Paradepl., CH-8022, tel. 01/2115360, fax 01/2111467. 112 rooms with bath. Facilities: 2 restaurants, café. AE, DC, MC, V.*

$$$ **Neues Schloss.** Headed by Bernard Seiler, an heir to the Zermatt hotel
★ dynasty, this small, discreet hotel in the business district (southeast of Paradeplatz) shows its bloodlines, offering a cordial welcome, good service, and the warmth of a tastefully furnished private home. Its restaurant, Le Jardin, is airy and floral, and popular at lunch. *Stockerstr. 17, CH-8022, tel. 01/2016550, fax 01/2016418. 59 rooms with bath. Facilities: restaurant. AE, DC, MC, V.*

$$$ **Splügenschloss.** Constructed at the turn of the century as a luxury apartment complex, this Relais et Châteaux property maintains an ornate and historic decor, with antiques in rooms and throughout public spaces. Some rooms have been paneled completely in Alpine-style pine; others are decorated in fussy florals. Its location southeast of the Neues Schloss may be a little out of the way for tourists, but atmosphere buffs will find it worth the effort. *Splügenstr. 2, CH-8002, tel. 01/2010800, fax 01/2014286. 55 rooms with bath. Facilities: restaurant, bar. AE, DC, MC, V.*

$$$ **Zum Storchen.** In a stunning central location, tucked between Fraumün-
★ ster and St. Peter on the gull-studded banks of the Limmat, this airy
600-year-old structure houses an impeccable modern hotel. It has
warmly appointed rooms, some with French windows that open over
the water, and a lovely terrace restaurant with river views, as well as
a cozy dining room reminiscent of a guild house. *Weinpl. 2, CH-8001,
tel. 01/2115510 or 800/413–8877, fax 01/2116451. 77 rooms with
bath. Facilities: restaurant, bar, café, snack bar. AE, DC, MC, V.*

$$–$$$ **City.** Near the Bahnhofstrasse, the train station, and the Löwenstrasse
shopping district, this is a hotel in miniature, with small furnishings
and baths and a high proportion of single rooms. It's recently been re-
newed to chic pastel polish, and some rooms have become rather
pricey. *Löwenstr. 34, CH-8021, tel. 01/2112055, fax 01/2120036. 83
rooms with bath. Facilities: restaurant, bar. AE, DC, MC, V.*

$$ **Rössli.** Young, trendy, and completely high-tech, this hip spot in Ober-
★ dorf, near the Grossmünster, offers a refreshing antidote to Zürich's
medievalism. Decor is white-on-white, with metallic-tiled baths, vivid
lithographs, and splashy fabrics; hair dryers, robes, and fax connections keep services above average, especially for the price. The adjoining
bar is very popular with young locals. *Rösslig. 7, CH-8001, tel.
01/2522121, fax 01/2522131. 12 rooms with bath. Facilities: bar. AE,
DC, MC, V.*

$$ **Sonnenberg.** If you're traveling by car and want to avoid the urban
★ rush, escape to this hillside refuge east of town. Run by the Wismer
family, it offers breathtaking views of the city, lake, and mountains,
and landscaped grounds with a lovely terrace restaurant. The wood,
stone, and beam decor reinforces the resort atmosphere. Take Tram 3
or 8 to Klusplatz, then walk 10 minutes uphill. *Aurorastr. 98, CH-8030,
tel. 01/2620062, fax 01/2620633. 35 rooms with bath. Facilities:
restaurant, café. AE, DC, MC, V.*

$$ **Wellenberg.** Another effort at high style, but not as effective as the Rössli,
this new, central hotel sports a postmodern retro look, with burled wood,
black lacquer, art deco travel posters, and Hollywood photos. The staff
is friendly, rooms are relatively spacious, if occasionally garish, and the
location—on Niederdorf's Hirschenplatz—is superb. Some rooms are
expensive. *Niederdorfstr. 10, CH-8001, tel. 01/2624300, fax
01/2513130. 46 rooms with bath. Breakfast room, conference room.
AE, DC, MC, V.*

$ **St. Georges.** This simple former pension has a fresh, bright lobby and
breakfast room, but guest rooms and corridors are considerably more
spare, with toothpaste-green walls, red linoleum floors, and '60s pine
furniture. Rooms are available with and without showers. Take Tram
3 or 14 from the station to Stauffacher, west of the center; it's another
five minutes on foot. *Weberstr. 11, CH-8004, tel. 01/2411144, fax
01/2411142. 44 rooms, 4 with bath. Facilities: breakfast room. AE,
DC, MC, V.*

$ **Vorderer Sternen.** On the edge of the Old Town and near the lake, this
plain but adequate establishment takes in the bustle (and noise) of the
city. It's steps from the opera house, theaters, art galleries, cinemas, and
a shopping area; it's also close to the Bellevueplatz tram junction.
There's a dependable and popular restaurant downstairs with moderate standards. *Theaterstr. 22, CH-8001, tel. 01/2514949, fax 01/2529063.
15 rooms without bath. Facilities: restaurant. AE, DC, MC, V.*

The Arts

Pick up *Zürich News*, published each week by the tourist office, to check
what's on. Ticket reservations can be made through the **Billetzentrale**

(Werdmühlepl., tel. 01/2212283; open weekdays 10–6:30, Sat. 10–2). **Musik Hug** (Limmatquai 26, tel. 01/2212540) and **Jecklin** (Rämistr. 30, tel. 01/2617733) are good ticket sources as well.

The **Zürich Tonhalle Orchestra** (Claridenstr. 7, tel. 01/2063434) ranks among Europe's best. The **Opernhaus** (Falkenstr., tel. 01/2620909) is renowned for its adventurous opera, operetta, and ballet productions. The **Schauspielhaus** (Rämistr. 34, tel. 01/2655858) is one of the finest German-speaking theaters in the world. Zürich has 40 movie theaters, with English-language films appearing regularly.

Nightlife

Zürich has a lively nightlife scene, largely centered in the Niederdorf, parallel to the Limmat and across from the Hauptbahnhof. Many spots are short-lived, so check in advance. Casual dress is acceptable in most places, but again, check to make sure. The hotel porter is a good source of information.

Bars and Lounges

The narrow bar at the **Kronenhalle** (Rämistr. 4, tel. 01/2511597) draws mobs of well-heeled locals and internationals for its prizewinning cocktails. The **Jules Verne Panorama Bar** (Uraniahaus, tel. 01/2111155) offers cocktails with a wraparound view of downtown Zürich. **Champagnertreff** in the Hotel Central (Central 1, tel. 01/2515555) is a popular deco-style piano bar with several champagnes available by the glass. **Odeon** (Am Bellevue, tel. 01/2511650) serves a young, arty set until 4 AM. Some beer halls, including **Bierhalle Kropf** (In Gassen 16, tel. 01/2211805) and **Zeughauskeller** (Bahnhofstr. 28, tel. 01/2112690), serve a variety of draft beers in an old-Zürich atmosphere.

Cabaret/Nightclubs

There's a variety show with dancers and magicians at **Polygon** (Marktg. 17, tel. 01/2521110). There are strip shows all over town, as well as the traditional nightclub atmosphere at **Le Privé** (Stauffacherstr. 106, tel. 01/2416487), **Moulin Rouge** (Mühleg. 14, tel. 01/2620730), and the slightly more sophisticated **Terrace** (Limmatquai 3, tel. 01/2511074). Expect to pay dearly for your evening pleasures.

Discos

Mascotte (Theaterstr. 10, tel. 01/2524481) is, at the moment, popular with all ages on weeknights, but caters to young crowds on weekends. **Le Petit Prince** (Bleicherweg 21, tel. 01/2011739) attracts an upscale crowd. Even more exclusive is **Diagonal,** at the Hotel Baur au Lac (Talstr. 1, tel. 01/2117396), where you must be a hotel guest—or the guest of one. **Rasputine's** (Schützeng. 16, tel. 01/2115058) offers 40 different kinds of vodka.

Jazz

Jazz clubs **Casa Bar** (Münsterg. 30, tel. 01/2612002) and **Moods** (Schlamtstr. 5, tel. 01/2018130) offer jazz into the wee hours.

Excursion from Zürich: Liechtenstein

For an international day trip out of Zürich, dip a toe into tiny Liechtenstein: There isn't room for much more. Just 80 kilometers (50 miles) southeast on the Austrian border, this miniature principality covers a scant 158 square kilometers (61 square miles). An independent nation since 1719, Liechtenstein has a customs union with Switzerland, which means they share trains, currency, and diplomats—but not stamps, which is why collectors prize the local releases. It's easiest to get there by car, since Liechtenstein is so small that Swiss trains pass through without stopping. If you're using a train pass, ride to Sargans or Buchs. From there, local postbuses deliver mail and passengers across the border to Liechtenstein's capital, Vaduz.

Tourist Information

The principal tourist office in Liechtenstein is at Städtle 37, Box 139, FL 9490, Vaduz, tel. 075/2321443. It's open weekdays 8–5:30, Sat. 9–4.

Exploring Liechtenstein

Green and mountainous, with vineyards lining its banks, greater Liechtenstein is best seen by car. But if you're on foot, you won't be stuck: The postbuses are prompt and take you everywhere at a scenic snail's pace.

In fairy-tale **Vaduz**, Prince Johannes Adam Pius still lives in **Vaduz Castle,** a massive 16th-century fortress perched high on the cliff over the city. Only honored guests of the prince tour the interior, but its exterior and the views from the grounds are worth the climb. In the modern center of town, head for the tourist information office to have your passport stamped with the Liechtenstein crown. Upstairs, the **Prince's Art Gallery and the State Art Collection** showcase various sectors of the vast collection. *Städtle 37, tel. 075/2322341. Admission: 5 SF adults, 2 SF children. Open Apr.–Oct., daily 10–noon and 1:30–5:30; Nov.–Mar., daily 10–noon and 1:30–5.*

On the same floor, the **Postage Stamp Museum** attracts philatelists from all over the world to see the 300 frames of beautifully designed and relatively rare stamps. Place subscriptions here for future first-day covers. *Städtle 37, tel. 075/2366109. Admission free. Open Apr.–Oct., daily 10–noon and 1:30–5:30; Nov.–Mar., 10–noon and 1:30–5.*

Next, move on to the **Liechtenstein National Museum** (closed until mid-1997), which houses historical artifacts, church carvings, ancient coins, and arms from the prince's collection. *Städtle 43, tel. 075/22310. Admission: 2 SF. Open May–Sept., daily 10–noon and 1:30–5:30; Oct.–Apr., Tues.–Sun. 2–5:30.*

In **Schaan,** just north of Vaduz, visit the Roman excavations and the parish church built on the foundations of a Roman fort. Or drive up to the chalets of picturesque **Triesenberg** for spectacular views of the Rhine Valley. Higher still, **Malbun** is a sun-drenched ski bowl with comfortable slopes and a low-key family ambience.

Dining

For details and price-category definitions, *see* Dining in Staying in Switzerland, *above.*

$ **Wirthschaft zum Löwen.** Though there's plenty of French, Swiss, and
★ Austrian influence, Liechtenstein has a cuisine of its own, and this is the place to try it. In a wood-shingle farmhouse on the Austrian border, the friendly Biedermann family serves tender homemade *Schwartenmagen* (the pressed-pork mold known unfortunately as headcheese in English), pungent *Sauerkäse* (sour cheese), and *Käseknöpfli* (cheese dumplings), plus lovely meats and the local crusty, chewy bread. *Schellenberg, tel. 075/3731162. Reservations advised. V.*

Dining and Lodging

For details and price-category definitions, *see* Dining and Lodging *in* Staying in Switzerland, *above.*

$$$$ **Real.** Surrounded by slick, new decor, you'll find rich, old-style Aus-
★   trian-French cuisine in all its buttery glory, prepared these days by Mar-
       tin Real, son of the unpretentious former chef, Felix Real—who, in his
       retirement, presides over the 20,000-bottle cellar. The menu offers
       game, seafood, generous seasonal salads, soufflés, and an extraordi-
       nary wine list. Downstairs is a more casual Stübli for those who don't
       feel like getting dressed up. There are 11 small but fresh decked rooms
       upstairs, with new tile baths. *Städtle 21, Vaduz, tel. 075/2322222. Reser-
       vations advised. AE, DC, MC, V.*

$$ **Engel.** Directly on the main tourist street, its café bulging with bus-tour
       crowds, this simple hotel/restaurant manages to maintain a local, com-
       fortable ambience. The Huber family oversees the easygoing pub down-
       stairs; the restaurant upstairs serves Chinese food. *Städtle 13, Vaduz,
       tel. 075/2320313, fax 075/2331159. 17 rooms with bath. Facilities:
       restaurant, café. AE, DC, MC, V.*

$ **Alpenhotel.** Well above the mists of the Rhine in sunny Malbun, this
       82-year-old chalet has been remodeled and a modern wing added. The
       old rooms are small and cozy; the higher-priced new rooms are mod-
       ern and spare. The Vögeli family's welcoming smiles and good food
       have made it a local institution. *Triesen, FL 9497, Maldun, Tel. 075/
       2631181, fax 075/2639646. 25 rooms with bath. Facilities: restaurant,
       café, indoor pool. AE, DC, MC, V.*

Lodging

For details and price-category definitions, *see* Lodging *in* Staying in
Switzerland, *above.*

$$$$ **Park-Hotel Sonnenhof.** A garden oasis commanding a superb view
       over the valley and mountains beyond, this hillside retreat in a resi-
       dential district offers discreet luxury minutes from downtown Vaduz.
       Some rooms open directly onto the lawns; others have balconies. The
       excellent restaurant, open only to guests, offers a five-course tasting
       menu for 100 SF, as well as more modest entrés. *Mareestr. 29, Vaduz
       FL-9490, tel. 075/2321192, fax 075/2320053. 29 rooms with bath.
       Facilities: restaurant. indoor pool, sauna. AE, DC, MC, V.*

GENEVA

Arriving and Departing

By Plane

Cointrin (tel. 022/7993111), Geneva's airport, is served by several air-
lines that fly directly to the city from New York; Washington, DC;
Toronto; or London. Swissair also has flights from Chicago and Los
Angeles. Check with individual airlines for their schedules.

Swissair ticket holders departing from Cointrin can check their lug-
gage through to the airplane from 120 rail and postbus stations, and
also get their boarding passes at eight train stations.

BETWEEN THE AIRPORT AND DOWNTOWN
Cointrin has a direct rail link with Cornavin (tel. 022/7316450), the
city's main train station, which is in the center of town. Trains run about
every 10 minutes from 5:30 AM to midnight. The trip takes about six
minutes, and the fare is 5 SF for second class.

There is regular city bus service from the airport to the center of
Geneva. The bus takes about 20 minutes, and the fare is 3 SF. Some
hotels have their own bus service.

Taxis, though plentiful, are very expensive, charging at least 30 SF to the city center. Tips are expected only for luggage.

By Train

All services—domestic and international—use Cornavin Station in the center of the city. For information, dial 022/7316450.

By Bus

Buses generally arrive at and depart from the bus station at Place Dorcière, behind the English Church in the city center.

By Car

Since Geneva sits on France's doorstep, entry from France, just a few minutes away, is very convenient. Or enter from the north via Lausanne.

Getting Around

By Bus and Streetcar

There are scheduled services by local buses and trains every few minutes on all routes. Before you board, you must buy your ticket from the machines at the stops (they have English instructions). For 2 SF you can use the system for one hour, changing as often as you like. Save money and buy a ticket covering unlimited travel all day within the city center for 6 SF. If you have a **Swiss Pass,** you can travel free (*see* Getting Around Switzerland by Train, *above*).

By Taxi

Taxis are extremely expensive; use them only if there's no alternative. There is a 5 SF minimum charge per passenger just to get into the cab plus a charge of 2 SF per kilometer.

Guided Tours

Orientation Tours

Bus tours around Geneva are operated by **Key Tours** (tel. 022/7314140). They leave from the bus station in place Dorcière, behind the English Church, at 2 (also at 10 AM in high season). These tours, which involve some walking in the Old Town, last about two hours and cost 27 SF for adults, 14 SF for children under 14.

Special-Interest Tours

The United Nations organizes tours around the Palais des Nations. Take Bus 8 or F past Nations to the Appia stop. Enter by the Pregny Gate in the avenue de la Paix. Tours, lasting about an hour, are given regularly from January through March and November to mid-December, weekdays 10–noon and 2–4; April through June, September, and October, daily 10–noon and 2–4; July and August, daily 9–noon and 2–6. They cost 8 SF for adults, 3.50 SF for children 6–18.

The tourist office will provide you with an audio-guided tour (in English) of the Old Town that covers 26 points of interest, complete with map, cassette, and player; rental is 10 SF. A refundable deposit of 50 SF is required.

Excursions

There are bus excursions from Geneva to Lausanne, Montreux, the Mont Blanc area, the Jura, and the Bernese Oberland. They vary considerably according to the weather and time of year, so inquire locally.

Boat excursions vary for the same reasons. When the weather is good, take one of the delightful day trips that stop at some of the waterside villages on the vineyard-fringed lake; some trips also pass by or stop at the 13th-century Château de Chillon, the inspiration for Byron's *The*

Prisoner of Chillon. Full details are available from **Mouettes Genevoises** (tel. 022/7322944), **Swissboat** (tel. 022/7367935), **Compagnie de Navigation** (tel. 022/3112521), or from the tourist office.

Tourist Information

The **Office du Tourisme de Genève** (Cornavin Station, tel. 022/7385200; open mid-Sept.–mid-June, Mon.–Sat. 9–6; mid-June–mid-Sept., weekdays 8–8, weekends 8–6). For information by mail, contact the administration at 1 rue de la Tour de l'Ile, Case Postale 5230, CH-1211 Genève. **Thomas Cook** (64 rue de Lausanne, tel. 022/7324555).

Exploring Geneva

Draped at the foot of the Jura and the Alps on the westernmost tip of Lake Geneva (or Lac Léman, as the natives know it), Geneva is the most cosmopolitan and graceful of Swiss cities and the stronghold of the French-speaking territory. Just a stone's throw from the French border and 160 kilometers (100 miles) or so from Lyon, its grand mansarded mansions stand guard beside the River Rhône, where yachts bob, gulls dive, and Rolls-Royces purr beside manicured promenades. The combination of Swiss efficiency and French savoir faire gives the city a chic polish, and the infusion of international blood from the United Nations adds a heterogeneity that is rare in cities with a population of only 160,000.

Headquarters of the World Health Organization and the International Red Cross, Geneva has always been a city of humanity and enlightenment, offering refuge to writers Voltaire, Hugo, Dumas, Balzac, and Stendhal, as well as to religious reformers Calvin and Knox. Byron, Shelley, Wagner, and Liszt all fled from scandals to Geneva's sheltering arms.

A Roman seat for 500 years (from 120 BC), then home to early Burgundians, Geneva flourished under bishop-princes into the 11th century, fending off the greedy dukes of Savoy in conflicts that lasted into the 17th century. Under the guiding fervor of Calvin, Geneva rejected Catholicism and became a stronghold of Protestant reforms. In 1798 it fell to the French, but joined the Swiss Confederation as a canton in 1815, shortly after Napoleon's defeat. The French accent remains nonetheless.

Numbers in the margin correspond to points of interest on the Geneva map.

❶ Start your walk from Gare de Cornavin (Cornavin Station) and head down the rue du Mont-Blanc to the **Pont du Mont-Blanc,** which spans the westernmost point of Lac Léman as it squeezes back into the Rhône. From the middle of the bridge (if it's clear) you can see the snowy peak of Mont Blanc itself, and from March through October you'll have a fine view of the **Jet d'Eau,** Europe's highest fountain, gushing 475 feet into the air.

❷ Back at the foot of the bridge, turn right onto quai du Mont-Blanc to reach the **Monument Brunswick,** the high-Victorian tomb of a duke of Brunswick who left his fortune to Geneva in 1873. Just north are the city's grandest hotels, overlooking a manicured garden walk and the embarkation points for excursion boats. If you continue north a considerable distance through elegant parks and turn inland on the avenue ❸ de la Paix, you'll reach the enormous **International Complex,** where the **Palais des Nations** houses the European seat of the United Nations.

(You can also reach it by taking Bus 8 or F from the train station. For guided tour information, *see* Special-Interest Tours, *above*.)

Or turn left from the Pont du Mont-Blanc and walk down the elegant
4 quai des Bergues. In the center of the Rhône is the **Ile Rousseau** (Rousseau Island), with a statue of the Swiss-born philosopher. Turn
5 left onto the **Pont de l'Ile,** where the tall Tour de l'Ile, once a medieval prison, houses the tourist office. Turn left again and cross the place Bel-Air, the center of the business and banking district, and follow the
6 rue de la Corraterie to the **place Neuve.** Here you'll see the **Grand Théâtre,** which hosts opera, ballet, and sometimes the Orchestre de la Suisse Romande (it also performs at nearby Victoria Hall), and the **Conservatoire de Musique.** Also at this address is the **Musée Rath,** with top-notch temporary exhibitions. *Tel. 022/3105270. Admission and hours vary with exhibition; check local listings.*

Above the ancient ramparts on your left are some of the wealthiest old homes in Geneva. The Parc des Bastions, behind imposing gates, is the
7 site of Geneva University. Keep left until you see the famous **Monument de la Réformation,** which pays homage to such Protestant pioneers as Bèze, Calvin, Farel, and Knox. Passing the uphill ramp and continuing to the farther rear gate, take the park exit just beyond the monument and turn left on the rue St-Leger, passing through the ivy-covered arch and winding into the **Vieille Ville,** or Old Town.

When you reach the ancient place du Bourg-de-Four, once a Roman
8 forum, turn right on rue des Chaudronniers and head for the **Musée d'Art et Histoire,** with its fine collection of paintings, sculpture, and archaeological relics. *2 rue Charles-Galland, tel. 022/3114340. Admission free. Open Tues.–Sun. 10–5.*

9 Just beyond are the spiraling cupolas of the **Eglise Russe** (Russian
10 Church) and the **Collection Baur** of Oriental arts. *8 rue Munier-Romilly, tel. 022/3461729. Admission: 5 SF. Open Tues.–Sun. 2–6.*

Alternatively, from the place du Bourg-de-Four, head left up any num-
11 ber of narrow streets and stairs toward the **Cathédrale St-Pierre,** with its schizophrenic mix of Classical and Gothic styles. Under its nave (entrance outside) is concealed one of the biggest **archaeological digs** in Europe, a massive excavation of the cathedral's early Christian predecessors, now restored as a stunning maze of backlit walkways over mosaics, baptisteries, and ancient foundations. *Tel. 022/7385650. Admission to site: 5 SF. Open Tues.–Sun. 10–1 and 2–6.*

12 Calvin worshiped in the cathedral; he made the **Temple de l'Auditoire,** a small Gothic church just south of the cathedral toward place du Bourg-de-Four, into his lecture hall, where he taught missionaries his doctrines of reform. *Place de la Taconnerie, tel. 022/7385650. Open Oct.–May, weekdays 9–noon and 2–5, Sat. 9:30–12:30 and 2–5, Sun. 2–5; June–Sept., weekdays 9–noon and 2–6, Sat. 9:30–12:30 and 2–6, Sun. 2–6.*

Behind the Temple de l'Auditoire, on the rue de l'Hôtel de Ville, is the
13 16th-century **Hôtel de Ville,** where in 1864, in the Alabama Hall, the Geneva Convention was signed by 16 countries, laying the foundations for the International Red Cross. *Individual visits by request. Guided group tours by advance arrangement, tel. 022/3272202.*

The winding, cobbled streets leading from the cathedral down to the modern city are lined with antiques shops, galleries, and unique but often expensive boutiques. The medieval Grand' Rue is the oldest in Geneva, the rue de l'Hôtel de Ville features lovely 17th-century homes,

1092

Cathédrale
St-Pierre, **11**
Collection Baur, **10**
Confédération-
Centre, **15**
Eglise Russe, **9**
Hôtel de Ville, **13**
Ile Rousseau, **4**
International Com-
plex, **3**
Jardin Anglais, **16**
Maison Tavel, **14**
Monument
Brunswick, **2**
Monument de la
Réformation, **7**
Musée d'Art et His-
toire, **8**
Place Neuve, **6**
Pont de l'Ile, **5**
Pont du Mont-Blanc, **1**
Temple de
l'Auditoire, **12**

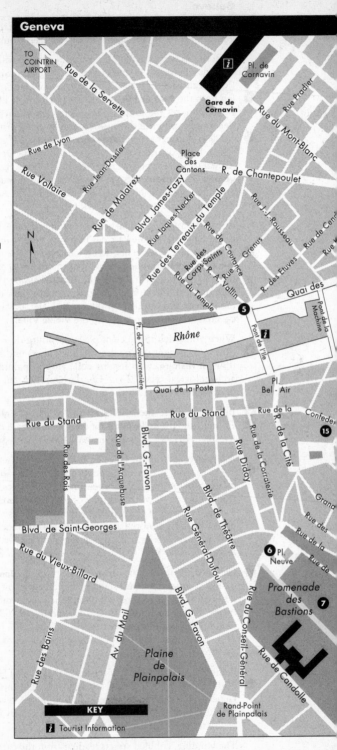

Geneva

Rue de Berne
Rue Rossi
Rue des Pâquis
Rue Ph. Plantamour

3

Rue des Alpes

Pl. des
Alpes

Rue Adhémar-Fabri

2

Square du
Mont-Blanc

Quai du Mont-Blanc

Lac Léman

0   220 yards
0   200 meters

endrier
Rue du
Mont-Blanc

e Kléberg

Pl. des
Bergues

1

Bergues

Pont des

Bergues

Pont du Mont-Blanc

4

Ile
Rousseau

Promenade du Lac

Quai Gustav-Ador

Rue du lac

Pl. de la
Fusterie

Rue du Rhône

Pl. du
Port

Jardin
Anglais

16

Quai Général - Guisan

R. de la Scie

Rue Muzy

Place de
Molard

Pl.
Longemalle

R. des Eaux-Vives

eration R. du Marché

Rue de la Croix d'Or

Rue de Rive

Rue Versonnex

Rue de la Rôtisserie

Rue d'Italie

Rue P.-Fatio

Pl. des
Eaux
Vives

Ave. Picet de
Rochemont

Rue Jean-Calvin

nd-Rue

Rue de la Fontaine

Blvd. Helvétique

Pl. du Pré-
l'Évêque

14

Rue du Puits
St-Pierre

11

Rue Verdaine

Rond-Point
de Rive

Rue de la Terrassière

Granges

Treille

Rue de l'Hôtel de Ville

12

13

Rue des
Chaudronniers
Pl. du Bourg-
de-Four

Rue Ferdinand-Hodler

R. d. Glacis-de-Rive

R. A. Lachenal

la Croix-Rouge

8

Rue Jaques-Dalcroze

Rue Charles-Galland

Rue Toepffer

R. Sturm

Route de

Rue de Villereuse

St-Léger R. de l'Athénée

9

Malagnou

Blvd. Jaques-Dalcroze

Blvd. Helvétique

R. Munier
Romilly

Place
Emile-Gayénot

Rue
des Bastions

Cours

-le-Fort

-le-Fort

Blvd. des
Tranchées

10

and the rue Calvin has noble mansions of the 18th century (No. 11 is on the site of Jean Calvin's house). No. 6 on the rue du Puits-St-Pierre ⓮ is the **Maison Tavel,** the oldest building in town and home of a vivid, intimate re-creation of daily life and urban history. *Tel. 022/3102900. Admission free. Open Tues.–Sun. 10–5.*

Down the hill, plunge back into the new city and one of the most luxurious shopping districts in Europe, which stretches temptingly between the quai Général-Guisan, rue du Rhône, rue de la Croix d'Or, and rue du Marché. It's tough enough to resist top-name *prêt-à-porter* (ready-to-wear clothing), dazzling jewelry and watches, luscious chocolates, and luxurious furs and leathers, but the glittering boutiques of the new ⓯ three-story **Confédération-Centre**—where all the above are concentrated with a vengeance—could melt the strongest resolve. Escape across the quai, head back toward the lake, and come to your senses ⓰ in the **Jardin Anglais,** where the famous floral clock will tell you that it's time to stop.

Dining

Perch fresh from Lac Léman, cream-sauced *omble chevalier* (a kind of salmon trout), Lyonnaise *cardon* (a celerylike vegetable often served in casseroles), pigs' feet, and the famous cheese fondue are specialties of this most French of Swiss cities. Be warned: Many restaurants close on weekends. For details and price-category definitions, *see* Dining *in* Staying in Switzerland, *above.*

$$$$ **Le Béarn.** This elegant and formal little Empire-style restaurant, dressed ★ up with pretty porcelain and crystal, features modern, light, and creative cuisine: ravioli stuffed with Scotch salmon and oysters, preserved rabbit in green mustard sauce, and any number of truffle specialties, including a spectacular truffle soufflé. There are excellent Swiss and French wines. *4 quai de la Poste, tel. 022/3210028. Reservations required. AE, MC, V. Closed Sun. No lunch Sat.*

$$$$ **Les Continents.** It's often a shock to find exceptional restaurants in modern business hotels, but this one—at the base of the Inter-Continental's 18 stories—serves contemporary French cuisine prepared by Irish super-chef Tommy Byrne. Try the warm salad of scallops with Oriental spices, pigeon pie, or grilled foie gras. All the international heads of state have met here during the peace conferences of the past 25 years. *7–9 ch. du Petit-Saconnex, tel. 022/7346091. Reservations required. AE, DC, MC, V. Closed Sat. No dinner Sun.*

$$$ **La Cassolette.** Located in the heart of Carouge, the picturesque *cité sarde* ★ (Sardinian city) of old houses, tiny streets, and ancient courtyards, this modern and colorful upscale bistro features the imaginative cuisine of young chef Réné Fracheboud. Novel specialties—salmon and zucchini with dried tomatoes and curry oil, or veal sweetbreads and duck liver in bitter cocoa and Arabian coffee—are served on Miami-bright triangular platters, in high contrast to the very pink decor. *31 rue Jacques Dalphin, Carouge, tel. 022/3420318. Reservations advised. No credit cards. Closed weekends.*

$$$ **La Mère Royaume.** Only in Geneva could you find good, classic French cooking served in a pseudo-historic setting under the careful direction of a charming Italian couple. Even the name is Genevois: La Mère Royaume was a kind of Genevois Joan of Arc, who in 1602 repulsed the army of the duke of Savoy by dumping hot soup on the soldiers' heads. The formal main restaurant serves French standards—duck liver with raspberries, rack of lamb with garlic confit—but the rustic bistro offers inexpensive plats du jour. *9 rue des Corps-Saints, tel. 022/7327008. Reservations advised. AE, DC, MC, V. Closed Sun. No lunch Sat.*

$$ Boeuf Rouge. Despite its kitschy decor this cozy and popular spot de-
★ livers the real thing: rich, unadulterated Lyon cuisine, from the bacon, egg, and greens *salade Lyonnaise* to the homemade pistachio sausage with lentil salad; *boudin noir* (blood sausage) with apples; *andouillettes* (spicy pork sausages) in mustard sauce; and authentic *tarte tatin* (the French version of apple pie). *17 rue Alfred-Vincent, tel. 022/7327537. Reservations advised. V. Closed weekends.*

$$ La Favola. Run by a young Ticinese couple from Locarno, this quirky
★ little restaurant may be the most picturesque in town. The tiny dining room, at the top of a vertiginous spiral staircase, strikes a delicate balance between rustic and fussy, with its lace window panels, embroidered cloths, polished parquet, and rough-beamed ceiling sponge-painted in Roman shades of ochre and rust. The food finds the same delicate balance between country simple and city chic: carpaccio with olive paste or white truffles, rabbit in Gorgonzola. *15 rue Jean Calvin, tel. 022/3117437. Reservations advised. MC, V. Closed weekends.*

$$ Le Pied-de-Cochon. While visiting antiques shops and art galleries in the Vielle Ville, stop for lunch or supper in this old bistro, which retains its original beams and zinc-top bar. Crowded, noisy, smoky, lively, it faces the Palais de Justice and shelters famous lawyers who plead celebrated causes; there are artists and workers as well. The good, simple fare includes *pieds de cochon* (pigs' feet), of course, either grilled, with mushrooms, with lentils, or *désossés* (boned), as well as simple Lyonnais dishes. *4 pl. du Bourg-de-Four, tel. 022/3104797. Reservations advised. AE, DC, MC, V. Closed weekends.*

$ Les Armures. In the picturesque and historic hotel at the summit of the
★ Old Town (*see* Lodging, *below*) and two steps from the Cathédrale St-Pierre, this atmospheric restaurant has several dining halls, all decorated with authentic arms from the Middle Ages. The broad menu of Swiss specialties ranges from fondue to *choucroute* (sauerkraut) to Rösti, but some of the dishes are pure Genevois. There also are inexpensive pizzas and a good selection of salads and fruit tarts. Everyone comes here, from workers to politicians. *1 rue du Puits-St-Pierre, tel. 022/3103442. Reservations advised. AE, DC, MC, V.*

$ Taverne de la Madeleine. Tucked into the commercial maze between
★ the Rue de la Croix d'Or and the Old Town, by l'Eglise de la Madeleine, this casual, alcohol-free café claims to be the oldest eatery in Geneva. It's run by the city's temperance league, and thus loses the business clientele who insist on a pitcher of Fendant with their meals: All the more room for you to relax over homemade choucroute, perch, or fresh-baked fruit tarts in the charming Victorian dining room upstairs. There are big, fresh salads, vegetable plates, and a variety of loose-leaf teas. *20 rue Toutes-âmes, tel. 022/3106070. Reservations advised. No credit cards.*

Lodging

For details and price-category definitions, *see* Lodging *in* Staying in Switzerland, *above.*

$$$$ Beau-Rivage. Hushed and genteel, this grand old Victorian palace has been largely restored to its 1865 splendor: It's all velvet, parquet, and frescoes, and there's a marble fountain in the lobby. Front rooms take in magnificent Right Bank views, as does the terrace restaurant on the first floor, over the prestigious French restaurant Le Chat Botté. In 1898, Empress Elizabeth of Austria died here after being stabbed only 300 feet away. *13 quai du Mont-Blanc, CH-1201, tel. 022/7310221, fax*

022/7389847. *115 rooms with bath. Facilities: 2 restaurants, bar, café, in-room VCRs. AE, DC, MC, V.*

$$$$ **Le Richemond.** Under the management of the Armleder family since
★ 1875, this Right Bank luxury landmark maintains its Victorian presence without looking like a museum. Nor does it feel like one: This is a lively, thriving, contemporary inn, proud of recent guests (Michael Jackson) as well as past ones (Colette, Miró, Chagall). Only the restaurant Le Gentilhomme indulges in museumlike conservatism: Amid pompous red velvet, crystal, and gilt, you can indulge in a meal Escoffier would have relished. There's classic but showy French cuisine, old wines, brandy, cigars, and your share of the 8 kilos of caviar they serve every day. *Jardin Brunswick, CH-1211, tel. 022/7311400, fax 022/7316709. 98 rooms with bath. Facilities: 2 restaurants, bar, café, hair salon. AE, DC, MC, V.*

$$$ **Les Armures.** In the heart of the Old Town, this 17th-century architectural treasure has been restored; now its charming original stonework, frescoes, and stenciled beams accompany impeccable modern comforts. Its few rooms are intimate, combining appropriate Old World furnishings with slick marble baths. Its casual restaurant is an Old Town must (*see* Dining, *above*). Approach by car can be difficult, and the nearest parking is three blocks away. *1 rue du Puits-St-Pierre, CH-1204, tel. 022/3109172, fax 022/3109846. 28 rooms with bath. Facilities: restaurant, bar, in-room VCRs. AE, DC, MC, V.*

$$$ **Metropole.** Built in 1855, lent to the city of Geneva to house Red Cross
★ archives for prisoners of war and now lovingly restored by its management of 27 years, the Metropole has as much riverside splendor as its Right Bank sisters—at a lower price. There's a relaxed, unfussy ambience despite the grand scale, with leather and hunting prints mixed in with discreet pastels. Riverside rooms are noisier, over traffic, but the view compensates; ask for the quieter third or fourth floors. It's seconds from the best shopping and minutes from the Old Town. *34 quai Général-Guisan, CH-1204, tel. 022/3111344, fax 022/3111350. 140 rooms with bath. Facilities: 2 restaurants, bar, café. AE, DC, MC, V.*

$$ **Strasbourg-Univers.** A stylish oasis in the slightly sleazy train-station neighborhood, this just-renovated spot offers sleek decor, convenience, and four-star quality at a three-star price. The new look is marble and faux exotic wood; a few older, less flashy rooms, redone eight years ago, still don't show the wear. *10 rue Pradier, CH-1201, tel. 022/7322562, fax 022/7384208. 58 rooms with bath or shower. Facilities: restaurant, bar, café. AE, DC, MC, V.*

$$ **Touring-Balance.** Renovations have given this 19th-century hotel a
★ modern, contemporary look; ask to stay in the slick, solid, high-tech rooms on the higher floors, where gallery-quality lithos hang. The restaurant offers a straightforward French menu, with entrées around 45 SF. You can't beat this location for shopping and sightseeing. *13 pl. Longemalle, CH-1204, tel. 022/287122, fax 022/3104045. 64 rooms with bath. Facilities: restaurant, café. AE, DC, MC, V.*

$ **De la Cloche.** This once-luxurious walk-up has tidy, tasteful new
★ decor that hasn't altered its period details, and the courtyard setting is so quiet you can hear birds in the garden. Good-size rooms with high ceilings share baths down the hall. The prices, which include breakfast, are still the lowest in town. *6 rue de la Cloche, CH-1201, tel. 022/7329481. 8 rooms without bath. Facilities: breakfast room. No credit cards.*

$ **Des Tourelles.** Once worthy of a czar, now host to the backpacking crowd, this fading Victorian offers enormous bay-windowed corner rooms, many with marble fireplaces, French doors, and views over the Rhône. Several rooms have been renovated to include a modern shower and toilet, and those on the street side have double-glazed windows to keep the street noise out. The staff is young and friendly, and the breakfast—included in the price of a night—is an all-you-can-eat backpacker's delight. *2 blvd. James-Fazy, CH-1201, tel. 022/7324423, fax 022/7327620. 25 rooms, some with shower. Facilities: breakfast room. AE, DC, MC, V.*

LUZERN

Arriving and Departing

By Plane
The nearest international airport is **Kloten** in **Zürich**, approximately 54 kilometers (33 miles) from Luzern. **Swissair** flies in most often from the United States and the United Kingdom. Easy rail connections, departing hourly, whisk you on to Luzern within 50 minutes.

By Car
It's easy to reach Luzern from Zürich by road, approaching from national expressway N3 south, connecting to N4 via the secondary E41, in the direction of Zug, and continuing on N4 to the city. Approaching from the southern, St. Gotthard Pass route, or after cutting through the Furka Pass by rail ferry, you descend below Andermatt to Altdorf, where a view-stifling tunnel sweeps you through to the shores of the lake and on to the city. Arriving from Basel in the northwest, it's a clean sweep by N2 into Luzern.

By Train
Luzern functions as a rail crossroads, with express trains connecting hourly from Zürich and every two hours from Geneva, the latter with a change at Bern. For rail information, call the station (tel. 041/1573333).

Getting Around

Luzern's modest scale allows you to explore most of the city easily on foot, but you will want to resort to mass transit to visit far-flung attractions like the Verkehrshaus (Swiss Transport Museum) and nearby Alpine viewpoints.

By Bus
The city bus system offers easy access throughout the urban area. If you're staying in a Luzern hotel, you will be eligible for a special **Guest-Ticket,** offering unlimited rides for two days for a minimal fee of 5 SF.

By Taxi
Given the small scale of the Old Town and the narrowness of most of its streets, taxis can prove a pricey encumbrance.

By Boat
It's a crime to see this city and the surrounding mountainous region only from the shore; some of its most impressive landscapes can be seen from the decks of one of the cruise ships that ply the Vierwaldstättersee (Lake Luzern). The boats of the Schiffahrtsgesellschaft des Vierwaldstättersee (tel. 041/404540) operate on a standardized, mass-transit-style schedule, crisscrossing the lake and stopping at scenic resorts and historic sites. Rides are included in a Swiss Pass or Swiss Boat Pass (*see* Getting Around in Switzerland, *above*).

Important Addresses and Numbers

Tourist Information

The city tourist office, near the Bahnhof (Frankenstr. 1, tel. 041/517171), offers information April–October, weekdays 8:30–6, Saturday 9–5; May–October, Sunday 9–1 as well; and November–March, weekdays 8:30–noon and 2–6, Saturday 9–1. Another tourist information center has opened at Schweizerhofquai 2 (open May and Oct., weekdays 9–noon and 1–7, Sat. 9–noon and 1–4; June–Sept., weekdays 9–5, Sat. 9–4). There is also an accommodations service.

Emergencies

Police (tel. 117). **Medical, dental, and pharmacy referral** (tel. 111). **Auto breakdown:** Tourist Club of Switzerland (tel. 140), Swiss Automobile Club (tel. 041/231000).

Guided Tours

Orientation Tours

The Luzern tourist office offers a two-hour guided walking tour of Luzern, departing from the office daily at 9:30; from May through September, there are 2 PM tours as well. The 15 SF price includes a drink.

Excursions

You may want to take a high-altitude day trip to **Mount Pilatus, Mount Rigi,** or—if you're bound for the highest—the **Titlis,** above Engelberg. All can be accomplished by combination train and cog-railway travel, though to mount the Titlis you must complete the journey by a series of cable car rides. For information, check at the Central Switzerland regional tourist office (Verkehrsverband Zentralschweiz, Alpenstr. 1, Luzern, tel. 041/511891) or at the city tourist office. Boat and bus trips to William Tell country—**Altdorf** and **Bürglen**—make the most of both scenery and local legend.

Exploring Luzern

Where the River Reuss flows out of the Vierwaldstättersee, Luzern's old town straddles the narrowed waters with the greater concentration of city life lying on the river's right bank. To get a feel for this riverfront center, start at the right-bank end of the prominent **Kapell-brücke,** with its flanking water tower. Stay on this side for the moment and head down the **Rathausquai,** lined with hotels and cafés on the right, a sloping reinforced bank on the left. Facing the end of a modern bridge (the Rathaus-Steg) stands the **Altes Rathaus** (Old Town Hall), built between 1599 and 1606 in the late-Renaissance style.

Numbers in the margin correspond to points of interest on the Luzern map.

❶ Just to the right of the Rathaus, the **Am Rhyn-Haus** contains an impressive collection of late paintings by Picasso. *Furreng., tel. 041/511773. Admission: 6 SF adults, 3 SF students. Open Apr.–Oct., daily 10–6; Nov.–Mar., daily 11–1 and 2–4.*

Turn right and climb the stairs past the ornately frescoed **Zunfthaus zur Pfistern,** a guild hall dating from the late 15th and early 16th centuries, to the Kornmarkt, former site of the local grain market. Cross the square and cut left into the **Weinmarkt,** the loveliest of Luzern's several squares. Its Gothic central fountain depicts St. Mauritius, patron saint of warriors, and its surrounding buildings are flamboyantly frescoed in 16th-century style.

② Leave the square from its west end, turn right on Kramgasse, and cross the Mühlenplatz to the **Spreuerbrücke,** a narrow, weathered covered wooden bridge dating from 1408. Its interior gables frame a series of eerie, well-preserved paintings (by Kaspar Meglinger) of the Dance of Death; they date from the 17th century, though their style and inspiration—tracing to the plague that devastated Luzern and all of Europe in the 14th century—is medieval.

③ At the other end of the bridge, on the left bank, stands the stylish **Historisches Museum** (Historical Museum). Its exhibitions of city sculptures, Swiss arms and flags, and reconstructed rooms depict rural and urban life. The late-Gothic building was an armory, dating from 1567. *Pfisterg. 24, tel. 041/245424. Admission: 4 SF. Open Tues.–Fri. 10– noon and 2–5, weekends 10–5.*

TIME OUT Follow Baselstrasse west to a funicular that carries you up (2 SF) to the **Château Gütsch,** where you can have a drink on the panoramic terrace and take in a bird's-eye view of the old town, the river, and the fortification walls—a must for photographers.

④ From the end of the Spreuerbrücke, cut back upstream along Pfistergasse and turn left onto Bahnhofstrasse to reach the Baroque **Jesuitenkirche** (Jesuit Church), constructed 1667–78. Its symmetrical entrance is flanked by two onion-domed towers, added in 1893. Do not fail to go inside: Its vast interior, restored to mint condition, is a rococo explosion of gilt, marble, and epic frescoes.

⑤ Continue past the Rathaus-Steg bridge, but before you enter the **Kapellbrücke** (Chapel Bridge), take a look at its exterior from the right. It snakes diagonally across the water and, when it was built in the early 14th century, served as the division between the lake and the river. Its shingled roof and grand stone water tower (now housing a souvenir stand) are to Luzern what the Matterhorn is to Zermatt—but considerably more vulnerable, as a 1993 fire proved: Almost 80% of this fragile monument was destroyed, including many of the 17th-century paintings inside; restorations are still in progress. Still, if you walk the length of this dark, creaky landmark you'll see polychrome copies of the 112 gable panels painted by Heinrich Wägmann in the 17th century, depicting Luzern and Swiss history, stories of St. Leodegar and St. Mauritius, Luzern's patron saints, and coats of arms from local patrician families.

Now break away from the old town and work through thick pedestrian and bus traffic at Schwanenplatz to Haldenstrasse. Turn left on Zürichstrasse or Löwenstrasse and continue to **Löwenplatz,** which is dominated by an enormous conical wooden structure, like a remnant
⑥ of a Victorian world's fair. That's its spirit: The **Bourbaki-Panorama** was created between 1876 and 1878 as a genuine, step-right-up tourist attraction. The conical roof covers a sweeping, wraparound epic painting of the French Army of the East retreating into Switzerland at Verrières—a famous episode in the Franco-Prussian War. *Löwenpl., tel. 041/529942. Admission: 3 SF. Open May–Sept., daily 9–6; Mar.–Apr. and Oct., daily 9–5.*

Just beyond lies yet another 19th-century wonder, a Luzern landmark that is certainly one of the world's most evocative public sculptures:
⑦ the **Löwendenkmal** (Lion Monument). Designed by Danish sculptor Berthel Thorvaldsen and carved out of a sheer sandstone face by Lucas Ahorn of Konstanz, it's a simple image of a dying lion, his chin sagging on his shield, a broken stump of spear in his side. It commemo-

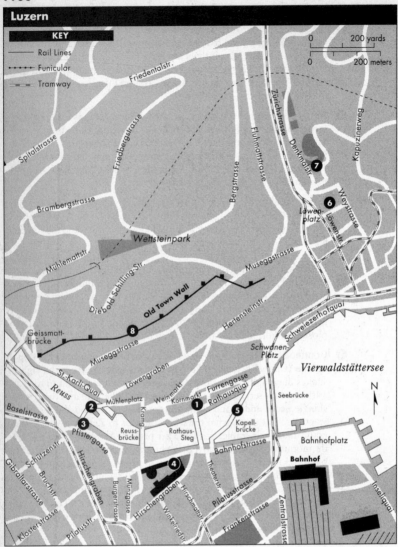

Luzern

KEY

— Rail Lines
•••• Funicular
╌╫╌ Tramway

0 — 200 yards
0 — 200 meters

Friedentalstr.

Spitalstrasse

Brambergstrasse

Friedbergstrasse

Mühlemattstr.

Wettsteinpark

Muleggstrasse

Diebold Schilling-Str.

Old Town Wall

Musegggstrasse

Hertensteinstr.

Bergstrasse

Fluhmattstrasse

Zürichstrasse

Denkmalstr.

Kapuzinerweg

❼

❻
Löwen-
platz

Weystrasse
Löwenstr.

Schweizerhofquai

Schwanen-
Platz

Vierwaldstättersee

N

Geissmatt-
brücke

❽

Reuss

St.-Karli-Quai

Baselstrasse

Pfistergasse

Mühlenplatz

Löwengraben

Kramg.

Weinmarkt

Kornmarkt

❷

❸

Reuss-
brücke

Rathaus-
Steg

❶

Furrengasse

Rathausquai

❺

Kapell-
brücke

Seebrücke

Bahnhofstrasse

Bahnhofplatz

Bahnhof

Schützenstr.

Gibraltarstrasse

Bruchstr.

Klosterstrasse

Pilotusstr.

Hirschengraben

Burgerstrasse

Münzgasse

Hirschengraben

❹

Winkelriedstr.

Hirschmatstr.

Theaterstr.

Pilatusstrasse

Frankenstrasse

Zentralstrasse

Inseliquai

Am Rhyn-Haus, **1**
Bourbaki-
Panorama, **6**
Historisches Mu-
seum, **3**
Jesuitenkirche, **4**
Kapellbrücke, **5**
Löwendenkmal, **7**
Spreuerbrücke, **2**
Zytturm, **8**

rates the 760 Swiss guards and their officers who died defending Louis XVI of France at the Tuileries in Paris in 1792.

Return down Löwenstrasse and, at Löwenplatz, turn right on Museggstrasse. This long street cuts through an original city gate and runs parallel to the **watchtowers** and **crenellated walls** of Old Luzern, constructed around 1400. The clock in the **Zytturm,** the fourth of the towers, was made in Basel in 1385 and still keeps time.

Off the Beaten Track

Not easily included in a walking tour of central Luzern but one of the city's (if not Switzerland's) greater attractions, the **Verkehrshaus** (Swiss Transport Museum) can be reached by steamer, car, or city bus. It's almost a world's fair in itself, with a complex of buildings and exhibitions both indoors and out, including dioramas, live demonstrations, and a "Swissorama" (360-degree screen) film about Switzerland. Every mode of transit is discussed, from stagecoaches and bicycles to jumbo jets and space capsules. *Lidostr. 5, tel. 041/314444. Admission: 15 SF adults, 8 SF children under 16. Open Mar.–Oct., daily 9–6; Nov.–Feb., weekdays 10–4, Sun. 10–5.*

Shopping

Luzern offers a good concentration of general Swiss goods: At **Sturzenegger** (Schwanenpl. 7, tel. 041/511958), you'll find fine St.-Gallen-made linens and embroidered niceties; at **Mühlebach & Birrer** (Kapellpl., tel. 041/516673) there's a selection of Alpen-style (although Austrian-made) Geiger clothing (boiled-wool jackets, edelweiss-embroidered sweaters) as well as Swiss-made handkerchiefs. **Schmid-Linder** (Denkmalstr. 9, tel. 041/514346) sells a comprehensive line of Swiss kitsch: cuckoo clocks, cowbells, embroidery, and a large stock of wood carvings from Brienz, in the Berner Oberland. **Innerschweizer Heimatwerk** (Franziskanerpl. 14, tel. 041/236944) sells nothing but local crafts—mostly contemporary rather than traditional—from handwoven items to ceramics and wooden toys. Watch dealers are unusually competitive, and the two enormous patriarchs of the business—**Gübelin** (Schweizerhofquai, tel. 041/515142) and **Bucherer** (Schwanenpl., tel. 041/437700) advertise heavily and offer inexpensive souvenirs to lure shoppers into their luxurious showrooms. Gübelin is the exclusive source for Audemars Piguet, Patek Philippe, and its own house brand; Bucherer represents Piaget and Rolex. An abundance of small shops carry Tissot, Rado, Corum, and others—but prices are controlled by the manufacturers, and discounts are rare. Watch for closeouts on out-of-date models.

Dining

Rooted in the German territory of Switzerland and the surrounding farmlands, Central Switzerland's native cuisine is down-home and hearty. Luzern takes pride in its *Kügelipaschtetli,* puff pastry nests filled with tiny veal meatballs, mushrooms, cream sauce, occasionally raisins, and bits of chicken, pork, or sweetbreads. Watch for lake fish such as *Egli* (perch), *Hecht* (pike), *Forelle* (trout), and *Felchen* (whitefish). Though most often served baked or fried, a Luzern tradition offers them sautéed and sauced with tomatoes, mushrooms, and capers. After your meal here, have a steaming mug of coffee laced with *Träsch,* a harsh schnapps blended from the dregs of other eaux-de-vie; the locals leave their spoons in their cups as they drink. For details and price-category definitions, *see* Dining *in* Staying in Switzerland, *above.*

$$$$ **Wilden Mann.** You may choose the ancient original Bürgerstube, all
★ dark beams and family crests, its origins as a rest-stop for St. Gotthard
travelers traced back to 1517; or you may opt for the more formal adjoining Liedertafel dining room, with wainscoting, vaulting, and candlelight. On either side, the menu and prices are the same (with
additional soup, salad, and sausage options in the Stube)—and the cooking is outstanding. *Bahnhofstr. 30, tel. 041/231666. Reservations advised. AE, DC, MC, V.*

$$$–$$$$ **La Vague (Hotel des Balances).** This chic combination upscale restau-
★ rant and casual bistro offers soigné decor, a shimmering riverside view,
and adventurous, worldly cuisine that features local fish. A typical three-
course dinner may include salmon carpaccio marinated with herbs, fol-
lowed by duck with port and fig sauce, topped off with a kirsch-doused
chestnut parfait. A house specialty is light, fresh fish fondue for two.
Weinmarkt, tel. 041/511851. Reservations advised. AE, DC, MC, V.

$$ **Galliker.** Step past the ancient facade into an all-wood room roaring
★ with local action, where Luzerners drink, smoke, and bask in their culi-
nary roots. Brisk, motherly waitresses serve the dishes Mutti used to
make: Fresh *Kutteln* (tripe) in rich white wine sauce with cumin seeds;
real *Kalbskopf* (chopped fresh veal head) served with heaps of green
onions and warm vinaigrette; authentic Luzerner Kügelipaschtetli; and
their famous simmered-beef pot-au-feu, served only on Tuesday,
Wednesday, and Saturday. *Schützenstr. 1, tel. 041/221002. Reservations advised. AE, MC, V. Closed Sun., Mon., and mid-July–mid-Aug.*

$$ **Rebstock/Hofstube.** Across from the Hofkirche and at the opposite end
of the culinary spectrum from Galliker, this up-to-date kitchen offers
modern, international fare, including rabbit, lamb, and organic vege-
tarian specialties. The lively bentwood brasserie hums with locals
lunching by the bar, while the more formal, old-style restaurant glows
with wood and brass under a low-beamed herringbone ceiling. Out-
door seating is available in the garden and on the terrace. *St.-Leode-
garstr. 3, tel. 041/4103581. Reservations advised. AE, DC, MC, V.*

$ **Zur Pfistern.** One of the architectural focal points of the Old Town wa-
terfront, this floridly decorated former guildhouse, whose origins can be
traced back to 1341, offers a good selection of moderate meals in addi-
tion to higher-priced standards. Lake fish and *pastetli* (Cornish pasty-
like meat pies made with puff pastry) are good local options. In summer
the small first-floor balcony may provide the best seat in town for a post-
card waterfront view. *Kornmarkt 4, tel. 041/513650. AE, DC, MC, V.*

Lodging

Luzern provides a convenient home base for excursions around the Vier-
waldstättersee and all over the region. Unlike most Swiss cities, Luzern
has high and low seasons, and drops prices considerably in winter. For
details and price-category definitions, *see* Lodging *in* Staying in Switzer-
land, *above.*

$$$$ **Chateau Gütsch.** Any antiquity in this "castle" built as a hotel in 1888
is strictly contrived, but honeymooners, groups, and determined ro-
mantics seeking out storybook Europe enjoy the Disneyland-like ex-
perience: the turrets and towers worthy of Mad Ludwig of Bavaria,
the cellars, crypts, and corridors lined with a hodgepodge of relics—
not to mention the magnificent hilltop site above Luzern, once a look-
out point, and the private forest beyond. An extravagant renovation,
reducing the number of fantasy-style rooms but enlarging them con-
siderably, has bumped this lodging-attraction into the deluxe cate-
gory. *Kanonenstr., CH-6003, tel. 041/220272, fax 041/220252. 49
rooms. Facilities: restaurant, outdoor pool. AE, DC, MC, V.*

$$$$ **Palace.** Brilliantly refurbished and subtly modernized to take in broader lake views, the Palace sports a classic look with a touch of postmodern. Built in 1906 and regularly updated, the hotel has a recently renovated fifth floor, and an entire sixth floor consists of spacious new rooms with views of the lake and the mountains. *Haldenstr. 10, CH-6003, tel. 041/502222, fax 041/516976. 185 rooms. Facilities: restaurant, bar, health club, 2 saunas, steam room, parking. AE, DC, MC, V.*

$$$ ★ **Des Balances.** Restored and renewed, outside and in, this riverfront property built in the 19th century on the site of an ancient guildhouse gleams with style. State-of-the-art tile baths, up-to-date pastel decor, and one of the best locations in town make this the slickest in its price class. Nearly every window frames a period scene outdoors, including the Chapel Bridge and the Jesuit Church. *Metzgerrainle 7, CH-6003, tel. 041/511851, fax 041/516451. 57 rooms with bath. Facilities: 2 restaurants, piano bar. AE, DC, MC, V.*

$$$ ★ **Wilden Mann.** Living up to its reputation, the city's best-known hotel offers its guests a gracious and authentic experience of Old Luzern. Joining several old houses that once were part of the town wall, the structure has been renewed to maintain its Reformation ambience, with stone, beams, brass, hand-painted tiles, and burnished wood everywhere. Standard rooms have a prim 19th-century look. *Bahnhofstr. 30, CH-6003, tel. 041/231666, fax 041/231629. 43 rooms. Facilities: 2 restaurants. AE, DC, MC, V.*

$$ **Des Alpes.** With a terrific riverfront location in the bustling heart of the Old Town, this historic hotel has been completely renovated inside to look like a laminate-and-vinyl chain motel. Rooms are generously proportioned, tidy, and sleek; front doubles, several with balconies, overlook the water and promenade. Cheaper back rooms face the Old Town. *Rathausquai 5, CH-6003, tel. 041/515825, fax 041/517451. 45 rooms with bath. Facilities: restaurant, café. AE, DC, MC, V.*

$$ ★ **Zum Weissen Kreuz.** Now renovated and upgraded, this former bargain hotel on the waterfront is slick, bright, and airtight, with tile, stucco, oak, and pine to soften the modern edges. Some rooms face the lake, others the Old Town. The restaurant, Al Forno, serves pasta and pizzas. *Furreng. 19, CH-6003, tel. 041/514040, fax 041/514060. 22 rooms with bath. Facilities: restaurant. AE, DC, MC, V.*

$ **Schlüssel.** On the Franziskanerplatz, with several rooms overlooking the Franciscan church and fountain, this spare, no-nonsense little lodging attracts young bargain hunters. It's a pleasant combination of tidy new touches (quarry tile, white paint) and antiquity: You can have dinner in a low, cross-vaulted "crypt" and admire the fine old lobby beams. *Franziskanerpl. 12, CH-6003, tel. 041/231061, fax 041/231021. 11 rooms, most with bath. Facilities: restaurant. MC, V.*

$ ★ **SSR Touristen.** Despite its friendly collegiate atmosphere, this cheery dormlike spot is anything but a backpackers' flophouse. It has a terrific setting on the Reuss, around the corner from the Old Town. Sleep in a dormitory room with 10 beds, or one of several rooms with four beds—some with bath, some without. *12 St. Karli Quai, CH-6003, tel. 041/512474, fax 041/528414. 100 beds. AE, DC, MC, V.*

The Arts

Luzern hosts the **International Music Festival** for three weeks in August every year. Performances take place at the **Kunsthaus** (Frohburgstr. 6, tel. 041/233880). For more information, contact Internationale Musikfestwochen (Postfach, CH-6002, Luzern, tel. 041/235272). The **Allgemeine Musikgesellschaft Luzern** (AML), the local orchestra in residence, offers a season of concerts from October through June, also in the Kunsthaus.

Nightlife

Bars and Lounges
Des Balances hotel has a hip, upscale piano bar (Metzgerrainle 7, tel. 041/511851), and **Château Gütsch** (Kanonenstr.) draws a sedate dinner-and-dancing crowd. **Mr. Pickwick** (Rathausquai 6, tel. 041/515927) is a Swiss version of an English pub.

Casinos
The most sophisticated nightlife in Luzern is found in the **Casino** (Haldenstr. 6, tel. 041/512751), on the northern shore by the grand hotels. You can play *boules* in the Gambling Room (5 SF federally imposed betting limit), dance in the **Babilonia** club, watch a strip show in the **Red Rose**, or have a Swiss meal in **Le Chalet** while watching a folklore display.

Discos
Flora Club (Seidenhofstr. 5, tel. 041/244444) mixes dancing with folklore shows.

Folklore
Besides the shows at the Casino and Flora Club, **Stadtkeller** (Sternenpl. 3, tel. 041/514733) transports you to the Valais Alps for cheese, yodeling, and dirndled dancers. **Nightboat** (Landungsbrücke 6, tel. 041/404540) sails every evening May through September at 8:45, offering drinks, meals, and a mid-cruise folklore show.

LUGANO

Arriving and Departing

By Plane
There are short connecting flights by **Crossair**—the Swiss domestic network—to Lugano Airport (tel. 091/505001) from Zürich, Geneva, Basel, and Bern, as well as from Paris, Nice, Rome, Florence, and Venice. The nearest intercontinental airport is at Milan, Italy, about 56 kilometers (35 miles) away.

BETWEEN THE AIRPORT AND DOWNTOWN
There is no longer a regular bus service between the local airport and central Lugano, 7 kilometers (4 miles) away; taxis, costing about 30 SF to the center, are the only option.

By Train
There's a train from Zürich seven minutes past every hour; the trip takes about three hours. If you're coming from Geneva, you can catch the Milan express at various times, changing at Domodossola and Bellinzona. Daytimes, there's a train 25 minutes past every hour from Milan's Centrale Station; the trip takes about 1½ hours. Always keep passports handy and confirm times with the SNTO. For train information in Lugano, tel. 091/226502.

By Car
There are fast, direct highways from Milan and from Zürich. If you are planning to come from Geneva, check the weather conditions with the automobile associations beforehand.

Getting Around

By Bus
Well-integrated services run regularly on all local routes. You must buy your ticket from the machine at the stop before you board.

By Train
With or without a Swiss Pass, get a **Regional Holiday Season Ticket** for Lugano from the tourist office. One of these gives unlimited free travel for seven consecutive days on most rail and steamer routes and a 50% or 25% discount on longer trips. It costs 96 SF for adults (88 SF for Swiss Pass holders) and 45 SF for children 6–16. The newest version offers any three out of seven days free on most routes, with 50% or 25% reductions on the remaining four days. It costs 70 SF for adults, 62 SF for Swiss Pass holders, and 30 SF for children.

By Taxi
Though less expensive than in Zürich or Geneva, taxis are still not cheap, with a 10 SF minimum. In a pinch, call 091/512121 or 091/519191.

By Boat
The **Navigation Company of Lake Lugano** (tel. 091/515223) offers cruise-boat excursions around the bay to the romantic fishing village of Gandria and toward the Villa Favorita. Use it like public transit, following a schedule and paying according to distance, or look into special tickets: Seven consecutive days' unlimited travel cost 50 SF, three days within a week cost 44 SF; an all-day pass costs 30 SF.

Guided Tours

The tourist office is the best source of information about hiking tours into the mountains surrounding Lugano; it offers several topographical maps and suggested itineraries. There are bus trips to Locarno, Ascona, Lake Como, Lake Maggiore, Milan, Venice, St. Moritz, Florence, the Alpine passes, and the Italian market in Como. A free guided walking tour of Lugano leaves the tourist office every Tuesday at 9:30 AM from April through October.

Tourist Information

Ente Turistico Lugano (Riva Albertolli 5, CH-6901, tel. 091/214664; open Oct.–June, weekdays 9–6; July–Sept., weekdays 9–6:30; April–Oct., Saturday 9–5).

Exploring Lugano

Its sparkling bay, with dark, conical mountains rising from the beautiful Lago di Lugano, has earned Lugano the nickname "Rio of the Old World." The largest city in the Ticino—the Italian-speaking corner of Switzerland—Lugano has not escaped some of the inevitable overdevelopment of a successful resort town. There's thick traffic, right up to the waterfront, much of it manic Italian-style, and it has more than its share of concrete waterfront high-rise hotels, with balconies skewed to claim rooms with a view no matter what the aesthetic cost.

But the view from the waterfront is unforgettable, the boulevards are fashionable, and the old quarter is still reminiscent of sleepy old towns in Italy. And the sacred *passeggiata*—the afternoon stroll to see and be seen that winds down every Italian day—asserts the city's true personality as a graceful, sophisticated Old World resort—not Swiss, not Italian . . . just Lugano.

Numbers in the margin correspond to points of interest on the Lugano map.

Start your walk under the broad porticoes of the tourist office and cross over to the tree-lined promenade, where you can stroll along the waterfront and take in stunning mountain views. Head left into the **Parco Civico,** with its cacti, exotic shrubs, and more than 1,000 varieties of roses. There's an aviary, a tiny "deer zoo," and a fine view of the bay from its peninsula. The **Villa Ciani,** temporarily closed for renovations, contains paintings and sculpture from Tintoretto to Giacometti.

There's also the canton's **Museo Cantonale di Storia Naturale** (Museum of Natural History), which contains exhibits on animals, plants, and mushrooms. *Viale Cattaneo 4, tel. 091/237827. Admission free. Open Tues.–Sat. 9–noon and 2–5.*

If you continue left along the waterfront, you'll find the **Lido,** with a stretch of sandy beach, several swimming pools, and a restaurant. *Admission: 5 SF adults, 2 SF children 2–14.*

Or follow the promenade right until you reach the **Imbarcadero Centrale,** where steamers launch into the bay, and turn inland to the **Piazza della Riforma,** the scene of Lugano's Italian culture, where the modish locals socialize in outdoor cafés. From here, enter the **Old Town** and follow the steep, narrow streets lined with chic Italian clothing shops and small markets offering pungent local cheeses and porcini mushrooms.

On the street of the same name, you'll find the **Cathedral San Lorenzo,** with its graceful Renaissance facade and noteworthy frescoes inside.

Then shop your way down the Via Nassa until you reach the **Church of Santa Maria degli Angioli** in Piazza Luini, started in 1455. Within, you'll find a splendid fresco of the *Passion and Crucifixion* by Bernardino Luini (1475–1532).

Across the street, the waterfront **Giardino Belvedere** (Belvedere Gardens) frame 12 modern sculptures with palms, camellias, oleanders, and magnolias. At the far end, there's **public bathing** on the Riva Caccia. *Admission (bathing): 5 SF, 3 SF children. Open mid-May–mid-Sept.*

If you want to see more of Lugano's luxurious parklands, take the funicular from the Old Town to the train station: Behind the station, deer greet you as you enter the floral **Parco Tassino.** Or take Bus 2 east to the San Domenico stop in Castagnola to reach the **Parco degli Ulivi** (Olive Park), where you can climb the olive-lined slopes of Monte Brè for views of the surrounding mountains.

The dust has finally settled at the **Villa Favorita,** owned by the art baron and *real* Baron Heinrich von Thyssen, and you'll find the villa not only completely renovated but also with a portion of its magnificent art collection back on the walls. Artists represented include Thomas Hart Benton, Giorgio de Chirico, Frederic Church, Lucien Freud, Edward Hopper, Franz Marc, Jackson Pollock, and Andrew Wyeth. *Strada Castagnola, tel. 091/516152. Admission: 14 SF. Open Easter–Oct., Fri.–Sun. 10–5; during special exhibitions, Tues.–Sun. 10–5.*

Dining

The Ticinese were once poor mountain people, so their cuisine shares the earthy delights of the Piemontese: polenta, gnocchi, game, and mushrooms. But as in all prosperous resorts, the mink-and-Vuarnets set draws the best in upmarket international cooking. Prix-fixe lunches are al-

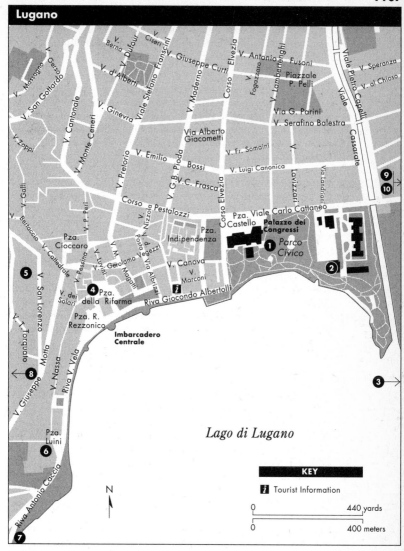

Lugano

Cathedral San
Lorenzo, **5**

Church of Santa
Maria degli Angioli, **6**

Giardino Belvedere, **7**

Lido, **3**

Museo Cantonale di
Storia Naturale, **2**

Parco Civico, **1**

Parco Tassino, **8**

Parco degli Ulivi, **9**

Piazza della
Riforma, **4**

Villa Favorita, **10**

most always cheaper, so dine as the Luganese do—before your siesta. That way you can sleep off the fruity local merlot wine before the requisite passeggiata. For details and price-category definitions, *see* Dining *in* Staying in Switzerland, *above*.

$$$$ Al Portone. With silver and lace dressing up the stucco and stone, the
★ settings are formal, but the ambience is strictly easy. Chef Roberto Galizzi pursues *nuova cucina* (nouvelle cuisine, Italian-style) with ambition and flair, putting local spins on classics: roast veal kidneys with balsamic vinegar, pasta with white beans and lobster, seafood carpaccio, or the simple luxury of creamed potatoes with white truffles. *Viale Cassarate 3, tel. 091/9235511, fax 091/9716505. Reservations required. AE, DC, MC, V. Closed Sun. and Mon.*

$$$$ Santabbondio. Ancient stone and terra-cotta blend with pristine pas-
★ tels in this upgraded grotto, where superb and imaginative new Franco-Italian dishes are served in intimate, formal little dining rooms and on a flower-filled terrace. Watch for lobster risotto, eggplant ravioli, or scallops in orange-basil sauce to confirm what locals assert—that chef and owner Martin Dalsass is the region's best. It's a cab ride from town, toward the airport, but worth the trip. *Via ai Grotti di Gentilino, Lugano/Sorengo, tel. 091/9932388, fax 091/9943237. Reservations advised. AE, DC, MC, V. Closed Mon. and first wk in Jan. No lunch Sat., no dinner Sun.*

$$$ Galleria. Though the setting aspires to formal hauteur, with contemporary appointments, modern art, and jacket-clad guests, family warmth and vigor peek through the chinks in the facade, and in the end this is a comfortable source of good, middle-class Italian cooking. *Via Vegezzi, tel. 091/9236288. Reservations advised. AE, DC, MC, V. Closed Sun.*

$$$ Locanda del Boschetto. The grill is the first thing you see in this no-
★ nonsense restaurant, a specialist in simple but sensational seafood *alla griglia* (grilled). Crisp linens contrast with rustic wood touches, and the low-key service is helpful and down-to-earth. *Via Boschetto 8, tel. 091/99442493. Reservations advised. AE, DC, MC, V. Closed Mon.*

$$ Al Barilotto. Despite its generic pizzeria decor and American-style salad
★ bar, this restaurant draws local crowds for grilled meats, homemade pasta, and wood-oven pizza. Take Bus 10 from the center. *Hôtel de la Paix, Via Calloni 18, tel. 091/9942331. Reservations advised. AE, DC, MC, V.*

$ La Tinera. This tiny tavern crowds loyal locals, tourists, and families
★ onto wooden benches for authentic regional specialties, hearty meats, and pastas. It's tucked down an alley off Via Pessina in the Old Town. Regional wine is served in traditional ceramic bowls. *Via dei Gorini 2, tel. 091/9235219. Reservations advised. AE, DC, MC, V.*

$ Sayonara. There's nothing Japanese about it: This is a modern urban pizzeria with several rooms that are crowded at lunchtime with a mix of tourists and shoppers. The old copper polenta pot automatically stirs polenta, which is offered in several combinations, one of them with mountain hare. *Via F. Soave 10, tel. 091/9220170. AE, DC, MC, V.*

Lodging

There are few inexpensive hotels in the downtown area, but a brief drive into the surrounding countryside increases your options. Since this is a summer resort, many hotels close for the winter, so call ahead. For details and price-category definitions, *see* Lodging *in* Staying in Switzerland, *above*.

$$$$ **Ticino.** In this warmly appointed, 16th-century house in the heart of
★ the Old Town, shuttered windows look out from every room onto a
glassed-in garden and courtyard, and vaulted halls are lined with art
and antiques. This member of the Romantik Hotels is steps away from
the funicular to the station. *Piazza Cioccaro 1, CH-6901, tel. 091/
9227772, fax 091/9236278. 23 rooms with bath. Facilities: restaurant.
AE, DC, MC, V.*

$$$$ **Villa Principe Leopoldo.** With exorbitant prices to match its Old World
★ service and splendor, this sumptuously appointed Relais et Château garden mansion sits on a hillside high over the lake. There is free transportation to the airport and town, and a 19-hole golf course 5 kilometers
away. *Via Montalbano 5, CH-6900, tel. 091/9858855, fax 091/9858825.
24 suites. Facilities: restaurant, bar, outdoor pool, health club, tennis
courts, hot tub, massage, sauna, free parking. AE, DC, MC, V.*

$$$ **Alba.** This solid little hotel, surrounded by landscaped grounds and
★ an interior that is lavish in the extreme, is ideal for lovers with a sense
of camp or honeymooners looking for romantic privacy. Mirrors, gilt,
plush, and crystal fill the public areas, and the beds are all ruffles and
swags. *Via delle Scuole 11, CH-6902, tel. 091/9943731, fax
091/9944523. 25 rooms with bath. Facilities: restaurant, bar. AE, DC,
MC, V.*

$$$ **Du Lac.** This discreet and simple hotel offers you more lakefront lux-
ury for your money than the glossier Grand Eden down the same beach.
All rooms face the lake, but the sixth floor is the quietest. The hotel has
a private swimming area on the lake. *Riva Paradiso 3, CH-6902, tel.
091/9941921, fax 091/9946173. 53 rooms with bath. Facilities: restaurant, bar, outdoor pool, massage, sauna. AE, DC, MC, V.*

$$$ **International au Lac.** This is a big, old-fashioned, friendly city hotel,
half a block from the lake, with many lake-view rooms. It's next to
Santa Maria degli Angioli, on the edge of the shopping district and the
Old Town. The restaurant serves primarily Italian fare, with a smat-
tering of continental dishes. *Via Nassa 68, CH-6901, tel. 091/9227541,
fax 091/9227544. 86 rooms with bath. Facilities: restaurant, outdoor
pool. AE, DC, MC, V. Closed Nov.–Mar.*

$$$ **Park-Hotel Nizza.** This former villa, modernized in 1974 and refurbished
★ every winter, affords panoramic views from its spot on the lower slopes
of San Salvatore; perched high above the lake, it's an uphill hike from
town. The mostly small rooms are decorated with antique reproductions; there is no extra charge for lake views. An ultramodern bar overlooks the lake, and a good restaurant serves vegetables (and even wine)
from its own garden—al fresco, when weather permits. There's a
weekly barbecue with the owners presiding. A shuttle provides service
to Paradiso. *Via Guidino 14, CH-6902, tel. 091/9941771, fax
091/9941773. 30 rooms with bath. Facilities: restaurant, bar, outdoor
pool. AE, DC, MC, V. Closed Nov.–Mar.*

$$ **San Carlo.** The San Carlo offers one of the better deals in a high-priced
town: It's small, clean, freshly furnished, and right on the main pedes-
trian shopping street, a block from the waterfront. It's also 150 yards
from the funicular that takes you to the railway station. There are no
frills, but the atmosphere is friendly. *Via Nassa 28, CH-6901, tel.
091/9227107, fax 091/9228022. 22 rooms with bath. Facilities: break-
fast room, free parking.*

$ **Flora.** Though it's one of the cheapest hotels in town, this 70-year-old,
★ family-owned lodging has been reasonably well maintained. The room
decor is minimal, a holdover from the '60s (red-orange prints, wood-
grain Formica), and the once-elegant dining hall has seen better days.
But some rooms have balconies, and there's a sheltered garden terrace
for balmy nights. *Via Geretta 16, CH-6902, tel. 091/9941671, fax*

091/9942738. 33 rooms with bath. Facilities: restaurant, bar, outdoor pool. AE, DC, MC, V.

$ **Zurigo.** Ideally placed behind the tourist office and handy to parks, shopping, and promenades, this spartan hotel near the Palais Congrès offers quiet comfort at rock-bottom rates, even in high season. Several rooms have full bathrooms. *Corso Pestalozzi 13, CH–6900, tel. and fax 091/9234343. 25 rooms. Facilities: breakfast room. No credit cards.*

BERN

Arriving and Departing

By Plane
Belp (tel. 031/9615516) is a small airport, 9 kilometers (6 miles) south of the city, with flights to and from most European capitals. A bus from the airport to the train station costs 12 SF, a taxi about 35 SF.

By Train
Bern is a major link between Geneva, Zürich, and Basel, with fast connections running usually every hour from the enormous central station. The high-speed French **Train de Grande Vitesse** (TGV) gets to Paris in 4½ hours.

By Car
The Geneva-Zürich expressway runs by Bern, with crossroads leading to Basel and Lugano as well.

Getting Around

By Bus and Tram
Bern is a small, concentrated city, and it's easy to get around on foot. There are 6½ kilometers (4 miles) of covered shopping arcades in the center. Bus and tram service is excellent, however, if you don't feel like walking. Fares range from 1.50 SF to 2.40 SF Buy individual tickets from the dispenser at the tram or bus stop; the posted map will tell you the cost. Tourist cards for unlimited rides are available at 5 SF for one day, 7 SF for two, and 10 SF for three. Buy them at the Bahnhof (train station) tourist office or from the public-transportation ticket office in the subway leading down to the main station (take the escalator in front of Loeb's department store and turn right through the Christoffel Tower). A **Swiss Pass** will allow you to travel free.

By Taxi
This extravagant alternative to walking costs between 6 SF and 15 SF across town.

Important Addresses and Numbers

Tourist Information
The tourist office is located at Bahnhofplatz (tel. 031/3116611); it's open June–Sept., daily 9–8:30; Oct.–May, Mon.–Sat. 9–6:30 and Sun. 10–5.

Embassies
U.S. (Jubiläumsstr. 93, tel. 031/3517011). **Canadian** (88 Kirchenfeldstr., tel. 031/3526381). **U.K.** (Thunstr. 50, tel. 031/3525021).

Emergencies
Police (tel. 117). **Ambulance** (tel. 144). **Doctor/Dentist** (tel. 3119211). **All-night pharmacy** (tel. 3119211).

Guided Tours

Walking Tours

A two-hour tour around the Old Town, covering all the principal sights, is offered by the tourist office from May to October, daily 10 and 2; from November to March, Saturday at 2; and in April, Monday to Saturday at 2 for 20F.

Excursions

Bern prides itself on its central location, and offers easy access to Zürich and Geneva as well as to the remote farmlands of the Bernese Mittelland, where you can visit the Emmental Valley. The most popular (though expensive) outing is up into the heights of the Jungfrau in the Alpine Bernese Oberland. The train passes through Interlaken, Lauterbrunne, Wengen, and Kleine Scheidegg to the Jungfraujoch, which, at 11,525 feet, has the highest rail station in Europe.

Exploring Bern

No cosmopolitan nonsense here: The local specialties are fatback and sauerkraut, the annual fair features the humble onion, and the president takes the tram to work. Walking down broad, medieval streets past squares teeming with farmers' markets and cafés full of shirt-sleeved politicos, you might forget that Bern is the federal capital—indeed, the geographic and political hub—of a sophisticated and prosperous nation.

It earned its pivotal position through a history of power and influence that dates from the 12th century, when Berchtold V of the Holy Roman Empire established a fortress on this gooseneck in the River Aare. By the 15th century the Bernese had overcome the Burgundians to expand their territories west to Geneva. Napoleon held them briefly—from 1798 until his defeat in 1815—but by 1848 Bern was back in charge, as the capital of the Swiss Confederation.

Today it's not the massive Bundeshaus (Capitol) that dominates the city, but the perfectly preserved arcades, the fountains, and the thick, sturdy towers of the Middle Ages. They're the reason UNESCO granted Bern World Landmark status, ranking it with the Pyramids and the Taj Mahal.

Numbers in the margin correspond to points of interest on the Bern map.

①② Start on the busy **Bahnhofplatz** in front of the grand old Schweizerhof hotel, facing the station. To your left is the **Heiliggeistkirche** (Church of the Holy Spirit), finished in 1729 and at odds with both the modern and the medieval in Bern. Head right up Bollwerk and turn right into Kleeplatz

③ and Hodlerstrasse, where you'll come to the **Kunstmuseum Bern** on your left. Originally dedicated to collecting Swiss art, it houses an exceptional group of works by Ferdinand Hodler, including some enormous, striking allegories; there are landscapes and portraits as well. The museum's pride—and its justified claim to fame—is its collection of more than 2,000 works by Paul Klee, who lived in Bern. *Hodlerstr. 8–12, tel. 031/3110944. Admission: 6 SF. Open Tues. 10–9; Wed.–Sun. 10–5.*

④ Head for the **Pfeiferbrunnen** (Bagpiper Fountain), the first of the city's many signature fountains, erected between 1539 and 1546, and the

⑤ **Käfigturm** (Prison Tower), which dates from the 13th and 14th centuries. There's a small museum of economic and cultural life inside. *Tel. 031/3112306. Admission free. Open Tues.–Fri. 9–1 and 2–6.*

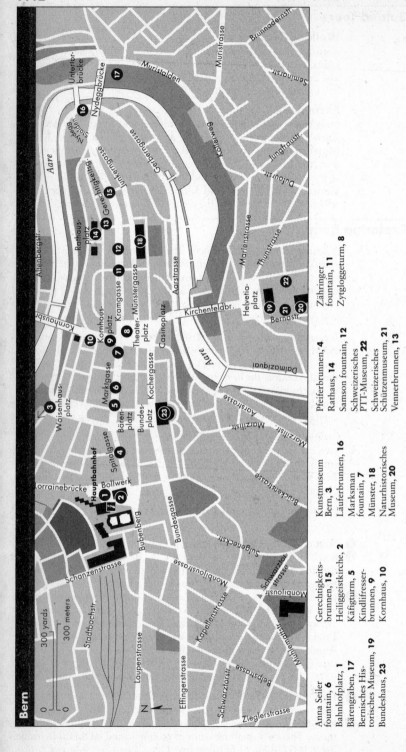

Bern

Anna Seiler fountain, **6**
Bahnhofplatz, **1**
Bärengraben, **17**
Bernisches Historisches Museum, **19**
Bundeshaus, **23**

Gerechtigkeitsbrunnen, **15**
Heiliggeistkirche, **2**
Käfigturm, **5**
Kindlifresserbrunnen, **9**
Kornhaus, **10**

Kunstmuseum Bern, **3**
Läuferbrunnen, **16**
Marksman fountain, **7**
Münster, **18**
Naturhistorisches Museum, **20**

Pfeiferbrunnen, **4**
Rathaus, **14**
Samson fountain, **12**
Schweizerisches PTT-Museum, **22**
Schweizerisches Schützenmuseum, **21**
Vennerbrunnen, **13**

Zähringer fountain, **11**
Zytgloggeturm, **8**

⑥ ⑦ Continue down Marktgasse past the **Anna Seiler** and **Marksman foun-**
⑧ **tains** to the **Zytgloggeturm** (clock tower), built as a city gate in 1191
but transformed by the addition of an astronomical clock in 1530. To
⑨ your right is the Theaterplatz, to your left the **Kindlifresserbrunnen** (Ogre
Fountain) and the Kornhausplatz, where you will see the imposing 18th-
⑩ century **Kornhaus** (granary), its magnificent vaulted cellar a popular
beer hall today. Now walk past the clock tower and observe the clock
from the east side. At four minutes before every hour, you can see the
famous mechanical puppet bears perform their ancient dance.

Continue down Kramgasse, past fine 18th-century houses and the
⑪ ⑫ **Zähringer** and **Samson fountains.** Turn left at the next small intersec-
⑬ tion and head for Rathausplatz, with its **Vennerbrunnen** (Ensign Foun-
⑭ tain), and the late-Gothic **Rathaus** (city hall), where the city and
cantonal governments meet.

Head back to the main route, here named Gerechtigkeitsgasse, and con-
⑮ tinue past the **Gerechtigkeitsbrunnen** (Justice Fountain) and lovely patrician houses. Artisan shops, galleries, and antiquaries line this leg of
the endless arcades. Turn left at the bottom and head down the steep
Nydegg Stalden through one of the city's oldest sections, past the
⑯ **Läuferbrunnen** (Messenger Fountain), to the River Aare. Here the
Nydeggkirche (Nydegg Church), on the right, was built from 1341 to
1571 on the foundations of Berchtold V's ruined fortress.

Cross the river by the **Untertorbrücke** (Bridge under the Gate), then
⑰ turn right and climb up to the **Nydeggbrücke.** Here you'll find the **Bären-**
graben (Bear Pits), where Bern keeps its famous live mascots. According to legend, Berchtold named the town after the first animal he
killed while hunting—a bear, since the woods were thick with them.

Now cross the bridge and head back into town, turning left up Junkern-
⑱ gasse to the magnificent Gothic **Münster** (cathedral), begun in 1421.
It features a fine portal (1490) depicting the Last Judgment, recently
restored and repainted in extravagant hues. There also are stunning
stained-glass windows, both originals and period reproductions.

Arty boutiques line the Münstergasse, leading to the **Casino,** which houses
a concert hall and restaurants, but no casino. If you head even farther
south (across the river yet again), you'll find Helvetiaplatz, a historic
⑲ square surrounded by museums. The **Bernisches Historisches Museum**
(Bern Historical Museum) has a prehistoric collection, 15th-century Flemish tapestries, and Bernese sculptures. *Helvetiapl. 5, tel. 031/3511811.
Admission: 5 SF. Open Tues.–Sun. 10–5.*

⑳ The **Naturhistorisches Museum** is one of Europe's major natural history museums. It features enormous wildlife dioramas and a splendid
collection of Alpine minerals. *Bernastr. 15, tel. 031/3507111. Admission: 3 SF. Open Mon. 2–5, Tues.–Sat. 9–5, and Sun. 10–5.*

㉑ The **Schweizerisches Schützenmuseum** (Swiss Shooting Museum) traces
the development of firearms from 1817 and celebrates Swiss marksmanship
beyond the apple-splitting accuracy of William Tell. It's between the History and Natural History museums. *Bernastr. 5, tel. 031/3510127. Admission free. Open Tues.–Sat. 2–4, Sun. 10–noon and 2–4.*

㉒ **The Schweizerisches PTT-Museum** (Swiss Postal and Telecommunications Museum), now housed in its striking new building behind the Historical Museum, offers detailed documents, art, and artifacts of early
technology to trace the history of the mail system in Switzerland. *Hel-
vetiastr. 16, tel. 031/3387777. Admission: 2 SF adults. Open Tues.–Sun.
10–5.*

Alternatively, head back from the Casino on Kochergasse past the
㉓ enormous domed **Bundeshaus** (Capitol). By night, be sure to stick to
Kochergasse instead of the river-view promenade behind the capitol
building; some visitors have been annoyed by obvious drug traffic.

Dining

Although Bern teeters between two cultures politically, Teutonic con-
quers Gallic when it comes to cuisine. Dining in Bern is usually a
down-to-earth affair, with Italian home cooking as a popular alternative to the local standard fare of meat and potatoes. Specialties include
the famous *Bernerplatte* (sauerkraut with boiled beef, fatty pork,
sausages, ham, and tongue), *Buurehamme* (hot smoked ham), and
Ratsherrentopf (Rösti with roast veal, beef, liver, and sausage). Coffee and *Kuchen* (pastry) are the four-o'clock norm. For details and price-
category definitions, *see* Dining *in* Staying in Switzerland, *above.*

$$$$ **Bellevue-Grill.** When Parliament is in town, this haute-cuisine landmark
★ is transformed from a local gourmet mecca to a political clubhouse where
the movers and shakers put their heads together over healthy portions
of updated classics such as chopped veal liver Geschnetzeltes with
raspberries. *Kochergasse 3–5, tel. 031/3204545. Reservations advised. AE, DC, MC, V.*

$$$$ **Schultheissenstube.** The intimate, rustic dining room, with a clublike
★ bar in the center and an adjoining all-wood Stübli, looks less like a gastronomic haven than a country pub, and the folksy music furthers the
delusion. Yet the cooking is sophisticated, international, and imaginative—duck breast in hazelnut vinaigrette, oyster-and-champagne
risotto, seafood lasagna with saffron, Cornish hen with goose-liver sauce.
*Hotel Schweizerhof, Bahnhofpl. 11, tel. 031/3114501. Reservations
advised. AE, DC, MC, V. Closed Sun.*

$$$ **Jack's Brasserie.** In the Hotel Schweizerhof, this street-level restaurant,
with high ceilings, wainscoting, and roomy banquettes, is airy and
bustling, frequented by shoppers, Parliament members, and business-
people who enjoy its urbane, slightly formal atmosphere. You can
enjoy a drink here by day or settle in at mealtime for a smartly served
menu of French classics with a light touch. *Hotel Schweizerhof, Bahn-
hofpl. 11, tel. 031/3114501. Reservations advised. AE, DC, MC, V.*

$$$ **Zum Rathaus.** Across from the Rathaus in the Old Town, this atmo-
spheric, all-wood landmark has been a restaurant since 1863, though
the row house dates from the 17th century. Downstairs, the setting is
casual and comfortable, while the upstairs "Marcuard-Stübli" is considerably more formal; during the summer, opt for the outdoor café
on the Rathausplatz. The cooking ranges from local meat standards
to game, salmon, and hearty pastries. *Rathauspl. 5, tel. 031/3116183.
Upstairs reservations advised. AE, DC, MC, V. Closed Sun. and Mon.*

$$ **Della Casa.** You can stay downstairs in the steamy, rowdy Stübli,
★ where necktied businessmen roll up their sleeves and play cards, or you
can head up to the restaurant, where they leave their jackets on. It's
an unofficial Parliament headquarters, with generous local and Ital-
ian specialties. *Schauplatzg. 16, tel. 031/3112142. Reservations advised.
DC, MC, V. No credit cards downstairs. Closed Sun. No dinner Sat.*

$$ **Lorenzini.** In a town where the cozy or stuffy holds sway, this hip, bright
★ spot stands apart. Delicious homemade pasta and changing menus fea-
turing the specialties of different Italian regions are served with authentic,
contemporary flair. The clientele is a mix of voguish yuppies; the café-
bar downstairs draws the young and even more seriously chic. *Markt-
gasse-Passage 3, tel. 031/3117850. Reservations advised. DC, MC, V.*

$$ **Zunft zur Webern.** Founded as a weavers' guildhouse and built in 1704, this classic building has been renovated on the ground floor in a slick but traditional style, with gleaming new wood and bright lighting. The cuisine reflects the sophisticated decor, with generous portions of such upgraded standards as lamb stew with saffron. *Gerechtigkeitsg. 68, tel. 031/3114258. MC, V.*

$ **Brasserie zum Bärengraben.** Directly across from the bear pits, this
★ popular, easygoing little local institution, with the thinnest veneer of a French accent, serves inexpensive lunch specials to shoppers, tourists, businesspeople, and retirees, who settle in with a newspaper and a *dezi* (deciliter) of wine. The menu offers many old-style basics—Kalbskopf Vinaigrette, pigs' feet, stuffed cabbage—and wonderful pastries. À la carte dining can be more expensive. *Muristalden 1, tel. 031/3314218. Reservations advised. No credit cards.*

$ **Harmonie.** Run by the same family since 1900, this leaded-glass and old-wood café-restaurant serves inexpensive basics alongside pricier heavy-meat dinners: sausage-and-Rösti, *Käseschnitte* (cheese toast), *Bauern* omelets (farm-style, with bacon, potatoes, onions, and herbs), and fondue. It's lively and a little dingy, very friendly, and welcoming to foreigners. *Hotelg. 3, tel. 031/3113840. No credit cards.*

$ **Klötzlikeller.** A cozy, quiet, muraled wine cellar, this is much more in-
★ timate than the famous Kornhauskeller and just as lovely. Its history as a wine bar dates back to 1635, when there were as many as 250 in Bern. True to its heritage, it is able to secure the limited wine of Bern, which is sold by the glass. There's also a good, if limited, menu of meat specialties. *Gerechtigkeitsg. 62, tel. 031/3117456. AE, MC, V.*

$ **Kornhauskeller.** This spectacular vaulted old wine cellar, under the
★ Kornhaus granary, is now a popular beer hall with live music on weekends. Drinkers and revelers take tables in the upstairs galleries while diners in the vast main hall below gaze up at the ceiling frescoes. The Swiss fare satisfies the largest of appetites, but the historic ambience is the real reason to come. *Kornhauspl. 18, tel. 031/3111133. AE, DC, MC, V.*

Lodging

For details and price-category definitions, *see* Lodging *in* Staying in Switzerland, *above.*

$$$$ **Bären/Bristol.** These neighboring properties have been twinned as dependable business-class hotels, with modern interiors and first-class comforts. The Bärenbar, where bears figure heavily in the decor, serves drinks and snacks. *Schauplatzg. 4–10, CH-3001, tel. 031/3113367, fax 031/3116983 (Bären); tel. 031/3110101, fax 031/3119479 (Bristol). 149 rooms, 91 with bath. Facilities: bar/café, in-room VCRs, sauna. AE, DC, MC, V.*

$$$$ **Bellevue Palace.** This is a palace indeed, with a view that gives it an advantage over its friendly rival in luxury, the Schweizerhof. It is 75 years old, with art nouveau details that include a sweeping staircase and a spectacular stained-glass ceiling in the lobby. Decor in the rooms varies greatly, but each is deluxe. Rooms in the back face the river and the distant snowcapped Alps, including the Eiger and the Jungrau. Next to the parliament building, it hosts its fair share of politicos. *Kocherg. 3–5, CH-3001, tel. 031/3204545, fax 031/3114743. 155 rooms with bath. Facilities: 2 restaurants, bar, café, grill. AE, DC, MC, V.*

$$$$ **Schweizerhof.** The quarters are roomy and luxuriously appointed (most double rooms are the size of junior suites and, starting at 350 SF, represent a great value); halls are decorated with antiques from the collection of the Gauer family, the hotel's owners; and service is excellent.

The brasserie of this grand, graceful landmark by the Bahnhof is a great place for meeting friends. *Bahnhofpl. 11, CH-3001, tel. 031/3114501, fax 031/3122179. 94 rooms with bath. Facilities: 3 restaurants, bar, café, deli, nightclub, meeting rooms. AE, DC, MC, V.*

$$$ **Belle Epoque.** This relatively new hotel with period furnishings is more
★ suggestive of fin de siècle Paris than you might expect in Germanic Bern: Every inch of the arcaded row house is filled with authentic Art Nouveau and Jugendstil antiques. Despite the historic look, amenities, including white-tile baths and electric blinds, are state-of-the-art. The bar, off the lobby, is a congenial place for a rendezvous. *Gerechtigkeitsg. 18, CH-3011, tel. 031/3114336, fax 031/3113936. 17 rooms with bath. Facilities: breakfast room, piano bar. AE, DC, MC, V.*

$$$ **Bern.** Behind a spare and imposing neoclassical facade, this former theater and formerly modest hotel has been transformed into a sleek, modern gem, with an air-shaft garden "courtyard" lighting the better rooms. *Zeughausg. 9, CH-3011, tel. 031/3121021, fax 031/3121147. 96 rooms with bath. Facilities: 2 restaurants, café, piano bar. AE, DC, MC, V.*

$$$ **Innere Enge.** Opened in December 1992, this renovated early 18th-century inn has been transformed into a slick, deluxe business hotel. Spacious, light, and airy thanks to generous windows that face the Bernese Alps, it's outside the city center. Marian's Jazzroom, in the Louis Armstrong Bar, features top jazz acts. Take Bus 21 ("Bremgarten") from the train station. *Engestr. 54, CH-3012, tel. 031/3096111, fax 031/3096112. 26 rooms with bath. Facilities: restaurant, café, piano. AE, DC, MC, V.*

$$ **Goldener Adler.** The exterior of this 1764 building is a magnificent pa-
★ trician town house, but its interior is modern and modest, with linoleum baths and severe Formica furniture. The ambience is comfortable and familial nonetheless: Peter Balz runs the kitchen while his wife Verni manages the front. Simple continental fare is served in the restaurant; for value, take the menu of the day for 15 SF. *Gerechtigkeitsg. 7, CH-3011, tel. 031/3111725, fax 031/3113761. 16 rooms with bath. Facilities: restaurant (closed Sun.), café. AE, DC, MC, V.*

$$ **Krebs.** A classic, small, Swiss hotel, Krebs is impeccable and solid, man-
★ aged with an eye on every detail. The spare decor is warmed with wood and made comfortable by the personal, friendly service of the Buri family. A handful of inexpensive rooms without bath offer excellent value. *Genferg. 8, CH-3001, tel. 031/3114942, fax 031/3111035. 44 rooms, 41 with shower. Facilities: restaurant. AE, DC, MC, V.*

$ **Glocke.** Though it's very plain and occasionally shabby, there's a young, friendly management team and two lively restaurants, one a "Swiss Chalet," with dancing and folklore shows, the other an Italian trattoria with a small group of musicians. The rooms have a fresh paint job, tile baths, and homey, unmatched towels. A few rooms without baths cost less. *Rathausg. 75, CH-3011, tel. 031/3113771, fax 031/3111008. 20 rooms, some with bath. Facilities: 2 restaurants. AE, DC, MC, V.*

$ **Goldener Schlüssel.** This is a bright, tidy spot with wood, crisp linens, and tiled baths. It's in the heart of the Old Town, so the rooms are quieter in the back. Two good restaurants serve Swiss and international specialties. *Rathausg. 72, CH-3011, tel. 031/3110216, fax 031/3115688. 29 rooms, some with shower. Facilities: 2 restaurants. DC, MC, V.*

$ **Hospiz zur Heimat.** The elegant 18th-century exterior belies the dor-
★ mitory gloom inside, but the baths are new and the rooms are immaculate. It's in an excellent Old Town location. *Gerechtigkeitsg. 50, CH-3011, tel. 031/3110436, fax 031/3123386. 40 rooms, some with bath. Breakfast room. AE, DC, MC, V.*

$ **Jardin.** In a commercial neighborhood far above the Old Town, this is a solid, roomy middle-class hotel, with fresh decor and baths in every room. It's easily reached by Tram 9 to Breitenrainplatz. *Militärstr. 38, CH-3014, tel. 031/3330117, fax 031/3330943. 17 rooms with bath. Facilities: restaurant. AE, DC, MC, V.*

$ **Marthahaus.** Take Bus 20 over the Kornhaus Bridge to this spare, old-style pension in a residential neighborhood north of the Old Town, where rates are low and the service is friendly. *Wyttenbachstr. 22a, CH-3014, tel. 031/3324135. 20 rooms, 6 with bath. Facilities: breakfast room. MC, V.*

ZERMATT

Lying at an altitude of 5,300 feet, Zermatt offers the ultimate Swiss-Alpine experience: spectacular mountains, a roaring stream, state-of-the-art transport facilities, and a broad range of high-quality accommodations, some of them radiating rustic atmosphere, plus 230 kilometers (143 miles) of downhill runs and 7 kilometers (4 miles) of cross-country trails. But its greatest claim to fame remains the **Matterhorn** (14,690 feet), which attracts swarms of package-tour sightseers pushing shoulder to shoulder to get yet another shot of this genuine wonder of the Western world.

Arriving and Departing

Zermatt is a car-free resort isolated at the end of the Mattertal, a rugged valley at the eastern end of the Alpine canton of Valais. A good mountain highway and the Brig-Visp-Zermatt Railway cut south through the valley from Visp, the crossroads of the main Valais east–west routes. The airports of Zürich and Geneva are roughly equidistant from Brig, but by approaching from Geneva you can avoid crossing mountain passes.

By Train

The Brig-Visp-Zermatt Railway, a private narrow-gauge system, runs from Brig to Visp, connecting on to Zermatt. All major rail routes connect through Brig, whether you approach from Geneva or Lausanne in the west, from the Lötschberg line that tunnels through from Kandersteg and the Bernese Oberland, or from the Simplon Pass that connects from Italy.

By Car

You may drive up the Mattertal as far as Täsch, where you must abandon your car in a large parking lot and catch the train as it completes its climb into Zermatt.

Getting Around

Because Zermatt permits no private cars, your only means of transit are electric taxis that shuttle arriving guests to their hotels and back. The village is relatively small and easily covered on foot.

By Cable Car and Mountain Rail

Hiking and skiing are Zermatt's raisons d'être, but you may want to get a head start into the heights by riding part of the sophisticated network of cable cars, lifts, cog railways, and even an underground metro that carry you above the village center into the wilderness. Excursions to the Klein, Matterhorn, and Gornergrat are particularly spectacular.

Important Addresses and Numbers

Tourist Information

The main tourist office, the **Verkehrsbüro Zermatt,** is across from the train station (Bahnhofpl., CH-3920 tel. 028/661181).

Emergencies

Police (tel. 027/225656). **Ambulance** (tel. 028/672000).

Exploring Zermatt

Zermatt lies in a hollow of meadows and trees ringed by mountains— among them the broad **Monte Rosa** (14,940 feet) and its tallest peak, the **Dufourspitze** (at 15,200 feet, the highest point in Switzerland)— of which visitors hear relatively little, so all-consuming is the cult of the Matterhorn. But the Matterhorn deserves the idolatry: Though it has become an almost self-parodying icon, like the Eiffel Tower or the Statue of Liberty, this distinctive snaggle-toothed pyramid, isolated on all sides from surrounding peaks, is larger than life.

Despite its celebrity mountain, Zermatt remains a resort with its feet on the ground, protecting its regional quirks along with its wildlife and its tumbledown *mazots* (little grain-storage sheds raised on mush-roomlike stone bases to keep the mice away), which crowd between glass-and-concrete chalets like old tenements between skyscrapers. Streets twist past weathered wood walls, flower boxes, and haphaz-ard stone roofs until they break into open country that inevitably slopes uphill.

In 1891, the cog railway between Visp and Zermatt took its first sum-mer run and began disgorging tourists with profitable regularity—though it didn't plow through in wintertime until 1927. But what really drew the first tourists and made Zermatt a household word was Edward Whymper's spectacular—and catastrophic—conquering of the Mat-terhorn in 1865. Whymper and his band of six made the successful trek to the mountain's summit before tragedy struck. During the treach-erous descent, four of the men slid against one another and fell 4,000 feet to their death. The body of one was never recovered, but the oth-ers lie in the grim little cemetery behind the Zermatt church in the vil-lage center.

If you want to gain the broader perspective of high altitudes without risking life or limb, take the trip up the Gornergrat—the train is used for excursions as well as ski transport. Part of the rail system completed in 1898 and the highest open-air rail system in Europe (the tracks to the Jungfraujoch, though higher, bore through the face of the Eiger), it connects out of the main Zermatt train station and climbs slowly up the valley to the **Riffelberg,** which at 8,471 feet offers wide-open views of the Matterhorn. From **Rotenboden,** at 9,248 feet, a short downhill walk leads to the **Riffelsee,** which obligingly provides photographers with a postcard-perfect reflection of the famous peak. At the end of the 9-kilometer (6-mile) line, the train stops at the summit station of **Gornergrat** (10,269 feet), and passengers pour onto the observation terraces to take in the majestic views of the Matterhorn, Monte Rosa, Gorner glacier, and scores of other peaks and glaciers. There are de-partures every 24 minutes between 8 AM and 7 PM. The round-trip fare is 53 SF. Bring warm clothes, sunglasses, and sturdy shoes.

Dining

Located at the German end of the mostly French canton of Valais, Zermatt offers a variety of French and German cooking, from veal and Rösti to raclette and fondue. Specialties often feature pungent mountain cheese: *Käseschnitte*, for instance, are substantial little casseroles of bread, cheese, and often ham, baked until the whey saturates the crusty bread and the cheese browns to gold. Air-dried beef is another Valais treat: The meat is pressed into a dense brick and dried in mountain breezes. It is served in thin, translucent slices, with gherkins and crisp pickled onions. Alas, McDonald's has infiltrated this once-isolated retreat, and you now have to climb or ski to find memorable, cut-above dining. For details and price-category definitions, *see* Dining *in* Staying in Switzerland, *above*. Since Zermatt is for the most part a one-street town, street addresses are not always used.

$$$ **Findlerhof.** Whether for long lunches between sessions on the slopes
★ or for the traditional wind-down après-ski, this mountain restaurant in tiny Findeln, between the Sunnegga and Blauherd ski areas, is still de rigueur, especially with the hip young English and Americans. The Matterhorn views are astonishing, the decor stylish, the staff chic— and the food surprisingly fine. Traditional hot dishes and nontraditional pastas share billing with good homemade desserts. *Findeln, tel. 028/672588. No credit cards. Closed May–mid-June, Oct.–Nov.*

$$$ **Zum See.** Beyond Findeln, in a tiny village by the same name, Zum See
★ has become something of an institution, serving light meals of a quality and level of invention that would merit acclaim even if the restaurant weren't in the middle of nowhere at 5,794 feet. In summer its shaded picnic tables draw hikers who reward themselves with homemade pasta and fresh-cranked sorbet at the finish of a day's climb; in winter its low, cozy log dining room gives skiers a glow with a fine assortment of brandies. *Tel. 028/672045. Dinner reservations advised. No credit cards. Closed May–June, Oct.–mid-Nov.*

$ **Elsie's Bar.** Directly across from the church, this popular, central après-ski haunt looks like a log cabin inside, and draws an international crowd into its barroom for cocktails, American-style. Light meals include cheese specialties and snails. *Tel. 028/672431. AE, DC, MC, V.*

Lodging

At high season—Christmas and New Year's, Easter, and late summer—Zermatt's high prices rival those of Zürich and Geneva. But read the fine print carefully when you plan your visit: Most hotels include half pension in their price, offering breakfast and your choice of a noon or evening meal. Hotels that call themselves "garni" do not offer pension dining plans. For details and price-category definitions, *see* Lodging *in* Staying in Switzerland, *above*.

$$$$ **Mont Cervin.** One of the flagships of the Seiler dynasty, this is a sleek,
★ luxurious, and urbane mountain hotel. Built in 1852, it's unusually low-slung for a grand hotel, with dark beams and classic decor; a few rooms are full of rustic stucco and carved blond wood. Jacket and tie are required in the guests' dining hall, and for the Friday gala buffet, it's black tie only. *CH-3920, tel. 028/668888, fax 028/672878. 143 rooms with bath. Facilities: restaurant, grill, indoor pool, sauna, health club, disco. AE, DC, MC, V. Closed May–mid-June and mid-Oct.–Nov.*

$$$$ **Zermatterhof.** The Cervin's rival for five-star luxury, this 19th-century hotel has recently undergone major renovations to better emphasize its rustic beginnings. Some of the suites now have fireplaces and whirlpool tubs; many also have balconies facing the Matterhorn. Both restaurants, including the elegant newer one opened in 1993, are for guests only, with breakfast included in the price. *CH-3920, tel. 028/661100, fax 028/674842. 93 rooms with bath. Facilities: 2 restaurants, indoor pool, sauna, health club. AE, DC, MC, V.*

$$$ **Hotel Simi.** Run by the Biner-Simon family, the Simi is a friendly inn-style hotel where creature comforts are taken seriously: From the sauna to the intimate bar to the huge buffet breakfast, the Biner-Simons make you feel you're at home. On a quiet side street in the center of town, the location is ideal. Rooms are simply furnished, with pine-paneled walls, twin beds, and light-color fabrics; the lobby lounge has comfortable couches and a small bar. *CH-3920, tel. 028/674656, fax 028/674861. 45 rooms with bath. Facilities: lobby lounge, sauna. MC, V.*

$$$ **Monte Rosa.** Behind its graceful shuttered facade you will find flag-★ stone floors, brass, stained and beveled glass, pine, fireplaces, and an elaborate Victorian dining hall, fully restored. Dinner is a five-course affair better suited to hearty appetites than seekers of innovative cuisine. The bar is an après-ski must. Guests have access to the Mont Cervin pool. *CH-3920, tel. 028/661131, fax 028/671160. 51 rooms with bath. Facilities: restaurant, sauna. AE, DC, MC, V.*

$$$ **Pollux.** Constructed in 1978 and renovated in 1989, this simple but chic modern hotel is on the main pedestrian shopping street. If you're looking for quiet, reserve a room at the back of the hotel; the front rooms are good for people-watching. A French restaurant serves seafood specialties, and an appealing old-fashioned Stübli draws locals for its low-price lunches, snacks, and Valais cheese specialties; the terrace café sits directly on the busy street. *CH-3920, tel. 028/671946, fax 028/675426. 32 rooms with bath. Facilities: restaurant, Stübli, sauna, disco. AE, DC, MC, V.*

$$$ **Julen.** Its 1937 chalet-style construction, knotty-pine decor, and im-★ peccable 1981 renovation qualify this lodge for membership in the Romantik chain, which assures guests of authentic regional comforts. The main restaurant offers French cooking, and the welcoming Stübli serves lamb specialties from locally raised flocks. *CH-3920, tel. 028/672481, fax 028/671481. 37 rooms with bath. Facilities: restaurant, café, sauna. AE, DC, MC, V.*

$$$ **Romantica.** Among the scores of anonymous modern hotels around Zermatt, this modest structure offers an exceptional location directly above the town center. Its tidy gardens and flower boxes, game trophies, and old-style stove soften the cookie-cutter look, and its plain rooms benefit from big windows and balconies. Views take in the mountains (though not the Matterhorn) over a graceful clutter of stone roofs. *CH-3920, tel. 028/671505, fax 028/675815. 14 rooms with bath. Facilities: bar. AE, MC, V.*

$ **Alphubel.** Although it is surrounded by other hotels and is steps from the main street, this modest, comfortable pension feels off the beaten track—and it offers large sunny balconies in its south-side rooms. The interior reflects the 1954 construction—a little institutional—but there's a sauna in the basement guests can use for a slight surcharge. *CH-3920, tel. 028/673003, fax 028/676684. 32 rooms, 16 with bath. Facilities: restaurant, sauna. AE, MC, V.*

$ **Mischabel.** This proud old budget pension—run by the same family ★ for 40 years—provides comfort, atmosphere, and a central location few places could match at twice the price, with balconies on the south side framing a perfect Matterhorn view. Creaky, homey, and covered with knotty pine aged to the color of toffee, its rooms have sinks only, though you'll find linoleum-lined showers on every floor. *CH-3920, tel. 028/*

671131, *fax 028/676507. 28 rooms without bath. Facilities: restaurant. No credit cards.*

$ **Touring.** Its reassuringly traditional architecture and snug, sunny al-
★ pine rooms, combined with an elevated location outside town and excellent Matterhorn views, make this an appealing choice for travelers
who wish to avoid the chic "downtown" scene. Built in 1958 and tastefully updated in 1989, it's family-run, and rooms with Matterhorn views
cost only 2 SF extra. *CH-3920, tel. 028/671177, fax 028/674601. 24
rooms, 10 with bath. Facilities: restaurant, Stübli. MC, V.*

29 Turkey

TURKEY IS ONE PLACE to which the phrase "East meets West" really applies, both literally and figuratively. It is in Turkey's largest city, Istanbul, that the continents of Europe and Asia meet, separated only by the Bosporus, which flows 29 kilometers (18 miles) from the Black Sea to the Sea of Marmara. On the vibrant streets of this city of 12 million people, miniskirts and trendy boots mingle with head scarves and prayer beads. People from as far away as Ghana, Sri Lanka and the Philippines and as nearby as the Central Asian republics and the former Soviet Union make their way to Istanbul in search of better lives.

Although most of Turkey's landmass is in Asia, Turkey has faced West politically since 1923, when Mustapha Kemal, better known as Atatürk, founded the modern republic. He transformed the remnants of the shattered Ottoman Empire into a secular state with a Western outlook. So thorough was this changeover—culturally, politically, and economically— that in 1987, 49 years after Atatürk's death, Turkey applied to the European Community (EC) for full membership. It has been a member of the North Atlantic Treaty Organization (NATO) since 1952.

For 16 centuries Istanbul, originally known as Byzantium, played a major part in world politics, first as the capital of the Eastern Roman Empire, when it was known as Constantinople, then as capital of the Ottoman Empire, the most powerful Islamic empire in the world, when it was renamed Istanbul. Atatürk moved the capital to Ankara at the inception of the Turkish Republic.

The legacies of the Greeks, Romans, Ottomans, and numerous other civilizations have made the country a vast outdoor museum. The most spectacular of the reconstructed classical sites are along the western Aegean coast and the southwest Mediterranean coast, which are lined with magnificent sandy beaches and sleepy little fishing villages, as well as busy holiday spots with sophisticated facilities for travelers.

For those with more time, an extra five to seven days, an excursion inland to central Anatolia and the eroded lunar valleys of the Cappadocia area will show some of the enormous diversity of the landscapes and people of Turkey.

ESSENTIAL INFORMATION

Before You Go

When to Go
The height of the tourist season runs from April through October. July and August are the busiest and warmest months. April through June and September and October are the best months to visit archaeological sites or Istanbul and the Marmara area because the days are cooler and the crowds are smaller.

CLIMATE
The Mediterranean and Aegean coasts have mild winters and hot summers. You can swim in the sea from late April through October. The Black Sea coast is mild and damp, with a rainfall of 228 centimeters (90 inches) a year.

The following are the average daily maximum and minimum temperatures for Istanbul.

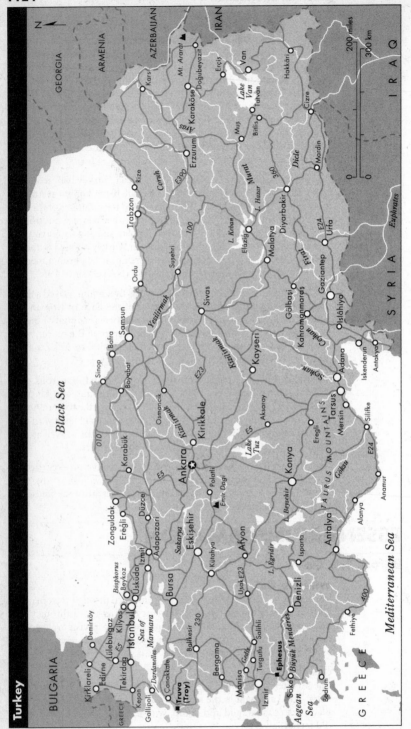

Turkey

Jan.	46F	8C	May	69F	21C	Sept.	76F	24C
	37	3		53	12		61	16
Feb.	47F	9C	June	77F	25C	Oct.	68F	20C
	36	2		60	16		55	13
Mar.	51F	11C	July	82F	28C	Nov.	59F	15C
	38	3		65	18		48	9
Apr.	60F	16C	Aug.	82F	28C	Dec.	51F	11C
	45	7		66	19		41	5

Currency

The monetary unit is the Turkish lira (TL), which comes in bank notes of 20,000, 50,000, 100,000, 250,000, and 500,000. Coins come in denominations of 500, 1,000, 2,500, 5,000 and 10,000. At press time (spring 1995), the exchange rate was 38,400 TL to the dollar and 64,860 TL to the pound sterling. These rates are subject to wide fluctuation, so check close to your departure. Major credit cards and traveler's checks are widely accepted in hotels, shops, and expensive restaurants in cities and resorts, but rarely in villages and small shops and restaurants.

Be certain to retain your original exchange slips when you convert money into Turkish lira—you will need them to reconvert the money. Because the Turkish lira is worth a lot less than most currencies, it's best to convert only what you plan to spend.

What It Will Cost

Turkey is the least expensive of the Mediterranean countries. Inflation, which has hovered between 50% and 70% for many years, soared to 149% in 1994, but frequent devaluations of the lira keep prices fairly stable when measured against foreign currencies. Prices in this chapter are quoted in dollars, which indicate the real cost to the tourist more accurately than do the constantly increasing lira prices.

SAMPLE PRICES

Coffee can range from about 30¢ to $2.50 a cup, depending on whether it's the less expensive Turkish coffee or American-style coffee and whether it's served in a luxury hotel or a café; tea, 20¢ to $2.50 a glass; local beer, $1–$3; soft drinks, $1–$4; lamb shish kebab, $1.50–$7; taxi, less than $1 for 1 mile (prices are 50% higher between midnight and 6 AM).

Customs

ON ARRIVAL

Turkish customs officials rarely look through tourists' luggage on arrival. You are allowed to take in 400 cigarettes, 50 cigars, 200 grams of tobacco, 1.5 kilograms of instant coffee, 500 grams of tea, and 2.5 liters of alcohol. An additional 600 cigarettes, 100 cigars, or 500 grams of tobacco may be imported if purchased at the Turkish duty-free shops on arrival. Register all valuable personal items in your passport on entry. Items at duty-free shops in airports are usually less expensive here than in duty-free shops in other European airports or in in-flight offerings.

ON DEPARTURE

You must keep receipts of your purchases, especially for such items as carpets, as proof that they were bought with legally exchanged currency. Also, it cannot be emphasized strongly enough that Turkey is extremely tough on anyone attempting to export antiques without authorization or anyone caught with illegal drugs, regardless of the amount.

Language

Atatürk launched language reforms that replaced Arabic script with the Latin-based alphabet. English and German are widely spoken in cities and resorts. In the villages or in remote areas, you'll have a hard time finding anyone who speaks anything but Turkish. Try learning a few basic Turkish words; the Turks will love you for it.

Getting Around

By Car

ROAD CONDITIONS

Turkey has excellent roads—25,000 miles of well-maintained, paved highways—but signposts are few, lighting is scarce, and city traffic is chaotic. City streets and highways are jammed with vehicles operated by high-speed drivers who constantly blast their horns. In Istanbul, it's safer and faster to drive on the modern highways. Avoid the many small one-way streets, since you never know when someone is going to barrel down one of them in the wrong direction. Better yet, use public transportation or take taxis. Parking is a big problem in the cities and larger towns.

RULES OF THE ROAD

The best way to see Turkey is by car, but be warned that it has one of the highest accident rates in Europe. In general, Turkish driving conforms to Mediterranean customs, with driving on the right and passing on the left. But watch out for drivers passing on a curve or on the top of a hill. Other hazards are peasant carts and motorcycles weaving in and out of traffic. Archaeological and historical sites are indicated by yellow signposts.

GASOLINE

Throughout the country Mobil, Shell, and British Petroleum, as well as two Turkish oil companies, have gas stations that are open 24 hours on the main highways. Others are open from 6 AM to 10 PM.

BREAKDOWNS

Before you start out, check with your hotel or a tourist information office about how, in case of an emergency, to contact one of the road rescue services available on some highways. Turkish mechanics in the villages will usually manage to get you going again, at least until you reach a city for full repairs. In the cities, entire streets are given over to car-repair shops. Prices are not high, but it's good to give a small tip to the person who does the actual repair work. If you're not in the shop during the repairs, take all the car documents with you. **The Touring and Automobile Club (TTOK,** tel. 212/282–8140) gives information about driving in Turkey and offers a repair service.

By Train

Although there are express trains in Turkey, the term is usually a misnomer. These trains ply several long-distance routes, but they tend to be slow. The best daily trains between Istanbul and Ankara are the Başkent Expres and the Faith Expres. The overnight Yatakli Ankara Expres has luxurious sleeper cars while the Anadolu Expres offers cheaper bunk beds. There are overnight trains to Pamukkale as well as daily trains to Edirne from Sirkeci station in Istanbul. Dining cars on some trains have waiter service and serve surprisingly good and inexpensive food.

FARES

Train fares tend to be less expensive than bus fares. Seats on the best trains, as well as those with sleeping berths, should be reserved in advance. There are 10% student discounts (30% Dec.–May) and 30%

discounts for groups of 24 or more. In railroad stations, buy tickets at windows marked ANAHAT GISELERI. Travel agencies carrying the TCDD (State Railways) sign and post offices sell train tickets too.

By Bus

Buses, which are run by private companies, are much faster than trains and provide excellent, inexpensive service. Buses are available, virtually around the clock, between all cities and towns. They are fairly comfortable and many are air-conditioned. Companies have their own fixed fares for different routes. Istanbul to Ankara, for instance, varies from $8 to $13; Istanbul to İzmir varies from $11 to $16. *Şişe suyu* (bottled water) is included in the fare. You can purchase tickets at stands in a town's *otogar* (central bus terminal) or at branch offices in city centers. All seats are reserved. Fares vary among competing companies, but most buses between major cities are double-deckers and have toilets. Companies such as Varan, Ulusoy, and Pamukkale offer no-smoking seating. For very short trips, or getting around within a city, take minibuses or a *dolmuş* (shared taxi). Both are inexpensive and comfortable.

By Plane

Turkish Airlines (THY) operates an extensive domestic network. There are at least nine flights daily on weekdays between Istanbul and Ankara. During the summer, many flights between the cities and coastal resorts are added. Try to arrive at the airport at least 45 minutes before your flight because security checks, which are rigidly enforced without exception, can be time-consuming. Checked luggage is placed on trolleys on the tarmac and must be identified by boarding passengers before it is put on the plane. Unidentified luggage is left behind and checked for bombs or firearms.

THY offers several discounts on domestic flights: 10% for families; 50% for children under 13; 90% for children under two; and 50% for sports groups of seven or more. The THY sales office is at Taksim Square (tel. 212/252–1106; reservations by phone, tel. 212/663–6363).

By Boat

Turkish Maritime Lines operates car ferry and cruise services from Istanbul. Cruises are in great demand, so make your reservations well in advance, either through the head office in Istanbul (Rihtim Cad. 1, Karaköy, tel. 212/249–9222 or through **Sunquest Holidays Ltd.** in London (Aldine House, Aldine St., London W12 8AW, tel. 0181/800–5455).

The **Black Sea Ferry** sails from May through September from Istanbul to Samsun and Trabzon and back, from Karaköy Dock in Istanbul. One-way fares to Trabzon are about $30 for a reclining seat, $38 to $94 for cabins, and $50 for cars. The Istanbul-to-İzmir car ferry departs three days a week. The price of a one-way ticket with no meals included varies between $38 and $122, and $40 for a car.

Staying in Turkey

Telephones

Note: All telephone numbers in Turkey now have seven local digits plus three-digit city codes. Intercity calls are preceded by 0.

Most pay phones are yellow, push-button models, although a few older, operator-controlled telephones are still in use. Multilingual directions are posted in phone booths.

LOCAL CALLS

Public phones use *jetons* (tokens), which can be purchased for 2,000 TL at post offices and street booths. If you need operator assistance for long-distance calls within Turkey, dial 131. For intercity automatic calls, dial 0, then dial the city code and the number. Jetons are available for 8,000 TL for long-distance calls. Far more practical than the jetons are telephone cards, available at post offices for 48,000 TL, 96,000 TL, and 160,000 TL.

Telephone numbers in European and Asian Istanbul have been assigned different codes: the code for European Istanbul (for numbers beginning with 2, 5, or 6) is 0/212; for Asian Istanbul (for numbers beginning with 3 or 4), dial 0/216.

INTERNATIONAL CALLS
For all international calls dial 00, then dial the country code, area or city code, and the number. You can use the higher-price cards for this, or reach an international operator by dialing 132. To reach an **AT&T** long distance operator, dial 00800-12277, for **MCI**, dial 00800-11177, and for **Sprint**, 00800-14477. The country code for Turkey is 90.

Mail
Post offices are painted bright yellow and have PTT (Post, Telegraph, and Telephone) signs on the front. The major ones are open Monday–Saturday from 8 AM to 9 PM, Sundays from 9 to 7. Smaller branches are open Monday–Saturday 8:30–5.

RECEIVING MAIL
If you're uncertain where you'll be staying, have mail addressed to "post restante" and sent to Merkez Postanesi (central post office) in the town of your choice.

Shopping
BARGAINING
The best part of shopping in Turkey is visiting the *bedestans* (bazaars), all brimming with copper and brass items, hand-painted ceramics, alabaster and onyx goods, fabrics, richly colored carpets, and relics and icons trickling in from the former Soviet Union. The key word for shopping in the bazaars is "bargain." You must be willing to bargain, and bargain hard. It's great fun once you get the hang of it. As a rule of thumb, offer 50% less after you're given the initial price and be prepared to go up by about 25% to 30% of the first asking price. It's both bad manners and bad business to underbid grossly or to start bargaining if you're not serious about buying. Outside the bazaars prices are usually fixed, although in resort areas some shopkeepers may be willing to bargain if you ask for a "better price." Part of the fun of roaming through the bazaars is having a free glass of *çay* (tea), which vendors will offer you whether you're a serious shopper or just browsing. Beware of antiques: Chances are you will end up with an expensive fake, but even if you do find the genuine article, it's illegal to export antiques of any type.

VAT REFUNDS
Value-added tax (VAT) is nearly always included in the price. You can claim back the VAT if you buy articles from authorized shops. The net total value of articles subject to VAT on your invoice must be over a specified amount, depending on the nature of the goods, and these articles must be exported within three months of purchase. The invoice must be stamped by customs. Otherwise, mail the stamped invoice back to the dealer within one month of departure and the dealer will send back a check.

Opening and Closing Times
Banks are open weekdays, 8:30–noon and 1:30–5.

Mosques are usually open to the public, except during *namaz* (prayer hours), which are observed five times a day. These times are based on the position of the sun, so they vary throughout the seasons between the following hours: sunrise (5–7), lunchtime (noon–1), afternoon (3–4), sunset (5–7), bedtime (9–10). Prayers last 30–40 minutes.

Museums are generally open Tuesday–Sunday, 9:30–4:30, and closed Monday. **Palaces,** open the same hours, are closed Thursday instead of Monday.

Shops are closed daily from 1 PM to 2 PM and all day Sunday. Generally they're open Monday–Saturday, 9:30–1 and 2–7. There are some exceptions in the resort areas, where shops stay open until 9 PM and are often open on Sunday.

National Holidays

January 1; February 22–24 (Şeker Bayram, "sugar feast," a three-day feast marking the end of Ramadan); April 23 (National Sovereignty and Children's Day); May 1–3 (Kurban Bayram, an important sacrificial feast celebrating Abraham's willingness to sacrifice his son to God); May 19 (National Youth and Sports Day); August 30 (Victory Day); October 28–29 (Republic Day); November 10 (Atatürk's Commemoration).

Dining

The Turkish people are justly proud of their cuisine. In addition to the blends of spices used, the food is also extremely healthful, full of fresh vegetables, yogurt, legumes, and grains, not to mention fresh seafood, roast lamb, and kebabs made of lamb, beef, or chicken. The old cliché about it being hard to find a bad meal in Paris more aptly describes dining in Istanbul, where even the tiniest little hole-in-the-wall serves delicious food. Because Turkey is predominantly Muslim, pork is not readily available. But there's plenty of alcohol, including local beer and wine, which are excellent and inexpensive. Particularly good wines are Villa Doluca and Kavaklidere, available in *beyaz* (white) and *kirmizi* (red). The most popular local beer is Efes Pilsen. The national alcoholic drink, raki, is made from grapes and aniseed. Turks mix it with water or ice and sip it throughout their meal or serve it as an aperitif.

Hotel restaurants have English-language menus and usually serve a bland version of Continental cuisine. Far more adventurous and tasty are meals in *restorans* and in *lokantas* (Turkish restaurants). Most lokantas do not have menus because they serve only what's fresh and in season, which varies daily. At lokantas, you simply sit back and let the waiter bring food to your table, beginning with a tray of mezes. You point to the dishes that look inviting and take as many as you want. Then you select your main course from fresh meat or fish—displayed in glass-covered refrigerated units—which is then cooked to order, or from a steam table laden with casseroles and stews. For lighter meals there are *kebabcis*, tiny restaurants specializing in kebabs served with salad and yogurt, and *pidecis*, selling *pides*, a pizzalike snack of flat bread topped with butter, cheese, egg, or ground lamb and baked in a wood-burning oven.

MEALTIMES

Lunch is generally served from noon to 3 and dinner from 7 to 10. In the cities you can find restaurants or cafés open virtually anytime of day or night, but in the villages, finding a restaurant open at odd hours can be a problem.

WHAT TO WEAR

Except for the pricier restaurants, where formal dress is appropriate, informal dress is acceptable at restaurants in all price categories.

PRECAUTIONS

Although tap water is heavily chlorinated, it is not safe to drink in cities and resorts. It's best to play it safe and drink *maden suyu* (bottled mineral water) or regular *şişe suyu,* which is better tasting and inexpensive.

RATINGS

Prices are per person and include an appetizer, main course, and dessert. Wine and gratuities are not included. Highly recommended restaurants are indicated by a star ★.

CATEGORY	MAJOR CITIES	OTHER AREAS
$$$$	over $40	over $30
$$$	$25–$40	$20–$30
$$	$12–$25	$10–$20
$	under $12	under $10

Lodging

Hotels are officially classified in Turkey as HL (luxury), H1 to H5 (first- to fifth-class); motels, M1 to M2 (first- to second-class); and P, *pansiyons* (guest houses). The classification is misleading because the lack of a restaurant or a lounge automatically relegates the establishment to the bottom of the ratings. A lower-grade hotel may actually be far more charming and comfortable than one with a higher rating. There are also many local establishments that are licensed but not included in the official ratings list. You can obtain their names from local tourist offices.

Accommodations range from international luxury chains in Istanbul, Ankara, and İzmir to comfortable, family-run pansiyons. Plan ahead for the peak summer season, when resort hotels are often booked solid by tour companies. Turkey does not have central hotel reservations offices.

Rates vary from $10 to more than $200 a night for a double room. In the less expensive hotels, the plumbing and furnishings will probably leave much to be desired. You can find very acceptable, clean double rooms with bath for between $30 and $70, with breakfast included. Room rates are displayed in the reception area. It is accepted practice in Turkey to ask to see the room in advance.

RATINGS

Prices are for two people in a double room, including 20% VAT and a 10–15% service charge. Highly recommended lodgings are indicated by a star ★.

CATEGORY	MAJOR CITIES	OTHER AREAS
$$$$	over $200	over $150
$$$	$100–$200	$100–$150
$$	$60–$100	$50–$100
$	under $60	under $50

Tipping

Except at the cheapest restaurants, a 10% to 15% charge is added to the bill. Since the money does not necessarily find its way to the waiter, leave an additional 10% on the table or hand it to the waiter. In the top restaurants, waiters expect tips of between 10% and 15%. Hotel porters expect between $2 and $5, and the chambermaid, about $2 a day. Taxi drivers don't expect tips, although they are becoming accustomed to foreigners giving them something. Round off the fare to the nearest 5,000 TL. At Turkish baths, the staff that attends you expects to share a tip of 30% to 35% of the bill. Don't worry about missing them—they'll be lined up expectantly on your departure.

ISTANBUL

Arriving and Departing

By Plane

All international and domestic flights arrive at Istanbul's Atatürk Airport. For arrival and departure information, call the individual airline or the airport's information desk (tel. 212/663–6400).

BETWEEN THE AIRPORT AND DOWNTOWN
Shuttle buses run from the airport's international and domestic terminals to the Turkish Airlines (THY) terminal in downtown Istanbul, at Meşrutiyet Caddesi, near the Galata Tower. Buses depart for the airport at the same address every hour from 6 AM to 11 PM. After that, departure time depends on demand. Allow at least 45 minutes for the bus ride. Plan to be at the airport two hours before your international flight because of the lengthy security and check-in procedures. The ride from the airport into town takes from 30 to 40 minutes, depending on traffic. Taxis charge about $15 to Taksim Square and $11 to Sultanahmet.

By Train

Trains from the west arrive at Sirkeci station (tel. 212/527–0050 or 0051) in Old Istanbul. Eastbound trains to Anatolia depart from Haydarpasa station (tel. 216/348–8020) on the Asian side.

By Bus

The destination for buses arriving in Istanbul is the newly built Esenler terminal northwest of the city center. From the terminal, bus companies offer free minibus service to centers such as Sultanahmet, Taksim and Aksaray. There is also the Hizli Tren (rapid train) connecting the terminal to Aksaray. A few buses from Anatolia arrive at Harem terminal, on the eastern shore of the Bosporus. Some bus companies have *servis arabasi* (minibus services) to the hotel areas of Taksim Square and Aksaray. If you arrive with baggage, it is much easier to take a taxi, which will cost about $8 to Taksim from the bus terminals and about $5 to Old Istanbul.

By Car

If you drive in from the west, take the busy E5 highway, also called Londra Asfalti, which leads from Edirne to Atatürk Airport and on through the city walls at Cannon Gate (Topkapı). E5 heading out of Istanbul leads into central Anatolia and on to Iran and Syria. An alternative to E5, when leaving the city, is to take one of the numerous car ferries that ply the Sea of Marmara and the Dardanelles from Kabataş Dock, or try the overnight ferry to İzmir, which leaves from Sarayburnu.

Getting Around

The best way to get around all the magnificent monuments in Sultanahmet in Old Istanbul is to walk. They're all within easy distance of each other, along streets filled with peddlers, shoe-shine boys, children playing, and craftsmen working. To get to other areas, you can take a bus or one of the many ferries that steam between the Asian and European continents; *deniz otobüsü* (sea buses) running between the continents, as well as to destinations such as the Princes' Islands, are fast and efficient. Dolmuş vehicles and taxis are plentiful, inexpensive, and more comfortable than city buses. A new tram system runs from Topkapı, via Sultanahmet, to Sirkeci. Subway system construction is underway between Taksim and Levent, and there is the Tünel, a tiny underground train that's handy for getting up the steep hill from Karaköy to the bottom of Is-tiklâl Caddesi. It runs every 10 minutes and costs about 25¢.

By Bus

Buy a ticket before boarding a bus. You can buy tickets, individually or in books of 10, at ticket stands around the city. Shoe-shine boys or men on the street will also sell them to you for a few cents more. Fares are about 25¢ per ride. On the city's orange privatized buses (Halk Otobüsü) as well as on the city's new double deckers, pay for tickets on the bus. The London-style double deckers now operate along a scenic route between Sultanahmet and Emigran on the Bosporus.

By Dolmuş

These are shared taxis operating between set destinations throughout the city. Dolmuş stops are indicated by a blue and white sign with a large D. The destination is shown either on a roof sign or a card in the front window. Many of them are classic American cars from the 1950s but are gradually being replaced by modern vans.

By Taxi

Taxis are inexpensive. Since most drivers do not speak English and may not know the street names, write down the street you want, the nearby main streets, and the name of the area. Taxis are metered. Although tipping is not expected, you should round off the fare to the nearest 5,000 TL.

By Boat

For a fun and inexpensive ride, take the *Anadolu Kavaği* boat along the Bosporus to its mouth at the Black Sea. The boat leaves year-round from the Eminönü Docks, next to the Galata Bridge on the Old Istanbul side, at 10:30 AM and 1:30 PM, with two extra trips on weekdays and four extra trips on Sundays from April to September. The fare is $6 (round-trip). The trip takes 1¾ hours one way. You can disembark at any of the stops and return by land if you wish. Regular ferries depart from Kabataş Dock, near Dolmabahçe Palace on the European side, to Üsküdar on the Asian side; and also from Eminönü Docks 1 and 2, near Sirkeci station.

Important Addresses and Numbers

Tourist Information

Official tourist information offices are at **Atatürk Airport** (tel. 212/663–6400); the **Hilton Hotel** (tel. 212/233–0592); **Karaköy Yolcu Salonu,** International Maritime Passenger Terminal (tel. 212/249–5776); and in a pavilion in the **Sultanahmet** district of Old Istanbul (Divan Yolu Cad. 3, tel. 212/518–1802 and 518-8754).

Consulates

U.S. (Meşrutiyet Cad. 147, Tepebaşi, Beyoğlu, tel. 212/251–3602). **Canadian** (Büyükdere Cad. 107/3, Bengün Han, tel. 212/272–5174). **U.K.** (Meşrutiyet Cad. 34, Tepebaşi, Beyoğlu, tel. 212/293–7540).

Emergencies

Tourism Police (212/527–4503) They are well-equipped for dealing with travelers' problems. **Ambulance** (tel. 112). **Doctors:** For an English-speaking doctor, call the American Hospital (Güzelbahçe Sok. 20, Nişantaşi, tel. 212/231–4050/69) or the International Hospital (Yesilyurt, tel. 212/663–3000). **Pharmacies:** There is one on duty 24 hours in every neighborhood; tel. 118 for details. Consult the notice in the window of any pharmacy for the name and address of the nearest all-night shop.

One that's centrally located is **Taksim** in the Taksim district (Istiklal Cad. 17, tel. 212/249–2252).

English-Language Bookstores
Dünya Aktuel Bookshop (Istiklal Cad. 469, tel. 212/249–1006) has several branches, including one each in the Hilton and the Swissôtel. **Net** (Yerebatan Cad. 15/3, Sultanahmet, tel. 212/520–8406) publishes tourism guides and **ABC Bookshop** (Istiklâl Cad. 461, tel. 249–2414) sells English-language books and magazines. **Robinson Crusoe** (Istiklal Caddessi 389, Tunel, tel. 212/293–6968 or 293–6977) carries books in major European languages. For English-speakers, there is a fiction section and many coffee-table books about Turkey.

Travel Agencies
Most are concentrated along Cumhuriyet Caddesi, off Taksim Square, in the hotel area. They include **American Express** (Hilton Hotel, Cumhuriyet Cad., Harbiye, tel. 212/241–0248 or 212/241–0249); **Intra** (Halaskargazi Cad. 111/2, Harbiye, tel. 212/247–8174 or 212/240–3891); **Setur** (Cumhuriyet Cad. 107, Harbiye, tel. 212/230–0336); and **Vitur** (Cumhuriyet Cad. 269/4, Harbiye, tel. 212/230–0895). **Istanbul Vision** (Cumhuriyet Cad. No: 12/C, Elmadağ, tel. 212/241–3935) offers a range of tours around Istanbul and into Anatolia; **Fest** (Dikilitaś, Tenigelin Sok., Meksan Binasi, No. 1, 7th Floor, Beśiktaś, tel. 212/258–2589 or 258–2573) specializes in expeditions to less-touristed sections of the city.

Guided Tours

Tours are arranged through travel agencies (*see* Travel Agencies, above). Choices include a half- or full-day "Classical Tour." The full-day guided "Classical Tour" by private car costs between $60 and $90 per person. The half-day tour costs $25 and includes Hagia Sophia, the Museum of Turkish and Islamic Arts, the Hippodrome, Yerebatan Sarayi, and the Blue Mosque; the full-day tour costs $50, and, in addition to the above sights, includes Topkapı Palace, the Süleymaniye Mosque, the Covered or Egyptian Bazaar, and lunch. The "Bosporus Tour" costs $25 for a half day or $50 for a full day, and includes lunch at Sariyer and visits to the Dolmabahçe and Beylerbeyi palaces. The "Night Tour" costs $50 and includes dinner and drinks at Kervansaray or Galata, where there is a show.

Exploring Istanbul

Istanbul is noisy, chaotic, and exciting. Spires and domes of mosques and medieval palaces dominate the skyline. At dawn, when the muezzin's call to prayer rebounds from ancient minarets, many people are making their way home from the nightclubs and bars, while others are kneeling on their prayer rugs, facing Mecca.

Day and night, Istanbul has a schizophrenic air to it. Women in jeans, business suits, or elegant designer outfits pass women wearing the long skirts and head coverings that villagers have worn for generations. Donkey-drawn carts vie with old Chevrolets and Pontiacs or shiny Toyotas and BMWs for dominance of the loud, narrow streets, and the world's most fascinating Oriental bazaar competes with Western boutiques for the time and attention of both tourists and locals.

Ironically, Istanbul's Asian side is filled with Western-style sprawling suburbs, while its European side contains Old Istanbul—an Oriental wonderland of mosques, opulent palaces, and crowded bazaars. The Golden Horn, an inlet 6½ kilometers (4 miles) long, flows off the Bosporus on the European side, separating Old Istanbul from New Town.

The center of New Town is Beyoğlu, a district filled with a combination of modern and turn-of-the-century hotels, banks, and shops grouped around Taksim Square. There are three bridges spanning the Golden Horn: the Atatürk, the Galata, and the Haliç. The historic Galata Bridge, which has been replaced by a modern drawbridge, is a central landmark and a good place to get your bearings. From here, you can see the city's layout and its seven hills. The bridge will also give you a taste of Istanbul's frenetic street life. It's filled with peddlers selling everything from pistachio nuts and spices to curly-toed slippers fancy enough for a sultan; fishermen grill their catch on coal braziers and sell them to passersby. None of this sits well with motorists, who blast their horns constantly, usually to no avail. If you want to orient yourself in a quieter way, take a boat trip from the docks on the Eminönü side of the Galata Bridge up the Bosporus.

Numbers in the margin correspond to points of interest on the Istanbul map.

Old Istanbul (Sultanahmet)

① The number-one attraction in Istanbul is **Topkapı Palace** (Topkapı Saray), located on Seraglio Point in Old Istanbul, known as Sultanahmet. The palace, which dates from the 15th century, was the residence of a number of sultans and their harems until the mid-19th century. To avoid the crowds, try to get there by 9 AM, when the gates open. If you're arriving by taxi, tell the driver you want the Topkapı *Saray* (palace) in Sultanahmet, or you could end up at the remains of the former Topkapı bus terminal on the outskirts of town.

Sultan Mehmet II built the first palace during the 1450s, shortly after the Ottoman conquest of Constantinople. Over the centuries, sultan after sultan added ever more elaborate architectural fantasies, until the palace eventually ended up with more than four courtyards and some 5,000 residents, many of them concubines and eunuchs. Topkapı was the residence and center of bloodshed and drama for the Ottoman rulers until the 1850s, when Sultan Abdül Mecit moved with his harem to the European-style Dolmabahçe Palace farther up the Bosporus coast.

② In Topkapı's outer courtyard are the **Church of St. Irene** (Aya Irini), open **③** only during festival days for concerts, and the **Court of the Janissaries** (Merasim Avlusu), originally for members of the sultan's elite guard.

Adjacent to the ticket office is the **Bab-i-Selam** (Gate of Salutation), built in 1524 by Suleyman the Magnificent, who was the only person allowed to pass through it. In the towers on either side, prisoners were kept until they were executed beside the fountain outside the gate in the first courtyard. In the second courtyard, amid the rose gardens, is the **Divan-i-Humayun,** the assembly room of the council of state, once presided over by the grand vizier (prime minister). The sultan would sit behind a latticed window, hidden by a curtain so no one would know when he was listening, although occasionally he would pull the curtain aside to comment.

One of the most popular tours in Topkapı is the **Harem,** a maze of nearly 400 halls, terraces, rooms, wings, and apartments grouped around the sultan's private quarters on the west side of the second courtyard. Forty rooms are restored and open to the public. Next to the entrance are the quarters of the eunuchs and about 200 of the lesser concubines, who were lodged in tiny cubicles, as cramped and uncomfortable as the main rooms of the Harem are large and opulent. Tours begin every half hour.

In the third courtyard is the **Treasury** (Hazine Dairesi), four rooms filled with jewels, including two uncut emeralds, each weighing 3½ kilograms (7.7 pounds), that once hung from the ceiling. Here, too, you will be dazzled by the emerald dagger used in the movie *Topkapı* and the 84-carat "Spoonmaker" diamond that, according to legend, was found by a pauper and traded for three wooden spoons.

TIME OUT Just past the Treasury, on the right side of the courtyard, are steps leading to a 19th-century rococo Mecidiye pavilion, now the **Konyali Restaurant** (tel. 212/513-9696), which serves excellent Turkish food and has a magnificent view of the seraglio and the Golden Horn. On a terrace below is an outdoor café with an even better view. Go early or reserve a table to beat the tour-group crush. *Open Wed.–Mon. Lunch only.*

In the fourth and last courtyard of the Topkapı Palace are small, elegant summer houses, mosques, fountains, and reflecting pools scattered amid the gardens on different levels. Here you will find the **Erivan Kiosk,** also known as the Revan Kiosk, built by Murat IV in 1636 to commemorate the successful Erivan campaign. In another kiosk in the gardens, called the **Golden Cage** (Iftariye), the closest relatives of the reigning sultan lived in strict confinement under what amounted to house arrest. The custom began during the 1800s after the old custom of murdering all possible rivals to the throne had been abandoned. The confinement of the heirs apparently helped keep the peace, but it deprived them of any chance to prepare themselves for the formidable task of ruling a great empire. *Topkapı Palace, tel. 212/512–0480. Admission: $4.25, harem $1. Open Wed.–Mon. 9:30–5:30.*

To the left as you enter the outer courtyard, a lane slopes downhill to three museums grouped together: the **Archaeological Museum** (Arkeoloji Müzesi), which houses a fine collection of Greek and Roman antiquities, including finds from Ephesus and Troy; the **Museum of the Ancient Orient** (Eski Şark Eserleri Müzesi), with Sumerian, Babylonian, and Hittite treasures; and the **Tiled Pavilion** (Çinili Köşkü), which houses ceramics from the early Seljuk and Osmanli empires. The admission price covers all three museums. *Tel. 212/520–7740. Admission: $2. Open Tues.–Sun. 9:30–5.*

Just outside the walls of Topkapı Palace is **Hagia Sophia** (Church of the Divine Wisdom), one of the world's greatest examples of Byzantine architecture. Built in AD 532 under the supervision of Emperor Justinian, it took 10,000 men six years to complete. Hagia Sophia is made of ivory from Asia, marble from Egypt, and columns from the ruins of Ephesus. The dome was the world's largest until the dome at St. Peter's Basilica was built in Rome 1,000 years later. Hagia Sophia was the cathedral of Constantinople for 900 years, surviving earthquakes and looting Crusaders until 1453, when it was converted into a mosque by Mehmet the Conqueror. Minarets were added by succeeding sultans. Hagia Sophia originally had many mosaics depicting Christian scenes, which were plastered over by Suleyman I, who felt they were inappropriate for a mosque. In 1935, Atatürk converted Hagia Sophia into a museum. Shortly after that, American archaeologists discovered the mosaics, which were restored and are now on display.

According to legend, the **Sacred Column,** in the north aisle of the mosque, "weeps water" that can work miracles. It's so popular that, over the centuries, believers have worn a hole through the marble and brass column. You can stick your finger in it and make a wish. *Ayasofya Meyd., tel. 212/522-1750. Admission: $4.25. Open Tues.–Sun. 9:30–5.*

1136

Archaeological Museum, **4**

Blue Mosque, **6**

Church of St. Irene, **2**

Cistern Basilica, **9**

Court of the Janissaries, **3**

Dolmabahçe Mosque, **16**

Dolmabahçe Palace, **17**

Egyptian Bazaar, **13**

Flower Arcade, **15**

Galata Tower, **14**

Grand Bazaar, **10**

Hagia Sophia, **5**

Hippodrome, **7**

Istanbul University, **11**

Museum of Turkish and Islamic Arts, **8**

Süleymaniye Mosque, **12**

Topkapi Palace, **1**

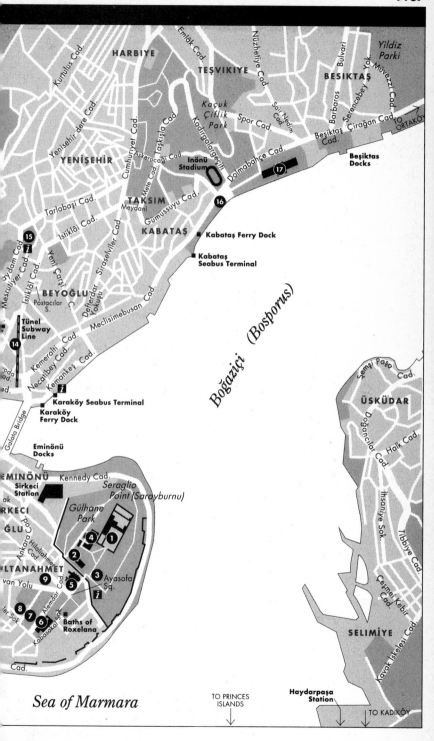

HARBIYE

Kurtulus Cad.

Emlâk Cad.

Nüzhetiye Cad.

Yildiz Parki

TEŞVIKIYE

Barbaros Bulvari

BEŞIKTAŞ

TO ORTAKÖY

Kaçuk Çiflik Park

Spor Cad.

Sair Nedim Cad.

Müvezzi Cad.

Serencebey Yok.

Yenisehir dere Cad.

Cumhuriyet Cad.

Askerocagi Cad.

Taşkisla Cad.

Kadirgalargecti

Beşiktaş Cad.

Ciragan Cad.

YENIŞEHIR

Inönü Stadium

Dolmabahçe Cad.

Beşiktas Docks

Tarlabaşi Cad.

Taksim Meydani

Gumussuyu Cad.

17

Mate Cad.

16

Istiklâl Cad.

Siraselviler Cad.

TAKSIM

Yeni Çarsi

KABATAŞ

Kabataş Ferry Dock

15

i

Meşrutiyet Cad.

Istiklâl Cad.

Kabataş Seabus Terminal

BEYOĞLU

Postacilar S.

Defterdar Yokusu

Meclisimebusan Cad.

Boğaziçi (Bosporus)

Tünel Subway Line

14

Kemeralti Cad.

Necatibey Cad.

Kemankes

Meclisimebusan Cad.

i

Şemsi Paşa Cad.

ÜSKÜDAR

oda.
ad.

Karaköy Seabus Terminal

Karaköy Ferry Dock

Doğancilar Cad.

Halk Cad.

Galata Bridge

Eminönü Docks

Ihsaniye Sok.

EMINÖNÜ

Kennedy Cad.

Seraglio Point (Sarayburnu)

Sirkeci Station

ak

Gülhane Park

Tibbiye Cad.

Çesmei Kebir Cad.

RKECI

ĞLU

Ankara Cad.

Hilalahmer Cad.

4

1

2

LTANAHMET

9

3

Ayasofa Sq.

5

i

van Yolu

Alemdar Cad.

SELIMIYE

8

7

6

Kabasakal Sok.

Baths of Roxelana

er Sok.

Kavak Iskelesi Cad.

Cad.

Sea of Marmara

TO PRINCES ISLANDS

Haydarpaşa Station

TO KADIKÖY

6 Across from Hagia Sophia is the **Blue Mosque** (Sultan Ahmet Camii), with its shimmering blue tiles, 260 stained-glass windows, and six minarets, as grand and beautiful a monument to Islam as Hagia Sophia was to Christianity. Mehmet Aga, also known as Sedefkar (Worker of Mother of Pearl) built the mosque during the reign of Sultan Ahmet I in eight years, beginning in 1609, nearly 1,100 years after the completion of Hagia Sophia. His goal was to surpass Justinian's masterpiece, and many in the world believe he succeeded.

Press through the throngs and enter the mosque at the side entrance that faces Hagia Sophia. Remove your shoes and leave them at the entrance. Immodest clothing is not allowed, but an attendant will lend you a robe if he feels you are not dressed appropriately. *Admission free. Open daily 9–5.*

The **Carpet and Kilim museums** (Hünkar Kasri) are in the mosque's stone-vaulted cellars and upstairs at the end of a stone ramp, where the sultans rested before and after their prayers. *Tel. 212/518–1330. Admission: $1.50 adults, 25¢ students. Open Tues.–Sat. 9–4.*

7 The **Hippodrome** is a long park directly in front of the Blue Mosque. As a Roman stadium with 100,000 seats, it was once the focal point for city life, including chariot races, circuses and public executions. What remain today are an **Egyptian Obelisk** (Dikilitas), the **Column of Constantinos** (Örme Sütun), and the **Serpentine Column** (Yilanli Sütun) taken from the Temple of Apollo at Delphi in Greece.

On the western side of the Hippodrome is **Ibrahim Paşa Palace,** the grandiose residence of the son-in-law and grand vizier of Suleyman the Magnificent. Ibrahim Paşa was executed when he became too powerful for Suleyman's liking.
8 The palace now houses the **Museum of Turkish and Islamic Arts,** which gives a superb insight into the lifestyles of Turks of every level of society, from the 8th century to the present. *Şifahane Sok, across from the Blue Mosque, in line with the Serpentine Column, tel. 212/518–1385 or 212/518–1805. Admission: $2.50. Open Tues.–Sun. 9:30–5.*

Walk back along the length of the Hippodrome and cross the busy main road, Divan Yolu. Turn left onto Hilaliahmer Caddesi. On your left is
9 the **Cistern Basilica** (Yerebatan Sarayı). This is an underground network of waterways first excavated by Emperor Constantine in the 3rd century and then by Emperor Justinian in the 6th century. It has 336 marble columns rising 8 meters (26 feet) to support Byzantine arches and domes. The cistern was always kept full as a precaution against long sieges. *Yerebatan Cad., tel. 212/522–1259. Admission: $2. Open Wed.–Mon. 9–5.*

TIME OUT For a real treat, spend an hour in a Turkish bath. One of the best is **Cağaloğlu Hamamı,** near Hagia Sophia in a magnificent 18th-century building. This establishment also offers luxurious massages, and you can nibble or sip something at the bar as you mellow out after your bath. *Ismail Gürkan Cad. 34, tel. 212/522–2424. Admission: $8 for self-service bath, $15 for full service, $24 for deluxe Ottoman massage. Open daily 8–8 for women; 7 am–10 pm for men.*

10 The shopper's paradise, the **Grand Bazaar** (Kapali Çarşışi) lies about a 1/4 mile northwest of the Hippodrome (a 15-minute walk or 5-minute taxi ride). Also called the Covered Bazaar, this maze of 65 winding, covered streets, hides 4,000 shops, tiny cafés, and restaurants. Originally built by Mehmet the Conqueror in the 1450s, it was ravaged by two modern-day fires, one in 1954 that virtually destroyed it, and a smaller one in 1974. In both cases, the bazaar was quickly rebuilt. It's filled with thousands of curios, including carpets, fabrics, clothing, brass ware, furniture, icons, and gold jewelry. *Yeniçeriler Cad. and Fuatpaşa Cad. Admission free. Open Apr.–Oct., Mon.–Sat. 8:30–7; Nov.–Mar., Mon.–Sat. 8:30–6:30.*

⑪ When you leave the bazaar, cross Fuatpaşa Caddesi and walk around the grounds of **Istanbul University,** which has a magnificent gateway facing Beyazit Square. Follow Besim Ömer Paşa Caddesi, the western border of the university, to the right to the 16th-century **Süleymaniye** **⑫** **Mosque.** The mosque was designed by Sinan, the architectural genius who masterminded more than 350 buildings and monuments under the direction of Suleyman the Magnificent. This is Sinan's grandest and most famous monument, and the burial site of both himself and his patron, Suleyman. *Admission free. Open daily outside prayer hours.*

⑬ The Grand Bazaar isn't the only bazaar in Istanbul. Another one worth visiting is the **Egyptian Bazaar** (Misir Çarşışı). You reach it by walking down Çarşi Caddesi to Çakmakçilar Yokuşu and Firincilar Sokak, and then into Sabunchani Sokak, where you will see the back of the bazaar. It was built in the 17th century as a means of rental income for the upkeep of the Yeni Mosque. The bazaar was once a vast pharmacy, filled with burlap bags overflowing with herbs and spices for folk remedies. Today, you're more likely to see bags full of fruit, nuts, Royal Jelly from the beehives of the Aegean coast, and white sacks spilling over with culinary spices. Some shopkeepers will offer you tastes of energizing pastes, such as *macun*, as well as dried fruits or other Turkish delights. Nearby are equally colorful fruit and fish markets. *Next to Yeni Cami. Open Mon.–Sat. 8–7.*

TIME OUT **Pandeli.** Savory food is served in this frenetic turn-of-the-century restaurant, with its domed alcoves. Try the *kağitta levrek* (paper-wrapped grilled sea bass). It is up two flights of stairs over the arched gateway to the Egyptian Bazaar. *Misir Carsişi, Eminönü, tel. 212/527–3909. AE, DC, MC, V. Lunch only. Closed Sun. $$*

New Town
New Town is the area on the northern shore of the Golden Horn, the waterway that cuts through Istanbul and divides Europe from Asia. **⑭** The area's most prominent landmark is the **Galata Tower,** built by the Genoese in 1349 as part of their fortifications. In this century, it served as a fire lookout until 1960. Today it houses a restaurant and nightclub (*see* Nightlife, *below*), and a viewing tower. *Büyük Hendek Cad. Admission: $1. Open daily 9–8.*

⑮ North of the tower is the **Flower Arcade** (Çiçek Pasaji), off Istiklâl Caddesi, a lively blend of tiny restaurants, bars, and street musicians. Strolling further on Istiklâl Caddesi is an experience in itself. The busy pedestrian road is lined with shops, restaurants, banks and cafés in turn-of-the-century buildings. The restored original 19th century tram still carries people from Tunel to Taksim Square. On the side streets you'll find Greek and Armenian churches, bars and other establishments; in the narrow, poorer residential alleys, you'll see laundry hanging between the old buildings, as you dodge through the children at play.

Next head for Dolmabahçe Mosque and Dolmabahçe Palace, which are reached by following Istiklâl Caddesi to Taksim Square and then taking Inönü (Gümüssuyu) Caddesi around the square downhill to a **⑯** junction. You will see the **Dolmabahçe Mosque** on your right and the clock tower and gateway to Dolmabahçe Palace on your left. The mosque is a separate building from the palace. It was founded by Valide Sultan Bezmialem, mother of Abdül Mecit I, and was completed in 1853. *Admission free. Open daily outside prayer hours.*

⑰ The **Dolmabahçe Palace** was also built in 1853 and, until the declaration of the modern republic in 1923, was the residence of the last sultans of the Ottoman Empire. It was also the residence of Atatürk, who died here in 1938. The palace, floodlit at night, is an extraordinary mixture of Hindu, Turkish, and European styles of architecture and interior design. Queen Victoria's contribution to the lavishness was a chandelier weighing 4½ tons. Guided tours of the palace take about 80 minutes. *Gümüssuyu Cad., tel. 212/258–5544. Admission: $4.80. Open Apr.–Oct. 9–4; Nov.–Mar. 9–3. Closed Mon.*

Shopping

Gift Ideas

The **Grand Bazaar** (*see* Exploring Istanbul, *above*) is a what it sounds like: a smattering of all things Turkish—carpets, brass, copper, jewelry, textiles, and leather goods. Tünel Square, a quick short metro ride up from Karaköy, is a quaint group of stores with old prints, books, and artifacts.

Stores

Stores and boutiques are located in New Town on such streets as **Istiklâl Caddesi**, which runs off Taksim Square, and **Rumeli, Halaskargazi,** and **Valikonagi Caddeleri,** north of the Hilton Hotel. Two streets in the Kadiköy area that offer good shopping are **Bağdat** and **Bahariye Caddeleri.** In Altunizade on the Asian side, **Capitol,** a new and slick mall, offers shoppers movies and entertainment, too. **Ataköy Shopping and Tourism Center** is a large shopping and leisure mall near the airport, while **Akmerkez,** the newest of the malls in Etiler, draws those who like luxury and designer wear.

Markets

Balikpazari (fish market) is in Beyoğlu Caddesi, off Istiklâl Caddesi. Despite its name, you will find anything connected with food at this market. A **flea market** is held in Beyazit Square, near the Grand Bazaar, every Sunday from about 10 AM. A crafts market, with street entertainment, is open on Sundays along the Bosporus at Ortaköy. A weekend crafts market is also held on Bekar Sokak, off Istiklal Caddesi.

Dining

Istanbul has a wide range of eating establishments, with prices to match. Most of the major hotels have dining rooms serving rather bland international cuisine. It's far more rewarding to eat in Turkish restaurants. For details and price-category definitions, *see* Dining *in* Staying in Turkey, *above.*

$$$$ **Körfez.** The specialty here is seafood dishes such as bass baked in salt. The restaurant boat ferries guests across the Bosporus from Rumeli Hisari. *Kanlica, tel. 216/413–4098. Reservations advised. AE, DC, MC, V. Closed Mon. and Nov.–Apr.*

$$$$ **Tugra.** Located in the historic Çiragan Palace, this spacious and luxurious restaurant serves the most delectable of long-savored Ottoman recipes, including stuffed bluefish and Circassian chicken. The Bosporus view is framed by the palace's marble columns; high ceilings carry dazzlingly crafted glass chandeliers. *Ciraǧan Cad. 84, Beşiktaş, tel. 212/258–3377, ext. 7684. Reservations advised. AE, DC, MC, V.*

$$$$ **Ulus 29.** Seafood is the specialty at this chic restaurant tucked away in a park in the upscale Ulus district. The terrace has spectacular views spanning both Bosporus bridges. In the summer, guests are ferried across to the Bosporus site, Çubuklu 29, which is reminiscent of a Roman villa. *Ahmet Adnan Saygun Cad., Ulus Park, tel. 212/265–6181 in spring, fall and winter; Paşabahçe Yolu, Çubuklu, tel. 216/322–3888 in summer. Reservations required. Dinner only. AE, DC, MC, V.*

$$$ **Divan.** You'll enjoy gourmet Turkish and international cuisine, elegant surroundings, and excellent service at this restaurant in the Divan hotel. *Cumhuriyet Cad. 2, Elmadağ, tel. 212/231–4100. Reservations advised. AE, DC, MC, V. Closed Sun.*

$$$ **Gelik.** This restaurant in a two-story 19th-century villa is usually packed, often with people who want to savor its specialty: various meats cooked in deep wells. *Sahil Yolu, Ataköy, tel. 212/560–7284. Reservations advised. AE, DC, MC, V.*

$$$ **Urcan.** A dramatic array of fresh fish and lobsters welcome you to this Bosporus fish restaurant, one of the finest in town. It's one of those places where locals bring visitors they want to impress, so you may see some visiting dignitary or celebrity. The decor is heavily nautical. *Orta Çeşme Cad., 2/1, Sariyer, tel. 212/242–0367. Reservations advised. AE, DC, V.*

$$ **Borsa Lokantasi.** This unpretentious restaurant serves some of the best
★ food in Turkey. The baked lamb in eggplant purée and the stuffed artichokes are not to be missed. *Yaliköskü Cad. Yaliköskü Han 60–62, Eminönü, tel. 212/522–4173. Lunch only. No credit cards. Closed Sun. Another branch at Halaskargazi Cad. 90/1, Osmanbey, tel. 212/232–4200. AE, DC, MC, V.*

$$ **Dört Mevsim.** Located in a large Victorian building, Dört Mevsim is noted for its blend of Turkish and French cuisine and for its owners, Gay and Musa, an Anglo-Turkish couple who opened it in 1965. On any given day, you'll find them in the kitchen overseeing such delights as shrimp in cognac sauce and baked marinated lamb. *Istiklâl Cad. 509, Beyoğlu, tel. 212/293–3941. Reservations advised. AE, DC, MC, V. Closed Sun.*

$$ **Dunya.** The frenetic traffic of the adjacent Ortaköy Square and waiters balancing appetizer trays is countered by the picturesque Bosporus view, which on summer nights includes many passing pleasure boats. The grilled *cupra* (breem) is a must, while mezes are always fresh and sumptuous. *Salhane Sok. 10, Ortaköy, tel. 212/258–6385. Reservations advised. No credit cards.*

$$ **Hanedan.** The emphasis is on kebabs, all kinds, all excellent; there are better-than-average mezes, too. The setting is lively, by the Besiktas ferry terminal. *Çiğdem Sok. 27, Besiktas, tel. 212/260–4854. Reservations advised. AE, MC, V.*

$ **Hacibaba.** This is a large, cheerful-looking place, with a terrace overlooking a churchyard. Fish, meat, and a wide variety of vegetable dishes are on display for your selection. Before you choose your main course, you'll be offered a tray of mezes that can be a meal in themselves. *Istiklal Cad. 49, Taksim, tel. 212/244–1886. Reservations advised. AE, DC, MC, V.*

$ **Haci Salih.** A tiny, family-run restaurant, Haci Salih has only 10 ta-
★ bles, so you may have to line up and wait—but it's worth it. Traditional Turkish food is the fare here, with special emphasis on vegetable dishes and lamb. Alcohol is not served, but you can bring your own. *Anadolu Han 201, off Istiklâl Cad., Beyoğlu, tel. 212/243–4528. Lunch only. No credit cards. Closed Sun.*

$ **Rejans.** Founded by two Russians and a Crimean fleeing the Bolshevik revolution, this restaurant offers traditional East European decor and excellent Russian food and vodka. With its Old World atmosphere and eccentric waiters, this has become an Istanbul institution. *Istiklal Cad., Olivo Gecidi 15, Galatasaray, tel. 212/244–1610. Reservations advised. V. Closed Sun.*

$ Yakup. This cheery hole-in-the-wall is smoky and filled with locals rather than tourists, and it can get loud, especially if there is a football (soccer) match on television. From the stuffed peppers to the *tereyağli borek* (buttered pastries) and octopus salad, the mezes are above average. *Asmali Mescit Sok. 35–37, Beyoğlu, tel. 212/249–2925. Reservations advised. AE, MC, V.*

Lodging

The top hotels are located mainly around Taksim Square in New Town. Hotels generally include the 15% VAT and a service charge of 10–15% in the rate. Modern, middle-range hotels usually have a friendly staff, which compensates for the generally bland architecture and interiors. In Old Istanbul, the Aksaray, Laleli, Sultanahmet, and Beyazit areas have many conveniently located, inexpensive small hotels and family-run pansiyons. Istanbul has a chronic shortage of beds, so plan ahead. For details and price-category definitions, *see* Lodging *in* Staying in Turkey, *above.*

$$$$ Çirağan Palace. This 19th-century Ottoman palace is the city's most
★ luxurious—and expensive—hotel. The swimming pool is right at the edge of the Bosporus. Guest rooms in the palace have a view of the new hotel and the rooms in the new hotel have a view of the palace (and are cheaper). *Çirağan Cad. 84, Beşiktaş, tel. 212/258–3377, fax 212/259–6687. 340 rooms with bath. Facilities: 4 restaurants, bar, Turkish bath, health spa, pool, casino, shops. AE, DC, MC, V.*

$$$$ Hilton. Lavishly decorated with Turkish rugs and large brass urns, this is one of the best Hiltons in the chain. Ask for a room overlooking the Bosporus. *Cumhuriyet Cad., Harbiye, tel. 212/231–4646, fax 212/240–4165. 510 rooms with bath. Facilities: restaurant, rooftop bar, conference facilities, Turkish baths, pool, tennis, squash, beauty and health spa, shop, casino. AE, DC, MC, V.*

$$$$ Hyatt Regency. This massive but tasteful pink building, reminiscent of Ottoman splendor, houses one of the city's newer five-star hotels. Many rooms have views of the Bosporus. The interior has plush carpeting and the decor is combination of earth tones in many textures. The restaurants serve a range of Asian, Turkish, and Italian foods. *Taşkişla Cad., Taksim, tel. 212/225–7000, fax 212/225–7007. 360 rooms with bath. Facilities: 2 restaurants, bar, café, pool, tennis courts, health club, business center, baby-sitting service. AE, DC, MC, V.*

$$$$ Pera Palace. A grand hotel with a genuinely Turkish feel, the Pera Palace
★ was built in 1892 to accommodate guests arriving on the *Orient Express.* Although it has been modernized for comfort, the hotel has lost none of its original Victorian opulence. The likes of Atatürk, Agatha Christie, and even Greta Garbo once slept here. There is talk of turning the legendary building into a Cultural Ministry Museum. *Meşrutiyet Cad. 98, Tepebaşi, tel. 212/251–4560, fax 212/251–4089. 145 rooms with bath. Facilities: bar. AE, DC, MC, V.*

$$$$ Sheraton. Taksim Park provides a splendid setting for this hotel and all rooms have views of the Bosporus or the square. For a night's spree, try the rooftop restaurant and nightclub. *Taksim Park, Taksim, tel. 212/231–2121, fax 212/231–2180. 437 rooms with bath. Facilities: restaurant, bar, nightclub, pool, health and beauty spa. AE, DC, MC, V.*

$$$ Ayasofia Pansiyons. These guest houses are part of an imaginative project undertaken by the Touring and Automobile Club to restore a little street of historic wooden houses along the outer wall of Topkapı

Palace. One of the houses has been converted into a library and two into pansiyons, furnished in late Ottoman style, with excellent dining rooms. During the summer, tea and refreshments are served in the gardens to guests and nonguests alike. *Soğukçeşme Sok., Sultanahmet, tel. 212/513–3660, fax 212/512–3669. 63 rooms with bath. Facilities: restaurant, café, bar, Turkish bath. AE, MC, V.*

$$$ Divan. Quiet, but close enough to Taksim Square, this old hotel has recently been renovated; some rooms have private terraces overlooking the Bosporus. The restaurant here is renowned for impeccably prepared Turkish and international dishes. *Cumhuriyet Cad. 2, Şişli, tel. 212/231–4100, fax 212/248–8527. 180 rooms with bath. Facilities: restaurant, bar, tea shop, beauty salon. AE, DC, MC.*

$$$ Yeşil Ev (Green House). Practically next door to the Blue Mosque, this
★ 19th-century building is decorated in old-fashioned Ottoman style with lace curtains and latticed shutters. Its high-walled garden restaurant is a verdant and peaceful oasis in the midst of frenetic Istanbul. *Kabasakal Sok. 5, Sultanahmet, tel. 212/517–6785, fax 212/517–6780. 20 rooms with bath. Facilities: restaurant and garden. AE, MC, V.*

$$ Barin. Modern, clean, and comfortable, with good, friendly service, the Barin caters to business travelers as well as tourists. *Fevziye Cad. 7, Şehzadebaşi, tel. 212/513–9100, fax 212/526–4440. 65 rooms with bath. AE, DC, MC, V.*

$$ Barut's Guesthouse. Quiet and secluded and in the heart of Old Istanbul,
★ Barut's has a peaceful roof terrace overlooking the Sea of Marmara. The hotel also has a modern art gallery in its foyer. *Ishakpaşa Cad. 8, Sultanahmet, tel. 212/516–0357, fax 212/516–2944. 23 rooms with bath. MC, V.*

$$ Büyük Londra. This is another Victorian hotel, similar to the Pera Palace—not quite as grand—that has grown old gracefully. *Meşrutiyet Cad. 117, Tepebaşi, tel. 212/293–1619 or 249–1025, fax 212/245–0671. 54 rooms with bath. AE, MC, V.*

$$ Richmond. A turn-of-the-century building on Istiklâl Caddesi was renovated to create this comfortable hotel. Downstairs is the Lebon patisserie, which is a remake of the 19th century pastry shop that once operated there. *Istiklâl Cad. 445, tel. 212/252–5460, fax 212/252–9707. 101 rooms with bath. Facilities: restaurant, bar, café. AE, V.*

$ Berk Guest House. An English-speaking couple, Güngör and Nevin Evrensel run this tidy little inn. Two rooms have balconies overlooking a garden. *Kutlugün Sok. 27, Cankurtaran, Sultanahmet, tel. 212/516–9671, fax 212/517–7715. 7 rooms with bath. No credit cards.*

$ Hotel Empress Zoe. Named after an empress who ruled Byzantium in the 11th century, this unusual property is decorated with murals and paintings in that era's style. Rooms, which are of varying configurations, are brightened with colorful embroidered textiles—some have views. The American owner, Ann Nevans, is a graceful manager and can help out with personalized itineraries of the nearby Sultanahmet sights and beyond. *Akbik Cad., Adliye Sok. 10, Sultanahmet, tel. 212/518–2504, fax 212/518–5699. 12 rooms with bath. MC, V.*

The Arts

Entertainment in Istanbul ranges from the **Istanbul International Festival**—held late-June through mid-July and attracting internationally renowned artists and performers—to local folklore and theatrical groups, some amateur, some professional. Because there is no central ticket agency, ask your hotel for help. You can also pick up tickets at the box office or through a local tourist office.

For tickets to the Istanbul International Festival, apply to the **Istanbul Foundation for Culture and Arts** (Kültür ve Sanat Vakfi, Yildiz, Besiktaş, tel. 212/260–4533). Tickets can also be purchased at the Marmara Hotel, in Taksim Square, tel. 212/251–4696. Performances, which include modern and classical music, ballet, opera, and theater, are given throughout the city in historic buildings, such as the Church of St. Irene and Rumeli Castle. The highlight of the festival is the performance of Mozart's opera *Abduction from the Seraglio,* at Topkapı Palace, the site that inspired the opera. The season at the City of Istanbul's **Cemal Resit Rey Concert Hall** (tel. 212/248–9404 or 212/248–5392) runs from September through May and includes classical and jazz music, as well as ballet performed by visiting and local groups.

Concerts

Tickets for performances at the main concert hall, **Atatürk Kültür Merkezi,** are available from the box office at Taksim Square (tel. 212/251–5600). From October through May, the **Istanbul State Symphony** gives performances here. Ballet and dance companies also perform at this hall.

Nightlife

Bars and Nightclubs

Bebek Bar (Bebek Ambassadeurs Hotel, Cevdet Paşa Cad. 113, Bebek, tel. 212/263–3000) has views over the Bosporus. The crowd here includes locals from the neighborhood and nearby Bosporus University. Open daily until 1 AM.

Beyoğlu Pub (Istiklâl Cad. 140/7, Beyoğlu, tel. 212/252–3842) is behind an arcade off Istiklal in a pleasant garden and frequented by moviegoers and an expatriate crowd.

Cuba Bar (Vapur Iskelesi Sok. 20, Ortaköy, tel. 212/260–0550) is for those who like their drinks to the swing of Latin music, often live. **Kepkedi** (Birinci Cad. 17/1, Arnavutköy, tel. 212/263–3234) is a waterfront bar on the Bosporus where cat lovers and others congregate for drinks and live music between the cat paraphernalia-cluttered walls. (The name of the bar means "very cat.")

Orient Express Bar (Pera Palace Hotel, Meşrutiyet Cad. 98, Tepebaşi, tel. 212/251–4560) distills the atmosphere of old Istanbul with the lingering presence of the rich, powerful, and famous (from Atatürk to Italian King Victor Emmanuel to Josephine Baker) who once played here.

Tribunal (Istiklâl Cad. Muammer Karaca Cikmazi 3, tel. 212/249–7179) once served as a French court and retains the original inlaid brick ceiling. Live bands perform authentic gypsy, Greek, or Latin music after 11 PM. On weekends, the bar is open until 4 AM.

A well-established nightclub is **Kervansaray** (Cumhuriyet Cad. 30, Elmadağ, tel. 212/247–1630), where you can dine, dance, and watch bellydancing shows every evening until midnight. Two other good places for floor shows are **Balim** (Kemerhatun Mah. Hamalbaşi Cad. 8, Beyoğlu, tel. 212/249–5608) and **Olimpia** (Acar Sok. Tomtom Mah., off Istiklâl Cad., tel. 212/244–9456). **Galata Tower** (Kuledibi, tel. 212/245–1160) offers dinner between 8:30 and 10, with a Turkish show and dancing from 10 PM to 1 AM.

Jazz

Hayal Kahvesi (Büyük Parmakkapi Sok. 19, Beyoğlu, tel. 212/244–2558) is a bohemian side-street bar with wooden furniture and lace curtains. Local groups perform jazz, blues, and rock; Tuesday and Friday are jazz nights.

Tepe Bar Lounge (Marmara Hotel, Taksim Square, tel. 212/251–4696) is on the top floor of the Marmara Hotel and has a 360-degree view of Istanbul. Local and visiting musicians play every evening from 11 to 1 PM.

Discos

The hottest place in town is **2019** (Oto Sanayi Sitesi, Maslak, tel. 212/285–1896), a dramatic outdoor junkyard-turned-disco, reminiscent of a *Mad Max* movie set. **Memo's** (Salhane Sok. 10, Ortaköy, tel. 212/261–8304) is also located near the hopping Ortaköy square and is home to a faithful yuppie clientele. The disco gets rolling around 11 PM. **Cities** (Nispetiye Cad. 29, Etiler, tel. 212/263–5411) is a posh and trendy bar, recently renovated in Viennese style, that turns into a disco after 11 PM. **Çubuklu 29** (Bahçeburun, Çubuklu, tel. 212/331–2829), situated by the Bosporus on the Asian side, is open from mid-June through September. **Şaziye** (Eytam Cad. 21, Maçka tel. 212/232–4155 or 212/231–1401) turns into a popular disco after 11:30 PM.

THE AEGEAN COAST

Some of the finest reconstructed Greek and Roman cities, including the fabled Pergamum, Ephesus, Aphrodisias, and Troy, are found in this region of Turkey. Bright yellow road signs pointing to historical sites or to those currently undergoing excavation are everywhere here. There are so many Greek and Roman ruins, in fact, that some haven't yet been excavated and others are going to seed.

Grand or small, all the sites are steeped in atmosphere and are best explored early in the morning or late in the afternoon, when there are fewer crowds. You can escape the heat of the day on one of the sandy beaches that line the coast.

Getting Around

The E24 from Çanakkale follows the coast until it turns inland at Kuşadasi to meet the Mediterranean again at Antalya. All the towns on the itinerary are served by direct bus routes, and there are connecting services to the ancient sites.

Guided Tours

The travel agencies in all the major towns offer tours of the historical sites. **Troy-Anzac Tours** (tel. 286/217–5849 or 286/217–5847), in central Çanakkale, has guided tours of the battlefields at Gallipoli. The tour takes about four hours and costs about $11 per person, including breakfast. Travel agencies along Teyyare Caddesi in Kuşadasi offer escorted tours to Ephesus; Priene, Miletus, and Didyma; and Aphrodisias and Pamukkale.

Tourist Information

Contact the tourist office in each town for names of travel agencies and licensed tour guides.

Ayvalık (Yat Limani Karşisi, tel. 266/312–2122).
Bergama (Zafer Mah. İzmir Cad. 54, tel. 232/633–1862).
Bursa (Ulu Cami Parki, Atatürk Cad. 1, tel. 224/221–2359).
Çanakkale (İskele Meyd. 67, tel. 286/217–1187).
Çeşme (İskele Meyd. 8, tel. 232/712–6653).

İzmir (Atatürk Cad. 418, Alsancak, tel. 232/422–0207; Gaziosman-pasa Bul. 1/C, tel. 232/484–2147).
Kuşadasi (Iskele Meyd. tel. 256/614–1103).

Exploring the Aegean Coast

Bursa

Bursa, the first capital of the Ottoman Empire, is known as Yeşil (Green) Bursa, not only because of its many trees and parks but also because of its **Yeşil Cami** (Green Mosque) and **Yeşil Türbe** (Green Mausoleum). Both the mosque and mausoleum derive their names from the green tiles that line their interiors. They are across from each other on Yeşil Caddesi (the appropriately-named "Green Avenue"). *Admission free. Open daily outside prayer hours.*

Bursa is also the site of **Uludağ** (the Great Mountain), Turkey's most popular ski resort. To fully appreciate why the town is called Green Bursa, take a ride on the *teleferik* (cable car) from Namazgah Caddesi up the mountain for a panoramic view.

The town square is called **Heykel,** which means "statue," and is named for its statue of Atatürk. Off Heykel, along Atatürk Caddesi, is the **Ulu Cami** (Great Mosque) with its distinctive silhouette of 20 domes. *Admission free. Open daily outside prayer hours.*

Troy

Long thought to be simply an imaginary city from Homer's *Iliad,* **Troy** was excavated in the 1870s by Heinrich Schliemann, a German amateur archaeologist who also found the remains of nine successive civilizations, one on top of the other, dating back 5,000 years. Considering Troy's fame, the site is surprisingly small. It's best to take a guided tour to appreciate fully the significance of this discovery and the unwavering passion of the man who proved that Troy was not just another ancient myth. *Admission: $2.50. Open daily 8–7.*

The E24 highway leads around the **Gulf of Edremit,** a glorious area of olive groves, pine forests, and small seaside resorts. **Ayvalık,** 5 kilometers (3 miles) off the main bus route, between Çanakkale and İzmir, is an ideal place to stay while visiting the ruins of ancient Pergamum, 40 kilometers (24 miles) away. From Ayvalık you can take boats to **Ali Bey Adası,** a tiny island with pleasant waterfront restaurants, and to the Greek island of Lesbos.

Pergamum

Pergamum is reached by driving southeast along E24 following the signs toward Bergama, the modern-day name of the ancient Greek-Roman site. If you're traveling by bus, be certain it is going all the way to Bergama, or you'll find yourself dropped off at the turn-in, 8 kilometers (5 miles) from the site.

Because the ruins of Pergamum are spread out over several miles, it's best to take a taxi from one site to the next. The most noteworthy places are the Asklepieion, the Ethnological Museum, the Red Hall, and the **Acropolis.** *Admission: $2.50. Open Apr.–Oct., daily 8:30–6:30; Nov.–Mar., daily 8:30–5:30.*

Pergamum's glory peaked during the Greek Attalid dynasty (241–133 BC), when it was one of the world's most magnificent architectural and artistic centers—especially so under the rule of Eumenes II, who lavished his great wealth on the city. Greek rule continued until 133 BC, when the mad Attalus III died, bequeathing the entire kingdom to Rome.

The Aegean Coast

The most famous building at the acropolis is the **library,** which once contained a collection of 200,000 books, all on papyrus. The library's collection was second only to the one in Alexandria, Egypt. When the troops of Julius Caesar burned down the library in Alexandria, Mark Antony consoled Cleopatra by shipping the entire collection of books from Pergamum to Alexandria. These, too, went up in flames 400 years later, in wars between Muslims and Christians.

İzmir

The coastal area between Bergama and **İzmir,** 104 kilometers (64 miles), was once thick with ancient Greek settlements. Today only İzmir remains. Called Smyrna by the Greeks, it was a vital trading port that was often ravaged by wars and earthquakes. İzmir was completely destroyed by a fire in 1922 following Turkey's War of Independence against Greece. The war was a bloody battle to win back the Aegean coast, which had been given to the Greeks in the 1920 Treaty of Sèvres. Atatürk was in İzmir helping to celebrate the victory when celebrations soon turned to horror as the fire engulfed the city.

The city was quickly rebuilt, and it then became known by its Turkish name, İzmir. It's a lively, modern city filled with wide boulevards and apartment houses and office buildings. The center of the city is **Kültürpark,** a large green park that is the site of İzmir's industrial fair from late August to late September (a time when most hotels are full).

On top of İzmir's highest hill is the **Kadifekale** (Velvet Fortress), built in the 3rd century BC by Lysimachos. It is easily reached by dolmuş and is one of the few ancient ruins that was not destroyed in the fire. At the foot of the hill is the restored **Agora,** the market of ancient Smyrna. The modern-day marketplace is in **Konak Square,** a maze of tiny streets filled with shops and covered stalls. *Open 8–8. Closed Sun.*

Kuşadası

Kuşadası, about 80 kilometers (50 miles) south of İzmir on Route 300, has grown since the late 1970s from a fishing village into a sprawling, hyperactive town geared to serving thousands of tourists who visit the nearby ruins and beaches. Still, the busy town maintains an easy pace.

Ephesus

The major attraction near Kuşadası is **Ephesus,** a city created by the Ionians in the 11th century BC and now one of the grandest reconstructed ancient sites in the world. It is the showpiece of Aegean archaeology. Ephesus was a powerful trading port and the sacred center for the cult of Artemis, Greek goddess of chastity, the moon, and hunting. The Ionians built a temple in her honor, one of the Seven Wonders of the Ancient World. During the Roman period, it became a shrine for the Roman goddess Diana. Today, waterlogged foundations are all that remain of the temple.

Allow yourself one full day for Ephesus. The city is especially appealing out of season, when it can seem like a ghost town, with its shimmering, long, white marble road grooved by chariot wheels.

Some of the splendors you can see here include the two-story **Library of Celsus;** houses of nobles, with their terraces and courtyards; a 25,000-seat **amphitheater,** still used today during the Selçuk Ephesus Festival of Culture and Art; remains of the municipal baths; and a brothel. *Admission: $5.50. Admission to the houses on the slopes: $1.20. Open daily 8:30–6 (summer), 8:30–5 (winter).*

Selçuk

On Ayasoluk Hill in **Selçuk,** 4 kilometers (2½ miles) from Ephesus, is the restored **Basilica of St. John** (St. Jean Aniti), containing the tomb of the apostle. Near the entrance to the basilica is the **Ephesus Museum,** with two statues of Artemis. The museum also has marvelous frescoes and mosaics among its treasures. *Admission: $2.50. Basilica and museum open Tues.–Sun. 8:30–6.*

St. Paul and St. John preached in both Ephesus and Selçuk and changed the cult of Artemis into the cult of the Virgin Mary. **Meryemana,** 5 kilometers (3 miles) from Ephesus, has the **House of Mary,** thought to have been the place where St. John took the mother of Jesus after the crucifixion and where some believe she ascended to heaven. *Admission $1.20. Open daily 7:30–sunset.*

Priene, Miletus, and Didyma

Priene and Miletus, 40 kilometers (25 miles) from Kuşadası, are sister cities, also founded by the Ionians in the 11th century BC. Nearby is **Didyma,** a holy sanctuary dedicated to Apollo. **Priene,** on top of a steep hill, was an artistic and cultural center. Its main attraction is the **Temple of Athena,** a spectacular sight, with its five fluted columns and its backdrop of mountains and the fertile plains of the Meander River. You can also see the city's small amphitheater, gymnasium, council chambers, marketplace, and stadium. *Admission: $1.20. Open daily 8:30–6.*

Nearby, **Miletus,** once a prosperous port, was the first Greek city to use coins for money. It also became an Ionian intellectual center and home to such philosophers as Thales, Anaximander, and Anaximenes, all of whom made contributions to mathematics and the natural sciences. The city's most magnificent building is the **Great Theater,** a remarkably intact 25,000-seat amphitheater built by the Ionians and kept up by the Romans. Climb to the highest seats in the amphitheater for a view across the city to the bay. *Admission: ruins $1.20, museum $1.20. Open Tues.–Sun. 8:30–6.*

Didyma

The temple of **Didyma** is reached by a 32-kilometer (20-mile) road called the **Sacred Way,** starting from Miletus at the bay. The temple's oracles were as revered as those of Delphi. Under the courtyard is a network of corridors whose walls would throw the oracle's voice into deep and ghostly echoes. The messages would then be interpreted by the priests. Fragments of bas-relief include a gigantic head of Medusa and a small statue of Poseidon and his wife, Amphitrite. *Admission: $1.20. Open daily 8:30–6.*

Pamukkale

East of Kuşadasıı, 215 kilometers (133 miles) away, is **Pamukkale,** which first appears as an enormous chalky white cliff rising some 330 feet from the plains. Mineral-rich volcanic spring water cascades over basins and natural terraces, crystallizing into white stalactites—curtains of solidified water seemingly suspended in air. The hot springs in the area were popular with the ancient Romans, who believed them to have curative powers. You can see the remains of Roman baths among the ruins of nearby **Hierapolis.** The village of Pamukkale has many small hotels surrounding the hot springs, which are used today by people who still believe that they cure a variety of problems, including rheumatism. Farther down in the village are inexpensive pansiyons, some also with hot springs. It's best to stay in Pamukkale overnight before heading on to the ruins of **Aphrodisias,** a city of 60,000 dedicated to Aphrodite, the Greek goddess of love and fertility. It thrived from 100 BC to AD 500. Aphrodisias is reached via **Karacasu,** a good place to stop for lunch; fresh trout is the local specialty. Aphrodisias is filled with marble baths, temples, and theaters, all overrun with wild blackberries and pomegranates. Across a field sprinkled with poppies and sunflowers is a well-preserved **stadium,** which was built for 30,000 spectators.

Dining and Lodging

For details and price-category definitions, *see* Dining and Lodging *in* Staying in Turkey, *above.*

Ayvalık
LODGING
Büyük Berk. Part of a larger complex, this modern hotel sits on Ayvalık's best beach, about 3¼ kilometers (2 miles) from the center of town. *Sarimsakli Mev., tel. 266/324–1045, fax 266/324–1194. 180 rooms with bath. Facilities: restaurant, disco, outdoor pool. $$*
Ankara Oteli. Located on Sarimsakli beach, just a few feet from the surf, the Ankara Oteli gives excellent value for the money. *Sarimsakli Mev., tel. 266/324–1195 or 266/324–1048, fax 266/324–0022. 104 rooms with bath. Facilities: restaurant, café, bar, game room. No credit cards. $*

Bergama
LODGING
Hotel Iskender. The 1990 structure is plain, modern (air conditioning against the hot summers, etc.) and conveniently situated in the center of town. An outdoor restaurant serves tasty fresh mezes and grilled foods. *İzmir Cad. Ilica Önü Mevkii, tel. 232/633–1245, fax 232/633–1245. 60 rooms with bath. Facilities: 2 restaurants, bar. No credit cards. $$*
Tusan Bergama Moteli. The rooms here are simple, clean, and just off the main road to Bergama. While the location is not that convenient

if you don't have a car, the facilities are enough for a one-night stay. The real draw, though, is a pool fed by hot springs. *İzmir Yolu, Çati Mev., tel. and fax 232/633–1938. 42 rooms with bath. Facilities: restaurant, swimming pool. No credit cards. $$*

Bursa

DINING

Cumurcul. A converted old house has become a local favorite, where grilled meats and fish are both attentively prepared. *Çekirge Cad., tel. 224/235–3707. Reservations advised. V. $$*

Kebabcı Iskender. Bursa is famous for the dish served here, *Iskender Kebab* (Alexander's kebab), slivers of skewer-grilled meat served with tomato sauce and yogurt. *Ünlü Cad. 7, Heykel, tel. 224/221–4615. No credit cards. $*

LODGING

★ **Celik Palace.** After guests have indulged at the hotel's restaurant, casino, and clubs, they can enjoy the crowning luxury: a dip in the domed, Roman-style pool fed by hot springs. *Çekirge Cad. 79, tel. 224/233–3800, fax 224/236–1910. 173 rooms with bath. Facilities: restaurant, bar, pool, meeting room, casino, nightclub, disco. AE, DC, MC, V. $$$*

Ada Palas. As at many properties in this region, guests here have use of a thermal pool. This comfortable hotel is just a short walk from the shore and is near Kültür Park, the center of town. *Murat Cad. 21, tel. 224/236–3990, fax 224/236–4656. 39 rooms with bath. Facilities: restaurant. V. $$*

Çanakkale and Troy

LODGING

Akol. This modern hotel is perched on the waterfront in Çanakkale; ask for a room with a terrace overlooking the Dardanelles. *Kordonboyu, tel. 286/217–9456, fax 286/217–2897. 138 rooms with bath. Facilities: restaurant, bar, outdoor pool, disco, meeting room. AE, MC, V. $$*

Büyük Truva. Near the center of Çanakkale, the Truva is an excellent base for sightseeing. *Kordonboyu, tel. 286/217–1024, fax 286/217–0903. 66 rooms with bath. Facilities: restaurant, bar. No credit cards. $$*

Tusan. Along the beachfront north of Troy at Güzelyali, and framed by a pine forest, the Tusan is one of the most popular hotels in the area. Be certain to reserve well in advance. *Güzelyali, tel. 286/232–8210 or 286/232–8273, fax 286/232–8226. 64 rooms with bath. Facilities: restaurant, bar, disco. MC, V. Closed Oct.–Feb. $*

Çeşme

LODGING

Kanuni Kervansaray. Built in 1528 during the reign of Suleyman the Magnificent, the Kervansaray is decorated in traditional Turkish style. It has an excellent restaurant, with outdoor dining in an ancient courtyard. Adjacent to the hotel is a medieval castle. *Çarşi Cad., tel. 232/712–7177 or 232/712–6491, fax 232/712–6492. 32 rooms with bath. Facilities: restaurant, bar. AE, DC, MC, V. $$$*

İzmir

LODGING

İzmir Hilton. At 34 stories, the Hilton is one of the tallest buildings on the Aegean coast. Striking and modern, the 1992 structure looms over the city center. From the 10-story atrium to the elegant rooftop restaurant, the public spaces are suitably grand. Guest rooms are plush with their thick floral comforters and matching drapes. *Gazi Osman Pasa Bul. 7, tel. 232/441–6060, fax 232/441–2277. 381 rooms with bath.*

Facilities: 4 restaurants, 2 bars, casino, pool, business center, shopping mall. AE, DC, MC, V. $$$$

Kismet. Tastefully decorated, the Kismet is a quiet, comfortable hotel with friendly service. *1377 Sok. 9, tel. 232/463–3853, fax 232/421–4856. 68 rooms with bath. Facilities: restaurant, bar, sauna. AE, MC, V. $$*

Kuşadası

DINING

★ **Sultan Han.** Full of atmosphere, with excellent food to boot, Sultan Han is an old house built around a courtyard, where the focal point is a gigantic tree. You can dine in the courtyard or upstairs in small rooms. One of the specialties is fresh seafood, which you select from platters piled high with fish and shellfish of every possible variety. Ask to have your after-dinner coffee served upstairs, where you can sit on cushions at low brass tables. *Bahar Sok. 8, tel. 256/614–6380. Reservations required. No credit cards. $$$*

Ali Baba Restaurant. With a peaceful view of the bay, this waterfront spot engages a simple style, with starched white tablecloths and wooden chairs. The focus is on the fish: try the marinated octopus salad or the fried calamari, followed by a grilled version of whatever has just been caught. *Belediye Turistik Carsisi, tel. 256/614–1551. Reservations strongly advised. MC, V. $$*

Ada Restaurant. The setting for this outdoor restaurant is a terrace on Guvercinada, the small island attached to Kuşadası. Fresh bass and turbot, as well as kebabs and appetizers, are displayed at the entrance. *Guvercin Adasi, tel. 256/614–1725. Reservations advised for groups. AE, MC, V. $*

LODGING

Club Kervansaray. A refurbished, 300-year-old caravansary, this hotel is decorated in the Ottoman style and loaded with charm and atmosphere. It's in the center of town and features a restaurant with a floor show. There's dancing after dinner in the courtyard, where the camels were once kept. *Atatürk Bul. 2, tel. 256/614–4115, fax 256/614–2423. 40 rooms with bath. Facilities: restaurant, bar, café, nightclub. AE, DC, MC, V. $$$*

★ **Kismet.** Although it's a small hotel, Kismet is run on a grand scale, surrounded by beautifully maintained gardens on a promontory overlooking the marina on one side and the Aegean on the other. Ask for rooms in the garden annex. Its popularity makes reservations a must. *Akyar Mev., Tükmen Mahallesi, tel. 256/614–2005, fax 256/614–4914. 98 rooms with bath. Facilities: restaurant, private beach. AE, MC, V. Closed Nov.–Mar. $$$*

Liman Hotel. Opened in 1993, this whitewashed building is dramatic, with black cast-iron balconies and black window frames. The upstairs summer terrace is a nice place to cool off and watch the town and port. The front rooms also offer panoramic views. *Kibris Cad., Buyral Sok. 4, tel. and fax 256/612–3149. 16 rooms with shower. Facilities: café, bar. No credit cards. $*

Pamukkale

LODGING

Tusan. The best feature of the Tusan is its pool, one of the most inviting in the area. The rooms are basic and comfortable. The one-story building is at the top of a steep hill. *Tel. 258/272–2010, fax 258/272–2059. 47 rooms with bath. Facilities: restaurant, outdoor pool. AE, DC, MC, V. $$*

Selçuk

Hülya. This is a pleasant, family-run pansiyon, where one of the family members is a fisherman who sometimes brings in some of his daily catch. Rooms are typically bare. There's a kitchen where you can cook if necessary. The down-to-earth owners serve meals in the lemon blossom-scented courtyard. *Atatürk Cad., Özgür Sok. 15, tel. 232/892–2120. 8 rooms with bath. No credit cards. $*

Kale Han. In a refurbished stone building is one of the nicest hotels in town, managed by a very welcoming family. Rooms are simple, with bare, whitewashed walls and dark timber beams. The restaurant serves excellent food around the clock. *Atatürk Cad. 49, tel. 232/892–6154, fax 232/892–2169. 52 rooms with shower. Facilities: restaurant, pool. MC, V. $*

THE MEDITERRANEAN COAST

Until the mid-1970s, Turkey's southwest coast was inaccessible to all but the most determined travelers—those intrepid souls in four-wheel-drive vehicles or on the backs of donkeys. Today well-maintained highways wind through the area and jets full of tourists arrive at the new Dalaman Airport.

Thanks to strict developmental control, the area has maintained its Turkish flavor, with low, whitewashed buildings and tiled roofs. The beaches are clean, and you can swim and snorkel in turquoise waters so clear that it is possible to see fish 20 feet below. There are excellent outdoor cafés and seafood restaurants in which to dine, and there's no shortage of bars, discos, or nightclubs.

Getting Around

By Car

Although the highways between towns are well maintained, the smaller roads are usually unpaved and very rough.

By Boat

There are many coves and picnic areas accessible only by boat. For a small fee, local fishermen will take you to and from the coves; also, you can take one of the many water taxis. Or charter a small yacht, with or without skipper, at the marinas of Bodrum and Marmaris. Many people charter boats and join small flotillas that leave the marinas daily for sightseeing in the summer. One of the most enjoyable ways to see the coast is to take a one- or two-week **Blue Voyage** cruise on a *gulet,* a wooden craft with a full crew. There are also three-night mini Blue Voyage trips for scuba divers and snorkelers. For information, contact the following Blue Voyage agencies: in the United States, **Club Voyages,** Box 7648, Shrewsbury, NJ 07702, tel. 908/291–8228; in the United Kingdom, **Explore,** 1 Frederick Street, Aldershot, Hants GU11 1LQ, tel. 012/5231–9448; **Simply Turkey,** 8 Chiswick Terrace, Acton Lane, London W4, tel. 0181/747–1011; **Falcon Sailing,** 13 Hillgate Street, London W8, tel. 0171/727–0232.

Guided Tours and Tourist Information

Local tourist offices list all the guided tours for the area and will also arrange for local guides.

Bodrum (Baris Meyd. 12, tel. 252/316–1091).
Dalaman (Dalaman Airport, tel. 252/692-5291).

Datça (Iskele Mah. Hükümet Binasi, tel. 252/712–3163 or 252/712–3546).

Kaş (Cumhuriyet Meyd. 5, tel. 242/836–1238).

Marmaris (Iskele Meyd. 2, tel. 252/412–1035).

Exploring the Mediterranean Coast

Bodrum

Sitting between two crescent-shaped bays, **Bodrum** has for years been the favorite haunt of the Turkish upper classes. Today the elite are joined by thousands of foreign visitors, and the area is rapidly filling with hotels and guest houses, cafés, restaurants, and discos. Many compare it to St. Tropez on the French Riviera. Fortunately, it is still beautiful and unspoiled, with gleaming whitewashed buildings covered with bougainvillea and magnificent unobstructed vistas of the bays. People flock to Bodrum not for its beach, which is a disappointment, but for its fine dining and nightlife. You'll find beautiful beaches in the outlying villages on the peninsula—**Torba, Türkbükü, Yalikavak, Turgutreis, Akyarlar, Ortakent, Bitez,** and **Gümbet.** Easy to reach by minibus or dolmuş, these villages are about an hour's drive away and have clean hotels and plenty of outdoor restaurants. One of the outstanding sights in Bodrum is **Bodrum Castle,** known as the **Castle of St. Peter.** Located between the two bays, the castle was built by crusaders in the 11th century. It has beautiful gardens and a **Museum of Underwater Archaeology.** *Castle and museum admission: $2.50. Open Tues.–Sun. 8:30–noon and 1–5.*

The peninsula is downright littered with ancient Greek and Roman ruins, although getting to some of them involves driving over rough dirt roads. Five kilometers (3 miles) from Bodrum is **Halikarnas,** a well-preserved 10,000-seat Greek amphitheater built in the 1st century BC and still used for town festivals. *Admission free. Open daily 8:30–sunset.*

Marmaris

Another beach resort between two bays is **Marmaris,** which has some of the best sailing on the Mediterranean. It is 178 kilometers (111 miles) from Bodrum via Muğla along Route 400. You'll climb steep, winding mountain passes, with cliffs that drop straight into the sea. The final 30 kilometers (19 miles) into Marmaris is a broad boulevard lined with eucalyptus trees. Marmaris, like Bodrum, is a sophisticated resort with boutiques, elegant restaurants, and plenty of nightlife. Nearby are quiet villages that are easy to reach by boat or taxi. One of these is **Knidos,** where you can see the ruins of Aphrodite's circular temple and an ancient theater. By road, Knidos is a very rough 108 kilometers (67 miles) from Marmaris. It's easier and quicker to take a boat. Another town is **Turunç,** worth a day's visit, especially for its beaches.

Freshwater **Lake Köyceğiz** can be reached by boat through the reed beds of the **Dalyan delta.** This entire area is a wildlife preserve, filled with such birds as kingfishers, kestrels, egrets, and cranes. Köyceğiz and **Dalyan** villages, both 20 minutes' drive from Dalaman Airport, are good stopping-off places for exploring the area. It costs about $20 to rent a boat with a boatman to sail from Dalyan to the ruins and beach.

Ölü Deniz

One of Turkey's greatest natural wonders is **Ölü Deniz,** an azure lagoon flanked by long, white beaches. The area is about 145 kilometers (90 miles) from Koyceğiz. There are a few wooden chalets in camping grounds and one beachfront hotel. Opposite the beach, you'll find small restaurants with rooftop bars, many with live music that goes on all night.

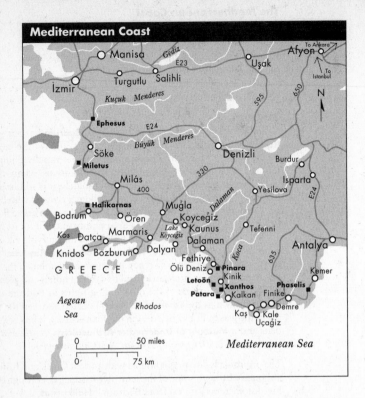

Mediterranean Coast

Southeast of Fethiye, near Route 400, are several ancient sites, including the ruins of **Pinara,** one of the most important cities of the former Roman province of Lycia. Near Pinara, up a steep and strenuous dirt road, you'll find nearly 200 Roman tombs cut honeycomb-fashion into the face of the cliffs. *Admission: $1.20. Open daily 8:30–sunset.*

Xanthos

Return to Route 400 and head 18 kilometers (11 miles) south toward the village of Kinik. At Kinik leave the main highway and take a mile-long bumpy road to **Xanthos,** another major city of ancient Lycia. It was excavated in 1838; much of what was found here is now in the British Museum in London. What's left is still well worth the bumpy ride: the acropolis, the Tomb of Harpies, some plaster-cast reliefs, and ruins of some Byzantine buildings. *Admission: $1.20. Open daily 8:30–sunset.*

Patara and Kalkan

Ten minutes from Xanthos is **Patara,** once the city's port. Here you'll find ruins scattered around the marshes and sand dunes. The area's long, wide beaches remain beautiful and unspoiled, despite the fact that they attract hundreds of Turkish families and tourists. The nearest place to stay is **Kalkan,** a fishing village 20 minutes away by minibus.

Kaş

Kaş, 30 kilometers (18 miles) from Kalkan, is another fishing village that has become a popular resort and is also developing into a major yachting center. Although luxury hotels have replaced many of the tiny houses on the hills, there are still plenty of old-fashioned pansiyons for those on a budget. One of the attractions here is a day trip by boat to the underwater city of **Kekova,** where you can look overboard and see ancient Roman and Greek columns that were once part of a thriving city before the area was flooded. Kekova is especially popular with scuba divers and snorkelers, but to scuba-dive or fish in this area, a permit must be obtained from the directorate of the harbor and from the directorate of the ministry of tourism. Boats leave daily at 9:30 and cost about $15.

For romantic ruins, it would be hard to beat **Phaselis.** The Roman agora, theater, aqueduct, and a necropolis with fine sarcophagi are scattered throughout the pine woods that surround the Temple of Athena. Overgrown streets descend to the translucent water, which is ideal for swimming.

Kemer is the center of intensive tourist development, with hotels and restaurants, a well-equipped marina, and club-style holiday villages that make you forget you're in Turkey. The remaining 35 kilometers (26 miles) are increasingly occupied by villas and motels along the smooth pebbles of Konyalti Beach, which stretches to the outskirts of Antalya.

Antalya

The resort of **Antalya,** on the Mediterranean, is a good base for several worthwhile excursions. The city is on a beautifully restored harbor and is filled with narrow streets lined with small houses, restaurants, and pansiyons. On the hilltop are tea gardens where you can enjoy tea made in an old-fashioned samovar and look across the bay to the Taurus Mountains, which parallel the coast. To the right of the port is the 13th-century **Yivli Minare** (Fluted Minaret). The Hisar Café, Tophane tea garden, and Mermerli tea garden all overlook Antalya's harbor.

Dining and Lodging

For details and price-category definitions, *see* Dining and Lodging *in* Staying in Turkey, *above.*

Antalya

DINING

Hisar Restaurant. Built into the 700-year-old walls of an old fortress, the Hisar is hard to beat for atmosphere. The inside is dominated by wood paneling through which it is possible to get a glimpse of the city wall and a view of the harbor. The mezes are above average and even the standard items are served with a twist: Try the tenderized steak rolled in cheese, mushrooms and ham. *Cumhuriyet Meydani, tel. 242/241–5281. Reservations advised. AE, V. $–$$*

LODGING

★ **Talya.** This is a luxurious resort hotel with its own beach that you reach by taking an elevator down the side of the cliff. From every angle there's a view of the sea. It gets booked up quickly in high season. *Fevzi Çakmak Cad., tel. 242/248–6800, fax 242/241–5400. 204 rooms with bath. Facilities: restaurant, disco, pool, game room, fitness room, private beach. AE, DC, MC, V. $$$$*

Tütav Türk Evleri. Part of the old Kaleiçi district, this hotel consists of a row of tastefully restored Turkish houses joined together. There are well-tended gardens surrounding the inn and its popular restaurant, which is known for its delectable fish stew. *Mermerli Sok. 2, tel. 242/248–6591, fax 242/241–9419. 20 rooms with bath. Facilities: restaurant, bar, garden, sauna, pool. MC, V. $$*

Natali Pansiyon. Each room is different in this small, odd pansiyon in the Kaleiçi district, but if you're feeling game, ask for the one with the enormous tiled bathroom (which is bigger than the bedroom). Breakfast is served on a terrace with a view over the old town. *İzmir Ali Efendi*

Sok. 13, Kaleiçi, tel. 242/247–7821. 7 rooms, 3 with bath. No credit cards. $

Bodrum

DINING

Club Pirinç. This restaurant has a pleasant bar, nine guest rooms, a swimming pool, and offers Turkish-French cuisine. *Akçabuk Mev., Kumbahçe, tel. 252/316–2902. No credit cards. $$$*

Restaurant No. 7. Octopus casseroles are a specialty. *Eski Banka Sok. 7. $$$*

Balik Restaurant. Specialties include fish, meat, and chicken kebabs. *Yeniçarşi 28, tel. 252/316–1454. No credit cards. $$*

Korfez Restaurant. This is a seaside fish restaurant with white tablecloths and candles, overlooking the bay. Try the calamari and octopus salad. *Cumhuriyet Cad. 32, tel. 252/316–1300 or 316–1241. AE, V. $$*

LODGING

Manastır Hotel. The name comes from the fact that part of this hotel was once a monastery. The atmosphere is Aegean, with the pink and green of bougainvillea blowing against the whitewashed walls. The restaurant serves grilled fish and spectacular Turkish salads. At peak times you may have to pay half-board. *Bariş Sitesi Mevkii, Kumbahçe, tel. 252/316–1719, fax 252/316–1720. 59 rooms with bath. Facilities: 2 restaurants, 2 bars, meeting room, swimming pools, tennis, sauna, fitness center. AE, MC, V. $$$*

Hotel Anka. This hilltop hotel, just a mile from the city center, commands stunning views of the Bodrum bay. Rooms with balconies in whitewashed bungalows are simple and clean, and the staff is warm. Although the hotel is now reasonably-priced, the owners are considering renovating and going deluxe—check before you go. *Eskiçeşme Mah. Asarlik Mevkii, Gümbet, tel. 252/316–8217, fax 252/316–6194. 85 rooms with bath. Facilities: restaurant, bars, disco, private beach, swimming pool. AE, DC, MC, V. $*

Dalyan

DINING

Yali Restaurant. This is a waterside eatery reached by a short boat ride from Dalyan. It's also a good stopping-off point if you're planning a walk to the Kaunus ruins. *Tel. 252/284–1150. No credit cards. $*

LODGING

Hotel Turtle. A quiet 10-room hotel tucked away in a bay of orchards on the lakeside provides a peaceful getaway. The hotel boat picks up guests from Dalyan. Vefa Ülkü, the owner, cooks excellent dishes served under a big plane tree. *Kücük Karaağac, Sultaniye Köyü, Köyceğiz, tel. 252/284–1487. 10 rooms. No credit cards. $$*

Kalkan

LODGING

Kalkan Han. A rambling old house in the back part of the village, the Kalkan Han has a special treat for visitors: a roof terrace with sweeping views of the bay, a perfect place to enjoy breakfast. *Köyiçi Mev., tel. 242/844–3151, fax 242/844–2048. 16 rooms with bath. Facilities: restaurant, bar. No credit cards. Closed Nov.–Apr. $$*

Balikçi Han. This delightful pansiyon is in a converted 19th-century inn, directly on the waterfront. *Tel. 242/844–1075. 7 rooms with bath. No credit cards. $*

Kaş

DINING

Mercan. On the eastern side of the harbor, the Mercan serves good, basic Turkish food in an attractive open-air setting. The water is so close you can actually hear fish jumping. The menu includes whole lamb on a spit, fish, and lobster, as well as vegetarian choices. *Hukumet Cad., tel. 242/836–1209. MC, V. $$*

LODGING

Kaş Oteli. There's good swimming off the rocks in front of the hotel, or you can laze in the sun with drinks and snacks from the bar or restaurant. There are also wonderful views of the Greek island of Kastellorizo. *Hastane Cad. 15, tel. 242/836–1271, fax 242/836–1368. Facilities: restaurant, bar. No credit cards. Closed Nov.–Apr. $$*

Mimosa. Conveniently located on a hill near the bus station, this small property has plain but perfectly adequate rooms, all with balconies and views. *Elmali Cad., tel. 242/836–1272, fax 242/836–1272. 26 rooms with bath. Facilities: swimming pool. No credit cards. $$*

Medusa Hotel. Set on a cliff overlooking the sea, this picturesque hotel is also a diving school. Front rooms have expansive ocean views, while back rooms face the mountains. *Küçükçakil, tel. 242/836–1440, fax 242/836–1441. 40 rooms with bath. Facilities: 2 restaurants, 2 bars, pool, garden, diving school. No credit cards. $*

Köyceğiz

LODGING

Hotel Özay. This lakeside hotel is quiet, modern, and efficiently run. The setting is smothered in lush greenery and palm trees. Daily boat tours of the lake are available and Turkish belly dancing shows take place at night. *Kordon Boyu 11, Köyceğiz, tel. 252/262–4300, fax 252/262–2000. 34 rooms with bath. Facilities: restaurant, bar, swimming pool. AE, DC, MC, V. $$$*

Kaunos Hotel. Ask for front rooms with lake views at this small, modern hotel set right on the water. *Cengiz Topel Cad., tel. 252/262–4288, fax 252/262–4836. 44 rooms with bath. Facilities: restaurant, bar, pool, disco, Turkish show. No credit cards. $*

Ölü Deniz

DINING

★ **Beyaz Yunus.** Wicker chairs and wooden floors fill this domed restaurant, whose name means "white dolphin." The most elegant restaurant in the area, it's situated on a promontory near Padirali and serves Continental and Turkish cuisines imaginatively prepared and presented. *Tel. 252/616–6036. No credit cards. $$$$*

Kebabcı Salonu. You can grill meat at your table in this outdoor restaurant, where tables and chairs are clustered around trees in a field. Meals are served with mezes, salad, and wine. *Behind Han Camp, no phone. No credit cards. $*

LODGING

Meri Oteli. Located on a steep incline above the lagoon, this is a series of bungalows, with rooms a bit down-at-the-heel but clean. These are the only accommodations at the lagoon. *Tel. 252/616–6060, fax 252/616–6456. 75 rooms with bath. Facilities: restaurant. AE, DC, MC, V. $$*

CENTRAL ANATOLIA AND CAPPADOCIA

Cappadocia, an area filled with ruins of ancient civilizations, is in the eastern part of Anatolia and has changed little over the centuries. People still travel between their farms and villages in horse-drawn carts, women drape their houses with strings of apricots and paprika for drying in the sun, and nomads pitch their black tents beside sunflower fields and cook on tiny fires that send smoke billowing through the tops of the tents.

Getting Around

By Car
There are good roads between Istanbul and the main cities of Anatolia—Ankara (the capital of Turkey), Konya, and Kayseri. The highways are generally well maintained and lead to all the major sites. Minor roads are full of potholes and are very rough. On narrow, winding roads, look out for oncoming trucks, whose drivers apparently don't believe in staying on their side of the road.

By Bus
There is a good interlinking bus network between most towns and cities, and fares are reasonable.

By Train
Though there are frequent trains between the main cities, they are almost nonexistent between small towns. It's much quicker to take a bus.

By Taxi
Drivers are usually willing to take you to historical sites out of town for reasonable fares.

Guided Tours

As the Cappadocia area is so vast, you'll need at least two days to see the main sights. If you are driving, consider hiring a guide for about $15–$30 a day. Local tourist offices and hotels will be able to recommend guides and excursions.

Tourist Information

Check with local tourist offices for names of travel agencies and English-speaking guides.

Ankara (Gazi Mustafa Kemal Bul. 121, Tandoğan, tel. 312/229–2631).
Aksaray (Ankara Cad. Dinçer Apt. 2/2, tel. 382/213–2474).
Kayseri (Kagni Pazari 61, tel. 352/222–3903).
Konya (Mevlana Cad. 21, tel. 332/351–1074).
Nevşehir (Atatürk Cad. Hastane Yani, tel. 384/213–1137).
Ürgüp (Kayseri Cad. 37, tel. 384/341–4059).

Exploring Central Anatolia and Cappadocia

An hour's drive, 30 kilometers (19 miles), to the northwest of Antalya is **Termessos**, which has an almost complete Roman amphitheater built on a mountainside, and the unexcavated remains of a Roman city on the other side of the mountain. There are organized tours to Termessos from Antalya. *Admission free. Open daily 9–5:30.*

Perge, 19 kilometers (11 miles) east of Antalya, has many Roman ruins to explore. You can climb up a 22,000-seat amphitheater, walk down a restored colonnaded street, visit well-preserved thermal baths and a Roman basilica, and see the spot where St. Paul preached his first sermon in AD 45. *Admission: $2.50. Open daily 9–5:30.*

Nearby is **Aspendos**, 44 kilometers (23 miles) to the east of Antalya, which contains Turkey's best-preserved amphitheater. The acoustics are

Central Anatolia & Cappadocia

Mediterranean Sea

so fine that modern-day performers don't need microphones or amplifiers. *Admission: $2.50. Open daily 9–5:30.*

Konya

Konya, home of the Whirling Dervishes, is reached by driving 427 kilometers (267 miles) northeast of Antalya past **Lake Beyşehir.** There is also a longer and more difficult road via **Lake Eğridir.** The Whirling Dervishes belong to a religious order founded in the 13th century by Celaleddin Rumi, or Mevlana, a Muslim mystic, who said, "There are many ways of knowing God. I choose the dance and music." You can see the dervishes whirl to the sounds of a flute at the annual commemorative rites held in Konya in early December. Tickets are available from travel agencies or from the Konya tourist information office (*see above*).

Sultan Han, 95 kilometers (59 miles) northeast of Konya, is Anatolia's largest and best-preserved caravansary, once a place of rest and shelter for travelers and their camels plying the ancient trade routes.

Cappadocia

Cappadocia roughly forms the triangular area between **Kayseri, Nevşehir,** and **Niğde.** Most of the main sights are within an even smaller triangular area linked by Ürgüp, Göreme, and Avanos. **Ürgüp** is the center from which to explore the villages and the best place to shop, as well as to arrange tours.

The softness of the rock in this area was ideal for hollowing out cave dwellings and forming defenses from invading armies. The Cappadocians carved out about 40 underground cities, with some structures as deep as 20 stories underground. The largest of these cities housed 20,000 people. Each had dormitories, dining halls, sewage disposal systems, ventilation chimneys, a cemetery, and a prison. Large millstones sealed off the entrances from enemies. Two of these cities are open to the public, one at **Derinkuyu,** 21 kilometers (13 miles) south of Nevşehir, and the other at **Kaymakli,** 30 kilometers (9 miles) south of Nevşehir. *Admission: $2.50. Open daily 8–sunset.*

The Christians also hid in these underground cities when the Islamic forces swept through Cappadocia in the 7th century. Some of the earliest relics of Christianity are to be found in the **Göreme Valley,** a few miles east of Nevşehir. There are dozens of old churches and monasteries covered with frescoes. For a history of the area, visit the **Göreme Open-Air Museum,** 1 kilometer (.62 miles) outside of Göreme village on the Ürgüp road. *Admission free. Open daily 8:30–5:30.*

Dining and Lodging

For details and price-category definitions, *see* Dining and Lodging *in* Staying in Turkey, *above.*

Avanos

LODGING
Zelve. This is a small modern hotel in the center of town. *Hükümet Meydani, tel. 384/511–4524, fax 384/511–4687. 29 rooms with bath. Facilities: restaurant, bar. AE, DC, MC, V. $*

Göreme

DINING AND LODGING
Ataman Hotel. Run by tourist guide Abbas and his wife Şermin, this atmospheric hotel and restaurant is built into the face of a rock facing the lush Göreme valley. The large restaurant specializes in seafood and French cuisine. The cozy rooms have been decorated in Seljuk style, with mother-of-pearl candle sconces, fireplaces and tile decorations hanging on the walls. *Göreme, tel. 384/271–2310, fax 384/271–2313. 38 rooms with bath. Facilities: 2 restaurants. MC, V. $*

Konya

DINING
Ali Baba Kebapçısı. This restaurant serves good kebabs and is famous for its Firin kebab, cooked over an open charcoal fire. *Eski Avukatlar Sok. 11/A, tel. 332/351–0307. No credit cards. $*
Bolu Restaurant. You can eat dishes here for which Konya is renowned: *etli ekmek* (flat bread with ground lamb) and *tereyağli borek* (buttered pastries). *Pürçüklü Mah. 31/c, tel. 332/352–4533. $*

LODGING
Balikçilar Hotel. Conveniently located across from Konya's main sight, Mevlana, this hotel has air-conditioned and spare but comfortable rooms. Many of the employees are trainees from tourism schools and can be helpful in planning local outings. *Mevlana Karşisi 1, tel. 332/350–9470, fax 332/351–3259. 48 rooms with bath. Facilities: 2 restaurants, 2 bars, Turkish bath, meeting room. MC, V. $$*

Ürgüp

DINING
Hanedan. In the cellar of an old Greek house, the Hanedan is on a hill a short distance from town. You can sit on the terrace and watch the sun set across the plains toward the mountains. The food is very good and is presented with flair. *Nevşehir Yolu Üzeri, tel. 384/341–4266. Group reservations required. DC, MC, V. $$*

LODGING
Büyük Almira. This centrally located hotel, renovated and expanded in 1994, has comfortable rooms overlooking an outdoor swimming

pool. The biggest and most popular disco in town is also here. *Kayseri Cad. 43, tel. 384/341–8999. 101 rooms with bath. Facilities: 2 restaurants, 3 bars, pool, disco, garden, meeting room. MC, V. $$*

Hitit. The family-run Hitit is a comfortable, small hotel with a restaurant that serves basic but enjoyable food. *Dumlupinar Cad. 54, tel. 384/341–1481. 15 rooms without bath. No credit cards. Closed Nov.–Mar. $*

INDEX

A

Air travel, 2–3, 19–20, 21, 22–23, 25
American Express, 9–26
Amsterdam, 568–585
Ann Frankhuis, 574
arts in, 583–584
ballet in, 576, 584
bars in, 584, 585
Begijnhof, 574–575
bookstores in, 569
casinos in, 585
Centraal Station, 570
Concertgebouw, 577–578, 583
Dam, 570–571, 574
Dam Palace, 574
Dokwerker, 576
emergencies in, 569
film in, 584
flower market, 575
gay and lesbian bars, 585
Golden Bend, 575
Haalemmerstraat 75, 578
Heineken Brewery, 578
Historisch Museum, 574
hotels in, 575, 581–583
Jewish Amsterdam, 575–577
Joods Historisch Museum, 576–577
Jordaan area of, 578
Koninklijk Paleis, 574
Kromhout Museum, 578
Leidseplein, 575
Maritime Quarter, 578
metro in, 568
Muntplein, 575
Museum Amstelkring, 571
Museum Boat, 569, 570
Museum Het Rembrandthuis, 576
music in, 576, 577–578, 583–584
Muziektheater/Stadhuis, 576
Netherlands Theater Institut, 575
Nieuwe Kerk, 571
nightlife in, 584–585
Nooderkerk, 574
opera in, 576, 584
Oude Kerk, 571
Portuguese Synagogue, 576
restaurants in, 574, 575, 579–581

Rijksmuseum, 577
Rijksmuseum Nederlands Scheepvaart, 578
Rijksmuseum Vincent van Gogh, 577
Royal Palace at Amsterdam, 574
St. Nicolasskerk, 570
Schreierstoren, 570–571
shopping in, 579
Singel 460, 578
Spui, 575
Stedelijk Museum, 577
theater in, 575, 576, 584
tourist information in, 569
Vondelpark, 578
Westerkerk, 574
Westermarkt, 574
Andorra, 32–41
Andorro La Vella, 38, 39–40
Can Pal, 39
Casa de la Vall, 38
churches in, 36, 38, 39
La Cortinada, 39
emergencies in, 38
Encamp, 38
Les Escaldes, 38, 40
hotels in, 36–37, 40, 41
La Massana, 38–39
Ordino, 39, 40
Pas de la Casa, 39, 41
Pont de St. Antoni, 38
restaurants in, 36, 39–40, 41
Sanctuary of Meritxell, 38
Santa Coloma, 39, 41
Santa Julià de Loria, 39, 41
Sant Joan des Caselles, 38
Sant Miguel d'Engolasters, 38
Sant Romà de les Bons, 38
shopping in, 39
tourist information in, 37
Antwerp, 106–112
boat excursion from, 108
Centraalstation, 107
Diamond Quarter, 107
Diamondland, 107
Grote Markt, 108
hotels in, 111–112
Koninklijk Museum voor Schone Kunsten, 108
Meir, 107
Museum Mayer van den Bergh, 108
Onze Lieve Vrouwekathe-draal, 108

Plantin-Moretus Museum, 108
Provinciaal Diamant Museum, 107
restaurants in, 110–111
Rubenshuis, 107–108
St. Annatunnel, 108
Steen, 188
Torengebouw, 108
tourist information in, 177
vogelmarkt, 110
zoo, 107
Apartment rentals, 8–9, 26
Athens, 520–538
Academy, 528
Acropolis, 525
Acropolis Museum, 525, 528
Agora, 528
Areopagus, 528
arts in, 536–537
bookstore in, 523
bouzoukias in, 537
Byzantine Museum, 529
Cathedral of Athens, 528
Cathedral Square, 528
concerts in, 536
emergencies in, 523
Erechtheion temple, 525
Evzone guards, 524, 529
film in, 536–537
Glyfada, 530
Hadrian's Arch, 524
Hephaisteion, 528
hotels in, 533–526
Kaisariani monastery, 529
Kolonaki, 529 Little Cathedral, 528
metro in, 522
Mikrolimano, 530
Mount Lycabettus, 529
Museum of the Agora Excavations, 528
Museum of Cycladic Art, 529
National Archaeological Museum, 528–529
National Gardens, 524
National Library, 528
nightlife in, 537–538
Odeon of Herodes Atticus, 525
opera in, 536
Panathenaic Stadium, 524–525
Parliament Building, 524
Parthenon, 525

Plaka, 528
Presidential Palace, 529
Propylaea, 525
restaurants in, 529, 531–533
Senate House of the University, 528
shopping in, 530–531
sound and light, shows, 536
Syntagma Square, 524
tavernas, 538
Temple of Olympian Zeus, 524
Temple of Wingless Victory, 525
Theater of Dionysos, 525
theater in, 525
Tomb of the Unknown Soldier, 524
tourist information in, 522
Austria, 42–82. See also Innsbruck; Salzburg; Vienna
Burg Kreuzenstein, 69
churches in, 56, 58, 59–60, 68, 72, 73, 78
Danube Valley of, 67–70
Dürnstein, 69
gardens in, 71
Göttweig, 67
hotels in, 49–50, 69–70
Imperial Toll House, 69
Klosterneuburg, 68
Krems, 70
Langelebarn, 70
Mautern, 70
Melk, 67, 68
Minoritenkirche, 69
museums in, 48–49, 56–57, 58, 59, 60–61, 71, 72, 75, 78
opera in, 57, 66, 76
restaurants in, 49, 68, 69–70
shopping in, 61–62
Stein, 69
Stift Göttweig, 68
tourist information in, 15, 68, 71, 78
Tulln, 68
zoos, 60, 75, 80
Auto clubs, 6
Auto rentals, 3, 30–31

B

Baggage insurance, 8, 25
Barcelona, 985–1000
Ajuntament, 989
arts in, 998–999
Barceloneta, 993

bars in, 997–998
beaches in, 999–1000
bookstores in, 987
bullfighting in, 994
cafés in, 997–998
casino in, 999
Cathedral, 988
Columbus Monument, 989
concerts in, 998
dance in, 998
Dreta de l'Eixample, 993
Eixample, 992
emergencies in, 987
film in, 999
Flamenco in, 999
Funicular in, 986
Gran Teatre del Liceu, 989
harbor trips in, 986
hotels in, 996–997
Major de Gràcia, 993
Mançana de la Discòrdia, 992
Maritime Museum, 989
metro in, 985–986
Miró Foundation, 993
Montjuïc, 992–993
Museu Frederic Marès, 998
Museum of Catalan Art, 993
music in, 998, 999
nightlife in, 999
Palau de la Generalitat, 989
Palau de la Virreina, 992
Palau Güell, 989
Picasso Museum, 988
Plaça de Catalunya, 992
Plaça del Rei, 988
Plaça Reial, 989
Plaça Sant Jaume, 989
Porta de L'Angel, 992
ports and beaches, 999–1000
Rambla, 989
restaurants in, 988, 989, 992, 994–996
Saló de Tinell, 988
Santa María del Mar, 988
Shoe Museum, 993
shopping in, 993–994
Temple Expiatori de la Sagrada Família, 992
theater in, 998–999
tourist information in, 986–987
Bath, 479–481, 487–489
Assembly Rooms, 487
Holburne Museum and Crafts Study Centre, 487
hotels in, 489
restaurants in, 487–489
Roman Baths Museum, 487

Royal Crescent, 487
tourist information in, 479
Baths and spas
in Bath, 487
in Czech Republic, 176–180
in Germany, 396
in Hungary, 628, 630
in Portugal, 903
in Rome, 714
Belgium, 83–116. See also Antwerp; Brugge; Brussels
camping in, 90
churches in, 95, 98, 108, 113
hotels in, 90
museums in, 99, 93–94, 95, 99–99, 100, 107, 108
restaurants in, 89–90
shopping in, 88–89, 100–101
tourist offices of, 15
youth hostels in, 90
Berlin, 402–421
Ägyptisches Museum, 410
Altes Museum, 411
arts in, 420
ballet in, 420
Berlin cathedral, 413
Berlin Philharmonic, 406, 420
Berlin Wall, 407
Bodemuseum, 413
bookstores in, 405
Brandenburger Tor, 4078, 411
Checkpoint Charlie, 411
Checkpoint Charlie Museum, 407
churches in, 406, 411, 413
concerts in, 420
Deutsches Historisches Museum, 411
Deutsche Staatsoper, 411
East Berlin, 410–414
emergencies in, 405
Fischerinsel, 413–414
Gemäldegalerie, 410
Grunewald, 410
hotels in, 417–420
Huguenot Museum, 411
Humboldt University, 411
Jewish Quarter, 414
Kaiser Wilhelm Gedächtniskirche, 406
Kunstgewerbe-Museum, 406
Museumsinsel, 411
Nationalgalerie, 413
Neue Nationalgalerie, 406
nightlife in, 420–421
Nikolaikirche, 413
opera in, 411, 420
Palast der Republik, 413

Pergamon Museum, 413
Potsdamer Platz, 407
public transportation in, 403–404
Rathaus, 413
Rathaus Schöneberg, 407, 410
Reichstag, 407
restaurants in, 407, 413, 415–417
St. Hedwigs Kathedrale, 411
Schauspielhaus, 411
Schloss Charlottenburg, 410
shopping in, 414–415
Siegessäule, 406
Soviet Victory Monument, 407
synagogue, 414
Tiergarten Park, 406
tourist information in, 404
TV tower, 413
West Berlin, 406–410
Zoologischer Garten, 406
Bern, 1110–1117
Bahnofplatz, 1111
Bärengraben, 1113
Bernisches Historisches Museum, 1113
casino, 1113
emergencies in, 1110
fountains in, 1113
Heilggeistkirche, 1111
hotels in, 1115–1117
Kornhaus, 1113
Kunstmuseum Bern, 1111
Münster, 1113
Naturhistorisches Museum, 1113
Pfeiferbrunnen, 1111
restaurants in, 1114–1115
Schweizerisches PTT-Museum, 1113
Schweizerisches Schützenmuseum, 1113
tourist information in, 1110
Better Business Bureau, 3
Bratislava, 937–942
Dóm svätého Martina, 940
emergencies in, 938–939
hotels in, 942
Hrad, 940
Hurbanovo námestie, 939
Jezuitský kostol, 941
Most SNP, 940
museums in, 940–941
Námestie SNP, 939
Palác Uhorskej kráľoveskej komory, 939–940

pharmacies, 939
Primaciálny palác, 941
restaurants in, 940, 941–942
Stará radnica, 941
tourist information in, 938
Židovská ulica, 941
Brugge, 112–116
Begijnhof, 115
Belfort, 113
Brangwyn Museum, 113
Burg, 112
Dijver, 113
Groeninge Museum, 113
Gruuthuse Museum, 113
Heilig-Bloed Basiliek, 113
hotels in, 116
Markt, 113
Memling Museum, 113–115
Minnewater Park, 115
Onze Lieve Vrouwekerk, 115
Oude Griffie, 113
Proostdijg, 113
Provinciaal Hof, 113
restaurants in, 115–116
Stadthius, 113
tourist information in, 112
Brussels, 91–106
arts in, 105
Atomium, 99
Autoworld Museum, 98–99
Bibliothèque Nationale, 94
Black Tower, 98
bookstores in, 92
Bourse, 98
Brussels Trade, 99
Butte de Lion, 99
Cathédrale de St. Michel et Ste-Gudule, 98
Centre Belge de laBande Dessinée, 99–100
Chunnel, 91
Cinquantenaire, 98
City Museum, 93–94
dance in, 105
emergencies in, 92
European Commission Headquarters, 98
film in, 105
Galeries St-Hubert, 94
Grand' Place, 93–94
Grand Sablon, 95
Heysel Stadium, 99
Hôtel de Ville, 93
hotels in, 103–105
Maison d'Erasme, 99
Maison du Roi, 93
Manneken Pis, 94
Marolles, 95

métro in, 91–92
Mini-Europe, 99
Musée d'Art Moderne, 94
Musée des Sciences Naturelles, 98
Musée Horta, 100
Musée Instrumental, 95
Musée Royale d'Art Ancien, 94
music, 105
nightlife in, 105–106
Notre Dame de la Chapelle, 95
Notre Dame du Sablon, 95
opera in, 105
Palais d'Egmont, 95
Palais de Justice, 95
Palais de la Nation, 98
Palais Royale, 98
Parc de Bruxelles, 98
Petit Sablon, 95
place des Martyrs, 98
place du Jeu de Balle, 95
place Royale, 94–95
restaurants in, 94, 95, 98, 99, 101–102
Royal Museums of Art and History, 98
shopping in, 100–101
theater in, 105
tourist information in, 92
Waterloo, 99
Wellington's headquarters, 99
Bucharest, 917–926
Arcul de Triumf, 923
arts in, 925–926
Ateneul Român, 922
Biserica din Curtea Veche, 919
Biserica Ortodoxa, 922
Columna Traiană, 922
Crețulescu Church, 922
Curtea Veche, 919
emergencies in, 918
Hanul lui Manuc, 919
hotels in, 924–925
Museul de Artă al Romniei, 922
music in, 925
Muzeul Curtea Veche-Palatul Voievodal, 919
Muzeul National de Istorie, 922
Muzeul Satului Romanesc, 923
Muzeul Tăranului Român, 922–923
Natural History Museum, 922
nightlife in, 926
restaurants in, 923–924

shopping in, 923
tourist information in, 918
Treasury, 922
Budapest, 610–625
Állami Operaház, 618
arts in, 624
Belvárosi plébánia templom,
617
bookstores in, 612
Budapest Történeti Múzeum,
613
concerts, 624
emergencies in, 611–612
Hadtörténeti Múzeum, 616
Halászbástya, 616
hotels in, 621–623
Jánoshegy, 619
Királyi Palota, 613
Kiscelli Múzeum, 619
Korzó, 616
Legújabbkori Történeti
Múzeum, 613
Ludwig Múzeum, 613
Március 15 Tér, 617
Mátyás templom, 612, 616
medieval synagogue, 616
Mezögazdasági Múzeum,
618–619
Millenniumi Emlékmü, 618
Mücsárnok, 618
National Gallery, 613
National Museum, 617
Néprajzi Múzeum, 617
nightlife in, 624–615
opera in, 618
Parliament, 617
public transportation in, 611
restaurants in, 616, 617, 619–
621
Roosevelt Tér, 616
shopping in, 619
Szépmüvészeti Múzeum, 618
Szent István Bazilika, 618
tourist information in, 611
Vajdahunyad Castle, 618
Várhegy (Castle Hill), 613
Városliget, 618
Zenetörténeti Múzeum, 616
Bulgaria, 117–144. See also
Sofia
Aladja Rock Monastery, 136
Albena, 137–138
Archaeological Museum, 136
Balčik, 136–137
Baldwin's Tower, 140
Black Sea, Golden Coast of,
134–139
Borovec, 142

Botanical Gardens, 137
Burgas, 137, 138
camping in, 125
churches in, 127, 129, 130,
136, 140–141
Copernicus Astronomy Com-
plex, 136
Djuni, 137
emergencies in, 126
Etur, 141
Forty Martyrs church, 140
gardens in, 129, 136, 137
Georgiadi House, 142
Hadji Nikoli, 141
hotels in, 124–125, 137–139,
143–144
Inland Bulgaria, 139–144
Kapana District, 142
Kazanlak, 141–142
Koprivshtitsa, 140, 143
Madara Horseman, 141
Marine Gardens, 136
Maritime Park, 137
mosques in, 130
museums in, 123, 127, 129,
136, 142
National Archaeological Mu-
seum, 142
National Ethnographical Mu-
seum, 142
Naval Museum, 136
Nesebâr, 137
Old Clock Tower, 136
Pliska, 141
Plovdiv, 141, 142, 143
restaurants in, 124–124, 137–
139, 143–144
Rila Monastery, 142
Roman ruins in, 136, 142
Saint Dimitrius, church of, 141
Saints Peter and Paul Church,
140–141
Shipka Pass, 141
shopping in, 130
Slânčev Brjag, 137, 138
Sozopol, 137
Stoyan Bucharov National
Theater, 136
Strumna Street, 142
Šumen, 141
Sunny Beach, 137, 138
Sveti Konstantin and Golden
Sands, 136–137, 138–139
tourist information in, 135,
140
Trojan Monastery, 140
Tsarevec, 140
Valley of Roses, 142

Varna, 135–136, 139
Veliki Preslav, 141
Veliko Târnovo, 140–142,
143–144
Zlatni Pjasâci, 136
Bullfighting
Museum of, 1007, 1017
in Spain, 969, 994, 1014
Buses
from United Kingdom to
Europe, 3
within Europe, 21

C

Cambridge, 491–497
Clare College, 493
Downing College, 493
Emmanuel College, 496
Fitzwilliam Museum, 493
hotels in, 497
Kettle's Yard, 493
King's College, 492–493
Magdalene College, 493
Mathematical Bridge, 493
Pembroke College, 493
Pepys Library, 493
Peterhouse, 493
Queen's College, 493
restaurants in, 493, 496
St. John's College, 493
tourist information in, 492
Trinity College, 493
Camcorders, 22
Cameras, 9, 21–22
Canadian citizens
customs and duties for, 5
passports and visas for, 29
Car rental, 30–31
Cash machines, 9, 26
Castles. See also Palaces
in Austria, 69, 73, 80
in Bohemia, 177–179
in Bratislava, 940
in Copenhagen, 192–193
in Cork, 680, 682
in Cyprus, 153, 158
in Czech Republic, 172, 177–
179
in Denmark, 192–193, 199,
212
in Edinburgh, 505
in Finland, 229, 242
in France, 280, 313, 314–315
in Germany, 385, 386–387
in Gibraltar, 1019
in Great Britain, 429, 480–
481, 486, 502, 505

in Hungary, 613, 618, 630
in Innsbruck, 80
in Ireland, 670, 682, 686, 690,
in Italy, 744
in Kraków, 866
in Liechtenstein, 1087
in Lisbon, 884
in Luxembourg, 795, 797
in Milan, 755
in Oslo, 825
in Poland, 869
in Portugal, 897, 902
in Prague, 172
in Rome, 716, 718
in Salzburg, 73
in Slovakia, 944–945
in Spain, 1019
in Stockholm, 1048
in Sweden, 1058, 1059
in Turkey, 1153
in Warsaw, 857
Channel Tunnel, 4, 22
Children, traveling with, 4–5,
22-23
Churches and cathedrals
in Andorra, 36, 38, 39
in Antwerp, 108
in Austria, 68, 78
in Barcelona, 988, 992
in Belgium, 95, 98, 188, 113
in Berlin, 406, 411, 413
in Bern, 1111, 1113
in Bratislava, 940, 941
in Brugge, 113
in Brussels, 95, 98
in Bucharest, 919, 922
in Budapest, 613
in Bulgaria, 127, 129, 130,
136, 140–141
in Copenhagen, 193, 196,
197
in Cork, 681
in Cyprus, 150, 151, 152, 153
in Czech Republic, 169, 172
in Delft, 596
in Denmark, 193, 196, 197,
199, 212–213
in Dublin, 665, 669–670, 671
in Edinburgh, 505, 506
in Finland, 228, 241, 224
in Florence, 731, 733, 736,
737
in France, 269, 270, 271, 277,
279, 292, 298–299, 305–
306, 307, 308, 313, 314,
315, 320, 321, 323
in Frankfurt, 363, 366
in Geneva, 1091

in Germany, 346, 363, 366,
376, 383, 384, 385, 386,
387, 388, 393, 395, 406,
411, 413, 424, 425, 426
in Gibraltar, 1019
in Great Britain, 453, 456,
457–458, 461, 462–463,
480, 495, 498
in Greece, 528, 541, 548
in Hamburg, 376
in Helsinki, 228, 232
in Holland, 570, 571, 574,
587, 588, 590, 594, 596
in Hungary, 613, 617, 618,
629
in Innsbruck, 78
in Ireland, 680, 681
in Italy, 703, 714, 715, 716–
719, 731, 733, 736, 737,
744–745, 746, 747, 748,
749, 755, 757, 765, 768,
769, 778, 780, 781
in Kraków, 864, 866
in London, 453, 456, 457–
458, 461, 462–463
in Lugano, 1106
in Luxembourg, 793, 796
in Luzern, 1099
in Malta, 805, 807, 810, 811
in Milan, 755, 757
in Nicosia, 150
in Norway, 825, 836, 843
in Paris, 269, 270, 271, 277,
279
in Poland, 857, 864, 866
in Portugal, 884, 886, 896,
901, 902, 903
in Prague, 172
in Reykjavík, 640, 642
in Romania, 919, 922
in Rome, 714, 715, 716–719
in Salzburg, 72, 73
in Slovakia, 943–944, 945
in Sofia, 127, 129, 130
in Spain, 980–981, 1002,
1005, 1007, 1009, 1018,
1019
in Sweden, 1044, 1057–1058
in Switzerland, 1099, 1106
in Toledo, 978
in Turkey, 1134, 1135, 1148
in Tuscany, 744, 745, 746–
747, 748, 749
in Uppsala, 1057–1058
in Valletta, 807
in Venice, 765, 768, 769
in Vienna, 56, 58, 59–60
in Warsaw, 857

in York, 498
in Zürich, 1079–1080
Climate, 18
Clothing, 28–29
Computers, 21
Copenhagen, 189–205
Amaliehavn, 196
Amalienborg, 196
arts in, 204
bookstores in, 191
Børsen, 193
Botanisk Have, 197–198
Christianborg-Slot, 192–193
concerts in, 204
Den Lille Havfrue, 197
Det Kongelige Bibliotek, 193
emergencies in, 191
excursions from, 199–200
Folketinget, 196–197
Frihedsmuseet, 196–197
Gammeltorv and Nytorv
square, 192
gardens in, 197–198
Helligånds Kirken, 193
Hirschprung Collection, 198
hotels in, 202–204
Kastellet, 197
Københavns Råhus, 192
Københavns Synagogue, 197
Kongelig Teater, 196
Kongens Nytorv, 196
Kunstindustrimuseet, 196
The Little Mermaid, 197
Lurblæserne, 192
Marmorkirken, 196
museums in, 192, 193, 198
Nationalmuseet, 192
nightlife in, 204–205
Nikolaj Kirke, 193, 196
Ny Carlsberg Glypotek, 198
Nyhavn, 196
Rådhus, 192
restaurants in, 196, 198, 200–
202
Rosenborg Slot, 197
Rundetårn, 197
Russiske Ortodoks Kirke, 196
shopping in, 200
Statens Museum for Kunst,
198
S-trains in, 190
Strøget, 192
synagogue in, 197
Teaterhistorisk Museum, 193
theater in, 196, 204
Thorvaldsens Museum, 193
Tivoli, 198
Tøjhusetmuseet, 193

tourist information in, 190
Tycho Brahe Planetarium, 198
university of, 197
Vor Frelser's Kirke, 193
Vor Frue Kirke, 197
Cork, 682–689
Blarney Castle, 682
Crawford Art Gallery, 681
Fota Island, 681–682
hotels in, 682–683, 687–689
Patrick Street, 680
restaurants in, 682–683, 687–
689
St. Anne's Church, 680
Shandon Steeple, 680
shopping in, 680–681
tourist information in, 679,
684
Currency, 9, 26
Customs and duties, 5, 23–24
Cyprus, 145–158. See also
Nicosia
Abbey of Bellapais, 158
amphitheater, 153
Ayia Napa, 152, 155
Ayios Lazarus, 151
Bellapais, 158
Byzantine Museum, 152
Castle of St. Hilarion, 158
churches in, 150, 151, 152,
153
Curium, 153
Cyprus Medieval Museum,
152–153
emergencies in, 150
Ethnographical Museum, 152
Famagusta, 158
Gazimagusa, 158
Girne, 157–158
Green Line, 150
Hala Sultan Tekke, 152
hotels in, 155–156
KEO Winery, 153
Kition, 151
Kolossi Castle, 153
Kykko Monastery, 153
Kyrenia, 157–158
Lala Mustafa Pasha Mosque,
158
Larnaca, 151–152, 154, 155
Latchi, 153
Lefkoşa, 157
Limassol, 152–153, 154, 155
Mevlevi Tekkeve Etnografy
Müzesi, 157
mosques in, 152, 157, 158
museums in, 149, 150, 151,
152–153, 157, 158

Northern Cyprus, 156–158
Old City, 157
Panayia Angelktistos Church,
152
Paphos, 152, 154, 156
Perides Collection, 151
Republic of, 148–156
restaurants in, 153–154
Roman ruins in, 152, 153
St. Hilarion, 158
Salamis, 158
Salt Lake, 152
Sanctuary of Apollo Hylates,
153
Selimiyre Mosque, 157
Shipwreck Museum, 158
shopping in, 149
Stavrovouni Monastery, 153
Tombs of the Kings, 152
tourist offices of, 16, 149–
150, 157
Troodos Mountains, 153
Turkish fort in, 151
Villa of Eustolios, 153
Czech Republic, 159–180. See
also Prague
Bohemian spas and castles,
176–180
camping in, 166
Çeské Budějovice, 179
Çesky Krumlov, 178–179
Chod Museum, 178
churches in, 169, 172
Domažlice, 178
Egon SchieleCenter, 179
gardens in, 172
hotels in, 165–166, 179–
180
Hussite Museum, 179
Karlovy Vary, 177, 179–180
Karlštejn, 177
Křivoklát, 177
Kvilda, 178
Lipno, 178
Mariánské Lázné, 177–178,
180
museums in, 161, 164, 169,
178, 179
Přemysla Otakara II Square,
179
restaurants in, 164–165, 179–
180
shopping in, 164, 173
Šumava mountains, 178
Tábor, 179
tourist information in, 16,
167, 177
Vltava River, 178

D

Delft, 592–593, 596–597,
598–599
hotels in, 598–599
Lambert van Meerten Mu-
seum, 597
Nieuwe Kerk, 596
Oude Kerk, 596
Prinsehof, 596
restaurants in, 598–599
tourist information in, 593
Denmark, 181–216. See also
Copenhagen
Aalborg, 213, 214–215
Ærøskøbing, 208
Århus, 212, 215
Auning, 213
Billund, 214
Brandt's Passage, 207
Budolfi Kirke, 213
camping in, 189
Carl-Henning Pederson and
Else Afelt Museum, 214
Carl Nielsen Museum, 207
churches in, 193, 196, 197,
199, 212–213
Den Fynske Landsby, 207
Den Gamla Gård, 207
Den Gamle By, 213
Den Georgrafiske Have, 212
Dollerup Bakker, 214
Domkirke (Århus), 212
Domkirke (Roskilde), 199
Domkirke (Viborg), 214
Egeskov Slot, 208
Fåborg, 207, 209
Fåborg Museum for Fynsk
Malerkunst, 207
farm vacations in, 188–189
ferry travel in, 186
Funen and CentralIslands,
205–210
Gammel Estrup, 213
gardens in, 197–198, 212
Graphic Museum, 207
Haervejen, 214
Hald Sø, 214
Hans Christian Anderson Mu-
seum, 207
Helligandsklosteret, 213
Helsingør-Kronborg Castle,
199
Herning, 214
hotels in, 188–189, 202–204,
208–210, 214–216
inns in, 188
Jelling, 212

Jens Bangs Stenhus, 213
Jutland and the Lakes, 210–216
Kerteminde, 206
Kolding, 212
Koldinghus castle, 212
Ladbyskibet, 206
Langeland, 208
Legoland, 214
Louisiana, 199
Moesgård Prehistoric Museum, 213
Møntegården, 207
Museum for Photographic Art, 207
museums in, 187, 192–193, 198, 199, 207, 212, 213, 214
Nyborg, 206, 209
Nyborg Slot, 206
Odense, 207, 209
Randers, 213
restaurants in, 187–188, 200–202, 208–, 210, 214–216
Ribe, 214, 215
Roskilde, 199
Rungstedlund, 199–200
shopping in, 187, 200
Silkeborg, 212
Silkeborg Kulturhistoriske Museum, 212
Skagen, 213, 215
Skagens Museum, 213
Svendborg, 208, 210
Tåsinge, 208
tourist information in, 16, 206, 210, 212
Troense, 208, 210
Valdemars Slot, 208 Vejle, 212, 216
Viborg, 213–214
Viking Ship Museum, 199
Vor Frue Kirke, 213
youth hostels in, 189
Disabilities, travelers with, 5–6, 24
Discounts, travel, 6, 24
Doctors, 7–8, 26
Driving, 6, 24–25
Dublin, 661–678
Abbey Theatre, 665, 678
Archbishop Marsh's Library, 669
arts in, 678
Book of Kells, 668
Brown Thomas, 669
Charlemont House, 664
Christ Church Cathedral, 670

City Hall, 670
Civic Museum, 669
Custom House, 671
Dublin Castle, 670
Dublin Writers Museum, 664
emergencies in, 662
Four Courts, 671
Gate Theater, 664
Genealogical Office, 669
General Post Office, 664
Grafton Street, 669
Gresham Hotel, 664
Guinness Brewery, 670
Ha'penny Bridge, 671
Heraldic Museum, 669
hotels in, 675–678
Howth, 671
Hugh Lane Municipal Gallery of Modern Art, 664
Irish Jewish Museum, 672
Irish Museum of Modern Art, 671
Irish Whiskey Corner, 671
Joyce Museum, 672
Kilkenny Design Workshops, 668
Leinster House, 668
Liffey (river), 670–671
Mansion House, 669
Merrion Square, 668
National Gallery, 668
National Library, 669
National Museum, 669
nightlife in, 678
O'Connell Bridge, 663
O'Connell Street, 663–665
Parliament House, 665
Parnell Square, 664
Phoenix Park, 670–671
Powerscourt Town House, 669
pubs in, 675, 678
restaurants in, 665, 668, 669, 672–675
Rotunda, 664
Royal Hospital Kilmainham, 671
Royal Irish Academy, 669
St. Mary's Pro Cathedral, 665
St. Michan's, 671
St. Patrick's Cathedral, 669–670
Sandycove, 671
shopping in, 672
Stephen's Green, 665, 668–669
Temple Bar, 670
theater in, 664, 678

tourist information in, 662
Trinity College, 665, 668

E

Edinburgh, 504–510
Arthur's Seat, 508
Calton Hill, 508
Canongate, 506
Canongate Kirk, 506
Castle Esplanade, 506
Charlotte Square, 508
Crown Room, 505
Edinburgh Castle, 505–506
Edinburgh International Festival, 508–509
Festival Fringe, 508–509
Georgian House, 508
Gladstone's Land, 506
High Kirk of St. Giles, 506
Holyrood Park, 508
hotels in, 509–510
Huntly House, 506
John Knox's House, 506
Lady Stair's House, 506
National Gallery of Scotland, 508
Netherbow Arts Centre, 506
Old Parliament Hall, 505
Palace of Holyroodhouse, 506, 508
Queen Mary's Apartments, 505
restaurants in, 508, 509
Royal Mile, 505–506, 508–509
St. Andrew Square, 508
St. Margaret's Chapel, 505
Scott Monument, 508
Scottish National War Memorial, 505
Tolbooth, 506
tourist information in, 505
Writers' Museum, 506
Electricity, 6, 28–29
Emergencies, 7–8, 26
in Amsterdam, 569
in Andorra, 38
in Athens, 523
in Barcelona, 987
in Berlin, 405
in Bern, 1110
in Bratislava, 938–939
in Brussels, 92
in Bucharest, 918
in Budapest, 611–612
in Cyprus, 150
in Denmark, 191

in Dublin, 662
in Florence, 729
in Frankfurt, 361
in Hamburg, 371
in Helsinki, 226
in Instanbul, 1132–1133
in Lisbon, 882
in London, 450
in Luxembourg, 792
in Luzern, 1098
in Madrid, 961
in Milan, 754
in Munich, 344
in Oslo, 823
in Paris, 265
in Prague, 167
in Reykjavík, 639
in Rome, 709
in Sofia, 126
in Stockholm, 1042
in Valletta, 806
in Venice, 763
in Vienna, 52
in Warsaw, 856
in Zermatt, 1118
in Zürich, 1078
England. See Great Britain
EurailPasses, 9–10

F

Ferries
from United Kingdom to Europe, 7
within Europe, 25
Film, 9, 21–22
Finland, 217–250. See also Helsinki
Amuri Museum of Workers' Housing, 241
aquarium, 241
Arctic Highway, 247–248
Arktikum, 246
camping in, 225
churches in, 228, 241, 242
farmhouses in, 224
Finnish Glass Museum, 242
Gold Museum, 247
Häme Castle, 242
Hämeenlinna, 242–243
Hattula Church, 242
hotels in, 224–225, 235–237, 239, 242–244, 246, 248–250
Iittala Glassworks, 242
Inari, 248
Ivalo, 248–250
Ivalo River, 248

Kaleva Church, 241
Kuopio, 239–240, 243
Lake Inari, 248
Lakelands of, 238–244
Lapland, Finnish, 245–250
Lappia Hall, 246
Lenin Museum, 241
Levitunturi, 249
Lintula convent, 240
Luostotunturi, 249
Menesjärvi, 248
Mikko (ship), 239
Monastery of Valamo, 239–240
Museum of the Province of Lapland, 246
museums in, 233, 239–240, 241, 242, 246, 247, 248
Näsinnuela Observation Tower, 241
Olavinlinna, 239
opera in, 232
Orthodox Church Museum, 239–240
planetarium, 241
Poet's Way, 242
Pöykköla Museum, 246
Puijo Tower, 240
Punkaharju, 239
Pyynikki, 241
reindeer roundups in, 245
rental houses in, 224
restaurants in, 223–224, 229, 232, 233–235, 242–244
Retretti, 239
Riihimäki, 242
Rovaniemi, 246, 249–250
Saariselkä, 247–248, 250
Salama (ship), 239
Sami Museum, 248
Santa Claus's Village, 247
Sarah Hildén Art Museum, 241
Savonlinna, 238–239, 243–244
Sevettijärui, 248shopping in, 223, 232–233
Sibelius birthplace, 242
Sodankylä, 246
Taidekeskus Retretti, 239
Tammerkoski Rapids, 241
Tampere, 240–242, 244
Tankavaara, 247, 250
tourist information in, 16, 238, 246
Urho Kekkonen National Park, 248
youth hostels in, 224

Flight insurance, 25
Florence, 728–743
Accademia Gallery, 732
arts in, 742
ballet in, 742
Baptistry, 731
Bargello, 733
Barrett-Browning house, 737
Bell Tower, 731
Boboli Gardens, 737
bookstores in, 729
Casa Buonarroti, 738
Casa Guidi, 737
Church of San Lorenzo, 733
Davanzati Museum, 737–738
emergencies in, 729
English Cemetery, 737
Gallery of Modern Art, 736
hotels in, 740–742
Jewish Museum, 738
Loggia del Mercato Nuovo, 732
Medici Chapel, 733
Museo Archeologico, 732
Museo dell'Opera del Duomo, 731
Museo di San Marco, 732–733
Museo Nazionale, 733
Museum of Santa Maria Novella, 733
nightlife in, 742–743
Orsanmichele, 731
Ospedale degli Innocenti, 732
Palatine Gallery, 736
Palazzo Medici Riccardi, 733, 737
Palazzo Pitti, 736
Palazzo Vecchio, 732
Piazza del Duomo, 731
Piazza della Signoria, 731–732
Ponte Vecchio, 736
restaurants in, 732, 733, 737, 739–740
San Lorenzo Market, 733
San Miniato al Monte, 738
Santa Croce, 736
Santa Maria del Carmine, 737
Santa Maria del Fiore, 731
Santa Maria Novella, 733
Santo Spirito, 737
shopping in, 738–739
Stibbert Museum, 738
synagogue in, 738
tourist information in, 729
Uffizi Gallery, 732

France, 251–327. See also
   Paris
Abbaye St-Ouen, 298
Aiguille, 299
Alabaster coast, 296
Amboise, 313–314, 315
Ancienne Auberge du Père
   Ganne, 293
Les Andelys, 298
Angers, 315, 316
Antibes, 320, 321, 325
Arronmanches, 300
Autun, 307
Auxerre, 305, 308–309
Avallon, 306, 309
Azay-le-Rideau, 314
Barbizon, 293–294, 295
Basilica of St-Andoche, 306
Bayeux, 300–301, 302
Beauce, 311
Beaune, 307, 309
bed-and-breakfasts in, 261
Blois, 313, 316
Burgundy, 304–311
Caen, 300, 302
Cagnes, 325–326
camping in, 262
Cannes, 320, 326
Cathédrale Notre-Dame
   (Bayeux), 300
Cathédrale Notre-Dame
   (Rouen), 298
Cathédrale St-Etienne (Aux-
   erre), 305
Cathédrale St-Etienne (Sens),
   305
Cathedral of St-Bénigne, 307
Cathedral of St-Gatien, 314
Chablis, 305, 310
Chambord, 313, 316
Chartres, 292, 295
Chartreuse de Champmol, 307
château of Chaumont, 313
château of Chenonceau, 314
Château du Clos de Vougeot,
   307
Châteaudun, 312–313
Château Gaillard, 298
Château Grimaldi, 321
château of Sully, 307
Chinon, 314–315, 317
churches in, 269, 270, 271,
   277, 279, 292, 298–299,
   305–306, 307, 308, 313,
   314, 315, 320, 321, 323
Clamecy, 305–307
Clos-Lucé, 313–314
Cluny, 308, 310

D-Day, 300–301
Deauville, 300, 302
Dijon, 307, 310
Disneyland Paris, 294, 295
Eglise de la Trinité (Fécamp),
   299
Eglise de la Trinité (Vendôme),
   313
Eglise Jeanne d'Arc, 298
Eglise St-Godard, 298
Eglise St-Maclou, 298
Etretat, 299, 302
Fécamp, 299, 303
film in, 288, 320
Fontainebleau, 293, 295
Fontevraud, 315
Fréjus, 320
Gassin, 320
Giverny, 298
Gorges d'Apremont, 293
Grasse, 320, 326
Honfleur, 299–300, 303
hotels in, 261–262, 277, 284–
   287, 294–296, 301–304,
   308–311, 315–318, 325–
   327
Ile de France, 289–296
Jardin Exotique, 325
Jumièges Abbey, 298
Landings Museum, 303
Langeais, 314
Loire Valley, 311–318
Lyon, 304–311, 308
Mâcon, 308
Maeght Foundation, 318
Mémorial, 300
Menton, 325, 326
Monaco, 323–325, 326–327
Mont St-Michel, 301, 303–
   304
Morvan Regional Park, 306
Mougins, 320, 327
Musée Archéologique, 321–
   322
Musée Baron Gérard, 300
Musée Chagall, 321
Musée d'Art et Histoire
   Romain Rolland, 305
Musée de la Bataille de Nor-
   mandie, 300
Musée de la Céramique, 298
Musée de l'Ecole de Barbizon,
   293
Musée de l'Annonciade, 320
Musée des Arts Décoratifs,
   315
Musée des Beaux-Arts (Lyon),
   308

Musé des Beaux-Arts Jules
   Chéret, 321
Musée des Beaux-Arts
   (Rouen), 298
Musée du Cheval, 315
Musée du Gros-Horloge, 298
Musée du Vin de Bourgogne,
   307
Musée Historial des Princes de
   Monaco, 323
Musée Jean Cocteau, 325
Musée Le Secq des Tournelles,
   298
Musée National des Auto-
   mates et Poupées d'Autre-
   fois, 323
Musée Océanographique, 323,
   325
Musée Ochier, 308
Musée Picasso, 321
Musée Rolin, 307
museums in, 260, 269, 270,
   271, 274, 276–277, 279,
   293, 298, 300–301, 305,
   306–307, 308, 315, 320,
   321, 323
Nice, 321–323, 327
Normandy, 296–304
Notre-Dame de Chartres, 292
Palais des Ducs, 307
Palais de Justice, 298
Palais du Prince, 323
Palais Synodal, 305
place Garibaldi, 321
place Masséna, 321
Port Grimaud, 320
Puits de Moïse, 307
Quarré-les-Tombes, 306
Ramatuelle, 320
Rambouillet, 292, 296
restaurants in, 260–261, 269,
   278, 282–284, 294–296,
   301–304, 308–311, 315–
   318, 325–327
Riviera, 327
Rocher de la Pérouse, 306
Rochers des Demoiselles,
   293
Roman ruins in, 307
Rouen, 298–299, 304
St-François-de-Paule, 321
St-Lazarus Church (Autun),
   307
St-Lazarus Church (Avallon),
   306
St-Martin Church, 305
St-Martin Garden, 323
St. Paul de Vence, 318, 319

St-Tropez, 319–320, 327
St-Wandrille Abbey, 298–299
Saulieu, 306
Saumur, 315, 317
Sens, 305, 311
shopping in, 259–260, 277, 278, 281–282
Siene Valley, 296
tourist information in, 16, 291, 297–298, 305, 312, 319
Tours, 314, 317–318
Les Trianons, 291
Trouville, 300
Ussé, 314
Vaux-le-Vicomte, 293–294
Vendôme, 313
Versailles, 291–292, 296
Vézelay, 305–306, 311
Villandry, 314
villas in, 262
William the Conqueror Cultural Center, 300
youth hostels in, 261–262
Frankfurt, 360–370
Alte Brücke, 367
Alte Oper, 366
bookstores in, 361
Börse, 366
Carmelite Monastery, 366
Eiserne Steg, 363
emergencies in, 361
Fountain of Justitia, 363
Goethehaus und Goethemuseum, 366
Hauptwache, 363
hotels in, 369–370
Jewish Museum, 367
Kaiserdom, 363
Kaisersaal, 363
Karmeliterkloster, 366
Katerinenkirche, 363
Kuhhirtenturm, 367
Leonhardskirche, 366
Museum of Modern Art, 366
Museum of Prehistoryand Early History, 366
Nikolaikirche, 363
Paulskirche, 363
Rententurm, 363
restaurants in, 367–368
Römer, 363
Römerberg Square, 363
Sachsenhausen, 367
Schaumainkai, 367
Städelsches Kunstinstitut and Städische Galerie, 367
tourist information in, 361

G

Gay and Lesbian Travelers, 7
Gdąsk, 868–871
hotels in, 870–871
restaurants in, 870–871
Solidarity Monument, 869
tourist information in, 868
Geneva, 1088–1097
Cathédral St-Pierre, 1091
Confédération Centre, 1094
Conservatoire de Musique, 1091
Grand Théâtre, 1091
Hôtel de Ville, 1091
hotels in, 1095–1097
International Complex, 1090
Jardin Anglais, 1094
Jet D'Eau, 1090
Maison Tavel, 1090
Monument Brunswick, 1090
Musée d'Art et Histoire, 1091
Musée Rath, 1091
opera in, 1091
Pont de l'Ile, 1091
Pont du Mont Blanc, 1090
Reformation Monument, 1091
restaurants in, 1094–1095
Rousseau Island, 1091
Russian church, 1091
Temple de l'Auditoire, 1091
tourist information in, 1090
Germany, 328–431. See also Berlin; Frankfurt; Hamburg; Munich; Saxony and Thuringia
Achkarren, 396
Alpirsbach, 395
Bacharach, 387, 388
Baden-Baden, 396, 397–398
Bad Godesberg, 385
Bad Liebenzell, 393, 398
Baiersbronn, 398–399
Black Forest, 392–402
Bonn, 384, 388–389
Boppard, 386, 389
Burg Gutenfels, 387
Burg Katz, 386–387
Burg Maus, 386–387
Calw, 399
camping in, 342
castles in, 385, 386–387
churches in, 346, 363, 366, 376, 383, 384, 385, 386, 387, 388, 393, 395, 406, 411, 413, 424, 425, 426
Deutsches Eck, 385
Drachenfels, 385

Ehrenbreitstein, 385
farm vacations in, 341–342
Freiburg, 395, 399–400
Freudenstadt, 394–395, 400–401
Gutach, 401
Gutachtal Valley, 395
Himmelreich, 395
Hinterzarten, 401
hotels in, 340–342, 356–358, 369–370, 378–380, 388–392, 397–402, 417–420
Kaub, 387, 389
Koblenz, 385–386, 389–390
Köln, 386, 390–391
Königswinter, 385, 391
Landesmuseum, 385–386
Lorelei rock, 387
Ludwig Museum, 386
Mainz, 387–388, 391
Mittelrhein Museum, 386
Mummelsee Lake, 396
Museum Ludwig, 383
museums in, 338, 350–351, 366, 367, 376, 383, 384, 385–386, 387, 388, 393, 395, 396, 406, 410, 411, 425, 426, 428
Nagold, 401
Neubulach silver mine, 394
Oberwesel, 387
Pfalzgrafenstein, 387
Pforzheim, 393, 401–402
rentals in, 341
restaurants in, 339–340, 353–356, 367–368, 377–378, 388–392, 394, 395–396, 397–402, 407, 413, 415–417
Reuchlinhaus, 393
Rheinfels Castle, 386
Rhine region, 380–392
Roman ruins in, 396–397
Römisch-Germanisches Museum, 383, 388
Rüdesheim, 391–392
St. Goar, 386, 392
St. Goarshausen, 386, 392
Schluchsee, 395
shopping in, 338, 352–353, 366, 383, 414–415
Siebengebirge, 385
Staufen, 396
telephones in, 337–338
Titisee, 395, 401
tourist information in, 16, 382, 393
Triberg, 395, 402

Wallraf-Richartz Museum, 383
Wine Road, 396
Wolfach, 395
youth hostels in, 342
Gibraltar, 1018–1020, 1021
Apes' Den, 1019
casino in, 1019
Catalan Bay, 1018
Cathedral of the Holy Trinity, 1019
Cathedral of St. Mary the Crowned, 1019
Europa Point, 1019
Gibraltar Museum, 1019
Governor's Residence, 1019
Holyland Tunnel, 1019
hotels in, 1021
Jews Gate, 1019
Koehler Gun, 1020
Law Courts, 1019
Moorish Castle, 1019
Nefusot Yehudada Synagogue, 1020
Nuns Well, 1019
Our Lady of Europe, 1019
restaurants in, 1021
Rosia Bay, 1019
St. Michael's Cave, 1019
Sandy Bay, 1018
tourist office, 16
Tower of Homage, 1019
Upper Nature Preserve, 1019
Wall of Charles V, 1019
Great Britain, 432–510. See also Bath; Cambridge; Edinburgh; London; Oxford; York
Abbeygate Street, 495
Angel Hill, 495
Anne Hathaway's Cottage, 486
bed-and-breakfasts in, 443
Bladon, 484
Blenheim Palace, 482, 484
Bolton Abbey, 501
Bury St. Edmund's, 495–496
camping in, 444
Castle Howard, 502
Chantry House, 481
Cheltenham, 487
Chipping Campden, 486
Christ Church, 482
churches in, 453, 456, 457–458, 461, 462–463, 480, 495, 498
Cotswolds, 487
Ely, 495
Eton, 481, 491

farmhouses in, 443–444
Fountains Abbey and Studley Royal, 501
gardens in, 459, 486
Grantchester, 493
Grassington, 501
Hall's Croft, 484
Helmsley, 501
Henley, 481
Hidcote Manor Garden, 486
historic buildings, 444
holiday cottages in, 444
Holy Trinity Church, 486
horse racing in, 495
hotels in, 443–445, 472–476, 488–491, 497, 503–504
Magdalen College, 484
Manor House Museum, 495
Marlow, 481
Mary Arden's House, 484
Museum of Eton Life, 481
museums in, 442, 453, 457, 459–460, 461–462, 463, 466, 481, 482, 484, 486, 487, 493, 495, 498, 499
National Horseracing Museum, 495
National Park Centre, 501
National Stud, 495
Newby Hall, 501
Newmarket, 495
North York Moors, 501
Nunnington Hall, 501–502
Queen Mary's Doll's House, 481
restaurants in, 442–443, 453, 459, 460, 461, 463, 467–472, 481, 484, 486, 488–491, 493, 495, 496, 499, 502–503
Rievaulx Abbey, 501
Roman ruins in, 487
Royal Shakespeare Theatre, 484–485
St. George's Chapel, 480
Shakespeare Birthplace Trust, 484
shopping in, 442, 458, 459, 466–467
Stained-Glass Museum, 495
Stratford, 479, 490–491
Stratford-upon-Avon, 484–486
Strid, 501
Swan, 485
theater in, 482, 484–485
Theater Royal, 496
tourist information in, 16, 479, 492, 498

university housing in, 444
Warwick Castle, 486
Windsor, 479–481, 491
Woolstaplers Hall, 486
Yorkshire Dales, 499, 501
youth hostels in, 444
Greece, 511–558. See also Athens
Acrocorinth, 540
Akrotiri, 554
Ancient Thira, 554
Arahova, 546
Arch of the Emperor Galerius, 548
Archaeological Museum, 548
Argos, 540
arts in, 536–537, 544–545
Cathedral of St. Andrew's, 541
churches in, 528, 541, 548
Corinth, 540
Crete, 555–556
The Cyclades, 552–554
Daphni, 539
Delos, 553
Delphi, 546–547, 549–550
Delphi Museum, 547
The Dodecanese, 554–555
Doric Temple of Apollo, 540
Eleusis, 540
Epidauros, 541
hotels in, 519–520, 533–536, 542–544, 549–551, 555–558
islands of, 552–558
Kalambaka, 547–548, 550
Kamenes, 554
Knights' Hospital, 554
Lindos, 555
Lion Gate, 540
Livadia, 546
mainland Greece, 545–551
Mallia, 555
Megalopolis, 541
Meteora, 547
monasteries in, 548
Monastery of Hosios Loukas, 546
Mount Olympus, 512, 545
Mount Parnassus, 512, 545
Museum of the Olympic Games, 541
museums in, 518, 525, 528, 529, 541, 547, 548, 553, 554, 555
Mycenae, 540
Mykonos, 552–553, 556–557
Nauplio, 541, 542–543
Olympia, 541, 543–544

Palace of the Grand Masters, 554
Palace of Knossos, 555
Patras, 541–542, 544
Peloponnese, 538–545
restaurants in, 519, 529, 531–533, 542–544, 549–551, 555–558
Rhodes, 554–556, 557–558
Santorini, 553–554, 558
shopping in, 518, 530–531
Temple of Apollo, 546
Terrace of the Lions, 553
theater in, 541
Thebes, 546
Thessaloniki, 548–549, 550–551
Tiryns, 540
tourist information in, 16, 539, 546, 552
volcanoes, 552, 554
White Tower, 548

H

The Hague, 592–596, 599
Haags Gemeentemuseum, 595
hotels in, 595, 599
International Court of Justice, 595
Kloosterkerk, 594
Kurhaus area, 595–596
Madurodam, 595
Mauritshuis, 593
Omniversum, 595
Panorama Mesdag, 594
Parliament Buildings, 593
The Pier, 596
restaurants in, 599
Ridderzaal, 593
Rijksmuseum H. W. Mesdag, 594–595
Scheveningen, 595
Sea Life Center, 596
Supreme Court, 594
tourist information in, 593
Vredespaleis, 595
Hamburg, 370–380
Alter Botanischer Garten, 373
Aussenalster, 377
Binnenalster, 377
Bismarck Memorial, 376
Blankenese, 373
bookstores in, 371
emergencies in, 371
Fischmarkt, 373
Grosse Wallanlagen, 373
Hauptbahnhof, 373

hotels in, 378–380
Jungfernstieg, 376
Kunsthalle, 377
Landungsbrücken, 373
Museum für Hamburgische Geschichte, 376
nightlife in, 380
Platen un Blomen, 373
Rathaus, 376
Rathausmarkt, 376
Reeperbahn, 373, 380
restaurants in, 377–378
St. Michael's Church, 376
tourist information in, 371
Wallringpark, 373
Health and accident insurance, 8, 25
Health issues, 7–8, 26
Helsinki, 225–238
Akseli Gallen Kallela's studio, 232
arts in, 237
bookstores, 227
concerts in, 237
emergencies in, 226
Finlandiatalo, 232
Havis Amanda statue, 228
hotels in, 235–237
Kaivopuisto, 229
Katajanokka, 228
Kauppatori, 228
Lutheran Cathedral, 228
Makasiini Terminal, 229
Mannerheim statue, 232
Market Hall, 229
National Museum, 232
National Theater, 229
nightlife in, 237–238
Nordic Arts Center, 229
Olympia Terminal, 229
Parliament House, 232
Pohjoisesplanadi, 228
Pohjoismainen Taidekeskus, 229
Presidentinlinna, 228
restaurants in, 229, 232, 233–235
Senaatintori, 228
shopping in, 232–233
Stockmann's, 229
Suomen Kansallismuseo, 232
Suomen Kansallisoppera, 232
Suomenlinna, 229
Swedish Theater, 229
Tapiola, 232
Temppeliaukion Church, 232
theater in, 237
tourist information in, 226

Tuomiokirkko, 228
Uspenskin Katedraali, 228
Valtion Taidemuseo Ateneum, 229
Holland, 559–600. See also Amsterdam; Delft; The Hague
Aalsmeer, 589
Amersfoort, 585–586
Apeldoorn, 586–587, 590
Arnhem, 587
Bloemenveiling, 589
Boymans-van Beuningen Museum, 598
Centraal Museum, 587–588
churches in, 570, 571, 574, 587, 588, 590, 594, 596
Domkerk, 587
Euromast, 597
Europoort, 597
Frans Hals Museum, 590
gardens in, 589
Gouda, 588, 590–591
Grote Kerk, 590
Haarlem, 589–590, 591
Hortus Botanicus gardens, 589
hotels in, 567–568, 581–583, 591–592, 595, 598–600
Keukenhof Gardens, 589
Kijk-Kubus, 597
Koopelport, 586
Kröller-Muller Museum, 586–587
Kunsthal, 598
Lakenhal, 588
Leiden, 588–589, 591
Lisse, 589
Molenmuseum De Valk, 588
Museum Flehite, 586
museums in, 563, 566, 569, 570, 571, 574, 576–578, 586–587, 588, 590, 594–595, 597, 598
Nederlands Architectuur in, 598
Nederlands Openluchtmuseum, 587
Pieterskerk, 587
Pilgrim Fathers Documentatie Centrum, 589
Prins Hendrik Maritime Museum, 598
restaurants in, 566–567, 574, 579–581, 591–592, 598–600
Rietveld-Schröder House, 588
Rijksmuseum Het Catharijneconvent, 587

Rijksmuseum Paleis Het Loo, 586

Rijkmuseumvan Oudheden, 589

Rijksmuseum van Speelklok tot Pierement, 587

Rotterdam, 592–593, 597–598, 599–600

St. Pieterskerk, 588

Scheveningen, 595

shopping in, 566, 579

Stedelijk Museum Het Catharina Gasthuis, 588

Teylers Museum, 590

tourist information in, 569, 585, 593

Utrecht, 587–588, 591–592

Home exchanges, 9, 26

Hostels, 10, 11

for older travelers, 10

for student travelers, 11

Hungary, 601–632. See also Budapest

Aquincum, 626

Balatonfüred, 628–629, 630, 631

camping in, 609

churches in, 613, 617, 618, 629

Danube Bend, 625–628

Esztergom, 627–628

guest houses in, 609

Herend, 630

hotels in, 608–610, 621–623, 627–628, 631–632

Keresztény Múzeum, 627

Lake Balaton, 628–632

Margit Kovács Pottery Museum, 626–627

museums in, 608, 613, 616, 617, 618–619, 626–627, 630

Nagyvázsony castle, 630

Nemesvámos, 629

parks in, 618

rentals in, 608–609

restaurants in, 608, 616, 617, 619–621, 627–628, 629–630, 631–632

shopping in, 619

Szabadtéri Néprajzi Múzeum, 627

Szentendre, 626, 628

Tihany, 630, 631–632

tourist information in, 17, 611, 626, 629

Veszprém, 629, 632

Visegrád, 627, 628

I

Iceland, 633–650. See also Reykjavík

Akureuyri, 646–647, 648, 650

Blönduós, 647, 648

Borgarnes, 647, 648

botanic gardens, 647

Breiddalsvik, 646, 648

Búðir, 648

churches in, 640, 642

countryside of, 644–650

Dettifoss waterfall, 647

Djúpivogur, 648, 650

Egilsstaðir, 646, 648, 650

Goðafoss waterfall, 647

Hallormsstaððarskógur, 646, 648

Höfn, 646, 648

hotels in, 638, 644, 649–650

Húsavík, 647, 649

Hveragerðði, 645, 649, 650

Ísafjörður, 649

Jökulsárlón, 646

Kirkjubæjarklaustur, 646, 649

Lake Mývatn, 646, 645

midnight sun in, 647

museums in, 637, 640, 642

Mývatn, 649

Ólafsvík, 647, 649

restaurants in, 637–638, 640, 643, 647–649

Sauððárkrókur, 649

Selfoss, 645

Seydðisfjörðður, 646, 649

shopping in, 643

Skaftafell National Park, 646, 650

Skógar, 645–646, 649

Snæfellsnes, 647

telephones in, 637

Tjörnes, 647

tourist information in, 17, 639, 645

Vatnajökull, 646

Vestfirððir, 647

Innsbruck, 77–82

Alpine Zoo, 80

Annasäule, 78

arts in, 82

churches in, 78

Ferdinandeum, 78

Goldenes Dachl, 78

Grassmayr Bell Foundry, 80

Hofburg, 78

Hofkirche, 78

hotels in, 81–82

Olympic Museum, 78

restaurants in, 78, 80–81

Schloss Ambras, 80

Tiroler Volkskunstmuseum, 78

tourist information in, 78

Triumphpforte, 78

Insurance, 8, 25–26

for rental cars, 31

Ireland, 651–694. See also Cork; Dublin

Ailwee Cave, 687

Aran Islands, 687

Ballyporeen, 680

bed-and-breakfasts in, 660–661

Belleek, 692

Blasket Islands, 686

Bundoran, 691

Bunratty Castle, 686

Cahir, 680, 682

camping in, 661

Cashel, 680, 682

Cashel Bay, 692

castles in, 670, 682, 686, 690

Cavan, 692

churches in, 665, 669–670, 671, 680, 681

Claddagh, 690

Clare Heritage Center, 686

Clarinbridge, 687

Clifden, 690, 692

Cliffs of Moher, 687

Cobb, 681

Collooney, 692

Cong, 693

Connemara, 690

Connemara National Park, 690

Croagpatrick, 691

Curragh, 679

Derrynane House, 685

Dingle Peninsula, 686, 687

Donegal, 691

Doolin, 687

Ennis, 687–688

Gaelteacht, 684

Galway City, 690, 693

guest houses in, 660

horse racing in, 679–680

hotels in, 660–661, 675–678, 682–683, 687–689

Inishmaan, 690

Innisfree, 691

Japanese Gardens, 680

Kells, 692

Kenmare, 685, 688

Kerry, 684

Kildare, 680

Killarney, 684, 688

Knappogue castle, 686
Lahinch, 688
Limerick, 686, 688–689
Lisdoonvarna, 686–687, 689
Lissadell House, 691
Lynch's Castle, 690
Moycullen, 693
Muckross, 684
museums in, 659, 664, 668,
    669, 671, 672, 680, 691
Naas, 679
National Stud and Horse Mu-
    seum, 680
Northwest, 689–694
Oughterand, 690, 693
The Pale, 679
parks in, 670–671, 684
pubs in, 675, 678
restaurants in, 659–660, 665,
    668, 669, 672–675, 682–
    683, 687–689
Ring of Kerry, 684–685
Rock of Cashel, 680
Rossaveale, 690
Salthill Promenade, 690
shopping in, 659, 672, 680–
    681
Skellig Rocks, 685
Sligo Town, 691, 693
Sneem, 685
Tara, hill of, 692
Tarbet, 686
tourist information in, 17,
    662, 679, 684, 689
Tralee, 686
Waterville, 685
Westport, 691, 694
Istanbul, 1131–114
Archaeological Museum, 1135
arts in, 1143–1144
Bab-i-Salam, 1134
bars in, 1144
Blue Mosque, 1138
bookstores in, 1133
Carpet Museum, 1138
Church of St. Irene, 1134
churches in, 1134, 1135
Cistern Basilica, 1138
Column of Constantinos, 1138
concerts in, 1144
Divan-i-Humayun, 1134
Dolmabahçe Mosque, 1139–
    1140
Dolmabahçe Palace, 1139,
    1140
Dolmuş in, 1132
Egyptian Bazaar, 1139
Egyptian Obelisk, 1138

emergencies, 1132–1133
Erivan Kiosk, 1135
Flower Arcade, 1139
Galata Tower, 1139
Golden Cage, 1135
Grand Bazaar, 1138–1139
Hagia Sophia, 1135
Harem, 1134
Hippodrome, 1138
hotels in, 1142–1143
Ibrahim Paşa Palace, 1138
Istanbul University, 1139
Kilim Museum, 1138
Museum of the Ancient Ori-
    ent, 1135
Museum of Turkish and Is-
    lamic Arts, 1138
New Town, 1139–1140
nightlife in, 1144–1145
opera in, 1144
restaurants in, 1135, 1140–
    1142
Sacred Column, 1135
Serpentine Column, 1138
shopping in, 1140
Süleymaniye Mosque, 1139
theater in, 1144
Tiled Pavilion, 1135
Topkapı Palace, 1134
tourist information in, 1132
tours of, 1133
Treasury, 1135
Turkish baths, 1138
Italy, 695–784. See also Flo-
    rence; Milan; Rome; Venice
Amalfi, 780, 781–782
Anacapri, 780
Arezzo, 748–749, 750
Baptistery (Pisa), 746–747
Campania region of, 776–784
camping in, 705
Capri, 780, 782
Castel Nuovo, 777–778
Certaldo, 747
Certosa di San Martino, 778
churches in, 703, 714, 715,
    716–719, 731, 733, 736
    737, 744–745, 746, 747,
    748, 749, 755, 757, 765,
    768, 769, 778, 780, 781
Collegiata, Church of the, 748
Cortona, 749, 750
Crypt of St. Peter's, 717
Duomo (Lucca), 746
Duomo (Pisa), 746
Duomo (Pistoia), 745
Duomo (Prato), 744
Duomo (Siena), 747

gardens in, 718, 746, 780
Gesù, 778
Grotto Azzurra, 780
Herculaneum, 779
hotels in, 704–706, 715, 725–
    726, 740–742, 749–753,
    759–760, 768, 773–775,
    781–785
Leaning Tower (Pisa), 746
Lucca, 745–746, 750
Montepulciano, 751
Museo Archeologico, 748
Museo Archeologico
    Nazionale, 778–779
Museo Correale, 780
Museo dell'Accademia Etrus-
    ca, 749
Museo dell'Opera del Duomo,
    744
Museo di Capodimonte, 779
Museo Diocesano, 749
museums in, 703, 711, 718,
    721, 731, 732–733, 736,
    737–738, 744, 748, 749,
    765, 770, 768, 778–779,
    780
Naples, 777–779, 782–783
Palazzo Reale, 777
Petrarch's House, 748
Piazza del Campo, 747
Piazza Grande, 748–749
Pievescola, 751
Pisa, 746–747, 751
Pistoia, 745, 751
Pompeii, 779
Positano, 780, 783–784
Prato, 744–745, 752
Ravello, 781, 784
rentals in, 705
restaurants in, 704, 711, 714,
    719, 720, 722–724, 732,
    733, 736, 737, 739–740,
    747, 749–753, 757–759,
    768, 771–773, 778, 781–
    785
Roman ruins in, 748
San Francesco (Arezzo), 748
San Francesco (Sorrento), 780
San Gimignano, 748, 752
San Giovanni Fuorcivitas, 745
Santa Chiara, 778
Santa Maria del Calcinaio,
    749
Santa Maria della Carceri, 744
Santa Maria della Pieve, 749
Sant'Andrea, 745
shopping in, 703–704, 721–
    722, 738–739, 757, 771

Siena, 747, 752–753
Sorrento, 779–780, 784–785
tourist information in, 17,
    697, 708, 729, 744, 754,
    763, 777
Tuscany region of, 743–753
Villa Cimbrone, 781
Villa Reale, 746
Villa Rufolo, 781

K

Kraków, 863–868
Auschwitz, 866
Barbakan, 864
Church of the Virgin Mary,
    864
hotels in, 867–868
Jagiellonian University, 864,
    866
Main Market, 864
Planty, 864
restaurants in, 864, 867-868
St. Florian's Gate, 864
Sukiennice, 864
tourist information in, 864
Wadowice, 866–867
Wawel Castleland Cathedral.
    866
Wieliczka, 866

L

Laptop computers, 21
Lefkosa. See Nicosia
Liechtenstein, 1086–1088
hotels in, 1087–1088
Liechtenstein National Mu-
    seum, 1087
Malbun, 1087
Postage Stamp Museum, 1087
Prince's Art Gallery and the
    State Art Collection, 1087
restaurants in, 1087-1088
Schaan, 1087
tourist information in, 1087
Triesenberg, 1087
Vaduz, 1087
Vaduz Castle, 1087
Lisbon, 881–894
arts in, 893
Alfama, 884
Avenida da Liberdade, 884,
    886
Bairro Alta, 886–887
Baixa, 884
ballet in, 893
Belém, 887–889
Castelo de São Jorge, 884

emergencies in, 882
Fundação Calouste Gul-
    benkian, 886
hotels in, 891–893
Igreja de São Roque, 886
Igreja do Carmo, 887
Instituto do Vinhodo Porto,
    886
Largo do Chiado, 886
Monument to the Discoveries,
    887
Mosteiro dos Jerónimos, 887
Museu da Artes Decorativas,
    884
Museu da Marioneta, 884
Museu de Arte Antiga, 889
Museu de Arte Sacra, 886
Museu de Marinha, 887
Museu Nacional do Coches,
    888
nightlife in, 893–894
opera in, 893
Palácio da Ajuda, 888
Palácio da Fronteira, 888–889
Parque Eduardo VII, 884
restaurants in, 887, 890–891
Rossio, 884
Sé, 884
shopping in, 889–890
theater in, 893
Torre de Belém, 888
tourist information in, 882
London, 445–479
Admiralty Arch, 453
Albert Memorial, 460
arts in, 476–478
ballet in, 478
Bank of England, 464
Banqueting House, 458
The Barbican, 463
Bayswater, 472–473
Belgravia, 474–475
Berkeley Square, 459
Big Ben, 457
Birdcage Walk, 456
Bloomsbury, 461–462, 467–
    468, 473
British Museum, 461–462
Buckingham Palace, 456
Burlington Arcade, 459
Burlington House, 459
buses in, 446, 449
Cabinet War Rooms, 457
Camden Lock, 465
Carlton House Terrace, 456
Cenotaph, 458
Changing of the Guard, 456
Chapel Royal, 456

Chapter House, 458
Cheapside, 463
Chelsea, 468, 473–474
The City, 462–465, 468
Clarence House, 456
concerts, 477
Cornhill, 464
Covent Garden, 461, 468–
    469
Crown Jewels, 465
Downing Street, 458
emergencies in, 450
film in, 478
Flower Walk, 460
Greenwich, 465–466
Guards Museum, 457
Guildhall, 463
Hampstead, 465
Hampstead Heath, 467
Henry VII's Chapel, 457–458
Horse Guards Parade, 458
hotels in, 472–476
Hyde Park, 459–460
Hyde Park Corner, 459
Jermyn Street, 459
Keats Grove, 465
Kensington, 469–470, 473–
    474
Kensington Gardens, 459
Kensington Palace, 460
Kenwood House, 465
Knightsbridge, 470, 474–475
Lancaster House, 456
Leadenhall Market, 464
Lloyd's of London, 464
London International Finan-
    cial Futures Exchange, 464
London Transport Museum,
    461
London Wall, 463
The Mall, 453
Mansion House, 464
Mayfair, 458–459, 470
Museum of London, 463
Museum of Mankind, 459
National Gallery, 453
National Maritime Museum,
    466
National Portrait Gallery, 453
National Theatre, 476
Natural History Museum, 460
nightlife in, 478–479
Notting Hill, 460, 471
Old Royal Observatory, 466
opera in, 461, 477
Palace of Westminster, 457
Parliament Square, 457
pharmacies in, 450

Piccadilly, 458
Pyx Chamber, 458
Queen's Gallery, 456
Regent's Park, 473
restaurants in, 453, 459, 460, 461, 467–472
Rotten Row, 459
Royal Academy, 460
Royal Exchange, 464
Royal Mews, 456
Royal Naval College, 466
Royal Opera House, 461
St. James's, 458–459, 472
St. James's Church, 458
St. James's Palace, 456
St. James Park, 453
St. Martin-in-the-Fields Church, 453
St. Mary-le-Bow, 463
St. Paul's Cathedral, 462–463
St. Paul's Church, 461
St. Stephen's Tower, 457
Science Museum, 459–460
Serpentine, 459
Shepherd Market, 459
shopping in, 458, 459, 466–467
Sir John Soane's Museum, 462
Soho, 471–472
10 Downing Street, 458
theater in, 476–477
Theatre Museum, 461
Theatre Royal Drury Lane, 461
tourist information in, 449–450
Tower of London, 464–465
Trafalgar Square, 453
Undercroft, 458
Underground in, 446–449
Victoria, 474–475
Victoria and Albert Museum, 460
Victoria Tower, 457
Wellington Barracks, 456–457
West End, 475–476
Westminster, 453, 456–458
Westminster Abbey, 457–458
Whispering Gallery, 463
Whitehall, 458
York House, 456
Lugano, 1104–1110
Belvedere Gardens, 1106
Cathedral of San Lorenzo, 1106
Church of Santa Maria degli Angioli, 1106
hotels in, 1108–1110

Lido, 1106
Museum of Natural History, 1106
Old Town, 1106
Parco degli Ulivi, 1106
Parco Tassino, 1106
restaurants in, 1106, 1108
tourist information in, 1105
Villa Ciani, 1106
Villa Favorita, 1106
Luggage, 29
Luxembourg, 786–800
camping in, 790
castles in, 795, 797
churches in, 793, 796
Diekirch, 796
Echternach, 797
holidays in, 789–790
hotels in, 790, 799–800
museums in, 789
restaurants in, 790, 795, 797–799
shopping in, 789, 796
tourist offices of, 17, 791–792
youth hostels in, 790
Vianden, 797
Luxembourg City, 790–800
Bock promontory, 795
bookstores in, 792
Cathédrale Notre-Dame, 793
Chapel of St-Quirin, 796
Citadelle du St-Ésprit, 793
emergencies in, 792
Grand Ducal Palace, 795
hotels in, 799–800
Maquette, 795
Monument de la Solidarité Nationale, 793
Musée d'Histoire dela Ville de Luxembourg, 793
Musée National, 795
Passerelle, 793
place de la Constitution, 793
place Guillaume, 795
Plateau Kirchberg, 796
restaurants in, 795, 797–799
St-Michel, 795
shopping in, 796
tourist information in, 791–792
Trois Tours, 795
Luzern, 1097–1104
Altes Rathaus, 1098
Am Rhyn-Haus, 1098
arts in, 1103–1104
casinos in, 1104
emergencies, 1098
Historisches Museum, 1099

hotels in, 1102–1103
Jesuitenkirche, 1099
Kapellbrücke, 1098, 1099
Löwendenkmal, 1099, 1101
Löwenplatz, 1099
nightlife in, 1104
restaurants in, 1099, 1101–1102
shopping in, 1101
Spreuerbrücke, 1099
tourist information in, 1098
Verkehrshaus, 1101
Zunfthaus zur Pfistern, 1098

M

Madrid, 959–976
arts in, 974–975
bookstores in, 961
bullfighting in, 969
cafés in, 974
Calle Mayor, 965
Casa Cisneros, 965
Casa de la Villa, 965
casino in, 976
Chueca, 968
Cibeles Fountain, 964
Convento de las Descalzas Reales, 965
dance in, 975
emergencies in, 961
environs of, 976–985
Flamenco in, 975
hotels in, 972–974
Lavapiés Quarter, 968
metro in, 960
Monument to the Fallen Angel, 964
Museo Thyssen-Bornemisza, 963–964
nightlife in, 975–976
opera in, 974–975
Plaza de la Cibeles, 964
Plaza de la Villa, 965
Plaza Mayor, 965
Prado Museum, 963
Puerta de Alcalá, 964
Puerta del Sol, 964–965
Real Academia de San Fernando, 964
Reina Sofia Arts Center, 963
restaurants in, 964, 965, 968, 969–972
Retiro Park, 964
Royal Carriage Museum, 968
Royal Palace, 965, 968
shopping in, 968–969
theater in, 975

tourist information in, 961
Zarzuela in, 975
Malta, 801–812. See also
  Valletta
Blue Grotto, 810
Buskett, 810
catacombs, 810
churches in, 805, 807, 810, 811
Folklore Museum, 811
Ggantija Prehistoric Temples,
  811
Ghar Dalam, 810
Gozo, 811
hotels in, 805–806, 809, 811–
  812
Hypogeum, 809
Marsaxlokk, 812
Mdina, 810
Mosta, 811
museums in, 804, 807, 808
Qawra, 812
Rabat, 810, 812
restaurants in, 805, 811-812
St. Julians, 812
Tarxien, 809–810
tourist offices of, 17
Xaghra, 811
Milan, 753–760
arts in, 760
ballet in, 760
Castello Sforzesco, 755
concerts in, 760
Duomo, 755
emergencies in, 754
Galleria, 755
hotels in, 759–760
Madonnina, 755
opera in, 755, 760
Piazza della Scala, 755
Pinacoteca di Brera, 755
restaurants in, 757–759, 808–
  809
San Lorenzo Maggiore, 757
San Satiro, 757
Santa Maria delle Grazie, 755,
  757
Sant'Ambrogio, 757
shopping in, 757
Teatro alla Scala, 755, 760
tourist information in, 754
Monaco, 17, 323–325, 326–
  327
Money, 9, 26
Munich, 343–360
Alte Peterskirche, 352
Alte Pinakothek, 350–351
Altes Rathaus, 346
Amalienburg, 351

arts in, 358–359
Asamkirche, 347
bookstores in, 345
Bürgersaal, 346
concerts in, 358–359
Dachau, 352
Dachau Concentration Camp
  Memorial, 351
dance in, 359
emergencies in, 344
Englischer Garten, 350
Feldherrnhalle, 350
film, 359
Frauenkirche, 346
Glockenspiel, 346–347
Hauptbahnhof, 346
Haus der Kunst, 350
Hertie, 346
Hofgarten, 347
hotels in, 356–358
jazz clubs in, 359–360
Justizpalast, 346
Karlsplatz, 346
Karlstor, 346
Leopoldstrasse, 350
Ludwigstrasse, 350
Marienplatz, 346
Marstallmuseum, 351
Michaelskirche, 346
museums in, 350–351
Neue Pinakothek, 351
Neues Rathaus, 346
nightlife in, 359–360
Nymphenburg, 351
Olympic Park, 351
opera in, 359
restaurants in, 347, 350, 353–
  356
Schloss Nymphenburg, 351
Schwabing, 350
shopping in, 352–353
Siegestor, 350
theater in, 359
Theatinerkirche, 350
tourist information in, 344
Viktualienmarkt, 347
Wienerplatz, 352
Museums
in Amsterdam, 569, 570, 571,
  574, 576–578
in Antwerp, 107, 108
in Athens, 525, 528, 529
in Austria, 48–49, 56–57, 58,
  59, 60–61, 71, 72, 75, 78
in Barcelona, 988, 989, 993
in Belgium, 89, 93–94, 95,
  98–99, 100, 107, 108
in Berlin, 406, 410, 411, 413

in Bern, 1111, 1113
in Bratislava, 940–941
in Brugge, 113, 115
in Brussels, 93–94, 95, 98–
  99, 100
in Bucharest, 919, 922–923
in Budapest, 613, 616, 617,
  618–619
in Bulgaria, 123, 127, 129,
  136, 142
in Copenhagen, 192, 193,
  198
in Cyprus, 149, 150, 152–
  153, 157, 158
in Czech Republic, 161, 164,
  169, 178, 179
in Delft, 597
in Denmark, 187, 192, 193,
  198, 199, 207, 212, 213,
  214
in Dresden, 423–424, 425
in Dublin, 664, 668, 669, 671,
  672
in Edinburgh, 505–506, 508
in Finland, 223, 239, 241,
  242, 246, 247, 248
in Florence, 731, 732–733,
  736, 737–738
in France, 260, 269, 270, 271,
  274, 276–277, 278–279,
  293, 298, 300, 301, 306–
  307, 308, 315, 320, 321,
  323, 325
in Frankfurt, 366
in Geneva, 1091
in Germany, 338, 350–351,
  366, 367, 376, 383, 384,
  385–386, 387, 388, 393,
  395, 396, 406, 410, 411,
  413, 425, 426, 428
in Great Britain, 442, 481,
  482, 484, 486, 487, 493,
  495, 498, 499
in Greece, 518, 525, 528, 529,
  541, 547, 548, 553, 554,
  555
in The Hague, 594–595
in Hamburg, 376, 377
in Helsinki, 229, 232
in Holland, 563, 566, 569,
  570, 571, 574, 576–578,
  586–587, 588, 589, 590,
  594–595, 597, 598
in Hungary, 608, 626–627,
  630
in Iceland, 637
in Innsbruck, 79
in Ireland, 659, 680, 691

in Istanbul, 1135, 1138
in Italy, 703, 711, 718, 721,
  731, 732–733, 736, 737–
  738, 744, 748–749, 765,
  770, 768, 778–779, 780
in Liechtenstein, 1087
in Lisbon, 884, 886, 887, 888,
  889
in London, 453, 457, 459–
  460, 461–462, 463, 466
in Lugano, 1106
in Luxembourg, 789, 793, 795
in Luzern, 1099
in Madrid, 963–964, 968
in Malta, 805, 807
in Nicosia, 150
in Norway, 820, 834, 835,
  836, 839, 840, 843, 844
in Oslo, 824, 825, 828, 829
in Paris, 269, 270, 271, 274,
  276–277, 278, 279
in Poland, 851, 853, 857, 870
in Portugal, 879, 896, 897,
  901, 902
in Prague, 169
in Reykjavík, 640, 642
in Romania, 915, 927, 928
in Rome, 711, 718, 721
in Salzburg, 71, 72, 75
in Slovakia, 936, 944
in Sofia, 127, 129
in Spain, 956, 1007, 1016,
  1017
in Stockholm, 1045
in Sweden, 1038, 1058, 1059,
  1063–1064
in Toledo, 978
in Turkey, 1153, 1160
in Tuscany, 744, 748, 749
in Uppsala, 1058, 1059
in Valletta, 807, 808
in Venice, 765, 770, 768
in Vienna, 53, 56–57, 58, 59,
  60–61
in Warsaw, 857
in York, 498, 499
in Zürich, 1080–1081

N

Netherlands. See Holland
Nicosia, 150–151, 157
Archbishop Makarios III Cul-
  tural Foundation, 150
Byzantine Art Museum, 150
Cyprus Folk Art Museum, 151
Cyprus Museum, 151
Famagusta Gate, 151

Greek War of Independence
  Gallery, 150–151
hotels in, 156
Laiki Yitonia, 150
Leventis Museum, 150
Municipal Gardens, 151
Municipal Theatre, 151
Museum of the National
  Struggle, 151
restaurants in, 154
St. John's Cathedral, 151
Tripiotis Church, 159
Norway, 813–846. See also
  Oslo
Ålesund, 843, 844–845
Åmot, 839
Arendal, 835, 837
Åsgårdstrand, 834
Bergen, 838–841
Bergenhus, 840
Bodø, 843, 845
Bragernes Hill, 834
camping in, 821
Christiansholm Fort, 835
churches in, 825, 836, 843
Dalen, 839
Drammen, 834, 837
Egersund, 836
Eidsborg, 839
Flekkefjord, 836
Hammerfest, 844, 845
Hanseatisk Museum, 840
Heddal, 839
hotels in, 820–821, 831–833,
  837–838, 841–842, 844–
  846
Jæren, 836
Kardemomme By, 835–836
Kinsarvik, 839, 840, 841
Kirkenes, 842
Kongsberg, 839, 842
Kragerø, 835
Kristiansand, 835, 837
Larvik, 834, 837
Lofoten islands, 844
maelstrom in, 843
Mandal, 836
Maritime Museum (Larvik),
  834
Morgedal, 839
museums in, 820, 824, 825,
  828, 829, 834, 835, 836,
  839, 840, 843, 844
Narvik, 844, 845
Nidaros Cathedral, 843
Norheimsund, 840
Norsk Bergverksmuseum, 839
Olav Bjåland's Museum, 839

rentals in, 821
restaurants in, 820, 825, 828,
  830-831, 837–838, 841–
  842, 843, 844–846
Risør, 835
Røldal, 839
Ryfylke fjords, 836–837
Sandefjord, 834, 837–838
Seljord, 839
shopping in, 819–820, 830
Stavanger, 836, 838,
Stiftsgården, 843
Svolvær, 845
Telemark area, 838–842
Tønsberg, 834
Tønsberghus, 834
tourist information in, 17,
  822–823, 834, 839, 843
Troldhaugen, 841
Tromsø, 844, 846
Trondheim, 843, 846
Tvedestrand, 835
Utne, 842
youth hostels in, 821
zoo, 835–836

O

Older travelers, 10, 31
Oslo, 822–833
arts in, 833
Aker Brygge, 825
Akershus Castle, 825
bookstores in, 823
concerts, 833
Contemporary Art Museum,
  825, 833
Domkirke, 825
Ekebergseletta Park, 829
emergencies in, 823
forests in, 829
Forsvarsmuseet, 825
Fram-museet, 828
Henie, Sonja, 833
Historisk Museum, 824
Hjemmefrontmuseum, 825
Holmenkollen ski jump, 829
hotels in, 831–833
Karl Johans gate, 824
Kon-Tiki Museum, 828
Lillehammer, 829
Munch-Museet, 828
Nasjonalgalleriet, 824
Nationalteatret, 824, 833
nightlife in, 833
Norsk Folkemuseum, 828
Oslo Ladegård, 829
Rådhuset, 825

restaurants in, 825, 828, 830–831

shopping in, 830

Slottet, 824

Stortinget, 825

tourist information in, 822-823

Tøyen, 828

Universitet, 824

Vigelandsparken, 829

Vikingskiphuset, 828

Oxford, 482–483, 489–490

Ashmolean Museum, 484

Balliol College, 482

Christ Church, 482

hotels in, 489–490

Magdalen College, 482

Oxford Story, 482

restaurants in, 482, 489–490

St. Edmund Hall, 482

Sheldonian Theatre, 482

P

Palaces. See also Castles

in Amsterdam, 574

in Bratislava, 939–940, 941

in Brussels, 93, 95, 98

in Budapest, 613

in Copenhagen, 196

in France, 270–271, 275, 278, 305

in Great Britain, 456, 457, 482, 484

in Greece, 554, 555

in Holland, 586

in Innsbruck, 78

in Istanbul, 1134, 1138, 1140

in Italy, 710, 711, 715–716, 720, 732, 733, 737, 777

in London, 456, 457

in Luxembourg City, 795

in Malta, 807–808

in Munich, 351

in Oslo, 824

in Paris, 270–271, 275, 278

in Portugal, 888–889, 896, 897, 901

in Prague, 177

in Rome, 710–711

in Spain, 964, 965, 968, 979, 988, 989, 992

in Stockholm, 1044, 1048

in Venice, 765, 768, 770

in Vienna, 56, 60, 72

in Warsaw, 857, 860

Paris, 262–289

American Center, 281

Arc de Triomphe, 275

arts in, 287–288

Arènes de Lutèce, 270

Beaubourg, 278

Beaux Quartiers, 281

Bercy, 280–281

Bois de Boulogne, 274

Bois de Vincennes, 280

bookstores in, 265

Bourse du Commerce, 278

Canal St-Martin, 280

Centre Pompidou, 278

Champs-Elysées, 275

Château de Vincennes, 280

Chinatown, 281

Conciergerie, 279

dance in, 288

Eglise de la Madeleine, 279

Eglise St-Séverin, 269

Eiffel Tower, 274

emergencies in, 265

film in, 288

Galeries Lafayette, 278

gardens in, 270, 275–276

Genitron, 278

Grand Palais, 275

Grande Galerie del'Evolution, 270

guillotine, 275

Les Halles, 278

Hôtel de Cluny, 269

Hôtel des Invalides, 271

Hôtel de Ville, 279

Hôtel Drouot, 280

hotels in, 277, 284–287

Ile de la Cité, 269

Ile St-Louis, 269

Jardin des Plantes, 270

Jardin des Tuileries, 275–276

Jeu de Paume, 276

L'Etoile, 275

Louvre, 276–277

Louvre des Antiquaires, 278

Maison de Victor Hugo, 279

Marais quarter, 279

métro in, 264

Montmarte, 277

Moulin Rouge cabaret, 277

Musé Cognacq-Jay, 279

Musée de l'Armée, 271, 274

Musée des Plans-Reliefs, 274

Musée d'Orsay, 271

Musée Marmottan, 276

Musé National du Moyen-Age, 269

Museum of Modern Art, 278

Musée Picasso, 279

Musée Rodin, 274

museums in, 269, 270, 271, 274, 276–277, 278, 279

nightlife in, 288–289

Notre Dame Cathedral, 269

Opéra, 278

opera in, 278, 287–288

Opéra Comique, 288

Opéra de la Bastille, 279

Orangerie, 276

Palais Bourbon, 271

Palais de Justice, 279

Palais de la Découverte, 275

Palais du Luxembourg, 270–271

Palais Omnisports, 280

Palais-Royal, 278

Panthéon, 270

Père Lachaise, 280

Petit Palais, 275

place Charles de Gaulle, 275

place de la Bastille, 279

place des Vosges, 279

place du Tertre, 277

place Pigalle, 277

place Vendôme, 277

Pont Alexandre III, 271

Printemps, 278

restaurants in, 269, 278, 282–284

rue de la Paix, 277

Sacré-Coeur, 277

Sainte-Chapelle, 279

St-Augustin, 277

St-Etienne du Mont, 270

St-Eustache, 278

St-Germain-des-Prés, 271

Saint-Paul-Saint-Louis, 279

St-Sulpice, 271

shopping in, 277, 278281–282

Sorbonne, 269–270

square du Vert Galant, 280

square Stravinsky, 278–279

theater in, 287

Tour de l'Horloge, 279

tourist information in, 265

Tour St-Jacques, 279

Val de Grâce, 270

Passports and visas, 9, 29–30

Photography, 9, 21–22

Poland, 847–871. See also Gdaąsk; Kraków; Warsaw

Auschwitz, 866

churches in, 857, 864, 866

Częstochowa, 866, 867

Elbląg, 870

Grunwald, site of battle of, 870
hotels in, 854–855, 861–862, 867–868, 870–871
Malbork, 869
museums in, 851, 853, 857, 870
Olsztyn, 870–871
Olsztynek, 870
Ostróda, 871
Płock, 868
restaurants in, 853–854, 861, 864, 867–868, 870–871
shopping in, 860
Sopot, 869
Toruą, 868–869, 871
tourist information in, 17, 856, 864, 868
Wadowice, 866–867
Wieliczka, 866
Portugal, 872–907. See also Lisbon
Albufeira, 902, 903–904
Algarve, 899–907
Almansil, 902
Alvor, 904
Armação de Pêrá, 902, 904–905
Boca do Inferno, 896
Cabo da Roca, 896
Cabo São Vincente, 903
Caldas de Monchique, 905
camping in, 881
Cascais, 895–896, 897–898
casino, 895
Castelo dos Mouros, 897
churches in, 884, 886, 896, 901, 902, 903
Estói, 901
Estoril, 895, 898
fairs in, 897
Faro, 901–902, 905
Ferragudo, 902–903
hotels in, 880–881, 891–893, 897–899, 903–907
Lagoa, 902
Lagos, 903, 905
Loulé, 901
Monchique, 906
Monserrate, 896
Monte Gordo, 900–901, 906
Museu Arqueologia, 902
Museu Conde de Castro Guimarães, 896
Museu do Brinquedo, 897
Museu do Etnografia Regional, 901

Museu Martimo, 901
museums in, 879, 884, 886, 887, 888, 889, 896, 897, 901, 902
Museu Municipal, 901
Olhão, 901
Olhos d'Agua, 906
Palácio do Visconde de Estói, 901
Palácio Nacional de Pena, 897
Palácio Nacional de Queluz, 897
Palácio Nacional de Sintra, 896
parks in, 896
Parque do Marachel Carmona, 896
Penedo, 896
Portimão, 902–903, 906
Praia de Rocha, 903, 906–907
Quarteira, 902
Queluz, 897, 898–899
Riviera, 894–899
Roman ruins in, 901
restaurants in, 879–880, 887, 890–891, 896, 897–899, 903–907
Sagres, 903, 907
Santa Barbara de Nexe, 907
Serra de Sintra, 896
shopping in, 879, 889–890
Silves, 902
Sintra, 896–897, 899
Tavira, 901
tourist information in, 17, 882, 894, 900
Vale de Lobo, 902, 907
Vilamoura, 902, 907
Vila Real de Santo António, 900, 907
zoo, 896
Prague, 166–176
ballet in, 176
Betlémeska kaple, 169
bookstores in, 167
Charles Bridge, 169
Chrám svatého Mikuláše, 169, 172
Clock Tower, 169
concerts in, 175–176
emergencies in, 167
hotels in, 174–175
Josefov, 169
Kafka, 169, 173
Kinského Zahrada, 172
Královský palác (Royal Palace), 172

Letenské Sady, 172
Loreto, 172
Malá Strana, 169–170
Mozart, 173
Národní Muzeum, 169
nightlife in, 176
Old Jewish Quarter, 169
opera in, 176
Prašná brána, 169
Pražsky hrad (Prague Castle), 172
puppet shows in, 176
restaurants in, 173–174
St. Vitus Cathedral, 172
Sts. Peter and Paul Church, 172
shopping in, 173
Staroměstske náměští, 169
synagogues in, 169
theater in, 176
tourist information in, 167
Václavské náměští, 169
Vyšehrad Castle, 172
Wallenstein Gardens, 172
Židowské muzeum, 169

R

Rail travel, 9–10, 30
Reykjavík, 638–644
Arbæjarsafn, 640
Arnarhóll Hill, 640
Ásgrímur Jónsson Museum, 642
Ásmundur Sveinsson Gallery, 640
Austurvöllur, 640
Bernhöfstorfa, 640
bookstores in, 639
cathedral, 640
Einar Jónsson Museum, 642
emergencies in, 639
Government House, 640
Hallgrímskirkja, 642
hotels in, 644
Kjarvalsstaðir gallery, 642
Miklatún, 642
Museum of Natural History, 640
National Library, 642
National Gallery, 640
National Museum, 642
National Theatre, 642
Nordic House, 642
Opera, 642
Parliament building, 640
Perlan, 642

restaurants in, 640, 643

shopping in, 643

tourist information in, 639

Romania, 908–930. See also
  Bucharest

Babadag, 928

Black Sea Coast of, 927–930

Callatis, 929

churches in, 919, 922

Constanţa, 928–929

Crişan, 929

Danube Delta, 927–928

hotels in, 916, 924–925, 929–
  930

Istria, 928

Mamaia, 928, 929

Mangalia, 929

museums in, 915, 919, 922–
  923, 927, 928

rentals in, 916

restaurants in, 915–916, 923–
  924, 929–930

Roman ruins in, 928

shopping in, 923

spas in, 928–929

tourist information in, 17,
  918, 927

Tulcea, 927, 930

Venus, 930

Roman ruins

in Austria, 59

in Bulgaria, 136, 142

in Cyprus, 152, 153

in France, 308

in Germany, 386

in Great Britain, 487

in Hungary, 626

in Italy, 711, 748

in Portugal, 901

in Romania, 928

in Spain, 979, 1005

in Turkey, 1146, 1149, 1153,
  1154, 1155

in Vienna, 59

Rome, 706–728

Aracoeli, 711

Arch of Constantine, 714

arts in, 726–727

Augusteo, 716

Baths of Caracalla, 714

bookstores in, 709

Campidoglio, 710

Campo dei Fiori, 720

Castel Gandolfo, 718

Castel Sant'Angelo, 716

Church of the Gesù, 719

Church of Santa Maria dela
  Concezione, 715

Circus Maximus, 711

Colosseum, 711

emergencies in, 709

Fabricio Bridge, 721

Fontana di Trevi, 714–715

Forum, 711

Fountain of the Barcaccia, 714

Fountain of the Bees, 715

Fountain of the Four Rivers,
  720

Fountain of the Tartarughe,
  721

Galleria Borghese, 706

Galleria Doria Pamphii, 721

Galleria Nazionale di Arte Antica, 715

hotels in, 715, 725–726

Keats and Shelley Memorial
  House, 714

metro in, 707–708

Museo Capitolino, 711

Museo Nazionale di Villa Giulia, 721

nightlife in, 727–728

opera in, 727

Ostia Antica, 721

Palatine Hill, 711

Palazzo Barberini, 706

Palazzo dei Conservatori, 711

Palazzo della Cancelleria, 720

Palazzo Farnese, 720

Palazzo Senatorio, 710

Palazzo Spada, 720

Pantheon, 719

Pasetto, 716

Piazza Barberini, 715

Piazza del Popolo, 714

Piazza di Spagna, 714

Piazza Farnese, 720

Piazza Navona, 720

Piazza San Pietro, 707

Piazza Venezia, 710

Ponte Sant'Angelo, 716

Porta Pinciana, 715

restaurants in, 711, 714, 719,
  720, 722–724

Roman Forum, 711

St. Peter's Basilica, 717

St. Peter's Square, 716

San Luigi dei Francesi, 720

Sant'Agnese in Agone, 720

Santa Maria del Popolo, 714

Santa Maria Sopra Minerva,
  719

shopping in, 721–722

Sistine Chapel, 718–719

Spanish Steps, 714

Teatro di Marcello, 721

Terrazza del Pincio, 721

Tiberina Island, 721

tourist information in, 708

Trinità dei Monti, 714

Triton, 715

Vatican City, 716–717

Vatican Museums, 718

Vatican Palace, 716–717,
  718

Villa Borghese, 715

S

Salzburg, 70–77

Alter Markt, 73

arts in, 76–77

Baroque Museum, 71

Bürgerspital, 72

Carolino Augusteum Museum,
  72

churches in, 72, 73

Dom, 72

Festspielhaus, 72

Festung Hohensalzburg, 73

fiakers in, 71

Franziskanerkirche, 72

hotels in, 75–76

Kapuzinerberg, 71

Kollegienkirche, 72

Landestheater, 71

Mirabell gardens, 71

Mozarteum, 72

Mozart's birthplace, 73

Mozart's Wohnhaus, 71

opera in, 76–77

Pferdeschwemme, 72

Residenz, 73

Residenzgalerie, 73

restaurants in, 72–73, 75

St. George's Chapel, 73

Schloss Hellbrunn, 85

Schloss Mirabell, 72

Stiftskirche St. Peter, 73

theater in, 76

Tiergarten, 75

tourist information in, 71

Wasserspiele, 73

Saxony and Thuringia, 421–
  431

Albertinum, 424

Altes Rathaus, 426

Buchenwald, 428

Deutsches Hygiene Museum,
  425

Dresden, 423–425, 429

Exhibition Pavilion, 426–427

Goethehaus, 427

Grassimuseum, 426

Herderkirche, 428
Historischer Friedhof, 428
hotels in, 428–431
Katholische Hofkirche, 425
Kirms-Krackow house, 428
Leipzig, 425–427, 429–430
Museum der Bildenden Kun-
   ste, 426
Nikolaikirche, 426
opera in, 423, 426
restaurants in, 426, 428–431
Schillerhaus, 427–428
Schloss Belvedere, 428
Schloss Pillnitz, 425
Semper Opera house, 423
Sempergalerie, 423–424
Stadtschloss, 428
Thomaskirche, 426
tourist information in, 422–
   423
Weimar, 427–428, 430–431
Wittumspalais, 427
Zwinger, 423–424
Scotland. *See* Great Britain
Ship travel, 10–11
Singles, tours for, 28
Slovakia, 931–946. *See also*
   Bratislava
Bardejov, 945
Bodružal, 945
churches in, 940, 941, 943–
   944, 945
High Tatras, 944
hotels in, 937, 942, 945–946
Hvervartov, 945
Levoča, 944-945
museums in, 936, 940–941,
   944
Museum of the Tatra National
   Park, 944
Poprad, 943
Prešov, 945
restaurants in, 936, 940, 941–
   942, 945–946
shopping in, 936
Smokovec, 944, 945–946
Spiš, 943–944
Spiš Castle, 944–945
Spišská Sobota, 943
Štrbské Pleso, 944
Sv. Jakub, 944
Sv. Juraj, 943–944
Svidník, 945
Tatranská Lomnica, 944,
   946
tourist information in, 18,
   938, 943
Zochová Chata, 943

Sofia, 125–134
Aleko, 130
art galleries in, 129, 133
arts in, 133
Banya Bashi Djamiya, 130
Borisova Grodina, 129
Boyana, 130
casino in, 134
Crypt Museum, 129
Dragalevci Monastery, 130
emergencies in, 126
hotels in, 132–133
Hram-pametnik Alexander
   Nevski, 129
Mavsolei Georgi Dimitrov,
   129
Natzionalen Archeologicheski
   Musei, 127–129
Natzionalen Dvoretz na Kul-
   turata, 129–130
Natzionalen Etnografski
   Musei, 129
Natzionalen Istoricheski
   Musei, 127
Natzionalna Hudozhestvena
   Galeria, 129
nightlife in, 134
Partiyniyat Dom, 127
Plodshtad Sveta Nedelya, 127
puppet theater in, 133
restaurants in, 130, 131–132
Rotonda Sveti Georgi, 127
shopping in, 130
tourist information in, 126
Tsentralen Universalen Maga-
   zin, 130
Tsentralni Hali, 130
Tzarkva Sveta Nedelya, 127
Tzarkva Sveta Nikolai, 129
Tzarkva Sveta Sovia, 129
Spain, 947–1030. *See also*
   Barcelona; Gibraltar;
   Madrid; Toledo
Alba de Tormes, 981–982
Alcaicería, 1009
Alcazaba, 1016
Alcázar (Segovia), 980
Alcázar (Seville), 1002, 1004
Alhambra, 1009
Alpujarras, 1009
Andalusia, 1000–1014
Ávila, 980–981, 982
Baena, 1007
Barrio de Santa Cruz, 1004
Basilica of San Vicente, 981
Benalmádena, 1016
bullfighting in, 969, 994,
   1007, 1014, 1017

camping in, 958
Canary Islands, 1025–1030
Carmona, 1005, 1010
Casares, 1018
churches in, 978, 980–981,
   988, 992, 1002, 1005,
   1007, 1009, 1018, 1019
Córdoba, 1005–1007, 1010–
   1011
Costa del Sol, 1014, 1025
Ecija, 1005
El Escorial, 979, 982–983
Estepona, 1017–1018, 1020–
   1021
Flamenco in, 1013–1014
Fuengirola, 1016
Fuerteventura, 1028
Generalife, 1009
Gibraltar, 1018–1020, 1021
Giralda, 1002
La Gomera, 1028
Gran Canaria, 1027–1028,
   1029
Granada, 1007–1010, 1011–
   1012, 1013–1014
La Granja, 979
El Hierro, 1028
hotels in, 957–958, 972–974,
   982–985, 996–997, 1010–
   1013, 1020–1025, 1028–
   1030
Lanzarote, 1028, 1029
Málaga, 1016, 1021–1022
Marbella, 1017, 1022–1023
María Luisa park, 1004
Mijas, 1016–1017, 1023–
   1024
Moorish, 1000–1014
mosques in, 1005
Museum of Bullfighting, 1007,
   1017
museums in, 956, 963–964,
   968, 978, 988, 989, 993,
   1007, 1016, 1017
Navacerrada pass, 979
Nerja, 1016, 1024
Ojén, 1017
La Palma, 1028
paradors in, 958
parks in, 1004
Puente Nuevo, 1017
Puerto de Sotogrande, 1018
restaurants in, 956–957, 964,
   965, 968, 969–972, 982–
   985, 988, 989, 992, 994–
   996, 1010–1013,
   1020–1025, 1028–1029
Ronda, 1017, 1024

Salamanca, 981–982, 983
Segovia, 979–980, 983–984
Seville, 1002–1005, 1012–
   1013, 1014
shopping in, 955, 968–969,
   993–994
Sierra Nevada, 1009
synagogues in, 1007, 1020
Tenerife, 1027, 1029–1030
Toledo, 977–979, 984–985
Torre de Oro, 1004
Torremolinos, 1016, 1024–
   1025
tourist information in, 18,
   961, 976, 986–987, 1001,
   1015, 1025
Trevélez, 1010
Valley of the Fallen, 979
villas in, 958
Spas. See Baths and spas
Stockholm, 1040–1057
arts in, 1055–1056
bars in, 1056–1057
Bergranska Botanical Garden,
   1049
bookstores in, 1042
City Hall, 1044
concerts, 1056
Djurgården, 1045
emergencies in, 1042
Fjäderholmarna, 1049
Gamla Stan, 1044
Gripsholm Castle, 1048
Gröna Lund Tivoli, 1045
hotels in, 1052–1055
Kaknas TV Tower, 1048–1049
Kungstrågården, 1044–1045
Mariefred (ship), 1048
Museum of National Antiqui-
   ties, 1045
nightlife in, 1056–1057
Nordic Museum, 1045
opera in, 1056
restaurants in, 1045, 1050–
   1052
Riddarholm Church, 1044
Royal Armory, 1044
Royal Palace, 1044
shopping in, 1049–1050
Skansen, 1045
Skokloster Palace, 1048
Stockholm archipelago, 1048
subways in, 1041–1042
theater in, 1056
tourist information in, 1042
Treasury, 1044
Vasamuseet, 1045
zoo, 1045

Student travel, 11, 31
Sweden, 1031–1066. See also
   Stockholm; Uppsala
camping in, 1040
churches in, 1044, 1057–1058
Dalarna, 1059
Emigrants' House, 1063–
   1064
Falun, 1058, 1060
folklore district of, 1057–
   1061
Glass Country of, 1061–1066
Göteborgskortet, 1062
Gothenburg, 1062, 1064–
   1065
hotels in, 1039–1040, 1052–
   1055, 1060–1061, 1064–
   1066
Jönköping, 1063, 1065
Kalmar, 1064, 1065–1066
Lake Hjälmaren, 1059
Lake Siljan, 1058
Lake Vattern, 1063
Ludvika, 1059, 1060
Matchstick Museum, 1063
Mora, 1058, 1060
museums in, 1038, 1045,
   1058, 1059, 1063–1064
Nusnäs, 1059
Örebro, 1059, 1060–1061
Rättvik, 1058
restaurants in, 1038–1039,
   1045, 1050–1052, 1060–
   1061, 1064–1066
Säter, 1058
shopping in, 1037–1038,
   1049–1050
Sundborn, 1058
Tällberg, 1058, 1061
tourist information in, 18,
   1042, 1057, 1062
Trädgårdsföreningen, 1062
Växjö, 1063, 1066
Wadköping, 1060
west coast of, 1061–1066
Switzerland, 1067–1121. See
   also Bern; Geneva; Lugano;
   Luzern; Zürich
churches in, 1079–1080,
   1091, 1099, 1106, 1111,
   1113
emergencies in, 1118
gardens in, 1106
hotels in, 1075, 1084–1085,
   1087–1088, 1095–1097,
   1102–1103, 1108–1110,
   1115–1117, 1119–1121
Liechtenstein, 1086–1088

Luzern, 1097–1104
Matterhorn, 1117
museums in, 1080–1081,
   1091, 1099, 1106, 1111,
   1113
rental chalets in, 1076
restaurants in, 1075, 1079,
   1082–1083, 1087–1088,
   1094–1095, 1101–1102,
   1106, 1108, 1114–1115,
   1119
shopping in, 1074, 1081, 1101
tourist information in, 1078,
   1087, 1090, 1098, 1105,
   1110, 1118
Zermatt, 1117–1121

T

Taxes, 11, 31
Telephones, 12, 31
Toledo, 977–979, 984–985
Cambrón Gate, 978
cathedral in, 978
Chapel of Santo Tomé, 978
El Greco's house, 978
Hill of the Angels, 977
Hospital de Tavera, 979
Museum of Santa Cruz, 978
Plaza Zocodover, 977
San Juan de los Reyes, 978
Santa María la Blanca, 978
Sephardic Museum, 978
Sinagoga del Tránsito, 978
Tour operators, 12–15
for gay and lesbian travelers, 7
packages and tours, 27–28
Train travel, 9–10, 30
Travel agencies, 15, 28
for gay and lesbian travelers, 6
for travelers with disabilities, 7
Travel briefings, U.S. govern-
   ment, 15
Traveler's checks, 26–27
Trip cancellation insurance, 8
Trip insurance, 8, 25–26
Turkey, 1122–1161. See also
   Istanbul
Acropolis, 1146, 1147
Aegean Coast, 1145–1152
Aksaray, 1158
Ankara, 1158
Antalya, 1155–1156
Aphrodisias, 1149
Aspendos, 1158–1159
Avanos, 1160
Ayvalik, 1146, 1149
Bergama, 1145, 1149–1150

Bodrum, 1153, 1156
Bursa, 1146, 1150
Çankkale, 1150
Cappadocia, 1157–1161
Castle of St. Peter, 1153
Central Anatolia, 1157–1161
Çesme, 1145, 1150
churches in, 1148
Dalaman, 1152
Dalyan, 1153, 1156
Datça, 1153
Derinkuyu, 1160
Didyma, 1148, 1149
Ephesus, 1148
Ephesus Museum, 1148
Göreme, 1160
Göreme Open-Air Museum, 1160
Gulf of Edremit, 1146
Halikarnas, 1153
Hierapolis, 1149
hotels in, 1130, 1142–1143, 1149–1152, 1155–1157
House of Mary, 1148
İzmir, 1147, 1150–1151
Kadifekale, 1147
Kalkan, 1154, 1156
Kaş, 1154–1155, 1157
Kaymakli, 1160
Kayseri, 1159
Kekova, 1154–1155
Kemer, 1155
Knidos, 1153
Konya, 1159, 1160
Köyceğiz, 1157
Kuşadasi, 1148, 1151
Marmaris, 1153
Mediterranean Coast, 1152–1157
Miletus, 1148–1149
mosques in, 1138, 1139–1140, 1146
museums in, 1129, 1135, 1138, 1153, 1160
Museum of Underwater Archaeology, 1153
Nevşehir, 1159
Olü Deniz, 1153–1154, 1157
Pammukale, 1149, 1151
Patara, 1154
Pergamum, 1146–1147
Perge, 1158
Phaselis, 1155
Pinara, 1154
Priene, 1148
restaurants in, 1129–1130, 1135, 1140–1142, 1151–1152, 1155–1157

Roman ruins in, 1146, 1149, 1153, 1158
Selçuk, 1148, 1152
shopping in, 1128, 1140
Sultan Han, 1159
Temple of Athena, 1148
Termessos, 1158
tourist information in, 18, 1132, 1145–1146, 1152–1153, 1158
Troy, 1146, 1150
Turunç, 1153
Ulu Cami, 1146
Uludağ, 1146
Ürgüp, 1159, 1160–1161
Xanthos, 1154

U

United Kingdom. See Great Britain
Uppsala, 1057–1061
cathedral, 1057–1058
Cathedral Museum, 1058
hotels in, 1061
restaurants in, 1061
Uppsala Castle, 1058

V

Valleta, 806–809
Armoury of the Knights, 807–808
City Gate, 807
emergencies in, 806
Fort St. Elmo, 808
Government Craft Center, 807
Grand Master's Palace, 807
Hospital of the Order, 808
hotels in, 809
National Museum of Archaeology, 807
National Museum of Fine Art, 808
restaurants in, 808–809
St. John's Co-Cathedral, 807
tourist information in, 806
Upper Barracca Gardens, 808
War Museum, 808
Value-added tax (VAT), 11, 31
Venice, 761–776
Accademia Gallery, 768, 770
arts in, 775
Basilica di San Marco, 765
Ca' Rezzonico, 770
Campanile di San Marco, 768
concerts, 775
emergencies in, 763
Frari, 769

Ghetto, 770
gondolas in, 763
Grand Canal, 770
hotels in, 768, 773–775
Museo Correr, 765
Museo Ebraico, 770
nightlife in, 776
opera in, 775
Palazzo Ducale, 765, 768
Palazzo Labia, 771
Palazzo Venier dei Leoni, 770
Peggy Guggenheim Museum, 770
Piazza San Marco, 765
restaurants in, 768, 771–773
Rialto Bridge, 769
San Moisè, 768
Santa Maria dei Miracoli, 769
Santa Maria del Giglio, 768
Santa Maria Formosa, 769
San Zanipolo, 769,
Scuoli di San Rocco, 768–769
shopping in, 771
Torcello, 771
tourist information in, 763
Traghettos in, 763
Vaporettos in, 762
water taxis in, 762
Video recorders, 22
Videotape, 22
Vienna, 50–67
Albertina, 53
Am Hof, 59
Anker-Uhr, 59
arts in, 66–67
Augustinerkirche, 53
Bermuda Triangle, 61
bookstores in, 52
Café Central, 59
churches in, 56, 58, 59–60
Court Silver and Tableware Museum, 56–57
Doll and Toy Museum, 61
Donner Brunnen, 58
emergencies in, 52
Freud's apartment, 61
Gloriette, 60
Hofburg, 56
Hofburgkapelle, 56
Hoher Markt, 59
hotels in, 58, 64–66
Hundertwasserhaus, 61
Jewish Museum, 58
Kaisergruft, 58
Kapuzinerkirche, 58
Karlskirche, 57
Kirche am Hof, 59
Kunst-Haus Wien Museum, 61

Kunsthistoriches Museum, 57
Loos building, 56
Maria am Gestade, 59
Michaelertor, 56
Mozart Erinnerungsräume, 59
Nationalbibliothek, 65
Naturhistorisches Museum, 57
Neue Hofburg Museums, 57
nightlife in, 67
opera in, 57, 66
Palais Ferstl, 59
Palais Harrach, 59
Pestsäule, 58
Peterskirche, 58
restaurants in, 56, 57, 58, 59,
   62–64
Ring, 53
Roman ruins, 59
Ruprechtskirche, 59–60
Sacher Hotel, 58
Schatzkammer, 56
Schloss Belvedere, 60
Schönbrunn Palace, 60
Schottenkirche, 59
shopping in, 61–62
Spanische Reitschule, 56
Staatsoper, 57, 66
Stephansdom, 58
streetcars in, 51
subways in, 51
Tabak Museum, 57
theater in, 66
Theater Museum, 53
Tiegarten, 60
tourist information in, 52
20th Century Museum, 60–61
Uhrenmuseum, 59
Vienna Woods, 61
Wagenburg, 60
wine taverns in, 67
Villa rentals, 8–9, 26
Visas, 9, 29–30
Visitor information, 15–18

W

Warsaw, 855–863
arts in, 862–863
Barbakan, 857
Belvedere Palace, 857
concerts in, 862–863
emergencies in, 856
*Heroes of the Warsaw Ghetto
   monument,* 860
Holy Cross Church, 857
hotels in, 861–862
Đazienkowski Palace, 860
Đazienkowski Park, 860
*Muzeum Marii-Skłodowskeij-
   Curie,* 857
nightlife in, 863
Nowe Miasto, 857
Old Town, 857
opera in, 863
Palace of Culture and Science,
   860
restaurants in, 861
Rynek Starego Miasta, 857
shopping in, 860
theater in, 862
tourist information in, 856
trams in, 855
University of Warsaw, 857
Wilanów, 860
Zamek Królowski, 857
Weather, 18

Y

York, 497–504
Castle Museum, 499
Chapter House, 498
hotels in, 503–504
Jorvik Viking Centre, 498–
   499
Merchant Adventurers' Hall,
   499
Minster, 498

National Railway Museum,
   499
restaurants in, 499, 502–503
The Shambles, 499
Stonegate, 499
tourist information in, 498
*Undercroft Museum and Trea-
   sury,* 498
walls of, 499

Z

Zürich, 1077–1086
Altstadt, 1080
arts in, 1085–1086
Bahnhofstrasse, 1079
bookstores in, 1078
E. G. Bührle Collection, 1081
emergencies in, 1078
Fraumünster, 1079
Graphiksammlung, 1081
Grossmünster, 1079
Haus zum Ruden, 1079–1080
hotels in, 1084–1085
Kunsthaus, 1079
Liechtenstein, 1086–1088
Limmatquai, 1079
Lindenhof, 1079
Museum Rietberg, 1081
Niederdorf, 1080
nightlife in, 1086
Peterskirche, 1079
Quai Bridge, 1079
Rathaus, 1080
restaurants in, 1079, 1082–
   1083
*Schweizerishes Landesmu-
   seum,* 1080–1081
shopping in, 1081
tourist information in, 1078
Wasserkirche, 1079

Your guide to a picture-perfect vacation

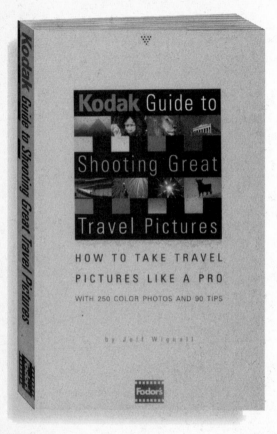

Kodak and Fodor's join together to create the guide that travelers everywhere have been asking for—one that covers the terms and techniques, the equipment and etiquette for taking first-rate travel photographs.

The most authoritative and up-to-date book of its kind, **The Kodak Guide to Shooting Great Travel Pictures** includes over 200 color photographs and spreads on 100 points of photography important to travelers, such as landscape basics, under sea shots, wildlife, city street, close-ups, photographing in museums and more.

$16.50 ($22.95 Canada)

At bookstores everywhere, or call 1-800-533-6478.

Fodor's. The name that means smart travel.™

Fodor's Travel Publications

Available at bookstores everywhere, or call 1–800–533–6478, 24 hours a day.

Gold Guides

U.S.

Alaska	Florida	New Orleans	Santa Fe, Taos, Albuquerque
Arizona	Hawaii	New York City	Seattle & Vancouver
Boston	Las Vegas, Reno, Tahoe	Pacific North Coast	The South
California	Los Angeles	Philadelphia & the Pennsylvania Dutch Country	U.S. & British Virgin Islands
Cape Cod, Martha's Vineyard, Nantucket	Maine, Vermont, New Hampshire	The Rockies	USA
The Carolinas & the Georgia Coast	Maui	San Diego	Virginia & Maryland
Chicago	Miami & the Keys	San Francisco	Waikiki
Colorado	New England		Washington, D.C.

Foreign

Australia & New Zealand	Egypt	London	Provence & the Riviera
Austria	Europe	Madrid & Barcelona	Scandinavia
The Bahamas	Florence, Tuscany & Umbria	Mexico	Scotland
Bermuda	France	Montréal & Québec City	Singapore
Budapest	Germany	Moscow, St. Petersburg, Kiev	South America
Canada	Great Britain	The Netherlands, Belgium & Luxembourg	South Pacific
Cancún, Cozumel, Yucatán Peninsula	Greece		Southeast Asia
Caribbean	Hong Kong	New Zealand	Spain
China	India	Norway	Sweden
Costa Rica, Belize, Guatemala	Ireland	Nova Scotia, New Brunswick, Prince Edward Island	Switzerland
Cuba	Israel		Thailand
The Czech Republic & Slovakia	Italy	Paris	Tokyo
	Japan		Toronto
Eastern Europe	Kenya & Tanzania	Portugal	Turkey
	Korea		Vienna & the Danube

Fodor's Special-Interest Guides

Branson	Fodor's London Companion	Kodak Guide to Shooting Great Travel Pictures	Walt Disney World for Adults
Caribbean Ports of Call	France by Train	Shadow Traffic's New York Shortcuts and Traffic Tips	Where Should We Take the Kids? California
The Complete Guide to America's National Parks	Halliday's New England Food Explorer	Sunday in New York	Where Should We Take the Kids? Northeast
Condé Nast Traveler Caribbean Resort and Cruise Ship Finder	Healthy Escapes	Sunday in San Francisco	
	Italy by Train		
Cruises and Ports of Call		Walt Disney World, Universal Studios and Orlando	

Before Catching Your Flight, Catch Up With Your World.

Fueled by the global resources of CNN and available in major airports across America, CNN Airport Network provides a live source  of current domestic and international news, 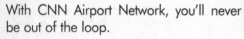 sports, business, weather and lifestyle programming. Plus two daily Fodor's features for the facts you need: "Travel Fact," a useful and creative mix of travel trivia; and "What's Happening," a comprehensive round-up of upcoming events in major cities 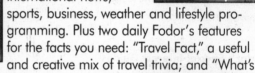 around the world.

With CNN Airport Network, you'll never  be out of the loop.

CNN
Airport Network
A CNN NETWORK

HERE'S YOUR OWN PERSONAL VIEW OF THE WORLD.

Here's the easiest way to get up-to-the-minute, objective, personalized information about what's going on in the city you'll be visiting—before you leave on your trip! Unique information you could get only if you knew someone personally in each of 160 destinations around the world. Everything from special places to dine to local events only a local would know about.

It's all yours—in your Travel Update from Worldview, the leading provider of time-sensitive destination information.

Review the following order form and fill it out by indicating your destination(s)

and travel dates and by checking off up to eight interest categories. Then mail or fax your order form to us, or call your order in. (We're here to help you 24 hours a day.)

Within 48 hours of receiving your order, we'll mail your convenient, pocket-sized custom guide to you, packed with information to make your travel more fun and interesting. And if you're in a hurry, we can even fax it.

Have a great trip with your Fodor's Worldview Travel Update!

Fodor's WORLDVIEW TRAVEL UPDATE

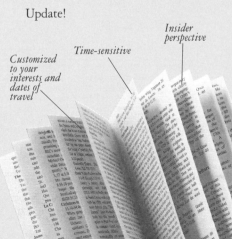

Insider perspective

Time-sensitive

Customized to your interests and dates of travel

DESTINATIONS

Worldview covers more than 160 destinations worldwide. Choose the destination(s) that match your itinerary from the list below:

Europe
- Amsterdam
- Athens
- Barcelona
- Berlin
- Brussels
- Budapest
- Copenhagen
- Dublin
- Edinburgh
- Florence
- Frankfurt
- French Riviera
- Geneva
- Glasgow
- Lausanne
- Lisbon
- London
- Madrid
- Milan
- Moscow
- Munich
- Oslo
- Paris
- Prague
- Provence
- Rome
- Salzburg
- Seville
- St. Petersburg
- Stockholm
- Venice
- Vienna
- Zurich

United States (Mainland)
- Albuquerque
- Atlanta
- Atlantic City
- Baltimore
- Boston
- Branson, MO
- Charleston, SC
- Chicago
- Cincinnati
- Cleveland
- Dallas/Ft. Worth
- Denver
- Detroit
- Houston
- Indianapolis
- Kansas City
- Las Vegas
- Los Angeles
- Memphis
- Miami
- Milwaukee
- Minneapolis/St. Paul
- Nashville
- New Orleans
- New York City
- Orlando
- Palm Springs
- Philadelphia
- Phoenix
- Pittsburgh
- Portland
- Reno/Lake Tahoe
- St. Louis
- Salt Lake City
- San Antonio
- San Diego
- San Francisco
- Santa Fe
- Seattle
- Tampa
- Washington, DC

Alaska
- Alaskan Destinations

Hawaii
- Honolulu
- Island of Hawaii
- Kauai
- Maui

Canada
- Quebec City
- Montreal
- Ottawa
- Toronto
- Vancouver

Bahamas
- Abaco
- Eleuthera/ Harbour Island
- Exuma
- Freeport
- Nassau & Paradise Island

Bermuda
- Bermuda Countryside
- Hamilton

British Leeward Islands
- Anguilla
- Antigua & Barbuda
- St. Kitts & Nevis

British Virgin Islands
- Tortola & Virgin Gorda

British Windward Islands
- Barbados
- Dominica
- Grenada
- St. Lucia
- St. Vincent
- Trinidad & Tobago

Cayman Islands
- The Caymans

Dominican Republic
- Santo Domingo

Dutch Leeward Islands
- Aruba
- Bonaire
- Curacao

Dutch Windward Island
- St. Maarten/St. Martin

French West Indies
- Guadeloupe
- Martinique
- St. Barthelemy

Jamaica
- Kingston
- Montego Bay
- Negril
- Ocho Rios

Puerto Rico
- Ponce
- San Juan

Turks & Caicos
- Grand Turk/ Providenciales

U.S. Virgin Islands
- St. Croix
- St. John
- St. Thomas

Mexico
- Acapulco
- Cancun & Isla Mujeres
- Cozumel
- Guadalajara
- Ixtapa & Zihuatanejo
- Los Cabos
- Mazatlan
- Mexico City
- Monterrey
- Oaxaca
- Puerto Vallarta

South/Central America
- Buenos Aires
- Caracas
- Rio de Janeiro
- San Jose, Costa Rica
- Sao Paulo

Middle East
- Istanbul
- Jerusalem

Australia & New Zealand
- Auckland
- Melbourne
- South Island
- Sydney

China
- Beijing
- Guangzhou
- Shanghai

Japan
- Kyoto
- Nagoya
- Osaka
- Tokyo
- Yokohama

Pacific Rim/Other
- Bali
- Bangkok
- Hong Kong & Macau
- Manila
- Seoul
- Singapore
- Taipei